1987

HISTORY

OF THE

CONQUEST OF MEXICO

AND

HISTORY

OF THE

CONQUEST OF PERU

HISTORY OF THE
CONQUEST OF MEXICO

AND

HISTORY OF THE
CONQUEST OF PERU

BY
WILLIAM H. PRESCOTT

THE MODERN LIBRARY

NEW YORK

Distributed in Canada
by Random House of Canada Limited, Toronto.

THE MODERN LIBRARY
is published by
RANDOM HOUSE, INC.

New York, New York

Manufactured in the United States of America

WILLIAM HICKLING PRESCOTT
(1796-1859)

A NOTE ON THE AUTHOR OF "HISTORY OF THE CONQUEST OF MEXICO" AND "HISTORY OF THE CONQUEST OF PERU"

Perhaps because it represents an heroic struggle against adversity, William Hickling Prescott's triumph over blindness often has been given more emphasis than his preëminence as an American historian. The accident he suffered while a student at Harvard College was, it is true, a determining factor in the choice of his career. He was struck by a crust of hard bread and the sight of his left eye was destroyed. After graduation, when his right eye began to fail, he abandoned the practice of law in his father's office to seek medical advice in Europe. Living for almost all the rest of his life in a darkened room, he devoted himself to literary research. His first great work was *History of the Reign of Ferdinand and Isabella*. After working for a time on a life of Molière, he forsook it for his preparatory work on his *History of the Conquest of Mexico*. Washington Irving, who was doing research in the same field, withdrew in Prescott's favor. Because of his failing sight, he developed a phenomenal memory, upon which he depended during the time of his monumental labors. Undeterred by his affliction, he undertook, after the completion of his *Conquest of Peru*, to revise Ticknor's *History of Spanish Literature*. His last work was the first two volumes of his unfinished *History of Philip II*, published in 1856. He died, in his sixty-third year, in 1859.

GENERAL CONTENTS

HISTORY OF THE CONQUEST OF MEXICO

BOOK I
INTRODUCTION—VIEW OF THE AZTEC CIVILIZATION

BOOK II
DISCOVERY OF MEXICO

BOOK III
MARCH TO MEXICO

BOOK IV
RESIDENCE IN MEXICO

BOOK V
EXPULSION FROM MEXICO

BOOK VI
SIEGE AND SURRENDER OF MEXICO

BOOK VII
CONCLUSION—SUBSEQUENT CAREER OF CORTÉS

APPENDIX

CONTENTS

BOOK I
INTRODUCTION—VIEW OF THE AXTEC CIVILIZATION

CHAPTER I

ANCIENT MEXICO—CLIMATE AND PRODUCTS—PRIMITIVE RACES—AZTEC EMPIRE

CHAPTER II

SUCCESSION TO THE CROWN—AZTEC NOBILITY—JUDICIAL SYSTEM—
LAWS AND REVENUES—MILITARY INSTITUTIONS

PAGE

CHAPTER III

MEXICAN MYTHOLOGY—THE SACERDOTAL ORDER—THE TEMPLES—
HUMAN SACRIFICES

CHAPTER IV

MEXICAN HIEROGLYPHICS—MANUSCRIPTS—ARITHMETIC—
CHRONOLOGY—ASTRONOMY

CHAPTER V

AZTEC AGRICULTURE—MECHANICAL ARTS—MERCHANTS—
DOMESTIC MANNERS

CHAPTER VI

TEZCUCANS—THEIR GOLDEN AGE—ACCOMPLISHED PRINCES— DECLINE OF THEIR MONARCHY

BOOK II

DISCOVERY OF MEXICO

CHAPTER I

SPAIN UNDER CHARLES V—PROGRESS OF DISCOVERY—COLONIAL POLICY—CONQUEST OF CUBA—EXPEDITIONS TO YUCATAN

CHAPTER II

HERNANDO CORTÉS—HIS EARLY LIFE—VISITS THE NEW WORLD—HIS RESIDENCE IN CUBA—DIFFICULTIES WITH VELASQUEZ—ARMADA IN- TRUSTED TO CORTÉS

CHAPTER III

JEALOUSY OF VELASQUEZ—CORTÉS EMBARKS—EQUIPMENT OF HIS FLEET
—HIS PERSON AND CHARACTER—RENDEZVOUS AT HAVANA—STRENGTH
OF HIS ARMAMENT

CHAPTER IV

VOYAGE TO COZUMEL—CONVERSION OF THE NATIVES—JERONIMO DE
AGUILAR—ARMY ARRIVES AT TABASCO—GREAT BATTLE WITH THE IN-
DIANS—CHRISTIANITY INTRODUCED

CHAPTER V

VOYAGE ALONG THE COAST—DOÑA MARINA—SPANIARDS LAND IN
MEXICO—INTERVIEW WITH THE AZTECS

CHAPTER VI

ACCOUNT OF MONTEZUMA—STATE OF HIS EMPIRE—STRANGE PROGNOS-
TICS—EMBASSY AND PRESENTS—SPANISH ENCAMPMENT

CONTENTS

CHAPTER VII

TROUBLES IN THE CAMP—PLAN OF A COLONY—MANAGEMENT OF CORTÉS —MARCH TO CEMPOALLA—PROCEEDINGS WITH THE NATIVES—FOUNDATION OF VERA CRUZ

CHAPTER VIII

ANOTHER AZTEC EMBASSY—DESTRUCTION OF THE IDOLS—DESPATCHES SENT TO SPAIN—CONSPIRACY IN THE CAMP—THE FLEET SUNK

BOOK III

MARCH TO MEXICO

CHAPTER I

PROCEEDINGS AT CEMPOALLA—THE SPANIARDS CLIMB THE TABLE-LAND —PICTURESQUE SCENERY—TRANSACTIONS WITH THE NATIVES—EMBASSY TO TLASCALA

CHAPTER II

REPUBLIC OF TLASCALA—ITS INSTITUTIONS—EARLY HISTORY—DISCUSSIONS IN THE SENATE—DESPERATE BATTLES

CHAPTER III

DECISIVE VICTORY—INDIAN COUNCIL—NIGHT ATTACK— NEGOTIATIONS WITH THE ENEMY—TLASCALAN HERO

CHAPTER IV

DISCONTENTS IN THE ARMY—TLASCALAN SPIES—PEACE WITH THE REPUBLIC—EMBASSY FROM MONTEZUMA

CHAPTER V

SPANIARDS ENTER TLASCALA—DESCRIPTION OF THE CAPITAL—ATTEMPTED CONVERSION—AZTEC EMBASSY—INVITED TO CHOLULA

CHAPTER VI

CITY OF CHOLULA—GREAT TEMPLE—MARCH TO CHOLULA—RECEPTION
OF THE SPANIARDS—CONSPIRACY DETECTED

CHAPTER VII

TERRIBLE MASSACRE—TRANQUILLITY RESTORED—REFLECTIONS ON THE
MASSACRE—FURTHER PROCEEDINGS—ENVOYS FROM MONTEZUMA

CHAPTER VIII

MARCH RESUMED—ASCENT OF THE GREAT VOLCANO—VALLEY OF MEXICO
—IMPRESSION ON THE SPANIARDS—CONDUCT OF MONTEZUMA—THEY
DESCEND INTO THE VALLEY

CHAPTER IX

ENVIRONS OF MEXICO—INTERVIEW WITH MONTEZUMA—ENTRANCE INTO
THE CAPITAL—HOSPITABLE RECEPTION—VISIT TO THE EMPEROR

BOOK IV

RESIDENCE IN MEXICO

CHAPTER I

TEZCUCAN LAKE—DESCRIPTION OF THE CAPITAL—PALACES AND MUSEUMS—ROYAL HOUSEHOLD—MONTEZUMA'S WAY OF LIFE

CHAPTER II

MARKET OF MEXICO—GREAT TEMPLE—INTERIOR SANCTUARIES— SPANISH QUARTERS

CHAPTER III

ANXIETY OF CORTÉS—SEIZURE OF MONTEZUMA—HIS TREATMENT BY THE SPANIARDS—EXECUTION OF HIS OFFICERS—MONTEZUMA IN IRONS— REFLECTIONS

CHAPTER IV

CHAPTER V

CHAPTER VI

CHAPTER VII

addresses the Aztecs—Spirit of the Aztecs—The Spaniards dismayed—
Distresses of the Garrison—Military Machine of Cortés—Impeded by
the Canals—Sharp Combats in the City—Bold Bearing of Cortés—Ap-
parition of St. James—Attempt to convert Montezuma—Its Failure—
Last Hours of Montezuma—His Character—His Posterity—Effect of his
Death on the Spaniards—Interment of Montezuma 424

CHAPTER III

COUNCIL OF WAR—SPANIARDS EVACUATE THE CITY—NOCHE TRISTE, OR
THE "MELANCHOLY NIGHT"—TERRIBLE SLAUGHTER—HALT FOR THE
NIGHT—AMOUNT OF LOSSES

Council of War—Predictions of the Astrologer—Their Effect on Cortés—He
decides to abandon the Capital—Arranges his Order of March—Spaniards
leave the City—Noche Triste, or the "Melancholy Night"—The Capital
is roused—Spaniards assailed on the Causeway—The Bridge wedged in
the Stones—Despair of the Spaniards—Fearful Carnage—Wreck of
Bodies and Treasure—Spaniards arrive at the third Breach—The Cavaliers return to the Rescue—Condition of the Rear—Alvarado's Leap—
Sad Spectacle of the Survivors—Feelings of Cortés—Spaniards defile
through Tacuba—Storm the Temple—Halt for the Night—Reflections of
the General—The Loss of the Spaniards 441

CHAPTER IV

RETREAT OF THE SPANIARDS—DISTRESSES OF THE ARMY—PYRAMIDS OF
TEOTIHUACAN—GREAT BATTLE OF OTUMBA

Quiet of the Mexicans—The Spaniards resume their Retreat—Distresses of
the Army—Their heroic Fortitude—Pyramids of Teotihuacan—Account
of them—Their probable Destination—The *Micoatl* or Path of the Dead
—The Races who reared them—Indian Host in the Valley of Otumba—
Sensations of the Spaniards—Instructions of Cortés—He leads the Attack
—Great Battle of Otumba—Gallantry of the Spaniards—Their Forces in
Disorder—Desperate Effort of Cortés—The Aztec Chief is slain—The
Barbarians put to Flight—Rich Spoil for the Victors—Reflections on the
Battle 454

CHAPTER V

ARRIVAL IN TLASCALA—FRIENDLY RECEPTION—DISCONTENTS OF THE
ARMY—JEALOUSY OF THE TLASCALANS—EMBASSY FROM MEXICO

Spaniards Arrive at Tlascala—Friendly Reception—Feelings of the Tlascalans
—Spaniards recruit their Strength—Their further Misfortunes—Tidings
from Villa Rica—Indomitable Spirit of Cortés—Discontents of the
Army—Their Remonstrance—The General's resolute Reply—Jealousy of
the Tlascalans—Cortés strives to allay it—Events in Mexico—Preparations for Defence—Aztec Embassy to Tlascala—Stormy Debate in the
Senate—Mexican Alliance rejected 466

CHAPTER VI

CHAPTER VII

BOOK VI

SIEGE AND SURRENDER OF MEXICO

CHAPTER I

CHAPTER II

CORTÉS RECONNOITRES THE CAPITAL—OCCUPIES TACUBA—SKIRMISHES
WITH THE ENEMY—EXPEDITION OF SANDOVAL—ARRIVAL OF REINFORCE-
MENTS

CHAPTER III

SECOND RECONNOITRING EXPEDITION—ENGAGEMENTS ON THE SIERRA—
CAPTURE OF CUERNAVACA—BATTLES AT XOCHIMILCO—NARROW ESCAPE
OF CORTÉS—HE ENTERS TACUBA

CHAPTER IV

CONSPIRACY IN THE ARMY—BRIGANTINES LAUNCHED—MUSTER OF
FORCES—EXECUTION OF XICOTENCATL—MARCH OF THE ARMY—BEGIN-
NING OF THE SIEGE

CHAPTER V

INDIAN FLOTILLA DEFEATED—OCCUPATION OF THE CAUSEWAYS—DES-
PERATE ASSAULTS—FIRING OF THE PALACES—SPIRIT OF THE BESIEGED
—BARRACKS FOR THE TROOPS

CHAPTER VI

GENERAL ASSAULT ON THE CITY—DEFEAT OF THE SPANIARDS—THEIR
DISASTROUS CONDITION—SACRIFICE OF THE CAPTIVES—DEFECTION OF
THE ALLIES—CONSTANCY OF THE TROOPS

CHAPTER VII

SUCCESSES OF THE SPANIARDS—FRUITLESS OFFERS TO GUATEMOZIN—
BUILDINGS RAZED TO THE GROUND—TERRIBLE FAMINE—THE TROOPS
GAIN THE MARKET-PLACE—BATTERING ENGINE

CHAPTER VIII

DREADFUL SUFFERINGS OF THE BESIEGED—SPIRIT OF GUATEMOZIN—
MURDEROUS ASSAULTS—CAPTURE OF GAUTEMOZIN—EVACUATION OF THE
CITY—TERMINATION OF THE SIEGE—REFLECTIONS

BOOK VII

CONCLUSION—SUBSEQUENT CAREER OF CORTÉS

CHAPTER I

TORTURE OF GUATEMOZIN—SUBMISSION OF THE COUNTRY—REBUILDING
OF THE CAPITAL—MISSION TO CASTILE—COMPLAINTS AGAINST CORTÉS—
HE IS CONFIRMED IN HIS AUTHORITY

CHAPTER II

MODERN MEXICO—SETTLEMENT OF THE COUNTRY—CONDITION OF THE
NATIVES—CHRISTIAN MISSIONARIES—CULTIVATION OF THE SOIL—VOY-
AGES AND EXPEDITIONS

CHAPTER III

CHAPTER IV

CHAPTER V

APPENDIX; PART I

ORIGIN OF THE MEXICAN CIVILIZATION—ANALOGIES WITH THE OLD WORLD

APPENDIX, PART II

ORIGINAL DOCUMENTS

GENERAL CONTENTS

HISTORY OF THE CONQUEST OF PERU

BOOK I
INTRODUCTION—VIEW OF THE CIVILIZATION OF THE INCAS

BOOK II
DISCOVERY OF PERU

BOOK III
CONQUEST OF PERU

BOOK IV
CIVIL WARS OF THE CONQUERORS

BOOK V
SETTLEMENT OF THE COUNTRY

BOOK I

INTRODUCTION—VIEW OF THE CIVILIZATION OF THE INCAS

CHAPTER I

PHYSICAL ASPECT OF THE COUNTRY—SOURCES OF PERUVIAN CIVILIZA-
TION—EMPIRE OF THE INCAS—ROYAL FAMILY—NOBILITY

CHAPTER II

ORDERS OF THE STATE—PROVISIONS FOR JUSTICE—DIVISION OF LANDS—
REVENUES AND REGISTERS—GREAT ROADS AND POSTS—MILITARY TACTICS
AND POLICY

CHAPTER III

PERUVIAN RELIGION—DEITIES—GORGEOUS TEMPLES—FESTIVALS—
VIRGINS OF THE SUN—MARRIAGE

CHAPTER IV

EDUCATION—QUIPUS—ASTRONOMY—AGRICULTURE—AQUEDUCTS—
GUANO—IMPORTANT ESCULENTS

CHAPTER V

PERUVIAN SHEEP—GREAT HUNTS—MANUFACTURES—MECHANICAL
SKILL—ARCHITECTURE—CONCLUDING REFLECTIONS

BOOK II

DISCOVERY OF PERU

CHAPTER I

CHAPTER II

CHAPTER III

CHAPTER IV

INDIGNATION OF THE GOVERNOR—STERN RESOLUTION OF PIZARRO— PROSECUTION OF THE VOYAGE—BRILLIANT ASPECT OF TUMBEZ—DISCOVERIES ALONG THE COAST—RETURN TO PANAMA—PIZARRO EMBARKS FOR SPAIN

BOOK III

CONQUEST OF PERU

CHAPTER I

PIZARRO'S RECEPTION AT COURT—HIS CAPITULATION WITH THE CROWN —HE VISITS HIS BIRTHPLACE—RETURNS TO THE NEW WORLD—DIFFICULTIES WITH ALMAGRO—HIS THIRD EXPEDITION—RICH INDIAN BOOTY —BATTLES IN THE ISLE OF PUNÁ

CHAPTER II

CHAPTER III

CHAPTER IV

CHAPTER V

DESPERATE PLAN OF PIZARRO—ATAHUALLPA VISITS THE SPANIARDS—
HORRIBLE MASSACRE—THE INCA A PRISONER—CONDUCT OF THE CON-
QUERORS—SPLENDID PROMISES OF THE INCA—DEATH OF HUASCAR

PAGE

Disposition of the Spanish Troops—Religious Ceremonies—Approach of the
Inca—Designs not to enter the Town—Disappointment of the Spaniards
—Atahuallpa changes his Purpose—Leaves his Warriors behind—Enters
the great Square—Urged to embrace Christianity—He rejects it with
Disdain—General Attack of the Spaniards—Bloody Massacre of the
Peruvians—Seizure of Atahuallpa—Dispersion of his Army—Demeanor
of the Captive Monarch—His probable Designs—Courteously treated by
Pizarro—Indian Prisoners—Rich Spoils of the Inca—Magnificent Offer
of Atahuallpa—Accepted by Pizarro—Inca's Mode of Life in Captivity—
Refuses to embrace Christianity—Assassination of his Brother Huascar .

CHAPTER VI

GOLD ARRIVES FOR THE RANSOM—VISIT TO PACHACAMAC—DEMOLITION
OF THE IDOL—THE INCA'S FAVORITE GENERAL—THE INCA'S LIFE IN
CONFINEMENT—ENVOY'S CONDUCT IN CUZCO—ARRIVAL OF ALMAGRO

Slow Arrival of the Ransom—Rumors of an Indian Rising—Emissaries sent
to Cuzco—City and Temple of Pachacamac—Hernando Pizarro's March
thither—Great Road of the Incas—Herds of Llamas—Rich Cultivation
of the Valleys—Hernando's Arrival at the City—Forcible Entry into the
Temple—Horror of the Natives—Destruction of the Indian Idol—Small
Amount of Booty—Hernando marches against Challcuchima—Persuades
him to visit Caxamalca—Interview of Atahuallpa with his General—
The Inca's absolute Authority—His Personal Habits and Appearance—
Return of the Emissaries from Cuzco—Magnificent Reports of the City
—They strip the Gold from the Temples—Their Insolence and
Rapacity—Return with Loads of Treasure—Almagro arrives in Peru—
Brings a large Reinforcement—Joins Pizarro's Camp—Superstitious Bod-
ings of Atahuallpa . . . .

CHAPTER VII

IMMENSE AMOUNT OF TREASURE—ITS DIVISION AMONG THE TROOPS—
RUMORS OF A RISING—TRIAL OF THE INCA—HIS EXECUTION—
REFLECTIONS

Division of the Inca's Ransom—Hernando takes the Royal Fifth to Spain
—His Jealousy of Almagro—Enormous Amount of the Treasure—Difficulties in its Distribution—Shares of the Pizarros—Those of the Soldiers—Exclusion of Almagro and his Followers—Preparations for the
March to Cuzco—The Inca demands his Liberty—Equivocal Conduct
of Pizarro—The Interpreter Felipillo—The Inca charged with exciting
Insurrection—His Protestations of Innocence—His Apprehensions—Fears
and Murmurs of the Spaniards—They demand the Inca's Death—He is
brought to Trial—Charges against him—Condemned to be burnt alive—
Some protest against the Sentence—The Inca entirely unmanned—His

CHAPTER VIII

DISORDERS IN PERU—MARCH TO CUZCO—ENCOUNTER WITH THE NATIVES
—CHALLCUCHIMA BURNT—ARRIVAL IN CUZCO—DESCRIPTION OF THE
CITY—TREASURE FOUND THERE

CHAPTER IX

NEW INCA CROWNED—MUNICIPAL REGULATIONS—TERRIBLE MARCH OF
ALVARADO—INTERVIEW   WITH   PIZARRO—FOUNDATION   OF   LIMA—
HERNANDO PIZARRO REACHES SPAIN—SENSATION AT COURT—FEUDS OF
ALMAGRO AND THE PIZARROS

CHAPTER X

BOOK IV

CIVIL WARS OF THE CONQUERORS

CHAPTER I

CHAPTER V

CHAPTER VI

CHAPTER VII

CHAPTER VIII

CHAPTER IX

BOOK V

SETTLEMENT OF THE COUNTRY

CHAPTER I

CHAPTER II

CHAPTER III

CHAPTER IV

EXECUTION OF CARBAJAL—GONZALO PIZARRO BEHEADED—SPOILS OF VICTORY—WISE REFORMS BY GASCA—HE RETURNS TO SPAIN—HIS DEATH
AND CHARACTER

HISTORY
OF THE
CONQUEST OF MEXICO

"Victrices aquilas alium laturus in orbem."
LUCAN, Pharsalia, lib. v., v. 238

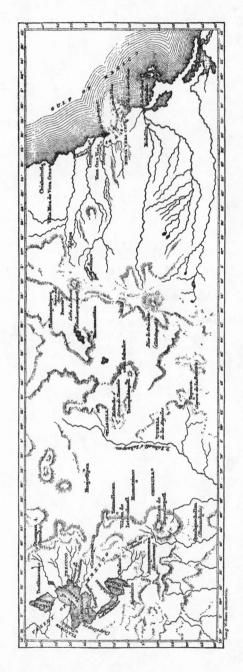

MAP OF THE COUNTRY TRAVERSED BY THE SPANIARDS ON THEIR MARCH TO MEXICO

PREFACE

As the Conquest of Mexico has occupied the pens Solís and of Robertson, two of the ablest historians of their respective nations, it might seem that little could remain at the present day to be gleaned by the historical inquirer. But Robertson's narrative is necessarily brief, forming only a part of a more extended work; and neither the British, nor the Castilian author, was provided with the important materials for relating this event, which have been since assembled by the industry of Spanish scholars. The scholar who led the way in these researches was Don Juan Baptista Muñoz, the celebrated historiographer of the Indies, who, by a royal edict, was allowed free access to the national archives, and to all libraries, public, private, and monastic, in the kingdom and its colonies. The result of his long labors was a vast body of materials, of which unhappily he did not live to reap the benefit himself. His manuscripts were deposited, after his death, in the archives of the Royal Academy of History at Madrid; and that collection was subsequently augmented by the manuscripts of Don Vargas Ponçe, President of the Academy, obtained, like those of Muñoz, from different quarters, but especially from the archives of the Indies at Seville.

On my application to the Academy, in 1838, for permission to copy that part of this inestimable collection relating to Mexico and Peru, it was freely acceded to, and an eminent German scholar, one of their own number, was appointed to superintend the collation and transcription of the manuscripts and this, it may be added, before I had any claim on the courtesy of that respectable body, as one of its associates. This conduct shows the advance of a liberal spirit in the Peninsula since the time of Dr. Robertson, who complains that he was denied admission to the most important public repositories. The favor with which my own application was regarded, however, must chiefly be attributed to the kind offices of the venerable President of the Academy, Don Martin Fernandez de Navarrette; a scholar whose personal character has secured to him the same high consideration at home, which his literary labors have obtained abroad. To this eminent person I am under still further obligations, for the free use which he has allowed me to make of his own mansuscripts, —the fruits of a life of accumulation, and the basis of those valuable publications, with which he has at different times illustrated the Spanish colonial history.

From these three magnificent collections, the result of half a century's careful researches, I have obtained a mass of unpublished documents, relating to the Conquest and Settlement of Mexico and of Peru, compris-

ing altogether about eight thousand folio pages. They consist of instructions of the Court, military and private journals, correspondence of the
great actors in the scenes, legal instruments, contemporary chronicles,
and the like, drawn from all the principal places in the extensive colonial
empire of Spain, as well as from the public archives in the Peninsula.

I have still further fortified the collection, by gleaning such materials
from Mexico itself as had been overlooked by my illustrious predecessors in these researches. For these I am indebted to the courtesy of
Count Cortina, and, yet more, to that of Don Lucas Alaman, Minister of
Foreign Affairs in Mexico; but, above all, to my excellent friend, Don
Angel Calderon de la Barca, late Minister Plenipotentiary to that country for the Court of Madrid,—a gentleman whose high and estimable
qualities, even more than his station, secured him the public confidence,
and gained him free access to every place of interest and importance in
Mexico.

I have also to acknowledge the very kind offices rendered to me by
the Count Camaldoli at Naples; by the Duke of Serradifalco in Sicily, a
nobleman, whose science gives additional lustre to his rank; and by the
Duke of Monteleone, the present representative of Cortés, who has courteously opened the archives of his family to my inspection. To these
names must also be added that of Sir Thomas Phillips, Bart., whose precious collection of manuscripts probably surpasses in extent that of any
private gentleman in Great Britain, if not in Europe; that of Mons.
Ternaux-Compans, the proprietor of the valuable literary collection of
Don Antonio Uguina, including the papers of Muñoz, the fruits of which
he is giving to the world in his excellent translations; and, lastly, that of
my friend and countryman, Arthur Middleton, Esq., late Chargé d'Af-
faires from the United States at the Court of Madrid, for the efficient
aid he has afforded me in prosecuting my inquiries in that capital.

In addition to this stock of original documents obtained through these
various sources, I have diligently provided myself with such printed
works as have reference to the subject, including the magnificent publications, which have appeared both in France and England, on the Antiquities of Mexico, which, from their cost and colossal dimensions, would
seem better suited to a public than to a private library.

Having thus stated the nature of my materials, and the sources
whence they are derived, it remains for me to add a few observations on
the general plan and composition of the work.—Among the remarkable
achievements of the Spaniards in the sixteenth century, there is no one
more striking to the imagination than the conquest of Mexico. The subversion of a great empire by a handful of adventurers, taken with all its
strange and picturesque accompaniments, has the air of romance rather
than of sober history; and it is not easy to treat such a theme according
to the severe rules prescribed by historical criticism. But, notwithstanding the seductions of the subject, I have conscientiously endeavored to
distinguish fact from fiction, and to establish the narrative on as broad
a basis as possible of contemporary evidence; and I have taken occasion

to corroborate the text by ample citations from authorities, usually in the original, since few of them can be very accessible to the reader. In these extracts I have scrupulously conformed to the ancient orthography, however obsolete and even barbarous, rather than impair in any degree the integrity of the original document.

Although the subject of the work is, properly, only the Conquest of Mexico, I have prepared the way for it by such a view of the Civilization of the ancient Mexicans, as might acquaint the reader with the character of this extraordinary race, and enable him to understand the difficulties which the Spaniards had to encounter in their subjugaton. This Introductory part of the work, with the essay in the Appendix which properly belongs to the Introduction, although both together making only half a volume, has cost me as much labor, and nearly as much time, as the remainder of the history. If I shall have succeeded in giving the reader a just idea of the true nature and extent of the civilization to which the Mexicans had attained, it will not be labor lost.

The story of the Conquest terminates with the fall of the capital. Yet I have preferred to continue the narrative to the death of Cortés, relying on the interest which the development of his character in his military career may have excited in the reader. I am not insensible to the hazard I incur by such a course. The mind, previously occupied with one great idea, that of the subversion of the capital, may feel the prolongation of the story beyond that point superfluous, if not tedious; and may find it difficult, after the excitement caused by witnessing a great national catastrophe, to take an interest in the adventures of a private individual. Solís took the more politic course of concluding his narrative with the fall of Mexico, and thus leaves his readers with the full impression of that memorable event, undisturbed, on their minds. To prolong the narrative is to expose the historian to the error so much censured by the French critics in some of their most celebrated dramas, where the author by a premature *dénouement* has impaired the interest of his piece. It is the defect that necessarily attaches, though in a greater degree, to the history of Columbus, in which petty adventures among a group of islands make up the sequel of a life that opened with the magnificent discovery of a World; a defect, in short, which has required all the genius of Irving and the magical charm of his style perfectly to overcome.

Notwithstanding these objections, I have been induced to continue the narrative, partly from deference to the opinion of several Spanish scholars, who considered that the biography of Cortés had not been fully exhibited, and partly from the circumstances of my having such a body of original materials for this biography at my command. And I cannot regret that I have adopted this course; since, whatever lustre the Conquest may reflect on Cortés as a military achievement, it gives but an imperfect idea of his enlightened spirit, and of his comprehensive and versatile genius.

To the eye of the critic there may seem some incongruity in a plan which combines objects so dissimilar as those embraced by the present history; where the Introduction, occupied with the antiquities and origin of a nation, has somewhat the character of a *philosophic* theme, while the conclusion is strictly *biographical*, and the two may be supposed to match indifferently with the main body, or *historical* portion of the work. But I may hope that such objections will be found to have less weight in practice than in theory; and, if properly managed, that the general views of the Introduction will prepare the reader for the particulars of the Conquest, and that the great public events narrated in this will, without violence, open the way to the remaining personal history of the hero who is the soul of it. Whatever incongruity may exist in other respects, I may hope that the *unity of interest,* the only unity held of much importance by modern critics, will be found still to be preserved.

The distance of the present age from the period of the narrative might be presumed to secure the historian from undue prejudice or partiality. Yet to American and English readers, acknowledging so different a moral standard from that of the sixteenth century, I may possibly be thought too indulgent to the errors of the Conquerors; while to a Spaniard, accustomed to the undiluted panegyric of Solís, I may be deemed to have dealt too hardly with them. To such I can only say, that, while, on the one hand, I have not hesitated to expose in their strongest colors the excesses of the Conquerors; on the other, I have given them the benefit of such mitigating reflections as might be suggested by the circumstances and the period in which they lived. I have endeavored not only to present a picture true in itself, but to place it in its proper light, and to put the spectator in a proper point of view for seeing it to the best advantage. I have endeavored, at the expense of some repetition, to surround him with the spirit of the times, and, in a word, to make him, if I may so express myself, a contemporary of the sixteenth century. Whether, and how far, I have succeeded in this, he must determine.

For one thing, before I conclude, I may reasonably ask the reader's indulgence. Owing to the state of my eyes, I have been obliged to use a writing-case made for the blind, which does not permit the writer to see his own manuscript. Nor have I ever corrected, or even read, my own original draft. As the chirography, under these disadvantages, has been too often careless and obscure, occasional errors, even with the utmost care of my secretary, must have necessarily occurred in the transcription, somewhat increased by the barbarous phraseology imported from my Mexican authorities. I cannot expect that these errors have always been detected even by the vigilant eye of the perspicacious critic to whom the proof-sheets have been subjected.

In the Preface to the "History of Ferdinand and Isabella," I lamented, that, while occupied with that subject, two of its most attractive parts had engaged the attention of the most popular of American authors, Washington Irving. By a singular chance, something like the reverse of this has taken place in the composition of the present history, and I have found myself unconsciously taking up ground which he was preparing to occupy. It was not till I had become master of my rich collection of materials, that I was acquainted with this circumstance; and, had he persevered in his design, I should unhesitatingly have abandoned my own, if not from courtesy, at least from policy; for, though armed with the weapons of Achilles, this could give me no hope of success in a competition with Achilles himself. But no sooner was that distinguished writer informed of the preparations I had made, than, with the gentlemanly spirit which will surprise no one who has the pleasure of his acquaintance, he instantly announced to me his intention of leaving the subject open to me. While I do but justice to Mr. Irving by this statement, I feel the prejudice it does to myself in the unavailing regret I am exciting in the bosom of the reader.

I must not conclude this Preface, too long protracted as it is already, without a word of acknowledgment to my friend George Ticknor, Esq., —the friend of many years,—for his patient revision of my manuscript; a labor of love, the worth of which those only can estimate, who are acquainted with his extraordinary erudition and his nice critical taste. If I have reserved his name for the last in the list of those to whose good offices I am indebted, it is most assuredly not because I value his services least.

WILLIAM H. PRESCOTT

Boston, October 1, 1843.

BOOK I

INTRODUCTION

VIEW OF THE AZTEC CIVILIZATION

CHAPTER I

ANCIENT MEXICO—CLIMATE AND PRODUCTS—PRIMITIVE RACES—
AZTEC EMPIRE

OF all that extensive empire which once acknowledged the authority of Spain in the New World, no portion, for interest and importance, can be compared with Mexico;—and this equally, whether we consider the variety of its soil and climate; the inexhaustible stores of its mineral wealth; its scenery, grand and picturesque beyond example; the character of its ancient inhabitants, not only far surpassing in intelligence that of the other North American races, but reminding us, by their monuments, of the primitive civilization of Egypt and Hindostan; or lastly, the peculiar circumstances of its Conquest, adventurous and romantic as any legend devised by Norman or Italian bard of chivalry. It is the purpose of the present narrative to exhibit the history of this Conquest, and that of the remarkable man by whom it was achieved.

But, in order that the reader may have a better understanding of the subject, it will be well, before entering on it, to take a general survey of the political and social institutions of the races who occupied the land at the time of its discovery.

The country of the ancient Mexicans, or Aztecs as they were called, formed but a very small part of the extensive territories comprehended in the modern republic of Mexico.[1] Its boundaries cannot be defined with certainty. They were much enlarged in the latter days of the empire, when they may be considered as reaching from about the eighteenth degree north, to the twenty-first, on the Atlantic; and from the fourteenth to the nineteenth, including a very narrow strip, on the Pacific.[2] In its greatest breadth, it could not exceed five degrees and a half,

[1] Extensive indeed, if we may trust Archbishop Lorenzana, who tells us, "It is doubtful if the country of New Spain does not border on *Tartary* and Greenland; —by the way of California, on the former, and by New Mexico, on the latter!" Historia de Nueva España, (México, 1770,) p. 38, nota.

[2] I have conformed to the limits fixed by Clavigero. He has, probably, examined the subject with more thoroughness and fidelity than most of his countrymen, who

o

dwindling, as it approached its south-eastern limits, to less than two. It covered, probably, less than sixteen thousand square leagues.[3] Yet such is the remarkable formation of this country, that, though not more than twice as large as New England, it presented every variety of climate, and was capable of yielding nearly every fruit, found between the equator and the Arctic circle.

All along the Atlantic, the country is bordered by a broad tract, called the *tierra caliente,* or hot region, which has the usual high temperature of equinoctial lands. Parched and sandy plains are intermingled with others, of exuberant fertility, almost impervious from thickets of aromatic shrubs and wild flowers, in the midst of which tower up trees of that magnificent growth which is found only within the tropics. In this wilderness of sweets lurks the fatal *malaria,* engendered, probably, by the decomposition of rank vegetable substances in a hot and humid soil. The season of the bilious fever,—*vómito,* as it is called,—which scourges these coasts, continues from the spring to the autumnal equinox, when it is checked by the cold winds that descend from Hudson's Bay. These winds in the winter season frequently freshen into tempests, and, sweeping down the Atlantic coast, and the winding Gulf of Mexico, burst with the fury of a hurricane on its unprotected shores, and on the neighboring West India islands. Such are the mighty spells with which Nature has surrounded this land of enchantment, as if to guard the golden treasures locked up within its bosom. The genius and enterprise of man have proved more potent than her spells.

After passing some twenty leagues across this burning region, the

---

differ from him, and who assign a more liberal extent to the monarchy. (See his Storia Antica del Messico, (Cesena, 1780,) dissert. 7.) The Abbé, however, has not informed his readers on what frail foundations his conclusions rest. The extent of the Aztec empire is to be gathered from the writings of historians since the arrival of the Spaniards, and from the picture-rolls of tribute paid by the conquered cities; both sources extremely vague and defective. See the MSS. of the Mendoza collection, in Lord Kingsborough's magnificent publication (Antiquities of Mexico, comprising Facsimiles of Ancient Paintings and Hieroglyphics, together with the Monuments of New Spain. London, 1830). The difficulty of the inquiry is much increased by the fact of the conquests having been made, as will be seen hereafter, by the united arms of three powers, so that it is not always easy to tell to which party they eventually belonged. The affair is involved in so much uncertainty, that Clavigero, notwithstanding the positive assertions in his text, has not ventured, in his map, to define the precise limits of the empire, either towards the north, where it mingles with the Tezcucan empire, or towards the south, where, indeed, he has fallen into the egregious blunder of asserting, that, while the Mexican territory reached to the fourteenth degree, it did not include any portion of Guatemala. (See tom. I. p. 29, and tom. IV. dissert. 7.) The Tezcucan chronicler, Ixtlilxochitl, puts in a sturdy claim for the paramount empire of his own nation. Historia Chichemeca, MS., cap. 39, 53, et alibi.

[3] Eighteen to twenty thousand, according to Humboldt, who considers the Mexican territory to have been the same with that occupied by the modern intendancies of Mexico, Puebla, Vera Cruz, Oaxaca, and Valladolid. (Essai Politique sur le Royaume de Nouvelle Espagne, (Paris, 1825,) tom. I. p. 196.) This last, however, was all, or nearly all, included in the rival kingdom of Mechoacan, as he himself more correctly states in another part of his work. Comp. tom. II. p. 164.

traveller finds himself rising into a purer atmosphere. His limbs recover their elasticity. He breathes more freely, for his senses are not now oppressed by the sultry heats and intoxicating perfumes of the valley. The aspect of nature, too, has changed, and his eye no longer revels among the gay variety of colors with which the landscape was painted there. The vanilla, the indigo, and the flowering cacao-groves disappear as he advances. The sugar-cane and the glossy-leaved banana still accompany him; and, when he has ascended about four thousand feet, he sees in the unchanging verdure, and the rich foliage of the liquid-amber tree, that he has reached the height where clouds and mists settle, in their passage from the Mexican Gulf. This is the region of perpetual humidity; but he welcomes it with pleasure, as announcing his escape from the influence of the deadly *vómito*.[4] He has entered the *tierra templada,* or temperate region, whose character resembles that of the temperate zone of the globe. The features of the scenery become grand, and even terrible. His road sweeps along the base of mighty mountains, once gleaming with volcanic fires, and still resplendent in their mantles of snow, which serve as beacons to the mariner, for many a league at sea. All around he beholds traces of their ancient combustion, as his road passes along vast tracts of lava, bristling in the innumerable fantastic forms into which the fiery torrent has been thrown by the obstacles in its career. Perhaps, at the same moment, as he casts his eye down some steep slope, or almost unfathomable ravine, on the margin of the road, he sees their depths glowing with the rich blooms and enamelled vegetation of the tropics. Such are the singular contrasts presented at the same time, to the senses, in this picturesque region!

Still pressing upwards, the traveller mounts into other climates, favorable to other kinds of cultivation. The yellow maize, or Indian corn, as we usually call it, has continued to follow him up from the lowest level; but he now first sees fields of wheat, and the other European grains brought into the country by the Conquerors. Mingled with them, he views the plantations of the aloe or maguey (*agave Americana*), applied to such various and important uses by the Aztecs. The oaks now acquire a sturdier growth, and the dark forests of pine announce that he has entered the *tierra fria,* or cold region,—the third and last of the great natural terraces into which the country is divided. When he has climbed to the height of between seven and eight thousand feet, the weary traveller sets his foot on the summit of the Cordillera of the Andes,— the colossal range, that, after traversing South America and the Isthmus of Darien, spreads out, as it enters Mexico, into that vast sheet of table-

---

[4] The traveller, who enters the country across the dreary sand-hills of Vera Cruz, will hardly recognise the truth of the above description. He must look for it in other parts of the *tierra caliente.* Of recent tourists, no one has given a more gorgeous picture of the impressions made on his senses by these sunny regions than Latrobe, who came on shore at Tampico; (Rambler in Mexico, (New York, 1836,) chap. 1;) a traveller, it may be added, whose descriptions of a man and nature, in our own country, where we can judge, are distinguished by a sobriety and fairness that en title him to confidence in his delineation of other countries.

land, which maintains an elevation of more than six thousand feet, for the distance of nearly two hundred leagues, until it gradually declines in the higher latitudes of the north.[5]

Across this mountain rampart a chain of volcanic hills stretches, in a westerly direction, of still more stupendous dimensions, forming, indeed, some of the highest land on the globe. Their peaks, entering the limits of perpetual snow, diffuse a grateful coolness over the elevated *plateaus* below; for these last, though termed 'cold', enjoy a climate, the mean temperature of which is not lower than that of the central parts of Italy.[6] The air is exceedingly dry; the soil, though naturally good, is rarely clothed with the luxuriant vegetation of the lower regions. It frequently, indeed, has a parched and barren aspect, owing partly to the greater evaporation which takes places on these lofty plains, through the diminished pressure of the atmosphere; and partly, no doubt, to the want of trees to shelter the soil from the fierce influence of the summer sun. In the time of the Aztecs, the table-land was thickly covered with larch, oak, cypress, and other forest trees, the extraordinary dimensions of some of which, remaining to the present day, show that the curse of barrenness in later times is chargeable more on man than on nature. Indeed, the early Spaniards made as indiscriminate war on the forest as did our Puritan ancestors, though with much less reason. After once conquering the country, they had no lurking ambush to fear from the submissive, semicivilized Indian, and were not, like our forefathers, obliged to keep watch and ward for a century. This spoliation of the ground, however, is said to have been pleasing to their imaginations, as it reminded them of the plains of their own Castile,—the table-land of Europe;[7] where the nakedness of the landscape forms the burden of every traveller's lament, who visits that country.

Midway across the continent, somewhat nearer the Pacific than the Atlantic ocean, at an elevation of nearly seven thousand five hundred feet, is the celebrated Valley of Mexico. It is of an oval form, about sixty-seven leagues in circumference,[8] and is encompassed by a towering

[5] This long extent of country varies in elevation from 5570 to 8856 feet,—equal to the height of the passes of Mount Cenis, or the Great St. Bernard. The table-land stretches still three hundred leagues further, before it declines to a level of 2624 feet. Humboldt, Essai Politique, tom. I. pp. 157, 255.

[6] About 62° Fahrenheit, or 17° Réaumur. (Humboldt, Essai Politique, tom I. p. 273.) The more elevated plateaus of the table-land, as the Valley of Toluca, about 8500 feet above the sea, have a stern climate, in which the thermometer, during a great part of the day, rarely rises beyond 45° F. Idem, (loc. cit.,) and Malte-Brun, (Universal Geography, Eng. Trans., book 83,) who is, indeed, in this part of his work, but an echo of the former writer.

[7] The elevation of the Castiles, according to the authority repeatedly cited, is about 350 toises, or 2100 feet above the ocean. (Humboldt's Dissertation, apud Laborde, Itinéraire Descriptif de l'Espagne, (Paris, 1827,) tom I. p. 5.) It is rare to find plains in Europe of so great a height.

[8] Archbishop Lorenzana estimates the circuit of the Valley at ninety leagues, correcting at the same time the statement of Cortés, which puts it at seventy, very near the truth, as appears from the result of M. de Humboldt's measurement, cited in the text. Its length is about eighteen leagues, by twelve and a half in breadth. (Hum-

rampart of porphyritic rock, which nature seems to have provided, though ineffectually, to protect it from invasion.

The soil, once carpeted with a beautiful verdure, and thickly sprinkled with stately trees, is often bare, and, in many places, white with the incrustation of salts, caused by the draining of the waters. Five lakes are spread over the Valley, occupying one tenth of its surface.[9] On the opposite borders of the largest of these basins, much shrunk in its dimensions [10] since the days of the Aztecs, stood the cities of Mexico and Tezcuco, the capitals of the two most potent and flourishing states of Anahuac, whose history, with that of the mysterious races that preceded them in the country, exhibits some of the nearest approaches to civilization to be met with anciently on the North American continent.

Of these races the most conspicuous were the Toltecs. Advancing from a northerly direction, but from what region is uncertain, they entered the territory of Anahuac,[11] probably before the close of the seventh century. Of course, little can be gleaned, with certainty, respecting a people, whose written records have perished, and who are known to us only through the traditionary legends of the nations that succeeded them.[12] By the

boldt, Essai Politique, tom. II. p. 29.—Lorenzana, Hist. de Nueva España, p. 101.) Humboldt's map of the Valley of Mexico forms the third in his "Atlas Geographique et Physique," and, like all the others in the collection, will be found of inestimable value to the traveller, the geologist, and the historian.

[9] Humboldt, Essai Politique, tom. II. pp. 29, 44-49.—Malte Brun, book 85. This latter geographer assigns only 6700 feet for the level of the Valley, contradicting himself, (Comp. book 83,) or rather, Humboldt, to whose pages he helps himself, *plenis manibus,* somewhat too liberally, indeed, for the scanty references at the bottom of his page.

[10] Torquemada accounts, in part, for this diminution, by supposing, that, as God permitted the waters, which once covered the whole earth, to subside, after mankind had been nearly exterminated for their iniquities, so he allowed the waters of the Mexican lake to subside in token of good-will and reconciliation, after the idolatrous races of the land had been destroyed by the Spaniards! (Monarchía Indiana, (Madrid, 1723,) tom. I. p. 309.) Quite as probable, if not as orthodox an explanation, may be found in the active evaporation of these upper regions, and in the fact of an immense drain having been constructed, during the lifetime of the good father, to reduce the waters of the principal lake, and protect the capital from inundation.

[11] Anahuac, according to Humboldt, comprehended only the country between the 14th and 21st degrees of N. latitude. (Essai Politique, tom. I. p. 197.) According to Clavigero, it included nearly all since known as New Spain. (Stor. del Messico, tom. I. p. 27.) Veytia uses it, also, as synonymous with New Spain. (Historia Antigua de Méjico, (Méjico, 1836,) tom. I. cap. 12) The first of these writers probably allows too little, as the latter do too much, for its boundaries. Ixtlilxochitl says it extended four hundred leagues south of the Otomie country. (Hist. Chichemeca, MS., cap. 73.) The word Anahuac signifies *near the water.* It was, probably, first applied to the country around the lakes in the Mexican Valley, and gradually extended to the remoter regions occupied by the Aztecs, and the other semicivilized races. Or, possibly, the name may have been intended, as Veytia suggests, (Hist. Antig., lib. 1, cap. 1,) to denote the land between the waters of the Atlantic and Pacific.

[12] Clavigero talks of Boturini's having written "on the faith of the Toltec historians." (Stor. del Messico, tom. I. p. 128.) But that scholar does not pretend to have ever met with a Toltec manuscript, himself, and had heard of only one in the possession of Ixtlilxochitl. (See his Idea de una Nueva Historia de la América Septentrional, (Madrid, 1746,) p. 110.) The latter writer tells us, that his account of the

general agreement of these, however, the Toltecs were well instructed in agriculture, and many of the most useful mechanic arts; were nice workers of metals; invented the complex arrangement of time adopted by the Aztecs; and, in short, were the true fountains of the civilization which distinguished this part of the continent in later times.[13] They established their capital at Tula, north of the Mexican Valley, and the remains of extensive buildings were to be discerned there at the time of the Conquest.[14] The noble ruins of religious and other edifices, still to be seen in various parts of New Spain, are referred to this people, whose name, *Toltec*, has passed into a synonyme for *architect*.[15] Their shadowy history reminds us of those primitive races, who preceded the ancient Egyptians in the march of civilization; fragments of whose monuments, as they are seen at this day, incorporated with the buildings of the Egyptians themselves, give to these latter the appearance of almost modern constructions.[16]

After a period of four centuries, the Toltecs, who had extended their sway over the remotest borders of Anahuac,[17] having been greatly re-duced, it is said, by famine, pestilence, and unsuccessful wars, disap-peared from the land as silently and mysteriously as they had entered it. A few of them still lingered behind, but much the greater number, probably, spread over the region of Central America and the neighbor-ing isles; and the traveller now speculates on the majestic ruins of Mitla and Palenque, as possibly the work of this extraordinary people.[18]

After the lapse of another hundred years, a numerous and rude tribe, called the Chichemecs, entered the deserted country from the regions of the far Northwest. They were speedily followed by other races, of higher civilization, perhaps of the same family with the Toltecs, whose language they appear to have spoken. The most noted of these were the Aztecs or Mexicans, and the Acolhuans. The latter, better known in later times

---

Toltec and Chichemec races was "derived from interpretation," (probably, of the Texcucan paintings,) "and from the traditions of old men"; poor authority for events which had passed, centuries before. Indeed, he acknowledges that their nar-ratives were so full of absurdity and falsehood, that he was obliged to reject nine-tenths of them. (See his Relaciones, MS., no. 5.) The cause of truth would not have suffered much, probably, if he had rejected nine-tenths of the remainder.

[13] Ixtlilxochitl, Hist. Chich., MS., cap. 2.—Idem, Relaciones, MS., no. 2.—Saha-gun, Historia General de las Cosas de Nueva España, (México, 1829,) lib. 10, cap. 29.—Veytia, Hist. Antig., lib. 1, cap. 27.

[14] Sahagun, Hist. de Nueva España, lib. 10, cap. 29.

[15] Idem, ubi supra.—Torquemada, Monarch. Ind., lib. 1, cap. 14.

[16] Description de l'Egypte, (Paris, 1809,) Antiquités, tom. I. cap. 1. Veytia has traced the migrations of the Toltecs with sufficient industry, scarcely rewarded by the necessarily doubtful credit of the results. Hist. Antig., lib. 2, cap. 21-33.

[17] Ixtlilxochitl, Hist. Chich. MS., cap. 73.

[18] Veytia, Hist. Antig., lib. 1, cap. 33.—Ixtlilxochitl, Hist. Chich., MS., cap. 3.—Idem, Relaciones, MS., no. 4, 5.—Father Torquemada—perhaps misinterpreting the Texcucan hieroglyphics—has accounted for this mysterious disappearance of the Tol-tecs, by such *fee-faw-fum* stories of giants and demons, as show his appetite for the marvellous was fully equal to that of any of his calling. See his Monarch. Ind., lib. 1, cap. 14.

by the name of Tezcucans, from their capital, Tezcuco,[19] on the eastern border of the Mexican lake, were peculiarly fitted, by their comparatively mild religion and manners, for receiving the tincture of civilization which could be derived from the few Toltecs that still remained in the country. This, in their turn, they communicated to the barbarous Chichemecs, a large portion of whom became amalgamated with the new settlers as one nation.[20]

Availing themselves of the strength derived, not only from this increase of numbers, but from their own superior refinement, the Acolhuans gradually stretched their empire over the ruder tribes in the north; while their capital was filled with a numerous population, busily employed in many of the more useful and even elegant arts of a civilized community. In this palmy state, they were suddenly assaulted by a warlike neighbor, the Tepanecs, their own kindred, and inhabitants of the same valley as themselves. Their provinces were overrun, their armies beaten, their king assassinated, and the flourishing city of Tezcuco became the prize of the victor. From this abject condition the uncommon abilities of the young prince, Nezahualcoyotl, the rightful heir to the crown, backed by the efficient aid of his Mexican allies, at length, redeemed the state, and opened to it a new career of prosperity, even more brilliant than the former.[21]

The Mexicans, with whom our history is principally concerned, came, also, as we have seen, from the remote regions of the North,—the populous hive of nations in the New World, as it has been in the Old. They arrived on the borders of Anahuac, towards the beginning of the thirteenth century, some time after the occupation of the land by the kindred races. For a long time they did not establish themselves in any permanent residence; but continued shifting their quarters to different parts of the Mexican Valley, enduring all the casualties and hardships of a migratory life. On one occasion, they were enslaved by a more powerful tribe; but their ferocity soon made them formidable to their masters.[22] After a series of wanderings and adventures, which need not shrink from comparison with the most extravagant legends of the heroic ages of antiquity, they at length halted on the southwestern borders of the principal lake, in the year 1325. They there beheld, perched on the stem of a prickly pear, which shot out from the crevice of a rock that was washed by the waves, a royal eagle of extraordinary size and beauty, with a serpent in his talons, and his broad wings opened to the rising

---

[19] *Tezcuco* signifies "place of detention"; as several of the tribes who successively occupied Anahuac were said to have halted some time at the spot. Ixtlilxochitl, Hist. Chich., MS., cap. 10.

[20] The historian speaks, in one page, of the Chichemecs' burrowing in caves, or, at best, in cabins of straw;—and, in the next, talks gravely of their *señoras, infantas,* and *caballeros!* Ibid., cap. 9, et seq.—Veytia, Hist. Antig., lib. 2. cap. 1-10.—Camargo, Historia de Tlascala, MS.

[21] Ixtlilxochitl, Hist. Chich. MS., cap. 9-20.—Veytia, Hist. Antig., lib. 2, cap. 29-54.

[22] These were the Colhuans, not Acolhuans, with whom Humboldt, and most writers since, have confounded them. See his Essai Politique, tom. I. p. 414, II. p. 37.

sun. They hailed the auspicious omen, announced by the oracle, as indicating the site of their future city, and laid its foundations by sinking
piles into the shallows; for the low marshes were half buried under
water. On these they erected their light fabrics of reeds and rushes; and
sought a precarious subsistence from fishing, and from the wild fowl
which frequented the waters, as well as from the cultivation of such
simple vegetables as they could raise on their floating gardens. The place
was called Tenochtitlan, in token of its miraculous origin, though only
known to Europeans by its other name of Mexico, derived from their
war-god, Mexitli.[23] The legend of its foundation is still further commemorated by the device of the eagle and the cactus, which form the arms of
the modern Mexican republic. Such were the humble beginnings of the
Venice of the Western World.[24]

The forlorn condition of the new settlers was made still worse by
domestic feuds. A part of the citizens seceded from the main body, and
formed a separate community on the neighboring marshes. Thus divided,
it was long before they could aspire to the acquisition of territory on the
main land. They gradually increased, however, in numbers, and strengthened themselves yet more by various improvements in their polity and
military discipline, while they established a reputation for courage as
well as cruelty in war, which made their name terrible throughout the
Valley. In the early part of the fifteenth century, nearly a hundred years
from the foundation of the city, an event took place which created an
entire revolution in the circumstances, and, to some extent, in the character of the Aztecs. This was the subversion of the Tezcucan monarchy
by the Tepanecs, already noticed. When the oppressive conduct of the
victors had at length aroused a spirit of resistance, its prince, Nezahual-

---

[23] Clavigero gives good reasons for preferring the etymology of Mexico above
noticed, to various others. (See his Stor. del Messico, tom. I. p. 168, nota.) The name
Tenochtitlan signifies *tunal* (a cactus) *on a stone*. Esplicacion de la Col. de Mendoza, apud Antiq. of Mexico, vol. IV.

[24] "Datur hæc venia antiquitati," says Livy, "ut, miscendo humana divinis, prim-
ordia urbium augustiora faciat." Hist., Præf.—See, for the above paragraph, Col.
de Mendoza, plate 1, apud Antiq. of Mexico, vol. I.,—Ixtlilxochitl, Hist. Chich., MS.,
cap. 10,—Toribio, Historia de los Indios, MS., Parte 3, cap. 8,—Veytia, Hist. Antig.,
lib. 2, cap. 15.—Clavigero, after a laborious examination, assigns the following dates
to some of the prominent events noticed in the text. No two authorities agree on
them; and this is not strange, considering that Clavigero—the most inquisitive of all
—does not always agree with himself. (Compare his dates for the coming of the
Acolhuans; tom. I. p. 147, and tom. IV. dissert. 2.)—

	A. D.
The Toltecs arrived in Anahuac	648
They abandoned the country	1051
The Chichemecs arrived	1170
The Acolhuans arrived about	1200
The Mexicans reached Tula	1196
They founded Mexico	1325

See his dissert. 2, sec. 12. In the last date, the one of most importance, he is confirmed by the learned Veytia, who differs from him in all the others. Hist. Antig.,
lib. 2, cap. 15.

coyotl, succeeded, after incredible perils and escapes, in mustering such a force, as, with the aid of the Mexicans, placed him on a level with his enemies. In two successive battles, these were defeated with great slaughter, their chief slain, and their territory, by one of those sudden reverses which characterize the wars of petty states, passed into the hands of the conquerors. It was awarded to Mexico, in return for its important services.

Then was formed that remarkable league, which, indeed, has no parallel in history. It was agreed between the states of Mexico, Tezcuco, and the neighboring little kingdom of Tlacopan, that they should mutually support each other in their wars, offensive and defensive, and that, in the distribution of the spoil, one fifth should be assigned to Tlacopan, and the remainder be divided, in what proportions is uncertain, between the other powers. The Tezcucan writers claim an equal share for their nation with the Aztecs. But this does not seem to be warranted by the immense increase of territory subsequently appropriated by the latter. And we may account for any advantage conceded to them by the treaty, on the supposition, that, however inferior they may have been originally, they were, at the time of making it, in a more prosperous condition than their allies, broken and dispirited by long oppression. What is more extraordinary than the treaty itself, however, is the fidelity with which it was maintained. During a century of uninterrupted warfare that ensued, no instance occurred where the parties quarrelled over the division of the spoil, which so often makes shipwreck of similar confederacies among civilized states.[25]

The allies for some time found sufficient occupation for their arms in their own valley; but they soon overleaped its rocky ramparts, and by the middle of the fifteenth century under the first Montezuma had spread down the sides of the table-land to the borders of the Gulf of Mexico. Tenochtitlan, the Aztec capital, gave evidence of the public prosperity. Its frail tenements were supplanted by solid structures of stone and lime. Its population rapidly increased. Its old feuds were healed. The citizens who had seceded were again brought under a common government with the main body and the quarter they occupied was permanently connected with the parent city; the dimensions of which, covering the

---

[25] The loyal Tezcucan chronicler claims the supreme dignity for his own sovereign, if not the greatest share of the spoil, by this imperial compact. (Hist. Chich., cap. 32.) Torquemada, on the other hand, claims one half of all the conquered lands for Mexico. (Monarch. Ind., lib. 2, cap. 40.) All agree in assigning only one fifth to Tlacopan; and Veytia (Hist. Antig., lib. 3, cap. 3) and Zurita (Rapport sur les Différentes Classes de Chefs de la Nouvelle Espagne, trad. de Ternaux, (Paris, 1840,) p. 11), both very competent critics, acquiesce in an equal division between the two principal states in the confederacy. An ode, still extant, of Nezahualcoyotl, in its Castilian version, bears testimony to the singular union of the three powers.

"solo se acordarán en las Naciones
lo bien que gobernáron
las *tres Cabezas* que el Imperio honráron."

CANTARES DEL EMPERADOR NEZAHUALCOYOTL, MS.

same ground, were much larger than those of the modern capital oi Mexico.[26]

Fortunately, the throne was filled by a succession of able princes, who knew how to profit by their enlarged resources and by the martial enthusiasm of the nation. Year after year saw them return, loaded with the spoils of conquered cities, and with throngs of devoted captives, to their capital. No state was able long to resist the accumulated strength of the confederates. At the beginning of the sixteenth century, just before the arrival of the Spaniards, the Aztec dominion reached across the continent, from the Atlantic to the Pacific; and, under the bold and bloody Ahuitzotl, its arms had been carried far over the limits already noticed as defining its permanent territory, into the farthest corners of Guatemala and Nicaragua. This extent of empire, however limited in comparison with that of many other states, is truly wonderful, considering it as the acquisition of a people whose whole population and resources had so recently been comprised within the walls of their own petty city; and considering, moreover, that the conquered territory was thickly settled by various races, bred to arms like the Mexicans, and little inferior to them in social organization. The history of the Aztecs suggests some strong points of resemblance to that of the ancient Romans, not only in their military successes, but in the policy which led to them.[27]

The most important contribution, of late years, to the early history of Mexico is the *Historia Antigua* of the Lic. Don Mariano Veytia, published in the city of Mexico, in 1836. This scholar was born of an ancient and highly respectable family at Puebla, 1718. After finishing his academic education, he went to Spain, where he was kindly received at court. He afterwards visited several other countries of Europe, made himself acquainted with their languages, and returned home well stored with the fruits of a discriminating observation and diligent study. The rest of his life he devoted to letters; especially to the illustration of the national history and antiquities. As the executor of the unfortunate Boturini, with whom he had contracted an intimacy in Madrid, he obtained access to his valuable collection of manuscripts in Mexico, and from them, and every other source which his position in society and his eminent character opened to him, he composed various works, none of which, however, except the one before us, has been admitted to the honors of the press. The time of his death is not given by his editor, but it was probably not later than 1780.

Veytia's history covers the whole period, from the first occupation of Anahuac to the middle of the fifteenth century, at which point his labors were unfortunately

---

[26] See the plans of the ancient and modern capital, in Bullock's "Mexico," first edition. The original of the ancient map was obtained by that traveller from the collection of the unfortunate Boturini; if, as seems probable, it is the one indicated on page 13 of his Catalogue, I find no warrant for Mr. Bullock's statement, that it was the same prepared for Cortés by the order of Montezuma.

[27] Clavigero, Stor. del Messico, tom. I. lib. 2.—Torquemada, Monarch. Ind., tom. I. lib. 2.—Boturini, Idea, p. 146.—Col. of Mendoza, Part 1, and Codex Telleriano-Remensis, apud Antiq. of Mexico, vols. I., VI.

Machiavelli has noticed it as one great cause of the military successes of the Romans, "that they associated themselves, in their wars, with other states, as the principal"; and expresses his astonishment that a similar policy should not have been adopted by ambitious republics in later times. (See his Discorsi sopra T. Livio, lib. 2, cap. 4, apud Opere (Geneva, 1798).) This, as we have seen above, was the very course pursued by the Mexicans.

terminated by his death. In the early portion he has endeavored to trace the migratory movements and historical annals of the principal races who entered the country. Every page bears testimony to the extent and fidelity of his researches; and, if we feel but moderate confidence in the results, the fault is not imputable to him, so much as to the dark and doubtful nature of the subject. As he descends to later ages, he is more occupied with the fortunes of the Tezcucan than with those of the Aztec dynasty, which have been amply discussed by others of his countrymen. The premature close of his labors prevented him, probably, from giving that attention to the domestic institutions of the people he describes, to which they are entitled as the most important subject of inquiry to the historian. The deficiency has been supplied by his judicious edior, Orteaga, from other sources. In the early part of his work, Veytia has explained the chronological system of the Aztecs, but, like most writers preceding the accurate Gama, with indifferent success. As a critic, he certainly ranks much higher than the annalists who preceded him; and, when his own religion is not involved, shows a discriminating judgment. When it is, he betrays a full measure of the credulity which still maintains its hold on too many even of the well informed of his countrymen. The editor of the work has given a very interesting letter from the Abbé Clavigero to Veytia, written when the former was a poor and humble exile, and in the tone of one addressing a person of high standing and literary eminence. Both were employed on the same subject. The writings of the poor Abbé, published again and again, and translated into various languages, have spread his fame throughout Europe, while the name of Veytia, whose works have been locked up in their primitive manuscript, is scarcely known beyond the boundaries of Mexico.

SUCCESSION TO THE CROWN—AZTEC NOBILITY—JUDICIAL SYSTEM—LAWS AND REVENUES—MILITARY INSTITUTIONS

THE form of government differed in the different states of Anahuac. With the Aztecs and Tezcucans it was monarchical and nearly absolute. The two nations resembled each other so much, in their political institutions, that one of their historians has remarked, in too unqualified a manner indeed, that what is told of one may be always understood as applying to the other.[1] I shall direct my inquiries to the Mexican polity, borrowing an illustration occasionally from that of the rival kingdom.

The government was an elective monarchy. Four of the principal nobles, who had been chosen by their own body in the preceding reign, filled the office of electors, to whom were added, with merely an honorary rank however, the two royal allies of Tezcuco and Tlacopan. The sovereign was selected from the brothers of the deceased prince, or, in default of them, from his nephews. Thus the election was always restricted to the same family. The candidate preferred must have distinguished himself in war, though, as in the case of the last Montezuma he were a member of the priesthood.[2] This singular mode of supplying the throne had some advantages. The candidates received an education which fitted them for the royal dignity, while the age, at which they were chosen, not only secured the nation against the evils of minority, but afforded ample means for estimating their qualifications for the office. The result, at all events, was favorable; since the throne, as already noticed, was filled by a succession of able princes, well qualified to rule over a warlike and ambitious people. The scheme of election, however defective, argues a more refined and calculating policy than was to have been expected from a barbarous nation.[3]

The new monarch was installed in his regal dignity with much parade of religious ceremony; but not until, by a victorious campaign he had

[1] Ixtlilxochitl, Hist. Chich. MS., cap. 36.
[2] This was an exception.—In Egypt, also, the king was frequently taken from the warrior caste, though obliged afterwards to be instructed in the mysteries of the priesthood: ὁ δὲ ἐκ μαχίμων ἀποδεδειγμένος εὐθὺς ἐγίνετο τῶν ἱερῶν. Plutarch, de Isid. et Osir., sec. 9.
[3] Torquemada, Monarch. Ind., lib. 2, cap. 18; lib. 11, cap. 27.—Clavigero, Stor. del Messico, tom. II. p. 112.—Acosta, Naturall and Morall Historie of the East and West Indies, Eng. trans. (London, 1604.)
According to Zurita, an election by the nobles took place only in default of heirs of the deceased monarch. (Rapport, p. 15.) The minute historical investigation of Clavigero may be permitted to outweigh this general assertion.

obtained a sufficient number of captives to grace his triumphal entry into the capital, and to furnish victims for the dark and bloody rites which stained the Aztec superstition. Amidst this pomp of human sacrifice, he was crowned. The crown, resembling a mitre in its form, and curiously ornamented with gold, gems, and feathers, was placed on his head by the lord of Tezcuco, the most powerful of his royal allies. The title of *King*, by which the earlier Aztec princes are distinguished by Spanish writers, is supplanted by that of *Emperor* in the later reigns, intimating, perhaps, his superiority over the confederated monarchies of Tlacopan and Tezcuco.[4]

The Aztec princes, especially towards the close of the dynasty, lived in a barbaric pomp, truly Oriental. Their spacious palaces were provided with halls for the different councils, who aided the monarch in the transaction of business. The chief of these was a sort of privy council, composed in part, probably, of the four electors chosen by the nobles after the accession, whose places, when made vacant by death, were immediately supplied as before. It was the business of this body, so far as can be gathered from the very loose accounts given of it, to advise the king, in respect to the government of the provinces, the administration of the revenues, and, indeed, on all great matters of public interest.[5]

In the royal buildings were accommodations, also, for a numerous body-guard of the sovereign, made up of the chief nobility. It is not easy to determine with precision, in these barbarian governments, the limits of the several orders. It is certain, there was a distinct class of nobles, with large landed possessions, who held the most important offices near the person of the prince, and engrossed the administration of the provinces and cities.[6] Many of these could trace their descent from the founders of the Aztec monarchy. According to some writers of authority, there were thirty great *caciques*, who had their residence, at least a part of the year, in the capital, and who could muster a hundred thousand vassals each on their estates.[7] Without relying on such wild statements, it is clear, from the testimony of the Conquerors, that the country was occupied by numerous powerful chieftains, who lived like independent princes on their domains. If it be true that the kings encouraged, or, indeed, exacted, the residence of these nobles in the capital, and required

[4] Sahagun, Hist. de Nueva España, lib. 6, cap. 9, 10, 14; lib. 8, cap. 31, 34.—See, also, Zurita, Rapport, pp. 20-23.
Ixtlilxochitl stoutly claims this supremacy for his own nation. (Hist. Chich., MS., cap. 34.) His assertions are at variance with facts stated by himself elsewhere, and are not countenanced by any other writer whom I have consulted.

[5] Sahagun, who places the elective power in a much larger body, speaks of four senators, who formed a state council. (Hist. de Nueva España, lib. 8, cap. 30.) Acosta enlarges the council beyond the number of the electors. (Lib. 6, ch. 26.) No two writers agree.

[6] Zurita enumerates four orders of chiefs, all of whom were exempted from imposts, and enjoyed very considerable privileges. He does not discriminate the several ranks with much precision. Rapport, p. 47, et seq.

[7] See, in particular, Herrera, Historia General de los Hechos de los Castellanos en las Islas y Tierra Firme del Mar Océano, (Madrid, 1730,) dec. 2, lib. 7, cap. 12.

hostages in their absence, it is evident that their power must have been very formidable.[8]

Their estates appear to have been held by various tenures, and to have been subject to different restrictions. Some of them, earned by their own good swords or received as the recompense of public services, were held without any limitation, except that the possessors could not dispose of them to a plebeian.[9] Others were entailed on the eldest male issue and, in default of such, reverted to the crown. Most of them seem to have been burdened with the obligation of military service. The principal chiefs of Tezcuco, according to its chronicler, were expressly obliged to support their prince with their armed vassals, to attend his court, and aid him in the council. Some, instead of these services, were to provide for the repairs of his buildings, and to keep the royal demesnes in order, with an annual offering, by way of homage, of fruits and flowers. It was usual, if we are to believe historians, for a new king, on his accession, to confirm the investiture of estates derived from the crown.[10]

It cannot be denied that we recognise, in all this, several features of the feudal system, which, no doubt, lose nothing of their effect, under the hands of the Spanish writers, who are fond of tracing analogies to European institutions. But such analogies lead sometimes to very erroneous conclusions. The obligation of military service, for instance, the most essential principle of a fief, seems to be naturally demanded by every government from its subjects. As to minor points of resemblance, they fall far short of that harmonious system of reciprocal service and protection, which embraced, in nice gradation, every order of a feudal monarchy. The kingdoms of Anahuac were, in their nature, despotic, attended, indeed, with many mitigating circumstances unknown to the despotisms of the East; but it is chimerical to look for much in common —beyond a few accidental forms and ceremonies—with those aristocratic institutions of the Middle Ages, which made the court of every petty baron the precise image in miniature of that of his sovereign.

The legislative power, both in Mexico and Tezcuco, resided wholly with the monarch. This feature of despotism, however, was, in some

---

[8] Carta de Cortés, ap. Lorenzana, Hist. de Nueva España, p. 110.—Torquemada, Monarch. Ind., lib. 2, cap. 89; lib. 14, cap. 6.—Clavigero, Stor. del Messico, tom. II. p. 121.—Zurita, Rapport, pp. 48, 65.

Ixtlilxochitl (Hist. Chich., MS., cap. 34) speaks of thirty great feudal chiefs, some of them Tezcucan and Tlacopan, whom he styles "grandees of the empire!" He says nothing of the great *tail* of 100,000 vassals to each, mentioned by Torquemada and Herrera.

[9] *Macehual,*—a word equivalent to the French word *roturier*. Nor could fiefs originally be held by plebeians in France. See Hallam's Middle Ages, (London, 1918,) vol. II. p. 207.

[10] Ixtlilxochitl, Hist. Chich., MS., ubi supra.—Zurita, Rapport, ubi supra.—Clavigero, Stor. del Messico, tom. II. pp. 122-124.—Torquemada, Monarch. Ind., lib. 14, cap. 7.—Gomara. Crónica de Nueva España, cap. 199, ap. Barcia, tom. II.

Boturini (Idea, p. 165) carries back the origin of *fiefs* in Anahuac, to the twelfth century. Carli says, "Le système politique y étoit féodal." In the next page he tells us, "Personal merit alone made the distinction of the nobility!" (Lettres Américaines, trad. Fr., (Paris, 1788,) tom. I, let. 11.) Carli was a writer of a lively imagination

measure, counteracted by the constitution of the judicial tribunals,—of more importance, among a rude people, than the legislative, since it is easier to make good laws for such a community, than to enforce them, and the best laws, badly administered, are but a mockery. Over each of the principal cities, with its dependent territories, was placed a supreme judge, appointed by the crown, with original and final jurisdiction in both civil and criminal cases. There was no appeal from his sentence to any other tribunal, nor even to the king. He held his office during life; and any one, who usurped his ensigns, was punished with death.[11]

Below this magistrate was a court, established in each province, and consisting of three members. It held concurrent jurisdiction with the supreme judge in civil suits, but, in criminal, an appeal lay to his tribunal. Besides these courts, there was a body of inferior magistrates, distributed through the country, chosen by the people themselves in their several districts. Their authority was limited to smaller causes, while the more important were carried up to the higher courts. There was still another class of subordinate officers, appointed also by the people, each of whom was to watch over the conduct of a certain number of families, and report any disorder or breach of the laws to the higher authorities.[12]

In Tezcuco the judicial arrangements were of a more refined character;[13] and a gradation of tribunals finally terminated in a general meeting or parliament, consisting of all the judges, great and petty, throughout the kingdom, held every eighty days in the capital, over which the king presided in person. This body determined all suits, which, from their importance, or difficulty, had been reserved for its consideration by the lower tribunals. It served, moreover, as a council of state, to assist the monarch in the transaction of public business.[14]

[11] This magistrate, who was called *cihuacoatl*, was also to audit the accounts of the collectors of the taxes in his district. (Clavigero, Stor. del Messico, tom. II. p. 127.—Torquemada, Monarch. Ind., lib. 11, cap. 25.) The Mendoza Collection contains a painting of the courts of justice, under Montezuma, who introduced great changes in them. (Antiq. of Mexico, vol. I., Plate 70.) According to the interpreter, an appeal lay from them, in certain cases, to the king's council. Ibid., vol. VI. p. 79.

[12] Clavigero, Stor. del Messico, tom. II. pp. 127, 128.—Torquemada, Monarch. Ind., ubi supra.

In this arrangement of the more humble magistrates we are reminded of the Anglo-Saxon hundreds and tithings, especially the latter, the members of which were to watch over the conduct of the families in their districts, and bring the offenders to justice. The hard penalty of mutual responsibility was not known to the Mexicans.

[13] Zurita, so temperate, usually, in his language, remarks, that, in the capital, "Tribunals were instituted which might compare in their organization with the royal audiences of Castile." (Rapport, p. 93.) His observations are chiefly drawn from the Tezcucan courts, which, in their forms of procedure, he says, were like the Aztec. (Loc. cit.)

[14] Boturini, Idea, p. 87. Torquemada, Monarch. Ind., lib. 11, cap. 26.

Zurita compares this body to the Castilian córtes. It would seem, however, according to him, to have consisted only of twelve principal judges, besides the king. His meaning is somewhat doubtful. (Rapport, pp. 94, 101, 106.) M. de Humboldt, in his account of the Aztec courts, has confounded them with the Tezcucan. Comp. Vues des Cordillères et Monument des Peuples Indigènes de l'Amérique, (Paris, 1810,) p. 55, and Clavigero, Stor. del Messico, tom. II. pp. 128, 129.

Such are the vague and imperfect notices that can be gleaned, respecting the Aztec tribunals, from the hieroglyphical paintings still preserved, and from the most accredited Spanish writers. These, being usually ecclesiastics, have taken much less interest in this subject, than in matters connected with religion. They find some apology, certainly, in the early destruction of most of the Indian paintings, from which their information was, in part, to be gathered.

On the whole, however, it must be inferred, that the Aztecs were sufficiently civilized to evince a solicitude for the rights both of property and of persons. The law, authorizing an appeal to the highest judicature in criminal matters only, shows an attention to personal security, rendered the more obligatory by the extreme severity of their penal code, which would naturally have made them more cautious of a wrong conviction. The existence of a number of coördinate tribunals, without a central one of supreme authority to control the whole, must have given rise to very discordant interpretations of the law in different districts. But this is an evil which they shared in common with most of the nations of Europe.

The provision for making the superior judges wholly independent of the crown was worthy of an enlightened people. It presented the strongest barrier, that a mere constitution could afford, against tyranny. It is not, indeed, to be supposed, that, in a government otherwise so despotic, means could not be found for influencing the magistrate. But it was a great step to fence round his authority with the sanctions of the law; and no one of the Aztec monarchs, as far as I know, is accused of an attempt to violate it.

To receive presents or a bribe, to be guilty of collusion in any way with a suitor, was punished, in a judge, with death. Who, or what tribunal, decided as to his guilt, does not appear. In Tezcuco this was done by the rest of the court. But the king presided over that body. The Tezcucan prince, Nezahualpilli, who rarely tempered justice with mercy, put one judge to death for taking a bribe, and another for determining suits in his own house,—a capital offence, also, by law.[15]

The judges of the higher tribunals were maintained from the produce of a part of the crown lands, reserved for this purpose. They, as well as the supreme judge, held their offices for life. The proceedings in the courts were conducted with decency and order. The judges wore an appropriate dress, and attended to business both parts of the day, dining, always, for the sake of despatch, in an apartment of the same building where they held their session; a method of proceedings much commended by the Spanish chroniclers, to whom despatch was not very familiar in their own tribunals. Officers attended to preserve order, and others summoned the parties, and produced them in court. No counsel was employed; the parties stated their own case, and supported it by their wit-

---

[15] "Ah! si esta se repitiera hoy, que bueno seria!" exclaims Sahagun's Mexican editor. Hist. de Nueva España, tom. II. p. 304, nota.—Zurita, Rapport, p. 102.—Torquemada, Monarch. Ind., ubi supra.—Ixtlilxochitl, Hist. Chich., MS., cap. 67.

nesses. The oath of the accused was also admitted in evidence. The statement of the case, the testimony, and the proceedings of the trial, were all set forth by a clerk, in hieroglyphical paintings, and handed over to the court. The paintings were executed with so much accuracy, that, in all suits respecting real property, they were allowed to be produced as good authority in the Spanish tribunals, very long after the Conquest; and a chair for their study and interpretation was established at Mexico in 1553, which has long since shared the fate of most other provisions for learning in that unfortunate country.[16]

A capital sentence was indicated by a line traced with an arrow across the portrait of the accused. In Tezcuco, where the king presided in the court, this, according to the national chronicler, was done with extra-ordinary parade. His description, which is of rather a poetical cast, I give in his own words. "In the royal palace of Tezcuco was a court-yard, on the opposite sides of which were two halls of justice. In the principal one, called the 'tribunal of God,' was a throne of pure gold, inlaid with turquoises and other precious stones. On a stool, in front, was placed a human skull, crowned with an immense emerald, of a pyramidal form, and surmounted by an aigrette of brilliant plumes and precious stones. The skull was laid on a heap of military weapons, shields, quivers, bows, and arrows. The walls were hung with tapestry, made of the hair of different wild animals, of rich and various colors, festooned by gold rings, and embroidered with figures of birds and flowers. Above the throne was a canopy of variegated plumage, from the centre of which shot forth resplendent rays of gold and jewels. The other tribunal called 'the King's,' was also surmounted by a gorgeous canopy of feathers, on which were emblazoned the royal arms. Here the sovereign gave public audience, and communicated his despatches. But, when he decided important causes, or confirmed a capital sentence, he passed to the 'tribunal of God,' attended by the fourteen great lords of the realm, marshalled according to their rank. Then, putting on his mitred crown, incrusted with precious stones, and holding a golden arrow, by way of sceptre, in his left hand, he laid his right upon the skull, and pronounced judgment." [17] All this looks rather fine for a court of justice, it must be owned. But it is certain, that the Tezcucans, as we shall see hereafter, possessed both the materials, and the skill requisite to work them up in this manner. Had they been a little further advanced in refinement, one might well doubt their having the bad taste to do so.

The laws of the Aztecs were registered, and exhibited to the people, in their hieroglyphical paintings. Much the larger part of them, as in

---

[16] Zurita, Rapport, pp. 95, 100, 103.—Sahagun, Hist. de Nueva España, loc. cit.—Humboldt, Vues des Cordillères, pp. 55, 56.—Torquemada, Monarch. Ind., lib. 11, cap. 25.

Clavigero says, the accused might free himself by oath; Il reo poteva purgarsi col giuramento." (Stor. del Messico, tom. II. p. 129.) What rogue, then, could ever have been convicted?

[17] Ixtlilxochitl, Hist. Chich., MS., cap. 36.

These various objects had a symbolical meaning, according to Boturini, Idea, p. 84

every nation imperfectly civilized, relates rather to the security of persons, than of property. The great crimes against society were all made
capital. Even the murder of a slave was punished with death. Adulterers,
as among the Jews, were stoned to death. Thieving, according to the
degree of the offence, was punished by slavery or death. Yet the Mexicans could have been under no great apprehension of this crime, since
the entrances to their dwellings were not secured by bolts, or fastenings
of any kind. It was a capital offence to remove the boundaries of another's lands; to alter the established measures; and for a guardian not
to be able to give a good account of his ward's property. These regulations evince a regard for equity in dealings, and for private rights, which
argues a considerable progress in civilization. Prodigals, who squandered
their patrimony, were punished in like manner; a severe sentence, since
the crime brought its adequate punishment along with it. Intemperance,
which was the burden, moreover, of their religious homilies, was visited
with the severest penalties; as if they had foreseen in it the consuming
canker of their own, as well as of the other Indian races in later times.
It was punished in the young with death, and in older persons with loss
of rank and confiscation of property. Yet a decent conviviality was not
meant to be proscribed at their festivals, and they possessed the means
of indulging it, in a mild fermented liquor, called *pulque*, which is still
popular, not only with the Indian, but the European population of the
country.[18]

The rites of marriage were celebrated with as much formality as in
any Christian country; and the institution was held in such reverence,
that a tribunal was instituted for the sole purpose of determining questions relating to it. Divorces could not be obtained, until authorized by
a sentence of this court, after a patient hearing of the parties.

But the most remarkable part of the Aztec code was that relating to
slavery. There were several descriptions of slaves: prisoners taken in
war, who were almost always reserved for the dreadful doom of sacrifice;
criminals, public debtors, persons who, from extreme poverty, voluntarily resigned their freedom, and children who were sold by their own
parents. In the last instance, usually occasioned also by poverty, it was
common for the parents, with the master's consent, to substitute others
of their children successively, as they grew up; thus distributing the
burden, as equally as possible, among the different members of the fam-

[18] Paintings of the Mendoza Collection, Pl. 72, and Interpretation, ap. Antiq. of
Mexico, vol. VI. p. 87.—Torquemada, Monarch. Ind., ab. 12, cap. 7.—Clavigero,
Stor. del Messico, tom. II. pp. 130-134.—Camargo, Hist. de Tlascala, MS.

They could scarcely have been an intemperate people, with these heavy penalties
hanging over them. Indeed, Zurita bears testimony that those Spaniards, who
thought they were, greatly erred. (Rapport, p. 112.) Mons. Ternaux's translation
of a passage of the Anonymous Conqueror, "aucun peuple n'est aussi sobre." (Re-
cueil de Pièces Relatives à la Conquête du Mexique, ap. Voyages, &c., (Paris, 1838,)
p. 54,) may give a more favorable impression, however, than that intended by his
original, whose remark is confined to abstemiousness in eating. See the Relatione,
ap. Ramusio, Raccolta delle Navigationi et Viaggi. (Venetia, 1554-1565.)

ily. The willingness of freemen to incur the penalties of this condition is explained by the mild form in which it existed. The contract of sale was executed in the presence of at least four witnesses. The services to be exacted were limited with great precision. The slave was allowed to have his own family, to hold property, and even other slaves. His children were free. No one could be born to slavery in Mexico; [19] an honorable distinction, not known, I believe, in any civilized community where slavery has been sanctioned.[20] Slaves were not sold by their masters, unless when these were driven to it by poverty. They were often liberated by them at their death, and sometimes, as there was no natural repugnance founded on difference of blood and race, were married to them. Yet a refractory or vicious slave might be led into the market, with a collar round his neck, which intimated his bad character, and there be publicly sold, and, on a second sale, reserved for sacrifice.[21]

Such are some of the most striking features of the Aztec code, to which the Tezcucan bore great resemblance.[22] With some exceptions, it is stamped with the severity, the ferocity, indeed, of a rude people, hardened by familiarity with scenes of blood, and relying on physical, instead of moral means, for the correction of evil.[23] Still, it evinces a profound respect for the great principles of morality, and as clear a perception of these principles as is to be found in the most cultivated nations.

The royal revenues were derived from various sources. The crown lands, which appear to have been extensive, made their returns in kind. The places in the neighborhood of the capital were bound to supply workmen and materials for building the king's palaces, and keeping them in repair. They were also to furnish fuel, provisions, and whatever was necessary for his ordinary domestic expenditure, which was certainly on no stinted scale.[24] The principal cities, which had numerous villages

[19] In Ancient Egypt the child of a slave was born free, if the father were free. (Diodorus, Bibl. Hist., lib. 1, sec. 80.) This, though more liberal than the code of most countries fell short of the Mexican.

[20] In Egypt the same penalty was attached to the murder of a slave, as to that of a freeman. (Ibid., lib. 1, sec. 77.) Robertson speaks of a class of slaves held so cheap in the eye of the Mexican law, that one might kill them with impunity. (History of America, (ed. London, 1776,) vol. III. p. 164.) This, however, was not in Mexico, but in Nicaragua, (see his own authority, Herrera, Hist. General, des. 3, lib. 4, cap. 2,) a distant country, not incorporated in the Mexican empire, and with laws and institutions very different from those of the latter.

[21] Torquemada, Monarch. Ind., lib. 12, cap. 15; lib. 14, cap. 16, 17.—Sahagun, Hist. de Nueva España, lib. 8, cap. 14.—Clavigero, Stor. del Messico, tom. II. pp. 134-136.

[22] Ixtlilxochitl, Hist. Chich., MS., cap. 38, and Relaciones, MS.

The Tezcucan code, indeed, as digested under the great Nezahualcoyotl, formed the basis of the Mexican, in the latter days of the empire. Zurita, Rapport, p. 95.

[23] In this, at least, they did not resemble the Romans; of whom their countryman could boast, "Gloriari licet, nulli gentium mitiores placuisse pœnas." Livy, Hist., lib. 1, cap. 28.

[24] The Tezcucan revenues were, in like manner, paid in the produce of the country. The various branches of the royal expenditure were defrayed by specified towns and districts; and the whole arrangements here, and in Mexico, bore a remarkable resemblance to the financial regulations of the Persian empire, as reported by the Greek writers; (see Herodotus, Clio, sec. 192;) with this difference, however, that

and a large territory dependent on them, were distributed into districts, with each a share of the lands allotted to it, for its support. The inhabitants paid a stipulated part of the produce to the crown. The vassals of the great chiefs, also, paid a portion of their earnings into the public treasury; an arrangement not at all in the spirit of the feudal institutions.[25]

In addition to this tax on all the agricultural produce of the kingdom, there was another on its manufactures. The nature and variety of the tributes will be best shown by an enumeration of some of the principal articles. These were cotton dresses, and mantles of featherwork exquisitely made; ornamented armor; vases and plates of gold; gold dust, bands and bracelets; crystal, gilt, and varnished jars and goblets; bells, arms, and utensils of copper, reams of paper; grain, fruits, copal, amber, cochineal, cacao, wild animals and birds, timber, lime, mats, &c.[26] In this curious medley of the most homely commodities, and the elegant superfluities of luxury, it is singular that no mention should be made of silver, the great staple of the country in later times, and the use of which was certainly known to the Aztecs.[27]

the towns of Persia proper were not burdened with tributes, like the conquered cities. Idem, Thalia, sec. 97.

[25] Lorenzana, Hist. de Nueva España, p. 172.—Torquemada, Monarch. Ind., lib. 2, cap. 89; lib. 14, cap. 7.—Boturini, Idea, p. 166.—Camargo, Hist. de Tlascala, MS.—Herrera, Hist. General, dec. 2, lib. 7, cap. 13.

The people of the provinces were distributed into *calpulli* or tribes who held the lands of the neighborhood in common. Officers of their own appointment parcelled out these lands among the several families of the *calpulli;* and, on the extinction or removal of a family, its lands reverted to the common stock, to be again distributed. The individual proprietor had no power to alienate them. The laws regulating these matters were very precise, and had existed ever since the occupation of the country by the Aztecs. Zurita, Rapport, pp. 51-62.

[26] The following items of the tribute furnished by different cities will give a more precise idea of its nature:—20 chests of ground chocolate; 40 pieces of armor, of a particular device; 2400 loads of large mantles, of twisted cloth; 800 loads of small mantles, of rich wearing apparel; 5 pieces of armor, of rich feathers; 60 pieces of armor, of common feathers; a chest of beans; a chest of *chian;* a chest of maize; 8000 reams of paper; likewise 2000 loaves of very white salt, refined in the shape of a mould, for the consumption only of the lords of Mexico; 8000 lumps of unrefined copal; 400 small baskets of white refined copal; 100 copper axes; 80 loads of red chocolate; 800 *xícaras,* out of which they drank chocolate; a little vessel of small turquoise stones; 4 chests of timber, full of maize; 4000 loads of lime; tiles of gold, of the size of an oyster, and as thick as the finger; 40 bags of cochineal; 20 bags of gold dust, of the finest quality; a diadem of gold, of a specified pattern; 20 lip-jewels of clear amber, ornamented with gold; 200 loads of chocolate; 100 pots or jars of liquid-amber; 8000 *handfuls* of rich scarlet feathers; 40 tiger-skins; 1600 bundles of cotton, &c., &c. Col. de Mendoza, part 2, ap. Antiq. of Mexico, vols. I., VI.

[27] Mapa de Tributos, ap. Lorenzana, Hist. de Nueva España.—Tribute-roll, ap. Antiq. of Mexico, vol. I., and Interpretation, vol. VI., pp. 17-44.

The Mendoza Collection, in the Bodleian Library at Oxford, contains a roll of the cities of the Mexican empire, with the specific tributes exacted from them. It is a copy made after the Conquest, with a pen, on European paper (See Foreign Quarterly Review, No. XVII. Art. 4.) An original painting of the same roll was in Boturini's museum. Lorenzana has given us engravings of it, in which the outlines of the Oxford copy are filled up, though somewhat rudely. Clavigero considers the explana-

Garrisons were established in the larger cities,—probably those at a distance, and recently conquered,—to keep down revolt, and to enforce the payment of the tribute.[28] Tax-gatherers were also distributed throughout the kingdom, who were recognised by their official badges, and dreaded from the merciless rigor of their exactions. By a stern law, every defaulter was liable to be taken and sold as a slave. In the capital were spacious granaries and warehouses for the reception of the tributes. A receiver-general was quartered in the palace, who rendered in an exact account of the various contributions, and watched over the conduct of the inferior agents, in whom the least malversation was summarily punished. This functionary was furnished with a map of the whole empire, with a minute specification of the imposts assessed on every part of it. These imposts, moderate under the reigns of the early princes, became so burdensome under those at the close of the dynasty, being rendered still more oppressive by the manner of collection, that they bred disaffection throughout the land, and prepared the way for its conquest by the Spaniards.[29]

Communication was maintained with the remotest parts of the country by means of couriers. Post-houses were established on the great roads about two leagues distant from each other. The courier, bearing his despatches in the form of a hieroglyphical painting, ran with them to the first station, where they were taken by another messenger and carried forward to the next, and so on till they reached the capital. These couriers, trained from childhood, travelled with incredible swiftness; not four or five leagues an hour, as an old chronicler would make us believe, but with such speed that despatches were carried from one to two hundred miles a day.[30] Fresh fish was frequently served at Montezuma's table in twenty-four hours from the time it had been taken in the Gulf of Mexico, two hundred miles from the capital. In this way

tions in Lorenzana's edition very inaccurate, (Stor. del Messico, tom. I. p. 25,) a judgment confirmed by Aglio, who has transcribed the entire collection of the Mendoza papers, in the first volume of the Antiquities of Mexico. It would have much facilitated reference to his plates, if they had been numbered;—a strange omission!

[28] The caciques, who submitted to the allied arms, were usually confirmed in their authority, and the conquered places allowed to retain their laws and usages. (Zurita, Rapport, p. 67.) The conquests were not always partitioned, but sometimes, singularly enough, were held in common by the three powers. Ibid., p. 11.

[29] Collec. of Mendoza, ap. Antiq. of Mexico, vol. VI. p. 17.—Carta de Cortés, ap Lorenzana, Hist. de Nueva España, p. 110.—Torquemada, Monarch. Ind., lib. 14, cap. 6, 8.—Herrera, Hist. General, dec. 2, lib. 7, cap. 13.—Sahagun, Hist. de Nueva España, lib. 8, cap. 18, 19.

[30] The Hon. C. A. Murray whose imperturbable good-humor under real troubles forms a contrast, rather striking, to the sensitiveness of some of his predecessors to imaginary ones, tells us, among other marvels, that an Indian of his party travelled a hundred miles in four and twenty hours. (Travels in N. America, (New York, 1839,) vol. I, p. 193.) The Greek, who according to Plutarch, brought the news of victory to Platæa, a hundred and twenty-five miles, in a day, was a better traveller still. Some interesting facts on the pedestrian capabilities of man in the savage state are collected by Buffon, who concludes, truly enough, "L'homme civilisé ne connait pas ses forces." (Histoire Naturelle; De la Jeunesse.)

intelligence of the movements of the royal armies was rapidly brought to court; and the dress of the courier, denoting by its color that of his tidings, spread joy or consternation in the towns through which he passed.[31]

But the great aim of the Aztec institutions, to which private discipline and public honors were alike directed, was the profession of arms. In Mexico, as in Egypt, the soldier shared with the priest the highest consideration. The king, as we have seen, must be an experienced warrior. The tutelary deity of the Aztecs was the god of war. A great object of their military expeditions was, to gather hecatombs of captives for his altars. The soldier who fell in battle, was transported at once to the region of ineffable bliss in the bright mansions of the Sun.[32] Every war, therefore, became a crusade; and the warrior, animated by a religious enthusiasm, like that of the early Saracen, or the Christian crusader, was not only raised to a contempt of danger, but courted it, for the imperishable crown of martyrdom. Thus we find the same impulse acting in the most opposite quarters of the globe, and the Asiatic, the European, and the American, each earnestly invoking the holy name of religion in the perpetration of human butchery.

The question of war was discussed in a council of the king and his chief nobles. Ambassadors were sent, previously to its declaration, to require the hostile state to receive the Mexican gods, and to pay the customary tribute. The persons of ambassadors were held sacred throughout Anahuac. They were lodged and entertained in the great towns at the public charge and were everywhere received with courtesy, so long as they did not deviate from the highroads on their route. When they did, they forfeited their privileges. If the embassy proved unsuccessful, a defiance, or open declaration of war, was sent; quotes were drawn from the conquered provinces, which were always subjected to military service, as well as the payment of taxes; and the royal army, usually with the monarch at his head, began its march.[33]

The Aztec princes made use of the incentive employed by European monarchs to excite the ambition of their followers. They established

---

[31] Torquemada, Monarch. Ind., lib. 14, cap. 1.

The same wants led to the same expedients in ancient Rome, and still more ancient Persia. "Nothing in the world is borne so swiftly," says Herodotus, "as messages by the Persian couriers"; which his commentator, Valckenaer, prudently qualifies by the exception of the carrier pigeon. (Herodotus, Hist., Urania, sec. 98, nec non Adnot. ed. Schweighäuser.) Couriers are noticed, in the thirteenth century, in China, by Marco Polo. Their stations were only three miles apart, and they accomplished five days' journey in one. (Viaggi di Marco Polo, lib. 2, cap. 29, ap. Ramusio, tom. II.) A similar arrangement for posts subsists there at the present day, and excites the admiration of a modern traveller. (Anderson, British Embassy to China, (London 1796,) p. 282.) In all these cases, the posts were for the use of government only.

[32] Sahagun, Hist. de Nueva España, lib. 3, Apend., cap. 3.

[33] Zurita, Rapport, pp. 68, 120.—Col. of Mendoza, ap. Antiq. of Mexico, vol. I. Pl. 67; vol. VI. p. 74.—Torquemada, Monarch. Ind., lib. 14, cap. 1.

The reader will find a remarkable resemblance to these military usages, in those of the early Romans. Comp. Liv., Hist., lib. 1, cap. 32; lib. 4, cap. 30. et alibi.

various military orders, each having its privileges and peculiar insignia. There seems, also, to have existed a sort of knighthood, of inferior degree. It was the cheapest reward of material prowess and whoever had not reached it was excluded from using ornaments on his arms or his person, and obliged to wear a coarse white stuff, made from the threads of the aloe, called *nequen*. Even the members of the royal family were not excepted from this law, which reminds one of the occasional practice of Christian knights, to wear plain armor, or shields without device, till they had achieved some doughty feat of chivalry. Although the military orders were thrown open to all, it is probable that they were chiefly filled with persons of rank, who, by their previous training and connections, were able to come into the fiield under peculiar advantages.[34]

The dress of the higher warriors was picturesque and often magnificent. Their bodies were covered with a close vest of quilted cotton, so thick as to be impenetrable to the light missiles of Indian warfare. This garment was so light and serviceable, that it was adopted by the Spaniards. The wealthier chiefs sometimes wore, instead of this cotton mail, a cuirass made of thin plates of gold, or silver. Over it was thrown a surcoat of the gorgeous feather-work in which they excelled.[35] Their helmets were sometimes of wood, fashioned like the heads of wild animals, and sometimes of silver, on the top of which waved a *panache* of variegated plumes, sprinkled with precious stones and ornaments of gold. They wore also collars, bracelets, and earrings, of the same rich materials.[36]

Their armies were divided into bodies of eight thousand men; and these, again, into companies of three or four hundred, each with its own commander. The national standard, which has been compared to the ancient Roman, displayed, in its embroidery of gold and feather-work, the armorial ensigns of the state. These were significant of its name, which, as the names of both persons and places were borrowed from some material object, was easily expressed by hieroglyphical symbols. The companies and the great chiefs had also their appropriate banners

---

[34] Ibid., lib. 14, cap. 4, 5.—Acosta, lib. 6, ch. 26.—Collec. of Mendoza, ap. Antiq. of Mexico, vol. I. Pl. 65; vol. VI. p. 72.—Camargo, Hist, de Tlascala, MS.

[35] "Their mail, if mail it may be called, was woven
Of vegetable down, like finest flax,
Bleached to the whiteness of new-fallen snow.
. . . .
Others, of higher office, were arrayed
In ieathery breastplates, of more gorgeous hue
Than the gay plumage of the mounttain-cock,
Than the pheasant's glittering pride. But what were these,
Or what the thin gold hauberk, when opposed
To arms like ours in battle?"

MADOC, P. 1, canto 7.

Beautiful painting! One may doubt, however, the propriety of the Welshman's vaunt, before the use of fire-arms.

[36] Sahagun, Hist. de Nueva España, lib. 2, cap. 27; lib. 8, cap. 12.—Relatione d'un gentil' huomo, ap. Ramusío, tom. III. p. 305.—Torquemada, Monarch. Ind., ubi supra.

and devices, and the gaudy hues of their many-colored plumes gave a dazzling splendor to the spectacle.

Their tactics were such as belong to a nation, with whom war, though a trade, is not elevated to the rank of a science. They advanced singing, and shouting their war-cries, briskly charging the enemy, as rapidly retreating, and making use of ambuscades, sudden surprises, and the light skirmish of guerilla warfare. Yet their discipline was such as to draw forth the encomiums of the Spanish conquerors. "A beautiful sight it was," says one of them, "to see them set out on their march, all moving forward so gayly, and in so admirable order!" [37] In battle, they did not seek to kill their enemies, so much as to take them prisoners; and they never scalped, like other North American tribes. The valor of a warrior was estimated by the number of his prisoners; and no ransom was large enough to save the devoted captive.[38]

Their military code bore the same stern features as their other laws. Disobedience of orders was punished with death. It was death, also, for a soldier to leave his colors, to attack the enemy before the signal was given, or to plunder another's booty or prisoners. One of the last Tezcucan princes, in the spirit of an ancient Roman, put two sons to death,—after having cured their wounds,—for violating the last-mentioned law.[39]

I must not omit to notice here an institution, the introduction of which, in the Old World, is ranked among the beneficent fruits of Christianity. Hospitals were established in the principal cities, for the cure of the sick, and the permanent refuge of the disabled soldier; and surgeons were placed over them, "who were so far better than those in Europe," says an old chronicler, "that they did not protract the cure, in order to increase the pay." [40]

Such is the brief outline of the civil and military polity of the ancient Mexicans; less perfect than could be desired, in regard to the former, from the imperfection of the sources whence it is drawn. Whoever has had occasion to explore the early history of modern Europe has found how vague and unsatisfactory is the political information which can be gleaned from the gossip of monkish annalists. How much is the difficulty increased in the present instance, where this information, first recorded in the dubious language of hieroglyphics, was interpreted in an-

[37] Relatione d'un gentil' huomo, ubi supra.

[38] Col. of Mendoza, ap. Antiq. of Mexico, vol. I. Pl. 65, 66; vol. VI. p. 73.—Sahagun, Hist. de Nueva España, lib. 8, cap. 12.—Toribio, Hist. de los Indios, MS., Parte I. cap. 7.—Torquemada, Monarch. Ind., lib. 14, cap. 3.—Relatione d'un gentil' huomo, ap. Ramusio, loc. cit.

Scalping may claim high authority, or, at least, antiquity. The Father of History gives an account of it among the Scythians, showing that they performed the operation, and wore the hideous trophy, in the same manner as our North American Indians. (Herodot., Hist., Melpomene, sec. 64.) Traces of the same savage custom are also found in the laws of the Visigoths, among the Franks, and even the Anglo-Saxons. See Guizot, Cours d'Histoire Moderne, (Paris, 1829,) tom. I. p. 283.

[39] Ixtlilxochitl, Hist. Chich., MS., cap. 67.

[40] Torquemada, Monarch. Ind., lib. 12, cap. 6; lib. 14, cap. 3.—Ixtlilxochitl, Hist. Chich., MS. cap. 36.

other language, with which the Spanish chroniclers were imperfectly acquainted, while it related to institutions of which their past experience enabled them to form no adequate conception! Amidst such uncertain lights, it is in vain to expect nice accuracy of detail. All that can be done is, to attempt an outline of the more prominent features, that a correct impression, so far as it goes, may be produced on the mind of the reader.

Enough has been said, however, to show that the Aztec and Tezcucan races were advanced in civilization very far beyond the wandering tribes of North America.[41] The degree of civilization which they had reached, as inferred by their political institutions, may be considered, perhaps, not much short of that enjoyed by our Saxon ancestors, under Alfred. In respect to the nature of it, they may be better compared with the Egyptians; and the examination of their social relations and culture may suggest still stronger points of resemblance to that ancient people.

Those familiar with the modern Mexicans will find it difficult to conceive that the nation should ever have been capable of devising the enlightened polity which we have been considering. But they should remember that in the Mexicans of our day they see only a conquered race; as different from their ancestors as are the modern Egyptians from those who built,—I will not say, the tasteless pyramids,—but the temples and palaces, whose magnificent wrecks strew the borders of the Nile, at Luxor and Karnac. The difference is not so great as between the ancient Greek, and his degenerate descendant, lounging among the masterpieces of art which he has scarcely taste enough to admire,—speaking the language of those still more imperishable monuments of literature which he has hardly capacity to comprehend. Yet he breathes the same atmosphere, is warmed by the same sun, nourished by the same scenes, as those who fell at Marathon, and won the trophies of Olympic Pisa.

[41] Zurita is indignant at the epithet of *barbarians* bestowed on the Aztecs; an epithet, he says, "which could come from no one who had personal knowledge of the capacity of the people, or their institutions, and which, in some respects, is quite as well merited by the European nations." (Rapport, p. 200, et seq.) This is strong language. Yet no one had better means of knowing than this eminent jurist, who, for nineteen years, held a post in the royal *audiences* of New Spain. During his long residence in the country he had ample opportunity of acquainting himself with its usages, both through his own personal observation and intercourse with the natives, and through the first missionaries who came over after the Conquest. On his return to Spain, probably about 1560, he occupied himself with an answer to queries which had been propounded by the government, on the character of the Aztec laws and institutions, and on that of the modifications introduced by the Spaniards. Much of his treatise is taken up with the latter subject. In what relates to the former he is more brief than could be wished, from the difficulty, perhaps, of obtaining full and satisfactory information as to the details. As far as he goes, however, he manifests a sound and discriminating judgment. He is very rarely betrayed into the extravagance of expression so visible in the writers of the time; and this temperance, combined with his uncommon sources of information, makes his work one of highest authority on the limited topics within its range.—The original manuscript was consulted by Clavigero, and, indeed, has been used by other writers. The work is now accessible to all, as one of the series of translations from the pen of the indefatigable Ternaux.

The same blood flows in his veins that flowed in theirs. But ages of
tyranny have passed over him; he belongs to a conquered race.

The American Indian has something peculiarly sensitive in his nature.
He shrinks instinctively from the rude touch of a foreign hand. Even
when this foreign influence comes in the form of civilization, he seems
to sink and pine away beneath it. It has been so with the Mexicans.
Under the Spanish domination, their numbers have silently melted away.
Their energies are broken. They no longer tread their mountain plains
with the conscious independence of their ancestors. In their faltering
step, and meek and melancholy aspect, we read the sad characters of
the conquered race. The cause of humanity, indeed, has gained. They
live under a better system of laws, a more assured tranquillity, a purer
faith. But all does not avail. Their civilization was of the hardy character which belongs to the wilderness. The fierce virtues of the Aztec
were all his own. They refused to submit to European culture,—to be
engrafted on a foreign stock. His outward form, his complexion, his
lineaments, are substantially the same. But the moral characteristics
of the nation, all that constituted its individuality as a race, are effaced
for ever.

Two of the principal authorities for this Chapter are Torquemada and Clavigero.
The former, a Provincial of the Franciscan order, came to the New World about the
middle of the sixteenth century. As the generation of the Conquerors had not then
passed away, he had ample opportunities of gathering the particulars of their enterprise from their own lips. Fifty years, during which he continued in the country,
put him in possession of the traditions and usages of the natives, and enabled him to
collect their history from the earliest missionaries, as well as from such monuments as
the fanaticism of his own countrymen had not then destroyed. From these ample
sources he compiled his bulky tomes, beginning, after the approved fashion of the
ancient Castilian chroniclers, with the creation of the world, and embracing the
whole circle of the Mexican institutions, political, religious, and social, from the
earliest period to his own time. In handling these fruitful themes, the worthy father
has shown a full measure of the bigotry which belonged to his order at that period.
Every page, too, is loaded with illustrations from Scripture or profane history, which
form a whimsical contrast to the barbaric staple of his story; and he has sometimes
fallen into serious errors, from his misconception of the chronological system of the
Aztecs. But, notwithstanding these glaring defects in the composition of the work,
the student, aware of his author's infirmities, will find few better guides than Torquemada in tracing the stream of historic truth up to the fountain head; such is his
manifest integrity, and so great were his facilities for information on the most
curious points of Mexican antiquity. No work, accordingly, has been more largely
consulted and copied, even by some, who, like Herrera, have affected to set little
value on the sources whence its information was drawn.—(Hist. General, dec. 6, lib.
6, cap. 19.) The *Monarchia Indiana* was first published at Seville, 1615, (Nic. Antonio, Bibliotheca Nova, (Matriti, 1783,) tom. II. p. 787,) and since, in a better
style, in three volumes folio, at Madrid, in 1723.

The other authority, frequently cited in the preceding pages, is the Abbé Clavigero's *Storia Antica del Messico*. It was originally printed towards the close of the
last century, in the Italian language, and in Italy, whither the author, a native of
Vera Cruz, and a member of the order of the Jesuits, had retired, on the expulsion
of that body from America, in 1767. During a residence of thirty-five years in his
own country, Clavigero had made himself intimately acquainted with its antiquities,
by the careful examination of paintings, manuscripts, and such other remains as were
to be found in his day. The plan of his work is nearly as comprehensive as that of

his predecessor, Torquemada; but the later and more cultivated period, in which he wrote, is visible in the superior address with which he has managed his complicated subject. In the elaborate disquisitions in his concluding volume, he has done much to rectify the chronology, and the various inaccuracies of preceding writers. Indeed, an avowed object of his work was, to vindicate his countrymen from what he conceived to be the misrepresentations of Robertson, Raynal, and De Pau. In regard to the last two, he was perfectly successful. Such an ostensible design might naturally suggest unfavorable ideas of his impartiality. But, on the whole, he seems to have conducted the discussion with good faith; and, if he has been led by national zeal to overcharge the picture with brilliant colors, he will be found much more temperate, on this score, than those who preceded him, while he has applied sound principles of criticism, of which they were incapable. In a word, the diligence of his researches has gathered into one focus the scattered lights of tradition and antiquarian lore, purified in a great measure from the mists of superstition which obscure the best productions of an earlier period. From these causes, the work, notwithstanding its occasional prolixity, and the disagreeable aspect given to it by the profusion of uncouth names in the Mexican orthography, which bristle over every page, has found merited favor with the public, and created something like a popular interest in the subject. Soon after its publication at Cesena, in 1780, it was translated into English, and more lately, into Spanish and German.

CHAPTER III

MEXICAN MYTHOLOGY—THE SACERDOTAL ORDER—THE TEMPLES—
HUMAN SACRIFICES

THE civil polity of the Aztecs is so closely blended with their religion, that, without understanding the latter, it is impossible to form correct ideas of their government or their social institutions. I shall pass over, for the present, some remarkable traditions, bearing a singular resemblance to those found in the Scriptures, and endeavour to give a brief sketch of their mythology, and their careful provisions for maintaining a national worship.

Mythology may be regarded as the poetry of religion,—or rather as the poetic development of the religious principle in a primitive age. It is the effort of untutored man to explain the mysteries of existence, and the secret agencies by which the operations of nature are conducted. Although the growth of similar conditions of society, its character must vary with that of the rude tribes in which it originates; and the ferocious Goth, quaffing mead from the skulls of his slaughtered enemies, must have a very different mythology from that of the effeminate native of Hispaniola, loitering away his hours in idle pastimes, under the shadow of his bananas.

At a later and more refined period, we sometimes find these primitive legends combined into a regular system under the hands of the poet, and the rude outline moulded into forms of ideal beauty, which are the objects of adoration in a credulous age, and the delight of all succeeding ones. Such were the beautiful inventions of Hesiod and Homer, "who," says the Father of History, "created the theogony of the Greeks"; an assertion not to be taken too literally, since it is hardly possible that any man should create a religious system for his nation.[1] They only filled up the shadowy outlines of tradition with the bright touches of their own imaginations, until they had clothed them in beauty which kindled the imaginations of others. The power of the poet, indeed, may be felt in a similar way in a much riper period of society. To say nothing of the "Divina Commedia," who is there that rises from the perusal of "Paradise Lost," without feeling his own conceptions of the angelic hierarchy quickened by those of the inspired artist, and a new and

[1] ποιήσαντες θεογονίην Ἕλλησι. Herodotus, Euterpe, sec. 53.—Heeren hazards a remark equally strong, respecting the epic poets of India, "who," says he, "have supplied the numerous gods that fill her Pantheon." Historical Researches, Eng. trans., (Oxford, 1833,) vol. III. p. 139.

sensible form, as it were, given to images which had before floated dim and undefined before him?

The last-mentioned period is succeeded by that of philosophy; which, disclaiming alike the legends of the primitive age, and the poetical embellishments of the succeeding one, seeks to shelter itself from the charge of impiety by giving an allegorical interpretation to the popular mythology, and thus to reconcile the latter with the genuine deductions of science.

The Mexican religion had emerged from the first of the periods we have been considering, and, although little affected by poetical influences, had received a peculiar complexion from the priests, who had digested as thorough and burdensome a ceremonial, as ever existed in any nation. They had, moreover, thrown the veil of allegory over early tradition, and invested their deities with attributes, savoring much more of the grotesque conceptions of the eastern nations in the Old World, than of the lighter fictions of Greek mythology, in which the features of humanity, however exaggerated, were never wholly abandoned.[2]

In contemplating the religious system of the Aztecs, one is struck with its apparent incongruity, as if some portion of it had emanated from a comparatively refined people, open to gentle influences, while the rest breathes a spirit of unmitigated ferocity. It naturally suggests the idea of two distinct sources, and authorizes the belief that the Aztecs had inherited from their predecessors a milder faith, on which was afterwards engrafted their own mythology. The latter soon become dominant, and gave its dark coloring to the creeds of the conquered nations,—which the Mexicans, like the ancient Romans, seem willingly to have incorporated into their own,—until the same funereal superstition settled over the farthest borders of Anahuac.

The Aztecs recognised the existence of a supreme Creator and Lord of the universe. They addressed him, in their prayers, as "the God by whom we live," "omnipresent, that knoweth all thoughts, and giveth all gifts," "without whom man is as nothing," "invisible, incorporeal, one God, of *perfect perfection* and purity," "under whose wings we find repose and a sure defence." These sublime attributes infer no inadequate conception of the true God. But the idea of unity—of a being, with whom volition is action, who has no need of inferior ministers to execute his purposes—was too simple, or too vast, for their understandings; and they sought relief, as usual, in a plurality of deities, who presided over the elements, the changes of the seasons, and the various occupations of man.[3] Of these,

---

[2] The Hon. Mountstuart Elphinstone has fallen into a similar train of thought, in a comparison of the Hindoo and Greek Mythology, in his "History of India," published since the remarks in the text were written. (See Book I. ch. 4.) The same chapter of this truly philosophic work suggests some curious points of resemblance to the Aztec religious institutions, that may furnish pertinent illustrations to the mind bent on tracing the affinities of the Asiatic and American races.

[3] Ritter has well shown, by the example of the Hindoo system, how the idea of unity suggests, of itself, that of plurality. History of Ancient hilosophy, Eng. trans., (Oxford, 1838.) book 2, ch. 1.

there were thirteen principal deities, and more than two hundred infe‑
rior; to each of whom some special day, or appropriate festival, was con‑
secrated.[4]

At the head of all stood the terrible Huitzilopotchli, the Mexican
Mars; although it is doing injustice to the heroic war-god of antiquity to
identify him with this sanguinary monster. This was the patron deity of
the nation. His fantastic image was loaded with costly ornaments. His
temples were the most stately and august of the public edifices; and his
altars reeked with the blood of human hecatombs in every city of the em‑
pire. Disastrous, indeed, must have been the influence of such a super‑
stition on the character of the people.[5]

A far more interesting personage in their mythology was Quetzalcoatl,
god of the air, a divinity who, during his residence on earth, instructed

[4] Sahagan, Hist. de Nueva España, lib. 6, passim.—Acosta, lib 5, ch. 9.—Boturini,
Idea, p. 8, et seq.—Ixtlilxochitl, Hist. Chich., MS., cap. 1.—Camargo, Hist. de
Tlascala, MS.

The Mexicans, according to Clavigero, believed in an evil Spirit, the enemy of the
human race, whose barbarous name signified "Rational Owl." (Stor. del Messico,
tom. II. p. 2.) The curate Bernaldez speaks of the Devil being embroidered on the
dresses of Columbus's Indians, in the likeness of an owl. (Historia de los Reyes
Católicos, MS., cap. 131.) This must not be confounded, however, with the evil
Spirit in the mythology of the North American Indians, (see Heckewelder's Account,
ap. Transactions of the American Philosophical Society, Philadelphia, vol. I. p. 205,)
still less, with the evil Principle of the Oriental nations of the Old World. It was only
one among many deities, for evil was found too liberally mingled in the natures of
most of the Aztec gods,—in the same manner as with the Greek,—to admit of its
personification by any one.

[5] Sahagun, Hist. de Nueva España, lib 3, cap. 1, et seq.—Acosta, lib. 5, ch. 9.—
Torquemada, Monarch. Ind., lib. 6, cap. 21.—Boturini, Idea, pp. 27, 28.

Huitzilopotchli is compounded of two words, signifying "humming-bird," and
"left," from his image having the feathers of this bird on its left foot; (Clavigero,
Stor. del Messico, tom. II. p. 17;) an amiable etymology for so ruffian a deity.—The
fantastic forms of the Mexican idols were in the highest degree symbolical. See
Gama's learned exposition of the devices on the statue of the goddess found in the
great square of Mexico. (Descripcion de las Dos Piedras, (México, 1832,) Parte 1,
pp. 34-44.) The tradition respecting the origin of this god, or, at least, his appear‑
ance on earth, is curious. He was born of a woman. His mother, a devout person,
one day, in her attendance on the temple, saw a ball of bright-colored feathers float‑
ing in the air. She took it, and deposited it in her bosom. She soon after found her‑
self pregnant, and the dread deity was born, coming into the world, like Minerva, all
armed,—with a spear in the right hand, a shield in the left, and his head surmounted
by a crest of green plumes. (See Clavigero, Stor. del Messico, tom. II. p. 19, et seq.)
A similar notion in respect to the incarnation of their principal deity existed among
the people of India beyond the Ganges, of China, and of Thibet. "Budh," says Mil‑
man, in his learned and luminous work on the History of Christianity, "according to
a tradition known in the West, was born of a virgin. So were the Fohi of China, and
the Schakaof of Thibet, no doubt the same, whether a mythic or a real personage.
The Jesuits in China, says Barrow, were appalled at finding in the mythology of
that country the counterpart of the Virgo Deipara." (Vol. I. p. 99, note.) The exis‑
tence of similar religious ideas in remote regions, inhabited by different races, is an
interesting subject of study; furnishing, as it does, one of the most important links
in the great chain of communication which binds together the distant families of
nations.

the natives in the use of metals, in agriculture, and in the arts of government. He was one of those benefactors of their species, doubtless, who
have been deified by the gratitude of posterity. Under him, the earth
teemed with fruits and flowers, without the pains of culture. An ear of
Indian corn was as much as a single man could carry. The cotton, as it
grew, took, of its own accord, the rich dyes of human art. The air was
filled with intoxicating perfumes and the sweet melody of birds. In short,
these were the halcyon days, which find a place in the mythic systems of
so many nations in the Old World. It was the *golden age* of Anahuac.

From some cause, not explained, Quetzalcoatl incurred the wrath of
one of the principal gods and was compelled to abandon the country. On
his way, he stopped at the city of Cholula, where a temple was dedicated
to his worship, the massy ruins of which still form one of the most interesting relics of antiquity in Mexico. When he reached the shores of the
Mexican Gulf, he took leave of his followers, promising that he and his
descendants would revisit them hereafter, and then, entering his wizard
skiff, made of serpents' skins, embarked on the great ocean for the fabled
land of Tlapallan. He was said to have been tall in stature, with a white
skin, long, dark hair, and a flowing beard. The Mexicans looked confidently to the return of the benevolent deity; and this remarkable tradition, deeply cherished in their hearts, prepared the way, as we shall see
hereafter, for the future success of the Spaniards.[6]

We have not space for further details respecting the Mexican divinities,
the attributes of many of whom were carefully defined, as they descended,
in regular gradation, to the *penates* or household gods, whose little images
were to be found in the humblest dwelling.

The Aztecs felt the curiosity, common to man in almost every stage of
civilization, to lift the veil which covers the mysterious past, and the more
awful future. They sought relief, like the nations of the Old Continent,
from the oppressive idea of eternity, by breaking it up into distinct cycles,
or periods of time, each of several thousand years' duration. There were
four of these cycles, and at the end of each, by the agency of the ele-

[6] Codex Vaticanus, Pl. 15, and Codex Telleriano-Remensis, Part 2, Pl. 2, ap. Antiq.
of Mexico, vols. I., VI.—Sahagun, Hist. de Nueva España, lib. 3 cap. 3, 4, 13, 14.—
Torquemada, Monarch. Ind., lib. 6, cap. 24.—Ixtlilxochitl, Hist. Chich., MS., cap. 1.
—Gomara, Crónica de la Nueva España, cap. 222, ap. Barcia, Historiadores Primitivos de las Indias Occidentales, (Madrid, 1749,) tom. II.

Quetzalcoatl signifies "feathered serpent." The last syllable means, likewise, a
"twin"; which furnished an argument for Dr. Siguenza to identify this god with the
apostle Thomas, (Didymus signifying also a twin,) who, he supposes, came over to
America to preach the gospel. In this rather startling conjecture he is supported by
several of his devout countrymen, who appear to have as little doubt of the fact as
of the advent of St. James, for a similar purpose, in the mother country. See the
various authorities and arguments set forth with becoming gravity in Dr. Mier's
dissertation in Bustamante's edition of Sahagun, (lib. 3, Suplem.,) and Veytia, (tom.
I. pp. 160-200.) Our ingenious countryman, McCulloh, carries the Aztec god up to a
still more respectable antiquity, by identifying him with the patriarch Noah. Researches, Philosophical and Antiquarian, concerning the Aboriginal History of
America, (Baltimore, 1829,) p. 232

ments, the human family was swept from the earth, and the sun blotted
out from the heavens, to be again rekindled.[7]

They imagined three separate states of existence in the future life. The
wicked, comprehending the greater part of mankind, were to expiate
their sins in a place of everlasting darkness. Another class, with no other
merit than that of having died of certain diseases, capriciously selected,
were to enjoy a negative existence of indolent contentment. The highest
place was reserved, as in most warlike nations, for the heroes who fell in
battle, or in sacrifice. They passed, at once, into the presence of the Sun,
whom they accompanied with songs and choral dances, in his bright progress through the heavens; and, after some years, their spirits went to
animate the clouds and singing birds of beautiful plumage, and to revel
amidst the rich blossoms and odors of the gardens of paradise.[8] Such was
the heaven of the Aztecs; more refined in its character than that of the
more polished pagan, whose elysium reflected only the martial sports, or
sensual gratifications, of this life.[9] In the destiny they assigned to the
wicked, we discern similar traces of refinement; since the absence of all
physical torture forms a striking contrast to the schemes of suffering so
ingeniously devised by the fancies of the most enlightened nations.[10] In

[7] Cod. Vat., Pl. 7-10, ap. Antiq. of Mexico, vols. I., VI.—Ixtlilxochitl, Hist. Chich.,
MS., cap 1.
M. de Humboldt has been at some pains to trace the analogy between the Aztec
cosmogony and that of Eastern Asia. He has tried, though in vain, to find a multiple
which might serve as the key to the calculations of the former. (Vues des Cordilléres,
pp. 202-212.) In truth, there seems to be a material discordance in the Mexican
statements, both in regard to the number of revolutions and their duration. A manuscript before me, of Ixtlilxochitl, reduces them to three, before the present state of
the world, and allows only 4394 years for them; (Sumaria Relacion, MS., No. 1;)
Gama, on the faith of an ancient Indian MS., in Boturini's Catalogue, (VIII. 13,)
reduces the duration still lower; (Descripcion de las Dos Piedras, Parte 1, p. 49, et
seq.;) while the cycles of the Vatican paintings take up near 18,000 years.—It is interesting to observe how the wild *conjectures* of an ignorant age have been confirmed
by the more recent *discoveries* in geology, making it probable that the earth has experienced a number of convulsions, possibly thousands of years distant from each
other, which have swept away the races then existing, and given a new aspect to the
globe.
[8] Sahagun, Hist. de Nueva España, lib. 3, Apend.—Cod. Vat., ap. Antiq. of Mexico, Pl. 1-5.—Torquemada, Monarch, Ind., lib. 13, cap. 48.
The last writer assures us, "that, as to what the Aztecs said of their going to hell,
they were right; for, as they died in ignorance of the true faith, they have, without
question, all gone there to suffer everlasting punishment!" Ubi supra.
[9] It conveys but a poor idea of these pleasures, that the shade of Achilles can say,
"he had rather be the slave of the meanest man on earth, than sovereign among the
dead." (Odyss. A. 488-490.) The Mahometans believe that the souls of martyrs pass,
after death, into the bodies of birds, that haunt the sweet waters and bowers of
Paradise. (Sale's Koran, (London, 1825,) vol. I. p. 106).—The Mexican heaven may
remind one of Dante's, in its *material* enjoyments; which, in both, are made up of
light, music, and motion. The sun, it must also be remembered, was a spiritual
conception with the Aztec;
"He sees with other eyes than theirs; where they
Behold a sun, he spies a deity."
[10] It is singular that the Tuscan bard, while exhausting his invention in devising
modes of bodily torture, in his "Inferno," should have made so little use of the *mor*

all this, so contrary to the natural suggestions of the ferocious Aztec, we see the evidences of a higher civilization, inherited from their predecessors in the land.

Our limits will allow only a brief allusion to one or two of their most interesting ceremonies. On the death of a person, his corpse was dressed in the peculiar habiliments of his tutelar deity. It was strewed with pieces of paper, which operated as charms against the dangers of the dark road he was to travel. A throng of slaves, if he were rich, was sacrificed at his obsequies. His body was burned, and the ashes, collected in a vase, were preserved in one of the apartments of his house. Here we have successively the usages of the Roman Catholic, the Mussulman, the Tartar, and the Ancient Greek and Roman; curious coincidences, which may show how cautious we should be in adopting conclusions founded on analogy.[11]

A more extraordinary coincidence may be traced with Christian rites, in the ceremony of naming their children. The lips and bosom of the infant were sprinkled with water, and "the Lord was implored to permit the holy drops to wash away the sin that was given to it before the foundation of the world; so that the child might be born anew." [12] We are reminded of Christian morals, in more than one of their prayers, in which they used regular forms. "Wilt thou blot us out, O Lord, for ever? Is this punishment intended, not for our reformation, but for our destruction?" Again, "Impart to us, out of thy great mercy, thy gifts, which we are not worthy to receive through our own merits." "Keep peace with all," says another petition; "bear injuries with humility; God, who sees, will avenge you." But the most striking parallel with Scripture is in the remarkable declaration, that "he, who looks too curiously on a woman, commits adultery with his eyes." These pure and elevated maxims, it is true, are mixed up with others of a puerile, and even brutal character, arguing that confusion of the moral perceptions, which is natural in the twilight of civilization. One would not expect, however, to meet, in such a state of society, with doctrines as sublime as any inculcated by the enlightened codes of ancient philosophy.[13]

al sources of misery. That he has not done so might be reckoned a strong proof of the rudeness of the time, did we not meet with examples of it in a later day; in which a serious and sublime writer, like Dr. Watts, does not disdain to employ the same coarse machinery for moving the conscience of the reader.

[11] Carta del Lic. Zuazo, (Nov., 1521,) MS.—Acosta, lib. 5, cap. 8.—Torquemada, Monarch. Ind., lib. 13, cap. 45.—Sahagun, Hist. de Nueva España, lib. 3, Apend.

Sometimes the body was buried entire, with valuable treasures, if the deceased was rich. The "Anonymous Conqueror," as he is called, saw gold to the value of 3000 castellanos drawn from one of these tombs. Relatione d' un gentil' huomo, ap. Ramusio, tom. III. p. 310.

[12] This interesting rite, usually solemnized with great formality, in the presence of the assembled friends and relatives, is detailed with minuteness by Sahagun, (Hist. de Nueva España, lib. 6, cap. 37,) and by Zuazo, (Carta, MS.,) both of them eyewitnesses. For a version of part of Sahagun's account, see *Appendix, Part 1. note 26.*

[13] ¿ Es posible que este azote y este castigo no se nos da para nuestra correccion y enmienda, sino para total destruccion y asolamiento?" (Sahagun, Hist. de Nueva España, lib. 6, cap. 1.) "Ye esto por sola vuestra liberalidad y magnificencia lo habeis de hacer, que ninguno es digno ni merecedor de recibir vuestras larguezas por su

But, although the Aztec mythology gathered nothing from the beauti‑ful inventions of the poet, nor from the refinements of philosophy, it was much indebted, as I have noticed, to the priests, who endeavoured to dazzle the imagination of the people by the most formal and pompous ceremonial. The influence of the priesthood must be greatest in an imper‑fect state of civilization, where it engrosses all the scanty science of the time in its own body. This is particularly the case, when the science is of that spurious kind which is less occupied with the real phenomena of na‑ture, than with the fanciful chimeras of human superstition. Such are the sciences of astrology and divination, in which the Aztec priests were well initiated; and, while they seemed to hold the keys of the future in their own hands, they impressed the ignorant people with sentiments of super‑stitious awe, beyond that which has probably existed in any other coun‑try,—even in ancient Egypt.

The sacerdotal order was very numerous; as may be inferred from the statement, that five thousand priests were, in some way or other, attached to the principal temple in the capital. The various ranks and functions of this multitudinous body were discriminated with great exactness. Those best instructed in music took the management of the choirs. Others ar‑ranged the festivals conformably to the calendar. Some superintended the education of youth, and others had charge of the hieroglyphical paintings and oral traditions; while the dismal rites of sacrifice were re‑served for the chief dignitaries of the order. At the head of the whole establishment were two high-priests, elected from the order, as it would seem, by the king and principal nobles, without reference to birth, but solely for their qualifications, as shown by their previous conduct in a subordinate station. They were equal in dignity, and inferior only to the sovereign, who rarely acted without their advice in weighty matters of public concern.[14]

The priests were each devoted to the service of some particular deity, and had quarters provided within the spacious precincts of their temple; at least, while engaged in immediate attendance there,—for they were allowed to marry, and have families of their own. In this monastic resi‑

dignidad y merecimiento, sino que por vuestra benignidad." (Ibid., lib. 6, cap. 2.) 'Sed sufridos y reportados, que Dios bien os vé y responderá por vosotros, y él os vengará (á) sed humildes con todos, y con esto os hará Dios merced y tambien honra." (Ibid., lib. 6, cap. 17.) "Tampoco mires con curiosidad el gesto y disposicion de la gente principal, mayormente de las mugeres, y sobre todo de las casadas, porque dice el refran que él que curiosamente mira á la muger adultera con la vista." (Ibid., lib. 6, cap. 22.)

[14] Sahagun, Hist. de Nueva España, lib. 2, Apend; lib. 3, cap. 9.—Torquemada, Monarch. Ind., lib. 8, cap. 20; lib. 9, cap. 3, 56.—Gomara Crón., cap. 215, ap. Barcia, tom. II.—Toribio, Hist. de los Indios, MS., Parte 1, cap. 4.

Clavigero says that the high-priest was necessarily a person of rank. (Stor. del Messico, tom. II. p. 37.) I find no authority for this, not even in his oracle, Tor‑quemada, who expressly says, "There is no warrant for the assertion, however prob‑able the fact may be." (Monarch. Ind., lib. 9, cap. 5.) It is contradicted by Sahagun, whom I have followed as the highest authority in these matters. Clavigero had no other knowledge of Sahagun's work than what was filtered through the writings of Torquemada, and later authors.

dence they lived in all the stern severity of conventual discipline. Thrice during the day, and once at night, they were called to prayers. They were frequent in their ablutions and vigils, and mortified the flesh by fasting and cruel penance,—drawing blood from their bodies by flagellation, or by piercing them with the thorns of the aloe; in short, by practising all those austerities to which fanaticism (to borrow the strong language of the poet) has resorted, in every age of the world,

"In hopes to merit heaven by making earth a hell." [15]

The great cities were divided into districts, placed under the charge of a sort of parochial clergy, who regulated every act of religion within their precincts. It is remarkable that they administered the rites of confession and absolution. The secrets of the confessional were held inviolable, and penances were imposed of much the same kind as those enjoined in the Roman Catholic Church. There were two remarkable peculiarities in the Aztec ceremony. The first was, that, as the repetition of an offence, once atoned for, was deemed inexpiable, confession was made but once in a man's life, and was usually deferred to a late period of it, when the penitent unburdened his conscience, and settled, at once, the long arrears of iniquity. Another peculiarity was, that priestly absolution was received in place of the legal punishment of offences, and authorized an acquittal in case of arrest. Long after the Conquest, the simple natives, when they came under the arm of the law, sought to escape by producing the certificate of their confession. [16]

One of the most important duties of the priesthood was that of education, to which certain buildings were appropriated within the inclosure of the principal temple. Here the youth of both sexes, of the higher and middling orders, were placed at a very tender age. The girls were intrusted to the care of priestesses; for women were allowed to exercise sacerdotal functions, except those of sacrifice. [17] In these institutions the

[15] Sahagun, Hist. de Nueva España, ubi supra.—Torquemada, Monarch. Ind., lib 9, cap. 25.—Gomara, Crón., ap. Barcia, ubi supra.—Acosta, lib. 5, cap. 14, 17.

[16] Sahagun, Hist. de Nueva España, lib. 1, cap. 12; lib. 6, cap. 7.
The address of the confessor, on these occasions, contains some things too remarkable to be omitted. "O merciful Lord," he says in his prayer, "thou who knowest the secrets of all hearts, let thy forgiveness and favor descend, like the pure waters of heaven, to wash away the stains from the soul. Thou knowest that this poor man *has sinned, not from his own free will,* but from the influence of the sign under which he was born." After a copious exhortation to the penitent, enjoining a variety of mortifications and minute ceremonies by way of penance, and particularly urging the necessity of instantly procuring *a slave for sacrifice* to the Deity, the priest concludes with inculcating charity to the poor. "Clothe the naked and feed the hungry, whatever privations it may cost thee; for remember, *their flesh is like thine, and they are men like thee.*" Such is the strange medley of truly Christian benevolence and heathenish abominations which pervades the Aztec litany,—intimating sources widely different.

[17] The Egyptian gods were also served by priestesses. (See Herodotus, Euterpe, sec. 54.) Tales of scandal similar to those which the Greeks circulated respecting them, have been told of the Aztec virgins. (See Le Noir's dissertation, ap. Antiquités Mexicaines, (Paris, 1834,) tom. II. p. 7, note.) The early missionaries, credu

boys were drilled in the routine of monastic discipline; they decorated
the shrines of the gods with flowers, fed the sacred fires, and took part
in the religious chants and festivals. Those in the higher school—the *Cal-
mecac*, as it was called—were initiated in their traditionary lore, the mysteries of hieroglyphics, the principles of government, and such branches
of astronomical and natural science as were within the compass of the
priesthood. The girls learned various feminine employments, especially
to weave and embroider rich coverings for the altars of the gods. Great
attention was paid to the moral discipline of both sexes. The most perfect decorum prevailed; and offences were punished with extreme rigor,
in some instances with death itself. Terror, not love, was the spring of
education with the Aztecs.[18]

At a suitable age for marrying, or for entering into the world, the
pupils were dismissed, with much ceremony, from the convent, and the
recommendation of the principal often introduced those most competent
to responsible situations in public life. Such was the crafty policy of the
Mexican priests, who, by reserving to themselves the business of instruction, were enabled to mould the young and plastic mind according to
their own wills, and to train it early to implicit reverence for religion
and its ministers; a reverence which still maintained its hold on the iron
nature of the warrior, long after every other vestige of education had
been effaced by the rough trade to which he was devoted.

To each of the principal temples, lands were annexed for the maintenance of the priests. These estates were augmented by the policy or devotion of successive princes, until, under the last Montezuma, they had
swollen to an enormous extent, and covered every district of the empire.
The priests took the management of their property into their own hands;
and they seem to have treated their tenants with the liberality and indulgence characteristic of monastic corporations. Besides the large supplies drawn from this source, the religious order was enriched with the
first-fruits, and such other offerings as piety or superstition dictated. The
surplus beyond what was required for the support of the national worship
was distributed in alms among the poor; a duty strenuously prescribed
by their moral code. Thus we find the same religion inculcating lessons
of pure philanthropy, on the one hand, and of merciless extermination,
as we shall soon see, on the other. The inconsistency will not appear in-

lous enough certainly, give no countenance to such reports; and father Acosta, on
the contrary, exclaims, "In truth, it is very strange to see that this false opinion of
religion hath so great force among these young men and maidens of Mexico, that
they will serve the Divell with so great rigor and austerity, which many of us doe
not in the service of the most high God; the which is a great shame and confusion."
Eng. Trans., lib. 5, cap. 16.

[18] Toribio, Hist. de los Indios, MS., Parte 1, cap. 9.—Sahagun, Hist. de Nueva España, lib. 2, Apend.; lib. 3, cap. 4-8.—Zurita, Rapport, pp. 123-126.—Acosta, lib.
5, cap. 15, 16.—Torquemada, Monarch. Ind., lib. 9, cap. 11-14, 30, 31.

"They were taught," says the good father last cited, "to eschew vice, and cleave
to virtue,—*according to their notions of them;* namely, to abstain from wrath, to
offer violence and do wrong to no man,—in short, to perform the duties plainly
pointed out by natural religion."

credible to those who are familiar with the history of the Roman Catholic Church, in the early ages of the Inquisition.[19]

The Mexican temples—*teocallis*, "houses of God," as they were called —were very numerous. There were several hundreds in each of the principal cities, many of them, doubtless, very humble edifices. They were solid masses of earth, cased with brick, or stone, and in their form somewhat resembled the pyramidal structures of ancient Egypt. The bases of many of them were more than a hundred feet square, and they towered to a still greater height. They were distributed into four or five stories, each of smaller dimensions than that below. The ascent was by a flight of steps, at an angle of the pyramid, on the outside. This led to a sort of terrace, or gallery, at the base of the second story, which passed quite round the building to another flight of stairs, commencing also at the same angle as the preceding and directly over it, and leading to a similar terrace; so that one had to make the circuit of the temple several times, before reaching the summit. In some instances the stairway led directly up the centre of the western face of the building. The top was a broad area, on which were erected one or two towers, forty or fifty feet high, the sanctuaries in which stood the sacred images of the presiding deities. Before these towers stood the dreadful stone of sacrifice, and two lofty altars, on which fires were kept, as inextinguishable as those in the temple of Vesta. There were said to be six hundred of these altars, on smaller buildings within the inclosure of the great temple of Mexico, which, with those on the sacred edifices in other parts of the city, shed a brilliant illumination over its streets, through the darkest night.[20]

From the construction of their temples, all religious services were public. The long processions of priests, winding round their massive sides, as they rose higher and higher towards the summit, and the dismal rites of sacrifice performed there, were all visible from the remotest corners of the capital, impressing on the spectator's mind a superstitious veneration for the mysteries of his religion, and for the dread ministers by whom they were interpreted.

This impression was kept in full force by their numerous festivals.

[19] Torquemada, Monarch. Ind., lib. 8, cap. 20, 21.—Camargo, Hist. de Tlascala, MS.

It is impossible not to be struck with the great resemblance, not merely in a few empty forms, but in the whole way of life, of the Mexican and Egyptian priesthood. Compare Herodotus (Euterpe, passim) and Diodorus (lib. 1, sec. 73, 81). The English reader may consult, for the same purpose, Heeren, (Hist. Res., vol. V. chap. 2,) Wilkinson, (Manners and Customs of the Ancient Egyptians, (London, 1837,) vol. I. pp. 257-279,) the last writer especially,—who has contributed, more than all others, towards opening to us the interior of the social life of this interesting people.

[20] Rel. d' un gent., ap. Ramusio, tom. III. fol. 307.—Camargo, Hist. de Tlascala, MS.—Acosta, lib. 5, cap. 13.—Gomara, Crón., cap. 80, ap. Barcia, tom. II.—Toribio, Hist. de los Indios, MS., Parte 1, cap. 4.—Carta del Lic. Zuazo, MS.

This last writer, who visited Mexico immediately after the Conquest, in 1521, assures us that some of the smaller temples, or pyramids, were filled with earth impregnated with odoriferous gums and gold dust; the latter, sometimes in such quantities as probably to be worth a million of *castellanos!* (Ubi supra.) These were the temples of Mammon, indeed! But I find no confirmation of such golden reports.

Every month was consecrated to some protecting deity; and every week, nay, almost every day, was set down in their calendar for some appropriate celebration; so that it is difficult to understand how the ordinary business of life could have been compatible with the exactions of religion. Many of their ceremonies were of a light and cheerful complexion, consisting of the national songs and dances, in which both sexes joined. Processions were made of women and children crowned with garlands and bearing offerings of fruits, the ripened maize, or the sweet incense of copal and other odoriferous gums, while the altars of the deity were stained with no blood save that of animals.[21] These were the peaceful rites derived from their Toltec predecessors, on which the fierce Aztecs engrafted a superstition too loathsome to be exhibited in all its nakedness, and one over which I would gladly draw a veil altogether, but that it would leave the reader in ignorance of their most striking institution, and one that had the greatest influence in forming the national character.

Human sacrifices were adopted by the Aztecs early in the fourteenth century, about two hundred years before the Conquest.[22] Rare at first, they became more frequent with the wider extent of their empire; till, at length, almost every festival was closed with this cruel abomination. These religious ceremonials were generally arranged in such a manner as to afford a type of the most prominent circumstances in the character or history of the deity who was the object of them. A single example will suffice.

One of their most important festivals was that in honor of the god, Tezcatlipoca, whose rank was inferior only to that of the Supreme Being. He was called "the soul of the world," and supposed to have been its creator. He was depicted as a handsome man, endowed with perpetual youth. A year before the intended sacrifice, a captive, distinguished for his personal beauty, and without a blemish on his body, was selected to represent this deity. Certain tutors took charge of him, and instructed him how to perform his new part with becoming grace and dignity. He was arrayed in a splendid dress, regaled with incense and with a profusion of sweet-scented flowers, of which the ancient Mexicans were as fond as their descendants at the present day. When he went abroad, he was attended by a train of the royal pages, and, as he halted in the streets to play some favorite melody, the crowd prostrated themselves before him, and did him homage as the representative of their good deity. In this way he led an easy, luxurious life, till within a month of his sacrifice. Four beautiful girls, bearing the names of the principal goddesses, were

[21] Cod. Tel.-Rem., Pl. 1, and Cod. Vat., passim, ap. Antiq. of Mexico, vols. I., VI. —Torquemada, Monarch. Ind., lib. 10, cap. 10, et seq.—Sahagun, Hist. de Nueva España, lib. 2, passim.

Among the offerings, quails may be particularly noticed, for the incredible quantities of them sacrificed and consumed at many of the festivals.

[22] The traditions of their origin have somewhat of a fabulous tinge. But, whether true or false, they are equally indicative of unparalleled ferocity in the people who could be the subject of them. Clavigero, Stor. del Messico, tom. I. p. 167, et seq.; also Humboldt. (who does not appear to doubt them,) Vues des Cordillères, p. 95.

then selected to share the honors of his bed; and with them he continued to live in idle dalliance, feasted at the banquets of the principal nobles, who paid him all the honors of a divinity.

At length the fatal day of sacrifice arrived. The term of his short-lived glories was at an end. He was stripped of his gaudy apparel, and bade adieu to the fair partners of his revelries. One of the royal barges transported him across the lake to a temple which rose on its margin, about a league from the city. Hither the inhabitants of the capital flocked, to witness the consummation of the ceremony. As the sad procession wound up the sides of the pyramid, the unhappy victim threw away his gay chaplets of flowers, and broke in pieces the musical instruments with which he had solaced the hours of captivity. On the summit he was received by six priests, whose long and matted locks flowed disorderly over their sable robes, covered with hieroglyphic scrolls of mystic import. They led him to the sacrificial stone, a huge block of jasper, with its upper surface somewhat convex. On this the prisoner was stretched. Five priests secured his head and his limbs; while the sixth, clad in a scarlet mantle, emblematic of his bloody office, dexterously opened the breast of the wretched victim with a sharp razor *itztli*,—a volcanic substance, hard as flint,—and, inserting his hand in the wound, tore out the palpitating heart. The minister of death, first holding this up towards the sun, an object of worship throughout Anahuac, cast it at the feet of the deity to whom the temple was devoted, while the multitudes below prostrated themselves in humble adoration. The tragic story of this prisoner was expounded by the priests as the type of human destiny, which, brilliant in its commencement, too often closes in sorrow and disaster.[23]

Such was the form of human sacrifice usually practised by the Aztecs. It was the same that often met the indignant eyes of the Europeans, in their progress through the country, and from the dreadful doom of which they themselves were not exempted. There were, indeed, some occasions when preliminary tortures, of the most exquisite kind,—with which it is unnecessary to shock the reader,—were inflicted, but they always terminated with the bloody ceremony above described. It should be remarked, however, that such tortures were not the spontaneous suggestions of cruelty, as with the North American Indians; but were all rigorously prescribed in the Aztec ritual, and doubtless were often inflicted with the same compunctious visitings which a devout familiar of the Holy Office might at times experience in executing its stern decrees.[24] Women, as

---

[23] Sahagun, Hist. de Nueva España, lib. 2, cap. 2, 5, 24, et alibi.—Herrera, Hist. General, dec. 3, lib. 2, cap. 16.—Torquemada, Monarch. Ind., lib. 7, cap. 19; lib. 10, cap. 14.—Rel. d' un gent., ap. Ramusio, tom. III. fol. 307.—Acosta, lib. 5, cap. 9–21 —Carta del Lic. Zuazo, MS.—Relacion por el Regimiento de Vera Cruz, (Julio 1519,) MS.

Few readers, probably, will sympathize with the sentence of Torquemada, who concludes his tale of woe by coolly dismissing "the soul of the victim, to sleep with those of his false gods, in hell!" Lib. 10, cap. 23.

[24] Sahagun, Hist. de Nueva España, lib. 2, cap. 10, 29.—Gomara, Crón., cap. 219, ap. Barcia, tom. II.—Toribio, Hist. de los Indios, MS., Parte 1, cap. 6-11.

The reader will find a tolerably exact picture of the nature of these tortures in

well as the other sex, were sometimes reserved for sacrifice. On some occasions, particularly in seasons of drought, at the festival of the insatiable Tlaloc, the god of rain, children, for the most part infants, were offered up. As they were borne along in open litters, dressed in their festal robes, and decked with the fresh blossoms of spring, they moved the hardest heart to pity, though their cries were drowned in the wild chant of the priests, who read in their tears a favorable augury for their petition. These innocent victims were generally bought by the priests of parents who were poor, but who stifled the voice of nature, probably less at the suggestions of poverty, than of a wretched superstition.[25]

The most loathsome part of the story—the manner in which the body of the sacrificed captive was disposed of—remains yet to be told. It was delivered to the warrior who had taken him in battle, and by him, after being dressed, was served up in an entertainment to his friends. This was not the coarse repast of famished cannibals, but a banquet teeming with delicious beverages and delicate viands, prepared with art, and attended by both sexes, who, as we shall see hereafter, conducted themselves with all the decorum of civilized life. Surely, never were refinement and the extreme of barbarism brought so closely in contact with each other! [26]

Human sacrifices have been practised by many nations, not excepting the most polished nations of antiquity; [27] but never by any, on a scale to be compared with those in Anahuac. The amount of victims immolated on its accursed altars would stagger the faith of the least scrupulous believer. Scarcely any author pretends to estimate the yearly sacrifices throughout the empire at less than twenty thousand, and some carry the number as high as fifty! [28]

the twenty-first canto of the "Inferno." The fantastic creations of the Florentine poet were nearly realized, at the very time he was writing, by the barbarians of an unknown world. One sacrifice, of a less revolting character, deserves to be mentioned. The Spaniards called it the "gladiatorial sacrifice," and it may remind one of the bloody games of antiquity. A captive of distinction was sometimes furnished with arms, and brought against a number of Mexicans in succession. If he defeated them all, as did occasionally happen, he was allowed to escape. If vanquished, he was dragged to the block and sacrificed in the usual manner. The combat was fought on a huge circular stone, before the assembled capital. Sahagun, Hist. de Nueve España, lib. 2, cap. 21.—Rel. d'un gent., ap. Ramusio, tom. III, fcl. 305.

[25] Sahagun, Hist. de Nueve España, lib. 2, cap. 1, 4, 21, et alibi.—Torquemada, Monarch. Ind., lib. 10, cap. 10.—Clavigero, Stor. del Messico, tom. II. pp. 76, 82.

[26] Carte del Lic. Zuazo, MS.—Torquemada, Monarch. Ind., lib. 7, cap. 19.—Herrera, Hist. General, dec. 3, lib. 2, cap. 17.—Sahagun, Hist. de Nueve España, lib. 2, cap. 21, et alibi.—Toribio, Hist. de los Indios, MS., Parte 1, cap. 2.

[27] To say nothing of Egypt, where, notwithstanding the indications on the monuments, there is strong reason for doubting it. (Comp. Herodotus, Euterpe, sec. 45.) It was of frequent occurrence among the Greeks, as every schoolboy knows. In Rome, it was so common as to require to be interdicted by an express law, less than a hundred years before the Christian era,—a law recorded in a very honest strain of exultation by Pliny; (Hist. Nat., lib. 30, sec. 3, 4;) notwithstanding which, traces of the existence of the practice may be discerned to a much later period. See, among others, Horace, Epod., In Canidiam.

[28] See Clavigero, Stor. del Messico, tom. II, p. 49.

Bishop Zumarraga, in a letter written a few years after the Conquest, states that

On great occasions, as the coronation of a king, or the consecration of a temple, the number becomes still more appalling. At the dedication of the great temple of Huitzilopotchli, in 1486, the prisoners, who for some years had been reserved for the purpose, were drawn from all quarters to the capital. They were ranged in files, forming a procession nearly two miles long. The ceremony consumed several days, and seventy thousand captives are said to have perished at the shrine of this terrible deity! But who can believe that so numerous a body would have suffered themselves to be led unresistingly like sheep to the slaughter? Or how could their remains, too great for consumption in the ordinary way, be disposed of, without breeding a pestilence in the capital? Yet the event was of recent date, and is unequivocally attested by the best informed historians.[29] One fact may be considered certain. It was customary to preserve the skulls of the sacrificed, in buildings appropriated to the purpose. The companions of Cortés counted one hundred and thirty-six thousand in one of these edifices![30] Without attempting a precise calculation, therefore, it is safe to conclude that thousands were yearly offered up, in the different cities of Anahuac, on the bloody altars of the Mexican divinities.[31]

Indeed, the great object of war, with the Aztecs, was quite as much to

[29] 20,000 victims were yearly slaughtered in the capital. Torquemada turns this into 20,000 *infants*. (Monarch. Ind., lib. 7, cap. 21.) Herrera, following Acosta, says 20,000 victims on a specified day of the year, throughout the kingdom. (Hist. General, dec. 2, lib. 2, cap. 16.) Clavigero, more cautious, infers that this number may have been sacrificed annually throughout Anahuac. (Ubi supra.) Las Casas, however, in his reply to Sepulveda's assertion, that no one who had visited the New World put the number of yearly sacrifices at less than 20,000, declares that "this is the estimate of brigands, who wish to find an apology for their own atrocities, and that the real number was not above 50!" (Œuvres, ed. Llorente, (Paris, 1822,) tom. I. pp. 365, 386.) Probably the good Bishop's arithmetic, here, as in most other instances, came more from his heart than his head. With such loose and contradictory *data*, it is clear that any specific number is mere conjecture, undeserving the name of calculation.

[29] I am within bounds. Torquemada states the number, most precisely, at 72,344 (Monarch. Ind., lib. 2, cap. 63.) Ixtlilxochitl, with equal precision, at 80,400. (Hist. Chich., MS.) ¿Quien sabe? The latter adds, that the captives massacred in the capital, in the course of that memorable year, exceeded 100,000! (Loc. cit.) One, however, has to read but a little way, to find out that the science of numbers—at least, where the party was not an eyewitness—is any thing but an exact science with these ancient chroniclers. The Codex Tel.-Rememsis, written some fifty years after the Conquest, reduces the amount to 20,000. (Antiq. of Mexico, vol. I. Pl. 19; vol. VI. p. 141, Eng. note.) Even this hardly warrants the Spanish interpreter in calling king Ahuitzotl a man "of a mild and moderate disposition," *templada y benigna condicion!* Ibid., vol. V. p. 49.

[30] Gomara states the number on the authority of two soldiers, whose names he gives, who took the trouble to count the grinning horrors in one of these Golgothas, where they were so arranged as to produce the most hideous effect. The existence of these conservatories is attested by every writer of the time.

[31] The "Anonymous Conqueror" assures us, as a fact beyond dispute, that the Devil introduced himself into the bodies of the idols, and persuaded the silly priests that his only diet was human hearts! It furnishes a very satisfactory solution, to his mind, of the frequency of sacrifices in Mexico. Rel. d' un gent., ap. Ramusio, tom III. fol. 307.

gather victims for their sacrifices, as to extend their empire. Hence it was, that an enemy was never slain in battle, if there were a chance of taking him alive. To this circumstance the Spaniards repeatedly owed their preservation. When Montezuma was asked, "why he had suffered the republic of Tlascala to maintain her independence on his borders," he replied, "that she might furnish him with victims for his gods!" As the supply began to fail, the priests, the Dominicans of the New World, bellowed aloud for more, and urged on their superstitious sovereign by the denunciations of celestial wrath. Like the militant churchmen of Christendom in the Middle Ages, they mingled themselves in the ranks, and were conspicuous in the thickest of the fight, by their hideous aspect and frantic gestures. Strange, that, in every country, the most fiendish passions of the human heart have been those kindled in the name of religion! [32]

The influence of these practices on the Aztec character was as disastrous as might have been expected. Familiarity with the bloody rites of sacrifice steeled the heart against human sympathy, and begat a thirst for carnage, like that excited in the Romans by the exhibitions of the circus. The perpetual recurrence of ceremonies, in which the people took part, associated religion with their most intimate concerns, and spread the gloom of superstition over the domestic hearth, until the character of the nation wore a grave and even melancholy aspect, which belongs to their descendants at the present day. The influence of the priesthood, of course, became unbounded. The sovereign thought himself honored by being permitted to assist in the services of the temple. Far from limiting the authority of the priests to spiritual matters, he often surrendered his opinion to theirs, where they were least competent to give it. It was their opposition that prevented the final capitulation which would have saved the capital. The whole nation, from the peasant to the prince, bowed their necks to the worst kind of tyranny, that of a blind fanaticism.

In reflecting on the revolting usages recorded in the preceding pages, one finds it difficult to reconcile their existence with any thing like a regular form of government, or an advance in civilization. Yet the Mexicans had many claims to the character of a civilized community. One may, perhaps, better understand the anomaly, by reflecting on the condition of some of the most polished countries in Europe, in the sixteenth cen-

---

[32] The Tezcucan priests would fain have persuaded the good king Nezahualcoyotl, on occasion of a pestilence, to appease the gods by the sacrifice of some of his own subjects, instead of his enemies; on the ground, that, not only they would be obtained more easily, but would be fresher victims, and more acceptable. (Ixlilxochitl, Hist. Chich., MS., cap. 41.) This writer mentions a cool arrangement entered into by the allied monarchs with the republic of Tlascala and her confederates. A battlefield was marked out, on which the troops of the hostile nations were to engage at stated seasons, and thus supply themselves with subjects for sacrifice. The victorious party was not to pursue his advantage by invading the other's territory, and they were to continue, in all other respects, on the most amicable footing. (Ubi supra.) The historian, who follows in the track of the Tezcucan Chronicler, may often find occasion to shelter himself, like Ariosto, with
"Bettendolo Turpin, lo metto anch'io."

tury, after the establishment of the modern Inquisition; an institution, which yearly destroyed its thousands, by a death more painful than the Aztec sacrifices; which armed the hand of brother against brother, and, setting its burning seal upon the lip, did more to stay the march of improvement than any other scheme ever devised by human cunning.

Human sacrifice, however cruel, has nothing in it degrading to its victim. It may be rather said to ennoble him by devoting him to the gods. Although so terrible with the Aztecs, it was sometimes voluntarily embraced by them, as the most glorious death, and one that opened a sure passage into paradise.[33] The Inquisition, on the other hand, branded its victims with infamy in this world, and consigned them to everlasting perdition in the next.

One detestable feature of the Aztec superstition, however, sunk it far below the Christian. This was its cannibalism; though, in truth, the Mexicans were not cannibals, in the coarsest acceptation of the term. They did not feed on human flesh merely to gratify a brutish appetite, but in obedience to their religion. Their repasts were made of the victims whose blood had been poured out on the altar of sacrifice. This is a distinction worthy of notice.[34] Still, cannibalism, under any form, or whatever sanction, cannot but have a fatal influence on the nation addicted to it. It suggests ideas so loathsome, so degrading to man, to his spiritual and immortal nature, that it is impossible the people who practise it should make any great progress in moral or intellectual culture. The Mexicans furnish no exception to this remark. The civilization, which they possessed, descended from the Toltecs, a race who never stained their altars, still less their banquets, with the blood of man. All that deserved the name of science in Mexico came from this source; and the crumbling ruins of edifices, attributed to them, still extant in various parts of New Spain, show a decided superiority in their architecture over that of the later races of Anahuac. It is true, the Mexicans made great proficiency in many of the social and mechanic arts, in that material culture,—if I may so call it,—the natural growth of increasing opulence, which ministers to the gratification of the senses. In purely intellectual progress, they were behind the Tezcucans, whose wise sovereigns came into the abominable rites of their neighbors with reluctance, and practised them on a much more moderate scale.[35]

In this state of things, it was beneficently ordered by Providence that the land should be delivered over to another race, who would rescue it from the brutish superstitions that daily extended wider and wider, with

[33] Rel. d' un gent., ap. Ramusio, tom. III. fol. 307.

Among other instances, is that of Chimalpopoca, third king of Mexico, who doomed himself, with a number of his lords, to this death, to wipe off an indignity offered him by a brother monarch. (Torquemada, Monarch. Ind., lib. 2, cap. 28.) This was the law of honor with the Aztecs.

[34] Voltaire, doubtless, intends this, when he says, "Ils n'étaient point anthropophages, comme un très-petit nombre de peuplades Américaines." (Essai sur les Mœurs, chap. 147.)

[35] Ixtlilxochitl, Hist. Chich., MS., cap. 45, et alibi.

extent of empire.[36] The debasing institutions of the Aztecs furnish the best apology for their conquest. It is true, the conquerors brought along with them the Inquisition. But they also brought Christianity, whose benign radiance would still survive, when the fierce flames of fanaticism should be extinguished; dispelling those dark forms of horror which had so long brooded over the fair regions of Anahuac.

The most important authority in the preceding chapter, and, indeed, wherever the Aztec religion is concerned, is Bernardino de Sahagun, a Franciscan friar, contemporary with the Conquest. His great work, *Historia Universal de Nueva España,* has been recently printed for the first time. The circumstances attending its compilation and subsequent fate form one of the most remarkable passages in literary history.

Sahagun was born in a place of the same name, in old Spain. He was educated at Salamanca, and, having taken the vows of St. Francis, came over as a missionary to Mexico in the year 1529. Here he distinguished himself by his zeal, the purity of his life, and his unwearied exertions to spread the great truths of religion among the natives. He was the guardian of several conventual houses, successively, until he relinquished these cares, that he might devote himself more unreservedly to the business of preaching, and of compiling various works designed to illustrate the antiquities of the Aztecs. For these literary labors he found some facilities in the situation which he continued to occupy, of reader, or lecturer, in the College of Santa Cruz, in the capital.

The "Universal History" was concocted in a singular manner. In order to secure to it the greatest possible authority, he passed some years in a Tezcucan town, where he conferred daily with a number of respectable natives unacquainted with Castilian. He propounded to them queries, which they, after deliberation, answered in thir usual method of writing, by hieroglyphical paintings. These he submitted to other natives, who had been educated under his own eye in the college of Santa Cruz; and the latter, after a consultation among themselves, gave a written version, in the Mexican tongue, of the hieroglyphics. This process he repeated in another place, in some part of Mexico, and subjected the whole to a still further revision by a third body in another quarter. He finally arranged the combined results into a regular history, in the form it now bears; composing it in the Mexican language, which he could both write and speak with great accuracy and elegance,—greater, indeed, than any Spaniard of the time.

The work presented a mass of curious information, that attracted much attention among his brethren. But they feared its influence in keeping alive in the natives a too vivid reminiscence of the very superstitions which it was the great object of the Christian clergy to eradicate. Sahagun had views more liberal than those of his order, whose blind zeal would willingly have annihilated every monument of art and human ingenuity, which had not been produced under the influence of Christianity. They refused to allow him the necessary aid to transcribe his papers, which he had been so many years in preparing, under the pretext that the expense was too great for their order to incur. This occasioned a further delay of several years. What was worse, his provincial got possession of his manuscripts, which were soon scattered among the different religious houses in the country.

In this forlorn state of his affairs, Sahagun drew up a brief statement of the nature and contents of his work, and forwarded it to Madrid. It fell into the hands of Don Juan de Ovando, president of the Council for the Indies, who was so much interested in it, that he ordered the manuscripts to be restored to their author, with

---

[36] No doubt the ferocity of character engendered by their sanguinary rites greatly facilitated their conquests. Machiavelli attributes to a similar cause, in part, the military successes of the Romans. (Discorsi sopra T. Livio. lib. 2, cap. 2.) The same chapter contains some ingenious reflections—much more ingenious than candid—on the opposite tendencies of Christianity.

the request that he would at once set about translating them into Castilian. This was accordingly done. His papers were recovered, though not without the menace of ecclesiastical censures; and the octogenarian author began the work of translation from the Mexican, in which they had been originally written by him thirty years before. He had the satisfaction to complete the task, arranging the Spanish version in a parallel column with the original, and adding a vocabulary, explaining the difficult Aztec terms and phrases; while the text was supported by the numerous paintings on which it was founded. In this form, making two bulky volumes in folio, it was sent to Madrid. There seemed now to be no further reason for postponing its publication, the importance of which could not be doubted. But from this moment it disappears; and we hear nothing further of it, for more than two centuries, except only as a valuable work, which had once existed, and was probably buried in some one of the numerous cemeteries of learning in which Spain abounds.

At length, towards the close of the last century, the indefatigable Muñoz succeeded in disinterring the long lost manuscript from the place tradition had assigned to it,—the library of a convent at Tolosa, in Navarre, the northern extremity of Spain. With his usual ardor, he transcribed the whole work with his own hands, and added it to the inestimable collection, of which, alas! he was destined not to reap the full benefit himself. From this transcript Lord Kingsborough was enabled to procure the copy which was published in 1830, in the sixth volume of his magnificent compilation. In it he expresses an honest satisfaction at being the first to give Sahagun's work to the world. But in this supposition he was mistaken. The very year preceding, an edition of it, with annotations, appeared in Mexico, in three volumes 8vo. It was prepared by Bustamante,—a scholar to whose editorial activity his country is largely indebted,—from a copy of the Muñoz manuscript which came into his possession. Thus this remarkable work, which was denied the honors of the press during the author's lifetime, after passing into oblivion, reappeared, at the distance of nearly three centuries, not in his own country, but in foreign lands widely remote from each other, and that, almost simultaneously. The story is extraordinary, though unhappily not so extraordinary in Spain as it would be elsewhere.

Sahagun divided his history into twelve books. The first eleven are occupied with the social institutions of Mexico, and the last with the Conquest. On the religion of the country he is particularly full. His great object evidently was, to give a clear view of its mythology, and of the burdensome ritual which belonged to it. Religion entered so intimately into the most private concerns and usages of the Aztecs, that Sahagun's work must be a text-book for every student of their antiquities. Torquemada availed himself of a manuscript copy, which fell into his hands before it was sent to Spain, to enrich his own pages,—a circumstance more fortunate for his readers than for Sahagun's reputation, whose work, now that it is published, loses much of the originality and interest which would otherwise attach to it. In one respect it is invaluable; as presenting a complete collection of the various forms of prayer, accommodated to every possible emergency, in use by the Mexicans. They are often clothed in dignified and beautiful language, showing, that sublime speculative tenets are quite compatible with the most degrading practices of superstition. It is much to be regretted that we have not the eighteen hymns, inserted by the author in his book, which would have particular interest, as the only specimen of devotional poetry preserved of the Aztecs. The hieroglyphical paintings, which accompanied the text, are also missing. If they have escaped the hands of fanaticism, both may reappear at some future day.

Sahagun produced several other works, of a religious or philological character. Some of these were voluminous, but none have been printed. He lived to a very advanced age, closing a life of activity and usefulness, in 1590, in the capital of Mexico. His remains were followed to the tomb by a numerous concourse of his own countrymen, and of the natives, who lamented in him the loss of unaffected piety, benevolence, and learning.

CHAPTER IV

MEXICAN HIEROGLYPHICS—MANUSCRIPTS—ARITHMETIC— CHRONOLOGY—ASTRONOMY

IT is a relief to turn from the gloomy pages of the preceding chapter, to a brighter side of the picture, and to contemplate the same nation in its generous struggle to raise itself from a nation of barbarism, and to take a positive rank in the scale of civilization. It is not the less interesting, that these efforts were made on an entirely new theatre of action, apart from those influences that operate in the Old World; the inhabitants of which, forming one great brotherhood of nations, are knit together by sympathies, that make the faintest spark of knowledge, struck out in one quarter, spread gradually wider and wider, until it has diffused a cheering light over the remotest. It is curious to observe the human mind, in this new position, conforming to the same laws as on the ancient continent, and taking a similar direction in its first inquiries after truth,—so similar, indeed, as, although not warranting, perhaps, the idea of imitation, to suggest, at least, that of a common origin.

In the eastern hemisphere, we find some nations, as the Greeks, for instance, early smitten with such a love of the beautiful as to be unwilling to dispense with it, even in the graver productions of science, and other nations, again, proposing a severer end to themselves, to which even imagination and elegant art were made subservient. The productions of such a people must be criticized, not by the ordinary rules of taste, but by their adaptation to the peculiar end for which they were designed. Such were the Egyptians in the Old World,[1] and the Mexicans in the New. We have already had occasion to notice the resemblance borne by the latter nation to the former in their religious economy. We shall be more struck with it in their scientific culture, especially their hieroglyphical writings and their astronomy.

To describe actions and events by delineating visible objects seems to be a natural suggestion, and is practised, after a certain fashion, by the rudest savages. The North American Indian carves an arrow on the bark of trees to show his followers the direction of his march, and some other sign to show the success of his expeditions. But to paint intelligibly a consecutive series of these actions—forming what Warburton has hap-

---

[1] "An Egyptian temple," says Denon, strikingly, "is an open volume, in which the teachings of science, morality, and the arts are recorded. Every thing seems to speak one and the same language, and breathes one and the same spirit." The passage is cited by Heeren, Hist. Res., vol. V. p. 178.

pily called *picture-writing* [2]—requires a combination of ideas, that amounts to a positively intellectual effort. Yet further, when the object of the painter, instead of being limited to the present, is, to penetrate the past, and to gather from its dark recesses lessons of instruction for coming generations, we see the dawnings of a literary culture,—and recognise the proof of a decided civilization in the attempt itself, however imperfectly it may be executed. The literal imitation of objects will not answer for this more complex and extended plan. It would occupy too much space, as well as time, in the execution. It then becomes necessary to abridge the pictures, to confine the drawing to outlines, or to such prominent parts of the bodies delineated, as may readily suggest the whole. This is the *representative* or *figurative* writing, which forms the lowest stage of hieroglyphics.

But there are things which have no type in the material world; abstract ideas, which can only be represented by visible objects supposed to have some quality analogous to the idea intended. This constitutes *symbolical* writing, the most difficult of all to the interpreter, since the analogy between the material and immaterial object is often purely fanciful, or local in its application. Who, for instance, could suspect the association which made a beetle represent the universe, as with the Egyptians, or a serpent typify time, as with the Aztecs?

The third and last division is the *phonetic*, in which signs are made to represent sounds, either entire words, or parts of them. This is the nearest approach of the hieroglyphical series to that beautiful invention, the alphabet, by which language is resolved into its elementary sounds, and an apparatus supplied for easily and accurately expressing the most delicate shades of thought.

The Egyptians were well skilled in all three kinds of hieroglyphics. But, although their public monuments display the first class, in their ordinary intercourse and written records, it is now certain, they almost wholly relied on the phonetic character. Strange, that, having thus broken down the thin partition which divided them from an alphabet, their latest monuments should exhibit no nearer approach to it than their earliest.[3] The Aztecs, also, were acquainted with the several varieties of

[2] Divine Legation, ap. Works, (London, 1811,) vol. IV. b. 4, sec. 4.
The bishop of Gloucester, in his comparison of the various hieroglyphical systems of the world, shows his characteristic sagacity and boldness by announcing opinions little credited then, though since established. He affirmed the existence of an Egyptian alphabet, but was not aware of the phonetic property of hiero-glyphics,—the great literary discovery of our age.
[3] It appears that the hieroglyphics on the most recent monuments of Egypt contain no larger infusion of phonetic characters than those which existed eighteen centuries before Christ; showing no advance, in this respect, for twenty-two hundred years! (See Champollion, Précis du Système Hiéroglyphique des Anciens Egyptiens, (Paris, 1824,) pp. 242, 281.) It may seem more strange that the enchorial alphabet, so much more commodious, should not have been substituted. But the Egyptians were familiar with their hieroglyphics from infancy, which, moreover, took the fancies of the most illiterate, probably in the same manner as our children are attracted and taught by the picture-alphabets in an ordinary spelling-book.

hieroglyphics. But they relied on the figurative infinitely more than on the others. The Egyptians were at the top of the scale, the Aztecs at the bottom.

In casting the eye over a Mexican manuscript, or map, as it is called, one is struck with the grotesque caricatures it exhibits of the human figure; monstrous, overgrown heads, on puny, misshapen bodies, which are themselves hard and angular in their outlines, and without the least skill in composition. On closer inspection, however, it is obvious that it is not so much a rude attempt to delineate nature, as a conventional symbol, to express the idea in the most clear and forcible manner; in the same way as the pieces of similar value on a chess-board, while they correspond with one another in form, bear little resemblance, usually, to the objects they represent. Those parts of the figure are most distinctly traced, which are the most important. So, also, the coloring, instead of the delicate gradations of nature, exhibits only gaudy and violent contrasts, such as may produce the most vivid impression. "For even colors," as Gama observes, "speak in the Aztec hieroglyphics." [4]

But in the execution of all this the Mexicans were much inferior to the Egyptians. The drawings of the latter, indeed, are exceedingly defective, when criticised by the rules of art; for they were as ignorant of perspective as the Chinese, and only exhibited the head in profile, with the eye in the centre, and with total absence of expression. But they handled the pencil more gracefully than the Aztecs, were more true to the natural forms of objects, and, above all, showed great superiority in abridging the original figure by giving only the outline, or some characteristic or essential feature. This simplified the process, and facilitated the communication of thought. An Egyptian text has almost the appearance of alphabetical writing in its regular lines of minute figures. A Mexican text looks usually like a collection of pictures, each one forming the subject of a separate study. This is particularly the case with the delineations of mythology; in which the story is told by a conglomeration of symbols, that may remind one more of the mysterious anaglyphs sculptured on the temples of the Egyptians, than of their written records.

The Aztecs had various emblems for expressing such things as, from their nature, could not be directly represented by the painter; as, for example, the years, months, days, the seasons, the elements, the heavens, and the like. A "tongue" denoted speaking; a "foot-print," travelling; a "man sitting on the ground," an earthquake. These symbols were often very arbitrary, varying with the caprice of the writer; and it requires a nice discrimination to interpret them, as a slight change in the form or position of the figure intimated a very different meaning.[5] An ingenious

---

[4] Descripcion Histórica y Cronológica de las Dos Piedras, (México, 1832,) Parte 2, p. 39.
[5] Ibid., pp. 32, 44.—Acosta, lib. 6, cap. 7.
The continuation of Gama's work, recently edited by Bustamante, in Mexico, contains, among other things, some interesting remarks on the Aztec hieroglyphics. The editor has rendered a good service by this further publication of the writings

writer asserts that the priests devised secret symbolic characters for the record of their religious mysteries. It is possible. But the researches of Champollion lead to the conclusion, that the similar opinion, formerly entertained respecting the Egyptian hieroglyphics, is without foundation.[6]

Lastly, they employed, as above stated, phonetic signs, though these were chiefly confined to the names of persons and places; which, being derived from some circumstance, or characteristic quality, were accommodated to the hieroglyphical system. Thus the town *Cimatlan* was compounded of *cimatl*, a "root, which grew near it, and *tlan*, signifying "near"; *Tlaxcallan* meant "the place of bread," from its rich fields of corn; *Huexotzinco*, "a place surrounded by willows." The names of persons were often significant of their adventures and achievements. That of the great Tezcucan prince, Nezahualcoyotl, signified "hungry fox," intimating his sagacity, and his distresses in early life.[7] The emblems of such names were no sooner seen, than they suggested to every Mexican the person and place intended; and, when painted on their shields, or embroidered on their banners, became the armorial bearings, by which city and chieftain were distinguished, as in Europe, in the age of chivalry.[8]

But, although the Aztecs were instructed in all the varieties of hieroglyphical painting, they chiefly resorted to the clumsy method of direct representation. Had their empire lasted, like the Egyptian, several thousand, instead of the brief space of two hundred years, they would, doubtless, like them, have advanced to the more frequent use of the phonetic writing. But, before they could be made acquainted with the capabilities of their own system, the Spanish Conquest, by introducing the European alphabet, supplied their scholars with a more perfect contrivance for expressing thought, which soon supplanted the ancient pictorial character.[9]

Clumsy as it was, however, the Aztec picture-writing seems to have

of this estimable scholar, who has done more than any of his countrymen to explain the mysteries of Aztec science.

[6] Gama, Descripcion, Parte 2, p. 32.

Warburton, with his usual penetration, rejects the idea of mystery in the figurative hieroglyphics. (Divine Legation, b. 4, sec. 4.) If there was any mystery reserved for the initiated, Champollion thinks it may have been the system of the anaglyphs. (Précis, p. 360.) Why may not this be true, likewise, of the monstrous symbolical combinations which represented the Mexican deities?

[7] Boturini, Idea, pp. 77-83.—Gama, Descripcion, Parte 2, pp. 34-43.

Heeren is not aware, or does not allow, that the Mexicans used phonetic characters of any kind. (Hist. Res., vol. V p. 45.) They, indeed, reversed the usual order of proceeding, and, instead of adapting the hieroglyphic to the name of the object, accommodated the name of the object to the hieroglyphic. This, of course, could not admit of great extension. We find phonetic characters, however, applied, in some instances, to common, as well as proper names.

[8] Boturini, Idea, ubi supra.

[9] Clavigero has given a catalogue of the Mexican historians of the sixteenth century,—some of whom are often cited in this history,—which bears honorable testimony to the literary ardor and intelligence of the native races. Stor. del Messico, tom. I., Pref.—Also, Gama, Descripcion. Parte 1, passim.

been adequate to the demands of the nation, in their imperfect state of civilization. By means of it were recorded all their laws, and even their regulations for domestic economy; their tribute-rolls, specifying the imposts of the various towns; their mythology, calendars, and rituals; their political annals, carried back to a period long before the foundation of the city. They digested a complete system of chronology, and could specify with accuracy the dates of the most important events in their history; the year being inscribed on the margin, against the particular circumstance recorded. It is true, history, thus executed, must necessarily be vague and fragmentary. Only a few leading incidents could be presented. But in this it did not differ much from the monkish chronicles of the dark ages, which often dispose of years in a few brief sentences;—quite long enough for the annals of barbarians.[10]

In order to estimate aright the picture-writing of the Aztecs, one must regard it in connection with oral tradition, to which it was auxiliary. In the colleges of the priests the youth were instructed in astronomy, history, mythology, &c.; and those who were to follow the profession of hieroglyphical painting were taught the application of the characters appropriated to each of these branches. In an historical work, one had charge of the chronology, another of the events. Every part of the labor was thus mechanically distributed.[11] The pupils, instructed in all that was before known in their several departments, were prepared to extend still further the boundaries of their imperfect science. The hieroglyphics served as a sort of stenography, a collection of notes, suggesting to the initiated much more than could be conveyed by a literal interpretation. This combination of the written and the oral comprehended what may be called the literature of the Aztecs.[12]

[10] M. de Humboldt's remark, that the Aztec annals, from the close of the eleventh century, "exhibit the greatest method, and astonishing minuteness," (Vues des Cordillères, p. 137,) must be received with some qualification. The reader would scarcely understand from it, that there are rarely more than one or two facts recorded in any year, and sometimes not one in a dozen or more. The necessary looseness and uncertainty of these historical records are made apparent by the remarks of the Spanish interpreter of the Mendoza codex, who tells us that the natives, to whom it was submitted, were very long in coming to an agreement about the proper signification of the paintings. Antiq. of Mexico, vol. VI. p. 87.

[11] Gama, Descripcion, Parte 2, p. 30.—Acosta, lib. 6, cap. 7.

"Tenian para cada género," says Ixtlilxochitl, "sus Escritores, unos que trataban de los Anales, poniendo por su órden las cosas que acaecian en cada un año, con dia, mes, y hora; otros tenian á su cargo las Genealogías, y descendencia de los Reyes, Señores, y Personas de linaje, asentando por cuenta y razon los que nacian, y borraban los que morian con la misma cuenta. Unos tenian cuidado de las pinturas, de los términos, límites, y mojoneras de las Ciudades, Provincias, Pueblos, y Lugares, y de las suertes, y repartimiento de las tierras cuyas eran, y á quien pertenecian; otros de los libros de Leyes, ritos, y seremonias que usaban." Hist. Chich., MS., Prólogo.

[12] According to Boturini, the ancient Mexicans were acquainted with the Peruvian method of recording events, by means of the *quipp s*;—knotted strings of various colors,—which were afterwards superseded by hieroglyphical painting. (Idea, p. 86.) He could discover, however, but a single specimen, which he met with in Tlascala, and that had nearly fallen to pieces with age. McCulloh suggests that it

Their manuscripts were made of different materials,—of cotton cloth, or skins nicely prepared; of a composition of silk and gum; but, for the most part, of a fine fabric from the leaves of the aloe, *agave Americana*, called by the natives, *maguey*, which grows luxuriantly over the table-lands of Mexico. A sort of paper was made from it, resembling somewhat the Egyptian *papyrus*,[13] which, when properly dressed and polished, is said to have been more soft and beautiful than parchment. Some of the specimens, still existing, exhibit their original freshness, and the paintings on them retain their brilliancy of colors. They were sometimes done up into rolls, but more frequently into volumes, of moderate size, in which the paper was shut up, like a folding-screen, with a leaf or tablet of wood at each extremity, that gave the whole, when closed, the appearance of a book. The length of the strips was determined only by convenience. As the pages might be read and referred to separately, this form had obvious advantages over the rolls of the ancients.[14]

At the time of the arrival of the Spaniards, great quantities of these manuscripts were treasured up in the country. Numerous persons were employed in painting, and the dexterity of their operations excited the astonishment of the Conquerors. Unfortunately, this was mingled with other, and unworthy feelings. The strange, unknown characters inscribed on them excited suspicion. They were looked on as magic scrolls; and were regarded in the same light with the idols and temples, as the symbols of a pestilent superstition, that must be extirpated. The first archbishop of Mexico, Don Juan de Zumarraga,—a name that should be as immortal as that of Omar,—collected these paintings from every quarter, especially from Tezcuco, the most cultivated capital in Anahuac, and the great depository of the national archives. He then caused them to be piled up in a "mountain-heap,"—as it is called by the Spanish writers themselves,—in the market-place of Tlatelolco, and reduced them all to

may have been only a wampum belt, such as is common among our North American Indians. (Researches, p. 201.) The conjecture is plausible enough. Strings of wampum, of various colors, were used by the latter people for the similar purpose of registering events. The insulated fact, recorded by Boturini, is hardly sufficient—unsupported, as far as I know, by any other testimony—to establish the existence of *quippus* among the Aztecs, who had but little in common with the Peruvians.

[13] Pliny, who gives a minute account of the *papyrus* reed of Egypt, notices the various manufactures obtained from it, as ropes, cloth, paper, &c. It also served as a thatch for the roofs of houses, and as food and drink for the natives. (Hist. Nat., lib. 11, cap. 20–22.) It is singular that the American *agave*, a plant so totally different, should also have been applied to all these various uses.

[14] Lorenzana, Hist. de Nueva España, p. 8.—Boturini, Idea, p. 96.—Humboldt, Vues des Cordillères, p. 52.—Peter Martyr Anglerius, De Orbe Novo, (Compluti, 1530,) dec. 3, cap. 8; dec. 5, cap. 10.

Martyr has given a minute description of the Indian maps, sent home soon after the invasion of New Spain. His inquisitive mind was struck with the evidence they afforded of a positive civilization. Ribera, the friend of Cortés, brought back a story, that the paintings were designed as patterns for embroiderers and jewelers. But Martyr had been in Egypt, and he felt little hesitation in placing the Indian drawings in the same class with those he had seen on the obelisks and temples of that country.

ashes! [15] His greater countryman, Archbishop Ximenes, had celebrated a similar *auto-da-fe* of Arabic manuscripts, in Granada, some twenty years before. Never did fanaticism achieve two more signal triumphs, than by the annihilation of so many curious monuments of human ingenuity and learning! [16]

The unlettered soldiers were not slow in imitating the example of their prelate. Every chart and volume which fell into their hands was wantonly destroyed; so that, when the scholars of a later and more enlightened age anxiously sought to recover some of these memorials of civilization, nearly all had perished, and the few surviving were jealously hidden by the natives.[17] Through the indefatigable labors of a private individual, however, a considerable collection was eventually deposited in the archives of Mexico; but was so little heeded there, that some were plundered, others decayed piecemeal from the damps and mildews, and others, again, were used up as waste-paper! [18] We contemplate with indignation the cruelties inflicted by the early conquerors. But indignation is qualified with contempt, when we see them thus ruthlessly trampling out the spark of knowledge, the common boon and property of all mankind. We may well doubt, which has the strongest claims to civilization, the victor, or the vanquished.

A few of the Mexican manuscripts have found their way, from time to time, to Europe, and are carefully preserved in the public libraries of its capitals. They are brought together in the magnificent work of Lord Kingsborough; but not one is there from Spain. The most important of them, for the light it throws on the Aztec institutions, is the Mendoza Codex; which, after its mysterious disappearance for more than a century, has at length reappeared in the Bodleian library at Oxford. It has been several times engraved.[19] The most brilliant in coloring, probably,

[15] Ixtlilxochitl, Hist. Chich., MS., Prólogo.—Idem, Sum. Relac., MS.
Writers are not agreed whether the conflagration took place in the square of Tlatelolco or Tezcuco. Comp. Clavigero, Stor. del Messico, tom. II. p. 188, and Bustamante's Pref. to Ixtlilxochitl, Cruantés des Conquérans, trad. de Ternaux, p. xvii.

[16] It has been my lot to record both these displays of human infirmity, so humbling to the pride of intellect. See the History of Ferdinand and Isabella, Part 2, Chap. 6.

[17] Sahagun, Hist. de Nueva España, lib. 10, cap. 27.—Bustamante, Mañanas de Alameda, (México, 1836,) tom. II., Prólogo.

[18] The enlightened governor, Don Lorenzo Zavala sold the documents in the archives of the Audience of Mexico, according to Bustamante, as wrapping-paper, to apothecaries, shopkeepers, and rocket-makers! Boturini's noble collection has not fared much better.

[19] The history of this famous collection is familiar to scholars. It was sent to the Emperor Charles the Fifth, not long after the Conquest, by the viceroy Mendoza, Marques de Mondejar. The vessel fell into the hands of a French cruiser, and the manuscript was taken to Paris. It was afterwards bought by the chaplain of the English embassy, and, coming into the possession of the antiquary Purchas, was engraved, *in extenso*, by him, in the third volume of his "Pilgrimage." After its publication, in 1625, the Aztec original lost its importance, and fell into oblivion so completely, that, when at length the public curiosity was excited in regard to its fate, no trace of it could be discovered. Many were the speculations of

is the Borgian collection, in Rome.[20] The most curious, however, is the Dresden Codex, which has excited less attention than it deserves. Although usually classed among Mexican manuscripts, it bears little resemblance to them in its execution; the figures of objects are more delicately drawn, and the characters, unlike the Mexican, appear to be purely arbitrary, and are possibly phonetic.[21] Their regular arrangement is quite equal to the Egyptian. The whole infers a much higher civilization than the Aztec, and offers abundant food for curious speculation.[22]

scholars, at home and abroad, respecting it, and Dr. Robertson settled the question as to its existence in England, by declaring that there was no Mexican relic in that country, except a golden goblet of Montezuma. (History of America, (London, 1796,) vol. III. p. 370.) Nevertheless, the identical Codex, and several other Mexican paintings, have been since discovered in the Bodleian library. The circumstance has brought some obloquy on the historian, who, while prying into the collections of Vienna and the Escurial, could be so blind to those under his own eyes. The oversight will not appear so extraordinary to a thorough-bred collector, whether of manuscripts, or medals, or any other rarity. The Mendoza Codex is, after all, but a copy, coarsely done with a pen on European paper. Another copy, from which Archbishop Lorenzana engraved his tribute-rolls in Mexico, existed in Boturini's collection. A third is in the Escurial, according to the Marques of Spineto. (Lectures on the Elements of Hieroglyphics, (London,) lect. 7.) This may possibly be the original painting. The entire Codex, copied from the Bodleian maps, with its Spanish and English interpretations, is included in the noble compilation of Lord Kingsborough. (Vols. I., V., VI.) It is distributed into three parts; embracing the civil history of the nation, the tributes paid by the cities, and the domestic economy and discipline of the Mexicans; and, from the fulness of the interpretation, is of much importance in regard to these several topics.

[20] It formerly belonged to the Giustiniani family; but was so little care(for, that it was suffered to fall into the mischievous hands of the domestics' children, who made sundry attempts to burn it. Fortunately it was painted on deerskin, and, though somewhat singed, was not destroyed. (Humboldt, Vues des Cordillères, p. 89, et seq.) It is impossible to cast the eye over this brilliant assemblage of forms and colors without feeling how hopeless must be the attempt to recover a key to the Aztec mythological symbols; which are here distributed with the symmetry, indeed, but in all the endless combinations, of the kaleidoscope. It is in the third volume of Lord Kingsborough's work.

[21] Humboldt, who has copied some pages of it in his "Atlas Pittoresque," intimates no doubt of its Aztec origin. (Vues des Cordillères, pp. 266, 267.) M. Le Noir even reads in it an exposition of Mexican Mythology, with occasional analogies to that of Egypt and of Hindostan. (Antiquités Mexicaines, tom. II., Introd.) The fantastic forms of hieroglyphic symbols may afford analogies for almost any thing.

[22] The history of this Codex, engraved entire in the third volume of the "Antiquities of Mexico," goes no further back than 1739, when it was purchased at Vienna for the Dresden library. It is made of the American agave. The figures painted on it bear little resemblance, either in feature or form, to the Mexican. They are surmounted by a sort of headgear, which looks something like a modern peruke. On the chin of one we may notice a beard, a sign often used after the Conquest to denote a European. Many of the persons are sitting crosslegged. The profiles of the faces, and the whole contour of the limbs, are sketched with a spirit and freedom, very unlike the hard, angular outlines of the Aztecs. The characters, also, are delicately traced, generally in an irregular, but circular form, and are very minute. They are arranged, like the Egyptian, both horizontally and perpendicularly, mostly in the former manner, and, from the prevalent direction of the profiles, would seem to have been read from right to left. Whether phonetic or ideographic, they are of that compact and purely conventional sort which belongs

Some few of these maps have interpretations annexed to them, which were obtained from the natives after the Conquest.[23] The greater part are without any, and cannot now be unriddled. Had the Mexicans made free use of a phonetic alphabet, it might have been originally easy, by mastering the comparatively few signs employed in this kind of communication, to have got a permanent key to the whole.[24] A brief inscription has furnished a clue to the vast labyrinth of Egyptian hieroglyphics. But the Aztec characters, representing individuals, or, at most, species, require to be made out separately; a hopeless task, for which little aid is to be expected from the vague and general tenor of the few interpretations now existing. There was, as already mentioned, until late in the last century, a professor in the University of Mexico, especially devoted to the study of the national picture-writing. But, as this was with a view to legal proceedings, his information, probably, was limited to deciphering title. In less than a hundred years after the Conquest, the knowledge of the hieroglyphics had so far declined, that a diligent Tezcucan writer complains he could find in the country only two persons, both very aged, at all competent to interpret them.[25]

It is not probable, therefore, that the art of reading these picture-writings will ever be recovered; a circumstance certainly to be regretted. Not that the records of a semi-civilized people would be likely to contain any new truth or discovery important to human comfort or progress; but they could scarcely fail to throw some additional light on the previous history of the nation, and that of the more polished people who be-

to a well-digested system for the communication of thought. One cannot but regret, that no trace should exist of the quarter whence this MS. was obtained; perhaps, some part of Central America; from the region of the mysterious races who built the monuments of Mitla and Palenque. Though, in truth, there seems scarcely more resemblance in the symbols to the Palenque *bas-reliefs*, than to the Aztec paintings.

[23] There are three of these; the Mendoza Codex; the Telleriano-Remensis,—formerly the property of Archbishop Tellier,—in the Royal library of Paris; and the Vatican MS., No. 3738. The interpretation of the last bears evident marks of its recent origin; probably as late as the close of the sixteenth, or the beginning of the seventeenth century, when the ancient hieroglyphics were read with the eye of faith, rather than of reason. Whoever was the commentator, (comp. Vues des Cordillères, pp. 203, 204; and Antiq. of Mexico, vol. VI. pp. 155, 222,) he has given such an exposition, as shows the old Aztecs to have been as orthodox Christians, as any subjects of the Pope.

[24] The total number of Egyptian hieroglyphics discovered by Champollion amounts to 864; and of these 130 only are phonetic, notwithstanding that this kind of character is used far more frequently than both the others. Précis, p. 263; —also Spineto, Lectures, lect. 3.

[25] Ixtlilxochitl, Hist. Chich., MS., Dedic.

Boturini, who travelled through every part of the country, in the middle of the last century, could not meet with an individual who could afford him the least clue to the Aztec hieroglyphics. So completely had every vestige of their ancient language been swept away from the memory of the natives. (Idea, p. 116.) If we are to believe Bustamante, however, a complete key to the whole system is, at this moment, *somewhere* in Spain. It was carried home, at the time of the process against father Mier, in 1795. The name of the Mexican Champollion who discovered it is Borunda. Gama, Descripcion, tom. II. p. 33, nota.

fore occupied the country. This would be still more probable, if any literary relics of their Toltec predecessors were preserved; and, if report be true, an important compilation from this source was extant at the time of the invasion, and may have perhaps contributed to swell the holocaust of Zumarraga.[26] It is no great stretch of fancy, to suppose that such records might reveal the successive links in the mighty chain of migration of the primitive races, and, by carrying us back to the seat of their possessions in the Old World, have solved the mystery which has so long perplexed the learned, in regard to the settlement and civilization of the New.

Besides the hieroglyphical maps, the traditions of the country were embodied in the songs and hymns, which, as already mentioned, were carefully taught in the public schools. These were various, embracing the mythic legends of a heroic age, the warlike achievements of their own, or the softer tales of love and pleasure.[27] Many of them were composed by scholars and persons of rank, and are cited as affording the most authentic record of events.[28] The Mexican dialect was rich and expressive, though inferior to the Tezcucan, the most polished of the idioms of Anahuac. None of the Aztec compositions have survived, but we can form some estimate of the general state of poetic culture from the odes which have come down to us from the royal house of Tezcuco.[29] Sahagun has furnished us with translations of their more elaborate prose, consisting of prayers and public discourses, which give a favorable idea of their eloquence, and show that they paid much attention to rhetorical effect. They are said to have had, also, something like theatrical exhibitions, of a pantomimic sort, in which the faces of the performers were covered with masks, and the figures of birds or animals were frequently represented; an imitation, to which they may have been led by the familiar delineation of such objects in their hieroglyphics.[30] In all this we see the

[26] *Teoamoxtli,* "the divine book," as it was called. According to Ixtlilxochitl, it was composed by a Tezcucan doctor, named Huèmatzin, towards the close of the seventh century. (Relaciones, MS.) It gave an account of the migrations of his nation from Asia, of the various stations on their journey, of their social and religious institutions, their science, arts, &c., &c., a good deal too much for one book. *Ignotum pro magnifico.* It has never been seen by a European. A copy is said to have been in possession of the Tezcucan chroniclers, on the taking of their capital. (Bustamante, Crónica Mexicana, (México, 1822,) carta 3.) Lord Kingsborough, who can scent out a Hebrew root, be it buried never so deep, has discovered that the *Teoamoxtli* was the Pentateuch. Thus,—*teo* means "divine," *amotl,* "paper" or "book," and *moxtli* "*appears* to be Moses,"—"Divine Book of Moses"! Antiq. of Mexico, vol. VI. p. 204, nota.

[27] Boturini, Idea, pp. 90-97.—Clavigero, Stor. del Messico, tom. II. pp. 174-178.

[28] "Los cantos con que las observaban Autores muy graves en su modo de ciencia y facultad, pues fuéron los mismos Reyes, y de la gente mas ilustre y entendida, que siempre observáron y adquiriéron la verdad, y esta con tanta, y razon, quanta pudiéron tener los mas graves y fidedignos Autores." Ixtlilxochitl, Hist. Chich., MS., Prólogo.

[29] See Chap. 6, of this Introduction.

[30] See some account of these mummeries in Acosta, (lib. 5, cap. 30,)—also Clavigero (Stor. del Messico, ubi supra). Stone models of masks are sometimes found among the Indian ruins, and engravings of them are both in Lord Kingsborough's work, and in the Antiquités Mexicaines.

dawning of a literary culture, surpassed, however, by their attainments in the severer walks of mathematical science.

They devised a system of notation in their arithmetic, sufficiently simple. The first twenty numbers were expressed by a corresponding number of dots. The first five had specific names; after which they were represented by combining the fifth with one of the four preceding; as five and one for six, five and two for seven, and so on. Ten and fifteen had each a separate name, which was also combined with the first four, to express a higher quantity. These four, therefore, were the radical characters of their oral arithmetic, in the same manner as they were of the written with the ancient Romans; a more simple arrangement, probably, than any existing among Europeans.[31] Twenty was expressed by a separate hieroglyphic,—a flag. Larger sums were reckoned by twenties, and, in writing, by repeating the number of flags. The square of twenty, four hundred, had a separate sign, that of a plume, and so had the cube of twenty, or eight thousand, which was denoted by a purse, or sack. This was the whole arithmetical apparatus of the Mexicans, by the combination of which they were enabled to indicate any quantity. For greater expedition, they used to denote fractions of the larger sums by drawing only a part of the object. Thus, half or three fourths of a plume, or of a purse, represented that proportion of their respective sums, and so on.[32] With all this, the machinery will appear very awkward to us, who perform our operations with so much ease, by means of the Arabic, or, rather, Indian ciphers. It is not much more awkward, however, than the system pursued by the great mathematicians of antiquity, unacquainted with the brilliant invention, which has given a new aspect to mathematical science, of determining the value, in a great measure, by the relative position of the figures.

In the measurement of time, the Aztecs adjusted their civil year by the solar. They divided it into eighteen months of twenty days each. Both months and days were expressed by peculiar hieroglyphics,—those of the former often intimating the season of the year, like the French months, at the period of the Revolution. Five complementary days, as in Egypt,[33] were added, to make up the full number of three hundred and sixty-five. They belonged to no month, and were regarded as peculiarly unlucky. A month was divided into four weeks, of five days each, on the last of which was the public fair, or market day.[34] This arrangement, dif-

---

[31] Gama, Descripcion, Parte 2, Apend. 2.

Gama, in comparing the language of Mexican notation with the decimal system of the Europeans, and the ingenious binary system of Leibnitz, confounds oral with written arithmetic.

[32] Ibid., ubi supra.

This learned Mexican has given a very satisfactory treatise on the arithmetic of the Aztecs, in his second part.

[33] Herodotus, Euterpe, sec. 4.

[34] Sahagun, Hist. de Nueva España, lib. 4, Apend.

According to Clavigero, the fairs were held on the days bearing the sign of the year. Stor. del Messico, tom. II. p. 62.

fering from that of the nations of the Old Continent, whether of Europe
or Asia,[35] has the advantage of giving an equal number of days to each
month, and of comprehending entire weeks, without a fraction, both in
the months and in the year.[36]

As the year is composed of nearly six hours more than three hundred
and sixty-five days, there still remained an excess, which, like other na·
tions who have framed a calendar, they provided for by intercalation;
not, indeed, every fourth year, as the Europeans,[37] but at longer inter·
vals, like some of the Asiatics.[38] They waited till the expiration of fifty-
two vague years, when they interposed thirteen days, or rather twelve
and a half, this being the number which had fallen in arrear. Had they
inserted thirteen, it would have been too much, since the annual excess
over three hundred and sixty-five is about eleven minutes less than six
hours. But, as their calendar, at the time of the Conquest, was found to
correspond with the European, (making allowance for the subsequent
Gregorian reform,) they would seem to have adopted the shorter period
of twelve days and a half,[39] which brought them, within an almost inap-

[35] The people of Java, according to Sir Stamford Raffles, regulated their mar·
kets, also, by a week of five days. They had, besides, our week of seven. (History
of Java, (London, 1830,) vol. I., pp. 531, 532.) The latter division of time, of
general use throughout the East, is the oldest monument existing of astronomical
science. See La Place, Exposition due Système du Monde, (Paris, 1808,) lib. 5
chap. 1.

[36] Veytia, Historia Antigua de Méjico, (Méjico, 1806,) tom. I. cap. 6, 7.—Gama,
Descripcion, Parte 1, pp. 33, 34, et alibi.—Boturini, Idea, pp. 4, 44, et seq.—Cod.
Tel.-Rem., ap. Antiq. of Mexico, vol. VI. p. 104.—Camargo, Hist. de Tlascala,
MS.—Toribio, Hist. de los Indios, MS., Parte 1, cap. 5.

[37] Sahagun intimates doubts of this. "Otra fiesta hacian de cuatro en cuatro
años á honra de fuego, y en esta fiesta *es verosimil, y hay congeturas* que hacian
su visiesto contando seis dias de *nemontemi*"; the five unlucky complementary days
were so called. (Hist. de Nueva España, lib. 4, Apend.) But this author, however
good an authority for the superstitions, is an indifferent one for the science of the
Mexicans.

[38] The Persians had a cycle of one hundred and twenty years, of three hundred
and sixty-five days each, at the end of which they intercalated thirty days. (Humboldt, Vues des Cordillères, p. 177.) This was the same as thirteen after the cycle
of fifty-two years of the Mexicans; but was less accurate than their probable intercalation of twelve days and a half. It is obviously indifferent, as far as ac·
curacy is concerned, which multiple of four is selected to form the cycle; though,
the shorter the interval of intercalation, the less, of course, will be the temporary
departure from the true time.

[39] This is the conclusion to which Gama arrives, after a very careful investigation of the subject. He supposes that the "bundles," or cycles, of fifty-two years,
—by which, as we shall see, the Mexicans computed time,—ended, alternately, at
midnight and midday. (Descripcion, Parte 1, p. 52, et seq.) He finds some warrant for this in Acosta's account (lib. 6, cap. 2) though contradicted by Torquemada, (Monarch. Ind., lib. 5, cap. 33,) and, as it appears, by Sahagun,—whose
work, however, Gama never saw,—(Hist. de Nueva España, lib. 7, cap. 9,) both of
whom place the close of the year at midnight. Gama's hypothesis derives confirmation from a circumstance I have not seen noticed. Besides the "bundle" of fifty-
two years, the Mexicans had a larger cycle of one hundred and four years, called
"an old age." As this was not used in their reckonings, which were carried on by
their "bundles," it seems highly probable that it was designed to express the period

preciable fraction, to the exact length of the tropical year, as established by the more accurate observations.[40] Indeed, the intercalation of twenty-five days, in every hundred and four years, shows a nicer adjustment of civil to solar time than is presented by any European calendar; since more than five centuries must elapse, before the loss of an entire day.[41] Such was the astonishing precision displayed by the Aztecs, or, perhaps, by their more polished Toltec predecessors, in these computations, so difficult as to have baffled, till a comparatively recent period, the most enlightened nations of Christendom! [42]

The chronological system of the Mexicans, by which they determined the date of any particular event, was, also, very remarkable. The epoch, from which they reckoned, corresponded with the year 1091, of the Christian era. It was the period of the reform of their calendar, soon after their migration from Aztlan. They threw the years, as already noticed, into great cycles, of fifty-two each, which they called "sheafs," or "bundles," and represented by a quantity of reeds bound together by a string. As often as this hieroglyphic occurs in their maps, it shows the number

which would bring round the commencement of the smaller cycles to the same hour, and in which the intercalary days, amounting to twenty-five, might be comprehended without a fraction.

[40] This length, as computed by Zach, at 365d. 5h. 48m. 48sec., is only 2m. 9sec. longer than the Mexican; which corresponds to the celebrated calculation of the astronomers of the Caliph Almamon, that fell short about two minutes of the true time. See La Place, Exposition, p. 350.

[41] "El corto exceso de 4hor. 38min. 40seg., que hay de mas de los 25 dias en el período de 104 años, no puede componer un dia entero, hasta que pasen mas de cinco de estos períodos máximos ó 538 años." (Gama, Descripcion, Parte 1, p. 23.) Gama estimates the solar year at 365d. 5h. 48m. 50sec.

[42] The ancient Etruscans arranged their calendar in cycles of 110 solar years, and reckoned the year at 365d. 5h. 40m.; at least, this seems probable, says Niebuhr. (History of Rome, Eng. trans., (Cambridge, 1828,) vol. I. pp. 113, 238.) The early Romans had not wit enough to avail themselves of this accurate measurement, which came within nine minutes of the true time. The Julian reform, which assumed 365d. 5¼h. as the length of the year, erred as much, or rather more, on the other side. And when the Europeans, who adopted this calendar, landed in Mexico, their reckoning was nearly eleven days in advance of the exact time,—or, in other words, of the reckoning of the barbarous Aztecs; a remarkable fact.

Gama's researches lead to the conclusion, that the year of the new cycle began with the Aztecs on the ninth of January; a date considerably earlier than that usually assigned by the Mexican writers. (Descripcion, Parte 1, pp. 49-52.) By postponing the intercalation to the end of fifty-two years, the annual loss of six hours made every fourth year begin a day earlier. Thus, the cycle commencing on the ninth of January, the fifth year of it began on the eighth, the ninth year on the seventh, and so on; so that the last day of the series of fifty-two years fell on the twenty-sixth of December, when the intercalation of thirteen days rectified the chronology, and carried the commencement of the new year to the ninth of January again. Torquemada, puzzled by the irregularity of the new year's day, asserts that the Mexicans were unacquainted with the annual excess of six hours, and therefore never intercalated! (Monarch. Ind., lib. 10, cap. 36.) The interpreter of the Vatican Codex has fallen into a series of blunders on the same subject, still more ludicrous. (Antiq. of Mexico, vol. VI. Pl. 16.) So soon had Aztec science fallen into oblivion, after the Conquest!

of half centuries. To enable them to specify any particular year, they divided the great cycle into four smaller cycles, or indictions, of thirteen years each. They then adopted two periodical series of signs, one consist-ing of their numerical dots, up to thirteen, the other, of four hieroglyphics of the years.[43] These latter they repeated in regular succession, setting against each one a number of the corresponding series of dots, continued also in regular succession up to thirteen. The same system was pursued through the four indictions, which thus, it will be observed, began always with a different hieroglyphic of the year from the preceding; and in this way, each of the hieroglyphics was made to combine successively with each of the numerical signs, but never twice with the same; since four, and thirteen, the factors of fifty-two,—the number of years in the cycle, —must admit of just as many combinations as are equal to their product. Thus every year had its appropriate symbol, by which it was, at once, recognised. And this symbol, preceded by the proper number of "bundles," indicating the half centuries, showed the precise time which had elapsed since the national epoch of 1091.[44] The ingenious contrivance of a periodical series, in place of the cumbrous system of hieroglyphical no-tation, is not peculiar to the Aztecs, and is to be found among various people, on the Asiatic continent,—the same in principle, though varying materially in arrangement.[45]

The solar calendar, above described, might have answered all the pur-poses of the nation; but the priests chose to construct another for them-selves. This was called a "lunar reckoning," though nowise accommo-

[43] These hieroglyphics were a "rabbit," a "reed," a "flint," a "house." They were taken as symbolical of the four elements, air, water, fire, earth, according to Vey-tia. (Hist. Antig., tom. 1. cap. 5.) It is not easy to see the connexion between the terms "rabbit" and "air," which lead the respective series.

[44] The following table of two of the four indictions of thirteen years each will make the text more clear. The first column shows the actual year of the great cycle, or "bundle." The second, the numerical dots used in their arithmetic. The third is composed of their hieroglyphics for rabbit, reed, flint, house, in their regular order.

By pursuing the combinations through the two remaining indictions, it will be found that the same number of dots will never coincide with the same hiero-glyphic.

These tables are generally thrown into the form of wheels, as are those, also, of their months and days, having a very pretty effect. Several have been published, at different times, from the collections of Siguenza and Boturini. The wheel of the great cycle of fifty-two years is encompassed by a serpent, which was also the symbol of "an age," both with the Persians and Egyptians. Father Toribio seems to misapprehend the nature of these chronological wheels; "Tenian rodelas y escudos, y en ellas pintadas las figuras y armas de sus Demonios con su blason." Hist. de los Indios, MS., Parte 1. cap. 4.

[45] Among the Chinese, Japanese, Moghols, Mantchous, and other families of the Tartar race. Their series are composed of symbols of their five elements, and the twelve zodiacal signs, making a cycle of sixty years' duration. Their several sys-tems are exhibited, in connection with the Mexican, in the luminous pages of Hum-boldt, (Vues des Cordillères, p. 149,) who draws important consequences from the comparison, to which we shall have occasion to return hereafter.

dated to the revolutions of the moon.[46] It was formed, also, of two periodical series, one of them consisting of thirteen numerical signs, or dots,
the other, of the twenty hieroglyphics of the days. But, as the product of
these combinations would only be 260, and, as some confusion might arise
from the repetition of the same terms for the remaining 105 days of the
years, they invented a third series, consisting of nine additional hiero-

First Indiction.			Second Indiction.		
Year of the Cycle.			Year of the Cycle.		
1.	.	🐇	14.	.	🪶
2.	. .	🪶	15.	. .	🔱
3.	. . .	🔱	16.	. . .	🏛
4.	. . . .	🏛	17.	. . . .	🐇
5.	. . . . .	🐇	18.	. . . . .	🪶
6.	:	🪶	19.	:	🔱
7.	: : . . .	🔱	20.	:	🏛
8.	: : : . .	🏛	21.	: : .	🐇
9.	: : : . .	🐇	22.	: : . .	🪶
10.	: : : : .	🪶	23.	: : . . .	🔱
11.	:	🔱	24.	: : . .	🏛
12.	: : . . .	🏛	25.	: : : . .	🐇
13.	: : : . .	🐇	26.	: : : : .	🪶

In this calendar, the months of the tropical year were distributed into cycles
of thirteen days, which, being repeated twenty times,—the number of days in a
solar month,—completed the lunar, or astrological, year of 260 days; when the
reckoning began again. "By the contrivance of these *trecenas* (terms of thirteen
days) and the cycle of fifty-two years," says Gama, "they formed a luni-solar
period, most exact for astronomical purposes." (Descripcion, Parte 1, p. 27.) He
adds, that these *trecenas* were suggested by the periods in which the moon is visible
before and after conjunction. (Loc. cit.) It seems hardly possible that a people,

glyphics, which, alternating with the two preceding series, rendered it impossible that the three should coincide twice in the same year, or indeed in less than 2340 days; since 20 $\times$ 13 $\times$ 9=2340.[47] Thirteen was a mystic number, of frequent use in their tables.[48] Why they resorted to that of nine, on this occasion, is not so clear.[49]

This second calendar rouses a holy indignation in the early Spanish missionaries, and father Sahagun loudly condemns it, as "most unhallowed, since it is founded neither on natural reason, nor on the influence of the planets, nor on the true course of the year; but is plainly the work of necromancy, and the fruit of a compact with the Devil!" [50] One may doubt, whether the superstition of those who invented the scheme was greater than that of those who thus impugned it. At all events, we may,

capable of constructing a calendar so accurately on the true principles of solar time, should so grossly err as to suppose, that, in this reckoning, they really "represented the daily revolutions of the moon." "The whole Eastern world," says the learned Niebuhr, "has followed the moon in its calendar; the free scientific division of a vast portion of time is peculiar to the West. Connected with the West is that primeval extinct world which we call the New." History of Rome, vol. I. p. 239.

[47] They were named "companions," and "lords of the night," and were supposed to preside over the night, as the other signs did over the day. Boturini, Idea, p. 57.

[48] Thus, their astrological year was divided into months of thirteen days, there were thirteen years in their indictions, which contained each three hundred and sixty-five periods of thirteen days, &c. It is a curious fact, that the number of lunar months of thirteen days, contained in a cycle of fifty-two years, with the intercalation, should correspond precisely with the number of years in the great Sothic period of the Egyptians, namely, 1491; a period, in which the seasons and festivals came round to the same place in the year again. The coincidence may be accidental. But a people employing periodical series, and astrological calculations, have generally some meaning in the numbers they select and the combinations to which they lead.

[49] According to Gama, (Descripcion, Parte 1, pp. 75, 76,) because 360 can be divided by nine without a fraction; the nine "companions" not being attached to the five complementary days. But 4, a mystic number much used in their arithmetical combinations, would have answered the same purpose, equally well. In regard to this, McCulloh oberves, with much shrewdness, "It seems impossible that the Mexicans, so careful in constructing their cycle, should abruptly terminate it with 360 revolutions, whose natural period of termination is 2340." And he supposes the nine "companions" were used in connection with the cycles of 260 days, in order to throw them into the larger ones, of 2340; eight of which, with a ninth of 260 days, he ascertains to be equal to the great solar period of 52 years. (Researches, pp. 207, 208.) This is very plausible. But in fact the combinations of the two first series, forming the cycle of 260 days, were always interrupted at the end of the year, since each new year began with the same hieroglyphic of the days. The third series of the "companions" was intermitted, as above stated, on the five unlucky days which closed the year, in order, if we may believe Boturini, that the first day of the solar year might have annexed to it the first of the nine "companions," which signified "lord of the year"; (Idea, p. 57;) a result which might have been equally well secured, without any intermission at all, by taking 5, another favorite number, instead of 9, as the divisor. As it was, however, the cycle, as far as the third series was concerned, did terminate with 360 revolutions. The subject is a perplexing one; and I can hardly hope to have presented it in such a manner as to make it perfectly clear to the reader.

[50] Hist. de Nueva España, lib. 4, Introd.

without having recourse to supernatural agency, find in the human heart
a sufficient explanation of its origin; in that love of power, that has led
the priesthood of many a faith to affect a mystery, the key to which was
in their own keeping.

By means of this calendar, the Aztec priests kept their own records,
regulated the festivals and seasons of sacrifice, and made all their astrological calculations.[51] The false science of astrology is natural to a state
of society partially civilized, where the mind, impatient of the slow and
cautious examination by which alone it can arrive at truth, launches, at
once, into the regions of speculation, and rashly attempts to lift the veil,
—the impenetrable veil, which is drawn around the mysteries of nature.
It is the characteristic of true science, to discern the impassable, but not
very obvious, limits which divide the province of reason from that of
speculation. Such knowledge comes tardily. How many ages have rolled
away in which powers, that, rightly directed, might have revealed the
great laws of nature, have been wasted in brilliant, but barren, reveries
on alchemy and astrology!

The latter is more particularly the study of a primitive age; when the
mind, incapable of arriving at the stupendous fact that the myriads of
minute lights, glowing in the firmament, are the centres of systems as
glorious as our own, is naturally led to speculate on their probable uses,
and to connect them in some way or other with man, for whose convenience every other object in the universe seems to have been created. As
the eye of the simple child of nature watches, through the long nights,
the stately march of the heavenly bodies, and sees the bright hosts coming up, one after another, and changing with the changing seasons of the
year, he naturally associates them with those seasons, as the periods over
which they hold a mysterious influence. In the same manner, he connects
their appearance with any interesting event of the time, and explores, in
their flaming characters, the destinies of the new-born infant.[52] Such is
the origin of astrology, the false lights of which have continued from
the earliest ages to dazzle and bewilder mankind, till they have faded
away in the superior illumination of a comparatively recent period.

The astrological scheme of the Aztecs was founded less on the plane-
tary influences, than on those of the arbitrary signs they had adopted

---

[51] "Dans les pays les plus différents," says Benjamin Constant, concluding some
sensible reflections on the sources of the sacerdotal power, "chez les peuples de
mœurs les plus opposées, le sacerdoce a dû au culte des éléments et des astres un
pouvoir dont aujourd'hui nous concevons à peine l'idée." De la Religion, (Paris,
1825,) lib. 3, ch. 5.

[52] "It is a gentle and affectionate thought,
    That, in immeasurable heights above us,
    At our first birth the wreath of love was woven
    With sparkling stars for flowers."
                    COLERIDGE, Translation of Wallenstein, Act 2, sec. 4.

Schiller is more true to poetry than history, when he tells us, in the beautiful
passage of which this is part, that the worship of the stars took the place of classic mythology. It existed long before it.

for the months and days. The character of the leading sign, in each lunar cycle of thirteen days, gave a complexion to the whole; though this was qualified, in some degree, by the signs of the succeeding days, as well as by those of the hours. It was in adjusting these conflicting forces that the great art of the diviner was shown. In no country, not even in ancient Egypt, were the dreams of the astrologer more implicitly deferred to. On the birth of a child, he was instantly summoned. The time of the event was accurately ascertained; and the family hung in trembling suspense, as the minister of Heaven cast the horoscope of the infant, and unrolled the dark volume of destiny. The influence of the priest was confessed by the Mexican, in the very first breath which he inhaled.[53]

We know little further of the astronomical attainments of the Aztecs. That they were acquainted with the cause of eclipses is evident from the representation, on their maps, of the disk of the moon projected on that of the sun.[54] Whether they had arranged a system of constellations is uncertain; though, that they recognised some of the most obvious, as the Pleiades, for example, is evident from the fact that they regulated their festivals by them. We know of no astronomical instruments used by them, except the dial.[55] An immense circular block of carved stone, disinterred in 1790, in the great square of Mexico, has supplied an acute and learned scholar with the means of establishing some interesting facts in regard to Mexican science.[56] This colossal fragment, on which the calendar is engraved, shows that they had the means of settling the hours of

---

[53] Gama has given us a complete almanac of the astrological year, with the appropriate signs and divisions, showing with what scientific skill it was adapted to its various uses. (Descripcion, Parte 1, pp. 25-31; 62-76.) Sahagun has devoted a whole book to explaining the mystic import and value of these signs, with a minuteness that may enable one to cast up a scheme of nativity for himself. (Hist. de Nueva España, lib. 4.) It is evident he fully believed the magic wonders which he told. "It was a deceitful art," he says, "pernicious and idolatrous; and was never contrived by human reason." The good father was certainly no philosopher.

[54] See, among others, the Cod. Tel.-Rem., Part 4, Pl. 22, ap. Antiq. of Mexico, vol. I.

[55] "It can hardly be doubted," says Lord Kingsborough, "that the Mexicans were acquainted with many scientifical instruments of strange invention, as compared with our own; whether the *telescope* may not have been of the number is uncertain; but the thirteenth plate of M. Dupaix's *Monuments*, Part Second, which represents a man holding something of a similar nature to his eye, affords reason to suppose that they knew how to improve the powers of vision." (Antiq. of Mexico, vol. VI. p. 15, note.) The instrument alluded to is rudely carved on a conical rock. It is raised no higher than the neck of the person who holds it, and looks—to my thinking—as much like a musket as a telescope; though I shall not infer the use of firearms among the Aztecs from this circumstance. (See vol. IV. Pl. 15.) Captain Dupaix, however, in his commentary on the drawing, sees quite as much in it as his Lordship. Ibid., vol. V. p. 241.

[56] Gama, Descripcion, Parte 1, sec. 4; Parte 2, Apend.
Besides this colossal fragment, Gama met with some others, designed, probably, for similar scientific uses, at Chapoltepec. Before he had leisure to examine them, however, they were broken up for materials to build a furnace! A fate not unlike that which has too often befallen the monuments of ancient art in the Old World.

the day with precision, the period of the solstices and of the equinoxes, and that of the transit of the sun across the zenith of Mexico.[57]

We cannot contemplate the astronomical science of the Mexicans, so disproportioned to their progress in other walks of civilization, without astonishment. An acquaintance with some of the more obvious principles of astronomy is within the reach of the rudest people. With a little care, they may learn to connect the regular changes of the seasons with those of the place of the sun at his rising and setting. They may follow the march of the great luminary through the heavens, by watching the stars that first brighten on his evening track, or fade in his morning beams. They may measure a revolution of the moon, by marking her phases, and may even form a general idea of the number of such revolutions in a solar year. But that they should be capable of accurately adjusting their festivals by the movements of the heavenly bodies, and should fix the true length of the tropical year, with a precision unknown to the great philosophers of antiquity, could be the result only of a long series of nice and patient observations, evincing no slight progress in civilization.[58] But whence could the rude inhabitants of these mountain regions have derived this curious erudition? Not from the barbarous hordes who roamed over the higher latitudes of the North; nor from the more polished races on the Southern continent, with whom, it is apparent, they had no intercourse. If we are driven, in our embarrassment, like the greatest astronomer of our age, to seek the solution among the civilized communities of Asia, we shall still be perplexed by finding, amidst general resemblance of outline, sufficient discrepancy in the details, to vindicate, in the judgments of many, the Aztec claim to originality.[59]

I shall conclude the account of Mexican science, with that of a remarkable festival, celebrated by the natives at the termination of the great cycle of fifty-two years. We have seen, in the preceding chapter, their tradition of the destruction of the world at four successive epochs. They looked forward confidently to another such catastrophe, to take place, like the preceding, at the close of a cycle, when the sun was to be effaced from the heavens, the human race, from the earth, and when the

[57] In his second treatise on the cylindrical stone, Gama dwells more at large on its scientific construction, as a vertical sun-dial, in order to dispel the doubts of some sturdy skeptics on this point. (Descripcion, Parte 2, Apend. 1.) The civil day was distributed by the Mexicans into sixteen parts; and began, like that of most of the Asiatic nations, with sunrise. M. de Humboldt, who probably never saw Gama's second treatise, allows only eight intervals. Vues des Cordillères, p. 128.

[58] "Un calendrier," exclaims the enthusiastic Carli, "qui est réglé sur la révolution annuelle du soleil, non seulement par l'addition de cinq jours tous les ans, mais encore par la correction du bissextile, doit sans doute être regardé comme une opération déduite d'une étude réfléchie, et d'une grande combinaison. Il faut donc supposer chez ces peuples une suite d'observations astronomiques, une idée distincte de la sphère, de la déclinaison de l'écliptique, et l'usage d'un calcul concernant les jours et les heures des apparitions solaires." Lettres Américaines, tom. I. let. 23.

[59] La Place, who suggests the analogy, frankly admits the difficulty. Système du Monde, lib. 5, ch. 3.

darkness of chaos was to settle on the habitable globe. The cycle would end in the latter part of December, and, as the dreary season of the winter solstice approached, and the diminished light of day gave melancholy presage of its speedy extinction, their apprehensions increased; and, on the arrival of the five "unlucky" days which closed the year, they abandoned themselves to despair.[60] They broke in pieces the little images of their household gods, in whom they no longer trusted. The holy fires were suffered to go out in the temples, and none were lighted in their own dwellings. Their furniture and domestic utensils were destroyed; their garments torn in pieces; and every thing was thrown into disorder, for the coming of the evil genii who were to descend on the desolate earth.

On the evening of the last day, a procession of priests, assuming the dress and ornaments of their gods, moved from the capital towards a lofty mountain, about two leagues distant. They carried with them a noble victim, the flower of their captives, and an apparatus for kindling the *new fire*, the success of which was an augury of the renewal of the cycle. On reaching the summit of the mountain, the procession paused till midnight; when, as the constellation of the Pleiades approached the zenith,[61] the *new fire* was kindled by the friction of the sticks placed on the wounded breast of the victim.[62] The flame was soon communicated to a funeral pile, on which the body of the slaughtered captive was thrown. As the light streamed up towards heaven, shouts of joy and triumph burst forth from the countless multitudes who covered the hills, the terraces of the temples, and the house-tops, with eyes anxiously bent on the mount of sacrifice. Couriers, with torches lighted at the blazing beacon, rapidly bore them over every part of the country; and the cheering element was seen brightening on altar and hearth-stone, for the circuit of many a league, long before the sun, rising on his accustomed track, gave assurance that a new cycle had commenced its march, and that the laws of nature were not to be reversed for the Aztecs.

The following thirteen days were given up to festivity. The houses

[60] M. Jomard errs in placing the *new fire*, with which ceremony the old cycle properly concluded, at the winter solstice. It was not till the 26th of December, if Gama is right. The cause of M. Jomard's error is his fixing it before, instead of after, the complementary days. See his sensible letter on the Aztec calendar, in the Vues des Cordillères, p. 309.

[61] At the actual moment of their culmination, according to both Sahagun (Hist. de Nueva España, lib. 4, Apend.) and Torquemada (Monarch. Ind., lib. 10, cap. 33, 36). But this could not be, as that took place at midnight, in November; so late as the last secular festival, which was early in Montezuma's reign, in 1507. (Gama, Descripcion, Parte 1, p. 50, nota.—Humboldt, Vues des Cordillères, pp. 181. 182.) The longer we postpone the beginning of the new cycle, the greater still must be the discrepancy.

[62] "On his bare breast the cedar boughs are laid;
On his bare breast, dry sedge and odorous gums
Laid ready to receive the sacred spark,
And blaze, to herald the ascending Sun,
Upon his living altar."

SOUTHEY'S MADOC, part 2, canto 26

were cleansed and whitened. The broken vessels were replaced by new ones. The people, dressed in their gayest apparel, and crowned with garlands and chaplets of flowers, thronged in joyous procession, to offer up their oblations and thanksgivings in the temples. Dances and games were instituted, emblematical of the regeneration of the world. It was the carnival of the Aztecs; or rather the national jubilee, the great secular festival, like that of the Romans, or ancient Etruscans, which few alive had witnessed before,—or could expect to see again.[63]

M. de Humboldt remarked, many years ago, "It were to be wished that some government would publish at its own expense the remains of the ancient American civilization; for it is only by the comparison of several monuments, that we can succeed in discovering the meaning of these allegories, which are partly astronomical, and partly mystic." This enlightened wish has now been realized, not by any government, but by a private individual, Lord Kingsborough. The great work, published under his auspices, and so often cited in this Introduction, appeared in London in 1830. When completed, it will reach to nine volumes, seven of which are now before the public. Some idea of its magnificence may be formed by those who have not seen it, from the fact, that copies of it, with colored plates, sold originally at £175, and, with uncolored, at £120. The price has been since much reduced. It is designed to exhibit a complete view of the ancient Aztec MSS., with such few interpretations as exist; the beautiful drawings of Castañeda relating to Central America, with the commentary of Dupaix; the unpublished history of father Sahagun; and, last, not least, the copious annotations of his Lordship.

Too much cannot be said of the mechanical execution of the book,—its splendid typography, the apparent accuracy and the delicacy of the drawings, and the sumptuous quality of the materials. Yet the purchaser would have been saved some superfluous expense, and the reader much inconvenience, if the letter-press had been in volumes of an ordinary size. But it is not uncommon, in works on this magnificent plan, to find utility in some measure sacrificed to show.

The collection of Aztec MSS., if not perfectly complete, is very extensive, and reflects great credit on the diligence and research of the compiler. It strikes one as strange, however, that not a single document should have been drawn from Spain. Peter Martyr speaks of a number having been brought thither in his time. (De Insulis nuper Inventis, p. 368.) The Marquis Spineto examined one in the Escurial, being the same with the Mendoza Codex, and perhaps the original, since that at Oxford is but a copy. (Lectures, lec. 7.) Mr. Waddilove, chaplain of the British embassy to Spain, gave a particular account of one to Dr. Robertson, which he saw in the same library, and considered an Aztec calendar. Indeed, it is scarcely possible, that the frequent voyagers to the New World should not have furnished the mother-country with abundant specimens of this most interesting feature of Aztec civilization. Nor should we fear that the present liberal government would seclude these treasures from the inspection of the scholar.

Much cannot be said in favor of the arrangement of these codices. In some of them, as the Mendoza Codex, for example, the plates are not even numbered; and

---

[63] I borrow the words of the summons by which the people were called to the *ludi seculares,* the secular games of ancient Rome, *"quos nec spectâsset quisquam, nec spectaturus esset."* (Suetonius, Vita Tib. Claudii, lib. 5.) The old Mexican chroniclers warm into something like eloquence in their descriptions of the Aztec festival. (Torquemada, Monarch. Ind., lib. 10, cap. 33.—Toribio, Hist. de los Indios, MS., Parte 1, cap. 5.—Sahagun, Hist. de Nueva España lib. 7, cap. 9-12. See, also, Gama, Descripcion, Parte 1, pp. 52-54,—Clavigero, Stor. del Messico, tom. II. pp. 84-86.) The English reader will find a more brilliant coloring of the same scene in the canto of Madoc, above cited,—"On the Close of the Century."

one, who would study them by the corresponding interpretation, must often bewilder himself in the maze of hieroglyphics, without a clue to guide him. Neither is there any attempt to enlighten us as to the positive value and authenticity of the respective documents, or even their previous history, beyond a barren reference to the particular library from which they have been borrowed. Little light, indeed, can be expected on these matters; but we have not that little.—The defect of arrangement is chargeable on other parts of the work. Thus, for instance, the sixth book of Sahagun is transferred from the body of the history to which it belongs, to a preceding volume; while the grand hypothesis of his lordship, for which the work was concocted, is huddled into notes, hitched on random passages of the text, with a good deal less connection than the stories of queen Scheherazade, in the "Arabian Nights," and not quite so entertaining.

The drift of Lord Kingsborough's speculations is, to establish the colonization of Mexico by the Israelites. To this the whole battery of his logic and learning is directed. For this, hieroglyphics are unriddled, manuscripts compared, monuments delineated. His theory, however, whatever be its merits, will scarcely become popular; since, instead of being exhibited in a clear and comprehensive form, readily embraced by the mind, it is spread over an infinite number of notes, thickly sprinkled with quotations, from languages ancient and modern, till the weary reader, floundering about in the ocean of fragments, with no light to guide him, feels like Milton's Devil, working his way through chaos,—

> "neither sea,
> Nor good dry land; nigh foundered, on he fares."

It would be unjust, however, not to admit that the noble author, if his logic is not always convincing, shows much acuteness in detecting analogies; that he displays familiarity with his subject, and a fund of erudition, though it often runs to waste; that, whatever be the defects of arrangement, he has brought together a most rich collection of unpublished materials to illustrate the Aztec, and, in a wider sense, American antiquities; and that, by this munificent undertaking, which no government, probably, would have, and few individuals could have, executed, he has entitled himself to the lasting gratitude of every friend of science.

Another writer, whose works must be diligently consulted by every student of Mexican antiquities, is Antonio Gama. His life contains as few incidents as those of most scholars. He was born at Mexico, in 1735, of a respectable family, and was bred to the law. He early showed a preference for mathematical studies, conscious that in this career lay his strength. In 1771, he communicated his observations on the eclipse of that year to the French astronomer M. de Lalande, who published them in Paris, with high commendations of the author. Gama's increasing reputation attracted the attention of government; and he was employed by it, in various scientific labors of importance. His great passion, however, was the study of Indian antiquities. He made himself acquainted with the history of the native races, their traditions, their languages, and, as far as possible, their hieroglyphics. He had an opportunity of showing the fruits of this preparatory training, and his skill as an antiquary, on the discovery of the great calendar-stone, in 1790. He produced a masterly treatise on this, and another Aztec monument, explaining the objects to which they were devoted, and pouring a flood of light on the astronomical science of the Aborigines, their mythology, and their astrological system. He afterwards continued his investigations in the same path, and wrote treatises on the dial, hieroglyphics, and arithmetic of the Indians. These, however, were not given to the world till a few years since, when they were published, together with a reprint of the former work, under the auspices of the industrious Bustamante. Gama died in 1802; leaving behind him a reputation for great worth in private life; one, in which the bigotry, that seems to enter too frequently into the character of the Spanish-Mexican, was tempered by the liberal feelings of a man of science. His reputation as a writer stands high for patient acquisition, accuracy, and acuteness. His conclusions are neither warped by the love of theory so common in the philosopher, nor by the easy credulity so natural to the antiquary. He feels his way with the caution of a mathematician, whose steps are demonstrations. M. de Humboldt was largely indebted to his first work, as he has emphatically acknowledged. But, notwithstanding the eulogiums of this popular writer, and his own merits, Gama's treatises are rarely met with out of New Spain, and his name can hardly be said to have a transatlantic reputation.

CHAPTER V

AZTEC AGRICULTURE—MECHANICAL ARTS—MERCHANTS—
DOMESTIC MANNERS

IT is hardly possible that a nation, so far advanced as the Aztecs in mathematical science, should not have made considerable progress in the mechanical arts, which are so nearly connected with it. Indeed, intellectual progress of any kind implies a degree of refinement, that requires a certain cultivation of both useful and elegant art. The savage, wandering through the wide forest, without shelter for his head, or raiment for his back, knows no other wants than those of animal appetites; and, when they are satisfied, seems to himself to have answered the only ends of existence. But man, in society, feels numerous desires, and artificial tastes spring up, accommodated to the various relations in which he is placed, and perpetually stimulating his invention to devise new expedients to gratify them.

There is a wide difference in the mechanical skill of different nations; but the difference is still greater in the inventive power which directs this skill, and makes it available. Some nations seem to have no power beyond that of imitation; or, if they possess invention, have it in so low a degree, that they are constantly repeating the same idea, without a shadow of alteration or improvement; as the bird builds precisely the same kind of nest which those of its own species built at the beginning of the world. Such, for example, are the Chinese, who have, probably, been familiar for ages with the germs of some discoveries, of little practical benefit to themselves, but which, under the influence of European genius, have reached a degree of excellence, that has wrought an important change in the constitution of society.

Far from looking back, and forming itself slavishly on the past, it is characteristic of the European intellect to be ever on the advance. Old discoveries become the basis of new ones. It passes onward from truth to truth, connecting the whole by a succession of links, as it were, into the great chain of science which is to encircle and bind together the universe. The light of learning is shed over the labors of art. New avenues are opened for the communication both of person and of thought. New facilities are devised for subsistence. Personal comforts, of every kind, are inconceivably multiplied, and brought within the reach of the poorest. Secure of these, the thoughts travel into a nobler region than that of the senses; and the appliances of art are made to minister to the demands of an elegant taste, and a higher moral culture.

The same enlightened spirit, applied to agriculture, raises it from a mere mechanical drudgery, or the barren formula of traditional precepts, to the dignity of a science. As the composition of the earth is analyzed, man learns the capacity of the soil that he cultivates; and, as his empire is gradually extended over the elements of nature, he gains the power to stimulate her to her most bountiful and various production. It is with satisfaction that we can turn to the land of our fathers, as the one in which the experiment has been conducted on the broadest scale, and attended with results that the world has never before witnessed. With equal truth, we may point to the Anglo-Saxon race in both hemispheres, as that whose enterprising genius has contributed most essentially to the great interests of humanity, by the application of science to the useful arts.

Husbandry, to a very limited extent, indeed, was practised by most of the rude tribes of North America. Whenever a natural opening in the forest, or a rich strip of *interval*, met their eyes, or a green slope was found along the rivers, they planted it with beans and Indian corn.[1] The cultivation was slovenly in the extreme, and could not secure the improvident natives from the frequent recurrence of desolating famines. Still, that they tilled the soil at all was a peculiarity which honorably distinguished them from other tribes of hunters, and raised them one degree higher in the scale of civilization.

Agriculture in Mexico was in the same advanced state as the other arts of social life. In few countries, indeed, has it been more respected. It was closely interwoven with the civil and religious institutions of the nation. There were peculiar deities to preside over it; the names of the months and of the religious festivals had more or less reference to it. The public taxes, as we have seen, were often paid in agricultural produce. All, except the soldiers and great nobles, even the inhabitants of the cities, cultivated the soil. The work was chiefly done by the men; the women scattering the seed, husking the corn, and taking part only in the lighter labors of the field.[2] In this they presented an honorable contrast to the other tribes of the continent, who imposed the burden of agriculture, severe as it is in the North, on their women.[3] Indeed, the sex was as

---

[1] This latter grain, according to Humboldt, was found by the Europeans in the New World, from the South of Chili to Pennsylvania; (Essai Politique, tom. II. p. 408;) he might have added, to the St. Lawrence. Our Puritan fathers found it in abundance on the New England coast, wherever they landed. See Morton, New England's Memorial, (Boston, 1826,) p. 68.—Gookin, Massachusetts Historical Collections, chap. 3.

[2] Torquemada, Monarch. Ind., lib. 13, cap. 31.

"Admirable example for our times," exclaims the good father, "when women are not only unfit for the labors of the field, but have too much levity to attend to their own household!"

[3] A striking contrast also to the Egyptians, with whom some antiquaries are disposed to identify the ancient Mexicans. Sophocles notices the effeminacy of the men in Egypt, who stayed at home tending the loom, while their wives were employed in severe labors out of doors.

" Ὦ πάντ' ἐκείνω τοῖς ἐν Αἰγύπτῳ νόμοις
Φύσιν κατεικασθέντε καὶ βίου τροφάς.
Ἐκεῖ γὰρ οἱ μὲν ἄρσενεσκατὰ στέγας
Θακοῦσιν ἱστουργοῦντες · αἱ δὲ σύννομος
Τἄξω βίου τροφεῖα ποσύνους' ἀεί."

SOPHOCL., Œdip. Col., v. 337-341.

tenderly regarded by the Aztecs in this matter, as it is, in most parts of Europe, at the present day.

There was no want of judgment in the management of their ground. When somewhat exhausted, it was permitted to recover by lying fallow. Its extreme dryness was relieved by canals, with which the land was partially irrigated; and the same end was promoted by severe penalties against the destruction of the woods, with which the country, as already noticed, was well covered before the Conquest. Lastly, they provided for their harvests ample granaries, which were admitted by the Conquerors to be of admirable construction. In the provision we see the forecast of civilized man.[4]

Among the most important articles of husbandry, we may notice the banana, whose facility of cultivation and exuberant returns are so fatal to habits of systematic and hardy industry.[5] Another celebrated plant was the cacao, the fruit of which furnished the chocolate,—from the Mexican *chocolatl*,—now so common a beverage throughout Europe.[6] The vanilla, confined to a small district of the seacoast, was used for the same purposes, of flavoring their food and drink, as with us.[7] The great staple of the country, as, indeed, of the American continent, was maize, or Indian corn, which grew freely along the valleys, and up the steep sides of the Cordilleras to the high level of the table-land. The Aztecs were as curious in its preparation, and as well instructed in its manifold uses, as the most expert New England housewife. Its gigantic stalks, in these equinoctial regions, afford a saccharine matter, not found to the same extent in northern latitudes, and supplied the natives with sugar little inferior to that of the cane itself, which was not introduced among them till after the Conquest.[8] But the miracle of nature was the great Mexican aloe, or *maguey*, whose clustering pyramids of flowers, towering above their dark coronals of leaves, were seen sprinkled over many a broad acre of the table-land. As we have already noticed its bruised leaves af-

[4] Torquemada, Monarch. Ind., lib. 13, cap. 32.—Clavigero, Stor. del Messico, tom. II. pp. 153-155.

"Jamas padeciéron hambre," says the former writer, "sino en pocas ocasiones." If these famines were rare, they were very distressing, however, and lasted very long. Comp. Ixtlilxochitl, Hist. Chich., MS., cap. 41, 71, et alibi.

[5] Oviedo considers the *musa* an imported plant; and Hernandez, in his copious catalogue, makes no mention of it at all. But Humboldt, who has given much attention to it, concludes, that, if some species were brought into the country, others were indigenous. (Essai Politique, tom. II. pp. 382-388.) If we may credit Clavigero, the banana was the forbidden fruit, that tempted our poor mother Eve! Stor. del Messico, tom. I. p. 49, nota.

[6] Rel. d'un gent., ap. Ramusio, tom. III. fol. 306.—Hernandez, de Historiâ Plantarum Novæ Hispaniæ, (Matriti, 1790,) lib. 6, cap. 87.

[7] Sahagun, Hist. de Nueva España, lib. 8, cap. 13, et alibi.

[8] Carta del. Lic. Zuazo, MS.

He extols the honey of the maize, as equal to that of the bees. (Also Oviedo, Hist. Natural de las Indias, cap. 4, ap. Barcia, tom. I.) Hernandez, who celebrates the manifold ways in which the maize was prepared, derives it from the Haytian word, *makiz*. Hist. Plantarum, lib. 6, cap. 44, 45.

forded a paste from which paper was manufactured; [9] its juice was fermented into an intoxicating beverage, *pulque*, of which the natives, to this day, are excessively fond; [10] its leaves further supplied an impenetrable thatch for the more humble dwellings; thread, of which coarse stuffs were made, and strong cords, were drawn from its tough and twisted fibres; pins and needles were made of the thorns at the extremity of its leaves; and the root, when properly cooked, was converted into a palatable and nutritious food. The *agave*, in short, was meat, drink, clothing, and writing materials, for the Aztec! Surely, never did Nature enclose in so compact a form so many of the elements of human comfort and civilization! [11]

It would be obviously out of place to enumerate in these pages all the varieties of plants, many of them of medicinal virtue, which have been introduced from Mexico into Europe. Still less can I attempt a catalogue of its flowers, which, with their variegated and gaudy colors, form the greatest attraction of our greenhouses. The opposite climates embraced within the narrow latitudes of New Spain have given to it, probably, the richest and most diversified Flora to be found in any country on the globe. These different products were systematically arranged by the Aztecs, who understood their properties, and collected them into nurseries, more extensive than any then existing in the Old World. It is not improb-

[9] And is still, in one spot at least, San Angel,—three leagues from the capital. Another mill was to have been established, a few years since, in Puebla. Whether this has actually been done I am ignorant. See the Report of the Committee on Agriculture to the Senate of the United States, March 12, 1838.

[10] Before the Revolution, the duties on the *pulque* formed so important a branch of revenue, that the cities of Mexico, Puebla, and Toluca alone, paid $817,739 to government. (Humboldt, Essai Politique, tom. II. p. 47.) It requires time to reconcile Europeans to the peculiar flavor of this liquor, on the merits of which they are consequently much divided. There is but one opinion among the natives. The English reader will find a good account of its manufacture in Ward's Mexico, vol. II. pp. 55-60.

[11] Hernandez enumerates the several species of the maguey, which are turned to these manifold uses, in his learned work, De Hist. Plantarum. (Lib. 7, cap. 71 et seq.) M. de Humboldt considers them all varieties of the *agave Americana,* familiar in the southern parts, both of the United States and Europe. (Essai Politique, tom. II. p. 487 et seq.) This opinion has brought on him a rather sour rebuke from our countryman, the late Dr. Perrine, who pronounces them a distinct species from the American *agave;* and regards one of the kinds, the *pita,* from which the fine thread is obtained, as a totally distinct genus. (See the Report of the Committee on Agriculture.) Yet the Baron may find authority for all the properties ascribed by him to the maguey, in the most accredited writers, who have resided more or less time in Mexico. See, among others, Hernandez, ubi supra.—Sahagun, Hist. de Nueva España, lib. 9, cap. 2; lib. 11, cap. 7.—Toribio, Hist. de los Indios, MS., Parte 3, cap. 19.—Carta del Lic. Zuazo, MS. The last, speaking of the maguey, which produces the fermented drink, says expressly, "De lo que queda de las dichas hojas se aprovechan, como de lino mui delgado, ó de Olanda, de que hacen lienzos mui primos para vestir, é bien delgados." It cannot be denied, however, that Dr. Perrine shows himself intimately acquainted with the structure and habits of the tropical plants, which, with such patriotic spirit, he proposed to introduce into Florida.

able that they suggested the idea of those "gardens of plants" which were introduced into Europe not many years after the Conquest.[12]

The Mexicans were as well acquainted with the mineral, as with the vegetable treasures of their kingdom. Silver, lead, and tin they drew from the mines of Tasco; copper from the mountains of Zacotollan. These were taken, not only from the crude masses on the surface, but from veins wrought in the solid rock, into which they opened extensive galleries. In fact, the traces of their labors furnished the best indications for the early Spanish miners. Gold, found on the surface, or gleaned from the beds of rivers, was cast into bars, or, in the form of dust, made parts of the regular tribute of the southern provinces of the empire. The use of iron, with which the soil was impregnated, was unknown to them. Notwithstanding its abundance, it demands so many processes to prepare it for use, that it has commonly been one of the last metals pressed into the service of man. The age of iron has followed that of brass, in fact as well as in fiction.[13]

They found a substitute in an alloy of tin and copper; and, with tools made of this bronze, could cut not only metals, but, with the aid of a silicious dust, the hardest substances, as basalt, porphyry, amethysts, and emeralds.[14] They fashioned these last, which were found very large, into many curious and fantastic forms. They cast, also, vessels of gold and silver, carving them with their metallic chisels in a very delicate manner. Some of the silver vases were so large that a man could not encircle them with his arms. They imitated very nicely the figures of animals, and, what was extraordinary, could mix the metals in such a manner, that the feathers of a bird, or the scales of a fish, should be alternately of gold and silver. The Spanish goldsmiths admitted their superiority over them selves in these ingenious works.[15]

---

[12] The first regular establishment of this kind, according to Carli, was at Padua, in 1545. Lettres Améric., tom. I, chap. 21.

[13] P. Martyr, De Orbe Novo, Decades, (Compluti, 1530,) dec. 5, p. 191.—Acosta, lib. 4, cap. 3.—Humboldt Essai Politique, tom. III. pp. 114-125.—Torquemada, Monarch. Ind., lib. 13, cap. 34.
"Men wrought in brass," says Hesiod, "when iron did not exist."

Χαλκῷ δ᾽ ἐργάζοντο · μέλας δ᾽ οὐκ ἔσκε σίδηρος.
HESIOD, Ἔργα καὶ Ἡμέραι.

The Abbé Raynal contends that the ignorance of iron must necessarily have kept the Mexicans in a low state of civilization, since without it "they could have produced no work in metal, worth looking at, no masonry nor architecture, engraving, nor sculpture." (History of the Indies, Eng. trans., vol. III. b. 6.) Iron, however, if known, was little used by the Ancient Egyptians, whose mighty monuments were hewn with bronze tools, while their weapons and domestic utensils were of the same material, as appears from the green color given to them in their paintings.

[14] Gama, Descripcion, Parte 2, pp. 25-29.—Torquemada, Monarch. Ind., ubi supra.

[15] Sahagun, Hist. de Nueva España, lib. 9, cap. 15-17.—Boturini, Idea, p. 77.—Torquemada, Monarch. Ind., loc. cit.
Herrera, who says they could also enamel, commends the skill of the Mexican goldsmiths in making birds and animals with movable wings and limbs, in a most

They employed another tool, made of *itztli*, or obsidian, a dark transparent mineral, exceedingly hard, found in abundance in their hills. They made it into knives, razors, and their serrated swords. It took a keen edge, though soon blunted. With this they wrought the various stones and alabasters employed in the construction of their public works and principal dwellings. I shall defer a more particular account of these to the body of the narrative, and will only add here, that the entrances and angles of the buildings were profusely ornamented with images, sometimes of their fantastic deities, and frequently of animals.[16] The latter were executed with great accuracy. "The former," according to Torquemada, "were the hideous reflection of their own souls. And it was not till after they had been converted to Christianity, that they could model the true figure of a man." [17] The old chronicler's facts are well founded, whatever we may think of his reasons. The allegorical phantasms of his religion, no doubt, gave a direction to the Aztec artist, in his delineation of the human figure; supplying him with an imaginary beauty in the personification of divinity itself. As these superstitions lost their hold on his mind, it opened to the influences of a purer taste; and, after the Conquest, the Mexicans furnished many examples of correct, and some of beautiful portraiture.

Sculptured images were so numerous, that the foundations of the cathedral in the *plaza mayor*, the great square of Mexico, are said to be entirely composed of them.[18] This spot may, indeed, be regarded as the Aztec forum,—the great depository of the treasures of ancient sculpture, which now lie hid in its bosom. Such monuments are spread all over the capital, however, and a new cellar can hardly be dug, or foundation laid, without turning up some of the mouldering relics of barbaric art. But they are little heeded, and, if not wantonly broken in pieces at once, are usually worked into the rising wall, or supports of the new edifice.[19] Two celebrated bas-reliefs, of the last Montezuma and his father, cut in the solid rock, in the beautiful groves of Chapoltepec, were deliberately destroyed, as late as the last century, by order of the government! [20] The

curious fashion. (Hist. General, dec. 2. lib. 7, cap. 15.) Sir John Maundeville, as usual,

"with his hair on end
At his own wonders,"

notices the "gret marvayle" of similar pieces of mechanism, at the court of the grand Chane of Cathay. See his Voiage and Travaile, chap. 20.

[16] Herrera, Hist. General, dec. 2, lib. 7, cap. 11.—Torquemada, Monarch. Ind., lib. 13, cap. 34.—Gama, Descripcion, Parte 2, pp. 27, 28.

[17] "Parece, que permitia Dios, que la figura de sus cuerpos se asimilase á la que tenian sus almas, por el pecado, en que siempre permanecian." Monarch. Ind., lib. 13, cap. 34.

[18] Clavigero, Stor. del Messico, tom. II. p. 195.

[19] Gama, Descripcion, Parte 1, p. 1. Besides the *plaza mayor*, Gama points out the Square of Tlatelolco, as a great cemetery of ancient relics. It was the quarter to which the Mexicans retreated, on the siege of the capital.

[20] Torquemada, Monarch. Ind., lib. 13, cap. 34.—Gama, Descripcion, Parte 2, pp. 81-83.

These statues are repeatedly noticed by the old writers. The last was destroyed in 1754, when it was seen by Gama, who highly commends the execution of it. Ibid

monuments of the barbarian meet with as little respect from civilized man, as those of the civilized man from the barbarian.[21]

The most remarkable piece of sculpture yet disinterred is the great calendar-stone, noticed in the preceding chapter. It consists of dark porphyry, and, in its original dimensions, as taken from the quarry, is computed to have weighed nearly fifty tons. It was transported from the mountains beyond Lake Chalco, a distance of many leagues, over a broken country intersected by water-courses and canals. In crossing a bridge which traversed one of these latter, in the capital, the support gave way and the huge mass was precipitated into the water, whence it was with difficulty recovered. The fact, that so enormous a fragment of porphyry could be thus safely carried for leagues, in the face of such obstacles, and without the aid of cattle,—for the Aztecs, as already mentioned, had no animals of draught,— suggests to us no mean ideas of their mechanical skill, and of their machinery; and implies a degree of cultivation, little inferior to that demanded for the geometrical and astronomical science displayed in the inscriptions on this very stone.[22]

The ancient Mexicans made utensils of earthen ware for the ordinary purposes of domestic life, numerous specimens of which still exist.[23] They made cups and vases of a lackered or painted wood, impervious to wet and gaudily colored. Their dyes were obtained from both mineral and vegetable substances. Among them was the rich crimson of the cochineal, the modern rival of the famed Tyrian purple. It was introduced into Europe from Mexico, where the curious little insect was nourished with great care on plantations of cactus, since fallen into neglect.[24] The natives were thus enabled to give a brilliant coloring to the webs, which were manufactured of every degree of fineness, from the cotton raised in abundance throughout the warmer regions of the country. They had the art, also, of interweaving with these the delicate hair of rabbits and other animals, which made a cloth of great warmth as well as beauty, of a kind

---

[21] This wantonness of destruction provokes the bitter animadversion of Martyr, whose enlightened mind respected the vestiges of civilization wherever found. "The conquerors," he says, "seldom repaired the buildings that were defaced. They would rather sack twenty stately cities, than erect one good edifice." De Orbe Novo, dec. 5, cap. 10.

[22] Gama, Descripcion, Parte 1, pp. 110-114.—Humboldt, Essai Politique, tom. II. p. 40.

Ten thousand men were employed in the transportation of this enormous mass, according to Tezozomoc, whose narrative, with all the accompanying prodigies, is minutely transcribed by Bustamante. The Licentiate shows an appetite for the marvellous, which might excite the envy of a monk of the Middle Ages. (See Descripcion, nota, loc. cit.) The English traveller, Latrobe, accommodates the wonders of nature and art very well to each other, by suggesting that these great masses of stone were transported by means of the mastodon, whose remains are occasionally disinterred in the Mexican Valley. Rambler in Mexico, p. 145.

[23] A great collection of ancient pottery, with various other specimens of Aztec art, the gift of Messrs. Poinsett and Keating, is deposited in the Cabinet of the American Philosophical Society, at Philadelphia. See the Catalogue, ap. Transactions, vol III, p. 510.

[24] Hernandez, Hist. Plantarum, lib. 6, cap. 116.

altogether original; and on this they often laid a rich embroidery, of birds, flowers, or some other fanciful device.[25]

But the art in which they most delighted was their *plumaje*, or feather-work. With this they could produce all the effect of a beautiful mosaic. The gorgeous plumage of the tropical birds, especially of the parrot tribe, afforded every variety of color; and the fine down of the humming-bird, which revelled in swarms among the honeysuckle bowers of Mexico, supplied them with soft aërial tints that gave an exquisite finish to the picture. The feathers, pasted on a fine cotton web, were wrought into dresses for the wealthy, hangings for apartments, and ornaments for the temples. No one of the American fabrics excited such admiration in Europe, whither numerous specimens were sent by the Conquerors. It is to be regretted, that so graceful an art should have been suffered to fall into decay.[26]

There were no shops in Mexico, but the various manufactures and agricultural products were brought together for sale in the great market-places of the principal cities. Fairs were held there every fifth day, and were thronged by a numerous concourse of persons, who came to buy or sell from all the neighbouring country. A particular quarter was allotted to each kind of article. The numerous transactions were conducted without confusion, and with entire regard to justice, under the inspection of magistrates appointed for the purpose. The traffic was carried on partly by barter, and partly by means of a regulated currency, of different values. This consisted of transparent quills of gold dust; of bits of tin, cut in the form of a **T** and of bags of cacao, containing a speci-·fied number of grains. "Blessed money," exclaims Peter Martyr, "which exempts its possessors from avarice, since it cannot be long hoarded, nor hidden under ground!" [27]

[25] Carta del Lic. Zuazo, MS.—Herrera, Hist. General, dec. 2, lib. 7, cap. 15.—Boturini, Idea, p. 77.

It is doubtful how far they were acquainted with the manufacture of silk. Carli supposes that what Cortés calls silk was only the fine texture of hair, or down, mentioned in the text. (Lettres Améric., tom. I. let. 21.) But it is certain they had a species of caterpillar, unlike our silkworm, indeed, which spun a thread that was sold in the markets of ancient Mexico. See the Essai Politique, (tom. III. pp. 66-69,) where M. de Humboldt has collected some interesting facts in regard to the culture of silk by the Aztecs. Still, that the fabric should be a matter of uncertainty at all shows that it could not have reached any great excellence or extent.

[26] Carta del Lic. Zuazo, MS.—Acosta, lib. 4, cap. 37.—Sahagun, Hist. de Nueva España, lib. 9, cap. 18-21.—Toribio, Hist. de los Indios, MS., Parte 1, cap. 15.—Rel. d' un gent., ap. Ramusio, tom. III. fol. 306.

Count Carli is in raptures with a specimen of feather-painting which he saw in Strasbourg. "Never did I behold any thing so exquisite," he says, "for brilliancy and nice gradation of color, and for beauty of design. No European artist could have made such a thing." (Lettres Améric., let. 21, note.) There is still one place, Patzquaro, where, according to Bustamante, they preserve some knowledge of this interesting art, though it is practised on a very limited scale, and at great cost. Sahagun, ubi supra, nota.

[27] "O felicen monetam, quæ suavem utilemque præbet humano generi potum, et a tartareâ peste avaritiæ suos immunes servat possessores, quod suffodi aut diu servari nequeat!" De Orbe Novo, dec. 5, cap. 4.—(See, also, Carta de Cortés, ap. Lorenza-

There did not exist in Mexico that distinction of castes found among the Egyptian and Asiatic nations. It was usual, however, for the son to follow the occupation of his father. The different trades were arranged into something like guilds; having, each, a particular district of the city appropriated to it, with its own chief, its own tutelar deity, its peculiar festivals, and the like. Trade was held in avowed estimation by the Aztecs. "Apply thyself, my son," was the advice of an aged chief, "to agriculture, or to feather-work, or some other honorable calling. Thus did your ancestors before you. Else, how would they have provided for themselves and their families? Never was it heard, that nobility alone was able to maintain its prossessor." [28] Shrewd maxims, that must have sounded somewhat strange in the ear of a Spanish *hidalgo!* [29]

But the occupation peculiarly respected was that of the merchant. It formed so important and singular a feature of their social economy, as to merit a much more particular notice than it has received from historians. The Aztec merchant was a sort of itinerant trader, who made his journeys to the remotest borders of Anahuac, and to the countries beyond, carrying with him merchandise of rich stuffs, jewelry, slaves, and other valuable commodities. The slaves were obtained at the great market of Azcapozalco, not many leagues from the capital, where fairs were regularly held for the sale of these unfortunate beings. They were brought thither by their masters, dressed in their gayest apparel, and instructed to sing, dance, and display their little stock of personal accomplishments, so as to recommend themselves to the purchaser. Slave-dealing was an honorable calling among the Aztecs.[30]

With this rich freight, the merchant visited the different provinces, always bearing some present of value from his own sovereign to the chiefs, and usually receiving others in return, with a permission to trade. Should this be denied him, or should he meet with indignity or violence, he had the means of resistance in his power. He performed his journeys with a number of companions of his own rank, and a large body of inferior attendants who were employed to transport the goods. Fifty or sixty pounds were the usual load for a man. The whole caravan went armed, and so well provided against sudden hostilities, that they could make good their defence, if necessary, till reinforced from home. In one instance, a body of these militant traders stood a siege of four years in

na, p. 100 et seq.—Sahagun, Hist. de Nueva España, lib. 8, cap. 36.—Toribio, Hist. de los Indios, MS., Parte 3, cap. 8.—Carta del Lic. Zuazo, MS.) The substitute for money throughout the Chinese empire was equally simple in Marco Polo's time, consisting of bits of stamped paper, made from the inner bark of the mulberry-tree. See Viaggi di Messer Marco Polo, gentil' huomo Venetiano, lib. 2, cap. 18, ap. Ramusio, tom. II.

[28] "Procurad de saber algun *oficio honroso*, como es el hacer obras de pluma y otros oficios mecánicos. . . . . . Mirad que tengais cuidado de lo tocante á la agricultura. . . . . En ninguna parte he visto que alguno se mantenga por su nobleza." Sahagun, Hist. de Nueva España, lib. 6, cap. 17.

[29] Col. de Mendoza, ap. Antiq. of Mexico, vol. I. Pl. 71; vol. VI. p. 86.—Torquemada, Monarch. Ind., lib. 2, cap. 41.

[30] Sahagun, Hist. de Nueva España, lib. 9, cap. 4, 10-14.

the town of Ayotlan which they finally took from the enemy.[31] Their own government, however, was always prompt to embark in a war on this ground, finding it a very convenient pretext for extending the Mexican empire. It was not unusual to allow the merchants to raise levies themselves, which were placed under their command. It was, moreover, very common for the prince to employ the merchants as a sort of spies, to furnish him information of the state of the countries through which they passed, and the dispositions of the inhabitants towards himself.[32]

Thus their sphere of action was much enlarged beyond that of a humble trader, and they acquired a high consideration in the body politic. They were allowed to assume insignia and devices of their own. Some of their number composed what is called by the Spanish writers a council of finance; at least, this was the case in Tezcuco.[33] They were much consulted by the monarch, who had some of them constantly near his person; addressing them by the title of "uncle," which may remind one of that of *primo*, or "cousin," by which a grandee of Spain is saluted by his sovereign. They were allowed to have their own courts, in which civil and criminal cases, not excepting capital, were determined; so that they formed an independent community, as it were, of themselves. And, as their various traffic supplied them with abundant stores of wealth, they enjoyed many of the most essential advantages of an hereditary aristocracy.[34]

That trade should prove the path of eminent political preferment in a nation but partially civilized, where the names of soldier and priest are usually the only titles to respect, is certainly an anomaly in history. It forms some contrast to the standard of the more polished monarchies of the Old World, in which rank is supposed to be less dishonored by a life of idle ease or frivolous pleasure, than by those active pursuits which promote equally the prosperity of the state and of the individual. If civilization corrects many prejudices, it must be allowed that it creates others.

We shall be able to form a better idea of the actual refinement of the

[31] Ibid., lib. 9, cap. 2.
[32] Ibid., lib. 9, cap. 2, 4.
In the Mendoza Codex is a painting, representing the execution of a cacique and his family, with the destruction of his city, for maltreating the persons of some Aztec merchants. Antiq. of Mexico, vol. I. Pl. 67.
[33] Torquemada, Monarch. Ind., lib. 2, cap. 41.
Ixtlilxochitl gives a curious story of one of the royal family of Tezcuco, who offered, with two *other* merchants, *otros mercaderes*, to visit the court of a hostile cacique, and bring him dead or alive to the capital. They availed themselves of a drunken revel, at which they were to have been sacrificed, to effect their object. Hist. Chich. MS., cap. 62.
[34] Sahagun, Hist. de Nueva España, lib. 9, cap. 2, 5.
The ninth book is taken up with an account of the merchants, their pilgrimages, the religious rites on their departure, and the sumptuous way of living on their return. The whole presents a very remarkable picture, showing they enjoyed a consideration, among the half-civilized nations of Anahuac, to which there is no parallel, unless it be that possessed by the merchant-princes of an Italian republic, or the princely merchants of our own.

natives, by penetrating into their domestic life and observing the inter-course between the sexes. We have fortunately the means of doing this. We shall there find the ferocious Aztec frequently displaying all the sensibility of a cultivated nature; consoling his friends under affliction, or congratulating them on their good fortune, as on occasion of a mar-riage, or of the birth or the baptism of a child, when he was punctilious in his visits, bringing presents of costly dresses and ornaments, or the more simple offering of flowers, equally indicative of his sympathy. The visits, at these times, though regulated with all the precision of Oriental courtesy, were accompanied by expressions of the most cordial and affectionate regard.[35]

The discipline of children, especially at the public schools, as stated in a previous chapter, was exceedingly severe.[36] But after she had come to a mature age, the Aztec maiden was treated by her parents with a tenderness, from which all reserve seemed banished. In the counsels to a daughter about to enter into life, they conjured her to preserve simplicity in her manners and conversation, uniform neatness in her attire, with strict attention to personal cleanliness. They inculcated modesty, as the great ornament of a woman, and implicit reverence for her husband; softening their admonitions by such endearing epithets, as showed the fulness of a parent's love.[37]

Polygamy was permitted among the Mexicans, though chiefly con-fined, probably, to the wealthiest classes.[38] And the obligations of the

---

[35] Sahagun, Hist. de Nueva España, lib. 6, cap. 23-37.—Camargo, Hist. de Tlascala, MS.

These complimentary attentions were paid at stated seasons, even during preg-nancy. The details are given with abundant gravity and minuteness by Sahagun, who descends to particulars, which his Mexican editor, Bustamante, has excluded, as somewhat too unreserved for the public eye. If they were more so than some of the editor's own notes, they must have been very communicative indeed.

[36] Zurita, Rapport, pp. 112-134.

The Third Part of the Col. de Mendoza (Antiq. of Mexico, vol. I.) exhibits the various ingenious punishments devised for the refractory child. The flowery path of knowledge was well strewed with thorns for the Mexican tyro.

[37] Zurita, Rapport, pp. 151-160.

Sahagun has given us the admonitions of both father and mother to the Aztec maiden, on her coming to years of discretion. What can be more tender than the be-ginning of the mother's exhortation? "Hija mia muy amada, muy querida palo-mita: ya has oido y notado las palabras que tu señor padre te ha dicho; ellas son palabras preciosas, y que raramente se dicen ni se oyen, las quales han procedido de las entrañas y corazon en que estaban atesoradas; y tu muy amado padre bien sabe que eres su hija, engendrada de él, eres su sangre y su carne, y sabe Dios nuestro señor que es así; aunque eres muger, é imágen de tu padre ¿ que mas te puedo decir, hija mia, de lo que ya esta dicho?" (Hist. de Nueva España, lib. 6, cap. 19.) The reader will find this interesting document, which enjoins so much of what is deemed most essential among civilized nations, translated entire in the *Appendix, Part 2, No. 1.*

[38] Yet we find the remarkable declaration, in the counsels of a father to his son, that, for the multiplication of the species, God ordained one man only for one woman "Nota, hijo mio, lo que te digo, mira que el mundo ya tiene este estilo de engendrar y multiplicar, y para esta generacion y multiplicacion, ordenó Dios que una muger usase de un varon, y una varon de una muger." Ibid. lib. 6, cap. 21.

marriage vow, which was made with all the formality of a religious ceremony, were fully recognised, and impressed on both parties. The women are described by the Spaniards as pretty, unlike their unfortunate descendants, of the present day, though with the same serious and rather melancholy cast of countenance. Their long black hair, covered, in some parts of the country, by a veil made of the fine web of the *pita*, might generally be seen wreathed with flowers, or, among the richer people, with strings of precious stones, and pearls from the Gulf of California. They appear to have been treated with much consideration by their husbands; and passed their time in indolent tranquillity, or in such feminine occupations as spinning, embroidery, and the like; while their maidens beguiled the hours by the rehearsal of traditional tales and ballads.[39]

The women partook equally with the men of social festivities and entertainments. These were often conducted on a large scale, both as regards the number of guests and the costliness of the preparations. Numerous attendants, of both sexes, waited at the banquet. The halls were scented with perfumes, and the courts strewed with odoriferous herbs and flowers, which were distributed in profusion among the guests, as they arrived. Cotton napkins and ewers of water were placed before them, as they took their seats at the board; for the venerable ceremony of ablution,[40] before and after eating, was punctiliously observed by the Aztecs.[41] Tobacco was then offered to the company, in pipes, mixed up with aromatic substances, or in the form of cigars, inserted in tubes of tortoise-shell or silver. They compressed the nostrils with the fingers, while they inhaled the smoke, which they frequently swallowed. Whether the women, who sat apart from the men at table, were allowed

---

[39] Ibid., lib. 6, cap. 21-23; lib. 8, cap. 23.—Rel. d' un gent., ap Ramusio, tom. III. fol. 305.—Carta del Lic. Zuazo, MS.

[40] As old as the heroic age of Greece, at least. We may fancy ourselves at the table of Penelope, where water in golden ewers was poured into silver basins for the accommodation of her guests, before beginning the repast.

"Χέρνιβα δ' ἀμφίπολος προχόῳ ἐπέχευε φέρουσα
Καλῇ, χρυσείῃ, ὑπὲρ ἀργυρέοιο λέβητος,
Νίψασθαι" παρὰ δὲ ξεστὴν ἐτάνυσσε τράπεζαν."

ΟΔΥΣΣ. Α.

The feast affords many other points of analogy to the Aztec, inferring a similar stage of civilization in the two nations. One may be surprised, however, to find a greater profusion of the precious metals in the barren isle of Ithaca, than in Mexico. But the poet's fancy was a richer mine than either.

[41] Sahagun, Hist. de Nueva España, lib. 6, cap. 22.

Amidst some excellent advice of a parent to his son, on his general deportment, we find the latter punctiliously enjoined not to take his seat at the board till he has washed his face and hands, and not to leave it till he has repeated the same thing, and *cleansed his teeth*. The directions are given with a precision worthy of an Asiatic. "Al principio de la comida labarte has las manos y la boca, y donde te juntares con otras á comer, no te sientes luego; mas antes tomarás el agua y la jícara para que se laben los otros, y echarles has agua á los manos, y despues de esto, cojerás lo que se ha caido por el suelo y barrerás el lugar de la comida, y tambien despues de comer lavarás te las manos y la boca, y limpiarás los dientes." Ibid., loc. cit.

the indulgence of the fragrant weed, as in the most polished circles of modern Mexico, is not told us. It is a curious fact, that the Aztecs also took the dried leaf in the pulverized form of snuff.[42]

The table was well provided with substantial meats, especially game; among which the most conspicuous was the turkey, erroneously sup‧ posed, as its name imports, to have come originally from the East.[43] These more solid dishes were flanked by others of vegetables and fruits, of every delicious variety found on the North American continent. The different viands were prepared in various ways, with delicate sauces and seasoning, of which the Mexicans were very fond. Their palate was still further regaled by confections and pastry, for which their maize-flour and sugar supplied ample materials. One other dish, of a disgusting nature, was sometimes added to the feast, especially when the celebration partook of a religious character. On such occasions a slave was sacrificed, and his flesh, elaborately dressed, formed one of the chief ornaments of the banquet. Cannibalism, in the guise of an Epicurean science, becomes even the more revolting.[44]

[42] Rel. d' un gent., ap. Ramusio, tom. III. fol. 306. ‑Sahagun, Hist. de Nueva Es‑ paña, lib. 4, cap. 37.—Torquemada, Monarch. Ind., lib. 13, cap. 23.—Clavigero, Stor. del Messico, tom. II. p. 227.

The Aztecs used to smoke after dinner, to prepare for the *siesta*, in which they indulged themselves as regularly as an old Castilian.—Tobacco, in Mexican *yetl*, is derived from a Haytian word, *tabaco*. The natives of Hispaniola, being the first with whom the Spaniards had much intercourse, have supplied Europe with the names of several important plants.—Tobacco, in some form or other, was used by almost all the tribes of the American continent, from the North-west Coast to Patagonia. (See McCulloh, Researches, pp. 91-94.) Its manifold virtues, both social and medicinal, are profusely panegyrized by Hernandez, in his Hist. Plantarum, lib. 2, cap. 109.

[43] This noble bird was introduced into Europe from Mexico. The Spaniards called it *gallopavo,* from its resemblance to the peacock. See Rel. d' un gent., ap. Ramusio, (tom. III. fol. 306) ; also Oviedo, (Rel. Sumaria, cap. 38,) the earliest naturalist who gives an account of the bird, which he saw soon after the Conquest, in the West Indies, whither it had been brought, as he says, from New Spain. The Europeans, however, soon lost sight of its origin, and the name "turkey" intimated the popular belief of its Eastern origin. Several eminent writers have maintained its Asiatic or African descent; but they could not impose on the sagacious and better instructed Buffon. (See Histoire Naturelle, Art. *Dindon*.) The Spaniards saw immense numbers of turkeys in the domesticated state, on their arrival in Mexico. where they were more common than any other poultry. They were found wild, not only in New Spain, but all along the continent, in the less frequented places, from the North-western territory of the United States to Panamá. The wild turkey is larger, more beautiful, and every way an incomparably finer bird, than the tame. Franklin, with some point, as well as pleasantry, insists on its preference to the bald eagle, as the national anthem. (See his Works, vol. X. p 63, in Sparks's excellent edition.) Interesting notices of the history and habits of the wild turkey may be found in the Ornithology both of Buonaparte and of that enthusiastic lover of nature, Audubon, *vox Meleagris, Gallopavo.*

[44] Sahagun, Hist. de Nueva España, lib. 4, cap. 37 ; lib. 8, cap. 13 ; lib. 9, cap. 10-14. —Torquemada, Monarch. Ind., lib. 13, cap. 23.—Rel. d' un gent., ap. Ramusio, tom. III. fol. 306.

Father Sahagun has gone into many particulars of the Aztec *cuisine*, and the mode of preparing sundry savory messes, making, all together, no despicable contribution to the noble science of gastronomy.

The meats were kept warm by chafing-dishes. The table was ornamented with vases of silver, and sometimes gold, of delicate workmanship. The drinking cups and spoons were of the same costly materials,
and likewise of tortoise shell. The favorite beverage was the *chocolatl*,
flavored with vanilla and different spices. They had a way of preparing
the froth of it, so as to make it almost solid enough to be eaten, and took
it cold.[45] The fermented juice of the maguey, with a mixture of sweets
and acids, supplied, also, various agreeable drinks, of different degrees
of strength, and formed the chief beverage of the elder part of the
company.[46]

As soon as they had finished their repast, the young people rose from
the table, to close the festivities of the day with dancing. They danced
gracefully, to the sound of various instruments, accompanying their
movements with chants, of a pleasing, though somewhat plaintive character.[47] The older guests continued at table, sipping *pulque*, and gossiping about other times, till the virtues of the exhilarating beverage put
them in good-humor with their own. Intoxication was not rare in this
part of the company, and, what is singular, was excused in them, though
severely punished in the younger. The entertainment was concluded by
a liberal distribution of rich dresses and ornaments among the guests,
when they withdrew, after midnight, "some commending the feast, and
others condemning the bad taste or extravagance of their host, in the
same manner," says an old Spanish writer, "as with us." [48] Human nature is, indeed, much the same all the world over.

[45] The froth, delicately flavored with spices and some other ingredients, was taken
cold by itself. It had the consistency almost of a solid; and the "Anonymous Conqueror" is very careful to inculcate the importance of "opening the mouth wide, in
order to facilitate deglutition, that the foam may dissolve gradually, and descend
imperceptibly, as it were, into the stomach." It was so nutritious that a single cup
of it was enough to sustain a man through the longest day's march. (Fol. 306.)
The old soldier discusses the beverage *con amore*.

[46] Sahagun, Hist. de Nueva España, lib. 4, cap. 37; lib. 8, cap. 13.—Torquemada,
Monarch. Ind., lib. 13, cap. 23.—Rel. d' un gent., ap. Ramusio, tom. III. fol. 306.

[47] Herrera, Hist. General, dec. 2, lib. 7, cap. 8.—Torquemada, Monarch. Ind., lib.
14, cap. 11.
The Mexican nobles entertained minstrels in their houses, who composed ballads
suited to the times, or the achievements of their lord, which they chanted, to the ac-
companiment of instruments, at the festivals and dances. Indeed, there was more or
less dancing at most of the festivals, and it was performed in the court-yards of the
houses, or in the open squares of the city. (Ibid., ubi supra.) The principal men had,
also, buffoons and jugglers in their service, who amused them, and astonished the
Spaniards by their feats of dexterity and strength; (Acosta, lib. 6, cap. 28;) also
Clavigero, (Stor. del Messico, tom. II, pp. 179-186,) who has designed several representations of their exploits, truly surprising. It is natural that a people of limited refinement should find their enjoyment in material, rather than intellectual pleasures,
and, consequently, should excel in them. The Asiatic nations, as the Hindoos and
Chinese, for example, surpass the more polished Europeans in displays of agility
and legerdemain.

[48] "Y de esta manera pasaban gran rato de la noche, y se despedian, é iban á sus
casas, unos alabando la fiesta, y otros murmurando de las demasías, y excesos; cosa
mui ordinaria en los que á semejantes actos se juntan." Torquemada, Monarch. Ind.,
lib. 13, cap. 23.—Sahagun, Hist. de Nueva España, lib. 9. cap. 10-14.

In this remarkable picture of manners, which I have copied faithfully from the records of earliest date after the Conquest, we find no resemblance to the other races of North American Indians. Some resemblance we may trace to the general style of Asiatic pomp and luxury. But, in Asia, woman, far from being admitted to unreserved intercourse with the other sex, is too often jealously immured within the walls of the harem. European civilization, which accords to this loveliest portion of creation her proper rank in the social scale, is still more removed from some of the brutish usages of the Aztecs. That such usages should have existed with the degree of refinement they showed in other things is almost inconceivable. It can only be explained as the result of religious superstition; superstition which clouds the moral perception, and perverts even the natural senses, till man, civilized man, is reconciled to the very things which are most revolting to humanity. Habits and opinions founded on religion must not be taken as conclusive evidence of the actual refinement of a people.

The Aztec character was perfectly original and unique. It was made up of incongruities apparently irreconcilable. It blended into one the marked peculiarities of different nations, not only of the same phase of civilization, but as far removed from each other as the extremes of barbarism and refinement. It may find a fitting parallel in their own wonderful climate, capable of producing, on a few square leagues of surface, the boundless variety of vegetable forms, which belong to the frozen regions of the North, the temperate zone of Europe, and the burning skies of Arabia and Hindostan!

One of the works repeatedly consulted and referred to in this Introduction is Boturini's *Idea de una nueva Historia General de la América Septentrional.* The singular persecutions sustained by its author, even more than the merits of his book, have associated his name inseparably with the literary history of Mexico. The Chevalier Lorenzo Boturini Benaduci was a Milanese by birth, of an ancient family, and possessed of much learning. From Madrid, where he was residing, he passed over to New Spain, in 1735, on some business of the countess of Santibañez, a lineal descendant of Montezuma. While employed on this, he visited the celebrated shrine of Our Lady of Guadaloupe, and, being a person of devout and enthusiastic temper, was filled with the desire of collecting testimony to establish the marvellous fact of her apparition. In the course of his excursions, made with this view, he fell in with many relics of Aztec antiquity, and conceived—what to a Protestant, at least, would seem much more rational—the idea of gathering together all the memorials he could meet with of the primitive civilization of the land.

In pursuit of this double object, he penetrated into the remotest parts of the country, living much with the natives, passing his nights sometimes in their huts, sometimes in caves, and the depths of the lonely forests. Frequently months would elapse, without his being able to add any thing to his collection; for the Indians had suffered too much, not to be very shy of Europeans. His long intercourse with them, however, gave him ample opportunity to learn their language and popular traditions, and, in the end, to amass a large stock of materials, consisting of hieroglyphical charts on cotton, skins, and the fibre of the maguey; besides a considerable body of Indian manuscripts, written after the Conquest. To all these must be added the precious documents for placing beyond controversy the miraculous apparition of the Virgin. With this treasure he returned, after a pilgrimage of eight years, to the capital.

His zeal, in the mean while, had induced him to procure from Rome a bull authorizing the coronation of the sacred image at Guadaloupe. The bull, however, though sanctioned by the Audience of New Spain, had never been approved by the Council of the Indies. In consequence of this informality, Boturini was arrested in the midst of his proceedings, his papers were taken from him, and, as he declined to give an inventory of them, he was thrown into prison, and confined in the same apartment with two criminals! Not long afterward he was sent to Spain. He there presented a memorial to the Council of the Indies, setting forth his manifold grievances, and soliciting redress. At the same time, he drew up his "Idea," above noticed, in which he displayed the catalogue of his *museum* in New Spain, declaring, with affecting earnestness, that "he would not exchange these treasures for all the gold and silver, diamonds and pearls, in the New World."

After some delay, the Council gave an award in his favor; acquitting him of any intentional violation of the law, and pronouncing a high encomium on his deserts. His papers, however, were not restored. But his Majesty was graciously pleased to appoint him Historiographer General of the Indies, with a salary of one thousand dollars *per annum*. The stipend was too small to allow him to return to Mexico. He remained in Madrid, and completed there the first volume of a "General History of North America," in 1749. Not long after this event, and before the publication of the work, he died. The same injustice was continued to his heirs; and, notwithstanding repeated applications in their behalf, they were neither put in possession of their unfortunate kinsman's collection, nor received a remuneration for it. What was worse,—as far as the public was concerned,—the collection itself was deposited in apartments of the Vice-regal palace at Mexico, so damp, that they gradually fell to pieces, and the few remaining were still further diminished by the pilfering of *the curious*. When Baron Humboldt visited Mexico, not one eighth of this inestimable treasure was in existence!

I have been thus particular in the account of the unfortunate Boturini as affording, on the whole, the most remarkable example of the serious obstacles and persecutions, which literary enterprise, directed in the path of the national antiquities, has, from some cause or other, been exposed to in New Spain.

Boturini's manuscript volume was never printed, and probably never will be, if, indeed, it is in existence. This will scarcely prove a great detriment to science, or to his own reputation. He was a man of a zealous temper, strongly inclined to the marvellous, with little of that acuteness requisite for penetrating the tangled mazes of antiquity, or of the philosophic spirit fitted for calmly weighing its doubts and difficulties. His "Idea" affords a sample of his peculiar mind. With abundant learning, ill-assorted and ill-digested, it is a jumble of fact and puerile fiction, interesting details, crazy dreams, and fantastic theories. But it is hardly fair to judge by the strict rules of criticism a work, which, put together hastily, as a catalogue of literary treasures, was designed by the author rather to show what might be done, than that he could do it himself.—It is rare that talents for action and contemplation are united in the same individual. Boturini was eminently qualified, by his enthusiasm and perseverance, for collecting the materials necessary to illustrate the antiquities of the country. It requires a more highly gifted mind to avail itself of them.

CHAPTER VI

TEZCUCANS—THEIR GOLDEN AGE—ACCOMPLISHED PRINCES—DECLINE
OF THEIR MONARCHY

THE reader would gather but an imperfect notion of the civilization of
Anahuac, without some account of the Acolhuans, or Tezcucans, as they
are usually called: a nation of the same great family with the Aztecs,
whom they rivalled in power, and surpassed in intellectual culture and
the arts of social refinement. Fortunately, we have ample materials for
this in the records left by Ixtlilxochitl, a lineal descendant of the royal
line of Tezcuco, who flourished in the century of the Conquest. With
every opportunity for information he combined much industry and
talent, and, if his narrative bears the high coloring of one who would
revive the faded glories of an ancient, but dilapidated house, he has been
uniformly commended for his fairness and integrity, and has been followed without misgiving by such Spanish writers as could have access
to his manuscripts.[1] I shall confine myself to the prominent features of
the two reigns which may be said to embrace the golden age of Tezcuco;
without attempting to weigh the probability of the details, which I will
leave to be settled by the reader, according to the measure of his faith.

The Acolhuans came into the Valley, as we have seen, about the close
of the twelfth century. and built their capital of Tezcuco on the eastern
borders of the lake, opposite to Mexico. From this point they gradually
spread themselves over the northern portion of Anahuac, when their
career was checked by an invasion of a kindred race, the Tepanecs, who,
after a desperate struggle, succeeded in taking their city, slaying their
monarch, and entirely subjugating his kingdom.[2] This event took place
about 1418; and the young prince, Nezahualcoyotl, the heir to the crown,
then fifteen years old, saw his father butchered before his eyes, while he
himself lay concealed among the friendly branches of a tree, which
overshadowed the spot.[3] His subsequent history is as full of romantic
daring, and perilous escapes, as that of the renowned Scanderbeg, or of
the "young Chevalier."[4]

---

[1] For a criticism on this writer, see the Postscript to this Chapter.
[2] See Chapter First of this Introduction, p. 15.
[3] Ixtlilxochitl, Relaciones, MS., No. 9.—Idem, Hist. Chich., MS., cap. 19.
[4] The adventures of the former hero are told with his usual spirit by Sismondi
(Républiques Italiennes, chap. 79). It is hardly necessary, for the latter, to refer
the English reader to Chambers's "History of the Rebellion of 1745"; a work which
proves how thin is the partition in human life, which divides romance from reality.

Not long after his flight from the field of his father's blood, the Tez-cucan prince fell into the hands of his enemy, was borne off in triumph to his city, and was thrown into a dungeon. He effected his escape, however, through the connivance of the governor of the fortress, an old servant of his family, who took the place of the royal fugitive, and paid for his loyalty with his life. He was at length permitted, through the intercession of the reigning family in Mexico, which was allied to him, to retire to that capital, and subsequently to his own, where he found a shelter in his ancestral palace. Here he remained unmolested for eight years, pursuing his studies under an old preceptor, who had had the care of his early youth, and who instructed him in the various duties befitting his princely station.[5]

At the end of this period the Tepanec usurper died, bequeathing his empire to his son, Maxtla, a man of fierce and suspicious temper. Neza-hualcoyotl hastened to pay his obeisance to him, on his accession. But the tyrant refused to receive the little present of flowers which he laid at his feet, and turned his back on him in presence of his chieftains. One of his attendants, friendly to the young prince, admonished him to provide for his own safety, by withdrawing, as speedily as possible, from the palace, where his life was in danger. He lost no time, consequently, in retreating from the inhospitable court, and returned to Tezcuco. Maxtla, however, was bent on his destruction. He saw with jealous eye the opening talents and popular manners of his rival, and the favor he was daily winning from his ancient subjects.[6]

He accordingly laid a plan for making way with him at an evening entertainment. It was defeated by the vigilance of the prince's tutor, who contrived to mislead the assassins, and to substitute another victim in the place of his pupil.[7] The baffled tyrant now threw off all disguise, and sent a strong party of soldiers to Tezcuco, with orders to enter the palace, seize the person of Nezahualcoyotl, and slay him on the spot. The prince, who became acquainted with the plot through the watchful-ness of his preceptor, instead of flying, as he was counselled, resolved to await his enemy. They found him playing at ball, when they arrived, in the court of his palace. He received them courteously, and invited them in, to take some refreshments after their journey. While they were occupied in this way, he passed into an adjoining saloon, which excited no suspicion, as he was still visible through the open doors by which the apartments communicated with each other. A burning censer stood in the passage, and, as it was fed by the attendants, threw up such clouds of incense as obscured his movements from the soldiers. Under this friendly veil he succeeded in making his escape by a secret passage, which

[5] Ixtlilxochitl, Relaciones, MS., No. 10.
[6] Idem, Relaciones, MS., No. 10.—Hist. Chich., MS., cap. 20-24.
[7] Idem, Hist. Chich., MS., cap. 25. The contrivance was effected by means of an extraordinary personal resemblance of the parties; a fruitful source of comic,—as very reader of the drama knows,—though rarely of tragic interest.

communicated with a large earthen pipe formerly used to bring water to the palace.[8] Here he remained till night-fall, when, taking advantage of the obscurity, he found his way into the suburbs, and sought a shelter in the cottage of one of his father's vassals.

The Tepanec monarch, enraged at this repeated disappointment, or· dered instant pursuit. A price was set on the head of the royal fugitive. Whoever should take him, dead or alive, was promised, however humble his degree, the hand of a noble lady, and an ample domain along with it. Troops of armed men were ordered to scour the country in every direction. In the course of the search, the cottage, in which the prince had taken refuge, was entered. But he fortunately escaped detection by being hid under a heap of maguey fibres used for manufacturing cloth. As this was no longer a proper place of concealment, he sought a retreat in the mountainous and woody district lying between the borders of his own state and Tlascala.[9]

Here he led a wretched, wandering life, exposed to all the inclemencies of the weather, hiding himself in deep thickets and caverns, and stealing out, at night, to satisfy the cravings of appetite; while he was kept in constant alarm by the activity of his pursuers, always hovering on his track. On one occasion he sought refuge from them among a small party of soldiers, who proved friendly to him, and concealed him in a large drum around which they were dancing. At another time, he was just able to turn the crest of a hill, as his enemies were climbing it on the other side, when he fell in with a girl who was reaping *chian*,— a Mexican plant, the seed of which was much used in the drinks of the country. He persuaded her to cover him up with the stalks she had been cutting. When his pursuers came up, and inquired if she had seen the fugitive, the girl coolly answered that she had, and pointed out a path as the one he had taken. Notwithstanding the high rewards offered, Nezahualcoyotl seems to have incurred no danger from treachery, such was the general attachment felt to himself and his house. "Would you not deliver up the prince, if he came in your way?" he inquired of a young peasant who was unacquainted with his person. "Not I," replied the other. "What, not for a fair lady's hand, and a rich dowry beside?" rejoined the prince. At which the other only shook his head and laughed.[10] On more than one occasion, his faithful people submitted to

[8] It was customary, on entering the presence of a great lord, to throw aromatics into the censer. "Hecho en el brasero incienso, y copal, que era uso y costumbre donde estaban los Reyes y Señores, cada vez que los criados entraban con mucha reverencia y acamiento echaban sahumerio en el brasero; y así con este perfume se obscurecia algo la sala." Ixtlilxochitl, Relaciones, MS., No. 11.

[9] Idem, Hist. Chich., MS., cap. 26.—Relaciones, MS., No. 11.—Veytia, Hist. Antig., lib. 2, cap. 47.

[10] "Nezahualcoiotzin le dixo, que si viese á quien buscaban, si lo iría á denunciar? respondió, que no; tornándole á replicar diciéndole, que haria mui mal en perder una muger hermosa, y lo demas, que el rey Maxtla prometia, el mancebo se rió de todo, no haciendo caso ni de lo uno, ni de lo otro." Ixtlilxochitl, Hist. Chich., MS., cap. 27.

torture, and even to lose their lives, rather than disclose the place of his retreat.[11]

However gratifying such proofs of loyalty might be to his feelings, the situation of the prince in these mountain solitudes became every day more distressing. It gave a still keener edge to his own sufferings to witness those of the faithful followers who chose to accompany him in his wanderings. "Leave me," he would say to them, "to my fate! Why should you throw away your own lives for one whom fortune is never weary of persecuting?" Most of the great Tezcucan chiefs had consulted their interests by a timely adhesion to the usurper. But some still clung to their prince, preferring proscription, and death itself, rather than desert him in his extremity.[12]

In the mean time, his friends at a distance were active in measures for his relief. The oppressions of Maxtla, and his growing empire, had caused general alarm in the surrounding states, who recalled the mild rule of the Tezcucan princes. A coalition was formed, a plan of operations concerted, and, on the day appointed for a general rising, Nezahualcoyotl found himself at the head of a force sufficiently strong to face his Tepanec adversaries. An engagement came on, in which the latter were totally discomfited; and the victorious prince, receiving everywhere on his route the homage of his joyful subjects, entered his capital, not like a proscribed outcast, but as the rightful heir, and saw himself once more enthroned in the halls of his fathers.

Soon after, he united his forces with the Mexicans, long disgusted with the arbitrary conduct of Maxtla. The allied powers, after a series of bloody engagements with the usurper, routed him under the walls of his own capital. He fled to the baths, whence he was dragged out, and sacrificed with the usual cruel ceremonies of the Aztecs; the royal city of Azcapozalco was razed to the ground, and the wasted territory was henceforth reserved as the great slave-market for the nations of Anahuac.[13]

These events were succeeded by the remarkable league among the three powers of Tezcuco, Mexico, and Tlacopan, of which some account has been given in a previous chapter.[14] Historians are not agreed as to the precise terms of it; the writers of the two former nations, each, insisting on the paramount authority of his own in the coalition. All agree in the subordinate position of Tlacopan, a state, like the others, bordering on the lake. It is certain, that in their subsequent operations, whethei of peace or war, the three states shared in each other's councils, embarked in each other's enterprises, and moved in perfect concert together till just before the coming of the Spaniards.

The first measure of Nezahualcoyotl, on returning to his dominions,

[11] Ibid., MS., cap. 26, 27.—Relaciones, MS., No. 11.—Veytia, Hist. Antig., lib. 2, cap. 47, 48.

[12] Ixtlilxochitl, MSS., ubi supra.—Veytia, ubi supra.

[13] Ixtlilxochitl, Hist. Chich., MS., cap. 28-31.—Relaciones, MS., No. 11.—Veytia Hist. Antig., lib. 2, cap. 51-54.

[14] See page 17 of this volume.

was a general amnesty. It was his maxim, "that a monarch might punish, but revenge was unworthy of him." [15] In the present instance, he was averse even to punish, and not only freely pardoned his rebel nobles, but conferred on some, who had most deeply offended, posts of honor and confidence. Such conduct was doubtless politic, especially as their alienation was owing, probably, much more to fear of the usurper, than to any disaffection towards himself. But there are some acts of policy which a magnanimous spirit only can execute.

The restored monarch next set about repairing the damages sustained under the late mis..le, and reviving, or rather remodelling, the various departments of government. He framed a concise, but comprehensive, code of laws, so well suited, it was thought to the exigencies of the times, that it was adopted as their own by the two other members of the triple alliance. It was written in blood, and entitled the author to be called the Draco, rather than "the Solon of Anahuac," as he is fondly styled by his admirers.[16] Humanity is one of the best fruits of refinement. It is only with increasing civilization that the legislator studies to economize human suffering, even for the guilty; to devise penalties, not so much by way of punishment for the past, as of reformation for the future.[17]

He divided the burden of government among a number of departments, as the council of war, the council of finance, the council of justice. This last was a court of supreme authority, both in civil and criminal matters, receiving appeals from the lower tribunals of the provinces, which were obliged to make a full report, every four months, or eighty days, of their own proceedings to this higher judicature. In all these bodies, a certain number of citizens were allowed to have seats with the nobles and professional dignitaries. There was, however, another body, a council of state, for aiding the king in the despatch of business, and advising him in matters of importance, which was drawn altogether from the highest order of chiefs. It consisted of fourteen members; and they had seats provided for them at the royal table.[18]

Lastly, there was an extraordinary tribunal, called the council of music, but which, differing from the import of its name, was devoted to the encouragement of science and art. Works on astronomy, chronology,

---

[15] "Que venganza no es justo la procuren los Reyes, sino castigar al que lo mereciere." MS., de Ixtlilxochitl.

[16] See Clavigero, Stor. del Messico, tom. I. p. 247.
Nezahualcoyotl's code consisted of eighty laws, of which thirty-four only have come down to us, according to Veytia. (Hist. Antig., tom. III. p. 224, nota.) Ixtlilxochitl enumerates several of them. Hist. Chich., MS., cap. 38, and Relaciones, MS., Ordenanzas.

[17] Nowhere are these principles kept more steadily in view than in the various writings of our adopted countryman, Dr. Lieber, having more or less to do with the theory of legislation. Such works could not have been produced before the nineteenth century.

[18] Ixtlilxochitl, Hist. Chich., MS., cap. 36.—Veytia, Hist. Antig., lib. 3, cap. 7.
According to Zurita, the principal judges, at their general meetings every four months, constituted also a sort of parliament or córtes, for advising the king on matters of state. See his Rapport, p. 106; also Ante, p. 30.

history, or any other science, were required to be submitted to its judg. ment, before they could be made public. This censorial power was of some moment, at least with regard to the historical department, where the wilful perversion of truth was made a capital offence by the bloody code of Nezahualcoyotl. Yet a Tezcucan author must have been a bungler, who could not elude a conviction under the cloudy veil of hieroglyphics. This body, which was drawn from the best instructed persons in the kingdom, with little regard to rank, had supervision of all the productions of art, and of the nicer fabrics. It decided on the qualifications of the professors in the various branches of science, on the fidelity of their instructions to their pupils, the deficiency of which was severely punished, and it instituted examinations of these latter. In short, it was a general board of education for the country. On stated days, historical compositions, and poems treating of moral or traditional topics, were recited before it by their authors. Seats were provided for the three crowned heads of the empire, who deliberated with the other members on the respective merits of the pieces, and distributed prizes of value to the successful competitors.[19]

Such are the marvellous accounts transmitted to us of this institution; an institution certainly not to have been expected among the Aborigines of America. It is calculated to give us a higher idea of the refinement of the people, than even the noble architectural remains, which still cover some parts of the continent. Architecture is, to a certain extent, a sensual gratification. It addresses itself to the eye, and affords the best scope for the parade of barbaric pomp and splendor. It is the form in which the revenues of a semi-civilized people are most likely to be lavished. The most gaudy and ostentatious specimens of it, and sometimes the most stupendous, have been reared by such hands. It is one of the first steps in the great march of civilization. But the institution in question was evidence of still higher refinement. It was a literary luxury; and argued the existence of a taste in the nation, which relied for its gratification on pleasures of a purely intellectual character.

The influence of this academy must have been most propitious to the capital, which became the nursery, not only of such sciences as could be compassed by the scholarship of the period, but of various useful and ornamental arts. Its historians, orators, and poets were celebrated throughout the country.[20] Its archives, for which accommodations were

[19] Ixtlilxochitl, Hist. Chich., MS., cap. 36.—Clavigero, Stor. del Messico, tom. II. p. 137.—Veytia, Hist. Antig., lib. 3, cap. 7.

"Concurrian á este consejo las tres cabezas del imperio, en ciertos dias, á oir cantar las poesías históricas antiguas y modernas, para instruirse de toda su historia, y tambien cuando habia algun nuevo invento en cualquiera facultad, para examinarlo, aprobarlo, ó reprobarlo. Delante de las sillas de los reyes habia una gran mesa cargada de joyas de oro y plata, pedrería, plumas, y otras cosas estimables, y en los rincones de la sala muchas de mantas de todas calidades, para premios de las habilidades y estímulo de los profesores, las cuales alhajas repartian los reyes, en los dias que concurrian, á los que se aventajaban en el ejercicio de sus facultades." Ibid.

[20] Veytia, Hist. Antig., lib. 3, cap. 7.—Clavigero, Stor. del Messico, tom. I. p. 247. The latter author enumerates four historians, some of much repute, of the royal

provided in the royal palace, were stored with the records of primitive ages.[21] Its idiom, more polished than the Mexican, was, indeed, the purest of all the Nahuatlac dialects; and continued, long after the Conquest, to be that in which the best productions of the native races were composed. Tezcuco claimed the glory of being the Athens of the Western World.[22]

Among the most illustrious of her bards was the emperor himself,— for the Tezcucan writers claim this title for their chief, as head of the imperial alliance. He, doubtless, appeared as a competitor before that very academy where he so often sat as a critic. Many of his odes descended to a late generation, and are still preserved, perhaps, in some of the dusty repositories of Mexico or Spain.[23] The historian, Ixtilxochitl, has left a translation, in Castilian, of one of the poems of his royal ancestor. It is not easy to render his version into corresponding English rhyme, without the perfume of the original escaping in this double filtration.[24] They remind one of the rich breathings of Spanish-Arab poetry, in which an ardent imagination is tempered by a not unpleasing and moral melancholy.[25] But, though sufficiently florid in diction, they are generally free from the meretricious ornaments and hyperbole with which the minstrelsy of the East is usually tainted. They turn on the vanities and mutability of human life; a topic very natural for a monarch who had himself experienced the strangest mutations of fortune. There is mingled in the lament of the Tezcucan bard, however, an Epicurean philosophy, which seeks relief from the fears of the future in the joys of the present. "Banish care," he says; "if there are bounds to

house of Tezcuco, descendants of the great Nezahualcoyotl. See his Account of Writers, tom. I. pp. 6-21.

[21] "En la ciudad de Tezcuco estaban los Archivos Reales de todas las cosas referidas, por haver sido la Metrópoli de todas las ciencias, usos, y buenas costumbres, porque los Reyes que fuéron de ella se preciáron de esto." (Ixtlilxochitl, Hist. Chich., MS., Prólogo.) It was from the poor wreck of these documents, once so carefully preserved by his ancestors, that the historian gleaned the materials, as he informs us, for his own works.

[22] "Aunque es tenida la lengua Mejicana por materna, y la Tezcucana por mas cortesana y pulida." (Camargo, Hist. de Tlascala, MS.) "Tezcuco," says Boturini, "donde los Señores de la Tierra embiaban á sus hijos para aprehender *lo mas pulido de la Lengua Nàhautl,* la Poesía, Filosofia Moral, la Theología Gentilica, la Astronomía, Medicina, y la Historia." Idea, p. 142.

[23] "Compuso LX. cantares," says the author last quoted, "que quizas tambien havrán perecido en las manos incendiarias de los ignorantes." (Idea, p. 79.) Boturini had translations of two of these in his museum, (Catálogo, p. 8,) and another has since come to light.

[24] Difficult as the task may be, it has been executed by the hand of a fair friend, who, while she has adhered to the Castilian with singular fidelity, has shown a grace and flexibility in her poetical movements, which the Castilian version, and probably the Mexican original, cannot boast. See both translations in *Appendix, Part 2, No. 2.*

[25] Numerous specimens of this may be found in Condé's "Dominacion de los Arabes en España." None of them are superior to the plaintive strains of the royal Abderahman on the solitary palm-tree, which reminded him of the pleasant land of his birth. See Parte 2, cap. 9.

pleasure, the saddest life must also have an end. Then weave the chaplet of flowers, and sing thy songs in praise of the all-powerful God; for the glory of this world soon fadeth away. Rejoice in the green freshness of thy spring; for the day will come when thou shalt sigh for these joys in vain; when the sceptre shall pass from thy hands, thy servants shall wander desolate in thy courts, thy sons, and the sons of thy nobles, shall drink the dregs of distress, and all the pomp of thy victories and triumphs shall live only in their recollection. Yet the remembrance of the just shall not pass away from the nations, and the good thou hast done shall ever be held in honor. The goods of this life, its glories and its riches, are but lent to us, its substance is but an illusory shadow, and the things of to-day shall change on the coming of the morrow. Then gather the fairest flowers from thy gardens, to bind round thy brow, and seize the joys of the present, ere they perish." [26]

But the hours of the Tezcucan monarch were not all passed in idle dalliance with the Muse, nor in the sober contemplations of philosophy, as at a later period. In the freshness of youth and early manhood he led the allied armies in their annual expeditions, which were certain to result in a wider extent of territory to the empire.[27] In the intervals of peace he fostered those productive arts which are the surest sources of public prosperity. He encouraged agriculture above all; and there was scarcely a spot so rude, or a steep so inaccessible, as not to confess the power of cultivation. The land was covered with a busy population, and towns

[26] "Io tocaré cantando
El músico instrumento sonoroso,
Tú de flores gozando
Danza, y festeja á Dios que es poderoso;
O gozemos de esta gloria,
Porque la humana vida es transitoria."

MS. DE IXTLILXOCHITL.

The sentiment, which is common enough, is expressed with uncommon beauty by the English poet, Herrick;

"Gather the rosebud while you may,
Old Time is still a flying;
The fairest flower that blooms to-day,
To-morrow may be dying."

And with still greater beauty, perhaps, by Racine;

"Rions, chantons, dit cette troupe impie;
De fleurs en fleurs, de plaisirs en plaisirs,
                    Promenons nos désirs.
Sur l'avenir insensé qui se fie.
De nos ans passagers le nombre est incertain.
Hâtons-nous aujourd'hui de jouir de la vie;
Qui sait si nous serons demain?"

ATHALIE, Acte 2.

It is interesting to see under what different forms the same sentiment is developed by different races, and in different languages. It is an Epicurean sentiment, indeed, but its universality proves its truth to nature.

[27] Some of the provinces and places thus conquered were held by the allied powers in common; Tlacopan, however, only receiving one fifth of the tribute. It was more usual to annex the vanquished territory to that one of the two great states, to which it lay nearest. See Ixtlilxochitl, Hist. Chich., MS., cap. 38.—Zurita, Rapport, p. 11

and cities sprung up in places since deserted, or dwindled into miserable villages.[28]

From resources thus enlarged by conquest and domestic industry, the monarch drew the means for the large consumption of his own numerous household,[29] and for the costly works which he executed for the convenience and embellishment of the capital. He filled it with stately edifices for his nobles, whose constant attendance he was anxious to secure at his court.[30] He erected a magnificent pile of buildings which might serve both for a royal residence and for the public offices. It extended, from east to west, twelve hundred and thirty-four yards, and from north to south, nine hundred and seventy-eight. It was encompassed by a wall of unburnt bricks and cement, six feet wide and nine high, for one half of the circumference, and fifteen feet high for the other half. Within this inclosure were two courts. The outer one was used as the great market-place of the city; and continued to be so until long after the Conquest,—if, indeed, it is not now. The interior court was surrounded by the council-chambers and halls of justice. There were also accommodations there for the foreign ambassadors; and a spacious saloon, with apartments opening into it, for men of science and poets, who pursued their studies in this retreat, or met together to hold converse under its marble porticos. In this quarter, also, were kept the public archives; which fared better under the Indian dynasty, than they have since under their European successors.[31]

Adjoining this court were the apartments of the king, including those for the royal harem, as liberally supplied with beauties as that of an

[28] Ixlilxochitl, Hist. Chich., MS., cap. 41. The same writer, in another work, calls the population of Tezcuco, at this period, double of what it was at the Conquest; founding his estimate on the royal registers, and on the numerous remains of edifices still visible in his day, in places now depopulated. "Parece en las historias que en este tiempo, antes que se destruyesen, havia doblado mas gente de las que halló al tiempo que vino Cortés, y los demas Españoles: porque yo hallo en los padrones reales, que el menor pueblo tenia 1100 vecinos, y de allí para arriba, y ahora no tienen 200 vecinos, y aun en algunas partes de todo punto see han acabado. . . . . . Como se hecha de ver en las ruinas, hasta los mas altos montes y sierras tenian sus sementeras, y casas principales para vivir y morar." Relaciones, MS., No. 9.

[29] Torquemada has extracted the particulars of the yearly expenditure of the palace from the royal account-book, which came into the historian's possession. The following are some of the items, namely; 4,900,300 fanegas of maize; (the *fanega* is equal to about one hundred pounds;) 2,744,000 fanegas of cacao; 8000 turkeys; 1300 baskets of salt; besides an incredible quantity of game of every kind, vegetables, condiments, &c. (Monarch, Ind., lib. 2, cap. 53.) See, also, Ixtlilxochitl, Hist. Chich., MS., cap. 35.

[30] There were more than four hundred of these lordly residences. "Así mismo hizo edificar muchos casas y palacios para los señores y cavalleros, que asistian en su corte, cada uno conforme á la calidad y méritos de su persona, las quales llegáron á ser mas de quatrocientas casas de señores y cavalleros de solar conocido." Ibid., cap. 38.

[31] Ibid., cap. 36 "Esta plaza cercada de portales, y tenia así mismo por la parte del poniente otra sala grande, y muchos quartos á la redonda, que era la universidad, en donde asistian todos los poetas, históricos, y philósophos del reyno, divididos en sus claves, y academias, conforme era la facultad de cada uno, y así mismo estaban aqui los archivos reales."

Eastern sultan. Their walls were incrusted with alabasters, and richly tinted stucco, or hung with gorgeous tapestries of variegated feather-work. They led through long arcades, and through intricate labyrinths of shrubbery, into gardens, where baths and sparkling fountains were overshadowed by tall groves of cedar and cypress. The basins of water were well stocked with fish of various kinds, and the aviaries with birds glowing in all the gaudy plumage of the tropics. Many birds and animals, which could not be obtained alive, were represented in gold and silver so skilfully, as to have furnished the great naturalist, Hernandez, with models for his work.[32]

Accommodations on a princely scale were provided for the sovereigns of Mexico and Tlacopan, when they visited the court. The whole of this lordly pile contained three hundred apartments, some of them fifty yards square.[33] The height of the building is not mentioned. It was probably not great; but supplied the requisite room by the immense extent of ground which it covered. The interior was doubtless constructed of light materials, especially of the rich woods, which, in that country, are remarkable, when polished, for the brilliancy and variety of their colors. That the more solid materials of stone and stucco were also liberally employed is proved by the remains at the present day; remains, which have furnished an inexhaustible quarry for the churches and other edifices since erection by the Spaniards on the site of the ancient city.[34]

We are not informed of the time occupied in building this palace.

---

[32] This celebrated naturalist was sent by Philip II. to New Spain, and he employed several years in compiling a voluminous work on its various natural productions, with drawings illustrating them. Although the government is said to have expended sixty thousand ducats in effecting this great object, the volumes were not published till long after the author's death. In 1651 a mutilated edition of the part of the work relating to medical botany appeared at Rome. The original MSS. were supposed to have been destroyed by the great fire in the Escurial, not many years after. Fortunately, another copy, in the author's own hand, was detected by the indefatigable Muñoz, in the library of the Jesuits' College at Madrid, in the latter part of the last century; and a beautiful edition, from the famous press of Ibarra, was published in that capital, under the patronage of government, in 1790. (Hist. Plantarum, Præfatio.—Nic. Antonio, Bibliotheca Hispana Nova, (Matriti, 1790,) tom. II. p. 432.)

The work of Hernandez is a monument of industry and erudition, the more remarkable, as being the first on this difficult subject. And after all the additional light from the labors of later naturalists, it still holds its place as a book of the highest authority, for the perspicuity, fidelity, and thoroughness, with which the multifarious topics in it are discussed.

[33] Ixtlilxochitl, Hist. Chich., MS., cap. 36.

[34] "Some of the terraces on which it stood," says Mr. Bullock, speaking of this palace, "are still entire, and covered with cement, very hard, and equal in beauty to that found in ancient Roman buildings. . . . . . The great church, which stands close by, is almost entirely built of the materials taken from the palace, many of the sculptured stones from which may be seen in the walls, though most of the ornaments are turned inwards. Indeed, our guide informed us, that whoever built a house at Tezcuco made the ruins of the palace serve as his quarry." (Six Months in Mexico, chap. 26.) Torquemada notices the appropriation of the materials to the same purpose. Monarch. Ind., lib. 2, cap. 45.

But two hundred thousand workmen, it is said, were employed on it![35] However this may be, it is certain that the Tezcucan monarchs, like those of Asia, and ancient Egypt, had the control of immense masses of men, and would sometimes turn the whole population of a conquered city, including the women, into the public works.[36]—The most gigantic monuments of architecture which the world has witnessed would never have been reared by the hands of freemen.

Adjoining the palace were buildings for the king's children, who, by his various wives, amounted to no less than sixty sons and fifty daughters.[37] Here they were instructed in all the exercises and accomplishments suited to their station; comprehending, what would scarcely find a place in a royal education on the other side of the Atlantic, the arts of working in metals, jewelry, and feather-mosaic. Once in every four months, the whole household, not excepting the youngest, and including all the officers and attendants on the king's person, assembled in a grand saloon of the palace, to listen to a discourse from an orator, probably one of the priesthood. The princes, on this occasion, were all dressed in *nequen*, the coarsest manufacture of the country. The preacher began by enlarging on the obligations of morality, and of respect for the gods, especially important in persons whose rank gave such additional weight to example. He occasionally seasoned his homily with a pertinent application to his audience, if any member of it had been guilty of a notorious delinquency. From this wholesome admonition the monarch himself was not exempted, and the orator boldly reminded him of his paramount duty to show respect for his own laws. The king so far from taking umbrage, received the lesson with humility; and the audience, we are assured, were often melted into tears by the eloquence of the preacher.[38] This curious scene may remind one of similar usages in the Asiatic and Egyptian despotisms, where the sovereign occasionally condescended to stoop from his pride of place, and allow his memory to be refreshed with the conviction of his own mortality.[39] It soothed the feelings of the subject, to find himself thus placed, though but for a moment, on a level with his king; while it cost little to the latter, who was removed too far from his people, to suffer any thing by this short-lived

[35] Ixtlilxochitl, MS., ubi supra.

[36] Thus, to punish the Chalcas for their rebellion, the whole population were compelled, women as well as men, says the chronicler so often quoted, to labor on the royal edifices, for four years together; and large granaries were provided with stores for their maintenance, in the mean time. Idem, Hist. Chich., MS., cap. 46.

[37] If the people in general were not much addicted to polygamy, the sovereign, it must be confessed,—and it was the same, we shall see, in Mexico,—made ample amends for any self-denial on the part of his subjects.

[38] Ixtlilxochitl, Hist. Chich., MS., cap. 37.

[39] The Egyptian priests managed the affair in a more courtly style, and, while they prayed that all sorts of kingly virtues might descend on the prince, they threw the blame of actual delinquencies on his ministers; thus, "not by the bitterness of reproof," says Diodorus, "but by the allurements of praise, enticing him to an honest way of life." Lib. i, cap. 70.

familiarity. It is probable that such an act of public humiliation would have found less favor with a prince less absolute.

Nezahualcoyotl's fondness for magnificence was shown in his numerous villas, which were embellished with all that could make a rural retreat delightful. His favorite residence was at Tezcotzinco; a conical hill about two leagues from the capital.[40] It was laid out in terraces, or hanging gardens, having a flight of steps five hundred and twenty in number, many of them hewn in the natural porphyry.[41] In the garden on the summit was a reservoir of water, fed by an aqueduct that was carried over hill and valley, for several miles, on huge buttresses of masonry. A large rock stood in the midst of this basin, sculptured with the hieroglyphics representing the years of Nezahualcoyotl's reign and his principal achievements in each.[42] On a lower level were three other reservoirs, in each of which stood a marble statue of a woman, emblematic of the three states of the empire. Another tank contained a winged lion, (?) cut out of the solid rock, bearing in his mouth the portrait of the emperor.[43] His likeness had been executed in gold, wood, feather-work, and stone, but this was the only one which pleased him.

From these copious basins the water was distributed in numerous channels through the gardens, or was made to tumble over the rocks in cascades, shedding refreshing dews on the flowers and odoriferous shrubs below. In the depths of this fragrant wilderness, marble porticos and pavilions were erected, and baths excavated in the solid porphyry, which are still shown by the ignorant natives, as the "Baths of Montezuma"![44] The visitor descended by steps cut in the living stone, and polished so bright as to reflect like mirrors.[45] Towards the base of the hill in the

[40] Ixtlilxochitl, Hist. Chich., MS., cap. 42.

[41] "Quinientos y veynte escalones." Davila Padilla, Historia de la Provincia de Santiago, (Madrid, 1596,) lib. 2, cap. 81.

This writer, who lived in the sixteenth century, counted the steps himself. Those which were not cut in the rock were crumbling into ruins, as, indeed, every part of the establishment was even then far gone to decay.

[42] On the summit of the mount, according to Padila, stood an image of a *coyotl*, —an animal resembling a fox,—which, according to tradition, represented an Indian famous for his fasts. It was destroyed by that stanch iconoclast, Bishop Zumarraga, as a relic of idolatry. (Hist. de Santiago, lib. 2, cap. 81.) This figure was, no doubt, the emblem of Nezahualcoyotl himself, whose name, as elsewhere noticed, signified "hungry fox."

[43] "Hecho de un peña un leon de mas de dos brazas de largo con sus alas y plumas: estaba hechado y mirando á la parte del oriente, en cuia boca asomaba un rostro, que era el mismo retrato del Rey." Ixtlilxochitl, Hist. Chich., MS., cap. 42.

[44] Bullock speaks of a "beautiful basin, twelve feet long by eight wide, having a well five feet by four, deep in the centre," &c., &c. Whether truth lies in the bottom of this well is not so clear. Latrobe describes the paths as "two singular basins, perhaps two feet and a half in diameter, not large enough for any monarch bigger than Oberon to take a duck in." (Comp. Six Months in Mexico, chap. 26; and Rambler in Mexico, let. 7.) Ward speaks much to the same purpose, (Mexico in 1827, (London, 1828,) vol. II. p. 296,) which agrees with verbal accounts I have received of the same spot.

[45] "Gradas hechas de la misma peña tan bien gravadas y lizas que parecian espejos." (Ixtlilxochitl, MS., ubi supra.) The travellers just cited notice the beautiful polish still visible in the porphyry.

midst of cedar groves, whose gigantic branches threw a refreshing coolness over the verdure in the sultriest seasons of the year,[46] rose the royal villa, with its light arcades and airy halls, drinking in the sweet perfumes of the gardens. Here the monarch often retired, to throw off the burden of state, and refresh his wearied spirits in the society of his favorite wives, reposing during the noontide heats in the embowering shades of his paradise, or mingling, in the cool of the evening, in their festive sports and dances. Here he entertained his imperial brothers of Mexico and Tlacopan, and followed the hardier pleasures of the chase in the noble woods that stretched for miles around his villa, flourishing in all their primeval majesty. Here, too, he often repaired in the latter days of his life, when age had tempered ambition and cooled the ardor of his blood, to pursue in solitude the studies of philosophy and gather wisdom from meditation.

The extraordinary accounts of the Tezcucan architecture are confirmed, in the main, by the relics which still cover the hill of Tezcotzinco, or are half buried beneath its surface. They attract little attention, indeed, in the country, where their true history has long since passed into oblivion;[47] while the traveller, whose curiosity leads him to the spot, speculates on their probable origin, and, as he stumbles over the huge fragments of sculptured porphyry and granite, refers them to the primitive races who spread their colossal architecture over the country, long before the coming of the Acolhuans and the Aztecs.[48]

The Tezcucan princes were used to entertain a great number of concubines. They had but one lawful wife, to whose issue the crown descended.[49] Nezahualcoyotl remained unmarried to a late period. He was disappointed in an early attachment, as the princess, who had been educated in privacy to be the partner of his throne, gave her hand to another. The injured monarch submitted the affair to the proper tri-

[46] Padilla saw entire pieces of cedar among the ruins, ninety feet long, and four in diameter. Some of the massive portals, he observed, were made of a single stone. (Hist. de Santiago, lib. 11, cap. 81.) Peter Martyr notices an enormous wooden beam, used in the construction of the palaces of Texcuco, which was one hundred and twenty feet long by eight feet in diameter! The accounts of this and similar huge pieces of timber were so astonishing, he adds, that he could not have received them except on the most unexceptionable testimony. De Orbe Novo, dec. 5, cap. 10.

[47] It is much to be regretted that the Mexican government should not take a deeper interest in the Indian antiquities. What might not be effected by a few hands drawn from the idle garrisons of some of the neighbouring towns, and employed in excavating this ground, "the Mount Palatine" of Mexico! But, unhappily, the age of violence has been succeeded by one of apathy.

[48] "They are, doubtless," says Mr. Latrobe, speaking of what he calls, "these inexplicable ruins,"—"rather of Toltec than Aztec origin, and, perhaps, with still more probability, attributable to a people of an age yet more remote." (Rambler in Mexico, let. 7.) "I am of opinion," says Mr. Bullock, "that these were antiquities prior to the discovery of America, and erected by a people whose history was lost even before the building of the city of Mexico.—Who can solve this difficulty?" (Six Months in Mexico, ubi supra.) The reader who takes Ixtlilxochitl for his guide will have no great trouble in solving it. He will find here, as he might, probably, in some other instances, that one need go little higher than the Conquest, for the origin of antiquities, which claim to be coeval with Phœnicia and Ancient Egypt.

[49] Zurita, Rapport, p. 12.

bunal. The parties, however, were proved to have been ignorant of the destination of the lady, and the court, with an independence which reflects equal honor on the judges who could give, and the monarch who could receive the sentence, acquitted the young couple. This story is sadly contrasted by the following.[50]

The king devoured his chagrin in the solitude of his beautiful villa of Tezcotzinco, or sought to divert it by travelling. On one of his journeys he was hospitably entertained by a potent vassal, the old lord of Tepechpan, who, to do his sovereign more honor, caused him to be attended at the banquet by a noble maiden, betrothed to himself, and who, after the fashion of the country, had been educated under his own roof. She was of the blood royal of Mexico, and nearly related, moreover, to the Tezcucan monarch. The latter, who had all the amorous temperament of the South, was captivated by the grace and personal charms of the youthful Hebe, and conceived a violent passion for her. He did not disclose it to any one, however, but, on his return home, resolved to gratify it, though at the expense of his own honor, by sweeping away the only obstacle which stood in his path.

He accordingly sent an order to the chief of Tepechpan to take command of an expedition set on foot against the Tlascalans. At the same time he instructed two Tezcucan chiefs to keep near the person of the old lord, and bring him into the thickest of the fight, where he might lose his life. He assured them, this had been forfeited by a great crime, but that, from regard for his vassal's past services, he was willing to cover up his disgrace by an honorable death.

The veteran, who had long lived in retirement on his estates, saw himself, with astonishment, called so suddenly and needlessly into action, for which so many younger men were better fitted. He suspected the cause, and, in the farewell entertainment to his friends, uttered a presentiment of his sad destiny. His predictions were too soon verified and a few weeks placed the hand of his virgin bride at her own disposal.

Nezahualcoyotl did not think it prudent to break his passion publicly to the princess, so soon after the death of his victim. He opened a correspondence with her through a female relative, and expressed his deep sympathy for her loss. At the same time, he tendered the best consolation in his power, by an offer of his heart, and hand. Her former lover had been too well stricken in years for the maiden to remain long inconsolable. She was not aware of the perfidious plot against his life; and, after a decent time, she was ready to comply with her duty, by placing herself at the disposal of her royal kinsman.

It was arranged by the king, in order to give a more natural aspect to the affair, and prevent all suspicion of the unworthy part he had acted, that the princess should present herself in his grounds at Tezcotzinco, to witness some public ceremony there. Nezahualcoyotl was standing in a balcony of the palace, when she appeared, and inquired, as if struck with her beauty for the first time, "who the lovely young creature was,

[50] Ixtlilxochitl, Hist. Chich., MS., cap. 43.

in his gardens." When his courtiers had acquainted him with her name and rank, he ordered her to be conducted to the palace, that she might receive the attentions due to her station. The interview was soon followed by a public declaration of his passion; and the marriage was celebrated not long after, with great pomp, in the presence of his court, and of his brother monarchs of Mexico and Tlacopan.[51]

This story, which furnishes so obvious a counterpart to that of David and Uriah, is told with great circumstantiality, both by the king's son and grandson, from whose narratives Ixtlilxochitl derived it.[52] They stigmatize the action as the basest in their great ancestor's life. It is indeed too base not to leave an indelible stain on any character, however pure in other respects, and exalted.

The king was strict in the execution of his laws, though his natural disposition led him to temper justice with mercy. Many anecdotes are told of the benevolent interest he took in the concerns of his subjects, and of his anxiety to detect and reward merit, even in the most humble. It was common for him to ramble among them in disguise, like the celebrated caliph in the "Arabian Nights," mingling freely in conversation, and ascertaining their actual condition with his own eyes.[53]

On one such occasion, when attended only by a single lord, he met with a boy who was gathering sticks in a field for fuel. He inquired of him "why he did not go into the neighbouring forest, where he would find a plenty of them." To which the lad answered, "It was the king's wood, and he would punish him with death, if he trespassed there." The royal forests were very extensive in Tezcuco, and were guarded by laws full as severe as those of the Norman tyrants in England. "What kind of man is your king?" asked the monarch, willing to learn the effect of these prohibitions on his own popularity. "A very hard man," answered the boy, "who denies his people what God has given them." [54] Nezahualcoyotl urged him not to mind such arbitrary laws, but to glean his sticks in the forest, as there was no one present who would betray him. But the boy sturdily refused, bluntly accusing the disguised king, at the same time, of being a traitor, and of wishing to bring him into trouble.

Nezahualcoyotl, on returning to the palace, ordered the child and his parents to be summoned before him. They received the orders with astonishment, but, on entering the presence, the boy at once recognised the person with whom he had discoursed so unceremoniously, and he was filled with consternation. The good-natured monarch, however, relieved his apprehensions, by thanking him for the lesson he had given him, and, at the same time, commended his respect for the laws, and praised his parents for the manner in which they had trained their son. He then

[51] Idem, Hist. Chich., MS., cap. 43.

[52] Idem, ubi supra.

[53] "En traje de cazador, (que lo acostumbraba á hacer muy de ordinario,) saliendo á solas, y disfrazado para que no fuese conocido, á reconocer las faltas y necesidad que havia en la república para remediarlas." Idem, Hist. Chich., MS., cap. 46.

[54] Un hombresillo miserable, pues quita á los hombres lo que Dios á manos llenas les da." Ibid., loc. cit.

dismissed the parties with a liberal largess; and afterwards mitigated the severity of the forest laws, so as to allow persons to gather any wood they might find on the ground, if they did not meddle with the standing timber.[55]

Another adventure is told of him, with a poor woodman and his wife, who had brought their little load of billets for sale to the market-place of Tezcuco. The man was bitterly lamenting his hard lot, and the difficulty with which he earned a wretched subsistence, while the master of the palace before which they were standing lived an idle life, without toil, and with all the luxuries in the world at his command.

He was going on in his complaints, when the good woman stopped him, by reminding him he might be overheard. He was so, by Nezahualcoyotl himself, who, standing, screened from observation, at a latticed window, which overlooked the market, was amusing himself, as he was wont, with observing the common people chaffering in the square. He immediately ordered the querulous couple into his presence. They appeared trembling and conscience-struck before him. The king gravely inquired what they had said. As they answered him truly, he told them they should reflect, that, if he had great treasures at his command, he had still greater calls for them; that, far from leading an easy life, he was oppressed with the whole burden of government; and concluded by admonishing them "to be more cautious in future, as walls had ears." [56] He then ordered his officers to bring a quantity of cloth, and a generous supply of cacao, (the coin of the country,) and dismissed them. "Go," said he; "with the little you now have, you will be rich; while, with all my riches, I shall still be poor." [57]

It was not his passion to hoard. He dispensed his revenues munificently, seeking out poor, but meritorious objects, on whom to bestow them. He was particularly mindful of disabled soldiers, and those who had in any way sustained loss in the public service; and, in case of their death, extended assistance to their surviving families. Open mendicity was a thing he would never tolerate, but chastised it with exemplary rigor.[58]

It would be incredible, that a man of the enlarged mind and endowments of Nezahualcoyotl should acquiesce in the sordid superstitions of his countrymen, and still more in the sanguinary rites borrowed by them from the Aztecs. In truth, his humane temper shrunk from these cruel ceremonies, and he strenuously endeavoured to recall his people to the more pure and simple worship of the ancient Toltecs. A circumstance produced a temporary change in his conduct.

He had been married some years to the wife he had so unrighteously obtained, but was not blessed with issue. The priests represented that it was owing to his neglect of the gods of his country, and that his only

[55] Ibid., cap. 46.
[56] "Porque las paredes oian." (Ibid.) A European proverb among the American Aborigines looks too strange, not to make one suspect the hand of the chronicler.
[57] "Le dijo, que con aquello poco le bastaba, y viviria bien aventurado; y él, con toda la máquina que le parecia que tenia arto, no tenia nada; y así lo despidió." Ibid
[58] Ibid.

remedy was, to propitiate them by human sacrifice. The king reluctantly consented, and the altars once more smoked with the blood of slaughtered captives. But it was all in vain; and he indignantly exclaimed, "These idols of wood and stone can neither hear nor feel; much less could they make the heavens, and the earth, and man, the lord of it. These must be the work of the all-powerful, unknown God, Creator of the universe, on whom alone I must rely for consolation and support." [59]

He then withdrew to his rural palace of Tezcotzinco, where he remained forty days, fasting and praying at stated hours, and offering up no other sacrifice, than the sweet incense of copal, and aromatic herbs and gums. At the expiration of this time, he is said to have been comforted by a vision assuring him of the success of his petition. At all events, such proved to be the fact; and this was followed by the cheering intelligence of the triumph of his arms in a quarter where he had lately experienced some humiliating reverses. [60]

Greatly strengthened in his former religious convictions, he now openly professed his faith, and was more earnest to wean his subjects from their degrading superstitions, and to substitute nobler and more spiritual conceptions of the Deity. He built a temple in the usual pyramidal form, and on the summit a tower nine stories high, to represent the nine heavens; a tenth was surmounted by a roof painted black, and profusely gilded with stars, on the outside, and incrusted with metals and precious stones within. He dedicated this to *"the unknown God, the Cause of causes."* [61] It seems probable, from the emblem on the tower, as well as from the complexion of his verses, as we shall see, that he mingled with his reverence for the Supreme the astral worship which existed among the Toltecs. [62] Various musical instruments were placed on the top of the tower, and the sound of them, accompanied by the ringing of a sonorous metal struck by a mallet, summoned the worshippers to prayers, at regular seasons. [63] No image was allowed in the edifice, as un-

---

[59] "Verdaderamente los Dioses que io adoro, que son ídolos de piedra que no hablan, ni sienten, no pudiéron hacer ni formar la hermosura del cielo, el sol, luna, y estrellas que lo hermosean, y dan luz á la tierra, rios, aguas, y fuentes, árboles, y plantas que la hermosean, las gentes que la poseen, y todo lo criado; algun Dios muy poderoso, oculto, y no conocido es el Criador de todo el universo. El solo es él que puede consolarme en mi afliccion, y socorrerme en tan grande angustia como mi corazon siente." MS. de Ixtlilxochitl.

[60] MS. de Ixtlilxochitl.
The manuscript here quoted is one of the many left by the author on the antiquities of his country, and forms part of a voluminous compilation made in Mexico by father Vega, in 1792, by order of the Spanish government. See *Appendix, Part 2, No. 2.*

[61] "Al Dios no conocido, causa de las causas." MS. de Ixtlilxochitl.

[62] Their earliest temples were dedicated to the Sun. The Moon tney worshipped as his wife, and the Stars as his sisters. (Veytia, Hist. Antig., tom. 1, cap. 25.) The ruins still existing at Teotihuacan, about seven leagues from Mexico, are supposed to have been temples, raised by this ancient people, in honor of the two great deities. Boturini, Idea, p. 42.

[63] MS. de Ixtlilxochitl.
"This was evidently a *gong*," says Mr. Ranking, who treads with enviable confi-

suited to the "invisible God"; and the people were expressly prohibited from profaning the altars with blood, or any other sacrifices than that of the perfume of flowers and sweet-scented gums.

The remainder of his days was chiefly spent in his delicious solitudes of Tezcotzinco, where he devoted himself to astronomical and, probably, astrological studies, and to meditation on his immortal destiny,—giving utterance to his feelings in songs, or rather hymns, of much solemnity and pathos. An extract from one of these will convey some idea of his religious speculations. The pensive tenderness of the verses quoted in a preceding page is deepened here into a mournful, and even gloomy coloring; while the wounded spirit, instead of seeking relief in the convivial sallies of a young and buoyant temperament, turns for consolation to the world beyond the grave.

"All things on earth have their term, and, in the most joyous career of their vanity and splendor, their strength fails, and they sink into the dust. All the round world is but a sepulchre; and there is nothing, which lives on its surface, that shall not be hidden and entombed beneath it. Rivers, torrents, and streams move onward to their destination. Not one flows back to its pleasant source. They rush onward, hastening to bury themselves in the deep bosom of the ocean. The things of yesterday are no more to-day; and the things of to-day shall cease, perhaps, on the morrow.[64] The cemetery is full of the loathsome dust of bodies once quickened by living souls, who occupied thrones, presided over assemblies, marshalled armies, subdued provinces, arrogated to themselves worship, were puffed up with vainglorious pomp, and power, and empire.

"But these glories have all passed away, like the fearful smoke that issues from the throat of Popocatepetl, with no other memorial of their existence than the record on the page of the chronicler.

"The great, the wise, the valiant, the beautiful—alas! where are they now? They are all mingled with the clod; and that which has befallen them shall happen to us, and to those that come after us. Yet let us take courage, illustrious nobles and chieftains, true friends and loyal subjects, —*let us aspire to that heaven, where all is eternal, and corruption cannot come.*[65] The horrors of the tomb are but the cradle of the Sun, and the dark shadows of death are brilliant lights for the stars." [66] The mys-

dence over the "suppositos cineres," in the path of the antiquary. See his Historical Researches on the Conquest of Peru, Mexico, &c., by the Mongols, (London, 1827,) p. 310.

[64] "Toda la redondez de la tierra es un sepulcro: no hay cosa que sustente que con título de piedad no la esconda y entierre. Corren los rios, los arroyos, las fuentes, y las aguas, y ningunas retroceden para sus alegres nacimientos: aceleranse con ansia para los vastos dominios de Tlulóca [Neptuno], y cuanto mas se arriman á sus dilatadas márgenes, tanto mas van labrando las melancólicas urnas para sepultarse. Lo que fué ayer no es hoy, ni lo de hoy se afianza que será mañana."

[65] "Aspiremos al cielo, que allí todo es terno y nada se corrompe."

[66] "El horror del sepulcro es lisongera cuna para él, y las funestas sombras, brillantes luces para los astros."

The original text and a Spanish translation of this poem first appeared, I believe, in a work of Granados y Galvez. (Tardes Americanas, (México, 1778,) p. 90 et seq.)

tic import of the last sentence seems to point to that superstition respecting the mansions of the Sun, which forms so beautiful a contrast to the dark features of the Aztec mythology.

At length, about the year 1470,[67] Nezahualcoyotl, full of years and honors, felt himself drawing near his end. Almost half a century had elapsed since he mounted the throne of Tezcuco. He had found the kingdom dismembered by faction, and bowed to the dust beneath the yoke of a foreign tyrant. He had broken that yoke; had breathed new life into the nation, renewed its ancient institutions, extended wide its domain; had seen it flourishing in all the activity of trade and agriculture, gathering strength from its enlarged resources, and daily advancing higher and higher in the great march of civilization. All this he had seen, and might fairly attribute no small portion of it to his own wise and beneficent rule. His long and glorious day was now drawing to its close; and he contemplated the event with the same serenity, which he had shown under the clouds of its morning and in its meridian splendor.

A short time before his death, he gathered around him those of his children in whom he most confided, his chief counsellors, the ambassadors of Mexico, and Tlacopan, and his little son, the heir to the crown, his only offspring by the queen. He was then not eight years old; but had already given, as far as so tender a blossom might, the rich promise of future excellence.[68]

After tenderly embracing the child, the dying monarch threw over him the robes of sovereignty. He then gave audience to the ambassadors, and, when they had retired, made the boy repeat the substance of the conversation. He followed this by such counsels as were suited to his comprehension, and which, when remembered through the long vista of after years, would serve as lights to guide him in his government of the kingdom. He besought him not to neglect the worship of "the unknown God," regretting that he himself had been unworthy to know him, and intimating his conviction that the time would come when he should be known and worshipped throughout the land.[69]

The original is in the Otomie tongue, and both, together with a French version, have been inserted by M. Ternaux-Compans in the Appendix to his translation of Ixtlil-xochitl's Hist. des Chichimêques (tom. I. pp. 359-367.) Bustamante, who has, also, published the Spanish version in his Galería de Antiguos Príncipes Mejicanos, (Puebla, 1821, (pp. 16, 17),) calls it the "Ode of the Flower," which was recited at a banquet of the great Tezcucan nobles. If this last, however, be the same mentioned by Torquemada, (Monarch. Ind., lib. 2, cap. 45,) it must have been written in the Tezcucan tongue; and, indeed, it is not probable that the Otomie, an Indian dialect, so distinct from the languages of Anahuac, however well understood by the royal poet, could have been comprehended by a miscellaneous audience of his countrymen.

[67] An approximation to a date is the most one can hope to arrive at with Ixtlil-xochitl, who has entangled his chronology in a manner beyond my skill to unravel. Thus, after telling us that Nezahualcoyotl was fifteen years old when his father was slain in 1418, he says he died at the age of seventy-one, in 1462. *Instar omnium.* Comp. Hist. Chich., MS., cap. 18, 19, 49.

[68] MS. de Ixtlilxochitl,—also, Hist. Chich., MS., cap. 49.

[69] "No consentiendo que haya sacrificios de gente humana, que Dios se enoja de ello, castigando con rigor á los que lo hicieren; que el dolor que llevo es no tener luz.

He next addressed himself to that one of his sons, in whom he placed the greatest trust, and whom he had selected as the guardian of the realm. "From this hour," said he to him, "you will fill the place that I have filled, of father to this child; you will teach him to live as he ought; and by your counsels he will rule over the empire. Stand in his place, and be his guide, till he shall be of age to govern for himself." Then, turning to his other children, he admonished them to live united with one another, and to show all loyalty to their prince, who, though a child, already manifested a discretion far above his years. "Be true to him," he added, "and he will maintain you in your rights and dignities." [70]

Feeling his end approaching, he exclaimed, "Do not bewail me with idle lamentations. But sing the song of gladness, and show a courageous spirit, that the nations I have subdued may not believe you disheartened, but may feel that each one of you is strong enough to keep them in obedience!" The undaunted spirit of the monarch shone forth even in the agonies of death. That stout heart, however, melted, as he took leave of his children and friends, weeping tenderly over them, while he bade each a last adieu. When they had withdrawn, he ordered the officers of the palace to allow no one to enter it again. Soon after, he expired, in the seventy-second year of his age, and the forty-third of his reign. [71]

Thus died the greatest monarch, and, if one foul blot could be effaced, perhaps the best, who ever sat upon an Indian throne. His character is delineated with tolerable impartiality by his kinsman, the Tezcucan chronicler. "He was wise, valiant, liberal; and, when we consider the magnanimity of his soul, the grandeur and success of his enterprises, his deep policy, as well as daring, we must admit him to have far surpassed every other prince and captain of this New World. He had few failings himself, and rigorously punished those of others. He preferred the public to his private interest; was most charitable in his nature, often buying articles, at double their worth, of poor and honest persons, and giving them away again to the sick and infirm. In seasons of scarcity he was particularly bountiful, remitting the taxes of his vassals, and supplying their wants from the royal granaries. He put no faith in the idolatrous worship of the country. He was well instructed in moral science, and sought, above all things, to obtain light for knowing the true God. He believed in one God only, the Creator of heaven and earth, by whom we have our being, who never revealed himself to us in human form, nor in any other; with whom the souls of the virtuous are to dwell after death, while the wicked will suffer pains unspeakable. He invoked the Most High, as 'He by whom we live,' and 'Who has all things in himself.' He recognised the Sun for his father, and the Earth for his

---

ni conocimiento, ni ser merecedor de conocer tan gran Dios, el qual tengo por cierto que ya que los presentes no lo conozcan, *ha de venir tiempo en que sea conocido y adorado en esta tierra.*" MS. de Ixtlilxochitl.

[70] Idem, ubi supra; also Hist. Chich., cap. 40.

[71] Hist. Chich., cap. 49.

mother. He taught his children not to confide in idols, and only to con-
form to the outward worship of them with deference to public opinion.[72]
If he could not entirely abolish human sacrifices, derived from the
Aztecs, he, at least, restricted them to slaves and captives." [73]

I have occupied so much space with this illustrious prince, that but
little remains for his son and successor, Nezahualpilli. I have thought it
better, in our narrow limits, to present a complete view of a single epoch,
the most interesting in the Tezcucan annals, than to spread the inquiries
over a broader, but comparatively barren field. Yet Nezahualpilli, the
heir to the crown, was a remarkable person, and his reign contains many
incidents, which I regret to be obliged to pass over in silence.[74]

He had, in many respects, a taste similar to his father's, and, like
him, displayed a profuse magnificence in his way of living and in his
public edifices. He was more severe in his morals; and, in the execution
of justice, stern even to the sacrifice of natural affection. Several remarkable instances of this are told; one, among others, in relation to his
eldest son, the heir to the crown, a prince of great promise. The young
man entered into a poetical correspondence with one of his father's concubines, the lady of Tula, as she was called, a woman of humble origin,
but of uncommon endowments. She wrote verses with ease, and could
discuss graver matters with the king and his ministers. She maintained a
separate establishment, where she lived in state, and acquired, by her
beauty and accomplishments, great ascendency over her royal lover.[75]
With this favorite the prince carried on a correspondence in verse,—
whether of an amorous nature does not appear. At all events, the offence
was capital. It was submitted to the regular tribunal, who pronounced
sentence of death on the unfortunate youth; and the king, steeling his
heart against all entreaties and the voice of nature, suffered the cruel
judgment to be carried into execution. We might, in this case, suspect
the influence of baser passions on his mind, but it was not a solitary
instance of his inexorable justice towards those most near to him. He

---

[72] "Solia amonestar á sus hijos en secreto que no adorasen á aquellas figuras de
ídolos, y que aquello que hiciesen en público fuese *solo por cumplimiento.*" Ibid.

[73] Idem, ubi supra.

[74] The name *Nezahualpilli* signifies "the prince for whom one has fasted,"—in allusion, no doubt, to the long fast of his father previous to his birth. (See Ixtlilxochitl, Hist. Chich., MS., cap. 45.) I have explained the meaning of the equally
euphonious name of his parent, Nezahualcoyotl. (Ante, ch. 4.) If it be true, that
"Cæsar or Epaminondas
Could ne'er without names have been known to us."
it is no less certain that such names as those of the two Tezcucan princes, so difficult
to be pronounced or remembered by a European, are most unfavorable to immortality.

[75] "De las concubinas la que mas privó con el rey, fué la que llamaban la Señora
de Tula, no por linage, sino porque era hija de un mercader, y era tan sabia que
competia con el rey y con los mas sabios de su reyno, y era en la poesía muy
aventajada, que con estas gracias y dones naturales tenia al rey muy sugeto á su
voluntad de tal manera que lo que queria alcanzaba de él, y así vivia sola por sí
con grande aparato y magestad en unos palacios que el rey le mandó edificar."
Ixtlilxochitl, Hist. Chich., MS., cap. 57.

had the stern virtue of an ancient Roman, destitute of the softer graces which make virtue attractive. When the sentence was carried into effect, he shut himself up in his palace for many weeks, and commanded the doors and windows of his son's residence to be walled up, that it might never again be occupied.[76]

Nezahualpilli resembled his father in his passion for astronomical studies, and is said to have had an observatory on one of his palaces.[77] He was devoted to war in his youth, but, as he advanced in years, resigned himself to a more indolent way of life, and sought his chief amusement in the pursuit of his favorite science, or in the soft pleasures of the sequestered gardens of Tezcotzinco. This quiet life was ill suited to the turbulent temper of the times, and of his Mexican rival, Montezuma. The distant provinces fell off from their allegiance; the army relaxed its discipline; disaffection crept into its ranks; and the wily Montezuma, partly by violence, and partly by stratagems unworthy of a king, succeeded in plundering his brother monarch of some of his most valuable domains. Then it was, that he arrogated to himself the title and supremacy of emperor, hitherto borne by the Tezcucan princes, as head of the alliance. Such is the account given by the historians of that nation, who, in this way, explain the acknowledged superiority of the Aztec sovereign, both in territory and consideration, on the landing of the Spaniards.[78]

These misfortunes pressed heavily on the spirits of Nezahaulpilli. Their effect was increased by certain gloomy prognostics of a near calamity which was to overwhelm the country.[79] He withdrew to his retreat, to brood in secret over his sorrows. His health rapidly declined; and in the year 1515, at the age of fifty-two, he sunk into the grave;[80] happy, at least, that, by this timely death, he escaped witnessing the fulfilment

[76] Ibid., cap. 67.
The Tezcucan historian records several appalling examples of this severity;—one in particular, in relation to his guilty wife. The story, reminding one of the tales of an Oriental harem, has been translated for the *Appenaix, Part 2, No. 3.* See also Torquemada, (Monarch. Ind., lib. 2, cap. 66,) ana Zurita (Rapport, pp. 108, 109). He was the terror, in particular, of all unjust magistrates. They had little favor to expect from the man who could stifle the voice or nature in his own bosom, in obedience to the laws. As Suetonius said of a prince who had not his virtue, "Vehemens et in coercendis quidem delictis immodicus." Vita Galbæ, sec. 9.

[77] Torquemada saw the remains of this, *or what passea for such,* in his day. Monarch. Ind., lib. 2, cap. 64.

[78] Ixtlilxochitl, Hist. Chich., MS., cap. 73, 74.
This sudden transfer of empire from the Tezcucans, at the close of the reigns of two of their ablest monarchs, is so improbable, that one cannot but doubt if they ever possessed it,—at least, to the extent claimed by the patriotic historian. See Ante, Chap. 1, note 25, and the corresponding text.

[79] Ixtlilxochitl, Hist. Chich., MS., cap. 72.
The reader will find a particular account of these prodigies, better authenticated than most miracles, in a future page of this History.

[80] Ibid., cap. 75.—Or, rather, at the age of fifty, if the historian is right, in placing his birth, as he does, in a preceding chapter, in 1465. (See cap. 46.) It is not easy to decide what is true, when the writer does not take the trouble to be true to himself

of his own predictions, in the ruin of his country, and the extinction of the Indian dynasties, for ever.[81]

In reviewing the brief sketch here presented of the Tezcucan monarchy, we are strongly impressed with the conviction of its superiority, in all the great features of civilization, over the rest of Anahuac. The Mexicans showed a similar proficiency, no doubt, in the mechanic arts, and even in mathematical science. But in the science of government, in legislation, in speculative doctrines of a religious nature, in the more elegant pursuits of poetry, eloquence, and whatever depended on refinement of taste and a polished idiom, they confessed themselves inferior, by resorting to their rivals for instruction, and citing their works as the masterpieces of their tongue. The best histories, the best poems, the best code of laws, the purest dialect, were all allowed to be Tezcucan. The Aztecs rivalled their neighbours in splendor of living, and even in the magnificence of their structures. They displayed a pomp and ostentatious pageantry, truly Asiatic. But this was the development of the material, rather than the intellectual principle. They wanted the refinement of manners essential to a continued advance in civilization. An insurmountable limit was put to theirs, by that bloody mythology, which threw its withering taint over the very air that they breathed.

The superiority of the Tezcucans was owing, doubtless, in a great measure, to that of the two sovereigns whose reigns we have been depicting. There is no position, which affords such scope for ameliorating the condition of man, as that occupied by an absolute ruler over a nation imperfectly civilized. From his elevated place, commanding all the resources of his age, it is in his power to diffuse them far and wide among his people. He may be the copious reservoir on the mountain top, drinking in the dews of heaven, to send them in fertilizing streams along the lower slopes and valleys, clothing even the wilderness in beauty. Such were Nezahualcoyotl, and his illustrious successor, whose enlightened policy, extending through nearly a century, wrought a most salutary revolution in the condition of their country. It is remarkable that we, the inhabitants of the same continent, should be more familiar with the history of many a barbarian chief, both in the Old and New World, than with that of these truly great men, whose names are identified with the most glorious period in the annals of the Indian races.

What was the actual amount of the Tezcucan civilization, it is not easy to determine, with the imperfect light afforded us. It was certainly far below any thing, which the word conveys, measured by a European standard. In some of the arts, and in any walk of science, they could only have made, as it were, a beginning. But they had begun in the right

[81] His obsequies were celebrated with sanguinary pomp. Two hundred male and one hundred female slaves were sacrificed at his tomb. His body was consumed, amidst a heap of jewels, precious stuffs, and incense, on a funeral pile; and the ashes, deposited in a golden urn, were placed in the great temple of Huitzilopotchli, for whose worship the king, notwithstanding the lessons of his father, had some partiality. Ibid.

way, and already showed a refinement in sentiment and manners, a capacity for receiving instruction, which, under good auspices, might have led them on to infinite improvement. Unhappily, they were fast falling under the dominion of the warlike Aztecs. And that people repaid the benefits received from their more polished neighbors by imparting to them their own ferocious superstition, which, falling like a mildew on the land, would soon have blighted its rich blossoms of promise, and turned even its fruits to dust and ashes.

Fernando de Alva Ixtlilxochitl, who flourished in the beginning of the sixteenth century, was a native of Tezcuco, and descended in a direct line from the sovereigns of that kingdom. The royal posterity became so numerous in a few generations, that it was common to see them reduced to great poverty, and earning a painful subsistence by the most humble occupations. Ixtlilxochitl, who was descended from the principal wife or queen of Nezahualpilli, maintained a very respectable position. He filled the office of interpreter to the viceroy, to which he was recommended by his acquaintance with the ancient hieroglyphics, and his knowledge of the Mexican and Spanish languages. His birth gave him access to persons of the highest rank in his own nation, some of whom occupied important civil posts under the new government, and were thus enabled to make large collections of Indian manuscripts, which were liberally opened to him. He had an extensive library of his own, also, and with these means diligently pursued the study of the Tezcucan antiquities. He deciphered the hieroglyphics, made himself master of the songs and traditions, and fortified his narrative by the oral testimony of some very aged persons, who had themselves been acquainted with the Conquerors. From such authentic sources he composed various works in the Castilian, on the primitive history of the Toltec and the Tezcucan races, continuing it down to the subversion of the empire by Cortés. These various accounts, compiled under the title of *Relaciones*, are, more or less, repetitions and abridgments of each other; nor is it easy to understand why they were thus composed. The *Historia Chichemeca* is the best digested and most complete of the whole series; and as such has been the most frequently consulted, for the preceding pages.

Ixtlilxochitl's writings have many of the defects belonging to his age. He often crowds the page with incidents of a trivial, and sometimes improbable character. The improbability increases with the distance of the period; for distance, which diminishes objects to the natural eye, exaggerates them to the mental. His chronology, as I have more than once noticed, is inextricably entangled. He has often lent a too willing ear to traditions and reports which would startle the more skeptical criticism of the present time. Yet there is an appearance of good faith and simplicity in his writings, which may convince the reader, that, when he errs, it is from no worse cause than national partiality. And surely such partiality is excusable in the descendant of a proud line, shorn of its ancient splendors, which it was soothing to his own feelings to revive again,—though with something more than their legitimate lustre,—on the canvas of history. It should also be considered, that, if his narrative is sometimes startling, his researches penetrate into the mysterious depths of antiquity, where light and darkness meet and melt into each other; and when everything is still further liable to distortion, as seen through the misty medium of hieroglyphics.

With these allowances, it will be found that the Tezcucan historian has just claims to our admiration for the compass of his inquiries, and the sagacity with which they have been conducted. He has introduced us to the knowledge of the most polished people of Anahuac, whose records, if preserved, could not, at a much later period, have been comprehended; and he has thus afforded a standard of comparison, which much raises our ideas of American civilization. His language is simple, and, occasionally, eloquent and touching. His descriptions are highly picturesque. He abounds in familiar anecdote; and the natural graces of his manner, in detailing the more striking events of history, and the personal adventures of his heroes, entitle him to the name of the Livy of Anahuac.

I shall be obliged to enter hereafter into his literary merits, in connection with the narrative of the Conquest; for which he is a prominent authority. His earlier annals—though no one of his manuscripts has been printed—have been diligently studied by the Spanish writers in Mexico, and liberally transferred to their pages; and his reputation, like Sahagun's, has doubtless suffered by the process. His *Historia Chichemeca* is now turned into French by M. Ternaux-Compans, forming part of that inestimable series of translations from unpublished documents, which have so much enlarged our acquaintaince with the early American history. I have had ample opportunity of proving the merits of his version of Ixtlilxochitl; and am happy to bear my testimony to the fidelity and elegance with which it is executed.

NOTE. It was my intention to conclude this Introductory portion of the work with an inquiry into the *Origin of the Mexican Civilization.* "But the general question of the origin of the inhabitants of a continent," says Humboldt, "is beyond the limits prescribed to history; perhaps it is not even a philosophic question." "For the majority of readers," says Livy, "the origin and remote antiquities of a nation can have comparatively little interest." The criticism of these great writers is just and pertinent; and, on further consideration, I have thrown the observations on this topic, prepared with some care, into the *Appendix (Part* 1); to which those, who feel sufficient curiosity in the discussion, can turn before entering on the narrative of the Conquest.

BOOK II

DISCOVERY OF MEXICO

CHAPTER I

Spain under Charles V—Progress of Discovery—Colonial Policy
—Conquest of Cuba—Expedition to Yucatan

1516 — 1518

In the beginning of the sixteenth century, Spain occupied perhaps the most prominent position in the theatre of Europe. The numerous states, into which she had been so long divided, were consolidated into one monarchy. The Moslem crescent, after reigning there for eight centuries, was no longer seen on her borders. The authority of the crown did not, as in later times, overshadow the inferior orders of the state. The people enjoyed the inestimable privilege of political representation, and exercised it with manly independence. The nation at large could boast as great a degree of constitutional freedom, as any other, at that time, in Christendom. Under a system of salutary laws and an equitable administration domestic tranquillity was secured, public credit established, trade, manufactures, and even the more elegant arts, began to flourish; while a higher education called forth the first blossoms of that literature, which was to ripen into so rich a harvest, before the close of the century. Arms abroad kept pace with arts at home. Spain found her empire suddenly enlarged by important acquisitions both in Europe and Africa, while a New World beyond the waters poured into her lap treasures of countless wealth, and opened an unbounded field for honorable enterprise.

Such was the condition of the kingdom at the close of the long and glorious reign of Ferdinand and Isabella, when, on the 23d of January, 1516, the sceptre passed into the hands of their daughter Joanna, or rather their grandson, Charles the Fifth, who alone ruled the monarchy during the long and imbecile existence of his unfortunate mother. During the two years following Ferdinand's death, the regency, in the absence of Charles, was held by Cardinal Ximenes, a man whose intrepidity, extraordinary talents, and capacity for great enterprises were accompanied by a haughty spirit, which made him too indifferent as to the means of their execution. His administration, therefore, notwithstanding the uprightness of his intentions, was, from his total disregard of forms, unfavorable to constitutional liberty; for respect for forms is an essential

element of freedom. With all his faults, however, Ximenes was a Spaniard; and the object he had at heart was the good of his country.

It was otherwise on the arrival of Charles, who, after a long absence,
came as a foreigner into the land of his fathers. (November, 1517.) His
manners, sympathies, even his language, were foreign, for he spoke the
Castilian with difficulty. He knew little of his native country, of the
character of the people or their institutions. He seemed to care still less
for them; while his natural reserve precluded that freedom of communication, which might have counteracted to some extent, at least, the
errors of education. In everything, in short, he was a foreigner, and resigned himself to the direction of his Flemish counsellors with a docility
that gave little augury of his future greatness.

On his entrance into Castile, the young monarch was accompanied
by a swarm of courtly sycophants, who settled, like locusts, on every
place of profit and honor throughout the kingdom. A Fleming was made
grand chancellor of Castile; another Fleming was placed in the archie-·
piscopal see of Toledo. They even ventured to profane the sanctity of the
córtes by intruding themselves on its deliberations. Yet that body did
not tamely submit to these usurpations, but gave vent to its indignation
in tones becoming the representatives of a free people.[1]

The deportment of Charles, so different from that to which the Spaniards had been accustomed under the benign administration of Ferdi·
nand and Isabella, closed all hearts against him; and, as his character
came to be understood, instead of the spontaneous outpourings of loyalty, which usually greet the accession of a new and youthful sovereign,
he was everywhere encountered by opposition and disgust. In Castile,
and afterwards in Aragon, Catalonia, and Valencia, the commons hesitated to confer on him the title of *King* during the lifetime of his
mother; and, though they eventually yielded this point, and associated his name with hers in the sovereignty, yet they reluctantly granted
the supplies he demanded, and, when they did so, watched over their
appropriation with a vigilance which left little to gratify the cupidity of
the Flemings. The language of the legislature on these occasions, though
temperate and respectful, breathes a spirit of resolute independence not
to be found, probably, on the parliamentary records of any other nation
at that period. No wonder that Charles should have early imbibed a
disgust for these popular assemblies,—the only bodies whence truths so

---

[1] The following passage—one among many—from that faithful mirror of the
times, Peter Martyr's correspondence, does ample justice to the intemperance, avarice, and intolerable arrogance of the Flemings. The testimony is worth the more, as
coming from one who, though resident in Spain, waꞏ not a Spaniard. "Crumenas
auro fulcire inhiant; huic uni studio invigilant. Nec detrectat ju venis Rex. Farcit
quacunque posse datur; non satiat tamen. Quæ qualisve sit gens hæc, depingere
adhuc nescio. Insufflat vulgus hic in omne genus hominum non arctoum. Minores
faciunt Hispanos, quam si nati essent inter eorum cloacas. Rugiunt jam Hispani,
labra mordent, submurmurant taciti, fatorum vices tales esse conqueruntur, quod
ipsi domitores regnorum ita floccifiant ab his, quorum Deus unicus (sub rege tem-
perato) Bacchus est cum Citherea." Opus Epistolarum, (Amstelodami, 1610,) ep
608.

unpalatable could find their way to the ears of the sovereign! [2] **Unfor-**
tunately, they had no influence on his conduct; till the discontent, long
allowed to fester in secret, broke out into that sad war of the *comunidades,* which shook the state to its foundations, and ended in the subversion of its liberties.

The same pestilent foreign influence was felt, though much less sensibly, in the Colonial administration. This had been placed, in the preceding reign, under the immediate charge of the two great tribunals,
the Council of the Indies, and the *Casa de Contratacion,* or India House,
at Seville. It was their business to further the progress of discovery,
watch over the infant settlements, and adjust the disputes which grew
up in them. But the licenses granted to private adventurers did more
for the cause of discovery, than the patronage of the crown or its officers. The long peace, enjoyed with slight interruption by Spain in the
early part of the sixteenth century, was most auspicious for this; and
the restless cavalier, who could no longer win laurels on the fields of
Africa or Europe, turned with eagerness to the brilliant career opened
to him beyond the ocean.

It is difficult for those of our time, as familiar from childhood with the
most remote places on the globe as with those in their own neighborhood,
to picture to themselves the feelings of the men who lived in the sixteenth
century. The dread mystery, which had so long hung over the great deep,
had, indeed, been removed. It was no longer beset with the same undefined horrors as when Columbus launched his bold bark on its dark and
unknown waters. A new and glorious world had been thrown open. But
as to the precise spot where that world lay, its extent, its history, whether
it were island or continent,—of all this, they had very vague and confused conceptions. Many, in their ignorance, blindly adopted the erroneous conclusion into which the great Admiral had been led by his superior science,—that the new countries were a part of Asia; and, as the mariner wandered among the Bahamas, or steered his caravel across the
Caribbean seas, he fancied he was inhaling the rich odors of the spice-
islands in the Indian Ocean. Thus every fresh discovery, interpreted by
this previous delusion, served to confirm him in his error, or, at least,
to fill his mind with new perplexities.

The career thus thrown open had all the fascinations of a desperate
hazard, on which the adventurer staked all his hopes of fortune, fame,
and life itself. It was not often indeed, that he won the rich prize which
he most coveted; but then he was sure to win the meed of glory, scarcely
less dear to his chivalrous spirit; and, if he survived to return to his
home, he had wonderful stories to recount, of perilous chances among

[2] Yet the nobles were not all backward in manifesting their disgust. When Charles
would have conferred the famous Burgundian order of the Golden Fleece on the
Count of Benavente, that lord refused it, proudly telling him, "I am a Castilian.
I desire no honors but those of my own country, in my opinion, quite as good as—
indeed, better than those of any other." Sandoval, Historia de la Vida y Hechos del
Emperador Cárlos V., (Ambéres, 1681,) tom. I. p. 102.

the strange people he had visited, and the burning climes, whose rank fertility and magnificence of vegetation so far surpassed any thing he had witnessed in his own. These reports added fresh fuel to imaginations already warmed by the study of those tales of chivalry which formed the favorite reading of the Spaniards, at that period. Thus romance and reality acted on each other, and the soul of the Spaniard was exalted to that pitch of enthusiasm, which enabled him to encounter the terrible trials that lay in the path of the discoverer. Indeed, the life of the cavalier of that day was romance put into action. The story of his adventures in the New World forms one of the most remarkable pages in the history of man.

Under this chivalrous spirit of enterprise, the progress of discovery had extended, by the beginning of Charles the Fifth's reign, from the Bay of Honduras, along the winding shores of Darien, and the South American continent, to the Rio de la Plata. The mighty barrier of the Isthmus had been climbed, and the Pacific descried, by Nuñez de Balboa, second only to Columbus in this valiant band of "ocean chivalry." The Bahamas and Caribbee Islands had been explored, as well as the Peninsula of Florida on the northern continent. To this latter point Sebastian Cabot had arrived in his descent along the coast from Labrador, in 1497. So that before 1518, the period when our narrative begins, the eastern borders of both the great continents had been surveyed through nearly their whole extent. The shores of the great Mexican Gulf, however, sweeping with a wide circuit far into the interior, remained still concealed, with the rich realms that lay beyond, from the eye of the navigator. The time had now come for their discovery.

The business of colonization had kept pace with that of discovery. In several of the islands, and in various parts of Terra Firma, and in Darien, settlements had been established, under the control of governors who affected the state and authority of viceroys. Grants of land were assigned to the colonists, on which they raised the natural products of the soil, but gave still more attention to the sugar-cane, imported from the Canaries. Sugar, indeed, together with the beautiful dye-woods of the country and the precious metals, formed almost the only articles of export in the infancy of the colonies, which had not yet introduced those other staples of the West Indian commerce, which, in our day, constitute its principal wealth. Yet the precious metals, painfully gleaned from a few scanty sources, would have made poor returns, but for gratuitous labor of the Indians.

The cruel system of *repartimientos*, or distribution of the Indians as slaves among the conquerors, had been suppressed by Isabella. Although subsequently countenanced by the government, it was under the most careful limitations. But it is impossible to license crime by halves,—to authorize injustice at all, and hope to regulate the measure of it. The eloquent remonstrances of the Dominicans,—who devoted themselves to the good work of conversion in the New World with the same zeal that they showed for persecution in the Old,—but, above all, those of Las Casas, induced the regent, Ximenes, to send out a commission with full powers to inquire into the alleged grievances, and to redress them. It had authority, moreover, to investigate the conduct of the civil officers, and to reform any abuses in their administration. This extraordinary commission consisted of three Hieronymite friars and an eminent jurist, all men of learning and unblemished piety.

They conducted the inquiry in a very dispassionate manner; but, after long deliberation, came to a conclusion most unfavorable to the demands of Las Casas, who insisted on the entire freedom of the natives. This conclusion they justified on the grounds, that the Indians would not labor without compulsion, and that, unless they labored, they could not be brought into communication with the whites, nor be converted to Christianity. Whatever we may think of this argument, it was doubtless urged with sincerity by its advocates, whose conduct through their whole administration places their motives above suspicion. They accompanied it with many careful provisions for the protection of the natives. But in vain. The simple people, accustomed all their days to a life of indolence and ease, sunk under the oppressions of their masters, and the population wasted away with even more frightful rapidity than did the Aborigines in our own country, under the operation of other causes. It is not necessary to pursue these details further, into which I have been led by the desire to put the reader in possession of the general policy and state of affairs in the New World, at the period when the present narrative begins.[3]

Of the islands, Cuba was the second discovered; but no attempt had been made to plant a colony there during the lifetime of Columbus; who, indeed, after skirting the whole extent of its southern coast, died in the conviction that it was part of the continent.[4] At length, in 1511, Diego, the son and successor of the "Admiral," who still maintained the seat of government in Hispaniola, finding the mines much exhausted there, proposed to occupy the neighboring island of Cuba, or Fernandina, as it was called, in compliment to the Spanish monarch.[5] He prepared a small force for the conquest, which he placed under the command of Don Diego Velasquez; a man described by a contemporary, as "possessed of considerable experience in military affairs, having served seventeen years in the European wars; as honest, illustrious by his line-

---

[3] I will take the liberty to refer the reader, who is desirous of being more minutely acquainted with the Spanish colonial administration and the state of discovery previous to Charles V., to the "History of the Reign of Ferdinand and Isabella," (Part 2, ch. 9, 26,) where the subject is treated *in extenso*.

[4] See the curious document attesting this, and drawn up by order of Columbus. ap. Navarrete, Coleccion de los Viages y de Descubrimientos, (Madrid, 1825,) tom. II. Col. Dip., No. 76.

[5] The island was originally called by Columbus, Juana, in honor of prince John, heir to the Castilian crown. After his death, it received the name of Fernandina, at the king's desire. The Indian name has survived both. Herrera, Hist. General. Descrip., cap. 6.

age and reputation, covetous of glory, and somewhat more covetous of wealth." [6] The portrait was sketched by no unfriendly hand.

Velasquez, or rather, his lieutenant, Narvaez, who took the office on himself of scouring the country, met with no serious opposition from the inhabitants, who were of the same family with the effeminate natives of Hispaniola. The conquest, through the merciful interposition of Las Casas, "the protector of the Indians," who accompanied the army in its march, was effected without much bloodshed. One chief, indeed, named Hatuey, having fled originally from St. Domingo to escape the oppression of its invaders, made a desperate resistance, for which he was condemned by Velasquez to be burned alive. It was he who made that memorable reply, more eloquent than a volume of invective. When urged at the stake to embrace Christianity, that his soul might find admission into heaven, he inquired if the white men would go there. On being answered in the affirmative, he exclaimed, "Then I will not be a Christian; for I would not go again to a place where I must find men so cruel!"[7]

After the conquest, Velasquez, now appointed governor, diligently occupied himself with measures for promoting the prosperity of the Island. He formed a number of settlements, bearing the same names with the modern towns, and made St. Jago, on the south-east corner, the seat of government.[8] He invited settlers by liberal grants of land and slaves. He encouraged them to cultivate the soil, and gave particular attention to the sugar-cane, so profitable an article of commerce in later times. He was, above all, intent on working the gold mines, which promised better returns than those in Hispaniola. The affairs of his government did not prevent him, meanwhile, from casting many a wistful glance at the discoveries going forward on the continent, and he longed for an opportunity to embark in these golden adventures himself. Fortune gave him the occasion he desired.

An *hidalgo* of Cuba, named Hernandez de Cordova, sailed with three vessels on an expedition to one of the neighboring Bahama Islands, in quest of Indian slaves. (February 8, 1517.) He encountered a succession of heavy gales which drove him far out of his course, and at the end of three weeks he found himself on a strange and unknown coast. On landing and asking the name of the country, he was answered by the natives, "*Tectetan,*" meaning "I do not understand you,"—but which the Spaniards, misinterpreting into the name of the place, easily corrupted into

---

[6] "Erat Didacus, ut hoc in loco de eo semel tantum dicamus, veteranus miles, rei militaris gnarus, quippe qui septem et decem annos in Hispania militiam exercitus fuerat, homo probus, opibus, genere et fama clarus, honoris cupidus, pecuniæ aliquanto cupidior." De Rebus Gestis Ferdinandi Cortesii, MS.

[7] The story is told by Las Casas in his appalling record of the cruelties of his countrymen in the New World, which charity—and common sense—may excuse us for believing the good father has greatly overcharged. Brevissima Relacion de la Destruycion de las Indias, (Venetia, 1643,) p. 28.

[8] Among the most ancient of these establishments we find in Havana, Puerto del Príncipe, Trinidad, St. Salvador, and Matanzas, or *the Slaughter,* so called from a massacre of the Spaniards there by the Indians. Bernal Diaz, Hist. de la Conquista, cap. 8.

Yucatan. Some writers give a different etymology.[9] Such mistakes, however, were not uncommon with the early discoverers, and have been the
origin of many a name on the American continent.[10]

Cordova had landed on the north-eastern end of the peninsula, at
Cape Catoche. He was astonished at the size and solid materials of the
buildings constructed of stone and lime, so different from the frail tenements of reeds and rushes which formed the habitations of the islanders.
He was struck, also, with the higher cultivation of the soil, and with the
delicate texture of the cotton garments and gold ornaments of the natives. Every thing indicated a civilization far superior to any thing he
had before witnessed in the New World. He saw the evidence of a different race, moreover, in the warlike spirit of the people. Rumors of the
Spaniards had, perhaps, preceded them, as they were repeatedly asked
if they came from the east; and, wherever they landed, they were met
with the most deadly hostility. Cordova himself, in one of his skirmishes
with the Indians, received more than a dozen wounds, and one only of
his party escaped unhurt. At length, when he had coasted the peninsula
as far as Campeachy, he returned to Cuba, which he reached after an
absence of several months, having suffered all the extremities of ill,
which these pioneers of the ocean were sometimes called to endure, and
which none but the most courageous spirit could have survived. As it
was, half the original number, consisting of one hundred and ten men,
perished, including their brave commander, who died soon after his return. The reports he had brought back of the country, and, still more,
the specimens of curiously wrought gold, convinced Velasquez of the importance of this discovery, and he prepared with all despatch to avail
himself of it.[11]

He accordingly fitted out a little squadron of four vessels for the
newly discovered lands, and placed it under the command of his nephew,
Juan de Grijalva, a man on whose probity, prudence, and attachment
to himself he knew he could rely. The fleet left the port of St. Jago de
Cuba, May 1, 1518.[12] It took the course pursued by Cordova, but was

[9] Gomara, Historia de las Indias, cap. 52, ap. Barcia, tom. II.

Bernal Diaz says the word came from the vegetable *yuca*, and *tale* the name for a
hillock in which it is planted. (Hist. de la Conquista, cap. 6.) M. Waldeck finds a
much more plausible derivation in the Indian word *Ouyouckatan*, "listen to what
they say." Voyage Pittoresque, p. 25.

[10] Two navigators, Solís and Pinzon, had descried the coast as far back as 1506,
according to Herrera, though they had not taken possession of it. (Hist. General,
dec. 1, lib. 6, cap. 17.) It is, indeed, remarkable it should so long have eluded discovery, considering that it is but two degrees distant from Cuba.

[11] Oviedo, General y Natural Historia de las Indias, MS., lib. 33, cap. 1.—De Rebus Gestis, MS.—Carta de Cabido de Vera Cruz, (July 10, 1519,) MS.

Bernal Diaz denies that the original object of the expedition, in which he took
part, was to procure slaves, though Velasquez had proposed it. (Hist. de la Conquista, cap. 2.) But he is contradicted in this by the other contemporary records
above cited.

[12] Itinerario de la isola de Iucha than, novamente ritrovata per il signor Joan de
Grijalva, per il suo capellano, MS.

The chaplain's word may be taken for the date, which is usually put at the eighth
of April.

driven somewhat to the south, the first land that it made being the island of Cozumel. From this quarter Grijalva soon passed over to the continent and coasted the peninsula, touching at the same places as his predecessor. Everywhere he was struck, like him, with the evidences of a higher civilization, especially in the architecture; as he well might be, since this was the region of those extraordinary remains which have become recently the subject of so much speculation. He was astonished, also at the sight of large stone crosses, evidently objects of worship, which he met with in various places. Reminded by these circumstances of his own country, he gave the peninsula the name of "New Spain," a name since appropriated to a much wider extent of territory.[13]

Wherever Grijalva landed, he experienced the same unfriendly reception as Cordova, though he suffered less, being better prepared to meet it. In the *Rio de Tabasco*, or *Grijalva*, as it is often called, after him, he held an amicable conference with a chief who gave him a number of gold plates fashioned into a sort of armor. As he wound round the Mexican coast, one of his captains, Pedro de Alvarado, afterwards famous in the Conquest, entered a river, to which he, also, left his own name. In a neighboring stream, called the *Rio de Vanderas*, or "River of Banners," from the ensigns displayed by the natives on its borders, Grijalva had the first communications with the Mexicans themselves.

The cacique who ruled over this province had received notice of the approach of the Europeans, and of their extraordinary appearance. He was anxious to collect all the information he could respecting them and the motives of their visit, that he might transmit them to his master, the Aztec emperor.[14] A friendly conference took place between the parties on shore, where Grijalva landed with all his force, so as to make a suitable impression on the mind of the barbaric chief. The interview lasted some hours, though, as there was no one on either side to interpret the language of the other, they could communicate only by signs. They, however, interchanged presents, and the Spaniards had the satisfaction of receiving, for a few worthless toys and trinkets, a rich treasure of jewels, gold ornaments and vessels, of the most fantastic forms and workmanship.[15]

Grijalva now thought that in this successful traffic—successful beyond his most sanguine expectations—he had accomplished the chief object of his mission. He steadily refused the solicitations of his followers to plant a colony on the spot,—a work of no little difficulty in so populous and powerful a country as this appeared to be. To this, indeed, he was inclined, but deemed it contrary to his instructions, which limited

---

[13] De Rebus Gestis, MS.—Itinerario del Capellano, MS.

[14] According to the Spanish authorities, the cacique was sent with these presents from the Mexican sovereign, who had received previous tidings of the approach of the Spaniards. I have followed Sahagun, who obtained his intelligence directly from the natives. Historia de la Conquista, MS., cap. 2.

[15] Gomara has given the *per* and *contra* of this negotiation, in which gold and jewels, of the value of fifteen or twenty thousand *pesos de oro*, were exchanged for glass beads, pins, scissors, and other trinkets common in an assorted cargo for savages. Crónica, cap. 6.

him to barter with the natives. He therefore despatched Alvarado in one of the caravels back to Cuba, with the treasure and such intelligence as he had gleaned of the great empire in the interior, and then pursued his voyage along the coast.

He touched at San Juan de Ulua, and at the *Isla de los Sacrificios*, so called by him from the bloody remains of human victims found in one of the temples. He then held on his course as far as the province of Panuco, where finding some difficulty in doubling a boisterous headland, he returned on his track, and, after an absence of nearly six months, reached Cuba in safety. Grijalva has the glory of being the first navigator who set foot on the Mexican soil, and opened an intercourse with the Aztecs.[16]

On reaching the island, he was surprised to learn, that another and more formidable armament had been fitted out to follow up his own discoveries, and to find orders, at the same time, from the governor, couched in no very courteous language, to repair at once to St. Jago. He was received by that personage, not merely with coldness, but with reproaches for having neglected so fair an opportunity of establishing a colony in the country he had visited. Velasquez was one of those captious spirits, who, when things do not go exactly to their minds, are sure to shift the responsibility of the failure from their own shoulders, where it should lie, to those of others. He had an ungenerous nature, says an old writer, credulous, and easily moved to suspicion.[17] In the present instance it was most unmerited. Grijalva, naturally a modest, unassuming person, had acted in obedience to the instructions of his commander, given before sailing; and had done this in opposition to his own judgment and the importunities of his followers. His conduct merited any thing but censure from his employer.[18]

When Alvarado had returned to Cuba with his golden freight, and the accounts of the rich empire of Mexico which he had gathered from the natives, the heart of the governor swelled with rapture as he saw his dreams of avarice and ambition so likely to be realized. Impatient of the long absence of Grijalva, he despatched a vessel in search of him under the command of Olid, a cavalier who took an important part afterwards in the Conquest. Finally he resolved to fit out another armament on a sufficient scale to insure the subjugation of the country.

He previously solicited authority for this from the Hieronymite commission in St. Domingo. He then despatched his chaplain to Spain with the royal share of the gold brought from Mexico, and a full account of the intelligence gleaned there. He set forth his own manifold services, and solicited from the court full powers to go on with the conquest and

---

[16] Itinerario del Capellano, MS.—Carta de Vera Cruz, MS.

[17] "Hombre de terrible condicion," says Herrera, citing the good Bishop of Chiapa, "para los que le servian, i aiudaban, i que facilmente se indignaba contra aquellos." Hist. General, dec. 2, lib. 3, cap. 10.

[18] At least, such is the testimony of Las Casas, who knew both the parties well, and had often conversed with Grijalva upon his voyage. Historia General de las Indias, MS., lib. 3, cap. 113.

colonization of the newly discovered regions.[19] Before receiving an answer, he began his preparations for the armament, and, first of all, endeavoured to find a suitable person to share the expense of it, and to take the command. Such a person he found, after some difficulty and delay, in Hernando Cortés; the man of all others best calculated to achieve this great enterprise,—the last man, to whom Velasquez, could he have foreseen the results, would have confided it.

[19] Itinerario del Capellano, MS.—Las Casas, Hist. de las Indias, MS., lib. 3, cap. 113.

The most circumstantial account of Grijalva's expedition is to be found in the *Itinerary* of his chaplain above quoted. The original is lost, but an indifferent Italian version was published at Venice, in 1522. A copy, which belonged to Ferdinand Columbus, is still extant in the library of the great church of Seville. The book had become so exceedingly rare, however, that the historiographer, Muñoz, made a transcript of it with his own hand, and from his manuscript that in my possession was taken.

HERNANDO CORTÉS—HIS EARLY LIFE—VISITS THE NEW WORLD—HIS RESIDENCE IN CUBA—DIFFICULTIES WITH VELASQUEZ—ARMADA INTRUSTED TO CORTÉS

1518

HERNANDO CORTÉS was born at Medellin, a town in the south-east corner of Estremadura, in 1485.[1] He came of an ancient and respectable family; and historians have gratified the national vanity by tracing it up to the Lombard kings, whose descendants crossed the Pyrenees, and established themselves in Aragon under the Gothic monarchy.[2] This royal genealogy was not found out till Cortés had acquired a name which would confer distinction on any descent, however noble. His father, Martin Cortés de Monroy, was a captain of infantry, in moderate circumstances, but a man of unblemished honor; and both he and his wife, Doña Catalina Pizarro Altamirano, appear to have been much regarded for their excellent qualities.[3]

In his infancy Cortés is said to have had a feeble constitution, which strengthened as he grew older. At fourteen, he was sent to Salamanca, as his father, who conceived great hopes from his quick and showy parts, proposed to educate him for the law, a profession which held out better inducements to the young aspirant than any other. The son, however, did not conform to these views. He showed little fondness for books, and, after loitering away two years at college, returned home, to the great chagrin of his parents. Yet his time had not been wholly misspent,

[1] Gomara, Crónica, cap. 1.—Bernal Diaz, Hist. de la Conquista, cap. 203. I find no more precise notice of the date of his birth; except, indeed, by Pizarro y Orellana, who tells us "that Cortés came into the world the same day that that *infernal beast, the false heretic Luther,* entered it,—by way of compensation, no doubt, since the labors of the one to pull down the true faith were counterbalanced by those of the other to maintain and extend it"! (Varones Ilustres del Nuevo Mundo, (Madrid, 1639,) p. 66.) But this statement of the good cavalier, which places the birth of our hero in 1483, looks rather more like a zeal for "the true faith," than for historic.

[2] Argensola, in particular, has bestowed great pains on the *prosapia* of the house of Cortés; which he traces up, nothing doubting, to Narnes Cortés, king of Lombardy and Tuscany. Anales de Aragon, (Zaragoza, 1630,) pp. 621-625.—Also, Caro de Torres, Historia de las Órdenes Militares, (Madrid, 1629,) fol. 103.

[3] De Rebus Gestis, MS.

Las Casas, who knew the father, bears stronger testimony to his poverty than to his noble birth. "Un escudero," he says of him, "que yo concí harto pobre y humilde, aunque Christiano, viejo *y dizen que hidalgo.*" Hist. de las Índias, MS., lib 3, cap. 27.

since he had laid up a little store of Latin, and learned to write good prose, and even verses "of some estimation, considering"—as an old writer quaintly remarks—"Cortés as the author." [4] He now passed his days in the idle, unprofitable manner of one who, too wilful to be guided by others, proposes no object to himself. His buoyant spirits were continually breaking out in troublesome frolics and capricious humors, quite at variance with the orderly habits of his father's household. He showed a particular inclination for the military profession, or rather for the life of adventure to which in those days it was sure to lead. And when, at the age of seventeen, he proposed to enrol himself under the banners of the Great Captain, his parents, probably thinking a life of hardship and hazard abroad preferable to one of idleness at home, made no objection.

The youthful cavalier, however, hesitated whether to seek his fortunes under that victorious chief, or in the New World, where gold as well as glory was to be won, and where the very dangers had a mystery and romance in them inexpressibly fascinating to a youthful fancy. It was in this direction, accordingly, that the hot spirits of that day found a vent, especially from that part of the country where Cortés lived, the neighborhood of Seville and Cádiz, the focus of nautical enterprise. He decided on this latter course, and an opportunity offered in the splendid armament fitted out under Don Nicholas de Ovando, successor to Columbus. An unlucky accident defeated the purpose of Cortés.[5]

As he was scaling a high wall, one night, which gave him access to the apartment of a lady with whom he was engaged in an intrigue, the stones gave way, and he was thrown down with much violence and buried under the ruins. A severe contusion, though attended with no other serious consequences, confined him to his bed till after the departure of the fleet.[6]

Two years longer he remained at home, profiting little, as it would seem, from the lesson he had received. At length he availed himself of another opportunity presented by the departure of a small squadron of vessels bound to the Indian islands. He was nineteen years of age, when he bade adieu to his native shores in 1504,—the same year in which Spain lost the best and greatest in the long line of princes, Isabella the Catholic.

The vessel in which Cortés sailed was commanded by one Alonso Quintero. The fleet touched at the Canaries, as was common in the outward passage. While the other vessels were detained there taking in supplies, Quintero secretly stole out by night from the island, with the

---

[4] Argensola, Anales, p. 220.

Las Casas and Bernal Diaz both state that he was Bachelor of Laws at Salamanca. (Hist. de las Indias, MS., ubi supra.—Hist. de la Conquista, cap. 203.) The degree was given probably in later life, when the University might feel a pride in claiming nim among her sons.

[5] De Rebus Gestis, MS.—Gomara, Crónica, cap. 1.

[6] De Rebus Gestis, MS.—Gomara, Ibid.

Argensola states the cause of his detention concisely enough; "Suspendió el viaje, por enamora, do y por quartanario." Anales, p. 621.

design of reaching Hispaniola, and securing the market, before the arrival of his companions. A furious storm, which he encountered, however, dismasted his ship, and he was obliged to return to port and refit.
The convoy consented to wait for their unworthy partner, and after a
short detention they all sailed in company again. But the faithless Quintero, as they drew near the Islands, availed himself once more of the
darkness of the night, to leave the squadron with the same purpose as
before. Unluckily for him, he met with a succession of heavy gales and
head winds, which drove him from his course, and he wholly lost his
reckoning. For many days the vessel was tossed about, and all on board
were filled with apprehensions, and no little indignation against the author of their calamities. At length they were cheered one morning with
the sight of a white dove, which, wearied by its flight, lighted on the
topmast. The biographers of Cortés speak of it as a miracle.[7] Fortunately it was no miracle, but a very natural occurrence, showing incon-
testably that they were near land. In a short time, by taking the direction of the bird's flight, they reached the island of Hispaniola; and, on
coming into port, the worthy master had the satisfaction to find his
companions arrived before him, and their cargoes already sold.[8]

Immediately on landing, Cortés repaired to the house of the governor,
to whom he had been personally known in Spain. Ovando was absent on
an expedition into the interior, but the young man was kindly received
by the secretary, who assured him there would be no doubt of his obtaining a liberal grant of land to settle on. "But I came to get gold,"
replied Cortés, "not to till the soil, like a peasant."

On the governor's return, Cortés consented to give up his roving
thoughts, at least for a time, as the other labored to convince him that
he would be more likely to realize his wishes from the slow, indeed, but
sure, returns of husbandry, where the soil and the laborers were a free
gift to the planter, than by taking his chance in the lottery of adventure,
in which there were so many blanks to a prize. He accordingly received
a grant of land, with a *repartimiento* of Indians, and was appointed
notary of the town or settlement of Açua. His graver pursuits, however,
did not prevent his indulgence of the amorous propensities which belong
to the sunny clime where he was born; and this frequently involved him
in affairs of honor, from which, though an expert swordsman, he carried
away scars that accompanied him to his grave.[9] He occasionally, moreover, found the means of breaking up the monotony of his way of life
by engaging in the military expeditions, which, under the command of
Ovando's lieutenant, Diego Velasquez, were employed to suppress the
insurrections of the natives. In this school the young adventurer first

[7] Some thought it was the Holy Ghost in the form of this dove; "Sanctum esse
Spiritum, qui, in illius alitis specie, ut mœstos et afflictos solaretur, venire erat dig-
natus"; (De Rebus Gestis, MS.;) a conjecture which seems very reasonable to
Pizarro y Orellana, since the expedition was to "redound so much to the spread of
the Catholic faith, and the Castilian monarchy!" Varones Ilustres, p. 70.

[8] Gomara, Crónica, cap. 2.

[9] Bernal Diaz, Hist. de la Conquista, cap. 203.

studied the wild tactics of Indian warfare; he became familiar with toil and danger, and with those deeds of cruelty which have too often, alas! stained the bright scutcheons of the Castilian chivalry in the New World. He was only prevented by illness—a most fortunate one, on this occasion—from embarking in Nicuessa's expedition, which furnished a tale of woe, not often matched in the annals of Spanish discovery. Providence reserved him for higher ends.

At length, in 1511, when Velasquez undertook the conquest of Cuba, Cortés willingly abandoned his quiet life for the stirring scenes there opened, and took part in the expedition. He displayed, throughout the invasion, an activity and courage that won him the approbation of the commander; while his free and cordial manners, his good-humor, and lively sallies of wit made him the favorite of the soldiers. "He gave little evidence," says a contemporary, "of the great qualities which he afterwards showed." It is probable these qualities were not known to himself; while to a common observer his careless manners and jocund repartees might well seem incompatible with any thing serious or profound; as the real depth of the current is not suspected under the light play and sunny sparkling of the surface.[10]

After the reduction of the island, Cortés seems to have been held in great favor by Velasquez, now appointed its governor. According to Las Casas, he was made one of his secretaries.[11] He still retained the same fondness for gallantry, for which his handsome person afforded obvious advantages, but which had more than once brought him into trouble in earlier life. Among the families who had taken up their residence in Cuba was one of the name of Xuarez, from Granada in Old Spain. It consisted of a brother, and four sisters remarkable for their beauty. With one of them, named Catalina, the susceptible heart of the young soldier became enamoured.[12] How far the intimacy was carried is not quite certain. But it appears he gave his promise to marry her,—a promise, which, when the time came, and reason, it may be, had got the better of passion, he showed no alacrity in keeping. He resisted, indeed, all remonstrances to this effect, from the lady's family, backed by the governor, and somewhat sharpened, no doubt, in the latter by the particular interest he took in one of the fair sisters, who is said not to have repaid it with ingratitude.

Whether the rebuke of Velasquez, or some other cause of disgust, rankled in the breast of Cortés, he now became cold toward his patron,

---

[10] De Rebus Gestis, MS.—Gomara, Crónica, cap. 3, 4.—Las Casas, Hist. de las Indias, MS., lib. 3, cap. 27.

[11] Hist. de las Indias, MS., loc. cit.

"Res omnes arduas difficilesque per Cortesium, quem in dies magis magisque amplectebatur, Velasquius agit. Ex eo ducis favore et gratiâ magnâ Cortesio invidia est orta." De Rebus Gestis, MS.

[12] Solís has found a patent of nobility for this lady also,—"doncella noble y recatada." (Historia de la Conquista de Méjico, (Paris, 1838,) lib. 1, cap. 9.) Las Casas treats her with less ceremony. "Una hermana de un Juan Xuarez, gente pobre." Hist. de las Indias, MS., lib. 3, cap. 17

and connected himself with a disaffected party tolerably numerous in the island. They were in the habit of meeting at his house and brooding over their causes of discontent, chiefly founded, it would appear, on what they conceived an ill requital of their services in the distribution of lands and offices. It may well be imagined, that it could have been no easy task for the ruler of one of these colonies, however discreet and well intentioned, to satisfy the indefinite cravings of speculators and adventurers, who swarmed, like so many famished harpies, in the track of discovery in the New World.[13]

The malecontents determined to lay their grievances before the higher authorities in Hispaniola, from whom Velasquez had received his commission. The voyage was one of some hazard, as it was to be made in an open boat, across an arm of the sea eighteen leagues wide; and they fixed on Cortés, with whose fearless spirit they were well acquainted, as the fittest man to undertake it. The conspiracy got wind, and came to the governor's ears before the departure of the envoy, whom he instantly caused to be seized, loaded with fetters, and placed in strict confinement. It is even said, he would have hung him, but for the interposition of his friends.[14] The fact is not incredible. The governors of these little territories, having entire control over the fortunes of their subjects, enjoyed an authority far more despotic than that of the sovereign himself. They were generally men of rank and personal consideration; their distance from the mother country withdrew their conduct from searching scrutiny, and, when that did occur, they usually had interest and means of corruption at command, sufficient to shield them from punishment. The Spanish colonial history, in its earlier stages, affords striking instances of the extraordinary assumption and abuse of powers by these petty potentates; and the sad fate of Vasquez Nuñez de Balboa, the illustrious discoverer of the Pacific, though the most signal, is by no means a solitary example, that the greatest services could be requited by persecution and an ignominious death.

The governor of Cuba, however, although irascible and suspicious in his nature, does not seem to have been vindictive, nor particularly cruel. In the present instance, indeed, it may well be doubted whether the blame would not be more reasonably charged on the unfounded expectations of his followers than on himself.

Cortés did not long remain in durance. He contrived to throw back one of the bolts of his fetters; and, after extricating his limbs, succeeded in forcing open a window with the irons so as to admit of his escape. He was lodged on the second floor of the building, and was able to let himself down to the pavement without injury, and unobserved. He then made the best of his way to a neighboring church, where he claimed the privilege of sanctuary.

[13] Gomara, Crónica, cap. 4.—Las Casas, Hist. de las Indias, MS., ubi supra.— De Rebus Gestis, MS.—Memorial de Benito Martinez, capellan de D. Velasquez contra H. Cortés, MS.
[14] Las Casas, Hist. de las Indias, MS., ubi supra.

Velasquez, though incensed at his escape, was afraid to violate the
sanctity of the place by employing force. But he stationed a guard in
the neighborhood, with orders to seize the fugitive, if he should forget
himself so far as to leave the sanctuary. In a few days this happened. As
Cortés was carelessly standing without the walls in front of the building,
an *alguacil* suddenly sprung on him from behind and pinioned his arms,
while others rushed in and secured him. This man, whose name was
Juan Escudero, was afterwards hung by Cortés for some offence in New
Spain.[15]

The unlucky prisoner was again put in irons, and carried on board a
vessel to sail the next morning for Hispaniola, there to undergo his trial.
Fortune favored him once more. He succeeded, after much difficulty
and no little pain, in passing his feet through the rings which shackled
them. He then came cautiously on deck, and, covered by the darkness
of the night, stole quietly down the side of the ship into a boat that lay
floating below. He pushed off from the vessel with as little noise as possible. As he drew near the shore, the stream became rapid and turbulent.
He hesitated to trust his boat to it; and as he was an excellent swimmer
prepared to breast it himself, and boldly plunged into the water. The
current was strong, but the arm of a man struggling for life was stronger;
and after buffeting the waves till he was nearly exhausted, he succeeded
in gaining a landing; when he sought refuge in the same sanctuary which
had protected him before. The facility with which Cortés a second time
effected his escape may lead one to doubt the fidelity of his guards; who
perhaps looked on him as the victim of persecution, and felt the influence of those popular manners which seem to have gained him friends
in every society into which he was thrown.[16]

For some reason not explained,—perhaps from policy,—he now relinquished his objections to the marriage with Catalina Xuarez. He thus
secured the good offices of her family. Soon afterwards the governor
himself relented, and became reconciled to his unfortunate enemy. A
strange story is told in connection with this event. It is said his proud
spirit refused to accept the proffers of reconciliation made him by
Velasquez; and that one evening, leaving the sanctuary, he presented
himself unexpectedly before the latter in his own quarters, when on a
military excursion at some distance from the capital. The governor,
startled by the sudden apparition of his enemy completely armed before
him, with some dismay inquired the meaning of it. Cortés answered by
insisting on a full explanation of his previous conduct. After some hot
discussion the interview terminated amicably; the parties embraced, and,
when a messenger arrived to announce the escape of Cortés, he found
him in the apartments of his Excellency, where, having retired to rest,

---

[15] Las Casas, Hist. de las Indias, MS., loc. cit.—Memorial de Martinez, MS.
[16] Gomara, Crónica, cap. 4.
Herrera tells a silly story of his being unable to swim, and throwing himself on a
plank, which, after being carried out to sea, was washed ashore with him at flood
tide. Hist. General, dec. 1, lib. 9, cap. 8.

both were actually sleeping in the same bed! The anecdote is repeated without distrust by more than one biographer of Cortés.[17] It is not very probable, however, that a haughty, irascible man like Velasquez should have given such uncommon proofs of condescension and familiarity to one, so far beneath him in station, with whom he had been so recently in deadly feud; nor, on the other hand, that Cortés should have had the silly temerity to brave the lion in his den, where a single nod would have sent him to the gibbet,—and that, too, with as little compunction or fear of consequences, as would have attended the execution of an Indian slave.[18]

The reconciliation with the governor, however brought about, was permanent. Cortés, though not reëstablished in the office of secretary, received a liberal *repartimiento* of Indians, and an ample territory in the neighborhood of St. Jago, of which he was soon after made *alcalde*. He now lived almost wholly on his estate, devoting himself to agriculture with more zeal than formerly. He stocked his plantation with different kinds of cattle, some of which were first introduced by him into Cuba.[19] He wrought, also, the gold mines which fell to his share, and which in this island promised better returns than those in Hispaniola. By this course of industry he found himself, in a few years, master of some two or three thousand *castellanos,* a large sum for one in his situation. "God, who alone knows at what cost of Indian lives it was obtained," exclaims Las Casas, "will take account of it!" [20] His days glided smoothly away in these tranquil pursuits, and in the society of his beautiful wife, who, however ineligible as a connection, from the inferiority of her condition, appears to have fulfilled all the relations of a faithful and affectionate partner. Indeed, he was often heard to say at this time, as the good bishop above quoted remarks, "that he lived as happily with her as if she had been the daughter of a duchess." Fortune gave him the means in after life of verifying the truth of his assertion.[21]

Such was the state of things, when Alvarado returned with the tidings of Grijalva's discoveries, and the rich fruits of his traffic with the natives.

---

[17] Gomara, Crónica, cap. 4.
"Cœnat cubatque Cortesius cum Velasquio eodem in lecto. Qui postero die fugæ Cortesii nuntius venerat, Velasquium et Cortesium juxta accubantes intuitus, miratur." De Rebus Gestis, MS.

[18] Las Casas, who remembered Cortés at this time "so poor and lowly that he would have gladly received any favor from the least of Velasquez' attendants," treats the story of the bravado with contempt. "Por lo qual si él [Velasquez] sintiera de Cortés una puncta de alfiler de cerviguillo ó presuncion, ó lo ahorcara ó á lo menos lo echara de la tierra y lo sumiera en ella sin que alzara cabeza en su vida." Hist. de las Indias, MS., lib. 3, cap. 27.

[19] "Pecuariam primus quoque habuit, in insulamque induxit, omni pecorum genere ex Hispania petito." De Rebus Gestis, MS.

[20] "Los que por sacarle el oro muriéon Dios abrá tenido mejor cuenta que yo.ᴿ Hist. de las Indias, MS., lib. 3, cap. 27. The text is a free translation.

[21] "Estando conmigo, me lo dixo que estava tan contento con ella como si fuera hija de una Duquessa." Hist. de las Indias, MS., ubi supra.—Gomara, Crónica. cap. 4.

The news spread like wildfire throughout the island; for all saw in it the promise of more important results than any hitherto obtained. The governor, as already noticed, resolved to follow up the track of discovery with a more considerable armament; and he looked around for a proper person to share the expense of it, and to take the command.

Several hidalgos presented themselves, whom, from want of proper qualifications, or from his distrust of their assuming an independence of their employer, he one after another rejected. There were two persons in St. Jago in whom he placed great confidence,—Amador de Lares, the *contador*, or royal treasurer,[22] and his own secretary, Andres de Duero. Cortés was also in close intimacy with both these persons; and he availed himself of it to prevail on them to recommend him as a suit- able person to be intrusted with the expedition. It is said, he reinforced the proposal, by promising a liberal share of the proceeds of it. However this may be, the parties urged his selection by the governor with all the eloquence of which they were capable. That officer had had ample ex- perience of the capacity and courage of the candidate. He knew, too, that he had acquired a fortune which would enable him to coöperate materially in fitting out the armament. His popularity in the island would speedily attract followers to his standard.[23] All past animosities had long since been buried in oblivion, and the confidence he was now to repose in him would insure his fidelity and gratitude. He lent a will- ing ear, therefore, to the recommendation of his counsellors, and, send- ing for Cortés, announced his purpose of making him Captain-General of the Armada.[24]

Cortés had now attained the object of his wishes,—the object for which his soul had panted, ever since he had set foot in the New World. He was no longer to be condemned to a life of mercenary drudgery; nor to be cooped up within the precincts of a petty island. But he was to be placed in a new and independent theatre of action, and a boundless per- spective was opened to his view, which might satisfy not merely the wildest cravings of avarice, but, to a bold, aspiring spirit like his, the far more importunate cravings of ambition. He fully appreciated the importance of the late discoveries, and read in them the existence of the great empire in the far West, dark hints of which had floated, from time to time, to the Islands, and of which more certain glimpses had been caught by those who had reached the continent. This was the country intimated to the "Great Admiral" in his visit to Honduras in 1502, and which he might have reached, had he held on a northern course, instead of striking to the south in quest of an imaginary strait. As it was, "he

[22] The treasurer used to boast he had passed some two and twenty years in the wars of Italy. He was a shrewd personage, and Las Casas, thinking that country a slippery school for morals, warned the governor, he says, more than once "to be- ware of the twenty-two years in Italy." Hist. de las Indias, MS., lib. 3, cap. 113.

[23] "Si él no fuera por Capitan, que no fuera la tercera parte de la gente que con él fué " Declaracion de Puertocarrero, MS. (Coruña, 30 de Abril, 1520.)

[24] Bernal Diaz, Hist. de la Conquista, cap. 19.—De Rebus Gestis, MS.—Gomara Crónica, cap. 7.—Las Casas, Hist. General de las Indias, MS., lib. 3, cap. 113.

had but opened the gate," to use his own bitter expression, "for others to enter." The time had at length come, when they were to enter it; and the young adventurer, whose magic lance was to dissolve the spell which had so long hung over these mysterious regions, now stood ready to assume the enterprise.

From this hour the deportment of Cortés seemed to undergo a change. His thoughts, instead of evaporating in empty levities or idle flashes of merriment, were wholly concentrated on the great object to which he was devoted. His elastic spirits were shown in cheering and stimulating the companions of his toilsome duties, and he was roused to a generous enthusiasm, of which even those who knew him best had not conceived him capable. He applied at once all the money in his possession to fitting out the armament. He raised more by the mortgage of his estates, and by giving his obligations to some wealthy merchants of the place, who relied for their reimbursement on the success of the expedition; and, when his own credit was exhausted, he availed himself of that of his friends.

The funds thus acquired he expended in the purchase of vessels, provisions, and military stores, while he invited recruits by offers of assistance to such as were too poor to provide for themselves, and by the additional promise of a liberal share of the anticipated profits.[25]

All was now bustle and excitement in the little town of St. Jago. Some were busy in refitting the vessels and getting them ready for the voyage; some in providing naval stores; others in converting their own estates into money in order to equip themselves; every one seemed anxious to contribute in some way or other to the success of the expedition. Six ships, some of them of a large size, had already been procured; and three hundred recruits enrolled themselves in the course of a few days, eager to seek their fortunes under the banner of this daring and popular chieftain.

How far the governor contributed towards the expenses of the outfit is not very clear. If the friends of Cortés are to be believed, nearly the whole burden fell on him; since, while he supplied the squadron without remuneration, the governor sold many of his own stores at an exorbitant profit.[26] Yet it does not seem probable that Velasquez, with such ample means at his command, should have thrown on his deputy the burden of

[25] Declaracion de Puertocarrero, MS.—Carta de Vera Cruz, MS.—Probanza en la Villa Segura, MS. (4 de Oct., 1520.)

[26] The letter from the Municipality of Vera Cruz, after stating that Velasquez bore only one third of the original expense, adds, "Y sepan Vras. Magestades que la mayor parte de la dicha tercia parte que el dicho Diego Velasquez gastó en ahcer la dicha armada fué, emplear sus dineros en vinos y en ropas, y en otras cosas de poco valor para nos lo vender acá en mucha mas cantidad de lo que á él le costó, por manera que podemos decir que entre nosotros los Españoles vasallos de Vras. Realus Altezas ha hecho Diego Velasquez su rescate y granosea de sus dineros cobrandolos muy bien." (Carta de Vera Cruz, MS.) Puertocarrero y Montejo, also, in their depositions taken in Spain, both speak of Cortés' having furnished two thirds of the cost of the flotilla. (Declaracion de Puertocarrero, MS.—Declaracion de Montejo, MS. (29 de Abril, 1520.).) The letter from Vera Cruz, however, was prepared under the eye of Cortés; and the two last were his confidential officers.

the expedition, nor that the latter—had he done so—could have been in a condition to meet these expenses, amounting, as we are told, to more than twenty thousand gold ducats. Still it cannot be denied that an ambitious man like Cortés, who was to reap all the glory of the enterprise, would very naturally be less solicitous to count the gains of it, than his employer, who, inactive at home, and having no laurels to win, must look on the pecuniary profits as his only recompense. The question gave rise, some years later, to a furious litigation between the parties, with which it is not necessary at present to embarrass the reader.

It is due to Velasquez to state that the instructions delivered by him for the conduct of the expedition cannot be charged with a narrow or mercenary spirit. The first object of the voyage was to find Grijalva, after which the two commanders were to proceed in company together. Reports had been brought back by Cordova, on his return from the first visit to Yucatan, that six Christians were said to be lingering in captivity in the interior of the country. It was supposed they might belong to the party of the unfortunate Nicuessa, and orders were given to find them out, if possible, and restore them to liberty. But the great object of the expedition was barter with the natives. In pursuing this, special care was to be taken that they should receive no wrong, but be treated with kindness and humanity. Cortés was to bear in mind, above all things, that the object which the Spanish monarch had most at heart was the conversion of the Indians. He was to impress on them the grandeur and goodness of his royal master, to invite them "to give in their allegiance to him, and to manifest it by regaling him with such comfortable presents of gold, pearls, and precious stones as, by showing their own good-will, would secure his favor and protection." He was to make an accurate survey of the coast, sounding its bays and inlets for the benefit of future navigators. He was to acquaint himself with the natural products of the country, with the character of its different races, their institutions and progress in civilization; and he was to send home minute accounts of all these, together with such articles as he should obtain in his intercourse with them. Finally, he was to take *the most careful care* to omit nothing that might redound to the service of God or his sover-- eign.[27]

Such was the general tenor of the instructions given to Cortés, and they must be admitted to provide for the interests of science and humanity, as well as for those which had reference only to a commercial speculation. It may seem strange, considering the discontent shown by Velasquez with his former captain, Grijalva, for not colonizing, that no directions should have been given to that effect here. But he had not yet received from Spain the warrant for investing his agents with such powers; and that which had been obtained from the Hieronymite fathers

---

[27] The instrument is often referred to by writers who never saw it, as the Agreement between Cortés and Velasquez. It is, in fact, only the instructions given by this latter to his officer, who was no party to it.

in Hispaniola conceded only the right to traffic with the natives. The commission at the same time recognised the authority of Cortés as Captain-General of the expedition.[28]

[28] Declaracion de Puertocarrero, MS.—Gomara, Crónica, cap. 7.

Velasquez soon after obtained from the crown authority to colonize the new countries, with the title of *adelantado* over them. The instrument was dated at Barcelona, Nov. 13th, 1518. (Herrera, Hist. General, dec. 2, lib. 3, cap. 8.) Empty privileges! Las Casas gives a caustic etymology of the title of *adelantado*, so often granted to the Spanish discoverers. "Adelantados porque se adelantaran en hazer males y daños tan gravísimos á gentes pacíficas." Hist. de las Indias, MS., lib. 3, cap. 117.

CHAPTER III

JEALOUSY OF VELASQUEZ—CORTÉS EMBARKS—EQUIPMENT OF HIS
FLEET—HIS PERSON AND CHARACTER—RENDEZVOUS AT HAVANA
—STRENGTH OF HIS ARMAMENT

1519

THE importance given to Cortés by his new position, and, perhaps, a
somewhat more lofty bearing, gradually gave uneasiness to the naturally
suspicious temper of Velasquez, who became apprehensive that his officer, when away where he would have the power, might also have the
inclination, to throw off his dependence on him altogether. An accidental
circumstance at this time heightened these suspicions. A mad fellow, his
jester, one of those crack-brained wits,—half wit, half fool,—who formed
in those days a common appendage to every great man's establishment,
called out to the governor, as he was taking his usual walk one morning
with Cortés towards the port, "Have a care, master Velasquez, or we
shall have to go a hunting, some day or other, after this same captain of
ours!" "Do you hear what the rogue says?" exclaimed the governor to
his companion. "Do not heed him," said Cortés, "he is a saucy knave,
and deserves a good whipping." The words sunk deep, however, in the
mind of Velasquez,—as, indeed, true jests are apt to stick.

There were not wanting persons about his Excellency, who fanned the
latent embers of jealousy into a blaze. These worthy gentlemen, some of
them kinsmen of Velasquez, who probably felt their own deserts somewhat thrown into the shade by the rising fortunes of Cortés, reminded
the governor of his ancient quarrel with that officer, and of the little
probability that affronts so keenly felt at the time could ever be forgotten. By these and similar suggestions, and by misconstructions of the
present conduct of Cortés, they wrought on the passions of Velasquez
to such a degree, that he resolved to intrust the expedition to other
hands.[1]

He communicated his design to his confidential advisers, Lares and
Duero, and these trusty personages reported it without delay to Cortés,
although, "to a man of half his penetration," says Las Casas, "the thing
would have been readily divined from the governor's altered demean-

---

[1] "Deterrebat," says the anonymous biographer, "eum Cortesii natura imperii
avida, fiducia sui ingens, et nimius sumptus in classe parandâ. Timere itaque Velasquius cœpit, si Cortesius cum eâ classe iret, nihil ad se vel honoris vel lucri redi-
turum." De Rebus Gestis, MS.—Bernal Diaz, Hist. de la Conquista, cap. 19.—Las
Casas, Hist. de las Indias, MS., cap. 114.

or." [2] The two functionaries advised their friend to expedite matters as much as possible, and to lose no time in getting his fleet ready for sea, if he would retain the command of it. Cortés showed the same prompt decision on this occasion, which more than once afterwards in a similar crisis gave the direction to his destiny.

He had not yet got his complement of men, nor of vessels; and was very inadequately provided with supplies of any kind. But he resolved to weigh anchor that very night. He waited on his officers, informed them of his purpose, and probably of the cause of it; and at midnight, when the town was hushed in sleep, they all went quietly on board, and the little squadron dropped down the bay. First, however, Cortés had visited the person whose business it was to supply the place with meat, and relieved him of all his stock on hand, notwithstanding his complaint that the city must suffer for it on the morrow, leaving him, at the same time, in payment, a massive gold chain of much value, which he wore round his neck.[3]

Great was the amazement of the good citizens of St. Jago, when, at dawn, they saw that the fleet, which they knew was so ill prepared for the voyage, had left its moorings and was busily getting under way. The tidings soon came to the ears of his Excellency, who, springing from his bed, hastily dressed himself, mounted his horse, and, followed by his retinue, galloped down to the quay. Cortés, as soon as he descried their approach, entered an armed boat, and came within speaking distance of the shore. "And is it thus you part from me!" exclaimed Velasquez; "a courteous way of taking leave, truly!" "Pardon me," answered Cortés, "time presses, and there are some things that should be done before they are even thought of. Has your Excellency any commands?" But the mortified governor had no commands to give; and Cortés, politely waving his hand, returned to his vessel, and the little fleet instantly made sail for the port of Macaca, about fifteen leagues distant. (November 18, 1518.) Velasquez rode back to his house to digest his chagrin as he best might; satisfied, probably, that he had made at least two blunders; one in appointing Cortés to the command,—the other in attempting to deprive him of it. For, if it be true, that, by giving our confidence by halves, we can scarcely hope to make a friend, it is equally true, that, by withdrawing it when given, we shall make an enemy.[4]

---

[2] "Cortés no avia menester mas para entendello de mirar el gesto á Diego Velasquez segun su astuta viveza y mundana sabiduría." Hist. de las Indias, MS., cap. 114.

[3] Las Casas had the story from Cortés' own mouth. Hist. de las Indias, MS., cap. 114.—Gomara, Crónica, cap. 7.—De Rebus Gestis, MS.

[4] Las Casas, Hist. de las Indias, MS., cap. 114.—Herrera, Hist. General, dec. 2, lib. 3, cap. 12.

Solís, who follows Bernal Diaz in saying that Cortés parted openly and amicably from Velasquez, seems to consider it a great slander on the character of the former to suppose that he wanted to break with the governor so soon, when he had received so little provocation. (Conquista, lib. 1, cap. 10.) But it is not necessary to suppose that Cortés intended a rupture with his employer by this clandestine move.

This clandestine departure of Cortés has been severely criticized by some writers, especially by Las Casas.[5] Yet much may be urged in vindication of his conduct. He had been appointed to the command by the voluntary act of the governor, and this had been fully ratified by the authorities of Hispaniola. He had at once devoted all his resources to the undertaking, incurring, indeed, a heavy debt in addition. He was now to be deprived of his commission, without any misconduct having been alleged or at least proved against him. Such an event must overwhelm him in irretrievable ruin, to say nothing of the friends from whom he had so largely borrowed, and the followers who had embarked their fortunes in the expedition on the faith of his commanding it. There are few persons, probably, who, under these circumstances, would have felt called tamely to acquiesce in the sacrifice of their hopes to a groundless and arbitrary whim. The most to have been expected from Cortés was, that he should feel obliged to provide faithfully for the interests of his employer in the conduct of the enterprise. How far he felt the force of this obligation will appear in the sequel.

From Macaca, where Cortés laid in such stores as he could obtain from the royal farms, and which, he said, he considered as "a loan from the king," he proceeded to Trinidad; a more considerable town, on the southern coast of Cuba. Here he landed, and, erecting his standard in front of his quarters, made proclamation, with liberal offers to all who would join the expedition. Volunteers came in daily, and among them more than a hundred of Grijalva's men, just returned from their voyage, and willing to follow up the discovery under an enterprising leader. The fame of Cortés attracted, also, a number of cavaliers of family and distinction, some of whom, having accompanied Grijalva, brought much information valuable for the present expedition. Among these hidalgos may be mentioned Pedro de Alvarado and his brothers, Cristóval de Olid, Alonso de Avila, Juan Velasquez de Leon, a near relation of the governor, Alonso Hernandez de Puertocarrero, and Gonzalo de Sandoval, —all of them men who took a most important part in the Conquest. Their presence was of great moment, as giving consideration to the enterprise; and, when they entered the little camp of the adventurers, the latter turned out to welcome them amidst lively strains of music and joyous salvos of artillery.

Cortés meanwhile was active in purchasing military stores and provisions. Learning that a trading vessel laden with grain and other commodities for the mines was off the coast, he ordered out one of his caravels to seize her and bring her into port. He paid the master in bills for both cargo and ship, and even persuaded this man, named Sedeño, who was wealthy, to join his fortunes to the expedition. He also despatched one of his officers, Diego de Ordaz, in quest of another ship, of

ment; but only to secure himself in the command. At all events, the text conforms in every particular to the statement of Las Casas, who, as he knew both the parties well, and resided on the island at the time, had ample means of information.

[5] Hist. de las Indias, MS., cap. 114.

which he had tidings, with instructions to seize it in like manner, and to meet him with it off Cape St. Antonio, the westerly point of the island.[6] By this he effected another object, that of getting rid of Ordaz, who was one of the governor's household, and an inconvenient spy on his own actions.

While thus occupied, letters from Velasquez were received by the commander of Trinidad, requiring him to seize the person of Cortés and to detain him, as he had been deposed from the command of the fleet, which was given to another. This functionary communicated his instructions to the principal officers in the expedition, who counselled him not to make the attempt, as it would undoubtedly lead to a commotion among the soldiers, that might end in laying the town in ashes. Verdugo thought it prudent to conform to this advice.[7]

As Cortés was willing to strengthen himself by still further reinforcements, he ordered Alvarado with a small body of men to march across the country to the Havana, while he himself would sail round the westerly point of the island, and meet him there with the squadron. In this port he again displayed his standard, making the usual proclamation. He caused all the large guns to be brought on shore, and, with the small arms and crossbows, to be put in order. As there was abundance of cotton raised in this neighborhood, he had the jackets of the soldiers thickly quilted with it, for a defence against the Indian arrows, from which the troops in the former expeditions had grievously suffered. He distributed his men into eleven companies, each under the command of an experienced officer; and it was observed, that, although several of the cavaliers in the service were the personal friends and even kinsmen of Velasquez, he appeared to treat them all with perfect confidence.

His principal standard was of black velvet embroidered with gold, and emblazoned with a red cross amidst flames of blue and white, with this motto in Latin beneath; "Friends, let us follow the Cross; and under this sign, if we have faith, we shall conquer." He now assumed more state in his own person and way of living, introducing a greater number of domestics and officers into his household, and placing it on a footing becoming a man of high station. This state he maintained through the rest of his life.[8]

Cortés at this time was thirty-three, or perhaps thirty-four years of age. In stature he was rather above the middle size. His complexion was pale; and his large dark eye gave an expression of gravity to his coun-

---

[6] Las Casas had this, also, from the lips of Cortés in later life. "Todo esto me dixo el mismo Cortés, con otras cosas çerca dello despues de Marques; . . . . . reindo y mofando é con estas formales palabras, *A la mi fée andube por alli como un gentil cosario.*" Hist. de las Indias, MS., cap. 115.

[7] De Rebus Gestis, MS.—Gomara, Crónica, cap. 8.—Las Casas, Hist. de las Indias, MS., cap. 114, 115.

[8] Bernal Diaz, Hist. de la Conquista, cap. 24.—De Rebus Gestis, MS.—Gomara Crónica, cap. 8.—Las Casas, Hist. de las Indias, MS., cap. 115.

The legend on the standard was, doubtless, suggested by that on the *labarum,*—the sacred banner of Constantine.

tenance, not to have been expected in one of his cheerful temperament. His figure was slender, at least until later life; but his chest was deep, his shoulders broad, his frame muscular and well proportioned. It pre· sented the union of agility and vigor which qualified him to excel in fencing, horsemanship, and the other generous exercises of chivalry. In his diet he was temperate, careless of what he ate, and drinking little; while to toil and privation he seemed perfectly indifferent. His dress, for he did not disdain the impression produced by such adventitious aids, was such as to set off his handsome person to advantage; neither gaudy nor striking, but rich. He wore few ornaments, and usually the same; but those were of great price. His manners, frank and soldierlike, con· cealed a most cool and calculating spirit. With his gayest humor there mingled a settled air of resolution, which made those who approached him feel they must obey; and which infused something like awe into the attachment of his most devoted followers. Such a combination, in which love was tempered by authority, was the one probably best calculated to inspire devotion in the rough and turbulent spirits among whom his lot was to be cast.

The character of Cortés seems to have undergone some change of cir· cumstances; or, to speak more correctly, the new scenes in which he was placed called forth qualities which before lay dormant in his bosom. There are some hardy natures that require the heats of excited action to unfold their energies; like the plants, which, closed to the mild influence of a temperate latitude, come to their full growth, and give forth their fruits only in the burning atmosphere of the tropics.—Such is the por· trait left to us by his contemporaries of this remarkable man; the in· strument selected by Providence to scatter terror among the barbarian monarchs of the Western World, and lay their empires in the dust.[9]

Before the preparations were fully completed at the Havana, the commander of the place, Don Pedro Barba, received despatches from Velasquez ordering him to apprehend Cortés, and to prevent the depar· ture of his vessels; while another epistle from the same source was de· livered to Cortés himself, requesting him to postpone his voyage till the governor could communicate with him, as he proposed, in person. "Never," exclaims Las Casas, "did I see so little knowledge of affairs shown, as in this letter of Diego Velasquez,—that he should have ima· gined, that a man, who had so recently put such an affront on him, would defer his departure at his bidding!"[10] It was, indeed, hoping to stay the flight of the arrow by a word, after it had left the bow.

The Captain-General, however, during his short stay, had entirely conciliated the good-will of Barba. And, if that officer had had the in· clination, he knew he had not the power, to enforce his principal's

[9] The most minute notices of the person and habits of Cortés are to be gathered from the narrative of the old cavalier Bernal Diaz, who served so long under him, and from Gomara, the general's chaplain. See in particular the last chapter of Go· mara's Crónica, and cap. 203 of the Hist. de la Conquista.
[10] Las Casas, Hist. de las Indias, MS., cap. 115.

orders, in the face of a resolute soldiery, incensed at this ungenerous persecution of their commander, and "all of whom," in the words of the honest chronicler who bore part in the expedition, "officers and privates, would have cheerfully laid down their lives for him." [11] Barba contented himself, therefore, with explaining to Velasquez the impracticability of the attempt, and at the same time endeavored to tranquillize his apprehensions by asserting his own confidence in the fidelity of Cortés. To this the latter added a communication of his own, couched "in the soft terms he knew so well how to use," [12] in which he implored his Excellency to rely on his devotion to his interests, and concluded with the comfortable assurance that he and the whole fleet, God willing, would sail on the following morning.

Accordingly on the 10th of February, 1519, the little squadron got under way, and directed its course towards Cape St. Antonio, the appointed place of rendezvous. When all were brought together, the vessels were found to be eleven in number; one of them, in which Cortés himself went, was of a hundred tons, burden, three others were from seventy to eighty tons; the remainder were caravels and open brigantines. The whole was put under the direction of Antonio de Alaminos, as chief pilot; a veteran navigator, who had acted as pilot to Columbus in his last voyage, and to Cordova and Grijalva in the former expeditions to Yucatan.

Landing on the Cape and mustering his forces, Cortés found they amounted to one hundred and ten mariners, five hundred and fifty-three soldiers, including thirty-two crossbowmen, and thirteen arquebusiers, besides two hundred Indians of the island, and a few Indian women for menial offices. He was provided with ten heavy guns, four lighter pieces called falconets, and with a good supply of ammunition.[13] He had besides sixteen horses. They were not easily procured; for the difficulty of transporting them across the ocean in the flimsy craft of that day made them rare and incredibly dear in the Islands.[14] But Cortés rightfully estimated

[11] Bernal Diaz, Hist. de la Conquista, cap. 24.
[12] Ibid., loc. cit.
[13] Bernal Diaz, Hist. de la Conquista, cap. 26.
There is some discrepancy among authorities, in regard to the numbers of the army. The Letter from Vera Cruz, which should have been exact, speaks in round terms of only four hundred soldiers. (Carta de Vera Cruz, MS.) Velasquez himself, in a communication to the Chief Judge of Hispaniola, states the number at six hundred. (Carta de Diego Velasquez al Lic. Figueroa, MS.) I have adopted the estimates of Bernal Diaz, who, in his long service, seems to have become intimately acquainted with every one of his comrades, their persons, and private history.
[14] Incredibly dear indeed, since, from the statements contained in the depositions at Villa Segura, it appears that the cost of the horses for the expedition was from four to five hundred *pesos de oro* each! "Si saben que de caballos que el dicho Señor Capitan General Hernando Cortés ha comprado para servir en la dicha Conquista, que som diez ó ocho, que le han costado á quatrocientos cinquenta é á quinientos pesos ha pagado, é que deve mas de ocho mil pesos de oro dellos." (Probanza en Villa Segura, MS.) The estimation of these horses is sufficiently shown by the minute information Bernal Diaz has thought proper to give of every one of them; minute enough for the pages of a sporting calendar. See Hist. de la Conquista, cap. 23.

the importance of cavalry, however small in number, both for their actual service in the field, and for striking terror into the savages. With so
paltry a force did he enter on a Conquest which even his stout heart
must have shrunk from attempting with such means, had he but foreseen half its real difficulties!

Before embarking, Cortés addressed his soldiers in a short but animated harangue. He told them they were about to enter on a noble enterprise, one that would make their name famous to after ages. He was
leading them to countries more vast and opulent than any yet visited by
Europeans. "I hold out to you a glorious prize," continued the orator,
"but it is to be won by incessant toil. Great things are achieved only by
great exertions, and glory was never the reward of sloth.[15] If I had
labored hard and staked my all on this undertaking, it is for the love of
that renown, which is the noblest recompense of man. But, if any among
you covet riches more, be but true to me, as I will be true to you and to
the occasion, and I will make you masters of such as our countrymen
have never dreamed of! You are few in number, but strong in resolution; and, if this does not falter, doubt not but that the Almighty, who
has never deserted the Spaniard in his contest with the infidel, will shield
you, though encompassed by a cloud of enemies; for your cause is a *just
cause*, and you are to fight under the banner of the Cross. Go forward,
then," he concluded, "with alacrity and confidence, and carry to a
glorious issue the work so auspiciously begun." [16]

The rough eloquence of the general, touching the various chords of
ambition, avarice, and religious zeal, sent a thrill through the bosoms
of his martial audience; and receiving it with acclamations, they seemed
eager to press forward under a chief who was to lead them not so much
to battle, as to triumph.

Cortés was well satisfied to find his own enthusiasm so largely shared
by his followers. Mass was then celebrated with the solemnities usual
with the Spanish navigators, when entering on their voyages of discovery. The fleet was placed under the immediate protection of St. Peter,
the patron saint of Cortés; and weighing anchor, took its departure on
the eighteenth day of February, 1519, for the coast of Yucatan.[17]

[15] "Io vos propongo grandes premios, mas embueltos en grandes trabajos; pero la
virtud no quiere ociosidad." (Gomara, Crónica, cap. 9.) It is the thought so finely
expressed by Thomson;
      "For sluggard's brow the laurel never grows;
      Renown is not the child of indolent repose."
[16] The text is a very condensed abridgment of the original speech of Cortés,—or
of his chaplain, as the case may be. See it, in Gomara, Crónica, cap. 9.
[17] Las Casas, Hist. de las Indias, MS., cap. 115.—Gomara, Crónica, cap. 10.—De
Rebus Gestis, MS.

"Tantus fuit armorum apparatus," exclaims the author of the last work, "quo
alterum terrarum orbem bellis Cortesius concutit; ex tam parvis opibus tantum imperium Carolo facit; aperitque omnium primus Hispanæ genti Hispaniam novam!"
The author of this work is unknown. It seems to have been part of a great compilation "De Orbe Novo," written, probably, on the plan of a series of biographical
sketches, as the introduction speaks of a life of Columbus preceding this of Cortés
It was composed, as it states, while many of the old Conquerors were still surviving

and is addressed to the son of Cortés. The historian, therefore, had ample means of verifying the truth of his own statements, although they too often betray, in his partiality for his hero, the influence of the patronage under which the work was produced. It runs into a prolixity of detail which, however tedious, has its uses in a contemporary document. Unluckily, only the first book was finished, or, at least, has survived; terminating with the events of this Chapter. It is written in Latin, in a pure and perspicuous style; and is conjectured with some plausibility to be the work of Calvet de Estrella, Chronicler of the Indies. The original exists in the Archives of Simancas, where it was discovered and transcribed by Muñoz from whose copy that in my library was taken.

CHAPTER IV

VOYAGE TO COZUMEL—CONVERSION OF THE NATIVES—JERÓNIMO DE
AGUILAR—ARMY ARRIVES AT TABASCO—GREAT BATTLE WITH THE
INDIANS—CHRISTIANITY INTRODUCED

1519

ORDERS were given for the vessels to keep as near together as possible,
and to take the direction of the *capitanía,* or admiral's ship, which carried a beacon light in the stern during the night. But the weather, which
had been favorable, changed soon after their departure, and one of those
tempests set in, which at this season are often found in the latitudes of
the West Indies. It fell with terrible force on the little navy, scattering it
far asunder, dismantling some of the ships, and driving them all considerably south of their proposed destination.

Cortés, who had lingered behind to convoy a disabled vessel, reached
the island of Cozumel last. On landing, he learned that one of his captains, Pedro de Alvarado, had availed himself of the short time he had
been there, to enter the temples, rifle them of their few ornaments, and,
by his violent conduct, so far to terrify the simple natives, that they had
fled for refuge into the interior of the island. Cortés, highly incensed at
these rash proceedings, so contrary to the policy he had proposed, could
not refrain from severely reprimanding his officer in the presence of the
army. He commanded two Indian captives, taken by Alvarado, to be
brought before him, and explained to them the pacific purpose of his
visit. This he did through the assistance of his interpreter, Melchorejo, a
native of Yucatan, who had been brought back by Grijalva, and who,
during his residence in Cuba, had picked up some acquaintance with the
Castilian. He then dismissed them loaded with presents, and with an
invitation to their countrymen to return to their homes without fear of
further annoyance. This humane policy succeeded. The fugitives, reassured, were not slow in coming back; and an amicable intercourse was
established, in which Spanish cutlery and trinkets were exchanged for
the gold ornaments of the natives; a traffic in which each party congratulated itself—a philosopher might think with equal reason—on outwit-
ting the other.

The first object of Cortés was, to gather tidings of the unfortunate
Christians who were reported to be still lingering in captivity on the
neighboring continent. From some traders in the island, he obtained
such a confirmation of the report, that he sent Diego de Ordaz with
two brigantines to the opposite coast of Yucatan, with instructions to

remain there eight days. Some Indians went as messengers in the vessels, who consented to bear a letter to the captives informing them of the arrival of their countrymen in Cozumel, with a liberal ransom for their release. Meanwhile the general proposed to make an excursion to the different parts of the island, that he might give employment to the restless spirits of the soldiers, and ascertain the resources of the country.

It was poor and thinly peopled. But everywhere he recognised the vestiges of a higher civilization than what he had before witnessed in the Indian islands. The houses were some of them large, and often built of stone and lime. He was particularly struck with the temples, in which were towers constructed of the same solid materials, and rising several stories in height. In the court of one of these he was amazed by the sight of a cross, of stone and lime, about ten palms high. It was the emblem of the God of rain. Its appearance suggested the wildest conjectures, not merely to the unlettered soldiers, but subsequently to the European scholar, who speculated on the character of the races that had introduced there the sacred symbol of Christianity. But no such inference, as we shall see hereafter, could be warranted.[1] Yet it must be regarded as a curious fact, that the Cross should have been venerated as the object of religious worship both in the New World, and in regions of the Old, where the light of Christianity had never risen.[2]

The first object of Cortés was to reclaim the natives from their gross idolatry and to substitute a purer form of worship. In accomplishing this he was prepared to use force, if milder measures should be ineffectual. There was nothing which the Spanish government had more earnestly at heart, than the conversion of the Indians. It forms the constant burden of their instructions, and gave to the military expeditions in this western hemisphere somewhat of the air of a crusade. The cavalier who embarked in them entered fully into these chivalrous and devotional feelings. No doubt was entertained of the efficacy of conversion, however sudden might be the change, or however violent the means. The sword was a good argument, when the tongue failed; and the spread of Mahometanism had shown that seeds sown by the hand of violence, far

---

[1] See *Appendix, Part 1, Note 27.*

[2] Carta de Vera Cruz, MS.—Bernal Diaz, Hist. de la Conquista, cap. 25, et seq.—Gomara, Crónica, cap. 10, 15.—Las Casas, Hist. de las Indias, MS., lib. 3, cap. 115.—Herrera, Hist. General, dec. 2, lib. 4, cap. 6.—Martyr, de Insulis nuper inventis, (Coloniæ, 1547,) p. 344.

While these pages were passing through the press, but not till two years after they were written, Mr. Stephens' important and interesting volumes appeared, containing the account of his second expedition to Yucatan. In the latter part of the work, he describes his visit to Cozumel, now an uninhabited island covered with impenetrable forests. Near the shore he saw the remains of ancient Indian structures, which he conceives may possibly have been the same that met the eyes of Grijalva and Cortés, and which suggest to him some important inferences. He is led into further reflections on the existence of the cross as a symbol of worship among the islanders. (Incidents of Travel in Yucatan, (New York, 1843,) vol. II. chap. 20.) As the discussion of these matters would lead me too far from the track of our narrative, I shall take occasion to return to them hereafter, when I treat of the architectural remains of the country.

from perishing in the ground, would spring up and bear fruit to after time. If this were so in a bad cause, how much more would it be true in a good one. The Spanish cavalier felt he had a high mission to accomplish as a soldier of the Cross. However unauthorized or unrighteous the war into which he had entered may seem to us, to him it was a holy war. He was in arms against the infidel. Not to care for the soul of his benighted enemy was to put his own in jeopardy. The conversion of a single soul might cover a multitude of sins. It was not for morals that he was concerned, but for *the faith.* This, though understood in its most literal and limited sense, comprehended the whole scheme of Christian morality. Whoever died in the faith, however immoral had been his life, might be said to die in the Lord. Such was the creed of the Castilian knight of that day, as imbibed from the preachings of the pulpit, from cloisters and colleges at home, from monks and missionaries abroad,—from all save one, whose devotion, kindled at a purer source, was not, alas! permitted to send forth its radiance far into the thick gloom by which he was encompassed.[3]

No one partook more fully of the feelings above described than Hernan Cortés. He was, in truth, the very mirror of the times in which he lived, reflecting its motley characteristics, its speculative devotion and practical license,—but with an intensity all his own. He was greatly scandalized at the exhibition of the idolatrous practices of the people of Cozumel, though untainted, as it would seem, with human sacrifices. He endeavored to persuade them to embrace a better faith, through the agency of two ecclesiastics who attended the expedition,—the licentiate Juan Diaz and father Bartolomé de Olmedo. The latter of these godly men afforded the rare example—rare in any age—of the union of fervent zeal with charity, while he beautifully illustrated in his own conduct the precepts which he taught. He remained with the army through the whole expedition, and by his wise and benevolent counsels was often enabled to mitigate the cruelties of the Conquerors, and to turn aside the edge of the sword from the unfortunate natives.

These two missionaries vainly labored to persuade the people of Cozumel to renounce their abominations, and to allow the Indian idols, in which the Christians recognised the true lineaments of Satan,[4] to be thrown down and demolished. The simple natives, filled with horror at the proposed profanation, exclaimed that these were the gods who sent them the sunshine and the storm, and, should any violence be offered, they would be sure to avenge it by sending their lightnings on the heads of its perpetrators.

Cortés was probably not much of a polemic. At all events, he preferred on the present occasion action to argument; and thought that the best

[3] See the biographical sketch of the good bishop Las Casas, the "Protector of the Indians," in the Postscript at the close of the present Book.

[4] "Fuese que el Demonio se les aparecia como es, y dejaba en su imaginacion aquellas especies; con que seria primorosa imitacion del artífice la fealdad del simulacro." Solís, Conquista, p. 39.

way to convince the Indians of their error was to prove the falsehood of the prediction. He accordingly, without further ceremony, caused the venerated images to be rolled down the stairs of the great temple, amidst the groans and lamentations of the natives. An altar was hastily constructed, an image of the Virgin and Child placed over it, and mass was performed by father Olmedo and his reverend companion for the first time within the walls of a temple in New Spain. The patient ministers tried once more to pour the light of the gospel into the benighted understandings of the islanders, and to expound the mysteries of the Catholic faith. The Indian interpreter must have afforded rather a dubious channel for the transmission of such abstruse doctrines. But they at length found favor with their auditors, who, whether overawed by the bold bearing of the invaders, or convinced of the impotence of deities that could not shield their own shrines from violation, now consented to embrace Christianity.[5]

While Cortés was thus occupied with the triumphs of the Cross, he received intelligence that Ordaz had returned from Yucatan without tidings of the Spanish captives. Though much chagrined, the general did not choose to postpone longer his departure from Cozumel. The fleet had been well stored with provisions by the friendly inhabitants, and, embarking his troops, Cortés, in the beginning of March, took leave of its hospitable shores. The squadron had not proceeded far, however, before a leak in one of the vessels compelled them to return to the same port. The detention was attended with important consequences; so much so, indeed, that a writer of the time discerns in it "a great mystery and a miracle." [6]

Soon after landing, a canoe with several Indians was seen making its way from the neighboring shores of Yucatan. On reaching the island, one of the men inquired, in broken Castilian, "if he were among Christians"; and, being answered in the affirmative, threw himself on his knees and returned thanks to Heaven for his delivery. He was one of the unfortunate captives for whose fate so much interest had been felt. His name was Jerónimo de Aguilar, a native of Ecija, in Old Spain, where he had been regularly educated for the church. He had been estab-

---

[5] Carta de Vera Cruz, MS.—Gomara, Crónica, cap. 13.—Herrera, Hist. General, dec. 2, lib. 4, cap. 7.—Ixtlilxochitl, Hist. Chich., MS., cap. 78.

Las Casas, whose enlightened views in religion would have done honor to the present age, insists on the futility of these forced conversions, by which it is proposed in a few days to wean men from the idolatry which they had been taught to reverence from the cradle. "The only way of doing this," he says, "is, by long, assiduous, and faithful preaching, until the heathen shall gather some ideas of the true nature of the Deity and of the doctrines they are to embrace. Above all, the lives of the Christians should be such as to exemplify the truth of these doctrines, that, seeing this, the poor Indian may glorify the Father, and acknowledge him, who has such worshippers, for the true and only God."

[6] "Muy gran misterio y milagro de Dios." Carta de Vera Cruz, MS.

lished with the colony at Darien, and on a voyage from that place to
Hispaniola, eight years previous, was wrecked near the coast of Yucatan. He escaped with several of his companions in the ship's boat, where
some perished from hunger and exposure, while others were sacrificed,
on their reaching land, by the cannibal natives of the peninsula. Aguilar
was preserved from the same dismal fate by escaping into the interior,
where he fell into the hands of a powerful cacique, who, though he
spared his life, treated him at first with great rigor. The patience of the
captive, however, and his singular humility, touched the better feelings
of the chieftain, who would have persuaded Aguilar to take a wife among
his people, but the ecclesiastic steadily refused, in obedience to his
vows. This admirable constancy excited the distrust of the cacique, who
put his virtue to a severe test by various temptations, and much of the
same sort as those with which the Devil is said to have assailed St.
Anthony.[7] From all these fiery trials, however, like his ghostly predecessor, he came out unscorched. Continence is too rare and difficult a
virtue with barbarians, not to challenge their veneration, and the practice of it has made the reputation of more than one saint in the Old as
well as the New World. Aguilar was now intrusted with the care of his
master's household and his numerous wives. He was a man of discretion, as well as virtue; and his counsels were found so salutary, that he
was consulted on all important matters. In short, Aguilar became a great
man among the Indians.

It was with much regret, therefore, that his master received the proposals for his return to his countrymen, to which nothing but the rich
treasure of glass beads, hawk-bells, and other jewels of like value, sent
for his ransom, would have induced him to consent. When Aguilar
reached the coast, there had been so much delay, that the brigantines
had sailed, and it was owing to the fortunate return of the fleet to Cozumel, that he was enabled to join it.

On appearing before Cortés, the poor man saluted him in the Indian
style, by touching the earth with his hand, and carrying it to his head.
The commander, raising him up, affectionately embraced him, covering
him at the same time with his own cloak, as Aguilar was simply clad in
the habiliments of the country, somewhat too scanty for a European eye.
It was long, indeed, before the tastes which he had acquired in the
freedom of the forest could be reconciled to the constraints either of
dress or manners imposed by the artificial forms of civilization. Aguilar's
long residence in the country had familiarized him with the Mayan dialects of Yucatan, and, as he gradually revived his Castilian, he became
of essential importance as an interpreter. Cortés saw the advantage of

---

[7] They are enumerated by Herrera with a minuteness which may claim, at least,
the merit of giving a much higher notion of Aguilar's virtue than the barren generalities of the text. (Hist. General, dec. 2, lib. 4, cap. 6-8.) The story is prettily told by
Washington Irving. Voyages and Discoveries of the Companions of Columbus,
(London, 1883,) p. 263, et seq.

this from the first, but he could not fully estimate all the consequences that were to flow from it.[8]

The repairs of the vessels being at length completed, the Spanish commander once more took leave of the friendly natives of Cozumel, and set sail on the 4th of March. Keeping as near as possible to the coast of Yucatan, he doubled Cape Catoche, and with flowing sheets swept down the broad bay of Campeachy, fringed with the rich dye-woods which have since furnished so important an article of commerce to Europe. He passed Potonchan, where Cordova had experienced a rough reception from the natives; and soon after reached the mouth of the *Rio de Tabasco*, or *Grijalva*, in which that navigator had carried on so lucrative a traffic. Though mindful of the great object of his voyage,—the visit to the Aztec territories,—he was desirous of acquainting himself with the resources of this country, and determined to ascend the river and visit the great town on its borders.

The water was so shallow, from the accumulation of sand at the mouth of the stream, that the general was obliged to leave the ships at anchor, and to embark in the boats with a part only of his forces. The banks were thickly studded with mangrove trees, that, with their roots shooting up and interlacing one another, formed a kind of impervious screen or net-work, behind which the dark forms of the natives were seen glancing to and fro with the most menacing looks and gestures. Cortés, much surprised at these unfriendly demonstrations, so unlike what he had had reason to expect, moved cautiously up the stream. When he had reached an open place, where a large number of Indians were assembled, he asked, through his interpreter, leave to land, explaining at the same time his amicable intentions. But the Indians, brandishing their weapons, answered only with gestures of angry defiance. Though much chagrined, Cortés thought it best not to urge the matter further that evening, but withdrew to a neighboring island, where he disembarked his troops, resolved to effect a landing on the following morning.

When day broke, the Spaniards saw the opposite banks lined with a much more numerous array than on the preceding evening, while the canoes along the shore were filled with bands of armed warriors. Cortés now made his preparations for the attack. He first landed a detachment of a hundred men under Alonso de Avila, at a point somewhat lower down the stream, sheltered by a thick grove of palms, from which a road, as he knew, led to the town of Tabasco, giving orders to his officer to march at once on the place, while he himself advanced to assault it in front.[9]

[8] Camargo, Historia de Tlascaa, MS.—Oviedo, Hist. de las Ind., MS., lib. 33, cap. 1.—Martyr, De Insulis, p. 347.—Bernal Diaz, Hist. de la Conquista, cap. 29.— Carta de Vera Cruz, MS.—Las Casas, Hist. de las Indias, MS., lib. 3, cap. 115, 116.
[9] Bernal Diaz, Hist. de la Conquista, cap. 31.—Carta de Vera Cruz, MS.—Gomara, Crónica, cap. 18.—Las Casas, Hist. de las Indias, MS., lib. 3, cap. 118.— Martyr, De Insulis, p. 348.
There are some discrepancies between the statements of Bernal Diaz, and the Letter from Vera Cruz; both by parties who were present.

Then embarking the remainder of his troops, Cortés crossed the river
in face of the enemy; but, before commencing hostilities, that he might
"act with entire regard to justice, and in obedience to the instructions
of the Royal Council," [10] he first caused proclamation to be made through
the interpreter, that he desired only a free passage for his men; and that
he proposed to revive the friendly relations which had formerly subsisted between his countrymen and the natives. He assured them that
if blood were spilt, the sin would lie on their heads, and that resistance
would be useless, since he was resolved at all hazards to take up his
quarters that night in the town of Tabasco. This proclamation, delivered
in lofty tone, and duly recorded by the notary, was answered by the
Indians—who might possibly have comprehended one word in ten of it
—with shouts of defiance and a shower of arrows.[11]

Cortés, having now complied with all the requisitions of a loyal cavalier, and shifted the responsibility from his own shoulders to those of the
Royal Council, brought his boats alongside of the Indian canoes. They
grappled fiercely together, and both parties were soon in the water,
which rose above the girdle. The struggle was not long, though desperate.
The superior strength of the Europeans prevailed, and they forced the
enemy back to land. Here, however, they were supported by their countrymen, who showered down darts, arrows, and blazing billets of wood
on the heads of the invaders. The banks were soft and slippery, and it
was with difficulty the soldiers made good their footing. Cortés lost a
sandal in the mud, but continued to fight barefoot, with great exposure
of his person, as the Indians, who soon singled out the leader, called to
one another, "Strike at the chief!"

At length the Spaniards gained the bank, and were able to come into
something like order, when they opened a brisk fire from their arquebuses and crossbows. The enemy, astounded by the roar and flash of the
fire-arms, of which they had had no experience, fell back, and retreated
behind a breastwork of timber thrown across the way. The Spaniards, hot
in the pursuit, soon carried these rude defences, and drove the Tabascans
before them towards the town, where they again took shelter behind
their palisades.

Meanwhile Avila had arrived from the opposite quarter, and the natives taken by surprise made no further attempt at resistance, but aban-

---

[10] Carta de Vera Cruz, MS.—Bernal Diaz, Hist. de la Conquista, cap. 31.

[11] "See," exclaims the Bishop of Chiapa, in his caustic vein, "the reasonableness of
this 'requisition,' or, to speak more correctly, the folly and insensibility of the
Royal Council, who could find, in the refusal of the Indians to receive it, a good
pretext for war." (Hist. de las Indias, MS., lib. 3, cap. 118.) In another place, he
pronounces an animated invective against the iniquity of those who covered up
hostilities under this empty form of words, the import of which was utterly incomprehensible to the barbarians. (Ibid., lib. 3, cap. 57.) The famous formula, used by
the Spanish conquerors on this occasion, was drawn up by Dr. Palacios Reubios, a
man of letters, and a member of the King's council. "But I laugh at him and his
letters," exclaims Oviedo, "if he thought a word of it could be comprehended by
the untutored Indians!" (Hist. de las Ind., MS., lib. 29, cap. 7.) The regular Manifesto, *requirimiento*, may be found translated in the concluding pages of Irving's
"Voyages of the Companions of Columbus."

doned the place to the Christians. They had previously removed their families and effects. Some provisions fell into the hands of the victors, but little gold, "a circumstance," says Las Casas, "which gave them no particular satisfaction." [12] It was a very populous place. The houses were mostly of mud; the better sort of stone and lime; affording proofs in the inhabitants of a superior refinement to that found in the Islands, as their stout resistance had given evidence of superior valor.[13]

Cortés, having thus made himself master of the town, took formal possession of it for the crown of Castile. He gave three cuts with his sword on a large *ceiba* tree, which grew in the place, and proclaimed aloud, that he took possession of the city in the name and behalf of the Catholic sovereigns, and would maintain and defend the same with sword and buckler against all who should gainsay it. The same vaunting declaration was also made by the soldiers, and the whole was duly recorded and attested by the notary. This was the usual simple, but chivalric form, with which the Spanish cavaliers asserted the royal title to the conquered territories in the New World. It was a good title, doubtless, against the claims of any other European potentate.

The general took up his quarters that night in the court-yard of the principal temple. He posted his sentinels, and took all the precautions practised in wars with a civilized foe. Indeed, there was reason for them. A suspicious silence seemed to reign through the place and its neighborhood; and tidings were brought that the interpreter, Melchorejo, had fled, leaving his Spanish dress hanging on a tree. Cortés was disquieted by the desertion of this man, who would not only inform his countrymen of the small number of the Spaniards, but dissipate any illusions that might be entertained of their superior natures.

On the following morning, as no traces of the enemy were visible, Cortés ordered out a detachment under Alvarado, and another under Francisco de Lujo, to reconnoitre. The latter officer had not advanced a league, before he learned the position of the Indians, by their attacking him in such force, that he was fain to take shelter in a large stone building, where he was closely besieged. Fortunately the loud yells of the assailants, like most barbarous nations seeking to strike terror by their ferocious cries, reached the ears of Alvarado and his men, who, speedily

---

[12] "Halláronlas llenas de maiz é gallinas y otros vastimentos, oro ninguno, de lo que ellos no resciviéron mucho plazer." Hist. de las Ind., MS., ubi supra.

[13] Peter Martyr gives a glowing picture of this Indian capital. "Ad fluminis ripam protentum dicunt esse oppidum, quantum non ausim dicere: mille quingentorum passuum, ait Alaminus nauclerus, et domorum quinque ac viginti millium: stringunt alij, ingens tamen fatentur et celebre. Hortis intersecantur domus, quæ sunt *egregiè lapidibus et calce fabrefactæ, maximâ industriâ et architectorum arte.*" (De Insulis, p. 349.) With his usual inquisitive spirit, he gleaned all the particulars from the old pilot Alaminos, and from two of the officers of Cortés who revisited Spain in the course of that year. Tabasco was in the neighborhood of those ruined cities of Yucatan, which have lately been the theme of so much speculation. The encomiums of Martyr are not so remarkable as the apathy of other contemporary chroniclers.

advancing to the relief of their comrades, enabled them to force a passage through the enemy. Both parties retreated, closely pursued, on the town, when Cortés, marching out to their support, compelled the Tabascans to retire.

A few prisoners were taken in this skirmish. By them Cortés found his worst apprehensions verified. The country was everywhere in arms. A force consisting of many thousands had assembled from the neighboring provinces, and a general assault was resolved on for the next day. To the general's inquiries why he had been received in so different a manner from his predecessor, Grijalva, they answered, that "the conduct of the Tabascans then had given great offence to the other Indian tribes, who taxed them with treachery and cowardice; so that they had promised, on any return of the white men, to resist them in the same manner that their neighbors had done." [14]

Cortés might now well regret that he had allowed himself to deviate from the direct object of his enterprise, and to become entangled in a doubtful war which could lead to no profitable result. But it was too late to repent. He had taken the step, and had no alternative but to go forward. To retreat would dishearten his own men at the outset, impair their confidence in him as their leader, and confirm the arrogance of his foes, the tidings of whose success might precede him on his voyage, and prepare the way for greater mortifications and defeats. He did not hesitate as to the course he was to pursue; but, calling his officers together, announced his intention to give battle the following morning.[15]

He sent back to the vessels such as were disabled by their wounds, and ordered the remainder of the forces to join the camp. Six of the heavy guns were also taken from the ships, together with all the horses. The animals were stiff and torpid from long confinement on board; but a few hours' exercise restored them to their strength and usual spirit. He gave the command of the artillery—if it may be dignified with the name—to a soldier named Mesa, who had acquired some experience as an engineer in the Italian wars. The infantry he had under the orders of Diego de Ordaz, and took charge of the cavalry himself. It consisted of some of the most valiant gentlemen of his little band, among whom may be mentioned Alvarado, Velasquez de Leon, Avila, Puertocarrero, Olid, Montejo. Having thus made all the necessary arrangements, and settled his plan of battle, he retired to rest,—but not to slumber. His feverish mind, as may well be imagined, was filled with anxiety for the morrow, which might decide the fate of his expedition; and, as was his wont on such occasions, he was frequently observed, during the night, going the

---

[14] Bernal Diaz, Hist. de la Conquista, cap. 31, 32.—Gomara, Crónica, cap. 18.—Las Casas, Hist. de las Indias, MS., lib. 3, cap. 118, 119.—Ixtlilxochitl, Hist. Chich MS., cap. 78, 79.

[15] According to Solís, who quotes the address of Cortés on the occasion, he summoned a council of his captains to advise him as to the course he should pursue (Conquista, cap. 19.) It is possible; but I find no warrant for it anywhere.

rounds, and visiting the sentinels, to see that no one slept upon his post

At the first glimmering of light he mustered his army, and declared his purpose not to abide, cooped up in the town, the assault of the enemy, but to march at once against him. For he well knew that the spirits rise with action, and that the attacking party gathers a confidence from the very movement, which is not felt by the one who is passively, perhaps anxiously, awaiting the assault. The Indians were understood to be encamped on a level ground a few miles distant from the city, called the plain of Ceutla. The general commanded that Ordaz should march with the foot, including the artillery, directly across the country, and attack them in front, while he himself would fetch a circuit with the horse, and turn their flank when thus engaged, or fall upon their rear.

These dispositions being completed, the little army heard mass and then sallied forth from the wooden walls of Tabasco. It was Lady-day, the twenty-fifth of March,—long memorable in the annals of New Spain. The district around the town was chequered with patches of maize, and, on the lower level, with plantations of cacao,—supplying the beverage, and perhaps the coin of the country, as in Mexico. These plantations, requiring constant irrigation, were fed by numerous canals and reservoirs of water, so that the country could not be traversed without great toil and difficulty. It was, however, intersected by a narrow path or causeway, over which the cannon could be dragged.

The troops advanced more than a league on their laborious march, without descrying the enemy. The weather was sultry, but few of them were embarrassed by the heavy mail worn by the European cavaliers at that period. Their cotton jackets, thickly quilted, afforded a tolerable protection against the arrows of the Indian, and allowed room for the freedom and activity of movement essential to a life of rambling adventure in the wilderness.

At length they came in sight of the broad plains of Ceutla, and beheld the dusky lines of the enemy stretching, as far as the eye could reach, along the edge of the horizon. The Indians had shown some sagacity in the choice of their position; and, as the weary Spaniards came slowly on, floundering through the morass, the Tabascans set up their hideous battle-cries, and discharged volleys of arrows, stones, and other missiles, which rattled like hail on the shields and helmets of the assailants. Many were severely wounded before they could gain the firm ground, where they soon cleared a space for themselves, and opened a heavy fire of artillery and musketry on the dense columns of the enemy, which presented a fatal mark for the balls. Numbers were swept down at every discharge; but the bold barbarians, far from being dismayed, threw up dust and leaves to hide their losses, and, sounding their war instruments, shot off fresh flights of arrows in return.

They even pressed closer on the Spaniards, and, when driven off by a vigorous charge, soon turned again, and, rolling back like the waves of the ocean, seemed ready to overwhelm the little band by weight of numbers. Thus cramped, the latter had scarcely room to perform their necessary evolutions, or even to work their guns with effect.[16] The engagement had now lasted more than an hour, and the Spaniards, sorely pressed, looked with great anxiety for the arrival of the horse,— which some unaccountable impediments must have detained,—to relieve them from their perilous position. At this crisis, the furthest columns of the Indian army were seen to be agitated and thrown into a disorder that rapidly spread through the whole mass. It was not long before the ears of the Christians were saluted with the cheering war-cry of "San Jago and San Pedro!" and they beheld the bright helmets and swords of the Castilian chivalry flashing back the rays of the morning sun, as they dashed through the ranks of the enemy, striking to the right and left, and scattering dismay around them. The eye of faith, indeed, could discern the patron Saint of Spain, himself, mounted on his grey war-horse, heading the rescue and trampling over the bodies of the fallen infidels! [17]

The approach of Cortés had been greatly retarded by the broken nature of the ground. When he came up, the Indians were so hotly engaged, that he was upon them before they observed his approach. He ordered his men to direct their lances at the faces of their opponents,[18] who, terrified at the monstrous apparition,—for they supposed the rider and the horse, which they had never before seen, to be one and the same,[19]—were seized with a panic. Ordaz availed himself of it to command a general charge along the line, and the Indians, many of them throwing away their arms, fled without attempting further resistance.

Cortés was too content with the victory, to care to follow it up by dipping his sword in the blood of the fugitives. He drew off his men to a copse of palms which skirted the place, and under their broad canopy the soldiers offered up thanksgivings to the Almighty for the victory vouchsafed them. The field of battle was made the site of a town, called, in honor of the day on which the action took place, *Santa María de la Vitoria,* long afterwards the capital of the Province.[20] The number of

[16] Las Casas, Hist. de las Indias, MS., lib. 3, cap. 119.—Gomara, Crónica, cap. 19, 20.—Herrera, Hist. General, dec. 2, lib. 4, cap. 11.—Martyr, De Insulis, p. 350. —Ixtlilxochitl, Hist. Chich., MS., cap. 79.—Bernal Diaz, Hist. de la Conquista, cap. 33, 36.—Carta de Vera Cruz, MS.

[17] Ixtlilxochitl, Hist. Chich., MS., cap. 79.

"Cortés supposed it was his own tutelar saint, St. Peter," says Pizarro y Orellana; "but the common and indubitable opinion is, that it was our glorious apostle St. James, the bulwark and safeguard of our nation." (Varones Ilustres, p. 73.) "Sinner that I am," exclaims honest Bernal Diaz, in a more skeptical vein, "it was not permitted to me to see either the one or the other of the Apostles on this occasion." Hist. de la Conquista, cap. 34.

[18] It was the order—as the reader may remember—given by Cæsar to his followers in his battle with Pompey;

"Adversosque jubet ferror confundere vultus."
LUCAN, Pharsalia, lib. 7, v. 575.

[19] "Equites," says Paolo Giovio, "unum integrum Centaurorum specie animæ esse existimarent." Elogia Virorum Illustrium, (Basil 1696,) lib. 6, p. 229.

[20] Clavigero, Stor. del Messico, tom. III. p. 11.

those who fought or fell in the engagement is altogether doubtful. Nothing, indeed, is more uncertain than numerical estimates of barbarians. And they gain nothing in probability, when they come, as in the present instance, from the reports of their enemies. Most accounts, however, agree that the Indian force consisted of five squadrons of eight thousand men each. There is more discrepancy as to the number of slain, varying from one to thirty thousand! In the monstrous discordance, the common disposition to exaggerate may lead us to look for truth in the neighborhood of the smallest number. The loss of the Christians was inconsiderable; not exceeding—if we receive their own reports, probably, from the same causes, much diminishing the truth—two killed and less than a hundred wounded! We may readily comprehend the feelings of the Conquerors, when they declared, that "Heaven must have fought on their side, since their own strength could never have prevailed against such a multitude of enemies!" [21]

Several prisoners were taken in the battle, among them two chiefs. Cortés gave them their liberty, and sent a message by them to their countrymen, "that he would overlook the past, if they would come in at once, and tender their submission. Otherwise he would ride over the land, and put every living thing in it, man, woman and child, to the sword!" With this formidable menace ringing in their ears, the envoys departed.

But the Tabascans had no relish for further hostilities. A body of inferior chiefs appeared the next day, clad in dark dresses of cotton, intimating their abject condition, and implored leave to bury their dead. It was granted by the general, with many assurances of his friendly disposition; but at the same time he told them, he expected their principal caciques, as he would treat with none other. These soon presented themselves, attended by a numerous train of vassals, who followed with timid curiosity to the Christian camp. Among their propitiatory gifts were twenty female slaves, which, from the character of one of them, proved of infinitely more consequence than was anticipated by either Spaniards or Tabascans. Confidence was soon restored; and was succeeded by a friendly intercourse, and the interchange of Spanish toys for the rude commodities of the country, articles of food, cotton, and a few gold ornaments of little value. When asked where the precious metal was procured, they pointed to the west, and answered "Culhua," "Mexico." The Spaniards saw this was no place for them to traffic, or to tarry in.—Yet here, they were not many leagues distant from a potent and opulent city, or what once had been so, the ancient Palenque. But

[21] "Crean Vras. Reales Altezas por cierto, que esta batalla fué vencida mas por voluntad de Dios que por nras. fuerzas, porque para con quarenta mil hombres de guerra, poca defensa fuera quatrozientos que nosotros eramos." (Carta de Vera Cruz, MS.—Gomara, Crónica, cap. 20.—Bernal Diaz, Hist. de la Conquista, cap. 35.) It is Las Casas, who, regulating his mathematics, as usual, by his feelings, rates the Indian loss at the exorbitant amount cited in the text. "This," he concludes dryly, "was the first preaching of the Gospel by Cortés in New Spain!" Hist. de las Indias, MS., lib. 3, cap. 119.

its glory may have even then passed away, and its name have been forgotten by the surrounding nations.

Before his departure the Spanish commander did not omit to provide for one great object of his expedition, the conversion of the Indians. He first represented to the caciques, that he had been sent thither by a powerful monarch on the other side of the water, to whom he had now a right to claim their allegiance. He then caused the reverend fathers Olmedo and Diaz to enlighten their minds, as far as possible, in regard to the great truths of revelation, urging them to receive these in place of their own heathenish abominations. The Tabascans, whose perceptions were no doubt materially quickened by the discipline they had undergone, made but a faint resistance to either proposal. The next day was Palm Sunday, and the general resolved to celebrate their conversion by one of those pompous ceremonials of the Church, which should make a lasting impression on their minds.

A solemn procession was formed of the whole army with the ecclesiastics at their head, each soldier bearing a palm-branch in his hand. The concourse was swelled by thousands of Indians of both sexes, who followed in curious astonishment at the spectacle. The long files bent their way through the flowery savannas that bordered the settlement, to the principal temple, where an altar was raised, and the image of the presiding deity was deposed to make room for that of the Virgin with the infant Saviour. Mass was celebrated by father Olmedo, and the soldiers who were capable joined in the solemn chant. The natives listened in profound silence, and, if we may believe the chronicler of the event who witnessed it, were melted into tears, while their hearts were penetrated with reverential awe for the God of those terrible beings who seemed to wield in their own hands the thunder and the lightning.[22]

The Roman Catholic communion has, it must be admitted, some decided advantages over the Protestant, for the purposes of proselytism. The dazzling pomp of its service and its touching appeal to the sensibilities affect the imagination of the rude child of nature much more powerfully than the cold abstractions of Protestantism, which, addressed to the reason, demand a degree of refinement and mental culture in the audience to comprehend them. The respect, moreover, shown by the Catholic for the material representations of Divinity, greatly facilitates the same object. It is true, such representations are used by him only as incentives, not as the objects of worship. But this distinction is lost on the savage, who finds such forms of adoration too analogous to his own to impose any great violence on his feelings. It is only required of him to transfer his homage from the image of Quetzalcoatl, the benevolent deity who walked among men, to that of the Virgin or the Redeemer; from the Cross, which he has worshipped as the emblem of the God of rain, to the same Cross, the symbol of salvation.

These solemnities concluded, Cortés prepared to return to his ships,

---

[22] Gomara, Crónica, cap. 21, 22.—Carta de Vera Cruz, MS.—Martyr, De Insulis, p. 351.—Las Casas, Hist. de las Indias, MS., ubi supra.

well satisfied with the impression made on the new converts, and with
the conquests he had thus achieved for Castile and Christianity. The
soldiers, taking leave of their Indian friends, entered the boats with the
palm-branches in their hands, and descending the river reëmbarked on
board their vessels, which rode at anchor at its mouth. A favorable breeze
was blowing, and the little navy, opening its sails to receive it, was
soon on its way again to the golden shores of Mexico

CHAPTER V

VOYAGE ALONG THE COAST—DOÑA MARINA—SPANIARDS LAND IN
MEXICO—INTERVIEW WITH THE AZTECS

1519

THE fleet held its course so near the shore, that the inhabitants could be
seen on it; and, as it swept along the winding borders of the Gulf, the
soldiers, who had been on the former expedition with Grijalva, pointed
out to their companions the memorable places on the coast. Here was
the *Rio de Alvarado,* named after the gallant adventurer, who was present, also, in this expedition; there the *Rio de Vanderas,* in which Grijalva
had carried on so lucrative a commerce with the Mexicans; and there
the *Isla de los Sacrificios,* where the Spaniards first saw the vestiges of
human sacrifice on the coast. Puertocarrero, as he listened to these reminiscences of the sailors, repeated the words of the old ballad of Montesinos, "Here is France, there is Paris, and there the waters of the
Duero," [1] &c. "But I advise you," he added, turning to Cortés, "to look
out only for the rich lands, and the best way to govern them." "Fear
not," replied his commander, "if Fortune but favors me as she did Or-
lando, and I have such gallant gentlemen as you for my companions, I
shall understand myself very well." [2]

The fleet had now arrived off San Juan de Ulua, the island so named
by Grijalva. The weather was temperate and serene, and crowds of natives were gathered on the shore of the main land, gazing at the strange
phenomenon, as the vessels glided along under easy sail on the smooth
bosom of the waters. It was the evening of Thursday in Passion Week.
The air came pleasantly off the shore, and Cortés, liking the spot,
thought he might safely anchor under the lee of the island, which would
shelter him from the *nortes* that sweep over these seas with fatal violence
in the winter, sometimes even late in the spring.

The ships had not been long at anchor, when a light pirogue, filled
with natives, shot off from the neighboring continent, and steered for

[1] "Cata Francia, Montesinos,
Cata Paris la ciudad,
Cata las aguas de Duero
Do van á dar en la mar."

They are the words of the popular old ballad, first published, I believe. in the Ro-
mancero de Ambéres, and lately by Duran, Romances Caballerescos é Históricos,
Parte 1, p. 82.
[2] Bernal Diaz, Hist. de la Conquista, cap. 37.

the general's vessel, distinguished by the royal ensign of Castile floating from the mast. The Indians came on board with a frank confidence, inspired by the accounts of the Spaniards spread by their countrymen who had traded with Grijalva. They brought presents of fruit and flowers and little ornaments of gold, which they gladly exchanged for the usual trinkets. Cortés was baffled in his attempts to hold a conversation with his visitors by means of the interpreter, Aguilar, who was ignorant of the language; the Mayan dialects, with which he was conversant, bearing too little resemblance to the Aztec. The natives supplied the deficiency, as far as possible, by the uncommon vivacity and significance of their gestures—the hieroglyphics of speech,—but the Spanish commander saw with chagrin the embarrassments he must encounter in future for want of a more perfect medium of communication.[8] In this dilemma, he was informed that one of the female slaves given to him by the Tabascan chiefs was a native Mexican, and understood the language. Her name—that given to her by the Spaniards—was Marina; and, as she was to exercise a most important influence on their fortunes, it is necessary to acquaint the reader with something of her character and history.

She was born at Painalla, in the province of Coatzacualco, on the south-eastern borders of the Mexican empire. Her father, a rich and powerful cacique, died when she was very young. Her mother married again, and, having a son, she conceived the infamous idea of securing to this offspring of her second union Marina's rightful inheritance. She accordingly feigned that the latter was dead, but secretly delivered her into the hands of some itinerant traders of Xicallanco. She availed herself, at the same time, of the death of a child of one of her slaves, to substitute the corpse for that of her own daughter, and celebrated the obsequies with mock solemnity. These particulars are related by the honest old soldier, Bernal Diaz, who knew the mother, and witnessed the generous treatment of her afterwards by Marina. By the merchants the Indian maiden was again sold to the cacique of Tabasco, who delivered her, as we have seen, to the Spaniards.

From the place of her birth she was well acquainted with the Mexican tongue, which, indeed, she is said to have spoken with great elegance. Her residence in Tabasco familiarized her with the dialects of that country, so that she could carry on a conversation with Aguilar, which he in turn rendered into the Castilian. Thus a certain, though somewhat circuitous channel was opened to Cortés for communicating with the Aztecs; a circumstance of the last importance to the success of his enterprise. It was not very long, however, before Marina, who had a lively genius, made herself so far mistress of the Castilian as to supersede the

---

[8] Las Casas notices the significance of the Indian gestures as implying a most active imagination. "Señas é meneos con que los Yndios mucho mas que otras generaciones entienden y se dan á entender, por tener muy bivos los sentidos exteriores y tambien los interiores, mayormente ques admirable su imaginacion." Hist. de las Indias, MS., lib. 3, cap. 120.

necessity of any other linguist. She learned it the more readily, as it was to her the language of love.

Cortés, who appreciated the value of her services from the first, made her his interpreter, then his secretary, and, won by her charms, his mistress. She had a son by him, Don Martin Cortés, *commendador* of the Military Order of St. James, less distinguished by his birth than his unmerited persecutions.

Marina was at this time in the morning of life. She is said to have possessed uncommon personal attractions,[4] and her open, expressive features indicated her generous temper. She always remained faithful to the countrymen of her adoption; and her knowledge of the language and customs of the Mexicans, and often of their designs, enabled her to extricate the Spaniards, more than once, from the most embarrassing and perilous situations. She had her errors, as we have seen. But they should be rather charged to the defects of early education, and to the evil influence of him to whom in the darkness of her spirit she looked with simple confidence for the light to guide her. All agree that she was full of excellent qualities, and the important services which she rendered the Spaniards have made her memory deservedly dear to them; while the name of Malinche—the name by which she is still known in Mexico—was pronounced with kindness by the conquered races, with whose misfortunes she showed an invariable sympathy.[5]

With the aid of his two intelligent interpreters, Cortés entered into conversation with his Indian visitors. He learned that they were Mexicans, or rather subjects of the great Mexican empire, of which they own their own province formed one of the comparatively recent conquests. The country was ruled by a powerful monarch, called Moctheuzoma,

[4] "Hermosa como Diosa," *beautiful as a goddess,* says Camargo of her. (Hist. de Tlascala, MS.) A modern poet pays her charms the following not inelegant tribute;
"Admira tan lúcida cabalgada
Y espectáculo tal Doña Marina,
India noble al caudillo presentada,
De fortuna y belleza peregrina.
* * * * *
Con despejado espíritu y viveza
Gira la vista en el concurso mudo;
Rico manto de extrema sutileza
Con chapas de oro autorizarla pudo,
Prendido con bizarra gentileza
Sobre los pechos en ayroso nudo;
Reyna parece de la Indiana Zona,
Varonil y hermosísima Amazona."
MORATIN, Las Naves de Cortés
Destruidas.
[5] Las Casas, Hist. de las Indias, MS., lib. 3, cap. 120.—Gomara Crónica, cap. 25, 26.—Clavigero, Stor. del Messico, tom. III. pp. 12-14.—Oviedo, Hist. de las Ind., MS., lib. 33, cap. 1.—Ixtlilxochitl, Hist. Chich., MS., cap. 79.—Camargo, Hist. de Tlascala, MS.—Bernal Diaz, Hist. de la Conquista, cap. 37, 38.
There is some discordance in the notices of the early life of Marina. I have followed Bernal Diaz,—from his means of observation, the best authority. There is happily no difference in the estimate of her singular merits and services.

or by Europeans more commonly Montezuma,[6] who dwelt on the moun-tain plains of the interior, nearly seventy leagues from the coast; their own province was governed by one of his nobles, named Teuhtlile, whose residence was eight leagues distant. Cortés acquainted them in turn with his own friendly views in visiting their country, and with his desire of an interview with the Aztec governor. He then dismissed them loaded with presents, having first ascertained that there was abundance of gold in the interior, like the specimens they had brought.

Cortés, pleased with the manners of the people, and the goodly re-ports of the land, resolved to take up his quarters here for the present. The next morning, April 21, being Good Friday, he landed, with all his force, on the very spot where now stands the modern city of Vera Cruz. Little did the Conqueror imagine that the desolate beach, on which he first planted his foot, was one day to be covered by a flourishing city, the great mart of European and Oriental trade, the commercial capital of New Spain.[7]

It was a wide and level plain, except where the sand had been drifted into hillocks by the perpetual blowing of the *norte*. On these sand-hills he mounted his little battery of guns, so as to give him the command of the country. He then employed the troops in cutting down small trees and bushes which grew near, in order to provide a shelter from the weather. In this he was aided by the people of the country, sent, as it appeared, by the governor of the district to assist the Spaniards. With their help stakes were firmly set in the earth, and covered with boughs, and with mats and cotton carpets, which the friendly natives brought with them. In this way they secured, in a couple of days, a good defence against the scorching rays of the sun, which beat with intolerable fierce-ness on the sands. The place was surrounded by stagnant marshes, the exhalations from which, quickened by the heat into the pestilent malaria, have occasioned in later times wider mortality to Europeans than all the hurricanes on the coast. The bilious disorders, now the terrible scourge of the *tierra caliente*, were little known before the Conquest. The seeds of the poison seem to have been scattered by the hand of civil-ization; for it is only necessary to settle a town, and draw together a busy European population, in order to call out the malignity of the venom which had before lurked innoxious in the atmosphere.[8]

[6] The name of the Aztec monarch, like those of most persons and places in New Spain, has been twisted into all possible varieties of orthography. Modern Spanish historians usually call him Motezuma. But as there is no reason to suppose that this is correct, I have preferred to conform to the name by which he is usually known to English readers. It is the one adopted by Bernal Diaz, and by no other contemporary, as far as I know.

[7] Ixtlilxochitl, Hist. Chich., MS., cap. 79.—Clavigero, Stor. del Messico, tom. III. p. 16.

New Vera Cruz, as the present town is called, is distinct, as we shall here-after, from that established by Cortés, and was not founded till the close of the six-teenth century, by the Conde de Monterey, viceroy of Mexico. It received its privi-leges as a city from Philip III. in 1615. Ibid., tom. III. p. 30, nota.

[8] The epidemic of the *matlazahuatl*, so fatal to the Aztecs, is shown by M. de

While these arrangements were in progress, the natives flocked in from the adjacent district, which was tolerably populous in the interior, drawn by a natural curiosity to see the wonderful strangers. They brought with them fruits, vegetables, flowers in abundance, game, and many dishes cooked after the fashion of the country, with little articles of gold and other ornaments. They gave away some as presents, and bar, tered others for the wares of the Spaniards; so that the camp, crowded with a motley throng of every age and sex, wore the appearance of a fair. From some of his visitors Cortés learned the intention of the governor to wait on him the following day.

This was Easter. Teuhtlile arrived, as he had announced, before noon. He was attended by a numerous train, and was met by Cortés, who conducted him with much ceremony to his tent, where his principal officers were assembled. The Aztec chief returned their salutations with polite, though formal courtesy. Mass was said by father Olmedo, and the service was listened to by Teuhtlile and his attendants with decent reverence. A collation was afterwards served, at which the general entertained his guest with Spanish wines and confections. The interpreters were then introduced, and a conversation commenced between the parties.

The first inquiries of Teuhtlile were respecting the country of the strangers, and the purport of their visit. Cortés told him, that "he was the subject of a potent monarch beyond the seas, who ruled over an immense empire, and had kings and princes for his vassals; that, acquainted with the greatness of the Mexican emperor, his master had desired to enter into a communication with him, and had sent him as his envoy to wait on Montezuma with a present in token of his good-will, and a message which he must deliver in person." He concluded by inquiring of Teuhtlile when he could be admitted to his sovereign's presence.

To this the Aztec noble somewhat haughtily replied, "How is it, that you have been here only two days, and demand to see the emperor?" He then added, with more courtesy, that "he was surprised to learn there was another monarch as powerful as Montezuma; but that, if it were so, he had no doubt his master would be happy to communicate with him. He would send his couriers with the royal gift brought by the Spanish commander, and, so soon as he had learned Montezuma's will, would communicate it."

Humboldt to be essentially different from the *vómito*, or bilious fever of our day. Indeed, this disease is not noticed by the early conquerors and colonists; and, Clavi-gero asserts, was not known in Mexico, till 1725. (Stor. del Messico, tom. I. p. 117 nota.) Humboldt, however, arguing that the same physical causes must have produced similar results, carries the disease back to a much higher antiquity, of which he discerns some traditional and historic vestiges. "Il ne faut pas confondre l'époque," he remarks with his usual penetration, "á laquelle une maladie a été décrite pour la première fois, parce qu'elle a fait de grands ravages dans un court espace de temps, avec l'époque de sa première apparition." Essai Politique, tom. IV p. 161 et seq., and 179.

Teuhtlile then commanded his slaves to bring forward the present intended for the Spanish general. It consisted of ten loads of fine cottons, several mantles of that curious feather-work whose rich and delicate dyes might vie with the most beautiful painting, and a wicker basket filled with ornaments of wrought gold, all calculated to inspire the Spaniards with high ideas of the wealth and mechanical ingenuity of the Mexicans.

Cortés received these presents with suitable acknowledgments, and ordered his own attendants to lay before the chief the articles designed for Montezuma. These were an arm-chair richly carved and painted, a crimson cap of cloth, having a gold medal emblazoned with St. George and the dragon, and a quantity of collars, bracelets, and other ornaments of cut glass, which, in a country where glass was not to be had, might claim to have the value of real gems, and no doubt passed for such with the inexperienced Mexican. Teuhtlile observed a soldier in the camp with a shining gilt helmet on his head, which he said reminded him of one worn by the god Quetzalcoatl in Mexico; and he showed a desire that Montezuma should see it. The coming of the Spaniards, as the reader will soon see, was associated with some traditions of this same deity. Cortés expressed his willingness that the casque should be sent to the emperor, intimating a hope that it would be returned filled with the gold dust of the country, that he might be able to compare its quality with that in his own! He further told the governor, as we are informed by his chaplain, "that the Spaniards were troubled with a disease of the heart, for which gold was a specific remedy"! [9] "In short," says Las Casas, "he contrived to make his want of gold very clear to the governor." [10]

While these things were passing, Cortés observed one of Teuhtlile's attendants busy with a pencil, apparently delineating some object. On looking at his work, he found that it was a sketch on canvass of the Spaniards, their costumes, arms, and, in short, different objects of interest, giving to each its appropriate form and color. This was the celebrated picture-writing of the Aztecs, and, as Teuhtlile informed him, this man was employed in portraying the various objects for the eye of Montezuma, who would thus gather a more vivid notion of their appearance than from any description by words. Cortés was pleased with the idea; and, as he knew how much the effect would be heightened by converting still life into action, he ordered out the cavalry on the beach, the wet sands of which afforded a firm footing for the horses. The bold and rapid movements of the troops, as they went through their military exercises; the apparent ease with which they managed the fiery animals on which they were mounted; the glancing of their weapons, and the shrill cry of the trumpet, all filled the spectators with astonishment; but when they heard the thunders of the cannon, which Cortés ordered to be fired at the same time, and witnessed the volumes of smoke and flame

[9] Gomara, Crónica, cap. 26.
[10] Las Casas, Hist. de las Indias. MS.. lib. 3, cap. 119.

issuing from these terrible engines, and the rushing sound of the balls, as they dashed through the trees of the neighboring forest, shivering their branches into fragments, they were filled with consternation, from which the Aztec chief himself was not wholly free.

Nothing of all this was lost on the painters, who faithfully recorded, after their fashion, every particular; not omitting the ships, "the water-houses,"—as they called them,—of the strangers, which, with their dark hulls and snow-white sails reflected from the water, were swinging lazily at anchor on the calm bosom of the bay. All was depicted with a fidelity, that excited in their turn the admiration of the Spaniards, who, doubtless unprepared for this exhibition of skill, greatly overestimated the merits of the execution.

These various matters completed, Teuhtlile with his attendants withdrew from the Spanish quarters, with the same ceremony with which he had entered them; leaving orders that his people should supply the troops with provisions and other articles requisite for their accommodation, till further instructions from the capital.[11]

[11] Ixtlilxochitl, Relaciones, MS., No. 13.—Idem, Hist. Chich., MS., cap. 79.—Gomara, Crónica, cap. 25, 26.—Bernal Diaz, Hist. de la Conquista, cap. 38.—Herrera, Hist. General, dec. 2, lib. 5, cap. 4.—Carta de Vera Cruz, MS.—Torquemada. Monarch. Ind., lib. 4, cap. 13-15.—Tezozomoc, Crón. Mexicana. MS., cap. 107.

CHAPTER VI

ACCOUNT OF MONTEZUMA—STATE OF HIS EMPIRE—STRANGE PROG-
NOSTICS—EMBASSY AND PRESENTS—SPANISH ENCAMPMENT

1519

WE must now take leave of the Spanish camp in the *tierra caliente*, and
transport ourselves to the distant capital of Mexico, where no little sensation was excited by the arrival of the wonderful strangers on the coast.
The Aztec throne was filled at that time by Montezuma the Second,
nephew of the last, and grandson of a preceding monarch. He had been
elected to the regal dignity in 1502, in preference to his brothers, for his
superior qualifications, both as a soldier and a priest,—a combination of
offices sometimes found in the Mexican candidates, as it was, more
frequently, in the Egyptian. In early youth, he had taken an active part
in the wars of the empire, though of late he had devoted himself more
exclusively to the services of the temple; and he was scrupulous in his
attentions to all the burdensome ceremonial of the Aztec worship. He
maintained a grave and reserved demeanor, speaking little and with
prudent deliberation. His deportment was well calculated to inspire ideas
of superior sanctity.[1]

When his election was announced to him, he was found sweeping
down the stairs in the great temple of the national war-god. He received
the messengers with a becoming humility, professing his unfitness for so
responsible a station. The address delivered as usual on the occasion was
made by his relative Nezahualpilli, the wise king of Tezcuco.[2] It has
fortunately been preserved, and presents a favorable specimen of Indian
eloquence. Towards the conclusion, the orator exclaims, "Who can
doubt that the Aztec empire has reached the zenith of its greatness,
since the Almighty has placed over it one whose very presence fills
every beholder with reverence? Rejoice, happy people, that you have
now a sovereign who will be to you a steady column of support; a father
in distress, a more than brother in tenderness and sympathy; one whose
aspiring soul will disdain all the profligate pleasures of the senses, and
the wasting indulgence of sloth. And thou, illustrious youth, doubt not
that the Creator, who has laid on thee so weighty a charge, will also give

---

[1] His name suited his nature; Montezuma, according to Las Casas. signifying, in
the Mexican, "sad or severe man." Hist. de las Indias, MS., lib. 3, cap. 120.—Ixtlilxochitl, Hist. Chich., MS., cap. 70.—Acosta, lib. 7, cap. 20.—Col. de Mendoza,
pp. 13-16; Codex Tel.-Rem., p. 143, ap. Antiq. of Mexico, vol. VI.

[2] For a full account of this prince, see Book I., chap. 6.

strength to sustain it; that He, who has been so liberal in times past.
will shower yet more abundant blessings on thy head, and keep thee
firm in thy royal seat through many long and glorious years."—These
golden prognostics, which melted the royal auditor into tears, were not
destined to be realized.[3]

Montezuma displayed all the energy and enterprise in the commencement of his reign, which had been anticipated from him. His first expedition against a rebel province in the neighborhood was crowned with
success, and he led back in triumph a throng of captives for the bloody
sacrifice that was to grace his coronation. This was celebrated with uncommon pomp. Games and religious ceremonies continued for several
days, and among the spectators who flocked from distant quarters were
some noble Tlascalans, the hereditary enemies of Mexico. They were in
disguise, hoping thus to elude detection. They were recognised, however, and reported to the monarch. But he only availed himself of the
information to provide them with honorable entertainment, and a good
place for witnessing the games. This was a magnanimous act, considering
the long cherished hostility between the nations.

In his first years, Montezuma was constantly engaged in war, and frequently led his armies in person. The Aztec banners were seen in the
furthest provinces on the Gulf of Mexico, and the distant regions of
Nicaragua and Honduras. The expeditions were generally successful; and
the limits of the empire were more widely extended than at any preceding period.

Meanwhile the monarch was not inattentive to the interior concerns
of the kingdom. He made some important changes in the courts of justice; and carefully watched over the execution of the laws, which he enforced with stern severity. He was in the habit of patrolling the streets
of his capital in disguise, to make himself personally acquainted with the
abuses in it. And with more questionable policy, it is said, he would
sometimes try the integrity of his judges by tempting them with large
bribes to swerve from their duty, and then call the delinquent to strict
account for yielding to the temptation.

He liberally recompensed all who served him. He showed a similar
munificent spirit in his public works, constructing and embellishing the
temples, bringing water into the capital by a new channel, and establishing a hospital, or retreat for invalid soldiers, in the city of Colhuacan.[4]

These acts, so worthy of a great prince, were counterbalanced by
others of an opposite complexion. The humility, displayed so ostentatiously before his elevation, gave way to an intolerable arrogance. In

[3] The address is fully reported by Torquemada, (Monarch. Ind., lib. 3, cap. 68,)
who came into the country little more than half a century after its delivery. It has
been recently republished by Bustamante. Tezcuco en los Últimos Tiempos, (México, 1826,) pp. 256-258.

[4] Acosta, lib. 7, cap. 22.—Sahagun, Hist. de Nueva España, lib. 8, Prólogo, et cap.
1.—Torquemada, Monarch. Ind., lib. 3, cap. 73, 74, 81.—Col. de Mendoza, pp. 14,
85, ap. Antiq. of Mexico, vol. VI.

his pleasure-houses, domestic establishment, and way of living, he assumed a pomp unknown to his predecessors. He secluded himself from public observation, or, when he went abroad, exacted the most slavish homage; while in the palace he would be served only, even in the most menial offices, by persons of rank. He, further, dismissed several plebeians, chiefly poor soldiers of merit, from the places they had occupied near the person of his predecessor, considering their attendance a dishonor to royalty. It was in vain that his oldest and sagest counsellors remonstrated on a conduct so impolitic.

While he thus disgusted his subjects by his haughty deportment, he alienated their affections by the imposition of grievous taxes. These were demanded by the lavish expenditure of his court. They fell with peculiar heaviness on the conquered cities. This oppression led to frequent insurrection and resistance; and the latter years of his reign present a scene of unintermitting hostility, in which the forces of one half of the empire were employed in suppressing the commotions of the other. Unfortunately there was no principle of amalgamation by which the new acquisitions could be incorporated into the ancient monarchy, as parts of one whole. Their interests, as well as sympathies, were different. Thus the more widely the Aztec empire was extended, the weaker it became; resembling some vast and ill-proportioned edifice, whose disjointed materials, having no principle of cohesion, and tottering under their own weight, seem ready to fall before the first blast of the tempest.

In 1516, died the Tezcucan king, Nezahualpilli: in whom Montezuma lost his most sagacious counsellor. The succession was contested by his two sons, Cacama and Ixtlilxochitl. The former was supported by Montezuma. The latter, the younger of the princes, a bold, aspiring youth, appealing to the patriotic sentiment of his nation, would have persuaded them that his brother was too much in the Mexican interests to be true to his own country. A civil war ensued, and ended by a compromise, by which one half of the kingdom, with the capital, remained to Cacama, and the northern portion to his ambitious rival. Ixtlilxochitl became from that time the mortal foe of Montezuma.[5]

A more formidable enemy still was the little republic of Tlascala, lying midway between the Mexican Valley and the coast. It had maintained its independence for more than two centuries against the allied forces of the empire. Its resources were unimpaired, its civilization scarcely below that of its great rival states, and for courage and military prowess it had established a name inferior to none other of the nations of Anahuac.

Such was the condition of the Aztec monarchy, on the arrival of Cortés;—the people disgusted with the arrogance of the sovereign; the provinces and distant cities outraged by fiscal exactions; while potent enemies in the neighborhood lay watching the hour when they might assail their formidable rival with advantage. Still the kingdom was

[5] Clavigero, Stor. del Messico, tom. I. pp. 267, 274, 275.—Ixtlilxochitl, Hist. Chich., MS., cap. 70-76.—Acosta, lib. 7, cap. 21.

strong in its internal resources, in the will of its monarch, in the long habitual deference to his authority,—in short, in the terror of his name, and in the valor and discipline of his armies, grown grey in active service, and well drilled in all the tactics of Indian warfare. The time had now come, when these imperfect tactics and rude weapons of the barbarian were to be brought into collision with the science and enginery of the most civilized nations of the globe.

During the latter years of his reign, Montezuma had rarely taken part in his military expeditions, which he left to his captains, occupying himself chiefly with his sacerdotal functions. Under no prince had the priesthood enjoyed greater consideration and immunities. The religious festivals and rites were celebrated with unprecedented pomp. The oracles were consulted on the most trivial occasions; and the sanguinary deities were propitiated by hecatombs of victims dragged in triumph to the capital from the conquered or rebellious provinces. The religion, or, to speak correctly, the superstition of Montezuma proved a principal cause of his calamities.

In a preceding chapter I have noticed the popular traditions respecting Quetzalcoatl, that deity with a fair complexion and flowing beard, so unlike the Indian physiognomy, who, after fulfilling his mission of benevolence among the Aztecs, embarked on the Atlantic Sea for the mysterious shores of Tlapallan.[6] He promised, on his departure, to return at some future day with his posterity, and resume the possession of his empire. That day was looked forward to with hope or with apprehension, according to the interest of the believer, but with general confidence throughout the wide borders of Anahuac. Even after the Conquest, it still lingered among the Indian races, by whom it was as fondly cherished, as the advent of their king Sebastian continued to be by the Portuguese, or that of the Messiah by the Jews.[7]

A general feeling seems to have prevailed in the time of Montezuma, that the period for the return of the deity, and the full accomplishment of his promise, was near at hand. This conviction is said to have gained ground from various preternatural occurrences, reported with more or less detail by all the most ancient historians.[8] In 1510, the great lake of Tezcuco, without the occurrence of a tempest, or earthquake, or any other visible cause, became violently agitated, overflowed its banks, and, pouring into the streets of Mexico, swept off many of the buildings by the fury of the waters. In 1511, one of the turrets of the great temple took

---

[6] Ante, Book I., chap. 3, pp. 38, 39, and note 6.

[7] Tezozomoc, Crón. Mexicana, MS., cap. 107.—Ixtlilxochitl, Hist. Chich., MS., cap. 1.—Torquemada, Monarch. Ind., lib. 4, cap. 14; lib. 6, cap. 24.—Codex Vaticanus, ap. Antiq. of Mexico, vol. VI.—Sahagun, Hist. de Nueva España, lib. 8, cap. 7.—Ibid., MS., lib. 12, cap. 3, 4.

[8] "Tenia por cierto," says Las Casas of Montezuma, "segun sus prophetas ó agoreros le avian certificado, que su estado é rriquezas y prosperidad avia de perezer dentro de pocos años por çiertas gentes que avian de venir en sus dias, que de su felicidad lo derrocase, y por esto vivia siempre con temor y en tristeça y sobresaltado." Hist. de las Indias, MS., lib. 3, cap. 120.

fire, equally without any apparent cause, and continued to burn in defiance of all attempts to extinguish it. In the following years, three comets were seen; and not long before the coming of the Spaniards a strange light broke forth in the east. It spread broad at its base on the horizon, and rising in a pyramidal form tapered off as it approached the zenith. It resembled a vast sheet or flood of fire, emitting sparkles, or, as an old writer expresses, it, "seemed thickly powdered with stars." [9] At the same time, low voices were heard in the air, and doleful wailings, as if to announce some strange, mysterious calamity! The Aztec monarch, terrified at the apparitions in the heavens, took counsel of Nezahualpilli, who was a great proficient in the subtle science of astrology. But the royal sage cast a deeper cloud over his spirit, by reading in these prodigies the speedy downfall of the empire.[10]

Such are the strange stories reported by the chroniclers, in which it is not impossible to detect the glimmerings of truth.[11] Nearly thirty years had elapsed since the discovery of the Islands by Columbus, and more than twenty since his visit to the American continent. Rumors, more or less distinct, of this wonderful appearance of the white men, bearing in their hands the thunder and the lightning, so like in many respects to the traditions of Quetzalcoatl, would naturally spread far and wide among the Indian nations. Such rumors, doubtless, long before the landing of the Spaniards in Mexico, found their way up the grand plateau, filling the minds of men with anticipations of the near coming of the period when the great deity was to return and receive his own again.

In the excited state of their imaginations, prodigies became a familiar occurrence. Or rather, events not very uncommon in themselves, seen through the discolored medium of fear, were easily magnified into prodigies; and the accidental swell of the lake, the appearance of a comet, and the conflagration of a building were all interpreted as the special annunciations of Heaven.[12] Thus it happens in those great political convulsions which shake the foundations of society,—the mighty events that cast their shadows before them in their coming. Then it is that the atmos-

---

[9] Camargo, Hist. de Tlascala, MS.—The Interpreter of the Codex Tel.-Rem. intimates that this scintillating phenomenon was probably nothing more than an eruption of one of the great volcanoes of Mexico. Antiq. of Mexico, vol. VI. p. 144.

[10] Sahagun, Hist. de Nueva España, MS., lib. 12, cap. 1.—Camargo, Hist. de Tlascala, MS.—Acosta, lib. 7, cap. 23.—Herrera, Hist. General, dec. 2, lib. 5, cap. 5. —Ixtlilxochitl, Hist. Chich., MS., cap. 74.

[11] I omit the most extraordinary miracle of all,—though legal attestations of its truth were furnished the Court of Rome, (see Clavigero, Stor. del Messico, tom. I p. 289,)—namely, the resurrection of Montezuma's sister, Papantzin, four days after her burial, to warn the monarch of the approaching ruin of his empire. It finds credit with one writer, at least, in the nineteenth century! See the note of Sahagun's Mexican editor, Bustamante, Hist. de Nueva España, tom. II. p. 270.

[12] Lucan gives a fine enumeration of such prodigies witnessed in the Roman capital in a similar excitement. (Pharsalia, lib. 1, v. 523, et seq.) Poor human nature is much the same everywhere. Machiavelli has thought the subject worthy of a separate chapter in his Discourses. The philosopher intimates a belief even in the existence of beneficent intelligences who send these portents as a sort of *premonitories.* to warn mankind of the coming tempest. Discorsi sopra Tito Livio, lib. 1, cap. 56

phere is agitated with the low, prophetic murmurs, with which Nature, in the moral as in the physical world, announces the march of the hurricane;

> "When from the shores
> And forest-rustling mountains comes a voice,
> That, solemn sounding, bids the world prepare!"

When tidings were brought to the capital, of the landing of Grijalva on the coast, in the preceding year, the heart of Montezuma was filled with dismay. He felt as if the destinies which had so long brooded over the royal line of Mexico were to be accomplished, and the sceptre was to pass away from his house for ever. Though somewhat relieved by the departure of the Spaniards, he caused sentinels to be stationed on the heights; and, when the Europeans returned under Cortés, he doubtless received the earliest notice of the unwelcome event. It was by his orders, however, that the provincial governor had prepared so hospitable a reception for them. The hieroglyphical report of these strange visitors, now forwarded to the capital, revived all his apprehensions. He called, without delay, a meeting of his principal counsellors, including the kings of Tezcuco and Tlacopan, and laid the matter before them.[13]

There seems to have been much division of opinion in that body. Some were for resisting the strangers, at once, whether by fraud, or by open force. Others contended, that, if they were supernatural beings, fraud and force would be alike useless. If they were, as they pretended, ambassadors from a foreign prince, such a policy would be cowardly and unjust. That they were not of the family of Quetzalcoatl was argued from the fact, that they had shown themselves hostile to his religion; for tidings of the proceedings of the Spaniards in Tabasco, it seems, had already reached the capital. Among those in favor of giving them a friendly and honorable reception was the Tezcucan king, Cacama.

But Montezuma, taking counsel of his own ill-defined apprehensions, preferred a half-way course,—as usual, the most impolitic. He resolved to send an embassy, with such a magnificent present to the strangers, as should impress them with high ideas of his grandeur and resources; while, at the same time, he would forbid their approach to the capital This was to reveal, at once, both his wealth and his weakness.[14]

While the Aztec court was thus agitated by the arrival of the Spaniards, they were passing their time in the *tierra caliente*, not a little annoyed by the excessive heats and suffocating atmosphere of the sandy waste on which they were encamped. They experienced every alleviation that could be derived from the attentions of the friendly natives. These, by the governor's command, had constructed more than a thousand huts

---

[13] Las Casas, Hist. de las Indias, MS., lib. 3, cap. 120.—Ixtlilxochitl, Hist. Chich., MS., cap. 80.—Idem, Relaciones, MS.—Sahagun, Hist. de Nueva España, MS., lib. 12, cap. 3, 4.—Tezozomoc, Crón. Mexicana, MS., cap. 108.

[14] Tezozomoc, Crón. Mexicana, MS., loc. cit.—Camargo, Hist. de Tlascala, MS.—Ixtlilxochitl, Hist. Chich., MS., cap. 80.

or booths of branches and matting, which they occupied in the neighborhood of the camp. Here they prepared various articles of food for the tables of Cortés and his officers, without any recompense; while the common soldiers easily obtained a supply for themselves, in exchange for such trifles as they brought with them for barter. Thus the camp was liberally provided with meat and fish dressed in many savory ways, with cakes of corn, bananas, pine-apples, and divers luscious vegetables of the tropics, hitherto unknown to the Spaniards. The soldiers contrived, moreover, to obtain many little bits of gold, of no great value, indeed, from the natives; a traffic very displeasing to the partisans of Velasquez, who considered it an invasion of his rights. Cortés, however, did not think it prudent, in this matter, to balk the inclinations of his followers.[15]

At the expiration of seven, or eight days at most, the Mexican embassy presented itself before the camp. It may seem an incredibly short space of time, considering the distance of the capital was near seventy leagues. But it may be remembered that tidings were carried there by means of posts, as already noticed, in the brief space of four and twenty hours;[16] and four or five days would suffice for the descent of the envoys to the coast, accustomed as the Mexicans were to long and rapid travelling. At all events, no writer states the period, occupied by the Indian emissaries on this occasion, as longer than that mentioned.

The embassy, consisting of two Aztec nobles, was accompanied by the governor, Teuhtlile, and by a hundred slaves, bearing the princely gifts of Montezuma. One of the envoys had been selected on account of the great resemblance which, as appeared from the painting representing the camp, he bore to the Spanish commander. And it is a proof of the fidelity of the painting, that the soldiers recognised the resemblance, and always distinguished the chief by the name of the "Mexican Cortés."

On entering the general's pavilion, the ambassadors saluted him and his officers with the usual signs of reverence to persons of great consideration, touching the ground with their hands and then carrying them to their heads, while the air was filled with clouds of incense, which rose up from the censers borne by their attendants. Some delicately wrought mats of the country (*petates*) were then unrolled, and on them the slaves displayed the various articles they had brought. They were of the most miscellaneous kind; shields, helmets, cuirasses, embossed with plates and ornaments of pure gold; collars and bracelets of the same metal, sandals, fans, *panaches* and crests of variegated feathers, intermingled with gold and silver thread, and sprinkled with pearls and precious stones; imitations of birds and animals in wrought and cast gold and silver, of exquisite workmanship; curtains, coverlets, and robes of cotton, fine as silk, of rich and various dyes, interwoven with feather-work that rivalled

---

[15] Bernal Diaz, Hist. de la Conquista, cap. 39.—Gomara, Crónica, cap. 27, ap Barcia, tom. II.

[16] Ante, Book i, Chap. 2, p. 29.

the delicacy of painting.[17] There were more than thirty loads of cotton cloth in addition. Among the articles was the Spanish helmet sent to the capital, and now returned filled to the brim with grains of gold. But the things which excited the most admiration were two circular plates of gold and silver, "as large as carriage-wheels." One, representing the sun, was richly carved with plants and animals,—no doubt, denoting the Aztec century. It was thirty palms in circumference, and was valued at twenty thousand *pesos de oro*. The silver wheel, of the same size, weighed fifty marks.[18]

The Spaniards could not conceal their rapture at the exhibition of treasures which so far surpassed all the dreams in which they had indulged. For, rich as were the materials, they were exceeded—according to the testimony of those who saw these articles afterwards in Seville, where they could coolly examine them—by the beauty and richness of the workmanship.[19]

[17] From the chequered figure of some of these colored cottons, Peter Martyr infers, the Indians were acquainted with chess! He notices a curious fabric made of the hair of animals, feathers, and cotton thread, interwoven together. "Plumas illas et concinnant inter cuniculorum villos interque gosampij stamina ordiuntur, et intexunt operose adeo, ut quo pacto id faciant non bene intellexerimus." De orbe Novo, (Parisiis, 1587,) dec. 5, cap. 10.

[18] Bernal Diaz, Hist. de la Conquista, cap. 39.—Oviedo, Hist. de las Ind., MS., lib. 33, cap. 1.—Las Casas, Hist. de las Indias, MS., lib. 3, cap. 120.—Gomara, Crónica, cap. 27, ap. Barcia, tom. II.—Carta de Vera Cruz, MS.—Herrera, Hist General, dec. 2, lib. 5, cap. 5.

Robertson cites Bernal Diaz as reckoning the value of the silver plate at 20,000 *pesos*, or about £5,000. (History of America, Vol. II. note 75.) But Bernal Diaz speaks only of the value of the gold plate, which he estimates at 20,000 *pesos de oro*, a different affair from the *pesos*, dollars, or ounces of silver, with which the historian confounds them. As the mention of the *peso de oro* will often recur in these pages, it will be well to make the reader acquainted with its probable value.

Nothing is more difficult than to ascertain the actual value of the currency of a distant age; so many circumstances occur to embarrass the calculation, besides the general depreciation of the precious metals, such as the adulteration of specific coins, and the like.

Señor Clemencin, the Secretary of the Royal Academy of History, in the sixth volume of its *Memorias,* has computed with great accuracy the value of the different denominations of the Spanish currency at the close of the fifteenth century, the period just preceding that of the conquest of Mexico. He makes no mention of the *peso de oro* in his tables. But he ascertains the precise value of the gold ducat, which will answer our purpose as well. (Memorias de la Real Academia de Historia, (Madrid, 1821,) tom. VI. Ilust. 20.) Oviedo, a contemporary of the Conquerors, informs us that the *peso de oro* and the *castellano* were of the same value, and that was precisely one third greater than the value of the ducat. (Hist. del Ind., lib. 6, cap. 8, ap. Ramusio, Navigationi et Viaggi, (Venetia, 1565,) tom. III.) Now the ducat, as appears from Clemencin, reduced to our own currency, would be equal to eight dollars and seventy-five cents. *The peso de oro, therefore, was equal to eleven dollars and sixty-seven cents, or two pounds, twelve shillings, and six-pence sterling.* Keeping this in mind, it will be easy for the reader to determine the actual value, in *pesos de oro*, of any sum that may be hereafter mentioned.

[19] "Cierto cosas de ver!" exclaims Las Casas, who saw them with the Emperor Charles V. in Seville, in 1520. "Quedáron todos los que viéron aquestas cosas tan ricas y tan bien artifiçiadas y ermosísimas como de cosas nunca vistas," &c. (Hist.

When Cortés and his officers had completed their survey, the ambassadors courteously delivered the message of Montezuma. "It gave their master great pleasure," they said, "to hold this communication with so powerful a monarch as the King of Spain, for whom he felt the most profound respect. He regretted much that he could not enjoy a personal interview with the Spaniards, but the distance of his capital was too great; since the journey was beset with difficulties, and with too many dangers from formidable enemies, to make it possible. All that could be done, therefore, was for the strangers to return to their own land, with the proofs thus afforded them of his friendly disposition."

Cortés, though much chagrined at this decided refusal of Montezuma to admit his visit, concealed his mortification as he best might, and politely expressed his sense of the emperor's munificence. "It made him only the more desirous," he said, "to have a personal interview with him. He should feel it, indeed, impossible to present himself again before his own sovereign, without having accomplished this great object of his voyage; and one, who had sailed over two thousand leagues of ocean, held lightly the perils and fatigues of so short a journey by land." He once more requested them to become the bearers of his message to their master, together with a slight additional token of his respect.

This consisted of a few fine Holland shirts, a Florentine goblet, gilt and somewhat curiously enamelled, with some toys of little value,—a sorry return for the solid magnificence of the royal present. The ambassadors may have thought as much. At least, they showed no alacrity in charging themselves either with the present or the message; and, on quitting the Castilian quarters, repeated their assurance that the general's application would be unavailing.[20]

The splendid treasure, which now lay dazzling the eyes of the Spaniards, raised in their bosoms very different emotions, according to the difference of their characters. Some it stimulated with the ardent desire to strike at once into the interior, and possess themselves of a country which teemed with such boundless stores of wealth. Others looked on it as the evidence of a power altogether too formidable to be encountered with their present insignificant force. They thought, therefore, it would be most prudent to return and report their proceedings to the governor of Cuba, where preparations could be made commensurate with so vast an undertaking. There can be little doubt as to the impression made on

de las Indias, MS., lib. 3, cap. 120.) "Muy hermosas"; says Oviedo, who saw them in Valladolid, and describes the great wheels more minutely; "todo era mucho de ver!" (Hist. de las Indias, MS., loc. cit.) The inquisitive Martyr, who examined them carefully, remarks, yet more emphatically, "Si quid unquam honoris humana ingenia in huiuscemodi artibus sunt adepta, principatum iure merito ista consequentur. Aurum, gemmasque non admiror quidem, quâ industriâ, quó studio superet opus materiam, stupeo. Mille figuras et facies mille prospexi quæ scribere nequeo. Quid oculos hominum suâ pulchritudine æque possit allicere meo iudicio vidi nunquam." De Orbe Novo, dec. 4, cap. 9.

[20] Las Casas, Hist. de las Indias, MS., lib. 3, cap. 121.—Bernal Diaz, Hist. de la Conquista, cap. 39.—Ixtlilxochitl, Hist. Chich., MS., cap. 80.—Gomara, Crónica, cap. 27, ap. Barcia, tom. II.

the bold spirit of Cortés, on which difficulties ever operated as incentives, rather than discouragements, to enterprise. But he prudently said nothing,—at least in public,—preferring that so important a movement should flow from the determination of his whole army, rather than from his own individual impulse.

Meanwhile the soldiers suffered greatly from the inconveniences of their position amidst burning sands and the pestilent effluvia of the neighboring marshes, while the venomous insects of these hot regions left them no repose, day or night. Thirty of their number had already sickened and died; a loss that could ill be afforded by the little band. To add to their troubles, the coldness of the Mexican chiefs had extended to their followers; and the supplies for the camp were not only much diminished, but the prices set on them were exorbitant. The position was equally unfavorable for the shipping, which lay in an open roadstead, exposed to the fury of the first *norte* which should sweep the Mexican Gulf.

The general was induced by these circumstances to despatch two vessels, under Francisco de Montejo, with the experienced Alaminos for his pilot, to explore the coast in a northerly direction, and see if a safer port and more commodious quarters for the army could not be found there.

After the lapse of ten days the Mexican envoys returned. They entered the Spanish quarters with the same formality as on the former visit, bearing with them an additional present of rich stuffs and metallic ornaments, which, though inferior in value to those before brought, were estimated at three thousand ounces of gold. Besides these, there were four precious stones, of a considerable size, resembling emeralds, called by the natives *chalchuites*, each of which, as they assured the Spaniards, was worth more than a load of gold, and was designed as a mark of particular respect for the Spanish monarch.[21] Unfortunately they were not worth as many loads of earth in Europe.

Montezuma's answer was in substance the same as before. It contained a positive prohibition for the strangers to advance nearer to the capital; and expressed the confidence, that, now they had obtained what they had most desired, they would return to their own country without unnecessary delay. Cortés received this unpalatable response courteously, though somewhat coldly, and, turning to his officers, exclaimed, "This is a rich and powerful prince indeed; yet it shall go hard, but we will one day pay him a visit in his capital!"

While they were conversing, the bell struck for vespers. At the sound, the soldiers, throwing themselves on their knees, offered up their orisons

---

[21] Bernal Diaz, Hist. de la Conquista, cap. 40.

Father Sahagun thus describes these stones, so precious in Mexico that the use of them was interdicted to any but the nobles. "Las *chalchuites* son verdes y no transparentes mezcladas de blanco, usanlas mucho los principales, trayéndolas á las muñecas atadas en hilo, y aquello es señal de que es persona noble el que las trae," Hist. de Nueva España, lib. 11, cap. 8.

before the large wooden cross planted in the sands. As the Aztec chiefs gazed with curious surprise, Cortés thought it a favorable occasion to impress them with what he conceived to be a principal object of his visit to the country. Father Olmedo accordingly expounded, as briefly and clearly as he could, the great doctrines of Christianity, touching on the atonement, the passion, and the resurrection, and concluding with assuring his astonished audience, that it was their intention to extirpate the idolatrous practices of the nation, and to subsitute the pure worship of the true God. He then put into their hands a little image of the Virgin with the infant Redeemer, requesting them to place it in their temples instead of their sanguinary deities. How far the Aztec lords comprehended the mysteries of the faith, as conveyed through the double version of Aguilar and Marina, or how well they perceived the subtle distinctions between their own images and those of the Roman Church, we are not informed. There is reason to fear, however, that the seed fell on barren ground; for, when the homily of the good father ended, they withdrew with an air of dubious reserve very different from their friendly manners on the first interview. The same night every hut was deserted by the natives, and the Spaniards saw themselves suddenly cut off from supplies in the midst of a desolate wilderness. The movement had so suspicious an appearance, that Cortés apprehended an attack would be made on his quarters, and took precautions accordingly. But none was meditated.

The army was at length cheered by the return of Montejo from his exploring expedition, after an absence of twelve days. He had run down the Gulf as far as Panuco, where he experienced such heavy gales, in attempting to double that headland, that he was driven back, and had nearly foundered. In the whole course of the voyage he had found only one place tolerably sheltered from the north winds. Fortunately, the adjacent country, well watered by fresh, running streams, afforded a favorable position for the camp; and thither, after some deliberation, it was determined to repair.[22]

[22] Camargo, Hist. de Tlascala, MS.—Las Casas, Hist. de las Indias, MS., lib. 3, cap. 121.—Bernal Diaz, Hist. de la Conquista, cap. 40, 41.—Herrera, Hist. General, dec. 2, lib. 5, cap. 6.—Gomara, Crónica, cap. 29, ap. Barcia, tom. II.

CHAPTER VII

TROUBLES IN THE CAMP—PLAN OF A COLONY—MANAGEMENT OF COR-
TÉS—MARCH TO CEMPOALLA—PROCEEDINGS WITH THE NATIVES—
FOUNDATIONS OF VERA CRUZ

1519

THERE is no situation which tries so severely the patience and discipline
of a soldier, as a life of idleness in camp, where his thoughts, instead of
being bent on enterprise and action, are fastened on himself and the
inevitable privations and dangers of his condition. This was particularly the case in the present instance, where, in addition to the evils of a
scanty subsistence, the troops suffered from excessive heat, swarms of
venomous insects, and the other annoyances of a sultry climate. They
were, moreover, far from possessing the character of regular forces,
trained to subordination under a commander whom they had long been
taught to reverence and obey. They were soldiers of fortune, embarked
with him in an adventure in which all seemed to have an equal stake,
and they regarded their captain—the captain of the day—as little more
than an equal.

There was a growing discontent among the men at their longer residence in this strange land. They were still more dissatisfied on learning
the general's intention to remove to the neighborhood of the port discovered by Montejo. "It was time to return," they said, "and report
what had been done to the governor of Cuba, and not linger on these
barren shores until they had brought the whole Mexican empire on their
heads!" Cortés evaded their importunities as well as he could, assuring
them there was no cause for despondency. "Every thing so far had gone
on prosperously, and, when they had taken up a more favorable position, there was no reason to doubt they might still continue the same
profitable intercourse with the natives."

While this was passing, five Indians made their appearance in the
camp one morning, and were brought to the general's tent. Their dress
and whole appearance were different from those of the Mexicans. They
wore rings of gold, and gems of a bright blue stone in their ears and nostrils, while a gold leaf delicately wrought was attached to the under lip
Marina was unable to comprehend their language, but, on her addressing them in Aztec, two of them, it was found, could converse in that
tongue. They said they were natives of Cempoalla, the chief town of the
Totonacs, a powerful nation who had come upon the great plateau many
centuries back, and descending its eastern slope, settled along the sierras

and broad plains which skirt the Mexican Gulf towards the north. Their
country was one of the recent conquests of the Aztecs, and they experienced such vexatious oppressions from their conquerors as made them
very impatient of the yoke. They informed Cortés of these and other
particulars. The fame of the Spaniards had reached their master, who
sent these messengers to request the presence of the wonderful strangers
in his capital.

This communication was eagerly listened to by the general, who, it
will be remembered, was possessed of none of those facts, laid before the
reader, respecting the internal condition of the kingdom, which he had
no reason to suppose other than strong and united. An important truth
now flashed on his mind; as his quick eye descried in this spirit of discontent a potent lever, by the aid of which he might hope to overturn
this barbaric empire.—He received the mission of the Totonacs most
graciously, and, after informing himself, as far as possible, of their dispositions and resources, dismissed them with presents, promising soon to
pay a visit to their lord.[1]

Meanwhile, his personal friends, among whom may be particularly
mentioned Alonso Hernandez Puertocarrero, Christóval de Olid, Alonso
de Avila, Pedro de Alvarado and his brothers, were very busy in persuading the troops to take such measures as should enable Cortés to go
forward in those ambitious plans, for which he had no warrant from the
powers of Velasquez. "To return now," they said, "was to abandon the
enterprise on the threshold, which, under such a leader, must conduct to
glory and incalculable riches. To return to Cuba would be to surrender
to the greedy governor the little gains they had already got. The only
way was to persuade the general to establish a permanent colony in
the country, the government of which would take the conduct of matters into its own hands, and provide for the interests of its members. It
was true, Cortés had no such authority from Velasquez. But the interests of the Sovereigns, which were paramount to every other, imperatively demanded it."

These conferences could not be conducted so secretly, though held by
night, as not to reach the ears of the friends of Velasquez.[2] They remonstrated against the proceedings, as insidious and disloyal. They accused the general of instigating them; and, calling on him to take
measures without delay for the return of the troops to Cuba, announced
their own intention to depart, with such followers as still remained true
to the governor.

Cortés, instead of taking umbrage at this high-handed proceeding, or
even answering in the same haughty tone, mildly replied, "that nothing
was further from his desire than to exceed his instructions. He, indeed,

---

[1] Bernal Diaz, Hist. de la Conquista, cap. 41.—Las Casas, Hist. de las Indias, MS.,
lib. 3, cap. 121.—Gomara Crónica, cap. 28.
[2] The letter from the *cabildo* of Vera Cruz says nothing of these midnight conferences. Bernal Diaz, who was privy to them is a sufficient authority. See Hist. de
la Conquista, cap. 42.

preferred to remain in the country, and continue his profitable intercourse with the natives. But, since the army thought otherwise, he
should defer to their opinion, and give orders to return, as they desired."
On the following morning, proclamation was made for the troops to hold
themselves in readiness to embark at once on board the fleet, which was
to sail for Cuba.[3]

Great was the sensation caused by their general's order. Even many
of those before clamorous for it, with the usual caprice of men whose
wishes are too easily gratified, now regretted it. The partisans of Cortés
were loud in their remonstrances. "They were betrayed by the general,"
they cried, and, thronging round his tent, called on him to countermand
his orders. "We came here," said they, "expecting to form a settlement,
if the state of the country authorized it. Now it seems you have no warrant from the governor to make one. But there are interests, higher than
those of Velasquez, which demand it. These territories are not his property, but were discovered for the Sovereigns;[4] and it is necessary to plant
a colony to watch over their interests, instead of wasting time in idle
barter, or, still worse, of returning, in the present state of affairs, to
Cuba. If you refuse," they concluded, "we shall protest against your
conduct as disloyal to their Highnesses."

Cortés received this remonstrance with the embarrassed air of one by
whom it was altogether unexpected. He modestly requested time for deliberation, and promised to give his answer on the following day. At the
time appointed, he called the troops together, and made them a brief
address. "There was no one," he said, "if he knew his own heart, more
deeply devoted than himself to the welfare of his sovereigns, and the
glory of the Spanish name. He had not only expended his all, but incurred heavy debts, to meet the charges of this expedition, and had hoped
to reimburse himself by continuing his traffic with the Mexicans. But,
if the soldiers thought a different course advisable, he was ready to postpone his own advantage to the good of the state."[5] He concluded by

[3] Gomara, Crónica, cap. 30.—Las Casas, Hist. de las Indias, MS., lib. 3, cap. 121.
—Ixtlilxochitl, Hist. Chich., MS., cap. 80.—Bernal Diaz, Ibid., loc. cit.—Declaracion de Puertocarrero, MS.
The deposition of a respectable person like Puertocarrero, taken in the course of
the following year after his return to Spain, is a document of great authority.

[4] Sometimes we find the Spanish writers referring to "the sovereigns," sometimes
to "the emperor"; in the former case, intending queen Joanna, the crazy mother of
Charles V., as well as himself. Indeed, all public acts and ordinances ran in the
name of both. The title of "Highness," which, until the reign of Charles V., had usually—not uniformly, as Robertson imagines (History of Charles V., vol. II. p. 59)
—been applied to the sovereign, now gradually gave way to that of "Majesty,"
which Charles affected after his election to the imperial throne. The same title is
occasionally found in the correspondence of the Great Captain, and other courtiers
of the reign of Ferdinand and Isabella.

[5] According to Robertson, Cortés told his men that he had proposed to establish
a colony on the coast, before marching into the country; but he abandoned his design, at their entreaties to set out at once on the expedition. In the very next page,
we find him organizing this same colony. (History of America, vol. II. pp. 241, 242.)

declaring his willingness to take measures for settling a colony *in the name of the Spanish sovereigns,* and to nominate a magistracy to preside over it.[6]

For the *alcaldes* he selected Puertocarrero and Montejo, the former cavalier his fast friend, and the latter the friend of Velasquez, and chosen for that very reason; a stroke of policy which perfectly succeeded. The *regidores, alguacil,* treasurer, and other functionaries, were then appointed, all of them his personal friends and adherents. They were regularly sworn into office, and the new city received the title of *Villa Rica de Vera Cruz,* "The Rich Town of the True Cross"; a name which was considered as happily intimating that union of spiritual and temporal interests to which the arms of the Spanish adventurers in the New World were to be devoted.[7] Thus, by a single stroke of the pen, as it were, the camp was transformed into a civil community, and the whole framework and even title of the city were arranged, before the site of it had been settled.

The new municipality were not slow in coming together; when Cortés presented himself, cap in hand, before that august body, and, laying the powers of Velasquez on the table, respectfully tendered the resignation of his office of Captain-General, "which, indeed," he said, "had necessarily expired, since the authority of the governor was now superseded by that of the magistracy of Villa Rica de Vera Cruz." He then, with a profound obeisance, left the apartment.[8]

The council, after a decent time spent in deliberation, again requested his presence. "There was no one," they said, "who, on mature reflection, appeared to them so well qualified to take charge of the interests of the community, both in peace and in war, as himself; and they unanimously named him, in behalf of their Catholic Highnesses, Captain General and Chief Justice of the colony." He was further empowered to draw, on his own account, one fifth of the gold and silver which might hereafter be obtained by commerce or conquest from the natives.[9] Thus clothed with

The historian would have been saved this inconsistency, if he had followed either of the authorities whom he cites, Bernal Diaz and Herrera, or the letter from Vera Cruz, of which he had a copy. They all concur in the statement in the next.

[6] Las Casas, Hist. de las Indias, MS., lib. 3, cap. 122.—Carta de Vera Cruz, MS. —Declaracion de Montejo, MS.—Declaracion de Puertocarrero, MS.

"Our general, after some urging, acquiesced," says the blunt old soldier, Bernal Diaz; "for, as the proverb says, 'You ask me to do what I have already made up my mind to.'" *Tu me lo ruegas, é yo me lo quiero.* Hist. de la Conquista, cap. 42.

[7] According to Bernal Diaz, the title of "Vera Cruz" was intended to commemorate their landing on Good Friday. Hist. de la Conquista, cap. 42.

[8] Solís, whose taste for speech-making might have satisfied even the Abbé Mably, (See his Treatise, "De la Manière d'écrire l'Histoire,") has put a very flourishing harangue on this occasion into the mouth of his hero, of which there is not a vestige in any contemporary account. (Conquista, lib. 2, cap. 7.) Dr. Robertson has transferred it to his own eloquent pages, without citing his author, indeed, who, considering he came a century and a half after the Conquest, must be allowed to be not the best, especially when the only voucher for a fact.

[9] "Lo peorde todo que le otorgámos," says Bernal Diaz, somewhat peevishly, was, "que le dariamos el quinto del oro de lo que se huuiesse, despues de sacado el Real

supreme civil and military jurisdiction, Cortés was not backward in exerting his authority. He found speedy occasion for it.

The transactions above described had succeeded each other so rapidly, that the governor's party seemed to be taken by surprise, and had formed no plan of opposition. When the last measure was carried, however, they broke forth into the most indignant and opprobrious invectives, denouncing the whole as a systematic conspiracy against Velasquez. These accusations led to recrimination from the soldiers of the other side, until from words they nearly proceeded to blows. Some of the principal cavaliers, among them Velasquez de Leon, a kinsman of the governor, Escobar, his page, and Diego de Ordaz, were so active in instigating these turbulent movements, that Cortés took the bold measure of putting them all in irons, and sending them on board the vessels. He then dispersed the common file by detaching many of them with a strong party under Alvarado to forage the neighboring country, and bring home provisions for the destitute camp.

During their absence, every argument that cupidity or ambition could suggest was used to win the retractory to his views. Promises, and even gold, it is said, were liberally lavished; till, by degrees, their understandings were opened to a clearer view of the merits of the case. And when the foraging party reappeared with abundance of poultry and vegetables, and the cravings of the stomach—that great laboratory of disaffection, whether in camp or capital—were appeased, good-humor returned with good cheer, and the rival factions embraced one another as companions in arms, pledged to a common cause. Even the high-mettled hidalgos on board the vessels did not long withstand the general tide of reconciliation, but one by one gave in their adhesion to the new government. What is more remarkable is that this forced conversion was not a hollow one, but from this time forward several of these very cavaliers became the most steady and devoted partisans of Cortés.[10]

Such was the address of this extraordinary man, and such the ascendency which in a few months he had acquired over these wild and turbulent spirits! By this ingenious transformation of a military into a civil

quinto." (Hist. de la Conquista, cap. 42.) The letter from Vera Cruz says nothing of this fifth.

[10] Carta de Vera Cruz, MS.—Gomara, Crónica, cap. 30, 31.—Las Casas, Hist. de las Indias, MS., lib. 3, cap. 122.—Ixtlilxochitl, Hist. Chich., MS., cap. 80.—Bernal Diaz, Hist. de la Conquista, cap. 42.—Declaraciones de Montejo y Puertocarrero, MSS

In the process of Narvaez against Cortés, the latter is accused of being possessed with the Devil, as only Lucifer could have gained him thus the affections of the soldiery. (Demanda de Narvaez, MS.) Solís, on the other hand, sees nothing but good faith and loyalty in the conduct of the general, who acted from a sense of duty! (Conquista, lib. 2, cap. 6, 7.) Solís is even a more steady apologist for his hero, than his own chaplain, Gomara, or the worthy magistrates of Vera Cruz. A more impartial testimony than either, probably, may be gathered from honest Bernal Diaz, so often quoted. A hearty champion of the cause, he was by no means blind to the defects nor the merits of his leader.

community, he had secured a new and effectual basis for future operations. He might now go forward without fear of check or control from a
superior,—at least from any other superior than the Crown, under which
alone he held his commission. In accomplishing this, instead of incurring
the charge of usurpation, or of transcending his legitimate powers, he
had transferred the responsibility, in a great measure, to those who had
imposed on him the necessity of action. By this step, moreover, he had
linked the fortunes of his followers indissolubly with his own. They had
taken their chance with him, and, whether for weal or for woe, must
abide the consequences. He was no longer limited to the narrow concerns of a sordid traffic, but, sure of their coöperation, might now boldly
meditate, and gradually disclose, those lofty schemes which he had
formed in his own bosom for the conquest of an empire.[11]

Harmony being thus restored, Cortés sent his heavy guns on board
the fleet, and ordered it to coast along the shore to the north as far as
Chiahuitztla, the town near which the destined port of the new city was
situated; proposing, himself, at the head of his troops, to visit Cempoalla,
on the march. The road lay for some miles across the dreary plains in
the neighborhood of the modern Vera Cruz. In this sandy waste no
signs of vegetation met their eyes, which, however, were occasionally refreshed by glimpses of the blue Atlantic, and by the distant view of the
magnificent Orizaba, towering, with his spotless diadem of snow, far
above his colossal brethren of the Andes.[12] As they advanced, the country gradually assumed a greener and richer aspect. They crossed a river,
probably a tributary of the *Rio de la Antigua*, with difficulty, on rafts,
and on some broken canoes that were lying on the banks. They now
came in view of very different scenery,—wide-rolling plains covered
with a rich carpet of verdure, and overshadowed by groves of cocoas
and feathery palms, among whose tall, slender stems were seen deer,
and various wild animals with which the Spaniards were unacquainted.
Some of the horsemen gave chase to the deer, and wounded, but did not

[11] This may appear rather indifferent logic to those who consider that Cortés appointed the very body, who, in turn, appointed him to the command. But the affectation of legal forms afforded him a thin varnish for his proceedings, which served
his purpose, for the present, at least, with the troops. For the future, he trusted to
his good star,—in other words, to the success of his enterprise,—to vindicate his
conduct to the Emperor. He did not miscalculate.

[12] The name of the mountain is not given, and probably was not known, but the
minute description in the MS. of Vera Cruz leaves no doubt that it was the one
mentioned in the text. "Entre las quales así una que excede en mucha altura á todas
las otras y de ella se vee y descubre gran parte de la mar y de la tierra, y es tan
alta, que si el dia no es bien claro, no se puede divisar ni ver lo alto de ella, porque
de la mitad arriba está toda cubierta de nubes; y algunos veces, cuando hace muy
claro dia, se vee por cima de las dichas nubes lo alto de ella, y está tan blanco, que lo
jusgamos por nieve." (Carta de Vera Cruz, MS.) This huge volcano was called
Citlaltepetl, or "Star-mountain," by the Mexicans,—perhaps from the fire which
once issued from its conical summit, far above the clouds. It stands in the intendancy
of Vera Cruz, and rises, according to Humboldt's measurement, to the enormous
height of 17,368 feet above the ocean. (Essai Politique, tom. I. p. 265.) It is the
highest peak but one in the whole range of the Mexican Cordilleras.

succeed in killing them. They saw, also, pheasants and other birds; among them the wild turkey, the pride of the American forest, which the Spaniards described as a species of peacock.[13]

On their route they passed through some deserted villages, in which were Indian temples, where they found censers, and other sacred utensils, and manuscripts of the *agave* fibre, containing the picture-writing, in which, probably, their religious ceremonies were recorded. They now beheld, also, the hideous spectacle, with which they became afterwards familiar, of the mutilated corpses of victims who had been sacrificed to the accursed deities of the land. The Spaniards turned with loathing and indignation from a display of butchery, which formed so dismal a contrast to the fair scenes of nature by which they were surrounded.

They held their course along the banks of the river, towards its source, when they were met by twelve Indians, sent by the cacique of Cempoalla to show them the way to his residence. At night they bivouacked in an open meadow, where they were well supplied with provisions by their new friends. They left the stream on the following morning, and, striking northerly across the country, came upon a wide expanse of luxuriant plains and woodland, glowing in all the splendor of tropical vegetation. The branches of the stately trees were gayly festooned with clustering vines of the dark-purple grape, variegated convolvuli, and other flowering parasites of the most brilliant dyes. The undergrowth of prickly aloe, matted with wild rose and honeysuckle, made in many places an almost impervious thicket. Amid this wilderness of sweet-smelling buds and blossoms, fluttered numerous birds of the parrot tribe, and clouds of butterflies, whose gaudy colors, nowhere so gorgeous as in the *tierra caliente*, rivalled those of the vegetable creation; while birds of exquisite song, the scarlet cardinal, and the marvellous mocking-bird, that comprehends in his own notes the whole music of a forest, filled the air with delicious melody.—The hearts of the stern Conquerors were not very sensible to the beauties of nature. But the magical charms of the scenery drew forth unbounded expressions of delight, and as they wandered through this "terrestrial paradise," as they called it, they fondly compared it to the fairest regions of their own sunny land.[14]

[13] Carta de Vera Cruz, MS.—Bernal Diaz, Hist. de la Conquista, cap. 44.

[14] Gomara, Crónica, cap. 32, ap. Barcia, tom. II.—Herrera, Hist. General, dec. 2, lib. 5, cap. 8.—Oviedo, Hist. de las Ind., MS., lib. 33, cap. 1.

"Mui hermosas vegas y riberas tales y tan hermosas que en toda España no pueden ser mejores ansí de apaçibles á la vista como de fructíferas." (Carta de Vera Cruz, MS.) The following poetical apostrophe, by Lord Morpeth, to the scenery of Cuba, equally applicable to that of the *tierra caliente*, will give the reader a more animated picture of the glories of these sunny climes, than my own prose can. The verses, which have never been published, breathe the generous sentiment characteristic of their noble author.

"Ye tropic forests of unfading green,
    Where the palm tapers and the orange glows,
Where the light bamboo weaves her feathery screen,
    And her far shade the matchless *ceiba* throws!

"Ye cloudless ethers of unchanging blue,

As they approached the Indian city, they saw abundant signs of cul-tivation, in the trim gardens and orchards that lined both sides of the road. They were now met by parties of the natives of either sex, who increased in numbers with every step of their progress. The women, as well as men, mingled fearlessly among the soldiers, bearing bunches and wreaths of flowers, with which they decorated the neck of the general's charger, and hung a chaplet of roses about his helmet. Flowers were the delight of this people. They bestowed much care in their cultivation, in which they were well seconded by a climate of alternate heat and moist-ure, stimulating the soil to the spontaneous production of every form of vegetable life. The same refined taste, as we shall see, prevailed among the warlike Aztecs, and has survived the degradation of the nation in their descendants of the present day.[15]

Many of the women appeared, from their richer dress and numerous attendants, to be persons of rank. They were clad in robes of fine cotton, curiously colored, which reached from the neck—in the inferior orders, from the waist—to the ankles. The men wore a sort of mantle of the same material, *á la Morisca,* in the Moorish fashion, over their shoulders, and belts or sashes about the loins. Both sexes had jewels and ornaments of gold round their necks, while their ears and nostrils were perforated with rings of the same metal.

Just before reaching the town, some horsemen who had rode in advance returned with the amazing intelligence, "that they had been near enough to look within the gates, and found the houses all plated with burnished silver!" On entering the place, the silver was found to be nothing more than a brilliant coating of stucco, with which the principal buildings were covered; a circumstance which produced much merri-ment among the soldiers at the expense of their credulous comrades. Such ready credulity is a proof of the exalted state of their imaginations, which were prepared to see gold and silver in every object around them.[16] The edifices of the better kind were of stone and lime, or bricks dried in the sun; the poorer were of clay and earth. All were thatched with palm-leaves, which, though a flimsy roof, apparently, for such structures, were so nicely interwoven as to form a very effectual protection against the weather.

> Save where the rosy streaks of eve give way
> To the clear sapphire of your midnight hue,
>   The burnished azure of your perfect day.
>
> "Yet tell me not my native skies are bleak,
>   That flushed with liquid wealth no cane fields wave;
> For virtue pines and Manhood dares not speak,
>   And Nature's glories brighten round the Slave."

[15] "The same love of flowers," observes one of the most delightful of modern trav-ellers, "distinguishes the natives now, as in the times of Cortés. And it presents a strange anomaly," she adds, with her usual acuteness; "this love of flowers having existed along with their sanguinary worship and barbarous sacrifices." Madame Cal-deron de la Barca, Life in Mexico, vol. I. let. 12.

[16] "Con la imaginacion que llevaban, i buenos deseos, todo se les antojaba plata *i* oro lo que relucia." Gomara, Crónica, cap. 32, ap. Barcia, tom. II.

The city was said to contain from twenty to thirty thousand inhabitants. This is the most moderate computation, and not improbable.[17]
Slowly and silently the little army paced the narrow and now crowded
streets of Cempoalla, inspiring the natives with no greater wonder than
they themselves experienced at the display of a policy and refinement so
far superior to any thing they had witnessed in the New World.[18] The
cacique came out in front of his residence to receive them. He was a tall
and very corpulent man, and advanced leaning on two of his attendants.
He received Cortés and his followers with great courtesy; and, after a
brief interchange of civilities, assigned the army its quarters in a neighboring temple, into the spacious court-yard of which a number of apartments opened, affording excellent accommodations for the soldiery.

Here the Spaniards were well supplied with provisions, meat cooked
after the fashion of the country, and maize made into bread-cakes. The
general received, also, a present of considerable value from the cacique,
consisting of ornaments of gold and fine cottons. Notwithstanding these
friendly demonstrations, Cortés did not relax his habitual vigilance, nor
neglect any of the precautions of a good soldier. On his route, indeed,
he had always marched in order of battle, well prepared against surprise.
In his present quarters, he stationed his sentinels with like care, posted
his small artillery so as to command the entrance, and forbade any
soldier to leave the camp without orders, under pain of death.[19]

The following morning, Cortés, accompanied by fifty of his men, paid
a visit to the lord of Cempoalla in his own residence. It was a building of
stone and lime, standing on a steep terrace of earth, and was reached
by a flight of stone steps. It may have borne resemblance in its structure
to some of the ancient buildings found in Central America. Cortés, leaving his soldiers in the court-yard, entered the mansion with one of his
officers, and his fair interpreter, Doña Marina.[20] A long conference ensued, from which the Spanish general gathered much light respecting the
state of the country. He first announced to the chief, that he was the subject of a great monarch who dwelt beyond the waters; that he had come
to the Aztec shores, to abolish the inhuman worship which prevailed
there, and to introduce the knowledge of the true God. The cacique
replied, that their gods, who sent them the sunshine and the rain, were
good enough for them; that he was the tributary of a powerful monarch

[17] This is Las Casas' estimate. (Hist. de las Ind., MS., lib. 3, cap. 121.) Torquemada hesitates between twenty, fifty, and one hundred and fifty thousand, each of
which he names at different times! (Clavigero, Stor. del Messico, tom. III. p. 26.
nota.) The place was gradually abandoned, after the Conquest, for others, in a more
favorable position, probably, for trade. Its ruins were visible at the close of the
last century. See Lorenzana, Hist. de Nueva España, p. 39, nota.

[18] "Porque viven mas política y rasonablemente que ninguna de las gentes que
hasta oy en estas partes se ha visto." Carta de Vera Cruz, MS.

[19] Las Casas, Hist. de las Indias, MS., lib. 3, cap. 121.—Carta de Vera Cruz, MS.
—Gomara, Crónica, cap. 33, ap. Barcia, tom. II.—Oviedo, Hist. de las Ind., MS.,
lib. 33, cap. 1.

[20] The courteous title of *doña* is usually given by the Spanish chroniclers to the
accomplished Indian.

also, whose capital stood on a lake far off among the mountains; a stern prince, merciless in his exactions, and, in case of resistance, or any offence, sure to wreak his vengeance by carrying off their young men and maidens to be sacrificed to his deities. Cortés assured him that he would never consent to such enormities; he had been sent by his sovereign to redress abuses and to punish the oppressor;[21] and, if the Totonacs would be true to him, he would enable them to throw off the detested yoke of the Aztecs.

The cacique added, that the Totonac territory contained about thirty towns and villages, which could muster a hundred thousand warriors,— a number much exaggerated.[22] There were other provinces of the empire, he said, where the Aztec rule was equally odious; and between him and the capital lay the warlike republic of Tlascala, which had always maintained its independence of Mexico. The fame of the Spaniards had gone before them, and he was well acquainted with their terrible victory at Tabasco. But still he looked with doubt and alarm to a rupture with "the great Montezuma," as he always styled him; whose armies, on the least provocation, would pour down from the mountain regions of the West, and, rushing over the plains like a whirlwind, sweep off the wretched people to slavery and sacrifice!

Cortés endeavoured to reassure him, by declaring that a single Spaniard was stronger than a host of Aztecs. At the same time, it was desirable to know what nations would coöperate with him, not so much on his account, as theirs, that he might distinguish friend from foe, and know whom he was to spare in this war of extermination. Having raised the confidence of the admiring chief by this comfortable and polite vaunt, he took an affectionate leave, with the assurance that he would shortly return and concert measures for their future operations, when he had visited his ships in the adjoining port, and secured a permanent settlement there.[23]

The intelligence gained by Cortés gave great satisfaction to his mind. It confirmed his former views, and showed, indeed, the interior of the monarchy to be in a state far more distracted than he had supposed. If he had before scarcely shrunk from attacking the Aztec empire in the true spirit of a knight-errant, with his single arm, as it were, what had he now to fear, when one half of the nation could be thus marshalled against the other? In the excitement of the moment, his sanguine spirit kindled with an enthusiasm which overleaped every obstacle. He communicated his own feelings to the officers about him, and, before a blow

[21] "No venia, sino á deshacer agravios, i favorecer los presos, aiudar á los mezquinos, i quitar tiranías." (Gomara, Crónica, cap. 33, ap. Barcia, tom. II.) Are we reading the adventures—it is the language—of Don Quixote, or Amadis de Gaula?

[22] Ibid., cap. 36.

Cortés, in his Second Letter to the emperor Charles V., estimates the number of fighting men at 50,000. Relacion Segunda, ap. Lorenzana, p. 40.

[23] Las Casas, Hist. de las Indias, MS., lib. 3, cap. 121.—Ixtlilxochitl, Hist. Chich., MS., cap. 81.—Oviedo, Hist. de las Ind., MS., lib. 33, cap. 1.

was struck, they already felt as if the banners of Spain were waving in triumph from the towers of Montezuma! But many a bloody field was to be fought, many a peril and privation to be encountered, before that consummation could be attained.

Taking leave of the hospitable Indian, on the following day, the Spaniards took the road to Chiahuitztla,[24] about four leagues distant, near which was the port discovered by Montejo, where their ships were now riding at anchor. They were provided by the cacique with four hundred Indian porters, *tamanes*, as they were called, to transport the baggage. These men easily carried fifty pounds' weight, five or six leagues in a day. They were in use all over the Mexican empire, and the Spaniards found them of great service, henceforth, in relieving the troops from this part of their duty. They passed through a country of the same rich, voluptuous character as that which they had lately traversed; and arrived early next morning at the Indian town, perched like a fortress on a bold, rocky eminence that commanded the Gulf. Most of the inhabitants had fled, but fifteen of the principal men remained, who received them in a friendly manner, offering the usual compliments of flowers and incense. The people of the place, losing their fears, gradually returned. While conversing with the chiefs, the Spaniards were joined by the worthy cacique of Cempoalla, borne by his men on a litter. He eagerly took part in their deliberations. The intelligence gained here by Cortés confirmed the accounts already gathered of the feelings and resources of the Totonac nation.

In the midst of their conference, they were interrupted by a movement among the people, and soon afterwards five men entered the great square or market-place, where they were standing. By their lofty port, their peculiar and much richer dress, they seemed not to be of the same race as these Indians. Their dark, glossy hair was tied in a knot on the top of the head. They had bunches of flowers in their hands, and were followed by several attendants, some bearing wands with cords, others fans, with which they brushed away the flies and insects from their lordly masters. As these persons passed through the place, they cast a haughty look on the Spaniards, scarcely deigning to return their salutations. They were immediately joined, in great confusion, by the Totonac chiefs, who seemed anxious to conciliate them by every kind of attention.

The general, much astonished, inquired of Marina, what it meant. She informed him, they were Aztec nobles, empowered to receive the tribute for Montezuma. Soon after, the chiefs returned with dismay painted on their faces. They confirmed Marina's statement, adding, that the Aztecs greatly resented the entertainment afforded the Spaniards

[24] The historian, with the aid of Clavigero, himself a Mexican, may rectify frequent blunders of former writers, in the orthography of Aztec names. Both Robertson and Solís spell the name of this place *Quiabislan*. Blunders in such a barbarous nomenclature must be admitted to be very pardonable.

without the Emperor's permission; and demanded in expiation twenty young men and women for sacrifice to the gods. Cortés showed the strongest indignation at this insolence. He required the Totonacs not only to refuse the demand, but to arrest the persons of the collectors, and throw them into prison. The chiefs hesitated, but he insisted on it so peremptorily, that they at length complied, and the Aztecs were seized, bound hand and foot, and placed under a guard.

In the night, the Spanish general procured the escape of two of them, and had them brought secretly before him. He expressed his regret at the indignity they had experienced from the Totonacs; told them, he would provide means for their flight, and to-morrow would endeavor to obtain the release of their companions. He desired them to report this to their master, with assurances of the great regard the Spaniards entertained for him, notwithstanding his ungenerous behaviour in leaving them to perish from want on his barren shores. He then sent the Mexican nobles down to the port, whence they were carried to another part of the coast by water, for fear of the violence of the Totonacs. These were greatly incensed at the escape of the prisoners, and would have sacrificed the remainder, at once, but for the Spanish commander, who evinced the utmost horror at the proposal, and ordered them to be sent for safe custody on board the fleet. Soon after, they were permitted to join their companions.—This artful proceeding, so characteristic of the policy of Cortés, had, as we shall see, hereafter, all the effect intended on Montezuma. It cannot be commended, certainly, as in the true spirit of chivalry. Yet it has not wanted its panegyrist among the national historians![25]

By order of Cortés, messengers were despatched to the Totonac towns, to report what had been done, calling on them to refuse the payment of further tribute to Montezuma. But there was no need of messengers. The affrighted attendants of the Aztec lords had fled in every direction, bearing the tidings, which spread like wildfire through the country, of the daring insult offered to the majesty of Mexico. The astonished Indians, cheered with the sweet hope of regaining their ancient liberty, came in numbers to Chiahuitztla, to see and confer with the formidable strangers. The more timid, dismayed at the thoughts of encountering the power of Montezuma, recommended an embassy to avert his displeasure by timely concessions. But the dexterous management of Cortés had committed them too far to allow any reasonable expectation of indulgence from this quarter. After some hesitation, therefore, it was determined to embrace the protection of the Spaniards, and to make one bold effort for the recovery of freedom. Oaths of allegiance were taken by the chiefs to the Spanish sovereigns, and duly recorded by Godoy, the royal notary. Cortés, satisfied with the important acquisition of so many vassals to the crown, set out soon after for the destined port, having first

<hr/>

[25] "Grande artífice," exclaims Solís, "de medir lo que disponia con lo que recelaba; y prudente capitan él que sabe caminar en alcance de las contingencias"! Conquista, lib. 2, cap. 9

promised to revisit Cempoalla, where his business was but partially accomplished.[26]

The spot selected for the new city was only half a league distant, in a wide and fruitful plain, affording a tolerable haven for the shipping. Cortés was not long in determining the circuit of the walls, and the sites of the fort, granary, town-house, temple, and other public buildings. The friendly Indians eagerly assisted, by bringing materials, stone, lime, wood, and bricks dried in the sun. Every man put his hand to the work. The general labored with the meanest of the soldiers, stimulating their exertions by his example, as well as voice. In a few weeks, the task was accomplished, and a town rose up, which, if not quite worthy of the aspiring name it bore, answered most of the purposes for which it was intended. It served as a good *point d'appui* for future operations; a place of retreat for the disabled, as well as for the army in case of reverses; a magazine for stores, and for such articles as might be received from or sent to the mother country; a port for the shipping; a position of sufficient strength to overawe the adjacent country.[27]

It was the first colony—the fruitful parent of so many others—in New Spain. It was hailed with satisfaction by the simple natives, who hoped to repose in safety under its protecting shadow. Alas! they could not read the future, or they would have found no cause to rejoice in this harbinger of a revolution more tremendous than any predicted by their bards and prophets. It was not the good Quetzalcoatl, who had returned to claim his own again, bringing peace, freedom, and civilization in his train. Their fetters, indeed, would be broken; and their wrongs be amply avenged on the proud head of the Aztec. But it was to be by that strong arm, which should bow down equally the oppressor and the oppressed. The light of civilization would be poured on their land. But it would be the light of a consuming fire, before which their barbaric glory, their institutions, their very existence and name as a nation, would wither and become extinct! Their doom was sealed, when the white man had set his foot on their soil.

[26] Ixtlilxochitl, Hist. Chich., MS., cap. 81.—Rel. Seg. de Cortés, ap. Lorenzana, p. 40.—Gomara, Crónica, cap. 34-36, ap. Barcia, tom. II.—Bernal Diaz, Conquista, cap. 46, 47.—Herrera, Hist. General, dec. 2, lib. 5, cap. 10, 11.

[27] Carta de Vera Cruz, MS.—Bernal Diaz, Conquista, cap. 48.—Oviedo, Hist. de las Ind., MS., lib. 33, cap. 1.—Declaracion de Montejo, MS.

Notwithstanding the advantages of its situation, La Villa Rica was abandoned in a few years for a neighboring position to the south, not far from the mouth of the Antigua. This second settlement was known by the name of *Vera Cruz Vieja*, "Old Vera Cruz." Early in the 17th century this place, also, was abandoned for the present city, *Nueva Vera Cruz*, or New Vera Cruz, as it is called. (See Ante, chap. 5, note 7.) Of the true cause of these successive migrations we are ignorant. If, as is pretended, it was on account of the *vómito*, the inhabitants, one would suppose, can have gained little by the exchange. (See Humboldt, Essai Politique, tom. II. p. 210.) A want of attention to these changes has led to much confusion and inaccuracy in the ancient maps. Lorenzana has not escaped them in his chart and topographical account of the route of Cortés.

CHAPTER VIII

ANOTHER AZTEC EMBASSY—DESTRUCTION OF THE IDOLS—DESPATCHES
SENT TO SPAIN—CONSPIRACY IN THE CAMP—THE FLEET SUNK

1519

WHILE the Spaniards were occupied with their new settlement, they
were surprised by the presence of an embassy from Mexico. The account
of the imprisonment of the royal collectors had spread rapidly through
the country. When it reached the capital, all were filled with amazement at the unprecedented daring of the strangers. In Montezuma every
other feeling, even that of fear, was swallowed up in indignation; and
he showed his wonted energy in the vigorous preparations which he instantly made, to punish his rebellious vassals, and to avenge the insult
offered to the majesty of the empire. But when the Aztec officers liberated
by Cortés reached the capital, and reported the courteous treatment they
had received from the Spanish commander, Montezuma's anger was
mitigated, and his superstitious fears, getting the ascendency again, induced him to resume his former timid and conciliatory policy. He accordingly sent an embassy, consisting of two youths, his nephews, and
four of the ancient nobles of his court, to the Spanish quarters. He provided them, in his usual munificent spirit, with a princely donation of
gold, rich cotton stuffs, and beautiful mantles of the *plumaje*, or feather
embroidery. The envoys, on coming before Cortés, presented him with
the articles, at the same time offering the acknowledgments of their
master for the courtesy he had shown in liberating his captive nobles.
He was surprised and afflicted, however, that the Spaniards should have
countenanced his faithless vassals in their rebellion. He had no doubt
they were the strangers whose arrival had been so long announced by
the oracles, and of the same lineage with himself.[1] From deference to
them he would spare the Totonacs, while they were present. But the time
for vengeance would come.

Cortés entertained the Indian chieftains with frank hospitality. At the
same time, he took care to make such a display of his resources, as, while
it amused their minds, should leave a deep impression of his power. He
then, after a few trifling gifts, dismissed them with a conciliatory message to their master, and the assurance that he should soon pay his re-

[1] "Teniendo respeto á que tiene por cierto, que somos los que sus antepassados les
auian dicho, que auian de venir á sus tierras, é que deuemos de ser de sus linages."
Bernal Diaz, Hist. de la Conquista, cap. 48.

spects to him in his capital, where all misunderstanding between them would be readily adjusted.

The Totonac allies could scarcely credit their senses, when they gathered the nature of this interview. Notwithstanding the presence of the Spaniards, they had looked with apprehension to the consequences of their rash act; and their feelings of admiration were heightened into awe, for the strangers who, at this distance, could exercise so mysterious an influence over the terrible Montezuma.[2]

Not long after, the Spaniards received an application from the cacique of Cempoalla to aid him in a dispute in which he was engaged with a neighboring city. Cortés marched with a part of his forces to his support. On the route, one Morla, a common soldier, robbed a native of a couple of fowls. Cortés, indignant at this violation of his orders before his face, and aware of the importance of maintaining a reputation for good faith with his allies, commanded the man to be hung up, at once, by the roadside, in face of the whole army. Fortunately for the poor wretch, Pedro de Alvarado, the future conqueror of Quiché, was present, and ventured to cut down the body, while there was yet life in it. He, probably, thought enough had been done for example, and the loss of a single life, unnecessarily, was more than the little band could afford. The anecdote is characteristic, as showing the strict discipline maintained by Cortés over his men, and the freedom assumed by his captains, who regarded him on terms nearly of equality,—as a fellow-adventurer with themselves. This feeling of companionship led to a spirit of insubordination·among them, which made his own post as commander the more delicate and difficult.

On reaching the hostile city, but a few leagues from the coast, they were received in an amicable manner; and Cortés, who was accompanied by his allies, had the satisfaction of reconciling these different branches of the Totonac family with each other, without bloodshed. He then returned to Cempoalla, where he was welcomed with joy by the people, who were now impressed with as favorable an opinion of his moderation and justice, as they had before been of his valor. In token of his grati-tude, the Indian cacique delivered to the general eight Indian maidens richly dressed, wearing collars and ornaments of gold, with a number of female slaves to wait on them. They were daughters of the principal chiefs, and the cacique requested that the Spanish captains might take them as their wives. Cortés received the damsels courteously, but told the cacique they must first be baptized, as the sons of the Church could have no commerce with idolaters.[3] He then declared that it was a great object of his mission to wean the natives from their heathenish abominations, and besought the Totonac lord to allow his idols to be cast down, and the symbols of the true faith to be erected in their place.

---

[2] Gomara, Crónica, cap. 37.—Ixtlilxochitl, Hist. Chich., MS., cap. 82.

[3] "De buena gana recibirian las Doncellas como fuesen Christianos; porque de otra manera, no era permitido á hombres, hijos de la Iglesia de Dios, tener comercio con idólatras." Herrera, Hist. General, dec. 2, lib. 5, cap. 13.

To this the other answered as before, that his gods were good enough for him; nor could all the persuasion of the general, nor the preaching of father Olmedo, induce him to acquiesce. Mingled with his polytheism, he had conceptions of a Supreme and Infinite Being, Creator of the Universe, and his darkened understanding could not comprehend how such a Being could condescend to take the form of humanity, with its infirmities and ills, and wander about on earth, the voluntary victim of persecution from the hands of those whom his breath had called into existence.[4] He plainly told the Spaniards that he would resist any violence offered to his gods, who would, indeed, avenge the act themselves, by the instant destruction of their enemies.

But the zeal of the Christians had mounted too high to be cooled by remonstrance or menace. During their residence in the land, they had witnessed more than once the barbarous rites of the natives, their cruel sacrifices of human victims, and their disgusting cannibal repasts.[5] Their souls sickened at these abominations, and they agreed with one voice to stand by their general, when he told them, that "Heaven would never smile on their enterprise, if they countenanced such atrocities, and that, for his own part, he was resolved the Indian idols should be demolished that very hour, if it cost him his life." To postpone the work of conversion was a sin. In the enthusiasm of the moment, the dictates of policy and ordinary prudence were alike unheeded.

Scarcely waiting for his commands, the Spaniards moved towards one of the principal *teocallis,* or temples, which rose high on a pyramidal foundation, with a steep ascent of stone steps in the middle. The cacique, divining their purpose, instantly called his men to arms. The Indian warriors gathered from all quarters, with shrill cries and clashing of weapons; while the priests, in their dark cotton robes, with dishevelled tresses matted with blood, flowing wildly over their shoulders, rushed frantic among the natives, calling on them to protect their gods from violation! All was now confusion, tumult, and warlike menace, where so lately had been peace and the sweet brotherhood of nations.

Cortés took his usual prompt and decided measures. He caused the cacique and some of the principal inhabitants and priests to be arrested by his soldiers. He then commanded them to quiet the people, for, if an arrow was shot against a Spaniard, it should cost every one of them

---

[4] Ibid., dec. 2, lib. 5, cap. 13.—Las Casas, Hist. de las Indias, MS., lib. 3, cap. 122.
Herrera has put a very edifying harangue, on this occasion, into the mouth of Cortés, which savors much more of the priest than the soldier. Does he not confound him with father Olmedo?

[5] "Esto habemos visto," says the Letter of Vera Cruz, "algunos de nosotros, y los que lo han visto dizen que es la mas terrible y la mas espantosa cosa de ver que jamas han visto." Still more strongly speaks Bernal Diaz. (Hist. de la Conquista, cap. 51.) The Letter computes that there were fifty or sixty persons thus butchered in each of the *teocallis* every year, giving an annual consumption, in the countries which the Spaniards had then visited, of three or four thousand victims! (Carta de Vera Cruz, MS.) However loose this arithmetic may be, the general fact is appalling.

his life. Marina, at the same time, represented the madness of resistance, and reminded the cacique, that, if he now alienated the affections of the Spaniards, he would be left without a protector against the terrible vengeance of Montezuma. These temporal considerations seem to have had more weight with the Totonac chieftain, than those of a more spiritual nature. He covered his face with his hands, exclaiming, that the gods would avenge their own wrongs.

The Christians were not slow in availing themselves of his tacit acquiescence. Fifty soldiers, at a signal from their general, sprang up the great stairway of the temple, entered the building on the summit, the walls of which were black with human gore, tore the huge wooden idols from their foundations, and dragged them to the edge of the terrace. Their fantastic forms and features, conveying a symbolic meaning, which was lost on the Spaniards, seemed in their eyes only the hideous lineaments of Satan. With great alacrity they rolled the colossal monsters down the steps of the pyramid, amidst the triumphant shouts of their own companions, and the groans and lamentations of the natives. They then consummated the whole by burning them in the presence of the assembled multitude.

The same effect followed as in Cozumel. The Totonacs, finding their deities incapable of preventing or even punishing this profanation of their shrines, conceived a mean opinion of their power, compared with that of the mysterious and formidable strangers. The floor and walls of the *teocalli* were then cleansed, by command of Cortés, from their foul impurities; a fresh coating of stucco was laid on them by the Indian masons; and an altar was raised, surmounted by a lofty cross, and hung with garlands of roses. A procession was next formed, in which some of the principal Totonac priests, exchanging their dark mantles for robes of white, carried lighted candles in their hands; while an image of the Virgin, half smothered under the weight of flowers, was borne aloft, and, as the procession climbed the steps of the temple, was deposited above the altar. Mass was performed by father Olmedo, and the impressive character of the ceremony and the passionate eloquence of the good priest touched the feelings of the motley audience, until Indians as well as Spaniards, if we may trust the chronicler, were melted into tears and audible sobs. The Protestant missionary seeks to enlighten the understanding of his convert by the pale light of reason. But the bolder Catholic, kindling the spirit by the splendor of the spectacle and by the glowing portrait of an agonized Redeemer, sweeps along his hearers in a tempest of passion, that drowns every thing like reflection. He has secured his convert, however, by the hold on his affections,—an easier and more powerful hold with the untutored savage, than reason.

An old soldier named Juan de Torres, disabled by bodily infirmity, consented to remain and watch over the sanctuary, and instruct the natives in its services. Cortés then, embracing his Totonac allies, now brothers in religion as in arms, set out once more for the Villa Rica.

where he had some arrangements to complete, previous to his departure for the capital.[6]

He was surprised to find that a Spanish vessel had arrived there in his absence, having on board twelve soldiers and two horses. It was under the command of a captain named Saucedo, a cavalier of the ocean, who had followed in the track of Cortés in quest of adventure. Though a small, they afforded a very seasonable body of recruits for the little army. By these men, the Spaniards were informed that Velasquez, the governor of Cuba, had lately received a warrant from the Spanish government to establish a colony in the newly discovered countries.

Cortés now resolved to put a plan in execution which he had been some time meditating. He knew that all the late acts of the colony, as well as his own authority, would fall to the ground without the royal sanction. He knew, too, that the interest of Velasquez, which was great at court, would, so soon as he was acquainted with his secession, be wholly employed to circumvent and crush him. He resolved to anticipate his movements, and to send a vessel to Spain, with despatches addressed to the emperor himself, announcing the nature and extent of his discoveries, and to obtain, if possible, the confirmation of his proceedings. In order to conciliate his master's good-will, he further proposed to send him such a present, as should suggest lofty ideas of the importance of his own services to the crown. To effect this, the royal fifth he considered inadequate. He conferred with his officers, and persuaded them to relinquish their share of the treasure. At his instance, they made a similar application to the soldiers; representing that it was the earnest wish of the general, who set the example by resigning his own fifth, equal to the share of the crown. It was but little that each man was asked to surrender, but the whole would make a present worthy of the monarch for whom it was intended. By this sacrifice, they might hope to secure his indulgence for the past, and his favor for the future; a temporary sacrifice, that would be well repaid by the security of the rich possessions which awaited them in Mexico. A paper was then circulated among the soldiers, which, all who were disposed to relinquish their shares, were requested to sign. Those who declined should have their claims respected, and receive the amount due to them. No one refused to sign; thus furnishing another example of the extraordinary power obtained by Cortés over these rapacious spirits, who, at his call, surrendered up the very treasures which had been the great object of their hazardous enterprise![7]

[6] Las Casas, Hist. de las Indias, MS., lib. 3, cap. 122.—Bernal Diaz, Hist. de la Conquista, cap. 51, 52.—Gomara, Crónica, cap. 43.—Herrera, Hist. General, dec. 2, lib. 5, cap. 13, 14.—Ixtlilxochitl, Hist. Chich., MS., cap. 83.

[7] Bernal Diaz, Hist. de la Conquista, cap. 53.—Ixtlilxochitl, Hist. Chich., MS., cap. 82.—Carta de Vera Cruz, MS.

A complete inventory of the articles received from Montezuma is contained in the *Carta de Vera Cruz.*—The following are a few of the items.

Two collars made of gold and precious stones.

He accompanied this present with a letter to the emperor, in which he gave a full account of all that had befallen him since his departure from Cuba; of his various discoveries, battles, and traffic with the natives; their conversion to Christianity; his strange perils and sufferings; many particulars respecting the lands he had visited, and such as he could collect in regard to the great Mexican monarchy and its sovereign. He stated his difficulties with the governor of Cuba, the proceedings of the army in reference to colonization, and besought the emperor to confirm their acts, as well as his own authority, expressing his entire confidence that he should be able, with the aid of his brave followers, to place the Castilian crown in possession of this great Indian empire.[8]

This was the celebrated *First Letter*, as it is called, of Cortés, which has hitherto eluded every search that has been made for it in the libraries of Europe.[9] Its existence is fully established by references to it, both in his own subsequent letters, and in the writings of contemporaries.[10] Its

A hundred ounces of gold ore, that their Highnesses might see in what state the gold came from the mines.

Two birds made of green feathers, with feet, beaks, and eyes of gold,—and, in the same piece with them, animals of gold, resembling snails.

A large alligator's head of gold.

A bird of green feathers, with feet, beak, and eyes of gold.

Two birds made of thread and feather-work having the quills of their wings and tails, their feet, eyes, and the ends of their beaks, of gold,—standing upon two reeds covered with gold, which are raised on balls of feather-work and gold embroidery, one white and the other yellow, with seven tassels of feather-work hanging from each of them.

A large wheel of silver weighing forty marks, and several smaller ones of the same metal.

A box of feather-work embroidered on leather, with a large plate of gold, weighing seventy ounces, in the midst.

Two pieces of cloth woven with feathers; another with variegated colors; and another worked with black and white figures.

A large wheel of gold, with figures of strange animals on it, and worked with tufts of leaves; weighing three thousand, eight hundred ounces.

A fan of variegated feather-work, with thirty-seven rods plated with gold.

Five fans of variegated feathers—four of which have ten, and the other thirteen, rods embossed with gold.

Sixteen shields of precious stones, with feathers of various colors hanging from their rims.

Two pieces of cotton very richly wrought with black and white embroidery.

Six shields, each covered with a plate of gold, with something resembling a golden mitre in the centre.

[8] "Una muy larga Carta," says Gomara, in his loose analysis of it. Crónica, cap. 40.

[9] Dr. Robertson states that the Imperial Library at Vienna was examined for this document, at his instance, but without success. (History of America, vol. II. note 70.) I have not been more fortunate in the researches made for me in the British Museum, the Royal Library of Paris, and that of the Academy of History at Madrid. The last is a great depository for the colonial historical documents; but a very thorough inspection of its papers makes it certain that this is wanting to the collection. As the emperor received it on the eve of his embarkation for Germany, and the Letter of Vera Cruz, forwarded at the same time, is in the library of Vienna, this would seem, after all, to be the most probable place of its retreat.

[10] "En una nao," says Cortés, in the very first sentence of his Second Letter to the emperor, "que de esta Nueva España de Vuestra Sacra Magestad despaché á 16

general purport is given by his chaplain, Gomara. The importance of the document has doubtless been much overrated; and, should it ever come to light, it will probably be found to add little of interest to the matter contained in the letter from Vera Cruz, which has formed the basis of the preceding portion of our narrative. He had no sources of information beyond those open to the authors of the latter document. He was even less full and frank in his communications, if it be true, that he suppressed all notice of the discoveries of his two immediate predecessors.[11]

The magistrates of the Villa Rica, in their epistle, went over the same ground with Cortés; concluding with an emphatic representation of the misconduct of Velasquez, whose venality, extortion, and selfish devotion to his personal interests, to the exclusion of those of his sovereigns as well as of his own followers, they placed in a most clear and unenviable light.[12] They implored the government not to sanction his interference with the new colony, which would be fatal to its welfare, but to commit the undertaking to Hernando Cortés, as the man most capable, by his experience and conduct, of bringing it to a glorious termination.[13]

With this letter went also another in the name of the citizen-soldiers of Villa Rica, tendering their dutiful submission to the sovereigns, and requesting the confirmation of their proceedings, above all, that of Cortés as their general.

The selection of the agents for the mission was a delicate matter, as

de Julio de el año 1519 embié á Vuestra Alteza muy larga y particular Relacion de las cosas hasta aquella sazon despues que yo á ella vine en ella sucedidas." (Rel. Seg. de Cortés, ap. Lorenzana, p. 38.) "Cortés escriuió," says Bernal Diaz, "segun él nos dixo, con recta relacion, mas no vímos su carta." (Hist. de la Conquista, cap. 53.) (Also, Oviedo, Hist. de las Ind., MS., lib. 33, cap. 1, and Gomara, ut supra.) Were it not for these positive testimonies, one might suppose that the Carta de Vera Cruz had suggested an *imaginary* letter of Cortés. Indeed, the copy of the former document, belonging to the Spanish Academy of History,—and perhaps the original at Vienna,—bears the erroneous title of "Primera Relacion de Cortés."

[11] This is the imputation of Bernal Diaz, reported on hearsay, as he admits he never saw the letter himself. Ibid., cap. 54.

[12] "Fingiendo mill cautelas," says Las Casas, politely, of this part of the letter, "y afirmando otras muchas falsedades é mentiras"! Hist. de las Indias, MS., lib. 3, cap. 122.

[13] This document is of the greatest value and interest, coming as it does from the best instructed persons in the camp. It presents an elaborate record of all then known of the countries they had visited, and of the principal movements of the army, to the time of the foundation of the Villa Rica. The writers conciliate our confidence by the circumspect tone of their narration. "Querer dar," they say, "á Vuestra Magestad todas las particularidades de esta tierra y gente de ella, podria ser que en algo se errase la relacion, porque muchas de ellas no se han visto mas de por informaciones de los naturales de ella, y por esto no nos entremetemos á dar mas de aquello que por muy cierto y verdadero Vras. Reales Altezas podrán mandar tener." The account given of Velasquez, however, must be considered as an *ex parte* testimony, and, as such, admitted with great reserve. It was essential to their own vindication, to vindicate Cortés. The letter has never been printed. The original exists, as above stated, in the Imperial Library at Vienna. The copy in my possession, covering more than sixty pages folio, is taken from that of the Academy of History at Madrid.

on the result might depend the future fortunes of the colony and its commander. Cortés intrusted the affair to two cavaliers on whom he could rely; Francisco de Montejo, the ancient partisan of Velasquez, and Alonso Hernandez de Puertocarrero. The latter officer was a near kinsman of the count of Medellin, and it was hoped his high connections might secure a favorable influence at court.

Together with the treasure, which seemed to verify the assertion that "the land teemed with gold as abundantly as that whence Solomon drew the same precious metal for his temple," [14] several Indian manuscripts were sent. Some were of cotton, others of the Mexican *agave*. Their unintelligible characters, says a chronicler, excited little interest in the Conquerors. As evidence of intellectual culture, however, they formed higher objects of interest to a philosophic mind, than those costly fabrics which attested only the mechanical ingenuity of the nation.[15] Four Indian slaves were added as specimens of the natives. They had been rescued from the cages in which they were confined for sacrifice. One of the best vessels of the fleet was selected for the voyage, manned by fifteen seamen, and placed under the direction of the pilot Alaminos. He was directed to hold his course through the Bahama channel, north of Cuba, or Fernandina, as it was then called, and on no account to touch at that island, or any other in the Indian ocean. With these instructions, the good ship took its departure on the 26th of July, freighted with the treasures and the good wishes of the community of the Villa Rica de Vera Cruz.

After a quick run the emissaries made the island of Cuba, and, in direct disregard of orders, anchored before Marien, on the northern side of the island. This was done to accommodate Montejo, who wished to visit a plantation owned by him in the neighborhood. While off the port, a sailor got on shore, and, crossing the island to St. Jago, the capital, spread everywhere tidings of the expedition, until they reached the ears of Velasquez. It was the first intelligence which had been received of the armament since its departure; and, as the governor listened to the recital, it would not be easy to paint the mingled emotions of curiosity, astonishment, and wrath which agitated his bosom. In the first sally of passion, he poured a storm of invective on the heads of his secretary and treasurer, the friends of Cortés, who had recommended him as the leader of the expedition. After somewhat relieving himself in this way, he despatched two fast-sailing vessels to Marien with orders to seize the rebel ship, and, in case of her departure, to follow and overtake her.

But before the ships could reach that port, the bird had flown, and

[14] "Á nuestra parecer se debe creer, que ai en esta tierra tanto quanto en aquella de donde se dize aver llevado Salomon el oro para el templo." Carta de Vera Cruz, MS.

[15] Peter Martyr, preëminent above his contemporaries for the enlightened views he took of the new discoveries, devotes half a chapter to the Indian manuscripts, in which he recognized the evidence of a civilization analogous to the Egyptian. De Orbe Novo, dec. 4, cap. 8.

was far on her way across the broad Atlantic. Stung with mortification
at this fresh disappointment, Velasquez wrote letters of indignant complaint to the government at home, and to the fathers of St. Jerome, in
Hispaniola, demanding redress. He obtained little satisfaction from the
last. He resolved, however, to take it into his own hands, and set about
making formidable preparations for another squadron, which should be
more than a match for that under his rebellious officer. He was indefatigable in his exertions, visiting every part of the island, and straining
all his resources to effect his purpose. The preparations were on a scale
that necessarily consumed many months.

Meanwhile the little vessel was speeding her prosperous way across
the waters; and, after touching at one of the Azores, came safely into
the harbor of St. Lucar, in the month of October. However long it may
appear, in the more perfect nautical science of our day, it was reckoned
a fair voyage for that. Of what befell the commissioners on their arrival,
their reception at court, and the sensation caused by their intelligence,
I defer the account to a future chapter.[16]

Shortly after the departure of the commissioners, an affair occurred of
a most unpleasant nature. A number of persons, with the priest Juan
Diaz at their head, ill-affected, from some cause or other, towards the
administration of Cortés, or not relishing the hazardous expedition before them, laid a plan to seize one of the vessels, make the best of their
way to Cuba, and report to the governor the fate of the armament. It
was conducted with so much secrecy, that the party had got their provisions, water, and everything necessary for the voyage, on board, without detection; when the conspiracy was betrayed, on the very night they
were to sail, by one of their own number, who repented the part he had
taken in it. The general caused the persons implicated to be instantly
apprehended. An examination was instituted. The guilt of the parties
was placed beyond a doubt. Sentence of death was passed on two of the
ringleaders; another, the pilot, was condemned to lose his feet, and
several others to be whipped. The priest, probably the most guilty of
the whole, claiming the usual benefit of clergy, was permitted to escape.
One of those condemned to the gallows was named Escudero, the very
alguacil who, the reader may remember, so stealthily apprehended
Cortés before the sanctuary in Cuba.[17] The general, on signing the
death-warrants, was heard to exclaim, "Would that I had never learned
to write!" It was not the first time, it was remarked, that the exclamation had been uttered in similar circumstances.[18]

[16] Bernal Diaz, Hist. de la Conquista, cap. 54-57.—Gomara, Crónica, cap. 40.—
Herrera, Hist. General, dec. 2, lib. 5, cap. 14.—Carta de Vera Cruz, MS.
    Martyr's copious information was chiefly derived from his conversations with
Alaminos and the two envoys, on their arrival at court. De Orbe Novo, dec. 4, cap.
6, et alibi; also Idem, Opus Epistolarum, (Amstelodami, 1670,) ep. 650.
    [17] See Ante, p. 133.
    [18] Bernal Diaz, Hist. de la Conquista, cap. 57.—Oviedo, Hist. de las Ind., MS., lib.
33, cap. 2.—Las Casas, Hist. de las Indias, MS., lib. 3, cap. 122.—Demanda de Narvaez, MS.—Rel. Seg. de Cortés, ap. Lorenzana, p. 41.
    It was the exclamation of Nero, as reported by Suetonius. "Et cum de supplicio

The arrangements being now finally settled at the Villa Rica, Cortés sent forward Alvarado, with a large part of the army, to Cempoalla, where he soon after joined them with the remainder. The late affair of the conspiracy seems to have made a deep impression on his mind. It showed him, that there were timid spirits in the camp on whom he could not rely, and who, he feared, might spread the seeds of disaffection among their companions. Even the more resolute, on any occasion of disgust or disappointment hereafter, might falter in purpose, and, getting possession of the vessels, abandon the enterprise. This was already too vast, and the odds were too formidable, to authorize expectation of success with diminution of numbers. Experience showed that this was always to be apprehended, while means of escape were at hand.[19] The best chance for success was to cut off these means.—He came to the daring resolution to destroy the fleet, without the knowledge of his army.

When arrived at Cempoalla, he communicated his design to a few of his devoted adherents, who entered warmly into his views. Through them he readily persuaded the pilots, by means of those golden arguments which weigh more than any other with ordinary minds, to make such a report of the condition of the fleet as suited his purpose. The ships, they said, were grievously racked by the heavy gales they had encountered, and, what was worse, the worms had eaten into their sides and bottoms until most of them were not sea-worthy, and some, indeed, could scarcely now be kept afloat.

Cortés received the communication with surprise; "for he could well dissemble," observes Las Casas, with his usual friendly comment, "when it suited his interests." "If it be so," he exclaimed, "we must make the best of it! Heaven's will be done!"[20] He then ordered five of the worst conditioned to be dismantled, their cordage, sails, iron, and whatever was movable, to be brought on shore, and the ships to be sunk. A survey was made of the others, and, on a similar report, four more were condemned in the same manner. Only one small vessel remained!

When the intelligence reached the troops in Cempoalla, it caused the deepest consternation. They saw themselves cut off by a single blow from friends, family, country! The stoutest hearts quailed before the prospect of being thus abandoned on a hostile shore, a handful of men arrayed against a formidable empire. When the news arrived of the destruction of the five vessels first condemned, they had acquiesced in it as a necessary measure, knowing the mischievous activity of the insects in

cujusdam capite damnati ut ex more subscriberet, admoneretur, 'Quam vellem,' inquit, 'nescire literas!' " Lib. 6. cap. 10.

[19] "Y porque," says Cortés, "demas de los que por ser criados y amigos de Diego Velasquez tenian voluntad de salir de la Tierra, habia otros, que por verla tan grande, y de tanta gente, y tal, y ver los pocos Españoles que eramos, esta ban del mismo propósito; creyen do, que si allí los navíos dejasse, se me alzarian con ellos, y yéndose todos los que de esta voluntad estavan, yo quedaria casi solo."

[20] "Mostró quando se lo dixéron mucho sentimiento Cortés, porque savia bien haçer fingimienños quando le era provechoso, y rrespondióles que mirasen vien en ello, é que si no estavan para navegar que diesen gracias á Dios por ello, pues no se podia hacer mas." Las Casas, Hist. de las Indias, MS., lib. 3, cap. 122.

these tropical seas. But, when this was followed by the loss of the remaining four, suspicions of the truth flashed on their minds. They felt they were betrayed. Murmurs, at first deep, swelled louder and louder, menacing open mutiny. "Their general," they said, "had led them like cattle to be butchered in the shambles!" [21] The affair wore a most alarming aspect. In no situation was Cortés ever exposed to greater danger from his soldiers.[22]

His presence of mind did not desert him at this crisis. He called his men together, and, employing the tones of persuasion rather than authority, assured them, that a survey of the ships showed they were not fit for service. If he had ordered them to be destroyed, they should consider, also, that his was the greatest sacrifice, for they were his property, —all, indeed, he possessed in the world. The troops, on the other hand, would derive one great advantage from it, by the addition of a hundred able-bodied recruits, before required to man the vessels. But, even if the fleet had been saved, it could have been of little service in their present expedition; since they would not need it if they succeeded, while they would be too far in the interior to profit by it if they failed. He besought them to turn their thoughts in another direction. To be thus calculating chances and means of escape was unworthy of brave souls. They had set their hands to the work; to look back, as they advanced, would be their ruin. They had only to resume their former confidence in themselves and their general, and success was certain. "As for me," he concluded, "I have chosen my part. I will remain here, while there is one to bear me company. If there be any so craven, as to shrink from sharing the dangers of our glorious enterprise, let them go home, in God's name. There is still one vessel left. Let them take that and return to Cuba. They can tell there, how they have deserted their commander and their comrades, and patiently wait till we return loaded with the spoils of the Aztecs." [23]

The politic orator had touched the right chord in the bosoms of the soldiers. As he spoke, their resentment gradually died away. The faded visions of future riches and glory, rekindled by his eloquence, again floated before their imaginations. The first shock over, they felt ashamed of their temporary distrust. The enthusiasm for their leader revived, for they felt that under his banner only they could hope for victory; and, as he concluded, they testified the revulsion of their feelings by making the air ring with their shouts, "To Mexico! to Mexico!"

The destruction of his fleet by Cortés is, perhaps, the most remark-

---

[21] "Decian, que los queria meter en el matadero." Gomara, Crónica, cap. 42.

[22] "Al cavo lo oviéron de sentir la gente y ayna se le amotinaran muchos, y esta fué uno de los peligros que pasáron por Cortés de muchos que para matallo de los mismos Españoles estuvo." Las Casas, Hist. de las Indias, MS., lib. 3, cap. 122.

[23] "Que ninguno seria tan cobarde y tan pusilánime que queria estimar su vida mas que la suya, ni de tan debil corazon que dudase de ir con él á México, donde tanto bien le estaba aparejado, y que si acaso se determinaba alguno de dejar de hacer este se podia ir bendito de Dios á Cuba en el navío que habia dexado, de que antes de mucho se arrepentiria, y pelaria las barbas, viendo la buena ventura que esperaba le sucederia." Ixtlilxochitl, Hist. Chich., MS., cap. 82.

able passage in the life of this remarkable man. History, indeed, affords examples of a similar expedient in emergencies somewhat similar; but none where the chances of success were so precarious, and defeat would be so disastrous.[24] Had he failed, it might well seem an act of madness. Yet it was the fruit of deliberate calculation. He had set fortune, fame, life itself, all upon the cast, and must abide the issue. There was no alternative in his mind but to succeed or perish. The measure he adopted greatly increased the chance of success. But to carry it into execution, in the face of an incensed and desperate soldiery, was an act of resolution that has few parallels in history.[25]

Fray Bartolomé de las Casas, bishop of Chiapa, whose "History of the Indies" forms an important authority for the preceding pages, was one of the most remarkable men of the sixteenth century. He was born at Seville in 1474. His father accompanied Columbus, as a common soldier, in his first voyage to the New World; and he acquired wealth enough by his vocation to place his son at the University of Salamanca. During his residence there, he was attended by an Indian page, whom his father had brought with him from Hispaniola. Thus the uncompromising advocate for freedom began his career as the owner of a slave himself. But he did not long

[24] Perhaps the most remarkable of these examples is that of Julian, who, in his unfortunate Assyrian invasion, burnt the fleet which had carried him up the Tigris. The story is told by Gibbon, who shows very satisfactorily that the fleet would have proved a hinderance rather than a help to the emperor in his further progress. See History of the Decline and Fall, (vol. IX, p. 177,) of Milman's excellent edition.

[25] The account given in the text of the destruction of the fleet is not that of Bernal Diaz, who states it to have been accomplished, not only with the knowledge, but entire approbation of the army, though at the suggestion of Cortés. (Hist. de la Conquista, cap. 58). This version is sanctioned by Dr. Robertson (History of America, vol. II. pp. 253, 254). One should be very slow to depart from the honest record of the old soldier, especially when confirmed by the discriminating judgment of the Historian of America. But Cortés expressly declares in his letter to the emperor, that he ordered the vessels to be sunk, without the knowledge of his men, from the apprehension, that, if the means of escape were open, the timid and disaffected might, at some future time, avail themselves of them. (Rel. Seg. de Cortés, ap. Lorenzana, p. 41.) The cavaliers Montejo y Puertocarrero, on their visit to Spain, stated, in their depositions, that the general destroyed the fleet on information received from the pilots. (Declaraciones, MSS.) Narvaez in his accusation of Cortés, and Las Casas, speak of the act in terms of unqualified reprobation, charging him, moreover, with bribing the pilots to bore holes in the bottoms of the ships, in order to disable them. (Demanda de Narvaez, MS.—Hist. de las Indias, MS., lib. 3, cap. 122.) The same account of the transaction, though with a very different commentary as to its merits, is repeated by Oviedo, (Hist. de las Ind., MS., lib. 33, cap. 2,) Gomara, (Crónica, cap. 42,) and Peter Martyr, (De Orbe Novo, dec. 5, cap. 1,) all of whom had access to the best sources of information.
The affair, so remarkable as the act of one individual, becomes absolutely incredible, when considered as the result of so many independent wills. It is not improbable, that Bernal Diaz, from his known devotion to the cause, may have been one of the few to whom Cortés confided his purpose. The veteran, in writing his narrative, many years after, may have mistaken a part for the whole, and in his zeal to secure to the army a full share of the glory of the expedition, too exclusively appropriated by the general, (a great object, as he tells us, of his history,) may have distributed among his comrades the credit of an exploit which, in this instance, at least, properly belonged to their commander.—Whatever be the cause of the discrepancy, his solitary testimony can hardly be sustained against the weight of contemporary evidence from such competent sources.

remain so, for his slave was one of those subsequently liberated by the generous commands of Isabella.

In 1498, he completed his studies in law and divinity, took his degree of licentiate, and, in 1502, accompanied Oviedo, in the most brilliant armada which had been equipped for the Western World. Eight years after, he was admitted to priest's orders in St. Domingo, an event somewhat memorable, since he was the first person consecrated in that holy office in the colonies. On the occupation of Cuba by the Spaniards, Las Casas passed over to that island, where he obtained a curacy in a small settlement. He soon, however, made himself known to the governor, Velasquez, by the fidelity with which he discharged his duties, and especially by the influence which his mild and benevolent teaching obtained for him over the Indians. Through his intimacy with the governor, Las Casas had the means of ameliorating the condition of the conquered race, and from this time he may be said to have consecrated all his energies to this one great object. At this period, the scheme of *repartimientos,* introduced soon after the discoveries of Columbus, was in full operation, and the Aboriginal population of the Islands was rapidly melting away under a system of oppression, which has been seldom paralleled in the annals of mankind. Las Casas, outraged at the daily exhibition of crime and misery, returned to Spain to obtain some redress from government. Ferdinand died soon after his arrival. Charles was absent, but the reins were held by Cardinal Ximenes, who listened to the complaints of the benevolent missionary, and, with his characteristic vigor, instituted a commission of three Hieronomite friars, with full authority, as already noticed in the text, to reform abuses. Las Casas was honored, for his exertions, with the title of "Protector General of the Indians."

The new commissioners behaved with great discretion. But their office was one of consummate difficulty, as it required time to introduce important changes in established institutions. The ardent and impetuous temper of Las Casas, disdaining every consideration of prudence, overleaped all these obstacles, and chafed under what he considered the lukewarm and temporizing policy of the commissioners. As he was at no pains to conceal his disgust, the parties soon came to a misunderstanding with each other; and Las Casas again returned to the mother country, to stimulate the government, if possible, to more effectual measures for the protection of the natives.

He found the country under the administration of the Flemings, who discovered from the first a wholesome abhorrence of the abuses practised in the colonies, and who, in short, seemed inclined to tolerate no peculation or extortion, but their own. They acquiesced, without much difficulty, in the recommendations of Las Casas, who proposed to relieve the natives by sending out Castilian laborers, and by importing Negro slaves into the Islands. This last proposition has brought heavy obloquy on the head of its author, who has been freely accused of having thus introduced Negro slavery into the New World. Others, with equal groundlessness, have attempted to vindicate his memory from the reproach of having recommended the measure at all. Unfortunately for the latter assertion, Las Casas, in his History of the Indies, confesses, with deep regret and humiliation, his advice on this occasion, founded on the most erroneous views, as he frankly states; since, to use his own words, "the same law applies equally to the Negro as to the Indian." But so far from having introduced slavery by this measure into the Islands, the importation of blacks there dates from the beginning of the century. It was recommended by some of the wisest and most benevolent persons in the colony, as the means of diminishing the amount of human suffering; since the African was more fitted by his constitution to endure the climate and the severe toil imposed on the slave than the feeble and effeminate islander. It was a suggestion of humanity, however mistaken, and, considering the circumstances under which it occurred, and the age, it may well be forgiven in Las Casas, especially taking into view, that, as he became more enlightened himself, he was so ready to testify his regret at having unadvisedly countenanced the measure.

The experiment recommended by Las Casas was made, but, through the apathy of Fonseca, president of the Indian Council, not heartily,—and it failed. The good missionary now proposed another, and much bolder scheme. He requested that a large tract of country in Tierra Firme, in the neighborhood of the famous pearl fisheries, might be ceded to him for the purpose of planting a colony there, and of converting the natives to Christianity. He required that none of the authorities of the Islands, and no military force, especially, should be allowed to interfere with his movements. He pledged himself by peaceful means alone to accomplish all that had been done by violence in other quarters. He asked only that a certain number of laborers should attend him, invited by a bounty from government, and that he might further be accompanied by fifty Dominicans, who were to be distinguished like himself by a peculiar dress, that should lead the natives to suppose them a different race of men from the Spaniards. This proposition was denounced as chimerical and fantastic by some, whose opportunities of observation entitled their judgment to respect. These men declared the Indian, from his nature, incapable of civilization. The question was one of such moment, that Charles the Fifth ordered the discussion to be conducted before him. The opponent of Las Casas was first heard, when the good missionary, in answer, warmed by the noble cause he was to maintain, and nothing daunted by the august presence in which he stood, delivered himself with a fervent eloquence that went directly to the hearts of his auditors. "The Christian religion," he concluded, "is equal in its operation, and is accommodated to every nation on the globe. It robs no one of his freedom, violates none of his inherent rights, on the ground that he is a slave by nature, as pretended; and it well becomes your Majesty to banish so monstrous an oppression from your kingdoms in the beginning of your reign, that the Almighty may make it long and glorious."

In the end Las Casas prevailed. He was furnished with the men and means for establishing his colony; and, in 1520, embarked for America. But the result was a lamentable failure. The country assigned to him lay in the neighborhood of a Spanish settlement, which had already committed some acts of violence on the natives. To quell the latter, now thrown into commotion, an armed force was sent by the young "Admiral" from Hispaniola. The very people, among whom Las Casas was to appear as the messenger of peace, were thus involved in deadly strife with his countrymen. The enemy had been before him in his own harvest. While waiting for the close of these turbulent scenes, the laborers, whom he had taken out with him, dispersed, in despair of effecting their object. And after an attempt to pursue, with his faithful Dominican brethren, the work of colonization further, other untoward circumstances compelled them to abandon the project altogether. Its unfortunate author, overwhelmed with chagrin, took refuge in the Dominican monastery in the island of Hispaniola.—The failure of the enterprise should, no doubt, be partly ascribed to circumstances beyond the control of its projector. Yet it is impossible not to recognise, in the whole scheme, and in the conduct of it, the hand of one much more familiar with books than men, who, in the seclusion of the cloister, had meditated and matured his benevolent plans, without fully estimating the obstacles that lay in their way, and who counted too confidently on meeting the same generous enthusiasm in others, which glowed in his own bosom.

He found, in his disgrace, the greatest consolation and sympathy from the brethren of St. Dominic, who stood forth as the avowed champions of the Indians on all occasions, and showed themselves as devoted to the cause of freedom in the New World, as they had been hostile to it in the Old. Las Casas soon became a member of their order, and, in his monastic retirement, applied himself for many years to the performance of his spiritual duties, and the composition of various works, all directed, more or less, to vindicate the rights of the Indians. Here, too, he commenced his great work, the "Historia General de las Indias," which he pursued, at intervals of leisure, from 1527 till a few years before his death. His time, however, was not wholly absorbed by these labors; and he found means to engage in several laborious missions. He preached the gospel among the natives of Nicaragua, and Guatemala; and succeeded in converting and reducing to obedience some wild tribes in the latter province, who had defied the arms of his countrymen. In all these pious labors, he was sustained by his Dominican brethren. At length, in 1539, he crossed the waters again, to seek further assistance and recruits among the members of his order.

A great change had taken place in the board that now presided over the colonial

department. The cold and narrow-minded Fonseca, who, during his long administration, had, it may be truly said, shown himself the enemy of every great name
and good measure connected with the Indians, had died. His place, as president of
the Indian Council, was filled by Loaysa, Charles's confessor. This functionary, general of the Dominicans, gave ready audience to Las Casas, and showed a good-will
to his proposed plans of reform. Charles, too, now grown older, seemed to feel
more deeply the responsibility of his station, and the necessity of redressing the
wrongs, too long tolerated, of his American subjects. The state of the colonies became a common topic of discussion, not only in the council, but in the court; and
the representations of Las Casas made an impression that manifested itself in the
change of sentiment more clearly every day. He promoted this by the publication of
some of his writings at this time, and especially of his "Brevísima Relacion," or
Short Account of the Destruction of the Indies, in which he sets before the reader
the manifold atrocities committed by his countrymen in different parts of the New
World in the prosecution of their conquests. It is a tale of woe. Every line of the
work may be said to be written in blood. However good the motives of its author,
we may regret that the book was ever written. He would have been certainly right
not to spare his countrymen; to exhibit their misdeeds in their true colors, and by
this appalling picture—for such it would have been—to have recalled the nation,
and those who governed it, to a proper sense of the iniquitous career it was pursuing on the other side of the water. But, to produce a more striking effect, he has
lent a willing ear to every tale of violence and rapine, and magnified the amount
to a degree which borders on the ridiculous. The wild extravagance of his numerical
estimates is of itself sufficient to shake confidence in the accuracy of his statements
generally. Yet the naked truth was too startling in itself to demand the aid of
exaggeration. The book found great favor with foreigners; was rapidly translated
into various languages, and ornamented with characteristic designs, which seemed
to put into action all the recorded atrocities of the text. It excited somewhat different feelings in his own countrymen, particularly the people of the colonies, who
considered themselves the subjects of a gross, however undesigned, misrepresentation; and, in his future intercourse with them, it contributed, no doubt, to diminish
his influence and consequent usefulness, by the spirit of alienation, and even resentment, which it engendered.

Las Casas' honest intentions, his enlightened views and long experience, gained
him deserved credit at home. This was visible in the important regulations made
at this time for the better government of the colonies, and particularly in respect
to the Aborigines. A code of laws, *Las Nuevas Leyes*, was passed, having for their
avowed object the enfranchisement of this unfortunate race; and, in the wisdom
and humanity of its provisions, it is easy to recognise the hand of the Protector of
the Indians. The history of Spanish colonial legislation is the history of the impotent struggles of the government in behalf of the natives, against the avarice and
cruelty of its subjects. It proves that an empire powerful at home—and Spain then
was so—may be so widely extended, that its authority shall scarcely be felt in its
extremities.

The government testified their sense of the signal services of Las Casas, by
promoting him to the bishopric of Cuzco, one of the richest sees in the colonies.
But the disinterested soul of the missionary did not covet riches or preferment.
He rejected the proffered dignity without hesitation. Yet he could not refuse the
bishopric of Chiapa, a country, which, from the poverty and ignorance of its inhabitants, offered a good field for his spiritual labors. In 1544, though at the advanced age of seventy, he took upon himself these new duties, and embarked, for
the fifth and last time, for the shores of America. His fame had preceded him. The
colonists looked on his coming with apprehension, regarding him as the real author
of the new code, which struck at their ancient immunities, and which he would be
likely to enforce to the letter. Everywhere he was received with coldness. In some
places his person was menaced with violence. But the venerable presence of the
prelate, his earnest expostulations, which flowed so obviously from conviction, and
his generous self-devotion, so regardless of personal considerations, preserved him

from this outrage. Yet he showed no disposition to conciliate his opponents by what he deemed an unworthy concession; and he even stretched the arm of authority so far as to refuse the sacraments to any, who still held an Indian in bondage. This high-handed measure not only outraged the planters, but incurred the disapprobation of his own brethren in the Church. Three years were spent in disagreeable altercation without coming to any decision. The Spaniards, to borrow their accustomed phraseology on these occasions, "obeying the law, but not fulfilling it," applied to the Court for further instruction; and the bishop, no longer supported by his own brethren, thwarted by the colonial magistrates, and outraged by the people, relinquished a post where his presence could be no further useful, and returned to spend the remainder of his days in tranquillity at home.

Yet, though withdrawn to his Dominican convent, he did not pass his hours in slothful seclusion. He again appeared as the champion of Indian freedom in the famous controversy with Sepulveda, one of the most acute scholars of the time, and far surpassing Las Casas in elegance and correctness of composition. But the Bishop of Chiapa was his superior in argument, at least in this discussion, where he had right and reason on his side. In his "Thirty Propositions," as they are called, in which he sums up the several points of his case, he maintains, that the circumstance of infidelity in religion cannot deprive a nation of its political rights; that the Holy See, in its grant of the New World to the Catholic sovereigns, designed only to confer the right of converting its inhabitants to Christianity, and of thus winning a peaceful authority over them; and that no authority could be valid, which rested on other foundations. This was striking at the root of the colonial empire, as assumed by Castile. But the disinterested views of Las Casas, the respect entertained for his principles, and the general conviction, it may be, of the force of his arguments, prevented the Court from taking umbrage at their import, or from pressing them to their legitimate conclusion. While the writings of his adversary were interdicted from publication, he had the satisfaction to see his own printed and circulated in every quarter.

From this period his time was distributed among his religious duties, his studies, and the composition of his works, especially his History. His constitution, naturally excellent, had been strengthened by a life of temperance and toil; and he retained his faculties unimpaired to the last. He died after a short illness, July, 1566, at the great age of ninety-two, in his monastery at Atocha, at Madrid.

The character of Las Casas may be inferred from his career. He was one of those, to whose gifted minds are revealed those glorious moral truths, which, like the lights of heaven, are fixed and the same for ever; but which, though now familiar, were hidden from all but a few penetrating intellects by the general darkness of the time in which he lived. He was a reformer, and had the virtues and errors of a reformer. He was inspired by one great and glorious idea. This was the key to all his thoughts, all that he said and wrote, to every act of his long life. It was this which urged him to lift the voice of rebuke in the presence of princes, to brave the menaces of an infuriated populace, to cross seas, to traverse mountains and deserts, to incur the alienation of friends, the hostility of enemies, to endure obloquy, insult, and persecution. It was this, too, which made him reckless of obstacles, led him to count too confidently on the coöperation of others, animated his discussion, sharpened his invective, too often steeped his pen in the gall of personal vituperation, led him into gross exaggeration and over-coloring in his statements, and a blind credulity of evil that rendered him unsafe as a counsellor, and unsuccessful in the practical concerns of life. His motives were pure and elevated. But his manner of enforcing them was not always so commendable. This may be gathered not only from the testimony of the colonists generally, who, as parties interested, may be supposed to have been prejudiced; but from that of the members of his own profession, persons high in office, and of integrity beyond suspicion, not to add that of missionaries engaged in the same good work with himself. These, in their letters and reported conversations, charged the Bishop of Chiapa with an arrogant, uncharitable temper, which deluded his judgment, and vented itself in unwarrantable crimination against such as resisted his projects, or differed from him in opinion.

Las Casas, in short, was a man. But, if he had the errors of humanity, he had virtues that rarely belong to it. The best commentary on his character is the estimation which he obtained in the court of his sovereign. A liberal pension was settled on him after his last return from America, which he chiefly expended on charitable objects. No measure of importance, relating to the Indians, was taken without his advice. He lived to see the fruits of his efforts in the positive amelioration of their condition, and in the popular admission of those great truths which it had been the object of his life to unfold. And who shall say how much of the successful efforts and arguments since made in behalf of persecuted humanity may be traced to the example and the writings of this illustrious philanthropist?

His compositions were numerous, most of them of no great length. Some were printed in his time; others have since appeared, especially in the French translation of Llorente. His great work, which occupied him at intervals for more than thirty years, the *Historia General de las Indias,* still remains in manuscript. It is in three volumes, divided into as many parts, and embraces the colonial history from the discovery of the country by Columbus to the year 1520. The style of the work, like that of all his writings, is awkward, disjointed, and excessively diffuse; abounding in repetitions, irrelevant digressions, and pedantic citations. But it is sprinkled over with passages of a different kind; and, when he is roused by the desire to exhibit some gross wrong to the natives, his simple language kindles into eloquence, and he expounds those great and immutable principles of natural justice, which, in his own day, were so little understood. His defect as a historian is, that he wrote history, like every thing else, under the influence of one dominant idea. He is always pleading the cause of the persecuted native. This gives a coloring to events which passed under his own eyes, and filled him with a too easy confidence in those which he gathered from the reports of others. Much of the preceding portion of our narrative which relates to affairs in Cuba must have come under his personal observation. But he seems incapable of shaking off his early deference to Velasquez, who, as we have noticed, treated him, while a poor curate in the island, with peculiar confidence. For Cortés, on the other hand, he appears to have felt a profound contempt. He witnessed the commencement of his career, when he was standing, cap in hand, as it were, at the proud governors's door, thankful even for a smile of recognition. Las Casas remembered all this, and, when he saw the Conqueror of Mexico rise into a glory and renown that threw his former patron into the shade,—and most unfairly, as Las Casas deemed, at the expense of that patron, —the good bishop could not withhold his indigation; nor speak of him otherwise than with a sneer, as a mere upstart adventurer.

It was the existence of defects like these, and the fear of the misconception likely to be produced by them, that have so long prevented the publication of his history. At his death, he left it to the convent of San Gregorio, at Valladolid, with directions that it should not be printed for forty years, nor be seen during that time by any layman or member of the fraternity. Herrera, however, was permitted to consult it, and he liberally transferred its contents to his own volumes, which appeared in 1601. The Royal Academy of History revised the first volume of Las Casas some years since, with a view to the publication of the whole work. But the indiscreet and imaginative style of the composition, according to Navarrete, and the consideration that its most important facts were already known through other channels, induced that body to abandon the design. With deference to their judgment, it seems to me a mistake. Las Casas, with every deduction, is one of the great writers of the nation; great from the important truths which he discerned when none else could see them, and from the courage with which he proclaimed them to the world. They are scattered over his History as well as his other writings. They are not, however, the passages transcribed by Herrera. In the statement of fact, too, however partial and prejudiced, no one will impeach his integrity; and, as an enlightened contemporary, his evidence is of undeniable value. It is due to the memory of Las Casas, that, if his work be given to the public at all, it should not be through the garbled extracts of one who was no fair interpreter of his opinions. Las Casas does not speak for himself in the courtly pages of Herrera. Yet the History should not be published without a suitable commentary to enlighten the student, and guard him against any undue prejudices in the writer. We may hope that the entire manuscript will one day be given to the world under the auspices of that distinguished body, which has already done so much in this way for the illustration of the national annals.

The life of Las Casas has been several times written. The two memoirs most worthy of notice are that by Llorente, late Secretary of the Inquisition, prefixed to his French translation of the Bishop's controversial writings, and that by Quintana, in the third volume of his "Epañoles Célebres," where it presents a truly noble specimen of biographical composition, enriched by a literary criticism as acute as it is candid.—I have gone to the greater length in this notice, from the interesting character of the man, and the little that is known of him to the English reader. I have also transferred a passage from his work in the original to the Appendix, that the Spanish scholar may form an idea of his style of composition. He ceases to be an authority for us hereafter, as his account of the expedition of Cortés terminates with the destruction of the navy.

BOOK III

MARCH TO MEXICO

CHAPTER I

PROCEEDINGS AT CEMPOALLA—THE SPANIARDS CLIMB THE TABLELAND
—PICTURESQUE SCENERY—TRANSACTIONS WITH THE NATIVES—
EMBASSY TO TLASCALA

WHILE at Cempoalla, Cortés received a message from Escalante, his commander at Villa Rica, informing him there were four strange ships hovering off the coast, and that they took no notice of his repeated signals. This intelligence greatly alarmed the general, who feared they might be a squadron sent by the govenor of Cuba, to interfere with his movements. In much haste, he set out at the head of a few horsemen, and, ordering a party of light infantry to follow, posted back to Villa Rica. The rest of the army he left in charge of Alvarado and of Gonzalo de Sandoval, a young officer, who had begun to give evidence of the uncommon qualiites which have secured to him so distinguished a rank among the conquerors of Mexico.

Escalante would have persuaded the general, on his reaching the town, to take some rest, and allow him to go in search of the strangers. But Cortés replied with the homely proverb, "A wounded hare takes no nap," [1] and, without stopping to refresh himself or his men, pushed on three or four leagues to the north, where he understood the ships were at anchor. On the way, he fell in with three Spaniards, just landed from them. To his eager inquiries whence they came, they replied that they belonged to a squadron fitted out by Francisco de Garay, governor of Jamaica. This person, the year previous, had visited the Florida coast, and obtained from Spain—where he had some interest at court—authority over the countries he might discover in that vicinity. The three men, consisting of a notary and two witnesses, had been sent on shore to warn their countrymen under Cortés to desist from what was considered an encroachment on the territories of Garay. Probably neither the governor of Jamaica, nor his officers, had any very precise notion of the geography and limits of these territories.

Cortés saw at once there was nothing to apprehend from this quarter. He would have been glad, however, if he could, by any means, have in-

[1] "Cabra coxa no tenga siesta."

duced the crews of the ships to join his expedition. He found no difficulty in persuading the notary and his companions. But when he came in sight of the vessels, the people on board, distrusting the good terms on which their comrades appeared to be with the Spaniards, refused to send their boat ashore. In this dilemma, Cortés had recourse to a stratagem.

He ordered three of his own men to exchange dresses with the new comers. He then drew off his little band in sight of the vessels, affecting to return to the city. In the night, however, he came back to the same place, and lay in ambush, directing the disguised Spaniards, when the morning broke, and they could be discerned, to make signals to those on board. The artifice succeeded. A boat put off, filled with armed men, and three or four leaped on shore. But they soon detected the deceit, and Cortés, springing from his ambush, made them prisoners. Their comrades in the boat, alarmed, pushed off, at once, for the vessels, which soon got under way, leaving those on shore to their fate. Thus ended the affair. Cortés returned to Cempoalla, with the addition of half a dozen able-bodied recruits, and, what was of more importance, relieved in his own mind from the apprehension of interference with his operations.[2]

He now made arrangements for his speedy departure from the Totonac capital. The forces reserved for the expedition amounted to about four hundred foot and fifteen horse, with seven pieces of artillery. He obtained, also, thirteen hundred Indian warriors, and a thousand *tamanes*, or porters, from the cacique of Cempoalla, to drag the guns, and transport the baggage. He took forty more of their principal men as hostages, as well as to guide him on the way, and serve him by their counsels among the strange tribes he was to visit. They were, in fact, of essential service to him throughout the march.[3]

The remainder of his Spanish force he left in garrison at Villa Rica de Vera Cruz, the command of which he had intrusted to the alguacil, Juan de Escalante, an officer devoted to his interests. The selection was judicious. It was important to place there a man who would resist any hostile interference from his European rivals, on the one hand, and maintain the present friendly relations with the natives, on the other. Cortés recommended the Totonac chiefs to apply to this officer, in case of any difficulty, assuring them, that, so long as they remained faithful to their new sovereign and religion, they should find a sure protection in the Spaniards.

Before marching, the general spoke a few words of encouragement to his own men. He told them, they were now to embark, in earnest, on an enterprise which had been the great object of their desires; and that the

---

[2] Oviedo, Hist. de las Ind., MS., lib. 33, cap. 1.—Rel. Seg. de Cortés, ap. Lorenzana, pp. 42-45.—Bernal Diaz, Hist. de la Conquista, cap. 59, 60.

[3] Gomara, Crónica, cap. 44.—Ixtlilxochitl, Hist. Chich., MS., cap. 83.—Bernal Diaz, Hist. de la Conquista, cap. 61.

The number of the Indian auxiliaries stated in the text is much larger than that allowed by either Cortés or Diaz. But both these actors in the drama show too obvious a desire to magnify their own prowess, by exaggerating the numbers of their foes, and diminishing their own, to be entitled to much confidence in their estimates

blessed Saviour would carry them victorious through every battle with their enemies. "Indeed," he added, "this assurance must be our stay, for every other refuge is now cut off, but that afforded by the Providence of God, and your own stout hearts." [4] He ended by comparing their achievements to those of the ancient Romans, "in phrases of honeyed eloquence far beyond any thing I can repeat," says the brave and simple-hearted chronicler who heard them. Cortés was, indeed, master of that eloquence which went to the soldiers' hearts. For their sympathies were his, and he shared in that romantic spirit of adventure which belonged to them. "We are ready to obey you," they cried as with one voice. "Our fortunes, for better or worse, are cast with yours." [5] Taking leave, therefore, of their hospitable Indian friends, the little army, buoyant with high hopes and lofty plans of conquest, set forward on the march to Mexico.

It was the sixteenth of August, 1519. During the first day, their road lay through the *tierra caliente*, the beautiful land where they had been so long lingering; the land of the vanilla, cochineal, cacao, (not till later days of the orange and the sugar-cane,) products which, indigenous to Mexico, have now become the luxuries of Europe; the land where the fruits and the flowers chase one another in unbroken circle through the year; where the gales are loaded with perfumes till the sense aches at their sweetness; and the groves are filled with many-colored birds, and insects whose enamelled wings glisten like diamonds in the bright sun of the tropics. Such are the magical splendors of this paradise of the senses. Yet Nature, who generally works in a spirit of compensation, has provided one here; since the same burning sun, which quickens into life these glories of the vegetable and animal kingdoms, calls forth the pestilent *malaria*, with its train of bilious disorders, unknown to the cold skies of the North. The season in which the Spaniards were there, the rainy months of summer, was precisely that in which the *vómito* rages with greatest fury; when the European stranger hardly ventures to set his foot on shore, still less to linger there a day. We find no mention made of it in the records of the Conquerors, nor any notice, indeed, of an uncommon mortality. The fact doubtless corroborates the theory of those who postpone the appearance of the yellow fever till long after the occupation of the country by the whites. It proves, at least, that, if existing before, it must have been in a very much mitigated form.

After some leagues of travel over roads made nearly impassable by the summer rains, the troops began the gradual ascent—more gradual on the eastern than the western declivities of the Cordilleras—which leads up to the table-land of Mexico. At the close of the second day, they reached Xalapa, a place still retaining the same Aztec name, that it has communicated to the drug raised in its environs, the medicinal virtues of which

---

[4] "No teniamos otro socorro, ni ayuda sino el de Dios; porque ya no teniamos nauíos para ir á Cuba, salvo neustro buen pelear, y coraçones fuertes." Bernal Diaz. Hist. de la Conquista, cap. 59.

[5] "Y todos á vna le respondímos, que hariamos lo que ordenasse, que echada estaua la suerte de la buena, ó mala ventura." Loc. cit.

are now known throughout the world.[6] This town stands midway up the long ascent, at an elevation where the vapors from the ocean, touching in their westerly progress, maintain a rich verdure throughout the year. Though somewhat infected with these marine fogs, the air is usually bland and salubrious. The wealthy resident of the lower regions retires here for safety in the heats of summer, and the traveller hails its groves of oak with delight, as announcing that he is above the deadly influence of the *vómito*.[7] From this delicious spot, the Spaniards enjoyed one of the grandest prospects in nature. Before them was the steep ascent,— much steeper after this point,—which they were to climb. On the right rose the *Sierra Madre*, girt with its dark belt of pines, and its long lines of shadowy hills stretching away in the distance. To the south, in brilliant contrast, stood the mighty Orizaba, with his white robe of snow descending far down his sides, towering in solitary grandeur, the giant spectre of the Andes. Behind them, they beheld, unrolled at their feet, the magnificent *tierra caliente*, with its gay confusion of meadows, streams, and flowering forests, sprinkled over with shining Indian villages, while a faint line of light on the edge of the horizon told them that there was the ocean, beyond which were the kindred and country—they were many of them never more to see.

Still winding their way upward, amidst scenery as different as was the temperature from that of the regions below, the army passed through settlements containing some hundreds of inhabitants each, and on the fourth day reached a "strong town," as Cortés terms it, standing on a rocky eminence, supposed to be that now known by the Mexican name of Naulinco. Here they were hospitably entertained by the inhabitants, who were friends of the Totonacs. Cortés endeavored, through father Olmedo, to impart to them some knowledge of Christian truths, which were kindly received, and the Spaniards were allowed to erect a cross in the place, for the future adoration of the natives. Indeed, the route of the army might be tracked by these emblems of man's salvation, raised wherever a willing population of Indians invited it, suggesting a very different idea from what the same memorials intimate to the traveller in these mountain solitudes in our day.[8]

The troops now entered a rugged defile, the Bishop's Pass,[9] as it is

<hr>

[6] Jalap, *Convolvulus jalapæ*. The *x* and *j* are convertible consonants in the Castilian.

[7] The heights of Xalapa are crowned with a convent dedicated to St. Francis, erected in later days by Cortés, showing, in its solidity, like others of the period built under the same auspices, says an agreeable traveller, a military as well as religious design. Tudor's Travels in North America, (London, 1834,) vol. II. p. 186.

[8] Oviedo, Hist. de las Ind., MS., lib. 33, cap. 1.—Rel. Seg. de Cortés, ap, Lorenzana, p. 40.—Gomara, Crónica, cap. 44.—Ixtlilxochitl, Hist. Chich., MS., cap. 83.

"Every hundred yards of our route," says the traveller last quoted, speaking of this very region, "was marked by the melancholy erection of a wooden cross, denoting, according to the custom of the country, the commission of some horrible murder on the spot where it was planted." Travels in North America, vol. II. p. 188.

[9] *El Paso del Obispo*. Cortés named it *Puerto del Nombre de Dios*. Viaje, ap Lorenzana, p. ii.

called, capable of easy defence against an army. Very soon they experienced a most unwelcome change of climate. Cold winds from the mountains, mingled with rain, and, as they rose still higher, with driving sleet
and hail, drenched their garments, and seemed to penetrate to their very
bones. The Spaniards, indeed, partially covered by their armor and thick
jackets of quilted cotton, were better able to resist the weather, though
their long residence in the sultry regions of the valley made them still
keenly sensible to the annoyance. But the poor Indians, natives of the
tierra caliente, with little protection in the way of covering, sunk under
the rude assault of the elements, and several of them perished on the
road.

The aspect of the country was as wild and dreary as the climate. Their
route wound along the spur of the huge Cofre de Perote, which borrows
its name, both in Mexican and Castilian, from the coffer-like rock on its
summit.[10] It is one of the great volcanoes of New Spain. It exhibits now,
indeed, no vestige of a crater on its top, but abundant traces of volcanic
action at its base, where acres of lava, blackened scoriæ, and cinders, proclaim the convulsions of nature, while numerous shrubs and mouldering
trunks of enormous trees, among the crevices, attest the antiquity of
these events. Working their toilsome way across this scene of desolation,
the path often led them along the borders of precipices, down whose sheer
depths of two or three thousand feet the shrinking eye might behold another climate, and see all the glowing vegetation of the tropics choking
up the bottom of the ravines.

After three days of this fatiguing travel, the way-worn army emerged
through another defile, the *Sierra del Agua*.[11] They soon came upon an
open reach of country, with a genial climate, such as belongs to the temperate latitudes of southern Europe. They had reached the level of more
than seven thousand feet above the ocean, where the great sheet of table-
land spreads out for hundreds of miles along the crests of the Cordilleras.
The country showed signs of careful cultivation, but the products were,
for the most part, not familiar to the eyes of the Spaniards. Fields and
hedges of the various tribes of the cactus, the towering organum, and
plantations of aloes with rich yellow clusters of flowers on their tall
stems, affording drink and clothing to the Aztec, were everywhere seen.
The plants of the torrid and temperate zones had disappeared, one after
another, with the ascent into these elevated regions. The glossy and dark-
leaved banana, the chief, as it is the cheapest, aliment of the countries
below, had long since faded from the landscape. The hardy maize, however, still shone with its golden harvests in all the pride of cultivation,
the great staple of the higher, equally with the lower terraces of the
plateau.

[10] The Aztec name is Nauhcampatepetl, from *nauhcampa*, "any thing square,"
and *tepetl*, "a mountain."—Humboldt, who waded through forests and snows to its
summit, ascertained its height to be 4,089 metres = 13,414 feet, above the sea. See
his Vues des Cordillères, p. 234, and Essai Politique, vol. I. p. 266.

[11] The same mentioned in Cortés' Letter as the *Puerto de la Leña*. Viaje, ap. Lorenzana, p. iii.

Suddenly the troops came upon what seemed the environs of a populous city, which, as they entered it, appeared to surpass even that of
Cempoalla in the size and solidity of its structures.[12] These were of stone
and lime, many of them spacious and tolerably high. There were thirteen
teocallis in the place; and in the suburbs they had seen a receptacle, in
which, according to Bernal Diaz, were stored a hundred thousand skulls
of human victims, all piled and ranged in order! He reports the number
as one he had ascertained by counting them himself.[13] Whatever faith we
may attach to the precise accuracy of his figures, the result is almost
equally startling. The Spaniards were destined to become familiar with
this appalling spectacle, as they approached nearer to the Aztec capital.

The lord of the town ruled over twenty thousand vassals. He was
tributary to Montezuma, and a strong Mexican garrison was quartered
in the place. He had probably been advised of the approach of the Spaniards, and doubted how far it would be welcome to his sovereign. At all
events, he gave them a cold reception, the more unpalatable after the extraordinary sufferings of the last few days. To the inquiry of Cortés,
whether he were subject to Montezuma, he answered, with real or affected surprise, "Who is there that is not a vassal to Montezuma?" [14]
The general told him, with some emphasis, that he was not. He then explained whence and why he came, assuring him that he served a monarch
who had princes for his vassals as powerful as the Aztec monarch himself.

The cacique in turn fell nothing short of the Spaniard, in the pompous
display of the grandeur and resources of the Indian emperor. He told his
guest that Montezuma could muster thirty great vassals, each master of
a hundred thousand men! [15] His revenues were immense, as every subject, however poor, paid something. They were all expended on his magnificent state, and in support of his armies. These were continually in the
field, while garrisons were maintained in most of the large cities of the
empire. More than twenty thousand victims, the fruit of his wars, were
annually sacrificed on the altars of his gods! His capital, the cacique
said, stood in a lake, in the centre of a spacious valley. The lake was

[12] Now known by the euphonious Indian name of Tlatlauqnitepec. (Viaje, ap.
Lorenzana, p. iv.) It is the *Cocotlan* of Bernal Diaz. (Hist. de la Conquista, cap.
61.) The old Conquerors made sorry work with the Aztec names, both of places
and persons, for which they must be allowed to have had ample apology.

[13] Puestos tantos rimeros de calaueras de muertos, que se podian bien contar,
segun el concierto con que estauan puestas, que me parece que eran mas de cien mil,
y digo otra vez sobre cien mil." Ibid., ubi supra.

[14] "El qual casi admirado de lo que le preguntaba, me respondió, diciendo; ¿que
quien no era vasallo de Muctezuma? quieriendo decir, que allí era Señor del Mundo." Rel. Seg. de Cortés, ap. Lorenzana, p. 47.

[15] "Tiene mas de 30 Príncipes á sí subjectos, que cada uno dellos tiene cient mill
hombres é mas de pelea." (Oviedo, Hist. de las Ind., MS., lib. 33, cap. 1.) This marvellous tale is gravely repeated by more than one Spanish writer, in their accounts
of the Aztec monarchy, not as the assertion of this chief, but as a veritable piece of
statistics. See, among others, Herrera, Hist. General, dec. 2, lib. 7, cap. 12,—Solís,
Conquista, lib. 3, cap. 16.

commanded by the emperor's vessels, and the approach to the city was by means of causeways, several miles long, connected in parts by wooden bridges, which, when raised, cut off all communication with the country. Some other things he added, in answer to queries of his guest, in which, as the reader may imagine, the crafty, or credulous cacique varnished over the truth with a lively coloring of romance. Whether romance, or reality, the Spaniards could not determine. The particulars they gleaned were not of a kind to tranquillize their minds, and might well have made bolder hearts than theirs pause, ere they advanced. But far from it. "The words which we heard," says the stout old cavalier, so often quoted, "however they may have filled us with wonder, made us—such is the temper of the Spaniard—only the more earnest to prove the adventure, desperate as it might appear." [16]

In a further conversation Cortés inquired of the chief, whether his country abounded in gold, and intimated a desire to take home some, as specimens to his sovereign. But the Indian lord declined to give him any, saying it might displease Montezuma. "Should he command it," he added, "my gold, my person, and all I possess, shall be at your disposal." The general did not press the matter further.

The curiosity of the natives was naturally excited by the strange dresses, weapons, horses, and dogs of the Spaniards. Marina, in satisfying their inquiries, took occasion to magnify the prowess of her adopted countrymen, expatiating on their exploits and victories, and stating the extraordinary marks of respect they had received from Montezuma. This intelligence seems to have had its effect; for soon after, the cacique gave the general some curious trinkets of gold, of no great value, indeed, but as a testimony of his good-will. He sent him, also, some female slaves to prepare bread for the troops, and supplied the means of refreshment and repose, more important to them, in the present juncture, than all the gold of Mexico.[17]

The Spanish general, as usual, did not neglect the occasion to inculcate the great truths of revelation on his host, and to display the atrocity of the Indian superstitions. The cacique listened with civil, but cold indifference. Cortés, finding him unmoved, turned briskly round to his soldiers, exclaiming that now was the time to plant the Cross! They eagerly seconded his pious purpose, and the same scenes might have been enacted as at Cempoalla, with, perhaps, very different results, had not father Olmedo, with better judgment, interposed. He represented that to introduce the Cross among the natives, in their present state of ignorance and incredulity, would be to expose the sacred symbol to desecration, so soon as the backs of the Spaniards were turned. The only way was to wait

[16] Bernal Diaz, Hist. de la Conquista, cap. 61.

There is a slight ground-swell of glorification in the Captain's narrative, which may provoke a smile,—not a sneer, for it is mingled with too much real courage, and simplicity of character.

[17] For the preceding pages, besides authorities cited in course, see Peter Martyr, De Orbe Novo, dec. 5, cap. 1,—Ixtlilxochitl, Hist. Chich., MS., cap. 83,—Gomara, Crónica, cap. 44,—Torquemada, Monarch. Ind., lib. 4, cap. 26.

patiently the season when more leisure should be afforded to instil into their minds a knowledge of the truth. The sober reasoning of the good father prevailed over the passions of the martial enthusiasts.

It was fortunate for Cortés that Olmedo was not one of those frantic friars, who would have fanned his fiery temper on such occasions into a blaze. It might have had a most disastrous influence on his fortunes; for he held all temporal consequences light in comparison with the great work of conversion, to effect which the unscrupulous mind of the soldier, trained to the stern discipline of the camp, would have employed force, whenever fair means were ineffectual.[18] But Olmedo belonged to that class of benevolent missionaries—of whom the Roman Catholic church, to its credit, has furnished many examples—who rely on spiritual weapons for the great work, inculcating those doctrines of love and mercy which can best touch the sensibilities and win the affections of their rude audience. These, indeed, are the true weapons of the Church, the weapons employed in the primitive ages, by which it has spread its peaceful banners over the farthest regions of the globe. Such were not the means used by the conquerors of America, who, rather adopting the policy of the victorious Moslems in their early career, carried with them the sword in one hand and the Bible in the other. They imposed obedience in matters of faith, no less than of government, on the vanquished, little heeding whether the conversion were genuine, so that it conformed to the outward observances of the Church. Yet the seeds thus recklessly scattered must have perished but for the missionaries of their own nation, who, in later times, worked over the same ground, living among the Indians as brethren, and, by long and patient culture, enabling the germs of truth to take root and fructify in their hearts.

The Spanish commander remained in the city four or five days to recruit his fatigued and famished forces; and the modern Indians still point out, or did, at the close of the last century, a venerable cypress, under the branches of which was tied the horse of the *Conquistador,*—the Conqueror, as Cortés was styled, *par excellence.*[19] Their route now opened on a broad and verdant valley, watered by a noble stream,—a circumstance of not too frequent occurrence on the parched table-land of New Spain. The soil was well protected by woods, a thing still rarer at the present day; since the invaders, soon after the Conquest, swept away the magnificent growth of timber, rivalling that of our Southern and Western States in variety and beauty, which covered the plateau under the Aztecs.[20]

---

[18] The general clearly belonged to the church militant, mentioned by Butler;
"Such as do build their faith upon
The holy text of pike and gun;
And prove their doctrines orthodox
By apostolic blows and knocks."

[19] "Arbol grande, diche *ahuhuete.*" (Viaje, ap. Lorenzana, p. iii.) The *cupressu disticha* of Linnæus. See Humboldt, Essai Politique, tom. II. p. 54, note.

[20] It is the same taste which has made the Castiles, the table-land of the Peninsula, so naked of wood. Prudential reasons, as well as taste, however, seem to have

All along the river, on both sides of it, an unbroken line of Indian dwellings, "so near as almost to touch one another," extended for three or four leagues; arguing a population much denser than at present.[21] On a rough and rising ground stood a town, that might contain five or six thousand inhabitants, commanded by a fortress, which, with its walls and trenches, seemed to the Spaniards quite "on a level with similar works in Europe." Here the troops again halted, and met with friendly treatment.[22]

Cortés now determined his future line of march. At the last place he had been counselled by the natives to take the route of the ancient city of Cholula, the inhabitants of which, subjects of Montezuma, were a mild race, devoted to mechanical and other peaceful arts, and would be likely to entertain him kindly. Their Cempoallan allies, however, advised the Spaniards not to trust the Cholulans, "a false and perfidious people," but to take the road to Tlascala, that valiant little republic, which had so long maintained its independence against the arms of Mexico. The people were frank as they were fearless, and fair in their dealings. They had always been on terms of amity with the Totonacs, which afforded a strong guaranty for their amicable disposition on the present occasion.

The arguments of his Indian allies prevailed with the Spanish commander, who resolved to propitiate the good-will of the Tlascalans by an embassy. He selected four of the principal Cempoallans for this, and sent by them a martial gift,—a cap of crimson cloth, together with a sword and a crossbow, weapons which, it was observed, excited general admiration among the natives. He added a letter, in which he asked permission to pass through their country. He expressed his admiration of the valor of the Tlascalans, and of their long resistance to the Aztecs, whose proud empire he designed to humble.[23] It was not to be expected that this epistle, indited in good Castilian, would be very intelligible to the Tlascalans. But Cortés communicated its import to the ambassadors. Its mysterious characters might impress the natives with an idea of superior in-

operated in New Spain. A friend of mine on a visit to a noble *hacienda,* but uncommonly barren of trees, was informed by the proprietor that they were cut down to prevent the lazy Indians on the plantation from wasting their time by loitering in their shade!

[21] It confirms the observations of M. de Humboldt. "Sans doute lors de la première arrivée des Espagnols, toute cette côte, depuis la rivière de Papaloapan (Alvarado) jusqu'à Huaxtecapan, était plus habitée et mieux cultivée qu'elle ne l'est aujourd'hui. Cependant à mesure que les conquérans montèrent au plateau, ils trouvèrent les villages plus rapprochés les uns des autres, les champs divisés en portions plus petites, le peuple plus policé." Humboldt, Essai Politique, tom. II. p. 202.

[22] The correct Indian name of the town, *Yxtacamaxtitlan, Yztacmastitan* of Cortés, will hardly be recognised in the *Xalacingo* of Diaz. The town was removed, in 1601, from the top of the hill to the plain. On the original site are still visible remains of carved stones of large dimensions, attesting the elegance of the ancient fortress or palace of the cacique. Viaje, ap. Lorenzana, p. v.

[23] "Estas cosas y otras de gran persuasion contenia la carta, pero como no sabian leer no pudiéron entender lo que contenia." Camargo, Hist. de Tlascala, MS.

telligence, and the letter serve instead of those hieroglyphical missives which formed the usual credentials of an Indian ambassador.[24]

The Spaniards remained three days in this hospitable place, after the departure of the envoys, when they resumed their progress. Although in a friendly country, they marched always as if in a land of enemies, the horse and light troops in the van, with the heavy-armed and baggage in the rear, all in battle array. They were never without their armor, waking or sleeping, lying down with their weapons by their sides. This unintermitting and restless vigilance was, perhaps, more oppressive to the spirits that even bodily fatigue. But they were confident in their superiority in a fair field, and felt that the most serious danger they had to fear from Indian warfare was surprise. "We are few against many, brave companions," Cortés would say to them; "be prepared, then, not as if you were going to battle, but as if actually in the midst of it!" [25]

The road taken by the Spaniards was the same which at present leads to Tlascala; not that, however, usually followed in passing from Vera Cruz to the capital, which makes a circuit considerably to the south, towards Puebla, in the neighborhood of the ancient Cholula. They more than once forded the stream that rolls through this beautiful plain, lingering several days on the way, in hopes of receiving an answer from the Indian republic. The unexpected delay of the messengers could not be explained, and occasioned some uneasiness.

As they advanced into a country of rougher and bolder features, their progress was suddenly arrested by a remarkable fortification. It was a stone wall nine feet in height, and twenty in thickness, with a parapet, a foot and a half broad, raised on the summit for the protection of those who defended it. It had only one opening, in the centre, made by two semicircular lines of wall overlapping each other for the space of forty paces, and affording a passage-way between, ten paces wide, so contrived, therefore, as to be perfectly commanded by the inner wall. This fortification, which extended more than two leagues, rested at either end on the bold natural buttresses formed by the sierra. The work was built of immense blocks of stones nicely laid together without cement;[26] and the remains still existing, among which are rocks of the whole breadth of the rampart, fully attest its solidity and size.[27]

---

[24] For an account of the diplomatic usages of the people of Anahuac, see Ante, p. 30.

[25] "Mira, señores compañeros, ya veis que somos pocos, hemos de estar siempre tan apercebidos, y aparejados, como si aora viessemos venir los contrarios á pelear, y no solamente vellos venir, sino hazer cuenta que estamos ya en la batalla con ellos." Bernal Diaz, Hist. de la Conquista, cap. 62.

[26] According to the writer last cited, the stones were held by a cement so hard that the men could scarcely break it with their pikes. (Hist. de la Conquista, cap. 62.) But the contrary statement, in the general's letter, is confirmed by the present appearance of the wall. Viaje, ap. Lorenzana, p. vii.

[27] Viaje, ap. Lorenzana, p. vii.
The attempts of the Archbishop to identify the route of Cortés have been very successful. It is a pity, that his map illustrating the itinerary should be so worthless

This singular structure marked the limits of Tlascala, and was in‧tended, as the natives told the Spaniards, as a barrier against the Mexican invasions. The army paused, filled with amazement at the contemplation of this Cyclopean monument, which naturally suggested reflections on the strength and resources of the people who had raised it. It caused them, too, some painful solicitude as to the probable result of their mission to Tlascala, and their own consequent reception there. But they were too sanguine to allow such uncomfortable surmises long to dwell in their minds. Cortés put himself at the head of his cavalry, and calling out, "Forward, soldiers, the Holy Cross is our banner, and under that we shall conquer," led his little army through the undefended passage, and in a few moments they trod the soil of the free republic of Tlascala.[28]

[28] Camargo, Hist. de Tlascala, MS.—Gomara, Crónica, cap. 44, 45.—Ixtlilxochitl Hist. Chich., MS., cap. 83.—Herrera, Hist. General, dec. 2, lib. 6, cap. 3.—Oviedo Hist. de las Ind., MS., lib. 33, cap. 2.—Peter Martyr, De Orbe Novo, dec. 5, cap. 1

REPUBLIC OF TLASCALA—ITS INSTITUTIONS—EARLY HISTORY—
DISCUSSIONS IN THE SENATE—DESPERATE BATTLES

1519

BEFORE advancing further with the Spaniards into the territory of Tlascala, it will be well to notice some traits in the character and institutions
of the nation, in many respects, the most remarkable in Anahuac. The
Tlascalans belonged to the same great family with the Aztecs.[1] They
came on the grand plateau about the same time with the kindred races,
at the close of the twelfth century, and planted themselves on the western
borders of the lake of Tezcuco. Here they remained many years engaged
in the usual pursuits of a bold and partially civilized people. From some
cause or other, perhaps their turbulent temper, they incurred the enmity
of surrounding tribes. A coalition was formed against them; and a bloody
battle was fought on the plains of Poyauhtlan, in which the Tlascalans
were completely victorious.

Disgusted, however, with their residence among nations with whom
they found so little favor, the conquering people resolved to migrate.
They separated into three divisions, the largest of which, taking a southern course by the great *volcan* of Mexico, wound round the ancient city
of Cholula, and finally settled in the district of country overshadowed by
the sierra of Tlascala. The warm and fruitful valleys, locked up in the
embraces of this rugged brotherhood of mountains, afforded means of
subsistence for an agricultural people, while the bold eminences of the
sierra presented secure positions for their towns.

After the lapse of years, the institutions of the nation underwent an
important change. The monarchy was divided first into two, afterwards
into four separate states, bound together by a sort of federal compact,
probably not very nicely defined. Each state, however, had its lord or
supreme chief, independent in his own territories, and possessed of co-
ordinate authority with the others in all matters concerning the whole

[1] The Indian chronicler, Camargo, considers his nation a branch of the Chichemec. (Hist. de Tlascala, MS.) So, also, Torquemada. (Monarch. Ind., lib. 3, cap. 9.)
Clavigero, who has carefully investigated the antiquities of Anahuac, calls it one
of the seven Nahuatlac tribes. (Stor. del Messico, tom. I. p. 153, nota.) The fact is
not of great moment, since they were all cognate races, speaking the same tongue,
and, probably, migrated from their country in the far North at nearly the same
time.

republic. The affairs of government, especially all those relating to peace and war, were settled in a senate or council, consisting of the four lords with their inferior nobles.

The lower dignitaries held of the superior, each in his own district, by a kind of feudal tenure, being bound to supply his table, and enable him to maintain his state in peace, as well as to serve him in war.[2] In return, he experienced the aid and protection of his suzerain. The same mutual obligations existed betwen him and the followers among whom his own territories were distributed.[3] Thus a chain of feudal dependencies was established, which, if not contrived with all the art and legal refinements of analogous institutions in the Old World, displayed their most prominent characteristics in its personal relations, the obligations of military service on the one hand, and protection on the other. This form of government, so different from that of the surrounding nations, subsisted till the arrival of the Spaniards. And it is certainly evidence of considerable civilization, that so complex a polity should have so long continued, undisturbed by violence or faction in the confederate states, and should have been found competent to protect the people in their rights, and the country from foreign invasion.

The lowest order of the people, however, do not seem to have enjoyed higher immunities than under the monarchical governments; and their rank was carefully defined by an appropriate dress, and by their exclusion from the insignia of the aristocratic orders.[4]

The nation, agricultural in its habits, reserved its highest honors, like most other rude—unhappily also, civilized—nations, for military prowess. Public games were instituted, and prizes decreed to those who excelled in such manly and athletic exercises, as might train them for the fatigues of war. Triumphs were granted to the victorious general, who entered the city, leading his spoils and captives in long procession, while his achievements were commemorated in national songs, and his effigy,

---

[2] The descendants of these petty nobles attached as great value to their pedigrees, as any Biscayan or Asturian in Old Spain. Long after the Conquest, they refused, however needy, to dishonor their birth by resorting to mechanical or other plebeian occupations, *oficios viles y bajos.* "Los descendientes de estos son estimados por hombres calificados, que aunque sean probrísimos no usan oficios mecánicos ni tratos bajos ni viles, ni jamas se permiten cargar ni cabar con coas y azadones, diciendo que son hijos Idalgos en que no han de aplicarse á estas cosas soeces y bajas, sino servir en guerras y fronteras, como Idalgos, y morir como hombres peleando." Camargo, Hist. de Tlascala, MS.

[3] "Cualquier Tecuhtli que formaba un Tecalli, que es casa de Mayorazgo, todas aquellas tierras que le caian en suerte de repartimiento, con montes, fuentes, rios, ó lagunas tomase para la casa principal la mayor y mejor suerte ó pagos de tierra, y luego las demas que quedaban se partian por sus soldados amigos y parientes, igualmente, y todos estos están obligados á reconocer la casa mayor y acudir á ella, á alzarla y repararla, y á ser continuos en re conocer á ella de aves, caza, flores, y ramos para el sustento de la casa del Mayorazgo, y el que lo es está obligado á sustentarlos y á regalarlos como amigos de aquella casa y parientes de ella." Ibid., MS.

[4] Camargo, Hist. de Tlascala, MS.

whether in wood or stone, was erected in the temples. It was truly in the martial spirit of republican Rome.[5]

An institution not unlike knighthood was introduced, very similar to one existing also among the Aztecs. The aspirant to the honors of this barbaric chivalry watched his arms and fasted fifty or sixty days in the temple, then listened to a grave discourse on the duties of his new profession. Various whimsical ceremonies followed, when his arms were restored to him; he was led in solemn procession through the public streets, and the inauguration was concluded by banquets and public rejoicings.— The new knight was distinguished henceforth by certain peculiar privileges, as well as by a badge intimating his rank. It is worthy of remark, that this honor was not reserved exclusively for military merit; but was the recompense, also, of public services of other kinds, as wisdom in council, or sagacity and success in trade. For trade was held in as high estimation by the Tlascalans, as by the other people of Anahuac.[6]

The temperate climate of the table-land furnished the ready means for distant traffic. The fruitfulness of the soil was indicated by the name of the country,—*Tlascala* signifying the "land of bread." Its wide plains, to the slopes of its rocky hills, waved with yellow harvests of maize, and with the bountiful maguey, a plant, which, as we have seen, supplied the materials for some important fabrics. With these, as well as the products of agricultural industry, the merchant found his way down the sides of the Cordilleras, wandered over the sunny regions at their base, and brought back the luxuries which nature had denied to his own.[7]

The various arts of civilization kept pace with increasing wealth and public prosperity; at least, these arts were cultivated to the same limited extent, apparently, as among the other people of Anahuac. The Tlascalan tongue, says the national historian, simple as beseemed that of a mountain region, was rough compared with the polished Tezcucan, or the popular Aztec dialect, and therefore, not so well fitted for composition. But they made like proficiency with the kindred nations in the rudiments of science. Their calendar was formed on the same plan. Their religion, their architecture, many of their laws and social usages were the same, arguing a common origin for all. Their tutelary deity was the same ferocious war-god as that of the Aztecs, though with a different name; their temples, in like manner, were drenched with the blood of human victims, and their boards groaned with the same cannibal repasts.[8]

---

[5] "Los grandes recibimientos que hacian á los capitanes que venian y alcanzaban victoria en las guerras, las fiestas y solenidades con que se solenizaban á manera de triunfo, que los metian en andas en su puebla, trayendo consigo á los vencidos; y por eternizar sus hazañas se las cantaban publicamente, y ansí quedaban memoradas y con estatuas que les ponian en los templos." Ibid., MS.

[6] The whole ceremony of inauguration, it seems, has especial reference to the merchant-knights.

[7] "Ha bel paese," says the Anonymous Conqueror, speaking of Tlascala, at the time of the invasion, "di pianure et mōtagne, et è provincia popolosa et vi si raccoglie molto pane." Rel. d'un gent., ap. Ramusio, tom. III. p. 308.

[8] A full account of the manners, customs, and domestic policy of Tlascala is given

Though not ambitious of foreign conquest, the prosperity of the Tlas calans, in time, excited the jealousy of their neighbors, and especially of the opulent state of Cholula. Frequent hostilities arose between them, in which the advantage was almost always on the side of the former. A still more formidable foe appeared in later days in the Aztecs; who could ill brook the independence of Tlascala, when the surrounding nations had acknowledged, one after another, their influence, or their empire. Under the ambitious Axayacatl, they demanded of the Tlascalans the same tribute and obedience rendered by other people of the country. If it were refused, the Aztecs would raze their cities to their foundations, and deliver the land to their enemies.

To this imperious summons, the little republic proudly replied, "Neither they nor their ancestors had ever paid tribute or homage to a foreign power, and never would pay it. If their country was invaded, they knew how to defend it, and would pour out their blood as freely in defence of their freedom now, as their fathers did of yore, when they routed the Aztecs on the plains of Poyauhtlan!" [9]

This resolute answer brought on them the forces of the monarchy. A pitched battle followed, and the sturdy republicans were victorious. From this period, hostilities between the two nations continued with more or less activity, but with unsparing ferocity. Every captive was mercilessly sacrificed. The children were trained from the cradle to deadly hatred against the Mexicans; and, even in the brief intervals of war, none of those intermarriages took place between the people of the respective countries, which knit together in social bonds most of the other kindred races of Anahuac.

In this struggle, the Tlascalans received an important support in the accession of the Othomis, or Otomies,—as usually spelt by Castilian writers,—a wild and warlike race originally spread over the table-land north of the Mexican Valley. A portion of them obtained a settlement in the republic, and were speedily incorporated in its armies. Their courage and fidelity to the nation of their adoption showed them worthy of trust, and the frontier places were consigned to their keeping. The mountain barriers, by which Tlascala is encompassed, afforded many strong natural positions for defence against invasion. The country was open towards the east, where a valley, of some six miles in breadth, invited the approach of an enemy. But here it was, that the jealous Tlascalans erected the formidable rampart which had excited the admiration of the Spaniards, and which they manned with a garrison of Otomies.

Efforts for their subjugation were renewed on a greater scale, after the accession of Montezuma. His victorious arms had spread down the declivities of the Andes to the distant provinces of Vera Paz and Nicaragua,[10] and his haughty spirit was chafed by the opposition of a petty

by the national historian, throwing much light on the other states of Anahuac, whose social institutions seem to have been all cast in the same mould.

[9] Camargo, Hist. de Tlascala, MS.—Torquemada, Monarch. Ind. lib. 2, cap. 70.

[10] Camargo (Hist. de Tlascala, MS.) notices the extent of Montezuma's conquests,—a debatable ground for the historian.

state, whose territorial extent did not exceed ten leagues in breadth by fifteen in length.[11] He sent an army against them under the command of a favorite son. His troops were beaten, and his son was slain. The enraged and mortified monarch was roused to still greater preparations. He enlisted the forces of the cities bordering on his enemy, together with those of the empire, and with this formidable army swept over the devoted valleys of Tlascala. But the bold mountaineers withdrew into the recesses of their hills, and, coolly awaiting their opportunity, rushed like a torrent on the invaders, and drove them back, with dreadful slaughter, from their territories.

Still, notwithstanding the advantages gained over the enemy in the field, the Tlascalans were sorely pressed by their long hostilities with a foe so far superior to themselves in numbers and resources. The Aztec armies lay between them and the coast, cutting off all communication with that prolific region, and thus limited their supplies to the products of their own soil and manufacture. For more than half a century they had neither cotton, nor cacao, nor salt. Indeed, their taste had been so far affected by long abstinence from these articles, that it required the lapse of several generations after the Conquest, to reconcile them to the use of salt at their meals.[12] During the short intervals of war, it is said, the Aztec nobles, in the true spirit of chivalry, sent supplies of these commodities as presents, with many courteous expressions of respect, to the Tlascalan chiefs. This intercourse, we are assured by the Indian chronicler, was unsuspected by the people. Nor did it lead to any further correspondence, he adds, between the parties, prejudicial to the liberties of the republic, "which maintained its customs and good government inviolate, and the worship of its gods." [13]

Such was the condition of Tlascala, at the coming of the Spaniards; holding, it might seem, a precarious existence under the shadow of the formidable power which seemed suspended like an avalanche over her head, but still strong in her own resources, stronger in the indomitable temper of her people; with a reputation established throughout the land, for good faith and moderation in peace, for valor in war, while her uncompromising spirit of independence secured the respect even of her enemies. With such qualities of character, and with an animosity sharpened by long, deadly hostility with Mexico, her alliance was obviously of

---

[11] Torquemada, Monarch. Ind., lib. 3, cap. 16.—Solís says, "The Tlascalan territory was fifty leagues in circumference, ten long, from east to west, and four broad, from north to south." (Conquista de Méjico, lib. 3, cap. 3.) It must have made a curious figure in geometry!

[12] Camargo, Hist. de Tlascala, MS.

[13] "Los Señores Mejicanos y Tezcucanos en tiempo que ponian treguas por algunas temporadas embiaban á los Señores de Tlaxcalla grandes presentes y dádivas de oro, ropa, y cacao, y sal, y de todas las cosas de que carecian, sin que la gente plebeya lo entendiese, y se saludaban secretamente, guardándose el decoro que se debian: mas con todos estos trabajos la órden de su república jamas se dejaba de gobernar con la rectitud de sus costumbres guardando inviolablemente el culto de sus Dioses." Ibid., MS.

the last importance to the Spaniards, in their present enterprise. It was not easy to secure it.[14]

The Tlascalans had been made acquainted with the advance and vic-torious career of the Christians, the intelligence of which had spread far and wide over the plateau. But they do not seem to have anticipated the approach of the strangers to their own borders. They were now much em-barrassed by the embassy demanding a passage through their territories. The great council was convened, and a considerable difference of opinion prevailed in its members. Some, adopting the popular superstition, sup-posed the Spaniards might be the white and bearded men foretold by the oracles.[15] At all events, they were the enemies of Mexico, and as such might coöperate with them in their struggle with the empire. Others argued that the strangers could have nothing in common with them. Their march throughout the land might be tracked by the broken images of the Indian gods, and desecrated temples. How did the Tlascalans even know that they were foes to Montezuma? They had received his em-bassies, accepted his presents, and were now in the company of his vas-sals on the way to his capital.

These last were the reflections of an aged chief, one of the four who presided over the republic. His name was Xicoténcatl. He was nearly blind, having lived, as is said, far beyond the limits of a century.[16] His son, an impetuous young man of the same name with himself, command-ed a powerful army of Tlascalan and Otomie warriors, near the eastern frontier. It would be best, the old man said, to fall with this force at once on the Spaniards. If victorious, the latter would then be in their power. If defeated, the senate could disown the act as that of the general, not of the republic.[17] The cunning counsel of the chief found favor with his hearers, though assuredly not in the spirit of chivalry, nor of the good faith for which his countrymen were celebrated. But with an Indian, force and stratagem, courage and deceit, were equally admissible in war, as they were among the barbarians of ancient Rome.[18]—The Cempoallan envoys were to be detained under pretence of assisting at a religious sacrifice.

Meanwhile, Cortés and his gallant band, as stated in the preceding

---

[14] The Tlascalan chronicler discerns in this deep-rooted hatred of Mexico the hand of Providence, who wrought out of it an important means for subverting the Aztec empire. Hist. de Tlascala, MS.

[15] "Si bien os acordais, como tenemos de nuestra antiguedad como han de venir gentes á la parte donde sale el sol, y que han de emparentar con nosotros, y que hemos de ser todos unos; y que han de ser blancos y barbudos." Ibid., MS.

[16] To the ripe age of one hundred and forty! if we may credit Camargo. Solís, who confounds this veteran with his son, has put a flourishing harangue in the mouth of the latter, which would be a rare gem of Indian eloquence,—were it not Castilian. Conquista, lib. 2, cap. 16.

[17] Camargo, Hist. de Tlascala, MS.—Herrera, Hist. General, dec. 2, lib. 6, cap. 3. —Torquemada, Monarch. Ind., lib. 4, cap. 27.

There is sufficient contradiction, as well as obscurity, in the proceedings reported of the council, which it is not easy to reconcile altogether with subsequent events.

[18] "——Dolus an virtus, quis in hosta requirat?"

chapter, had arrived before the rocky rampart on the eastern confines of Tlascala. From some cause or other, it was not manned by its Otomie garrison, and the Spaniards passed in, as we have seen, without resistance. Cortés rode at the head of his body of horse, and, ordering the infantry to come on at a quick pace, went forward to reconnoitre. After advancing three or four leagues, he descried a small party of Indians, armed with sword and buckler, in the fashion of the country. They fled at his approach. He made signs for them to halt, but, seeing that they only fled the faster, he and his companions put spurs to their horses, and soon came up with them. The Indians, finding escape impossible, faced round, and, instead of showing the accustomed terror of the natives at the strange and appalling aspect of a mounted trooper, they commenced a furious assault on the cavaliers. The latter, however, were too strong for them, and would have cut their enemy to pieces without much difficulty, when a body of several thousand Indians appeared in sight, and coming briskly on to the support of their countrymen.

Cortés, seeing them, despatched one of his party, in all haste, to accelerate the march of his infantry. The Indians, after discharging their missiles, fell furiously on the little band of Spaniards. They strove to tear the lances from their grasp, and to drag the riders from the horses. They brought one cavalier to the ground, who afterwards died of his wounds, and they killed two of the horses, cutting through their necks with their stout broadswords—if we may believe the chronicler—at a blow! [19] In the narrative of these campaigns, there is sometimes but one step—and that a short one—from history to romance. The loss of the horses, so important and so few in number, was seriously felt by Cortés, who could have better spared the life of the best rider in the troop.

The struggle was a hard one. But the odds were as overwhelming as any recorded by the Spaniards in their own romances, where a handful of knights is arrayed against legions of enemies. The lances of the Christians did terrible execution here also; but they had need of the magic lance of Astolpho, that overturned myriads with a touch, to carry them safe through so unequal a contest. It was with no little satisfaction, therefore, that they beheld their comrades rapidly advancing to their support.

No sooner had the main body reached the field of battle, than, hastily forming, they poured such a volley from their muskets and crossbows as staggered the enemy. Astounded, rather than intimidated, by the terrible report of the fire-arms, now heard for the first time in these regions, the Indians made no further effort to continue the fight, but drew off in good order, leaving the road open to the Spaniards. The latter, too well satisfied to be rid of the annoyance, to care to follow the retreating foe, again held on their way.

Their route took them through a country sprinkled over with Indian cottages, amidst flourishing fields of maize and maguey, indicating an in-

[19] "I les matáron dos Caballos, de dos cuchilladas, i segun algunos, que lo viéron, sortáron á cercen de un golpe cada pescueço, con riendas, i todas." Gomara, Crónica cap. 45.

dustrious and thriving peasantry. They were met here by two Tlascalar envoys, accompanied by two of the Cempoallans. The former, presenting themselves before the general, disavowed the assault on his troops, as an unauthorized act, and assured him of a friendly reception at their capital. Cortés received the communication in a courteous manner, affecting to place more confidence in its good faith, than he probably felt.

It was now growing late, and the Spaniards quickened their march, anxious to reach a favorable ground for encampment before nightfall. They found such a spot on the borders of a stream that rolled sluggishly across the plain. A few deserted cottages stood along the banks, and the fatigued and famished soldiers ransacked them in quest of food. All they could find was some tame animals resembling dogs. These they killed and dressed without ceremony, and, garnishing their unsavory repast with the fruit of the *tuna*, the Indian fig, which grew wild in the neighborhood, they contrived to satisfy the cravings of appetite. A careful watch was maintained by Cortés, and companies of a hundred men each relieved each other in mounting guard through the night. But no attack was made. Hostilities by night were contrary to the system of Indian tactics.[20]

By break of day on the following morning, it being the second of September, the troops were under arms. Besides the Spaniards, the whole number of Indian auxiliaries might now amount to three thousand; for Cortés had gathered recruits from the friendly places on his route; three hundred from the last. After hearing mass, they resumed their march. They moved in close array; the general had previously admonished the men not to lag behind, or wander from the ranks a moment, as stragglers would be sure to be cut off by their stealthy and vigilant enemy. The horsemen rode three abreast, the better to give one another support; and Cortés instructed them, in the heat of fight to keep together, and never to charge singly. He taught them how to carry their lances, that they might not be wrested from their hands by the Indians, who constantly attempted it. For the same reason, they should avoid giving thrusts, but aim their weapons steadily at the faces of their foes.[21]

They had not proceeded far, when they were met by the two remaining Cempoallan envoys, who with looks of terror informed the general that they had been treacherously seized and confined, in order to be sacrificed at an approaching festival of the Tlascalans, but in the night had succeeded in making their escape. They gave the unwelcome tidings, also, that a large force of the natives was already assembled to oppose the progress of the Spaniards.

Soon after, they came in sight of a body of Indians, about a thousand,

[20] Rel. Seg. de Cortés, ap. Lorenzana, p. 50.—Camargo, Hist. de Tlascala, MS.—Bernal Diaz, Hist. de la Conquista, cap. 62.—Gomara, Crónica, cap. 45.—Oviedo, Hist. de las Ind., MS., lib. 33, cap. 3; 41.—Sahagun, Hist. de Nueva España, MS., lib. 12, cap. 10.

[21] "Que quando rompiessemos por los esquadrones, que lleuassen las lanças por las caras, y no parassen á dar lançadas, porque no les echassen mano dellas." Bernal Diaz, Hist. de la Conquista, cap. 62.

apparently, all armed and brandishing their weapons, as the Christians approached, in token of defiance. Cortés, when he had come within hearing, ordered the interpreters to proclaim that he had no hostile intentions; but wished only to be allowed a passage through their country, which he had entered as a friend. This declaration he commanded the royal notary, Godoy, to record on the spot, that, if blood were shed, it might not be charged on the Spaniards. This pacific proclamation was met, as usual on such occasions, by a shower of darts, stones, and arrows, which fell like rain on the Spaniards, rattling on their stout harness, and in some instances penetrating to the skin. Galled by the smart of their wounds, they called on the general to lead them on, till he sounded the well known battle-cry, "St. Jago, and at them!" [22]

The Indians maintained their ground for a while with spirit, when they retreated with precipitation, but not in disorder.[23] The Spaniards, whose blood was heated by the encounter, followed up their advantage with more zeal than prudence, suffering the wily enemy to draw them into a narrow glen or defile, intersected by a little stream of water, where the broken ground was impracticable for artillery, as well as for the movements of cavalry. Pressing forward with eagerness, to extricate themselves from their perilous position, to their great dismay, on turning an abrupt angle of the pass, they came in presence of a numerous army, choking up the gorge of the valley, and stretching far over the plains beyond. To the astonished eyes of Cortés, they appeared a hundred thousand men, while no account estimates them at less than thirty thousand.[24]

They presented a confused assemblage of helmets, weapons, and many-colored plumes, glancing bright in the morning sun, and mingled with banners, above which proudly floated one that bore as a device the heron on a rock. It was the well known ensign of the house of Titcala, and, as well as the white and yellow stripes on the bodies, and the like colors on the feather-mail of the Indians, showed that they were the warriors of Xicotencatl.[25]

As the Spaniards came in sight, the Tlascalans set up a hideous war-cry, or rather whistle, piercing the ear with its shrillness, and which, with

---

[22] "Entonces dixo Cortés, 'Santiago, y á ellos.'" Ibid., cap. 63.

[23] "Una gentil contienda," says Gomara of this skirmish. Crónica, cap. 46.

[24] Rel. Seg. de Cortés, ap. Lorenzana, p. 51. According to Gomara, (Crónica, cap. 46,) the enemy mustered 80,000. So, also, Ixtlilxochitl. (Hist. Chich., MS., cap. 83.) Bernal Diaz says, more than 40,000. (Hist. de la Conquista, cap. 63.) But Herrera (Hist. General, dec. 2, lib. 6, cap. 5) and Torquemada (Monarch. Ind., lib. 4, cap. 20) reduce them to 30,000. One might as easily reckon the leaves in a forest, as the numbers of a confused throng of barbarians. As this was only one of several armies kept on foot by the Tlascalans, the smallest amount is, probably, too large. The whole population of the state, according to Clavigero, who would not be likely to underrate it, did not exceed half a million at the time of the invasion. Stor. del Messico, tom. I. p. 156.

[25] "La divisa y armas de la casa y cabecera de Titcala es una garga blanca sobre un peñasco." (Camargo, Hist. de Tlascala, MS.) "El capitan general," says Bernal Diaz 'que se dezia Xicotenga, y con sus diuisas de blanco y colorado, porque aquella diuisa y iibrea era de aquel Xicotenga." Hist. de la Conquista, cap. 63.

the beat of their melancholy drums, that could be heard for half a league or more,[26] might well have filled the stoutest heart with dismay. This formidable host came rolling on towards the Christians, as if to overwhelm them by their very numbers. But the courageous band of warriors, closely serried together and sheltered under their strong panoplies, received the shock unshaken, while the broken masses of the enemy, chafing and heaving tumultuously around them, seemed to recede only to return with new and accumulated force.

Cortés, as usual, in the front of danger, in vain endeavored, at the head of the horse, to open a passage for the infantry. Still his men, both cavalry and foot, kept their array unbroken, offering no assailable point to their foe. A body of the Tlascalans, however, acting in concert, assaulted a soldier named Moran, one of the best riders in the troop. They succeeded in dragging him from his horse, which they despatched with a thousand blows. The Spaniards, on foot, made a desperate effort to rescue their comrade from the hands of the enemy,—and from the horrible doom of the captive. A fierce struggle now began over the body of the prostrate horse. Ten of the Spaniards were wounded, when they succeeded in retrieving the unfortunate cavalier from his assailants, but in so disastrous a plight that he died on the following day. The horse was borne off in triumph by the Indians, and his mangled remains were sent, a strange trophy, to the different towns of Tlascala. The circumstance troubled the Spanish commander, as it divested the animal of the supernatural terrors with which the superstition of the natives had usually surrounded it. To prevent such a consequence, he had caused the two horses, killed on the preceding day, to be secretly buried on the spot.

The enemy now began to give ground gradually, borne down by the riders, and trampled under the hoofs of their horses. Through the whole of this sharp encounter, the Indian allies were of great service to the Spaniards. They rushed into the water, and grappled their enemies, with the desperation of men who felt that "their only safety was in the despair of safety." [27] "I see nothing but death for us," exclaimed a Cempoallan chief to Marina; "we shall never get through the pass alive." "The God of the Christians is with us," answered the intrepid woman; "and He will carry us safely through." [28]

Amidst the din of battle, the voice of Cortés was heard, cheering on his soldiers. "If we fail now," he cried, "the cross of Christ can never be

---

[26] "Llaman Teponaztle ques de un trozo de madero concavado y de una pieza rollizo y, como decimos, hueco por de dentro, que suena algunas veces mas de media legua y con el atambor hace estrañía y suave consonancia." (Camargo, Hist. de Tlascala, MS.) Clavigero, who gives a drawing of this same drum, says it is still used by the Indians, and may be heard two or three miles. Stor. del Messico, tom. II. p. 179.

[27] "Una illis fuit spes salutis, desperâsse de salute." (P. Martyr, De Orbe Novo, dec. 1, cap. 1.) It is said with the classic energy of Tacitus.

[28] "Respondióle Marina, que no tuviese miedo, porque el Dios de los Christianos, que es muy poderoso, i los queria mucho, los sacaria de peligro." Herrera, Hist. General, dec. 2, lib. 6, cap. 5.

planted in the land. Forward, comrades! When was it ever known that a Castilian turned his back on a foe?" [29] Animated by the words and heroic bearing of their general, the soldiers, with desperate efforts, at length succeeded in forcing a passage through the dark columns of the enemy, and emerged from the defile on the open plain beyond.

Here they quickly recovered their confidence with their superiority. The horse soon opened a space for the manœuvres of the artillery. The close files of their antagonists presented a sure mark; and the thunders of the ordnance vomiting forth torrents of fire and sulphurous smoke, the wide desolation caused in their ranks, and the strangely mangled carcasses of the slain, filled the barbarians with consternation and horror. They had no weapons to cope with these terrible engines, and their clumsy missiles, discharged from uncertain hands, seemed to fall ineffectual on the charmed heads of the Christians. What added to their embarrassment was, the desire to carry off the dead and wounded from the field, a general practice among the people of Anahuac, but which necessarily exposed them, while thus employed, to still greater loss.

Eight of their principal chiefs had now fallen; and Xicotencatl, finding himself wholly unable to make head against the Spaniards in the open field, ordered a retreat. Far from the confusion of a panic-struck mob, so common among barbarians, the Tlascalan force moved off the ground with all the order of a well disciplined army. Cortés, as on the preceding day, was too well satisfied with his present advantage to desire to follow it up. It was within an hour of sunset, and he was anxious before nightfall to secure a good position, where he might refresh his wounded troops, and bivouac for the night.[30]

Gathering up his wounded, he held on his way, without loss of time; and before dusk reached a rocky eminence, called *Tzompachtepetl*, or "the hill of Tzompach." It was crowned by a sort of tower or temple, the remains of which are still visible.[31] His first care was given to the wounded, both men and horses. Fortunately, an abundance of provisions was found in some neighboring cottages; and the soldiers, at least, all who were not disabled by their injuries, celebrated the victory of the day with feasting and rejoicing.

As to the number of killed or wounded on either side, it is matter of loosest conjecture. The Indians must have suffered severely, but the practice of carrying off the dead from the field made it impossible to know to what extent. The injury sustained by the Spaniards appears to have been principally in the number of their wounded. The great object of the natives of Anahuac in their battles was, to make prisoners, who might grace their triumphs, and supply victims for sacrifice. To this brutal superstition the Christians were indebted, in no slight degree,

---

[29] Ibid., ubi supra.
[30] Oviedo, Hist. de las Ind., MS., lib. 33, cap. 3, 45.—Ixtlilxochitl, Hist. Chich., MS., cap. 8?.—Rel. Seg. de Cortés, ap. Lorenzana, p. 51.—Bernal Diaz, Hist. de la Conquista, cap. 63.—Gomara, Crónica, cap. 40.
[31] Viaje de Cortés, ap. Lorenzana, p. ix.

for their personal preservation. To take the reports of the Conquerors, their own losses in action were always inconsiderable. But whoever has had occasion to consult the ancient chroniclers of Spain in relation to its wars with the infidel, whether Arab or American, will place little confidence in numbers.[32]

The events of the day had suggested many topics for painful reflection to Cortés. He had nowhere met with so determined a resistance within the borders of Anahuac; nowhere had he encountered native troops so formidable for their weapons, their discipline, and their valor. Far from manifesting the superstitious terrors felt by the other Indians, at the strange arms and aspect of the Spaniards, the Tlascalans had boldly grappled with their enemy, and only yielded to the inevitable superiority of his military science. How important would the alliance of such a nation be in a struggle with those of their own race,—for example, with the Aztecs! But how was he to secure this alliance? Hitherto, all overtures had been rejected with disdain; and it seemed probable, that every step of his progress in this populous land was to be fiercely contested. His army, especially the Indians, celebrated the events of the day with feasting and dancing, songs of merriment, and shouts of triumph. Cortés encouraged it, well knowing how important it was to keep up the spirits of his soldiers. But the sounds of revelry at length died away; and in the still watches of the night, many an anxious thought must have crowded on the mind of the general, while his little army lay buried in slumber in its encampment around the Indian hill.

[33] According to Cortés not a Spaniard fell,—though many were wounded,—in this action so fatal to the infidel! Diaz allows one. In the famous battle of Navas de Tolosa, between the Spaniards and Arabs, in 1212, equally matched in military science at that time, there were left 200,000 of the latter on the field; and, to balance this bloody roll, only five and twenty Christians! See the estimate in Alfonso IX.'s veracious letter, ap. Mariana (Hist. de España, lib. 2, cap. 24). The official returns of the old Castilian crusaders, whether in the Old World or the New, are scarcely more trustworthy than a French *imperial* bulletin in our day.

CHAPTER III

DECISIVE VICTORY—INDIAN COUNCIL—NIGHT ATTACK—NEGOTIA‐
TIONS WITH THE ENEMY—TLASCALAN HERO

1519

THE Spaniards were allowed to repose undisturbed the following day,
and to recruit their strength after the fatigue and hard fighting of the
preceding. They found sufficient employment, however, in repairing and
cleaning their weapons, replenishing their diminished stock of arrows,
and getting every thing in order for further hostilities, should the severe
lesson they had inflicted on the enemy prove insufficient to discourage
him. On the second day, as Cortés received no overtures from the Tlas‐
calans, he determined to send an embassy to their camp, proposing a
cessation of hostilities, and expressing his intention to visit their capital
as a friend. He selected two of the principal chiefs taken in the late en‐
gagement, as the bearers of the message.

Meanwhile, averse to leaving his men longer in a dangerous state of
inaction, which the enemy might interpret as the result of timidity or
exhaustion, he put himself at the head of the cavalry and such light
troops as were most fit for service, and made a foray into the neighbor‐
ing country. It was a mountainous region, formed by a ramification of
the great sierra of Tlascala, with verdant slopes and valleys teeming
with maize and plantations of maguey, while the eminences were
crowned with populous towns and villages. In one of these, he tells us,
he found three thousand dwellings.[1] In some places he met with a reso‐
lute resistance, and on these occasions took ample vengeance by laying
the country waste with fire and sword. After a successful inroad he re‐
turned laden with forage and provisions, and driving before him several
hundred Indian captives. He treated them kindly, however, when ar‐
rived in camp, endeavoring to make them understand that these acts
of violence were not dictated by his own wishes, but by the unfriendly
policy of their countrymen. In this way he hoped to impress the nation
with the conviction of his power on the one hand, and of his amicable
intentions, if met by them in the like spirit, on the other.

[1] Rel. Seg. de Cortés, ap. Lorenzana, p. 52.
Oviedo, who made free use of the manuscripts of Cortés, writes thirty-nine
houses. (Hist. de las Ind., MS., lib. 33, cap. 3.) This may, perhaps, be explained by
the sign for a thousand, in Spanish notation, bearing great resemblance to the figure
9. Martyr, who had access, also, to the Conqueror's manuscript, confirms the larger,
and, *a priori*, less probable number.

On reaching his quarters, he found the two envoys returned from the Tlascalan camp. They had fallen in with Xicotencatl at about two leagues' distance, where he lay encamped with a powerful force. The cacique gave them audience at the head of his troops. He told them to return with the answer, "That the Spaniards might pass on as soon as they chose to Tlascala; and, when they reached it, their flesh would be hewn from their bodies, for sacrifice to the gods! If they preferred to remain in their own quarters, he would pay them a visit there the next day." [2] The ambassadors added, that the chief had an immense force with him, consisting of five battalions of ten thousand men each. They were the flower of the Tlascalan and Otomie warriors, assembled under the banners of their respective leaders, by command of the senate, who were resolved to try the fortunes of the state in a pitched battle, and strike one decisive blow for the extermination of the invaders.[3]

This bold defiance fell heavily on the ears of the Spaniards, not prepared for so pertinacious a spirit in their enemy. They had had ample proof of his courage and formidable prowess. They were now, in their crippled condition, to encounter him with a still more terrible array of numbers. The war, too, from the horrible fate with which it menaced the vanquished, wore a peculiarly gloomy aspect, that pressed heavily on their spirits. "We feared death," says the lion-hearted Diaz, with his usual simplicity, "for we were men." There was scarcely one in the army, that did not confess himself that night to the reverend father Olmedo, who was occupied nearly the whole of it with administering absolution, and with the other solemn offices of the Church. Armed with the blessed sacraments, the Catholic soldier lay tranquilly down to rest, prepared for any fate that might betide him under the banner of the Cross.[4]

As a battle was now inevitable, Cortés resolved to march out and meet the enemy in the field. This would have a show of confidence, that might serve the double purpose of intimidating the Tlascalans, and inspiriting his own men, whose enthusiasm might lose somewhat of its heat, if compelled to await the assault of their antagonists, inactive in their own intrenchments. The sun rose bright on the following morning, the 5th of September, 1519, an eventful day in the history of the Spanish Conquest. The general reviewed his army, and gave them, pre-

---

[2] "Que fuessemos á su pueblo adonde está su padre, q̃ allá harian las pazes cõ hartarse de nuestras carnes, y honrar sus dioses con nuestros coraçones, y sangre, é que para otro dia de mañana veriamos su respuesta." Bernal Diaz, Hist. de la Conquista, cap. 64.

[3] More than one writer repeats a story of the Tlascalan general's sending a good supply of provisions, at this time, to the famished army of the Spaniards; to put them in stomach, it may be, for the fight. (Gomara, Crónica, cap. 46.—Ixtlilxochitl, Hist. Chich., MS., cap. 83.) This ultra-chivalrous display from the barbarian is not very probable, and Cortés' own account of his successful foray may much better explain the abundance which reigned in his camp.

[4] Rel. Seg. de Cortés, ap. Lorenzana, p. 52.—Ixtlilxochitl, Hist. Chich., MS., cap. 83.—Gomara, Crónica, cap. 46, 47.—Oviedo, Hist. de las Ind., MS., lib. 33, cap. 3.—Bernal Diaz, Hist. de la Conquista, cap. 64.

ɔaratory to marching, a few words of encouragement and advice. The infantry he instructed to rely on the point rather than the edge of their swords, and to endeavour to thrust their opponents through the body. The horsemen were to charge at half speed, with their lances aimed at the eyes of the Indians. The artillery, the arquebusiers, and crossbow-men, were to support one another, some loading while others discharged their pieces, that there should be an unintermitted firing kept up through the action. Above all, they were to maintain their ranks close and unbroken, as on this depended their preservation.

They had not advanced a quarter of a league, when they came in sight of the Tlascalan army. Its dense array stretched far and wide over a vast plain or meadow ground, about six miles square. Its appearance justified the report which had been given of its numbers.[5] Nothing could be more picturesque than the aspect of these Indian battalions, with the naked bodies of the common soldiers gaudily painted, the fantastic helmets of the chiefs glittering with gold and precious stones, and the glowing panoplies of feather-work, which decorated their persons.[6] Innumerable spears and darts tipped with points of transparent *itzli*, fiery copper, sparkled bright in the morning sun, like the phosphoric gleams playing on the surface of a troubled sea, while the rear of the mighty host was dark with the shadows of banners, on which were emblazoned the armorial bearings of the great Tlascalan and Otomie chieftains.[7] Among these, the white heron on the rock, the cognizance of the house of Xicotencatl, was conspicuous, and, still more, the golden eagle with outspread wings, in the fashion of a Roman *signum*, richly orna-

---

[5] Through the magnifying lens of Cortés, they appeared to be 150,000 men; (Rel. Seg., ap. Lorenzana, p. 52;) a number usually preferred by succeeding writers.

[6] "Not half so gorgeous, for their May-day mirth
   All wreathed and ribanded, our youths and maids,
   As these stern *Tlascalans* in war attire!
   The golden glitterance, and the feathermail
   More gay than glittering gold; and round the helm
   A coronal of high upstanding plumes,
   Green as the spring grass in a sunny shower;
   Or scarlet bright, as in the wintry wood
   The clustered holly; or of purple tint;
   Whereto shall that be likened? to what gem
   Indiademed, what flower, what insect's wing?
   With war songs and wild music they came on;
   We, the while kneeling, raised with one accord
   The hymn of supplication."
                              SOUTHEY'S Madoc, Part i, canto 7.

[7] The standards of the Mexicans were carried in the centre, those of the Tlas calans in the rear of the army. (Clavigero, Stor. del Messico, vol. II. p. 145.) According to the Anonymous Conqueror, the banner staff was attached to the back of the ensign, so that it was impossible to be torn away. "Ha ogni cōpagnia il suo Alfiere con la sua insegna inhastata, et in tal modo ligata sopra le spalle, che non gli da alcun disturbo di poter combattere ne far ció che vuole, e la porta cosi ligata bene al corpo, che se nō fanno del suo corpo pezzi, non se gli puo sligare, ne torglielᴀ mai." Rel. d' un gent., ap. Ramusio, tom. III. fol. 305.

mented with emeralds and silver-work, the great standard of the re
public of Tlascala.[8]

The common file wore no covering except a girdle round the loins.
Their bodies were painted with the appropriate colors of the chieftain
whose banner they followed. The feather-mail of the higher class of warriors exhibited, also, a similar selection of colors for the like object, in
the same manner as the color of the tartan indicates the peculiar clan of
the Highlander.[9] The caciques and principal warriors were clothed in a
quilted cotton tunic, two inches thick, which, fitting close to the body,
protected, also, the thighs and the shoulders. Over this the wealthier
Indians wore cuirasses of thin gold plate, or silver. Their legs were
defended by leathern boots or sandals, trimmed with gold. But the
most brilliant part of their costume was a rich mantle of the *plumaje* or
feather-work, embroidered with curious art, and furnishing some resemblance to the gorgeous surcoat worn by the European knight over
his armor in the Middle Ages. This graceful and picturesque dress was
surmounted by a fantastic head-piece made of wood or leather, representing the head of some wild animal, and frequently displaying a formidable array of teeth. With this covering the warrior's head was enveloped, producing a most grotesque and hideous effect.[10] From the
crown floated a splendid panache of the richly variegated plumage of
the tropics, indicating, by its form and colors, the rank and family of
the wearer. To complete their defensive armor, they carried shields or
targets, made sometimes of wood covered with leather, but more usually
of a light frame of reeds quilted with cotton, which were preferred, as
tougher and less liable to fracture than the former. They had other
bucklers, in which the cotton was covered with an elastic substance,
enabling them to be shut up in a more compact form, like a fan or um-
brella. These shields were decorated with showy ornaments, according
to the taste or wealth of the wearer, and fringed with a beautiful pendant
of feather-work.

Their weapons were slings, bows and arrows, javelins, and darts.

[8] Camargo, Hist. de Tlascala, MS.—Herrera, Hist. General, dec. 2, lib. 6, cap. 6.—
Gomara, Crónica, cap. 46.—Bernal Diaz, Hist. de la Conquista, cap. 64.—Oviedo,
Hist. de las Ind., MS., lib. 33, cap. 45.

The two last authors speak of the device of "a white bird like an ostrich," as that
of the republic. They have evidently confounded it with that of the Indian general.
Camargo, who has given the heraldic emblems of the four great families of Tlascala,
notices the white heron, as that of Xicotencatl.

[9] The accounts of the Tlascalan chronicler are confirmed by the Anonymous Conqueror and by Bernal Diaz, both eyewitnesses; though the latter frankly declares,
that, had he not seen them with his own eyes, he should never have credited the
existence of orders and badges among the barbarians, like those found among the
civilized nations of Europe. Hist. de la Conquista, cap. 64, et alibi.—Camargo, Hist.
de Tlascala, MS.—Rel. d' un gent., ap. Ramusio, tom. III. fol. 305.

[10] "Portano in testa," says the Anonymous Conqueror, "per difesa una cosa come
teste di serpēti, ò di tigri, ò di leoni, ò di lupi, che ha le mascelle, et è la testa dell'
huomo messa nella testa di q̄sto animale com se lo volesse diuorare: sono di legno,
et sopra vi é a pēna, et di piastra d' oro et di pietro preciose copte, che è cosa
marauigliosa da vedere." Rel. d' un gent., ap. Ramusio, tom. III. fol. 305.

They were accomplished archers, and would discharge two or even three arrows at a time. But they most excelled in throwing the javelin. One species of this, with a thong attached to it, which remained in the slinger's hand, that he might recall the weapon, was especially dreaded by the Spaniards. These various weapons were pointed with bone, or the mineral *itztli*, (obsidian,) the hard vitreous substance, already noticed, as capable of taking an edge like a razor, though easily blunted. Their · spears and arrows were also frequently headed with copper. Instead of a sword, they bore a two handed staff, about three feet and a half long, in which, at regular distances, were inserted, transversely, sharp blades of *itztli*,—a formidable weapon, which, an eyewitness assures us, he had seen fell a horse at a blow.[11]

Such was the costume of the Tlascalan warrior, and, indeed, of that great family of nations generally, who occupied the plateau of Anahuac. Some parts of it, as the targets and the cotton mail or *escaupil*, as it was called in Castilian, were so excellent, that they were subsequently adopted by the Spaniards, as equally effectual in the way of protection, and superior, on the score of lightness and convenience, to their own. They were of sufficient strength to turn an arrow, or the stroke of a javelin, although impotent as a defence against fire-arms. But what armor is not? Yet it is probably no exaggeration to say, that, in convenience, gracefulness, and strength, the arms of the Indian warrior were not very inferior to those of the polished nations of antiquity.[12]

As soon as the Castilians came in sight, the Tlascalans set up their yell of defiance, rising high above the wild barbaric minstrelsy of shell, atabal, and trumpet, with which they proclaimed their triumphant anticipations of victory over the paltry forces of the invaders. When the latter had come within bowshot, the Indians hurled a tempest of missiles, that darkened the sun for a moment as with a passing cloud, strewing the earth around with heaps of stones and arrows.[13] Slowly and steadily the little band of Spaniards held on its way amidst their arrowy shower, until it reached what appeared the proper distance for delivering its fire with full effect. Cortés then halted, and, hastily forming his troops, opened a general well-directed fire along the whole line. Every shot bore its errand of death; and the ranks of the Indians were mowed down faster than their comrades in the rear could carry off their bodies, according to custom, from the field. The balls in their passage through the

[11] "Io viddi che cōbattēdosi un dì, diede un Indiano una cortellata a un cauallo sopra il qual era un caualliero cō chi cōbatteua, nel petto, che glielo aperse fin alle ĩteriora, et cadde icōtanēte morto, et il medesimo giorno viddi che un altro Indiano diede un altra cortellata a un altro cauallo su il collo che se lo gettó morto a i piedi." Rel. d' un gent., ap. Ramusio, tom. III. fol. 305.

[12] Particular notices of the military dress and appointments of the American tribes on the plateau may be found in Camargo, Hist. de Tlascala, MS.,—Clavigero, Stor. del Messico, tom. II. p. 101, et seq.,—Acosta, lib. 6, cap. 26,—Rel. d' un gent., ap. Ramusio, tom. III. fol. 305, et auct. al.

[13] "Que granizo de piedra de los honderos! Pues flechas todo el suelo hecho parva de varas todas de á dos gajos, que passan qualquiera arma, y las entrañas adonde no ay defensa." Bernal Diaz, Hist. de la Conquista, cap. 65.

crowded files, bearing splinters of the broken harness, and mangled limbs of the warriors, scattered havoc and desolation in their path. The mob of barbarians stood petrified with dismay, till, at length, galled to desperation by their intolerable suffering, they poured forth simultaneously their hideous war-shriek, and rushed impetuously on the Christians.

On they came like an avalanche, or mountain torrent, shaking the solid earth, and sweeping away every obstacle in its path. The little army of Spaniards opposed a bold front to the overwhelming mass. But no strength could withstand it. They faltered, gave way, were borne along before it, and their ranks were broken and thrown into disorder. It was in vain, the general called on them to close again and rally. His voice was drowned by the din of fight and the fierce cries of the assailants. For a moment, it seemed that all was lost. The tide of battle had turned against them, and the fate of the Christians was sealed.

But every man had that within his bosom, which spoke louder than the voice of the general. Despair gave unnatural energy to his arm. The naked body of the Indian afforded no resistance to the sharp Toledo steel; and with their good swords, the Spanish infantry at length succeeded in staying the human torrent. The heavy guns from a distance thundered on the flank of the assailants, which, shaken by the iron tempest, was thrown into disorder. Their very numbers increased the confusion, as they were precipitated on the masses in front. The horses at the same moment, charging gallantly under Cortés, followed up the advantage, and at length compelled the tumultuous throng to fall back with greater precipitation and disorder than that with which they had advanced.

More than once in the course of the action, a similar assault was attempted by the Tlascalans, but each time with less spirit, and greater loss. They were too deficient in military science to profit by their vast superiority in numbers. They were distributed into companies, it is true, each serving under its own chieftain and banner. But they were not arranged by rank and file, and moved in a confused mass, promiscuously heaped together. They knew not how to concentrate numbers on a given point, or even how to sustain an assault, by employing successive detachments to support and relieve one another. A very small part only of their array could be brought into contact with an enemy inferior to them in amount of forces. The remainder of the army, inactive and worse than useless, in the rear, served only to press tumultuously on the advance, and embarrass its movements by mere weight of numbers, while, on the least alarm, they were seized with a panic and threw the whole body into inextricable confusion. It was, in short, the combat of the ancient Greeks and Persians over again.

Still, the great numerical superiority of the Indians might have enabled them, at a severe cost of their own lives, indeed, to wear out, in time, the constancy of the Spaniards, disabled by wounds and incessant fatigue. But, fortunately for the latter, dissensions arose among their enemies. A Tlascalan chieftain, commanding one of the great divisions, had taken umbrage at the haughty demeanor of Xicotencatl, who had charged him with misconduct or cowardice in the late action. The injured cacique challenged his rival to single combat. This did not take place. But, burning with resentment, he chose the present occasion to indulge it, by drawing off his forces, amounting to ten thousand men from the field. He also persuaded another of the commanders to follow his example.

Thus reduced to about half his original strength, and that greatly crippled by the losses of the day, Xicotencatl could no longer maintain his ground against the Spaniards. After disputing the field with admirable courage for four hours, he retreated and resigned it to the enemy. The Spaniards were too much jaded, and too many were disabled by wounds, to allow them to pursue; and Cortés, satisfied with the decisive victory he had gained, returned in triumph to his position on the hill of Tzompach.

The number of killed in his own ranks had been very small, notwithstanding the severe loss inflicted on the enemy. These few he was careful to bury where they could not be discovered, anxious to conceal not only the amount of the slain, but the fact that the whites were mortal.[14] But very many of the men were wounded, and all the horses. The trouble of the Spaniards was much enhanced by the want of many articles important to them in their present exigency. They had neither oil, nor salt, which, as before noticed, was not to be obtained in Tlascala. Their clothing, accommodated to a softer climate, was ill adapted to the rude air of the mountains; and bows and arrows, as Bernal Diaz sarcastically remarks, formed an indifferent protection against the inclemency of the weather.[15]

Still, they had much to cheer them in the events of the day; and they might draw from them a reasonable ground for confidence in their own resources, such as no other experience could have supplied. Not that the results could authorize any thing like contempt for their Indian foe. Singly and with the same weapons, he might have stood his ground against the Spaniard.[16] But the success of the day established the super-

---

[14] So says Bernal Diaz; who, at the same time, by the epithets, *los muertos, los cuerpos*, plainly contradicts his previous boast that only one Christian fell in the fight. (Hist. de la Conquista, cap. 65.) Cortés has not the grace to acknowledge that one.

[15] Oviedo, Hist. de las Ind., MS., lib. 33, cap. 3.—Rel. Seg. de Cortés, ap. Lorenzana, p. 52.—Herrera, Hist. General, dec. 2, lib. 6, cap. 6.—Ixtlilxochitl, Hist. Chich., MS., cap. 83.—Gomara, Crónica, cap. 46.—Torquemada, Monarch. Ind., lib. 4, cap 32.—Bernal Diaz, Hist. de la Conquista, cap. 65, 66.

The warm chivalrous glow of feeling, which colors the rude composition of the last chronicler, makes him a better painter than his more correct and classical rivals. And, if there is somewhat too much of the self-complacent tone of the *quorum pars magna fui* in his writing, it may be pardoned in the hero of more than a hundred battles, and almost as many wounds.

[16] The Anonymous Conqueror bears emphatic testimony to the valor of the Indians, specifying instances in which he had seen a single warrior defend himself for a long time against two, three, and even four Spaniards! "Sono fra loro di valětissimi huomini et che ossano morir ostinatissimamēte Et io ho veduto un d' essi difendersi

iority of science and discipline over mere physical courage and numbers. It was fighting over again, as we have said, the old battle of the European and the Asiatic. But the handful of Greeks who routed the hosts of Xerxes and Darius, it must be remembered, had not so obvious an advantage on the score of weapons, as was enjoyed by the Spaniards in these wars. The use of fire-arms gave an ascendency which cannot easily be estimated; one so great, that a contest between nations equally civilized, which should be similar in all other respects to that between the Spaniards and the Tlascalans, would probably be attended with a similar issue. To all this must be added the effect produced by the cavalry. The nations of Anahuac had no large domesticated animals, and were unacquainted with any beast of burden. Their imaginations were bewildered, when they beheld the strange apparition of the horse and his rider moving in unison and obedient to one impulse, as if possessed of a common nature; and as they saw the terrible animal, with his "neck clothed in thunder," bearing down their squadrons and trampling them in the dust, no wonder they should have regarded him with the mysterious terror felt for a supernatural being. A very little reflection on the manifold grounds of superiority, both moral and physical, possessed by the Spaniards in this contest, will surely explain the issue, without any disparagement to the courage or capacity of their opponents.[17]

Cortés, thinking the occasion favorable, followed up the important blow he had struck by a new mission to the capital, bearing a message of similar import with that recently sent to the camp. But the senate was not yet sufficiently humbled. The late defeat caused, indeed, general consternation. Maxixcatzin, one of the four great lords who presided over the republic, reiterated with greater force the arguments before urged by him for embracing the proffered alliance of the strangers. The armies of the state had been beaten too often to allow any reasonable hope of successful resistance; and he enlarged on the generosity shown by the politic Conqueror to his prisoners,—so unusual in Anahuac,—as an additional motive for an alliance with men who knew how to be friends as well as foes.

But in these views he was overruled by the war-party, whose animosity was sharpened, rather than subdued, by the late discomfiture. Their hostile feelings were further exasperated by the younger Xicotencatl, who burned for an opportunity to retrieve his disgrace, and to wipe away the stain which had fallen for the first time on the arms of the republic.

In their perplexity, they called in the assistance of the priests, whose authority was frequently invoked in the deliberations of the American

valetemente da duoi caualli leggieri, et un altro da tre, et quattro." Rel. d' un gent., ap. Ramusio, tom. III. fol. 305.

[17] The appalling effect of the cavalry on the natives reminds one of the confusion into which the Roman legions were thrown by the strange appearance of the elephants in their first engagements with Pyrrhus, as told by Plutarch in his life of that prince.

chiefs. The latter inquired, with some simplicity, of these interpreters of fate, whether the strangers were supernatural beings, or men of flesh and blood like themselves. The priests, after some consultation, are said to have made the strange answer, that the Spaniards, though not gods, were children of the Sun; that they derived their strengh from that luminary, and, when his beams were withdrawn, their powers would also fail. They recommended a night attack, therefore, as one which afforded the best chance of success. This apparently childish response may have had in it more of cunning than credulity. It was not improbably suggested by Xicotencatl himself, or by the caciques in his interest, to reconcile the people to a measure, which was contrary to the military usages,—indeed, it may be said, to the public law of Anahuac. Whether the fruit of artifice or superstition, it prevailed; and the Tlascalan general was empowered, at the head of a detachment of ten thousand warriors, to try the effect of an assault by night on the Christian camp.

The affair was conducted with such secrecy, that it did not reach the ears of the Spaniards. But their general was not one who allowed himself, sleeping or waking, to be surprised on his post. Fortunately, the night appointed was illumined by the full beams of an autumnal moon; and one of the videttes preceived by its light, at a considerable distance, a large body of Indians moving towards the Christian lines. He was not slow in giving the alarm to the garrison.

The Spaniards slept, as has been said, with their arms by their side; while their horses, picketed near them, stood ready saddled, with the bridle hanging at the bow. In five minutes, the whole camp was under arms; when they beheld the dusky columns of the Indians cautiously advancing over the plain, their heads just peering above the tall maize with which the land was impartially covered. Cortés determined not to abide the assault in his intrenchments, but to sally out and pounce on the enemy when he had reached the bottom of the hill.

Slowly and stealthily the Indians advanced, while the Christian camp, hushed in profound silence, seemed to them buried in slumber. But no sooner had they reached the slope of the rising ground, than they were astounded by the deep battle-cry of the Spaniards, followed by the instantaneous apparition of the whole army, as they sallied forth from the works, and poured down the sides of the hill. Brandishing aloft their weapons, they seemed to the troubled faces of the Tlascalans, like so many spectres or demons hurrying to and fro in mid air, while the uncertain light magnified their numbers, and expanded the horse and his rider into gigantic and unearthly dimensions.

Scarcely waiting the shock of their enemy, the panic-struck barbarians let off a feeble volley of arrows, and, offering no other resistance, fled rapidly and tumultuously across the plain. The horse easily overtook the fugitives, riding them down and cutting them to pieces without mercy, until Cortés, weary with slaughter, called off his men, leaving the field loaded with the bloody trophies of victory.[18]

[18] Rel. Seg. de Cortés, ap. Lorenzana, pp. 53, 54.—Oviedo, Hist. de las Ind., MS.,

The next day, the Spanish commander, with his usual policy after a decisive blow had been struck, sent a new embassy to the Tlascalan capital. The envoys received their instructions through the interpreter, Marina. That remarkable woman had attracted general admiration by the constancy and cheerfulness with which she endured all the privations of the camp. Far from betraying the natural weakness and timidity of her sex, she had shrunk from no hardship herself, and had done much to fortify the drooping spirits of the soldiers; while her sympathies, whenever occasion offered, had been actively exerted in mitigating the calamities of her Indian countrymen.[19]

Through his faithful interpreter, Cortés communicated the terms of his message to the Tlascalan envoys. He made the same professions of amity as before, promising oblivion to all past injuries; but, if this proffer were rejected, he would visit their capital as a conqueror, raze every house in it to the ground, and put every inhabitant to the sword! He then dismissed the ambassadors with the symbolical presents of a letter in one hand, and an arrow in the other.

The envoys obtained respectful audience from the council of Tlascala, whom they found plunged in deep dejection by their recent reverses. The failure of the night attack had extinguished every spark of hope in their bosoms. Their armies had been beaten again and again, in the open field and in secret ambush. Stratagem and courage, all their resources, had alike proved ineffectual against a foe whose hand was never weary, and whose eye was never closed. Nothing remained but to submit. They selected four principal caciques, whom they intrusted with a mission to the Christian camp. They were to assure the strangers of a free passage through the country, and a friendly reception in the capital. The proffered friendship of the Spaniards was cordially embraced, with many awkward excuses for the past. The envoys were to touch at the Tlascalan camp on their way, and inform Xicotencatl of their proceedings. They were to require him, at the same time, to abstain from all further hostilities, and to furnish the white men with an ample supply of provisions.

But the Tlascalan deputies, on arriving at the quarters of that chief, did not find him in the humor to comply with these instructions. His repeated collisions with the Spaniards, or, it may be, his constitutional courage, left him inaccessible to the vulgar terrors of his countrymen. He regarded the strangers not as supernatural beings, but as men like himself. The animosity of a warrior had rankled into a deadly hatred from the mortifications he had endured at their hands, and his head

---

lib. 33, cap. 3.—P. Martyr, De Orbe Novo, dec. 2, cap. 2.—Torquemada, Monarch. Ind., lib. 4, cap. 32.—Herrera, Hist. General, dec. 2, lib. 6, cap. 8.—Bernal Diaz, Hist. de la Conquista, cap. 66.

[19] "Digamos como Doña Marina, con ser muger de la tierra, que esfuerço tan varonil tenia, que con oir cada dia que nos auian de matar, y comer nuestras carnes, y auernos visto cercados en las batallas passadas, y que aora todos estauamos heridos, y dolientes, jamas vímos flaqueza en ella, sino muy mayor esfuerço que de muger." Bernal Diaz, Hist. de ia Conquista, cap. 66.

æemed with plans for recovering his fallen honors, and for taking vengeance on the invaders of his country. He refused to disband any of the
force, still formidable, under his command; or to send supplies to the
enemy's camp. He further induced the ambassadors to remain in his
quarters, and relinquish their visit to the Spaniards. The latter, in consequence, were kept in ignorance of the movements in their favor,
which had taken place in the Tlascalan capital.[20]

The conduct of Xicotencatl is condemned by Castilian writers, as
that of a ferocious and sanguinary barbarian. It is natural they should
so regard it. But those, who have no national prejudice to warp their
judgments, may come to a different conclusion. They may find much
to admire in that high, unconquerable spirit, like some proud column,
standing alone in its majesty amidst the fragments and ruins around it.
They may see evidences of a clear-sighted sagacity, which, piercing the
thin vein of insidious friendship proffered by the Spaniards, and penetrating the future, discerned the coming miseries of his country; the
noble patriotism of one who would rescue that country at any cost, and,
amidst the gathering darkness, would infuse his own intrepid spirit
into the hearts of his nation, to animate them to a last struggle for independence.

[20] Ibid., cap. 67.—Camargo, Hist. de Tlascala, MS.—Ixtlilxochitl, Hist. Chich.,
MS., cap. 83

CHAPTER IV

DISCONTENTS IN THE ARMY—TLASCALAN SPIES—PEACE WITH THE RE-
PUBLIC—EMBASSY FROM MONTEZUMA

1519

DESIROUS to keep up the terror of the Castilian name, by leaving the
enemy no respite, Cortés, on the same day that he despatched the embassy to Tlascala, put himself at the head of a small corps of cavalry
and light troops to scour the neighboring country. He was at that time
so ill from fever, aided by medical treatment,[1] that he could hardly keep
his seat in the saddle. It was a rough country, and the sharp winds from
the frosty summits of the mountains pierced the scanty covering of the
troops, and chilled both men and horses. Four or five of the animals
gave out, and the general, alarmed for their safety, sent them back to
the camp. The soldiers, discouraged by this ill omen, would have persuaded him to return. But he made answer, "We fight under the banner
of the Cross; God is stronger than nature," [2] and continued his march.

It led through the same kind of chequered scenery of rugged hill
and cultivated plain as that already described, well covered with towns
and villages, some of them the frontier posts occupied by the Otomies.
Practising the Roman maxim of lenity to the submissive foe, he took
full vengeance on those who resisted, and, as resistance too often occurred, marked his path with fire and desolation. After a short absence,
he returned in safety, laden with the plunder of a successful foray. It
would have been more honorable to him, had it been conducted with
less rigor. The excesses are imputed by Bernal Diaz to the Indian allies,
whom in the heat of victory it was found impossible to restrain.[3] On
whose head soever they fall, they seem to have given little uneasiness
to the general, who declares in his letter to the Emperor Charles the

[1] The effect of the medicine—though rather a severe dose, according to the precise
Diaz—was suspended during the general's active exertions. Gomara, however, does
not consider this a miracle. (Crónica, cap. 49.) Father Sandoval does. (Hist. de
Cárlos Quinto, tom. I. p. 127.) Solís, after a conscientious inquiry into this perplexing matter, decides—strange as it may seem—against the father! Conquista, lib. 2,
cap. 20.

[2] "Dios es sobre natura." Rel. Seg. de Cortés, ap. Lorenzana, p. 54.

[3] Hist. de la Conquista, cap. 64.
Not so Cortés, who says boldly, "Quemé mas de diez pueblos." (Ibid., p. 52.) His
reverend commentator specifies the localities of the Indian towns destroyed by him,
in his forays. Viaje, ap. Lorenzana, pp. ix-xi.

244

Fifth, "As we fought under the standard of the Cross,[4] for the true Faith, and the service of your Highness, Heaven crowned our arms with such success, that, while multitudes of the infidel were slain, little loss was suffered by the Castilians." [5] The Spanish Conquerors, to judge from their writings, unconscious of any worldly motive lurking in the bottom of their hearts, regarded themselves as soldiers of the Church, fighting the great battle of Christianity; and in the same edifying and comfortable light are regarded by most of the national historians of a later day.[6]

On his return to the camp, Cortés found a new cause of disquietude in discontents which had broken out among the soldiery. Their patience was exhausted by a life of fatigue and peril to which there seemed to be no end. The battles they had won against such tremendous odds had not advanced them a jot. The idea of their reaching Mexico, says the old soldier so often quoted, "was treated as a jest by the whole army"; [7] and the indefinite prospect of hostilities with the ferocious people among whom they were now cast, threw a deep gloom over their spirits.

Among the malcontents were a number of noisy, vaporing persons, such as are found in every camp, who, like empty bubbles, are sure to rise to the surface and make themselves seen in seasons of agitation. They were, for the most part, of the old faction of Velasquez, and had estates in Cuba, to which they turned many a wistful glance as they receded more and more from the coast. They now waited on the general not in a mutinous spirit of resistance, (for they remembered the lesson in Villa Rica,) but with the design of frank expostulation, as with a brother adventurer in a common cause.[8] The tone of familiarity thus assumed was eminently characteristic of the footing of equality on which the parties in the expedition stood with one another.

Their sufferings, they told him, were too great to be endured. All the men had received one, most of them, two or three wounds. More than fifty had perished, in one way or another, since leaving Vera Cruz. There was no beast of burden but led a life preferable to theirs. For,

[4] The famous banner of the Conqueror, with the Cross emblazoned on it, has been preserved in Mexico to our day.

[5] "É como trayamos la Bandera de la Cruz, y puñabamos por nuestra Fe, y por servicio de Vuestra Sacra Magestad, en su muy Real ventura nos dió Dios tanta victoria, que les matámos mucha gente, sin que los nuestros recibiessen daño." Rel Seg. de Cortés, ap. Lorenzana, p. 52.

[6] "Y fué cosa notable," exclaims Herrera, "con quanta humildad, i devocion, bolvian todos alabando á Dios, que tan milagrosas victorias les daba; de donde se conocia claro, que los favorecia con su Divina asistencia."

[7] "Porque entrar en México, teníamoslo por cosa de risa, á causa de sus grandes fuerças." Bernal Diaz, Hist. de la Conquista, cap. 66.

[8] Diaz indignantly disclaims the idea of mutiny, which Gomara attached to this proceeding. "Las palabras que le dezian era por via de acôsejarle, y porque les parecia que eran bien dichas, y no por otra via, porque siempre le siguiéron muy bien, y lealmête; y no es mucho que en los exércitos algunos buenos soldados aconsejen á su Capitan, y mas si se ven tan trabaiados como nosotros andauamos." Ibid., cap. 71.

when the night came, the former could rest from his labors; but they, fighting or watching, had no rest, day nor night. As to conquering Mexico, the very thought of it was madness. If they had encountered such opposition from the petty republic of Tlascala, what might they not expect from the great Mexican empire? There was now a temporary suspension of hostilities. They should avail themselves of it, to retrace their steps to Vera Cruz. It is true, the fleet there was destroyed; and by this act, unparalleled for rashness even in Roman annals, the general had become responsible for the fate of the whole army. Still there was one vessel left. That might be despatched to Cuba, for reinforcements and supplies; and, when these arrived, they would be enabled to resume operations with some prospect of success.

Cortés listened to this singular expostulation with perfect composure. He knew his men, and, instead of rebuke or harsher measures, replied in the same frank and soldier-like vein which they had affected.

There was much truth, he allowed, in what they said. The sufferings of the Spaniards had been great; greater than those recorded of any heroes in Greek or Roman story. So much the greater would be their glory. He had often been filled with admiration as he had seen his little host encircled by myriads of barbarians, and felt that no people but Spaniards could have triumphed over such formidable odds. Nor could they, unless the arm of the Almighty had been over them. And they might reasonably look for his protection hereafter; for was it not in his cause they were fighting? They had encountered dangers and difficulties, it was true. But they had not come here expecting a life of idle dalliance and pleasure. Glory, as he had told them at the outset, was to be won only by toil and danger. They would do him the justice to acknowledge, that he had never shrunk from his share of both.—This was a truth, adds the honest chronicler who heard and reports the dialogue, which no one could deny.—But, if they had met with hardships, he continued, they had been everywhere victorious. Even now, they were enjoying the fruits of this, in the plenty which reigned in the camp. And they would soon see the Tlascalans, humbled by their late reverses, suing for peace on any terms. To go back now was impossible. The very stones would rise up against them. The Tlascalans would hunt them in triumph down to the water's edge. And how would the Mexicans exult at this miserable issue of their vainglorious vaunts! Their former friends would become their enemies; and the Totonacs, to avert the vengeance of the Aztecs, from which the Spaniards could no longer shield them, would join in the general cry. There was no alternative, then, but to go forward in their career. And he besought them to silence their pusillanimous scruples, and, instead of turning their eyes toward Cuba, to fix them on Mexico, the great object of their enterprise.

While this singular conference was going on, many other soldiers had gathered round the spot; and the discontented party, emboldened by the presence of their comrades, as well as by the general's forbearance, replied, that they were far from being convinced. Another such victory as the last would be their ruin. They were going to Mexico only to be slaughtered. Until, at length, the general's patience being exhausted, he cut the argument short, by quoting a verse from an old song, implying that it was better to die with honor, than to live disgraced, a sentiment which was loudly echoed by the greater part of his audience, who, notwithstanding their occasional murmurs, had no design to abandon the expedition, still less the commander, to whom they were passionately devoted. The malcontents, disconcerted by this rebuke, slunk back to their own quarters, muttering half-smothered execrations on the leader who had projected the enterprise, the Indians who had guided him, and their own countrymen who supported him in it.[9]

Such were the difficulties that lay in the path of Cortés: a wily and ferocious enemy; a climate uncertain, often unhealthy; illness in his own person, much aggravated by anxiety as to the manner in which his conduct would be received by his sovereign; last, not least, disaffection among his soldiers, on whose constancy and union he rested for the basis of his operations,—the great lever by which he was to overturn the empire of Montezuma.

On the morning following this event, the camp was surprised by the appearance of a small body of Tlascalans, decorated with badges, the white color of which intimated peace. They brought a quantity of provisions, and some trifling ornaments, which, they said, were sent by the Tlascalan general, who was weary of the war, and desired an accommodation with the Spaniards. He would soon present himself to arrange this in person. The intelligence diffused general joy, and the emissaries received a friendly welcome.

A day or two elapsed, and while a few of the party left the Spanish quarters, the others, about fifty in number, who remained, excited some distrust in the bosom of Marina. She communicated her suspicions to Cortés that they were spies. He caused several of them, in consequence, to be arrested, examined them separately, and ascertained that they were employed by Xicotencatl to inform him of the state of the Christian camp, preparatory to a meditated assault, for which he was mustering his forces. Cortés, satisfied of the truth of this, determined to make such an example of the delinquents, as should intimidate his enemy from repeating the attempt. He ordered their hands to be cut off, and in that condition sent them back to their countrymen, with the message, "that the Tlascalans might come by day or night; they would find the Spaniards ready for them."[10]

---

[9] This conference is reported, with some variety, indeed, by nearly every historian. (Rel. Seg. de Cortés, ap. Lorenzana, p. 55.—Oviedo, Hist. de las Ind., MS., lib. 33, cap. 3.—Gomara, Crónica, cap. 51, 52.—Ixtlilxochitl, Hist. Chich., MS., cap. 80.— Herrera, Hist. General, dec. 2, lib. 6, cap. 9.—P. Martyr, De Orbe Novo, dec. 5, cap. 2.) I have abridged the account given by Bernal Diaz, one of the audience, though not one of the parties to the dialogue,—for that reason, the better authority.

[10] Diaz says only seventeen lost their hands, the rest their thumbs. (Hist. de la Conquista, cap. 70,) Cortés does not flinch confessing, the hands of the whole fifty, "Los mandé tomar á todos cincuenta, y cortarles las manos, y los embié, que

The doleful spectacle of their comrades returning in this mutilated state filled the Indian camp with horror and consternation. The haughty crest of their chief was humbled. From that moment, he lost his wonted buoyancy and confidence. His soldiers, filled with superstitious fear, refused to serve longer against a foe who could read their very thoughts, and divine their plans before they were ripe for execution.[11]

The punishment inflicted by Cortés may well shock the reader by its brutality. But it should be considered in mitigation, that the victims of it were spies, and, as such, by the laws of war, whether among civilized or savage nations, had incurred the penalty of death. The amputation of the limbs was a milder punishment, and reserved for inferior offences. If we revolt at the barbarous nature of the sentence, we should reflect that it was no uncommon one at that day; not more uncommon, indeed, than whipping and branding with a hot iron were in our own country, at the beginning of the present century, or than cropping the ears was in the preceding one. A higher civilization, indeed, rejects such punishments, as pernicious in themselves, and degrading to humanity. But in the sixteenth century, they were openly recognised by the laws of the most polished nations in Europe. And it is too much to ask of any man, still less one bred to the iron trade of war, to be in advance of the refinement of his age. We may be content, if, in circumstances so unfavorable to humanity, he does not fall below it.

All thoughts of further resistance being abandoned, the four delegates of the Tlascalan republic were now allowed to proceed on their mission. They were speedily followed by Xicotencatl himself, attended by a numerous train of military retainers. As they drew near the Spanish lines, they were easily recognised by the white and yellow colors of their uniforms, the livery of the house of Titcala. The joy of the army was great at this sure intimation of the close of hostilities; and it was with difficulty that Cortés was enabled to restore the men to tranquillity, and the assumed indifference which it was proper to maintain in the presence of an enemy.

The Spaniards gazed with curious eye on the valiant chief who had so long kept his enemies at bay, and who now advanced with the firm and fearless step of one who was coming rather to bid defiance than to sue for peace. He was rather above the middle size, with broad shoulders, and a muscular frame intimating great activity and strength. His head was large, and his countenance marked with the lines of hard service rather than of age, for he was but thirty-five. When he entered the presence of Cortés, he made the usual salutation, by touching the ground with his hand, and carrying it to his head; while the sweet incense of aromatic gums rolled up in clouds from the censers carried by his slaves.

dixessen á su Señor, que de noche, y de dia, y cada, y quando él viniesse, verian quien eramos." Rel. Seg. de Cortés, ap. Lorenzana, p. 53.

[11] "De que los Tlascaltecas se admiráron, entendiendo que Cortés les entendia sus pensamientos." Ixtlilxochitl, Hist. Chich., MS., cap. 83.

Far from a pusillanimous attempt to throw the blame on the senate, he assumed the whole responsibility of the war. He had considered the white men, he said, as enemies, for they came with the allies and vassals of Montezuma. He loved his country, and wished to preserve the independence which she had maintained through her long wars with the Aztecs. He had been beaten. They might be the strangers, who, it had been so long predicted, would come from the east, to take possession of the country. He hoped they would use their victory with moderation, and not trample on the liberties of the republic. He came now in the name of his nation, to tender their obedience to the Spaniards, assuring them they would find his countrymen as faithful in peace as they had been firm in war.

Cortés, far from taking umbrage, was filled with admiration at the lofty spirit which thus disdained to stoop beneath misfortunes. The brave man knows how to respect bravery in another. He assumed, however, a severe aspect, as he rebuked the chief for having so long persisted in hostilities. Had Xicotencatl believed the word of the Spaniards, and accepted their proffered friendship sooner, he would have spared his people much suffering, which they well merited by their obstinacy. But it was impossible, continued the general, to retrieve the past. He was willing to bury it in oblivion, and to receive the Tlascalans as vassals to the emperor, his master. If they proved true, they should find him a sure column of support; if false, he would take such vengeance on them as he had intended to take on their capital, had they not speedily given in their submission.—It proved an ominous menace for the chief to whom it was addressed.

The cacique then ordered his slaves to bring forward some trifling ornaments of gold and feather-embroidery, designed as presents. They were of little value, he said, with a smile, for the Tlascalans were poor. They had little gold, not even cotton, nor salt. The Aztec emperor had left them nothing but their freedom and their arms. He offered this gift only as a token of his good-will. "As such I receive it," answered Cortés, "and coming from the Tlascalans, set more value on it, than I should from any other source, though it were a house full of gold";—a politic, as well as magnanimous reply, for it was by the aid of this good-will, that he was to win the gold of Mexico.[12]

Thus ended the bloody war with the fierce republic of Tlascala, during the course of which, the fortunes of the Spaniards, more than once, had trembled in the balance. Had it been persevered in but a little longer, it must have ended in their confusion and ruin, exhausted as they were by wounds, watching, and fatigues, with the seeds of disaffection rankling among themselves. As it was, they came out of the fearful contest with untarnished glory. To the enemy, they seemed invulnerable, bearing charmed lives, proof alike against the accidents of fortune and

[12] Rel. Seg. de Cortés, ap. Lorenzana, pp. 56, 57.—Oviedo, Hist. de las Ind., MS., lib. 33, cap. 3.—Gomara, Crónica, cap. 53.—Bernal Diaz, Hist. de la Conquista, cap. 71, et seq.—Sahagun, Hist. de Nueva España, MS., lib. 12, cap. 11.

the assaults of man. No wonder that they indulged a similar conceit in their own bosoms, and that the humblest Spaniard should have fancied himself the subject of a special interposition of Providence, which shielded him in the hour of battle, and reserved him for a higher destiny.

While the Tlascalans were still in the camp, an embassy was announced from Montezuma. Tidings of the exploits of the Spaniards had spread far and wide over the plateau. The emperor, in particular, had watched every step of their progress, as they climbed the steeps of the Cordilleras, and advanced over the broad table-land, on their summit. He had seen them, with great satisfaction, take the road to Tlascala, trusting, that, if they were mortal men, they would find their graves there. Great was his dismay, when courier after courier brought him intelligence of their successes, and that the most redoubtable warriors on the plateau had been scattered like chaff, by the swords of this handful of strangers.

His superstitious fears returned in full force. He saw in the Spaniards "the men of destiny," who were to take possession of his sceptre. In his alarm and uncertainty, he sent a new embassy to the Christian camp. It consisted of five great nobles of his court, attended by a train of two hundred slaves. They brought with them a present, as usual, dictated partly by fear, and, in part, by the natural munificence of his disposition. It consisted of three thousand ounces of gold, in grains, or in various manufactured articles, with several hundred mantles and dresses of embroidered cotton, and the picturesque feather-work. As they laid these at the feet of Cortés, they told him, they had come to offer the congratulations of their master on the late victories of the white men. The emperor only regretted that it would not be in his power to receive them in his capital, where the numerous population was so unruly, that their safety would be placed in jeopardy. The mere intimation of the Aztec emperor's wishes, in the most distant way, would have sufficed with the Indian nations. It had very little weight with the Spaniards; and the envoys, finding this puerile expression of them ineffectual, resorted to another argument, offering a tribute in their master's name to the Castilian sovereign, provided the Spaniards would relinquish their visit to his capital. This was a greater error; it was displaying the rich casket with one hand, which he was unable to defend with the other. Yet the author of this pusillanimous policy, the unhappy victim of superstition, was a monarch renowned among the Indian nations for his intrepidity and enterprise,—the terror of Anahuac!

Cortés, while he urged his own sovereign's commands as a reason for disregarding the wishes of Montezuma, uttered expressions of the most profound respect for the Aztec prince, and declared that if he had not the means of requiting his munificence, as he could wish, at present, he trusted *to repay him, at some future day, with good works!*[13]

---

[13] "Cortés recibió con alegría aquel presente, y dixo que se lo tenia en merced, y que él lo pagaria al señor Monteçuma en buenas obras." Bernal Diaz, Hist. de la Conquista, cap. 73.

The Mexican ambassadors were not much gratified with finding the war at an end, and a reconciliation established between their mortal enemies and the Spaniards. The mutual disgust of the two parties with each other was too strong to be repressed even in the presence of the general, who saw with satisfaction the evidences of a jealousy, which, undermining the strength of the Indian emperor, was to prove the surest source of his own success.[14]

Two of the Aztec mission returned to Mexico, to acquaint their sovereign with the state of affairs in the Spanish camp. The others remained with the army, Cortés being willing that they should be personal spectators of the deference shown him by the Tlascalans. Still he did not hasten his departure for their capital. Not that he placed reliance on the injurious intimations of the Mexicans respecting their good faith. Yet he was willing to put this to some longer trial, and, at the same time, to reëstablish his own health more thoroughly, before his visit. Meanwhile, messengers daily arrived from the city, pressing his journey, and were finally followed by some of the aged rulers of the republic, attended by a numerous retinue, impatient of his long delay. They brought with them a body of five hundred *tamanes,* or *men of burden,* to drag his cannon, and relieve his own forces from this fatiguing part of their duty. It was impossible to defer his departure longer; and after mass, and a solemn thanksgiving to the great Being who had crowned their arms with triumph, the Spaniards bade adieu to the quarters which they had occupied for nearly three weeks on the hill of Tzompach. The strong tower, or *teocalli,* which commanded it, was called, in commemoration of their residence, "the tower of victory"; and the few stones, which still survive of its ruins, point out to the eye of the traveller a spot ever memorable in history for the courage and constancy of the early Conquerors.[15]

[14] He dwells on it in his letter to the Emperor. "Vista la discordia y desconformidad de los unos y de los otros, no huve poco placer, porque me pareció hacer mucho á mi propósito, y que podria tener manera de mas aýna sojuzgarlos, é aun acordéme de una autoridad Evangélica, que dice: *Omne Regnum in seipsum divisum desolabitur:* y con los unos y con los otros maneaba, y á cada uno en secreto lo agradecia el aviso, que me daba, y le daba crédito de mas amistad que al otro." Rel. Seg. de Cortés, ap. Lorenzana, p. 61.

[15] Herrera, Hist. General, dec. 2, lib. 6, cap. 10.—Oviedo, Hist. de las Ind., MS., lib. 33, cap. 4.—Gomara, Crónica, cap. 54.—Martyr, De Orbe Novo, dec. 5, cap. 2.—Bernal Diaz, Hist. de la Conquista, cap. 72-74.—Ixtlilxochitl, Hist. Chich., MS., cap. 83.

CHAPTER V

SPANIARDS ENTER TLASCALA—DESCRIPTION OF THE CAPITAL—AT-
TEMPTED CONVERSION—AZTEC EMBASSY—INVITED TO CHOLULA

1519

THE city of Tlascala, the capital of the republic of the same name, lay
at the distance of above six leagues from the Spanish camp. The road
led into a hilly region, exhibiting in every arable patch of ground the
evidence of laborious cultivation. Over a deep *barranca*, or ravine they
crossed on a bridge of stone, which, according to tradition,—a slippery
authority,—is the same still standing, and was constructed originally for
the passage of the army.[1] They passed some considerable towns on their
route, where they experienced a full measure of Indian hospitality. As
they advanced, the approach to a populous city was intimated by the
crowds who flocked out to see and welcome the strangers; men and
women in their picturesque dresses, with bunches and wreaths of roses,
which they gave to the Spaniards, or fastened to the necks and caparisons
of their horses, in the same manner as at Cempoalla. Priests, with their
white robes, and long matted tresses floating over them, mingled in the
crowd, scattering volumes of incense from their burning censers. In this
way, the multitudinous and motley procession defiled through the gates
of the ancient capital of Tlascala. It was the twenty-third of September,
1519, the anniversary of which is still celebrated by the inhabitants, as
a day of jubilee.[2]

The press was now so great, that it was with difficulty the police of
the city could clear a passage for the army; while the *azoteas*, or flat
terraced roofs of the buildings, were covered with spectators, eager to
catch a glimpse of the wonderful strangers. The houses were hung with
festoons of flowers, and arches of verdant boughs, intertwined with

---

[1] "A distancia de un quarto de legua caminando á esta dicha ciudad se encuentra
una barranca honda, que tiene para pasar *un Puente de cal y canto de bóveda*, y es
tradicion en el pueblo de San Salvador, que se hizo en aquellos dias, que estubo allí
Cortés paraque pasasse." (Viaje, ap. Lorenzana, p. xi.) If the antiquity of this
arched stone bridge could be established, it would settle a point much mooted in
respect to Indian architecture. But the construction of so solid a work in so short
a time is a fact requiring a better voucher than the villagers of San Salvador.

[2] Clavigero, Stor. del Messico, tom. III. p. 53.

"Recibimiento el mas solene y famoso que en el mundo se ha visto," exclaims
the enthusiastic historian of the republic. He adds, that "more than a hundred
thousand men flocked out to receive the Spaniards; a thing that appears impossible,"
que parece cosa imposible! It does indeed. Camargo, Hist. de Tlascala, MS.

roses and honeysuckle, were thrown across the streets. The whole population abandoned itself to rejoicing; and the air was rent with songs and shouts of triumph mingled with the wild music of the national instruments, that might have excited apprehensions in the breasts of the soldiery, had they not gathered their peaceful import from the assurance of Marina, and the joyous countenances of the natives.

With these accompaniments, the procession moved along the principal streets to the mansion of Xicotencatl, the aged father of the Tlascalan general, and one of the four rulers of the republic. Cortés dismounted from his horse, to receive the old chieftain's embrace. He was nearly blind; and satisfied, as far as he could, a natural curiosity respecting the person of the Spanish general, by passing his hand over his features. He then led the way to a spacious hall in his palace, where a banquet was served to the army. In the evening, they were shown to their quarters, in the buildings and open ground surrounding one of the principal *teocallis;* while the Mexican ambassadors, at the desire of Cortés, had apartments assigned them next to his own, that he might the better watch over their safety, in this city of their enemies.[3]

Tlascala was one of the most important and populous towns on the table-land. Cortés, in his letter to the Emperor, compares it to Granada, affirming, that it was larger, stronger, and more populous than the Moorish capital, at the time of the conquest, and quite as well built.[4] But, notwithstanding we are assured by a most respectable writer at the close of the last century, that its remains justify the assertion,[5] we shall be slow to believe that its edifices could have rivalled those monuments of Oriental magnificence, whose light, aërial forms still survive after the lapse of ages, the admiration of every traveller of sensibility and taste. The truth is, that Cortés, like Columbus, saw objects through the warm medium of his own fond imagination, giving them a higher tone of coloring and larger dimensions than were strictly warranted by the fact. It was natural that the man who had made such rare discoveries should unconsciously magnify their merits to his own eyes, and to those of others.

The houses were built, for the most part, of mud or earth; the better sort of stone and lime, or bricks dried in the sun. They were unprovided with doors or windows, but in the apertures for the former hung mats fringed with pieces of copper or something which, by its tinkling sound, would give notice of any one's entrance. The streets were narrow and dark. The population must have been considerable, if, as Cortés asserts,

---

[3] Sahagun, Hist. de Nueva España, MS., lib. 12, cap. 11.—Rel. Seg. de Cortés, ap. Lorenzana, p. 59.—Camargo, Hist. de Tlascala, MS.—Gomara, Crónica, cap. 54.—Herrera, Hist. General, dec. 2, lib. 6, cap. 11.

[4] "La qual ciudad es tan grande, y de tanta admiracion, que aunque mucho de lo, que de ella podria decir, dexe, lo poco que diré creo es casi increible, porque es muy mayor que Granada, y muy mas fuerte, y de tan buenos Edificios y de muy mucha mas gente, que Granada tenia al tiempo que se ganó." Rel. Seg. de Cortés, ap. Lorenzana, p. 58.

[5] "En las Ruinas, que aun hoy se vén en Tlaxcala, se conoce, que no es ponderacion." Ibid., p. 58. Nota del editor, Lorenzana.

thirty thousand souls were often gathered in the market on a public day. These meetings were a sort of fairs, held, as usual in all the great towns, every fifth day, and attended by the inhabitants of the adjacent country, who brought there for sale every description of domestic produce and manufacture, with which they were acquainted. They peculiarly excelled in pottery, which was considered as equal to the best in Europe.[6] It is a further proof of civilized habits, that the Spaniards found barbers' shops, and baths both of vapor and hot water, familiarly used by the inhabitants. A still higher proof of refinement may be discerned in a vigilant police which repressed every thing like disorder among the people.[7]

The city was divided into four quarters, which might rather be called so many separate towns, since they were built at different times, and separated from each other by high stone walls, defining their respective limits. Over each of these districts ruled one of the four great chiefs of the republic, occupying his own spacious mansion, and surrounded by his own immediate vassals. Strange arrangement,—and more strange, that it should have been compatible with social order and tranquillity! The ancient capital, through one quarter of which flowed the rapid current of the Zahuatl, stretched along the summits and sides of hills, at whose base are now gathered the miserable remains of its once flourishing population.[8] Far beyond, to the south-east, extended the bold sierra of Tlascala, and the huge Malinche, crowned with the usual silver diadem of the highest Andes, having its shaggy sides clothed with dark-green forests of firs, gigantic sycamores, and oaks whose towering stems rose to the height of forty or fifty feet, unincumbered by a branch. The clouds, which sailed over from the distant Atlantic, gathered round the lofty peaks of the sierra, and, settling into torrents, poured over the plains in the neighborhood of the city, converting them, at such seasons, into swamps. Thunder storms, more frequent and terrible here, than in other parts of the table-land, swept down the sides of the mountains, and shook the frail tenements of the capital to their foundations. But, although the bleak winds of the sierra gave an austerity to the climate, unlike the sunny skies of genial temperature of the lower regions, it was far more favorable to the development of both the physical and moral energies. A bold and hardy peasantry was nurtured among the recesses

[6] "Nullum est fictile vas apud nos, quod arte superet ab illis vasa formata." Martyr, De Orbe Novo, dec. 5, cap. 2.
[7] Camargo, Hist. de Tlascala, MS.—Rel. Seg. de Cortés, ap. Lorenzana, p. 59.—Oviedo, Hist. de las Ind., MS., lib. 33, cap. 4.—Ixtlilxochitl, Hist. Chich., MS., cap. 83.
The last historian enumerates such a number of contemporary Indian authorities for his narrative, as of itself argues no inconsiderable degree of civilization in the people.
[8] Herrera, Hist. General, dec. 2, lib. 6, cap. 12.
The population of a place, which Cortés could compare with Granada, had dwindled by the beginning of the present century to 3,400 inhabitants, of which less than a thousand were of the Indian stock. See Humboldt, Essai Politique, tom. II. p. 158.

of the hills, fit equally to cultivate the land in peace, and to defend it in war. Unlike the spoiled child of Nature, who derives such facilities of subsistence from her too prodigal hand, as supersede the necessity of exertion on his own part, the Tlascalan earned his bread—from a soil not ungrateful, it is true—by the sweat of his brow. He led a life of temperance and toil. Cut off by his long wars with the Aztecs from commercial intercourse, he was driven chiefly to agricultural labor, the occupation most propitious to purity of morals and sinewy strength of constitution. His honest breast glowed with the patriotism,—or local attachment to the soil, which is the fruit of its diligent culture; while he was elevated by a proud consciousness of independence, the natural birthright of the child of the mountains.—Such was the race with whom Cortés was now associated, for the achievement of his great work.

Some days were given by the Spaniards to festivity, in which they were successively entertained at the hospitable boards of the four great nobles, in their several quarters of the city. Amidst these friendly demonstrations, however, the general never relaxed for a moment his habitual vigilance, or the strict discipline of the camp; and he was careful to provide for the security of the citizens by prohibiting, under severe penalties, any soldier from leaving his quarters without express permission. Indeed, the severity of his discipline provoked the remonstrance of more than one of his officers, as a superfluous caution; and the Tlascalan chiefs took some exception at it, as inferring an unreasonable distrust of them. But, when Cortés explained it, as in obedience to an established military system, they testified their admiration, and the ambitious young general of the republic proposed to introduce it, if possible, into his own ranks.[9]

The Spanish commander, having assured himself of the loyalty of his new allies, next proposed to accomplish one of the great objects of his mission, their conversion to Christianity. By the advice of father Olmedo, always opposed to precipitate measures, he had deferred this till a suitable opportunity presented itself for opening the subject. Such a one occurred when the chiefs of the state proposed to strengthen the alliance with the Spaniards, by the intermarriage of their daughters with Cortés and his officers. He told them, this could not be, while they continued in the darkness of infidelity. Then, with the aid of the good friar, he expounded as well as he could the doctrines of the Faith; and, exhibiting the image of the Virgin with the infant Redeemer, told them that there was the God, in whose worship alone they would find salvation, while that of their own false idols would sink them in eternal perdition.

It is unnecessary to burden the reader with a recapitulation of his homily, which contained, probably, dogmas quite as incomprehensible to the untutored Indian, as any to be found in his own rude mythology. But, though it failed to convince his audience, they listened with a deferential awe. When he had finished, they replied, they had no doubt that

[9] Sahagun, Hist. de Nueva España, MS., lib. 12, cap. 11.—Camargo, Hist. de Tlascala, MS.—Gomara, Crónica, cap. 54, 55.—Herrera, Hist. General, dec. 2, lib. 6, cap. 13.—Bernal Diaz, Hist. de la Conquista, cap. 75.

the God of the Christians must be a good and a great God, and as such they were willing to give him a place among the divinities of Tlascala. The polytheistic system of the Indians, like that of the ancient Greeks, was of that accommodating kind which could admit within its elastic folds the deities of any other religion, without violence to itself.[10] But every nation, they continued, must have its own appropriate and tutelary deities. Nor could they, in their old age, abjure the service of those who had watched over them from youth. It would bring down the vengeance of their gods, and of their own nation, who were as warmly attached to their religion as their liberties, and would defend both with the last drop of their blood!

It was clearly inexpedient to press the matter further, at present. But the zeal of Cortés, as usual, waxing warm by opposition, had now mounted too high for him to calculate obstacles; nor would he have shrunk, probably, from the crown of martyrdom in so good a cause. But, fortunately, at least for the success of his temporal cause, this crown was not reserved for him.

The good monk, his ghostly adviser, seeing the course things were likely to take, with better judgment interposed to prevent it. He had no desire, he said, to see the same scenes acted over again as at Cempoalla. He had no relish for forced conversions. They could hardly be lasting. The growth of an hour might well die with the hour. Of what use was it to overturn the altar, if the idol remained enthroned in the heart? or to destroy the idol itself, if it were only to make room for another? Better to wait patiently the effect of time and teaching to soften the heart and open the understanding, without which there could be no assurance of a sound and permanent conviction. These rational views were enforced by the remonstrances of Alvarado, Velasquez de Leon, and those in whom Cortés placed most confidence; till, driven from his original purpose, the military polemic consented to relinquish the attempt at conversion, for the present, and to refrain from a repetition of the scenes, which, considering the different mettle of the population, might have been attended with very different results from those at Cozumel and Cempoalla.[11]

---

[10] Camargo notices this elastic property in the religions of Anahuac. "Este modo de hablar y decir que les querrá dar otro Dios, es saber que cuando estas gentes tenian noticia de algun Dios de buenas propiedades y costumbres, que le rescibiesen admitiéndole por tal, porque otras gentes advenedizas trujéron muchos ídolos que tubiéron por Dioses, y á este fin y propósito decian, que Cortés las traia otro Dios." Hist. de Tlascala, MS.

[11] Ixtlilxochitl, Hist. Chich., MS., cap. 84.—Gomara, Crónica, cap. 56.—Bernal Diaz, Hist. de la Conquista, cap. 76, 77.

This is not the account of Camargo. According to him, Cortés gained his point; the nobles led the way by embracing Christianity, and the idols were broken. (Hist. de Tlascala, MS.) But Camargo was himself a Christianized Indian, who lived in the next generation after the Conquest; and may very likely have felt as much desire to relieve his nation from the reproach of infidelity, as a modern Spaniard would to scour out the stain—*mala raza y mancha*—of Jewish or Moorish lineage, from his escutcheon.

In the course of our narrative, we have had occasion to witness more than once the good effects of the interposition of father Olmedo. Indeed, it is scarcely too much to say, that his discretion in spiritual matters contributed as essentially to the success of the expedition, as did the sagacity and courage of Cortés in temporal. He was a true disciple in the school of Las Casas. His heart was unscathed by that fiery fanaticism which sears and hardens whatever it touches. It melted with the warm glow of Christian charity. He had come out to the New World, as a missionary among the heathen, and he shrunk from no sacrifice, but that of the welfare of the poor benighted flock to whom he had consecrated his days. If he followed the banners of the warrior, it was to mitigate the ferocity of war, and to turn the triumphs of the Cross to a good account for the natives themselves, by the spiritual labors of conversion. He afforded the uncommon example—not to have been looked for, certainly, in a Spanish monk of the sixteenth century—of enthusiasm controlled by reason, a quickening zeal tempered by the mild spirit of toleration.

But, though Cortés abandoned the ground of conversion for the present, he compelled the Tlascalans to break the fetters of the unfortunate victims reserved for sacrifice; an act of humanity unhappily only transient in its effects, since the prisons were filled with fresh victims, on his departure.

He also obtained permission for the Spaniards to perform the services of their own religion unmolested. A large cross was erected in one of the great courts or squares. Mass was celebrated every day in the presence of the army and of crowds of natives, who, if they did not comprehend its full import, were so far edified, that they learned to reverence the religion of their conquerors. The direct interposition of Heaven, however, wrought more for their conversion than the best homily of priest or soldier. Scarcely had the Spaniards left the city,—the tale is told on very respectable authority,—when a thin, transparent cloud descended and settled like a column on the cross, and, wrapping it round in its luminous folds, continued to emit a soft, celestial radiance through the night, thus proclaiming the sacred character of the symbol, on which was shed the halo of divinity! [12]

The principle of toleration in religious matters being established, the Spanish general consented to receive the daughters of the caciques. Five or six of the most beautiful of the Indian maidens were assigned to as many of his principal officers, after they had been cleansed from the stains of infidelity by the waters of baptism. They received, as usual, on this occasion, good Castilian names, in exchange for the barbarous nomenclature of their own vernacular.[13] Among them, Xicotencatl's

---

[12] The miracle is reported by Herrera, (Hist. General, dec. 2, lib. 6, cap. 15,) and *believed* by Solís. Conquista de Méjico, lib. 3, cap. 5.

[13] To avoid the perplexity of selection, it was common for the missionary to give the same names to all the Indians baptized on the same day. Thus, one day was set apart for the Johns, another for the Peters, and so on; an ingenious arrangement,

daughter, Doña Luisa, as she was called after her baptism, was a princess
of the highest estimation and authority in Tlascala. She was given by
her father to Alvarado, and their posterity intermarried with the noblest
families of Castile. The frank and joyous manners of this cavalier made
him a great favorite with the Tlascalans; and his bright, open countenance, fair complexion, and golden locks, gave him the name of *Tonatiuh*,
the "Sun." The Indians often pleased their fancies by fastening a *sobriquet*, or some characteristic epithet on the Spaniards. As Cortés was
always attended, on public occasions, by Doña Marina, or Malinche, as
she was called by the natives, they distinguished him by the same name.
By these epithets, originally bestowed in Tlascala, the two Spanish captains were popularly designated among the Indian nations.

While these events were passing, another embassy arrived from the
court of Mexico. It was charged, as usual, with a costly donative of embossed gold plate, and rich embroidered stuffs of cotton and feather-
work. The terms of the message might well argue a vacillating and timid
temper in the monarch, did they not mask a deeper policy. He now invited the Spaniards to his capital, with the assurance of a cordial welcome. He besought them to enter into no alliance with the base and
barbarous Tlascalans; and he invited them to take the route of the
friendly city of Cholula, where arrangements, according to his orders,
were made for their reception.[15]

The Tlascalans viewed with deep regret the general proposed visit to
Mexico. Their reports fully confirmed all he had before heard of the
power and ambition of Montezuma. His armies, they said, were spread
over every part of the continent. His capital was a place of great strength,
and as from its insular position, all communication could be easily cut
off with the adjacent country, the Spaniards, once entrapped there, would
be at his mercy. His policy, they represented, was as insidious, as his
ambition was boundless. "Trust not his fair words," they said, "his
courtesies, and his gifts. His professions are hollow, and his friendships
are false." When Cortés remarked, that he hoped to bring about a better

much more for the convenience of the clergy, than of the converts. See Camargo,
Hist. de Tlascala, MS.
[14] Ibid., MS.—Bernal Diaz, Hist. de la Conquista, cap. 74, 77.
    According to Camargo, the Tlascalans gave the Spanish commander three hundred
damsels to wait on Marina; and the kind treatment and instruction they received
led some of the chiefs to surrender their own daughters, "con propósito de que
si acoso algunas se empreñasen quedase entre ellos generacion de hombres tan
valientes y temidos."
[15] Bernal Diaz, Hist. de la Conquista, cap. 80.—Rel. Seg. de Cortés, ap. Lorenzana,
p. 60.—Martyr, De Orbe Novo, dec. 5, cap. 2.
    Cortés notices only one Aztec mission, while Diaz speaks of three. The former,
from brevity, falls so much short of the whole truth, and the latter, from forget-
fulness perhaps, goes so much beyond it, that it is not always easy to decide between
them. Diaz did not compile his narrative till some fifty years after the Conquest; a
lapse of time, which may excuse many errors, but must considerably impair our confidence in the minute accuracy of his details. A more intimate acquaintance with his
chronicle does not strengthen this confidence.

understanding between the emperor and them, they replied, it would be impossible; however smooth his words, he would hate them at heart.

They warmly protested, also, against the general's taking the route of Cholula. The inhabitants, not brave in the open field, were more dangerous from their perfidy and craft. They were Montezuma's tools, and would do his bidding. The Tlascalans seemed to combine with this distrust a superstitious dread of the ancient city, the headquarters of the religion of Anahuac. It was here that the god Quetzalcoatl held the pristine seat of his empire. His temple was celebrated throughout the land, and the priests were confidently believed to have the power, as they themselves boasted, of opening an inundation from the foundations of his shrine, which should bury their enemies in the deluge. The Tlascalans further reminded Cortés, that, while so many other and distant places had sent to him at Tlascala, to testify their good-will, and offer their allegiance to his sovereigns, Cholula, only six leagues distant, had done neither.—The last suggestion struck the general more forcibly than any of the preceding. He instantly despatched a summons to the city, requiring a formal tender of its submission.

Among the embassies from different quarters which had waited on the Spanish commander, while at Tlascala, was one from Ixtlilxochitl, son of the great Nezahualpilli, and an unsuccessful competitor with his elder brother—as noticed in a former part of our narrative—for the crown of Tezcuco.[16] Though defeated in his pretensions, he had obtained a part of the kingdom, over which he ruled with a deadly feeling of animosity towards his rival, and to Montezuma, who had sustained him. He now offered his services to Cortés, asking his aid, in return, to place him on the throne of his ancestors. The politic general returned such an answer to the aspiring young prince, as might encourage his expectations, and attach him to his interests. It was his aim to strengthen his cause, by attracting to himself every particle of disaffection that was floating through the land.

It was not long before deputies arrived from Cholula, profuse in their expressions of good-will, and inviting the presence of the Spaniards in their capital. The messengers were of low degree, far beneath the usual rank of ambassadors. This was pointed out by the Tlascalans; and Cortés regarded it as a fresh indignity. He sent in consequence a new summons, declaring, if they did not instantly send him a deputation of their principal men, he would deal with them as *rebels* to his own sovereign, the rightful lord of these realms![17] The menace had the desired effect.

[16] Ante, p. 170.

[17] "Si no viniessen, iria sobre ellos, y los destruiria, y procederia contra ellos como contra personas rebeldes; diciéndoles, como todas estas Partes, y otras muy mayores Tierras, y Señoríos eran de Vuestra Alteza." (Rel. Seg. de Cortés, ap. Lorenzana, p. 63.) "Rebellion" was a very convenient term, fastened in like manner by the countrymen of Cortés on the Moors, for defending the possessions which they had held for eight centuries in the Peninsula. It justified very rigorous reprisals.—(See the History of Ferdinand and Isabella, Part I. Chap. 13, et alibi.)

The Cholulans were not inclined to contest, at least, for the present, his magnificent pretensions. Another embassy appeared in the camp, consisting of some of the highest nobles; who repeated the invitation for the Spaniards to visit their city, and excused their own tardy appearance by apprehensions for their personal safety in the capital of their enemies. The explanation was plausible, and was admitted by Cortés.

The Tlascalans were now more than ever opposed to his projected visit. A strong Aztec force, they had ascertained, lay in the neighborhood of Cholula, and the people were actively placing their city in a posture of defence. They suspected some insidious scheme concerted by Montezuma to destroy the Spaniards.

These suggestions disturbed the mind of Cortés, but did not turn him from his purpose. He felt a natural curiosity to see the venerable city so celebrated in the history of the Indian nations. He had, besides, gone too far to recede, too far, at least, to do so without a show of apprehension, implying a distrust in his own resources, which could not fail to have a bad effect on his enemies, his allies, and his own men. After a brief consultation with his officers, he decided on the route to Cholula.[18]

It was now three weeks since the Spaniards had taken up their residence within the hospitable walls of Tlascala; and nearly six, since they entered her territory. They had been met on the threshold as an enemy, with the most determined hostility. They were now to part with the same people, as friends and allies; fast friends, who were to stand by them, side by side, through the whole of their arduous struggle. The result of their visit, therefore, was of the last importance; since on the coöperation of these brave and warlike republicans, greatly depended the ultimate success of the expedition.

[18] Rel. Seg. de Cortés, ap. Lorenzana, pp. 62, 63.—Oviedo, Hist. de las Ind., MS., lib. 33, cap. 4.—Ixtlilxochitl, Hist. Chich., MS., cap. 84.—Gomara, Crónica, cap. 58. —Martyr, De Orbe Novo, dec. 5, cap. 2.—Herrera, Hist. General, dec. 2, lib. 6, cap. 18.—Sahagun, Hist. de Nueva España, MS., lib. 12, cap 11.

CHAPTER VI

CITY OF CHOLULA—GREAT TEMPLE—MARCH TO CHOLULA—RECEP
TION OF THE SPANIARDS—CONSPIRACY DETECTED

1519

THE ancient city of Cholula, capital of the republic of that name, lay
nearly six leagues south of Tlascala, and about twenty east, or rather
southeast, of Mexico. It was said by Cortés to contain twenty thousand
houses within the walls, and as many more in the environs;[1] though now
dwindled to a population of less than sixteen thousand souls.[2] Whatever
was its real number of inhabitants, it was unquestionably, at the time of
the Conquest, one of the most populous and flourishing cities in New
Spain.

It was of great antiquity, and was founded by the primitive races
who overspread the land before the Aztecs.[3] We have few particulars of
its form of government, which seems to have been cast on a republican
model similar to that of Tlascala. This answered so well, that the state
maintained its independence down to a very late period, when, if not
reduced to vassalage by the Aztecs, it was so far under their control, as
to enjoy few of the benefits of a separate political existence. Their connection with Mexico brought the Cholulans into frequent collision with
their neighbors and kindred, the Tlascalans. But, although far superior
to them in refinement and the various arts of civilization, they were no
match in war for the bold mountaineers, the Swiss of Anahuac. The
Cholulan capital was the great commercial emporium of the plateau. The
inhabitants excelled in various mechanical arts, especially that of working in metals, the manufacture of cotton and agave cloths, and of a delicate kind of pottery, rivalling, it was said, that of Florence in beauty.[4]

[1] Rel. Seg., ap. Lorenzana, p. 67.
According to Las Casas, the place contained 30,000 *vecinos*, or about 150,000 inhabitants. (Brevissima Relatione della Distrutione dell' Indie Occidentale (Venetia,
1643).) This latter, being the smaller estimate, is *a priori* the most credible; especially—a rare occurrence—when in the pages of the good bishop of Chiapa.
[2] Humboldt, Essai Politique, tom. III. p. 159.
[3] Veytia carries back the foundation of the city to the Ulmecs, a people who preceded the Toltecs. (Hist. Antig., tom. I. cap. 13, 20.) As the latter, after occupying
the land several centuries, have left not a single written record, probably, of their
existence, it will be hard to disprove the licentiate's assertion,—still harder to prove
it.
[4] Herrera, Hist. General, dec. 2, lib. 7, cap. 1.

But such attention to the arts of a polished and peaceful community
naturally indisposed them to war, and disqualified them for coping with
those who made war the great business of life. The Cholulans were accused of effeminacy; and were less distinguished—it is the charge of
their rivals—by their courage, than their cunning.[5]

But the capital, so conspicuous for its refinement and its great antiquity, was even more venerable for the religious traditions which invested it. It was here that the god Quetzalcoatl paused in his passage to
the coast, and passed twenty years in teaching the Toltec inhabitants the
arts of civilization. He made them acquainted with better forms of government, and a more spiritualized religion, in which the only sacrifices
were the fruits and flowers of the season.[6] It is not easy to determine
what he taught, since his lessons have been so mingled with the licentious dogmas of his own priests, and the mystic commentaries of the
Christian missionary.[7] It is probable he was one of those rare and gifted
beings, who, dissipating the darkness of the age by the illumination of
their own genius, are deified by a grateful posterity, and placed among
the lights of heaven.

It was in honor of this benevolent deity, that the stupendous mound
was erected, on which the traveller still gazes with admiration as the
most colossal fabric in New Spain, rivalling in dimensions, and somewhat resembling in form, the pyramidal structures of ancient Egypt. The
date of its erection is unknown; for it was found there when the Aztecs
entered on the plateau. It had the form common to the Mexican *teocallis,*
that of a truncated pyramid, facing with its four sides the cardinal points,
and divided into the same number of terraces. Its original outlines,
however, have been effaced by the action of time and of the elements,
while the exuberant growth of shrubs and wild flowers, which have
mantled over its surface, give it the appearance of one of those symmetrical elevations thrown up by the caprice of nature, rather than by
the industry of man. It is doubtful, indeed, whether the interior be
not a natural hill, though it seems not improbable that it is an artificial
composition of stone and earth, deeply incrusted, as is certain, in every
part, with alternate strata of brick and clay.[8]

---

[5] Camargo, Hist. de Tlascala, MS.—Gomara, Crónica, cap. 58.—Torquemada,
Monarch. Ind., lib. 3, cap. 19.

[6] Veytia, Hist. Antig., tom. I. cap. 15, et seq.—Sahagun, Hist. de Nueva España,
lib. 1, cap. 5; lib. 3.

[7] Later divines have found in these teachings of the Toltec god, or high-priest, the
germs of some of the great mysteries of the Christian faith, as those of the Incarnation, and the Trinity, for example. In the teacher himself, they recognize no less a
person than St. Thomas, the Apostle! See the Dissertation of the irrefragable Dr.
Mier, with an edifying commentary by Señor Bustamante, ap. Sahagun. (Hist. de
Nueva España, tom. I. Suplemento.) The reader will find further particulars of this
matter in *Appendix, Part* 1, of this History.

[8] Such, on the whole, seems to be the judgment of M. de Humboldt, who has examined this interesting monument with his usual care. (Vues des Cordillères, p. 27,
et seq. Essai Politique, tom. II. p. 150, et seq.) The opinion derives strong confirma-

The perpendicular height of the pyramid is one hundred and seventy-seven feet. Its base is one thousand four hundred and twenty-three feet long, twice as long as that of the great pyramid of Cheops. It may give some idea of its dimensions to state, that its base, which is square, covers about forty-four acres, and the platform on its truncated summit embraces more than one. It reminds us of those colossal monuments of brick work, which are still seen in ruins on the banks of the Euphrates, and, in much higher preservation, on those of the Nile.[9]

On the summit stood a sumptuous temple, in which was the image of the mystic deity, "god of the air," with ebon features, unlike the fair complexion which he bore upon earth, wearing a mitre on his head waving with *plumes of fire*, with a resplendent collar of gold round his neck, pendants of mosaic turquoise in his ears, a jewelled sceptre in one hand, and a shield curiously painted, the emblem of his rule over the winds, in the other.[10] The sanctity of the place, hallowed by hoary tradition, and the magnificence of the temple and its services, made it an object of veneration throughout the land, and pilgrims from the furthest corners of Anahuac came to offer up their devotions at the shrine of Quetzalcoatl.[11] The number of these was so great, as to give an air of mendicity to the motley population of the city; and Cortés, struck with the novelty, tells us that he saw multitudes of beggars, such as are to be found in the enlightened capitals of Europe;[12]—a whimsical criterion of civilization, which must place our own prosperous land somewhat low in the scale.

Cholula was not the resort only of the indigent devotee. Many of the kindred races had temples of their own in the city, in the same manner as some Christian nations have in Rome, and each temple was provided with its own peculiar ministers for the service of the deity to whom it was consecrated. In no city was there seen such a concourse of priests, so many processions, such pomp of ceremonial, sacrifice, and religious

tion from the fact, that a road, cut some years since across the tumulus, laid open a large section of it, in which the alternate layers of brick and clay are distinctly visible. (Ibid., loc. cit.) The present appearance of this monument, covered over with the verdure and vegetable mould of centuries, excuses the skepticism of the more superficial traveller.

[9] Several of the pyramids of Egypt, and the ruins of Babylon, are, as is well known, of brick. An inscription on one of the former, indeed, celebrates this material as superior to stone. (Herodotus, Euterpe, sec. 136.)—Humboldt furnishes an apt illustration of the size of the Mexican *teocalli*, by comparing it to a mass of bricks covering a square four times as large as the *place* Vendôme, and of twice the height of the Louvre. Essai Politique, tom. II. p. 152.

[10] A minute account of the costume and insignia of Quetzalcoatl is given by father Sahagun, who saw the Aztec gods before the arm of the Christian convert had tumbled them from "their pride of place." See Hist. de Nueva España, lib. 1, cap. 3.

[11] They came from the distance of two hundred leagues, says Torquemada. Monarch. Ind., lib. 3, cap. 19.

[12] "Hay mucha gente pobre, y que piden entre los Ricos por las Calles, y por las Casas, y Mercados, como hacen los Pobres en España, y en otras partes que hay gente *de razon*." Rel. Seg., ap. Lorenzana, pp. 67, 68.

festivals. Cholula was, in short, what Mecca is among Mahometans, or Jerusalem among Christians; it was the Holy City of Anahuac.[13]

The religious rites were not performed, however, in the pure spirit originally prescribed by its tutelary deity. His altars, as well as those of the numerous Aztec gods, were stained with human blood; and six thousand victims *are said* to have been annually offered up at their sanguinary shrines![14] The great number of these may be estimated from the declaration of Cortés, that he counted four hundred towers in the city;[15] yet no temple had more than two, many only one. High above the rest rose the great "pyramid of Cholula," with its undying fires flinging their radiance far and wide over the capital, and proclaiming to the nations, that there was the mystic worship—alas! how corrupted by cruelty and superstition!—of the good deity who was one day to return and resume his empire over the land.

Nothing could be more grand than the view which met the eye from the area on the truncated summit of the pyramid. Toward the west stretched that bold barrier of porphyritic rock which nature has reared around the Valley of Mexico, with the huge Popocatepetl and Iztaccihuatl standing like two colossal sentinels to guard the entrance to the enchanted region. Far away to the east was seen the conical head of Orizaba soaring high into the clouds, and nearer, the barren, though beautifully shaped Sierra de Malinche, throwing its broad shadows over the plains of Tlascala. Three of these are volcanoes higher than the highest mountain peak in Europe, and shrouded in snows which never melt under the fierce sun of the tropics. At the foot of the spectator lay the sacred city of Cholula, with its bright towers and pinnacles sparkling in the sun, reposing amidst gardens and verdant groves, which then thickly studded the cultivated environs of the capital. Such was the magnificent prospect which met the gaze of the Conquerors, and may still, with slight change, meet that of the modern traveller, as from the platform of the great pyramid his eye wanders over the fairest portion of the beautiful plateau of Puebla.[16]

[13] Torquemada, Monarch. Ind., lib. 3, cap. 19.—Gomara, Crónica, cap. 61.—Camargo, Hist. de Tlascala, MS.

[14] Herrera, Hist. General, dec. 2, lib. 7, cap. 2.—Torquemada, Monarch. Ind., ubi supra.

[15] "É certifico á Vuestra Alteza, que yo conté desde una Mezquita quatrocientas, y tantas Torres en la dicha Ciudad, y todas son de Mezquitas." Rel. Seg., ap. Lorenzana, p. 67.

[16] The city of Puebla de los Angeles was founded by the Spaniards soon after the Conquest, on the site of an insignificant village in the territory of Cholula, a few miles to the east of that capital. It is, perhaps, the most considerable city in New Spain, after Mexico itself, which it rivals in beauty. It seems to have inherited the religious preëminence of the ancient Cholula, being distinguished, like her, for the number and splendor of its churches, the multitude of its clergy, and the magnificence of its ceremonies and festivals. These are fully displayed in the pages of travellers, who have passed through the place on the usual route from Vera Cruz to the capital. (See in particular, Bullock's Mexico, vol. I. chap. 6.) The environs of Cholula, still irrigated as in the days of the Aztecs, are equally remarkable for the

But it is time to return to Tlascala. On the appointed morning, the Spanish army took up its march to Mexico by the way of Cholula. It was followed by crowds of the citizens, filled with admiration at the intrepidity of men who, so few in number, would venture to brave the great Montezuma in his capital. Yet an immense body of warriors offered to share the dangers of the expedition; but Cortés, while he showed his gratitude for their good-will, selected only six thousand of the volunteers to bear him company.[17] He was unwilling to encumber himself with an unwieldy force that might impede his movements; and probably did not care to put himself so far in the power of allies, whose attachment was too recent to afford sufficient guaranty for their fidelity.

After crossing some rough and hilly ground, the army entered on the wide plain which spreads out for miles around Cholula. At the elevation of more than six thousand feet above the sea, they beheld the rich products of various climes growing side by side, fields of towering maize, the juicy aloe, the *chilli* or Aztec pepper, and large plantations of the cactus, on which the brilliant cochineal is nourished. Not a rood of land but was under cultivation;[18] and the soil—an uncommon thing on the table-land—was irrigated by numerous streams and canals, and well shaded by woods, that have disappeared before the rude axe of the Spaniards. Towards evening, they reached a small stream, on the banks of which Cortés determined to take up his quarters for the night, being unwilling to disturb the tranquillity of the city by introducing so large a force into it at an unseasonable hour.

Here he was soon joined by a number of Cholulan caciques and their attendants, who came to view and welcome the strangers. When they saw their Tlascalan enemies in the camp, however, they exhibited signs of displeasure, and intimated an apprehension that their presence in the town might occasion disorder. The remonstrance seemed reasonable to Cortés, and he accordingly commanded his allies to remain in their present quarters, and to join him as he left the city on the way to Mexico.

On the following morning, he made his entrance at the head of his army into Cholula, attended by no other Indians than those from Cempoalla, and a handful of Tlascalans, to take charge of the baggage. His allies, at parting, gave him many cautions respecting the people he was to visit, who, while they affected to despise them as a nation of traders,

---

fruitfulness of the soil. The best wheat lands, according to a very respectable auth.ority, yield in the proportion of eighty for one. Ward's Mexico, vol. II. p. 270.—See, also, Humboldt, Essai Politique, tom. II. p. 158; tom. IV. p. 330.

[17] According to Cortés, a hundred thousand men offered their services on this occasion! "E puesto que yo ge lo defendiesse, y rogué que no fuessen, porque no habia necesidad, todavía me siguiéron hasta cien mil Hombres muy bien aderezados de Guerra, y llegáron con migo hasta dos leguas de la Ciudad: y desde allí, por mucha importunidad mia se bolviéron, aunque todavía quedáron en mi compañía hasta cinco ó seis mil de ellos." (Rel. Seg., ap. Lorenzana, p. 64.) This, which must have been nearly the whole fighting force of the republic, does not startle Oviedo, (Hist. de las Ind., MS., cap. 4,) nor Gomara, Crónica, cap. 58.

[18] The words of the *Conquistador* are yet stronger. "Ni un *palmo* de tierra hay, que no esté labrada." Rel. Seg., ap. Lorenzana, p. 67.

employed the dangerous arms of perfidy and cunning. As the troops drew near the city, the road was lined with swarms of people of both sexes and every age, old men tottering with infirmity, women with children in their arms, all eager to catch a glimpse of the strangers, whose persons, weapons, and horses were objects of intense curiosity to eyes which had not hitherto ever encountered them in battle. The Spaniards, in turn, were filled with admiration at the aspect of the Cholulans, much superior in dress and general appearance to the nations they had hitherto seen. They were particularly struck with the costume of the higher classes, who wore fine embroidered mantles, resembling the graceful *albornoz*, or Moorish cloak, in their texture and fashion.[19] They showed the same delicate taste for flowers as the other tribes of the plateau, decorating their persons with them, and tossing garlands and bunches among the soldiers. An immense number of priests mingled with the crowd, swinging their aromatic censers, while music from various kinds of instruments gave a lively welcome to the visitors, and made the whole scene one of gay, bewildering enchantment. If it did not have the air of a triumphal procession as much as at Tlascala, where the melody of instruments was drowned by the shouts of the multitude, it gave a quiet assurance of hospitality and friendly feeling not less grateful.

The Spaniards were also struck with the cleanliness of the city, the width and great regularity of the streets, which seemed to have been laid out on a settled plan, with the solidity of the houses, and the number and size of the pyramidal temples. In the court of one of these, and its surrounding buildings, they were quartered.[20]

They were soon visited by the principal lords of the place, who seemed solicitous to provide them with accommodations. Their table was plentifully supplied, and, in short, they experienced such attentions as were calculated to dissipate their suspicions, and made them impute those of their Tlascalan friends to prejudice and old national hostility.

In a few days the scene changed. Messengers arrived from Montezuma,

---

[19] "Los honrados ciudadanos de ella todos trahen *albornoces,* encima de la otra ropa, aunque son diferenciados de los de África, porque tienen maneras; pero en la hechura y tela y los rapacejos son muy semejables." Rel. Seg. de Cortés, ap. Lorenzana, p. 67.

[20] Ibid., p. 67.—Ixtlilxochitl, Hist. Chich., MS., cap. 84.—Oviedo, Hist. de las Ind., MS., lib. 33, cap. 4.—Bernal Diaz, Hist. de la Conquista, cap. 82.

The Spaniards compared Cholula to the beautiful Valladolid, according to Herrera, whose description of the entry is very animated. "Saliéronle otro dia á recibir mas de diez mil ciudadanos en diversas tropas, con rosas, flores, pan, aves, i frutas, i mucha música. Llegaba vn esquadron á dar la bien llegada á Hernando Cortés, i con buena órden se iba apartando, dando lugar á que otro llegase. . . . . . . En llegando á la ciudad, que pareció mucho á los Castellanos, en el asiento, i perspectiva, á Valladolid, salió la demas gente, quedando mui espantada de ver las figuras, talles, i armas de los Castellanos. Saliéron los sacerdotes con vestiduras blancas, como sobrepellices, i algunas cerradas por delante, los braços defuera, confluecos de algodon en las orillas. Unos llevaban figuras de ídolos en las manos, otros sahumerios; otros tocaban cornetas, atabalejos, i diversas músicas, i todos iban cantando, i llegaban á encensar á los Castellanos. Con esta pompa entráron en Chulula." Hist. General, dec. 2, lib. 7, cap. 1.

who, after a short and unpleasant intimation to Cortés that his approach occasioned much disquietude to their master, conferred separately with the Mexican ambassadors still in the Castilian camp, and then departed, taking one of the latter along with them. From this time, the deportment of their Cholulan hosts underwent a visible alteration. They did not visit the quarters as before, and, when invited to do so, excused themselves on pretence of illness. The supply of provisions was stinted, on the ground that they were short of maize. These symptoms of alienation, independently of temporary embarrassment, caused serious alarm in the breast of Cortés, for the future. His apprehensions were not allayed by the reports of the Cempoallans, who told him, that in wandering round the city, they had seen several streets barricaded, the *azoteas,* or flat roofs of the houses, loaded with huge stones and other missiles, as if preparatory to an assault, and in some places they had found holes covered over with branches, and upright stakes planted within, as if to embarrass the movements of the cavalry.[21] Some Tlascalans coming in, also, from their camp, informed the general, that a great sacrifice, mostly of children, had been offered up in a distant quarter of the town, to propitiate the favor of the gods, apparently for some intended enterprise. They added, that they had seen numbers of the citizens leaving the city with their women and children, as if to remove them to a place of safety. These tidings confirmed the worst suspicions of Cortés, who had no doubt that some hostile scheme was in agitation. If he had felt any, a discovery by Marina, the good angel of the expedition, would have turned these doubts into certainty.

The amiable manners of the Indian girl had won her the regard of the wife of one of the caciques, who repeatedly urged Marina to visit her house, darkly intimating that in this way she would escape the fate that awaited the Spaniards. The interpreter, seeing the importance of obtaining further intelligence at once, pretended to be pleased with the proposal, and affected, at the same time, great discontent with the white men, by whom she was detained in captivity. Thus throwing the credulous Cholulan off her guard, Marina gradually insinuated herself into her confidence, so far as to draw from her a full account of the conspiracy.

It originated, she said, with the Aztec emperor, who had sent rich bribes to the great caciques, and to her husband among others, to secure them in his views. The Spaniards were to be assaulted as they marched out of the capital, when entangled in its streets, in which numerous impediments had been placed to throw the cavalry into disorder. A force of twenty thousand Mexicans was already quartered at no great distance

---

[21] Cortés, indeed, noticed these same alarming appearances on his entering the city, thus suggesting the idea of a premeditated treachery. "Y en el camino topámos muchas señales, de las que los Naturales de esta Provincia nos habian dicho: por que hallámos el camino real cerrado, y hecho otro, y algunos hoyos aunque no muchos, y algunas calles de la ciudad tapiadas, y muchas piedras en todas las Azoteas. Y con esto nos hiciéron estar mas sobre aviso, y á mavor recaudo." Rel. Seg., ap. Lorenzana, ᵃᵖ. 64.

from the city, to support the Cholulans in the assault. It was confidently expected that the Spaniards, thus embarrassed in their movements, would fall an easy prey to the superior strength of their enemy. A sufficient number of prisoners was to be reserved to grace the sacrifices of Cholula; the rest were to be led in fetters to the capital of Montezuma.

While this conversation was going on, Marina occupied herself with putting up such articles of value and wearing apparel as she proposed to take with her in the evening, when she could escape unnoticed from the Spanish quarters to the house of her Cholulan friend, who assisted her in the operation. Leaving her visitor thus employed, Marina found an opportunity to steal away for a few moments, and, going to the general's apartment, disclosed to him her discoveries. He immediately caused the cacique's wife to be seized, and, on examination, she fully confirmed the statement of his Indian mistress.

The intelligence thus gathered by Cortés filled him with the deepest alarm. He was fairly taken in the snare. To fight or to fly seemed equally difficult. He was in a city of enemies, where every house might be converted into a fortress, and where such embarrassments were thrown in the way, as might render the manœuvres of his artillery and horse nearly impracticable. In addition to the wily Cholulans, he must cope, under all these disadvantages, with the redoubtable warriors of Mexico. He was like a traveller who has lost his way in the darkness among precipices, where any step may dash him to pieces, and where to retreat or to advance is equally perilous.

He was desirous to obtain still further confirmation and particulars of the conspiracy. He accordingly induced two of the priests in the neighborhood, one of them a person of much influence in the place, to visit his quarters. By courteous treatment, and liberal largesses of the rich presents he had received from Montezuma,—thus turning his own gifts against the giver,—he drew from them a full confirmation of the previous report. The emperor had been in a state of pitiable vacillation since the arrival of the Spaniards. His first orders to the Cholulans were, to receive the strangers kindly. He had recently consulted his oracles anew, and obtained for answer, that Cholula would be the grave of his enemies; for the gods would be sure to support him in avenging the sacrilege offered to the Holy City. So confident were the Aztecs of success, that numerous manacles, or poles with thongs which served as such, were already in the place to secure the prisoners.

Cortés, now feeling himself fully possessed of the facts, dismissed the priests, with injunctions of secrecy, scarcely necessary. He told them it was his purpose to leave the city on the following morning, and requested that they would induce some of the principal caciques to grant him an interview in his quarters. He then summoned a council of his officers, though, as it seems, already determined as to the course he was to take.

The members of the council were differently affected by the startling intelligence, according to their different characters. The more timid, disheartened by the prospect of obstacles which seemed to multiply as they drew nearer the Mexican capital, were for retracing their steps, and seeking shelter in the friendly city of Tlascala. Others, more persevering, but prudent, were for taking the more northerly route, originally recommended by their allies. The greater part supported the general, who was ever of opinion that they had no alternative but to advance. Retreat would be ruin. Half-way measures were scarcely better; and would infer a timidity which must discredit them with both friend and foe. Their true policy was to rely on themselves; to strike such a blow, as should intimidate their enemies, and show them that the Spaniards were as incapable of being circumvented by artifice, as of being crushed by weight of numbers and courage in the open field.

When the caciques, persuaded by the priests, appeared before Cortés, he contented himself with gently rebuking their want of hospitality, and assured them the Spaniards would be no longer a burden to their city, as he proposed to leave it early on the following morning. He requested, moreover, that they would furnish a reinforcement of two thousand men to transport his artillery and baggage. The chiefs, after some consultation, acquiesced in a demand which might in some measure favor their own designs.

On their departure, the general summoned the Aztec ambassadors before him. He briefly acquainted them with his detection of the treacherous plot to destroy his army, the contrivance of which he said, was imputed to their master, Montezuma. It grieved him much, he added, to find the emperor implicated in so nefarious a scheme, and that the Spaniards must now march as enemies against the prince, whom they had hoped to visit as a friend.

The ambassadors, with earnest protestations, asserted their entire ignorance of the conspiracy; and their belief that Montezuma was equally innocent of a crime, which they charged wholly on the Cholulans. It was clearly the policy of Cortés to keep on good terms with the Indian monarch; to profit as long as possible by his good offices; and to avail himself of his fancied security—such feelings of security as the general could inspire him with—to cover his own future operations. He affected to give credit, therefore, to the assertion of the envoys, and declared his unwillingness to believe, that a monarch, who had rendered the Spaniards so many friendly offices, would now consummate the whole by a deed of such unparalleled baseness. The discovery of their twofold duplicity, he added, sharpened his resentment against the Cholulans, on whom he would take such vengeance as should amply requite the injuries done both to Montezuma and the Spaniards. He then dismissed the ambassadors, taking care, notwithstanding this show of confidence, to place a strong guard over them, to prevent communication with the citizens.[22]

[22] Bernal Diaz, Hist. de la Conquista, cap. 83.—Gomara, Crónica, cap. 59.—Rel. Seg. de Cortés, ap. Lorenzana, p 65.—Torquemada, Monarch. Ind., lib. 4, cap 39, —Oviedo, Hist. de las Ind., MS., lib. 83, cap. 4.—Martyr, De Orbe Novo, dec. 5, cap. 2.—Herrera, Hist. General, dec. 2, lib. 7, cap. 1.—Argensola, Anares, lib 1 cap. 85

That night was one of deep anxiety to the army. The ground they stood on seemed loosening beneath their feet, and any moment might be the one marked for their destruction. Their vigilant general took all possible precautions for their safety, increasing the number of the sentinels, and posting his guns in such a manner as to protect the approaches to the camp. His eyes, it may well be believed, did not close during the night. Indeed, every Spaniard lay down in his arms, and every horse stood saddled and bridled, ready for instant service. But no assault was meditated by the Indians, and the stillness of the hour was undisturbed except by the occasional sounds heard in a populous city, even when buried in slumber, and by the hoarse cries of the priests from the turrets of the *teocallis*, proclaiming through their trumpets the watches of the night.[23]

[23] "Las horas de la noche las regulaban por las estrellas, y tocaban los ministros del templo que estaban destinados para este fin, ciertos instrumentos como vocinas, con que hacian conocer al pueblo el tiempo." Gama, Descripcion, Parte i, p. 14.

CHAPTER VII

TERRIBLE MASSACRE—TRANQUILLITY RESTORED—REFLECTIONS ON
THE MASSACRE—FURTHER PROCEEDINGS—ENVOYS FROM MONTEZUMA

1519

WITH the first streak of morning light, Cortés was seen on horseback,
directing the movements of his little band. The strength of his forces he
drew up in the great square or court, surrounded partly by buildings, as
before noticed, and in part by a high wall. There were three gates of
entrance, at each of which he placed a strong guard. The rest of his
troops, with his great guns, he posted without the inclosure, in such a
manner as to command the avenues and secure those within from interruption in their bloody work. Orders had been sent the night before to
the Tlascalan chiefs to hold themselves ready, at a concerted signal, to
march into the city and join the Spaniards.

The arrangements were hardly completed, before the Cholulan caciques appeared, leading a body of levies, *tamanes*, even more numerous
than had been demanded. They were marched, at once, into the square,
commanded, as we have seen, by the Spanish infantry which was drawn
up under the walls. Cortés then took some of the caciques aside. With a
stern air, he bluntly charged them with the conspiracy, showing that he
was well acquainted with all the particulars. He had visited their city,
he said, at the invitation of their emperor; had come as a friend; had
respected the inhabitants and their property; and, to avoid all cause of
umbrage, had left a great part of his forces without the walls. They had
received him with a show of kindness and hospitality, and, reposing on
this, he had been decoyed into the snare, and found this kindness only
a mask to cover the blackest perfidy.

The Cholulans were thunderstruck at the accusation. An undefined
awe crept over them, as they gazed on the mysterious strangers, and felt
themselves in the presence of beings who seemed to have the power of
reading the thoughts scarcely formed in their bosoms. There was no use
in prevarication or denial before such judges. They confessed the whole,
and endeavored to excuse themselves by throwing the blame on Montezuma. Cortés, assuming an air of higher indignation at this, assured them
that the pretence should not serve, since, even if well founded, it would
be no justification; and he would now make such an example of them
for their treachery, that the report of it should ring throughout the wide
borders of Anahuac!

The fatal signal, the discharge of an arquebuse, was then given. In an instant every musket and crossbow was levelled at the unfortunate Cholulans in the court-yard, and a frightful volley poured into them as they stood crowded together like a herd of deer in the centre. They were taken by surprise, for they had not heard the preceding dialogue with the chiefs. They made scarcely any resistance to the Spaniards, who followed up the discharge of their pieces by rushing on them with their swords; and, as the half-naked bodies of the natives afforded no protection, they hewed them down with as much ease as the reaper mows down the ripe corn in harvest time. Some endeavored to scale the walls, but only afforded a surer mark to the arquebusiers and archers. Others threw themselves into the gateways, but were received on the long pikes of the soldiers who guarded them. Some few had better luck in hiding themselves under the heaps of slain with which the ground was soon loaded.

While this work of death was going on, the countrymen of the slaughtered Indians, drawn together by the noise of the massacre, had commenced a furious assault on the Spaniards from without. But Cortés had placed his battery of heavy guns in a position that commanded the avenues, and swept off the files of the assailants as they rushed on. In the intervals between the discharges, which, in the imperfect state of the science in that day, were much longer than in ours, he forced back the press by charging with the horse into the midst. The steeds, the guns, the weapons of the Spaniards were all new to the Cholulans. Notwithstanding the novelty of the terrific spectacle, the flash of fire-arms mingling with the deafening roar of the artillery as its thunders reverberated among the buildings, the despairing Indians pushed on to take the places of their fallen comrades.

While this fierce struggle was going forward, the Tlascalans, hearing the concerted signal, had advanced with quick pace into the city. They had bound, by order of Cortés, wreaths of sedge round their heads, that they might the more surely be distinguished from the Cholulans.[1] Coming up in the very heat of the engagement, they fell on the defenceless rear of the townsmen, who, trampled down under the heels of the Castilian cavalry on one side, and galled by their vindictive enemies on the other, could no longer maintain their ground. They gave way, some taking refuge in the nearest buildings, which, being partly of wood, were speedily set on fire. Others fled to the temples. One strong party, with a number of priests at its head, got possession of the great *teocalli*. There was a vulgar tradition, already alluded to, that, on removal of part of the walls, the god would send forth an inundation to overwhelm his enemies. The superstitious Cholulans with great difficulty succeeded in wrenching away some of the stones in the walls of the edifice. But dust,

---

[1] "Usáron los de Tlaxcalla de un aviso muy bueno y les dió Hernando Cortés porque fueran conocidos y no morir entre los enemigos por yerro, porque sus armas y divisas eran casi de una manera; . . . . . y ansí se pusiéron en las cabezas unas guirnaldas de esparto á manera de torzales, y con esto eran conocidos los de nuestra parcialidad que no fué pequeño aviso." Camargo, Hist. de Tlascala, MS.

not water, followed. Their false god deserted them in the hour of need. In despair they flung themselves into the wooden turrets that crowned the temple, and pouring down stones, javelins, and burning arrows on the Spaniards, as they climbed the great staircase, which, by a flight of one hundred and twenty steps, scaled the face of the pyramid. But the fiery shower fell harmless on the steel bonnets of the Christians, while they availed themselves of the burning shafts to set fire to the wooden citadel, which was speedily wrapt in flames. Still the garrison held out, and though quarter, *it is said,* was offered, only one Cholulan availed himself of it. The rest threw themselves headlong from the parapet, or perished miserably in the flames.[2]

All was now confusion and uproar in the fair city which had so lately reposed in security and peace. The groans of the dying, the frantic supplications of the vanquished for mercy, were mingled with the loud battle-cries of the Spaniards as they rode down their enemy, and with the shrill whistle of the Tlascalans, who gave full scope to the long cherished rancor of ancient rivalry. The tumult was still further swelled by the incessant rattle of musketry, and the crash of falling timbers, which sent up a volume of flame that outshone the ruddy light of morning, making all together a hideous confusion of sights and sounds, that converted the Holy City into a Pandemonium. As resistance slackened, the victors broke into the houses and sacred places, plundering them of whatever valuables they contained, plate, jewels, which were found in some quantity, wearing apparel and provisions, the two last coveted even more than the former by the simple Tlascalans, thus facilitating a division of the spoil much to the satisfaction of their Christian confederates. Amidst this universal license, it is worthy of remark, the commands of Cortés were so far respected that no violence was offered to women or children, though these, as well as numbers of the men, were made prisoners to be swept into slavery by the Tlascalans.[3] These scenes of violence had lasted some hours, when Cortés, moved by the entreaties of some Cholulan chiefs, who had been reserved from the massacre, backed by the prayers of the Mexican envoys, consented, out of regard, as he said, to the latter, the representatives of Montezuma, to call off the soldiers, and put a stop, as well as he could, to further outrage. Two of the caciques were, also, permitted to go to their countrymen with assurances of pardon and protection to all who would return to their obedience.

These measures had their effect. By the joint efforts of Cortés and the caciques, the tumult was with much difficulty appeased. The assailants, Spaniards and Indians, gathered under their respective banners, and the Cholulans, relying on the assurance of their chiefs, gradually returned to their homes.

---

[2] Camargo, Hist. de Tlascala, MS.—Oviedo, Hist. de las Ind., MS., lib. 33, cap. 4, 45.—Torquemada, Monarch. Ind., lib. 4, cap. 40.—Ixtlilxochitl, Hist. Chich., MS., cap. 84.—Gomara, Crónica, cap. 60.

[3] "Matáron casi seis mil personas sin tocar á niños ni mugeres, porque así se les ordenó." Herrera, Hist. General, dec. 2, lib. 7, cap. 2.

The first act of Cortés was, to prevail on the Tlascalan chiefs to lib‹ erate their captives.[4] Such was their deference to the Spanish commander that they acquiesced, though not without murmurs, contenting themselves, as they best could, with the rich spoil rifled from the Cholulans, consisting of various luxuries long since unknown in Tlascala. His next care was to cleanse the city from its loathsome impurities, particularly from the dead bodies which lay festering in heaps in the streets and great square. The general, in his letter to Charles the Fifth, admits three thousand slain, most accounts say six, and some swell the amount yet higher. As the eldest and principal cacique was among the number, Cortés assisted the Cholulans in installing a successor in his place.[5] By these pacific measures confidence was gradually restored. The people in the environs, reassured, flocked into the capital to supply the place of the diminished population. The markets were again opened; and the usual avocations of an orderly, industrious community were resumed. Still, the long piles of black and smouldering ruins proclaimed the hurricane which had so lately swept over the city, and the walls surrounding the scene of slaughter in the great square, which were standing more than fifty years after the event, told the sad tale of the Massacre of Cholula.[6]

[4] Bernal Diaz, Hist. de la Conquista, cap. 83.—Ixtlilxochitl, Hist. Chich., MS., ubi supra.
[5] Bernal Diaz, Hist. de la Conquista, cap. 83.
The descendants of the principal Cholulan cacique are living at this day in Puebla, according to Bustamante. See Gomara, Crónica, trad. de Chimalpain, (México, 1826,) tom. I. p. 98, nota.
[6] Rel. Seg. de Cortés, ap. Lorenzana, 66.—Camargo, Hist. de Tlascala, MS.—Ixtlilxochitl, Hist. Chich., MS., cap. 84.—Oviedo, Hist. de las Ind., MS., lib. 33, cap. 4. 45.—Bernal Diaz, Hist. de la Conquista, cap. 83.—Gomara, Crónica, cap. 60.—Sahagun, Hist. de Nueva España, MS., lib. 12, cap. 11.
Las Casas, in his printed treatise on the Destruction of the Indies, garnishes his account of these transactions with some additional and rather startling particulars. According to him, Cortés caused a hundred or more of the caciques to be impaled or roasted at the stake! He adds the report, that, while the massacre in the courtyard was going on, the Spanish general repeated a scrap of an old *romance*, describing Nero as rejoicing over the burning ruins of Rome;

"Mira Nero de Tarpeya,
Á Roma como se ardia.
Gritos dan niños y viejos,
Y él de nada se dolia."
(Brevísima Relacion, p. 46.)

This is the first instance, I suspect, on record, of any person being ambitious of finding a parallel for himself in that emperor! Bernal Diaz, who had seen "the interminable narrative," as he calls it, of Las Casas, treats it with great contempt. His own version—one of those chiefly followed in the text—was corroborated by the report of the missionaries, who, after the Conquest, visited Cholula, and investigated the affair with the aid of the priests and several old survivors who had witnessed it. It is confirmed in its substantial details by the other contemporary accounts. The excellent bishop of Chiapa wrote with the avowed object of moving the sympathies of his countrymen in behalf of the oppressed natives; a generous object, certainly, but one that has too often warped his judgment from the strict line of historic impartiality. He was not an eyewitness of the transactions in New Spain, and was much too willing to receive whatever would make for his case, and te

This passage in their history is one of those that have left a dark stain on the memory of the Conquerors. Nor can we contemplate at this day, without a shudder, the condition of this fair and flourishing capital thus invaded in its privacy, and delivered over to the excesses of a rude and ruthless soldiery. But, to judge the action fairly, we must transport ourselves to the age when it happened. The difficulty that meets us in the outset is, to find a justification of the right of conquest, at all. But it should be remembered, that religious infidelity, at this period, and till a much later, was regarded—no matter whether founded on ignorance or education, whether hereditary or acquired, heretical or Pagan—as a sin to be punished with fire and faggot in this world, and eternal suffering in the next. This doctrine, monstrous as it is, was the creed of the Romish, in other words, of the Christian Church,—the basis of the Inquisition, and of those other species of religious persecutions, which have stained the annals, at some time or other, of nearly every nation in Christendom.[7] Under this code, the territory of the heathen, wherever found, was regarded as a sort of religious waif, which, in default of a legal proprietor, was claimed and taken possession of by the Holy See, and as such was freely given away by the head of the Church, to any temporal potentate whom he pleased, that would assume the burden of conquest.[8] Thus, Alexander the Sixth, generously granted a large portion of the Western

"over-red," if I may so say, his argument with such details of blood and slaughter, as, from their very extravagance, carry their own refutation with them.

[7] For an illustration of the above remark the reader is referred to the closing pages of chap. 7, Part II., of the "History of Ferdinand and Isabella," where I have taken some pains to show how deep settled were these convictions in Spain, at the period with which we are now occupied. The world had gained little in liberality since the age of Dante, who could coolly dispose of the great and good of Antiquity in one of the circles of Hell, because—no fault of theirs, certainly—they had come into the world too soon. The memorable verses, like many others of the immortal bard, are a proof at once of the strength and weakness of the human understanding. They may be cited as a fair exponent of the popular feeling at the beginning of the sixteenth century.

> "Ch' ei non peccaro, e, s'egli hanno mercedi,
>   Non basta, *perch'* e' *non ebber battesmo,*
>   Ch' è porta della fede che tu credi.
> E, se furon dinanzi al Cristianesmo,
>   Non adorar debitamente Dio;
>   E di questi cotai son io medesmo
> Per tai difetti, e non per altro rio,
>   Semo perduti, e sol di tanto offesi
>   Che sanza speme vivemo in disio."

INFERNO, canto 4.

[8] It is in the same spirit that the laws of Oleron, the maritime code of so high authority in the Middle Ages, abandon the property of the infidel, in common with that of pirates, as fair spoil to the true believer! "S'ilz sont pyrates, pilleurs, ou escumeurs de mer, ou Turcs, *et autres contraires et ennemis de nostredicte foy catholicque,* chascun peut prendre sur telles manieres de gens, *comme sur chiens, et peut l'on les desrobber et spolier de lurs bins sans pugnition.* C'est le jugement." Jugemens d'Oleron. Art. 45, ap. Collection de Lois Maritimes, par J. M. Pardessus, (ed. Paris, 1828,) tom. I. p. 351.

hemisphere to the Spaniards, and of the Eastern to the Portuguese. These lofty pretensions of the successors of the humble fisherman of Galilee, far from being nominal, were acknowledged and appealed to as conclusive in controversies between nations.[9]

With the right of conquest, thus conferred, came, also, the obligation, on which it may be said to have been founded, to retrieve the nations sitting in darkness from eternal perdition. This obligation was acknowledged by the best and the bravest, the gownsman in his closet, the missionary, and the warrior in the crusade. However much it may have been debased by temporal motives and mixed up with worldly considerations of ambition and avarice, it was still active in the mind of the Christian conqueror. We have seen how far paramount it was to every calculation of personal interest in the breast of Cortés. The concession of the Pope, then, founded on, and enforcing, the imperative duty of conversion,[10] was the assumed basis—and, in the apprehension of that age, a sound one—of the right of conquest.[11]

[9] The famous bull of partition became the basis of the treaty of Tordesillas, by which the Castilian and Portuguese governments determined the boundary line of their respective discoveries; a line that secured the vast empire of Brazil to the latter, which from priority of occupation should have belonged to their rivals. See the History of Ferdinand and Isabella, Part I., chap. 18; Part II., chap. 9,—the closing pages of each.

[10] It is the condition, unequivocally expressed and reiterated, on which Alexander VI., in his famous bulls of May 3d and 4th, 1493, conveys to Ferdinand and Isabella full and absolute right over all such territories in the Western World, as may not have been previously occupied by Christian princes. See these precious documents, *in extenso*, apud Navarrete, Colleccion de los Viages y Descubrimientos, (Madrid, 1825,) tom. II. Nos. 17, 18.

[11] The ground on which Protestant nations assert a natural right to the fruits of their discoveries in the New World is very different. They consider that the earth was intended for cultivation; and that Providence never designed that hordes of wandering savages should hold a territory far more than necessary for their own maintenance, to the exclusion of civilized man. Yet it may be thought, as far as improvement of the soil is concerned, that this argument would afford us but an indifferent tenure for much of our own unoccupied and uncultivated territory, far exceeding what is demanded for our present or prospective support. As to a right founded on difference of civilization, this is obviously a still more uncertain criterion. It is to the credit of our Puritan ancestors, that they did not avail themselves of any such interpretation of the law of nature, and still less rely on the powers conceded by King James' patent, asserting rights as absolute, nearly, as those claimed by the Roman See. On the contrary, they established their title to the soil by fair purchase of the Aborigines; thus forming an honorable contrast to the policy pursued by too many of the settlers on the American continents. It should be remarked, that, whatever difference of opinion may have subsisted between the Roman Catholic,—or rather the Spanish and Portuguese nations,—and the rest of Europe, in regard to the true foundation of their titles in a moral view, they have always been content, in their controversies with one another, to rest them exclusively on priority of discovery. For a brief view of the discussion, see Vattel, (Droit des Gens, sec. 209,) and especially Kent, (Commentaries on American Law, vol. III. lec. 51,) where it is handled with much perspicuity and eloquence. The argument, as founded on the law of nations, may be found in the celebrated case of Johnson *v.* McIntosh. (Wheaton, Reports of Cases in the Supreme Court of the United States, vol. VIII. p. 543, et seq.) If it were not treating a grave discussion too lightly, I should crave leave to refer the reader to the renowned Diedrich Knickerbocker's

This right could not, indeed, be construed to authorize any unnecessary act of violence to the natives. The present expedition, up to the period of its history at which we are now arrived, had probably been stained with fewer of such acts than almost any similar enterprise of the Spanish discoveries in the New World. Throughout the campaign, Cortés had prohibited all wanton injuries to the natives, in person or property, and had punished the perpetrators of them with exemplary severity. He had been faithful to his friends, and, with perhaps a single exception, not unmerciful to his foes. Whether from policy or principle, it should be recorded to his credit; though, like every sagacious mind, he may have felt, that principle and policy go together.

He had entered Cholula as a friend, at the invitation of the Indian emperor, who had a real, if not avowed, control over the state. He had been received as a friend, with every demonstration of good-will; when, without any offence of his own or his followers, he found they were to be the victims of an insidious plot,—that they were standing on a mine which might be sprung at any moment, and bury them all in its ruins. His safety, as he truly considered, left no alternative but to anticipate the blow of his enemies. Yet who can doubt that the punishment thus inflicted was excessive,—that the same end might have been attained by directing the blow against the guilty chiefs, instead of letting it fall on the ignorant rabble, who but obeyed the commands of their masters? But when was it ever seen, that fear, armed with power, was scrupulous in the exercise of it? or that the passions of a fierce soldiery, inflamed by conscious injuries, could be regulated in the moment of explosion?

We shall, perhaps, pronounce more impartially on the conduct of the Conquerors, if we compare it with that of our own contemporaries under somewhat similar circumstances. The atrocities at Cholula were not so bad as those inflicted on the descendants of these very Spaniards, in the late war of the Peninsula, by the most polished nations of our time; by the British at Badajoz, for example,—at Taragona, and a hundred other places, by the French. The wanton butchery, the ruin of property, and, above all, those outrages worse than death, from which the female part of the population were protected at Cholula, show a catalogue of enormities quite as black as those imputed to the Spaniards, and without the same apology for resentment,—with no apology, indeed, but that afforded by a brave and patriotic resistance. The consideration of these events, which, from their familiarity, make little impression on our senses, should render us more lenient in our judgments of the past, showing, as they do, that man in a state of excitement, savage or civilized is much the same in every age. It may teach us,—it is one of the best lessons of history,—that, since such are the *inevitable* evils of war, even among the most polished people, those who hold the destinies of nations

History of New York, (book 1, chap. 5,) for a luminous disquisition on this knotty question. At all events, he will find there the popular arguments subjected to the test of ridicule; a test, showing, more than any reasoning can, how much, or rather how little, they are really worth.

in their hands, whether rulers or legislators, should submit to every sacrifice, save that of honor, before authorizing an appeal to arms. The extreme solicitude to avoid these calamities, by the aid of peaceful congresses and impartial mediation, is, on the whole, the strongest evidence, stronger than that afforded by the progress of science and art, of our boasted advance in civilization.

It is far from my intention to vindicate the cruel deeds of the old Conquerors. Let them lie heavy on their heads. They were an iron race, who periled life and fortune in the cause; and, as they made little account of danger and suffering for themselves, they had little sympathy to spare for their unfortunate enemies. But, to judge them fairly, we must not do it by the lights of our own age. We must carry ourselves back to theirs, and take the point of view afforded by the civilization of their time. Thus only can we arrive at impartial criticism in reviewing the generations that are past. We must extend to them the same justice which we shall have occasion to ask from Posterity, when, by the light of a higher civilization, it surveys the dark or doubtful passages in our own history, which hardly arrest the eye of the contemporary.

But, whatever be thought of this transaction in a moral view, as a stroke of policy, it was unquestionable. The nations of Anahuac had beheld, with admiration mingled with awe, the little band of Christian warriors steadily advancing along the plateau in face of every obstacle, overturning army after army with as much ease, apparently, as the good ship throws off the angry billows from her bows, or rather like the lava, which, rolling from their own volcanoes, holds on its course unchecked by obstacles, rock, tree, or building, bearing them along, or crushing and consuming them in its fiery path. The prowess of the Spaniards—"the white gods," as they were often called [12]—made them to be thought invincible. But it was not till their arrival at Cholula, that the natives learned how terrible was their vengeance,—and they trembled!

None trembled more than the Aztec emperor on his throne among the mountains. He read in these events the dark characters traced by the finger of Destiny.[13] He felt his empire melting away like a morning mist. He might well feel so. Some of the most important cities in the neighborhood of Cholula, intimidated by the fate of that capital, now sent their envoys to the Castilian camp, tendering their allegiance, and pro-

---

[12] *Los Dioses blancos.*—Camargo, Hist. de Tlascala, MS.—Torquemada, Monarch. Ind., lib. 4, cap. 40.

[13] Sahagun, Hist. de Nueva España, MS., lib. 12, cap. 11.

In an old Aztec harangue, made as a matter of form on the accession of a prince, we find the following remarkable prediction. "Perhaps ye are dismayed at the prospect of the terrible calamities that are one day to overwhelm us, calamities foreseen and foretold, though not felt, by our fathers! . . . . When the destruction and desolation of the empire shall come, when all shall be plunged in darkness, when the hour shall arrive in which they shall make us slaves throughout the land, and we shall be condemned to the lowest and most degrading offices!" (Ibid., lib. 6, cap. 16.) This random shot of prophecy, which I have rendered literally, shows how strong and settled was the apprehension of some impending revolution.

pitiating the favor of the strangers by rich presents of gold and slaves.[14] Montezuma, alarmed at these signs of defection, took counsel again of his impotent deities; but, although the altars smoked with fresh hecatombs of human victims, he obtained no cheering response. He determined, therefore, to send another embassy to the Spaniards, disavowing any participation in the conspiracy of Cholula.

Meanwhile Cortés was passing his time in that capital. He thought that the impression produced by the late scenes, and by the present restoration of tranquillity, offered a fair opportunity for the good work of conversion. He accordingly urged the citizens to embrace the Cross, and abandon the false guardians who had abandoned them in their extremity. But the traditions of centuries rested on the Holy City, shedding a halo of glory around it as "the sanctuary of the gods," the religious capital of Anahuac. It was too much to expect that the people would willingly resign this preëminence, and descend to the level of an ordinary community. Still Cortés might have pressed the matter, however unpalatable, but for the renewed interposition of the wise Olmedo, who persuaded him to postpone it till after the reduction of the whole country.[15]

The Spanish general, however, had the satisfaction to break open the cages in which the victims for sacrifice were confined, and to dismiss the trembling inmates to liberty and life. He also seized upon the great *teocalli,* and devoted that portion of the building, which, being of stone, had escaped the fury of the flames, to the purposes of a Christian church; while a crucifix of stone and lime, of gigantic dimensions, spreading out its arms above the city, proclaimed that the population below was under the protection of the Cross. On the same spot now stands a temple overshadowed by dark cypresses of unknown antiquity, and dedicated to Our Lady *de los Remedios.* An image of the Virgin presides over it, *said* to have been left by the Conqueror himself;[16] and an Indian ecclesiastic, a descendant of the ancient Cholulans, performs the peaceful services of the Roman Catholic communion, on the spot where his ancestors celebrated the sanguinary rites of the mystic Quetzalcoatl.[17]

During the occurrence of these events, envoys arrived from Mexico. They were charged, as usual, with a rich present of plate and ornaments of gold, among others, artificial birds in imitation of turkeys, with plumes of the same precious metal. To these were added fifteen hundred cotton dresses of delicate fabric. The emperor even expressed his regret at the catastrophe of Cholula, vindicated himself from any share in the conspiracy, which he said had brought deserved retribution on the heads of its authors, and explained the existence of an Aztec force in the neighborhood by the necessity of repressing some disorders there.[18]

[14] Herrera, Hist. General, dec. 2, lib. 7, cap. 3.
[15] Bernal Diaz, Hist. de la Conquista, cap. 83.
[16] Veytia, Hist. Antig., tom I. cap. 13.
[17] Humboldt, Vues des Cordillères, p. 32.
[18] Rel. Seg. de Cortés, ap. Lorenzana, p. 69.—Gomara, Crónica, cap. 63.—Oviedo, Hist de las Ind., MS., lib. 33, cap. 5.—Ixtlilxochitl, Hist. Chich., MS., cap. 84.

One cannot contemplate this pusillanimous conduct of Montezuma without mingled feelings of pity and contempt. It is not easy to reconcile his assumed innocence of the plot with many circumstances connected with it. But it must be remembered here and always, that his history is to be collected solely from Spanish writers and such of the natives as flourished after the Conquest, when the country had become a colony of Spain. Not an Aztec record of the primitive age survives, in a form capable of interpretation.[19] It is the hard fate of this unfortunate monarch, to be wholly indebted for his portraiture to the pencil of his enemies.

More than a fortnight had elapsed since the entrance of the Spaniards into Cholula, and Cortés now resolved without loss of time to resume his march towards the capital. His rigorous reprisals had so far intimidated the Cholulans, that he felt assured he should no longer leave an active enemy in his rear, to annoy him in case of retreat. He had the satisfaction, before his departure, to heal the feud—in outward appearance, at least—that had so long subsisted between the Holy City and Tlascala, and which, under the revolution which so soon changed the destinies of the country, never revived.

It was with some disquietude that he now received an application from his Cempoallan allies to be allowed to withdraw from the expedition, and return to their own homes. They had incurred too deeply the resentment of the Aztec emperor, by their insults to his collectors, and by their coöperation with the Spaniards, to care to trust themselves in his capital. It was in vain Cortés endeavored to reassure them, by promises of his protection. Their habitual distrust and dread of "the great Montezuma" were not to be overcome. The general learned their determination with regret, for they had been of infinite service to the cause by their stanch fidelity and courage. All this made it the more difficult for him to resist their reasonable demand. Liberally recompensing their services, there-fore, from the rich wardrobe and treasures of the emperor, he took leave of his faithful followers, before his own departure from Cholula. He availed himself of their return to send letters to Juan de Escalante, his lieutenant at Vera Cruz, acquainting him with the successful progress of the expedition. He enjoined on that officer to strengthen the fortifications

[19] The language of the text may appear somewhat too unqualified, considering that three Aztec codices exist with interpretations. (See Ante, Vol. I. pp. 60, 61.) But they contain very few and general allusions to Montezuma, and these strained through commentaries of Spanish monks, oftentimes manifestly irreconcilable with the genuine Aztec notions. Even such writers as Ixtlilxochitl and Camargo, from whom, considering their Indian descent, we might expect more independence, seem less solicitous to show this, than their loyalty to the new faith and country of their adoption. Perhaps the most honest Aztec record of the period is to be obtained from the volumes, the twelfth book, particularly, of father Sahagun, embodying the traditions of the natives soon after the Conquest. This portion of his great work was rewritten by its author, and considerable changes were made in it, at a later period of his life. Yet it may be doubted if the reformed version reflects the traditions of the country as faithfully as the original. which is still in manuscript, and which I have chiefly followed.

of that place, so as the better to resist any hostile interference from Cuba, —an event for which Cortés was ever on the watch,—and to keep down revolt among the natives. He especially commended the Totonacs to his protection, as allies whose fidelity to the Spaniards exposed them, in no slight degree, to the vengeance of the Aztecs.[20]

[20] Bernal Diaz, Hist. de la Conquista, cap. 84, 85.—Rel. Seg. de Cortés, ap. Lorenzana, p. 67.—Gomara, Crónica, cap. 60.—Oviedo, Hist. de las Ind., MS., lib. 33, cap. 5.

MARCH RESUMED—ASCENT OF THE GREAT VOLCANO—VALLEY OF MEXICO—IMPRESSION ON THE SPANIARDS—CONDUCT OF MONTEZUMA—THEY DESCEND INTO THE VALLEY

1519

EVERY thing being now restored to quiet in Cholula, the allied army of Spaniards and Tlascalans set forward in high spirits, and resumed the march on Mexico. The road lay through the beautiful savannas and luxuriant plantations that spread out for several leagues in every direction. On the march, they were met occasionally by embassies from the neighboring places, anxious to claim the protection of the white men, and to propitiate them by gifts, especially of gold, for which their appetite was generally known throughout the country.

Some of these places were allies of the Tlascalans, and all showed much discontent with the oppressive rule of Montezuma. The natives cautioned the Spaniards against putting themselves in his power, by entering his capital; and they stated, as evidence of his hostile disposition, that he had caused the direct road to it to be blocked up, that the strangers might be compelled to choose another, which, from its narrow passes and strong positions, would enable him to take them at great disadvantage.

The information was not lost on Cortés, who kept a strict eye on the movements of the Mexican envoys, and redoubled his own precautions against surprise.[1] Cheerful and active, he was ever where his presence was needed, sometimes in the van, at others in the rear, encouraging the weak, stimulating the sluggish, and striving to kindle in the breasts of others the same courageous spirit which glowed in his own. At night he never omitted to go the rounds, to see that every man was at his post. On one occasion, his vigilance had well-nigh proved fatal to him. He approached so near a sentinel, that the man, unable to distinguish his person in the dark, levelled his crossbow at him, when fortunately an exclamation of the general, who gave the watchword of the night, arrested a movement, which might else have brought the campaign to a close, and given a respite for some time longer to the empire of Montezuma.

The army came at length to the place mentioned by the friendly In-

---

[1] "Andauamos," says Diaz, in the homely, but expressive Spanish proverb, "la barba sobre el ombro." Hist. de la Conquista, cap. 86.

dians, where the road forked, and one arm of it was found, as they had
foretold, obstructed with large trunks of trees, and huge stones which had
been strewn across it. Cortés inquired the meaning of this from the
Mexican ambassadors. They said it was done by the emperor's orders,
to prevent their taking a route which, after some distance, they would
find nearly impracticable for the cavalry. They acknowledged, however,
that it was the most direct road; and Cortés declaring that this was
enough to decide him in favor of it, as the Spaniards made no account of
obstacles, commanded the rubbish to be cleared away. Some of the timber might still be seen by the road-side, as Bernal Diaz tells us, many
years after. The event left little doubt in the general's mind of the meditated treachery of the Mexicans. But he was too polite to betray his suspicions.[2]

They were now leaving the pleasant champaign country, as the road
wound up the bold sierra which separates the great plateaus of Mexico
and Puebla. The air, as they ascended, became keen and piercing; and
the blasts, sweeping down the frozen sides of the mountains, made the
soldiers shiver in their thick harness of cotton, and benumbed the limbs
of both men and horses.

They were passing between two of the highest mountains on the North
American continent; Popocatepetl, "the hill that smokes," and Iztaccihuatl, or "white woman," [3]—a name suggested, doubtless, by the bright
robe of snow spread over its broad and broken surface. A puerile superstition of the Indians regarded these celebrated mountains as gods, and
Iztaccihuatl as the wife of her more formidable neighbor.[4] A tradition
of a higher character described the northern volcano, as the abode of the
departed spirits of wicked rulers, whose fiery agonies, in their prison-
house, caused the fearful bellowings and convulsions in times of eruption. It was the classic fable of Antiquity.[5] These superstitious legends
had invested the mountain with a mysterious horror, that made the natives shrink from attempting its ascent, which, indeed, was from natural
causes a work of incredible difficulty.

The great *volcan*,[6] as Popocatepetl was called, rose to the enormous

[2] Ibid., ubi supra.—Rel. Seg. de Cortés, ap. Lorenzana, p. 70.—Torquemada,
Monarch. Ind., lib. 4, cap. 41.
[3] "Llamaban al volcan Popocatépetl, y á la sierra nevada Iztaccihuatl, que quiere
decir la sierra que humea, y la blanca muger." Camargo, Hist. de Tlascala, MS.
[4] "La Sierra nevada y el volcan los tenian por Dioses; y que el volcan y la Sierra
nevada eran marido y muger." Ibid., MS.
[5] Gomara, Crónica, cap. 62.
          "Ætna Giganteos nunquam tacitura triumphos,
          Enceladi bustum, qui saucia terga revinctus
          Spirat inexhaustum flagranti pectore sulphur."
                              CLAUDIAN, De Rapt. Pros., lib. 1, v. 152.
[6] The old Spaniards called any lofty mountain by that name, though never having
given signs of combustion. Thus, Chimborazo was called a *volcan de nieve*, or
'snow volcano'; (Humboldt, Essai Politique, tom. I, p. 162;) and that enterprising
traveller, Stephens, notices the *volcan de agua*, "water volcano," in the neighborhood of Antigua Guatemala. Incidents of Travel in Chiapas, Central America, and
Yucatan, (New York, 1841,) vol. I. chap. 17

height of 17,852 feet above the level of the sea; more than 2000 feet above the "monarch of mountains,"—the highest elevation in Europe.[7] During the present century, it has rarely given evidence of its volcanic origin, and "the hill that smokes" has almost forfeited its claim to the appellation. But at the time of the Conquest it was frequently in a state of activity, and raged with uncommon fury while the Spaniards were at Tlascala; an evil omen, it was thought, for the natives of Anahuac. Its head, gathered into a regular cone by the deposite of successive eruptions, wore the usual form of volcanic mountains, when not disturbed by the falling in of the crater. Soaring towards the skies, with its silver sheet of everlasting snow, it was seen far and wide over the broad plains of Mexico and Puebla, the first object which the morning sun greeted in his rising, the last where his evening rays were seen to linger, shedding a glorious effulgence over its head, that contrasted strikingly with the ruinous waste of sand and lava immediately below, and the deep fringe of funereal pines that shrouded its base.

The mysterious terrors which hung over the spot, and the wild love of adventure, made some of the Spanish cavaliers desirous to attempt the ascent, which the natives declared no man could accomplish and live. Cortés encouraged them in the enterprise, willing to show the Indians that no achievement was above the dauntless daring of his followers. One of his captains, accordingly, Diego Ordaz, with nine Spaniards, and several Tlascalans, encouraged by their example, undertook the ascent. It was attended with more difficulty than had been anticipated.

The lower region was clothed with a dense forest, so thickly matted, that in some places it was scarcely possible to penetrate it. It grew thinner, however, as they advanced, dwindling, by degrees, into a straggling, stunted vegetation, till, at the height of somewhat more than thirteen thousand feet, it faded away altogether. The Indians who had held on thus far, intimidated by the strange subterraneous sounds of the volcano, even then in a state of combustion, now left them. The track opened on a black surface of glazed volcanic sand and of lava, the broken fragments of which, arrested in its boiling progress in a thousand fantastic forms, opposed continual impediments to their advance. Amidst these, one huge rock, the *Pico del Fraile*, a conspicuous object from below, rose to the perpendicular height of a hundred and fifty feet, compelling them to take a wide circuit. They soon came to the limits of perpetual snow, where new difficulties presented themselves, as the treacherous ice gave an imperfect footing, and a false step might precipitate them into the frozen chasms that yawned around. To increase their distress, respiration in these aërial regions became so difficult, that every effort was attended with sharp pains in the head and limbs. Still they pressed on, till, drawing nearer the crater, such volumes of smoke, sparks and cinders were belched forth from its burning entrails, and driven down the sides of the

[7] Mont Blanc, according to M. de Saussure, is 15,670 feet high. For the estimate of Popocatepetl, see an elaborate communication in the *Revista Mexicana*, tom. II No. 4.

mountain, as nearly suffocated and blinded them. It was too much even for their hardy frames to endure, and, however reluctantly, they were compelled to abandon the attempt on the eve of its completion. They brought back some huge icicles,—a curious sight in these tropical regions, —as a trophy of their achievement, which, however imperfect, was sufficient to strike the minds of the natives with wonder, by showing that with the Spaniards the most appalling and mysterious perils were only as pastimes. The undertaking was eminently characteristic of the bold spirit of the cavalier of that day, who, not content with the dangers that lay in his path, seems to court them from the mere Quixotic love of adventure. A report of the affair was transmitted to the Emperor Charles the Fifth, and the family of Ordaz was allowed to commemorate the exploit by assuming a burning mountain on their escutcheon.[8]

The general was not satisfied with the result. Two years after, he sent up another party, under Francisco Montaño, a cavalier of determined resolution. The object was to obtain sulphur to assist in making gunpowder for the army. The mountain was quiet at this time, and the expedition was attended with better success. The Spaniards, five in number, climbed to the very edge of the crater, which presented an irregular ellipse at its mouth, more than a league in circumference. Its depth might be from eight hundred to a thousand feet. A lurid flame burned gloomily at the bottom, sending up a sulphureous steam, which, cooling as it rose, was precipitated on the sides of the cavity. The party cast lots, and it fell on Montaño himself, to descend in a basket into this hideous abyss, into which he was lowered by his companions to the depth of four hundred feet! This was repeated several times, till the adventurous cavalier had collected a sufficient quantity of sulphur for the wants of the army. This doughty enterprise excited general admiration at the time. Cortés concludes his report of it, to the emperor, with the judicious reflection, that it would be less inconvenient, on the whole, to import their powder from Spain.[9]

[8] Rel. Seg. de Cortés, ap. Lorenzana, p. 70.—Oviedo, Hist. de las Ind., MS., lib. 33, cap. 5.—Bernal Diaz, Hist. de la Conquista, cap. 78.
The latter writer speaks of the ascent as made when the army lay at Tlascala, and of the attempt as perfectly successful. The general's letter, written soon after the event, with no motive for misstatement, is the better authority. See, also, Herrera, Hist. General, dec. 2, lib. 6, cap. 18.—Rel. d' un gent., ap. Ramusio, tom. III. p. 308.—Gomara, Crónica, cap. 62.
[9] Rel. Ter. y Quarta de Cortés, ap. Lorenzana, pp. 318, 380.—Herrera, Hist. General, dec. 3, lib. 3, cap. 1.—Oviedo, Hist. de las Ind., MS., lib. 33, cap. 41.
M. de Humboldt doubts the fact of Montaño's descent into the crater, thinking it more probable that he obtained the sulphur through some lateral crevice in the mountain. (Essai Politique, tom. I. p. 164.) No attempt—at least, no successful one—has been made to gain the summit of Popocatepetl, since this of Montaño, till the present century. In 1827 it was reached in two expeditions, and again in 1833 and 1834. A very full account of the last, containing many interesting details and scientific observations, was written by Federico de Gerolt, one of the party, and published in the periodical already referred to. (Revista Mexicana, tom. I. pp. 461-482.) The party from the topmost peak, which commanded a full view of the less elevated Iztaccihuatl, saw no vestige of a crater in that mountain, contrary to the opinion usually received

But it is time to return from our digression, which may, perhaps, be excused, as illustrating, in a remarkable manner, the chimerical spirit of enterprise,—not inferior to that in his own romances of chivalry,—which glowed in the breast of the Spanish cavalier in the sixteenth century.

The army held on its march through the intricate gorges of the sierra. The route was nearly the same as that pursued at the present day by the courier from the capital to Puebla, by the way of Mecameca.[10] It was not that usually taken by travellers from Vera Cruz, who follow the more circuitous road round the northern base of Iztaccihuatl, as less fatiguing than the other, though inferior in picturesque scenery and romantic points of view. The icy winds, that now swept down the sides of the mountains, brought with them a tempest of arrowy sleet and snow, from which the Christians suffered even more than the Tlascalans, reared from infancy among the wild solitudes of their own native hills. As night came on, their sufferings would have been intolerable, but they luckily found a shelter in the commodious stone buildings which the Mexican government had placed at stated intervals along the roads for the accommodation of the traveller and their own couriers. It little dreamed it was providing a protection for its enemies.

The troops, refreshed by a night's rest, succeeded, early on the following day, in gaining the crest of the sierra of Ahualco, which stretches like a curtain between the two great mountains on the north and south. Their progress was now comparatively easy, and they marched forward with a buoyant step, as they felt they were treading the soil of Montezuma.

They had not advanced far, when, turning an angle of the sierra, they suddenly came on a view which more than compensated the toils of the preceding day. It was that of the Valley of Mexico, or Tenochtitlan, as more commonly called by the natives; which, with its picturesque assemblage of water, woodland, and cultivated plains, its shining cities and shadowy hills, was spread out like some gay and gorgeous panorama before them. In the highly rarefied atmosphere of these upper regions, even remote objects have a brilliancy of coloring and a distinctness of outline which seem to annihilate distance.[11] Stretching far away at their feet, were seen noble forests of oak, sycamore, and cedar, and beyond, yellow fields of maize and the towering maguey, intermingled with orchards and blooming gardens; for flowers, in such demand for their religious festivals, were even more abundant in this populous valley than in other parts of Anahuac. In the centre of the great basin were beheld the lakes, occupying then a much larger portion of its surface than at present; their borders thickly studded with towns and hamlets, and, in the midst,—like some Indian empress with her coronal of pearls,—the fair city of Mexico, with her white towers and pyramidal temples, reposing, as it were, on the bosom of the waters,—the far-famed "Venice of the Aztecs." High over

---

[10] Humboldt, Essaï Politique, tom. IV. p. 17.

[11] The lake of Tezcuco, on which stood the capital of Mexico, is 2277 metres, nearly 7500 feet, above the sea. Humboldt, Essaï Politique, tom. II. p. 45.

all rose the royal hill of Chapoltepec, the residence of the Mexican monarchs, crowned with the same grove of gigantic cypresses, which at this day fling their broad shadows over the land. In the distance beyond the blue waters of the lake, and nearly screened by intervening foliage, was seen a shining speck, the rival capital of Tezcuco, and, still further on, the dark belt of porphyry, girdling the Valley around, like a rich setting which Nature had devised for the fairest of her jewels.

Such was the beautiful vision which broke on the eyes of the Conquerors. And even now, when so sad a change has come over the scene; when the stately forests have been laid low, and the soil, unsheltered from the fierce radiance of a tropical sun, is in many places abandoned to sterility; when the waters have retired, leaving a broad and ghastly margin white with the incrustation of salts, while the cities and hamlets on their borders have mouldered into ruins;—even now that desolation broods over the landscape, so indestructible are the lines of beauty which Nature has traced on its features, that no traveller, however cold, can gaze on them with any other emotions than those of astonishment and rapture.[12]

What, then, must have been the emotions of the Spaniards, when, after working their toilsome way into the upper air, the cloudy tabernacle parted before their eyes, and they beheld these fair scenes in all their pristine magnificence and beauty! It was like the spectacle which greeted the eyes of Moses from the summit of Pisgah, and, in the warm glow of their feelings, they cried out, "It is the promised land!" [13]

But these feelings of admiration were soon followed by others of a very different complexion; as they saw in all this the evidences of a civilization and power far superior to any thing they had yet encountered. The more timid, disheartened by the prospect, shrunk from a contest so unequal, and demanded, as they had done on some former occasions, to be led back again to Vera Cruz. Such was not the effect produced on the sanguine spirit of the general. His avarice was sharpened by the display of the dazzling spoil at his feet; and, if he felt a natural anxiety at the formidable odds, his confidence was renewed, as he gazed on the lines of his veterans, whose weather-beaten visages and battered armor told of battles won and difficulties surmounted, while his bold barbarians, with appetites whetted by the view of their enemies' country, seemed like eagles on the mountains, ready to pounce upon their prey. By argument, entreaty, and menace, he endeavored to restore the faltering courage of the soldiers, urging them not to think of retreat, now that they had reached the goal for which they had panted, and the golden gates were

[12] It is unnecessary to refer to the pages of modern travellers, who, however they may differ in taste, talent, or feeling, all concur in the impressions produced on them by the sight of this beautiful valley.

[13] Torquemada, Monarch. Ind., lib. 4, cap. 41.

It may call to the reader's mind the memorable view of the fair plains of Italy which Hannibal displayed to his hungry barbarians, after a similar march through the wild passes of the Alps, as reported by the prince of historic painters. Livy, Hist., lib. 21, cap. 35.

opened to receive them. In these efforts, he was well seconded by the brave cavaliers, who held honor as dear to them as fortune; until the dullest spirits caught somewhat of the enthusiasm of their leaders, and the general had the satisfaction to see his hesitating columns, with their usual buoyant step, once more on their march down the slopes of the sierra.[14]

With every step of their progress, the woods became thinner; patches of cultivated land more frequent; and hamlets were seen in the green and sheltered nooks, the inhabitants of which, coming out to meet them, gave the troops a kind reception. Everywhere they heard complaints of Montezuma, especially of the unfeeling manner in which he carried off their young men to recruit his armies, and their maidens for his harem. These symptoms of discontent were noticed with satisfaction by Cortés, who saw that Montezuma's "mountain-throne," as it was called, was, indeed, seated on a volcano, with the elements of combustion so active within, that it seemed as if any hour might witness an explosion. He encouraged the disaffected natives to rely on his protection, as he had come to redress their wrongs. He took advantage, moreover, of their favorable dispositions, to scatter among them such gleams of spiritual light as time and the preaching of father Olmedo could afford.

He advanced by easy stages, somewhat retarded by the crowd of curious inhabitants gathered on the highways to see the strangers, and halting at every spot of interest or importance. On the road, he was met by another embassy from the capital. It consisted of several Aztec lords, freighted, as usual, with a rich largess of gold, and robes of delicate furs and feathers. The message of the emperor was couched in the same deprecatory terms as before. He even condescended to bribe the return of the Spaniards, by promising, in that event, four loads of gold to the general, and one to each of the captains,[15] with a yearly tribute to their sovereign. So effectually had the lofty and naturally courageous spirit of the barbarian monarch been subdued by the influence of superstition!

But the man, whom the hostile array of armies could not daunt, was not to be turned from his purpose by a woman's prayers. He received the embassy with his usual courtesy, declaring, as before, that he could not answer it to his own sovereign, if he were now to return without visiting the emperor in his capital. It would be much easier to arrange matters by a personal interview than by distant negotiation. The Spaniards came in the spirit of peace. Montezuma would so find it, but, should their presence prove burdensome to him, it would be easy for them to relieve him of it.[16]

---

[14] Torquemada, Monarch. Ind., ubi supra.—Herrera, Hist. General, dec. 2, lib. 7, cap. 3.—Gomara, Crónica, cap. 64.—Oviedo, Hist. de las Ind., MS., lib. 33, cap. 5.

[15] A load for a Mexican *tamane* was about fifty pounds, or eight hundred ounces. Clavigero, Stor. del Messico, tom. III. p. 69, nota.

[16] Sahagun, Hist. de Nueva España, MS., lib. 12, cap. 12.—Rel. Seg. de Cortés, ap. Lorenzana, p. 73.—Herrera, Hist. General, dec. 2, lib. 7, cap. 3.—Gomara, Crónica. cap. 64.—Oviedo, Hist. de las Ind., MS., lib. 33, cap. 5.—Bernal Diaz, Hist. de la Conquista, cap. 87.

The Aztec monarch, meanwhile, was a prey to the most dismal appre-- hensions. It was intended that the embassy above noticed should reach the Spaniards before they crossed the mountains. When he learned that this was accomplished, and that the dread strangers were on their march across the Valley, the very threshold of his capital, the last spark of hope died away in his bosom. Like one who suddenly finds himself on the brink of some dark and yawning gulf, he was too much bewildered to be able to rally his thoughts, or even to comprehend his situation. He was the victim of an absolute destiny; against which no foresight or precautions could have availed. It was as if the strange beings, who had thus invaded his shores, had dropped from some distant planet, so different were they from all he had ever seen, in appearance and manners; so superior— though a mere handful, in numbers—to the banded nations of Anahuac in strength and science, and all the fearful accompaniments of war! They were now in the Valley. The huge mountain screen, which nature had so kindly drawn around it, for its defence, had been overleaped. The golden visions of security and repose, in which he had so long indulged, the lordly sway descended from his ancestors, his broad imperial domain, were all to pass away. It seemed like some terrible dream,—from which he was now, alas! to awake to a still more terrible reality.

In a paroxysm of despair, he shut himself up in his palace, refused food, and sought relief in prayer and in sacrifice. But the oracles were dumb. He then adopted the more sensible expedient of calling a council of his principal and oldest nobles. Here was the same division of opinion which had before prevailed. Cacama, the young king of Tezcuco, his nephew, counselled him to receive the Spaniards courteously, as ambas- sadors, so styled by themselves of a foreign prince. Cuitlahua, Monte- zuma's more warlike brother, urged him to muster his forces on the in- stant, and drive back the invaders from his capital, or die in its defence. But the monarch found it difficult to rally his spirits for this final strug- gle. With downcast eye and dejected mien, he exclaimed, "Of what avail is resistance, when the gods have declared themselves against us![17] Yet I mourn most for the old and infirm, the women and children, too feeble to fight or to fly. For myself and the brave men around me, we must bare our breasts to the storm, and meet it as we may!" Such are the sorrow- ful and sympathetic tones in which the Aztec emperor is said to have uttered the bitterness of his grief. He would have acted a more glorious part, had he put his capital in a posture of defence, and prepared, like the last of the Palæologi, to bury himself under its ruins.[18]

He straightway prepared to send a last embassy to the Spaniards, with his nephew, the lord of Tezcuco, at its head, to welcome them to Mexico.

The Christian army, meanwhile, had advanced as far as Amaqueme-

---

[17] This was not the sentiment of the Roman hero.

"Victrix causa Diis placuit, sed victa Catoni!"

LUCAN, lib. i, v. 128.

[18] Sahagun, Hist. de Nueva España, MS., lib. 12, cap. 13.—Torquemada, Monarch ind., lib. 4, cap. 44.—Gomara, Crónica, cap. 63.

can, a well built town of several thousand inhabitants. They were kindly received by the cacique, lodged in large, commodious, stone buildings, and at their departure presented, among other things, with gold to the amount of three thousand *castellanos*.[19] Having halted there a couple of days, they descended among flourishing plantations of maize, and of maguey, the latter of which might be called the Aztec vineyards, towards the lake of Chalco. Their first resting-place was Ajotzinco, a town of considerable size, with a great part of it then standing on piles in the water. It was the first specimen which the Spaniards had seen of this maritime architecture. The canals which intersected the city, instead of streets, presented an animated scene, from the number of barks which glided up and down freighted with provisions and other articles for the inhabitants. The Spaniards were particularly struck with the style and commodious structure of the houses, built chiefly of stone, and with the general aspect of wealth and even elegance which prevailed there.

Though received with the greatest show of hospitality, Cortés found some occasion for distrust in the eagerness manifested by the people to see and approach the Spaniards.[20] Not content with gazing at them in the roads, some even made their way stealthily into their quarters, and fifteen or twenty unhappy Indians were shot down by the sentinels as spies. Yet there appears, as well as we can judge, at this distance of time, to have been no real ground for such suspicion. The undisguised jealousy of the Court, and the cautions he had received from his allies, while they very properly put the general on his guard, seem to have given an unnatural acuteness, at least in the present instance, to his perceptions of danger.[21]

Early on the following morning, as the army was preparing to leave the place, a courier came, requesting the general to postpone his departure till after the arrival of the king of Tezcuco, who was advancing to meet him. It was not long before he appeared, borne in a palanquin or litter, richly decorated with plates of gold and precious stones, having pillars curiously wrought, supporting a canopy of green plumes, a favorite color with the Aztec princes. He was accompanied by a numerous suite of nobles and inferior attendants. As he came into the presence of Cortés, the lord of Tezcuco descended from his palanquin, and the obsequious officers swept the ground before him as he advanced. He appeared

[19] "El señor de esta provincia y pueblo me dió hasta quarenta esclavas, y tres mil castellanos; y dos dias que allí estuye nos proveyó muy cumplidamente de todo lo necessario para nuestra comida." Rel. Seg. de Cortés, ap. Lorenzana, p. 74.

[20] "De todas partes era infinita la gente que de un cabo é de otro concurrian á mirar á los Españoles, é maravillábanse mucho de los ver. Tenian grande espacio é atencion en mirar los caballos; decian, 'Estos son Teules,' que quiere decir Demonios." Oviedo, Hist. de las Ind., MS., lib. 33, cap. 45.

[21] Cortés tells the affair coolly enough to the emperor. "É aquella noche tuve tal guarda, que assí de espías, que venian por el agua en canoas, como de otras, que por la sierra abajaban, á ver si habia aparejo para executar suvoluntad, amaneciéron casi quince, ó veinte, que las nuestras las habian tomado, y muerto. Por manera que pocas bolviéron á dar su respuesta de el aviso que venian á tomar." Rel. Seg. de Cortés, ap. Lorenzana, p. 74.

to be a young man of about twenty-five years of age, with a comely presence, erect and stately in his deportment. He made the Mexican salutation usually addressed to persons of high rank, touching the earth with his right hand, and raising it to his head. Cortés embraced him as he rose, when the young prince informed him that he came as the representative of Montezuma, to bid the Spaniards welcome to his capital. He then presented the general with three pearls of uncommon size and lustre. Cortés, in return, threw over Cacama's neck a chain of cut glass, which, where glass was as rare as diamonds, might be admitted to have a value as real as the latter. After this interchange of courtesies, and the most friendly and respectful assurances on the part of Cortés, the Indian prince withdrew, leaving the Spaniards strongly impressed with the superiority of his state and bearing over any thing they had hitherto seen in the country.[22]

Resuming its march, the army kept along the southern borders of the lake of Chalco, overshadowed, at that time, by noble woods, and by orchards glowing with autumnal fruits, of unknown names, but rich and tempting hues. More frequently it passed through cultivated fields waving with the yellow harvest, and irrigated by canals introduced from the neighboring lake; the whole showing a careful and economical husbandry, essential to the maintenance of a crowded population.

Leaving the main land, the Spaniards came on the great dike or causeway, which stretches some four or five miles in length, and divides lake Chalco from Xochicalco on the west. It was a lance in breadth in the narrowest part, and in some places wide enough for eight horsemen to ride abreast. It was a solid structure of stone and lime, running directly through the lake, and struck the Spaniards as one of the most remarkable works which they had seen in the country.

As they passed along, they beheld the gay spectacle of multitudes of Indians darting up and down in their light pirogues, eager to catch a glimpse of the strangers, or bearing the products of the country to the neighboring cities. They were amazed, also, by the sight of the *chinampas*, or floating gardens,—those wandering islands of verdure, to which we shall have occasion to return hereafter,—teeming with flowers and vegetables, and moving like rafts over the waters. All round the margin, and occasionally far in the lake, they beheld little towns and villages, which, half concealed by the foliage, and gathered in white clusters round the shore, looked in the distance like companies of wild swans riding quietly on the waves. A scene so new and wonderful filled their rude hearts with amazement. It seemed like enchantment; and they could find nothing to compare it with, but the magical pictures in the "Amadis de

---

[22] Rel. Seg. de Cortés, ap. Lorenzana, p. 75.—Gomara, Crónica, cap. 64.—Ixtlilxochitl, Hist. Chich., MS., cap. 85.—Oviedo Hist. de las Ind., MS., lib. 33, cap. 5.

"Llegó con el mayor fausto, y grandeza que ningun señor de los Mexicanos auiamos visto traer, ... y lo tuuímos por muy gran cosa: y platicámos entre nosotros, que quando aquel Cacique traia tanto triunfo, que haria el gran Monteçuma?" Bernal Diaz, Hist. de la Conquista, cap. 87.

Gaula."[23] Few pictures, indeed, in that or any other legend of chivalry, could surpass the realities of their own experience. The life of the adventurer in the New World was romance put into action. What wonder, then, if the Spaniard of that day, feeding his imagination with dreams of enchantment at home, and with its realities abroad, should have displayed a Quixotic enthusiasm,—a romantic exaltation of character, not to be comprehended by the colder spirits of other lands!

Midway across the lake the army halted at the town of Cuitlahuac, a place of moderate size, but distinguished by the beauty of the buildings, —the most beautiful, according to Cortés, that he had yet seen in the country.[24] After taking some refreshment at this place, they continued their march along the dike. Though broader in this northern section, the troops found themselves much embarrassed by the throng of Indians, who, not content with gazing on them from the boats, climbed up the causeway, and lined the sides of the road. The general, afraid that his ranks might be disordered, and that too great familiarity might diminish a salutary awe in the natives, was obliged to resort not merely to command, but menace, to clear a passage. He now found, as he advanced, a considerable change in the feelings shown towards the government. He heard only of the pomp and magnificence, nothing of the oppressions, of Montezuma. Contrary to the usual fact, it seemed that the respect for the court was greatest in its immediate neighborhood.

From the causeway, the army descended on that narrow point of land which divides the waters of the Chalco from the Tezcucan lake, but which in those days was overflowed for many a mile now laid bare.[25] Traversing this peninsula, they entered the royal residence of Iztapalapan, a place containing twelve or fifteen thousand houses, according to Cortés.[26] It

[23] "Nos quedámos admirados," exclaims Diaz, with simple wonder, "y deziamos que parecia á las casas de encantamento, que cuentan en libro de Amadis!" (Ibid., loc. cit.) An edition of this celebrated romance in its Castilian dress had appeared before this time, as the prologue to the second edition of 1521 speaks of a former one in the reign of the "Catholic Sovereigns." See Cervantes, Don Quixote, ed. Pellicer, (Madrid, 1797,) tom. I., Discurso Prelim.

[24] "Una ciudad, la mas hermosa, aunque pequeña, que hasta entonces habiamos visto, assí de muy bien obradas Casas, y Torres, como de la buena órden, que en el fundamento de ella habia por ser armada toda sobre Agua." (Rel. Seg. de Cortés, ap. Lorenzana, p. 76.) The Spaniards gave this aquatic city the name of Venezuela, or little Venice. Toribio, Hist. de los Indios, MS., Parte 2, cap. 4.

[26] M. de Humboldt has dotted the *conjectural* limits of the ancient lake in his admirable chart of the Mexican Valley. (Atlas Géographique et Physique de la Nouvelle Espagne, (Paris, 1811,) carte 3.) Notwithstanding his great care, it is not easy always to reconcile his topography with the itineraries of the Conquerors, so much has the face of the country been changed by natural and artificial causes. It is still less possible to reconcile their narratives with the maps of Clavigero, Lopez, Robertson, and others, defying equally topography and history.

[26] Several writers notice a visit of the Spaniards to Tezcuco on the way to the capital. (Torquemada, Monarch. Ind., lib. 4, cap. 42.—Solís, Conquista, lib. 3, cap. 9.—Herrera, Hist. General, dec. 2, lib. 7, cap. 4.—Clavigero, Stor. del Messico, tom. III. p. 74.) This improbable episode—which, it may be remarked, has led these authors into some geographical perplexities, not to say blunders—is altogether too remarkable to have been passed over in silence, in the minute relation of Bernal Diaz, and that of Cortés, neither of whom alludes to it.

was governed by Cuitlahua, the emperor's brother, who, to do greater honor to the general, had invited the lords of some neighboring cities, of the royal house of Mexico, like himself, to be present at the interview. This was conducted with much ceremony, and, after the usual present of gold and delicate stuffs,[27] a collation was served to the Spaniards in one of the great halls of the palace. The excellence of the architecture here, also, excited the admiration of the general, who does not hesitate, in the glow of his enthusiasm, to pronounce some of the buildings equal to the best in Spain.[28] They were of stone, and the spacious apartments had roofs of odorous cedar-wood, while the walls were tapestried with fine cottons stained with brilliant colors.

But the pride of Iztapalapan, on which its lord had freely lavished his care and his revenues, was its celebrated gardens. They covered an immense tract of land; were laid out in regular squares, and the paths intersecting them were bordered with trellises, supporting creepers and aromatic shrubs that loaded the air with their perfumes. The gardens were stocked with fruit-trees, imported from distant places, and with the gaudy family of flowers which belong to the Mexican Flora, scientifically arranged, and growing luxuriant in the equable temperature of the table-land. The natural dryness of the atmosphere was counteracted by means of aqueducts and canals that carried water into all parts of the grounds.

In one quarter was an aviary, filled with numerous kinds of birds, remarkable in this region both for brilliancy of plumage and of song. The gardens were intersected by a canal communicating with the lake of Tezcuco, and of sufficient size for barges to enter from the latter. But the most elaborate piece of work was a huge reservoir of stone, filled to a considerable height with water well supplied with different sorts of fish. This basin was sixteen hundred paces in circumference, and was surrounded by a walk, made also of stone, wide enough for four persons to go abreast. The sides were curiously sculptured, and a flight of steps led to the water below, which fed the aqueducts above noticed, or, collected into fountains, diffused a perpetual moisture.

Such are the accounts transmitted of these celebrated gardens, at a period when similar horticultural establishments were unknown in Europe;[29] and we might well doubt their existence in this semi-civilized land, were it not a matter of such notoriety at the time, and so explicitly attested by the invaders. But a generation had scarcely passed after the Conquest, before a sad change came over these scenes so beautiful. The town itself was deserted, and the shore of the lake was strewed with the wreck of buildings which once were its ornament and its glory. The gar-

[27] "É me diéron," says Cortés, "hasta tres, ó quatro mil Castellanos, y algunas Esclavas, y Ropa, é me hiciéron muy buen acogimiento." Rel. Seg., ap. Lorenzana, p. 76.

[28] "Tiene el Señor de ella unas Casas nuevas, que aun no están acabadas, que son tan buenas como las mejores de España, digo de grandes y bien labradas." Ibid., p. 77.

[29] The earliest instance of a Garden of Plants in Europe is said to have been at Padua, in 1545. Carli, Lettres Américaines, tom. I. let. 21.

dens shared the fate of the city. The retreating waters withdrew the means of nourishment, converting the flourishing plains into a foul and unsightly morass, the haunt of loathsome reptiles; and the water-fowl built her nest in what had once been the palaces of princes! [30]

In the city of Iztapalapan, Cortés took up his quarters for the night. We may imagine what a crowd of ideas must have pressed on the mind of the Conqueror, as, surrounded by these evidences of civilization, he prepared with his handful of followers to enter the capital of a monarch, who, as he had abundant reason to know, regarded him with distrust and aversion. This capital was now but a few miles distant, distinctly visible from Iztapalapan. And as its long lines of glittering edifices, struck by the rays of the evening sun, trembled on the dark-blue waters of the lake, it looked like a thing of fairy creation, rather than the work of mortal hands. Into this city of enchantment Cortés prepared to make his entry on the following morning.[31]

[30] Rel. Seg. de Cortés, ubi supra.—Herrera, Hist. General, dec. 2, lib. 7, cap. 44.—Sahagun, Hist. de Nueva España, MS., lib. 12, cap. 13.—Oviedo, Hist. de las Ind., MS., lib. 33, cap. 5.—Bernal Diaz, Hist. de la Conquista, cap. 87.
[31] "There Aztlan stood upon the farther shore;
Amid the shade of trees its dwellings rose,
Their level roofs with turrets set around,
And battlements all burnished white, which shone
Like silver in the sunshine. I beheld
The imperial city, her far-circling walls,
Her garden groves and stately palaces,
Her temples mountain size, her thousand roofs;
And when I saw her might and majesty,
My mind misgave me then."

SOUTHEY's Madoc, Part 1, canto 6.

CHAPTER IX

ENVIRONS OF MEXICO—INTERVIEW WITH MONTEZUMA—ENTRANCE
INTO THE CAPITAL—HOSPITABLE RECEPTION—VISIT TO THE EM-
PEROR.

1519

WITH the first faint streak of dawn, the Spanish general was up, mustering his followers. They gathered, with beating hearts, under their respective banners, as the trumpet sent forth its spirit-stirring sounds across
water and woodland, till they died away in distant echoes among the
mountains. The sacred flames on the altars of numberless *teocallis*, dimly
seen through the grey mists of morning, indicated the site of the capital.
till temple, tower, and palace were fully revealed in the glorious illumination which the sun, as he rose above the eastern barrier, poured over the
beautiful Valley. It was the eighth of November, 1519; a conspicuous
day in history, as that on which the Europeans first set foot in the capital
of the Western World.

Cortés with his little body of horse formed a sort of advanced guard to
the army. Then came the Spanish infantry, who in a summer's campaign
had acquired the discipline, and the weather-beaten aspect, of veterans.
The baggage occupied the centre; and the rear was closed by the dark
files of Tlascalan warriors. The whole number must have fallen short of
seven thousand; of which less than four hundred were Spaniards.[1]

For a short distance, the army kept along the narrow tongue of land
that divides the Tezcucan from the Chalcan waters, when it entered on
the great dike, which, with the exception of an angle near the commencement, stretches in a perfectly straight line across the salt floods of Tezcuco to the gates of the capital. It was the same causeway, or rather the
basis of that, which still forms the great southern avenue of Mexico.[2] The
Spaniards had occasion more than ever to admire the mechanical science
of the Aztecs, in the geometrical precision with which the work was exe-

[1] He took about 6000 warriors from Tlascala; and some few of the Cempoallan
and other Indian allies continued with him. The Spanish force on leaving Vera
Cruz amounted to about 400 foot and 15 horse. In the remonstrance of the disaffected soldiers, after the murderous Tlascalan combats, they speak of having lost
fifty of their number since the beginning of the campaign. Ante, Vol. I. p. 245.

[2] "La calzada d'Iztapalapan est fondée sur cette même digue ancienne, sur laquelle Cortéz fit des prodiges de valeur dans ses rencontres avec les assiégés." Humboldt, Essai Politique, tom. II. p. 57.

cuted, as well as the solidity of its construction. It was composed of huge stones well laid in cement; and wide enough, throughout its whole extent, for ten horsemen to ride abreast.

They saw, as they passed along, several large towns, resting on piles, and reaching far into the water,—a kind of architecture which found great favor with the Aztecs, being in imitation of that of their metropolis.[3] The busy population obtained a good subsistence from the manufacture of salt, which they extracted from the waters of the great lake. The duties on the traffic in this article were a considerable source of revenue to the crown.

Everywhere the Conquerors beheld the evidence of a crowded and thriving population, exceeding all they had yet seen. The temples and principal buildings of the cities were covered with a hard white stucco, which glistened like enamel in the level beams of the morning. The margin of the great basin was more thickly gemmed, than that of Chalco, with towns and hamlets.[4] The water was darkened by swarms of canoes filled with Indians,[5] who clambered up the sides of the causeway, and gazed with curious astonishment on the strangers. And here, also, they beheld those fairy islands of flowers, overshadowed occasionally by trees of considerable size, rising and falling with the gentle undulation of the billows. At the distance of half a league from the capital, they encountered a solid work or curtain of stone, which traversed the dike. It was twelve feet high, was strengthened by towers at the extremities, and in the centre was a battlemented gate-way, which opened a passage to the troops. It was called the Fort of Xoloc, and became memorable in aftertimes as the position occupied by Cortés in the famous siege of Mexico.

Here they were met by several hundred Aztec chiefs, who came out to announce the approach of Montezuma, and to welcome the Spaniards to his capital. They were dressed in the fanciful gala costume of the country, with the *maxtlatl*, or cotton sash, around their loins, and a broad mantle of the same material, or of the brilliant feather-embroidery, flowing gracefully down their shoulders. On their necks and arms they displayed collars and bracelets of turquoise mosaic, with which delicate

[3] Among these towns were several containing from three to five or six thousand dwellings, according to Cortés, whose barbarous orthography in proper names will not easily be recognized by Mexican or Spaniard. Rel. Seg., ap. Lorenzana, p. 78.

[4] Father Toribio Benavente does not stint his panegyric in speaking of the neighborhood of the capital, which he saw in its glory. "Creo, que en toda nuestra Europa hay pocas ciudades que tengan tal asiento y tal comarca, con tantos pueblos á la redonda de sí y tan bien asentados." Hist. de los Indios, MS., Parte 3, cap. 7.

[5] It is not necessary, however, to adopt Herrera's account of 50,000 canoes, which, he says, were constantly employed in supplying the capital with provisions! (Hist. General, dec. 2, lib. 7, cap. 14.) The poet-chronicler Saavedra is more modest in his estimate.

> "Dos mil y mas canoas cada dia
> Bastecen el gran pueblo Mexicano
> De la mas y la menos niñeria
> Que es necessario al alimento humano."
> EL PEREGRINO INDIANO, canto 11.

plumage was curiously mingled,[6] while their ears, under-lips, and occa-sionally their noses, were garnished with pendants formed of precious stones, or crescents of fine gold. As each cacique made the usual formal salutation of the country separately to the general, the tedious ceremony delayed the march more than an hour. After this, the army experienced no further interruption till it reached a bridge near the gates of the city. It was built of wood, since replaced by one of stone, and was thrown across an opening of the dike, which furnished an outlet to the waters, when agitated by the winds, or swollen by a sudden influx in the rainy season. It was a draw-bridge; and the Spaniards, as they crossed it, felt how truly they were committing themselves to the mercy of Montezuma, who, by thus cutting off their communications with the country, might hold them prisoners in his capital.[7]

In the midst of these unpleasant reflections, they beheld the glittering retinue of the emperor emerging from the great street which led then, as it still does, through the heart of the city.[8] Amidst a crowd of Indian nobles, preceded by three officers of state, bearing golden wands,[9] they saw the royal palanquin blazing with burnished gold. it was borne on the shoulders of nobles, and over it a canopy of gaudy feather-work, pow-dered with jewels, and fringed with silver, was supported by four atten-dants of the same rank. They were bare-footed, and walked with a slow, measured pace, and with eyes bent on the ground. When the train had come within a convenient distance, it halted, and Montezuma, descending from his litter, came forward leaning on the arms of the lords of Tezcuco and Iztapalapan, his nephew and brother, both of whom, as we have seen, had already been made known to the Spaniards. As the monarch ad-vanced under the canopy, the obsequious attendants strewed the ground with cotton tapestry, that his imperial feet might not be contaminated by the rude soil. His subjects of high and low degree, who lined the sides of the causeway, bent forward with their eyes fastened on the ground as he passed, and some of the humbler class prostrated themselves before him.[10]

---

[6] "Usaban unos brazaletes de musaico, hechos de turquezas con unas plumas ricas que salian de ellos, que eran mas altas que la cabeza, y bordadas con plumas ricas y con oro, y unas bandas de oro, que subian con las plumas." Sahagun, Hist. de Nueva España, lib. 8, cap. 9.

[7] Gonzalo de las Casas, Defensa, MS., Parte 1, cap. 24.—Gomara, Crónica, cap. 65. —Bernal Diaz, Hist. de la Conquista, cap. 88.—Oviedo, Hist. de las Ind., MS., lib. 33, cap. 5.—Rel. Seg. de Cortés, ap. Lorenzana, pp. 78, 79.—Ixtlilxochitl, Hist. Chich., MS., cap. 85.

[8] Cardinal Lorenzana says, the street intended, probably, was that crossing the city from the Hospital of San Antonio. (Rel. Seg. de Cortés, p. 79, nota.) This is confirmed by Sahagun. "Y así en aquel trecho que está desde la Iglesia de San An-tonio (que ellos llaman Xuluco) que va por cave las casas de Alvarado, hacia el Hospital de la Concepcion, salió Moctezuma á recibir de paz á D. Hernando Cor-tés." Hist. de Nueva España, MS., lib. 12, cap. 16.

[9] Carta del Lic. Zuazo, MS.

[10] "Toda la gente que estaba en las calles se le humiliaban y hacian profunda reverencia y grande acatamiento sin levantar los ojos á le mirar, sino que todos estaban hasta que él era pasado, tan inclinados como frayles en Gloria Patri." Tori-bio, Hist. de los Indios, MS., Parte 3, cap. 7.

Such was the homage paid to the Indian despot, showing that the slavish forms of Oriental adulation were to be found among the rude inhabitants of the Western World.

Montezuma wore the girdle and ample square cloak, *tilmatli*, of his nation. It was made of the finest cotton, with the embroidered ends gathered in a knot round his neck. His feet were defended by sandals having soles of gold, and the leathern thongs which bound them to his ankles were embossed with the same metal. Both the cloak and sandals were sprinkled with pearls and precious stones, among which the emerald and the *chalchivitl*—a green stone of higher estimation than any other among the Aztecs—were conspicuous. On his head he wore no other ornament than a *panache* of plumes of the royal green which floated down his back, the badge of military, rather than of regal, rank.

He was at this time about forty years of age. His person was tall and thin, but not ill-made. His hair, which was black and straight, was not very long; to wear it short was considered unbecoming persons of rank. His beard was thin; his complexion somewhat paler than is often found in his dusky, or rather copper-colored race. His features, though serious in their expression, did not wear the look of melancholy, indeed, of dejection, which characterizes his portrait, and which may well have settled on them at a later period. He moved with dignity, and his whole demeanor, tempered by an expression of benignity not to have been anticipated from the reports circulated of his character, was worthy of a great prince.—Such is the portrait left to us of the celebrated Indian emperor, in this his first interview with the white men.[11]

The army halted as he drew near. Cortés, dismounting, threw his reins to a page, and, supported by a few of the principal cavaliers, advanced to meet him. The interview must have been one of uncommon interest to both. In Montezuma, Cortés beheld the lord of the broad realms he had traversed, whose magnificence and power had been the burden of every tongue. In the Spaniard, on the other hand, the Aztec prince saw the strange being whose history seemed to be so mysteriously connected with his own; the predicted one of his oracles; whose achievements proclaimed

---

[11] For the preceding account of the equipage and appearance of Montezuma, see Bernal Diaz, Hist. de la Conquista, cap. 88,—Carta de Zuazo, MS.,—Ixtlilxochitl, Hist. Chich., MS., cap. 85,—Gomara, Crónica, cap. 65,—Oviedo, Hist. de las Ind., MS., ubi supra, et cap. 45,—Acosta, lib. 7, cap. 22,—Sahagun, Hist. de Nueva España, MS., lib. 12, cap. 16,—Toribio, Hist. de los Indios, MS., Parte 3, cap. 7.

The noble Castilian, or rather Mexican bard, Saavedra, who belonged to the generation after the Conquest, has introduced most of the particulars in his rhyming chronicle. The following specimen will probably suffice for the reader.

"Yva el gran Moteçuma atauiado
De manta açul y blanca con gran falda,
De algodon muy sutil y delicado,
Y al remate vna concha de esmeralda:
En la parte que el nudo tiene dado,
Y una tiara á modo de guirnalda,
Zapatos que de oro son las suelas
Asidos con muy ricas correhuelas."

EL PEREGRINO INDIANO, canto II.

him something more than human. But, whatever may have been the monarch's feelings, he so far suppressed them as to receive his guest with princely courtesy, and to express his satisfaction at personally seeing him in his capital.[12] Cortés responded by the most profound expressions of respect, while he made ample acknowledgments for the substantial proofs which the emperor had given the Spaniards of his munificence. He then hung round Montezuma's neck a sparkling chain of colored crystal, accompanying this with a movement as if to embrace him, when he was restrained by the two Aztecs lords, shocked at the menaced profanation of the sacred person of their master.[13] After the interchange of these civilities, Montezuma appointed his brother to conduct the Spaniards to their residence in the capital, and again entering his litter was borne off amidst prostrate crowds in the same state in which he had come. The Spaniards quickly followed, and with colors flying and music playing soon made their entrance into the southern quarter of Tenochtitlan.[14]

Here, again, they found fresh cause for admiration in the grandeur of the city, and the superior style of its architecture. The dwellings of the poorer class were, indeed, chiefly of reeds and mud. But the great avenue through which they were now marching was lined with the houses of the nobles, who were encouraged by the emperor to make the capital their residence. They were built of a red porous stone drawn from quarries in the neighborhood, and, though they rarely rose to a second story, often covered a large space of ground. The flat roofs, *azoteas*, were protected by stone parapets, so that every house was a fortress. Sometimes these roofs resembled parterres of flowers, so thickly were they covered with them, but more frequently these were cultivated in broad terraced gardens, laid out between the edifices.[15] Occasionally a great square or market-place intervened, surrounded by its porticos of stone and stucco; or a pyramidal temple reared its colossal bulk, crowned with its tapering sanctuaries, and altars blazing with inextinguishable fires. The great street facing the southern causeway, unlike most others in the place, was wide, and extended some miles in nearly a straight line, as before noticed, through the centre of the city. A spectator standing at one end of it, as his eye ranged along the deep vista of temples, terraces, and gardens, might clearly discern the other, with the blue mountains in the distance, which, in the transparent atmosphere of the table-land, seemed almost in contact with the buildings.

But what most impressed the Spaniards was the throngs of people who swarmed through the streets and on the canals, filling every door-way and window, and clustering on the roofs of the buildings. "I well remember

---

[12] "Satis vultu læto," says Martyr, "an stomacho sedatus, et an hospites per vim quis unquam libens susceperit, experti loquantur." De Orbe Novo, dec. 5, cap. 3.

[13] Rel. Seg. de Cortés, ap. Lorenzana, p. 79.

[14] "Entráron en la ciudad de Méjico á punto de guerra, tocando los atambores, y con banderas desplegadas," &c. Sahagun, Hist. de Nueva España, MS., lib. 12, cap. 15.

[15] "Et giardini alti et bassi, che era cosa maravigliosa da vedere." Rel. d' un gent. ap. Ramusio, tom. III. fol. 309.

the spectacle," exclaims Bernal Diaz; "it seems now, after so many years, as present to my mind, as if it were but yesterday." [16] But what must have been the sensations of the Aztecs themselves, as they looked on the portentous pageant! as they heard, now for the first time, the well-cemented pavement ring under the iron tramp of the horses,—the strange animals which fear had clothed in such supernatural terrors; as they gazed on the children of the East, revealing their celestial origin in their fair complexions; saw the bright falchions and bonnets of steel, a metal to them unknown, glancing like meteors in the sun, while sounds of unearthly music—at least, such as their rude instruments had never wakened—floated in the air! But every other emotion was lost in that of deadly hatred, when they beheld their detested enemy, the Tlascalan, stalking, in defiance, as it were, through their streets, and staring around with looks of ferocity and wonder, like some wild animal of the forest, who had strayed by chance from his native fastnesses into the haunts of civilization.[17]

As they passed down the spacious street, the troops repeatedly traversed bridges suspended above canals, along which they saw the Indian barks gliding swifty with their little cargoes of fruits and vegetables for the markets of Tenochtitlan.[18] At length, they halted before a broad area near the centre of the city, where rose the huge pyramidal pile dedicated to the patron war-god of the Aztecs, second only, in size, as well as sanctity, to the temple of Cholula, and covering the same ground now in part occupied by the great cathedral of Mexico.

Facing the western gate of the inclosure of the temple, stood a low range of stone buildings, spreading over a wide extent of ground, the palace of Axayacatl, Montezuma's father, built by that monarch about fifty years before.[19] It was appropriated as the barracks of the Spaniards. The emperor himself was in the court-yard, waiting to receive them. Approaching Cortés, he took from a vase of flowers, borne by one of his slaves, a massy collar, in which the shell of a species of craw-fish, much

---

[16] "¿Quien podrá," exclaims the old soldier, "dezir la multitud de hombres, y mugeres, y muchachos, que estauan en las calles, é açuteas, y en Canoas en aquellas acequias, que nos salian á mirar? Era cosa de notar, que agora que lo estoy escriuiendo, se me representa todo delante de mis ojos, como si ayer fuera quando esto passó." Hist. de la Conquista, cap. 88.

[17] "Ad spectaculum," says the penetrating Martyr, "tandem Hispanis placidum, quia diu optatum, Tenustiatanis prudentibus forte aliter, quia verentur fore, vt hi hospites quietem suam Elysiam veniant perturbaturi; de populo secus, qui nil sentit æque delectabile, quàm res novas ante oculos in presentiarum habere, de futuro nihil anxius." De Orbe Novo, dec. 5, cap. 3.

[18] The euphonious name of *Tenochtitlan* is commonly derived from Aztec words signifying "the *tuna,* or cactus, on a rock," the appearance of which, as the reader may remember, was to determine the site of the future capital. (Toribio, Hist. de los Indios, Parte 3, cap. 7.—Esplic. de la Colec: de Mendoza, ap. Antiq. of Mexico, vol. IV.) Another etymology derives the word from *Tenoch,* the name of one of the founders of the monarchy.

[19] Clavigero, Stor. del Messico, tom. III. p. 78.
It occupied what is now the corner of the streets, "Del Indio Triste" and "Tacuba." Humboldt, Vues des Cordillères, p. 7, et seq.

prized by the Indians, was set in gold, and connected by heavy links of the same metal. From this chain depended eight ornaments, also of gold, made in resemblance of the same shell-fish, a span in length each, and of delicate workmanship; [20] for the Aztec goldsmiths were confessed to have shown skill in their craft, not inferior to their brethren of Europe.[21] Montezuma, as he hung the gorgeous collar round the general's neck said, "This palace belongs to you, Malinche," [22] (the epithet by which he always addressed him,) "and your brethren. Rest after your fatigues, for you have much need to do so, and in a little while I will visit you again." So saying, he withdrew with his attendants, evincing, in this act, a delicate consideration not to have been expected in a barbarian.

Cortés' first care was to inspect his new quarters. The building, though spacious, was low, consisting of one floor, except, indeed, in the centre, where it rose to an additional story. The apartments were of great size, and afforded accommodations, according to the testimony of the Conquerors themselves, for the whole army! [23] The hardy mountaineers of Tlascala were, probably, not very fastidious, and might easily find a shelter in the out-buildings, or under temporary awnings in the ample courtyards. The best apartments were hung with gay cotton draperies, the floors covered with mats or rushes. There were, also, low stools made of single pieces of wood elaborately carved, and in most of the apartments beds made of the palm-leaf, woven into a thick mat, with coverlets, and sometimes canopies of cotton. These mats were the only beds used by the natives, whether of high or low degree.[24]

After a rapid survey of this gigantic pile, the general assigned his troops their respective quarters, and took as vigilant precautions for security, as if he had anticipated a siege, instead of a friendly entertainment. The place was encompassed by a stone wall of considerable thickness, with towers or heavy buttresses at intervals, affording a good means of defence. He planted his cannon so as to command the approaches, stationed his sentinels along the works, and, in short, enforced in every respect as strict military discipline as had been observed in any part of the march. He well knew the importance to his little band, at least for the present, of conciliating the good-will of the citizens; and, to avoid all possibility

[20] Rel. Seg. de Cortés, ap. Lorenzana, p. 88.—Gonzalo de las Casas, Defensa, MS., Parte 1, cap. 24.

[21] Boturini says, greater, by the acknowledgment of the goldsmiths themselves. "Los plateros de Madrid, viendo algunas Piezas, y Brazaletes de oro, con que se armaban en guerra los Reyes, y Capitanes Indianos, confessáron, que eran inimitables en Europa." (Idea, p. 78.) And Oviedo, speaking of their work in jewelry, remarks, "Io ví algunas piedras jaspes, calcidonias, jacintos, corniolas, é plasmas de esmeraldas, é otras de otras especies labradas é fechas, cabezas de Aves, é otras hechas animales é otras figuras, que dudo haber en España ni en Italia quien las supiera hacer con tanta perficion." Hist. de las Ind., MS., lib. 33, cap. 11.

[22] Ante, Vol. I. p. 258.

[23] Bernal Diaz, Hist. de la Conquista, cap. 88.—Rel. Seg. de Cortés, ap Lorenzana, p. 80.

[24] Bernal Diaz Ibid., loc. cit.—Oviedo, Hist. de las Ind., MS., lib. 33, cap. 5.— Sahagun, Hist. de Nueva España, MS., lib. 12, cap. 16.

of collision, he prohibited any soldier from leaving his quarters without orders, under pain of death. Having taken these precautions, he allowed his men to partake of the bountiful collation which had been prepared for them.

They had been long enough in the country to become reconciled to, if not to relish, the peculiar cooking of the Aztecs. The appetite of the soldier is not often dainty, and on the present occasion it cannot be doubted that the Spaniards did full justice to the savory productions of the royal kitchen. During the meal they were served by numerous Mexican slaves, who were, indeed, distributed through the palace, anxious to do the bidding of the strangers. After the repast was concluded, and they had taken their *siesta*, not less important to a Spaniard than food itself, the presence of the emperor was again announced.

Montezuma was attended by a few of his principal nobles. He was received with much deference by Cortés; and, after the parties had taken their seats, a conversation commenced between them, through the aid of Doña Marina, while the cavaliers and Aztec chieftains stood around in respectful silence.

Montezuma made many inquiries concerning the country of the Spaniards, their sovereign, the nature of his government, and especially their own motives in visiting Anahuac. Cortés explained these motives by the desire to see so distinguished a monarch, and to declare to him the true Faith professed by the Christians. With rare discretion, he contented himself with dropping this hint, for the present, allowing it to ripen in the mind of the emperor, till a future conference. The latter asked, whether those white men, who in the preceding year had landed on the eastern shores of his empire, were their countrymen. He showed himself well informed of the proceedings of the Spaniards from their arrival in Tabasco to the present time, information of which had been regularly transmitted in the hieroglyphical paintings. He was curious, also, in regard to the rank of his visitors in their own country; inquiring, if they were the kinsmen of the sovereign. Cortés replied, they were kinsmen of one another, and subjects of their great monarch, who held them all in peculiar estimation. Before his departure, Montezuma made himself acquainted with the names of the principal cavaliers, and the position they occupied in the army.

At the conclusion of the interview, the Aztec prince commanded his attendants to bring forward the presents prepared for his guests. They consisted of cotton dresses, enough to supply every man, it is said, including the allies, with a suit! [25] And he did not fail to add the usual accompani-

---

[25] "Muchas y diversas Joyas de Oro, y Plata, y Plumajes, y con fasta cinco ó seis mil Piezas de Ropa de Algodon muy ricas, y de diversas maneras texida, y labrada." (ReL Seg. de Cortés, ap. Lorenzana, p. 80.) Even this falls short of truth, according to Diaz. "Tenia apercebido el gran Monteçuma muy ricas joyas de oro, y de muchas hechuras, que dió á nuestro Capitan, é assí mismo á cada vno de nuestros Capitanes dió cositas de oro, y tres cargas de mantas de labores ricas de pluma, y entre todos los soldados tambien nos dió á cada vno á dos cargas de mantas, con

ment of gold chains and other ornaments, which he distributed in profusion among the Spaniards. He then withdrew with the same ceremony with which he had entered, leaving every one deeply impressed with his munificence and his affability so unlike what they had been taught to expect, by, what they now considered, an invention of the enemy.[26]

That evening, the Spaniards celebrated their arrival in the Mexican capital by a general discharge of artillery. The thunders of the ordnance reverberating among the buildings and shaking them to their foundations, the stench of the sulphureous vapor that rolled in volumes above the walls of the encampment, reminding the inhabitants of the explosions of the great *volcan*, filled the hearts of the superstitious Aztecs with dismay. It proclaimed to them, that their city held in its bosom those dread beings whose path had been marked with desolation, and who could call down the thunderbolts to consume their enemies! It was doubtless the policy of Cortés to strengthen this superstitious feeling as far as possible, and to impress the natives, at the outset, with a salutary awe of the supernatural powers of the Spaniards.[27]

On the following morning, the general requested permission to return the emperor's visit, by waiting on him in his palace. This was readily granted, and Montezuma sent his officers to conduct the Spaniards to his presence. Cortés dressed himself in his richest habit, and left the quarters attended by Alvarado, Sandoval, Velasquez and Ordaz, together with five or six of the common file.

The royal habitation was at no great distance. It stood on the ground, to the south-west of the cathedral, since covered in part by the *Casa del Estado*, the palace of the dukes of Monteleone, the descendants of Cortés.[28] It was a vast, irregular pile of low stone buildings, like that garrisoned by the Spaniards. So spacious was it, indeed, that, as one of the Conquerors assures us, although he had visited it more than once, for the express purpose, he had been too much fatigued each time by wandering through the apartments ever to see the whole of it.[29] It was built of the

alegría, y en todo parecia gran señor." (Hist. de la Conquista, cap. 89.) "Sex millia vestium, aiunt qui eas vidêre." Martyr, De Orbe Novo, dec. 5, cap. 3.

[26] Ixtlilxochitl, Hist. Chich., MS.; cap. 85.—Gomara, Crónica, cap. 66.—Herrera, Hist. General, dec. 2, lib. 7, cap. 6.—Bernal Diaz, Ibid., ubi supra.—Oviedo, Hist. de las Ind., MS., lib. 33, cap. 5.

[27] "La noche siguiente jugáron la artillería por la solemnidad de haber llegado sin daño á donde deseaban; pero los Indios como no usados á los truenos de la artillería, mal edor de la pólvora, recibiéron grande alteracion y miedo toda aquella noche." Sahagun, Hist. de Nueva España, MS., lib. 12, cap. 17.

[28] "C'est là que la famille construisit le bel édifice dans lequel se trouvent les archives del Estado, et qui est passfi avec tout l'héritage au duc Napolitain de Monteleone." (Humboldt, Essai Politique, tom. II. p. 72.) The inhabitants of modern Mexico have large obligations to this inquisitive traveller, for the care he has taken to identify the memorable localities of their capital. It is not often that a philosophical treatise is, also, a good *manuel du voyageur*.

[29] "Et io entrai più di quattro volte in una casa del gran Signor non per altro effetto che per vederla, et ogni volta vi camminauo tanto che mi stancauo, et mai la fini di vedere tutta." Rel. d' un gent., ap. Ramusio, tom III. fol. 309.

red porous stone of the country, *tetzontli*, was ornamented with marble, and on the façade over the principal entrance were sculptured the arms or device of Montezuma, an eagle bearing an ocelot in his talons.[30]

In the courts through which the Spaniards passed, fountains of crystal water were playing, fed from the copious reservoir on the distant hill of Chapoltepec, and supplying in their turn more than a hundred baths in the interior of the palace. Crowds of Aztec nobles were sauntering up and down in these squares, and in the outer halls, loitering away their hours in attendance on the court. The apartments were of immense size, though not lofty. The ceilings were of various sorts of odoriferous wood ingeniously carved; the floors covered with mats of the palm-leaf. The walls were hung with cotton richly stained, with the skins of wild animals, or gorgeous draperies of feather-work wrought in imitation of birds, insects, and flowers, with the nice art and glowing radiance of colors that might compare with the tapestries of Flanders. Clouds of incense rolled up from censers, and diffused intoxicating odors through the apartments. The Spaniards might well have fancied themselves in the voluptuous precincts of an Eastern harem, instead of treading the halls of a wild barbaric chief in the Western World.[31]

On reaching the hall of audience, the Mexican officers took off their sandals, and covered their gay attire with a mantle of *nequen*, a coarse stuff made of the fibres of the maguey, worn only by the poorest classes. This act of humiliation was imposed on all, except the members of his own family, who approached the sovereign.[32] Thus bare-footed, with down-cast eyes, and formal obeisance, they ushered the Spaniards into the royal presence.

They found Montezuma seated at the further end of a spacious saloon, and surrounded by a few of his favorite chiefs. He received them kindly, and very soon Cortés, without much ceremony, entered on the subject which was uppermost in his thoughts. He was fully aware of the importance of gaining the royal convert, whose example would have such an influence on the conversion of his people. The general, therefore, prepared to display the whole store of his theological science, with the most win-

---

[30] Gomara, Crónica, cap. 71.—Herrera, Hist. General, dec. 2, lib. 7, cap. 9.

The authorities call it "tiger," an animal not known in America. I have ventured to substitute the "ocelotl," *tlalocelotl* of Mexico, a native animal, which, being of the same family, might easily be confounded by the Spaniards with the tiger of the Old Continent.

[31] Toribio, Hist. de los Indios, MS., Parte 3, cap. 7.—Herrera, Hist. General, dec. 2, lib. 7, cap. 9.—Gomara, Crónica, cap. 71.—Bernal Diaz, Hist. de la Conquista, cap. 91.—Oviedo, Hist. de las Ind., MS., lib. 33, cap. 5, 46.—Rel. Seg. de Cortés, ap. Lorenzana, pp. 111-114.

[32] "Para entrar en su palacio, á que ellos llaman Tecpa, todos se descalzaban, y los que entraban á negociar con él habian de llevar mantas groseras encima de sí, y si eran grandes señores ó en tiempo de frio, sobre las mantas buenas que llevaban vestidas, ponian una manta grosera y pobre; y para hablarle, estaban muy humiliados y sin levantar los ojos." (Toribio, Hist. de los Indios, MS., Parte 3, cap. 7.) There is no better authority than this worthy missionary, for the usages of the ancient Aztecs, of which he had such large personal knowledge.

ning arts of rhetoric he could command, while the interpretation was conveyed through the silver tones of Marina, as inseparable from him on these occasions, as his shadow.

He set forth, as clearly as he could, the ideas entertained by the Church in regard to the holy mysteries of the Trinity, the Incarnation, and the Atonement. From this he ascended to the origin of things, the creation of the world, the first pair, paradise, and the fall of man. He assured Monte-zuma, that the idols he worshipped were Satan under different forms. A sufficient proof of it was the bloody sacrifices they imposed, which he contrasted with the pure and simple rite of the mass. Their worship would sink him in perdition. It was to snatch his soul, and the souls of his peo-ple, from the flames of eternal fire by opening to them a purer faith, that the Christians had come to his land. And he earnestly besought him not to neglect the occasion, but to secure his salvation by embracing the Cross, the great sign of human redemption.

The eloquence of the preacher was wasted on the insensible heart of his royal auditor. It, doubtless, lost somewhat of its efficacy, strained through the imperfect interpretation of so recent a neophyte as the In-dian damsel. But the doctrines were too abstruse in themselves to be comprehended at a glance by the rude intellect of a barbarian. And Mon-tezuma may have, perhaps, thought it was not more monstrous to feed on the flesh of a fellow-creature, than on that of the Creator himself.[33] He was, besides, steeped in the superstitions of his country from his cradle. He had been educated in the straitest sect of her religion; had been him-self a priest before his election to the throne; and was now the head both of the religion and the state. Little probability was there that such a man would be open to argument or persuasion, even from the lips of a more practised polemic than the Spanish commander. How could he abjure the faith that was intertwined with the dearest affections of his heart, and the very elements of his being? How could he be false to the gods who had raised him to such prosperity and honors, and whose shrines were in-trusted to his especial keeping?

He listened, however, with silent attention, until the general had con-cluded his homily. He then replied, that he knew the Spaniards had held this discourse wherever they had been. He doubted not their God was, as they said, a good being. His gods, also, were good to him. Yet what his visitor said of the creation of the world was like what he had been taught to believe.[34] It was not worth while to discourse further of the matter. His ancestors, he said, were not the original proprietors of the land. They had occupied it but a few ages, and had been led there by a great Being,

---

[33] The ludicrous effect—if the subject be not too grave to justify the expression—of a literal belief in the doctrine of Transubstantiation in the mother country, even at this day, is well illustrated by Blanco White, Letters from Spain, (London, 1822,) let. 1.

[34] "Y en esso de la creacion del mundo assí lo tenemos nosotros creido muchos tiempos passados." (Bernal Diaz, Hist. de la Conquista, cap. 90.) For some points of resemblance between the Aztec and Hebrew traditions, see Book 1, Ch. 3, and Appendix, Part 1. of this History.

who, after giving them laws and ruling over the nation for a time, had
withdrawn to the regions where the sun rises. He had declared, on his
departure, that he or his descendants would again visit them and resume
his empire.[35] The wonderful deeds of the Spaniards, their fair complexions, and the quarter whence they came, all showed they were his descendants. If Montezuma had resisted their visit to his capital, it was because he had heard such accounts of their cruelties,—that they sent the
lightning to consume his people, or crushed them to pieces under the hard
feet of the ferocious animals on which they rode. He was now convinced
that these were idle tales; that the Spaniards were kind and generous in
their natures; they were mortals of a different race, indeed, from the Aztecs, wiser, and more valiant,—and for this he honored them.

"You, too," he added, with a smile, "have been told, perhaps, that I
am a god, and dwell in palaces of gold and silver.[36] But you see it is false.
My houses, though large, are of stone and wood like those of others; and
as to my body," he said, baring his tawny arm, "you see it is flesh and
bone like yours. It is true, I have a great empire inherited from my ancestors; lands, and gold, and silver. But your sovereign beyond the
waters is, I know, the rightful lord of all. I rule in his name. You, Malinche, are his ambassador; you and your brethren shall share these things
with me. Rest now from your labors. You are here in your own dwellings,
and every thing shall be provided for your subsistence. I will see that
your wishes shall be obeyed in the same way as my own." [37] As the monarch concluded these words, a few natural tears suffused his eyes, while
the image of ancient independence, perhaps, flitted across his mind.[38]

Cortés, while he encouraged the idea that his own sovereign was the
great Being indicated by Montezuma, endeavored to comfort the monarch by the assurance that his master had no desire to interfere with his
authority, otherwise than, out of pure concern for his welfare, to effect
his conversion and that of his people to Christianity. Before the emperor
dismissed his visitors he consulted his munificent spirit, as usual, by distributing rich stuffs and trinkets of gold among them, so that the poorest

[35] "É siempre hemos tenido, que de los que de él descendiessen habian de venir á
sojuzgar esta tierra, y á nosotros como á sus Vasallos." Rel. Seg. de Cortés, ap.
Lorenzana, p. 81.

[36] "Y luego el Monteçuma dixo riendo, porque en todo era muy regozijado en su
hablar de gran señor: Malinche, bien sé que te han dicho essos de Tlascala, con
quien tanta amistad aueis tomado, que yo que soy como Dios, ó Teule, que quanto
ay en mis casas es todo oro, é plata, y piedras ricas." Bernal Diaz, Ibid., ubi supra.

[37] "É por tanto Vos sed cierto, que os obedecerémos, y ternémos por señor en lugar
de esse gran señor, que decis, y que en ello no habia falta, ni engaño alguno; é bien
podeis en toda la tierra, digo, que en la que yo en mi Señorío poseo, mandar á
vuestra voluntad, porque será obedecido y fecho, y todo lo que nosotros tenemos es
para lo que Vos de ello quisieredes disponer." Rel. Seg. de Cortés, ubi supra.

[38] Martyr, De Orbe Novo, dec. 5, cap. 3.—Gomara, Crónica, cap. 66.—Oviedo,
Hist. de las Ind., MS., lib. 33, cap. 5.—Gonzalo de las Casas, MS., Parte 1, cap. 24.

Cortés, in his brief notes of this proceeding, speaks only of the interview with
Montezuma in the Spanish quarters, which he makes the scene of the preceding
dialogue.—Bernal Diaz transfers this to the subsequent meeting in the palace. In the
only fact of importance, the dialogue itself, both substantially agree.

soldier, says Bernal Diaz, one of the party, received at least two heavy collars of the precious metal for his share. The iron hearts of the Spaniards were touched with the emotion displayed by Montezuma, as well as by his princely spirit of liberality. As they passed him, the cavaliers, with bonnet in hand, made him the most profound obeisance, and "on the way home," continues the same chronicler, "we could discourse of nothing but the gentle breeding and courtesy of the Indian monarch, and of the respect we entertained for him." [39]

Speculations of a graver complexion must have pressed on the mind of the general, as he saw around him the evidences of a civilization, and consequently power, for which even the exaggerated reports of the natives—discredited from their apparent exaggeration—had not prepared him. In the pomp and burdensome ceremonial of the court, he saw that nice system of subordination and profound reverence for the monarch which characterize the semi-civilized empires of Asia. In the appearance of the capital, its massy, yet elegant architecture, its luxurious social accommodations, its activity in trade, he recognised the proofs of the intellectual progress, mechanical skill, and enlarged resources of an old and opulent community; while the swarms in the streets attested the existence of a population capable of turning these resources to the best account.

In the Aztec he beheld a being unlike either the rude republican Tlascalan, or the effeminate Cholulan; but combining the courage of the one with the cultivation of the other. He was in the heart of a great capital, which seemed like an extensive fortification, with its dikes and its drawbridges, where every house might be easily converted into a castle. Its insular position removed it from the continent, from which, at the mere nod of the sovereign, all communication might be cut off, and the whole warlike population be at once precipitated on him and his handful of followers. What could superior science avail against such odds? [40]

As to the subversion of Montezuma's empire, now that he had seen him in his capital, it must have seemed a more doubtful enterprise than ever. The recognition which the Aztec prince had made of the feudal supremacy, if I may so say, of the Spanish sovereign, was not to be taken too literally. Whatever show of deference he might be disposed to pay the latter, under the influence of his present—perhaps temporary—delusion, it was not to be supposed that he would so easily relinquish his actual power and possessions, or that his people would consent to it. Indeed, his sensitive apprehensions in regard to this very subject, on the coming of

---

[39] "Assí nos despedímos con grandes cortesías dél, y nos fuýmos á nuestros aposentos, é ibamos platicando de la buena manera é criança que en todo tenia, é que nosotros en todo le tuuiessemos mucho acato, é con las gorras de armas colchadas quitadas, quando delante dél passassemos." Bernal Diaz, Hist. de la Conquista, cap. 90.

[40] "Y assí," says Toribio de Benavente, "estaba tan fuerte esta ciudad, que parecia no bastar poder humano para ganarla; porque además de su fuerza y municion que tenia, era cabeza y Señoría de toda la tierra, y el Señor de ella (Moteczuma) gloriábase en su silla y en la fortaleza de su ciudad, y en la muchedumbre de sus vassallos." Hist. de los Indios, MS., Parte 3, cap. 8.

the Spaniards, were sufficient proof of the tenacity with which he clung to his authority. It is true that Cortés had a strong lever for future operations in the superstitious reverence felt for himself both by prince and people. It was undoubtedly his policy to maintain this sentiment unimpaired in both, as far as possible.[41] But, before settling any plan of operations, it was necessary to make himself personally acquainted with the topography and local advantages of the capital, the character of its population, and the real nature and amount of its resources. With this view, he asked the emperor's permission to visit the principal public edifices.

Antonio de Herrera, the celebrated chronicler of the Indies, was born of a respectable family at Cuella in Old Spain, in 1549. After passing through the usual course of academic discipline in his own country, he went to Italy, to which land of art and letters the Spanish youth of that time frequently resorted to complete their education. He there became acquainted with Vespasian Gonzaga, brother of the duke of Mantua, and entered into his service. He continued with this prince after he was made viceroy of Navarre, and was so highly regarded by him, that, on his death-bed, Gonzaga earnestly commended him to the protection of Philip the Second. This penetrating monarch soon discerned the excellent qualities of Herrera, and raised him to the post of Historiographer of the Indies,—an office for which Spain is indebted to Philip. Thus provided with a liberal salary, and with every facility for pursuing the historical researches to which his inclination led him, Herrera's days glided peacefully away in the steady, but silent, occupations of a man of letters. He continued to hold the office of historian of the colonies through Philip the Second's reign, and under his successors, Philip the Third, and the Fourth; till in 1625 he died at the advanced age of seventy-six, leaving behind him a high character for intellectual and moral worth.

Herrera wrote several works, chiefly historical. The most important, that on which his reputation rests, is his *Historia General de las Indias Occidentales*. It extends from the year 1492, the time of the discovery of America, to 1554, and is divided into eight decades. Four of them were published in 1601, and the remaining four in 1615, making in all five volumes in folio. The work was subsequently republished in 1730, and has been translated into most of the languages of Europe. The English translator, Stevens, has taken great liberties with his original, in the way of abridgment and omission, but the execution of his work is on the whole superior to that of most of the old English versions of the Castilian chroniclers.

Herrera's vast subject embraces the whole colonial empire of Spain in the New World. The work is thrown into the form of annals, and the multifarious occurrences in the distant regions of which he treats are all marshalled with exclusive reference to their chronology, and made to move together *pari passu*. By means of this tasteless arrangement the thread of interest is perpetually snapped, the reader is hurried from one scene to another, without the opportunity of completing his survey of any. His patience is exhausted and his mind perplexed with partial and scattered glimpses, instead of gathering new light as he advances from the skilful development of a continuous and well digested narrative. This is the great defect of a plan founded on a slavish adherence to chronology. The defect becomes more serious, when the work, as in the present instance, is of vast compass and embraces a great variety of details, having little relation to each other. In such a work we feel the superiority of a plan like that which Robertson has pursued in his "History of America," where every subject is allowed to occupy its own independent place, proportioned to its importance, and thus to make a distinct and individual impression on the reader.

[41] "Many are of opinion," says Father Acosta, "that, if the Spaniards had continued the course they began, they might easily have disposed of Montezuma and his kingdom, and introduced the law of Christ without much bloodshed." Lib. 7, cap. 25.

Herrera's position gave him access to the official returns from the colonies, state papers, and whatever documents existed in the public offices for the illustration of the colonial history. Among these sources of information were some manuscripts, with which it is not now easy to meet; as, for example, the memorial of Alonso de Ojeda, one of the followers of Cortés, which has eluded my researches both in Spain and Mexico. Other writings, as those of father Sahagun, of much importance in the history of Indian civilization, were unknown to the historian. Of such manuscripts as fell into his hands, Herrera made the freest use. From the writings of Las Casas, in particular, he borrowed without ceremony. The bishop had left orders that his "History of the Indies" should not be published till at least forty years after his death. Before that period had elapsed, Herrera had entered on his labors, and, as he had access to the papers of Las Casas, he availed himself of it to transfer whole pages, nay, chapters, of his narrative in the most unscrupulous manner to his own work. In doing this, he made a decided improvement on the manner of his original, reduced his cumbrous and entangled sentences to pure Castilian, omitted his turgid declamation and his unreasonable invectives. But, at the same time, he also excluded the passages that bore hardest on the conduct of his countrymen, and those bursts of indignant eloquence, which showed a moral sensibility in the bishop of Chiapa that raised him so far above his age. By this sort of metempsychosis, if one may so speak, by which the letter and not the spirit of the good missionary was transferred to Herrera's pages, he rendered the publication of Las Casas' history, in some measure, superfluous; and this circumstance has, no doubt, been one reason for its having been so long detained in manuscript.

Yet, with every allowance for the errors incident to rapid composition, and to the pedantic chronological system pursued by Herrera, his work must be admitted to have extraordinary merit. It displays to the reader the whole progress of Spanish conquest and colonization in the New World, for the first sixty years after the discovery. The individual actions of his complicated story, though unskilfully grouped together, are unfolded in a pure and simple style, well suited to the gravity of his subject. If at first sight he may seem rather too willing to magnify the merits of the early discoverers, and to throw a veil over their excesses, it may be pardoned, as flowing, not from moral insensibility, but from the patriotic sentiment which made him desirous, as far as might be, to wipe away every stain from the escutcheon of his nation, in the proud period of her renown. It is natural that the Spaniard, who dwells on this period, should be too much dazzled by the display of her gigantic efforts, scrupulously to weigh their moral character, or the merits of the cause in which they were made. Yet Herrera's national partiality never makes him the apologist of crime; and, with the allowances fairly to be conceded, he may be entitled to the praise so often given him of integrity and candor.

It must not be forgotten, that, in addition to the narrative of the early discoveries of the Spaniards, Herrera has brought together a vast quantity of information in respect to the institutions and usages of the Indian nations, collected from the most authentic sources. This gives his work a completeness, beyond what is to be found in any other on the same subject. It is, indeed, a noble monument of sagacity and erudition; and the student of history, and still more the historical compiler, will find himself unable to advance a single step among the early colonial settlements of the New World without reference to the pages of Herrera.

Another writer on Mexico, frequently consulted in the course of the present narrative, is Toribio de Benavente, or *Motolinia*, as he is still more frequently called, from his Indian cognomen. He was one of the twelve Franciscan missionaries, who, at the request of Cortés, were sent out to New Spain immediately after the Conquest, in 1523. Toribio's humble attire, naked feet, and, in short, the poverty-stricken aspect which belongs to his order, frequently drew from the natives the exclamation of *Motolinia*, or "poor man." It was the first Aztec word, the signification of which the missionary learned, and he was so much pleased with it, as intimating his own condition, that he henceforth assumed it as his name. Toribio employed himself zealously with his brethren in the great object of their mission. He travelled on foot over various parts of Mexico, Guatemala, and Nicaragua. Wherever he went, he spared no pains to wean the natives from their dark idolatry, and to pour into their minds the light of revelation. He showed even a tender regard for their temporal as well as spiritual wants, and Bernal Diaz testifies that he has known him to give away his own robe to clothe a destitute and suffering Indian. Yet this charitable friar, so meek and conscientious in the discharge of his Christian duties, was one of the fiercest opponents of Las Casas, and sent home a remonstrance against the bishop of Chiapa, couched in terms the most opprobrious and sarcastic. It has led the bishop's biographer, Quintana, to suggest that the friar's threadbare robe may have covered somewhat of worldly pride and envy. It may be so. Yet it may also lead us to distrust the discretion of Las Casas himself, who could carry measures with so rude a hand as to provoke such unsparing animadversions from his fellow-laborers in the vineyard.

Toribio was made guardian of a Franciscan convent at Tezcuco. In this situation he continued active in good works, and, at this place, and in his different pilgrimages, is stated to have baptized more than four hundred thousand natives. His efficacious piety was attested by various miracles. One of the most remarkable was, when the Indians were suffering from great drought, which threatened to annihilate the approaching harvests. The good father recommended a solemn procession of the natives to the church of Santa Cruz, with prayers and a vigorous flagellation. The effect was soon visible in such copious rains as entirely relieved the people from their apprehensions, and in the end made the season uncommonly fruitful. The counterpart to this prodigy was afforded a few years later, while the country was laboring under excessive rains; when, by a similar remedy the evil was checked, and a like propitious influence exerted on the season as before. The exhibition of such miracles greatly edified the people, says his biographer, and established them firmly in the Faith. Probably Toribio's exemplary life and conversation, so beautifully illustrating the principles which he taught, did quite as much for the good cause as his miracles.

Thus passing his days in the peaceful and pious avocations of the Christian missionary, the worthy ecclesiastic was at length called from the scene of his earthly pilgrimage, in what year is uncertain, but at an advanced age, for he survived all the little band of missionaries who had accompanied him to New Spain. He died in the convent of San Francisco at Mexico, and his panegyric is thus emphatically pronounced by Torquemada, a brother of his own order: "He was a truly apostolic man, a great teacher of Christianity, beautiful in the ornament of every virtue, jealous of the glory of God, a friend of evangelical poverty, most true to the observance of his monastic rule, and zealous in the conversion of the heathen."

Father Toribio's long personal intercourse with the Mexicans, and the knowledge of their language, which he was at much pains to acquire, opened to him all the sources of information respecting them and their institutions, which existed at the time of the Conquest. The results he carefully digested in the work so often cited in these pages, the *Historia de los Indios de Nueva España*, making a volume of manuscript in folio. It is divided into three parts. 1. The religion, rites, and sacrifices of the Aztecs. 2. Their conversion to Christianity, and their manner of celebrating the festivals of the Church. 3. The genius and character of the nation, their chronology and astrology, together with notices of the principal cities and the staple productions of the country. Notwithstanding the methodical arrangement of the work, it is written in the rambling, unconnected manner of a common-place book, into which the author has thrown at random his notices of such matters as most interested him in his survey of the country. His own mission is ever before his eyes, and the immediate topic of discussion, of whatever nature it may be, is at once abandoned to exhibit an event or an anecdote that can illustrate his ecclesiastical labors. The most startling occurrences are recorded with all the credulous gravity which is so likely to win credit from the vulgar; and a stock of miracles is duly attested by the historian, of more than sufficient magnitude to supply the wants of the infant religious communities of New Spain.

Yet, amidst this mass of pious *incredibilia*, the inquirer into the Aztec antiquities will find much curious and substantial information. Toribio's long and intimate relations with the natives put him in possession of their whole stock of theology and science; and as his manner, though somewhat discursive, is plain and unaffected, there is no obscurity in the communication of his ideas. His inferences, colored by the superstitions of the age, and the peculiar nature of his profession, may be often received with distrust. But, as his integrity and his means of information were unquestionable, his work becomes of the first authority in relation to the antiquities of the country, and its condition at the period of the Conquest. As an educated man, he was enabled to penetrate deeper than the illiterate soldiers of Cortés, men given to action rather than to speculation.—Yet Toribio's manuscript, valuable as it is to the historian, has never been printed, and has too little in it of popular interest, probably, ever to be printed. Much that it contains has found its way, in various forms, into subsequent compilations. The work itself is very rarely to be found. Dr. Robertson had a copy, as it seems from the catalogue of MSS. published with his "History of America"; though the author's name is not prefixed to it. There is no copy, I believe, in the library of the Academy of History at Madrid; and for that in my possession I am indebted to the kindness of that curious bibliographer, Mr. O. Rich, now consul for the United States at Minorca.

Pietro Martire de Angleria, or Peter Martyr, as he is called by English writers, belonged to an ancient and highly respectable family of Arona in the north of Italy. In 1487 he was induced by the count of Tendilla, the Spanish ambassador at Rome, to return with him to Castile. He was graciously received by Queen Isabella, always desirous to draw around her enlightened foreigners who might exercise a salutary influence on the rough and warlike nobility of Castile. Martyr, who had been educated for the Church, was persuaded by the queen to undertake the instruction of the young nobles at the court. In this way he formed an intimacy with some of the most illustrious men of the nation, who seem to have cherished a warm personal regard for him through the remainder of his life. He was employed by the Catholic sovereigns in various concerns of public interest, was sent on a mission to Egypt, and was subsequently raised to a distinguished post in the cathedral of Granada. But he continued to pass much of his time at court, where he enjoyed the confidence of Ferdinand and Isabella, and of their successor, Charles the Fifth, till in 1525 he died, at the age of seventy.

Martyr's character combined qualities not often found in the same individual,— an ardent love of letters, with a practical sagacity that can only result from familiarity with men and affairs. Though passing his days in the gay and dazzling society of the capital, he preserved the simple tastes and dignified temper of a philosopher. His correspondence, as well as his more elaborate writings, if the term elaborate can be applied to any of his writings, manifests an enlightened and oftentimes independent spirit; though one would have been better pleased, had he been sufficiently independent to condemn the religious intolerance of the government. But Martyr, though a philosopher, was enough of a courtier to look with a lenient eye on the errors of princes. Though deeply imbued with the learning of Antiquity, and a scholar at heart, he had none of the feelings of the recluse, but took the most lively interest in the events that were passing around him. His various writings, including his copious correspondence, are for this reason the very best mirror of the age in which he lived.

His inquisitive mind was particularly interested by the discoveries that were going on in the New World. He was allowed to be present at the sittings of the Council of the Indies, when any communication of importance was made to it; and he was subsequently appointed a member of that body. All that related to the colonies passed through his hands. The correspondence of Columbus, Cortés, and the other discoverers, with the Court of Castile was submitted to his perusal. He became personally acquainted with these illustrious persons, on their return home, and frequently, as we find from his own letters, entertained them at his own table. With these advantages, his testimony becomes but one degree removed from that of the actors themselves in the great drama In one respect it is of a higher kind, since it is free from the prejudice and passion, which a personal interest in events is apt to beget. The testimony of Martyr is that of a philosopher, taking a clear and comprehensive survey of the ground, with such lights of previous knowledge to guide him, as none of the actual discoverers and conquerors could pretend to. It is true, this does not prevent his occasionally falling into errors; the errors of credulity,—not, however, of the credulity founded on superstition, but that which arises from the uncertain nature of the subject, where phenomena, so unlike any thing with which he had been familiar, were now first disclosed by the revelation of an unknown world.

He may be more fairly charged with inaccuracies of another description, growing out of haste and inadvertence of composition. But even here we should be charitable. For he confesses his sins with a candor that disarms criticism. In truth, he wrote rapidly, and on the spur of the moment, as occasion served. He shrunk from the publication of his writings, when it was urged on him, and his Decades *De Orbe Novo,* in which he embodied the results of his researches in respect to the American discoveries, were not published entire till after his death. The most valuable and complete edition of this work—the one referred to in the present pages—is the edition of Hakluyt, published at Paris, in 1587.

Martyr's works are all in Latin, and that not the purest; a circumstance rather singular, considering his familiarity with the classic models of Antiquity. Yet he evidently handled the dead languages with the same facility as the living. Whatever defects may be charged on his manner, in the selection and management of his topics he shows the superiority of his genius. He passes over the trivial details, which so often encumber the literal narratives of the Spanish voyagers, and fixes his attention on the great results of their discoveries,—the products of the country, the history and institutions of the races, their character and advance in civilization. In one respect his writings are of peculiar value. They show the state of feeling which existed at the Castilian court during the progress of discovery. They furnish, in short, the reverse side of the picture; and, when we have followed the Spanish conquerors in their wonderful career of adventure in the New World, we have only to turn to the pages of Martyr to find the impression produced by them on the enlightened minds of the Old. Such a view is necessary to the completeness of the historical picture.

If the reader is curious to learn more of this estimable scholar, he will find the particulars given in "The History of Ferdinand and Isabella," (Part I. chap. 14, Postscript, and chap. 19,) for the illustration of whose reign, his voluminous correspondence furnishes the most authentic materials.

BOOK IV

RESIDENCE IN MEXICO

CHAPTER I

Tezcucan Lake—Description of the Capital—Palaces and Museums—Royal Household—Montezuma's Way of Life

1519

The ancient city of Mexico covered the same spot occupied by the modern capital. The great causeways touched it in the same points; the streets ran in much the same direction, nearly from north to south and from east to west; the cathedral in the *plaza mayor* stands on the same ground that was covered by the temple of the Aztec war-god; and the four principal quarters of the town are still known among the Indians by their ancient names. Yet an Aztec of the days of Montezuma, could he behold the modern metropolis, which has risen with such phœnix-like splendor from the ashes of the old, would not recognise its site as that of his own Tenochtitlan. For the latter was encompassed by the salt floods of Tezcuco, which flowed in ample canals through every part of the city; while the Mexico of our day stands high and dry on the main land, nearly a league distant, at its centre, from the water. The cause of this apparent change in its position is the diminution of the lake, which, from the rapidity of evaporation in these elevated regions, had become perceptible before the Conquest, but which has since been greatly accelerated by artificial causes.[1]

The average level of the Tezcucan lake, at the present day, is but four feet lower than the great square of Mexico.[2] It is considerably lower than the other great basins of water which are found in the Valley. In the heavy swell sometimes caused by long and excessive rains, these latter reservoirs anciently overflowed into the Tezcuco, which, rising with the accumulated volume of waters, burst through the dikes, and, pouring into

---

[1] The lake, it seems, had perceptibly shrunk before the Conquest, from the testimony of Motilinia, who entered the country soon after. Toribio, Hist .de los Indios, MS., Parte 3, cap. 6.

[2] Humboldt, Essai Politique, tom. II. p. 95.

Cortés supposed there were regular tides in this lake. (Rel. Seg., ap. Lorenzana, p. 101.) This sorely puzzles the learned Martyr; (De Orbe Novo, dec. 5, cap. 3;) as it has more than one philosopher since, whom it has led to speculate on a subterraneous communication with the ocean! What the general called "tides" was probably the periodical swells caused by the prevalence of certain regular winds.

313

the streets of the capital, buried the lower part of the buildings under a deluge. This was comparatively a light evil, when the houses stood on piles so elevated that boats might pass under them; when the streets were canals, and the ordinary mode of communication was by water. But it became more disastrous, as these canals, filled up with the rubbish of the ruined Indian city, were supplanted by streets of solid earth, and the foundations of the capital were gradually reclaimed from the watery element. To obviate this alarming evil, the famous drain of Huehuetoca was opened, at an enormous cost, in the beginning of the seventeenth century, and Mexico, after repeated inundations, has been at length placed above the reach of the flood.[3] But what was gained to the useful, in this case, as in some others, has been purchased at the expense of the beautiful. By this shrinking of the waters, the bright towns and hamlets once washed by them have been removed some miles into the interior, while a barren strip of land, ghastly from the incrustation of salts formed on the surface, has taken the place of the glowing vegetation which once enamelled the borders of the lake, and of the dark groves of oak, cedar, and sycamore which threw their broad shadows over its bosom.

The *chinampas*, that archipelago of wandering islands, to which our attention was drawn in the last chapter, have, also, nearly disappeared. These had their origin in the detached masses of earth, which, loosening from the shores, were still held together by the fibrous roots with which they were penetrated. The primitive Aztecs, in their poverty of land, availed themselves of the hint thus afforded by nature. They constructed rafts of reeds, rushes, and other fibrous materials, which, tightly knit together, formed a sufficient basis for the sediment that they drew up from the bottom of the lake. Gradually islands were formed, two or three hundred feet in length, and three or four feet in depth, with a rich stimulated soil, on which the economical Indian raised his vegetables and flowers for the markets of Tenochtitlan. Some of these *chinampas* were even firm enough to allow the growth of small trees, and to sustain a hut for the residence of the person that had charge of it, who with a long pole, resting on the sides or the bottom of the shallow basin, could change the position of his little territory at pleasure, which with its rich freight of vegetable stores was seen moving like some enchanted island over the water.[4]

The ancient dikes were three in number. That of Iztapalapan, by which the Spaniards entered, approaching the city from the south. That of Tepejacac, on the north, which, continuing the principal street, might be regarded, also, as a continuation of the first causeway. Lastly, the dike of Tlacopan, connecting the island-city with the continent on the west. This last causeway, memorable for the disastrous retreat of the Span-

---

[3] Humboldt has given a minute account of this tunnel, which he pronounces one of the most stupendous hydraulic works in existence, and the completion of which, in its present form, does not date earlier than the latter part of the last century. See his Essai Politique, tom. II. p. 105, et seq.

[4] Ibid., tom. II. p. 87, et seq.—Clavigero, Stor. del Messico, tom. II. p. 153.

lards, was about two miles in length. They were all built in the same substantial manner, of lime and stone, were defended by draw-bridges, and were wide enough for ten or twelve horsemen to ride abreast.[5]

The rude founders of Tenochtitlan built their frail tenements of reeds and rushes on the group of small islands in the western part of the lake. In process of time, these were supplanted by more substantial buildings. A quarry in the neighborhood, of a red porous amygdaloid, *tetzontli*, was opened, and a light, brittle stone drawn from it and wrought with little difficulty. Of this their edifices were constructed, with some reference to architectural solidity, if not elegance. Mexico, as already noticed, was the residence of the great chiefs, whom the sovereign encouraged, or rather compelled, from obvious motives of policy, to spend part of the year in the capital. It was also the temporary abode of the great lords of Tezcuco and Tlacopan, who shared, nominally, at least, the sovereignty of the empire.[6] The mansions of these dignitaries, and of the principal nobles, were on a scale of rude magnificence, corresponding with their state. They were low, indeed; seldom of more than one floor, never exceeding two. But they spread over a wide extent of ground; were arranged in a quadrangular form, with a court in the centre, and were surrounded by porticos embellished with porphyry and jasper, easily found in the neighborhood, while not unfrequently a fountain of crystal water in the centre shed a grateful coolness over the atmosphere. The dwellings of the common people were also placed on foundations of stone, which rose to the height of a few feet, and were then succeeded by courses of unbaked bricks, crossed occasionally by wooden rafters.[7] Most of the streets were mean and narrow. Some few, however, were wide and of great length. The principal street, conducting from the great southern causeway, penetrated in a straight line the whole length of the city, and afforded a noble vista, in which the long lines of low stone edifices were broken occasionally by intervening gardens, rising on terraces, and displaying all the pomp of Aztec horticulture.

The great streets, which were coated with a hard cement, were intersected by numerous canals. Some of these were flanked by a solid way, which served as a foot-walk for passengers, and as a landing-place where boats might discharge their cargoes. Small buildings were erected at in-

[5] Toribio, Hist. de los Indios, MS., Parte 3, cap. 8.
Cortés, indeed, speaks of four causeways. (Rel. Seg., ap. Lorenzana, p. 102.) He may have reckoned an arm of the southern one leading to Cojohuacan, or possibly the great aqueduct of Chapoltepec.
[6] Ante, Vol. I. p. 17.
[7] Martyr gives a particular account of these dwellings, which shows that even the poorer classes were comfortably lodged. "Populares vero domus cingulo virili tenus lapideæ sunt et ipsæ, ob lacunæ incrementum per fluxum aut fluviorum in ea labentium alluvies. Super fundamentis illis magnis, lateribus tum coctis, tum æstivo sole siccatis, immixtis trabibus reliquam molem construunt; uno sunt communes domus contentæ tabulato. In solo parum hospitantur propter humiditatem, tecta non tegulis sed bitumine quodam terreo vestiunt; ad solem captandum commodior est ille modus, breviore tempore consumi debere credendum est." De Orbe Novo, dec. 5, cap. 10.

tervals, as stations for the revenue officers who collected the duties on different articles of merchandise. The canals were traversed by numerous bridges, many of which could be raised, affording the means of cutting off communication between different parts of the city.[8]

From the accounts of the ancient capital, one is reminded of those aquatic cities in the Old World, the positions of which have been selected from similar motives of economy and defence; above all, of Venice,[9]—if it be not rash to compare the rude architecture of the American Indian with the marble palaces and temples—alas, how shorn of their splendor! —which crowned the once proud mistress of the Adriatic.[10] The example of the metropolis was soon followed by the other towns in the vicinity. Instead of resting their foundations on *terra firma*, they were seen advancing far into the lake, the shallow waters of which in some parts do not exceed four feet in depth.[11] Thus an easy means of intercommunication was opened, and the surface of this island "sea," as Cortés styles it, was darkened by thousands of canoes[12]—an Indian term—industriously engaged in the traffic between these little communities. How gay and picturesque must have been the aspect of the lake in those days, with its shining cities, and flowering islets rocking, as it were, an anchor on the fair bosom of its waters!

The population of Tenochtitlan, at the time of the Conquest, is variously stated. No contemporary writer estimates it at less than sixty thou-

[8] Toribio, Hist. de los Indios, MS., Parte 3, cap. 8.—Rel. Seg. de Cortés, ap. Lorenzana, p. 108.—Oviedo, Hist. de las Ind., MS., lib. 33, cap. 10, 11.—Rel. d' un gent., ap. Ramusio, tom. III. fol. 309.

[9] Martyr was struck with the resemblance. "Uti de illustrissima civitate Venetiarum legitur, ad tumulum in ea sinus Adriatici parte visum, fuisse constructam." Martyr, De Orbe Novo, dec. 5, cap. 10.

[10] May we not apply, without much violence, to the Aztec capital, Giovanni della Casa's spirited sonnet, contrasting the origin of Venice with its meridian glory?

 "Questi Palazzi e queste logge or colte
  D'ostro, di marmo e di figure elette,
  Fur poche e basse case insieme accolte,
  Deserti lidi e povere Isolette.
 Ma genti ardite d'ogni vizio sciolte
  Premeano il mar con picciole barchette,
  Che qui non per domar provincie molte,
  Ma fuggir servitù s' eran ristrette
 Non era ambizion ne' petti loro;
  Ma 'l mentire abborrian più che la morte,
  Nè vi regnava ingorda fame d' oro.
 Se 'l Ciel v' ha dato più beata sorte,
  Non sien quelle virtù che tanto onoro,
  Dalle nuove ricchezze oppresse emorte."

[11] "Le lac de Tezcuco n'a généralement que trois à cinq mètres de profondeur. Dans quelques endroits le fond se trouve même déjà à moins d'un mètre." Humboldt, Essai Politique, tom. II. p. 49.

[12] "Y cada dia entran gran mutitud de Indios cargados de bastimentos y tributos, así por tierra como por agua, en acales ó barcas, que *en lengua de las Islas llaman Canoas.*" Toribio, Hist. de los Indios, MS., Parte 3, cap. 6.

sand houses, which, by the ordinary rules of reckoning, would give three hundred thousand souls.[13] If a dwelling often contained, as is asserted, several families, it would swell the amount considerably higher.[14] Nothing is more uncertain than estimates of numbers among barbarous communities, who necessarily live in a more confused and promiscuous manner than civilized, and among whom no regular system is adopted for ascertaining the population. The concurrent testimony of the Conquerors; the extent of the city, which was said to be nearly three leagues in circumference; [15] the immense size of its great market-place; the long lines of edifices, vestiges of whose ruins may still be found in the suburbs, miles from the modern city; [16] the fame of the metropolis throughout Anahuac, which, however, could boast many large and populous places; lastly, the economical husbandry and the ingenious contrivances to extract aliment from the most unpromising sources,[17]—all attest a numerous population, far beyond that of the present capital.[18]

A careful police provided for the health and cleanliness of the city. A thousand persons are said to have been daily employed in watering and sweeping the streets,[19] so that a man—to borrow the language of an old Spaniard—"could walk through them with as little danger of soiling his

[13] "Esta la cibdad de Méjico ó *Teneztutan,* que será de sesenta mil vecinos." (Carta de Lic. Zuazo, MS.) "Tenustitanam ipsam inquiunt sexaginta circiter esse millium domorum." (Martyr, De Orbe Novo, dec. 5, cap. 3.) "Era Méjico, quando Cortés entró, pueblo de sesenta mil casas." (Gomara, Crónica, cap. 78.) Toribio says, vaguely, "Los moradores y gente era innumerable." (Hist. de los Indios, MS., Parte 3, cap. 8.) The Italian translation of the "Anonymous Conqueror," who survives only in translation, says, indeed, "meglio di sessanta mila *habitatori"; (Rel. d'un gent., ap. Ramusio, tom. III. fol. 309;) owing, probably, to a blunder in rendering the word *vecinos,* the ordinary term in Spanish statistics, which, signifying *householders,* corresponds with the Italian *fuochi.* See, also, Clavigero. (Stor. del Messico, tom. III. p. 86, ncta.) Robertson rests *exclusively* on this Italian translation for his estimate. (History of America, vol. II. p. 281.) He cites, indeed, two other authorities in the same connection; Cortés, who says nothing of the population, and Herrera, who confirms the popular statement of "sesenta mil casas." (Hist. General, dec. 2, lib. 7, cap. 13.) The fact is of some importance.

[14] "En las casas, por pequeñas que eran, pocas veces dexaban de morar dos, quatro, y seis vecinos." Herrera, Hist. General, dec. 2, lib. 7, cap. 13.

[15] Rel. d'un gent., ap. Ramusio, tom. III. fol. 309.

[16] "C'est sur le chemin qui mène à Tanepantla et aux Ahuahuetes que l'on peut marcher plus d'une heure entre les ruines de l'ancienne ville. On y reconnaît, ainsi que sur la route de Tacuba et d'Iztapalapan, combien Mexico, rebâti par Cortés, est plus petit que l'était Tenochtitlan sous le dernier des Montezuma. L'énorme grandeur du marché de Tlatelolco, dont on reconnaît encore les limites, prouve combien la population de l'ancienne ville doit avoir été considérable." Humboldt, Essai Politique, tom. II. p. 43.

[17] A common food with the lower classes was a glutinous scum found in the lakes, which they made into a sort of cake, having a savor not unlike cheese. (Bernal Diaz, Hist. de la Conquista, cap. 92.)

[18] One is confirmed in this inference by comparing the two maps at the end of the first edition of Bullock's "Mexico"; one of the modern City, the other of the ancient, taken from Boturini's museum, and showing its regular arrangement of streets and canals; as regular, indeed, as the square on a chessboard.

[19] Clavigero, Stoi. del Messico, tom. I. p. 274.

feet as his hands." [20] The water, in a city washed on all sides by the salt floods, was extremely brackish. A liberal supply of the pure element, however, was brought from Chapoltepec, "the grasshopper's hill," less than a league distant. It was brought through an earthen pipe, along a dike constructed for the purpose. That there might be no failure in so essential an article, when repairs were going on, a double course of pipes was laid. In this way a column of water of the size of a man's body was conducted into the heart of the capital, where it fed the fountains and reservoirs of the principal mansions. Openings were made in the aqueduct as it crossed the bridges, and thus a supply was furnished to the canoes below, by means of which it was transported to all parts of city.[21]

While Montezuma encouraged a taste for architectural magnificence in his nobles, he contributed his own share towards the embellishment of the city. It was in his reign that the famous calendar-stone, weighing, probably, in its primitive state, nearly fifty tons, was transported from its native quarry, many leagues distant, to the capital, where it still forms one of the most curious monuments of Aztec science. Indeed, when we reflect on the difficulty of hewing such a stupendous mass from its hard basaltic bed without the aid of iron tools, and that of transporting it such a distance across land and water without the help of animals. we may well feel admiration at the mechanical ingenuity and enterprise of the people who accomplished it.[22]

Not content with the spacious residence of his father, Montezuma erected another on a yet more magnificent scale. It occupied, as before mentioned, the ground partly covered by the private dwellings on one side of the *plaza mayor* of the modern city. This building, or, as it might more correctly be styled, pile of buildings, spread over an extent of ground so vast, that, as one of the Conquerors assures us, its terraced roof might have afforded ample room for thirty knights to run their courses in a regular tourney.[23] I have already noticed its interior decorations, its fanciful draperies, its roofs inlaid with cedar and other odoriferous woods, held together without a nail, and, probably, without a knowledge of the arch,[24] its numerous and spacious apartments, which

---

[20] "Era tan barrido y el suelo tan asentado y liso, que aunque la planta del pie fuera tan delicada como la de la mano no recibiera el pie detrimento ninguno en andar descalzo." Toribio, Hist. de los Indios, MS., Parte 3, cap. 7.

[21] Rel. Seg. de Cortés, ap. Lorenzana, p. 108.—Carta del Lic. Zuazo, MS.—Rel. d'un gent., ap. Ramusio, tom. III. fol. 309.

[22] These immense masses, according to Martyr, who gathered his information from eyewitnesses, were transported by means of long files of men, who dragged them with ropes over huge wooden rollers. (De Orbe Novo, dec. 5, cap. 10.) It was the manner in which the Egyptians removed their enormous blocks of granite, as appears from numerous reliefs sculptured on their buildings.

[23] Rel. d'un gent., ap. Ramusio, tom. III. fol. 309.

[24] "Ricos edificios," says the Licentiate Zuazo, speaking of the buildings in Anahuac generally, "ecepto que no se halla alguno con *boveda*." (Carta, MS.) The writer made large and careful observation, the year after the Conquest. His assertion, if it be received, will settle a question much mooted among antiquaries.

Cortés, with enthusiastic hyperbole, does not hesitate to declare superior to any thing of the kind in Spain.[25]

Adjoining the principal edifice were others devoted to various objects One was an armory, filled with the weapons and military dresses worn by the Aztecs, all kept in the most perfect order, ready for instant use. The emperor was himself very expert in the management of the *maquahuitl*, or Indian sword, and took great delight in witnessing athletic exercises, and the mimic representation of war by his young nobility. Another build-ing was used as a granary, and others as warehouses for the different articles of food and apparel contributed by the districts charged with the maintenance of the royal household.

There were, also, edifices appropriated to objects of quite another kind. One of these was an immense aviary, in which birds of splendid plumage were assembled from all parts of the empire. Here was the scarlet cardi-nal, the golden pheasant, the endless parrot-tribe with their rainbow hues, (the royal green predominant,) and that miniature miracle of nature, the humming-bird, which delights to revel among the honeysuckle bowers of Mexico.[26] Three hundred attendants had charge of this aviary, who made themselves acquainted with the appropriate food of its inmates, often-times procured at great cost, and in the moulting season were careful to collect the beautiful plumage, which, with its many-colored tints, furn-ished the materials for the Aztec painter.

A separate building was reserved for the fierce birds of prey; the vora-cious vulture-tribes and eagles of enormous size, whose home was in the snowy solitudes of the Andes. No less than five hundred turkeys, the cheapest meat in Mexico, were allowed for the daily consumption of these tyrants of the feathered race.

Adjoining this aviary was a menagerie of wild animals, gathered from the mountain forests, and even from the remote swamps of the *tierra caliente*. The resemblance of the different species to those in the Old World, with which no one of them, however, was identical, led to a per-petual confusion in the nomenclature of the Spaniards, as it has since done in that of better instructed naturalists. The collection was still fur-ther swelled by a great number of reptiles and serpents remarkable for their size and venomous qualities, among which the Spaniards beheld the

[25] "Tenia dentro de la ciudad sus Casas de Aposentamiento, tales, y tan mara-villosas que me pareceria casi imposible poder decir la bondad y grandeza de ellas. É por tanto, no me porné en expresar cosa de ellas, mas dé que en España no hay su semejable." Rel. Seg., ap. Lorenzana, p. 111.

[26] Herrera's account of these feathered insects, if one may so style them, shows the fanciful errors into which even men of science were led in regard to the new tribes of animals discovered in America. "There are some birds in the country of the size of butterflies, with long beaks, brilliant plumage, much esteemed for the curious works made of them. Like the bees, they live on flowers, and the dew which settles on them; and when the rainy season is over, and the dry weather sets in, they fasten themselves to the trees by their beaks and soon die. But in the following year, when the new rains come, they come to life again"! Hist. General, dec. 2, lib. 10, cap. 21.

fiery little animal "with the castanets in his tail," the terror of the American wilderness.[27] The serpents were confined in long cages lined with down or feathers, or in troughs of mud and water. The beasts and birds of prey were provided with apartments large enough to allow of their moving about, and secured by a strong lattice-work, through which light and air were freely admitted. The whole was placed under the charge of numerous keepers, who acquainted themselves with the habits of their prisoners, and provided for their comfort and cleanliness. With what deep interest would the enlightened naturalist of that day—an Oviedo, or a Martyr, for example—have surveyed this magnificent collection, in which the various tribes which roamed over the Western wilderness, the unknown races of an unknown world, were brought into one view! How would they have delighted to study the peculiarities of these new species, compared with those of their own hemisphere, and thus have risen to some comprehension of the general laws by which Nature acts in all her works! The rude followers of Cortés did not trouble themselves with such refined speculations. They gazed on the spectacle with a vague curiosity not unmixed with awe; and, as they listened to the wild cries of the ferocious animals and the hissings of the serpents, they almost fancied themselves in the infernal regions.[28]

I must not omit to notice a strange collection of human monsters, dwarfs, and other unfortunate persons, in whose organization Nature had capriciously deviated from her regular laws. Such hideous anomalies were regarded by the Aztecs as a suitable appendage of state. It is even said, they were in some cases the results of artificial means, employed by unnatural parents desirous to secure a provision for their offspring by thus qualifying them for a place in the royal museum! [29]

Extensive gardens were spread out around these buildings, filled with fragrant shrubs and flowers, and especially with medicinal plants.[30] No country has afforded more numerous species of these last, than New Spain; and their virtues were perfectly understood by the Aztecs, with whom medical botany may be said to have been studied as a science. Amidst this labyrinth of sweet-scented groves and shrubberies, fountains

[27] "Pues mas tenian," says the honest Captain Diaz, "en aquella maldita casa muchas Víboras, y Culebras emponçoñadas, que traen en las colas vnos que suenan como cascabeles; estas son las peores Víboras de todas." Hist. de la Conquista, cap. 91.
[28] "Digamos aora," exclaims Captain Diaz, "las cosas infernales que hazian, quando bramauan los Tigres y Leones, y aullauan los Adiues y Zorros, y silbauan las Sierpes, era grima oirlo, y parecia infierno." Ibid., loc. cit.
[29] Ibid., ubi supra.—Rel. Seg. de Cortés, ap. Lorenzana, pp. 111-113.—Carta del Lic. Zuazo, MS.—Toribio, Hist. de los Indios, MS., Parte 3, cap. 7.—Oviedo, Hist. de las Ind., MS., lib. 33, cap. 11, 46.
[30] Montezuma, according to Gomara, would allow no fruit-trees, considering them as unsuitable to pleasure-grounds. (Crónica, cap. 75.) Toribio says, to the same effect, "Los Indios Señores no procuran árboles de fruta, porque se la traen sus vasallos, sino árboles de floresta, de donde cojan rosas, y adonde se crian aves, así para gozar del canto, como para las tirar con Cerbatana, de la cual son grandes tiradores." Hist. de los Indios, MS., Parte 3, cap. 6

of pure water might be seen throwing up their sparkling jets, and scattering refreshing dews over the blossoms. Ten large tanks, well stocked with fish, afforded a retreat on their margins to various tribes of water-fowl, whose habits were so carefully consulted, that some of these ponds were of salt water, as that which they most loved to frequent. A tessellated pavement of marble inclosed the ample basins, which were overhung by light and fanciful pavilions, that admitted the perfumed breezes of the gardens, and offered a grateful shelter to the monarch and his mistresses in the sultry heats of summer.[31]

But the most luxurious residence of the Aztec monarch, at that season, was the royal hill of Chapoltepec, a spot consecrated, moreover, by the ashes of his ancestors. It stood in a westerly direction from the capital, and its base was, in his day, washed by the waters of the Tezcuco. On its lofty crest of porphyritic rock, there now stands the magnificent, though desolate, castle erected by the young viceroy Galvez, at the close of the seventeenth century. The view from its windows is one of the finest in the environs of Mexico. The landscape is not disfigured here, as in many other quarters, by the white and barren patches, so offensive to the sight; but the eye wanders over an unbroken expanse of meadows and cultivated fields, waving with rich harvests of European grain. Montezuma's gardens stretched for miles around the base of the hill. Two statues of that monarch and his father, cut in *bas relief* in the porphyry, were spared till the middle of the last century; [32] and the grounds are still shaded by gigantic cypresses, more than fifty feet in circumference, which were centuries old at the time of the Conquest. The place is now a tangled wilderness of wild shrubs, where the myrtle mingles its dark, glossy leaves with the red berries and delicate foliage of the pepper-tree. Surely, there is no spot better suited to awaken meditation on the past; none, where the traveller, as he sits under those stately cypresses grey with the moss of ages, can so fitly ponder on the sad destinies of the Indian races and the monarch who once held his courtly revels under the shadow of their branches.

The domestic establishment of Montezuma was on the same scale of barbaric splendor as every thing else about him. He could boast as many wives as are found in the harem of an Eastern sultan.[33] They were lodged in their own apartments, and provided with every accommodation, according to their ideas, for personal comfort and cleanliness. They passed their hours in the usual feminine employments of weaving and embroidery, especially in the graceful feather-work, for which such rich materials were furnished by the royal aviaries. They conducted themselves with strict decorum, under the supervision of certain aged females, who acted in the respectable capacity of duennas, in the same manner as in

[31] Ibid., loc. cit.—Rel. Seg. de Cortés, ubi supra.—Oviedo, Hist. de las Ind., MS., lib. 33, cap. 11.

[32] Gama, a competent critic, who saw them just before their destruction, praises their execution. Gama, Descripcion, Parte 2, pp. 81-83.—Also, Ante, Vol. I. p. 82.

[33] No less than one thousand, if we believe Gomara; who adds the edifying intelligence, "quo huvo vez, yue tuvo ciento i cincuenta preñadas à un tiempo!"

th: religious houses attached to the *teocallis*. The palace was supplied with numerous baths, and Montezuma set the example, in his own person, of frequent ablutions. He bathed at least once, and changed his dress four times, it is said, every day.[34] He never put on the same apparel a second time, but gave it away to his attendants. Queen Elizabeth, with a similar taste for costume, showed a less princely spirit in hoarding her discarded suits. Her wardrobe was, probably, somewhat more costly than that of the Indian emperor.

Besides his numerous female retinue, the halls and antechambers were filled with nobles in constant attendance on his person, who served also as a sort of body-guard. It had been usual for plebeians of merit to fill certain offices in the palace. But the haughty Montezuma refused to be waited upon by any but men of noble birth. They were not unfrequently the sons of the great chiefs, and remained as hostages in the absence of their fathers; thus serving the double purpose of security and state.[35]

His meals the emperor took alone. The well-matted floor of a large saloon was covered with hundreds of dishes.[36] Sometimes Montezuma himself, but more frequently his steward, indicated those which he preferred, and which were kept hot by means of chafing-dishes.[37] The royal bill of fare comprehended, besides domestic animals, game from the distant forests, and fish which, the day before, was swimming in the Gulf of Mexico! They were dressed in manifold ways, for the Aztec *artistes*, as we have already had occasion to notice, had penetrated deep into the mysteries of culinary science.[38]

The meats were served by the attendant nobles, who then resigned the office of waiting on the monarch to maidens selected for their personal grace and beauty. A screen of richly gilt and carved wood was drawn

[34] "Vestíase todos los dias quatro maneras de vestiduras todas nuevas, y nunca mas se las vestia otra vez." Rel. Seg. de Cortés, ap. Lorenzana, p. 114.

[35] Bernal Diaz, Hist. de la Conquista, cap. 91.—Gomara, Crónica, cap. 67, 71, 76. —Rel. Seg. de Cortés, ap. Lorenzana, pp. 113, 114. Toribio, Hist. de los Indios, MS., Parte 3, cap. 7.

"Á la puerta de la sala estaba vn patio mui grande en que habia cien aposentos de 25 ó 30 pies de largo cada vno sobre sí en torno de dicho patio, é allí estaban los Señores principales aposentados como guardas del palacio ordinarias, y estos tales aposentos se llaman galpones, los quales á la contina ocupan mas de 600 hombres, que jamas se quitaban de allí, é cada vno de aquellos tenian mas de 30 servidores, de manera que á lo menos nunca faltaban 3000 hombres de guerra en esta guarda cotediana del palacio." (Oviedo, Hist. de las Ind., MS., lib. 33, cap. 46.) A very curious and full account of Montezuma's household is given by this author, as he gathered it from the Spaniards who saw it in its splendor. Oviedo's history still remains in manuscript.

[36] Bernal Diaz., Ibid., loc. cit.—Rel. Seg. de Cortés, ubi supra.

[37] "Y porque la Tierra es fria, trahian debaxo de cada plato y escudilla de manjar un braserico con brasa, porque no se enfriasse." Rel. Seg. de Cortés, ap. Lorenzana, p. 113.

[38] Bernal Diaz has given us a few items of the royal *carte*. The first cover is rather a startling one, being a fricassee or stew of little children! *"carnes de muchachos de poca edad."* He admits, however, that this is somewhat apocryphal. Ibid., ubi supra.

around him, so as to conceal him from vulgar eyes during the repast. He was seated on a cushion, and the dinner was served on a low table covered with a delicate cotton cloth. The dishes were of the finest ware of Cholula. He had a service of gold, which was reserved for religious celebrations. Indeed, it would scarcely have comported with even his princely revenues to have used it on ordinary occasions, when his table equipage was not allowed to appear a second time, but was given away to his attendants. The saloon was lighted by torches made of a resinous wood, which sent forth a sweet odor and, probably, not a little smoke, as they burned. At his meal, he was attended by five or six of his ancient counsellors, who stood at a respectful distance, answering his questions, and occasionally rejoiced by some of the viands with which he complimented them from his table.

This course of solid dishes was succeeded by another of sweetmeats and pastry, for which the Aztec cooks, provided with the important requisites of maize-flour, eggs, and the rich sugar of the aloe, were famous. Two girls were occupied at the further end of the apartment, during dinner, in preparing fine rolls and wafers, with which they garnished the board from time to time. The emperor took no other beverage than the *choçolatl*, a potation of chocolate, flavored with vanilla and other spices, and so prepared as to be reduced to a froth of the consistency of honey, which gradually dissolved in the mouth. This beverage, if so it could be called, was served in golden goblets, with spoons of the same metal or of tortoise-shell finely wrought. The emperor was exceedingly fond of it, to judge from the quantity,—no less than fifty jars or pitchers being prepared for his own daily consumption! [39] Two thousand more were allowed for that of his household. [40]

The general arrangement of the meal seems to have been not very unlike that of Europeans. But no prince in Europe could boast a dessert which could compare with that of the Aztec emperor. For it was gathered fresh from the most opposite climes; and his board displayed the products of his own temperate region, and the luscious fruits of the tropics, plucked, the day previous, from the green groves of the *tierra caliente*, and transmitted with the speed of steam, by means of couriers, to the capital. It was as if some kind fairy should crown our banquets with the spicy products that but yesterday were growing in a sunny isle of the far-off Indian seas!

After the royal appetite was appeased, water was handed to him by the female attendants in a silver basin, in the same manner as had been done before commencing his meal; for the Aztecs were as constant in their ablutions, at these times, as any nation of the East. Pipes were then brought, made of a varnished and richly gilt wood, from which he in-

[39] "*Lo que yo ví,*" says Diaz, speaking from his own observation, "que traian sobre cincuenta jarros grandes hechos de buen cacao con su espuma, y de lo que bebia." Ibid., cap. 91.

[40] Ibid., ubi supra.—Rel. Seg. de Cortés, ap. Lorenzana, pp. 113, 114.—Oviedo, Hist. de las Ind., MS., lib. 33, cap. 11, 46.—Gomara, Crónica, cap 67.

haled, sometimes through the nose, at others through the mouth, the fumes of an intoxicating weed, "called *tobacco*," [41] mingled with liquid-amber. While this soothing process of fumigation was going on, the emperor enjoyed the exhibitions of his mountebanks and jugglers, of whom a regular corps was attached to the palace. No people, not even those of China or Hindostan, surpassed the Aztecs in feats of agility and legerdemain.[42]

Sometimes he amused himself with his jester; for the Indian monarch had his jesters, as well as his more refined brethren of Europe, at that day. Indeed, he used to say, that more instruction was to be gathered from them than from wiser men, for they dared to tell the truth. At other times, he witnessed the graceful dances of his women, or took delight in listening to music,—if the rude minstrelsy of the Mexicans deserve that name,—accompanied by a chant, in slow and solemn cadence, celebrating the heroic deeds of great Aztec warriors, or of his own princely line.

When he had sufficiently refreshed his spirits with these diversions, he composed himself to sleep, for in his *siesta* he was as regular as a Spaniard. On awaking, he gave audience to ambassadors from foreign states, or his own tributary cities, or to such caciques as had suits to prefer to him. They were introduced by the young nobles in attendance, and, whatever might be their rank, unless of the blood royal, they were obliged to submit to the humiliation of shrouding their rich dresses under the coarse mantle of *nequen*, and entering barefooted, with downcast eyes, into the presence. The emperor addressed few and brief remarks to the suitors, answering them generally by his secretaries; and the parties retired with the same reverential obeisance, taking care to keep their faces turned towards the monarch. Well might Cortés exclaim, that no court, whether of the Grand Seignior or any other infidel, ever displayed so pompous and elaborate a ceremonial! [43]

Besides the crowd of retainers already noticed, the royal household was not complete without a host of artisans constantly employed in the erection or repair of buildings, besides a great number of jewellers and persons skilled in working metals, who found abundant demand for their trinkets among the dark-eyed beauties of the harem. The imperial mummers and jugglers were also very numerous, and the dancers belonging to the palace occupied a particular district of the city, appropriated exclusively to them.

[41] "Tambien le ponian en la mesa tres cañutos muy pintados, y dorados, y dentro traian liquidámbar, rebuelto con vnas yervas *que se dize tabaco.*" Bernal Diaz, Hist. de la Conquista, cap. 91.
[42] The feats of jugglers and tumblers were a favorite diversion with the Grand Khan of China, as Sir John Maundeville informs us. (Voiage and Travaille chap. 22.) The Aztec mountebanks had such repute, that Cortés sent two of them to Rome to amuse his Holiness, Clement VII. Clavigero, Stor. del Messico, tom. II. p. 186.
[43] "Ninguno de los Soldanes, ni otro ningun señor infiel, de los que hasta agora se tiene noticia, no creo, que tantas, ni tales ceremonias en servicio tengan." Rel. Seg. de Cortés, ap. Lorenzana, p. 115.

The maintenance of this little host, amounting to some thousands of individuals, involved a heavy expenditure, requiring accounts of a complicated, and, to a simple people, it might well be, embarrassing nature. Every thing, however, was conducted with perfect order; and all the various receipts and disbursements were set down in the picture-writing of the country. The arithmetical characters were of a more refined and conventional sort than those for narrative purposes; and a separate apartment was filled with hieroglyphical ledgers, exhibiting a complete view of the economy of the palace. The care of all this was intrusted to a treasurer, who acted as a sort of major-domo in the household, having a general superintendence over all its concerns. This responsible office, on the arrival of the Spaniards, was in the hands of a trusty cacique named Tapia.[44]

Such is the picture of Montezuma's domestic establishment and way of living, as delineated by the Conquerors and their immediate followers, who had the best means of information; [45] too highly colored, it may be, by the proneness to exaggerate, which was natural to those who first witnessed a spectacle so striking to the imagination, so new and unexpected. I have thought it best to present the full details, trivial though they may seem to the reader, as affording a curious picture of manners, so superior in point of refinement to those of the other Aboriginal tribes on the North American continent. Nor are they, in fact, so trivial, when we reflect, that, in these details of private life, we possess a surer measure of civilization, than in those of a public nature.

In surveying them we are strongly reminded of the civilization of the East; not of that higher, intellectual kind which belonged to the more polished Arabs and the Persians, but that semi-civilization which has distinguished, for example, the Tartar races, among whom art, and even science, have made, indeed, some progress in their adaptation to material wants and sensual gratification, but little in reference to the higher and more ennobling interests of humanity. It is characteristic of such a people, to find a puerile pleasure in a dazzling and ostentatious pageantry; to make show for substance; vain pomp for power; to hedge round the throne itself with a barren and burdensome ceremonial, the counterfeit of real majesty.

Even this, however, was an advance in refinement, compared with the rude manners of the earlier Aztecs. The change may, doubtless, be referred in some degree to the personal influence of Montezuma. In his younger days, he had tempered the fierce habits of the soldier with the milder profession of religion. In later life, he had withdrawn himself still more from the brutalizing occupations of war, and his manners acquired

[44] Bernal Diaz, Hist. de la Conquista, cap. 91.—Carta del Lic. Zuazo, MS.—Oviedo, Hist. de las Ind., MS., ubi supra.—Toribio, Hist. de los Indios, MS., Parte 3, cap. 7.—Rel. Seg. de Cortés, ap. Lorenzana, pp. 110-115.—Rel. d'un gent., ap. Ramusio, tom. III. fol. 306.
[45] If the historian will descend but a generation later for his authorities, he may find materials for as good a chapter as any in Sir John Maundeville or the Arabian Nights.

a refinement tinctured, it may be added, with an effeminacy, unknown to his martial predecessors.

The condition of the empire, too, under his reign, was favorable to this change. The dismemberment of the Tezcucan kingdom, on the death of the great Nezahualpilli, had left the Aztec monarchy without a rival; and it soon spread its colossal arms over the furthest limits of Anahuac. The aspiring mind of Montezuma rose with the acquisition of wealth and power; and he displayed the consciousness of new importance by the assumption of unprecedented state. He affected a reserve unknown to his predecessors; withdrew his person from the vulgar eye, and fenced himself round with an elaborate and courtly etiquette. When he went aboard, it was in state, on some public occasion, usually to the great temple, to take part in the religious services; and, as he passed along, he exacted from his people, as we have seen, the homage of an adulation worthy of an Oriental despot.[46] His haughty demeanor touched the pride of his more potent vassals, particularly those who, at a distance, felt themselves nearly independent of his authority. His exactions, demanded by the profuse expenditure of his palace, scattered broadcast the seeds of discontent; and, while the empire seemed towering in its most palmy and prosperous state, the canker had eaten deepest into its heart.

---

[46] "Referre in tanto rege piget superbam mutationem vestis, et desideratas humi jacentium adulationes." (Livy, Hist., lib. 9, cap. 18.) The remarks of the Roman historian in reference to Alexander, after he was infected by the manners of Persia, fit equally well the Aztec emperor.

CHAPTER II

MARKET OF MEXICO—GREAT TEMPLE—INTERIOR SANCTUARIES—
SPANISH QUARTERS

1519

FOUR days had elapsed since the Spaniards made their entry into Mexico. Whatever schemes their commander may have revolved in his mind, he felt that he could determine on no plan of operations till he had seen more of the capital, and ascertained by his own inspection the nature of its resources. He accordingly, as was observed at the close of the last Book, sent to Montezuma, asking permission to visit the great *teocalli*, and some other places in the city.

The friendly monarch consented without difficulty. He even prepared to go in person to the great temple to receive his guests there,—it may be, to shield the shrine of his tutelar deity from any attempted profanation. He was acquainted, as we have already seen, with the proceedings of the Spaniards on similar occasions in the course of their march.— Cortés put himself at the head of his little corps of cavalry, and nearly all the Spanish foot, as usual, and followed the caciques sent by Montezuma to guide him. They proposed first to conduct him to the great market of Tlatelolco in the western part of the city.

On the way, the Spaniards were struck, in the same manner as they had been on entering the capital, with the appearance of the inhabitants, and their great superiority in the style and quality of their dress, over the people of the lower countries.[1] The *tilmatli* or cloak thrown over the shoulders and tied round the neck, made of cotton of different degrees of fineness, according to the condition of the wearer, and the ample sash around the loins, were often wrought in rich and elegant figures, and edged with a deep fringe or tassel. As the weather was now growing cool, mantles of fur or of the gorgeous feather-work were sometimes substituted. The latter combined the advantage of great warmth with beauty.[2]

[1] "La Gente de esta Ciudad es de mas manera y primor en su vestido, y servicio, que no la otra de estas otras Provincias, y Ciudades: porque como allí estaba siempre este Señor Muteczuma, y todos los Señores sus Vasallos ocurrian siempre á la Ciudad, habia en ella mas manera, y policía en todas las cosas." Rel. Seg., ap. Lorenzana, p. 109.

[2] Zuazo, speaking of the beauty and warmth of this national fabric, says, "Ví muchas de á dos haces labradas de plumas de papos de aves tan suaves, que trayendo la mano por encima á pelo y á pospelo, no era mas que vna manta zebellina mui bien adobada: hice pesar vna dellas no peso mas de seis onzas. Dicen que en el tiempo del Ynbierno una abasta para encima de la camisa sin otro cobertor ni mas ropa encima de la cama." Carta, MS.

The Mexicans had also the art of spinning a fine thread of the hair of the rabbit and other animals, which they wove into a delicate web that took a permanent dye.

The women, as in other parts of the country, seemed to go about as freely as the men. They wore several skirts or petticoats of different lengths, with highly ornamented borders, and sometimes over them loose flowing robes, which reached to the ankles. These, also, were made of cotton, for the wealthier classes, of a fine texture, prettily embroidered.[3] No veils were worn here, as in some other parts of Anahuac, where they were made of the aloe thread, or of the light web of hair, above noticed. The Aztec women had their faces exposed; and their dark, raven tresses floated luxuriantly over their shoulders, revealing features, which, although of a dusky or rather cinnamon hue, were not unfrequently pleasing, while touched with the serious, even sad expression characteristic of the national physiognomy.[4]

On drawing near to the *tianguez*, or great market, the Spaniards were astonished at the throng of people pressing towards it, and, on entering the place, their surprise was still further heightened by the sight of the multitudes assembled there, and the dimensions of the inclosure, thrice as large as the celebrated square of Salamanca.[5] Here were met together traders from all parts, with the products and manufactures peculiar to their countries; the goldsmiths of Azcapozalco; the potters and jewellers of Cholula, the painters of Tezcuco, the stone-cutters of Tenajocan, the hunters of Xilotepec, the fishermen of Cuitlahuac, the fruiterers of the warm countries, the mat and chair-makers of Quauhtitlan, and the florists of Xochimilco,—all busily engaged in recommending their respective wares, and in chaffering with purchasers.[6]

The market-place was surrounded by deep porticos, and the several articles had each its own quarter allotted to it. Here might be seen cotton piled up in bales, or manufactured into dresses and articles of domestic use, as tapestry, curtains, coverlets, and the like. The richly stained and nice fabrics reminded Cortés of the *alcayceria*, or silk-market of Granada. There was the quarter assigned to the goldsmiths, where the purchaser might find various articles of ornament or use formed of the precious metals, or curious toys, such as we have already had occasion to notice, made in imitation of birds and fishes, with scales and feathers alternately of gold and silver, and with movable heads and

---

[3] "Sono lunghe & large, lauorate di bellisimi, & molto gentili lauori sparsi per esse, cō le loro frangie, ò orletti ben lauorati che compariscono benissimo." Rel. d'un gent., ap. Ramusio, tom. III. fol. 305.

[4] Ibid., fol. 305.

[5] Ibid., fol. 309.

[6] "Quivi concorrevano i Pentoai, ed i Giojellieri di Cholulla, gli Orefici d' Azcapozalco, i Pittori di Tezcuco, gli Scarpellini di Tenajocan, i Cacciatori di Xilotepec, i Pescatori di Cuitlahuac, i fruttajuoli de' paesi caldi, gli artefici di stuoje, e di scranne di Quauhtitlan ed i coltivatori de' fiori di Xochimilco." Clavigero, Stor. del Messico, tom. II. p. 165.

bodies. These fantastic little trinkets were often garnished with precious stones, and showed a patient, puerile ingenuity in the manufacture, like that of the Chinese.[7]

In an adjoining quarter were collected specimens of pottery coarse and fine, vases of wood elaborately carved, varnished or gilt, of curious and sometimes graceful forms. There were also hatchets made of copper alloyed with tin, the substitute, and, as it proved, not a bad one, for iron. The soldier found here all the implements of his trade. The casque fashioned into the head of some wild animal, with its grinning defences of teeth, and bristling crest dyed with the rich tint of the cochineal;[8] the *escaupil*, or quilted doublet of cotton, the rich surcoat of feather-mail, and weapons of all sorts, copper-headed lances and arrows, and the broad *maquahuitl*, the Mexican sword, with its sharp blades of *itztli*. Here were razors and mirrors of this same hard and polished mineral which served so many of the purposes of steel with the Aztecs.[9] In the square were also to be found booths occupied by barbers, who used these same razors in their vocation. For the Mexicans, contrary to the popular and erroneous notions respecting the Aborigines of the New World, had beards, though scanty ones. Other shops or booths were tenanted by apothecaries, well provided with drugs, roots, and different medicinal preparations. In other places, again, blank books or maps for the hieroglyphical picture-writing were to be seen, folded together like fans, and made of cotton, skins, or more commonly the fibres of the agave, the Aztec papyrus.

Under some of the porticos they saw hides raw and dressed, and various articles for domestic or personal use made of the leather. Animals, both wild and tame, were offered for sale, and near them, perhaps, a gang of slaves, with collars round their necks, intimating they were likewise on sale,—a spectacle unhappily not confined to the barbarian markets of Mexico, though the evils of their condition were aggravated there by

---

[7] "Oro y plata, piedras de valor, con otros plumajes é argenterías maravillosas, y con tanto primor fabricadas que excede todo ingenio humano para comprenderlas y alcanzarlas." (Carta del Lic. Zuazo, MS.) The licentiate then enumerates several of these elegant pieces of mechanism. Cortés is not less emphatic in his admiration; "Contrahechas de oro, y plata, y piedras y plumas, tan al natural lo de Oro, y Plata, que no hay Platero en el Mundo que mejor lo hiciesse, y lo de las Piedras, que no baste juicio comprehender con que Instrumentos se hiciesse tan perfecto, y lo de Pluma, que ni de Cera, ni en ningun broslado se podria hacer tan maravillosamente." (Rel. Seg., ap. Lorenzana, p. 110.) Peter Martyr, a less prejudiced critic than Cortés, and who saw and examined many of these golden trinkets afterwards in Castile, bears the same testimony to the exquisite character of the workmanship, which, he says, far surpassed the value of the material. De Orbe Novo, dec. 5, cap 10.

[8] Herrera makes the unauthorized assertion, repeated by Solís, that the Mexicans were unacquainted with the value of the cochineal, till it was taught them by the Spaniards. (Herrera, Hist. General, dec. 4, lib. 8, cap. 11.) The natives, on the contrary, took infinite pains to rear the insect on plantations of the cactus, and it formed one of the staple tributes to the crown from certain districts. See the tribute-rolls, ap. Lorenzana, Nos. 23, 24.—Hernandez, Hist. Plantarum, lib. 6, cap. 116.— Also, Clavigero, Stor. del Messico, tom I. p. 114, nota.

[9] Ante, Vol. I. p. 82.

the consciousness that a life of degradation might be consummated at any moment by the dreadful doom of sacrifice.

The heavier materials for building, as stone, lime, timber, were considered too bulky to be allowed a place in the square, and were deposited in the adjacent streets on the borders of the canals. It would be tedious to enumerate all the various articles, whether for luxury or daily use, which were collected from all quarters in this vast bazaar. I must not omit to mention, however, the display of provisions, one of the most attractive features of the *tianguez*; meats of all kinds, domestic poultry, game from the neighboring mountains, fish from the lakes and streams, fruits in all the delicious abundance of these temperate regions, green vegetables, and the unfailing maize. There was many a viand, too, ready dressed, which sent up its savory steams provoking the appetite of the idle passenger; pastry, bread of the Indian corn, cakes, and confectionary.[10] Along with these were to be seen cooling or stimulating beverages, the spicy foaming *chocolatl*, with its delicate aroma of vanilla, and the inebriating *pulque*, the fermented juice of the aloe. All these commodities, and every stall and portico, were set out, or rather smothered, with flowers, showing, on a much greater scale, indeed, a taste similar to that displayed in the markets of modern Mexico. Flowers seem to be the spontaneous growth of this luxuriant soil; which, instead of noxious weeds, as in other regions, is ever ready, without the aid of man, to cover up its nakedness with this rich and variegated livery of Nature.[11]

I will spare the reader the repetition of all the particulars enumerated by the bewildered Spaniards, which are of some interest as evincing the various mechanical skill and the polished wants, resembling those of a refined community, rather than of a nation of savages. It was the *material* civilization, which belongs neither to the one nor the other. The Aztec had plainly reached that middle station, as far above the rude races of the New World as it was below the cultivated communities of the Old.

As to the numbers assembled in the market, the estimates differ, as usual. The Spaniards often visited the place, and no one states the amount at less than forty thousand! Some carry it much higher.[12] With-

[10] Zuazo, who seems to have been nice in these matters, concludes a paragraph of dainties with the following tribute to the Aztec *cuisine*. "Vendense huebos asados, crudos, en tortilla, é diversidad de guisados que se suelen guisar, con otras cazuelas y parteles, que en el mal cocinado de Medina, ni en otros lugares de Tlamencos dicen que hai ni se pueden hallar tales trujamanes." Carta, MS.

[11] Ample details—many more than I have thought it necessary to give—of the Aztec market of Tlatelolco may be found in the writings of all the old Spaniards who visited the capital. Among others, see Rel. Seg. de Cortés, ap. Lorenzana, pp. 103-105.—Toribio, Hist. de los Indios, MS., Parte 3, cap. 7.—Carta del Lic. Zuazo, MS.—Rel. d'un gent., ap. Ramusio, tom. III. fol. 309.—Bernal Diaz, Hist. de la Conquista, cap. 92.

[12] Zuazo raises it to 80,000! (Carta, MS.) Cortés to 60,000. (Rel. Seg., ubi supra.) The most modest computation is that of the "Anonymous Conqueror," who says from 40,000 to 50,000. "Et il giorno del mercato, che si fa di cinque in cinque

out relying too much on the arithmetic of the Conquerors, it is certain that on this occasion, which occurred every fifth day, the city swarmed with a motley crowd of strangers, not only from the vicinity, but from many leagues around; the causeways were thronged, and the lake was darkened by canoes filled with traders flocking to the great *tianguez*. It resembled, indeed, the periodical fairs in Europe, not as they exist now, but as they existed in the Middle Ages, when, from the difficulties of intercommunication, they served as the great central marts for commercial intercourse, exercising a most important and salutary influence on the community.

The exchanges were conducted partly by barter, but more usually in the currency of the country. This consisted of bits of tin stamped with a character like a **T**, bags of cacao, the value of which was regulated by their size, and lastly quills filled with gold dust. Gold was part of the regular currency, it seems, in both hemispheres. In their dealings it is singular that they should have had no knowledge of scales and weights. The quantity was determined by measure and number.[13]

The most perfect order reigned throughout this vast assembly. Officers patrolled the square, whose business it was to keep the peace, to collect the duties imposed on the different articles of merchandise, to see that no false measures or fraud of any kind were used, and to bring offenders at once to justice. A court of twelve judges sat in one part of the *tianguez*, clothed with those ample and summary powers, which, in despotic countries, are often delegated even to petty tribunals. The extreme severity with which they exercised these powers, in more than one instance, proves that they were not a dead letter.[14]

The *tianguez* of Mexico was naturally an object of great interest, as well as wonder, to the Spaniards. For in it they saw converged into one focus, as it were, all the rays of civilization scattered throughout the land. Here they beheld the various evidences of mechanical skill, of domestic industry, the multiplied resources, of whatever kind, within the compass of the natives. It could not fail to impress them with high ideas of the magnitude of these resources, as well as of the commercial activity and social subordination by which the whole community was knit together; and their admiration is fully evinced by the minuteness and energy of their descriptions.[15]

---

giorni, vi sono da quaranta ò cinquanta mila persone", (Rel. d'un gent., ap. Ramusio, tom. III. fol. 309;) a confirmation, by the by, of the supposition that the estimated population of the capital, found in the Italian version of this author, is a misprint. (See the preceding chapter, note 13.) He would hardly have crowded an amount equal to the whole of it into the market.

[13] Ante, Vol. I. p. 84.

[14] Toribio, Hist. de los Indios, MS.. Parte 3, cap. 7.—Rel. Seg., ap. Lorenzana, p. 104.—Oviedo, Hist. de las Ind., MS., lib. 33, cap. 10.—Bernal Díaz, Hist. de la Conquista, loc. cit.

[15] "Entre nosotros," says Diaz. "huuo soldados que auian estado en muchas partes del mundo, y en Constantinopla, y en toda Italia y Roma, y dixéron, que plaça tan bien compassada, y con tanto concierto, y tamaña, y llena de tanta gente, no la auian visto." Ibid., ubi supra.

From this bustling scene, the Spaniards took their way to the great *teocalli*, in the neighborhood of their own quarters. It covered, with the subordinate edifices, as the reader has already seen, the large tract of ground now occupied by the cathedral, part of the market-place, and some of the adjoining streets.[16] It was the spot which had been consecrated to the same object, probably, ever since the foundation of the city. The present building, however, was of no great antiquity, having been constructed by Ahuitzon, who celebrated its dedication in 1486, by that hecatomb of victims, of which such incredible reports are to be found in the chronicles.[17]

It stood in the midst of a vast area, encompassed by a wall of stone and lime, about eight feet high, ornamented on the outer side by figures of serpents, raised in relief, which gave it the name of the *coatepantli*, or "wall of serpents." This emblem was a common one in the sacred sculpture of Anahuac, as well as of Egypt. The wall, which was quadrangular, was pierced by huge battlemented gateways, opening on the four principal streets of the capital. Over each of the gates was a kind of arsenal, filled with arms and warlike gear; and, if we may credit the report of the Conquerors, there were barracks adjoining, garrisoned by ten thousand soldiers, who served as a sort of military police for the capital, supplying the emperor with a strong arm in case of tumult or sedition.[18]

The *teocalli* itself was a solid pyramidal structure of earth and pebbles, coated on the outside with hewn stones probably of the light, porous kind employed in the buildings of the city.[19] It was probably square, with its sides facing the cardinal points.[20] It was divided into five bodies or stories, each one receding so as to be of smaller dimensions than that immediately below it; the usual form of the Aztec *teocallis*, as already described, and bearing obvious resemblance to some of the primitive pyramidal structures of the Old World.[21] The ascent was by a flight of

[16] Clavigero, Stor. del Messico, tom. II. p. 27.

[17] Ante, Vol. I. p. 49.

[18] "Et di più v'hauea vna guarnigione di dieci mila huomini di guerra, tutti eletti per huomini valenti, & questi accompagnauano & guardauano la sua persona, & quando si facea qualche rumore o ribellione nella città ò nel paese circumuicino, andauano questi, ò parte d'essi per Capitani." Rel. d'un gent., ap. Ramusio, tom. III. fol. 309.

[19] Humboldt, Essai Politique, tom. II. p. 40.

On paving the square, not long ago, round the modern cathedral, there were found large blocks of sculptured stone buried between thirty and forty feet deep in the ground. Ibid., loc. cit.

[20] Clavigero calls it oblong, on the alleged authority of the "Anonymous Conqueror." (Stor. del Messico, tom. II. p. 27, nota.) But the latter says not a word of the shape, and his contemptible woodcut is too plainly destitute of all proportion, to furnish an inference of any kind. (Comp. Rel. d'un gent., ap. Ramusio, tom. III. fol. 307.) Torquemada and Gomara both say, it was square; (Monarch. Ind., lib. 8, cap. 11;—Crónica, cap. 80;) and Toribio de Benavente, speaking generally of the Mexican temples, says, they had that form. Hist. de los. Ind., MS. Parte I, cap. 12.

[21] See *Appendix, Part 1.*

steps on the outside, which reached to the narrow terrace or platform
at the base of the second story, passing quite round the building, when
a second stairway conducted to a similar landing at the base of the
third. The breadth of this walk was just so much space as was left by
the retreating story next above it. From this construction the visitor was
obliged to pass round the whole edifice four times, in order to reach the
top. This had a most imposing effect in the religious ceremonials, when
the pompous procession of priests with their wild minstrelsy came sweeping round the huge sides of the pyramid, as they rose higher and higher,
in the presence of gazing multitudes, towards the summit.

The dimensions of the temple cannot be given with any certainty. The
Conquerors judged by the eye, rarely troubling themselves with any
thing like an accurate measurement. It was, probably, not much less than
three hundred feet square at the base;[22] and, as the Spaniards counted
a hundred and fourteen steps, was probably, less than one hundred feet
in height.[23]

When Cortés arrived before the *teocalli*, he found two priests and sev.
eral caciques commissioned by Montezuma to save him the fatigue of
the ascent by bearing him on their shoulders, in the same manner as had
been done to the emperor. But the general declined the compliment,
preferring to march up at the head of his men. On reaching the summit,
they found it a vast area, paved with broad flat stones. The first object
that met their view was a large block of jasper, the peculiar shape of
which showed it was the stone on which the bodies of the unhappy victims were stretched for sacrifice. Its convex surface, by raising the
breast, enabled the priest to perform his diabolical task more easily, of
removing the heart. At the other end of the area were the towers or
sanctuaries, consisting of three stories, the lower one of stone and stucco,
the two upper of wood elaborately carved. In the lower division stood
the images of their gods; the apartments above were filled with utensils

[22] Clavigero, calling it oblong, adopts Torquemada's estimate,—not Sahagun's, as
he pretends, which he never saw, and who gives no measurement of the building,—
for the length, and Gomara's estimate, which is somewhat less, for the breadth.
(Stor. del. Messico, tom. II. p. 28, nota.) As both his authorities make the building
square, this spirit of accommodation is whimsical enough. Toribio, who did measure
a *teocalli* of the usual construction in the town of Tenayuca, found it to be forty
brazas, or two hundred and forty feet square. (Hist. de los Ind., MS., Parte 1,
cap. 12.) The great temple of Mexico was undoubtedly larger, and, in the want of
better authorities, one may accept Torquemada, who makes it a little more than
three hundred and sixty Toledan, equal to three hundred and eight French feet,
square. (Monarch. Ind., lib. 8, cap. 11.) How can M. de Humboldt speak of the
"great concurrence of testimony" in regard to the dimensions of the temple? (Essai
Politique, tom. II. p. 41.) No two authorities agree.

[23] Bernal Diaz says he counted one hundred and fourteen steps. (Hist. de la Conquista, cap. 92.) Toribio says that more than one person who had numbered them
told him they exceeded a hundred. (Hist. de los Indios, MS., Parte 1, cap. 12.) The
steps could hardly have been less than eight or ten inches high, each; Clavigero assumes that they were a foot, and that the building, therefore, was a hundred and
fourteen feet high, precisely. (Stor. del Messico, tom. II. pp. 28, 29.) It is seldom
safe to use any thing stronger than *probably* in history.

for their religious services, and with the ashes of some of their Aztec princes, who had fancied this airy sepulchre. Before each sanctuary stood an altar with that undying fire upon it, the extinction of which boded as much evil to the empire, as that of the Vestal flame would have done in ancient Rome. Here, also, was the huge cylindrical drum made of serpents' skins, and struck only on extraordinary occasions, when it sent forth a melancholy sound that might be heard for miles,— a sound of woe in after-times to the Spaniards.

Montezuma, attended by the high-priest, came forward to receive Cortés as he mounted the area. "You are weary, Malinche," said he to him, "with climbing up our great temple." But Cortés, with a politic vaunt, assured him "the Spaniards were never weary!" Then, taking him by the hand, the emperor pointed out the localities of the neighborhood. The temple on which they stood, rising high above all other edifices in the capital, afforded the most elevated as well as central point of view. Below them, the city lay spread out like a map, with its streets and canals intersecting each other at right angles, its terraced roofs blooming like so many parterres of flowers. Every place seemed alive with business and bustle; canoes were glancing up and down the canals, the streets were crowded with people in their gay, picturesque costume, while from the market-place, they had so lately left, a confused hum of many sounds and voices rose upon the air.[24] They could distinctly trace the symmetrical plan of the city, with its principal avenues issuing, as it were, from the four gates of the *coatepantli;* and connecting themselves with the causeways, which formed the grand entrances to the capital. This regular and beautiful arrangement was imitated in many of the inferior towns, where the great roads converged towards the chief *teocalli*, or cathedral, as to a common focus.[25] They could discern the insular position of the metropolis, bathed on all sides by the salt floods of the Tezcuco, and in the distance the clear fresh waters of the Chalco; far beyond stretched a wide prospect of fields and waving woods, with the burnished walls of many a lofty temple rising high above the trees, and crowning the distant hill-tops.[26] The view reached in an unbroken line to

[24] "Tornámos á ver la gran plaça, y la multitud de gente que en ella auia, vnos comprādo, y otros vendiendo, que solamente el rumor, y zumbido de las vozes, y palabras que allí auia, sonaua mas que de vna legua!" Bernal Diaz, Hist. de la Conquista, cap. 92.

[25] "Y por honrar mas sus templos sacaban los caminos muy derechos por cordel de una y de dos leguas que era cosa harto de ver, desde lo Alto del principal templo, como venian de todos los pueblos menores y barrios; salian los caminos muy derechos y iban á dar al patio de los teocallis." Toribio, Hist. de los Indios, MS., Parte I, cap. 12.

[26] "No se contentaba el Demonio con los [Teucales] ya dichos, sino que en cada pueblo, en cada barrio, y á cuarto de legua, tenian otros patios pequeños adonde habia tres ó cuatro teocallis, y en algunos mas, en otras partes solo uno, y en cada Mogote ó Cerrejon uno ó dos, y por los caminos y entre los Maizales, habia otros muchos pequeños, y todos estaban blancos y encalados, que parecian y abultaban mucho, que en la tierra bien poblada parecia que todo estaba lleno de casas, en especial de los patios del Demonio, que eran muy de ver." Toribio, Hist. de los Indios, MS., ubi supra.

the very base of the circular range of mountains, whose frosty peaks glittered as if touched with fire in the morning ray; while long, dark wreaths of vapor, rolling up from the hoary head of Popocatepetl, told that the destroying element was, indeed, at work in the bosom of the beautiful Valley.

Cortés was filled with admiration at this grand and glorious spectacle, and gave utterance to his feelings in animated language to the emperor, the lord of these flourishing domains. His thoughts, however, soon took another direction; and, turning to father Olmedo, who stood by his side, he suggested that the area would afford a most conspicuous position for the Christian Cross, if Montezuma would but allow it to be planted there. But the discreet ecclesiastic, with the good sense which on these occasions seems to have been so lamentably deficient in his commander, reminded him, that such a request, at present, would be exceedingly ill-timed, as the Indian monarch had shown no dispositions as yet favorable to Christianity.[27]

Cortés then requested Montezuma to allow him to enter the sanctuaries, and behold the shrines of his gods. To this the latter, after a short conference with the priests, assented, and conducted the Spaniards into the building. They found themselves in a spacious apartment incrusted on the sides with stucco, on which various figures were sculptured, representing the Mexican calendar, perhaps, or the priestly ritual. At one end of the saloon was a recess with a roof of timber richly carved and gilt. Before the altar in this sanctuary, stood the colossal image of Huitzilopotchli, the tutelary deity and war-god of the Aztecs. His countenance was distorted into hideous lineaments of symbolical import. In his right hand he wielded a bow, and in his left a bunch of golden arrows, which a mystic legend had connected with the victories of his people. The huge folds of a serpent, consisting of pearls and precious stones, were coiled round his waist, and the same rich materials were profusely sprinkled over his person. On his left foot were the delicate feathers of the humming-bird, which, singularly enough, gave its name to the dread deity.[28] The most conspicuous ornament was a chain of gold and silver hearts alternate, suspended round his neck, emblematical of the sacrifice in which he most delighted. A more unequivocal evidence of this was afforded by three human hearts smoking and almost palpitating, as if recently torn from the victims, and now lying on the altar before him!

The adjoining sanctuary was dedicated to a milder deity. This was Tezcatlipoca, next in honor to that invisible Being, the Supreme God, who was represented by no image, and confined by no temple. It was Tezcatlipoca who created the world, and watched over it with a providential care. He was represented as a young man, and his image, of polished black stone, was richly garnished with gold plates and ornaments; among which a shield, burnished like a mirror, was the most characteristic emblem, as in it he saw reflected all the doings of the

[27] Bernal Diaz, Hist. de la Conquista, ubi supra.
[28] Ante, Vol. I. p. 38.

world. But the homage to this god was not always of a more refined or merciful character than that paid to his carnivorous brother; for five bleeding hearts were also seen in a golden platter on his altar.

The walls of both these chapels were stained with human gore. "The stench was more intolerable," exclaims Diaz, "than that of the slaughter-houses in Castile!" And the frantic forms of the priests, with their dark robes clotted with blood, as they flitted to and fro, seemed to the Span-iards to be those of the very ministers of Satan![29]

From this foul abode they gladly escaped into the open air; when Cortés, turning to Montezuma, said, with a smile, "I do not comprehend how a great and wise prince, like you, can put faith in such evil spirits as these idols, the representatives of the Devil! If you will but permit us to erect here the true Cross, and place the images of the blessed Virgin and her Son in your sanctuaries, you will soon see how your false gods will shrink before them!"

Montezuma was greatly shocked at this sacrilegious address. "These are the gods," he answered, "who have led the Aztecs on to victory since they were a nation, and who send the seed-time and harvest in their seasons. Had I thought you would have offered them this outrage, I would not have admitted you into their presence."

Cortés, after some expressions of concern at having wounded the feelings of the emperor, took his leave. Montezuma remained, saying that he must expiate, if possible, the crime of exposing the shrines of the divinities to such profanation by the strangers.[30]

On descending to the court, the Spaniards took a leisurely survey of the other edifices in the inclosure. The area was protected by a smooth stone pavement, so polished, indeed, that it was with difficulty the horses could keep their legs. There were several other *teocallis*, built generally on the model of the great one, though of much inferior size, dedicated to the different Aztec deities.[31] On their summits were the altars crowned with perpetual flames, which, with those on the numerous temples in other quarters of the capital, shed a brilliant illumination over its streets, through the long nights.[32]

[29] "Y tenia en las paredes tantas costras de sangre, y el suelo todo bañado dello, que en los mataderos de Castilla no auia tanto hedor." Bernal Diaz, Hist. de la Conquista, ubi supra.—Rel. Seg. de Cortés, ap. Lorenzana, pp. 105, 106.—Carta del Lic. Zuazo, MS.—See, also, for notices of these deities, Sahagun, lib. 3, cap. 1, et seq.,—Torquemada, Monarch. Ind., lib. 6, cap. 20, 21,—Acosta, lib. 5, cap. 9.

[30] Bernal Diaz, Ibid., ubi supra.

Whoever examines Cortés' great letter to Charles V. will be surprised to find it stated, that, instead of any acknowledgment to Montezuma, he threw down his idols and erected the Christian emblems in their stead. (Rel. Seg., ap. Lorenzana, p. 106.) This was an event of much later date. The *Conquistador* wrote his despatches too rapidly and concisely to give heed always to exact time and circumstance. We are quite as likely to find them attended to in the long-winded, gossiping,—inestimable chronicle of Diaz.

[31] "Quarenta torres muy altas y bien obradas." Rel. Seg. de Cortés, ap. Lorenzana, p. 105.

[32] "Delante de todos estos altares habia braçeros que toda la noche hardian, y en las salas tambien tenian sus fuegos." Teribio, Hist. de los Indios, MS., Parte 1, cap. 12.

Among the *teocallis* in the inclosure was one consecrated to Quet-zalcoatl, circular in its form, and having an entrance in imitation of a dragon's mouth, bristling with sharp fangs, and dropping with blood. As the Spaniards cast a furtive glance into the throat of this horrible monster, they saw collected there implements of sacrifice and other abominations of fearful import. Their bold hearts shuddered at the spec-tacle, and they designated the place not inaptly as the "Hell."[33]

One other structure may be noticed as characteristic of the brutish nature of their religion. This was a pyramidal mound or tumulus, having a complicated frame-work of timber on its broad summit. On this was strung an immense number of human skulls, which belonged to the victims, mostly prisoners of war, who had perished on the accursed stone of sacrifice. One of the soldiers had the patience to count the num-ber of these ghastly trophies, and reported it to be one hundred and thirty-six thousand![34] Belief might well be staggered, did not the Old World present a worthy counterpart in the pyramidal Golgothas which commemorated the triumphs of Tamerlane.[35]

There were long ranges of buildings in the inclosure, appropriated as the residence of the priests and others engaged in the offices of religion. The whole number of them was said to amount to several thousand. Here were, also, the principal seminaries for the instruction of youth of both sexes, drawn chiefly from the higher and wealthier classes. The girls were taught by elderly women who officiated as priestesses in the tem-ples, a custom familiar, also, to Egypt. The Spaniards admit that the greatest care for morals, and the most blameless deportment, were main-tained in these institutions. The time of the pupils was chiefly occupied, as in most monastic establishments, with the minute and burdensome cer-emonial of their religion. The boys were likewise taught such elements of science as were known to their teachers, and the girls initiated in the mysteries of embroidery and weaving, which they employed in decorating the temples. At a suitable age they generally went forth into the world to assume the occupations fitted to their condition, though some re-mained permanently devoted to the services of religion.[36]

[33] Bernal Diaz, Ibid., ubi supra.
Toribio, also, notices this temple with the same complimentary epithet.
"La boca hecha como de infierno y en ella pintada la boca de una temerosa Sierpe con terribles colmillos y dientes, y en algunas de estas los colmillos eran de bulto, que verlo y entrar dentro ponia gran temor y grima, en especial el infierno que estaba en México, que parecia traslado del verdadero infierno." Hist. de los Indios, MS., Parte 1, cap. 4.

[34] Bernal Diaz, ubi supra.
"Andres de Tapia, *que me to dijo*, i Gonçalo de Umbria, las contáron vn Dia, i halláron ciento i treinta i seis mil Calaveras, en las Vigas, i Gradas." Gomara, Cró-nica, cap. 82.

[35] Three collections, thus fancifully disposed, of these grinning horrors—in all 230,000—are noticed by Gibbon! (Decline and Fall, ed. Milman, vol. I. p. 52; vol. XII. p. 45.) A *European* scholar commends "the conqueror's piety, his modera-tion, and his justice!" Rowe's Dedication of "Tamerlane."

[36] Ante, Vol. I. pp. 43, 44.
The desire of presenting the reader with a complete view of the actual state of the capital, at the time of its occupation by the Spaniards, has led me in this and

The spot was also covered by edifices of a still different character. There were granaries filled with the rich produce of the church-lands, and with the first-fruits and other offerings of the faithful. One large mansion was reserved for strangers of eminence, who were on a pilgrimage to the great *teocalli*. The inclosure was ornamented with gardens, shaded by ancient trees and watered by fountains and reservoirs from the copious streams of Chapoltepec. The little community was thus provided with almost everything requisite for its own maintenance, and the services of the temple.[37]

It was a microcosm of itself, a city within a city; and, according to the assertion of Cortés, embraced a tract of ground large enough for five hundred houses.[38] It presented in this brief compass the extremes of barbarism, blended with a certain civilization, altogether characteristic of the Aztecs. The rude Conquerors saw only the evidence of the former. In the fantastic and symbolical features of the deities, they beheld the literal lineaments of Satan; in the rites and frivolous ceremonial, his own especial code of damnation; and in the modest deportment and careful nurture of the inmates of the seminaries, the snares by which he was to beguile his deluded victims![39] Before a century had elapsed, the descendants of these same Spaniards discerned in the mysteries of the Aztec religion the features, obscured and defaced, indeed, of the Jewish and Christian revelations![40] Such were the opposite conclusions of the unlettered soldier and of the scholar. A philosopher, untouched by superstition, might well doubt which of the two was the most extraordinary.

The sight of the Indian abominations seems to have kindled in the Spaniards a livelier feeling for their own religion; since, on the following day, they asked leave of Montezuma to convert one of the halls in their residence into a chapel, that they might celebrate the services of the Church there. The monarch, in whose bosom the feelings of resentment seem to have soon subsided, easily granted their request, and sent some of his own artisans to aid them in the work.

While it was in progress, some of the Spaniards observed what appeared to be a door recently plastered over. It was a common rumor that Montezuma still kept the treasures of his father, King Axayacatl, in this ancient palace. The Spaniards, acquainted with this fact, felt no scruple in gratifying their curiosity by removing the plaster. As was an-

the preceding chapter into a few repetitions of remarks on the Aztec institutions in the Introductory Book of this History.

[37] Toribio, Hist. de los Indios, MS., Parte 1, cap. 12.—Gomara, Crónica, cap. 80. —Rel. d'un gent., ap. Ramusio, tom. III. fol. 309.

[38] "Es tan grande que dentro del circuito de ella, que es todo cercado de Muro muy alto, se podia muy bien facer una Villa de quinientos Vecinos." Rel. Seg., ap. Lorenzana, p. 105.

[39] "Todas estas mugeres," says father Toribio, "estaban aquí sirviendo al demonio por sus propios intereses; las unas porque el Demonio las hiciese modestas," &c. Hist. de los Indios, MS., Parte 1, cap. 9.

[40] See *Appendix, Part 1.*

ticipated, it concealed a door. On forcing this, they found the rumor was no exaggeration. They beheld a large hall filled with rich and beautiful stuffs, articles of curious workmanship of various kinds, gold and silver in bars and in the ore, and many jewels of value. It was the private hoard of Montezuma, the contributions, it may be, of tributary cities, and once the property of his father. "I was a young man," says Diaz, who was one of those that obtained a sight of it, "and it seemed to me as if all the riches of the world were in that room!" [41] The Spaniards, notwithstanding their elation at the discovery of this precious deposit, seem to have felt some commendable scruples as to appropriating it to their own use, —at least for the present. And Cortés, after closing up the wall as it was before, gave strict injunctions that nothing should be said of the matter, unwilling that the knowledge of its existence by his guests should reach the ears of Montezuma.

Three days sufficed to complete the chapel; and the Christians had the satisfaction to see themselves in possession of a temple where they might worship God in their own way, under the protection of the Cross, and the blessed Virgin. Mass was regularly performed by the fathers Olmedo and Diaz, in the presence of the assembled army, who were most earnest and exemplary in their devotions, partly, says the chronicler above quoted, from the propriety of the thing, and partly for its edifying influence on the benighted heathen.[42]

[41] "Y luego lo supímos entre todos los demas Capitanes, y soldados, y lo entrámos á ver muy secretamente, y como yo lo ví, digo que me admiré, é como en aquel tiempo era mancebo, y no auia visto en mi vida riquezas como aquellas, tuue por cierto, que en el mundo nc deuiera auer otras tantas!" Hist. de la Conquista, cap. 93.
[42] Ibid., loc. cit.

CHAPTER III

ANXIETY OF CORTÉS—SEIZURE OF MONTEZUMA—HIS TREATMENT BY
THE SPANIARDS—EXECUTION OF HIS OFFICERS—MONTEZUMA IN
IRONS—REFLECTIONS

1519

THE Spaniards had been now a week in Mexico. During this time, they
had experienced the most friendly treatment from the emperor. But the
mind of Cortés was far from easy. He felt that it was quite uncertain how
long this amiable temper would last. A hundred circumstances might
occur to change it. He might very naturally feel the maintenance of so
large a body too burdensome on his treasury. The people of the capital
might become dissatisfied at the presence of so numerous an armed force
within their walls. Many causes of disgust might arise betwixt the soldiers
and the citizens. Indeed, it was scarcely possible that a rude, licentious
soldiery, like the Spaniards, could be long kept in subjection without
active employment.[1] The danger was even greater with the Tlascalans, a
fierce race now brought into daily contact with the nation who held
them in loathing and detestation. Rumors were already rife among the
allies, whether well-founded or not, of murmurs among the Mexicans,
accompanied by menaces of raising the bridges.[2]

Even should the Spaniards be allowed to occupy their present quarters
unmolested, it was not advancing the great object of the expedition.
Cortés was not a whit nearer gaining the capital, so essential to his meditated subjugation of the country; and any day he might receive tidings
that the Crown, or, what he most feared, the governor of Cuba, had sent
a force of superior strength to wrest from him a conquest but half
achieved. Disturbed by these anxious reflections, he resolved to extricate
himself from his embarrassment by one bold stroke. But he first sub-

[1] "Los Españoles," says Cortés frankly, of his countrymen, "somos algo incom-
portables, é importunos." Rel. Seg., ap. Lorenzana, p. 84.

[2] Gomara, Crónica, cap. 83.

There is reason to doubt the truth of these stories. "Segun una carta original que
tengo en mi poder firmada de las tres cabezas de la Nueva España en donde escriben á la Magestad del Emperador Nuestro Señor (que Dios tenga en su Santo
Reyno) disculpan en ella á Motecuhzoma y á los Mexicanos de esto, y de lo demas
que se les argulló, que lo cierto era que fué invencion de los Tlascaltecas, y de algunos de los Españoles que veian la hora de salirse de miedo de la Ciudad, y poner
en cobro innumerables riquezas que habian venido á sus manos." Ixtlilxochitl, Hist.
Chich., MS., cap. 85.

mitted the affair to a council of the officers in whom he most confided, desirous to divide with them the responsibility of the act, and, no doubt, to interest them more heartily in its execution, by making it in some measure the result of their combined judgments.

When the general had briefly stated the embarrassments of their position, the council was divided in opinion. All admitted the necessity of some instant action. One party were for retiring secretly from the city, and getting beyond the causeways before their march could be intercepted. Another advised that it should be done openly, with the knowledge of the emperor, of whose good-will they had had so many proofs. But both these measures seemed alike impolitic. A retreat under these circumstances, and so abruptly made, would have the air of a flight. It would be construed into distrust of themselves; and any thing like timidity on their part would be sure not only to bring on them the Mexicans, but the contempt of their allies, who would, doubtless, join in the general cry.

As to Montezuma, what reliance could they place on the protection of a prince so recently their enemy, and who, in his altered bearing, must have taken counsel of his fears, rather than his inclinations?

Even should they succeed in reaching the coast, their situation would be little better. It would be proclaiming to the world, that, after all their lofty vaunts, they were unequal to the enterprise. Their only hopes of their sovereign's favor, and of pardon for their irregular proceedings, were founded on success. Hitherto, they had only made the discovery of Mexico; to retreat would be to leave conquest and the fruits of it to another.—In short, to stay and to retreat seemed equally disastrous.

In this perplexity, Cortés proposed an expedient, which none but the most daring spirit, in the most desperate extremity, would have conceived. This was, to march to the royal palace, and bring Montezuma to the Spanish quarters, by fair means if they could persuade him, by force if necessary,—at all events, to get possession of his person. With such a pledge, the Spaniards would be secure from the assault of the Mexicans, afraid by acts of violence to compromise the safety of their prince. If he came by his own consent, they would be deprived of all apology for doing so. As long as the emperor remained among the Spaniards, it would be easy, by allowing him a show of sovereignty, to rule in his name, until they had taken measures for securing their safety, and the success of their enterprise. The idea of employing a sovereign as a tool for the government of his own kingdom, if a new one in the age of Cortés, is certainly not so in ours.[3]

[3] Rel. Seg. de Cortés, ap. Lorenzana, p. 84.—Ixtlilxochitl, Hist. Chich., MS., cap. 85.—P. Martyr, De Orbe Novo, dec. 5, cap. 3.—Oviedo, Hist. de las Ind., MS., lib. 33, cap. 6.
Bernal Diaz gives a very different report of this matter. According to him, a number of officers and soldiers, of whom he was one, suggested the capture of Montezuma to the general, who came into the plan with hesitation. (Hist. de la Conquista, cap. 93.) This is contrary to the character of Cortés, who was a man to lead, not to be led, on such occasions. It is contrary to the general report of

A plausible pretext for the seizure of the hospitable monarch—for the most barefaced action seeks to veil itself under some show of decency —was afforded by a circumstance of which Cortés had received intelligence at Cholula.[4] He had left, as we have seen, a faithful officer, Juan de Escalante, with a hundred and fifty men in garrison at Vera Cruz, on his departure for the capital. He had not been long absent, when his lieutenant received a message from an Aztec chief named Quauhpopoca, governor of a district to the north of the Spanish settlement, declaring his desire to come in person and tender his allegiance to the Spanish authorities at Vera Cruz. He requested that four of the white men might be sent to protect him against certain unfriendly tribes through which his road lay. This was not an uncommon request, and excited no suspicion in Escalante. The four soldiers were sent; and on their arrival two of them were murdered by the false Aztec. The other two made their way back to the garrison.[5]

The commander marched at once, with fifty of his men, and several thousand Indian allies, to take vengeance on the cacique. A pitched battle followed. The allies fled from the redoubted Mexicans. The few Spaniards stood firm, and with the aid of their fire-arms and the blessed Virgin, who was distinctly seen hovering over their ranks in the van, they made good the field against the enemy. It cost them dear, however; since seven or eight Christians were slain, and among them the gallant Escalante himself, who died of his injuries soon after his return to the fort. The Indian prisoners captured in the battle spoke of the whole proceeding as having taken place at the instigation of Montezuma.[6]

historians, though these, it must be confessed, are mainly built on the general's narrative. It is contrary to anterior probability; since, if the conception seems almost too desperate to have seriously entered into the head of any one man, how much more improbable is it, that it should have originated with a number! Lastly, it is contrary to the positive written statement of Cortés to the Emperor, publicly known and circulated, confirmed in print by his chaplain, Gomara, and all this when the thing was fresh, and when the parties interested were alive to contradict it. We cannot but think that the captain here, as in the case of the burning of the ships, assumes rather more for himself and his comrades, than the facts will strictly warrant; an oversight, for which the lapse of half a century—to say nothing of his avowed anxiety to show up the claims of the latter—may furnish some apology.

[4] Even Gomara has the candor to style it a "pretext"—*achaque*. Crónica, cap. 83.

[5] Bernal Diaz states the affair, also, differently. According to him, the Aztec governor was enforcing the payment of the customary tribute from the Totonacs, when Escalante, interfering to protect his allies, now subjects of Spain, was slain in an action with the enemy. (Hist. de la Conquista, cap. 93.) Cortés had the best means of knowing the facts, and wrote at the time. He does not usually shrink from avowing his policy, however severe, towards the natives; and I have thought it fair to give him the benefit of his own version of the story.

[6] Oviedo, Hist. de las Ind., MS., lib. 33, cap. 5.—Rel. Seg. de Cortés, ap Lorenzana, pp. 83, 84.

The apparition of the Virgin was seen only by the Aztecs, who, it is true, had to make out the best case for their defeat they could to Montezuma; a suspicious circumstance, which, however, did not stagger the Spaniards. "Y ciertamente, todos los soldados que passámos con Cortés tenemos muy creido, è assí es verdad, que la misericordia diuina, y Nuestra Señora la Vírgen María siempre era con nosotros." Bernal Diaz, Hist. de la Conquista, cap. 94.

One of the Spaniards fell into the hands of the natives, but soon after perished of his wounds. His head was cut off and sent to the Aztec emperor. It was uncommonly large and covered with hair; and, as Montezuma gazed on the ferocious features, rendered more horrible by death, he seemed to read in them the dark lineaments of the destined destroyers of his house. He turned from it with a shudder, and commanded that it should be taken from the city, and not offered at the shrine of any of his gods.

Although Cortés had received intelligence of this disaster at Cholula, he had concealed it within his own breast, or communicated it to very few only of his most trusty officers, from apprehension of the ill effect it might have on the spirits of the common soldiers.

The cavaliers whom Cortés now summoned to the council were men of the same mettle with their leader. Their bold, chivalrous spirits seemed to court danger for its own sake. If one or two, less adventurous, were startled by the proposal he made, they were soon overruled by the others, who, no doubt, considered that a desperate disease required as desperate a remedy.

That night, Cortés was heard pacing his apartment to and fro, like a man oppressed by thought, or agitated by strong emotion. He may have been ripening in his mind the daring scheme for the morrow.[7] In the morning the soldiers heard mass as usual, and father Olmedo invoked the blessing of Heaven on their hazardous enterprise. Whatever might be the cause in which he was embarked, the heart of the Spaniard was cheered with the conviction that the Saints were on his side![8]

Having asked an audience from Montezuma, which was readily granted, the general made the necessary arrangements for his enterprise. The principal part of his force was drawn up in the court-yard, and he stationed a considerable detachment in the avenues leading to the palace, to check any attempt at rescue by the populace. He ordered twenty-five or thirty of the soldiers to drop in at the palace, as if by accident, in groups of three or four at a time, while the conference was going on with Montezuma. He selected five cavaliers, in whose courage and coolness he placed the most trust, to bear him company; Pedro de Alvarado, Gonzalo de Sandoval, Francisco de Lujo, Velasquez de Leon, and Alonso de Avila,—brilliant names in the annals of the Conquest. All were clad, as well as the common soldiers, in complete armor, a circumstance of too familiar occurrence to excite suspicion.

The little party were graciously received by the emperor, who soon, with the aid of the interpreters, became interested in a sportive conversation with the Spaniards, while he indulged his natural munificence by

[7] "Paseóse vn gran rato solo, i cuidadoso de aquel gran hecho, que emprendia, i que aun á él mesmo le parecia temerario, pero necesario para su intento, andando." Gomara, Crónica, cap. 83.

[8] Diaz says, they were at prayer all night. "Toda la noche estuuimos en oracion con el Padre de la Merced, rogando á Dios que fuesse de tal modo, que redundasse para su santo servicio." Hist. de la Conquista, cap. 95.

giving them presents of gold and jewels. He paid the Spanish general the particular compliment of offering him one of his daughters as his wife; an honor which the latter respectfully declined, on the ground that he was already accommodated with one in Cuba, and that his religion forbade a plurality.

When Cortés perceived that a sufficient number of his soldiers were assembled, he changed his playful manner, and with a serious tone briefly acquainted Montezuma with the treacherous proceedings in the *tierra caliente*, and the accusation of him as their author. The emperor listened to the charge with surprise; and disavowed the act, which he said could only have been imputed to him by his enemies. Cortés expressed his belief in his declaration, but added, that, to prove it true, it would be necessary to send for Quauhpopoca and his accomplices, that they might be examined and dealt with according to their deserts. To this Montezuma made no objection. Taking from his wrist, to which it was attached, a precious stone, the royal signet, on which was cut the figure of the War-god,[9] he gave it to one of his nobles, with orders to show it to the Aztec governor, and require his instant presence in the capital, together with all those who had been accessory to the murder of the Spaniards. If he resisted, the officer was empowered to call in the aid of the neighboring towns, to enforce the mandate.

When the messenger had gone, Cortés assured the monarch that this prompt compliance with his request convinced him of his innocence. But it was important that his own sovereign should be equally convinced of it. Nothing would promote this so much as for Montezuma to transfer his residence to the palace occupied by the Spaniards, till on the arrival of Quauhpopoca the affair could be fully investigated. Such an act of condescension would, of itself, show a personal regard for the Spaniards, incompatible with the base conduct alleged against him, and would fully absolve him from all suspicion![10]

Montezuma listened to this proposal, and the flimsy reasoning with which it was covered, with looks of profound amazement. He became pale as death; but in a moment, his face flushed with resentment, as, with the pride of offended dignity, he exclaimed, "When was it ever heard that a great prince, like myself, voluntarily left his own palace to become a prisoner in the hands of strangers!"

Cortés assured him he would not go as a prisoner. He would experience nothing but respectful treatment from the Spaniards; would be surrounded by his own household, and hold intercourse with his people as usual. In short, it would be but a change of residence, from one of his palaces to another, a circumstance of frequent occurrence with him.—It was in vain. "If I should consent to such a degradation," he answered,

---

[9] According to Ixtlilxochitl, it was his own portrait. "Se quitó del brazo una rica piedra, donde está esculpido su rostro (que era lo mismo que un sello Real)." Hist Chich., MS., cap. 85.

[10] Rel. Seg. Cortés. ap. Lorenzana, p. 86.

"my subjects never would!" [11] When further pressed, he offered to give up one of his sons and of his daughters to remain as hostages with the Spaniards, so that he might be spared this disgrace.

Two hours passed in this fruitless discussion, till a high-mettled cavalier, Velasquez de Leon, impatient of the long delay, and seeing that the attempt, if not the deed, must ruin them, cried out, "Why do we waste words on this barbarian? We have gone too far to recede now. Let us seize him, and, if he resists, plunge our swords into his body!"[12] The fierce tone and menacing gestures, with which this was uttered, alarmed the monarch, who inquired of Marina what the angry Spaniard said. The interpreter explained it in as gentle a manner as she could, beseeching him "to accompany the white men to their quarters, where he would be treated with all respect and kindness, while to refuse them would but expose himself to violence, perhaps to death." Marina, doubtless, spoke to her sovereign as she thought, and no one had better opportunity of knowing the truth than herself.

This last appeal shook the resolution of Montezuma. It was in vain that the unhappy prince looked around for sympathy or support. As his eyes wandered over the stern visages and iron forms of the Spaniards, he felt that his hour was indeed come; and, with a voice scarcely audible from emotion, he consented to accompany the strangers,—to quit the palace, whither he was never more to return. Had he possessed the spirit of the first Montezuma, he would have called his guards around him, and left his life-blood on the threshold, sooner than have been dragged a dishonored captive across it. But his courage sunk under circumstances. He felt he was the instrument of an irresistible Fate![13]

No sooner had the Spaniards got his consent, than orders were given for the royal litter. The nobles, who bore and attended it, could scarcely believe their senses, when they learned their master's purpose. But pride now came to Montezuma's aid, and, since he must go, he preferred that it should appear to be with his own free will. As the royal retinue, escorted by the Spaniards, marched through the street with downcast eyes and dejected mien, the people assembled in crowds, and a

[11] "Quando Io lo consintiera, los mios no pasarian por ello." Ixtlilxochitl, Hist. Chich., MS., cap. 85.

[12] "¿Que haze v. m. ya con tantas palabras? Ó le lleuemos preso, ó le darémos de estocadas, por esso tornalde á dezir, que si da vozes, ó haze alboroto, que le matáreis, porque mas vale que desta vez asseguremos nuestras vidas, ó las perdamos." Bernal Diaz, Hist. de la Conquista, cap. 95.

[13] Oviedo has some doubts whether Montezuma's conduct is to be viewed as pusillanimous or as prudent. "Al coronista le parece, segun lo que se puede colegir de esta materia, que Montezuma era, ó mui falto de ánimo, ó pusilánimo, ó mui prudente, aunque en muchas cosas, los que le viéron lo loan de mui señor y mui liberal; y en sus razonamientos mostraba ser de buen juicio." He strikes the balance, however, in favor of pusillanimity. "Un Príncipe tan grande como Montezuma no se habia de dexar incurrir en tales términos, ni consentir ser detenido de tan poco número de Españoles, ni de otra generacion alguna; mas como Dios tiene ordenado lo que ha de ser, ninguno puede huir de su juicio." Hist. de las Ind., MS., lib. 33, cap 6.

rumor ran among them, that the emperor was carried off by force to the quarters of the white men. A tumult would have soon arisen but for the intervention of Montezuma himself, who called out to the people to disperse, as he was visiting his friends of his own accord; thus sealing his ignominy by a declaration which deprived his subjects of the only excuse for resistance. On reaching the quarters, he sent out his nobles with similar assurances to the mob, and renewed orders to return to their homes.[14]

He was received with ostentatious respect by the Spaniards, and selected the suite of apartments which best pleased him. They were soon furnished with fine cotton tapestries, feather-work, and all the elegancies of Indian upholstery. He was attended by such of his household as he chose, his wives and his pages, and was served with his usual pomp and luxury at his meals. He gave audience, as in his own palace, to his subjects, who were admitted to his presence, few, indeed, at a time, under the pretext of greater order and decorum. From the Spaniards themselves he met with a formal deference. No one, not even the general himself, approached him without doffing his casque, and rendering the obeisance due to his rank. Nor did they ever sit in his presence, without being invited by him to do so.[15]

With all this studied ceremony and show of homage, there was one circumstance which too clearly proclaimed to his people that their sovereign was a prisoner. In the front of the palace a patrol of sixty men was established, and the same number in the rear. Twenty of each corps mounted guard at once, maintaining a careful watch, day and night.[16] Another body, under command of Velasquez de Leon, was stationed in the royal antechamber. Cortés punished any departure from duty, or relaxation of vigilance, in these sentinels, with the utmost severity.[17] He felt, as, indeed, every Spaniard must have felt, that the escape of the emperor now would be their ruin. Yet the task of this unintermitting watch sorely added to their fatigues. "Better this dog of a king should die," cried a soldier one day, "than that we should wear out our lives in this manner." The words were uttered in the hearing of Montezuma, who gathered something of their import, and the offender was severely chastised by order of the general.[18] Such instances of disrespect, however,

[14] The story of the seizure of Montezuma may be found, with the usual discrepancies in the details, in Rel. Seg. de Cortés, ap. Lorenzana, pp. 84-86,—Bernal Diaz, Hist. de la Conquista, cap. 95,—Ixtlilxochitl, Hist. Chich., MS., cap. 85,—Oviedo, Hist. de las Ind., MS., lib. 33, cap. 6,—Gomara, Crónica, cap. 83,—Herrera, Hist. General, dec. 2, lib. 8, cap, 2, 3,—Martyr, De Orbe Novo, dec. 5, cap. 3.

[15] "Siempre que ante él passauamos, y aunque fuesse Cortés, le quitauamos los bonetes de armas ó cascos, que siempre estauamos armados, y él nos hazia gran mesura, y honra á todos. . . . . . Digo que no se sentauan Cortés, ni ningun Capitan, hasta que el Monteçuma les mandaua dar sus assentaderos ricos, y les mandaua assentar" Bernal Diaz, Hist. de la Conquista, cap. 95, 100.

[16] Herrera, Hist. General, dec. 2, lib. 8, cap. 3.

[17] On one occasion, three soldiers, who left their posts without orders, were sentenced to run the gantlet,—a punishment little short of death. Ibid., ubi supra.

[18] Bernal Diaz, Hist. de la Conquista, cap 97.

were very rare. Indeed, the amiable deportment of the monarch, who seemed to take pleasure in the society of his jailers, and who never allowed a favor or attention from the meanest soldier to go unrequited, inspired the Spaniards with as much attachment as they were capable of feeling—for a barbarian.

Things were in this posture, when the arrival of Quauhpopoca from the coast was announced. He was accompanied by his son and fifteen Aztec chiefs. He had travelled all the way, borne, as became his high rank, in a litter. On entering Montezuma's presence, he threw over his dress the coarse robe of *nequen*, and made the usual humiliating acts of obeisance. The poor parade of courtly ceremony was the more striking, when placed in contrast with the actual condition of the parties.

The Aztec governor was coldly received by his master, who referred the affair (had he the power to do otherwise?) to the examination of Cortés. It was, doubtless, conducted in a sufficiently summary manner. To the general's query, whether the cacique was the subject of Montezuma, he replied, "And what other sovereign could I serve?" implying that his sway was universal.[19] He did not deny his share in the transaction, nor did he seek to shelter himself under the royal authority, till sentence of death was passed on him and his followers, when they all laid the blame of their proceedings on Montezuma.[20] They were condemned to be burnt alive in the area before the palace. The funeral piles were made of heaps of arrows, javelins, and other weapons, drawn by the emperor's permission from the arsenals round the great *teocalli*, where they had been stored to supply means of defence in times of civic tumult or insurrection. By this politic precaution, Cortés proposed to remove a ready means of annoyance in case of hostilities with the citizens.

To crown the whole of these extraordinary proceedings, Cortés, while preparations for the execution were going on, entered the emperor's apartment, attended by a soldier bearing fetters in his hands. With a severe aspect, he charged the monarch with being the original contriver of the violence offered to the Spaniards, as was now proved by the declaration of his own instruments. Such a crime, which merited death in a subject, could not be atoned for, even by a sovereign, without some punishment. So saying, he ordered the soldier to fasten the fetters on Montezuma's ankles. He coolly waited till it was done; then, turning his back on the monarch, quitted the room.

Montezuma was speechless under the infliction of this last insult. He was like one struck down by a heavy blow, that deprives him of all his

---

[19] "Y despues que confesáron haber muerto los Españoles, les hice interrogar si ellos eran Vasallos de Muteczuma? Y el dicho Qualpopoca respondió, que si habia otro Señor, de quien pudiesse serlo? casi diciendo, que no habia otro, y que si eran." Rel. Seg. de Cortés, ap. Lorenzana, p. 87.

[20] "É assimismo les pregunté, si lo que allí se habia hecho si habia sido por su mandado? y dijéron que no, aunque despues, al tiempo que en ellos se executó la sentencia, que fuessen quemados, todos á una voz dijéron, que era verdad que el dicho Muteczuma se lo habia embiado á mandar, y que por su mandado lo habia hecho." Ibid., loc. cit.

faculties. He offered no resistance. But, though he spoke not a word, low, ill-suppressed moans, from time to time, intimated the anguish of his spirit. His attendants, bathed in tears, offered him their consolations. They tenderly held his feet in their arms, and endeavored, by inserting their shawls and mantles, to relieve them from the pressure of the iron. But they could not reach the iron which had penetrated into his soul. He felt that he was no more a king.

Meanwhile, the execution of the dreadful doom was going forward in the court-yard. The whole Spanish force was under arms, to check any interruption that might be offered by the Mexicans. But none was attempted. The populace gazed in silent wonder, regarding it as the sentence of the emperor. The manner of the execution, too, excited less surprise, from their familiarity with similar spectacles, aggravated, indeed, by additional horrors, in their own diabolical sacrifices. The Aztec lord and his companions, bound hand and foot to the blazing piles, submitted without a cry or a complaint to their terrible fate. Passive fortitude is the virtue of the Indian warrior; and it was the glory of the Aztec, as of the other races on the North American continent, to show how the spirit of the brave man may triumph over torture and the agonies of death.

When the dismal tragedy was ended, Cortés reentered Montezuma's apartment. Kneeling down, he unclasped his shackles with his own hand, expressing at the same time his regret that so disagreeable a duty as that of subjecting him to such a punishment had been imposed on him. This last indignity had entirely crushed the spirit of Montezuma; and the monarch, whose frown, but a week since, would have made the nations of Anahuac tremble to their remotest borders, was now craven enough to thank his deliverer for his freedom, as for a great and unmerited boon![21]

Not long after, the Spanish general, conceiving that his royal captive was sufficiently humbled, expressed his willingness that he should return, if he inclined, to his own palace. Montezuma declined it; alleging, it is said, that his nobles had more than once importuned him to resent his injuries by taking arms against the Spaniards; and that, were he in the midst of them, it would be difficult to avoid it, or to save his capital from bloodshed and anarchy.[22] The reason did honor to his heart, if it was the one which influenced him. It is probable that he did not care to trust his safety to those haughty and ferocious chieftains, who had wit-

---

[21] Gomara, Crónica, cap. 89.—Oviedo, Hist. de las Ind., MS., lib. 33, cap. 6.—Bernal Diaz, Hist. de la Conquista, cap. 95.

One may doubt whether pity or contempt predominates in Martyr's notice of this event. "Infelix tunc Muteczuma re adeo noua perculsus, formidine repletur, decidit animo, neque iam erigere caput audet, aut suorum auxilia implorare. Ille vero pœnam se meruisse fassus est, vti agnus mitis. Æquo animo pati videtur has regulas grammaticalibus duriores, imberbibus pueris dictatas, omnia placide fert, ne seditio ciuium et procerum oriatur." De Orbe Novo, dec. 5, cap. 3.

[22] Rel. Seg. de Cortés. an Lorenzana, p. 88.

nessed the degradation of their master, and must despise his pusillanimity, as a thing unprecedented in an Aztec monarch. It is also said, that,
when Marina conveyed to him the permission of Cortés, the other interpreter, Aguilar, gave him to understand the Spanish officers never
would consent that he should avail himself of it.[23]

Whatever were his reasons, it is certain that he declined the offer; and
the general, in a well-feigned, or real ecstasy, embraced him, declaring,
"that he loved him as a brother, and that every Spaniard would be
zealously devoted to his interests, since he had shown himself so mindful of theirs!" Honeyed words, "which," says the shrewd old chronicler
who was present, "Montezuma was wise enough to know the worth of."

The events recorded in this chapter are certainly some of the most
extraordinary on the page of history. That a small body of men, like
the Spaniards, should have entered the palace of a mighty prince, have
seized his person in the midst of his vassals, have borne him off a captive to their quarters,—that they should have put to an ignominious
death before his face his high officers, for executing, probably, his own
commands, and have crowned the whole by putting the monarch in
irons like a common malefactor,—that this should have been done, not to
a drivelling dotard in the decay of his fortunes, but to a proud monarch
in the plenitude of his power, in the very heart of his capital, surrounded
by thousands and tens of thousands, who trembled at his nod, and would
have poured out their blood like water in his defence,—that all this
should have been done by a mere handful of adventurers, is a thing too
extravagant, altogether too improbable, for the pages of romance! It is,
nevertheless, literally true. Yet we shall not be prepared to acquiesce in
the judgments of contemporaries who regarded these acts with admiration. We may well distrust any grounds on which it is attempted to justify the kidnapping of a friendly sovereign,—by those very persons, too,
who were reaping the full benefit of his favors.

To view the matter differently, we must take the position of the Conquerors, and assume with them the original right of conquest. Regarded
from this point of view, many difficulties vanish. If conquest were a duty,
whatever was necessary to effect it was right also. Right and expedient
become convertible terms. And it can hardly be denied, that the capture
of the monarch was expedient, if the Spaniards would maintain their
hold on the empire.[24]

The execution of the Aztec governor suggests other considerations.
If he were really guilty of the perfidious act imputed to him by Cortés,

---

[23] Bernal Diaz, Ibid., ubi supra.

[24] Archbishop Lorenzana, as late as the close of the last century, finds good Scripture warrant for the proceeding of the Spaniards. "Fué grande prudencia, y Arte
militar haber asegurado á el Emperador, porque sino quedaban expuestos Hernan
Cortés, y sus soldados á perecer á traycion, y teniendo seguro á el Emperador se
aseguraba á sí mismo, pues los Españoles no se confian ligeramente: Jonathas fué
muerto, y sorprendido por haberse confiado de Triphon." Rel. Seg. de Cortés, p.
84, nota.

and if Montezuma disavowed it, the governor deserved death, and the general was justified by the law of nations in inflicting it.[25] It is by no means so clear, however, why he should have involved so many in this sentence; most, perhaps all, of whom must have acted under his authority. The cruel manner of the death will less startle those who are familiar with the established penal codes in most civilized nations in the sixteenth century.

But, if the governor deserved death, what pretence was there for the outrage on the person of Montezuma? If the former was guilty, the latter surely was not. But, if the cacique only acted in obedience to orders, the responsibility was transferred to the sovereign who gave the orders. They could not both stand in the same category.

It is vain, however, to reason on the matter, on any abstract prin‑ ciples of right and wrong, or to suppose that the Conquerors troubled themselves with the refinements of casuistry. Their standard of right and wrong, in reference to the natives, was a very simple one. Despis‑ ing them as an outlawed race, without God in the world, they, in com‑ mon with their age, held it to be their "mission" (to borrow the cant phrase of our own day) to conquer and to convert. The measures they adopted certainly facilitated the first great work of conquest. By the execution of the caciques, they struck terror not only into the capital, but throughout the country. It proclaimed that not a hair of a Spaniard was to be touched with impunity! By rendering Montezuma contemptible in his own eyes and those of his subjects, Cortés deprived him of the support of his people, and forced him to lean on the arm of the stranger. It was a politic proceeding,—to which few men could have been equal, who had a touch of humanity in their natures.

A good criterion of the moral sense of the actors in these events is afforded by the reflections of Bernal Diaz, made some fifty years, it will be remembered, after the events themselves, when the fire of youth had become extinct, and the eye, glancing back through the vista of half a century, might be supposed to be unclouded by the passions and pre‑ judices which throw their mist over the present. "Now that I am an old man," says the veteran, "I often entertain myself with calling to mind the heroical deeds of early days, till they are as fresh as the events of yesterday. I think of the seizure of the Indian monarch, his confinement in irons, and the execution of his officers, till all these things seem act‑ ually passing before me. And, as I ponder on our exploits, I feel that it was not of ourselves that we performed them, but that it was the provi‑ dence of God which guided us. Much food is there here for medita‑ tion!"[26] There is so, indeed, and for a meditation not unpleasing, as we

[25] See Puffendorf, De Jure Naturæ et Gentium, lib. 8, cap. 6, sec. 10.—Vattel, Law of Nations, book 3, chap. 8, sec. 141.

[26] "Osar quemar sus Capitanes delante de sus Palacios, y echalle grillos entre tanto que se hazia la Justicia, que muchas vezes aora que soy viejo me paro á considerar las cosas heroicas que en aquel tiempo passámos, que me parece las veo presentes: Y digo que nuestros hechos, que no los haziamos nosotros, sino que venian todos

reflect on the advance, in speculative morality, at least, which the nineteenth century has made over the sixteenth. But should not the consciousness of this teach us charity? Should it not make us the more distrustful of applying the standard of the present to measure the actions of the past?

encaminados por Dios. . . . . . Porque ay mucho que ponderar en ello." Hist. de la Conquista, cap. 95.

CHAPTER IV

Montezuma's Deportment—His Life in the Spanish Quarters—
Meditated Insurrection—Lord of Tezcuco seized—Further
Measures of Cortés

1520

The settlement of La Villa Rica de Vera Cruz was of the last importance to the Spaniards. It was the port by which they were to communicate with Spain; the strong post on which they were to retreat in case of disaster, and which was to bridle their enemies and give security to their allies; the *point d'appui* for all their operations in the country. It was of great moment, therefore, that the care of it should be intrusted to proper hands.

A cavalier, named Alonso de Grado, had been sent by Cortés to take the place made vacant by the death of Escalante. He was a person of greater repute in civil than military matters, and would be more likely, it was thought, to maintain peaceful relations with the natives, than a person of more belligerent spirit. Cortés made—what was rare with him —a bad choice. He soon received such accounts of troubles in the settlement from the exactions and negligence of the new governor, that he resolved to supersede him.

He now gave the command to Gonzalo de Sandoval, a young cavalier, who had displayed, through the whole campaign, singular intrepidity united with sagacity and discretion; while the good-humor with which he bore every privation, and his affable manners, made him a favorite with all, privates, as well as officers. Sandoval accordingly left the camp for the coast. Cortés did not mistake his man a second time.

Notwithstanding the actual control exercised by the Spaniards through their royal captive, Cortés felt some uneasiness, when he reflected that it was in the power of the Indians, at any time, to cut off his communications with the surrounding country, and hold him a prisoner in the capital. He proposed, therefore, to build two vessels of sufficient size to transport his forces across the lake, and thus to render himself independent of the causeways. Montezuma was pleased with the idea of seeing those wonderful "water-houses," of which he had heard so much, and readily gave permission to have the timber in the royal forests felled for the purpose. The work was placed under the direction of Martin Lopez, an experienced ship-builder. Orders were also given to Sandoval to send up from the coast a supply of cordage, sails, iron, and other necessary materials, which had been judiciously saved on the destruction of the fleet.[1]

The Aztec emperor, meanwhile, was passing his days in the Spanish quarters in no very different manner from what he had been accustomed to in his own palace. His keepers were too well aware of the value of their prize, not to do every thing which could make his captivity comfortable, and disguise it from himself. But the chain will gall, though wreathed with roses. After Montezuma's breakfast, which was a light meal of fruits or vegetables, Cortés or some of his officers usually waited on him, to learn if he had any commands for them. He then devoted some time to business. He gave audience to those of his subjects who had petitions to prefer, or suits to settle. The statement of the party was drawn up on the hieroglyphic scrolls, which were submitted to a number of counsellors or judges, who assisted him with their advice on these occasions. Envoys from foreign states or his own remote provinces and cities were also admitted, and the Spaniards were careful that the same precise and punctilious etiquette should be maintained towards the royal puppet, as when in the plenitude of his authority.

After business was despatched, Montezuma often amused himself with seeing the Castilian troops go through their military exercises. He, too, had been a soldier, and in his prouder days had led armies in the field. It was very natural he should take an interest in the novel display of European tactics and discipline. At other times, he would challenge Cortés or his officers to play at some of the national games. A favorite one was called *totoloque*, played with golden balls aimed at a target or mark of the same metal. Montezuma usually staked something of value, —precious stones or ingots of gold. He lost with good-humor; indeed, it was of little consequence whether he won or lost, since he generally gave away his winnings to his attendants.[2] He had, in truth, a most munificent spirit. His enemies accused him of avarice. But, if he were avaricious, it could have been only that he might have the more to give away.

Each of the Spaniards had several Mexicans, male and female, who attended to his cooking and various other personal offices. Cortés, considering that the maintenance of this host of menials was a heavy tax on the royal exchequer, ordered them to be dismissed, excepting one to be retained for each soldier. Montezuma, on learning this, pleasantly remonstrated with the general on his careful economy, as unbecoming a royal establishment, and, countermanding the order, caused additional accommodations to be provided for the attendants, and their pay to be doubled.

On another occasion, a soldier purloined some trinkets of gold from the treasure kept in the chamber, which, since Montezuma's arrival in the Spanish quarters, had been reopened. Cortés would have punished the man for the theft, but the emperor interfering said to him, "Your

[1] Bernal Diaz, Hist. de la Conquista, cap. 96
[2] Ibid., cap. 97.

countrymen are welcome to the gold and other articles, if you will but spare those belonging to the gods." Some of the soldiers, making the most of his permission, carried off several hundred loads of fine cotton to their quarters. When this was represented to Montezuma, he only replied, "What I have once given, I never take back again." [3]

While thus indifferent to his treasures, he was keenly sensitive to personal slight or insult. When a common soldier once spoke to him angrily, the tears came into the monarch's eyes, as it made him feel the true character of his impotent condition. Cortés, on becoming acquainted with it, was so much incensed, that he ordered the soldier to be hanged; but, on Montezuma's intercession, commuted this severe sentence for a flogging. The general was not willing that any one but himself should treat his royal captive with indignity. Montezuma was desired to procure a further mitigation of the punishment. But he refused, saying, "that, if a similar insult had been offered by any one of his subjects to Malinche, he would have resented it in like manner." [4]

Such instances of disrespect were very rare. Montezuma's amiable and inoffensive manners, together with his liberality, the most popular of virtues with the vulgar, made him generally beloved by the Spaniards.[5] The arrogance, for which he had been so distinguished in his prosperous days, deserted him in his fallen fortunes. His character in captivity seems to have undergone something of that change which takes place in the wild animals of the forest, when caged within the walls of the menagerie.

The Indian monarch knew the name of every man in the army, and was careful to discriminate his proper rank.[6] For some he showed a strong partiality. He obtained from the general a favorite page, named Orteguilla, who, being in constant attendance on his person, soon learned enough of the Mexican language to be of use to his countrymen. Montezuma took great pleasure, also, in the society of Velasquez de Leon, the captain of his guard, and Pedro de Alvarado, *Tonatiuh*, or "the Sun," as he was called by the Aztecs, from his yellow hair and sunny countenance. The sunshine, as events afterwards showed, could sometimes be the prelude to a terrible tempest.

Notwithstanding the care taken to cheat him of the tedium of captivity, the royal prisoner cast a wistful glance, now and then, beyond the walls of his residence to the ancient haunts of business or pleasure. He intimated a desire to offer up his devotions at the great temple, where he was once so constant in his worship. The suggestion startled Cortés. It was too reasonable, however, for him to object to it, without wholly discarding the appearances which he was desirous to maintain. But he secured Montezuma's return by sending an escort with him of a hundred

[3] Gomara, Crónica, cap. 84.—Herrera, Hist. General, dec. 2, lib. 8, cap. 4.

[4] Ibid., dec. 2, lib. 8, cap. 5.

[5] "En esto era tan bien mirado, que todos le queriamos con gran amor, porque verdaderamente era gran señor en todas las cosas que le viamos hazer." Bernal Diaz, Hist. de la Conquista, cap. 100.

[6] "Y él bien conocia á todos, y sabia nuestros nombres, y aun calidades, y era tan bueno que á todos nos daua joyas, á otros mantas é Indias hermosas." Ibid., cap. 97.

and fifty soldiers under the same resolute cavaliers who had aided in his seizure. He told him, also, that in case of any attempt to escape, his life would instantly pay the forfeit. Thus guarded, the Indian prince visited the *teocalli*, where he was received with the usual state, and, after performing his devotions, he returned again to his quarters.[7]

It may well be believed that the Spaniards did not neglect the opportunity afforded by his residence with them, of instilling into him some notions of the Christine doctrine. Fathers Diaz and Olmedo exhausted all their battery of logic and persuasion, to shake his faith in his idols, but in vain. He, indeed, paid a most edifying attention, which gave promise of better things. But the conferences always closed with the declaration, that "the God of the Christians was good, but the gods of his own country were the true gods for him." [8] It is said, however, they extorted a promise from him, that he would take part in no more human sacrifices. Yet such sacrifices were of daily occurrence in the great temples of the capital; and the people were too blindly attached to their bloody abominations, for the Spaniards to deem it safe, for the present at least, openly to interfere.

Montezuma showed, also, an inclination to engage in the pleasures of the chase, of which he once was immoderately fond. He had large forests reserved for the purpose on the other side of the lake. As the Spanish brigantines were now completed Cortés proposed to transport him and his suite across the water in them. They were of a good size, strongly built. The largest was mounted with four falconets, or small guns. It was protected by a gayly-colored awning stretched over the deck, and the royal ensign of Castile floated proudly from the mast. On board of this vessel, Montezuma, delighted with the opportunity of witnessing the nautical skill of the white men, embarked with a train of Aztec nobles and a numerous guard of Spaniards. A fresh breeze played on the waters, and the vessel soon left behind it the swarms of light pirogues which darkened their surface. She seemed like a thing of life in the eyes of the astonished natives, who saw her, as if disdaining human agency, sweeping by with snowy pinions as if on the wings of the wind, while the thunders from her sides, now for the first time breaking on the silence of this "inland sea," showed that the beautiful phantom was clothed in terror.[9]

The royal chase was well stocked with game, some of which the emperor shot with arrows, and others were driven by the numerous attendants into nets.[10] In these woodland exercises, while he ranged over his

---

[7] Ibid., cap. 98.

[8] According to Solís, the Devil closed his heart against these good men; though, in the historian's opinion, there is no evidence that this evil counsellor actually appeared and conversed with Montezuma, after the Spaniards had displayed the Cross in Mexico. Conquista, lib. 3, cap. 20.

[9] Bernal Diaz, Hist. de la Conquista, cap. 99.—Rel. Seg. de Cortés, ap. Lorenzana, p. 88.

[10] He sometimes killed his game with a tube, a sort of air-gun, through which he blew little balls at birds and rabbits. "La Caça á que Moteçuma iba por la Laguna era á tirar á Pájaros, i á Conejos, con Cebratana, de la qual era diestro." Herrera Hist. General, dec. 2, lib. 8, cap. 4.

wild domain, Montezuma seemed to enjoy again the sweets of liberty. It was but the shadow of liberty, however; as in his quarters, at home, he enjoyed but the shadow of royalty. At home or abroad, the eye of the Spaniard was always upon him.

But, while he resigned himself without a struggle to his inglorious fate, there were others who looked on it with very different emotions. Among them was his nephew Cacama, lord of Tezcuco, a young man not more than twenty-five years of age, but who enjoyed great consideration from his high personal qualities, especially his intrepidity of character. He was the same prince who had been sent by Montezuma to welcome the Spaniards on their entrance into the Valley; and, when the question of their reception was first debated in the council, he had advised to admit them honorably as ambassadors of a foreign prince, and, if they should prove different from what they pretended, it would be time enough then to take up arms against them. That time, he thought, had now come.

In a former part of this work, the reader has been made acquainted with the ancient history of the Acolhuan or Tezcucan monarchy, once the proud rival of the Aztec in power, and greatly its superior in civilization.[11] Under its last sovereign, Nezahualpilli, its territory is said to have been grievously clipped by the insidious practices of Montezuma, who fomented dissensions and insubordination among his subjects. On the death of the Tezcucan prince, the succession was contested, and a bloody war ensued between his eldest son, Cacama, and an ambitious younger brother, Ixtlilxochitl. This was followed by a partition of the kingdom, in which the latter chieftain held the mountain districts north of the capital, leaving the residue to Cacama. Though shorn of a large part of his hereditary domain, the city was itself so important, that the lord of Tezcuco still held a high rank among the petty princes of the Valley. His capital, at the time of the Conquest, contained, according to Cortés, a hundred and fifty thousand inhabitants.[12] It was embellished with noble buildings, rivalling those of Mexico itself, and the ruins still to be met with on its ancient site attest that it was once the abode of princes.[13]

[11] Ante, Book I. Chap. 6.

[12] "É llámase esta Ciudad Tezcuco, y será de hasta treinta mil Vecinos." (Rel. Seg., ap. Lorenzana, p. 94.) According to the licentiate Zuazo, double that number, —*sesenta mil Vecinos*. (Carta, MS.) Scarcely probable, as Mexico had no more. Toribio speaks of it as covering a league one way by six another! (Hist. de los Indios, MS., Parte 3, cap. 7.) This must include the environs to a considerable extent. The language of the old chroniclers is not the most precise.

[13] A description of the capital in its glory is thus given by an eye-witness. "Esta Ciudad era la segunda cosa principal de la tierra, y así habia en Tezcuco muy grandes edificios de templos del Demonio, y muy gentiles casas y aposentos de Señores, entre los cuales, fué muy cosa de ver la casa del Señor principal, así la vieja con su huerta cercada de mas de mil cedros muy grandes y muy hermosos, de los cuales hoy dia están los mas en pie, aunque la casa está asolada, otra casa tenia que se podia aposentar en ella un egército, con muchos jardines, y un muy grande estanque, que por debajo de tierra solian entrar á él con barcas." (Toribio, Hist. de los Indios, MS., Parte 3, cap. 7.) The last relics of this palace were employed in the fortifications of the city in the revolutionary war of 1810. (Ixtlilxochitl, Venida de los Esp., p. 78. nota.) Tezcuco is now an insignificant little place, with a popula-

The young Tezcucan chief beheld, with indignation, and no slight con‹ tempt, the abject condition of his uncle. He endeavored to rouse him to manly exertion, but in vain. He then set about forming a league with several of the neighboring caciques to rescue his kinsman, and to break the detested yoke of the strangers. He called on the lord of Iztapalapan, Montezuma's brother, the lord of Tlacopan, and some others of most authority, all of whom entered heartily into his views. He then urged the Aztec nobles to join them, but they expressed an unwillingness to take any step not first sanctioned by the emperor.[14] They entertained, undoubtedly, a profound reverence for their master; but it seems probable that jealousy of the personal views of Cacama had its influence on their determination. Whatever were their motives, it is certain that, by this refusal, they relinquished the best opportunity ever presented for retrieving their sovereign's independence, and their own.

These intrigues could not be conducted so secretly as not to reach the ears of Cortés, who, with his characteristic promptness, would have marched at once on Tezcuco, and trodden out the spark of "rebellion," [15] before it had time to burst into a flame. But from this he was dissuaded by Montezuma, who represented that Cacama was a man of resolution, backed by a powerful force, and not to be put down without a desperate struggle. He consented, therefore, to negotiate, and sent a message of amicable expostulation to the cacique. He received a haughty answer in return. Cortés rejoined in a more menacing tone, asserting the supremacy of his own sovereign, the emperor of Castile. To this Cacama replied, "He acknowledged no such authority; he knew nothing of the Spanish sovereign nor his people, nor did he wish to know any thing of them." [16] Montezuma was not more successful in his application to Cacama to come to Mexico, and allow him to mediate his differences with the Span-

tion of a few thousand inhabitants. Its architectural remains, as still to be discerned, seem to have made a stronger impression on Mr. Bullock than on most travellers. Six Months in Mexico, chap. 27.

[14] "Cacama reprehendió asperamente á la Nobleza Mexicana porque consentia hacer semejantes desacatos á quatro Estrangeros y que no les mataban, se escusaban con decirles les iban á la mano y no les consentian tomar las Armas para libertarlo, y tomar sí una tan gran deshonra como era la que los Estrangeros les habian hecho en prender á su señor, y quemar á Quauhpopocatzin, los demas sus Hijos y Deudos sin culpa, con las Armas y Municion que tenian para la defenza y guarda de la ciudad, y de su autoridad tomar para sí los tesoros del Rey, y de los Dioses, y otras libertades y desvergüenzas que cada dia pasaban, y aunque todo esto vehian lo disimulaban por no enojar á Moteczuma que tan amigo y casado estaba con ellos." Ixtlilxochitl, Hist. Chich., MS., cap. 86.

[15] It is the language of Cortés. "Y esta señor *se rebeló,* assí contra el servicio de Vuestra Alteza, á quien se habia ofrecido, como contra el dicho Muteczuma." Rel. Seg., ap. Lorenzana, p. 95.—Voltaire, with his quick eye for the ridiculous, notices this arrogance in his tragedy of Alzire.

"Tu vois de ces tyrans la fureur despotique:
Ils pensent que pour eux le Ciel fit l'Amérique,
Qu'ils en sont nés les Rois; et Zamore à leurs yeux,
Tout souverain qu'il fut, n'est ~~'un séditieux."
ALZIRE, Act 4, sc. 3.

* Gomara, Crónica, cap. 91.

iards, with whom he assured the prince he was residing as a friend. But the young lord of Tezcuco was not to be so duped. He understood the position of his uncle, and replied, "that, when he did visit his capital it would be to rescue it, as well as the emperor himself, and their common gods, from bondage. He should come, not with his hand in his bosom, but on his sword,—to drive out the detested strangers who had brought such dishonor on their country!" [17]

Cortés, incensed at this tone of defiance, would again have put himself in motion to punish it, but Montezuma interposed with his more polite arts. He had several of the Tezcucan nobles, he said, in his pay;[18] and it would be easy, through their means, to secure Cacama's person, and thus break up the confederacy, at once, without bloodshed. The maintaining of a corps of stipendiaries in the courts of neighboring princes was a refinement which showed that the Western barbarian understood the science of political intrigue, as well as some of his royal brethren on the other side of the water.

By the contrivance of these faithless nobles, Cacama was induced to hold a conference, relative to the proposed invasion, in a villa which overhung the Tezcucan lake, not far from his capital. Like most of the principal edifices, it was raised so as to admit the entrance of boats beneath it. In the midst of the conference, Cacama was seized by the conspirators, hurried on board a bark in readiness for the purpose, and transported to Mexico. When brought into Montezuma's presence, the high-spirited chief abated nothing of his proud and lofty bearing. He taxed his uncle with his perfidy, and a pusillanimity so unworthy of his former character, and of the royal house from which he was descended. By the emperor he was referred to Cortés, who, holding royalty but cheap in an Indian prince, put him in fetters.[19]

There was at this time in Mexico a brother of Cacama, a stripling much younger than himself. At the instigation of Cortés, Montezuma, pretending that his nephew had forfeited the sovereignity by his late *rebellion,* declared him to be deposed, and appointed Cuicuitzca in his place. The Aztec sovereigns had always been allowed a paramount authority in questions relating to the succession. But this was a most unwarrantable exercise of it. The Tezcucans acquiesced, however, with a

---

[17] "I que para reparar la Religion, i restituir los Dioses, guardar el Reino, cobrar la fama, i libertad á él, i á México, iria de mui buena gana. mas no las manos en el seno, sino en la Espada, para matar los Españoles, que tanta mengua, i afrenta ha· .an hecho á la Nacion de Culhúa." Ibid., cap. 91.

[18] "Pero que él tenia en su Tierra de el dicho Cacamazin muchas Personas Principales, que vivian con él, y les daba su salario." Rel. Seg. de Cortés, ap. Lorenzana, p. 95.

[19] Ibid., pp. 95, 96.—Oviedo, Hist. de las Ind., MS., lib. 33, cap. 8.—Ixtlilxochitl, Hist. Chich., MS., cap. 86.

The latter author dismisses the capture of Cacama with the comfortable reflection, "that it saved the Spaniards much embarrassment, and greatly facilitated the introduction of the Catholic faith."

ready ductility, which showed their allegiance hung but lightly on them, or, what is more probable, that they were greatly in awe of the Spaniards; and the new prince was welcomed with acclamations to his capital.[20]

Cortés still wanted to get into his hands the other chiefs who had entered into the confederacy with Cacama. This was no difficult matter. Montezuma's authority was absolute, everywhere but in his own palace. By his command, the caciques were seized, each in his own city, and brought in chains to Mexico, where Cortés placed them in strict confinement with their leader.[21]

He had now triumphed over all his enemies. He had set his foot on the necks of princes; and the great chief of the Aztec empire was but a convenient tool in his hands, for accomplishing his purposes. His first use of this power was, to ascertain the actual resources of the monarchy. He sent several parties of Spaniards, guided by the natives, to explore the regions where gold was obtained. It was gleaned mostly from the beds of rivers, several hundred miles from the capital.

His next object was, to learn if there existed any good natural harbor for shipping on the Atlantic coast, as the road of Vera Cruz left no protection against the tempests that at certain seasons swept over these seas. Montezuma showed him a chart on which the shores of the Mexican Gulf were laid down with tolerable accuracy.[22] Cortés, after carefully inspecting it, sent a commission, consisting of ten Spaniards, several of them pilots, and some Aztecs, who descended to Vera Cruz, and made a careful survey of the coast for nearly sixty leagues south of that settlement, as far as the great river Coatzacualco, which seemed to offer the best, indeed, the only, accommodations for a safe and suitable harbor. A spot was selected as the site of a fortified post, and the general sent a detachment of a hundred and fifty men under Velasquez de Leon to plant a colony there.

He also obtained a grant of an extensive tract of land, in the fruitful province of Oaxaca, where he proposed to lay out a plantation for the Crown. He stocked it with the different kinds of domesticated animals peculiar to the country, and with such indigenous grains and plants as would afford the best articles for export. He soon had the estate under

[20] Cortés calls the name of this prince Cucuzca. (Rel. Seg. ap. Lorenzana, p. 96.) In the orthography of Aztec words, the general was governed by his ear; and was wrong nine times out of ten.—Bustamante, in his catalogue of Tezcucan monarchs, omits him altogether. He probably regards him as an intruder, who had no claim to be ranked among the rightful sovereigns of the land. (Galería de Antiguos Príncipes, (Puebla, 1821,) p. 21.) Sahagun has, in like manner, struck his name from the royal roll of Tezcuco. Hist. de Nueva España, lib. 8, cap. 3.

[21] The exceeding lenity of the Spanish commander, on this occasion, excited general admiration, if we are to credit Solís, throughout the Aztec empire! "Tuvo notable aplauso en todo el imperio este género de castigo sin sangre, que se atribuyó al superior juicio de los Españoles, porque no esperaban de Motezuma semejante moderacion." Conquista, lib. 4, cap. 2.

[22] Rel. Seg. de Cortés, ap Lorenzana, p. 91.

such cultivation, that he assured his master, the emperor, Charles the Fifth, it was worth twenty thousand ounces of gold.[23]

[23] "Damus quæ dant," says Martyr, briefly, in reference to this valuation. (De Orbe Novo, dec. 5, cap. 3.) Cortés notices the reports made by his people, of large and beautiful edifices in the province of Oaxaca. (Rel. Seg., ap. Lorenzana, p. 89.) It is here, also, that some of the most elaborate specimens of Indian architecture are still to be seen, in the ruins of Mitla.

CHAPTER V

MONTEZUMA SWEARS ALLEGIANCE TO SPAIN—ROYAL TREASURES—
THEIR DIVISION—CHRISTIAN WORSHIP IN THE TEOCALLI—DIS-
CONTENTS OF THE AZTECS

1520

CORTÉS now felt his authority sufficiently assured to demand from Montezuma a formal recognition of the supremacy of the Spanish emperor.
The Indian monarch had intimated his willingness to acquiesce in this, on
their very first interview. He did not object, therefore, to call together his
principal caciques for the purpose. When they were assembled, he made
them an address, briefly stating the object of the meeting. They were all
acquainted, he said, with the ancient tradition, that the great Being, who
had once ruled over the land, had declared, on his departure, that he
should return at some future time and resume his sway. That time had
now arrived. The white men had come from the quarter where the sun
rises, beyond the ocean, to which the good deity had withdrawn. They
were sent by their master to reclaim the obedience of his ancient subjects.
For himself he was ready to acknowledge his authority. "You have been
faithful vassals of mine," continued Montezuma, "during the many years
that I have sat on the throne of my fathers. I now expect that you will
show me this last act of obedience by acknowledging the great king beyond the waters to be your lord, also, and that you will pay him tribute
in the same manner as you have hitherto done to me." [1] As he concluded,
his voice was nearly stifled by his emotion, and the tears fell fast down
his cheeks.

His nobles, many of whom, coming from a distance, had not kept pace
with the changes which had been going on in the capital were filled with
astonishment, as they listened to his words, and beheld the voluntary
abasement of their master, whom they had hitherto reverenced as the
omnipotent lord of Anahuac. They were the more affected, therefore, by
the sight of his distress.[2] His will, they told him, had always been their

[1] "Y mucho os ruego, pues á todos os es notorio todo esto, que assí como hasta
aquí á mí me habeis tenido, y obedecido por Señor vuestro, de aquí adelante tengais,
y obedescais á este Gran Rey, pues él es vuestro natural Señor, y en su lugar tengais
á este su Capitan: y todos los Tributos, y Servicios, que fasta aquí á mí me haciades,
los haced, y dad á él, porque yo assimismo tengo de contribuir, y servir con todo lo
que me mandaré." Rel. Seg. de Cortés, ap. Lorenzana, p. 97.

[2] "Lo qual todo les dijo llorando, con las mayores lágrimas, y suspiros, que un
hombre podia manifestar; é assimismo todos aquellos Señores, que le estaban oiendo,
lloraban tanto, que en gran rato no le pudiéron responder." Ibid., loc. cit.

law. It should be so now; and, if he thought the sovereign of the strangers was the ancient lord of their country, they were willing to acknowledge him as such still. The oaths of allegiance were then administered with all due solemnity, attested by the Spaniards present, and a full record of the proceedings was drawn up by the royal notary, to be sent to Spain.[3] There was something deeply touching in the ceremony by which an independent and absolute monarch, in obedience less to the dictates of fear than of conscience, thus relinquished his hereditary rights in favor of an unknown and mysterious power. It even moved those hard men who were thus unscrupulously availing themselves of the confiding ignorance of the natives; and, though "it was in the regular way of their own business," says an old chronicler, "there was not a Spaniard who could look on the spectacle with a dry eye!"[4]

The rumor of these strange proceedings was soon circulated through the capital and the country. Men read in them the finger of Providence. The ancient tradition of Quetzalcoatl was familiar to all; and where it had slept scarcely noticed in the memory, it was now revived with many exaggerated circumstances. It was said to be part of the tradition, that the royal line of the Aztecs was to end with Montezuma; and his name, the literal signification of which is "sad" or "angry lord," was construed into an omen of his evil destiny.[5]

Having thus secured this great feudatory to the crown of Castile, Cortés suggested that it would be well for the Aztec chiefs to send his sovereign such a gratuity as would conciliate his good-will by convincing

[3] Solís regards this ceremony as supplying what was before defective in the title of the Spaniards to the country. The remarks are curious, even from a professed casuist. "Y siendo una como insinuacion misteriosa del título que se debió despues al derecho de las armas, sobre justa provocacion, como lo verémos en su lugar: circunstancia particular, que concurrió en la conquista de Méjico para mayor justificacion de aquel dominio, sobre las demas consideraciones generales que no solo hiciéron lícita la guerra en otras partes, sino legítima y razonable siempre que se puso en términos de medio necesario para la introduccion del Evangelio." Conquista, lib. 4, cap. 3.

[4] Bernal Diaz, Hist. de la Conquista, cap. 101.—Solís, Conquista, loc. cit.—Herrera, Hist. General, dec. 2, lib. 9, cap. 4.—Ixtlilxochitl, Hist. Chich., MS., cap. 87.

Oviedo considers the grief of Montezuma as sufficient proof that his homage, far from being voluntary, was extorted by necessity. The historian appears to have seen the drift of events more clearly than some of the actors in them. "Y en la verdad si como Cortés lo dice, ó escrivió, pasó en efecto, mui gran cosa me parece la conciencia y liberalidad de Montezuma en esta su restitucion é obediencia al Rey de Castilla, por la simple ó cautelosa informacion de Cortés, que le podia hacer para ello; Mas aquellas lágrimas que dice, que Montezuma hizo su oracion, é amonestamiento, despojándose de su señorío, é las de aquellos con que les respondiéron aceptando lo que les mandaba, y exortaba, y á mi parecer su llanto queria decir, ó enseñar otra cosa de lo que él, y ellos dixéron; porque las obediencias que se suelen dar á los Príncipes con riza, é con cámaras; é diversidad de Música, é leticia, enseñales de placer, se suele hacer; é no con lucto ni lágrimas, é sollozos, ni estando preso quien obedece; porque como dice Marco Varron: Lo que por fuerza se da no es servicio sino robo." Hist. de las Ind., MS., lib. 33, cap. 9.

[5] Gomara, Crónica, cap. 92.—Clavigero, Stor. del Messico, tom. II. p. 256.

him of the loyalty of his new vassals.[6] Montezuma consented that his collectors should visit the principal cities and provinces, attended by a number of Spaniards, to receive the customary tributes, in the name of the
Castilian sovereign. In a few weeks most of them returned, bringing back
large quantities of gold and silver plate, rich stuffs, and the various commodities in which the taxes were usually paid.

To this store Montezuma added, on his own account, the treasure of
Axayacatl, previously noticed, some part of which had been already given
to the Spaniards. It was the fruit of long and careful hoarding,—of extortion, it may be,—by a prince who little dreamed of its final destination,
When brought into the quarters, the gold alone was sufficient to make
three great heaps. It consisted partly of native grains; part had been
melted into bars; but the greatest portion was in utensils, and various
kinds of ornaments and curious toys, together with imitations of birds,
insects, or flowers, executed with uncommon truth and delicacy. There
were, also, quantities of collars, bracelets, wands, fans, and other trinkets,
in which the gold and feather-work were richly powdered with pearls and
precious stones. Many of the articles were even more admirable for the
workmanship than for the value of the materials;[7] such, indeed,—if we
may take the report of Cortés to one who would himself have soon an
opportunity to judge of its veracity, and whom it would not be safe to
trifle with,—as no monarch in Europe could boast in his dominions! [8]

Magnificent as it was, Montezuma expressed his regret that the treasure was no larger. But he had diminished it, he said, by his former gifts
to the white men. "Take it," he added, "Malinche, and let it be recorded
in your annals, that Montezuma sent this present to your master." [9]

The Spaniards gazed with greedy eyes on the display of riches,[10] now
their own, which far exceeded all hitherto seen in the New World, and fell
nothing short of the *El Dorado* which their glowing imaginations had depicted. It may be, that they felt somewhat rebuked by the contrast which
their own avarice presented to the princely munificence of the barbarian
chief. At least, they seemed to testify their sense of his superiority by the

[6] "Pareceria que ellos comenzaban á servir, y Vuestra Alteza tendria mas concepto
de las voluntades, que á su servicio mostraban." Rel. Seg. de Cortés, ap. Lorenzana,
p. 98.

[7] Peter Martyr, distrusting some extravagance in this statement of Cortés, found
it fully confirmed by the testimony of others. "Referunt non credenda. Credenda
tamen, quando vir talis ad Cæsarem et nostri collegii Indici senatores audeat ex-
scribere. Addes insuper se multa prætermittere, ne tanta recensendo sit molestus.
Idem affirmant qui ad nos inde regrediuntur." De Orbe Novo, dec. 5, cap. 3.

[8] "Las quales, demas de su valor, eran tales, y tan maravillosas, que consideradas
por su novedad, y estrañeza, no tenian precio, ni es de creer, que alguno de todos los
Príncipes del Mundo de quien se tiene noticia, las pudiesse tener tales, y de tal
calidad." Rel. Seg. de Cortés, ap. Lorenzana, p. 99.—See, also, Oviedo, Hist. de las
Ind., MS., lib. 33, cap. 9,—Bernal Diaz, Hist. de la Conquista, cap. 104.

[9] "Dezilde en vuestros anales y cartas: Esto os embia vuestro buen vassalio Monteçuma." Bernal Diaz, ubi supra.

[10] "Fluctibus auri
Expleri calor ille nequit."
CLAUDIAN, In Ruf., lib. 1.

respectful homage which they rendered him, as they poured forth the fulness of their gratitude.[11] They were not so scrupulous, however, as to manifest any delicacy in appropriating to themselves the donative, a small part of which was to find its way into the royal coffers. They clamored loudly for an immediate division of the spoil, which the general would have postponed till the tributes from the remoter provinces had been gathered in. The goldsmiths of Azcapozalco were sent for to take in pieces the larger and coarser ornaments, leaving untouched those of more delicate workmanship. Three days were consumed in this labor, when the heaps of gold were cast into ingots, and stamped with the royal arms.

Some difficulty occurred in the division of the treasure, from the want of weights, which, strange as it appears, considering their advancement in the arts, were, as already observed, unknown to the Aztecs. The deficiency was soon supplied by the Spaniards, however, with scales and weights of their own manufacture, probably not the most exact. With the aid of these they ascertained the value of the royal fifth to be thirty-two thousand and four hundred *pesos de oro*.[12] Diaz swells it to nearly four times that amount.[13] But their desire of securing the emperor's favor makes it improbable that the Spaniards should have defrauded the exchequer of any part of its due; while, as Cortés was responsible for the sum admitted in his letter, he would be still less likely to overstate it. His estimate may be received as the true one.

The whole amounted, therefore, to one hundred and sixty-two thousand *pesos de oro*, independently of the fine ornaments and jewelry, the value of which Cortés computes at five hundred thousand ducats more. There were, besides, five hundred marks of silver, chiefly in plate, drinking-cups, and other articles of luxury. The inconsiderable quantity of the silver, as compared with the gold, forms a singular contrast to the relative proportions of the two metals since the occupation of the country by the Europeans.[14] The whole amount of the treasure, reduced to our own cur-

---

[11] "Y quãdo aquello le oyó Cortés, y todos nosotros, estuvímos espantados de la gran bondad, y liberalidad del gran Monteçuma, y con mucho acato le quitámos todos las gorras de armas, y le dixímos, que se lo teniamos en merced, y con palabras de mucho amor," &c. Bernal Diaz, ubi supra.

[12] Rel. Seg. de Cortés, ap. Lorenzana, p. 99.
This estimate of the royal fifth is confirmed (with the exception of the four hundred ounces) by the affidavits of a number of witnesses cited on behalf of Cortés, to show the amount of the treasure. Among these witnesses we find some of the most respectable names in the army, as Olid, Ordaz, Avila, the priests Olmedo and Diaz,—the last, it may be added, not too friendly to the general. The instrument, which is without date, is in the collection of Vargas Ponçe. Probanza fecha á pedimento de Juan de Lexalde, MS.

[13] "Eran tres montones *de oro*, y pesado huvo en ellos sobre *seiscientos mil pesos*, como adelante diré, sin la plata, é otras muchas riquezas." Hist. de la Conquista, cap. 104.

[14] The quantity of silver taken from the American mines has exceeded that of gold in the ratio of forty-six to one. (Humboldt, Essai Politique, tom. III. p. 401.) The value of the latter metal, says Clemencin, which, on the discovery of the New World, was only eleven times greater than that of the former, has now come to be sixteen times. (Memorias de la Real Acad. de Hist., tom. VI. Ilust. 20.) This does

rency, and making allowance for the change in the value of gold since the beginning of the sixteenth century, was about six million three hundred thousand dollars, or one million four hundred and seventeen thousand pounds sterling; a sum large enough to show the incorrectness of the popular notion, that little or no wealth was found in Mexico.[15] It was, indeed, small in comparison with that obtained by the conquerors of Peru. But few European monarchs of that day could boast a larger treasure in their coffers.[16]

The division of the spoil was a work of some difficulty. A perfectly equal division of it among the Conquerors would have given them more than three thousand pounds sterling, apiece; a magnificent booty! But one fifth was to be deducted for the Crown. An equal portion was reserved for the general, pursuant to the tenor of his commission. A large sum was then allowed to indemnify him and the governor of Cuba, for the charges of the expedition and the loss of the fleet. The garrison of Vera Cruz was also to be provided for. Ample compensation was made to the principal cavaliers. The cavalry, arquebusiers, and crossbow-men, each received double pay. So that, when the turn of the common soldiers came, there remained not more than a hundred *pesos de oro* for each; a sum so insignificant, in comparison with their expectations, that several refused to accept it.[17]

Loud murmurs now rose among the men. "Was it for this," they said, "that we left our homes and families, perilled our lives, submitted to fatigue and famine, and all for so contemptible a pittance! Better to have stayed in Cuba, and contented ourselves with the gains of a safe and easy traffic. When we gave up our share of the gold at Vera Cruz, it was on the assurance that we should be amply requited in Mexico. We have, indeed, found the riches we expected; but no sooner seen, than they are snatched

not vary materially from Smith's estimate made after the middle of the last century. (Wealth of Nations, book 1, chap. 11.) The difference would have been much more considerable, but for the greater demand for silver for objects of ornament and use.

[15] Dr. Robertson, preferring the authority, it seems, of Diaz, speaks of the value of the treasure as 600,000 *pesos*. (History of America, vol. II. pp. 296, 298.) The value of the *peso* is an ounce of silver, or dollar, which, making allowance for the depreciation of silver, represented, in the time of Cortés, nearly four times its value at the present day. But that of the *peso de oro* was nearly three times that sum, or eleven dollars, sixty-seven cents. (See Ante, Book II. chap. 6, note 18.) Robertson makes his own estimate, so much reduced below that of his original, an argument for doubting the existence, in any great quantity, of either gold or silver in the country. In accounting for the scarcity of the former metal in this argument, he falls into an error in stating that gold was not one of the standards by which the value of other commodities in Mexico was estimated. Comp. Ante, p. 84.

[16] Many of them, indeed, could boast little or nothing in their coffers. Maximilian of Germany, and the more prudent Ferdinand of Spain, left scarcely enough to defray their funeral expenses. Even as late as the beginning of the next century, we find Henry IV of France embracing his minister Sully, with rapture, when he informed him, that, by dint of great economy, he had 36,000,000 livres, about 1,500,000 pounds sterling, in his treasury. See Mémoires du Duc de Sully, tom. III. liv. 27.

[17] "Por ser tan poco, muchos soldados huuo que no lo quisiéron recebir." Bernal Diaz, Hist. de la Conquista, cap. 105.

from us by the very men who pledged us their faith"! The malecontents even went so far as to accuse their leaders of appropriating to themselves several of the richest ornaments, before the partition had been made; an accusation that receives some countenance from a dispute which arose between Mexia, the treasurer for the Crown, and Velasquez de Leon, a relation of the governor, and a favorite of Cortés. The treasurer accused this cavalier of purloining certain pieces of plate before they were submitted to the royal stamp. From words the parties came to blows. They were good swordsmen; several wounds were given on both sides, and the affair might have ended fatally, but for the interference of Cortés, who placed both under arrest.

He then used all his authority and insinuating eloquence to calm the passions of his men. It was a delicate crisis. He was sorry, he said, to see them so unmindful of the duty of loyal soldiers, and cavaliers of the Cross, as to brawl like common banditti over their booty. The division, he assured them, had been made on perfectly fair and equitable principles. As to his own share, it was no more than was warranted by his commission. Yet, if they thought it too much, he was willing to forego his just claims, and divide with the poorest soldier. Gold, however welcome, was not the chief object of his ambition. If it were theirs, they should still reflect, that the present treasure was little in comparison with what awaited them hereafter; for had they not the whole country and its mine at their disposal? It was only necessary that they should not give an opening to the enemy, by their discord, to circumvent and to crush them. —With these honeyed words, of which he had good store for all fitting occasions, says an old soldier,[18] for whose benefit, in part, they were intended, he succeeded in calming the storm for the present; while in private he took more effectual means, by presents judiciously administered, to mitigate the discontents of the importunate and refractory. And, although there were a few of more tenacious temper, who treasured this in their memories against a future day, the troops soon returned to their usual subordination. This was one of those critical conjunctures which taxed all the address and personal authority of Cortés. He never shrunk from them, but on such occasions was true to himself. At Vera Cruz he had persuaded his followers to give up what was but the earnest of future gains. Here he persuaded them to relinquish these gains themselves. It was snatching the prey from the very jaws of the lion. Why did he not turn and rend him?

To many of the soldiers, indeed, it mattered little whether their share of the booty were more or less. Gaming is a deep-rooted passion in the Spaniard, and the sudden acquisition of riches furnished both the means and the motive for its indulgence. Cards were easily made out of old parchment drum-heads, and in a few days most of the prize-money, obtained with so much toil and suffering, had changed hands, and many of

[18] "Palabras muy melifluas; . . . . . razones mui bien dichas, que las sabia bien proponer." Ibid, ubi supra.

the improvident soldiers closed the campaign as poor as they had commenced it. Others, it is true, more prudent, followed the example of their officers, who, with the aid of the royal jewellers, converted their gold into chains, services of plate, and other portable articles of ornament or use.[19]

Cortés seemed now to have accomplished the great objects of the expedition. The Indian monarch had declared himself the feudatory of the Spanish. His authority, his revenues, were at the disposal of the general. The conquest of Mexico seemed to be achieved, and that without a blow. But it was far from being achieved. One important step yet remained to be taken, towards which the Spaniards had hitherto made little progress, —the conversion of the natives. With all the exertions of father Olmedo, backed by the polemic talents of the general,[20] neither Montezuma nor his subjects showed any disposition to abjure the faith of their fathers.[21] The bloody exercises of their religion, on the contrary, were celebrated with all the usual circumstance and pomp of sacrifice before the eyes of the Spaniards.

Unable further to endure these abominations, Cortés, attended by several of his cavaliers, waited on Montezuma. He told the emperor that the Christians could no longer consent to have the services of their religion shut up within the narrow walls of the garrison. They wished to spread its light far abroad, and to open to the people a full participation in the blessings of Christianity. For this purpose, they requested that the great *teocalli* should be delivered up, as a fit place where their worship might be conducted in the presence of the whole city.

Montezuma listened to the proposal with visible consternation. Amidst all his troubles he had leaned for support on his own faith, and, indeed, it was in obedience to it, that he had shown such deference to the Spaniards as the mysterious messengers predicted by the oracles. "Why," said he, "Malinche, why will you urge matters to an extremity, that must surely bring down the vengeance of our gods, and stir up an insurrection

---

[19] Ibid., cap. 105, 106.—Gomara, Crónica, cap. 93.—Herrera, Hist. General, dec. 2, lib. 8, cap. 5.

[20] "Ex jureconsulto Cortesius theologus effectus," says Martyr, in his pithy manner. De Orbe Novo, dec. 5, cap. 4.

[21] According to Ixtlilxochitl, Montezuma got as far on the road to conversion, as the *Credo* and the *Ave Maria*, both of which he could repeat; but his baptism was postponed, and he died before receiving it. That he ever consented to receive it is highly improbable. I quote the historian's words, in which he further notices the general's unsuccessful labors among the Indians. "Cortés comenzó á dar órden de la conversion de los Naturales, diciéndoles, que pues eran vasallos del Rey de España que se tornasen Cristianos como él lo era, y así se comenzáron á Bautizar algunos aunque fuéron muy pocos, y Motecuhzoma aunque pidió el Bautismo, y sabia algunas de las oraciones como eran el Ave María, y el Credo, se dilató por la Pasqua siguiente, que era la de Resurreccion, y fué tan desdichado que nunca alcanzó tanto bien y los Nuestros con la dilacion y aprieto en que se viéron, se descuidáron, de que pesó á todos mucho muriese sin Bautismo." Hist. Chich., MS. cap. 87.

among my people, who will never endure this profanation of their temples?" [22]

Cortés, seeing how greatly he was moved, made a sign to his officers to withdraw. When left alone with the interpreters, he told the emperor that he would use his influence to moderate the zeal of his followers, and persuade them to be contented with one of the sanctuaries of the *teocalli*. If that were not granted, they should be obliged to take it by force, and to roll down the images of his false deities in the face of the city. "We fear not for our lives," he added, "for, though our numbers are few, the arm of the true God is over us." Montezuma, much agitated, told him that he would confer with the priests.

The result of the conference was favorable to the Spaniards, who were allowed to occupy one of the sanctuaries as a place of worship. The tidings spread great joy throughout the camp. They might now go forth in open day and publish their religion to the assembled capital. No time was lost in availing themselves of the permission. The sanctuary was cleansed of its disgusting impurities. An altar was raised, surmounted by a crucifix and the image of the Virgin. Instead of the gold and jewels which blazed on the neighboring Pagan shrine, its walls were decorated with fresh garlands of flowers; and an old soldier was stationed to watch over the chapel, and guard it from intrusion.

When these arrangements were completed, the whole army moved in solemn procession up the winding ascent of the pyramid. Entering the sanctuary, and clustering round its portals, they listened reverentially to the service of the mass, as it was performed by the fahers Olmedo and Diaz. And, as the beautiful *Te Deum* rose towards heaven, Cortés and his soldiers, kneeling on the ground, with tears streaming from their eyes, poured forth their gratitude to the Almighty for this glorious triumph of the Cross.[23]

It was a striking spectacle,—that of these rude warriors lifting up their orisons on the summit of this mountain temple, in the very capital of Heathendom, on the spot especially dedicated to its unhallowed mysteries. Side by side, the Spaniard and the Aztec knelt down in prayer; and the Christian hymn mingled its sweet tones of love and mercy with the wild chant by the Indian priest in honor of the war-god of Anahuac! It was an unnatural union, and could not long abide.

[22] "O Malinche, y como nos quereis echar á perder á toda esta ciudad, porque estarán mui enojados nuestros Dioses contra nosotros, y aun vuestras vidas no sé en que pararán." Bernal Diaz, Hist. de la Conquista, cap. 107.

[23] This transaction is told with more discrepancy than usual by the different writers. Cortés assures the Emperor that he occupied the temple, and turned out the false gods by force, in spite of the menaces of the Mexicans. (Rel. Seg., ap. Lorenzana, p. 106.) The improbability of this Quixotic feat startles Oviedo, who nevertheless reports it. (Hist. de las Ind., MS., lib. 33, cap. 10.) It looks, indeed, very much as if the general was somewhat too eager to set off his militant zeal to advantage in the eyes of his master. The statements of Diaz, and of other chroniclers, conformably to that in the text, seem far the most probable. Comp. Diaz, Hist. de la Conquista, ubi supra.—Herrera. Hist. General, dec. 2, lib. 8, cap. 6.—Argensola, Anales, lib. 1, cap. 88.

A nation will endure any outrage sooner than that on its religion. This is an outrage both on its principles and its prejudices; on the ideas instilled into it from childhood, which have strengthened with its growth, until they become a part of its nature,—which have to do with its highest interests here, and with the dread hereafter. Any violence to the religious sentiment touches all alike, the old and the young, the rich and the poor, the noble and the plebeian. Above all, it touches the priests, whose personal consideration rests on that of their religion; and who, in a semi-civilized state of society, usually hold an unbounded authority. Thus it was with the Brahmins of India, the Magi of Persia, the Roman Catholic clergy in the Dark Ages, the priests of ancient Egypt and Mexico.

The people had borne with patience all the injuries and affronts hitherto put on them by the Spaniards. They had seen their sovereign dragged as a captive from his own palace; his ministers butchered before his eyes; his treasure seized and appropriated; himself in a manner deposed from his royal supremacy. All this they had seen without a struggle to prevent it. But the profanation of their temples touched a deeper feeling, of which the priesthood were not slow to take advantage.[24]

The first intimation of this change of feeling was gathered from Montezuma himself. Instead of his usual cheerfulness, he appeared grave and abstracted, and instead of seeking, as he was wont, the society of the Spaniards, seemed rather to shun it. It was noticed, too, that conferences were more frequent between him and the nobles, and especially the priests. His little page, Orteguilla, who had now picked up a tolerable acquaintance with the Aztec, contrary to Montezuma's usual practice, was not allowed to attend him at these meetings. These circumstances could not fail to awaken most uncomfortable apprehensions in the Spaniards.

Not many days elapsed, however, before Cortés received an invitation, or rather a summons, from the emperor, to attend him in his apartment. The general went with some feelings of anxiety and distrust, taking with him Olid, captain of the guard, and two or three other trusty cavaliers. Montezuma received them with cold civility, and, turning to the general, told him that all his predictions had come to pass. The gods of his country had been offended by the violation of their temples. They had threatened the priests, that they would forsake the city, if the sacrilegious strangers were not driven from it, or rather sacrificed on the altars, in expiation of their crimes.[25] The monarch assured the Christians, it was

[24] "Para mí yo tengo por marabilla, é grande, la mucha paciencia de Montezuma, y de los Indios principales, que assí viéron tratar sus Templos, é Ídolos: Mas su disimulacion adelante se mostró ser otra cosa viendo, que vna Gente Extrangera, é de tan poco número, les prendió su Señor é porque formas los hacia tributarios, é se castigaban é quemaban los principales, é se aniquilaban y disipaban sus templos, é hasta en aquellos y sus antecesores estaban. Recia cosa me parece soportarla con tana quietud; pero adelante, como lo dirá la Historia, mostró el tiempo lo que en el pecho estaba oculto en todos los Indios generalmente." Hist. de las Ind., MS., lib. 33, cap. 10.

[25] According to Herrera, it was the Devil himself who communicated this to Montezuma, and he reports the substance of the dialogue between the parties. (Hist. General, dec. 2, lib. 9, cap. 6.) Indeed, the apparition of Satan in his own bodily

from regard to their safety, that he communicated this; and, "if you have any regard for it yourselves," he concluded, "you will leave the country without delay. I have only to raise my finger, and every Aztec in the land will rise in arms against you." There was no reason to doubt his sincerity. For Montezuma, whatever evils had been brought on him by the white men, held them in reverence as a race more highly gifted than his own, while for several, as we have seen, he had conceived an attachment, flowing, no doubt, from their personal attentions and deference to himself.

Cortés was too much master of his feelings, to show how far he was startled by this intelligence. He replied with admirable coolness, that he should regret much to leave the capital so precipitately, when he had no vessels to take him from the country. If it were not for this, there could be no obstacle to his leaving it at once. He should also regret another step to which he should be driven, if he quitted it under these circumstances, —that of taking the emperor along with him.

Montezuma was evidently troubled by this last suggestion. He inquired how long it would take to build the vessels, and finally consented to send a sufficient number of workmen to the coast, to act under the orders of the Spaniards; meanwhile, he would use his authority to restrain the impatience of the people, under the assurance that the white men would leave the land, when the means for it were provided. He kept his word. A large body of Aztec artisans left the capital with the most experienced Castilian ship-builders, and, descending to Vera Cruz, began at once to fell the timber and build a sufficient number of ships to transport the Spaniards back to their own country. The work went forward with apparent alacrity. But those who had the direction of it, it is said, received private instructions from the general, to interpose as many delays as possible, in hopes of receiving in the mean time such reinforcements from Europe, as would enable him to maintain his ground.[26]

The whole aspect of things was now changed in the Castilian quarters. Instead of the security and repose in which the troops had of late in-

presence, on this occasion, is stoutly maintained by most historians of the time. Oviedo, a man of enlarged ideas on most subjects, speaks with a little more qualification on this. "Porque la Misa y Evangelio, que predicaban y decian los christianos, le [al Diablo] daban gran tormento; y débese pensar, si verdad es, que esas gentes tienen tanta conversacion y comunicacion con nuestro adversario, *como se tiene por cierto en estas Indias,* que no le podia á nuestro enemigo placer con los misterios y sacramentos de la sagrada religion christiana." Hist. de las Ind., MS., lib. 33, cap. 47.

[26] "É Cortés proveió de maestros é personas que entendiesen en la labor de los Navíos, é dixo despues á los Españoles desta manera: Señores y hermanos, este Señor Montezuma quiere que nos vamos de la tierra, y conviene que se hagan Navíos. Id con estos Indios é córtese la madera; é entretanto Dios nos proveherá de gente é socorro; por tanto, poned tal dilacion que parezca que haceis algo y se haga con ella lo que nos conviene; é siempre me escrivid éavisad que tales estáis en la Montaña, é que no sientan los Indios nuestra disimulacion. É así se puso por obra." (Oviedo, Hist. de las Ind., MS., lib. 33, cap. 47.) So, also, Gomara, (Crónica, cap. 95.) Diaz denies any such secret orders, alleging that Martin Lopez, the principal builder, assured him they made all the expedition possible in getting three ships on the stocks. Hist. de la Conquista, cap. 108.

dulged, they felt a gloomy apprehension of danger, not the less oppressive to the spirits, that it was scarcely visible to the eye;—like the faint speck just descried above the horizon by the voyager in the tropics, to the common gaze seeming only a summer cloud, but which to the experienced mariner bodes the coming of the hurricane. Every precaution that prudence could devise was taken to meet it. The soldier, as he threw himself on his mats for repose, kept on his armor. He ate, drank, slept, with his weapons by his side. His horse stood ready caparisoned, day and night, with the bridle hanging at the saddle-bow. The guns were carefully planted so as to command the great avenues. The sentinels were doubled, and every man, of whatever rank, took his turn in mounting guard. The garrison was in a state of siege.[27] Such was the uncomfortable position of the army, when, in the beginning of May, 1520, six months after their arrival in the capital, tidings came from the coast, which gave greater alarm to Cortés, than even the menaced insurrection of the Aztecs.

[27] "I may say without vaunting," observes our stout-hearted old chronicler, Bernal Diaz, "that I was so accustomed to this way of life, that since the conquest of the country I have never been able to lie down undressed, or in a bed; yet I sleep as sound as if I were on the softest down. Even when I make the rounds of my *encomienda,* I never take a bed with me; unless, indeed, I go in the company of other cavaliers, who might impute this to parsimony. But even then I throw myself on it with my clothes on. Another thing I must add, that I cannot sleep long in the night without getting up to look at the heavens and the stars, and stay a while in the open air, and this without a bonnet or covering of any sort on my head. And, thanks to God, I have received no harm from it. I mention these things, that the world may understand of what stuff we, the true Conquerors, were made, and how well drilled we were to arms and watching." Hist. de la Conquista, cap. 108.

CHAPTER VI

FATE OF CORTÉS' EMISSARIES—PROCEEDINGS IN THE CASTILIAN COURT
—PREPARATIONS OF VELASQUEZ—NARVAEZ LANDS IN MEXICO—
POLITIC CONDUCT OF CORTÉS—HE LEAVES THE CAPITAL

1520

BEFORE explaining the nature of the tidings alluded to in the preceding chapter, it will be necessary to cast a glance over some of the transactions of an earlier period. The vessel, which, as the reader may remember, bore the envoys Puertocarrero and Montejo with the despatches from Vera Cruz, after touching, contrary to orders, at the nothern coast of Cuba, and spreading the news of the late discoveries, held on its way uninterrupted towards Spain, and early in October, 1519, reached the little port of San Lucar. Great was the sensation caused by her arrival and the tidings which she brought; a sensation scarcely inferior to that created by the original discovery of Columbus. For now, for the first time, all the magnificent anticipations formed of the New World seemed destined to be realized.

ᛁ Unfortunately, there was a person in Seville, at this time, named Benito Martin, chaplain of Velasquez, the governor of Cuba. No sooner did this man learn the arrival of the envoys, and the particulars of their story, than he lodged a complaint with the *Casa de Contratacion,*—the Royal India House,—charging those on board the vessel with mutiny and rebellion against the authorities of Cuba, as well as with treason to the Crown.[1] In consequence of his representations, the ship was taken possession of by the public officers, and those on board were prohibited from removing their own effects, or anything else from her. The envoys were not even allowed the funds necessary for the expenses of the voyage, nor a considerable sum remitted by Cortés to his father, Don Martin. In this embarrassment they had no alternative but to present themselves, as speedily as possible, before the emperor, deliver the letters with which they had been charged by the colony, and seek redress for their own grievances. They first sought out Martin Cortés, residing at Medellin and with him made the best of their way to court.

Charles the Fifth was then on his first visit to Spain after his acces-

[1] In the collection of MSS., made by Don Vargas Ponçe, former President of the Academy of History, is a Memorial of this same Benito Martin to the Emperor, setting forth the services of Velasquez, and the ingratitude and revolt of Cortés and his followers. The paper is without date; written after the arrival of the envoys, probably at the close of 1519 or the beginning of the following year.

sion. It was not a long one; long enough, however, to disgust his sub-jects, and, in a great degree, to alienate their affections. He had lately received intelligence of his election to the imperial crown of Germany. From that hour, his eyes were turned to that quarter. His stay in the Peninsula was prolonged only that he might raise supplies for appearing with splendor in the great theatre of Europe. Every act showed too plainly that the diadem of his ancestors was held lightly in comparison with the imperial bauble in which neither his countrymen nor his own posterity could have the slightest interest. The interest was wholly per-sonal.

Contrary to established usage, he had summoned the Castilian córtes to meet at Compostella, a remote town in the North, which presented no other advantage than that of being near his place of embarkation.[2] On his way thither he stopped some time at Tordesillas, the residence of his unhappy mother, Joanna "the Mad." It was here that the envoys from Vera Cruz presented themselves before him, in March, 1520. At nearly the same time, the treasures brought over by them reached the court, where they excited unbounded admiration.[3] Hitherto, the returns from the New World had been chiefly in vegetable products, which, if the surest, are, also, the slowest sources of wealth. Of gold they had as yet seen but little, and that in its natural state or wrought into the rudest trinkets. The courtiers gazed with astonishment on the large masses of the precious metal, and the delicate manufacture of the various articles, especially of the richly tinted feather-work. And, as they listened to the accounts, written and oral, of the great Aztec empire, they felt assured that the Castilian ships had, at length, reached the golden Indies, which hitherto had seemed to recede before them.

In this favorable mood there is little doubt the monarch would have granted the petition of the envoys, and confirmed the irregular proceed-ings of the Conquerors, but for the opposition of a person who held the highest office in the Indian department. This was Juan Rodriguez de Fonseca, formerly dean of Seville, now bishop of Burgos. He was a man of noble family, and had been intrusted with the direction of the colonial concerns, on the discovery of the New World. On the establishment of the Royal Council of the Indies by Ferdinand the Catholic, he had been made its president, and had occupied that post ever since. His long con-tinuance in a position of great importance and difficulty is evidence of capacity for business. It was no uncommon thing in that age to find ec-clesiastics in high civil, and even military employment. Fonseca appears to have been an active, efficient person, better suited to a secular than to a religious vocation. He had, indeed, little that was religious in his tem-

---

[2] Sandoval, indeed, gives a singular reason,—that of being near the coast, so as to enable Chiévres, and the other Flemish blood-suckers, to escape suddenly, if need were, with their ill-gotten treasures, from the country. Hist. de Cárlos Quinto, tom. I. p. 203, ed. Pamplona, 1634.

[3] See the letter of Peter Martyr to his noble friend and pupil, the Marquis de Mondejar, written two months after the arrival of the vessel from Vera Cruz. Opus Epist., ep. 650.

per; quick to take offence and slow to forgive. His resentments seem to have been nourished and perpetuated like a part of his own nature. Unfortunately his peculiar position enabled him to display them towards some of the most illustrious men of his time. From pique at some real or fancied slight from Columbus, he had constantly thwarted the plans of the great navigator. He had shown the same unfriendly feeling towards the Admiral's son, Diego, the heir of his honors; and he now, and from this time forward, showed a similar spirit towards the Conqueror of Mexico. The immediate cause of this was his own personal relations with Velasquez, to whom a near relative was betrothed.[4]

Through this prelate's representations, Charles, instead of a favorable answer to the envoys, postponed his decision till he should arrive at Coruña, the place of embarkation.[5] But here he was much pressed by the troubles which his impolitic conduct had raised, as well as by preparations for his voyage. The transaction of the colonial business, which, long postponed, had greatly accumulated on his hands, was reserved for the last week in Spain. But the affairs of the "young admiral" consumed so large a portion of this, that he had no time to give to those of Cortés; except, indeed, to instruct the board at Seville to remit to the envoys so much of their funds as was required to defray the charges of the voyage. On the 16th of May, 1520, the impatient monarch bade adieu to his distracted kingdom without one attempt to settle the dispute between his belligerent vassals in the New World, and without an effort to promote the magnificent enterprise which was to secure to him the possession of an empire. What a contrast to the policy of his illustrious predecessors, Ferdinand and Isabella! [6]

The governor of Cuba, meanwhile, without waiting for support from home, took measures for redress into his own hands. We have seen, in a preceding chapter, how deeply he was moved by the reports of the proceedings of Cortés, and of the treasures which his vessel was bearing to Spain. Rage, mortification, disappointed avarice, distracted his mind. He could not forgive himself for trusting the affair to such hands. On the very week in which Cortés had parted from him to take charge of the fleet, a *capitulation* had been signed by Charles the Fifth, conferring on Velasquez the title of *adelantado*, with great augmentation of his original powers.[7] The governor resolved, without loss of time, to send such a force to the Aztec coast, as should enable him to assert his new authority to its

---

[4] Zuñiga, Anales Eclesiásticos y Seculares de Sevilla, (Madrid, 1677,) fol. 414.— Herrera, Hist. General, dec. 2, lib. 5, cap. 14; lib. 9, cap. 17, et alibi.

[5] Velasquez, it appears, had sent home an account of the doings of Cortés and of the vessel which touched with the treasures at Cuba, as early as October, 1519. Carta de Velasquez al Lic. Figueroa, MS., Nov. 17, 1519.

[6] "Con gran música," says Sandoval, bitterly, "de todos los ministriles y clarines, recogiendo las áncoras, diéron vela al viento con gran regozijo, dexando á la triste España cargada de duelos, y desventuras." Hist. de Cárlos Quinto, tom. I. p. 219.

[7] The instrument was dated at Barcelona, Nov. 13, 1518. Cortés left St. Jago the 18th of the same month. Herrera, Hist. General, dec. 2, lib. 3, cap. 11.

full extent, and to take vengeance on his rebellious officer. He began his preparations as early as October.[8] At first, he proposed to assume the command in person. But his unwieldy size, which disqualified him for the fatigues incident to such an expedition, or, according to his own account, tenderness for his Indian subjects, then wasted by an epidemic, induced him to devolve the command on another.[9]

The person whom he selected was a Castilian hidalgo, named Pánfilo de Narvaez. He had assisted Velasquez in the reduction of Cuba, where his conduct cannot be wholly vindicated from the charge of inhumanity, which too often attaches to the early Spanish adventurers. From that time he continued to hold important posts under the government, and was a decided favorite with Velasquez. He was a man of some military capacity, though negligent and lax in his discipline. He possessed undoubted courage, but it was mingled with an arrogance, or rather overweening confidence in his own powers, which made him deaf to the suggestions of others more sagacious than himself. He was altogether deficient in that prudence and calculating foresight demanded in a leader who was to cope with an antagonist like Cortés.[10]

The governor and his lieutenant were unwearied in their efforts to assemble an army. They visited every considerable town in the island, fitting out vessels, laying in stores and ammunition, and encouraging volunteers to enlist by liberal promises. But the most effectual bounty was the assurance of the rich treasures that awaited them in the golden regions of Mexico. So confident were they in this expectation, that all classes and ages vied with one another in eagerness to embark in the expedition, until it seemed as if the whole white population would desert the island, and leave it to its primitive occupants.[11]

The report of these proceedings soon spread through the Islands, and drew the attention of the Royal Audience of St. Domingo. This body was intrusted, at that time, not only with the highest judicial authority in the colonies, but with a civil jurisdiction, which, as "the Admiral" complained, encroached on his own rights. The tribunal saw with alarm the proposed expedition of Velasquez, which, whatever might be its issue in regard to the parties, could not fail to compromise the interests of the Crown. They chose accordingly one of their number, the licentiate Ayllon, a man of prudence and resolution, and despatched him to Cuba, with

---

[8] Gomara (Crónica, cap. 96) and Robertson (History of America, vol. II. pp. 304, 466) consider that the new dignity of *adelantado* stimulated the governor to this enterprise. By a letter of his own writing in the Muñoz collection, it appears he had begun operations some months previous to his receiving notice of his appointment. Carta de Velasquez al señor de Xêvres, Isla Fernandina, MS., Octubre 12, 1519.

[9] Carta de Velasquez al Lic. Figueroa, MS., Nov. 17, 1519.

[10] The person of Narvaez is thus whimsically described by Diaz. "He was tall, stout limbed, with a large head and red beard, an agreeable presence, a voice deep and sonorous, as if it rose from a cavern. He was a good horseman and valiant." Hist. de la Conquista, cap. 205.

[11] The danger of such a result is particularly urged in a memorandum of the licentiate Ayllon. Carta al Emperador, Guaniguanico, Marzo 4, 1520, MS.

instructions to interpose his authority, and stay, if possible, the proceedings of Velasquez.[12]

On his arrival, he found the governor in the western part of the island, busily occupied in getting the fleet ready for sea. The licentiate explained to him the purport of his mission, and the views entertained of the proposed enterprise by the Royal Audience. The conquest of a powerful country like Mexico required the whole force of the Spaniards, and, if one half were employed against the other, nothing but ruin could come of it. It was the governor's duty, as a good subject, to forego all private animosities, and to sustain those now engaged in the great work by sending them the necessary supplies. He might, indeed, proclaim his own powers, and demand obedience to them. But, if this were refused, he should leave the determination of his dispute to the authorized tribunals, and employ his resources in prosecuting discovery in another direction, instead of hazarding all by hostilities with his rival.

This admonition, however sensible and salutary, was not at all to the taste of the governor. He professed, indeed, to have no intention of coming to hostilities with Cortés. He designed only to assert his lawful jurisdiction over territories discovered under his own auspices. At the same time, he denied the right of Ayllon or of the Royal Audience to interfere in the matter. Narvaez was still more refractory; and, as the fleet was now ready, proclaimed his intention to sail in a few hours. In this state of things, the licentiate, baffled in his first purpose of staying the expedition, determined to accompany it in person, that he might prevent, if possible, by his presence, an open rupture between the parties.[13]

The squadron consisted of eighteen vessels, large and small. It carried nine hundred men, eighty of whom were cavalry, eighty more arquebusiers, one hundred and fifty crossbow-men, with a number of heavy guns, and a large supply of ammunition and military stores. There were, besides, a thousand Indians, natives of the island, who went probably in a menial capacity.[14] So gallant an armada—with one exception [15]—never before rode in the Indian seas. None to compare with it had ever been fitted out in the Western World.

Leaving Cuba early in March, 1520, Narvaez held nearly the same course as Cortés, and running down what was then called the "island of Yucatan," [16] after a heavy tempest, in which some of his smaller vessels

[12] Processo y Pesquiza hecha por la Real Audiencia de la Española, Santo Domingo, Diciembre 24, 1519, MS.

[13] Parecer del Lic. Ayllon al adelantado Diego Velasquez, Isla Fernandina, 1520, MS.

[14] Relacion del Lic. Ayllon, Santo Domingo, 30 de Agosto, 1520, MS.—Processo y Pesquiza por la R. Audiencia, MS.
According to Diaz, the ordnance amounted to twenty cannon. Hist. de la Conquista, cap. 109.

[15] The great fleet under Ovando, 1501, in which Cortés had intended to embark for the New World. Herrera, Hist. General, dec. 1, lib. 4, cap. 11.

[16] "De allí seguímos el viage por toda la costa de la Isla de Yucatan." Relacion del Lic. Ayllon, MS.

foundered, anchored, April 23, off San Juan de Ulua. It was the place where Cortés, also, had first landed; the sandy waste covered by the present city of Vera Cruz.

Here the commander met with a Spaniard, one of those sent by the general from Mexico, to ascertain the resources of the country, especially its mineral products. This man came on board the fleet, and from him the Spaniards gathered the particulars of all that had occurred since the departure of the envoys from Vera Cruz,—the march into the interior, the bloody battles with the Tlascalans, the occupation of Mexico, the rich treasures found in it, and the seizure of the monarch, by means of which, concluded the soldier, "Cortés rules over the land like its own sovereign, so that a Spaniard may travel unarmed from one end of the country to the other, without insult or injury." [17] His audience listened to this marvellous report with speechless amazement, and the loyal indignation of Narvaez waxed stronger and stronger, as he learned the value of the prize which had been snatched from his employer.

He now openly proclaimed his intention to march against Cortés, and punish him for his rebellion. He made this vaunt so loudly, that the natives, who had flocked in numbers to the camp, which was soon formed on shore, clearly comprehended that the new comers were not friends, but enemies, of the preceding. Narvaez determined, also,—though in opposition to the counsel of the Spaniard, who quoted the example of Cortés,—to establish a settlement on this unpromising spot; and he made the necessary arrangements to organize a municipality. He was informed by the soldier of the existence of the neighboring colony at Villa Rica, commanded by Sandoval, and consisting of a few invalids, who, he was assured, would surrender on the first summons. Instead of marching against the place, however, he determined to send a peaceful embassy to display his powers, and demand the submission of the garrison. [18]

These successive steps gave serious displeasure to Ayllon, who saw they must lead to inevitable collision with Cortés. But it was in vain he remonstrated, and threatened to lay the proceedings of Narvaez before the government. The latter, chafed by his continued opposition and sour rebuke, determined to rid himself of a companion who acted as a spy on his movements. He caused him to be seized and sent back to Cuba. The licentiate had the address to persuade the captain of the vessel to change her destination for St. Domingo; and, when he arrived there, a formal report of his proceedings, exhibiting in strong colors the disloyal conduct

[17] "La cual tierra sabe é ha visto este testigo, que el dicho Hernando Cortés tiene pacífica, é le sirven é obedecen todos los Indios; é que cree este testigo que lo hacen por cabsa que el dicho Hernando Cortés tiene preso á un Cacique que dicen Montesuma, que es Señor de lo mas de la tierra, á lo que este testigo alcanza, al cual los Indios obedecen, é facen lo que les manda, é los Cristianos andan por toda esta tierra seguros, é un solo Cristiano la ha atravesado toda sin temor." Processo y Pesquiza por la R. Audiencia, MS.

[18] Relacion del Lic. Ayllon, MS.—Demanda de Zavallos en nombre de Narvaez MS.

of the governor and his lieutenant, was prepared, and despatched by the Royal Audience to Spain.[19]

Sandoval meanwhile had not been inattentive to the movements of Narvaez. From the time of his first appearance on the coast, that vigilant officer, distrusting the object of the armament, had kept his eye on him. No sooner was he apprised of the landing of the Spaniards, than the commander of Villa Rica sent off his few disabled soldiers to a place of safety in the neighborhood. He then put his works in the best posture of defence that he could, and prepared to maintain the place to the last extremity. His men promised to stand by him, and, the more effectually to fortify the resolution of any who might falter, he ordered a gallows to be set up in a conspicuous part of the town! The constancy of his men was not put to the trial.

The only invaders of the place were a priest, a notary, and four other Spaniards, selected for the mission, already noticed, by Narvaez. The ecclesiastic's name was Guevara. On coming before Sandoval, he made him a formal address, in which he pompously enumerated the services and claims of Velasquez, taxed Cortés and his adherents with rebellion, and demanded of Sandoval to tender his submission, as a loyal subject, to the newly constituted authority of Narvaez.

The commander of La Villa Rica was so much incensed at this unceremonious mention of his companions in arms, that he assured the reverend envoy, that nothing but respect for his cloth saved him from the chastisement he merited. Guevara now waxed wroth in his turn, and called on the notary to read the proclamation. But Sandoval interposed, promising that functionary, that, if he attempted to do so, without first producing a warrant of his authority from the Crown, he should be soundly flogged. Guevara lost all command of himself at this, and stamping on the ground repeated his orders in a more peremptory tone than before. Sandoval was not a man of many words. He simply remarked, that the instrument should be read to the general himself in Mexico. At the same time, he ordered his men to procure a number of sturdy *tamanes,* or Indian porters, on whose backs the unfortunate priest and his companions were bound like so many bales of goods. They were then placed under a guard of twenty Spaniards, and the whole caravan took its march for the capital. Day and night they travelled, stopping only to obtain fresh relays of carriers; and as they passed through populous towns, forest, and cultivated fields, vanishing as soon as seen, the Spaniards, bewildered by the strangeness of the scene, as well as of their novel mode of conveyance, hardly knew whether they were awake or in a dream. In this way, at the end of the fourth day, they reached the Tezcucan lake in view of the Aztec capital.[20]

---

[19] This report is to be found among the MSS. of Vargas Ponçe, in the archives of the Royal Academy of History. It embraces a hundred and ten folio pages, and is entitled, "El Processo y Pesquiza hecha por la Real Audiencia de la Española é tierra nuevamente descubierta. Para el Consejo de su Majestad."

[20] "É iban espantados de que veian tātas ciudades y pueblos grandes, que les

Its inhabitants had already been made acquainted with the fresh ar·
rival of white men on the coast. Indeed, directly on their landing, intel·
ligence had been communicated to Montezuma, who is said (it does not
seem probable) to have concealed it some days from Cortés.[21] At length,
inviting him to an interview, he told him there was no longer any obstacle to his leaving the country, as a fleet was ready for him. To the inquiries of the astonished general, Montezuma replied by pointing to a
hieroglyphical map sent him from the coast, on which the ships, the
Spaniards themselves, and their whole equipment, were minutely delineated. Cortés, suppressing all emotions but those of pleasure, exclaimed,
"Blessed be the Redeemer for his mercies!" On returning to his quarters,
the tidings were received by the troops with loud shouts, the firing of
cannon, and other demonstrations of joy. They hailed the new comers as
a reinforcement from Spain. Not so their commander. From the first, he
suspected them to be sent by his enemy, the governor of Cuba. He communicated his suspicions to his officers, through whom they gradually
found their way among the men. The tide of joy was instantly checked.
Alarming apprehensions succeeded, as they dwelt on the probability of
this suggestion, and on the strength of the invaders. Yet their constancy
did not desert them; and they pledged themselves to remain true to their
cause, and, come what might, to stand by their leader. It was one of those
occasions that proved the entire influence which Cortés held over these
wild adventurers. All doubts were soon dispelled by the arrival of the
prisoners from Villa Rica.

One of the convoy, leaving the party in the suburbs, entered the city,
and delivered a letter to the general from Sandoval, acquainting him with
all the particulars. Cortés instantly sent to the prisoners, ordered them
to be released, and furnished them with horses to make their entrance
into the capital,—a more creditable conveyance than the backs of
tamanes. On their arrival, he received them with marked courtesy,
apologized for the rude conduct of his officers, and seemed desirous by
the most assiduous attentions to soothe the irritation of their minds. He
showed his good-will still further by lavishing presents on Guevara and
his associates, until he gradually wrought such a change in their dispositions, that, from enemies, he converted them into friends, and drew
forth many important particulars respecting not merely the designs of
their leader, but the feelings of his army. The soldiers, in general, they
said, far from desiring a rupture with those of Cortés, would willingly cooperate with them, were it not for their commander. They had no feelings
of resentment to gratify. Their object was gold. The personal influence of
Narvaez was not great, and his arrogance and penurious temper had already gone far to alienate from him the affections of his followers. These
hints were not lost on the general.

traian de comer, y vnos los dexavan, y otros los to mavan, y andar por su camino.
Dizē que iban pensando si era encantamiento, ó sueño." Bernal Diaz, Hist. de la
Conquista, cap. III.—Demanda de Zavallos, MS.
[21] "Ya auia tres dias que lo sabia el Monteçuma, y Cortés no sabia cosa ninguna."
Bernal Diaz, Hist. de la Conquista, cap. 110.

He addressed a letter to his rival in the most conciliatory terms. He besought him not to proclaim their animosity to the world, and, by kindling a spirit of insubordination in the natives, unsettle all that had been so far secured. A violent collision must be prejudicial even to the victor, and might be fatal to both. It was only in union that they could look for success. He was ready to greet Narvaez as a brother in arms, to share with him the fruits of conquest, and, if he could produce a royal commission, to submit to his authority.—Cortés well knew he had no such commission to show.[22]

Soon after the departure of Guevara and his comrades,[23] the general determined to send a special envoy of his own. The person selected for this delicate office was father Olmedo, who, through the campaign, had shown a practical good sense, and a talent for affairs, not always to be found in persons of his spiritual calling. He was intrusted with another epistle to Narvaez, of similar import with the preceding. Cortés wrote, also, to the licentiate Ayllon, with whose departure he was not acquainted, and to Andres de Duero, former secretary of Velasquez, and his own friend, who had come over in the present fleet. Olmedo was instructed to converse with these persons in private, as well as with the principal officers and soldiers, and, as far as possible, to infuse into them a spirit of accommodation. To give greater weight to his arguments, he was furnished with a liberal supply of gold.

During this time, Narvaez had abandoned his original design of planting a colony on the sea-coast, and had crossed the country to Cempoalla, where he had taken up his quarters. He was here, when Guevara returned, and presented the letter of Cortés.

Narvaez glanced over it with a look of contempt, which was changed into one of stern displeasure, as his envoy enlarged on the resources and formidable character of his rival, counselling him, by all means, to accept his proffers of amity. A different effect was produced on the troops, who listened with greedy ears to the accounts given of Cortés, his frank and liberal manners, which they involuntarily contrasted with those of their own commander, the wealth in his camp, where the humblest private could stake his ingot and chain of gold at play, where all revelled in plenty, and the life of the soldier seemed to be one long holiday. Guevara had been admitted only to the sunny side of the picture.

The impression made by these accounts was confirmed by the presence of Olmedo. The ecclesiastic delivered his missives, in like manner, to Narvaez, who ran through their contents with feelings of anger which found vent in the most opprobrious invectives against his rival; while one of his captains, named Salvatierra, openly avowed his intention to

---

[22] Oviedo, Hist. de las Ind., MS., lib. 33, cap. 47.—Rel. Seg. de Cortés, ap. Lorenzana, pp. 117-120.

[23] "Our commander said so many kind things to them," says Diaz, "and *anointed their fingers* so plentifully with gold, that, though they came like roaring lions, they went home perfectly tame"! Hist. de la Conquista, cap. 111.

cut off the rebel's ears, and broil them for his breakfast! [24] Such impotent sallies did not alarm the stout-hearted friar, who soon entered into communication with many of the officers and soldiers, whom he found better inclined to an accommodation. His insinuating eloquence, backed by his liberal largesses, gradually opened a way into their hearts, and a party was formed, under the very eye of their chief, better affected to his rival's interests than to his own. The intrigue could not be conducted so secretly as wholly to elude the suspicions of Narvaez, who would have arrested Olmedo and placed him under confinement, but for the interposition of Duero. He put a stop to his further machinations by sending him back again to his master. But the poison was left to do its work.

Narvaez made the same vaunt, as at his landing, of his design to march against Cortés and apprehend him as a traitor. The Cempoallans learned with astonishment that their new guests, though the countrymen, were enemies of their former. Narvaez, also, proclaimed his intention to release Montezuma from captivity, and restore him to his throne. It is said, he received a rich present from the Aztec emperor, who entered into a correspondence with him.[25] That Montezuma should have treated him with his usual munificence, supposing him to be the friend of Cortés, is very probable. But that he should have entered into a secret communication, hostile to the general's interests, is too repugnant to the whole tenor of his conduct, to be lightly admitted.

These proceedings did not escape the watchful eye of Sandoval. He gathered the particulars partly from deserters, who fled to Villa Rica, and partly from his own agents, who in the disguise of natives mingled in the enemy's camp. He sent a full account of them to Cortés, acquainted him with the growing defection of the Indians, and urged him to take speedy measures for the defence of Villa Rica, if he would not see it fall into the enemy's hands. The general felt that it was time to act.

Yet the selection of the course to be pursued was embarrassing in the extreme. If he remained in Mexico and awaited there the attack of his rival, it would give the latter time to gather round him the whole forces of the empire, including those of the capital itself, all willing, no doubt, to serve under the banners of a chief who proposed the liberation of their master. The odds were too great to be hazarded.

If he marched against Narvaez, he must either abandon the city and the emperor, the fruit of all his toils and triumphs, or, by leaving a garrison to hold them in awe, must cripple his strength already far too weak to cope with that of his adversary. Yet on this latter course he decided.

[24] Ibid., cap. 112.
[25] Ibid., cap. 111.
Oviedo says that Montezuma called a council of his nobles, in which it was decided to let the troops of Narvaez into the capital, and then to crush them at one blow, with those of Cortés! (Hist. de las Ind., MS., lib. 33, cap. 47.) Considering the awe in which the latter alone were held by the Mexicans, a more improbable tale could not be devised. But nothing is too improbable for history,—though, according to Boileau's maxim. it may be for fiction.

He trusted less, perhaps, to an open encounter of arms, than to the influence of his personal address and previous intrigues, to bring about an amicable arrangement. But he prepared himself for either result.

In the preceding chapter, it was mentioned that Velasquez de Leon was sent with a hundred and fifty men to plant a colony on one of the great rivers emptying into the Mexican Gulf. Cortés, on learning the arrival of Narvaez, had despatched a messenger to his officer, to acquaint him with the fact, and to arrest his further progress. But Velasquez had already received notice of it from Narvaez himself, who, in a letter written soon after his landing, had adjured him in the name of his kinsman, the governor of Cuba, to quit the banners of Cortés, and come over to him. That officer, however, had long since buried the feelings of resentment which he had once nourished against his general, to whom he was now devotedly attached, and who had honored him throughout the campaign with particular regard. Cortés had early seen the importance of securing this cavalier to his interests. Without waiting for orders, Velasquez abandoned his expedition, and commenced a countermarch on the capital, when he received the general's commands to wait him in Cholula.

Cortés had also sent to the distant province of Chinantla, situated far to the south-east of Cholula, for a reinforcement of two thousand natives. They were a bold race, hostile to the Mexicans, and had offered their services to him since his residence in the metropolis. They used a long spear in battle, longer, indeed, than that borne by the Spanish or German infantry. Cortés ordered three hundred of their double-headed lances to be made for him, and to be tipped with copper instead of *itztli*. With this formidable weapon he proposed to foil the cavalry of his enemy.

The command of the garrison, in his absence, he intrusted to Pedro de Alvarado,—the *Tonatiuh* of the Mexicans,—a man possessed of many commanding qualities, of an intrepid, though somewhat arrogant spirit, and his warm personal friend. He inculcated on him moderation and forbearance. He was to keep a close watch on Montezuma, for on the possession of the royal person rested all their authority in the land. He was to show him the deference alike due to his high station, and demanded by policy. He was to pay uniform respect to the usages and the prejudices of the people; remembering that though his small force would be large enough to overawe them in times of quiet, yet should they be once roused, it would be swept away like chaff before the whirlwind.

From Montezuma he exacted a promise to maintain the same friendly relations with his lieutenant which he had preserved towards himself. This, said Cortés, would be most grateful to his own master, the Spanish sovereign. Should the Aztec prince do otherwise, and lend himself to any hostile movement, he must be convinced that he would fall the first victim of it.

The emperor assured him of his continued goodwill. He was much perplexed, however, by the recent events. Were the Spaniards at his court, or those just landed, the true representatives of their sovereign? Cortés, who had hitherto maintained a reserve on the subject, now told him that the latter were indeed his countrymen, but traitors to his master. As such, it was his painful duty to march against them, and, when he had chastised their rebellion, he should return, before his departure from the land, in triumph to the capital. Montezuma offered to support him with five thousand Aztec warriors; but the general declined it, not choosing to encumber himself with a body of doubtful, perhaps disaffected, auxiliaries.

He left in garrison, under Alvarado, one hundred and forty men, two thirds of his whole force.[26] With these remained all the artillery, the greater part of the little body of horse, and most of the arquebusiers. He took with him only seventy soldiers, but they were men of the most mettle in the army and his stanch adherents. They were lightly armed and encumbered with as little baggage as possible. Every thing depended on celerity of movement.

Montezuma, in his royal litter borne on the shoulders of his nobles, and escorted by the whole Spanish infantry, accompanied the general to the causeway. There, embracing him in the most cordial manner, they parted, with all the external marks of mutual regard.—It was about the middle of May, 1520, more than six months since the entrance of the Spaniards into Mexico. During this time they had lorded it over the land with absolute sway. They were now leaving the city in hostile array, not against an Indian foe, but their own countrymen. It was the beginning of a long career of calamity,—chequered, indeed, by occasional triumphs,—which was yet to be run before the Conquest could be completed.[27]

[26] In the Mexican edition of the letters of Cortés, it is called five hundred men. (Rel. Seg., ap. Lorenzana, p. 122.) But this was more than his whole Spanish force. In Ramusio's version of the same letter, printed as early as 1565, the number is stated as in the text. (Navigationi et Viaggi, fol. 244.) In an instrument without date, containing the affidavits of certain witnesses as to the management of the royal fifth by Cortés, it is said, there were one hundred and fifty soldiers left in the capital under Alvarado. (Probanza fecha en la nueva España del mar océano á pedimento de Juan Ochoa de Lexalde, en nombre de Hernando Cortés, MS.) The account in the Mexican edition is unquestionably an error.

[27] Carta de Villa de Vera Cruz á el Emperador, MS. This letter without date was probably written in 1520.—See, also, for the preceding pages, Probanza fecha á pedimento de Juan Ochoa, MS.,—Herrera, Hist. General, dec. 2, lib. 9, cap. 1, 21; lib. 10, cap. 1,—Rel. Seg. de Cortés, ap. Lorenzana, pp. 119, 120,—Bernal Diaz, Hist. de la Conquista, cap. 112-115,—Oviedo, Hist. de las Ind., MS., lib. 33, cap. 47.

CHAPTER VII

CORTÉS DESCENDS FROM THE TABLE-LAND—NEGOTIATES WITH NAR-
VAEZ—PREPARES TO ASSAULT HIM—QUARTERS OF NARVAEZ—AT-
TACKED BY NIGHT—NARVAEZ DEFEATED

1520

TRAVERSING the southern causeway, by which they had entered the capital, the little party were soon on their march across the beautiful Valley.
They climbed the mountain screen which Nature has so ineffectually
drawn around it; passed between the huge volcanoes that, like faithless
watch-dogs on their posts, have long since been buried in slumber;
threaded the intricate defiles where they had before experienced such
bleak and tempestuous weather; and, emerging on the other side, descended the western slope which opens on the wide expanse of the fruitful
plateau of Cholula.

They heeded little of what they saw on their rapid march, nor whether
it was cold or hot. The anxiety of their minds made them indifferent to
outward annoyances; and they had fortunately none to encounter from
the natives, for the name of Spaniard was in itself a charm,—a better
guard than helm or buckler to the bearer.

In Cholula, Cortés had the inexpressible satisfaction of meeting Velasquez de Leon, with the hundred and twenty soldiers intrusted to his command for the formation of a colony. That faithful officer had been some
time at Cholula, waiting for the general's approach. Had he failed, the
enterprise of Cortés must have failed, also.[1] The idea of resistance, with
his own handful of followers, would have been chimerical. As it was, his
little band was now trebled, and acquired a confidence in proportion.

Cordially embracing their companions in arms, now knit together more
closely than ever by the sense of a great and common danger, the combined troops traversed with quick step the streets of the sacred city,
where many a dark pile of ruins told of their disastrous visit on the preceding autumn. They kept the high road to Tlascala; and, at not many
leagues' distance from that capital, fell in with father Olmedo and his
companions on their return from the camp of Narvaez, to which, it will
be remembered, they had been sent as envoys. The ecclesiastic bore a let-

---

[1] So says Oviedo—and with truth; "Si aquel capitan Juan Velasquez de Leon no
estubiera mal con su pariente Diego Velasquez, é se pasara con los 150 Hombres,
que havia llevado á Guaçacalco, á la parte de Pánfilo de Narvaez su cuñado, acabado
oviera Cortés su oficio." Hist. de las Ind., MS., lib. 33, cap. 12.

ter from that commander, in which he summoned Cortés and his followers to submit to his authority as captain-general of the country, menacing
them with condign punishment, in case of refusal or delay. Olmedo gave
many curious particulars of the state of the enemy's camp. Narvaez he
described as puffed up by authority, and negligent of precautions against
a foe whom he held in contempt. He was surrounded by a number of
pompous, conceited officers, who ministered to his vanity, and whose
braggart tones, the good father, who had an eye for the ridiculous, imitated, to the no small diversion of Cortés and the soldiers. Many of the
troops, he said, showed no great partiality for their commander, and were
strongly disinclined to a rupture with their countrymen; a state of feeling much promoted by the accounts they had received of Cortés, by his
own arguments and promises, and by the liberal distribution of the gold
with which he had been provided. In addition to these matters, Cortés
gathered much important intelligence respecting the position of the enemy's force, and his general plan of operations.

At Tlascala, the Spaniards were received with a frank and friendly
hospitality. It is not said, whether any of the Tlascalan allies had accompanied them from Mexico. If they did, they went no further than their
native city. Cortés requested a reinforcement of six hundred fresh troops
to attend him on his present expedition. It was readily granted, but, before the army had proceeded many miles on its route, the Indian auxiliaries fell off, one after another, and returned to their city. They had no
personal feeling of animosity to gratify in the present instance, as in a
war against Mexico. It may be, too, that, although intrepid in a contest
with the bravest of the Indian races, they had had too fatal experience of
the prowess of the white men, to care to measure swords with them again.
At any rate, they deserted in such numbers, that Cortés dismissed the remainder at once, saying, good-humoredly, "He had rather part with
them then, than in the hour of trial."

The troops soon entered on that wild district in the neighborhood of
Perote, strewed with the wreck of volcanic matter, which forms so singular a contrast to the general character of beauty with which the scenery is
stamped. It was not long before their eyes were gladdened by the approach of Sandoval and about sixty soldiers from the garrison of Vera
Cruz, including several deserters from the enemy. It was a most important reinforcement, not more on account of the numbers of the men than
of the character of the commander, in every respect one of the ablest captains in the service. He had been compelled to fetch a circuit, in order to
avoid falling in with the enemy, and had forced his way through thick
forests, and wild mountain-passes, till he had fortunately, without accident, reached the appointed place of rendezvous, and stationed himself
once more under the banner of his chieftain.[2]

At the same place, also, Cortés was met by Tobillos, a Spaniard whom
he had sent to procure the lances from Chinantla. They were perfectly

[2] Rel. Seg. de Cortés, ap. Lorenzana, pp. 123, 124.—Bernal Diaz, Hist. de la Conquista, cap. 115-117.—Oviedo, Hist. de las Ind., MS., lib. 33, cap. 12.

well made, after the pattern which had been given; double-headed spears, tipped with copper, and of great length. Tobillos drilled the men in the exercise of this weapon, the formidable uses of which, especially against horse, had been fully demonstrated, towards the close of the last century, by the Swiss battalions, in their encounters with the Burgundian chivalry, the best in Europe.[3]

Cortés now took a review of his army,—if so paltry a force may be called an army,—and found their numbers were two hundred and sixty-six, only five of whom were mounted. A few muskets and crossbows were sprinkled among them. In defensive armor they were sadly deficient. They were for the most part cased in the quilted doublet of the country, thickly stuffed with cotton, the *escaupil,* recommended by its superior lightness, but which, though competent to turn the arrow of the Indian, was ineffectual against a musket-ball. Most of this cotton mail was exceedingly out of repair, giving evidence, in its unsightly gaps, of much rude service, and hard blows. Few, in this emergency, but would have given almost any price—the best of the gold chains which they wore in tawdry display over their poor habiliments—for a steel morion or cuirass, to take the place of their own hacked and battered armor.[4]

Under this coarse covering, however, they bore hearts stout and courageous as ever beat in human bosoms. For they were the heroes, still invincible, of many a hard-fought field, where the odds had been incalculably against them. They had large experience of the country and of the natives; knew well the character of their own commander, under whose eye they had been trained, till every movement was in obedience to him. The whole body seemed to constitute but a single individual, in respect of unity of design and of action. Thus its real effective force was incredibly augmented; and, what was no less important, the humblest soldier felt it to be so.

The troops now resumed their march across the table-land, until, reaching the eastern slope, their labors were lightened, as they descended towards the broad plains of the *tierra caliente,* spread out like a boundless ocean of verdure below them. At some fifteen leagues' distance from Cempoalla, where Narvaez, as has been noticed, had established his quarters, they were met by another embassy from that commander. It consisted of the priest, Guevara, Andres de Duero, and two or three others. Duero, the fast friend of Cortés, had been the person most instrumental, originally, in obtaining him his commission from Velasquez. They now greeted each other with a warm embrace, and it was not till after much

---

[3] But, although irresistible against cavalry, the long pike of the German proved no match for the short sword and buckler of the Spaniard, in the great battle of Ravenna, fought a few years before this, 1512. Machiavelli makes some excellent reflections on the comparative merit of these arms. Arte della Guerra, lib. 2, ap. Opere, tom. IV. p. 67.

[4] Bernal Diaz, Hist. de la Conquista, cap. 118.

"Tambien quiero dezir la gran necessidad que teniamos de armas, que por vn peto, ó capacete, ó casco, ó babera de hierro, dieramos aquella noche quãto nos pidiera por ello, y todo quãto auiamos ganado." Cap. 122.

preliminary conversation on private matters, that the secretary disclosed the object of his visit.

He bore a letter from Narvaez, couched in terms somewhat different from the preceding. That officer required, indeed, the acknowledgment of his paramount authority in the land, but offered his vessels to transport all who desired it from the country, together with their treasures and effects, without molestation or inquiry. The more liberal tenor of these terms was, doubtless, to be ascribed to the influence of Duero. The secretary strongly urged Cortés to comply with them, as the most favorable that could be obtained, and as the only alternative affording him a chance of safety in his desperate condition. "For, however valiant your men may be, how can they expect," he asked, "to face a force so much superior in numbers and equipment as that of their antagonist?" But Cortés had set his fortunes on the cast, and he was not the man to shrink from it. "If Narvaez bears a royal commission," he returned, "I will readily submit to him. But he has produced none. He is a deputy of my rival, Velasquez. For myself, I am a servant of the king; I have conquered the country for him; and for him, I and my brave followers will defend it, be assured, to the last drop of our blood. If we fall, it will be glory enough to have perished in the discharge of our duty." [5]

His friend might have been somewhat puzzled to comprehend how the authority of Cortés rested on a different ground from that of Narvaez; and if they both held of the same superior, the governor of Cuba, why that dignitary should not be empowered to supersede his own officer in case of dissatisfaction, and appoint a substitute.[6] But Cortés here reaped the full benefit of that legal fiction, if it may be so termed, by which his commission, resigned to the self-constituted municipality of Vera Cruz, was again derived through that body from the Crown. The device, indeed, was too palpable to impose on any but those who chose to be blinded. Most of the army were of this number. To them it seemed to give additional confidence, in the same manner as a strip of painted can-

---

[5] "Yo les respondí, que no via provision de Vuestra Alteza, por donde le debiesse entregar la Tierra; é que si alguna trahia, que la presentasse ante mí, y ante el Cabildo de la Vera Cruz, segun órden, y costumbre de España, y que yo estaba presto de la obedecer, y cumplir; y que hasta tanto, por ningun interese, ni partido haria lo que él decia; ántes yo, y los que conmigo estaban, moririamos en defensa de la Tierra, pues la habiamos ganado, y tenido por Vuestra Magestad pacífica, y segura, y por no ser Traydores y desleales á nuestro Rey. . . . . . Considerando, que morir en servicio de mi Rey, y por defender, y amparar sus Tierras, y no las dejar usurpar, á mí, y á los de mi Compañía se nos seguia farta gloria." Rel. Seg. de Cortés, ap. Lorenzana, pp. 125-127.

[6] Such are the natural reflections of Oviedo, speculating on the matter some years later. "É tambien que me parece donaire, ó no bastante la escusa que Cortés da para fundar é justificar su ne gocio, que es decir, que el Narvaez presentase las provisiones que llevaba de S. M. Como si el dicho Cortés oviera ido á aquella tierra por mandado de S. M. ó con mas, ni tanta autoridad como llebaba Narvaez; pues que es claro é notorio, que el Adelantada Diego Velasquez, que embió á Cortés, era parte, segun derecho, para le embiar á remover, y el Cortés obligado á le obedecer. No quiero decir mas en esto por no ser odioso á ninguna de las partes." Hist. de las Ind., MS., lib. 33, cap. 1ᵒ

vass, when substituted, as it has sometimes been, for a real parapet of stone, has been found not merely to impose on the enemy, but to give a sort of artificial courage to the defenders concealed behind it.[7]

Duero had arranged with his friend in Cuba, when he took command of the expedition, that he himself was to have a liberal share of the profits. It is said that Cortés confirmed this arrangement at the present juncture, and made it clearly for the other's interest that he should prevail in the struggle with Narvaez. This was an important point, considering the position of the secretary.[8] From this authentic source the general derived much information respecting the designs of Narvaez, which had escaped the knowledge of Olmedo. On the departure of the envoys, Cortés intrusted them with a letter for his rival, a counterpart of that which he had received from him. This show of negotiation intimated a desire on his part to postpone, if not avoid hostilities, which might the better put Narvaez off his guard. In the letter he summoned that commander and his followers to present themselves before him without delay, and to acknowledge his authority as the representative of his sovereign. He should otherwise be compelled to proceed against them as rebels to the Crown! [9] With this missive, the vaunting tone of which was intended quite as much for his own troops as the enemy, Cortés dismissed the envoys. They returned to disseminate among their comrades their admiration of the general, and of his unbounded liberality, of which he took care they should experience full measure, and they dilated on the riches of his adherents, who, over their wretched attire, displayed, with ostentatious profusion, jewels, ornaments of gold, collars, and massive chains winding several times round their necks and bodies, the rich spoil of the treasury of Montezuma.

The army now took its way across the level plains of the *tierra caliente,* on which Nature has exhausted all the wonders of creation; it was covered more thickly then, than at the present day, with noble forests, where the towering cotton-wood tree, the growth of ages, stood side by side with the light bamboo, or banana, the product of a season, each in its way attesting the marvellous fecundity of the soil, while innumerable creeping flowers, muffling up the giant branches of the trees, waved in bright festoons above their heads, loading the air with odors. But the senses of the Spaniards were not open to the delicious influences of nature. Their minds were occupied by one idea.

---

[7] More than one example of this *ruse* is mentioned by Mariana in Spanish history, though the precise passages have escaped my memory.

[8] Bernal Diaz, Hist. de la Conquista, cap. 119.

[9] "É assimismo mandaba, y mandé por el dicho Mandamiento á todas las Personas, que con el dicho Narvaez estaban, que no tubiessen, ni obedeciessen al dicho Narvaez por tal Capitan, ni Justicia; ántes, dentro de cierto término, que en el dicho Mandamiento señalé, pareciessen ante mí, para que yo les dijesse, lo que debian hacer en servicio de Vuestra Alteza: con protestacion, que lo contrario haciendo, procederia contra ellos, como contra Traydores, y aleves, y malos Vasallos, que se rebelaban contra su Rey, y quieren usurpar sus Tierras, y Señoríos." Rel. Seg. de Cortés, ap. Lorenzana, p. 127.

Coming upon an open reach of meadow, of some extent, they were, at length, stopped by a river, or rather stream, called *Rio de Canoas*, "the River of Canoes," of no great volume ordinarily, but swollen at this time by excessive rains. It had rained hard that day, although at intervals the sun had broken forth with intolerable fervor, affording a good specimen of those alternations of heat and moisture, which give such activity to vegetation in the tropics, where the process of forcing seems to be always going on.

The river was about a league distant from the camp of Narvaez. Before seeking out a practicable ford, by which to cross it, Cortés allowed his men to recruit their exhausted strength by stretching themselves on the ground. The shades of evening had gathered round; and the rising moon, wading through dark masses of cloud, shone with a doubtful and interrupted light. It was evident that the storm had not yet spent its fury.[10] Cortés did not regret this. He had made up his mind to an assault that very night, and in the darkness and uproar of the tempest his movements would be most effectually concealed.

Before disclosing his design, he addressed his men in one of those stirring, soldierly harangues, to which he had recourse in emergencies of great moment, as if to sound the depths of their hearts, and, where any faltered, to reanimate them with his own heroic spirit. He briefly recapitulated the great events of the campaign, the dangers they had surmounted, the victories they had achieved over the most appalling odds, the glorious spoil they had won. But of this they were now to be defrauded; not by men holding a legal warrant from the Crown, but by adventurers, with no better title than that of superior force. They had established a claim on the gratitude of their country and their sovereign. This claim was now to be dishonored, their very services were converted into crimes, and their names branded with infamy as those of traitors. But the time had at last come for vengeance. God would not desert the soldier of the Cross. Those, whom he had carried victorious through great dangers would not be left to fail now. And, if they should fail, better to die like brave men on the field of battle, than, with fame and fortune cast away, to perish ignominiously like slaves on the gibbet.—This last point he urged home upon his hearers; well knowing there was not one among them so dull as not to be touched by it.

They responded with hearty acclamations, and Velasquez de Leon, and de Lugo, in the name of the rest, assured their commander. if they failed, it should be his fault, not theirs. They would follow wherever he led.— The general was fully satisfied with the temper of his soldiers, as he felt that his difficulty lay not in awakening their enthusiasm, but in giving it a right direction. One thing is remarkable. He made no allusion to the defection which he knew existed in the enemy's camp. He would have his soldiers, in this last pinch, rely on nothing but themselves.

---

[10] "Y aun llouia de rato en rato, y entonces salia la Luna, que quãdo allí llegámos hazia muy escuro, y llouia, y tambien la escuridad ayudó." Hist. de la Conquista, cap. 122.

He announced his purpose to attack the enemy that very night, when he should be buried in slumber, and the friendly darkness might throw a veil over their own movements, and conceal the poverty of their numbers. To this the troops, jaded though they were by incessant marching, and half famished, joyfully assented. In their situation, suspense was the worst of evils. He next distributed the commands among his captains. To Gonzalo de Sandoval he assigned the important office of taking Narvaez. He was commanded, as *alguacil mayor,* to seize the person of that officer as a rebel to his sovereign, and, if he made resistance, to kill him on the spot.[11] He was provided with sixty picked men to aid him in this difficult task, supported by several of the ablest captains, among whom were two of the Alvarados, de Avila, and Ordaz. The largest division of the force was placed under Christóval de Olid, or, according to some authorities, of Pizarro, one of that family so renowned in the subsequent conquest of Peru. He was to get possession of the artillery, and to cover the assault of Sandoval by keeping those of the enemy at bay, who would interfere with it. Cortés reserved only a body of twenty men for himself, to act on any point that occasion might require. The watch-word was *Espíritu Santo,* it being the evening of Whit-sunday. Having made these arrangements, he prepared to cross the river.[12]

During the interval thus occupied by Cortés, Narvaez had remained at Cempoalla, passing his days in idle and frivolous amusement. From this he was at length aroused, after the return of Duero, by the remonstrances of the old cacique of the city. "Why are you so heedless?" exclaimed the latter; "do you think Malinche is so? Depend on it, he knows your situation exactly, and, when you least dream of it, he will be upon you." [13]

Alarmed at these suggestions and those of his friends, Narvaez at length put himself at the head of his troops, and, on the very day on which Cortés arrived at the River of Canoes, sallied out to meet him. But, when he had reached this barrier, Narvaez saw no sign of an enemy. The rain, which fell in torrents, soon drenched the soldiers to the skin. Made somewhat effeminate by their long and luxurious residence at Cempoalla, they murmured at their uncomfortable situation. "Of what use was it to remain there fighting with the elements? There was no sign of an enemy, and little reason to apprehend his approach in such tempestuous weather.

---

[11] The Attorney of Narvaez, in his complaint before the Crown, expatiates on the diabolical enormity of these instructions. "El dho Fernando Corttés como traidor aleboso, sin apercibir al dho mi partte, con un diabólico pensamᵗᵒ é Infernal osadía, en contemtto é menosprecio de V. M. ó de sus provisiones R.ˢ, no mirando ni asattando la lealtad qᵉ debia á V. M., el dho Corttés dió un Mandamientto al dho Gonzalo de Sandobal para que prendiese al dho Pánfilo de Narvaez, é si se defendiese qᵉ lo mattase." Demanda de Zavallos en nombre de Narvaez, MS.

[12] Oviedo, Hist. de las Ind., MS., lib. 33, cap. 12, 47.—Bernal Diaz, Hist. de la Conquista, cap. 122.—Herrera, Hist. General, dec. 2, lib. 10, cap. 1.

[13] "Que hazeis, que estais mui descuidado? pensais que Malinche, y los Teules que trae Cõsigo, que son assí como vosotros? Pues yo os digo, que quãdo no os cataredes, será aquí, y os matará." Bernal Diaz, Hist. de la Conquista, cap. 121.

It would be wiser to return to Cempoalla, and in the morning they should be all fresh for action, should Cortés make his appearance."

Narvaez took counsel of these advisers, or rather of his own inclinations. Before retracing his steps, he provided against surprise, by stationing a couple of sentinels at no great distance from the river, to give notice of the approach of Cortés. He also detached a body of forty horse in another direction, by which he thought it not improbable the enemy might advance on Cempoalla. Having taken these precautions, he fell back again before night on his own quarters.

He there occupied the principal *teocalli*. It consisted of a stone building on the usual pyramidal basis; and the ascent was by a flight of steep steps on one of the faces of the pyramid. In the edifice or sanctuary above he stationed himself with a strong party of arquebusiers and crossbowmen. Two other *teocallis* in the same area were garrisoned by large detachments of infantry. His artillery, consisting of seventeen or eighteen small guns, he posted in the area below, and protected it by the remainder of his cavalry. When he had thus distributed his forces, he returned to his own quarters, and soon after to repose, with as much indifference as if his rival had been on the other side of the Atlantic, instead of a neighboring stream.

That stream was now converted by the deluge of waters into a furious torrent. It was with difficulty that a practicable ford could be found. The slippery stones, rolling beneath the feet, gave away at every step. The difficulty of the passage was much increased by the darkness and driving tempest. Still, with their long pikes, the Spaniards contrived to make good their footing, at least, all but two, who were swept down by the fury of the current. When they had reached the opposite side, they had new impediments to encounter, in traversing a road, never good, now made doubly difficulty by the deep mire, and the tangled brushwood with which it was overrun.

Here they met with a cross, which had been raised by them on their former march into the interior. They hailed it as a good omen; and Cortés, kneeling before the blessed sign, confessed his sins, and declared his great object to be the triumph of the holy Catholic faith. The army followed his example, and, having made a general confession, received absolution from father Olmedo, who invoked the blessing of Heaven on the warriors who had consecrated their swords to the glory of the Cross. Then rising up and embracing one another, as companions in the good cause, they found themselves wonderfully invigorated and refreshed. The incident is curious, and well illustrates the character of the time,—in which war, religion, and rapine were so intimately blended together. Adjoining the road was a little coppice; and Cortés, and the few who had horses, dismounted, fastening the animals to the trees, where they might find some shelter from the storm. They deposited there, too, their baggage, and such superfluous articles as would encumber their movements. The general then gave them a few last words of advice. "Every thing," said he, "depends on obedience. Let no man, from desire of distinguishing himself, break his ranks. On silence, despatch, and, above all, obedience to your officers, the success of our enterprise depends."

Silently and stealthily they held on their way without beat of drum, or sound of trumpet, when they suddenly came on the two sentinels who had been stationed by Narvaez to give notice of their approach. This had been so noiseless, that the videttes were both of them surprised on their post, and one only, with difficulty, effected his escape. The other was brought before Cortés. Every effort was made to draw from him some account of the present position of Narvaez. But the man remained obstinately silent; and, though threatened with the gibbet, and having a noose actually drawn round his neck, his Spartan heroism was not to be vanquished. Fortunately no change had taken place in the arrangements of Narvaez since the intelligence previously derived from Duero.

The other sentinel, who had escaped, carried the news of the enemy's approach to the camp. But his report was not credited by the lazy soldiers, whose slumbers he had disturbed. "He had been deceived by his fears," they said, "and mistaken the noise of the storm and the waving of the bushes, for the enemy. Cortés and his men were far enough on the other side of the river, which they would be slow to cross in such a night." Narvaez himself shared in the same blind infatuation, and the discredited sentinel slunk abashed to his own quarters, vainly menacing them with the consequences of their incredulity.[14]

Cortés, not doubting that the sentinel's report must alarm the enemy's camp, quickened his pace. As he drew near, he discerned a light in one of the lofty towers of the city. "It is the quarters of Narvaez," he exclaimed to Sandoval, "and that light must be your beacon." On entering the suburbs, the Spaniards were surprised to find no one stirring, and no symptom of alarm. Not a sound was to be heard, except the measured tread of their own footsteps, half-drowned in the howling of the tempest. Still they could not move so stealthily as altogether to elude notice, as they defiled through the streets of this populous city. The tidings were quickly conveyed to the enemy's quarters, where, in an instant, all was bustle and confusion. The trumpets sounded to arms. The dragoons sprang to their steeds, the artillery-men to their guns. Narvaez hastily buckled on his armor, called his men around him, and summoned those in the neighboring *teocallis* to join him in the area. He gave his orders with coolness; for, however wanting in prudence, he was not deficient in presence of mind, or courage.

All this was the work of a few minutes. But in those minutes the Spaniards had reached the avenue leading to the camp. Cortés ordered his men to keep close to the walls of the buildings, that the cannon-shot might have a free range.[15] No sooner had they presented themselves before the

---

[14] Rel. Seg. de Cortés, ap. Lorenzana, p. 128.—Oviedo, Hist. de las Ind., MS., lib. 33, cap. 47.—Herrera, Hist. General, dec. 2, lib. 10, cap. 2, 3.

[15] "Ya que se acercaban al Aposento de Narvaez, Cortés, que andaba reconociendo, i ordenando á todas partes, dixo á la Tropa de Sandoval: Señores, arrimaos á las dos aceras de la Calle, para que las balas del Artillería pasen por medio, sin hacer daño." Ibid., dec. 2, lib. 10, cap. 3.

inclosure, than the artillery of Narvaez opened a general fire. Fortunately the pieces were pointed so high that most of the balls passed over their heads, and three men only were struck down. They did not give the enemy time to reload. Cortés shouting the watch-word of the night, "Espíritu Santo! Espíritu Santo! Upon them!" in a moment Olid and his division rushed on the artillery-men, whom they pierced, or knocked down with their pikes, and got possession of their guns. Another division engaged the cavalry, and made a diversion in favor of Sandoval, who with his gallant little band sprang up the great stairway of the temple. They were received with a shower of missiles,—arrows, and musket-balls, which, in the hurried aim, and the darkness of the night, did little mischief. The next minute the assailants were on the platform, engaged hand to hand with their foes. Narvaez fought bravely in the midst, encouraging his followers. His standard-bearer fell by his side, run through the body. He himself received several wounds; for his short sword was no match for the long pikes of the assailants. At length, he received a blow from a spear, which struck out his left eye. "Santa María!" exclaimed the unhappy man, "I am slain!" The cry was instantly taken up by the followers of Cortés, who shouted, "Victory!"

Disabled, and half mad with agony from his wound, Narvaez was withdrawn by his men into the sanctuary. The assailants endeavored to force an entrance, but it was stoutly defended. At length a soldier, getting possession of a torch, or firebrand, flung it on the thatched roof, and in a few moments the combustible materials of which it was composed were in a blaze. Those within were driven out by the suffocating heat and smoke. A soldier named Farfan grappled with the wounded commander, and easily brought him to the ground; when he was speedily dragged down the steps, and secured with fetters. His followers, seeing the fate of their chief, made no further resistance.[16]

During this time, Cortés and the troops of Olid had been engaged with the cavalry, and had discomfited them, after some ineffectual attempts on the part of the latter to break through the dense array of pikes, by which several of their number were unhorsed and some of them slain. The general then prepared to assault the other *teocallis,* first summoning the garrisons to surrender. As they refused, he brought up the heavy guns to bear on them, thus turning the artillery against its own masters. He accompanied this menacing movement with offers of the most liberal import; an amnesty of the past, and a full participation in all the advantages of the Conquest. One of the garrisons was under the command of Salvatierra, the same officer who talked of cutting off the ears of Cortés. From the moment he had learned the fate of his own general, the hero was seized with a violent fit of illness which disabled him from further action. The garrison waited only for one discharge of the ordnance, when they accepted the terms of capitulation. Cortés, it is said, received, on this occasion, a support from an unexpected auxiliary. The air was filled

[16] Demanda de Zavallos en nombre de Narvaez, MS.—Oviedo, Hist. de las Ind.; MS., lib. 33, cap. 47.

with the *cocuyos*,—a species of large beetle which emits an intense phosphoric light from its body, strong enough to enable one to read by it.
These wandering fires, seen in the darkness of the night, were converted,
by the excited imaginations of the beseiged, into an army with match-
locks! Such is the report of an eyewitness.[17] But the facility with which
the enemy surrendered may quite as probably be referred to the cowardice of the commander, and the disaffection of the soldiers, not unwilling to come under the banners of Cortés.

The body of cavalry, posted, it will be remembered, by Narvaez on one
of the roads to Cempoalla, to intercept his rival, having learned what had
been passing, were not long in tendering their submission. Each of the
soldiers in the conquered army was required, in token of his obedience, to
deposit his arms in the hands of the alguacils, and to take the oaths to
Cortés as Chief Justice and Captain-General of the colony.

The number of the slain is variously reported. It seems probable that
not more than twelve perished on the side of the vanquished, and of the
victors half that number. The small amount may be explained by the
short duration of the action, and the random aim of the missiles in the
darkness. The number of the wounded was much more considerable.[18]

The field was now completely won. A few brief hours had sufficed to
change the condition of Cortés from that of a wandering outlaw at the
head of a handful of needy adventurers, a rebel with a price upon his
head, to that of an independent chief, with a force at his disposal strong
enough not only to secure his present conquests, but to open a career for
still loftier ambition. While the air rung with the acclamations of the soldiery, the victorious general, assuming a deportment corresponding with
his change of fortune, took his seat in a chair of state, and, with a rich,
embroidered mantle thrown over his shoulders, received, one by one, the
officers and soldiers, as they came to tender their congratulations. The
privates were graciously permitted to kiss his hand. The officers he noticed with words of compliment or courtesy; and, when Duero, Bermudez, the treasurer, and some others of the vanquished party, his old
friends, presented themselves, he cordially embraced them.[19]

[17] "Como hazia tan escuro auia muchos cocayos (ansí los llaman en Cuba) que
relumbrauan de noche, é los de Narvaez creyéron que erã muchas de las escopetas."
Bernal Diaz, Hist. de la Conquista, cap. 122.

[18] Narvaez, or rather his attorney, swells the amount of slain on his own side much
higher. But it was his cue to magnify the mischief sustained by his employer. The
collation of this account with those of Cortés and his followers affords the best
means of approximation to truth. "É allí le mattáron quince hombres qᵉ muriéron
de las feridas qᵉ les diéron é les quemáron seis hombres del dho Incendio qᵉ despues
pareciéron las cabezas de ellos quemadas, é pusiéron á sacomano todo quantto
ttenian los que benian con el dho mi partte como si fueran Moros y al dho mi partte
robáron é saqueáron todos sus vienes, oro, é Platta é Joyas." Demanda de Zavallos
en nombre de Narvaez, MS.

[19] "Entre ellos venia Andres de Duero, y Agustin Bermudez, y muchos amigos de
nuestro Capitã, y assí como veniã, ivan á besar las manos á Cortés, q̃ estaua sentado en vna silla de caderas, con vna ropa larga de color como narãjada, cõ sus
armas debaxo, acõpañado de nosotros. Pues ver la gracia con que les hablaua, y
abraçaua, y las palabras de tãtos cumplimiẽtos que les dezia, era cosa de ver que

Narvaez, Salvatierra, and two or three of the hostile leaders were led before him in chains. It was a moment of deep humiliation for the former commander, in which the anguish of the body, however keen, must have been forgotten in that of the spirit. "You have great reason, Señor Cortés," said the discomfited warrior, "to thank Fortune for having given you the day so easily, and put me in your power." "I have much to be thankful for," replied the general; "but for my victory over you, I esteem it as one of the least of my achievements since my coming into the country"! [20] He then ordered the wounds of the prisoners to be cared for, and sent them under a strong guard to Vera Cruz.

Notwithstanding the proud humility of his reply, Cortés could scarcely have failed to regard his victory over Narvaez as one of the most brilliant achievements in his career. With a few scores of followers, badly clothed, worse fed, wasted by forced marches, under every personal disadvantage, deficient in weapons and military stores, he had attacked in their own quarters, routed, and captured the entire force of the enemy, thrice his superior in numbers, well provided with cavalry and artillery, admirably equipped, and complete in all the munitions of war! The amount of troops engaged on either side was, indeed, inconsiderable. But the proportions are not affected by this; and the relative strength of the parties made a result so decisive one of the most remarkable events in the annals of war.

It is true there were some contingencies on which the fortunes of the day depended, that could not be said to be entirely within his control. Something was the work of chance. If Velasquez de Leon, for example, had proved false, the expedition must have failed.[21] If the weather, on the night of the attack, had been fair, the enemy would have had certain notice of his approach, and been prepared for it. But these are the

alegre estaua: y tenia mucha razon de verse en aquel pū to tan señor, y pujáte: y assí como le besaua la mano, se fuérō cada vno á su posada." Bernal Diaz, Hist. de la Conquista, cap. 122.

[20] Ibid., loc. cit.

"Díxose que como Narvaez vido á Cortés estando así preso le dixo: Señor Cortés, tened en mucho la ventura que habeis tenido, é lo mucho que habeis hecho en tener mi persona, ó en tomar mi persona. É que Cortés le respondió, é dixo: Lo menos que yo he hecho en esta tierra donde estais, es haberos prendido; é luego le hizo poner á buen recaudo é le tubo mucho tiempo preso." Oviedo, Hist. de las Ind., MS., lib. 33, cap. 47.

[21] Oviedo says, that military men discussed whether Velasquez de Leon should have obeyed the commands of Cortés rather than those of his kinsman, the governor of Cuba. They decided in favor of the former, on the ground of his holding his commission immediately from him. "Visto he platicar sobre esto á caballeros é personas militares sobre si este Juan Velasquez de Leon hizo lo que debia, en acudir ó no á Diego Velasquez, ó al Pánfilo en su nombre; É combienen los veteranos mílites é á mi parecer determinan bien la question, en que si Juan Velasquez tubo conducta de capitan para que con aquella Gente que él le dió ó toviese en aquella tierra como capitan particular le acudiese á él ó á quien le mandase. Juan Velasquez faltó á lo que era obligado en no pasar á Pánfilo de Narvaez siendo requerido de Diego Velasquez, mas si le hizo capitan Hernando Cortés, é le dió él la Gente, á él havia de acudir, como acudió, excepto si viera carta, á mandamiento expreso del Rey en contrario." Hist. de las Ind., MS., lib. 33, cap. 12.

chances that enter more or less into every enterprise. He is the skilful general, who knows how to turn them to account; to win the smiles of Fortune, and make even the elements fight on his side.

If Velasquez de Leon was, as it proved, the very officer whom the general should have trusted with the command, it was his sagacity which originally discerned this, and selected him for it. It was his address that converted this dangerous foe into a friend; and one so fast that in the hour of need he chose rather to attach himself to his desperate fortunes than to those of the governor of Cuba, powerful as the latter was, and his near kinsman. It was the same address which gained Cortés such an ascendency over his soldiers, and knit them to him so closely, that, in the darkest moment, not a man offered to desert him.[22] If the success of the assault may be ascribed mainly to the dark and stormy weather which covered it, it was owing to him that he was in a condition to avail himself of this. The shortest possible time intervened between the conception of his plan and its execution. In a very few days, he descended by extraordinary marches from the capital to the sea-coast. He came like a torrent from the mountains, pouring on the enemy's camp, and sweeping every thing away, before a barrier could be raised to arrest it. This celerity of movement, the result of a clear head and determined will, has entered into the strategy of the greatest captains, and forms a prominent feature in their most brilliant military exploits. It was undoubtedly in the present instance a great cause of success.

But it would be taking a limited view of the subject, to consider the battle which decided the fate of Narvaez, as wholly fought at Cempoalla. It was begun in Mexico. With that singular power which he exercised over all who came near him, Cortés converted the very emissaries of Narvaez into his own friends and agents. The reports of Guevara and his companions, the intrigues of father Olmedo, and the general's gold, were all busily at work to shake the loyalty of the soldiers, and the battle was half won before a blow had been struck. It was fought quite as much with gold as with steel. Cortés understood this so well, that he made it his great object to seize the person of Narvaez. In such an event, he had full confidence that indifference to their own cause and partiality to himself would speedily bring the rest of the army under his banner. He was not deceived. Narvaez said truly enough, therefore, some years after this event, that "he had been beaten by his own troops, not by those of his rival; that his followers had been bribed to betray him." [23] This affords

---

[22] This ascendency the thoughtful Oviedo refers to his dazzling and liberal manners, so strongly contrasted with those of the governor of Cuba. "En lo demas valerosa persona ha seido, é para mucho; y este deseo de mandar juntamente con que fué mui bien partido é gratificador de los que le viniéron, fué mucha causa juntamente con ser mal quisto Diego Velasquez, para que Cortés se saliese con lo que emprendió, é se quedase en el oficio, é governacion." Ibid., MS., lib. 33, cap. 12.

[23] It was in a conversation with Oviedo himself, at Toledo, in 1525, in which Narvaez descanted with much bitterness, as was natural, on his rival's conduct. The gossip, which has never appeared in print, may have some interest for the Spanish reader. "Que el año de 1525, estando Cesar en la cibdad de Toledo, ví allí al dicho

the only explanation of their brief and ineffectual resistance.

Narvaez, é publicamente decia, que Cortés era vn traidor: É que dándole S. M. licencia se lo haria conocer de su persona á la suya, é que era hombre sin verdad, é otras muchas é feas palabras llamándole alevoso é tirano, é ingrato á su Señor, é á quien le havia embiado á la Nueva España, que era el Adelantado Diego Velasquez á su propia costa, é se le havia alzado con la tierra, é con la Gente é Hacienda, é otras muchas cosas que mal sonaban. Y en la manera de su prision la contaba mui al reves de lo que está dicho. Lo que yo noto de esto es, que con todo lo que oí á Narvaez, (como yo se lo dixe) no puedo hallarle desculpa para su descuido, porque ninguna necesidad tenia de andar con Cortés en pláticas, sino estar en vela mejor que la que hizo. É á esto decia él que le havian vendido aquellos de quien se fiaba, que Cortés le havia sobornado." Ibid., lib. 33, cap. 12.

CHAPTER VIII

DISCONTENT OF THE TROOPS—INSURRECTION IN THE CAPITAL—RE-
TURN OF CORTÉS—GENERAL SIGNS OF HOSTILITY—MASSACRE BY
ALVARADO—RISING OF THE AZTECS

1520

THE tempest, that had raged so wildly during the night, passed away
with the morning, which rose bright and unclouded on the field of battle.
As the light advanced, it revealed more strikingly the disparity of the
two forces so lately opposed to each other. Those of Narvaez could not
conceal their chagrin, and murmurs of displeasure became audible, as
they contrasted their own superior numbers and perfect appointments
with the way-worn visages and rude attire of their handful of enemies! It
was with some satisfaction, therefore, that the general beheld his dusky
allies from Chinantla, two thousand in number, arrive upon the field.
They were a fine, athletic set of men; and, as they advanced in a sort of
promiscuous order, so to speak, with their gay banners of feather-work,
and their long lances tipped with *itztli* and copper, glistening in the morning sun, they had something of an air of military discipline. They came
too late for the action, indeed, but Cortés was not sorry to exhibit to his
new followers the extent of his resources in the country. As he had now
no occasion for his Indian allies, after a courteous reception and a liberal
recompense, he dismissed them to their homes.[1]

He then used his utmost endeavors to allay the discontent of the
troops. He addressed them in his most soft and insinuating tones, and was
by no means frugal of his promises.[2] He suited the action to the word.
There were few of them but had lost their accoutrements, or their baggage, or horses taken and appropriated by the victors. This last article
was in great request among the latter, and many a soldier, weary with
the long marches, hitherto made on foot, had provided himself, as he
imagined, with a much more comfortable as well as creditable conveyance for the rest of the campaign. The general now commanded every
thing to be restored.[3] "They were embarked in the same cause," he said,

[1] Herrera, Hist. General, dec. 2, lib. 10, cap. 6.—Oviedo, Hist. de las Ind., MS.,
lib. 33, cap. 47.—Bernal Diaz, Hist. de la Conquista, cap. 123.
[2] Diaz who had often listened to it, thus notices his eloquence. "Comenzó vn
parlamento por tan lindo estilo, y plática, tābiē dichas cierto otras palabras mas
sabrosas, y llenas de ofertas, q̄ yc aquí no sabré escriuir." Ibid., cap. 122.
[3] Captain Diaz had secured for nis share of the spoil of the Philistines, as he tells
us, a very good horse with all his accoutrements, a brace of swords, three daggers,
and a buckler,—a very beautiful outfit for the campaign. The general's orders were
naturally enough, not at all to his taste. Ibid., cap. 124.

"and should share with one another equally." He went still further; and distributed among the soldiers of Narvaez a quantity of gold and other precious commodities gathered from the neighboring tribes, or found in his rival's quarters.[4]

These proceedings, however politic in reference to his new followers, gave great disgust to his old. "Our commander," they cried, "has forsaken his friends for his foes. We stood by him in his hour of distress, and are rewarded with blows and wounds, while the spoil goes to our enemies!" The indignant soldiery commissioned the priest Olmedo and Alonso de Avila to lay their complaints before Cortés. The ambassadors stated them without reserve, comparing their commander's conduct to the ungrateful proceeding of Alexander, who, when he gained a victory, usually gave away more to his enemies than to the troops who enabled him to beat them. Cortés was greatly perplexed. Victorious or defeated, his path seemed equally beset with difficulties!

He endeavored to soothe their irritation by pleading the necessity of the case. "Our new comrades," he said, "are formidable from their numbers, so much so, that we are even now much more in their power than they are in ours. Our only security is to make them not merely confederates, but friends. On any cause of disgust, we shall have the whole battle to fight over again, and, if they are united, under a much greater disadvantage than before. I have considered your interests," he added, "as much as my own. All that I have is yours. But why should there be any ground for discontent, when the whole country, with its riches, is before us? And our augmented strength must henceforth secure the undisturbed control of it!"

But Cortés did not rely wholly on argument for the restoration of tranquillity. He knew this to be incompatible with inaction, and he made arrangements to divide his forces, at once, and to employ them on distant services. He selected a detachment of two hundred men, under Diego de Ordaz, whom he ordered to form the settlement before meditated on the Coatzacualco. A like number was sent with Velasquez de Leon, to secure the province of Panuco, some three degrees to the north, on the Mexican Gulf. Twenty in each detachment were drafted from his own veterans.

Two hundred men he despatched to Vera Cruz, with orders to have the rigging, iron, and every thing portable on board of the fleet of Narvaez, brought on shore, and the vessels completely dismantled. He appointed a person named Cavallero superintendent of the marine, with instructions, that, if any ships, hereafter, should enter the port, they should be dismantled in like manner, and their officers imprisoned on shore.[5]

---

[4] Narvaez alleges that Cortés plundered him of property to the value of 100,000 castellanos of gold! (Demanda de Zavallos en nombre de Narvaez, MS.) If so, the pillage of the leader may have supplied the means of liberality to the privates.

[5] Demanda de Zavallos en nombre de Narvaez, MS.—Bernal Diaz, Hist. de la Conquista, cap. 124.—Oviedo, Hist. de las Ind., MS., lib. 33, cap. 47.—Rel. Seg. de Cortés, ap. Lorenzana, p. 130.—Camargo, Hist. de Tlascala, MS.

The visit of Narvaez left melancholy traces among the natives, that made it long remembered. A Negro in his suite brought with him the small-pox. The disease

But, while he was thus occupied with new schemes of discovery and conquest, he received such astounding intelligence from Mexico, as compelled him to concentrate all his faculties and his forces on that one point. The city was in a state of insurrection. No sooner had the struggle with his rival been decided, than Cortés despatched a courier with the tidings to the capital. In less than a fortnight, the same messenger returned with letters from Alvarado, conveying the alarming information, that the Mexicans were in arms, and had vigorously assaulted the Spaniards in their own quarters. The enemy, he added, had burned the brigantines, by which Cortés had secured the means of retreat in case of the destruction of the bridges. They had attempted to force the defences, and had succeeded in partially undermining them, and they had overwhelmed the garrison with a tempest of missiles, which had killed several, and wounded a great number. The letter concluded with beseeching his commander to hasten to their relief, if he would save them, or keep his hold on the capital.

These tidings were a heavy blow to the general,—the heavier, it seemed, coming, as they did, in the hour of triumph, when he had thought to have all his enemies at his feet. There was no room for hesitation. To lose their footing in the capital, the noblest city in the Western World, would be to lose the country itself, which looked up to it as its head.[6] He opened the matter fully to his soldiers, calling on all who would save their countrymen to follow him. All declared their readiness to go; showing an alacrity, says Diaz, which some would have been slow to manifest, had they foreseen the future.

Cortés now made preparations for instant departure. He countermanded the orders previously given to Velasquez and Ordaz, and directed them to join him with their forces at Tlascala. He recalled the troops from Vera Cruz, leaving only a hundred men in garrison there, under command of one Rodrigo Rangre; for he could not spare the services of Sandoval at this crisis. He left his sick and wounded at Cempoalla, under charge of a small detachment, directing that they should follow as soon as they were in marching order. Having completed these arrangements, he set out from Cempoalla, well supplied with provisions by its hospitable cacique, who attended him some leagues on his way. The Totonac chief seems to have had an amiable facility of accommodating himself to the powers that were in the ascendant.

Nothing worthy of notice occurred during the first part of the march. The troops everywhere met with a friendly reception from the peasantry, who readily supplied their wants. Some time before reaching Tlascala, the route lay through a country thinly settled; and the army experienced considerable suffering from want of food, and still more from that of

spread rapidly in that quarter of the country, and great numbers of the Indian population soon fell victims to it. Herrera, Hist. General, dec. 2, lib. 10, cap. 6.

[6] "Se perdia la mejor, y mas Noble Ciudad de todo lo nuevamente descubierto del Mundo; y ella perdida, se perdia todo lo que estaba ganado, por ser la Cabeza d. todo, y á quien todos obedecian." Rel. Seg. de Cortés, ap. Lorenzana, p. 131.

water. Their distress increased to an alarming degree, as, in the hurry of their forced march, they travelled with the meridian sun beating fiercely on their heads. Several faltered by the way, and, throwing themselves down by the road-side, seemed incapable of further effort, and almost indifferent to life.

In this extremity, Cortés sent forward a small detachment of horse to procure provisions in Tlascala, and speedily followed in person. On arriving, he found abundant supplies already prepared by the hospitable natives. They were sent back to the troops; the stragglers were collected one by one; refreshments were administered; and the army, restored in strength and spirits, entered the republican capital.

Here they gathered little additional news respecting the events in Mexico, which a popular rumor attributed to the secret encouragement and machinations of Montezuma. Cortés was commodiously lodged in the quarters of Maxixca, one of the four chiefs of the republic. They readily furnished him with two thousand troops. There was no want of heartiness, when the war was with their ancient enemy, the Aztec.[7]

The Spanish commander, on reviewing his forces, after the junction with his two captains, found that they amounted to about a thousand foot, and one hundred horse, besides the Tlascalan levies.[8] In the infantry were nearly a hundred arquebusiers, with as many crossbow-men; and the part of the army brought over by Narvaez was admirably equipped. It was inferior, however, to his own veterans in what is better than any outward appointments,—military training, and familiarity with the peculiar service in which they were engaged.

Leaving these friendly quarters, the Spaniards took a more northerly route, as more direct than that by which they had before penetrated into the Valley. It was the road to Tezcuco. It still compelled them to climb the same bold range of the Cordilleras, which attains its greatest elevation in the two mighty *volcans* at whose base they had before travelled. The sides of the sierra were clothed with dark forests of pine, cypress, and cedar,[9] through which glimpses now and then opened into fathomless dells and valleys, whose depths, far down in the sultry climate of the tropics, were lost in a glowing wilderness of vegetation. From the crest

---

[7] Ibid., ubi supra.—Oviedo, Hist. de las Ind., MS., lib. 33, cap. 13, 14.—Bernal Diaz, Hist. de la Conquista, cap. 124, 125.—Peter Martyr, De Orbe Novo, dec. 5, cap. 5.—Camargo, Hist. de Tlascala, MS.

[8] Gomara, Crónica, cap. 103.—Herrera, Hist. General, dec. 2, lib. 10, cap. 7.

Bernal Diaz raises the amount to 1300 foot and 96 horse. (Ibid., cap. 125.) Cortés diminishes it to less than half that number. (Rel. Seg., ubi supra.) The estimate cited in the text from the two preceding authorities corresponds nearly enough with that already given from official documents of the forces of Cortés and Narvaez before the junction.

[9] "Las sierras altas de Tetzcuco á que le mostrasen desde la mas alta cumbre de aquellas montañas y sierras de Tetzcuco, que son las sierras de Tlallocan altísimas y umbrosas, en las cuales he estado y visto y puedo decir que son bastante para descubrir el un emisferio y otro, porque son los mayores puertos y mas altos de esta Nueva España, de árboles y montes de grandísima altura, de cedras, cipreses y pinares." Camargo, Hist. de Tlascala, MS.

of the mountain range the eye travelled over the broad expanse of country, which they had lately crossed, far away to the green plains of Cholula. Towards the west, they looked down on the Mexican Valley, from a
point of view wholly different from that which they had before occupied,
but still offering the same beautiful spectacle, with its lakes trembling in
the light, its gay cities and villas floating on their bosom, its burnished
teocallis touched with fire, its cultivated slopes and dark hills of porphyry
stretching away in dim perspective to the verge of the horizon. At their
feet lay the city of Tezcuco, which, modestly retiring behind her deep
groves of cypress, formed a contrast to her more ambitious rival on the
other side of the lake, who seemed to glory in the unveiled splendors of
her charms, as Mistress of the Valley.

As they descended into the populous plains, their reception by the natives was very different from that which they had experienced on the preceding visit. There were no groups of curious peasantry to be seen gazing
at them as they passed, and offering their simple hospitality. The supplies
they asked were not refused, but granted with an ungracious air, that
showed the blessing of the giver did not accompany them. This air of reserve became still more marked as the army entered the suburbs of the
ancient capital of the Acolhuans. No one came forth to greet them, and
the population seemed to have dwindled away,—so many of them were
withdrawn to the neighboring scene of hostilities at Mexico.[10] Their cold
reception was a sensible mortification to the veterans of Cortés, who,
judging from the past, had boasted to their new comrades of the sensation their presence would excite among the natives. The cacique of the
place, who, as it may be remembered, had been created through the influence of Cortés, was himself absent. The general drew an ill omen from
all these circumstances, which even raised an uncomfortable apprehension in his mind respecting the fate of the garrison in Mexico.[11]

But his doubts were soon dispelled by the arrival of a messenger in a
canoe from that city, whence he had escaped through the remissness of
the enemy, or, perhaps, with their connivance. He brought despatches
from Alvarado, informing his commander that the Mexicans had for the
last fortnight desisted from active hostilities, and converted their operations into a blockade. The garrison had suffered greatly, but Alvarado
expressed his conviction that the siege would be raised, and tranquillity
restored, on the approach of his countrymen. Montezuma sent a messenger, also, to the same effect. At the same time, he exculpated himself from
any part in the late hostilities, which he said had not only been conducted
without his privity, but contrary to his inclination and efforts.

[10] The historian partly explains the reason. "En la misma Ciudad de Tescuco
habia algunos apasionados de los deudos y amigos de los que mataron Pedro de
Alvarado y sus compañeros en México." Ixtlilxochitl, Hist. Chich., MS., cap. 88.
[11] "En todo el camino nunca me salió á recibir ninguna Persona de el dicho
Muteczuma, como ántes lo solian facer; y toda la Tierra estaba alborotada, y casi
despoblada: de que concebí mala sospecha, creyendo que los Españoles que en ia
dicha Ciudad habian quedado, eran muertos." Rel. Seg. de Cortés, ap Lorenzana,
p. 132.

The Spanish general, having halted long enough to refresh his wearied troops, took up his march along the southern margin of the lake, which led him over the same causeway by which he had before entered the capital. It was the day consecrated to St. John the Baptist, the 24th of June, 1520. But how different was the scene from that presented on his former entrance! [12] No crowds now lined the roads, no boats swarmed on the lake, filled with admiring spectators. A single pirogue might now and then be seen in the distance, like a spy stealthily watching their movements, and darting away the moment it had attracted notice. A deathlike stillness brooded over the scene,—a stillness that spoke louder to the heart, than the acclamations of multitudes.

Cortés rode on moodily at the head of his battalions, finding abundant food for meditation, doubtless, in this change of circumstances. As if to dispel these gloomy reflections, he ordered his trumpets to sound, and their clear, shrill notes, borne across the waters, told the inhabitants of the beleaguered fortress, that their friends were at hand. They were answered by a joyous peal of artillery, which seemed to give a momentary exhilaration to the troops, as they quickened their pace, traversed the great drawbridges, and once more found themselves within the walls of the imperial city.

The appearance of things here was not such as to allay their apprehensions. In some places they beheld the smaller bridges removed, intimating too plainly, now that their brigantines were destroyed, how easy it would be to cut off their retreat.[13] The town seemed even more deserted than Tezcuco. Its once busy and crowded population had mysteriously vanished. And, as the Spaniards defiled through the empty streets, the tramp of their horses' feet upon the pavement was answered by dull and melancholy echoes that fell heavily on their hearts. With saddened feelings they reached the great gates of the palace of Axayacatl. The gates were thrown open, and Cortés and his veterans, rushing in, were cordially embraced by their companions in arms, while both parties soon forgot the present in the interesting recapitulation of the past.[14]

The first inquiries of the general were respecting the origin of the tumult. The accounts were various. Some imputed it to the desire of the

---

[12] "Y como asomó á la vista de la Ciudad de México, parecióle que estaba toda yerma, y que no parecia persona por todos los caminos, ni casas, ni plazas, ni nadie le salió á recibir, ni de los suyos, ni de los enemigos; y fué esto señal de indignacion y enemistad por lo que habia pasado." Sahagun, Hist. de Nueva España, MS., lib. 12, cap. 19.

[13] "Pontes ligneos qui tractim lapideos intersecant, sublatos, ac vias aggeribus munitas reperit." P. Martyr, De Orbe Novo, dec. 5, cap. 5.

[14] Probanza á pedimento de Juan de Lexalde, MS.,—Rel. Seg. de Cortés, ap. Lorenzana, p. 133.

"Esto causó gran admiracion en todos los que venian, pero no dejáron de marchar, hasta entrar donde estaban los Españoles acorralados. Venian todos muy casados y muy fatigados y con mucho deseo de llegar á donde estaban sus hermanos; los de dentro cuando los viéron, recibiéron singular consolacion y esfuerzo y recibiéronlos con la artillería que tenian, saludándolos, y dándolos el parabien de su venida." Sahagun, Hist. de Nueva España, MS., lib. 12, cap. 22.

Mexicans to release their sovereign from confinement; others to the design of cutting off the garrison while crippled by the absence of Cortés and their countrymen. All agreed, however, in tracing the immediate cause to the violence of Alvarado. It was common for the Aztecs to celebrate an annual festival in May, in honor of their patron war-god. It was called the "incensing of Huitzilopotchli," and was commemorated by sacrifice, religious songs, and dances, in which most of the nobles engaged, for it was one of the great festivals which displayed the pomp of the Aztec ritual. As it was held in the court of the *teocalli*, in the immediate neighborhood of the Spanish quarters, and as a part of the temple itself was reserved for a Christian chapel, the caciques asked permission of Alvarado to perform their rites there. They requested also, it is said, to be allowed the presence of Montezuma. This latter petition Alvarado declined, in obedience to the injunctions of Cortés; but acquiesced in the former, on condition that the Aztecs should celebrate no human sacrifices, and should come without weapons.

They assembled accordingly on the day appointed, to the number of six hundred, at the smallest computation.[15] They were dressed in their most magnificent gala costumes, with their graceful mantles of featherwork, sprinkled with precious stones, and their necks, arms, and legs ornamented with collars and bracelets of gold. They had that love of gaudy splendor which belongs to semi-civilized nations, and on these occasions displayed all the pomp and profusion of their barbaric wardrobes.

Alvarado and his soldiers attended as spectators, some of them taking their station at the gates, as if by chance, and others mingling in the crowd. They were all armed, a circumstance, which, as it was usual, excited no attention. The Aztecs were soon engrossed by the exciting movement of the dance, accompanied by their religious chant and wild, discordant minstrelsy. While thus occupied, Alvarado and his men, at a concerted signal, rushed with drawn swords on their victims. Unprotected by armor or weapons of any kind, they were hewn down without resistance by their assailants, who, in their bloody work, says a contemporary, showed no touch of pity or compunction.[16] Some fled to the gates, but were caught on the long pikes of the soldiers. Others, who attempted to scale the *Coatepantli*, or Wall of Serpents, as it was called, which surrounded the area, shared the like fate, or were cut to pieces, or shot by the ruthless soldiery. The pavement, says a writer of the age, ran with streams of blood, like water in a heavy shower.[17] Not an Aztec, of all

[15] "É así los Indios, todos Señores, mas de 600 desnudos é con muchas joyas de oro é hermosos penachos, é muchas piedras preciosas, é como mas aderezados é gentiles hombres se pudiéron é supiéron aderezar, é sin arma alguna defensiva ni ofensiva bailaban é cantaban é hacian su areito é fiesta segun su costumbre." (Oviedo, Hist. de las Ind., MS., lib. 33, cap. 54.) Some writers carry the number as high as eight hundred or even one thousand. Las Casas, with a more modest exaggeration than usual, swells it only to two thousand. Brevíssima Relatione, p. 48.

[16] "Sin duelo ni piedad Christiana los acuchilló, i mató." Gomara, Crónica, cap. 104.

[17] "Fué tan grande el derramamiento de Sangre, que corrian arroyos de ella por el Patio, como agua cuando mucho llueve." Sahagun, Hist. de Nueva España, MS. lib. 12, cap. 20.

that gay company, was left alive! It was repeating the dreadful scene of Cholula, with the disgraceful addition, that the Spaniards, not content with slaughtering their victims, rifled them of the precious ornaments on their persons! On this sad day fell the flower of the Aztec nobility. Not a family of note, but had mourning and desolation brought within its walls. And many a doleful ballad, rehearsing the tragic incidents of the story, and adapted to the plaintive national airs, continued to be chanted by the natives long after the subjugation of the country.[18]

Various explanations have been given of this atrocious deed. But few historians have been content to admit that of Alvarado himself. According to this, intelligence had been obtained through his spies—some of them Mexicans—of an intended rising of the Indians. The celebration of this festival was fixed on, as the period for its execution, when the caciques would be met together, and would easily rouse the people to support them. Alvarado, advised of all this, had forbidden them to wear arms at their meeting. While affecting to comply, they had secreted their weapons in the neighboring arsenals, whence they could readily withdraw them. But his own blow, by anticipating theirs, defeated the design, and, as he confidently hoped, would deter the Aztecs from a similar attempt in future.[19]

Such is the account of the matter given by Alvarado. But, if true, why did he not verify his assertion by exposing the arms thus secreted? Why did he not vindicate his conduct in the eyes of the Mexicans generally, by publicly avowing the treason of the nobles, as was done by Cortés at Cholula? The whole looks much like an apology devised after the commission of the deed, to cover up its atrocity.

Some contemporaries assign a very different motive for the massacre, which, according to them, originated in the cupidity of the Conquerors, as shown by their plundering the bodies of their victims.[20] Bernal Diaz, who, though not present, had conversed familiarly with those who were, vindicates them from the charge of this unworthy motive. According to him, Alvarado struck the blow in order to intimidate the Aztecs from any

[18] "Y de aquí á que se acabe el mundo, ó ellos del todo se acaben, no dexarán de lamentar, y cantar en sus areytos, y bayles, como en romances, que acá dezimos, aquella calamidad, y perdida de la sucession de toda su nobleza, de que se preciauan de tantos años atras." Las Casas, Brevíssima Relatione, p. 49.

[19] See Alvarado's reply to queries of Cortés, as reported by Diaz, (Hist. de la Conquista, cap. 125,) with some additional particulars in Torquemada, (Monarch. Ind., lib. 4, cap. 66,) Solís, (Conquista, lib. 4, cap. 12,) and Herrera, (Hist. General, dec. 2, lib. 10, cap. 8,) who all seem content to endorse Alvarado's version of the matter. I find no other authority, of any weight, in the same charitable vein.

[20] Oviedo mentions a conversation which he had some years after this tragedy with a noble Spaniard, Don Thoan Cano, who came over in the train of Narvaez, and was present at all the subsequent operations of the army. He married a daughter of Montezuma, and settled in Mexico after the Conquest. Oviedo describes him as a man of sense and integrity. In answer to the historian's queries respecting the cause of the rising, he said, that Alvarado had wantonly perpetrated the massacre from pure avarice; and the Aztecs, enraged at such unprovoked and unmerited cruelty rose, as they well might, to avenge it. (Hist. de las Ind., MS., lib. 33, cap. 54.)

insurrectionary movement.[21] But whether he had reason to apprehend such, or even affected to do so before the massacre, the old chronicler does not inform us.

On reflection, it seems scarely possible that so foul a deed, and one involving so much hazard to the Spaniards themselves, should have been perpetrated from the mere desire of getting possession of the baubles worn on the persons of the natives. It is more likely this was an afterthought, suggested to the rapacious soldiery by the display of the spoil before them. It is not improbable that Alvarado may have gathered rumors of a conspiracy among the nobles,—rumors, perhaps, derived through the Tlascalans, their inveterate foes, and for that reason very little deserving of credit.[22] He proposed to defeat it by imitating the example of his commander at Cholula. But he omitted to imitate his leader in taking precautions against the subsequent rising of the populace. And he grievously miscalculated, when he confounded the bold and warlike Aztec with the effeminate Cholulan.

No sooner was the butchery accomplished, than the tidings spread like wildfire through the capital. Men could scarcely credit their senses. All they had hitherto suffered, the desecration of their temples, the imprisonment of their sovereign, the insults heaped on his person, all were forgotten in this one act.[23] Every feeling of long smothered hostility and rancor now burst forth in the cry for vengeance. Every former sentiment of superstitious dread was merged in that of inextinguishable hatred. It required no effort of the priests—though this was not wanting—to fan these passions into a blaze. The city rose in arms to a man; and on the

---

[21] "Verdaderamente dió en ellos por metelles temor." Hist. de la Conquista, cap. 125.

[22] Such, indeed, is the statement of Ixtlilxochitl, derived, as he says, from the native Tezcucan annalists. According to them, the Tlascalans, urged by their hatred of the Aztecs and their thirst for plunder, persuaded Alvarado, nothing loth, that the nobles meditated a rising on the occasion of these festivities. The testimony is important, and I give it in the author's words. "Fué que ciertos Tlascaltecas (segun las Historias de Tescuco que son las que Io sigo y la carta que otras veces he referido) por embidia lo uno acordándose que en semejante fiesta los Mexicanos solian sacrificar gran suma de cautivos de los de la Nacion Tlascalteca, y lo otro que era la mejor ocasion que ellos podian tener para poder hinchir las manos de despojos y hartar su codicia, y vengarse de sus Enemigos, (porque hasta entonces no habian tenido lugar, ni Cortés se les diera, ni admitiera sus dichos, porque siempre hacia las cosas con mucho acuerdo) fuéron con esta invencion al capitan Pedro de Albarado, que estaba en lugar de Cortés, el qual no fué menester mucho para darles crédito porque tan buenos filos, y pensamientos tenia como ellos, y mas viendo que allí en aquella fiesta habian acudido todos los Señores y Cabezas del Imperio y que muertos no tenian mucho trabajo en sojuzgarles." Hist. Chich., MS., cap. 88.

[23] Martyr well recapitulates these grievances, showing that they seemed such in the eyes of the Spaniards themselves,—of those, at least, whose judgment was not warped by a share in the transactions. "Emori statuerunt malle, quam diutius ferre tales hospites qui regem suum sub tutoris vitæ specie detineant, civitatem occupent, antiquos hostes Tascaltecanos et alios præterea in contumeliam ante illorum oculos ipsorum impensa conseruent; . . . . . qui demum simulachra deorum confregerint, et ritus veteres ac ceremonias antiquas illis abstulerint." De Orbe Novo, dec. 5 cap. 5.

following dawn, almost before the Spaniards could secure themselves in their defences, they were assaulted with desperate fury. Some of the assailants attempted to scale the walls; others succeeded in partially undermining and in setting fire to the works. Whether they would have succeeded in carrying the place by storm is doubtful. But, at the prayers of the garrison, Montezuma himself interfered, and mounting the battlements addressed the populace, whose fury he endeavored to mitigate by urging considerations for his own safety. They respected their monarch so far as to desist from further attempts to storm the fortress, but changed their operations into a regular blockade. They threw up works around the palace to prevent the egress of the Spaniards. They suspended the *tianguez,* or market, to preclude the possibility of their enemy's obtaining supplies; and they then quietly sat down, with feelings of sullen desperation, waiting for the hour when famine should throw their victims into their hands.

The condition of the besieged, meanwhile, was sufficiently distressing. Their magazines of provisions, it is true, were not exhausted; but they suffered greatly from want of water, which, within the inclosure, was exceedingly brackish, for the soil was saturated with the salt of the surrounding element. In this extremity, they discovered, it is said, a spring of fresh water in the area. Such springs were known in some other parts of the city; but, discovered first under these circumstances, it was accounted as nothing less than a miracle. Still they suffered much from their past encounters. Seven Spaniards, and many Tlascalans, had fallen, and there was scarcely one of either nation who had not received several wounds. In this situation, far from their own countrymen, without expectation of succour from abroad, they seemed to have no alternative before them, but a lingering death by famine, or one more dreadful on the altar of sacrifice. From this gloomy state they were relieved by the coming of their comrades.[24]

Cortés calmly listened to the explanation made by Alvarado. But, before it was ended, the conviction must have forced itself on his mind, that he had made a wrong selection for this important post. Yet the mistake was natural. Alvarado was a cavalier of high family, gallant and chivalrous, and his warm personal friend. He had talents for action, was possessed of firmness and intrepidity, while his frank and dazzling manners made the *Tonatiuh* an especial favorite with the Mexicans. But, underneath this showy exterior, the future conqueror of Guatemala concealed a heart rash, rapacious, and cruel. He was altogether destitute of that moderation, which, in the delicate position he occupied, was a quality of more worth than all the rest.

When Alvarado had concluded his answers to the several interrogatories of Cortés, the brow of the latter darkened, as he said to his lieutenant, "You have done badly. You have been false to your trust. Your con-

[24] Camargo, Hist. de Tlascala, MS.—Oviedo, Hist. de las Ind., MS., lib. 33, cap. 13, 47.—Gomara, Crónica. cap. 105.

duct has been that of a madman!" And, turning abruptly on his heel, he left him in undisguised displeasure.

Yet this was not a time to break with one so popular, and, in many respects, so important to him, as this captain, much less to inflict on him the punishment he merited. The Spaniards were like mariners laboring in a heavy tempest, whose bark nothing but the dexterity of the pilot, and the hearty coöperation of the crew, can save from foundering. Dissensions at such a moment must be fatal. Cortés, it is true, felt strong in his present resources. He now found himself at the head of a force which could scarcely amount to less than twelve hundred and fifty Spaniards, and eight thousand native warriors, principally Tlascalans.[25] But, though relying on this to overawe resistance, the very augmentation of numbers increased the difficulty of subsistence. Discontented with himself, disgusted with his officer, and embarrassed by the disastrous consequences in which Alvarado's intemperance had involved him, he became irritable, and indulged in a petulance by no means common; for, though a man of lively passions, by nature, he held them habitually under control.[26]

On the day that Cortés arrived, Montezuma had left his own quarters to welcome him. But the Spanish commander, distrusting, as it would seem, however unreasonably, his good faith, received him so coldly that the Indian monarch withdrew, displeased and dejected, to his apartment. As the Mexican populace made no show of submission, and brought no supplies to the army, the general's ill-humor with the emperor continued. When, therefore, Montezuma sent some of the nobles to ask an interview with Cortés, the latter, turning to his own officers, haughtily exclaimed, "What have I to do with this dog of a king who suffers us to starve before his eyes?"

His captains, among whom were Olid, de Avila, and Velasquez de Leon, endeavored to mitigate his anger, reminding him, in respectful terms, that, had it not been for the emperor, the garrison might even now have been overwhelmed by the enemy. This remonstrance only chafed him the more. "Did not the dog," he asked, repeating the opprobrious epithet, "betray us in his communications with Narvaez? And does he not now suffer his markets to be closed, and leave us to die of famine?" Then turning fiercely to the Mexicans, he said, "Go tell your master and his people to open the markets, or we will do it for them, at their cost!" The chiefs, who had gathered the import of his previous taunt on their sovereign, from his tone and gesture, or perhaps from some comprehension of his language, left his presence swelling with re-

---

[25] He left in garrison, on his departure from Mexico, 140 Spaniards and about 6500 Tlascalans, including a few Cempoallan warriors. Supposing five hundred of these—a liberal allowance—to have perished in battle and otherwise, it would still leave a number, which, with the reinforcement now brought, would raise the amount to that stated in the text.

[26] "Y viendo que todo estaua muy al contrario de sus pensamientos, q̃ aũ de comer no nos dauan, estaua muy airado, y sobervio cõ la mucha gẽte de Españoles que traia, y muy triste, y mohino." Bernal Diaz, Hist. de la Conquista cap. 126.

sentment; and, in communicating his message, took care it should lose
none of its effect.[27]

Shortly after, Cortés, at the suggestion, it is said, of Montezuma, released his brother Cuitlahua, lord of Iztapalapan, who, it will be remembered, had been seized on suspicion of coöperating with the chief of
Tezcuco in his meditated revolt. It was thought he might be of service
in allaying the present tumult, and bringing the populace to a better
state of feeling. But he returned no more to the fortress.[28] He was a bold,
ambitious prince, and the injuries he had received from the Spaniards
rankled deep in his bosom. He was presumptive heir to the crown, which,
by the Aztec laws of succession, descended much more frequently in a
collateral than in a direct line. The people welcomed him as the representative of their sovereign, and chose him to supply the place of Montezuma during his captivity. Cuitlahua willingly accepted the post of honor
and of danger. He was an experienced warrior, and exerted himself to
reorganize the disorderly levies, and to arrange a more efficient plan of
operations. The effect was soon visible.

Cortés meanwhile had so little doubt of his ability to overawe the
insurgents, that he wrote to that effect to the garrison of Villa Rica, by
the same despatches in which he informed them of his safe arrival in the
capital. But scarcely had his messenger been gone half an hour, when
he returned breathless with terror, and covered with wounds. "The city,"
he said, "was all in arms! The draw-bridges were raised, and the enemy
would soon be upon them!" He spoke truth. It was not long before a
hoarse, sullen sound became audible, like that of the roaring of distant
waters. It grew louder and louder; till, from the parapet surrounding
the inclosure, the great avenues which led to it might be seen dark with
the masses of warriors, who came rolling on in a confused tide towards
the fortress. At the same time, the terraces and *azoteas* or flat roofs, in
the neighborhood, were thronged with combatants brandishing their
missiles, who seemed to have risen up as if by magic! [29] It was a spectacle
to appall the stoutest.—But the dark storm to which it was the prelude,
and which gathered deeper and deeper round the Spaniards during the
remainder of their residence in the capital, must form the subject of a
separate Book.

Gonzalo Fernandez de Oviedo y Valdés was born in 1478. He belonged to an
ancient family of the Asturias. Every family, indeed, claims to be ancient in this

---

[27] The scene is reported by Diaz, who was present. (Ibid., cap. 126.) See, also, the
Chronicle of Gomara, the chaplain of Cortés. (Cap. 106.) It is further confirmed
by Don Thoan Cano, an eyewitness, in his conversation with Oviedo.

[28] Herrera, Hist. General, dec. 2, lib. 10, cap. 8.

[29] "El qual Mensajero bolvió dende á media hora todo descalabrado, y herido,
dando voces, que todos los Indios de la Ciudad venian de Guerra y que tenian todas
las Puentes alzadas; é junto tras él da sobre nosotros tanta multitud de Gente por
todas partes, que ni las calles ni Azoteas se parecian con Gente; la qual venia con
los mayores alaridos, y grita mas espantable, que en el Mundo se puede pensar."
Rel. Seg. de Cortés, ap. Lorenzana, p. 134.—Oviedo, Hist de las Ind., MS., lib. 33,
cap. 13.

last retreat of the intrepid Goths. He was early introduced at court, and was appointed page to Prince Juan, the only son of Ferdinand and Isabella, on whom
their hopes, and those of the nation, deservedly rested. Oviedo accompanied the
camp in the latter campaigns of the Moorish war, and was present at the memorable
siege of Granada. On the untimely death of his royal master in 1496, he passed over
to Italy and entered the service of King Frederick of Naples. At the death of that
prince he returned to his own country, and in the beginning of the sixteenth century we find him again established in Castile, where he occupied the place of keeper
of the crown jewels. In 1513, he was named by Ferdinand the Catholic *veedor*, or
inspector of the gold founderies in the American colonies. Oviedo, accordingly,
transported himself to the New World, where he soon took a commission under
Pedrarias, governor of Darien; and shared in the disastrous fortunes of that colony.
He obtained some valuable privileges from the Crown, built a fortress on Tierra
Firme and entered into traffic with the natives. In this we may presume he was
prosperous, since we find him at length established with a wife and family at Hispaniola, or Fernandina, as it was then called. Although he continued to make his
principal residence in the New World, he made occasional visits to Spain; and in
1526, published at Madrid his *Sumario*. It is dedicated to the Emperor Charles the
Fifth, and contains an account of the West Indies, their geography, climate, the
races who inhabited them, together with their animals and vegetable productions.
The subject was of great interest to the inquisitive minds of Europe, and one of
which they had previously gleaned but scanty information. In 1535, in a subsequent visit to Spain, Oviedo gave to the world the first volume of his great work,
which he had been many years in compiling,—the "Historia de las Indias Occidentales." In the same year, he was appointed by Charles the Fifth alcayde of the
fortress of Hispaniola. He continued in the island the ten following years, actively
engaged in the prosecution of his historical researches, and then returned for the
last time to his native land. The veteran scholar was well received at court, and
obtained the honorable appointment of Chronicler of the Indies. He occupied this
post until the period of his death, which took place at Valladolid in 1557, in the
seventy-ninth year of his age, at the very time when he was employed in preparing
the residue of his history for the press.

Considering the intimate footing on which Oviedo lived with the eminent persons of his time, it is singular that so little is preserved of his personal history
and his character. Nic. Antonio speaks of him as a "man of large experience, courteous in his manners, and of great probity." His long and active life is a sufficient
voucher for his experience, and one will hardly doubt his good breeding, when we
know the high society in which he moved. He left a large mass of manuscripts,
embracing a vast range both of civil and natural history. By far the most important is his *Historia General de las Indias*. It is divided into three parts, containing
fifty books. The first part, consisting of nineteen books, is the one already noticed
as having been published during his lifetime. It gives in a more extended form the
details of geographical and natural history embodied in his *Sumario*, with a narrative, moreover, of the discoveries and conquests of the Islands. A translation of
this portion of the work was made by the learned Ramusio, with whom Oviedo
was in correspondence, and is published in the third volume of his inestimable collection. The two remaining parts relate to the conquests of Mexico, of Peru, and
other countries of South America. It is that portion of the work consulted for these
pages. The manuscript was deposited, at his death, in the *Casa de la Contratacion*,
at Seville. It afterwards came into the possession of the Dominican monastery of
Monserrat. In process of time, mutilated copies found their way into several private
collections; when, in 1775, Don Francisco Cerda y Rico, an officer in the Indian
department, ascertained the place in which the original was preserved, and,
prompted by his literary zeal, obtained an order from the government for its publication. Under his supervision the work was put in order for the press, and Oviedo's
biographer, Alvarez y Baena, assures us that a complete edition of it, prepared with
the greatest care, would soon be given to the world. (Hijos de Madrid, (Madrid,
1790,) tom. II. pp. 354-361.) It still remains in manuscript.

No country has been more fruitful in the field of historical composition than Spain. Her ballads are chronicles done into verse. The chronicles themselves date from the twelfth and thirteenth centuries. Every city, every small town, every great family, and many a petty one, has its chronicler. These were often mere monkish chroniclers, who in the seclusion of the convent found leisure for literary occupation. Or, not unfrequently, they were men who had taken part in the affairs they described, more expert with the sword than with the pen. The compositions of this latter class have a general character of that indifference to fine writing, which shows a mind intent on the facts with which it is occupied, much more than on forms of expression. The monkish chroniclers, on the other hand, often make a pedantic display of obsolete erudition, which contrasts rather whimsically with the homely texture of the narrative. The chronicles of both the one and the other class of writers may frequently claim the merit of picturesque and animated detail, showing that the subject was one of living interest, and that the writer's heart was in his subject.

Many of the characteristic blemishes, of which I have been speaking, may be charged on Oviedo. His style is cast in no classic mould. His thoughts find themselves a vent in tedious, interminable sentences, that may fill the reader with despair; and the thread of the narrative is broken by impertinent episodes that lead to nothing. His scholarship was said to be somewhat scanty. One will hardly be led to doubt it, from the tawdry display of Latin quotations with which he garnishes his pages, like a poor gallant, who would make the most of his little store of finery. He affected to take the elder Pliny as his model, as appears from the preface to his *Sumario*. But his own work fell far short of the model of erudition and eloquence which that great writer of natural history has bequeathed to us.

Yet, with his obvious defects, Oviedo showed an enlightened curiosity, and a shrewd spirit of observation, which place him far above the ordinary range of chroniclers. He may even be said to display a philosophic tone in his reflections, though his philosophy must be regarded as cold and unscrupulous, wherever the rights of the Aborigines are in question. He was indefatigable in amassing materials for his narratives, and for this purpose maintained a correspondence with the most eminent men of his time, who had taken part in the transactions which he commemorates. He even condescended to collect information from more humble sources, from popular tradition and the reports of the common soldiers. Hence his work often presents a medley of inconsistent and contradictory details, which perplex the judgment, making it exceedingly difficult, at this distance of time, to disentangle the truth. It was, perhaps, for this reason, that Las Casas complimented the author by declaring, that "his works were a wholesale fabrication, as full of lies as of pages!" Yet another explanation of this severe judgment may be found in the different characters of the two men. Oviedo shared in the worldly feelings common to the Spanish Conquerors; and, while he was ever ready to magnify the exploits of his countrymen, held lightly the claims and the sufferings of the unfortunate Aborigines. He was incapable of appreciating the generous philanthropy of Las Casas, or of rising to his lofty views, which he doubtless derided as those of a benevolent, it might be, but visionary, fanatic. Las Casas, on the other hand, whose voice had been constantly uplifted against the abuses of the Conquerors, was filled with abhorrence at the sentiments avowed by Oviedo, and it was natural that his aversion to the principles should be extended to the person who professed them. Probably no two men could have been found less competent to form a right estimate of each other.

Oviedo showed the same activity in gathering materials for natural history, as he had done for the illustration of civil. He collected the different plants of the Islands in his garden, and domesticated many of the animals, or kept them in confinement under his eye, where he could study their peculiar habits. By this course, if he did not himself rival Pliny and Hernandez in science, he was, at least, enabled to furnish the man of science with facts of the highest interest and importance.

Besides these historical writings, Oviedo left a work in six volumes, called by the whimsical title of *Quincuagenas*. It consists of imaginary dialogues between the most eminent Spaniards of the time, in respect to their personal history, their families, and genealogy. It is a work of inestimable value to the historian of the times of Ferdinand and Isabella, and of Charles the Fifth. But it has attracted little attention in Spain, where it still remains in manuscript. A complete copy of Oviedo's History of the Indies is in the archives of the Royal Academy of History in Madrid, and it is understood that this body has now an edition prepared for the press. Such parts as are literally transcribed from preceding narratives, like the Letters of Cortés, which Oviedo transferred without scruple entire and unmutilated into his own pages, though enlivened, it is true, by occasional criticism of his own, might as well be omitted. But the remainder of the great work affords a mass of multifarious information which would make an important contribution to the colonial history of Spain.

An authority of frequent reference in these pages is Diego Muños Camargo. He was a noble Tlascalan *mestee,* and lived in the latter half of the sixteenth century. He was educated in the Christian faith, and early instructed in Castilian, in which tongue he composed his *Historia de Tlascala.* In this work he introduces the reader to the different members of the great Nahuatlac family, who came successively up the Mexican plateau. Born and bred among the Aborigines of the country, when the practices of the Pagan age had not wholly become obsolete, Camargo was in a position perfectly to comprehend the condition of the ancient inhabitants; and his work supplies much curious and authentic information respecting the social and religious institutions of the land at the time of the Conquest. His patriotism warms, as he recounts the old hostilities of his countrymen with the Aztecs, and it is singular to observe how the detestation of the rival nations survived their common subjection under the Castilian yoke.

Camargo embraces in his narrative an account of this great event, and of the subsequent settlement of the country. As one of the Indian family, we might expect to see his chronicle reflect the prejudices, or, at least, partialities, of the Indian. But the Christian convert yielded up his sympathies as freely to the Conquerors as to his own countrymen. The desire to magnify the exploits of the latter, and at the same time to do full justice to the prowess of the white men, produces occasionally a most whimsical contrast in his pages, giving the story a strong air of inconsistency. In point of literary execution the work has little merit; as great, however, as could be expected from a native Indian, indebted for his knowledge of the tongue to such imperfect instruction as he could obtain from the missionaries. Yet in style of composition it may compare not unfavorably with the writings of some of the missionaries themselves.

The original manuscript was long preserved in the convent of *San Felipe Neri* in Mexico, where Torquemada, as appears from occasional references, had access to it. It has escaped the attention of other historians, but was embraced by Muñoz in his magnificent collection, and deposited in the archives of the Royal Academy of History at Madrid; from which source the copy in my possession was obtained It bears the title of *Pedazo de Historia Verdadera,* and is without the author's name, and without division into books or chapters.

BOOK V

EXPULSION FROM MEXICO

CHAPTER I

DESPERATE ASSAULT ON THE QUARTERS—FURY OF THE MEXICANS—
SALLY OF THE SPANIARDS—MONTEZUMA ADDRESSES THE PEOPLE—
DANGEROUSLY WOUNDED

1520

THE palace of Axayacatl, in which the Spaniards were quartered, was, as the reader may remember, a vast, irregular pile of stone buildings, having but one floor, except in the centre, where another story was added, consisting of a suite of apartments which rose like turrets on the main building of the edifice. A vast area stretched around, encompassed by a stone wall of no great height. This was supported by towers or bulwarks at certain intervals, which gave it some degree of strength; not, indeed, as compared with European fortifications, but sufficient to resist the rude battering enginery of the Indians. The parapet had been pierced here and there with embrasures for the artillery, which consisted of thirteen guns; and smaller apertures were made in other parts for the convenience of the arquebusiers. The Spanish forces found accommodations within the great building; but the numerous body of Tlascalan auxiliaries could have had no other shelter than what was afforded by barracks or sheds hastily constructed for the purpose in the spacious court-yard. Most of them, probably, bivouacked under the open sky, in a climate milder than that to which they were accustomed among the rude hills of their native land. Thus crowded into a small and compact compass, the whole army could be assembled at a moment's notice; and, as the Spanish commander was careful to enforce the strictest discipline and vigilance, it was scarcely possible that he could be taken by surprise. No sooner, therefore, did the trumpet call to arms, as the approach of the enemy was announced, than every soldier was at his post, the cavalry mounted, the artillery-men at their guns, and the archers and arquebusiers stationed so as to give the assailants a warm reception

On they came, with the companies, or irregular masses, into which the multitude was divided, rushing forward each in its own dense column, with many a gay banner displayed, and many a bright gleam of light reflected from helmet, arrow, and spear-head, as they were tossed about in their disorderly array. As they drew near the inclosure, the Aztecs set up a hideous yell, or rather that shrill whistle used in fight by the nations of Anahuac, which rose far above the sound of shell and atabal, and their other rude instruments of warlike melody. They followed this by a tempest of missiles,—stones, darts, and arrows,—which fell thick as rain on the besieged, while volleys of the same kind descended from the crowded terraces in the neighborhood.[1]

The Spaniards waited until the foremost column had arrived within the best distance for giving effect to their fire, when a general discharge of artillery and arquebuses swept the ranks of the assailants, and mowed them down by hundreds.[2] The Mexicans were familiar with the report of these formidable engines, as they had been harmlessly discharged on some holiday festival; but never till now had they witnessed their murderous power. They stood aghast for a moment, as with bewildered looks they staggered under the fury of the fire; [3] but, soon rallying, the bold barbarians uttered a piercing cry, and rushed forward over the prostrate bodies of their comrades. A second and a third volley checked their career, and threw them into disorder, but still they pressed on, letting off clouds of arrows; while their comrades on the roofs of the houses took more deliberate aim at the combatants in the court-yard. The Mexicans were particularly expert in the use of the sling; [4] and the stones which they hurled from their elevated positions on the heads of their enemies did even greater execution than the arrows. They glanced, indeed, from the mail-covered bodies of the cavaliers, and from those who were sheltered under the cotton panoply, or *escaupil*. But some of the soldiers, especially the veterans of Cortés, and many of their Indian allies, had but slight defences, and suffered greatly under this stony tempest.

The Aztecs, meanwhile, had advanced close under the walls of the intrenchment; their ranks broken and disordered, and their limbs mangled by the unintermitting fire of the Christians. But they still pressed

---

[1] "Eran tantas las Piedras, que nos echaban con Hondas dentro en la Fortaleza que no parecia sino que el Cielo las llovia; é las Flechas, y Tiraderas eran tantas, que todas las paredes y Patios estaban llenos, que casi no podiamos andar con ellas." (Rel. Seg. de Cortés, ap. Lorenzana, p. 134.) No wonder that they should have found some difficulty in wading through the arrows, if Herrera's account be correct, that *forty cart-loads* of them were gathered up and burnt by the besieged every day! Hist. General, dec. 2, lib. 10, cap. 9.

[2] "Luego sin tardanza se juntáron los Mexicanos, en gran copia, puestos á punto de Guerra, que no parecia, sino que habian salido debajo de tierra todos juntos, y comenzáron luego á dar grita y pelear, y los Españoles les comenzáron á responder de dentro con toda la artillería que de nuebo habian traido, y con toda la gente que de nuevo habia venido, y los Españoles hiciéron gran destrozo en los Indios, con la artillería, arcabuzes, y ballestas y todo el otro artificio de pelear." (Sahagun, Hist. de Nueva España, MS., lib. 12, cap. 22.) The good father waxes eloquent in his description of the battle scene.

[3] The enemy presented so easy a mark, says Gomara, that the gunners loaded and fired with hardly the trouble of pointing their pieces. "Tan recio, que los artilleros sin asestar jugaban con los tiros." Crónica, cap. 106.

[4] "Hondas, que eran la mas fuerte arma de pelea que los Meji canos tenian." Camargo. Hist. de Tlascala. MS.

on, under the very muzzle of the guns. They endeavored to scale the parapet, which, from its moderate height, was in itself a work of no great difficulty. But the moment they showed their heads above the rampart, they were shot down by the unerring marksmen within, or stretched on the ground by a blow of a Tlascalan *maquahuitl*. Nothing daunted, others soon appeared to take the place of the fallen, and strove, by raising themselves on the writhing bodies of their dying comrades, or by fixing their spears in the crevices of the wall, to surmount the barrier. But the attempt proved equally vain.

Defeated here, they tried to effect a breach in the parapet by battering it with heavy pieces of timber. The works were not constructed on those scientific principles by which one part is made to overlook and protect another. The besiegers, therefore, might operate at their pleasure, with but little molestation from the garrison within, whose guns could not be brought into a position to bear on them, and who could mount no part of their own works for their defence, without exposing their persons to the missiles of the whole besieging army. The parapet, however, proved too strong for the efforts of the assailants. In their despair they endeavored to set the Christian quarters on fire, shooting burning arrows into them, and climbing up so as to dart their firebrands through the embrasures. The principal edifice was of stone. But the temporary defences of the Indian allies, and other parts of the exterior works, were of wood. Several of these took fire, and the flame spread rapidly among the light, combustible materials. This was a disaster for which the besieged were wholly unprepared. They had little water, scarcely enough for their own consumption. They endeavored to extinguish the flames by heaping on earth. But in vain. Fortunately the great building was of materials which defied the destroying element. But the fire raged in some of the outworks, connected with the parapet, with a fury which could only be checked by throwing down a part of the wall itself, thus laying open a formidable breach. This, by the general's order, was speedily protected by a battery of heavy guns, and a file of arquebusiers, who kept up an incessant volley through the opening on the assailants.[5]

The fight now raged with fury on both sides. The walls around the palace belched forth an unintermitting sheet of flame and smoke. The groans of the wounded and dying were lost in the fiercer battle-cries of the combatants, the roar of the artillery, the sharper rattle of the musketry, and the hissing sound of Indian missiles. It was the conflict of the European with the American; of civilized man with the barbarian; of the science of the one with the rude weapons and warfare of the other. And as the ancient walls of Tenochtitlan shook under the thunders

---

[5] "En la Fortaleza daban tan recio combate, que por muchas partes nos pusiéron fuego, y por la una se quemó mucha parte de ella, sin la poder remediar, hasta que la atajámos, cortando las paredes, y derrocando un pedazo que mató el fuego. É sí no fuera por la mucha Guarda, que allí puse de Escopeteros, y Ballesteros, y otros tiros de pólvora, nos entraran á escala vista, sin los poder resistir." Rel. Seg. de Cortés, ap. Lorenzana, p. 134.

of the artillery,—it announced that the white man, the destroyer, had set his foot within her precincts.[6]

Night at length came, and drew her friendly mantle over the contest. The Aztec seldom fought by night. It brought little repose, however, to the Spaniards, in hourly expectation of an assault; and they found abundant occupation in restoring the breaches in their defences, and in repairing their battered armor. The beleaguering host lay on their arms through the night, giving token of their presence, now and then, by sending a stone or shaft over the battlements, or by a solitary cry of defiance from some warrior more determined than the rest, till all other sounds were lost in the vague, indistinct murmurs which float upon the air in the neighborhood of a vast assembly.

The ferocity shown by the Mexicans seems to have been a thing for which Cortés was wholly unprepared. His past experience, his uninterrupted career of victory with a much feebler force at his command, had led him to underrate the military efficiency, if not the valor, of the Indians. The apparent facility, with which the Mexicans had acquiesced in the outrages on their sovereign and themselves, had led him to hold their courage, in particular, too lightly. He could not believe the present assault to be any thing more than a temporary ebullition of the populace, which would soon waste itself by its own fury. And he proposed, on the following day, to sally out and inflict such chastisement on his foes as should bring them to their senses, and show who was master in the capital.

With early dawn, the Spaniards were up and under arms; but not before their enemies had given evidence of their hostility by the random missiles, which, from time to time, were sent into the inclosure. As the grey light of morning advanced, it showed the besieging army far from being diminished in numbers, filling up the great square and neighboring avenues in more dense array than on the preceding evening. Instead of a confused, disorderly rabble, it had the appearance of something like a regular force, with its battalions distributed under their respective banners, the devices of which showed a contribution from the principal cities and districts in the Valley. High above the rest was conspicuous the ancient standard of Mexico, with its well known cognizance, an eagle pouncing on an ocelot, emblazoned on a rich mantle of featherwork. Here and there priests might be seen mingling in the ranks of the besiegers, and, with frantic gestures, animating them to avenge their insulted deities.

The greater part of the enemy had little clothing save the *maxtlatl*, or sash round the loins. They were variously armed, with long spears tipped with copper, or flint, or sometimes merely pointed and hardened in the fire. Some were provided with slings, and others with darts having two

[6] Ibid., ubi supra.—Gomara, Crónica, cap. 106.—Oviedo, Hist. de las Ind., MS., lib. 33, cap. 13.—Sahagun, Hist. de Nuevo España, MS., lib. 12, cap. 22.—Gonzalo de las Casas, Defensa, MS., Parte 1, cap. 26.—Bernal Diaz, Hist. de la Conquista, cap. 126.

or three points, with long strings attached to them, by which, when discharged, they could be torn away again from the body of the wounded. This was a formidable weapon, much dreaded by the Spaniards. Those of a higher order wielded the terrible *maquahuitl*, with its sharp and brittle blades of obsidian. Amidst the motley bands of warriors, were seen many whose showy dress and air of authority intimated persons of high military consequence. Their breasts were protected by plates of metal, over which was thrown the gay surcoat of feather-work. They wore casques resembling, in their form, the head of some wild and ferocious animal, crested with bristly hair, or overshadowed by tall and graceful plumes of many a brilliant color. Some few were decorated with the red fillet bound round the hair, having tufts of cotton attached to it, which denoted by their number that of the victories they had won, and their own preëminent rank among the warriors of the nation. The motley assembly plainly showed that priest, warrior, and citizen had all united to swell the tumult.

Before the sun had shot his beams into the Castilian quarters, the enemy were in motion, evidently preparing to renew the assault of the preceding day. The Spanish commander determined to anticipate them by a vigorous sortie, for which he had already made the necessary dispositions. A general discharge of ordnance and musketry sent death far and wide into the enemy's ranks, and, before they had time to recover from their confusion, the gates were thrown open, and Cortés, sallying out at the head of his cavalry, supported by a large body of infantry and several thousand Tlascalans, rode at full gallop against them. Taken thus by surprise, it was scarcely possible to offer much resistance. Those who did were trampled down under the horses' feet, cut to pieces with the broadswords, or pierced with the lances of the riders. The infantry followed up the blow, and the rout for the moment was general.

But the Aztecs fled only to take refuge behind a barricade, or strong work of timber and earth, which had been thrown across the great street through which they were pursued. Rallying on the other side, they made a gallant stand, and poured in turn a volley of their light weapons on the Spaniards, who, saluted with a storm of missiles at the same time, from the terraces of the houses, were checked in their career, and thrown into some disorder.[7]

Cortés, thus impeded, ordered up a few pieces of heavy ordnance, which soon swept away the barricades, and cleared a passage for the army. But it had lost the momentum acquired in its rapid advance. The enemy had time to rally and to meet the Spaniards on more equal terms. They were attacked in flank, too, as they advanced, by fresh battalions, who swarmed in from the adjoining streets and lanes. The canals were alive with boats filled with warriors, who, with their formidable darts searched every crevice or weak place in the armor of proof, and made havoc on the unprotected bodies of the Tlascalans. By repeated and vigorous charges, the Spaniards succeeded in driving the Indians before

[7] Carta del Exército, MS.

them; though many, with a desperation which showed they loved vengeance better than life, sought to embarrass the movements of their
horses by clinging to their legs, or, more successfully strove to pull the
riders from their saddles. And woe to the unfortunate cavalier who was
thus dismounted,—to be despatched by the brutal *maquahuitl*, or to be
dragged on board a canoe to the bloody altar of sacrifice!

But the greatest annoyance which the Spaniards endured was from the
missiles from the *azoteas*, consisting often of large stones, hurled with a
force that would tumble the stoutest rider from his saddle. Galled in the
extreme by these discharges, against which even their shields afforded no
adequate protection, Cortés ordered fire to be set to the buildings. This
was no very difficult matter, since, although chiefly of stone, they were
filled with mats, cane-work, and other combustible materials, which were
soon in a blaze. But the buildings stood separated from one another by
canals and drawbridges, so that the flames did not easily communicate
to the neighboring edifices. Hence, the labor of the Spaniards was incalculably increased, and their progress in the work of destruction—
fortunately for the city—was comparatively slow.[8] They did not relax
their efforts, however, till several hundred houses had been consumed,
and the miseries of a conflagration, in which the wretched inmates perished equally with the defenders, were added to the other horrors of the
scene.

The day was now far spent. The Spaniards had been everywhere victorious. But the enemy, though driven back on every point, still kept
the field. When broken by the furious charges of the cavalry, he soon
rallied behind the temporary defences, which, at different intervals, had
been thrown across the streets, and, facing about, renewed the fight
with undiminished courage, till the sweeping away of the barriers by
the cannon of the assailants left a free passage for the movements of
their horse. Thus the action was a succession of rallying and retreating,
in which both parties suffered much, although the loss inflicted on the
Indians was probably tenfold greater than that of the Spaniards. But
the Aztecs could better afford the loss of a hundred lives than their
antagonists that of one. And, while the Spaniards showed an array
broken, and obviously thinned in numbers, the Mexican army, swelled by
the tributary levies which flowed in upon it from the neighboring
streets, exhibited, with all its losses, no sign of diminution. At length,
sated with carnage, and exhausted by toil and hunger, the Spanish
commander drew off his men, and sounded a retreat.[9]

[8] Están todas en el agua, y de casa á casa vna puente leuadiza, passalla á nado, era
cosa muy peligrosa; porque desde las açuteas tirauan tanta piedra, y cantos, que era
cosa perdida ponernos en ello. Y demas desto, en algunas casas que les poniamos
fuego, tardaua vna casa é se quemar vn dia entero, y no se podia pegar fuego de vna
casa á otra; lo vno, por estar apartadas la vna de otra el agua en medio; y lo otro,
por ser de açuteas." Bernal Diaz, Hist. de la Conquista, cap. 126.

[9] "The Mexicans fought with such ferocity," says Diaz, "that, if we had had the
assistance on that day of ten thousand Hectors, and as many Orlandos, we should
have made no impression on them! There were several of our troops," he adds,

On his way back to his quarters, he beheld his friend, the secretary Duero, in a street adjoining, unhorsed, and hotly engaged with a body of Mexicans, against whom he was desperately defending himself with his poniard. Cortés, roused at the sight, shouted his war-cry, and, dash-ing into the midst of the enemy, scattered them like chaff by the fury of his onset; then, recovering his friend's horse, he enabled him to re-mount, and the two cavaliers, striking their spurs into their steeds, burst through their opponents and joined the main body of the army.[10] Such displays of generous gallantry were not uncommon in these en-gagements, which called forth more feats of personal adventure than battles with antagonists better skilled in the science of war. The chival-rous bearing of the general was emulated in full measure by Sandoval, De Leon, Olid, Alvarado, Ordaz, and his other brave companions, who won such glory under the eye of their leader, as prepared the way for the independent commands which afterwards placed provinces and kingdoms at their disposal.

The undaunted Aztecs hung on the rear of their retreating foes, annoy-ing them at every step by fresh flights of stones and arrows; and, when the Spaniards had reëntered their fortress, the Indian host encamped around it, showing the same dogged resolution as on the preceding eve-ning. Though true to their ancient habits of inaction during the night, they broke the stillness of the hour by insulting cries and menaces, which reached the ears of the besieged. "The gods have delivered you, at last, into our hands," they said; "Huitzilopotchli has long cried for his vic-tims. The stone of sacrifice is ready. The knives are sharpened. The wild beasts in the palace are roaring for their offal. And the cages," they added, taunting the Tlascalans with their leanness, "are waiting for the false sons of Anahuac, who are to be fattened for the festival!" These dismal menaces, which sounded fearfully in the ears of the besieged, who understood too well their import, were mingled with piteous lamenta-tions for their sovereign, whom they called on the Spaniards to deliver up to them.

Cortés suffered much from a severe wound which he had received in the hand in the late action. But the anguish of his mind must have been still greater, as he brooded over the dark prospect before him. He had mistaken the character of the Mexicans. Their long and patient endur-ance had been a violence to their natural temper, which, as their whole history proves, was arrogant and ferocious beyond that of most of the races of Anahuac. The restraint, which, in deference to their monarch, more than to their own fears, they had so long put on their natures, being

"who had served in the Italian wars, but neither there nor in the battles with the Turk had they ever seen any thing like the desperation shown by these Indians." Hist. de la Conquista, cap. 126.

See, also, for the last pages, Rel. Seg. de Cortés, ap. Lorenzana, p. 135,—Ixtlil-xochitl, Relaciones, MS.,—Probanza á pedimento de Juan de Lexalde, MS.,—Oviedo, Hist. de las Ind., MS., lib. 33, cap. 13,—Gomara, Crónica, cap. 196.

[10] Herrera, Hist. General, dec. 2, lib. 10, cap. 9.—Torquemada, Monarch. Ind. lib. 4, cap. 69.

once removed, their passions burst forth with accumulated violence. The Spaniards had encountered in the Tlascalan an open enemy, who had no grievance to complain of, no wrong to redress. He fought under the vague apprehension only of some coming evil to his country. But the Aztec, hitherto the proud lord of the land, was goaded by insult and injury, till he had reached that pitch of self-devotion, which made life cheap, in comparison with revenge. Armed thus with the energy of despair, the savage is almost a match for the civilized man; and a whole nation, moved to its depths by a common feeling, which swallows up all selfish considerations of personal interest and safety, becomes, whatever be its resources, like the earthquake and the tornado, the most formidable among the agencies of nature.

Considerations of this kind may have passed through the mind of Cortés, as he reflected on his own impotence to restrain the fury of the Mexicans, and resolved, in despite of his late supercilious treatment of Montezuma, to employ his authority to allay the tumult,—an authority so successfully exerted in behalf of Alvarado, at an earlier stage of the insurrection. He was the more confirmed in his purpose, on the following morning, when the assailants, redoubling their efforts, succeeded in scaling the works in one quarter, and effecting an entrance into the inclosure. It is true, they were met with so resolute a spirit, that not a man, of those who entered, was left alive. But, in the impetuosity of the assault, it seemed, for a few moments, as if the place was to be carried by storm.[11]

Cortés now sent to the Aztec emperor to request his interposition with his subjects in behalf of the Spaniards. But Montezuma was not in the humor to comply. He had remained moodily in his quarters ever since the general's return. Disgusted with the treatment he had received, he had still further cause for mortification in finding himself the ally of those who were the open enemies of his nation. From his apartment he had beheld the tragical scenes in his capital, and seen another, the presumptive heir to his throne, taking the place which he should have occupied at the head of his warriors, and fighting the battles of his country.[12] Distressed by his position, indignant at those who had placed him in it, he coldly answered, "What have I to do with Malinche? I do not wish to hear from him. I desire only to die. To what a state has my willingness to serve him reduced me!"[13] When urged still further to comply by Olid and father Olmedo, he added, "It is of no use. They will neither believe me, nor the false words and promises of Malinche. You will never

---

[11] Bernal Diaz, Hist. de la Conquista, cap. 126.—Oviedo, Hist. de las Ind., MS., lib. 33, cap. 13.—Gomara, Crónica, cap. 107.

[12] Cortés sent Marina to ascertain from Montezuma the name of the gallant chief, who could be easily seen from the walls animating and directing his countrymen. The emperor informed him that it was his brother Cuitlahua, the presumptive heir to his crown, and the same chief whom the Spanish commander had released a few days previous. Herrera, Hist. General, dec. 2, lib. 10, cap. 10.

[13] "¿Que quiere de mí ya Malinche, que yo no deseo viuir ni oille? pues en tal estado por su causa mi ventura me ha traido." Bernal Diaz, Hist. de la Conquista, cap. 126.

leave these walls alive." On being assured, however, that the Spaniards would willingly depart, if a way were opened to them by their enemies, he at length—moved, probably, more by a desire to spare the blood of his subjects, than of the Christians—consented to expostulate with his people.[14]

In order to give the greater effect to his presence, he put on his imperial robes. The *tilmatli*, his mantle of white and blue, flowed over his shoulders, held together by its rich clasp of the green *chalchivitl*. The same precious gem, with emeralds of uncommon size, set in gold, profusely ornamented other parts of his dress. His feet were shod with the golden sandals, and his brows covered by the *copilli*, or Mexican diadem, resembling in form the pontifical tiara. Thus attired, and surrounded by a guard of Spaniards and several Aztec nobles, and preceded by the golden wand, the symbol of sovereignty, the Indian monarch ascended the central turret of the palace. His presence was instantly recognised by the people, and, as the royal retinue advanced along the battlements, a change, as if by magic, came over the scene. The clang of instruments, the fierce cries of the assailants, were hushed, and a death-like stillness pervaded the whole assembly, so fiercely agitated, but a few moments before, by the wild tumult of war! Many prostrated themselves on the ground; others bent the knee; and all turned with eager expectation towards the monarch, whom they had been taught to reverence with slavish awe, and from whose countenance they had been wont to turn away as from the intolerable splendors of divinity! Montezuma saw his advantage; and, while he stood thus confronted with his awe-struck people, he seemed to recover all his former authority and confidence, as he felt himself to be still a king. With a calm voice, easily heard over the silent assembly, he is said by the Castilian writers to have thus addressed them.

"Why do I see my people here in arms against the palace of my fathers? Is it that you think your sovereign a prisoner, and wish to release him? If so, you have acted rightly. But you are mistaken. I am no prisoner. The strangers are my guests. I remain with them only from choice, and can leave them when I list. Have you come to drive them from the city? That is unnecessary. They will depart of their own accord, if you will open a way for them. Return to your homes, then. Lay down your arms. Show your obedience to me who have a right to it. The white men shall go back to their own land; and all shall be well again within the walls of Tenochtitlan."

As Montezuma announced himself the friend of the detested strangers, a murmur ran through the multitude; a murmur of contempt for the pusillanimous prince who could show himself so insensible to the insults and injuries for which the nation was in arms! The swollen tide of their passions swept away all the barriers of ancient reverence, and, taking a new direction, descended on the head of the unfortunate monarch, so far degenerated from his warlike ancestors. "Base Aztec," they exclaimed,

[14] Ibid., ubi supra.—Ixtlilxochitl, Hist. Chich., MS., cap. 88.

"woman, coward, the white men have made you a woman,—fit only to weave and spin!" These bitter taunts were soon followed by still more hostile demonstrations. A chief, it is said, of high rank, bent a bow or brandished a javelin with an air of defiance against the emperor,[15] when, in an instant, a cloud of stones and arrows descended on the spot where the royal train was gathered. The Spaniards appointed to protect his person had been thrown off their guard by the respectful deportment of the people during their lord's address. They now hastily interposed their bucklers. But it was too late. Montezuma was wounded by three of the missiles, one of which, a stone, fell with such violence on his head, near the temple, as brought him senseless to the ground. The Mexicans, shocked at their own sacrilegious act, experienced a sudden revulsion of feeling, and, setting up a dismal cry, dispersed panic-struck, in different directions. Not one of the multitudinous array remained in the great square before the palace!

The unhappy prince, meanwhile was borne by his attendants to his apartments below. On recovering from the insensibility caused by the blow, the wretchedness of his condition broke upon him. He had tasted the last bitterness of degradation. He had been reviled, rejected, by his people. The meanest of the rabble had raised their hands against him. He had nothing more to live for. It was in vain that Cortés and his officers endeavored to soothe the anguish of his spirit and fill him with better thoughts. He spoke not a word in answer. His wound, though dangerous, might still, with skilful treatment, not prove mortal. But Montezuma refused all the remedies prescribed for it. He tore off the bandages as often as they were applied, maintaining, all the while, the most determined silence. He sat with eyes dejected, brooding over his fallen fortunes, over the image of ancient majesty, and present humiliation. He had survived his honor. But a spark of his ancient spirit seemed to kindle in his bosom, as it was clear he did not mean to survive his disgrace.—From this painful scene the Spanish general and his followers were soon called away by the new dangers which menaced the garrison.[16]

[15] Acosta reports a tradition, that Guatemozin, Montezuma's nephew, who himself afterwards succeeded to the throne, was the man that shot the first arrow. Lib. 7, cap. 26.

[16] I have reported this tragical event, and the circumstances attending it, as they are given, in more or less detail, but substantially in the same way, by the most accredited writers of that and the following age,—several of them eyewitnesses. (See Bernal Diaz, Hist. de la Conquista, cap. 126.—Oviedo, Hist. de las Ind., MS., lib. 33, cap. 47.—Rel. Seg. de Cortés, ap. Lorenzana, p. 136.—Camargo, Hist. de Tlascala, MS.—Ixtlilxochitl, Hist. Chich., MS., cap. 88.—Herrera, Hist. General, dec. 2, lib. 10, cap. 10.—Torquemada, Monarch, Ind., lib. 4, cap. 70.—Acosta, ubi supra.—Martyr, De Orbe Novo, dec. 5, cap. 5.) It is also confirmed by Cortés in the instrument granting to Montezuma's favorite daughter certain estates by way of dowry. Don Thoan Cano, indeed, who married this princess, assured Oviedo that the Mexicans respected the person of the monarch so long as they saw him, and were not aware, when they discharged their missiles, that he was present, being hid from sight by the shields of the Spaniards. This improbable statement is repeated by the chaplain Gomara. (Crónica, cap. 107.) It is rejected by Oviedo, however, who says, that Alvarado, himself present at the scene, in a conversation with him after-

wards, explicitly confirmed the narrative given in the text. (Hist. de las Ind., Ms, lib. 33, cap. 47.) The Mexicans gave a very different account of the transaction. According to them, Montezuma, together with the lords of Tezcuco and Tlatelolco, then detained as prisoners in the fortress by the Spaniards, were all strangled by means of the *garrote*, and their dead bodies thrown over the walls to their countrymen. I quote the original of father Sahagun, who gathered the story from the Aztecs themselves.

"De esta manera se determináron los Españoles á morir ó vencer varonilmente; y así habláron á todos los amigos Indios, y todos ellos estuviéron firmes en esta determinacion: y lo primero que hiciéron fué que diéron garrote á todos los Señores que tenian presos, y los echáron muertos fuera del fuerte: y antes que esto hiciesen les dijéron muchas cosas, y les hiciéron saber su determinacion, y que de ellos habia de comenzar esta obra, y luego todos los demas habian de ser muertos á sus manos, dijéronles, no es posible que vuestros Ídolos os libren de nuestras manos. Y desque les hubiéron dado Garrote, y viéron que estaban muertos, mandáronlos echar por las azoteas, fuera de la casa, en un lugar que se llama Tortuga de Piedra, porque alli estaba una piedra labrada á manera de Tortuga. Y desque supiéron y viéron los de á fuera, que aquellos Señores tan principales habian sido muertos por las manos de los Españoles, luego tomáron los cuerpos, y les hiciéron sus exequias, al modo de su Idolatría, y quemáron sus cuerpos, y tomáron sus cenizas, y las pusiéron en lugares apropiadas á sus dignidades y valor." Hist. de Nueva España, MS., lib. 12, cap. 23.

It is hardly necessary to comment on the absurdity of this monstrous imputation, which, however, has found favor with some later writers. Independently of all other considerations, the Spaniards would have been slow to compass the Indian monarch's death, since, as the Tezcucan Ixtlilxochitl truly observes, it was the most fatal blow which could befall them, by dissolving the last tie which held them to the Mexicans. Hist. Chich., MS., ubi supra.

STORMING OF THE GREAT TEMPLE—SPIRIT OF THE AZTECS—DISTRESSES OF THE GARRISON—SHARP COMBATS IN THE CITY—DEATH OF MONTEZUMA

1520

OPPOSITE to the Spanish quarters, at only a few rods' distance, stood the great *teocalli* of Huitzilopotchli. This pyramidal mound, with the sanctuaries that crowned it, rising altogether to the height of near a hundred and fifty feet, afforded an elevated position that completely commanded the palace of Axayacatl, occupied by the Christians. A body of five or six hundred Mexicans, many of them nobles and warriors of the highest rank, had got possession of the *teocalli*, whence they discharged such a tempest of arrows on the garrison, that no one could leave his defences for a moment without imminent danger; while the Mexicans, under shelter of the sanctuaries, were entirely covered from the fire of the besieged. It was obviously necessary to dislodge the enemy, if the Spaniards would remain longer in their quarters.

Cortés assigned this service to his chamberlain, Escobar, giving him a hundred men for the purpose, with orders to storm the *teocalli*, and set fire to the sanctuaries. But that officer was thrice repulsed in the attempt, and, after the most desperate efforts, was obliged to return with considerable loss, and without accomplishing his object.

Cortés, who saw the immediate necessity of carrying the place, determined to lead the storming party himself. He was then suffering much from the wound in his left hand, which had disabled it for the present. He made the arm serviceable, however, by fastening his buckler to it,[1] and, thus crippled, sallied out at the head of three hundred chosen cavaliers, and several thousand of his auxiliaries.

In the court-yard of the temple he found a numerous body of Indians prepared to dispute his passage. He briskly charged them, but the flat, smooth stones of the pavement were so slippery, that the horses lost their footing, and many of them fell. Hastily dismounting, they sent back the animals to their quarters, and, renewing the assault, the Spaniards succeeded without much difficulty in dispersing the Indian warriors, and opening a free passage for themselves to the *teocalli*. This building, as

---

[1] "Salí fuera de la Fortaleza, aunque manco de la mano izquierda de una herida que el primer dia me habian dado: y liada la rodela en el brazo fuý á la Torre con algunos Españoles, que me siguiéron." Rel. Seg. de Cortés, ap. Lorenzana, p. 138.

the reader may remember, was a huge pyramidal structure, about three hundred feet square at the base. A flight of stone steps on the outside, at one of the angles of the mound, led to a platform, or terraced walk, which passed round the building until it reached a similar flight of stairs directly over the preceding, that conducted to another landing as before. As there were five bodies or divisions of the *teocalli*, it became necessary to pass round its whole extent four times, or nearly a mile, in order to reach the summit, which, it may be recollected, was an open area, crowned only by the two sanctuaries dedicated to the Aztec deities.[2]

Cortés, having cleared a way for the assault, sprang up the lower stair-way, followed by Alvarado, Sandoval, Ordaz, and the other gallant cavaliers of his little band, leaving a file of arquebusiers and a strong corps of Indian allies to hold the enemy in check at the foot of the monument. On the first landing, as well as on the several galleries above, and on the summit, the Aztec warriors were drawn up to dispute his passage. From their elevated position they showered down volleys of lighter missiles, together with heavy stones, beams, and burning rafters, which, thundering along the stairway, overturned the ascending Spaniards, and carried desolation through their ranks. The more fortunate, eluding or springing over these obstacles, succeeded in gaining the first terrace; where, throwing themselves on their enemies, they compelled them, after a short resistance, to fall back. The assailants pressed on, effectually supported by a brisk fire of the musketeers from below, which so much galled the Mexicans in their exposed situation, that they were glad to take shelter on the broad summit of the *teocalli*.

Cortés and his comrades were close upon their rear, and the two parties soon found themselves face to face on this aërial battle-field, engaged in mortal combat in presence of the whole city, as well as of the troops in the court-yard, who paused, as if by mutual consent, from their own hostilities, gazing in silent expectation on the issue of those above. The area, though somewhat smaller than the base of the *teocalli*, was large enough to afford a fair field of fight for a thousand combatants. It was paved with broad, flat stones. No impediment occurred over its surface, except the huge sacrificial block, and the temples of stone which rose to the height of forty feet, at the further extremity of the arena. One of these had been consecrated to the Cross. The other was still occupied by the Mexican war-god. The Christian and the Aztec contended for their religions under the very shadow of their respective shrines; while the Indian priests, running to and fro, with their hair wildly streaming over their sable mantles, seemed hovering in mid air, like so many demons of darkness urging on the work of slaughter!

The parties closed with the desperate fury of men who had no hope but in victory. Quarter was neither asked nor given; and to fly was im-

---

[2] See Ante, pp. 332-334.

I have ventured to repeat the description of the temple here, as it is important that the reader, who may perhaps not turn to the preceding pages, should have a distinct image of it in his own mind, before beginning the combat.

possible. The edge of the area was unprotected by parapet or battlement. The least slip would be fatal; and the combatants, as they struggled in mortal agony, were sometimes seen to roll over the sheer sides of the precipice together.[3] Cortés himself is said to have had a narrow escape from this dreadful fate. Two warriors, of strong, muscular frames, seized on him, and were dragging him violently towards the brink of the pyramid. Aware of their intention, he struggled with all his force, and, before they could accomplish their purpose, succeeded in tearing himself from their grasp, and hurling one of them over the walls with his own arm! The story is not improbable in itself, for Cortés was a man of uncommon agility and strength. It has been often repeated; but not by contemporary history.[4]

The battle lasted with unintermitting fury for three hours. The number of the enemy was double that of the Christians; and it seemed as if it were a contest which must be determined by numbers and brute force, rather than by superior science. But it was not so. The invulnerable armor of the Spaniard, his sword of matchless temper, and his skill in the use of it, gave him advantages which far outweighed the odds of physical strength and numbers. After doing all that the courage of despair could enable men to do, resistance grew fainter and fainter on the side of the Aztecs. One after another they had fallen. Two or three priests only survived to be led away in triumph by the victors. Every other combatant was stretched a corpse on the bloody arena, or had been hurled from the giddy heights. Yet the loss of the Spaniards was not inconsiderable. It amounted to forty-five of their best men, and nearly all the remainder were more or less injured in the desperate conflict.[5]

[3] Many of the Aztecs, according to Sahagun, seeing the fate of such of their comrades as fell into the hands of the Spaniards, on the narrow terrace below, voluntarily threw themselves headlong from the lofty summit and were dashed in pieces on the pavement. "Y los de arriba viendo á los de abajo muertos, y á los de arriba que los iban matando los que habian subido, comenzáron á arrojarse del cu abajo, desde lo alto, los cuales todos morian despeñados, quebrados brazos y piernas, y hechos pedazos, porque el cu era muy alto; y otros los mesmos Españoles los arrojaban de lo alto del cu, y así todos cuantos allá habian subido de los Mexicanos, muriéron mala muerte." Sahagun, Hist. de Nueva España, MS., lib. 12, cap. 22.

[4] Among others, see Herrera, Hist. General, dec. 2, lib. 10, cap. 9,—Torquemada, Monarch. Ind., lib. 4, cap. 69,—and Solís, very circumstantially, as usual, Conquista, lib. 4, cap. 16.

The first of these authors had access to some contemporary sources the chronicle of the old soldier, Ojeda, for example, not now to be met with. It is strange, that so valiant an exploit should not have been communicated by Cortés himself, who cannot be accused of diffidence in such matters.

[5] Captain Diaz, a little loth sometimes, is emphatic in his encomiums on the valor shown by his commander on this occasion. "Aquí se mostró Cortés mui varō, como siēpre lo fué. O que pelear, y fuerte batalla q̃ aquí tuuímos! era cosa de notar vernos á todos corriendo sangre, y llenos de heridas, é mas de quarenta soldados muertos." (Hist. de la Conquista, cap. 126.) The pens of the old chroniclers keep pace with their swords in the display of this brilliant exploit;—"colla penna e colla spada," equally fortunate. See Rel. Seg. de Cortés, ap. Lorenzana, p. 138.—Gomara, Crónica, cap. 106.—Sahagun, Hist. de Nueva España, MS., lib. 12, cap. 22.—Herrera, Hist. General, dec. 2, lib. 10, cap. 9.—Oviedo, Hist. de las Ind., MS., lib. 33, cap. 13.—Torquemada, Monarch. Ind., lib. 4, cap. 6ᶜ

The victorious cavaliers now rushed towards the sanctuaries. The lower story was of stone; the two upper were of wood. Penetrating into their recesses, they had the mortification to find the image of the Virgin and the Cross removed.[6] But in the other edifice they still beheld the grim figure of Huitzilopotchli, with his censer of smoking hearts, and the walls of his oratory reeking with gore,—not improbably of their own countrymen! With shouts of triumph the Christians tore the uncouth monster from his niche, and tumbled him, in the presence of the horror-struck Aztecs, down the steps of the *teocalli*. They then set fire to the accursed building. The flames speedily ran up the slender towers, sending forth an ominous light over city, lake, and valley, to the remotest hut among the mountains. It was the funeral pyre of Paganism, and proclaimed the fall of that sanguinary religion which had so long hung like a dark cloud over the fair regions of Anahuac![7]

Having accomplished this good work, the Spaniards descended the winding slopes of the *teocalli* with more free and buoyant step, as if conscious that the blessing of Heaven now rested on their arms. They passed through the dusky files of Indian warriors in the court-yard, too much dismayed by the appalling scenes they had witnessed to offer resistance; and reached their own quarters in safety. That very night they followed up the blow by a sortie on the sleeping town, and burned three hundred houses, the horrors of conflagration being made still more impressive by occurring at the hour when the Aztecs, from their own system of warfare, were least prepared for them.[8]

Hoping to find the temper of the natives somewhat subdued by these reverses, Cortés now determined, with his usual policy, to make them a vantage-ground for proposing terms of accommodation. He accordingly invited the enemy to a parley, and, as the principal chiefs, attended by their followers, assembled in the great square, he mounted the turret before occupied by Montezuma, and made signs that he would address

[6] Archbishop Lorenzana is of opinion that this image of the Virgin is the same now seen in the church of *Nuestra Señora de los Remedios!* (Rel. Seg. de Cortés, ap. Lorenzana, p. 138, nota.) In what way the Virgin survived the sack of the city, and was brought to light again, he does not inform us. But the more difficult to explain, the more undoubted the miracle.

[7] No achievement in the war struck more awe into the Mexicans, than this storming of the great temple, in which the white men seemed to bid defiance equally to the powers of God and man. Hieroglyphical paintings minutely commemorating it were to be frequently found among the natives after the Conquest. The sensitive Captain Diaz intimates that those which he saw made full as much account of the wounds and losses of the Christians as the facts would warrant. (Ibid., ubi supra.) It was the only way in which the conquered could take their revenge.

[8] "Sequenti nocte, nostri erumpentes in vna viarum arci vicina, domos combussêre tercentum: in altera plerasque e quibus acri molestia fiebat. Ita nunc trucidando, nunc diruendo, et interdum vulnera recipiendo, in pontibus et in viis, diebus noctibusque multis laboratum est utrinque." (Martyr, De Orbe Novo, dec. 5, cap. 6.) In the number of actions and their general result, namely, the victories, barren victories, of the Christians, all writers are agreed. But as to time, place, circumstance, or order, no two hold together. How shall the historian of the present day make a harmonious tissue out of these motley and many-colored threads?

them. Marina, as usual, took her place by his side, as his interpreter. The multitude gazed with earnest curiosity on the Indian girl, whose influence with the Spaniards was well known, and whose connection with the general, in particular, had led the Aztecs to designate him by her Mexican name of Malinche.[9] Cortés, speaking through the soft, musical tones of his mistress, told his audience they must now be convinced, that they had nothing further to hope from opposition to the Spaniards. They had seen their gods trampled in the dust, their altars broken, their dwellings burned, their warriors falling on all sides. "All this," continued he, "you have brought on yourselves by your rebellion. Yet for the affection the sovereign, whom you have so unworthily treated, still bears you, I would willingly stay my hand, if you will lay down your arms, and return once more to your obedience. But, if you do not," he concluded, "I will make your city a heap of ruins, and leave not a soul alive to mourn over it!"

But the Spanish commander did not yet comprehend the character of the Aztecs, if he thought to intimidate them by menaces. Calm in their exterior and slow to move, they were the more difficult to pacify when roused; and now that they had been stirred to their inmost depths, it was no human voice that could still the tempest. It may be, however, that Cortés did not so much misconceive the character of the people. He may have felt that an authoritative tone was the only one he could assume with any chance of effect, in his present position, in which milder and more conciliatory language would, by intimating a consciousness of inferiority, have too certainly defeated its own object.

It was true, they answered, he had destroyed their temples, broken in pieces their gods, massacred their countrymen. Many more, doubtless, were yet to fall under their terrible swords. But they were content so long as for every thousand Mexicans they could shed the blood of a single white man! [10] "Look out," they continued, "on our terraces and streets, see them still thronged with warriors as far as your eyes can reach. Our numbers are scarcely diminished by our losses. Yours, on the contrary, are lessening every hour. You are perishing from hunger and sickness. Your provisions and water are falling. You must soon fall into our hands. *The bridges are broken down, and you cannot escape!* [11] There will be too few of you left to glut the vengeance of our Gods!" As they concluded, they sent a volley of arrows over the battlements, which compelled the Spaniards to descend and take refuge in their defences.

The fierce and indomitable spirit of the Aztecs filled the besieged with

[9] It is the name by which she is still celebrated in the popular minstrelsy of Mexico. Was the famous Tlascalan mountain, *sierra de Malinche,*—anciently "Mattalcueye,"—named in compliment to the Indian damsel? At all events, it was an honor well merited from her adopted countrymen.

[10] According to Cortés, they boasted, in somewhat loftier strain, they could spare twenty-five thousand for one, "á morir veinte y cinco mil de ellos, y uno de los nuestros." Rel. Seg. de Cortés, ap. Lorenzana, p. 139.

[11] "Que todas las calzadas de las entradas de la ciudad eran deshechas, como de hecho passaba." Ibid., loc. cit.—Oviedo, Hist. de las Ind., MS., iib. 33, cap. 13.

dismay. All, then, that they had done and suffered, their battles by day, their vigils by night, the perils they had braved, even the victories they had won, were of no avail. It was too evident that they had no longer the spring of ancient superstition to work upon, in the breasts of the natives, who, like some wild beast that has burst the bonds of his keeper, seemed now to swell and exult in the full consciousness of their strength. The annunciation respecting the bridges fell like a knell on the ears of the Christians. All that they had heard was too true,—and they gazed on one another with looks of anxiety and dismay.

The same consequences followed, which sometimes take place among the crew of a shipwrecked vessel. Subordination was lost in the dreadful sense of danger. A spirit of mutiny broke out, especially among the recent levies drawn from the army of Narvaez. They had come into the country from no motive of ambition, but attracted simply by the glowing reports of its opulence, and they had fondly hoped to return in a few months with their pockets well lined with the gold of the Aztec monarch. But how different had been their lot! From the first hour of their landing, they had experienced only trouble and disaster, privations of every description, sufferings unexampled, and they now beheld in perspective a fate yet more appalling. Bitterly did they lament the hour when they left the sunny fields of Cuba for these cannibal regions! And heartily did they curse their own folly in listening to the call of Velasquez, and still more, in embarking under the banner of Cortés! [12]

They now demanded with noisy vehemence to be led instantly from the city, and refused to serve longer in defence of a place where they were cooped up like sheep in the shambles, waiting only to be dragged to slaughter. In all this they were rebuked by the more orderly, soldier-like conduct of the veterans of Cortés. These latter had shared with their general the day of his prosperity, and they were not disposed to desert him in the tempest. It was, indeed, obvious, on a little reflection, that the only chance of safety, in the existing crisis, rested on subordination and union; and that even this chance must be greatly diminished under any other leader than their present one.

Thus pressed by enemies without and by factions within, that leader was found, as usual, true to himself. Circumstances so appalling, as would have paralyzed a common mind, only stimulated his to higher action, and drew forth all its resources. He combined what is most rare, singular coolness and constancy of purpose, with a spirit of enterprise that might well be called romantic. His presence of mind did not now desert him. He calmly surveyed his condition, and weighed the difficulties which surrounded him, before coming to a decision. Independently of the hazard of a retreat in the face of a watchful and desperate foe, it was a deep mortification to surrender up the city, where he had so long

[12] "Pues tambien quiero dezir las maldiciones que los de Narvaez echauan á Cortés, y las palabras que dezian, que renegauan dél, y de la tierra, y aun de Diego Velasquez, que acá les embió, que bien pacíficos estauan en sus casas en la Isla de Cuba, y estavan embelesados, y sin sentido." Bernal Diaz, Hist. de la Conquista, ubi supra.

lorded it as a master; to abandon the rich treasures which he had secured to himself and his followers; to forego the very means by which he hoped to propitiate the favor of his sovereign, and secure an amnesty for his irregular proceedings. This, he well knew, must, after all, be dependent on success. To fly now was to acknowledge himself further removed from the conquest than ever. What a close was this to a career so auspiciously begun! What a contrast to his magnificent vaunts! What a triumph would it afford to his enemies! The governor of Cuba would be amply revenged.

But, if such humiliating reflections crowded on his mind, the alternative of remaining, in his present crippled condition, seemed yet more desperate.[13] With his men daily diminishing in strength and numbers, their provisions reduced so low that a small daily ration of bread was all the sustenance afforded to the soldier under his extraordinary fatigues,[14] with the breaches every day widening in his feeble fortifications, with his ammunition, in fine, nearly expended, it would be impossible to maintain the place much longer—and none but men of iron constitutions and tempers, like the Spaniards, could have held it out so long—against the enemy. The chief embarrassment was as to the time and manner in which it would be expedient to evacuate the city. The best route seemed to be that of Tlacopan (Tacuba). For the causeway, the most dangerous part of the road, was but two miles long in that direction, and would, therefore, place the fugitives, much sooner than either of the other great avenues, on terra firma. Before his final departure, however, he proposed to make another sally in that direction, in order to reconnoitre the ground, and, at the same time, divert the enemy's attention from his real purpose by a show of active operations.

For some days, his workmen had been employed in constructing a military machine of his own invention. It was called a *manta*, and was contrived somewhat on the principle of the mantelets used in the wars of the Middle Ages. It was, however, more complicated, consisting of a tower made of light beams and planks, having two chambers, one over the other. These were to be filled with musketeers, and the sides were provided with loop-holes, through which a fire could be kept up on the enemy. The great advantage proposed by this contrivance was, to afford a defence to the troops against the missiles hurled from the terraces. These machines, three of which were made, rested on rollers, and were provided with strong ropes, by which they were to be dragged along the streets by the Tlascalan auxiliaries.[15]

[13] Notwithstanding this, in the petition or letter from Vera Cruz, addressed by the army to the Emperor Charles V., after the Conquest, the importunity of the soldiers is expressly stated as the principal motive that finally induced their general to abandon the city. Carta del Exército, MS.

[14] "La hambre era tanta, que á los Indios no se daba mas de *vna Tortilla de racion, i á los Castellanos cinquenta granos de Maiz.*" Herrera, Hist. General, dec. 2, lib. 10, cap. 9.

[15] Rel. Seg. de Cortés, ap. Lorenzana, p. 135.—Gomara, Crónica, cap. 106

Dr. Bird, in his picturesque romance of "Calavar," has made good use of these

The Mexicans gazed with astonishment on this warlike machinery, and, as the rolling fortresses advanced, belching forth fire and smoke from their entrails, the enemy, incapable of making an impression on those within, fell back in dismay. By bringing the *mantas* under the walls of the houses, the Spaniards were enabled to fire with effect on the mischievous tenants of the *azoteas*, and when this did not silence them, by letting a ladder, or light drawbridge, fall on the roof from the top of the *manta*, they opened a passage to the terrace, and closed with the combatants hand to hand. They could not, however, thus approach the higher buildings, from which the Indian warriors threw down such heavy masses of stone and timber as dislodged the planks that covered the machines, or, thundering against their sides, shook the frail edifices to their foundation, threatening all within with indiscriminate ruin. Indeed, the success of the experiment was doubtful, when the intervention of a canal put a stop to their further progress.

The Spaniards now found the assertion of their enemies too well confirmed. The bridge which traversed the opening had been demolished; and, although the canals which intersected the city were, in general, of no great width or depth, the removal of the bridges not only impeded the movements of the general's clumsy machines, but effectually disconcerted those of his cavalry. Resolving to abandon the *mantas*, he gave orders to fill up the chasm with stone, timber, and other rubbish drawn from the ruined buildings, and to make a new passage-way for the army. While this labor was going on, the Aztec slingers and archers on the other side of the opening kept up a galling discharge on the Christians, the more defenceless from the nature of their occupation. When the work was completed, and a safe passage secured, the Spanish cavaliers rode briskly against the enemy, who, unable to resist the shock of the steel-clad column, fell back with precipitation to where another canal afforded a similar strong position for defence.[16]

There were no less than seven of these canals, intersecting the great street of Tlacopan,[17] and at every one the same scene was renewed, the Mexicans making a gallant stand, and inflicting some loss, at each, on

mantas, better, indeed, than can be permitted to the historian. He claims the privilege of the romancer; though it must be owned he does not abuse this privilege, for he has studied with great care the costume, manners, and military usages of the natives. He has done for them what Cooper has done for the wild tribes of the North, —touched their rude features with the bright coloring of a poetic fancy. He has been equally fortunate in his delineation of the picturesque scenery of the land. If he has been less so in attempting to revive the antique dialogue of the Spanish cavalier, we must not be surprised. Nothing is more difficult than the skilful execution of a modern antique. It requires all the genius and learning of Scott to execute it so that the connoisseur shall not detect the counterfeit.

[16] Carta del Exército, MS.—Rel. Seg. de Cortés, ap. Lorenzana, p. 140.—Gomara Crónica, cap. 109.

[17] Clavigero is mistaken in calling this the street of Iztapalapan. (Stor. del Messico, tom. III., p. 120.) It was not the street by which the Spaniards entered, but by which they finally left the city, and is correctly indicated by Lorenzana, as that of Tlacopan,—or rather, Tacuba, into which the Spaniards corrupted the name. See p 140, note.

their persevering antagonists. These operations consumed two days, when, after incredible toil, the Spanish general had the satisfaction to find the line of communication completely reëstablished through the whole length of the avenue, and the principal bridges placed under strong detachments of infantry. At this juncture, when he had driven the foe before him to the furthest extremity of the street, where it touches on the causeway, he was informed, that the Mexicans, disheartened by their reverses, desired to open a parly with him respecting the terms of an accommodation, and that their chiefs awaited his return for that purpose at the fortress. Overjoyed at the intelligence, he instantly rode back, attended by Alvarado, Sandoval, and about sixty of the cavaliers, to his quarters.

The Mexicans proposed that he should release the two priests captured in the temple, who might be the bearers of his terms, and serve as agents for conducting the negotiation. They were accordingly sent with the requisite instructions to their countrymen. But they did not return. The whole was an artifice of the enemy, anxious to procure the liberation of their religious leaders, one of whom was their *teoteuctli*, or high-priest, whose presence was indispensable in the probable event of a new coronation.

Cortés, meanwhile, relying on the prospects of a speedy arrangement, was hastily taking some refreshment with his officers, after the fatigues of the day; when he received the alarming tidings, that the enemy were in arms again, with more fury than ever; that they had overpowered the detachments posted under Alvarado at three of the bridges, and were busily occupied in demolishing them. Stung with shame at the facility with which he had been duped by his wily foe, or rather by his own sanguine hopes, Cortés threw himself into the saddle, and, followed by his brave companions, galloped back at full speed to the scene of action. The Mexicans recoiled before the impetuous charge of the Spaniards. The bridges were again restored; and Cortés and his chivalry rode down the whole extent of the great street, driving the enemy, like frightened deer, at the points of their lances. But, before he could return on his steps, he had the mortification to find that the indefatigable foe, gathering from the adjoining lanes and streets, had again closed on his infantry, who, worn down by fatigue, were unable to maintain their position at one of the principal bridges. New swarms of warriors now poured in on all sides, overwhelming the little band of Christian cavaliers with a storm of stones, darts, and arrows, which rattled like hail on their armor and on that of their well-barbed horses. Most of the missiles, indeed, glanced harmless from the good panoplies of steel, or thick quilted cotton, but, now and then, one better aimed penetrated the joints of the harness, and stretched the rider on the ground.

The confusion became greater around the broken bridge. Some of the horsemen were thrown into the canal, and their steeds floundered wildly about without a rider. Cortés himself, at this crisis, did more than any other to cover the retreat of his followers. While the bridge was repairing, he plunged boldly into the midst of the barbarians, striking down an enemy at every vault of his charger, cheering on his own men, and spreading terror through the ranks of his opponents by the well-known sound of his battle-cry. Never did he display greater hardihood, or more freely expose his person, emulating, says an old chronicler, the feats of the Roman Cocles.[18] In this way he stayed the tide of assailants, till the last man had crossed the bridge, when, some of the planks having given way, he was compelled to leap a chasm of full six feet in width, amidst a cloud of missiles, before he could place himself in safety.[19] A report ran through the army that the general was slain. It soon spread through the city, to the great joy of the Mexicans, and reached the fortress, where the besieged were thrown into no less consternation. But, happily for them, it was false. He, indeed, received two severe contusions on the knee, but in other respects remained uninjured. At no time, however, had he been in such extreme danger; and his escape, and that of his companions, was esteemed little less than a miracle. More than one grave historian refers the preservation of the Spaniards to the watchful care of their patron Apostle, St. James, who, in these desperate conflicts, was beheld careering on his milk-white steed at the head of the Christian squadrons, with his sword flashing lightning, while a lady robed in white—supposed to be the Virgin—was distinctly seen by his side, throwing dust in the eyes of the infidel! The fact is attested both by Spaniards and Mexicans,—by the latter after their conversion to Christianity. Surely, never was there a time when the interposition of their tutelar saint was more strongly demanded.[20]

---

[18] It is Oviedo who finds a parallel for his hero in the Roman warrior; the same, to quote the spirit-stirring legend of Macaulay,

"who kept the bridge so well
In the brave days of old."

"Mui digno es Cortés que se compare este fecho suyo desta jornada al de Oracio Cocles, que se tocó de suso, porque con su esfuerzo, é lanza sola dió tanto lugar, que los caballos pudieran pasar, é hizo desembarazar la puente é pasó, á pesar de los Enemigos, aunque con harto trabajo." Hist. de las Ind., MS., lib. 33, cap. 13.

[19] It was a fair leap, for a knight and horse in armor. But the general's own assertion to the Emperor (Rel. Seg., ap. Lorenzana, p. 142) is fully confirmed by Oviedo, who tells us he had it from several who were present. "Y segun lo que yo he entendido de algunos que presentes se hallárn, demas de la resistencia de aquellos havia de la vna parte á la otra casi vn estado de saltar con el caballo sin le faltar muchas pedradas de diversas partes, é manos, é por ir él, é su caballo bien armados no los hiriérn; pero no dexó de quedar atormentado de los golpes que le diéron." Hist. de las Ind., MS., ubi supra.

[20] Truly, "dignus vindice nodus"! The intervention of the celestial chivalry on these occasions is testified in the most unqualified manner by many respectable authorities. It is edifying to observe the combat going on in Oviedo's mind between the dictates of strong sense and superior learning, and those of the superstition of the age. It was an unequal combat, with odds sorely against the former, in the sixteenth century. I quote the passage as characteristic of the times. "Afirman que se vido el Apóstol Santiago á caballo peleando sobre vn caballo blanco en favor de los Christianos; é decian los Indios que el caballo con los pies y manos é con la boca mataba muchos dellos, de forma, que en poco discurso de tiempo no pareció Indio, é reposáron los Christianos lo restante de aquel dia. Ya sé que los incrédulos ó poco

The coming of night dispersed the Indian battalions, which, vanishing like birds of ill omen from the field, left the well-contested pass in possession of the Spaniards. They returned, however, with none of the joyous feelings of conquerors to their citadel, but with slow step and dispirited, with weapons hacked, armor battered, and fainting under the loss of blood, fasting, and fatigue. In this condition they had yet to learn the tidings of a fresh misfortune in the death of Montezuma.[21]

The Indian monarch had rapidly declined, since he had received his injury, sinking, however, quite as much under the anguish of a wounded spirit, as under disease. He continued in the same moody state of insensibility as that already described; holding little communication with those around him, deaf to consolation, obstinately rejecting all medical remedies as well as nourishment. Perceiving his end approach, some of the cavaliers present in the fortress, whom the kindness of his manners had personally attached to him, were anxious to save the soul of the dying prince from the sad doom of those who perish in the darkness of unbelief. They accordingly waited on him, with father Olmedo at their head, and in the most earnest manner implored him to open his eyes to the error of his creed, and consent to be baptized. But Montezuma—whatever may have been suggested to the contrary—seems never to have faltered in his hereditary faith, or to have contemplated becoming an apostate; for surely he merits that name in its most odious application, who, whether Christian or pagan, renounces his religion without conviction of its falsehood.[22] Indeed, it was a too implicit reliance on its oracles, which had led him to give such easy confidence to the Spaniards. His intercourse with them had, doubtless, not sharpened his desire to embrace their communion; and the calamities of his country he might consider as sent by his

---

devotos dirán, que mi ocupacion en esto destos miraglos, pues no los ví, es superflua, ó perder tiempo novelando, y yo hablo, que esto é mas se puede creer; pues que los gentiles é sin fé, é Idólatras escriben, que ovo grandes misterios é miraglos en sus tiempos, é aquellos sabemos que eran causados é fechos por el Diablo, pues mas fácil cosa es á Dios é á la inmaculata Vírgin Nuestra Señor é al glorioso Apóstol Santiago, é á los santos é amigos de Jesu Christo hacer esos miraglos, que de suso estan dichos, é otros maiores." Hist. de las Ind., MS., lib. 33, cap. 47.

[21] "Multi restiterunt lapidibus et iaculis confossi, fuit et Cortesius grauiter percussus, pauci eva serunt incolumes, et hi adeò languidi, vt neque lacertos erigere quirent. Postquam vero se in arcem receperunt, non commodè satis conditas dapes, quibus reficerentur, inuenerunt, nec fortè asperi maiicii panis bucellas, aut aquam potabilem, de vino aut carnibus sublata erat cura." (Martyr, De Orbe Novo, dec. 5, cap. 6.) See also, for the hard fighting in the last pages, Oviedo, Hist. de las Ind., MS., lib. 33, cap. 13,—Rel. Seg. de Cortés, ap. Lorenzana, pp. 140-142,—Carta del Exército, MS.,—Gonzalo de las Casas, Defensa, MS., Parte 1. cap. 26,—Herrera, Hist. General, dec. 2, lib. 10, cap. 9, 10,—Gomara Crónica, cap. 107.

[22] The sentiment is expressed with singular energy in the verses of Voltaire;
"Mais renoncer aux dieux que l'on croit dans son cœur,
C'est le crime d'un lâche, et non pas une erreur;
C'est trahir à la fois, sous un masque hypocrite,
Et le dieu qu'on préfère, et le dieu que l'on quitte:
C'est mentir au Ciel même, à l'univers, à soi."
ALZIRE, Acte 5, sc. 5.

gods to punish him for his hospitality to those who had desecrated and destroyed their shrines.[23]

When father Olmedo, therefore, kneeling at his side, with the uplifted crucifix, affectionately besought him to embrace the sign of man's redemption, he coldly repulsed the priest, exclaiming, "I have but a few moments to live; and will not at this hour desert the faith of my fathers." [24] One thing, however, seemed to press heavily on Montezuma's mind. This was the fate of his children, especially of three daughters, whom he had by his two wives; for there were certain rites of marriage, which distinguished the lawful wife from the concubine. Calling Cortés to his bedside, he earnestly commended these children to his care, as "the most precious jewels that he could leave him." He besought the general to interest his master, the emperor, in their behalf, and to see that they should not be left destitute, but be allowed some portion of their rightful inheritance. "Your lord will do this," he concluded, "if it were only for the friendly offices I have rendered the Spaniards, and for the love I have shown them,—though it has brought me to this condition! But for this I bear them no ill-will." [25] Such, according to Cortés himself, were the

[23] Camargo, the Tlascalan convert, says, he was told by several of the Conquerors, that Montezuma was baptized at his own desire in his last moments, and that Cortés and Alvarado stood sponsors on the occasion. "Muchos afirman de los conquistadores que yo conocì, que estando en el artículo de la muerte, pidió agua de batismo é que fué batizado y murió Cristiano, aunque en esto hay grandes dudas y diferentes paresceres; mas como digo que de personas fidedignas conquistadores de los primeros desta tierra de quien fuimos informados, supímos que murió batizado y Cristiano, é que fuéron sus padrinos del batismo Fernando Cortés y Don Pedro de Alvarado." (Hist. de Tlascala, MS.) According to Gomara, the Mexican monarch desired to be baptized before the arrival of Narvaez. The ceremony was deferred till Easter, that it might be performed with greater effect. But in the hurry and bustle of the subsequent scenes it was forgotten, and he died without the stain of infidelity having been washed away from him. (Crónica, cap. 107.) Torquemada, not often a Pyrrhonist where the honor of the faith is concerned, rejects these tales as irreconcilable with the subsequent silence of Cortés himself, as well as of Alvarado, who would have been loud to proclaim an event so long in vain desired by them. (Monarch. Ind., lib. 4, cap. 70.) The criticism of the father is strongly supported by the fact, that neither of the preceding accounts is corroborated by writers of any weight, while they are contradicted by several, by popular tradition, and, it may be added, by one another.

[24] "Respondió, Que por la media hora que le quedaba de vida, no se queria apartar de la religion de sus Padres." (Herrera, Hist. General, dec. 2, lib. 10, cap. 10.) "Ya he dicho," says Diaz, "la tristeza que todos nosotros huví, mos por ello, y aun al Frayle de la Merced, que siempre estaua con él, y no le pudo atraer á que so bolviesse Christiano." Hist. de la Conquista, cap. 127.

[25] *Aunque no le pesaba dello;* literally, "although he did not repent of it." But this would be rather too much for human nature to assert; and it is probable the language of the Indian prince underwent some little change, as it was sifted through the interpretation of Marina. The Spanish reader will find the original conversation, as reported by Cortés himself, in the remarkable document (*Appendix, Part 2, No.* 12).—The general adds, that he faithfully complied with Montezuma's request, receiving his daughters, after the Conquest, into his own family, where, *agreeably to their royal father's desire, they were baptized,* and instructed in the doctrines and usages of the Christian faith. They were afterwards married to Castilian hidalgos, and handsome dowries were assigned them by the government. See note 36 of this Chapter.

words of the dying monarch. Not long after, on the 30th of June, 1520,[26] he expired in the arms of some of his own nobles, who still remained faithful in their attendance on his person. "Thus," exclaims a native historian, one of his enemies, a Tlascalan, "thus died the unfortunate Montezuma, who had swayed the sceptre with such consummate policy and wisdom; and who was held in greater reverence and awe than any other prince of his lineage, or any, indeed, that ever sat on a throne in this Western World. With him may be said to have terminated the royal line of the Aztecs, and the glory to have passed away from the empire, which under him had reached the zenith of its prosperity." [27] "The tidings of his death," says the old Castilian chronicler, Diaz, "were received with real grief by every cavalier and soldier in the army who had had access to his person; for we all loved him as a father,—and no wonder, seeing how good he was." [28] This simple, but emphatic, testimony to his desert, at such a time, is in itself the best refutation of the suspicions occasionally entertained of his fidelity to the Christians.[29]

[26] I adopt Clavigero's chronology, which cannot be far from truth. (Stor. del Messico, tom. III. p. 131.) And yet there are reasons for supposing he must have died at least a day sooner.

[27] "De suerte que le tiráron una pedrada con una honda y le diéron en la cabeza de que vino á morir el desdichado Rey, habiendo gobernado este nuevo Mundo con la mayor prudencia y gobierno que se puede imaginar, siendo el mas tenido y reverenciado y adorado Señor que en el mundo ha habido, y en su linaje, como es cosa pública y notoria en toda la maquina deste Nuevo Mundo, donde con la muerte de tan gran Señor se acabáron los Reyes Culhuaques Mejicanos, y todo su poder y mando, estando en la mayor felicidad de su monarquía; y ansí no hay de que fiar en las cosas desta vida sino en solo Dios." Hist. de Tlascala, MS.

[28] "Y Cortés lloró por él, y todos nuestros Capitanes, y soldados: é hombres huvo entre nosotros de los que le conociamos, y tratauamos, que tan llorado fué, como si fuera nuestro padre, y no nos hemos de maravillar dello, viendo que tan bueno era." Hist. de la Conquista, cap. 126.

[29] "He loved the Christians," says Herrera, "as well as could be judged from appearances." (Hist. General, dec. 2, lib. 10, cap. 10.) "They say," remarks the general's chaplain, "that Montezuma, though often urged to it, never consented to the death of a Spaniard, nor to the injury of Cortés, whom he loved exceedingly. But there are those who dispute this." (Gomara, Crónica, cap. 107.) Don Thoan Cano assured Oviedo, that, during all the troubles of the Spaniards with the Mexicans, both in the absence of Cortés, and after his return, the emperor did his best to supply the camp with provisions. And finally, Cortés himself, in an instrument already referred to, dated six years after Montezuma's death, bears emphatic testimony to the good-will he had shown to Spaniards, and particularly acquits him of any share in the late rising, which, says the Conqueror, "I had trusted to suppress through his assistance."

The Spanish historians, in general,—notwithstanding an occasional intimation of a doubt as to his good faith towards their countrymen,—make honorable mention of the many excellent qualities of the Indian prince. Solís, however, the most eminent of all, dismisses the account of his death with the remark, that "his last hours were spent in breathing vengeance and maledictions against his people; until he surrendered up to Satan—with whom he had frequent communication in his lifetime —the eternal possession of his soul!" (Conquista de México, lib. 4, cap. 15.) Fortunately, the historiographer of the Indians could know as little of Montezuma's fate in the next world, as he appears to have known of it in this. Was it bigotry, or a desire to set his own hero's character in a brighter light, which led him thus unworthily to darken that of his Indian rival?

It is not easy to depict the portrait of Montezuma in its true colors, since it has been exhibited to us under two aspects, of the most opposite and contradictory character. In the accounts gathered of him by the Spaniards, on coming into the country, he was uniformly represented as bold and warlike, unscrupulous as to the means of gratifying his ambition, hollow and perfidious, the terror of his foes, with a haughty bearing which made him feared even by his own people. They found him, on the contrary, not merely affable and gracious, but disposed to waive all the advantages of his own position, and to place them on a footing with himself; making their wishes his law; gentle even to effeminacy in his deportment, and constant in his friendship, while his whole nation was in arms against them.—Yet these traits, so contradictory, were truly enough drawn. They are to be explained by the extraordinary circumstances of his position.

When Montezuma ascended the throne, he was scarcely twenty-three years of age. Young, and ambitious of extending his empire, he was continually engaged in war, and is said to have been present himself in nine pitched battles.[30] He was greatly renowned for his martial prowess, for he belonged to the *Quachictin,* the highest military order of his nation, and one into which but few even of its sovereigns had been admitted.[31] In later life, he preferred intrigue to violence, as more consonant to his character and priestly education. In this he was as great an adept as any prince of his time, and, by arts not very honorable to himself, succeeded in filching away much of the territory of his royal kinsman of Tezcuco. Severe in the administration of justice, he made important reforms in the arrangement of the tribunals. He introduced other innovations in the royal household, creating new offices, introducing a lavish magnificence and forms of courtly etiquette unknown to his ruder predecessors. He was, in short, most attentive to all that concerned the exterior and pomp of royalty.[32] Stately and decorous, he was careful of his own dignity, and might be said to be as great an "actor of majesty" among the barbarian potentates of the New World, as Louis the Fourteenth was among the polished princes of Europe.

He was deeply tinctured, moreover, with that spirit of bigotry, which threw such a shade over the latter days of the French monarch. He received the Spaniards as the beings predicted by his oracles. The anxious dread, with which he had evaded their proffered visit, was founded on the same feelings which led him so blindly to resign himself to them on their approach. He felt himself rebuked by their superior genius. He at once

---

[30] "Dicen que venció nueve Batallas, i otros nueve Campos, en desafío vno á vno." Gomara, Crónica, cap. 107.

[31] One other only of his predecessors, Tizoc, is shown by the Aztec Paintings to have belonged to this knightly order, according to Clavigero. Stor. del Messico, tom II. p. 140.

[32] "Era mas cauteloso, y ardidoso, que valeroso. En las Armas, y modo de su govierno, fué muy justiciero; en las cosas tocantes á ser estimado y tenido en su Dignidad y Majestad Real de condicion muy severo, aunque cuerdo y gracioso." Ixtlilxochitl, Hist. Chich., MS., cap. 88.

conceded all that they demanded,—his treasures, his power, even his person. For their sake, he forsook his wonted occupations, his pleasures, his most familiar habits. He might be said to forego his nature; and, as his subjects asserted, to change his sex and become a woman. If we cannot refuse our contempt for the pusillanimity of the Aztec monarch, it should be mitigated by the consideration, that his pusillanimity sprung from his superstition, and that superstition in the savage is the substitute for religious principle in the civilized man.

It is not easy to contemplate the fate of Montezuma without feelings of the strongest compassion;—to see him thus borne along the tide of events beyond his power to avert or control; to see him, like some stately tree, the pride of his own Indian forests, towering aloft in the pomp and majesty of its branches, by its very eminence a mark for the thunderbolt, the first victim of the tempest which was to sweep over its native hills! When the wise king of Tezcuco addressed his royal relative at his coronation, he exclaimed, "Happy the empire, which is now in the meridian of its prosperity, for the sceptre is given to one whom the Almighty has in his keeping; and the nations shall hold him in reverence!" [33] Alas! the subject of this auspicious invocation lived to see his empire melt away like the winter's wreath; to see a strange race drop as it were, from the clouds on his land; to find himself a prisoner in the palace of his fathers, the companion of those who were the enemies of his gods and his people; to be insulted, reviled, trodden in the dust, by the meanest of his subjects, by those who, a few months previous, had trembled at his glance; drawing his last breath in the halls of the stranger,—a lonely outcast in the heart of his own capital! He was the sad victim of destiny,—a destiny as dark and irresistible in its march, as that which broods over the mythic legends of Antiquity! [34]

Montezuma at the time of his death, was about forty-one years old, of which he reigned eighteenth. His person and manners have been already described. He left a numerous progeny by his various wives, most of whom, having lost their consideration after the Conquest, fell into obscurity, as they mingled with the mass of the Indian population.[35] Two of them, however, a son and a daughter, who embraced Christianity, became founders of noble houses in Spain.[36] The government, willing to show its

[33] The whole address is given by Torquemada, Monarch. Ind., lib. 4, cap. 68.

[34] "Τέχνη δ' ἀνάγκης ἀσθενεστέρα μακρῷ.
Τίς οὖν ἀνάγκης ἐστὶν οἰακοστρόφος;
Μοῖραι τρίμορφοι, μνήμονές τ' Ἐρινύες.
Τούτων ἄρ' ὁ Ζεύς ἐστιν ἀσθενέστερος;
Οὔκουν ἂν ἐκφύγοι γε τὴν πεπρωμένην."
ÆSCHYL., Prometh., v. 514-518.

[35] Señor de Calderon, the late Spanish minister at Mexico, informs me, that he has more than once passed by an Indian dwelling, where the Indians in his suite made a reverence, saying it was occupie by a descendant of Montezuma.

[36] This son, baptized by the name of Pedro, was descended from one of the royal concubines. Montezuma had two lawful wives. By the first of these, named Teçalco, he had a son, who perished in the flight from Mexico; and a daughter named Tecuichpo, who embraced Christianity, and received the name of Isabella. She was

gratitude for the large extent of empire derived from their ancestor, conferred on them ample estates and important hereditary honors; and the Counts of Montezuma and Tula, intermarrying with the best blood of Castile, intimated by their names and titles their illustrious descent from the royal dynasty of Mexico.[37]

Montezuma's death was a misfortune to the Spaniards. While he lived, they had a precious pledge in their hands, which, in extremity, they might possibly have turned to account. Now the last link was snapped which connected them with the natives of the country. But independently of interested feelings, Cortés and his officers were much affected by his death from personal considerations, and, when they gazed on the cold remains of the ill-starred monarch, they may have felt a natural compunction, as they contrasted his late flourishing condition with that to which his friendship for them had now reduced him.

The Spanish commander showed all respect for his memory. His body, arrayed in its royal robes, was laid decently on a bier, and borne on the shoulders of his nobles to his subjects in the city. What honors, if any, indeed, were paid to his remains, is uncertain. A sound of wailing, distinctly heard in the western quarters of the capital, was interpreted by the Spaniards into the moans of a funeral procession, as it bore the body to be laid among those of his ancestors, under the princely shades of

married, when very young to her cousin Guatemozin; and lived long enough after his death to give her hand to three Castilians, all of honorable family. From two of these, Don Pedro Gallejo, and Don Thoan Cano, descended the illustrious families of the Andrada and Cano Montezuma.

Montezuma, by his second wife, the princess Acatlan, left two daughters, named, after their conversion, Maria and Leonor. The former died without issue. Doña Leonor married with a Spanish cavalier, Cristóval de Valderrama, from whom descended the family of the Sotelos de Montezuma. To which of these branches belonged the counts of Miravalle, noticed by Humboldt, (Essai Politique, tom. II. p. 73, note,) I am ignorant.

The royal genealogy is minutely exhibited in a Memorial, setting forth the claims of Montezuma's grandsons to certain property in right of their respective mothers. The document, which is without date, is among the MSS. of Muñoz.

[37] It is interesting to know that a descendant of the Aztec emperor, Don Joseph Sarmiento Valladares, Count of Montezuma, ruled as viceroy, from 1697 to 1701, over the dominions of his barbaric ancestors. (Humboldt, Essai Politique, tom. II. p. 93, note.) Solís speaks of this noble house, grandees of Spain, who intermingled their blood with that of the Guzmans and the Mendozas. Clavigero has traced their descent from the emperor's son Iohualicahua, or Don Pedro Montezuma, as he was called after his baptism, down to the close of the eighteenth century. (See Solís, Conquista, lib. 4, cap. 15.—Clavigero, Stor. del Messico, tom. I. p. 302, tom. III. p. 132.) The last of the line, of whom I have been able to obtain any intelligence, died not long since in this country. He was very wealthy, having large estates in Spain,—but was not, as it appears, very wise. When seventy years old or more, he passed over to Mexico, in the vain hope, that the nation, in deference to his descent, might place him on the throne of his Indian ancestors, so recently occupied by the presumptuous Iturbide. But the modern Mexicans, with all their detestation of the old Spaniards, showed no respect for the royal blood of the Aztecs. The unfortunate nobleman retired to New Orleans, where he soon after put an end to his existence by blowing out his brains,—not for ambition, however, if report be true, but disappointed love!

Chapoltepec.[38] Others state, that it was removed to a burial-place in the city named Copalco and there burnt with the usual solemnities and signs of lamentation by his chiefs, but not without some unworthy insults from the Mexican populace.[39] Whatever be the fact, the people, occupied with the stirring scenes in which they were engaged, were probably not long mindful of the monarch, who had taken no share in their late patriotic movements. Nor is it strange that the very memory of his sepulchre should be effaced in the terrible catastrophe which afterwards over-whelmed the capital, and swept away every landmark from its surface.

[38] Gomara, Crónica, cap. 107.—Herrera, Hist. General, dec. 2, lib. 10, cap. 10.
[39] Torquemada, Monarch. Ind., lib. 4, cap. 7.

CHAPTER III

COUNCIL OF WAR—SPANIARDS EVACUATE THE CITY—NOCHE TRISTE, OR
"THE MELANCHOLY NIGHT"—TERRIBLE SLAUGHTER—HALT FOR
THE NIGHT—AMOUNT OF LOSSES

1520

THERE was no longer any question as to the expediency of evacuating
the capital. The only doubt was as to the time of doing so, and the route.
The Spanish commander called a council of officers to deliberate on these
matters. It was his purpose to retreat on Tlascala, and in that capital to
decide according to circumstances on his future operations. After some
discussion, they agreed on the causeway of Tlacopan as the avenue by
which to leave the city. It would, indeed, take them back by a circuitous
route, considerably longer than either of those by which they had approached the capital. But, for that reason, it would be less likely to be
guarded, as least suspected; and the causeway itself, being shorter than
either of the other entrances, would sooner place the army in comparative security on the main land.

There was some difference of opinion in respect to the hour of departure. The day-time, it was argued by some, would be preferable, since it
would enable them to see the nature and extent of their danger, and to
provide against it. Darkness would be much more likely to embarrass
their own movements than those of the enemy, who were familiar with
the ground. A thousand impediments would occur in the night, which
might prevent their acting in concert, or obeying, or even ascertaining,
the orders of the commander. But, on the other hand, it was urged, that
the night presented many obvious advantages in dealing with a foe who
rarely carried his hostilities beyond the day. The late active operations
of the Spaniards had thrown the Mexicans off their guard, and it was improbable they would anticipate so speedy a departure of their enemies.
With celerity and caution, they might succeed, therefore, in making their
escape from the town, possibly over the causeway, before their retreat
should be discovered; and, could they once get beyond that pass of peril,
they felt little apprehension for the rest.

These views were fortified it is said, by the counsels of a soldier named
Botello, who professed the mysterious science of judicial astrology. He
had gained credit with the army by some predictions which had been verified by the events; those lucky hits which make chance pass for calcula-

tion with the credulous multitude.[1] This man recommended to his countrymen by all means to evacuate the place in the night, as the hour most propitious to them, although he should perish in it. The event proved the astrologer better acquainted with his own horoscope than with that of others.[2]

It is possible Botello's predictions had some weight in determining the opinion of Cortés. Superstition was the feature of the age, and the Spanish general, as we have seen, had a full measure of its bigotry. Seasons of gloom, moreover, dispose the mind to a ready acquiescence in the marvellous. It is, however, quite as probable that he made use of the astrologer's opinion, finding it coincided with his own, to influence that of his men, and inspire them with higher confidence. At all events, it was decided to abandon the city that very night.

The general's first care was to provide for the safe transportation of the treasure. Many of the common soldiers had converted their share of the prize, as we have seen, into gold chains, collars, or other ornaments, which they easily carried about their persons. But the royal fifth, together with that of Cortés himself, and much of the rich booty of the principal cavaliers, had been converted into bars and wedges of solid gold and deposited in one of the strong apartments of the palace. Cortés delivered the share belonging to the Crown to the royal officers, assigning them one of the strongest horses, and a guard of Castilian soldiers, to transport it.[3] Still, much of the treasure, belonging both to the Crown and to individuals, was necessarily abandoned, from the want of adequate means of conveyance. The metal lay scattered in shining heaps along the floor, exciting the cupidity of the soldiers. "Take what you will of it," said Cortés to his men. "Better you should have it, than these Mexican hounds.[4]

---

[1] Oviedo, Hist. de las Ind., MS., lib. 33, cap. 47.

The astrologer predicted that Cortés would be reduced to the greatest extremity of distress, and afterwards come to great honor and fortune. (Bernal Diaz, Hist. de la Conquista, cap. 128.) He showed himself as cunning in his art, as the West Indian sybil who foretold the destiny of the unfortunate Josephine.

[2] "Pues al astrólogo Botello, no le aprouechó su astrología, que tambien allí murió." Ibid., ubi supra.

[3] The disposition of the treasure has been stated with some discrepancy, though all agree as to its ultimate fate. The general himself did not escape the imputation of negligence, and even peculation, most unfounded, from his enemies. The account in the text is substantiated by the evidence, under oath, of the most respectable names in the expedition, as given in the instrument already more than once referred to. "Hizo sacar el oro é joyas de sus Altezas é le dió é entregó á los otros oficiales, Alcaldes é Regidores, é les dixo á la rason que así se lo entregó, que todos viesen el mejor modo é manera que habia para lo poder salvar, que él allí estaba para por su parte hacer lo que fuese posible é poner su persona á qualquier trance é riesgo que sobre lo salvar le viniese. . . . . . El qual les dió para ello una muy buena yegua, é quatro ó cinco Españoles de mucha confianza, á quien se encargó la dha yegua cargado con el otro oro." Probanza á pedimento de Juan de Lexalde.

[4] "Desde aquí se o doi, como se ha de quedar aquí perdido entre estos perros." Bernal Diaz, Hist. de la Conquista, cap. 128.—Oviedo, Hist. de las Ind., MS., lib. 33, cap. 47.

But be careful not to overload yourselves. He travels safest in the dark night who travels lightest." His own more wary followers took heed to his counsel, helping themselves to a few articles of least bulk, though, it might be, of greatest value.[5] But the troops of Narvaez, pining for riches, of which they had heard so much, and hitherto seen so little, showed no such discretion. To them it seemed as if the very mines of Mexico were turned up before them, and, rushing on the treacherous spoil, they greed-ily loaded themselves with as much of it, not merely as they could accom-modate about their persons, but as they could stow away in wallets, box-es, or any other mode of conveyance at their disposal.[6]

Cortés next arranged the order of march. The van, composed of two hundred Spanish foot, he placed under the command of the valiant Gon-zalo de Sandoval, supported by Diego de Ordaz, Francisco de Lujo, and about twenty other cavaliers. The rear-guard, constituting the strength of the infantry, was intrusted to Pedro de Alvarado, and Velasquez de Leon. The general himself took charge of the "battle," or centre, in which went the baggage, some of the heavy guns, most of which, however, re-mained in the rear, the treasure, and the prisoners. These consisted of a son and two daughters of Montezuma, Cacama, the deposed lord of Tezcuco, and several other nobles, whom Cortés retained as important pledges in his future negotiations with the enemy. The Tlascalans were distributed pretty equally among the three divisions; and Cortés had un-der his immediate command a hundred picked soldiers, his own veterans most attached to his service, who, with Christóval de Olid, Francisco de Morla, Alonso de Avila, and two or three other cavaliers, formed a select corps, to act wherever occasion might require.

The general had already superintended the construction of a portable bridge to be laid over the open canals in the causeway. This was given in charge to an officer named Magarino, with forty soldiers under his orders, all pledged to defend the passage to the last extremity. The bridge was to be taken up when the entire army had crossed one of the breaches, and transported to the next. There were three of these openings in the cause-way, and most fortunate would it have been for the expedition, if the foresight of the commander had provided the same number of bridges. But the labor would have been great, and time was short.[7]

At midnight the troops were under arms, in readiness for the march. Mass was performed by father Olmedo, who invoked the protection of the Almighty through the awful perils of the night. The gates were thrown open, and, on the first of July, 1520, the Spaniards for the last

---

[5] Captain Diaz tells us, that he contented himself with four *chalchivitl*,—the green stone so much prized by the natives,—which he cunningly picked out of the royal coffers before Cortés' majordomo had time to secure them. The prize proved of great service, by supplying him the means of obtaining food and medicine, when in great extremity, afterwards, from the people of the country. Ibid., loc. cit.

[6] Oviedo, Hist. de las Ind., MS., ubi supra.

[7] Gomara, Crónica, cap. 109.—Re.. Seg. de Cortés, ap. Lorenzana, p. 143.—Oviedo, Hist. de las Ind., MS., lib. 33, cap. 13, 47.

time sallied forth from the walls of the ancient fortress, the scene of so much suffering and such indomitable courage.[8]

The night was cloudy, and a drizzling rain, which fell without inter mission, added to the obscurity. The great square before the palace was deserted, as, indeed, it had been since the fall of Montezuma. Steadily, and as noiselessly as possible, the Spaniards held their way along the great street of Tlacopan, which so lately had resounded to the tumult of battle. All was now hushed in silence; and they were only reminded of the past by the occasional presence of some solitary corpse, or a dark heap of the slain, which too plainly told where the strife had been hottest. As they passed along the lanes and alleys which opened into the great street, or looked down the canals, whose polished surface gleamed with a sort of ebon lustre through the obscurity of night, they easily fancied that they discerned the shadowy forms of their foe lurking in ambush, and ready to spring on them. But it was only fancy; and the city slept undisturbed even by the prolonged echoes of the tramp of the horses, and the hoarse rumbling of the artillery and baggage trains. At length, a lighter space beyond the dusky line of buildings showed the van of the army that it was emerging on the open causeway. They might well have congratulated themselves on having thus escaped the dangers of an as-sault in the city itself, and that a brief time would place them in compar-ative safety on the opposite shore.—But the Mexicans were not all asleep.

As the Spaniards drew near the spot where the street opened on the causeway, and were preparing to lay the portable bridge across the un-covered breach, which now met their eyes, several Indian sentinels, who had been stationed at this, as at the other approaches to the city, took the alarm, and fled, rousing their countrymen by their cries. The priests, keeping their night watch on the summit of the *teocallis*, instantly caught the tidings and sounded their shells, while the huge drum in the desolate temple of the war-god sent forth those solemn tones, which, heard only in seasons of calamity, vibrated through every corner of the capital. The Spaniards saw that no time was to be lost. The bridge was brought for-ward and fitted with all possible expedition. Sandoval was the first to try its strength, and, riding across, was followed by his little body of chiv-alry, his infantry, and Tlascalan allies, who formed the first division of the army. Then came Cortés and his squadrons, with the baggage, ammu-nition wagons, and a part of the artillery. But before they had time to de-

[8] There is some difficulty in adjusting the precise date of their departure, as, in-deed, of most events in the Conquest; attention to chronology being deemed some-what superfluous by the old chroniclers. Ixtlilxochitl, Gomara, and others fix the date at July 10th. But this is wholly contrary to the letter of Cortés, which states, that the army reached Tlascala on the eighth of July, not the tenth, as Clavigero misquotes him; (Stor. del Messico, tom. III. pp. 135, 136, nota;) and from the general's accurate account of their progress each day, it appears that they left the capital on the last night of June, or rather the morning of July 1st. It was the night, he also adds, following the affair of the bridges in the city. Comp. Rel. Seg., ap. Lorenzana, pp. 142-149

tle across the narrow passage, a gathering sound was heard, like that of a mighty forest agitated by the winds. It grew louder and louder, while on the dark waters of the lake was heard a plashing noise, as of many oars. Then came a few stones and arrows striking at random among the hurrying troops. They fell every moment faster and more furious, till they thickened into a terrible tempest, while the very heavens were rent with the yells and war-cries of myriads of combatants, who seemed all at once to be swarming over land and lake!

The Spaniards pushed steadily on through this arrowy sleet, though the barbarians, dashing their canoes against the sides of the causeway, clambered up and broke in upon their ranks. But the Christians, anxious only to make their escape, declined all combat except for self-preservation. The cavaliers, spurring forward their steeds, shook off their assailants, and rode over their prostrate bodies, while the men on foot with their good swords or the butts of their pieces drove them headlong again down the sides of the dike.

But the advance of several thousand men, marching, probably, on a front of not more than fifteen or twenty abreast, necessarily required much time, and the leading files had already reached the second breach in the causeway before those in the rear had entirely traversed the first. Here they halted; as they had no means of effecting a passage, smarting all the while under unintermitting volleys from the enemy, who were clustered thick on the waters around this second opening. Sorely distressed, the van-guard sent repeated messages to the rear to demand the portable bridge. At length the last of the army had crossed, and Magarino and his sturdy followers endeavored to raise the ponderous framework. But it stuck fast in the sides of the dike. In vain they strained every nerve. The weight of so many men and horses, and above all of the heavy artillery, had wedged the timbers so firmly in the stones and earth, that it was beyond their power to dislodge them. Still they labored amidst a torrent of missiles, until, many of them slain, and all wounded, they were obliged to abandon the attempt.

The tidings soon spread from man to man, and no sooner was their dreadful import comprehended, than a cry of despair arose, which for a moment drowned all the noise of conflict. All means of retreat were cut off. Scarcely hope was left. The only hope was in such desperate exertions as each could make for himself. Order and subordination were at an end. Intense danger produced intense selfishness. Each thought only of his own life. Pressing forward, he trampled down the weak and the wounded, heedless whether it were friend or foe. The leading files, urged on by the rear, were crowded on the brink of the gulf. Sandoval, Ordaz, and the other cavaliers dashed into the water. Some succeeded in swimming their horses across. Others failed, and some, who reached the opposite bank, being overturned in the ascent, rolled headlong with their steeds into the lake. The infantry followed pellmell, heaped promiscuously on one another, frequently pierced by the shafts, or struck down by the war-clubs of the Aztecs; while many an unfortunate victim was dragged half-stunned on board their canoes, to be reserved for a protracted, but more dreadful death.[9]

The carnage raged fearfully along the length of the causeway. Its shadowy bulk presented a mark of sufficient distinctness for the enemy's missiles, which often prostrated their own countrymen in the blind fury of the tempest. Those nearest the dike, running their canoes alongside, with a force that shattered them to pieces, leaped on the land, and grappled with the Christians, until both came rolling down the side of the causeway together. But the Aztec fell among his friends, while his antagonist was borne away in triumph to the sacrifice. The struggle was long and deadly. The Mexicans were recognised by their white cotton tunics, which showed faint through the darkness. Above the combatants rose a wild and discordant clamor, in which horrid shouts of vengeance were mingled with groans of agony, with invocations of the saints and the blessed Virgin, and with the screams of women; [10] for there were several women, both natives and Spaniards, who had accompanied the Christian camp. Among these, one named María de Estrada is particularly noticed for the courage she displayed, battling with broadsword and target like the stanchest of the warriors.[11]

The opening in the causeway, meanwhile, was filled up with the wreck of matter which had been forced into it, ammunition-wagons, heavy guns, bales of rich stuffs scattered over the waters, chests of solid ingots, and bodies of men and horses, till over this dismal ruin a passage was gradually formed, by which those in the rear were enabled to clamber to the other side.[12] Cortés, it is said, found a place that was fordable, where, halting, with the water up to his saddle-girths, he endeavored to check the confusion, and lead his followers by a safer path to the opposite bank. But his voice was lost in the wild uproar, and finally, hurrying on with the tide, he pressed forwards with a few trusty cavaliers, who remained near his person, to the van; but not before he had seen his favor-

[9] Ibid., p. 143.—Camargo, Hist. de Tlascala, MS. Bernal Diaz, Hist. de la Conquista, cap. 128.—Oviedo, Hist. de las Ind., MS., lib. 33, cap. 13, 47.—Sahagun, Hist. de Nueva España, MS., lib. 12, cap. 24.—Martyr, De Orbe Novo, dec. 5, cap. 6.—Herrera, Hist. General, dec. 2, lib. 10, cap. 4.—Probanza en la Villa Segura, MS.

[10] "Pues la grita, y lloros, y lástimas q̃ deziã demãdando socorro: Ayudadme, q̃ me ahogo, otros: Socorredme, q̃ me matã, otros demãdando ayuda á N. Señora Santa María, y á Señor Santiago." Bernal Diaz, Ibid., cap. 128.

[11] "Y asimismo se mostró mui valerosa en este aprieto, y conflicto María de Estrada, la qual con vna Espada, y vna Rodela en las Manos, hiço hechos maravillosos, y se entraba por los Enemigos con tanto corage, y ánimo, como si fuera vno de los mas valientes Hombres de el Mundo, olvidada de que era Muger. . . . . . Casó esta Señora con Pedro Sanchez Farfan, y diéronle en Encomienda el Pueblo de Tetela." Torquemada, Monarch. Ind., lib. 4, cap. 72.

[12] Camargo, Hist. de Tlascala, MS.—Bernal Diaz, Hist. de la Conquista, cap. 128. "Por la gran priesa que daban de ambas partes de el camino, comenzáron á caer en aquel foso, y cayéron juntos, que de Españoles, que de Indios y de caballos, y de cargas, el foso se hinchó hasta arriba, cayendo los unos sobre los otros, y los otros sobre los otros, de manera que todos los del bagage quedáron allí ahogados, y los de la retaguardia pasáron sobre los muertos." Sahagun, Hist. de Nueva España, MS., lib. 12, cap. 24.

ite page, Juan de Salazar, struck down, a corpse, by his side. Here he found Sandoval and his companions, halting before the third and last breach, endeavoring to cheer on their followers to surmount it. But their resolution faltered. It was wide and deep; though the passage was not so closely beset by the enemy as the preceding ones. The cavaliers again set the example by plunging into the water. Horse and foot followed as they could, some swimming, others with dying grasp clinging to the manes and tails of the struggling animals. Those fared best, as the general had predicted, who travelled lightest; and many were the unfortunate wretches, who, weighed down by the fatal gold which they loved so well, were buried with it in the salt floods of the lake.[13] Cortés, with his gallant comrades, Olid, Morla, Sandoval, and some few others, still kept in the advance, leading his broken remnant off the fatal causeway. The din of battle lessened in the distance; when the rumor reached them, that the rearguard would be wholly overwhelmed without speedy relief. It seemed almost an act of desperation; but the generous hearts of the Spanish cavaliers did not stop to calculate danger, when the cry for succour reached them. Turning their horses' bridles, they galloped back to the theatre of action, worked their way through the press, swam the canal, and placed themselves in the thick of the *mêlée* on the opposite bank.[14]

The first grey of the morning was now coming over the waters. It showed the hideous confusion of the scene which had been shrouded in the obscurity of night. The dark masses of combatants, stretching along the dike, were seen struggling for mastery, until the very causeway on which they stood appeared to tremble, and reel to and fro, as if shaken by an earthquake; while the bosom of the lake, as far as the eye could reach, was darkened by canoes crowded with warriors, whose spears and bludgeons, armed with blades of "volcanic glass," gleamed in the morning light.

The cavaliers found Alvarado unhorsed, and defending himself with a poor handful of followers against an overwhelming tide of the enemy. His good steed, which had borne him through many a hard fight, had fallen under him.[15] He was himself wounded in several places, and was striving in vain to rally his scattered column, which was driven to the verge of the canal by the fury of the enemy, then in possession of the whole rear of the causeway, where they were reinforced every hour by fresh combatants from the city. The artillery in the earlier part of the engagement had not been idle, and its iron shower, sweeping along the dike, had mowed

---

[13] "É los que habian ido con Narvaez arrojáronse en la sala, é cargáronse de aquel oro é plata quanto pudiéron; pero los menos lo gozáron, porque la carga no los dexaba pelear, é los Indios los tomaban vivos cargados; é á otros llevaban arrastrando, é á otros mataban allí; É así no se salváron sino los desocupados é que iban en la delantera." Oviedo, Hist. de las Ind., MS., lib. 33, cap. 47.

[14] Herrera, Hist. General, dec. 2, lib. 10, cap. 11.—Oviedo, Hist. de las Ind., MS., lib. 33, cap. 13.—Bernal Diaz, Hist. de la Conquista, cap. 128.

[15] "Luego encontráron con Pedro de Alvarado bien herido con vna lança en la mano á pie, que la yegua alaçana ya se la auian muerto." Bernal Diaz, Hist. de la Conquista, cap. 128.

down the assailants by hundreds. But nothing could resist their impetuosity. The front ranks, pushed on by those behind, were at length forced up to the pieces, and, pouring over them like a torrent, overthrew men and guns in one general ruin. The resolute charge of the Spanish cavaliers, who had now arrived, created a temporary check, and gave time for their countrymen to make a feeble rally. But they were speedily borne down by the returning flood. Cortés and his companions were compelled to plunge again into the lake,—though all did not escape. Alvarado stood on the brink for a moment, hesitating what to do. Unhorsed as he was, to throw himself into the water, in the face of the hostile canoes that now swarmed around the opening, afforded but a desperate chance of safety. He had but a second for thought. He was a man of powerful frame, and despair gave him unnatural energy. Setting his long lance firmly on the wreck which strewed the bottom of the lake, he sprung forward with all his might, and cleared the wide gap at a leap! Aztecs and Tlascalans gazed in stupid amazement, exclaiming, as they beheld the incredible feat, "This is truly the *Tonatiuh*,—the child of the Sun!"[16]—The breadth of the opening is not given. But it was so great, that the valorous captain Diaz, who well remembered the place, says the leap was impossible to any man.[17] Other contemporaries, however, do not discredit the story.[18] It was, beyond doubt, matter of popular belief at the time; it is to this day familiarly known to every inhabitant of the capital; and the name of the *Salto de Alvarado,* "Alvarado's Leap," given to the spot, still commemorates an exploit which rivalled those of the demi-gods of Grecian fable.[19]

[16] "Y los amigos vista tan gran hazaña quedáron maravillados, y al instante que esto viéron se arrojáron por el suelo postrados por tierra en señal de hecho tan heroico, espantable y raro, que ellos no habian visto hacer á ningun hombre, y ansi adoráron al Sol, comiendo puñados de tierra, arrancando yervas del campo, diciendo á grandes voces, verdaderamente que este hombre es *hijo del Sol.*" (Camargo, Hist. de Tlascala, MS.) This writer consulted the process instituted by Alvarado's heirs, in which they set forth the merits of their ancestor, as attested by the most valorous captains of the Tlascalan nation, present at the Conquest. It *may be* that the famous leap was among these "merits," of which the historian speaks. M. de Humboldt, citing Camargo, so considers it. (Essai Politique, tom. II. p. 75.) This would do more than any thing else to establish the fact. But Camargo's language does not seem to me necessarily to warrant the inference.
[17] "Se llama aora la puente del salto de Alvarado: y platicauamos muchos soldados sobre ello, y no hallavamos razon, ni soltura de vn hombre que tal saltasse." Hist. de la Conquista, cap. 128.
[18] Gomara, Crónica, cap. 109.—Camargo, Ibid., ubi supra.—Oviedo, Hist. de las Ind., MS., lib. 33, cap. 47.—Which last author, however, frankly says, that many, who had seen the place, declared it seemed to them impossible. "Fué tan estremado de grande el salto, que á muchos hombres que han visto aquello, he oido decir que parece cosa imposible haberlo podido saltar ninguno hombre humano. En fin él lo saltó é ganó por ello la vida, é perdiéronla muchos que atras quedaban."
[19] The spot is pointed out to every traveller. It is where a ditch, of no great width, is traversed by a small bridge not far from the western extremity of the Alameda. As the place received its name in Alvarado's time, the story could scarcely have been discountenanced by him. But, since the length of the leap, strange to say, is nowhere given, the reader can have no means of passing his own judgment on its probabilit͏y

Cortés and his companions now rode forward to the front, where the troops, in a loose, disorderly manner, were marching off the fatal cause-way. A few only of the enemy hung on their rear, or annoyed them by occasional flights of arrows from the lake. The attention of the Aztecs was diverted to the rich spoil that strewed the battle-ground; fortunately for the Spaniards, who, had their enemy pursued with the same ferocity with which he had fought, would, in their crippled condition, have been cut off probably, to a man. But little molested, therefore, they were allowed to defile through the adjacent village, or suburbs, it might be called, of Popotla.[20]

The Spanish commander there dismounted from his jaded steed, and, sitting down on the steps of an Indian temple, gazed mournfully on the broken files as they passed before him. What a spectacle did they present! The cavalry, most of them dismounted, were mingled with the infantry, who dragged their feeble limbs along with difficulty; their shattered mail and tattered garments dripping with the salt ooze, showing through their rents many a bruise and ghastly wound; their bright arms soiled, their proud crests and banners gone, the baggage, artillery, all, in short, that constitutes the pride and panoply of glorious war, for ever lost. Cortés, as he looked wistfully on their thinned and disordered ranks, sought in vain for many a familiar face, and missed more than one dear companion who had stood side by side with him through all the perils of the Conquest. Though accustomed to control his emotions, or, at least, to conceal them, the sight was too much for him. He covered his face with his hands, and the tears, which trickled down, revealed too plainly the anguish of his soul.[21]

He found some consolation, however, in the sight of several of the cavaliers on whom he most relied. Alvarado, Sandoval, Olid, Ordaz, Avila, were yet safe. He had the inexpressible satisfaction, also, of learning the safety of the Indian interpreter, Marina, so dear to him, and so important to the army. She had been committed, with a daughter of a Tlascalan chief, to several of that nation. She was fortunately placed in the van, and her faithful escort had carried her securely through all the dangers of the night. Aguilar, the other interpreter, had also escaped. And it was with no less satisfaction, that Cortés learned the safety of the ship-builder, Martin Lopez.[22] The general's solicitude for the fate of this man, so indispensable, as he proved, to the success of his subsequent operations, showed, that, amidst all his affliction, his indomitable spirit was looking forward to the hour of vengeance.

Meanwhile, the advancing column had reached the neighboring city

---

[20] "Fué Dios servido de que los Mejicanos se ocupasen en recojer los despojos de los muertos, y las riquezas de oro y piedras que llevaba el bagage, y de sacar los muertos de aquel acequia, y á los caballos y otros bestias. Y por esto no siguiéron el alcanze, y los Españoles pudiéron ir poco á poco por su camino sin tener mucha molestia de enemigos." Sahagun, Hist. de Nueva España, MS., lib. 12, cap. 25.

[21] Oviedo, Hist. de las Ind., MS., lib. 33, cap. 47.—Ixtlilxochitl, Hist. Chich., MS., cap. 89.—Gomara, Crónica, cap. 109.

[22] Herrera, Hist. General, dec. 2, lib. 10, cap. 12.

of Tlacopan, (Tacuba,) once the capital of an independent principality. There it halted in the great street, as if bewildered and altogether uncertain what course to take; like a herd of panic-struck deer, who, flying from the hunters, with the cry of hound and horn still ringing in their ears, look wildly around for some glen or copse in which to plunge for concealment. Cortés, who had hastily mounted and rode on to the front again, saw the danger of remaining in a populous place, where the inhabitants might sorely annoy the troops from the *azoteas,* with little risk to themselves. Pushing forward, therefore, he soon led them into the country. There he endeavored to reform his disorganized battalions, and bring them to something like order.[23]

Hard by, at no great distance on the left, rose an eminence, looking towards a chain of mountains which fences in the Valley on the west. It was called the Hill of Otoncalpolco, and sometimes the Hill of Montezuma.[24] It was crowned with an Indian *teocalli,* with its large outworks of stone covering an ample space, and by its strong position, which commanded the neighboring plain, promised a good place of refuge for the exhausted troops. But the men, disheartened and stupefied by their late reverses, seemed for the moment incapable of further exertion; and the place was held by a body of armed Indians. Cortés saw the necessity of dislodging them, if he would save the remains of his army from entire destruction. The event showed he still held a control over their wills stronger than circumstances themselves. Cheering them on, and supported by his gallant cavaliers, he succeeded in infusing into the most sluggish something of his own intrepid temper, and led them up the ascent in face of the enemy. But the latter made slight resistance, and, after a few feeble volleys of missiles which did little injury, left the ground to the assailants.

It was covered by a building of considerable size, and furnished ample accommodations for the diminished numbers of the Spaniards. They found there some provisions; and more, it is said, were brought to them, in the course of the day, from some friendly Otomie villages in the neighborhood. There was, also, a quantity of fuel in the courts, destined to the use of the temple. With this they made fires to dry their drenched garments, and busily employed themselves in dressing one another's wounds, stiff and extremely painful from exposure and long exertion. Thus refreshed, the weary soldiers threw themselves down on the floor

[23] "Tacuba," says that interesting traveller, Latrobe, "lies near the foot of the hills, and is at the present day chiefly noted for the large and noble church which was erected there by Cortés. And hard by, you trace the lines of a Spanish encampment. I do not hazard the opinion, but it might appear by the coincidence, that this was the very position chosen by Cortés for his intrenchment, after the retreat just mentioned, and before he commenced his painful route towards Otumba." (Rambler in Mexico, letter 5.) It is evident, from our text, that Cortés could have thrown up no intrenchment here, at least on his retreat from the capital.

[24] Lorenzana, Viage, p. xiii

and courts of the temple, and soon found the temporary oblivion,—which Nature seldom denies even in the greatest extremity of suffering.[25]

There was one eye in that assembly, however, which we may well believe did not so speedily close. For what agitating thoughts must have crowded on the mind of their commander, as he beheld his poor remnant of followers thus huddled together in this miserable bivouac! And this was all that survived of the brilliant array with which but a few weeks since he had entered the capital of Mexico! Where now were his dreams of conquest and empire? And what was he but a luckless adventurer, at whom the finger of scorn would be uplifted as a madman? Whichever way he turned, the horizon was almost equally gloomy, with scarcely one light spot to cheer him. He had still a weary journey before him, through perilous and unknown paths, with guides of whose fidelity he could not be assured. And how could he rely on his reception at Tlascala, the place of his destination; the land of his ancient enemies; where, formerly as a foe, and now as a friend, he had brought desolation to every family within its borders?

Yet these agitating and gloomy reflections, which might have crushed a common mind, had no power over that of Cortés; or rather, they only served to renew his energies, and quicken his perceptions, as the war of the elements purifies and gives elasticity to the atmosphere. He looked with an unblenching eye on his past reverses; but, confident in his own resources, he saw a light through the gloom which others could not. Even in the shattered relics which lay around him, resembling in their haggard aspect and wild attire a horde of famished outlaws, he discerned the materials out of which to reconstruct his ruined fortunes. In the very hour of discomfiture and general despondency, there is no doubt that his heroic spirit was meditating the plan of operations which he afterwards pursued with such dauntless constancy.

The loss sustained by the Spaniards on this fatal night, like every other event in the history of the Conquest, is reported with the greatest discrepancy. If we believe Cortés' own letter, it did not exceed one hundred and fifty Spaniards, and two thousand Indians. But the general's bulletins, while they do full justice to the difficulties to be overcome, and the importance of the results, are less scrupulous in stating the extent either of his means or of his losses. Thoan Cano, one of the cavaliers present, estimates the slain at eleven hundred and seventy Spaniards, and eight thousand allies. But this is a greater number than we have allowed for the whole army. Perhaps we may come nearest the truth by taking the computation of Gomara, who was the chaplain of Cortés, and who had free access, doubtless, not only to the general's papers, but to other authentic sources of information. According to him, the number of

[25] Sahagun, Hist. de Nueva España, MS., lib. 12, cap. 24.—Bernal Diaz, Hist. de la Conquista, cap. 128.—Camargo, Hist. de Tlascala, MS.—Ixtlilxochitl, Hist Chich., MS., cap. 89.

452   THE CONQUEST OF MEXICO

Christians killed and missing was four hundred and fifty, and that of
natives four thousand. This, with the loss sustained in the conflicts of the
previous week, may have reduced the former to something more than a
third and the latter to a fourth, or, perhaps, fifth, of the original force
with which they entered the capital.[26] The brunt of the action fell on
the rear-guard, few of whom escaped. It was formed chiefly of the soldiers
of Narvaez, who fell the victims, in some measure, of their cupidity.[27]
Forty-six of the cavalry were cut off, which with previous losses reduced
the number in this branch of the service to twenty-three, and some of
these in very poor condition. The greater part of the treasure, the baggage, the general's papers, including his accounts, and a minute diary of
transactions since leaving Cuba,—which, to posterity, at least, would
have been of more worth than the gold,—had been swallowed up by the
waters.[28] The ammunition, the beautiful little train of artillery, with
which Cortés had entered the city, were all gone. Not a musket even remained, the men having thrown them away, eager to disencumber themselves of all that might retard their escape on that disastrous night.
Nothing, in short, of their military apparatus was left, but their swords,

---

[26] The table below may give the reader some idea of the discrepancies in numerical
estimates, even among eyewitnesses, and writers who, having access to the actors,
are nearly of equal authority.

Cortés, ap. Lorenzana, p. 145,	150 Spaniards,	2000 Indians, killed and missing.		
Cano, ap. Oviedo, lib. 33, cap. 54,	1170 "	8000 "	" "	"
Probanza, &c.,	200 "	2000 "	" "	"
Oviedo, Hist. de las Ind., lib. 33,				
cap. 13,	150 "	2000 "	" "	"
Camargo,	450 "	4000 "	" "	"
Gomara, cap. 109,	450 "	4000 "	" "	"
Ixtlilxochitl, Hist. Chich., cap. 88,	450 "	4000 "	" "	"
Sahagun, lib. 12, cap. 24,	300 "	2000 "	" "	"
Herrera, dec. 2, lib. 10, cap. 12,	150 "	4000 "	" "	"

Bernal Diaz does not take the trouble to agree with himself. After stating that
the rear, on which the loss fell heaviest, consisted of 120 men, he adds, in the same
paragraph, that 150 of these were slain, which number swells to 200 in a few lines
further! Falstaff's men in buckram! See Hist. de la Conquista, cap. 128.

Cano's estimate embraces, it is true, those—but their number was comparatively
small—who perished subsequently on the march. The same authority states, that
270 of the garrison, ignorant of the proposed departure of their countrymen, were
perfidiously left in the palace of Axayacatl, where they surrendered on terms, but
were subsequently all sacrificed by the Aztecs! The improbability of this monstrous
story, by which the army with all its equipage could leave the citadel without the
knowledge of so many of their comrades,—and this be permitted, too, at a juncture,
which made every man's coöperation so important,—is too obvious to require
refutation. Herrera records, what is much more probable, that Cortés gave particular orders to the captain, Ojeda, to see that none of the sleeping or wounded should,
in the hurry of the moment, be overlooked in their quarters. Hist. General, dec. 2,
lib. 10, cap. 11.

[27] "Pues de los de Narvaez, todos los mas en las puentes quedáron, cargados de
oro." Bernal Diaz, Hist. de la Conquista, cap. 128.

[28] According to Diaz, part of the gold intrusted to the *Tlascalan* convoy was preserved. (Hist. de la Conquista, cap. 136.) From the document already cited,—Probanza de Villa Segura, MS.,—it appears, that it was a Castilian guard who had
charge of it.

their crippled cavalry, and a few damaged crossbows, to assert the superiority of the European over the barbarian.

The prisoners, including, as already noticed, the children of Montezuma and the cacique of Tezcuco, all perished by the hands of their ignorant countrymen, it is said, in the indiscriminate fury of the assault. There were, also, some persons of consideration among the Spaniards, whose names were inscribed on the same bloody roll of slaughter. Such was Francisco de Morla, who fell by the side of Cortés, on returning with him to the rescue. But the greatest loss was that of Juan Velasquez de Leon, who, with Alvarado, had command of the rear. It was the post of danger on that night, and he fell, bravely defending it at an early part of the retreat. He was an excellent officer, possessed of many knightly qualities, though somewhat haughty in his bearing, being one of the best connected cavaliers in the army. The near relation of the governor of Cuba, he looked coldly, at first, on the pretentions of Cortés; but, whether from a conviction that the latter had been wronged, or from personal preference, he afterwards attached himself zealously to his leader's interests. The general requited this with a generous confidence, assigning him, as we have seen, a separate and independent command, where misconduct, or even a mistake, would have been fatal to the expedition. Velasquez proved himself worthy of the trust; and there was no cavalier in the army, with the exception, perhaps, of Sandoval and Alvarado, whose loss would have been so deeply deplored by the commander.—Such were the disastrous results of this terrible passage of the causeway; more disastrous than those occasioned by any other reverse which has stained the Spanish arms in the New World; and which have branded the night on which it happened, in the national annals, with the name of the *noche triste*, "the sad or melancholy night." [29]

[29] Gomara. Crónica, cap. 109.—Oviedo, Hist. de las Ind., MS., lib. 33, cap. 13.—Probanza en la Villa Segura, MS.—Bernal Diaz, Hist. de la Conquista, cap. 128.

CHAPTER IV

RETREAT OF THE SPANIARDS—DISTRESSES OF THE ARMY—PYRAMIDS OF
TEOTIHUACAN—GREAT BATTLE OF OTUMBA

1520

THE Mexicans, during the day which followed the retreat of the Spaniards, remained, for the most part, quiet in their own capital, where they
found occupation in cleansing the streets and causeways from the dead,
which lay festering in heaps that might have bred a pestilence. They
may have been employed, also, in paying the last honors to such of their
warriors as had fallen, solemnizing the funeral rites by the sacrifice of
their wretched prisoners, who, as they contemplated their own destiny,
may well have envied the fate of their companions who left their bones
on the battle-field. It was most fortunate for the Spaniards, in their extremity, that they had this breathing-time allowed them by the enemy.
But Cortés knew that he could not calculate on its continuance, and,
feeling how important it was to get the start of his vigilant foe, he ordered his troops to be in readiness to resume their march by midnight.
Fires were left burning, the better to deceive the enemy; and at the appointed hour, the little army, without sound of drum or trumpet, but
with renewed spirits, sallied forth from the gates of the *teocalli*, within
whose hospitable walls they had found such seasonable succour. The
place is now indicated by a Christian church, dedicated to the Virgin,
under the title of *Nuestra Señora de los Remedios*, whose miraculous
image—the very same, *it is said,* brought over by the followers of Cortés [1]—still extends her beneficent sway over the neighboring capital;
and the traveller, who pauses within the precincts of the consecrated fane,
may feel that he is standing on the spot made memorable by the refuge
it afforded to the Conquerors in the hour of their deepest despondency.[2]

It was arranged that the sick and wounded should occupy the centre,
transported on litters, or on the backs of the *tamanes*, while those who
were strong enough to keep their seats should mount behind the cavalry
The able-bodied soldiers were ordered to the front and rear, while others
protected the flanks, thus affording all the security possible to the in
valids.

[1] Lorenzana, Viage, p. xiii.
[2] The last instance, I believe, of the direct interposition of the Virgin in behalf of
the metropolis was in 1833, when she was brought into the city to avert the cholera.
She refused to pass the night in town, however, but was found the next morning in
her own sanctuary at Los Remedios, showing, by the mud with which she was
plentifully bespattered, that she must have performed the distance—several leagues
—through the miry ways on foot! See Latrobe, Rambler in Mexico, letter 5.

The retreating army held on its way unmolested under cover of the darkness. But, as morning dawned, they beheld parties of the natives moving over the heights, or hanging at a distance, like a cloud of locusts, on their rear. They did not belong to the capital; but were gathered from the neighboring country, where the tidings of their rout had already penetrated. The charm, which had hitherto covered the white men, was gone. The dread *Teules* were no longer invincible.[3]

The Spaniards, under the conduct of their Tlascalan guides, took a circuitous route to the north, passing through Quauhtitlan, and round lake Tzompanco, (Zumpango,) thus lengthening their march, but keeping a distance from the capital. From the eminences, as they passed along, the Indians rolled down heavy stones, mingled with volleys of darts and arrows, on the heads of the soldiers. Some were even bold enough to descend into the plain and assault the extremities of the column. But they were soon beaten off by the horse, and compelled to take refuge among the hills, where the ground was too rough for the rider to follow. Indeed, the Spaniards did not care to do so, their object being rather to fly than to fight.

In this way they slowly advanced, halting at intervals to drive off their assailants when they became too importunate, and greatly distressed by their missiles and their desultory attacks. At night, the troops usually found shelter in some town or hamlet, whence the inhabitants, in anticipation of their approach, had been careful to carry off all the provisions. The Spaniards were soon reduced to the greatest straits for subsistence. Their principal food was the wild cherry, which grew in the woods, or by the roadside. Fortunate were they, if they found a few ears of corn unplucked. More frequently nothing was left but the stalks; and with them, and the like unwholesome fare, they were fain to supply the cravings of appetite. When a horse happened to be killed, it furnished an extraordinary banquet; and Cortés himself records the fact of his having made one of a party who thus sumptuously regaled themselves, devouring the animal eve nto his hide.[4]

---

[3] The epithet by which, according to Diaz, the Castilians were constantly addressed by the natives; and which—whether correctly or not—he interprets into *gods*, or *divine beings*. (See Hist. de la Conquista, cap. 48, et alibi.) One of the stanzas of Ercilla intimates the existence of a similar delusion among the South American Indians,—and a similar cure of it.

> "Por dioses, como dixe, eran tenidos
> de los Indios los nuestros ;pero oliéron
> que de muger y hombre eran nacidos,
> y todas sus flaquezas entendiéron
> viéndolos á miserias sometidos,
> el error ignorante conociéron,
> ardiendo en viva rabia avergonzados
> por verse de mortales conquistados."
> LA ARAUCANA, Parte 1, Canto 2

[4] Rel. Seg. de Cortés, ap. Lorenzana, p. 147.

Hunger furnished them a sauce, says Oviedo, which made their horse-flesh as relishing as the far-famed sausages of Naples, the delicate kid of Avila, or the savory veal of Saragossa! "Con la carne del caballo tubiéron buen pasto, é se

The wretched soldiers, faint with famine and fatigue, were some-times seen to drop down lifeless on the road. Others loitered behind, un-able to keep up with the march, and fell into the hands of the enemy, who followed in the track of the army like a flock of famished vultures, eager to pounce on the dying and the dead. Others, again, who strayed too far, in their eagerness to procure sustenance, shared the same fate. The number of these, at length, and the consciousness of the cruel lot for which they were reserved, compelled Cortés to introduce stricter dis-cipline, and to enforce it by sterner punishments than he had hitherto done,—though too often ineffectually, such was the indifference to dan-ger, under the overwhelming pressure of present calamity.

In their prolonged distresses, the soldiers ceased to set a value on those very things for which they had once been content to hazard life itself. More than one, who had brought his golden treasure safe through the perils of the *noche triste*, now abandoned it as an intolerable bur-den; and the rude Indian peasant gleaned up, with wondering delight, the bright fragments of the spoils of the capital.[5]

Through these weary days Cortés displayed his usual serenity and fortitude. He was ever in the post of danger, freely exposing himself in encounters with the enemy; in one of which he received a severe wound in the head, that afterwards gave him much trouble.[6] He fared no better than the humblest soldier, and strove, by his own cheerful countenance and counsels, to fortify the courage of those who faltered, assuring them that their sufferings would soon be ended by their arrival in the hospit-able "land of bread." [7] His faithful officers cooperated with him in these efforts; and the common file, indeed, especially his own veterans, must be allowed, for the most part, to have shown a full measure of the con-stancy and power of endurance so characteristic of their nation,—justify-ing the honest boast of an old chronicler, "that there was no people so capable of supporting hunger as the Spaniards, and none of them who were ever more severely tried than the soldiers of Cortés." [8] A similar fortitude was shown by the Tlascalans, trained in a rough school that made them familiar with hardship and privations. Although they some-

consoláron ó mitigáron en parte su hambre, é se lo comiéron sin dexar cuero, ni otra cosa dél sino los huesos é las vñas, y el pelo ; é aun las tripas no les pareció de menos buen gusto que las sobreasados de Nápoles, ó los gentiles cabritos de Abila, ó las sabrosas Terneras de Zaragosa, segun la estrema necesidad que llevaban ; por que despues que de la gran cibdad de Temixtitan havian salido, ninguna otra cosa comiéron sino mahiz tostado, é cocido, é yervas del campo, y desto no tanto quan-to quisieran ó ovieran menester." Hist. de las Ind., MS., lib. 33, cap. 13.

[5] Herrera mentions one soldier who had succeeded in carrying off his gold to the value of 3,000 *castellanos* across the causeway, and afterwards flung it away by the advice of Cortés. "The devil take your gold," said the commander bluntly to him, "if it is to cost you your life." Hist. General, dec. 2, lib. 10, cap. 11.

[6] Gomara, Crónica, cap. 110.

[7] The meaning of the word *Tlascala*, and so called from the abundance of maize raised in the country. Boturini, Idea, p. 78.

[8] "Empero la Nacion nuestra Española sufre mas hambre que otra ninguna, i estos de Cortés mas que todos." Gomara, Crónica, cap. 110.

times threw themselves on the ground, in the extremity of famine, imploring their gods not to abandon them, they did their duty as warriors, and, far from manifesting coldness towards the Spaniards as the cause of their distresses, seemed only the more firmly knit to them by the sense of a common suffering.

On the seventh morning, the army had reached the mountain rampart which overlooks the plains of Otompan, or Otumba, as commonly called, from the Indian city,—now a village,—situated in them. The distance from the capital is hardly nine leagues. But the Spaniards had travelled more than thrice that distance, in their circuitous march round the lakes. This had been performed so slowly, that it consumed a week; two nights of which had been passed in the same quarters, from the absolute necessity of rest. It was not, therefore, till the 7th of July, that they reached the heights commanding the plains which stretched far away towards the territory of Tlascala, in full view of the venerable pyramids of Teotihuacan, two of the most remarkable monuments of the antique American civilization now existing north of the Isthmus. During all the preceding day, they had seen parties of the enemy hovering like dark clouds above the highlands, brandishing their weapons, and calling out in vindictive tones, "Hasten on! You will soon find yourselves where you cannot escape!" words of mysterious import, which they were made fully to comprehend on the following morning.[9]

The monuments of San Juan Teotihuacan are, with the exception of the temple of Cholula, the most ancient remains, probably, on the Mexican soil. They were found by the Aztecs, according to their traditions, on their entrance into the country, when Teotihuacan, *the habitation of the gods*, now a paltry village, was a flourishing city, the rival of Tula, the great Toltec capital.[10] The two principal pyramids were dedicated to *Tonatiuh*, the Sun, and *Meztli*, the Moon. The former, which is considerably the larger, is found by recent measurements to be six hundred and eighty-two feet long at the base, and one hundred and eighty feet high, dimensions not inferior to those of some of the kindred monuments of Egypt.[11] They were divided into four stories, of which three are now discernible, while the vestiges of the intermediate gradations are nearly effaced. In fact, time has dealt so roughly with them, and the materials have been so much displaced by the treacherous vegetation of the tropics, muffling up with its flowery mantle the ruin which it causes, that it is

[9] For the concluding pages, see Camargo, Hist. de Tlascala, MS.,—Bernal Diaz, Hist. de la Conquista, cap. 128,—Oviedo, Hist. de las Ind., MS., lib. 33, cap. 13,—Gomara, Crónica, ubi supra,—Ixtlilxochitl, Hist. Chich., MS., cap. 89,—Martyr, De Orbe Novo, dec. 5, cap. 6,—Rel. Seg. de Cortés, ap. Lorenzana, pp. 147, 148,—Sahagun, Hist. de Nueva España, MS., lib. 12, cap. 25, 26.

[10] "Su nombre, que quiere decir *habitacion de los Dioses*, y que ya por estos tiempos era ciudad tan famosa, que no solo competia, pero excedia con muchas ventajas á la corte de Tollan." Veytia, Hist. Antig., tom. I. cap. 27.

[11] The pyramid of Mycerinos is 280 feet only at the base, and 162 feet in height. The great pyramid of Cheops is 728 feet at the base, and 448 feet high. See Denon Egypt Illustrated, (London, 1825,) p. 9.

not easy to discern, at once, the pyramidal form of the structures.[12] The
huge masses bear such resemblance to the North American mounds, that
some have fancied them to be only natural eminences shaped by the
hand of man into a regular form, and ornamented with the temples and
terraces, the wreck of which still covers their slopes. But others, seeing
no example of a similar elevation in the wide plain in which they stand,
infer, with more probability, that they are wholly of an artificial construction.[13]

The interior is composed of clay mixed with pebbles, incrusted on the
surface with the light porous stone *tetzontli*, so abundant in the neighboring quarries. Over this was a thick coating of stucco, resembling, in
its reddish color, that found in the ruins of Palenque. According to tradition, the pyramids are hollow, but hitherto the attempt to discover the
cavity in that dedicated to the Sun has been unsuccessful. In the smaller
mound, an aperture has been found on the southern side, at two thirds
of the elevation. It is formed by a narrow gallery, which, after penetrating to the distance of several yards, terminates in two pits or wells.
The largest of these is about fifteen feet deep;[14] and the sides are faced
with unbaked bricks; but to what purpose it was devoted, nothing is left
to show. It may have been to hold the ashes of some powerful chief, like
the solitary apartment discovered in the great Egyptian pyramid. That
these monuments were dedicated to religious uses, there is no doubt;
and it would be only conformable to the practice of Antiquity in the
eastern continent, that they should have served for tombs, as well as
temples.[15]

Distinct traces of the latter destination are said to be visible on the
summit of the smaller pyramid, consisting of the remains of stone walls
showing a building of considerable size and strength.[16] There are no remains on the top of the pyramid of the Sun. But the traveller, who will
take the trouble to ascend its bald summit, will be amply compensated
by the glorious view it will open to him;—towards the south-east, the

[12] "It requires a particular position," says Mr. Tudor, "united with some little
faith, to discover the pyramidal form at all." (Tour in North America, vol. II. p.
277.) Yet Mr. Bullock says, "The general figure of the square is as perfect as the
great pyramid of Egypt." (Six Months in Mexico, vol. II. chap. 26.) Eyewitnesses
both. This historian must often content himself with repeating, in the words of the
old French lay,—

> "Si com je l'ai trové escrite,
> Vos conterai la verité."

[13] This is M. de Humboldt's opinion. (See his Essai Politique, tom. II. pp. 66-70.)
He has also discussed these interesting monuments in his Vues des Cordillères p. 25,
et seq.

[14] Latrobe gives the description of this cavity, into which he and his fellow-
travellers penetrated, Rambler in Mexico, let. 7.

[15] "Et tot templa deûm Romæ, quot in urbe sepulcra
Heroum numerare licet: quos fabula manes
Nobilitat, noster populus veneratus adorat."

PRUDENTIUS, Contra Sym., lib. I.

[16] The dimensions are given by Bullock, (Six Months in Mexico, vol. II. chap. 26,)
who has sometimes seen what has eluded the optics of other travellers.

hills of Tlascala, surrounded by their green plantations and cultivated corn-fields, in the midst of which stands the little village, once the proud capital of the republic. Somewhat further to the south, the eye passes across the beautiful plains lying around the city of Puebla de los Ángeles, founded by the old Spaniards, and still rivalling, in the splendor of its churches, the most brilliant capitals of Europe; and far in the west he may behold the Valley of Mexico, spread out like a map, with its diminished lakes, its princely capital rising in still greater glory from its ruins, and its rugged hills gathering darkly around it, as in the days of Montezuma.

The summit of this larger mound is said to have been crowned by a temple, in which was a colossal statue of its presiding deity, the Sun, made of one entire block of stone, and facing the east. Its breast was protected by a plate of burnished gold and silver, on which the first rays of the rising luminary rested.[17] An antiquary, in the early part of the last century, speaks of having seen some fragments of the statue. It was still standing, according to report, on the invasion of the Spaniards, and was demolished by the indefatigable Bishop Zumarraga, whose hand fell more heavily than that of Time itself on the Aztec monuments.[18]

Around the principal pyramids are a great number of smaller ones, rarely exceeding thirty feet in height, which, according to tradition, were dedicated to the stars, and served as sepulchres for the great men of the nation. They are arranged symmetrically in avenues terminating at the sides of the great pyramids, which face the cardinal points. The plain on which they stand was called *Micoatl*, or "Path of the Dead." The laborer, as he turns up the ground, still finds there numerous arrowheads, and blades of obsidian, attesting the warlike character of its primitive population.[19]

What thoughts must crowd on the mind of the traveller, as he wanders amidst these memorials of the past; as he treads over the ashes of the generations who reared these colossal fabrics, which take us from the present into the very depths of time! But who were their builders? Was it the shadowy Olmecs, whose history, like that of the ancient Titans, is lost in the mists of fable? or, as commonly reported, the peaceful and industrious Toltecs, of whom all that we can glean rests on traditions hardly more secure? What has become of the races who built them? Did they remain on the soil, and mingle and become incorporated with the fierce Aztecs who succeeded them? Or did they pass on to the South, and find a wider field for the expansion of their civilization, as shown by the higher character of the architectural remains in the distant regions

[17] Such is the account given by the cavalier Boturini. Idea, pp. 42, 43.

[18] Both Ixtlilxochitl and Boturini, who visited these monuments, one, early in the seventeenth, the other in the first part of the eighteenth century, testify to their having seen the remains of this statue. They had entirely disappeared by 1757, when Veytia examined the pyramid. Hist. Antig., tom. I. cap. 26.

[19] "Agricola, incurvo terram molitus aratro,
Exesa inveniet scabra rubigine pila," &c.

GEORG., lib. I

of Central America and Yucatan? It is all a mystery,—over which Time has thrown an impenetrable veil, that no mortal hand may raise. A nation has passed away,—powerful, populous, and well advanced in refinement, as attested by their monuments,—but it has perished without a name. It has died and made no sign!

Such speculations, however, do not seem to have disturbed the minds of the Conquerors, who have not left a single line respecting these time-honored structures, though they passed in full view of them,—perhaps, under their very shadows. In the sufferings of the present, they had little leisure to bestow on the past. Indeed, the new and perilous position, in which at this very spot they found themselves, must naturally have excluded every other thought from their bosoms, but that of self-preservation.

As the army was climbing the mountain steeps which shut in the Valley of Otompan, the videttes came in with the intelligence, that a powerful body was encamped on the other side, apparently awaiting their approach. The intelligence was soon confirmed by their own eyes, as they turned the crest of the sierra, and saw spread out, below, a mighty host, filling up the whole depth of the valley, and giving to it the appearance, from the white cotton mail of the warriors, of being covered with snow.[20] It consisted of levies from the surrounding country, and especially the populous territory of Tezcuco, drawn together at the instance of Cuitlahua, Montezuma's successor, and now concentrated on this point to dispute the passage of the Spaniards. Every chief of note had taken the field with his whole array gathered under his standard, proudly displaying all the pomp and rude splendor of his military equipment. As far as the eye could reach, were to be seen shields and waving banners, fantastic helmets, forests of shining spears, the bright feather-mail of the chief, and the coarse cotton panoply of his follower, all mingled together in wild confusion, and tossing to and fro like the billows of a troubled ocean.[21] It was a sight to fill the stoutest heart among the Christians with dismay, heightened by the previous expectation of soon reaching the friendly land which was to terminate their wearisome pilgrimage. Even Cortés, as he contrasted the tremendous array before him with his own diminished squadrons, wasted by disease and enfeebled by hunger and fatigue, could not escape the conviction that his last hour had arrived.[22]

But his was not the heart to despond; and he gathered strength from the very extremity of his situation. He had no room for hesitation; for there was no alternative left to him. To escape was impossible. He could

---

[20] "Y como iban vestidos de blanco, parecia el campo nevado." Herrera, Hist. General, dec. 2, lib. 10, cap. 13.

[21] "Vistosa confusion," says Solís, "de armas y penachos, en que tenian su hermosura los horrores." (Conquista, lib. 4, cap. 20.) His painting shows the hand of a great artist,—which he certainly was. But he should not have put fire arms into the hands of his countrymen, on this occasion.

[22] "Y cierto creímos ser aquel el último de nuestros dias." Rel. Seg. de Cortés, ap Lorenzana, p. 148

not retreat on the capital, from which he had been expelled. He must advance,—cut through the enemy, or perish. He hastily made his dispositions for the fight. He gave his force as broad a front as possible, protecting it on each flank by his little body of horse, now reduced to twenty. Fortunately, he had not allowed the invalids, for the last two days, to mount behind the riders, from a desire to spare the horses, so that these were now in tolerable condition; and, indeed, the whole army had been refreshed by halting, as we have seen, two nights and a day in the same place, a delay, however, which had allowed the enemy time to assemble in such force to dispute its progress.

Cortés instructed his cavaliers not to part with their lances, and to direct them at the face. The infantry were to thrust, not strike, with their swords; passing them, at once, through the bodies of their enemies. They were, above all, to aim at the leaders, as the general well knew how much depends on the life of the commander in the wars of barbarians, whose want of subordination makes them impatient of any control but that to which they are accustomed.

He then addressed to his troops a few words of encouragement, as customary with him on the eve of an engagement. He reminded them of the victories they had won with odds nearly as discouraging as the present; thus establishing the superiority of science and discipline over numbers. Numbers, indeed, were of no account, where the arm of the Almighty was on their side. And he bade them have full confidence, that He, who had carried them safely through so many perils, would not now abandon them and his own good cause, to perish by the hand of the infidel. His address was brief, for he read in their looks that settled resolve which rendered words unnecessary. The circumstances of their position spoke more forcibly to the heart of every soldier than any eloquence could have done, filling it with that feeling of desperation, which makes the weak arm strong, and turns the coward into a hero. After they had earnestly commended themselves, therefore, to the protection of God, the Virgin, and St. James, Cortés led his battalions straight against the enemy.[23]

It was a solemn moment,—that, in which the devoted little band, with steadfast countenances, and their usual intrepid step, descended on the plain, to be swallowed up, as it were, in the vast ocean of their enemies. The latter rushed on with impetuosity to meet them, making the mountains ring to their discordant yells and battle-cries, and sending forth volleys of stones and arrows which for a moment shut out the light of day. But, when the leading files of the two armies closed, the superiority of the Christians was felt, as their antagonists, falling back before the

---

[23] Camargo, Hist. de Tlascala, MS.—Oviedo, Hist. de las Ind., MS., lib. 33, cap. 14.—Bernal Diaz, Hist. de la Conquista, cap. 128.—Sahagun, Hist. de Nueva España, MS., lib. 12, cap. 27.

Cortés might have addressed his troops, as Napoleon did his in the famous battle with the Mamelukes: "From yonder pyramids forty centuries look down upon you." But the situation of the Spaniards was altogether too serious for theatrical display.

charges of cavalry, were thrown into confusion by their own numbers who pressed on them from behind. The Spanish infantry followed up the blow, and a wide lane was opened in the ranks of the enemy, who, receding on all sides, seemed willing to allow a free passage for their opponents. But it was to return on them with accumulated force, as rallying they poured upon the Christians, enveloping the little army on all sides, which, with its bristling array of long swords and javelins, stood firm,—in the words of a contemporary,—like an islet against which the breakers, roaring and surging, spend their fury in vain.[24] The struggle was desperate of man against man. The Tlascalan seemed to renew his strength, as he fought almost in view of his own native hills; as did the Spaniard, with the horrible doom of the captive before his eyes. Well did the cavaliers do their duty on that day; charging, in little bodies of four or five abreast, deep into the enemy's ranks, riding over the broken files, and by their temporary advantage giving strength and courage to the infantry. Not a lance was there which did not reek with the blood of the infidel. Among the rest, the young captain Sandoval is particularly commemorated for his daring prowess. Managing his fiery steed with easy horsemanship, he darted, when least expected, into the thickest of the *mêlée*, overturning the stanchest warriors, and rejoicing in danger, as if it were his natural element.[25]

But these gallant displays of heroism served only to ingulf the Spaniards deeper and deeper in the mass of the enemy, with scarcely any more chance of cutting their way through his dense and interminable battalions, than of hewing a passage with their swords through the mountains. Many of the Tlascalans and some of the Spaniards had fallen, and not one but had been wounded. Cortés himself had received a second cut on the head, and his horse was so much injured that he was compelled to dismount, and take one from the baggage train, a strong-boned animal, who carried him well through the turmoil of the day.[26] The contest had now lasted several hours. The sun rode high in the heavens, and shed an intolerable fervor over the plain. The Christians, weakened

---

[24] It is Sahagun's simile. "Estaban los Españoles como una Isleta en el mar, combatida de las olas por todas partes." (Hist. de Nueva España, MS., lib. 12, cap. 27.) The venerable missionary gathered the particulars of the action, as he informs us, from several who were present in it.

[25] The epic bard Ercilla's spirited portrait of the young warrior Tucapél may apply without violence to Sandoval, as described by the Castilian chroniclers.

> "Cubierto Tucapél de fina malla
> saltó como un libero y suelto pardo
> en medio de la tímida canalla,
> haciendo plaza el bárbaro gallardo:
> con silvos grita en desigual batalla:
> con piedra, palo, flecha, lanza y dardo
> le persigue la gente de manera
> como si fuera toro, ó brava fiera."
> LA ARAUCANA, Parte 1, canto 8.

[26] Herrera, Hist. General, dec. 2, lib. 10, cap. 13.

"Este caballo harriero," says Camargo, "le sirvió en la conquista de Méjico. y er la última guerra que se dió se la matáron." Hist. de Tlascala, MS.

by previous sufferings and faint with loss of blood, began to relax in their desperate exertions. Their enemies, constantly supported by fresh relays from the rear, were still in good heart, and, quick to perceive their advantage, pressed with redoubled force on the Spaniards. The horse fell back, crowded on the foot; and the latter, in vain seeking a passage amidst the dusky throngs of the enemy, who now closed up the rear, were thrown into some disorder. The tide of battle was setting rapidly against the Christians. The fate of the day would soon be decided; and all that now remained for them seemed to be to sell their lives as dearly as possible.

At this critical moment, Cortés, whose restless eye had been roving round the field in quest of any object that might offer him the means of arresting the coming ruin, rising in his stirrups, descried at a distance, in the midst of the throng, the chief who from his dress and military *cortège* he knew must be the commander of the barbarian forces. He was covered with a rich surcoat of feather-work; and a panache of beautiful plumes, gorgeously set in gold and precious stones, floated above his head. Rising above this, and attached to his back, between the shoulders, was a short staff bearing a golden net for a banner,—the singular, but customary, symbol of authority for an Aztec commander. The cacique, whose name was Cihuaca, was borne on a litter, and a body of young warriors, whose gay and ornamented dresses showed them to be the flower of the Indian nobles, stood round as a guard of his person and the sacred emblem.

The eagle eye of Cortés no sooner fell on this personage, than it lighted up with triumph. Turning quickly round to the cavaliers at his side, among whom were Sandoval, Olid, Alvarado, and Avila, he pointed out the chief, exclaiming, "There is our mark! Follow and support me!" Then crying his war-cry, and striking his iron heel into his weary steed, he plunged headlong into the thickest of the press. His enemies fell back, taken by surprise and daunted by the ferocity of the attack. Those who did not were pierced through with his lance, or borne down by the weight of his charger. The cavaliers followed close in the rear. On they swept, with the fury of a thunderbolt, cleaving the solid ranks asunder, strewing their path with the dying and the dead, and bounding over every obstacle in their way. In a few minutes they were in the presence of the Indian commander, and Cortés, overturning his supporters, sprung forward with the strength of a lion, and striking him through with his lance, hurled him to the ground. A young cavalier, Juan de Salamanca, who had kept close by his general's side, quickly dismounted and despatched the fallen chief. Then tearing away his banner, he presented it to Cortés, as a trophy to which he had the best claim.[27] It was all the work of a moment. The guard, overpowered by the suddenness of the onset, made little resistance, but, flying, communicated their own panic

---

[27] The brave cavalier was afterwards permitted by the Emperor Charles V. to assume this trophy on his own escutcheon, in commemoration of his exploit. Bernal Diaz, Hist. de la Conquista, cap. 128.

to their comrades. The tidings of the loss soon spread over the field. The Indians, filled with consternation, now thought only of escape. In their blind terror, their numbers augmented their confusion. They trampled on one another, fancying it was the enemy in their rear.[28]

The Spanish and Tlascalans were not slow to avail themselves of the marvellous change in their affairs. Their fatigue, their wounds, hunger, thirst, all were forgotten in the eagerness for vengeance; and they followed up the flying foe, dealing death at every stroke, and taking ample retribution for all they had suffered in the bloody marshes of Mexico.[29] Long did they pursue, till, the enemy having abandoned the field, they returned sated with slaughter to glean the booty which he had left. It was great, for the ground was covered with the bodies of chiefs, at whom the Spaniards, in obedience to the general's instructions, had particularly aimed; and their dresses displayed all the barbaric pomp of ornament, in which the Indian warrior delighted.[30] When his men had thus indemnified themselves, in some degree, for their late reverses, Cortés called them again under their banners; and, after offering up a grateful acknowledgement to the Lord of Hosts for their miraculous preservation,[31] they renewed their march across the now deserted valley. The sun was declining in the heavens, but, before the shades of evening had gathered around, they reached an Indian temple on an eminence, which afforded a strong and commodious position for the night.

Such was the famous battle of Otompan,—or Otumba, as commonly called, from the Spanish corruption of the name. It was fought on the

---

[28] The historians all concur in celebrating this glorious achievement of Cortés; who, concludes Gomara, "by his single arm saved the whole army from destruction." See Crónica, cap. 110.—Also Sahagun, Hist. de Nueva España, MS., lib. 12, cap. 27. —Camargo, Hist. de Tlascala, MS.—Bernal Diaz, Hist. de la Conquista, cap. 128.— Oviedo, Hist. de las Ind., MS., lib. 33, cap. 47.—Herrera, Hist. General, dec. 2, lib. 10, cap. 13.—Ixtlilxochitl, Hist. Chich., MS., cap. 89.

The brief and extremely modest notice of the affair in the general's own letter forms a beautiful contrast to the style of panegyric by others. "É con este trabajo fuímos mucha parte de el dia, hasta que quiso Dios, que murió una Persona de ellos, que debia ser tan Principal, que con su muerte cesó toda aquella Guerra." Rel. Seg., ap. Lorenzana, p. 148.

[29] "Pues á nosotros," says the doughty Captain Diaz, "no nos dolian las heridas, ni teniamos hambre, ni sed, sino que parecia que no auiamos auido, ni passado ningun mal trabajo. Seguímos la vitoria matando, é hiriendo. Pues nuestros amigos los de Tlascala estavan hechos vnos leones, y con sus espadas, y montantes, y otras armas que allí apañáron, hazíanlo muy bië y esforçadamente." Hist. de la Conquista, loc. cit.

[30] Ibid., ubi supra.

[31] The belligerent apostle St. James, riding, as usual, his milk-white courser, came to the rescue on this occasion; an event commemorated by the dedication of a hermitage to him, in the neighborhood. (Camargo, Hist. de Tlascala.) Diaz, a skeptic on former occasions, admits his indubitable appearance on this. (Ibid., ubi supra.) According to the Tezcucan chronicler, he was supported by the Virgin and St. Peter. (Hist. Chich., MS., cap. 89.) Voltaire sensibly remarks, "Ceux qui ont fait les relations de ces étranges événemens les ont voulu relever par des miracles, qui ne servent en effet qu'à les rabaisser. Le vrai miracle fut la conduite de Cortés." Voltaire, Essai sur les Mœurs, chap. 147.

8th of July, 1520. The whole amount of the Indian force is reckoned by Castilian writers at two hundred thousand! that of the slain at twenty thousand! Those who admit the first part of the estimate will find no difficulty in receiving the last.[32] It is about as difficult to form an accurate calculation of the numbers of a disorderly savage multitude, as of the pebbles on the beach, or the scattered leaves in autumn. Yet it was, undoubtedly, one of the most remarkable victories ever achieved in the New World. And this, not merely on account of the disparity of the forces, but of their unequal condition. For the Indians were in all their strength, while the Christians were wasted by disease, famine, and long protracted sufferings; without cannon or firearms, and deficient in the military apparatus which had so often struck terror into their barbarian foe,—deficient even in the terrors of a victorious name. But they had discipline on their side, desperate resolve, and implicit confidence in their commander. That they should have triumphed against such odds furnishes an inference of the same kind as that established by the victories of the European over the semi-civilized hordes of Asia.

Yet even here all must not be referred to superior discipline and tactics. For the battle would certainly have been lost, had it not been for the fortunate death of the Indian general. And, although the selection of the victim may be called the result of calculation, yet it was by the most precarious chance that he was thrown in the way of the Spaniards. It is, indeed, one among many examples of the influence of fortune in determining the fate of military operations. The star of Cortés was in the ascendant. Had it been otherwise, not a Spaniard would have survived that day, to tell the bloody tale of the battle of Otumba.

[33] See Oviedo, Hist. de las Ind., MS., lib. 33, cap. 47.—Herrera, Hist. General dec. 2, lib. 10, cap. 13.—Gomara, Crónica, cap. 110.

CHAPTER V

ARRIVAL IN TLASCALA--FRIENDLY RECEPTION—DISCONTENTS OF THE
ARMY—JEALOUSY OF THE TLASCALANS—EMBASSY FROM MEXICO

1520

ON the following morning, the army broke up its encampment at an
early hour. The enemy do not seem to have made an attempt to rally.
Clouds of skirmishers, however, were seen during the morning, keeping at
a respectful distance, though occasionally venturing near enough to
salute the Spaniards with a volley of missiles.

On a rising ground they discovered a fountain, a blessing not too often
met with in these arid regions, and gratefully commemorated by the
Christians, for the refreshment afforded by its cool and abundant waters.[1]
A little further on they descried the rude works which served as the
bulwark and boundary of the Tlascalan territory. At the sight, the allies
sent up a joyous shout of congratulation, in which the Spaniards heartily
joined, as they felt they were soon to be on friendly and hospitable
ground.

But these feelings were speedily followed by others of a different nature; and, as they drew nearer the territory, their minds were disturbed
with the most painful apprehensions as to their reception by the people
among whom they were bringing desolation and mourning, and who
might so easily, if ill-disposed, take advantage of their present crippled
condition. "Thoughts like these," says Cortés, "weighed as heavily on my
spirit as any which I ever experienced in going to battle with the Aztecs." [2] Still, he put, as usual, a good face on the matter, and encouraged
his men to confide in their allies, whose past conduct had afforded every
ground for trusting to their fidelity in future. He cautioned them, however, as their own strength was so much impaired, to be most careful to
give no umbrage, or ground for jealousy, to their high-spirited allies.
"Be but on your guard," continued the intrepid general, "and we have

[1] Is it not the same fountain of which Toribio makes honorable mention in his
topographical account of the country? "Nace en Tlaxcala una fuente grande á la
parte del Norte, cinco leguas de la principal ciudad; nace en un pueblo que se llama
Azumba, que en su lengua quiere decir *cabeza*, y así es, porque esta fuente es cabeza
y principio del mayor rio de los que entran en la mar del Sur, el cual entra en la
mar por Zacatula." Hist. de los Indios, MS., Parte 3, cap. 16.
[2] "El qual pensamiento, y sospecha nos púso en tanta afliccion, quanta trahíamos
viniendo peleando con los de Culúa." Rel. Seg. de Cortés, ap. Lorenzana. p. 149.

still stout hearts and strong hands to carry us through the midst of them!"[3] With these anxious surmises, bidding adieu to the Aztec domain, the Christian army crossed the frontier, and once more trod the soil of the Republic.

The first place at which they halted was the town of Huejotlipan, a place of about twelve or fifteen thousand inhabitants.[4] They were kindly greeted by the people, who came out to receive them, inviting the troops to their habitations, and administering all the relief of their simple hospitality. Yet this was not so disinterested, according to some of the Spaniards, as to prevent their expecting in requital a share of the plunder taken in the late action.[5] Here the weary forces remained two or three days, when the news of their arrival having reached the capital, not more than four or five leagues distant, the old chief, Maxixca, their efficient friend on their former visit, and Xicotencatl, the young warrior, who, it will be remembered, had commanded the troops of his nation in their bloody encounters with the Spaniards, came with a numerous concourse of the citizens to welcome the fugitives to Tlascala. Maxixca, cordially embracing the Spanish commander, testified the deepest sympathy for his misfortunes. That the white men could so long have withstood the confederated power of the Aztecs was proof enough of their marvellous prowess. "We have made common cause together," said the lord of Tlascala, "and we have common injuries to avenge; and, come weal or come woe, be assured we will prove true and loyal friends, and stand by you to the death."[6]

This cordial assurance and sympathy, from one who exercised a control over the public counsels beyond any other ruler, effectually dispelled the doubts that lingered in the mind of Cortés. He readily accepted his invitation to continue his march, at once, to the capital, where he would find so much better accommodations for his army, than in a small town on the frontier. The sick and wounded, placed in hammocks, were borne on the shoulders of the friendly natives; and, as the troops drew near the city, the inhabitants came flocking out in crowds to meet them, rending the air with joyous acclamations, and wild bursts of their rude Indian minstrelsy. Amidst the general jubilee, however, were heard sounds of wailing and sad lament, as some unhappy relative or friend, looking earnestly into the diminished files of their countrymen, sought

---

[3] "Y mas dixo, que tenia esperança en Dios que los hallariamos buenos, y leales; é que si otra cosa fuesse, lo que Dios no permita, que nos han de tornar á andar los puños con coraçones fuertes, y braços vigorosos, y que para esso fuessemos muy apercibidos." Bernal Diaz, Hist. de la Conquista, cap. 128.

[4] Called Gualipan by Cortés. (Ibid., p. 149.) An Aztec would have found it hard to trace the route of his enemies by their itineraries.

[5] Ibid., ubi supra.

Thoan Cano, however, one of the army, denies this, and asserts that the natives received them like their children, and would take no recompense. (See *Appendix, Part 2, No. 11.*)

[6] "Y que tubiesse por cierto, que me serian muy ciertos, y verdaderos Amigos hasta la muerte." Rel. Seg. de Cortés, ap. Lorenzana, p. 150.

in vain for some dear and familiar countenance, and, as they turned dis-appointed away, gave utterance to their sorrow in tones that touched the heart of every soldier in the army. With these mingled accompaniments of joy and woe,—the motley web of human life,—the way-worn columns of Cortés at length reëntered the republican capital.[7]

The general and his suite were lodged in the rude, but spacious, palace of Maxixca. The rest of the army took up their quarters in the district over which the Tlascalan lord presided. Here they continued several weeks, until, by the attentions of the hospitable citizens, and such med-ical treatment as their humble science could supply, the wounds of the soldiers were healed, and they recovered from the debility to which they had been reduced by their long and unparalleled sufferings. Cortés was one of those who suffered severely. He lost the use of two of the fingers of his left hand.[8] He had received, besides, two injuries on the head; one of which was so much exasperated by his subsequent fatigues and ex-citement of mind, that it assumed an alarming appearance. A part of the bone was obliged to be removed.[9] A fever ensued, and for several days the hero, who had braved danger and death in their most terrible forms, lay stretched on his bed, as helpless as an infant. His excellent constitu-tion, however, got the better of disease, and he was, at length, once more enabled to resume his customary activity.—The Spaniards, with politic generosity, requited the hospitality of their hosts by sharing with them the spoils of their recent victory, and Cortés especially rejoiced the heart of Maxixca, by presenting him with the military trophy which he had won from the Indian commander.[10]

But while the Spaniards were thus recruiting their health and spirits under the friendly treatment of their allies, and recovering the confi-dence and tranquillity of mind which had sunk under their hard reverses, they received tidings, from time to time, which showed that their late disaster had not been confined to the Mexican capital. On his descent

[7] Camargo, Hist. de Tlascala, MS.—Bernal Diaz, Hist. de la Conquista, ubi supra —"Sobreviniéron las mugeres Tlascaltecas, y todas puestas de luto, y llorando á donde estaban los Españoles, las unas preguntaban por sus maridos, las otras por sus hijos y hermanos, las otras por sus parientes que habian ido con los Españoles, y quedaban todos allá muertos: no es menos, sino que de esto llanto causó gran sentimiento en el corazon del Capitan, y de todos los Españoles, y él procuró lo mejor que pudo consolarles por medio de sus Intérpretes." Sahagun, Hist. de Nueva España, MS., lib. 12, cap. 28.

[8] "Yo assimismo quedé manco de dos dedos de la mano izquierda"—is Cortés' own expression in his letter to the emperor. (Rel. Seg., ap. Lorenzana, p. 152.) Don Thoan Cano, however, whose sympathies—from his Indian alliance, perhaps—seem to have been quite as much with the Aztecs as with his own countrymen, assured Oviedo, who was lamenting the general's loss, that he might spare his regrets, since Cortés had as many fingers on his hand, at that hour, as when he came from Cas-tile. May not the word *manco*, in his letter, be rendered by "maimed" ?

[9] "Hiriéron á Cortés con Honda tan mal, que se le pasmó la Cabeça, ó porque no le curáron bien, sacándole Cascos, ó por el demasiado trabajo que pasó." Gomara Crónica, cap. 110.

[10] Herrera, Hist. General, dec. 2, lib. 10, cap. 13.—Bernal Diaz, Ibid., ubi supra.

from Mexico to encounter Narvaez, Cortés had brought with him a quantity of gold, which he left for safe keeping at Tlascala. To this was added a considerable sum, collected by the unfortunate Velasquez de Leon, in his expedition to the coast, as well as contributions from other sources. From the unquiet state of the capital, the general thought it best, on his return there, still to leave the treasure under the care of a number of invalid soldiers, who, when in marching condition, were to rejoin him in Mexico. A party from Vera Cruz, consisting of five horsemen and forty foot, had since arrived at Tlascala, and, taking charge of the invalids and treasure, undertook to escort them to the capital. He now learned that they had been intercepted on the route, and all cut off, with the entire loss of the treasure. Twelve other soldiers, marching in the same direction, had been massacred in the neighboring province of Tepeaca; and accounts continually arrived of some unfortunate Castilian, who, presuming on the respect hitherto shown to his countrymen, and ignorant of the disasters in the capital, had fallen a victim to the fury of the enemy.[11]

These dismal tidings filled the mind of Cortés with gloomy apprehensions for the fate of the settlement at Villa Rica,—the last stay of their hopes. He despatched a trusty messenger, at once, to that place; and had the inexpressible satisfaction to receive a letter in return from the commander of the garrison, acquainting him with the safety of the colony, and its friendly relations with the neighbouring Totonacs. It was the best guaranty of the fidelity of the latter, that they had offended the Mexicans too deeply to be forgiven.

While the affairs of Cortés wore so gloomy an aspect without, he had to experience an annoyance scarcely less serious from the discontents of his followers. Many of them had fancied that their late appalling reverses would put an end to the expedition; or, at least, postpone all thoughts of resuming it for the present. But they knew little of Cortés who reasoned thus. Even while tossing on his bed of sickness, he was ripening in his mind fresh schemes for retrieving his honor, and for recovering the empire which had been lost more by another's rashness than his own. This was apparent, as he became convalescent, from the new regulations he made respecting the army, as well as from the orders sent to Vera Cruz for fresh reinforcements.

The knowledge of all this occasioned much disquietude to the disaffected soldiers. They were, for the most part, the ancient followers of Narvaez, on whom, as we have seen, the brunt of the war had fallen the heaviest. Many of them possessed property in the Islands, and had embarked on this expedition chiefly from the desire of increasing it. But they

[11] Rel. Seg. de Cortés, ap. Lorenzana, p. 150.—Oviedo, Hist. de las Ind., MS., lib. 33, cap. 15.

Herrera gives the following inscription, cut on the bark of a tree by some of these unfortunate Spaniards. "By this road passed Juan Juste and his wretched companions, who were so much pinched by hunger, that they were obliged to give a solid bar of gold, weighing eight hundred ducats, for a few cakes of maize bread." Hist. General, dec. 2, lib. 10, cap. 13.

had gathered neither gold nor glory in Mexico. Their present service filled them only with disgust; and the few, comparatively, who had been so fortunate as to survive, languished to return to their rich mines and pleasant farms in Cuba, bitterly cursing the day when they had left them.

Finding their complaints little heeded by the general, they prepared a written remonstrance, in which they made their demand more formally. They represented the rashness of persisting in the enterprise in his present impoverished state, without arms or ammunition, almost without men; and this, too, against a powerful enemy, who had been more than a match for him with all the strength of his late resources. It was madness to think of it. The attempt would bring them all to the sacrifice-block. Their only course was to continue their march to Vera Cruz. Every hour of delay might be fatal. The garrison in that place might be overwhelmed from want of strength to defend itself; and thus their last hope would be annihilated. But, once there, they might wait in comparative security for such reinforcements as would join them from abroad; while in case of failure they could the more easily make their escape. They concluded, with insisting on being permitted to return, at once, to the port of Villa Rica. This petition, or rather remonstrance, was signed by all the disaffected soldiers, and, after being formally attested by the royal notary, was presented to Cortés.[12]

It was a trying circumstance for him. What touched him most nearly was, to find the name of his friend, the secretary Duero, to whose good offices he had chiefly owed his command, at the head of the paper. He was not, however, to be shaken from his purpose for a moment; and while all outward resources seemed to be fading away, and his own friends faltered, or failed him, he was still true to himself. He knew that to retreat to Vera Cruz would be to abandon the enterprise. Once there, his army would soon find a pretext and a way for breaking up and returning to the Islands. All his ambitious schemes would be blasted. The great prize, already once in his grasp, would then be lost for ever. He would be a ruined man.

In his celebrated letter to Charles the Fifth, he says, that, in reflecting on his position, he felt the truth of the old adage, "that fortune favors the brave." The Spaniards were the followers of the Cross; and, trusting in the infinite goodness and mercy of God, he could not believe that He would suffer them and his own good cause thus to perish among the heathen.[13] He was resolved, therefore, not to descend to the coast,

[12] One is reminded of the similar remonstrance made by Alexander's soldiers to him, on reaching the Hystaspis,—but attended with more success; as, indeed, was reasonable. For Alexander continued to advance from the ambition of indefinite conquest, while Cortés was only bent on carrying out his original enterprise. What was madness in the one was heroism in the other.

[13] "Acordándome, que siempre á los osados ayuda la fortuna, y que eramos Christianos y confiando en la grandíssima Bondad, y Misericordia de Dios, que no permitiria, que del todo pereciessemos, y se perdiesse tanta, y tan noble Tierra." Rel. Seg., ap. Lorenzana, p. 152.

but at all hazards to retrace his steps and beard the enemy again in his capital.

It was in the same resolute tone that he answered his discontented followers.[14] He urged every argument which could touch their pride or honor as cavaliers. He appealed to that ancient Castilian valor which had never been known to falter before an enemy; besought them not to discredit the great deeds which had made their name ring throughout Europe; not to leave the emprise half achieved, for others more daring and adventurous to finish. How could they with any honor, he asked, desert their allies whom they had involved in the war, and leave them unprotected to the vengeance of the Aztecs? To retreat but a single step towards Villa Rica would be to proclaim their own weakness. It would dishearten their friends, and give confidence to their foes. He implored them to resume the confidence in him which they had ever showed, and to reflect, that, if they had recently met with reverses, he had up to that point accomplished all, and more than all, that he had promised. It would be easy now to retrieve their losses, if they would have patience, and abide in this friendly land until the reinforcements, which would be ready to come in at his call, should enable them to act on the offensive. If, however, there were any so insensible to the motives which touch a brave man's heart, as to prefer ease at home, to the glory of this great achievement, he would not stand in their way. Let them go in God's name. Let them leave their general in his extremity. He should feel stronger in the service of a few brave spirits, than if surrounded by a host of the false or the faint-hearted.[15]

The disaffected party, as already noticed, was chiefly drawn from the troops of Narvaez. When the general's own veterans heard this appeal,[16] their blood warmed with indignation at the thoughts of abandoning him or the cause, at such a crisis. They pledged themselves to stand by him to the last; and the malcontents, silenced, if not convinced, by this generous expression of sentiment from their comrades, consented to postpone their departure for the present, under the assurance, that no obstacle should be thrown in their way, when a more favorable season should present itself.[17]

[14] This reply, exclaims Oviedo, showed a man of unconquerable spirit, and high destinies. "Paréceme que la respuesta que á esto les dió Hernando Cortés, é lo que hizo en ello, fué vna cosa de ánimo invencible, é de varon de mucha suerte é valor." Hist. de las Ind., MS., lib. 33, cap. 15.

[15] "É no me hable ninguno en otra cosa; y él que desta opinion no estubiere váyase en buen hora, que mas holgaré de quedar con los pocos y osados, que en compañía de muchos, ni de ninguno cobarde, ni desacordado de su propia honra." Hist. de las Ind., MS., loc. cit.

[16] Oviedo has expanded the harangue of Cortés into several pages, in the course of which the orator quotes Xenophon, and borrows largely from the old Jewish history, a style of eloquence savoring much more of the closet than the camp. Cortés was no pedant, and his soldiers were no scholars.

[17] For the account of this turbulent transaction, see Bernal Diaz, Hist. de la Conquista, cap. 129,—Rel. Seg. de Cortés, ap. Lorenzana, p. 152,—Oviedo, Hist. de las

Scarcely was this difficulty adjusted, when Cortés was menaced with one more serious, in the jealousy springing up between his soldiers and their Indian allies. Notwithstanding the demonstrations of regard by Maxixca and his immediate followers, there were others of the nation who looked with an evil eye on their guests, for the calamities in which they had involved them; and they tauntingly asked, if, in addition to this, they were now to be burdened by the presence and maintenance of the strangers? These sallies of discontent were not so secret as altogether to escape the ears of the Spaniards, in whom they occasioned no little disquietude. They proceeded, for the most part, it is true, from persons of little consideration, since the four great chiefs of the republic appear to have been steadily secured to the interests of Cortés. But they derived some importance from the countenance of the warlike Xicotencatl, in whose bosom still lingered the embers of that implacable hostility which he had displayed so courageously on the field of battle; and sparkles of this fiery temper occasionally gleamed forth in the intimate intercourse into which he was now reluctantly brought with his ancient opponents.

Cortés, who saw, with alarm, the growing feelings of estrangement, which must sap the very foundations on which he was to rest the lever for future operations, employed every argument which suggested itself, to restore the confidence of his own men. He reminded them of the good services they had uniformly received from the great body of the nation. They had a sufficient pledge of the future constancy of the Tlascalans in their long cherished hatred of the Aztecs, which the recent disasters they had suffered from the same quarter could serve only to sharpen. And he urged with much force, that, if any evil designs had been meditated by them against the Spaniards, the Tlascalans would, doubtless, have taken advantage of their late disabled condition, and not waited till they had recovered their strength and means of resistance.[18]

While Cortés was thus endeavoring, with somewhat doubtful success, to stifle his own apprehensions, as well as those in the bosoms of his followers, an event occurred which happily brought the affair to an issue, and permanently settled the relations in which the two parties were to stand to each other. This will make it necessary to notice some events which had occurred in Mexico, since the expulsion of the Spaniards.

On Montezuma's death, his brother, Cuitlahua, lord of Iztapalapan, conformably to the usage regulating the descent of the Aztec crown, was chosen to succeed him. He was an active prince, of large experience in military affairs, and, by the strength of his character, was well fitted to sustain the tottering fortunes of the monarchy. He appears, moreover, to

Ind., MS., lib. 33, cap. 15,—Gomara, Crónica, cap. 112, 113,—Herrera, Hist. General, dec. 2, lib. 10, cap. 14.

Diaz is exceedingly wroth with the chaplain, Gomara, for not discriminating between the old soldiers and the levies of Narvaez, whom he involves equally in the sin of rebellion. The captain's own version seems a fair one, and I have followed it, therefore, in the text.

[18] Oviedo, Hist. de las Ind., MS., lib. 33, cap. 15.—Herrera, Hist. General, dec. 2, lib. 10, cap. 14.—Sahagun, Hist. de Nueva España, MS., lib. 12, cap. 29.

have been a man of liberal, and what may be called enlightened, taste, to judge from the beautiful gardens which he had filled with rare exotics, and which so much attracted the admiration of the Spaniards in his city of Iztapalapan. Unlike his predecessor, he held the white men in detestation; and had, probably, the satisfaction of celebrating his own coronation by the sacrifice of many of them. From the moment of his release from the Spanish quarters, where he had been detained by Cortés, he entered into the patriotic movements of his people. It was he who conducted the assaults both in the streets of the city, and on the "Melancholy Night"; and it was at his instigation, that the powerful force had been assembled to dispute the passage of the Spaniards in the Vale of Otumba.[19]

Since the evacuation of the capital, he had been busily occupied in repairing the mischief it had received,—restoring the buildings and the bridges, and putting it in the best posture of defence. He had endeavored to improve the discipline and arms of his troops. He introduced the long spear among them, and, by attaching the sword-blades taken from the Christians to long poles, contrived a weapon that should be formidable against the cavalry. He summoned his vassals, far and near, to hold themselves in readiness to march to the relief of the capital, if necessary, and, the better to secure their good-will, relieved them from some of the burdens usually laid on them. But he was now to experience the instability of a government which rested not on love, but on fear. The vassals in the neighborhood of the Valley remained true to their allegiance; but others held themselves aloof, uncertain what course to adopt; while others, again, in the more distant provinces, refused obedience altogether, considering this a favorable moment for throwing off the yoke which had so long galled them.[20]

In this emergency, the government sent a deputation to its ancient enemies, the Tlascalans. It consisted of six Aztec nobles, bearing a present of cotton cloth, salt, and other articles rarely seen, of late years, in the republic. The lords of the state, astonished at this unprecedented act of condescension in their ancient foe, called the council or senate of the great chiefs together, to give the envoys audience.

Before this body, the Aztecs stated the purpose of their mission. They invited the Tlascalans to bury all past grievances in oblivion, and to enter into a treaty with them. All the nations of Anahuac should make common cause in defence of their country against the white men. The Tlascalans would bring down on their own heads the wrath of the gods, if they longer harbored the strangers who had violated and destroyed

[19] Oviedo, Hist. de las Ind., MS., lib. 33, cap. 47.—Rel. Seg. de Cortés, ap. Lorenzana, p. 166.—Sahagun, Hist. de Nueva España, MS., lib. 12, cap. 27, 29.

Or rather, it was "at the instigation of the great Devil, the captain of all the devils, called Satan, who regulated every thing in New Spain by his free will and pleasure, before the coming of the Spaniards," according to father Sahagun, who begins his chapter with this eloquent exordium.

[20] Ixtlilxochitl, Hist. Chich., MS., cap. 88.—Sahagun, Hist. de Nueva España, MS., lib. 12, cap. 29.—Herrera, Hist. General, dec. 2, lib. 10, cap. 19.

their temples. If they counted on the support and friendship of their guests, let them take warning from the fate of Mexico, which had received them kindly within its walls, and which, in return, they had filled with blood and ashes. They conjured them, by their reverence for their common religion, not to suffer the white men, disabled as they now were, to escape from their hands, but to sacrifice them at once to the gods, whose temples they had profaned. In that event, they proffered them their alliance, and the renewal of that friendly traffic which would restore to the republic the possession of the comforts and luxuries of which it had been so long deprived.

The proposals of the ambassadors produced different effects on their audience. Xicotencatl was for embracing them at once. Far better was it, he said, to unite with their kindred, with those who held their own language, their faith and usages, than to throw themselves into the arms of the fierce strangers, who, however they might talk of religion, worshipped no god but gold. This opinion was followed by that of the younger warriors, who readily caught the fire of his enthusiasm. But the elder chiefs, especially his blind old father, one of the four rulers of the state, who seem to have been all heartily in the interests of the Spaniards, and one of them, Maxixca, their stanch friend, strongly expressed their aversion to the proposed alliance with the Aztecs. They were always the same, said the latter,—fair in speech, and false in heart. They now proffered friendship to the Tlascalans. But it was fear which drove them to it, and, when that fear was removed, they would return to their old hostility. Who was it, but these insidious foes, that had so long deprived the country of the very necessaries of life, of which they were now so lavish in their offers? Was it not owing to the white men, that the nation at length possessed them? Yet they were called on to sacrifice the white men to the gods!—the warriors who, after fighting the battles of the Tlascalans, now threw themselves on their hospitality. But the gods abhorred perfidy. And were not their guests the very beings whose coming had been so long predicted by the oracles? Let us avail ourselves of it, he concluded, and unite and make common cause with them, until we have humbled our haughty enemy.

This discourse provoked a sharp rejoinder from Xicotencatl, till the passion of the elder chieftain got the better of his patience, and, substituting force for argument, he thrust his younger antagonist, with some violence, from the council chamber. A proceeding so contrary to the usual decorum of Indian debate astonished the assembly. But, far from bringing censure on its author, it effectually silenced opposition. Even the hot-headed followers of Xicotencatl shrunk from supporting a leader who had incurred such a mark of contemptuous displeasure from the ruler whom they most venerated. His own father openly condemned him; and the patriotic young warrior, gifted with a truer foresight into futurity than his countrymen, was left without support in the council, as he had formerly been on the field of battle.—The proffered alliance of the Mexicans was unanimously rejected; and the envoys, fearing that even the sacred character with which they were invested might not protect them from violence, made their escape secretly from the capital.[21]

The result of the conference was of the last importance to the Spaniards, who, in their present crippled condition, especially if taken unawares, would have been, probably, at the mercy of the Tlascalans. At all events, the union of these latter with the Aztecs would have settled the fate of the expedition; since, in the poverty of his own resources, it was only by adroitly playing off one part of the Indian population against the other, that Cortés could ultimately hope for success.

[21] The proceedings in the Tlascalan senate are reported in more or less detail, but substantially alike, by Camargo, Hist. de Tlascala, MS.,—Sahagun, Hist. de Nueva España, MS., lib. 12, cap. 29,—Herrera, Hist. General, dec. 2, lib. 12, cap. 14.

See, also, Bernal Diaz, Hist. de la Conquista, cap. 129,—Gomara, Crónica, cap. III.

CHAPTER VI

WAR WITH THE SURROUNDING TRIBES—SUCCESSES OF THE SPANIARDS—
DEATH OF MAXIXCA—ARRIVAL OF REINFORCEMENTS—RETURN IN
TRIUMPH TO TLASCALA

1520

THE Spanish commander, reassured by the result of the deliberations in
the Tlascalan senate, now resolved on active operations, as the best means
of dissipating the spirit of faction and discontent inevitably fostered by a
life of idleness. He proposed to exercise his troops, at first, against some
of the neighboring tribes who had laid violent hands on such of the
Spaniards as, confiding in their friendly spirit, had passed through their
territories. Among these were the Tepeacans, a people often engaged in
hostility with the Tlascalans, and who, as mentioned in a preceding
Chapter, had lately massacred twelve Spaniards in their march to the
capital. An expedition against them would receive the ready support of
his allies, and would assert the dignity of the Spanish name, much
dimmed in the estimation of the natives by the late disasters.

The Tepeacans were a powerful tribe of the same primitive stock as
the Aztecs, to whom they acknowledged allegiance. They had transferred this to the Spaniards, on their first march into the country, intimidated by the bloody defeats of their Tlascalan neighbors. But, since the
troubles in the capital, they had again submitted to the Aztec sceptre.
Their capital, now a petty village, was a flourishing city at the time of the
Conquest, situated in the fruitful plains that stretch far away towards
the base of Orizaba.[1] The province contained, moreover, several towns
of considerable size, filled with a bold and warlike population.

As these Indians had once acknowledged the authority of Castile, Cortés and his officers regarded their present conduct in the light of rebellion, and, in a council of war, it was decided that those engaged in the
late massacre had fairly incurred the doom of slavery.[2] Before proceeding against them, however, the general sent a summons requiring their

---

[1] The Indian name of the capital,—the same as that of the province,—*Tepejacac*,
was corrupted by the Spaniards into *Tepeaca*. It must be admitted to have gained
by the curruption.

[2] "Y como aquello vió Cortés, comunicólo con todos nuestros Capitanes, y soldados: y fué acordado, que se hiziesse vn auto por ante Escriuano, que diesse fe de
todo lo passado, y que se diessen por esclauos." Bernal Diaz, Hist. de la Conquista,
cap. 130.

submission, and offering full pardon for the past, but, in case of refusal, menacing them with the severest retribution To this the Indians, now in arms, returned a contemptuous answer, challenging the Spaniards to meet them in fight, as they were in want of victims for their sacrifices.

Cortés, without further delay, put himself at the head of his small corps of Spaniards, and a large reinforcement of Tlascalan warriors. They were led by the younger Xicotencatl, who now appeared willing to bury his recent animosity, and desirous to take a lesson in war under the chief who had so often foiled him in the field.[3]

The Tepeacans received their enemy on their borders. A bloody battle followed, in which the Spanish horse were somewhat embarrassed by the tall maize that covered part of the plain. They were successful in the end, and the Tepeacans, after holding their ground like good warriors, were at length routed with great slaughter. A second engagement, which took place a few days after, was followed by like decisive results; and the victorious Spaniards with their allies, marching straightway on the city of Tepeaca, entered it in triumph.[4] No further resistance was attempted by the enemy, and the whole province, to avoid further calamities, eagerly tendered its submission. Cortés, however, inflicted the meditated chastisement on the places implicated in the massacre. The inhabitants were branded with a hot iron as slaves, and, after the royal fifth had been reserved, were distributed between his own men and the allies.[5] The Spaniards were familiar with the system of *repartimientos* established in the Islands; but this was the first example of slavery in New Spain. It was justified, in the opinion of the general and his military casuists, by the aggravated offences of the party. The sentence, however, was not countenanced by the Crown,[6] which, as the colonial legislation abundantly shows, was ever at issue with the craving and mercenary spirit of the colonist.

Satisfied with this display of his vengeance, Cortés now established his head-quarters at Tepeaca, which, situated in a cultivated country, afforded easy means for maintaining an army, while its position on the Mexican frontier made it a good *point d'appui* for future operations.

The Aztec government, since it had learned the issue of its negotiations at Tlascala, had been diligent in fortifying its frontier in that quarter. The garrisons usually maintained there were strengthened, and large

---

[3] The chroniclers estimate his army at 50,000 warriors; one half, according to Horibio, of the disposable military force of the republic. "De la cual, (Tlascala,) como ya tengo dicho, solian salir cien mil hombres de pelea." Hist. de los Indios, MS., Parte 3, cap. 16.

[4] "That night," says the credulous Herrera, speaking of the carouse that followed one of their victories, "the Indian allies had a grand supper of legs and arms; for, besides an incredible number of roasts on wooden spits, they had fifty thousand pots of stewed human flesh!!" (Hist. General, dec. 2, lib. 10, cap. 15.) Such a banquet would not have smelt savory in the nostrils of Cortés.

[5] "Y allí hiziéron hazer el hierro con que se auian de herrar los que se tomauan por esclauos, que era una G., que quiere decir *guerra*." Bernal Diaz, Hist. de la Conquista, cap. 130.

[6] Solís, Conquista, lib. 5, cap. 3.

bodies of men were marched in the same direction, with orders to occupy the strong positions on the borders. The conduct of these troops was in their usual style of arrogance and extortion, and greatly disgusted the inhabitants of the country.

Among the places thus garrisoned by the Aztecs was Quauhquechollan,[7] a city containing thirty thousand inhabitants, according to the historians, and lying to the south-west twelve leagues or more from the Spanish quarters. It stood at the extremity of a deep valley, resting against a bold range of hills, or rather, mountains, and flanked by two rivers with exceedingly high and precipitous banks. The only avenue, by which the town could be easily approached, was protected by a stone wall more than twenty feet high and of great thickness.[8] Into this place, thus strongly defended by art as well as by nature, the Aztec emperor had thrown a garrison of several thousand warriors, while a much more formidable force occupied the heights commanding the city.

The cacique of this strong post, impatient of the Mexican yoke, sent to Cortés, inviting him to march to his relief, and promising a coöperation of the citizens in an assault on the Aztec quarters. The general eagerly embraced the proposal, and detached Christóval de Olid, with two hundred Spaniards and a strong body of Tlascalans, to support the friendly cacique.[9] On the way, Olid was joined by many volunteers from the Indian city and from the neighboring capital of Cholula, all equally pressing their services. The number and eagerness of these auxiliaries excited suspicions in the bosom of the cavalier. They were strengthened by the surmises of the soldiers of Narvaez, whose imaginations were still haunted, it seems, by the horrors of the *noche triste*, and who saw in the friendly alacrity of their new allies evidence of an insidious understanding with the Aztecs. Olid, catching this distrust, made a countermarch on Cholula, where he seized the suspected chiefs, who had been most forward in offering their services, and sent them under a strong guard to Cortés.

The general, after a careful examination, was satisfied of the integrity of the suspected parties. He, expressing his deep regret at the treatment they had received, made them such amends as he could by liberal presents; and, as he now saw the impropriety of committing an affair of such importance to other hands, put himself at the head of his remaining force, and effected a junction with his officer in Cholula.

[7] Called by the Spaniards *Huacachula*, and spelt with every conceivable diversity by the old writers, who may be excused for stumbling over such a confusion of consonants.

[8] "Y toda la Ciudad está cercada de muy fuerte Muro de cal y canto, tan alto, como quatro estados por de fuera de la Ciudad: é por de dentro está casi igual con el suelo. Y por toda la Muralla va su petril, tan alto, como medio estado, para pelear, tiene quatro entradas, tan anchas, como uno puede entrar á Caballo." Rel. Seg., p. 162.

[9] This cavalier's name is usually spelt Olid by the Chroniclers. In a copy of his own signature, I find it written Oli.

He had arranged with the cacique of the city against which he was marching, that, on the appearance of the Spaniards, the inhabitants should rise on the garrison. Every thing succeeded as he had planned. No sooner had the Christian battalions defiled on the plain before the town, than the inhabitants attacked the garrison with the utmost fury. The latter, abandoning the outer defences of the place, retreated to their own quarters in the principal *teocalli*, where they maintained a hard struggle with their adversaries. In the heat of it, Cortés, at the head of his little body of horse, rode into the place, and directed the assault in person. The Aztecs made a fierce defence. But fresh troops constantly arriving to support the assailants, the works were stormed, and every one of the garrison was put to the sword.[10]

The Mexican forces, meanwhile, stationed on the neighboring eminences, had marched down to the support of their countrymen in the town, and formed in order of battle in the suburbs, where they were encountered by the Tlascalan levies. "They mustered," says Cortés, speaking of the enemy, "at least thirty thousand men, and it was a brave sight for the eye to look on,—such a beautiful array of warriors glistening with gold and jewels and variegated feather-work!"[11] The action was well contested between the two Indian armies. The suburbs were set on fire, and, in the midst of the flames, Cortés and his squadrons, rushing on the enemy, at length broke their array, and compelled them to fall back in disorder into the narrow gorge of the mountain, from which they had lately descended. The pass was rough and precipitous. Spaniards and Tlascalans followed close in the rear, and the light troops, scaling the high wall of the valley, poured down on the enemy's flanks. The heat was intense, and both parties were so much exhausted by their efforts, that it was with difficulty, says the chronicler, that the one could pursue, or the other fly.[12] They were not too weary, however, to slay. The Mexicans were routed with terrible slaughter. They found no pity from their Indian foes, who had a long account of injuries to settle with them. Some few sought refuge by flying higher up into the fastnesses of the sierra. They were followed by their indefatigable enemy, until, on the bald summit of the ridge, they reached the Mexican encampment. It covered a wide tract of ground. Various utensils, ornamented dresses, and articles of luxury, were scattered round, and the number of slaves in attendance showed the barbaric pomp with which the nobles of Mexico went to their

[10] "I should have been very glad to have taken some alive,' says Cortés, "who could have informed me of what was going on in the great city, and who had been lord there since the death of Montezuma. But I succeeded in saving only one,—and he was more dead than alive." Rel. Seg. de Cortés, ap. Lorenzana, p. 159.

[11] "Y á ver que cosa era aquella, los quales eran mas de treinta mil Hombres, y la mas lúcida Gente, que hemos visto, porque trahian muchas Joyas de Oro, y Plata y Plumajes." Ibid., p. 160.

[12] "Alcanzando muchos por una Cuesta arriba muy agra; y tal, que quando acabámos de encumbrar la Sierra, ni los Enemigos, ni nosotros podiamos ir atras, ni adelante: é assí caiéron muchos de ellos muertos, y ahogados de la calor, sin herida ninguna." Ibid., p. 160.

campaigns.[13] It was a rich booty for the victors, who spread over the deserted camp, and loaded themselves with the spoil, until the gathering darkness warned them to descend.[14]

Cortés followed up the blow by assaulting the strong town of Itzocan, held, also, by a Mexican garrison, and situated in the depths of a green valley watered by artificial canals, and smiling in all the rich abundance of this fruitful region of the plateau.[15] The place, though stoutly defended, was stormed and carried; the Aztecs were driven across a river which ran below the town, and, although the light bridges that traversed it were broken down in the flight, whether by design or accident, the Spaniards, fording and swimming the stream as they could, found their way to the opposite bank, following up the chase with the eagerness of bloodhounds. Here, too, the booty was great; and the Indian auxiliaries flocked by thousands to the banners of the chief who so surely led them on to victory and plunder.[16]

Soon afterwards, Cortés returned to his headquarters at Tepeaca. Thence he detached his officers on expeditions which were usually successful. Sandoval, in particular, marched against a large body of the enemy lying between the camp and Vera Cruz; defeated them in two decisive battles, and thus restored the communications with the port.

The result of these operations was the reduction of that populous and cultivated territory which lies between the great *volcan*, on the west, and the mighty skirts of Orizaba, on the east. Many places, also, in the neighboring province of Mixtecapan acknowledged the authority of the Spaniards, and others from the remote region of Oaxaca sent to claim their protection. The conduct of Cortés towards his allies had gained

---

[13] "Porque demas de la Gente de Guerra, tenian mucho aparato de Servidores, y fornecimiento para su Real." Ibid., p. 160.

[14] The story of the capture of this strong post is told very differently by Captain Diaz. According to him, Olid, when he had fallen back on Cholula, in consequence of the refusal of his men to advance, under the strong suspicion which they entertained of some foul practice from their allies, received such a stinging rebuke from Cortés, that he compelled his troops to resume their march, and, attacking the enemy, "with the fury of a tiger," totally routed them. (Hist. de la Conquista, cap. 132.) But this version of the affair is not endorsed, so far as I am aware, by any contemporary. Cortés is so compendious in his report, that it is often necessary to supply the omissions with the details of other writers. But where he is positive in his statements,—unless there be some reason to suspect a bias,—his practice of writing on the spot, and the peculiar facilities for information afforded by his position, make him decidedly the best authority.

[15] Cortés, with an eye less sensible to the picturesque than his great predecessor in the track of discovery, Columbus, was fully as quick in detecting the capabilities of the soil. "Tiene un Valle redondo muy fertil de Frutas, y Algodon, que en ninguna parte de los Puertos arriba se hace por la gran frialdad: y allí es Tierra caliente, y caúsalo, que está muy abrigada de Sierras; todo este Valle se riega por muy buenas Azequias, que tienen muy bien sacadas, y concertadas." Ibid., pp. 164, 165.

[16] So numerous, according to Cortés, that they covered hill and dale, as far as the eye could reach, mustering more than a hundred and twenty thousand strong! (Ibid., p. 162.) When the Conquerors attempt any thing like a precise numeration, it will be as safe to substitute "a multitude," "a great force," &c., trusting the amount to the reader's own imagination.

him great credit for disinterestedness and equity. The Indian cities in the adjacent territory appealed to him, as their umpire, in their differ ences with one another, and cases of disputed succession in their govern ments were referred to his arbitration. By his discreet and moderate pol· icy, he insensibly acquired an ascendency over their counsels, which had been denied to the ferocious Aztec. His authority extended wider and wider every day; and a new empire grew up, in the very heart of the land, forming a counterpoise to the colossal power which had so long over-shadowed it.[17]

Cortés now felt himself strong enough to put in execution the plans for recovering the capital, over which he had been brooding ever since the hour of his expulsion. He had greatly undervalued the resources of the Aztec monarchy. He was now aware, from bitter experience, that, to vanquish it, his own forces, and all he could hope to muster, would be incompetent, without a very extensive support from the Indians themselves. A large army would, moreover, require large supplies for its maintenance, and these could not be regularly obtained, during a protracted siege, without the friendly coöperation of the natives. On such support he might now safely calculate from Tlascala, and the other Indian territories, whose warriors were so eager to serve under his banners. His past acquaintance with them had instructed him in their national character and system of war; while the natives who had fought under his command, if they had caught little of the Spanish tactics, had learned to act in concert with the white men, and to obey him implicitly as their commander. This was a considerable improvement in such wild and disor· derly levies, and greatly augmented the strength derived from numbers.

Experience showed, that, in a future conflict with the capital, it would not do to trust to the causeways, but that, to succeed, he must command the lake. He proposed, therefore, to build a number of vessels like those constructed under his orders in Montezuma's time, and afterwards destroyed by the inhabitants. For this he had still the services of the same experienced ship-builder, Martin Lopez, who, as we have seen, had fortunately escaped the slaughter of the "Melancholy Night." Cortés now sent this man to Tlascala, with orders to build thirteen brigantines, which might be taken to pieces and carried on the shoulders of the Indians to be launched on the waters of Lake Tezcuco. The sails, rigging, and iron work, were to be brought from Vera Cruz, where they had been stored since their removal from the dismantled ships. It was a bold conception, that of constructing a fleet to be transported across forest and mountain before it was launched on its destined waters! But it suited the daring genius of Cortés, who, with the coöperation of his stanch Tlascalan confederates, did not doubt his ability to carry it into execution.

---

[17] For the hostilities with the Indian tribes, noticed in the preceding pages, see, in addition to the Letter of Cortés, so often cited, Oviedo, Hist. de las Ind., MS., lib. 33, cap. 15,—Herrera, Hist. General, dec. 2, lib. 10, cap. 15, 16,—Ixtlilxochitl, Hist. Chich. MS. cap. 90,—Bernal Diaz, Hist. de la Conquista, cap. 130, 132, 134, —Gomara, Crónica, cap. 114-117,—P. Martyr, De Orbe Novo, dec. 5, cap. 6,— Camargo, Hist. de Tlascala, MS.

It was with no little regret, that the general learned at this time the death of his good friend Maxixca, the old lord of Tlascala, who had stood by him so steadily in the hour of adversity. He had fallen a victim to that terrible epidemic, the smallpox, which was now sweeping over the land like fire over the prairies, smiting down prince and peasant, and adding another to the long train of woes that followed the march of the white men. It was imported into the country, it is said, by a Negro slave, in the fleet of Narvaez.[18] It first broke out in Cempoalla. The poor natives, ignorant of the best mode of treating the loathsome disorder, sought relief in their usual practice of bathing in cold water, which greatly aggravated their trouble. From Cempoalla it spread rapidly over the neighboring country, and, penetrating through Tlascala, reached the Aztec capital, where Montezuma's successor, Cuitlahua, fell one of its first victims. Thence it swept down towards the borders of the Pacific, leaving its path strewn with the dead bodies of the natives, who, in the strong language of a contemporary, perished in heaps like cattle stricken with the murrain.[19] It does not seem to have been fatal to the Spaniards, many of whom, probably, had already had the disorder, and who were, at all events, acquainted with the proper method of treating it.

The death of Maxixca was deeply regretted by the troops, who lost in him a true and most efficient ally. With his last breath, he commended them to his son and successor, as the great beings whose coming into the country had been so long predicted by the oracles.[20] He expressed a desire to die in the profession of the Christian faith. Cortés no sooner learned his condition than he despatched father Olmedo to Tlascala. The friar found that Maxixca had already caused a crucifix to be placed before his sick couch, as the object of his adoration. After explaining, as intelligibly as he could, the truths of revelation, he baptized the dying chieftain; and the Spaniards had the satisfaction to believe that the soul of their benefactor was exempted from the doom of eternal perdition, that hung over the unfortunate Indian who perished in his unbelief.[21]

Their late brilliant successes seem to have reconciled most of the disaffected soldiers to the prosecution of the war. There were still a few among them, the secretary Duero, Bermudez the treasurer, and others high in office, or wealthy hidalgos, who looked with disgust on another campaign, and now loudly reiterated their demand of a free passage to

---

[18] "La primera fué de viruela, y comenzó de esta manera. Siendo Capitan y Governador Hernando Cortés al tiempo que el Capitan Pánfilo de Narvaez desembarcó en esta tierra, en uno de sus navíos vino un negro herido de viruelas, la cual enfermedad nunca en esta tierra se habia visto, y esta sazon estaba esta nueva España en estremo muy llena de gente." Toribio, Hist. de los Indios, MS, Parte 1, cap. 1.

[19] "Morian como chinches á montones." (Ibid., ubi supra.) "Eran tantos los difuntos que morian de aquella enfermedad, que no habia quien los enterrase, por lo cual en México los echaban en las azequias, porque entónces habia muy grande copia de aguas y era muy grande hedor el que salia de los cuerpos muertos." Sahagun, Hist. de Nueva España, lib. 8, cap. 1.

[20] Bernal Diaz, Hist. de la Conquista, cap. 136.

[21] Ibid., ubi supra.—Herrera, Hist. General, dec. 2, lib. 10, cap. 19.—Sahagun, Hist. de Nueva España, MS., lib. 12, cap. 39.

Cuba. To this Cortés, satisfied with the support on which he could safely count, made no further objection. Having once given his consent, he did all in his power to facilitate their departure, and provide for their comfort. He ordered the best ship at Vera Cruz to be placed at their disposal, to be well supplied with provisions and every thing necessary for the voyage, and sent Alvarado to the coast to superintend the embarkation. He took the most courteous leave of them, with assurances of his own unalterable regard. But, as the event proved, those who could part from him at this crisis had little sympathy with his fortunes; and we find Duero not long afterwards in Spain, supporting the claims of Velasquez before the emperor, in opposition to those of his former friend and commander.

The loss of these few men was amply compensated by the arrival of others, whom Fortune—to use no higher term—most unexpectedly threw in his way. The first of these came in a small vessel sent from Cuba by the governor, Velasquez, with stores for the colony at Vera Cruz. He was not aware of the late transactions in the country, and of the discomfiture of his officer. In the vessel came despatches, it is said, from Fonseca, bishop of Burgos, instructing Narvaez to send Cortés, if he had not already done so, for trial to Spain.[22] The alcalde of Vera Cruz, agreeably to the general's instructions, allowed the captain of the bark to land, who had no doubt that the country was in the hands of Narvaez. He was undeceived by being seized, together with his men, so soon as they had set foot on shore. The vessel was then secured; and the commander and his crew, finding out their error, were persuaded without much difficulty to join their countrymen in Tlascala.

A second vessel, sent soon after by Velasquez, shared the same fate, and those on board consented, also, to take their chance in the expedition under Cortés.

About the same time, Garay, the governor of Jamaica, fitted out three ships with an armed force to plant a colony on the Panuco, a river which pours into the Gulf a few degrees north of Villa Rica. Garay persisted in establishing this settlement, in contempt of the claims of Cortés, who had already entered into a friendly communication with the inhabitants of that region. But the crews experienced such a rough reception from the natives on landing, and lost so many men, that they were glad to take to their vessels again. One of these foundered in a storm. The others put into the port of Vera Cruz to restore the men, much weakened by hunger and disease. Here they were kindly received, their wants supplied, their wounds healed; when they were induced, by the liberal promises of Cortés, to abandon the disastrous service of their employer, and enlist under his own prosperous banner. The reinforcements obtained from these sources amounted to full a hundred and fifty men well provided with arms and ammunition, together with twenty horses. By this strange concurrence of circumstances, Cortés saw himself in possession of the

supplies he most needed; that, too, from the hands of his enemies, whose
costly preparations were thus turned to the benefit of the very man whom
they were designed to ruin.

His good fortune did not stop here. A ship from the Canaries touched
at Cuba, freighted with arms and military stores for the adventurers in
the New World. Their commander heard there of the recent discoveries
in Mexico, and, thinking it would afford a favorable market for him,
directed his course to Vera Cruz. He was not mistaken. The alcalde, by
the general's orders, purchased both ship and cargo; and the crews, catching the spirit of adventure, followed their countrymen into the interior.
There seemed to be a magic in the name of Cortés, which drew all who
came within hearing of it under his standard.[23]

Having now completed the arrangements for settling his new conquests, there seemed to be no further reason for postponing his departure
to Tlascala. He was first solicited by the citizens of Tepeaca to leave a
garrison with them, to protect them from the vengeance of the Aztecs.
Cortés acceded to the request, and, considering the central position of the
town favorable for maintaining his conquests, resolved to plant a colony
there. For this object he selected sixty of his soldiers, most of whom were
disabled by wounds or infirmity. He appointed the alcaldes, regidores,
and other functionaries of a civic magistracy. The place he called *Segura
de la Frontera,* or Security of the Frontier.[24] It received valuable privili-
ges as a city, a few years later, from the emperor Charles the Fifth; [25]
and rose to some consideration in the age of the Conquest. But its consequences soon after declined. Even its Castilian name, with the same
caprice which has decided the fate of more than one name in our own
country, was gradually supplanted by its ancient one, and the little village of Tepeaca is all that now commemorates the once flourishing Indian
capital, and the second Spanish colony in Mexico.

While at Segura, Cortés wrote that celebrated letter to the emperor,—
the second in the series,—so often cited in the preceding pages. It takes up
the narrative with the departure from Vera Cruz, and exhibits in a brief
and comprehensive form the occurrences up to the time at which we are
now arrived. In the concluding page, the general, after noticing the embarrassments under which he labors, says, in his usual manly spirit, that
he holds danger and fatigue light in comparison with the attainment of
his object; and that he is confident a short time will restore the Spaniards
to their former position, and repair all their losses.[26]

He notices the resemblance of Mexico, in many of its features and
productions, to the mother country, and requests that it may henceforth

[23] Ibid., cap. 131, 133, 136.—Herrera, Hist. General, ubi supra.—Rel. Seg. de
Cortés, ap. Lorenzana, pp. 154, 167.—Oviedo, Hist. de las Ind., MS., lib. 33, cap. 16.
[24] Rel. Seg. de Cortés, ap. Lorenzana, p. 156.
[25] Clavigero, Stor. del Messico, tom. 3, p. 153.
[26] "É creo, como ya á Vuestra Magestad he dicho, que en muy breve tomará al
estado, en que antes yo la tenia, é se restaurarán las pérdidas pasadas." Rel. Seg.,
ap. Lorenzana, p. 167.

be called, "New Spain of the Ocean Sea." [27] He finally requests that a commission may be sent out, at once, to investigate his conduct, and to verify the accuracy of his statements.

This letter, which was printed at Seville the year after its reception, has been since reprinted, and translated, more than once.[28] It excited a great sensation at the court, and among the friends of science generally. The previous discoveries in the New World had disappointed the expectations which had been formed after the solution of the grand problem of its existence. They had brought to light only rude tribes, which, however gentle and inoffensive in their manners, were still in the primitive stages of barbarism. Here was an authentic account of a vast nation, potent and populous, exhibiting an elaborate social polity, well advanced in the arts of civilization, occupying a soil that teemed with mineral treasures and with a boundless variety of vegetable products, stores of wealth both natural and artificial, that seemed, for the first time, to realize the golden dreams in which the great discoverer of the New World had so fondly, and in his own day so fallaciously, indulged. Well might the scholar of that age exult in the revelation of these wonders, which so many had long, but in vain, desired to see.[29]

With this letter went another to the emperor, signed, as it would seem, by nearly every officer and soldier in the camp. It expatiated on the obstacles thrown in the way of the expedition by Velasquez and Narvaez, and the great prejudice this had caused to the royal interests. It then set forth the services of Cortés, and besought the emperor to confirm him in his authority, and not to allow any interference with one who, from his personal character, his intimate knowledge of the land and its people, and the attachment of his soldiers, was the man best qualified in all the world to achieve the conquest of the country.[30]

[27] "Me pareció, que el mas conveniente nombre para esta dicha Tierra, era llamarse *la Nueva España del Mar Océano:* y assí en nombre de Vuestra Magestad se le puso aqueste nombre; humildemente suplico á Vuestra Alteza lo tenga por bien, y mande, que se nombre assí." (Ibid., p. 169.) The name of "New Spain," without other addition, had been before given by Grijalva to Yucatan. Ante, Book 2, Chapter 1.

[28] It was dated, "De la Villa Segura de la Frontera de esta Nueva España, á treinta de Octubre de mil quinientos veinte años." But, in consequence of the loss of the ship intended to bear it, the letter was not sent till the spring of the following year; leaving the nation still in ignorance of the fate of the gallant adventurers in Mexico, and the magnitude of their discoveries.

[29] The state of feeling occasioned by these discoveries may be seen in the correspondence of Peter Martyr, then residing at the court of Castile. See, in particular, his epistle, dated March, 1521, to his noble pupil, the Marques de Mondejar, in which he dwells with unbounded satisfaction on all the rich stores of science which the expedition of Cortés had thrown open to the world. Opus Epistolarum, ep. 771.

[30] This memorial is in that part of my collection made by the former President of the Spanish Academy, Vargas Ponçe. It is signed by four hundred and forty-four names; and it is remarkable that this roll, which includes every other familiar name in the army, should not contain that of Bernal Diaz del Castillo. It can only be accounted for by his illness; as he tells us he was confined to his bed by a fever about this time. Hist. de la Conquista, cap. 134.

It added not a little to the perplexities of Cortés, that he was still in entire ignorance of the light in which his conduct was regarded in Spain. He had not even heard whether his despatches, sent the year preceding from Vera Cruz, had been received. Mexico was as far removed from all intercourse with the civilized world, as if it had been placed at the antipodes. Few vessels had entered, and none had been allowed to leave its ports. The governor of Cuba, an island distant but a few days' sail, was yet ignorant, as we have seen, of the fate of his armament. On the arrival of every new vessel or fleet on these shores, Cortés might well doubt whether it brought aid to his undertaking, or a royal commission to supersede him. His sanguine spirit relied on the former; though the latter was much the more probable, considering the intimacy of his enemy, the governor, with Bishop Fonseca, a man jealous of his authority, and one who, from his station at the head of the Indian department, held a predominant control over the affairs of the New World. It was the policy of Cortés, therefore, to lose no time; to push forward his preparations, lest another should be permitted to snatch the laurel now almost within his grasp. Could he but reduce the Aztec capital, he felt that he should be safe; and that, in whatever light his irregular proceedings might now be viewed, his services in that event would far more than counterbalance them in the eyes both of the Crown and of the country.

The general wrote, also, to the Royal Audience at St. Domingo, in order to interest them in his cause. He sent four vessels to the same island, to obtain a further supply of arms and ammunition; and, the better to stimulate the cupidity of adventurers, and allure them to the expedition, he added specimens of the beautiful fabrics of the country, and of its precious metals.[31] The funds for procuring these important supplies were, probably, derived from the plunder gathered in the late battles, and the gold which, as already remarked, had been saved from the general wreck by the Castilian convoy.

It was the middle of December, when Cortés, having completed all his arrangements, set out on his return to Tlascala, ten or twelve leagues distant. He marched in the van of the army, and took the way of Cholula. How different was his condition from that in which he had left the republican capital not five months before! His march was a triumphal procession, displaying the various banners and military ensigns taken from the enemy, long files of captives, and all the rich spoils of conquest gleaned from many a hard-fought field. As the army passed through the towns and villages, the inhabitants poured out to greet them, and, as they drew near to Tlascala, the whole population, men, women, and children, came forth celebrating their return with songs, dancing, and music. Arches dec-

---

[31] Rel. Terc. de Cortés, ap. Lorenzana, p. 179.—Herrera, Hist. General, dec. 2, lib. 10, cap. 18.

Alonso de Avila went as the bearer of despatches to St. Domingo. Bernal Diaz, who is not averse, now and then, to a fling at his commander, says, that Cortés was willing to get rid of this gallant cavalier, because he was too independent and plainspoken. Hist. de la Conquista, cap. 136.

orated with flowers were thrown across the streets through which they passed, and a Tlascalan orator addressed the general, on his entrance into the city, in a lofty panegyric on his late achievements, proclaiming him the "avenger of the nation." Amidst this pomp and triumphal show, Cortés and his principal officers were seen clad in deep mourning in honor of their friend Maxixca. And this tribute of respect to the memory of their venerated ruler touched the Tlascalans more sensibly than all the proud display of military trophies.[32]

The general's first act was to confirm the son of his deceased friend in the succession, which had been contested by an illegitimate brother. The youth was but twelve years of age; and Cortés prevailed on him without difficulty to follow his father's example, and receive baptism. He afterwards knighted him with his own hand; the first instance, probably, of the order of chivalry being conferred on an American Indian.[33] The elder Xicotencatl was also persuaded to embrace Christianity, and the example of their rulers had its obvious effect in preparing the minds of the people for the reception of the truth. Cortés, whether from the suggestions of Olmedo, or from the engrossing nature of his own affairs, did not press the work of conversion further, at this time, but wisely left the good seed, already sown, to ripen in secret, till time should bring forth the harvest.

The Spanish commander, during his short stay in Tlascala, urged forward the preparations for the campaign. He endeavored to drill the Tlascalans, and to give them some idea of European discipline and tactics. He caused new arms to be made, and the old ones to be put in order. Powder was manufactured with the aid of sulphur obtained by some adventurous cavaliers from the smoking throat of Popocatepetl.[34] The construction of the brigantines went forward prosperously under the direction of Lopez, with the aid of the Tlascalans.[35] Timber was cut in the forests, and pitch, an article unknown to the Indians, was obtained from the pines on the neighboring Sierra de Malinche. The rigging and other appurtenances were transported by the Indian *tamanes* from Villa Rica; and by Christmas, the work was so far advanced, that it was no longer necessary for Cortés to delay the march to Mexico.

[32] Bernal Diaz, Hist. de la Conquista, cap. 136.—Herrera, Hist. General, dec. 2, lib. 10, cap. 19.

[33] Ibid., ubi supra.

"Híçolo," says Herrera, "i armóle caballero, al vso de Castilla: i porque lo fuese de Jesu-Christo, le hiço bautiçar, i se llamó D. Lorenço Maxiscatzin."

[34] For an account of the manner in which this article was procured by Montaño and his doughty companions, see Ante, p. 285.

[35] "Ansí se hiciéron trece bergantines en el barrio de Atempa, junto á una hermita que se llama San Buenaventura, los quales hizo y otro Martin Lopez uno de los primeros conquistadores, y le ayudó Neguez Gomez." Hist. de Tlascala, MS.

GUATEMOZIN, EMPEROR OF THE AZTECS—PREPARATIONS FOR THE MARCH—MILITARY CODE—SPANIARDS CROSS THE SIERRA—ENTER TEZCUCO—PRINCE IXTLILXOCHITL

1520

WHILE the events related in the preceding Chapter were passing, an important change had taken place in the Aztec monarchy. Montezuma's brother and successor, Cuitlahua, had suddenly died of the small-pox, after a brief reign of four months,—brief, but glorious, for it had witnessed the overthrow of the Spaniards and their expulsion from Mexico.[1] On the death of their warlike chief, the electors were convened, as usual, to supply the vacant throne. It was an office of great responsibility in the dark hour of their fortunes. The *teoteuctli,* or high-priest, invoked the blessing of the supreme God on their deliberations. His prayer is still extant. It was the last one ever made on a similar occasion in Anahuac, and a few extracts from it may interest the reader, as a specimen of Aztec eloquence.

"O Lord! thou knowest that the days of our sovereign are at an end, for thou hast placed him beneath thy feet. He abides in the place of his retreat; he has trodden the path which we are all to tread; he has gone to the house whither we are all to follow,—the house of eternal darkness, where no light cometh. He is gathered to his rest, and no one henceforth shall disquiet him. . . . . . All these were the princes, his predecessors, who sat on the imperial throne, directing the affairs of thy kingdom; for thou art the universal lord and emperor, by whose will and movement the whole world is directed; thou needest not the counsel of another. They laid down the intolerable burden of government, and left it to him, their successor. Yet he sojourned but a few days in his kingdom,—but a few days had we enjoyed his presence, when thou summonedst him away

[1] Solís dismisses this prince with the remark, "that he reigned but a few days; long enough, however, for his indolence and apathy to efface the memory of his name among the people." (Conquista, lib. 4, cap. 16.) Whence the historiographer of the Indies borrowed the coloring for this portrait I cannot conjecture; certainly not from the ancient authorities, which uniformly delineate the character and conduct of the Aztec sovereign in the light represented in the text. Cortés, who ought to know, describes him "as held to be very wise and valiant." Rel. Seg., ap. Lorenzana, p. 166.—See, also, Sahagun, Hist. de Nueva España, MS., lib. 12, cap. 29,—Herrera, Hist. General, dec. 2, lib. 10, cap. 19,—Ixtlilxochitl, Hist. Chich., MS., cap. 88,—Oviedo, Hist. de las Ind., MS., lib. 33, cap. 16,—Gomara, Crónica, cap. 118.

to follow those who had ruled over the land before him. And great cause
has he for thankfulness, that thou hast relieved him from so grievous a
load, and placed him in tranquillity and rest. . . . . . Who now shall
order matters for the good of the people and the realm? Who shall appoint the judges to administer justice to thy people? Who now shall bid
the drum and the flute to sound, and gather together the veteran soldiers
and the men mighty in battle? Our Lord and our Defence! wilt thou, in
thy wisdom, elect one who shall be worthy to sit on the throne of thy
kingdom; one who shall bear the grievous burden of government; who
shall comfort and cherish thy poor people, even as the mother cherisheth
her offspring? . . . . . O Lord most merciful! pour forth thy light and
thy splendor over this thine empire! . . . . . Order it so that thou shalt
be served in all, and through all." [2]

The choice fell on Quauhtemotzin, or Guatemozin, as euphoniously
corrupted by the Spaniards.[3] He was nephew to the two last monarchs,
and married his cousin, the beautiful princess Tecuichpo, Montezuma's
daughter. "He was not more than twenty-five years old, and elegant in

---

[2] The reader of Spanish will see, that, in the version in the text, I have condensed
the original, which abounds in the tautology and repetitions characteristic of the
compositions of a rude people.

"Señor nuestro! ya V. M. sabe como es muerto nuestro N.: ya lo habeis puesto
debajo de vuestros pies: ya está en su recogimiento, y es ido por el camino que
todos hemos de ir y á la casa donde hemos de morar, casa de perpetuas tinieblas,
donde ni hay ventana, ni luz alguna: ya está en el reposo donde nadie le desasose-
gará. . . . . . Todos estos señores y reyes rigiéron, gobernáron, y gozáron del señorío
y dignidad real, y del trono y sitial del imperio, los cuales ordenáron y concertáron
las cosas de vuestro reino, que sois el universal señor y emperador, por cuyo albe-
drio y motivo se rige todo el universo, y que no teneis necesidad de consejo de ningun otro. Ya estos dichos dejáron la carga intolerable del gobierno que tragéron
sobre sus hombros, y lo dejáron á su succesor N., el cual por algunos pocos dias
tuvo en pie su señoría y reino, y ahora ya se ha ido en pos de ellos al otro mundo,
porque vos le mandásteis que fuese y le llamásteis, y por haberle descargado de
tan gran carga, y quitado tan gran trabajo, y haberle puesto en paz y en reposo,
está muy obligado á daros gracias. Algunos pocos dias le lográmos, y ahora para
siempre se ausentó de nosotros para nunca mas volver al mundo. . . . . . ¿Quien
ordenará y dispondrá las cosas necesarias al bien del pueblo, señorio y reino?
¿Quien elegirá á los jueces particulares, que tengan carga de la gente baja por los
barrios? ¿Quien mandará tocar el atambor y pífano para juntar gente para la
guerra? ¿Y quien reunirá y acaudillará á los soldados viejos, y hombres diestros en
la pelea? Señor nuestro y amparador nuestro! tenga por bien V. M. de elegir, y
señalar alguna persona suficiente para que tenga vuestro trono, y lleve á cuestas
la carga pesada del régimen de la república, regocige y regale á los populares, bien
así como la madre regala á su hijo, poniéndole en su regazo. . . . . . O señor nuestro
humanísimo! dad lumbre y resplandor de vuestra mano á esto reino! . . . . . Hágase
como V. M. fuere servido en todo, y por todo." Sahagun, Hist. de Nueva España,
lib. 6, cap. 5.

[3] The Spaniards appear to have changed the *Qua,* beginning Aztec names, into
Gua, in the same manner as, in the mother country, they changed the *Wad* at the
beginning of Arabic names into *Guad.* (See Condé, El Nubiense, Descripcion de
España, notas, passim.) The Aztec *tzin* was added to the names of sovereigns and
great lords, as a mark of reverence. Thus Cuitlahua was called Cuitlahuatzin. This
termination, usually dropped by the Spaniards, has been retained from accident, or,
perhaps, for the sake of euphony, in Guatemozin's name.

his person for an Indian." says one who had seen him often; "valiant, and so terrible, that his followers trembled in his presence."[4] He did not shrink from the perilous post that was offered to him; and, as he saw the tempest gathering darkly around, he prepared to meet it like a man. Though young, he had ample experience in military matters, and had distinguished himself above all others in the bloody conflicts of the capital. He bore a sort of religious hatred to the Spaniards, like that which Hannibal is said to have sworn, and which he certainly cherished, against his Roman foes.

By means of his spies, Guatemozin made himself acquainted with the movements of the Spaniards, and their design to besiege the capital. He prepared for it by sending away the useless part of the population, while he called in his potent vassals from the neighborhood. He continued the plans of his predecessor for strengthening the defences of the city, reviewed his troops, and stimulated them by prizes to excel in their exercises. He made harangues to his soldiers to rouse them to a spirit of desperate resistance. He encouraged his vassals throughout the empire to attack the white men wherever they were to be met with, setting a price on their heads, as well as on the persons of all who should be brought alive to him in Mexico.[5] And it was no uncommon thing for the Spaniards to find hanging up in the temples of the conquered places the arms and accoutrements of their unfortunate countrymen who had been seized and sent to the capital for sacrifice.[6]—Such was the young monarch who was now called to the tottering throne of the Aztecs; worthy, by his bold and magnanimous nature, to sway the sceptre of his country, in the most flourishing period of her renown; and now, in her distress, devoting himself in the true spirit of a patriot prince to uphold her falling fortunes, or bravely perish with them.[7]

We must now return to the Spaniards in Tlascala, where we left them preparing to resume their march on Mexico. Their commander had the satisfaction to see his troops tolerably complete in their appointments; varying, indeed, according to the condition of the different reinforcements which had arrived from time to time; but, on the whole, superior to those of the army with which he had first invaded the country. His whole force fell little short of six hundred men; forty of whom were cavalry, together with eighty arquebusiers and crossbow-men. The rest were

[4] "Mancebo de hasta veynte y cinco años, bien gentil hombre para ser Indio, y muy esforçado, y se hizo temer de tal manera, que todos los suyos temblauan dél; y estaua casado con vna hija de Monteçuma, bien hermosa muger para ser India." Bernal Diaz, Hist. de la Conquista, cap. 130.

[5] Herrera, Hist. General, dec. 2, lib. 10, cap. 19.

[6] Bernal Diaz, Hist. de la Conquista, cap. 134.

[7] One may call to mind the beautiful invocation which Racine has put into the mouth of Joad;

> "Venez, cher rejeton d'une vaillante race,
> Remplir vos défenseurs d'une nouvelle audace;
> Venez du diadême à leurs yeux vous couvrir,
> Et périssez du moins en roi, s'il faut périr."
> ATHALIE, acte 4, scène 5.

armed with sword and target, and with the copper-headed pike of Chin-antla. He had nine cannon of moderate calibre, and was indifferently sup-plied with powder.[8]

As his forces were drawn up in order of march, Cortés rode through the ranks, exhorting his soldiers, as usual with him on these occasions, to be true to themselves, and the enterprise in which they were embarked. He told them, they were to march against *rebels,* who had once acknowl-edged allegiance to the Spanish sovereign; [9] against barbarians, the ene-mies of their religion. They were to fight the battles of the Cross and of the crown; to fight their own battles, to wipe away the stain from their arms, to avenge their injuries, and the loss of the dear companions who had been butchered on the field or on the accursed altar of sacrifice. Never was there a war which offered higher incentives to the Christian cavalier; a war which opened to him riches and renown in this life, and an imperishable glory in that to come.[10]

Thus did the politic chief touch all the secret springs of devotion, honor, and ambition in the bosoms of his martial audience, waking the mettle of the most sluggish before leading him on the perilous emprise. They answered with acclamations, that they were ready to die in defence of the Faith; and would either conquer, or leave their bones with those of their countrymen in the waters of the Tezcuco.

The army of the allies next passed in review before the general. It is variously estimated by writers from a hundred and ten to a hundred and fifty thousand soldiers! The palpable exaggeration, no less than the dis-crepancy, shows that little reliance can be placed on any estimate. It is certain, however, that it was a multitudinous array, consisting not only of the flower of the Tlascalan warriors, but of those of Cholula, Tepeaca, and the neighboring territories, which had submitted to the Castilian crown.[11]

They were armed, after the Indian fashion, with bows and arrows, the glassy *maquahuitl,* and the long pike, which formidable weapon, Cortés, as we have seen, had introduced among his own troops. They were div-ided into battalions, each having its own banner, displaying the appro-priate arms or emblem of its company. The four great chiefs of the nation marched in the van; three of them venerable for their years, and show-ing, in the insignia which decorated their persons, the evidence of many

---

[8] Rel. Tercera de Cortés, ap. Lorenzana, p. 183.

Most, if not all, of the authorities,—a thing worthy of note,—concur in this estimate of the Spanish forces.

[9] "Y como sin causa ninguna todos los Naturales de Colúa, que son los de la gran Ciudad de Temixtitan, y los de todas las otras Provincias á ellas sujetas, no solamente se habian *rebelado* contra Vuestra Magestad." Ibid., ubi supra.

[10] Rel. Terc. de Cortés, ap. Lorenzana, p. 184.

"Porque demas del premio, que les davia en el cielo, se les seguirian en esto mun-do grandíssima honra, riquezas inestimables." Ixtlilxochitl, Hist. Chichimeca, MS., cap. 91.

[11] "Cosa muy de ver," says father Sahagun, without hazarding any precise num-ber, "en la cantidad y en los aparejos que llevaban." Hist. de Nueva España, lib. 12, cap. 30, M.S.

a glorious feat in arms. The panache of many-colored plumes floated
from their casques, set in emeralds or other precious stones. Their *escaupil,* or stuffed doublet of cotton, was covered with the graceful surcoat of
feather-work, and their feet were protected by sandals embossed with
gold. Four young pages followed, bearing their weapons, and four others
supported as many standards, on which were emblazoned the armorial
bearings of the four great divisions of the republic.[12] The Tlascalans,
though frugal in the extreme, and rude in their way of life, were as ambitious of display in their military attire as any of the races on the plateau.
As they defiled before Cortés, they saluted him by waving their banners
and by a flourish of their wild music, which the general acknowledged by
courteously raising his cap as they passed.[13] The Tlascalan warriors, and
especially the younger Xicotencatl, their commander, affected to imitate
their European masters, not merely in their tactics, but in minuter matters of military etiquette.

Cortés, with the aid of Marina, made a brief address to his Indian allies. He reminded them that he was going to fight their battles against
their ancient enemies. He called on them to support him in a manner
worthy of their renowned republic. To those who remained at home, he
committed the charge of aiding in the completion of the brigantines, on
which the success of the expedition so much depended; and he requested
that none would follow his banner, who were not prepared to remain till
the final reduction of the capital.[14] This address was answered by shouts,
or rather yells, of defiance, showing the exultation felt by his Indian confederates at the prospect of at last avenging their manifold wrongs, and
humbling their haughty enemy.

Before setting out on the expedition, Cortés published a code of ordinances, as he terms them, or regulations for the army, too remarkable to
be passed over in silence. The preamble sets forth, that in all institutions,
whether divine or human,—if the latter have any worth,—order is the
great law. The ancient chronicles inform us, that the greatest captains in
past times owed their successes quite as much to the wisdom of their ordinances, as to their own valor and virtue. The situation of the Spaniards
eminently demanded such a code; a mere handful of men as they were, in
the midst of countless enemies, most cunning in the management of their
weapons and in the art of war. The instrument then reminds the army
that the conversion of the heathen is the work most acceptable in the eye
of the Almighty, and one that will be sure to receive his support. It calls
on every soldier to regard this as the prime object of the expedition,
*without which the war would be manifestly unjust, and every acquisition
made by it, a robbery.*[15]

[12] Herrera, Hist. General, dec. 2, lib. 10, cap. 20.

[13] Ibid., ubi supra.

[14] Ibid., loc. cit.

[15] "Que su principal motivo é intencion sea apartar y desarraigar de las dichas
idolatrías á todos los naturales destas partes y reducillos ó á lo menos desear su
salvacion y que sean reducidos al conocimiento de Dios y de su Santa Fe católica:

The general solemnly protests, that the principal motive, which operates in his own bosom, is the desire to wean the natives from their gloomy idolatry, and to impart to them the knowledge of a purer faith; and next, to recover for his master, the emperor, the dominions which of right belong to him.[16]

The ordinances then prohibit all blasphemy against God or the saints; a vice much more frequent among Catholic than Protestant nations, arising, perhaps, less from difference of religion, than of physical temperament,—for the warm sun of the South, under which Catholicism prevails, stimulates the sensibilities to the more violent expression of passion.[17]

Another law is directed against gaming, to which the Spaniards, in all ages, have been peculiarly addicted. Cortés, making allowance for the strong national propensity, authorizes it under certain limitations; but prohibits the use of dice altogether.[18] Then follow other laws against brawls and private combats, against personal taunts and the irritating sarcasms of rival companies; rules for the more perfect discipline of the troops, whether in camp or the field. Among others, is one prohibiting any captain, under pain of death, from charging the enemy without orders; a practice, noticed as most pernicious and of too frequent occurrence,—showing the impetuous spirit and want of true military subordination in the bold cavaliers who followed the standard of Cortés.

The last ordinance prohibits any man, officer or private, from securing to his own use any of the booty taken from the enemy, whether it be gold, silver, precious stones, feather-work, stuffs, slaves, or other commodity, however or wherever obtained, in the city or in the field; and requires him to bring it forthwith to the presence of the general, or the officer appointed to receive it. The violation of this law was punished with

porque si con otra intencion se hiciese la dicha guerra seria injusta y todo lo que en ella se oviese Onoloxio é obligado á restitucion." Ordenanzas Militares, M.S.

[16] "É desde ahora protesto en nombre de S. M. que mi principal intencion é motivo es facer esta guerra é las otras que ficiese por traer y reducir á los dichos naturales al dicho conocimiento de nuestra Santa Fe é creencia; y despues por los sozjugar é supeditar debajo del yugo é dominio imperial é real de su Sacra Magestad, á quien juridicamente el Señorío de todas estas partes." Ordenanzas Militares, MS.

[17] "Ce n'est qu'en Espagne et en Italie," says the penetrating historian of the Italian Republics, "qu'on rencontre cette habitude vicieuse, absolument inconnue aux peuples protestans, et qu'il ne faut point confondre avec les grossiers juremens que le peuple en tout pays mêle à ses discours. Dans tous les accès de colère des peuples du Midi, ils s' attaquent aux objets de leur culte, ils les menacent, et ils accablent de paroles outrageantes la Divinité elle-même, le Rédempteur ou ses saints." Sismondi, Républiques Italiennes, cap. 126.

[18] Lucio Marineo, who witnessed all the dire effects of this national propensity at the Castilian court, where he was residing at this time, breaks out into the following animated apostrophe against it: "El jugador es el que dessea y procura la muerte de sus padres, el que jura falso por Dios y por la vida de su Rey y Señor, el que mata á su ánima, y la echa en el infierno: ¿y que no hará el jugador q̃ no avergüença de perder sus dineros, de perder el tiempo, perder el sueño, perder la fama, perder la honra, y perder finalmente la vida? Por lo cual como ya gran parte de los hombres siempre y donde quiera continuamente juegan, parésceme verdadera la opinion de aquellos que dizen el infierno estar lleno de jugadores." Cosas Memorables de Espagña, (ed. Sevilla, 1539,) fol. 165.

death and confiscation of property. So severe an edict may be thought to prove, that, however much the *Conquistador* may have been influenced by spiritual considerations, he was by no means insensible to those of a temporal character.[19]

These provisions were not suffered to remain a dead letter. The Spanish commander, soon after their proclamation, made an example of two of his own slaves, whom he hanged for plundering the natives. A similar sentence was passed on a soldier for the like offence, though he allowed him to be cut down before the sentence was entirely executed. Cortés knew well the character of his followers; rough and turbulent spirits, who required to be ruled with an iron hand. Yet he was not eager to assert his authority on light occasions. The intimacy into which they were thrown by their peculiar situation, perils, and sufferings, in which all equally shared, and a common interest in the adventure, induced a familiarity between men and officers, most unfavorable to military discipline. The general's own manners, frank and liberal, seemed to invite this freedom, which, on ordinary occasions, he made no attempt to repress; perhaps finding it too difficult, or at least impolitic, since it afforded a safety-valve for the spirits of a licentious soldiery, that, if violently coerced, might have burst forth into open mutiny. But the limits of his forbearance were clearly defined; and any attempt to overstep them, or to violate the established regulations of the camp, brought a sure and speedy punishment on the offender. By thus tempering severity with indulgence, masking an iron will under the open bearing of a soldier,—Cortés established a control over his band of bold and reckless adventurers, such as a pedantic martinet, scrupulous in enforcing the minutiæ of military etiquette, could never have obtained.

The ordinances, dated on the twenty-second of December, were proclaimed to the assembled army on the twenty-sixth. Two days afterwards, the troops were on their march, and Cortés, at the head of his battalions, with colors flying and music playing, issued forth from the gates of the republican capital, which had so generously received him in his distress, and which now, for the second time, supplied him with the means for consummating his great enterprise. The population of the city, men, women, and children, hung on the rear of the army, taking a last leave of their countrymen, and imploring the gods to crown their arms with victory.

Notwithstanding the great force mustered by the Indian confederates, the Spanish general allowed but a small part of them now to attend him. He proposed to establish his head-quarters at some place on the Tezcucan lake, whence he could annoy the Aztec capital, by reducing the sur-

---

[19] These regulations are reported with much uniformity by Herrera, Solís, Clavigero, and others, but with such palpable inaccuracy, that it is clear they never could have seen the original instrument. The copy in my possession was taken from the Muñoz collection. As the document, though curious and highly interesting, has never been published, I have given it entire in the *Appendix, Part* 2, *No.* 13.

ᵣ ounding country, cutting off the supplies, and thus placing the city in a state of blockade.[20]

The direct assault on Mexico itself he intended to postpone, until the arrival of the brigantines should enable him to make it with the greatest advantage. Meanwhile, he had no desire to encumber himself with a superfluous multitude, whom it would be difficult to feed; and he preferred to leave them at Tlascala, whence they might convey the vessels, when completed, to the camp, and aid him in his future operations.

Three routes presented themselves to Cortés, by which he might penetrate into the Valley. He chose the most difficult, traversing the bold sierra which divides the eastern plateau from the western, and so rough and precipitous, as to be scarcely practicable for the march of an army. He wisely judged, that he should be less likely to experience annoyance from the enemy in this direction, as they might naturally confide in the difficulties of the ground for their protection.

The first day, the troops advanced five or six leagues, Cortés riding in the van, at the head of his little body of cavalry. They halted at the village of Tetzmellocan, at the base of the mountain chain which traverses the country, touching, at its southern limit, the mighty Iztaccihuatl, or "White Woman,"—white with the snows of ages.[21] At this village they met with a friendly reception, and on the following morning began the ascent of the sierra.

The path was steep and exceedingly rough. Thick matted bushes covered its surface, and the winter torrents had broken it into deep stony channels, hardly practicable for the passage of artillery, while the straggling branches of the trees, flung horizontally across the road, made it equally difficult for cavalry. The cold, as they rose higher, became intense. It was keenly felt by the Spaniards, accustomed of late to a warm, or, at least, temperate climate; though the extreme toil, with which they forced their way upward, furnished the best means of resisting the weather. The only vegetation to be seen in these higher regions was the pine, dark forests of which clothed the sides of the mountains, till even these dwindled into a thin and stunted growth. It was night before the way-worn soldiers reached the bald crest of the sierra, where they lost no time in kindling their fires; and, huddling round their bivouacs, they warmed their frozen limbs and prepared their evening repast.

With the earliest dawn, the troops were again in motion. Mass was said, and they began their descent, more difficult and painful than their ascent on the day preceding; for, in addition to the natural obstacles of

[20] Herrera, Hist. General, dec. 2, lib. 10, cap. 20.—Bernal Diaz, Hist. de la Conquista, cap. 127. The former historian states the number of Indian allies who followed Cortés, at eighty thousand; the latter at ten thousand! *¿Quien sabe?*

[21] This mountain, which, with its neighbor Popocatepetl, forms the great barrier—the *Herculis columnæ*—of the Mexican Valley, has been fancifully likened, from its long dorsal swell, to the back of a dromedary. (Tudor's Tour in North America, let. 22.) It rises far above the limits of perpetual snow in the tropics, and its huge crest and sides, enveloped in its silver drapery, form one of the most striking objects in the magnificent *coup d'œil* presented to the inhabitants of the capital

the road, they found it strewn with huge pieces of timber and trees, obviously felled for the purpose by the natives. Cortés ordered up a body of light troops to clear away the impediments, and the army again resumed its march, but with the apprehension that the enemy had prepared an ambuscade, to surprise them when they should be entangled in the pass. They moved cautiously forward, straining their vision to pierce the thick gloom of the forests, where the wily foe might be lurking. But they saw no living thing, except only the wild inhabitants of the woods, and flocks of the *zopilote*, the voracious vulture of the country, which, in anticipation of a bloody banquet, hung, like a troop of evil spirits, on the march of the army.

As they descended, the Spaniards felt a sensible and most welcome change in the temperature. The character of the vegetation changed with it, and the funereal pine, their only companion of late, gave way to the sturdy oak, to the sycamore, and, lower down, to the graceful pepper-tree mingling its red berry with the dark foliage of the forest; while, in still lower depths, the gaudy-colored creepers might be seen flinging their gay blossoms over the branches, and telling of a softer and more luxurious climate.

At length, the army emerged on an open level, where the eye, unobstructed by intervening wood or hill-top, could range, far and wide, over the Valley of Mexico. There it lay bathed in the golden sunshine, stretched out, as it were, in slumber, in the arms of the giant hills, which clustered, like a phalanx of guardian genii, around it. The magnificent vision, new to many of the spectators, filled them with rapture. Even the veterans of Cortés could not withhold their admiration, though this was soon followed by a bitter feeling, as they recalled the sufferings which had befallen them within these beautiful, but treacherous, precincts. It made us feel, says the lion-hearted Conqueror, in his Letters, that "we had no choice but victory or death;—and, our minds once resolved, we moved forward with as light a step, as if we had been going on an errand of certain pleasure." [22]

As the Spaniards advanced, they beheld the neighboring hill-tops blazing with beacon fires, showing that the country was already alarmed and mustering to oppose them. The general called on his men to be mindful of their high reputation; to move in order, closing up their ranks, and to obey implicitly the commands of their officers.[23] At every turn among the hills, they expected to meet the forces of the enemy drawn up to dispute their passage. And, as they were allowed to pass the defiles unmolested, and drew near to the open plains, they were prepared to see them occupied by a formidable host, who would compel them to fight

[22] "Y prometímos todos de nunca de ella salir, sin Victoria, ó dejar allí las vidas. Y con esta determinacion ibamos todos tan alegres, como si fueramos á cosa de mucho placer." Rel. Terc., ap. Lorenzana, p. 188.

[23] "Y yo torné á rogar, y encomendar mucho á los Españoles, que hiciessen, como siempre habian hecho y como se esperaba de sus Personas; y que nadie no se desmandasse, y que fuessen con mucho concierto, y órden por su Camino." Ibid., ubi supra.

over again the battle of Otumba. But, although clouds of dusky warriors were seen from time to time, hovering on the highlands, as if watching their progress, they experienced no interruption, till they reached a *barranca*, or deep ravine, through which flowed a little river, crossed by a bridge partly demolished. On the opposite side a considerable body of Indians was stationed, as if to dispute the passage; but, whether distrusting their own numbers, or intimidated by the steady advance of the Spaniards, they offered them no annoyance, and were quickly dispersed by a few resolute charges of cavalry. The army then proceeded, without molestation, to a small town, called Coatepec, where they halted for the night. Before retiring to his own quarters, Cortés made the rounds of the camp, with a few trusty followers, to see that all was safe.[24] He seemed to have an eye that never slumbered, and a frame incapable of fatigue. It was the indomitable spirit within, which sustained him.[25]

Yet he may well have been kept awake through the watches of the night, by anxiety and doubt. He was now but three leagues from Tezcuco, the far-famed capital of the Acolhuans. He proposed to establish his head-quarters, if possible, at this place. Its numerous dwellings would afford ample accommodations for his army. An easy communication with Tlascala, by a different route from that which he had traversed, would furnish him with the means of readily obtaining supplies from that friendly country, and for the safe transportation of the brigantines, when finished, to be launched on the waters of the Tezcuco. But he had good reason to distrust the reception he should meet with in the capital; for an important revolution had taken place there, since the expulsion of the Spaniards from Mexico, of which it will be necessary to give some account.

The reader will remember that the cacique of that place, named Cacama, was deposed by Cortés, during his first residence in the Aztec metropolis, in consequence of a projected revolt against the Spaniards, and that the crown had been placed on the head of a younger brother, Cuicuitzca. The deposed prince was among the prisoners carried away by Cortés, and perished with the others, in the terrible passage of the causeway, on the *noche triste*. His brother, afraid, probably, after the flight of the Spaniards, of continuing with his own vassals, whose sympathies were altogether with the Aztecs, accompanied his friends in their retreat, and was so fortunate as to reach Tlascala in safety.

Meanwhile, a second son of Nezahualpilli, named Coanaco, claimed

---

[24] "É como la Gente de pie venia algo cansada, y se hacia tarde, dormímos en una Poblacion, que se dice Coatepeque......É yo con diez de Caballo comenzé la Vela, y Ronda de la prima, y hice, que toda la Gente estubiesse muy apercibida." Ibid., pp. 188, 189.

[25] For the preceding pages, giving the account of the march, besides the Letter of Cortés, so often quoted, see Gomara, Crónica, cap. 121,—Oviedo, Hist. de las Ind., MS., lib. 33, cap. 18,—Bernal Diaz, Hist. de la Conquista, cap. 137,—Camargo, Hist. de Tlascala, MS.,—Herrera, Hist. General, dec. 2, lib. 10, cap. 20,—Ixtlilxochitl, Relacion de la Venida de los Españoles y Principio de la Ley Evangélica, (México, 1829,) p. 9.

the crown, on his elder brother's death, as his own rightful inheritance. As he heartily joined his countrymen and the Aztecs in their detestation of the white men, his claims were sanctioned by the Mexican emperor. Soon after his accession, the new lord of Tezcuco had an opportunity of showing his loyalty to his imperial patron in an effectual manner.

A body of forty-five Spaniards, ignorant of the disasters in Mexico, were transporting thither a large quantity of gold, at the very time their countrymen were on the retreat to Tlascala. As they passed through the Tezcucan territory, they were attacked by Coanaco's orders, most of them massacred on the spot, and the rest sent for sacrifice to Mexico. The arms and accoutrements of these unfortunate men were hung up as trophies in the temples, and their skins, stripped from their dead bodies, were suspended over the bloody shrines, as the most acceptable offering to the offended deities.[26]

Some months after this event, the exiled prince, Cuicuitzca, wearied with his residence in Tlascala, and pining for his former royal state, made his way back secretly to Tezcuco, hoping, it would seem, to raise a party there in his favor. But, if such were his expectations, they were sadly disappointed; for no sooner had he set foot in the capital, than he was betrayed to his brother, who, by the advice of Guatemozin, put him to death, as a traitor to his country.[27]—Such was the posture of affairs in Tezcuco, when Cortés, for the second time, approached its gates; and well might he doubt, not merely the nature of his reception there, but whether he would be permitted to enter at all, without force of arms.

These apprehensions were dispelled the following morning, when, before the troops were well under arms, an embassy was announced from the lord of Tezcuco. It consisted of several nobles, some of whom were known to the companions of Cortés. They bore a golden flag in token of amity, and a present of no great value to Cortés. They brought also a message from the cacique, imploring the general to spare his territories, inviting him to take up his quarters in his capital, and promising on his arrival to become the vassal of the Spanish sovereign.

Cortés dissembled the satisfaction with which he listened to these overtures, and sternly demanded of the envoys an account of the Spaniards who had been massacred, insisting, at the same time, on the immediate restitution of the plunder. But the Indian nobles excused themselves, by throwing tne whole blame upon the Aztec emperor, by whose orders the deed had been perpetrated, and who now had possession of the treasure. They urged Cortés not to enter the city that day, but to pass the night in the suburbs, that their master might have time to prepare

---

[26] See Ante, p. 469.

The skins of those immolated on the sacrificial stone were a common offering in the Indian temples, and the mad priests celebrated many of their festivals by publicly dancing with their own persons enveloped in these disgusting spoils of their victims. See Sahagun, Hist. de Nueva España, passim.

[27] Rel. Terc. de Cortés, ap. Lorenzana, p. 187.—Oviedo, Hist. de las Ind., MS., lib. 33, cap. 19.

suitable accommodations for him. The Spanish commander, however, gave no heed to this suggestion, but pushed forward his march, and at noon, on the thirty-first of December, 1520, entered, at the head of his legions, the venerable walls of Tezcuco, "the place of rest," as not inaptly denominated.[28]

He was struck, as when he before visited this populous city, with the solitude and silence which reigned throughout its streets. He was conducted to the palace of Nezahualpilli, which was assigned as his quarters. It was an irregular pile of low buildings, covering a wide extent of ground, like the royal residence occupied by the troops in Mexico. It was spacious enough to furnish accommodations, not only for all the Spaniards, says Cortés, but for twice their number.[29] He gave orders, on his arrival, that all regard should be paid to the persons and property of the citizens; and forbade any Spaniard to leave his quarters under pain of death.

His commands were not effectual to suppress some excesses of his Indian allies, if the report of the Tezcucan chronicler be correct, who states that the Tlascalans burned down one of the royal palaces, soon after their arrival. It was the depository of the national archives; and the conflagration, however it may have occurred, may well be deplored by the antiquary, who might have found in its hieroglyphic records some clue to the migrations of the mysterious races which first settled on the highlands of Anahuac.[30]

Alarmed at the apparent desertion of the place, as well as by the fact that none of its principal inhabitants came to welcome him, Cortés ordered some soldiers to ascend the neighboring *teocalli* and survey the city. They soon returned with the report, that the inhabitants were leaving it in great numbers, with their families and effects, some in canoes upon the lake, others on foot towards the mountains. The general now comprehended the import of the cacique's suggestion, that the Spaniards should pass the night in the suburbs,—in order to secure time for evacuating the city. He feared that the chief himself might have fled. He lost no time in detaching troops to secure the principal avenues, where they were to turn back the fugitives, and arrest the cacique, if he were among the number. But it was too late. Coanaco was already far on his way across the lake to Mexico.

Cortés now determined to turn this event to his own account, by placing another ruler on the throne, who should be more subservient to

[28] Tezcuco, a Chichemec name, according to Ixtlilxochitl, signifying "place of detention or rest," because the various tribes from the North halted there on their entrance into Anahuac. Hist. Chich., MS., cap. 10.

[29] "La qual es tan grande, que aunque fueramos doblados los Españoles, nos pudieramos aposentar bien á placer en ella." Rel. Terc., ap. Lorenzana, p. 191.

[30] "De tal manera que se quemáron todos los Archivos Reales de toda la Nueva España, que fué una de las mayores pérdidas que tuvo esta tierra, porque con esto toda la memoria de sus antiguayas y otras cosas que eran como Escrituras y recuerdos pereciéron desde este tiempo. La obra de las Casas era la mejor y la mas artificiosa que hubo en esta tierra." Ixtlilxochitl, Hist. Chich., MS., cap. 91.

his interests. He called a meeting of the few principal persons still re-maining in the city, and by their advice, and ostensible election, ad-vanced a brother of the late sovereign to the dignity, which they declared vacant. This prince, who consented to be baptized, was a willing instru-ment in the hands of the Spaniards. He survived but a few months,[31] and was succeeded by another member of the royal house, named Ixtlil-xochitl, who, indeed, as general of his armies, may be said to have held the reins of government in his hands during his brother's lifetime. As this person was intimately associated with the Spaniards in their subse-quent operations, to the success of which he essentially contributed, it is proper to give some account of his earlier history, which, in truth, is as much enveloped in the marvellous, as that of any fabulous hero of antiquity.[32]

He was son, by a second queen, of the great Nezahualpilli. Some alarming prodigies at his birth, and the gloomy aspect of the planets, led the astrologers, who cast his horoscope, to advise the king, his father, to take away the infant's life since, if he lived to grow up, he was destined to unite with the enemies of his country, and overturn its institutions and religion. But the old monarch replied, says the chronicler, that "the time had arrived when the sons of Quetzalcoatl were to come from the East to take possession of the land; and, if the Almighty had selected his child to coöperate with them in the work, His will be done." [33]

As the boy advanced in years, he exhibited a marvellous precocity not merely of talent, but of michievous activity, which afforded an alarming prognostic for the future. When about twelve years old, he formed a little corps of followers of about his own age, or somewhat older, with whom he practised the military exercises of his nation, conducting mimic fights and occasionally assaulting the peaceful burghers, and throwing the

[31] The historian Ixtlilxochitl pays the following high tribute to the character of his royal kinsman, whose name was Tecocol. Strange that this name is not to be found—with the exception of Sahagun's work—in any contemporary record! "Fué el primero que lo fué en Tezcoco, con harta pena de los Españoles, porque fué nobilísimo y los quiso mucho. Fué D. Fernando Tecocoltzin muy gentil hombre, alto de cuerpo y muy blanco, tanto cuanto podia ser cualquier Español por muy blanco que fuese, y que mostraba su persona y término descender, y ser del linage que era. Supo la lengua Castellana, y así casi las mas noches despues de haber cen-ado, trataban él y Cortés de todo lo que se debia hacer acerca de las guerras." Ixtlilxochitl, Venida de los Esp., pp. 12, 13.

[32] The accession of Tecocol, as, indeed, his existence, passes unnoticed by some historians, and by others is mentioned in so equivocal a manner,—his Indian name being omitted,—that it is very doubtful if any other is intended than his younger brother Ixtlilxochitl. The Tezcucan chronicler, bearing this last melodious name, has alone given the particulars of his history. I have followed him, as, from his personal connections, having had access to the best sources of information; though, it must be confessed, he is far too ready to take things on trust, to be always the best authority.

[33] "Él respondió, que era por demas ir contra lo determinado por el Dios Criador de todas las cosas, pues no sin misterio y secreto juicio suyo le daba tal hijo al tiempo y quando se acercaban las profecías de sus Antepasados, que havíase venir nuevas Gentes á poseer la Tierra, como eran los hijos de Quetzalcoatl que aguarda-ban suvenida de la parte oriental." Ixtlilxochitl, Hist. Chich., M.S., cap. 69.

whole city as well as palace into uproar and confusion. Some of his father's ancient counsellors, connecting this conduct with the predictions at his birth, saw in it such alarming symptoms, that they repeated the advice of the astrologers, to take away the prince's life, if the monarch would not see his kingdom one day given up to anarchy. This unpleasant advice was reported to the juvenile offender, who was so much exasperated by it, that he put himself at the head of a party of his young desperadoes, and, entering the houses of the offending counsellors, dragged them forth, and administered to them the *garrote*,—the mode in which capital punishment was inflicted in Tezcuco.

He was seized and brought before his father. When questioned as to his extraordinary conduct, he coolly replied, "that he had done no more than he had a right to do. The guilty ministers had deserved their fate, by endeavoring to alienate his father's affections from him, for no other reason, than his too great fondness for the profession of arms,— the most honorable profession in the state, and the one most worthy of a prince. If they had suffered death, it was no more than they had intended for him." The wise Nezahualpilli, says the chronicler, found much force in these reasons; and, as he saw nothing low and sordid in the action, but rather the ebullition of a daring spirit, which in after life might lead to great things, he contented himself with bestowing a grave admonition on the juvenile culprit.[34] Whether this admonition had any salutary effect on his subsequent demeanor, we are not informed. It is said, however, that, as he grew older, he took an active part in the wars of his country, and, when no more than seventeen, had won for himself the insignia of a valiant and victorious captain.[35]

On his father's death, he disputed the succession with his elder brother, Cacama. The country was menaced with a civil war, when the affair was compromised by his brother's ceding to him that portion of his territories, which lay among the mountains. On the arrival of the Spaniards, the young Chieftain—for he was scarcely twenty years of age—made, as we have seen, many friendly demonstrations towards them, induced, no doubt, by his hatred of Montezuma, who had supported the pretensions of Cacama.[36] It was not, however, till his advancement to the lordship of Tezcuco, that he showed the full extent of his good-will. From that hour, he became the fast friend of the Christians, supporting them

---

[34] "Con que el Rey no supo con que ocacion poderle castigar, porque lo pareciéron sus razones tan vivas y fundadas que su parte no habia hecho cosa indebida ni vileza para poder ser castigado, mas tan solo una ferocidad de ánimo; pronóstico de lo mucho que habia de venir á saber por las Armas, y así el Rey dijo, que se fuese á la mano." Ixtlilxochitl, Hist. Chich., M. S., cap. 69.

[35] Ibid., ubi supra.

Among other anecdotes recorded of the young prince's early development is one of his having, when only three years old, pitched his nurse into a well, as she was drawing water, to punish her for certain improprieties of conduct of which he had been witness. But I spare the reader the recital of these astonishing proofs of precocity, as it is very probable, his appetite for the marvellous may not keep pace with that of the chronicler of Tezcuco.

[36] Ante, p. 170.

with his personal authority, and the whole strength of his military array and resources, which, although much shorn of their ancient splendor
since the days of his father, were still considerable, and made him a most
valuable ally. His important services have been gratefully commemorated by the Castilian historians; and history should certainly not defraud him of his just meed of glory,—the melancholy glory of having
contributed more than any other chieftain of Anahuac to rivet the
chains of the white man round the necks of his countrymen.

The two pillars, on which the story of the Conquest mainly rests, are the Chronicles of Gomara and of Bernal Diaz, two individuals having as little resemblance to
each other as the courtly and cultivated churchman has to the unlettered soldier.

The first of these, Francisco Lopez de Gomara, was a native of Seville. On the return of Cortés to Spain after the Conquest, Gomara became his chaplain; and on
his patron's death continued in the service of his son, the second Marquess of the
Valley. It was then that he wrote his Chronicle; and the circumstances under which
it was produced might lead one to conjecture, that the narrative would not be conducted on the strict principles of historic impartiality. Nor would such a conjecture
be without foundation. The history of the Conquest is necessarily that of the great
man who achieved it. But Gomara has thrown his hero's character into so bold relief, that it has entirely overshadowed that of his brave companions in arms; and,
while he has tenderly drawn the veil over the infirmities of his favorite, he is ever
studious to display his exploits in the full blaze of panegyric. His situation may in
some degree excuse his partiality. But it did not vindicate him in the eyes of the
honest Las Casas, who seldom concludes a chapter of his own narrative of the
Conquest without administering a wholesome castigation to Gomara. He even
goes so far as to tax the chaplain with "downright falsehood," assuring us "that he
had neither eyes nor ears but for what his patron chose to dictate to him." That
this is not literally true is evident from the fact that the narrative was not written
till several years after the death of Cortés. Indeed, Gomara, derived his information from the highest sources; not merely from his patron's family, but also from
the most distinguished actors in the great drama, with whom his position in society placed him in intimate communication.

The materials thus obtained he arranged with a symmetry little understood by
the chroniclers of the time. Instead of their rambling incoherencies, his style displays
an elegant brevity; it is as clear as it is concise. If the facts are somewhat too thickly
crowded on the reader, and occupy the mind too busily for reflection, they at least
all tend to a determinate point, and the story, instead of dragging its slow length
along till our patience and interest are exhausted, steadily maintains its onward
march. In short, the execution of the work is not only superior to that of most contemporary narratives, but, to a certain extent, may aspire to the rank of a classical
composition.

Owing to these circumstances, Gomara's History soon obtained general circulation
and celebrity; and, while many a letter of Cortés, and the more elaborate compositions of Oviedo and Las Casas, were suffered to slumber in manuscript, Gomara's
writings were printed and reprinted in his own day, and translated into various
languages of Europe. The first edition of the Crónica de la Nueva España appeared
at Medina, in 1553; it was republished at Antwerp the following year. It has since
been incorporated in Barcia's collection, and lastly, in 1826, made its appearance
on this side of the water from the Mexican press. The circumstances attending this
last edition are curious. The Mexican government appropriated a small sum to defray the expense of translating what was supposed to be an original chronicle of
Chimalpain, an Indian writer who lived at the close of the sixteenth century. The
care of the translation was committed to the laborious Bustamante. But this scholar
had not proceeded far in his labor, when he ascertained that the supposed original
was itself an Aztec translation of Gomara's Chronicle. He persevered, however, in

his editorial labors, until he had given to the public an American edition of Gomara. It is a fact more remarkable, that the editor in his different compilations constantly refers to this same work as the Chronicle of Chimalpain.

The other authority to which I have adverted is Bernal Diaz del Castillo, a native of Medina del Campo in Old Castile. He was born of a poor and humble family,
and in 1514 came over to seek his fortunes in the New World. He embarked as a
common soldier under Cordova in the first expedition to Yucatan. He accompanied
Grijalva in the following year to the same quarter; and finally enlisted under the
banner of Cortés. He followed this victorious chief in his first march up the great
plateau; descended with him to make the assault on Narvaez; shared the disasters
of the *noche triste;* and was present at the siege and surrender of the capital. In
short, there was scarcely an event or an action of importance in the whole war in
which he did not bear a part. He was engaged in a hundred and nineteen different
battles and rencontres, in several of which he was wounded, and in more than one
narrowly escaped falling into the enemy's hands. In all these Bernal Diaz displayed
the old Castilian valor, and a loyalty which made him proof against the mutinous
spirit that too often disturbed the harmony of the camp. On every occasion he was
found true to his commander and to the cause in which he was embarked. And his
fidelity is attested not only by his own report, but by the emphatic commendations
of his general; who selected him on this account for offices of trust and responsibility, which furnished the future chronicler with access to the best means of information in respect to the Conquest.

On the settlement of the country, Bernal Diaz received his share of the *repartimientos* of land and laborers. But the arrangement was not to his satisfaction; and
he loudly murmurs at the selfishness of his commander, too much engrossed by the
care for his own emoluments to think of his followers. The division of spoil is usually an unthankful office.—Diaz had been too long used to a life of adventure to be
content with one of torpid security. He took part in several expeditions conducted
by the captains of Cortés, and he accompanied that chief in his terrible passage
through the forests of Honduras. At length, in 1568, we find the veteran established
as regidor of the city of Guatemala, peacefully employed in recounting the valorous
achievements of his youth. It was then nearly half a century after the Conquest.
He had survived his general and nearly all his ancient companions in arms. Five
only remained of that gallant band who had accompanied Cortés on his expedition
from Cuba; and those five, to borrow the words of the old chronicler, were "poor,
aged, and infirm, with children and grandchildren looking to them for support, but
with scarcely the means of affording it,—ending their days, as they had begun
them, in toil and trouble." Such was the fate of the Conquerors of golden Mexico.

The motives which induced Bernal Diaz to take up his pen, at so late a period of
life, were to vindicate for himself and his comrades that share of renown in the
Conquest, which fairly belonged to them. Of this they had been deprived, as he
conceived, by the exaggerated reputation of their general; owing, no doubt, in part,
to the influence of Gomara's writings. It was not, however, till he had advanced
beyond the threshold of his own work, that Diaz met with that of the chaplain.
The contrast presented by his own homely diction to the clear and polished style
of his predecessor filled him with so much disgust, that he threw down his pen in
despair. But, when he had read further, and saw the gross inaccuracies and what he
deemed disregard of truth in his rival, he resumed his labors, determined to exhibit
to the world a narrative which should, at least, have the merit of fidelity. Such was
the origin of the *Historia Verdadera de la Conquista de la Nueva España.*

The chronicler may be allowed to have succeeded in his object. In reading his
pages, we feel, that, whatever are the errors into which he has fallen, from oblivion
of ancient transactions, or from unconscious vanity,—of which he had full measure,
—or from credulity, or any other cause, there is nowhere a wilful perversion of
truth. Had he attempted it, indeed, his very simplicity would have betrayed him.
Even in relation to Cortés, while he endeavors to adjust the true balance between
his pretensions and those of his followers, and while he freely exposes his cunning
or cupidity, and sometimes his cruelty, he does ample justice to his great and heroic

qualities. With all his defects, it is clear that he considers his own chief as superior to any other of ancient or modern times. In the heat of remonstrance, he is ever ready to testify his loyalty and personal attachment. When calumnies assail his commander, or he experiences unmerited slight or indignity, the loyal chronicler is prompt to step forward and shield him. In short, it is evident, that, however much he may at times censure Cortés, he will allow no one else to do it.

Bernal Diaz, the untutored child of nature, is a most true and literal copyist of nature. He transfers the scenes of real life by a sort of *daguerreotype* process, if I may say so, to his pages. He is among chroniclers what De Foe is among novelists. He introduces us into the heart of the camp, we huddle round the bivouac with the soldiers, loiter with them on their wearisome marches, listen to their stories, their murmurs of discontent, their plans of conquest, their hopes, their triumphs, their disappointments. All the picturesque scenes and romantic incidents of the campaign are reflected in his page as in a mirror. The lapse of fifty years has had no power over the spirit of the veteran. The fire of youth glows in every line of his rude history, and, as he calls up the scenes of the past, the remembrance of the brave companions who are gone gives, it may be, a warmer coloring to the picture, than if it had been made at an earlier period. Time, and reflection, and the apprehensions for the future, which might steal over the evening of life, have no power over the settled opinions of his earlier days. He has no misgivings as to the right of conquest, or as to the justice of the severities inflicted on the natives. He is still the soldier of the Cross; and those who fell by his side in the fight were martyrs for the faith. "Where are now my companions?" he asks; "they have fallen in battle or been devoured by the cannibal, or been thrown to fatten the wild beasts in their cages! they whose remains should rather have been gathered under monuments emblazoned with their achievements, which deserve to be commemorated in letters of gold; for they died in the service of God and of his Majesty, and to give light to those who sat in darkness,—*and also to acquire that wealth which most men covet.*" The last motive—thus tardily and incidentally expressed—may be thought by some to furnish a better key than either of the preceding to the conduct of the Conquerors. It is, at all events, a specimen of that *naïveté* which gives an irresistible charm to the old chronicler; and which, in spite of himself, unlocks his bosom, as it were, and lays it open to the eye of the reader.

It may seem extraordinary, that, after so long an interval, the incidents of his campaigns should have been so freshly remembered. But we must consider that they were of the most strange and romantic character, well fitted to make an impression on a young and susceptible imagination. They had probably been rehearsed by the veteran again and again to his family and friends, until every passage of the war was as familiar to his mind as the "tale of Troy" to the Greek rhapsodist, or the interminable adventures of Sir Lancelot or Sir Gawain to the Norman minstrel. The throwing of his narrative into the form of chronicle was but repeating it once more.

The literary merits of the work are of a very humble order; as might be expected from the condition of the writer. He has not even the art to conceal his own vulgar vanity, which breaks out with a truly comic ostentation in every page of the narrative. And yet we should have charity for this, when we find that it is attended with no disposition to depreciate the merits of others, and that its display may be referred in part to the singular simplicity of the man. He honestly confesses his infirmity, though, indeed, to excuse it. "When my chronicle was finished," he says, "I submitted it to two licentiates, who were desirous of reading the story, and for whom I felt all the respect which an ignorant man naturally feels for a scholar. I besought them, at the same time, to make no change or correction in the manuscript, as all there was set down in good faith. When they had read the work, they much commended me for my wonderful memory. The language, they said, was good old Castilian, without any of the flourishes and finicalities so much affected by our fine writers. But they remarked, that it would have been as well, if I had not praised myself and my comrades so liberally, but had left that to others. To this I answered, that it was common for neighbors and kindred to speak kindly of one another; and, if we did not speak well of ourselves, who would? Who else witnessed our exploits and our battles,—unless, indeed, the clouds in the sky, and the birds that were flying over our heads?"

Notwithstanding the liberal encomiums passed by the licentiates on our author's style, it is of a very homely texture; abounding in colloquial barbarisms, and seasoned occasionally by the piquant sallies of the camp. It has the merit, however, of clearly conveying the writer's thoughts, and is well suited to their simple character. His narrative is put together with even less skill than is usual among his craft, and abounds in digressions and repetitions, such as vulgar gossips are apt to use in telling their stories. But it is superfluous to criticize a work by the rules of art, which was written manifestly in total ignorance of those rules; and which, however we may criticize it, will be read and re-read by the scholar and the schoolboy, while the compositions of more classic chroniclers sleep undisturbed on their shelves.

In what, then, lies the charm of the work? In that spirit of truth which pervades it; which shows us situations as they were, and sentiments as they really existed in the heart of the writer. It is this which imparts a living interest to his story; and which is more frequently found in the productions of the untutored penman solely intent upon facts, than in those of the ripe and fastidious scholar occupied with the mode of expressing them.

It was by a mere chance that this inimitable chronicle was rescued from the oblivion into which so many works of higher pretensions have fallen in the Peninsula. For more than sixty years after its composition, the manuscript lay concealed in the obscurity of a private library, when it was put into the hands of Father Alonso Remon, Chronicler General of the Order of Mercy. He had the sagacity to discover, under its rude exterior, its high value in illustrating the history of the Conquest. He obtained a license for the publication of the work, and under his auspices it appeared at Madrid in 1632,—the edition used in the preparation of these volumes.

BOOK VI

CHAPTER I

ARRANGEMENTS AT TEZCUCO—SACK OF IZTAPALAPAN—ADVANTAGES OF
THE SPANIARDS—WISE POLICY OF CORTÉS—TRANSPORTATION OF
THE BRIGANTINES

1521

THE city of Tezcuco was the best position, probably, which Cortés
could have chosen for the headquarters of the army. It supplied all the
accommodations for lodging a numerous body of troops, and all the
facilities for subsistence, incident to a large and populous town.[1] It furnished, moreover, a multitude of artisans and laborers for the uses of the
army. Its territories, bordering on the Tlascalan, afforded a ready means
of intercourse with the country of his allies, while its vicinity to Mexico
enabled the general, without much difficulty, to ascertain the movements
in that capital. Its central situation, in short, opened facilities for communication with all parts of the Valley, and made it an excellent *point
d'appui* for his future operations.

The first care of Cortés was to strengthen himself in the palace assigned to him, and to place his quarters in a state of defence, which might
secure them against surprise, not only from the Mexicans, but from the
Tezcucans themselves. Since the election of their new ruler, a large part
of the population had returned to their homes, assured of protection in
person and property. But the Spanish general, notwithstanding their
show of submission, very much distrusted its sincerity; for he knew that
many of them were united too intimately with the Aztecs, by marriage
and other social relations, not to have their sympathies engaged in their
behalf.[2] The young monarch, however, seemed wholly in his interests;

---

[1] "Así mismo hizo juntar todos los bastimentos que fuéron necesarios para sus-
tentar el Exército y Guarniciones de Gente que andaban en favor de Cortés, y así
hizo traer á la Ciudad de Tezcuco el Maiz que habia en las Troxes y Graneros de
las Provincias sugetas al Reyno de Tezcuco." Ixtlilxochitl, Hist. Chich., MS., cap. 91.

[2] "No era de espantar que tuviese este recelo, porque sus Enemigos, y los de esta
Ciudad eran todos Deudos y Parientes mas cercanos, mas despues el tiempo lo
desengañó, y vido la gran lealtad de Ixtlilxochitl, y de todos." Ixtlilxochitl, Hist.
Chich., MS., cap. 92.

and, to secure him more effectually, Cortés placed several Spaniards near his person, whose ostensible province it was to instruct him in their language and religion, but who were in reality to watch over his conduct and prevent his correspondence with those who might be unfriendly to the Spanish interests.[3]

Tezcuco stood about half a league from the lake. It would be necessary to open a communication with it, so that the brigantines, when put together in the capital, might be launched upon its waters. It was proposed, therefore, to dig a canal, reaching from the gardens of Nezahualcoyotl, as they were called, from the old monarch who planned them, to the edge of the basin. A little stream or rivulet, which flowed in that direction, was to be deepened sufficiently for the purpose; and eight thousand Indian laborers were forthwith employed on this great work, under the direction of the young Ixtlilxochitl.[4]

Meanwhile Cortés received messages from several places in the neighborhood, intimating their desire to become the vassals of his sovereign, and to be taken under his protection. The Spanish commander required, in turn, that they should deliver up every Mexican who should set foot in their territories. Some noble Aztecs, who had been sent on a mission to these towns, were consequently delivered into his hands. He availed himself of it to employ them as bearers of a message to their master, the emperor. In it he deprecated the necessity of the present hostilities. Those who had most injured him, he said, were no longer among the living. He was willing to forget the past; and invited the Mexicans, by a timely submission, to save their capital from the horrors of a siege.[5] Cortés had no expectation of producing any immediate result by this appeal. But he thought it might lie in the minds of the Mexicans, and that, if there was a party among them disposed to treat with him, it might afford them encouragement, as showing his own willingness to coöperate with their views. At this time, however, there was no division of opinion in the capital. The whole population seemed animated by a spirit of resistance, as one man.

In a former page I have mentioned that it was the plan of Cortés, on entering the Valley, to commence operations by reducing the subordinate cities before striking at the capital itself, which, like some goodly tree, whose roots had been severed one after another, would be thus left without support against the fury of the tempest. The first point of attack which he selected was the ancient city of Iztapalapan; a place containing fifty thousand inhabitants, according to his own account, and situated about six leagues distant, on the narrow tongue of land, which divides the waters of the great salt lake from those of the fresh. It was

[3] Bernal Diaz, Hist. de la Conquista, cap. 137.

[4] Ibid., ubi supra.—Ixtlilxochitl, Hist. Chich., MS., cap. 91.

[5] "Los principales, que habian sido en hacerme la Guerra pasada, eran ya muertos; y que lo pasado fuesse pasado, y que no quisiessen dar causa á que destruyesse sus Tierras, y Ciudades, porque me pesaba mucho de ello." Rel. Terc. de Cortés, ap. Lorenzana, p. 193.

the private domain of the last sovereign of Mexico; where, as the reader may remember, he entertained the white men, the night before their entrance into the capital, and astonished them by the display of his princely gardens. To this monarch they owed no good-will, for he had conducted the operations on the *noche triste*. He was, indeed, no more; but the people of his city entered heartily into his hatred of the strangers, and were now the most loyal vassals of the Mexican crown.

In a week after his arrival at his new quarters, Cortés, leaving the command of the garrison to Sandoval, marched against this Indian city, at the head of two hundred Spanish foot, eighteen horse, and between three and four thousand Tlascalans. Their route lay along the eastern border of the lake, gemmed with many a bright town and hamlet, or, unlike its condition at the present day, darkened with overhanging groves of cypress and cedar, and occasionally opening a broad expanse to their view, with the Queen of the Valley rising gloriously from the waters, as if proudly conscious of her supremacy over the fair cities around her. Further on, the eye ranged along the dark line of causeway connecting Mexico with the mainland, and suggesting many a bitter recollection to the Spaniards.

They quickened their step, and had advanced within two leagues of their point of destination, when they were encountered by a strong Aztec force, drawn up to dispute their progress. Cortés instantly gave them battle. The barbarians showed their usual courage; but, after some hard fighting, were compelled to give way before the steady valor of the Spanish infantry, backed by the desperate fury of the Tlascalans, whom the sight of an Aztec seemed to inflame almost to madness. The enemy retreated in disorder, closely followed by the Spaniards. When they had arrived within half a league of Iztapalapan, they observed a number of canoes filled with Indians, who appeared to be laboring on the mole which hemmed in the waters of the salt lake. Swept along in the tide of pursuit, they gave little heed to it, but, following up the chase, entered pell-mell with the fugitives into the city.

The houses stood some of them on dry ground, some on piles in the water. The former were deserted by the inhabitants, most of whom had escaped in canoes across the lake, leaving, in their haste, their effects behind them. The Tlascalans poured at once into the vacant dwellings and loaded themselves with booty; while the enemy, making the best of their way through this part of the town, sought shelter in the buildings erected over the water, or among the reeds which sprung from its shallow bottom. In the houses were many of the citizens also, who still lingered with their wives and children, unable to find the means of transporting themselves from the scene of danger.

Cortés, supported by his own men, and by such of the allies as could be brought to obey his orders, attacked the enemy in this last place of their retreat. Both parties fought up to their girdles in the water. A desperate struggle ensued; as the Aztec fought with the fury of a tiger driven to bay by the huntsmen. It was all in vain. The enemy was overpowered in every quarter. The citizen shared the fate of the soldier, and a pitiless massacre succeeded, without regard to sex or age. Cortés endeavored to stop it. But it would have been as easy to call away the starving wolf from the carcass he was devouring, as the Tlascalan who had once tasted the blood of an enemy. More than six thousand, including women and children, according to the Conqueror's own statement, perished in the conflict.[6]

Darkness meanwhile had set in; but it was dispelled in some measure by the light of the burning houses, which the troops had set on fire in different parts of the town. Their insulated position, it is true, prevented the flames from spreading from one building to another, but the solitary masses threw a strong and lurid glare over their own neighborhood, which gave additional horror to the scene. As resistance was now at an end, the soldiers abandoned themselves to pillage, and soon stripped the dwellings of every portable article of any value.

While engaged in this work of devastation, a murmuring sound was heard as of the hoarse rippling of waters, and a cry soon arose among the Indians that the dikes were broken! Cortes now comprehended the business of the men whom he had seen in the canoes at work on the mole which fenced in the great basin of Lake Tezcuco.[7] It had been pierced by the desperate Indians, who thus laid the country under an inundation, by suffering the waters of the salt lake to spread themselves over the lower level, through the opening. Greatly alarmed, the general called his men together, and made all haste to evacuate the city. Had they remained three hours longer, he says, not a soul could have escaped.[8] They came staggering under the weight of booty, wading with difficulty through the water, which was fast gaining upon them. For some distance, their path was illumined by the glare of the burning buildings. But, as the light faded away in distance, they wandered with uncertain steps, sometimes up to their knees, at others up to their waists, in the water, through which they floundered on with the greatest difficulty. As they reached the opening in the dike, the stream became deeper, and flowed out with such a current that the men were unable to maintain their footing. The Spaniards, breasting the flood, forced their way through; but many of the Indians, unable to swim, were borne down by the waters. All the plunder was lost. The powder was spoiled; the arms and clothes of the soldiers were saturated with the brine, and the cold night-wind, as it blew over them, benumbed their weary limbs till they could scarcely drag them along. At dawn they beheld the lake swarming with canoes,

[6] "Muriéron de ellos mas de seis mil ánimas, entre Hombres, y Mugeres, y Niños; porque los Indios nuestros Amigos, vista la Victoria, que Dios nos daba, no entendian en otra cosa, sino en matar á diestro y á siniestro." Ibid., p. 195.

[7] "Estándolas quemando, pareció que Nuestro Señor me inspiró, y trujo á la memoria la Calzada, ó Presa, que habia visto rota en el Camino, y representóseme el gran daño, que era." Ibid., loc. cit.

[8] "Y certifico á Vuestra Magestad, que si aquella noche no pasaramos el Agua, ó aguardaramos tres horas mas, que ninguno de nosotros escapara, porque quedabamos cercados de Agua, sin tener paso por parte ninguna." Ibid., ubi supra.

full of Indians, who had anticipated their disaster, and who now saluted them with showers of stones, arrows, and other deadly missiles. Bodies of light troops, hovering in the distance, disquieted the flanks of the army in like manner. The Spaniards had no desire to close with the enemy. They only wished to regain their comfortable quarters in Tezcuco, where they arrived on the same day, more disconsolate and fatigued than after many a long march and hard-fought battle.[9]

The close of the expedition, so different from its brilliant commencement, greatly disappointed Cortés. His numerical loss had, indeed, not been great; but this affair convinced him how much he had to apprehend from the resolution of a people, who, with a spirit worthy of the ancient Hollanders, were prepared to bury their country under water, rather than to submit. Still the enemy had little cause for congratulation; since, independently of the number of slain, they had seen one of their most flourishing cities sacked, and in part, at least, laid in ruins,—one of those, too, which in its public works displayed the nearest approach to civilization. Such are the triumphs of war!

The expedition of Cortés, notwithstanding the disasters which chequered it, was favorable to the Spanish cause. The fate of Iztapalapan struck a terror throughout the Valley. The consequences were soon apparent in the deputations sent by the different places eager to offer their submission. Its influence was visible, indeed, beyond the mountains. Among others, the people of Otumba, the town near which the Spaniards had gained their famous victory, sent to tender their allegiance and to request the protection of the powerful strangers. They excused themselves, as usual, for the part they had taken in the late hostilities, by throwing the blame on the Aztecs.

But the place of most importance, which thus claimed their protection, was Chalco, situated on the eastern extremity of the lake of that name. It was an ancient city, peopled by a kindred tribe of the Aztecs, and once their formidable rival. The Mexican emperor, distrusting their loyalty, had placed a garrison within their walls to hold them in check. The rulers of the city now sent a message secretly to Cortés, proposing to put themselves under his protection, if he would enable them to expel the garrison.

The Spanish commander did not hesitate; but instantly detached a considerable force under Sandoval for this object. On the march, his rear-guard, composed of Tlascalans, was roughly handled by some light troops of the Mexicans. But he took his revenge in a pitched battle which took place with the main body of the enemy at no great distance from Chalco. They were drawn up on a level ground, covered with green crops of maize and maguey. The field is traversed by the road which at

[9] The general's own Letter to the Emperor is so full and precise, that it is the very best authority for this event. The story is told also by Bernal Diaz, Hist. de la Conquista, cap. 138.—Oviedo, Hist. de las Ind., MS., lib. 33, cap. 18,—Ixtlilxochitl, Hist. Chich., MS., cap. 92,—Herrera, Hist. General, dec. 3, lib. 1, cap. 2, et auct. aliis.

this day leads from the last mentioned city to Tezcuco.[10] Sandoval, charging the enemy at the head of his cavalry, threw them into disorder. But they quickly rallied, formed again, and renewed the battle with greater spirit than ever. In a second attempt he was more fortunate; and, breaking through their lines by a desperate onset, the brave cavalier succeeded, after a warm, but ineffectual, struggle on their part, in completely routing and driving them from the field. The conquering army continued its march to Chalco, which the Mexican garrison had already evacuated, and was received in triumph by the assembled citizens, who seemed eager to testify their gratitude for their deliverance from the Aztec yoke. After taking such measures as he could for the permanent security of the place, Sandoval returned to Tezcuco, accompanied by the two young lords of the city, sons of the late cacique.

They were courteously received by Cortés; and they informed him that their father had died full of years, a short time before. With his last breath he had expressed his regret that he should not have lived to see Malinche. He believed that the white men were the beings predicted by the oracles, as one day to come from the East and take possession of the land;[11] and he enjoined it on his children, should the strangers return to the Valley, to render them their homage and allegiance. The young caciques expressed their readiness to do so; but, as this must bring on them the vengeance of the Aztecs, they implored the general to furnish a sufficient force for their protection.[12]

Cortés received a similar application from various other towns, which were disposed, could they do so with safety, to throw off the Mexican yoke. But he was in no situation to comply with their request. He now felt, more sensibly than ever, the incompetency of his means to his undertaking. "I assure your Majesty," he writes in his letter to the Emperor, "the greatest uneasiness which I feel, after all my labors and fatigues, is from my inability to succour and support our Indian friends, your Majesty's loyal vassals."[13] Far from having a force competent to this, he had scarcely enough for his own protection. His vigilant enemy had an eye on all his movements, and, should he cripple his strength by sending away too many detachments or by employing them at too great a distance, would be prompt to take advantage of it. His only expeditions, hitherto, had been in the neighborhood, where the troops, after striking some sudden and decisive blow, might speedily regain their quarters.

[10] Lorenzana, p. 199, nota.

[11] "Porque ciertamente sus antepassados les auian dicho, que auian de señorear aquellas tierras hombres que vernian con barbas de hazia donde sale el Sol, y que por las cosas que han visto, eramos nosotros." Bernal Diaz, Hist. de la Conquista, cap. 139.

[12] Ibid., ubi supra.—Rel. Terc. de Cortés, ap. Lorenzana, p. 200.—Gomara, Crónica, cap. 122.—Venida de los Esp., p. 15.

[13] "Y certifico á Vuestra Magestad, allende de nuestro trabajo y necesidad, la mayor fatiga, que tenia, era no poder ayudar, y socorrer á los Indios nuestros Amigos, que por ser Vasallos de Vuestra Magestad, eran molestados y trabajados de los de Culua." Rel Terc., ap. Lorenzana, p. 204.

The utmost watchfulness was maintained there, and the Spaniards lived in as constant preparation for an assault, as if their camp was pitched under the walls of Mexico.

On two occasions the general had sallied forth and engaged the enemy in the environs of Tezcuco. At one time a thousand canoes, filled with Aztecs, crossed the lake to gather in a large crop of Indian corn nearly ripe, on its borders. Cortés thought it important to secure this for himself. He accordingly marched out and gave battle to the enemy, drove them from the field, and swept away the rich harvest to the granaries of Tezcuco. Another time a strong body of Mexicans had established themselves in some neighboring towns friendly to their interests. Cortés, again sallying, dislodged them from their quarters, beat them in several skirmishes, and reduced the places to obedience. But these enterprises demanded all his resources, and left him nothing to spare for his allies. In this exigency, his fruitful genius suggested an expedient for supplying the deficiency of his means.

Some of the friendly cities without the Valley, observing the numerout beacon-fires on the mountains, inferred that the Mexicans were mustering in great strength, and that the Spaniards must be hard pressed in their new quarters. They sent messengers to Tezcuco expressing their apprehension, and offering reinforcements, which the general, when he set out on his march, had declined. He returned many thanks for the proffered aid; but, while he declined it for himself, as unnecessary, he indicated in what manner their services might be effectual for the defence of Chalco and the other places which had invoked his protection. But his Indian allies were in deadly feud with these places, whose inhabitants had too often fought under the Aztec banner not to have been engaged in repeated wars with the people beyond the mountains.

Cortés set himself earnestly to reconcile these differences. He told the hostile parties that they should be willing to forget their mutual wrongs, since they had entered into new relations. They were now vassals of the same sovereign, engaged in a common enterprise against the formidable foe who had so long trodden them in the dust. Singly they could do little, but united they might protect each other's weakness and hold their enemy at bay, till the Spaniards could come to their assistance. These arguments finally prevailed; and the politic general had the satisfaction to see the high-spirited and hostile tribes forego their long-cherished rivalry, and, resigning the pleasures of revenge, so dear to the barbarian, embrace one another as friends and champions in a common cause. To this wise policy the Spanish commander owed quite as much of his subsequent successes, as to his arms.[14]

Thus the foundations of the Mexican empire were hourly loosening, as the great vassals, around the capital, on whom it most relied, fell off one after another from their allegiance. The Aztecs, properly so called, formed but a small part of the population of the Valley. This was prin-

---

[14] Ibid., pp. 204, 205.—Oviedo, Hist. de las Ind., MS., lib. 33, cap. 19.

cipally composed of cognate tribes, members of the same great family of the Nahuatlacs, who had come upon the plateau at nearly the same time. They were mutual rivals, and were reduced one after another by the more warlike Mexican, who held them in subjection, often by open force, always by fear. Fear was the great principle of cohesion which bound together the discordant members of the monarchy, and this was now fast dissolving before the influence of a power more mighty than that of the Aztec. This, it is true, was not the first time that the conquered races had attempted to recover their independence. But all such attempts had failed for want of concert. It was reserved for the commanding genius of Cortés to extinguish their old hereditary feuds, and, combining their scattered energies, to animate them with a common principle of action.[15]

Encouraged by this state of things, the Spanish general thought it a favorable moment to press his negotiations with the capital. He availed himself of the presence of some noble Mexicans, taken in the late action with Sandoval, to send another message to their master. It was in substance a repetition of the first, with a renewed assurance, that if the city would return to its allegiance to the Spanish crown, the authority of Guatemozin should be confirmed, and the persons and property of his subjects be respected. To this communication no reply was made. The young Indian emperor had a spirit as dauntless as that of Cortés himself. On his head descended the full effects of that vicious system of government bequeathed to him by his ancestors. But, as he saw his empire crumbling beneath him, he sought to uphold it by his own energy and resources. He anticipated the defection of some vassals by establishing garrisons within their walls. Others he conciliated by exempting them from tributes or greatly lightening their burdens, or by advancing them to posts of honor and authority in the state. He showed, at the same time, his implacable animosity towards the Christians, by commanding that every one taken within his dominions should be straightway sent to the

---

[15] Oviedo, in his admiration of his hero, breaks out into the following panegyric on his policy, prudence, and military science, which, as he truly predicts, must make his name immortal. It is a fair specimen of the manner of the sagacious old chronicler.

"Sin dubda alguna la habilidad y esfuerzo, é prudencia de Hernando Cortés mui dignas son que entre los cavalleros, é gente militar en nuestros tiempos se tengan en mucha estimacion, y en los venideros nunca se desacuerden. Por causa suya me acuerdo muchas veces de aquellas cosas que se escriven del capitan Viriato nuestro Español y Estremeño; y por Hernando Cortés me ocurren al sentido las muchas fatigas de aquel espejo de caballería Julio César dictador, como parece por sus comentarios, é por Suetonio é Plutarco é otros autores que en conformidad escriviéron los grandes hechos suyos. Pero los de Hernando Cortés en un Mundo nuevo, é tan apartadas provincias de Europa, é con tantos trabajos é necesidades é pocas fuerzas, é con gente tan innumerable, é tan bárbara é bellicosa, é apacentada en carne humana, é aun habida por excelente é sabroso manjar entre sus adversarios; é faltándole á él ó á sus mílites el pan é vino é los otros mantenimientos todos de España, y en tan diferenciadas regiones é aires é tan desviado é léjos de socorro é de su príncipe, cosas son de admiracion." Hist. de las Ind., MS., lib. 33, cap. 20.

capital, where he was sacrificed, with all the barbarous ceremonies prescribed by the Aztec ritual.[16]

While these occurrences were passing, Cortés received the welcome intelligence, that the brigantines were completed and waiting to be transported to Tezcuco. He detached a body for the service, consisting of two hundred Spanish foot and fifteen horse, which he placed under the command of Sandoval. This cavalier had been rising daily in the estimation both of the general and of the army. Though one of the youngest officers in the service, he possessed a cool head and a ripe judgment, which fitted him for the most delicate and difficult undertakings. There were others, indeed, as Alvarado and Olid, for example, whose intrepidity made them equally competent to achieve a brilliant *coup-de-main.* But the courage of Alvarado was too often carried to temerity, or perverted by passion; while Olid, dark and doubtful in his character, was not entirely to be trusted. Sandoval was a native of Medellin, the birth-place of Cortés himself. He was warmly attached to his commander, and had on all occasions proved himself worthy of his confidence. He was a man of few words, showing his worth rather by what he did, than what he said. His honest, soldierlike deportment made him a favorite with the troops, and had its influence even on his enemies. He unfortunately died in the flower of his age. But he discovered talents and military skill, which, had

[16] Among other chiefs, to whom Guatemozin applied for assistance in the perilous state of his affairs, was Tangapan, lord of Michuacan, an independent and powerful state in the West, which had never been subdued by the Mexican army. The accounts which the Aztec emperor gave him, through his ambassadors, of the white men, were so alarming, according to Ixtlilxochitl, who tells the story, that the king's sister voluntarily starved herself to death, from her apprehensions of the coming of the terrible strangers. Her body was deposited, as usual, in the vaults reserved for the royal household, until preparations could be made for its being burnt. On the fourth day, the attendants, who had charge of it, were astounded by seeing the corpse exhibit signs of returning life. The restored princess, recovering her speech, requested her brother's presence. On his coming, she implored him not to think of hurting a hair of the heads of the mysterious visitors. She had been permitted, she said, to see the fate of the departed in the next world. The souls of all her ancestors she had beheld tossing about in unquenchable fire; while those who embraced the faith of the strangers were in glory. As a proof of the truth of her assertion, she added, that her brother would see, on a great festival, near at hand, a young warrior, armed with a torch brighter than the sun, in one hand, and a flaming sword, like that worn by the white men, in the other, passing from east to west over the city.

Whether the monarch waited for the vision, or ever beheld it, is not told us by the historian. But relying, perhaps, on the miracle of her resurrection, as quite a sufficient voucher, he disbanded a very powerful force, which he had assembled on the plains of Avalos, for the support of his brother of Mexico.

This narrative, with abundance of supernumerary incidents, not necessary to repeat, was commemorated in the Michuacan picture-records, and reported to the historian of Tezcuco himself, by the grandson of Tangapan. (See Ixtlilxochitl, Hist. Chich., MS., cap. 91.)—Whoever reported it to him, it is not difficult to trace the same pious fingers in it, which made so many wholesome legends for the good of the Church on the Old Continent, and which now found, in the credulity of the New, a rich harvest for the same godly work.

he lived to later life, would undoubtedly have placed his name on the roll with those of the greatest captains of his nation.

Sandoval's route was to lead him by Zoltepec, a small city where the massacre of the forty-five Spaniards, already noticed, had been perpetrated. The cavalier received orders to find out the guilty parties, if possible, and to punish them for their share in the transaction.

When the Spaniards arrived at the spot, they found that the inhabitants, who had previous notice of their approach, had all fled. In the deserted temples they discovered abundant traces of the fate of their countrymen; for, besides their arms and clothing, and the hides of their horses, the heads of several soldiers, prepared in such a way that they could be well preserved, were found suspended as trophies of the victory. In a neighboring building, traced with charcoal on the walls, they found the following inscription in Castilian: "In this place the unfortunate Juan Juste, with many others of his company, was imprisoned." [17] This hidalgo was one of the followers of Narvaez, and had come with him into the country in quest of gold, but had found, instead, an obscure and inglorious death. The eyes of the soldiers were suffused with tears, as they gazed on the gloomy record, and their bosoms swelled with indignation, as they thought of the horrible fate of the captives. Fortunately the inhabitants were not then before them. Some few, who subsequently fell into their hands, were branded as slaves. But the greater part of the population, who threw themselves, in the most abject manner, on the mercy of the conquerors, imputing the blame of the affair to the Aztecs, the Spanish commander spared, from pity, or contempt.[18]

He now resumed his march on Tlascala; but scarcely had he crossed the borders of the republic, when he descried the flaunting banners of the convoy which transported the brigantines, as it was threading its way through the defiles of the mountains. Great was his satisfaction at the spectacle, for he had feared a detention of some days at Tlascala, before the preparations for the march could be completed.

There were thirteen vessels in all, of different sizes. They had been constructed under the direction of the experienced ship-builder, Martin Lopez, aided by three or four Spanish carpenters and the friendly natives, some of whom showed no mean degree of imitative skill. The brigantines, when completed, had been fairly tried on the waters of the Zahuapan. They were then taken to pieces, and, as Lopez was impatient of delay, the several parts, the timbers, anchors, iron-work, sails, and cordage were placed on the shoulders of the *tamanes,* and, under a numerous military escort, were thus far advanced on the way to Tezcuco.[19] Sandoval dismissed a part of the Indian convoy, as superfluous.

[17] "Aquí estuvo ⌐reso el sin ventura de Juã Iuste cõ otros muchos que traia en mi compañía." Bernal Diaz, Hist. de la Conquista, cap. 140.

[18] Ibid., ubi supra.—Oviedo, Hist. de las Ind., MS., lib. 33, cap. 19.—Rel. Terc. de Cortés, ap. Lorenzana, p. 206.

[19] "Y despues de hechos por órden de Cortés, y probados en el rio que llaman de Tlaxcalla Zahuapan, que se atajó para probarlos los bergantines, y los tornáron á

Twenty thousand warriors he retained, dividing them into two equal bodies for the protection of the *tamanes* in the centre.[20] His own little body of Spaniards he distributed in like manner. The Tlascalans in the van marched under the command of a chief who gloried in the name of Chichemecatl. For some reason Sandoval afterwards changed the order of march, and placed this division in the rear,—an arrangement which gave great umbrage to the doughty warrior that led it, who asserted his right to the front, the place which he and his ancestors had always occupied, as the post of danger. He was somewhat appeased by Sandoval's assurance that it was for that very reason he had been transferred to the rear, the quarter most likely to be assailed by the enemy. But even then he was greatly dissatisfied, on finding that the Spanish commander was to march by his side, grudging, it would seem, that any other should share the laurel with himself.

Slowly and painfully, encumbered with their heavy burden, the troops worked their way over steep eminences and rough mountain-passes, presenting, one might suppose, in their long line of march, many a vulnerable point to an enemy. But, although small parties of warriors were seen hovering, at times, on their flanks and rear, they kept at a respectful distance, not caring to encounter so formidable a foe. On the fourth day the warlike caravan arrived in safety before Tezcuco.

Their approach was beheld with joy by Cortés and the soldiers, who hailed it as the signal of a speedy termination of the war. The general, attended by his officers, all dressed in their richest attire, came out to welcome the convoy. It extended over a space of two leagues, and so slow was its progress that six hours elapsed before the closing files had entered the city.[21] The Tlascalan chiefs displayed all their wonted bravery of apparel, and the whole array, composed of the flower of their warriors, made a brilliant appearance. They marched by the sound of atabal and cornet, and, as they traversed the streets of the capital amidst the acclamations of the soldiery, they made the city ring with the shouts of "Castile and Tlascala, long live our sovereign, the emperor!"[22]

"It was a marvellous thing," exclaims the Conqueror, in his Letters,

desbaratar por llevarlos á cuestas sobre hombros de los de Tlaxcalla á la ciudad de Tetzcuco, donde se echáron en la laguna, y se armáron de artillería y municion." Camargo, Hist. de Tlascala, MS.

[*] Rel. Terc. de Cortés, ap. Lorenzana, p. 207.
Bernal Diaz says sixteen thousand. (Ibid., ubi supra.) There is a wonderful agreement between the several Castilian writers as to the number of forces, the order of march, and the events that occurred on it.

[21] "Estendíase tanto la Gente, que dende que los primeros comenzáron á entrar, hasta que los postreros hobiéron acabado, se pasáron mas de seis horas; sin quebrar el hilo de la Gente." Rel. Terc. de Cortés, ap. Lorenzana, p. 208.

[22] Dando vozes y silvos y diziendo: Viua, viua el Emperador, nuestro Señor, y Castilla, Castilla, y Tlascala, Tlascala." (Bernal Diaz, Hist. de la Conquista, cap. 140.) For the particulars of Sandoval's expedition, see, also, Oviedo, Hist. de las Ind., MS., lib. 33, cap. 19,—Gomara, Crónica, cap. 124,—Torquemada, Monarch. Ind., lib. 4, cap. 84,—Ixtlilxochitl, Hist. Chich., MS., cap. 92,—Herrera, Hist. General, dec. 3, lib. 1, cap. 2.

"that few have seen, or even heard of,—this transportation of thirteen vessels of war on the shoulders of men, for nearly twenty leagues across the mountains!" [23] It was, indeed, a stupendous achievement, and not easily matched in ancient or modern story; one which only a genius like that of Cortés could have devised, or a daring spirit like his have so successfully executed. Little did he foresee, when he ordered the destruction of the fleet which first brought him to the country, and with his usual forecast commanded the preservation of the iron-work and rigging,— little did he foresee the important uses for which they were to be reserved. So important, that on their preservation may be said to have depended the successful issue of his great enterprise.[24]

He greeted his Indian allies with the greatest cordiality, testifying his sense of their services by those honors and attentions which he knew would be most grateful to their ambitious spirits. "We come," exclaimed the hardy warriors, "to fight under your banner; to avenge our common quarrel, or to fall by your side"; and, with their usual impatience, they urged him to lead them at once against the enemy. "Wait," replied the general, bluntly, "till you are rested, and you shall have your hands full.[25]

[23] "Que era cosa maravillosa de ver, y assí me parece que es de oir, llevar trece Fustas diez y ocho leguas por Tierra." (Rel. Terc. de Cortés, ap. Lorenzana, p. 207.) "En rem Romano populo," exclaims Martyr, "quando illustris res illorum vigebant, non facilem!" De Orbe Novo, dec. 5, cap. 8.

[24] Two memorable examples of a similar transportation of vessels across the land are recorded, the one in ancient, the other in modern history; and both, singularly enough, at the same place, Tarentum, in Italy. The first occurred at the siege of that city by Hannibal; (see Polybius, lib. 8;) the latter some seventeen centuries later, by the Great Captain, Gonsalvo de Cordova. But the distance they were transported was inconsiderable. A more analogous example is that of Balboa, the bold discoverer of the Pacific. He made arrangements to have four brigantines transported a distance of twenty-two leagues across the Isthmus of Darien, a stupendous labor, and not entirely successful, as only two reached their point of destination. (See Herrera, Hist. General, dec. 2, lib. 2, cap. 11.) This took place in 1516, in the neighborhood, as it were, of Cortés, and may have suggested to his enterprising spirit the first idea of his own more successful, as well as more extensive, undertaking.

[25] "Y ellos me dijéron, que trahian deseo de se ver con los de Culúa, y que viesse lo que mandaba, que ellos, y aquella Gente venian con deseos, y voluntad de se vengar, ó morir con nosotros; y yo les dí las gracias, y les dije, que reposassen, y que presto les daria las manos llenas." Rel. Terc., ap. Lorenzana, p. 208.

CHAPTER II

1521

In the course of three or four days, the Spanish general furnished the
Tlascalans with the opportunity so much coveted, and allowed their
boiling spirits to effervesce in active operations. He had, for some time,
meditated an expedition to reconnoitre the capital and its environs, and
to chastise, on the way, certain places, which had sent him insulting
messages of defiance, and which were particularly active in their hostilities. He disclosed his design to a few only of his principal officers, from
his distrust of the Tezcucans, whom he suspected to be in correspondence
with the enemy.

Early in the spring, he left Tezcuco, at the head of three hundred and
fifty Spaniards and the whole strength of his allies. He took with him
Alvarado and Olid, and entrusted the charge of the garrison to Sandoval.
Cortés had had practical acquaintance with the incompetence of the first
of these cavaliers for so delicate a post, during his short, but disastrous,
rule in Mexico.

But all his precautions had not availed to shroud his designs from the
vigilant foe, whose eye was on all his movements; who seemed even to
divine his thoughts, and to be prepared to thwart their execution. He
had advanced but a few leagues, when he was met by a considerable
body of Mexicans, drawn up to dispute his progress. A sharp skirmish
took place, in which the enemy were driven from the ground, and the
way was left open to the Christians. They held a circuitous route to the
north, and their first point of attack was the insular town of Xaltocan,
situated on the northern extremity of the lake of that name, now called
San Christóbal. The town was entirely surrounded by water, and communicated with the main land by means of causeways, in the same manner as the Mexican capital. Cortés, riding at the head of his cavalry, advanced along the dike, till he was brought to a stand by finding a wide
opening in it, through which the waters poured so as to be altogether impracticable, not only for horse, but for infantry. The lake was covered
with canoes, filled with Aztec warriors, who, anticipating the movement
of the Spaniards, had come to the aid of the city. They now began a furious discharge of stones and arrows on the assailants, while they were
themselves tolerably well protected from the musketry of their enemy by

the light bulwarks, with which, for that purpose, they had fortified their canoes.

The severe volleys of the Mexicans did some injury to the Spaniards and their allies, and began to throw them into disorder, crowded as they were on the narrow causeway, without the means of advancing, when Cortés ordered a retreat. This was followed by renewed tempests of missiles, accompanied by taunts and fierce yells of defiance. The battle-cry of the Aztec, like the war-whoop of the North American Indian, was an appalling note, according to the Conqueror's own acknowledgment, in the ears of the Spaniards.[1] At this juncture, the general fortunately obtained information from a deserter, one of the Mexican allies, of a ford, by which the army might traverse the shallow lake, and penetrate into the place. He instantly detached the greater part of the infantry on the service, posting himself with the remainder and with the horse at the entrance of the passage, to cover the attack and prevent any interruption in the rear.

The soldiers, under the direction of the Indian guide, forded the lake without much difficulty, though in some places the water came above their girdles. During the passage, they were annoyed by the enemy's missiles; but, when they had gained the dry level, they took ample revenge, and speedily put all who resisted to the sword. The greater part, together with the townsmen, made their escape in the boats. The place was now abandoned to pillage. The troops found in it many women who had been left to their fate; and these, together with a considerable quantity of cotton stuffs, gold, and articles of food, fell into the hands of the victors, who, setting fire to the deserted city, returned in triumph to their comrades.[2]

Continuing his circuitous route, Cortés presented himself successively before three other places, each of which had been deserted by the inhabitants in anticipation of his arrival.[3] The principal of these, Azcapozalco, had once been the capital of an independent state. It was now the great slave-market of the Aztecs, where their unfortunate captives were brought, and disposed of at public sale. It was also the quarter occupied by the jewellers; and the place whence the Spaniards obtained the gold-smiths who melted down the rich treasures received from Montezuma. But they found there only a small supply of the precious metals, or, indeed, of any thing else of value, as the people had been careful to remove their effects. They spared the buildings, however, in consideration of their having met with no resistance.

[1] "De lejos comenzáron á gritar, como lo suelen hacer en la Guerra, que cierto es cosa espantosa oillos." Rel. Terc., ap. Lorenzana, p. 209.
[2] Ibid., loc. cit.—Bernal Diaz, Hist. de la Conquista, cap. 141.—Oviedo, Hist. de las Ind., MS., lib. 33, cap. 20.—Ixtlilxochitl, Venida de los Esp., pp. 13, 14.—Idem, Hist. Chich., MS., cap. 92.—Gomara, Crónica, cap. 125.
[3] These towns rejoiced in the melodious names of Tenajoccan, Quauhtitlan and Azcapozalco. I have constantly endeavoured to spare the reader, in the text, any unnecessary accumulation of Mexican names, which, as he is aware by this time, have not even brevity to recommend them.

During the nights, the troops bivouacked in the open fields, maintain-ing the strictest watch, for the country was all in arms, and beacons were flaming on every hill-top, while dark masses of the enemy were occasion-ally descried in the distance. The Spaniards were now traversing the most opulent region of Anahuac. Cities and villages were scattered over hill and valley, with cultivated environs blooming around them, all giving token of a dense and industrious population. In the centre of this bril-liant circumference stood the Indian metropolis, with its gorgeous tiara of pyramids and temples, attracting the eye of the soldier from every other object, as he wound round the borders of the lake. Every inch of ground, which the army trod, was familiar to them,—familiar as the scenes of childhood, though with very different associations, for it had been written on their memories in characters of blood. On the right rose the Hill of Montezuma, crowned by the *teocalli,* under the roof of which the shattered relics of the army had been gathered, on the day following the flight from the capital. In front lay the city of Tacuba, through whose inhospitable streets they had hurried in fear and consternation, and away to the east of it, stretched the melancholy causeway.

It was the general's purpose to march at once on Tacuba, and estab-lish his quarters in that ancient capital for the present. He found a strong force encamped under its walls, prepared to dispute his entrance. With-out waiting for their advance, he rode at full gallop against them with his little body of horse. The arquebuses and crossbows opened a lively volley on their extended wings, and the infantry, armed with their swords and copper-headed lances, and supported by the Indian battalions, followed up the attack of the horse with an alacrity which soon put the enemy to flight. The Spaniards usually opened the combat with a charge of cav-alry. But, had the science of the Aztecs been equal to their courage, they might with their long spears have turned the scale of battle, sometimes at least, in their own favor; for it was with the same formidable weapon, that the Swiss mountaineers, but a few years before this period of our history, broke and completely foiled the famous *ordonnance* of Charles the Bold, the best appointed cavalry of their day. But the barbarians were ignorant of the value of this weapon when opposed to cavalry. And, indeed, the appalling apparition of the war-horse and his rider still held a mysterious power over their imaginations, which contributed, perhaps, quite as much as the effective force of the cavalry itself, to their discom-fiture.—Cortés led his troops without further opposition into the suburbs of Tacuba, the ancient Tlacopan, where he established himself for the night.

On the following morning, he found the indefatigable Aztecs again under arms, and, on the open ground before the city, prepared to give him battle. He marched out against them, and, after an action, hotly contested, though of no long duration, again routed them. They fled to-wards the town, but were driven through the streets at the point of the lance, and were compelled, together with the inhabitants, to evacuate the place. The city was then delivered over to pillage; and the Indian allies, not content with plundering the houses of every thing portable within them, set them on fire, and in a short time a quarter of the town—the poorer dwellings, probably, built of light, combustible materials—was in flames. Cortés and his troops did all in their power to stop the conflagration, but the Tlascalans were a fierce race, not easily guided at any time, and, when their passions were once kindled, it was impossible, even for the general himself, to control them. They were a terrible auxiliary, and, from their insubordination, as terrible sometimes to friend as to foe.[4]

Cortés proposed to remain in his present quarters for some days, during which time he established his own residence in the ancient palace of the lords of Tlacopan. It was a long range of low buildings, like most of the royal residences in the country, and offered good accommodations for the Spanish forces. During his halt here, there was not a day on which the army was not engaged in one or more rencontres with the enemy. They terminated almost uniformly in favor of the Spaniards, though with more or less injury to them and to their allies. One encounter, indeed, had nearly been attended with more fatal consequences.

The Spanish general, in the heat of pursuit, had allowed himself to be decoyed upon the great causeway,—the same which had once been so fatal to his army. He followed the flying foe, until he had gained the further side of the nearest bridge, which had been repaired since the disastrous action of the *noche triste*. When thus far advanced, the Aztecs, with the rapidity of lightning, turned on him, and he beheld a large reinforcement in their rear, all fresh on the field, prepared to support their countrymen. At the same time, swarms of boats, unobserved in the eagerness of the chase, seemed to start up as if by magic, covering the waters around. The Spaniards were now exposed to a perfect hail-storm of missiles, both from the causeway and the lake; but they stood unmoved amidst the tempest, when Cortés, too late perceiving his error, gave orders for the retreat. Slowly, and with admirable coolness, his men receded, step by step, offering a resolute front to the enemy.[5] The Mexicans came on with their usual vociferation, making the shores echo to their war-cries, and striking at the Spaniards with their long pikes, and with poles, to which the swords taken from the Christians had been fastened. A cavalier, named Volante, bearing the standard of Cortés, was felled by one of their weapons, and, tumbling into the lake, was picked up by the Mexican boats. He was a man of a muscular frame, and, as the enemy

---

[4] They burned this place, according to Cortés, in retaliation of the injuries inflicted by the inhabitants on their countrymen in the retreat. "Y en amaneciendo los Indios nuestros Amigos comenzáron á saquear, y quemar toda la Ciudad, salvo el Aposento donde estabamos, y pusiéron tanta diligencia, que aun de él se quemó un Quarto; y esto se hizo, porque quando salímos la otra vez desbaratados de Temixtitan, pasando por esta Ciudad, los Naturales de ella juntamente con los de Temixtitan nos hiciéron muy cruel Guerra, y nos matáron muchos Españoles." Rel. Terc., ap. Lorenzana, p. 210.

[5] "Luego mandó, que todos se retraxessen; y con el mejor concierto que pudo, y no bueltas las espaldas, sino los rostros á los contrarios, pie contra pie, como quien haze represas." Bernal Diaz. Hist. de la Conquista, cap. 141.

were dragging him off, he succeeded in extricating himself from their grasp, and, clenching his colors in his hand, with a desperate effort sprang back upon the causeway. At length, after some hard fighting, in which many of the Spaniards were wounded, and many of their allies slain, the troops regained the land, where Cortés, with a full heart, returned thanks to Heaven for what he might well regard as a providential deliverance.[6] It was a salutary lesson; though he should scarcely have needed one, so soon after the affair with Iztapalapan, to warn him of the wily tactics of his enemy.

It had been one of Cortés' principal objects in this expedition to obtain an interview, if possible, with the Aztec emperor, or with some of the great lords at his court, and to try if some means for an accommodation could not be found, by which he might avoid the appeal to arms. An occasion for such a parley presented itself, when his forces were one day confronted with those of the enemy, with a broken bridge interposed between them. Cortés, riding in advance of his people, intimated by signs his peaceful intent, and that he wished to confer with the Aztecs. They respected the signal, and, with the aid of his interpreter, he requested, that, if there were any great chief among them, he would come forward and hold a parley with him. The Mexicans replied, in derision, they were all chiefs, and bade him speak openly whatever he had to tell them. As the general returned no answer, they asked, why he did not make another visit to the capital, and, tauntingly, added, "Perhaps Malinche does not expect to find there another Montezuma, as obedient to his commands as the former." [7] Some of them complimented the Tlascalans with the epithet of *women*, who, they said, would never have ventured so near the capital, but for the protection of the white men.

The animosity of the two nations was not confined to these harmless, though bitter, jests, but showed itself in regular cartels of defiance, which daily passed between the principal chieftains. These were followed by combats, in which one or more champions fought on a side, to vindicate the honor of their respective countries. A fair field of fight was given to the warriors, who conducted those combats, *à l'outrance*, with the punctilio of a European tourney; displaying a valor worthy of the two boldest of the races of Anahuac, and a skill in the management of their weapons, which drew forth the admiration of the Spaniards.[8]

Cortés had now been six days in Tacuba. There was nothing further to detain him, as he had accomplished the chief objects of his expedition. He had humbled several of the places which had been most active in their hostility; and he had revived the credit of the Castilian arms, which

---

[6] "Desta manera se escapó Cortés aquella vez del poder de México, y quando se vió en tierra firme, dió muchas gracias á Dios.' Ibid., ubi supra.

[7] "Pensais, que hay agora otro Muteczuma, para que haga todo, lo que quisieredes?" Rel. Terc. de Cortés, ap. Lorenzana, p. 211.

[8] "Y peleaban los unos con los otros muy hermosamente." Ibid., ubi supra.— Oviedo, Hist. de las Ind., MS., lib. 33, cap. 20.

had been much tarnished by their former reverses in this quarter of the Valley. He had also made himself acquainted with the condition of the capital, which he found in a better posture of defence than he had imagined. All the ravages of the preceding year seemed to be repaired, and there was no evidence, even to his experienced eye, that the wasting hand of war had so lately swept over the land. The Aztec troops, which swarmed through the Valley, seemed to be well appointed, and showed an invincible spirit, as if prepared to resist to the last. It is true, they had been beaten in every encounter. In the open field they were no match for the Spaniards, whose cavalry they could never comprehend, and whose firearms easily penetrated the cotton mail, which formed the stoutest defence of the Indian warrior. But, entangled in the long streets and narrow lanes of the metropolis, where every house was a citadel, the Spaniards, as experience had shown, would lose much of their superiority. With the Mexican emperor, confident in the strength of his preparations, the general saw there was no probability of effecting an accommodation. He saw, too, the necessity of the most careful preparations on his own part, indeed, that he must strain his resources to the utmost, before he could safely venture to rouse the lion in his lair.

The Spaniards returned by the same route by which they had come. Their retreat was interpreted into a flight by the natives, who hung on the rear of the army, uttering vainglorious vaunts, and saluting the troops with showers of arrows, which did some mischief. Cortés resorted to one of their own stratagems to rid himself of this annoyance. He divided his cavalry into two or three small parties, and concealed them among some thick shrubbery, which fringed both sides of the road. The rest of the army continued its march. The Mexicans followed, unsuspicious of the ambuscade, when the horse, suddenly darting from their place of concealment, threw the enemy's flanks into confusion, and the retreating columns of infantry, facing about suddenly, commenced a brisk attack, which completed their consternation. It was a broad and level plain, over which the panic-struck Mexicans made the best of their way, without attempting resistance; while the cavalry, riding them down and piercing the fugitives with their lances, followed up the chase for several miles, in what Cortés calls a truly beautiful style.[9] The army experienced no further annoyance from the enemy.

On their arrival at Tezcuco, they were greeted with joy by their comrades, who had received no tidings of them during the fortnight which had elapsed since their departure. The Tlascalans, immediately on their return, requested the general's permission to carry back to their own country the valuable booty which they had gathered in their foray,—a request, which, however unpalatable, he could not refuse.[10]

[9] "Y comenzámos á lanzear en ellos, y duró el alcanze cerca de dos leguas todas llanas, como la palma, que fué muy hermosa cosa." Rel. Terc., ap. Lorenzana, p. 212.
[10] For the particulars of this expedition of Cortés, see, besides his own Commentaries so often quoted, Oviedo, Hist. de las Ind., MS., lib. 33, cap. 20,—Torque-

The troops had not been in quarters more than two or three days, when an embassy arrived from Chalco, again soliciting the protection of the Spaniards against the Mexicans, who menaced them from several points in their neighborhood. But the soldiers were so much exhausted by unintermitted vigils, forced marches, battles, and wounds, that Cortés wished to give them a breathing-time to recruit, before engaging in a new expedition. He answered the application of the Chalcans, by sending his missives to the allied cities, calling on them to march to the assistance of their confederate. It is not to be supposed, that they could comprehend the import of his despatches. But the paper, with its mysterious characters, served for a warrant to the officer who bore it, as the interpreter of the general's commands.

But, although these were implicitly obeyed, the Chalcans felt the danger so pressing, that they soon repeated their petition for the Spaniards to come in person to their relief. Cortés no longer hesitated; for he was well aware of the importance of Chalco, not merely on its own account, but from its position, which commanded one of the great avenues to Tlascala, and to Vera Cruz, the intercourse with which should run no risk of interruption. Without further loss of time, therefore, he detached a body of three hundred Spanish foot and twenty horse, under the command of Sandoval, for the protection of the city.

That active officer soon presented himself before Chalco, and, strengthened by the reinforcement of its own troops and those of the confederate towns, directed his first operations against Huaxtepec, a place of some importance, lying five leagues or more to the south among the mountains. It was held by a strong Mexican force, watching their opportunity to make a descent upon Chalco. The Spaniards found the enemy drawn up at a distance from the town, prepared to receive them. The ground was broken and tangled with bushes, unfavorable to the cavalry, which, in consequence, soon fell into disorder; and Sandoval, finding himself embarrassed by their movements, ordered them, after sustaining some loss, from the field. In their place he brought up his musketeers and crossbow-men, who poured a rapid fire into the thick columns of the Indians. The rest of the infantry, with sword and pike, charged the flanks of the enemy, who, bewildered by the shock, after sustaining considerable slaughter, fell back in an irregular manner, leaving the field of battle to the Spaniards.

The victors proposed to bivouac there, for the night. But, while engaged in preparations for their evening meal, they were aroused by the cry of "To arms, to arms! the enemy is upon us!" In an instant, the trooper was in his saddle, the soldier grasped his musket or his good Toledo, and the action was renewed with greater fury than before. The Mexicans had received a reinforcement from the city. But their second attempt was not more fortunate than their first; and the victorious Spaniards, driving their antagonists before them, entered and took possession

mada, Monarch. Ind., lib. 4, cap. 85,—Gomara, Crónica, cap. 125,—Ixtlilxochitl, Venida de los Esp., pp. 13, 14,—Bernal Diaz, Hist. de la Conquista, cap. 141.

of the town itself, which had already been evacuated by the inhabitants.[11]

Sandoval took up his quarters in the dwelling of the lord of the place, surrounded by gardens, which rivalled those of Iztapalapan in magnificence, and surpassed them in extent. They are said to have been two leagues in circumference, having pleasure houses, and numerous tanks stocked with various kinds of fish; and they were embellished with trees, shrubs, and plants, native and exotic, some selected for their beauty and fragrance, others for their medicinal properties. They were scientifically arranged; and the whole establishment displayed a degree of horticultural taste and knowledge, of which it would not have been easy to find a counterpart, at that day, in the more civilized communities of Europe.[12] Such is the testimony not only of the rude Conquerors, but of men of science, who visited these beautiful repositories in the day of their glory.[13]

After halting two days to refresh his forces in this agreeable spot, Sandoval marched on Jacapichtla, about twelve miles to the eastward. It was a town, or rather fortress, perched on a rocky eminence, almost inaccessible from its steepness. It was garrisoned by a Mexican force, who rolled down on the assailants, as they attempted to scale the heights, huge fragments of rock, which, thundering over the sides of the precipice, carried ruin and desolation in their path. The Indian confederates fell back in dismay from the attempt. But Sandoval, indignant that any achievement should be too difficult for a Spaniard, commanded his cavaliers to dismount, and, declaring that he "would carry the place or die in the attempt," led on his men with the cheering cry of "St. Iago." [14] With renewed courage, they now followed their gallant leader up the ascent, under a storm of lighter missiles, mingled with huge masses of stone, which, breaking into splinters, overturned the assailants, and made fearful havoc in their ranks. Sandoval, who had been wounded on

[11] Rel. Terc. de Cortés, ap. Lorenzana, pp. 214, 215.—Gomara, Crónica, cap. 146. —Bernal Diaz, Hist. de la Conquista, cap. 142.—Oviedo, Hist. de las Ind., MS., lib. 33, cap. 21.

[12] "La qual Huerta," says Cortés, who afterwards passed a day there, "es la mayor, y mas hermosa, y fresca, que nunca se vió, porque tiene dos leguas de circuito, y por medio de ella va una muy gentil Ribera de Agua, y de trecho á trecho, cantidad de dos tiros de Ballesta, hay Aposentamientos, y Jardines muy frescos, y infinitos Árboles de diversas Frutas, y muchas Yervas, y Flores olorosas, que cierto es cosa de admiracion ver la gentileza, y grandeza de toda esta Huerta." (Rel. Terc., ap. Lorenzana, pp. 221, 222.) Bernal Diaz is not less emphatic in his admiration. Hist. de la Conquista, cap. 142.

[13] The distinguished naturalist, Hernandez, has frequent occasion to notice this garden, which furnished him with many specimens for his great work. It had the good fortune to be preserved after the Conquest, when particular attention was given to its medicinal plants, for the use of a great hospital established in the neighborhood. See Clavigero, Stor. del Messico, tom. II. p. 153.

[14] "É como esto vió el dicho Alguacil Mayor, y los Españoles, determináron de morir, ó subilles por fuerza á lo alto del Pueblo, y con el apellido de Señor Santiago comenzáron á subir." Rel. Terc. de Cortés, ap. Lorenzana, p. 214,—Oviedo, Hist. de las Ind., MS., lib. 33, cap. 21.

the preceding day, received a severe contusion on the head, while more
than one of his brave comrades were struck down by his side. Still they
clambered up, sustaining themselves by the bushes or projecting pieces
of rock, and seemed to force themselves onward as much by the energy
of their wills, as by the strength of their bodies.

After incredible toil, they stood on the summit, face to face with the
astonished garrison. For a moment they paused to recover breath, then
sprang furiously on their foes. The struggle was short, but desperate.
Most of the Aztecs were put to the sword. Some were thrown headlong
over the battlements, and others, letting themselves down the precipice,
were killed on the borders of a little stream that wound round its base,
the waters of which were so polluted with blood, that the victors were
unable to slake their thirst with them for a full hour! [15]

Sandoval, having now accomplished the object of his expedition, by
reducing the strong-holds which had so long held the Chalcans in awe,
returned in triumph to Tezcuco. Meanwhile, the Aztec emperor, whose
vigilant eye had been attentive to all that had passed, thought that the
absence of so many of its warriors afforded a favorable opportunity for
recovering Chalco. He sent a fleet of boats, for this purpose, across the
lake, with a numerous force under the command of some of his most
valiant chiefs.[16] Fortunately the absent Chalcans reached their city before the arrival of the enemy; but, though supported by their Indian
allies, they were so much alarmed by the magnitude of the hostile array,
that they sent again to the Spaniards, invoking their aid.

The messengers arrived at the same time with Sandoval and his
army. Cortés was much puzzled by the contradictory accounts. He suspected some negligence in his lieutenant, and, displeased with his precipitate return in this unsettled state of the affair, ordered him back at once,
with such of his forces as were in fighting condition. Sandoval felt deeply
injured by this proceeding, but he made no attempt at exculpation, and,
obeying his commander in silence, put himself at the head of his troops,
and made a rapid countermarch on the Indian city.[17]

Before he reached it, a battle had been fought between the Mexicans
and the confederates, in which the latter, who had acquired unwonted
confidence from their recent successes, were victorious. A number of
Aztec nobles fell into their hands in the engagement, whom they delivered to Sandoval to be carried off as prisoners to Tezcuco. On his
arrival there, the cavalier, wounded by the unworthy treatment he had

[15] So says the *Conquistador*. (Rel. Terc., ap. Lorenzana, p. 215.) Diaz, who will
allow no one to hyperbolize but himself, says, "For as long as one might take to
say an Ave Maria!" (Hist. de la Conquista, cap. 142.) Neither was present.

[16] The gallant Captain Diaz, who affects a sobriety in his own estimates, which
often leads him to disparage those of the chaplain, Gomara, says, that the force
consisted of 20,000 warriors in 2000 canoes. Ibid., loc. cit.

[17] "El Cortés no le quiso escuchar á Sandoual de enojo, creyendo que por su
culpa, ó descuido, recibiā mala obra nuestros amigos los de Chalco; y luego sin
mas dilacion, ni le oyr, le mandó bolver." Ibid., ubi supra.

received, retired to his own quarters without presenting himself before his chief.

During his absence, the inquiries of Cortés had satisfied him of his own precipitate conduct, and of the great injustice he had done his lieutenant. There was no man in the army, on whose services he set so high a value, as the responsible situations in which he had placed him plainly showed; and there was none, for whom he seemed to have enter‹ tained a greater personal regard. On Sandoval's return, therefore, Cor‧ tés instantly sent to request his attendance; when, with a soldier's frank‧ ness, he made such an explanation, as soothed the irritated spirit of the cavalier,—a matter of no great difficulty, as the latter had too generous a nature, and too earnest a devotion to his commander and the cause in which they were embarked, to harbor a petty feeling of resentment in his bosom.[18]

During the occurrence of these events, the work was going forward actively on the canal, and the brigantines were within a fortnight of their completion. The greatest vigilance was required, in the mean time, to prevent their destruction by the enemy, who had already made three ineffectual attempts to burn them on the stocks. The precautions, which Cortés thought it necessary to take against the Tezcucans themselves, added not a little to his embarrassment.

At this time he received embassies from different Indian states, some of them on the remote shores of the Mexican Gulf, tendering their allegiance and soliciting his protection. For this he was partly indebted to the good offices of Ixtlilxochitl, who, in consequence of his brother's death, was now advanced to the sovereignty of Tezcuco. This important position greatly increased his consideration and authority through the country, of which he freely availed himself to bring the natives under the dominion of the Spaniards.[19]

The general received also at this time the welcome intelligence of the arrival of three vessels at Villa Rica, with two hundred men on board, well provided with arms and ammunition, and with seventy or eighty horses. It was a most seasonable reinforcement. From what quarter it came is uncertain; most probably, from Hispaniola. Cortés, it may be remembered, had sent for supplies to that place; and the authorities of the island, who had general jurisdiction over the affairs of the colonies, had shown themselves, on more than one occasion, well inclined towards him, probably considering him, under all circumstances, as better fitted

[18] Besides the authorities already quoted for Sandoval's expedition, see Gomara, Crónica, cap. 126,—Ixtlilxochitl, Hist. Chich., MS., cap. 92,—Torquemada, Monarch. Ind., lib. 4, cap. 86.

[19] "Ixtlilxochitl procuraba siempre traer á la devocion y amistad de los Cristianos no tan solamente á los de el Reyno de Tezcuco sino aun los de las Provincias remotas, rogándoles que todos se procurasen dar de paz al Capitan Cortés, y que aunque de las guerras pasadas algunos tuviesen culpa, era tan afable y deseaba tanto la paz que luego al punto los reciviria en su amistad." Ixtlilxochitl, Hist. Chich., MS., cap. 92.

than any other man to achieve the conquest of the country.[20]

The new recruits soon found their way to Tezcuco; as the communications with the port were now open and unobstructed. Among them were several cavaliers of consideration, one of whom, Julian de Alderete, the royal treasurer, came over to superintend the interests of the Crown.

There was also in the number a Dominican friar, who brought a quantity of pontifical bulls, offering indulgences to those engaged in war against the infidel. The soldiers were not slow to fortify themselves with the good graces of the Church; and the worthy father, after driving a prosperous traffic with his spiritual wares, had the satisfaction to return home, at the end of a few months, well freighted, in exchange, with the more substantial treasures of the Indies.[21]

---

[20] Cortés speaks of these vessels, as coming at the same time, but does not intimate from what quarter. (Rel. Terc., ap. Lorenzana, p. 216.) Bernal Diaz, who notices only one, says it came from Castile. (Hist. de la Conquista, cap. 143.) But the old soldier wrote long after the events he commemorates, and may have confused the true order of things. It seems hardly probable that so important a reinforcement should have arrived from Castile, considering that Cortés had yet received none of the royal patronage, or even sanction, which would stimulate adventurers in the mother country to enlist under his standard.

[21] Bernal Diaz, Hist. de la Conquista, cap. 143.—Oviedo, Hist. de las Ind., MS., lib. 33, cap. 21.—Herrera, Hist. General, dec. 3, lib. 1, cap. 6.

CHAPTER III

SECOND RECONNOITRING EXPEDITION—ENGAGEMENTS ON THE SIERRA—
CAPTURE OF CUERNAVACA—BATTLES AT XOCHIMILCO—NARROW
ESCAPE OF CORTÉS—HE ENTERS TACUBA

1521

NOTWITHSTANDING the relief which had been afforded to the people of
Chalco, it was so ineffectual, that envoys from that city again arrived at
Tezcuco, bearing a hieroglyphical chart, on which were depicted several
strong places in their neighborhood, garrisoned by the Aztecs, from
which they expected annoyance. Cortés determined, this time, to take
the affair into his own hands, and to scour the country so effectually, as
to place Chalco, if possible, in a state of security. He did not confine
himself to this object, but proposed, before his return, to pass quite
round the great lakes, and reconnoitre the country to the south of them,
in the same manner as he had before done to the west. In the course of
his march, he would direct his arms against some of the strong places
from which the Mexicans might expect support in the siege. Two or
three weeks must elapse before the completion of the brigantines; and,
if no other good resulted from the expedition, it would give active occupation to his troops, whose turbulent spirits might fester into discontent in the monotonous existence of a camp.

He selected for the expedition thirty horse and three hundred Spanish infantry, with a considerable body of Tlascalan and Tezcucan warriors. The remaining garrison he left in charge of the trusty Sandoval,
who, with the friendly lord of the capital, would watch over the construction of the brigantines, and protect them from the assaults of the
Aztecs.

On the fifth of April he began his march, and on the following day
arrived at Chalco, where he was met by a number of the confederate
chiefs. With the aid of his faithful interpreters, Doña Marina and Aguilar, he explained to them the objects of his present expedition; stated
his purpose soon to enforce the blockade of Mexico, and required their
coöperation with the whole strength of their levies. To this they readily
assented; and he soon received a sufficient proof of their friendly disposition in the forces which joined him on the march, amounting, according to one of the army, to more than had ever before followed his banner.[1]

---

[1] "Viniéron tantos, que en todas las entradas que yo auia ido, despues que en la
Nueua España entré, nunca ví tanta gente de guerra de nuestros amigos, como aora
fuéron en nuestra compañía." Bernal Diaz, Hist. de la Conquista, cap. 144.

Taking a southerly direction, the troops, after leaving Chalco, struck into the recesses of the wild sierra, which, with its bristling peaks, serves as a formidable palisade to fence round the beautiful Valley; while, within its rugged arms, it shuts up many a green and fruitful pasture of its own. As the Spaniards passed through its deep gorges, they occasionally wound round the base of some huge cliff or rocky eminence, on which the inhabitants had built their towns, in the same manner as was done by the people of Europe in the feudal ages; a position, which, however favorable to the picturesque, intimates a sense of insecurity as the cause of it, which may reconcile us to the absence of this striking appendage of the landscape in our own more fortunate country.

The occupants of these airy pinnacles took advantage of their situation, to shower down stones and arrows on the troops, as they defiled through the narrow passes of the sierra. Though greatly annoyed by their incessant hostilities, Cortés held on his way, till, winding round the base of a castellated cliff, occupied by a strong garrison of Indians, he was so severely pressed, that he felt, to pass on without chastising the aggressors would imply a want of strength, which must disparage him in the eyes of his allies. Halting in the valley, therefore, he detached a small body of light troops to scale the heights, while he remained with the main body of the army below, to guard against surprise from the enemy.

The lower region of the rocky eminence was so steep, that the soldiers found it no easy matter to ascend, scrambling, as well as they could, with hand and knee. But, as they came into the more exposed view of the garrison, the latter rolled down huge masses of rock, which, bounding along the declivity, and breaking into fragments, crushed the foremost assailants, and mangled their limbs in a frightful manner. Still they strove to work their way upward, now taking advantage of some gulley, worn by the winter torrent, now sheltering themselves behind a projecting cliff, or some straggling tree, anchored among the crevices of the mountain. It was all in vain. For no sooner did they emerge again into open view, than the rocky avalanche thundered on their heads with a fury, against which steel helm and cuirass were as little defence as gossamer. All the party were more or less wounded. Eight of the number were killed on the spot,—a loss the little band could ill afford,—and the gallant ensign, Corral, who led the advance, saw the banner in his hand torn into shreds.[2] Cortés, at length, convinced of the impracticability of the attempt, at least without a more severe loss than he was disposed to incur, commanded a retreat. It was high time; for a large body of the enemy were on full march across the valley to attack him.

He did not wait for their approach, but, gathering his broken files together, headed his cavalry, and spurred boldly against them. On the level plain, the Spaniards were on their own ground. The Indians, unable to sustain the furious onset, broke, and fell back before it. The

---

[2] "Todos descalabrados, y corriendo sangre. y las vanderas rotas, y ocho, muertos." Ibid., ubi supra.

the present day of sober, practical reality. The Spaniard, with his nice point of honor, high romance, and proud, vainglorious vaunt, was the true representative of that age. The Europeans, generally, had not yet learned to accommodate themselves to a life of literary toil, or to the drudgery of trade, or the patient tillage of the soil. They left these to the hooded inmate of the cloister, the humble burgher, and the miserable serf. Arms was the only profession worthy of gentle blood,—the only career which the high-mettled cavalier could tread with honor. The New World, with its strange and mysterious perils, afforded a noble theatre for the exercise of his calling; and the Spaniard entered on it with all the enthusiasm of a paladin of romance.

Other nations entered on it also, but with different motives. The French sent forth their missionaries to take up their dwelling among the heathen, who, in the good work of winning souls to Paradise, were content to wear—nay, sometimes seemed to court—the crown of martyr· dom. The Dutch, too, had their mission, but it was one of worldly lucre, and they found a recompense for toil and suffering in their gainful traffic with the natives. While our own Puritan fathers, with the true Anglo Saxon spirit, left their pleasant homes across the waters, and pitched their tents in the howling wilderness, that they might enjoy the sweets of civil and religious freedom. But the Spaniard came over to the New World in the true spirit of a knight-errant, courting adventure however perilous, wooing danger, as it would seem, for its own sake. With sword and lance, he was ever ready to do battle for the Faith; and, as he raised his old war-cry of "St. Jago," he fancied himself fighting under the banner of the military apostle, and felt his single arm a match for more than a hundred infidels!—It was the expiring age of chivalry; and Spain, romantic Spain, was the land where its light lingered longest above the horizon.

It was not yet dusk when Cortés and his followers reëntered the city; and the general's first act was to ascend a neighboring *teocalli* and reconnoitre the surrounding country. He there beheld a sight which might have troubled a bolder spirit than his. The surface of the salt lake was darkened with canoes, and the causeway, for many a mile, with Indian squadrons, apparently on their march towards the Christian camp. In fact, no sooner had Guatemozin been apprised of the arrival of the white men at Xochimilco, than he mustered his levies in great force to relieve the city. They were now on their march, and, as the capital was but four leagues distant, would arrive soon after nightfall.[14]

Cortés made active preparations for the defence of his quarters. He stationed a corps of pikemen along the landing where the Aztecs would be likely to disembark. He doubled the sentinels, and, with his principal officers, made the rounds repeatedly in the course of the night. In addi-

---

[14] "Por el Agua á una muy grande flota de Canoas, que creo, que pasaban de dos mil; y en ellas venian mas de doce mil Hombres de Guerra; é por la Tierra llegó tanta multitud de Gente, que todos los Campos cubrian." Rel. Terc. de Cortés, ap Lorenzana, p. 227.

made so stout a resistance on the morning of the preceding day, to tender their submission.[4]

After a halt of two days in this sequestered region, the army resumed
its march in a south-westerly direction on Huaxtepec, the same city which
had surrendered to Sandoval. Here they were kindly received by the
cacique, and entertained in his magnificent gardens, which Cortés and
his officers, who had not before seen them, compared with the best in
Castile.[5] Still threading the wild mountain mazes, the army passed
through Jauhtepec and several other places, which were abandoned at
their approach. As the inhabitants, however, hung in armed bodies on
their flanks and rear, doing them occasionally some mischief, the Spaniards took their revenge by burning the deserted towns.

Thus holding on their fiery track, they descended the bold slope of
the Cordilleras, which, on the south, are far more precipitous than on the
Atlantic side. Indeed, a single day's journey is sufficient to place the
traveller on a level several thousand feet lower than that occupied by
him in the morning; thus conveying him, in a few hours, through the
climates of many degrees of latitude. The route of the army led them
across many an acre, covered with lava and blackened scoriæ, attesting
the volcanic character of the region; though this was frequently relieved by patches of verdure, and even tracts of prodigal fertility, as if
Nature were desirous to compensate by these extraordinary efforts for
the curse of barrenness, which elsewhere had fallen on the land. On the
ninth day of their march, the troops arrived before the strong city of
Quauhnahuac, or Cuernavaca, as since called by the Spaniards.[6] It was
the ancient capital of the Tlahuicas, and the most considerable place
for wealth and population in this part of the country. It was tributary to
the Aztecs, and a garrison of this nation was quartered within its walls.
The town was singularly situated, on a projecting piece of land, encompassed by *barrancas*, or formidable ravines, except on one side, which
opened on a rich and well cultivated country. For, though the place
stood at an elevation of between five and six thousand feet above the
level of the sea, it had a southern exposure so sheltered by the mountain

---

[4] Cortés, according to Bernal Diaz, ordered the troops, who took possession of
the second fortress, "not to meddle with a grain of maize belonging to the besieged." Diaz, giving this a very liberal interpretation, proceeded forthwith to load
his Indian *tamanes* with everything but maize, as fair booty. He was interrupted
in his labors, however, by the captain of the detachment, who gave a more narrow
construction to his general's orders, much to the dissatisfaction of the latter, if we
may trust the doughty chronicler. Ibid., ubi supra.

[5] "Adonde estaua la huerta que he dicho, que es la mejor que auia visto en toda
mi vida, y ansí lo torno á dezir, que Cortés, y el Tesorero Alderete, desque entonces
le viéron, y passeáron algo de ella, se admiráron, y dixéron, que mejor cosa de huerta
no auian visto en Castilla." Ibid., loc. cit.

[6] This barbarous Indian name is tortured into all possible variations by the old
chroniclers. The town soon received from the Spaniards the name which it now
bears, of Cuernavaca, and by which it is indicated on modern maps. "Prevalse
poi quello di *Cuernabaca,* col quale é presentemente conosciuta dagli Spagnuoli."
Clavigero, Stor. del Messico tom. III. p. 185, nota

barrier on the north, that its climate was as soft and genial as that of a much lower region.

The Spaniards, on arriving before this city, the limit of their southerly progress, found themselves separated from it by one of the vast barrancas before noticed, which resembled one of those frightful rents not unfrequent in the Mexican Andes, the result, no doubt, of some terrible convulsion in earlier ages. The rocky sides of the ravine sunk perpendicularly down, and so bare as scarcely to exhibit even a vestige of the cactus, or of the other hardy plants with which Nature in these fruitful regions so gracefully covers up her deformities. The bottom of the chasm, however, showed a striking contrast to this, being literally choked up with a rich and spontaneous vegetation; for the huge walls of rock, which shut in these barrancas, while they screen them from the cold winds of the Cordilleras, reflect the rays of a vertical sun, so as to produce an almost suffocating heat in the inclosure, stimulating the soil to the rank fertility of the *tierra caliente*. Under the action of this forcing apparatus,—so to speak,—the inhabitants of the towns on their margin above may with ease obtain the vegetable products which are to be found on the sultry level of the lowlands.

At the bottom of the ravine was seen a little stream, which, oozing from the stony bowels of the sierra, tumbled along its narrow channel, and contributed by its perpetual moisture to the exuberant fertility of the valley. This rivulet, which at certain seasons of the year was swollen to a torrent, was traversed, at some distance below the town, where the sloping sides of the barranca afforded a more practicable passage, by two rude bridges, both of which had been broken, in anticipation of the coming of the Spaniards. The latter had now arrived on the brink of the chasm, which intervened between them and the city. It was, as has been remarked, of no great width, and the army drawn up on its borders was directly exposed to the archery of the garrison, on whom its own fire made little impression, protected as they were by their defences.

The general, annoyed by his position, sent a detachment to seek a passage lower down, by which the troops might be landed on the other side. But, although the banks of the ravine became less formidable as they descended, they found no means of crossing the river, till a path unexpectedly presented itself, on which, probably, no one before had ever been daring enough to venture.

From the cliffs on the opposite sides of the barranca, two huge trees shot up to an enormous height, and, inclining towards each other, interlaced their boughs so as to form a sort of natural bridge. Across this avenue, in mid air, a Tlascalan conceived it would not be difficult to pass to the opposite bank. The bold mountaineer succeeded in the attempt, and was soon followed by several others of his countrymen, trained to feats of agility and strength among their native hills. The Spaniards imitated their example. It was a perilous effort for an armed man to make his way over this aërial causeway, swayed to and fro by the wind, where the brain might become giddy, and where a single false movement of hand or foot would plunge him in the abyss below. Three of the soldiers lost their hold and fell. The rest, consisting of some twenty or thirty Spaniards, and a considerable number of Tlascalans, alighted in safety on the other bank.[7] There hastily forming, they marched with all speed on the city. The enemy, engaged in their contest with the Castilians on the opposite brink of the ravine, were taken by surprise,—which, indeed, could scarcely have been exceeded, if they had seen their foe drop from the clouds on the field of battle.

They made a brave resistance, however, when fortunately the Spaniards succeeded in repairing one of the dilapidated bridges in such a manner as to enable both cavalry and foot to cross the river, though with much delay. The horse, under Olid and Andres de Tapia, instantly rode up to the succour of their countrymen. They were soon followed by Cortés at the head of the remaining battalions, and the enemy, driven from one point to another, were compelled to evacuate the city, and to take refuge among the mountains. The buildings in one quarter of the town were speedily wrapt in flames. The place was abandoned to pillage, and, as it was one of the most opulent marts in the country, it amply compensated the victors for the toil and danger they had encountered. The trembling caciques, returning, soon after, to the city, appeared before Cortés, and, deprecating his resentment, by charging the blame, as usual, on the Mexicans, threw themselves on his mercy. Satisfied with their submission, he allowed no further violence to the inhabitants.[8]

Having thus accomplished the great object of his expedition across the mountains, the Spanish commander turned his face northwards, to recross the formidable barrier which divided him from the Valley. The ascent, steep and laborious, was rendered still more difficult by fragments of rock and loose stones, which encumbered the passes. The mountain sides and summits were shaggy with thick forests of pine and stunted oak, which threw a melancholy gloom over the region, still further heightened at the present day by its being a favorite haunt of banditti.

The weather was sultry, and, as the stony soil was nearly destitute of water, the troops suffered severely from thirst. Several of them, indeed, fainted on the road, and a few of the Indian allies perished from exhaustion.[9] The line of march must have taken the army across the eastern shoulder of the mountain, called the *Cruz del Marques*, or Cross of the Marquess, from a huge stone cross, erected there to indicate the boundary

---

[7] The stout-hearted Diaz was one of those who performed this dangerous feat, though his head swam so, as he tells us, that he scarcely knew how he got on. "Porque de mí digo, que verdaderamēte quando passaua, q̃ lo ví mui peligroso, é malo de passar, y se me desvanecia la cabeça, y todavía passé yo, y otros veinte, ó treinta soldados, y muchos Tlascatecas." Ibid., ubi supra.

[8] For the preceding account of the capture of Cuernavaca, see Bernal Diaz, ubi supra,—Oviedo, Hist. de las Ind., MS., lib. 33, cap. 21,—Ixtlilxochitl, Hist. Chich., MS., cap. 93,—Herrera, Hist. General, dec. 3, lib. 1, cap. 8,—Torquemada, Monarch. Ind., lib. 4, cap. 87,—Rel. Terc. de Cortés, ap. Lorenzana, pp. 223, 224.

[9] "Una Tierra de Pinales, despoblada, y sin ninguna agua, la qual y un Puerto passámos con grandíssimo trabajo, y sin beber: tanto, que muchos de los Indios que iban con nosotros pereciéron de sed." Rel. Terc. de Cortés, ap. Lorenzana, p. 224

of the territories granted by the Crown to Cortés, as Marquess of the Valley. Much, indeed, of the route lately traversed by the troops lay across the princely domain subsequently assigned to the Conqueror.[10]

The Spaniards were greeted from these heights with a different view from any which they had before had of the Mexican Valley, made more attractive in their eyes, doubtless, by contrast with the savage scenery in which they had lately been involved. It was its most pleasant and populous quarter, for nowhere did its cities and villages cluster together in such numbers as round the lake of sweet water. From whatever quarter seen, however, the enchanting region presented the same aspect of natural beauty and cultivation, with its flourishing villas, and its fair lake in the centre, whose dark and polished surface glistened like a mirror, deep set in the huge frame-work of porphyry, in which nature had enclosed it.

The point of attack selected by the general was Xochimilco, or "the field of flowers," as its name implies, from the floating gardens which rode at anchor, as it were on the neighboring waters.[11] It was one of the most potent and wealthy cities in the Valley, and a stanch vassal of the Aztec crown. It stood, like the capital itself, partly in the water, and was approached in that quarter by causeways of no great length. The town was composed of houses like those of most other places of like magnitude in the country, mostly of cottages or huts made of clay and the light bamboo, mingled with aspiring *teocallis*, and edifices of stone, belonging to the more opulent classes.

As the Spaniards advanced, they were met by skirmishing parties of the enemy, who, after dismissing a light volley of arrows, rapidly retreated before them. As they took the direction of Xochimilco, Cortés inferred that they were prepared to resist him in considerable force. It exceeded his expectations.

On traversing the principal causeway, he found it occupied, at the further extremity, by a numerous body of warriors, who, stationed on the opposite side of a bridge, which had been broken, were prepared to dispute his passage. They had constructed a temporary barrier of palisades, which screened them from the fire of the musketry. But the water in its neighborhood was very shallow, and the cavaliers and infantry, plunging into it, soon made their way, swimming or wading, as they could, in face of a storm of missiles, to the landing near the town. Here they closed with the enemy, and, hand to hand, after a sharp struggle, drove them back on the city; a few, however, taking the direction of the open country, were followed up by the cavalry. The great mass, hotly pursued by the infantry, were driven through street and lane, without

[10] The city of Cuernavaca was comprehended in the patrimony of the dukes of Monteleone, descendants and heirs of the *Conquistador.*—The Spaniards, in their line of march towards the north, did not deviate far, probably, from the great road which now leads from Mexico to Acapulco, still exhibiting in this upper portion of it the same characteristic features as at the period of the Conquest.

[11] Clavigero, Stor. del Messico, tom. III. p. 187, nota.

much further resistance. Cortés, with a few followers, disengaging him-self from the tumult, remained near the entrance of the city. He had not been there long, when he was assailed by a fresh body of Indians, who suddenly poured into the place from a neighboring dike. The general, with his usual fearlessness, threw himself into the midst, in hopes to check their advance. But his own followers were too few to support him, and he was overwhelmed by the crowd of combatants. His horse lost his footing and fell; and Cortés, who received a severe blow on the head before he could rise, was seized and dragged off in triumph by the In-dians. At this critical moment, a Tlascalan, who perceived the general's extremity, sprang, like one of the wild ocelots of his own forests, into the midst of the assailants, and endeavored to tear him from their grasp. Two of the general's servants also speedily came to the rescue, and Cortés, with their aid and that of the brave Tlascalan, succeeded in regaining his feet and shaking off his enemies. To vault into the saddle and brandish his good lance was but the work of a moment. Others of his men quickly came up, and the clash of arms reaching the ears of the Spaniards, who had gone in pursuit, they returned, and, after a desperate conflict, forced the enemy from the city. Their retreat, however, was intercepted by the cavalry, returning from the country, and, thus hemmed in between the opposite columns, they were cut to pieces, or saved them-selves only by plunging into the lake.[12]

This was the greatest personal danger which Cortés had yet encoun-tered. His life was in the power of the barbarians, and had it not been for their eagerness to take him prisoner, he must undoubtedy have lost it. To the same cause may be frequently attributed the preservation of the Spaniards in these engagements. The next day, he sought, it is said, for the Tlascalan who came so boldly to his rescue, and, as he could learn nothing of him, he gave the credit of his preservation to his patron, St. Peter.[13] He may well be excused for presuming the interposition of his good Genius, to shield him from the awful doom of the captive,—a doom not likely to be mitigated in his case. That heart must have been a bold one, indeed, which, from any motive, could voluntarily encounter such a peril! Yet his followers did as much, and that, too, for a much inferior reward.

The period which we are reviewing was still the age of chivalry; that stirring and adventurous age, of which we can form little conception in

---

[12] Rel. Terc. de Cortés, ap. Lorenzana, p. 226.—Herrera, Hist. General, dec. 3, lib. 1, cap. 8.—Oviedo, Hist. de las Ind., MS., lib. 33, cap. 21.

This is the general's own account of the matter. Diaz, however, says, that he was indebted for his rescue to a Castilian, named Olea, supported by some Tlasca-lans, and that his preserver received three severe wounds himself, on the occasion. (Hist. de la Conquista, cap. 145.) This was an affair, however, in which Cortés ought to be better informed than any one else, and one, moreover, not likely to slip his memory. The old soldier has probably confounded it with another and similar adventure of his commander.

[13] "Otra Dia buscó Cortés al Indio, que le socorrió, i muerto, ni vivo no pareició; i Cortés, por la devocion de San Pedro, juzgó que él le avia aiudado." Terrera, Hist. General, dec. 3, lib. 1, cap. 8.

flight soon became a rout, and the fiery cavaliers, dashing over them at full gallop, or running them through with their lances, took some revenge for their late discomfiture. The pursuit continued for some miles, till the nimble foe made their escape into the rugged fastnesses of the sierra, where the Spaniards did not care to follow. The weather was sultry, and, as the country was nearly destitute of water, the men and horses suffered extremely. Before evening they reached a spot overshadowed by a grove of wild mulberry trees, in which some scanty springs afforded a miserable supply to the army.

Near the place rose another rocky summit of the sierra, garrisoned by a stronger force than the one which they had encountered in the former part of the day; and at no great distance stood a second fortress at a still greater height, though considerably smaller than its neighbor. This was also tenanted by a body of warriors, who, as well as those of the adjoining cliff, soon made active demonstration of their hostility by pouring down missiles on the troops below. Cortés, anxious to retrieve the disgrace of the morning, ordered an assault on the larger, and, as it seemed, more practicable eminence. But, though two attempts were made with great resolution, they were repulsed with loss to the assailants. The rocky sides of the hill had been artificially cut and smoothed, so as greatly to increase the natural difficulties of the ascent.—The shades of evening now closed around; and Cortés drew off his men to the mulberry grove, where he took up his bivouac for the night, deeply chagrined at having been twice foiled by the enemy on the same day.

During the night, the Indian force, which occupied the adjoining height, passed over to their brethren, to aid them in the encounter, which they foresaw would be renewed on the following morning. No sooner did the Spanish general, at the break of day, become aware of this manœuvre, than, with his usual quickness, he took advantage of it. He detached a body of musketeers and crossbow-men to occupy the deserted eminence, purposing, as soon as this was done, to lead the assault in person against the other. It was not long before the Castilian banner was seen streaming from the rocky pinnacle, when the general instantly led up his men to the attack. And, while the garrison were meeting them resolutely on that quarter, the detachment on the neighboring heights poured into the place a well-directed fire, which so much distressed the enemy, that, in a very short time, they signified their willingness to capitulate.[3]

On entering the place, the Spaniards found that a plain of some extent ran along the crest of the sierra, and that it was tenanted, not only by men, but by women and their families, with their effects. No violence was offered by the victors to the property or persons of the vanquished, and the knowledge of this lenity induced the Indian garrison, who had

---

[3] For the assault on the rocks,—the topography of which it is impossible to verify from the narratives of the Conquerors,—see Bernal Diaz, Hist. de la Conquista, cap. 144,—Rel. Terc. de Cortés, ap. Lorenzana, pp. 218-221,—Gomara, Crónica, cap. 127,—Ixtlilxochitl, Venida de los Esp., pp. 16, 17,—Oviedo, Hist. de las Ind., MS., lib. 33, cap. 21.

tion to other causes for watchfulness, the bolts of the crossbowmen were nearly exhausted, and the archers were busily employed in preparing and adjusting shafts to the copper heads, of which great store had been provided for the army. There was little sleep in the camp that night.[15]

It passed away, however, without molestation from the enemy. Though not stormy, it was exceedingly dark. But, although the Spaniards on duty could see nothing, they distinctly heard the sound of many oars in the water, at no great distance from the shore. Yet those on board the canoes made no attempt to land, distrusting, or advised, it may be, of the preparations made for their reception. With early dawn, they were under arms, and, without waiting for the movement of the Spaniards, poured into the city and attacked them in their own quarters.

The Spaniards, who were gathered in the area round one of the *teocallis*, were taken at disadvantage in the town, where the narrow lanes and streets, many of them covered with a smooth and slippery cement, offered obvious impediments to the manœuvres of cavalry. But Cortés hastily formed his musketeers and crossbow-men, and poured such a lively, well-directed fire into the enemy's ranks, as threw him into disorder, and compelled him to recoil. The infantry, with their long pikes, followed up the blow; and the horse, charging at full speed, as the retreating Aztecs emerged from the city, drove them several miles along the main land.

At some distance, however, they were met by a strong reinforcement of their countrymen, and, rallying, the tide of battle turned, and the cavaliers, swept along by it, gave the rein to their steeds, and rode back at full gallop towards the town. They had not proceeded very far, when they came upon the main body of the army, advancing rapidly to their support. Thus strengthened, they once more returned to the charge, and the rival hosts met together in full career, with the shock of an earthquake. For a time, victory seemed to hang in the balance, as the mighty press reeled to and fro under the opposite impulse, and a confused shout rose up towards heaven, in which the war-whoop of the savage was mingled with the battle-cry of the Christian,—a still stranger sound on these sequestered shores. But, in the end, Castilian valor, or rather Castilian arms and discipline, proved triumphant. The enemy faltered, gave way, and, recoiling step by step, the retreat soon terminated in a rout, and the Spaniards, following up the flying foe, drove them from the field, with such dreadful slaughter, that they made no further attempt to renew the battle.

The victors were now undisputed masters of the city. It was a wealthy place, well stored with Indian fabrics, cotton, gold, feather-work, and other articles of luxury and use, affording a rich booty to the soldiers.

<hr>

[15] "Y acordóse que huviesse mui buena vela en todo nuestro Real, repartida á los puertos, é azequias por donde auian de venir á desembarcar, y los de acauallo mui á punto toda la noche ensillados y enfrenados, aguardando en la calçada, y tierra firme, y todos los Capitanes, y Cortés con ellos, haziendo vela y ronda toda la noche." Bernal Diaz. Hist. de la Conquista, cap. 145.

While engaged in the work of plunder, a party of the enemy, landing from their canoes, fell on some of the stragglers, laden with merchandise, and made four of them prisoners. It created a greater sensation among the troops than if ten times that number had fallen on the field. Indeed, it was rare that a Spaniard allowed himself to be taken alive. In the present instance the unfortunate men were taken by surprise. They were hurried to the capital, and soon after sacrificed; when their arms and legs were cut off, by the command of the ferocious young chief of the Aztecs, and sent round to the different cities, with the assurance, that this should be the fate of the enemies of Mexico![16]

From the prisoners taken in the late engagement, Cortés learned, that the forces already sent by Guatemozin formed but a small part of his levies; that his policy was to send detachment after detachment, until the Spaniards, however victorious they might come off from the contest with each individually, would, in the end succumb from mere exhaustion, and thus be vanquished, as it were, by their own victories.

The soldiers having now sacked the city, Cortés did not care to await further assaults from the enemy in his present quarters. On the fourth morning after his arrival, he mustered his forces on a neighboring plain. They came, many of them reeling under the weight of their plunder. The general saw this with uneasiness. They were to march, he said, through a populous country, all in arms to dispute their passage. To secure their safety, they should move as light and unencumbered as possible. The sight of so much spoil would sharpen the appetite of their enemies, and draw them on, like a flock of famished eagles after their prey. But his eloquence was lost on his men; who plainly told him they had a right to the fruit of their victories, and that what they had won with their swords, they knew well enough how to defend with them.

Seeing them thus bent on their purpose, the general did not care to balk their inclinations. He ordered the baggage to the centre, and placed a few of the cavalry over it; dividing the remainder between the front and rear, in which latter post, as that most exposed to attack, he also stationed his arquebusiers and cross-bow men. Thus prepared, he resumed his march; but first set fire to the combustible buildings of Xochimilco, in retaliation for the resistance he had met there.[17] The light of the burning city streamed high into the air, sending its ominous glare far

---

[16] Diaz, who had an easy faith, states, as a fact, that the limbs of the unfortunate men were cut off *before* their sacrifice. "Manda cortar pies y braços á los tristes nuestros compañeros, y las embia por muchos pueblos nuestros amigos de los q̃ nes auian venido de paz, y les embia á dezir, que antes que bolvamos á Tezcuco, piensa no quedará ninguno de nosotros á vida, y con los coraçones y sangre hizo sacrificio á sus ídolos." (Hist. de la Conquista, cap. 145.)—This is not very probable. The Aztecs did not, like our North American Indians, torture their enemies from mere cruelty, but in conformity to the prescribed regulations of their ritual. The captive was a religious victim.

[17] "Y al cabo dejándola toda quemada y asolada nos partímos; y cierto era mucho par ver, porque tenia muchas Casas, y Torres de sus Idolos de cal y canto." Rel. Terc. de Cortés, ap. Lorenzana, p. 228

and wide across the waters, and telling the inhabitants on their margin
that the fatal strangers, so long predicted by their oracles, had descended like a consuming flame upon their borders.[18]

Small bodies of the enemy were seen occasionally at a distance, but
they did not venture to attack the army on its march, which, before noon,
brought them to Cojohuacan, a large town about two leagues distant
from Xochimilco. One could scarcely travel that distance in this populous quarter of the Valley without meeting with a place of considerable
size, oftentimes the capital of what had formerly been an independent
state. The inhabitants, members of different tribes, and speaking dialects somewhat different, belonged to the same great family of nations,
who had come from the real, or imaginary region of Aztlan, in the far
North-west. Gathered round the shores of their Alpine sea, these petty
communities continued, after their incorporation with the Aztec monarchy, to maintain a spirit of rivalry in their intercourse with one another, which—as with the cities on the Mediterranean, in the feudal
ages—quickened their mental energies, and raised the Mexican Valley
higher in the scale of civilization than most other quarters of Anahuac.

The town at which the army had now arrived was deserted by its inhabitants; and Cortés halted two days there to restore his troops, and
give the needful attention to the wounded.[19] He made use of the time
to reconnoitre the neighboring ground, and, taking with him a strong
detachment, descended on the causeway which led from Cojohuacan to
the great avenue of Iztapalapan.[20] At the point of intersection, called

---

[18] For other particulars of the actions at Xochimilco, see Oviedo, Hist. de las
Ind., MS., lib. 23, cap. 21,—Herrera, Hist. General, dec. 3, lib. 1, cap. 8, 11,—
Ixtlilxochitl, Venida de los Esp. p. 18,—Torquemada, Monarch. Ind., lib. 4, cap
87, 88,—Bernal Diaz, Hist. de la Conquista, cap. 145.
   The Conqueror's own account of these engagements has not his usual perspicuity,
perhaps from its brevity. A more than ordinary confusion, indeed, prevails in the
different reports of them, even those proceeding from contemporaries, making it
extremely difficult to collect a probable narrative from authorities, not only contradicting one another, but themselves. It is rare, at any time, that two accounts
of a battle coincide in all respects; the range of observation for each individual is
necessarily so limited and different, and it is so difficult to make a cool observation
at all, in the hurry and heat of conflict. Any one, who has conversed with the survivors, will readily comprehend this, and be apt to conclude, that, wherever he
may look for truth, it will hardly be on the battle-ground.
[19] This place, recommended by the exceeding beauty of its situation, became, after
the Conquest, a favorite residence of Cortés, who founded a nunnery in it, and
commanded in his will, that his bones should be removed thither, from any part of
the world in which he might die. "Que mis huesos—los lleven á la mi Villa de
Coyoacan, y allí les den tierra en el Monesterio de Monjas, que mando hacer y
edificar en la dicha mi Villa." Testamento de Hernan Cortés, MS.
[20] This, says archbishop Lorenzana, was the modern *calzada de la Piedad*. (Rel.
Terc. de Cortés, p. 229, nota.) But it is not easy to reconcile this with the elaborate
chart which M. de Humboldt has given of the Valley. A short arm, which reached
from this city in the days of the Aztecs, touched obliquely the great southern avenue, by which the Spaniards first entered the capital. As the waters, which once
entirely surrounded Mexico, have shrunk into their narrow basin, the face of the
country has undergone a great change, and, though the foundations of the principal
causeways are still maintained, it is not always easy to discern vestiges of the
ancient avenues.

Xoloc, he found a strong barrier or fortification, behind which a Mexican force was intrenched. Their archery did some mischief to the Spaniards. as they came within bowshot. But the latter, marching intrepidly forward in face of the arrowy shower, stormed the works, and, after an obstinate struggle, drove the enemy from their position.[21] Cortés then advanced some way on the great causeway of Iztapalapan; but he beheld the further extremity darkened by a numerous array of warriors, and, as he did not care to engage in unnecessary hostilities, especially as his ammunition was nearly exhausted, he fell back and retreated to his own quarters.

The following day, the army continued its march, taking the road to Tacuba, but a few miles distant. On the way it experienced much annoyance from straggling parties of the enemy, who, furious at the sight of the booty which the invaders were bearing away, made repeated attacks on their flanks and rear. Cortés retaliated, as on the former expedition, by one of their own stratagems, but with less success than before; for, pursuing the retreating enemy too hotly, he fell with his cavalry into an ambuscade, which they had prepared for him in their turn. He was not yet a match for their wily tactics. The Spanish cavaliers were enveloped in a moment by their subtle foe, and separated from the rest of the army. But, spurring on their good steeds, and charging in a solid column together, they succeeded in breaking through the Indian array, and in making their escape, except two individuals, who fell into the enemy's hands. They were the general's own servants, who had followed him faithfully through the whole campaign, and he was deeply affected by their loss; rendered the more distressing by the consideration of the dismal fate that awaited them. When the little band rejoined the army, which had halted, in some anxiety at their absence, under the walls of Tacuba, the soldiers were astonished at the dejected mien of their commander, which too visibly betrayed his emotion.[22]

The sun was still high in the heavens, when they entered the ancient capital of the Tepanecs. The first care of Cortés was to ascend the principal *teocalli*, and survey the surrounding country. It was an admirable point of view, commanding the capital, which lay but little more than a league distant, and its immediate environs. Cortés was accompanied by Alderete, the treasurer, and some other cavaliers, who had lately joined his banner. The spectacle was still new to them; and, as they gazed on the stately city, with its broad lake covered with boats and barges hurrying to and fro, some laden with merchandise, or fruits and vegetables, for the markets of Tenochtitlan, others crowded with warriors, they could not withhold their admiration at the life and activity of the scene, de-

---

[21] "Y llegámos á una Albarrada, que tenian hecha en la Calzada, y los Peones comenzáronla á combatir; y aunque fué muy re cia, y hubo mucha resistencia, y hiriéron diez Españoles, al fin se la ganáron, y matáron muchos de los Enemigos. aunque los Ballesteros, y Escopeteros quedáron sin Pólvora, y sin Saetas." Ibid., ubi supra.

[22] "Y estando en esto viene Cortés, con el qual nos alegrámos, puesto que él venia muy triste y como lloroso." Bernal Díaz, Hist. de la Conquista, cap. 145.

claring that nothing but the hand of Providence could have led thei°
countrymen safe through the heart of this powerful empire.[23]

In the midst of the admiring circle, the brow of Cortés alone was observed to be overcast, and a sigh, which now and then stole audibly from
his bosom, showed the gloomy working of his thoughts.[24] "Take comfort," said one of the cavaliers, approaching his commander, and wishing
to console him in his rough way for his recent loss, "you must not lay
these things so much to heart; it is, after all, but the fortune of war."
The general's answer showed the nature of his meditations. "You are my
witness," said he, "how often I have endeavored to persuade yonder
capital peacefully to submit. It fills me with grief, when I think of the
toil and the dangers my brave followers have yet to encounter before
we can call it ours. But the time is come when we must put our hands
to the work." [25]

There can be no doubt, that Cortés, with every other man in his army,
felt he was engaged on a holy crusade, and that, independently of personal considerations, he could not serve Heaven better, than by planting
the Cross on the blood-stained towers of the heathen metropolis. But it
was natural that he should feel some compunction, as he gazed on the
goodly scene, and thought of the coming tempest, and how soon the
opening blossoms of civilization which there met his eye must wither under the rude breath of War. It was a striking spectacle, that of the great
Conqueror, thus brooding in silence over the desolation he was about to
bring on the land! It seems to have made a deep impression on his soldiers, little accustomed to such proofs of his sensibility; and it forms the
burden of some of those *romances*, or national ballads, with which the
Castilian minstrel, in the olden time, delighted to commemorate the favorite heroes of his country, and which, coming mid-way between oral
tradition and chronicle, have been found as imperishable a record as
chronicle itself.[26]

---

[23] "Pues quando viéron la gran ciudad de México, y la laguna, y tanta multitud
de canoas, que vnas ivan cargadas con bastimentos, y otras ivan á pescar, y otras
valdías, mucho mas se espantáron, porque no las auian visto, hasta en aquella
saçon: y dixéron, que nuestra venida en esta Nueua España, que no eran cosas de
hombres humanos, sino que la gran misericordia de Dios era quiē nos sostenia" Ibid.,
ubi supra.

[24] "En este instante suspiró Cortés cõ vna muy grã tristeza, mui mayor q̃ la q̃ de
antes traia." Ibid., loc. cit.

[25] "Y Cortés le dixo, que ya veia quantas vezes auia embiado á México á rogalles
con la paz, y que la tristeza no la tenia por sola vna cosa, sino en pensar en los
grandes trabajos en que nos auiamos de ver, hasta tornar á señorear; y que con la
ayuda de Dios presto lo porniamos por la obra." Ibid., ubi supra.

[26] Diaz gives the opening *redondillas* of the *romance*, which I have not been able
to find in any of the printed collections.

> "En Tacuba está Cortés,
> cõ su esquadron esforçado,
> triste estaua, y muy penoso,
> triste, y con gran cuidado,
> la vna mano en la mexilla,
> y la otra en en costado," &c.

Tacuba was the point which Cortés had reached on his former expedition round the northern side of the Valley. He had now, therefore, made the entire circuit of the great lake; had reconnoitred the several approaches to the capital, and inspected with his own eyes the dispositions made on the opposite quarters for its defence. He had no occasion to prolong his stay in Tacuba, the vicinity of which to Mexico must soon bring on him its whole warlike population.

Early on the following morning, he resumed his march, taking the route pursued in the former expedition north of the small lakes. He met with less annoyance from the enemy, than on the preceding days; a circumstance owing in some degree, perhaps, to the state of the weather, which was exceedingly tempestuous. The soldiers, with their garments heavy with moisture, ploughed their way with difficulty through miry roads flooded by the torrents. On one occasion, as their military chronicler informs us, the officers neglected to go the rounds of the camp, at night, and the sentinels to mount guard, trusting to the violence of the storm for their protection. Yet the fate of Narvaez might have taught them not to put their faith in the elements.

At Acolman, in the Acolhuan territory, they were met by Sandoval, with the friendly cacique of Tezcuco, and several cavaliers, among whom were some recently arrived from the Islands. They cordially greeted their countrymen, and communicated the tidings, that the canal was completed, and that the brigantines, rigged and equipped, were ready to be launched on the bosom of the lake. There seemed to be no reason, therefore, for longer postponing operations against Mexico.—With this welcome intelligence, Cortés and his victorious legions made their entry for the last time into the Acolhuan capital, having consumed just three weeks in completing the circuit of the Valley.

It may be thus done into pretty literal doggerel:

> In Tacuba stood Cortés,
>   With many a care opprest,
> Thoughts of the past came o'er him,
>   And he bowed his haughty crest.
> One hand upon his cheek he laid,
>   The other on his breast,
> While his valiant squadrons round him, &c.

CHAPTER IV

CONSPIRACY IN THE ARMY—BRIGANTINES LAUNCHED—MUSTER OF
FORCES—EXECUTION OF XICOTENCATL—MARCH OF THE ARMY—
BEGINNING OF THE SIEGE

1521

AT the very time when Cortés was occupied with reconnoitring the Valley, preparatory to his siege of the capital, a busy faction in Castile was
laboring to subvert his authority and defeat his plans of conquest altogether. The fame of his brilliant exploits had spread not only through
the Isles, but to Spain and many parts of Europe, where a general admiration was felt for the invincible energy of the man, who, with his single
arm, as it were, could so long maintain a contest with the powerful Indian
empire. The absence of the Spanish monarch from his dominions, and the
troubles of the country, can alone explain the supine indifference shown
by the government to the prosecution of this great enterprise. To the
same causes it may be ascribed, that no action was had in regard to the
suits of Velasquez and Narvaez, backed, as they were, by so potent an
advocate as Bishop Fonseca, president of the Council of the Indies. The
reins of government had fallen into the hands of Adrian of Utrecht,
Charles's preceptor, and afterwards Pope,—a man of learning, and not
without sagacity, but slow and timid in his policy, and altogether incapable of that decisive action which suited the bold genius of his predecessor, Cardinal Ximenes.

In the spring of 1521, however, a number of ordinances passed the
Council of the Indies, which threatened an important innovation in the
affairs of New Spain. It was decreed, that the Royal Audience of Hispaniola should abandon the proceedings already instituted against Narvaez, for his treatment of the commissioner Ayllon; that that unfortunate commander should be released from his confinement at Vera
Cruz; and that an arbitrator should be sent to Mexico, with authority to
investigate the affairs and conduct of Cortés, and to render ample justice to the governor of Cuba. There were not wanting persons at court,
who looked with dissatisfaction on these proceedings, as an unworthy
requital of the services of Cortés, and who thought the present moment,
at any rate, not the most suitable for taking measures, which might discourage the general, and, perhaps, render him desperate. But the arrogant temper of the bishop of Burgos overruled all objections; and the
ordinances having been approved by the Regency, were signed by that
body, April 11, 1521. A person named Tapia, one of the functionaries of

the Audience at St. Domingo, was selected as the new commissioner to be despatched to Vera Cruz. Fortunately circumstances occurred, which postponed the execution of the design for the present, and permitted Cortés to go forward unmolested in his career of conquest.[1]

But, while thus allowed to remain, for the present at least, in possession of authority, he was assailed by a danger nearer home, which menaced not only his authority, but his life. This was a conspiracy in the army, of a more dark and dangerous character than any hitherto formed there. It was set on foot by a common soldier, named Antonio Villafaña, a native of Old Castile, of whom nothing is known but his share in this transaction. He was one of the troop of Narvaez,—that leaven of disaffection, which had remained with the army, swelling with discontent on every light occasion, and ready, at all times, to rise into mutiny. They had voluntarily continued in the service, after the secession of their comrades at Tlascala; but it was from the same mercenary hopes with which they had originally embarked in the expedition,—and in these they were destined still to be disappointed. They had little of the true spirit of adventure, which distinguished the old companions of Cortés; and they found the barren laurels of victory but a sorry recompense for all their toils and sufferings.

With these men were joined others, who had causes of personal disgust with the general; and others, again, who looked with distrust on the result of the war. The gloomy fate of their countrymen, who had fallen into the enemy's hands, filled them with dismay. They felt themselves the victims of a chimerical spirit in their leader, who, with such inadequate means, was urging to extremity so ferocious and formidable a foe; and they shrunk with something like apprehension from thus pursuing the enemy into his own haunts, where he would gather tenfold energy from despair.

These men would have willingly abandoned the enterprise, and returned to Cuba; but how could they do it? Cortés had control over the whole route from the city to the sea-coast; and not a vessel could leave its ports without his warrant. Even if he were put out of the way, there were others, his principal officers, ready to step into his place, and avenge the death of their commander. It was necessary to embrace these, also, in the scheme of destruction; and it was proposed, therefore, together with Cortés, to assassinate Sandoval, Olid, Alvarado, and two or three others most devoted to his interests. The conspirators would then raise the cry of liberty, and doubted not that they should be joined by the greater part of the army, or enough, at least, to enable them to work their own pleasure. They proposed to offer the command, on Cortés' death, to Francisco Verduga, a brother-in-law of Velasquez. He was an honorable cavalier, and not privy to their design. But they had little doubt that he would acquiesce in the command, thus, in a manner, forced upon him, and this would secure them the protection of the governor of

---

[1] Herrera, Hist. General, dec. 3, lib. 1, cap. 15.—Relacion de Alonso de Verzara, Escrivano Público de Vera Cruz, MS., dec. 21.

Cuba, who, indeed, from his own hatred of Cortés, would be disposed to look with a lenient eye on their proceedings.

The conspirators even went so far as to appoint the subordinate officers, an *alguacil mayor* in place of Sandoval, a quartermaster-general to succeed Olid, and some others.[2] The time fixed for the execution of the plot was soon after the return of Cortés from his expedition. A parcel, pretended to have come by a fresh arrival from Castile, was to be presented to him while at table, and, when he was engaged in breaking open the letters, the conspirators were to fall on him and his officers, and despatch them with their poniards. Such was the iniquitous scheme devised for the destruction of Cortés and the expedition. But a conspiracy, to be successful, especially when numbers are concerned, should allow but little time to elapse between its conception and its execution.

On the day previous to that appointed for the perpetration of the deed, one of the party, feeling a natural compunction at the commission of the crime, went to the general's quarters, and solicited a private interview with him. He threw himself at his commander's feet, and revealed all the particulars relating to the conspiracy, adding, that in Villafaña's possession a paper would be found, containing the names of his accomplices. Cortés, thunder-struck at the disclosure, lost not a moment in profiting by it. He sent for Alvarado, Sandoval, and one or two other officers marked out by the conspirator, and, after communicating the affair to them, went at once with them to Villafaña's quarters, attended by four alguacils.

They found him in conference with three or four friends, who were instantly taken from the apartment, and placed in custody. Villafaña, confounded at this sudden apparition of his commander, had barely time to snatch a paper, containing the signatures of the confederates, from his bosom, and attempt to swallow it. But Cortés arrested his arm, and seized the paper. As he glanced his eye rapidly over the fatal list, he was much moved at finding there the names of more than one, who had some claim to consideration in the army. He tore the scroll in pieces, and ordered Villafaña to be taken into custody. He was immediately tried by a military court hastily got together, at which the general himself presided. There seems to have been no doubt of the man's guilt. He was condemned to death, and, after allowing him time for confession and absolution, the sentence was executed by hanging him from the window of his own quarters.[3]

Those ignorant of the affair were astonished at the spectacle; and the remaining conspirators were filled with consternation, when they saw that their plot was detected, and anticipated a similar fate for themselves. But they were mistaken. Cortés pursued the matter no further. A

---

[2] "Haziã Alguazil mayor é Alférez, y Alcaldes, y Regidores, y Contador, y Tesorero, y Ueedor, y otras cosas deste arte, y aun repartido entre ellos nuestros bienes, y cauallos." Bernal Diaz, Hist. de la Conquista, cap. 146.

[3] Ibid., loc. cit.—Oviedo, Hist. de las Ind., MS., lib. 33, cap. 48.—Herrera. Hist. General, dec. 3, lib. 1, cap. 1.

little reflection convinced him, that to do so would involve him in the most disagreeable, and even dangerous, perplexities. And, however much the parties implicated in so foul a deed might deserve death, he could ill afford the loss even of the guilty, with his present limited numbers. He resolved, therefore, to content himself with the punishment of the ring-leader.

He called his troops together, and briefly explained to them the nature of the crime for which Villafaña had suffered. He had made no confession, he said, and the guilty secret had perished with him. He then expressed his sorrow, that any should have been found in their ranks capable of so base an act, and stated his own unconsciousness of having wronged any individual among them; but, if he had done so, he invited them frankly to declare it, as he was most anxious to afford them all the redress in his power.[4]—But there was no one of his audience, whatever might be his grievances, who cared to enter his complaint at such a moment; least of all were the conspirators willing to do so, for they were too happy at having, as they fancied, escaped detection, to stand forward now in the ranks of the malecontents. The affair passed off, therefore, without further consequences.

The conduct of Cortés, in this delicate conjuncture, shows great coolness, and knowledge of human nature. Had he suffered his detection, or even his suspicion, of the guilty parties to take air, it would have placed him in hostile relations with them for the rest of his life. It was a disclosure of this kind, in the early part of Louis the Eleventh's reign, to which many of the troubles of his later years were attributed.[5] The mask once torn away, there is no longer occasion to consult even appearances. The door seems to be closed against reform. The alienation, which might have been changed by circumstances, or conciliated by kindness, settles into a deep and deadly rancor. And Cortés would have been surrounded by enemies in his own camp, more implacable than those in the camp of the Aztecs.

As it was, the guilty soldiers had suffered too serious apprehensions to place their lives hastily in a similar jeopardy. They strove, on the contrary, by demonstrations of loyalty, and the assiduous discharge of their duties, to turn away suspicion from themselves. Cortés, on his part, was careful to preserve his natural demeanor, equally removed from distrust, and—what was perhaps more difficult—that studied courtesy, which intimates, quite as plainly, suspicion of the party who is the object of it. To do this required no little address. Yet he did not forget the past. He had, it is true, destroyed the scroll containing the list of the conspirators. But the man, that has once learned the names of those

---

[4] Ibid., ubi supra.

[5] So says M. de Barante in his picturesque *rifacimento* of the ancient chronicles. "Les procès du connétable et de monsieur de Némours, bien d'autres révélations, avaient fait éclater leur mauvais vouloir, ou du moins leur peu de fidélité pour le roi; ils ne pouvaient donc douter qu'il désirât ou complotât leur ruine." *Histoire des Ducs de Bourgogne*, (Paris 1838,) tom. XI. p. 169.

who have conspired against his life, had no need of a written record to keep them fresh in his memory. Cortés kept his eye on all their movements, and took care to place them in no situation, afterwards, where they could do him injury.[6]

This attempt on the life of their commander excited a strong sensation in the army, with whom his many dazzling qualities and brilliant military talents had made him a general favorite. They were anxious to testify their reprobation of so foul a deed, coming from their own body, and they felt the necessity of taking some effectual measures for watching over the safety of one, with whom their own destinies, as well as the fate of the enterprise, were so intimately connected. It was arranged, therefore, that he should be provided with a guard of soldiers, who were placed under the direction of a trusty cavalier named Antonio de Quiñones. They constituted the general's body-guard, during the rest of the campaign, watching over him day and night, and protecting him from domestic treason, no less than from the sword of the enemy.

As was stated at the close of the last Chapter, the Spaniards, on their return to quarters, found the construction of the brigantines completed, and that they were fully rigged, equipped, and ready for service. The canal, also, after having occupied eight thousand men for nearly two months, was finished.

It was a work of great labor; for it extended half a league in length, was twelve feet wide, and as many deep. The sides were strengthened by palisades of wood, or solid masonry. At intervals, dams and locks were constructed, and part of the opening was through the hard rock. By this avenue the brigantines might now be safely introduced on the lake.[7]

Cortés was resolved that so auspicious an event should be celebrated with due solemnity. On the 28th of April, the troops were drawn up under arms, and the whole population of Tezcuco assembled to witness the ceremony. Mass was performed, and every man in the army, together with the general, confessed and received the sacrament. Prayers were offered up by father Olmedo, and a benediction invoked on the little navy, the first—worthy of the name—ever launched on American waters.[8] The signal was given by the firing of a cannon, when the vessels, dropping down the canal, one after another, reached the lake in good order; and, as they emerged on its ample bosom, with music sounding, and the royal ensign of Castile proudly floating from their masts, a shout of admira-

---

[6] "Y desde allı adelante, aunque mostraua gran voluntad á las personas que eran en la cōjuraciō, siempre se rezelaua dellos." Bernal Diaz, Hist. de la Conquista, cap. 146.

[7] Ixtlilxochitl, Venida de los Esp., p. 19.—Rel. Terc. de Cortés, ap. Lorenzana, p. 234.
"Obra grandíssima," exclaims the Conqueror, "y mucho para ver."—"Fuéron en guarde de estos bergantines," adds Camargo, "mas de diez mil hombres de guerra con los maestros dellas, hasta que los armáron y echáron en el agua y laguna de Méjico, que fué obra de mucho efecto para tomarse Méjico." Hist. de Tlascala, MS.

[8] The brigantines were still to be seen, preserved, as precious memorials, long after the Conquest, in the dockyards of Mexico. Toribio. Hist. de los Indios, MS Parte 1, cap. 1

tion arose from the countless multitudes of spectators, which mingled
with the roar of artillery and musketry from the vessels and the shore![9]
It was a novel spectacle to the simple natives; and they gazed with wonder on the gallant ships, which, fluttering like sea-birds on their snowy
pinions, bounded lightly over the waters, as if rejoicing in their element.
It touched the stern hearts of the Conquerors with a glow of rapture, and,
as they felt that Heaven had blessed their undertaking, they broke forth,
by general accord, into the noble anthem of the *Te Deum*. But there was
no one of that vast multitude for whom the sight had deeper interest
than their commander. For he looked on it as the work, in a manner, of
his own hands; and his bosom swelled with exultation, as he felt he was
now possessed of a power strong enough to command the lake, and to
shake the haughty towers of Tenochtitlan.[10]

The general's next step was to muster his forces in the great square of
the capital. He found they amounted to eighty-seven horse, and eight
hundred and eighteen foot, of which one hundred and eighteen were arquebusiers and crossbow-men. He had three large field-pieces of iron,
and fifteen lighter guns or falconets of brass.[11] The heavier cannon had
been transported from Vera Cruz to Tezcuco, a little while before, by
the faithful Tlascalans. He was well supplied with shot and balls, with
about ten hundred weight of powder, and fifty thousand copper-headed
arrows, made after a pattern furnished by him to the natives.[12] The number and appointments of the army much exceeded what they had been at
any time since the flight from Mexico, and showed the good effects of
the late arrivals from the Islands. Indeed, taking the fleet into the account, Cortés had never before been in so good a condition for carrying
on his operations. Three hundred of the men were sent to man the vessels, thirteen, or rather twelve, in number, one of the smallest having
been found, on trial, too dull a sailor to be of service. Half of the crews
were required to navigate the ships. There was some difficulty in finding
hands for this, as the men were averse to the employment. Cortés selected those who came from Palos, Moguer, and other maritime towns, and,
notwithstanding their frequent claims of exemption, as hidalgos, from

[9] "Deda la señal, soltó la Presa, fuéron saliendos los Vergantines, sin tocar vno á
otro, i apartándose por la Laguna, desplegáron las Vanderas, tocó la Música, dis-
paráron su Artillería, respondió la del Exército, así de Castellanos, como de Indios."
Herrera, Hist. General, dec. 3, lib. 1, cap. 6.

[10] Ibid., ubi supra.—Rel. Terc. de Cortés, ap. Lorenzana, p. 234.—Ixtlilxochitl,
Venida de los Esp., p. 19.—Oviedo, Hist. de las Ind., MS., lib. 33, cap. 48.
The last-mentioned chronicler indulges in no slight swell of exultation at this
achievement of his hero, which in his opinion throws into shade the boasted exploits
of the great Sesostris. "Otras muchas é notables cosas, cuenta este actor que he dicho
de aqueste Rey Sesori, en que no me quiero detener, ni las tengo en tanto como
esta tranchea, ó canja que es dicho, y los Vergantines de que tratamos, los quales
diéron ocasion á que se oviesen mayores Thesoros é Provincias, é Reynos, que no
tuvo Sesori, para la corona Real de Castilla por la industria de Hernando Cortés."
Ibid., lib. 33, cap. 22.

[11] Rel. Terc. de Cortés, ap. Lorenzana, p. 234.

[12] Bernal Diaz, Hist. de la Conquista. cap. 147.

this menial occupation, he pressed them into the service.[13] Each vessel mounted a piece of heavy ordnance, and was placed under an officer of respectability, to whom Cortés gave a general code of instructions for the government of the little navy, of which he proposed to take the command in person.

He had already sent to his Indian confederates, announcing his purpose of immediately laying siege to Mexico, and called on them to furnish their promised levies, within the space of ten days at furthest. The Tlascalans he ordered to join him in Tezcuco; the others were to assemble at Chalco, a more convenient place of rendezvous for the operations in the southern quarter of the Valley. The Tlascalans arrived within the time prescribed, led by the younger Xicotencatl, supported by Chichemecatl, the same doughty warrior who had convoyed the brigantines to Tezcuco. They came fifty thousand strong, according to Cortés,[14] making a brilliant show with their military finery, and marching proudly forward under the great national banner, emblazoned with a spread eagle, the arms of the republic.[15] With as blithe and many a step, as if they were going to the battle-ground, they defiled through the gates of the capital, making its walls ring with the friendly shouts of "Castile and Tlascala."

The observations, which Cortés had made in his late tour of *reconnaissance*, had determined him to begin the siege by distributing his forces into three separate camps, which he proposed to establish at the extremities of the principal causeways. By this arrangement the troops would be enabled to move in concert on the capital, and be in the best position to intercept its supplies from the surrounding country. The first of these points was Tacuba, commanding the fatal causeway of the *noche triste*. This was assigned to Pedro de Alvarado, with a force consisting, according to Cortés' own statement, of thirty horse, one hundred and sixty-eight Spanish infantry, and five and twenty thousand Tlascalans. Chiistóval de Olid had command of the second army, of much the same magnitude, which was to take up its position at Cojohuacan, the

---

[13] Ibid., ubi supra.

Hidalguia, besides its legal privileges, brought with it some fanciful ones to its possessor; if, indeed, it be considered a privilege to have excluded him from many a humble, but honest, calling, by which the poor man might have gained his bread. (From an amusing account of these, see Doblado's Letters from Spain, let. 2.) In no country has the *poor gentleman* afforded so rich a theme for the satirist, as the writings of Le Sage, Cervantes, and Lope de Vega abundantly show.

[14] "Y los Capitanes de Tascaltecal con toda su gente, muy lúcida, y bien armada, ... y segun la cuenta, que los Capitanes nos diéron, pasaban de cinquenta mil Hombres de Guerra." (Rel. Terc. de Cortés, ap. Lorenzana, p. 236.) "I toda la Gente," adds Herrera, "tardó tres Dias en entrar, segun en sus Memoriales dice Alonso de Ojeda, ni con ser Tezcuco tan gran Ciudad, cabian en ella." Hist. General, dec. 3, lib. 1, cap. 13.

[15] "Y sus vãderas tẽdidas, y el aue blãca q̃ tienen por armas, q̃ parece águila, con sus alas tendidas." (Bernal Diaz, Hist. de la Conquista, cap. 149.) A spread eagle of gold, Clavigero considers as the arms of the republic. (Clavigero, Stor. del Messico, tom. II. p. 145.) But, as Bernal Diaz speaks of it as "white," it may have been the white heron, which belonged to the house of Xicotencatl.

city, it will be remembered, overlooking the short causeway connected with that of Iztapalapan. Gonzalo de Sandoval had charge of the third division, of equal strength with each of the two preceding, but which was to draw its Indian levies from the forces assembled at Chalco. This officer was to march on Iztapalapan, and complete the destruction of that city, begun by Cortés soon after his entrance into the Valley. It was too formidable a post to remain in the rear of the army. The general intended to support the attack with his brigantines, after which the subsequent movements of Sandoval would be determined by circumstances.[16]

Having announced his intended dispositions to his officers, the Spanish commander called his troops together, and made one of those brief and stirring harangues, with which he was wont on great occasions to kindle the hearts of his soldiery. "I have taken the last step," he said; "I have brought you to the goal for which you have so long panted. A few days will place you before the gates of Mexico,—the capital from which you were driven with so much ignominy. But we now go forward under the smiles of Providence. Does any one doubt it? Let him but compare our present condition with that in which we found ourselves not twelve months since, when, broken and dispirited, we sought shelter within the walls of Tlascala; nay, with that in which we were but a few months since, when we took up our quarters in Tezcuco.[17] Since that time our strength has been nearly doubled. We are fighting the battles of the Faith, fighting for our honor, for riches, for revenge. I have brought you face to face with your foe. It is for you to do the rest." [18]

The address of the bold chief was answered by the thundering acclamations of his followers, who declared that every man would do his duty under such a leader; and they only asked to be led against the enemy.[19] Cortés then caused the regulations for the army, published at Tlascala, to be read again to the troops, with the assurance that they should be enforced to the letter.

[16] The precise amount of each division, as given by Cortés, was,—in that of Alvarado, 30 horse, 168 Castilian infantry, and 25,000 Tlascalan; in that of Olid, 33 horse, 178 infantry, 20,000 Tlascalans; and in Sandoval's, 24 horse, 167 infantry, 30,000 Indians.—(Rel. Terc., ap. Lorenzana, p. 236.) Diaz reduces the number of native troops to one third. Hist. de la Conquista, cap. 150.

[17] "Que se alegrassen, y esforzassen mucho, pues que veian, que nuestro Señor nos encaminaba para haber victoria de nuestros Enemigos: porque bien sabian, que quando habiamos entrado en Tesaico, no habiamos trahido mas de quarenta de Caballo, y que Dios nos habia socorrido mejor, que lo habiamos pensado." Rel. Terc. de Cortés, ap. Lorenzana, p. 235.

[18] Oviedo expands, what he, nevertheless, calls the "brebe é substancial oracion" of Cortés, into treble the length of it, as found in the general's own pages; in which he is imitated by most of the other chroniclers. Hist. de las Ind., MS., lib. 33, cap. 22.

[19] "Y con estas últimas palabras cesó; y todos respondiéron sin discrepancia, é á una voce dicentes: Sirvanse Dios y el Emperador nuestro Señor de tan bien capitan, y de nosotros, que así lo harémos todos como quien somos, y como se debe esperar de buenos Españoles, y con tanta voluntad, y deseo, dicho que parecia que cada hora les era perder vn año de tiempo por estar y á las manos con los Enemigos." Oviedo, Hist. de las Ind., MS., ubi supra.

It was arranged, that the Indian forces should precede the Spanish by a day's march, and should halt for their confederates on the borders of the Tezcucan territory. A circumstance occurred soon after their departure, which gave bad augury for the future. A quarrel had arisen in the camp at Tezcuco, between a Spanish soldier and a Tlascalan chief, in which the latter was badly hurt. He was sent back to Tlascala, and the matter was hushed up, that it might not reach the ears of the general, who, it was known, would not pass it over lightly. Xicotencatl was a near relative of the injured party, and, on the first day's halt, he took the opportunity to leave the army, with a number of his followers, and set off for Tlascala. Other causes are assigned for his desertion.[20] It is certain, that, from the first, he had looked on the expedition with an evil eye, and had predicted that no good would come of it. He came into it with reluctance, as, indeed, he detested the Spaniards in his heart.

His partner in the command instantly sent information of the affair to the Spanish general, still encamped at Tezcuco. Cortés, who saw at once the mischievous consequences of this defection at such a time, detached a party of Tlascalan and Tezcucan Indians after the fugitive, with instructions to prevail on him, if possible, to return to his duty. They overtook him on the road, and remonstrated with him on his conduct, contrasting it with that of his countrymen generally, and of his own father in particular, the steady friend of the white men. "So much the worse," replied the chieftain; "if they had taken my counsel, they would never have become the dupes of the perfidious strangers." [21] Finding their remonstrances received only with anger or contemptuous taunts, the emissaries returned without accomplishing their object.

Cortés did not hesitate on the course he was to pursue. "Xicotencatl," he said, "had always been the enemy of the Spaniards, first in the field, and since in the council-chamber; openly, or in secret, still the same,— their implacable enemy. There was no use in parleying with the false-hearted Indian." He instantly despatched a small body of horse with an alguacil to arrest the chief, wherever he might be found, even though it were in the streets of Tlascala, and to bring him back to Tezcuco. At the same time, he sent information of Xicotencatl's proceedings to the Tlascalan senate, adding, that desertion among the Spaniards was punished with death.

The emissaries of Cortés punctually fulfilled his orders. They arrested the fugitive chief,—whether in Tlascala or in its neighborhood is uncertain,—and brought him a prisoner to Tezcuco, where a high gallows,

---

[20] According to Diaz, the desire to possess himself of the lands of his comrade Chichemecatl, who remained with the army; (Hist. de la Conquista, cap. 150;) according to Herrera, it was an amour that carried him home. (Hist. General, dec. 3, lib. 1, cap. 17.) Both and all agree on the chief's aversion to the Spaniards, and to the war.

[21] "Y la respuesta que le embió á dezir fué, que si el viejo de su padre, y Masse Escaci le huvieran creido, que no se huvieran señoreado tanto dellos, que les haze hazer todo lo que quiere: *y por no gastar mas palabras, dixo, que no queria venir*" Bernal Diaz, Hist. de la Conquista, cap. 150.

erected in the great square, was prepared for his reception. He was instantly led to the place of execution; his sentence and the cause for which he suffered were publicly proclaimed, and the unfortunate cacique expiated his offence by the vile death of a malefactor. His ample property, consisting of lands, slaves, and some gold, was all confiscated to the Castilian crown.[22]

Thus perished Xicotencatl, in the flower of his age,—as dauntless a warrior as ever led an Indian army to battle. He was the first chief who successfully resisted the arms of the invaders; and, had the natives of Anahuac, generally, been animated with a spirit like his, Cortés would probably never have set foot in the capital of Montezuma. He was gifted with a clearer insight into the future than his countrymen; for he saw that the European was an enemy far more to be dreaded than the Aztec. Yet, when he consented to fight under the banner of the white men, he had no right to desert it, and he incurred the penalty prescribed by the code of savage as well as of civilized nations. It is said, indeed, that the Tlascalan senate aided in apprehending him, having previously answered Cortés, that his crime was punishable with death by their own laws.[23] It was a bold act, however, thus to execute him in the midst of his people. For he was a powerful chief, heir to one of the four seigniories of the republic. His chivalrous qualities made him popular, especially with the younger part of his countrymen; and his garments were torn into shreds at his death, and distributed as sacred relics among them. Still, no resistance was offered to the execution of the sentence, and no commotion followed it. He was the only Tlascalan who ever swerved from his loyalty to the Spaniards.

According to the plan of operations settled by Cortés, Sandoval, with his division, was to take a southern direction, while Alvarado and Olid would make the northern circuit of the lakes. These two cavaliers, after getting possession of Tacuba, were to advance to Chapoltepec, and demolish the great aqueduct there, which supplied Mexico with water. On the 10th of May, they commenced their march; but at Acolman, where they halted for the night, a dispute arose between the soldiers of the two divisions, respecting their quarters. From words they came to

[22] So says Herrera, who had the Memorial of Ojeda in his possession, one of the Spaniards employed to apprehend the chieftain. (Hist. General, dec. 3, lib. 1, cap. 17, and Torquemado, Monarch. Ind., lib. 4, cap. 90.) Bernal Diaz, on the other hand, says, that the Tlascalan chief was taken and executed on the road. (Hist. de la Conquista, cap. 150.) But the latter chronicler was probably absent at the time with Alvarado's division, in which he served.—Solís, however, prefers his testimony, on the ground, that Cortés would not have hazarded the execution of Xicotencatl before the eyes of his own troops. (Conquista, lib. 5, cap. 19.) But the Tlascalans were already well on their way towards Tacuba. A very few only could have remained in Tezcuco, which was occupied by the citizens and the Castilian army,—neither of them very likely to interfere in the prisoner's behalf. His execution there would be an easier matter than in the territory of Tlascala, which he had probably reached before his apprehension.

[23] Herrera, Hist. General, dec. 3, lib. 1, cap. 17.—Torquemada, Monarch. Ind., lib. 4, cap. 90.

blows, and a defiance was even exchanged between the leaders, who entered into the angry feelings of their followers.[24] Intelligence of this was
soon communicated to Cortés, who sent at once to the fiery chiefs, imploring them, by their regard for him and the common cause, to lay aside
their differences, which must end in their own ruin, and that of the expedition. His remonstrance prevailed, at least, so far as to establish a show
of reconciliation between the parties. But Olid was not a man to forget,
or easily to forgive; and Alvarado, though frank and liberal, had an impatient temper much more easily excited than appeased. They were never
afterwards friends.[25]

The Spaniards met with no opposition on their march. The principal
towns were all abandoned by the inhabitants, who had gone to strengthen
the garrison of Mexico, or taken refuge with their families among the
mountains. Tacuba was in like manner deserted, and the troops once
more established themselves in their old quarters in the lordly city of
the Tepanecs.[26]

Their first undertaking was, to cut off the pipes that conducted the
water from the royal streams of Chapoltepec to feed the numerous tanks
and fountains which sparkled in the court-yards of the capital. The
aqueduct, partly constructed of brickwork, and partly of stone and mortar, was raised on a strong, though narrow, dike, which transported it
across an arm of the lake; and the whole work was one of the most pleasing monuments of Mexican civilization. The Indians, well aware of its
importance, had stationed a large body of troops for its protection. A
battle followed, in which both sides suffered considerably, but the Spaniards were victorious. A part of the aqueduct was demolished, and during the siege no water found its way again to the capital through this
channel.

On the following day, the combined forces descended on the fatal
causeway, to make themselves masters, if possible, of the nearest bridge.
They found the dike covered with a swarm of warriors, as numerous as
on the night of their disaster, while the surface of the lake was dark with
the multitude of canoes. The intrepid Christians strove to advance under
a perfect hurricane of missiles from the water and the land, but they
made slow progress. Barricades thrown across the causeway embarrassed
the cavalry, and rendered it nearly useless. The sides of the Indian boats

[24] "Y sobre ello ya auiamos echado mano á las armas los de nuestra Capitanía
contra los de Christóual de Oli, y aun los Capitanes desafiados." Bernal Diaz, Hist
de la Conquista, cap. 150.

[25] Ibid., loc. cit.—Rel. Terc. de Cortés, ap. Lorenzana, p. 237.—Gomara, Crónica,
cap. 130.—Oviedo, Hist. de las Ind., MS., lib. 33, cap. 22.

[26] The Tepanec capital, shorn of its ancient splendors, is now only interesting
from its historic associations. "These plains of Tacuba," says the spirited author of
"Life in Mexico," "once the theatre of fierce and bloody conflicts, and where, during the siege of Mexico, Alvarado "of the leap" fixed his camp, now present a very
tranquil scene. Tacuba itself is now a small village of mud huts, with some fine old
trees, a few very old ruined houses, a ruined church, and some traces of a building,
which ——— assured us had been the palace of their last monarch; whilst others
declare it to have been the site of the Spanish encampment." Vol. I. let. 13.

were fortified with bulwarks, which shielded the crews from the arque-buses and crossbows; and, when the warriors on the dike were hard pushed by the pike-men, they threw themselves fearlessly into the water, as if it were their native element, and, reappearing along the sides of the dike, shot off their arrows and javelins with fatal execution. After a long and obstinate struggle, the Christians were compelled to fall back on their own quarters with disgrace, and—including the allies—with nearly as much damage as they had inflicted on the enemy. Olid, disgusted with the result of the engagement, inveighed against his companion, as having involved them in it by his wanton temerity, and drew off his forces the next morning to his own station at Cojohuacan.

The camps, separated by only two leagues, maintained an easy com-munication with each other. They found abundant employment in for-aging the neighboring country for provisions, and in repelling the active sallies of the enemy; on whom they took their revenge by cutting off his supplies. But their own position was precarious, and they looked with impatience for the arrival of the brigantines under Cortés. It was in the latter part of May, that Olid took up his quarters at Cojohuacan; and from that time may be dated the commencement of the siege of Mexico.[27]

[27] Rel. Terc. de Cortés, ap. Lorenzana, pp. 237-239.—Ixtlilxochitl, Hist. Chich., MS., cap. 94.—Oviedo, Hist. de las Ind., MS., lib. 33, cap. 22.—Bernal Diaz, Hist. de la Conquista, cap. 50.—Gomara, Crónica, cap. 130.

Clavigero settles this date at the day of Corpus Christi, May 30th. (Clavigero, Stor. del Messico, tom. III. p. 196.) But the Spaniards left Tezcuco, May 10th, according to Cortés: and three weeks could not have intervened between their de-parture, and their occupation of Cojohuacan. Clavigero disposes of this difficulty, it is true, by dating the beginning of their march on the 20th, instead of the 10th of May; following the chronology of Herrera, instead of that of Cortés. Surely, the general is the better authority of the two.

CHAPTER V

INDIAN FLOTILLA DEFEATED—OCCUPATION OF THE CAUSEWAYS—DES-
PERATE ASSAULTS—FIRING OF THE PALACES—SPIRIT OF THE BE-
SIEGED—BARRACKS FOR THE TROOPS

1521

No sooner had Cortés received intelligence that his two officers had established themselves in their respective posts, than he ordered Sandoval to
march on Iztapalapan. The cavalier's route led him through a country
for the most part friendly; and at Chalco his little body of Spaniards was
swelled by the formidable muster of Indian levies who awaited there his
approach. After this junction, he continued his march without opposition
till he arrived before the hostile city, under whose walls he found a large
force drawn up to receive him. A battle followed, and the natives, after
maintaining their ground sturdily for some time, were compelled to give
way, and to seek refuge either on the water, or in that part of the town
which hung over it. The remainder was speedily occupied by the Spaniards.

Meanwhile Cortés had set sail with his flotilla, intending to support his
lieutenant's attack by water. On drawing near the southern shore of the
lake, he passed under the shadow of an insulated peak, since named from
him the "Rock of the Marquess." It was held by a body of Indians, who
saluted the fleet, as it passed, with showers of stones and arrows. Cortés,
resolving to punish their audacity, and to clear the lake of his troublesome enemy, instantly landed with a hundred and fifty of his followers.
He placed himself at their head, scaled the steep ascent, in the face of
a driving storm of missiles, and, reaching the summit, put the garrison
to the sword. There was a number of women and children, also, gathered
in the place, whom he spared.[1]

On the top of the eminence was a blazing beacon, serving to notify to
the inhabitants of the capital when the Spanish fleet weighed anchor.
Before Cortés had regained his brigantine, the canoes and *piraguas* of
the enemy had left the harbors of Mexico, and were seen darkening
the lake for many a rood. There were several hundred of them, all crowd-

---

[1] "It was a beautiful victory," exclaims the Conqueror. "É entrámoslos de tal manera, que ninguno de ellos se escapó, excepto las Mugeres, y Niños; y en este
combate me hiriéron veinte y cinco Españoles, pero fué muy hermosa Victoria."
Rel. Terc., ap. Lorenzana, p. 241.

ed with warriors, and advancing rapidly by means of their oars over the calm bosom of the waters.[2]

Cortés, who regarded his fleet, to use his own language, as "the key of the war," felt the importance of striking a decisive blow in the first encounter with the enemy.[3] It was with chagrin, therefore, that he found his sails rendered useless by the want of wind. He calmly waited the approach of the Indian squadron, which, however, lay on their oars, at something more than musket-shot distance, as if hesitating to encounter these leviathans of their waters. At this moment, a light air from land rippled the surface of the lake; it gradually freshened into a breeze, and Cortés, taking advantage of the friendly succour, which he may be excused, under all the circumstances, for regarding as especially sent him by Heaven, extended his line of battle, and bore down, under full press of canvass, on the enemy.[4]

The latter no sooner encountered the bows of their formidable opponents, than they were overturned and sent to the bottom by the shock, or so much damaged that they speedily filled and sank. The water was covered with the wreck of broken canoes, and with the bodies of men struggling for life in the waves, and vainly imploring their companions to take them on board their over-crowded vessels. The Spanish fleet, as it dashed through the mob of boats, sent off its volleys to the right and left with a terrible effect, completing the discomfiture of the Aztecs. The latter made no attempt at resistance, scarcely venturing a single flight of arrows, but strove with all their strength to regain the port from which thy had so lately issued. They were no match in the chase, any more than in the fight, for their terrible antagonist, who, borne on the wings of the wind, careered to and fro at his pleasure, dealing death widely around him, and making the shores ring with the thunders of his ordnance. A few only of the Indian flotilla succeeded in recovering the port, and, gliding up the canals, found a shelter in the bosom of the city, where the heavier burden of the brigantines made it impossible for them to follow. This victory, more complete than even the sanguine temper of Cortés had prognosticated, proved the superiority of the Spaniards, and left them, henceforth, undisputed masters of the Aztec sea.[5]

[2] About five hundred boats, according to the general's own estimate; (Ibid., loc. cit.;) but more than four thousand, according to Bernal Diaz; (Hist. de la Conquista, cap. 150;) who, however, was not present.

[3] "Y como yo deseaba mucho, que el primer reencuentro, que con ellos obiessemos, fuesse de mucha victoria; y se hiciesse de manera, que ellos cobrassen mucho temor de los bergantines, porque la llave de toda la Guerra estaba en ellos." Rel. Terc., ap. Lorenzana, pp. 241, 242.

[4] "Plugo á nuestro Señor, que estándonos mirando los unos á los otros, vino un viento de la Tierra muy favorable para embestir con ellos." Ibid., p. 242.

[5] Ibid., loc. cit.—Oviedo, Hist. de las Ind., MS., lib. 33, cap. 48.—Sahagun, Hist. de Nueva España, MS., lib. 12, cap. 32.

I may be excused for again quoting a few verses from a beautiful description in "Madoc," and one as pertinent as it is beautiful.

> "Their thousand boats, and the ten thousand oars
> From whose broad bowls the waters fall and flash,

It was nearly dusk, when the squadron, coasting along the great southern causeway, anchored off the point of junction, called Xoloc, where the
branch from Cojohuacan meets the principal dike. The avenue widened
at this point, so as to afford room for two towers, or turreted temples,
built of stone, and surrounded by walls of the same material, which
presented altogether a position of some strength, and, at the present moment, was garrisoned by a body of Aztecs. They were not numerous, and
Cortés, landing with his soldiers, succeeded without much difficulty in
dislodging the enemy, and in getting possession of the works.

It seems to have been originally the general's design, to take up his
own quarters with Olid at Cojohuacan. But, if so, he now changed his
purpose, and wisely fixed on this spot, as the best position for his encampment. It was but half a league distant from the capital; and, while
it commanded its great southern avenue, had a direct communication
with the garrison at Cojohuacan, through which he might receive supplies from the surrounding country. Here, then, he determined to establish his headquarters. He at once caused his heavy iron cannon to be
transferred from the brigantines to the causeway, and sent orders to Olid
to join him with half his force, while Sandoval was instructed to abandon
his present quarters, and advance to Cojohuacan, whence he was to detach fifty picked men of his infantry to the camp of Cortés. Having made
these arrangements, the general busily occupied himself with strengthening the works at Xoloc, and putting them in the best posture of defence.

During the first five or six days after their encampment, the Spaniards
experienced much annoyance from the enemy, who too late endeavored
to prevent their taking up a position so near the capital, and which, had
they known much of the science of war, they would have taken better
care themselves to secure. Contrary to their usual practice, the Indians
made their attacks by night as well as by day. The water swarmed with
canoes, which hovered at a distance in terror of the brigantines, but still
approached near enough, especially under cover of the darkness, to send
showers of arrows into the Christian camp, that fell so thick as to hide
the surface of the ground, and impede the movements of the soldiers.
Others ran along the western side of the causeway, unprotected, as it
was, by the Spanish fleet, and plied their archery with such galling effect,
that the Spaniards were forced to make a temporary breach in the dike,
wide enough to admit two of their own smaller vessels, which, passing
through, soon obtained as entire command of the interior basin, as they
before had of the outer. Still, the bold barbarians, advancing along the

> And twice ten thousand feathered helms, and shields,
> Glittering with gold and scarlet plumery.
> Onward they come with song and swelling horn;
> .   .   .   .   . On the other side
> Advance the *British* barks; the freshening breeze
> Fills the broad sail; around the rushing keel
> The waters sing, while proudly they sail on,
> Lords of the water."
>
> MADOC, Part 2, canto 25

causeway, marched up within bow-shot of the Christian ramparts, sending forth such yells and discordant battle-cries, that it seemed, in the words of Cortés, "as if heaven and earth were coming together." But they were severely punished for their temerity, as the batteries, which commanded the approaches to the camp, opened a desolating fire, that scattered the assailants, and drove them back in confusion to their own quarters.[6]

The two principal avenues to Mexico, those on the south and the west, were now occupied by the Christians. There still remained a third, the great dike of Tepejacac, on the north, which, indeed, taking up the principal street, that passed in a direct line through the heart of the city, might be regarded as a continuation of the dike of Iztapalapan. By this northern route a means of escape was still left open to the besieged, and they availed themselves of it, at present, to maintain their communications with the country, and to supply themselves with provisions. Alvarado, who observed this from his station at Tacuba, advised his commander of it, and the latter instructed Sandoval to take up his position on the causeway. That officer, though suffering, at the time, from a severe wound, received from a lance in one of the late skirmishes, hastened to obey; and thus, by shutting up its only communication with the surrounding country, completed the blockade of the capital.[7]

But Cortés was not content to wait patiently the effects of a dilatory blockade, which might exhaust the patience of his allies, and his own resources. He determined to support it by such active assaults on the city, as should still further distress the besieged, and hasten the hour of surrender. For this purpose, he ordered a simultaneous attack, by the two commanders at the other stations, on the quarters nearest their encampments.

On the day appointed, his forces were under arms with the dawn. Mass, as usual, was performed; and the Indian confederates, as they listened with grave attention to the stately and imposing service, regarded with undisguised admiration the devotional reverence shown by the Christians, whom, in their simplicity, they looked upon as little less than divinities themselves.[8] The Spanish infantry marched in the van, led on by Cortés, attended by a number of cavaliers, dismounted like himself. They had not moved far upon the causeway, when they were brought to a stand by

---

[6] "Y era tanta la multitud," says Cortés, "que por el Agua, y por la Tierra no viamos sino Gente, y daban tantas gritas, y alaridos, que parecia que se hundia el Mundo." Ibid., p. 245.—Oviedo, Hist. de las Ind., MS., lib. 33, cap. 23.—Ixtlilxochitl, Hist. Chich., MS., cap. 95.—Sahagun, Hist. de Nueva España, MS., lib. 12, cap. 32.

[7] Rel. Terc. de Cortés, ap. Lorenzana, pp. 246, 247.—Bernal Diaz, Hist. de la Conquista, cap. 150.—Herrera, Hist. de las Ind., dec. 3, lib. 1, cap. 17.—Defensa MS., cap. 28.

[8] "Asi como fué de dia se dixo vna misa de Espíritu Santo, que todos los Christianos oyéron con mucha devocion; é aun los Indios, como simples, é no entendientes de tan alto misterio, con admiracion estaban atentos notando el silencio de los cathólicos y el acatamiento que al altar, y al sacerdote los Christianos toviéron hasta receivia la benedicion." Oviedo, Hist. de las Ind., MS., lib. 33, cap. 24.

one of the open breaches, that had formerly been traversed by a bridge. On the further side a solid rampart of stone and lime had been erected, and behind this a strong body of Aztecs were posted, who discharged on the Spaniards, as they advanced, a thick volley of arrows. The latter vainly endeavored to dislodge them with their fire-arms and crossbows; they were too well secured behind their defences.

Cortés then ordered two of the brigantines, which had kept along, one on each side of the causeway, in order to coöperate with the army, to station themselves so as to enfilade the position occupied by the enemy. Thus placed between two well directed fires, the Indians were compelled to recede. The soldiers on board the vessels, springing to land, bounded like deer up the sides of the dike. They were soon followed by their countrymen, under Cortés, who, throwing themselves into the water, swam the undefended chasm, and joined in pursuit of the enemy. The Mexicans fell back, however, in something like order, till they reached another opening in the dike, like the former, dismantled of its bridge, and fortified in the same manner by a bulwark of stone, behind which the retreating Aztecs, swimming across the chasm, and reinforced by fresh bodies of their countrymen, again took shelter.

They made good their post, till, again assailed by the cannonade from the brigantines, they were compelled to give way. In this manner breach after breach was carried, and, at every fresh instance of success, a shout went up from the crews of the vessels, which, answered by the long files of the Spaniards and their confederates on the causeway, made the Valley echo to its borders.

Cortés had now reached the end of the great avenue, where it entered the suburbs. There he halted to give time for the rear-guard to come up with him. It was detained by the labor of filling up the breaches, in such a manner as to make a practicable passage for the artillery and horse, and to secure one for the rest of the army on its retreat. This important duty was intrusted to the allies, who executed it by tearing down the ramparts on the margins, and throwing them into the chasms, and, when this was not sufficient,—for the water was deep around the southern causeway,—by dislodging the great stones and rubbish from the dike itself, which was broad enough to admit of it, and adding them to the pile, until it was raised above the level of the water.

The street, on which the Spaniards now entered, was the great avenue that intersected the town from north to south, and the same by which they had first visited the capital. It was broad and perfectly straight, and, in the distance, dark masses of warriors might be seen gathering to the support of their countrymen, who were prepared to dispute the further progress of the Spaniards. The sides were lined with buildings, the terraced roofs of which were also crowded with combatants, who, as the army advanced, poured down a pitiless storm of missiles on their heads, which glanced harmless, indeed, from the coat of mail, but too often found their way through the more common *escaupil* of the soldier, already gaping with many a ghastly rent. Cortés, to rid himself of this an-

noyance for the future, ordered his Indian pioneers to level the principal buildings, as they advanced; in which work of demolition, no less
than in the repair of the breaches, they proved of inestimable service.[9]

The Spaniards, meanwhile, were steadily, but slowly advancing, as
the enemy recoiled before the rolling fire of musketry, though turning,
at intervals, to discharge their javelins and arrows against their pursuers.
In this way they kept along the great street, until their course was interrupted by a wide ditch or canal, once traversed by a bridge, of which
only a few planks now remained. These were broken by the Indians, the
moment they had crossed, and a formidable array of spears was instantly
seen bristling over the summit of a solid rampart of stone, which protected the opposite side of the canal. Cortés was no longer supported by
his brigantines, which the shallowness of the canals prevented from penetrating into the suburbs. He brought forward his arquebusiers, who,
protected by the targets of their comrades, opened a fire on the enemy.
But the balls fell harmless from the bulwarks of stone; while the assailants presented but too easy a mark to their opponents.

The general then caused the heavy guns to be brought up, and opened
a lively cannonade, which soon cleared a breach in the works, through
which the musketeers and crossbow-men poured in their volleys thick as
hail. The Indians now gave way in disorder, after having held their antagonists at bay for two hours.[10] The latter, jumping into the shallow
water, scaled the opposite bank without further resistance, and drove the
enemy along the street towards the square, where the sacred pyramid
reared its colossal bulk high over the other edifices of the city.

It was a spot too familiar to the Spaniards. On one side stood the
palace of Axayacatl, their old quarters, the scene to many of them of so
much suffering. Opposite was the pile of low, irregular buildings, once
the residence of the unfortunate Montezuma; while a third side of the
square was flanked by the *Coatepantli*, or Wall of Serpents, which encompassed the great *teocalli* with its little city of holy edifices. The Spaniards halted at the entrance of the square, as if oppressed, and for the

[9] Sahagun, Hist. de Nueva España, MS., lib. 12, cap. 32.—Ixtlilxochitl, Hist.
Chich., MS., cap. 95.—Oviedo, Hist. de las Ind., MS., lib. 33, cap. 23.—Rel. Terc.
de Cortés, ap. Lorenzana, pp. 247, 248.

[10] Ibid., ubi supra.—Ixtlilxochitl, Hist. Chich., MS., cap. 95.

Here terminates the work last cited of the Tezcucan chronicler; who has accompanied us from the earliest period of our narrative down to this point in the final
siege of the capital. Whether the concluding pages of the manuscript have been lost,
or whether he was interrupted by death, it is impossible to say. But the deficiency
is supplied by a brief sketch of the principal events of the siege, which he has left
in another of his writings. He had, undoubtedly, uncommon sources of information
in his knowledge of the Indian languages and picture-writing, and in the oral testimony which he was at pains to collect from the actors in the scenes he describes.
All these advantages are too often counterbalanced by a singular incapacity for
discriminating—I will not say, between historic truth and falsehood (for what is
truth?)—but between the probable, or rather the possible, and the impossible. One
of the generation of primitive converts to the Romish faith, he lived in a state of
twilight civilization, when, if miracles were not easily wrought, it was at least easy
to believe them.

moment overpowered, by the bitter recollections that crowded on their minds. But their intrepid leader, impatient at their hesitation, loudly called on them to advance before the Aztecs had time tó rally; and, grasping his target in one hand, and waving his sword high above his head with the other, he cried his war-cry of "St. Iago," and led them at once against the enemy.[11]

The Mexicans, intimidated by the presence of their detested foe, who, in spite of all their efforts, had again forced his way into the heart of their city, made no further resistance, but retreated, or rather fled, for refuge into the sacred inclosure of the *teocalli*, where the numerous build-ings scattered over its ample area afforded many good points of defence. A few priests, clad in their usual wild and blood-stained vestments, were to be seen lingering on the terraces which wound round the stately sides of the pyramid, chanting hymns in honor of their god, and encouraging the warriors below to battle bravely for his altars.[12]

The Spaniards poured through the open gates into the area, and a small party rushed up the winding corridors to its summit. No vestige now remained there of the Cross, or of any other symbol of the pure faith to which it had been dedicated. A new effigy of the Aztec war-god had taken the place of the one demolished by the Christians, and raised its fantastic and hideous form in the same niche which had been occu-pied by its predecessor. The Spaniards soon tore away its golden mask and the rich jewels with which it was bedizened, and, hurling the strug-gling priests down the sides of the pyramid, made the best of their way to their comrades in the area. It was full time.[13]

The Aztecs, indignant at the sacrilegious outrage perpetrated before their eyes, and gathering courage from the inspiration of the place, un-der the very presence of their deities, raised a yell of horror and vindic-tive fury, as, throwing themselves into something like order, they sprang, by a common impulse, on the Spaniards. The latter, who had halted near the entrance, though taken by surprise, made an effort to maintain their position at the gateway. But in vain; for the headlong rush of the assail-ants drove them at once into the square, where they were attacked by other bodies of Indians, pouring in from the neighboring streets. Broken, and losing their presence of mind, the troops made no attempt to rally, but, crossing the square, and abandoning the cannon, planted there, to the enemy, they hurried down the great street of Iztapalapan.

[11] "I con todo eso no se determinaban los Christianos de entrar en la Plaça; por lo qual diciendo Hernando Cortés, que no era tiempo de mostrar cansancio, ni cobardía, con vna Rodela en la mano, apellidando Santiago, arremetió el primero." Herrera, Hist. General, dec. 3. lib. 1, cap. 18.

[12] Sahagun, Hist. de Nueva España, MS., lib. 12, cap. 32.

[13] Ixtlilxochitl, in his Thirteenth Relation, embracing among other things a brief notice of the capture of Mexico, of which an edition has been given to the world by the industrious Bustamante, bestows the credit of this exploit on Cortés himself. "En la capilla mayor donde estaba Huitzilopoxctli, que llegáron Cortés é Ixtlil-xuchitl á un tiempo, y ambos embistiéron con el ídolo. *Cortés cogió la máscara de oro que tenia puesta este idolo* con ciertas piedras preciosas que estaban engastadas en ella." Venida de los Esp., p. 29.

Here they were soon mingled with the allies, who choked up the way and who, catching the panic of the Spaniards, increased the confusion, while the eyes of the fugitives, blinded by the missiles that rained on them from the *azoteas*, were scarcely capable of distinguishing friend from foe. In vain Cortés endeavored to stay the torrent, and to restore order. His voice was drowned in the wild uproar, as he was swept away, like drift-wood, by the fury of the current.

All seemed to be lost;—when suddenly sounds were heard in an adjoining street, like the distant tramp of horses galloping rapidly over the pavement. They drew nearer and nearer, and a body of cavalry soon emerged on the great square. Though but a handful in number, they plunged boldly into the thick of the enemy. We have often had occasion to notice the superstitious dread entertained by the Indians of the horse and his rider. And, although the long residence of the cavalry in the capital had familiarized the natives, in some measure, with their presence, so long a time had now elapsed since they had beheld them, that all their former mysterious terrors revived in full force; and, when thus suddenly assailed in flank by the formidable apparition, they were seized with a panic, and fell into confusion. It soon spread to the leading files, and Cortés, perceiving his advantage, turned with the rapidity of lightning, and, at this time supported by his followers, succeeded in driving the enemy with some loss back into the inclosure.

It was now the hour of vespers, and, as night must soon overtake them, he made no further attempt to pursue his advantage. Ordering the trumpets, therefore, to sound a retreat, he drew off his forces in good order, taking with him the artillery, which had been abandoned in the square. The allies first went off the ground, followed by the Spanish infantry, while the rear was protected by the horse, thus reversing the order of march on their entrance. The Aztecs hung on the closing files, and though driven back by frequent charges of the cavalry, still followed in the distance, shooting off their ineffectual missiles, and filling the air with wild cries and howlings, like a herd of ravenous wolves disappointed of their prey. It was late before the army reached its quarters at Xoloc.[14]

Cortés had been well supported by Alvarado and Sandoval in this assault on the city; though neither of these commanders had penetrated the suburbs, deterred, perhaps, by the difficulties of the passage, which, in Alvarado's case, were greater than those presented to Cortés, from the greater number of breaches with which the dike in his quarter was intersected. Something was owing, too, to the want of brigantines, until Cortés supplied the deficiency by detaching half of his little navy to the support of his officers. Without their coöperation, however, the general

[14] "Los de Caballo revolvian sobre ellos, que siempre alanceaban, ó mataban algunos; é como la Calle era muy larga, hubo lugar de hacerce esto quatro, ó cinco veces. É aunque los Enemigos vian que recibian daño, venian los Perros tan rabiosos, en ninguna manera los podiamos detener, ni que nos dejassen de seguir." Rel. Terc de Cortés, ap. Lorenzana, p. 250.—Herrera, Hist. General, dec. 3, lib. 1, cap. 18.—Sahagun, Hist. de Nueva España, MS., lib. 2 cap. 32.—Oviedo, Hist. de las Ind. MS., lib. 33. cap. 23.

himself could not have advanced so far, nor, perhaps, have succeeded at all in setting foot within the city. The success of this assault spread consternation not only among the Mexicans, but their vassals, as they saw that the formidable preparations for defence were to avail little against the white man, who had so soon, in spite of them, forced his way into the very heart of the capital. Several of the neighboring places, in consequence, now showed a willingness to shake off their allegiance, and claimed the protection of the Spaniards. Among these, were the territory of Xochimilco, so roughly treated by the invaders, and some tribes of Otomies, a rude but valiant people, who dwelt on the western confines of the Valley.[15] Their support was valuable, not so much from the additional reinforcements which it brought, as from the greater security it gave to the army, whose outposts were perpetually menaced by these warlike barbarians.

The most important aid, which the Spaniards received at this time, was from Tezcuco, whose prince, Ixtlilxochitl, gathered the whole strength of his levies, to the number of fifty thousand, if we are to credit Cortés, and led them in person to the Christian camp. By the general's orders, they were distributed among the three divisions of the besiegers.[16]

Thus strengthened, Cortés prepared to make another attack upon the capital, and that before it should have time to recover from the former. Orders were given to his lieutenants on the other causeways, to march at the same time, and coöperate with him, as before, in the assault. It was conducted in precisely the same manner as on the previous entry, the infantry taking the van, and the allies and cavalry following. But, to the great dismay of the Spaniards, they found two thirds of the breaches restored to their former state, and the stones and other materials, with which they had been stopped, removed by the indefatigable enemy. They were again obliged to bring up the cannon, the brigantines ran alongside, and the enemy was dislodged, and driven from post to post, in the same manner as on the preceding attack. In short, the whole work was to be done over again. It was not till an hour after noon, that the army had won a footing in the suburbs.

Here their progress was not so difficult as before; for the buildings,

---

[15] The great mass of the Otomies were an untamed race, who roamed over the broad tracks of the plateau, far away to the north. But many of them, who found their way into the Valley, became blended with the Tezcucan, and even with the Tlascalan nation, making some of the best soldiers in their armies.

[16] "Istrisuchil, [Ixtlilxochitl,] que es de edad de veinte y tres, ó veinte y quatro años, muy esforzado, amado, y temido de todos." (Rel. Terc., de Cortés, ap. Lorenzana, p. 251). The greatest obscurity prevails among historians in respect to this prince, whom they seem to have confounded very often with his brother and predecessor on the throne of Tezcuco. It is rare, that either of them is mentioned by any other than his baptismal name of Hernando; and, if Herrera is correct in the assertion, that this name was assumed by both, it may explain in some degree the confusion. (Hist. General, dec. 3, lib. 1, cap. 18.) I have conformed in the main to the old Tezcucan chronicler, who gathered his account of his kinsman, as he tells us, from the records of his nation, and from the oral testimony of the contemporaries of the prince himself. Venida de los Esp., pp. 30, 31.

from the terraces of which they had experienced the most annoyance, had been swept away. Still it was only step by step that they forced a passage in face of the Mexican militia, who disputed their advance with the same spirit as before. Cortés, who would willingly have spared the inhabitants, if he could have brought them to terms, saw them with regret, as he says, thus desperately bent on a war of extermination. He conceived that there would be no way more likely to affect their minds, than by destroying at once some of the principal edifices, which they were accustomed to venerate as the pride and ornament of the city.[17]

Marching into the great square, he selected, as the first to be destroyed, the old palace of Axayacatl, his former barracks. The ample range of low buildings was, it is true, constructed of stone; but the interior, as well as the outworks, its turrets, and roofs, were of wood. The Spaniards, whose associations with the pile were of so gloomy a character, sprang to the work of destruction with a satisfaction, like that which the French mob may have felt in the demolition of the Bastile. Torches and firebrands were thrown about in all directions; the lower parts of the building were speedily on fire, which, running along the inflammable hangings and wood-work of the interior, rapidly spread to the second floor. There the element took freer range, and, before it was visible from without, sent up from every aperture and crevice a dense column of vapor, that hung like a funereal pall over the city. This was dissipated by a bright sheet of flame, which enveloped all the upper regions of the vast pile, till, the supporters giving way, the wide range of turreted chambers fell, amidst clouds of dust and ashes, with an appalling crash, that for a moment stayed the Spaniards in the work of devastation.

It was but for a moment. On the other side of the square, adjoining Montezuma's residence, were several buildings, as the reader is aware, appropriated to animals. One of these was now marked for destruction,—the House of Birds, filled with specimens of all the painted varieties which swarmed over the wide forests of Mexico. It was an airy and elegant building, after the Indian fashion, and, viewed in connection with its object, was undoubtedly a remarkable proof of refinement and intellectual taste in a barbarous monarch. Its light, combustible materials of wood and bamboo formed a striking contrast to the heavy stone edifices around it, and made it obviously convenient for the present purpose of the invaders. The torches were applied, and the fanciful structure was soon wrapped in flames, that sent their baleful splendors, far and wide, over city and lake. Its feathered inhabitants either perished in the fire, or those of stronger wing, bursting the burning lattice-work of the aviary, soared high into the air, and fluttering for a while over the devoted city, fled with loud screams to their native forests beyond the mountains.

[17] "Daban ocasion, y nos forzaban á que totalmente les destruyessemos. É de esta postrera tenia mas sentimiento, y me pesaba en el alma, y pensaba que forma ternia para los atemorizar, de manera, que viniessen en conocimiento de su yerro, y de el daño, que podian recibir de nosotros, y no hacia sinc quemalles, y derrocalles las Torres de sus Idolos, y sus Casas." Rel. Terc. de Cortés, ap. Lorenzana, p. 254.

The Aztecs gazed with inexpressible horror on this destruction of the venerable abode of their monarchs, and of the monuments of their luxury and splendor. Their rage was exasperated almost to madness, as they beheld their hated foes, the Tlascalans, busy in the work of desolation, and aided by the Tezcucans, their own allies, and not unfrequently their kinsmen. They vented their fury in bitter execrations, especially on the young prince Ixtlilxochitl, who, marching side by side with Cortés, took his full share in the dangers of the day. The warriors from the housetops poured the most opprobrious epithets on him, as he passed, denouncing him as a false-hearted traitor; false to his country and his blood,—reproaches not altogether unmerited, as his kinsman, who chronicles the circumstance, candidly confesses.[18] He gave little heed to their taunts, however, holding on his way with the dogged resolution of one true to the cause in which he was embarked; and, when he entered the great square, he grappled with the leader of the Aztec forces, wrenched a lance from his grasp, won by the latter from the Christians, and dealt him a blow with his mace, or *maquahuitl*, which brought him lifeless to the ground.[19]

The Spanish commander, having accomplished the work of destruction, sounded a retreat, sending on the Indian allies, who blocked up the way before him. The Mexicans, maddened by their losses, in wild transports of fury hung close on his rear, and, though driven back by the cavalry, still returned, throwing themselves desperately under the horses, striving to tear the riders from their saddles, and content to throw away their own lives for one blow at their enemy. Fortunately the greater part of their militia was engaged with the assailants on the opposite quarters of the city, but, thus crippled, they pushed the Spaniards under Cortés so vigorously, that few reached the camp that night without bearing on their bodies some token of the desperate conflict.[20]

On the following day, and indeed, on several days following, the general repeated his assaults with as little care for repose, as if he and his men had been made of iron. On one occasion he advanced some way down the street of Tacuba, in which he carried three of the bridges, desirous, if possible, to open a communication with Alvarado, posted on the contiguous causeway. But the Spaniards in that quarter had not penetrated beyond the suburbs, still impeded by the severe character of the ground, and wanting, it may be, somewhat of that fiery impetuosity, which the soldier feels, who fights under the eye of his chief.

In each of these assaults, the breaches were found more or less restored to their original state by the pertinacious Mexicans, and the materials,

[18] "Y desde las azoteas deshonrarle llamándole de traidor contra su patria y deudos, y otras razones pesadas, que á la verdad *á ellos les sobraba la razon;* mas Ixtlilxochitl callaba y peleaba, que mas estimaba la amistad y salud de los Cristianos, que todo esto." Venida de los Esp., p. 32.
[19] Ibid. p. 29.
[20] For the preceding pages relating to this second assault, see Rel. Terc. de Cortés, ap. Lorenzana, pp. 254-256,—Sahagun, Hist. de Nueva Esp., MS., lib. 12, cap. 33,—Oviedo, Hist. de las Ind., MS., lib. 33, cap. 24.—Defensa, MS., cap. 28.

which had been deposited in them with so much labor, again removed. It may seem strange, that Cortés did not take measures to guard against the repetition of an act which caused so much delay and embarrassment to his operations. He notices this in his Letter to the Emperor, in which he says, that to do so would have required, either that he should have established his quarters in the city itself, which would have surrounded him with enemies, and cut off his communications with the country; or that he should have posted a sufficient guard of Spaniards—for the natives were out of the question—to protect the breaches by night, a duty altogether beyond the strength of men engaged in so arduous service through the day.[21]

Yet this was the course adopted by Alvarado; who stationed, at night, a guard of forty soldiers for the defence of the opening nearest to the enemy. This was relieved by a similar detachment, in a few hours, and this again by a third, the two former still lying on their post; so that, on an alarm, a body of one hundred and twenty soldiers was ready on the spot to repel an attack. Sometimes, indeed, the whole division took up their bivouac in the neighborhood of the breach, resting on their arms, and ready for instant action.[22]

But a life of such incessant toil and vigilance was almost too severe even for the stubborn constitutions of the Spaniards. "Through the long night," exclaims Diaz, who served in Alvarado's division, "we kept our dreary watch; neither wind, nor wet, nor cold availing anything. There we stood, smarting, as we were, from the wounds we had received in the fight of the preceding day." [23] It was the rainy season, which continues in that country from July to September; and the surface of the causeways, flooded by the storms, and broken up by the constant movement of such large bodies of men, was converted into a marsh, or rather quagmire, which added inconceivably to the distresses of the army.

The troops under Cortés were scarcely in a better situation. But few of them could find shelter in the rude towers that garnished the works of Xoloc. The greater part were compelled to bivouac in the open air, exposed to all the inclemency of the weather. Every man, unless his wounds prevented it, was required by the camp regulations to sleep on his arms; and they were often roused from their hasty slumbers by the midnight call to battle. For Guatemozin, contrary to the usual practice of his countrymen, frequently selected the hours of darkness to aim a blow at

[21] Rel. Terc., ap. Lorenzana, p. 259.

[22] Bernal Diaz, Hist. de la Conquista, cap. 151.

According to Herrera, Alvarado and Sandoval did not conceal their disapprobation of the course pursued by their commander in respect to the breaches. "I Alvarado, i Sandoval, por su parte, tambien lo hiciéron mui bien, culpando á Hernando Cortés por estas retiradas, queriendo muchos que se quedara en lo ganado, por no bolver tantas veces á ello." Hist. General, dec. 3, lib. 1, cap. 19.

[23] "Porque como era de noche, no aguardauan mucho, y desta manera que he dicho velauamos, que ni porque llouiesse, ni vientos, ni frios, y aunque estauamos metidos en medio de grandes lodos, y heridos, allí auiamos de estar." Hist. de la Conquista, cap. 151.

the enemy. "In short," exclaims the veteran soldier above quoted, "so unintermitting were our engagements, by day and by night, during the three months in which we lay before the capital, that to recount them all would but exhaust the reader's patience, and make him to fancy he was perusing the incredible feats of a knight-errant of romance." [24]

The Aztec emperor conducted his operations on a systematic plan, which showed some approach to military science. He not unfrequently made simultaneous attacks on the three several divisions of the Spaniards established on the causeways, and on the garrisons at their extremities. To accomplish this, he enforced the service not merely of his own militia of the capital, but of the great towns in the neighborhood, who all moved in concert, at the well-known signal of the beacon-fire, or of the huge drum struck by the priests on the summit of the temple. One of these general attacks, it was observed, whether from accident or design, took place on the eve of St. John the Baptist, the anniversary of the day on which the Spaniards made their second entry into the Mexican capital.[25]

Notwithstanding the severe drain on his forces by this incessant warfare, the young monarch contrived to relieve them in some degree by different detachments, who took the place of one another. This was apparent from the different uniforms and military badges of the Indian battalions, who successively came, and disappeared from the field. At night a strict guard was maintained in the Aztec quarters, a thing not common with the nations of the plateau. The outposts of the hostile armies were stationed within sight of each other. That of the Mexicans was usually placed in the neighborhood of some wide breach, and its position was marked by a large fire in front. The hours for relieving guard were intimated by the shrill Aztec whistle, while bodies of men might be seen moving behind the flame, which threw a still ruddier glow over the cinnamon-colored skins of the warriors.

While thus active on land, Guatemozin was not idle on the water. He was too wise, indeed, to cope with the Spanish navy again in open battle; but he resorted to stratagem, so much more congenial to Indian warfare. He placed a large number of canoes in ambuscade among the tall reeds which fringed the southern shores of the lake, and caused piles, at the same time, to be driven into the neighboring shallows. Several *piraguas,* or boats of a larger size, then issued forth, and rowed near the spot where the Spanish brigantines were moored. Two of the smallest vessels, supposing the Indian barks were conveying provisions to the besieged, instantly stood after them, as had been foreseen. The Aztec boats fled for shelter to the reedy thicket, where their companions lay in ambush. The Spaniards, following, were soon entangled among the palisades under the

[24] "Porque nouenta y tres dias estuuímos sobre esta tan fuerte ciudad, cada dia é de noche teniamos guerras, y combates; é no lo pongo aquí por capítulos lo que cada dia haziamos, porque me parece que seria gran proligidad, é seria cosa para nunca acabar, y pareceria á los libros de Amadis, é de otros corros de caualleros." Ibid., ubi supra.

[25] Ibid., ubi supra.—Sahagun, Hist. de Nueva Esp., MS., lib. 12. cap. 33.

water. They were instantly surrounded by the whole swarm of Indian canoes, most of the men were wounded, several, including the two commanders, slain, and one of the brigantines fell—a useless prize—into the hands of the victors. Among the slain was Pedro Barba, captain of the crossbow-men, a gallant officer, who had highly distinguished himself in the Conquest. This disaster occasioned much mortification to Cortés. It was a salutary lesson, that stood him in good stead during the remainder of the war.[26]

Thus the contest was waged by land and by water,—on the causeway, the city, and the lake. Whatever else might fail, the capital of the Aztec empire was true to itself; and, mindful of its ancient renown, opposed a bold front to its enemies in every direction. As in a body, whose extremities have been struck with death, life still rallied in the heart, and seemed to beat there, for the time, with even a more vigorous pulsation than ever.

It may appear extraordinary, that Guatemozin should have been able to provide for the maintenance of the crowded population now gathered in the metropolis, especially as the avenues were all in the possession of the besieging army.[27] But, independently of the preparations made with this view before the siege, and of the loathsome sustenance daily furnished by the victims for sacrifice, supplies were constantly obtained from the surrounding country across the lake. This was so conducted, for a time, as, in a great measure, to escape observation; and even when the brigantines were commanded to cruise day and night, and sweep the waters of the boats employed in this service, many still contrived, under cover of the darkness, to elude the vigilance of the cruisers, and brought their cargoes into port. It was not till the great towns in the neighborhood cast off their allegiance, that the supply began to fail, from the failure of its sources. This defection was more frequent, as the inhabitants became convinced that the government, incompetent to its own defence, must be still more so to theirs; and the Aztec metropolis saw its great vassals fall off, one after another, as the tree, over which decay is stealing, parts with its leaves at the first blast of the tempest.[28]

The cities, which now claimed the Spanish general's protection, supplied the camp with an incredible number of warriors; a number, which, if we admit Cortés' own estimate, one hundred and fifty thousand,[29] could have only served to embarrass his operations on the long extended causeways. Yet it is true, that the Valley, teeming with towns and villages, swarmed with a population—and one, too, in which every man

---

[26] Ibid., loc. cit.—Sahagun, Hist. de Nueva Esp., MS., lib. 12, cap. 34.

[27] I recollect meeting with no estimate of their numbers; nor, in the loose arithmetic of the Conquerors, would it be worth much. They must, however, have been very great, to enable them to meet the assailants so promptly and efficiently on every point.

[28] Defensa, MS., cap. 28.—Sahagun, Hist. de Nueva Esp., MS., lib. 12, cap. 34.

The principal cities were Mexicaltzinco, Cuitlahuac, Iztapalapan, Mizquiz, Huitzilopochco, Colhuacan.

[29] "Y como aquel dia llevabamos mas de ciento y cincuenta mil Hombres de Guerra." Rel. Terc., ap. Lorenzana, p. 280.

was a warrior—greatly exceeding that of the present day. These levies were distributed among the three garrisons at the terminations of the causeways; and many found active employment in foraging the country for provisions, and yet more in carrying on hostilities against the places still unfriendly to the Spaniards.

Cortés found further occupation for them in the construction of barracks for his troops, who suffered greatly from exposure to the incessant rains of the season, which were observed to fall more heavily by night than by day. Quantities of stone and timber were obtained from the buildings that had been demolished in the city. They were transported in the brigantines to the causeway, and from these materials a row of huts or barracks was constructed, extending on either side of the works of Xoloc. It may give some idea of the great breadth of the causeway at this place, one of the deepest parts of the lake, to add, that, although the barracks were erected in parallel lines on the opposite sides of it, there still remained space enough for the army to defile between.[30]

By this arrangement, ample accommodations were furnished for the Spanish troops and their Indian attendants, amounting in all to about two thousand. The great body of the allies, with a small detachment of horse and infantry, were quartered at the neighboring post of Cojohuacan, which served to protect the rear of the encampment, and to maintain its communications with the country. A similar disposition of forces took place in the other divisions of the army, under Alvarado and Sandoval, though the accommodations provided for the shelter of the troops on their causeways were not so substantial as those for the division of Cortés.

The Spanish camp was supplied with provisions from the friendly towns in the neighborhood, and especially from Tezcuco.[31] They consisted of fish, the fruits of the country, particularly a sort of fig borne by the *tuna*, (*cactus opuntia*,) and a species of cherry, or something much resembling it, which grew abundant at this season. But their principal food was the tortillas, cakes of Indian meal, still common in Mexico, for which bakehouses were established, under the care of the natives, in the garrison towns commanding the causeways.[32] The allies, as appears too

---

[30] "Y vea Vuestra Magestad," says Cortés to the Emperor, "que tan ancha puede ser la Calzada, que va por lo mas hondo de la Laguna, que de la una parte, y de la otra iban estas Casas, y quedaba en medio hecha Calle, que muy á placer á pie, y á caballo ibamos, y veniamos por ella." Ibid., p. 260.

[31] The greatest difficulty, under which the troops labored, according to Diaz, was that of obtaining the requisite medicaments for their wounds. But this was in a great degree obviated by a Catalan soldier, who, by virtue of his prayers and incantations, wrought wonderful cures both on the Spaniards, and their allies. The latter, as the more ignorant, flocked in crowds to the tent of this military Æsculapius, whose success was doubtless in a direct ratio to the faith of his patients. Hist. de la Conquista, ubi supra.

[32] Diaz mourns over this unsavory diet. (Ibid., loc. cit.) Yet the Indian fig is an agreeable, nutritious fruit; and the *tortilla*, made of maize flour, with a slight infusion of lime, though not precisely a *morceau friand*, might pass for very tolerable camp fare. According to the lively Author of "Life in. Mexico," it is made now, precisely as it was in the days of the Aztecs.—If so, a cooking receipt is almost the only thing that has not changed in this country of revolutions.

probable, reinforced their frugal fare with an occasional banquet on human flesh, for which the battle-field unhappily afforded them too much facility, and which, however shocking to the feelings of Cortés, he did not consider himself in a situation, at that moment, to prevent.[33]

Thus the tempest, which had been so long mustering, broke, at length, in all its fury, on the Aztec capital. Its unhappy inmates beheld the hostile legions encompassing them about, with their glittering files stretching as far as the eye could reach. They saw themselves deserted by their allies and vassals in their utmost need; the fierce stranger penetrating into their secret places, violating their temples, plundering their palaces, wasting the fair city by day, firing its suburbs by night, and intrenching himself in solid edifices under their walls, as if determined never to withdraw his foot while one stone remained upon another. All this they saw, yet their spirits were unbroken; and, though famine and pestilence were beginning to creep over them, they still showed the same determined front to their enemies. Cortés, who would gladly have spared the town and its inhabitants, beheld this resolution with astonishment. He intimated more than once, by means of the prisoners whom he released, his willingness to grant them fair terms of capitulation. Day after day, he fully expected his proffers would be accepted. But day after day he was disappointed [34] He had yet to learn how tenacious was the memory of the Aztecs; and that, whatever might be the horrors of their present situation, and their fears for the future, they were all forgotten in their hatred of the white man.

[33] "Quo strages," says Martyr, "erat crudelior, eo magis copisoe ac opipare cœnabant Guazuzingui & Tascaltecani, cæterique prouinciales auxiliarii, qui soliti sunt hostes in prœlio cadentes intra suos ventres sepelire; nec vetare ausus fuisset Cortesius." (De Orbe Novo, dec. 5, cap. 8). "Y los otros les mostraban los de su Ciudad hechos pedazos, diciéndoles, que los habian de cenar aquella noche, y almorzar otro dia, como de hecho lo hacian." (Rel. Terc. de Cortés, ap. Lorenzana, p. 256.) Yet one may well be startled by the assertion of Oviedo, that the carniverous monsters fished up the bloated bodies of those drowned in the lake to swell their repast! "Ni podian ver los ojos de los Christianos, é Cathólicos, mas espantable é aborrecida cosa, que ver en el Real de los Amigos confederados el continuo exercicio de comer carne asada, ó cocida de los Indios enemigos, é aun de los que mataban en las canoas, ó se ahogaban, é despues, el agua los echaba en la superficie de la laguna, ó en la costa, no los dexaban de pescar, é aposentar en sus vientres." Hist. de las Ind., MS., lib. 33, cap. 24.

[34] "Y sin duda el dia pasado, y aqueste yo tenia por cierto, que vinieran de Paz, de la qual yo siempre con Victoria, y sin ella hacia todas las muestras, que podia. Y nunca por esso en ellos hallabamos alguna señal de Paz." Rel. Terc. de Cortés, ap. Lorenzana, p. 261.

CHAPTER VI

GENERAL ASSAULT ON THE CITY—DEFEAT OF THE SPANIARDS—THEIR
DISASTROUS CONDITION—SACRIFICE OF THE CAPTIVES—DEFEC-
TION OF THE ALLIES—CONSTANCY OF THE TROOPS

1521

FAMINE was now gradually working its way into the heart of the beleaguered city. It seemed certain, that, with this strict blockade, the
crowded population must in the end be driven to capitulate, though no
arm should be raised against them. But it required time; and the Spaniards, though constant and enduring by nature, began to be impatient of
hardships scarcely inferior to those experienced by the besieged. In some
respects their condition was even worse, exposed, as they were, to the
cold, drenching rains, which fell with little intermission, rendering their
situation dreary and disastrous in the extreme.

In this state of things, there were many who would willingly have
shortened their sufferings, and taken the chance of carrying the place by
a *coup de main*. Others thought it would be best to get possession of the
great market of Tlatelolco, which, from its situation in the north-western
part of the city, might afford the means of communication with the
camps of both Alvarado and Sandoval. This place, encompassed by spacious porticos, would furnish accommodations for a numerous host; and,
once established in the capital, the Spaniards would be in a position to
follow up the blow with far more effect than at a distance.

These arguments were pressed by several of the officers, particularly
by Alderete, the royal treasurer, a person of much consideration, not only
from his rank, but from the capacity and zeal he had shown in the service.
In deference to their wishes, Cortés summoned a council of war, and laid
the matter before it. The treasurer's views were espoused by most of the
high-mettled cavaliers, who looked with eagerness to any change of their
present forlorn and wearisome life; and Cortés, thinking it, probably,
more prudent to adopt the less expedient course, than to enforce a cold
and reluctant obedience to his own opinion, suffered himself to be overruled.[1]

A day was fixed for the assault, which was to be made simultaneously

---

[1] Such is the account explicitly given by Cortés to the Emperor. (Rel. Terc., ap
Lorenzana, p. 264.) Bernal Diaz, on the contrary, speaks of the assault as first
conceived by the general himself. (Hist. de la Conquista, cap. 151.) Yet Diaz had
not the best means of knowing; and Cortés would hardly have sent home a palpable misstatement that could have been so easily exposed.

by the two divisions under Alvarado and the commander-in-chief. Sando-val was instructed to draw off the greater part of his forces from the northern causeway, and to unite himself with Alvarado, while seventy picked soldiers were to be detached to the support of Cortés.

On the appointed morning, the two armies, after the usual celebration of mass, advanced along their respective causeways against the city.[2] They were supported, in addition to the brigantines, by a numerous fleet of Indian boats, which were to force a passage up the canals, and by a countless multitude of allies, whose very numbers served in the end to embarrass their operations. After clearing the suburbs, three avenues presented themselves, which all terminated in the square of Tlatelolco. The principal one, being of much greater width than the other two, might rather be called a causeway than a street, since it was flanked by deep canals on either side. Cortés divided his force into three bodies. One of them he placed under Alderete, with orders to occupy the principal street. A second he gave in charge to Andres de Tapia and Jorge de Alva-rado; the former a cavalier of courage and capacity, the latter, a younger brother of Don Pedro, and possessed of the intrepid spirit which belonged to that chivalrous family. These were to penetrate by one of the parallel streets, while the general himself, at the head of the third division, was to occupy the other. A small body of cavalry, with two or three field-pieces, was stationed as a reserve in front of the great street of Tacuba, which was designated as the rallying point for the different divisions.[3]

Cortés gave the most positive instructions to his captains, not to ad-vance a step without securing the means of retreat, by carefully filling up the ditches, and the openings in the causeway. The neglect of this pre-caution by Alvarado, in an assault which he had made on the city but a few days before, had been attended with such serious consequences to his army, that Cortés rode over, himself, to his officer's quarters, for the purpose of publicly reprimanding him for his disobedience of orders. On his arrival at the camp, however, he found that his offending captain had conducted the affair with so much gallantry, that the intended repri-mand—though well deserved—subsided into a mild rebuke.[4]

The arrangements being completed, the three divisions marched at

[2] This punctual performance of mass by the army, in storm and in sunshine, by day and by night, among friends and enemies, draws forth a warm eulogium from the archiepiscopal editor of Cortés. "En el Campo, en una Calzada, entre Enemigos, trabajando dia, y noche nunca se omitia la Missa, páraque toda la obra se atrib-uyesse á Dios, y mas en unos Meses, en que incomodan las Agua las Habitaciones, ó malas Tiendas." Lorenzana, p 266, nota.

[3] In the treasurer's division, according to the general's Letter, there were 70 Span-ish foot, 7 or 8 horse, and 15,000 or 20,000 Indians; in Tapia's, 80 foot, and 10,000 allies, and in his own, 8 horse, 100 infantry, and "an infinite number of allies." (Ibid., ubi supra.) The looseness of the language shows that a few thou-sands, more or less, were of no great moment in the estimate of the Indian forces.

[4] "Otro dia de mañana acordé de ir á su Real para le reprehender lo pasador. . . . . . Y visto, no les imputé tanta culpa, como antes parecia tener, y platicado cerca de lo que habia de hacer, yo me bolví á nuestro Real aquel dia." Ibid., pp. 263, 264.

once up the several streets. Cortés, dismounting, took the van of his own squadron, at the head of his infantry. The Mexicans fell back as he advanced, making less resistance than usual. The Spaniards pushed on, carrying one barricade after another, and carefully filling up the gaps with rubbish, so as to secure themselves a footing. The canoes supported the attack, by moving along the canals, and grappling with those of the enemy; while numbers of the nimble-footed Tlascalans, scaling the terraces, passed on from one house to another, where they were connected, hurling the defenders into the streets below. The enemy, taken apparently by surprise, seemed incapable of withstanding for a moment the fury of the assault; and the victorious Christians, cheered on by the shouts of triumph which arose from their companions in the adjoining streets, were only the more eager to be first at the destined goal.

Indeed, the facility of his success led the general to suspect that he might be advancing too fast; that it might be a device of the enemy to draw them into the heart of the city, and then surround or attack them in the rear. He had some misgivings, moreover, lest his too ardent officers, in the heat of the chase, should, notwithstanding his commands, have overlooked the necessary precaution of filling up the breaches. He, accordingly, brought his squadron to a halt, prepared to baffle any insidious movement of his adversary. Meanwhile he received more than one message from Alderete, informing him that he had nearly gained the market. This only increased the general's apprehension, that, in the rapidity of his advance, he might have neglected to secure the ground. He determined to trust no eyes but his own, and, taking a small body of troops, proceeded at once to reconnoitre the route followed by the treasurer.

He had not proceeded far along the great street, or causeway, when his progress was arrested by an opening ten or twelve paces wide, and filled with water, at least two fathoms deep, by which a communication was formed between the canals on the opposite sides. A feeble attempt had been made to stop the gap with the rubbish of the causeway, but in too careless a manner to be of the least service; and a few straggling stones and pieces of timber only showed that the work had been abandoned almost as soon as begun.[5] To add to his consternation, the general observed that the sides of the causeway in this neighborhood had been pared off, and, as was evident, very recently. He saw in all this the artifice of the cunning enemy; and had little doubt that his hot-headed officer had rushed into a snare deliberately laid for him. Deeply alarmed, he set about repairing the mischief as fast as possible, by ordering his men to fill up the yawning chasm.

But they had scarcely begun their labors, when the hoarse echoes of

---

[5] "Y hallé, que habian pasado una quebrada de la Calle, que era de diez, ó doce pasos de ancho; y el Agua, que por ella pasaba, era de hondura de mas de dos estados, y al tiempo que la pasáron habian echado en ella madera, y cañas de carrizo, y como pasaban pocos á pocos, y con tiento, no se habia hundido la madera y cañas." Ibid., p. 268.—See also Oviedo, Hist. de las Ind., MS., lib. 33, cap. 48.

conflict in the distance were succeeded by a hideous sound of mingled yells and war-whoops, that seemed to rend the very heavens. This was followed by a rushing noise, as of the tread of thronging multitudes, showing that the tide of battle was turned back from its former course, and was rolling on towards the spot where Cortés and his little band of cavaliers were planted.

His conjecture proved too true. Alderete had followed the retreating Aztecs with an eagerness which increased with every step of his advance. He had carried the barricades, which had defended the breach, without much difficulty, and, as he swept on, gave orders that the opening should be stopped. But the blood of the high-spirited cavaliers was warmed by the chase, and no one cared to be detained by the ignoble occupation of filling up the ditches, while he could gather laurels so easily in the fight; and they all pressed on, exhorting and cheering one another with the assurance of being the first to reach the square of Tlatelolco. In this way they suffered themselves to be decoyed into the heart of the city; when suddenly the horn of Guatemozin—the sacred symbol, heard only in seasons of extraordinary peril—sent forth a long and piercing note from the summit of a neighboring *teocalli*. In an instant, the flying Aztecs, as if maddened by the blast, wheeled about, and turned on their pursuers. At the same time, countless swarms of warriors from the adjoining streets and lanes poured in upon the flanks of the assailants, filling the air with the fierce, unearthly cries which had reached the ears of Cortés, and drowning, for a moment, the wild dissonance which reigned in the other quarters of the capital.[6]

The army, taken by surprise, and shaken by the fury of the assault, were thrown into the utmost disorder. Friends and foes, white men and Indians, were mingled together in one promiscuous mass. Spears, swords, and war-clubs were brandished together in the air. Blows fell at random. In their eagerness to escape, they trod down one another. Blinded by the missiles, which now rained on them from the *azoteas*, they staggered on, scarcely knowing in what direction, or fell, struck down by hands which they could not see. On they came like a rushing torrent sweeping along some steep declivity, and rolling in one confused tide towards the open breach, on the further side of which stood Cortés and his companions, horror-struck at the sight of the approaching ruin. The foremost files soon plunged into the gulf, treading one another under the flood, some striving ineffectually to swim, others, with more success, to clamber over the heaps of their suffocated comrades. Many, as they attempted to scale

[6] Gomara, Crónica, cap. 138.—Ixtlilxochitl, Venida de los Esp., p. 37.—Oviedo, Hist. de las Ind., MS., lib. 33, cap. 26.

Guatemozin's horn rung in the ears of Bernal Diaz, for many a day after the battle. "Guatemuz y manda tocar su corneta, q̃ era vna señal q̃ quando aquella se tocasse, era q̃ auian de pelear sus Capitanes de manera, q̃ hiziessen presa, ó morir sobre ello; y retumbaua el sonido, q̃ se metia en los oidos, y de q̃ lo oyérõ aquellos sus esquadrones, y Capitanes: saber yo aqui dezir aora, con q̃ ra bia, y esfuerço se metian entre nosotros á nos echar mano, es cosa de espanto." Hist. de la Conquista, cap. 152.

the opposite sides of the slippery dike, fell into the water, or were hurried off by the warriors in the canoes, who added to the horrors of the
rout by the fresh storm of darts and javelins, which they poured on the
fugitives.

Cortés, meanwhile, with his brave followers, kept his station undaunted on the other side of the breach. "I had made up my mind," he says,
"to die, rather than desert my poor followers in their extremity!" [7] With
outstretched hands he endeavored to rescue as many as he could from
the watery grave, and from the more appalling fate of captivity. He as
vainly tried to restore something like presence of mind and order among
the distracted fugitives. His person was too well known to the Aztecs,
and his position now made him a conspicuous mark for their weapons.
Darts, stones, and arrows fell around him thick as hail, but glanced
harmless from his steel helmet and armor of proof. At length a cry of
"Malinche," "Malinche," arose among the enemy; and six of their number, strong and athletic warriors, rushing on him at once, made a violent
effort to drag him on board their boat. In the struggle he received a
severe wound in the leg, which, for the time, disabled it. There seemed
to be no hope for him; when a faithful follower, Christóval de Olea, perceiving his general's extremity, threw himself on the Aztecs, and with a
blow cut off the arm of one savage, and then plunged his sword in the
body of another. He was quickly supported by a comrade named Lerma,
and by a Tlascalan chief, who, fighting over the prostrate body of Cortés, despatched three more of the assailants, though the heroic Olea paid
dearly for his self-devotion, as he fell mortally wounded by the side of
his general.[8]

[7] "É como el negocio fué tan de súpito, y ví que mataban la Gente, determiné
de me quedar allí, y morir peleando." Rel. Terc. ap. Lorenzana, p. 268.

[8] Ixtlilxochitl, who would fain make his royal kinsman a sort of residuary legatee
for all unappropriated, or even doubtful, acts of heroism, puts in a sturdy claim
for him on this occasion. A painting, he says, on one of the gates of a monastery
of Tlatelolco, long recorded the fact, that it was the Tezcucan chief who saved the
life of Cortés (Venida de los Esp., p. 38.) But Camargo gives the full credit of it
to Olea, on the testimony of "a famous Tlascalan warrior," present in the action,
who reported it to him. (Hist. de Tlascala, MS.) The same is stoutly maintained by
Bernal Diaz, the townsman of Olea, to whose memory he pays a hearty tribute, as
one of the best men and bravest soldiers in the army. (Hist. de la Conquista, cap.
152, 204.) Saavedra, the poetic chronicler,—something more of chronicler than
poet,—who came on the stage before all that had borne arms in the Conquest had
left it, gives the laurel also to Olea, whose fate he commemorates in verses, that, at
least, aspire to historic fidelity.

> "Túvole con las manos abraçado,
> Y Francisco de Olea el valeroso,
> Vn valiente Español, y su criado,
> Le tiró vn tajo brauo y riguroso:
> Las dos manos á cercen le ha cortado
> Y él le libró del trance trabajoso.
> Huuo muy gran rumor, porque dezian,
> Que ya en prision amarga le tenian.
>
> "Llegáron otros Indios arriscados,

The report soon spread among the soldiers, that their commander was taken; and Quiñones, the captain of his guard, with several others, pouring in to the rescue, succeeded in disentangling Cortés from the grasp of his enemies who were struggling with him in the water, and, raising him in their arms, placed him again on the causeway. One of his pages, meanwhile, had advanced some way through the press, leading a horse for his master to mount. But the youth received a wound in the throat from a javelin, which prevented him from effecting his object. Another of his attendants was more successful. It was Guzman, his chamberlain; but, as he held the bridle, while Cortés was assisted into the saddle, he was snatched away by the Aztecs, and, with the swiftness of thought, hurried off by their canoes. The general still lingered, unwilling to leave the spot, while his presence could be of the least service. But the faithful Quiñones, taking his horse by the bridle, turned his head from the breach, exclaiming, at the same time, that "his master's life was too important to the army to be thrown away there." [9]

Yet it was no easy matter to force a passage through the press. The surface of the causeway, cut up by the feet of men and horses, was knee-deep in mud, and in some parts was so much broken, that the water from the canals flowed over it. The crowded mass, in their efforts to extricate themselves from their perilous position, staggered to and fro like a drunken man. Those on the flanks were often forced by the lateral pressure of their comrades down the slippery sides of the dike, where they were picked up by the canoes of the enemy, whose shouts of triumph proclaimed the savage joy with which they gathered in every new victim for the sacrifice. Two cavaliers, riding by the general's side, lost their footing, and rolled down the declivity into the water. One was taken and his horse killed. The other was happy enough to escape. The valiant ensign, Corral, had a similar piece of good fortune. He slipped into the canal, and the enemy felt sure of their prize, when he again succeeded in recovering the causeway with the tattered banner of Castile still flying above his head. The barbarians set up a cry of disappointed rage, as they lost possession of a trophy, to which the people of Anahuac attached, as we have seen, the highest importance, hardly inferior in their eyes to the capture of the commander-in-chief himself.[10]

> Y á Olea matáron en vn punto,
> Cercáron á Cortés por todos lados,
> Y al miserable cuerpo ya difunto:
> Y viendo sus sentidos recobrados,
> Puso mano á la espada y daga junto.
> Antonio de Quiñones llegó luego,
> Capitan de la guarda ardiendo en fuego."
>   EL PEREGRINO INDIANO, Canto 20.

[9] "É aquel Capitan que estaba con el General, que se decia Antonio de Quiñones, díxole: Vamos, Señor, de aquí, y salvemos vuestra Persona, pues que ya esto está de manera, que es morir desperado atender; é sin vos, ninguno de nosotros puede escapar, que no es esfuerzo, sino poquedad, porfiar aquí otra cosa." Oviedo, Hist. de las Ind., MS., lib. 33, cap. 26.

[10] It may have been the same banner which is noticed by Mr. Bullock, as treas-

Cortés at length succeeded in regaining the firm ground, and reaching the open place before the great street of Tacuba. Here, under a sharp fire of the artillery, he rallied his broken squadrons, and, charging at the head of the little body of horse, which, not having been brought into action, were still fresh, he beat off the enemy. He then commanded the retreat of the two other divisions. The scattered forces again united; and the general, sending forward his Indian confederates, took the rear with a chosen body of cavalry to cover the retreat of the army, which was effected with but little additional loss.[11]

Andres de Tapia was despatched to the western causeway to acquaint Alvarado and Sandoval with the failure of the enterprise. Meanwhile the two captains had penetrated far into the city. Cheered by the triumphant shouts of their countrymen in the adjacent streets, they had pushed on with extraordinary vigor, that they might not be outstripped in the race of glory. They had almost reached the market-place, which lay nearer to their quarters than to the general's, when they heard the blast from the dread horn of Guatemozin,[12] followed by the overpowering yell of the barbarians, which had so startled the ears of Cortés; till at length the sounds of the receding conflict died away in the distance. The two captains now understood that the day must have gone hard with their countrymen. They soon had further proof of it, when the victorious Aztecs, returning from the pursuit of Cortés, joined their forces to those engaged with Sandoval and Alvarado, and fell on them with redoubled fury. At the same time they rolled on the ground two or three of the bloody heads of the Spaniards, shouting the name of "Malinche." The captains, struck with horror at the spectacle,—though they gave little credit to the words of the enemy,—instantly ordered a retreat. Indeed, it was not in their power to maintain their ground against the furious assaults of the besieged, who poured on them, swarm after swarm, with a desperation, of which, says one who was there, "although it seems as if it were now present to my eyes, I can give but a faint idea to the reader, God alone could have brought us off safe from the perils of that day."[13]

ured up in the Hospital of Jesus, "where," says he, "we beheld the identical embroidered standard, under which the great captain wrested this immense empire from the unfortunate Montezuma." Six Months in Mexico, vol. I, chap. 10.

[11] For this disastrous affair, besides the Letter of Cortés, and the Chronicle of Diaz, so often quoted, see Sahagun, Hist. de Nueva Esp., MS., lib. 12, cap. 33,—Camargo, Hist. de Tlascala, MS.,—Gomara, Crónica, cap. 138,—Torquemada, Monarch. Ind., lib. 4, cap. 94,—Oviedo, Hist. de las Ind., MS., lib. 33, cap. 26, 48.

[12] "El resonido de la corneta de Guatemuz."—Astolfo's magic horn was not more terrible.

> "Dico che 'l corno è di sì orribil suono,
> Ch' ovunque s' oda, fa fuggir la gente.
> Non può trovarsi al mondo un cor sì buono,
> Che possa non fuggir come lo sente.
> Rumor di vento e di tremuoto, e 'l tuono,
> A par del suon di questo, era niente."
> ORLANDO FURIOSO, Canto 15, st. 15.

[13] "Por q̃ yo lo sé aqui escriuir q̃ aora q̃ me pongo á pensar en ello, es como si visiblemente lo viesse, mas bueluo á dezir, y ansí es verdad, q̃ si Dios no nos diera

The fierce barbarians followed up the Spaniards to their very intrenchments. But here they were met, first by the cross fire of the brigantines,
which, dashing through the palisades planted to obstruct their movements, completely enfiladed the causeway, and next by that of the small
battery erected in front of the camp, which, under the management of a
skilful engineer, named Medrano, swept the whole length of the defile.
Thus galled in front and on flank, the shattered columns of the Aztecs
were compelled to give way and take shelter under the defences of the
city.

The greatest anxiety now prevailed in the camp, regarding the fate of
Cortés; for Tapia had been detained on the road by scattered parties of
the enemy, whom Guatemozin had stationed there to interrupt the communications between the camps. He arrived, at length, however, though
bleeding from several wounds. His intelligence, while it reassured the
Spaniards as to the general's personal safety, was not calculated to allay
their uneasiness in other respects.

Sandoval, in particular, was desirous to acquaint himself with the
actual state of things, and the further intentions of Cortés. Suffering as
he was from three wounds, which he had received in that day's fight, he
resolved to visit in person the quarters of the commander-in-chief. It was
mid-day,—for the busy scenes of the morning had occupied but a few
hours,—when Sandoval remounted the good steed, on whose strength
and speed he knew he could rely. It was a noble anmial, well-known
throughout the army, and worthy of its gallant rider, whom it had carried safe through all the long marches and bloody battles of the conquest.[14] On the way he fell in with Guatemozin's scouts, who gave him
chase, and showered around him volleys of missiles, which fortunately
found no vulnerable point in his own harness, or that of his well-barbed
charger.

On arriving at the camp, he found the troops there much worn and
dispirited by the disaster of the morning. They had good reason to be so.
Besides the killed, and a long file of wounded, sixty-two Spaniards, with
a multitude of allies, had fallen alive into the hands of the enemy,—an
enemy who was never known to spare a captive. The loss of two field-
pieces and seven horses crowned their own disgrace and the triumphs of
the Aztecs. This loss, so insignificant in European warfare, was a great
one here, where both horses and artillery, the most powerful arms of
war against the barbarians, were not to be procured without the greatest
cost and difficulty.[15]

esfuerço, segun estauamos todos heridos: él nos saluó q̃ de otra manera no nos
podiamos llegar á nuestros ranchos." Bernal Diaz, Hist. de la Conquista, cap. 152.

[14] This renowned steed, who might rival the Babieca of the Cid, was named
Motilla, and, when one would pass unqualified praise on a horse, he would say
"He is as good as Motilla." So says that prince of chroniclers, Diaz, who takes care
that neither beast nor man shall be defrauded of his fair guerdon in these campaigns
against the infidel. He was of a chestnut color, it seems, with a star in his forehead,
and, luckily for his credit, with only one foot white. See Hist. de la Conquista, cap.
152, 205.

[15] The cavaliers might be excused for not wantonly venturing their horses, if, as

Cortés, it was observed, had borne himself throughout this trying day with his usual intrepidity and coolness. The only time he was seen to falter was when the Mexicans threw down before him the heads of several Spaniards, shouting, at the same time, "Sandoval," "Tonatiuh," the well-known epithet of Alvarado. At the sight of the gory trophies, he grew deadly pale,—but, in a moment recovering his usual confidence, he endeavored to cheer up the drooping spirits of his followers. It was with a cheerful countenance, that he now received his lieutenant; but a shade of sadness was visible through this outward composure, showing how the catastrophe of the *puente cuidada*, "the sorrowful bridge," as he mournfully called it, lay heavy at his heart.

To the cavalier's anxious inquiries, as to the cause of the disaster, he replied: "It is for my sins, that it has befallen me, son Sandoval"; for such was the affectionate epithet with which Cortés often addressed his best-beloved and trusty officer. He then explained to him the immediate cause, in the negligence of the treasurer. Further conversation followed, in which the general declared his purpose to forego active hostilities for a few days. "You must take my place," he continued, "for I am too much crippled at present to discharge my duties. You must watch over the safety of the camps. Give especial heed to Alvarado's. He is a gallant soldier, I know it well; but I doubt the Mexican hounds may, some hour, take him at disadvantage."[16] These few words showed the general's own estimate of his two lieutenants; both equally brave and chivalrous; but the one uniting with these qualities the circumspection so essential to success in perilous enterprises, in which the other was signally deficient. The future conqueror of Guatemala had to gather wisdom, as usual, from the bitter fruits of his own errors. It was under the training of Cortés that he learned to be a soldier.—The general, having concluded his instructions, affectionately embraced his lieutenant, and dismissed him to his quarters.

It was late in the afternoon when he reached them; but the sun was still lingering above the western hills, and poured his beams wide over the Valley, lighting up the old towers and temples of Tenochtitlan with a mellow radiance, that little harmonized with the dark scenes of strife, in which the city had so lately been involved. The tranquillity of the hour, however, was, on a sudden, broken by the strange sounds of the great drum in the temple of the war-god,—sounds which recalled the *noche triste*, with all its terrible images, to the minds of the Spaniards,

---

Diaz asserts, they could only be replaced at an expense of eight hundred, or a thousand dollars apiece. "Porque costaua en aquella sazon vn cauallo ochocientos pesos, y aun algunos costauan á mas de mil." Hist. de la Conquista, cap. 151. See, also, Ante, Book II, chap. 3, note 14.

[16] "Mira pues veis que yo no puedo ir á todas partes, á vos os encomiendo estos trabajos, pues veis q̃ estoy herido y coxo; ruego os pongais cobro en estos tres reales; bien sé q̃ Pedro de Aluarado, y sus Capitanes, y soldados aurán batallado, y hecho como caualleros, mas temo el gran poder destos perros no les ayan desbaratado." Ibid., cap. 152.

for that was the only occasion on which they had ever heard them.[17] They intimated some solemn act of religion within the unhallowed precincts of the *teocalli*; and the soldiers, startled by the mournful vibrations, which might be heard for leagues across the Valley, turned their eyes to the quarter whence they proceeded. They there beheld a long procession winding up the huge sides of the pyramid; for the camp of Alvarado was pitched scarcely a mile from the city, and objects are distinctly visible, at a great distance, in the transparent atmosphere of the table-land.

As the long file of priests and warriors reached the flat summit of the *teocalli*, the Spaniards saw the figures of several men stripped to their waists, some of whom, by the whiteness of their skins, they recognised as their own countrymen. They were the victims for sacrifice. Their heads were gaudily decorated with coronals of plumes, and they carried fans in their hands. They were urged along by blows, and compelled to take part in the dances in honor of the Aztec war-god. The unfortunate captives, then stripped of their sad finery, were stretched, one after another, on the great stone of sacrifice. On its convex surface, their breasts heaved up conveniently for the diabolical purpose of the priestly executioner, who cut asunder the ribs by a strong blow with his sharp razor of *itztli*, and, thrusting his hand into the wound, tore away the heart, which, hot and reeking, was deposited on the golden censer before the idol. The body of the slaughtered victim was then hurled down the steep stairs of the pyramid, which, it may be remembered, were placed at the same angle of the pile, one flight below another; and the mutilated remains were gathered up by the savages beneath, who soon prepared with them the cannibal repast which completed the work of abomination! [18]

We may imagine with what sensations the stupefied Spaniards must have gazed on this horrid spectacle, so near that they could almost recognise the persons of their unfortunate friends, see the struggles and writhing of their bodies, hear—or fancy that they heard—their screams of agony! yet so far removed, that they could render them no assistance. Their limbs trembled beneath them, as they thought what might one day be their own fate; and the bravest among them, who had hith-

[17] "Vn atambor de muy triste sonido, enfin como instrumento de demonios, y retumbaua tanto, que se oia dos, ó tres leguas." Ibid., loc. cit.

[18] Ibid., ubi supra.—Oviedo, Hist. de las Ind., MS., lib. 33, cap. 48.

"Sacándoles los corazones, sobre una piedra que era como un pilar cortado, tan grueso como un hombre y algo mas, y tan alto como medio estadio; allí á cada uno echado de espaldas sobre aquella piedra, que se llama Techcatl, uno le tiraba por un brazo, y otro por el otro, y tambien por las piernas otros dos, y venia uno de aquellos Sátrapas, con un pedernal, como un hierro de lanza enhastado, en un palo de dos palmos de largo, le daba un golpe con ambas manos en el pecho; y sacando aquel pedernal, por la misma llaga metia la mano, y arrancábale el corazon, y luego fregaba con él la boca del Idolo; y echaba á rodar el cuerpo por las gradas abajo, que serian como cinquenta ó sesenta gradas, por allí abajo iba quebrando las piernas y los brazos, y dando cabezasos con la cabeza, *hasta que llegaba abajo aun vivo.*" Sahagun, Hist. de Nueva Esp., MS., lib. 12, cap. 35.

erto gone to battle, as careless and light-hearted, as to the banquet or the ball-room, were unable, from this time forward, to encounter their ferocious enemy without a sickening feeling, much akin to fear, coming over them.[19]

Such was not the effect produced by this spectacle on the Mexican forces, gathered at the end of the causeway. Like vultures maddened by the smell of distant carrion, they set up a piercing cry, and, as they shouted that "such should be the fate of all their enemies," swept along in one fierce torrent over the dike. But the Spaniards were not to be taken by surprise; and, before the barbarian horde had come within their lines, they opened such a deadly fire from their battery of heavy guns, supported by the musketry and crossbows, that the assailants were compelled to fall back slowly, but fearfully mangled, to their former position.

The five following days passed away in a state of inaction, except, indeed, so far as was necessary to repel the *sorties*, made from time to time, by the militia of the capital. The Mexicans, elated with their success, meanwhile, abandoned themselves to jubilee; singing, dancing, and feasting on the mangled relics of their wretched victims. Guatemozin sent several heads of the Spaniards, as well as of the horses, round the country, calling on his old vassals to forsake the banners of the white men, unless they would share the doom of the enemies of Mexico. The priests now cheered the young monarch and the people with the declaration, that the dread Huitzilopochtli, their offended deity, appeased by the sacrifices offered up on his altars, would again take the Aztecs under his protection, and deliver their enemies, before the expiration of eight days, into their hands.[20]

This comfortable prediction, confidently believed by the Mexicans, was thundered in the ears of the besieging army in tones of exultation and defiance. However it may have been contemned by the Spaniards, it had a very different effect on their allies. The latter had begun to be disgusted with a service so full of peril and suffering, and already pro-

---

[19] At least, such is the honest confession of Captain Diaz, as stout-hearted a soldier as any in the army. He consoles himself, however, with the reflection, that the tremor of his limbs intimated rather an excess of courage than a want of it, since it arose from a lively sense of the great dangers into which his daring spirit was about to hurry him! The passage in the original affords a good specimen of the inimitable *naïveté* of the old chronicler. "Digan agora todos aquellos caualleros, que desto del militar entienden, y se han hallado en trances peligrosos de muerte, á que fin echarán mi temor, si es á mucha flaqueza de ánimo, ó á mucho esfuerço, porque como he dicho, sentia yo en mi pensamiento, que auia de poner por mi persona, batallando en parte que por fuerça, auia de temer la muerte mas que otras vezes, y por esto me temblaua el coraçon, y temia la muerte." Hist. de la Conquista, cap. 156.

[20] Herrera, Hist. General, dec. 3, lib. 2, cap. 20.—Ixtlilxochitl, Venida de los Esp., pp. 41, 42.

"Y nos dezian, que de ai á ocho dias no auia de quedar ninguno de nosotros á vida, porque assí se lo auian prometido la noche antes sus Dioses." Bernal Diaz, Hist. de la Conquista, cap. 153.

tracted far beyond the usual term of Indian hostilities. They had less confidence than before in the Spaniards. Experience had shown that they were neither invincible nor immortal, and their recent reverses made them even distrust the ability of the Christans to reduce the Aztec metropolis. They recalled to mind the ominous words of Xicotencatl, that "so sacrilegious a war could come to no good for the people of Anahuac." They felt that their arm was raised against the gods of their country. The prediction of the oracle fell heavy on their hearts. They had little doubt of its fulfilment, and were only eager to turn away the bolt from their own heads by a timely secession from the cause.

They took advantage, therefore, of the friendly cover of night to steal away from their quarters. Company after company deserted in this manner, taking the direction of their respective homes. Those belonging to the great towns of the Valley, whose allegiance was the most recent, were the first to cast it off. Their example was followed by the older confederates, the militia of Cholula, Tepeaca, Tezcuco, and even the faithful Tlascala. There were, it is true, some exceptions to these, and, among them, Ixtlilxochitl, the young lord of Tezcuco, and Chichemecatl, the valiant Tlascalan chieftain, who, with a few of their immediate followers, still remained true to the banner under which they had enlisted. But their number was insignificant.—The Spaniards beheld with dismay the mighty array, on which they relied for support, thus silently melting away before the breath of superstition. Cortés alone maintained a cheerful countenance. He treated the prediction with contempt, as an invention of the priests, and sent his messengers after the retreating squadrons, beseeching them to postpone their departure, or at least to halt on the road, till the time, which would soon elapse, should show the falsehood of the prophecy.

The affairs of the Spaniards, at this crisis, must be confessed to have worn a gloomy aspect. Deserted by their allies, with their ammunition nearly exhausted, cut off from the customary supplies from the neighborhood, harassed by unintermitting vigils and fatigues, smarting under wounds, of which every man in the army had his share, with an unfriendly country in their rear, and a mortal foe in front, they might well be excused for faltering in their enterprise. They found abundant occupation by day in foraging the country, and in maintaining their position on the causeways against the enemy, now made doubly daring by success, and by the promises of their priests; while at night their slumbers were disturbed by the beat of the melancholy drum, the sounds of which, booming far over the waters, tolled the knell of their murdered comrades. Night after night fresh victims were led up to the great altar of sacrifice; and, while the city blazed with the illumination of a thousand bonfires on the terraced roofs of the dwellings, and in the areas of the temples, the dismal pageant, showing through the fiery glare like the work of the ministers of hell, was distinctly visible from the camp below. One of the last of the sufferers was Guzman, the unfortunate chamberlain of Cortés, who lingered in captivity eighteen days before he met his doom.[21]

Yet in this hour of trial the Spaniards did not falter. Had they faltered, they might have learned a lesson of fortitude from some of their own wives, who continued with them in the camp, and who displayed a heroism, on this occasion, of which history has preserved several examples. One of these, protected by her husband's armor, would frequently mount guard in his place, when he was wearied. Another, hastily putting on a soldier's *escaupil*, and seizing a sword and lance, was seen, on one occasion, to rally their retreating countrymen, and lead them back against the enemy. Cortés would have persuaded these Amazonian dames to remain at Tlascala; but they proudly replied, "It was the duty of Castilian wives not to abandon their husbands in danger, but to share it with them, —and die with them, if necessary." And well did they do their duty.[22]

Amidst all the distresses and multiplied embarrassments of their situation, the Spaniards still remained true to their purpose. They relaxed in no degree the severity of the blockade. Their camps still occupied the only avenues to the city; and their batteries, sweeping the long defiles at every fresh assault of the Aztecs, mowed down hundreds of the assailants. Their brigantines still rode on the waters, cutting off the communication with the shore. It is true, indeed, the loss of the auxiliary canoes left a passage open for the occasional introduction of supplies to the capital.[23] But the whole amount of these supplies was small; and its crowded population, while exulting in their temporary advantage, and the delusive assurances of their priests, were beginning to sink under the withering grasp of an enemy within, more terrible than the one which lay before their gates.

[21] Sahagun, Hist. de Nueva Esp., MS., lib. 12, cap. 36.—Ixtlilxochitl, Venida de los Esp., pp. 41, 42.

The Castilian scholar will see that I have not drawn on my imagination for the picture of these horrors. "Digamos aora lo que los Mexicanos hazian de noche en sus grandes, y altos Cues; y es, q̃ tañian su maldito atambor, que dixe otra vez que era el de mas maldito sonido, y mas triste q̃ se podia inuétar, y sonaua muy lexos; y tañian otros peores instrumentos. En fin, cosas diabólicas, y teniã grandes lumbres, y dauã grãdíssimos gritos, y siluos, y en aquel instãte estauan sacrificando de nuestros cõpañeros, de los q̃ tomárõ á Cortés, que supímos q̃ sacrificáron diez dias arreo, hasta que los acabáron, y el postrero dexárõ á Christonal de Guzman, q̃ viuo lo tuuiéron diez y ocho dias, segun dixérõ tres Capitanes Mexicanos q̃ prẽdímos." Bernal Diaz, Hist. de la Conquista, cap. 153.

[22] "Que no era bien, que Mugeres Castellanas dexasen á sus Maridos, iendo á la Guerra, i que adonde ellos muriesen, moririan ellas." (Herrera, Hist. General, dec. 3, lib. 1, cap. 22.) The historian has embalmed the names of several of these heroines in his pages, who are, doubtless, well entitled to share the honors of the Conquest; Beatriz de Palacios, María de Estrada, Juana Martin, Isabel Rodriguez, and Beatriz Bermudez.

[23] Ibid, ubi supra.

CHAPTER VII

SUCCESSES OF THE SPANIARDS—FRUITLESS OFFERS TO GUATEMOZIN—
BUILDINGS RAZED TO THE GROUND—TERRIBLE FAMINE—THE
TROOPS GAIN THE MARKET-PLACE—BATTERING ENGINE

1521

THUS passed away the eight days prescribed by the oracle; and the sun, which rose upon the ninth, beheld the fair city still beset on every side by the inexorable foe. It was a great mistake of the Aztec priests,—one not uncommon with false prophets, anxious to produce a startling impression on their followers,—to assign so short a term for the fulfillment of their prediction.[1]

The Tezcucan and Tlascalan chiefs now sent to acquaint their troops with the failure of the prophecy, and to recall them to the Christian camp. The Tlascalans, who had halted on the way, returned, ashamed of their credulity, and with ancient feelings of animosity, heightened by the artifice of which they had been the dupes. Their example was followed by many of the other confederates, with the levity natural to a people whose convictions are the result, not of reason, but of superstition. In a short time the Spanish general found himself at the head of an auxiliary force, which, if not so numerous as before, was more than adequate to all his purposes. He received them with politic benignity; and, while he reminded them that they had been guilty of a great crime in thus abandoning their commander, he was willing to overlook it in consideration of their past services. They must be aware that these services were not necessary to the Spaniards, who had carried on the siege with the same vigor during their absence, as when they were present. But he was unwilling that those, who had shared the dangers of the war with him, should not also partake its triumphs, and be present at the fall of their enemy, which, he promised, with a confidence better founded than that of the priests in their prediction, should not be long delayed.

Yet the menaces and machinations of Guatemozin were still not without effect in the distant provinces. Before the full return of the confederates, Cortés received an embassy from Cuernavaca, ten or twelve leagues distant, and another from some friendly towns of the Otomies, still further off, imploring his protection against their formidable neigh-

[1] And yet the priests were not so much to blame, if, as Solís assures us, "the Devil went about very industriously in those days, insinuating into the ears of his flock, what he could not into their hearts." Conquista, lib. 5, cap. 22.

bors, who menaced them with hostilities, as allies of the Spaniards. As
the latter were then situated, they were in a condition to receive succour much more than to give it.[2] Most of the officers were accordingly
opposed to granting a request, the compliance with which must still further impair their diminished strength. But Cortés knew the importance,
above all, of not betraying his own inability to grant it. "The greater
our weakness," he said, "the greater need have we to cover it under a
show of strength."[3]

He immediately detached Tapia with a body of about a hundred men
in one direction, and Sandoval with a somewhat larger force in the other,
with orders that their absence should not in any event be prolonged beyond ten days.[4] The two captains executed their commission promptly
and effectually. They each met and defeated his adversary in a pitched
battle; laid waste the hostile territories, and returned within the time
prescribed. They were soon followed by ambassadors from the conquered places, soliciting the alliance of the Spaniards; and the affair
terminated by an accession of new confederates, and, what was more
important, a conviction in the old, that the Spaniards were both willing
and competent to protect them.

Fortune, who seldom dispenses her frowns or her favors single-handed,
further showed her good-will to the Spaniards, at this time, by sending a
vessel into Vera Cruz laden with ammunition and military stores. It was
part of the fleet destined for the Florida coast by the romantic old knight,
Ponce de Leon. The cargo was immediately taken by the authorities of
the port, and forwarded, without delay, to the camp, where it arrived
most seasonably, as the want of powder, in particular, had begun to be
seriously felt.[5] With strength thus renovated, Cortés determined to resume active operations, but on a plan widely differing from that pursued
before.

In the former deliberations on the subject, two courses, as we have
seen, presented themselves to the general. One was, to intrench himself
in the heart of the capital, and from this point carry on hostilities; the
other was the mode of proceeding hitherto followed. Both were open to
serious objections, which he hoped would be obviated by the one now
adopted. This was, to advance no step without securing the entire safety

---

[2] "Y teniamos necesidad antes de ser socorridos, que de dar socorro." Rel. Terc.
de Cortés, ap. Lorenzana, p. 272.

[3] "God knows," says the general, "the peril in which we all stood; pero como nos
convenia mostrar mas esfuerzo y ánimo, que nunca, y morir peleando, disimula-
bamos nuestra flaqueza assí con los Amigos como con los Enemigos." Ibid., p. 275.

[4] Tapia's force consisted of 10 horse and 80 foot; the chief alguacil, as Sandoval
was styled, had 18 horse and 100 infantry. Ibid., loc. cit.—Also Oviedo, Hist. de
las Ind., MS., lib. 33, cap. 26.

[5] "Pólvora y Ballestas, de que teniamos muy estrema necesidad." (Rel. Terc. de
Cortés, ap. Lorenzana, p. 278.) It was probably the expedition in which Ponce de
Leon lost his life; an expedition to the very land which the chivalrous cavalier had
himself first visited in quest of the Fountain of Health. The story is pleasantly told
by Irving, as the reader may remember, in his "Companions of Columbus."

of the army, not only on its immediate retreat, but in its future inroads. Every breach in the causeway, every canal in the streets, was to be filled up in so solid a manner, that the work should not be again disturbed. The materials for this were to be furnished by the buildings, every one of which, as the army advanced, whether public or private, hut, temple, or palace, was to be demolished! Not a building in their path was to be spared. They were all indiscriminately to be levelled, until, in the Conqueror's own language, "the water should be converted into dry land," and a smooth and open ground be afforded for the manœuvres of the cavalry and artillery! [6]

Cortés came to this terrible determination with great difficulty. He sincerely desired to spare the city, "the most beautiful thing in the world," [7] as he enthusiastically styles it, and which would have formed the most glorious trophy of his conquest. But, in a place, where every house was a fortress, and every street was cut up by canals so embarrassing to his movements, experience proved it was vain to think of doing so, and becoming master of it. There was as little hope of a peaceful accommodation with the Aztecs, who, so far from being broken by all they had hitherto endured, and the long perspective of future woes, showed a spirit as haughty and implacable as ever.[8]

The general's intentions were learned by the Indian allies with unbounded satisfaction; and they answered his call for aid by thousands of pioneers, armed with their *coas*, or hoes of the country, all testifying the greatest alacrity in helping on the work of destruction.[9] In a short time the breaches in the great causeways were filled up so effectually that they were never again molested. Cortés, himself, set the example by carrying stones and timber with his own hands.[10] The buildings in the suburbs were then thoroughly levelled, the canals were filled up with the rubbish, and a wide space around the city was thrown open to the manœuvres of the cavalry, who swept over it free and unresisted. The Mexicans did not look with indifference on these preparations to lay waste their town, and leave them bare and unprotected against the enemy. They made incessant efforts to impede the labors of the besiegers; but the latter, under

[6] The calm and simple manner, in which the *Conquistador*, as usual, states this in his *Commentaries*, has something appalling in it from its very simplicity. "Acordé de tomar un medio para nuestra seguridad, y para poder mas estrechar á los Enemigos; y fué, que como fuessemos ganando por las Calles de la Ciudad, que fuessen derrocando todas las Casas de ellas, del un lado, y del otro; por manera, que no fuessemos un paso adelante, sin lo dejar todo asolado, y lo que era Agua, hacerlo Tierra-firme, aunque hobiesse toda la dilacion, que se pudiesse seguir." Rel. Terc., ap. Lorenzana. p. 279.

[7] "Porque era la mas hermosa cosa del Mundo." Ibid., p. 278.

[8] "Mas antes en el pelear, y en todos sus ardides, los hallabamos con mas ánimo, que nunca." Ibid, p. 279.

[9] Yet we shall hardly credit the Tezcucan historians' assertion, that a hundred thousand Indians flocked to the camp for this purpose! "Viniesen todos los labradores con sus coas para este efecto con toda brevedad: . . . . . llegáron *mas de cien mil de ellos*." Ixtlilxochitl, Venida de los Esp., p. 42.

[10] Bernal Diaz, Hist. de la Conquista, cap. 153.

cover of their guns, which kept up an unintermitting fire, still advanced in the work of desolation.[11]

The gleam of fortune, which had so lately broken out on the Mexicans, again disappeared; and the dark mist, after having been raised for a moment, settled on the doomed capital more heavily than before. Famine, with all her hideous train of woes, was making rapid strides among its accumulated population. The stores provided for the siege were exhausted. The casual supply of human victims, or that obtained by some straggling pirogue from the neighboring shores, was too inconsiderable to be widely felt.[12] Some forced a scanty sustenance from a mucilaginous substance, gathered in small quantities on the surface of the lake and canals.[13] Others appeased the cravings of appetite by devouring rats, lizards, and the like loathsome reptiles, which had not yet deserted the starving city. Its days seemed to be already numbered. But the page of history has many an example, to show that there are no limits to the endurance of which humanity is capable, when animated by hatred and despair.

With the sword thus suspended over it, the Spanish commander, desirous to make one more effort to save the capital, persuaded three Aztec nobles, taken in one of the late actions, to bear a message from him to Guatemozin; though they undertook it with reluctance, for fear of the consequences to themselves. Cortés told the emperor, that all had now been done that brave men could do in defence of their country. There remained no hope, no chance of escape, for the Mexicans. Their provisions were exhausted; their communications were cut off; their vassals had deserted them; even their gods had betrayed them. They stood alone, with the nations of Anahuac banded against them. There was no hope, but in immediate surrender. He besought the young monarch to take compassion on his brave subjects, who were daily perishing before his eyes; and on the fair city, whose stately buildings were fast crumbling into ruins. "Return to the allegiance," he concludes, "which you once proffered to the sovereign of Castile. The past shall be forgotten. The persons and property, in short, all the rights, of the Aztecs shall be re-

[11] Sahagun, who gathered the story from the actors, and from the aspect of the scene, before the devastation had been wholly repaired, writes with the animation of an eye-witness. "La guerra por agua y por tierra fué tan por fiada y tan sangrienta, que era espanto de verla, y no hay posibilidad, para decir las particularidades que pasaban; eran tan espesas las saetas, y dardos, y piedras, y palos, que se arrojavan los unos á los otros, que quitavan la claridad del sol; era tan grande la vocería, y grita, de hombres y mugeres, y niños que voceaban y lloraban, que era cosa de grima; era tan grande la polvareda, y ruido, en derrocar y quemar casas, y robar lo que en ellas habia, y cautivar niños y mugeres, *que parecia un juicio.*" Hist. de Nueva Esp., MS., lib. 12, cap. 38.

[12] The flesh of the Christians failed to afford them even the customary nourishment, since the Mexicans said it was intolerably bitter; a miracle, considered by Captain Diaz, as expressly wrought for this occasion. Ibid., cap. 153.

[13] Ibid., ubi supra.

When dried in the sun, this slimy deposit had a flavor not unlike that of cheese, and formed part of the food of the poorer classes at all times, according to Clavigero. Stor. del Messico. tom. 2, p. 222.

spected. You shall be confirmed in your authority, and Spain will once more take your city under her protection." [14]

The eye of the young monarch kindled, and his dark cheek flushed with sudden anger, as he listened to proposals so humiliating. But, though his bosom glowed with the fiery temper of the Indian, he had the qualities of a "gentle cavalier," says one of his enemies, who knew him well.[15] He did no harm to the envoys; but, after the heat of the moment had passed off, he gave the matter a calm consideration, and called a council of his wise men and warriors to deliberate upon it. Some were for accepting the proposals, as offering the only chance of preservation. But the priests took a different view of the matter. They knew that the ruin of their own order must follow the triumph of Christianity. "Peace was good," they said, "but not with the white men." They reminded Guatemozin of the fate of his uncle Montezuma, and the requital he had met with for all his hospitality; of the seizure and imprisonment of Cacama, the cacique of Tezcuco; of the massacre of the nobles by Alvarado; of the insatiable avarice of the invaders, which had stripped the country of its treasures; of their profanation of the temples; of the injuries and insults which they had heaped without measure on the people and their religion. "Better," they said, "to trust to the promises of their own gods, who had so long watched over the nation. Better, if need be, give up our lives at once for our country, than drag them out in slavery and suffering among the false strangers." [16]

The eloquence of the priests, artfully touching the various wrongs of his people, roused the hot blood of Guatemozin. "Since it is so," he abruptly exclaimed, "let us think only of supplying the wants of the people. Let no man, henceforth, who values his life, talk of surrender. We can at least die like warriors." [17]

The Spaniards waited two days for the answer to their embassy. At length, it came in a general sortie of the Mexicans, who, pouring through every gate of the capital, like a river that has burst its banks, swept on, wave upon wave, to the very intrenchments of the besiegers, threatening to overwhelm them by their numbers! Fortunately, the position of the latter on the dikes secured their flanks, and the narrowness of the defile gave their small battery of guns all the advantages of a larger one. The fire of artillery and musketry blazed without intermission along the several causeways, belching forth volumes of sulphurous smoke, that, roll-

[14] Bernal Diaz, Ibid., cap. 154.
[15] "Mas como el Guatemuz era mancebo, *y muy gentil-hombre* y de buena disposicion." Ibid., loc. cit.
[16] "Mira primero lo que nuestros Dioses te han prometido, toma buen consejo sobre ello y no te fies de Malinche, ni de sus palabras, que mas vale que todos muramos en esta ciudad peleando, que no vernos en poder de quiẽ nos harán esclauos, y nos atormentarán." Ibid., ubi supra.
[17] "Y entonces el Guatemuz medio enojado les dixo: Pues assí quereis que sea, guardad mucho el maiz, y bastimentos que tenemos, y muramos todos peleando: y desde aquí adelante ninguno sea osado á me demander pazes, si no yo le mataré: y allí todos prometiéron de pelear noches, y dias, y morir en la defensa de su ciudad.' Ibid., ubi supra.

ing heavily over the waters, settled dark around the Indian city, and hid it from the surrounding country. The brigantines thundered, at the same time, on the flanks of the columns, which, after some ineffectual efforts to maintain themselves, rolled back in wild confusion, till their impotent fury died away in sullen murmurs within the capital.

Cortés now steadily pursued the plan he had laid down for the devastation of the city. Day after day the several armies entered by their respective quarters; Sandoval probably directing his operations against the north-eastern district. The buildings, made of porous *tetzontli*, though generally low, were so massy and extensive, and the canals were so numerous, that their progress was necessarily slow. They, however, gathered fresh accessions of strength every day from the numbers who flocked to the camp from the surrounding country, and who joined in the work of destruction with a hearty good-will, which showed their eagerness to break the detested yoke of the Aztecs. The latter raged with impotent anger, as they beheld their lordly edifices, their temples, all they had been accustomed to venerate, thus ruthlessly swept away; their canals, constructed with so much labor, and what to them seemed science, filled up with rubbish; their flourishing city, in short, turned into a desert, over which the insulting foe now rode triumphant. They heaped many a taunt on the Indian allies. "Go on," they said, bitterly; "the more you destroy, the more you will have to build up again hereafter. If we conquer, you shall build for us; and, if your white friends conquer, they will make you do as much for them." [18] The event justified the prediction.

In their rage they rushed blindly on the corps which covered the Indian pioneers. But they were as often driven back by the impetuous charge of the cavalry, or received on the long pikes of Chinantla, which did good service to the besiegers in their operations. At the close of day, however, when the Spaniards drew off their forces, taking care to send the multitudinous host of confederates first from the ground, the Mexicans usually rallied for a more formidable attack. Then they poured out from every lane and by-way, like so many mountain streams, sweeping over the broad level cleared by the enemy, and falling impetuously on their flanks and rear. At such times, they inflicted considerable loss in their turn, till an ambush, which Cortés laid for them among the buildings adjoining the great temple, did them so much mischief, that they were compelled to act with more reserve.

At times the war displayed something of a chivalrous character, in the personal rencontres of the combatants. Challenges passed between them, and especially between the native warriors. These combats were usually conducted on the *azoteas*, whose broad and level surface afforded a good field of fight. On one occasion, a Mexican of powerful frame, brandish-

---

[18] "Los de la Ciudad como veian tanto estrago, por esforzarse, decian á nuestros Amigos, que no ficiessen sino quemar, y destruir, que ellos se las harian tornar á hacer de nuevo, porque si ellos eran vencedores, ya ellos sabian, que habia de see assí, y si no, que las habian de hacer para nosotros." Rel. Terc. de Cortés, ap. Lorenzana, p. 286.

ing a sword and buckler, which he had won from the Christians, defied his enemies to meet him in single fight. A young page of Cortés', named Nuñez, obtained his master's permission to accept the vaunting chal· lenge of the Aztec; and, springing on the *azotea*, succeeded after a hard struggle in discomfiting his antagonist, who fought at a disadvantage with weapons in which he was unpractised, and, running him through the body, brought off his spoils in triumph, and laid them at the general's feet.[19]

The division of Cortés had now worked its way as far north as the great street of Tacuba, which opened a communication with Alvarado's camp, and near which stood the palace of Guatemozin. It was a spacious stone pile, that might well be called a fortress. Though deserted by its royal master, it was held by a strong body of Aztecs, who made a tem· porary defence, but of little avail against the battering enginery of the besiegers. It was soon set on fire, and its crumbling walls were levelled in the dust, like those other stately edifices of the capital, the boast and admirations of the Aztecs, and some of the fairest fruits of their civiliza· tion. "It was a sad thing to witness their destruction," exclaims Cortés; "but it was part of our plan of operations, and we had no alternative." [20]

These operations had consumed several weeks, so that it was now drawing towards the latter part of July. During this time, the blockade had been maintained with the utmost rigor, and the wretched inhabitants were suffering all the extremities of famine. Some few stragglers were taken, from time to time, in the neighborhood of the Christian camp, whither they had wandered in search of food. They were kindly treated by command of Cortés, who was in hopes to induce others to follow their example, and thus to afford a means of conciliating the inhabitants, which might open the way to their submission. But few were found will· ing to leave the shelter of the capital, and they preferred to take their chance with their suffering countrymen, rather than trust themselves to the mercies of the besiegers.

From these few stragglers, however, the Spaniards heard a dismal tale of woe, respecting the crowded population in the interior of the city. All the ordinary means of sustenance had long since failed, and they now supported life as they could, by means of such roots as they could dig from the earth, by gnawing the bark of trees, by feeding on the grass,— on anything, in short, however loathsome, that could allay the craving of appetite. Their only drink was the brackish water of the soil saturated with the salt lake.[21] Under this unwholesome diet, and the diseases

[19] Ibid., pp. 282–284.—Herrera, Hist. General, dec. 3, lib. 1, cap. 22, lib. 2, cap. 2. —Gomara, Crónica, cap. 140.—Oviedo, Hist. de las Ind., MS., lib. 33, cap. 28.— Ixtlilxochitl, Venida de los Esp., p. 43.

[20] "No se entendió sino en que mar, y hallanar Casas, que era lástima cierto de lo ver; pero como no nos convenia hacer otra cosa, eramos forzado seguir aquella ór· den." Ibid., p. 286.

[21] "No tenian agua dulce para beber, ni para de ninguna manera de comer; bebian del agua salada y hedionda, comian ratones y lagartijas, y cortezas de árboles, y otras cosas no comestibles; y de esta causa enfermáron muchos, y muriéron much·

THE CONQUEST OF MEXICO

engendered by it, the population was gradually wasting away. Men sickened and died every day, in all the excruciating torments produced by
hunger, and the wan and emaciated survivors seemed only to be waiting
for their time.

The Spaniards had visible confirmation of all this, as they penetrated
deeper into the city and approached the district of Tlatelolco, now occupied by the besieged. They found the ground turned up in quest of
roots and weeds, the trees stripped of their green stems, their foliage, and
their bark. Troops of famished Indians flitted in the distance, gliding like
ghosts among the scenes of their former residence. Dead bodies lay unburied in the streets and court-yards, or filled up the canals. It was a
sure sign of the extremity of the Aztecs; for they held the burial of the
dead as a solemn and imperative duty. In the early part of the siege,
they had religiously attended to it. In its later stages, they were still careful to withdraw the dead from the public eye, by bringing their remains
within the houses. But the number of these, and their own sufferings, had
now so fearfully increased, that they had grown indifferent to this, and
they suffered their friends and their kinsmen to lie and moulder on the
spot where they drew their last breath![22]

As the invaders entered the dwellings, a more appalling spectacle presented itself;—the floors covered with the prostrate forms of the miserable inmates, some in the agonies of death, others festering in their
corruption; men, women, and children, inhaling the poisonous atmosphere, and mingled promiscuously together; mothers, with their
infants in their arms perishing of hunger before their eyes, while they
were unable to afford them the nourishment of nature; men crippled by
their wounds, with their bodies frightfully mangled, vainly attempting
to crawl away, as the enemy entered. Yet, even in this state, they scorned
to ask for mercy, and glared on the invaders with the sullen ferocity of
the wounded tiger, that the huntsmen have tracked to his forest cave.
The Spanish commander issued strict orders that mercy should be shown
to these poor and disabled victims. But the Indian allies made no distinction. An Aztec, under whatever circumstances, was an enemy; and, with
hideous shouts of triumph, they pulled down the burning buildings on
their heads, consuming the living and the dead in one common funeral
pile!

Yet the sufferings of the Aztecs, terrible as they were, did not incline

os." Sahagun, Hist. de Nueva Esp., MS., lib. 12, cap. 39.—Also Rel. Terc. de Cortés,
ap. Lorenzana, p. 289.

[22] "Y es verdad y juro amen, que toda la laguna, y casas, y barbacoas estauan
llenas de cuerpos, y cabeças de hombres muertos, que yo no sé de que manera lo
escriua." (Bernal Diaz, Hist. de la Conquista, cap. 156.) Clavigero considers that it
was a scheme of the Mexicans to leave the dead unburied, in order that the stench
might annoy and drive off the Spaniards. (Stor. del Messico, tom. III. p. 231, nota.)
But this policy would have operated much more to the detriment of the besieged
than of the besiegers, whose presence in the capital was but transitory. It is much
more natural to refer it to the same cause which has led to a similar conduct under
similar circumstances elsewhere, whether occasioned by pestilence or famine.

them to submission. There were many, indeed, who, from greater strength of constitution, or from the more favorable circumstances in which they were placed, still showed all their wonted energy of body and mind, and maintained the same undaunted and resolute demeanor as before. They fiercely rejected all the overtures of Cortés, declaring they would rather die than surrender, and adding, with a bitter tone of exultation, that the invaders would be at least disappointed in their expectations of treasure, for it was buried where they could never find it! [23]

The women, it is said, shared in this desperate—it should rather be called heroic—spirit. They were indefatigable in nursing the sick, and dressing their wounds; they aided the warriors in battle, by supplying them with the Indian ammunition of stones and arrows, prepared their slings, strung their bows, and displayed, in short, all the constancy and courage shown by the noble maidens of Saragossa in our day, and by those of Carthage in the days of antiquity.[24]

Cortés had now entered one of the great avenues leading to the market-place of Tlatelolco, the quarter, towards which the movements of Alvarado were also directed. A single canal only lay in his way, but this was of great width and stoutly defended by the Mexican archery. At this crisis, the army one evening, while in their intrenchments on the causeway, were surprised by an uncommon light, that arose from the huge *teocalli* in that part of the city, which, being at the north, was the most distant from their own position. This temple, dedicated to the dread war-god, was inferior only to the pyramid in the great square; and on it the Spaniards had more than once seen their unhappy countrymen led to slaughter. They now supposed that the enemy were employed in some of their diabolical ceremonies, when the flame, mounting higher and higher, showed that the sanctuaries themselves were on fire. A shout of exultation at the sight broke forth from the assembled soldiers, as they assured one another that their countrymen under Alvarado had got possession of the building.

It was indeed true. That gallant officer, whose position on the western causeway placed him near the district of Tlatelolco, had obeyed his commander's instructions to the letter, razing every building to the ground in his progress, and filling up the ditches with their ruins. He, at length, found himself before the great *teocalli* in the neighborhood of the market. He ordered a company, under a cavalier named Gutierre de Badajoz, to storm the place, which was defended by a body of warriors,

[23] Gonzalo de las Casas, Defensa, MS., cap. 28.—Martyr, De Orbe Novo, dec. 5, cap. 8.—Ixtlilxochitl, Venida de los Esp., p. 45.—Rel. Terc. de Cortés, ap. Lorenzana, p. 289.—Oviedo, Hist. de las Ind., MS., lib. 33, cap. 29.

[24] "Muchas cosas acaeciéron en este cerco, que entre otras generaciones estobieran discantadas é tenidas en mucho, en especial de las Mugeres de Temixtitan, de quien ninguna mencion se ha fecho. Y soy certificado, que fué cosa maravillosa y para espantar, ver la prontitud y constancia que tobiéron en servir á sus maridos, y en curar los heridos, e en el labrar de las piedras para los que tiraban con hondas, é en otros oficios para mas que mugeres." Oviedo, Hist. de las Ind., MS., lib 33, cap. 48.

mingled with priests, still more wild and ferocious than the soldiery. The garrison, rushing down the winding terraces, fell on the assailants with such fury, as compelled them to retreat in confusion, and with some loss. Alvarado ordered another detachment to their support. This last was engaged, at the moment, with a body of Aztecs, who hung on its rear as it wound up the galleries of the *teocalli*. Thus hemmed in between two enemies, above and below, the position of the Spaniards was critical. With sword and buckler, they plunged desperately on the ascending Mexicans, and drove them into the court-yard below, where Alvarado plied them with such lively volleys of musketry, as soon threw them into disorder and compelled them to abandon the ground. Being thus rid of annoyance in the rear, the Spaniards returned to the charge. They drove the enemy up the heights of the pyramid, and, reaching the broad summit, a fierce encounter followed in mid-air,—such an encounter as takes place where death is certain consequence of defeat. It ended, as usual, in the discomfiture of the Aztecs, who were either slaughtered on the spot still wet with the blood of their own victims, or pitched headlong down the sides of the pyramid.

The area was covered with the various symbols of the barbarous worship of the country, and with two lofty sanctuaries, before whose grinning idols were displayed the heads of several Christian captives, who had been immolated on their altars. Although overgrown by their long, matted hair and bushy beards, the Spaniards could recognise, in the livid countenances, their comrades who had fallen into the hands of the enemy. Tears fell from their eyes, as they gazed on the melancholy spectacle, and thought of the hideous death which their countrymen had suffered. They removed the sad relics with decent care, and after the Conquest deposited them in consecrated ground, on a spot since covered by the Church of the Martyrs.[25]

They completed their work by firing the sanctuaries, that the place might be no more polluted by these abominable rites. The flame crept slowly up the lofty pinnacles, in which stone was mingled with wood, till, at length, bursting into one bright blaze, it shot up its spiral volume to such a height, that it was seen from the most distant quarters of the Valley. It was this which had been hailed by the soldiery of Cortés, and it served as the beacon-light to both friend and foe, intimating the progress of Christian arms.

The commander-in-chief and his division, animated by the spectacle, made, in their entrance on the following day, more determined efforts to place themselves alongside of their companions under Alvarado. The broad canal, above noticed as the only impediment now lying in his way, was to be traversed; and on the further side the emaciated figures of the Aztec warriors were gathered in numbers to dispute the passage, like the gloomy shades that wander—as ancient poets tell us—on the banks of the infernal river. They poured down, however, a storm of

[25] Oviedo, Hist. de las Ind., MS., lib. 33, cap. 29.—Bernal Diaz, Hist. de la Conquista, cap. 155.—Rel. Terc. de Cortés, ap. Lorenzana, pp. 287–289.

missiles, which were no shades, on the heads of the Indian laborers, while occupied with filling up the wide gap with the ruins of the surrounding buildings. Still they toiled on in defiance of the arrowy shower, fresh numbers taking the place of those who fell. And when at length the work was completed, the cavalry rode over the rough plain at full charge against the enemy, followed by the deep array of spearmen, who bore down all opposition with their invincible phalanx.

The Spaniards now found themselves on the same ground with Alvarado's division. Soon afterwards, the chief, attended by several of his staff, rode into their lines, and cordially embraced his countrymen and companions in arms, for the first time since the beginning of the siege. They were now in the neighborhood of the market. Cortés, taking with him a few of his cavaliers, galloped into it. It was a vast inclosure, as the reader has already seen, covering many an acre.[26] Its dimensions were suited to the immense multitudes who gathered there from all parts of the Valley in the flourishing days of the Aztec monarchy. It was surrounded by porticos and pavilions for the accommodation of the artisans and traders, who there displayed their various fabrics and articles of merchandise. The flat roofs of the piazzas were now covered with crowds of men and women, who gazed in silent dismay on the steel-clad horsemen, that profaned these precincts with their presence, for the first time since their expulsion from the capital. The multitude, composed, for the most part, probably, of unarmed citizens, seemed taken by surprise; at least, they made no show of resistance; and the general, after leisurely viewing the ground, was permitted to ride back unmolested to the army.

On arriving there, he ascended the *teocalli*, from which the standard of Castile, supplanting the memorials of Aztec superstition, was now triumphantly floating. The Conqueror, as he strode among the smoking embers on the summit, calmly surveyed the scene of desolation below. The palaces, the temples, the busy marts of industry and trade, the glittering canals, covered with their rich freights from the surrounding country, the royal pomp of groves and gardens, all the splendors of the imperial city, the capital of the Western World, forever gone,—and in their place a barren wilderness! How different the spectacle which the year before had met his eyes, as it wandered over the same scenes from the heights of the neighboring *teocalli*, with Montezuma at his side! Seven eighths of the city were laid in ruins, with the occasional excep-

[26] Ante, p. 328.
The *tianguez* still continued of great dimensions, though with faded magnificence, after the Conquest, when it is thus noticed by father Sahagun. "Entráron en la plaza ó Tianguez de este Tlaltilulco (lugar muy espacioso mucho mas de lo que ahora es) el cual se podia llamar emporio de toda esta nueva España: al cual venian á tratar gentes de toda esta nueva España, y aun de los Reinos a ella contiguos, y donde se vendian y compraban todas cuantas cosas hay en toda esta tierra, y en los Reinos de Quahtimalla y Xalisco, (cosa cierto mucho de ver,) yo lo ví por muchos años morando en esta Casa del Señor Santiago, aunque ya no era tanto como antes de la Conquista." Hist. de Nueva Esp., MS., lib. 12, cap. 37.

tion, perhaps, of some colossal temple, that it would have required too
much time to demolish.[27] The remaining eighth, comprehending the district of Tlatelolco, was all that now remained to the Aztecs, whose
population—still large after its losses—was crowded into a compass that
would hardly have afforded accommodations for a third of their numbers.
It was the quarter lying between the great northern and western causeways, and is recognised in the modern capital as the *Barrio de San Jago*
and its vicinity. It was the favorite residence of the Indians after the
Conquest,[28] though at the present day thinly covered with humble
dwellings, forming the straggling suburbs, as it were, of the metropolis.
Yet it still affords some faint vestiges of what it was in its prouder days;
and the curious antiquary, and occasionally the laborer, as he turns up
the soil, encounters a glittering fragment of obsidian, or the mouldering
head of a lance, or arrow, or some other warlike relic, attesting that on
this spot the retreating Aztecs made their last stand for the independence
of their country.[29]

On the day following Cortés, at the head of his battalions, made a
second entry into the great *tianguez*. But this time the Mexicans were
better prepared for his coming. They were assembled in considerable
force in the spacious square. A sharp encounter followed; but it was
short. Their strength was not equal to their spirit, and they melted away
before the rolling fire of musketry, and left the Spaniards masters of the
inclosure.

The first act was to set fire to some temples of no great size within the
market-place, or more probably on its borders. As the flames ascended,
the Aztecs, horror-struck, broke forth into piteous lamentations at the destruction of the deities on whom they relied for protection.[30]

The general's next step was at the suggestion of a soldier named
Sotelo, a man who had served under the Great Captain in the Italian
wars, where he professed to have gathered knowledge of the science of
engineering, as it was then practised. He offered his services to construct
a sort of catapult, a machine for discharging stones of great size, which

[27] "É yo miré dende aquella Torre, lo que teniamos ganado de la Ciudad, que sin
duda de ocho partes teniamos ganado las siete." Rel. Terc. de Cortés, ap. Lorenzana,
p. 289.
[28] Toribio, Hist. de los Ind., MS., Parte 3, cap. 7.
The remains of the ancient foundations may still be discerned in this quarter,
while in every other *etiam periêre ruinæ!*
[29] Bustamante, the Mexican editor of Sahagun, mentions that he has now in his
possession several of these military spoils. "Toda la llanura del Santuario de nuestra
Señor de los Ángeles y de Santiago Tlaltilolco se ve sembrada de fragmentos de
lanzas cortantes, de macanas, y flechas de piedra obsidiana, de que usaban los Mexicanos ó sea Chinapos, y yo he recogido no pocos que conservo en mi poder." Hist.
de Nueva Esp., lib. 12, nota 21.
[30] "Y como comenzó á arder, levantóse una llama tan alta que parecia llegar al
cielo, al espectáculo de esta quema, todos los hombres y mugeres que se habian
acogido á las tiendas que cercaban todo el Tianguez comenzáron á llorar á voz en
grito, que fué cosa de espanto oirlos; porque quemado aquel delubro satánico luego
entendiéron que habian de ser del todo destruidos v robados." Sahagun, Hist. de
Nueva Esp., MS., lib. 12, cap. 37.

might take the place of the regular battering-train, in demolishing the buildings. As the ammunition, notwithstanding the liberal supplies, which, from time to time, had found their way into the camp, now began to fail, Cortés eagerly acceded to a proposal so well suited to his exigencies. Timber and stone were furnished, and a number of hands were employed, under the direction of the self-styled engineer, in constructing the ponderous apparatus, which was erected on a solid platform of masonry, thirty paces square, and seven or eight feet high, that covered the centre of the market-place. It was the work of the Aztec princes, and was used as a scaffolding, on which mountebanks and jugglers might exhibit their marvellous feats for the amusement of the populace, who took great delight in these performances.[31]

The erection of the machine consumed several days, during which hostilities were suspended, while the artisans were protected from interruption by a strong corps of infantry. At length the work was completed; and the besieged, who, with silent awe, had beheld from the neighboring *azoteas* the progress of the mysterious engine, which was to lay the remainder of their capital in ruins, now looked with terror for its operation. A stone of huge size was deposited on the timber. The machinery was set in motion; and the rocky fragment was discharged with a tremendous force from the catapult. But, instead of taking the direction of the Aztec buildings, it rose high and perpendicularly into the air, and descending whence it sprung, broke the ill-omened machine into splinters! It was a total failure. The Aztecs were released from their apprehensions, and the soldiery made many a merry jest on the catastrophe, somewhat at the expense of their commander, who testified no little vexation at the disappointment, and still more at his own credulity.[32]

[31] Vestiges of the work are still visible, according to M. de Humboldt, within the limits of the porch of the chapel of St. Jago Essai Politique, tom. II. p. 44.
[32] Bernal Diaz, Hist. de la Conquista, cap. 155.—Rel. Terc. de Cortés, ap. Lorenzana, p. 290.—Sahagun, Hist. de Nueva España, MS., lib. 12, cap. 37.

CHAPTER VIII

Dreadful Sufferings of the Besieged—Spirit of Guatemozin—
Murderous Assaults—Capture of Gautemozin—Evacuation
of the City—Termination of the Siege—Reflections

1521

THERE was no occasion to resort to artificial means to precipitate the ruin of the Aztecs. It was accelerated every hour by causes more potent than those arising from mere human agency. There they were,—pent up in their close and suffocating quarters, nobles, commoners, and slaves, men, women, and children, some in houses, more frequently in hovels,—for this part of the city was not the best,—others in the open air in canoes, or in the streets, shivering in the cold rains of night, and scorched by the burning heat of the day.[1] An old chronicler mentions the fact of two women of rank remaining three days and nights up to their necks in the water among the reeds, with only a handful of maize for their support.[2] The ordinary means of sustaining life were long since gone. They wandered about in search of any thing, however unwholesome or revolting, that might mitigate the fierce gnawings of hunger. Some hunted for insects and worms on the borders of the lake, or gathered the salt weeds and moss from its bottom, while at times they might be seen casting a wistful look at the green hills beyond, which many of them had left to share the fate of their brethren in the capital.

To their credit, it is said by the Spanish writers, that they were not driven, in their extremity, to violate the laws of nature by feeding on one another.[3] But unhappily this is contradicted by the Indian authorities, who state that many a mother, in her agony, devoured the offspring which she had no longer the means of supporting. This is recorded of more than one siege in history; and it is the more probable here, where the sensibilities must have been blunted by familiarity with the brutal practices of the national superstition.[4]

[1] "Estaban los tristes Mejicanos, hombres y mugeres, niños y niñas, viejos y viejas, heridos y enfermos en un lugar bien estrecho, y bien apretados los unos con los otros, y con grandísima falta de bastimentos, y al calor del Sol, y al frio de la noche, y cada hora esperando la muerte." Sahagun, Hist. de Nueva Esp., MS., lib. 12, cap. 39.
[2] Torquemada had the anecdote from a nephew of one of the Indian matrons, then a very old man himself. Monarch. Ind., lib. 4, cap. 102.
[3] Ibid., ubi supra.—Bernal Diaz, Hist. de la Conquista, cap. 156.
[4] "De los niños, no quedó nadie, que las mismas m~dr~~ ~ ~~dres los ~~mian (que

598

But all was not sufficient, and hundreds of famished wretches died every day from the extremity of suffering. Some dragged themselves into the houses, and drew their last breath alone, and in silence. Others sank down in the public streets. Wherever they died, there they were left. There was no one to bury, or to remove them. Familiarity with the spec‹ tacle made men indifferent to it. They looked on in dumb despair, waiting for their own turn. There was no complaint, no lamentation, but deep, un‹ utterable woe.

If in other quarters of the town the corpses might be seen scattered over the streets, here they were gathered in heaps. "They lay so thick," says Bernal Diaz, "that one could not tread except among the bodies."[5] "A man could not set his foot down," says Cortés, yet more strongly, "un‹ less on the corpse of an Indian!"[6] They were piled one upon another, the living mingled with the dead. They stretched themselves on the bodies of their friends, and lay down to sleep there. Death was everywhere. The city was a vast charnel-house, in which all was hastening to decay and decomposition. A poisonous steam arose from the mass of putrefaction, under the action of alternate rain and heat, which so tainted the whole atmosphere, that the Spaniards, including the general himself, in their brief visits to the quarter, were made ill by it, and it bred a pestilence that swept off even greater numbers than the famine.[7]

Men's minds were unsettled by these strange and accumulated horrors. They resorted to all the superstitious rites prescribed by their religion, to stay the pestilence. They called on their priests to invoke the gods in their behalf. But the oracles were dumb, or gave only gloomy responses. Their deities had deserted them, and in their place they saw signs of celestial wrath, telling of still greater woes in reserve. Many, after the siege, declared, that, among other prodigies, they beheld a stream of light, of a blood-red color, coming from the north in the direction of Tepejacac, with a rushing noise, like that of a whirlwind, which swept round the district of Tlatelolco, darting out sparkles and flakes of fire, till it shot far into the centre of the lake![8] In the disordered state of their nerves, a

---

era gran lástima de ver, y mayormente de sufrir)." (Sahagun, Hist. de Nueva Esp., MS., lib. 12, cap. 39.) The historian derived his accounts from the Mexicans them-selves, soon after the event.—One is reminded of the terrible denunciations of Moses: "The tender and delicate woman among you, which would not adventure to set the sole of her foot upon the ground for delicateness and tenderness, her eye shall be evil toward . . . . . her children which she shall bear; for she shall eat them, for want of all things, secretly, in the siege and straitness wherewith thine enemy shall distress thee in thy gates." Deuteronomy, chap. 28, vs. 56, 57.

[5] "No podiamos andar sino entre cuerpos, y cabeças de Indios muertos." Hist. de la Conquista, cap. 156.

[6] "No tenian donde estar sino sobre los cuerpos muertos de los suyos." Rel. Terc., ap. Lorenzana, p. 291.

[7] Bernal Diaz, Ibid., ubi supra.—Herrera, Hist. General, dec. 3, lib. 2, cap. 8.— Sahagun, Hist. de Nueva Esp., MS., lib. 12, cap. 41.—Gonzalo de Las Casas, Defen-sa, MS., cap. 28.

[8] "Un torbellino de fuego como sangre embuelto en brasas y en centellas, que partia de hacia Tepeacac (que es donde está ahora Santa María de Guadalupe) y fué

mysterious fear took possession of their senses. Prodigies were of familiar occurence, and the most familiar phenomena of nature were converted
into prodigies.[9] Stunned by their calamities, reason was bewildered, and
they became the sport of the wildest and most superstitious fancies.

In the midst of these awful scenes, the young emperor of the Aztecs
remained, according to all accounts, calm and courageous. With his fair
capital laid in ruins before his eyes, his nobles and faithful subjects dying
around him, his territory rent away, foot by foot, till scarce enough remained for him to stand on, he rejected every invitation to capitulate, and
showed the same indomitable spirit, as at the commencement of the siege.
When Cortés, in the hope that the extremities of the besieged would
incline them to listen to an accommodation, persuaded a noble prisoner to
bear to Guatemozin his proposals to that effect; the fierce young monarch, according to the general, ordered him at once to be sacrificed.[10] It
is a Spaniard, we must remember, who tells the story.

Cortés, who had suspended hostilities for several days, in the vain hope
that the distresses of the Mexicans would bend them to submission, now
determined to drive them to it by a general assault. Cooped up, as they
were, within a narrow quarter of the city, their position favored such an
attempt. He commanded Alvarado to hold himself in readiness, and directed Sandoval—who, besides the causeway, had charge of the fleet,
which lay off the Tlatelolean district—to support the attack by a cannonade on the houses near the water. He then led his forces into the city, or
rather across the horrid waste that now encircled it.

On entering the Indian precincts, he was met by several of the chiefs,
who, stretching forth their emaciated arms, exclaimed, "You are the
children of the Sun. But the Sun is swift in his course. Why are you, then,
so tardy? Why do you delay so long to put an end to our miseries? Rather
kill us at once, that we may go to our god Huitzilopochtli, who waits for
us in heaven to give us rest from our sufferings!"[11]

Cortés was moved by their piteous appeal, and answered, that he desired not their death, but their submission. "Why does your master refuse to treat with me," he said, "when a single hour will suffice for me to
crush him and all his people?" He then urged them to request Guate-

haciendo gran ruido, hacia donde estaban acorralados los Mejicanos y Tlaltilul-
canos; y dió una vuelta para enrededor de ellos, y no dicen si los empeció algo, sino
que habiendo dado aquella vuelta, se entró por la laguna adelante; y allí desapare-
ció." Sahagun, Hist. de Nueva Esp., MS., lib. 12, cap. 40.

[9] "Inclinatis ad credendum animis," says the philosophic Roman historian, "loco
ominum etiam fortuita." Tacitus, Hist., lib. 2, sec. 1.

[10] "Y como lo lleváron delante de Guatimucin su Señor, y él le comenzó á hablar
sobre la Paz, dizque luego lo mandó matar y sacrificar." Rel. Terc., ap. Lorenzana,
p. 293.

[11] "Que pues ellos me tenian por Hijo del Sol, y el Sol en tanta brevedad como era
en un dia y una noche daba vuelta á todo el Mundo, que porque yo assí brevemente
no los acababa de matar, y los quitaba de penar tanto, porque ya ellos tenian deseos
de morir, y irse al Cielo para su Ochilobus. [Huitzilopochtli,] que los estaba esperando para descansar." Ibid., p. 292.

mozin to confer with him, with the assurance that he might do it in safety, as his person should not be molested.

The nobles, after some persuasion, undertook the mission; and it was received by the young monarch in a manner which showed—if the anecdote before related of him be true—that misfortune had, at length, asserted some power over his haughty spirit. He consented to the interview, though not to have it take place on that day, but the following, in the great square of Tlatelolco. Cortés, well satisfied, immediately withdrew from the city, and resumed his position on the causeway.

The next morning he presented himself at the place appointed, having previously stationed Alvarado there with a strong corps of infantry, to guard against treachery. The stone platform in the centre of the square was covered with mats and carpets, and a banquet was prepared to refresh the famished monarch, and his nobles. Having made these arrangements, he awaited the hour of the interview.

But Guatemozin, instead of appearing himself, sent his nobles, the same who had brought to him the general's invitation, and who now excused their master's absence on the plea of illness. Cortés, though disappointed, gave a courteous reception to the envoys, considering that it might still afford the means of opening a communication with the emperor. He persuaded them, without much entreaty, to partake of the good cheer spread before them, which they did with a voracity that told how severe had been their abstinence. He then dismissed them with a seasonable supply of provisions for their master, pressing him to consent to an interview, without which it was impossible their differences could be adjusted.

The Indian envoys returned in a short time, bearing with them a present of fine cotton fabrics, of no great value, from Guatemozin, who still declined to meet the Spanish General. Cortés, though deeply chagrined, was unwilling to give up the point. "He will surely come," he said to the envoys, "when he sees that I suffer you to go and come unharmed, you who have been my steady enemies, no less than himself, throughout the war. He has nothing to fear from me." [12] He again parted with them, promising to receive their answer the following day.

On the next morning, the Aztec chiefs, entering the Christian quarters, announced to Cortés that Guatemozin would confer with him at noon in the market-place. The general was punctual at the hour; but without success. Neither monarch, nor ministers appeared there. It was plain that the Indian prince did not care to trust the promises of his enemy. A thought of Montezuma may have passed across his mind. After he had waited three hours, the general's patience was exhausted, and, as he

[12] "Y yo les torné á repetir, que no sabia la causa, porque él se recelaba venir ante mí, pues veia que á ellos, que yo sabia q̃ habian sido los causadores principales de la Guerra, y que los habian sustentado, les hacia buen tratamiento, que los dejaba ir, y venir seguramente, sin recibir enojo alguno; que les rogaba, que le tornassen á hablar, y mirassen mucho en esto de su venida, pues á él le convenia, y yo lo haraí por su provecho." Ibid., pp. 294, 295.

learned that the Mexicans were busy in preparations for defence, he made immediate dispositions for the assault.[13]

The confederates had been left without the walls, for he did not care to bring them in sight of the quarry, before he was ready to slip the leash. He now ordered them to join him; and, supported by Alvarado's division, marched at once into the enemy's quarters. He found them prepared to receive him. Their most able-bodied warriors were thrown into the van, covering their feeble and crippled comrades. Women were seen occasionally mingled in the ranks, and, as well as children, thronged the *azoteas*, where, with famine-stricken visages, and haggard eyes, they scowled defiance and hatred on their invaders.

As the Spaniards advanced, the Mexicans set up a fierce war-cry, and sent off clouds of arrows with their accustomed spirit, while the women and boys rained down darts and stones from their elevated position on the terraces. But the missiles were sent by hands too feeble to do much damage; and, when the squadrons closed, the loss of strength became still more sensible in the Aztecs. Their blows fell feebly and with doubtful aim, though some, it is true, of stronger constitution, or gathering strength from despair, maintained to the last a desperate fight.

The arquebusiers now poured in a deadly fire. The brigantines replied by successive volleys, in the opposite quarter. The besieged, hemmed in, like deer surrounded by the huntsmen, were brought down on every side. The carnage was horrible. The ground was heaped up with slain, until the maddened combatants were obliged to climb over the human mounds to get at one another. The miry soil was saturated with blood, which ran off like water, and dyed the canals themselves with crimson.[14] All was uproar and terrible confusion. The hideous yells of the barbarians; the oaths and execrations of the Spaniards; the cries of the wounded; the shrieks of women and children; the heavy blows of the Conquerors; the death-struggle of their victims; the rapid, reverberating echoes of musketry; the hissing of innumerable missiles; the crash and crackling of blazing buildings, crushing hundreds in their ruins; the blinding volumes of dust and sulphurous smoke shrouding all in their gloomy canopy,— made a scene appalling even to the soldiers of Cortés, steeled as they were by many a rough passage of war, and by long familiarity with blood and violence. "The piteous cries of the women and children, in particular," says the general, "were enough to break one's heart."[15] He com-

---

[13] The testimony is most emphatic and unequivocal to these repeated efforts on the part of Cortés to bring the Aztecs peaceably to terms. Besides his own Letter to the Emperor, see Bernal Diaz, cap. 155,—Herrera, Hist. General, lib. 2, cap. 6, 7,—Torquemada, Monarch. Ind., lib. 4, cap. 100,—Ixtlilxochitl, Venida de los Esp., pp. 44–48,—Oviedo, Hist. de las Ind., MS., lib. 33, cap. 29, 30.

[14] "Corrian Arroios de Sangre por las Calles, como pueden correr de Agua, quando llueve, y con ímpetu, y fuerça." Torquemada, Monarch. Ind., lib 4, cap. 103.

[15] "Era tanta la grita, y lloro de los Niños, y Mugeres, que no habia Persona, á quien no quebrantasse el corazon." (Rel. Terc., ap. Lorenzana, p. 296.) They were a rash and stiff-necked race, exclaims his reverend editor, the archbishop, with a charitable commentary! *"Gens durae cervicis. gens absque consilio."* Nota.

manded that they should be spared, and that all, who asked it, should receive quarter. He particularly urged this on the confederates, and placed men among them to restrain their violence.[16] But he had set an engine in motion too terrible to be controlled. It were as easy to curb the hurricane in its fury, as the passions of an infuriated horde of savages. "Never did I see so pitiless a race," he exclaims, "or anything wearing the form of man so destitute of humanity." [17] They made no distinction of sex or age, and in this hour of vengeance seemed to be requiting the hoarded wrongs of a century. At length, sated with slaughter, the Span-ish commander sounded a retreat. It was full time, if, according to his own statement,—we may hope it is an exaggeration,—forty thousand souls had perished! [18] Yet their fate was to be envied, in comparison with that of those who survived.

Through the long night which followed, no movement was perceptible in the Aztec quarter. No light was seen there, no sound was heard, save the low moaning of some wounded or dying wretch, writhing in his agony. All was dark and silent,—the darkness of the grave. The last blow seemed to have completely stunned them. They had parted with hope, and sat in sullen despair, like men waiting in silence the stroke of the execu-tioner. Yet, for all this, they showed no disposition to submit. Every new injury had sunk deeper into their souls, and filled them with a deeper hatred of their enemy. Fortune, friends, kindred, home,—all were gone. They were content to throw away life itself, now that they had nothing more to live for.

Far different was the scene in the Christian camp, where, elated with their recent successes, all was alive with bustle, and preparation for the morrow. Bonfires were seen blazing along the causeways, lights gleamed from tents and barracks, and the sounds of music and merriment, borne over the waters, proclaimed the joy of the soldiers, at the prospect of so soon terminating their wearisome campaign.

On the following morning the Spanish commander again mustered his forces, having decided to follow up the blow of the preceding day, before the enemy should have time to rally, and, at once, to put an end to the war. He had arranged with Alvarado, on the evening previous, to occupy the market-place of Tlatelolco; and the discharge of an arquebuse was to be the signal for a simultaneous assault. Sandoval was to hold the northern causeway, and, with the fleet, to watch the movements of the Indian emperor, and to intercept the flight to the main land, which

[16] "Como la gente de la Cibdad se salia á los nuestros habia el general proveido que por todas las calles estubiesen Españoles para estorvar á los amigos, que no matasen aquellos tristes, que eran sin número. É tambien dixo á todos los amigos capitanes, que no consintiesen á su gente que matasen á ninguno de los que salian Oviedo, Hist. de las Ind., MS., lib. 33, cap. 30.

[17] "La qual crueldad nunca en Generacion tan recia se vió, ni tan fuera de toda órden de naturaleza, como en los Naturales de estas partes." Rel. Terc. de Cortés, ap. Lorenzana, p. 296.

[18] Ibid., ubi supra.—Ixtlilxochitl says, 50,000 were slain and taken in this dreadfu' onslaught. Vendia de los Esp., p. 48.

Cortés knew he meditated. To allow him to effect this would be to leave a formidable enemy in his own neighborhood, who might at any time kindle the flame of insurrection throughout the country. He ordered Sandoval, however, to do no harm to the royal person, and not to fire on the enemy at all, except in self-defence.[19]

It was the memorable 13th of August, 1521, the day of St. Hypolito,— from this circumstance selected as the patron saint of modern Mexico,— that Cortés led his warlike array for the last time across the black and blasted environs which lay around the Indian capital. On entering the Aztec precincts, he paused, willing to afford its wretched inmates one more chance of escape, before striking the fatal blow. He obtained an interview with some of the principal chiefs, and expostulated with them on the conduct of their prince. "He surely will not," said the general, "see you all perish, when he can so easily save you." He then urged them to prevail on Guatemozin to hold a conference with him, repeating the assurances of his personal safety.

The messengers went on their mission, and soon returned with the cihuacoatl at their head, a magistrate of high authority among the Mexicans. He said, with a melancholy air, in which his own disappointment was visible, that "Guatemozin was ready to die where he was, but would hold no interview with the Spanish commander"; adding, in a tone of resignation, "it is for you to work your pleasure." "Go, then," replied the stern Conqueror, "and prepare your countrymen for death. Their hour is come."[20]

He still postponed the assault for several hours. But the impatience of his troops at this delay was heightened by the rumor, that Guatemozin and his nobles were preparing to escape with their effects in the *piraguas* and canoes which were moored on the margin of the lake. Convinced of the fruitlessness and impolicy of further procrastination, Cortés made his final dispositions for the attack, and took his own station on an *azotea*, which commanded the theatre of operations.

When the assailants came into presence of the enemy, they found them huddled together in the utmost confusion, all ages and sexes, in masses so dense that they nearly forced one another over the brink of the causeways into the water below. Some had climbed on the terraces, others feebly supported themselves against the walls of the buildings. Their squalid and tattered garments gave a wildness to their appearance, which still further heightened the ferocity of their expression, as they glared

[19] "Adonde estauan retraidos el Guatemuz con toda la flor de sus Capitanes, y personas mas nobles que en México auia, y le mandó que no matasse, ni hiriesse á ningunos Indios, saluo si no le diessen guerra, é que aunque se la diessen, que solamente se defendiesse." Bernal Diaz, Hist. de la Conquista, cap. 156.

[20] "Y al fin me dijo, que en ninguna manera el Señor vernia ante mí; y antes queria por allá morir, y que á él pesaba mucho de esto, que hiciesse yo lo que quisiesse; y como ví en esto su determinacion, yo le dije; que se bolviesse á los supos, y que él, y ellos se aparejassen, porque los queria combatir, y acabar de matar, y assí se fué." Rel. Terc. de Cortés, ap. Lorenzana, p. 298.

on their enemy with eyes in which hate was mingled with despair. When the Spaniards had approached within bowshot, the Aztecs let off a flight of impotent missiles, showing, to the last, the resolute spirit, though they had lost the strength, of their better days. The fatal signal was then given by the discharge of an arquebuse,—speedily followed by peals of heavy ordnance, the rattle of fire-arms, and the hellish shouts of the confederates, as they sprang upon their victims. It is unnecessary to stain the page with a repetition of the horrors of the preceding day. Some of the wretched Aztecs threw themselves into the water, and were picked up by the canoes. Others sunk and were suffocated in the canals. The number of these became so great, that a bridge was made of their dead bodies, over which the assailants could climb to the opposite banks. Others again, especially the women, begged for mercy, which, as the chroniclers assure us, was everywhere granted by the Spaniards, and, contrary to the instructions and entreaties of Cortés, everywhere refused by the confederates.[21]

While this work of butchery was going on, numbers were observed pushing off in the barks that lined the shore, and making the best of their way across the lake. They were constantly intercepted by the brigantines, which broke through the flimsy array of boats; sending off their volleys to the right and left, as the crews of the latter hotly assailed them. The battle raged as fiercely on the lake as on the land. Many of the Indian vessels were shattered and overturned. Some few, however, under cover of the smoke, which rolled darkly over the waters, succeeded in clearing themselves of the turmoil, and were fast nearing the opposite shore.

Sandoval had particularly charged his captains to keep an eye on the movements of any vessel in which it was at all probable that Guatemozin might be concealed. At this crisis, three or four of the largest *piraguas* were seen skimming over the water, and making their way rapidly across the lake. A captain, named Garci Holguin, who had command of one of the best sailers in the fleet, instantly gave them chase. The wind was favorable, and, every moment, he gained on the fugitives, who pulled their oars with a vigor that despair alone could have given. But it was in vain; and, after a short race, Holguin, coming alongside of one of the *pirgaguas*, which, whether from its appearance, or from information he had received, he conjectured might bear the Indian emperor, ordered his men to level their crossbows at the boat. But, before they could discharge them, a cry arose from those in it, that their lord was on board. At the same moment, a young warrior, armed with buckler and *maquahuitl*, rose up, as if to beat off the assailants. But, as the Spanish captain ordered his men not to shoot, he dropped his weapons, and ex-

[21] Oviedo, Hist. de las Ind., MS., lib. 33, cap. 30.—Ixtlilxochitl, Venida de los Esp., p. 48.—Herrera, Hist. General, dec. 3, lib. 2, cap. 7.—Rel. Terc. de Cortés, ap. Lorenzana, pp. 297. 298.—Gomara, Crónica, cap. 142.

claimed, "I am Guatemozin; lead me to Malinche, I am his prisoner; but let no harm come to my wife and my followers." [22]

Holguin assured him, that his wishes should be respected, and assisted him to get on board the brigantine, followed by his wife and attendants. These were twenty in number, consisting of Coanaco, the deposed lord of Tezcuco, the lord of Tlacopan, and several other caciques and dignitaries, whose rank, probably, had secured them some exemption from the general calamities of the siege. When the captives were seated on the deck of his vessel, Holguin requested the Aztec prince to put an end to the combat by commanding his people in the other canoes to surrender. But, with a dejected air, he replied, "It is not necessary. They will fight no longer, when they see that their prince is taken." He spoke truth. The news of Guatemozin's capture spread rapidly through the fleet, and on shore, where the Mexicans were still engaged in conflict with their enemies. It ceased, however, at once. They made no further resistance; and those on the water quickly followed the brigantines, which conveyed their captive monarch to land. It seemed as if the fight had been maintained thus long, the better to divert the enemy's attention, and cover their master's retreat.[23]

Meanwhile Sandoval, on receiving tidings of the capture, brought his own brigantine alongside of Holguin's, and demanded the royal prisoner to be surrendered to him. But his captain claimed him as his prize. A dispute arose between the parties, each anxious to have the glory of the deed, and perhaps the privilege of commemorating it on his escutcheon. The controversy continued so long that it reached the ears of Cortés, who, in his station on the *azotea*, had learned, with no little satisfaction, the capture of his enemy. He instantly sent orders to his wrangling officers, to bring Guatemozin before him, that he might adjust the difference between them.[24] He charged them, at the same time, to treat their

---

[22] Ixtlilxochitl, Venida de los Esp., p. 49.

"No me tiren, que yo soy el Rey de México, y desta tierra, y lo que te ruego es, que no me llegues á mi muger, ni á mis hijos; ni á ninguna muger, ni á ninguna cosa de lo que aquí traygo, sino que me tomes á mí, y me lleues á Malinche." (Bernal Diaz, Hist. de la Conquista, cap. 156.) M. de Humboldt has taken much pains to identify the place of Guatemozin's capture,—now become dry land,—which he considers to have been somewhere between the Garita del Peralvillo, the square of St. Iago de Tlaltelolco, and the bridge of Amaxac. Essai Politique, tom. II, p. 76.

[23] For the preceding account of the capture of Guatemozin, told with little discrepancy, though with more or less minuteness by the different writers, see Bernal Diaz, Ibid., ubi supra,—Rel. Terc. de Cortés, p. 299,—Gonzalo de las Casas, Defensa, MS.,—Oviedo, Hist. de las Ind., MS., lib. 33, cap. 30,—Torquemada, Monarch. Ind., lib. 4, cap. 101.

[24] The general, according to Diaz, rebuked his officers for their ill-timed contention, reminding them of the direful effects of a similar quarrel between Marius and Sylla, respecting Jugurtha. (Hist. de la Conquista, cap. 156.) This piece of pedantry savors much more of the old chronicler than his commander. The result of the whole —not an uncommon one in such cases—was, that the Emperor granted to neither of the parties, but to Cortés, the exclusive right of commemorating the capture of Guatemozin, by placing his head, together with the heads of seven other captive princes, on the border of his shield.

prisoner with respect. He then made preparations for the interview; caused the terrace to be carpeted with crimson cloth and matting, and a table to be spread with provisions, of which the unhappy Aztecs stood so much in need.[25] His lovely Indian mistress, Doña Marina, was present to act as interpreter. She had stood by his side through all the troubled scenes of the Conquest, and she was there now to witness its triumphant termination.

Guatemozin, on landing, was escorted by a company of infantry to the presence of the Spanish commander. He mounted the *azotea* with a calm and steady step, and was easily to be distinguished from his attendant nobles, though his full, dark eye was no longer lighted up with its accustomed fire, and his features wore an expression of passive resignation, that told little of the fierce and fiery spirit that burned within. His head was large, his limbs well proportioned, his complexion fairer than those of his bronze-colored nation, and his whole deportment singularly mild and engaging.[26]

Cortés came forward with a dignified and studied courtesy to receive him. The Aztec monarch probably knew the person of his conqueror, for he first broke silence by saying; "I have done all that I could, to defend myself and my people. I am now reduced to this state. You will deal with me, Malinche, as you list." Then, laying his hand on the hilt of a poniard, stuck in the general's belt, he added, with vehemence, "Better despatch me with this, and rid me of life at once." [27] Cortés was filled with admiration at the proud bearing of the young barbarian, showing in his reverses a spirit worthy of an ancient Roman. "Fear not," he replied, "you shall be treated with all honor. You have defended your capital like a brave warrior. A Spaniard knows how to respect valor even in an enemy." [28] He then inquired of him, where he had left the princess, his wife; and, being informed that she still remained under protection of a Spanish guard on board the brigantine, the general sent to have her escorted to his presence.

[25] Sahagun, Hist. de Nueva Esp., lib. 12, cap. 40, MS.

[26] For the portrait of Guatemozin, I again borrow the faithful pencil of Diaz, who knew him—at least his person—well. "Guatemuz era de muy gentil disposicion, assí de cuerpo, como de fayciones, y la cata algo larga, y alegre, y los ojos mas parecian que quando miraua, que eran con grauedad, y halagüeños, y no auia falta en ellos, y era de edad de veinte y tres, ó veinte y quatro años, y el color tiraua mas á blanco, que al color, y matiz de essotros Indios morenos." Hist. de la Conquista, cap. 156.

[27] "Llegóse á mi, y díjome en su lengua: que ya él habia hecho todo, lo que de su parte era obligado para defenderse á sí, y á los suyos, hasta venir en aquel estado; que ahora ficiesse de él lo que yo quisiesse; y puso la mano en un puñal, que yo tenia diciéndome, que le diesse de puñaladas, y le matasse." (Rel. Terc. de Cortés, ap. Lorenzana, p. 300.) This remarkable account by the Conqueror himself is confirmed by Diaz, who does not appear to have seen this letter of his commander. Hist. de la Conquista, cap. 156.

[28] Ibid., cap. 156.—Also Oviedo, Hist. de las Ind., MS., lib. 33, cap. 48,—and Martyr, (De Orbe Novo, dec. 5, cap. 8,) who, by the epithet of *magnanimo regi*, testifies the admiration which Guatemozin's lofty spirit excited in the court of Castile.

She was the youngest daughter of Montezuma, and was hardly yet on the verge of womanhood. On the accession of her cousin, Guatemozin, to the throne, she had been wedded to him as his lawful wife.[29] She is celebrated by her contemporaries for her personal charms; and the beautiful princess, Tecuichpo, is still commemorated by the Spaniards, since from her, by a subsequent marriage, are descended some of the illustrious families of their own nation.[30] She was kindly received by Cortés, who showed her the respectful attentions suited to her rank. Her birth, no doubt, gave her an additional interest in his eyes, and he may have felt some touch of compunction, as he gazed on the daughter of the unfortunate Montezuma. He invited his royal captives to partake of the refreshments, which their exhausted condition rendered so necessary. Meanwhile the Spanish commander made his dispositions for the night, ordering Sandoval to escort the prisoners to Cojohuacan, whither he proposed, himself, immediately to follow. The other captains, Olid and Alvarado, were to draw off their forces to their respective quarters. It was impossible for them to continue in the capital, where the poisonous effluvia from the unburied carcasses loaded the air with infection. A small guard only was stationed to keep order in the wasted suburbs.—It was the hour of vespers when Guatemozin surrendered,[31] and the siege might be considered as then concluded. The evening set in dark, and the rain began to fall, before the several parties had evacuated the city.[32]

During the night, a tremendous tempest, such as the Spaniards had rarely witnessed, and such as is known only within the tropics, burst

[29] The ceremony of marriage, which distinguished the "lawful wife" from the concubine, is described by Don Thoan Cano, in his conversation with Oviedo. According to this, it appears that the only legitimate offspring, which Montezuma left at his death, was a son and a daughter, this same princess.

[30] For a further account of Montezuma's daughter, see Book VII., Chapter III. of this History.

[31] The event is annually commemorated, or rather was, under the colonial government, by a solemn procession round the walls of the city. It took place on the 13th of August, the anniversary of the surrender, and consisted of the principal cavaliers and citizens on horseback, headed by the viceroy, and displaying the venerable standard of the Conqueror.

[32] Toribio, Hist. de los Ind., MS., Parte 3, cap. 7.—Sahagun, Hist. de Nueva Esp., MS., lib. 12, cap. 42.—Bernal Diaz, Hist. de la Conquista, cap. 156.

"The lord of Mexico having surrendered," says Cortés, in his letter to the Emperor, "the war, by the blessing of Heaven, was brought to an end, on Wednesday, the 13th day of August, 1521. So that from the day when we first sat down before the city, which was the 30th of May, until its final occupation, seventy-five days elapsed." (Rel. Terc., ap. Lorenzana, p. 300.) It is not easy to tell what event occurred on May 30th, to designate the beginning of the siege. Clavigero considers it the occupation of Cojohuacan by Olid. (Stor. del Messico, tom. III. p. 196.) But I know not on what authority. Neither Bernal Diaz, nor Herrera, nor Cortés, so fixes the date. Indeed, Clavigero says, that Alvarado and Olid left Tezcuco May 20, while Cortés says May 10. Perhaps Cortés dates from the time when Sandoval established himself on the northern causeway, and when the complete investment of the capital began.—Bernal Diaz, more than once, speaks of the siege as lasting three months, computing, probably, from the time when his own division, under Alvarado, took up its position at Tacuba.

over the Mexican Valley. The thunder, reverberating from the rocky amphitheatre of hills, bellowed over the waste of waters, and shook the *teocallis* and crazy tenements of Tenochtitlan—the few that yet survived—to their foundations. The lightning seemed to cleave asunder the vault of heaven, as its vivid flashes wrapped the whole scene in a ghastly glare, for a moment, to be again swallowed up in darkness. The war of elements was in unison with the fortunes of the ruined city. It seemed as if the deities of Anahuac, scared from their ancient abodes, were borne along shrieking and howling in the blast, as they abandoned the fallen capital to its fate! [33]

On the day following the surrender, Guatemozin requested the Spanish commander to allow the Mexicans to leave the city, and to pass unmolested into the open country. To this Cortés readily assented, as, indeed, without it he could take no steps for purifying the capital. He gave his orders, accordingly, for the evacuation of the place, commanding that no one, Spaniard or confederate, should offer violence to the Aztecs, or in any way obstruct their departure. The whole number of these is variously estimated at from thirty to seventy thousand, beside women and children, who had survived the sword, pestilence, and famine.[34] It is certain they were three days in defiling along the several causeways,—a mournful train; [35] husbands and wives, parents and children, the sick and the wounded, leaning on one another for support, as they feebly tottered along, squalid, and but half covered with rags, that disclosed at every step hideous gashes, some recently received, others festering from long neglect, and carrying with them an atmosphere of contagion. Their wasted forms and famine-stricken faces told the whole history of the siege; and, as the straggling files gained the opposite shore, they were observed to pause from time to time, as if to take one more look at the spot so lately crowned by the imperial city, once their pleasant home, and endeared to them by many a glorious recollection.

On the departure of the inhabitants, measures were immediately taken to purify the place, by means of numerous fires kept burning day and night, especially in the infected quarter of Tlatelolco, and by collecting the heaps of dead, which lay mouldering in the streets, and consigning them to the earth.—Of the whole number, who perished in the course

---

[33] It did not, apparently, disturb the slumbers of the troops, who had been so much deafened by the incessant noises of the siege, that, now these had ceased, "we felt," says Diaz, in his homely way, "like men suddenly escaped from a belfry, where we had been shut up for months with a chime of bells ringing in our ears!" Ibid., ubi supra.

[34] Herrera (Hist. General, dec. 3, lib. 2, cap. 7) and Torquemada (Monarch. Ind., lib. 4, cap. 101) estimate them at 30,000. Ixtlilxochitl says that 60,000 fighting men laid down their arms; (Venida de los Esp. p. 49;) and Oviedo swells the amount still higher, to 70,000. (Hist. de las Ind., MS., lib. 33, cap. 48.)—After the losses of the siege, these numbers are startling.

[35] "Digo que en tres dias con sus noches iban todas tres calçadas llenas de Indios, é Indias, y muchachos, llenas de bote en bote, que nunca dexauan de salir, y tan flacos, y suzios, é amarillos, é hediondos, que era lástima de los ver." Bernal Diaz, Hist. de la Conquista, cap. 156.

of the siege, it is impossible to form any probable computation. The ac-counts range widely from one hundred and twenty thousand, the lowest estimate, to two hundred and forty thousand.[36] The number of the Span-iards who fell was comparatively small, but that of the allies must have been large, if the historian of Tezcuco is correct in asserting, that thirty thousand perished of his own countrymen alone.[37] That the number of those destroyed within the city was immense cannot be doubted, when we consider, that, besides its own redundant population, it was thronged with that of the neighboring towns, who, distrusting their strength to resist the enemy, sought protection within its walls.

The booty found there—that is, the treasures of gold and jewels, the only booty of much value in the eyes of the Spaniards—fell far below their expectations. It did not exceed, according to the general's state-ment, a hundred and thirty thousand *castellanos* of gold, including the sovereign's share, which, indeed, taking into account many articles of curious and costly workmanship, voluntarily relinquished by the army, greatly exceeded his legitimate fifth.[38] Yet the Aztecs must have been in possession of a much larger treasure, if it were only the wreck of that recovered from the Spaniards on the night of the memorable flight from Mexico. Some of the spoil may have been sent away from the capital; some spent in preparations for defence, and more of it buried in the earth, or sunk in the water of the lake. Their menaces were not without a meaning. They had, at least, the satisfaction of disappointing the avarice of their enemies.

Cortés had no further occasion for the presence of his Indian allies. He assembled the chiefs of the different squadrons, thanked them for their services, noticed their valor in flattering terms, and, after distributing presents among them, with the assurance that his master, the Emperor,

[36] Cortés estimates the losses of the enemy in the three several assaults at 67,000, which, with 50,000, whom he reckons to have perished from famine and disease, would give 117,000. (Rel. Terc., ap. Lorenzana, p. 298, et alibi.) But this is exclu-sive of those who fell previously to the commencement of the vigorous plan of operations for demolishing the city. Ixtlilxochitl, who seldom allows any one to beat him in figures, puts the dead, in round numbers, at 240,000, comprehending the flower of the Aztec nobility. (Venida de los Esp., p. 51.) Bernal Diaz observes, more generally, "I have read the story of the destruction of Jerusalem, but I doubt if there was as great mortality there as in this siege; for there was assembled in the city an immense number of Indian warriors from all the provinces and towns sub-ject to Mexico, the most of whom perished." (Hist. de la Conquista, cap. 156.) "I have conversed," says Oviedo, "with many hidalgos and other persons, and have heard them say that the number of the dead was incalculable,—greater than that at Jerusalem, as described by Josephus." (Hist. de las Ind., MS., lib. 30, cap. 30.) As the estimate of the Jewish historian amounts to 1,100,000, (Antiquities of the Jews, Eng. tr., Book VII. chap. XVII.,) the comparison may stagger the most accommo-dating faith. It will be safer to dispense with arithmetic, where the data are too loose and slippery to afford a foothold for getting at truth.

[37] Ibid., ubi supra.

[38] Rel. Terc., ap. Lorenzana, p. 301.

Oviedo goes into some further particulars respecting the amount of the treasure, and especially of the imperial fifth, to which I shall have occasion to advert here-after. Hist. de las Ind., MS., lib. 33, cap. 31.

would recompense their fidelity yet more largely, dismissed them to their own homes. They carried off a liberal share of the spoils, of which they had plundered the dwellings,—not of a kind to excite the cupidity of the Spaniards,— and returned in triumph, short-sighted triumph! at the success of their expedition, and the downfall of the Aztec dynasty.

Great, also, was the satisfaction of the Spaniards at this brilliant termination of their long and laborious campaign. They were, indeed, disappointed at the small amount of treasure found in the conquered city. But the soldier is usually too much absorbed in the present to give much heed to the future; and, though their discontent showed itself afterwards in a more clamorous form, they now thought only of their triumph, and abandoned themselves to jubilee. Cortés celebrated the event by a banquet, as sumptuous as circumstances would permit, to which all the cavaliers and officers were invited. Loud and long was their revelry, which was carried to such an excess, as provoked the animadversion of father Olmedo, who intimated that this was not the fitting way to testify their sense of the favors shown them by the Almighty. Cortés admitted the justice of the rebuke, but craved some indulgence for a soldier's license in the hour of victory. The following day was appointed for the commemoration of their successes in a more suitable manner.

A procession of the whole army was then formed with father Olmedo at its head. The soiled and tattered banners of Castile, which had waved over many a field of battle, now threw their shadows on the peaceful array of the soldiery, as they slowly moved along, rehearsing the litany, and displaying the image of the Virgin and the blessed symbol of man's redemption. The reverend father pronounced a discourse, in which he briefly reminded the troops of their great cause for thankfulness to Providence for conducting them safe through their long and perilous pilgrimage; and, dwelling on the responsibility incurred by their present position, he besought them not to abuse the rights of conquest, but to treat the unfortunate Indians with humanity. The sacrament was then administered to the commander-in-chief and the principal cavaliers, and the services concluded with a solemn thanksgiving to the God of battles, who had enabled them to carry the banner of the Cross triumphant over this barbaric empire.[39]

Thus, after a siege of nearly three months' duration, unmatched in history for the constancy and courage of the besieged, seldom surpassed for the severity of its sufferings, fell the renowned capital of the Aztecs. Unmatched, it may be truly said, for constancy and courage, when we recollect that the door of capitulation on the most honorable terms was left open to them throughout the whole blockade, and that, sternly rejecting every proposal of their enemy, they, to a man, preferred to die rather than surrender. More than three centuries had elapsed, since the Aztecs,

[39] Herrera, Hist. General, dec. 3, lib. 2, cap. 8.—Bernal Diaz, Hist. de la Conquista, cap. 156.—Sahagun, Hist. de Nueva Esp., MS., lib. 12, cap. 42.—Oviedo, Hist de las Ind., MS., lib ͡ 2. cap. 30.—Ixtlilxochitl, Venida de los Esp., pp. 51, 52.

a poor and wandering tribe from the far North-west had come on the plateau. There they built their miserable collection of huts on the spot— as tradition tells us—prescribed by the oracle. Their conquests, at first confined to their immediate neighborhood, gradually covered the Valley, then, crossing the mountains, swept over the broad extent of the table-land, descended its precipitous sides, and rolled onwards to the Mexican Gulf, and the distant confines of Central America. Their wretched capital, meanwhile, keeping pace with the enlargement of territory, had grown into a flourishing city, filled with buildings, monuments of art, and a numerous population, that gave it the first rank among the capitals of the Western World. At this crisis, came over another race from the remote East, strangers like themselves, whose coming had also been predicted by the oracle, and, appearing on the plateau, assailed them in the very zenith of their prosperity, and blotted them out from the map of nations for ever! The whole story has the air of fable, rather than of history! a legend of romance,—a tale of the genii!

Yet we cannot regret the fall of an empire, which did so little to promote the happiness of its subjects, or the real interests of humanity. Notwithstanding the lustre thrown over its latter days by the glorious defence of its capital, by the mild munificence of Montezuma, by the dauntless heroism of Guatemozin, the Aztecs were emphatically a fierce and brutal race, little calculated, in their best aspects, to excite our sympathy and regard. Their civilization, such as it was, was not their own, but reflected, perhaps imperfectly, from a race whom they had succeeded in the land. It was, in respect to the Aztecs, a generous graft on a vicious stock, and could have brought no fruit to perfection. They ruled over their wide domains with a sword, instead of a sceptre. They did nothing to ameliorate the condition, or in any way promote the progress, of their vassals. Their vassals were serfs, used only to minister to their pleasure, held in awe by armed garrisons, ground to the dust by imposts in peace, by military conscriptions in war. They did not, like the Romans, whom they resembled in the nature of their conquests, extend the rights of citizenship to the conquered. They did not amalgamate them into one great nation, with common rights and interests. They held them as aliens, —even those, who in the Valley were gathered round the very walls of the capital. The Aztec metropolis, the heart of the monarchy, had not a sympathy, not a pulsation, in common with the rest of the body politic. It was a stranger in its own land.

The Aztecs not only did not advance the condition of their vassals, but, morally speaking, they did much to degrade it. How can a nation, where human sacrifices prevail, and especially when combined with cannibalism, further the march of civilization? How can the interests of humanity be consulted, where man is levelled to the rank of the brutes that perish? The influence of the Aztecs introduced their gloomy superstition into lands before unacquainted with it, or where, at least, it was not established in any great strength. The example of the capital was contagious. As the latter increased in opulence, the religious celebrations

were conducted with still more terrible magnificence; in the same manner, as the gladiatorial shows of the Romans increased in pomp with
the increasing splendor of the capital. Men became familiar with scenes
of horror and the most loathsome abominations. Women and children—
the whole nation became familiar with, and assisted at them. The heart
was hardened, the manners were made ferocious, the feeble light of civilization, transmitted from a milder race, was growing fainter and fainter,
as thousands and thousands of miserable victims, throughout the empire,
were yearly fattened in its cages, sacrificed on its altars, dressed and
served at its banquets! The whole land was converted into a vast human
shambles! The empire of the Aztecs did not fall before its time.

Whether these unparalleled outrages furnish a sufficient plea to the
Spaniards for their invasion, whether, with the Protestant, we are content to find a warrant for it in the natural rights and demands of civilization, or, with the Roman Catholic, in the good pleasure of the Pope,—
on the one or other of which grounds, the conquests by most Christian
nations in the East and the West have been defended,—it is unnecessary
to discuss, as it has already been considered in a former Chapter. It is
more material to inquire, whether, assuming the right, the conquest of
Mexico was conducted with a proper regard to the claims of humanity.
And here we must admit, that, with all allowance for the ferocity of the
age and the laxity of its principles, there are passages which every Spaniard, who cherishes the fame of his countrymen, would be glad to see
expunged from their history; passages not to be vindicated on the score
of self-defence, or of necessity of any kind, and which must forever leave
a dark spot on the annals of the Conquest. And yet, taken as a whole,
the invasion, up to the capture of the capital, was conducted on principles less revolting to humanity, than most, perhaps than any, of the
other conquests of the Castilian crown in the New World.

It may seem slight praise to say, that the followers of Cortés used no
blood-hounds to hunt down their wretched victims, as in some other
parts of the Continent, nor exterminated a peaceful and submissive population in mere wantonness of cruelty, as in the Islands. Yet it is something, that they were not so far infected by the spirit of the age, and that
their swords were rarely stained with blood, unless it was indispensable
to the success of their enterprise. Even in the last siege of the capital,
the sufferings of the Aztecs, terrible as they were, do not imply any unusual cruelty in the victors; they were not greater than those inflicted
on their own countrymen at home, in many a memorable instance, by the
most polished nations, not merely of ancient times, but of our own. They
were the inevitable consequences which follow from war, when, instead
of being confined to its legitimate field, it is brought home to the hearth-
stone, to the peaceful community of the city,—its burghers untrained to
arms, its women and children yet more defenceless. In the present instance, indeed, the sufferings of the besieged were in a great degree to be
charged on themselves,—on their patriotic, but desperate, self-devotion
It was not the desire, as certainly it was not the interest, of the Span

iards, to destroy the capital, or its inhabitants. When any of these fell into their hands, they were kindly entertained, their wants supplied, and every means taken to infuse into them a spirit of conciliation; and this, too, it should be remembered, in despite of the dreadful doom to which they consigned their Christian captives. The gates of a fair capitulation were kept open, though unavailingly, to the last hour.

The right of conquest necessarily implies that of using whatever force may be necessary for overcoming resistance to the assertion of that right. For the Spaniards to have done otherwise than they did would have been to abandon the siege, and, with it, the conquest of the country. To have suffered the inhabitants, with their high-spirited monarch, to escape, would but have prolonged the miseries of war by transferring it to another and more inaccessible quarter. They literally, as far as the success of the expedition was concerned, had no choice. If our imagination is struck with the amount of suffering in this, and in similar scenes of the Conquest, it should be borne in mind, that it is a natural result of the great masses of men engaged in the conflict. The amount of suffering does not of itself show the amount of cruelty which caused it; and it is but justice to the Conquerors of Mexico to say, that the very brilliancy and importance of their exploits have given a melancholy celebrity to their misdeeds, and thrown them into somewhat bolder relief than strictly belongs to them.—It is proper that thus much should be stated, not to excuse their excesses, but that we may be enabled to make a more impartial estimate of their conduct, as compared with that of other nations under similar circumstances, and that we may not visit them with peculiar obloquy for evils which necessarily flow from the condition of war.[40] I have not drawn a veil over these evils; for the historian should not shrink from depicting, in their true colors, the atrocities of a condition, over which success is apt to throw a false halo of glory, but which, bursting asunder the strong bonds of human fellowship, purchases its triumphs by arming the hand of man against his brother, makes a savage of the civilized, and kindles the fires of hell in the bosom of the savage.

Whatever may be thought of the Conquest in a moral view, regarded as a military achievement it must fill us with astonishment. That a handful of adventurers, indifferently armed and equipped, should have landed

[40] By none has this obloquy been poured with such unsparing hand on the heads of the old Conquerors, as by their own descendants, the modern Mexicans. Ixtlilxochitl's editor, Bustamante, concludes an animated invective against the invaders, with recommending that a monument should be raised on the spot,—now dry land, —where Guatemozin was taken, which, as the proposed inscription itself intimates, should "devote to eternal execration the detested memory of these banditti!" (Venida de los Esp., p. 52, nota.) One would suppose that the pure Aztec blood, uncontaminated by a drop of Castilian, flowed in the veins of the indignant editor and his compatriots; or, at least, that their sympathies for the conquered race would make them anxious to reinstate them in their ancient rights. Notwithstanding these bursts of generous indignation, however, which plentifully season the writings of the Mexicans of our day, we do not find, that the Revolution, or any of its numerous brood of *pronunciamientos*, has resulted in restoring them to an acre of their ancient territory.

on the shores of a powerful empire inhabited by a fierce and warlike race, and, in defiance of the reiterated prohibitions of its sovereign, have forced their way into the interior;—that they should have done this, without knowledge of the language or of the land, without chart or compass to guide them, without any idea of the difficulties they were to encounter, totally uncertain whether the next step might bring them on a hostile nation, or on a desert, feeling their way along in the dark, as it were;—that, though nearly overwhelmed by their first encounter with the inhabitants, they should have still pressed on to the capital of the empire, and, having reached it, thrown themselves unhesitatingly into the midst of their enemies;—that, so far from being daunted by the extraordinary spectacle there exhibited of power and civilization, they should have been but the more confirmed in their original design;—that they should have seized the monarch, have executed his ministers before the eyes of his subjects, and, when driven forth with ruin from the gates, have gathered their scattered wreck together, and, after a system of operations, pursued with consummate policy and daring, have succeeded in overturning the capital, and establishing their sway over the country;—that all this should have been so effected by a mere handful of indigent adventurers, is a fact little short of the miraculous,—too startling for the probabilities demanded by fiction, and without a parallel in the pages of history.

Yet this must not be understood too literally; for it would be unjust to the Aztecs themselves, at least to their military prowess, to regard the Conquest as directly achieved by the Spaniards alone. This would indeed be to arm the latter with the charmed shield of Ruggiero, and the magic lance of Astolfo, overturning its hundreds at a touch. The Indian empire was in a manner conquered by Indians. The first terrible encounter of the Spaniards with the Tlascalans, which had nearly proved their ruin, did in fact insure their success. It secured to them a strong native support, on which to retreat in the hour of trouble, and round which they could rally the kindred races of the land for one great and overwhelming assault. The Aztec monarchy fell by the hands of its own subjects, under the direction of European sagacity and science. Had it been united, it might have bidden defiance to the invaders. As it was, the capital was dissevered from the rest of the country, and the bolt, which might have passed off comparatively harmless, had the empire been cemented by a common principle of loyalty and patriotism, now found its way into every crack and crevice of the ill-compacted fabric, and buried it in its own ruins.—Its fate may serve as a striking proof, that a government, which does not rest on the sympathies of its subjects, cannot long abide; that human institutions, when not connected with human prosperity and progress, must fall,—if not before the increasing light of civilization, by the hand of violence; by violence from within, if not from without. And who shall lament their fall?

With the events of this Book terminates the history. by Solis, of the *Conquista de Méjico;* a history, in many points of view, the most remarkable in the Castilian language.—Don Antonio de Solís was born of a respectable family, in October, 1610, at Alcalá de Henares, the nursery of science, and the name of which is associated in Spain with the brightest ornaments of both church and state. Solís, while very young, exhibited the sparks of future genius, especially in the vivacity of his imagination and a sensibility to the beautiful. He showed a decided turn for dramatic composition, and produced a comedy, at the age of seventeen, which would have reflected credit on a riper age. He afterwards devoted himself with assiduity to the study of ethics, the fruits of which are visible in the moral reflections which give a didactic character to the lightest of his compositions.

At the usual age he entered the University of Salamanca, and went through the regular course of the canon and civil law. But the imaginative spirit of Solís took much more delight in the soft revels of the Muses than in the severe discipline of the schools; and he produced a number of pieces for the theatre, much esteemed for the richness of the diction, and for the ingenious and delicate texture of the intrigue. His taste for dramatic composition was, no doubt, nourished by his intimacy with the great Calderon, for whose dramas he prepared several *loas,* or prologues. The amiable manners and brilliant acquisitions of Solís recommended him to the favor of the Conde de Oropesa, viceroy of Navarre, who made him his secretary. The letters written by him, while in the service of this nobleman, and afterwards, have some of them been given to the public, and are much commended for the suavity and elegance of expression, characteristic of all the writings of their author.

The increasing reputation of Solís attracted the notice of the Court, and, in 1661, he was made secretary of the queen dowager,—an office which he had declined under Philip the Fourth,—and he was also preferred to the still more important post of Historiographer of the Indies, an appointment which stimulated his ambition to a bold career, different from any thing he had yet attempted. Five years after this event, at the age of fifty-six, he made a most important change in his way of life, by embracing the religious profession, and was admitted to priest's orders in 1666. From this time, he discontinued his addresses to the comic Muse; and, if we may credit his biographers, even refused, from conscientious scruples, to engage in the composition of the religious dramas, styled *autos sacramentales,* although the field was now opened to him by the death of the poet Calderon. But such tenderness of conscience it seems difficult to reconcile with the publication of his various comedies, which took place in 1681. It is certain, however, that he devoted himself zealously to his new profession, and to the historical studies in which his office of chronicler had engaged him. At length, the fruits of these studies were given to the world in his *Conquista de Méjico,* which appeared at Madrid in 1684. He designed, it is said, to continue the work to the times after the Conquest. But, if so, he was unfortunately prevented by his death, which occurred about two years after the publication of his history, on the 13th of April, 1686. He died at the age of seventy-six, much regarded for his virtues, and admired for his genius, but in that poverty with which genius and virtue are too often requited.

The miscellaneous poems of Solís were collected and published a few years after his death, in one volume quarto; which has since been reprinted. But his great work, that on which his fame is permanently to rest, is his *Conquista de Méjico.* Notwithstanding the field of history had been occupied by so many eminent Spanish scholars, there was still a new career open to Solís. His predecessors, with all their merits, had shown a strange ignorance of the principles of art. They had regarded historical writing, not as a work of art, but as a science. They had approached it on that side only, and thus divorced it from its legitimate connection with *belles-lettres.* They had thought only of the useful, and nothing of the beautiful; had addressed themselves to the business of instruction, not to that of giving pleasure; to the man of letters, studious to hive up knowledge, not to the man of leisure, who turns to books as a solace or a recreation. Such writers are never in the hands of the many, —not even of the cultivated many. They are condemned to the closet of the student, painfully toiling after truth, and little mindful of the coarse covering under which she may be wrapped. Some of the most distinguished of the national historio-graphers, as, for example, Herrera and Zurita, two of the greatest names in Castile and Aragon, fall under this censure. They display acuteness, strength of argument, judicious criticism, wonderful patience and industry in accumulating details for their varied and voluminous compilations; but in all the graces of composition,— in elegance of style, skilful arrangement of the story, and in selection of incidents, they are lamentably deficient. With all their high merits, intellectually considered, they are so defective on the score of art, that they can neither be popular, nor reverenced as the great classics of the nation.

Solís saw that the field was unappropriated by his predecessors, and had the address to avail himself of it. Instead of spreading himself over a vast range, where he must expend his efforts on cold and barren generalities, he fixed his attention on one great theme,—one, that, by its picturesque accompaniments, the romantic incidents of the story, the adventurous character of the actors, and their exploits, associated with many a proud and patriotic feeling in the bosom of the Spaniard,— one, in fine, that, by the brilliant contrast it afforded of European civilization to the barbaric splendors of an Indian dynasty, was remarkably suited to the kindling imagination of the poet. It was accordingly under its poetic aspect, that the eye of Solís surveyed it. He distributed the whole subject with admirable skill, keeping down the subordinate parts, bringing the most important into high relief, and, by a careful study of its proportions, giving an admirable symmetry to the whole. Instead of bewildering the attention by a variety of objects, he presented to it one great and predominant idea, which shed its light, if I may so say, over his whole work. Instead of the numerous episodes, leading, like so many blind galleries, to nothing, he took the student along a great road, conducting straight towards the mark. At every step which we take in the narrative, we feel ourselves on the advance. The story never falters or stands still. That admirable *liaison* of the parts is maintained, by which one part is held to another, and each preceding event prepares the way for that which is to follow. Even those occasional interruptions, the great stumbling-block of the historian, which cannot be avoided, in consequence of the important bearing which the events that cause them have on the story, are managed with such address, that, if the interest is suspended, it is never snapped. Such halting-places, indeed, are so contrived, as to afford a repose not unwelcome after the stirring scenes in which the reader has been long involved; as the traveller, exhausted by the fatigues of his journey, finds refreshment at places, which, in their own character, have little to recommend them.

The work, thus conducted, affords the interest of a grand spectacle,—of some well-ordered drama, in which scene succeeds to scene, act to act, each unfolding and preparing the mind for the one that is to follow, until the whole is consummated by the grand and decisive *dénouement*. With this *dénouement*, the fall of Mexico, Solís has closed his history, preferring to leave the full impression unbroken on the reader's mind, rather than to weaken it by prolonging the narrative to the Conqueror's death. In this he certainly consulted effect.

Solís used the same care in regard to style, that he showed in the arrangement of his story. It is elaborated with nicest art, and displays that varied beauty and brilliancy which remind us of those finely variegated woods, which, under a high polish, display all the rich tints that lie beneath the surface. Yet this style finds little favor with foreign critics, who are apt to condemn it as tumid, artificial, and verbose. But let the foreign critic beware how he meddles with style, that impalpable essense which surrounds thought as with an atmosphere, giving to it its life and peculiar tone of color, differing in different nations, like the atmospheres which envelope the different planets of our system, and which require to be comprehended, that we may interpret the character of the objects seen through their medium. None but a native can pronounce with any confidence upon style, affected, as it is, by so many casual and local associations, that determine its propriety and its elegance. In the judgment of eminent Spanish critics, the style of Solís claims the merits of perspicuity, copiousness, and classic elegance. Even the foreigner will not be insensible to its power of conveying a living picture to the eye. Words are the colors of the writer, and Solís uses them with the skill of a consummate artist; now displaying the dark tumult of battle, and now refreshing the mind by scenes of quiet magnificence, or of soft luxury and repose.

Solís formed himself, to some extent, on the historical models of Antiquity. He introduced set speeches into the mouths of his personages, speeches of his own composing. The practice may claim high authority among moderns as well as ancients, especially among the great Italian historians. It has its advantages, in enabling the writer to convey, in a dramatic form, the sentiments of the actors, and thus to maintain the charm of historic illusion by never introducing the person of the historian. It has also another advantage, that of exhibiting the author's own sentiments under cover of his hero's,—a more effective mode than if they were introduced as his own. But, to one trained in the school of the great English historians, the practice has something in it unsatisfactory and displeasing. There is something like deception in it. The reader is unable to determine what are the sentiments of the characters and what those of the author. History assumes the air of romance, and the bewildered student wanders about in an uncertain light, doubtful whether he is treading on fact or fiction.

It is open to another objection, when, as it frequently does, it violates the propriety of costume. Nothing is more difficult than to preserve the keeping of the piece, when the new is thus laid on the old,—the imitation of the antique on the antique itself. The declamations of Solís are much prized as specimens of eloquence. But they are too often misplaced; and the rude characters, into whose mouths they are inserted, are as little in keeping with them, as were the Roman heroes with the fashionable wig and sword, with which they strutted on the French stage in Louis the Fourteenth's time.

As to the value of the researches made by Solís in the compilation of his work it is not easy to speak, for the page is supported by none of the notes and references which enable us to track the modern author to the quarry whence he has drawn his materials. It was not the usage of the age. The people of that day, and, indeed, of preceding times, were content to take the author's word for his facts. They did not require to know why he affirmed this thing or doubted that; whether he built his story on the authority of a friend, or of a foe, of a writer of good report, or of evil report. In short, they did not demand a reason for their faith. They were content to take it on trust. This was very comfortable to the historian. It saved him a world of trouble in the process, and it prevented the detection of error, or, at least, of negligence. It prevented it with all who did not carefully go over the same ground with himself. They who have occasion to do this with Solís will probably arise from the examination with no very favorable idea of the extent of his researches; they will find, that, though his situation gave him access to the most valuable repositories in the kingdom, he rarely ascends to original documents, but contents himself with the most obvious and accessible; that he rarely discriminates between the contemporary testimony, and that of later date; in a word, that, in all that constitutes the *scientific* value of history, he falls far below his learned predecessor, Herrera,—rapid as was the composition of this last.

Another objection that may be made to Solís is his bigotry, or rather his fanaticism. This defect, so repugnant to the philosophic spirit which should preside over the labors of the historian, he possessed, it is true, in common with many of his countrymen. But in him it was carried to an uncommon height; and it was peculiarly unfortunate, since his subject, being the contest between the Christian and the Infidel, naturally drew forth the full display of this failing. Instead of regarding the benighted heathen with the usual measure of aversion in which they were held in the Peninsula, after the subjugation of Granada, he considered them as part of the grand confederacy of Satan, not merely breathing the spirit and acting under the invisible influence of the Prince of Darkness, but holding personal communication with him; he seems to have regarded them, in short, as his regular and organized militia. In this view, every act of the unfortunate enemy was a crime. Even good ᴀcts were misrepresented, or referred to evil motives; for how could goodness. originate with the Spirit of Evil? No better evidence of the results of this way of thinking need be given, than that afforded by the ill-favored and unauthorized portrait which the historian has left us of Montezuma,—even in his dying hours. The war of the Conquest was, in short, in the historian's eye, a conflict between light and darkness, between the good principle and the evil principle, between the soldiers of Satan and the chivalry of the Cross. It was a Holy War, in which the sanctity of the cause covered up the sins of the Conquerors; and every one—the meanest soldier who fell in it—might aspire to the crown of martyrdom. With sympathies thus preoccupied, what room was there for that impartial criticism which is the life of history?

The historian's overweening partiality to the Conquerors is still further heightened by those feelings of patriotism,—a bastard patriotism,—which, identifying the writer's own glory with that of his countrymen, makes him blind to their errors. This partiality is especially shown in regard to Cortés, the hero of the piece. The lights and shadows of the picture are all disposed with reference to this principal character. The good is ostentatiously paraded before us, and the bad is winked out of sight. Solís does not stop here, but, by the artful gloss which makes the worse appear the better cause, he calls on us to admire his hero sometimes for his very transgressions. No one, not even Gomara himself, is such a wholesale encomiast of the great Conqueror; and, when his views are contradicted by the statements of honest Diaz, Solís is sure to find a motive for the discrepancy in some sinister purpose of the veteran. He knows more of Cortés, of his actions and his motives, than his companion in arms, or his admiring chaplain.

In this way Solís has presented a beautiful image of his hero,—but it is a hero of romance; a character without a blemish. An eminent Castilian critic has commended him for "having conducted his history with so much art, that it has become a panegyric." This may be true; but, if history be panegyric, panegyric is not history.

Yet, with all these defects,—the existence of which no candid critic will be disposed to deny,—the History of Solís has found such favor with his own countrymen, that it has been printed and reprinted, with all the refinements of editorial luxury. It has been translated into the principal languages of Europe; and such is the charm of its composition, and its exquisite finish as a work of art, that it will doubtless be as imperishable as the language in which it is written, or the memory of the events which it records.

At this place, also, we are to take leave of father Sahagun, who has accompanied us through our narrative. As his information was collected from the traditions of the natives, the contemporaries of the Conquest, it has been of considerable importance in corroborating or contradicting the statements of the Conquerors. Yet its value in this respect is much impaired by the wild and random character of many of the Aztec traditions,—so absurd, indeed, as to carry their own refutation with them. Where the passions are enlisted, what is too absurd to find credit?

The Twelfth Book—as it would appear from his Preface, the Ninth Book originally—of his *Historia de la Nueva España* is devoted to the account of the Conquest. In 1585, thirty years after the first draft, he rewrote this part of his great work, moved to it, as he tells us, "by the desire to correct the defects of the first account, in which some things had found their way that had better been omitted, and other things omitted which were well deserving of record." * It might be supposed, that the obloquy, which the missionary had brought on his head by his honest recital of the Aztec traditions, would have made him more circumspect in this *rifacimento* of his former narrative. But I have not found it so; or that there has been any effort to mitigate the statements that bore hardest on his countrymen. As this manuscript copy must have been that which the author himself deemed the most correct, since. it is his last revision, and as it is more copious than the printed narrative. I have been usually guided by it.

Señor de Bustamante is mistaken in supposing that the edition of this Twelfth Book, which he published in Mexico, in 1829, is from the *reformed* copy of Sahagun. The manuscript cited in these pages is undoubtedly a transcript of that copy. For in the Preface to it, as we have seen, the author himself declares it.—In the intrinsic value of the two drafts there is, after all, but little difference.

* "En el libro nono, donde se trata esta Conquista, se hiciéron ciertos defectos; y fué, que algunas cosas se pusiéron en la narracion de este Conquista que fuéron mal puestas; y otras se calláron, que fuéron mal calladas. Por esta causa, este año de mil quinientos ochenta y cinco, enmende este Libro." MS.

BOOK VII

CONCLUSION
SUBSEQUENT CAREER OF CORTÉS

CHAPTER I

Torture of Guatemozin—Submission of the Country—·Rebuild-
ing of the Capital—Mission to Castile—Complaints against
Cortés—He is confirmed in his Authority

1521—1522

The history of the Conquest of Mexico terminates with the surrender
of the capital. But the history of the Conquest is so intimately blended
with that of the extraordinary man who achieved it, that there would
seem to be an incompleteness in the narrative, if it were not continued
to the close of his personal career. This part of the subject has been very
imperfectly treated by preceding writers. I shall therefore avail myself
of the authentic materials in my possession to give a brief sketch of the
brilliant, but chequered, fortunes which marked the subsequent career
of Cortés.

The first ebullition of triumph was succeeded in the army by very different feelings, as they beheld the scanty spoil gleaned from the conquered city, and as they brooded over the inadequate compensation they
were to receive for all their toils and sufferings. Some of the soldiers of
Narvaez, with feelings of bitter disappointment, absolutely declined to
accept their shares. Some murmured audibly against the general, and
others against Guatemozin, who, they said, could reveal, if he chose, the
place where the treasures were secreted. The white walls of the barracks
were covered with epigrams and pasquinades levelled at Cortés, whom
they accused of taking "one fifth of the booty as Commander-in-chief,
and another fifth as King." As Guatemozin refused to make any revelation in respect to the treasure, or rather declared there was none to make,
the soldiers loudly insisted on his being put to the torture. But for this act
of violence, so contrary to the promise of protection recently made to the
Indian prince, Cortés was not prepared; and he resisted the demand,
until the men, instigated, it is said, by the royal treasurer, Alderete, accused the general of a secret understanding with Guatemozin, and of a
design to defraud the Spanish sovereigns and themselves. These un
merited taunts stung Cortés to the quick, and in an evil hour he delivered

the Aztec prince into the hands of his enemies to work their pleasure
on him.

But the hero, who had braved death in its most awful forms, was not
to be intimidated by bodily suffering. When his companion, the cacique
of Tacuba, who was put to torture with him, testified his anguish by his
groans, Guatemozin coldly rebuked him by exclaiming, "And do you
think I, then, am taking my pleasure in my bath!" [1] At length Cortés,
ashamed of the base part he was led to play, rescued the Aztec prince
from his tormentors before it was too late;—not, however, before it was
too late for his own honor, which has suffered an indelible stain from
this treatment of his royal prisoner.

All that could be wrung from Guatemozin by the extremity of his sufferings was the confession, that much gold had been thrown into the
water. But, although the best divers were employed, under the eye of
Cortés himself, to search the oozy bed of the lake, only a few articles of
inconsiderable value were drawn from it. They had better fortune in
searching a pond in Guatemozin's gardens, where a sun, as it is called,
probably one of the Aztec calendar wheels, made of pure gold, of great
size and thickness, was discovered. The cacique of Tacuba had confessed
that a quantity of treasure was buried in the ground at one of his own
villas. But, when the Spaniards carried him to the spot, he alleged that
"his only motive for saying so was the hope of dying on the road!" The
soldiers, disappointed in their expectations, now, with the usual caprice
of an unlicensed mob, changed their tone, and openly accused their commander of cruelty to his captive. The charge was well deserved,—but not
from them. [2]

The tidings of the fall of Mexico were borne on the wings of the wind
over the plateau, and down the broad sides of the Cordilleras. Many an
envoy made his appearance from the remote Indian tribes, anxious to
learn the truth of the astounding intelligence, and to gaze with their own
eyes on the ruins of the detested city. Among these were ambassadors
from the kingdom of Michuacan, a powerful and independent state, inhabited by one of the kindred Nahuatlac races, and lying between the
Mexican Valley and the Pacific. The embassy was soon followed by the
king of the country in person, who came in great state to the Castilian
quarters. Cortés received him with equal parade, astonished him by the
brilliant evolutions of his cavalry, and by the thunders of his ordnance,
and escorted him in one of the brigantines round the fallen city, whose
pile of smouldering palaces and temples was all that now remained of
the once dread capital of Anahuac. The Indian monarch gazed with silent
awe on the scene of desolation, and eagerly craved the protection of the

---

[1] "¿Estoi yo en algun deleite, ó baño?" (Gomara, Crónica, cap. 145.) The literal
version is not so poetical as "the bed of flowers," into which this exclamation of
Guatemozin is usually rendered.

[2] The most particular account of this disgraceful transaction is given by Bernai
Diaz, one of those selected to accompany the lord of Tacuba to his villa. (Hist. de
la Conquista, cap. 157.) He notices the affair with becoming indignation, but excuses Cortés from a voluntary part in it.

invincible beings who had caused it.[3] His example was followed by ambassadors from the remote regions which had never yet had intercourse with the Spaniards. Cortés, who saw the boundaries of his empire thus rapidly enlarging, availed himself of the favorable dispositions of the natives to ascertain the products and resources of their several countries.

Two small detachments were sent into the friendly state of Michuacan, through which country they penetrated to the borders of the great Southern ocean. No European had as yet descended on its shores so far north of the equator. The Spaniards eagerly advanced into its waters, erected a cross on the sandy margin, and took possession of it, with all the usual formalities, in the name of their Most Catholic Majesties. On their return, they visited some of the rich districts towards the north, since celebrated for their mineral treasures, and brought back samples of gold and Californian pearls, with an account of their discovery of the Ocean. The imagination of Cortés was kindled, and his soul swelled with exultation at the splendid prospects which their discoveries unfolded. "Most of all," he writes to the emperor, "do I exult in the tidings brought me of the Great Ocean. For in it, as cosmographers, and those learned men who know most about the Indies, inform us, are scattered the rich isles teeming with gold and spices and precious stones." [4] He at once sought a favorable spot for a colony on the shores of the Pacific, and made arrangements for the construction of four vessels to explore the mysteries of these unknown seas. This was the beginning of his noble enterprises for discovery in the Gulf of California.

Although the greater part of Anahuac, overawed by the successes of the Spaniards, had tendered their allegiance, there were some, especially on the southern slopes of the Cordilleras, who showed a less submissive disposition. Cortés instantly sent out strong detachments under Sandoval and Alvarado to reduce the enemy and establish colonies in the conquered provinces. The highly colored reports, which Alvarado, who had a quick scent for gold, gave of the mineral wealth of Oaxaca, no doubt operated with Cortés in determining him to select this region for his own particular domain.

The commander-in-chief, with his little band of Spaniards, now daily recruited by reinforcements from the Islands, still occupied the quarters

---

[3] Rel. Terc. de Cortés, ap. Lorenzana, p. 308.

The simple statement of the Conqueror contrasts strongly with the pompous narrative of Herrera, (Hist. General, dec. 3, lib. 3, cap. 3,) and with that of father Cavo, who may draw a little on his own imagination. "Cortés en una canoa ricamente entapizada, llevó á el Rey Vehichilze, y á los nobles de Michoacan á México. Este es uno de los palacios de Moctheuzoma (les decia) ; allí está el gran templo de Huitzilopuctli; estas ruinas son del grande edificio de Quauhtemoc, aquellos de la gran plaza del mercado. Conmovido Vehichilzi de este espectáculo, se le saltáron las lágrimas." Los Tres Siglos de México, (México, 1836,) tom. I, p. 13.

[4] "Que todos los que tienen alguna ciencia, y experiencia en la Navegacion de las Indias, han tenido por muy cierto, que descubriendo por estas Partes la Mar del Sur, se habian de hallar muchas Islas ricas de Oro, y Perlas, y Piedras preciosas, y Especería, y se habian de descubrir y hallar otros muchos secretos y cosas admirables." Rel. Terc. de Cortés, ap. Lorenzana, pp. 302, 303.

of Cojohuacan, which they had taken up at the termination of the siege. Cortés did not immediately decide in what quarter of the Valley to establish the new capital which was to take the place of the ancient Tenochtitlan. The situation of the latter, surrounded by water and exposed to occasional inundations, had some obvious disadvantages. But there was no doubt that in some part of the elevated and central plateau of the Valley the new metropolis should be built, to which both European and Indian might look up as to the head of the colonial empire of Spain. At length he decided on retaining the site of the ancient city, moved to it, as he says, "by its past renown, and the memory"—not an enviable one, surely—"in which it was held among the nations"; and he made preparations for the reconstruction of the capital on a scale of magnificence, which should, in his own language, "raise her to the rank of Queen of the surrounding provinces, in the same manner as she had been of yore." [5]

The labor was to be performed by the Indian population, drawn from all quarters of the Valley, and including the Mexicans themselves, great numbers of whom still lingered in the neighborhood of their ancient residence. At first they showed reluctance, and even symptoms of hostility, when called to this work of humiliation by their conquerors. But Cortés had the address to secure some of the principal chiefs in his interests, and, under their authority and direction, the labor of their countrymen was conducted. The deep groves of the Valley and the forests of the neighboring hills supplied cedar, cypress, and other durable woods, for the interior of the buildings, and the quarries of *tetzontli* and the ruins of the ancient edifices furnished abundance of stone. As there were no beasts of draught employed by the Aztecs, an immense number of hands was necessarily required for the work. All within the immediate control of Cortés were pressed into the service. The spot so recently deserted now swarmed with multitudes of Indians of various tribes, and with Europeans, the latter directing, while the others labored. The prophecy of the Aztecs was accomplished.[6] And the work of reconstruction went forward with a rapidity like that shown by an Asiatic despot, who concentrates the population of an empire on the erection of a favorable capital.[7]

Yet the condition of Cortés, notwithstanding the success of his arms, suggested many causes for anxiety. He had not received a word of encouragement from home,—not a word, indeed, of encouragement or cen-

[5] "Y crea Vuestra Magestad, que cada dia se irá ennobleciendo en tal manera, que como antes fué Principal, y Señora de todas estas Provincias, que lo será tambien de aquí adelante." Ibid., p. 307.

[6] Ante, p. 590.

[7] Herrera, Hist. General, dec. 3, lib. 4, cap. 8.—Oviedo, Hist. de las Ind., MS., lib. 33, cap. 32.—Camargo, Hist. de Tlascala, MS.—Gomara, Crónica, cap. 162.

"En la cual (la edificacion de la ciudad) los primeros años andaba mas gente que en la edificacion del templo de Jerusalem, porque era tanta la gente que andaba en las obras, que apénas podia hombre romper por algunas calles y calzadas, aunque son muy anchas." (Toribio, Hist. de los Indios, MS., Parte 1, cap. 1.) Ixtlilxochitl supplies any blank which the imagination might leave, by filling it up with 400,000, as the number of natives emploved in this work by Cortés! Venida de los Esp., p. 60.

suie. In what light his irregular course was regarded by the government or the nation was still matter of painful uncertainty. He now prepared another Letter to the emperor, the Third in the published series, written in the same simple and energetic style which has entitled his Commentaries, as they may be called, to a comparison with those of Cæsar. It was dated at Cojohuacan, May 15th, 1522, and in it he recapitulated the events of the final siege of the capital, and his subsequent operations, accompanied by many sagacious reflections, as usual, on the character and resources of the country. With this letter he purposed to send the royal fifth of the spoils of Mexico, and a rich collection of fabrics, especially of gold and jewelry wrought into many rare and fanciful forms. One of the jewels was an emerald, cut in a pyramidal shape, of so extraordinary a size, that the base was as broad as the palm of the hand! [8] The collection was still further augmented by specimens of many of the natural products, as well as of animals peculiar to the country.

The army wrote a letter to accompany that of Cortés, in which they expatiated on his manifold services, and besought the emperor to ratify his proceedings and confirm him in his present authority. The important mission was intrusted to two of the general's confidential officers, Quiñones and Avila. It proved to be unfortunate. The agents touched at the Azores, where Quiñones lost his life in a brawl. Avila, resuming his voyage, was captured by a French privateer, and the rich spoils of the Aztecs went into the treasury of his Most Christian Majesty. Francis the First gazed with pardonable envy on the treasures which his Imperial rival drew from his colonial domains and he intimated his discontent by peevishly expressing a desire "to see the clause in Adam's testament which entitled his brothers of Castile and Portugal to divide the New World between them." Avila found means, through a private hand, of transmitting his letters, the most important part of his charge, to Spain, where they reached the court in safety.[9]

While these events were passing, affairs in Spain had been taking an unfavorable turn for Cortés. It may seem strange, that the brilliant exploits of the Conqueror of Mexico should have attracted so little notice from the government at home. But the country was at that time distracted by the dismal feuds of the *comunidades*. The sovereign was in Germany, too much engrossed by the cares of the empire to allow leisure for those of his own kingdom. The reins of government were in the hands of Adrian, Charles's preceptor; a man whose ascetic and studious habits better qualified him to preside over a college of monks, than to fill, as he successively did, the most important posts in Christendom,—first as Regent of Castile, afterwards as Head of the Church. Yet the slow and

[8] "Sirviéron al Emperador con muchas piedras, i entre ellas con una esmeralda fina, como la palma, pero quadrada, i que se remataba en punta como pirámide." (Gomara, Crónica, cap. 146.) Martyr confirms the account of this wonderful emerald, which, he says, "was reported to the king and council to be nearly as broad as the palm of the hand, and which those, who had seen it, thought could not be procured for any sum." De Orbe Novo, dec. 8, cap. 4.

[9] Ibid., ubi supra.—Bernal Diaz, Hist. de la Conquista, cap. 169.

hesitating Adrian could not have so long passed over in silence the important services of Cortés, but for the hostile interference of Velasquez,
the governor of Cuba, sustained by Fonseca, bishop of Burgos, the chief
person in the Spanish colonial department. This prelate, from his elevated station, possessed paramount authority in all matters relating to
the Indies, and he had exerted it from the first, as we have already seen,
in a manner most prejudicial to the interests of Cortés. He had now the
address to obtain a warrant from the regent, which was designed to ruin
the Conqueror at the very moment when his great enterprise had been
crowned with success. The instrument, after recapitulating the offences of
Cortés in regard to Velasquez, appoints a commissioner with full powers
to visit the country, to institute an inquiry into the general's conduct, to
suspend him from his functions, and even to seize his person and sequestrate his property, until the pleasure of the Castilian court could be
known. The warrant was signed by Adrian, at Burgos, on the 11th of
April, 1521, and countersigned by Fonseca.[10]

The individual selected for the delicate task of apprehending Cortés
and bringing him to trial, in the theatre of his own discoveries and in
the heart of his own camp, was named Christóval de Tapia, *veedor*, or inspector of the gold foundries in St. Domingo. He was a feeble, vacillating
man, as little competent to cope with Cortés in civil matters, as Narvaez
had shown himself to be in military.

The commissioner, clothed in his brief authority, landed, in December,
at Villa Rica. But he was coldly received by the magistrates of the city.
His credentials were disputed, on the ground of some technical informality. It was objected, moreover, that his commission was founded on obvious misrepresentations to the government; and, notwithstanding a most
courteous and complimentary epistle which he received from Cortés, congratulating him, as an old friend, on his arrival, the *veedor* soon found
that he was neither to be permitted to penetrate far into the country, nor
to exercise any control there. He loved money, and, as Cortés knew the
weak side of his "old friend," he proposed to purchase his horses, slaves,
and equipage, at a tempting price. The dreams of disappointed ambition
were gradually succeeded by those of avarice; and the discomfited commissioner consented to reëmbark for Cuba, well freighted with gold, if
not with glory, and provided with fresh matter of accusation against the
high-handed measures of Cortés.[11]

[10] The instrument also conferred similar powers in respect to an inquiry into
Narvaez's treatment of the licentiate Ayllon. The whole document is cited in a
deposition drawn up by the notary, Alonso de Vergara, setting forth the proceedings of Tapia and the municipality of Villa Rica, dated at Cempoalla, Dec. 24th,
1521. The MS. forms part of the collection of Don Vargas Ponçe, in the archives of
the Academy of History at Madrid.

[11] Relacion de Vergara, MS.—Rel Terc. de Cortés, ap. Lorenzana, pp. 309–314.—
Bernal Diaz, Hist. de la Conquista, cap. 158.

The *regidores* of Mexico and other places remonstrated against Cortés' leaving
the Valley to meet Tapia, on the ground that his presence was necessary to overawe
the natives. (MS., Coyoacan, Dec. 12, 1521.) The general acquiesced in the force of
a remonstrance, which, it is not improbable, was made at his own suggestion.

Thus left in undisputed possession of authority, the Spanish commander went forward with vigor in his plans for the settlement of his conquests. The Panuchese, a fierce people on the borders of the Panuco, on the Atlantic coast, had taken up arms against the Spaniards. Cortés marched at the head of a considerable force into their country, defeated them in two pitched battles, and, after a severe campaign, reduced the warlike tribe to subjection.

A subsequent insurrection was punished with greater severity. They rose on the Spaniards, massacred five hundred of their oppressors, and menaced with destruction the neighboring settlement of San Estévan. Cortés ordered Sandoval to chastise the insurgents; and that officer, after a campaign of incredible hardship, completely routed the barbarians, captured four hundred of their chiefs, and, after the affected formalities of a trial, sentenced every man of them to the stake or the gibbet. "By which means," says Cortés, "God be praised! the safety of the Spaniards was secured, and the province once more restored to tranquillity and peace." [12] He had omitted to mention in his Letter his ungenerous treatment of Guatemozin. But the undisguised and *naïve* manner, so to speak, in which he details these circumstances to the emperor, shows that he attached no discredit to the deed. It was the just recompense of *rebellion;* a word that has been made the apology for more atrocities than any other word,—save *religion.*

During this interval, the great question in respect to Cortés and the colony had been brought to a decisive issue. The general must have succumbed under the insidious and implacable attacks of his enemies, but for the sturdy opposition of a few powerful friends zealously devoted to his interests. Among them may be mentioned his own father, Don Martin Cortés, a discreet and efficient person,[13] and the Duke de Bejar, a powerful nobleman, who from an early period had warmly espoused the cause of Cortés. By their representations the timid regent was at length convinced that the measures of Fonseca were prejudicial to the interests of the Crown, and an order was issued interdicting him from further interference in any matters in which Cortés was concerned.

While the exasperated prelate was chafing under this affront, both the commissioners Tapia and Narvaez arrived in Castile. The latter had been ordered to Cojohuacan after the surrender of the capital, where his cringing demeanor formed a striking contrast to the swaggering port which he had assumed on first entering the country. When brought into the presence of Cortés, he knelt down and would have kissed his hand, but the latter raised him from the ground, and, during his residence in his quarters, treated him with every mark of respect. The general soon

---

[12] "Como ya (loado nuestro Señor) estaba toda la Provincia muy pacífica, y segura." Rel. Quarta de Cortés, ap. Lorenzana, p. 367.

[13] The Muñoz collection of MSS. contains a power of attorney given by Cortés to his father, authorizing him to manage all negotiations with the emperor, and with private persons, to conduct all lawsuits on his behalf, to pay over and receive money, &c.

afterwards permitted his unfortunate rival to return to Spain, where h.
proved, as might have been anticipated, a most bitter and implacable
enemy.[14]

These two personages, reinforced by the discontented prelate, brought
forward their several charges against Cortés with all the acrimony which
mortified vanity and the thirst of vengeance could inspire. Adrian was no
longer in Spain, having been called to the chair of St. Peter; but Charles
the Fifth, after his long absence, had returned to his dominions, in July,
1522. The royal ear was instantly assailed with accusations of Cortés on
the one hand and his vindication on the other, till the young monarch,
perplexed, and unable to decide on the merits of the question, referred
the whole subject to the decision of a board selected for the purpose. It
was drawn partly from the members of his privy council, and partly from
the Indian department, with the Grand Chancellor of Naples as its president; and constituted altogether a tribunal of the highest respectability
for integrity and wisdom.[15]

By this learned body a patient and temperate hearing was given to
the parties. The enemies of Cortés accused him of having seized and finally destroyed the fleet intrusted to him by Velasquez, and fitted out at
the governor's expense; of having afterwards usurped powers in contempt
of the royal prerogative; of the unjustifiable treatment of Narvaez and
Tapia, when they had been lawfully commissioned to supersede him; of
cruelty to the natives, and especially to Guatemozin; of embezzling the
royal treasures, and remitting but a small part of its dues to the Crown;
of squandering the revenues of the conquered countries in useless and
wasteful schemes, and particularly in rebuilding the capital on a plan of
unprecedented extravagance; of pursuing, in short, a system of violence
and extortion, without respect to the public interest, or any other end
than his own selfish aggrandizement.

In answer to these grave charges, the friends of Cortés adduced evidence to show, that he had defrayed with his own funds two thirds of
the cost of the expedition. The powers of Velasquez extended only to
traffic, not to establish a colony. Yet the interests of the Crown required
the latter. The army had therefore necessarily assumed this power to
themselves; but, having done so, they had sent intelligence of their proceedings to the emperor and solicited his confirmation of them. The rupture with Narvaez was that commander's own fault; since Cortés would
have met him amicably, had not the violent measures of his rival, threatening the ruin of the expedition, compelled him to an opposite course.
The treatment of Tapia was vindicated on the grounds alleged to that
officer by the municipality at Cempoalla. The violence to Guatemozin

[14] Bernal Diaz, Hist. de la Conquista, cap. 158.
[15] Sayas, Annales de Aragon, (Zaragoza, 1666,) cap. 63, 78.
It is sufficient voucher for the respectability of this court, that we find in it the
name of Dr. Galindez de Carbajal, an eminent Castilian jurist, grown grey in the
service of Ferdinand and Isabella, whose confidence he enjoyed in the highest degree.

was laid at the door of Alderete, the royal treasurer, who had instigated the soldiers to demand it. The remittances to the Crown, it was clearly proved, so far from falling short of the legitimate fifth, had considerably exceeded it. If the general had expended the revenues of the country on costly enterprises and public works, it was for the interest of the country that he did so, and he had incurred a heavy debt by straining his own credit to the utmost for the same great objects. Neither did they deny, that, in the same spirit, he was now rebuilding Mexico on a scale which should be suited to the metropolis of a vast and opulent empire.

They enlarged on the opposition he had experienced, throughout his whole career, from the governor of Cuba, and still more from the bishop of Burgos, which latter functionary, instead of affording him the aid to have been expected, had discouraged recruits, stopped his supplies, sequestered such property as, from time to time, he had sent to Spain, and falsely represented his remittances to the Crown, as coming from the governor of Cuba. In short, such and so numerous were the obstacles thrown in his path, that Cortés had been heard to say, "he had found it more difficult to contend against his own countrymen than against the Aztecs." They concluded with expatiating on the brilliant results of his expedition, and asked if the council were prepared to dishonor the man, who, in the face of such obstacles, and with scarcely other resources than what he found in himself, had won an empire for Castile, such as was possessed by no European potentate! [16]

This last appeal was irresistible. However irregular had been the manner of proceeding, no one could deny the grandeur of the results. There was not a Spaniard that could be insensible to such services, or that would not have cried out, "Shame!" at an ungenerous requital of them. There were three Flemings in the council; but there seems to have been no difference of opinion in the body. It was decided, that neither Velasquez nor Fonseca should interfere further in the concerns of New Spain. The difficulties of the former with Cortés were regarded in the nature of a private suit; and, as such, redress must be sought by the regular course of law. The acts of Cortés were confirmed in their full extent. He was constituted Governor, Captain-General, and Chief Justice of New Spain, with power to appoint to all offices, civil and military, and to order any person to leave the country, whose residence there he might deem prejudicial to the interests of the Crown. This judgment of the council was ratified by Charles the Fifth, and the commission investing Cortés with these ample powers was signed by the emperor at Valladolid, October 15th, 1522. A liberal salary was provided, to enable the governor of New Spain to maintain his office with suitable dignity. The principal officers were recompensed with honors and substantial emoluments; and the troops, together with some privileges, grateful to the vanity of the soldier, received the promise of liberal grants of land. The emperor still further

---

[16] Sayas, Annales de Aragon, cap. 78.—Herrera, Hist. General, dec. 3, lib. 4, cap. 3.—Probanza en la Villa Segura, MS.—Declaraciones de Puertocarrero y de Montejo, MSS.

complimented them by a letter written to the army with his own hand, in which he acknowledged its services in the fullest manner.[17]

From this hour the influence of Fonseca in the Indian department was at an end. He did not long survive his chagrin, as he died in the following year. No man was in a situation to do more for the prosperity of his country than the bishop of Burgos. For more than thirty years, ever since the first dawn of discovery under Columbus, he had held supreme control over colonial affairs; and it lay with him, therefore, in an especial degree, to give ardor to enterprise, and to foster the youthful fortunes of the colonies. But he lay like a blight upon them. He looked with an evil eye on the most illustrious of the Spanish discoverers, and sought only to throw impediments in their career. Such had been his conduct towards Columbus, and such to Cortés. By a wise and generous policy, he might have placed his name among the great lights of his age. As it was, he only served to bring these into greater lustre by contrast with his own dark and malignant nature. His career shows the overweening ascendency which the ecclesiastical profession possessed in Castile in the sixteenth century; when it could raise a man to so important a station, for which he was totally unfit,—and keep him there after he had proved himself to be so.[18]

The messengers, who bore the commission of Cortés to Mexico, touched on their way at Cuba, where the tidings were proclaimed by sound of trumpet. It was a death-blow to the hopes of Velasquez. Exasperated by the failure of his schemes, impoverished by the expense of expeditions of which others had reaped the fruits, he had still looked forward to eventual redress, and cherished the sweet hope of vengeance, —long delayed. That hope was now gone. There was slight chance of redress, he well knew, in the tedious and thorny litigation of the Castilian courts. Ruined in fortune, dishonored before the nation, the haughty spirit of the governor was humbled in the dust. He would take no comfort, but fell into a sullen melancholy, and in a few months died—if report be true—of a broken heart.[19]

The portrait usually given of Velasquez is not favorable. Yet Las Casas speaks kindly of him, and, when his prejudices are not involved, there can be no better authority. But Las Casas knew him, when, in his earlier days, the missionary first landed in Cuba. The governor treated him with courtesy, and even confidence; and it was natural, that the condescension of a man of high family and station should have made its impression on the feelings of the poor ecclesiastic. In most accounts he

[17] Nombramiento de Governador y Capitan General y Justicia Mayor de Nueva España, MS.—Also Bernal Diaz, Hist. de la Conquista, cap. 168.

[18] The character of Fonseca has been traced by the same hand which has traced that of Columbus. (Irving's Life and Voyages of Columbus, Appendix, No. 32.) Side by side they will go down to posterity in the beautiful page of the historian, though the characters of the two individuals have been inscribed with pens as different from each other as the golden and iron pen which Poalo Giovio tells us he employed in his compositions.

[19] Bernal Diaz, Hist. de la Conquista, cap. 158.

is depicted as a haughty, irascible person, jealous of authority, and covetous of wealth. He quarrelled with Grijalva, Cortés' predecessor, apparently without cause. With as little reason, he broke with Cortés before he left the port. He proposed objects to himself in their nature incompatible. He proposed that others should fight his battles, and that he should win the laurels; that others should make discoveries, and that he should reap the fruits of them. None but a weak mind would have conformed to his conditions, and a weak mind could not have effected his objects. His appointment of Cortés put him in a false position for the rest of his life. His efforts to retrieve his position only made things worse. The appointment of Cortés to the command was scarcely a greater error, than the subsequent appointment of Narvaez and of Tapia. The life of Velasquez was a series of errors.

The announcement of the emperor's commission, confirming Cortés in the supreme authority of New Spain, was received there with general acclamation. The army rejoiced in having, at last, secured not merely an amnesty for their irregular proceedings, but a distinct acknowledgment of their services. The nomination of Cortés to the supreme command put his mind at ease as to the past, and opened to him a noble theatre for future enterprise. The soldiers congratulated themselves on the broad powers conferred on their commander, and, as they reckoned up their scars and their services, indulged in golden dreams and the most vague and visionary expectations. It is not strange that their expectations should have been disappointed.

CHAPTER II

MODERN MEXICO—SETTLEMENT OF THE COUNTRY—CONDITION OF THE
NATIVES—CHRISTIAN MISSIONARIES—CULTIVATION OF THE SOIL—
VOYAGES AND EXPEDITIONS

1522—1524

IN less than four years from the destruction of Mexico, a new city had
risen on its ruins, which, if inferior to the ancient capital in extent, surpassed it in magnificence and strength. It occupied so exactly the same
site as its predecessor, that the *plaza mayor*, or great square, was the
same spot which had been covered by the huge *teocalli* and the palace of
Montezuma; while the principal streets took their departure as before
from this central point, and, passing through the whole length of the city,
terminated at the principal causeways. Great alterations, however, took
place in the fashion of the architecture. The streets were widened, many
of the canals were filled up, and the edifices were constructed on a plan
better accommodated to European taste and the wants of a European
population.

On the site of the temple of the Aztec war-god rose the stately cathedral dedicated to St. Francis; and, as if to complete the triumphs of the
Cross, the foundations were laid with the broken images of the Aztec
gods.[1] In a corner of the square, on the ground once covered by the
House of Birds, stood a Franciscan convent, a magnificent pile, erected
a few years after the Conquest by a lay brother, Pedro de Gante, a natural son, it is said, of Charles the Fifth.[2] In an opposite quarter of the
same square Cortés caused his own palace to be constructed. It was built
of hewn stone, and seven thousand cedar beams are said to have been
used for the interior.[3] The government afterwards appropriated it to the
residence of the viceroys; and the Conqueror's descendants, the dukes of
Monteleone, were allowed to erect a new mansion in another part of the
plaza, on the spot which, by an ominous coincidence, had been covered
by the palace of Montezuma.[4]

The houses occupied by the Spaniards were of stone, combining with
elegance a solid strength which made them capable of defence like so

[1] Herrera, Hist. General, dec. 3, lib. 4, cap. 8.
[2] Clavigero, Stor. del Messico, tom. I. p. 271.—Humboldt. Essai Politique. tom.
II. p. 58.
[3] Herrera, Hist. General, ubi supra.
[4] Humboldt, Essai Politique, tom. II. p. 72.

many fortresses.[5] The Indian buildings were for the most part of an inferior quality. They were scattered over the ancient district of Tlatelolco, where the nation had made its last stand for freedom. This quarter was also provided with a spacious cathedral; and thirty inferior churches attested the care of the Spaniards for the spiritual welfare of the natives.[6] It was in watching over his Indian flock, and in the care of the hospitals with which the new capital was speedily endowed, that the good father Olmedo, when oppressed by growing infirmities, spent the evening of his days.[7]

To give greater security to the Spaniards, Cortés caused a strong fortress to be erected in a place since known as the *Matadero*.[8] It was provided with a dock-yard, and the brigantines, which had served in the siege of Mexico, were long preserved there as memorials of the Conquest. When the fortress was completed, the general, owing to the evil offices of Fonseca, found himself in want of artillery and ammunition for its defence. He supplied the former deficiency by causing cannon to be cast in his own founderies, made of the copper which was common in the country, and tin which he obtained with more difficulty from the mines of Tasco. By this means, and a contribution which he received from the shipping, he contrived to mount his walls with seventy pieces of ordnance. Stone balls, used much in that age, could easily be made; but for the manufacture of his powder, although there was nitre in abundance, he was obliged to seek the sulphur by a perilous expedition into the bowels of the great *volcan*.[9] Such were the resources displayed by Cortés, enabling him to supply every deficiency, and to triumph over every obstacle which the malice of his enemies had thrown in his path.

The general's next care was to provide a population for the capital. He invited the Spaniards thither by grants of lands and houses, while the Indians, with politic liberality, were permitted to live under their own chiefs as before, and to enjoy various immunities. With this encouragement, the Spanish quarter of the city in the neighborhood of the great square could boast in a few years two thousand families; while the Indian district of Tlatelolco included no less than thirty thousand.[10] The various trades and occupations were resumed; the canals were again covered with barges; two vast markets in the respective quarters of the capital displayed all the different products and manufactures of the surrounding country; and the city swarmed with a busy, industrious population, in which the white man and the Indian, the conqueror and the conquered, mingled together promiscuously in peaceful and picturesque confusion. Not twenty years had elapsed since the Conquest, when a missionary

[5] Rel. d' un gent., ap. Ramusio, tom. III. fol. 309.
[6] Ibid., ubi supra.
[7] Bernal Diaz, Hist. de la Conquista, cap. 177.
[8] Rel. Quarta de Cortés, ap. Lorenzana, p. 376, nota.
[9] For an account of this singular enterprise, see Ante, p. 285.
[10] Cortés, reckoning only the Indian population, says *treinta mil vecinos*. (Rel. Quarta, ap. Lorenzana, p. 375.) Gomara, speaking of Mexico some years later, estimates the number of Spanish householders as in the text. Crónica, cap. 162.

who visited it had the confidence, or the credulity, to assert, that "Europe could not boast a single city so fair and opulent as Mexico." [11]

The metropolis of our day would seem to stand in a different situation from that reared by the Conquerors; for the waters no longer flow through its streets, nor wash the ample circumference of its walls. These waters have retreated within the diminished basin of Tezcuco; and the causeways, which anciently traversed the depths of the lake, are not now to be distinguished from the other avenues to the capital. But the city, embellished, it is true, by the labors of successive viceroys, is substantially the same as in the days of the Conquerors; and the massive grandeur of the few buildings that remain of the primitive period, and the general magnificence and symmetry of its plan, attest the far-sighted policy of its founder, which looked beyond the present to the wants of coming generations.

The attention of Cortés was not confined to the capital. He was careful to establish settlements in every part of the country which afforded a favorable position for them. He founded Zacatula on the shores of the miscalled Pacific, Coliman in the territory of Michuacan, San Estéban on the Atlantic coast, probably not far from the site of Tampico, Medellin (so called after his own birth-place) in the neighborhood of the modern Vera Cruz, and a port near the river Antigua, from which it derived its name. It was designed to take the place of Villa Rica, which, as experience had shown, from its exposed situation, afforded no protection to shipping against the winds that sweep over the Mexican Gulf. Antigua, sheltered within the recesses of a bay, presented a more advantageous position. Cortés established there a board of trade, connected the settlement by a highway with the capital, and fondly predicted that his new city would become the great emporium of the country.[12] But in this he was mistaken. From some cause not very obvious, the port of entry was removed, at the close of the sixteenth century, to the modern Vera Cruz; which, without any superiority, probably, of topographical position, or even of salubrity of climate, has remained ever since the great commercial capital of New Spain.

Cortés stimulated the settlement of his several colonies by liberal grants of land and municipal privileges. The great difficulty was to induce women to reside in the country, and without them he felt that the colonies, like a tree without roots, must soon perish. By a singular provision he required every settler, if a married man, to bring over his wife within eighteen

[11] Toribio, Hist. de los Indios, MS., Parte 3, cap. 7.

Yet this is scarcely stronger language than that of the Anonymous Conqueror; "Cosí ben ordinato et di si belle piazze et strade, quanto d' altre città che siano al mondo." Rel. d' un gent., ap. Ramusio, tom. III. fol. 309.

[12] "Y tengo por cierto, que aquel Pueblo ha de ser, despues de esta Ciudad, el mejor que obiere en esta Nueva España." (Rel. Quarta, ap. Lorenzana, p. 382.) The archbishop confounds this town with the modern Vera Cruz. But the general's description of the port refutes this supposition, and confirms our confidence in Clavigero's statement, that the present city was founded by the Conde de Monterey, at the time mentioned in the text. See p. 191, note.

.nonths on pain of forfeiting his estate. If he were too poor to do this himself, the government would assist him. Another law imposed the same penalty on all bachelors who did not provide themselves with wives with· in the same period! The general seems to have considered celibacy as too great a luxury for a young country.[13]

His own wife, Doña Catalina Xuarez, was among those who came over from the Islands to New Spain. According to Bernal Diaz, her coming gave him no particular satisfaction.[14] It is possible; since his marriage with her seems to have been entered into with reluctance, and her lowly condition and connections stood somewhat in the way of his future advancement. Yet they lived happily together for several years, according to the testimony of Las Casas;[15] and, whatever he may have felt, he had the generosity, or the prudence, not to betray his feelings to the world. On landing, Doña Catalina was escorted by Sandoval to the capital, where she was kindly received by her husband, and all the respect paid to her, to which she was entitled by her elevated rank. But the climate of the table-land was not suited to her constitution, and she died in three months after her arrival.[16] An event so auspicious to his worldly prospects did not fail, as we shall see hereafter, to provoke the tongue of scandal to the most malicious, but it is scarcely necessary to say, unfounded inferences.

[13] Ordenanzas Municipales, Tenochtitlan, Marzo, 1524, MS.

The Ordinances made by Cortés, for the government of the country during his viceroyalty, are still preserved in Mexico; and the copy in my possession was transmitted to me from that capital. They give ample evidence of the wise and penetrating spirit which embraced every object worthy of the attention of an enlightened ruler; and I will quote, in the original, the singular provisions mentioned in the text.

"Item. Por que mas se manifieste la voluntad que los pobladores de estas partes tienen de residir y permanecer en ellas, mando que todas las personas que tuvieren Indios, que fueren casados en Castilla ó en otras partes, que traigan sus mugeres dentro de un año y medio primero siguientes de como estas ordenanzas fueren pregonadas, so pena de perder los Indios, y todo lo con ellos adquirido é grangeado; y por que muchas personas podrian poner por achaque aunque tuviesen aparejo de decir que no tienen dineros para enviar por ellas, por hende las tales personas que tuvieran esta necesidad parescan ante el R°. P°. Fray Juan de Teto y ante Alonso de Estrada, tesorero de su Magestad, á les informar de su necesidad, para que ellos la comuniquen á mí, y su necesidad se remedie; y si algunas personas hay que casados y no tienen sus mugeres en esta tierra, y quisieran traerlas, sepan que trayéndolas serán ayudadas así mismo para las traer dando fianzas.

"Item. Por quanto en esta tierra hay muchas personas que tienen Indios de en comienda y no son casados, por hende por que conviene así para *la salud de sus conciencias de los tales* por estar en buen estado, como por la poblacion é noblecimiento de sus tierras, mando que las tales personas se casen, traigan y tengan sus mugeres en esta tierra dentro de un año y medio, des pues que fueren pregonadas estas dichas Ordenanzas, é que no haciendo lo por el mismo caso sean privados y pierdan los tales Indios que así tienen."

[14] Bernal Diaz, Hist. de la Conquista, cap. 160.

[15] Ante, p. 134.

[16] Of asthma, according to Bernal Diaz; (Hist. de la Conquista, ubi supra;) but her death seems to have been too sudden to be attributed to that disease. I shall return to the subject hereafter.

In the distribution of the soil among the Conquerors, Cortés adopted the vicious system of *repartimientos*, universally practised among his countrymen. In a letter to the emperor, he states, that the superior capacity of the Indians in New Spain had made him regard it as a grevious thing to condemn them to servitude, as had been done in the Islands. But, on further trial, he had found the Spaniards so much harassed and impoverished, that they could not hope to maintain themselves in the land without enforcing the services of the natives, and for this reason he had at length waived his own scruples in compliance with their repeated remonstrances.[17] This was the wretched pretext used on the like occasions by his countrymen to cover up this flagrant act of injustice. The Crown, however, in its instructions to the general, disavowed the act and annulled the *repartimientos*.[18] It was all in vain. The necessities, or rather the cupidity, of the colonists, easily evaded the royal ordinances. The colonial legislation of Spain shows, in the repetition of enactments against slavery, the perpetual struggle that subsisted between the Crown and the colonists, and the impotence of the former to enforce measures repugnant to the interests, at all events to the avarice, of the latter. New Spain furnishes no exception to the general fact.

The Tlascalans, in gratitude for their signal services, were exempted, at the recommendation of Cortés, from the doom of slavery. It should be added, that the general, in granting the *repartimientos*, made many humane regulations for limiting the power of the master, and for securing as many privileges to the native as were compatible with any degree of compulsory service.[19] These limitations, it is true, were too often disregarded; and in the mining districts, in particular, the situation of the poor Indian was often deplorable. Yet the Indian population, clustering together in their own villages, and living under their own magistrates, have continued to prove by their numbers, fallen as these have below their primitive amount, how far superior was their condition to that in most other parts of the vast colonial empire of Spain.[20] This condition has been gradually ameliorated, under the influence of higher moral views and larger ideas of government; until the servile descendants of the ancient lords of the soil have been permitted, in republican Mexico, to rise—nominally, at least—to a level with the children of their conquerors.

Whatever disregard he may have shown to the political rights of the natives, Cortés manifested a commendable solicitude for their spiritual

[17] Rel. Terc., ap. Lorenzana, pp. 319, 320.

[18] Herrera, Hist. General, dec. 3, lib. 5, cap. 1.

[19] Ibid., dec. 4, lib. 6, cap. 5.—Ordenanzas, MS.

The ordinances prescribe the service of the Indians, the hours they may be employed, their food, compensation, and the like. They require the *encomendero* to provide them with suitable means of religious instruction and places of worship.— But what avail good laws, which, in their very nature, imply the toleration of a great abuse?

[20] The whole population of New Spain, in 1810, is estimated by Don Francisco Navarro y Noriega at about 6,000,000; of which more than half were pure Indians. The author had the best means for arriving at a correct result. See Humboldt, Essai Politique, tom. I. pp. 318, 319, note.

welfare. He requested the emperor to send out holy men to the country; not bishops and pampered prelates, who too often squandered the substance of the Church in riotous living, but godly persons, members of religious fraternities, whose lives might be a fitting commentary on their teaching. Thus only, he adds,—and the remark is worthy of note,—can they exercise any influence over the natives, who have been accustomed to see the least departure from morals in their own priesthood punished with the utmost rigor of the law.[21] In obedience to these suggestions twelve Franciscan friars embarked for New Spain, which they reached early in 1524. They were men of unblemished purity of life, nourished with the learning of the cloister, and, like many others whom the Romish Church has sent forth on such apostolic missions, counted all personal sacrifices as little in the sacred cause to which they were devoted.[22]

The presence of the reverend fathers in the country was greeted with general rejoicing. The inhabitants of the towns through which they passed came out in a body to welcome them; processions were formed of the natives bearing wax tapers in their hands, and the bells of the churches rung out a joyous peal in honor of their arrival. Houses of refreshment were provided for them along their route to the capital; and, when they entered it, they were met by a brilliant cavalcade of the principal cavaliers and citizens, with Cortés at their head. The general, dismounting, and bending one knee to the ground, kissed the robes of father Martin of Valencia, the principal of the fraternity. The natives, filled with amazement at the viceroy's humiliation before men whose naked feet and tattered garments gave them the aspect of mendicants, henceforth regarded them as beings of a superior nature. The Indian chronicler of Tlascala does not conceal his admiration of this edifying condescension of Cortés, which he pronounces "one of the most heroical acts of his life!" [23]

The missionaries lost no time in the good work of conversion. They began their preaching through interpreters, until they had acquired a

[21] Rel. Quarta, ap. Lorenzana, pp. 391-394.

The petition of the Conquerors was acceded to by government, which further prohibited "attorneys and men learned in the law from setting foot in the country, on the ground that experience had shown, they would be sure by their evil practices to disturb the peace of the community." (Herrera, Hist. General, dec. 3, lib. 5, cap. 2.) These enactments are but an indifferent tribute to the character of the two professions in Castile.

[22] Toribio, Hist. de los Indios, MS., Parte 1, cap. 1.—Camargo, Hist. de Tlascala, MS.

[23] "Cuyo hecho del rotísimo y humilde recebimiento fué uno de los heroicos hechos que este Capitan hizo, porque fué documento para que con mayor fervor los naturales desta tierra viniesen á la conversion de nuestra fee." (Camargo, Hist. de Tlascala, MS.—See also Bernal Diaz, Hist. de la Conquista, cap. 171.) Archbishop Lorenzana falls nothing short of the Tlascalan historian in his admiration of the religious zeal of the great *Conquistador,* which, he assures us, "entirely overwhelms him, as savoring so much more of the apostolic missionary than of the soldier!" Lorenzana, n 203. nota.

competent knowledge of the language themselves. They opened schools
and founded colleges, in which the native youth were instructed in profane as well as Christian learning. The ardor of the Indian neophyte
emulated that of his teacher. In a few years every vestige of the primitive *teocallis* was effaced from the land. The uncouth idols of the country,
and unhappily the hieroglyphical manuscripts, shared the same fate.
Yet the missionary and the convert did much to repair these losses by
their copious accounts of the Aztec institutions, collected from the most
authentic sources.[24]

The business of conversion went on prosperously among the several
tribes of the great Nahuatlac family. In about twenty years from the
first advent of the missionaries, one of their body could make the pious
vaunt, that nine millions of converts—a number probably exceeding the
population of the country—had been admitted within the Christian
fold![25] The Aztec worship was remarkable for its burdensome ceremonial,
and prepared its votaries for the pomp and splendors of the Romish ritual. It was not difficult to pass from the fasts and festivals of the one religion to the fasts and festivals of the other; to transfer their homage
from the fantastic idols of their own creation to the beautiful forms in
sculpture and in painting which decorated the Christian cathedral. It is
true, they could have comprehended little of the dogmas of their new
faith, and little, it may be, of its vital spirit. But, if the philosopher may
smile at the reflection, that conversion, under these circumstances, was
one of form rather than of substance, the philanthropist will console
himself by considering how much the cause of humanity and good morals
must have gained by the substitution of these unsullied rites for the brutal abominations of the Aztecs.

The Conquerors settled in such parts of the country as best suited their
inclinations. Many occupied the south-eastern slopes of the Cordilleras
towards the rich valley of Oaxaca. Many more spread themselves over
the broad surface of the table-land, which, from its elevated position, reminded them of the plateau of their own Castiles. Here, too, they were
in the range of those inexhaustible mines which have since poured their
silver deluge over Europe. The mineral resources of the land were not,
indeed, fully explored or comprehended till at a much later period; but

[24] Toribio, Hist. de los Indios, MS., Parte 3, cap. 1.

Father Sahagun, who has done better service in this way than any other of his
order, describes with simple brevity the rapid process of demolition. "We took the
children of the caciques," he says, "into our schools, where we taught them to read,
write, and to chant. The children of the poorer natives were brought together in
the court-yard, and instructed there in the Christian faith. After our teaching, one
or two brethren took the pupils to some neighboring *teocalli,* and, by working at it
for a few days, they levelled it to the ground. In this way they demolished, in a
short time, all the Aztec temples, great and small, *so that not a vestige of them remained."* (Hist. de Nueva España, tom. III. p. 77.) This passage helps to explain
why so few architectural relics of the Indian era still survive in Mexico.

[25] "De manera que á mi juicio y verdaderamente serán bautizados en este tiempo
que digo, que serán quince años, mas de nueve millones de ánimas de Indios." Toribio, Hist. de los Indios, MS., Parte 2, cap. 3.

some few, as the mines of Zacatecas, Guanuaxato, and Tasco,—the last of which was also known in Montezuma's time,—had begun to be wrought within a generation after the Conquest.[26]

But the best wealth of the first settlers was in the vegetable products of the soil, whether indigenous, or introduced from abroad by the wise economy of Cortés. He had earnestly recommended the Crown to require all vessels coming to the country to bring over a certain quantity of seeds and plants.[27] He made it a condition of the grants of land on the plateau, that the proprietor of every estate should plant a specified number of vines in it.[28] He further stipulated, that no one should get a clear title to his estate until he had occupied it eight years.[29] He knew that permanent residence could alone create that interest in the soil, which would lead to its efficient culture; and that the opposite system had caused the impoverishment of the best plantations in the Islands. His various regulations, some of them not a little distasteful to the colonists, augmented the agricultural resources of the country by the addition of the most important European grains and other vegetables, for which the diversified climate of New Spain was admirably adapted. The sugar-cane was transplanted from the neighboring islands to the lower level of the country, and, together with indigo, cotton, and cochineal, formed a more desirable staple for the colony than its precious metals. Under the sun of the tropics, the peach, the almond, the orange, the vine, and the olive, before unknown there, flourished in the gardens of the tableland, at an elevation twice as great, as that at which the clouds are suspended in summer above our heads. The importation of a European fruit or vegetable was hailed by the simple colonists with delight. The first produce of the exotic was celebrated by a festival, and the guests greeted each other, as on the appearance of an old familiar friend, who called up the remembrance of the past, and the tender associations of their native land.

While thus occupied with the internal economy of the country, Cortés was still bent on his great schemes of discovery and conquest. In the preceding Chapter we have seen him fitting out a little fleet at Zacatula, to explore the shores of the Pacific. It was burnt in the dock-yard, when nearly completed. This was a serious calamity, as most of the materials were to be transported across the country from Villa Rica. Cortés, however, with his usual promptness, took measures to repair the loss. He writes to the emperor, that another squadron will soon be got ready at the same port, and, "he doubts not, will put his Majesty in possession of

[26] Clavigero, Stor. del Messico, tom. I. p. 43.—Humboldt, Essai Politique, tom. III. pp. 115, 145.—Esposicion de Don Lúcas Alaman, (México, 1828,) p. 59.
[27] "Páraque cada Navío traiga cierta cantidad de Plantas, y que no pueda salir sin ellas, porque será mucha causa para la Poblacion, y perpetuacion de ella." Rel. Quarta de Cortés, ap. Lorenzana, p. 397.
[28] "Item, que cualquier vesino que tubiere Indios de repartimiento sea obligado á poner en ellos en cada un año con cada cien Indios de los que tuvieren de repartimiento mil sarmientos, encogiendo la mejor que pudiese hallar." Ordenanzas Municipales, año de 1524, MS.
[29] Ordenanzas Municipales, año de 1524, MS.

more lands and kingdoms, than the nation has ever heard of!" [30] This magnificent vaunt shows the common sentiment of the Spaniards at that time, who looked on the Pacific as the famed Indian Ocean, studded with golden islands, and teeming with the rich treasures of the East.

A principal object of this squadron was the discovery of a strait which should connect the Atlantic with the Pacific. Another squadron, consisting of five vessels, was fitted out in the Gulf of Mexico, to take the direction of Florida, with the same view of detecting a strait. For Cortés trusted— we, at this day, may smile at the illusion—that one might be found in that direction, which should conduct the navigator to those waters which had been traversed by the keels of Magellan! [31]

The discovery of a strait was the great object to which nautical enterprise in that day was directed, as it had been ever since the time of Columbus. It was in the sixteenth century what the discovery of the North-west passage has been in our own age; the great *ignis fatuus* of navigators. The vast extent of the American continent had been ascertained by the voyages of Cabot in the North, and of Magellan very recently in the South. The proximity, in certain quarters, of the two great oceans that washed its eastern and western shores had been settled by the discoveries both of Balboa and of Cortés. European scholars could not believe, that Nature had worked on a plan so repugnant, apparently, to the interests of humanity, as to interpose, through the whole length of the great continent, such a barrier to communication between the adjacent waters. The correspondence of men of science,[32] the instructions of the Court, the letters of Cortés, like those of Columbus, touch frequently on this favorite topic. "Your Majesty may be assured," he writes, "that, as I know how much you have at heart the discovery of *this great secret of a strait*, I shall postpone all interests and projects of my own, some of them of the highest moment, for the fulfilment of this great object." [33]

It was partly with the same view, that the general caused a considerable armament to be equipped and placed under the command of Christóval de Olid, the brave officer, who, as the reader will remember, had charge of one of the great divisions of the besieging army. He was to steer for Honduras, and plant a colony on its northern coast. A detachment of Olid's squadron was afterwards to cruise along its southern shore towards Darien in search of the mysterious strait. The country was reported to be full of gold; so full, that "the fishermen used gold weights for their nets." The life of the Spanish discoverers was one long day-dream. Illusion after illusion chased one another like the bubbles which the child throws

---

[30] "Tengo de ser causa, que Vuestra Cesarea Magestad sea en estas partes Señor de mas Reynos, y Señoríos que los que hasta hoy en nuestra Nacion se tiene noticia." Rel. Quarta de Cortés, ap. Lorenzana, p. 374.

[31] "Much as I esteem Hernando Cortés," exclaims Oviedo, "for the greatest captain and most practised in military matters of any we have known, I think such an opinion shows he was no great cosmographer." (Hist. de las Ind., MS., lib. 33, cap. 41.) Oviedo had lived to see its fallacy.

[32] Martyr, Opus Epist., ep. 811.

[33] Rel. Quarta, ap. Lorenzana, p. 385.

off from his pipe, as bright, as beautiful, and as empty. They lived in a world of enchantment.[34]

Together with these maritime expeditions Cortés fitted out a powerful expedition by land. It was intrusted to Alvarado, who, with a large force of Spaniards and Indians, was to descend the southern slant of the Cordilleras, and penetrate into the countries that lay beyond the rich valley of Oaxaca. The campaigns of this bold and rapacious chief terminated in the important conquest of Guatemala. The general required his captains to send him minute accounts of the countries which they visited, the productions of the soil, and their general resources. The result was several valuable and interesting communications.[35] In his instructions for the conduct of these expeditions, he enjoined a considerate treatment of the natives, and inculcated a policy which may be called humane, as far as humanity is compatible with a system of subjugation.[36] Unfortunately, the character of his officers too often rendered these instructions unavailing.

In the prosecution of his great enterprises, Cortés, within three short years after the Conquest, had reduced under the dominion of Castile an extent of country more than four hundred leagues in length, as he affirms, on the Atlantic coast, and more than five hundred on the Pacific; and, with the exception of a few interior provinces of no great importance, had brought them to a condition of entire tranquillity.[37] In accomplishing this, he had freely expended the revenues of the Crown, drawn from tributes similar to those which had been anciently paid by the natives to their own sovereigns; and he had, moreover, incurred a large debt on his own account, for which he demanded remuneration from government. The celebrity of his name, and the dazzling reports of the conquered countries, drew crowds of adventurers to New Spain, who furnished the general with recruits for his various enterprises.

Whoever would form a just estimate of this remarkable man must not confine himself to the history of the Conquest. His military career, indeed, places him on a level with the greatest captains of his age. But the

---

[34] The illusion at home was kept up, in some measure, by the dazzling display of gold and jewels remitted from time to time, wrought into fanciful and often fantastic forms. One of the articles sent home by Cortés was a piece of ordnance, made of gold and silver, of very fine workmanship, the metal of which alone cost 25,500 *pesos de oro.* Oviedo, who saw it in the palace, speaks with admiration of this magnificent toy. Hist. de las Ind., MS., lib. 33, cap. 41.

[35] Among these may be particularly mentioned the Letters of Alvarado and Diego de Godoy, transcribed by Oviedo in his Hist. de las Ind., MS., (lib. 33, cap. 42-44,) and translated by Ramusio, for his rich collection, Viaggi, tom. III.

[36] See, among others, his orders to his kinsman, Francis Cortés,—"Instruccion Civil y Militar por la Expedicion de la Costa de Colima." The paper is dated in 1524, and forms part of the Muñoz collection of MSS.

[37] Rel. Quarta, ap. Lorenzana, p. 371.

"Well may we wonder," exclaims his archiepiscopal editor, "that Cortés and his soldiers could have overrun and subdued, in so short a time, countries, many of them so rough and difficult of access, that, even at the present day, we can hardly penetrate them!" Ibid., nota.

period subsequent to the Conquest affords different, and in some respects nobler, points of view for the study of his character. For we then see him devising a system of government for the motley and antagonist races, so to speak, now first brought under a common dominion; repairing the mischiefs of war; and employing his efforts to detect the latent resources of the country, and to stimulate it to its highest power of production. The narrative may seem tame, after the recital of exploits as bold and adventurous as those of a paladin of romance. But it is only by the perusal of this narrative, that we can form an adequate conception of the acute and comprehensive genius of Cortés.

CHAPTER III

DEFECTION OF OLID—DREADFUL MARCH TO HONDURAS—EXECUTION
OF GUATEMOZIN—DOÑA MARINA—ARRIVAL AT HONDURAS

1524—1526

IN the last Chapter we have seen that Christóval de Olid was sent by Cortés to plant a colony in Honduras. The expedition was attended with consequences which had not been foreseen. Made giddy by the possession of power, Olid, when he had reached his place of destination, determined to assert an independent jurisdiction for himself. His distance from Mexico, he flattered himself, might enable him to do so with impunity. He misunderstood the character of Cortés, when he supposed that any distance would be great enough to shield a rebel from his vengeance.

It was long before the general received tidings of Olid's defection. But no sooner was he satisfied of this, than he despatched to Honduras a trusty captain and kinsman, Francisco de las Casas, with directions to arrest his disobedient officer. Las Casas was wrecked on the coast, and fell into Olid's hands; but eventually succeeded in raising an insurrection in the settlement, seized the person of Olid, and beheaded that unhappy delinquent in the market-place of Naco.[1]

Of these proceedings, Cortés learned only what related to the shipwreck of his lieutenant. He saw all the mischievous consequences that must arise from Olid's example, especially if his defection were to go unpunished. He determined to take the affair into his own hands, and to lead an expedition in person to Honduras. He would thus, moreover, be enabled to ascertain from personal inspection the resources of the country, which were reputed great on the score of mineral wealth; and would, perhaps, detect the point of communication between the great oceans, which had so long eluded the efforts of the Spanish discoverers. He was still further urged to this step by the uncomfortable position in which he had found himself of late in the capital. Several functionaries had recently been sent from the mother country for the ostensible purpose of administering the colonial revenues. But they served as spies on the general's conduct, caused him many petty annoyances, and sent back to court the most malicious reports of his purposes and proceedings. Cortés, in short, now that he was made Governor-General of the country, had less real power than when he held no legal commission at all.

[1] Carta Quinta de Cortés. MS.

The Spanish force which he took with him did not probably exceed a hundred horse and forty or perhaps fifty foot; to which were added about three thousand Indian auxiliaries.[2] Among them were Guatemozin and the cacique of Tacuba, with a few others of highest rank, whose consideration with their countrymen would make them an obvious nucleus, round which disaffection might gather. The general's personal retinue consisted of several pages, young men of good family, and among them Montejo, the future conqueror of Yucatan; a butler and stewart; several musicians, dancers, jugglers, and buffoons, showing, it might seem, more of the effeminacy of an Oriental satrap, than the hardy valor of a Spanish cavalier.[3] Yet the imputation of effeminacy is sufficiently disproved by the terrible march which he accomplished.

On the 12th of October, 1524, Cortés commenced his march. As he descended the sides of the Cordilleras, he was met by many of his old companions in arms, who greeted their commander with a hearty welcome, and some of them left their estates to join the expedition.[4] He halted in the province of Coatzacualco, (Huasacualco,) until he could receive intelligence respecting his route from the natives of Tabasco. They furnished him with a map, exhibiting the principal places whither the Indian traders, who wandered over these wild regions, were in the habit of resorting. With the aid of this map, a compass, and such guides as from time to time he could pick up on his journey, he proposed to traverse that broad and level tract which forms the base of Yucatan, and spreads from the Coatzacualco river to the head of the Gulf of Honduras. "I shall give your Majesty," he begins his celebrated Letter to the emperor, describing this expedition, "an account, as usual, of the most remarkable events of my journey, every one of which might form the subject of a separate narration." Cortés did not exaggerate.[5]

The beginning of the march lay across a low and marshy level, intersected by numerous little streams, which form the head waters of the *Rio de Tabasco*, and of the other rivers that discharge themselves, to the north, into the Mexican Gulf. The smaller streams they forded, or passed

[2] Carta de Albornos, MS., Mexico, Dec. 15, 1525.—Carta Quinta de Cortés, MS.
The authorities do not precisely agree as to the numbers, which were changing, probably, with every step of their march across the table-land.
[3] Bernal Diaz, Hist. de la Conquista, cap. 174.
[4] Among these was Captain Diaz, who, however, left the pleasant farm, which he occupied in the province of Coatzacualco, with a very ill grace, to accompany the expedition. "But Cortés commanded it, and we dared not say no," says the veteran. Ibid., cap. 175.
[5] This celebrated Letter, which has never been published, is usually designated as the *Carta Quinta*, or "Fifth Letter," of Cortés. It is nearly as long as the longest of the printed letters of the Conqueror, is written in the same clear, simple, business-like manner, and is as full of interest as any of the preceding. It gives a minute account of the expedition to Honduras, together with events that occurred in the year following. It bears no date, but was probably written in that year from Mexico. The original manuscript is in the Imperial Library at Vienna, which, as the German sceptre was swayed at that time by the same hand which held the Castilian, contains many documents of value for the illustration of Spanish history.

in canoes, suffering their horses to swim across as they held them by the bridle. Rivers of more formidable size they crossed on floating bridges. It gives one some idea of the difficulties they had to encounter in this way, when it is stated, that the Spaniards were obliged to construct no less than fifty of these bridges in a distance of less than a hundred miles![6] One of them was more than nine hundred paces in length. Their troubles were much augmented by the difficulty of obtaining subsistence, as the natives frequently set fire to the villages on their approach, leaving to the way-worn adventurers only a pile of smoking ruins.

It would be useless to encumber the page with the names of Indian towns which lay in the route of the army, but which may be now obsolete, and, at all events, have never found their way into a map of the country.[7] The first considerable place which they reached was Iztapan, pleasantly situated in the midst of a fruitful region, on the banks of one of the tributaries of the Rio de Tabasco. Such was the extremity to which the Spaniards had already, in the course of a few weeks, been reduced by hunger and fatigue, that the sight of a village in these dreary solitudes was welcomed by his followers, says Cortés, "with a shout of joy that was echoed back from all the surrounding woods." The army was now at no great distance from the ancient city of Palenque, the subject of so much speculation in our time. The village of *Las Tres Cruzes*, indeed, situated between twenty and thirty miles from Palenque, is said still to commemorate the passage of the Conquerors by the existence of three crosses which they left there. Yet no allusion is made to the ancient capital. Was it then the abode of a populous and flourishing community, such as once occupied it, to judge from the extent and magnificence of its remains? Or was it, even then, a heap of mouldering ruins, buried in a wilderness of vegetation, and thus hidden from the knowledge of the surrounding country? If the former, the silence of Cortés is not easy to be explained.

On quitting Iztapan, the Spaniards struck across a country having the same character of a low and marshy soil, chequered by occasional patches of cultivation, and covered with forests of cedar and Brazil wood, which seemed absolutely interminable. The overhanging foliage threw so deep a shade, that, as Cortés says, the soldiers could not see where to set their feet.[8] To add to their perplexity, their guides deserted them; and, when

[6] "Es tierra mui baja y de muchas sienegas, tanto que en tiempo de invierno no se puede andar, ni se sirve sino en canoas, y con pasarla yo en tiempo de seca, desde la entrada hasta la salida de ella, que puede aver veinti leguas, se hiziéron mas de cinquenta puentes, que sin se hazer, fuera imposible pasar." Carta Quinta de Cortés, MS.

[7] I have examined some of the most ancient maps of the country, by Spanish, French, and Dutch cosmographers, in order to determine the route of Cortés. An inestimable collection of these maps, made by the learned German, Ebeling, is to be found in the library of Harvard University. I can detect on them only four or five of the places indicated by the general. They are the places mentioned in the text, and, though few, may serve to show the general direction of the march of the army.

[8] "Donde se ponian los pies en el suelo açia arriba la claridad del cielo no se veia, tanta era la espesura y alteza de los árboles, que aunque se subian en algunos, no podian descubrir un tiro de piedra." Carta Quinta de Cortés, MS.

they climbed to the summits of the tallest trees, they could see only the same cheerless, interminable line of waving woods. The compass and the map furnished the only clue to extricate them from this gloomy labyrinth; and Cortés and his officers, among whom was the constant Sandoval, spreading out their chart on the ground, anxiously studied the probable direction of their route. Their scanty supplies meanwhile had entirely failed them, and they appeased the cravings of appetite by such roots as they dug out of the earth, or by the nuts and berries that grew wild in the woods. Numbers fell sick, and many of the Indians sank by the way, and died of absolute starvation.

When, at length, the troops emerged from these dismal forests, their path was crossed by a river of great depth, and far wider than any which they had hitherto traversed. The soldiers, disheartened, broke out into murmurs against their leader, who was plunging them deeper and deeper in a boundless wilderness, where they must lay their bones. It was in vain that Cortés encouraged them to construct a floating bridge, which might take them to the opposite bank of the river. It seemed a work of appalling magnitude, to which their wasted strength was unequal. He was more successful in his appeal to the Indian auxiliaries, till his own men, put to shame by the ready obedience of the latter, engaged in the work with a hearty good-will, which enabled them, although ready to drop from fatigue, to accomplish it at the end of four days. It was, indeed, the only expedient by which they could hope to extricate themselves from their perilous situation. The bridge consisted of one thousand pieces of timber, each of the thickness of a man's body and full sixty feet long.[9] When we consider that the timber was all standing in the forest at the commencement of the labor, it must be admitted to have been an achievement worthy of the Spaniards. The well-compacted beams presented a solid structure, which nothing, says Cortés, but fire could destroy. It excited the admiration of the natives, who came from a great distance to see it; and "the bridge of Cortés" remained for many a year the enduring monument of that commander's energy and perseverance.

The arrival of the army on the opposite bank of the river involved them in new difficulties. The ground was so soft and saturated with water, that the horses floundered up to their girths, and, sometimes plunging into quagmires, were nearly buried in the mud. It was with the greatest difficulty that they could be extricated by covering the wet soil with the foliage and the boughs of trees, when a stream of water, which forced its way through the heart of the morass, furnished the jaded animals with the means of effecting their escape by swimming.[10] As the Spaniards

[9] "Porque lleva mas que mil bigas, que la menor es casi tan gorda como un cuerpo de un hombre, y de nueve y diez brazas en largo." Carta Quinta de Cortés, MS.

[10] "Pasada toda la gente y cavallos de la otra parte del alcon dímos luego en una gran çienega, que durava bien tres tiros de ballesta, la cosa mas espantosa que jamas las gentes viéron, donde todos los cavallos desençillados se sumiéron hasta las orejas sin parecerse otra cosa, y querer forçejar á salir, sumianse mas, de manera que allí perdímos toda la esperanza de poder escapar cavallos ningunos, pero todavía comenzámos á trabajar y componerles haçes de yerba y ramas grandes de baio, sobre que

emerged from these slimy depths, they came on a broad and rising ground, which, by its cultivated fields teeming with maize, *agi*, or pepper of the country, and the *yuca* plant, intimated their approach to the capital of the fruitful province of Aculan. It was in the beginning of Lent, 1525, a period memorable for an event of which I shall give the particulars from the narrative of Cortés.

The general at this place was informed by one of the Indian converts in his train, that a conspiracy had been set on foot by Guatemozin, with the cacique of Tacuba, and some other of the principal Indian nobles, to massacre the Spaniards. They would seize the moment when the army should be entangled in the passage of some defile, or some frightful morass like that from which it had just escaped, where, taken at disadvantage, it could be easily overpowered by the superior number of the Mexicans. After the slaughter of the troops, the Indians would continue their march to Honduras, and cut off the Spanish settlements there. Their success would lead to a rising in the capital, and, indeed, throughout the land, until every Spaniard should be exterminated, and the vessels in the ports be seized, and secured from carrying the tidings across the waters.

No sooner had Cortés learned the particulars of this formidable plot, than he arrested Guatemozin and the principal Aztec lords in his train. The latter admitted the fact of the conspiracy, but alleged, that it had been planned by Guatemozin, and that they had refused to come into it. Guatemozin and the chief of Tacuba neither admitted nor denied the truth of the accusation, but maintained a dogged silence.—Such is the statement of Cortés.[11] Bernal Diaz, however, who was present in the expedition, assures us, that both Guatemozin and the cacique of Tacuba avowed their innocence. They had, indeed, they said, talked more than once together of the sufferings they were then enduring, and had said, that death was preferable to seeing so many of their poor followers dying daily around them. They admitted, also, that a project for rising on the Spaniards had been discussed by some of the Aztecs; but Guatemozin had discouraged it from the first, and no scheme of the kind could have been put into execution without his knowledge and consent.[12] These protestations did not avail the unfortunate princes; and Cortés, having satisfied, or affected to satisfy, himself of their guilt, ordered them to immediate execution.

When brought to the fatal tree, Guatemozin displayed the intrepid spirit worthy of his better days. "I knew what it was," said he, "to trust to your false promises, Malinche; I knew that you had destined me to this fate, since I did not fall by my own hand when you entered my city of Tenochtitlan. Why do you slay me so unjustly, God will demand it of

se sostuviesen y no se sumiesen, remediávanse algo, y andando trabajando y yendo y viniendo de la una parte á la otra, abrióse por medio de un calejon de agua y çieno, que los cavallos comenzáron algo á nadar, y con esto plugo á nuestro Señor que saliéron todos sin peligro ninguno." Carta Quinta de Cortés, MS.

[11] Carta Quinta de Cortés, MS.

[12] Hist. de la Conquista, cap. 177.

you!"[13] The cacique of Tacuba, protesting his innocence, declared, that he desired no better lot than to die by the side of his lord. The unfortunate princes, with one or more inferior nobles, (for the number is uncertain,) were then executed by being hung from the huge branches of a *ceiba* tree, which overshadowed the road.[14]

Such was the sad end of Guatemozin, the last emperor of the Aztecs, if we might not rather call him "the last of the Aztecs"; since, from this time, broken in spirit and without a head, the remnant of the nation resigned itself, almost without a struggle, to the stern yoke of its oppressors. Among all the names of barbarian princes, there are few entitled to a higher place on the roll of fame than that of Guatemozin. He was young, and his public career was not long; but it was glorious. He was called to the throne in the convulsed and expiring hours of the monarchy, when the banded nations of Anahuac and the fierce European were thundering at the gates of the capital. It was a post of tremendous responsibility; but Guatemozin's conduct fully justified the choice of him to fill it. No one can refuse his admiration to the intrepid spirit which could prolong a defence of his city, while one stone was left upon another; and our sympathies, for the time, are inevitably thrown more into the scale of the rude chieftain, thus battling for his country's freedom, than into that of his civilized and successful antagonist.[15]

In reviewing the circumstances of Guatemozin's death, one cannot attach much weight to the charge of conspiracy brought against him. That the Indians, brooding over their wrongs and present sufferings, should have sometimes talked of revenge would not be surprising. But that any chimerical scheme of an insurrection, like that above mentioned, should have been set on foot, or even sanctioned by Guatemozin, is altogether improbable. That prince's explanation of the affair, as given by Diaz, is, to say the least, quite as deserving of credit as the accusation of the Indian informer.[16] The defect of testimony and the

---

[13] Ibid., ubi supra.

[14] According to Diaz, both Guatemozin and the prince of Tacuba had embraced the religion of their conquerors, and were confessed by a Franciscan friar before their execution. We are further assured by the same authority, that "they were, *for Indians,* very good Christians, and believed well and truly." (Ibid., loc. cit.) One is reminded of the last hours of Caupolican, converted to Christianity by the same men who tied him to the stake. See the scene, painted in the frightful coloring of a master hand, in the Araucana, Canto 34.

[15] Guatemozin's beautiful wife, the princess Tecuichpo, the daughter of Montezuma, lived long enough after his death to give her hand to three Castilians, all of noble descent. (See Ante, pp. 438, 439, note 36.) She is described as having been as well instructed in the Catholic faith as any woman in Castile, as most gracious and winning in her deportment, and as having contributed greatly, by her example, and the deference with which she inspired the Aztecs, to the tranquillity of the conquered country.—This pleasing portrait, it may be well enough to mention, is by the hand of her husband, Don Thoan Cano.

[16] The Indian chroniclers regard the pretended conspiracy of Guatemozin as an invention of Cortés. The informer himself, when afterwards put to the torture by the cacique of Tezcuco, declared that he had made no revelation of this nature to the Spanish commander. Ixtlilxochitl vouches for the truth of this story. (Venida de los Esp., pp. 83-93.) But who will vouch for Ixtlilxochitl?

distance of time make it difficult for us, at the present day, to decide
the question. We have a surer criterion of the truth in the opinion of
those who were eyewitnesses of the transaction. It is given in the words
of the old chronicler, so often quoted. "The execution of Guatemozin,"
says Diaz, "was most unjust; and was thought wrong by all of us." [17]

The most probable explanation of the affair seems to be, that Guatemozin was a troublesome and, indeed, formidable captive. Thus much is
intimated by Cortés himself, in his Letter to the emperor.[18] The fallen
sovereign of Mexico, by the ascendency of his character, as well as by his
previous station, maintained an influence over his countrymen, which
would have enabled him with a breath, as it were, to rouse their smothered, not extinguished, animosity into rebellion. The Spaniards, during
the first years after the Conquest, lived in constant apprehension of a
rising of the Aztecs. This is evident from numerous passages in the
writings of the time. It was under the same apprehension, that Cortés
consented to embarrass himself with his royal captive on this dreary expedition. And in such distrust did he hold him, that, even while in Mexico, he neither rode abroad, nor walked to any great distance, according
to Gomara, without being attended by Guatemozin.[19]

Parties standing in such relations to each other could have been the
objects only of mutual distrust and aversion. The forlorn condition of
the Spaniards on the present march, which exposed them, in a peculiar
degree, to any sudden assault from their wily Indian vassals, increased
the suspicions of Cortés. Thus predisposed to think ill of Guatemozin,
the general lent a ready ear to the first accusation against him. Charges
were converted into proofs, and condemnation followed close upon the
charges. By a single blow he proposed to rid himself and the state for ever
of a dangerous enemy,—the more dangerous, that he was an enemy in
disguise. Had he but consulted his own honor and his good name, Guatemozin's head should have been the last on which he should have suffered
an injury to fall. "He should have cherished him," to borrow the homely
simile of his encomiast, Gomara, "like gold in a napkin, as the best trophy
of his victories." [20]

Whatever may have been the real motives of his conduct in this affair, it seems to have left the mind of Cortés but ill at ease. For a long
time he was moody and irritable, and found it difficult to sleep at night.
On one occasion, as he was pacing an upper chamber of a *teocalli* in
which he was quartered, he missed his footing in the dark, and was precipitated from a height of some twelve feet to the ground, which occa-

---

[17] "Y fué esta muerte que les diéron muy injustamente dada, y pareció mal á
todos los que ibamos aquella jornada." Hist. de la Conquista, cap. 177.

[18] "Guatemazin, Señor que fué de esta Ciudad de Temixtitan, á quien yo despues
que la gané he tenido siempre preso, teniéndole por hombre bullicioso, y le llevé
conmigo." Carta Quinta, MS.

[19] "Y le hacian aquella mesma reverencia, i ceremonias, que á Motecçuma, i creo
que por eso le llevaba siempre consigo por la Ciudad á Caballo, si cavalgaba, i sino á
pie como él iba." Crónica, cap. 170.

[20] "I Cortés debiera guardarlo vivo, como Oro en paño, que era el triumpho, i
gloria de sus Victorias." Crónica, cap. 170.

sioned him a severe contusion on the head,—a thing too palpable to be concealed, though he endeavored, says the gossiping Diaz, to hide the knowledge of it, as well as he could, from the soldiers.[21]

It was not long after the sad scene of Guatemozin's execution, that the wearied troops entered the head town of the great province of Aculan; a thriving community of traders, who carried on a profitable traffic with the furthest quarters of Central America. Cortés notices in general terms the excellence and beauty of the buildings, and the hospitable reception which he experienced from the inhabitants.

After renewing their strength in these comfortable quarters, the Spaniards left the capital of Aculan, the name of which is to be found on no map, and held on their toilsome way in the direction of what is now called the Lake of Peten. It was then the property of an emigrant tribe of the hardy Maya family, and their capital stood on an island in the lake, "with its houses and lofty *teocallis* glistening in the sun," says Bernal Diaz, "so that it might be seen for the distance of two leagues." [22] These edifices, built by one of the races of Yucatan, displayed, doubtless, the same peculiarities of construction as the remains still to be seen in that remarkable peninsula. But, whatever may have been their architectural merits, they are disposed of in a brief sentence by the Conquerors.

The inhabitants of the island showed a friendly spirit, and a docility unlike the warlike temper of their countrymen of Yucatan. They willingly listened to the Spanish missionaries who accompanied the expedition, as they expounded the Christian doctrines through the intervention of Marina. The Indian interpreter was present throughout this long march, the last in which she remained at the side of Cortés. As this, too, is the last occasion on which she will appear in these pages, I will mention, before parting with her, an interesting circumstance that occurred when the army was traversing the province of Coatzacualco. This, it may be remembered, was the native country of Marina, where her infamous mother sold her, when a child, to some foreign traders, in order to secure her inheritance to a younger brother. Cortés halted for some days at this place, to hold a conference with the surrounding caciques, on matters of government and religion. Among those summoned to this meeting was Marina's mother, who came, attended by her son. No sooner did they make their appearance, than all were struck with the great resemblance of the cacique to her daughter. The two parties recognised each other, though they had not met since their separation. The mother, greatly terrified, fancied that she had been decoyed into a snare, in order to punish her inhuman conduct. But Marina instantly ran up to her, and endeavored to allay her fears, assuring her that she should receive no harm, and, addressing the by-standers, said, "that she was sure her mother knew not what she did, when she sold her to the traders, and that she forgave her." Then tenderly embracing her unnatural parent, she gave her such

[21] Hist. de la Conquista, ubi supra.
[22] Ibid., cap. 178.

jewels and other little ornaments as she wore about her own person, to win back, as it would seem, her lost affection. Marina added, that "she felt much happier than before, now that she had been instructed in the Christian faith, and given up the bloody worship of the Aztecs." [23]

In the course of the expedition to Honduras, Cortés gave Marina away to a Castilian knight, Don Juan Xamarillo, to whom she was wedded as his lawful wife. She had estates assigned to her in her native province, where she probably passed the remainder of her days. From this time, the name of Marina disappears from the page of history. But it has been always held in grateful remembrance by the Spaniards, for the important aid which she gave them in effecting the Conquest, and by the natives, for the kindness and sympathy which she showed them in their misfortunes. Many an Indian ballad commemorates the gentle virtues of Malinche—her Aztec epithet. Even now her spirit, if report be true, watches over the capital which she helped to win; and the peasant is occasionally startled by the apparition of an Indian princess, dimly seen through the evening shadows, as it flits among the groves and grottos of the royal Hill of Chapoltepec.[24]

By the Conqueror, Marina left one son, Don Martin Cortés. He rose to high consideration, and was made a *comendador* of the order of St. Jago. He was subsequently suspected of treasonable designs against the government; and neither his parents' extraordinary services, nor his own deserts, could protect him from a cruel persecution; and in 1568, the son of Hernando Cortés was shamefully subjected to torture in the very capital which his father had acquired for the Castilian Crown!

The inhabitants of the isles of Peten—to return from our digression—listened attentively to the preaching of the Franciscan friars, and consented to the instant demolition of their idols, and the erection of the Cross upon their ruins.[25] A singular circumstance showed the value of these hurried conversions. Cortés, on his departure, left among this friendly people one of his horses, who had been disabled by an injury in the foot. The Indians felt a reverence for the animal, as in some way connected with the mysterious power of the white men. When their visitors had gone, they offered flowers to the horse, and, as it is said, prepared for him many savory messes of poultry, such as they would have administered to their own sick. Under this extraordinary diet the poor animal pined away and died. The affrighted Indians raised his effigy in stone,

[23] Diaz, who was present, attests the truth of this account by the most solemn adjuration. "Y todo esto que digo, se lo oí muy certificadamente y se lo juro amen." Ibid., cap. 37.

[24] Life in Mexico, let. 8.
The fair author does not pretend to have been favored with a sight of the apparition.

[25] Villagutierre says, that the Iztacs, by which name the inhabitants of these islands were called, did not destroy their idols while the Spaniards remained there. (Historia de la Conquista de la Provincia de el Itza, (Madrid, 1701,) pp. 49, 50.) The historian is wrong, since Cortés expressly asserts, that the images were broken and burnt in his presence. Carta Quinta, MS.

and, placing it in one of their *teocallis*, did homage to it, as to a deity. In 1618, when two Franciscan friars came to preach the Gospel in these regions, then scarcely better known to the Spaniards than before the time of Cortés, one of the most remarkable objects which they found was this statue of a horse, receiving the homage of the Indian worshippers, as the god of thunder and lightning! [26]

It would be wearisome to recount all the perils and hardships endured by the Spaniards in the remainder of their journey. It would be repeating only the incidents of the preceding narrative, the same obstacles in their path, the same extremities of famine and fatigue,—hardships more wearing on the spirits than encounters with an enemy, which, if more hazardous, are also more exciting. It is easier to contend with man than with Nature. Yet I must not omit to mention the passage of the *Sierra de los Pedernales*, "the Mountain of Flints," which, though only twenty-four miles in extent, consumed no less than twelve days in crossing it! The sharp stones cut the horses' feet to pieces, while many were lost down the precipices and ravines; so that, when they had reached the opposite side, sixty-eight of these valuable animals had perished, and the remainder were, for the most part, in an unserviceable condition! [27]

The rainy season had now set in, and torrents of water, falling day and night, drenched the adventurers to the skin, and added greatly to their distresses. The rivers, swollen beyond their usual volume, poured along with a terrible impetuosity that defied the construction of bridges; and it was with the greatest difficulty, that, by laying trunks of trees from one huge rock to another, with which these streams were studded, they effected a perilous passage to the opposite banks. [28]

At length the shattered train drew near the Golfo Dolce, at the head of the Bay of Honduras. Their route could not have been far from the site of Copan, the celebrated city whose architectural ruins have furnished such noble illustration for the pencil of Catherwood. But the Spaniards passed on in silence. Nor, indeed, can we wonder, that, at this stage of the enterprise, they should have passed on without heeding the vicinity of a city in the wilderness, though it were as glorious as the capital of Zenobia; for they were arrived almost within view of the Spanish settlements, the object of their long and wearisome pilgrimage.

The place which they were now approaching was Naco, or San Gil de Buena Vista, a Spanish settlement on the Golfo Dolce. Cortés advanced

---

[26] The fact is recorded by Villagutierre, Conquista de el Itza, pp. 100-102, and Co-jullado, Hist. de Yucathan, lib. 1, cap. 16.

[27] "Y querer dezir la aspereza y fragosidad de este Puerto y sierras, ni quien lo dixese lo sabria significar, ni quien lo oyese podria entender, sino que sepa V. M. que en ocho leguas que duró hasta este puerto estuvímos en las andar doze dias, digo los postreros en llegar al cabo de él, en que muriéron sesenta y ocho cavallos despeñados y desxaretados, y todos los demas viniéron heridos y tan lastimados que no pensámos aprovecharnos de ninguno." Carta Quinta de Cortés, MS.

[28] "If any unhappy wretch had become giddy in this transit," says Cortés, "he must inevitably have been precipitated into the gulf and perished. There were upwards of twenty of these frightful passes." Carta Quinta, MS.

cautiously, prepared to fall on the town by surprise. He had held on his way with the undeviating step of the North American Indian, who, traversing morass and mountain and the most intricate forests, guided by the instinct of revenge, presses straight towards the mark, and, when he has reached it, springs at once on his unsuspecting victim. Before Cortés made his assault, his scouts fortunately fell in with some of the inhabitants of the place, from whom they received tidings of the death of Olid, and of the reëstablishment of his own authority. Cortés, therefore, entered the place like a friend, and was cordially welcomed by his countrymen, greatly astonished, says Diaz, "by the presence among them of the general so renowned throughout these countries." [29]

The colony was at this time sorely suffering from famine; and to such extremity was it soon reduced, that the troops would probably have found a grave in the very spot to which they had looked forward as the goal of their labors, but for the seasonable arrival of a vessel with supplies from Cuba. With a perseverance which nothing could daunt, Cortés made an examination of the surrounding country, and occupied a month more in exploring dismal swamps, steaming with unwholesome exhalations, and infected with bilious fevers, and with swarms of venomous insects which left peace neither by day nor night. At length he embarked with a part of his forces on board of two brigantines, and, after touching at one or two ports in the Bay, anchored off Truxillo, the principal Spanish settlement on that coast. The surf was too high for him easily to effect a landing; but the inhabitants, overjoyed at his arrival, rushed into the shallow water and eagerly bore back the general in their arms to the shore.[30]

After he had restored the strength and spirits of his men, the indefatigable commander prepared for a new expedition, the object of which was to explore and to reduce the extensive province of Nicaragua. One may well feel astonished at the adventurous spirit of the man, who, unsubdued by the terrible sufferings of his recent march, should so soon be prepared for another enterprise equally appalling. It is difficult, in this age of sober sense, to conceive the character of a Castilian cavalier of the sixteenth century, a true counterpart of which it would not have been easy to find in any other nation, even at that time,—or anywhere, indeed, save in those tales of chivalry, which, however wild and extravagant they may seem, were much more true to character than to situation. The mere excitement of exploring the strange and the unknown was a sufficient compensation to the Spanish adventurer for all his toils and trials. It seems to have been ordered by Providence, that such a race of men should exist contemporaneously with the discovery of the New World, that those regions should be brought to light which were beset with dangers and difficulties so appalling as might have tended to overawe and to

[29] "Espantáronse en gran manera, y como supiéron que era Cortés q̃ tan nombrado era en todas estas partes de las Indias, y en Castilla, no sabiã que se hazer de placer." Hist. de la Conquista, cap. 179.
[30] Ibid., cap. 179 et seq.—Herrera, Hist. Gen., dec. 3, lib. 8, cap. 3, 4.—Carta Quinta de Cortés, MS.

discourage the ordinary spirit of adventure. Yet Cortés, though filled with this spirit, proposed nobler ends to himself than those of the mere vulgar adventurer. In the expedition to Nicaragua, he designed, as he had done in that to Honduras, to ascertain the resources of the country in general, and, above all, the existence of any means of communication between the great oceans on its borders. If none such existed, it would at least establish this fact, the knowledge of which, to borrow his own language, was scarcely less important.

The general proposed to himself the further object of enlarging the colonial empire of Castile. The conquest of Mexico was but the commencement of a series of conquests. To the warrior who had achieved this nothing seemed impracticable; and scarcely would any thing have been so, had he been properly sustained. It is no great stretch of imagination, to see the Conqueror of Mexico advancing along the provinces of the vast Isthmus,—Nicaragua, Costa Rica, and Darien, until he had planted his victorious banner on the shores of the Gulf of Panamá; and, while it was there fanned by the breezes from the golden South, a land of the Incas, to see him gathering such intelligence of this land as would stimulate him to carry his arms still further, and to anticipate, it might be, the splendid career of Pizarro!

But from these dreams of ambition Cortés was suddenly aroused by such tidings as convinced him, that his absence from Mexico was already too far prolonged, and that he must return without delay, if he would save the capital or the country.

CHAPTER IV

DISTURBANCES IN MEXICO—RETURN OF CORTÉS—DISTRUST OF THE
COURT—CORTÉS RETURNS TO SPAIN—DEATH OF SANDOVAL—BRIL-
LIANT RECEPTION OF CORTÉS—HONORS CONFERRED ON HIM

1526—1530

THE intelligence alluded to in the preceding Chapter was conveyed in a
letter to Cortés from the licentiate Zuazo, one of the functionaries to
whom the general had committed the administration of the country during his absence. It contained full particulars of the tumultuous proceedings in the capital. No sooner had Cortés quitted it, than dissensions
broke out among the different members of the provisional government.
The misrule increased as his absence was prolonged. At length tidings
were received, that Cortés with his whole army had perished in the mo-
rasses of Chiapa. The members of the government showed no reluctance
to credit this story. They now openly paraded their own authority, proclaimed the general's death; caused funeral ceremonies to be performed
in his honor; took possession of his property wherever they could meet
with it, piously devoting a small part of the proceeds to purchasing
masses for his soul, while the remainder was appropriated to pay off what
was called his debt to the state. They seized, in like manner, the property of other individuals engaged in the expedition. From these outrages they proceeded to others against the Spanish residents in the city,
until the Franciscan missionaries left the capital in disgust, while the Indian population were so sorely oppressed, that great apprehensions were
entertained of a general rising. Zuazo, who communicated these tidings,
implored Cortés to quicken his return. He was a temperate man, and the
opposition which he had made to the tyrannical measures of his comrades had been rewarded with exile.[1]

The general, greatly alarmed by this account, saw that no alternative
was left but to abandon all further schemes of conquest, and to return at
once, if he would secure the preservation of the empire which he had won.
He accordingly made the necessary arrangements for settling the administration of the colonies at Honduras, and embarked with a small number
of followers for Mexico.

He had not been long at sea, when he encountered such a terrible
tempest as seriously damaged his vessel, and compelled him to return to

[1] Carta Quinta de Cortés, MS.—Bernal Diaz, Hist. de la Conquista, cap. 185.—
Relacion del Tesorero Strada, MS., México, 1526.

port and refit. A second attempt proved equally unsuccessful; and Cortés, feeling that his good star had deserted him, saw, in this repeated disaster, an intimation from Heaven that he was not to return.[2] He contented himself, therefore, with sending a trusty messenger to advise his friends of his personal safety in Honduras. He then instituted processions and public prayers to ascertain the will of Heaven, and to deprecate its anger. His health now showed the effects of his recent sufferings, and declined under a wasting fever. His spirits sank with it, and he fell into a state of gloomy despondency. Bernal Diaz, speaking of him at this time, says, that nothing could be more wan and emaciated than his person, and that so strongly was he possessed with the idea of his approaching end, that he procured a Franciscan habit,—for it was common to be laid out in the habit of some one or other of the monastic orders,—in which to be carried to the grave.[3]

From this deplorable apathy Cortés was roused by fresh advices urging his presence in Mexico, and by the judicious efforts of his good friend Sandoval, who had lately returned, himself, from an excursion into the interior. By his persuasion, the general again consented to try his fortunes on the seas. He embarked on board of a brigantine, with a few followers, and bade adieu to the disastrous shores of Honduras, April 25, 1526. He had nearly made the coast of New Spain, when a heavy gale threw him off his course, and drove him to the island of Cuba. After staying there some time to recruit his exhausted strength, he again put to sea on the 16th of May, and in eight days landed near San Juan de Ulua, whence he proceeded about five leagues on foot to Medellin.

Cortés was so much changed by disease, that his person was not easily recognised. But no sooner was it known, that the general had returned, than crowds of people, white men and natives, thronged from all the neighboring country to welcome him. The tidings spread far and wide on the wings of the wind, and his progress to the capital was a triumphal procession. The inhabitants came from the distance of eighty leagues to have a sight of him; and they congratulated one another on the presence of the only man who could rescue the country from its state of anarchy. It was a resurrection of the dead,—so industriously had the reports of his death been circulated, and so generally believed.[4]

At all the great towns where he halted he was sumptuously entertained. Triumphal arches were thrown across the road, and the streets were strewed with flowers as he passed. After a night's repose at Tezcuco, he made his entrance in great state into the capital. The municipality came out to welcome him, and a brilliant cavalcade of armed citizens formed his escort; while the lake was covered with barges of the Indians, all fancifully decorated with their gala dresses, as on the day of his first arrival among them. The streets echoed to music, and dancing, and sounds

[2] Carta Quinta de Cortés, MS.

[3] Hist. de la Conquista, cap. 184, et seq.—Carta Quinta de Cortés, MS.

[4] Carta Quinta de Cortés, MS.—Bernal Diaz, Hist. de la Conquista, cap. 189, 190 Carta de Cortés al Emperador, MS., México, Set. 11. 1526.

of jubilee, as the procession held on its way to the great convent of St Francis, where thanksgivings were offered up for the safe return of the general, who then proceeded to take up his quarters once more in his own princely residence.[5]—It was in June, 1526, when Cortés reëntered Mexico; nearly two years had elapsed since he had left it, on his difficult march to Honduras,—a march which led to no important results, but which consumed nearly as much time, and was attended with sufferings quite as severe, as the conquest of Mexico itself.[6]

Cortés did not abuse his present advantage. He, indeed, instituted proceedings against his enemies; but he followed them up so languidly, as to incur the imputation of weakness. It is the only instance in which he has been accused of weakness; and, since it was shown in the prosecution of his own injuries, it may be thought to reflect no discredit on his character.[7]

He was not permitted long to enjoy the sweets of triumph. In the month of July, he received advices of the arrival of a *juez de residencia* on the coast, sent by the court of Madrid to supersede him temporarily in the government. The Crown of Castile, as its colonial empire extended, became less and less capable of watching over its administration. It was therefore obliged to place vast powers in the hands of its viceroys; and, as suspicion naturally accompanies weakness, it was ever prompt to listen to accusations against these powerful vassals. In such cases the government adopted the expedient of sending out a commissioner, or *juez de residencia*, with authority to investigate the conduct of the accused, to suspend him in the mean while from his office, and, after a judicial examination, to reinstate him in it, or to remove him altogether, according to the issue of the trial. The enemies of Cortés had been, for a long time, busy in undermining his influence at court, and in infusing suspicions of his loyalty in the bosom of the emperor. Since his elevation to the government of the country, they had redoubled their mischievous activity, and they assailed his character with the foulest imputations. They charged him with appropriating to his own use the gold which belonged

[5] Carta de Ocaño, MS., Agosto 31, 1526.—Carta Quinta de Cortés, MS.

[6] "What Cortés suffered," says Dr. Robertson, "on this march, a distance, according to Gomara, of 3000 miles,"—(the distance must be greatly exaggerated,)—"from famine, from the hostility of the natives, from the climate, and from hardships of every species, has nothing in history parallel to it, but what occurs in the adventures of the other discoverers and conquerors of the New World. Cortés was employed in this dreadful service above two years; and, though it was not distinguished by any splendid event, he exhibited, during the course of it, greater personal courage, more fortitude of mind, more perseverance and patience, than in any other period or scene in his life." (Hist. of America, Note 96.) The historian's remarks are just; as the passages, which I have borrowed from the extraordinary record of the Conqueror, may show. Those, who are desirous of seeing something of the narrative told in his own way, will find a few pages of it translated in the *Appendix, Part 2, No.* 14.

[7] "Y esto yo lo oí dezir á los del Real Consejo de Indias, estando presente el señor Obispo Fray Bartolomé de las Casas, que se descuidó mucho Cortés en ello, ʺ se lo tuviéron á floxedad." Bernal Diaz, Hist. de la Conquista, cap. 190.

to the Crown, and especially with secreting the treasures of Montezuma. He was said to have made false reports of the provinces he had conquered, that he might defraud the exchequer of its lawful revenues. He had distributed the principal offices among his own creatures; and had acquired an unbounded influence, not only over the Spaniards, but the natives, who were all ready to do his bidding. He had expended large sums in fortifying both the capital and his own palace; and it was evident, from the magnitude of his schemes and his preparations, that he designed to shake off his allegiance, and to establish an independent sovereignty in New Spain.[8]

The government, greatly alarmed by these formidable charges, the probability of which they could not estimate, appointed a commissioner with full powers to investigate the matter. The person selected for this delicate office was Luis Ponce de Leon, a man of high family, young for such a post, but of a mature judgment, and distinguished for his moderation and equity. The nomination of such a minister gave assurance, that the Crown meant to do justly by Cortés.

The emperor wrote at the same time with his own hand to the general, advising him of this step, and assuring him, that it was taken, not from distrust of his integrity, but to afford him the opportunity of placing that integrity in a clear light before the world.[9]

Ponce de Leon reached Mexico in July, 1526. He was received with all respect by Cortés and the municipality of the capital; and the two parties interchanged those courtesies with each other, which gave augury that the future proceedings would be conducted in a spirit of harmony. Unfortunately, this fair beginning was blasted by the death of the commissioner in a few weeks after his arrival, a circumstance which did not fail to afford another item in the loathsome mass of accusation heaped upon Cortés. The commissioner fell the victim of a malignant fever, which carried off a number of those who had come over in the vessel with him.[10]

On his death-bed, Ponce de Leon delegated his authority to an infirm old man, who survived but a few months, and transmitted the reins of government to a person named Estrada or Strada, the royal treasurer, one of the officers sent from Spain to take charge of the finances, and who was personally hostile to Cortés. The Spanish residents would have persuaded Cortés to assert for himself at least an equal share of the authority, to which they considered Estrada as having no sufficient title. But the general, with singular moderation, declined a competition in this matter, and determined to abide a more decided expression of his sovereign's will. To his mortification, the nomination of Estrada was confirmed, and this dignitary soon contrived to inflict on his rival all those

[8] Memorial de Luis Cardenas, MS.—Carta de Diego de Ocaña, MS.—Herrera. Hist. Gen., dec. 3, lib. 8, cap. 14, 15.

[9] Carta del Emperador, MS., Toledo, Nov. 4, 1525.

[10] Bernal Diaz, Hist. de la Conquista, cap. 192.—Carta de Cortés al Emp., MS., México, Set. 11, 1526.

annoyances by which a little mind, in possession of unexpected power, endeavors to make his superiority felt over a great one. The recommendations of Cortés were disregarded; his friends mortified and insulted; his attendants outraged by injuries. One of the domestics of his friend Sandoval, for some slight offence, was sentenced to lose his hand; and, when the general remonstrated against these acts of violence, he was preemptorily commanded to leave the city! The Spaniards, indignant at this outrage, would have taken up arms in his defence; but Cortés would allow no resistance, and, simply remarking, "that it was well, that those, who, at the price of their blood, had won the capital, should not be allowed a footing in it," withdrew to his favorite villa of Cojohuacan, a few miles distant, to wait there the result of these strange proceedings.[11]

The suspicions of the Court of Madrid, meanwhile, fanned by the breath of calumny, had reached the most preposterous height. One might have supposed, that it fancied the general was organizing a revolt throughout the colonies, and meditated nothing less than an invasion of the mother country. Intelligence having been received, that a vessel might speedily be expected from New Spain, orders were sent to the different ports of the kingdom, and even to Portugal, to sequestrate the cargo, under the expectation that it contained remittances to the general's family which belonged to the Crown; while his letters, affording the most luminous account of all his proceedings and discoveries, were forbidden to be printed. Fortunately, however, three letters, constituting the most important part of the Conqueror's correspondence, had been given to the public, some years previous, by the indefatigable press of Seville.

The Court, moreover, made aware of the incompetency of the treasurer, Estrada, to the present delicate conjuncture, now intrusted the whole affair of the inquiry to a commission dignified with the title of the Royal Audience of New Spain. This body was clothed with full powers to examine into the charges against Cortés, with instructions to send him back, as a preliminary measure, to Castile,—peacefully if they could, but forcibly if necessary. Still afraid that its belligerent vassal might defy the authority of this tribunal, the government resorted to artifice to effect his return. The president of the Indian Council was commanded to write to him, urging his presence in Spain to vindicate himself from the charges of his enemies, and offering his personal coöperation in his defence. The emperor further wrote a letter to the Audience, containing his commands for Cortés to return, as the government wished to consult him on matters relating to the Indies, and to bestow on him a recompense suited to his high deserts. This letter was intended to be shown to Cortés.[12]

But it was superfluous to put in motion all this complicated machinery to effect a measure on which Cortés was himself resolved. Proudly conscious of his own unswerving loyalty, and of the benefits he had rendered to his country, he felt deeply sensible to this unworthy requital of them,

[11] Bernal Diaz, Hist. de la Conquista, cap. 194.—Carta de Cortés al Emp., MS, Set. 11, 1526.

[12] Herrera, Hist. General, dec. 4, lib. 2, cap. 1; and lib. 3, cap. 8.

especially in the very theatre of his achievements. He determined to abide no longer where he was exposed to such indignities; but to proceed at once to Spain, present himself before his sovereign, boldly assert his innocence, and claim redress for his wrongs, and a just reward for his services. In the close of his letter to the emperor, detailing the painful expedition to Honduras, after enlarging on the magnificent schemes he had entertained of discovering in the South Sea, and vindicating himself from the charge of a too lavish expenditure, he concludes with the lofty, yet touching declaration, "that he trusts his Majesty will in time acknowledge his deserts; but, if that unhappily shall not be, the world at least will be assured of his loyalty, and he himself shall have the conviction of having done his duty; and no better inheritance than this shall he ask for his children." [13]

No sooner was the intention of Cortés made known, than it excited a general sensation through the country. Even Estrada relented; he felt that he had gone too far, and that it was not his policy to drive his noble enemy to take refuge in his own land. Negotiations were opened, and an attempt at a reconciliation was made, through the bishop of Tlascala. Cortés received these overtures in a courteous spirit, but his resolution was unshaken. Having made the necessary arrangements, therefore, in Mexico, he left the Valley, and proceeded at once to the coast. Had he entertained the criminal ambition imputed to him by his enemies, he might have been sorely tempted by the repeated offers of support, which were made to him, whether in good or in bad faith, on the journey, if he would but reassume the government, and assert his independence of Castile. But these disloyal advances he rejected with the scorn they merited.[14]

On his arrival at Villa Rica, he received the painful tidings of the death of his father, Don Martin Cortés, whom he had hoped so soon to embrace, after his long and eventful absence. Having celebrated his obsequies with every mark of filial respect, he made preparations for his speedy departure. Two of the best vessels in the port were got ready and provided with every thing requisite for a long voyage. He was attended by his friend, the faithful Sandoval, by Tapia, and some other cavaliers, most attached to his person. He also took with him several Aztec and Tlascalan chiefs, and among them a son of Montezuma, and another of Maxixca, the friendly old Tlascalan lord, both of whom were desirous to accompany the general to Castile. He carried home a large collection of plants and minerals, as specimens of the natural resources of the country; several wild animals and birds of gaudy plumage; various fabrics of delicate workmanship, especially the gorgeous feather-work; and a number

---

[13] "Todas estas entradas están ahora para partir casi á una, plega á Dios de los guiar como él se sirva, que yo aunque V. M. mas me mande desfavoreçer no tengo de dejar de servir, que no es posible, que por tiempo V. M. no conosca mis servicios, y ya que esto no sea, yo me satisfago con hazer lo que debo, y con saber que á todo el mundo tengo satisfecho, y les son notorios mis servicios y ealdad, con que los hago, y no quiero otro mayorasgo sino este." Carta Quinta, MS.

[14] Bernal Diaz, Hist. de la Conquista, cap. 194.—Carta de Ocaña, MS., Agosto 31, 1526.

of jugglers, dancers, and buffoons, who greatly astonished the Europeans by the marvellous facility of their performances, and were thought a suitable present for his Holiness, the Pope.[15] Lastly, Cortés displayed his magnificence in a rich treasure of jewels, among which were emeralds of extraordinary size and lustre, gold to the amount of two hundred thousand *pesos de oro*, and fifteen hundred marks of silver. "In fine," says Herrera, "he came in all the state of a great lord." [16]

After a brief and prosperous voyage, Cortés came in sight once more of his native shores, and, crossing the bar of Saltes, entered the little port of Palos in May, 1528,—the same spot where Columbus had landed five and thirty years before, on his return from the discovery of the Western World. Cortés was not greeted with the enthusiasm and public rejoicings which welcomed the great navigator; and, indeed, the inhabitants were not prepared for his arrival. From Palos he soon proceeded to the convent of La Rabida, the same place also, within the hospitable walls of which Columbus had found a shelter. An interesting circumstance is mentioned by historians, connected with his short stay at Palos. Francisco Pizarro, the Conqueror of Peru, had arrived there, having come to Spain to solicit aid for his great enterprise.[17] He was then in the commencement of his brilliant career, as Cortés might be said to be at the close of his. He was an old acquaintance, and a kinsman, as is affirmed, of the general, whose mother was a Pizarro.[18] The meeting of these two extraordinary men, the Conquerors of the North and of the South, in the New World, as they set foot, after their eventful absence, on the shores of their native land, and that, too, on the spot consecrated by the presence of Columbus, has something in it striking to the imagination. It has accordingly attracted the attention of one of the most illustrious of living poets, who, in a brief, but beautiful sketch, has depicted the scene in the genuine coloring of the age.[19]

While reposing, from the fatigues of his voyage, at La Rabida, an event occurred which afflicted Cortés deeply, and which threw a dark cloud over his return. This was the death of Gonzalo de Sandoval, his trusty friend, and so long the companion of his fortunes. He was taken ill in a wretched inn at Palos, soon after landing; and his malady gained ground so rapidly, that it was evident his constitution, impaired, probably, by the extraordinary fatigues he had of late years undergone, would be un-

---

[15] The Pope, who was of the joyous Medici family, Clement VII., and the cardinals, were greatly delighted with the feats of the Indian jugglers, according to Diaz; and his Holiness, who, it may be added, received at the same time from Cortés a substantial donative of gold and jewels, publicly testified, by prayers and solemn processions, his great sense of the services rendered to Christianity by the Conquerors of Mexico, and generously requited them by bulls, granting plenary absolution from their sins. Hist. de la Conquista, cap. 195.

[16] "Y en fin venia como gran Señor." Hist. Gen. dec. 4, lib. 3, cap. 8.

[17] Herrera, Hist. Gen., dec. 4, lib. 4, cap. 1.—Cavo, Los Tres Siglos de Méx., tom. I. p. 78.

[18] Pizarro y Orellana, Varones Ilustres, p. 121.

[19] See the conclusion of Rogers' Voyage of Columbus

able to resist it. Cortés was instantly sent for, and arrived in time to ad
minister the last consolations of friendship to the dying cavalier. Sandoval met his approaching end with composure, and, having given the attention, which the short interval allowed, to the settlement of both his
temporal and spiritual concerns, he breathed his last in the arms of his
commander.

Sandoval died at the premature age of thirty-one.[29] He was in many
respects the most eminent of the great captains formed under the eye of
Cortés. He was of good family, and a native of Medellin, also the birth-
place of the general, for whom he had the warmest personal regard. Cortés soon discerned his uncommon qualities, and proved it by uniformly
selecting the young officer for the most difficult commissions. His conduct on these occasions fully justified the preference. He was a decided
favorite with the soldiers; for, though strict in enforcing discipline, he
was careful of their comforts and little mindful of his own. He had nothing of the avarice so common in the Castilian cavalier; and seemed to
have no other ambition than that of faithfully discharging the duties of
his profession. He was a plain man, affecting neither the showy manners
nor the bravery in costume which distinguished Alvarado, the Aztec
Tonatiuh. The expression of his countenance was open and manly; his
chestnut hair curled close to his head; his frame was strong and sinewy.
He had a lisp in his utterance, which made his voice somewhat indistinct.
Indeed, he was no speaker; but, if slow of speech, he was prompt and
energetic in action. He had precisely the qualities which fitted him for
the perilous enterprise in which he was embarked. He had accomplished
his task; and, after having escaped death, which lay waiting for him in
every step of his path, had come home, as it would seem, to his native
land, only to meet it there.

His obsequies were performed with all solemnity by the Franciscan
friars of La Rabida, and his remains were followed to their final resting-
place by the comrades who had so often stood by his side in battle. They
were laid in the cemetery of the convent, which, shrouded in its forest of
pines, stood, and may yet stand, on the bold eminence that overlooks
the waste of waters so lately traversed by the adventurous soldier.[21]

It was not long after this melancholy event, that Cortés and his suite
began their journey into the interior. The general stayed a few days at
the castle of the duke of Medina Sidonia, the most powerful of the Andalusian lords, who hospitably entertained him, and, at his departure, presented him with several noble Arabian horses. Cortés first directed his
steps towards Guadaloupe, where he passed nine days, offering up prayers
and causing masses to be performed at Our Lady's shrine for the soul of
his departed friend.

Before his departure from La Rabida, he had written to the Court,
informing it of his arrival in the country. Great was the sensation caused

---

[20] Bernal Diaz says, that Sandoval was twenty-two years old, when he first came
to New Spain in 1519.—Hist. de la Conquista, cap. 205.

[21] Ibid., cap. 195.

there by the intelligence; the greater, that the late reports of his treasonable practices had made it wholly unexpected. His arrival produced an immediate change of feeling. All cause of jealousy was now removed; and, as the clouds, which had so long settled over the royal mind, were dispelled, the emperor seemed only anxious to show his sense of the distinguished services of his so dreaded vassal. Orders were sent to different places on the route to provide him with suitable accommodations, and preparations were made to give him a brilliant reception in the capital.

Meanwhile Cortés had formed the acquaintance at Guadaloupe of several persons of distinction, and among them of the family of the *comendador* of Leon, a nobleman of the highest consideration at court. The general's conversation, enriched with the stores of a life of adventure, and his manners, in which the authority of habitual command was tempered by the frank and careless freedom of the soldier, made a most favorable impression on his new friends; and their letters to the court, where he was yet unknown, heightened the interest already felt in this remarkable man. The tidings of his arrival had by this time spread far and wide, throughout the country; and, as he resumed his journey, the roads presented a spectacle such as had not been seen since the return of Columbus. Cortés did not usually affect an ostentation of dress, though he loved to display the pomp of a great lord in the number and magnificence of his retainers. His train was now swelled by the Indian chieftains, who, by the splendors of their barbaric finery, gave additional brilliancy, as well as novelty, to the pageant. But his own person was the object of general curiosity. The houses and the streets of the great towns and villages were thronged with spectators, eager to look on the hero, who, with his single arm, as it were, had won an empire for Castile, and who, to borrow the language of an old historian, "came in the pomp and glory, not so much of a great vassal, as of an independent monarch." [22]

As he approached Toledo, then the rival of Madrid, the press of the multitude increased, till he was met by the duke de Bejar, the count de Aguilar, and others of his steady friends, who, at the head of a large body of the principal nobility and cavaliers of the city, came out to receive him, and attended him to the quarters prepared for his residence. It was a proud moment for Cortés; and distrusting, as he well might, his reception by his countrymen, it afforded him a greater satisfaction than the brilliant entrance, which, a few years previous, he had made into the capital of Mexico.

The following day he was admitted to an audience by the emperor, and Cortés, gracefully kneeling to kiss the hand of his sovereign, presented to him a memorial which succinctly recounted his services and the requital he had received for them. The emperor graciously raised him,

[22] "Vino de las Indias despues de la conquista de México, con tanto acompañamiento y magestad, que mas parecia de Príncipe, ó señor poderosíssimo, que de Capitan y vasallo de algun Rey ó Emperador." Lanuza, Historias Ecclesiásticas y Seculares de Aragon (Zaragoza, 1622,) lib. 3, cap. 14.

and put many questions to him respecting the countries he had conquered. Charles was pleased with the general's answers, and his intelligent mind took great satisfaction in inspecting the curious specimens of Indian ingenuity which his vassal had brought with him from New Spain. In subsequent conversations the emperor repeatedly consulted Cortés on the best mode of administering the government of the colonies; and by his advice introduced some important regulations, especially for ameliorating the condition of the natives, and for encouraging domestic industry.

The monarch took frequent opportunity to show the confidence which he now reposed in Cortés. On all public occasions he appeared with him by his side; and once, when the general lay ill of a fever, Charles paid him a visit in person, and remained some time in the apartment of the invalid. This was an extraordinary mark of condescension in the haughty court of Castile; and it is dwelt upon with becoming emphasis by the historians of the time, who seem to regard it as an ample compensation for all the sufferings and services of Cortés.[23]

The latter had now fairly triumphed over opposition. The courtiers, with that ready instinct which belongs to the tribe, imitated the example of their master; and even envy was silent, amidst the general homage that was paid to the man who had so lately been a mark for the most envenomed calumny. Cortés, without a title, without a name but what he had created for himself, was at once, as it were, raised to a level with the proudest nobles in the land.

He was so still more effectually by the substantial honors which were accorded to him by his sovereign in the course of the following year. By an instrument, dated July 6th, 1529, the emperor raised him to the dignity of the Marquess of the Valley of Oaxaca;[24] and the title of "marquess," when used without the name of the individual, has been always appropriated in the colonies, in an especial manner to Cortés, as the title of "admiral" was to Columbus.[25]

Two other instruments, dated in the same month of July, assigned to Cortés a vast tract of land in the rich province of Oaxaca, together with large estates in the city of Mexico, and other places in the Valley.[26] The princely domain thus granted comprehended more than twenty large towns and villages, and twenty-three thousand vassals. The language in which the gift was made greatly enhanced its value. The preamble of the instrument, after enlarging on the "good services rendered by Cortés in

[23] Gomara, Crónica, cap. 183.—Herrera, Hist. Gen., dec. 4, lib. 4, cap. 1.—Bernal Diaz, Hist. de la Conquista, cap. 195.
[24] Título de Marques, MS., Barcelona, 6 de Julio, 1529.
[25] Humboldt, Essai Politique, tom. II. p. 30, note.
According to Lanuza, he was offered by the emperor the Order of St. Jago. but declined it, because no *encomienda* was attached to it. (Hist. de Aragon, tom. I. lib. 3, cap. 14.) But Caro de Torres, in his History of the Military Orders of Castile, enumerates Cortés among the members of the Compostellan fraternity. Hist. de las Ord. Militares, (Madrid, 1629,) fol. 103, et seq.
[26] Merced de Tierras Immediatas á México, MS., Barcelona, 23 de Julio, 1529.— Merced de los Vasallos, MS., Barcelona, 6 de Julio, 1529.

the Conquest, and the great benefits resulting therefrom, both in respect to the increase of the Castile empire, and the advancement of the Holy Catholic Faith," acknowledges "the sufferings he had undergone in accomplishing this glorious work, and the fidelity and obedience, with which, as a good and trusty vassal, he had ever served the Crown." [27] It declares, in conclusion, that it grants this recompense of his deserts, because it is "the duty of princes to honor and reward those who serve them well and loyally, in order that the memory of their great deeds should be perpetuated, and others be incited by their example to the performance of the like illustrious exploits." The unequivocal testimony thus borne by his sovereign to his unwavering loyalty was most gratifying to Cortés;—how gratifying, every generous soul, who has been the subject of suspicion undeserved, will readily estimate. The language of the general in after time shows how deeply he was touched by it.[28]

Yet there was one degree in the scale, above which the royal gratitude would not rise. Neither the solicitations of Cortés, nor those of the duke de Bejar, and his other powerful friends, could prevail on the emperor to reinstate him in the government of Mexico. The country, reduced to tranquillity, had no longer need of his commanding genius to control it; and Charles did not care to place again his formidable vassal in a situation which might revive the dormant spark of jealousy and distrust. It was the policy of the Crown to employ one class of its subjects to effect its conquests, and another class to rule over them. For the latter it selected men in whom the fire of ambition was tempered by a cooler judgment naturally, or by the sober influence of age. Even Columbus, notwithstanding the terms of his original "capitulation" with the Crown, had not been permitted to preside over the colonies; and still less likely would it be to concede this power to one possessed of the aspiring temper of Cortés.

But, although the emperor refused to commit the civil government of the colony into his hands, he reinstated him in his military command. By a royal ordinance, dated also in July, 1529, the marquess of the Valley was named Captain-General of New Spain, and of the coasts of the South Sea. He was empowered to make discoveries in the Southern Ocean, with the right to rule over such lands as he should colonize,[29] and by a subse-

[27] É nos habemos recibido y tenemos de vos por bien servido en ello, y acatando los grandes provechos que de vuestros servicios han redundado, ansí para el servicio de Nuestro Señor y aumento de su santa fe católica, y en las dichas tierras que estaban sin conocimiento ni fe se han plantado, como el acrecentamiento que dello ha redundado á nuestra corona real destos reynos, y los trabajos que en ello habeis pasado, y la fidelidad y obediencia con que siempre nos habeis servido como bueno é fiel servidor y vasallo nuestro, de que somos ciertos y confiados." Merced de los Vasallos, MS.

[28] "The benignant reception which I experienced, on my return, from your Majesty," says Cortés, "your kind expressions and generous treatment, make me not only forget all my toils and sufferings, but even cause me regret that I have not been called to endure more in your service." (Carta de Cortés al Lic. Nuñez, MS., 1535.) This memorial, addressed to his agent in Castile, was designed for the emperor.

[29] Título de Capitan General de la Nueva España y Costa del Sur, MS., Barcelona 6 de Julio, 1529.

quent grant he was to become proprietor of one twelfth of all his dis-coveries.[30] The government had no design to relinquish the services of so able a commander. But it warily endeavored to withdraw him from the scene of his former triumphs, and to throw open a new career of ambi-tion, that might stimulate him still further to enlarge the dominions of the Crown.

Thus gilded by the sunshine of royal favor, "rivalling," to borrow the homely comparison of an old chronicler, "Alexander in the fame of his exploits, and Crassus in that of his riches," [31] with brilliant manners, and a person, which, although it showed the effects of hard service, had not yet lost all the attractions of youth, Cortés might now be regarded as offering an enviable alliance for the best houses in Castile. It was not long before he paid his addresses, which were favorably received, to a mem-ber of that noble house, which had so steadily supported him in the dark hour of his fortunes. The lady's name was Doña Juana de Zuñiga, daughter of the second count de Aguilar, and niece of the duke de Be-jar.[32] She was much younger than himself, beautiful, and, as events showed, not without spirit. One of his presents to his youthful bride excited the admiration and envy of the fairer part of the court. This was five emeralds, of wonderful size and brilliancy. These jewels had been cut by the Aztecs into the shapes of flowers, fishes, and into other fanciful forms, with an exquisite style of workmanship which enhanced their original value.[33] They were, not improbably, part of the treasure of the unfortunate Montezuma, and, being easily portable, may have escaped the general wreck of the *noche triste*. The Queen of Charles the Fifth, it is said,—it may be the idle gossip of a court,—had intimated a willing-ness to become proprietor of some of these magnificent baubles; and the preference which Cortés gave to his fair bride caused some feelings of estrangement in the royal bosom, which had an unfavorable influence on the future fortunes of the Marquess.

[30] Asiento y Capitulacion que hizo con el Emperador Don H. Cortés, MS., Madrid, 27 de Oct., 1529.

[31] "Que, segun se dezia, excedia en las hazañas á Alexandro Magno, y en las riquezas á Crasso." (Lanuza, Hist. de Aragon, lib. 3, cap. 14.) The rents of the marquess of the Valley, according to L. Marineo Siculo, who lived at the court at this time, were about 60,000 ducats a year. Cosas Memorables de España, (Al-calá de Henares, 1539,) fol. 24.

[32] Doña Juana was of the house of Arellano, and of the royal lineage of Navarre. Her father was not a very wealthy noble. L. Marineo Siculo, Cosas Mem., fol. 24, 25.

[33] One of these precious stones was as valuable as Shylock's turquoise. Some Gen-oese merchants in Seville offered Cortés, according to Gomara, 40,000 ducats for it. The same author gives a more particular account of the jewels, which may interest some readers. It shows the ingenuity of the artist, who, without steel, could so nicely cut so hard a material. One emerald was in the form of a rose; the second in that of a horn; a third, like a fish, with eyes of gold; the fourth was like a little bell, with a fine pearl for the tongue, and on the rim was this inscription, in Span-ish, *Blessed is he who created thee*. The fifth, which was the most valuable, was a small cup with a foot of gold, and with four little chains, of the same metal, attached to a large pearl as a button. The edge of the cup was of gold, on which was en-graven this Latin sentence, *Inter natos mulierum non surrexit major*. Gomara, Cró-nica, cap. 184.

Late in the summer of 1529, Charles the Fifth left his Spanish dominions for Italy. Cortés accompanied him on his way, probably to the place of embarkation; and in the capital of Aragon we find him, according to the national historian, exciting the same general interest and admiration among the people as he had done in Castile. On his return, there seemed no occasion for him to protract his stay longer in the country. He was weary of the life of idle luxury which he had been leading for the last year, and which was so foreign to his active habits and the stirring scenes to which he had been accustomed. He determined, therefore, to return to Mexico, where his extensive property required his presence, and where a new field was now opened to him for honorable enterprise.

CHAPTER V

CORTÉS REVISITS MEXICO—RETIRES TO HIS ESTATES—HIS VOY-
AGES OF DISCOVERY—FINAL RETURN TO CASTILE—COLD RECEP-
TION—DEATH OF CORTÉS—HIS CHARACTER

1530—1547

EARLY in the spring of 1530, Cortés embarked for New Spain. He was
accompanied by the marchioness, his wife, together with his aged mother,
who had the good fortune to live to see her son's elevation, and by a magnificent retinue of pages and attendants, such as belonged to the household of a powerful noble. How different from the forlorn condition, in
which, twenty-six years before, he had been cast loose, as a wild adventurer, to seek his bread upon the waters!

The first point of his destination was Hispaniola, where he was to remain until he received tidings of the organization of the new government
that was to take charge of Mexico.[1] In the preceding Chapter it was
stated, that the administration of the country had been intrusted to a
body called the Royal Audience; one of whose first duties it was to investigate the charges brought against Cortés. Nuñez de Guzman, his
avowed enemy, was placed at the head of this board; and the investigation was conducted with all the rancor of personal hostility. A remarkable document still exists, called the *Pesquisa Secreta*, or "Secret Inquiry," which contains a record of the proceedings against Cortés. It was
prepared by the secretary of the Audience, and signed by the several
members. The document is very long, embracing nearly a hundred folio
pages. The name and the testimony of every witness are given, and the
whole forms a mass of loathsome details such as might better suit a prosecution in a petty municipal court than that of a great officer of the Crown.

The charges are eight in number; involving, among other crimes, that
of a deliberate design to cast off his allegiance to the Crown; that of the
murder of two of the commissioners who had been sent out to supersede
him; of the murder of his own wife, Catalina Xuarez;[2] of extortion, and

---

[1] Carta de Cortés al Emperador, MS., Tezcuco, 10 de Oct., 1530.
[2] Doña Catalina's death happened so opportunely for the rising fortunes of Cortés, that this charge of murder by her husband has found more credit with the vulgar than the other accusations brought against him. Cortés, from whatever reason,
perhaps from the conviction that the charge was too monstrous to obtain credit,
never condescended to vindicate his innocence. But, in addition to the arguments
mentioned in the text for discrediting the accusation generally, we should consider

of licentious practices,—of offences, in short, which, from their private
nature, would seem to have little to do with his conduct as a public man.
The testimony is vague and often contradictory; the witnesses are for
the most part obscure individuals, and the few persons of consideration
among them appear to have been taken from the ranks of his decided
enemies. When it is considered, that the inquiry was conducted in the
absence of Cortés, before a court, the members of which were personally
unfriendly to him, and that he was furnished with no specification of the
charges, and had no opportunity, consequently, of disproving them, it is
impossible, at this distance of time, to attach any importance to this
paper as a legal document. When it is added, that no action was taken on
it by the government, to whom it was sent, we may be disposed to regard
it simply as a monument of the malice of his enemies. It has been drawn
by the curious antiquary from the obscurity to which it had been so long
consigned in the Indian archives at Seville; but it can be of no further
use to the historian, than to show, that a great name in the sixteenth century exposed its possessor to calumnies as malignant as it has at any
time since.[3]

The high-handed measures of the Audience, and the oppressive conduct of Guzman, especially towards the Indians, excited general indignation in the colony, and led to serious apprehensions of an insurrection.
It became necessary to supersede an administration so reckless and un-

that this particular charge attracted so little attention in Castile, where he had
abundance of enemies, that he found no difficulty, on his return there, seven years
afterwards, in forming an alliance with one of the noblest houses in the kingdom;
that no writer of that day, (except Bernal Diaz, who treats it as a base calumny,)
not even Las Casas, the stern accuser of the Conquerors, intimates a suspicion of
his guilt; and that, lastly, no allusion whatever is made to it in the suit, instituted,
some years after her death, by the relatives of Doña Catalina, for the recovery of
property from Cortés, pretended to have been derived through her marriage with
him,—a suit conducted with acrimony, and protracted for several years. I have not
seen the documents connected with this suit, which are still preserved in the archives of the house of Cortés, but the fact has been communicated to me by a distinguished Mexican, who has carefully examined them, and I cannot but regard it
as of itself conclusive, that the family, at least, of Doña Catalina, did not attach
credit to the accusation.

Yet so much credit has been given to this in Mexico, where the memory of the
old Spaniards is not held in especial favor, at the present day, that it has formed the
subject of an elaborate discussion in the public periodicals of that city.

[3] This remarkable paper, forming part of the valuable collection of Don Vargas
Ponçe, is without date. It was doubtless prepared in 1529, during the visit of Cortés
to Castile. The following Title is prefixed to it.
"Pesquisa secreta.
Relacion de los cargos que resultan de la pesquisa secreta contra Don Hernando
Cortés, de los quales no se le dió copia ni translado á la parte del dicho Don Hernando, así por ser los dichos cargos de la calidad que son, como por estar la persona
del dicho Don Hernando ausente como está. Los quales yo Gregorio de Saldaña,
escribano de S. M. y escribano de la dicha Residencia, saqué de la dicha pesquisa
secreta por mandado de los Señores, Presidente y Oidores de la Audiencia y Chan-
cillería Real que por mandado de S. M. en esta Nueva España reside. Los quales
dichos Señores, Presidente y Oidores, envian á S. M. para que los mande ver, y vis-
tos mande proveer lo que á su servicio convenga." MS.

principled. But Cortés was detained two months at the island, by the slow movements of the Castilian court, before tidings reached him of the appointment of a new Audience for the government of the country. The person selected to preside over it was the bishop of St. Domingo, a prelate whose acknowledged wisdom and virtue gave favorable augury for the conduct of his administration. After this, Cortés resumed his voyage, and landed at Villa Rica on the 15th of July, 1530.

After remaining for a time in the neighborhood, where he received some petty annoyances from the Audience, he proceeded to Tlascala, and publicly proclaimed his powers as Captain-General of New Spain and the South Sea. An edict, issued by the empress during her husband's absence, had interdicted Cortés from approaching within ten leagues of the Mexican capital, while the present authorities were there.[4] The empress was afraid of a collision between the parties. Cortés, however, took up his residence on the opposite side of the lake, at Tezcuco.

No sooner was his arrival there known in the metropolis, than multitudes, both of Spaniards and natives, crossed the lake to pay their respects to their old commander, to offer him their services, and to complain of their manifold grievances. It seemed as if the whole population of the capital was pouring into the neighboring city, where the marquess maintained the state of an independent potentate. The members of the Audience, indignant at the mortifying contrast which their own diminished court presented, imposed heavy penalties on such of the natives as should be found in Tezcuco; and, affecting to consider themselves in danger, made preparations for the defence of the city. But these belligerent movements were terminated by the arrival of the new Audience; though Guzman had the address to maintain his hold on a northern province, where he earned a reputation for cruelty and extortion, unrivalled even in the annals of the New World.

Every thing seemed now to assure a tranquil residence to Cortés. The new magistrates treated him with marked respect, and took his advice on the most important measures of government. Unhappily this state of things did not long continue; and a misunderstanding arose between the parties, in respect to the enumeration of the vassals assigned by the Crown to Cortés, which the marquess thought was made on principles prejudicial to his interests, and repugnant to the intentions of the grant.[5] He was still further displeased by finding that the Audience were intrusted, by their commission, with a concurrent jurisdiction with himself in military affairs.[6] This led, occasionally, to an interference, which the proud spirit of Cortés, so long accustomed to independent rule, could ill brook. After submitting to it for a time, he left the capital in disgust, no

---

[4] MS., Tordelaguna, 22 de Marzo, 1530.

[5] The principal grievance alleged was, that slaves, many of them held temporarily by their masters, according to the old Aztec usage, were comprehended in the census. The complaint forms part of a catalogue of grievances embodied by Cortés in a memorial to the emperor. It is a clear and business-like paper. Carta de Cortés á Nuñez, MS.

[6] Ibid., MS.

more to return there, and took up his residence in his city of Cuernavaca. It was the place won by his own sword from the Aztecs, previous to the siege of Mexico. It stood on the southern slope of the Cordilleras, and overlooked a wide expanse of country, the fairest and most flourishing portion of his own domain. He had erected a stately palace on the spot, and henceforth made this city his favorite residence.[7] It was well situated for superintending his vast estates, and he now devoted himself to bring them into proper cultivation. He introduced the sugar-cane from Cuba, and it grew luxuriantly in the rich soil of the neighboring lowlands. He imported large numbers of merino sheep and other cattle, which found abundant pastures in the country around Tehuantepec. His lands were thickly sprinkled with groves of mulberry-trees, which furnished nourishment for the silk-worm. He encouraged the cultivation of hemp and flax, and, by his judicious and enterprising husbandry, showed the capacity of the soil for the culture of valuable products before unknown in the land; and he turned these products to the best account, by the erection of sugar-mills, and other works for the manufacture of the raw material. He thus laid the foundation of an opulence for his family, as substantial, if not as speedy, as that derived from the mines. Yet this latter source of wealth was not neglected by him, and he drew gold from the region of Tehuantepec, and silver from that of Zacatecas. The amount derived from these mines was not so abundant as at a later day. But the expense of working them, on the other hand, was much less in the earlier stages of the operation, when the metal lay so much nearer the surface.[8]

But this tranquil way of life did not long content his restless and adventurous spirit; and it sought a vent by availing itself of his new charter of discovery to explore the mysteries of the great Southern Ocean. In 1527, two years before his return to Spain, he had sent a little squadron to the Moluccas. The expedition was attended with some important consequences; but, as they do not relate to Cortés, an account of it will find a more suitable place in the maritime annals of Spain, where it has been given by the able hand which has done so much for the country in this department.[9]

Cortés was preparing to send another squadron of four vessels in the

[7] The palace has crumbled into ruins, and the spot is now only remarkable for its natural beauty and its historic associations. "It was the capital," says Madame de Calderon, "of the Tlahuica nation, and, after the Conquest, Cortés built here a splendid palace, a church, and a convent for Franciscans, believing that he had laid the foundation of a great city. . . . . . It is, however, a place of little importance, though so favored by nature; and the Conqueror's palace is a half-ruined barrack, though a most picturesque object, standing on a hill, behind which starts up the great white volcano. There are some good houses, and the remains of the church which Cortés built, celebrated for its bold arch." Life in Mexico, vol. II. let. 31.

[8] These particulars, respecting the agricultural economy of Cortés, I have derived, in part, from a very able argument, prepared, in January, 1828, for the Mexican Chamber of Deputies, by Don Lúcas Alaman, in defence of the territorial rights possessed at this day by the Conqueror's descendant, the duke of Monteleone.

[9] Navarrete, Coleccion de los Viages y descubrimientos, (Madrid, 1837,) tom. V., Viages al Maluco.

same direction, when his plans were interrupted by his visit to Spain; and his unfinished little navy, owing to the malice of the Royal Audience, who drew off the hands employed in building it, went to pieces on the stocks. Two other squadrons were now fitted out by Cortés, in the years 1532 and 1533, and sent on a voyage of discovery to the North-west.[10] They were unfortunate, though, in the latter expedition, the Californian peninsula was reached, and a landing effected on its southern extremity at Santa Cruz, probably the modern port of La Paz. One of the vessels, thrown on the coast of New Galicia, was seized by Guzman, the old enemy of Cortés, who ruled over that territory, the crew were plundered, and the ship was detained as a lawful prize. Cortés, indignant at the outrage, demanded justice from the Royal Audience; and, as that body was too feeble to enforce its own decrees in his favor, he took redress into his own hands.[11]

He made a rapid but difficult march on Chiametla, the scene of Guzman's spoliation; and, as the latter did not care to face his incensed antagonist, Cortés recovered his vessel, though not the cargo. He was then joined by the little squadron which he had fitted out from his own port of Tehuantepec,—a port, which, in the sixteenth century, promised to hold the place since occupied by that of Acapulco.[12] The vessels were provided with every thing requisite for planting a colony in the newly discovered region, and transported four hundred Spaniards and *three hundred negro slaves*, which Cortés had assembled for that purpose. With this intention he crossed the Gulf, the Adriatic—to which an old writer compares it—of the Western World.

Our limits will not allow us to go into the details of this disastrous expedition, which was attended with no important results either to its projector or to science. It may suffice to say, that, in the prosecution of it, Cortés and his followers were driven to the last extremity by famine; that he again crossed the Gulf, was tossed about by terrible tempests, without a pilot to guide him, was thrown upon the rocks, where his shattered vessel nearly went to pieces, and, after a succession of dangers and disasters as formidable as any which he had ever encountered on land, succeeded, by means of his indomitable energy, in bringing his crazy bark safe into the same port of Santa Cruz from which he had started.

While these occurrences were passing, the new Royal Audience, after a faithful discharge of its commission, had been superseded by the arrival of a Viceroy, the first ever sent to New Spain. Cortés, though invested with similar powers, had the title only of Governor. This was the commencement of the system, afterwards pursued by the Crown, of intrusting the colonial administration to some individual, whose high rank and personal consideration might make him the fitting representative of

---

[10] Instruccion que dió Marques del Valle á Juan de Avellaneda, &c., MS.

[11] Provision sobre los Descubrimientos del Sur, MS., Setiembre, 1534.

[12] The river Huasacualco furnished great facilities for transporting, across the isthmus, from Vera Cruz, materials to build vessels on the Pacific. Humboldt, Essai Politique, tom IV. p. 50.

majesty. The jealousy of the Court did not allow the subject clothed with such ample authority to remain long enough in the same station to form dangerous schemes of ambition, but at the expiration of a few years he was usually recalled, or transferred to some other province of the vast colonial empire. The person now sent to Mexico was Don Antonio de Mendoza, a man of moderation and practical good sense, and one of that illustrious family who in the preceding reign furnished so many distinguished ornaments to the Church, to the camp, and to letters.

The long absence of Cortés had caused the deepest anxiety in the mind of his wife, the marchioness of the Valley. She wrote to the viceroy immediately on his arrival, beseeching him to ascertain, if possible, the fate of her husband, and, if he could be found, to urge his return. The viceroy, in consequence, despatched two ships in search of Cortés, but whether they reached him before his departure from Santa Cruz is doubtful. It is certain, that he returned safe, after his long absence, to Acapulco, and was soon followed by the survivors of his wretched colony.

Undismayed by these repeated reverses, Cortés, still bent on some discovery worthy of his reputation, fitted out three more vessels, and placed them under the command of an officer named Ulloa. This expedition, which took its departure in July, 1539, was attended with more important results. Ulloa penetrated to the head of the Gulf; then, returning and winding round the coast of the peninsula, doubled its southern point, and ascended as high as the twenty-eight or twenty-ninth degree of north latitude on its western borders. After this, sending home one of the squadron, the bold navigator held on his course to the north, but was never more heard of.[13]

Thus ended the maritime enterprises of Cortés; sufficiently disastrous in a pecuniary view, since they cost him three hundred thousand *castellanos* of gold, without the return of a ducat.[14] He was even obliged to borrow money, and to pawn his wife's jewels, to procure funds for the last enterprise;[15] thus incurring a debt, which, increased by the great charges of his princely establishment, hung about him during the remainder of his life. But, though disastrous in an economical view, his generous efforts added important contributions to science. In the course of these expeditions, and those undertaken by Cortés previous to his visit to Spain, the Pacific had been coasted from the Bay of Panamá to the Rio

[13] Instruccion del Marques del Valle, MS.

The most particular and authentic account of Ulloa's cruise will be found in Ramusio. (Tom. III. pp. 340-354.) It is by one of the officers of the squadron.— My limits will not allow me to give the details of the voyages made by Cortés, which, although not without interest, were attended with no permanent consequences. A good summary of his expeditions in the Gulf has been given by Navarrete in the Introduction to his Relacion del Viage hecho por las Goletas Sutil y Mexicana, (Madrid, 1802,) pp. vi.–xxvi.; and the English reader will find a brief account of them in Greenhow's valuable Memoir on the Northwest Coast of North America, (Washington, 1840) pp. 22-27.

[14] Memorial al Rey del Marques del Valle, MS., 25 de Junio, 1540.

[15] Provision sobre los Descubrimientos del Sur, MS.

Colorado. The great peninsula of California had been circumnavigated as far as to the isle of Cedros, or Cerros, into which the name has since been corrupted. This vast tract, which had been supposed to be an archipelago of islands, was now discovered to be a part of the continent; and its general outline, as appears from the maps of the time, was nearly as well understood as at the present day.[16] Lastly, the navigator had explored the recesses of the Californian Gulf, or *Sea of Cortés*, as, in honor of the great discoverer, it is with more propriety named by the Spaniards; and he had ascertained, that, instead of the outlet before supposed to exist towards the north, this unknown ocean was locked up within the arms of the mighty continent. These were results that might have made the glory and satisfied the ambition of a common man; but they are lost in the brilliant renown of the former achievements of Cortés.

Notwithstanding the embarrassments of the marquess of the Valley, he still made new efforts to enlarge the limits of discovery, and prepared to fit out another squadron of five vessels, which he proposed to place under the command of a natural son, Don Luis. But the viceroy Mendoza, whose imagination had been inflamed by the reports of an itinerant monk respecting an *El Dorado* in the north, claimed the right of discovery in that direction. Cortés protested against this, as an unwarrantable interference with his own powers. Other subjects of collision arose between them; till the marquess, disgusted with this perpetual check on his authority and his enterprises, applied for redress to Castile.[17] He finally determined to go there to support his claims in person, and to obtain, if possible, remuneration for the heavy charges he had incurred by his maritime expeditions, as well as for the spoliation of his property by the Royal Audience, during his absence from the country; and, lastly, to procure an assignment of his vassals on principles more conformable to the original intentions of the grant. With these objects in view, he bade adieu to his family, and, taking with him his eldest son and heir, Don Martin, then only eight years of age, he embarked at Mexico in 1540, and, after a favorable voyage, again set foot on the shores of his native land.

The emperor was absent from the country. But Cortés was honorably received in the capital, where ample accommodations were provided for him and his retinue. When he attended the Royal Council of the Indies, to urge his suit, he was distinguished by uncommon marks of respect. The president went to the door of the hall to receive him, and a seat was provided for him among the members of the Council.[18] But all evaporated in this barren show of courtesy. Justice, proverbially slow in Spain, did

[16] See the map prepared by the pilot Domingo del Castillo, in 1541, ap. Lorenzana, p. 328.
[17] In the collection of Vargas Ponçe is a petition of Cortés, setting forth his grievances, and demanding an investigation of the vice-king's conduct. It is without date. Peticion contra Don Antonio de Mendoza Virrey, pediendo residencia contra él, MS.
[18] Bernal Diaz, Hist de la Conquista, cap. 200.

aot mend her gait for Cortés; and at the expiration of a year, he found himself no nearer the attainment of his object than on the first week after his arrival in the capital.

In the following year, 1541, we find the marquess of the Valley embarked as a volunteer in the memorable expedition against Algiers. Charles the Fifth, on his return to his dominions, laid siege to that stronghold of the Mediterranean corsairs. Cortés accompanied the forces destined to meet the emperor, and embarked on board the vessel of the Admiral of Castile. But a furious tempest scattered the navy, and the admiral's ship was driven a wreck upon the coast. Cortés and his son escaped by swimming, but the former, in the confusion of the scene, lost the inestimable set of jewels noticed in the preceding chapter; "a loss," says an old writer, "that made the expedition fall more heavily on the marquess of the Valley, than on any other man in the kingdom, except the emperor." [19]

It is not necessary to recount the particulars of this disastrous siege, in which Moslem valor, aided by the elements, set at defiance the combined forces of the Christians. A council of war was called, and it was decided to abandon the enterprise and return to Castile. This determination was indignantly received by Cortés, who offered, with the support of the army, to reduce the place himself; and he only expressed the regret, that he had not a handful of those gallant veterans by his side who had served him in the conquest of Mexico. But his offers were derided, as those of a romantic enthusiast. He had not been invited to take part in the discussions of the council of war. It was a marked indignity; but the courtiers, weary of the service, were too much bent on an immediate return to Spain, to hazard the opposition of a man, who, when he had once planted his foot, was never known to raise it again, till he had accomplished his object.[20]

On arriving in Castile, Cortés lost no time in laying his suit before the emperor. His applications were received by the monarch with civility,— a cold civility, which carried no conviction of its sincerity. His position was materially changed since his former visit to the country. More than ten years had elapsed, and he was now too well advanced in years to give promise of serviceable enterprise in future. Indeed, his undertakings of late had been singularly unfortunate. Even his former successes suffered the disparagement natural to a man of declining fortunes. They were already eclipsed by the magnificent achievements in Peru, which had poured a golden tide into the country, that formed a striking contrast to the streams of wealth, that, as yet, had flowed in but scantily from the silver mines of Mexico. Cortés had to learn, that the gratitude of a Court has reference to the future much more than to the past. He stood in the position of an importunate suitor, whose claims, however just, are

[19] Gomara, Crónica, cap. 237.
[20] Sandoval, Hist. de Cárlos V., lib. 12, cap. 25.—Ferreras, (trad. d'Hermilly,) Hist. d'Espagne, tom. IX. p. 231.

too large to be readily allowed. He found, like Columbus, that it was possible to deserve too greatly.[21]

In the month of February, 1544, he addressed a letter to the emperor.
—it was the last he ever wrote him,—soliciting his attention to his suit.
He begins, by proudly alluding to his past services to the Crown. "He had hoped, that the toils of youth would have secured him repose in his old age. For forty years he had passed his life with little sleep, bad food, and with his arms constantly by his side. He had freely exposed his person to peril, and spent his substance in exploring distant and unknown regions, that he might spread abroad the name of his sovereign, and bring under his sceptre many great and powerful nations. All this he had done, not only without assistance from home, but in the face of obstacles thrown in his way by rivals and by enemies who thirsted like leeches for his blood. He was now old, infirm, and embarrassed with debt. Better had it been for him not to have known the liberal intentions of the emperor, as intimated by his grants; since he should then have devoted himself to the care of his estates, and not have been compelled, as he now was, to contend with the officers of the Crown, against whom it was more difficult to defend himself than to win the land from the enemy." He concluded with beseeching his sovereign to "order the Council of the Indies, with the other tribunals which had cognizance of his suits, to come to a decision; since he was too old to wander about like a vagrant, but ought rather, during the brief remainder of his life, to stay at home and settle his account with Heaven, occupied with the concerns of his soul, rather than with his substance."[22]

This appeal to his sovereign, which has something in it touching from a man of the haughty spirit of Cortés, had not the effect to quicken the determination of his suit. He still lingered at the court from week to week, and from month to month, beguiled by the deceitful hopes of the litigant, tasting all that bitterness of the soul which arises from hope deferred. After three years more, passed in this unprofitable and humiliating occupation, he resolved to leave his ungrateful country and return to Mexico.

He had proceeded as far as Seville, accompanied by his son, when he fell ill of an indigestion, caused, probably, by irritation and trouble of mind. This terminated in dysentery, and his strength sank so rapidly under the disease, that it was apparent his mortal career was drawing towards its close. He prepared for it by making the necessary arrangements for the settlement of his affairs. He had made his will some time

[21] Voltaire tells us, that, one day, Cortés, unable to obtain an audience of the emperor, pushed through the press surrounding the royal carriage, and mounted the steps; and, when Charles inquired "who that man was," he replied, "One who has given you more kingdoms than you had towns before." (Essai sur les Mœurs, chap. 147.) For this most improbable anecdote I have found no authority whatever. It served, however, very well to point a moral,—the main thing with the philosopher of Ferney.

[22] The Letter is dated February 3, 1544. Valladolid.

before; and he now executed it. It is a very long document, and in some respects a remarkable one.

The bulk of his property was entailed to his son, Don Martin, then fifteen years of age. In the testament he fixes his majority at twenty-five; but at twenty his guardians were to allow him his full income, to maintain the state becoming his rank. In a paper accompanying the will, Cortés specified the names of the agents to whom he had committed the management of his vast estates scattered over many different provinces; and he requests his executors to confirm the nomination, as these agents have been selected by him from a knowledge of their peculiar qualifications. Nothing can better show the thorough supervision, which, in the midst of pressing public concerns, he had given to the details of his widely extended property.

He makes a liberal provision for his other children, and a generous allowance to several old domestics and retainers in his household. By another clause he gives away considerable sums in charity, and he applies the revenues of his estates in the city of Mexico to establish and permanently endow three public institutions,—a hospital in the capital, which was to be dedicated to Our Lady of the Conception, a college in Cojohuacan for the education of missionaries to preach the gospel among the natives, and a convent, in the same place, for nuns. To the chapel of this convent, situated in his favorite town, he orders that his own body shall be transported for burial, in whatever quarter of the world he may happen to die.

After declaring that he has taken all possible care to ascertain the amount of the tributes formerly paid by his Indian vassals to their native sovereigns, he enjoins on his heir, that, in case those which they have hitherto paid shall be found to exceed the right valuation, he shall restore them a full equivalent. In another clause, he expresses a doubt whether it is right to exact personal service from the natives; and commands that a strict inquiry shall be made into the nature and value of such services as he had received, and that, in all cases, a fair compensation shall be allowed for them. Lastly, he makes this remarkable declaration: "It has long been a question, whether one can conscientiously hold property in Indian slaves. Since this point has not yet been determined, I enjoin it on my son Martin and his heirs, that they spare no pains to come to an exact knowledge of the truth; as a matter which deeply concerns the conscience of each of them, no less than mine." [23]

Such scruples of conscience, not to have been expected in Cortés, were

[23] "Item. Porque acerca de los esclavos naturales de la dicha Nueva España, así de guerra como de rescate, ha habido y hay muchas dudas y opiniones sobre si se han podido tener con buena conciencia ó no, y hasta ahora no está determinado: Mando que todo aquello que generalmente se averiguare, que en este caso se debe hacer para descargo de las conciencias en lo que toca á estos esclavos de la dicha Nueva España que se haya y cumpla entodos los que yo tengo, é encargo. Y mando á D. Martin mi hijo subcesor, y á los que despues dél subcedieren en mi Estado, que para averiguar esto hagan todas las diligencias que combengan al descargo de mi conciencia y suyas." Testamento de Hernan Cortés, MS

still less likely to be met with in the Spaniards of a later generation. The state of opinion in respect to the great question of slavery, in the sixteenth century, at the commencement of the system, bears some resemblance to that which exists in our time, when we may hope it is approaching its conclusion. Las Casas and the Dominicans of the former age, the abolitionists of their day, thundered out their uncompromising invectives against the system, on the broad ground of natural equity and the rights of man. The great mass of proprietors troubled their heads little about the question of right, but were satisfied with the expediency of the institution. Others more considerate and conscientious, while they admitted the evil, found an argument for its toleration in the plea of necessity, regarding the constitution of the white man as unequal, in a sultry climate, to the labor of cultivating the soil.[24] In one important respect, the condition of slavery, in the sixteenth century, differed materially from its condition in the nineteenth. In the former, the seeds of the evil, but lately sown, might have been, with comparatively little difficulty, eradicated. But in our time they have struck their roots deep into the social system, and cannot be rudely handled without shaking the very foundations of the political fabric. It is easy to conceive, that a man, who admits all the wretchedness of the institution and its wrong to humanity, may nevertheless hesitate to adopt a remedy, until he is satisfied that the remedy itself is not worse than the disease. That such a remedy will come with time, who can doubt, that has confidence in the ultimate prevalence of the right, and the progressive civilization of his species?

Cortés names, as his executors, and as guardians of his children, the duke of Medina Sidonia, the marquess of Astorga, and the count of Aguilar. For his executors in Mexico, he appoints his wife, the marchioness, the archbishop of Toledo, and two other prelates. The will was executed at Seville, October 11th, 1547.[25]

Finding himself much incommoded, as he grew weaker, by the presence of visitors, to which he was necessarily exposed at Seville, he withdrew to the neighboring village of Castilleja de la Cuesta, attended by his son, who watched over his dying parent with filial solicitude. Cortés seems to have contemplated his approaching end with the composure not always to be found in those who have faced death with indifference on the field of battle. At length, having devoutly confessed his sins and received the sacrament, he expired on the 2d of December, 1547, in the sixty-third year of his age.[26]

[24] This is the argument controverted by Las Casas in his elaborate Memorial addressed to the government, in 1542, on the best method of arresting the destruction of the Aborigines.

[25] This interesting document is in the Royal Archives of Seville; and a copy of it forms part of the valuable collection of Don Vargas Ponçe.

[26] Zuñiga, Annales de Sevilla, p. 504.—Gomara, Crónica, cap. 237.

In his last letter to the emperor, dated in February, 1544, he speaks of himself as being "sixty years of age." But he probably did not mean to be exact to a year. Gomara's statement, that he was born in the year 1485, (Crónica, cap. 1,) was confirmed by Diaz, who tells us, that Cortés used to say, that, when he first came over

The inhabitants of the neighboring country were desirous to show every mark of respect to the memory of Cortés. His funeral obsequies were celebrated with due solemnity by a long train of Andalusian nobles, and of the citizens of Seville, and his body was transported to the chapel of the monastery, San Isidro, in that city, where it was laid in the family vault of the duke of Medina Sidonia.[27] In the year 1562, it was removed, by order of his son, Don Martin, to New Spain, not, as directed by his will, to Cojohuacan, but to the monastery of St. Francis, in Tezcuco, where it was laid by the side of a daughter, and of his mother, Doña Catalina Pizarro. In 1629, the remains of Cortés were again removed; and on the death of Don Pedro, fourth marquess of the Valley, it was decided by the authorities of Mexico to transfer them to the church of St. Francis, in that capital. The ceremonial was conducted with the pomp suited to the occasion. A military and religious procession was formed, with the archbishop of Mexico at its head. He was accompanied by the great dignitaries of church and state, the various associations with their respective banners, the several religious fraternities, and the members of the Audience. The coffin, containing the relics of Cortés, was covered with black velvet, and supported by the judges of the Royal tribunals. On either side of it was a man in complete armor, bearing, on the right, a standard of pure white, with the arms of Castile embroidered in gold, and, on the left, a banner of black velvet, emblazoned in like manner with the armorial ensigns of the house of Cortés. Behind the corpse came the viceroy and a numerous escort of Spanish cavaliers, and the rear was closed by a battalion of infantry, armed with pikes and arquebuses, and with their banners trailing on the ground. With this funeral pomp, by the sound of mournful music, and the slow beat of the muffled drum, the procession moved forward, with measured pace, till it reached the capital, when the gates were thrown open to receive the mortal remains of the hero, who, a century before, had performed there such prodigies of valor.

Yet his bones were not permitted to rest here undisturbed; and in 1794 they were removed to the Hospital of Jesus of Nazareth. It was a more fitting place, since it was the same institution, which, under the name of "Our Lady of Conception," had been founded and endowed by Cortés, and which, with a fate not too frequent in similar charities, has been administered to this day on the noble principles of its foundation. The mouldering relics of the warrior, now deposited in a crystal coffin secured by bars and plates of silver, were laid in the chapel, and over them was raised a simple monument, displaying the arms of the family, and surmounted by a bust of the Conqueror, executed in bronze by Tolsa, a sculptor worthy of the best period of the arts.[28]

to Mexico, in 1519, he was thirty-four years old. (Hist. de la Conquista, cap. 205.) This would coincide with the age mentioned in the text.

[27] Noticia del Archivero de la Santa Eclesia de Sevilla, MS.

[28] The full particulars of the ceremony described in the text may be found in a copy of the original document, existing in the Archives of the Hospital of Jesus, in Mexico.

Unfortunately for Mexico, the tale does not stop here. In 1823, **the** patriot mob of the capital, in their zeal to commemorate the era of the national independence, and their detestation of the "old Spaniards," prepared to break open the tomb which held the ashes of Cortés, and to scatter them to the winds! The authorities declined to interfere on the occasion; but the friends of the family, as is commonly reported, entered the vault by night, and, secretly removing the relics, prevented the commission of a sacrilege, which must have left a strain, not easy to be effaced, on the scutcheon of the fair city of Mexico.—Humboldt, forty years ago, remarked, that "we may traverse Spanish America from Buenos Aires to Monterey, and in no quarter shall we meet with a national monument which the public gratitude has raised to Christopher Columbus, or Hernando Cortés." [29] It was reserved for our own age to conceive the design of violating the repose of the dead, and insulting their remains! Yet the men who meditated this outrage were not the descendants of Montezuma, avenging the wrongs of their fathers, and vindicating their own rightful inheritance. They were the descendants of the old Conquerors, and their countrymen, depending on the right of conquest for their ultimate title to the soil.

Cortés had no children by his first marriage. By his second he left four; a son, Don Martin,—the heir of his honors, and of persecutions even more severe than those of his father,[30]—and three daughters, who formed splendid alliances. He left, also, several natural children, whom he particularly mentions in his testament and honorably provides for. Two of these, Don Martin, the son of Marina, and Don Luis Cortés, attained considerable distinction, and were created *comendadores* of the Order of St. Jago.

The male line of the marquesses of the Valley became extinct in the fourth generation. The title and estates descended to a female, and by her marriage were united with those of the house of Terranova, descendants of the "Great Captain," Gonsalvo de Cordova. By a subsequent marriage they were carried into the family of the duke of Monteleone, a Neapolitan noble. The present proprietor of these princely honors and of vast domains, both in the Old and the New World, dwells in Sicily, and boasts a descent—such as few princes can boast—from two of the most

---

[29] Essai Politique, tom. II. p. 60.

[30] Don Martin Cortéz, second marquess of the Valley, was accused, like his father, of an attempt to establish an independent sovereignty in New Spain. His natural brothers, Don Martin and Don Luis, were involved in the same accusation with himself, and the former—as I have elsewhere remarked—was in consequence subjected to the torture. Several others of his friends, on charge of abetting his treasonable designs, suffered death. The marquess was obliged to remove with his family to Spain, where the investigation was conducted; and his large estates in Mexico were sequestered until the termination of the process, a period of seven years, from 1567 to 1574, when he was declared innocent. But his property suffered irreparable injury, under the wretched administration of the royal officers, during the term of sequestration.

illustrious commanders of the sixteenth century, the "Great Captain,"
and the Conqueror of Mexico.

The personal history of Cortés has been so minutely detailed in the
preceding narrative, that it will be only necessary to touch on the more
prominent features of his character. Indeed, the history of the Conquest,
as I have already had occasion to remark, is necessarily that of Cortés,
who is, if I may so say, not merely the soul, but the body, of the enterprise, present everywhere in person, in the thick of the fight, or in the
building of the works, with his sword or with his musket, sometimes
leading his soldiers, and sometimes directing his little navy. The negotiations, intrigues, correspondence, are all conducted by him; and, like
Cæsar, he wrote his own Commentaries in the heat of the stirring scenes
which form the subject of them. His character is marked with the most
opposite traits, embracing qualities apparently the most incompatible. He
was avaricious, yet liberal; bold to desperation, yet cautious and calculating in his plans; magnanimous, yet very cunning; courteous and affable
in his deportment, yet inexorably stern; lax in his notions of morality,
yet (not uncommon) a sad bigot. The great feature in his character was
constancy of purpose; a constancy not to be daunted by danger, nor
baffled by disappointment, nor wearied out by impediments and delays.

He was a knight-errant, in the literal sense of the word. Of all the band
of adventurous cavaliers, whom Spain, in the sixteenth century, sent
forth on the career of discovery and conquest, there was none more
deeply filled with the spirit of romantic enterprise than Hernando Cortés.
Dangers and difficulties, instead of deterring, seemed to have a charm in
his eyes. They were necessary to rouse him to a full consciousness of his
powers. He grappled with them at the outset, and, if I may so express myself, seemed to prefer to take his enterprises by the most difficult side. He
conceived, at the first moment of his landing in Mexico, the design of its
conquest. When he saw the strength of its civilization, he was not turned
from his purpose. When he was assailed by the superior force of Narvaez,
he still persisted in it; and, when he was driven in ruin from the capital,
he still cherished his original idea. How successfully he carried it into
execution, we have seen. After the few years of repose which succeeded
the Conquest, his adventurous spirit impelled him to that dreary march
across the marshes of Chiapa; and, after another interval, to seek his
fortunes on the stormy Californian Gulf. When he found that no other
continent remained for him to conquer, he made serious proposals to the
emperor to equip a fleet at his own expense, with which he would sail to
the Moluccas, and subdue the Spice-Islands for the Crown of Castile! [31]

[31] "Yo me ofresco á descubrir por aquí to da la especería, y otras Islas si huviere
cerca de Moluco, ó Melaca, y la China, y aun de dar tal órden que V. M. no aiga la
especería por via de rescate, como la ha el Rey de Portugal, sino que la tenga por
cosa propria, y los naturales de aquellas Islas le reconoscan y sirvan como á su Rey
y señor natural, porque yo me ofresco con el dicho additamento de embiar á ellas
tal armada, ó *ir yo con mi persona por manera que la sojusge y pueble.*" Carta
Quinta de Cortés. MS.

This spirit of knight-errantry might lead us to undervalue his talents as a general, and to regard him merely in the light of a lucky adventurer. But this would be doing him injustice; for Cortés was certainly a great general, if that man be one, who performs great achievements with the resources which his own genius has created. There is probably no instance in history, where so vast an enterprise has been achieved by means apparently so inadequate. He may be truly said to have effected the Conquest by his own resources. If he was indebted for his success to the coöperation of the Indian tribes, it was the force of his genius that obtained command of such materials. He arrested the arm that was lifted to smite him, and made it do battle in his behalf. He beat the Tlascalans, and made them his stanch allies. He beat the soldiers of Narvaez, and doubled his effective force by it. When his own men deserted him, he did not desert himself. He drew them back by degrees, and compelled them to act by his will, till they were all as one man. He brought together the most miscellaneous collection of mercenaries who ever fought under one standard; adventurers from Cuba and the Isles, craving for gold; hidalgos, who came from the old country to win laurels; broken-down cavaliers, who hoped to mend their fortunes in the New World; vagabonds flying from justice; the grasping followers of Narvaez, and his own reckless veterans,—men with hardly a common tie, and burning with the spirit of jealousy and faction; wild tribes of the natives from all parts of the country, who had been sworn enemies from their cradles, and who had met only to cut one another's throats, and to procure victims for sacrifice; men, in short, differing in race, in language, and in interests, with scarcely any thing in common among them. Yet this motley congregation was assembled in one camp, compelled to bend to the will of one man, to consort together in harmony, to breathe, as it were, one spirit, and to move on a common principle of action! It is in this wonderful power over the discordant masses thus gathered under his banner, that we recognise the genius of the great commander, no less than in the skill of his military operations.

His power over the minds of his soldiers was a natural result of their confidence in his abilities. But it is also to be attributed to his popular manners,—that happy union of authority and companionship, which fitted him for the command of a band of roving adventurers. It would not have done for him to have fenced himself round with the stately reserve of a commander of regular forces. He was embarked with his men in a common adventure, and nearly on terms of equality, since he held his commission by no legal warrant. But, while he indulged this freedom and familiarity with his soldiers, he never allowed it to interfere with their strict obedience, nor to impair the severity of discipline. When he had risen to higher consideration, although he affected more state, he still admitted his veterans to the same intimacy. "He preferred," says Diaz, "to be called 'Cortés' by us, to being called by any title; and with good reason," continues the enthusiastic old cavalier, "for the name of Cortés is as famous in our day as was that of Cæsar among the Romans, or of

Hannibal among the Carthaginians." [32] He showed the same kind regard towards his ancient comrades in the very last act of his life. For he appropriated a sum by his will for the celebration of two thousand masses for the souls of those who had fought with him in the campaigns of Mexico.[33]

His character has been unconsciously traced by the hand of a master.

> "And oft *the chieftain* deigned to aid
> And mingle in the mirth they made;
> For, though, with men of high degree,
> The proudest of the proud was he,
> Yet, trained in camps, he knew the art
> To win the soldiers' hardy heart.
> They love a captain to obey,
> Boisterous as March, yet fresh as May;
> With open hand, and brow as free,
> Lover of wine, and minstrelsy;
> Ever the first to scale a tower,
> As venturous in a lady's bower;—
> Such buxom chief shall lead his host
> From India's fires to Zembla's frost."

Cortés, without much violence, might have sat for this portrait of Marmion.

Cortés was not a vulgar conqueror. He did not conquer from the mere ambition of conquest. If he destroyed the ancient capital of the Aztecs, it was to build up a more magnificent capital on its ruins. If he desolated the land, and broke up its existing institutions, he employed the short period of his administration in digesting schemes for introducing there a more improved culture and a higher civilization. In all his expeditions he was careful to study the resources of the country, its social organization, and its physical capacities. He enjoined it on his captains to attend particularly to these objects. If he was greedy of gold, like most of the Spanish cavaliers in the New World, it was not to hoard it, nor merely to lavish it in the support of a princely establishment, but to secure funds for prosecuting his glorious discoveries. Witness his costly expeditions to the Gulf of California. His enterprises were not undertaken solely for

[32] The comparison to Hannibal is better founded than the old soldier probably imagined. Livy's description of the Carthaginian warrior has a marvellous application to Cortés,—better, perhaps, than that of the imaginary personage quoted a few lines below in the text. "Plurimum audaciæ ad pericula capessenda, plurimum consilii iner ipsa pericula erat: nullo labore aut corpus fatigari, aut animus vinci poterat. Caloris ac frigoris patientia par: cibi potionisque desiderio naturali, non voluptate, modus finitus: vigiliarum somnique nec die, nec nocte discriminata tempora. Id, quod gerendis rebus superesset, quieti datum; ea neque molli strato, neque silentio arcessita. Multi sæpe militari sagulo opertum, humi jacentem, inter custodias stationesque militum, conspexerunt. Vestitus nihil inter æquales excellens; arma atque equi conspiciebantur. Equitum peditumque idem longe primus erat; princeps in prœlium ibat; ultimus conserto prœlio excedebat." (Hist., lib. xxi, sec. 5.) The reader, who reflects on the face of Guatemozin, may possibly think that the extract should have embraced the "perfidia plus quám Punica," in the succeeding sentence.

[33] Testamente de Hernan Cortés, MS.

mercenary objects; as is shown by the various expeditions he set on foot for the discovery of a communication between the Atlantic and the Pacific. In his schemes of ambition he showed a respect for the interests of science, to be referred partly to the natural superiority of his mind, but partly, no doubt, to the influence of early education. It is, indeed, hardly possible, that a person of his wayward and mercurial temper should have improved his advantages at the University, but he brought away from it a tincture of scholarship, seldom found among the cavaliers of the period, and which had its influence in enlarging his own conceptions. His celebrated Letters are written with a simple elegance, that, as I have already had occasion to remark, have caused them to be compared to the military narrative of Cæsar. It will not be easy to find in the chronicles of the period a more concise, yet comprehensive, statement, not only of the events of his campaigns, but of the circumstances most worthy of notice in the character of the conquered countries.

Cortés was not cruel; at least, not cruel as compared with most of those who followed his iron trade. The path of the conqueror is necessarily marked with blood. He was not too scrupulous, indeed, in the execution of his plans. He swept away the obstacles which lay in his track; and his fame is darkened by the commission of more than one act which his boldest apologists will find it hard to vindicate. But he was not wantonly cruel. He allowed no outrage on his unresisting foes. This may seem small praise, but it is an exception to the usual conduct of his countrymen in their conquests, and it is something to be in advance of one's time. He was severe, it may be added, in enforcing obedience to his orders for protecting their persons and their property. With his licentious crew, it was, sometimes, not without hazard that he was so. After the Conquest, he sanctioned the system of *repartimientos;* but so did Columbus. He endeavored to regulate it by the most humane laws, and continued to suggest many important changes for ameliorating the condition of the natives. The best commentary on his conduct, in this respect, is the deference that was shown him by the Indians, and the confidence with which they appealed to him for protection in all their subsequent distresses.

In private life he seems to have had the power of attaching to himself, warmly, those who were near his person. The influence of this attachment is shown in every page of Bernal Diaz, though his work was written to vindicate the claims of the soldiers, in opposition to those of the general. He seems to have led a happy life with his first wife, in their humble retirement in Cuba; and regarded the second, to judge from the expressions in his testament, with confidence and love. Yet he cannot be acquitted from the charge of those licentious gallantries which entered too generally into the character of the military adventurer of that day. He would seem also, by the frequent suits in which he was involved, to have been of an irritable and contentious spirit. But much allowance must be made for the irritability of a man who had been too long accustomed to independent sway, patiently to endure the checks and control of the petty spirits who were incapable of comprehending the noble character of his enterprises. "He thought," says an eminent writer, "to silence his enemies by the brilliancy of the new career on which he had entered. He did not reflect, that these enemies had been raised by the very grandeur and rapidity of his success." [34] He was rewarded for his efforts by the misinterpretation of his motives; by the calumnious charges of squandering the public revenues and of aspiring to independent sovereignty. But, although we may admit the foundation of many of the grievances alleged by Cortés, yet when we consider the querulous tone of his correspondence and the frequency of his litigation, we may feel a natural suspicion that his proud spirit was too sensitive to petty slights, and too jealous of imaginary wrongs.

One trait more remains to be noticed in the character of this remarkable man; that is, his bigotry, the failing of the age,—for, surely, it should be termed only a failing.[35] When we see the hand, red with the blood of the wretched native, raised to invoke the blessing of Heaven on the cause which it maintains, we experience something like a sensation of disgust at the act, and a doubt of its sincerity. But this is unjust. We should throw ourselves back (it cannot be too often repeated) into the age; the age of the Crusades. For every Spanish cavalier, however sordid and selfish might be his private motives, felt himself to be the soldier of the Cross. Many of them would have died in defence of it. Whoever has read the correspondence of Cortés, or, still more, has attended to the circumstances of his career, will hardly doubt that he would have been among the first to lay down his life for the Faith. He more than once perilled life, and fortune, and the success of his whole enterprise, by the premature and most impolitic manner in which he would have forced conversion on the natives.[36] To the more rational spirit of the present day, enlightened by a purer Christianity, it may seem difficult to reconcile gross deviations from morals with such devotion to the cause of religion. But the religion taught in that day was one of form and elaborate ceremony. In the punctilious attention to discipline, the spirit of Christianity was permitted to evaporate. The mind, occupied with forms, thinks little of substance. In a worship that is addressed too exclusively to the senses, it is often the case, that morality becomes divorced from religion, and

[34] Humboldt, Essai Politique, tom. II. p. 267.

[35] An extraordinary anecdote is related by Cavo, of this bigotry (shall we call it policy?) of Cortés. "In Mexico," says the historian, "it is commonly reported, that, after the Conquest, he commanded, that on Sundays and holidays all should attend, under pain of a certain number of stripes, to the expounding of the Scriptures. The general was himself guilty of an omission, on one occasion, and, after having listened to the admonition of the priest, submitted, with edifying humility, to be chastised by him, to the unspeakable amazement of the Indians!" Hist. de los Tres Siglos, tom. I. p. 151.

[36] "Al Rey infinitas tierras,
    Y á Dios infinitas almas,"
says Lope de Vega, commemorating in this couplet the double glory of Cortés. It is the light in which the Conquest was viewed by every devout Spaniard of the sixteenth century.

the measure of righteousness is determined by the creed rather than by the conduct.

In the earlier part of the History, I have given a description of the person of Cortés.[37] It may be well to close this review of his character by the account of his manners and personal habits left us by Bernal Diaz, the old chronicler, who has accompanied us through the whole course of our narrative, and who may now fitly furnish the conclusion of it. No man knew his commander better; and, if the avowed object of his work might naturally lead to a disparagement of Cortés, this is more than counterbalanced by the warmth of his personal attachment, and by that *esprit de corps* which leads him to take a pride in the renown of his general.

"In his whole appearance and presence," says Diaz, "in his discourse, his table, his dress, in everything, in short, he had the air of a great lord. His clothes were in the fashion of the time; he set little value on silk, damask, or velvet, but dressed plainly and exceedingly neat;[38] nor did he wear massy chains of gold, but simply a fine one, of exquisite workmanship, from which was suspended a jewel having the figure of our Lady the Virgin and her precious Son, with a Latin motto cut upon it. On his finger he wore a splendid diamond ring; and from his cap which, according to the fashion of that day, was of velvet, hung a medal, the device of which I do not remember. He was magnificently attended, as became a man of his rank, with chamberlains and major-domos and many pages; and the service of his table was splendid, with a quantity of both gold and silver plate. At noon he dined heartily, drinking about a pint of wine mixed with water. He supped well, though he was not dainty in regard to his food, caring little for the delicacies of the table, unless, indeed, on such occasions as made attention to these matters of some consequence.[39]

"He was acquainted with Latin, and, as I have understood, was made Bachelor of Laws; and, when he conversed with learned men who addressed him in Latin, he answered them in the same language. He was also something of a poet; his conversation was agreeable, and he had a pleasant elocution. In his attendance on the services of the Church he was most punctual, devout in his manner, and charitable to the poor.[40]

"When he swore, he used to say, 'On my conscience'; and when he was vexed with any one, 'Evil betide you.' With his men he was very patient; and they were sometimes impertinent and even insolent. When very angry, the veins in his throat and forehead would swell, but he uttered no reproaches against either officer or soldier.

"He was fond of cards and dice, and, when he played, was always in

---

[37] Ante, p. 142.

[38] So Gomara: "Vestia mas pulido que rico. Era hombre limpísimo." Crónica, cap. 238.

[39] "Fué mui gran comedor, i templado en el beber, teniendo abundancia. Sufria mucho la hambre con necesidad." Ibid., ubi supra.

[40] He dispensed a thousand ducats every year in his ordinary charities, according to Gomara. "Grandísimo limosnero; daba cada un año mil ducados de limosna ordinaria." Ibid., ubi supra.

good humor, indulging freely in jests and repartees. He was affable with his followers, especially with those who came over with him from Cuba. In his campaigns he paid strict attention to discipline, frequently going the rounds himself during the night, and seeing that the sentinels did their duty. He entered the quarters of his soldiers without ceremony, and chided those whom he found without their arms and accoutrements, saying, 'It was a bad sheep that could not carry its own wool.' On the expedition to Honduras he acquired the habit of sleeping after his meals, feeling unwell if he omitted it; and, however sultry or stormy the weather, he caused a carpet or his cloak to be thrown under a tree, and slept soundly for some time. He was frank and exceedingly liberal in his disposition, until the last few years of his life, when he was accused of parsimony. But we should consider that his funds were employed on great and costly enterprises; and that none of these, after the Conquest, neither his expedition to Honduras, nor his voyages to California, were crowned with success. It was perhaps intended that he should receive his recompense in a better world; and I fully believe it; for he was a good cavalier, most true in his devotions to the Virgin, to the Apostle St. Peter, and to all the other Saints." [41]

Such is the portrait, which has been left to us by the faithful hand most competent to trace it, of Hernando Cortés, the Conqueror of Mexico.

[41] Hist. de la Conquista, cap. 203.

PRELIMINARY NOTICE

THE following Essay was originally designed to close the Introductory Book, to which it properly belongs. It was written three years since, at the same time with that part of the work. I know of no work of importance, having reference to the general subject of discussion, which has appeared since that period, except Mr. Bradford's valuable treatise on *American Antiquities*. But, in respect to that part of the discussion which treats of American Architecture, a most important contribution has been made by Mr. Stephens's two works, containing the account of his visits to Central America and Yucatan, and especially by the last of these publications. Indeed, the ground, before so imperfectly known, has now been so diligently explored, that we have all the light, which we can reasonably expect, to aid us in making up our opinion in regard to the mysterious monuments of Yucatan. It only remains, that the exquisite illustrations of Mr. Catherwood should be published on a larger scale, like the great works on the subject in France and England, in order to exhibit to the eye a more adequate representation of these magnificent ruins, than can be given in the limited compass of an octavo page.

But, notwithstanding the importance of Mr. Stephens's researches, I have not availed myself of them to make any additions to the original draft of this Essay, nor have I rested my conclusions in any instance on his authority. These conclusions had been formed from a careful study of the narratives of Dupaix and Waldeck, together with that of their splendid illustrations of the remains of Palenque and Uxmal, two of the principal places explored by Mr. Stephens; and the additional facts, collected by him from the vast field which he has surveyed, so far from shaking my previous deductions, have only served to confirm them. The only object of my speculations on these remains was, to ascertain their probable origin, or rather to see what light, if any, they could throw on the origin of Aztec Civilization. The reader, on comparing my reflections with those of Mr. Stephens in the closing chapters of his two works, will see that I have arrived at inferences, as to the origin and probable antiquity of these structures, precisely the same as his. Conclusions, formed under such different circumstances, serve to corroborate each other; and, although the reader will find here some things which would have been different, had I been guided by the light now thrown on the path, yet I prefer not to disturb the foundations on which the argument stands, nor to impair its value,—if it has any,—as a distinct and independent testimony.

APPENDIX, PART I

ORIGIN OF THE MEXICAN CIVILIZATION—ANALOGIES WITH THE OLD WORLD

When the Europeans first touched the shores of America, it was as if they had alighted on another planet,—every thing there was so different from what they had before seen. They were introduced to new varieties of plants, and to unknown races of animals; while man, the lord of all, was equally strange, in complexion, language, and institutions.[1] It was what they emphatically styled it, a New World. Taught by their faith to derive all created beings from one source, they felt a natural perplexity as to the manner in which these distant and insulated regions could have obtained their inhabitants. The same curiosity was felt by their country-men at home, and the European scholars bewildered their brains with speculations on the best way of solving this interesting problem.

In accounting for the presence of animals there, some imagined that the two hemispheres might once have been joined in the extreme North, so as to have afforded an easy communication.[2] Others, embarrassed by the difficulty of transporting inhabitants of the tropics across the Arctic regions, revived the old story of Plato's Atlantis, that huge island, now submerged, which might have stretched from the shores of Africa to the eastern borders of the new continent; while they saw vestiges of a similar convulsion of nature in the green islands sprinkled over the Pacific, once the mountain summits of a vast continent, now buried beneath the waters.[3] Some, distrusting the existence of revolutions, of which no record was preserved, supposed that animals might have found their way across the ocean by various means; the birds of stronger wing by flight over the narrowest spaces; while the tamer kinds of quadrupeds might easily have been transported by men in boats, and even the most fero-

---

[1] The names of many animals in the New World, indeed, have been frequently borrowed from the Old; but the species are very different. "When the Spaniards landed in America," says an eminent naturalist, "they did not find a single animal they were acquainted with; not one of the quadrupeds of Europe, Asia, or Africa." Lawrence, Lectures on Physiology, Zoology, and the Natural History of Man, (London, 1819,) p. 250.

[2] Acosta, lib. 1, cap. 16.

[3] Count Carli shows much ingenuity and learning in support of the famous Egyptian tradition, recorded by Plato, in his "Timæus,"—of the good faith of which the Italian philosopher nothing doubts. Lettres Améric., tom. II. let. 36-39

cious, as tigers, bears, and the like, have been brought over in the same
manner, when young, "for amusement and the pleasure of the chase!" [4]
Others, again, maintained the equally probable opinion, that angels, who
had, doubtless, taken charge of them in the ark, had also superintended
their distribution afterwards over the different parts of the globe.[5] Such
were the extremities to which even thinking minds were reduced, in their
eagerness to reconcile the literal interpretation of Scripture with the phenomena of nature! The philosophy of a later day conceives that it is no
departure from this sacred authority to follow the suggestions of science,
by referring the new tribes of animals to a creation, since the deluge, in
those places for which they were clearly intended by constitution and
habits.[6]

Man would not seem to present the same embarrassments, in the discussion, as the inferior orders. He is fitted by nature for every climate,
the burning sun of the tropics and the icy atmosphere of the North. He
wanders indifferently over the sands of the desert, the waste of polar
snows, and the pathless ocean. Neither mountains nor seas intimidate
him, and, by the aid of mechanical contrivances, he accomplishes journeys which birds of boldest wing would perish in attempting. Without
ascending to the high northern latitudes, where the continents of Asia
and America approach within fifty miles of each other, it would be easy
for the inhabitant of Eastern Tartary or Japan to steer his canoe from
islet to islet, quite across to the American shore, without ever being on
the ocean more than two days at a time.[7] The communication is somewhat more difficult on the Atlantic side. But even there, Iceland was occupied by colonies of Europeans many hundreds years before the discovery by Columbus; and the transit from Iceland to America is comparatively easy.[8] Independently of these channels, others were opened in the
southern hemisphere, by means of the numerous islands in the Pacific.
The population of America is not nearly so difficult a problem, as that of
these little spots. But experience shows how practicable the communica-

[4] Garcia, Orígen de los Indios de el Nuevo Mundo (Madrid, 1729,) cap. 4.
[5] Torquemada Monarch. Ind., lib. 1, cap. 8.
[6] Prichard, Researches into the Physical History of Mankind, (London, 1826,)
vol. I, p. 81, et seq.
He may find an orthodox authority of respectable antiquity, for a similar hypothesis, in St. Augustine, who plainly intimates his belief, that, "as by God's command, at the time of the creation, the earth brought forth the living creature after
his kind, so a similar process must have taken place after the deluge, in islands too
remote to be reached by animals from the continent." De Civitate Dei, ap. Opera,
(Parisiis, 1636,) tom. V. p. 987.
[7] Beechey, Voyage to the Pacific and Beering's Strait, (London, 1831,) Part 2,
Appendix.—Humboldt, Examen Critique de l'Histoire de la Géographie du Nouveau Continent, (Paris, 1837,) tom. II. p. 58.
[8] Whatever skepticism may have been entertained as to the visit of the Northmen,
in the eleventh century, to the coasts of the great continent, it is probably set at
rest in the minds of most scholars, since the publication of the original documents,
by the Royal Society at Copenhagen. (See, in particular. Antiquitates Americanæ,
[Hafuiæ, 1837,] pp. 79-200.) How far south they penetrated is not so easily settled.

tion may have been, even with such sequestered places.[9] The savage has been picked up in his canoe, after drifting hundreds of leagues on the open ocean, and sustaining life, for months, by the rain from heaven, and such fish as he could catch.[10] The instances are not very rare; and it would be strange, if these wandering barks should not sometimes have been intercepted by the great continent, which stretches across the globe, in unbroken continuity, almost from pole to pole. No doubt, history could reveal to us more than one example of men, who, thus driven upon the American shores, have mingled their blood with that of the primitive races who occupied them.

The real difficulty is not, as with the animals, to explain how man could have reached America, but from what quarter he actually has reached it. In surveying the whole extent of the New World, it was found to contain two great families, one in the lowest stage of civilization, composed of hunters, and another nearly as far advanced in refinement as the semi-civilized empires of Asia. The more polished races were probably unacquainted with the existence of each other, on the different continents of America, and had as little intercourse with the barbarian tribes, by whom they were surrounded. Yet they had some things in common both with these last and with one another, which remarkably distinguished them from the inhabitants of the Old World. They had a common complexion and physical organization,—at least, bearing a more uniform character than is found among the nations of any other quarter of the globe. They had some usages and institutions in common, and spoke languages of similar construction, curiously distinguished from those on the eastern hemisphere.

Whence did the refinement of these more polished races come? Was it only a higher development of the same Indian character, which we see, in the more northern latitudes, defying every attempt at permanent civilization? Was it engrafted on a race of higher order in the scale originally, but self-instructed, working its way upward by its own powers? Was it, in short, an indigenous civilization? or was it borrowed in some degree from the nations in the Eastern World? If indigenous, how are we to explain the singular coincidence with the East in institutions and opin-

[9] The most remarkable example, probably, of a direct intercourse between remote points, is furnished us by Captain Cook, who found the inhabitants of New Zealand not only with the same religion, but speaking the same language, as the people of Otaheite, distant more than 2,000 miles. The comparison of the two vocabularies establishes the fact. Cook's Voyages, (Dublin, 1784,) vol. I. book 1, chap. 8.

[10] The eloquent Lyell closes an enumeration of some extraordinary and well-attested instances of this kind with remarking, "Were the whole of mankind now cut off, with the exception of one family, inhabiting the old or new continent, or Australia, or even some coral islet of the Pacific, we should expect their descendants, though they should never become more enlightened than the South-Sea Islanders or the Esquimaux, to spread, in the course of ages, over the whole earth, diffused partly by the tendency of population to increase beyond the means of subsistence in a limited district, and partly by the accidental drifting of canoes by tides and currents to distant shores." Principles of Geology, (London, 1832,) vol. II. p. 121.

ions? If Oriental, how shall we account for the great dissimilarity in language, and for the ignorance of some of the most simple and useful arts, which, once known, it would seem scarcely possible should have been forgotten? This is the riddle of the Sphinx, which no Œdipus has yet had the ingenuity to solve. It is, however, a question of deep interest to every curious and intelligent observer of his species. And it has accordingly occupied the thoughts of men, from the first discovery of the country to the present time; when the extraordinary monuments brought to light in Central America have given a new impulse to inquiry, by suggesting the probability,—the possibility, rather,—that surer evidences than any hitherto known might be afforded for establishing the fact of a positive communication with the other hemisphere.

It is not my intention to add many pages to the volumes already written on this inexhaustible topic. The subject—as remarked by a writer, of a philosophical mind himself, and who has done more than any other for the solution of the mystery—is of too speculative a nature for history, almost a philosophy.[11] But this work would be incomplete, without affording the reader the means of judging for himself as to the true sources of the peculiar civilization already described, by exhibiting to him the alleged points of resemblance with the ancient continent. In doing this, I shall confine myself to my proper subject, the Mexicans, or to what, in some way or other, may have a bearing on this subject; proposing to state only real points of resemblance, as they are supported by evidence, and stripped, as far as possible, of the illusions with which they have been invested by the pious credulity of one party, and the visionary system-building of another.

An obvious analogy is found in *cosmogonal traditions*, and *religious usages*. The reader has already been made acquainted with the Aztec system of four great cycles, at the end of each of which the world was destroyed, to be again regenerated.[12] The belief in these periodical convulsions of nature, through the agency of some one or other of the elements, was familiar to many countries in the eastern hemisphere; and, though varying in detail, the general resemblance of outline furnishes an argument in favor of a common origin.[13]

No tradition has been more widely spread among nations than that of a Deluge. Independently of tradition, indeed, it would seem to be naturally suggested by the interior structure of the earth, and by the elevated

---

[11] "La question générale de la première origine des habitans d'un continent est au-delà des limites prescrites à l'histoire; peutêtre même n'est elle pas une question philosophique." Humboldt, Essai Politique, tom. I. p. 349.

[12] Ante, p. 39.

[13] The fanciful division of time into four or five cycles or ages was found among the Hindoos, (Asiatic Researches, vol. II. mem. 7,) the Thibetians, (Humboldt, Vues des Cordillères, p. 210,) the Persians, (Bailly, Traité de l'Astronomie, (Paris, 1787,) tom. I. discours préliminaire,) the Greeks, (Hesiod, "Εργα καὶ Ἡμέραι, v. 108, et seq.,) and other people, doubtless. The five ages in the Grecian cosmogony had reference to moral, rather than physical phenomena,—a proof of higher civilization.

places on which marine substances are found to be deposited. It was the received notion, under some form or other, of the most civilized people in the Old World, and of the barbarians of the New.[14] The Aztecs combined with this some particular circumstances of a more arbitrary character, resembling the accounts of the East. They believed that two persons survived the deluge, a man, named Coxcox, and his wife. Their heads are represented in ancient paintings, together with a boat floating on the waters, at the foot of a mountain. A dove is also depicted, with the hiero-glyphical emblem of languages in his mouth, which he is distributing to the children of Coxcox, who were born dumb.[15] The neighboring people of Michuacan, inhabiting the same high plains of the Andes, had a still further tradition, that the boat, in which Tezpi, their Noah, escaped, was filled with various kinds of animals and birds. After some time, a vulture was sent out from it, but remained feeding on the dead bodies of the giants, which had been left on the earth, as the waters subsided. The little humming-bird, *huitzitzilin*, was sent forth, and returned with a twig in its mouth. The coincidence of both these accounts with the Hebrew and Chaldean narratives is obvious. It were to be wished that the authority for the Michuacan version were more satisfactory.[16]

On the way between Vera Cruz and the capital, not far from the modern city of Puebla, stands the venerable relic,—with which the reader has become familiar in the course of the narrative,—called the temple of

---

[14] The Chaldean and Hebrew accounts of the Deluge are nearly the same. The parallel is pursued in Palfrey's ingenious Lectures on the Jewish Scriptures and Antiquities, (Boston, 1840,) vol. II. lect. 21, 22. Among the Pagan writers, none approach so near to the Scripture narrative as Lucian, who, in his account of the Greek traditions, speaks of the ark, and the pairs of different kinds of animals. (De Deâ Syriâ, sec. 12.) The same thing is found in the Bhagawatn Purana, a Hindoo poem of great antiquity. (Asiatic Researches, vol. II. mem. 7.) The simple tradition of a universal inundation was preserved among most of the Aborigines, probably, of the Western World. See McCulloh, Researches, p. 147.

[15] This tradition of the Aztecs is recorded in an ancient hieroglyphical map, first published in Gemelli Carreri's Giro del Mondo. (See tom. VI. p. 38, ed. Napoli, 1700.) Its authenticity, as well as the integrity of Carreri himself, on which some suspicions have been thrown, (see Robertson's America, (London, 1796,) vol. III. note 26,) has been successfully vindicated by Boturini, Clavigero, and Humboldt, all of whom trod in the steps of the Italian traveller. (Boturini, Idea, p. 54.—Humboldt, Vues des Cordillères, pp. 223, 224.—Clavigero, Stor. del Messico, tom. I. p. 24.) The map is a copy from one in the curious collection of Siguenza. It has all the character of a genuine Aztec picture, with the appearance of being retouched, especially in the costumes, by some later artist. The painting of the four ages, in the Vatican Codex, No. 3730, represents, also, the two figures in the boat, escaping the great cataclysm. Antiq. of Mexico, vol. I. Pl. 7.

[16] I have met with no other voucher for this remarkable tradition than Clavigero; (Stor. del Messico, dissert. 1;) a good, though certainly not the best, authority, when he gives us no reason for our faith. Humboldt, however, does not distrust the tradition. (See Vues des Cordillères, p. 226.) He is not so skeptical as Vater; who, in allusion to the stories of the Flood, remarks, "I have purposely omitted noticing the resemblance of religious notions, for I do not see how it is possible to separate from such views every influence of Christian ideas, if it be only from an imperceptible confusion in the mind of the narrator." Mithridates, oder allgemeine Sprachenkunde, (Berlin, 1812,) theil III. abtheil 3, p. 82, note.

Cholula. It is, as he will remember, a pyramidal mound, built, or rather cased, with unburnt brick, rising to the height of nearly one hundred and eighty feet. The popular tradition of the natives is, that it was erected by a family of giants, who had escaped the great inundation, and designed to raise the building to the clouds; but the gods, offended with their presumption, sent fires from heaven on the pyramid, and compelled them to abandon the attempt.[17] The partial coincidence of this legend with the Hebrew account of the tower of Babel, received, also, by other nations of the East, cannot be denied.[18] But one, who has not examined the subject, will scarcely credit what bold hypotheses have been reared on this slender basis.

Another point of coincidence is found in the goddess Cioacoatl, "our lady and mother"; "the first goddess who brought forth"; "who bequeathed the sufferings of childbirth to women, as the tribute of death"; "by whom sin came into the world." Such was the remarkable language applied by the Aztecs to this venerated deity. She was usually represented with a serpent near her; and her name signified the "serpent-woman." In all this we see much to remind us of the mother of the human family, the Eve of the Hebrew and Syrian nations.[19]

[17] This story, so irreconcilable with the vulgar Aztec tradition, which admits only two survivors of the Deluge, was still lingering among the natives of the place, on M. de Humboldt's visit there. (Vues des Cordillères, pp. 31, 32.) It agrees with that given by the interpreter of the Vatican Codex; (Antiq. of Mexico, vol. VI. p. 192, et seq.;) a writer,—probably a monk of the sixteenth century,—in whom ignorance and dogmatism contend for mastery. See a precious specimen of both, in his account of the Aztec chronology, in the very pages above referred to.

[18] A tradition, very similar to the Hebrew one, existed among the Chaldeans and the Hindoos. (Asiatic Researches, vol. III. mem. 16.) The native of Chiapa, also, according to the bishop Nuñez de la Vega, had a story, cited as genuine by Humboldt, (Vues des Cordillères, p. 148,) which not only agrees with the Scripture account of the manner in which Babel was built, but with that of the subsequent dispersion, and the confusion of tongues. A very marvellous coincidence! But who shall vouch for the authenticity of the tradition? The bishop flourished towards the close of the seventeenth century. He drew his information from hieroglyphical maps, and an Indian MS., which Boturini in vain endeavored to recover. In exploring these, he borrowed the aid of the natives, who, as Boturini informs us, frequently led the good man into errors and absurdities; of which he gives several specimens. (Idea, p. 116, et seq.)—Boturini himself has fallen into an error equally great, in regard to a map of this same Cholulan pyramid, which Clavigero shows, far from being a genuine antique, was the forgery of a later day. (Stor. del Mesico, tom. I, p. 130, nota.) It is impossible to get a firm footing in the quicksands of tradition. The further we are removed from the Conquest, the more difficult it becomes to decide what belongs to the primitive Aztec, and what to the Christian convert.

[19] Sahagun, Hist. de Nueva España, lib. 1, cap. 6; lib. 6, cap. 28, 33.

Torquemada, not content with the honest record of his predecessor, whose MS. lay before him, tells us, that the Mexican Eve had two sons, Cain and Abel. (Monarch. Ind., lib. 6, cap. 31.) The ancient interpreters of the Vatican and Tellerian Codices add the further tradition, of her bringing sin and sorrow into the world by plucking the forbidden *rose*; (Antiq. of Mexico, vol VI., explan. of Pl. 7, 20;) and Veytia remembers to have seen a Toltec or Aztec map, representing a garden with a single tree in it, round which was coiled the serpent with a human face! (Hist. Antig., lib. 1, cap. 1.) After this we may be prepared for Lord Kings-

But none of the deities of the country suggested such astonishing analogies with Scripture, as Quetzalcoatl, with whom the reader has already been made acquainted.[20] He was the white man, wearing a long beard, who came from the East; and who, after presiding over the golden age of Anahuac, disappeared as mysteriously as he had come, on the great Atlantic Ocean. As he promised to return at some future day, his reappearance was looked for with confidence by each succeeding generation. There is little in these circumstances to remind one of Christianity. But the curious antiquaries of Mexico found out, that to this god were to be referred the institution of ecclesiastical communities, reminding one of the monastic societies of the Old World; that of the rites of confession and penance; and the knowledge even of the great doctrines of the Trinity and the Incarnation! [21] One party, with pious industry, accumulated proofs to establish his identity with the Apostle St. Thomas;[22] while another, with less scrupulous faith, saw, in his anticipated advent to regenerate the nation, the type, dim-veiled, of the Messiah![23]

Yet we should have charity for the missionaries who first landed in this world of wonders; where, while man and nature wore so strange an aspect, they were astonished by occasional glimpses of rites and ceremonies, which reminded them of a purer faith. In their amazement, they did not reflect, whether these things were not the natural expression of the religious feeling common to all nations who have reached even a moderate civilization. They did not inquire, whether the same things were not practised by other idolatrous people. They could not suppress their wonder, as they beheld the Cross, the sacred emblem of their own faith, raised as an object of worship in the temples of Anahuac. They met with it in various places; and the image of a cross may be seen at this day, sculptured in bas-relief, on the walls of one of the buildings of Palenque, while a figure bearing some resemblance to that of a child is held up to it, as if in adoration.[24]

borough's deliberate conviction, that the "Aztecs had a clear knowledge of the Old Testament, and, most probably, of the New, though somewhat corrupted by time, and hieroglyphics"! Antiq. of Mexico, vol. VI. p. 409.

[20] Ante, pp. 38, 39.

[21] Veytia, Hist. Antig., lib. 1, cap. 15.

[22] Ibid., lib. 1, cap. 19.—A sorry argument, even for a casuist. See, also, the elaborate dissertation of Dr. Mier, (apud Sahagun, lib. 3, Suplem.,) which settles the question entirely to the satisfaction of his reporter, Bustamante.

[23] See, among others, Lord Kingsborough's reading of the Borgian codex, and the interpreters of the Vatican, (Antiq. of Mexico, Vol. VI., explan. of Pl. 3, 10, 41,) equally well skilled with his lordship,—and Sir Hudibras,—in unravelling mysteries:
"Whose primitive tradition reaches,
As far as Adam's first green breeches."

[24] Antiquités Mexicaines, exped. 3, Pl. 36.

The figures are surrounded by hieroglyphics of most arbitrary character, perhaps phonetic. (See also Herrera Hist. General, dec. 2, lib. 3, cap. 1.—Gomara, Crónica de la Nueva España, cap. 15, ap. Barcia, tom. II.) [Mr. Stephens considers that the celebrated "Cozumel Cross," preserved at Merida, which claims the credit of being the same originally worshipped by the natives of Cozumel, is, after all, nothing but a cross that was erected by the Spaniards in one of their own temples

Their surprise was heightened, when they witnessed a religious rite which reminded them of the Christian communion. On these occasions, an image of the tutelary deity of the Aztecs was made of the flour of maize, mixed with blood, and, after consecration by the priests, was distributed among the people, who, as they ate it, "showed signs of humiliation and sorrow, declaring it was the flesh of the deity!" [25] How could the Roman Catholic fail to recognise the awful ceremony of the Eucharist?

With the same feelings they witnessed another ceremony, that of the Aztec baptism; in which, after a solemn invocation, the head and lips of the infant were touched with water, and a name was given to it; while the goddess Cioacoatl, who presided over childbirth, was implored, "that the sin, which was given to us before the beginning of the world, might not visit the child, but that, cleansed by these waters, it might live and be born anew!" [26]

in that island after the Conquest. This fact he regards as "completely invalidating the strongest proof offered at this day, that the Cross was recognised by the Indians as a symbol of worship." (Travels in Yucatan, vol. II. chap. 20.) But, admitting the truth of this statement, that the Cozumel Cross is only a Christian relic, which the ingenious traveller has made extremely probable, his inference is by no means admissible. Nothing could be more natural than that the friars in Merida should endeavor to give celebrity to their convent by making it the possessor of so remarkable a monument as the very relic which proved, in their eyes, that Christianity had been preached at some earlier date among the natives. But the real proof of the existence of the Cross, as an object of worship, in the New World, does not rest on such spurious monuments as these, but on the unequivocal testimony of the Spanish discoverers themselves.]

[25] "Lo recibian con gran reverencia, humiliacion, y lágrimas, diciendo que comian la carne de su Dios." Veytia, Hist. Antig., lib. 1, cap. 18.—Also, Acosta, lib. 5, cap. 24.

[26] Ante, p. 41.—Sahagun, Hist. de Nueva España, lib. 6, cap. 37.

That the reader may see, for himself, how like, yet how unlike, the Aztec rite was to the Christian, I give the translation of Sahagun's account, at length.

"When every thing necessary for the baptism has been made ready, all the relations of the child were assembled, and the midwife, who was the person that performed the rite of baptism, was summoned. At early dawn, they met together in the court-yard of the house. When the sun had risen, the midwife, taking the child in her arms, called for a little earthen vessel of water, while those about her placed the ornaments which had been prepared for the baptism in the midst of the court. To perform the rite of baptism, she placed herself with her face towards the west, and immediately began to go through certain ceremonies. . . . . . After this she sprinkled water on the head of the infant, saying, 'O, my child! take and receive the water of the Lord of the world, which is our life, and is given for the increasing and renewing of our body. It is to wash and to purify. I pray that these heavenly drops may enter into your body, and dwell there; that they may destroy and remove from you all the evil and sin which was given to you before the beginning of the world; since all of us are under its power, being all the children of Chalchivitlycue' [the goddess of water]. She then washed the body of the child with water, and spoke in this manner: 'Whencesoever thou comest, thou that art hurtful to this child; leave him and depart from him, for he now liveth anew, and is born anew; now is he purified and cleansed afresh, and our mother Chalchivitlycue again bringeth him into the world.' Having thus prayed, the midwife took the child in both hands, and, lifting him towards heaven, said, 'O Lord, thou seest here thy creature, whom thou hast sent into this world, this place of sorrow, suffering, and penitence. Grant him O Lord, thy gifts, and thine inspiration, for thou art the Great God, and

It is true, these several rites were attended with many peculiarities, very unlike those in any Christian church. But the fathers fastened their eyes exclusively on the points of resemblance. They were not aware, that the Cross was the symbol of worship, of the highest antiquity, in Egypt and Syria;[27] and that rites, resembling those of communion[28] and baptism, were practised by Pagan nations, on whom the light of Christianity had never shone.[29] In their amazement, they not only magnified what they saw, but were perpetually cheated by the illusions of their own heated imaginations. In this they were admirably assisted by their Mexican converts, proud to establish—and half believing it themselves—a correspondence between their own faith, and that of their conquerors.[30]

The ingenuity of the chronicler was taxed to find out analogies between the Aztec and Scripture histories, both old and new. The migration from Aztlan to Anahuac was typical of the Jewish exodus.[31] The places, where the Mexicans halted on the march, were identified with those in the journey of the Israelites;[32] and the name of Mexico itself was found to be

---

with thee is the great goddess.' Torches of pine were kept burning during the performance of these ceremonies. When these things were ended, they gave the child the name of some one of his ancestors, in the hope that he might shed a new lustre over it. The name was given by the same midwife, or priestess, who baptized him."

[27] Among Egyptian symbols, we meet with several specimens of the Cross. One, according to Justus Lipsius, signified "life to come." (See his treatise, De Cruce, (Lutetiæ Parisiorum, 1598,) lib. 3, cap. 8.) We find another in Champollion's catalogue, which he interprets, "support or saviour." (Précis, tom. II., Tableau Gén., Nos. 277, 348.) Some curious examples of the reverence paid to this sign by the ancients have been collected by McCulloh, (Researches, p. 330, et seq.,) and by Humboldt, in his late work, Géographie du Nouveau Continent, tom. II. p. 354, et seq.

[28] "Ante, Deos homini quod conciliare valeret
      Far erat,"

says Ovid. (Fastorum, lib. 1, v. 337.) Count Carli has pointed out a similar use of consecrated bread, and wine or water, in the Greek and Egyptian mysteries. (Lettres Améric., tom. I. let. 27.) See, also, McCulloh, Researches, p. 240, et seq.

[29] Water for purification and other religious rites is frequently noticed by the classical writers. Thus Euripides;

" Ἀγνοῖς καθαρμοῖς πρῶτά νιν νίψαι θέλω.
  Θάλασσα κλύζει πάντα τάνθρώπων κακά."

IPHIG. IN TAUR., vv. 1192, 1194.

The notes on this place in the admirable Variorum edition of Glasgow, 1821, contain references to several passages of similar import in different authors.

[30] The difficulty of obtaining any thing like a faithful report from the natives is the subject of complaint from more than one writer, and explains the great care taken by Sahagun, to compare their narratives with each other. See Hist. de Nueva España, Prólogo.—Ixtlilxochitl, Hist. Chich., MS., Pról.—Boturini, Idea, p. 116.

[31] The parallel was so closely pressed by Torquemada, that he was compelled to suppress the chapter containing it, on the publication of his book. See the Proemio to the edition of 1723, sec. 2.

[32] "The Devil," says Herrera, "chose to imitate, in every thing, the departure of the Israelites from Egypt, and their subsequent wanderings." (Hist. General, dec. 3, lib. 3, cap. 10.) But all that has been done by monkish annalist and missionary, to establish the parallel with the children of Israel, falls far short of Lord Kingsborough's learned labors, spread over nearly two hundred folio pages. (See Antiq. of Mexico, tom. VI. pp. 282-410.) *Quantum inane!*

nearly identical with the Hebrew name for the Messiah.[33] The Mexican hieroglyphics afforded a boundless field for the display of this critical acuteness. The most remarkable passages in the Old and New Testaments were read in their mysterious characters; and the eye of faith could trace there the whole story of the Passion, the Saviour suspended from the cross, and the Virgin Mary with her attendant angels! [34]

The Jewish and Christian schemes were strangely mingled together, and the brains of the good fathers were still further bewildered by the mixture of heathenish abominations, which were so closely intertwined with the most orthodox observances. In their perplexity, they looked on the whole as the delusion of the Devil, who counterfeited the rites of Christianity and the traditions of the chosen people, that he might allure his wretched victims to their own destruction.[35]

But, although it is not necessary to resort to this startling supposition, nor even to call up an apostle from the dead, or any later missionary, to explain the coincidences with Christianity; yet these coincidences must be allowed to furnish an argument in favor of some primitive communication with that great brotherhood of nations on the old continent, among whom similar ideas have been so widely diffused. The probability of such a communication, especially with Eastern Asia, is much strengthened by the resemblance of sacerdotal institutions, and of some religious rites, as those of marriage,[36] and the burial of the dead;[37] by the practice of human sacrifices, and even of cannibalism, traces of which are discernible in the Mongol races;[38] and, lastly, by a conformity of social usages and manners, so striking that the description of Montezuma's court may

[33] The word משיח, from which is derived *Christ,* "the anointed," is still more nearly—not "precisely," as Lord Kingsborough states (Antiq. of Mexico, vol. VI. p. 186)—identical with that of Mexi, or Mesi, the chief who was said to have led the Aztecs on the plains of Anahuac.

[34] Interp. of Cod. Tel.-Rem., et Vat., Antiq. of Mexico, vol. VI.—Sahagun, Hist. de Nueva España, lib. 3, Suplem.—Veytia, Hist. Antig., lib. 1. cap. 16.

[35] This opinion finds favor with the best Spanish and Mexican writers, from the Conquest downwards. Solís sees nothing improbable in the fact, "that a malignant influence, so frequently noticed in sacred history, should be found equally in profane." Hist. de la Conquista, lib. 2, cap. 4.

[36] The bridal ceremony of the Hindoos, in particular, contains curious points of analogy with the Mexican. (See Asiatic Researches, vol. VII. mem. 9.) The institution of a numerous priesthood, with the practices of confession and penance, was familiar to the Tartar people. (Maundeville, Voiage, chap. 23.) And monastic establishments were found in Thibet and Japan, from the earliest ages. Humboldt, Vues des Cordillères, p. 179.

[37] "Doubtless," says the ingenious Carli, "the fashion of burning the corpse, collecting the ashes in a vase, burying them under pyramidal mounds with the immolation of wives and servants at the funeral, all remind one of the customs of Egypt and Hindostan." Lettres Améric., tom. II. let. 10.

[38] Marco Polo notices a civilized people in South-eastern China, and another in Japan, who drank the blood and ate the flesh of their captives; esteeming it the most savory food in the world,—"la più saporita et migliore, che si possa truovar al mondo." (Viaggi, lib. 2, cap. 75; lib. 3, 13, 14.) The Mongols, according to Sir John Maundeville, regarded the ears "sowced in vynegre," as a particular dainty. Voiage, chap. 23.

well pass for that of the Grand Khan's, as depicted by Maundeville and Marco Polo.[39] It would occupy too much room to go into details in this matter, without which, however, the strength of the argument cannot be felt, nor fully established. It has been done by others; and an occasional coincidence has been adverted to in the preceding chapter.

It is true, we should be very slow to infer identity, or even correspondence, between nations, from a partial resemblance of habits and institutions. Where this relates to manners, and is founded on caprice, it is not more conclusive than when it flows from the spontaneous suggestions of nature, common to all. The resemblance, in the one case, may be referred to accident; in the other, to the constitution of man. But there are certain arbitrary peculiarities, which, when found in different nations, reasonably suggest the idea of some previous communicaton between them. Who can doubt the existence of an affinity, or, at least, intercourse, between tribes, who had the same strange habit of burying the dead in a sitting posture, as was practised, to some extent, by most, if not all, of the Aborigines, from Canada to Patagonia?[40] The habit of burning the dead, familiar to both Mongols and Aztecs, is, in itself, but slender proof of a common origin. The body must be disposed of in some way; and this, perhaps, is as natural as any other. But, when to this is added the circumstance of collecting the ashes in a vase, and depositing the single article of a precious stone along with them, the coincidence is remarkable.[41] Such minute coincidences are not unfrequent; while the accumulation of those of a more general character, though individually of little account, greatly strengthens the probability of a communication with the East.

A proof of a higher kind is found in the analogies of *science*. We have seen the peculiar chronological system of the Aztecs; their method of distributing the years into cycles, and of reckoning by means of periodical series, instead of numbers. A similar process was used by the various Asiatic nations of the Mongol family, from India to Japan. Their cycles, indeed, consisted of sixty, instead of fifty-two years; and for the terms

[39] Marco Polo, Viaggi, lib. 2, cap. 10.—Maundeville, Voiage, cap. 20, et alibi.
See, also, a striking parallel between the Eastern Asiatics and Americans, in the Supplement to Ranking's "Historical Researches"; a work embodying many curious details of Oriental history and manners, in support of a whimsical theory.

[40] Morton, Crania Americana, (Philadelphia, 1839,) pp. 224-246.
The industrious author establishes this singular fact, by examples drawn from a great number of nations in North and South America.

[41] Gomara, Crónica de la Nueva España, cap. 202, ap. Barcia, tom. II.—Clavigero, Stor. del Messico, tom. I. pp. 94, 95.—McCulloh, (Researches, p. 198,) who cites the Asiatic Researches.
Dr. McCulloh, in his single volume, has probably brought together a larger mass of materials for the illustration of the aboriginal history of the continent, than any other writer in the language. In the selection of his facts, he has shown much sagacity, as well as industry; and, if the formal and somewhat repulsive character of the style has been unfavorable to a popular interest, the work must always have an interest for those who are engaged in the study of the Indian antiquities. His fanciful speculations on the subject of Mexican mythology may amuse those whom they fail to convince.

of their periodical series, they employed the names of the elements, and the signs of the zodiac, of which latter the Mexicans, probably, had no knowledge. But the principle was precisely the same.[42]

A correspondence quite as extraordinary is found between the hieroglyphics used by the Aztecs for the signs of the days, and those zodiacal signs which the Eastern Asiatics employed as one of the terms of their series. The symbols in the Mongolian calendar are borrowed from animals. Four of the twelve are the same as the Aztec. Three others are as nearly the same as the different species of animals in the two hemispheres would allow. The remaining five refer to no creature then found in Anahuac.[43] The resemblance went as far as it could.[44] The similarity of these conventional symbols, among the several nations of the East, can hardly fail to carry conviction of a common origin for the system, as regards them. Why should not a similar conclusion be applied to the Aztec calendar, which, although relating to days, instead of years, was, like the Asiatic, equally appropriated to chronological uses, and to those of divination?[45]

I shall pass over the further resemblance to the Persians, shown in the adjustment of time by a similar system of intercalation;[46] and to the

[42] Ante, p. 64, et seq.

[43] This will be better shown by enumerating the zodiacal signs, used as the *names of the years* by the Eastern Asiatics. Among the Mongols, these were, 1. mouse, 2. ox, 3. leopard, 4. hare, 5. crocodile, 6. serpent, 7. horse, 8. sheep, 9. monkey, 10. hen, 11. dog, 12. hog. The Mantchou Tartars, Japanese, and Thibetians, have nearly the same terms, substituting, however, for No. 3, tiger; 5, dragon; 8, goat. In the Mexican signs, for the names of the days, we also meet with *hare, serpent, monkey, dog*. Instead of the "leopard," "crocodile," and "her.,"—neither of which animals were known in Mexico, at the time of the Conquest,—we find the *ocelotl*, the *lizard*, and the *eagle*.

The lunar calendar of the Hindoos exhibits a correspondence equally extraordinary. Seven of the terms agree with those of the Aztecs, namely, *serpent, cane, razor, path of the sun, dog's tail, house*. (Humboldt, Vues des Cordillères, p. 152.) These terms, it will be observed, are still more arbitrarily selected, not being confined to animals; as, indeed, the hieroglyphics of the Aztec calendar were derived indifferently from them, and other objects, like the signs of our zodiac.

These scientific analogies are set in the strongest light by M. de Humboldt, and occupy a large, and, to the philosophical inquirer, the most interesting, portion of his great work. (Vues des Cordillères, pp. 125-194.) He has not embraced in his tables, however, the Mongol calendar, which affords even a closer approximation to the Mexican, than that of the other Tartar races. Comp. Ranking, Researches, pp. 370, 371, note.

[44] There is some inaccuracy in Humboldt's definition of the *ocelotl*, as "the tiger," "the jaguar." (Ibid., p. 159.) It is smaller than the jaguar, though quite as ferocious, and is as graceful and beautiful as the leopard, which it more nearly resembles. It is a native of New Spain, where the tiger is not known. (See Buffon, Histoire Naturelle, (Paris, An. 8,) tom. II., *vox, Ocelotl*. The adoption of this latter name, therefore, in the Aztec calendar, leads to an inference somewhat exaggerated.

[45] Both the Tartars and the Aztecs indicated the year by its sign; as the "year of the hare," or "rabbit," &c. The Asiatic signs, likewise, far from being limited to the years and months, presided, also, over days, and even hours. (Humboldt, Vues des Cordillères, p. 165.) The Mexicans had also astrological symbols appropriated to the hours. Gama, Descripcion, Parte 2, p. 117.

[46] Ante, p. 65, note.

Egyptians, in the celebration of the remarkable festival of the winter solstice;[47] since, although sufficiently curious, the coincidences might be accidental, and add little to the weight of evidence offered by an agreement in combinations, of so complex and artificial a character, as those before stated.

Amidst these intellectual analogies, one would expect to meet with that of *language*, the vehicle of intellectual communication, which usually exhibits traces of its origin, even when the science and literature, that are embodied in it, have widely diverged. No inquiry, however, has led to less satisfactory results. The languages spread over the western continent far exceed in number those found in any equal population in the eastern.[48] They exhibit the remarkable anomaly of differing as widely in etymology as they agree in organization; and, on the other hand, while they bear some slight affinity to the languages of the Old World in the former particular, they have no resemblance to them whatever in the latter.[49] The Mexican was spoken for an extent of three hundred leagues. But within the boundaries of New Spain more than twenty languages were found; not simply dialects, but, in many instances, radically different.[50] All these idioms, however, with one exception, conformed to that peculiar synthetic structure, by which every Indian dialect appears to have been fashioned, from the land of the Esquimaux to Terra del Fuego;[51] a system, which, bringing the greatest number of ideas within the smallest possible compass, condenses whole sentences into a single

[47] Achilles Tatius notices a custom of the Egyptians,—who, as the sun descended towards Capricorn, put on mourning; but, as the days lengthened, their fears subsided, they robed themselves in white, and, crowned with flowers, gave themselves up to jubilee, like the Aztecs.—This account, transcribed by Carli's French translator, and by M. de Humboldt, is more fully criticized by M. Jomard in the Vues des Cordillères, p. 309, et seq.

[48] Jefferson, (Notes on Virginia, (London, 1787,) p. 164,) confirmed by Humboldt (Essai Politique, tom. I. p. 353). Mr. Gallatin comes to a different conclusion. (Transactions of American Antiquarian Society, (Cambridge, 1836, vol. II. p. 161.) The great number of American dialects and languages is well explained by the unsocial nature of a hunter's life, requiring the country to be parcelled out into small and separate territories for the means of subsistence.

[49] Philologists have, indeed, detected two curious exceptions, in the Congo and primitive Basque; from which, however, the Indian languages differ in many essential points. See Du Ponceau's Report, ap. Transactions of the Lit. and Hist. Committee of the Am. Phil. Society, vol. I.

[50] Vater, (Mithridates, theil III. abtheil 3, p. 70,) who fixes on the Rio Gila and the Isthmus of Darien, as the boundaries, within which traces of the Mexican language were to be discerned. Clavigero estimates the number of dialects at thirty-five. I have used the more guarded statement of M. de Humboldt, who adds, that fourteen of these languages have been digested into dictionaries and grammars. Essai Politique, tom. I. p. 352.

[51] No one has done so much towards establishing this important fact, as that estimable scholar, Mr. Du Ponceau. And the frankness, with which he has admitted the exception that disturbed his favorite hypothesis, shows that he is far more wedded to science than to system. See an interesting account of it, in his prize essay before the Institute. Mémoire sur le Système Grammaticale des Langues de quelques Nations Indiennes de l'Amérique. (Paris, 1838.)

word,[52] displaying a curious mechanism, in which some discern the hand of the philosopher, and others only the spontaneous efforts of the savage.[53]

The etymological affinities detected with the ancient continent are not very numerous, and they are drawn indiscriminately from all the tribes scattered over America. On the whole, more analogies have been found with the idioms of Asia, than of any other quarter. But their amount is too inconsiderable to balance the opposite conclusion inferred by a total dissimilarity of structure.[54] A remarkable exception is found in the Othomi or Otomie language, which covers a wider territory than any other but the Mexican, in New Spain;[55] and which, both in its monosyllabic composition, so different from those around it, and in its vocabulary, shows a very singular affinity to the Chinese.[56] The existence of this insulated idiom, in the heart of this vast continent, offers a curious theme for speculation, entirely beyond the province of history.

The American languages, so numerous and widely diversified, present an immense field of inquiry, which, notwithstanding the labors of several distinguished philologists, remains yet to be explored. It is only after a wide comparison of examples, that conclusions founded on analogy can be trusted. The difficulty of making such comparisons increases with time, from the facility which the peculiar structure of the Indian languages affords for new combinations; while the insensible influence of contact with civilized man, in producing these, must lead to a still further distrust of our conclusions.

[52] The Mexican language, in particular, is most flexible; admitting of combinations so easily, that the most simple ideas are often buried under a load of accessories. The forms of expression, though picturesque, were thus made exceedingly cumbrous. A "priest," for example, was called, *notlazomahuizteopixcatatzin*, meaning, "venerable minister of God, that I love as my father." A still more comprehensive word is *amatlacuilolitquitcatlaxtlahuitli*, signifying, "the reward given to a messenger who bears a hieroglyphical map conveying intelligence."

[53] See, in particular, for the latter view of the subject, the arguments of Mr. Gallatin, in his acute and masterly disquisition on the Indian tribes; a disquisition, that throws more light on the intricate topics of which it treats, than whole volumes that have preceded it. Transactions of the American Antiquarian Society, vol. II., Introd., sec. 6.

[54] This comparative anatomy of the languages of the two hemispheres, begun by Barton, (Origin of the tribes and Nations of America, (Philadelphia, 1797,)) has been extended by Vater (Mithridates, theil III. abtheil 1, p. 348, et seq.). A selection of the most striking analogies may be found, also, in Malte Brun, book 75, table.

[55] *Othomi*, from *otho*, "stationary," and *mi*, "nothing." (Najera, Dissert., *ut infra*.) The etymology intimates the condition of this rude nation of warriors, who, imperfectly reduced by the Aztec arms, roamed over the high lands north of the Valley of Mexico.

[56] See Najera's Dissertatio *De Lingua Othomitorum*, ap. Transactions of the American Philosophical Society, vol. V. New Series.

The author, a learned Mexican, has given a most satisfactory analysis of this remarkable language, which stands alone among the idioms of the New World, as the Basque—the solitary wreck, perhaps, of a primitive age—exists among those of the Old.

The theory of an Asiatic origin for Aztec civilization derives stronger confirmation from the light of *tradition*, which, shining steadily from the far North-west, pierces through the dark shadows that history and mythology have alike thrown around the antiquities of the country. Traditions of a Western, or North-western origin were found among the more barbarous tribes,[57] and by the Mexicans were preserved both orally and in their hieroglyphical maps, where the different stages of their migration are carefully noted. But who, at this day, shall read them? [58] They are admitted to agree, however, in representing the populous North as the prolific hive of the American races.[59] In this quarter were placed their Aztlan, and their Huehuetapallan; the bright abodes of their ancestors, whose warlike exploits rivalled those which the Teutonic nations have recorded of Odin and the mythic heroes of Scandinavia. From this quarter the Toltecs, the Chichemecs, and the kindred races of the Nahuatlacs, came successively up the great plateau of the Andes, spreading over its hills and valleys, down to the Gulf of Mexico.[60]

Antiquaries have industriously sought to detect some still surviving traces of these migrations. In the north-western districts of New Spain, at a thousand miles' distance from the capital, dialects have been discovered, showing intimate affinity with the Mexican.[61] Along the Rio

[57] Barton, p. 92.—Heckewelder, chap. 1, ap. Transactions of the Hist. and Lit. Committee of the Am. Phil. Soc., vol. I.
The various traditions have been assembled by M. Warden, in the Antiquités Mexicaines, part 2, p. 185, et seq.

[58] The recent work of Mr. Delafield (Inquiry into the Origin of the Antiquities of America (Cincinnati, 1839,)) has an engraving of one of these maps, said to have been obtained by Mr. Bullock, from Boturini's collection. Two such are specified on page 10 of that antiquary's Catalogue. This map has all the appearance of a genuine Aztec painting, of the rudest character. We may recognise, indeed, the symbols of some dates and places, with others denoting the aspect of the country, whether fertile or barren, a state of war or peace, &c. But it is altogether too vague, and we know too little of the allusions, to gather any knowledge from it of the course of the Aztec migration.
Gemelli Carreri's celebrated chart contains the names of many places on the route, interpreted, perhaps, by Siguenza himself, to whom it belonged; (Giro del Mondo, tom. VI. p. 56;) and Clavigero has endeavored to ascertain the various localities with some precision. (Stor. del Messico, tom. I. p. 160, et seq.) But, as they are all within the boundaries of New Spain, and, indeed, south of the Rio Gila, they throw little light, of course, on the vexed question of the primitive abodes of the Aztecs.

[59] This may be fairly gathered from the agreement of the *traditionary* interpretations of the maps of the various people of Anahuac, according to Veytia; who, however, admits, that it is "next to impossible," with the lights of the present day, to determine the precise route taken by the Mexicans. (Hist. Antig., tom. I. cap. 2.) Lorenzana is not so modest. "Los Mexicanos por tradicion viniéron por el norte," says he, "y se saben ciertaments sus mansiones." (Hist. de Nueva España, p. 81, nota.) There are some antiquaries who see best in the dark.

[60] Ixtlilxochitl, Hist. Chich., MS., cap. 2, et seq.—Idem, Relaciones, MS.—Veytia, Hist. Antig., ubi supra.—Torquemada, Monarch. Ind., tom. I. lib. 1.

[61] In the province of Sonora, especially along the California Gulf. The Cora language, above all, of which a regular grammar has been published, and which is spoken in New Biscay, about 30° north, so much resembles the Mexican, that Vater refers them both to a common stock. Mithridates, theil III. abtheil 3, p. 143.

Gila, remains of populous towns are to be seen, quite worthy of the Aztecs in their style of architecture.[62] The country north of the great Rio
Colorado has been imperfectly explored; but, in the higher latitudes, in
the neighborhood of Nootka, tribes still exist, whose dialects, both in the
termination and general sound of the words, bear considerable resemblance to the Mexican.[63] Such are the vestiges, few, indeed, and feeble,
that still exist to attest the truth of traditions, which themselves have
remained steady and consistent, through the lapse of centuries, and the
migrations of successive races.

The conclusions suggested by the intellectual and moral analogies with
Eastern Asia derive considerable support from those of a *physical nature*. The Aborigines of the Western World were distinguished by certain
peculiarities of organization, which have led physiologists to regard them
as a separate race. These peculiarities are shown in their reddish complexion, approaching a cinnamon color; their straight, black, and exceedingly glossy hair; their beard thin, and usually eradicated;[64] their high
cheek-bones, eyes obliquely directed towards the temples, prominent
noses, and narrow foreheads falling backwards with a greater inclination than those of any other race except the African.[65] From this general
standard, however, there are deviations, in the same manner, if not to
the same extent, as in other quarters of the globe, though these deviations
do not seem to be influenced by the same laws of local position.[66] Anato-

---

[62] On the southern bank of this river are ruins of large dimensions, described by
the missionary Pedro Font, on his visit there, in 1775. (Antiq. of Mexico, vol. VI.
p. 538.)—At a place of the same name, Casas Grandes, about 33° north, and, like
the former, a supposed station of the Aztecs, still more extensive remains are to be
found; large enough, indeed, according to a late traveller, Lieut. Hardy, for a population of 20,000 or 30,000 souls. The country for leagues is covered with these remains, as well as with utensils of earthen ware, obsidian, and other relics. A drawing, which the author has given of a painted jar or vase, may remind one of the
Etruscan. "There were, also, good specimens of earthen images in the Egyptian
style," he observes, "which are, to *me, at least, so perfectly uninteresting*, that I
was at no pains to procure any of them." (Travels in the Interior of Mexico, (London, 1829,) pp. 464-466.) The Lieutenant was neither a Boturini nor a Belzoni.

[63] Vater has examined the languages of three of these nations, between 50° and
60° north, and collated their vocabularies with the Mexican, showing the probability
of a common origin of many of the words in each. Mithridates, theil III. abtheil 3,
p. 212.

[64] The Mexicans are noticed by M. de Humboldt, as distinguished from the
other Aborigines, whom he had seen, by the quantity both of beard and mous-
taches. (Essai Politique, tom. I. p. 361.) The modern Mexican, however, broken in
spirit and fortunes, bears as little resemblance, probably, in physical, as in moral
characteristics, to his ancestors, the fierce and independent Aztecs.

[65] Prichard, Physical History, vol. I. pp. 167-169, 182, et seq.—Morton, Crania
Americana, p. 66.—McCulloh, Researches, p. 18.—Lawrence, Lectures, pp. 317, 565.

[66] Thus we find amidst the generally prevalent copper or cinnamon tint, nearly all
gradations of color, from the European white, to a black, almost African; while
the complexion capriciously varies among different tribes, in the neighborhood of
each other. See examples in Humboldt, (Essai Politique, tom. I. pp. 358, 359,) also
Prichard, (Physical History, vol. II. pp. 452, 522, et alibi,) a writer, whose various
research and dispassionate judgment have made his work a text-book in this department of science.

mists, also, have discerned in crania disinterred from the mounds, and in those of the inhabitants of the high plains of the Cordilleras, an obvi ous difference from those of the more barbarous tribes. This is seen espe cially in the ampler forehead, intimating a decided intellectual superior ity.[67] These characteristics are found to bear a close resemblance to those of the Mongolian family, and especially to the people of Eastern Tar tary;[68] so that, notwithstanding certain differences recognised by physi ologists, the skulls of the two races could not be readily distinguished from one another by a common observer. No inference can be surely drawn, however, without a wide range of comparison. That hitherto made has been chiefly founded on specimens from the barbarous tribes.[69] Per haps a closer comparison with the more civilized may supply still stronger evidence of affinity.[70]

In seeking for analogies with the Old World, we should not pass by in silence the *architectural remains* of the country, which, indeed, from their resemblance to the pyramidal structures of the East, have suggested to more than one antiquary the idea of a common origin.[71] The Spanish in--

[67] Such is the conclusion of Dr. Warren, whose excellent collection has afforded him ample means for study and comparison. (See his Remarks before the British Association for the Advancement of Science, ap. London Athenæum, Oct., 1837.) In the specimens collected by Dr. Morton, however, the barbarous tribes would seem to have a somewhat larger facial angle, and a greater quantity of brain, than the semi-civilized. Crania Americana, p. 259.

[68] "On ne peut se refuser d'admettre que l'espèce humaine n'offre pas de races plus voisines que le sont celles des Américains, des Mongols, des Mantchoux, et des Malais." Humboldt, Essai Politique, tom. I. p. 367.—Also, Prichard, Physical His tory, vol. I. pp. 184-186; vol. II. pp. 365-367.—Lawrence, Lectures, p. 365.

[69] Dr. Morton's splendid work on American crania has gone far to supply the requisite information. Out of about one hundred and fifty specimens of skulls, of which he has ascertained the dimensions with admirable precision, one third belong to the semi-civilized races; and of them thirteen are Mexican. The number of these last is too small to found any general conclusions upon, considering the great di versity found in individuals of the same nation, not to say kindred.—Blumenbach's observations on American skulls were chiefly made, according to Prichard, (Physical History, vol. I. pp. 183, 184,) from specimens of the Carib tribes, as unfavorable, perhaps, as any on the continent.

[70] Yet these specimens are not so easy to be obtained. With uncommon advantages for procuring these myself in Mexico, I have not succeeded in obtaining any speci mens of the genuine Aztec skull. The difficulty of this may be readily compre hended by any one who considers the length of time that has elapsed since the Conquest, and that the burial-places of the ancient Mexicans have continued to be used by their descendants. Dr. Morton more than once refers to his specimens, as those of the "genuine Toltec skull, from cemeteries in Mexico, older than the Con quest." (Crania Americana, pp. 152, 155, 231, et alibi.) But how does he know that the heads are Toltec? That nation is reported to have left the country about the middle of the eleventh century, nearly eight hundred years ago,—according to Ixtlilxochitl, indeed, a century earlier; and it seems much more probable, that the specimens now found in these burial-places should belong to some of the races who have since occupied the country, than to one so far removed. The presumption is manifestly too feeble to authorize any positive inference.

[71] The tower of Belus, with its retreating stories, described by Herodotus, (Clio, sec. 181,) has been selected as the model of the *teocalli;* which leads Vater some what shrewdly to remark, that it is strange, no evidence of this should appear in

vaders, it is true, assailed the Indian buildings, especially those of a religious character, with all the fury of fanaticism. The same spirit survived
in the generations which succeeded. The war has never ceased against
the monuments of the country; and the few that fanaticism has spared
have been nearly all demolished to serve the purposes of utility. Of all
the stately edifices, so much extolled by the Spaniards who first visited
the country, there are scarcely more vestiges at the present day than are
to be found in some of those regions of Europe and Asia, which once
swarmed with populous cities, the great marts of luxury and commerce.[72]
Yet some of these remains, like the temple of Xochicalco,[73] the palaces
of Tezcotzinco,[74] the colossal calendar-stone in the capital, are of sufficient magnitude, and wrought with sufficient skill, to attest mechanical

the erection of similar structures by the Aztecs, in the whole course of their journey
to Anahuac. (Mithridates, theil III. abtheil 3, pp. 74, 75.) The learned Niebuhr
finds the elements of the Mexican temple in the mythic tomb of Porsenna. (Roman
History, Eng. trans., (London, 1827,) vol. I. p. 88.) The resemblance to the accumulated pyramids, composing this monument, is not very obvious. Comp. Pliny
(Hist. Nat., lib. 36, sec. 19). Indeed, the antiquarian may be thought to encroach on
the poet's province, when he finds in Etruscan *fable*,—"cúm omnia excedat fabulosi-
tas," as Pliny characterizes this,—the origin of Aztec science.

[72] See the powerful description of Lucan, Pharsalia, lib. 9, v. 966.
The Latin bard has been surpassed by the Italian, in the beautiful stanza, beginning *Giace l' alta Cartago*, (Gierusalemme Liberata, C. 15, s. 20,) which may be
said to have been expanded by Lord Byron into a canto,—the fourth of Childe
Harold.

[73] The most remarkable remains on the proper Mexican soil are the temple or
fortress of Xochicalco, not many miles from the capital. It stands on a rocky eminence, nearly a league in circumference, cut into terraces faced with stone. The building on the summit is seventy-five feet long, and sixty-six broad. It is of hewn granite, put together without cement, but with great exactness. It was constructed in
the usual pyramidal, terraced form, rising by a succession of stories, each smaller
than that below it. The number of these is now uncertain; the lower one alone remaining entire. This is sufficient, however, to show the nice style of execution, from
the sharp, salient cornices, and the hieroglyphical emblems with which it is covered, all cut in the hard stone. As the detached blocks found among the ruins are
sculptured with bas-reliefs in like manner, it is probable that the whole building
was covered with them. It seems probable, also, as the same pattern extends over
different stones, that the work was executed after the walls were raised.
In the hill beneath, subterraneous galleries, six feet wide and high, have been cut
to the length of one hundred and eighty feet, where they terminate in two halls,
the vaulted ceilings of which connect by a sort of tunnel with the buildings above.
These subterraneous works are also lined with hewn stone. The size of the blocks,
and the hard quality of the granite of which they consist, have made the buildings
of Xochicalco a choice quarry for the proprietors of a neighboring sugar-refinery,
who have appropriated the upper stories of the temple to this ignoble purpose!
The Barberini at least built palaces, beautiful themselves, as works of art, with the
plunder of the Coliseum.
See the full description of this remarkable building, both by Dupaix and Alzate.
(Antiquités Mexicaines, tom. I. Exp. 1, pp. 15-20; tom. III. Exp. 1, Pl. 33.) A recent investigation has been made by order of the Mexican government, the report
of which differs, in some of its details, from the preceding. Revista Mexicana, tom.
I. mem. 5.

[74] Ante, pp. 104, 105.

powers in the Aztecs not unworthy to be compared with those of the ancient Egyptians.

But, if the remains on the Mexican soil are so scanty, they multiply as we descend the south-eastern slopes of the Cordilleras, traverse the rich Valley of Oaxaca, and penetrate the forests of Chiapa and Yucatan. In the midst of these lonely regions, we meet with the ruins, recently discovered, of several ancient cities, Mitla, Palenque, and Itzalana or Ux- mal,[75] which argue a higher civilization than any thing yet found on the American continent; and, although it was not the Mexicans who built these cities, yet as they are probably the work of cognate races, the pres- ent inquiry would be incomplete without some attempt to ascertain what light they can throw on the origin of the Indian, and consequently of the Aztec, civilization.[76]

Few works of art have been found in the neighborhood of any of the ruins. Some of them, consisting of earthen or marble vases, fragments of statues, and the like, are fantastic, and even hideous; others show much grace and beauty of design, and are apparently well executed.[77] It may seem extraordinary, that no iron in the buildings themselves, nor iron tools, should have been discovered, considering that the materials used are chiefly granite, very hard, and carefully hewn and polished. Red cop- per chisels and axes have been picked up in the midst of large blocks of granite imperfectly cut, with fragments of pillars and architraves, in the quarries near Mitla.[78] Tools of a similar kind have been discovered, also, in the quarries near Thebes, and the difficulty, nay, impossibility, of cut- ting such masses from the living rock, with any tools which we possess, except iron, has confirmed an ingenious writer in the supposition, that this metal must have been employed by the Egyptians, but that its tend- ency to decomposition, especially in a nitrous soil, has prevented any

[75] It is impossible to look at Waldeck's finished drawings of buildings, where Time seems scarcely to have set his mark on the nicely chiselled stone, and the clear tints are hardly defaced by a weather-stain, without regarding the artist's work as a *restoration;* a picture, true, it may be, of those buildings in the day of their glory, but not of their decay.—Cogolludo, who saw them in the middle of the seventeenth century, speaks of them with admiration, as works of "accomplished architects," of whom history has preserved no tradition. Historia de Yucatan, (Madrid, 1688,) lib. 4, cap. 2.

[76] In the original text is a description of some of these ruins, especially of those of Mitla and Palenque. It would have had novelty at the time in which it was written, since the only accounts of these buildings were in the colossal publications of Lord Kingsborough, and in the Antiquités Mexicaines, not very accessible to most readers. But it is unnecessary to repeat descriptions, now familiar to every one, and so much better executed than they can be by me, in the spirited pages of Stephens.

[77] See, in particular, two terra-cotta busts with helmets, found in Oaxaca, which might well pass for Greek, both in the style of the heads, and the casques that cover them. Antiquités Mexicaines, tom. III. Exp. 2, Pl. 36.

[78] Dupaix speaks of these tools, as made of pure copper. But doubtless there was some alloy mixed with it, as was practised by the Aztecs and Egyptians; otherwise, their edges must have been easily turned by the hard substances on which they were employed.

specimens of it from being preserved.[79] Yet iron has been found, after the lapse of some thousands of years, in the remains of antiquity; and it is certain, that the Mexicans, down to the time of the Conquest, used only copper instruments, with an alloy of tin, and a siliceous powder, to cut the hardest stones and some of them of enormous dimensions.[80] This fact, with the additional circumstance, that only similar tools have been found in Central America, strengthens the conclusion, that iron was neither known there, nor in ancient Egypt.

But what are the nations of the Old Continent, whose style of architecture bears most resemblance to that of the remarkable monuments of Chiapa and Yucatan? The points of resemblance will, probably, be found neither numerous nor decisive. There is, indeed, some analogy both to the Egyptian and Asiatic style of architecture in the pyramidal, terrace-formed bases on which the buildings repose, resembling, also, the Toltec and Mexican *teocalli*. A similar care, also, is observed in the people of both hemispheres, to adjust the position of their buildings by the cardinal points. The walls in both are covered with figures and hieroglyphics, which, on the American, as on the Egyptian, may be designed, perhaps, to record the laws and historical annals of the nation. These figures, as well as the buildings themselves, are found to have been stained with various dyes, principally vermilion;[81] a favorite color with the Egyptians, also, who painted their colossal statues and temples of granite.[82] Notwithstanding these points of similarity, the Palenque architecture has little to remind us of the Egyptian, or of the Oriental. It is, indeed, more conformable, in the perpendicular elevation of the walls, the moderate size of the stones, and the general arrangement of the parts, to the European. It must be admitted, however, to have a character of originality peculiar to itself.

More positive proofs of communication with the East might be looked for in their sculpture, and in the conventional forms of their hieroglyphics. But the sculptures on the Palenque buildings are in relief, unlike the Egyptian, which are usually in *intaglio*. The Egyptians were not very successful in their representations of the human figure, which are on the same invariable model, always in profile, from the greater facility of execution this presents over the front view; the full eye is placed on the side of the head, while the countenance is similar in all, and perfectly destitute of expression.[83] The Palenque artists were equally awkward in

[79] Wilkinson, Ancient Egyptians, vol. III. pp. 246-254.

[80] Ante, p. 81.

[81] Waldeck, Atlas Pittoresque, p. 73.

The fortress of Xochicalco was also colored with a red paint; (Antiquités Mexicaines, tom. I. p. 20;) and a cement of the same color covered the Toltec pyramid at Teotihuacan, according to Mr. Bullock, Six Months in Mexico, vol. II. p. 143.

[82] Description de l'Égypte, Antiq., tom. II. cap. 9, sec. 4.

The huge image of the Sphinx was originally colored red (Clarke's Travels, vol. V. p. 202.) Indeed, many of the edifices, as well as statues, of ancient Greece, also, still exhibit traces of having been painted.

[83] The various causes of the stationary condition of art in Egypt, for so many

representing the various attitudes of the body, which they delineated also in profile. But the parts are executed with much correctness, and sometimes gracefully, the costume is rich and various; and the ornamented head-dress, typical, perhaps, like the Aztec, of the name and condition of the party, conforms in its magnificence to the Oriental taste. The countenance is various, and often expressive. The contour of the head is, indeed, most extraordinary, describing almost a semicircle from the forehead to the tip of the nose, and contracted towards the crown, whether from the artificial pressure practised by many of the Aborigines, or from some preposterous notion of ideal beauty.[84] But, while superior in the execution of the details, the Palenque artist was far inferior to the Egyptian in the number and variety of the objects displayed by him, which, on the Theban temples, comprehend animals as well as men, and almost every conceivable object of use, or elegant art.

The hieroglyphics are too few on the American buildings to authorize any decisive inference. On comparing them, however, with those of the Dresden Codex, probably from this same quarter of the country,[85] with those on the monument of Xochicalco, and with the ruder picture-writing of the Aztecs, it is not easy to discern any thing which indicates a common system. Still less obvious is the resemblance to the Egyptian characters, whose refined and delicate abbreviations approach almost to the simplicity of an alphabet. Yet the Palenque writing shows an advanced stage of the art; and, though somewhat clumsy, intimates, by the conventional and arbitrary forms of the hieroglyphics, that it was symbolical, and perhaps phonetic, in its character.[86] That its mysterious import will ever be deciphered is scarcely to be expected. The language of the race who employed it, the race itself, is unknown. And it is not likely that another Rosetta stone will be found, with its trilingual inscription, to supply the means of comparison, and to guide the American Champollion in the path of discovery.

It is impossible to contemplate these mysterious monuments of a lost

---

ages, are clearly exposed by the duke di Serradifalco, in his *Antichità della Sicilia;* (Palermo, 1834, tom. II. pp. 33, 34;) a work in which the author, while illustrating the antiquities of a little island, has thrown a flood of light on the arts and literary culture of ancient Greece.

[84] "The ideal is not always the beautiful," as Winckelmann truly says, referring to the Egyptian figures. (Historie de l'Art chez les Anciens, liv. 4, chap. 2, trad. Fr.) It is not impossible, however, that the portraits mentioned in the text may be copies from life. Some of the rude tribes of America distorted their infants' heads into forms quite as fantastic, and Garcilaso de la Vega speaks of a nation discovered by the Spaniards in Florida, with a formation apparently not unlike the Palenque. *"Tienen cabezas increiblemente largas, y ahusadas para arriba,* que las ponen así con artificio, atándoselas desde el punto, que nascen las criaturas, hasta que son de nueve ó diez años." La Florida, (Madrid, 1723,) p. 190.

[85] For a notice of this remarkable codex, see Ante, p. 61. There is, indeed, a resemblance, in the use of straight lines and dots, between the Palenque writing and the Dresden MS. Possibly these dots denoted years, like the rounds in the Mexican system.

[86] The hieroglyphics are arranged in perpendicular lines. The heads are uniformly turned towards the right, as in the Dresden MS.

civilization, without a strong feeling of curiosity as to who were their architects, and what is their probable age. The data, on which to rest our conjectures of their age, are not very substantial; although some find in them a warrant for an antiquity of thousands of years, coeval with the architecture of Egypt and Hindostan.[87] But the interpretation of hieroglyphics, and the apparent duration of trees, are vague and unsatisfactory.[88] And how far can we derive an argument from the discoloration and dilapidated condition of the ruins, when we find so many structures of the Middle Ages dark and mouldering with decay, while the marbles of the Acropolis, and the grey stone of Pæstum, still shine in their primitive splendor?

There are, however, undoubted proofs of considerable age to be found there. Trees have shot up in the midst of the buildings, which measure, it is said, more than nine feet in diameter.[89] A still more striking fact is the accumulation of vegetable mould in one of the courts, to the depth of nine feet above the pavement.[90] This in our latitude would be decisive of a very great antiquity. But, in the rich soil of Yucatan, and under the ardent sun of the tropics, vegetation bursts forth with irrepressible exuberance, and generations of plants succeed each other without intermission, leaving an accumulation of deposits, that would have perished under a northern winter. Another evidence of their age is afforded by the circumstance, that, in one of the courts of Uxmal, the granite pavement, on which the figures of tortoises were raised in relief, is worn nearly smooth by the feet of the crowds who have passed over it;[91] a curious fact, suggesting inferences both in regard to the age and population of the place. Lastly, we have authority for carrying back the date of many of these

[87] "Les ruines," says the enthusiastic chevalier Le Noir, "sans nom, à qui l'on a donné celui de *Palenque*, peuvent remonter comme les plus anciennes ruines du monde à trois mille ans. Ceci n'est point mon opinion seule; c'est celle de *tous* les voyageurs qui ont vu les ruines dont il s'agit, de *tous* les archéologues qui en ont examiné les dessins ou lu les descriptions, enfin des historiens qui ont fait des recherches, et qui n'ont rien trouvé dans les annales du monde qui fasse soupçonner l'époque de la fondation de tels monuments, dont l'origine se perd dans la nuit des temps." (Antiquités Mexicaines, tom. II., Examen, p. 73.) Colonel Galindo, fired with the contemplation of the American ruins, pronounces this country the true cradle of civilization, whence it passed over to China, and latterly to Europe, which, whatever "its foolish vanity" may pretend, has but just started in the march of improvement! See his Letter on Copan, ap. Trans. of Am. Ant. Soc., vol. II.

[88] From these sources of information, and especially from the number of the concentric rings in some old trees, and the incrustation of stalactites found on the ruins of Palenque, Mr. Waldeck computes their age at between two and three thousand years. (Voyage en Yucatan, p. 78.) The criterion, as far as the trees are concerned, cannot be relied on in an advanced stage of their growth; and as to the stalactite formations, they are obviously affected by too many casual circumstances, to afford the basis of an accurate calculation.

[89] Waldeck, Voyage en Yucatan, ubi supra.

[90] Antiquités Mexicaines, Examen, p. 76.

Hardly deep enough, however, to justify Captain Dupaix's surmise of the antediluvian existence of these buildings; especially, considering that the accumulation was in the sheltered position of an interior court.

[91] Waldeck, Voyage en Yucatan, p. 97.

ruins to a certain period, since they were found in a deserted, and probably dilapidated, state by the first Spaniards who entered the country. Their notices, indeed, are brief and casual, for the old Conquerors had little respect for works of art;[92] and it is fortunate for these structures, that they had ceased to be the living temples of the gods, since no merit of architecture, probably, would have availed to save them from the general doom of the monuments of Mexico.

If we find it so difficult to settle the age of these buildings, what can we hope to know of their architects? Little can be gleaned from the rude people by whom they are surrounded. The old Tezcucan chronicler, so often quoted by me, the best authority for the traditions of his country, reports, that the Toltecs, on the breaking up of their empire,—which he places, earlier than most authorities, in the middle of the tenth century, —migrating from Anahuac, spread themselves over Guatemala, Tecuantepec, Campeachy, and the coasts and neighboring isles on both sides of the Isthmus.[93] This assertion, important, considering its source, is confirmed by the fact, that several of the nations in that quarter adopted systems of astronomy and chronology, as well as sacerdotal institutions, very similar to the Aztec,[94] which, as we have seen, were also probably

---

[92] The chaplain of Grijalva speaks with admiration of the "lofty towers of stone and lime, some of them very ancient," found in Yucatan. (Itinerario, MS. (1518).) Bernal Diaz, with similar expressions of wonder, refers the curious antique relics found there to the Jews. (Hist. de la Conquista, cap. 2, 6.) Alvarado, in a letter to Cortés, expatiates on the "maravillosos et grandes edificios," to be seen in Guatemala. (Oviedo, Hist. de las Ind., MS., lib. 33, cap. 42.) According to Cogolludo, the Spaniards, who could get no tradition of their origin, referred them to the Phœnicians or Carthaginians. (Hist. de Yucatan, lib. 4, cap. 2.) He cites the following emphatic notice of these remains from Las Casas: "Ciertamente la tierra de Yucatan da á entender cosas mui especiales, y de mayor antiguedad, por las grandes, admirables, y excessivas maneras de edificios, y letreros de ciertos caracteres, que en otra ninguna parte se hallan." (Loc. cit.) Even the inquisitive Martyr has collected no particulars respecting them, merely noticing the buildings of this region with general expressions of admiration. (De Insulis nuper Inventis, pp. 334-340.) What is quite as surprising is the silence of Cortés, who traversed the country forming the base of Yucatan, in his famous expedition to Honduras, of which he has given many details we would gladly have exchanged for a word respecting these interesting memorials. Carta Quinta de Cortés, MS.

I must add, that some remarks in the above paragraph in the text would have been omitted, had I enjoyed the benefit of Mr. Stephens' researches, when it was originally written. This is especially the case with the reflections on the probable condition of these structures at the time of the Conquest; when some of them would appear to have been still used for their original purposes.

[93] "Asimismo los Tultecas que escapáron se fuéron por las costas del Mar del Sur y Norte, como, son Huatimala, Tecuantepec, Cuauhzacualco, Campechy, Tecolotlan, y los de las Islas y Costas de una mar y otra, que despues se viniéron á multiplicar." Ixtlilxochitl, Relaciones, MS., No. 5.

[94] Herrera, Hist. General, dec. 4, lib. 10, cap. 1-4.—Cogolludo, Hist. de Yucatan, lib. 4, cap. 5.—Pet Martyr, De Insulis, ubi supra.

M. Waldeck comes to just the opposite inference, namely, that the inhabitants of Yucatan were the true sources of the Toltec and Aztec civilization. (Voyage en Yucatan. p. 72.) "Doubt must be our lot in every thing," exclaims the honest Captain Dupaix,—"*The true faith always excepted.*" Antiquités Mexicaines, tom. I. p. 21.

derived from the Toltecs, their more polished predecessors in the land.

If so recent a date for the construction of the American buildings be thought incompatible with this oblivion of their origin, it should be remembered how treacherous a thing is tradition, and how easily the links of the chain are severed. The builders of the pyramids had been forgotten before the time of the earliest Greek historians.[95] The antiquary still disputes, whether the frightful inclination of that architectural miracle, the tower of Pisa, standing, as it does, in the heart of a populous city, was the work of accident or design. And we have seen how soon the Tezcucans, dwelling amidst the ruins of their royal palaces, built just before the Conquest, had forgotten their history, while the more inquisitive traveller refers their construction to some remote period before the Aztecs.[96]

The reader has now seen the principal points of coincidence insisted on between the civilization of ancient Mexico, and the eastern hemisphere. In presenting them to him, I have endeavored to confine myself to such as rest on sure historic grounds; and not so much to offer my own opinion, as to enable him to form one for himself. There are some material embarrassments in the way to this, however, which must not be passed over in silence. These consist, not in explaining the fact, that, while the mythic system and the science of the Aztecs afford some striking points of analogy with the Asiatic, they should differ in so many more; for the same phenomenon is found among the nations of the Old World, who seem to have borrowed from one another those ideas, only, best suited to their peculiar genius and institutions. Nor does the difficulty lie in accounting for the great dissimilarity of the American languages to those in the other hemisphere; for the difference with these is not greater than what exists among themselves; and no one will contend for a separate origin for each of the Aboriginal tribes.[97] But it is scarcely possible to reconcile the knowledge of Oriental science with the total ignorance of some of the most serviceable and familiar arts, as the use of milk, and iron, for example; arts so simple, yet so important to domestic comfort, that, when once acquired, they could hardly be lost.

The Aztecs had no useful domesticated animals. And we have seen that they employed bronze, as a substitute for iron, for all mechanical purposes. The bison, or wild cow of America, however, which ranges in countless herds over the magnificent prairies of the west, yields milk like the tame animal of the same species, in Asia and Europe;[98] and iron was

[95] "Inter omnes eos non constat a quibus factæ sint, justissimo casu, obliteratis tantæ vanitatis auctoribus." Pliny, Hist. Nat., lib. 36, cap. 17.

[96] Ante, p. 105.

[97] At least, this is true of the etymology of these languages, and, as such, was adduced by Mr. Edward Everett, in his Lectures on the Aboriginal civilization of America, forming part of a course delivered some years since by that acute and highly accomplished scholar.

[98] The mixed breed, from the buffalo and the European stock, was known formerly in the northwestern counties of Virginia, says Mr. Gallatin; (Synopsis, sec. 5;) who is, however, mistaken in asserting, that "the bison is not known to have ever been domesticated by the Indians." (Ubi supra.) Gomara speaks of a nation,

scattered in large masses over the surface of the table-land. Yet there have been people considerably civilized in Eastern Asia, who were almost equally strangers to the use of milk.[99] The buffalo range was not so much on the western coast, as on the eastern slopes of the Rocky Mountains;[100] and the migratory Aztec might well doubt, whether the wild, uncouth monsters, whom he occasionally saw bounding with such fury over the distant plains, were capable of domestication, like the meek animals which he had left grazing in the green pastures of Asia. Iron, too, though met with on the surface of the ground, was more tenacious, and harder to work, than copper, which he also found in much greater quantities on his route. It is possible, moreover, that his migration may have been previous to the time when iron was used by his nation; for we have seen more than one people in the Old World employing bronze and copper, with entire ignorance, apparently, of any more serviceable metal.[101]—Such is the explanation, unsatisfactory, indeed, but the best that suggests itself, of this curious anomaly.

The consideration of these and similar difficulties has led some writers to regard the antique American civilization as purely indigenous. Whichever way we turn, the subject is full of embarrassment. It is easy, indeed,

---

dwelling about 40° north latitude, on the north-western borders of New Spain, whose chief wealth was in droves of these cattle, (*buyes con una giba sobre la cruz*, "oxen with a hump on the shoulders,") from which they got their clothing, food, and drink, which last, however, appears to have been only the blood of the animal. —Historia de las Indias, cap. 214, ap. Barcia, tom. II.

[99] The people of parts of China, for example, and, above all, of Cochin China, who never milk their cows, according to Macartney, cited by Humboldt, Essai Politique, tom. III. p. 58, note.—See, also, p. 118.

[100] The native regions of the buffalo were the vast prairies of the Missouri, and they wandered over the long reach of country east of the Rocky Mountains, from 55° north, to the head-waters of the streams between the Mississippi and the Rio del Norte. The Columbia plains, says Gallatin, were as naked of game as of trees. (Synopsis, sec. 5.) That the bison was sometimes found, also, on the other side of the mountains, is plain from Gomara's statement. (Hist. de las Ind., loc. cit.) See, also, Laet, who traces their southern wanderings to the river Vaquimi, (?) in the province of Cinaloa, on the California Gulf. Novus Orbis, (Lug. Bat. 1633,) p. 286.

[101] Ante, p. 81.

Thus, Lucretius,

> "Et prior æris erat, quam ferri cognitus usus,
> Quo facilis magis est natura, et copia maior.
> Ære solum terræ tractabant, æreque belli
> Miscebant fluctus."
>
> DE RERUM NATURA, lib. 5.

According to Carli, the Chinese were acquainted with iron 3,000 years before Christ. (Lettres Améric., tom. II. p. 63.) Sir J. G. Wilkinson, in an elaborate inquiry into its first appearance among the people of Europe and Western Asia, finds no traces of it earlier than the sixteenth century before the Christian era. (Ancient Egyptians, vol. III. pp. 241–246.) The origin of the most useful arts is lost in darkness. Their very utility is one cause of this, from the rapidity with which they are diffused among distant nations. Another cause is, that, in the first ages of the discovery, men are more occupied with availing themselves of it than with recording its history; until time turns history into fiction. Instances are familiar to every schoolboy

by fastening the attention on one portion of it, to come to a conclusion. In this way, while some feel little hesitation in pronouncing the American civilization orignal; others, no less certainly, discern in it a Hebrew, or an Egyptian, or a Chinese, or a Tartar origin, as their eyes are attracted by the light of analogy too exclusively to this or the other quarter. The number of contradictory lights, of itself, perplexes the judgment, and prevents us from arriving at a precise and positive inference. Indeed, the affectation of this, in so doubtful a matter, argues a most unphilosophical mind. Yet, where there is most doubt, there is often the most dogmatism.

The reader of the preceding pages may, perhaps, acquiesce in the general conclusions,—not startling by their novelty,—

First, that the coincidences are sufficiently strong to authorize a belief, that the civilization of Anahuac was, in some degree, influenced by that of Eastern Asia.

And, secondly, that the discrepancies are such as to carry back the communication to a very remote period; so remote, that this foreign influence has been too feeble to interfere materially with the growth of what may be regarded, in its essential features, as a peculiar and indigenous civilization.

APPENDIX, PART II

ORIGINAL DOCUMENTS

No. I.—See p. 87

ADVICE OF AN AZTEC MOTHER TO HER DAUGHTER; TRANSLATED FROM SAHAGUN'S "HISTORIA DE NUEVA ESPAÑA," LIB. VI., CAP. XIX

[I have thought it best to have this translation made in the most literal manner, that the reader may have a correct idea of the strange mixture of simplicity, approaching to childishness, and moral sublimity, which exist together in the original. It is the product of the twilight of civilization.]

My beloved daughter, very dear little dove, you have already heard and attended to the words which your father has told you. They are precious words, and such as are rarely spoken or listened to, and which have proceeded from the bowels and heart, in which they were treasured up; and your beloved father well knows that you are his daughter, begotten of him, are his blood, and his flesh; and God our Lord knows that it is so. Although you are a woman, and are *the image of your father,* what more can I say to you than has already been said? What more can you hear than what you have heard from your lord and father? who has fully told you what it is becoming for you to do and to avoid, nor is there any thing remaining. which concerns you, that he has not touched upon. Nevertheless, that I may do towards you my whole duty, I will say to you some few words.—The first thing that I earnestly charge upon you is, that you observe and do not forget what your father has now told you, since it is all very precious; and persons of his condition rarely publish such things; for they are the words which belong to the noble and wise,—valuable as rich jewels. See, then, that you take them and lay them up in your heart, and write them in your bowels. If God gives you life, with these same words will you teach your sons and daughters, if God shall give you them.—The second thing that I desire to say to you, is that I love you much, that you are my dear daughter. Remember that nine months I bore you in my womb, that you were born and brought up in my arms. I placed you in your cradle, and in my lap, and with my milk I nursed you. This I tell you, in order that you may know that I and your father are the source of your being; it is we who now instruct you. See that you receive our words, and treasure them in your breast.—Take care that your garments are such as are decent and proper; and observe that you do not adorn yourself with much finery, since this is a mark of vanity and of folly. As little becoming is it, that your dress should be very mean, dirty, or ragged; since rags are a mark of the low, and of those who are held in contempt. Let your clothes be becoming and neat, that you may neither appear fantastic nor mean. When you speak, do not hurry your words from uneasiness, but speak deliberately and calmly. Do not raise your voice very high, nor speak very low, but in a moderate tone. Neither mince, when you speak, nor when you salute, nor speak through your nose; but let your words be proper, of a good sound, and your voice gentle. Do not be nice in the choice of your words. In walking, my daughter, see that you behave becomingly, neither going with haste, nor too slowly; since it is an evidence of being puffed up, to walk too slowly, and walking hastily causes a vicious habit of restlessness and instability. Therefore neither walk very fast, nor very slow; yet, when it shall be necessary to go with haste, do so,—in this use your discretion. And when you may be obliged to jump over a pool of water, do it with decency, that you may neither appear clumsy nor light. When you are in the street, do not carry your head much inclined, or your body bent; nor as little go with your head very much raised; since it is a mark of ill breeding; walk erect, and with your head slightly inclined. Do not have your mouth covered, or your face, from shame, nor go looking like a near-sighted person, nor, on your way, make fantastic movements with your feet. Walk through the street quietly, and with propriety. Another thing that you must attend to, my daughter, is, that, when you are in the street, you do not go looking hither and thither, nor turning your head to look at this and that; walk neither looking at the skies, nor on the ground. Do not look upon those whom you meet with the eyes of an offended person, nor have the appearance of being uneasy; but of one who looks upon all with a serene countenance; doing this, you will give no one occasion of being offended with you. Show a becoming countenance; that you may neither appear morose, nor, on the other hand, too complaisant. See, my daughter, that you give yourself no concern about the words you may hear, in going through the street, nor pay any regard to them, let those who come and go say what they will. Take care that you neither answer nor speak, but act as if you neither heard nor understood them; since, doing in this manner, no one will be able to say with truth that you have said any thing amiss. See, likewise, my daughter, that you never paint your face, or stain it or your lips with colors, in order to appear well; since this is a mark of vile and unchaste women. Paints and coloring are things which bad women use,—the immodest, who have lost all shame and even sense, who are like fools and drunkards, and are called *rameras* [prostitutes]. But, that your husband may not dislike you, adorn yourself, wash yourself, and cleanse your clothes; and let this be done with moderation; since, if every day you wash yourself and your clothes, it will be said of you, that you are overnice,—too delicate; they will call you *tapepetzon tinemaxoch*.—My daughter, this is the course you are to take; since in this manner the ancestors from whom you spring brought us up. Those noble and venerable dames, your grandmothers, told us not so many things as I have told you,—they said but few words, and spoke thus: "Listen, my daughters; in this world, it is necessary to live with much prudence and circumspection. Hear this allegory, which I shall now tell you, and preserve it, and take from it a warning and example for living aright. Here, in this world, we travel by a very narrow, steep, and dangerous road, which is as a lofty mountain ridge, on whose top passes a narrow path; on either side is a great gulf without bottom, and, if you deviate from the path, you will fall into it. There is need, therefore, of much discretion in pursuing the road." My tenderly loved daughter, my little dove, keep this illustration in your heart, and see that you do not forget it,—it will be to you as a lamp and a beacon, so long as you shall live in this world.—Only one thing remains to be said, and I have done. If God shall give you life, if you shall continue some years upon the earth, see that you guard yourself carefully, that no stain come upon you; should you forfeit your chastity, and afterwards be asked in marriage and should marry any one, you will never be fortunate, nor have true love,—he will always remember that you were not a virgin, and this will be the cause of great affliction and distress; you will never be at peace, for your husband will always be suspicious of you. O, my dearly beloved daughter, if you shall live upon the earth, see that not more than one man approaches you; and observe what I now shall tell you, as a strict command. When it shall please God that you receive a husband, and you are placed under his authority, be free from arrogance, see that you do not neglect him, nor allow your heart to be in opposition to him. Be not disrespectful to him. Beware, that, in no time or place, you commit the treason against him called adultery. See that you give no favor to another; since this, my dear and much loved daughter, is to fall into a pit without bottom, from which there will be no escape. According to the custom of the world, if it shall be known, for this crime they will kill you, they will throw you into the street, for an exampl„ to all the people, where your head will be crushed and dragged upon the ground. Of these says a proverb: "You will be stoned and dragged upon the earth, and others will take warning at your death." From this will arise a stain and dishonor upon our ancestors, the nobles and senators from whom we are descended. You will tarnish their illustrious fame, and their glory, by the filthiness and impurity of your sin. You will, likewise, lose your reputation, your nobility, and honor of birth; your name will be forgotten and abhorred. Of you will it be said, that you were buried in the dust of your sins. And remember, my daughter, that, though no man shall see you, nor your husband ever know what happens, *God, who is in every place, sees you*, will be angry with you, and will also excite the indignation of the people against you, and will be avenged upon you as he shall see fit. By his command, you shall either be maimed, or struck blind, or your body will wither, or you will come to extreme poverty, for daring to injure your husband. Or, perhaps, he will give you to death, and put you under his feet, sending you to the place of torment. Our Lord is compassionate; but, if you commit treason against your husband, God, who is in every place, shall take vengeance on your sin, and will permit you to have neither contentment, nor repose, nor a peaceful life; and he will excite your husband to be always unkind towards you, and always to speak to you with anger. My dear daughter, whom I tenderly love, see that you live in the world in peace, tranquillity, and contentment, all the days that you shall live. See that you disgrace not yourself, that you stain not your honor, nor pollute the lustre and fame of your ancestors. See that you honor me and your father, and reflect glory on us by your good life. May God prosper you, my first-born, and may you come to God, who is in every place.

No. II.—See p. 99

A CASTILIAN AND AN ENGLISH TRANSLATION OF A POEM ON THE MU-TABILITY OF LIFE, BY NEZAHUALCOYOTL, LORD OF TEZCUCO

[This poem was fortunately rescued from the fate of too many of the Indian MSS., by the chevalier Boturini, and formed part of his valuable *Muséo*. It was subsequently incorporated in the extensive collection of documents made by father Manuel de la Vega, in Mexico, 1792. This magnificent collection was made in obedience to an enlightened order of the Spanish government, "that all such MSS. as could be found in New Spain, fitted to illustrate the antiquities, geography, civil, ecclesiastical and natural history of America, should be copied and transmitted to Madrid." This order was obeyed, and the result was a collection of thirty, two volumes in folio, which, amidst much that is trivial and of little worth, contains also a mass of original materials, of inestimable value to the historian of Mexico and of the various races who occupied the country of New Spain.]

Un rato cantar quiero,
pues la ocasion y el tiempo se ofrece;
ser admitido espero,
si intento lo merece;
y comienzo mi canto,
aunque fuera mejor llamarle llanto.
Y tú, querido Amigo,
goza la amenidad de aquestas flores.
alégrate conmigo;

desechemos de pena los temores,
que el gusto trae medida,
por ser al fin con fin la mala vida.
    Io tocaré cantando
el músico instrumento sonoroso,
tú de flores gozando
danza, y festeja á Dios que es Poderoso;
gocemos de esta gloria,
porque la humana vida es transitoria.
    De Ocblehacan pusíste
en esta noble Corte, y siendo tuyo,
tus sillas, y quisiste
vestirlas; donde arguyo,
que con grandeza tanta
el Imperio se aumenta y se levanta.
    Oyoyotzin prudente,
famoso Rey y singular Monarca,
goza del bien presente,
que lo presente lo florido abarca;
porque vendrá algun dia
que busques este gusto y alegría.
    Entonces tu Fortuna
te ha de quitar el Cetro de la mano,
ha de menguar tu Luna,
no te verás tan fuerte y tan ufano;
entonces tus criados
de todo bien serán desamparados.
    Y en tan triste suceso
los nobles descendientes de tu nido,
de Príncipes el peso,
los que de nobles Padres han nacido,
laltando tú Cabeza,
gustarán la amargura de pobreza.
    Y traerán á la memoria
quien fuíste en pompa de todos envidiada
tus triunfos y victoria;
y con la gloria y Magestad pasada
cotejando pesares,
de lágrimas harán crecidas Mares.
    Y estos tus descendientes,
que te sirven de pluma y de corona,
de tí viéndose ausentes,
de Culhuacan estrañarán la cuna,
y tenidos por tales
con sus desdichas crecerán sus males.
    Y de esta grandeza rara,
digna de mil coronas y blasones,
será la fama avara;
solo se acordarán en las naciones,
lo bien que governáron,
las tres Cabezas que el imperio honráron
    En México famosa
Moctezumá, valor de pecho Indiano;
á Culhuacan dichosa
de Neçahualcoyotl rigió la mano;
Acatlapan la fuerte
Totoquilhuastli le salió por suerte
    Y ningun olvido temo

de lo bien que tu reyno dispusíste,
estando en el supremo
lugar, que de la mano recibíste
de aquel Señor del Mundo,
factor de aquestas cosas sin segundo.
 Y goza pues muy gustoso,
O Neçahualcoyotl, lo que agora tienes;
con flores de este hermoso
jardin corona tus ilustres sienes;
oye mi canto, y lira
que á darte gustos y placeres tira.
 Y los gustos de esta vida,
sus riquezas, y mandos son prestados,
son sustancia fingida,
con apariencias solo matizados;
y es tan gran verdad esta,
que á una pregunta me has de dar respuesta.
 ¿Y que es de Cihuapan,
y Quantzintecomtzin el valiente,
y Conahuatzin;
que es de toda esa gente?
sus voces; ¡agora acaso!
ya están en la otra vida, este es el caso.
 ¡Ojala los, que agora
juntos los tiene del amor el hilo,
que amistad atesora,
vieramos de la muerte el duro filo!
porque no hay bien seguro.
que siempre trae mudanza á lo futuro.

Now would I sing, since time and place
  Are mine,—and oh! with thee
May this my song obtain the grace
  My purpose claims for me.
I wake these notes on song intent,
But call it rather a lament.
Do thou, beloved, now delight
In these my flowers, pure and bright,
  Rejoicing with thy friend;
Now let us banish pain and fear,
For, if our joys are measured here,
  Life's sadness hath its end.

And I will strike, to aid my voice,
  The deep, sonorous chord;
Thou, dancing, in these flowers rejoice,
  And feast Earth's mighty Lord;
Seize we the glories of to-day,
For mortal life fleets fast away.—
In Ocblehacan, all thine own,
Thy hand hath placed the noble throne,
  Which thou hast richly dressed;
From whence I argue, that thy sway
Shall be augmented day by day,
  In rising greatness blessed.

**Wise Oyoyotzin! prudent king!
Unrivalled Prince, and great!**

Enjoy the fragrant flowers that spring
    Around thy kingly state;
A day will come which shall destroy
Thy present bliss,—thy present joy,—
When fate the sceptre of command
Shall wrench from out thy royal hand,—
    Thy moon diminished rise;
And, as thy pride and strength are quenched,
From thy adherents shall be wrenched
    All that they love or prize.

When sorrows shall my truth attest,
    And this thy throne decline,—
The birds of thy ancestral nest,
    The princes of thy line,—
The mighty of thy race,—shall see
The bitter ills of poverty;—
And then shall memory recall
Thy envied greatness, and on all
    Thy brilliant triumphs dwell;
And as they think on by-gone years,
Compared with present shame, their tears
    Shall to an ocean swell.

And those, who, though a royal band,
    Serve thee for crown, or plume,
Remote from Culhuacan's land
    Shall find the exile's doom.
Deprived of thee,—their rank forgot,
Misfortune shall o'erwhelm their lot.
Then fame shall grudgingly withhold
Her meed to greatness, which of old
    Blazons and crowns displayed;
The people will retain alone
Remembrance of that *triple throne*
    Which this our land obeyed.

Brave Moctezuma's Indian land
    Was Mexico the great,
And Nezahualcoyotl's hand
    Blessed Culhuacan's state,
Whilst Totoquil his portion drew
In Acatlapan, strong and true;
But no oblivion can I fear,
Of good by thee accomplished here,
    Whilst high upon thy throne;
That station, which, to match thy worth,
Was given by the Lord of Earth,
    Maker of good alone!

Then, Nezahualcoyotl,—now,
    In what thou *hast,* delight;
And wreathe around thy royal brow
    Life's garden blossoms bright;
List to my lyre and my lay,
Which aim to please thee, and obey.
The pleasures, which our lives present,—
Earth's sceptres, and its wealth,—are lent,
    Are shadows fleeting by;

Appearance colors all our bliss;
A truth so great, that now to this
One question, make reply.

What has become of Cihuapan,
Quantzintecomtzin brave,
And Conahuatzin, mighty man;
Where are they? In the grave!
Their names remain, but they are fled,
Forever numbered with the dead.
Would that those now in friendship bound,
We whom Love's thread encircles round,
Death's cruel edge might see!
Since good on earth is insecure,
And all things must a change endure
In dark futurity!

No. III.—See p. 113

TRANSLATION FROM IXTLILXOCHITL'S "HISTORIA CHICHIMECA," MS., CAP. LXIV.

OF THE EXTRAORDINARY SEVERITY WITH WHICH THE KING NEZAHUALPILLI PUNISHED THE MEXICAN QUEEN FOR HER ADULTERY AND TREASON

When Axaiacatzin, king of Mexico, and other lords, sent their daughters to king Nezahualpilli, for him to choose one to be his queen and lawful wife, whose son might succeed to the inheritance, she who had highest claims among them, from nobility of birth and rank, was Chachiuhnenetzin, daughter of the Mexican king. But, being at that time very young, she was brought up by the monarch in a separate palace, with great pomp and numerous attendants, as became the daughter of so great a king. The number of servants attached to her household exceeded two thousand. Young as she was, she was yet exceedingly artful and vicious; so that, finding herself alone, and seeing that her people feared her, on account of her rank and importance, she began to give way to the unlimited indulgence of her lust. Whenever she saw a young man who pleased her fancy, she gave secret orders to have him brought to her, and, having satisfied her desires, caused him to be put to death. She then ordered a statue or effigy of his person to be made, and, adorning it with rich clothing, gold and jewelry, had it placed in the apartment in which she lived. The number of statues of those whom she thus put to death was so great as almost to fill the apartment. When the king came to visit her, and inquired respecting these statues, she answered, that they were her gods; and he, knowing how strict the Mexicans were in the worship of their false deities, believed her. But, as no iniquity can be long committed with entire secrecy, she was finally found out in this manner. Three of the young men, for some reason or other, she had left alive. Their names were Chicuhcoatl, Huitzilimitzin, and Maxtla, one of whom was lord of Tesoyucan, and one of the grandees of the kingdom; and the other two, nobles of high rank. It happened, that one day the king recognised on one of these a very precious jewel, which he had given to the queen; and, although he had no fear of treason on her part, it gave him some uneasiness. Proceeding to visit her that night, her attendants told him that she was asleep, supposing that the king would then return, as he had done at other times. But the affair of the jewel made him insist on entering the chamber in which she slept; and, going to awake her, he found only a statue in the bed, adorned with her hair, and closely resembling her. This being seen by the king, and, also, that the attendants around were in much trepidation and alarm, he called his guards, and, assembling all the people of the house, made a general search for the queen, who was shortly found, at an entertainment with the three young lords, who were likewise arrested with her. The king referred the case to the judges of his court, in order that they might make an inquiry into the matter, and examine the parties implicated. These discovered many individuals, servants of the queen, who had in some way or other been accessory to her crimes, workmen who had been engaged in making and adorning the statues, others who had aided in introducing the young men into the palace, and others again who had put them to death, and concealed their bodies. The case having been sufficiently investigated, he despatched ambassadors to the kings of Mexico and Tlacopan, giving them information of the event, and signifying the day on which the punishment of the queen and her accomplices was to take place; and he likewise sent through the empire to summon all the lords to bring their wives and their daughters, however young they might be, to be witnesses of a punishment which he designed for a great example. He also made a truce with all the enemies of the empire, in order that they might come freely to see it. The time being arrived, so great was the concourse of people gathered on the occasion, that, large as was the city of Tezcuco, they could scarcely all find room in it. The execution took place publicly in sight of the whole city. The queen was put to the *garrote,* [a method of strangling by means of a rope twisted round a stick,] as well as her three gallants; and, from their being persons of high birth, their bodies were burned, together with the effigies before mentioned. The other parties who had been accessory to the crime, who were more than two thousand persons, were also put to the *garrote,* and buried in a pit made for the purpose in a ravine near a temple of the Idol of Adulterers. All applauded so severe and exemplary a punishment, except the Mexican lords, the relations of the queen, who were much incensed at so public an example, and, although for the present they concealed their resentment, meditated future revenge. It was not without cause that the king experienced this disgrace in his household, since he was thus punished for the unworthy means made use of by his father to obtain his mother as a wife.

HISTORY

OF THE

CONQUEST OF PERU

"Congestæ cumulantur opes, orbisque rapinas
Accipit."

CLAUDIAN, In Ruf., lib. i., v. 194.

"So color de religion
Van a buscar plata y oro
Del encubierto tesoro."

LOPE DE VEGA, El Nuevo Mundo, Jorn. I.

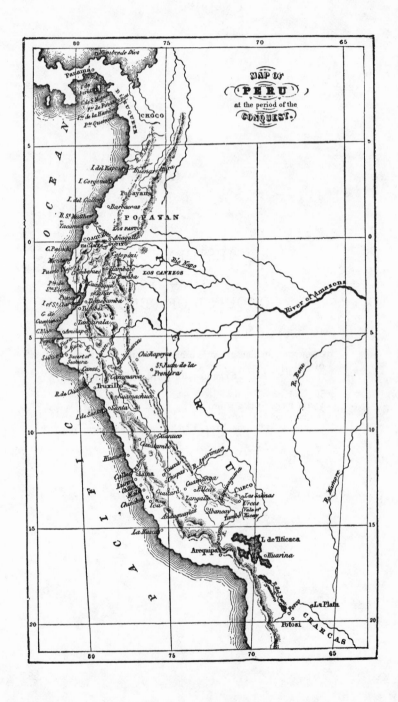

MAP OF
PERU
at the period of the
CONQUEST.

PREFACE

THE most brilliant passages in the history of Spanish adventure in the New World are undoubtedly afforded by the conquests of Mexico and Peru,—the two states which combined with the largest extent of empire a refined social polity, and considerable progress in the arts of civilization. Indeed, so prominently do they stand out on the great canvas of history, that the name of the one, notwithstanding the contrast they exhibit in their respective institutions, most naturally suggests that of the other; and when I sent to Spain to collect materials for an account of the Conquest of Mexico, I included in my researches those relating to the Conquest of Peru.

The larger part of the documents, in both cases, was obtained from the same great repository,—the archives of the Royal Academy of History at Madrid; a body specially intrusted with the preservation of whatever may serve to illustrate the Spanish colonial annals. The richest portion of its collection is probably that furnished by the papers of Muñoz. This eminent scholar, historiographer of the Indies, employed nearly fifty years of his life in amassing materials for a history of Spanish discovery and conquest in America. For this, as he acted under the authority of the government, every facility was afforded him; and public offices and private depositories, in all the principal cities of the empire, both at home and throughout the wide extent of its colonial possessions, were freely opened to his inspection. The result was a magnificent collection of manuscripts, many of which he patiently transcribed with his own hand. But he did not live to reap the fruits of his persevering industry. The first volume, relative to the voyages of Columbus, were scarcely finished when he died; and his manuscripts, at least that portion of them which have reference to Mexico and Peru, were destined to serve the uses of another, an inhabitant of that New World to which they related.

Another scholar, to whose literary stores I am largely indebted, is Don Martin Fernandez de Navarrete, late Director of the Royal Academy of History. Through the greater part of his long life he was employed in assembling original documents to illustrate the colonial annals. Many of these have been incorporated in his great work, "Coleccion de los Viages y Descubrimientos," which, although far from being completed after the original plan of its author, is of inestimable service to the historian. In following down the track of discovery, Navarrete turned aside from the conquests of Mexico and Peru, to exhibit the voyages of his countrymen in the Indian seas. His manuscripts, relating to the two former countries, he courteously allowed to be copied for me. Some of them have since appeared in print, under the auspices of his learned coadjutors, Salvà and Baranda, associated with him in the Academy; but the documents placed in my hands form a most important contribution to my materials for the present history.

The death of this illustrious man, which occurred some time after the present work was begun, has left a void in his country not easy to be filled; for he was zealously devoted to letters, and few have done more to extend the knowledge of her colonial history. Far from an exclusive solicitude for his own literary projects, he was ever ready to extend his sympathy and assistance to those of others. His reputation as a scholar was enhanced by the higher qualities which he possessed as a man,—by his benevolence, his simplicity of manners, and unsullied moral worth. My own obligations to him are large; for from the publication of my first historical work, down to the last week of his life, I have constantly received proofs from him of his hearty and most efficient interest in the prosecution of my historical labors; and I now the more willingly pay this well-merited tribute to his deserts, that it must be exempt from all suspicion of flattery.

In the list of those to whom I have been indebted for materials, I must, also, include the name of M. Ternaux-Compans, so well known by his faithful and elegant French versions of the Muñoz manuscripts; and that of my friend Don Pascual de Gayangos, who, under the modest dress of translation, has furnished a most acute and learned commentary on Spanish Arabian history,—securing for himself the foremost rank in that difficult department of letters, which has been illumined by the labors of a Masdeu, a Casiri, and a Conde.

To the materials derived from these sources, I have added some manuscripts of an important character from the library of the Escurial. These, which chiefly relate to the ancient institutions of Peru, formed part of the splendid collection of Lord Kingsborough, which has unfortunately shared the lot of most literary collections, and been dispersed since the death of its noble author. For these I am indebted to that industrious bibliographer, Mr. O. Rich, now resident in London. Lastly, I must not omit to mention my obligations, in another way, to my friend Charles Folsom, Esq., the learned librarian of the Boston Athenæum; whose minute acquaintance with the grammatical structure and the true idiom of our English tongue has enabled me to correct many inaccuracies into which I had fallen in the composition both of this and of my former works.

From these different sources I have accumulated a large amount of manuscripts, of the most various character, and from the most authentic sources; royal grants and ordinances, instructions of the Court, letters of the Emperor to the great colonial officers, municipal records, personal diaries and memoranda, and a mass of private correspondence of the principal actors in this turbulent drama. Perhaps it was the turbulent state of the country which led to a more frequent correspondence between the government at home and the colonial officers. But, whatever be the cause, the collection of manuscript materials in reference to Peru is fuller and more complete than that which relates to Mexico; so that there is scarcely a nook or corner so obscure, in the path of the adventurer, that some light has not been thrown on it by the written correspondence of the period. The historian has rather had occasion to complain of the *embarras des richesses;* for, in the multiplicity of contradictory testimony, it is not always easy to detect the truth, as the multiplicity of cross-lights is apt to dazzle and bewilder the eye of the spectator.

The present History has been conducted on the same general plan with that of the Conquest of Mexico. In an Introductory Book, I have endeavored to portray the institutions of the Incas, that the reader may be acquainted with the character and condition of that extraordinary race, before he enters on the story of their subjugation. The remaining books are occupied with the narrative of the Conquest. And here, the subject, it must be allowed, notwithstanding the opportunities it presents for the display of character, strange, romantic incident, and picturesque scenery, does not afford so obvious advantages to the historian, as the Conquest of Mexico. Indeed, few subjects can present a parallel with that, for the purposes either of the historian or the poet. The natural development of the story, there, is precisely what would be prescribed by the severest rules of art. The conquest of the country is the great end always in the view of the reader. From the first landing of the Spaniards on the soil, their subsequent adventures, their battles and negotiations, their ruinous retreat, their rally and final siege, all tend to this grand result, till the long series is closed by the downfall of the capital. In the march of events, all moves steadily forward to this consummation. It is a magnificent epic, in which the unity of interest is complete.

In the "Conquest of Peru," the action, so far as it is founded on the subversion of the Incas, terminates long before the close of the narrative. The remaining portion is taken up with the fierce feuds of the Conquerors, which would seem, from their very nature, to be incapable of being gathered round a central point of interest. To secure this, we must look beyond the immediate overthrow of the Indian empire. The conquest of the natives is but the first step, to be followed by the conquest of the Spaniards,—the rebel Spaniards, themselves,—till the supremacy of the Crown is permanently established over the country. It is not till this period, that the acquisition of this Transatlantic empire can be said to be completed; and, by fixing the eye on this remoter point, the successive steps of the narrative will be found leading to one great result, and that unity of interest preserved which is scarcely less essential to historic than dramatic composition. How far this has been effected, in the present work, must be left to the judgment of the reader.

No history of the conquest of Peru, founded on original documents, and aspiring to the credit of a classic composition, like the "Conquest of Mexico" by Solís, has been attempted, as far as I am aware, by the Spaniards. The English possess one of high value, from the pen of

Robertson, whose masterly sketch occupies its due space in his great work on America. It has been my object to exhibit this same story, in all its romantic details; not merely to portray the characteristic features of the Conquest, but to fill up the outline with the coloring of life, so as to present a minute and faithful picture of the times. For this purpose, I have, in the composition of the work, availed myself freely of my manuscript materials, allowed the actors to speak as much as possible for themselves, and especially made frequent use of their letters; for nowhere is the heart more likely to disclose itself, than in the freedom of private correspondence. I have made liberal extracts from these authorities in the notes, both to sustain the text, and to put in a printed form those productions of the eminent captains and statesmen of the time, which are not very accessible to Spaniards themselves.

M. Amédée Pichot, in the Preface to the French translation of the "Conquest of Mexico," infers from the plan of the composition, that I must have carefully studied the writings of his countryman, M. de Barante. The acute critic does me but justice in supposing me familiar with the principles of that writer's historical theory, so ably developed in the Preface to his "Ducs de Bourgogne." And I have had occasion to admire the skilful manner in which he illustrates this theory himself, by constructing out of the rude materials of a distant time a monument of genius that transports us at once into the midst of the Feudal Ages,—and this without the incongruity which usually attaches to a modern-antique. In like manner, I have attempted to seize the characteristic expression of a distant age, and to exhibit it in the freshness of life. But in an essential particular, I have deviated from the plan of the French historian. I have suffered the scaffolding to remain after the building has been completed. In other words, I have shown to the reader the steps of the process by which I have come to my conclusions. Instead of requiring him to take my version of the story on trust, I have endeavored to give him a reason for my faith. By copious citations from the original authorities, and by such critical notices of them as would explain to him the influences to which they were subjected, I have endeavored to put him in a position for judging for himself, and thus for revising, and, if need be, reversing, the judgments of the historian. He will, at any rate, by this means, be enabled to estimate the difficulty of arriving at truth amidst the conflict of testimony; and he will learn to place little reliance on those writers who pronounce on the mysterious past with what Fontenelle calls "a frightful degree of certainty,"—a spirit the most opposite to that of the true philosophy of history.

Yet it must be admitted, that the chronicler who records the events of an earlier age has some obvious advantages in the store of manuscript materials at his command,—the statements of friends, rivals, and enemies, furnishing a wholesome counterpoise to each other; and also, in the general course of events, as they actually occurred, affording the best commentary on the true motives of the parties. The actor, engaged in the heat of the strife, finds his view bounded by the circle around him, and his vision blinded by the smoke and dust of the conflict; while the spectator, whose eye ranges over the ground from a more distant and elevated point, though the individual objects may lose somewhat of their vividness, takes in at a glance all the operations of the field. Paradoxical as it may appear, truth founded on contemporary testimony would seem, after all, as likely to be attained by the writer of a later day, as by contemporaries themselves.

Before closing these remarks, I may be permitted to add a few of a personal nature. In several foreign notices of my writings, the author has been said to be blind; and more than once I have had the credit of having lost my sight in the composition of my first history. When I have met with such erroneous accounts, I have hastened to correct them. But the present occasion affords me the best means of doing so; and I am the more desirous of this, as I fear some of my own remarks, in the Prefaces to my former histories, have led to the mistake.

While at the University, I received an injury in one of my eyes, which deprived me of the sight of it. The other, soon after, was attacked by inflammation so severely, that, for some time, I lost the sight of that also; and though it was subsequently restored, the organ was so much disordered as to remain permanently debilitated, while twice in my life, since, I have been deprived of the use of it for all purposes of reading and writing, for several years together. It was during one of these periods that I received from Madrid the materials for the "History of Ferdinand and Isabella," and in my disabled condition, with my Transatlantic treasures lying around me, I was like one pining from hunger in the midst of abundance. In this state, I resolved to make the ear, if possible, do the work of the eye. I procured the services of a secretary, who read to me the various authorities; and in time I became so far familiar with the sounds of the different foreign languages (to some of which, indeed, I had been previously accustomed by a residence abroad), that I could comprehend his reading without much difficulty. As the reader proceeded, I dictated copious notes; and, when these had swelled to a considerable amount, they were read to me repeatedly, till I had mastered their contents sufficiently for the purposes of composition. The same notes furnished an easy means of reference to sustain the text.

Still another difficulty occurred, in the mechanical labor of writing, which I found a severe trial to the eye. This was remedied by means of a writing-case, such as is used by the blind, which enabled me to commit my thoughts to paper without the aid of sight, serving me equally well in the dark as in the light. The characters thus formed made a near approach to hieroglyphics; but my secretary became expert in the art of deciphering, and a fair copy—with a liberal allowance for unavoidable blunders—was transcribed for the use of the printer. I have described the process with more minuteness, as some curiosity has been repeatedly expressed in reference to my *modus operandi* under my privations, and the knowledge of it may be of some assistance to others in similar circumstances.

Though I was encouraged by the sensible progress of my work, it was necessarily slow. But in time the tendency to inflammation diminished, and the strength of the eye was confirmed more and more. It was at length so far restored, that I could read for several hours of the day; though my labors in this way necessarily terminated with the daylight. Nor could I ever dispense with the services of a secretary, or with the writing-case; for, contrary to the usual experience, I have found writing a severer trial to the eye than reading,—a remark, however, which does not apply to the reading of manuscript; and to enable myself, therefore, to revise my composition more carefully, I caused a copy of the "History of Ferdinand and Isabella" to be printed for my own inspection, before it was sent to the press for publication. Such as I have described was the improved state of my health during the preparation of the "Conquest of Mexico"; and, satisfied with being raised so nearly to a level with the rest of my species, I scarcely envied the superior good fortune of those who could prolong their studies into the evening, and the later hours of the night.

But a change has again taken place during the last two years. The sight of my eye has become gradually dimmed, while the sensibility of the nerve has been so far increased, that for several weeks of the last year I have not opened a volume, and through the whole time I have not had the use of it, on an average, for more than an hour a day. Nor can I cheer myself with the delusive expectation, that, impaired as the organ has become, from having been tasked, probably, beyond its strength, it can ever renew its youth, or be of much service to me hereafter in my literary researches. Whether I shall have the heart to enter, as I had proposed, on a new and more extensive field of historical labor, with these impediments, I cannot say. Perhaps long habit, and a natural desire to follow up the career which I have so long pursued, may make this, in a manner, necessary, as my past experience has already proved that it is practicable.

From this statement—too long, I fear, for his patience—the reader, who feels any curiosity about the matter, will understand the real extent of my embarrassments in my historical pursuits. That they have not been very light will be readily admitted, when it is considered that I have had but a limited use of my eye, in its best state, and that much of the time I have been debarred from the use of it altogether. Yet the difficulties I have had to contend with are very far inferior to those which fall to the lot of a blind man. I know of no historian, now alive, who can claim the glory of having overcome such obstacles, but the author of "La Conquête de l'Angleterre par les Normands"; who, to use his own touching and beautiful language, "has made himself the friend of darkness"; and who, to a profound philosophy that requires no light but that from within, unites a capacity for extensive and various research, that might well demand the severest application of the student.

The remarks into which I have been led at such length will, I trust, not be set down by the reader to an unworthy egotism, but to their true source, a desire to correct a misapprehension to which I may have unintentionally given rise myself, and which has gained me the credit with some—far from grateful to my feelings, since undeserved—of having surmounted the incalculable obstacles which lie in the path of the blind man.

BOSTON, April 2, 1847.

BOOK I

INTRODUCTION

VIEW OF THE CIVILIZATION OF THE INCAS

CHAPTER I

PHYSICAL ASPECT OF THE COUNTRY—SOURCES OF PERUVIAN CIVILIZA-
TION—EMPIRE OF THE INCAS—ROYAL FAMILY—NOBILITY

OF the numerous nations which occupied the great American continent
at the time of its discovery by the Europeans, the two most advanced in
power and refinement were undoubtedly those of Mexico and Peru. But,
though resembling one another in extent of civilization, they differed
widely as to the nature of it; and the philosophical student of his species
may feel a natural curiosity to trace the different steps by which these
two nations strove to emerge from the state of barbarism, and place
themselves on a higher point in the scale of humanity.—In a former work
I have endeavored to exhibit the institutions and character of the ancient Mexicans, and the story of their conquest by the Spaniards. The
present will be devoted to the Peruvians; and, if their history shall be
found to present less strange anomalies and striking contrasts than that
of the Aztecs, it may interest us quite as much by the pleasing picture it
offers of a well-regulated government and sober habits of industry under
the patriarchal sway of the Incas.

The empire of Peru, at the period of the Spanish invasion, stretched
along the Pacific from about the second degree north to the thirty-seventh
degree of south latitude; a line, also, which describes the western boundaries of the modern republics of Ecuador, Peru, Bolivia, and Chili. Its
breadth cannot so easily be determined; for, though bounded everywhere by the great ocean on the west, towards the east it spread out, in
many parts, considerably beyond the mountains, to the confines of barbarous states, whose exact position is undetermined, or whose names are
effaced from the map of history. It is certain, however, that its breadth
was altogether disproportioned to its length.[1]

[1] Sarmiento, Relacion, MS., cap. 65.—Cieza de Leon, Cronica del Peru, (Anvers,
1554,) cap. 41.—Garcilasso de la Vega, Commentarios Reales, (Lisboa, 1609,) Parte
1, lib. 1, cap. 8.

According to the last authority, the empire, in its greatest breadth, did not exceed one hundred and twenty leagues. But Garcilasso's geography will not bear
criticism.

The topographical aspect of the country is very remarkable. A strip of land, rarely exceeding twenty leagues in width, runs along the coast, and is hemmed in through its whole extent by a colossal range of mountains, which, advancing from the Straits of Magellan, reaches its highest elevation—indeed, the highest on the American continent—about the seventeenth degree south,[2] and, after crossing the line, gradually subsides into hills of inconsiderable magnitude, as it enters the Isthmus of Panamá. This is the famous Cordillera of the Andes, or "copper mountains," [3] as termed by the natives, though they might with more reason have been called "mountains of gold." Arranged sometimes in a single line, though more frequently in two or three lines running parallel or obliquely to each other, they seem to the voyager on the ocean but one continuous chain; while the huge volcanoes, which to the inhabitants of the table-land look like solitary and independent masses, appear to him only like so many peaks of the same vast and magnificent range. So immense is the scale on which Nature works in these regions, that it is only when viewed from a great distance, that the spectator can, in any degree, comprehend the relation of the several parts to the stupendous whole. Few of the works of Nature, indeed, are calculated to produce impressions of higher sublimity than the aspect of this coast, as it is gradually unfolded to the eye of the mariner sailing on the distant waters of the Pacific; where mountain is seen to rise above mountain, and Chimborazo, with its glorious canopy of snow, glittering far above the clouds, crowns the whole as with a celestial diadem.[4]

The face of the country would appear to be peculiarly unfavorable to the purposes both of agriculture and of internal communication. The sandy strip along the coast, where rain never falls, is fed only by a few scanty streams, that furnish a remarkable contrast to the vast volumes of water which roll down the eastern sides of the Cordilleras into the Atlantic. The precipitous steeps of the sierra, with its splintered sides of porphyry and granite, and its higher regions wrapped in snows that never melt under the fierce sun of the equator, unless it be from the desolating action of its own volcanic fires, might seem equally unpropitious to the labors of the husbandman. And all communication between the parts of the long-extended territory might be thought to be precluded by the sav-

[2] According to Malte-Brun, it is under the equator that we meet with the loftiest summits of this chain. (Universal Geography, Eng. trans. book 86.) But more recent measurements have shown this to be between fifteen and seventeen degrees south, where the Nevada de Sorata rises to the enormous height of 25,250 feet, and the Illimani to 24,300.

[3] At least, the word *anta*, which has been thought to furnish the etymology of *Andes*, in the Peruvian tongue, signified "copper." Garcilasso, Com. Real., Parte 1, lib. 5, cap. 15.

[4] Humboldt, Vues des Cordillères et Monumens des Peuples Indigènes de l'Amérique, (Paris, 1810,) p. 106.—Malte-Brun, book 88.

The few brief sketches which M. de Humboldt has given of the scenery of the Cordilleras, showing the hand of a great painter, as well as of a philosopher, make us regret the more, that he has not given the results of his observations in this interesting region as minutely as he has done in respect to Mexico.

age character of the region, broken up by precipices, furious torrents, and impassable *quebradas*,—those hideous rents in the mountain chain, whose depths the eye of the terrified traveller, as he winds along his aërial pathway, vainly endeavors to fathom.[5] Yet the industry, we might almost say, the genius, of the Indian was sufficient to overcome all these impediments of Nature.

By a judicious system of canals and subterraneous aqueducts, the waste places on the coast were refreshed by copious streams, that clothed them in fertility and beauty. Terraces were raised upon the steep sides of the Cordillera; and, as the different elevations had the effect of difference of latitude, they exhibited in regular gradation every variety of vegetable form, from the stimulated growth of the tropics, to the temperate products of a northern clime; while flocks of *llamas*—the Peruvian sheep—wandered with their shepherds over the broad, snow-covered wastes on the crests of the sierra, which rose beyond the limits of cultivation. An industrious population settled along the lofty regions of the plateaus, and towns and hamlets, clustering amidst orchards and wide-spreading gardens, seemed suspended in the air far above the ordinary elevation of the clouds.[6] Intercourse was maintained between these numerous settlements by means of great roads which traversed the mountain passes, and opened an easy communication between the capital and the remotest extremities of the empire.

The source of this civilization is traced to the valley of Cuzco, the central region of Peru, as its name implies.[7] The origin of the Peruvian empire, like the origin of all nations, except the very few which, like our own, have had the good fortune to date from a civilized period and people, is lost in the good mists of fable, which, in fact, have settled as darkly round its history as round that of any nation, ancient or modern, in the Old World. According to the tradition most familiar to the European scholar, the time was, when the ancient races of the continent were all plunged in deplorable barbarism; when they worshipped nearly every object in nature indiscriminately; made war their pastime, and feasted on the flesh of their slaughtered captives. The Sun, the great luminary and parent of mankind, taking compassion on their degraded condition, sent two of his children, Manco Capac and Mama Oello Huaco, to gather the natives into communities, and teach them the arts of civilized life. The celestial pair, brother and sister, husband and wife, advanced along the high plains in the neigh-

---

[5] "These crevices are so deep," says M. de Humboldt, with his usual vivacity of illustration, "that if Vesuvius or the Puy de Dôme were seated in the bottom of them, they would not rise above the level of the ridges of the neighboring sierra." Vues des Cordillères, p. 9.

[6] The plains of Quito are at the height of between nine and ten thousand feet above the sea. (See Condamine, Journal d'un Voyage à L'Equateur, (Paris, 1751,) p. 48.) Other valleys or plateaus in this vast group of mountains reach a still higher elevation.

[7] "*Cuzco*, in the language of the Incas," says Garcilasso, "signifies *navel*." Com Real., Parte 1, lib. 1, cap. 18.

borhood of Lake Titicaca, to about the sixteenth degree south. They bore with them a golden wedge, and were directed to take up their residence on the spot where the sacred emblem should without effort sink into the ground. They proceeded accordingly but a short distance, as far as the valley of Cuzco, the spot indicated by the performance of the miracle, since there the wedge speedily sank into the earth and disappeared for ever. Here the children of the Sun established their residence, and soon entered upon their beneficent mission among the rude inhabitants of the country; Manco Capac teaching the men the arts of agriculture, and Mama Oello [8] initiating her own sex in the mysteries of weaving and spinning. The simple people lent a willing ear to the messengers of Heaven, and, gathering together in considerable numbers, laid the foundations of the city of Cuzco. The same wise and benevolent maxims, which regulated the conduct of the first Incas,[9] descended to their successors, and under their mild sceptre a community gradually extended itself along the broad surface of the table-land, which asserted its superiority over the surrounding tribes. Such is the pleasing picture of the origin of the Peruvian monarchy, as portrayed by Garcilasso de la Vega, the descendant of the Incas, and through him made familiar to the European reader.[10]

But this tradition is only one of several current among the Peruvian Indians, and probably not the one most generally received. Another legend speaks of certain white and bearded men, who, advancing from the shores of Lake Titicaca, established an ascendency over the natives, and imparted to them the blessings of civilization. It may remind us of the tradition existing among the Aztecs in respect to Quetzalcoatl, the good deity, who with a similar garb and aspect came up the great plateau from the east on a like benevolent mission to the natives. The analogy is the more remarkable, as there is no trace of any communication with, or even knowledge of, each other to be found in the two nations.[11]

[8] *Mama*, with the Peruvians, signified "mother." (Garcilasso, Com. Real., Parte 1, lib. 4, cap. 1.) The identity of this term with that used by Europeans is a curious coincidence. It is scarcely less so, however, than that of the corresponding word, *papa*, which with the ancient Mexicans denoted a priest of high rank; reminding us of the *papa*, "pope," of the Italians. With both, the term seems to embrace in its most comprehensive sense the paternal relation, in which it is more familiarly employed by most of the nations of Europe. Nor was the use of it limited to modern times, being applied in the same way both by Greeks and Romans; "Πάππα Φίλε," says Nausikaa, addressing her father, in the simple language which the modern versifiers have thought too simple to render literally.

[9] *Inca* signified *king* or *lord*. Capac meant *great* or *powerful*. It was applied to several of the successors of Manco, in the same manner as the epithet *Yupanqui*, signifying *rich in all virtues*, was added to the names of several Incas. (Cieza de Leon, Cronica, cap. 41.—Garcilasso, Com. Real., Parte 1, lib. 2, cap. 17.) The good qualities commemorated by the cognomens of most of the Peruvian princes afford an honorable, though not altogether unsuspicious, tribute to the excellence of their characters.

[10] Com. Real., Parte 1, lib. 1, cap. 9–16.

[11] These several traditions, all of a very puerile character, are to be found in Ondegardo, Relacion Segunda, MS.,—Sarmiento, Relacion, MS., cap. 1,—Cieza de Leon, Cronica, cap. 105,—Conquista i Poblacion del Piru, MS.,—Declaracion de los

The date usually assigned for these extraordinary events was about four hundred years before the coming of the Spaniards, or early in the twelfth century.[12] But, however pleasing to the imagination, and however popular, the legend of Manco Capac, it requires but little reflection to show its improbability, even when divested of supernatural accompaniments. On the shores of Lake Titicaca extensive ruins exist at the present day, which the Peruvians themselves acknowledge to be of older date than the pretended advent of the Incas, and to have furnished them with the models of their architecture.[13] The date of their appearance, indeed, is manifestly irreconcilable with their subsequent history. No account assigns to the Inca dynasty more than thirteen princes before the Conquest. But this number is altogether too small to have spread over four hundred years, and would not carry back the foundations of the monarchy, on any probable computation, beyond two centuries and a half,— an antiquity not incredible in itself, and which, it may be remarked, does not precede by more than half a century the alleged foundation of the capital of Mexico. The fiction of Manco Capac and his sister-wife was devised, no doubt, at a later period, to gratify the vanity of the Peruvian monarchs, and to give additional sanction to their authority by deriving it from a celestial origin.

We may reasonably conclude that there existed in the country a race advanced in civilization before the time of the Incas; and, in conformity with nearly every tradition, we may derive this race from the neighbor-

Presidente é Oydores de la Audiencia Reale del Peru, MS.,—all of them authorities contemporary with the Conquest. The story of the bearded white men finds its place in most of their legends.

[12] Some writers carry back the date 500, or even 550, years before the Spanish invasion. (Balboa, Histoire du Perou, chap. 1.—Velasco, Histoire de Royaume de Quito, tom. I. p. 81.—Ambo auct. ap. Relations et Mémoires Originaux pour servir à l'Histoire de la Découverte de l'Amérique, par Ternaux-Compans, (Paris, 1840.)) In the Report of the Royal Audience of Peru, the epoch is more modestly fixed at 200 years before the Conquest. Dec. de la Aud. Real., MS.

[13] "Otras cosas ay mas que dezir deste Tiaguanaco, que passo por no detenerme: concluyédo que yo para mi tengo esta antigualla por la mas antigua de todo el Peru. Y assi se tiene que antes q̄ los Ingas reynassen con muchos tiempos estavan hechos algunos edificios destos: porque yo he oydo afirmar a Indios, que los Ingas hizieron los edificios grandes del Cuzco por la forma que vieron tener la muralla o pared que se vee en este pueblo." (Cieza de Leon, Cronica, cap. 105.) See also Garcilasso, (Com. Real., Parte 1, lib. 3, cap 1,) who gives an account of these remains, on the authority of a Spanish ecclesiastic, which might compare, for the marvellous, with any of the legends of his order. Other ruins of similar traditional antiquity are noticed by Herrera, (Historia General de los Hechos de los Castellanos en las Islas y Tierra Firme del Mar Océano, (Madrid, 1730,) dec. 6, lib. 6, cap. 9.) McCulloh, in some sensible reflections on the origin of the Peruvian civilization, adduces, on the authority of Garcilasso de la Vega, the famous temple of Pachacamac, not far from Lima, as an example of architecture more ancient than that of the Incas. (Researches, Philosophical and Antiquarian, concerning the Aboriginal History of America, (Baltimore, 1829,) p. 405.) This, if true, would do much to confirm the views in our text. But McCulloh is led into an error by his blind guide, Rycaut, the translator of Garcilasso, for the latter does not speak of the temple as existing before the time of the Incas, but before the time when the country was conquered by the Incas. Com. Real. Parte 1, lib. 6, cap. 30.

hood of Lake Titicaca;[14] a conclusion strongly confirmed by the imposing architectural remains which still endure, after the lapse of so many
years, on its borders. Who this race were, and whence they came, may
afford a tempting theme for inquiry to the speculative antiquarian. But it
is a land of darkness that lies far beyond the domain of history.[15]

The same mists that hang round the origin of the Incas continue to
settle on their subsequent annals; and, so imperfect were the records
employed by the Peruvians, and so confused and contradictory their traditions, that the historian finds no firm footing on which to stand till
within a century of the Spanish conquest.[16] At first, the progress of the
Peruvians seems to have been slow, and almost imperceptible. By their
wise and temperate policy, they gradually won over the neighboring
tribes to their dominion, as these latter became more and more convinced
of the benefits of a just and well-regulated government. As they grew
stronger, they were enabled to rely more directly on force; but, still
advancing under cover of the same beneficent pretexts employed by their
predecessors, they proclaimed peace and civilization at the point of the
sword. The rude nations of the country, without any principle of cohesion among themselves, fell one after another before the victorious arm
of the Incas. Yet it was not till the middle of the fifteenth century that
the famous Topa Inca Yupanqui, grandfather of the monarch who occu-

---

[14] Among other authorities for this tradition, see Sarmiento, Relacion, MS., cap.
3, 4,—Herrera, Hist. General, dec. 5, lib. 3, cap. 6,—Conq. i Pob. del Piru, MS.,—
Zarate, Historia del Descubrimiento y de la Conquista del Peru, lib. 1, cap. 10, ap.
Barcia, Historiadores Primitivos de las Indias Occidentales, (Madrid, 1749,) tom. 3.

In most, not all, of the traditions, Manco Capac is recognized as the name of the
founder of the Peruvian monarchy, though his history and character are related with
sufficient discrepancy.

[15] Mr. Ranking,

> "Who can deep mysteries unriddle,
> As easily as thread a needle,"

finds it "highly probable that the first Inca of Peru was a son of the Grand Khan
Kublai!" (Historical Researches on the Conquest of Peru, &c., by the Moguls,
(London, 1827,) p. 170.) The coincidences are curious, though we shall hardly
jump at the conclusion of the adventurous author. Every scholar will agree with
Humboldt, in the wish that "some learned traveller would visit the borders of the
lake of Titicaca, the district of Callao, and the high plains of Tiahuanaco, the
theatre of the ancient American civilization." (Vues des Cordillères, p. 199.) And
yet the architectural monuments of the aborigines, hitherto brought to light, have
furnished few materials for a bridge of communication across the dark gulf that
still separates the Old World from the New.

[16] A good deal within a century, to say truth. Garcilasso and Sarmiento, for example, the two ancient authorities in highest repute, have scarcely a point of contact in their accounts of the earlier Peruvian princes; the former representing the
sceptre as gliding down in peaceful succession from hand to hand, through an unbroken dynasty, while the latter garnishes his tale with as many conspiracies, depositions, and revolutions, as belong to most barbarous, and, unhappily, most civilized communities. When to these two are added the various writers, contemporary
and of the succeeding age, who have treated of the Peruvian annals, we shall find
ourselves in such a conflict of traditions that criticism is lost in conjecture. Yet this
uncertainty as to historical events fortunately does not extend to the history of
arts and institutions, which were in existence on the arrival of the Spaniards.

oied the throne at the coming of the Spaniards, led his armies across the terrible desert of Atacama, and, penetrating to the southern region of Chili, fixed the permanent boundary of his dominions at the river Maule. His son, Huayna Capac, possessed of ambition and military talent fully equal to his father's, marched along the Cordillera towards the north, and, pushing his conquests across the equator, added the powerful kingdom of Quito to the empire of Peru.[17]

The ancient city of Cuzco, meanwhile, had been gradually advancing in wealth and population, till it had become the worthy metropolis of a great and flourishing monarchy. It stood in a beautiful valley on an elevated region of the plateau, which, among the Alps, would have been buried in eternal snows, but which within the tropics enjoyed a genial and salubrious temperature. Towards the north it was defended by a lofty eminence, a spur of the great Cordillera; and the city was traversed by a river, or rather a small stream, over which bridges of timber, covered with heavy slabs of stone, furnished an easy means of communication with the opposite banks. The streets were long and narrow; the houses low, and those of the poorer sort built of clay and reeds. But Cuzco was the royal residence, and was adorned with the ample dwellings of the great nobility; and the massy fragments still incorporated in many of the modern edifices bear testimony to the size and solidity of the ancient.[18]

The health of the city was promoted by spacious openings and squares, in which a numerous population from the capital and the distant country assembled to celebrate the high festivals of their religion. For Cuzco was the "Holy City";[19] and the great temple of the Sun, to which pilgrims resorted from the furthest borders of the empire, was the most magnificent structure in the New World, and unsurpassed, probably, in the costliness of its decorations by any building in the Old.

[17] Sarmiento, Relacion, MS., cap. 57, 64.—Conq. i Pob. del Piru, MS.—Velasco, Hist. de Quito, p. 59.—Dec. de la Aud. Real., MS.—Garcilasso, Com. Real., Parte i, lib. 7, cap. 18, 19; lib. 8, cap. 5-8.
The last historian, and, indeed, some others, refer the conquest of Chili to Yupanqui, the father of Topa Inca. The exploits of the two monarchs are so blended together by the different annalists, as in a manner to confound their personal identity.
[18] Garcilasso, Com. Real., lib. 7, cap. 8-11.—Cieza de Leon, Cronica, cap. 92.
"El Cuzco tuuo gran manera y calidad, deuio ser fundada por gente de gran ser. Auia grandes calles, saluo q̄ erā angostas, y las casas hechas de piedra pura cō tan lindas junturas, q̄ illustra el antiguedad del edificio, pues estauan piedras tan grādes muy bien assentadas." (Ibid., ubi supra.) Compare with this Miller's account of the city, as existing at the present day. "The walls of many of the houses have remained unaltered for centuries. The great size of the stones, the variety of their shapes, and the inimitable workmanship they display, give to the city that interesting air of antiquity and romance, which fills the mind with pleasing though painful veneration." Memoirs of Gen. Miller in the Service of the Republic of Peru, (London, 1829, 2d ed.) vol. II. p. 225.
[19] "La Imperial Ciudad de Cozco, que la adoravan los Indios, como á Cosa Sagrada." Garcilasso. Com. Real.. Parte i, lib. 3, cap. 20.—Also Ondegardo, Rel. Seg., MS

Towards the north, on the sierra or rugged eminence already noticed, rose a strong fortress, the remains of which at the present day, by their vast size, excite the admiration of the traveller.[20] It was defended by a single wall of great thickness, and twelve hundred feet long on the side facing the city, where the precipitous character of the ground was of itself almost sufficient for its defence. On the other quarter, where the approaches were less difficult, it was protected by two other semicircular walls of the same length as the preceding. They were separated, a considerable distance from one another and from the fortress; and the intervening ground was raised so that the walls afforded a breastwork for the troops stationed there in times of assault. The fortress consisted of three towers, detached from one another. One was appropriated to the Inca, and was garnished with the sumptuous decorations befitting a royal residence, rather than a military post. The other two were held by the garrison, drawn from the Peruvian nobles, and commanded by an officer of the blood royal; for the position was of too great importance to be intrusted to inferior hands. The hill was excavated below the towers, and several subterraneous galleries communicated with the city and the palaces of the Inca.[21]

The fortress, the walls, and the galleries were all built of stone, the heavy blocks of which were not laid in regular courses, but so disposed that the small ones might fill up the interstices between the great. They formed a sort of rustic work, being rough-hewn except towards the edges, which were finely wrought; and, though no cement was used, the several blocks were adjusted with so much exactness and united so closely, that it was impossible to introduce even the blade of a knife between them.[22] Many of these stones were of vast size; some of them being full thirty-eight feet long, by eighteen broad, and six feet thick.[23]

We are filled with astonishment, when we consider, that these enormous masses were hewn from their native bed and fashioned into shape,

[20] See, among others, the Memoirs, above cited, of Gen. Miller, which contain a minute and very interesting notice of modern Cuzco. (Vol. II. p. 223, et seq.) Ulloa, who visited the country in the middle of the last century, is unbounded in his expressions of admiration. Voyage to South America, Eng. trans., (London, 1806,) book VII. ch. 12.

[21] Betanzos, Suma y Narracion de los Yngas, MS., cap. 12.—Garcilasso, Com. Real., Parte 1, lib. 7, cap. 27-29.

The demolition of the fortress, begun immediately after the Conquest, provoked the remonstrance of more than one enlightened Spaniard, whose voice, however, was impotent against the spirit of cupidity and violence. See Sarmiento, Relacion, MS., cap. 48.

[22] Ibid., ubi supra.—Inscripciones, Medallas, Templos, Edificios, Antiguedades, y Monumentos del Peru, MS. This manuscript, which formerly belonged to Dr. Robertson, and which is now in the British Museum, is the work of some unknown author, somewhere probably about the time of Charles III.; a period when, as the sagacious scholar to whom I am indebted for a copy of it remarks, a spirit of sounder criticism was visible in the Castilian historians.

[23] Acosta, Naturall and Morall Historie of the East and West Indies, Eng. trans., (London, 1604,) lib. 6, cap. 14.—He measured the stones himself.—See also Garcilasso, Com. Real., loc. cit.

by a people ignorant of the use of iron; that they were brought from quarries, from four to fifteen leagues distant,[24] without the aid of beasts of burden; were transported across rivers and ravines, raised to their elevated position on the sierra, and finally adjusted there with the nicest accuracy, without the knowledge of tools and machinery familiar to the European. Twenty thousand men are said to have been employed on this great structure, and fifty years consumed in the building.[25] However this may be, we see in it the workings of a despotism which had the lives and fortunes of its vassals at its absolute disposal, and which, however mild in its general character, esteemed these vassals, when employed in its service, as lightly as the brute animals for which they served as a substitute.

The fortress of Cuzco was but part of a system of fortifications established throughout their dominions by the Incas. This system formed a prominent feature in their military policy; but before entering on this latter, it will be proper to give the reader some view of their civil institutions and scheme of government.

The sceptre of the Incas, if we may credit their historian, descended in unbroken succession from father to son, through their whole dynasty. Whatever we may think of this, it appears probable that the right of inheritance might be claimed by the eldest son of the *Coya*, or lawful queen, as she was styled, to distinguish her from the host of concubines who shared the affections of the sovereign.[26] The queen was further distinguished, at least in later reigns, by the circumstance of being selected from the sisters of the Inca, an arrangement which, however revolting to the ideas of civilized nations, was recommended to the Peruvians by its securing an heir to the crown of the pure heaven-born race, uncontaminated by any mixture of earthly mould.[27]

In his early years, the royal offspring was intrusted to the care of the *amautas*, or "wise men," as the teachers of Peruvian science were called,

---

[24] Cieza de Leon, Cronica, cap. 93.—Ondegardo, Rel. Seg., MS.

Many hundred blocks of granite may still be seen, it is said, in an unfinished state, in a quarry near Cuzco.

[25] Sarmiento, Relacion, MS., cap. 48.—Ondegardo, Rel. Seg., MS.—Garcilasso, Com. Real., Parte 1, lib. 7, cap. 27, 28.

The Spaniards, puzzled by the execution of so great a work with such apparently inadequate means, referred it all, in their summary way, to the Devil; an opinion which Garcilasso seems willing to indorse. The author of the Antig. y Monumentos del Peru, MS., rejects this notion with becoming gravity.

[26] Sarmiento, Relacion, MS., cap. 7.—Garcilasso, Com. Real., Parte 1, lib. 1, cap. 26.

Acosta speaks of the eldest brother of the Inca as succeeding in preference to the son. (lib. 6, cap. 12.) He may have confounded the Peruvian with the Aztec usage. The Report of the Royal Audience states that a brother succeeded in default of a son. Dec. de la Aud. Real., MS.

[27] *"Et soror et conjux."*—According to Garcilasso, the heir-apparent *always* married a sister. (Com. Real., Parte 1, lib. 4, cap. 9.) Ondegardo notices this as an innovation at the close of the fifteenth century. (Relacion Primera, MS.) The historian of the Incas, however, is confirmed in his extraordinary statement by Sarmiento Relacion, MS., cap. 7.

who instructed him in such elements of knowledge as they possessed, and especially in the cumbrous ceremonial of their religion, in which he was to take a prominent part. Great care was also bestowed on his military education, of the last importance in a state which, with its professions of peace and good-will, was ever at war for the acquisition of empire.

In this military school he was educated with such of the Inca nobles as were nearly of his own age; for the sacred name of Inca—a fruitful source of obscurity in their annals—was applied indifferently to all who descended by the male line from the founder of the monarchy.[28] At the age of sixteen the pupils underwent a public examination, previous to their admission to what may be called the order of chivalry. This examination was conducted by some of the oldest and most illustrious Incas. The candidates were required to show their prowess in the athletic exercises of the warrior; in wrestling and boxing, in running such long courses as fully tried their agility and strength, in severe fasts of several days' duration, and in mimic combats, which, although the weapons were blunted, were always attended with wounds, and sometimes with death. During this trial, which lasted thirty days, the royal neophyte fared no better than his comrades, sleeping on the bare ground, going unshod, and wearing a mean attire,—a mode of life, it was supposed, which might tend to inspire him with more sympathy with the destitute. With all this show of impartiality, however, it will probably be doing no injustice to the judges to suppose that a politic discretion may have somewhat quickened their perceptions of the real merits of the heir-apparent.

At the end of the appointed time, the candidates selected as worthy of the honors of their barbaric chivalry were presented to the sovereign, who condescended to take a principal part in the ceremony of inauguration. He began with a brief discourse, in which, after congratulating the young aspirants on the proficiency they had shown in martial exercises, he reminded them of the responsibilities attached to their birth and station; and, addressing them affectionately as "children of the Sun," he exhorted them to imitate their great progenitor in his glorious career of beneficence to mankind. The novices then drew near, and, kneeling one by one before the Inca, he pierced their ears with a golden bodkin; and this was suffered to remain there till an opening had been made large enough for the enormous pendants which were peculiar to their order, and which gave them, with the Spaniards, the name of *orejones*.[29] This

---

[28] Garcilasso, Com. Real., Parte 1, lib. 1, cap. 26.

[29] From *oreja*, "ear."—"Los caballeros de la sangre Real tenian orejas horadadas, y de ellas colgando grandes rodetes de plata y oro: llamaronles por esto los *orejones* los Castellaños la primera vez que los vieron." (Montesinos, Memorias Antiguas Historiales del Peru, MS., lib. 2, cap. 6.) The ornament, which was in the form of a wheel, did not depend on the ear, but was inserted in the gristle of it, and was as large as an orange. "La hacen tan ancha como una gran rosca de naranja; los Señores i Principales traian aquellas roscas de oro fino en las orejas." (Conq. i Pob. del Piru, MS.—Also Garcilasso, Com. Real., Parte 1, lib. 1, cap. 22.) "The larger the hole," says one of the old Conquerors, "the more of a gentleman!" Pedro Pizarro, Descub. y Conq., MS.

ornament was so massy in the ears of the sovereign, that the cartilage was distended by it nearly to the shoulder, producing what seemed a monstrous deformity in the eyes of the Europeans, though, under the magical influence of fashion, it was regarded as a beauty by the natives.

When this operation was performed, one of the most venerable of the nobles dressed the feet of the candidates in the sandals worn by the order, which may remind us of the ceremony of buckling on the spurs of the Christian knight. They were then allowed to assume the girdle or sash around the loins, corresponding with the *toga virilis* of the Romans, and intimating that they had reached the season of manhood. Their heads were adorned with garlands of flowers, which, by their various colors, were emblematic of the clemency and goodness that should grace the character of every true warrior; and the leaves of an evergreen plant were mingled with the flowers, to show that these virtues should endure without end.[30] The prince's head was further ornamented by a fillet, or tasselled fringe, of a yellow color, made of the fine threads of the vicuña wool, which encircled the forehead as the peculiar insignia of the heir-apparent. The great body of the Inca nobility next made their appearance, and, beginning with those nearest of kin, knelt down before the prince, and did him homage as successor to the crown. The whole assembly then moved to the great square of the capital, where songs, and dances, and other public festivities closed the important ceremonial of the *huaracu*.[31]

The reader will be less surprised by the resemblance which this ceremonial bears to the inauguration of a Christian knight in the feudal ages, if he reflects that a similar analogy may be traced in the institutions of other people more or less civilized; and that it is natural that nations, occupied with the one great business of war, should mark the period, when the preparatory education for it was ended, by similar characteristic ceremonies.

Having thus honorably passed through his ordeal, the heir-apparent was deemed worthy to sit in the councils of his father, and was employed in offices of trust at home, or, more usually, sent on distant expeditions to practise in the field the lessons which he had hitherto studied only in the mimic theatre of war. His first campaigns were conducted under the renowned commanders who had grown grey in the service of his father; until, advancing in years and experience, he was placed in command himself, and, like Huayna Capac, the last and most illustrious of his line, carried the banner of the rainbow, the armorial ensign of his house, far over the borders, among the remotest tribes of the plateau.

The government of Peru was a despotism, mild in its character, but in

---

[30] Garcilasso, Com. Real., Parte 1, lib. 6, cap. 27.

[31] Ibid., Parte 1, lib. 6, cap. 24-28.

According to Fernandez, the candidates wore white shirts, with something like a cross embroidered in front! (Historia del Peru, (Sevilla, 1571,) Parte 2, lib. 3, cap. 6.) We may fancy ourselves occupied with some chivalrous ceremonial of the Middle Ages.

its form a pure and unmitigated despotism. The sovereign was placed at an immeasurable distance above his subjects. Even the proudest of the Inca nobility, claiming a descent from the same divine original as himself, could not venture into the royal presence, unless barefoot, and bearing a light burden on his shoulders in token of homage.[32] As the representative of the Sun, he stood at the head of the priesthood, and presided at the most important of the religious festivals.[33] He raised armies, and usually commanded them in person. He imposed taxes, made laws, and provided for their execution by the appointment of judges, whom he removed at pleasure. He was the source from which every thing flowed,—all dignity, all power, all emolument. He was, in short, in the well-known phrase of the European despot, "himself the state." [34]

The Inca asserted his claims as a superior being by assuming a pomp in his manner of living well calculated to impose on his people. His dress was of the finest wool of the vicuña, richly dyed, and ornamented with a profusion of gold and precious stones. Round his head was wreathed a turban of many-colored folds, called the *llautu;* and a tasselled fringe, like that worn by the prince, but of a scarlet color, with two feathers of a rare and curious bird, called the *coraquenque,* placed upright in it, were the distinguishing insignia of royalty. The birds from which these feathers were obtained were found in a desert country among the mountains; and it was death to destroy or to take them, as they were reserved for the exclusive purpose of supplying the royal head-gear. Every succeeding monarch was provided with a new pair of these plumes, and his credulous subjects fondly believed that only two individuals of the species had ever existed to furnish the simple ornament for the diadem of the Incas.[35]

Although the Peruvian monarch was raised so far above the highest of

---

[32] Zarate, Conq. del Peru, lib. 1, cap. 11.—Sarmiento, Relacion, MS., cap. 7.

"Porque verdaderamente á lo que yo he averiguado toda la pretension de los Ingas fue una subjeccion en toda la gente, qual yo nunca he oido decir de ninguna otra nacion en tanto grado, que por muy principal que un Señor fuese, dende que entrava cerca del Cuzco en cierta señal que estava puesta en cada camino de quatro que hay, havia dende alli de venir cargado hasta la presencia del Inga, y alli dejava la carga y hacia su obediencia." Ondegardo, Rel. Prim., MS.

[33] It was only at one of these festivals, and hardly authorizes the sweeping assertion of Carli, that the royal and sacerdotal authority were blended together in Peru. We shall see, hereafter, the important and independent position occupied by the high-priest. "La Sacerdoce et l'Empire étoient divisés au Mexique; au lieu qu'ils étoient réunis au Pérou, comme au Tibet et à la Chine, et comme il le fut à Rome, lorsqu' Auguste jetta les fondemens de l'Empire, en y réunissant le Sacerdoce ou la dignité de Souverain Pontife." Lettres Américaines, (Paris, 1788,) trad. Franç., tom. I. let. 7.

[34] "Porque el Inga dava á entendër que era hijo del Sol, con este titulo se hacia adorar, i governava principalmente en tanto grado que nadie se le atrevia, i su palabra era ley, i nadie osaba ir contra su palabra ni voluntad; aunque obiese de matar cient mill Indios, no havia ninguno en su Reino que le osase decir que no lo hiciese." Conq. i Pob. del Piru, MS.

[35] Cieza de Leon, Cronica, cap. 114.—Garcilasso, Com. Real., Parte 1, lib. 1, cap. 22; lib. 6, cap. 28.—Acosta, lib. 6, cap. 12.

his subjects, he condescended to mingle occasionally with them, and took great pains personally to inspect the condition of the humbler classes. He presided at some of the religious celebrations, and on these occasions entertained the great nobles at his table, when he complimented them, after the fashion of more civilized nations, by drinking the health of those whom he most delighted to honor.[36]

But the most effectual means taken by the Incas for communicating with their people were their progresses through the empire. These were conducted, at intervals of several years, with great state and magnificence. The sedan, or litter, in which they travelled, richly emblazoned with gold and emeralds, was guarded by a numerous escort. The men who bore it on their shoulders were provided by two cities, specially appointed for the purpose. It was a post to be coveted by no one, if, as is asserted, a fall was punished by death.[37] They travelled with ease and expedition, halting at the *tambos*, or inns, erected by government along the route, and occasionally at the royal palaces, which in the great towns afforded ample accommodations to the whole of the monarch's retinue. The noble roads which traversed the table-land were lined with people, who swept away the stones and stubble from their surface, strewing them with sweet-scented flowers, and vying with each other in carrying forward the baggage from one village to another. The monarch halted from time to time to listen to the grievances of his subjects, or to settle some points which had been referred to his decision by the regular tribunals. As the princely train wound its way along the mountain passes, every place was thronged with spectators eager to catch a glimpse of their sovereign; and, when he raised the curtains of his litter, and showed himself to their eyes, the air was rent with acclamations as they invoked blessings on his head.[38] Tradition long commemorated the spots at which

[36] One would hardly expect to find among the American Indians this social and kindly custom of our Saxon ancestors,—now fallen somewhat out of use, in the capricious innovations of modern fashion. Garcilasso is diffuse in his account of the forms observed at the royal table. (Com. Real., Parte 1, lib. 6, cap. 23.) The only hours of eating were at eight or nine in the morning, and at sunset, which took place at nearly the same time, in all seasons, in the latitude of Cuzco. The historian of the Incas admits that, though temperate in eating, they indulged freely in their cups, frequently prolonging their revelry to a late hour of the night. Ibid., Parte 1, lib. 6, cap. 1.

[37] "In lecticâ, aureo tabulato constratâ, humeris ferebant; in ummâ, ea erat observantia, vt vultum ejus intueri maxime incivile putarent, et inter baiulos, quicunque vel leviter pede offenso hæsitaret, e vestigio interficerent." Levinus Apollonius, De Peruviæ Regionis Inventione, et Rebus in eâdem gestis, (Antverpiæ, 1567,) fol. 37.—Zarate, Conq. del Peru, lib. 1, cap. 11.

According to this writer, the litter was carried by the nobles; one thousand of whom were specially reserved for the humiliating honor. Ubi supra.

[38] The acclamations must have been potent indeed, if, as Sarmiento tells us, they sometimes brought the birds down from the sky! "De esta manera eran tan temidos los Reyes que si salian por el Reyno y permitian alzar algun paño de los que iban en las andas para dejarse ver de sus vasallos, alzaban tan gran alarido que hacian caer las aves de lo alto donde iban volando á ser tomadas á manos." (Relacion, MS., cap. 10.)

he halted, and the simple people of the country held them in reverence as places consecrated by the presence of an Inca.[39]

The royal palaces were on a magnificent scale, and, far from being confined to the capital or a few principal towns, were scattered over all the provinces of their vast empire.[40] The buildings were low, but covered a wide extent of ground. Some of the apartments were spacious, but they were generally small, and had no communication with one another, except that they opened into a common square or court. The walls were made of blocks of stone of various sizes, like those described in the fortress of Cuzco, rough-hewn, but carefully wrought near the line of junction, which was scarcely visible to the eye. The roofs were of wood or rushes, which have perished under the rude touch of time, that has shown more respect for the walls of the edifices. The whole seems to have been characterized by solidity and strength, rather than by any attempt at architectural elegance.[41]

But whatever want of elegance there may have been in the exterior of the imperial dwellings, it was amply compensated by the interior, in which all the opulence of the Peruvian princes was ostentatiously displayed. The sides of the apartments were thickly studded with gold and silver ornaments. Niches, prepared in the walls, were filled with images of animals and plants curiously wrought of the same costly materials; and even much of the domestic furniture, including the utensils devoted to the most ordinary menial services, displayed the like wanton magnificence![42] With these gorgeous decorations were mingled richly colored stuffs of the delicate manufacture of the Peruvian wool, which were of so beautiful a texture, that the Spanish sovereigns, with all the luxuries of Europe and Asia at their command, did not disdain to use them.[43] The royal household consisted of a throng of menials, supplied by the neighboring towns and villages, which, as in Mexico, were bound to

[39] Garcilasso, Com. Real., Parte 1, lib. 3, cap. 14; lib. 6, cap. 3.—Zarate, Conq. del Peru, lib. 1, cap. 11.

[40] Velasco has given some account of several of these palaces situated in different places in the kingdom of Quito. Hist. de Quito, tom. I. pp. 195-197.

[41] Cieza de Leon, Cronica, cap. 44.—Antig. y Monumentos del Peru, MS.—See, among others, the description of the remains still existing of the royal buildings at Callo, about ten leagues south of Quito, by Ulloa, Voyage to S. America, book 6, ch. 11, and since, more carefully, by Humboldt, Vues des Cordillères, p. 197.

[42] Garcilasso, Com. Real., Parte 1, lib. 6, cap. 1.

"Tanto que todo el servicio de la Casa del Rey así de cantaras para su vino, *como de cozina,* todo era oro y plata, y esto no en un lugar y en una parte lo tenia, sino en muchas." (Sarmiento, Relacion, MS., cap. 11.) See also the flaming accounts of the palaces of Bilcas, to the west of Cuzco, by Cieza de Leon, as reported to him by Spaniards who had seen them in their glory. (Cronica, cap. 89.) The niches are still described by modern travellers as to be found in the walls. (Humboldt, Vues des Cordillères, p. 197.)

[43] "La ropa de la cama toda era de mantas, y freçadas de lana de Vicuña, que es tan fina, y tan regalada, que entre otras cosas preciadas de aquellas Tierras, se las han traido para la cama del Rey Don Phelipe Segundo." Garcilasso, Com. Real., Parte 1, lib. 6, cap. 1.

furnish the monarch with fuel and other necessaries for the consumption of the palace.

But the favorite residence of the Incas was at Yucay, about four leagues distant from the capital. In this delicious valley, locked up within the friendly arms of the sierra, which sheltered it from the rude breezes of the east, and refreshed by gushing fountains and streams of running water, they built the most beautiful of their palaces. Here, when wearied with the dust and toil of the city, they loved to retreat, and solace themselves with the society of their favorite concubines, wandering amidst groves and airy gardens, that shed around their soft, intoxicating odors, and lulled the senses to voluptuous repose. Here, too, they loved to indulge in the luxury of their baths, replenished by streams of crystal water which were conducted through subterraneous silver channels into basins of gold. The spacious gardens were stocked with numerous varieties of plants and flowers that grew without effort in this *temperate* region of the tropics, while parterres of a more extraordinary kind were planted by their side, glowing with the various forms of vegetable life skilfully imitated in gold and silver! Among them the Indian corn, the most beautiful of American grains, is particularly commemorated, and the curious workmanship is noticed with which the golden ear was half disclosed amidst the broad leaves of silver, and the light tassel of the same material that floated gracefully from its top.[44]

If this dazzling picture staggers the faith of the reader, he may reflect that the Peruvian mountains teemed with gold; that the natives understood the art of working the mines, to a considerable extent; that none of the ore, as we shall see hereafter, was converted into coin, and that the whole of it passed into the hands of the sovereign for his own exclusive benefit, whether for purposes of utility or ornament. Certain it is that no fact is better attested by the Conquerors themselves, who had ample means of information, and no motive for misstatement.—The Italian poets, in their gorgeous pictures of the gardens of Alcina and Morgana, came nearer the truth than they imagined.

Our surprise, however, may reasonably be excited, when we consider that the wealth displayed by the Peruvian princes was only that which each had amassed individually for himself. He owed nothing to inheritance from his predecessors. On the decease of an Inca, his palaces were abandoned, all his treasures, except what were employed in his obsequies, his furniture and apparel, were suffered to remain as he left them, and his mansions, save one, were closed up for ever. The new sovereign was to provide himself with every thing new for his royal state. The reason of this was the popular belief, that the soul of the departed monarch

---

[44] Garcilasso, Com. Real., Parte 1, lib. 5, cap. 26; lib. 6, cap. 2.—Sarmiento, Relacion, MS., cap. 24.—Cieza de Leon, Cronica, cap. 94.

The last writer speaks of a cement, made in part of liquid gold, as used in the royal buildings of Tambo, a valley not far from Yucay! (Ubi supra.) We may excuse the Spaniards for demolishing such edifices,—if they ever met with them

would return after a time to reänimate his body on earth; and they wished that he should find every thing to which he had been used in life prepared for his reception.[45]

When an Inca died, or, to use his own language, "was called home to the mansions of his father, the Sun," [46] his obsequies were celebrated with great pomp and solemnity. The bowels were taken from the body, and deposited in the temple of Tampu, about five leagues from the capital. A quantity of his plate and jewels was buried with them, and a number of his attendants and favorite concubines, amounting sometimes, it is said, to a thousand, were immolated on his tomb.[47] Some of them showed the natural repugnance to the sacrifice occasionally manifested by the victims of a similar superstition in India. But these were probably the menials and more humble attendants; since the women have been known, in more than one instance, to lay violent hands on themselves, when restrained from testifying their fidelity by this act of conjugal martyrdom. This melancholy ceremony was followed by a general mourning throughout the empire. At stated intervals, for a year, the people assembled to renew the expressions of their sorrow, processions were made, displaying the banner of the departed monarch; bards and minstrels were appointed to chronicle his achievements, and their songs continued to be rehearsed at high festivals in the presence of the reigning monarch,—thus stimulating the living by the glorious example of the dead.[48]

The body of the deceased Inca was skilfully embalmed, and removed to the great temple of the Sun at Cuzco. There the Peruvian sovereign, on entering the awful sanctuary, might behold the effigies of his royal ancestors, ranged in opposite files,—the men on the right, and their queens on the left, of the great luminary which blazed in refulgent gold on the walls of the temple. The bodies, clothed in the princely attire which they had been accustomed to wear, were placed on chairs of gold, and sat with their heads inclined downward, their hands placidly crossed over their bosoms, their countenances exhibiting their natural dusky hue,—less liable to change than the fresher coloring of a European complexion,—and their hair of raven black, or silvered over with age, according to the period at which they died! It seemed like a company of solemn worshippers fixed in devotion,—so true were the forms and lineaments to life. The Peruvians were as successful as the Egyptians in the miserable attempt to perpetuate the existence of the body beyond the limits assigned to it by nature.[49]

[45] Acosta, lib. 6, cap. 12.—Garcilasso, Com. Real., Parte 1, lib. 6, cap. 4.

[46] The Aztecs, also, believed that the soul of the warrior who fell in battle went to accompany the Sun in his bright progress through the heavens. (See Conquest of Mexico, book 1, chap. 3.)

[47] Conq. i Pob. del Piru, MS.—Acosta, lib. 5, cap. 6.

Four thousand of these victims, according to Sarmiento,—we may hope it is an exaggeration,—graced the funeral obsequies of Huayna Capac, the last of the Incas before the coming of the Spaniards. Relacion, MS., cap. 65.

[48] Cieza de Leon, Cronica, cap. 62.—Garcilasso, Com. Real., Parte 1, lib. 6, cap. 5.—Sarmiento, Relacion, MS. cap. 8.

[49] Ondegardo, Rel. Prim., MS.—Garcilasso, Com. Real., Parte 1, lib. 5, cap. 29.

The Peruvians secreted these mummies of their sovereigns after the Conquest, that

They cherished a still stranger illusion in the attentions which they continued to pay to these insensible remains, as if they were instinct with life. One of the houses belonging to a deceased Inca was kept open and occupied by his guard and attendants, with all the state appropriate to royalty. On certain festivals, the revered bodies of the sovereigns were brought out with great ceremony into the public square of the capital. Invitations were sent by the captains of the guard of the respective Incas to the different nobles and officers of the court; and entertainments were provided in the names of their masters, which displayed all the profuse magnificence of their treasures,—and "such a display," says an ancient chronicler, "was there in the great square of Cuzco, on this occasion, of gold and silver plate and jewels, as no other city in the world ever witnessed." [50] The banquet was served by the menials of the respective households, and the guests partook of the melancholy cheer in the presence of the royal phantom with the same attention to the forms of courtly etiquette as if the living monarch had presided! [51]

The nobility of Peru consisted of two orders, the first and by far the most important of which was that of the Incas, who, boasting a common descent with their sovereign, lived, as it were, in the reflected light ol his glory. As the Peruvian monarchs availed themselves of the right of polygamy to a very liberal extent, leaving behind them families of one or even two hundred children,[52] the nobles of the blood royal, though comprehending only their descendants in the male line, came in the course of years to be very numerous.[53] They were divided into different lineages,

they might not be profaned by the insults of the Spaniards. Ondegardo, when *corregidor* of Cuzco, discovered five of them, three male and two female. The former were the bodies of Viracocha, of the great Tupac Inca Yupanqui, and of his son Huayna Capac. Garcilasso saw them in 1560. They were dressed in their regal robes, with no insignia but the *llautu* on their heads. They were in a sitting posture, and, to use his own expression, "perfect as life, without so much as a hair or an eyebrow wanting." As they were carried through the streets, decently shrouded with a mantle, the Indians threw themselves on their knees, in sign of reverence, with many tears and groans, and were still more touched as they beheld some of the Spaniards themselves doffing their caps, in token of respect to departed royalty. (Ibid., ubi supra.) The bodies were subsequently removed to Lima; and Father Acosta, who saw them there some twenty years later, speaks of them as still in perfect preservation.

[50] "Tenemos por muy cierto que ni en Jerusalem, Roma, ni en Persia, ni en ninguna parte del mundo por ninguna Republica ni Rey de el, se juntaba en un lugar tanta riqueza de Metales de oro y Plata y Pedreria como en esta Plaza del Cuzco; quando estas fiestas y otras semejantes se hacian." Sarmiento, Relacion, MS., cap. 27.

[51] Idem, Relacion, MS., cap. 8, 27.—Ondegardo, Rel. Seg., MS.

It was only, however, the great and good princes that were thus honored, according to Sarmiento, "whose souls the silly people fondly believed, on account of their virtues, were in heaven, although, in truth," as the same writer assures us, "they were all the time burning in the flames of hell!" "Digo los que haviendo sido en vida buenos y valerosos, generosos con los Indios en les hacer mercedes, perdonadores de injurias, porque á estos tales canonizaban en su ceguedad por Santos y honrraban sus huesos, sin entender que las animas ardian en los Ynfiernos y creian que estaban en el Cielo." Ibid., ubi supra.

[52] Garcilasso says over three hundred! (Com. Real., Parte 1, lib. 3, cap. 19.) The fact, though rather startling, is not incredible, if, like Huayna Capac, they counted seven hundred wives in their seraglio. See Sarmiento, Relacion, MS., cap. 7.

[53] Garcilasso mentions a class of Incas *por privilegio,* who were allowed to possess

each of which traced its pedigree to a different member of the royal dynasty, though all terminated in the divine founder of the empire.

They were distinguished by many exclusive and very important privileges; they wore a peculiar dress; spoke a dialect, if we may believe the chronicler, peculiar to themselves;[54] and had the choicest portion of the public domain assigned for their support. They lived, most of them, at court, near the person of the prince, sharing in his counsels, dining at his board, or supplied from his table. They alone were admissible to the great offices in the priesthood. They were invested with the command of armies, and of distant garrisons, were placed over the provinces, and, in short, filled every station of high trust and emolument.[55] Even the laws, severe in their general tenor, seem not to have been framed with reference to them; and the people, investing the whole order with a portion of the sacred character which belonged to the sovereign, held that an Inca noble was incapable of crime.[56]

The other order of nobility was the *Curacas*, the caciques of the conquered nations, or their descendants. They were usually continued by the government in their places, though they were required to visit the capital occasionally, and to allow their sons to be educated there as the pledges of their loyalty. It is not easy to define the nature or extent of their privileges. They were possessed of more or less power, according to the extent of their patrimony, and the number of their vassals. Their authority was usually transmitted from father to son, though sometimes the successor was chosen by the people.[57] They did not occupy the highest posts of state, or those nearest the person of the sovereign, like the nobles of the blood. Their authority seems to have been usually local, and always in subordination to the territorial jurisdiction of the great provincial governors, who were taken from the Incas.[58]

the name and many of the immunities of the blood royal, though only descended from the great vassals that first served under the banner of Manco Capac. (Com. Real., Parte 1, lib. 1, cap. 22.) This important fact, to which he often refers, one would be glad to see confirmed by a single authority.

[54] "Los Incas tuvieron otra Lengua particular, que hablavan entre ellos, que no la entendian los demàs Indios, ni les era licito aprenderla, como Lenguage Divino. Esta me escriven del Perù, que se ha perdido totalmente; porque como pereciò la Republica particular de los Incas, pereciò tambien el Lenguage dellos." Garcilasso, Com. Real., Parte 1, lib. 7, cap. 1.

[55] "Una sola gente hallo yo que era exenta, que eran los Ingas del Cuzco y por alli al rededor de ambas parcialidades, porque estos no solo no pagavan tributo, pero aun comian de lo que traian al Inga de todo el reino, y estos eran por la mayor parte los Governadores en todo el reino, y por donde quiera que iban se les hacia mucha honrra." Ondegardo, Rel. Prim., MS.

[56] Garcilasso, Com. Real., Parte 1, lib. 2, cap. 15.

[57] In this event, it seems, the successor named was usually presented to the Inca for confirmation. (Dec. de la Aud. Real., MS.) At other times, the Inca himself selected the heir from among the children of the deceased Curaca. "In short," says Ondegardo, "there was no rule of succession so sure, but it might be set aside by the supreme will of the sovereign." Rel. Prim., MS.

[58] Garcilasso, Com. Real., Parte 1, lib. 4, cap. 10.—Sarmiento, Relacion, MS., cap. 11.—Dec. de la Aud. Real., MS.—Cieza de Leon. Cronica, cap. 93.—Conq. i Pob. del Piru, MS.

It was the Inca nobility, indeed, who constituted the real strength of the Peruvian monarchy. Attached to their prince by ties of consanguinity, they had common sympathies and, to a considerable extent, common interests with him. Distinguished by a peculiar dress and insignia, as well as by language and blood, from the rest of the community, they were never confounded with the other tribes and nations who were incorporated into the great Peruvian monarchy. After the lapse of centuries, they still retained their individuality as a peculiar people. They were to the conquered races of the country what the Romans were to the barbarous hordes of the Empire, or the Normans to the ancient inhabitants of the British Isles. Clustering around the throne, they formed an invincible phalanx, to shield it alike from secret conspiracy and open insurrection. Though living chiefly in the capital, they were also distributed throughout the country in all its high stations and strong military posts, thus establishing lines of communication with the court, which enabled the sovereign to act simultaneously and with effect on the most distant quarters of his empire. They possessed, moreover, an intellectual preëminence, which, no less than their station, gave them authority with the people. Indeed, it may be said to have been the principal foundation of their authority. The crania of the Inca race show a decided superiority over the other races of the land in intellectual power;[59] and it cannot be denied that it was the fountain of that peculiar civilization and social polity, which raised the Peruvian monarchy above every other state in South America. Whence this remarkable race came, and what was its early history, are among those mysteries that meet us so frequently in the annals of the New World, and which time and the antiquary have as yet done little to explain.

[59] Dr. Morton's valuable work contains several engravings of both the Inca and the common Peruvian skull, showing that the facial angle in the former, though by no means great, was much larger than that in the latter, which was singularly flat and deficient in intellectual character. Crania Americana, (Philadelphia, 1829.)

CHAPTER II

ORDERS OF THE STATE—PROVISIONS FOR JUSTICE—DIVISION OF LANDS
—REVENUES AND REGISTERS—GREAT ROADS AND POSTS—MILI-
TARY TACTICS AND POLICY

IF we are surprised at the peculiar and original features of what may be
called the Peruvian aristocracy, we shall be still more so as we descend to
the lower orders of the community, and see the very artificial character
of their institutions,—as artificial as those of ancient Sparta, and, though
in a different way, quite as repugnant to the essential principles of our
nature. The institutions of Lycurgus, however, were designed for a petty
state, while those of Peru, although originally intended for such, seemed,
like the magic tent in the Arabian tale, to have an indefinite power of
expansion, and were as well suited to the most flourishing condition of the
empire as to its infant fortunes. In this remarkable accommodation to
change of circumstances we see the proofs of a contrivance that argues
no slight advance in civilization.

The name of Peru was not known to the natives. It was given by the
Spaniards, and originated, it is said, in a misapprehension of the Indian
name of "river." [1] However this may be, it is certain that the natives had
no other epithet by which to designate the large collection of tribes and
nations who were assembled under the sceptre of the Incas, than that of
Tavantinsuyu, or "four quarters of the world." [2] This will not surprise a
citizen of the United States, who has no other name by which to class
himself among nations than what is borrowed from a quarter of the globe.[3]
The kingdom, conformably to its name, was divided into four parts, distinguished each by a separate title, and to each of which ran one of the
four great roads that diverged from Cuzco, the capital or *navel* of the

[1] Pelu, according to Garcilasso, was the Indian name for "river," and was given
by one of the natives in answer to a question put to him by the Spaniards, who conceived it to be the name of the country. (Com. Real., Parte 1, lib. 1, cap. 6.) Such
blunders have led to the names of many places both in North and South America.
Montesinos, however, denies that there is such an Indian term for "river." (Mem.
Antiguas, MS., lib. 1, cap. 2.) According to this writer, Peru was the ancient *Ophir*,
whence Solomon drew such stores of wealth; and which, by a very *natural* transition, has in time been corrupted into *Phiru, Piru, Peru!* The first book of the Memorias, consisting of thirty-two chapters, is devoted to this precious discovery.

[2] Ondegardo, Rel. Prim., MS.—Garcilasso, Com. Real., Parte 1, lib. 2, cap. 11.

[3] Yet an *American* may find food for his vanity in the reflection, that the name of
a quarter of the globe, inhabited by so many civilized nations, has been exclusively
conceded to him.—Was it conceded or assumed?

Peruvian monarchy. The city was in like manner divided into four quarters; and the various races, which gathered there from the distant parts of the empire, lived each in the quarter nearest to its respective province. They all continued to wear their peculiar national costume, so that it was easy to determine their origin; and the same order and system of arrangement prevailed in the motley population of the capital, as in the great provinces of the empire. The capital, in fact, was a miniature image of the empire.[4]

The four great provinces were each placed under a viceroy or governor, who ruled over them with the assistance of one or more councils for the different departments. These viceroys resided, some portion of their time, at least, in the capital, where they constituted a sort of council of state to the Inca.[5] The nation at large was distributed into decades, or small bodies of ten; and every tenth man, or head of a decade, had supervision of the rest,—being required to see that they enjoyed the rights and immunities to which they were entitled, to solicit aid in their behalf from government, when necessary, and to bring offenders to justice. To this last they were stimulated by a law that imposed on them, in case of neglect, the same penalty that would have been incurred by the guilty party. With this law hanging over his head, the magistrate of Peru, we may well believe, did not often go to sleep on his post.[6]

The people were still further divided into bodies of fifty, one hundred, five hundred, and a thousand, with each an officer having general supervision over those beneath, and the higher ones possessing, to a certain extent, authority in matters of police. Lastly, the whole empire was distributed into sections or departments of ten thousand inhabitants, with a governor over each, from the Inca nobility, who had control over the *curacas* and other territorial officers in the district. There were, also, regular tribunals of justice, consisting of magistrates in each of the towns or small communities, with jurisdiction over petty offences, while those of a graver character were carried before superior judges, usually the governors or rulers of the districts. These judge all held their authority and received their support from the Crown, by which they were appointed and removed at pleasure. They were obliged to determine every suit in five days from the time it was brought before them; and there was no

[4] Ibid., parte 1, cap. 9, 10.—Cieza de Leon, Cronica, cap. 93.
The capital was further divided into two parts, the Upper and Lower town, founded, as pretended, on the different origin of the population; a division recognized also in the inferior cities. Ondegardo, Rel. Seg., MS.

[5] Dec. de la Aud. Real., MS.—Garcilasso, Com. Real., Parte 1, lib. 2, cap. 15.
For this account of the councils I am indebted to Garcilasso, who frequently fills up gaps that have been left by his fellow-laborers. Whether the filling up will, in all cases, bear the touch of time, as well as the rest of his work, one may doubt.

[6] Dec. de la Aud. Real., MS.—Montesinos, Mem. Antiguas, MS., lib. 2, cap. 6.—Ondegardo, Rel. Prim., MS.
How analogous is the Peruvian to the Anglo-Saxon division into hundreds and tithings! But the Saxon law was more humane, which imposed only a fine on the district, in case of a criminal's escape.

appeal from one tribunal to another. Yet there were important provisions for the security of justice. A committee of visitors patrolled the kingdom at certain times to investigate the character and conduct of the magistrates; and any neglect or violation of duty was punished in the most exemplary manner. The inferior courts were also required to make monthly returns of their proceedings to the higher ones, and these made reports in like manner to the viceroys; so that the monarch, seated in the centre of his dominions, could look abroad, as it were, to the most distant extremities, and review and rectify any abuses in the administration of the law.[7]

The laws were few and exceedingly severe. They related almost wholly to criminal matters. Few other laws were needed by a people who had no money, little trade, and hardly any thing that could be called fixed property. The crimes of theft, adultery, and murder were all capital; though it was wisely provided that some extenuating circumstances might be allowed to mitigate the punishment.[8] Blasphemy against the Sun, and malediction of the Inca,—offences, indeed, of the same complexion,— were also punished with death. Removing landmarks, turning the water away from a neighbor's land into one's own, burning a house, were all severely punished. To burn a bridge was death. The Inca allowed no obstacle to those facilities of communication so essential to the maintenance of public order. A rebellious city or province was laid waste, and its inhabitants exterminated. Rebellion against the "Child of the Sun," was the greatest of all crimes.[9]

The simplicity and severity of the Peruvian code may be thought to infer a state of society but little advanced; which had few of those complex interests and relations that grow up in a civilized community, and which had not proceeded far enough in the science of legislation to economize human suffering by proportioning penalties to crimes. But the Peruvian institutions must be regarded from a different point of view

[7] Dec. de la Aud. Real., MS.—Ondegardo, Rel. Prim. et Seg., MSS.—Garcilasso, Com. Real., Parte 1, lib. 2, cap. 11-14.—Montesinos, Mem. Antiguas, MS., lib. 2, cap. 6.

The accounts of the Peruvian tribunals by the early authorities are very meagre and unsatisfactory. Even the lively imagination of Garcilasso has failed to supply the blank.

[8] Ondegardo, Rel. Prim., MS.—Herrera, Hist. General, dec. 5, lib. 4, cap. 3.

Theft was punished less severely, if the offender had been really guilty of it to supply the necessities of life. It is a singular circumstance, that the Peruvian law made no distinction between fornication and adultery, both being equally punished with death. Yet the law could hardly have been enforced, since prostitutes were assigned, or at least allowed, a residence in the suburbs of the cities. See Garcilasso, Com. Real., Parte 1, lib. 4, cap. 34.

[9] Sarmiento, Relacion, MS., cap. 23.

"I los traidores entre ellos llamava *aucaes,* i esta palabra es la mas abiltada de todas quantas pueden decir aun Indio del Pirú, que quiere decir traidor á su Señor." (Conq. i Pob. del Pirú, MS.) "En las rebeliones y alzamientos se hicieron los castigos tan asperos que algunas veces asolaron las provincias de todos los varones de edad sin quedar ninguno." Ondegardo, Rel. Prim., MS.

from that in which we study those of other nations. The laws emanated from the sovereign, and that sovereign held a divine commission, and was possessed of a divine nature. To violate the law was not only to insult the majesty of the throne, but it was sacrilege. The slightest offence, viewed in this light, merited death; and the gravest could incur no heavier penalty.[10] Yet, in the infliction of their punishments, they showed no unnecessary cruelty; and the sufferings of the victim were not prolonged by the ingenious torments so frequent among barbarous nations.[11]

These legislative provisions may strike us as very defective, even as compared with those of the semi-civilized races of Anahuac, where a gradation of courts, moreover, with the right of appeal, afforded a tolerable security for justice. But in a country like Peru, where few but criminal causes were known, the right of appeal was of less consequence. The law was simple, its application easy; and, where the judge was honest, the case was as likely to be determined correctly on the first hearing as on the second. The inspection of the board of visitors, and the monthly returns of the tribunals, afforded no slight guaranty for their integrity. The law which required a decision within five days would seem little suited to the complex and embarrassing litigation of a modern tribunal. But, in the simple questions submitted to the Peruvian judge, delay would have been useless; and the Spaniards, familiar with the evils growing out of long-protracted suits, where the successful litigant is too often a ruined man, are loud in their encomiums of this swift-handed and economical justice.[12]

The fiscal regulations of the Incas, and the laws respecting property, are the most remarkable features in the Peruvian polity. The whole territory of the empire was divided into three parts, one for the Sun, another for the Inca, and the last for the people. Which of the three was the largest is doubtful. The proportions differed materially in different provinces. The distribution, indeed, was made on the same general principle, as each new conquest was added to the monarchy; but the proportion varied according to the amount of population, and the greater or

---

[10] "El castigo era reguroso, que por la mayor parte era de muerte, por liviano que fuese el delito; porque decian, que no los castigavan por el delito que avian hecho, ni por la ofensa agena, sino por aver quebrantado el mandamiento, y rompido la palabra del Inca, que lo respetavan como á Dios." Garcilasso, Com. Real., Parte 1, lib. 2, cap. 12.

[11] One of the punishments most frequent for minor offences was to carry a stone on the back. A punishment attended with no suffering but what arises from the disgrace attached to it is very justly characterized by McCulloh as a proof of sensibility and refinement. Researches, p. 361.

[12] The Royal Audience of Peru under Philip II.—there cannot be a higher authority—bears emphatic testimony to the cheap and efficient administration of justice under the Incas. "De suerte que los vicios eran bien castigados y la gente estaba bien sujeta y obediente; y aunque en las dichas penas havia esceso, redundaba en buen govierno y policia suya, y mediante ella eran aumentados. . . . . . Porque los Yndios alababan la governacion del Ynga, y aun los Españoles que algo alcanzan de ella, es porque todas las cosas susodichas se determinaban sin hacerles costas." Dec. de la Aud. Real., MS.

less amount of land consequently required for the support of the inhabi‧tants.[13]

The lands assigned to the Sun furnished a revenue to support the tem‧ples, and maintain the costly ceremonial of the Peruvian worship and the multitudinous priesthood. Those reserved for the Inca went to sup‧port the royal state, as well as the numerous members of his household and his kindred, and supplied the various exigencies of government. The remainder of the lands was divided, *per capita,* in equal shares among the people. It was provided by law, as we shall see hereafter, that every Peruvian should marry at a certain age. When this event took place, the community or district in which he lived furnished him with a dwelling, which, as it was constructed of humble materials, was done at little cost. A lot of land was then assigned to him sufficient for his own maintenance and that of his wife. An additional portion was granted for every child, the amount allowed for a son being the double of that for a daughter. The division of the soil was renewed every year, and the possessions of the tenant were increased or diminished according to the numbers in his family.[14] The same arrangement was observed with reference to the curacas, except only that a domain was assigned to them corresponding with the superior dignity of their stations.[15]

A more thorough and effectual agrarian law than this cannot be imag‧ined. In other countries where such a law has been introduced, its opera‧tion, after a time, has given way to the natural order of events, and, un‧der the superior intelligence and thrift of some and the prodigality of others, the usual vicissitudes of fortune have been allowed to take their course, and restore things to their natural inequality. Even the iron law of Lycurgus ceased to operate after a time, and melted away before the spirit of luxury and avarice. The nearest approach to the Peruvian con‧stitution was probably in Judea, where, on the recurrence of the great national jubilee, at the close of every half-century, estates reverted to

---

[13] Acosta, lib. 6, cap. 15.—Garcilasso, Com. Real., Parte 1, lib. 5, cap. 1.

"Si estas partes fuesan iguales, o qual fuese mayor, yo lo he procurado averiguar, y en unas es diferente de otras, y finalm^te yo tengo entendido que se hacia conforme á la disposicion de la tierra y a la calidad de los Indios." Ondegardo, Rel. Prim., MS.

[14] Ondegardo, Rel. Prim., MS.—Garcilasso, Com. Real., Parte 1, lib. 5, cap. 2.

The portion granted to each new-married couple, according to Garcilasso, was a *fanega* and a half of land. A similar quantity was added for each male child that was born; and half of the quantity for each female. The *fanega* was as much land as could be planted with a hundred weight of Indian corn. In the fruitful soil of Peru, this was a liberal allowance for a family.

[15] Ibid., Parte 1, lib. 5, cap. 3.

It is singular, that while so much is said of the Inca sovereign, so little should be said of the Inca nobility, of their estates, or the tenure by which they held them. Their historian tells us, that they had the best of the lands, wherever they resided, besides the interest which they had in those of the Sun and the Inca, as children of the one, and kinsmen of the other. He informs us, also, that they were supplied from the royal table, when living at court. (lib. 6, cap. 3.) But this is very loose language. The student of history will learn, on the threshold, that he is not to expect precise, or even very consistent, accounts of the institutions of a barbarous age and people, from contemporary annalists.

their original proprietors. There was this important difference in Peru; that not only did the lease, if we may so call it, terminate with the year, but during that period the tenant had no power to alienate or to add to his possessions. The end of the brief term found him in precisely the same condition that he was in at the beginning. Such a state of things might be supposed to be fatal to any thing like attachment to the soil, or to that desire of improving it, which is natural to the permanent proprietor, and hardly less so to the holder of a long lease. But the practical operation of the law seems to have been otherwise; and it is probable, that, under the influence of that love of order and aversion to change which marked the Peruvian institutions, each new partition of the soil usually confirmed the occupant in his possession, and the tenant for a year was converted into a proprietor for life.

The territory was cultivated wholly by the people. The lands belonging to the Sun were first attended to. They next tilled the lands of the old, of the sick, of the widow and the orphan, and of soldiers engaged in actual service; in short, of all that part of the community who, from bodily infirmity or any other cause, were unable to attend to their own concerns. The people were then allowed to work on their own ground, each man for himself, but with the general obligation to assist his neighbor, when any circumstance—the burden of a young and numerous family, for example—might demand it.[16] Lastly, they cultivated the lands of the Inca. This was done, with great ceremony, by the whole population in a body. At break of day, they were summoned together by proclamation from some neighboring tower or eminence, and all the inhabitants of the district, men, women, and children, appeared dressed in their gayest apparel, bedecked with their little store of finery and ornaments, as if for some great jubilee. They went through the labors of the day with the same joyous spirit, chanting their popular ballads which commemorated the heroic deeds of the Incas, regulating their movements by the measure of the chant, and all mingling in the chorus, of which the word *hailli*, or "triumph," was usually the burden. These national airs had something soft and pleasing in their character, that recommended them to the Spaniards; and many a Peruvian song was set to music by them after the Conquest, and was listened to by the unfortunate natives with melancholy satisfaction, as it called up recollections of the past, when their days glided peacefully away under the sceptre of the Incas.[17]

A similar arrangement prevailed with respect to the different manufactures as to the agricultural products of the country. The flocks of llamas, or Peruvian sheep, were appropriated exclusively to the Sun and to the Inca.[18] Their number was immense. They were scattered over the

[16] Garcilasso relates that an Indian was hanged by Huayna Capac for tilling a curaca's ground, his near relation, before that of the poor. The gallows was erected on the curaca's own land. Ibid., Parte 1, lib. 5, cap. 2.
[17] Ibid., Parte 1, lib. 5, cap. 1–3.—Ondegardo, Rel. Seg., MS.
[18] Ondegardo, Rel. Prim., MS.
Yet sometimes the sovereign would recompense some great chief, or even some one among the people, who had rendered him a service, by the grant of a small num-

different provinces, chiefly in the colder regions of the country, where they were intrusted to the care of experienced shepherds, who conducted them to different pastures according to the change of season. A large number was every year sent to the capital for the consumption of the Court, and for the religious festivals and sacrifices. But these were only the males, as no female was allowed to be killed. The regulations for the care and breeding of these flocks were prescribed with the greatest minuteness, and with a sagacity which excited the admiration of the Spaniards, who were familiar with the management of the great migratory flocks of merinos in their own country.[19]

At the appointed season, they were all sheared, and the wool was deposited in the public magazines. It was then dealt out to each family in such quantities as sufficed for its wants, and was consigned to the female part of the household, who were well instructed in the business of spinning and weaving. When this labor was accomplished, and the family was provided with a coarse but warm covering, suited to the cold climate of the mountains,—for, in the lower country, cotton, furnished in like manner by the Crown, took the place, to a certain extent, of wool,—the people were required to labor for the Inca. The quantity of the cloth needed, as well as the peculiar kind and quality of the fabric, was first determined at Cuzco. The work was then apportioned among the different provinces. Officers, appointed for the purpose, superintended the distribution of the wool, so that the manufacture of the different articles should be intrusted to the most competent hands.[20] They did not leave the matter here, but entered the dwellings, from time to time, and saw that the work was faithfully executed. This domestic inquisition was not confined to the labors for the Inca. It included, also, those for the several families; and care was taken that each household should employ the materials furnished for its own use in the manner that was intended, so that no one should be unprovided with necessary apparel.[21] In this domestic labor aii the female part of the establishment was expected to join. Occupation was found for all, from the child five years old to the aged matron not too infirm to hold a distaff. No one, at least none but the decrepit and the sick, was allowed to eat the bread of idleness in Peru. Idleness was a crime in the eye of the law, and, as such, severely punished; while industry was publicly commended and stimulated by rewards.[22]

ber of llamas,—never many. These were not to be disposed of or killed by their owners, but descended as common property to their heirs. This strange arrangement proved a fruitful source of litigation after the Conquest. Ibid., ubi supra.

[19] See especially the account of the Licentiate Ondegardo, who goes into more detail than any contemporary writer, concerning the management of the Peruvian flocks. Rel. Seg., MS.

[20] Ondegardo, Rel. Prim. et Seg., MSS.

The manufacture of cloths for the Inca included those for the numerous persons of the blood royal, who wore garments of a finer texture than was permitted to any other Peruvian. Garcilasso, Com. Real., Parte 1, lib. 5, cap. 6.

[21] Ondegardo, Rel. Seg., MS.—Acosta, lib. 6, cap. 15.

[22] Ondegardo, Rel. Seg., MS.—Garcilasso, Com. Real., Parte 1, lib. 5, cap. 11

The like course was pursued with reference to the other requisitions of the government. All the mines in the kingdom belonged to the Inca. They were wrought exclusively for his benefit, by persons familiar with this service, and selected from the districts where the mines were situated.[23] Every Peruvian of the lower class was a husbandman, and, with the exception of those already specified, was expected to provide for his own support by the cultivation of his land. A small portion of the community, however, was instructed in mechanical arts; some of them of the more elegant kind, subservient to the purposes of luxury and ornament. The demand for these was chiefly limited to the sovereign and his Court; but the labor of a larger number of hands was exacted for the execution of the great public works which covered the land. The nature and amount of the services required were all determined at Cuzco by commissioners well instructed in the resources of the country, and in the character of the inhabitants of different provinces.[24]

This information was obtained by an admirable regulation, which has scarcely a counterpart in the annals of a semi-civilized people. A register was kept of all the births and deaths throughout the country, and exact returns of the actual population were made to government every year, by means of the *quipus*, a curious invention, which will be explained hereafter.[25] At certain intervals, also, a general survey of the country was made, exhibiting a complete view of the character of the soil, its fertility, the nature of its products, both agricultural and mineral,—in short, of all that constituted the physical resources of the empire.[26] Furnished with these statistical details, it was easy for the government, after determining the amount of requisitions, to distribute the work among the respective provinces best qualified to execute it. The task of apportioning the labor was assigned to the local authorities, and great care was taken that it should be done in such a manner, that, while the most competent hands were selected, it should not fall disproportionately heavy on any.[27]

[23] Garcilasso would have us believe that the Inca was indebted to the curacas for his gold and silver, which were furnished by the great vassals as presents. (Com. Real., Parte 1, lib. 5, cap. 7.) This improbable statement is contradicted by the Report of the Royal Audience, MS., by Sarmiento, (Relacion, MS., cap. 15,) and by Ondegardo, (Rel. Prim., MS.) who all speak of the mines as the property of the government, and wrought exclusively for its benefit. From this reservoir the proceeds were liberally dispensed in the form of presents among the great lords, and still more for the embellishment of the temples.

[24] Garcilasso, Com. Real., Parte 1, lib. 5, cap. 13-16.—Ondegardo, Rel. Prim. et Seg., MSS.

[25] Montesinos, Mem. Antiguas, MS., lib. 2, cap. 6.—Pedro Pizarro, Relacion del Descubrimiento y Conquista de los Reynos del Perú, MS.

"Cada provincia, en fin del año, mandava asentar en los quipos, por la cuenta de sus nudos, todos los hombres que habian muerto en ella en aquel año, y por el consiguiente los que habian nacido, y por principio del año que entraba, venian con los quipos al Cuzco." Sarmiento, Relacion, MS., cap. 16.

[26] Garcilasso, Com. Real., Parte 1, lib. 2, cap. 14.

[27] Ondegardo, Rel. Prim., MS.—Sarmiento, Rel., MS., cap. 15.

"Presupuesta y entendida la dicha division que el Inga tenia hecha de su gente, y orden que tenia puesta en el govierno de ella, era muy facil haverla en la division y

The different provinces of the country furnished persons peculiarly suited to different employments, which, as we shall see hereafter, usually descended from father to son. Thus, one district supplied those most skilled in working the mines, another the most curious workers in metals, or in wood, and so on.[28] The artisan was provided by government with the materials; and no one was required to give more than a stipulated portion of his time to the public service. He was then succeeded by another for the like term; and it should be observed, that all who were engaged in the employment of the government—and the remark applies equally to agricultural labor—were maintained, for the time, at the public expense.[29] By this constant rotation of labor, it was intended that no one should be overburdened, and that each man should have time to provide for the demands of his own household. It was impossible—in the judgment of a high Spanish authority—to improve on the system of distribution, so carefully was it accommodated to the condition and comfort of the artisan.[30] The security of the working classes seems to have been ever kept in view in the regulations of the government; and these were so discreetly arranged, that the most wearing and unwholesome labors, as those of the mines, occasioned no detriment to the health of the laborer; a striking contrast to his subsequent condition under the Spanish rule.[31]

A part of the agricultural produce and manufactures was transported to Cuzco, to minister to the immediate demands of the Inca and his Court. But far the greater part was stored in magazines scattered over the different provinces. These spacious buildings, constructed of stone, were divided between the Sun and the Inca, though the greater share seems to have been appropriated by the monarch. By a wise regulation, any deficiency in the contributions of the Inca might be supplied from the granaries of the Sun.[32] But such a necessity could rarely have happened; and the providence of the government usually left a large surplus in the royal depositories, which was removed to a third class of magazines, whose design was to supply the people in seasons of scarcity, and, occasionally, to furnish relief to individuals, whom sickness or misfortune had reduced to poverty; thus, in a manner, justifying the assertion

cobranza de los dichos tributos; porque era claro y cierto lo que á cada uno cabia sin que hubiese desigualdad ni engaño." Dec. de la Aud. Real., MS.

[28] Sarmiento, Relacion, MS., cap. 15.—Ondegardo, Rel. Seg., MS.

[29] Ondegardo, Rel. Prim., MS.—Garcilasso, Com. Real., Parte 1, lib. 5, cap. 5.

[30] "Y tambien se tenia cuenta que el trabajo que pasavan fuese moderado, y con el menos riesgo que fuese posible. . . . . . Era tanta la orden que tuvieron estos Indios, que a mi parecer aunque mucho se piense en ello seria dificultoso mejorarla conocida su condicion y costumbres." Ondegardo, Rel. Prim., MS.

[31] "The working of the mines," says the President of the Council of the Indies, "was so regulated that no one felt it a hardship, much less was his life shortened by it." (Sarmiento, Relacion, MS., cap. 15.) It is a frank admission for a Spaniard.

[32] Garcilasso, Com. Real., Parte 1, lib. 5, cap. 34.—Ondegardo, Rel. Prim., MS.

"E asi esta parte del Inga no hay duda sino que de todas tres era la mayor, y en los depositos se parece bien que yó visité muchos en diferentes partes, é son mayores ὲ ᴤas largos que nó los de su religion sin comparasion." Idem, Rel. Seg., MS.

of a Castilian document, that a large portion of the revenues of the Inca found its way back again, through one channel or another, into the hands of the people.[33] These magazines were found by the Spaniards, on their arrival, stored with all the various products and manufactures of the country,—with maize, *coca, quinua,* woolen and cotton stuffs of the finest quality, with vases and utensils of gold, silver, and copper, in short, with every article of luxury or use within the compass of Peruvian skill.[34] The magazines of grain, in particular, would frequently have sufficed for the consumption of the adjoining district for several years.[35] An inventory of the various products of the country, and the quarters whence they were obtained, was every year taken by the royal officers, and recorded by the *quipucamayus* on their registers, with surprising regularity and precision. These registers were transmitted to the capital, and submitted to the Inca, who could thus at a glance, as it were, embrace the whole results of the national industry, and see how far they corresponded with the requisitions of government.[36]

Such are some of the most remarkable features of the Peruvian institutions relating to property, as delineated by writers who, however contradictory in the details, have a general conformity of outline. These institutions are certainly so remarkable, that it is hardly credible they should ever have been enforced throughout a great empire, and for a long period of years. Yet we have the most unequivocal testimony to the fact from the Spaniards, who landed in Peru in time to witness their operation; some of whom, men of high judicial station and character, were commissioned by the government to make investigations into the state of the country under its ancient rulers.

The impositions on the Peruvian people seem to have been sufficiently heavy. On them rested the whole burden of maintaining, not only their own order, but every other order in the state. The members of the royal house, the great nobles, even the public functionaries, and the numerous

---

[33] "Todos los dichos tributos y servicios que el Inga imponia y llevaba como dicho es eran con color y para efecta del govierno y pro comun de todos asi como lo que se ponia en depositos todo se combertia y distribuia entre los mismos naturales." Dec de la Aud. Real., MS.

[34] Acosta, lib. 6, cap. 15.
"No podre decir," says one of the Conquerors, "los depositos. Vide de rropas y de todos generos de rropas y vestidos que en este reino se hacian y vsavan que faltava tiempo para vello y entendimiento para comprender tanta cosa, muchos depositos de barretas de cobre para las minas y de costales y sogas de vasos de palo y platos del oro y plata que aqui se hallo hera cosa despanto." Pedro Pizarro, Descub. y Conq., MS.

[35] For ten years, sometimes, if we may credit Ondegardo, who had every means of knowing. "É ansi cuando nó era menester se estaba en los depositos é habia algunas vezes comida de diez años. . . . . Los cuales todos se hallaron llenos cuando llegaron los Españoles desto y de todas las cosas necesarias para la vida humana." Rel. Seg., MS.

[36] Ondegardo, Rel. Prim., MS.
"Por tanta orden é cuenta que seria dificultoso creerlo ni darlo á entender como ellos lo tienen en su cuenta é por registros é por menudo lo manifestaron que se pudiera por estenso." Idem, Rel. Seg., MS.

body of the priesthood, were all exempt from taxation.[37] The whole duty
of defraying the expenses of the government belonged to the people. Yet
this was not materially different from the condition of things formerly
existing in most parts of Europe, where the various privileged classes
claimed exemption—not always with success, indeed—from bearing part
of the public burdens. The great hardship in the case of the Peruvian was,
that he could not better his condition. His labors were for others, rather
than for himself. However industrious, he could not add a rood to his own
possessions, nor advance himself one hair's breadth in the social scale.
The great and universal motive to honest industry, that of bettering one's
lot, was lost upon him. The great law of human progress was not for him.
As he was born, so he was to die. Even his time he could not properly call
his own. Without money, with little property of any kind, he paid his
taxes in labor.[38] No wonder that the government should have dealt with
sloth as a crime. It was a crime against the state, and to be wasteful of
time was, in a manner, to rob the exchequer. The Peruvian, laboring all
his life for others, might be compared to the convict in a treadmill, going
the same dull round of incessant toil, with the consciousness, that, however profitable the results to the state, they were nothing to him.

But this is the dark side of the picture. If no man could become rich in
Peru, no man could become poor. No spendthrift could waste his substance in riotous luxury. No adventurous schemer could impoverish his
family by the spirit of speculation. The law was constantly directed to enforce a steady industry and a sober management of his affairs. No mendicant was tolerated in Peru. When a man was reduced by poverty or misfortune, (it could hardly be by fault,) the arm of the law was stretched out
to minister relief; not the stinted relief of private charity, nor that which
is doled out, drop by drop, as it were, from the frozen reservoirs of "the
parish," but in generous measure, bringing no humiliation to the object
of it, and placing him on a level with the rest of his countrymen.[39]

No man could be rich, no man could be poor, in Peru; but all might
enjoy, and did enjoy, a competence. Ambition, avarice, the love of
change, the morbid spirit of discontent, those passions which most agi-

---

[37] Garcilasso, Com. Real., Parte 1, lib. 5, cap. 15.

[38] "Solo el trabajo de las personas era el tributo que se dava, porque ellos no po-
seian otra cosa." Ondegardo, Rel. Prim., MS.

[39] "Era tanta la orden que tenia en todos sus Reinos y provincias, que no consentia
haver ningun Indio pobre ni menesteroso, porque havia orden i formas para ello sin
que los pueblos reciviesen vexacion ni molestia, porque el Inga lo suplia de sus tributos." (Conq. i Pob. del Piru, MS.) The Licentiate Ondegardo sees only a device of
Satan in these provisions of the Peruvian law, by which the old, the infirm, and the
poor were rendered, in a manner, independent of their children, and those nearest of
kin, on whom they would naturally have leaned for support; no surer way to harden
the heart, he considers, than by thus disengaging it from the sympathies of humanity;
and no circumstance has done more, he concludes, to counteract the influence and
spread of Christianity among the natives. (Rel. Seg., MS.) The views are ingenious;
but, in a country where the people had no property, as in Peru, there would seem to
be no alternative for the supernumeraries, but to receive support from government
or to starve

tate the minds of men, found no place in the bosom of the Peruvian. The very condition of his being seemed to be at war with change. He moved on in the same unbroken circle in which his fathers had moved before him, and in which his children were to follow. It was the object of the Incas to infuse into their subjects a spirit of passive obedience and tranquillity,—a perfect acquiescence in the established order of things. In this they fully succeeded. The Spaniards who first visited the country are emphatic in their testimony, that no government could have been better suited to the genius of the people; and no people could have appeared more contented with their lot, or more devoted to their government.[40]

Those who may distrust the accounts of Peruvian industry will find their doubts removed on a visit to the country. The traveller still meets, especially in the central regions of the table-land, with memorials of the past, remains of temples, palaces, fortresses, terraced mountains, great military roads, aqueducts, and other public works, which, whatever degree of science they may display in their execution, astonish him by their number, the massive character of the materials, and the grandeur of the design. Among them, perhaps the most remarkable are the great roads, the broken remains of which are still in sufficient preservation to attest their former magnificence. There were many of these roads, traversing different parts of the kingdom; but the most considerable were the two which extended from Quito to Cuzco, and, again diverging from the capital, continued in a southern direction towards Chili.

One of these roads passed over the grand plateau, and the other along the lowlands on the borders of the ocean. The former was much the more difficult achievement, from the character of the country. It was conducted over pathless sierras buried in snow; galleries were cut for leagues through the living rock; rivers were crossed by means of bridges that swung suspended in the air; precipices were scaled by stairways hewn out of the native bed; ravines of hideous depth were filled up with solid masonry; in short, all the difficulties that beset a wild and mountainous region, and which might appall the most courageous engineer of modern times, were encountered and successfully overcome. The length of the road, of which scattered fragments only remain, is variously estimated, from fifteen hundred to two thousand miles; and stone pillars, in the manner of European milestones, were erected at stated intervals of somewhat more than a league, all along the route. Its breadth scarcely exceeded twenty feet.[41] It was built of heavy flags of freestone, and in some parts, at least, covered with a bituminous cement, which time has made

---

[40] Acosta, lib 6, cap. 12, 15.—Sarmiento, Relacion, MS., cap. 10.

[41] Dec. de la Aud. Real., MS.

"Este camino hecho por valles ondos y por sierras altas, por montes de nieve, por tremedales de agua y por peña viva y junto á rios furiosos por estas partes y ballano y empedrado por las laderas, bien sacado por las sierras, deshechado, por laspeñas socavado, por junto á los Rios sus paredes, entre nieves con escalones y descanso, por todas partes limpio barrido descombrado, lleno de aposentos, de depositos de tesoros, de Templos del Sol, de Postas que havia en este camino." Sarmiento, Relacion, MS., cap. 60.

harder than the stone itself. In some places, where the ravines had been filled up with masonry, the mountain torrents, wearing on it for ages, have gradually eaten a way through the base, and left the superincumbent mass—such is the cohesion of the materials—still spanning the valley like an arch! [42]

Over some of the boldest streams it was necessary to construct suspension bridges, as they are termed, made of the tough fibres of the maguey, or of the osier of the country, which has an extraordinary degree of tenacity and strength. These osiers were woven into cables of the thickness of a man's body. The huge ropes, then stretched across the water, were conducted through rings or holes cut in immense buttresses of stone raised on the opposite banks of the river, and there secured to heavy pieces of timber. Several of these enormous cables, bound together, formed a bridge, which, covered with planks, well secured and defended by a railing of the same osier materials on the sides, afforded a safe passage for the traveller. The length of this aërial bridge, sometimes exceeding two hundred feet, caused it, confined, as it was, only at the extremities, to dip with an alarming inclination towards the centre, while the motion given to it by the passenger occasioned an oscillation still more frightful, as his eye wandered over the dark abyss of waters that foamed and tumbled many a fathom beneath. Yet these light and fragile fabrics were crossed without fear by the Peruvians, and are still retained by the Spaniards over those streams which, from the depth or impetuosity of the current, would seem impracticable for the usual modes of conveyance. The wider and more tranquil waters were crossed on *balsas*—a kind of raft still much used by the natives—to which sails were attached, furnishing the only instance of this higher kind of navigation among the American Indians. [43]

The other great road of the Incas lay through the level country between the Andes and the ocean. It was constructed in a different manner, as demanded by the nature of the ground, which was for the most part low, and much of it sandy. The causeway was raised on a high embankment of earth, and defended on either side by a parapet or wall of clay; and trees and odoriferous shrubs were planted along the margin, regaling the sense of the traveller with their perfumes, and refreshing him by their shades, so grateful under the burning sky of the tropics. In the strips of sandy waste, which occasionally intervened, where the light and volatile

[42] "On avait comblé les vides et les ravins par de grandes masses de maçonnerie. Les torrents qui descendent des hauteurs après des pluies abondantes, avaient creusé les endroits les moins solides, et s'etaient frayé une voie sous le chemin, le laissant ainsi suspendu en l'air comme un pont fait d'une seule pièce." (Velasco, Hist. de Quito, tom. I. p. 206.) This writer speaks from personal observation, having examined and measured different parts of the road, in the latter part of the last century.

[43] Garcilasso, Com. Real., Parte 1, lib. 3, cap. 7.

A particular account of these bridges, as they are still to be seen in different parts of Peru, may be found in Humboldt. (Vues des Cordillères, p. 230 et seq.) The *balsas* are described with equal minuteness by Stevenson. Residence in America, vol. II. p. 222, et. seq.

soil was incapable of sustaining a road, huge piles, many of them to be seen at this day, were driven into the ground to indicate the route to the traveller.[44]

All along these highways, caravansaries, or *tambos*, as they were called, were erected, at the distance of ten or twelve miles from each other, for the accommodation, more particularly, of the Inca and his suite, and those who journeyed on the public business. There were few other travellers in Peru. Some of these buildings were on an extensive scale, consisting of a fortress, barracks, and other military works, surrounded by a parapet of stone, and covering a large tract of ground. These were evidently destined for the accommodation of the imperial armies, when on their march across the country.—The care of the great roads was committed to the districts through which they passed, and a large number of hands was constantly employed under the Incas to keep them in repair. This was the more easily done in a country where the mode of travelling was altogether on foot; though the roads are said to have been so nicely constructed, that a carriage might have rolled over them as securely as on any of the great roads of Europe.[45] Still, in a region where the elements of fire and water are both actively at work in the business of destruction, they must, without constant supervision, have gradually gone to decay. Such has been their fate under the Spanish conquerors, who took no care to enforce the admirable system for their preservation adopted by the Incas. Yet the broken portions that still survive, here and there, like the fragments of the great Roman roads scattered over Europe, bear evidence to their primitive grandeur, and have drawn forth the eulogium from a discriminating traveller, usually not too profuse in his panegyric, that "the roads of the Incas were among the most useful and stupendous works ever executed by man." [46]

The system of communication through their dominions was still further improved by the Peruvian sovereigns, by the introduction of posts, in the same manner as was done by the Aztecs. The Peruvian posts, however, established on all the great routes that conducted to the capital, were on a much more extended plan than those in Mexico. All along these routes, small buildings were erected, at the distance of less than five miles asunder,[47] in each of which a number of runners, or *chasquis*, as

[44] Cieza de Leon, Cronica, cap. 60.—Relacion del Primer Descubrimiento de la Costa y Mar del Sur, MS.

This anonymous document of one of the early Conquerors contains a minute and probably trustworthy account of both the high roads, which the writer saw in their glory, and which he ranks among the greatest wonders of the world.

[45] Relacion del Primer Descub., MS.—Cieza de Leon, Cronica, cap. 37.—Zarate, Conq. del Peru, lib. 1, cap. 11.—Garcilasso, Com. Real., Parte 1, lib. 9, cap. 13.

[46] "Cette chaussée, bordée de grandes pierres de taille, peut être comparée aux plus belles routes des Romaines que j'aie vues en Italie, en France et en Espagne. . . . . . Le grand chemin de l'Inca, un des ouvrages les plus utiles, et en même temps des plus gigantesques que les hommes aient exécuté." Humboldt, Vues des Cordillères, p. 294.

[47] The distance between the posthouses is variously stated; most writers not estimating it at more than three fourths of a league. I have preferred the authority of Ondegardo, who usually writes with more conscientiousness and knowledge of his ground than most of his contemporaries.

they were called, were stationed to carry forward the despatches of government.[48] These despatches were either verbal, or conveyed by means of *quipus*, and sometimes accompanied by a thread of the crimson fringe worn round the temples of the Inca, which was regarded with the same implicit deference as the signet ring of an Oriental despot.[49]

The *chasquis* were dressed in a peculiar livery, intimating their profession. They were all trained to the employment, and selected for their speed and fidelity. As the distance each courier had to perform was small, and as he had ample time to refresh himself at the stations, they ran over the ground with great swiftness, and messages were carried through the whole extent of the long routes, at the rate of a hundred and fifty miles a day. The office of the *chasquis* was not limited to carrying despatches. They frequently brought various articles for the use of the Court; and in this way, fish from the distant ocean, fruits, game, and different commodities from the hot regions on the coast, were taken to the capital in good condition, and served fresh at the royal table.[50] It is remarkable that this important institution should have been known to both the Mexicans and the Peruvians without any correspondence with one another; and that it should have been found among two barbarian nations of the New World, long before it was introduced among the civilized nations of Europe.[51]

By these wise contrivances of the Incas, the most distant parts of the long-extended empire of Peru were brought into intimate relations with each other. And while the capitals of Christendom, but a few hundred miles apart, remained as far asunder as if seas had rolled between them, the great capitals Cuzco and Quito were placed by the high roads of the Incas in immediate correspondence. Intelligence from the numerous

[48] The term *chasqui*, according to Montesinos, signifies "one that receives a thing." (Mem. Antiguas, MS., cap. 7.) But Garcilasso, a better authority for his own tongue, says it meant "one who makes an exchange." Com. Real., Parte 1, lib. 6, cap. 8.

[49] "Con vn hilo de esta Borla, entregado á uno de aquellos Orejones governaban la Tierra, i proveian lo que querian con maior obediencia, que en ninguna Provincia del Mundo se ha visto tener á las Provissiones de su Rei." Zarate, Conq. del Peru, lib. 1, cap. 9.

[50] Sarmiento, Relacion, MS., cap. 18.—Dec. de la Aud. Real., MS.

If we may trust Montesinos, the royal table was served with fish, taken a hundred leagues from the capital, in twenty-four hours after it was drawn from the ocean! (Mem. Antiguas, MS., lib. 2, cap. 7.) This is rather too expeditious for any thing but rail-cars.

[51] The institution of the Peruvian posts seems to have made a great impression on the minds of the Spaniards who first visited the country; and ample notices of it may be found in Sarmiento, Relacion, MS., cap. 15.—Dec. de la Aud. Real., MS.—Fernandez, Hist. del Peru, Parte 2, lib. 3, cap. 5.—Conq. i Pob. del Piru, MS., et auct. plurimis.

The establishment of posts is of old date among the Chinese and, probably, still older among the Persians. (See Herodotus, Hist., Urania, sec. 98.) It is singular, that an invention designed for the uses of a despotic government should have received its full application only under a free one. For in it we have the germ of that beautiful system of intercommunication, which binds all the nations of Christendom together as one vast commonwealth.

provinces was transmitted on the wings of the wind to the Peruvian metropolis, the great focus to which all the lines of communication con,
verged. Not an insurrectionary movement could occur, not an invasion
on the remotest frontier, before the tidings were conveyed to the capital,
and the imperial armies were on their march across the magnificent roads
of the country to suppress it. So admirable was the machinery contrived
by the American despots for maintaining tranquillity throughout their
dominions! It may remind us of the similar institutions of ancient Rome,
when, under the Cæsars, she was mistress of half the world.

A principal design of the great roads was to serve the purposes of military communication. It formed an important item of their military policy,
which is quite as well worth studying as their municipal.

Notwithstanding the pacific professions of the Incas, and the pacific
tendency, indeed, of their domestic institutions, they were constantly at
war. It was by war that their paltry territory had been gradually enlarged to a powerful empire. When this was achieved, the capital, safe
in its central position, was no longer shaken by these military movements,
and the country enjoyed, in a great degree, the blessings of tranquillity
and order. But, however tranquil at heart, there is not a reign upon record in which the nation was not engaged in war against the barbarous
nations on the frontier. Religion furnished a plausible pretext for incessant aggression, and disguised the lust of conquest in the Incas, probably,
from their own eyes, as well as from those of their subjects. Like the followers of Mahomet, bearing the sword in one hand and the Koran in the
other, the Incas of Peru offered no alternative but the worship of the
Sun or war.

It is true, their fanaticism—or their policy—showed itself in a milder
form than was found in the descendants of the Prophet. Like the great
luminary which they adored, they operated by gentleness more potent
than violence.[52] They sought to soften the hearts of the rude tribes
around them, and melt them by acts of condescension and kindness. Far
from provoking hostilities, they allowed time for the salutary example
of their own institutions to work its effect, trusting that their less civilized
neighbors would submit to their sceptre, from a conviction of the blessings it would secure to them. When this course failed, they employed
other measures, but still of a pacific character; and endeavored by negotiation, by conciliatory treatment, and by presents to the leading men,
to win them over to their dominion. In short, they practised all the arts
familiar to the most subtle politician of a civilized land to secure the
acquisition of empire. When all these expedients failed, they prepared
for war.

Their levies were drawn from all the different provinces; though from
some, where the character of the people was particularly hardy, more

---

[52] "Mas se hicieron Señores al principio por maña, que por fuerza." Ondegardo,
Rel. Prim., MS.

than from others.[53] It seems probable that every Peruvian, who had reached a cerain age, might be called to bear arms. But the rotation of military service, and the regular drills, which took place twice or thrice in a month, of the inhabitants of every village, raised the soldiers gener- ally above the rank of a raw militia. The Peruvian army, at first incon- siderable, came, with the increase of population, in the latter days of the empire, to be very large, so that their monarchs could bring into the field, as contemporaries assure us, a force amounting to two hundred thousand men. They showed the same skill and respect for order in their military organization, as in other things. The troops were divided into bodies corresponding with our battalions and companies, led by officers, that rose, in regular gradation, from the lowest subaltern to the Inca noble, who was intrusted with the general command.[54]

Their arms consisted of the usual weapons employed by nations, whether civilized or uncivilized, before the invention of powder,—bows and arrows, lances, darts, a short kind of sword, a battle-axe or partisan, and slings, with which they were very expert. Their spears and arrows were tipped with copper, or, more commonly, with bone, and the weap- ons of the Inca lords were frequently mounted with gold or silver. Their heads were protected by casques made either of wood or of the skins of wild animals, and sometimes richly decorated with metal and with pre- cious stones, surmounted by the brilliant plumage of the tropical birds. These, of course, were the ornaments only of the higher orders. The great mass of the soldiery were dressed in the peculiar costume of their provinces, and their heads were wreathed with a sort of turban or roll of different-colored cloths, that produced a gay and animating effect. Their defensive armor consisted of a shield or buckler, and a close tunic of quilted cotton, in the same manner as with the Mexicans. Each company had its particular banner, and the imperial standard, high above all, dis- played the glittering device and the rainbow,—the armorial ensign of the Incas, intimating their claims as children of the skies.[55]

By means of the thorough system of communication established in the country, a short time sufficed to draw the levies together from the most distant quarters. The army was put under the direction of some exper- ienced chief, of the blood royal, or, more frequently, headed by the Inca in person. The march was rapidly performed, and with little fatigue to the soldier; for, all along the great routes, quarters were provided for him, at regular distances, where he could find ample accommodations. The country is still covered with the remains of military works, con-

[53] Idem, Rel. Prim., MS.—Dec. de la Aud. Real., MS.
[54] Gomara, Cronica, cap. 195.—Conq. i Pob. del Piru, MS.
[55] Gomara, Cronica. ubi supra.—Sarmiento, Relacion, MS., cap. 20.—Velasco, Hist. de Quito, tom. I. pp. 176–179.
This last writer gives a minute catalogue of the ancient Peruvian arms, compre- hending nearly every thing familiar to the European soldier, except fire-arms.—it was judicious in him to omit these.

structed of porphyry or granite, which tradition assures us were designed to lodge the Inca and his army.[56]

At regular intervals, also, magazines were established, filled with grain, weapons, and the different munitions of war, with which the army was supplied on its march. It was the especial care of the government to see that these magazines, which were furnished from the stores of the Incas, were always well filled. When the Spaniards invaded the country, they supported their own armies for a long time on the provisions found in them.[57] The Peruvian soldier was forbidden to commit any trespass on the property of the inhabitants whose territory lay in the line of march. Any violation of this order was punished with death.[58] The soldier was clothed and fed by the industry of the people, and the Incas rightly resolved that he should not repay this by violence. Far from being a tax on the labors of the husbandman, or even a burden on his hospitality, the imperial armies traversed the country, from one extremity to the other, with as little inconvenience to the inhabitants, as would be created by a procession of peaceful burghers, or a muster of holiday soldiers for a review.

From the moment war was proclaimed, the Peruvian monarch used all possible expedition in assembling his forces, that he might anticipate the movements of his enemies, and prevent a combination with their allies. It was, however, from the neglect of such a principle of combination, that the several nations of the country, who might have prevailed by confederated strength, fell one after another under the imperial yoke. Yet, once in the field the Inca did not usually show any disposition to push his advantages to the utmost, and urge his foe to extremity. In every stage of the war, he was open to propositions for peace; and although he sought to reduce his enemies by carrying off their harvests and distressing them by famine, he allowed his troops to commit no unnecessary outrage on person or property. "We must spare our enemies," one of the Peruvian princes is quoted as saying, "or it will be our loss, since they and all that belong to them must soon be ours." [59] It was a wise

[56] Zarate, Conq. del Peru, lib. 1, cap. 11.—Sarmiento, Relacion, MS., cap. 60.

Condamine speaks of the great number of these fortified places, scattered over the country between Quito and Lima, which he saw in his visit to South America in 1737; some of which he has described with great minuteness. Mémoire sur Quelques Anciens Monumens du Pérou, du Tems des Incas, ap. Histoire de l'Académie Royale des Sciences et de Belles Lettres, (Berlin, 1748,) tom. II. p. 438.

[57] "E ansi cuando," says Ondegardo, speaking from his own personal knowledge, "el Señor Presidente Gasca passó con la gente de castigo de Gonzalo Pizarro por el valle de Jauja, estuvo alli siete semanas á lo que me acuerdo, se hallaron en deposito maiz de cuatro y de tres y de dos años mas de 15 ☿. hanegas junto al camino, é alli comió la gente, y se entendió que si fuera menester muchas mas nó faltaran en el valle en aquellos depositos, conforme á la orden antigua, porque á mi cargo estubo el repartirlas y hacer la cuenta para pagarlas." Rel. Seg., MS.

[58] Pedro Pizarro, Descub. y Conq., MS.—Cieza de Leon, Cronica, cap. 44.—Sarmiento, Relacion, MS., cap. 14.

[59] "Mandabase que en los mantenimientos y casas de los enemigos se hiciese poco

maxim, and, like most other wise maxims, founded equally on benevolence and prudence. The Incas adopted the policy claimed for the Romans by their countryman, who tells us that they gained more by clemency to the vanquished than by their victories.[60]

In the same considerate spirit, they were most careful to provide for the
security and comfort of their own troops; and, when a war was long protracted, or the climate proved unhealthy, they took care to relieve their
men by frequent reinforcements, allowing the earlier recruits to return to
their homes.[61] But while thus economical of life, both in their own followers and in the enemy, they did not shrink from sterner measures when
provoked by the ferocious or obstinate character of the resistance; and
the Peruvian annals contain more than one of those sanguinary pages
which cannot be pondered at the present day without a shudder. It should
be added, that the beneficent policy, which I have been delineating as
characteristic of the Incas, did not belong to all; and that there was more
than one of the royal line who displayed a full measure of the bold and
unscrupulous spirit of the vulgar conqueror.

The first step of the government, after the reduction of a country, was
to introduce there the worship of the Sun. Temples were erected, and
placed under the care of a numerous priesthood, who expounded to the
conquered people the mysteries of their new faith, and dazzled them by
the display of its rich and stately ceremonial.[62] Yet the religion of the
conquered was not treated with dishonor. The Sun was to be worshipped
above all; but the images of their gods were removed to Cuzco and established in one of the temples, to hold their rank among the inferior deities
of the Peruvian Pantheon. Here they remained as hostages, in some sort,
for the conquered nation, which would be the less inclined to forsake its
allegiance, when by doing so it must leave its own gods in the hands of
its enemies.[63]

The Incas provided for the settlement of their new conquests, by ordering a census to be taken of the population, and a careful survey to be
made of the country, ascertaining its products, and the character and
capacity of its soil.[64] A division of the territory was then made on the
same principle with that adopted throughout their own kingdom; and
their respective portions were assigned to the Sun, the sovereign, and the
people. The amount of the last was regulated by the amount of the population, but the share of each individual was uniformly the same. It may
seem strange, that any people should patiently have acquiesced in an arrangement which involved such a total surrender of property. But it was

daño, diciendoles el Señor, presto serán estos nuestros como los que ya lo son; como
esto tenian conocido, procuraban que la guerra fuese la mas liviana que ser pudiese."
Sarmiento, Relacion, MS., cap. 14.

[60] "Plus pene parcendo victis, quàm vincendo imperium auxisse." Livy, lib. 30,
cap. 42.

[61] Garcilasso, Com. Real., Parte 1, lib. 6, cap. 18.

[62] Sarmiento, Relacion, MS., cap. 14.

[63] Acosta, lib. 5, cap. 12.—Garcilasso, Com. Real., Parte 1, lib. 5, cap. 12.

[64] Ibid.. Parte 1, lib. 5, cap. 13, 14.—Sarmiento, Relacion, MS., cap. 15.

a conquered nation that did so, held in awe, on the least suspicion of meditating resistance, by armed garrisons, who were established at various commanding points throughout the country.[65] It is probable, too, that the Incas made no greater changes than was essential to the new arrangement, and that they assigned estates, as far as possible, to their former proprietors. The curacas, in particular, were confirmed in their ancient authority; or, when it was found expedient to depose the existing curaca, his rightful heir was allowed to succeed him.[66] Every respect was shown to the ancient usages and laws of the land, as far as was compatible with the fundamental institutions of the Incas. It must also be remembered, that the conquered tribes were, many of them, too little advanced in civilization to possess that attachment to the soil which belongs to a cultivated nation.[67] But, to whatever it be referred, it seems probable that the extraordinary institutions of the Incas were established with little opposition in the conquered territories.[68]

Yet the Peruvian sovereigns did not trust altogether to this show of obedience in their new vassals; and, to secure it more effectually, they adopted some expedients too remarkable to be passed by in silence.— Immediately after a recent conquest, the curacas and their families were removed for a time to Cuzco. Here they learned the language of the capital, became familiar with the manners and usages of the court, as well as with the general policy of government, and experienced such marks of favor from the sovereign as would be most grateful to their feelings, and might attach them most warmly to his person. Under the influence of these sentiments, they were again sent to rule over their vassals, but still leaving their eldest sons in the capital, to remain there as a guaranty for their own fidelity, as well as to grace the court of the Inca.[69]

Another expedient was of a bolder and more original character. This was nothing less than to revolutionize the language of the country. South America, like North, was broken up into a great variety of dialects, or rather languages, having little affinity with one another. This circumstance occasioned great embarrassment to the government in the administration of the different provinces, with whose idioms they were unacquainted. It was determined, therefore, to substitute one universal lan-

[65] Sarmiento, Relacion, MS., cap. 19.

[66] Fernandez, Hist. del Peru, Parte 2, lib. 3, cap. 11.

[67] Sarmiento has given a very full and interesting account of the singularly humane policy observed by the Incas in their conquests, forming a striking contrast with the usual course of those scourges of mankind, whom mankind are wise enough to requite with higher admiration even, than it bestows on its benefactors. Sarmiento, who was President of the Royal Council of the Indies, and came into the country soon after the Conquest, is a high authority, and his work, lodged in the dark recesses of the Escurial, is almost unknown.

[68] According to Velasco, even the powerful state of Quito, sufficiently advanced in civilization to have the law of property well recognized by its people, admitted the institutions of the Incas, "not only without repugnance, but with joy." (Hist. de Quito, tom. II. p. 183.) But Velasco, a modern authority, believed easily,—or reckoned on his readers' doing so.

[69] Garcilasso. Com. Real., Parte 1, lib. 5, cap. 12; lib. 7, cap. 2.

guage, the *Quichua*,—the language of the court, the capital, and the surrounding country,—the richest and most comprehensive of the South American dialects. Teachers were provided in the towns and villages throughout the land, who were to give instruction to all, even the humblest classes; and it was intimated at the same time, that no one should be raised to any office of dignity or profit, who was unacquainted with this tongue. The curacas and other chiefs, who attended at the capital, became familiar with this dialect in their intercourse with the Court, and, on their return home, set the example of conversing in it among themselves. This example was imitated by their followers, and the Quichua gradually became the language of elegance and fashion, in the same manner as the Norman French was affected by all those who aspired to any consideration in England, after the Conquest. By this means, while each province retained its peculiar tongue, a beautiful medium of communication was introduced, which enabled the inhabitants of one part of the country to hold intercourse with every other, and the Inca and his deputies to communicate with all. This was the state of things on the arrival of the Spaniards. It must be admitted, that history furnishes few examples of more absolute authority than such a revolution in the language of an empire, at the bidding of a master.[70]

Yet little less remarkable was another device of the Incas for securing the loyalty of their subjects. When any portion of the recent conquests showed a pertinacious spirit of disaffection, it was not uncommon to cause a part of the population, amounting, it might be, to ten thousand inhabitants or more, to remove to a distant quarter of the kingdom, occupied by ancient vassals of undoubted fidelity to the crown. A like number of these last was transplanted to the territory left vacant by the emigrants. By this exchange, the population was composed of two distinct races, who regarded each other with an eye of jealousy, that served as an effectual check on any mutinous proceeding. In time, the influence of the well-affected prevailed, supported, as they were, by royal authority, and by the silent working of the national institutions, to which the strange races became gradually accustomed. A spirit of loyalty sprang up by degrees in their bosoms, and, before a generation had passed away, the different tribes mingled in harmony together as members of the same community.[71] Yet the different races continued to be distinguished by difference of dress; since, by the law of the land, every citizen was required to wear the costume of his native province.[72] Neither could the colonist, who had

[70] Ibid., Parte 1, lib. 6, cap. 35; lib. 7, cap. 1, 2.—Ondegardo, Rel. Seg., MS.—Sarmiento, Relacion, MS., cap. 55.

"Aun la Criatura no hubiese dejado el Pecho de su Madre quando le comenzasen á mostrar le Lenguaque havia de saber; y aunque al principio fué dificultoso, é muchos se pusieron en no querer deprender mas lenguas de las suyas propias, los Reyes pudieron tanto que salieron con su intencion y ellos tubieron por bien de cumplir su mandado y tan de veras se entendió en ello que en tiempo de pocos años se savia y usaba una lengua en mas de mil y doscientas leguas." Ibid., cap. 21.

[71] Ondegardo, Rel. Prim., MS.—Fernandez, Hist. del Peru, Parte 2, lib. 3, cap. 11.

[72] "This regulation," says Father Acosta, "the Incas held to be of great importance to the order and right government of the realm." lib. 6, cap. 16.

been thus unceremoniously transplanted, return to his native district For, by another law, it was forbidden to any one to change his resi-dence without license.[73] He was settled for life. The Peruvian government ascribed to every man his local habitation, his sphere of action, nay, the very nature and quality of that action. He ceased to be a free agent; it might be almost said, that it relieved him of personal responsibility.

In following out this singular arrangement, the Incas showed as much regard for the comfort and convenience of the colonist as was compatible with the execution of their design. They were careful that the *mitimaes,* as these emigrants were styled, should be removed to climates most con-genial with their own. The inhabitants of the cold countries were not transplanted to the warm, nor the inhabitants of the warm countries to the cold.[74] Even their habitual occupations were consulted, and the fish-erman was settled in the neighborhood of the ocean, or the great lakes; while such lands were assigned to the husbandman as were best adapted to the culture with which he was most familiar.[75] And, as migration by many, perhaps by most, would be regarded as a calamity, the govern-ment was careful to show particular marks of favor to the *mitimaes,* and, by various privileges and immunities, to ameliorate their condition, and thus to reconcile them, if possible, to their lot.[76]

The Peruvian institutions, though they may have been modified and matured under successive sovereigns, all bear the stamp of the same orig-inal,—were all cast in the same mould. The empire, strengthening and enlarging at every successive epoch of its history, was, in its latter days, but the development, on a great scale, of what it was in miniature at its commencement, as the infant germ is said to contain within itself all the ramifications of the future monarch of the forest. Each succeeding Inca seemed desirous only to tread in the path, and carry out the plans, of his predecessor. Great enterprises, commenced under one, were continued by another, and completed by a third. Thus, while all acted on a regular plan, without any of the eccentric or retrograde movements which betray the agency of different individuals, the state seemed to be under the di-rection of a single hand, and steadily pursued, as if through one long reign, its great career of civilization and of conquest.

The ultimate aim of its institutions was domestic quiet. But it seemed as if this were to be obtained only by foreign war. Tranquillity in the heart of the monarchy, and war on its borders, was the condition of Peru. By this war it gave occupation to a part of its people, and, by the re-duction and civilization of its barbarous neighbors, gave security to all.

[73] Conq. i Pob. del Piru, MS.

[74] "Trasmutaban de las tales Provincias la cantidad de gente de que de ella parecia convenir que saliese, á los cuales mandaban pasar a poblar otra tierra del temple y manera de donde salian, si fria fria, si caliente caliente, en donde les daban tierras, y campos, y casas, tanto, y mas como dejaron." Sarmiento, Relacion, MS., cap. 19.

[75] Ondegardo, Rel. Prim., MS.

[76] The descendants of these *mitimaes* are still to be found in Quito, or were so at the close of the last century, according to Velasco, distinguished by this name from the rest of the population. Hist. de Quito, tom. I. p. 175.

Every Inca sovereign, however mild and benevolent in his domestic rule, was a warrior, and led his armies in person. Each successive reign extended still wider the boundaries of the empire. Year after year saw the victorious monarch return laden with spoils, and followed by a throng of tributary chieftains to his capital. His reception there was a Roman triumph. The whole of its numerous population poured out to welcome him, dressed in the gay and picturesque costumes of the different provinces, with banners waving above their heads, and strewing branches and flowers along the path of the conqueror. The Inca, borne aloft in his golden chair on the shoulders of his nobles, moved in solemn procession, under the triumphal arches that were thrown across the way, to the great temple of the Sun. There, without attendants,—for all but the monarch were excluded from the hallowed precincts,—the victorious prince, stripped of his royal insignia, barefooted, and with all humility, approached the awful shrine, and offered up sacrifice and thanksgiving to the glorious Deity who presided over the fortunes of the Incas. This ceremony concluded, the whole population gave itself up to festivity; music, revelry, and dancing were heard in every quarter of the capital, and illuminations and bonfires commemorated the victorious campaign of the Inca, and the accession of a new territory to his empire.[77]

In this celebration we see much of the character of a religious festival. Indeed, the character of religion was impressed on all the Peruvian wars. The life of an Inca was one long crusade against the infidel, to spread wide the worship of the Sun, to reclaim the benighted nations from their brutish superstitions, and impart to them the blessings of a well-regulated government. This, in the favorite phrase of our day, was the "mission" of the Inca. It was also the mission of the Christian conqueror who invaded the empire of this same Indian potentate. Which of the two executed his mission most faithfully, history must decide.

Yet the Peruvian monarchs did not show a childish impatience in the acquisition of empire. They paused after a campaign, and allowed time for the settlement of one conquest before they undertook another; and, in this interval, occupied themselves with the quiet administration of their kingdom, and with the long progresses, which brought them into nearer intercourse with their people. During this interval, also, their new vassals had begun to accommodate themselves to the strange institutions of their masters. They learned to appreciate the value of a government which raised them above the physical evils of a state of barbarism, secured them protection of person, and a full participation in all the privileges enjoyed by their conquerors; and, as they became more familiar with the peculiar institutions of the country, habit, that second nature, attached them the more strongly to these institutions, from their very peculiarity. Thus, by degrees, and without violence, arose the great fabric of the Peruvian empire, composed of numerous independent and even hostile tribes, yet, under the influence of a common religion, common

[77] Sarmiento, Relacion, MS., cap. 55.—Garcilasso, Com. Real., Parte I, lib. 3, cap. 11, 17; lib. 6, cap. 16.

language, and common government, knit together as one nation, animated by a spirit of love for its institutions and devoted loyalty to its sovereign. What a contrast to the condition of the Aztec monarchy, on the neighboring continent, which, composed of the like heterogeneous materials, without any internal principle of cohesion, was only held together by the stern pressure, from without, of physical force!—Why the Peruvian monarchy should have fared no better than its rival, in its conflict with European civilization, will appear in the following pages.

CHAPTER III

PERUVIAN RELIGION—DEITIES—GORGEOUS TEMPLES—FESTIVALS—
VIRGINS OF THE SUN—MARRIAGE

IT is a remarkable fact, that many, if not most, of the rude tribes inhabiting the vast American continent, however disfigured their creeds may
have been in other respects by a childish superstition, had attained to
the sublime conception of one Great Spirit, the Creator of the Universe,
who, immaterial in his own nature, was not to be dishonored by an attempt at visible representation, and who, pervading all space, was not to
be circumscribed within the walls of a temple. Yet these elevated ideas,
so far beyond the ordinary range of the untutored intellect, do not seem
to have led to the practical consequences that might have been expected;
and few of the American nations have shown much solicitude for the maintenance of a religious worship, or found in their faith a powerful spring
of action.

But, with progress in civilization, ideas more akin to those of civilized communities were gradually unfolded; a liberal provision was made,
and a separate order instituted, for the services of religion, which were
conducted with a minute and magnificent ceremonial, that challenged
comparison, in some respects, with that of the most polished nations of
Christendom. This was the case with the nations inhabiting the table-land
of North America, and with the natives of Bogotá, Quito, Peru, and the
other elevated regions on the great Southern continent. It was, above all,
the case with the Peruvians, who claimed a divine original for the founders of their empire, whose laws all rested on a divine sanction, and whose
domestic institutions and foreign wars were alike directed to preserve and
propagate their faith. Religion was the basis of their polity, the very condition, as it were, of their social existence. The government of the Incas,
in its essential principles, was a theocracy.

Yet, though religion entered so largely into the fabric and conduct of
the political institutions of the people, their mythology, that is, the traditionary legends by which they affected to unfold the mysteries of the
universe, was exceedingly mean and puerile. Scarce one of their traditions—except the beautiful one respecting the founders of their royal
dynasty—is worthy of note, or throws much light on their own antiquities, or the primitive history of man. Among the traditions of importance
is one of the deluge, which they held in common with so many of the

nations in all parts of the globe, and which they related with some particulars that bear resemblance to a Mexican legend.[1]

Their ideas in respect to a future state of being deserve more attention. They admitted the existence of a soul hereafter, and connected with this a belief in the resurrection of the body. They assigned two distinct places for the residence of the good and of the wicked, the latter of which they fixed in the centre of the earth. The good they supposed were to pass a luxurious life of tranquillity and ease, which comprehended their highest notions of happiness. The wicked were to expiate their crimes by ages of wearisome labor. They associated with these ideas a belief in an evil principle or spirit, bearing the name of Cupay, whom they did not attempt to propitiate by sacrifices, and who seems to have been only a shadowy personification of sin, that exercised little influence over their conduct.[2]

It was this belief in the resurrection of the body, which led them to preserve the body with so much solicitude, by a simple process, however, that, unlike the elaborate embalming of the Egyptians, consisted in exposing it to the action of the cold, exceedingly dry, and highly rarefied atmosphere of the mountains.[3] As they believed that the occupations in the future world would have great resemblance to those of the present, they buried with the deceased noble some of his apparel, his utensils, and, frequently, his treasures; and completed the gloomy ceremony by sacrificing his wives and favorite domestics, to bear him company and do him service in the happy regions beyond the clouds.[4] Vast mounds of an irregular, or, more frequently, oblong shape, penetrated by galleries running at right angles to each other, were raised over the dead, whose dried bodies or mummies have been found in considerable numbers, sometimes erect, but more often in the sitting posture, common to the Indian tribes

---

[1] They related, that, after the deluge, seven persons issued from a cave where they had saved themselves, and by them the earth was repeopled. One of the traditions of the Mexicans deduced their descent, and that of the kindred tribes, in like manner, from seven persons who came from as many caves in Aztlan. (Conf. Acosta, lib. 6, cap. 19; lib. 7, cap. 2.—Ondegardo, Rel. Prim., MS.) The story of the deluge is told by different writers with many variations, in some of which it is not difficult to detect the plastic hand of the Christian convert.

[2] Ondegardo, Rel. Seg., MS.—Gomara, Hist. de las Ind., cap. 123.—Garcilasso, Com. Real., Parte 1, lib. 2, cap. 2, 7.

One might suppose that the educated Peruvians—if I may so speak—imagined the common people had no souls, so little is said of their opinions as to the condition of these latter in a future life, while they are diffuse on the prospects of the higher orders, which they fondly believed were to keep pace with their condition here.

[3] Such, indeed, seems to be the opinion of Garcilasso, though some writers speak of resinous and other applications for embalming the body. The appearance of the royal mummies found at Cuzco, as reported both by Ondegardo and Garcilasso, makes it probable that no foreign substance was employed for their preservation.

[4] Ondgardo, Rel. Seg. MS.

The Licentiate says, that this usage continued even after the Conquest; and that he had saved the life of more than one favorite domestic, who had fled to him for protection, as they were about to be sacrificed to the Manes of their deceased lords. Ibid., ubi supra.

of both continents. Treasures of great value have also been occasionally drawn from these monumental deposits, and have stimulated speculators to repeated excavations with the hope of similar good-fortune. It was a lottery like that of searching after mines, but where the chances have proved still more against the adventurers.[5]

The Peruvians, like so many other of the Indian races, acknowledged a Supreme Being, the Creator and Ruler of the Universe, whom they adored under the different names of Pachacamac and Viracocha.[6] No temple was raised to this invisible Being, save one only in the valley which took its name from the deity himself, not far from the Spanish city of Lima. Even this temple had existed there before the country came under the sway of the Incas, and was the great resort of Indian pilgrims from remote parts of the land; a circumstance which suggests the idea, that the worship of this Great Spirit, though countenanced, perhaps, by their accommodating policy, did not originate with the Peruvian princes.[7]

The deity whose worship they especially inculcated, and which they never failed to establish wherever their banners were known to penetrate, was the Sun. It was he, who, in a particular manner, presided over the destinies of man; gave light and warmth to the nations, and life to the vegetable world; whom they reverenced as the father of their royal dynasty, the founder of their empire; and whose temples rose in every city and almost every village throughout the land, while his altars smoked with burnt offerings,—a form of sacrifice peculiar to the Peruvians among the semi-civilized nations of the New World.[8]

Besides the Sun, the Incas acknowledged various objects of worship in some way or other connected with this principal deity. Such was the Moon, his sister-wife; the Stars, revered as part of her heavenly train,— though the fairest of them, Venus, known to the Peruvians by the name

[5] Yet these sepulchral mines have sometimes proved worth the digging. Sarmiento speaks of gold to the value of 100,000 *castellanos,* as occasionally buried with the Indian lords; (Relacion, MS., cap. 57;) and Las Casas—not the best authority in numerical estimates—says that treasures worth more than half a million of ducats had been found, within twenty years after the Conquest, in the tombs near Truxillo. (Œuvres, ed. par Llorente, (Paris, 1822,) tom. II. p. 192.) Baron Humboldt visited the sepulchre of a Peruvian prince in the same quarter of the country, whence a Spaniard in 1576 drew forth a mass of gold worth a million of dollars! Vues des Cordillères, p. 29.

[6] *Pachacamac* signifies "He who sustains or gives life to the universe." The name of the great deity is sometimes expressed by both Pachacamac and Viracocha combined. (See Balboa, Hist. du Pérou, chap. 6.—Acosta, lib. 6, cap. 21.) An old Spaniard finds in the popular meaning of *Viracocha,* "foam of the sea," an argument for deriving the Peruvian civilization from some voyager from the Old World. Conq. i Pob. del Piru, MS.

[7] Pedro Pizarro, Descub. y. Conq., MS.—Sarmiento, Relacion, MS., cap. 27.

Ulloa notices the extensive ruins of brick, which mark the probable site of the temple of Pachacamac, attesting by their present appearance its ancient magnificence and strength, Mémoires Philosophiques, Historiques, Physiques, (Paris, 1787,) trad. Fr., p. 78.

[8] At least, so says Dr. McCulloh; and no better authority can be required on American antiquities. (Researches, p. 392.) Might he not have added *barbarous* nations, also?

of Chasca, or the "youth with the long and curling locks," was adored as the page of the Sun, whom he attends so closely in his rising and in his setting. They dedicated temples also to the Thunder and Lightning,[9] in whom they recognized the Sun's dread ministers, and to the Rainbow, whom they worshipped as a beautiful emanation of their glorious deity.[10]

In addition to these, the subjects of the Incas enrolled among their inferior deities many objects in nature, as the elements, the winds, the earth, the air, great mountains and rivers, which impressed them with ideas of sublimity and power, or were supposed in some way or other to exercise a mysterious influence over the destinies of man.[11] They adopted also a notion, not unlike that professed by some of the schools of ancient philosophy, that every thing on earth had its archetype or idea, its *mother*, as they emphatically styled it, which they held sacred, as, in some sort, its spiritual essence.[12] But their system, far from being limited even to these multiplied objects of devotion, embraced within its ample folds the numerous deities of the conquered nations, whose images

[9] Thunder, Lightning, and Thunderbolt, could be all expressed by the Peruvians in one word, *Illapa*. Hence some Spaniards have inferred a knowledge of the Trinity in the natives! "The Devil stole all he could," exclaims Herrera, with righteous indignation. (Hist. General, dec. 5, lib. 4, cap. 5.) These, and even rasher conclusions, (see Acosta, lib. 5, cap. 28,) are scouted by Garcilasso, as inventions of Indian converts, willing to please the imaginations of their Christian teachers. (Com. Real., Parte 1. lib. 2, cap. 5, 6; lib. 3, cap. 21.) Imposture, on the one hand, and credulity on the other, have furnished a plentiful harvest of absurdities, which has been diligently gathered in by the pious antiquary of a later generation.

[10] Garcilasso's assertion, that these heavenly bodies were objects of reverence as holy things, but not of worship, (Com. Real., Parte 1, lib. 2, cap. 1, 23,) is contradicted by Ondegardo, Rel. Seg., MS.,— Dec. de la Aud. Real. MS.,—Herrera, Hist. General, dec. 5, lib. 4, cap. 4,—Gomara, Hist. de las Ind. cap. 121,—and, I might add, by almost every writer of authority whom I have consulted. It is contradicted, in a manner, by the admission of Garcilasso himself, that these several objects were all personified by the Indians as living beings, and had temples dedicated to them as such, with their effigies delineated in the same manner as was that of the Sun in his dwelling. Indeed, the effort of the historian to reduce the worship of the Incas to that of the Sun alone is not very reconcilable with what he elsewhere says of the homage paid to Pachacamac, above all, and to Rimac, the great oracle of the common people. The Peruvian mythology was, probably, not unlike that of Hindostan, where, under two, or at most three, principal deities, were assembled a host of inferior ones, to whom the nation paid religious homage, as personifications of the different objects in nature.

[11] Ondegardo, Rel. Seg., MS.

These consecrated objects were termed *huacas*,—a word of most prolific import; since it signified a temple, a tomb, any natural object remarkable for its size or shape, in short, a cloud of meanings, which by their contradictory sense have thrown incalculable confusion over the writings of historians and travellers.

[12] "La orden por donde fundavan sus huacas que ellos llamavan á las Idolatrias hera porque decian que todas criava el sol i que les dava madre por madre que mostravan á la tierra, porque decian que tenia madre, i tenian léwecho su vulto i sus adoratorios, i al fuego decian que tambien tenia madre i al mais i á las otras sementeras i á las ovejas iganado decian que tenian madre, i a la chocha ques el brevaje que ellos usan decian que el vinagre della hera la madre i lo reverenciavan i llamavan mama agua madre del vinagre, i á cada cosa adoravan destas de su manera." Cenq. i Pob. del Piru. MS.

were transported to the capital, where the burdensome charges of their worship were defrayed by their respective provinces. It was a rare stroke of policy in the Incas, who could thus accommodate their religion to their interests.[13]

But the worship of the Sun constituted the peculiar care of the Incas, and was the object of their lavish expenditure. The most ancient of the many temples dedicated to this divinity was in the Island of Titicaca, whence the royal founders of the Peruvian line were said to have proceeded. From this circumstance, this sanctuary was held in peculiar veneration. Every thing which belonged to it, even the broad fields of maize, which surrounded the temple, and formed part of its domain, imbibed a portion of its sanctity. The yearly produce was distributed among the different public magazines, in small quantities to each, as something that would sanctify the remainder of the store. Happy was the man who could secure even an ear of the blessed harvest for his own granary! [14]

But the most renowned of the Peruvian temples, the pride of the capital, and the wonder of the empire, was at Cuzco, where, under the munificence of successive sovereigns, it had become so enriched, that it received the name of *Coricancha*, or "the Place of Gold." It consisted of a principal building and several chapels and inferior edifices, covering a large extent of ground in the heart of the city, and completely encompassed by a wall, which, with the edifices, was all constructed of stone. The work was of the kind already described in the other public buildings of the country, and was so finely executed, that a Spaniard, who saw it in its glory, assures us, he could call to mind only two edifices in Spain, which, for their workmanship, were at all to be compared with it.[15] Yet this substantial, and, in some respects, magnificent structure, was thatched with straw!

The interior of the temple was the most worthy of admiration. It was literally a mine of gold. On the western wall was emblazoned a representation of the deity, consisting of a human countenance, looking forth

[13] Pedro Pizarro, Descub. y Conq., MS.
So it seems to have been regarded by the Licentiate Ondegardo. "E los Idolos estaban en aq¹ *galpon* grande de la casa del Sol, y cada Idolo destos tenia su servicio y gastos y mugeres, y en la casa del Sol le iban á hacer reverencia los que venian de su provincia, para lo qual é sacrificios que se hacian proveian de su misma tierra ordinaria é muy abundantemente por la misma orden que lo hacian quando estaba en la misma provincia, que daba gran autoridad á mi parecer é aun fuerza á estos Ingas que cierto me causó gran admiracion." Rel. Seg., MS.

[14] Garcilasso, Com. Real., Parte I, lib. 3, cap. 25.

[15] "Tenia este Templo en circuito mas de quatro cientos pasos, todo cercado de una muralla fuerte, labrado todo el edificio de cantera muy excelente de fina piedra, muy bien puesta y asentada, y algunas piedras eran muy grandes y soberbias, no tenian mezcla de tierra ni cal, sino con el betun que ellos suelen hacer sus edificios, y estan tan bien labradas estas piedras que no se les parece mezcla ni juntura ninguna. En toda España no he visto cosa que pueda comparar á estas paredes y postura de piedra, sino a la torre que llaman la Calahorra que está junto con la puente de Cordoba, y à una obra que vi en Toledo, cuando fui a presentar la primera parte de mi Cronica al Principe Dⁿ Felipe." Sarmiento, Relacion, MS., cap. 24.

from amidst innumerable rays of light, which emanated from it in every direction, in the same manner as the sun is often personified with us. The figure was engraved on a massive plate of gold of enormous dimensions, thickly powdered with emeralds and precious stones.[16] It was so situated in front of the great eastern portal, that the rays of the morning sun fell directly upon it at its rising, lighting up the whole apartment with an effulgence that seemed more than natural, and which was reflected back from the golden ornaments with which the walls and ceiling were everywhere in crusted. Gold, in the figurative language of the people was "the tears wept by the sun," [17] and every part of the interior of the temple glowed with burnished plates and studs of the precious metal. The cornices, which surrounded the walls of the sanctuary, were of the same costly material; and a broad belt or frieze of gold, let into the stonework, encompassed the whole exterior of the edifice.[18]

Adjoining the principal structure were several chapels of smaller dimensions. One of them was consecrated to the Moon, the deity held next in reverence, as the mother of the Incas. Her effigy was delineated in the same manner as that of the Sun, on a vast plate that nearly covered one side of the apartment. But this plate, as well as all the decorations of the building, was of silver, as suited to the pale, silvery light of the beautiful planet. There were three other chapels, one of which was dedicated to the host of Stars, who formed the bright court of the Sister of the Sun; another was consecrated to his dread ministers of vengeance, the Thunder and the Lightning; and a third, to the Rainbow, whose many-colored arch spanned the walls of the edifice with hues almost as radiant as its own. There were besides several other buildings, or insulated apartments, for the accommodation of the numerous priests who officiated in the services of the temple.[19]

All the plate, the ornaments, the utensils of every description, appropriated to the uses of religion, were of gold or silver. Twelve immense vases of the latter metal stood on the floor of the great saloon, filled with grain of the Indian corn;[20] the censers for the perfumes, the ewers which

---

[16] Conq. i Pob. del Piru, MS.—Cieza de Leon, Cronica, cap. 44, 92.

"La figura del Sol, muy grande, hecha de oro obrada muy primamente engastonada en muchas piedras ricas." Sarmiento, Relacion, MS., cap. 24.

[17] "I al oro asimismo decian que era lagrimas que el Sol llorava." Conq. i Pob. del Piru, MS.

[18] Sarmiento, Relacion, MS., cap. 24.—Antig. y Monumentos del Peru, MS.

"Cercada junto á la techumbre de una plancha de oro de palmo i medio de ancho i lo mismo tenian por de dentro en cada bohio ó casa i aposento." (Conq. i Pob. del Piru, MS.) "Tenia una cinta de planchas de oro de anchor de mas de un palmo enlazadas en las piedras." Pedro Pizarro, Descub. y Conq., MS.

[19] Sarmiento, Relacion, MS., cap. 24.—Garcilasso, Com. Real., Parte i, lib. 3, cap. 21.—Pedro Pizarro, Descub. y Conq., MS.

[20] "El bulto del Sol tenian mui grande de oro, i todo el servicio desta casa era de plata i oro, i tenian doze horones de plata blanca que dos hombres no abrazarian cada uno quadrados, i eran mas altos que un buena pica donde hechavan el maiz que havian de dar al Sol, segun ellos decian que comiese." Conq. i Pob. del Piru, MS.

The original, as the Spanish reader perceives, says each of these silver vases or bins

held the water for sacrifice, the pipes which conducted it through sub terraneous channels into the buildings, the reservoirs that received it, even the agricultural implements used in the gardens of the temple, were all of the same rich materials. The gardens, like those described, belonging to the royal palaces, sparkled with flowers of gold and silver, and various imitations of the vegetable kingdom. Animals, also, were to be found there,—among which the llama, with its golden fleece, was most conspicuous,—executed in the same style, and with a degree of skill, which, in this instance, probably, did not surpass the excellence of the material.[21]

If the reader sees in this fairy picture only the romantic coloring of some fabulous *El Dorado,* he must recall what has been said before in reference to the palaces of the Incas, and consider that these "Houses of the Sun," as they were styled, were the common reservoir into which flowed all the streams of public and private benefaction throughout the empire. Some of the statements, through credulity, and others, in the desire of exciting admiration, may be greatly exaggerated; but, in the coincidence of contemporary testimony, it is not easy to determine the exact line which should mark the measure of our skepticism. Certain it is, that the glowing picture I have given is warranted by those who saw these buildings in their pride, or shortly after they had been despoiled by the cupidity of their countrymen. Many of the costly articles were buried by the natives, or thrown into the waters of the rivers and the lakes; but enough remained to attest the unprecedented opulence of these religious establishments. Such things as were in their nature portable were speedily removed, to gratify the craving of the Conquerors, who even tore away the solid cornices and frieze of gold from the great temple, filling the vacant places with the cheaper, but—since it affords no temptation to avarice—more durable, material of plaster. Yet even thus shorn of their splendor, the venerable edifices still presented an attraction to the spoiler, who found in their dilapidated walls an inexhaustable quarry for the erection of other buildings. On the very ground once crowned by the gorgeous Coricancha rose the stately church of St. Dominic, one of the most magnificent structures of the New World. Fields of maize and lu-

---

was as high as a good lance, and so large that two men with outspread arms could barely encompass them! As this might, perhaps, embarrass even the most accommodating faith, I have preferred not to become responsible for any particular dimensions.

[21] Levinus Apollonius, fol. 38.—Garcilasso, Com. Real., Parte 1, lib. 3, cap. 24.—Pedro Pizarro, Descub. y Conq., MS.

"Tenian un Jardin que los Terrones eran pedazos de oro fino y estaban artificiosamente sembrado de maizales los quales eran oro asi las Cañas de ello como las ojas y mazorcas, y estaban tan bien plantados que aunque hiciesen recios bientos no se arrancaban, Sin todo esto tenian hechas mas de veinte obejas de oro con sus Corderos y los Pastores con sus ondas y cayados que las guardaban hecho de este metal; havia mucha cantidad de Tinajas de oro y de Plata y esmeraldas, vasos, ollas y todo genero de vasijas todo de oro fino; por otras Paredes tenian esculpidas y pintadas otras mayores cosas, en fin era uno de los ricos Templos que huho en el mundo." Sarmiento, Relacion, MS., cap. 24.

cerne now bloom on the spot which glowed with the golden gardens of the temple; and the friar chants his orisons within the consecrated precincts once occupied by the Children of the Sun.[22]

Besides the great temple of the Sun, there was a large number of inferior temples and religious houses in the Peruvian capital and its environs, amounting, as is stated, to three or four hundred.[23] For Cuzco was a sanctified spot, venerated not only as the abode of the Incas, but of all those deities who presided over the motley nations of the empire. It was the city beloved of the Sun; where his worship was maintained in its splendor; "where every fountain, pathway, and wall," says an ancient chronicler, "was regarded as a holy mystery." [24] And unfortunate was the Indian noble who, at some period or other of his life, had not made his pilgrimage to the Peruvian Mecca.

Other temples and religious dwellings were scattered over the provinces; and some of them constructed on a scale of magnificence, that almost rivalled that of the metropolis. The attendants on these composed an army of themselves. The whole number of functionaries, including those of the sacerdotal order, who officiated at the Coricancha alone, was no less than four thousand.[25]

At the head of all, both here and throughout the land, stood the great High-Priest, or Villac Vmu, as he was called. He was second only to the Inca in dignity, and was usually chosen from his brothers or nearest kindred. He was appointed by the monarch, and held his office for life; and he, in turn, appointed to all the subordinate stations of his own order. This order was very numerous. Those members of it who officiated in the House of the Sun, in Cuzco, were taken exclusively from the sacred race of the Incas. The ministers in the provincial temples were drawn from the families of the curacas; but the office of high-priest in each district was reserved for one of the blood royal. It was designed by this regulation to preserve the faith in its purity, and to guard against any departure from the stately ceremonial which it punctiliously prescribed.[26]

[22] Miller's Memoirs, vol. II. pp. 223, 224.

[23] Herrera, Hist. General, dec. 5, lib. 4, cap. 8.
"Havia en aquella ciudad y legua y media de la redonda quatrocientos y tantos lugares, donde se hacian sacrificios, y se gastava mucha suma de hacienda en ellos." Ondegardo, Rel. Prim., MS.

[24] "Que aquella ciudad del Cuzco era casa y morada de Dioses, é ansi nó habia en toda ella fuente ni paso ni pared que nó dixesen que tenia misterio." Ondegardo, Rel. Seg., MS.

[25] Conq. i Pob. del Piru, MS.
An army, indeed, if, as Cieza de Leon states, the number of priests and menials employed in the famous temple of Bilcas, on the route to Chili, amounted to 40,000! (Cronica, cap. 89.) Every thing relating to these Houses of the Sun appears to have been on a grand scale. But we may easily believe this a clerical error for 4,000.

[26] Sarmiento, Relacion, MS., cap. 27.—Conq. i Pob. del Piru, MS.
It was only while the priests were engaged in the service of the temples, that they were maintained, according to Garcilasso, from the estates of the Sun. At other times, they were to get their support from their own lands, which, if he is correct, were assigned to them in the same manner as to the other orders of the nation. Com Real., Parte 1, lib. 5, cap. 8.

The sacerdotal order, though numerous, was not distinguished by any peculiar badge or costume from the rest of the nation. Neither was it the sole depository of the scanty science of the country, nor was it charged with the business of instruction, nor with those parochial duties, if they may so be called, which bring the priest in contact with the great body of the people,—as was the case in Mexico. The cause of this peculiarity may probably be traced to the existence of a superior order, like that of the Inca nobles, whose sanctity of birth so far transcended all human appointments, that they in a manner engrossed whatever there was of religious veneration in the people. They were, in fact, the holy order of the state. Doubtless, any of them might, as very many of them did, take on themselves the sacerdotal functions; and their own insignia and peculiar privileges were too well understood to require any further badge to separate them from the people.

The duties of the priest were confined to ministration in the temple. Even here his attendance was not constant, as he was relieved after a stated interval by other brethren of his order, who succeeded one another in regular rotation. His science was limited to an acquaintance with the fasts and festivals of his religion, and the appropriate ceremonies which distinguished them. This, however frivolous might be its character, was no easy acquisition; for the ritual of the Incas involved a routine of observances, as complex and elaborate as ever distinguished that of any nation, whether pagan or Christian. Each month had its appropriate festival, or rather festivals. The four principal had reference to the Sun, and commemorated the great periods of his annual progress, the solstices and equinoxes. Perhaps the most magnificent of all the national solemnities was the feast of Raymi, held at the period of the summer solstice, when the Sun, having touched the southern extremity of his course, retraced his path, as if to gladden the hearts of his chosen people by his presence. On this occasion, the Indian nobles from the different quarters of the country thronged to the capital to take part in the great religious celebration.

For three days previous, there was a general fast, and no fire was allowed to be lighted in the dwellings. When the appointed day arrived, the Inca and his court, followed by the whole population of the city, assembled at early dawn in the great square to greet the rising of the Sun. They were dressed in their gayest apparel, and the Indian lords vied with each other in the display of costly ornaments and jewels on their persons, while canopies of gaudy feather-work and richly tinted stuffs, borne by the attendants over their heads, gave to the great square, and the streets that emptied into it, the appearance of being spread over with one vast and magnificent awning. Eagerly they watched the coming of their deity, and, no sooner did his first yellow rays strike the turrets and loftiest buildings of the capital, than a shout of gratulation broke forth from the assembled multitude, accompanied by songs of triumph, and the wild melody of barbaric instruments, that swelled louder and louder as his bright orb, rising above the mountain range towards the east, shone in full splendor on his votaries. After the usual ceremonies of adoration, a libation was offered to the great deity by the Inca, from a huge golden vase, filled with the fermented liquor of maize or of maguey, which, after the monarch had tasted it himself, he dispensed among his royal kindred. These ceremonies completed, the vast assembly was arranged in order of procession, and took its way towards the Coricancha.[27]

As they entered the street of the sacred edifice, all divested themselves of their sandals, except the Inca and his family, who did the same on passing through the portals of the temple, where none but these august personages were admitted.[28] After a decent time spent in devotion, the sovereign, attended by his courtly train, again appeared, and preparations were made to commence the sacrifice. This, with the Peruvians, consisted of animals, grain, flowers, and sweet-scented gums; sometimes of human beings, on which occasions a child or beautiful maiden was usually selected as the victim. But such sacrifices were rare, being reserved to celebrate some great public event, as a coronation, the birth of a royal heir, or a great victory. They were never followed by those cannibal repasts familiar to the Mexicans, and to many of the fierce tribes conquered by the Incas. Indeed, the conquests of these princes might well be deemed a blessing to the Indian nations, if it were only from their suppression of cannibalism, and the diminution, under their rule, of human sacrifices.[29]

At the feast of Raymi, the sacrifice usually offered was that of the llama; and the priest, after opening the body of his victim, sought in the appearances which it exhibited to read the lesson of the mysterious future. If the auguries were unpropitious, a second victim was slaught-

---

[27] Dec. de la Aud. Real., MS.—Sarmiento, Relacion, MS., cap. 27.

The reader will find a brilliant, and not very extravagant, account of the Peruvian festivals in Marmontel's romance of *Les Incas*. The French author saw in their gorgeous ceremonial a fitting introduction to his own literary pageant. Tom. I. chap. 1–4.

[28] "Ningun Indio comun osaba pasar por la calle del Sol calzado; ni ninguno, aunque fuese mui grand Señor, entrava en las casas del Sol con zapatos." Conq. i Pob. del Piru, MS.

[29] Garcilasso de la Vega flatly denies that the Incas were guilty of human sacrifices; and maintains, on the other hand, that they uniformly abolished them in every country they subdued, where they had previously existed. (Com. Real., Parte I, lib. 2, cap. 9, et alibi.) But in this material fact he is unequivocally contradicted by Sarmiento, Relacion, MS., cap. 22,—Dec. de la Aud. Real., MS.,—Montesinos, Mem. Antiguas, MS., lib. 2, cap. 8,—Balboa, Hist. du Perou, chap. 5, 8,—Cieza de Leon. Cronica, cap. 72,—Ondegardo, Rel. Seg., MS.,—Acosta, lib. 5, cap. 19,—and I might add, I suspect, were I to pursue the inquiry, by nearly every ancient writer of authority; some of whom, having come into the country soon after the Conquest, while its primitive institutions were in vigor, are entitled to more deference in a matter of this kind than Garcilasso himself. It was natural that the descendant of the Incas should desire to relieve his race from so odious an imputation; and we must have charity for him, if he does show himself, on some occasions, where the honor of his country is at stake, "high gravel blind." It should be added, in justice to the Peruvian government, that the best authorities concur in the admission, that the sacrifices were few, both in number and in magnitude, being reserved for such extraordinary occasions as those mentioned in the text.

ered, in the hope of receiving some more comfortable assurance. The Peruvian augur might have learned a good lesson of the Roman,—to consider every omen as favorable, which served the interests of his country.[30]

A fire was then kindled by means of a concave mirror of polished metal, which, collecting the rays of the sun into a focus upon a quantity of dried cotton, speedily set it on fire. It was the expedient used on the like occasions in ancient Rome, at least under the reign of the pious Numa. When the sky was overcast, and the face of the good deity was hidden from his worshippers, which was esteemed a bad omen, fire was obtained by means of friction. The sacred flame was intrusted to the care of the Virgins of the Sun, and if, by any neglect, it was suffered to go out in the course of the year, the event was regarded as a calamity that boded some strange disaster to the monarchy.[31] A burnt offering of the victims was then made on the altars of the deity. This sacrifice was but the prelude to the slaughter of a great number of llamas, part of the flocks of the Sun, which furnished a banquet not only for the Inca and his Court, but for the people, who made amends at these festivals for the frugal fare to which they were usually condemned. A fine bread or cake, kneaded of maize flour by the fair hands of the Virgins of the Sun, was also placed on the royal board, where the Inca, presiding over the feast, pledged his great nobles in generous goblets of the fermented liquor of the country, and the long revelry of the day was closed at night by music and dancing. Dancing and drinking were the favorite pastimes of the Peruvians. These amusements continued for several days, though the sacrifices terminated on the first.—Such was the great festival of Raymi; and the recurrence of this and similar festivities gave relief to the monotonous routine of toil prescribed to the lower orders of the community.[32]

In the distribution of bread and wine at this high festival, the orthodox Spaniards, who first came into the country, saw a striking resemblance to the Christian communion; [33] as in the practice of confession and penance, which, in a most irregular form, indeed, seems to have been used

---

[30] "Augurque cum esset, dicere ausus est, optimis auspiciis ea geri, quæ pro reipublicæ salute gererentur." Cicero, De Senectute.

This inspection of the entrails of animals for the purposes of divination is worthy of note, as a most rare if not a solitary, instance of the kind among the nations of the New World, though so familiar in the ceremonial of sacrifice among the pagan nations of the Old.

[31] "Vigilemque sacraverat ignem,
Excubias divûm ærnas."

Plutarch, in his life of Numa, describes the reflectors used by the Romans for kindling the sacred fire, as concave instruments of brass, though not spherical like the Peruvian, but of a triangular form.

[32] Acosta, lib. 5, cap. 28, 29.—Garcilasso, Com. Real., Parte I, lib. 6, cap. 23.

[33] "That which is most admirable in the hatred and presumption of Satan is, that he not only counterfeited in idolatry and sacrifices, but also in certain ceremonies, our sacraments, which Jesus Christ our Lord instituted, and the holy Church uses, having especially pretended to imitate, in some sort, the sacrament of the communion, which is the most high and divine of all others." Acosta, lib. 5, cap. 23.

by the Peruvians, they discerned a coincidence with another of the sacraments of the Church.[34] The good fathers were fond of tracing such coincidences, which they considered as the contrivance of Satan, who thus endeavored to delude his victims by counterfeiting the blessed rites of Christianity.[35] Others, in a different vein, imagined that they saw in such analogies the evidence, that some of the primitive teachers of the Gospel, perhaps an apostle himself, had paid a visit to these distant regions, and scattered over them the seeds of religious truth.[36] But it seems hardly necessary to invoke the Prince of Darkness, or the intervention of the blessed saints, to account for coincidences which have existed in countries far removed from the light of Christianity, and in ages, indeed, when its light had not yet risen on the world. It is much more reasonable to refer such casual points of resemblance to the general constitution of man, and the necessities of his moral nature.[37]

Another singular analogy with Roman Catholic institutions is presented by the Virgins of the Sun, the "elect," as they were called,[38] to whom I have already had occasion to refer. These were young maidens, dedicated to the service of the deity, who, at a tender age, were taken from their homes, and introduced into convents, where they were placed under the care of certain elderly matrons, *mamaconas*, who had grown grey within their walls.[39] Under these venerable guides, the holy virgins were instructed in the nature of their religious duties. They were employed in spinning and embroidery, and, with the fine hair of the vicuña, wove the hangings for the temples, and the apparel for the Inca and his

[34] Herrera, Hist. General, dec. 5, lib. 4, cap. 4.—Ondegardo, Rel. Prim., MS.
"The father of lies would likewise counterfeit the sacrament of Confession, and in his idolatries sought to be honored with ceremonies very like to the manner of Christians." Acosta, lib. 5, cap. 25.

[35] Cieza de Leon, not content with many marvellous accounts of the influence and real apparition of Satan in the Indian ceremonies, has garnished his volume with numerous wood-cuts representing the Prince of Evil in bodily presence with the usual accompaniments of tail, claws, &c., as if to reënforce the homilies in his text! The Peruvian saw in his idol a god. His Christian conqueror saw in it the Devil. One may be puzzled to decide which of the two might lay claim to the grossest superstition.

[36] Piedrahita, the historian of the Muyscas, is satisfied that this apostle must have been St. Bartholomew, whose travels were known to have been extensive. (Conq. de Granada, Parte 1, lib. 1, cap. 3.) The Mexican antiquaries consider St. Thomas as having had charge of the mission to the people of Anahuac. These two apostles, then, would seem to have divided the New World, at least the civilized portions of it, between them. How they came, whether by Behring's Straits, or directly across the Atlantic, we are not informed. Velasco—a writer of the eighteenth century!—has little doubt that they did really come. Hist. de Quito, tom. I. pp. 89, 90.

[37] The subject is illustrated by some examples in the "History of the Conquest of Mexico," vol. III., *Appendix, No. 1.*; since the same usages in that country led to precisely the same rash conclusions among the Conquerors.

[38] Llamavase Casa de Escogidas; porque las escogian, ó por Linage, ó por Hermosura." Garcilasso, Com. Real., Parte 1, lib. 4, cap. 1.

[39] Ondegardo, Rel. Prim., MS.
The word *mamacona* signified "matron;" *mama,* the first half of this compound word, as already noticed, meaning "mother." See Garcilasso, Com. Real., Parte 1, lib. 4, cap. 1.

household.[40] It was their duty, above all, to watch over the sacred fire
obtained at the festival of Raymi. From the moment they entered the
establishment, they were cut off from all connection with the world, even
with their own family and friends. No one but the Inca, and the Coya or
queen, might enter the consecrated precincts. The greatest attention was
paid to their morals, and visitors were sent every year to inspect the institutions, and to report on the state of their discipline.[41] Woe to the unhappy maiden who was detected in an intrigue! By the stern law of the
Incas, she was to be buried alive, her lover was to be strangled, and the
town or village to which he belonged was to be razed to the ground, and
"sowed with stones," as if to efface every memorial of his existence [42]
One is astonished to find so close a resemblance between the institutions
of the American Indian, the ancient Roman, and the modern Catholic!
Chastity and purity of life are virtues in woman, that would seem to
be of equal estimation with the barbarian and with the civilized.—Yet
the ultimate destination of the inmates of these religious houses was materially different.

The great establishment at Cuzco consisted wholly of maidens of the
royal blood, who amounted, it is said, to no less than fifteen hundred.
The provincial convents were supplied from the daughters of the curacas
and inferior nobles, and, occasionally, where a girl was recommended by
great personal attractions, from the lower classes of the people.[43] The
"Houses of the Virgins of the Sun" consisted of low ranges of stone buildings, covering a large extent of ground, surrounded by high walls, which
excluded those within entirely from observation. They were provided
with every accommodation for the fair inmates, and were embellished in
the same sumptuous and costly manner as the palaces of the Incas, and
the temples; for they received the particular care of government, as an
important part of the religious establishment.[44]

Yet the career of all the inhabitants of these cloisters was not confined
within their narrow walls. Though Virgins of the Sun, they were brides
of the Inca, and, at a marriageable age, the most beautiful among them

[40] Pedro Pizarro, Descub. y Conq., MS.

[41] Dec. de la Aud. Real., MS.

[42] Balboa, Hist. du Pérou, chap. 9.—Fernandez, Hist. del Peru, Parte 2, lib. 3, cap.
11.—Garcilasso, Com. Real., Parte 1. lib. 4, cap. 3.

According to the historian of the Incas, the terrible penalty was never incurred by
a single lapse on the part of the fair sisterhood; though, if it had been, the sovereign,
he assures us, would have "exacted it to the letter, with as little compunction as he
would have drowned a puppy." (Com. Real., Parte 1, lib. 4, cap. 3.) Other writers
contend, on the contrary, that these Virgins had very little claim to the reputation of
Vestals. (See Pedro Pizarro, Descub. y Conq., MS.—Gomara, Hist. de las Ind., cap.
121.) Such imputations are common enough on the inhabitants of religious houses,
whether pagan or Christian. They are contradicted in the present instance by the
concurrent testimony of most of those who had the best opportunity of arriving at
truth, and are made particularly improbable by the superstitious reverence entertained for the Incas.

[43] Pedro Pizarro, Descub. y Conq., MS.—Garcilasso, Com. Real., Parte 1, lib. 4,
cap. 1.

[44] Ibid., Parte 1, lib. 4, cap. 5.—Cieza de Leon, Cronica, cap. 44.

were selected for the honors of his bed, and transferred to the royal seraglio. The full complement of this amounted in time not only to hundreds, but thousands, who all found accommodations in his different palaces throughout the country. When the monarch was disposed to lessen the number of his establishment, the concubine with whose society he was willing to dispense returned, not to her former monastic residence, but to her own home; where, however humble might be her original condition, she was maintained in great state, and, far from being dishonored by the situation she had filled, was held in universal reverence as the Inca's bride.[45]

The great nobles of Peru were allowed, like their sovereign, a plurality of wives. The people, generally, whether by law, or by necessity stronger than law, were more happily limited to one. Marriage was conducted in a manner that gave it quite as original a character as belonged to the other institutions of the country. On an appointed day of the year, all those of a marriageable age—which, having reference to their ability to take charge of a family, in the males was fixed at not less than twenty-four years, and in the women at eighteen or twenty—were called together in the great squares of their respective towns and villages, throughout the empire. The Inca presided in person over the assembly of his own kindred, and taking the hands of the different couples who were to be united, he placed them within each other, declaring the parties man and wife. The same was done by the curacas towards all persons of their own or inferior degree in their several districts. This was the simple form of marriage in Peru. No one was allowed to select a wife beyond the community to which he belonged, which generally comprehended all his own kindred; [46] nor was any but the sovereign authorized to dispense with the law of nature—or at least, the usual law of nations—so far as to marry his own sister.[47] No marriage was esteemed valid without the consent of the parents; and the preference of the parties, it is said, was also to be consulted; though, considering the barriers imposed by the prescribed age of the candidates, this must have been within rather narrow and whimsical limits. A dwelling was got ready for the new-married pair at the charge of the district, and the prescribed portion of land assigned for their maintenance. The law of Peru provided for the future, as well as for the present. It left nothing to chance.—The simple ceremony of marriage was followed by general festivities among the friends of the parties, which lasted several days; and as every wedding took place on the same

[45] Dec. de la Aud. Real., MS.—Garcilasso, Com. Real., Parte 1, lib. 4, cap. 4.—Montesinos, Mem. Antiguas, MS., lib. 2, cap. 19.

[46] By the strict letter of the law, according to Garcilasso, no one was to marry out of his own lineage. But this narrow rule had a most liberal interpretation, since all of the same town, and even province, he assures us, were reckoned of kin to one another. Com. Real., Parte 1, lib. 4, cap. 8.

[47] Fernandez, Hist. del Peru, Parte 2, lib. 3, cap. 9.

This practice, so revolting to our feelings that it might well be deemed to violate the law of nature must not, however, be regarded as altogether peculiar to the Incas, since it was countenanced by some of the most polished nations of antiquity.

day, and as there were few families who had not someone of their members or their kindred personally interested, there was one universal bridal
jubilee throughout the empire.[48]

The extraordinary regulations respecting marriage under the Incas are
eminently characteristic of the genius of the government; which, far from
limiting itself to matters of public concern, penetrated into the most private recesses of domestic life, allowing no man, however humble, to act
for himself, even in those personal matters in which none but himself,
or his family at most, might be supposed to be interested. No Peruvian
was too low for the fostering vigilance of government. None was so high
that he was not made to feel his dependence upon it in every act of his
life. His very existence as an individual was absorbed in that of the community. His hopes and his fears, his joys and his sorrows, the tenderest
sympathies of his nature, which would most naturally shrink from observation, were all to be regulated by law. He was not allowed even to
be happy in his own way. The government of the Incas was the mildest,
—but the most searching of despotisms.

[48] Ondegardo, Rel. Seg., MS.—Garcilasso, Com. Real., Parte 1, lib. 6, cap. 36.—
Dec. de la Aud. Real., MS.—Montesinos, Mem. Antiguas, MS., lib. 2, cap. 6.

CHAPTER IV

EDUCATION—QUIPUS—ASTRONOMY—AGRICULTURE—AQUEDUCTS
—GUANO—IMPORTANT ESCULENTS

"SCIENCE was not intended for the people; but for those of generous blood. Persons of low degree are only puffed up by it, and rendered vain and arrogant. Neither should such meddle with the affairs of government; for this would bring high offices into disrepute, and cause detriment to the state." [1] Such was the favorite maxim, often repeated, of Tupac Inca Yupanqui, one of the most renowned of the Peruvian sovereigns. It may seem strange that such a maxim should ever have been proclaimed in the New World, where popular institutions have been established on a more extensive scale than was ever before witnessed; where government rests wholly on the people; and education—at least, in the great northern division of the continent—is mainly directed to qualify the people for the duties of government. Yet this maxim was strictly conformable to the genius of the Peruvian monarchy, and may serve as a key to its habitual policy; since, while it watched with unwearied solicitude over its subjects, provided for their physical necessities, was mindful of their morals, and showed, throughout, the affectionate concern of a parent for his children, it yet regarded them only as children, who were never to emerge from the state of pupilage, to act or to think for themselves, but whose whole duty was comprehended in the obligation of implicit obedience.

Such was the humiliating condition of the people under the Incas, while the numerous families of the blood royal enjoyed the benefit of all the light of education, which the civilization of the country could afford; and, long after the Conquest, the spots continued to be pointed out where the seminaries had existed for their instruction. These were placed under the care of the *amautas,* or "wise men," who engrossed the scanty stock of science—if science it could be called—possessed by the Peruvians, and who were the sole teachers of youth. It was natural that the monarch should take a lively interest in the instruction of the young nobility, his own kindred. Several of the Peruvian princes are said to have built their palaces in the neighborhood of the schools, in order that they might the

---

[1] "No es licito, que enseñen à los hijos de los Plebeios, las Ciencias, que pertenescen à los Generosos, y no mas; porque como Gente baja, no se eleven, y ensobervezcan, y menoscaben, y apoquen la Republica: bastales, que aprendan los Oficios de sus Padres; que el Mandar, y Governar no es de Plebeios, que es hacer agravio al Oficio, y à la Republica, encomendarsela à Gente comun." Garcilasso, Com. Real., Parte 1, lib. 8, cap. 8.

more easily visit them and listen to the lectures of the amautas, which they occasionally reinforced by a homily of their own.[2] In these schools, the royal pupils were instructed in all the different kinds of knowledge in which their teachers were versed, with especial reference to the stations they were to occupy in after-life. They studied the laws, and the principles of administering the government, in which many of them were to take part. They were initiated in the peculiar rites of their religion, most necessary to those who were to assume the sacerdotal functions. They learned also to emulate the achievements of their royal ancestors by listening to the chronicles compiled by the amautas. They were taught to speak their own dialect with purity and elegance; and they became acquainted with the mysterious science of the quipus, which supplied the Peruvians with the means of communicating their ideas to one another, and of transmitting them to future generations.[3]

The quipu was a cord about two feet long, composed of different colored threads tightly twisted together, from which a quantity of smaller threads were suspended in the manner of a fringe. The threads were of different colors and were tied into knots. The word *quipu*, indeed, signifies *a knot*. The colors denoted sensible objects; as, for instance, *white* represented *silver*, and *yellow*, *gold*. They sometimes also stood for abstract ideas. Thus, *white* signified *peace*, and *red*, *war*. But the quipus were chiefly used for arithmetical purposes. The knots served instead of ciphers, and could be combined in such a manner as to represent numbers to any amount they required. By means of these they went through their calculations with great rapidity, and the Spaniards who first visited the country bear testimony to their accuracy.[4]

Officers were established in each of the districts, who, under the title of *quipucamayus*, or "keepers of the quipus," were required to furnish the government with information on various important matters. One had charge of the revenues, reported the quantity of raw material distributed among the laborers, the quality and quantity of the fabrics made from it, and the amount of stores, of various kinds, paid into the royal magazines. Another exhibited the register of births and deaths, the marriages, the number of those qualified to bear arms, and the like details in reference to the population of the kingdom. These returns were annually forwarded to the capital, where they were submitted to the inspection of officers acquainted with the art of deciphering these mystic records. The government was thus provided with a valuable mass of statistical information, and the skeins of many-colored threads, collected and care-

---

[2] Ibid., Parte i, lib. 7, cap. 10.

The descendant of the Incas notices the remains, visible in his day, of two of the palaces of his royal ancestors, which had been built in the vicinity of the schools, for more easy access to them.

[3] Ibid., Parte i, lib. 4, cap. 19.

[4] Conq. i Pob. del Piru, MS.—Sarmiento, Relacion, MS., cap. 9.—Acosta, lib. 6 cap. 8.—Garcilasso Parte i, lib. 6, cap 8

fully preserved, constituted what might be called the national archives.[5]

But, although the quipus sufficed for all the purposes of arithmetical computation demanded by the Peruvians, they were incompetent to represent the manifold ideas and images which are expressed by writing. Even here, however, the invention was not without its use. For, independently of the direct representation of simple objects, and even of abstract ideas, to a very limited extent, as above noticed, it afforded great help to the memory by way of association. The peculiar knot or color, in this way, suggested what it could not venture to represent; in the same manner—to borrow the homely illustration of an old writer—as the number of the Commandment calls to mind the Commandment itself. The quipus, thus used, might be regarded as the Peruvian system of mnemonics.

Annalists were appointed in each of the principal communities, whose business it was to record the most important events which occurred in them. Other functionaries of a higher character, usually the amavtas, were intrusted with the history of the empire, and were selected to chronicle the great deeds of the reigning Inca, or of his ancestors.[6] The narrative, thus concocted, could be communicated only by oral tradition; but the quipus served the chronicler to arrange the incidents with method, and to refresh his memory. The story, once treasured up in the mind, was indelibly impressed there by frequent repetition. It was repeated by the amauta to his pupils, and in this way history, conveyed partly by oral tradition, and partly by arbitrary signs, was handed down from generation to generation, with sufficient discrepancy of details, but with a general conformity of outline to the truth.

The Peruvian quipus were, doubtless, a wretched substitute for that beautiful contrivance, the alphabet, which, employing a few simple characters as the representatives of sounds, instead of ideas, is able to convey the most delicate shades of thought that ever passed through the mind of man. The Peruvian invention, indeed, was far below that of the hieroglyphics, even below the rude picture-writing of the Aztecs; for the latter art, however incompetent to convey abstract ideas, could depict sensible objects with tolerable accuracy. It is evidence of the total ignorance in which the two nations remained of each other, that the Peruvians should have borrowed nothing of the hieroglyphical system of the Mex-

---

[5] Ondegardo expresses his astonishment at the variety of objects embraced by these simple records, "hardly credible by one who had not seen them." "En aquella ciudad se hallaron muchos viejos oficiales antiguos del Inga, asi de la religion, como del Govierno, y otra cosa que no pudiera creer sino la viera, que por hilos y nudos se hallan figuradas las leyes, y estatutos asi de lo uno como de lo otro, y las sucesiones de los Reyes y tiempo que governaron: y hallose lo que todo esto tenian a su cargo que no fue poco, y aun tube alguna claridad de los estatutos que en tiempo de cada uno se havian puesto." (Rel. Prim., MS.) (See also Sarmiento, Relacion, MS., cap. 9.—Acosta, lib. 6, cap. 8.—Garcilasso, Parte 1, lib. 6, cap. 8, 9.) A vestige of the quipus is still to be found in some parts of Peru, where the shepherds keep the tallies of their numerous flocks by means of this ancient arithmetic

[6] Ibid., ubi supra.

icans, and this, notwithstanding that the existence of the maguey plant, *agave*, in South America might have furnished them with the very material used by the Aztecs for the construction of their maps.[7]

It is impossible to contemplate without interest the struggles made by different nations, as they emerge from barbarism, to supply themselves with some visible symbols of thought,—that mysterious agency by which the mind of the individual may be put in communication with the minds of a whole community. The want of such a symbol is itself the greatest impediment to the progress of civilization. For what is it but to imprison the thought, which has the elements of immortality, within the bosom of its author, or of the small circle who come in contact with him, instead of sending it abroad to give light to thousands, and to generations yet unborn! Not only is such a symbol an essential element of civilization, but it may be assumed as the very criterion of civilization; for the intellectual advancement of a people will keep pace pretty nearly with its facilities for intellectual communication.

Yet we must be careful not to underrate the real value of the Peruvian system; nor to suppose that the quipus were as awkward an instrument, in the hand of a practised native, as they would be in ours. We know the effect of habit in all mechanical operations, and the Spaniards bear constant testimony to the adroitness and accuracy of the Peruvians in this. Their skill is not more surprising than the facility with which habit enables us to master the contents of a printed page, comprehending thousands of separate characters, by a single glance, as it were, though each character must require a distinct recognition by the eye, and that, too, without breaking the chain of thought in the reader's mind. We must not hold the invention of the quipus too lightly, when we reflect that they supplied the means of calculation demanded for the affairs of a great nation, and that, however insufficient, they afforded no little help to what aspired to the credit of literary composition.

The office of recording the national annals was not wholly confined to the amautas. It was assumed in part by the *haravecs*, or poets, who selected the most brilliant incidents for their songs or ballads, which were chanted at the royal festivals and at the table of the Inca.[8] In this manner, a body of traditional minstrelsy grew up, like the British and Spanish ballad poetry, by means of which the name of many a rude chieftain, that might have perished for want of a chronicler, has been borne down the tide of rustic melody to later generations.

---

[7] Ibid., ubi supra.—Dec. de la Aud. Real., MS.—Sarmiento, Relacion, MS., cap. 9.
  Yet the quipus must be allowed to bear some resemblance to the belts of wampum—made of colored beads strung together—in familiar use among the North American tribes, for commemorating treaties, and for other purposes.
  [8] Dec. de la Aud. Real., MS.—Garcilasso, Com. Real., Parte i, lib. 2, cap. 27.
  The word *haravec* signified "inventor" or finder"; and in his title, as well as in his functions, the minstrel-poet may remind us of the Norman *trouvère*. Garcilasso has translated one of the little lyrical pieces of his countrymen. It is light and lively; but one short specimen affords no basis for general criticism.

Yet history may be thought not to gain much by this alliance with poetry; for the domain of the poet extends over an ideal realm peopled with the shadowy forms of fancy, that bear little resemblance to the rude realities of life. The Peruvian annals may be deemed to show somewhat of the effects of this union, since there is a tinge of the marvellous spread over them down to the very latest period, which, like a mist before the reader's eye, makes it difficult to distinguish between fact and fiction.

The poet found a convenient instrument for his purposes in the beautiful Quichua dialect. We have already seen the extraordinary measures taken by the Incas for propagating their language throughout their empire. Thus naturalized in the remotest provinces, it became enriched by a variety of exotic words and idioms, which, under the influence of the Court and of poetic culture, if I may so express myself, was gradually blended, like some finished mosaic made up of coarse and disjointed materials, into one harmonious whole. The Quichua became the most comprehensive and various, as well as the most elegant, of the South American dialects.[9]

Besides the compositions already noticed, the Peruvians, it is said, showed some talent for theatrical exhibitions; not those barren pantomimes which, addressed simply to the eye, have formed the amusement of more than one rude nation. The Peruvian pieces aspired to the rank of dramatic compositions, sustained by character and dialogue, founded sometimes on themes of tragic interest, and at others on such as, from their light and social character, belong to comedy.[10] Of the execution of these pieces we have now no means of judging. It was probably rude enough, as befitted an unformed people. But, whatever may have been the execution, the mere conception of such an amusement is a proof of refinement that honorably distinguishes the Peruvian from the other American races, whose pastime was war, or the ferocious sports that reflect the image of it.

The intellectual character of the Peruvians, indeed, seems to have been marked rather by a tendency to refinement than by those hardier qual-

---

[9] Ondegardo, Rel. Prim., MS.

Sarmiento justly laments that his countrymen should have suffered this dialect, which might have proved so serviceable in their intercourse with the motley tribes of the empire, to fall so much out of use as it has done. "Y con tanto digo que fué harto beneficio para los Españoles haver esta lengua pues podian con ella andar por todas partes en algunas de las quales ya se vá perdiendo." Relacion, MS., cap. 21.

According to Velasco, the Incas, on arriving with their conquering legions at Quito, were astonished to find a dialect of the Quichua spoken there, although it was unknown over much of the intermediate country; a singular fact, if true. (Hist. de Quito, tom. I. p. 185.) The author, a native of that country, had access to some rare sources of information; and his curious volumes show an intimate analogy between the science and social institutions of the people of Quito and Peru. Yet his book betrays an obvious anxiety to set the pretensions of his own country in the most imposing point of view, and he frequently hazards assertions with a confidence that is not well calculated to secure that of his readers.

[10] Garcilasso, Com. Real., ubi supra.

ities which insure success in the severer walks of science. In these they were behind several of the semi-civilized nations of the New World. They had some acquaintance with geography, so far as related to their own empire, which was indeed extensive; and they constructed maps with lines raised on them to denote the boundaries and localities, on a similar principle with those formerly used by the blind. In astronomy, they appear to have made but moderate proficiency. They divided the year into twelve lunar months, each of which, having its own name, was distinguished by its appropriate festival.[11] They had, also, weeks; but of what length, whether of seven, nine, or ten days, is uncertain. As their lunar year would necessarily fall short of the true time, they rectified their calendar by solar observations made by means of a number of cylindrical columns raised on the high lands round Cuzco, which served them for taking azimuths; and, by measuring their shadows, they ascertained the exact times of the solstices. The period of the equinoxes they determined by the help of a solitary pillar, or gnomon, placed in the centre of a circle, which was described in the area of the great temple, and traversed by a diameter that was drawn from east to west. When the shadows were scarcely visible under the noontide rays of the sun, they said that "the god sat with all his light upon the column." [12] Quito, which lay immediately under the equator, where the vertical rays of the sun threw no shadow at noon, was held in especial veneration as the favored abode of the great deity. The period of the equinoxes was celebrated by public rejoicings. The pillar was crowned by the golden chair of the Sun, and, both then and at the solstices, the columns were hung with garlands, and offerings of flowers and fruits were made, while high festival was kept throughout the empire. By these periods the Peruvians regulated their religious rites and ceremonial, and prescribed the nature of their agricultural labors. The year itself took its departure from the date of the winter solstice.[13]

This meagre account embraces nearly all that has come down to us of Peruvian astronomy. It may seem strange that a nation, which had proceeded thus far in its observations, should have gone no farther; and that, notwithstanding its general advance in civilization, it should in this

[11] Ondegardo, Rel. Prim., MS.

Fernandez, who differs from most authorities in dating the commencement of the year from June, gives the names of the several months, with their appropriate occupations. Hist. del Peru, Parte 2, lib. 3, cap. 10.

[12] Garcilasso, Com. Real., Parte 1, lib. 2, cap. 22-26.

The Spanish conquerors threw down these pillars, as savouring of idolatry in the Indians. Which of the two were best entitled to the name of barbarians?

[13] Betanzos, Nar. de los Ingas, MS., cap. 16.—Sarmiento, Relacion, MS., cap. 23. —Acosta, lib. 6, cap. 3.

The most celebrated gnomon in Europe, that raised on the dome of the metropolitan church of Florence, was erected by the famous Toscanelli,—for the purpose of determining the solstices, and regulating the festivals of the Church,—about the year 1468; perhaps at no very distant date from that of the similar astronomical contrivance of the American Indian. See Tiraboschi, Historia della Letteratura Italiana, tom. VI. lib. 2, cap. 2, sec. 38.

science have fallen so far short, not only of the Mexicans, but of the Muyscas, inhabiting the same elevated regions of the great southern plateau with themselves. These latter regulated their calendar on the same general plan of cycles and periodical series as the Aztecs, approaching yet nearer to the system pursued by the people of Asia.[14]

It might have been expected that the Incas, the boasted children of the Sun, would have made a particular study of the phenomena of the heavens, and have constructed a calendar on principles as scientific as that of their semi-civilized neighbors. One historian, indeed, assures us that they threw their years into cycles of ten, a hundred, and a thousand years, and that by these cycles they regulated their chronology.[15] But this assertion—not improbable in itself—rests on a writer but little gifted with the spirit of criticism, and is counter-balanced by the silence of every higher and earlier authority, as well as by the absence of any monument, like those found among other American nations, to attest the existence of such a calendar. The inferiority of the Peruvians may be, perhaps, in part explained by the fact of their priesthood being drawn exclusively from the body of the Incas, a privileged order of nobility, who had no need, by the assumption of superior learning, to fence themselves round from the approaches of the vulgar. The little true science possessed by the Aztec priest supplied him with a key to unlock the mysteries of the heavens, and the false system of astrology which he built upon it gave him credit as a being who had something of divinity in his own nature. But the Inca noble was divine by birth. The illusory study of astrology, so captivating to the unenlightened mind, engaged no share of his attention. The only persons in Peru, who claimed the power of reading the mysterious future, were the diviners, men who, combining with their pretensions some skill in the healing art, resembled the conjurors found among many of the Indian tribes. But the office was held in little repute, except among the lower classes, and was abandoned to those whose age and infirmity disqualified them for the real business of life.[16]

[14] A tolerably meagre account—yet as full, probably, as authorities could warrant —of this interesting people has been given by Piedrahita, Bishop of Panamá, in the first two Books of his Historia General de las Conquistas del Nuevo Regno de Granada, (Madrid, 1688.)—M. de Humboldt was fortunate in obtaining a MS., composed by a Spanish ecclesiastic resident in Santa Fé de Bogota, in relation to the Muysca calendar, of which the Prussian philosopher has given a large and luminous analysis. Vues des Cordillères, p. 244.

[15] Montesinos, Mem. Antiguas, MS., lib. 2, cap. 7.

"Renovó la computacion de los tiempos, que se iba perdiendo, y se contaron en su Reynado los años por 365 dias y seis horas; á los años añadió decadas de diez años, á cada diez decadas una centuria de 100 años, y á cada diez centurias una capachoata ó Jutiphuacan, que son 1000 años, que quiere decir el grande año del Sol; asi contaban los siglos y los sucesos memorables de sus Reyes." Ibid., loc. cit.

[16] "Ansi mismo les hicieron señalar gente para hechizeros que tambien es entre ellos, oficio publico y conocido en todos, ... los diputados para ello no lo tenian por travajo, por que ninguno podia tener semejante oficio como los dichos

The Peruvians had knowledge of one or two constellations, and watched the motions of the planet Venus, to which, as we have seen, they dedicated altars. But their ignorance of the first principles of astronomical
science is shown by their ideas of eclipses, which, they supposed, denoted
some great derangement of the planet; and when the moon labored under one of these mysterious infirmities, they sounded their instruments,
and filled the air with shouts and lamentations, to rouse her from her
lethargy. Such puerile conceits as these form a striking contrast with
the real knowledge of the Mexicans, as displayed in their hieroglyphical
maps, in which the true cause of this phenomenon is plainly depicted.[17]

But, if less successful in exploring the heavens, the Incas must be admitted to have surpassed every other American race in their dominion
over the earth. Husbandry was pursued by them on principles that may
be truly called scientific. It was the basis of their political institutions.
Having no foreign commerce, it was agriculture that furnished them with
the means of their internal exchanges, their subsistence, and their revenues. We have seen their remarkable provisions for distributing the land
in equal shares among the people, while they required every man, except
the privileged orders, to assist in its cultivation. The Inca himself did not
disdain to set the example. On one of the great annual festivals, he proceeded to the environs of Cuzco, attended by his Court, and, in the presence of all the people, turned up the earth with a golden plough,—or an
instrument that served as such,—thus consecrating the occupation of the
husbandman as one worthy to be followed by the Children of the Sun.[18]

The patronage of the government did not stop with this cheap display
of royal condescension, but was shown in the most efficient measures for
facilitating the labors of the husbandman. Much of the country along
the sea-coast suffered from want of water, as little or no rain fell there,
and the few streams, in their short and hurried course from the mountains, exerted only a very limited influence on the wide extent of territory. The soil, it is true, was, for the most part, sandy and sterile; but
many places were capable of being reclaimed, and, indeed, needed only
to be properly irrigated to be susceptible of extraordinary production.
To these spots water was conveyed by means of canals and subterraneous
aqueducts, executed on a noble scale. They consisted of large slabs of
freestone nicely fitted together without cement, and discharged a volume

sino fuesen viejos é viejas, y personas inaviles para travajar, como mancos, cojos ó
contrechos, y gente asi á quien faltava las fuerzas para ello." Ondegardo, Rel. Seg.,
MS.
   [17] See Codex Tel.-Remensis, Part 4, Pl. 22, ap. Antiquities of Mexico, vol. I. London, 1829.
   [18] Sarmiento, Relacion, MS., cap. 16.
   The nobles, also, it seems, at this high festival, imitated the example of their
master. "Pasadas todas las fiestas, en la ultima llevavan muchos arados de manos,
los quales antiguamente heran de oro; i échos los oficios, tomava el Inga un arado
i comenzava con el a romper la tierra, i lo mismo los demas señores, para que de
alli adelante en todo su señorio hiciesen lo mismo, i sin que el Inga hiciese esto no
avia Indio que osase romper la tierra, ni pensavan que produjese si el Inga no la
rompia primero i esto vaste quante á las fiestas." Cono. i Pob. del Piru, MS.

of water sufficient, by means of latent ducts or sluices, to moisten the lands in the lower level, through which they passed. Some of these aqueducts were of great length. One that traversed the district of Condesuyu measured between four and five hundred miles. They were brought from some elevated lake or natural reservoir in the heart of the mountains, and were fed at intervals by other basins which lay in their route along the slopes of the sierra. In this descent, a passage was sometimes to be opened through rocks,—and this without the aid of iron tools; impracticable mountains were to be turned; rivers and marshes to be crossed; in short, the same obstacles were to be encountered as in the construction of their mighty roads. But the Peruvians seemed to take pleasure in wrestling with the difficulties of nature. Near Caxamarca, a tunnel is still visible, which they excavated in the mountains, to give an outlet to the waters of a lake, when these rose to a height in the rainy season that threatened the country with inundation.[19]

Most of these beneficent works of the Incas were suffered to go to decay by their Spanish conquerors. In some spots, the waters are still left to flow in their silent, subterraneous channels, whose windings and whose sources have been alike unexplored. Others, though partially dilapidated, and closed up with rubbish and the rank vegetation of the soil, still betray their course by occasional patches of fertility. Such are the remains in the valley of Nasca, a fruitful spot that lies between long tracts of desert; where the ancient water-courses of the Incas, measuring four or five feet in depth by three in width, and formed of large blocks of uncemented masonry, are conducted from an unknown distance.

The greatest care was taken that every occupant of the land through which these streams passed should enjoy the benefit of them. The quantity of water alloted to each was prescribed by law; and royal overseers superintended the distribution, and saw that it was faithfully applied to the irrigation of the ground.[20]

The Peruvians showed a similar spirit of enterprise in their schemes for introducing cultivation into the mountainous parts of their domain. Many of the hills, though covered with a strong soil, were too precipitous to be tilled. These they cut into terraces, faced with rough stone, diminishing in regular gradation towards the summit; so that, while the lower strip, or *anden*, as it was called by the Spaniards, that belted round the base of the mountain, might comprehend hundreds of acres, the upper-

[19] Sarmiento, Relacion, MS., cap. 21.—Garcilasso, Com. Real., Parte 1, lib. 5, cap. 24.—Stevenson Narrative of a Twenty Years' Residence in S. America, (London, 1829,) vol. I. p. 412; II. pp. 173, 174.

"Sacauan acequias en cabos y por partes que es cosa estraña afirmar lo: porque las echauan por lugares altos y baxos: y por laderas de los cabeços y haldes de sierras q estan en los valles: y por ellos mismos atrauiessan muchas: unas por una parte, y otras por otra, que es gran delectaciō caminar por aquellos valles: porque parece que se anda entra huertas y florestas llenas de frescuras." Cieza de Leon, Cronica, cap. 66.

[20] Pedro Pizarro, Descub. y Conq., MS.—Memoirs of Gen. Miller, vol. II. p. 220.

most was only large enough to accommodate a few rows of Indian corn.[21] Some of the eminences presented such a mess of solid rock, that, after being hewn into terraces, they were obliged to be covered deep with earth, before they could serve the purpose of the husbandman. With such patient toil did the Peruvians combat the formidable obstacles presented by the face of their country! Without the use of tools or the machinery familiar to the European, each individual could have done little; but acting in large masses, and under a common direction, they were enabled by indefatigable perseverance to achieve results, to have attempted which might have filled even the European with dismay.[22]

In the same spirit of economical husbandry which redeemed the rocky sierra from the curse of sterility, they dug below the arid soil of the valleys, and sought for a stratum where some natural moisture might be found. These excavations, called by the Spaniards *hoyas*, or "pits," were made on a great scale, comprehending frequently more than an acre, sunk to the depth of fifteen or twenty feet, and fenced round within by a wall of *adobes*, or bricks baked in the sun. The bottom of the excavation, well prepared by a rich manure of the sardines,—a small fish obtained in vast quantities along the coast,—was planted with some kind or grain or vegetable.[23]

The Peruvian farmers were well acquainted with the different kinds of manures, and made large use of them; a circumstance rare in the rich lands of the tropics, and probably not elsewhere practised by the rude tribes of America. They made great use of *guano*, the valuable deposit of sea-fowl, that has attracted so much attention, of late, from the agriculturists both of Europe and of our own country, and the stimulating and nutritious properties of which the Indians perfectly appreciated. This was found in such immense quantities on many of the little islands along the coast, as to have the appeaarnce of lofty hills, which, covered with a white saline incrustation, led the Conquerors to give them the name of the *sierra nevada*, or "snowy mountains."

The Incas took their usual precautions for securing the benefits of this important article to the husbandman. They assigned the small islands on the coast to the use of the respective districts which lay adjacent to them. When the island was large, it was distributed among several districts, and the boundaries for each were clearly defined. All encroach-

---

[21] Miller supposes that it was from these *andenes* that the Spaniards gave the name of Andes to the South American Cordilleras. (Memoirs of Gen. Miller, vol. II. p. 219.) But the name is older than the Conquest, according to Garcilasso, who traces it to *Anti*, the name of a province that lay east of Cuzco. (Com. Real., Parte 1, lib. 2, cap. 11.) *Anta*, the word for copper, which was found abundant in certain quarters of the country, may have suggested the name of the province, if not immediately that of the mountains.

[22] Memoirs of Gen. Miller, ubi supra.—Garcilasso, Com. Real., Parte 1, lib. 5, cap. 1.

[23] Cieza de Leon, Cronica, cap. 73.

The remains of these ancient excavations still excite the wonder of the modern traveller. See Stevenson, Residence in S. America, vol. I. p. 359.—Also McCulloh, Researches, p. 358.

ment on the rights of another was severely punished. And they secured the preservation of the fowl by penalties as stern as those by which the Norman tyrants of England protected their own game. No one was allowed to set foot on the island during the season for breeding, under pain of death; and to kill the birds at any time was punished in the like manner.[24]

With this advancement in agricultural science, the Peruvians might be supposed to have had some knowledge of the plough, in such general use among the primitive nations of the eastern continent. But they had neither the iron ploughshare of the Old World, nor had they animals for draught, which, indeed, were nowhere found in the New. The instrument which they used was a strong, sharp-pointed stake, traversed by a horizontal piece, ten or twelve inches from the point, on which the ploughman might set his foot and force it into the ground. Six or eight strong men were attached by ropes to the stake, and dragged it forcibly along, —pulling together, and keeping time as they moved by chanting their national songs, in which they were accompanied by the women who followed in their train, to break up the sods with their rakes. The mellow soil offered slight resistance; and the laborer, by long practice, acquired a dexterity which enabled him to turn up the ground to the requisite depth with astonishing facility. This substitute for the plough was but a clumsy contrivance; yet it is curious as the only specimen of the kind among the American aborigines, and was perhaps not much inferior to the wooden instrument introduced in its stead by the European conquerors.[25]

It was frequently the policy of the Incas, after providing a deserted tract with the means for irrigation, and thus fitting it for the labors of the husbandman, to transplant there a colony of *mitimaes*, who brought it under cultivation by raising the crops best suited to the soil. While the peculiar character and capacity of the lands were thus consulted, a means of exchange of the different products was afforded to the neighboring provinces, which, from the formation of the country, varied much more than usual within the same limits. To facilitate these agricultural exchanges, fairs were instituted, which took place three times a month in some of the most populous places, where, as money was unknown, a rude kind of commerce was kept up by the barter of their respective products. These fairs afforded so many holidays for the relaxation of the industrious laborer.[26]

Such were the expedients adopted by the Incas for the improvement of their territory; and, although imperfect, they must be allowed to show an acquaintance with the principles of agricultural science, that gives them some claim to the rank of a civilized people. Under their patient and discriminating culture, every inch of good soil was tasked to its

[24] Acosta, lib. 4, cap. 36.—Garcilasso, Com. Real., Parte 1, lib. 5, cap. 3.
[25] Ibid., Parte 1, lib. 5, cap. 2.
[26] Sarmiento, Relacion, MS., cap. 19.—Garcilasso, Com. Real., Parte 1, lib. 6, cap 36; lib. 7, cap. 1.—Herrera, Hist. General, dec. 5, lib. 4, cap. 3.

greatest power of production; while the most unpromising spots were
compelled to contribute something to the subsistence of the people.
Everywhere the land teemed with evidence of agricultural wealth, from
the smiling valleys along the coast to the terraced steeps of the sierra,
which, rising into pyramids of verdure, glowed with all the splendors of
tropical vegetation.

The formation of the country was particularly favorable, as already
remarked, to an infinite variety of products, not so much from its ex‹
tent as from its various elevations, which, more remarkable, even, than
those in Mexico, comprehend every degree of latitude from the equator
to the polar regions. Yet, though the temperature changes in this region
with the degree of elevation, it remains nearly the same in the same spots
throughout the year; and the inhabitant feels none of those grateful vicissitudes of season which belong to the temperate latitudes of the globe.
Thus, while the summer lies in full power on the burning regions of the
palm and the cocoa-tree that fringe the borders of the ocean, the broad
surface of the table-land blooms with the freshness of perpetual spring,
and the higher summits of the Cordilleras are white with everlasting
winter.

The Peruvians turned this fixed variety of climate, if I may so say, to
the best account by cultivating the productions appropriate to each; and
they particularly directed their attention to those which afforded the most
nutriment to man. Thus, in the lower level were to be found the cassava-
tree and the banana, that bountiful plant, which seems to have relieved
man from the primeval curse—if it were not rather a blessing—of toiling
for his sustenance.[27] As the banana faded from the landscape, a good substitute was found in the maize, the great agricultural staple of both the
northern and southern divisions of the American continent; and which,
after its exportation to the Old World, spread so rapidly there, as to suggest the idea of its being indigenous to it.[28] The Peruvians were well
acquainted with the different modes of preparing this useful vegetable,
though it seems they did not use it for bread, except at festivals; and
they extracted a sort of honey from the stalk, and made an intoxicating
liquor from the fermented grain, to which, like the Aztecs, they were immoderately addicted.[29]

[27] The prolific properties of the banana are shown by M. de Humboldt, who
states that its productiveness, as compared with that of wheat, is as 133 to 1, and
with that of the potato, as 44 to 1. (Essai Politique sur le Royaume de la Nouvelle
Espagne, Paris, 1827, tom. II. p. 389.) It is a mistake to suppose that this plant was
not indigenous to South America. The banana-leaf has been frequently found in
ancient Peruvian tombs.
[28] The misnomer of *blé de Turquie* shows the popular error. Yet the rapidity of
its diffusion through Europe and Asia, after the discovery of America, is of itself
sufficient to show that it could not have been indigenous to the Old World, and
have so long remained generally unknown there.
[29] Acosta, lib. 4, cap. 16.
The saccharine matter contained in the maize-stalk is much greater in tropical
countries than in more northern latitudes; so that the natives in the former may be
seen sometimes sucking it like the sugar-cane. One kind of the fermented liquors,

The temperate climate of the table-land furnished them with the maguey, *agave Americana*, many of the extraordinary qualities of which they comprehended, though not its most important one of affording a material for paper. Tobacco, too, was among the products of this elevated region. Yet the Peruvians differed from every other Indian nation to whom it was known, by using it only for medicinal purposes, in the form of snuff.[30] They may have found a substitute for its narcotic qualities in the coca (*Erythroxylum Peruvianum*), or *cuca*, as called by the natives. This is a shrub which grows to the height of a man. The leaves when gathered are dried in the sun, and, being mixed with a little lime, form a preparation for chewing, much like the betel-leaf of the East.[31] With a small supply of this cuca in his pouch, and a handful of roasted maize, the Peruvian Indian of our time performs his wearisome journeys, day after day, without fatigue, or, at least, without complaint. Even food the most invigorating is less grateful to him than his loved narcotic. Under the Incas, it is said to have been exclusively reserved for the noble orders. If so, the people gained one luxury by the Conquest; and, after that period, it was so extensively used by them, that this article constituted a most important item of the colonial revenue of Spain.[32] Yet, with the soothing charms of an opiate, this weed so much vaunted by the natives, when used to excess, is said to be attended with all the mischievous effects of habitual intoxication.[33]

Higher up on the slopes of the Cordilleras, beyond the limits of the maize and of the *quinoa*,—a grain bearing some resemblance to rice, and largely cultivated by the Indians,—was to be found the potato, the introduction of which into Europe has made an era in the history of agriculture. Whether indigenous to Peru, or imported from the neighboring country of Chili, it formed the great staple of the more elevated plains, under the Incas, and its culture was continued to a height in the equatorial regions which reached many thousand feet above the limits of perpetual snow in the temperate latitudes of Europe.[34] Wild specimens

sora, made from the corn, was of such strength, that the use of it was forbidden by the Incas, at least to the common people. Their injunctions do not seem to have been obeyed so implicitly in this instance as usual.

[30] Garcilasso, Com. Real., Parte 1, lib. 2, cap. 25.

[31] The pungent leaf of the *betel* was in like manner mixed with lime when chewed. (Elphinstone, History of India, London, 1841, vol. I. p. 331.) The similarity of this social indulgence, in the remote East and West, is singular.

[32] Ondegardo, Rel. Seg., MS.—Acosta, lib. 4, cap. 22.—Stevenson, Residence in S. America, vol. II. p. 63.—Cieza de Leon, Cronica, cap. 96.

[33] A traveller (Poeppig) noticed in the Foreign Quarterly Review, (No. 33,) expatiates on the malignant effects of the habitual use of the *cuca*, as very similar to those produced on the chewer of opium. Strange that such baneful properties should not be the subject of more frequent comment with other writers! I do not remember to have seen them even adverted to.

[34] Malte-Brun, book 86.

The potato, found by the early discoverers in Chili, Peru, New Granada, and all along the Cordilleras of South America, was unknown in Mexico,—an additional proof of the entire ignorance in which the respective nations of the two continents remained of one another. M. de Humboldt, who has bestowed much attention on

of the vegetable might be seen still higher, springing up spontaneously amidst the stunted shrubs that clothed the lofty sides of the Cordilleras, till these gradually subsided into the mosses and the short yellow grass, *pajonal*, which, like a golden carpet, was unrolled around the base of the mighty cones, that rose far into the regions of eternal silence, covered with the snows of centuries.[35]

the early history of this vegetable, which has exerted so important an influence on European society, supposes that the cultivation of it in Virginia, where it was known to the early planters, must have been originally derived from the Southern Spanish colonies. Essai Politique, tom. II. p. 462.

[35] While Peru, under the Incas, could boast these indigenous products, and many others less familiar to the European, it was unacquainted with several of great importance, which, since the Conquest, have thriven there as on their natural soil. Such are the olive, the grape, the fig, the apple, the orange, the sugar-cane. None of the cereal grains of the Old World were found there. The first wheat was introduced by a Spanish lady of Trujillo, who took great pains to disseminate it among the colonists, of which the government, to its credit, was not unmindful. Her name was Maria de Escobar. History, which is so much occupied with celebrating the scourges of humanity, should take pleasure in commemorating one of its real benefactors.

CHAPTER V

PERUVIAN SHEEP—GREAT HUNTS—MANUFACTURES—MECHANICAL
SKILL—ARCHITECTURE—CONCLUDING REFLECTIONS

A NATION which had made such progress in agriculture might be reasonably expected to have made, also, some proficiency in the mechanical
arts,—especially when, as in the case of the Peruvians, their agricultural
economy demanded in itself no inconsiderable degree of mechanical skill.
Among most nations, progress in manufactures has been found to have
an intimate connection with the progress of husbandry. Both arts are directed to the same great object of supplying the necessaries, the comforts, or, in a more refined condition of society, the luxuries of life; and
when the one is brought to a perfection that infers a certain advance in
civilization, the other must naturally find a corresponding development
under the increasing demands and capacities of such a state. The subjects of the Incas, in their patient and tranquil devotion to the more
humble occupations of industry which bound them to their native soil,
bore greater resemblance to the Oriental nations, as the Hindoos and Chinese, than they bore to the members of the great Anglo-Saxon family,
whose hardy temper has driven them to seek their fortunes on the stormy
ocean, and to open a commerce with the most distant regions of the
globe. The Peruvians, though lining a long extent of sea-coast, had no
foreign commerce.

They had peculiar advantages for domestic manufacture in a material
incomparably superior to anything possessed by the other races of the
Western continent. They found a good substitute for linen in a fabric
which, like the Aztecs, they knew how to weave from the tough thread
of the maguey. Cotton grew luxuriantly on the low, sultry level of the
coast, and furnished them with a clothing suitable to the milder latitudes
of the country. But from the llama and the kindred species of Peruvian
sheep they obtained a fleece adapted to the colder climate of the table-
land, "more estimable," to quote the language of a well-informed writer,
"than the down of the Canadian beaver, the fleece of the *brebis des Cal-
moucks*, or of the Syrian goat." [1]

Of the four varieties of the Peruvian sheep, the llama, the one most
familiarly known, is the least valuable on account of its wool. It is chiefly
employed as a beast of burden, for which, although it is somewhat larger

---

[1] Walton, Historical and Descriptive Account of the Peruvian Sheep, (London,
1811,) p. 115. This writer's comparison is directed to the wool of the vicuña, the
most esteemed of the genus for its fleece.

than any of the other varieties, its diminutive size and strengui would seem to disqualify it. It carries a load of little more than a hundred pounds, and cannot travel above three or four leagues in a day. But all this is compensated by the little care and cost required for its manage-ment and its maintenance. It picks up an easy subsistence from the moss and stunted herbage that grow scantily along the withered sides and the steeps of the Cordilleras. The structure of its stomach, like that of the camel, is such as to enable it to dispense with any supply of water for weeks, nay, months together. Its spongy hoof, armed with a claw or pointed talon to enable it to take secure hold on the ice, never requires to be shod; and the load laid upon its back rests securely in its bed of wool, without the aid of girth or saddle. The llamas move in troops of five hundred or even a thousand, and thus, though each individual carries but little, the aggregate is considerable. The whole caravan travels on at its regular pace, passing the night in the open air without suffering from the coldest temperature, and marching in perfect order, and in obedience to the voice of the driver. It is only when overloaded that the spirited little animal refuses to stir, and neither blows nor caresses can induce him to rise from the ground. He is as sturdy in asserting his rights on this occasion, as he is usually docile and unresisting.[2]

The employment of domestic animals distinguished the Peruvians from the other races of the New World. This economy of human labor by the substitution of the brute is an important element of civilization, inferior only to what is gained by the substitution of machinery for both. Yet the ancient Peruvians seem to have made much less account of it than their Spanish conquerors, and to have valued the llama, in common with the other animals of that genus, chiefly for its fleece. Immense herds of these "large cattle," as they were called, and of the "smaller cattle,"[3] or *alpacas*, were held by the government, as already noticed, and placed under the direction of shepherds, who conducted them from one quarter of the country to another, according to the changes of the season. These migrations were regulated with all the precision with which the code of the *mesta* determined the migrations of the vast merino flocks in Spain; and the Conquerors, when they landed in Peru, were amazed at finding a race of animals so similar to their own in properties and habits, and under the control of a system of legislation which might seem to have been imported from their native land.[4]

[2] Ibid., p. 23, et seq.—Garcilasso, Com. Real., Parte 1, lib. 8, cap. 16.—Acosta, lib. 4, cap. 41.

Llama, according to Garcilasso de la Vega, is a Peruvian word signifying "flock." (Ibid., ubi supra.) The natives got no milk from their domesticated animals; nor was milk used, I believe, by any tribe on the American continent.

[3] *Ganado maior, ganado menor.*

[4] The judicious Ondegardo emphatically recommends the adoption of many of these regulations by the Spanish government, as peculiarly suited to the exigencies of the natives. "En esto de los ganados paresció haber hecho muchas constituciones en diferentes tiempos é algunas tan utiles é provechosas para su conservacion que convendria que tambien guardasen agora." Rel. Seg., MS.

But the richest store of wool was obtained, not from these domesticated animals, but from the two other species, the *huanacos* and the *vicuñas*, which roamed in native freedom over the frozen ranges of the Cordilleras; where not unfrequently they might be seen scaling the snow-covered peaks which no living thing inhabits save the condor, the huge bird of the Andes, whose broad pinions bear him up in the atmosphere to the height of more than twenty thousand feet above the level of the sea.[5] In these rugged pastures, "the flock without a fold" finds sufficient sustenance in the *ychu*, a species of grass which is found scattered all along the great ridge of the Cordilleras, from the equator to the southern limits of Patagonia. And as these limits define the territory traversed by the Peruvian sheep, which rarely, if ever, venture north of the line, it seems not improbable that this mysterious little plant is so important to their existence, that the absence of it is the principal reason why they have not penetrated to the northern latitudes of Quito and New Granada.[6]

But, although thus roaming without a master over the boundless wastes of the Cordilleras, the Peruvian peasant was never allowed to hunt these wild animals, which were protected by laws as severe as were the sleek herds that grazed on the more cultivated slopes of the plateau. The wild game of the forest and the mountain was as much the property of the government, as if it had been inclosed within a park, or penned within a fold.[7] It was only on stated occasions, at the great hunts, which took place once a year, under the personal superintendence of the Inca or his principal officers, that the game was allowed to be taken. These hunts were not repeated in the same quarter of the country oftener than once in four years, that time might be allowed for the waste occasioned by them to be replenished. At the appointed time, all those living in the district and its neighborhood, to the number, it might be, of fifty or sixty thousand men,[8] were distributed round, so as to form a cordon of immense extent, that should embrace the whole country which was to be hunted over. The men were armed with long poles and spears, with which they beat up game of every description lurking in the woods, the valleys, and the mountains, killing the beasts of prey without mercy, and driving the others, consisting chiefly of the deer of the country, and the huanacos and vicuñas, towards the centre of the wide-extended circle; until, as this gradually contracted, the timid inhabitants of the forest were concentrated on some spacious plain, where the eye of the hunter might range freely over his victims, who found no place for shelter or escape.

The male deer and some of the coarser kind of the Peruvian sheep

---

[5] Malte-Brun, book 86.

[6] *Ychu*, called in the Flora Peruana *Jarava;* Class, Monandria Digynia. See Walton, p. 17.

[7] Ondegardo, Rel. Prim., MS.

[8] Sometimes even a hundred thousand mustered, when the Inca hunted in person, if we may credit Sarmiento. "De donde haviendose ya juntado cinquenta ó sesenta mil Personas ó cien mil si mandado les era." Relacion, MS., cap. 13.

were slaughtered; their skins were reserved for the various useful manufactures to which they are ordinarily applied, and their flesh, cut into
thin slices, was distributed among the people, who converted it into
charqui, the dried meat of the country, which constituted then the sole,
as it has since the principal, animal food of the lower classes of Peru.[9]

But nearly the whole of the sheep, amounting usually to thirty or forty
thousand, or even a larger number, after being carefully sheared, were
suffered to escape and regain their solitary haunts among the mountains.
The wool thus collected was deposited in the royal magazines, whence,
in due time, it was dealt out to the people. The coarser quality was worked up into garments for their own use, and the finer for the Inca; for
none but an Inca noble could wear the fine fabric of the vicuña.[10]

The Peruvians showed great skill in the manufacture of different
articles for the royal household from this delicate material, which, under
the name of *vigonia* wool, is now familiar to the looms of Europe. It was
wrought into shawls, robes, and other articles of dress for the monarch,
and into carpets, coverlets, and hangings for the imperial palaces and the
temples. The cloth was finished on both sides alike; [11] the delicacy of the
texture was such as to give it the lustre of silk; and the brilliancy of the
dyes excited the admiration and the envy of the European artisan.[12]
The Peruvians produced also an article of great strength and durability
by mixing the hair of animals with wool; and they were expert in the
beautiful feather-work, which they held of less account than the Mexicans from the superior quality of the materials for other fabrics, which
they had at their command.[13]

The natives showed a skill in other mechanical arts similar to that displayed by their manufactures of cloth. Every man in Peru was expected
to be acquainted with the various handicrafts essential to domestic comfort. No long apprenticeship was required for this, where the wants were
so few as among the simple peasantry of the Incas. But, if this were all,
it would imply but a very moderate advancement in the arts. There were

[9] Ibid., ubi supra.
Charqui; hence, probably, says McCulloh, the term "jerked," applied to the dried
beef of South America. Researches, p. 377.
[10] Sarmiento, Relacion, MS., loc. cit.—Cieza de Leon, Cronica, cap. 81.—Garcilasso, Com. Real., Parte 1, lib. 6, cap. 6.
[11] Acosta, lib. 4, cap. 41.
[12] "Ropas finisimas para los Reyes, que lo eran tanto que parecian de sarga de
seda y con colores tan perfectos quanto se puede afirmar." Sarmiento, Relacion.
MS., cap. 13.
[13] Pedro Pizarro, Descub. y Conq., MS.
"Ropa finissima para los señores Ingas de lana de las Vicunias. Y cierto fue tan
prima esta ropa, como auran visto en España: por alguna que alla fue luego que se
gano este reyno. Los vestidos destos Ingas eran camisetas desta ropa; vnas pobla-
das de argenteria de oro, otras de esmeraldas y piedras preciosas: y algunas de
plumas de aues: otras de solamente la manta. Para hazer estas ropas, tuuierō y
tienen tan perfetas colores de carmesi, azul, amarillo, negro, y de otras suertes: que
verdaderamente tienen ventaja a las de España." Cieza de Leon, Cronica, cap. 114

certain individuals, however, carefully trained to those occupations which minister to the demands of the more opulent classes of society. These occupations, like every other calling and office in Peru, always descended from father to son.[14] The division of castes, in this particular, was as precise as that which existed in Egypt or Hindostan. If this arrangement be unfavorable to originality, or to the development of the peculiar talent of the individual, it at least conduces to an easy and finished execution by familiarizing the artist with the practice of his art from chlidhood.[15]

The royal magazines and the *huacas* or tombs of the Incas have been found to contain many specimens of curious and elaborate workmanship. Among these are vases of gold and silver, bracelets, collars, and other ornaments for the person; utensils of every description, some of fine clay, and many more of copper; mirrors of a hard, polished stone, or burnished silver, with a great variety of other articles made frequently on a whimsical pattern, evincing quite as much ingenuity as taste or inventive talent.[16] The character of the Peruvian mind led to imitation, in fact, rather than invention, to delicacy and minuteness of finish, rather than to boldness or beauty of design.

That they should have accomplished these difficult works with such tools as they possessed, is truly wonderful. It was comparatively easy to cast and even sculpture metallic substances, both of which they did with consummate skill. But that they should have shown the like facility in cutting the hardest substances, as emeralds and other precious stones, is not easy to explain. Emeralds they obtained in considerable quantity from the barren district of Atacames, and this inflexible material seems to have been almost as ductile in the hands of the Peruvian artist as if it had been made of clay.[17] Yet the natives were unacquainted with the use of iron, though the soil was largely impregnated with it.[18] The tools used were of stone, or more frequently of copper. But the material on which they relied for the execution of their most difficult tasks was

---

[14] Ondegardo, Rel. Prim. et Seg., MSS.—Garcilasso, Com. Real., Parte 1, lib. 5, cap. 7, 9, 13.

[15] At least, such was the opinion of the Egyptians, who referred to this arrangement of castes as the source of their own peculiar dexterity in the arts. See Diodorus Sic., lib. 1, sec. 74.

[16] Ulloa, Not Amer., ent. 21.—Pedro Pizarro, Descub. y Conq., MS.—Cieza de Leon, Cronica, cap. 114.—Condamine, Mem. ap. Hist. de l'Acad. Royale de Berlin, tom. II. p. 454-456.

The last writer says, that a large collection of massive gold ornaments of very rich workmanship was long preserved in the royal treasury of Quito. But on his going there to examine them, he learned that they had just been melted down into ingots to send to Carthagena, then beseiged by the English! The art of war can flourish only at the expense of all the other arts.

[17] They had turquoises, also, and might have had pearls, but for the tenderness of the Incas, who were unwilling to risk the lives of their people in this perilous fishery! At least, so we are assured by Garcilasso, Com. Real., Parte 1, lib. 8, cap. 23.

[18] "No tenian herramientas de hierro ni azero." Ondegardo, Rel. Seg., MS.—Herrera, Hist. General, dec. 5, lib. 4, cap. 4.

formed by combining a very small portion of tin with copper.[19] This
composition gave a hardness to the metal which seems to have been little
inferior to that of steel. With the aid of it, not only did the Peruvian
artisan hew into shape porphyry and granite, but by his patient industry
accomplished works which the European would not have ventured to undertake. Among the remains of the monuments of Cannar may be seen
movable rings in the muzzles of animals, all nicely sculptured of one
entire block of granite.[20] It is worthy of remark, that the Egyptians, the
Mexicans, and the Peruvians, in their progress towards civilization,
should never have detected the use of iron, which lay around them in
abundance; and that they should each, without any knowledge of the
other, have found a substitute for it in such a curious composition of
metals as gave to their tools almost the temper of steel; [21] a secret that
has been lost—or, to speak more correctly, has never been discovered—
by the civilized European.

I have already spoken of the large quantity of gold and silver wrought
into various articles of elegance and utility for the Incas; though the
amount was inconsiderable, in comparison with what could have been afforded by the mineral riches of the land, and with what has since been
obtained by the more sagacious and unscrupulous cupidity of the white
man. Gold was gathered by the Incas from the deposits of the streams.
They extracted the ore also in considerable quantities from the valley
of Curimayo, northeast of Caxamarca, as well as from other places; and
the silver mines of Porco, in particular, yielded them considerable returns. Yet they did not attempt to penetrate into the bowels of the earth
by sinking a shaft, but simply excavated a cavern in the steep sides of
the mountain, or, at most, opened a horizonal vein of moderate depth.
They were equally deficient in the knowledge of the best means of detaching the precious metal from the dross with which it was united, and
had no idea of the virtues of quicksilver,—a mineral not rare in Peru,—
as an amalgam to effect this decomposition.[22] Their method of smelting
the ore was by means of furnaces built in elevated and exposed situations, where they might be fanned by the strong breezes of the mountains.
The subjects of the Incas, in short, with all their patient perseverance,
did little more than penetrate below the crust, the outer rind, as it were,
formed over those golden caverns which lie hidden in the dark depths of
the Andes. Yet what they gleaned from the surface was more than ade-

[19] M. de Humboldt brought with him back to Europe one of these metallic tools, a
chisel, found in a silver mine opened by the Incas not far from Cuzco. On an analysis, it was found to contain 0.94 of copper, and 0.06 of tin. See Vues des Cordillères,
p. 117.
[20] "Quoiqu'il en soit," says M. de la Condamine, "nous avons vû en quelques
autres ruïnes des ornemens du même granit, qui représentoient des mufles d'animaux,
dont les narines percées portoient des anneaux mobiles de la même pierre." Mem. ap.
Hist. de l'Acad. Royale de Berlin, tom. II. p. 452.
[21] See the History of the Conquest of Mexico, Book 1, chap. 5.
[22] Garcilasso, Com. Real., Parte 1, lib. 8, cap. 25.

quate for all their demands. For they were not a commercial people, and had no knowledge of money.[23] In this they differed from the ancient Mexicans, who had an established currency of a determinate value. In one respect, however, they were superior to their American rivals, since they made use of weights to determine the quantity of their commodities, a thing wholly unknown to the Aztecs. This fact is ascertained by the discovery of silver balances, adjusted with perfect accuracy, in some of the tombs of the Incas.[24]

But the surest test of the civilization of a people—at least, as sure as any—afforded by mechanical art is to be found in their architecture, which presents so noble a field for the display of the grand and the beautiful, and which, at the same time, is so intimately connected with the essential comforts of life. There is no object on which the resources of the wealthy are more freely lavished, or which calls out more effectually the inventive talent of the artist. The painter and the sculptor may display their individual genius in creations of surpassing excellence, but it is the great monuments of architectural taste and magnificence that are stamped in a peculiar manner by the genius of the nation. The Greek, the Egyptian, the Saracen, the Gothic,—what a key do their respective styles afford to the character and condition of the people! The monuments of China, of Hindostan, and of Central America are all indicative of an immature period, in which the imagination has not been disciplined by study, and which, therefore, in its best results, betrays only the ill-regulated aspirations after the beautiful, that belong to a semi-civilized people.

The Peruvian architecture, bearing also the general characteristics of an imperfect state of refinement, had still its peculiar character; and so uniform was that character, that the edifices throughout the country seem to have been all cast in the same mould.[25] They were usually built of porphyry or granite; not unfrequently of brick. This, which was formed into blocks or squares of much larger dimensions than our brick, was made of a tenacious earth mixed up with reeds or tough grass, and acquired a degree of hardness with age that made it insensible alike to the storms and the more trying sun of the tropics.[26] The walls were of great

[23] Ibid., Parte 1, lib. 5, cap. 7; lib. 6, cap. 8.—Ondegardo, Rel. Seg., MS.

This, which Bonaparte thought so incredible of the little island of Loo Choo, was still more extraordinary in a great and flourishing empire like Peru;—the country, too, which contained within its bowels the treasures that were one day to furnish Europe with the basis of its vast metallic currency.

[24] Ulloa, Not. Amer., ent. 21.

[25] It is the observation of Humboldt. "Il est impossible d'examiner attentivement un seul édifice du temps des Incas, sans reconnoître le même type dans tous les autres qui couvrent le dos des Andes, sur une longueur de plus de quatre cent cinquante lieues, depuis mille jusqu'à quatre mille mêtres d'élévation au-dessus du niveau de l'Océan. On dirait qu'un seul architecte a construit ce grand nombre de monumens." Vues des Cordillères, p. 197.

[26] Ulloa, who carefully examined these bricks, suggests that there must have been some secret in their composition,—so superior in many respects to our own manufacture,—now lost. Not. Amer., ent. 20.

thickness, but low, seldom reaching to more than twelve or fourteen feet in height. It is rare to meet with accounts of a building that rose to a second story.[27]

The apartments had no communication with one another, but usually opened into a court; and, as they were unprovided with windows, or apertures that served for them, the only light from without must have been admitted by the doorways. These were made with the sides approaching each other towards the top, so that the lintel was considerably narrower than the threshold, a peculiarity, also, in Egyptian architecture. The roofs have for the most part disappeared with time. Some few survive in the less ambitious edifices, of a singular bell-shape, and made of a composition of earth and pebbles. They are supposed, however, to have been generally formed of more perishable materials, of wood or straw. It is certain that some of the most considerable stone-buildings were thatched with straw. Many seem to have been constructed without the aid of cement; and writers have contended that the Peruvians were unacquainted with the use of mortar, or cement of any kind.[28] But a close, tenacious mould, mixed with lime, may be discovered filling up the interstices of the granite in some buildings; and in others, where the well-fitted blocks leave no room for this coarser material, the eye of the antiquary has detected a fine bituminous glue, as hard as the rock itself.[29]

The greatest simplicity is observed in the construction of the buildings, which are usually free from outward ornament; though in some the huge stones are shaped into a convex form with great regularity, and adjusted with such nice precision to one another, that it would be impossible, but for the flutings, to determine the line of junction. In others, the stone is rough, as it was taken from the quarry, in the most irregular forms, with the edges nicely wrought and fitted to each other. There is no appearance of columns or of arches; though there is some contradiction as to the latter point. But it is not to be doubted, that, although they may have made some approach to this mode of construction by the greater or less inclination of the walls, the Peruvian architects were wholly unacquainted with the true principle of the circular arch reposing on its key-stone.[30]

[27] Ibid., ubi supra.

[28] Among others, see Acosta, lib. 6, cap. 15.—Robertson, History of America, (London, 1796,) vol. III. p. 213.

[29] Ondegardo, Rel. Seg., MS.—Ulloa, Not. Amer., ent. 21.

Humboldt, who analyzed the cement of the ancient structures at Cannar, says that it is a true mortar, formed of a mixture of pebbles and a clayey marl. (Vues des Cordillères, p. 116.) Father Velasco is in raptures with an "almost imperceptible kind of cement" made of lime and a bituminous substance resembling glue, which incorporated with the stones so as to hold them firmly together like one solid mass, yet left nothing visible to the eye of the common observer. This glutinous composition, mixed with pebbles, made a sort of *Macadamized* road much used by the Incas, as hard and almost as smooth as marble. Hist. de Quito, tom. 1. pp. 126–128.

[30] Condamine, Mem. ap. Hist. de l'Acad. Royale de Berlin, tom. II. p. 448.—Antig. y Monumentos del Peru, MS.—Herrera, Hist. General, dec. 5, lib. 4, cap. 4.—Acosta, lib. 6, cap. 14.—Ulloa, Voyage to S. America, vol. I. p. 460.—Ondegardo, Rel. Seg., MS.

The architecture of the Incas is characterized, says an eminent travel-ler, "by simplicity, symmetry, and solidity." [31] It may seem unphilo-sophical to condemn the peculiar fashion of a nation as indicating want of taste, because its standard of taste differs from our own. Yet there is an incongruity in the composition of the Peruvian buildings which argues a very imperfect acquaintance with the first principles of architecture. While they put together their bulky masses of porphyry and granite with the nicest art, they were incapable of mortising their timbers, and, in their ignorance of iron, knew no better way of holding the beams together that tying them with thongs of maguey. In the same incongruous spirit, the building that was thatched with straw, and unilluminated by a win-dow, was glowing with tapestries of gold and silver! These are the incon-sistencies of a rude people, among whom the arts are but partially de-veloped. It might not be difficult to find examples of like inconsistency in the architecture and domestic arrangements of our Anglo-Saxon, and, at a still later period of our Norman ancestors.

Yet the buildings of the Incas were accommodated to the character of the climate, and were well fitted to resist those terrible convulsions which belong to the land of volcanoes. The wisdom of their plan is attested by the number which still survive, while the more modern constructions of the Conquerors have been buried in ruins. The hand of the Conquerors, indeed, has fallen heavily on these venerable monuments, and, in their blind and superstitious search for hidden treasure, has caused infinitely more ruin than time or the earthquake.[32] Yet enough of these monu-ments still remain to invite the researches of the antiquary. Those only in the most conspicuous situations have been hitherto examined. But, by

[31] "Simplicité, symétrie, et solidité, voil à les trois caractères par lesquels se distin-guent avantageusement tous les édifices péruviens." Humboldt, Vues des Cordillères. p. 115.

[32] The anonymous author of the Antig. y Monumentos del Peru, MS., gives us, at second hand, one of those golden traditions which, in early times, fostered the spirit of adventure. The tradition, in this instance, he thinks well entitled to credit. The reader will judge for himself.

"It is a well-authenticated report, and generally received, that there is a secret hall in the fortress of Cuzco, where an immense treasure is concealed, consisting of the statues of all the Incas, wrought in gold. A lady is still living, Doña Maria de Esquivel, the wife of the last Inca, who has visited this hall, and I have heard her relate the way in which she was carried to see it.

"Don Carlos, the lady's husband, did not maintain a style of living becoming his high rank. Doña Maria sometimes reproached him, declaring that she had been de-ceived into marrying a poor Indian under the lofty title of Lord or Inca. She said this so frequently, that Don Carlos one night exclaimed, 'Lady! do you wish to know whether I am rich or poor? You shall see that no lord nor king in the world has a larger treasure than I have.' Then covering her eyes with a handkerchief, he made her turn round two or three times, and, taking her by the hand, led her a short distance before he removed the bandage. On opening her eyes, what was her amazement! She had gone not more than two hundred paces, and descended a short flight of steps, and she now found herself in a large quadrangular hall, where, ranged on benches round the walls, she beheld the statues of the Incas, each of the size of a boy twelve years old, all of massive gold! She saw also many vessels of gold and silver 'In fact,' she said, 'it was one of the most magnificent treasures in the whole world!'"

the testimony of travellers, many more are to be found in the less frequented parts of the country; and we may hope they will one day call
forth a kindred spirit of enterprise to that which has so successfully explored the mysterious recesses of Central America and Yucatan.

I cannot close this analysis of the Peruvian institutions without a few
reflections on their general character and tendency, which, if they involve
some repetition of previous remarks, may, I trust, be excused, from my
desire to leave a correct and consistent impression on the reader. In this
survey, we cannot but be struck with the total dissimilarity between these
institutions and those of the Aztecs,—the other great nation who led in
the march of civilization on this western continent, and whose empire in
the northern portion of it was as conspicuous as that of the Incas in the
south. Both nations came on the plateau, and commenced their career
of conquest, at dates, it may be, not far removed from each other.[33] And
it is worthy of notice, that, in America, the elevated region along the
crests of the great mountain ranges should have been the chosen seat of
civilization in both hemispheres.

Very different was the policy pursued by the two races in their military
career. The Aztecs, animated by the most ferocious spirit, carried on a
war of extermination, signalizing their triumphs by the sacrifice of hecatombs of captives; while the Incas, although they pursued the game of
conquest with equal pertinacity, preferred a milder policy, substituting
negotiation and intrigue for violence, and dealt with their antagonists so
that their future resources should not be crippled, and that they should
come as friends, not as foes, into the bosom of the empire.

Their policy toward the conquered forms a contrast no less striking to
that pursued by the Aztecs. The Mexican vassals were ground by excessive imposts and military conscriptions. No regard was had to their welfare, and the only limit to oppression was the power of endurance. They
were over-awed by fortresses and armed garrisons, and were made to feel
every hour that they were not part and parcel of the nation, but held only
in subjugation as a conquered people. The Incas, on the other hand, admitted their new subjects at once to all the rights enjoyed by the rest of
the community; and, though they made them conform to the established
laws and usages of the empire, they watched over their personal security
and comfort with a sort of parental solicitude. The motley population,
thus bound together by common interest, was animated by a common
feeling of loyalty, which gave greater strength and stability to the empire, as it became more and more widely extended; while the various
tribes who successively came under the Mexican sceptre, being held together only by the pressure of external force, were ready to fall asunder
the moment that that force was withdrawn. The policy of the two nations displayed the principle of fear as contrasted with the principle of
love.

[33] Ante, chap. i.

The characteristic features of their religious systems had as little re-semblance to each other. The whole Aztec pantheon partook more or less of the sanguinary spirit of the terrible war-god who presided over it, and their frivolous ceremonial almost always terminated with human sacrifice and cannibal orgies. But the rites of the Peruvians were of a more in-nocent cast, as they tended to a more spiritual worship. For the worship of the Creator is most nearly approached by that of the heavenly bodies, which, as they revolve in their bright orbits, seem to be the most glorious symbols of his beneficence and power.

In the minuter mechanical arts, both showed considerable skill; but in the construction of important public works, of roads, aqueducts, canals, and in agriculture in all its details, the Peruvians were much superior. Strange that they should have fallen so far below their rivals in their ef-forts after a higher intellectual culture, in astronomical science, more especially, and in the art of communicating thought by visible symbols! When we consider the greater refinement of the Incas, their inferiority to the Aztecs in these particulars can be explained only by the fact, that the latter in all probability were indebted for their science to the race who preceded them in the land,—that shadowy race whose origin and whose end are alike veiled from the eye of the inquirer, but who possibly may have sought a refuge from their ferocious invaders in those regions of Central America the architectural remains of which now supply us with the most pleasing monuments of Indian civilization. It is with this more polished race, to whom the Peruvians seem to have borne some resem-blance in their mental and moral organization, that they should be com-pared. Had the empire of the Incas been permitted to extend itself with the rapid strides with which it was advancing at the period of the Span-ish conquest, the two races might have come into conflict, or, perhaps, into alliance with one another.

The Mexicans and Peruvians, so different in the character of their peculiar civilization, were, it seems probable, ignorant of each other's ex-istence; and it may appear singular, that, during the simultaneous contin-uance of their empires, some of the seeds of science and of art, which pass so imperceptibly from one people to another, should not have found their way across the interval which separated the two nations. They furnish an interesting example of the opposite directions which the human mind may take in its struggle to emerge from darkness into the light of civilization.

A closer resemblance—as I have more than once taken occasion to no-tice—may be found between the Peruvian institutions and some of the despotic governments of Eastern Asia; those governments where despot-ism appears in its more mitigated form, and the whole people, under the patriarchal sway of its sovereign, seem to be gathered together like the members of one vast family. Such were the Chinese, for example, whom the Peruvians resembled in their implicit obedience to authority, their mild yet somewhat stubborn temper, their solicitude for forms, their reverence for ancient usage, their skill in the minuter manufactures, their imitative rather than inventive cast of mind, and their invincible patience, which serves instead of a more adventurous spirit for the execution of difficult undertakings.[34]

A still closer analogy may be found with the natives of Hindostan in their division into castes, their worship of the heavenly bodies and the elements of nature, and their acquaintance with the scientific principles of husbandry. To the ancient Egyptians, also, they bore considerable resemblance in the same particulars, as well as in those ideas of a future existence which led them to attach so much importance to the permanent preservation of the body.

But we shall look in vain in the history of the East for a parallel to the absolute control exercised by the Incas over their subjects. In the East, this was founded on physical power,—on the external resources of the government. The authority of the Inca might be compared with that of the Pope in the day of his might, when Christendom trembled at the thunders of the Vatican, and the successor of St. Peter set his foot on the necks of princes. But the authority of the Pope was founded on opinion. His temporal power was nothing. The empire of the Incas rested on both. It was a theocracy more potent in its operation than that of the Jews; for, though the sanction of the law might be as great among the latter, the law was expounded by a human lawgiver, the servant and representative of Divinity. But the Inca was both the lawgiver and the law. He was not merely the representative of Divinity, or, like the Pope, its vicegerent, but he was Divinity itself. The violation of his ordinance was sacrilege. Never was there a scheme of government enforced by such terrible sanctions, or which bore so oppressively on the subjects of it. For it reached not only to the visible acts, but to the private conduct, the words, the very thoughts, of its vassals.

It added not a little to the efficacy of the government, that, below the sovereign, there was an order of hereditary nobles of the same divine original with himself, who, placed far below himself, were still immeasurably above the rest of the community, not merely by descent, but, as it would seem, by their intellectual nature. These were the exclusive depositaries of power, and, as their long hereditary training made them familiar with their vocation, and secured them implicit deference from the multitude, they became the prompt and well-practised agents for carrying out the executive measures of the administration. All that occurred throughout the wide extent of his empire—such was the perfect system of communication—passed in review, as it were, before the eyes of the monarch, and a thousand hands, armed with irresistible authority, stood

[34] Count Carli has amused himself with tracing out the different points of resemblance between the Chinese and the Peruvians. The emperor of China was styled the son of Heaven or of the Sun. He also held a plough once a year in presence of his people, to show his respect for agriculture. And the solstices and equinoxes were noted, to determine the periods of their religious festivals. The coincidences are curious. Lettres Américaines, tom. II. pp. 7. 8.

ready in every quarter to do his bidding. Was it not, as we have said, the most oppressive, though the mildest, of despotisms?

It was the mildest, from the very circumstance, that the transcendent rank of the sovereign, and the humble, nay, superstitious, devotion to his will make it superfluous to assert this will be acts of violence or rigor. The great mass of the people may have appeared to his eyes as but little removed above the condition of the brute, formed to minister to his pleasures. But, from their very helplessness, he regarded them with feelings of commiseration, like those which a kind master might feel for the poor animals committed to his charge, or—to do justice to the beneficent character attributed to many of the Incas—that a parent might feel for his young and impotent offspring. The laws were carefully directed to their preservation and personal comfort. The people were not allowed to be employed on works pernicious to their health, nor to pine—a sad contrast to their subsequent destiny—under the imposition of tasks too heavy for their powers. They were never made the victims of public or private extortion; and a benevolent forecast watched carefully over their necessities, and provided for their relief in seasons of infirmity, and for their sustenance in health. The government of the Incas, however arbitrary in form, was in its spirit truly patriarchal.

Yet in this there was nothing cheering to the dignity of human nature. What the people had was conceded as a boon, not as a right. When a nation was brought under the sceptre of the Inacs, it resigned every personal right, even the rights dearest to humanity. Under this extraordinary polity, a people advanced in many of the social refinements, well skilled in manufactures and agriculture, were unacquainted, as we have seen, with money. They had nothing that deserved to be called property. They could follow no craft, could engage in no labor, no amusement, but such as was specially provided by law. They could not change their residence or their dress without a license from the government. They could not even exercise the freedom which is conceded to the most abject in other countries, that of selecting their own wives. The imperative spirit of despotism would not allow them to be happy or miserable in any way but that established by law. The power of free agency—the inestimable and inborn right of every human being—was annihilated in Peru.

The astonishing mechanism of the Peruvian polity could have resulted only from the combined authority of opinion and positive power in the ruler to an extent unprecedented in the history of man. Yet that it should have so successfully gone into operation, and so long endured, in opposition to the taste, the prejudices, and the very principles of our nature, is a strong proof of a generally wise and temperate administration of the government.

The policy habitually pursued by the Incas for the *prevention* of evils that might have disturbed the order of things is well exemplified in their provisions against poverty and idleness. In these they rightly discerned the two great causes of disaffection in a populous community. The industry of the people was secured not only by their compulsory occupations at home, but by their employment on those great public works which covered every part of the country, and which still bear testimony in their decay to their primitive grandeur. Yet it may well astonish us to find, that the natural difficulty of these undertakings, sufficiently great in itself, considering the imperfection of their tools and machinery, was inconceivably enhanced by the politic contrivance of government. The royal edifices of Quito, we are assured by the Spanish conquerors, were constructed of huge masses of stone, many of which were carried all the way along the mountain roads from Cuzco, a distance of several hundred leagues.[35] The great square of the capital was filled to a considerable depth with mould brought with incredible labor up the steep slopes of the Cordilleras from the distant shores of the Pacific Ocean.[36] Labor was regarded not only as a means, but as an end, by the Peruvian law.

With their manifold provisions against poverty the reader has already been made acquainted. They were so perfect, that, in their wide extent of territory,—much of it smitten with the curse of barrenness,—no man, however humble, suffered from the want of food and clothing. Famine, so common a scourge in every other American nation, so common at that period in every country of civilized Europe, was an evil unknown in the dominions of the Incas.

The most enlightened of the Spaniards who first visited Peru, struck with the general appearance of plenty and prosperity, and with the astonishing order with which every thing throughout the country was regulated, are loud in their expressions of admiration. No better government, in their opinion, could have been devised for the people. Contented with their condition, and free from vice, to borrow the language of an eminent authority of that early day, the mild and docile character of the Peruvians would have well fitted them to receive the teachings of Chris-

[35] "Era muy principal intento que la gente no holgase, que dava causa a que despues que los Ingas estuvieron en paz hacer traer de Quito al Cuzco piedra que venia de provincia en provincia para hacer casas para si ó p^a el Sol en gran cantidad, y del Cuzco llevalla a Quito p^a el mismo efecto, ... y asi destas cosas hacian los Ingas muchas de poco provecho y de escesivo travajo en que traian ocupadas las provincias ordinariam^te, y en fin el travajo era causa de su conservacion." Ondegardo, Rel. Prim., MS.—Also Antig. y Monumentos del Peru, MS.

[36] This was literally gold dust; for Ondegardo states, that, when governor of Cuzco, he caused great quantities of gold vessels and ornaments to be disinterred from the sand in which they had been secreted by the natives. "Que toda aquella plaza del Cuzco le sacaron la tierra propia, y se llevó á otras partes por cosa de gran estima, é la hincheron de arena de la costa de la mar, como hasta dos palmos y medio en algunas partes, mas sembraron por toda ella muchos vasos de oro é plata, y hovejuelas y hombrecillos pequeños de lo mismo, lo cual se ha sacado en mucha cantidad, que todo lo hemos visto; desta arena estaba toda la plaza, quando yo fui á governar aquella Ciudad; é si fue verdad que aquella se trajo de ellos, afirman é tienen puestos en sus registros, paresceme que sea ansí, que toda la tierra junta tubo necesidad de entender en ello, por que la plaza es grande, y no tiene numero las cargas que en ella entraron; y la costa por lo mas cerca esta mas de nobenta leguas á lo que creo, y cierto yo me satisfice, porque todos dicen, que aquel genero de arena, no lo hay hasta la costa." Rel. Seg., MS.

tianity, had the love of conversion, instead of gold, animated the breasts of the Conquerors.[37] And a philosopher of a later time, warmed by the contemplation of the picture—which his own fancy had colored—of public prosperity and private happiness under the rule of the Incas, pronounces "the *moral* man in Peru far superior to the European." [38]

Yet such results are scarcely reconcilable with the theory of the government I have attempted to analyze. Where there is no free agency, there can be no morality. Where there is no temptation, there can be little claim to virtue. Where the routine is rigorously prescribed by law, the law, and not the man, must have the credit of the conduct. If that government is the best, which is felt the least, which encroaches on the natural liberty of the subject only so far as is essential to civil subordination, then of all governments devised by man the Peruvian has the least real claim to our admiration.

It is not easy to comprehend the genius and the full import of institutions so opposite to those of our own free republic, where every man, however humble his condition, may aspire to the highest honors of the state,—may select his own career, and carve out his fortune in his own way; where the light of knowledge, instead of being concentrated on a chosen few, is shed abroad like the light of day, and suffered to fall equally on the poor and the rich; where the collision of man with man wakens a generous emulation that calls out latent talent and tasks the energies to the utmost; where consciousness of independence gives a feeling of self-reliance unknown to the timid subjects of a despotism; where, in short, the government is made for man,—not as in Peru, where man seemed to be made only for the government. The New World is the theatre in which these two political systems, so opposite in their character, have been carried into operation. The empire of the Incas has passed away and left no trace. The other great experiment is still going on,—the experiment which is to solve the problem, so long contested in the Old

[37] "Y si Dios permitiera que tubieran quien con celo de Cristiandad, y no con ramo de codicia, en lo pasado, les dieran entera noticia de nuestra sagrada Religion, era gente en que bien imprimiera, segun vemos por lo que ahora con la buena orden que hay se obra." Sarmiento, Relacion, MS., cap. 22.

But the most emphatic testimony to the merits of the people is that afforded by Mancio Sierra Lejesema, the last survivor of the early Spanish Conquerors, who settled in Peru. In the preamble to his testament, made, as he states, to relieve his conscience, at the time of his death, he declares that the whole population, under the Incas, was distinguished by sobriety and industry; that such things as robbery and theft were unknown; that, far from licentiousness, there was not even a prostitute in the country; and that every thing was conducted with the greatest order, and entire submission to authority. The panegyric is somewhat too unqualified for a whole nation, and may lead one to suspect that the stings of remorse for his own treatment of the natives goaded the dying veteran into a higher estimate of their deserts than was strictly warranted by facts. Yet this testimony by such a man at such a time is too remarkable, as well as too honorable to the Peruvians, to be passed over in silence by the historian.

[38] "Sans doute l'homme moral du Pérou étoit infiniment plus perfectionné que l'Européen." Carli, Lettres Américaines, tom. I. p. 215.

World, of the capacity of man for self-government. Alas for humanity, if it should fail!

The testimony of the Spanish conquerors is not uniform in respect to the favorable influence exerted by the Peruvian institutions on the character of the people. Drinking and dancing are said to have been the pleasures to which they were immoderately addicted. Like the slaves and serfs in other lands, whose position excluded them from more serious and ennobling occupations, they found a substitute in frivolous or sensual indulgence. Lazy, luxurious, and licentious, are the epithets bestowed on them by one of those who saw them at the Conquest, but whose pen was not too friendly to the Indian.[39] Yet the spirit of independence could hardly be strong in a people who had no interest in the soil, no personal rights to defend; and the facility with which they yielded to the Spanish invader—after every allowance for their comparative inferiority—argues a deplorable destitution of that patriotic feeling which holds life as little in comparison with freedom.

But we must not judge too hardly of the unfortunate native, because he quailed before the civilization of the European. We must not be insensible to the really great results that were achieved by the government of the Incas. We must not forget, that, under their rule, the meanest of the people enjoyed a far greater degree of personal comfort, at least, a greater exemption from physical suffering, than was possessed by similar classes in other nations on the American continent,—greater, probably, than was possessed by these classes in most of the countries of feudal Europe. Under their sceptre, the higher orders of the state had made advances in many of the arts that belong to a cultivated community. The foundations of a regular government were laid, which, in an age of rapine, secured to its subjects the inestimable blessings of tranquillity and safety. By the well-sustained policy of the Incas, the rude tribes of the forest were gradually drawn from their fastnesses, and gathered within the folds of civilization; and of these materials was constructed a flourishing and populous empire, such as was to be found in no other quarter of the American continent. The defects of this government were those of over-refinement in legislation,—the last defects to have been looked for, certainly, in the American aborigines.

NOTE. I have not thought it necessary to swell this Introduction by an inquiry into the origin of Peruvian civilization, like that appended to the history of the Mexican. The Peruvian history doubtless suggests analogies with more than one na-

---

[39] "Heran muy dados á la lujuria y al bever, tenian acceso carnal con las hermanas y las mugeres de sus padres como no fuesen sus mismas madres, y aun algunos avia que con ellas mismas lo hacian y ansi mismo con sus hijas. Estando borrachos tocavan algunos en el pecado nefando, emborrachavanse muy á menudo, y estando borrachos todo lo que el demonio les traia á la voluntad hacian. Heran estos orejones muy soberbios y presuntuosos. . . . . . Tenian otras muchas maldades que por ser muchas no las digo." Pedro Pizarro, Descub. y Conq., MS.

These random aspersions of the hard conqueror show too gross an ignorance of the institutions of the people to merit much confidence as to what is said of their character.

tion in the East, some of which have been briefly adverted to in the preceding pages; although these analogies are adduced there not as evidence of a common origin, but as showing the coincidences which might naturally spring up among different nations under the same phase of civilization. Such coincidences are neither so numerous nor so striking as those afforded by the Aztec history. The correspondence presented by the astronomical science of the Mexicans is alone of more importance than all the rest. Yet the light of analogy, afforded by the institutions of the Incas, seems to point, as far as it goes, towards the same direction; and as the investigation could present but little substantially to confirm, and still less to confute, the views taken in the former disquisition, I have not thought it best to fatigue the reader with it.

Two of the prominent authorities on whom I have relied in this Introductory portion of the work, are Juan de Sarmiento and the Licentiate Ondegardo. Of the former I have been able to collect no information beyond what is afforded by his own writings. In the title prefixed to his manuscript, he is styled President of the Council of the Indies, a post of high authority, which infers a weight of character in the party, and means of information, that entitle his opinions on colonial topics to great deference.

These means of information were much enlarged by Sarmiento's visit to the colonies, during the administration of Gasca. Having conceived the design of compiling a history of the ancient Peruvian institutions, he visited Cuzco, as he tells us, in 1550, and there drew from the natives themselves the materials for his narrative. His position gave him access to the most authentic sources of knowledge, and from the lips of the Inca nobles, the best instructed of the conquered race, he gathered the traditions of their national history and institutions. The quipus formed, as we have seen, an imperfect system of mnemonics, requiring constant attention, and much inferior to the Mexican hieroglyphics. It was only by diligent instruction that they were made available to historical purposes; and this instruction was so far neglected after the Conquest, that the ancient annals of the country would have perished with the generation which was the sole depositary of them, had it not been for the efforts of a few intelligent scholars, like Sarmiento, who saw the importance, at this critical period, of cultivating an intercourse with the natives, and drawing from them their hidden stores of information.

To give still further authenticity to his work, Sarmiento travelled over the country, examined the principal objects of interest with his own eyes, and thus verified the accounts of the natives as far as possible by personal observation. The result of these labors was his work entitled, "Relacion de la sucesion y govierno de las Yngas Señores naturales que fueron de las Provincias del Peru y otras cosas tocantes á aquel Reyno, para el Iltmo. Señor Dⁿ Juan Sarmiento, Presidente del Consejo R¹ de Indias."

It is divided into chapters, and embraces about four hundred folio pages in manuscript. The introductory portion of the work is occupied with the traditionary tales of the origin and early period of the Incas; teeming, as usual, in the antiquities of a barbarous people, with legendary fables of the most wild and monstrous character. Yet these puerile conceptions afford an inexhaustible mine for the labors of the antiquarian, who endeavors to unravel the allegorical web which a cunning priesthood had devised as symbolical of those mysteries of creation that it was beyond their power to comprehend. But Sarmiento happily confines himself to the mere statement of traditional fables, without the chimerical ambition to explain them.

From this region of romance, Sarmiento passes to the institutions of the Peruvians, describes their ancient polity, their religion, their progress in the arts, especially agriculture; and presents, in short, an elaborate picture of the civilization which they reached under the Inca dynasty. This part of his work, resting, as it does, on the best authority, confirmed in many instances by his own observation, is of unquestionable value, and is written with an apparent respect for truth, that engages the confidence of the reader. The concluding portion of the manuscript is occupied with the civil history of the country. The reigns of the early Incas, which lie beyond the sober province of history, he despatches with commendable brevity. But on the three last reigns, and fortunately of the greatest princes who occupied the Peruvian throne, he is more diffuse. This was comparatively firm ground for the chronicler, for the events were too recent to be obscured by the vulgar legends that gather like moss round every incident of the older time. His account stops with the Spanish invasion: for this story, Sarmiento felt, might be safely left to his contemporaries who acted a part in it, but whose taste and education had qualified them but indifferently for exploring the antiquities and social institutions of the natives.

Sarmiento's work is composed in a simple, perspicuous style, without that ambition of rhetorical display too common with his countrymen. He writes with honest candor, and while he does ample justice to the merits and capacity of the conquered races, he notices with indignation the atrocities of the Spaniards and the demoralizing tendency of the Conquest. It may be thought, indeed, that he forms too high an estimate of the attainments of the nation under the Incas. And it is not improbable, that, astonished by the vestiges it afforded of an original civilization, he became enamoured of his subject, and thus exhibited it in colors somewhat too glowing to the eye of the European. But this was an amiable failing, not too largely shared by the stern Conquerors, who subverted the institutions of the country, and saw little to admire in it, save its gold. It must be further admitted, that Sarmiento has no design to impose on his reader, and that he is careful to distinguish between what he reports on hearsay, and what on personal experience. The Father of History himself does not discriminate between these two things more carefully.

Neither is the Spanish historian to be altogether vindicated from the superstition which belongs to his time; and we often find him referring to the immediate interposition of Satan those effects which might quite as well be charged on the perverseness of man. But this was common to the age, and to the wisest men in it; and it is too much to demand of a man to be wiser than his generation. It is sufficient praise of Sarmiento, that, in an age when superstition was too often allied with fanaticism, he seems to have had no tincture of bigotry in his nature. His heart opens with benevolent fulness to the unfortunate native; and his language, while it is not kindled into the religious glow of the missionary, is warmed by a generous ray of philanthropy that embraces the conquered, no less than the conquerors, as his brethren.

Notwithstanding the great value of Sarmiento's work for the information it affords of Peru under the Incas, it is but little known, has been rarely consulted by historians, and still remains among the unpublished manuscripts which lie, like uncoined bullion, in the secret chambers of the Escurial.

The other authority to whom I have alluded, the Licentiate Polo de Ondegardo, was a highly respectable jurist, whose name appears frequently in the affairs of Peru. I find no account of the period when he first came into the country. But he was there on the arrival of Gasca, and resided at Lima under the usurpation of Gonzalo Pizarro. When the artful Cepeda endeavored to secure the signatures of the inhabitants to the instrument proclaiming the sovereignty of his chief, we find Ondegardo taking the lead among those of his profession in resisting it. On Gasca's arrival, he consented to take a commission in his army. At the close of the rebellion he was made corregidor of La Plata, and subsequently of Cuzco, in which honorable station he seems to have remained several years. In the exercise of his magisterial functions, he was brought into familiar intercourse with the natives, and had ample opportunity for studying their laws and ancient customs. He conducted himself with such prudence and moderation, that he seems to have won the confidence not only of his countrymen but of the Indians; while the administration was careful to profit by his large experience in devising measures for the better government of the colony.

The *Relaciones*, so often cited in this History, were prepared at the suggestion of the viceroys, the first being addressed to the Marques de Cañete, in 1561, and the second, ten years later, to the Conde de Nieva. The two cover about as much ground as Sarmiento's manuscript; and the second memorial, written so long after the first, may be thought to intimate the advancing age of the author, in the greater carelessness and diffuseness of the composition.

As these documents are in the nature of answers to the interrogatories propound-

ed by government the range of topics might seem to be limited within narrower
bounds than the modern historian would desire. These queries, indeed, had particular
reference to the revenues, tributes,—the financial administration, in short, of the
Incas; and on these obscure topics the communication of Ondegardo is particularly
full. But the enlightened curiosity of government embraced a far wider range; and
the answers necessarily implied an acquaintance with the domestic policy of the
Incas, with their laws, social habits, their religion, science, and arts, in short, with
all that make up the elements of civilization. Ondegardo's memoirs, therefore, cover
the whole ground of inquiry for the philosophic historian.

In the management of these various subjects, Ondegardo displays both acuteness
and erudition. He never shrinks from the discussion, however difficult; and while
he gives his conclusions with an air of modesty, it is evident that he feels conscious
of having derived his information through the most authentic channels. He rejects
the fabulous with disdain; decides on the probabilities of such facts as he relates, and
candidly exposes the deficiency of evidence. Far from displaying the simple enthusiasm of the well-meaning but credulous missionary, he proceeds with the cool and
cautious step of a lawyer accustomed to the conflict of testimony and the uncertainty
of oral tradition. This circumspect manner of proceeding, and the temperate character of his judgments, entitle Ondegardo to much higher consideration as an authority than most of his countrymen who have treated of Indian antiquities.

There runs through his writings a vein of humanity, shown particularly in his
tenderness to the unfortunate natives, to whose ancient civilization he does entire,
but not extravagant, justice; while, like Sarmiento, he fearlessly denounces the excesses of his own countrymen, and admits the dark reproach they had brought on
the honor of the nation. But while this censure forms the strongest ground for condemnation of the Conquerors, since it comes from the lips of a Spaniard like themselves, it proves, also, that Spain in this age of violence could send forth from her
bosom wise and good men who refused to make common cause with the licentious
rabble around them. Indeed, proof enough is given in these very memorials of the
unceasing efforts of the colonial government, from the good viceroy Mendoza downwards, to secure protection and the benefit of a mild legislation to the unfortunate
natives. But the iron Conquerors, and the colonist whose heart softened only to the
touch of gold, presented a formidable barrier to improvement.

Ondegardo's writings are honorably distinguished by freedom from that superstition which is the debasing characteristic of the times; a superstition shown in the
easy credit given to the marvellous, and this equally whether in heathen or in
Christian story; for in the former the eye of credulity could discern as readily the
direct interposition of Satan, as in the latter the hand of the Almighty. It is this
ready belief in a spiritual agency, whether for good or for evil, which forms one of
the most prominent features in the writings of the sixteenth century. Nothing could
be more repugnant to the true spirit of philosophical inquiry or more irreconcilable
with rational criticism. Far from betraying such weakness, Ondegardo writes in a
direct and business-like manner, estimating things for what they are worth by the
plain rule of common-sense. He keeps the main object of his argument ever in view,
without allowing himself, like the garrulous chroniclers of the period, to be led
astray into a thousand rambling episodes that bewilder the reader and lead to nothing.

Ondegardo's memoirs deal not only with the antiquities of the nation, but with
its actual condition, and with the best means for redressing the manifold evils to
which it was subjected under the stern rule of its conquerors. His suggestions are
replete with wisdom, and a merciful policy, that would reconcile the interests of
government with the prosperity and happiness of its humblest vassal. Thus, while
his contemporaries gathered light from his suggestions as to the present condition
of affairs, the historian of later times is no less indebted to him for information in
respect to the past. His manuscript was freely consulted by Herrera and the reader,
as he peruses the pages of the learned historian of the Indies, is unconsciously enjoying the benefit of the researches of Ondegardo. His valuable *Relaciones* thus had
their uses for future generations, though they have never been admitted to the

honors of the press. The copy in my possession, like that of Sarmiento's manuscript, for which I am indebted to that industrious bibliographer, Mr. Rich, formed part of the magnificent collection of Lord Kingsborough,—a name ever to be held in honor by the scholar for his indefatigable efforts to illustrate the antiquities of America.

Ondegardo's manuscripts, it should be remarked, do not bear his signature. But they contain allusions to several actions of the writer's life, which identify them, beyond any reasonable doubt, as his production. In the archives of Simancas is a duplicate copy of the first memorial, *Relacion Primera,* though, like the one in the Escurial, without its author's name. Muñoz assigns it to the pen of Gabriel de Rojas, a distinguished cavalier of the Conquest. This is clearly an error; for the author of the manuscript identifies himself with Ondegardo, by declaring, in his reply to the fifth interrogatory, that he was the person who discovered the mummies of the Incas in Cuzco; an act expressly referred both by Acosta and Garcilasso, to the Licentiate Polo de Ondegardo, when corregidor of that city.—Should the *savans* of Madrid hereafter embrace among the publications of valuable manuscripts these *Relaciones,* they should be careful not to be led into an error here, by the authority of a critic like Muñoz, whose criticism is rarely at fault.

BOOK II

DISCOVERY OF PERU

CHAPTER I

ANCIENT AND MODERN SCIENCE—ART OF NAVIGATION—MARITIME DIS-
COVERY—SPIRIT OF THE SPANIARDS—POSSESSIONS IN THE NEW
WORLD—RUMORS CONCERNING PERU

WHATEVER difference of opinion may exist as to the comparative merit
of the ancients and the moderns in the arts, in poetry, eloquence, and all
that depends on imagination, there can be no doubt that in science the
moderns have eminently the advantage. It could not be otherwise. In the
early ages of the world, as in the early period of life, there was the freshness of a morning existence, when the gloss of novelty was on every thing
that met the eye; when the senses, not blunted by familiarity, were more
keenly alive to the beautiful, and the mind, under the influence of a
healthy and natural taste, was not perverted by philosophical theory;
when the simple was necessarily connected with the beautiful, and the
epicurean intellect, sated by repetition, had not begun to seek for stimulants in the fantastic and capricious. The realms of fancy were all un-
travelled, and its fairest flowers had not been gathered, nor its beauties
despoiled, by the rude touch of those who affected to cultivate them.
The wing of genius was not bound to the earth by the cold and conventional rules of criticism, but was permitted to take its flight far and wide
over the broad expanse of creation.

But with science it was otherwise. No genius could suffice for the creation of facts,—hardly for their detection. They were to be gathered in by
painful industry; to be collected from careful observation and experiment. Genius, indeed, might arrange and combine these facts into new
forms, and elicit from their combinations new and important inferences;
and in this process might almost rival in originality the creations of the
poet and the artist. But if the processes of science are necessarily slow,
they are sure. There is no retrograde movement in her domain. Arts may
fade, the Muse become dumb, a moral lethargy may lock up the faculties
of a nation, the nation itself may pass away and leave only the memory of
its existence. but the stores of science it has garnered up will endure for
ever. As other nations come upon the stage, and new forms of civilization
arise, the monuments of art and of imagination, productions of an older

time, will lie as an obstacle in the path of improvement. They cannot be built upon; they occupy the ground which the new aspirant for immortality would cover. The whole work is to be gone over again, and other forms of beauty—whether higher or lower in the scale of merit, but unlike the past—must arise to take a place by their side. But, in science, every stone that has been laid remains as the foundation for another. The coming generation takes up the work where the preceding left it. There is no retrograde movement. The individual nation may recede, but science still advances. Every step that has been gained makes the ascent easier for those who come after. Every step carries the patient inquirer after truth higher and higher towards heaven, and unfolds to him, as he rises, a wider horizon, and new and more magnificent views of the universe.

Geography partook of the embarrassments which belonged to every other department of science in the primitive ages of the world. The knowledge of the earth could come only from an extended commerce; and commerce is founded on artificial wants or an enlightened curiosity, hardly compatible with the earlier condition of society. In the infancy of nations, the different tribes, occupied with their domestic feuds, found few occasions to wander beyond the mountain chain or broad stream that formed the natural boundary of their domains. The Phœnicians, it is true, are said to have sailed beyond the Pillars of Hercules, and to have launched out on the great western ocean. But the adventures of these ancient voyagers belong to the mythic legends of antiquity, and ascend far beyond the domain of authentic record.

The Greeks, quick and adventurous, skilled in mechanical art, had many of the qualities of successful navigators, and within the limits of their little inland sea ranged fearlessly and freely. But the conquests of Alexander did more to extend the limits of geographical science, and opened an acquaintance with the remote countries of the East. Yet the march of the conqueror is slow in comparison with the movements of the unencumbered traveller. The Romans were still less enterprising than the Greeks, were less commercial in their character. The contributions to geographical knowledge grew with the slow acquisitions of empire. But their system was centralizing in its tendency; and instead of taking an outward direction and looking abroad for discovery, every part of the vast imperial domain turned towards the capital at its head and central point of attraction. The Roman conqueror pursued his path by land, not by sea. But the water is the great highway between nations, the true element for the discoverer. The Romans were not a maritime people. At the close of their empire, geographical science could hardly be said to extend farther than to an acquaintance with Europe,—and this not its more northern division,—together with a portion of Asia and Africa; while they had no other conception of a world beyond the western waters than was to be gathered from the fortunate prediction of the poet.[1]

---

[1] Seneca's well-known prediction, in his Medea, is, perhaps, the most remarkable random prophecy on record. For it is not a simple extension of the boundaries of the

Then followed the Middle Ages; the dark ages, as they are called, though in their darkness were matured those seeds of knowledge, which, in fulness of time, were to spring up into new and more glorious forms of civilization. The organization of society became more favorable to geographical science. Instead of one overgrown, lethargic empire, oppressing every thing by its colossal weight, Europe was broken up into various independent communities, many of which, adopting liberal forms of government, felt all the impulses natural to freemen; and the petty republics on the Mediterranean and the Baltic sent forth their swarms of seamen in a profitable commerce, that knit together the different countries scattered along the great European waters.

But the improvements which took place in the art of navigation, the more accurate measurement of time, and, above all, the discovery of the polarity of the magnet, greatly advanced the cause of geographical knowledge. Instead of creeping timidly along the coast, or limiting his expeditions to the narrow basins of inland waters, the voyager might now spread his sails boldly on the deep, secure of a guide to direct his bark unerringly across the illimitable waste. The consciousness of this power led thought to travel in a new direction; and the mariner began to look with earnestness for another path to the Indian Spice-islands than that by which the Eastern caravans had traversed the continent of Asia. The nations on whom the spirit of enterprise, at this crisis, naturally descended, were Spain and Portugal, placed, as they were, on the outposts of the European continent, commanding the great theatre of future discovery.

Both countries felt the responsibility of their new position. The crown of Portugal was constant in its efforts, through the fifteenth century, to find a passage round the southern point of Africa into the Indian Ocean; though so timid was the navigation, that every fresh headland became a formidable barrier; and it was not till the latter part of the century that the adventurous Diaz passed quite round the Stormy Cape, as he termed it, but which John the Second, with happier augury, called the Cape of Good Hope. But, before Vasco de Gama had availed himself of this discovery to spread his sails in the Indian seas, Spain entered on her glorious career, and sent Columbus across the western waters.

The object of the great navigator was still the discovery of a route to India, but by the west instead of the east. He had no expectation of meeting with a continent in his way, and, after repeated voyages, he remained in his original error, dying, as is well known, in the conviction that it was the eastern shore of Asia which he had reached. It was the same object

known parts of the globe that is so confidently announced, but the existence of a *New World* across the waters to be revealed in coming ages.
> "Quibus Oceanus
> Vincula rerum laxet, et ingens
> Pateat tellus, Typhisque Novos
> Detegat Orbes."

It was the lucky hit of the philosopher rather than the poet.

which directed the nautical enterprises of those who followed in the Admiral's track; and the discovery of a strait into the Indian Ocean was the burden of every order from the government, and the design of many an expedition to different points of the new continent, which seemed to stretch its leviathan length along from one pole to the other. The discovery of an Indian passage is the true key to the maritime movements of the fifteenth and the first half of the sixteenth centuries. It was the great leading idea that gave the character to the enterprise of the age.

It is not easy at this time to comprehend the impulse given to Europe by the discovery of America. It was not the gradual acquisition of some border territory, a province or a kingdom that had been gained, but a New World that was now thrown open to the Europeans. The races of animals, the mineral treasures, the vegetable forms, and the varied aspects of nature, man in the different phases of civilization, filled the mind with entirely new sets of ideas, that changed the habitual current of thought and stimulated it to indefinite conjecture. The eagerness to explore the wonderful secrets of the new hemisphere became so active, that the principal cities of Spain were, in a manner, depopulated, as emigrants thronged one after another to take their chance upon the deep.[2] It was a world of romance that was thrown open; for, whatever might be the luck of the adventurer, his reports on his return were tinged with a coloring of romance that stimulated still higher the sensitive fancies of his countrymen, and nourished the chimerical sentiments of an age of chivalry. They listened with attentive ears to tales of Amazons which seemed to realize the classic legends of antiquity, to stories of Patagonian giants, to flaming pictures of an *El Dorado*, where the sands sparkled with gems, and golden pebbles as large as birds' eggs were dragged in nets out of the rivers.

Yet that the adventurers were no impostors, but dupes, too easy dupes of their own credulous fancies, is shown by the extravagant character of their enterprises; by expeditions in search of the magical Fountain of Health, of the golden Temple of Doboyba, of the golden sepulchres of Zenu; for gold was ever floating before their distempered vision, and the name of *Castilla del Oro*, Golden Castile, the most unhealthy and unprofitable region of the Isthmus, held out a bright promise to the unfortunate settler, who too frequently, instead of gold, found there only his grave.

In this realm of enchantment, all the accessories served to maintain the illusion. The simple natives, with their defenceless bodies and rude weapons, were no match for the European warrior armed to the teeth in mail. The odds were as great as those found in any legend of chivalry, where the lance of the good knight overturned hundreds at a touch. The

---

[2] The Venetian ambassador, Andrea Navagiero, who travelled through Spain in 1525, near the period of the commencement of our narrative, notices the general fever of emigration. Seville, in particular, the great port of embarkation, was so stripped of its inhabitants, he says, "that the city was left almost to the women." Viaggio fatto in Spagna, (Vinegia, 1563,) fol. 15.

perils that lay in the discoverer's path, and the sufferings he had to sustain, were scarcely inferior to those that beset the knight-errant. Hunger and thirst and fatigue, the deadly effluvia of the morass with its swarms of venomous insects, the cold of mountain snows, and the scorching sun of the tropics, these were the lot of every cavalier who came to seek his fortunes in the New World. It was the reality of romance. The life of the Spanish adventurer was one chapter more—and not the least remarkable —in the chronicles of knight-errantry.

The character of the warrior took somewhat of the exaggerated coloring shed over his exploits. Proud and vainglorious, swelled with lofty anticipations of his destiny, and an invincible confidence in his own resources, no danger could appall and no toil could tire him. The greater the danger, indeed, the higher the charm; for his soul revelled in excitement, and the enterprise without peril wanted that spur of romance which was necessary to rouse his energies into action. Yet in the motives of action meaner influences were strangely mingled with the loftier, the temporal with the spiritual. Gold was the incentive and the recompense, and in the pursuit of it his inflexible nature rarely hesitated as to the means. His courage was sullied with cruelty, the cruelty that flowed equally—strange as it may seem—from his avarice and his religion; religion as it was understood in that age,—the religion of the Crusader. It was the convenient cloak for a multitude of sins, which covered them even from himself. The Castilian, too proud for hypocrisy, committed more cruelties in the name of religion than were ever practised by the pagan idolater or the fanatical Moslem. The burning of the infidel was a sacrifice acceptable to Heaven, and the conversion of those who survived amply atoned for the foulest offences. It is a melancholy and mortifying consideration, that the most uncompromising spirit of intolerance—the spirit of the Inquisitor at home, and of the Crusader abroad— should have emanated from a religion which preached peace upon earth and good-will towards man!

What a contrast did these children of Southern Europe present to the Anglo-Saxon races who scattered themselves along the great northern division of the western hemisphere! For the principle of action with these latter was not avarice, nor the more specious pretext of proselytism; but independence—independence religious and political. To secure this, they were content to earn a bare subsistence by a life of frugality and toil. They asked nothing from the soil, but the reasonable returns of their own labor. No golden visions threw a deceitful halo around their path, and beckoned them onwards through seas of blood to the subversion of an unoffending dynasty. They were content with the slow but steady progress of their social polity. They patiently endured the privations of the wilderness, watering the tree of liberty with their tears and with the sweat of their brow, till it took deep root in the land and sent up its branches high towards the heavens; while the communities of the neighboring continent, shooting up into the sudden splendors of a tropical vegetation, exhibited, even in their prime, the sure symptoms of decay.

It would seem to have been especially ordered by Providence that the discovery of the two great divisions of the American hemisphere should fail to the two races best fitted to conquer and colonize them. Thus the northern section was consigned to the Anglo-Saxon race, whose orderly, industrious habits found an ample field for development under its colder skies and on its more rugged soil; while the southern portion, with its rich tropical products and treasures of mineral wealth, held out the most attractive bait to invite the enterprise of the Spaniard. How different might have been the result, if the bark of Columbus had taken a more northerly direction, as he at one time meditated, and landed its band of adventurers on the shores of what is now Protestant America!

Under the pressure of that spirit of nautical enterprise which filled the maritime communities of Europe in the sixteenth century, the whole extent of the mighty continent, from Labrador to Terra del Fuego, was explored in less than thirty years after its discovery; and in 1521, the Portuguese Maghellan, sailing under the Spanish flag, solved the problem of the strait, and found a westerly way to the long sought Spice-islands of India,—greatly to the astonishment of the Portuguese, who, sailing from the opposite direction, there met their rivals, face to face, at the antipodes. But while the whole eastern coast of the American continent had been explored, and the central portion of it colonized,—even after the brilliant achievement of the Mexican conquest,—the veil was not yet raised that hung over the golden shores of the Pacific.

Floating rumors had reached the Spaniards, from time to time, of countries in the far west, teeming with the metal they so much coveted; but the first distinct notice of Peru was about the year 1511, when Vasco Nuñez de Balboa, the discoverer of the Southern Sea, was weighing some gold which he had collected from the natives. A young barbarian chieftain, who was present, struck the scales with his fist, and, scattering the glittering metal around the apartment, exclaimed,—"If this is what you prize so much that you are willing to leave your distant homes, and risk even life itself for it, I can tell you of a land where they eat and drink out of golden vessels, and gold is as cheap as iron is with you." It was not long after this startling intelligence that Balboa achieved the formidable adventure of scaling the mountain rampart of the Isthmus which divides the two mighty oceans from each other; when, armed with sword and buckler, he rushed into the waters of the Pacific, and cried out, in the true chivalrous vein, that "he claimed this unknown sea with all that it contained for the king of Castile, and that he would make good the claim against all, Christian or infidel, who dared to gainsay it!" [3] All the broad continent and sunny isles washed by the waters of the Southern Ocean! Little did the bold cavalier comprehend the full import of his magnificent vaunt.

On this spot he received more explicit tidings of the Peruvian empire, heard proofs recounted of its civilization, and was shown drawings of

[3] Herrera, Hist. General, dec. 1, lib. 10, cap. 2.—Quintana, Vidas de Españoles Celebres, (Madrid, 1830,) tom. II. p. 44.

the llama, which, to the European eye, seemed a species of the Arabian camel. But, although he steered his caravel for these golden realms, and even pushed his discoveries some twenty leagues south of the Gulf of St Michael, the adventure was not reserved for him. The illustrious discov-erer was doomed to fall a victim to that miserable jealousy with which a little spirit regards the achievements of a great one.

The Spanish colonial domain was broken up into a number of petty governments, which were dispensed sometimes to court favorites, though, as the duties of the post, at this early period, were of an arduous nature, they were more frequently reserved for men of some practical talent and enterprise. Columbus, by virtue of his original contract with the Crown, had jurisdiction over the territories discovered by himself, embracing some of the principal islands, and a few places on the continent. This jurisdiction differed from that of other functionaries, inasmuch as it was hereditary; a privilege found in the end too considerable for a subject, and commuted, therefore, for a title and a pension. These colonial gov-ernments were multiplied with the increase of empire, and by the year 1524, the period at which our narrative properly commences, were scat-tered over the islands, along the Isthmus of Darien, the broad tract of Terra Firma, and the recent conquests of Mexico. Some of these govern-ments were of no great extent. Others, like that of Mexico, were of the dimensions of a kingdom; and most had an indefinite range for discovery assigned to them in their immediate neighborhood, by which each of the petty potentates might enlarge his territorial sway, and enrich his fol-lowers and himself. This politic arrangement best served the ends of the Crown, by affording a perpetual incentive to the spirit of enterprise. Thus living on their own little domains at a long distance from the mother country, these military rulers held a sort of vice-regal sway, and too fre-quently exercised it in the most oppressive and tyrannical manner; op-pressive to the native, and tyrannical towards their own followers. It was the natural consequence, when men, originally low in station, and un-prepared by education for office, were suddenly called to the possession of a brief, but in its nature irresponsible, authority. It was not till after some sad experience of these results, that measures were taken to hold these petty tyrants in check by means of regular tribunals, or Royal Audiences, as they were termed, which, composed of men of character and learning, might interpose the arm of the law, or, at least, the voice of remonstrance, for the protection of both colonist and native.

Among the colonial governors, who were indebted for their situation to their rank at home, was Don Pedro Arias de Avila, or Pedrarias, as usually called. He was married to a daughter of Doña Beatriz de Boba-dilla, the celebrated Marchioness of Moya, best known as the friend of Isabella the Catholic. He was a man of some military experience and considerable energy of character. But, as it proved, he was of a malig-nant temper; and the base qualities, which might have passed unno-ticed in the obscurity of private life, were made conspicuous, and perhaps created in some measure, by sudden elevation to power; as the sun·

shine, which operates kindly on a generous soil, and stimulates it to production, calls forth from the unwholesome marsh only foul and pestilent vapors. This man was placed over the territory of *Castilla del Oro*, the ground selected by Nuñez de Balboa for the theatre of his discoveries. Success drew on this latter the jealousy of his superior, for it was crime enough in the eyes of Pedrarias to deserve too well. The tragical history of this cavalier belongs to a period somewhat earlier than that with which we are to be occupied. It has been traced by abler hands than mine, and, though brief, forms one of the most brilliant passages in the annals of the American conquerors.[4]

But though Pedrarias was willing to cut short the glorious career of his rival, he was not insensible to the important consequences of his dis-coveries. He saw at once the unsuitableness of Darien for prosecuting expeditions on the Pacific, and, conformably to the original suggestion of Balboa, in 1519, he caused his rising capital to be transferred from the shores of the Atlantic to the ancient site of Panamá, some distance east of the present city of that name.[5] This most unhealthy spot, the cemetery of many an unfortunate colonist, was favorably situated for the great object of maritime enterprise; and the port, from its central position, afforded the best point of departure for expeditions, whether to the north or south, along the wide range of undiscovered coast that lined the Southern Ocean. Yet in this new and more favorable position, several years were suffered to elapse before the course of discovery took the direction of Peru. This was turned exclusively towards the north, or rather west, in obedience to the orders of government, which had ever at heart the detection of a strait that, as was supposed, must intersect some part or other of the long-extended Isthmus. Armament after armament was fitted out with this chimerical object; and Pedrarias saw his domain extending every year farther and farther without deriving any considerable advantage from his acquisitions. Veragua, Costa Rica, Nicaragua, were successively occupied; and his brave cavaliers forced a way across forest and mountain and warlike tribes of savages, till, at Honduras, they came in collision with the companions of Cortés, the Conquerors of Mexico,

[4] The memorable adventures of Vasco Nuñez de Balboa have been recorded by Quintana, (Españoles Celebres, tom. II.) and by Irving in his Companions of Columbus.—It is rare that the life of an individual has formed the subject of two such elegant memorials produced at nearly the same time, and in different languages, without any communication between the authors.

[5] The Court gave positive instructions to Pedrarias to make a settlement in the Gulf of St. Michael, in obedience to the suggestion of Vasco Nuñez, that it would be the most eligible site for discovery and traffic in the South Sea. "El asiento que se oviere de hacer en el golfo de S. Miguel en la mar del sur debe ser en el puerto que mejor se hallare y mas convenibl para la contratacion de aquel golfo, porque segund lo que Vasco Nuñez escribe, seria muy necesario que allí haya algunos navíos, así para descubrir las cosas del golfo; y de la comarca dél, como para la contratacion de rescates de las otras cosas necesarias al buen proveimiento de aquello; é para que estoz naviós aprovechen es menester que se hagan allá." Capítulo de Carta escrita por el Rey Católico á Pedrarias Dávila, ap. Navarrete, Coleccion de íos Viages y Descu-brimientos (Madrid, 1829,) tom. III. No. 3.

who had descended from the great northern plateau on the regions of Central America, and thus completed the survey of this wild and mysterious land.

It was not till 1522 that a regular expedition was despatched in the direction south of Panamá, under the conduct of Pascual de Andagoya, a cavalier of much distinction in the colony. But that officer penetrated only to the Puerto de Piñas, the limit of Balboa's discoveries, when the oad state of his health compelled him to reëmbark and abandon his enterprise at its commencement.[6]

Yet the floating rumors of the wealth and civilization of a mighty nation at the South were continually reaching the ears and kindling the dreamy imaginations of the colonists; and it may seem astonishing that an expedition in that direction should have been so long deferred. But the exact position and distance of this fairy realm were matter of conjecture. The long tract of intervening country was occupied by rude and warlike races; and the little experience which the Spanish navigators had already had of the neighboring coast and its inhabitants, and still more, the tempestuous character of the seas—for their expeditions had taken place at the most unpropitious seasons of the year—enhanced the apparent difficulties of the undertaking, and made even their stout hearts shrink from it.

Such was the state of feeling in the little community of Panamá for several years after its foundation. Meanwhile, the dazzling conquest of Mexico gave a new impulse to the ardor of discovery, and, in 1524, three men were found in the colony, in whom the spirit of adventure triumphed over every consideration of difficulty and danger that obstructed the prosecution of the enterprise. One among them was selected as fitted by his character to conduct it to a successful issue. That man was Francisco Pizarro; and as he held the same conspicuous post in the Conquest of Peru that was occupied by Cortés in that of Mexico, it will be necessary to take a brief review of his early history.

[6] According to Montesinos, Andagoya received a severe injury by a fall from his horse, while showing off the high-mettled animal to the wondering eyes of the natives. (Annales del Peru, MS., año 1524.) But the Adelantado, in a memorial of his own discoveries, drawn up by himself, says nothing of this unlucky feat of horsemanship, but imputes his illness to his having fallen into the water, an accident by which he was near being drowned, so that it was some years before he recovered from the effects of it; a mode of accounting for his premature return, more soothing to his vanity probably, than the one usually received. This document, important as coming from the pen of one of the primitive discoverers, is preserved in the Indian Archives of Seville, and was published by Navarrete, Coleccion, tom. III. No. 7.

CHAPTER II

FRANCISCO PIZARRO—HIS EARLY HISTORY—FIRST EXPEDITION TO THE
SOUTH—DISTRESSES OF THE VOYAGERS—SHARP ENCOUNTERS—
RETURN TO PANAMÁ—ALMAGRO'S EXPEDITION

1524—1525

FRANCISCO PIZARRO was born at Truxillo, a city of Estremadura, in
Spain. The period of his birth is uncertain; but probably it was not far
from 1471.[1] He was an illegitimate child, and that his parents should not
have taken pains to perpetuate the date of his birth is not surprising.
Few care to make a particular record of their transgressions. His father,
Gonzalo Pizarro, was a colonel of infantry, and served with some distinction in the Italian campaigns under the Great Captain, and afterwards in the wars of Navarre. His mother, named Francisca Gonzales,
was a person of humble condition in the town of Truxillo.[2]

But little is told of Francisco's early years, and that little not always
deserving of credit. According to some, he was deserted by both his parents, and left as a foundling at the door of one of the principal churches
of the city. It is even said that he would have perished, had he not been
nursed by a sow.[3] This is a more discreditable fountain of supply than
that assigned to the infant Romulus. The early history of men who have
made their names famous by deeds in after-life, like the early history of
nations, affords a fruitful field for invention.

[1] The few writers who venture to assign the date of Pizarro's birth do it in so
vague and contradictory a manner as to inspire us with but little confidence in their
accounts. Herrera, it is true, says positively, that he was sixty-three years old at the
time of his death, in 1541. (Hist. General, dec. 6, lib. 10, cap. 6.) This would carry
back the date of his birth only to 1478. But Garcilasso de la Vega affirms that he
was more than fifty years old in 1525. (Com. Real., Parte 2, lib. 1, cap. 1.) This
would place his birth before 1475. Pizarro y Orellana, who, as a kinsman of the
Conqueror, may be supposed to have had better means of information, says he was
fifty-four years of age at the same date of 1525. (Varones Ilustres del Nuevo Mundo,
(Madrid, 1639,) p. 128.) But at the period of his death he calls him nearly eighty
years old! (p. 185.) Taking this latter as a round exaggeration for effect in the particular connection in which it is used, and admitting the accuracy of the former
statement, the epoch of his birth will conform to that given in the text. This makes
him somewhat late in life to set about the conquest of an empire. But Columbus,
when he entered on his career was still older.

[2] Xerez, Conquista del Peru, ap. Barcia, tom. III. p. 179.—Zarate, Conq. del Peru,
lib. 1, cap. 1.—Pizarro y Orellana, Varones Ilustres, p. 128.

[3] "Nació en Truxillo, i echaronlo à la puerta de la Iglesia, mamò una Puerca ciertos
Dias, no se hallando quien le quisiese dàr leche." Gomara, Hist. de las Ind., cap. 144.

It seems certain that the young Pizarro received little care from either of his parents, and was suffered to grow up as nature dictated. He was neither taught to read nor write, and his principal occupation was that of a swineherd. But this torpid way of life did not suit the stirring spirit of Pizarro, as he grew older, and listened to the tales, widely circulated and se captivating to a youthful fancy, of the New World. He shared in the popular enthusiasm, and availed himself of a favorable moment to abandon his ignoble charge, and escape to Seville, the port where the Spanish adventurers embarked to seek their fortunes in the West. Few of them could have turned their backs on their native land with less cause for regret than Pizarro.[4]

In what year this important change in his destiny took place we are not informed. The first we hear of him in the New World is at the island of Hispaniola, in 1510, where he took part in the expedition to Uraba in Terra Firma, under Alonzo de Ojeda, a cavalier whose character and achievements find no parallel but in the pages of Cervantes. Hernando Cortés, whose mother was a Pizarro, and related, it is said, to the father of Francis, was then in St. Domingo, and prepared to accompany Ojeda's expedition, but was prevented by a temporary lameness. Had he gone, the fall of the Aztec empire might have been postponed for some time longer, and the sceptre of Montezuma have descended in peace to his posterity. Pizarro shared in the disastrous fortunes of Ojeda's colony, and, by his discretion, obtained so far the confidence of his commander, as to be left in charge of the settlement, when the latter returned for supplies to the islands. The lieutenant continued at his perilous post for nearly two months, waiting deliberately until death should have thinned off the colony sufficiently to allow the miserable remnant to be embarked in the single small vessel that remained to it.[5]

After this, we find him associated with Balboa, the discoverer of the Pacific, and coöperating with him in establishing the settlement at Darien. He had the glory of accompanying this gallant cavalier in his terrible march across the mountains, and of being among the first Europeans, therefore, whose eyes were greeted with the long-promised vision of the Southern Ocean.

After the untimely death of his commander, Pizarro attached himself to the fortunes of Pedrarias, and was employed by that governor in several military expeditions, which, if they afforded nothing else, gave him the requisite training for the perils and privations that lay in the path of the future Conqueror of Peru.

In 1515, he was selected, with another cavalier named Morales, to

---

[4] According to the Comendador Pizarro y Orellana, Francis Pizarro served, while quite a stripling, with his father, in the Italian wars; and afterwards, under Columbus and other illustrious discoverers, in the New World, whose successes the author modestly attributes to his kinsman's valor, as a principal cause! Varones Ilustres, p. 187.
[5] Pizarro y Orellana, Varones Ilustres, pp. 121, 128.—Herrera Hist. Gen., dec. 1, lib. 7, cap. 14.—Montesinos, Annales, MS., año 1510.

cross the Isthmus and traffic with the natives on the shores of the Pacific. And there, while engaged in collecting his booty of gold and pearls from the neighbouring islands, as his eye ranged along the shadowy line of coast till it faded in the distance, his imagination may have been first fired with the idea of, one day, attempting the conquest of the mysterious regions beyond the mountains. On the removal of the seat of government across the Isthmus to Panamá, Pizarro accompanied Pedrarias, and his name became conspicuous among the cavaliers who extended the line of conquest to the north over the martial tribes of Veragua. But all these expeditions, whatever glory they may have brought him, were productive of very little gold; and, at the age of fifty, the captain Pizarro found himself in possession only of a tract of unhealthy land in the neighborhood of the capital, and of such *repartimientos* of the natives as were deemed suited to his military services.[6] The New World was a lottery, where the great prizes were so few that the odds were much against the player; yet in the game he was content to stake health, fortune, and, too often, his fair fame.

Such was Pizarro's situation when, in 1522, Andagoya returned from his unfinished enterprise to the south of Panamá, bringing back with him more copious accounts than any hitherto received of the opulence and grandeur of the countries that lay beyond.[7] It was at this time, too, that the splendid achievements of Cortés made their impression on the public mind, and gave a new impulse to the spirit of adventure. The southern expeditions became a common topic of speculation among the colonists of Panamá. But the region of gold, as it lay behind the mighty curtain of the Cordilleras, was still veiled in obscurity. No idea could be formed of its actual distance; and the hardships and difficulties encountered by the few navigators who had sailed in that direction gave a gloomy character to the undertaking, which had hitherto deterred the most daring from embarking in it. There is no evidence that Pizarro showed any particular alacrity in the cause. Nor were his own funds such as to warrant any expectation of success without great assistance from others. He found this in two individuals of the colony, who took too important a part in the subsequent transactions not to be particularly noticed.

One of them, Diego de Almagro, was a soldier of fortune, somewhat older, it seems probable, than Pizarro; though little is known of his birth, and even the place of it is disputed. It is supposed to have been the town of Almagro in New Castile, whence his own name, for want of

---

[6] "Teniendo su casa, i Hacienda, i Repartimiento de Indios como uno de los Principales de la Tierra; porque siempre lo fue." Xerez, Conq. del Peru, ap. Barcia, tom. III. p. 79.

[7] Andagoya says that he obtained, while at Birú, very minute accounts of the empire of the Incas, from certain itinerant traders who frequented that country. "En esta provincia supe y hube relacion, ansí de los señores como de mercaderes é intérpretes que ellos tenian, de toda la costa de todo lo que despues se ha visto hasta el Cuzco, particularmente de cada provincia la manera y gente della, porque estos alcanzaban por via de mercaduria mucha tierra." Navarrete, Coleccion, tom. III. No. 7

a better source, was derived; for, like Pizarro, he was a foundling.[8] Few particulars are known of him till the present period of our history; for he was one of those whom the working of turbulent times first throws upon the surface,—less fortunate, perhaps, than if left in their original obscurity. In his military career, Almagro had earned the reputation of a gallant soldier. He was frank and liberal in his disposition, somewhat hasty and ungovernable in his passions, but, like men of a sanguine temperament, after the first sallies had passed away, not difficult to be appeased. He had, in short, the good qualities and the defects incident to an honest nature, not improved by the discipline of early education or self-control.

The other member of the confederacy was Hernando de Luque, a Spanish ecclesiastic, who exercised the functions of vicar at Panamá, and had formerly filled the office of schoolmaster in the Cathedral of Darien. He seems to have been a man of singular prudence and knowledge of the world; and by his respectable qualities had acquired considerable influence in the little community to which he belonged, as well as the control of funds, which made his coöperation essential to the success of the present enterprise.

It was arranged among the three associates, that the two cavaliers should contribute their little stock towards defraying the expenses of the armament, but by far the greater part of the funds was to be furnished by Luque. Pizarro was to take command of the expedition, and the business of victualling and equipping the vessels was assigned to Almagro. The associates found no difficulty in obtaining the consent of the governor to their undertaking. After the return of Andagoya, he had projected another expedition, but the officer to whom it was to be intrusted died. Why he did not prosecute his original purpose, and commit the affair to an experienced captain like Pizarro, does not appear. He was probably not displeased that the burden of the enterprise should be borne by others, so long as a good share of the profits went into his own coffers. This he did not overlook in his stipulations.[9]

[8] "Decia el que hera de *Almagro*," says Pedro Pizarro, who knew him well. Relacion del Descubrimiento y Conquista de los Reynos del Peru, MS.—See also Zarate, Conq. del Peru, lib. 1, cap. 1.—Gomara, Hist. de las Ind., cap. 141.—Pizarro y Orellana, Varones Ilustres, p. 211.
The last writer admits that Almagro's parentage is unknown; but adds that the character of his early exploits infers an illustrious descent.—This would scarcely pass for evidence with the College of Heralds.
[9] "Asi que estos tres compañeros ya dichos Acordaron de yr á conquistar esta provincia ya dicha. Pues consultandolo con Pedro Arias de Avila que a la sazon hera governador en tierra firme. Vino en ello haziendo compañia con los dichos compañeros con condicion que Pedro Arias no havia de contribuir entonces con ningun dinero ni otra cosa sino de lo que se hallase en la tierra de lo que á el le cupiese por virtud de la compañia de alli se pagasen os gastos que á el le cupiesen. Los tres compañeros vinieron en ello por aver esta licencia porque de otra manera no la alcanzaran." (Pedro Pizarro, Descub. y Conq., MS.) Andagoya, however, affirms that the governor was interested equally with the other associates in the adventure, each taking a fourth part on himself. (Navarrete, Coleccion, tom. III. No. 7.) But whatever was the original interest of Pedrarias, it mattered little, as it was surrendered before any profits were realized from the expedition.

Thus fortified with the funds of Luque, and the consent of the governor, Almagro was not slow to make preparations for the voyage. Two small vessels were purchased, the larger of which had been originally built by Balboa, for himself, with a view to this same expedition. Since his death, it had lain dismantled in the harbor of Panamá. It was now refitted as well as circumstances would permit, and put in order for sea, while the stores and provisions were got on board with an alacrity which did more credit, as the event proved, to Almagro's zeal than to his forecast.

There was more difficulty in obtaining the necessary complement of hands; for a general feeling of distrust had gathered round expeditions in this direction, which could not readily be overcome. But there were many idle hangers-on in the colony, who had come out to mend their fortunes, and were willing to take their chance of doing so, however desperate. From such materials as these, Almagro assembled a body of somewhat more than a hundred men;[10] and every thing being ready, Pizarro assumed the command, and, weighing anchor, took his departure from the little port of Panamá, about the middle of November, 1524. Almagro was to follow in a second vessel of inferior size, as soon as it could be fitted out.[11]

The time of year was the most unsuitable that could have been selected for the voyage; for it was the rainy season, when the navigation to the south, impeded by contrary winds, is made doubly dangerous by the tempests that sweep over the coast. But this was not understood by the adventurers. After touching at the Isle of Pearls, the frequent resort of navigators, at a few leagues' distance from Panamá, Pizarro held his way across the Gulf of St. Michael, and steered almost due south for the Puerto de Piñas, a headland in the province of Biruquete, which marked the limit of Andagoya's voyage. Before his departure, Pizarro had obtained all the information which he could derive from that officer in respect to the country, and the route he was to follow. But the cavalier's own experience had been too limited to enable him to be of much assitance.

Doubling the Puerto de Piñas, the little vessel entered the river Birú, the misapplication of which name is supposed by some to have given rise

[10] Herrera, the most popular historian of these transactions estimates the number of Pizarro's followers only at eighty. But every other authority which I have consulted raises them to over a hundred. Father Naharro, a contemporary, and resident at Lima, even allows a hundred and twenty-nine. Relacion sumaria de la entrada de los Españoles en el Peru, MS.

[11] There is the usual discrepancy among authors about the date of this expedition. Most fix it at 1525. I have conformed to Xerez, Pizarro's secretary, whose narrative was published ten years after the voyage, and who could hardly have forgotten the date of so memorable an event, in so short an interval of time. (See his Conquista del Peru, ap. Barcia, tom. III. p. 179.)

The year seems to be settled by Pizarro's *Capitulacion* with the Crown, which I had not examined till after the above was written. This instrument, dated July, 1529, speaks of his first expedition as having take place about five years previous to that of the empire of the Incas.[12] After sailing up this stream for a couple of leagues, Pizarro came to anchor, and disembarking his whole force except the sailors, proceeded at the head of it to explore the coun try. The land spread out into a vast swamp, where the heavy rains had settled in pools of stagnant water, and the muddy soil afforded no foot ing to the traveller. This dismal morass was fringed with woods, through whose thick and tangled undergrowth they found it difficult to penetrate; and emerging from them, they came out on a hilly country, so rough and rocky in its character, that their feet were cut to the bone, and the weary soldier, encumbered with his heavy mail or thick-padded doublet of cotton, found it difficult to drag one foot after the other. The heat at times was oppressive; and, fainting with toil and famished for want of food, they sank down on the earth from mere exhaustion. Such was the ominous commencement of the expedition to Peru.

Pizarro, however, did not lose heart. He endeavored to revive the spirits of his men, and besought them not to be discouraged by difficulties which a brave heart would be sure to overcome, reminding them of the golden prize which awaited those who persevered. Yet it was obvious that nothing was to be gained by remaining longer in this desolate region. Returning to their vessel, therefore, it was suffered to drop down the river and proceed along its southern course on the great ocean.

After coasting a few leagues, Pizarro anchored off a place not very inviting in its appearance, where he took in a supply of wood and water. Then, stretching more towards the open sea, he held on in the same direction towards the south. But in this he was baffled by a succession of heavy tempests, accompanied with such tremendous peals of thunder and floods of rain as are found only in the terrible storms of the tropics. The sea was lashed into fury, and, swelling into mountain billows, threatened every moment to overwhelm the crazy little bark, which opened at every seam. For ten days the unfortunate voyagers were tossed about by the pitiless elements, and it was only by incessant exertions—the exertions of despair—that they preserved the ship from foundering. To add to their calamities, their provisions began to fail, and they were short of water, of which they had been furnished only with a small number of casks; for Almagro had counted on their recruiting their scanty supplies, from time to time, from the shore. Their meat was wholly consumed, and they were reduced to the wretched allowance of two ears of Indian corn a day for each man.

Thus harassed by hunger and the elements, the battered voyagers were too happy to retrace their course and regain the port where they had last taken in supplies of wood and water. Yet nothing could be more unpromising than the aspect of the country. It had the same character of low, swampy soil, that distinguished the former landing-place; while thick-matted forests, of a depth which the eye could not penetrate, stretched along the coast to an interminable length. It was in vain that the wearied Spaniards endeavored to thread the mazes of this tangled thicket, where the creepers and flowering vines, that shoot up luxuriant in a hot and humid atmosphere, had twined themselves round the huge trunks of the forest-trees, and made a network that could be opened only with the axe. The rain, in the mean time, rarely slackened, and the ground, strewed with leaves and saturated with moisture, seemed to slip away beneath their feet.

Nothing could be more dreary and disheartening than the aspect of these funereal forests; where the exhalations from the overcharged surface of the ground poisoned the air, and seemed to allow no life, except that, indeed, of myriads of insects, whose enamelled wings glanced to and fro, like sparks of fire, in every opening of the woods. Even the brute creation appeared instinctively to have shunned the fatal spot, and neither beast nor bird of any description was seen by the wanderers. Silence reigned unbroken in the heart of these dismal solitudes; at least, the only sounds that could be heard were the plashing of the rain-drops on the leaves, and the tread of the forlorn adventurers.[13]

Entirely discouraged by the aspect of the country, the Spaniards began to comprehend that they had gained nothing by changing their quarters from sea to shore, and they felt the most serious apprehensions of perishing from famine in a region which afforded nothing but such unwholesome berries as they could pick up here and there in the woods. They loudly complained of their hard lot, accusing their commander as the author of all their troubles, and as deluding them with promises of a fairy land, which seemed to recede in proportion as they advanced. It was of no use, they said, to contend against fate, and it was better to take their chance of regaining the port of Panamá in time to save their lives, than to wait where they were to die of hunger.

But Pizarro was prepared to encounter much greater evils than these, before returning to Panamá, bankrupt in credit, an object of derision as a vainglorious dreamer, who had persuaded others to embark in an adventure which he had not the courage to carry through himself. The present was his only chance. To return would be ruin. He used every argument, therefore, that mortified pride or avarice could suggest to turn his followers from their purpose; represented to them that these were the troubles that necessarily lay in the path of the discoverer; and called to mind the brilliant successes of their countrymen in other quarters, and the repeated reports, which they had themselves received, of the rich regions along the coast, of which it required only courage and constancy on their part to become the masters. Yet, as their present exigencies were pressing, he resolved to send back the vessel to the Isle of Pearls, to lay in a fresh stock of provisions for his company, which might enable them to go forward with renewed confidence. The distance was not great, and

[13] Xerez, Conq. del Peru, ap. Barcia, tom. III. p. 180.—Relacion del Primer. Descub., MS.—Montesinos, Annales, MS., año 1515.—Zarate, Conq. del Peru, lib. 1, cap. 1.—Garcilasso, Com. Real., Parte 2, lib. 1, cap. 7.—Herrera, Hist. General, dec. 3, lib. 6, cap. 13.

in a few days they would all be relieved from their perilous position. The officer detached on this service was named Montenegro; and taking with him nearly half the company, after receiving Pizarro's directions, he instantly weighed anchor, and steered for the Isle of Pearls.

On the departure of his vessel, the Spanish commander made an attempt to explore the country, and see if some Indian settlement might not be found, where he could procure refreshments for his followers. But his efforts were vain, and no trace was visible of a human dwelling; though, in the dense and impenetrable foliage of the equatorial regions, the distance of a few rods might suffice to screen a city from observation. The only means of nourishment left to the unfortunate adventurers were such shell-fish as they occasionally picked up on the shore, or the bitter buds of the palm-tree, and such berries and unsavory herbs as grew wild in the woods. Some of these were so poisonous, that the bodies of those who ate them swelled up and were tormented with racking pains. Others, preferring famine to this miserable diet, pined away from weakness and actually died of starvation. Yet their resolute leader strove to maintain his own cheerfulness and to keep up the drooping spirits of his men. He freely shared with them his scanty stock of provisions, was unwearied in his endeavors to procure them sustenance, tended the sick, and ordered barracks to be constructed for their accommodation, which might, at least, shelter them from the drenching storms of the season. By this ready sympathy with his followers in their sufferings, he obtained an ascendency over their rough natures, which the assertion of authority, at least in the present extremity, could never have secured to him.

Day after day, week after week, had now passed away, and no tidings were heard of the vessel that was to bring relief to the wanderers. In vain did they strain their eyes over the distant waters to catch a glimpse of their coming friends. Not a speck was to be seen in the blue distance, where the canoe of the savage dared not venture, and the sail of the white man was not yet spread. Those who had borne up bravely at first now gave way to despondency, as they felt themselves abandoned by their countrymen on this desolate shore. They pined under that sad feeling which "maketh the heart sick." More than twenty of the little band had already died, and the survivors seemed to be rapidly following.[14]

At this crisis reports were brought to Pizarro of a light having been seen through a distant opening in the woods. He hailed the tidings with eagerness, as intimating the existence of some settlement in the neighborhood; and, putting himself at the head of a small party, went in the direction pointed out, to reconnoitre. He was not disappointed, and, after extricating himself from a dense wilderness of underbrush and foliage, he emerged into an open space, where a small Indian village was planted. The timid inhabitants, on the sudden apparition of the strangers, quitted their huts in dismay; and the famished Spaniards, rushing in, eagerly made themselves masters of their contents. These consisted of different

[14] Ibid., ubi supra.—Relacion del Primer. Descub., MS.—Xerez, Conq. del Peru, ubi supra.

articles of food, chiefly maize and cocoanuts. The supply, though small, was too seasonable not to fill them with rapture.

The astonished natives made no attempt at resistance. But, gathering more confidence as no violence was offered to their persons, they drew nearer the white men, and inquired, "Why they did not stay at home and till their own lands, instead of roaming about to rob others who had never harmed them?" [15] Whatever may have been their opinion as to the question of right, the Spaniards, no doubt, felt then that it would have been wiser to do so. But the savages wore about their persons gold ornaments of some size, though of clumsy workmanship. This furnished the best reply to their demand. It was the golden bait which lured the Spanish adventurer to forsake his pleasant home for the trials of the wilderness. From the Indians Pizarro gathered a confirmation of the reports he had so often received of a rich country lying farther south; and at the distance of ten days' journey across the mountains, they told him, there dwelt a mighty monarch whose dominions had been invaded by another still more powerful, the Child of the Sun.[16] It may have been the invasion of Quito that was meant, by the valiant Inca Huayna Capac, which took place some years previous to Pizarro's expedition.

At length, after the expiration of more than six weeks, the Spaniards beheld with delight the return of the wandering bark that had borne away their comrades, and Montenegro sailed into port with an ample supply of provisions for his famishing countrymen. Great was his horror at the aspect presented by the latter, their wild and haggard countenances and wasted frames,—so wasted by hunger and disease, that their old companions found it difficult to recognize them. Montenegro accounted for his delay by incessant head winds and bad weather; and he himself had also a doleful tale to tell of the distress to which he and his crew had been reduced by hunger, on their passage to the Isle of Pearls.—It is minute incidents like these with which we have been occupied, that enable one to comprehend the extremity of suffering to which the Spanish adventurer was subjected in the prosecution of his great work of discovery.

Revived by the substantial nourishment to which they had so long been strangers, the Spanish cavaliers, with the buoyancy that belongs to men of a hazardous and roving life, forgot their past distresses in their

---

[15] "Porque decian à los Castellanos, que por què no sembraban, i cogian, sin andar tomando los Bastimentos agenos, pasando tantos trabajos?" Herrera, Hist. General, loc. cit.

[16] "Dioles noticia el viejo por medio del lengua, como diez soles de alli habia un Rey muy poderoso yendo por espesas montañas, y que otro mas poderoso hijo del sol habia venido de milagro á quitarle el Reino sobre que tenian mui sangrientas batallas." (Montesinos, Annales, MS., año 1525.) The conquest of Quito by Huayna Capac took place more than thirty years before this period in our history. But the particulars of this revolution, its time or precise theatre, were, probably, but very vaguely comprehended by the rude nations in the neighborhood of Panamá; and their allusion to it in an unknown dialect was as little comprehended by the Spanish voyagers who must have collected their information from signs much more than words.

eagerness to prosecute their enterprise. Reëmbarking therefore on board his vessel, Pizarro bade adieu to the scene of so much suffering, which he branded with the appropriate name of *Puerto de la Hambre*, the Port of Famine, and again opened his sails to a favorable breeze that bore him onwards towards the south.

Had he struck boldly out into the deep, instead of hugging the inhos·pitable shore, where he had hitherto found so little to recompense him, he might have spared himself the repetition of wearisome and unprofit-able adventures, and reached by a shorter route the point of his destina-tion. But the Spanish mariner groped his way along these unknown coasts, landing at every convenient headland, as if fearful lest some fruit-ful region or precious mine might be overlooked, should a single break occur in the line of survey. Yet it should be remembered, that, though the true point of Pizarro's destination is obvious to us, familiar with the topography of these countries, he was wandering in the dark, feeling his way along, inch by inch, as it were, without chart to guide him, without knowledge of the seas or of the bearings of the coast, and even with no better defined idea of the object at which he aimed than that of a land teeming with gold, that lay somewhere at the south! It was a hunt after an *El Dorado;* on information scarcely more circumstantial or authentic than that which furnished the basis of so many chimerical enterprises in this land of wonders. Success only, the best argument with the multi-tude, redeemed the expeditions of Pizarro from a similar imputation of extravagance.

Holding on his southerly course under the lee of the shore, Pizarro, after a short run, found himself abreast of an open reach of country, or at least one less encumbered with wood, which rose by a gradual swell, as it receded from the coast. He landed with a small body of men, and, advancing a short distance into the interior, fell in with an Indian hamlet. It was abandoned by the inhabitants, who, on the approach of the in-vaders, had betaken themselves to the mountains; and the Spaniards, entering their deserted dwellings, found there a good store of maize and other articles of food, and rude ornaments of gold of considerable value. Food was not more necessary for their bodies than was the sight of gold, from time to time, to stimulate their appetite for adventure. One spec-tacle, however, chilled their blood with horror. This was the sight of human flesh, which they found roasting before the fire, as the barbarians had left it, preparatory to their obscene repast. The Spaniards, conceiv-ing that they had fallen in with a tribe of Caribs, the only race in that part of the New World known to be cannibals, retreated precipitately to their vessel.[17] They were not steeled by sad familiarity with the spectacle, like the Conquerors of Mexico.

The weather, which had been favorable, now set in tempestuous, with heavy squalls, accompanied by incessant thunder and lightning, and the

[17] "I en las Ollas de la comida, que estaban al Fuego, entre la Carne, que sacaban, havia Pies i Manos de Hombres, de donde conocieron, que aquellos Indios eran Caribes." Herrera, Hist. General, dec. 3, lib. 8, cap. 11.

rain, as usual in these tropical tempests, descended not so much in drops as in unbroken sheets of water. The Spaniards, however, preferred to take their chance on the raging element rather than remain in the scene of such brutal abominations. But the fury of the storm gradually subsided, and the little vessel held on her way along the coast, till, coming abreast of a bold point of land named by Pizarro Punta Quemada, he gave orders to anchor. The margin of the shore was fringed with a deep belt of mangrove-trees, the long roots of which, interlacing one another, formed a kind of submarine lattice-work that made the place difficult of approach. Several avenues, opening through this tangled thicket, led Pizarro to conclude that the country must be inhabited, and he disembarked, with the greater part of his force, to explore the interior.

He had not penetrated more than a league, when he found his conjecture verified by the sight of an Indian town of larger size than those he had hitherto seen, occupying the brow of an eminence, and well defended by palisades. The inhabitants, as usual, had fled; but left in their dwellings a good supply of provisions and some gold trinkets, which the Spaniards made no difficulty of appropriating to themselves. Pizarro's flimsy bark had been strained by the heavy gales it had of late encountered, so that it was unsafe to prosecute the voyage further without more thorough repairs than could be given to her on this desolate coast. He accordingly determined to send her back with a few hands to be careened at Panamá, and meanwhile to establish his quarters in his present position, which was so favorable for defence. But first he despatched a small party under Montenegro to reconnoitre the country, and, if possible, to open a communication with the natives.

The latter were a warlike race. They had left their habitations in order to place their wives and children in safety. But they had kept an eye on the movements of the invaders, and, when they saw their forces divided, they resolved to fall upon each body singly before it could communicate with the other. So soon, therefore, as Montenegro had penetrated through the defiles of the lofty hills, which shoot out like spurs of the Cordilleras along this part of the coast, the Indian warriors, springing from their ambush, sent off a cloud of arrows and other missiles that darkened the air, while they made the forest ring with their shrill warwhoop. The Spaniards, astonished at the appearance of the savages, with their naked bodies gaudily painted, and brandishing their weapons as they glanced among the trees and straggling underbrush that choked up the defile, were taken by surprise and thrown for a moment into disarray. Three of their number were killed and several wounded. Yet, speedily rallying, they returned the discharge of the assailants with their cross-bows,—for Pizarro's troops do not seem to have been provided with muskets on this expedition,—and then gallantly charging the enemy, sword in hand, succeeded in driving them back into the fastnesses of the mountains. But it only led them to shift their operations to another quarter, and make an assault on Pizarro before he could be relieved by his lieutenant.

Availing themselves of their superior knowledge of the passes, they reached that commander's quarters long before Montenegro, who had commenced a countermarch in the same direction. And issuing from the woods, the bold savages saluted the Spanish garrison with a tempest of darts and arrows, some of which found their way through the joints of the harness and the quilted mail of the cavaliers. But Pizarro was too well practised a soldier to be off his guard. Calling his men about him, he resolved not to abide the assault tamely in the works, but to sally out, and meet the enemy on their own ground. The barbarians, who had advanced near the defences, fell back as the Spaniards burst forth with their valiant leader at their head. But, soon returning with admirable ferocity to the charge, they singled out Pizarro, whom, by his bold bearing and air of authority, they easily recognized as the chief; and, hurling at him a storm of missiles, wounded him, in spite of his armour, in no less than seven places.[18]

Driven back by the fury of the assault directed against his own person, the Spanish commander retreated down the slope of the hill, still defending himself as he could with sword and buckler, when his foot slipped and he fell. The enemy set up a fierce yell of triumph, and some of the boldest sprang forward to despatch him. But Pizarro was on his feet in an instant, and, striking down two of the foremost with his strong arm, held the rest at bay till his soldiers could come to the rescue. The barbarians, struck with admiration at his valor, began to falter, when Montenegro luckily coming on the ground at the moment, and falling on their rear, completed their confusion; and, abandoning the field, they made the best of their way into the recesses of the mountains. The ground was covered with their slain; but the victory was dearly purchased by the death of two more Spaniards and a long list of wounded.

A council of war was then called. The position had lost its charm in the eyes of the Spaniards, who had met here with the first resistance they had yet experienced on their expedition. It was necessary to place the wounded in some secure spot, where their injuries could be attended to. Yet it was not safe to proceed farther, in the crippled state of their vessel. On the whole, it was decided to return and report their proceedings to the governor; and, though the magnificent hopes of the adventurers had not been realized, Pizarro trusted that enough had been done to vindicate the importance of the enterprise, and to secure the countenance of Pedrarias for the further prosecution of it.[19]

Yet Pizarro could not make up his mind to present himself, in the present state of the undertaking, before the governor. He determined, therefore, to be set on shore with the principal part of his company at Chicamá, a place on the main land, at a short distance west of Panamá. From this place, which he reached without any further accident, he despatched the vessel, and in it his treasurer, Nicolas de Ribera, with the

[18] Naharro, Relacion Sumaria, MS.—Xerez, Conq. del Peru ap. Barcia, tom. III. p. 180.—Zarate, Conq. del Peru, lib. 1, cap. 1.—Balboa, Hist. du Perou, chap. 15.
[19] Herrera, Hist. General, dec. 3, lib. 8, cap. 11.—Xerez, ubi supra.

gold he had collected, and with instructions to lay before the governor a full account of his discoveries, and the result of the expedition.

While these events were passing, Pizarro's associate, Almagro, had been busily employed in fitting out another vessel for the expedition at the port of Panamá. It was not till long after his friend's departure that he was prepared to follow him. With the assistance of Luque, he at length succeeded in equipping a small caravel and embarking a body of between sixty and seventy adventurers, mostly of the lowest order of the colonists. He steered in the track of his comrade, with the intention of overtaking him as soon as possible. By a signal previously concerted of notching the trees, he was able to identify the spots visited by Pizarro,—Puerto de Piñas, Puerto de la Hambre, Pueblo Quemado,—touching successively at every point of the coast explored by his countrymen, though in a much shorter time. At the last-mentioned place he was received by the fierce natives with the same hostile demonstrations as Pizarro, though in the present encounter the Indians did not venture beyond their defences. But the hot blood of Almagro was so exasperated by this check, that he assaulted the place and carried it sword in hand, setting fire to the outworks and dwellings, and driving the wretched inhabitants into the forests.

His victory cost him dear. A wound from a javelin on the head caused an inflammation in one of his eyes, which, after great anguish, ended in the loss of it. Yet the intrepid adventurer did not hesitate to pursue his voyage, and, after touching at several places on the coast, some of which rewarded him with a considerable booty in gold, he reached the mouth of the *Rio de San Juan,* about the fourth degree of north latitude. He was struck with the beauty of the stream, and with the cultivation on its borders, which were sprinkled with Indian cottages showing some skill in their construction, and altogether intimating a higher civilization than any thing he had yet seen.

Still his mind was filled with anxiety for the fate of Pizarro and his followers. No trace of them had been found on the coast for a long time, and it was evident they must have foundered at sea, or made their way back to Panamá. This last he deemed most probable; as the vessel might have passed him unnoticed under the cover of the night, or of the dense fogs that sometimes hang over the coast.

Impressed with this belief, he felt no heart to continue his voyage of discovery, for which, indeed, his single bark, with its small complement of men, was altogether inadequate. He proposed, therefore, to return without delay. On his way, he touched at the Isle of Pearls, and there learned the result of his friend's expedition, and the place of his present residence. Directing his course, at once, to Chicamá, the two cavaliers soon had the satisfaction of embracing each other, and recounting their several exploits and escapes. Almagro returned even better freighted with gold than his confederate, and at every step of his progress he had collected fresh confirmation of the existence of some great and opulent empire in the South. The confidence of the two friends was much strengthened by their discoveries; and they unhesitatingly pledged themselves to one another to die rather than abandon the enterprise.[20]

The best means of obtaining the levies requisite for so formidable an undertaking—more formidable, as it now appeared to them, than before—were made the subject of long and serious discussion. It was at length decided that Pizarro should remain in his present quarters, inconvenient and even unwholesome as they were rendered by the humidity of the climate, and the pestilent swarms of insects that filled the atmosphere. Almagro would pass over to Panamá, lay the case before the governor, and secure, if possible, his good-will towards the prosecution of the enterprise. If no obstacle were thrown in their way from this quarter, they might hope, with the assistance of Luque, to raise the necessary supplies; while the results of the recent expedition were sufficiently encouraging to draw adventurers to their standard in a community which had a craving for excitement that gave even danger a charm, and which held life cheap in comparison with gold.

[20] Xerez, ubi supra.—Naharro, Relacion Sumaria, MS.—Zarate, Conq. del Peru, loc. cit.—Balboa, Hist. du Perou, chap. 15.—Relacion del Primer. Descub., MS.—Herrera, Hist. General, dec. 3, lib. 8, cap. 13.—Levins Apollonius, fol. 12.—Gomara, Hist. de las Ind., cap. 108.

THE FAMOUS CONTRACT—SECOND EXPEDITION—RUIZ EXPLORES THE COAST—PIZARRO'S SUFFERINGS IN THE FORESTS—ARRIVAL OF NEW RECRUITS—FRESH DISCOVERIES AND DISASTERS—PIZARRO ON THE ISLE OF GALLO

1526—1527

ON his arrival at Panamá, Almagro found that events had taken a turn less favorable to his views than he had anticipated. Pedrarias, the governor, was preparing to lead an expedition in person against a rebellious officer in Nicaragua; and his temper, naturally not the most amiable, was still further soured by this defection of his lieutenant, and the necessity it imposed on him of a long and perilous march. When, therefore, Almagro appeared before him with the request that he might be permitted to raise further levies to prosecute his enterprise, the governor received him with obvious dissatisfaction, listened coldly to the narrative of his losses, turned an incredulous ear to his magnificent promises for the future, and bluntly demanded an account of the lives, which had been sacrificed by Pizarro's obstinacy, but which, had they been spared, might have stood him in good stead in his present expedition to Nicaragua. He positively declined to countenance the rash schemes of the two adventurers any longer, and the conquest of Peru would have been crushed in the bud, but for the efficient interposition of the remaining associate, Fernando de Luque.

This sagacious ecclesiastic had received a very different impression from Almagro's narrative, from that which had been made on the mind of the irritable governor. The actual results of the enterprise in gold and silver, thus far, indeed, had been small,—forming a mortifying contrast to the magnitude of their expectations. But, in another point of view, they were of the last importance; since the intelligence which the adventurers had gained in every successive stage of their progress confirmed, in the strongest manner, the previous accounts, received from Andogoya and others, of a rich Indian empire at the south, which might repay the trouble of conquering it as well as Mexico had repaid the enterprise of Cortés. Fully entering, therefore, into the feelings of his military associates, he used all his influence with the governor to incline him to a more favorable view of Almagro's petition; and no one in the little community of Panamá exercised greater influence over the councils of the executive than Father Luque, for which he was indebted no less to his discretion and acknowledged sagacity than to his professional station.

But while Pedrarias, overcome by the arguments or importunity of the

848

churchman, yielded a reluctant assent to the application, he took care to testify his displeasure with Pizarro, on whom he particularly charged the loss of his followers, by naming Almagro as his equal in command in the proposed expedition. This mortification sunk deep into Pizarro's mind. He suspected his comrade, with what reason does not appear, of soliciting this boon from the governor. A temporary coldness arose between them, which subsided, in outward show, at least, on Pizarro's reflecting that it was better to have this authority conferred on a friend than on a stranger, perhaps an enemy. But the seeds of permanent distrust were left in his bosom, and lay waiting for the due season to ripen into a fruitful harvest of discord.[1]

Pedrarias had been originally interested in the enterprise, at least, so far as to stipulate for a share of the gains, though he had not contrib‑ uted, as it appears, a single ducat towards the expenses. He was at length, however, induced to relinquish all right to a share of the contingent profits. But, in his manner of doing so, he showed a mercenary spirit, better becoming a petty trader than a high officer of the Crown. He stip‑ ulated that the associates should secure to him the sum of one thousand *pesos de oro* in requital of his good‑will, and they eagerly closed with his proposal, rather than be encumbered with his pretensions. For so paltry a consideration did he resign his portion of the rich spoil of the Incas! [2] But the governor was not gifted with the eye of a prophet. His avarice was of that short‑sighted kind which defeats itself. He had sacrificed the chivalrous Balboa just as that officer was opening to him the conquest of Peru, and he would now have quenched the spirit of enterprise, that was taking the same direction, in Pizarro and his associates.

Not long after this, in the following year, he was succeeded in his gov‑ ernment by Don Pedro de los Rios, a cavalier of Cordova. It was the policy of the Castilian Crown to allow no one of the great colonial officers to occupy the same station so long as to render himself formidable by his authority.[3] It had, moreover, many particular causes of disgust with Ped‑ rarias. The functionary they sent out to succeed him was fortified with

---

[1] Xerez, Conq. del Peru, ap. Barcia, tom. III. p. 180.—Montesinos, Annales, MS., año 1526.—Herrera, Hist. General, dec. 3, lib. 8, cap. 12.

[2] Such is Oviedo's account, who was present at the interview between the gov‑ ernor and Almagro, when the terms of compensation were discussed. The dialogue is amusing enough, and well told by the old Chronicler. Another version of the af‑ fair is given in the *Relacion*, often quoted by me, of one of the Peruvian conquerors, in which Perarias is said to have gone out of the partnership voluntarily from his disgust at the unpromising state of affairs. "Vueltos con la dicha gente á Panamá, destrozados y gastados que ya no tenian haciendas para tornar con provisiones y gentes que todo lo habian gastado, el dicho Pedrarias de Avila les dijo, que ya el no queria mas hacer compañia con ellos en los gastos de la armada, que si ellos querian volver á su costa, que lo hiciesen; y ansi como gente que habia perdido todo lo que tenia y tanto habia trabajado, acordaron de tornar á proseguir su jornada y dar fin á las vidas y haciendas que les quedaba, ó descubrir aquella tierra, y cierta‑ mente ellos tubieron grande constancia y animo." Relacion del Primer. Descub., MS.

[3] This policy is noticed by the sagacious Martyr. "De mutandis namque plærisque gubernatoribus, ne longa nimis imperii assuetudine insolescant, cogitatur, qui præ‑ cipue non fuerint prouinciarum domitores, de hisce ducibus namque alia ratio non‑

ample instructions for the good of the colony, and especially of the natives, whose religious conversion was urged as a capital object, and whose
personal freedom was unequivocally asserted, as loyal vassals of the
Crown. It is but justice to the Spanish government to admit that its provisions were generally guided by a humane and considerate policy, which
was as regularly frustrated by the cupidity of the colonist, and the capricious cruelty of the conqueror. The few remaining years of Pedrarias were
spent in petty squabbles, both of a personal and official nature; for he was
still continued in office, though in one of less consideration than that
which he had hitherto filled. He survived but a few years, leaving behind
him a reputation not to be envied, of one who united a pusillanimous
spirit with uncontrollable passions; who displayed, notwithstanding, a
certain energy of character, or, to speak more correctly, an impetuosity
of purpose, which might have led to good results had it taken a right direction. Unfortunately, his lack of discretion was such, that the direction
he took was rarely of service to his country or to himself.

Having settled their difficulties with the governor, and obtained his
sanction to their enterprise, the confederates lost no time in making the
requisite preparations for it. Their first step was to execute the memorable contract which served as the basis of their future arrangements;
and, as Pizarro's name appears in this, it seems probable that that chief
had crossed over to Panamá so soon as the favorable disposition of Pedrarias had been secured.[4] The instrument, after invoking in the most
solemn manner the names of the Holy Trinity and Our Lady the Blessed
Virgin, sets forth, that, whereas the parties have full authority to discover
and subdue the countries and provinces lying south of the Gulf, belonging
to the empire of Peru, and as Fernando de Luque had advanced the funds
for the enterprise in bars of gold of the value of twenty thousand *pesos*,
they mutually bind themselves to divide equally among them the whole
of the conquered territory. This stipulation is reiterated over and over
again, particularly with reference to Luque, who, it is declared, is to be
entitled to one third of all lands, *repartimientos*, treasures of every kind,
gold, silver, and precious stones,—to one third even of all vassals, rents,
and emoluments arising from such grants as may be conferred by the
Crown on either of his military associates, to be held for his own use, or
for that of his heirs, assigns, or legal representative.

The two captains solemnly engage to devote themselves exclusively to

deratur." (De Orbe Novo, (Parisiis, 1587,) p. 498.) One cannot but regret that the
philosopher, who took so keen an interest in the successive revelations of the different portions of the New World, should have died before the empire of the Incas was
disclosed to Europeans. He lived to learn and to record the wonders of
   "Rich Mexico, the seat of Montezuma;
       Not Cuzco in Peru, the richer seat of Atabalipa."
   [4] In opposition to most authorities,—but not to the judicious Quintana,—I have
conformed to Montesinos, in placing the execution of the contract at the commencement of the second instead of the first, expedition. This arrangement coincides with
the date of the instrument itself, which, moreover, is reported *in extenso* by no ancient writer whom I have consulted except Montesinos.

the present undertaking until it is accomplished; and, in case of failure in their part of the covenant, they pledge themselves to reimburse Luque for his advances, for which all the property they possess shall be held responsible, and this declaration is to be a sufficient warrant for the execution of judgment against them, in the same manner as if it had proceeded from the decree of a court of justice.

The commanders, Pizarro and Almagro, made oath, in the name of God and the Holy Evangelists, sacredly to keep this covenant, swearing it on the missal, on which they traced with their own hands the sacred emblem of the cross. To give still greater efficacy to the compact, Father Luque administered the sacrament to the parties, dividing the consecrated wafer into three portions, of which each one of them partook; while the bystanders, says an historian, were affected to tears by this spectacle of the solemn ceremonial with which these men voluntarily devoted themselves to a sacrifice that seemed little short of insanity.[5]

The instrument, which was dated March 10, 1526, was subscribed by Luque, and attested by three respectable citizens of Panamá, one of whom signed on behalf of Pizarro, and the other for Almagro; since neither of these parties, according to the avowal of the instrument, was able to subscribe his own name.[6]

Such was the singular compact by which three obscure individuals coolly carved out and partitioned among themselves, an empire of whose extent, power, and resources, of whose situation, of whose existence, even, they had no sure or precise knowledge. The positive and unhesitating manner in which they speak of the grandeur of this empire, of its stores of wealth, so conformable to the event, but of which they could have really known so little, forms a striking contrast with the general skepticism and indifference manifested by nearly every other person, high and low, in the community of Panamá.[7]

The religious tone of the instrument is not the least remarkable feature in it, especially when we contrast this with the relentless policy, pursued by the very men who were parties to it, in their conquest of the country. "In the name of the Prince of Peace," says the illustrious historian of America, "they ratified a contract of which plunder and bloodshed were the objects." [8] The reflection seems reasonable. Yet, in criticizing what is done, as well as what is written, we must take into account the spirit of the times.[9] The invocation of Heaven was natural, where the object of

[5] This singular instrument is given at length by Montesinos. (Annales, MS., año 1526.)

[6] For some investigation of the fact, which has been disputed by more than one, of Pizarro's ignorance of the art of writing, see Book 4, chap. 5 of this History.

[7] The epithet of loco or "madman" was punningly bestowed on Father Luque, for his spirited exertions in behalf of the enterprise; *Padre Luque ò loco,* says Oviedo of him, as if it were synonymous. Historia de las Indias Islas e Tierra Firme del Mar Oceano, MS., Parte 3, lib. 8, cap. 1.

[8] Robertson, America, vol. III. p. 5.

[9] "A perfect judge will read each work of wit
With the same spirit that its author writ,"
says the great bard of Reason. A fair criticism will apply the same rule to action as

the undertaking was, in part, a religious one. Religion entered, more or less, into the theory, at least, of the Spanish conquests in the New World. That motives of a baser sort mingled largely with these higher ones, and in different proportions according to the character of the individual, no one will deny. And few are they that have proposed to themselves a long career of action without the intermixture of some vulgar personal motive, —fame, honors, or emolument. Yet that religion furnishes a key to the American crusades, however rudely they may have been conducted, is evident from the history of their origin; from the sanction openly given to them by the Head of the Church; from the throng of self-devoted missionaries, who followed in the track of the conquerors to garner up the rich harvest of souls; from the reiterated instructions of the Crown, the great object of which was the conversion of the natives; from those superstitious acts of the iron-hearted soldiery themselves, which, however they may be set down to fanaticism, were clearly too much in earnest to leave any ground for the charge of hypocrisy. It was indeed a fiery cross that was borne over the devoted land, scathing and consuming it in its terrible progress; but it was still the cross, the sign of man's salvation, the only sign by which generations and generations yet unborn were to be rescued from eternal perdition.

It is a remarkable fact, which has hitherto escaped the notice of the historian, that Luque was not the real party to this contract. He represented another, who placed in his hands the funds required for the undertaking. This appears from an instrument signed by Luque himself and certified before the same notary that prepared the original contract. The instrument declares that the whole sum of twenty thousand *pesos* advanced for the expedition was furnished by the Licientiate Gaspar de Espinosa, then at Panamá; that the vicar acted only as his agent and by his authority; and that, in consequence, the said Espinosa and no other was entitled to a third of all the profits and acquisitions resulting from the conquest of Peru. This instrument, attested by three persons, one of them the same who had witnessed the original contract, was dated on the 6th of August, 1531.[10] The Licentiate Espinosa was a respectable functionary, who had filled the office of principal alcalde in Darien, and since taken a conspicuous part in the conquest and settlement of Tierra Firme. He enjoyed much consideration for his personal character and station; and it is remarkable that so little should be known of the manner in which the covenant, so solemnly made, was executed in reference to him. As in the case of Columbus, it is probable that the unexpected magnitude of the results was such as to prevent a faithful adherence to the original stipula-

to writing, and, in the moral estimate of conduct will take largely into account the spirit of the age which prompted it.

[10] The instrument making this extraordinary disclosure is cited at length in a manuscript entitled Noticia General del Perú, Tierra Firme y Chili, by Francisco Lopez de Caravantes, a fiscal officer in these colonies. The MS., formerly preserved in the library of the great college of Cuença at Salamanca, is now to be found in her Majesty's library at Madrid. The passage is extracted by Quintana, Españoles Celebres, tom. II. Apend. No. 2, nota.

tion; and yet, from the same consideration, one can hardly doubt that the twenty thousand *pesos* of the bold speculator must have brought him a magnificent return. Nor did the worthy vicar of Panamá, as the history will show hereafter, go without his reward.

Having completed these preliminary arrangements, the three associates lost no time in making preparations for the voyage. Two vessels were purchased, larger and every way better than those employed on the former occasion. Stores were laid in, as experience dictated, on a larger scale than before, and proclamation was made of "an expedition to Peru." But the call was not readily answered by the skeptical citizens of Panamá. Of nearly two hundred men who had embarked on the former cruise, not more than three fourths now remained.[11] This dismal mortality, and the emaciated, poverty-stricken aspect of the survivors, spoke more eloquently than the braggart promises and magnificent prospects held out by the adventurers. Still there were men in the community of such desperate circumstances, that any change seemed like a chance of bettering their condition. Most of the former company also, strange to say, felt more pleased to follow up the adventure to the end than to abandon it, as they saw the light of a better day dawning upon them. From these sources the two captains succeeded in mustering about one hundred and sixty men, making altogether a very inadequate force for the conquest of an empire. A few horses were also purchased, and a better supply of ammunition and military stores than before, though still on a very limited scale. Considering their funds, the only way of accounting for this must be by the difficulty of obtaining supplies at Panamá, which, recently founded, and on the remote coast of the Pacific, could be approached only by crossing the rugged barrier of mountains, which made the transportation of bulky articles extremely difficult. Even such scanty stock of materials as it possessed was probably laid under heavy contribution, at the present juncture, by the governor's preparations for his own expedition to the north.

Thus indifferently provided, the two captains, each in his own vessel, again took their departure from Panamá, under the direction of Bartholomew Ruiz, a sagacious and resolute pilot, well experienced in the navigation of the Southern Ocean. He was a native of Moguer, in Andalusia, that little nursery of nautical enterprise, which furnished so many seamen for the first voyages of Columbus. Without touching at the intervening points of the coast, which offered no attraction to the voyagers, they stood farther out to sea, steering direct for the Rio de San Juan, the utmost limit reached by Almagro. The season was better selected than on the former occasion, and they were borne along by favorable breezes to the place of their destination, which they reached without accident in a few days. Entering the mouth of the river, they saw the banks well lined

[11] "Con ciento i diez Hombres saliò de Panamá, i fue donde estaba el Capitan Piçarro con otros cinquenta de los primeros cineto i diez, que con èl salieron, i de los setenta, quel el Capitan Almagro llevò quando le fue à buscar, que los ciento i treinta ià eran muertos." Xerez. Conq. del Peru, ap. Barcia, tom. III. p. 180.

with Indian habitations; and Pizarro, disembarking, at the head of a party of soldiers, succeeded in surprising a small village and carrying off a considerable booty of gold ornaments found in the dwellings, together with a few of the natives.[12]

Flushed with their success, the two chiefs were confident that the sight of the rich spoil so speedily obtained could not fail to draw adventurers to their standard in Panamá; and, as they felt more than ever the necessity of a stronger force to cope with the thickening population of the country which they were now to penetrate, it was decided that Almagro should return with the treasure and beat up for reinforcements, while the pilot Ruiz, in the other vessel, should reconnoitre the country towards the south, and obtain such information as might determine their future movements. Pizarro, with the rest of the force, would remain in the neighborhood of the river, as he was assured by the Indian prisoners, that not far in the interior was an open reach of country, where he and his men could find comfortable quarters. This arrangement was instantly put in execution. We will first accompany the intrepid pilot in his cruise towards the south.

Coasting along the great continent, with his canvas still spread to favorable winds, the first place at which Ruiz cast anchor was off the little island of Gallo, about two degrees north. The inhabitants, who were not numerous, were prepared to give him a hostile reception,—for tidings of the invaders had preceded them along the country, and even reached this insulated spot. As the object of Ruiz was to explore, not conquer, he did not care to entangle himself in hostilities with the natives; so, changing his purpose of landing, he weighed anchor, and ran down the coast as far as what is now called the Bay of St. Matthew. The country, which, as he advanced, continued to exhibit evidence of a better culture as well as of a more dense population than the parts hitherto seen, was crowded, along the shores, with spectators, who gave no signs of fear or hostility. They stood gazing on the vessel of the white men as it glided smoothly into the crystal waters of the bay, fancying it, says an old writer, some mysterious being descended from the skies.

Without staying long enough on this friendly coast to undeceive the simple people, Ruiz, standing off shore, struck out into the deep sea; but he had not sailed far in that direction, when he was surprised by the sight of a vessel, seeming in the distance like a caravel of considerable size, traversed by a large sail that carried it sluggishly over the waters. The old navigator was not a little perplexed by this phenomenon, as he was confident no European bark could have been before him in these latitudes, and no Indian nation, yet discovered, not even the civilized Mexican, was acquainted with the use of sails in navigation. As he drew near, he found it was a large vessel, or rather raft, called *balsa* by the natives, consisting of a number of huge timbers of a light, porous wood, tightly

[12] Ibid., pp. 180, 181.—Naharro, Relacion Sumaria, MS.—Zarate, Conq. del Peru, lib. 1, cap. 1.—Herrera, Hist. General, dec. 3, lib. 8, cap. 13.

lashed together, with a frail flooring of reeds raised on them by way of deck. Two masts or sturdy poles, erected in the middle of the vessel, sustained a large square-sail of cotton, while a rude kind of rudder and a movable keel, made of plank inserted between the logs, enabled the mariner to give a direction to the floating fabric, which held on its course without the aid of oar or paddle.[13] The simple architecture of this craft was sufficient for the purposes of the natives, and indeed has continued to answer them to the present day; for the *balsa,* surmounted by small thatched huts or cabins, still supplies the most commodious means for the transportation of passengers and luggage on the streams and along the shores of this part of the South American continent.

On coming alongside, Ruiz found several Indians, both men and women, on board, some with rich ornaments on their persons, besides several articles wrought with considerable skill in gold and silver, which they were carrying for purposes of traffic to the different places along the coast. But what most attracted his attention was the woollen cloth of which some of their dresses were made. It was of a fine texture, delicately embroidered with figures of birds and flowers, and dyed in brilliant colors. He also observed in the boat a pair of balances made to weigh the precious metals.[14] His astonishment at these proofs of ingenuity and civilization, so much higher than anything he had ever seen in the country, was heightened by the intelligence which he collected from some of these Indians. Two of them had come from Tumbez, a Peruvian port, some degrees to the south; and they gave him to understand, that in their neighborhood the fields were covered with large flocks of the animals from which the wool was obtained, and that gold and silver were almost as common as wood in the palaces of their monarch. The Spaniards listened greedily to reports which harmonized so well with their fond desires. Though half distrusting the exaggeration, Ruiz resolved to detain some of the Indians, including the natives of Tumbez, that they might repeat the wondrous tale to his commander, and at the same time, by learning the Castilian, might hereafter serve as interpreters with their countrymen. The rest of the party he suffered to proceed without further interruption on their voyage. Then holding on his course, the prudent pilot, without touching at any other point of the coast, advanced as far as the

[13] "Traia sus manteles y antenas de muy fina madera y velas de algodon del mismo talle de manera que los nuestros navios." Relacion de los Primeros Descubrimientos de F. Pizarro y Diego de Almagro, sacada del Codice, No. 120 de la Biblioteca Imperial de Vienna, MS.

[14] In a short notice of this expedition, written apparently at the time of it, or soon after, a minute specification is given of the several articles found in the *balsa;* among them are mentioned vases and mirrors of burnished silver, and curious fabrics both cotton and woollen. "Espejos guarnecidos de la dicha plata, y tasas y otras vasijas para beber, trahian muchas mantas de lana y de algodon, y camisas y aljubas y alcaçeres y alaremes, y otras muchas ropas, todo lo mas de ello muy labrado de labores muy ricas de colores de grana y carmisi y azul y amarillo, y de todas otras colores de diversas maneras de labores y figuras de aves y animales, y Pescados, y arbolesas y trahian unos pesos chiquitos de pesar oro como hechura de Romana, y otras muchas cosas." Relacion sacada de la Biblioteca Imperial de Vienna, MS.

Punta de Pasado, about half a degree south, having the glory of being the first European who, sailing in this direction on the Pacific, had crossed the equinoctial line. This was the limit of his discoveries; on reaching which he tacked about, and standing away to the north, succeeded, after an absence of several weeks, in regaining the spot where he had left Pizarro and his comrades.[15]

It was high time; for the spirits of that little band had been sorely tried by the perils they had encountered. On the departure of his vessels, Pizarro marched into the interior, in the hope of finding the pleasant champaign country which had been promised him by the natives. But at every step the forests seemed to grow denser and darker, and the trees towered to a height such as he had never seen, even in these fruitful regions, where Nature works on so gigantic a scale.[16] Hill continued to rise above hill, as he advanced, rolling onward, as it were, by successive waves to join that colossal barrier of the Andes, whose frosty sides, far away above the clouds, spread out like a curtain of burnished silver, that seemed to connect the heavens with the earth.

On crossing these woody eminences, the forlorn adventurers would plunge into ravines of frightful depth, where the exhalations of a humid soil steamed up amidst the incense of sweet-scented flowers, which shone through the deep glooms in every conceivable variety of color. Birds, especially of the parrot tribe, mocked this fantastic variety of nature with tints as brilliant as those of the vegetable world. Monkeys chattered in crowds above their heads, and made grimaces like the fiendish spirits of these solitudes; while hideous reptiles, engendered in the slimy depths of the pools, gathered round the footsteps of the wanderers. Here was seen the gigantic boa, coiling his unwieldy folds about the trees, so as hardly to be distinguished from their trunks, till he was ready to dart upon his prey; and alligators lay basking on the borders of the streams, or, gliding under the waters, seized their incautious victim before he was aware of their approach.[17] Many of the Spaniards perished miserably in this way, and others were waylaid by the natives, who kept a jealous eye on their movements, and availed themselves of every opportunity to take them at advantage. Fourteen of Pizarro's men were cut off at once in a canoe which had stranded on the bank of a stream.[18]

Famine came in addition to other troubles, and it was with difficulty

---

[15] Xerez, Conq. del Peru, ap. Barcia, tom. III. p. 181.—Relacion sacada de la Biblioteca Imperial de Vienna, MS.—Herrera, Hist. General, dec. 3, lib. 8, cap. 13.

One of the authorities speaks of his having been sixty days on this cruise. I regret not to be able to give precise dates of the events in these early expeditions. But chronology is a thing beneath the notice of these ancient chroniclers, who seem to think that the date of events, so fresh in their own memory, must be so in that of every one else.

[16] "Todo era montañas, con arboles hasta el cielo!" Herrera, Hist. General, ubi supra.

[17] Ibid., ubi supra.

[18] Ibid. loc. cit.—Gomara, Hist. de las Ind., cap. 108.—Naharro, Relacion Sumaria, MS.

that they found the means of sustaining life on the scanty fare of the forest,—occasionally the potato, as it grew without cultivation, or the wild cocoa-nut, or, on the shore, the salt and bitter fruit of the mangrove; though the shore was less tolerable than the forest, from the swarms of mosquitos which compelled the wretched adventurers to bury their bodies up to their very faces in the sand. In this extremity of suffering, they thought only of return; and all schemes of avarice and ambition—except with Pizarro and a few dauntless spirits—were exchanged for the one craving desire to return to Panamá.

It was at this crisis that the pilot Ruiz returned with the report of his brilliant discoveries; and, not long after, Almagro sailed into port with his vessel laden with refreshments, and a considerable reinforcement of volunteers. The voyage of that commander had been prosperous. When he arrived at Panamá, he found the government in the hands of Don Pedro de los Rios; and he came to anchor in the harbor, unwilling to trust himself on shore, till he had obtained from Father Luque some account of the dispositions of the executive. These were sufficiently favorable; for the new governor had particular instructions fully to carry out the arrangements made by his predecessor with the associates. On learning Almagro's arrival, he came down to the port to welcome him, professing his willingness to afford every facility for the execution of his designs. Fortunately, just before this period, a small body of military adventurers had come to Panamá from the mother country, burning with desire to make their fortunes in the New World. They caught much more eagerly than the old and wary colonists at the golden bait held out to them; and with their addition, and that of a few supernumerary stragglers who hung about the town, Almagro found himself at the head of a reinforcement of at least eighty men, with which, having laid in a fresh supply of stores, he again set sail for the Rio de San Juan.

The arrival of the new recruits all eager to follow up the expedition, the comfortable change in their circumstances produced by an ample supply of refreshments, and the glowing pictures of the wealth that awaited them in the south, all had their effect on the dejected spirits of Pizarro's followers. Their late toils and privations were speedily forgotten, and, with the buoyant and variable feelings incident to a freebooter's life, they now called as eagerly on their commander to go forward in the voyage, as they had before called on him to abandon it. Availing themselves of the renewed spirit of enterprise, the captains embarked on board their vessels, and, under the guidance of the veteran pilot, steered in the same track he had lately pursued.

But the favorable season for a southern course, which in these latitudes lasts but a few months in the year, had been suffered to escape. The breezes blew steadily towards the north, and a strong current, not far from shore, set in the same direction. The winds frequently rose into tempests, and the unfortunate voyagers were tossed about, for many days, in the boiling surges, amidst the most awful storms of thunder and lightning, until, at length, they found a secure haven in the island of Gallo.

already visited by Ruiz. As they were now too strong in numbers to apprehend an assault, the crews landed, and, experiencing no molestation from the natives, they continued on the island for a fortnight, refitting their damaged vessels, and recruiting themselves after the fatigues of the ocean. Then, resuming their voyage, the captains stood towards the south until they reached the Bay of St. Matthew. As they advanced along the coast, they were struck, as Ruiz had been before, with the evidences of a higher civilization constantly exhibited in the general aspect of the country and its inhabitants. The hand of cultivation was visible in every quarter. The natural appearance of the coast, too, had something in it more inviting; for, instead of the eternal labyrinth of mangrove-trees, with their complicated roots snarled into formidable coils under the water, as if to waylay and entangle the voyager, the low margin of the sea was covered with a stately growth of ebony, and with a species of mahogany, and other hard woods that take the most brilliant and variegated polish. The sandal-wood, and many balsamic trees of unknown names, scattered their sweet odors far and wide, not in an atmosphere tainted with vegetable corruption, but on the pure breezes of the ocean, bearing health as well as fragrance on their wings. Broad patches of cultivated land intervened, disclosing hill-sides covered with the yellow maize and the potato, or checkered, in the lower levels, with blooming plantations of cacao.[19]

The villages became more numerous; and, as the vessels rode at anchor off the port of Tacamez, the Spaniards saw before them a town of two thousand houses or more, laid out into streets, with a numerous population clustering around it in the suburbs.[20] The men and women displayed many ornaments of gold and precious stones about their persons, which may seem strange, considering that the Peruvian Incas claimed a monopoly of jewels for themselves and the nobles on whom they condescended to bestow them. But, although the Spaniards had now reached the outer limits of the Peruvian empire, it was not Peru, but Quito, and that portion of it but recently brought under the sceptre of the Incas, where the ancient usages of the people could hardly have been effaced under the oppressive system of the American despots. The adjacent country was, moreover, particularly rich in gold, which, collected from the washings of the streams, still forms one of the staple products of Barbacoas. Here, too, was the fair River of Emeralds, so called from the quarries of the beautiful gem on its borders, from which the Indian monarchs enriched their treasury.[21]

[19] Xerez, Conq. del Peru, ap. Barcia, tom. III. p. 181.—Relacion sacada de la Biblioteca Imperial de Vienna, MS.—Naharro, Relacion Summaria, MS.—Montesinos, Annales, MS., año 1526.—Zarate, Conq. del Peru, lib. 1, cap. 1.—Relcaion del Primer. Descub., MS.

[20] Pizarro's secretary speaks of one of the towns as containing 3,000 houses. "En esta Tierra havia muchos Mantenimientos, i la Gente tenia mui buena orden de vivir, los Pueblos con sus Calles, i Plaças: Pueblo havia que tenia mas de tres mil Casas, i otros havia menores." Conq. del Peru, ap. Barcia, tom. III. p. 181.

[21] Stevenson who visited this part of the coast early in the present century, is pro-

The Spaniards gazed with delight on these undeniable evidences of wealth, and saw in the careful cultivation of the soil a comfortable assurance that they had at length reached the land which had so long been seen in brilliant, though distant, perspective before them. But here again they were doomed to be disappointed by the warlike spirit of the people, who, conscious of their own strength, showed no disposition to quail before the invaders. On the contrary, several of their canoes shot out, loaded with warriors, who, displaying a gold mask as their ensign, hovered round the vessels with looks of defiance, and, when pursued, easily took shelter under the lee of the land.[22]

A more formidable body mustered along the shore, to the number, according to the Spanish accounts, of at least ten thousand warriors, eager, apparently, to come to close action with the invaders. Nor could Pizarro, who had landed with a party of his men in the hope of a conference with the natives, wholly prevent hostilities; and it might have gone hard with the Spaniards, hotly pressed by their resolute enemy so superior in numbers, but for a ludicrous accident reported by the historians as happening to one of the cavaliers. This was a fall from his horse, which so astonished the barbarians, who were not prepared for this division of what seemed one and the same being into two, that, filled with consternation, they fell back, and left a way open for the Christians to regain their vessels![23]

A council of war was now called. It was evident that the forces of the Spaniards were unequal to a contest with so numerous and well-appointed a body of natives; and, even if they should prevail here, they could have no hope of stemming the torrent which must rise against them in their progress—for the country was becoming more and more thickly settled, and towns and hamlets started into view at every new headland which

---

fuse in his description of its mineral and vegetable treasures. The emerald mine in the neighborhood of Las Esmeraldas, once so famous, is now placed under the ban of a superstition, more befitting the times of the Incas. "I never visited it," says the traveller, "owing to the superstitious dread of the natives, who assured me that it was enchanted, and guarded by an enormous dragon, which poured forth thunder and lightning on those who dared to ascend the river." Residence in South America, vol. II. p. 406.

[22] "Salieron á los dichos navios quatorce canoas grandes con muchos Indios dos armados de oro y plata, y trahian en la una canoa ó en estandarte y encima de él un bolto de un mucho desio de oro, y dieron una suelta á los navios por avisarlos en manera que no los pudiese enojar, y asi dieron vuelta acia á su pueblo, y los navios no los pudieron tomar porque se metieron en los baxos junto á la tierra." Relacion sacada de la Biblioteca Imperial de Vienna, MS.

[23] "Al tiempo del romper los unos con los otros, uno de aquellos de caballo cayó del caballo abajo; y como los Indios vieron dividirse aquel animal en dos partes, teniendo por cierto que todo era una cosa, fué tanto el miedo que tubieron que volvieron las espaldas dando voces á los suyos, diciendo, que se habia hecho dos haciendo admiracion dello: lo cual no fué sin misterio; porque á no acaecer esto se presume, que mataran todos los cristianos." (Relacion del Primer. Descub., MS.) This way of accounting for the panic of the barbarians is certainly quite as credible as the explanation, under similar circumstances, afforded by the apparition of the militant apostle St. James so often noticed by the historians of these wars.

they doubled. It was better, in the opinion of some,—the faint-hearted,—
to abandon the enterprise at once, as beyond their strength. But Almagro
took a different view of the affair. "To go home," he said, "with nothing
done, would be ruin, as well as disgrace. There was scarcely one but had
left creditors at Panamá, who looked for payment to the fruits of this
expedition. To go home now would be to deliver themselves at once into
their hands. It would be to go to prison. Better to roam a freeman, though
in the wilderness, than to lie bound with fetters in the dungeons of Panamá.[24] The only course for them," he concluded, "was the one lately pursued. Pizarro might find some more commodious place where he could
remain with part of the force while he himself went back for recruits to
Panamá. The story they had now to tell of the riches of the land, as they
had seen them with their own eyes, would put their expedition in a very
different light, and could not fail to draw to their banner as many volunteers as they needed."

But this recommendation, however judicious, was not altogether to the
taste of the latter commander, who did not relish the part, which constantly fell to him, of remaining behind in the swamps and forests of this
wild country. "It is all very well," he said to Almagro, "for you, who pass
your time pleasantly enough, careering to and fro in your vessel, or snug-
ly sheltered in a land of plenty at Panamá; but it is quite another matter
for those who stay behind to droop and die of hunger in the wilderness." [25] To this Almagro retorted with some heat, professing his own
willingness to take charge of the brave men who would remain with him,
if Pizarro declined it. The controversy assuming a more angry and menacing tone, from words they would have soon come to blows, as both,
laying their hands on their swords, were preparing to rush on each other,
when the treasurer Ribera, aided by the pilot Ruiz, succeeded in pacify-
ing them. It required but little effort on the part of these cooler counsellors to convince the cavaliers of the folly of a conduct which must at
once terminate the expedition in a manner little creditable to its projectors. A reconciliation consequently took place, sufficient, at least in outward show, to allow the two commanders to act together in concert. Al-

---

[24] "No era bien bolver pobres, á pedir limosna, i morir en las Carceles, los que
tenian deudas." Herrera, Hist. General, dec. 3, lib. 10, cap. 2.
[25] "Como iba, i venia en los Navios, adonde no le faltaba Vitualla, no padecia la
miseria de la hambre, i otras angustias que tenian, i ponian á todos en estrema
congoja." (Herrera, Hist. General, dec. 3, lib. 10, cap. 2.) The cavaliers of Cortés
and Pizarro however doughty their achievements, certainly fell short of those
knights-errant, commemorated by Hudibras, who
          "As some think,
Of old did neither eat nor drink;
Because, when thorough deserts vast
And regions desolate they past,
Unless they grazed, there's not one word
Of their provision on record;
Which made some confidently write,
They had no stomachs but to fight."

magro's plan was then adopted; and it only remained to find out the most secure and convenient spot for Pizarro's quarters.

Several days were passed in touching at different parts of the coast, as they retraced their course; but everywhere the natives appeared to have caught the alarm, and assumed a menacing, and from their numbers a formidable, aspect. The more northerly region, with its unwholesome fens and forests, where nature wages a war even more relentless than man, was not to be thought of. In this perplexity, they decided on the little island of Gallo, as being, on the whole, from its distance from the shore, and from the scantiness of its population, the most eligible spot for them in their forlorn and destitute condition.[26]

But no sooner was the resolution of the two captains made known, than a feeling of discontent broke forth among their followers, especially those who were to remain with Pizarro on the island, "What!" they exclaimed, "were they to be dragged to that obscure spot to die by hunger? The whole expedition had been a cheat and a failure, from beginning to end. The golden countries, so much vaunted, had seemed to fly before them as they advanced; and the little gold they had been fortunate enough to glean had all been sent back to Panamá to entice other fools to follow their example. What had they got in return for all their sufferings? The only treasures they could boast were their bows and arrows, and they were now to be left to die on this dreary island, without so much as a rood of consecrated ground to lay their bones in![27]

In this exasperated state of feeling, several of the soldiers wrote back to their friends, informing them of their deplorable condition, and complaining of the cold-blooded manner in which they were to be sacrificed to the obstinate cupidity of their leaders. But the latter were wary enough to anticipate this movement, and Almagro defeated it by seizing all the letters in the vessels, and thus cutting off at once the means of communication with their friends at home. Yet this act of unscrupulous violence, like most other similar acts, fell short of its purpose; for a soldier named Sarabia had the ingenuity to evade it by introducing a letter into a ball of cotton, which was to be taken to Panamá as a specimen of the products of the country, and presented to the governor's lady.[28]

[26] Pedro Pizarro, Descub. y Conq., MS.—Relacion sacada de la Biblioteca Imperial de Vienna, MS.—Naharro, Relacion Sumaria, MS.—Zarate, Conq. del Peru, lib. 1, cap. 1.—Herrera, Hist. General, dec. 3, lib. 10, cap. 2.

It was singularly unfortunate, that Pizarro, instead of striking farther south, should have so long clung to the northern shores of the continent. Dampier notices them as afflicted with incessant rain; while the inhospitable forests and the particularly ferocious character of the natives continued to make these regions but little known down to his time. See his Voyages and Adventures, (London, 1776,) vol. I. chap. 14.

[27] "Miserablemente morir adonde aun no havia lugar Sagrado, para sepultura de sus cuerpos." Herrera, Hist. General, dec. 3, lib. 10, cap. 3.

[28] "Metieron en un ovillo de algodon una carta firmada de muchos en que sumariamente daban cuenta de las hambres, muertes y desnudez que padecian, y que era cosa de risa todo, pues las riquezas se habian convertido en flechas, y no havia otra cosa." Montesinos, Annales, MS., año 1527.

The letter, which was signed by several of the disaffected soldiery besides the writer, painted in gloomy colors the miseries of their condition, accused the two commanders of being the authors of this, and called on the authorities of Panamá to interfere by sending a vessel to take them from the desolate spot, while some of them might still be found surviving the horrors of their confinement. The epistle concluded with a stanza, in which the two leaders were stigmatized as partners in a slaughter-house; one being employed to drive in the cattle for the other to butcher. The verses, which had a currency in their day among the colonists to which they were certainly not entitled by their poetical merits, may be thus rendered into corresponding doggerel:

> "Look out, Señor Governor,
> For the drover while he 's near;
> Since he goes home to get the sheep
> For the butcher who stays here." [29]

[29] Xerez, Conq. del Peru, ap. Barcia, tom. III. p. 181.—Naharro, Relacio. Sumaria, MS.—Balboa, Hist. du Perou, chap. 15.

"Al fin de la peticion que hacian en la carta al Governador puso Juan de Sarabia, natural de Trujillo, esta cuarteta:—
> Pues Señor Gobernador,
> Mireio bien por entero
> que alla va ei recogedor,
> y acá queda el carnicere."

Montesinos, Annales, MS. año 1527.

CHAPTER IV

INDIGNATION OF THE GOVERNOR—STERN RESOLUTION OF PIZARRO—
PROSECUTION OF THE VOYAGE—BRILLIANT ASPECT OF TUMBEZ—
DISCOVERIES ALONG THE COAST—RETURN TO PANAMÁ—PIZARRO
EMBARKS FOR SPAIN

1527—1528

NOT long after Almagro's departure, Pizarro sent off the remaining vessel, under the pretext of its being put in repair at Panamá. It probably relieved him of a part of his followers, whose mutinous spirit made them an obstacle rather than a help in his forlorn condition, and with whom he was the more willing to part from the difficulty of finding subsistence on the barren spot which he now occupied.

Great was the dismay occasioned by the return of Almagro and his followers, in the little community of Panamá; for the letter, surreptitiously conveyed in the ball of cotton, fell into the hands for which it was intended, and the contents soon got abroad with usual quantity of exaggeration. The haggard and dejected mien of the adventurers, of itself, told a tale sufficiently disheartening, and it was soon generally believed that the few ill-fated survivors of the expedition were detained against their will by Pizarro, to end their days with their disappointed leader on his desolate island.

Pedro de los Rios, the governor, was so much incensed at the result of the expedition, and the waste of life it had occasioned to the colony, that he turned a deaf ear to all the applications of Luque and Almagro for further countenance in the affair; he derided their sanguine anticipations of the future, and finally resolved to send an officer to the isle of Gallo, with orders to bring back every Spaniard whom he should find still living in that dreary abode. Two vessels were immediately despatched for the purpose, and placed under charge of a cavalier named Tafur, a native of Cordova.

Meanwhile Pizarro and his followers were experiencing all the miseries which might have been expected from the character of the barren spot on which they were imprisoned. They were, indeed, relieved from all apprehensions of the natives, since these had quitted the island on its occupation by the white men; but they had to endure the pains of hunger even in a greater degree than they had formerly experienced in the wild woods of the neighboring continent. Their principal food was crabs and such shell-fish as they could scantily pick up along the shores. Incessant

863

storms of thunder and lightning, for it was the rainy season, swept over the devoted island, and drenched them with a perpetual flood. Thus, half-naked, and pining with famine, there were few in that little company who did not feel the spirit of enterprise quenched within them, or who looked for any happier termination of their difficulties than that afforded by a return to Panamá. The appearance of Tafur, therefore, with his two vessels, well stored with provisions, was greeted with all the rapture that the crew of a sinking wreck might feel on the arrival of some unexpected succour; and the only thought, after satisfying the immediate cravings of hunger, was to embark and leave the detested isle forever.

But by the same vessel letters came to Pizarro from his two confederates, Luque and Almagro, beseeching him not to despair in his present extremity, but to hold fast to his original purpose. To return under the present circumstances would be to seal the fate of the expedition; and they solemnly engaged, if he would remain firm at his post, to furnish him in a short time with the necessary means for going forward.[1]

A ray of hope was enough for the courageous spirit of Pizarro. It does not appear that he himself had entertained, at any time, thoughts of returning. If he had, these words of encouragement entirely banished them from his bosom, and he prepared to stand the fortune of the cast on which he had so desperately ventured. He knew, however, that solicitations or remonstrances would avail little with the companions of his enterprise; and he probably did not care to win over the more timid spirits who, by perpetually looking back, would only be a clog on his future movements. He announced his own purpose, however, in a laconic but decided manner, characteristic of a man more accustomed to act than to talk, and well calculated to make an impression on his rough followers.

Drawing his sword, he traced a line with it on the sand from east to west. Then turning towards the south, "Friend and comrades!" he said, "on that side are toil, hunger, nakedness, the drenching storm, desertion, and death; on this side, ease and pleasure. There lies Peru with its riches; here, Panamá and its poverty. Choose, each man, what best becomes a brave Castilian. For my part, I go to the south." So saying, he stepped across the line.[2] He was followed by the brave pilot Ruiz; next by Pedro de Candia, a cavalier, born, as his name imports, in one of the isles of Greece. Eleven others successively crossed the line, thus intimating their

[1] Xerez, Conq. del Peru, ap. Barcia, tom. III. p. 182.—Zarate, Conq. del Peru, lib. 1, cap. 2.—Montesinos, Annales, MS., año 1527.—Herrera, Hist. General, dec. 3, lib. 10, cap. 3.—Naharro, Relacion Sumaria, MS.

[2] "Obedeciola Pizarro y antes que se egecutase sacó un Puñal, y con notable animo hizo con la punta una raya de Oriente á Poniente; y señalando al medio dia, que era la parte de su noticia, y derrotero dijo: camaradas y amigos esta parte es la de la muerte, de los trabajos, de las hambres, de la desnudez, de los aguaceros, y desamparos; la otra la del gusto: Por aqui se ba à Panama à ser pobres, por alla al Peru à ser ricos. Escoja el que fuere buen Castellano lo que mas bien le estubiere. Diciendo esto pasó la raya: siguieronle Barthome Ruiz natural de Moguer, Pedro de Candi Griego, natural de Candia." Montesinos, Annales, MS., año 1527.

willingness to abide the fortunes of their leader, for good or for evil.⁴
Fame, to quote the enthusiastic language of an ancient chronicler, has
commemorated the names of this little band, "who thus, in the face oɪ
difficulties unexampled in history, with death rather than riches for their
reward, preferred it all to abandoning their honor, and stood firm by
their leader as an example of loyalty to future ages." ⁴

But the act excited no such admiration in the mind of Tafur, who looked on it as one of gross disobedience to the commands of the governor,
and as little better than madness, involving the certain destruction of the
parties engaged in it. He refused to give any sanction to it himself by
leaving one of his vessels with the adventurers to prosecute their voyage,
and it was with great difficulty that he could be persuaded even to allow
them a part of the stores which he had brought for their support. This
had no influence on their determination, and the little party, bidding
adieu to their returning comrades, remained unshaken in their purpose
of abiding the fortunes of their commander.⁵

There is something striking to the imagination in the spectacle of these
few brave spirits, thus consecrating themselves to a daring enterprise,
which seemed as far above their strength as any recorded in the fabulous
annals of knight-errantry. A handful of men, without food, without clothing, almost without arms, without knowledge of the land to which they
were bound, without vessel to transport them, were here left on a lonely
rock in the ocean with the avowed purpose of carrying on a crusade
against a powerful empire, staking their lives on its success. What is there
in the legends of chivalry that surpasses it? This was the crisis of Pizarro's fate. There are moments in the lives of men, which, as they are
seized or neglected, decide their future destiny.⁶ Had Pizarro faltered

³ The names of these thirteen faithful companions are preserved in the conven-
tion made with the Crown two years later, where they are suitably commemorated
for their loyalty. Their names should not be omitted in a history of the Conquest
of Peru. They were "Bartolomé Ruiz, Cristoval de Peralta, Pedro de Candia, Domingo de Soria Luce, Nícolas de Ribera, Francisco de Cuellar, Alonso de Molina,
Pedro Alcon, Garcia de Jerez, Anton de Carrion, Alonso Briceño, Martin de Paz,
Joan de la Torre."

⁴ "Estos fueron los trece de la fama. Estos los que cercados de los mayores trabajos que pudo el Mundo ofrecer á hombres, y los que estando mas para esperar
la muerte que las riquezas que se les prometian, todo lo pospusieron á la honra,
y siguieron á su capitan y caudillo para egemplo de lealtad en lo futuro." Montesinos, Annales, MS., año 1527.

⁵ Zarate, Conq. del Peru, lib. 1, cap. 2.—Montesinos, Annales, MS., año 1527.—
Naharro, Relacion Sumaria, MS.—Herrera, Hist. General, dec. 3, lib. 10, cap. 3.

⁶ This common sentiment is expressed with uncommon beauty by the fanciful
Boiardo, where he represents Rinaldo as catching Fortune, under the guise of the
fickle fairy Morgana, by the forelock. The Italian reader may not be displeased to
refresh his memory with it.

"Chi cerca in questo mondo aver tesoro,
    O diletto, e piacere, honore, e stato,
    Ponga la mano a questa chioma d' oro,
    Ch' io porto in fronte, e lo farò beato;

from his strong purpose, and yielded to the occasion, now so temptingly presented, for extricating himself and his broken band from their desperate position, his name would have been buried with his fortunes, and the conquest of Peru would have been left for other and more successful adventurers. But his constancy was equal to the occasion, and his conduct here proved him competent to the perilous post he had assumed, and inspired others with a confidence in him which was the best assurance of success.

In the vessel that bore back Tafur and those who seceded from the expedition the pilot Ruiz was also permitted to return, in order to cooperate with Luque and Almagro in their application for further succour.

Not long after the departure of the ships, it was decided by Pizarro to abandon his present quarters, which had little to recommend them, and which, he reflected, might now be exposed to annoyance from the original inhabitants, should they take courage and return, on learning the diminished number of the white men. The Spaniards, therefore, by his orders, constructed a rude boat or raft, on which they succeeded in transporting themselves to the little island of Gorgona, twenty-five leagues to the north of their present residence. It lay about five leagues from the continent, and was uninhabited. It had some advantages over the isle of Gallo; for it stood higher above the sea, and was partially covered with wood, which afforded shelter to a species of pheasant, and the hare or rabbit of the country, so that the Spaniards, with their cross-bows, were enabled to procure a tolerable supply of game. Cool streams that issued from the living rock furnished abundance of water, though the drenching rains that fell, without intermission, left them in no danger of perishing by thirst. From this annoyance they found some protection in the rude huts which they constructed; though here, as in their former residence, they suffered from the no less intolerable annoyance of venomous insects, which multiplied and swarmed in the exhalations of the rank and stimulated soil. In this dreary abode Pizarro omitted no means by which to sustain the drooping spirits of his men. Morning prayers were duly said, and the evening hymn to the Virgin was regularly chanted; the festivals of the church were carefully commemorated, and every means taken by their commander to give a kind of religious characℯr to his enterprise, and to inspire his rough followers with a confidence in the protection of Heaven, that might support them in their perilous circumstances.[7]

In these uncomfortable quarters, their chief employment was to keep watch on the melancholy ocean, that they might hail the first signal of

> Ma quando ha in destro sì fatto lavoro,
> Non prenda indugio, che 'l tempo passato
> Perduto è tutto, e non ritorna mai,
> Ed io mi volto, e lui lascio con guai."
>   Orlando, Innamorato, lib. 2, canto 8.

[7] "Cada Mañana daban gracias á Dios: à las tardes decian la Salve, i otras Oraciones, por las Horas: sabian las Fiestas, i tenian cuenta con los Viernes i Domingos." Herrera, Hist. General, dec. 3, lib. 10, cap. 3.

the anticipated succour. But many a tedious month passed away, and no sign of it appeared. All around was the same wide waste of waters, except to the eastward, where the frozen crest of the Andes, touched with the ardent sun of the equator, glowed like a ridge of fire along the whole extent of the great continent. Every speck in the distant horizon was carefully noticed, and the drifting timber or masses of sea-weed, heaving to and fro on the bosom of the waters, was converted by their imaginations into the promised vessel; till, sinking under successive disappointments, hope gradually gave way to doubt, and doubt settled into despair.[8]

Meanwhile the vessel of Tafur had reached the port of Panamá. The tidings which she brought of the inflexible obstinacy of Pizarro and his followers filled the governor with indignation. He could look on it in no other light than as an act of suicide, and steadily refused to send further assistance to men who were obstinately bent on their own destruction. Yet Luque and Almagro were true to their engagements. They represented to the governor, that, if the conduct of their comrade was rash, it was at least in the service of the Crown, and in prosecuting the great work of discovery. Rios had been instructed, on his taking the government, to aid Pizarro in the enterprise; and to desert him now would be to throw away the remaining chance of success, and to incur the responsibility of his death and that of the brave men who adhered to him. These remonstrances, at length, so far operated on the mind of that functionary, that he reluctantly consented that a vessel should be sent to the island of Gorgona, but with no more hands than were necessary to work her, and with positive instructions to Pizarro to return in six months and report himself at Panamá, whatever might be the future results of his expedition.

Having thus secured the sanction of the executive, the two associates lost no time in fitting out a small vessel with stores and a supply of arms and ammunition, and despatched it to the island. The unfortunate tenants of this little wilderness, who had now occupied it for seven months,[9] hardly dared to trust their senses when they descried the white sails of the friendly bark coming over the waters. And although, when the vessel anchored off the shore, Pizarro was disappointed to find that it brought no additional recruits for the enterprise, yet he greeted it with joy, as affording the means of solving the great problem of the existence of the rich southern empire, and of thus opening the way for its future conquest. Two of his men were so ill, that it was determined to leave them in the care of some of the friendly Indians who had continued with him through the whole of his sojourn, and to call for them on his return. Taking with him the rest of his hardy followers and the natives of Tumbez, he em-

---

[8] "Al cabo de muchos Dias aguardando, estaban tan angustiados, que los salages, que se hacian bien dentro de la Mar, les parecia, que era el Navio." Herrera, Hist. General, dec. 3, lib. 10, cap. 4.

[9] "Estubieron con estos trabajos con igualdad de animo siete meses." Montesinos Annales, MS., año 1527.

barked, and, speedily weighing anchor, bade adieu to the "Hell," as it was called by the Spaniards, which had been the scene of so much suffering and such undaunted resolution.[10]

Every heart was now elated with hope, as they found themselves once more on the waters, under the guidance of the good pilot Ruiz, who, obeying the directions of the Indians, proposed to steer for the land of Tumbez, which would bring them at once into the golden empire of the Incas, —the El Dorado, of which they had been so long in pursuit. Passing by the dreary isle of Gallo, which they had such good cause to remember, they stood farther out to sea until they made Point Tacumez, near which they had landed on their previous voyage. They did not touch at any part of the coast, but steadily held on their way, though considerably impeded by the currents, as well as by the wind, which blew with little variation from the south. Fortunately, the wind was light, and, as the weather was favorable, their voyage, though slow, was not uncomfortable. In a few days, they came in sight of Point Pasado, the limit of the pilot's former navigation; and, crossing the line, the little bark entered upon those unknown seas which had never been ploughed by European keel before. The coast, they observed, gradually declined from its former bold and rugged character, gently sloping towards the shore, and spreading out into sandy plains, relieved here and there by patches of uncommon richness and beauty; while the white cottages of the natives glistening along the margin of the sea, and the smoke that rose among the distant hills, intimated the increasing population of the country.

At length, after the lapse of twenty days from their departure from the island, the adventurous vessel rounded the point of St. Helena, and glided smoothly into the waters of the beautiful gulf of Guayaquil. The country was here studded along the shore with towns and villages, though the mighty chain of the Cordilleras, sweeping up abruptly from the coast, left but a narrow strip of emerald verdure, through which numerous rivulets, spreading fertility around them, wound their way into the sea.

The voyagers were now abreast of some of the most stupendous heights of this magnificent range; Chimborazo, with its broad round summit, towering like the dome of the Andes, and Cotopaxi, with its dazzling cone of silvery white, that knows no change except from the action of its own volcanic fires; for this mountain is the most terrible of the American volcanoes, and was in formidable activity at no great distance from the period of our narrative. Well pleased with the signs of civilization that opened on them at every league of their progress, the Spaniards, at length, came to anchor, off the island of Santa Clara, lying at the entrance of the bay of Tumbez.[11]

---

[10] Xerez, Conq. del Peru, ap. Barcia, tom. III. p. 182.—Montesinos, Annales, MS., año 1527.—Naharro, Relacion Sumaria, MS.—Herrera, Hist. General, dec. 3, lib. 10, cap. 4.—Pedro Pizarro, Descub. y Conq., MS.

[11] According to Garcilasso, two years elapsed between the departure from Gorgona and the arrival at Tumbez. (Com. Real., Parte 2, lib. 1, cap. 11.) Such gross defiance of chronology is rather uncommon even in the narratives of these transac-

The place was uninhabited, but was recognized by the Indians on board, as occasionally resorted to by the warlike people of the neighboring isle of Puná, for purposes of sacrifice and worship. The Spaniards found on the spot a few bits of gold rudely wrought into various shapes, and probably designed as offerings to the Indian deity. Their hearts were cheered, as the natives assured them they would see abundance of the same precious metal in their own city of Tumbez.

The following morning they stood across the bay for this place. As they drew near, they beheld a town of considerable size, with many of the buildings apparently of stone and plaster, situated in the bosom of a fruitful meadow, which seemed to have been redeemed from the sterility of the surrounding country by careful and minute irrigation. When at some distance from shore, Pizarro saw standing towards him several large balsas, which were found to be filled with warriors going on an expedition against the island of Puná. Running alongside of the Indian flotilla, he invited some of the chiefs to come on board of his vessel. The Peruvians gazed with wonder on every object which met their eyes, and especially on their own countrymen, whom they had little expected to meet there. The latter informed them in what manner they had fallen into the hands of the strangers, whom they described as a wonderful race of beings, that had come thither for no harm, but solely to be made acquainted with the country and its inhabitants. This account was confirmed by the Spanish commander, who persuaded the Indians to return in their balsas and report what they had learned to their townsmen, requesting them at the same time to provide his vessel with refreshments, as it was his desire to enter into a friendly intercourse with the natives.

The people of Tumbez were gathered along the shore, and were gazing with unutterable amazement on the floating castle, which, now having dropped anchor, rode lazily at its moorings in their bay. They eagerly listened to the accounts of their countrymen, and instantly reported the affair to the *curaca* or ruler of the district, who, conceiving that the strangers must be beings of a superior order, prepared at once to comply with their request. It was not long before several balsas were seen steering for the vessel laden with bananas, plantains, yuca, Indian corn, sweet potatoes, pine-apples, cocoa-nuts, and other rich products of the bountiful vale of Tumbez. Game and fish, also, were added, with a number of llamas, of which Pizarro had seen the rude drawings belonging to Balboa, but of which till now he had met with no living specimen. He examined this curious animal, the Peruvian sheep,—or, as the Spaniards called it, the "little camel" of the Indians,—with much interest, greatly admiring the mixture of wool and hair which supplied the natives with the materials for their fabrics.

At that time there happened to be at Tumbez an Inca noble, or *orejon*, —for so, as I have already noticed, men of his rank were called by the

tions, where it is as difficult to fix a precise date, amidst the silence, rather than the contradictions. of contemporary statements, as if the events had happened before the deluge.

Spaniards, from the huge ornaments of gold attached to their ears. He expressed great curiosity to see the wonderful strangers, and had, accordingly, come out with the balsas for the purpose. It was easy to perceive from the superior quality of his dress, as well as from the deference paid to him by the others, that he was a person of consideration, and Pizarro received him with marked distinction. He showed him the different parts of the ship, explaining to him the uses of whatever engaged his attention, and answering his numerous queries, as well as he could, by means of the Indian interpreters. The Peruvian chief was especially desirous of knowing whence and why Pizarro and his followers had come to these shores. The Spanish captain replied, that he was the vassal of a great prince, the greatest and most powerful in the world, and that he had come to this country to assert his master's *lawful supremacy* over it. He had further come to rescue the inhabitants from the darkness of unbelief in which they were now wandering. They worshipped an evil spirit, who would sink their souls into everlasting perdition; and he would give them the knowledge of the true and only God, Jesus Christ, since to believe in him was eternal salvation.[12]

The Indian prince listened with deep attention and apparent wonder; but answered nothing. It may be, that neither he nor his interpreters had any very distinct ideas of the doctrines thus abruptly revealed to them. It may be that he did not believe there was any other potentate on earth greater than the Inca; none, at least, who had a better right to rule over his dominions. And it is very possible he was not disposed to admit that the great luminary whom he worshipped was inferior to the God of the Spaniards. But whatever may have passed in the untutored mind of the barbarian, he did not give vent to it, but maintained a discreet silence, without any attempt to controvert or to convince his Christian antagonist.

He remained on board the vessel till the hour of dinner, of which he partook with the Spaniards, expressing his satisfaction at the strange dishes, and especially pleased with the wine, which he pronounced far superior to the fermented liquors of his own country. On taking leave, he courteously pressed the Spaniards to visit Tumbez, and Pizarro dismissed him with the present, among other things, of an iron hatchet, which had greatly excited his admiration; for the use of iron, as we have seen, was as little known to the Peruvians as to the Mexicans.

On the day following, the Spanish captain sent one of his own men, named Alonso de Molina, on shore, accompanied by a negro who had come in the vessel from Panamá, together with a present for the curaca of some swine and poultry, neither of which were indigenous to the New World. Towards evening his emissary returned with a fresh supply of fruits and vegetables, that the friendly people sent to the vessel. Molina

---

[12] The text abridges somewhat the discourse of the military polemic; which is reported at length by Herrera, Hist. General, dec. 3, lib. 10, cap. 4.—See also Montesinos, Annales, MS., año 1527.—Conq. i. Pob. del Piru, MS.—Naharro, Relacion Sumaria, MS.—Relacion del Primer. Descub., MS

had a wondrous tale to tell. On landing, he was surrounded by the natives, who expressed the greatest astonishment at his dress, his fair complexion, and his long beard. The women, especially, manifested great curiosity in respect to him, and Molina seemed to be entirely won by their charms and captivating manners. He probably intimated his satisfaction by his demeanor, since they urged him to stay among them, promising in that case to provide him with a beautiful wife.

Their surprise was equally great at the complexion of his sable companion. They could not believe it was natural, and tried to rub off the imaginary dye with their hands. As the African bore all this with characteristic good-humor, displaying at the same time his rows of ivory teeth, they were prodigiously delighted.[13] The animals were no less above their comprehension; and, when the cock crew, the simple people clapped their hands, and inquired what he was saying.[14] Their intellects were so bewildered by sights so novel, that they seemed incapable of distinguishing between man and brute.

Molina was then escorted to the residence of the curaca, whom he found living in much state, with porters stationed at his doors, and with a quantity of gold and silver vessels, from which he was served. He was then taken to different parts of the Indian city, saw a fortress built of rough stone, and, though low, spreading over a large extent of ground.[15] Near this was a temple; and the Spaniard's description of its decorations, blazing with gold and silver, seemed so extravagant, that Pizarro, distrusting his whole account, resolved to send a more discreet and trustworthy emissary on the following day.[16]

The person selected was Pedro de Candia, the Greek cavalier mentioned as one of the first who intimated his intention to share the fortunes of his commander. He was sent on shore, dressed in complete mail as became a good knight, with his sword by his side, and his arquebuse on his shoulder. The Indians were even more dazzled by his appearance than by Molina's, as the sun fell brightly on his polished armour, and glanced from his military weapons. They had heard much of the formidable arquebuse from their townsmen who had come in the vessel, and they besought Candia "to let it speak to them." He accordingly set up a wooden board as a target, and, taking deliberate aim, fired off the musket. The flash of the powder and the startling report of the piece, as the board, struck by the ball, was shivered into splinters, filled the natives with dismay. Some fell on the ground, covering their faces with their

[13] "No se cansaban de mirarle, hacianle labar, para vèr si se le quitaba la Tinta negra, i èl lo hacia de buena gana, riendose, i mostrando sus Dientes blancos." Herrera, Hist. General, dec. 3, lib. 10, cap. 5.

[14] Ibid., ubi supra.

[15] "Cerca del solia estar una fortaleza muy fuerte y de linda obra, hecha por los Yngas reyes del Cuzco y señores de todo el Peru. . . . . . Ya esta el edificio desta fortaleza muy gastado y deshecho: mas no para que dexe de dar muestra de lo mucho que fue." Cieza de Leon, Cronica, cap. 4.

[16] Conq. i Pob. del Piru, MS.—Herrera, Hist. General, loc. cit.—Zarate, Conq del Peru, lib. 1, cap. 2.

hands, and others approached the cavalier with feelings of awe, which were gradually dispelled by the assurance they received from the smiling expression of his countenance.[17]

They then showed him the same hospitable attentions which they had paid to Molina; and his description of the marvels of the place, on his return, fell nothing short of his predecessor's. The fortress, which was surrounded by a triple row of wall, was strongly garrisoned. The temple he described as literally tapestried with plates of gold and silver. Adjoining this structure was a sort of convent appropriated to the Inca's destined brides, who manifested great curiosity to see him. Whether this was gratified is not clear; but Candia described the gardens of the convent, which he entered, as glowing with imitations of fruits and vegetables all in pure gold and silver![18] He had seen a number of artisans at work, whose sole business seemed to be to furnish these gorgeous decorations for the religious houses.

The reports of the cavalier may have been somewhat over-colored.[19] It was natural that men coming from the dreary wilderness, in which they had been buried the last six months, should have been vividly impressed by the tokens of civilization which met them on the Peruvian coast. But Tumbez was a favorite city of the Peruvian princes. It was the most important place on the northern borders of the empire, contiguous to the recent acquisition of Quito. The great Tupac Yupanqui had established a strong fortress there, and peopled it with a colony of *mitimaes*. The

---

[17] It is moreover stated that the Indians, desirous to prove still further the superhuman nature of the Spanish cavalier, let loose on him a tiger—a jaguar probably—which was caged in the royal fortress. But Don Pedro was a good Catholic, and he gently laid the cross which he wore round his neck on the animal's back, who, instantly forgetting his ferocious nature, crouched at the cavalier's feet, and began to play round him in innocent gambols. The Indians, now more amazed than ever, nothing doubted of the sanctity of their guest, and bore him in triumph on their shoulders to the temple.—This credible anecdote is repeated, without the least qualification or distrust, by several contemporary writers. (See Naharro, Relacion Sumaria, MS.—Herrera, Hist. General, dec. 3, lib. 10, cap. 5.—Cieza de Leon, Cronica, cap. 54.—Garcilasso, Com. Real., Parte 2, lib. 1, cap. 12.) This last author may have had his version from Candia's own son, with whom he tells us he was brought up at school. It will no doubt find as easy admission with those of the present day, who conceive that the age of miracles has not yet past.

[18] "Que habia visto un jardin donde las yerbas eran de oro imitando en un todo á las naturales, arboles con frutas de lo mismo, y otras muchas cosas á este modo, con que aficionó grandemente á sus compañeros á esta conquista." Montesinos, Annales, año 1527.

[19] The worthy knight's account does not seem to have found favor with the old Conqueror, so often cited in these pages, who says, that, when they afterwards visited Tumbez, the Spaniards found Candia's relation a lie from beginning to end, except, indeed, in respect to the temple; though the veteran acknowledges that what was deficient in Tumbez was more than made up by the magnificence of other places in the empire not then visited. "Lo cual fué mentira; porque despues que todos los Españoles entramos en ella, se vió por vista de ojos haber mentido en todo, salvo en lo del templo, que este era cosa de ver, aunque mucho mas de lo que aquel encareció, lo que faltó en esta ciudad, se halló despues en otras que muchas leguas mas adelante se descubrieron." Relacion del Primer. Descub., MS.

temple, and the house occupied by the Virgins of the Sun, had been erected by Huayna Capac, and were liberally endowed by that Inca, after the sumptuous fashion of the religious establishments of Peru. The town was well supplied with water by numerous aqueducts, and the fruitful valley in which it was embosomed, and the ocean which bathed its shores, supplied ample means of subsistence to a considerable population. But the cupidity of the Spaniards, after the Conquest, was not slow in despoiling the place of its glories; and the site of its proud towers and temples, in less than half a century after that fatal period, was to be traced only by the huge mass of ruins that encumbered the ground.[20]

The Spaniards were nearly mad with joy, says an old writer, at receiving these brilliant tidings of the Peruvian city. All their fond dreams were now to be realized, and they had at length reached the realm which had so long flitted in visionary splendor before them. Pizarro expressed his gratitude to Heaven for having crowned his labors with so glorious a result; but he bitterly lamented the hard fate which, by depriving him of his followers, denied him, at such a moment, the means of availing himself of his success. Yet he had no cause for lamentation; and the devout Catholic saw in this very circumstance a providential interposition which prevented the attempt at conquest, while such attempts would have been premature. Peru was not yet torn asunder by the dissensions of rival candidates for the throne; and, united and strong under the sceptre of a warlike monarch, she might well have bid defiance to all the forces that Pizarro could muster. "It was manifestly the work of Heaven," exclaims a devout son of the Church, "that the natives of the country should have received him in so kind and loving a spirit, as best fitted to facilitate the conquest; for it was the Lord's hand which led him and his followers to this remote region for the extension of the holy faith, and for the salvation of souls." [21]

Having now collected all the information essential to his object, Pizarro, after taking leave of the natives of Tumbez, and promising a speedy return, weighed anchor, and again turned his prow towards the south. Still keeping as near as possible to the coast, that no place of importance might escape his observation, he passed Cape Blanco, and, after sailing about a degree and a half, made the port of Payta. The inhabitants, who had notice of his approach, came out in their balsas to get sight of the wonderful strangers, bringing with them stores of fruits, fish, and vegetables, with the same hospitable spirit shown by their countrymen at Tumbez.

After staying here a short time, and interchanging presents of trifling value with the natives, Pizarro continued his cruise; and, sailing by the

---

[20] Cieza de Leon, who crossed this part of the country in 1548, mentions the wanton manner in which the hand of the Conqueror had fallen on the Indian edifices, which lay in ruin, even at that early period. Cronica, cap. 67.

[21] "I si le recibiesen con amor, hiciese su Mrd. lo que mas conveniente le pareciese al efecto de su conquista: porque tenia entendido, que el haverlos traido Dios erá para que su santa fé se dilatase i aquellas almas se salvasen." Naharro, Relacion Sumaria, MS.

sandy plains of Sechura for an extent of near a hundred miles, he doubled the Punta de Aguja, and swept down the coast as it fell off towards the east, still carried forward by light and somewhat variable breezes. The weather now became unfavorable, and the voyagers encountered a succession of heavy gales, which drove them some distance out to sea, and tossed them about for many days. But they did not lose sight of the mighty ranges of the Andes, which, as they proceeded towards the south, were still seen, at nearly the same distance from the shore, rolling onwards, peak after peak, with their stupendous surges of ice, like some vast ocean, that had been suddenly arrested and frozen up in the midst of its wild and tumultuous career. With this landmark always in view, the navigator had little need of star or compass to guide his bark on her course.

As soon as the tempest had subsided, Pizarro stood in again for the continent, touching at the principal points as he coasted along. Everywhere he was received with the same spirit of generous hospitality: the natives coming out in their balsas to welcome him, laden with their little cargoes of fruits and vegetables, of all the luscious varieties that grow in the *tierra caliente*. All were eager to have a glimpse of the strangers, the "Children of the Sun," as the Spaniards began already to be called, from their fair complexions, brilliant armour, and the thunderbolts which they bore in their hands.[22] The most favorable reports, too, had preceded them, of the urbanity and gentleness of their manners, thus unlocking the hearts of the simple natives, and disposing them to confidence and kindness. The iron-hearted soldier had not yet disclosed the darker side of his character. He was too weak to do so. The hour of Conquest had not yet come.

In every place Pizarro received the same accounts of a powerful monarch who ruled over the land, and held his court on the mountain plains of the interior, where his capital was depicted as blazing with gold and silver, and displaying all the profusion of an Oriental satrap. The Spaniards, except at Tumbez, seem to have met with little of the precious metals among the natives on the coast. More than one writer asserts that they did not covet them, or, at least, by Pizarro's orders, affected not to do so. He would not have them betray their appetite for gold, and actually refused gifts when they were proffered![23] It is more probable that they saw little display of wealth, except in the embellishments of the temples and other sacred buildings, which they did not dare to violate. The precious metals, reserved for the uses of religion and for persons of high degree, were not likely to abound in the remote towns and hamlets on the coast.

[22] "Que resplandecian como el Sol. Llamabanles hijos del Sol por esto." Montesinos, Annales, MS., año 1528.

[23] Pizarro wished the natives to understand, says Father Naharro, that their good alone and not the love of gold, had led him to their distant land! "Sin haver querido recibir el oro, plata i perlas que les ofrecieron, á fin de que conociesen no era codicia, sino deseo de su bien el que habia traido de tan lejas tierras á las suyas." Relacion Sumaria, MS.

Yet the Spaniards met with sufficient evidence of general civilization and power to convince them that there was much foundation for the reports of the natives. Repeatedly they saw structures of stone and plaster, and occasionally showing architectural skill in the execution, if not elegance of design. Wherever they cast anchor, they beheld green patches of cultivated country redeemed from the sterility of nature, and blooming with the variegated vegetation of the tropics; while a refined system of irrigation, by means of aqueducts and canals, seemed to be spread like a net-work over the surface of the country, making even the desert to blossom as the rose. At many places where they landed they saw the great road of the Incas which traversed the sea-coast, often, indeed, lost in the volatile sands, where no road could be maintained, but rising into a broad and substantial causeway, as it emerged on a firmer soil. Such a provision for internal communication was in itself no slight monument of power and civilization.

Still beating to the south, Pizarro passed the site of the future flourishing city of Truxillo, founded by himself some years later, and pressed on till he rode off the port of Santa. It stood on the banks of a broad and beautiful stream; but the surrounding country was so exceedingly arid that it was frequently selected as a burial-place by the Peruvians, who found the soil most favorable for the preservation of their mummies. So numerous, indeed, were the Indian *guacas*, that the place might rather be called the abode of the dead than of the living.[24]

Having reached this point, about the ninth degree of southern latitude, Pizarro's followers besought him not to prosecute the voyage farther. Enough and more than enough had been done, they said, to prove the existence and actual position of the great Indian empire of which they had so long been in search. Yet, with their slender force, they had no power to profit by the discovery. All that remained, therefore, was to return and report the success of their enterprise to the governor at Panamá. Pizarro acquiesced in the reasonableness of this demand. He had now penetrated nine degrees farther than any former navigator in these southern seas, and, instead of the blight which, up to this hour, had seemed to hang over his fortunes, he could now return in triumph to his countrymen. Without hesitation, therefore, he prepared to retrace his course, and stood again towards the north.

On his way, he touched at several places where he had before landed. At one of these, called by the Spaniards Santa Cruz, he had been invited on shore by an Indian woman of rank, and had promised to visit her on his return. No sooner did his vessel cast anchor off the village where she lived, than she came on board, followed by a numerous train of attendants. Pizarro received her with every mark of respect, and on her de-

---

[24] "Lo que mas me admiro, quando passe por este valle, fue ver la muchedumbre que tienen de sepolturas: y que por todas las sierras y secadales en los altos del valle: ay numero grande de apartados, hechos a su usança, todo cubiertas de huessos de muertos. De manera que loque ay en este valle mas que ver, es las sepolturas de los muertos, y los campos que labraron siendo vivos." Cieza de Leon, Cronica, Cap. 70

parture presented her with some trinkets which had a real value in the eyes of an Indian princess. She urged the Spanish commander and his companions to return the visit, engaging to send a number of hostages on board, as security for their good treatment. Pizarro assured her that the frank confidence she had shown towards them proved that this was unnecessary. Yet, no sooner did he put off in his boat, the following day, to go on shore, than several of the principal persons in the place came alongside of the ship to be received as hostages during the absence of the Spaniards,—a singular proof of consideration for the sensitive apprehensions of her guests.

Pizarro found that preparations had been made for his reception in a style of simple hospitality that evinced some degree of taste. Arbours were formed of luxuriant and wide-spreading branches, interwoven with fragrant flowers and shrubs that diffused a delicious perfume through the air. A banquet was provided, teeming with viands prepared in the style of the Peruvian cookery, and with fruits and vegetables of tempting hue and luscious to the taste, though their names and nature were unknown to the Spaniards. After the collation was ended, the guests were entertained with music and dancing by a troop of young men and maidens simply attired, who exhibited in their favorite national amusement all the agility and grace which the supple limbs of the Peruvian Indians so well qualified them to display. Before his departure, Pizarro stated to his kind host the motives of his visit to the country, in the same manner as he had done on other occasions, and he concluded by unfurling the royal banner of Castile, which he had brought on shore, requesting her and her attendants to raise it in token of their allegiance to his sovereign. This they did with great good-humor, laughing all the while, says the chronicler, and making it clear that they had a very imperfect conception of the serious nature of the ceremony. Pizarro was contented with this outward display of loyalty, and returned to his vessel well satisfied with the entertainment he had received, and meditating, it may be, on the best mode of repaying it, hereafter, by the subjugation and conversion of the country.

The Spanish commander did not omit to touch also at Tumbez, on his homeward voyage. Here some of his followers, won by the comfortable aspect of the place and the manners of the people, intimated a wish to remain, conceiving, no doubt, that it would be better to live where they would be persons of consequence than to return to an obscure condition in the community of Panamá. One of these men was Alonso de Molina, the same who had first gone on shore at this place, and been captivated by the charms of the Indian beauties. Pizarro complied with their wishes, thinking it would not be amiss to find, on his return, some of his own followers who would be instructed in the language and usages of the natives. He was also allowed to carry back in his vessel two or three Peruvians, for the similar purpose of instructing them in the Castilian. One of them, a youth named by the Spaniards Felipillo, plays a part of some importance in the history of subsequent events.

On leaving Tumbez, the adventurers steered directly for Panamá, touching only, on their way, at the ill-fated island of Gorgona to take on board their two companions who were left there too ill to proceed with them. One had died, and, receiving the other, Pizarro and his gallant little band continued their voyage; and, after an absence of at least eighteen months, found themselves once more safely riding at anchor in the harbor of Panamá.[25]

The sensation caused by their arrival was great, as might have been expected. For there were few, even among the most sanguine of their friends, who did not imagine that they had long since paid for their temerity, and fallen victims to the climate or the natives, or miserably perished in a watery grave. Their joy was proportionably great, therefore, as they saw the wanderers now returned, not only in health and safety, but with certain tidings of the fair countries which had so long eluded their grasp. It was a moment of proud satisfaction to the three associates, who, in spite of obloquy, derision, and every impediment which the distrust of friends or the coldness of government could throw in their way, had persevered in their great enterprise until they had established the truth of what had been so generally denounced as a chimera. It is the misfortune of those daring spirits who conceive an idea too vast for their own generation to comprehend, or, at least, to attempt to carry out, that they pass for visionary dreamers. Such had been the fate of Luque and his associates. The existence of a rich Indian empire at the south, which, in their minds, dwelling long on the same idea and alive to all the arguments in its favor, had risen to the certainty of conviction, had been derided by the rest of their countrymen as a mere *mirage* of the fancy, which, on nearer approach, would melt into air; while the projectors, who staked their fortunes on the adventure, were denounced as madmen. But their hour of triumph, their slow and hard-earned triumph, had now arrived.

Yet the governor, Pedro de los Rios, did not seem, even at this moment, to be possessed with a conviction of the magnitude of the discovery,—or, perhaps, he was discouraged by its very magnitude. When the associates, now with more confidence, applied to him for patronage in an undertaking too vast for their individual resources, he coldly replied, "He had no desire to build up other states at the expense of his own; nor would he be led to throw away more lives than had already been sacrificed by the cheap display of gold and silver toys and a few Indian sheep!"[26]

Sorely disheartened by this repulse from the only quarter whence

---

[25] Conq. i Pob. del Piru, MS.—Montesinos, Annales, MS., año 1528.—Naharro, Relacion Sumaria, MS.—Pedro Pizarro, Descub. y Conq., MS.—Herrera, Hist. General, dec. 4, lib. 2, cap. 6, 7.—Relacion del Primer. Descub., MS.

[26] "No entendia de despoblar su Governacion, para que se fuesen à poblar nuevas Tierras, muriendo en tal demanda mas Gente de la que havia muerto, cebando à los Hombres con la muestra de las Ovejas, Oro, i Plata, que havian traido." Herrera, Hist. General, dec. 4, lib. 3, cap. 1

effectual aid could be expected, the confederates, without funds, and with credit nearly exhausted by their past efforts, were perplexed in the extreme. Yet to stop now,—what was it but to abandon the rich mine which their own industry and perseverance had laid open, for others to work at pleasure? In this extremity the fruitful mind of Luque suggested the only expedient by which they could hope for success. This was to apply to the Crown itself. No one was so much interested in the result of the expedition. It was for the government, indeed, that discoveries were to be made, that the country was to be conquered. The government alone was competent to provide the requisite means, and was likely to take a much broader and more liberal view of the matter than a petty colonial officer.

But who was there qualified to take charge of this delicate mission? Luque was chained by his professional duties to Panamá; and his associates, unlettered soldiers, were much better fitted for the business of the camp than of the court. Almagro, blunt, though somewhat swelling and ostentatious in his address, with a diminutive stature and a countenance naturally plain, now much disfigured by the loss of an eye, was not so well qualified for the mission as his companion in arms, who, possessing a good person and altogether a commanding presence, was plausible, and, with all his defects of education, could, where deeply interested, be even eloquent in discourse. The ecclesiastic, however, suggested that the negotiation should be committed to the Licentiate Corral, a respectable functionary, then about to return on some public business to the mother country. But to this Almagro strongly objected. No one, he said, could conduct the affair so well as the party interested in it. He had a high opinion of Pizarro's prudence, his discernment of character, and his cool, deliberate policy.[27] He knew enough of his comrade to have confidence that his presence of mind would not desert him, even in the new, and therefore embarrassing, circumstances in which he would be placed at court. No one, he said, could tell the story of their adventures with such effect, as the man who had been the chief actor in them. No one could so well paint the unparalleled sufferings and sacrifices which they had encountered; no other could tell so forcibly what had been done, what yet remained to do, and what assistance would be necessary to carry it into execution. He concluded, with characteristic frankness, by strongly urging his confederate to undertake the mission.

Pizarro felt the force of Almagro's reasoning, and, though with undisguised reluctance, acquiesced in a measure which was less to his taste than an expedition to the wilderness. But Luque came into the arrangement with more difficulty. "God grant, my children," exclaimed the ecclesiastic, "that one of you may not defraud the other of his bless-

[27] "E por pura importunacion de Almagro cupole á Pizarro, porque siempre Almagro le tubo respeto, é deseó honrarle." Oviedo, Hist. de las Indias MS., Parte 3, lib. 8, cap. 1.

ing!" [28] Pizarro engaged to consult the interests of his associates equally with his own. But Luque, it is clear, did not trust Pizarro.

There was some difficulty in raising the funds necessary for putting the envoy in condition to make a suitable appearance at court; so low had the credit of the confederates fallen, and so little confidence was yet placed in the result of their splendid discoveries. Fifteen hundred ducats were at length raised; and Pizarro, in the spring of 1528, bade adieu to Panamá, accompanied by Pedro de Candia.[29] He took with him, also, some of the natives, as well as two or three llamas, various nice fabrics of cloth, with many ornaments and vases of gold and silver, as specimens of the civilization of the country, and vouchers for his wonderful story.

Of all the writers on ancient Peruvian history, no one has acquired so wide celebrity, or been so largely referred to by later compilers, as the Inca Garcilasso de la Vega. He was born at Cuzco, in 1540; and was a *mestizo*, that is of mixed descent, his father being European, and his mother Indian. His father, Garcilasso de la Vega, was one of that illustrious family whose achievements, both in arms and letters, shed such lustre over the proudest period of the Castilian annals. He came to Peru, in the suite of Pedro de Alvarado, soon after the country had been gained by Pizarro. Garcilasso attached himself to the fortunes of this chief, and, after his death, to those of his brother Gonzalo,—remaining constant to the latter, through his rebellion, up to the hour of his rout at Xaquixaguana, when Garcilasso took the same course with most of his faction, and passed over to the enemy. But this demonstration of loyalty, though it saved his life, was too late to redeem his credit with the victorious party; and the obloquy which he incurred by his share in the rebellion threw a cloud over his subsequent fortunes, and even over those of his son, as it appears, in after years.

The historian's mother was of the Peruvian blood royal. She was niece of Huayna Capac, and granddaughter of the renowned Tupac Inca Yupanqui. Garcilasso, while he betrays obvious satisfaction that the blood of the civilized European flows in his veins shows himself not a little proud of his descent from the royal dynasty of Peru; and this he intimated by combining with his patronymic the distinguishing title of the Peruvian princes,—subscribing himself always Garcilasso Inca de la Vega.

His early years were passed in his native land, where he was reared in the Roman Catholic faith, and received the benefit of as good an education as could be obtained amidst the incessant din of arms and civil commotion. In 1560, when twenty years of age, he left America, and from that time took up his residence in Spain. Here he entered the military service, and held a captain's commission in the war against the Moriscos, and, afterwards, under Don John of Austria. Though he acquitted himself honorably in his adventurous career, he does not seem to have been satisfied with the manner in which his services were requited by the government. The old reproach of the father's disloyalty still clung to the son and Garcilasso assures us that this circumstance defeated all his efforts to recover the large inheritance of landed property belonging to his mother, which had escheated to the Crown. "Such were the prejudices against me," says he, "that I could not urge my ancient claims or expectations; and I left the army so poor and so much in debt, that I did not care to show myself again at court; but was obliged to withdraw into an obscure

[28] "Plegue à Dios, Hijos, que no os hurteis la bendicion el uno al otro, que yo todavia holgaria, que à lo menos fuerades entrambos." Herrera, Hist. General, dec. 4, lib. 3, cap. 1.

[29] "Juntaronle mil y quinientos pesos de oro, que dió de buena voluntad Dr Fernando de Luque." Montesinos, Annales, MS., año 1528.

solitude, where I lead a tranquil life for the brief space that remains to me, no longer deluded by the world or its vanities."

The scene of this obscure retreat was not, however, as the reader might imagine from this tone of philosophic resignation, in the depths of some rural wilderness, but in Cordova, once the gay capital of Moslem science, and still the busy haunt of men. Here our philosopher occupied himself with literary labors, the more sweet and soothing to his wounded spirit, that they tended to illustrate the faded glories of his native land, and exhibit them in their primitive splendor to the eyes of his adopted countrymen. "And I have no reason to regret," he says in his Preface to his account of Florida, "that Fortune has not smiled on me, since this circumstance has opened a literary career which, I trust, will secure to me a wider and more enduring fame than could flow from any worldly prosperity."

In 1609, he gave to the world the First Part of his great work, the *Commentarios Reales,* devoted to the history of the country under the Incas; and in 1616, a few months before his death, he finished the Second Part, embracing the story of the Conquest, which was published at Cordova the following year. The chronicler, who thus closed his labors with his life, died at the ripe old age of seventy-six. He left a considerabe sum for the purchase of masses for his soul, showing that the complaints of his poverty are not to be taken literally. His remains were interred in the cathedral church of Cordova, in a chapel which bears the name of Garcilasso; and an inscription was placed on his monument, intimating the high respect in which the historian was held both for his moral worth and his literary attainments.

The First Part of the *Commentarios Reales* is occupied, as already noticed, with the ancient history of the country, presenting a complete picture of its civilization under the Incas,—far more complete than has been given by any other writer. Garcilasso's mother was but ten years old at the time of her cousin Atahuallpa's accession, or rather usurpation, as it is called by the party of Cuzco. She had the good fortune to escape the massacre which, according to the chronicler, befell most of her kindred, and with her brother continued to reside in their ancient capital after the Conquest. Their conversations naturally turned to the good old times of the Inca rule, which, colored by their fond regrets, may be presumed to have lost nothing as seen through the magnifying medium of the past. The young Garcilasso listened greedily to the stories which recounted the magnificence and prowess of his royal ancestors, and though he made no use of them at the time, they sunk deep into his memory, to be treasured up for a future occasion. When he prepared, after the lapse of many years, in his retirement at Cordova, to compose the history of his country, he wrote to his old companions and schoolfellows, of the Inca family, to obtain fuller information than he could get in Spain on various matters of historical interest. He had witnessed in his youth the ancient ceremonies and usages of his countrymen, understood the science of their quipus, and mastered many of their primitive traditions. With the assistance he now obtained from his Peruvian kindred, he acquired a familiarity with the history of the great Inca race, and of their national institutions, to an extent that no person could have possessed, unless educated in the midst of them, speaking the same language, and with the same Indian blood flowing in his veins. Garcilasso, in short, was the representative of the conquered race; and we might expect to find the lights and shadows of the picture disposed under his pencil so as to produce an effect very different from that which they had hitherto exhibited under the hands of the Conquerors.

Such, to a certain extent, is the fact; and this circumstance affords a means of comparison which would alone render his works of great value in arriving at just historic conclusions. But Garcilasso wrote late in life, after the story had been often told by Castilian writers. He naturally deferred much to men, some of whom enjoyed high credit on the score both of their scholarship and their social position. His object, he professes, was not so much to add any thing new of his own, as to correct their errors and the misconceptions into which they had been brought by their ignorance of the Indian languages and the usages of his people. He does, in fact, however, go far beyond this; and the stores of information which he has collected have made his work a large repository, whence later laborers in the same field have drawn copious materials. He writes from the fulness of his heart, and illuminates every topic that he touches with a variety and richness of illustration, that leave little to be desired by the most importunate curiosity. The difference between reading his Commentaries and the accounts of European writers is the difference that exists between reading a work in the original and in a bald translation. Garcilasso's writings are an emanation from the Indian mind.

Yet his Commentaries are open to a grave objection,—and one naturally suggested by his position. Addressing himself to the cutivated European, he was most desirous to display the ancient glories of his people, and still more of the Inca race, in their most imposing form. This, doubtless, was the great spur to his literary labors, for which previous education, however good for the evil time on which he was cast, had far from qualified him. Garcilasso, therefore, wrote to effect a particular object. He stood forth as counsel for his unfortunate countrymen, pleading the cause of that degraded race before the tribunal of posterity. The exaggerated tone of panegyric consequent on this becomes apparent in every page of his work. He pictures forth a state of society such as an Utopian philosopher would hardly venture to depict. His royal ancestors became the types of every imaginery excellence, and the golden age is revived for a nation, which, while the war of proselytism is raging on its borders, enjoys within all the blessings of tranquillity and peace. Even the material splendors of the monarchy, sufficiently great in this land of gold, become heightened, under the glowing imagination of the Inca chronicler, into the gorgeous illusions of a fairy tale.

Yet there is truth at the bottom of his wildest conceptions, and it would be unfair to the Indian historian to suppose that he did not himself believe most of the magic marvels which he describes. There is no credulity like that of a Christian convert,—one newly converted to the faith. From long dwelling in the darkness of paganism, his eyes, when first opened to the light of truth, have not acquired the power of discriminating the just proportions of objects, of distinguishing between the real and the imaginary. Garcilasso was not a convert indeed, for he was bred from infancy in the Roman Catholic faith. But he was surrounded by converts and neophytes,—by those of his own blood, who, after practising all their lives the rites of paganism, were now first admitted into the Christian fold. He listened to the teachings of the missionary, learned from him to give implicit credit to the marvellous legends of the Saints, and the no less marvellous accounts of his own victories in his spiritual warfare for the propagation of the faith. Thus early accustomed to such large drafts on his credulity, his reason lost its heavenly power of distinguishing truth from error, and he became so familiar with the miraculous, that the miraculous was no longer a miracle.

Yet, while large deductions are to be made on this account from the chronicler's reports, there is always a germ of truth which it is not difficult to detect, and even to disengage from the fanciful covering which envelopes it; and after every allowance for the exaggerations of national vanity, we shall find an abundance of genuine information in respect to the antiquities of his country, for which we shall look in vain in any European writer.

Garcilasso's work is the reflection of the age in which he lived. It is addressed to the imagination, more than to sober reason. We are dazzled by the gorgeous spectacle it perpetually exhibits, and delighted by the variety of amusing details and animated gossip sprinkled over its pages. The story of the action is perpetually varied by discussions on topics illustrating its progress, so as to break up the monotony of the narrative, and afford an agreeable relief to the reader. This is true of the First Part of his great work. In the Second there was no longer room for such discussion. But he has supplied the place by garrulous reminiscences, personal anecdotes, incidental adventures, and a host of trivial details,—trivial in the eyes of the pedant,—which historians have been too willing to discard, as below the dignity of history. We have the actors in this great drama in their private dress, become acquainted with their personal habits, listen to their familiar sayings, and, in short, gather up those minutiæ which in the aggregate make up so much of life, and not less of character.

It is this confusion of the great and the little, thus artlessly blended together, that constitutes one of the charms of the old romantic chronicle,—not the less true that, in this respect, it approaches nearer to the usual tone of romance. It is in such writings that we may look to find the form and pressure of the age. The worm-eaten state-papers, official correspondence, public records, are all serviceable, indispensable, to history. They are the framework on which it is to repose; the skeleton of facts which gives it its strength and proportions. But they are as worthless as the dry bones of the skeleton, unless clothed with the beautiful form and garb of humanity, and instinct with the spirit of the age.—Our debt is large to the antiquarian, who with conscientious precision lays broad and deep the foundations of historic truth; and no less to the philosophic annalist who exhibits man in the dress of public life,—man in masquerade; but our gratitude must surely not be withheld from those, who, like Garcilasso de la Vega, and many a romancer of the Middle Ages, have held up the mirror—distorted though it may somewhat be—to the interior of life, reflecting every object, the great and the mean the beautiful and the deformed, with their natural prominence and their vivacity of coloring, to the eye of the spectator. As a work of art, such a production may be thought to be below criticism. But, although it defy the rules of art in its composition, it does not necessarily violate the principles of taste; for it conforms in its spirit to the spirit of the age in which it was written. And the critic, who coldly condemns it on the severe principles of art, will find a charm in its very simplicity, that will make him recur again and again to its pages, while more correct and classical compositions are laid aside and forgotten.

I cannot dismiss this notice of Garcilasso, though already long protracted, without some allusion to the English translation of his Commentaries. It appeared in James the Second's reign, and is the work of Sir Paul Rycaut, Knight. It was printed at London in 1688, in folio, with considerable pretension in its outward dress, well garnished with wood-cuts, and a frontispiece displaying the gaunt and rather sardonic features, not of the author, but his translator. The version keeps pace with the march of the original, corresponding precisely in books and chapters, and seldom, though sometimes, using the freedom, so common in these ancient versions, of abridgment and omission. Where it does depart from the original, it is rather from ignorance than intention. Indeed, as far as the plea of ignorance will avail him, the worthy knight may urge it stoutly in his defence. No one who reads the book will doubt his limited acquaintance with his own tongue, and no one who compares it with the original will deny his ignorance of the Castilian. It contains as many blunders as paragraphs, and most of them such as might shame a schoolboy. Yet such are the rude charms of the original, that this ruder version of it has found considerable favor with readers; and Sir Paul Rycaut's translation, old as it is, may still be met with in many a private, as well as public library.

BOOK III

CONQUEST OF PERU

CHAPTER I

PIZARRO'S RECEPTION AT COURT—HIS CAPITULATION WITH THE CROWN
—HE VISITS HIS BIRTHPLACE—RETURNS TO THE NEW WORLD—
DIFFICULTIES WITH ALMAGRO—HIS THIRD EXPEDITION—ADVEN-
TURES ON THE COAST—BATTLES IN THE ISLE OF PUNÁ

1528—1531

PIZARRO and his officer, having crossed the Isthmus, embarked at Nombre de Dios for the old country, and, after a good passage, reached Seville
early in the summer of 1528. There happened to be at that time in port a
person well known in the history of Spanish adventure as the Bachelor
Enciso. He had taken an active part in the colonization of Tierra Firme,
and had a pecuniary claim against the early colonists of Darien, of whom
Pizarro was one. Immediately on the landing of the latter, he was seized
by Enciso's orders, and held in custody for the debt. Pizarro, who had
fled from his native land as a forlorn and houseless adventurer, after an
absence of more than twenty years, passed, most of them, in unprecedented toil and suffering, now found himself on his return the inmate
of a prison. Such was the commencement of those brilliant fortunes
which, as he had trusted, awaited him at home. The circumstance excited general indignation; and no sooner was the Court advised of his
arrival in the country, and the great purpose of his mission, than orders
were sent for his release, with permission to proceed at once on his
journey.

Pizarro found the emperor at Toledo, which he was soon to quit, in
order to embark for Italy. Spain was not the favorite residence of Charles
the Fifth, in the earlier part of his reign. He was now at that period of it
when he was enjoying the full flush of his triumphs over his gallant rival
of France, whom he had defeated and taken prisoner at the great battle
of Pavia; and the victor was at this moment preparing to pass into Italy
to receive the imperial crown from the hands of the Roman Pontiff.
Elated by his successes and his elevation to the German throne, Charles
made little account of his hereditary kingdom, as his ambition found so
splendid a career thrown open to it on the wide field of European politics.

He had hitherto received too inconsiderable returns from his transatlantic possessions to give them the attention they deserved. But, as
the recent acquisition of Mexico and the brilliant anticipations in respect to the southern continent were pressed upon his notice, he felt their
importance as likely to afford him the means of prosecuting his ambitious
and most expensive enterprises.

Pizarro, therefore, who had now come to satisfy the royal eyes, by
visible proofs, of the truth of the golden rumors which, from time to time,
had reached Castile, was graciously received by the emperor. Charles examined the various objects which his officer exhibited to him with great
attention. He was particularly interested by the appearance of the llama,
so remarkable as the only beast of burden yet known on the new continent; and the fine fabrics of woollen cloth, which were made from its
shaggy sides, gave it a much higher value, in the eyes of the sagacious
monarch, than what it possessed as an animal for domestic labor. But the
specimens of gold and silver manufacture, and the wonderful tale which
Pizarro had to tell of the abundance of the precious metals, must have
satisfied even the cravings of royal cupidity.

Pizarro, far from being embarrassed by the novelty of his situation,
maintained his usual self-possession, and showed that decorum and even
dignity in his address which belong to the Castilian. He spoke in a simple
and respectful style, but with the earnestness and natural eloquence of
one who had been an actor in the scenes he described, and who was conscious that the impression he made on his audience was to decide his future destiny. All listened with eagerness to the account of his strange adventures by sea and land, his wanderings in the forests, or in the dismal
and pestilent swamps on the sea-coast, without food, almost without raiment, with feet torn and bleeding at every step, with his few companions
becoming still fewer by disease and death, and yet pressing on with unconquerable spirit to extend the empire of Castile, and the name and
power of her sovereign; but when he painted his lonely condition on the
desolate island, abandoned by the government at home, deserted by all
but a handful of devoted followers, his royal auditor, though not easily
moved, was affected to tears. On his departure from Toledo, Charles
commended the affairs of his vassal in the most favorable terms to the
consideration of the Council of the Indies.[1]

There was at this time another man at court, who had come there on
a similar errand from the New World, but whose splendid achievements
had already won for him a name that threw the rising reputation of
Pizarro comparatively into the shade. This man was Hernando Cortés,

[1] Pedro Pizarro, Descub. y Conq., MS.—Naharro, Relacion Sumaria, MS.—Conq.
i Pob. del Piru, MS.

"Hablaba tan bien en la materia, que se llevó los aplausos y atencion en Toledo
donde el Emperador estaba diole audiencia con mucho gusto, tratolo amoroso, y
oyole tierno, especialmente cuando le hizo relacion de su consistencia y de los
trece compañeros en la Isla en medio de tantos trabajos." Montesinos, Annales, MS.,
año 1528.

the Conqueror of Mexico. He had come home to lay an empire at the feet of his sovereign, and to demand in return the redress of his wrongs, and the recompense of his great services. He was at the close of his career, as Pizarro was at the commencement of his; the Conqueror of the North and of the South; the two men appointed by Providence to overturn the most potent of the Indian dynasties, and to open the golden gates by which the treasures of the New World were to pass into the coffers of Spain.

Notwithstanding the emperor's recommendation, the business of Pizarro went forward at the tardy pace with which affairs are usually conducted in the court of Castile. He found his limited means gradually sinking under the expenses incurred by his present situation, and he represented, that, unless some measures were speedily taken in reference to his suit, however favorable they might be in the end, he should be in no condition to profit by them. The queen, accordingly, who had charge of the business, on her husband's departure, expedited the affair, and on the twenty-sixth of July, 1529, she executed the memorable *Capitulation*, which defined the powers and privileges of Pizarro.

The instrument secured to that chief the right of discovery and conquest in the province of Peru, or New Castile,—as the country was then called, in the same manner as Mexico had received the name of New Spain,—for the distance of two hundred leagues south of Santiago. He was to receive the titles and rank of Governor and Captain-General of the province, together with those of Adelantado, and Alguacil Mayor, for life; and he was to have a salary of seven hundred and twenty-five thousand maravedis, with the obligation of maintaining certain officers and military retainers, corresponding with the dignity of his station. He was to have the right to erect certain fortresses, with the absolute government of them; to assign *encomiendas* of Indians, under the limitations prescribed by law; and, in fine, to exercise nearly all the prerogatives incident to the authority of a viceroy.

His associate, Almagro, was declared commander of the fortress of Tumbez, with an annual rent of three hundred thousand maravedis, and with the further rank and privileges of an hidalgo. The reverend Father Luque received the reward of his services in the Bishopric of Tumbez, and he was also declared Protector of the Indians of Peru. He was to enjoy the yearly stipend of a thousand ducats,—to be derived, like the other salaries and gratuities in this instrument, from the revenues of the conquered territory.

Nor were the subordinate actors in the expedition forgotten. Ruiz received the title of Grand Pilot of the Southern Ocean, with a liberal provision; Candia was placed at the head of the artillery; and the remaining eleven companions on the desolate island were created hidalgos and cavalleros, and raised to certain municipal dignities,—in prospect.

Several provisions of a liberal tenor were also made, to encourage emigration to the country. The new settlers were to be exempted from some of the most onerous, but customary taxes, as the *alcabala*, or to be subject to them only in a mitigated form. The tax on the precious metals drawn from mines was to be reduced, at first, to one tenth, instead of the fifth imposed on the same metals when obtained by barter or by rapine.

It was expressly enjoined on Pizarro to observe the existing regulations for the good government and protection of the natives; and he was required to carry out with him a specified number of ecclesiastics, with whom he was to take counsel in the conquest of the country, and whose efforts were to be dedicated to the service and conversion of the Indians; while lawyers and attorneys, on the other hand, whose presence was considered as boding ill to the harmony of the new settlements, were strictly prohibited from setting foot in them.

Pizarro, on his part, was bound, in six months from the date of the instrument, to raise a force, well equipped for the service, of two hundred and fifty men, of whom one hundred might be drawn from the colonies; and the government engaged to furnish some trifling assistance in the purchase of artillery and military stores. Finally, he was to be prepared, in six months after his return to Panamá, to leave that port and embark on his expedition.[2]

Such are some of the principal provisions of this Capitulation, by which the Castilian government, with the sagacious policy which it usually pursued on the like occasions, stimulated the ambitious hopes of the adventurer by high-sounding titles, and liberal promises of reward contingent on his success, but took care to stake nothing itself on the issue of the enterprise. It was careful to reap the fruits of his toil, but not to pay the cost of them.

A circumstance, that could not fail to be remarked in these provisions, was the manner in which the high and lucrative posts were accumulated on Pizarro, to the exclusion of Almagro, who, if he had not taken as conspicuous a part in personal toil and exposure, had, at least, divided with him the original burden of the enterprise, and, by his labors in another direction, had contributed quite as essentially to its success. Almagro had willingly conceded the post of honor to his confederate; but it had been stipulated, on Pizarro's departure for Spain, that, while he solicited the office of Governor and Captain-General for himself, he should secure that of Adelantado for his companion. In like manner, he had engaged to apply for the see of Tumbez for the vicar of Panamá, and the office of Alguacil Mayor for the pilot Ruiz. The bishopric took the direction that was concerted, for the soldier could scarcely claim the mitre of the prelate; but the other offices, instead of their appropriate distribution, were all concentred in himself. Yet it was in reference to his application for his friends, that Pizarro had promised on his departure to deal fairly and honorably by them all.[3]

---

[2] This remarkable document, formerly in the archives of Simancas, and now transferred to the *Archivo General de las Indias* in Seville, was transcribed for the rich collection of the late Don Martin Fernandez de Navarrete, to whose kindness I am indebted for a copy of it.

"Al fin se capituló, que Francisco Piçarro negociase la **Governacion** para si: &

It is stated by the military chronicler, Pedro Pizarro, that his kinsman did, in fact, urge the suit strongly in behalf of Almagro; but that he was refused by the government, on the ground that offices of such paramount importance could not be committed to different individuals. The ill effects of such an arrangement had been long since felt in more than one of the Indian colonies, where it had led to rivalry and fatal collision.[4] Pizarro, therefore, finding his remonstrances unheeded, had no alternative but to combine the offices in his own person, or to see the expedition fall to the ground. This explanation of the affair has not received the sanction of other contemporary historians. The apprehensions expressed by Luque, at the time of Pizarro's assuming the mission, of some such result as actually occurred, founded, doubtless, on a knowledge of his associate's character, may warrant us in distrusting the alleged vindication of his conduct, and our distrust will not be diminished by familiarity with his subsequent career. Pizarro's virtue was not of a kind to withstand temptation,—though of a much weaker sort than that now thrown in his path.

The fortunate cavalier was also honored with the habit of St. Jago;[5] and he was authorized to make an important innovation in his family escutcheon,—for by the father's side he might claim his armorial bearings. The black eagle and the two pillars emblazoned on the royal arms were incorporated with those of the Pizarros; and an Indian city, with a vessel in the distance on the waters, and the llama of Peru, revealed the theatre and the character of his exploits; while the legend announced, that "under the auspices of Charles, and by the industry, the genius, and the resources of Pizarro, the country had been discovered and reduced to tranquillity,"—thus modestly intimating both the past and prospective services of the Conqueror.[6]

These arrangements having been thus completed to Pizarro's satisfaction, he left Toledo for Truxillo, his native place, in Estremadura, where he thought he should be most likely to meet with adherents for his new enterprise, and where it doubtless gratified his vanity to display himself

para Diego de Almagro, el Adelantamiento: i para Hernando de Luque, el Obispado: i para Bartolomé Ruiz, el Alguacilazgo Maior: i Mercedes para los que quedaban vivos, de los trece Compañeros, afirmando siempre Francisco Piçarro, que todo lo queria para ellos, i prometiendo, que negociaria lealmente, i sin ninguna cautela." Hierra, Hist. General, dec. 4, lib. 3, cap. 1.

[4] "Y don Francisco Piçarro pidio conforme á lo que llevava capitulado y hordenado con sus compañeros ya dicho, y en el con sejo se le rrespondio que no avia lugar de dar governacion á dos compañeros, á caussa de que en santa marta se avia dado ansi á dos compañeros y el uno avia muerto al otro. . . . . . Pues pedido, como digo, muchas vezes por don Francisco Piçarro se les hiziese la merced á ambos compañeros, se le rrespondio la pidiesse parassi sino que se daria á otro, y visto que no avia lugar lo que pedia y queria pedio se le hiziese la merced á el, y ansi se le hizo." Descub. y Conq., MS.

[5] Xerez, Conq. del Peru, ap. Barcia, tom. III. p. 182.—Oviedo, Hist. de las Indias, MS., Parte 3, lib. 8, cap. 1.—Caro de Torres, Historia de las Ordenes Militares, (ed. Madrid, 1629,) p. 113.

[6] "Caroli Cæsaris auspicio, et labore, ingenio, ac impensa Ducis Picarro inventa, et pacata." Herrera, Hist. General, dec. 4, lib. 6, cap. 5.

in the palmy, or at least promising, state of his present circumstances. If vanity be ever pardonable, it is certainly in a man who, born in an obscure station in life, without family, interest, or friends to back him, has carved out his own fortunes in the world, and, by his own resources, triumphed over all the obstacles which nature and accident had thrown in his way. Such was the condition of Pizarro, as he now revisited the place of his nativity, where he had hitherto been known only as a poor outcast, without a home to shelter, a father to own him, or a friend to lean upon. But he now found both friends and followers, and some who were eager to claim kindred with him, and take part in his future fortunes. Among these were four brothers. Three of them, like himself, were illegitimate; one of whom, named Francisco Martin de Alcántara, was related to him by the mother's side; the other two, named Gonzalo and Juan Pizarro, were descended from the father. "They were all poor, and proud as they were poor," says Oviedo, who had seen them; "and their eagerness for gain was in proportion to their poverty." [7]

The remaining and eldest brother, named Hernando, was a legitimate son,—"legitimate," continues the same caustic authority, "by his pride, as well as by his birth." His features were plain, even disagreeably so; but his figure was good. He was large of stature, and, like his brother Francis, had on the whole an imposing presence.[8] In his character, he combined some of the worst defects incident to the Castilian. He was jealous in the extreme; impatient not merely of affront, but of the least slight, and implacable in his resentment. He was decisive in his measures, and unscrupulous in their execution. No touch of pity had power to arrest his arm. His arrogance was such, that he was constantly wounding the self-love of those with whom he acted; thus begetting an ill-will which unnecessarily multiplied obstacles in his path. In this he differed from his brother Francis, whose plausible manners smoothed away difficulties, and conciliated confidence and coöperation in his enterprises. Unfortunately, the evil counsels of Hernando exercised an influence over his brother which more than compensated the advantages derived from his singular capacity for business.

Notwithstanding the general interest which Pizarro's adventures excited in his country, that chief did not find it easy to comply with the provisions of the Capitulation in respect to the amount of his levies. Those who were most astonished by his narrative were not always most inclined to take part in his fortunes. They shrunk from the unparalleled hardships which lay in the path of the adventurer in that direction; and they listened with visible distrust to the gorgeous pictures of the golden

---

[7] "Trujo tres o cuatro hermanos suyos tan soberbios como pobres, é tan sin hacienda como deseosos de ancanzarla." Hist. de las Indias, MS., Parte 3, lib. 8, cap. 1

[8] Oviedo's portrait of him is by no means flattering. He writes like one too familiar with the original. "É de todos ellos el Hernando Pizarro solo era legitimo, é mas legitimado en la soberbia, hombre de alta estatura é grueso, la lengua é labios gordos, é la punta de la nariz con sobrada carne é encendida, y este fue el desavenidor y estorbador del sosiego de todos y en especial de los dos viejos compañeros Francisco Pizarra é Diego de Almagro." Hist. de las Indias, MS. ubi supra.

temple. and gardens of Tumbez, which they looked upon as indebted in some degree, at least, to the coloring of his fancy, with the obvious purpose of attracting followers to his banner. It is even said that Pizarro would have found it difficult to raise the necessary funds, but for the seasonable aid of Cortés, a native of Estremadura like himself, his companion in arms in early days, and, according to report, his kinsman.[9] No one was in a better condition to hold out a helping hand to a brother adventurer, and, probably, no one felt greater sympathy in Pizarro's fortunes, or greater confidence in his eventual success, than the man who had so lately trod the same career with renown.

The six months allowed by the Capitulation had elapsed, and Pizarro had assembled somewhat less than his stipulated complement of men, with which he was preparing to embark in a little squadron of three vessels at Seville; but, before they were wholly ready, he received intelligence that the officers of the Council of the Indies proposed to inquire into the condition of the vessels, and ascertain how far the requisitions had been complied with.

Without loss of time, therefore, Pizarro, afraid, if the facts were known, that his enterprise might be nipped in the bud, slipped his cables, and crossing the bar of San Lucar, in January, 1530, stood for the isle of Gomera,—one of the Canaries,—where he ordered his brother Hernando, who had charge of the remaining vessels, to meet him.

Scarcely had he gone, before the officers arrived to institute the search. But when they objected the deficiency of men, they were easily—perhaps willingly—deceived by the pretext that the remainder had gone forward in the vessel with Pizarro. At all events, no further obstacles were thrown in Hernando's way, and he was permitted, with the rest of the squadron, to join his brother, according to agreement, at Gomera.

After a prosperous voyage, the adventurers reached the northern coast of the great southern continent, and anchored off the port of Santa Marta. Here they received such discouraging reports of the countries to which they were bound, of forests teeming with insects and venomous serpents, of huge alligators that swarmed on the banks of the streams, and of hardships and perils such as their own fears had never painted, that several of Pizarro's men deserted; and their leader, thinking it no longer safe to abide in such treacherous quarters, set sail at once for Nombre de Dios.

Soon after his arrival there, he was met by his two associates, Luque and Almagro, who had crossed the mountains for the purpose of hearing from his own lips the precise import of the capitulation with the Crown. Great, as might have been expected, was Almagro's discontent at learning the result of what he regarded as the perfidious machinations of his associate. "Is it thus," he exclaimed, "that you have dealt with the friend who shared equally with you in the trials, the dangers, and the cost of the enterprise; and this, notwithstanding your solemn engagements on your

Pizarro y Orellana. Varones Ilustres, p. 143.

departure to provide for his interests as faithfully as your own? How could you allow me to be thus dishonored in the eyes of the world by so paltry a compensation, which seems to estimate my services as nothing in comparison with your own?" [10]

Pizarro, in reply, assured his companion that he had faithfully urged his suit, but that the government refused to confide powers which intrenched so closely on one another to different hands. He had no alternative, but to accept all himself or to decline all; and he endeavored to mitigate Almagro's displeasure by representing that the country was large enough for the ambition of both, and that the powers conferred on himself were, in fact, conferred on Almagro, since all that he had would ever be at his friend's disposal, as if it were his own. But these honeyed words did not satisfy the injured party; and the two captains soon after returned to Panamá with feelings of estrangement, if not hostility, towards one another, which did not augur well for their enterprise.

Still, Almagro was of a generous temper, and might have been appeased by the politic concessions of his rival, but for the interference of Hernando Pizarro, who, from the first hour of their meeting, showed respect for the veteran, which, indeed, the diminutive person of the latter was not calculated to inspire, and who now regarded him with particular aversion as an impediment to the career of his brother.

Almagro's friends—and his frank and liberal manners had secured him many—were no less disgusted than himself with the overbearing conduct of this new ally. They loudly complained that it was quite enough to suffer from the perfidy of Pizarro, without being exposed to the insults of his family, who had now come over with him to fatten on the spoils of conquest which belonged to their leader. The rupture soon proceeded to such a length, that Almagro avowed his intention to prosecute the expedition without further coöperation with his partner, and actually entered into negotiations for the purchase of vessels for that object. But Luque, and the Licentiate Espinosa, who had fortunately come over at that time from St. Domingo, now interposed to repair a breach which must end in the ruin of the enterprise, and the probable destruction of those most interested in its success. By their mediation, a show of reconciliation was at length effected between the parties, on Pizarro's assurance that he would relinquish the dignity of Adelantado in favor of his rival, and petition the emperor to confirm him in the possession of it;—an assurance, it may be remarked, not easy to reconcile with his former assertion in respect to the avowed policy of the Crown in bestowing this office. He was, moreover, to apply for a distinct government for his associate, so soon as he had become master of the country assigned to himself; and was to solicit no office for either of his own brothers, until Almagro had been first provided for. Lastly, the former contract in regard to the division of the spoil into three equal shares between the three original asso-

[10] Herrera, Hist. General, dec. 4, lib. 7, cap. 9.—Pedro Pizarro, Descub. y Conq. MS.

ciates was confirmed in the most explicit manner. The reconciliation thus effected among the parties answered the temporary purpose of enabling them to go forward in concert in the expedition. But it was only a thin scar that had healed over the wound, which, deep and rankling within, waited only fresh cause of irritation to break out with a virulence more fatal than ever.[11]

No time was now lost in preparing for the voyage. It found little encouragement, however, among the colonists of Panamá, who were too familiar with the sufferings on the former expeditions to care to undertake another, even with the rich bribe that was held out to allure them. A few of the old company were content to follow out the adventure to its close; and some additional stragglers were collected from the province of Nicaragua,—a shoot, it may be remarked, from the colony of Panamá. But Pizarro made slender additions to the force brought over with him from Spain, though this body was in better condition, and, in respect to arms, ammunition, and equipment generally, was on a much better footing than his former levies. The whole number did not exceed one hundred and eighty men, with twenty-seven horses for the cavalry. He had provided himself with three vessels, two of them of a good size, to take the place of those which he had been compelled to leave on the opposite side of the Isthmus at Nombre de Dios; an armament small for the conquest of an empire, and far short of that prescribed by the capitulation with the Crown. With this the intrepid chief proposed to commence operations, trusting to his own successes, and the exertions of Almagro, who was to remain behind, for the present, to muster reinforcements.[12]

On St. John the Evangelist's day, the banners of the company and the royal standard were consecrated in the cathedral church of Panamá; a sermon was preached before the little army by Fray Juan de Vargas, one of the Dominicans selected by the government for the Peruvian mission; and mass was performed, and the sacrament administered to every soldier previous to his engaging in the crusade against the infidel.[13] Having thus solemnly invoked the blessing of Heaven on the enterprise, Pizarro and

[11] Pedro Pizarro, Descub. y Conq., MS.—Naharro, Relacion Sumaria, MS.—Montesinos, Annales, MS., año 1529.—Relacion del Primer. Descub., MS.—Zarate, Conq. del Peru, lib. 1, cap. 3.—Oviedo, Hist. de las Indias, MS., Parte 3, lib. 8, cap. 1.
There seems to have been little good-will, at bottom, between any of the confederates; for Father Luque wrote to Oviedo that both of his partners had repaid his services with ingratitude.—"Padre Luque compañero de estos Capitanes, con cuya hacienda hicieron ellos sus hechos, puesto que el uno é el otro se lo pagaron con ingratitud segun a mi me lo escribió el mismo electo de su mano." Ibid., loc. cit.
[12] The numerical estimates differ, as usual. I conform to the statement of Pizarro's secretary, Xerez, Conq. del Peru, ap. Barcia, tom. III. p. 182.
[13] "El qual haviendo hecho bendecir en la Iglesia mayor las banderas i estandarte real dia de San Juan Evangelista de dicho año de 1530, i que todos los soldados confesasen i comulgasen en el con vento de Nuestra Señora de la Merced, dia de los Inocentes en la misa cantada que se celebró con toda solemnidad i sermon que predicó el P. Present^do Fr. Juan de Vargas, uno de los 5 religiosos que en cumplimiento de la obediencia de sus prelados i orden del Emperador pasaban à la conquista." Naharro, Relacion Sumaria, MS

his followers went on board their vessels, which rode at anchor in the Bay of Panamá, and early in January, 1531, sallied forth on his third and last expedition for the conquest of Peru.

It was his intention to steer direct for Tumbez, which held out so magnificent a show of treasure on his former voyage. But head winds and currents, as usual, baffled his purpose, and after a run of thirteen days, much shorter than the period formerly required for the same distance, his little squadron came to anchor in the Bay of St. Matthew, about one degree north; and Pizarro, after consulting with his officers, resolved to disembark his forces and advance along the coast, while the vessels, held their course at a convenient distance from the shore.

The march of the troops was severe and painful in the extreme; for the road was constantly intersected by streams, which, swollen by the winter rains, widened at their mouths into spacious estuaries. Pizarro, who had some previous knowledge of the country, acted as guide as well as commander of the expedition. He was ever ready to give aid where it was needed, encouraging his followers to ford or swim the torrents as they best could, and cheering the desponding by his own buoyant and courageous spirit.

At length they reached a thick-settled hamlet, or rather town, in the province of Coaque. The Spaniards rushed on the place, and the inhabitants, without offering resistance, fled in terror to the neighboring forests, leaving their effects—of much greater value than had been anticipated—in the hands of the invaders. "We fell on them, sword in hand," says one of the Conquerors, with some *naïveté*; "for, if we had advised the Indians of our approach, we should never have found there such store of gold and precious stones." [14] The natives, however, according to another authority, stayed voluntarily; "for, as they had done no harm to the white men, they flattered themselves none would be offered to them, but that there would be only an interchange of good offices with the strangers," [15]—an expectation founded, it may be, on the good character which the Spaniards had established for themselves on their preceding visit, but in which the simple people now found themselves most unpleasantly deceived.

Rushing into the deserted dwellings, the invaders found there, besides stuffs of various kinds, and food most welcome in their famished condition, a large quantity of gold and silver wrought into clumsy ornaments, together with many precious stones; for this was the region of the *esmeraldas*, or emeralds, where that valuable gem was most abundant. One of these jewels that fell into the hands of Pizarro, in this neighborhood, was as large as a pigeon's egg. Unluckily, his rude followers did not know the value of their prize; and they broke many of them in pieces by

---

[14] "Pues llegados á este pueblo de Coaque dieron de supito sin savello la gente del porque si estuvieran avisados. No se tomara la cantidad de oro y esmeraldas que en el se tomaron." Pedro Pizarro, Descub. y Conq., MS.

[15] Herrera, Hist. General, dec. 4, lib. 7, cap. 9.

pounding them with hammers.[16] They were led to this extraordinary proceeding, it is said, by one of the Dominican missionaries, Fray Reginaldo de Pedraza, who assured them that this was the way to prove the true emerald, which could not be broken. It was observed that the good father did not subject his own jewels to this wise experiment; but, as the stones, in consequence of it, fell in value, being regarded merely as colored glass, he carried back a considerable store of them to Panamá.[17]

The gold and silver ornaments rifled from the dwellings were brought together and deposited in a common heap; when a fifth was deducted for the Crown, and Pizarro distributed the remainder in due proportions among the officers and privates of his company. This was the usage invariably observed on the like occasions throughout the Conquest. The invaders had embarked in a common adventure. Their interest was common, and to have allowed every one to plunder on his own account would only have led to insubordination and perpetual broils. All were required, therefore, on pain of death, to contribute whatever they obtained, whether by bargain or by rapine, to the general stock; and all were too much interested in the execution of the penalty to allow the unhappy culprit, who violated the law, any chance of escape.[18]

Pizarro, with his usual policy, sent back to Panamá a large quantity of the gold, no less than twenty thousand *castellanos* in value, in the belief that the sight of so much treasure, thus speedily acquired, would settle the doubt of the wavering, and decide them on joining his banner.[19] He judged right. As one of the Conquerors piously expresses it, "It pleased the Lord that we should fall in with the town of Coaque, that the riches of the land might find credit with the people, and that they should flock to it." [20]

[16] Relacion del Primer. Descub., MS.—Zarate, Conq. del Peru, lib. i, cap. 4.
"Á lo que se ha entendido en las esmeraldas ovo gran hierro y torpedad en algunas Personas por no conoscellas. Aunque quieren decir que algunos que las conoscieron las guardaron. Pero ffinalmente muchos vbieron esmeraldes de mucho valor: vnos las provavan en yunques dandolas con martillos, diziendo que si hera esmeralda no se quebraria; otros las despreciaban, diziendo que era vidrio." Pedro Pizarro, Descub. y Conq., MS.

[17] Pedro Pizarro, Descub. y Conq., MS.—Herrera, Hist. General, dec. 4, lib. 7, cap. 9.

[18] "Los Españoles las rrecoxeron juntaron el oro y la plata, porque asi estava mandado y hordenado sopena de la vida el que otra cossa hiziese, porque todos lo avian de traer á monton para que de alli el governador lo rrepartiese, dando á cada uno confforme á su persona y meritos de servicios; y esta horden se guardo en toda esta tierra en la conquista della, y al que se le hallara oro ó plata escondido muriera por ello, y deste medio nadie oso escondello." Pedro Pizarro, Descub. y Conq., MS.

[19] The booty was great, indeed, if, as Pedro Pizarro, one of the Conquerors present, says, it amounted in value to 200,000 gold castellanos. "Aqui se hallo mucha chaquira de oro y de plata, muchas coronas hechas de oro á manera de imperiales, y otras muchas piezas en que se avaleo montar mas de dozientos mill castellanos." (Descub. y Conq., MS.) Naharro, Montesinos, and Herrera content themselves with stating that he sent back 20,000 castellanos in the vessels to Panamá.

[20] "Fueron a dar en vn pueblo que se dezia Coaque que fue nuestro Señor servido tapasen con el, porque con lo que en el se hallo se acredito la tierra y vino gente a ella." Pedro Pizarro, Descub. y Conq., MS.

Pizarro, having refreshed his men, continued his march along the coast, but no longer accompanied by the vessels, which had returned for recruits to Panamá. The road, as he advanced, was checkered with strips of sandy waste, which, drifted about by the winds, blinded the soldiers, and afforded only treacherous footing for man and beast. The glare was intense; and the rays of a vertical sun beat fiercely on the iron mail and the thick quilted doublets of cotton, till the fainting troops were almost suffocated with the heat. To add to their distresses, a strange epidemic broke out in the little army. It took the form of ulcers, or rather hideous warts of great size, which covered the body, and when lanced, as was the case with some, discharged such a quantity of blood as proved fatal to the sufferer. Several died of this frightful disorder, which was so sudden in its attack, and attended with such prostration of strength, that those who lay down well at night were unable to lift their hands to their heads in the morning.[21] The epidemic, which made its first appearance during this invasion, and which did not long survive it, spread over the country, sparing neither native nor white man.[22] It was one of those plagues from the vial of wrath, which the destroying angel, who follows in the path of the conqueror, pours out on the devoted nations.

The Spaniards rarely experienced on their march either resistance or annoyance from the inhabitants, who, instructed by the example of Coaque, fled with their effects into the woods and neighboring mountains. No one came out to welcome the strangers and offer the rites of hospitality, as on their last visit to the land. For the white men were no longer regarded as good beings that had come from heaven, but as ruthless destroyers, who, invulnerable to the assaults of the Indians, were borne along on the backs of fierce animals, swifter than the wind, with weapons in their hands, that scattered fire and desolation as they went. Such were the stories now circulated of the invaders, which, preceding them everywhere on their march, closed the hearts, if not the doors, of the natives against them. Exhausted by the fatigue of travel and by disease, and grievously disappointed at the poverty of the land, which now offered no compensation for their toils, the soldiers of Pizarro cursed the hour in which they had enlisted under his standard, and the men of Nicaragua, in particular, says the old chronicler, calling to mind their pleasant quarters in their luxurious land, sighed only to return to their Mahometan paradise.[23]

At this juncture the army was gladdened by the sight of a vessel from Panamá, which brought some supplies, together with the royal treasurer,

---

[21] Naharro, Relacion Sumaria, MS.—Pedro Pizarro, Descub. y Conq., MS.—Montesinos, Annales, MS., año 1530.

[22] Garcilasso, Com. Real., Parte 2, lib. 1, cap. 15.

[23] "Aunque ellos no ninguno por aver venido, porque como avian dexado el paraiso de mahoma que hera Nicaragua y hallaron la isla alzada y falta de comidas y la mayor parte de la gente enfferma y no oro ni plata como atras avian hallado, algunos y todos se holgaran de volver de adonde avian venido." Pedro Pizarro, Descub. v Conq., MS.

the *veedor* or inspector, the comptroller, and other high officers appointed by the Crown to attend the expedition. They had been left in Spain by Pizarro, in consequence of his abrupt departure from the country; and the Council of the Indies, on learning the circumstance, had sent instructions to Panamá to prevent the sailing of his squadron from that port. But the Spanish government, with more wisdom, countermanded the order, only requiring the functionaries to quicken their own departure, and take their place without loss of time in the expedition.

The Spaniards in their march along the coast had now advanced as far as Puerto Viejo. Here they were soon after joined by another small reinforcement of about thirty men, under an officer named Belalcazar, who subsequently rose to high distinction in this service. Many of the followers of Pizarro would now have halted at this spot and established a colony there. But that chief thought more of conquering than of colonizing, at least for the present; and he proposed, as his first step, to get possession of Tumbez, which he regarded as the gate of the Peruvian empire. Continuing his march, therefore, to the shores of what is now called the Gulf of Guayaquil, he arrived off the little island of Puná, lying at no great distance from the Bay of Tumbez. This island, he thought, would afford him a convenient place to encamp until he was prepared to make his descent on the Indian city.

The dispositions of the islanders seemed to favor his purpose. He had not been long in their neighborhood, before a deputation of the natives, with their cacique at their head, crossed over in their balsas to the main land to welcome the Spaniards to their residence. But the Indian interpreters of Tumbez, who had returned with Pizarro from Spain, and continued with the camp, put their master on his guard against the meditated treachery of the islanders, whom they accused of designing to destroy the Spaniards by cutting the ropes that held together the floats, and leaving those upon them to perish in the waters. Yet the cacique, when charged by Pizarro with this perfidious scheme, denied it with such an air of conscious innocence, that the Spanish commander trusted himself and his followers, without further hesitation, to his conveyance, and was transported in safety to the shores of Puná.

Here he was received in a hospitable manner, and his troops were provided with comfortable quarters. Well satisfied with his present position, Pizarro resolved to occupy it until the violence of the rainy season was passed, when the arrival of the reinforcements he expected would put him in better condition for marching into the country of the Inca.

The island, which lies in the mouth of the river of Guayaquil, and is about eight leagues in length by four in breadth, at the widest part, was at that time partially covered with a noble growth of timber. But a large portion of it was subjected to cultivation, and bloomed with plantations of cacao, of the sweet potato, and the different products of a tropical clime, evincing agricultural knowledge as well as industry in the population. They were a warlike race; but had received from their Peruvian foes the appellation of "perfidious." It was the brand fastened by the Roman historians on their Carthaginian enemies,—with perhaps no better reason. The bold and independent islanders opposed a stubborn resistance to the arms of the Incas; and, though they had finally yielded, they had been ever since at feud, and often in deadly hostility, with their neighbors of Tumbez.

The latter no sooner heard of Pizarro's arrival on the island than, trusting, probably, to their former friendly relations with him, they came over in some number to the Spanish quarters. The presence of their detested rivals was by no means grateful to the jealous inhabitants of Puná, and the prolonged residence of the white men on their island could not be otherwise than burdensome. In their outward demeanor they still maintained the same show of amity; but Pizarro's interpreters again put him on his guard against the proverbial perfidy of their hosts. With his suspicions thus roused, the Spanish commander was informed that a number of the chiefs had met together to deliberate on a plan of insurrection. Not caring to wait for the springing of the mine, he surrounded the place of meeting with his soldiers and made prisoners of the suspected chieftains. According to one authority, they confessed their guilt.[24] This is by no means certain. Nor is it certain that they meditated an insurrection. Yet the fact is not improbable, in itself; though it derives little additional probability from the assertion of the hostile interpreters. It is certain, however, that Pizarro was satisfied of the existence of a conspiracy; and, without further hesitation, he abandoned his wretched prisoners, ten or twelve in number, to the tender mercies of their rivals of Tumbez, who instantly massacred them before his eyes.[25]

Maddened by this outrage, the people of Puná sprang to arms, and threw themselves at once, with fearful yells and the wildest menaces of despair, on the Spanish camp. The odds of numbers were greatly in their favor, for they mustered several thousand warriors. But the more decisive odds of arms and discipline were on the side of their antagonists; and, as the Indians rushed forward in a confused mass to the assault, the Castilians coolly received them on their long pikes, or swept them down by the volleys of their musketry. Their ill-protected bodies were easily cut to pieces by the sharp sword of the Spaniard; and Hernando Pizarro, putting himself at the head of the cavalry, charged boldly into the midst, and scattered them far and wide over the field, until, panic-struck by the terrible array of steel-clad horsemen, and the stunning reports and the flash of fire-arms, the fugitives sought shelter in the depths of their forests. Yet the victory was owing, in some degree, at least,—if we may credit the Conquerors,—to the interposition of Heaven; for St. Michael and his legions were seen high in the air above the combatants, con-

[24] Xeres, Conq. del Peru, ap. Barcia, tom. III. p. 183.

[25] "Y el marques don Francisco Piçarro por tenellos por amigos y estuviesen de paz quando alla passasen, les dio algunos principales los quales ellos matavan en presencia de los españoles, cortandoles las cavezas por el cogote." Pedro Pizarro, Descub. y Conq., MS.

tending with the arch-enemy of man, and cheering on the Christians by their example! [26]

Not more than three or four Spaniards fell in the fight; but many were wounded, and among them Hernando Pizarro, who received a severe injury in the leg from a javelin. Nor did the war end here; for the implacable islanders, taking advantage of the cover of night, or of any remissness on the part of the invaders, were ever ready to steal out of their fastnesses and spring on their enemy's camp, while, by cutting off his straggling parties, and destroying his provisions, they kept him in perpetual alarm.

In this uncomfortable situation, the Spanish commander was gladdened by the appearance of two vessels off the island. They brought a reinforcement consisting of a hundred volunteers besides horses for the cavalry. It was commanded by Hernando de Soto, a captain afterwards famous as the discoverer of the Mississippi, which still rolls its majestic current over the place of his burial,—a fitting monument for his remains, as it is of his renown.[27]

The reinforcement was most welcome to Pizarro, who had been long discontented with his position on an island, where he found nothing to compensate the life of unintermitting hostility which he was compelled to lead. With these recruits, he felt himself in sufficient strength to cross over to the continent, and resume military operations in the proper theatre for discovery and conquest. From the Indians of Tumbez he learned that the country had been for some time distracted by a civil war between two sons of the late monarch, competitors for the throne. This intelligence he regarded as of the utmost importance, for he remembered the use which Cortés had made of similar dissensions among the tribes of Anahuac. Indeed, Pizarro seems to have had the example of his great predecessor before his eyes on more occasions than this. But he fell far short of his model; for, notwithstanding the restraint he sometimes put upon himself, his coarser nature and more ferocious temper often betrayed him into acts most repugnant to sound policy, which would never have been countenanced by the Conqueror of Mexico.

---

[26] The city of San Miguel was so named by Pizarro to commemorate the event —and the existence of such a city may be considered by some as establishing the truth of the miracle.—"En la batalla de Puná vieron muchos, ya de los Indios, ya de los nuestros, que habia en el aire otros dos campos, uno acaudillado por el Arcangel Sⁿ Miguel con espada y rodela, y otro, por Luzbel y sus secuaces; mas apenas cantaron los Castellanos la victoria huyeron los diablos, y formando un gran torvellino de viento se oyeron en el aire unas terribles voces que decian, Vencistenos! Miguel vencistenos! De aqui tornó Dⁿ Francisco Pizarro tanta devocion al sto Arcangel, que prometió llamar la primera ciudad que fundase de su nombre; cumpliolo asi como veremos adelante." Montesinos, Annales, MS., año 1530.

[27] The transactions in Puná are given at more or less length by Naharro, Relacion Sumaria, MS.—Conq. i Pob. del Peru, MS.—Pedro Pizarro, Descub. y Conq. MS.—Montesinos, Annales, MS., ubi supra.—Relacion del Primer. Descub. MS.— Xerez, Conq. del Peru, ap. Barcia, tom. III. pp. 182, 183.

CHAPTER II

PERU AT THE TIME OF THE CONQUEST—REIGN OF HUAYNA CAPAC—THE
INCA BROTHERS—CONQUEST FOR THE EMPIRE—TRIUMPH AND
CRUELTIES OF ATAHUALLPA

BEFORE accompanying the march of Pizarro and his followers into the
country of the Incas, it is necessary to make the reader acquainted with
the critical situation of the kingdom at that time. For the Spaniards arrived just at the consummation of an important revolution,—at a crisis
most favorable to their views of conquest, and but for which, indeed, the
conquest, with such a handful of soldiers, could never have been achieved.

In the latter part of the fifteenth century died Tupac Inca Yupanqui,
one of the most renowned of the "Children of the Sun," who, carrying
the Peruvian arms across the burning sands of Atacama, penetrated to
the remote borders of Chili, while in the opposite direction he enlarged
the limits of the empire by the acquisition of the southern provinces of
Quito. The war in this quarter was conducted by his son Huayna Capac,
who succeeded his father on the throne, and fully equalled him in military
daring and in capacity for government.

Under this prince, the whole of the powerful state of Quito, which
rivalled that of Peru itself in wealth and refinement, was brought under
the sceptre of the Incas; whose empire received, by this conquest, the
most important accession yet made to it since the foundation of the
dynasty of Manco Capac. The remaining days of the victorious monarch
were passed in reducing the independent tribes on the remote limits of
his territory, and, still more, in cementing his conquests by the introduction of the Peruvian polity. He was actively engaged in completing the
great works of his father, especially the high-roads which led from Quito
to the capital. He perfected the establishment of posts, took great pains
to introduce the Quichua dialect throughout the empire, promoted a better system of agriculture, and, in fine, encouraged the different branches
of domestic industry and the various enlightened plans of his predecessors
for the improvement of his people. Under his sway, the Peruvian monarchy reached its most palmy state; and under both him and his illustrious father it was advancing with such rapid strides in the march of
civilization as would soon have carried it to a level with the more refined
despotisms of Asia, furnishing the world, perhaps, with higher evidence of
the capabilities of the American Indian than is elsewhere to be found on
the great western continent.—But other and gloomier destinies were in
reserve for the Indian races.

The first arrival of the white men on the South American shores of the Pacific was about ten years before the death of Huayna Capac, when Balboa crossed the Gulf of St. Michael, and obtained the first clear report of the empire of the Incas. Whether tidings of these adventurers reached the Indian monarch's ears is doubtful. There is no doubt, however, that he obtained the news of the first expedition under Pizarro and Almagro, when the latter commander penetrated as far as the Rio de San Juan, about the fourth degree north. The accounts which he received made a strong impression on the mind of Huayna Capac. He discerned in the formidable prowess and weapons of the invaders proofs of a civilization far superior to that of his own people. He intimated his apprehension that they would return, and that at some day, not far distant, perhaps, the throne of the Incas might be shaken by these strangers, endowed with such incomprehensible powers.[1] To the vulgar eye, it was a little speck on the verge of the horizon; but that of the sagacious monarch seemed to descry in it the dark thunder-cloud, that was to spread wider and wider till it burst in fury on his nation!

There is some ground for believing thus much. But other accounts, which have obtained a popular currency, not content with this, connect the first tidings of the white men with predictions long extant in the country, and with supernatural appearances, which filled the hearts of the whole nation with dismay. Comets were seen flaming athwart the heavens. Earthquakes shook the land; the moon was girdled with rings of fire of many colors; a thunderbolt fell on one of the royal palaces and consumed it to ashes; and an eagle, chased by several hawks, was seen, screaming in the air, to hover above the great square of Cuzco, when, pierced by the talons of his tormentors, the king of birds fell lifeless in the presence of many of the Inca nobles, who read in this an augury of their own destruction! Huayna Capac himself, calling his great officers around him, as he found he was drawing near his end, announced the subversion of his empire by the race of white and bearded strangers, as the consummation predicted by the oracles after the reign of the twelfth Inca, and he enjoined it on his vassals not to resist the decrees of Heaven, but to yield obedience to its messengers.[2]

Such is the report of the impressions made by the appearance of the Spaniards in the country, reminding one of the similar feelings of superstitious terror occasioned by their appearance in Mexico. But the traditions of the latter land rest on much higher authority than those of the

---

[1] Sarmiento, an honest authority, tells us he had this from some of the Inca lords who heard it. Relacion, MS., cap. 65.

[2] A minute relation of these supernatural occurrences is given by the Inca Garcilasso de la Vega, (Com. Real., Parte 1, lib. 9, cap. 14,) whose situation opened to him the very best sources of information, which is more than counterbalanced by the defects in his own character as an historian,—his childish credulity, and his desire to magnify and mystify every thing relating to his own order, and, indeed, his nation. His work is the source of most of the facts—and the falsehoods—that have obtained circulation in respect to the ancient Peruvians. Unfortunately, at this distance of time, it is not always easy to distinguish the one from the other.

Peruvians, which, unsupported by contemporary testimony, rest almost wholly on the naked assertion of one of their own nation, who thought to find, doubtless, in the inevitable decrees of Heaven, the best apology for the supineness of his countrymen.

It is not improbable that rumors of the advent of a strange and mysterious race should have spread gradually among the Indian tribes along the great table-land ot the Cordilleras, and should have shaken the hearts of the stoutest warriors with feelings of undefined dread, as of some impending calamity. In this state of mind, it was natural that physical convulsions, to which that volcanic country is peculiarly subject, should have made an unwonted impression on their minds; and that the phenomena, which might have been regarded only as extraordinary, in the usual seasons of political security, should now be interpreted by the superstitious soothsayer as the handwriting on the heavens, by which the God of the Incas proclaimed the approaching downfall of their empire.

Huayna Capac had, as usual with the Peruvian princes, a multitude of concubines, by whom he left a numerous posterity. The heir to the crown, the son of his lawful wife and sister, was named Huascar.[3] At the period of the history at which we are now arrived, he was about thirty years of age. Next to the heir-apparent, by another wife, a cousin of the monarch's, came Manco Capac, a young prince who will occupy an important place in our subsequent story. But the best-beloved of the Inca's children was Atahuallpa. His mother was the daughter of the last *Scyri* of Quito, who had died of grief, it was said, not long after the subversion of his kingdom by Huayna Capac. The princess was beautiful, and the Inca, whether to gratify his passion, or, as the Peruvians say, willing to make amends for the ruin of her parents, received her among his concubines. The historians of Quito assert that she was his lawful wife; but this dignity, according to the usages of the empire, was reserved for maidens of the Inca blood.

The latter years of Huayna Capac were passed in his new kingdom of Quito. Atahuallpa was accordingly brought up under his own eye, accompanied him, while in his tender years, in his campaigns, slept in the same tent with his royal father, and ate from the same plate.[4] The vivacity of the boy, his courage and generous nature, won the affections of the old

---

[3] *Huascar,* in the Quichua dialect, signifies "a cable." The reason of its being given to the heir apparent is remarkable. Huayna Capac celebrated the birth of the prince by a festival, in which he introduced a massive gold chain for the nobles to hold in their hands as they performed their national dances. The chain was seven hundred feet in length, and the links nearly as big round as a man's wrist! (See Zarate, Conq. del Peru, lib. 1, cap. 14.—Garcilasso, Com. Real., Parte 1, lib. 9, cap. 1.) The latter writer had the particulars, he tells us, from his old Inca uncle,— who seems to have dealt largely in the marvellous; not too largely for his audience, however, as the story has been greedily circulated by most of the Castilian writers, both of that and of the succeeding age.

[4] "Atabalipa era bien quisto de los Capitanes viejos de su Padre y de los Soldados, porque andubo en la guerra en su niñez y porque él en vida le mostró tanto amor que no le dejaba comer otra cosa que lo que él le daba de su plato." Sarmiento, Relacion, MS., cap. 66.

monarch to such a degree, that he resolved to depart from the established usages of the realm, and divide his empire between him and his elder brother Huascar. On his death-bed, he called the great officers of the crown around him, and declared it to be his will that the ancient kingdom of Quito should pass to Atahuallpa, who might be considered as having a natural claim on it, as the dominion of his ancestors. The rest of the empire he settled on Huascar; and he enjoined it on the two brothers to acquiesce in this arrangement, and to live in amity with each other. This was the last act of the heroic monarch; doubtless, the most impolitic of his whole life. With his dying breath he subverted the fundamental laws of the empire; and, while he recommended harmony between the successors to his authority, he left in this very division of it the seeds of inevitable discord.[5]

His death took place, as seems probable, at the close of 1525, not quite seven years before Pizarro's arrival at Puná.[6] The tidings of his decease spread sorrow and consternation throughout the land; for, though stern and even inexorable to the rebel and the long-resisting foe, he was a brave and magnanimous monarch, and legislated with the enlarged views of a prince who regarded every part of his dominions as equally his concern. The people of Quito, flattered by the proofs which he had given of preference for them by his permanent residence in that country, and his embellishment of their capital, manifested unfeigned sorrow at his loss; and his subjects at Cuzco, proud of the glory which his arms and his abilities had secured for his native land, held him in no less admiration;[7] while the more thoughtful and the more timid, in both countries, looked with apprehension to the future, when the sceptre of the vast empire, instead of being swayed by an old and experienced hand, was to be consigned to rival princes, naturally jealous of one another, and, from their age, necessarily exposed to the unwholesome influence of crafty and ambitious counsellors. The people testified their regret by the unwonted honors paid to the memory of the deceased Inca. His heart was retained in Quito, and his body, embalmed after the fashion of the country, was transported

---

[5] Oviedo, Hist. de las Indias, MS., Parte 1, lib. 8, cap. 9.—Zarate, Conq. del Peru, lib. 1, cap. 12.—Sarmiento, Relacion, MS., cap. 65.—Xerez, Conq. del Peru, ap. Barcia, tom. III. p. 201.

[6] The precise date of this event, though so near the time of the Conquest, is matter of doubt. Balboa, a contemporary with the Conquerors, and who wrote at Quito, where the Inca died, fixes it at 1525. (Hist. du Perou, chap. 14.) Velasco, another inhabitant of the same place, after an investigation of the different accounts, comes to the like conclusion. (Hist. de Quito, tom. I. p. 232.) Dr. Robertson, after telling us that Huayna Capac died in 1529, speaks again of this event as having happened in 1527. (Conf. America, vol. III. pp. 25, 381.) Any one, who has been bewildered by the chronological snarl of the ancient chronicles will not be surprised at meeting occasionally with such inconsistencies in a writer who is obliged to take them as his guides.

[7] One cannot doubt this monarch's popularity with the female part of his subjects, at least, if, as the historian of the Incas tells us, "he was never known to refuse a woman, of whatever age or degree she might be, any favor that she asked of him!" Com. Real., Parte 1. lib. 8, cap. 7.

to Cuzco, to take its place in the great temple of the Sun, by the side of the remains of his royal ancestors. His obsequies were celebrated with sanguinary splendor in both the capitals of his far-extended empire; and several thousand of the imperial concubines, with numerous pages and officers of the palace, are said to have proved their sorrow, or their superstition, by offering up their own lives, that they might accompany their departed lord to the bright mansions of the Sun.[8]

For nearly five years after the death of Huayna Capac, the royal brothers reigned, each over his allotted portion of the empire, without distrust of one another, or, at least, without collision. It seemed as if the wish of their father was to be completely realized, and that the two states were to maintain their respective integrity and independence as much as if they had never been united into one. But, with the manifold causes for jealousy and discontent, and the swarms of courtly sycophants, who would find their account in fomenting these feelings, it was easy to see that this tranquil state of things could not long endure. Nor would it have endured so long, but for the more gentle temper of Huascar, the only party who had ground for complaint. He was four or five years older than his brother, and was possessed of courage not to be doubted; but he was a prince of a generous and easy nature, and perhaps, if left to himself, might have acquiesced in an arrangement which, however unpalatable, was the will of his deified father. But Atahuallpa was of a different temper. Warlike, ambitious, and daring, he was constantly engaged in enterprises for the enlargement of his own territory, though his crafty policy was scrupulous not to aim at extending his acquisitions in the direction of his royal brother. His restless spirit, however, excited some alarm at the court of Cuzco, and Huascar, at length, sent an envoy to Atahuallpa, to remonstrate with him on his ambitious enterprises, and to require him to render him homage for his kingdom of Quito.

This is one statement. Other accounts pretend that the immediate cause of rupture was a claim instituted by Huascar for the territory of Tumebamba, held by his brother as part of his patrimonial inheritance. It matters little what was the ostensible ground of collision between persons placed by circumstances in so false a position in regard to one another, that collision must, at some time or other, inevitably occur.

The commencement, and, indeed, the whole course, of hostilities which soon broke out between the rival brothers are stated with irreconcilable, and, considering the period was so near to that of the Spanish invasion, with unaccountable discrepancy. By some it is said, that, in Atahuallpa's first encounter with the troops of Cuzco, he was defeated and made prisoner near Tumebamba, a favorite residence of his father in the ancient territory of Quito, and in the district of Cañaris. From this disaster he recovered by a fortunate escape from confinement, when, regaining his capital, he soon found himself at the head of a numerous army, led by the most able and experienced captains in the empire. The liberal man-

---

[8] Sarmiento, Relacion, MS., cap. 65.—Herrera, Hist. General, dec. 5, lib. 3, cap. 17.

ners of the young Atahuallpa had endeared him to the soldiers, with whom, as we have seen, he served more than one campaign in his father's lifetime. These troops were the flower of the great army of the Inca, and some of them had grown gray in his long military career, which had left them at the north, where they readily transferred their allegiance to the young sovereign of Quito. They were commanded by two officers of great consideration, both possessed of large experience in military affairs, and high in the confidence of the late Inca. One of them was named Quizquiz; the other, who was the maternal uncle of Atahuallpa, was called Chalicuchima.

With these practised warriors to guide him, the young monarch put himself at the head of his martial array, and directed his march towards the south. He had not advanced farther than Ambato, about sixty miles distant from his capital, when he fell in with a numerous host, which had been sent against him by his brother, under the command of a distinguished chieftain, of the Inca family. A bloody battle followed, which lasted the greater part of the day; and the theatre of combat was the skirts of the mighty Chimborazo.[9]

The battle ended favorably for Atahuallpa, and the Peruvians were routed with great slaughter, and the loss of their commander. The prince of Quito availed himself of his advantage to push forward his march until he arrived before the gates of Tumebamba, which city, as well as the whole district of Cañaris, though an ancient dependency of Quito, had sided with his rival in the contest. Entering the captive city like a conqueror, he put the inhabitants to the sword, and razed it with all its stately edifices, some of which had been reared by his own father, to the ground. He carried on the same war of extermination, as he marched through the offending district of Cañaris. In some places, it is said, the women and children came out, with green branches in their hands, in melancholy procession, to deprecate his wrath; but the vindictive conqueror, deaf to their entreaties, laid the country waste with fire and sword, sparing no man capable of bearing arms who fell into his hands.[10]

---

[9] Garcilasso denies that anything but insignificant skirmishes took place before the decisive action fought on the plains of Cuzco. But the Licentiate Sarmiento, who gathered his accounts of these events, as he tells us, from the actors in them, walked over the field of battle at Ambato, when the ground was still covered with the bones of the slain. "Yo hé pasado por este Pueblo y he visto el Lugar donde dicen que esta Batalla se dió y cierto segun hay la osamenta devieron aun de morir mas gente de la que cuentan." Relacion, MS., cap. 69.

[10] "Cuentan muchos Indios á quien yo lo oi, que por amansar su ira, mandaron á un escuadron grande de niños y á otro de hombres de toda edad, que saliesen hasta las ricas andas donde venia con gran pompa, llevando en las manos ramos verdes y ojas de palma, y que le pidiesen la gracia y amistad suya para el pueblo, sin mirar la injuria pasada, y que en tantos clamores se lo suplicaron, y con tanta humildad, que bastara quebrantar corazones de piedra; mas poca impresion hicerion en el cruel de Atabalipa, porque dicen que mandó á sus capitanes y gentes que matasen á todos aquellos que habian venido, lo cual fué hecho, no perdonando sino á algunos miños y á las mugeres sagradas del Templo." Sarmiento, Relacion, MS, cap. 70.

The fate of Cañaris struck terror into the hearts of his enemies, and one place after another opened its gates to the victor, who held on his triumphant march towards the Peruvian capital. His arms experienced a temporary check before the island of Puná, whose bold warriors maintained the cause of his brother. After some days lost before this place, Atahuallpa left the contest to their old enemies, the people of Tumbez, who had early given in their adhesion to him, while he resumed his march and advanced as far as Caxamalca, about seven degrees south. Here he halted with a detachment of the army, sending forward the main body under the command of his two generals, with orders to move straight upon Cuzco. He preferred not to trust himself farther in the enemy's country, where a defeat might be fatal. By establishing his quarters at Caxamalca, he would be able to support his generals, in case of a reverse, or, at worst, to secure his retreat on Quito, until he was again in condition to renew hostilities.

The two commanders, advancing by rapid marches, at length crossed the Apurimac river, and arrived within a short distance of the Peruvian capital.—Meanwhile, Huascar had not been idle. On receiving tidings of the discomfiture of his army at Ambato, he made every exertion to raise levies throughout the country. By the advice, it is said, of his priests—the most incompetent advisers in times of danger—he chose to await the approach of the enemy in his own capital; and it was not till the latter had arrived within a few leagues of Cuzco, that the Inca, taking counsel of the same ghostly monitors, sallied forth to give him battle.

The two armies met on the plains of Quipaypan, in the neighborhood of the Indian metropolis. Their numbers are stated with the usual discrepancy; but Atahuallpa's troops had considerably the advantage in discipline and experience, for many of Huascar's levies had been drawn hastily together from the surrounding country. Both fought, however, with the desperation of men who felt that every thing was at stake. It was no longer a contest for a province, but for the possession of an empire. Atahuallpa's troops, flushed with recent success, fought with the confidence of those who relied on their superior prowess; while the loyal vassals of the Inca displayed all the self-devotion of men who held their own lives cheap in the service of their master.

The fight raged with the greatest obstinacy from sunrise to sunset; and the ground was covered with heaps of the dying and the dead, whose bones lay bleaching on the battle-field long after the conquest by the Spaniards. At length, fortune declared in favor of Atahuallpa; or rather, the usual result of superior discipline and military practice followed. The ranks of the Inca were thrown into irretrievable disorder, and gave way in all directions. The conquerors followed close on the heels of the flying. Huascar himself, among the latter, endeavored to make his escape with about a thousand men who remained round his person. But the royal fugitive was discovered before he had left the field; his little party was enveloped by clouds of the enemy, and nearly every one of the devoted band perished in defence of their Inca. Huascar was made prisoner,

and the victorious chiefs marched at once on his capital, which they occupied in the name of their sovereign.[11]

These events occurred in the spring of 1532, a few months before the
landing of the Spaniards. The tidings of the success of his arms and the
capture of his unfortunate brother reached Atahuallpa at Caxamalca. He
instantly gave orders that Huascar should be treated with the respect due
to his rank, but that he should be removed to the strong fortress of
Xauxa, and held there in strict confinement. His orders did not stop
here,—if we are to receive the accounts of Garcilasso de la Vega, himself
of the Inca race, and by his mother's side nephew of the great Huayna
Capac.

According to this authority, Atahuallpa invited the Inca nobles
throughout the country to assemble at Cuzco, in order to deliberate on
the best means of partitioning the empire between him and his brother.
When they had met in the capital, they were surrounded by the soldiery
of Quito, and butchered without mercy. The motive for this perfidious
act was to exterminate the whole of the royal family, who might each one
of them show a better title to the crown than the illegitimate Atahuallpa.
But the massacre did not end here. The illegitimate offspring, like himself, half-brothers of the monster, all, in short, who had any of the Inca
blood in their veins, were involved in it; and with an appetite for carnage unparalleled in the annals of the Roman Empire or of the French
Republic, Atahuallpa ordered all the females of the blood royal, his aunts,
nieces, and cousins, to be put to death, and that, too, with the most refined and lingering tortures. To give greater zest to his revenge, many of
the executions took place in the presence of Huascar himself, who was
thus compelled to witness the butchery of his own wives and sisters,
while, in the extremity of anguish, they in vain called on him to protect
them![12]

Such is the tale told by the historian of the Incas, and received by
him, as he assures us, from his mother and uncle, who, being children at
the time, were so fortunate as to be among the few that escaped the
massacre of their house.[13] And such is the account repeated by many a

[11] Cieza de Leon, Cronica, cap. 77.—Oviedo, Hist. de las Indias, MS., Parte 3,
lib. 8, cap. 9.—Xerez, Conq. del Peru, ap. Barcia, tom. III. p. 202.—Zarate, Conq.
del Peru, lib. 1, cap. 12.—Sarmiento, Relacion, MS., cap. 70.—Pedro Pizarro, Descub. y Conq., MS.

[12] Garcilasso, Com. Real., Parte 1, lib. 9, cap. 35-39.
"A las Mugeres, Hermanas, Tias, Sobrinas, Primas Hermanas, y Madrastras de
Atahuallpa, colgavan de los Arboles, y de muchas Horcas mui altas que hicieron: à
unas colgaron de los cabellos, à otras por debajo de los braços, y à otras de otras
maneras feas, que por la honestidad se callan: davanles sus hijuelos, que los tuviesen en braços, tenianlos hasta que se les caian, y se aporreavan." (Ibid., cap. 37.)
The variety of torture shows some invention in the writer, or, more probably, in
the writer's uncle, the ancient Inca, the *raconteur* of these Bluebeard butcheries.

[13] "Las crueldades que Atahuallpa en los de la Sangre Real hiço, diré de Re-
lacion de mi Madre, y de un Hermano suio, que se llamó Don Fernando Huallpa
Tupac Inca Yupanqui, que entonces eran Niños de menos de diez Años." Ibid.,
Parte 1, lib. 9, cap. 14.

Castilian writer since, without any symptom of distrust. But a tissue of unprovoked atrocities like these is too repugnant to the principles of human nature,—and, indeed, to common sense, to warrant our belief in them on ordinary testimony.

The annals of semi-civilized nations unhappily show that there have been instances of similar attempts to extinguish the whole of a noxious race, which had become the object of a tyrant's jealousy; though such an attempt is about as chimerical as it would be to extirpate any particular species of plant, the seeds of which had been borne on every wind¹ over the country. But, if the attempt to exterminate the Inca race was actually made by Atahuallpa, how comes it that so many of the pure descendants of the blood royal—nearly six hundred in number—are admitted by the historian to have been in existence seventy years after the imputed massacre?[14] Why was the massacre, instead of being limited to the legitimate members of the royal stock, who could show a better title to the crown than the usurper, extended to all, however remotely, or in whatever way, connected with the race? Why were aged women and young maidens involved in the proscription, and why were they subjected to such refined and superfluous tortures, when it is obvious that beings so impotent could have done nothing to provoke the jealousy of the tyrant? Why, when so many were sacrificed from some vague apprehension of distant danger, was his rival Huascar, together with his younger brother Manco Capac, the two men from whom the conqueror had most to fear, suffered to live? Why, in short, is the wonderful tale not recorded by others before the time of Garcilasso, and nearer by half a century to the events themselves?[15]

That Atahuallpa may have been guilty of excesses, and abused the rights of conquest by some gratuitous acts of cruelty, may be readily believed; for no one, who calls to mind his treatment of the Cañaris,—which his own apologists do not affect to deny,[16]—will doubt that he had a full measure of the vindictive temper which belongs to

> "Those souls of fire, and Children of the Sun,
> With whom revenge was virtue."

[14] This appears from a petition for certain immunities, forwarded to Spain in 1603, and signed by five hundred and sixty-seven Indians of the royal Inca race. (Ibid., Parte 3, lib. 9, cap. 40.) Oviedo says that Huayna Capac left a hundred sons and daughters and that *most of them were alive at the time of his writing*. "Tubo cien hijos y hijas, y la mayor parte de ellos son vivos." Hist. de las Indias, MS., Parte 3, lib. 8, cap. 9.

[15] I have looked in vain for some confirmation of this story in Oviedo, Sarmiento, Xerez, Cieza de Leon, Zarate, Pedro Pizarro, Gomara,—all living at the time, and having access to the best sources of information; and all, it may be added, disposed to do stern justice to the evil qualities of the Indian monarch.

[16] No one of the apologists of Atahuallpa goes quite so far as Father Velasco, who, in the over-flowings of his loyalty for a Quito monarch, regards his massacre of the Cañares as a very fair retribution for their offences. "Si les auteurs dont je viens de parler s'étaient trouvés dans les mênes circonstances qu' Atahuallpa et avient éprouvé autant d'offenses graves et de trahisons, je ne croirai jamais qu'ils eussent agi autrement"! Hist. de Quito, tom. I. p. 253.

But there is a wide difference between this and the monstrous and most unprovoked atrocities imputed to him; implying a diabolical nature not to be admitted on the evidence of an Indian partisan, the sworn foe of his house, and repeated by Castilian chroniclers, who may naturally seek, by blazoning the enormities of Atahuallpa, to find some apology for the cruelty of their countrymen towards him.

The news of the great victory was borne on the wings of the wind to Caxamalca; and loud and long was the rejoicing, not only in the camp of Atahuallpa, but in the town and surrounding country; for all now came in, eager to offer their congratulations to the victor, and do him homage. The prince of Quito no longer hesitated to assume the scarlet *borla*, the diadem of the Incas. His triumph was complete. He had beaten his enemies on their own ground; had taken their capital; had set his foot on the neck of his rival, and won for himself the ancient sceptre of the Children of the Sun. But the hour of triumph was destined to be that of his deepest humiliation. Atahuallpa was not one of those to whom, in the language of the Grecian bard, "the Gods are willing to reveal themselves." [17] He had not read the handwriting on the heavens. The small speck, which the clear-sighted eye of his father had discerned on the distant verge of the horizon, though little noticed by Atahuallpa, intent on the deadly strife with his brother, had now risen high towards the zenith, spreading wider and wider, till it wrapped the skies in darkness, and was ready to burst in thunders on the devoted nation.

[17] "Οὐ γάρ πω πάντεσσι θεοὶ φαίνονται ἐναργεῖς."
ΟΔΥΣ. π, v. 161.

CHAPTER III

THE SPANIARDS LAND AT TUMBEZ—PIZARRO RECONNOITRES THE COUN-
TRY—FOUNDATION OF SAN MIGUEL—MARCH INTO THE INTERIOR—
EMBASSY FROM THE INCA—ADVENTURES ON THE MARCH—REACH
THE FOOT OF THE ANDES

1532

WE left the Spaniards at the island of Puná, preparing to make their descent on the neighboring continent at Tumbez. This port was but a few
leagues distant, and Pizarro, with the greater part of his followers, passed
over in the ships, while a few others were to transport the commander's
baggage and the military stores on some of the Indian balsas. One of the
latter vessels which first touched the shore was surrounded, and three persons who were on the raft were carried off by the natives to the adjacent
woods and there massacred. The Indians then got possession of another
of the balsas, containing Pizarro's wardrobe; but, as the men who defended it raised loud cries for help, they reached the ears of Hernando
Pizarro, who, with a small body of horse, had effected a landing some way
farther down the shore. A broad tract of miry ground, overflowed at high
water, lay between him and the party thus rudely assailed by the natives. The tide was out, and the bottom was soft and dangerous. With
little regard to the danger, however, the bold cavalier spurred his horse
into the slimy depths, and followed by his men, with the mud up to their
saddle-girths, they plunged forward until they came into the midst of the
marauders, who, terrified by the strange apparition of the horsemen, fled
precipitately, without show of fight, to the neighboring forests.

This conduct of the natives of Tumbez is not easy to be explained;
considering the friendly relations maintained with the Spaniards on their
preceding visit, and lately renewed in the island of Puná. But Pizarro was
still more astonished, on entering their town, to find it not only deserted,
but, with the exception of a few buildings, entirely demolished. Four or
five of the most substantial private dwellings, the great temple, and the
fortress—and these greatly damaged, and wholly despoiled of their interior decorations—alone survived to mark the site of the city, and attest
its former splendor.[1] The scene of desolation filled the conquerors with

---

[1] Xerez, Conq. del Peru, ap. Barcia, tom. III. p. 185.

"Aunque lo del templo del Sol en quien ellos adoran era cosa de ver, porque
tenian grandes edificios, y todo el por de dentro y de fuera pintado de grandes
pinturas y ricos matizes de colores, porque los hay en aquella tierra." Relacion del
Primer. Descub., MS.

dismay; for even the raw recruits, who had never visited the coast before, had heard the marvellous stories of the golden treasures of Tumbez, and they had confidently looked forward to them as an easy spoil after all their fatigues. But the gold of Peru seemed only like a deceitful phantom, which, after beckoning them on through toil and danger, vanished the moment they attempted to grasp it.

Pizarro despatched a small body of troops in pursuit of the fugitives; and, after some slight skirmishing, they got possession of several of the natives, and among them, as it chanced, the curaca of the place. When brought before the Spanish commander, he exonerated himself from any share in the violence offered to the white men, saying that it was done by a lawless party of his people, without his knowledge at the time; and he expressed his willingness to deliver them up to punishment, if they could be detected. He explained the dilapidated condition of the town by the long wars carried on with the fierce tribes of Puná, who had at length succeeded in getting possession of the place, and driving the inhabitants into the neighboring woods and mountains. The Inca, to whose cause they were attached, was too much occupied with his own feuds to protect them against their enemies.

Whether Pizarro gave any credit to the cacique's exculpation of himself may be doubted. He dissembled his suspicions, however, and, as the Indian lord promised obedience in his own name, and that of his vassals, the Spanish general consented to take no further notice of the affair. He seems now to have felt for the first time, in its full force, that it was his policy to gain the good-will of the people among whom he had thrown himself in the face of such tremendous odds. It was, perhaps, the excesses of which his men had been guilty in the earlier stages of the expedition that had shaken the confidence of the people of Tumbez, and incited them to this treacherous retaliation.

Pizarro inquired of the natives who now, under promise of impunity, came into the camp, what had become of his two followers that remained with them in the former expedition. The answers they gave were obscure and contradictory. Some said, they had died of an epidemic; others, that they had perished in the war with Puná; and others intimated, that they had lost their lives in consequence of some outrage attempted on the Indian women. It was impossible to arrive at the truth. The last account was not the least probable. But, whatever might be the cause, there was no doubt they had both perished.

This intelligence spread an additional gloom over the Spaniards; which was not dispelled by the flaming pictures now given by the natives of the riches of the land, and of the state and magnificence of the monarch in his distant capital among the mountains. Nor did they credit the authenticity of a scroll of paper, which Pizarro had obtained from an Indian, to whom it had been delivered by one of the white men left in the country. "Know, whoever you may be," said the writing, "that may chance to set foot in this country, that it contains more gold and silver than there is iron in Biscay." This paper, when shown to the soldiers, excited only their ridicule, as a device of their captain to keep alive their chimerical hopes.[2]

Pizarro now saw that it was not politic to protract his stay in his present quarters, where a spirit of disaffection would soon creep into the ranks of his followers, unless their spirits were stimulated by novelty or a life of incessant action. Yet he felt deeply anxious to obtain more particulars than he had hitherto gathered of the actual condition of the Peruvian empire, of its strength and resources, of the monarch who ruled over it, and of his present situation. He was also desirous, before taking any decisive step for penetrating the country, to seek out some commodious place for a settlement, which might afford him the means of a regular communication with the colonies, and a place of strength, on which he himself might retreat in case of disaster.

He decided, therefore, to leave part of his company at Tumbez, including those who, from the state of their health, were least able to take the field, and with the remainder to make an excursion into the interior, and reconnoitre the land, before deciding on any plan of operations. He set out early in May, 1532; and, keeping along the more level regions himself, sent a small detachment under the command of Hernando de Soto to explore the skirts of the vast sierra.

He maintained a rigid discipline on the march, commanding his soldiers to abstain from all acts of violence, and punishing disobedience in the most prompt and resolute manner.[3] The natives rarely offered resistance. When they did so, they were soon reduced, and Pizarro, far from vindictive measures, was open to the first demonstrations of submission. By this lenient and liberal policy, he soon acquired a name among the inhabitants which effaced the unfavorable impressions made of him in the earlier part of the campaign. The natives, as he marched through the thick-settled hamlets which sprinkled the level region between the Cordilleras and the ocean, welcomed him with rustic hospitality, providing good quarters for his troops, and abundant supplies, which cost but little in the prolific soil of the *tierra caliente*. Everywhere Pizarro made proclamation that he came in the name of the Holy Vicar of God and of the sovereign of Spain, requiring the obedience of the inhabitants as true children of the Church, and vassals of his lord and master. And as the simple people made no opposition to a formula, of which they could not comprehend a syllable, they were admitted as good subjects of the Crown of Castile, and their act of homage—or what was readily interpreted as such—was duly recorded and attested by the notary.[4]

[2] For the account of the transactions in Tumbez, see Pedro Pisarro, Descub. y Conq. MS.—Oviedo, Hist. de las Indias, MS., Parte 3, lib. 8, cap. 1.—Relacion del Primer. Descub., MS.—Herrera, Hist. General, dec. 4, lib. 9, cap. 1, 2.—Xerez, Conq. del Peru, ap. Barcia, tom. III. p. 185.

[3] "Mando el Gobernador por pregon é so graves penas que no le fuese hecha fuerza ni descortesia é que se les hiciese muy buen tratamiento por los Españoles é sus criados." Oviedo, Hist. de las Indias, MS., Parte 3, lib. 8, cap. 2.

[4] "E mandabaies notificar ó dar á entender con las lenguas el requerimiento que su Magestad manda que se les haga á los Indios para traellos en conocimiento de

At the expiration of some three or four weeks spent in reconnoitring the country, Pizarro came to the conclusion that the most eligible site for his new settlement was in the rich valley of Tangarala, thirty leagues south of Tumbez, traversed by more than one stream that opens a communication with the ocean. To this spot, accordingly, he ordered the men left at Tumbez to repair at once in their vessels; and no sooner had they arrived, than busy preparations were made for building up the town in a manner suited to the wants of the colony. Timber was procured from the neighboring woods. Stones were dragged from their quarries, and edifices gradually rose, some of which made pretensions to strength, if not to elegance. Among them were a church, a magazine for public stores, a hall of justice, and a fortress. A municipal government was organized, consisting of regidores, alcaldes, and the usual civic functionaries. The adjacent territory was parcelled out among the residents, and each colonist had a certain number of the natives allotted to assist him in his labors; for, as Pizarro's secretary remarks, "it being evident that the colonists could not support themselves without the services of the Indians, the ecclesiastics and the leaders of the expedition all agreed that a *repartimiento* of the natives would serve the cause of religion, and tend greatly to their spiritual welfare, since they would thus have the opportunity of being initiated in the true faith." [5]

Having made these arrangements with such conscientious regard to the welfare of the benighted heathen, Pizarro gave his infant city the name of San Miguel, in acknowledgment of the service rendered him by that saint in his battles with the Indians of Puná. The site originally occupied by the settlement was afterward found to be so unhealthy, that it was abandoned for another on the banks of the beautiful Piura. The town is still of some note for its manufactures, though dwindled from its ancient importance; but the name of San Miguel de Piura, which it bears, still commemorates the foundation of the first European colony in the empire of the Incas.

Before quitting the new settlement, Pizarro caused the gold and silver ornaments which he had obtained in different parts of the country to be melted down into one mass, and a fifth to be deducted for the Crown. The

nuestra Santa fé catolica, y requiriendoles con la paz, é que obedezcan á la Iglesia e Apostolica de Roma, é en lo temporal den la obediencia á su Magestad é á los Reyes sus succesores en los regnos de Castilla i de Leon; respondieron que asi lo querian é harian, guardarian é cumplirian enteramente; e el Gobernador los recibio por tales vasallos de sus Magestades por auto publico de notarios." Ibid., MS., ubi supra.

[5] Pedro Pizarro, Descub. y Conq., MS.—Conq. i Pob. del Peru, MS.—Cieza de Leon, Cronica, cap. 55.—Relacion del Primer. Descub., MS.

"Porque los Vecinos, sin aiuda i servicios de los Naturales no se podian sostener, ni poblarse el Pueblo. . . . . . A esta causa, con acuerdo de el Religioso, i de los Oficiales que les parecio convenir asi al servicio de Dios, i bien de los Naturales, el Gobernador depositò los Caciques, i Indios en los Vecinos de este Pueblo, porque los aiudasen a sostener, i los Christianos los Doctrinasen en nuestra Santa Fè, conforme á los Mandamientos de su Magestad." Xerez, Conq. del Peru, ap. Barcia, tom. III. p. 187.

remainder, which belonged to the troops, he persuaded them to relinquish for the present; under the assurance of being repaid from the first spoils that fell into their hands.[6] With these funds, and other articles collected in the course of the campaign, he sent back the vessels to Panamá. The gold was applied to paying off the ship-owners, and those who had furnished the stores for the expedition. That he should so easily have persuaded his men to resign present possession for a future contingency is proof that the spirit of enterprise was renewed in their bosoms in all its former vigor, and that they looked forward with the same buoyant confidence to the results.

In his late tour of observation, the Spanish commander had gathered much important intelligence in regard to the state of the kingdom. He had ascertained the result of the struggle between the Inca brothers, and that the victor now lay with his army encamped at the distance of only ten or twelve days' journey from San Miguel. The accounts he heard of the opulence and power of that monarch, and of his great southern capital, perfectly corresponded with the general rumors before received; and contained, therefore, something to stagger the confidence, as well as to stimulate the cupidity, of the invaders.

Pizarro would gladly have seen his little army strengthened by reinforcements, however small the amount; and on that account postponed his departure for several weeks. But no reinforcement arrived; and, as he received no further tidings from his associates, he judged that longer delay would, probably, be attended with evils greater than those to be encountered on the march; that discontents would inevitably spring up in a life of inaction, and the strength and spirits of the soldier sink under the enervating influence of a tropical climate. Yet the force at his command, amounting to less than two hundred soldiers in all, after reserving fifty for the protection of the new settlement, seemed but a small one for the conquest of an empire. He might, indeed, instead of marching against the Inca, take a southerly direction towards the rich capital of Cuzco. But this would only be to postpone the hour of reckoning. For in what quarter of the empire could he hope to set his foot, where the arm of its master would not reach him? By such a course, moreover, he would show his own distrust of himself. He would shake that opinion of his invincible prowess, which he had hitherto endeavored to impress on the natives, and which constituted a great secret of his strength; which, in short, held sterner sway over the mind than the display of numbers and mere physical force. Worse than all, such a course would impair the confidence of his troops in themselves and their reliance on himself. This would be to palsy the arm of enterprise at once. It was not to be thought of.

But while Pizarro decided to march into the interior, it is doubtful whether he had formed any more definite plan of action. We have no means of knowing his intentions, at this distance of time, otherwise than

---

[6] "E sacado el quinto para su Magestad, lo restante que perteneció al Egercito de la Conquista, el Gobernador le tomó prestado de los compañeros para se lo pagar del primer oro que se obiese." Oviedo, Hist. de las Indias, MS., Parte 3, lib. 8, cap. 1.

as they are shown by his actions. Unfortunately, he could not write, and he has left no record, like the inestimable Commentaries of Cortés, to enlighten us as to his motives. His secretary, and some of his companions in arms, have recited his actions in detail; but the motives which led to them they were not always so competent to disclose.

It is possible that the Spanish general, even so early as the period of his residence at San Miguel, may have meditated some daring stroke, some effective *coup-de-main*, which, like that of Cortés, when he carried off the Aztec monarch to his quarters, might strike terror into the hearts of the people, and at once decide the fortunes of the day. It is more probable, however, that he now only proposed to present himself before the Inca, as the peaceful representative of a brother monarch, and, by these friendly demonstrations, disarm any feeling of hostility, or even of suspicion. When once in communication with the Indian prince, he could regulate his future course by circumstances.

On the 24th of September, 1532, five months after landing at Tumbez, Pizarro marched out at the head of his little body of adventurers from the gates of San Miguel, having enjoined it on the colonists to treat their Indian vassals with humanity, and to conduct themselves in such a manner as would secure the good-will of the surrounding tribes. Their own existence, and with it the safety of the army and the success of the undertaking, depended on this course. In the place were to remain the royal treasurer, the *veedor*, or inspector of metals, and other officers of the crown; and the command of the garrison was intrusted to the *contador*, Antonio Navarro.[7] Then putting himself at the head of his troops, the chief struck boldly into the heart of the country in the direction where, as he was informed, lay the camp of the Inca. It was a daring enterprise, thus to venture with a handful of followers into the heart of a powerful empire, to present himself, face to face, before the Indian monarch in his own camp, encompassed by the flower of his victorious army! Pizarro had already experienced more than once the difficulty of maintaining his ground against the rude tribes of the north, so much inferior in strength and numbers to the warlike legions of Peru. But the hazard of the game, as I have already more than once had occasion to remark, constituted its great charm with the Spaniard. The brilliant achievements of his countrymen, on the like occasions, with means so inadequate, inspired him with confidence in his own good star; and this confidence was one source of his success. Had he faltered for a moment, had he stopped to calculate chances, he must inevitably have failed; for the odds were too great to be combated by sober reason. They were only to be met triumphantly by the spirit of the knight-errant.

After crossing the smooth waters of the Piura, the little army continued to advance over a level district intersected by streams that descended from the neighboring Cordilleras. The face of the country was shagged over with forests of gigantic growth, and occasionally traversed

⁷ Xerez, Conq. del Peru, ap. Barcia, tom. III. p. 187.—Pedro Pizarro. Descub. y Conq., MS.—Oviedo, Hist. de las Indias, MS., Parte 3, lib. 8, cap. 10.

by ridges of barren land, that seemed like shoots of the adjacent Andes, breaking up the surface of the region into little sequestered valleys of singular loveliness. The soil, though rarely watered by the rains of heaven, was naturally rich, and wherever it was refreshed with moisture, as on the margins of the streams, it was enamelled with the brightest verdure. The industry of the inhabitants, moreover, had turned these streams to the best account, and canals and aqueducts were seen crossing the low lands in all directions, and spreading over the country, like a vast network, diffusing fertility and beauty around them. The air was scented with the sweet odors of flowers, and everywhere the eye was refreshed by the sight of orchards laden with unknown fruits, and of fields waving with yellow grain and rich in luscious vegetables of every description that teem in the sunny clime of the equator. The Spaniards were among a people who had carried the refinements of husbandry to a greater extent than any yet found on the American continent; and, as they journeyed through this paradise of plenty, their condition formed a pleasing contrast to what they had before endured in the dreary wilderness of the mangroves.

Everywhere, too, they were received with confiding hospitality by the simple people; for which they were no doubt indebted, in a great measure, to their own inoffensive deportment. Every Spaniard seemed to be aware, that his only chance of success lay in conciliating the good opinion of the inhabitants, among whom he had so recklessly cast his fortunes. In most of the hamlets, and in every place of considerable size, some fortress was to be found, or royal caravansary, destined for the Inca on his progresses, the ample halls of which furnished abundant accommodations for the Spaniards; who were thus provided with quarters along their route at the charge of the very government which they were preparing to overturn.[8]

On the fifth day after leaving San Miguel, Pizarro halted in one of these delicious valleys, to give his troops repose, and to make a more complete inspection of them. Their number amounted in all to one hundred and seventy-seven, of which sixty-seven were cavalry. He mustered only three arquebusiers in his whole company, and a few crossbow-men, altogether not exceeding twenty.[9] The troops were tolerably well equipped, and in good condition. But the watchful eye of their commander noticed with uneasiness, that, notwithstanding the general heartiness, in the cause manifested by his followers, there were some among them whose countenances lowered with discontent, and who, although they did not give vent to it in open murmurs, were far from moving with their wonted alacrity.

[8] Oviedo, Hist. de las Indias, MS., Parte 3, lib. 8, cap. 4.—Naharro, Relacion Sumaria, MS.—Conq. i Pob. del Piru, MS.—Relacion del Primer. Descub., MS.

[9] There is less discrepancy in the estimate of the Spanish force here than usual. The paucity of numbers gave less room for it. No account carries them as high as two hundred. I have adopted that of the Secretary Xerez, (Conq. del Peru, ap Barcia, tom. III. p. 187,) who has been followed by Oviedo, (Hist. de las Indias MS., Parte 3, lib. 1, cap. 3,) and by the judicious Herrera, Hist. General, dec. 5, lib. 1, cap. 2.

He was aware, that, if this spirit became contagious, it would be the ruin of the enterprise; and he thought it best to exterminate the gangrene; at once, and at whatever cost, than to wait until it had infected the whole system. He came to an extraordinary resolution.

Calling his men together, he told them that "a crisis had now arrived in their affairs, which it demanded all their courage to meet. No man should think of going forward in the expedition, who could not do so with his whole heart, or who had the least misgiving as to its success. If any repented of his share in it, it was not too late to turn back. San Miguel was but poorly garrisoned, and he should be glad to see it in greater strength. Those who chose might return to this place, and they should be entitled to the same proportion of lands and Indian vassals as the present residents. With the rest, were they few or many, who chose to take their chance with him, he should pursue the adventure to the end." [10]

It was certainly a remarkable proposal for a commander, who was ignorant of the amount of disaffection in his ranks, and who could not safely spare a single man from his force, already far too feeble for the undertaking. Yet, by insisting on the wants of the little colony of San Miguel, he afforded a decent pretext for the secession of the malecontents, and swept away the barrier of shame which might have still held them in the camp. Notwithstanding the fair opening thus afforded, there were but few, nine in all, who availed themselves of the general's permission. Four of these belonged to the infantry, and five to the horse. The rest loudly declared their resolve to go forward with their brave leader; and, if there were some whose voices were faint amidst the general acclamation, they, at least, relinquished the right of complaining hereafter, since they had voluntarily rejected the permission to return.[11] This stroke of policy in their sagacious captain was attended with the best effects. He had winnowed out the few grains of discontent, which, if left to themselves, might have fermented in secret till the whole mass had swelled into mutiny. Cortés had compelled his men to go forward heartily in his enterprise, by burning their vessels, and thus cutting off the only means of retreat. Pizarro, on the other hand, threw open the gates to the disaffected and facilitated their departure. Both judged right, under their peculiar circumstances, and both were perfectly successful.

Feeling himself strengthened, instead of weakened, by his loss, Pizarro now resumed his march, and, on the second day, arrived before a place called Zaran, situated in a fruitful valley among the mountains. Some of the inhabitants had been drawn off to swell the levies of Atahuallpa. The

[10] "Que todos los que quiriesen bolverse á la ciudad de San Miguel y avecindarse alli demas de los vecinos que alli quedaban el los depositaria repartimientos de Indios con que se sortubiesen como lo habia hecho con los otros vecinos; é que con los Españoles quedasen, pocos ó muchos, iria á conquistar é pacificar la tierra en demanda y persecucion del camino que llevaba." Oviedo, Hist. de las Indias, MS., Parte 3, lib. 8, cap. 3.

[11] Ibid., MS., loc. cit.—Herrera, Hist. General, dec. 5, lib. 1, cap. 2.—Xerez, Conq. del Peru, ap. Barcia, tom. III. p. 187.

Spaniards had repeated experience on their march of the oppressive ex-actions of the Inca, who had almost depopulated some of the valleys to obtain reinforcements for his army. The curaca of the Indian town, where Pizarro now arrived, received him with kindness and hospitality, and the troops were quartered as usual in one of the royal *tambos* or caravansaries, which were found in all the principal places.[12]

Yet the Spaniards saw no signs of their approach to the royal encamp-ment, though more time had already elapsed than was originally allowed for reaching it. Shortly before entering Zaran, Pizarro had heard that a Peruvian garrison was established in a place called Caxas, lying among the hills, at no great distance from his present quarters. He immediately despatched a small party under Hernando de Soto in that direction, to reconnoitre the ground, and bring him intelligence of the actual state of things, at Zaran, where he would halt until his officer's return.

Day after day passed on, and a week had elapsed before tidings were received of his companions, and Pizarro was becoming seriously alarmed for their fate, when on the eighth morning Soto appeared, bringing with him an envoy from the Inca himself. He was a person of rank, and was attended by several followers of inferior condition. He had met the Span-iards at Caxas, and now accompanied them on their return, to deliver his sovereign's message, with a present to the Spanish commander. The pres-ent consisted of two fountains, made of stone, in the form of fortresses; some fine stuffs of woollen embroidered with gold and silver; and a quan-tity of goose-flesh, dried and seasoned in a peculiar manner, and much used as a perfume, in a pulverized state, by the Peruvian nobles.[13] The Indian ambassador came charged also with his master's greeting to the strangers, whom Atahuallpa welcomed to his country, and invited to visit him in his camp among the mountains.[14]

Pizarro well understood that the Inca's object in this diplomatic visit was less to do him courtesy, than to inform himself of the strength and condition of the invaders. But he was well pleased with the embassy, and

---

[12] Conq. i Pob. del Piru, MS.

[13] "Dos Fortaleças, à manera de Fuente, figuradas en Piedra, con que beba, i dos cargas de Patos secos, desollados, para que hechos polvos, se sahume con ellos, porque asi se usa entre los Señores de su Tierra: i que le embiaba à decir, que èl tiene volun-tad de ser su Amigo, i esperalle de Paz en Caxamalca." Xerez, Conq. del Peru, ap. Barcia, tom. III. p. 189.

[14] Pedro Pizarro, Descub. y Conq., MS.—Oviedo, Hist. de las Indias, MS., Parte 3, lib. 8, cap. 3.—Relacion del Primer. Descub., MS.—Xerez, Conq. del Peru, ap. Barcia, tom. III. p. 189.

Garcilasso de la Vega tells us that Atahuallpa's envoy addressed the Spanish com-mander in the most humble and deprecatory manner, as Son of the Sun and of the great God Viracocha. He adds, that he was loaded with a prodigious present of all kinds of game, living and dead, gold and silver vases, emeralds, turquoises, &c., &c., enough to furnish out the finest chapter of the Arabian Nights. (Com. Real., Parte 2, lib. 1, cap. 19.) It is extraordinary that none of the Conquerors, who had a quick eye for these dainties, should allude to them! One cannot but suspect that the "old uncle" was amusing himself at his young nephew's expense; and, as it has proved, at the expense of most of his readers, who receive the Inca's fairy tales as historic facts.

dissembled his consciousness of its real purpose. He caused the Peruvian to be entertained in the best manner the camp could afford, and paid him the respect, says one of the Conquerors, due to the ambassador of so great a monarch.[15] Pizarro urged him to prolong his visit for some days, which the Indian envoy declined, but made the most of his time while there, by gleaning all the information he could in respect to the uses of every strange article which he saw, as well as the object of the white men's visit to the land, and the quarter whence they came.

The Spanish captain satisfied his curiosity in all these particulars. The intercourse with the natives, it may be here remarked, was maintained by means of two of the youths who had accompanied the Conquerors on their return home from their preceding voyage. They had been taken by Pizarro to Spain, and, as much pains had been bestowed on teaching them the Castilian, they now filled the office of interpreters, and opened an easy communication with their countrymen. It was of inestimable service; and well did the Spanish commander reap the fruits of his forecast.[16]

On the departure of the Peruvian messenger, Pizarro presented him with a cap of crimson cloth, some cheap but showy ornaments of glass, and other toys, which he had brought for the purpose from Castile. He charged the envoy to tell his master, that the Spaniards came from a powerful prince, who dwelt far beyond the waters; that they had heard much of the fame of Atahuallpa's victories, and were come to pay their respects to him, and to offer their services by aiding him with their arms against his enemies; and he might be assured, they would not halt on the road, longer than was necessary, before presenting themselves before him.

Pizarro now received from Soto a full account of his late expedition. That chief, on entering Caxas, found the inhabitants mustered in hostile array, as if to dispute his passage. But the cavalier soon convinced them of his pacific intentions, and, laying aside their menacing attitude, they received the Spaniards with the same courtesy which had been shown them in most places on their march.

Here Soto found one of the royal officers, employed in collecting the tribute for the government. From this functionary he learned that the Inca was quartered with a large army at Caxamalca, a place of considerable size on the other side of the Cordillera, where he was enjoying the luxury of the warm baths, supplied by natural springs, for which it was

[15] "I mandò, que le diesen de comer à el, i à los que con èl venian, i todo lo que huviesen menester, i fuesen bien aposentados, como Embajadores de tan Gran Señor." Xerez, Conq. del Peru, ap. Barcia, tom. III. p. 189.

[16] "Los Indios de la tierra se entendian muy bien con los Españoles, porque aquellos mochachos Indios que en el descubrimiento de la tierra Pizarro truxo á España, entendian muy bien nuestra lengua, y los tenia alli, con los cuales se entendia muy bien con todos los naturales de la tierra." (Relacion del Primer. Descub., MS.) Yet it is a proof of the ludicrous blunders into which the Conquerors were perpetually falling that Pizarro's secretary constantly confounds the Inca's name with that of his capital. Huayna Capac, he always styles "old Cuzco," and his son Huascar "young Cuzco."

then famous, as it is at the present day. The cavalier gathered, also, much important information in regard to the resources and the general policy of government, the state maintained by the Inca, and the stern severity with which obedience to the law was everywhere enforced. He had some opportunity of observing this for himself, as, on entering the village, he saw several Indians hanging dead by their heels, having been executed for some violence offered to the Virgins of the Sun, of whom there was a convent in the neighborhood.[17]

From Caxas, De Soto had passed to the adjacent town of Guancabamba, much larger, more populous, and better built than the preceding. The houses, instead of being made of clay baked in the sun, were many of them constructed of solid stone, so nicely put together, that it was impossible to detect the line of junction. A river, which passed through the town, was traversed by a bridge, and the high road of the Incas, which crossed this district, was far superior to that which the Spaniards had seen on the sea-board. It was raised in many places, like a causeway, paved with heavy stone flags, and bordered by trees that afforded a grateful shade to the passenger, while streams of water were conducted through aqueducts along the sides to slake his thirst. At certain distances, also, they noticed small houses, which, they were told, were for the accommodation of the traveller, who might thus pass, without inconvenience, from one end of the kingdom to the other.[18] In another quarter they beheld one of those magazines destined for the army, filled with grain, and with articles of clothing; and at the entrance of the town was a stone building, occupied by a public officer, whose business it was to collect the tolls or duties on various commodities brought into the place, or carried out of it.[19]—These accounts of De Soto not only confirmed all that the Spaniards had heard of the Indian empire, but greatly raised their ideas of its resources and domestic policy. They might well have shaken the confidence of hearts less courageous.

Pizarro, before leaving his present quarters, despatched a messenger to San Miguel with particulars of his movements, sending, at the same time, the articles received from the Inca, as well as those obtained at different places on the route. The skill shown in the execution of some of these fabrics excited great admiration, when sent to Castile. The fine woollen cloths, especially, with their rich embroidery, were pronounced equal to

[17] "A la entrada del Pueblo havia ciertos Indios ahorcados de los pies: i supo de este Principal, que Atabalipa los mandò matar, porque uno de ellos entrò en la Casa de las Mugeres à dormir con una: al qual, i à todos los porteros que consintieron, ahorcò." Xerez, Conq. del Peru, ap. Barcia, tom. III. p. 188.

[18] "Van por este camino caños de agua de donde los caminantes beben, traidos de sus nacimientos de otras partes, y a cada jornada una Casa á manera de Venta donde se aposentan los que van é vienen." Oviedo, Hist. de las Indias, MS., Parte 3, lib. 8, cap. 3.

[19] "A la entrada de este Camino en el Pueblo de Cajas esta una casa al principio de una puente donde reside una guarde que recibe el Portazgo de todos los que van e vienen, é paganló en la misma cosa que llevan, y ninguno puede sacar carga del Pueblo sino la mete, y esta costumbre es alli antigua." Oviedo, Hist. de las Indias, MS., ubi supra.

silk, from which it was not easy to distinguish them. It was probably the delicate wool of the vicuña, none of which had then been seen in Europe.[20]

Pizarro, having now acquainted himself with the most direct route to Caxamalca,—the Caxamarca of the present day,—resumed his march, taking a direction nearly south. The first place of any size at which he halted was Motupe, pleasantly situated in a fruitful valley, among hills of no great elevation, which cluster round the base of the Cordilleras. The place was deserted by its curaca, who, with three hundred of its warriors, had gone to join the standard of their Inca. Here the general, notwithstanding his avowed purpose to push forward without delay, halted four days. The tardiness of his movements can be explained only by the hope, which he may have still entertained of being joined by further reinforcements before crossing the Cordilleras. None such appeared, however; and advancing across a country in which tracts of sandy plain were occasionally relieved by a broad expanse of verdant meadow, watered by natural streams and still more abundantly by those brought through artificial channels, the troops at length arrived at the borders of a river. It was broad and deep, and the rapidity of the current opposed more than ordinary difficulty to the passage. Pizarro, apprehensive lest this might be disputed by the natives on the opposite bank, ordered his brother Hernando to cross over with a small detachement under cover of night, and secure a safe landing for the rest of the troops. At break of day Pizarro made preparations for his own passage, by hewing timber in the neighboring woods, and constructing a sort of floating bridge, on which before nightfall the whole company passed in safety, the horses swimming, being led by the bridle. It was a day of severe labor, and Pizarro took his own share in it freely, like a common soldier, having ever a word of encouragement to say to his followers.

On reaching the opposite side, they learned from their comrades that the people of the country, instead of offering resistance, had fled in dismay. One of them, having been taken and brought before Hernando Pizarro, refused to answer the questions put to him respecting the Inca and his army; till, being put to the torture, he stated that Atahuallpa was encamped, with his whole force, in three separate divisions, occupying the high grounds and plains of Caxamalca. He further stated, that the Inca was aware of the approach of the white men and of their small number, and that he was purposely decoying them into his own quarters, that he might have them more completely in his power.

This account, when reported by Hernando to his brother, caused the latter much anxiety. As the timidity of the peasantry, however, gradually wore off, some of them mingled with the troops, and among them the curaca or principal person of the village. He had himself visited the royal

[20] "Piezas de lana de la tierra, que era cosa mucho de ver segun su primer é gentileza, e no se sabian determinar si era seda ó lana segun su fineza con muchas labores i figuras de oro de martillo de tal manera asentado en la ropa que era cosa de marabillar." Oviedo, Hist. de las Indias, MS., Parte 3, lib. 8, cap. 4.

camp, and he informed the general that Atahuallpa lay at the strong town of Guamachucho, twenty leagues or more south of Caxamalca, with an army of at least fifty thousand men.

These contradictory statements greatly perplexed the chieftain; and he proposed to one of the Indians who had borne him company during a great part of the march, to go as a spy into the Inca's quarters, and bring him intelligence of his actual position, and, as far as he could learn them, of his intentions towards the Spaniards. But the man positively declined this dangerous service, though he professed his willingness to go as an authorized messenger of the Spanish commander.

Pizarro acquiesced in this proposal, and instructed his envoy to assure the Inca that he was advancing with all convenient speed to meet him. He was to acquaint the monarch with the uniformly considerate conduct of the Spaniards towards his subjects, in their progress through the land, and to assure him that they were now coming in full confidence of finding in him the same amicable feelings towards themselves. The emissary was particularly instructed to observe if the strong passes on the road were defended, or if any preparations of a hostile character were to be discerned. This last intelligence he was to communicate to the general by means of two or three nimble-footed attendants, who were to accompany him on his mission.[21]

Having taken this precaution, the wary commander again resumed his march, and at the end of three days reached the base of the mountain rampart, behind which lay the ancient town of Caxamalca. Before him rose the stupendous Andes, rock piled upon rock, their skirts below dark with evergreen forests, varied here and there by terraced patches of cultivated garden, with the peasant's cottage clinging to their shaggy sides, and their crests of snow glittering high in the heavens,—presenting altogether such a wild chaos of magnificence and beauty as no other mountain scenery in the world can show. Across this tremendous rampart, through a labyrinth of passes, easily capable of defence by a handful of men against an army, the troops were now to march. To the right ran a broad and level road, with its border of friendly shades, and wide enough for two carriages to pass abreast. It was one of the great routes leading to Cuzco, and seemed by its pleasant and easy access to invite the way-worn soldier to choose it in preference to the dangerous mountain defiles. Many were accordingly of opinion that the army should take this course, and abandon the original destination to Caxamalca. But such was not the decision of Pizarro.

The Spaniards had everywhere proclaimed their purpose, he said, to visit the Inca in his camp. This purpose had been communicated to the Inca himself. To take an opposite direction now would only be to draw on them the imputation of cowardice, and to incur Atahuallpa's contempt. No alternative remained but to march straight across the sierra to

[21] Oviedo, Hist. de las Indias, MS., Parte 3, lib. 8, cap. 4.—Conq. i Pob. del Piru, MS.—Relacion del Primer. Descub., MS.—Xerez. Conq. del Peru, ap Barcia, tom. III. p. 190.

his quarters "Let every one of you," said the bold cavalier, "take heart and go forward like a good soldier, nothing daunted by the smallness of your numbers. For in the greatest extremity God ever fights for his own; and doubt not he will humble the pride of the heathen, and bring him to the knowledge of the true faith, the great end and object of the Conquest." [22]

Pizarro, like Cortés, possessed a good share of that frank and manly eloquence which touches the heart of the soldier more than the parade of rhetoric or the finest flow of elocution. He was a soldier himself, and partook in all the feelings of the soldier, his joys, his hopes, and his disappointments. He was not raised by rank and education above sympathy with the humblest of his followers. Every chord in their bosoms vibrated with the same pulsations as his own, and the conviction of this gave him a mastery over them. "Lead on," they shouted, as he finished his brief but animating address, "lead on wherever you think best. We will follow with good-will, and you shall see that we can do our duty in the cause of God and the King!" [23] There was no longer hesitation. All thoughts were now bent on the instant passage of the Cordilleras.

[22] "Que todos se animasen y esforzasen á hacer como de ellos esperaba y como buenos españoles lo suelen hacer, é que no les pusiese temor la multitud que se decia que habia de gente ni el poco numero de los cristianos, que aunque menos fuesen é mayor el egercito contrario, la ayuda de Dios es mucho mayor, y en las mayores necesidades socorre y faborece a los suyos para desbaratar y abajar la soberbia de los infieles è traerlos en conocimiento de nuestra Sta fe catolica." Oviedo, Hist. de las Indias, MS., Parte 3, lib. 8, cap. 4.

[23] "Todos digeron que fuese por el Camino que quisiese i viese que mas convenia, que todos le seguirian con buena voluntad é obra al timepo del efecto, y veria lo que cada uno de ellos haria en servicio de Dios é de su Magestad." Ibid., MS., loc cit.

CHAPTER IV

SEVERE PASSAGE OF THE ANDES—EMBASSIES FROM ATAHUALLPA—THE
SPANIARDS REACH CAXAMALCA—EMBASSY TO THE INCA—INTER-
VIEW WITH THE INCA—DESPONDENCY OF THE SPANIARDS

1532

THAT night Pizarro held a council of his principal officers, and it was determined that he should lead the advance, consisting of forty horse and
sixty foot, and reconnoitre the ground; while the rest of the company,
under his brother Hernando, should occupy their present position till
they received further orders.

At early dawn the Spanish general and his detachment were under
arms, and prepared to breast the difficulties of the sierra. These proved
even greater than had been foreseen. The path had been conducted in the
most judicious manner round the rugged and precipitous sides of the
mountains, so as best to avoid the natural impediments presented by the
ground. But it was necessarily so steep, in many places, that the cavalry
were obliged to dismount, and, scrambling up as they could, to lead their
horses by the bridle. In many places, too, where some huge crag or eminence overhung the road, this was driven to the very verge of the precipice; and the traveller was compelled to wind along the narrow ledge of
rock, scarcely wide enough for his single steed, where a misstep would
precipitate him hundreds, nay, thousands, of feet into the dreadful abyss!
The wild passes of the sierra, practicable for the half-naked Indian, and
even for the sure and circumspect mule,—an animal that seems to have
been created for the roads of the Cordilleras,—were formidable to the
man-at-arms encumbered with his panoply of mail. The tremendous fis-
sures or *quebradas*, so frightful in this mountain chain, yawned open, as
if the Andes had been split asunder by some terrible convulsion, showing
a broad expanse of the primitive rock on their sides, partially mantled
over with the spontaneous vegetation of ages; while their obscure depths
furnished a channel for the torrents, that, rising in the heart of the sierra,
worked their way gradually into light, and spread over the savannas and
green valleys of the *tierra caliente* on their way to the great ocean.

Many of these passes afforded obvious points of defence; and the Spaniards, as they entered the rocky defiles, looked with apprehension lest
they might rouse some foe from his ambush. This apprehension was
heightened, as, at the summit of a steep and narrow gorge, in which they
were engaged, they beheld a strong work, rising like a fortress, and
frowning, as it were, in gloomy defiance on the invaders. As they drew
near this building, which was of solid stone, commanding an angle of the

road, they almost expected to see the dusky forms of the warriors rise over the battlements, and to receive their tempest of missiles on their bucklers; for it was in so strong a position, that a few resolute men might easily have held there an army at bay. But they had the satisfaction to find the place untenanted, and their spirits were greatly raised by the conviction that the Indian monarch did not intend to dispute their passage, when it would have been easy to do so with success.

Pizarro now sent orders to his brother to follow without delay; and, after refreshing his men, continued his toilsome ascent, and before nightfall reached an eminence crowned by another fortress, of even greater strength than the preceding. It was built of solid masonry, the lower part excavated from the living rock, and the whole work executed with skill not inferior to that of the European architect.[1]

Here Pizarro took up his quarters for the night. Without waiting for the arrival of the rear, on the following morning he resumed his march, leading still deeper into the intricate gorges of the sierra. The climate had gradually changed, and the men and horses, especially the latter, suffered severely from the cold, so long accustomed as they had been to the sultry climate of the tropics.[2] The vegetation also had changed its character; and the magnificent timber which covered the lower level of the country had gradually given way to the funereal forest of pine, and, as they rose still higher, to the stunted growth of numberless Alpine plants, whose hardy natures found a congenial temperature in the icy atmosphere of the more elevated regions. These dreary solitudes seemed to be nearly abandoned by the brute creation as well as by man. The light-footed vicuña, roaming in its native state, might be sometimes seen looking down from some airy cliff, where the foot of the hunter dared not venture. But instead of the feathered tribes whose gay plumage sparkled in the deep glooms of the tropical forests, the adventurers now beheld only the great bird of the Andes, the loathsome condor, who, sailing high above the clouds, followed with doleful cries in the track of the army, as if guided by instinct in the path of blood and carnage.

At length they reached the crest of the Cordillera, where it spreads out into a bold and bleak expanse, with scarce the vestige of vegetation, except what is afforded by the *pajonal*, a dried yellow grass, which, as it is seen from below, encircling the base of the snow-covered peaks, looks, with its brilliant straw-color lighted up in the rays of an ardent sun, like a setting of gold round pinnacles of burnished silver. The land was sterile, as usual in mining districts, and they were drawing near the once famous gold quarries on the way to Caxamalca;

> "Rocks rich in gems, and mountains big with mines,
> That on the high equator ridgy rise."

[1] "Tan ancha la Cerca como qualquier Fortaleça de España, con sus Puertas: que si en esta Tierra oviese los Maestros, i Herramientas de España, no pudiera ser mejor labrada la Cerca." Xerez, Conq. del Peru, ap. Barcia, tom. III. p. 192.

[2] "Es tanto el frio que hace en esta Sierra, que como los Caballos venian hechos al calor, que en los Valles hacia, algunos de ellos se resfriaron." Ibid., p. 191.

Here Pizarro halted for the coming up of the rear. The air was sharp and frosty; and the soldiers, spreading their tents, lighted fires, and, huddling round them, endeavored to find some repose after their laborious march.[3]

They had not been long in these quarters, when a messenger arrived, one of those who had accompanied the Indian envoy sent by Pizarro to Atahuallpa. He informed the general that the road was free from enemies, and that an embassy from the Inca was on its way to the Castilian camp. Pizarro now sent back to quicken the march of the rear, as he was unwilling that the Peruvian envoy should find him with his present diminished numbers. The rest of the army were not far distant, and not long after reached the encampment.

In a short time the Indian embassy also arrived, which consisted of one of the Inca nobles and several attendants, bringing a welcome present of llamas to the Spanish commander. The Peruvian bore, also, the greetings of his master, who wished to know when the Spaniards would arrive at Caxamalca, that he might provide suitable refreshments for them. Pizarro learned that the Inca had left Guamachucho, and was now lying with a small force in the neighborhood of Caxamalca, at a place celebrated for its natural springs of warm water. The Peruvian was an intelligent person, and the Spanish commander gathered from him many particulars respecting the late contests which had distracted the empire.

As the envoy vaunted in lofty terms the military prowess and resources of his sovereign, Pizarro thought it politic to show that it had no power to overawe him. He expressed his satisfaction at the triumphs of Atahuallpa, who, he acknowledged, had raised himself high in the rank of Indian warriors. But he was as inferior, he added with more policy than politeness, to the monarch who ruled over the white men, as the petty curacas of the country were inferior to him. This was evident from the ease with which a few Spaniards had overrun this great continent, subduing one nation after another, that had offered resistance to their arms. He had been led by the fame of Atahuallpa to visit his dominions, and to offer him his services in his wars; and, if he were received by the Inca in the same friendly spirit with which he came, he was willing, for the aid he could render him, to postpone awhile his passage across the country to the opposite seas. The Indian, according to the Castilian accounts, listened with awe to this strain of glorification from the Spanish commander. Yet it is possible that the envoy was a better diplomatist than they imagined; and that he understood it was only the game of brag at which he was playing with his more civilized antagonist.[4]

[3] "É aposentaronse los Españoles en sus toldos ó pabellones de algodon de la tierra que llevaban, é haciendo fuegos para defenderse del mucho frio que en aquella Sierra hacen, porque sin ellos no se pudieron valer sin padecer mucho trabajo; y segun à los cristianos les pareció, y aun como era lo cierto, no podia haber mas frio en parte de España en invierno." Oviedo, Hist. de las Indias, MS., Parte 3, lib. 8, cap. 4.

[4] Xerez, Conq. del Perú, ap. Barcia, tom. III. p. 193.—Oviedo, Hist. de las Indias MS., Parte 3, lib. 8, cap. 5.

On the succeeding morning, at an early hour, the troops were again on their march, and for two days were occupied in threading the airy defiles of the Cordilleras. Soon after beginning their descent on the eastern side, another emissary arrived from the Inca, bearing a message of similar import to the preceding, and a present, in like manner, of Peruvian sheep. This was the same noble that had visited Pizarro in the valley. He now came in more state, quaffing *chicha*—the fermented juice of the maize— from golden goblets borne by his attendants, which sparkled in the eyes of the rapacious adventurers.[5]

While he was in the camp, the Indian messenger, originally sent by Pizarro to the Inca, returned, and no sooner did he behold the Peruvian, and the honorable reception which he met with from the Spaniards, than he was filled with wrath, which would have vented itself in personal violence, but for the interposition of the by-standers. It was hard, he said, that this Peruvian dog should be thus courteously treated, when he himself had nearly lost his life on a similar mission among his countrymen. On reaching the Inca's camp, he had been refused admission to his presence, on the ground that he was keeping a fast and could not be seen. They had paid no respect to his assertion that he came as an envoy from the white men, and would, probably, not have suffered him to escape with life, if he had not assured them that any violence offered to him would be retaliated in full measure on the persons of the Peruvian envoys, now in the Spanish quarters. There was no doubt, he continued, of the hostile intentions of Atahuallpa; for he was surrounded with a powerful army, strongly encamped about a league from Caxamalca, while that city was entirely evacuated by its inhabitants.

To all this the Inca's envoy coolly replied, that Pizarro's messenger might have reckoned on such a reception as he had found, since he seemed to have taken with him no credentials of his mission. As to the Inca's fast, that was true; and, although he would doubtless have seen the messenger, had he known there was one from the strangers, yet it was not safe to disturb him at these solemn seasons, when engaged in his religious duties. The troops by whom he was surrounded were not numerous, considering that the Inca was at that time carrying on an important war; and as to Caxamalca, it was abandoned by the inhabitants in order to make room for the white men, who were so soon to occupy it.[6]

This explanation, however plausible, did not altogether satisfy the general; for he had too deep a conviction of the cunning of Atahuallpa,

---

[5] "Este Embajador traìa servicio de Señor, i cinco, ò seis Vasos de Oro fino, con que bebia, i con ellos daba à beber à los Españoles de la Chicha que traìa." Xerez, Conq. del Peru, ap. Barcia, tom. III, p. 193.—Oviedo, Hist. de las Indias, MS., ubi supra.

The latter author, in this part of his work, has done little more than make a transcript of that of Xerez. His indorsement of Pizarro's secretary, however, is of value, from the fact that, with less temptation to misstate or overstate he enjoyed excellent opportunities for information.

[6] Xerez, Conq. del Peru, ap. Barcia, tom. III. p. 194.—Oviedo, Hist. de las Indias, MS., ubi supra.

whose intentions towards the Spaniards he had long greatly distrusted. As he proposed, however, to keep on friendly relations with the monarch for the present, it was obviously not his cue to manifest suspicion. Affecting, therefore, to give full credit to the explanation of the envoy, he dismissed him with reiterated assurances of speedily presenting himself before the Inca.

The descent of the sierra, though the Andes are less precipitous on their eastern side than towards the west, was attended with difficulties almost equal to those of the upward march; and the Spaniards felt no little satisfaction, when, on the seventh day, they arrived in view of the valley of Caxamalca, which, enamelled with all the beauties of cultivation, lay unrolled like a rich and variegated carpet of verdure, in strong contrast with the dark forms of the Andes, that rose up everywhere around it. The valley is of an oval shape, extending about five leagues in length by three in breadth. It was inhabited by a population of a superior character to any which the Spaniards had met on the other side of the mountains, as was argued by the superior style of their attire, and the greater cleanliness and comfort visible both in their persons and dwellings.[7] As far as the eye could reach, the level tract exhibited the show of a diligent and thrifty husbandry. A broad river rolled through the meadows, supplying facilities for copious irrigation by means of the usual canals and subterraneous aqueducts. The land, intersected by verdant hedge-rows, was checkered with patches of various cultivation; for the soil was rich, and the climate, if less stimulating than that of the sultry regions of the coast, was more favorable to the hardy products of the temperate latitudes. Below the adventurers, with its white houses glittering in the sun, lay the little city of Caxamalca, like a sparkling gem on the dark skirts of the sierra. At the distance of about a league farther, across the valley, might be seen columns of vapor rising up towards the heavens, indicating the place of the famous hot baths, much frequented by the Peruvian princes. And here, too, was a spectacle less grateful to the eyes of the Spaniards; for along the slope of the hills a white cloud of pavilions was seen covering the ground, as thick as snow-flakes, for the space, apparently, of several miles. "It filled us all with amazement," exclaims one of the Conquerors, "to behold the Indians occupying so proud a position! So many tents, so well appointed, as were never seen in the Indies till now! The spectacle caused something like confusion and even fear in the stoutest bosom. But it was too late to turn back, or to betray the least sign of weakness, since the natives in our own company would, in such case, have been the first to rise upon us. So, with as bold a countenance as we could, after coolly surveying the ground, we prepared for our entrance into Caxamalca."[8]

[7] Xerez, Conq. del Peru, ap. Barcia, tom. III. p. 195.

[8] "Y eran tantas las tiendas que parecian, que cierto nos puso harto espanto, porque no pensabamos que Indios pudiesen tener tan soberbia estancia, ni tantas tiendas, ni tan á punto, lo cual hasta alli en las Indias nunca se vió, que nos causó á todos los Españoles harta confusion y temor; aunque no convenia mostrarse, no menos vol-

What were the feelings of the Peruvian monarch we are not informed, when he gazed on the martial cavalcade of the Christians, as, with banners streaming, and bright panoplies glistening in the rays of the evening sun, it emerged from the dark depths of the sierra, and advanced in hostile array over the fair domain, which, to this period, had never been trodden by other foot than that of the red man. It might be, as several of the reports had stated, that the Inca had purposely decoyed the adventurers into the heart of his populous empire, that he might envelope them with his legions, and the more easily become master of their property and persons.[9] Or was it from a natural feeling of curiosity, and relying on their professions of friendship, that he had thus allowed them, without any attempt at resistance, to come into his presence? At all events, he could hardly have felt such confidence in himself, as not to look with apprehension, mingled with awe, on the mysterious strangers, who, coming from an unknown world, and possessed of such wonderful gifts, had made their way across mountain and valley, in spite of every obstacle which man and nature had opposed to them.

Pizarro, meanwhile, forming his little corps into three divisions, now moved forward, at a more measured pace, and in order of battle, down the slopes that led towards the Indian city. As he drew near, no one came out to welcome him; and he rode through the streets without meeting with a living thing, or hearing a sound, except the echoes, sent back from the deserted dwellings, of the tramp of the soldiery.

It was a place of considerable size, containing about ten thousand inhabitants, somewhat more, probably, than the population assembled at this day within the walls of the modern city of Caxamalca.[10] The houses, for the most part, were built of clay, hardened in the sun; the roofs thatched, or of timber. Some of the more ambitious dwellings were of hewn stone; and there was a convent in the place, occupied by the Virgins of the Sun, and a temple dedicated to the same tutelar deity, which

ver atras, porque si alguna flaqueza en nosotros sintieran, los mismos Indios que llevabamos nos mataran, y ansi con animoso semblante, despues de haber muy bien atalayado el pueblo y tiendas que he dicho, abajamos por el valle abajo, y entramos en el pueblo de Cajamalca." Relacion del Primer. Descub., MS.

[9] This was evidently the opinion of the old Conqueror, whose imperfect manuscript forms one of the best authorities for this portion of our narrative. "Teniendonos en muy poco, y no haciendo cuenta que 190 hombres le habian de ofender, dió lugar y consintió que pasasemos por aquel paso y por otros muchos tan malos como él, porque realmente, á lo que despues se supo y averiguó, su intencion era vernos y preguntarnos, de donde veniamos? y quien nos habia hechado alli? y que queriamos? *Porque era muy sabio y discreto, y aunque sin luz ni escriptura, amigo de saber y de sotil entendimiento;* y despues de holgadose con nosotros, tomarnos los caballos y las cosas que á el mas le aplacian, y sacrificar á los demas." Relacion del Primer. Descub., MS.

[10] According to Stevenson, this population, which is of a very mixed character, amounts, or did amount some thirty years ago, to about seven thousand. That sagacious traveller gives an animated description of the city, in which he resided some time, and which he seems to have regarded with peculiar predilection. Yet it does not hold probably the relative rank at the present day, that it did in that of the Incas. Residence in South America, vol. II. p. 131.

last was hidden in the deep embowering shades of a grove on the skirts
of the city. On the quarter towards the Indian camp was a square—if
square it might be called, which was almost triangular in form—of an
immense size, surrounded by low buildings. These consisted of capacious
halls, with wide doors or openings communicating with the square. They
were probably intended as a sort of barracks for the Inca's soldiers.[11] At
the end of the *plaza*, looking towards the country, was a fortress of stone,
with a stairway leading from the city, and a private entrance from the
adjoining suburbs. There was still another fortress on the rising ground
which commanded the town, built of hewn stone, and encompassed by
three circular walls,—or rather one and the same wall, which wound up
spirally around it. It was a place of great strength, and the workmanship
showed a better knowledge of masonry, and gave a higher impression of
the architectural science of the people, than anything the Spaniards had
yet seen.[12]

It was late in the afternoon of the fifteenth of November, 1532, when
the Conquerors entered the city of Caxamalca. The weather, which had
been fair during the day, now threatened a storm, and some rain mingled
with hail—for it was unusually cold—began to fall.[13] Pizarro, however,
was so anxious to ascertain the dispositions of the Inca, that he determined to send an embassy, at once, to his quarters. He selected for this,
Hernando de Soto with fifteen horse, and, after his departure, conceiving
that the number was too small, in case of any unfriendly demonstrations
by the Indians, he ordered his brother Hernando to follow with twenty
additional troopers. This captain and one other of his party have left us
an account of the excursion.[14]

Between the city and the imperial camp was a causeway, built in a
substantial manner across the meadow land that intervened. Over this
the cavalry galloped at a rapid pace, and, before they had gone a league,
they came in front of the Peruvian encampment, where it spread along
the gentle slope of the mountains. The lances of the warriors were fixed in
the ground before their tents, and the Indian soldiers were loitering with-

[11] Carte de Hern. Pizarro, ap. Oviedo, Hist. de las Indias, MS., Parte 3, lib. 8, cap.
15.—Xerez, Conq. del Peru, ap. Barcia, tom. III. p. 195.

[12] "Fuerças son, que entre Indios no se han visto tales." Xerez, Conq. del Peru, ap.
Barcia, tom. III. p. 195.—Relacion del Primer. Descub., MS.

[13] "Desde à poco rato começo à llover, i caer graniço." (Xerez, Conq. del Peru,
ap. Barcia, tom. III. p. 195.) Caxamalca in the Indian tongue, signifies "place of
frost"; for the temperature, though usually bland and genial, is sometimes affected
by frosty winds from the east, very pernicious to vegetation. Stevenson, Residence
in South America, vol. II. p. 129.

[14] Carta de Hern. Pizarro, MS.

The Letter of Hernando Pizarro, addressed to the Royal Audience of St. Domingo,
gives a full account of the extraordinary events recorded in this and the ensuing
chapter, in which that cavalier took a prominent part. Allowing for the partialities
incident to a chief actor in the scenes he describes, no authority can rank higher.
The indefatigable Oviedo, who resided in St. Domingo, saw its importance, and
fortunately incorporated the document in his great work, Hist. de las Indias, MS.,
Parte 3, lib. 8 cap. 15.—The anonymous author of the Relacion del Primer. Descub.
MS., was also detached on this service.

out, gazing with silent astonishment at the Christian cavalcade, as with clangor of arms and shrill blast of trumpet it swept by, like some fearful apparition, on the wings of the wind.

The party soon came to a broad but shallow stream, which, winding through the meadow, formed a defence for the Inca's position. Across it was a wooden bridge; but the cavaliers, distrusting its strength, preferred to dash through the waters, and without difficulty gained the opposite bank. At battalion of Indian warriors was drawn up under arms on the farther side of the bridge, but they offered no molestation to the Spaniards; and these latter had strict orders from Pizarro—scarcely necessary in their present circumstances—to treat the natives with courtesy. One of the Indians pointed out the quarter occupied by the Inca.[15]

It was an open court-yard, with a light building or pleasure-house in the centre, having galleries running around it, and opening in the rear on a garden. The walls were covered with a shining plaster, both white and colored, and in the area before the edifice was seen a spacious tank or reservoir of stone, fed by aqueducts that supplied it with both warm and cold water.[16] A basin of hewn stone—it may be of a more recent construction—still bears, on the spot, the name of the "Inca's bath." [17] The court was filled with Indian nobles, dressed in gayly ornamented attire, in attendance on the monarch, and with women of the royal household. Amidst this assembly it was not difficult to distinguish the person of Atahuallpa, though his dress was simpler than that of his attendants. But he wore on his head the crimson *borla* or fringe, which, surrounding the forehead, hung down as low as the eyebrow. This was the well-known badge of Peruvian sovereignty, and had been assumed by the monarch only since the defeat of his brother Huascar. He was seated on a low stool or cushion, somewhat after the Morisco or Turkish fashion, and his nobles and principal officers stood around him, with great ceremony, holding the stations suited to their rank.[18]

The Spaniards gazed with much interest on the prince, of whose cruelty and cunning they had heard so much, and whose valor had secured to

[15] Pedro Pizarro, Descub. y Conq., MS.—Carta de Hern. Pizarro, MS.

[16] Xerez, Conq. del Peru, ap. Barcia, tom. III. p. 202.

"Y al estanque venian dos caños de agua, uno caliente y otro frio, y alli se templava la una con la otra, para quando el Señor se queria bañar ó sus mugeres que otra persona no osava entrar en el so pena de la vida." Pedro Pizarro Descub. y Conq., MS.

[17] Stevenson, Residence in South America, vol. II. p. 164.

[18] Xerez, Conq. del Peru, ap. Barcia, tom. III. p. 196.—Carta de Hern. Pizarro, MS.

The appearance of the Peruvian monarch is described in simple but animated style by the Conqueror so often quoted, one of the party. "Llegados al patio de la dicha casa que tenia delante della, vimos estar en medio de gran muchedumbre de Indios asentado aquel gran Señor Atabalica (de quien tanta noticia, y tantas cosas nos habian dicho) con una corona en la cabeza, y una borla que le salia della, y le cubria toda la frente, la cual era la insinia real, sentado en una sillecita muy baja del suelo, como los turcos y moros acostumbran sentarse, el cual estaba con tanta magestad y aparato cual nunca se ha visto jamas, porque estaba cercado de mas de seiscientos Señores de su tierra." Relacion del Primer. Descub., MS.

him the possession of the empire. But his countenance exhibited neither
the fierce passions nor the sagacity which had been ascribed to him; and,
though in his bearing he showed a gravity and a calm consciousness of
authority well becoming a king, he seemed to discharge all expression
from his features, and to discover only the apathy so characteristic of
the American races. On the present occasion, this must have been in part,
at least, assumed. For it is impossible that the Indian prince should not
have contemplated with curious interest a spectacle so strange, and, in
some respects, appalling, as that of these mysterious strangers, for
which no previous description could have prepared him.

Hernando Pizarro and Soto, with two or three only of their followers,
slowly rode up in front of the Inca; and the former, making a respectful
obeisance, but without dismounting, informed Atahuallpa that he came
as an ambassador from his brother, the commander of the white men, to
acquaint the monarch with their arrival in his city of Caxamalca. They
were the subjects of a mighty prince across the waters, and had come, he
said, drawn thither by the report of his great victories, to offer their services, and to impart to him the doctrines of the true faith which they
professed; and he brought an invitation from the general to Atahuallpa
that the latter would be pleased to visit the Spaniards in their present
quarters.

To all this the Inca answered not a word; nor did he make even a sign
of acknowledgment that he comprehended it; though it was translated
for him by Felipillo, one of the interpreters already noticed. He remained
silent, with his eyes fastened on the ground; but one of his nobles, standing by his side, answered, "It is well." [19] This was an embarrassing situation for the Spaniards, who seemed to be as wide from ascertaining the
real disposition of the Peruvian monarch towards themselves, as when the
mountains were between them.

In a courteous and respectful manner, Hernando Pizarro again broke
the silence by requesting the Inca to speak to them himself, and to inform
them what was his pleasure.[20] To this Atahuallpa condescended to reply,
while a faint smile passed over his features,—"Tell your captain that I
am keeping a fast, which will end to-morrow morning. I will then visit
him, with my chieftains. In the meantime, let him occupy the public
buildings on the square, and no other, till I come, when I will order what
shall be done." [21]

[19] "Las cuales por él oidas, con ser su inclinacion preguntarnos y saber de donde
veniamos, y que queriamos, y ver nuestras personas y caballos, tubo tanta serenidad
en el rostro, y tanta gravedad en su persona, que no quiso responder palabra á lo
que se le decia, salvo que un Señor de aquellos que estaban par de el respondia: bien
está." Relacion del Primer. Descub., MS.
[20] "Visto por el dicho Hernando Pizarro que él no hablaba, y que aquella tercera
persona respondia de suyo, tornó le á suplicar, que el hablase por su boca, y le
respondiese lo que quisiese." Ibid., MS., ubi supra.
[21] "El cual á esto volvió la cabeza á mirarle sonriendose y le dijo: Decid á ese
Capitan que os embia acá; que yo estoy en ayuno, y le acabo mañana, que en bebi-
endo una vez, yo iré con algunos destos principales mios á verme con el, que en tanto

Soto, one of the party present at this interview, as before noticed, was the best mounted and perhaps the best rider in Pizarro's troop. Observing that Atahuallpa looked with some interest on the fiery steed that stood before him, champing the bit and pawing the ground with the natural impatience of a war-horse, the Spaniard gave him the rein, and, striking his iron heel into his side, dashed furiously over the plain; then, wheeling him round and round, displayed all the beautiful movements of his charger, and his own excellent horsemanship. Suddenly checking him in full career, he brought the animal almost on his haunches, so near the person of the Inca, that some of the foam that flecked his horse's sides was thrown on the royal garments. But Atahuallpa maintained the same marble composure as before, though several of his soldiers, whom De Soto passed in the course, were so much disconcerted by it, that they drew back in manifest terror; an act of timidity for which they paid dearly, *if*, as the Spaniards assert, Atahuallpa caused them to be put to death that same evening for betraying such unworthy weakness to the strangers.[22]

Refreshments were now offered by the royal attendants to the Spaniards, which they declined, being unwilling to dismount. They did not refuse, however, to quaff the sparkling chicha from golden vases of extraordinary size, presented to them by the dark-eyed beauties of the harem.[23] Taking then a respectful leave of the Inca, the cavaliers rode back to Caxamalca, with many moody speculations on what they had seen; on the state and opulence of the Indian monarch; on the strength of his military array, their excellent appointments, and the apparent discipline in their ranks,—all arguing a much higher degree of civilization, and consequently of power, than anything they had witnessed in the lower regions of the country. As they contrasted all this with their own diminutive force, too far advanced, as they now were, for succour to reach them, they felt they had done rashly in throwing themselves into the midst of so formidable an empire, and were filled with gloomy forebodings of the result.[24] Their comrades in the camp soon caught the in-

él se aposente en esas casas que estan en la plaza que son comunes á todos, y que no entren en otra ninguna hasta que Yo vaya, que Yo mandaré lo que se ha de hacer." Ibid., MS., ubi supra.

In this singular interview I have followed the account of the cavalier who accompanied Hernando Pizarro, in preference to the latter, who represents himself as talking in a lordly key, that savours too much of the vaunt of the hidalgo.

[22] Pedro Pizarro, Descub. y Conq., MS.—Relacion del Primer. Descub., MS.

"I algunos Indios, con miedo, se desviaron de la Carrera, por lo qual Atabalipa los hiço luego matar." (Zarate, Conq. del Peru, lib. 2, cap. 4.)—Xerez states that Atahuallpa confessed this himself, in conversation with the Spaniards after he was taken prisoner.—Soto's charger might well have made the Indians start, if, as Balboa says, he took twenty feet at a leap, and this with a knight in armour on his back! Hist. du Perou, chap. 22.

[23] Relacion del Primer. Descub., MS.—Xerez, Conq. del Peru, ap. Barcia, tom. III. p. 196.

[24] "Hecho esto y visto y atalayado la grandeza del ejercito, y las tiendas que era bien de ver, nos bolvimos á donde el dicho capitan nos estabá esperando, harto espantados de lo que habiamos visto, habiendo y tomando entre nosotros muchos

fectious spirit of despondency, which was not lessened as night came on, and they beheld the watch-fires of the Peruvians lighting up the sides of the mountains, and glittering in the darkness, "as thick," says one who saw them, "as the stars of heaven." [25]

Yet there was one bosom in that little host which was not touched with the feeling either of fear or dejection. That was Pizarro's, who secretly rejoiced that he had now brought matters to the issue for which he had so long panted. He saw the necessity of kindling a similar feeling in his followers, or all would be lost. Without unfolding his plans, he went round among his men, beseeching them not to show faint hearts at this crisis, when they stood face to face with the foe whom they had been so long seeking. "They were to rely on themselves, and on that Providence which had carried them safe through so many fearful trials. It would not now desert them; and if numbers, however great, were on the side of their enemy, it mattered little when the arm of Heaven was on theirs." [26] The Spanish cavalier acted under the combined influence of chivalrous adventure and religious zeal. The latter was the most effective in the hour of peril; and Pizarro, who understood well the characters he had to deal with, by presenting the enterprise as a crusade, kindled the dying embers of enthusiasm in the bosoms of his followers, and restored their faltering courage.

He then summoned a council of his officers, to consider the plan of operations, or rather to propose to them the extraordinary plan on which he had himself decided. This was to lay an ambuscade for the Inca, and take him prisoner in the face of his whole army! It was a project full of peril,—bordering, as it might well seem, on desperation. But the circumstances of the Spaniards were desperate. Whichever way they turned, they were menaced by the most appalling dangers; and better was it bravely to confront the danger, than weakly to shrink from it, when there was no avenue for escape.

To fly was now too late. Whither could they fly? At the first signal of retreat, the whole army of the Inca would be upon them. Their movements would be anticipated by a foe far better acquainted with the intricacies of the sierra than themselves; the passes would be occupied, and they would be hemmed in on all sides; while the mere fact of this retro-

---

acuerdos y opiniones de lo que se debia hacer, estando todos con mucho temor por ser tan pocos, y estar tan metidos en la tierra donde no podiamos ser socorridos." (Relacion del Primer. Descub., MS.) Pedro Pizarro is honest enough to confirm this account of the consternation of the Spaniards. (Descub. y Conq., MS.) Fear was a strange sensation for the Castilian cavalier. But if he did not feel some touch of it on that occasion, he must have been akin to that doughty knight who, as Charles V. pronounced, "never could have snuffed a candle with his fingers.

[25] "Hecimos la guardia en la plaza, de donde se vian los fuegos del ejercito de los Indios, lo cual era cosa espantable, que como estaban en una ladera la mayor parte, y tan juntos unos de otros, no parecia sino un cielo muy estrellado." Relacion del Primer. Descub., MS.

[26] Xerez, Conq. del Peru, ap. Barcia, tom. III. p. 197.—Naharro, Relacion Sumaria, MS.

grade movement would diminish the confidence and with it the effective strength of his own men, while it doubled that of his enemy.

Yet to remain long inactive in his present position seemed almost equally perilous. Even supposing that Atahuallpa should entertain friendly feelings towards the Christians, they could not confide in the continuance of such feelings. Familiarity with the white men would soon destroy the idea of anything supernatural, or even superior, in their natures. He would feel contempt for their diminutive numbers. Their horses, their arms and showy appointments, would be an attractive bait in the eye of the barbaric monarch, and when conscious that he had the power to crush their possessors, he would not be slow in finding a pretext for it. A sufficient one had already occurred in the high-handed measures of the Conquerors, on their march through his dominions.

But what reason had they to flatter themselves that the Inca cherished such a disposition towards them? He was a crafty and unscrupulous prince, and, if the accounts they had repeatedly received on their march were true, had ever regarded the coming of the Spaniards with an evil eye. It was scarcely possible he should do otherwise. His soft messages had only been intended to decoy them across the mountains, where, with the aid of his warriors, he might readily overpower them. They were entangled in the toils which the cunning monarch had spread for them.

Their only remedy, then, was to turn the Inca's arts against himself; to take him, if possible, in his own snare. There was no time to be lost; for any day might bring back the victorious legions who had recently won his battles at the south, and thus make the odds against the Spaniards far greater than now.

Yet to encounter Atahuallpa in the open field would be attended with great hazard; and even if victorious, there would be little probability that the person of the Inca, of so much importance, would fall into the hands of the victors. The invitation he had so unsuspiciously accepted to visit them in their quarters afforded the best means for securing this desirable prize. Nor was the enterprise so desperate, considering the great advantages afforded by the character and weapons of the invaders, and the unexpectedness of the assault. The mere circumstance of acting on a concerted plan would alone make a small number more than a match for a much larger one. But it was not necessary to admit the whole of the Indian force into the city before the attack; and the person of the Inca once secured, his followers, astounded by so strange an event, were they few or many, would have no heart for further resistance;—and with the Inca once in his power, Pizarro might dictate laws to the empire.

In this daring project of the Spanish chief, it was easy to see that he had the brilliant exploit of Cortés in his mind, when he carried off the Aztec monarch in his capital. But that was not by violence,—at least not by open violence,—and it received the sanction, compulsory though it were, of the monarch himself. It was also true that the results in that case did not altogether justify a repetition of the experiment; since the people rose in a body to sacrifice both the prince and his kidnappers. Yet this was owing, in part, at least, to the indiscretion of the latter. The ex-periment in the outset was perfectly successful; and, could Pizarro once become master of the person of Atahuallpa, he trusted to his own discre-tion for the rest. It would, at least, extricate him from his present critical position, by placing in his power an inestimable guaranty for his safety; and if he could not make his own terms with the Inca at once, the arrival of reinforcements from home would, in all probability, soon enable him to do so.

Pizarro having concerted his plans for the following day, the council broke up, and the chief occupied himself with providing for the security of the camp during the night. The approaches to the town were defended; sentinels were posted at different points, especially on the summit of the fortress, where they were to observe the position of the enemy, and to re-port any movement that menaced the tranquillity of the night. After these precautions, the Spanish commander and his followers withdrew to their appointed quarters,—but not to sleep. At least, sleep must have come late to those who were aware of the decisive plan for the morrow; that morrow which was to be the crisis of their fate,—to crown their ambitious schemes with full success, or consign them to irretrievable ruin!

CHAPTER V

**⁂ESPERATE PLAN OF PIZARRO—ATAHUALLPA VISITS THE SPANIARDS—
HORRIBLE MASSACRE—THE INCA A PRISONER—CONDUCT OF THE
CONQUERORS—SPLENDID PROMISES OF THE INCA—DEATH OF
HUASCAR**

1532

THE clouds of the evening had passed away, and the sun rose bright on
the following morning, the most memorable epoch in the annals of Peru.
It was Saturday, the sixteenth of November, 1532. The loud cry of the
trumpet called the Spaniards to arms with the first streak of dawn; and
Pizarro, briefly acquainting them with the plan of the assault, made the
necessary dispositions.

The *plaza*, as mentioned in the preceding chapter, was defended on its
three sides by low ranges of buildings, consisting of spacious halls with
wide doors or vomitories opening into the square. In these halls he stationed his cavalry in two divisions, one under his brother Hernando, the
other under De Soto. The infantry he placed in another of the buildings,
reserving twenty chosen men to act with himself as occasion might require. Pedro de Candia, with a few soldiers and the artillery,—comprehending under this imposing name two small pieces of ordnance, called
falconets,—he established in the fortress. All received orders to wait at
their posts till the arrival of the Inca. After his entrance into the great
square, they were still to remain under cover, withdrawn from observation, till the signal was given by the discharge of a gun, when they were
to cry their war-cries, to rush out in a body from their covert, and, putting the Peruvians to the sword, bear off the person of the Inca. The
arrangement of the immense halls, opening on a level with the *plaza*,
seemed to be contrived on purpose for a *coup de théatre*. Pizarro particularly inculcated order and implicit obedience, that in the hurry of the
moment there should be no confusion. Everything depended on their acting with concert, coolness, and celerity.[1]

The chief next saw that their arms were in good order; and that the
breastplates of their horses were garnished with bells, to add by their
noise to the consternation of the Indians. Refreshments were, also, liberally provided, that the troops should be in condition for the conflict.
These arrangements being completed, mass was performed with great so-

[1] Pedro Pizarro, Descub. y Conq., MS.—Relacion del Primer. Descub., MS.—
Xerez, Conq. del Peru, ap. Barcia, tom. III. p. 197.—Carta de Hern. Pizarro, MS.—
Oviedo Hist. de las Indias, MS., Parte 3, lib. 8, cap. 7.

lemnity by the ecclesiastics who attended the expedition; the God or battles was invoked to spread his shield over the soldiers who were fighting to extend the empire of the Cross; and all joined with enthusiasm in the chant, *"Exsurge, Domine,"* "Rise, O Lord! and judge thine own cause." [2] One might have supposed them a company of martyrs, about to lay down their lives in defence of their faith, instead of a licentious band of adventurers, meditating one of the most atrocious acts of perfidy on the record of history! Yet, whatever were the vices of the Castilian cavalier, hypocrisy was not among the number. He felt that he was battling for the Cross, and under this conviction, exalted as it was at such a moment as this into the predominant impulse, he was blind to the baser motives which mingled with the enterprise. With feelings thus kindled to a flame of religious ardor, the soldiers of Pizarro looked forward with renovated spirits to the coming conflict; and the chieftain saw with satisfaction, that in the hour of trial his men would be true to their leader and themselves.

It was late in the day before any movement was visible in the Peruvian camp, where much preparation was making to approach the Christian quarters with due state and ceremony. A message was received from Atahuallpa, informing the Spanish commander that he should come with his warriors fully armed, in the same manner as the Spaniards had come to his quarters the night preceding. This was not an agreeable intimation to Pizarro, though he had no reason, probably, to expect the contrary. But to object might imply distrust, or, perhaps, disclose, in some measure, his own designs. He expressed his satisfaction, therefore, at the intelligence, assuring the Inca, that, come as he would, he would be received by him as a friend and brother.[3]

It was noon before the Indian procession was on its march, when it was seen occupying the great causeway for a long extent. In front came a large body of attendants, whose office seemed to be to sweep away every particle of rubbish from the road. High above the crowd appeared the Inca, borne on the shoulders of his principal nobles, while others of the same rank marched by the sides of his litter, displaying such a dazzling show of ornaments on their persons, that, in the language of one of the Conquerors, "they blazed like the sun." [4] But the greater part of the Inca's

---

[2] "Les Eclesiasticos i Religiosos se ocuparon toda aquella noche en oracion, pidiendo a Dios el mas conveniente suceso á su sagrado servicio, exaltacion de la fé é salvacion de tanto numero de almas, derramando muchas lagrimas i sangre en las disciplinas que tomaron. *Francisco Pizarro animó á los soldados con una mui cristiana platica que les hizo:* con que, i asegurarles los Eclesiasticos de parte de Dios i de su Madre Santisima la vitoria, amanecieron todos mui deseosos de dar la batalla, diciendo á voces, Exsurge Domine, et judica causam tuam." Naharro, Relacion Sumaria, MS.

[3] "El governador respondiò: Dì à tu Señor, que venga en hora buena como quisiere, que de la manera que viniere lo recebirè como Amigo, i Hermano." Xerez, Conq. del Peru, ap. Barcia, tom. III. p. 197.—Oviedo, Hist. de las Indias, MS., Parte 3, lib. 8, cap. 7.—Carta de Hern. Pizarro, MS.

[4] "Hera tanta la pateneria que traian d'oro y plata que hera cossa estraña lo que Reluzia con el Sol." Pedro Pizarro Descub. y Conq., MS.

forces mustered along the fields that lined the road, and were spread over
the broad meadows as far as the eye could reach.[5]

When the royal procession had arrived within half a mile of the city,
it came to a halt; and Pizarro saw with surprise that Atahuallpa was
preparing to pitch his tents, as if to encamp there. A messenger soon after
arrived, informing the Spaniards that the Inca would occupy his present
station the ensuing night, and enter the city on the following morning.

This intelligence greatly disturbed Pizarro, who had shared in the general impatience of his men at the tardy movements of the Peruvians. The
troops had been under arms since daylight, the cavalry mounted, and the
infantry at their post, waiting in silence the coming of the Inca. A profound stillness reigned throughout the town, broken only at intervals by
the cry of the sentinel from the summit of the fortress, as he proclaimed
the movements of the Indian army. Nothing, Pizarro well knew, was so
trying to the soldier as prolonged suspense, in a critical situation like the
present; and he feared lest his ardor might evaporate, and be succeeded
by that nervous feeling natural to the bravest soul at such a crisis, and
which, if not fear, is near akin to it.[6] He returned an answer, therefore,
to Atahuallpa, deprecating his change of purpose; and adding that he
had provided everything for his entertainment, and expected him that
night to sup with him.[7]

This message turned the Inca from his purpose; and, striking his tents
again, he resumed his march, first advising the general that he should
leave the greater part of his warriors behind, and enter the place with
only a few of them, and without arms,[8] as he preferred to pass the night
at Caxamalca. At the same time he ordered accommodations to be provided for himself, and his retinue in one of the large stone buildings, called, from a serpent sculptured on the walls, "the House of the Serpent." [9]
—No tidings could have been more grateful to the Spaniards. It seemed

[5] To the eye of the old Conqueror so often quoted, the number of Peruvian warriors appeared not less than 50,000; "mas de cincuenta mil que tenia de guerra."
(Relacion del Primer. Descub., MS.) To Pizarro's secretary, as they lay encamped
along the hills, they seemed about 30,000. (Xerez, Conq. del Peru, ap. Barcia, tom
III. p. 196.) However gratifying to the imagination to repose on some precise number, it is very rare that one can do so with safety, in estimating the irregular and
tumultuous levies of a barbarian host.

[6] Pedro Pizarro says that an Indian spy reported to Atahuallpa, that the white
men were all huddled together in the great halls on the square, in much consternation, *llenos de miedo,* which was not far from the truth, adds the cavalier. (Descub.
y Conq., MS.)

[7] Pedro Pizarro, Descub. y Conq., MS.

"Asentados sus toldos envió á decir al gobernador que ya era tarde, que él quería
dormir allí, que por la mañana vernía: el gobernador le envió á decir que le rogaba
que viniese luego, porque le esperaba á cenar, é que no habia de cenar, hasta que
fuese." Carta de Hern. Pizarro, MS.

[8] "Él queria vernir luego, é que venia sin armas. E luego Atabaliva se movió para
venir, é dejó allí la gente con las armas, é llevó consigo hasta cinco ó seis mil indios
sin armas, salvo que debajo de las camisetas traían unas porras pequeñas, é honda-
é bolsas con piedras." Carte de Hern Pizarro, MS.

[9] Xerez, Conq. del Peru, ap. Barcia, tom. III. p. 197.

as if the Indian monarch was eager to rush into the snare that had been spread for him! The fanatical cavalier could not fail to discern in it the immediate finger of Providence.

It is difficult to account for this wavering conduct of Atahuallpa, so different from the bold and decided character which history ascribes to him. There is no doubt that he made his visit to the white men in perfect good faith; though Pizarro was probably right in conjecturing that this amiable disposition stood on a very precarious footing. There is as little reason to suppose that he distrusted the sincerity of the strangers; or he would not thus unnecessarily have proposed to visit them unarmed. His original purpose of coming with all his force was doubtless to display his royal state, and perhaps, also, to show greater respect for the Spaniards; but when he consented to accept their hospitality, and pass the night in their quarters, he was willing to dispense with a great part of his armed soldiery, and visit them in a manner that implied entire confidence in their good faith. He was too absolute in his own empire easily to suspect; and he probably could not comprehend the audacity with which a few men, like those now assembled in Caxamalca, meditated an assault on a powerful monarch in the midst of his victorious army. He did not know the character of the Spaniard.

It was not long before sunset, when the van of the royal procession entered the gates of the city. First came some hundreds of the menials, employed to clear the path from every obstacle, and singing songs of triumph as they came, "which, in our ears," says one of the Conquerors, "sounded like the songs of hell!" [10] Then followed other bodies of different ranks, and dressed in different liveries. Some wore a showy stuff, checkered white and red, like the squares of a chess-board. [11] Others were clad in pure white, bearing hammers or maces of silver or copper; [12] and the guards, together with those in immediate attendance on the prince, were distinguished by a rich azure livery, and a profusion of gay ornaments, while the large pendants attached to the ears indicated the Peruvian noble.

Elevated high above his vassals came the Inca Atahuallpa, borne on a sedan or open litter, on which was a sort of throne made of massive gold of inestimable value. [13] The palanquin was lined with the richly colored plumes of tropical birds, and studded with shining plates of gold and silver. [14] The monarch's attire was much richer than on the preceding evening. Round his neck was suspended a collar of emeralds of uncom-

[10] Relacion del Primer. Descub. MS.

[11] "Blanca y colorada como las casas de un ajedrez." Ibid., MS.

[12] "Con martillos en las manos de cobre y plata." Ibid., MS.

[13] "El asiento que traia sobre las andas era un tablon de oro que pesó un quintal de oro segun dicen los historiadores 25,000 pesos ó ducados." Naharro, Relacion Sumaria, MS.

[14] "Luego vania mucha Gente con Armaduras, Paternas, i Coronas de oro i Plata: entre estos venia Atabaliba, en una Litera, aforrada de Pluma de Papagaios, de muchas colores, guarnecida de chapas de Oro, i Plata." Xerez, Conq. del Peru, ap Barcia, tom. III. p. 198.

mon size and brilliancy.[15] His short hair was decorated with golden ornaments, and the imperial *borla* encircled his temples. The bearing of the Inca was sedate and dignified; and from his lofty station he looked down on the multitudes below with an air of composure, like one accustomed to command.

As the leading files of the procession entered the great square, larger, says an old chronicler, than any square in Spain, they opened to the right and left for the royal retinue to pass. Everything was conducted with admirable order. The monarch was permitted to traverse the *plaza* in silence, and not a Spaniard was to be seen. When some five or six thousand of his people had entered the place, Atahuallpa halted, and, turning round with an inquiring look, demanded, "Where are the strangers?"

At this moment Fray Vicente de Valverde, a Dominican friar, Pizarro's chaplain, and afterward Bishop of Cuzco, came forward with his breviary, or, as other accounts say, a Bible, in one hand, and a crucifix in the other, and, approaching the Inca, told him, that he came by order of his commander to expound to him the doctrines of the true faith, for which purpose the Spaniards had come from a great distance to his country. The friar then explained, as clearly as he could, the mysterious doctrine of the Trinity, and, ascending high in his account, began with the creation of man, thence passed to his fall, to his subsequent redemption by Jesus Christ, to the crucifixion, and the ascension, when the Saviour left the Apostle Peter as his Vicegerent upon earth. This power had been transmitted to the successors of the Apostle, good and wise men, who, under the title of Popes, held authority over all powers and potentates on earth. One of the last of these Popes had commissioned the Spanish emperor, the most mighty monarch in the world, to conquer and convert the natives in this western hemisphere; and his general, Francisco Pizarro, had now come to execute this important mission. The friar concluded with beseeching the Peruvian monarch to receive him kindly; to abjure the errors of his own faith, and embrace that of the Christians now proffered to him, the only one by which he could hope for salvation; and, furthermore, to acknowledge himself a tributary of the Emperor Charles the Fifth, who, in that event, would aid and protect him as his loyal vassal.[16]

Whether Atahuallpa possessed himself of every link in the curious

[15] Pedro Pizarro, Descub. y Conq., MS.

"Venia la persona de Atabalica, la cual traian ochenta Señores en hombros todos bestidos de una librea azul muy rica, y el bestido su persona muy ricamente con su corona en la cabeza, y al cuello un collar de emeraldas grandes." Relacion del Primer. Descub., MS.

[16] Montesinos says that Valverde read to the Inca the regular formula used by the Spaniards in their Conquests. (Annales, MS., año 1533.) But that address, though absurd enough, did not comprehend the whole range of theology ascribed to the chaplain on this occasion. Yet it is not impossible. But I have followed the report of Fray Naharro who collected his information from the actors in the tragedy, and whose minuter statement is corroborated by the more general testimony of both the Pizarros and the secretary Xerez

chain of argument by which the monk connected Pizarro with St. Peter, may be doubted. It is certain, however, that he must have had very incorrect notions of the Trinity, if, as Garcilasso states, the interpreter Felipillo explained it by saying, that "the Christians believed in three Gods and one God, and that made four." [17] But there is no doubt he perfectly comprehended that the drift of the discourse was to persuade him to resign his sceptre and acknowledge the supremacy of another.

The eyes of the Indian monarch flashed fire, and his dark brow grew darker as he replied,—"I will be no man's tributary. I am greater than any prince upon earth. Your emperor may be a great prince; I do not doubt it, when I see that he has sent his subjects so far across the waters; and I am willing to hold him as a brother. As for the Pope of whom you speak, he must be crazy to talk of giving away countries which do not belong to him. For my faith," he continued, "I will not change it. Your own God, as you say, was put to death by the very men whom he created. But mine," he concluded, pointing to his Deity,—then, alas! sinking in glory behind the mountains,—"my God still lives in the heavens, and looks down on his children." [18]

He then demanded of Valverde by what authority he had said these things. The friar pointed to the book which he held, as his authority. Atahuallpa, taking it, turned over the pages a moment, then, as the insult he had received probably flashed across his mind, he threw it down with vehemence, and exclaimed,—"Tell your comrades that they shall give me an account of their doings in my land. I will not go from here, till they have made me full satisfaction for all the wrongs they have committed." [19]

The friar, greatly scandalized by the indignity offered to the sacred volume, stayed only to pick it up, and, hastening to Pizarro, informed him of what had been done, exclaiming, at the same time,—"Do you not see, that, while we stand here wasting our breath in talking with this dog, full of pride as he is, the fields are filling with Indians? Set on, at once; I absolve you." [20] Pizarro saw that the hour had come. He waved a white

[17] "Por dezir Dios trino y uno, dixo Dios tres y uno son quatro, sumando los numeros por darse á entender." Com. Real., Parte 2, lib. 1, cap. 23.

[18] Some accounts describe him as taxing the Spaniards in much more unqualified terms.

[19] According to some authorities, Atahuallpa let the volume drop by accident. (Montesinos, Anales, MS., año 1533.—Balboa, Hist. du Perou, chap. 22.) But the testimony, as far as we have it, of those present, concurs in representing it as stated in the text. And, if he spoke with the heat imputed to him, this act would only be in keeping.

[20] "Visto esto por el Frayle y lo poco que aprovechan sus palabras, tomó su libro, y abajó su cabeza, y fuese para donde estaba el dicho Pizarro, casi corriendo, y dijole: No veis lo que pasa: para que estais en comedimientos y requerimientos con este perro lleno de soberbia que vienen los campos llenos de Indios? Salid á el,—que yo os absuelvo." (Relacion del Primer. Descub., MS.) The historian should be slow in ascribing conduct so diabolical to Father Valverde, without evidence. Two of the conquerors present, Pedro Pizarro and Xerez, simply state that the monk reported to his commander the indignity offered to the sacred volume. But Hernando Pizarro and the author of the Relacion del Primer. Descub., both eyewitnesses, and Naharro

scarf in the air, the appointed signal. The fatal gun was fired from the fortress. Then, springing into the square, the Spanish captain and his followers shouted the old war-cry of "St. Jago and at them." It was answered by the battle-cry of every Spaniard in the city, as, rushing from the avenues of the great halls in which they were concealed, they poured into the *plaza*, horse and foot, each in his own dark column, and threw themselves into the midst of the Indian crowd. The latter, taken by surprise, stunned by the report of artillery and muskets, the echoes of which reverberated like thunder from the surrounding buildings, and blinded by the smoke which rolled in sulphurous volumes along the square, were seized with a panic. They knew not whither to fly for refuge from the coming ruin. Nobles and commoners,—all were trampled down under the fierce charge of the cavalry, who dealt their blows, right and left, without sparing; while their swords, flashing through the thick gloom, carried dismay into the hearts of the wretched natives, who now, for the first time, saw the horse and his rider in all their terrors. They made no resistance,—as, indeed, they had no weapons with which to make it. Every avenue to escape was closed, for the entrance to the square was choked up with the dead bodies of men who had perished in vain efforts to fly; and, such was the agony of the survivors under the terrible pressure of their assailants, that a large body of Indians, by their convulsive struggles, burst through the wall of stone and dried clay which formed part of the boundary of the *plaza!* It fell, leaving an opening of more than a hundred paces, through which multitudes now found their way into the country, still hotly pursued by the cavalry, who, leaping the fallen rubbish, hung on the rear of the fugitives, striking them down in all directions.[21]

Meanwhile the fight, or rather massacre, continued hot around the Inca, whose person was the great object of the assault. His faithful nobles, rallying about him, threw themselves in the way of the assailants, and strove, by tearing them from their saddles, or, at least, by offering their own bosoms as a mark for their vengeance, to shield their beloved master. It is said by some authorities, that they carried weapons concealed under their clothes. If so, it availed them little, as it is not pretended that they used them. But the most timid animal will defend itself when at bay. That they did not so in the present instance is proof that they had no weapons to use.[22] Yet they still continued to force back the

Zarate, Gomara, Balboa, Herrera, the Inca Titucussi Yupanqui, all of whom obtained their information from persons who were eyewitnesses, state the circumstance, with little variation, as in the text. Yet Oviedo indorses the account of Xerez, and Garcilasso de la Vega insists on Valverde's innocence of any attempt to rouse the passions of his comrades.

[21] Pedro Pizarro, Descub. y Conq., MS.—Xerez, Conq. del Peru, ap. Barcia, tom. III, p. 198.—Carta de Hern. Pizarro, MS.—Oviedo, Hist. de las Indias, MS., Parte 3, lib. 8, cap. 7.—Relacion del Primer. Descub., MS.—Zarate, Conq. del Peru, lib. 2, cap. 5.—Instruccion del Inga Titucussi Yupanqui, MS.

[22] The author of the Relacion del Primero Descubrimiento speaks of a few as having bows and arrows, and of others as armed with silver and copper mallets or

cavaliers, clinging to their horses with dying grasp, and, as one was cut down, another taking the place of his fallen comrade with a loyalty truly affecting.

The Indian monarch, stunned and bewildered, saw his faithful subjects falling round him without fully comprehending his situation. The litter on which he rode heaved to and fro, as the mighty press swayed backwards and forwards; and he gazed on the overwhelming ruin, like some forlorn mariner, who, tossed about in his bark by the furious elements, sees the lightning's flash and hears the thunder bursting around him with the consciousness that he can do nothing to avert his fate. At length, weary with the work of destruction, the Spaniards, as the shades of evening grew deeper, felt afraid that the royal prize might, after all, elude them; and some of the cavaliers made a desperate attempt to end the affray at once by taking Atahuallpa's life. But Pizarro, who was nearest his person, called out with stentorian voice, "Let no one, who values his life, strike at the Inca"; [23] and, stretching out his arm to shield him, received a wound on the hand from one of his own men,—the only wound received by a Spaniard in the action.[24]

The struggle now became fiercer than ever round the royal litter. It reeled more and more, and at length, several of the nobles who supported it having been slain, it was overturned, and the Indian prince would have come with violence to the ground, had not his fall been broken by the efforts of Pizarro and some other of the cavaliers, who caught him in their arms. The imperial *borla* was instantly snatched from his temples by a soldier named Estete,[25] and the unhappy monarch, strongly secured, was

maces, which may, however, have been more for ornament than for service in fight. —Pedro Pizarro and some later writers say that the Indians brought thongs with them to bind the captive white men.—Both Hernando Pizarro and the secretary Xerez agree that their only arms were secreted under their clothes; but as they do not pretend that these were used, and as it was announced by the Inca that he came without arms, the assertion may well be doubted,—or rather discredited. All authorities, without exception, agree that no attempt was made at resistance.

[23] "El marquez dio bozes diciendo. Nadie hiera al indio so pena de la vida." Pedro Pizarro, Descub. y Conq., MS.

[24] Whatever discrepancy exists among the Castilian accounts in other respects, *all* concur in this remarkable fact,—that no Spaniard, except their general, received a wound on that occasion. Pizarro saw in this a satisfactory argument for regarding the Spaniards, this day, as under the especial protection of Providence. See Xerez, Conq. del Peru, ap. Barcia, tom. III. p. 199.

[25] Miguel Estete, who long retained the silken diadem as a trophy of the exploit, according to Garcilasso de la Vega, (Com. Real., Parte 2, lib. 1, cap. 27,) an indifferent authority for any thing in this part of his history. This popular writer, whose work, from his superior knowledge of the institutions of the country, has obtained greater credit, even in what relates to the Conquest, than the reports of the Conquerors themselves, has indulged in the romantic vein to an unpardonable extent, in his account of the capture of Atahuallpa. According to him, the Peruvian monarch treated the invaders from the first with supreme deference, as descendants of Viracocha, predicted by his oracles as to come and rule over the land. But if this flattering homage had been paid by the Inca, it would never have escaped the notice of the Conquerors. Garcilasso had read the Commentaries of Cortéz, as he somewhere tells us; and it is probable that that general's account, well founded, it appears, of a

removed to a neighboring building, where he was carefully guarded. All attempt at resistance now ceased. The fate of the Inca soon spread over town and country. The charm which might have held the Peruvians together was dissolved. Every man thought only of his own safety. Even the soldiery encamped on the adjacent fields took the alarm, and, learning the fatal tidings, were seen flying in every direction before their pursuers, who in the heat of triumph showed no touch of mercy. At length night, more pitiful than man, threw her friendly mantle over the fugitives, and the scattered troops of Pizarro rallied once more at the sound of the trumpet in the bloody square of Caxamalca.

The number of slain is reported, as usual, with great discrepancy. Pizarro's secretary says two thousand natives fell.[26] A descendant of the Incas—a safer authority than Garcilasso—swells the number to ten thousand.[27] Truth is generally found somewhere between the extremes. The slaughter was incessant, for there was nothing to check it. That there should have been no resistance will not appear strange, when we consider the fact, that the wretched victims were without arms, and that their senses must have been completely overwhelmed by the strange and appalling spectacle which burst on them so unexpectedly. "What wonder was it," said an ancient Inca to a Spaniard, who repeats it, "what wonder that our countrymen lost their wits, seeing blood run like water, and the Inca, whose person we all of us adore, seized and carried off by a handful of men?"[28] Yet though the massacre was incessant, it was short in

similar superstition among the Aztecs suggested to the historian the idea of a corresponding sentiment in the Peruvians, which, while it flattered the vanity of the Spaniards, in some degree vindicated his own countrymen from the charge of cowardice, incurred by their too ready submission; for, however they might be called on to resist men it would have been madness to resist the decrees of Heaven. Yet Garcilasso's romantic version has something in it so pleasing to the imagination, that it has ever found favor with the majority of readers. The English student might have met with a sufficient corrective in the criticism of the sagacious and skeptical Robertson.

[26] Xerex, Conq. del Peru, ap. Barcia, tom. III, p. 199.

[27] "Los mataron á todos con los Cavallos con espadas con arcabuzes como quien mata ovejas—sin hacerles nadie resistencia que no se escaparon de mas de diez mil, doscientos." Instruc. del Inga Titucussi, MS.

This document, consisting of two hundred folio pages, is signed by a Peruvian Inca, grandson of the great Huayna Capac, and nephew, consequently of Atahuallpa. It was written in 1570, and designed to set forth to his Majesty Philip II. the claims of Titucussi and the members of his family to the royal bounty. In the course of the Memorial, the writer takes occasion to recapitulate some of the principal events in the latter years of the empire; and though sufficiently prolix to tax even the patience of Philip II., it is of much value as an historical document, coming from one of the royal race of Peru.

[28] Montesinos, Annales, MS., año 1532.

According to Naharro, the Indians were less astounded by the wild uproar caused by the sudden assault of the Spaniards, though "this was such that it seemed as if the very heavens were falling," than by a terrible apparition which appeared in the air during the onslaught. It consisted of a woman and a child, and, at their side, a horseman all clothed in white on a milk-white charger,—doubtless the valiant St. James,—who, with his sword glancing lightning, smote down the infidel host, and

duration. The whole time consumed by it, the brief twilight of the trop-ics, did not much exceed half an hour; a short period, indeed,—yet long enough to decide the fate of Peru, and to subvert the dynasty of the Incas.

That night Pizarro kept his engagement with the Inca, since he had Atahuallpa to sup with him. The banquet was served in one of the halls facing the great square, which a few hours before had been the scene of slaughter, and the pavement of which was still encumbered with the dead bodies of the Inca's subjects. The captive monarch was placed next his conqueror. He seemed like one who did not yet fully comprehend the extent of his calamity. If he did, he showed an amazing fortitude. "It is the fortune of war," he said; [29] and, if we may credit the Spaniards, he expressed his admiration of the adroitness with which they had contrived to entrap him in the midst of his own troops.[30] He added, that he had been made acquainted with the progress of the white men from the hour of their landing; but that he had been led to undervalue their strength from the insignificance of their numbers. He had no doubt he should be easily able to overpower them, on their arrival at Caxamalca, by his su-perior strength; and, as he wished to see for himself what manner of men they were, he had suffered them to cross the mountains, meaning to select such as he chose for his own service, and, getting possession of their wonderful arms and horses, put the rest to death.[31]

That such may have been Atahuallpa's purpose is not improbable. It explains his conduct in not occupying the mountain passes, which afford-ed such strong points of defence against invasion. But that a prince so astute, as by the general testimony of the Conquerors he is represented to have been, should have made so impolitic a disclosure of his hidden motives is not so probable. The intercourse with the Inca was carried on chiefly by means of the interpreter Felipillo, or *little Philip*, as he was called, from his assumed Christian name,—a malicious youth, as it ap-pears, who bore no good-will to Atahuallpa, and whose interpretations were readily admitted by the Conquerors, eager to find some pretext for their bloody reprisals.

Atahuallpa, as elsewhere noticed, was, at this time, about thirty years of age. He was well made, and more robust than usual with his country-men. His head was large, and his countenance might have been called handsome, but that his eyes, which were bloodshot, gave a fierce expres-sion to his features. He was deliberate in speech, grave in manner, and

---

rendered them incapable of resistance. This miracle the good father reports on the testimony of three of his Order who were present in the action, and who received it from numberless of the natives. Relacion Sumaria, MS.

[29] "Diciendo que era uso de Guerra vencei i ser vencido." Herrera, Hist. General, dec. 5, lib. 2, cap. 12.

[30] "Haciendo admiracion de la traza que tenia hecha." Relacion del Primer. Descub., MS.

[31] "And in my opinion," adds the Conqueror who reports the speech, "he had good grounds for believing he could do this, since nothing but the miraculous interposition of Heaven could have saved us." Ibid., MS.

towards his own people stern even to severity; though with the Spaniards he showed himself affable, sometimes even indulging in sallies of mirth.[32]

Pizarro paid every attention to his royal captive, and endeavored to lighten, if he could not dispel, the gloom which, in spite of his assumed equanimity, hung over the monarch's brow. He besought him not to be cast down by his reverses, for his lot had only been that of every prince who had resisted the white men. They had come into the country to proclaim the gospel, the religion of Jesus Christ; and it was no wonder they had prevailed, when his shield was over them. Heaven had permitted that Atahuallpa's pride should be humbled, because of his hostile intentions towards the Spaniards, and the insults he had offered to the sacred volume. But he bade the Inca take courage and confide in him, for the Spaniards were a generous race, warring only against those who made war on them, and showing grace to all who submitted![33]—Atahuallpa may have thought the massacre of that day an indifferent commentary on this vaunted lenity.

Before retiring for the night, Pizarro briefly addressed his troops on their present situation. When he had ascertained that not a man was wounded, he bade them offer up thanksgivings to Providence for so great a miracle; without its care, they could never have prevailed so easily over the host of their enemies; and he trusted their lives had been reserved for still greater things. But if they would succeed, they had much to do for themselves. They were in the heart of a powerful kingdom, encompassed by foes deeply attached to their own sovereign. They must be ever on their guard, therefore, and be prepared at any hour to be roused from their slumbers by the call of the trumpet.[34]—Having then posted his sentinels, placed a strong guard over the apartment of Atahuallpa, and taken all the precautions of a careful commander, Pizarro withdrew to repose; and, if he could really feel, that, in the bloody scenes of the past day, he had been fighting only the good fight of the Cross, he doubtless slept sounder than on the night preceding the seizure of the Inca.

On the following morning, the first commands of the Spanish chief were to have the city cleansed of its impurities; and the prisoners, of whom there were many in the camp, were employed to remove the dead, and give them decent burial. His next care was to despatch a body of about thirty horse to the quarters lately occupied by Atahuallpa at the baths, to take possession of the spoil, and disperse the remnant of the Peruvian forces which still hung about the place.

Before noon, the party which he had detached on this service returned with a large troop of Indians, men and women, among the latter of whom were many of the wives and attendants of the Inca. The Spaniards had met with no resistance; since the Peruvian warriors, though so superior

[3] Xerez, Conq. del Peru, ap. Barcia, tom. III. p. 203.

[33] Nosotros vsamos de piedad con nuestros Enemigos vencidos, i no hacemos Guerra, sino à los que nos la hacen, i pudiendolos destruir, no lo hacemos, antes los verdonamos." Ibid , tom. III. p. 199.

[34] Ibid., ubi supra.—Pedro Pizarro, Descub. i Conq., MS.

in number, excellent in appointments, and consisting mostly of able-bodied young men,—for the greater part of the veteran forces were with the Inca's generals at the south,—lost all heart from the moment of their sovereign's captivity. There was no leader to take his place; for they recognized no authority but that of the Child of the Sun, and they seemed to be held by a sort of invisible charm near the place of his confinement; while they gazed with superstitious awe on the white men, who could achieve so audacious an enterprise.[35]

The number of Indian prisoners was so great, that some of the Conquerors were for putting them all to death, or, at least, cutting off their hands, to disable them from acts of violence, and to strike terror into their countrymen.[36] The proposition, doubtless, came from the lowest and most ferocious of the soldiery. But that it should have been made at all shows what materials entered into the composition of Pizarro's company. The chief rejected it at once, as no less impolitic than inhuman, and dismissed the Indians to their several homes, with the assurance that none should be harmed who did not offer resistance to the white men. A sufficient number, however, were retained to wait on the Conquerors who were so well provided, in this respect, that the most common soldier was attended by a retinue of menials that would have better suited the establishment of a noble.[37]

The Spaniards had found immense droves of llamas under the care of their shepherds in the neighborhood of the baths, destined for the consumption of the Court. Many of them were now suffered to roam abroad among their native mountains; though Pizarro caused a considerable number to be reserved for the use of the army. And this was no small quantity, if, as one of the Conquerors says, a hundred and fifty of the Peruvian sheep were frequently slaughtered in a day.[38] Indeed, the Spaniards were so improvident in their destruction of these animals, that, in a few years, the superb flocks, nurtured with so much care by the Peruvian government, had almost disappeared from the land.[39]

[35] From this time, says Ondegardo, the Spaniards, who hitherto had been designated as the "men with beards," *barbudos,* were called by the natives, from their fair-complexioned deity, *Viracochas.* The people of Cuzco, who bore no good-will to the captive Inca, "looked upon the strangers," says the author, "as sent by Viracocha himself." (Rel. Prim., MS.) It reminds us of a superstition, or rather an amiable fancy, among the ancient Greeks, that "the stranger came from Jupiter."

"Πρὸς γὰρ Διός εἰσιν ἅπαντες Ξεῖνοί τε."
ΟΔΥΣ. ξ, v. 57.

[36] "Algunos fueron de opinion, que matasen à todos los Hombres de Guerra, ò les cortasen las manos." Xerez, Hist. del Peru, ap. Barcia, tom. III. p. 200.

[37] "Cada Español de los que alli ivan tomaron para si mui gran cantidad tanto que como andava todo a rienda suelta havia Español que tenia docientas piezas de Indios i Indias de servicio." Conq. i Pob. del Piru, MS.

[38] "Se matan cada Dia, ciento i cinquenta." Xerez, Conq. del Peru, ap. Barcia, tom. III. p. 202.

[39] Cieza de Leon, Cronica, cap. 80.—Ondegardo, Rel. Seg., MS.

"Hasta que los destruian todos sin haver Español ni Justicia que lo defendiese ni amparase." Conq. i Pob. del Piru, MS.

The party sent to pillage the Inca's pleasure-house brought back a rich booty in gold and silver, consisting chiefly of plate for the royal table, which greatly astonished the Spaniards by their size and weight. These, as well as some large emeralds obtained there, together with the precious spoils found on the bodies of the Indian nobles who had perished in the massacre, were placed in safe custody, to be hereafter divided. In the city of Caxamalca, the troops also found magazines stored with goods, both cotton and woollen, far superior to any they had seen, for fineness of texture, and the skill with which the various colors were blended. They were piled from the floors to the very roofs of the buildings, and in such quantity, that, after every soldier had provided himself with what he desired, it made no sensible diminution of the whole amount.[40]

Pizarro would now gladly have directed his march on the Peruvian capital. But the distance was great, and his force was small. This must have been still further crippled by the guard required for the Inca, and the chief feared to involve himself deeper in a hostile empire so populous and powerful, with a prize so precious in his keeping. With much anxiety, therefore, he looked for reinforcements from the colonies; and he despatched a courier to San Miguel, to inform the Spaniards there of his recent successes, and to ascertain if there had been any arrival from Panamá. Meanwhile he employed his men in making Caxamalca a more suitable residence for a Christian host, by erecting a church, or, perhaps, appropriating some Indian edifice to this use, in which mass was regularly performed by the Dominican fathers, with great solemnity. The dilapidated walls of the city were also restored in a more substantial manner than before, and every vestige was soon effaced of the hurricane that had so recently swept over it.

It was not long before Atahuallpa discovered, amidst all the show of religious zeal in his Conquerors, a lurking appetite more potent in most of their bosoms than either religion or ambition. This was the love of gold. He determined to avail himself of it to procure his own freedom. The critical posture of his affairs made it important that this should not be long delayed. His brother, Huascar, ever since his defeat, had been detained as a prisoner, subject to the victor's orders. He was now at Andamarca, at no great distance from Caxamalca; and Atahuallpa feared, with good reason, that, when his own imprisonment was known, Huascar would find it easy to corrupt his guards, make his escape, and put himself at the head of the contested empire, without a rival to dispute it.

In the hope, therefore, to effect his purpose by appealing to the avarice of his keepers, he one day told Pizarro, that, if he would set him free, he would engage to cover the floor of the apartment on which they stood

[40] Xerez, Conq. del Peru, ap. Barcia, tom. III. p. 200.

There was enough, says the anonymous Conqueror, for several ship-loads. "Todas estas cosas de tiendas y ropas de lana y algodon eran en tan gran cantidad, que à mi parecer fueran menester muchos navios en que supieran." Relacion del Primer. Descub., MS.

with gold. Those present listened with an incredulous smile; and, as the Inca received no answer, he said, with some emphasis, that "he would not merely cover the floor, but would fill the room with gold as high as he could reach"; and, standing on tiptoe, he stretched out his hand against the wall. All stared with amazement; while they regarded it as the insane boast of a man too eager to procure his liberty to weigh the meaning of his words. Yet Pizarro was sorely perplexed. As he had advanced into the country, much that he had seen, and all that he had heard, had confirmed the dazzling reports first received of the riches of Peru. Atahuallpa himself had given him the most glowing picture of the wealth of the capital, where the roofs of the temples were plated with gold, while the walls were hung with tapestry and the floors inlaid with tiles of the same precious metal. There must be some foundation for all this. At all events, it was safe to accede to the Inca's proposition; since, by so doing, he could collect, at once, all the gold at his disposal, and thus prevent its being purloined or secreted by the natives. He therefore acquiesced in Atahuallpa's offer, and, drawing a red line along the wall at the height which the Inca had indicated, he caused the terms of the proposal to be duly recorded by the notary. The apartment was about seventeen feet broad, by twenty-two feet long, and the line round the walls was nine feet from the floor.[41] This space was to be filled with gold; but it was understood that the gold was not to be melted down into ingots, but to retain the original form of the articles into which it was manufactured, that the Inca might have the benefit of the space which they occupied. He further agreed to fill an adjoining room of smaller dimensions twice full with silver, in like manner; and he demanded two months to accomplish all this.[42]

[41] I have adopted the dimensions given by the secretary Xerez, (Conq. del Peru, ap. Barcia, tom. III. p. 202.) According to Hernando Pizarro, the apartment was nine feet high, but thirty-five feet long by seventeen or eighteen feet wide. (Carta, MS.) The most moderate estimate is large enough.

Stevenson says that they still show "a large room, part of the old palace, and now the residence of the Cacique Astopilca, where the ill-fated Inca was kept a prisoner"; and he adds that the line traced on the wall is still visible. (Residence in South America, vol. II. p. 163.) Peru abounds in remains as ancient as the Conquest; and it would not be surprising that the memory of a place so remarkable as this should be preserved,—though any thing but a memorial to be cherished by the Spaniards.

[42] The facts in the preceding paragraph are told with remarkable uniformity by the ancient chroniclers. (Conf. Pedro Pizarro, Descub. y Conq., MS.—Carte de Hern. Pizarro, MS.—Xerez, Conq. del Peru, ap. Barcia, ubi supra.—Naharro, Relacion Sumaria, MS.—Zarate, Conq. del Peru, lib. 2, cap. 6.—Gomara, Hist. de las Ind., cap. 114.—Herrera, Hist. General, dec. 5, lib. 2, cap. 1.)

Both Naharro and Herrera state expressly that Pizarro promised the Inca his liberation on fulfilling the compact. This is not confirmed by the other chroniclers, who, however, do not intimate that the Spanish general declined the terms. And as Pizarro, by all accounts, encouraged his prisoner to perform his part of the contract, it must have been with the understanding implied, if not expressed, that he would abide by the other. It is most improbable that the Inca would have stripped himself of his treasures, if he had not so understood it.

No sooner was this arrangement made, than the Inca despatched couriers to Cuzco and the other principal places in the kingdom, with orders that the gold ornaments and utensils should be removed from the royal palaces, and from the temples and other public buildings, and transported without loss of time to Caxamalca. Meanwhile he continued to live in the Spanish quarters, treated with the respect due to his rank, and enjoying all the freedom that was compatible with the security of his person. Though not permitted to go abroad, his limbs were unshackled, and he had the range of his own apartments under the jealous *surveillance* of a guard, who knew too well the value of the royal captive to be remiss. He was allowed the society of his favorite wives, and Pizarro took care that his domestic privacy should not be violated. His subjects had free access to their sovereign, and every day he received visits from the Indian nobles, who came to bring presents, and offer condolence to their unfortunate master. On such occasions, the most potent of these great vassals never ventured into his presence, without first stripping off their sandals, and bearing a load on their backs in token of reverence. The Spaniards gazed with curious eyes on these acts of homage, or rather of slavish submission, on the one side, and on the air of perfect indifference with which they were received, as a matter of course, on the other; and they conceived high ideas of the character of a prince who, even in his present helpless condition, could inspire such feelings of awe in his subjects. The royal levee was so well attended, and such devotion was shown by his vassals to the captive monarch, as did not fail, in the end, to excite some feelings of distrust in his keepers.[43]

Pizarro did not neglect the opportunity afforded him of communicating the truths of revelation to his prisoner, and both he and his chaplain, Father Valverde, labored in the same good work. Atahuallpa listened with composure and apparent attention. But nothing seemed to move him so much as the argument with which the military polemic closed his discourse,—that it could not be the true God whom Atahuallpa worshipped, since he had suffered him to fall into the hands of his enemies. The unhappy monarch assented to the force of this, acknowledging that his Deity had indeed deserted him in his utmost need.[44]

Yet his conduct towards his brother Huascar, at this time, too clearly proves, that, whatever respect he may have shown for the teachers, the doctrines of Christianity had made little impression on his heart. No sooner had Huascar been informed of the capture of his rival, and of the large ransom he had offered for his deliverance, than, as the latter had foreseen, he made every effort to regain his liberty, and sent, or attempted to send, a message to the Spanish commander, that he would pay

---

[43] Relacion del Primer. Descub., MS.—Naharro, Relacion Sumaria, MS.—Zarate, Conq. del Peru, lib. 2, cap. 6.

[44] "I mas dijo Atabalipa, que estaba espantado de lo que el Governador le havia dicho: que bien conocia que aquel que hablaba en su Idolo, no es Dios verdadero, pues tan poco le aiudò." Xerez, Conq. del Peru, ap. Barcia, tom. III. p. 203.

a much larger ransom than that promised by Atahuallpa, who, never having dwelt in Cuzco, was ignorant of the quantity of treasure there, and where it was deposited.

Intelligence of all this was secretly communicated to Atahuallpa by the persons who had his brother in charge; and his jealousy, thus roused, was further heightened by Pizarro's declaration, that he intended to have Hauscar brought to Caxamalca, where he would himself examine into the controversy, and determine which of the two had best title to the sceptre of the Incas. Pizarro perceived, from the first, the advantages of a competition which would enable him, by throwing his sword into the scale he preferred, to give it a preponderance. The party who held the sceptre by his nomination would henceforth be a tool in his hands, with which to work his pleasure more effectually than he could well do in his own name. It was the game, as every reader knows, played by Edward the First in the affairs of Scotland, and by many a monarch, both before and since,—and though their examples may not have been familiar to the unlettered soldier, Pizarro was too quick in his perceptions to require, in this matter, at least, the teachings of history.

Atahuallpa was much alarmed by the Spanish commander's determination to have the suit between the rival candidates brought before him; for he feared, that, independently of the merits of the case, the decision would be likely to go in favor of Huascar, whose mild and ductile temper would make him a convenient instrument in the hands of his conquerors. Without further hesitation, he determined to remove this cause of jealousy for ever, by the death of his brother.

His orders were immediately executed, and the unhappy prince was drowned, as was commonly reported, in the river of Andamarca, declaring with his dying breath that the white men would avenge his murder, and that his rival would not long survive him.[45]—Thus perished the unfortunate Huascar, the legitimate heir of the throne of the Incas, in the very morning of life, and the commencement of his reign; a reign, however, which had been long enough to call forth the display of many excellent and amiable qualities, though his nature was too gentle to cope with the bold and fiercer temper of his brother. Such is the portrait we have of him from the Indian and Castilian chroniclers, though the former, it should be added, were the kinsmen of Huascar, and the latter certainly bore no good-will to Atahuallpa.[46]

[45] Both the place and the manner of Huascar's death are reported with much discrepancy by the historians. All agree in the one important fact, that he died a violent death at the instigation of his brother. Conf. Herrera, Hist. General, dec. 5, lib. 3, cap. 2.—Xerez, Conq. del Peru, ap. Barcia, tom. III. p. 204.—Pedro Pizarro, Descub. y Conq., MS.—Naharro, Relacion Sumaria, MS.—Zarate, Conq. del Peru, lib. 2, cap. 6.—Instruc. del Inga. Titucussi, MS.

[46] Both Garcilasso de la Vega and Titucussi Yupanque were descendants from Huayna Capac, of the pure Peruvian stock, the natural enemies, therefore, of their kinsman of Quito, whom they regarded as a usurper. Circumstances brought the Castilians into direct collision with Atahuallpa, and it was natural they should seek to darken his reputation by contrast with the fair character of his rival.

That prince received the tidings of Huascar's death with every mark of surprise and indignation. He immediately sent for Pizarro, and communicated the event to him with expressions of the deepest sorrow. The Spanish commander refused, at first, to credit the unwelcome news, and bluntly told the Inca, that his brother could not be dead, and that he should be answerable for his life.[47] To this Atahuallpa replied by renewed assurances of the fact, adding that the deed had been perpetrated, without his privity, by Huascar's keepers, fearful that he might take advantage of the troubles of the country to make his escape. Pizarro, on making further inquiries, found that the report of his death was but too true. That it should have been brought about by Atahuallpa's officers, without his express command, would only show, that, by so doing, they had probably anticipated their master's wishes. The crime, which assumes in our eyes a deeper dye from the relation of the parties, had not the same estimation among the Incas, in whose multitudinous families the bonds of brotherhood must have sat loosely,—much too loosely to restrain the arm of the despot from sweeping away any obstacle that lay in his path.

[47] "Sabido esto por el Gobernador, mostrò, que le pesaba mucho: i dijo que era mentira, que no le havian muerto, que lo trujesen luego vivo: i sino, que èl mandaria matar à Atabalipa." Xerez, Conq. del Peru, ap. Barcia, tom. III. p. 204.

Gold arrives for the Ransom—Visit to Pachacamac—Demolition
of the Idol—The Inca's favorite General—The Inca's Life
in Confinement—Envoys' Conduct in Cuzco—Arrival of Almagro

1533

Several weeks had now passed since Atahuallpa's emissaries had been
despatched for the gold and silver that were to furnish his ransom to the
Spaniards. But the distances were great, and the returns came in slowly.
They consisted, for the most part, of massive pieces of plate, some of
which weighed two or three *arrobas*,—a Spanish weight of twenty-five
pounds. On some days, articles of the value of thirty or forty thousand
pesos de oro were brought in, and, occasionally, of the value of fifty or
even sixty thousand *pesos*. The greedy eyes of the Conquerors gloated on
the shining heaps of treasure, which were transported on the shoulders
of the Indian porters, and, after being carefully registered, were placed
in safe deposit under a strong guard. They now began to believe that the
magnificent promises of the Inca would be fulfilled. But, as their avarice
was sharpened by the ravishing display of wealth, such as they had hardly dared to imagine, they became more craving and impatient. They
made no allowance for the distance and the difficulties of the way, and
loudly inveighed against the tardiness with which the royal commands
were executed. They even suspected Atahuallpa of devising this scheme
only to gain a pretext for communicating with his subjects in distant
places, and of proceeding as dilatorily as possible, in order to secure time
for the execution of his plans. Rumors of a rising among the Peruvians
were circulated, and the Spaniards were in apprehension of some general
and sudden assault on their quarters. Their new acquisitions gave them
additional cause for solicitude; like a miser, they trembled in the midst
of their treasures.[1]

Pizarro reported to his captive the rumors that were in circulation
among the soldiers, naming, as one of the places pointed out for the
rendezvous of the Indians, the neighboring city of Guamachucho. Atahuallpa listened with undisguised astonishment, and indignantly repelled
the charge, as false from beginning to end. "No one of my subjects," said

---

[1] Zarata, Conq. del Peru, lib. 2, cap. 6.—Naharro, Relacion Sumaria, MS.—Xerez,
Conq. del Peru, ap. Barcia, tom. III. p. 204.

he, "would dare to appear in arms, or to raise his finger, without my orders. You have me," he continued, "in your power. Is not my life at your disposal? And what better security can you have for my fidelity?" He then represented to the Spanish commander, that the distances of many of the places were very great; that to Cuzco, the capital, although a message might be sent by post, through a succession of couriers, in five days from Caxamalca, it would require weeks for a porter to travel over the same ground, with a heavy load on his back. "But that you may be satisfied I am proceeding in good faith," he added, "I desire you will send some of your own people to Cuzco. I will give them a safe-conduct, and, when there, they can superintend the execution of the commission, and see with their own eyes that no hostile movements are intended." It was a fair offer, and Pizarro, anxious to get more precise and authentic information of the state of the country, gladly availed himself of it.[2]

Before the departure of these emissaries, the general had despatched his brother Hernando with about twenty horse and a small body of infantry to the neighboring town of Guamachucho, in order to reconnoitre the country, and ascertain if there was any truth in the report of an armed force having assembled there. Hernando found every thing quiet, and met with a kind reception from the natives. But before leaving the place, he received further orders from his brother to continue his march to Pachacamac, a town situated on the coast, at least a hundred leagues distant from Caxamalca. It was consecrated at the seat of the great temple of the deity of that name, whom the Peruvians worshipped as the Creator of the world. It is said that they found there altars raised to this god, on their first occupation of the country; and, such was the veneration in which he was held by the natives, that the Incas, instead of attempting to abolish his worship, deemed it more prudent to sanction it conjointly with that of their own deity, the Sun. Side by side, the two temples rose on the heights that overlooked the city of Pachacamac, and prospered in the offerings of their respective votaries. "It was a cunning arrangement," says an ancient writer, "by which the great enemy of man secured to himself a double harvest of souls."[3]

But the temple of Pachacamac continued to maintain its ascendency; and the oracles, delivered from its dark and mysterious shrine, were held in no less repute among the natives of *Tavantinsuyu,* (or "the four quarters of the world," as Peru under the Incas was called,) than the oracles of Delphi obtained among the Greeks. Pilgrimages were made to the hallowed spot from the most distant regions, and the city of Pachacamac became among the Peruvians what Mecca was among the Mahometans, or Cholula with the people of Anahuac. The shrine of the deity, en-

---

[2] Pedro Pizarro, Descub. y Conq., MS.—Xerez, Conq. del Peru, ap. Barcia, tom. III. pp. 203, 204.—Naharro, Relacion Sumaria, MS.

[3] "El demonio Pachacama alegre con este concierto, afirman que mostraua en sus respuestas gran contento: pues con lo vno y lo otro era el seruido, y quedauan las animas de los simples malauenturados presas en su podor." Cieza de Leon, Croncia cap. ⁷⁰

riched by the tributes of the pilgrims, gradually became one of the most opulent in the land; and Atahuallpa, anxious to collect his ransom as speedily as possible, urged Pizarro to send a detachment in that direction, to secure the treasures before they could be secreted by the priests of the temple.

It was a journey of considerable difficulty. Two thirds of the route lay along the table-land of the Cordilleras, intersected occasionally by crests of the mountain range, that imposed no slight impediment to their progress. Fortunately, much of the way, they had the benefit of the great road to Cuzco, and "nothing in Christendom," exclaims Hernando Pizarro, "equals the magnificence of this road across the sierra." [4] In some places, the rocky ridges were so precipitous, that steps were cut in them for the travellers; and though the sides were protected by heavy stone balustrades or parapets, it was with the greatest difficulty that the horses were enabled to scale them. The road was frequently crossed by streams, over which bridges of wood and sometimes of stone were thrown; though occasionally, along the declivities of the mountains, the waters swept down in such furious torrents, that the only method of passing them was by the swinging bridges of osier, of which, till now, the Spaniards had had little experience. They were secured on either bank to heavy buttresses of stone. But as they were originally designed for nothing heavier than the foot-passenger and the llama, and, as they had something exceedingly fragile in their appearance, the Spaniards hesitated to venture on them with their horses. Experience, however, soon showed they were capable of bearing a much greater weight; and though the traveller, made giddy by the vibration of the long avenue, looked with a reeling brain into the torrent that was tumbling at the depth of a hundred feet or more below him, the whole of the cavalry effected their passage without an accident. At these bridges, it may be remarked, they found persons stationed whose business it was to collect toll for the government from all travellers. [5]

The Spaniards were amazed by the number as well as magnitude of the flocks of llamas which they saw browsing on the stunted herbage that grows in the elevated regions of the Andes. Sometimes they were gathered in inclosures, but more usually were roaming at large under the conduct of their Indian shepherds; and the Conquerors now learned, for the first time, that these animals were tended with as much care, and

---

[4] "El camino de las sierras es cosa de ver, porque en verdad en tierra tan fragosa en la cristiandad no se han visto tan hermosos caminos, toda la mayor parte de calzada." Carta, MS.

[5] "Todos los arroyos tienen puentes de piedra ó de madera: en un rio grande, que era muy caudaloso é muy grande, que pasamos dos veces, hallamos puentes de red, que es cosa maravillosa de ver; pasamos por ellas los caballos; tienen en cada pasaje dos puentes, la una por donde pasa la gente comun, la otra por donde pasa el señor de la tierra ó sus capitanes: esta tienen siempre cerrada é indios que la guardan; estos indios cobran portazgo de los que pasan." Carta de Hern. Pizarro, MS.—Also Relacion del Primer. Descub., MS.

their migrations as nicely regulated, as those of the vast flocks of merinos in their own country.[6]

The table-land and its declivities were thickly sprinkled with hamlets
and towns, some of them of considerable size; and the country in every
direction bore the marks of a thrifty husbandry. Fields of Indian corn
were to be seen in all its different stages, from the green and tender ear to
the yellow ripeness of harvest time. As they descended into the valleys
and deep ravines that divided the crests of the Cordilleras, they were surrounded by the vegetation of a warmer climate, which delighted the eye
with the gay livery of a thousand bright colors, and intoxicated the
senses with its perfumes. Everywhere the natural capacities of the soil
were stimulated by a minute system of irrigation, which drew the fertilizing moisture from every stream and rivulet that rolled down the declivities of the Andes; while the terraced sides of the mountains were clothed
with gardens and orchards that teemed with fruits of various latitudes.
The Spaniards could not sufficiently admire the industry with which the
natives had availed themselves of the bounty of Nature, or had supplied the deficiency where she had dealt with a more parsimonious hand.

Whether from the commands of the Inca, or from the awe which their
achievements had spread throughout the land, the Conquerors were received, in every place through which they passed, with hospitable kindness. Lodgings were provided for them, with ample refreshments from
the well-stored magazines, distributed at intervals along the route. In
many of the towns the inhabitants came out to welcome them with singing and dancing; and, when they resumed their march, a number of able-
bodied porters were furnished to carry forward their baggage.[7]

At length, after some weeks of travel, severe even with all these appliances, Hernando Pizarro arrived before the city of Pachacamac. It was a
place of considerable population, and the edifices were, many of them,
substantially built. The temple of the tutelar deity consisted of a vast
stone building, or rather pile of buildings, which, clustering around a
conical hill, had the air of a fortress rather than a religious establishment. But, though the walls were of stone, the roof was composed of a
light thatch, as usual in countries where rain seldom or never falls, and
where defence, consequently, is wanted chiefly against the rays of the sun.

Presenting himself at the lower entrance of the temple, Hernando

---

[6] A comical blunder has been made by the printer, in M. Ternaux-Compans's
excellent translation of Xerez, in the account of this expedition. "On trouve sur
toute la route beaucoup de porcs, de lamas." (Relation de la Conquête du Pérou, p.
157.) The substitution of *porcs* for *parcs* might well lead the reader into the error
of supposing that swine existed in Peru before the Conquest.

[7] Carta de Hern. Pizarro, MS.—Estete, ap. Barcia, tom. III. pp. 206, 207.—Relacion del Primer. Descub., MS.

Both the last-cited author and Miguel Estete, the royal *veedor* or inspector, accompanied Hernando Pizarro on this expedition, and, of course, were eyewitnesses,
like himself, of what they relate. Estete's narrative is incorporated by the secretary
Xerez in his own.

Pizarro was refused admittance by the guardians of the portal. But, exclaiming that "he had come too far to be stayed by the arm of an Indian priest," he forced his way into the passage, and, followed by his men, wound up the gallery which led to an area on the summit of the mount, at one end of which stood a sort of chapel. This was the sanctuary of the dread deity. The door was garnished with ornaments of crystal, and with turquoises and bits of coral.[8] Here again the Indians would have dissuaded Pizarro from violating the consecrated precincts, when, at that moment, the shock of an earthquake, that made the ancient walls tremble to their foundation, so alarmed the natives, both those of Pizarro's own company and the people of the place, that they fled in dismay, nothing doubting that their incensed deity would bury the invaders under the ruins, or consume them with his lightnings. But no such terror found its way into the breast of the Conquerors, who felt that here, at least, they were fighting the good fight of the Faith.

Tearing open the door, Pizarro and his party entered. But instead of a hall blazing, as they had fondly imagined, with gold and precious stones, offerings of the worshippers of Pachacamac, they found themselves in a small and obscure apartment, or rather den, from the floor and sides of which steamed up the most offensive odors,—like those of a slaughter-house. It was the place of sacrifice. A few pieces of gold and some emeralds were discovered on the ground, and, as their eyes became accommodated to the darkness, they discerned in the most retired corner of the room the figure of the deity. It was an uncouth monster, made of wood, with the head resembling that of a man. This was the god, through whose lips Satan had breathed forth the far-famed oracles which had deluded his Indian votaries! [9]

Tearing the idol from its recess, the indignant Spaniards dragged it into the open air, and there broke it into a hundred fragments. The place was then purified, and a large cross, made of stone and plaster, was erected on the spot. In a few years the walls of the temple were pulled down by the Spanish settlers, who found there a convenient quarry for their own edifices. But the cross still remained spreading its broad arms over the ruins. It stood where it was planted in the very heart of the stronghold of Heathendom; and, while all was in ruins around it, it proclaimed the permanent triumphs of the Faith.

The simple natives, finding that Heaven had no bolts in store for the Conquerors, and that their god had no power to prevent the profanation of his shrine, came in gradually and tendered their homage to the strang-

[8] "Esta puerta era muy tejida de diversas cosas de corales y turquesas y cristales y otras cosas." Relacion del Primer. Descub., MS.

[9] "Aquel era Pachacama, el cual les sanaba de sus enfermedades, y á lo que alli se entendió, el Demonio aparecia en aquella cueba á aquellos sacerdotes y hablaba con ellos, y estos entraban con las peticiones y ofrendas de los que venian en romeria, que es cierto que del todo el Señorio de Atabalica iban alli, como los Moros y Turcos van á la casa de Meca." Relacion del Primer. Descub., MS.—Also Estete, ap. Barcia, tom. III. p. 209.

ers, whom they now regarded with feelings of superstitious awe. Pizarro profited by this temper to wean them, if possible, from their idolatry; and though no preacher himself, as he tells us, he delivered a discourse as edifying, doubtless, as could be expected from the mouth of a soldier;[10] and, in conclusion, he taught them the sign of the cross, as an inestimable talisman to secure them against the future machinations of the Devil.[11]

But the Spanish commander was not so absorbed in his spiritual labors as not to have an eye to those temporal concerns for which he came into this quarter. He now found, to his chagrin, that he had come somewhat too late; and that the priests of Pachacamac, being advised of his mission, had secured much the greater part of the gold, and decamped with it before his arrival. A quantity was afterwards discovered buried in the grounds adjoining.[12] Still the amount obtained was considerable, falling little short of eighty thousand castellanos, a sum which once would have been deemed a compensation for greater fatigues than they had encountered. But the Spaniards had become familiar with gold; and their imaginations, kindled by the romantic adventures in which they had of late been engaged, indulged in visions which all the gold of Peru would scarcely have realized.

One prize, however, Hernando obtained by his expedition, which went far to console him for the loss of his treasure. While at Pachacamac, he learned that the Indian commander Challcuchima lay with a large force in the neighborhood of Xauxa, a town of some strength at a considerable distance among the mountains. This man, who was nearly related to Atahuallpa, was his most experienced general, and together with Quizquiz, now at Cuzco, had achieved those victories at the south which placed the Inca on the throne. From his birth, his talents, and his large experience, he was accounted second to no subject in the kingdom. Pizarro was aware of the importance of securing his person. Finding that the Indian noble declined to meet him on his return, he determined to march at once on Xauxa and take the chief in his own quarters. Such a scheme, considering the enormous disparity of numbers, might seem desperate even for Spaniards. But success had given them such confidence, that they hardly condescended to calculate chances.

The road across the mountains presented greater difficulties than those on the former march. To add to the troubles of the cavalry, the shoes of their horses were used up, and their hoofs suffered severely on the rough and stony ground. There was no iron at hand, nothing but gold and silver. In the present emergency they turned even these to account; and

[10] "É á falta de predicador les hice mi sermon, diciendo el engaño en que vivian." Carta de Hern. Pizarro, MS.

[11] Ibid., MS.—Relacion del Primer. Descub., MS.—Estete, ap. Barcia, tom. III. p 209.

[12] "Y andando los tiĕpos el capitan Rodrigo Orgoñez, y Francisco de Godoy, y otros sacaron grã summa de oro y plata de los enterramientos. Y aun se presume y tiene por cierto, que ay mucho mas: pero como no se sabe donde esta enterrado, s. pierde." Cieza de Leon, Cronica, cap. 72.

Pizarro caused the horses of the whole troop to be shod with silver The work was done by the Indian smiths, and it answered so well, that in this precious material they found a substitute for iron during the remainder of the march.[13]

Xauxa was a large and populous place; though we shall hardly credit the assertion of the Conquerors, that a hundred thousand persons assembled habitually in the great square of the city.[14] The Peruvian commander was encamped, it was said, with an army of five-and-thirty thousand men at only a few miles' distance from the town. With some difficulty he was persuaded to an interview with Pizarro. The latter addressed him courteously, and urged his return with him to the Castilian quarters in Caxamalca, representing it as the command of the Inca. Ever since the capture of his master, Challcuchima had remained uncertain what course to take. The capture of the Inca in this sudden and mysterious manner by a race of beings who seemed to have dropped from the clouds, and that too in the very hour of his triumph, had entirely bewildered the Peruvian chief. He had concerted no plan for the rescue of Atahuallpa, nor, indeed, did he know whether any such movement would be acceptable to him. He now acquiesced in his commands, and was willing, at all events, to have a personal interview with his sovereign. Pizarro gained his end without being obliged to strike a single blow to effect it. The barbarian, when brought into contact with the white man, would seem to have been rebuked by his superior genius, in the same manner as the wild animal of the forest is said to quail before the steady glance of the hunter.

Challcuchima came attended by a numerous retinue. He was borne in his sedan on the shoulders of his vassals; and, as he accompanied the Spaniards on their return through the country, received everywhere from the inhabitants the homage paid only to the favorite of a monarch. Yet all this pomp vanished on his entering the presence of the Inca, whom he approached with his feet bare, while a light burden, which he had taken from one of the attendants, was laid on his back. As he drew near, the old warrior, raising his hands to heaven, exclaimed,—"Would that I had been here!—this would not then have happened"; then, kneeling down, ne kissed the hands and feet of his royal master, and bathed them with his tears. Atahuallpa, on his part, betrayed not the least emotion, and showed no other sign of satisfaction at the presence of his favorite coun-

[13] "Hicieron hacer herrage de herraduras é claves para sus Caballos de Plata, los cuales hicieron los cien Indios fundidores muy buenos é cuantos quisieron de ellos, con el cual herrage andubieron dos meses." (Oviedo, Hist. de las Indias, MS., Parte 3, lib. 8, cap. 16.) The author of the Relacion del Primero Descubrimiento, MS., says they shod the horses with silver and copper. And another of the Peruvian Conquerors assures us they used gold and silver. (Relatione d'un Capitano Spagnuolo, ap. Ramusio, Navigationi et Viaggi, Venetia, 1565, tom. III. fol. 376.) All agree in the silver.

[14] "Era mucha la Gente de aquel Pueblo, i de sus Comarcas, que al parecer de los Españoles, se juntaban cada Dia en la Plaça Principal cien mil Personas." Estete ap. Barcia, tom. III. p. 230.

sellor, than by simply bidding him welcome. The cold demeanor of the monarch contrasted strangely with the loyal sensibility of the subject.[15]

The rank of the Inca placed him at an immeasurable distance above the proudest of his vassals; and the Spaniards had repeated occasion to admire the ascendency which, even in his present fallen fortunes, he maintained over his people, and the awe with which they approached him. Pedro Pizarro records an interview, at which he was present, between Atahuallpa and one of his great nobles, who had obtained leave to visit some remote part of the country on condition of returning by a certain day. He was detained somewhat beyond the appointed time, and, on entering the presence with a small propitiatory gift for his sovereign, his knees shook so violently, that it seemed, says the chronicler, as if he would have fallen to the ground. His master, however, received him kindly, and dismissed him without a word of rebuke.[16]

Atahuallpa in his confinement continued to receive the same respectful treatment from the Spaniards as hitherto. They taught him to play with dice, and the more intricate game of chess, in which the royal captive became expert, and loved to beguile with it the tedious hours of his imprisonment. Towards his own people he maintained as far as possible his wonted state and ceremonial. He was attended by his wives and the girls of his harem, who, as was customary, waited on him at table and discharged the other menial offices about his person. A body of Indian nobles were stationed in the antechamber, but never entered the presence unbidden; and when they did enter it, they submitted to the same humiliating ceremonies imposed on the greatest of his subjects. The service of his table was gold and silver plate. His dress, which he often changed, was composed of the wool of the vicuña wrought into mantles, so fine that it had the appearance of silk. He sometimes exchanged these for a robe made of the skins of bats, as soft and sleek as velvet. Round his head he wore the *llautu*, a woollen turban or shawl of the most delicate texture, wreathed in folds of various bright colors; and he still continued to encircle his temples with the *borla*, the crimson threads of which, mingled with gold, descended so as partly to conceal his eyes. The image of royalty had charms for him, when its substance had departed. No garment or utensil that had once belonged to the Peruvian sovereign could ever be used by another. When he laid it aside, it was carefully deposited in a chest, kept for the purpose, and afterwards burned. It would have been sacrilege to apply to vulgar uses that which had been consecrated by the touch of the Inca.[17]

Not long after the arrival of the party from Pachacamac, in the latter part of May, the three emissaries returned from Cuzco. They had been

[15] Pedro Pizarro, Descub. y Conq., MS.

"The like of it," exclaims Estete, "was never before seen since the Indies were discovered." Ibid., p. 231.

[16] Pedro Pizarro, Descub. y Conq., MS.

[17] This account of the personal habits of Atahuallpa is taken from Pedro Pizarro, who saw him often in his confinement

very successful in their mission. Owing to the Inca's order, and the awe which the white men now inspired throughout the country, the Spaniards had everywhere met with a kind reception. They had been carried on the shoulders of the natives in the *hamacas*, or sedans, of the country; and, as they had travelled all the way to the capital on the great imperial road, along which relays of Indian carriers were established at stated intervals, they performed this journey of more than six hundred miles, not only without inconvenience, but with the most luxurious ease. They passed through many populous towns, and always found the simple natives disposed to venerate them as beings of a superior nature. In Cuzco they were received with public festivities, were sumptuously lodged, and had every want anticipated by the obsequious devotion of the inhabitants.

Their accounts of the capital confirmed all that Pizarro had before heard of the wealth and population of the city. Though they had remained more than a week in this place, the emissaries had not seen the whole of it. The great temple of the Sun they found literally covered with plates of gold. They had entered the interior and beheld the royal mummies, seated each in his gold-embossed chair, and in robes profusely covered with ornaments. The Spaniards had the grace to respect these, as they had been previously enjoined by the Inca; but they required that the plates which garnished the walls should be all removed. The Peruvians most reluctantly acquiesced in the commands of their sovereign to desecrate the national temple, which every inhabitant of the city regarded with peculiar pride and veneration. With less reluctance they assisted the Conquerors in stripping the ornaments from some of the other edifices, where the gold, however, being mixed with a large proportion of alloy, was of much less value.[18]

The number of plates they tore from the temple of the Sun was seven hundred; and though of no great thickness, probably, they are compared in size to the lid of a chest, ten or twelve inches wide.[19] A cornice of pure gold encircled the edifice, but so strongly set in the stone, that it fortunately defied the efforts of the spoilers. The Spaniards complained of the want of alacrity shown by the Indians in the work of destruction, and said that there were other parts of the city containing buildings rich in gold and silver which they had not been allowed to see. In truth, their mission, which, at best, was a most ungrateful one, had been rendered doubly annoying by the manner in which they had executed it. The emissaries were men of a very low stamp, and, puffed up by the honors conceded to them by the natives, they looked on themselves as entitled to these, and contemned the poor Indians as a race immeasurably beneath the European. They not only showed the most disgusting rapacity,

---

[18] Rel. d'un Capitano Spagn., ap. Ramusio, tom. III. fol. 375.—Pedro Pizarro, Descub. y Conq., MS.—Herrera, Hist. General, dec. 5, lib. 2, cap. 12, 13.

[19] "I de las Chapas de oro, que esta Casa tenia, quitaron setecientas Planchas . . . . . à manera de Tablas de Caxas de à tres, i à quatro palmos de largo." Xerez, Conq. del Peru, ap. Barcia, tom. III. p. 232.

but treated the nighest nobles with wanton insolence. They even went so far, it is said, as to violate the privacy of the convents, and to outrage the religious sentiments of the Peruvians by their scandalous amours with the Virgins of the Sun. The people of Cuzco were so exasperated, that they would have laid violent hands on them, but for their habitual reverence for the Inca, in whose name the Spaniards had come there. As it was, the Indians collected as much gold as was necessary to satisfy their unworthy visitors, and got rid of them as speedily as possible.[20] It was a great mistake in Pizarro to send such men. There were persons, even in his company, who, as other occasions showed, had some sense of self-respect, if not respect for the natives.

The messengers brought with them, besides silver, full two hundred *cargas* or loads of gold.[21] This was an important accession to the con-tributions of Atahuallpa; and, although the treasure was still consider-ably below the mark prescribed, the monarch saw with satisfaction the time drawing nearer for the completion of his ransom.

Not long before this, an event had occurred which changed the con-dition of the Spaniards, and had an unfavorable influence on the for-tunes of the Inca. This was the arrival of Almagro at Caxamalca, with a strong reinforcement. That chief had succeeded, after great efforts, in equipping three vessels, and assembling a body of one hundred and fifty men, with which he sailed from Panamá, the latter part of the preceding year. On his voyage, he was joined by a small additional force from Nica-ragua, so that his whole strength amounted to one hundred and fifty foot and fifty horse, well provided with the munitions of war. His vessels were steered by the old pilot Ruiz; but after making the Bay of St. Matthew, he crept slowly along the coast, baffled as usual by winds and currents, and experiencing all the hardships incident to that protracted navigation. From some cause or other, he was not so fortunate as to obtain tidings of Pizarro; and so disheartened were his followers, most of whom were raw adventurers, that, when arrived at Puerto Viejo, they proposed to aban-don the expedition, and return at once to Panamá. Fortunately, one of the little squadron which Almagro had sent forward to Tumbez brought intelligence of Pizarro and of the colony he had planted at San Miguel. Cheered by the tidings, the cavalier resumed his voyage, and succeeded, at length, towards the close of December, 1532, in bringing his whole party safe to the Spanish settlement.

He there received the account of Pizarro's march across the moun-tains, his seizure of the Inca, and, soon afterwards, of the enormous ran-som offered for his liberation. Almagro and his companions listened with

[20] Herrera, Hist. General, ubi supra.

[21] So says Pizarro's secretary. "I vinieron docientas cargas de Oro, i veinte i cinco de Plata." (Xerez, Conq. del Peru, ap. Barcia, ubi supra.) A load, he says, was brought by four Indians. "Cargas de Paligueres, que las traen quatro Indios." The meaning of *paligueres*—not a Spanish word—is doubtful. Ternaux-Compans sup-poses, ingeniously enough, that it may have something of the same meaning with *palanquin*, to which it bears some resemblance.

undisguised amazement to this account of his associate, and of a change in his fortunes so rapid and wonderful that it seemed little less than magic. At the same time, he received a caution from some of the colonists not to trust himself in the power of Pizarro, who was known to bear him no good-will.

Not long after Almagro's arrival at San Miguel, advices were sent of it to Caxamalca, and a private note from his secretary Perez informed Pizarro that his associate had come with no purpose of coöperating with him, but with the intention to establish an independent government. Both of the Spanish captains seem to have been surrounded by mean and turbulent spirits, who sought to embroil them with each other, trusting, doubtless, to find their own account in the rupture. For once, however, their malicious machinations failed.

Pizarro was overjoyed at the arrival of so considerable a reinforcement, which would enable him to push his fortunes as he had desired, and go forward with the conquest of the country. He laid little stress on the secretary's communication, since, whatever might have been Almagro's original purpose, Pizarro knew that the richness of the vein he had now opened in the land would be certain to secure his coöperation in working it. He had the magnanimity, therefore,—for there is something magnanimous in being able to stifle the suggestions of a petty rivalry in obedience to sound policy,—to send at once to his ancient comrade, and invite him, with many assurances of friendship, to Caxamalca. Almagro, who was of a frank and careless nature, received the communication in the spirit in which it was made, and, after some necessary delay, directed his march into the interior. But before leaving San Miguel, having become acquainted with the treacherous conduct of his secretary, he recompensed his treason by hanging him on the spot.[22]

Almagro reached Caxamalca about the middle of February, 1533. The soldiers of Pizarro came out to welcome their countrymen, and the two captains embraced each other with every mark of cordial satisfaction. All past differences were buried in oblivion, and they seemed only prepared to aid one another in following up the brilliant career now opened to them in the conquest of an empire.

There was one person in Caxamalca on whom this arrival of the Spaniards produced a very different impression from that made on their own countrymen. This was the Inca Atahuallpa. He saw in the new-comers only a new swarm of locusts to devour his unhappy country; and he felt, that, with his enemies thus multiplying around him, the chances were diminished of recovering his freedom, or of maintaining it, if recovered. A little circumstance, insignificant in itself, but magnified by superstition into something formidable, occurred at this time to cast an additional gloom over his situation.

A remarkable appearance, somewhat of the nature of a meteor, or it

[22] Pedro Pizarro, Descub. y Conq., MS.—Xerez, Conq. del Peru, ap. Barcia, tom. III. pp. 204, 205.—Relacion Sumaria, MS.—Conq. i Pob. del Piru, MS.—Relacion del Primer. Descub., MS.—Herrera, Hist. General, dec. 5, lib. 3, cap. 1.

may have been a comet, was seen in the heavens by some soldiers and pointed out to Atahuallpa. He gazed on it with fixed attention for some minutes, and then exclaimed, with a dejected air, that "a similar sign had been seen in the skies a short time before the death of his father Huayna Capac." [23] From this day a sadness seemed to take possession of him, as he looked with doubt and undefined dread to the future.—Thus it is, that, in seasons of danger, the mind, like the senses, becomes morbidly acute in its perceptions; and the least departure from the regular course of nature, that would have passed unheeded in ordinary times, to the superstitious eye seems pregnant with meaning, as in some way or other connected with the destiny of the individual.

[23] Rel. d'un Capitano Spagn., ap. Ramusio, tom. III. fol. 377.—Cieza de Leon. Cronica, cap. 65.

CHAPTER VII

IMMENSE AMOUNT OF TREASURE—ITS DIVISION AMONG THE TROOPS—
RUMORS OF A RISING—TRIAL OF THE INCA—HIS EXECUTION—
REFLECTIONS

1533

THE arrival of Almagro produced a considerable change in Pizarro's
prospects, since it enabled him to resume active operations, and push forward his conquests in the interior. The only obstacle in his way was the
Inca's ransom, and the Spaniards had patiently waited, till the return of
the emissaries from Cuzco swelled the treasure to a large amount, though
still below the stipulated limit. But now their avarice got the better of
their forbearance, and they called loudly for the immediate division of
the gold. To wait longer would only be to invite the assault of their enemies, allured by a bait so attractive. While the treasure remained un-
counted, no man knew its value, nor what was to be his own portion. It
was better to distribute it at once, and let every one possess and defend
his own. Several, moreover, were now disposed to return home, and take
their share of the gold with them, where they could place it in safety.
But these were few, while much the larger part were only anxious to leave
their present quarters, and march at once to Cuzco. More gold, they
thought, awaited them in that capital, than they could get here by prolonging their stay; while every hour was precious, to prevent the inhabitants from secreting their treasures, of which design they had already
given indication.

Pizarro was especially moved by the last consideration; and he felt,
that, without the capital, he could not hope to become master of the empire. Without further delay, the division of the treasure was agreed upon.

Yet, before making this, it was necessary to reduce the whole to ingots
of a uniform standard, for the spoil was composed of an infinite variety
of articles, in which the gold was of very different degrees of purity.
These articles consisted of goblets, ewers, salvers, vases of every shape
and size, ornaments and utensils for the temples and the royal palaces,
tiles and plates for the decoration of the public edifices, curious imitations of different plants and animals. Among the plants, the most beautiful was the Indian corn, in which the golden ear was sheathed in its
broad leaves of silver, from which hung a rich tassel of threads of the
same precious metal. A fountain was also much admired, which sent up
a sparkling jet of gold, while birds and animals of the same material

played in the waters at its base. The delicacy of the workmanship of some of these, and the beauty and ingenuity of the design, attracted the admiration of better judges than the rude Conquerors of Peru.[1]

Before breaking up these specimens of Indian art, it was determined to send a quantity, which should be deducted from the royal fifth, to the Emperor. It would serve as a sample of the ingenuity of the natives, and would show him the value of his conquests. A number of the most beautiful articles was selected, to the amount of a hundred thousand ducats, and Hernando Pizarro was appointed to be the bearer of them to Spain. He was to obtain an audience of Charles, and, at the same time that he laid the treasures before him, he was to give an account of the proceedings of the Conquerors, and to seek a further augmentation of their powers and dignities.

No man in the army was better qualified for this mission, by his address and knowledge of affairs, than Hernando Pizarro; no one would be so likely to urge his suit with effect at the haughty Castilian court. But other reasons influenced the selection of him at the present juncture.

His former jealousy of Almagro still rankled in his bosom, and he had beheld that chief's arrival at the camp with feelings of disgust, which he did not care to conceal. He looked on him as coming to share the spoils of victory, and defraud his brother of his legitimate honors. Instead of exchanging the cordial greeting proffered by Almagro at their first interview, the arrogant cavalier held back in sullen silence. His brother Francis was greatly displeased at a conduct which threatened to renew their ancient feud, and he induced Hernando to accompany him to Almagro's quarters, and make some acknowledgment for his uncourteous behavior.[2] But, notwithstanding this show of reconciliation, the general thought the present a favorable opportunity to remove his brother from the scene of operations, where his factious spirit more than counterbalanced his eminent services.[3]

The business of melting down the plate was intrusted to the Indian goldsmiths, who were thus required to undo the work of their own hands. They toiled day and night, but such was the quantity to be recast, that it consumed a full month. When the whole was reduced to bars of a uniform standard, they were nicely weighed, under the superintendence of the royal inspectors. The total amount of the gold was found to be one mil-

---

[1] Relatione de Pedro Sancho, ap. Ramusio, Viaggi, tom. III. fol. 399.—Xerez, Conq. del Peru, ap. Barcia, tom. III. p. 233.—Zarate, Conq. del Peru, lib. 2, cap. 7.
  Oviedo saw at St. Domingo the articles which Ferdinand Pizarro was bearing to Castile; and he expatiates on several beautifully wrought vases, richly chased, of very fine gold, and measuring twelve inches in height and thirty round. Hist. de las Indias, MS., Parte 3, lib. 8, cap. 16.

[2] Herrera, Hist. General, dec. 5, lib. 2, cap. 3.

[3] According to Oviedo it was agreed that Hernando should have a share, much larger than he was entitled to, of the Inca's ransom, in the hope that he would feel so rich as never to desire to return again to Peru. "Trabajaron de le embiar rico por quitarle de entre ellos, y porque yendo muy rico como fue no tubiese voluntad de tornar á aquellas partes." Hist. de las Indias. MS., Parte 3, lib. 8, cap. 16.

lion, three hundred and twenty-six thousand, five hundred and thirty-nine *pesos de oro*, which, allowing for the greater value of money in the sixteenth century, would be equivalent, probably, at the present time, to near *three millions and a half of pounds sterling*, or somewhat less than *fifteen millions and a half of dollars*.[4] The quantity of silver was estimated at fifty-one thousand six hundred and ten marks. History affords no parallel of such a booty—and that, too, in the most convertible form, in ready money, as it were—having fallen to the lot of a little band of

---

[4] Acta de Reparticion del Rescate de Atahuallpa, MS.—Xerez, Conq. del Peru, ap. Barcia, tom. III. p. 232.

In reducing the sums mentioned in this work, I have availed myself—as I before did, in the History of the Conquest of Mexico—of the labors of Señor Clemencin, formerly Secretary of the Royal Academy of History at Madrid. This eminent scholar, in the sixth volume of the Memoirs of the Academy, prepared wholly by himself, has introduced an elaborate essay on the value of the currency in the reign of Ferdinand and Isabella. Although this period—the close of the fifteenth century—was somewhat earlier than that of the Conquest of Peru, yet his calculations are sufficiently near the truth for our purpose, since the Spanish currency had not as yet been much affected by that disturbing cause,—the influx of the precious metals from the New World.

In inquiries into the currency of a remote age, we may consider, in the first place, the specific value of the coin,—that is, the value which it derives from the weight, purity, &c., of the metal, circumstances easily determined. In the second place, we may inquire into the commercial or comparative worth of the money,—that is, the value founded on a comparison of the difference between the amount of commodities which the same sum would purchase formerly, and at the present time. The last inquiry is attended with great embarrassment, from the difficulty of finding any one article which may be taken as the true standard of value. Wheat, from its general cultivation and use, has usually been selected by political economists as this standard; and Clemencin has adopted it in his calculations. Assuming wheat as the standard, he has endeavored to ascertain the value of the principal coins in circulation, at the time of the "Catholic Kings." He makes no mention in his treatise of the *peso de oro,* by which denomination the sums in the early part of the sixteenth century were more frequently expressed than by any other. But he ascertains both the specific and the commercial value of the *castellano,* which several of the old writers, as Oviedo, Herrera, and Xerez, concur in stating as precisely equivalent to the *peso de oro*. From the results of his calculations, it appears that the specific value of the castellano, as stated by him in reals, is equal to *three dollars and seven cents of our own currency,* while the commercial value is nearly four times as great, or *eleven dollars sixty-seven cents, equal to two pounds twelve shillings and sixpence sterling.* By adopting *this as the approximate value of the peso de oro, in the early part of the sixteenth century,* the reader may easily compute for himself the value, at that period, of the sums mentioned in these pages; most of which are expressed in that denomination.

I have been the more particular in this statement, since, in my former work, I confined myself to the commercial value of the money, which, being much greater than the specific value founded on the quality and weight of the metal, was thought by an ingenious correspondent to give the reader an exaggerated estimate of the sums mentioned in the history. But it seems to me that it is only this comparative or commercial value with which the reader has any concern; indicating what amount of commodities any given sum represents, that he may thus know the real worth of that sum;—thus adopting the principle, though conversely stated, of the old Hudibrastic maxim,—

> "What is *worth* in any thing,
> But so much money as 't will bring?"

military adventurers, like the Conquerors of Peru. The great object of the Spanish expeditions in the New World was gold. It is remarkable that their success should have been so complete. Had they taken the track of the English, the French, or the Dutch, on the shores of the northern continent, how different would have been the result! It is equally worthy of remark, that the wealth thus suddenly acquired, by diverting them from the slow but surer and more permanent sources of national prosperity, has in the end glided from their grasp, and left them among the poorest of the nations of Christendom.

A new difficulty now arose in respect to the division of the treasure. Almagro's followers claimed to be admitted to a share of it; which, as they equalled, and indeed, somewhat exceeded in number Pizarro's company, would reduce the gains of these last very materially. "We were not here, it is true," said Almagro's soldiers to their comrades, "at the seizure of the Inca, but we have taken our turn in mounting guard over him since his capture, have helped you to defend your treasures, and now give you the means of going forward and securing your conquests. It is a common cause," they urged, "in which all are equally embarked, and the gains should be shared equally between us."

But this way of viewing the matter was not at all palatable to Pizarro's company, who alleged that Atahuallpa's contract had been made exclusively with them; that they had seized the Inca, had secured the ransom, had incurred, in short, all the risk of the enterprise, and were not now disposed to share the fruits of it with every one who came after them.— There was much force, it could not be denied, in this reasoning, and it was finally settled between the leaders, that Almagro's followers should resign their pretensions for a stipulated sum of no great amount, and look to the career now opened to them for carving out their fortunes for themselves.

This delicate affair being thus harmoniously adjusted, Pizarro prepared, with all solemnity, for a division of the imperial spoil. The troops were called together in the great square, and the Spanish commander, "with the fear of God before his eyes," says the record, "invoked the assistance of Heaven to do the work before him conscientiously and justly." [5] The appeal may seem somewhat out of place at the distribution of spoil so unrighteously acquired; yet, in truth, considering the magnitude of the treasure, and the power assumed by Pizarro to distribute it according to the respective deserts of the individuals, there were few acts of his life involving a heavier responsibility. On his present decision might be said to hang the future fortunes of each one of his followers,—poverty or independence during the remainder of his days.

The royal fifth was first deducted, including the remittance already sent to Spain. The share appropriated by Pizarro amounted to fifty-seven thousand two hundred and twenty-two pesos of gold, and two thousand

---

[5] "Segun Dios Nuestro Señor le diere á entender teniendo su conciencia y para lo mejor hazer pedia el ayuda de Dios Nuestro Señor, é imboco el auxilio divino." Acta de Reparticion del Rescate, MS.

three hundred and fifty marks of silver. He had besides this the great chair or throne of the Inca, of solid gold, and valued at twenty-five thousand *pesos de oro*. To his brother Hernando were paid thirty-one thousand and eighty pesos of gold, and two thousand three hundred and fifty marks of silver. De Soto received seventeen thousand seven hundred and forty pesos of gold, and seven hundred and twenty-four marks of silver. Most of the remaining cavalry, sixty in number, received each eight thousand eight hundred and eighty pesos of gold, and three hundred and sixty-two marks of silver, though some had more, and a few considerably less. The infantry mustered in all one hundred and five men. Almost one fifth of them were allowed, each, four thousand four hundred and forty pesos of gold, and one hundred and eighty marks of silver, half of the compensation of the troopers. The remainder received one fourth part less; though here again there were exceptions, and some were obliged to content themselves with a much smaller share of the spoil.[6]

The new church of San Francisco, the first Christian temple in Peru, was endowed with two thousand two hundred and twenty pesos of gold. The amount assigned to Almagro's company was not excessive, if it was not more than twenty thousand pesos;[7] and that reserved for the colonists of San Miguel, which amounted only to fifteen thousand pesos, was unaccountably small.[8] There were among them certain soldiers, who at an early period of the expedition, as the reader may remember, abandoned the march, and returned to San Miguel. These, certainly, had little claim to be remembered in the division of booty. But the greater part of the colony consisted of invalids, men whose health had been broken by their previous hardships, but who still, with a stout and willing heart, did good service in their military post on the sea-coast. On what grounds they had forfeited their claims to a more ample remuneration, it is not easy to explain.

Nothing is said, in the partition, of Almagro himself, who, by the terms of the original contract, might claim an equal share of the spoil with his associate. As little notice is taken of Luque, the remaining partner. Luque himself, was, indeed, no longer to be benefited by worldly treasure. He had died a short time before Almagro's departure from Panamá;[9] too soon to learn the full success of the enterprise, which, but for his exer-

---

[6] The particulars of the distribution are given in the *Acta de Reparticion del Rescate*, an instrument drawn up and signed by the royal notary. The document, which is therefore of unquestionable authority, is among the MSS. selected for me from the collection of Muñoz.

[7] "Se diese á la gente gue vino con el Capitan Diego de Almagro para ayuda á pagar sus deudas y fletes y suplir algunas necesidades que traian veinte mil pesos." (Acta de Reparticion del Rescate, MS.) Herrera says that 100,000 *pesos* were paid to Almagro's men. (Hist. General, dec. 5, lib. 2, cap. 3.) But it is not so set down in the instrument.

[8] "En treinta personas que quedaron en la ciudad de san Miguel de Piura dolientes y otros que no vinieron ni se hallaron en la prision de Atagualpa y toma del oro porque algunos son pobres y otros tienen necesidad señalaba 15,000 pˢ de oro para los repartir S. Señoria entre las dichas personas." Ibid., MS.

[9] Montesinos. Annales, MS., año 1533.

tions, must have failed; too soon to become acquainted with the achievements and the crimes of Pizarro. But the Licentiate Espinosa, whom he represented, and who, it appears, had advanced the funds for the expedition, was still living at St. Domingo, and Luque's pretensions were explicitly transferred to him. Yet it is unsafe to pronounce, at this distance of time, on the authority of mere negative testimony; and it must be admitted to form a strong presumption in favor of Pizarro's general equity in the distribution, that no complaint of it has reached us from any of the parties present, nor from contemporary chroniclers.[10]

The division of the ransom being completed by the Spaniards, there seemed to be no further obstacle to their resuming active operations, and commencing the march to Cuzco. But what was to be done with Atahuallpa? In the determination of this question, whatever was expedient was just.[11] To liberate him would be to set at large the very man who might prove their most dangerous enemy; one whose birth and royal station would rally round him the whole nation, place all the machinery of government at his control, and all its resources,—one, in short, whose bare word might concentrate all the energies of his people against the Spaniards, and thus delay for a long period, if not wholly defeat, the conquest of the country. Yet to hold him in captivity was attended with scarcely less difficulty; since to guard so important a prize would require such a division of their force as must greatly cripple its strength, and how could they expect, by any vigilance, to secure their prisoner against rescue in the perilous passes of the mountains?

The Inca himself now loudly demanded his freedom. The proposed amount of the ransom had, indeed, not been fully paid. It may be doubted whether it ever would have been, considering the embarrassments thrown in the way by the guardians of the temples, who seemed disposed to secrete the treasures, rather than despoil these sacred depositories to satisfy the cupidity of the strangers. It was unlucky, too, for the Indian monarch, that much of the gold, and that of the best quality, consisted of flat plates or tiles, which, however valuable, lay in a compact form that did little towards swelling the heap. But an immense amount had been already realized, and it would have been a still greater one, the Inca might allege, but for the impatience of the Spaniards. At all events, it was a magnificent ransom, such as was never paid by prince or potentate before.

These considerations Atahuallpa urged on several of the cavaliers, and especially on Hernando de Soto, who was on terms of more familiarity

---

[10] The "Spanish Captain," several times cited, who tells us he was one of the men appointed to guard the treasure, does indeed complain that a large quantity of gold vases and other articles remained undivided, a palpable injustice, he thinks, to the honest Conquerors, who had earned all by their hardships. (Rel. d'un Capitano Spagn., ap. Ramusio, tom. III. fol. 378, 379.) The writer, throughout his Relation, shows a full measure of the coarse and covetous spirit which marked the adventurers of Peru.

[11] "Y esto tenia por justo, pues era provechoso." It is the sentiment imputed to Pizarro by Herrera, Hist. General, dec. 5, lib. 3, cap. 4.

with him than Pizarro. De Soto reported Atahuallpa's demands to his leader; but the latter evaded a direct reply. He did not disclose the dark purposes over which his mind was brooding.[12] Not long afterward he caused the notary to prepare an instrument, in which he fully acquitted the Inca of further obligation in respect to the ransom. This he commanded to be publicly proclaimed in the camp, while at the same time he openly declared that the safety of the Spaniards required, that the Inca should be detained in confinement until they were strengthened by additional reinforcements.[13]

Meanwhile the old rumors of a meditated attack by the natives began to be current among the soldiers. They were repeated from one to another, gaining something by every repetition. An immense army, it was reported, was mustering at Quito, the land of Atahuallpa's birth, and thirty thousand Caribs were on their way to support it.[14] The Caribs were distributed by the early Spaniards rather indiscriminately over the different parts of America, being invested with peculiar horrors as a race of cannibals.

It was not easy to trace the origin of these rumors. There was in the camp a considerable number of Indians, who belonged to the party of Huascar, and who were, of course, hostile to Atahuallpa. But his worst enemy was Felipillo, the interpreter from Tumbez, already mentioned in these pages. This youth had conceived a passion, or, as some say, had been detected in an intrigue with, one of the royal concubines.[15] The circumstance had reached the ears of Atahuallpa, who felt himself deeply outraged by it. "That such an insult should have been offered by so base a person was an indignity," he said, "more difficult to bear than his imprisonment";[16] and he told Pizarro, "that, by the Peruvian law, it could

---

[12] "I como no ahondaban los designios que tenia le replicaban; pero èl respondia, que iba mirando en ello." Herrera, Hist. General, dec. 5, lib. 3, cap. 4.

[13] "Fatta quella fusione, il Governatore fece vn atto innanzi al notaro nel quale liberaua il Cacique Atabalipa et l'absolueua della promessa et parola che haueua data a gli Spagnuoli che lo presero della casa d'oro c'haueua lor côcessa, il quale fece publicar publicamête a suon di trombe nella piazza di quella città di Caxamalca." (Pedro Sancho, Rel., ap. Ramusio, tom. III. fol. 399.) The authority is unimpeachable,—for any fact, at least, that makes against the Conquerors,—since the *Relatione* was by one of Pizarro's own secretaries, and was authorized under the hands of the general and his great officers.

[14] "De la Gente Natural de Quito vienen docientos mil Hombres de Guerra, i treinta mil Caribes, que comen Carne Humana." Xerez, Conq. del Peru, ap. Barcia, tom. III. p. 233.—See also Pedro Sancho, Rel., ap. Ramusio, ubi supra.

[15] "Pues estando asi atravesose un demonio de una lengua que se dezia ffelipillo uno de los muchachos que el marquez avia llevado á España que al presente hera lengua y andava enamorado de una muger de Atabalipa." Pedro Pizarro, Descub. y Conq., MS.

The amour and the malice of Felipillo, which, Quintana seems to think, rest chiefly on Garcilasso's authority, (see Españoles Célebres, tom. II. p. 210, nota,) are stated very explicitly by Zarate, Naharro, Gomara, Balboa, all contemporaneous, though not, like Pedro Pizarro, personally present in the army.

[16] "Diciendo que sentia mas aquel desacato, que su prision." Zarate, Conq. del Peru, lib. 2, cap. 7.

be expiated, not by the criminal's own death alone, but by that of his whole family and kindred." [17] But Felipillo was too important to the Spaniards to be dealt with so summarily; nor did they probably attach such consequence to an offence which, if report be true, they had countenanced by their own example.[18] Felipillo, however, soon learned the state of the Inca's feelings towards himself, and from that moment he regarded him with deadly hatred. Unfortunately, his malignant temper found ready means for its indulgence.

The rumors of a rising among the natives pointed to Atahuallpa as the author of it. Challcuchima was examined on the subject, but avowed his entire ignorance of any such design, which he pronounced a malicious slander. Pizarro next laid the matter before the Inca himself, repeating to him the stories in circulation, with the air of one who believed them. "What treason is this," said the general, "that you have meditated against me,—me, who have ever treated you with honor, confiding in your words, as in those of a brother?" "You jest," replied the Inca, who, perhaps, did not feel the weight of this confidence; "you are always jesting with me. How could I or my people think of conspiring against men so valiant as the Spaniards? Do not jest with me thus, I beseech you."[19] "This," continues Pizarro's secretary, "he said in the most composed and natural manner, smiling all the while to dissemble his falsehood, so that we were all amazed to find such cunning in a barbarian." [20]

But it was not with cunning, but with the consciousness of innocence, as the event afterwards proved, that Atahuallpa thus spoke to Pizarro. He readily discerned, however, the causes, perhaps the consequences, of the accusation. He saw a dark gulf opening beneath his feet; and he was surrounded by strangers, on none of whom he could lean for counsel or protection. The life of the captive monarch is usually short; and Atahuallpa might have learned the truth of this, when he thought of Huascar. Bitterly did he now lament the absence of Hernando Pizarro, for, strange as it may seem, the haughty spirit of this cavalier had been touched by the condition of the royal prisoner, and he had treated him with a deference which won for him the peculiar regard and confidence of the Indian. Yet the latter lost no time in endeavoring to efface the general's suspicions, and to establish his own innocence. "Am I not," said he to Pizarro, "a poor captive in your hands? How could I harbor the designs you impute to me, when I should be the first victim of the outbreak? And you little know my people, if you think that such a movement would be made without my orders; when the very birds in my dominions," said

[17] Ibid., loc. cit.

[18] "È le habian tomado sus mugeres é repartidolas en su presencia é usaban de ellas de sus adulterios." Oviedo, Hist. de las Indias, MS., Parte 3, lib. 8, cap. 22.

[19] "Burlaste conmigo? siempre me hablas cosas de burlas? Què parte somos Yo, ¿ toda mi Gente, para enojar à tan valientes Hombres como vosotros? No me digas esas burlas." Xerez, Conq. del Peru, ap. Barcia, tom. III, p. 234.

[20] "De que los Españoles que se las han oido, estan espantados de vèr en vn Hombre Barbaro tanta prudencia." Ibid., loc. cit.

he, with somewhat of an hyperbole, "would scarcely venture to fly contrary to my will." [21]

But these protestations of innocence had little effect on the troops; among whom the story of a general rising of the natives continued to gain credit every hour. A large force, it was said, was already gathered at Guamachucho, not a hundred miles from the camp, and their assault might be hourly expected. The treasure which the Spaniards had acquired afforded a tempting prize, and their own alarm was increased by the apprehension of losing it. The patroles were doubled. The horses were kept saddled and bridled. The soldiers slept on their arms; Pizarro went the rounds regularly to see that every sentinel was on his post. The little army, in short, was in a state of preparation for instant attack.

Men suffering from fear are not likely to be too scrupulous as to the means of removing the cause of it. Murmurs, mingled with gloomy menaces, were now heard against the Inca, the author of these machinations. Many began to demand his life as necessary to the safety of the army. Among these, the most vehement were Almagro and his followers. They had not witnessed the seizure of Atahuallpa. They had no sympathy with him in his fallen state. They regarded him only as an incumbrance, and their desire now was to push their fortunes in the country, since they had got so little of the gold of Caxamalca. They were supported by Riquelme, the treasurer, and by the rest of the royal officers. These men had been left at San Miguel by Pizarro, who did not care to have such official spies on his movements. But they had come to the camp with Almagro, and they loudly demanded the Inca's death, as indispensable to the tranquillity of the country, and the interests of the Crown.[22]

To these dark suggestions Pizarro turned—or seemed to turn—an unwilling ear, showing visible reluctance to proceed to extreme measures with his prisoner.[23] There were some few, and among others Hernando de Soto, who supported him in these views, and who regarded such measures as not at all justified by the evidence of Atahuallpa's guilt. In this state of things, the Spanish commander determined to send a small detachment to Guamachucho, to reconnoitre the country and ascertain what ground there was for the rumors of an insurrection. De Soto was placed at the head of the expedition, which, as the distance was not great, would occupy but a few days.

After that cavalier's departure, the agitation among the soldiers, instead of diminishing, increased to such a degree, that Pizarro, unable to resist their importunities, consented to bring Atahuallpa to instant trial. It was but decent, and certainly safer, to have the forms of a trial. A

[21] "Pues si Yo no lo quiero, ni las Aves bolaràn en mi Tierra." Zarate, Conq. del Peru, lib. 2, cap. 7.

[22] Pedro Pizarro, Descub. y Conq., MS.—Relacion del Primer. Descub., MS.—Ped. Sancho, Rel., ap. Ramusio, tom. III. fol. 400.

These cavaliers were all present in the camp.

[23] "Aunque contra voluntad del dicho Gobernador, que nunca estubo bien en ello." Relacion del Primer. Descub., MS.—So also Pedro Pizarro, Descub. y Conq., MS.—Ped. Sancho, Rel., ap. Ramusio, ubi supra.

court was organized, over which the two captains, Pizarro and Almagro, were to preside as judges. An attorney-general was named to prosecute for the Crown, and counsel was assigned to the prisoner.

The charges preferred against the Inca, drawn up in the form of interrogatories, were twelve in number. The most important were, that he had usurped the crown and assassinated his brother Huascar; that he had squandered the public revenues since the conquest of the country by the Spaniards, and lavished them on his kindred and his minions; that he was guilty of idolatry, and of adulterous practices, indulging openly in a plurality of wives; finally, that he had attempted to excite an insurrection against the Spaniards.[24]

These charges, most of which had reference to national usages, or to the personal relations of the Inca, over which the Spanish conquerors had clearly no jurisdiction, are so absurd, that they might well provoke a smile, did they not excite a deeper feeling. The last of the charges was the only one of moment in such a trial; and the weakness of this may be inferred from the care taken to bolster it up with the others. The mere specification of the articles must have been sufficient to show that the doom of the Inca was already sealed.

A number of Indian witnesses were examined, and their testimony, filtrated through the interpretation of Felipillo, received, it is said, when necessary, a very different coloring from that of the original. The examination was soon ended, and "a warm discussion," as we are assured by one of Pizarro's own secretaries, "took place in respect to the probable good or evil that would result from the death of Atahuallpa." [25] It was a question of expediency. He was found guilty,—whether of all the crimes alleged we are not informed,—and he was sentenced to be burnt alive in the great square of Caxamalca. The sentence was to be carried into execution that very night. They were not even to wait for the return of De Soto, when the information he would bring would go far to establish the

---

[24] The specification of the charges against the Inca is given by Garcilasso de la Vega. (Com. Real., Parte 2, lib. 1, cap. 37.) One could have wished to find them specified by some of the actors in the tragedy. But Garcilasso had access to the best sources of information, and where there was no motive for falsehood, as in the present instance, his word may probably be taken.—The fact of a process being formally instituted against the Indian monarch is explicitly recognized by several contemporary writers, by Gomara, Oviedo, and Pedro Sancho. Oviedo characterizes it as "a badly contrived and worse written document, devised by a factious and unprincipled priest, a clumsy notary without conscience, and others of the like stamp, who were all concerned in this villainy." (Hist. de las Indias, MS., Parte 3, lib. 8, cap. 22.) Most authorities agree in the two principal charges,—the assassination of Huascar, and the conspiracy against the Spaniards.

[25] "Doppo l'essersi molto disputato, et ragionato del danno et vtile che saria potuto auuenire per il viuere o morire di Atabalipa, fu risoluto che si facesse giustitia di lui." (Ped. Sancho, Rel., ap. Ramusio, tom. III. fol. 400.) It is the language of a writer who may be taken as the mouthpiece of Pizarro himself. According to him, the conclave, which agitated this "question of expediency," consisted of the "officers of the Crown and those of the army, a certain doctor learned in the law, that chanced to be with them, and the reverend Father Vicente de Valverde."

truth or the falsehood of the reports respecting the insurrection of the natives. It was desirable to obtain the countenance of Father Valverde to these proceedings, and a copy of the judgment was submitted to the friar for his signature, which he gave without hesitation, declaring, that, "in his opinion, the Inca, at all events, deserved death." [26]

Yet there were some few in that martial conclave who resisted these high-handed measures. They considered them as a poor requital of all the favors bestowed on them by the Inca, who hitherto had received at their hands nothing but wrong. They objected to the evidence as wholly insufficient; and they denied the authority of such a tribunal to sit in judgment on a sovereign prince in the heart of his own dominions. If he were to be tried, he should be sent to Spain, and his cause brought before the Emperor, who alone had power to determine it.

But the great majority—and they were ten to one—overruled these objections, by declaring there was no doubt of Atahuallpa's guilt, and they were willing to assume the responsibility of his punishment. A full account of the proceedings would be sent to Castile, and the Emperor should be informed who were the loyal servants of the Crown, and who were its enemies. The dispute ran so high, that for a time it menaced an open and violent rupture; till, at length, convinced that resistance was fruitless, the weaker party, silenced, but not satisfied, contented themselves with entering a written protest against these proceedings, which would leave an indelible stain on the names of all concerned in them.[27]

When the sentence was communicated to the Inca, he was greatly overcome by it. He had, indeed, for some time, looked to such an issue as probable, and had been heard to intimate as much to those about him. But the probability of such an event is very different from its certainty, —and that, too, so sudden and speedy. For a moment, the overwhelming conviction of it unmanned him, and he exclaimed, with tears in his eyes,—"What have I done, or my children, that I should meet such a fate? And from your hands, too," said he, addressing Pizarro; "you, who have met with friendship and kindness from my people, with whom I have shared my treasures, who have received nothing but benefits from my hands!" In the most piteous tones, he then implored that his life might be spared, promising any guaranty that might be required for the safety of every Spaniard in the army,—promising double the ransom he had already paid, if time were only given him to obtain it.[28]

[26] "Respondió, que firmaria, que era bastante, para que el Inga fuese condenado à muerte, porque aun en lo exterior quisieron justificar su intento." Herrera, Hist. General, dec. 5, lib. 3, cap. 4.

[27] Garcilasso has preserved the names of some of those who so courageously, though ineffectually, resisted the popular cry for the Inca's blood. (Com. Real., Parte 2, lib. 1, cap. 37.) They were doubtless correct in denying the right of such a tribunal to sit in judgment on an independent prince, like the Inca of Peru; but not so correct in supposing that their master, the Emperor, had a better right. Vattel (Book II. ch. 4.) especially animadverts on this pretended trial of Atahuallpa, as a manifest outrage on the law of nations.

[28] Pedro Pizarro, Descub. y Conq., MS.—Herrera, Hist. General, dec. 5, lib. 3, cap. 4.—Zarate, Conq. del Peru, lib. 2, cap. 7.

An eyewitness assures us that Pizarro was visibly affected, as he turned away from the Inca, to whose appeal he had no power to listen, in opposition to the voice of the army, and to his own sense of what was due to the security of the country.[29] Atahuallpa, finding he had no power to turn his Conqueror from his purpose, recovered his habitual self-possession, and from that moment submitted himself to his fate with the courage of an Indian warrior.

The doom of the Inca was proclaimed by sound of trumpet in the great square of Caxamalca; and, two hours after sunset, the Spanish soldiery assembled by torch-light in the *plaza* to witness the execution of the sentence. It was on the twenty-ninth of August, 1533. Atahuallpa was led out chained hand and foot,—for he had been kept in irons ever since the great excitement had prevailed in the army respecting an assault. Father Vicente de Valverde was at his side, striving to administer consolation, and, if possible, to persuade him at this last hour to abjure his superstition and embrace the religion of his Conquerors. He was willing to save the soul of his victim from the terrible expiation in the next world, to which he had so cheerfully consigned his mortal part in this.

During Atahuallpa's confinement, the friar had repeatedly expounded to him the Christian doctrines, and the Indian monarch discovered much acuteness in apprehending the discourse of his teacher. But it had not carried conviction to his mind, and though he listened with patience, he had shown no disposition to renounce the faith of his fathers. The Dominican made a last appeal to him in this solemn hour; and, when Atahuallpa was bound to the stake, with the fagots that were to kindle his funeral pile lying around him, Valverde, holding up the cross, besought him to embrace it and be baptized, promising that, by so doing, the painful death to which he had been sentenced should be commuted for the milder form of the *garrote*,—a mode of punishment by strangulation, used for criminals in Spain.[30]

The unhappy monarch asked if this were really so, and, on its being confirmed by Pizarro, he consented to abjure his own religion, and receive baptism. The ceremony was performed by Father Valverde, and the new convert received the name of Juan de Atahuallpa,—the name of Juan being conferred in honor of John the Baptist, on whose day the event took place.[31]

---

[29] "I myself," says Pedro Pizarro, "saw the general weep." "*Yo vide llorar* al marques de pesar por no podelle dar la vida porque cierto temio los requirimientos y el rriezgo que avia en la tierra si se soltava." Descub. y Conq., MS.

[30] Xerez, Conq. del Peru, ap. Barcia, tom. III. p. 234.—Pedro Pizarro, Descub. y Conq., MS.—Conq. i Pob. del Piru, MS.—Ped. Sancho, Rel., ap. Ramusio, tom. III. fol. 400.

The *garrote* is a mode of execution by means of a noose drawn round the criminal's neck, to the back part of which a stick is attached. By twisting this stick, the noose is tightened and suffocation is produced. This was the mode, probably, of Atahuallpa's execution. In Spain, instead of the cord, an iron collar is substituted, which, by means of a screw, is compressed round the throat of the sufferer.

[31] Velasco, Hist. de Quito. tom. I. p. 372.

Atahuallpa expressed a desire that his remains might be transported to Quito, the place of his birth, to be preserved with those of his maternal ancestors. Then turning to Pizarro, as a last request, he implored him to take compassion on his young children, and receive them under his protection. Was there no other one in that dark company who stood grimly around him, to whom he could look for the protection of his offspring? Perhaps he thought there was no other so competent to afford it, and that the wishes so solemnly expressed in that hour might meet with respect even from his Conqueror. Then, recovering his stoical bearing, which for a moment had been shaken, he submitted himself calmly to his fate,— while the Spaniards, gathering around, muttered their *credos* for the salvation of his soul! [32] Thus by the death of a vile malefactor perished the last of the Incas!

I have already spoken of the person and the qualities of Atahuallpa. He had a handsome countenance, though with an expression somewhat too fierce to be pleasing. His frame was muscular and well-proportioned; his air commanding; and his deportment in the Spanish quarters had a degree of refinement, the more interesting that it was touched with melancholy. He is accused of having been cruel in his wars, and bloody in his revenge.[33] It may be true, but the pencil of an enemy would be likely to overcharge the shadows of the portrait. He is allowed to have been bold, high-minded, and liberal.[34] All agree that he showed singular penetration and quickness of perception. His exploits as a warrior had placed

---

[32] "Ma quando se lo vidde appressare per douer esser morto, disse che raccomandaua al Gouernatore i suoi piccioli figliuoli che volesse tenersegli appresso, & con queste vltime parole, & dicendo per l'anima sua li Spagnuoli che erano all' intorno il Credo, fu subito affogato." Ped. Sancho, Rel., ap. Ramusio, tom. III. fol. 399.

Xerez, Conq. del Peru, ap. Barcia, tom. III. p. 234.—Pedro Pizarro, Descub. y Conq., MS.—Naharro, Relacion Sumaria, MS.—Conq. i Pob. del Piru, MS.—Relacion del Primer. Descub., MS.—Zarate, Conq. del Peru, lib. 2, cap. 7.

The death of Atahuallpa has many points of resemblance with that of Caupolican, the great Araucanian chief, as described in the historical epic of Ercilla. Both embraced the religion of their conquerors at the stake, though Caupolican was so far less fortunate than the Peruvian monarch, that his conversion did not save him from the tortures of a most agonizing death. He was impaled and shot with arrows. The spirited verses reflect so faithfully the character of these early adventurers, in which the fanaticism of the Crusader was mingled with the cruelty of the conqueror, and they are so germane to the present subject, that I would willingly quote the passage were it not too long. See La Araucana, Parte 2, canto 24.

[33] "Thus he paid the penalty of his errors and cruelties," says Xerez, "for he was the greatest butcher, as all agree, that the world ever saw; making nothing of razing a whole town to the ground for the most trifling offence, and massacring a thousand persons for the fault of one!" (Conq. del Peru, ap. Barcia, tom. III. p. 234.) Xerez was the private secretary of Pizarro. Sancho, who, on the departure of Xerez for Spain, succeeded him in the same office, pays a more decent tribute to the memory of the Inca, who, he trusts, "is received into glory, since he died penitent for his sins, and in the true faith of a Christian." Ped. Sancho, Rel., ap. Ramusio, tom. III. fol. 399.

[34] "El hera muy regalado, y muy Señor," says Pedro Pizarro. (Descub. y Conq., MS.) "Mui dispuesto, sabio. animoso, franco," says Gomara. (Hist. de las Ind. cap. 118.)

his valor beyond dispute. The best homage to it is the reluctance shown by the Spaniards to restore him to freedom. They dreaded him as an enemy, and they had done him too many wrongs to think that he could be their friend. Yet his conduct towards them from the first had been most friendly; and they repaid it with imprisonment, robbery, and death.

The body of the Inca remained on the place of execution through the night. The following morning it was removed to the church of San Francisco, where his funeral obsequies were performed with great solemnity. Pizarro and the principal cavaliers went into mourning, and the troops listened with devout attention to the service of the dead from the lips of Father Valverde.[35] The ceremony was interrupted by the sound of loud cries and wailing, as of many voices at the doors of the church. These were suddenly thrown open, and a number of Indian women, the wives and sisters of the deceased, rushing up the great aisle, surrounded the corpse. This was not the way, they cried, to celebrate the funeral rites of an Inca; and they declared their intention to sacrifice themselves on his tomb, and bear him company to the land of spirits. The audience, outraged by this frantic behaviour, told the intruders that Atahuallpa had died in the faith of a Christian, and that the God of the Christians abhorred such sacrifices. They then caused the women to be excluded from the church, and several, retiring to their own quarters, laid violent hands on themselves, in the vain hope of accompanying their beloved lord to the bright mansions of the Sun.[36]

Atahuallpa's remains, notwithstanding his request, were laid in the cemetery of San Francisco.[37] But from thence, as is reported, after the Spaniards left Caxamalca, they were secretly removed, and carried, as he had desired, to Quito. The colonists of a later time supposed that some treasures might have been buried with the body. But, on excavating the ground, neither treasure nor remains were to be discovered.[38]

A day or two after these tragic events, Hernando de Soto returned from his excursion. Great was his astonishment and indignation at learn-

---

[35] The secretary Sancho seems to think that the Peruvians must have regarded these funeral honors as an ample compensation to Atahuallpa for any wrongs he may have sustained, since they at once raised him to a level with the Spaniards! Ibid., loc. cit.

[36] Relacion del Primer. Descub., MS.
See *Appendix, No.* 10, where I have cited in the original several of the contemporary notices of Atahuallpa's execution, which being in manuscript are not very accessible, even to Spaniards.

[37] "Oi dicen los indios que está su sepulcro junto á una Cruz de Piedra Blanca que esta en el Cementerio del Convento de Sⁿ Francisco." Montesinos, Annales, MS., año 1533.

[38] Oviedo, Hist. de las Indias, MS., Parte 3, lib. 8, cap. 22.
According to Stevenson, "In the chapel belonging to the common gaol, which was formerly part of the palace, the altar stands on the stone on which Atahuallpa was placed by the Spaniards and strangled, and under which he was buried." (Residence in South America, vol. II. p. 163.) Montesinos, who wrote more than a century after the Conquest, tells us that "spots of blood were still visible on a broad flagstone, in the prison of Caxamalca, on which Atahuallpa was *beheaded*." (Annales. MS.. año 1533.)—Ignorance and credulity could scarcely go farther.

ing what had been done in his absence. He sought out Pizarro at once, and found him, says the chronicler, "with a great felt hat, by way of mourning, slouched over his eyes," and in his dress and demeanor exhibiting all the show of sorrow.[39] "You have acted rashly," said De Soto to him bluntly; "Atahuallpa has been basely slandered. There was no enemy at Guamachucho; no rising among the natives. I have met with nothing on the road but demonstrations of good-will, and all is quiet. If it was necessary to bring the Inca to trial, he should have been taken to Castile and judged by the Emperor. I would have pledged myself to see him safe on board the vessel." [40] Pizarro confessed that he had been precipitate, and said that he had been deceived by Riquelme, Valverde, and the others. These charges soon reached the ears of the treasurer and the Dominican, who, in their turn, exculpated themselves, and upbraided Pizarro to his face, as the only one responsible for the deed. The dispute ran high; and the parties were heard by the by-standers to give one another the lie! [41] This vulgar squabble among the leaders, so soon after the event, is the best commentary on the iniquity of their own proceedings and the innocence of the Inca.

The treatment of Atahuallpa, from first to last, forms undoubtedly one of the darkest chapters in Spanish colonial history. There may have been massacres perpetrated on a more extended scale, and executions accompanied with a greater refinement of cruelty. But the blood-stained annals of the Conquest afford no such example of cold-hearted and systematic persecution, not of an enemy, but of one whose whole deportment had been that of a friend and a benefactor.

From the hour that Pizarro and his followers had entered within the sphere of Atahuallpa's influence, the hand of friendship had been extended to them by the natives. Their first act, on crossing the mountains, was to kidnap the monarch and massacre his people. The seizure of his person might be vindicated, by those who considered the end as justifying the means, on the ground that it was indispensable to secure the triumphs of the Cross. But no such apology can be urged for the massacre of the unarmed and helpless population,—as wanton as it was wicked.

The long confinement of the Inca had been used by the Conquerors to wring from him his treasures with the hard gripe of avarice. During the whole of this dismal period, he had conducted himself with singular generosity and good faith. He had opened a free passage to the Spaniards

[39] "Hallaronle monstrando mucho sentimiento con un gran sombrero de fieltro puesto en la cabeza por luto é muy calado sobre los ojos." Oviedo, Hist. de las Indias, MS., Parte 3, lib. 8, cap. 22.

[40] Ibid., MS., ubi supra.—Pedro Pizarro, Descub. y Conq., MS.

[41] This remarkable account is given by Oviedo, not in the body of his narrative, but in one of those supplementary chapters, which he makes the vehicle of the most miscellaneous, yet oftentimes important gossip, respecting the great transactions of his history. As he knew familiarly the leaders in these transactions, the testimony which he collected, somewhat at random, is of high authority. The reader will find Oviedo's account of the Inca's death extracted, in the original, among the other notices of this catastrophe, in Appendix, No. 10.

through every part of his empire; and had furnished every facility for the execution of their plans. When these were accomplished, and he remained an encumbrance on their hands, notwithstanding their engagement, expressed or implied, to release him,—and Pizarro, as we have seen, by a formal act, acquitted his captive of any further obligation on the score of the ransom,—he was arraigned before a mock tribunal, and, under pretences equally false and frivolous, was condemned to an excruciating death. From first to last, the policy of the Spanish conquerors towards their unhappy victim is stamped with barbarity and fraud.

It is not easy to acquit Pizarro of being in a great degree responsible for this policy. His partisans have labored to show, that it was forced on him by the necessity of the case, and that in the death of the Inca, especially, he yielded reluctantly to the importunities of others.[42] But weak as is this apology, the historian who has the means of comparing the various testimony of the period will come to a different conclusion. To him it will appear, that Pizarro had probably long felt the removal of Atahuallpa as essential to the success of his enterprise. He foresaw the odium that would be incurred by the death of his royal captive without sufficient grounds; while he labored to establish these, he still shrunk from the responsibility of the deed, and preferred to perpetrate it in obedience to the suggestions of others, rather than his own. Like many an unprincipled politician, he wished to reap the benefit of a bad act, and let others take the blame of it.

Almagro and his followers are reported by Pizarro's secretaries to have first insisted on the Inca's death. They were loudly supported by the treasurer and the royal officers, who considered it as indispensable to the interests of the Crown; and, finally, the rumors of a conspiracy raised the same cry among the soldiers, and Pizarro, with all his tenderness for his prisoner, could not refuse to bring him to trial.—The form of a trial was necessary to give an appearance of fairness to the proceedings. That it was only form is evident from the indecent haste with which it was conducted,—the examination of evidence, the sentence, and the execution, being all on the same day. The multiplication of the charges, designed to place the guilt of the accused on the strongest ground, had, from their very number, the opposite effect, proving only the determination to convict him. If Pizarro had felt the reluctance to his conviction which he pretended, why did he send De Soto, Atahuallpa's best friend, away, when the inquiry was to be instituted? Why was the sentence so summarily executed, as not to afford opportunity, by that cavalier's return, of disproving the truth of the principal charge,—the only one, in fact, with which the Spaniards had any concern? The solemn farce of

---

[42] "Contra su voluntad sentencio á muerte á Atabalipa." (Pedro Pizarro, Descub. y Conq., MS.) "Contra voluntad del dicho Gobernador." (Relacion del Primer. Descub. MS.) "Ancora che molto li dispiacesse di venir a questo atto." (Ped Sancho, Rel., ap. Ramusio, tom. III. fol. 399.) Even Oviedo seems willing to admit it possible that Pizarro may have been somewhat deceived by others. "Que tambien se puede creer que era engañado." Hist. de las Indias, MS., Parte 3, lib. 8, cap. 22.

mourning and deep sorrow affected by Pizarro, who by these honors to the dead would intimate the sincere regard he had entertained for the living, was too thin a veil to impose on the most credulous.

It is not intended by these reflections to exculpate the rest of the army, and especially its officers, from their share in the infamy of the transaction. But Pizarro, as commander of the army, was mainly responsible for its measures. For he was not a man to allow his own authority to be wrested from his grasp, or to yield timidly to the impulses of others. He did not even yield to his own. His whole career shows him, whether for good or for evil, to have acted with a cool and calculating policy.

A story has been often repeated, which refers the motives of Pizarro's conduct, in some degree at least, to personal resentment. The Inca had requested one of the Spanish soldiers to write the name of God on his nail. This the monarch showed to several of his guards successively, and, as they read it, and each pronounced the same word, the sagacious mind of the barbarian was delighted with what seemed to him little short of a miracle,—to which the science of his own nation afforded no analogy. On showing the writing to Pizarro, that chief remained silent; and the Inca, finding he could not read, conceived a contempt for the commander who was even less informed than his soldiers. This he did not wholly conceal, and Pizarro, aware of the cause of it, neither forgot nor forgave it.[43] The anecdote is reported not on the highest authority. It may be true; but it is unnecessary to look for the motives of Pizarro's conduct in personal pique, when so many proofs are to be discerned of a dark and deliberate policy.

Yet the arts of the Spanish chieftain failed to reconcile his countrymen to the atrocity of his proceedings. It is singular to observe the difference between the tone assumed by the first chroniclers of the transaction, while it was yet fresh, and that of those who wrote when the lapse of a few years had shown the tendency of public opinion. The first boldly avow the deed as demanded by expediency, if not necessity; while they deal in no measured terms of reproach with the character of their unfortunate victim.[44] The latter, on the other hand, while they extenuate the errors of the Inca, and do justice to his good faith, are unreserved in their condemnation of the Conquerors, on whose conduct, they say, Heaven set the seal of its own reprobation, by bringing them all to an

[43] The story is to be found in Garcilasso de la Vega, (Com. Real., Parte 2, cap. 38,) and in no other writer of the period, so far as I am aware.

[44] I have already noticed the lavish epithets heaped by Xerez on the Inca's cruelty. This account was printed in Spain, in 1534, the year after the execution. "The proud tyrant," says the other secretary, Sancho, "would have repaid the kindness and good treatment he had received from the governor and every one of us with the same coin with which he usually paid his own followers, without any fault on their part,—by putting them to death." (Ped. Sancho, Rel., ap. Ramusio, tom. III. fol. 399.) "He deserved to die," says the old Spanish Conqueror before quoted "and all the country was rejoiced that he was put out of the way." Rel. d'un Capitano Spagn., ap. Ramusio, tom. III. fol. 377.

untimely and miserable end.[45] The sentence of contemporaries has been fully ratified by that of posterity;[46] and the persecution of Atahuallpa is regarded with justice as having left a stain, never to be effaced, on the Spanish arms in the New World.

[45] "Las demostraciones que despues se vieron bien manifiestan lo mui injusta que fué, ... puesto que todos quantos entendieron en ella tuvieron despues mui desastradas muertes." (Naharro, Relacion Sumaria, MS.) Gomara uses nearly the same language. "No ai que reprehender à los que le mataron, pues el tiempo, i sus pecados los castigaron despues; cà todos ellos acabaron mal." (Hist. de las Ind., cap. 118.) According to the former writer, Felipillo paid the forfeit of his crimes sometime afterwards,—being hanged by Almagro on the expedition to Chili,—when, as *some say,* he confessed having perverted testimony given in favor of Atahuallpa's innocence, directly against that monarch." Oviedo, usually ready enough to excuse the excesses of his countrymen, is unqualified in his condemnation of this whole proceeding, (see *Appendix, No.* 10,) which, says another contemporary, "fills every one with pity who has a spark of humanity in his bosom." Conq. i Pob. del Piru, MS.

[46] The most eminent example of this is given by Quintana in his memoir of Pizarro, (Españoles Celebres, tom. II.,) throughout which the writer, rising above the mists of national prejudice, which too often blind the eyes of his countrymen, holds the scale of historic criticism with an impartial hand, and deals a full measure of reprobation to the actors in these dismal scenes.

CHAPTER VIII

DISORDERS IN PERU—MARCH TO CUZCO—ENCOUNTER WITH THE NA-
TIVES—CHALLCUCHIMA BURNT—ARRIVAL IN CUZCO—DESCRIP-
TION OF THE CITY—TREASURE FOUND THERE

1533—1534

THE Inca of Peru was its sovereign in a peculiar sense. He received an
obedience from his vassals more implicit than that of any despot; for
his authority reached to the most secret conduct,—to the thoughts of the
individual. He was reverenced as more than human.[1] He was not merely
the head of the state, but the point to which all its institutions converged,
as to a common centre,—the keystone of the political fabric, which must
fall to pieces by its own weight when that was withdrawn. So it fared on
the death of Atahuallpa.[2] His death not only left the throne vacant, without any certain successor, but the manner of it announced to the Peruvian people that a hand stronger than that of their Incas had now seized
the sceptre, and that the dynasty of the Children of the Sun had passed
away for ever.

The natural consequences of such a conviction followed. The beautiful order of the ancient institutions was broken up, as the authority which
controlled it was withdrawn. The Indians broke out into greater excesses
from the uncommon restraint to which they had been before subjected.
Villages were burnt, temples and palaces were plundered, and the gold
they contained was scattered or secreted. Gold and silver acquired an
importance in the eyes of the Peruvian, when he saw the importance attached to them by his conquerors. The precious metals, which before
served only for purposes of state or religious decoration, were now hoard-

[1] "Such was the awe in which the Inca was held," says Pizarro, "that it was only
necessary for him to intimate his commands to that effect, and a Peruvian would at
once jump down a precipice, hang himself, or put an end to his life in any way that
was prescribed." Descub. y Conq., MS.

[2] Oviedo tells us, that the Inca's right name was *Atabaliva,* and that the Spaniards
usually misspelt it, because they thought much more of getting treasure for themselves, than they did of the name of the person who owned it. (Hist. de las Indias,
MS., Parte 3, lib. 8, cap. 16.) Nevertheless, I have preferred the authority of Garcilasso, who, a Peruvian himself, and a near kinsman of the Inca, must be supposed to have been well informed. His countrymen, he says, pretended that the
cocks imported into Peru by the Spaniards, when they crowed, uttered the name
of Atahuallpa; "and I and the other Indian boys," adds the historian, "when we
were at school, used to mimic them." Com. Real., Parte 1, lib. 9, cap. 23.

ed up and buried in caves and forests. The gold and silver concealed by the natives were affirmed greatly to exceed in quantity that which fell into the hands of the Spaniards.[3] The remote provinces now shook off their allegiance to the Incas. Their great captains, at the head of distant armies, set up for themselves. Ruminavi, a commander on the borders of Quito, sought to detach that kingdom from the Peruvian empire, and to reassert its ancient independence. The country, in short, was in that state, in which old things are passing away, and the new order of things has not yet been established. It was in a state of revolution.

The authors of the revolution, Pizarro and his followers, remained meanwhile at Caxamalca. But the first step of the Spanish commander was to name a successor to Atahuallpa. It would be easier to govern under the venerated authority to which the homage of the Indians had been so long paid; and it was not difficult to find a successor. The true heir to the crown was a second son of Huayna Capac, named Manco, a legitimate brother of the unfortunate Huascar. But Pizarro had too little knowledge of the dispositions of this prince; and he made no scruple to prefer a brother of Atahuallpa, and to present him to the Indian nobles as their future Inca. We know nothing of the character of the young Toparca, who probably resigned himself without reluctance to a destiny which, however humiliating in some points of view, was more exalted than he could have hoped to obtain in the regular course of events. The ceremonies attending a Peruvian coronation were observed, as well as time would allow; the brows of the young Inca were encircled with the imperial *borla* by the hands of his conqueror, and he received the homage of his Indian vassals. They were the less reluctant to pay it, as most of those in the camp belonged to the faction of Quito.

All thoughts were now eagerly turned towards Cuzco, of which the most glowing accounts were circulated among the soldiers, and whose temples and royal palaces were represented as blazing with gold and silver. With imaginations thus excited, Pizarro and his entire company, amounting to almost five hundred men, of whom nearly a third, probably, were cavalry, took their departure early in September from Caxamalca,—a place ever memorable as the theatre of some of the most strange and sanguinary scenes recorded in history. All set forward in high spirits,—the soldiers of Pizarro from the expectation of doubling their present riches, and Almagro's followers from the prospect of sharing equally in the spoil with "the first conquerors." [4] The young Inca and the old chief Challcuchima accompanied the march in their litters, at-

[3] "That which the Inca gave the Spaniards, said some of the Indian nobles to Benalcazar, the conqueror of Quito, was but as a kernel of corn, compared with the heap before him." (Oviedo, Hist. de las Indias, MS., Parte 3, lib. 8, cap. 22.) See also Pedro Pizarro, Descub. y Conq., MS.—Relacion del Primer. Descub., MS.

[4] The "first conquerors," according to Garcilasso, were held in especial honor by those who came after them, though they were, on the whole, men of less consideration and fortune than the later adventurers. Com. Real., Parte 1, lib. 7, cap. 9.

tended by a numerous retinue of vassals, and moving in as much state and ceremony as if in the possession of real power.[5]

Their course lay along the great road of the Incas, which stretched across the elevated regions of the Cordilleras, all the way to Cuzco. It was of nearly a uniform breadth, though constructed with different degrees of care, according to the ground.[6] Sometimes it crossed smooth and level valleys, which offered of themselves little impediment to the traveller; at other times, it followed the course of a mountain stream that wound round the base of some beetling cliff, leaving small space for the foothold; at others, again, where the sierra was so precipitous that it seemed to preclude all further progress, the road, accommodated to the natural sinuosities of the ground, wound round the heights which it would have been impossible to scale directly.[7]

But although managed with great address, it was a formidable passage for the cavalry. The mountain was hewn into steps, but the rocky ledges cut up the hoofs of the horses; and, though the troopers dismounted and led them by the bridle, they suffered severely in their efforts to keep their footing.[8] The road was constructed for man and the light-footed llama; and the only heavy beast of burden at all suited to it was the sagacious and sure-footed mule, with which the Spanish adventurers were not then provided. It was a singular chance that Spain was the land of the mule; and thus the country was speedily supplied with the very animal which seems to have been created for the difficult passes of the Cordilleras.

Another obstacle, often occurring, was the deep torrents that rushed down in fury from the Andes. They were traversed by the hanging bridges of osier, whose frail materials were after a time broken up by the heavy tread of the cavalry, and the holes made in them added materially to the dangers of the passage. On such occasions, the Spaniards contrived to work their way across the rivers on rafts, swimming their horses by the bridle.[9]

All along the route, they found post-houses for the accommodation of the royal couriers, established at regular intervals; and magazines of grain and other commodities, provided in the principal towns for the Indian armies. The Spaniards profited by the prudent forecast of the Peruvian government.

Passing through several hamlets and towns of some note, the principal of which were Guamachucho and Guanuco, Pizarro, after a tedious march, came in sight of the rich valley of Xauxa. The march, though tedious, had been attended with little suffering, except in crossing the bristling crests of the Cordilleras, which occasionally obstructed their

[5] Pedro Pizarro, Descub. y Conq., MS.—Naharro, Relacion Sumaria, MS.—Ped. Sancho, Rel., ap. Ramusio, tom. III. fol. 400.

[6] "Va todo el camino de una traza y anchura hecho á mano." Relacion del Primer. Descub., MS.

[7] "En muchas partes viendo lo que está adelante, parece cosa impossible poderlo pasar." Ibid., MS.

[8] Ped. Sancho, Rel., ap. Ramusio, tom. III. fol. 404.

[9] Ibid., ubi supra.—Relacion del Primer. Descub., MS.

path,—a rough setting to the beautiful valleys, that lay scattered like gems along this elevated region. In the mountain passes they found some inconvenience from the cold; since, to move more quickly, they had disencumbered themselves of all superfluous baggage, and were even unprovided with tents.[10] The bleak winds of the mountains penetrated the thick harness of the soldiers; but the poor Indians, more scantily clothed and accustomed to a tropical climate, suffered most severely. The Spaniard seemed to have a hardihood of body, as of soul, that rendered him almost indifferent to climate.

On the march they had not been molested by enemies. But more than once they had seen vestiges of them in smoking hamlets and ruined bridges. Reports, from time to time, had reached Pizarro of warriors on his track; and small bodies of Indians were occasionally seen like dusky clouds on the verge of the horizon, which vanished as the Spaniards approached. On reaching Xauxa, however, these clouds gathered into one dark mass of warriors, which formed on the opposite bank of the river that flowed through the valley.

The Spaniards advanced to the stream, which, swollen by the melting of the snows, was now of considerable width, though not deep. The bridge had been destroyed; but the Conquerors, without hesitation, dashing boldly in, advanced, swimming and wading, as they best could, to the opposite bank. The Indians, disconcerted by this decided movement, as they had relied on their watery defences, took to flight, after letting off an impotent volley of missiles. Fear gave wings to the fugitives; but the horse and his rider were swifter, and the victorious pursuers took bloody vengeance on their enemy for having dared even to meditate resistance.

Xanxa was a considerable town. It was the place already noticed as having been visited by Hernando Pizarro. It was seated in the midst of a verdant valley, fertilized by a thousand little rills, which the thrifty Indian husbandman drew from the parent river that rolled sluggishly through the meadows. There were several capacious buildings of rough stone in the town, and a temple of some note in the times of the Incas. But the strong arm of Father Valverde and his countrymen soon tumbled the heathen deities from their pride of place, and established, in their stead, the sacred effigies of the Virgin and Child.

Here Pizarro proposed to halt for some days, and to found a Spanish colony. It was a favorable position, he thought, for holding the Indian mountaineers in check, while, at the same time, it afforded an easy communication with the sea-coast. Meanwhile he determined to send forward De Soto, with a detachment of sixty horse, to reconnoitre the country in advance, and to restore the bridges where demolished by the enemy.[11]

[10] "La notte dormirono tutti in quella campagna senza coperto alcuno, sopra la neue, ne pur hebber souuenimento di legne ne da mangiare." Ped. Sancho, Rel., ap. Ramusio, tom. III. fol. 401.
[11] Carta de la Justicia y Regimiento de la Ciudad de Xauja, MS.—Pedro Pizarro,

That active cavalier set forward at once, but found considerable impediments to his progress. The traces of an enemy became more frequent as he advanced. The villages were burnt, the bridges destroyed,
and heavy rocks and trees strewed in the path to impede the march of
the cavalry. As he drew near to Bilcas, once an important place, though
now effaced from the map, he had a sharp encounter with the natives, in
a mountain defile, which cost him the lives of two or three troopers. The
loss was light; but any loss was felt by the Spaniards, so little accustomed as they had been of late, to resistance.

Still pressing forward, the Spanish captain crossed the river Abancay,
and the broad waters of the Apurimac; and, as he drew near the sierra of
Vilcaconga, he learned that a considerable body of Indians lay in wait
for him in the dangerous passes of the mountains. The sierra was several
leagus from Cuzco; and the cavalier, desirous to reach the further side of
it before nightfall, incautiously pushed on his wearied horses. When he
was fairly entangled in its rocky defiles, a multitude of armed warriors,
springing, as it seemed, from every cavern and thicket of the sierra, filled
the air with their war-cries, and rushed down, like one of their own
mountain torrents, on the invaders, as they were painfully toiling up the
steeps. Men and horses were overturned in the fury of the assault, and
the foremost files, rolling back on those below, spread ruin and consternation in their ranks. De Soto in vain endeavored to restore order, and,
if possible, to charge the assailants. The horses were blinded and maddened by the missiles, while the desperate natives, clinging to their legs,
strove to prevent their ascent up the rocky pathway. De Soto saw, that,
unless he gained a level ground which opened at some distance before
him, all must be lost. Cheering on his men with the old battle-cry, that
always went to the heart of a Spaniard, he struck his spurs deep into the
sides of his wearied charger, and, gallantly supported by his troop, broke
through the dark array of warriors, and, shaking them off to the right
and left, at length succeeded in placing himself on the broad level.

Here both parties paused, as if by mutual consent, for a few moments.
A little stream ran through the plain, at which the Spaniards watered
their horses;[12] and the animals, having recovered wind, De Soto and
his men made a desperate charge on their assailants. The undaunted Indians sustained the shock with firmness; and the result of the combat was
still doubtful, when the shades of evening, falling thicker around them,
separated the combatants.

Both parties then withdrew from the field, taking up their respective
stations within bow-shot of each other, so that the voices of the warriors
on either side could be distinctly heard in the stillness of the night. But
very different were the reflections of the two hosts. The Indians, exulting in their temporary triumph, looked with confidence to the morrow
to complete it. The Spaniards, on the other hand, were proportionably

Descub. y Conq., MS.—Conq. i Pob. del Piru, MS.—Herrera, Hist. General, dec. 5,
lib. 4, cap. 10.—Relacion del Primer. Descub., MS.
  [12] Ped. Sancho, Rel., ap. Ramusio. tom. III. fol. 405.

discouraged. They were not prepared for this spirit of resistance in an enemy hitherto so tame. Several cavaliers had fallen; one of them by a blow from a Peruvian battle-axe, which clove his head to the chin, attesting the power of the weapon, and of the arm that used it.[13] Several horses, too, had been killed; and the loss of these was almost as severely felt as that of their riders, considering the great cost and difficulty of transporting them to these distant regions. Few either of the men or horses escaped without wounds, and the Indian allies suffered still more severely.

It seemed probable, from the pertinacity and a certain order maintained in the assault, that it was directed by some leader of military experience; perhaps the Indian commander Quizquiz, who was said to be hanging round the environs of Cuzco with a considerable force.

Notwithstanding the reasonable cause of apprehension for the morrow, De Soto, like a stout-hearted cavalier, as he was, strove to keep up the spirits of his followers. If they had beaten off the enemy when their horses were jaded, and their own strength nearly exhausted, how much easier it would be to come off victorious when both were restored by a night's rest; and he told them to "trust in the Almighty, who would never desert his faithful followers in their extremity." The event justified De Soto's confidence in this seasonable succour.

From time to time, on his march, he had sent advices to Pizarro of the menacing state of the country, till his commander, becoming seriously alarmed, was apprehensive that the cavalier might be overpowered by the superior numbers of the enemy. He accordingly detached Almagro with nearly all the remaining horse, to his support,—unencumbered by infantry, that he might move the lighter. That efficient leader advanced by forced marches, stimulated by the tidings which met him on the road; and was so fortunate as to reach the foot of the sierra of Vilcaconga the very night of the engagement.

There hearing of the encounter, he pushed forward without halting, though his horses were spent with travel. The night was exceedingly dark, and Almagro, afraid of stumbling on the enemy's bivouac, and desirous to give De Soto information of his approach, commanded his trumpets to sound, till the notes, winding through the defiles of the mountains, broke the slumbers of his countrymen, sounding like blithest music in their ears. They quickly replied with their own bugles, and soon had the satisfaction to embrace their deliverers.[14]

Great was the dismay of the Peruvian host, when the morning light discovered the fresh reinforcement of the ranks of the Spaniards. There was no use in contending with an enemy who gathered strength from the conflict, and who seemed to multiply his numbers at will. Without further attempt to renew the fight, they availed themselves of a thick fog, which hung over the lower slopes of the hills, to effect their retreat, and left the passes open to the invaders. The two cavaliers then continued

[13] Ibid., loc. cit.
[14] Pedro Pizarro, Descub. y Conq., MS.—Herrera. Hist. General, dec. 5, lib. 5, cap. 3.

their march until they extricated their forces from the sierra, when, taking up a secure position, they proposed to await there the arrival of Pizarro.[15]

The commander-in-chief, meanwhile, lay at Xauxa, where he was greatly disturbed by the rumors which reached him of the state of the country. His enterprise, thus far, had gone forward so smoothly, that he was no better prepared than his lieutenant to meet with resistance from the natives. He did not seem to comprehend that the mildest nature might at last be roused by oppression; and that the massacre of their Inca, whom they regarded with such awful veneration, would be likely, if any thing could do it, to wake them from their apathy.

The tidings which he now received of the retreat of the Peruvians were most welcome; and he caused mass to be said, and thanksgivings to be offered up to Heaven, "which had shown itself thus favorable to the Christians throughout this mighty enterprise." The Spaniard was ever a Crusader. He was, in the sixteenth century, what *Cœur de Lion* and his brave knights were in the twelfth, with this difference; the cavalier of that day fought for the Cross and for glory, while gold and the Cross were the watchwords of the Spaniard. The spirit of chivalry had waned somewhat before the spirit of trade; but the fire of religious enthusiasm still burned as bright under the quilted mail of the American Conqueror, as it did of yore under the iron panoply of the soldier of Palestine.

It seemed probable that some man of authority had organized, or at least countenanced, this resistance of the natives, and suspicion fell on the captive chief Challcuchima, who was accused of maintaining a secret correspondence with his confederate, Quizquiz. Pizarro waited on the Indian noble, and, charging him with the conspiracy, reproached him, as he had formerly done his royal master, with ingratitude towards the Spaniards, who had dealt with him so liberally. He concluded by the assurance, that, if he did not cause the Peruvians to lay down their arms, and tender their submission at once, he should be burnt alive, so soon as they reached Almagro's quarters.[16]

The Indian chief listened to the terrible menace with the utmost composure. He denied having had any communication with his countrymen, and said, that, in his present state of confinement, at least, he could have no power to bring them to submission. He then remained doggedly silent, and Pizarro did not press the matter further.[17] But he placed a strong guard over his prisoner, and caused him to be put in irons. It was an ominous proceeding, and had been the precursor of the death of Atahuallpa.

---

[15] The account of De Soto's affair with the natives is given in more or less detail, by Ped Sancho, Rel., ap. Ramusio, tom. III. fol. 405,—Conq. i Pob. del Piru, MS., —Relacion del Primer. Descub., MS.,—Pedro Pizarro, Descub. y Conq., MS.,— parties all present in the army.

[16] Pedro Pizarro, Descub. y Conq., MS.—Ped. Sancho, Rel., ap. Ramusio, tom. III. fol. 406.

[17] Ibid., ubi supra.

Before quitting Xauxa, a misfortune befell the Spaniards in the death of their creature, the young Inca Toparca. Suspicion, of course, fell on Challcuchima, now selected as the scape-goat for all the offences of his nation.[18] It was a disappointment to Pizarro, who hoped to find a convenient shelter for his future proceedings under this shadow of royalty.[19]

The general considered it most prudent not to hazard the loss of his treasures by taking them on the march, and he accordingly left them at Xauxa, under a guard of forty soldiers, who remained there in garrison. No event of importance occurred on the road, and Pizarro, having effected a junction with Almagro, their united forces soon entered the vale of Xaquixaguana, about five leagues from Cuzco. This was one of those bright spots, so often found embosomed amidst the Andes, the more beautiful from contrast with the savage character of the scenery around it. A river flowed through the valley, affording the means of irrigating the soil, and clothing it in perpetual verdure; and the rich and flowering vegetation spread out like a cultivated garden. The beauty of the place and its delicious coolness commended it as a residence for the Peruvian nobles, and the sides of the hills were dotted with their villas, which afforded them a grateful retreat in the heats of summer.[20] Yet the centre of the valley was disfigured by a quagmire of some extent, occasioned by the frequent overflowing of the waters; but the industry of the Indian architects had constructed a solid causeway, faced with heavy stone, and connected with the great road, which traversed the whole breadth of the morass.[21]

In this valley Pizarro halted for several days, while he refreshed his troops from the well-stored magazines of the Incas. His first act was to bring Challcuchima to trial; if trial that could be called, where sentence may be said to have gone hand in hand with accusation. We are not informed of the nature of the evidence. It was sufficient to satisfy the Spanish captains of the chieftain's guilt. Nor is it at all incredible that Challcuchima should have secretly encouraged a movement among the people, designed to secure his country's freedom and his own. He was condemned to be burnt alive on the spot. "Some thought it a hard measure," says Herrera; "but those who are governed by reasons of state policy are apt

---

[18] It seems, from the language of the letter addressed to the Emperor by the municipality of Xauxa, that the troops themselves were far from being convinced of Challcuchima's guilt. "Publico fue, aunque dello no ubo averiguacion in certenidad, que el capitan Chaliconiman le abia dado ierbas o a beber con que murio." Carta de la Just. y Reg. de Xauja, MS.

[19] According to Velasco, Toparca, whom, however, he calls by another name, tore off the diadem bestowed on him by Pizarro, with disdain, and died in a few weeks of chagrin. (Hist. de Quito, tom. I. p. 377.) This writer, a Jesuit of Quito, seems to feel himself bound to make out as good a case for Atahuallpa and his family, as if he had been expressly retained in their behalf. His vouchers—when he condescends to give any—too rarely bear him out in his statements to inspire us with much confidence in his correctness.

[20] "Auia en este valle muy sumptuosos aposentos y ricos adonde los señores del Cuzco salian a tomar sus plazeres y solazes." Cieza de Leon, Cronica, cap. 91.

[21] Ibid., ubi supra

to shut their eyes against every thing else." [22] Why this cruel mode of execution was so often adopted by the Spanish Conquerors is not obvious; unless it was that the Indian was an infidel, and fire, from ancient date, seems to have been considered the fitting doom of the infidel, as the type of that inextinguishable flame which awaited him in the regions of the damned.

Father Valverde accompanied the Peruvian chieftain to the stake. He seems always to have been present at this dreary moment, anxious to profit by it, if possible, to work the conversion of the victim. He painted in gloomy colors the dreadful doom of the unbeliever, to whom the waters of baptism could alone secure the ineffable glories of paradise.[23] It does not appear that he promised any commutation of punishment in this world. But his arguments fell on a stony heart, and the chief coldly replied, he "did not understand the religion of the white men." [24] He might be pardoned for not comprehending the beauty of a faith which, as it would seem, had borne so bitter fruits to him. In the midst of his tortures, he showed the characteristic courage of the American Indian, whose power of endurance triumphs over the power of persecution in his enemies, and he died with his last breath invoking the name of Pachacamac. His own followers brought the fagots to feed the flames that consumed him.[25]

Soon after this tragic event, Pizarro was surprised by a visit from a Peruvian noble, who came in great state, attended by a numerous and showy retinue. It was the young prince Manco, brother of the unfortunate Huascar, and the rightful successor to the crown. Being brought before the Spanish commander, he announced his pretensions to the throne, and claimed the protection of the strangers. It is said he had meditated resisting them by arms, and had encouraged the assaults made on them on their march; but, finding resistance ineffectual, he had taken this politic course, greatly to the displeasure of his more resolute nobles. However this may be, Pizarro listened to his application with singular contentment, for he saw in this new scion of the true royal stock, a more effectual instrument for his purposes than he could have found in the family of Quito, with whom the Peruvians had but little sympathy. He received the young man, therefore, with great cordiality, and did not hesitate to assure him that he had been sent into the country by his master, the Castilian sovereign, in order to vindicate the claims of Huascar to the crown, and to punish the usurpation of his rival.[26]

Taking with him the Indian prince, Pizarro now resumed his march. It was interrupted for a few hours by a party of the natives, who lay in

[22] Hist. General, dec. 5, lib. 6, cap. 3.

[23] Ped. Sancho, Rel., ap. Ramusio, tom. III. fol. 406.

[24] Ibid., loc. cit.

[25] Ibid., loc. cit.—Pedro Pizarro, Descub. y Conq., MS.

The MS. of the old Conqueror is so much damaged in this part of it, that much of his account is entirely effaced.

[26] Ped. Sancho, Rel. ap Ramusio, tom. III. fol. 406.—Pedro Pizarro, Descub. y Conq., MS.

wait for him in the neighboring sierra. A sharp skirmish ensued, in which the Indians behaved with great spirit, and inflicted some little in. jury on the Spaniards; but the latter, at length, shaking them off, made good their passage through the defile, and the enemy did not care to follow them into the open country.

It was late in the afternoon when the Conquerors came in sight of Cuzco.[27] The descending sun was streaming his broad rays full on the imperial city, where many an altar was dedicated to his worship. The low ranges of buildings, showing in his beams like so many lines of silvery light, filled up the bosom of the valley and the lower slopes of the moun· tains, whose shadowy forms hung darkly over the fair city, as if to shield it from the menaced profanation. It was so late, that Pizarro resolved to defer his entrance till the following morning.

That night vigilant guard was kept in the camp, and the soldiers slept on their arms. But it passed away without annoyance from the enemy, and early on the following day, November 15, 1533, Pizarro prepared for his entrance into the Peruvian capital.[28]

The little army was formed into three divisions, of which the centre, or "battle," as it was called, was led by the general. The suburbs were thronged with a countless multitude of the natives, who had flocked from the city and the surrounding country to witness the showy, and, to them, startling pageant. All looked with eager curiosity on the strangers, the fame of whose terrible exploits had spread to the remotest parts of the empire. They gazed with astonishment on their dazzling arms and fair complexions, which seemed to proclaim them the true Children of the Sun; and they listened with feelings of mysterious dread, as the trumpet sent forth its prolonged notes through the streets of the capital, and the solid ground shook under the heavy tramp of the cavalry.

The Spanish commander rode directly up the great square. It was surrounded by low piles of buildings, among which were several palaces of the Incas. One of these, erected by Huayna Capac, was surmounted by a tower, while the ground-floor was occupied by one or more immense halls, like those described in Caxamalca, where the Peruvian nobles held their *fêtes* in stormy weather. These buildings afforded convenient barracks for the troops, though, during the first few weeks, they remained under their tents in the open *plaza*, with their horses picketed by their side, ready to repulse any insurrection of the inhabitants.[29]

The capital of the Incas, though falling short of the *El Dorado* which had engaged their credulous fancies, astonished the Spaniards by the beauty of its edifices, the length and regularity of its streets, and the

[27] "Y dos horas antes que el Sol se pusiese, llegaron á vista de la ciudad del Cuzco." Relacion del Primer. Descub., MS.
[28] The chronicles differ as to the precise date. There can be no better authorities than Pedro Sancho's narrative and the Letter of the Magistrates of Xauxa, which I have followed in the text.
[29] Ped. Sancho, Rel., ap. Ramusio, tom. III. fol. 407.—Garcilasso, Com. Real. Parte I. lib. 7, cap. 10.—Relacion del Primer. Descub., MS

good order and appearance of comfort, even luxury, visible in its nu merous population. It far surpassed all they had yet seen in the New World. The population of the city is computed by one of the Conquerors at two hundred thousand inhabitants, and that of the suburbs at as many more.[30] This account is not confirmed, as far as I have seen, by any other writer. But however it may be exaggerated, it is certain that Cuzco was the metropolis of a great empire, the residence of the Court and the chief nobility; frequented by the most skilful mechanics and artisans of every description, who found a demand for their ingenuity in the royal precincts; while the place was garrisoned by a numerous soldiery, and was the resort, finally, of emigrants from the most distant provinces. The quarters whence this motley population came were indicated by their peculiar dress, and especially their head-gear, so rarely found at all on the American Indian, which, with its variegated colors, gave a picturesque effect to the groups and masses in the streets. The habitual order and decorum maintained in this multifarious assembly showed the excellent police of the capital, where the only sounds that disturbed the repose of the Spaniards were the noises of feasting and dancing, which the natives, with happy insensibility, constantly prolonged to a late hour of the night.[31]

The edifices of the better sort—and they were very numerous—were of stone, or faced with stone.[32] Among the principal were the royal residences; as each sovereign built a new palace for himself, covering, though low, a large extent of ground. The walls were sometimes stained or painted with gaudy tints, and the gates, we are assured, were sometimes of colored marble.[33] "In the delicacy of the stone-work," says another of the Conquerors, "the natives far excelled the Spaniards, though the roofs of their dwellings, instead of tiles, were only of thatch, but put together

---

[30] "Esta ciudad era muy grande i mui populosa de grandes edificios i comarcas, quando los Españoles entraron la primera vez en ella havia gran cantidad de gente, seria pueblo de mas de 40 mill. vecinos solamente lo que tomaba la ciudad, que arravalles i comarca en deredor del Cuzco á 10 ó 12 leguas creo yo que havia docientos mill. Indios porque esto era lo mas poblado de todos estos reinos." (Conq. i Pob. del Piru, MS.) The *vecino* or "householder" is computed, usually, as representing five individuals.—Yet Father Valverde, in a letter written a few years after this, speaks of the city as having only three or four thousand houses at the time of its occupation, and the suburbs as having nineteen or twenty thousand. (Carta al Emperador, MS., 20 de Marzo, 1539.) It is possible that he took into the account only the better kind of houses, not considering the mud huts, or rather hovels, which made so large a part of a Peruvian town, as deserving notice.

[31] "Heran tantos los atambores que de noche se oian por todas partes bailando y cantando y beviendo que toda la mayor parte de la noche se les pasava en esto cotidianamente." Pedro Pizarro, Descub. y Conq., MS.

[32] "La maggior parte di queste case sono di pietra, et l'altre hāno la metà della facciata di pietra." Ped. Sancho, Rel., ap. Ramusio, tom. III. fol. 413.

[33] "Che sono le principali della città dipinte et lauorate, et di pietra: et la miglior d'esse è la casa di Guainacaba Cacique vecchio, et la porta d'essa è di marmo bianco et rosso, et d'altri colori." (Ibid., ubi supra.) The buildings were usually of freestone. There may have been porphyry from the neighboring mountains mixed with this, which the Spaniards mistook for marble.

with the nicest art." [34] The sunny climate of Cuzco did not require a very substantial material for defence against the weather.

The most important building was the fortress, planted on a solid rock, that rose boldly above the city. It was built of hewn stone, so finely wrought that it was impossible to detect the line of junction between the blocks; and the approaches to it were defended by three semicircular parapets, composed of such heavy masses of rock, that it bore resemblance to the kind of work known to architects as the Cyclopean. The fortress was raised to a height rare in Peruvian architecture; and from the summit of the tower the eye of the spectator ranged over a magnificent prospect, in which the wild features of the mountain scenery, rocks, woods, and waterfalls, were mingled with the rich verdure of the valley, and the shining city filling up the foreground,—all blended in sweet harmony under the deep azure of a tropical sky.

The streets were long and narrow. They were arranged with perfect regularity, crossing one another at right angles; and from the great square diverged four principal streets connecting with the high roads of the empire. The square itself, and many parts of the city, were paved with a fine pebble.[35] Through the heart of the capital ran a river of pure water, if it might not be rather termed a canal, the banks or sides of which, for the distance of twenty leagues, were faced with stone.[36] Across this stream, bridges, constructed of similar broad flags, were thrown, at intervals, so as to afford an easy communication between the different quarters of the capital.[37]

The most sumptuous edifice in Cuzco, in the times of the Incas, was undoubtedly the great temple dedicated to the Sun, which, studded with gold plates, as already noticed, was surrounded by convents and dormi-

---

[34] "Todo labrado de piedra muy prima, que cierto toda la canteria desta cibdad hace gran ventaja á la de España, aunque carecen de teja que todas las casas sino es la fortaleza, que era hecha de azoteas son cubiertas de paja, aunque tan primamente puesta, que parece bien." Relacion del Primer. Descub., MS.

[35] Ped. Sancho, Rel., ap. Ramusio, tom. III., ubi supra.

A passage in the Letter of the Municipality of Xauxa is worth quoting, as confirming on the best authority some of the interesting particulars mentioned in the text. "Esta cibdad es la mejor e maior que en la tierra se ha visto, i aun en Yndias; e decimos a V.M. ques tan hermosa i de tan buenos edeficios que en España seria muy de ver; tiene las calles por mucho concierto en pedradas i por medio dellas un caño enlosado. la plaza es hecha en cuadra i empedrada de quijas pequeñas todas, todas las mas de las casas son de Señores Principales hechas de canteria. esta en una ladera de un zerro en el cual sobre el pueblo esta una fortaleza mui bien obrada de canteria, tan de ver que por Españoles que han andado Reinos estraños dicen no haver visto otro edeficio igual al della." Carta de la Just. y Reg. de Xauja, MS.

[36] "Un rio, el cual baja por medio de la cibdad y desde que nace, mas de veinte leguas por aquel valle abajo donde hay muchas poblaciones, va enlosado todo por el suelo, y las varrancas de una parte y de otra hechas de canteria labrada, cosa nunca vista, ni oida." Relacion del Primer. Descub., MS.

[37] The reader will find a few repetitions in this chapter of what I have already said, in the Introduction, of Cuzco under the Incas. But the facts here stated are for the most part drawn from other sources, and some repetition was unavoidable in order to give a distinct image of the capital.

tories for the priests, with their gardens and broad parterres sparkling with gold. The exterior ornaments had been already removed by the Conquerors,—all but the frieze of gold, which, imbedded in the stones, still encircled the principal building. It is probable that the tales of wealth, so greedily circulated among the Spaniards, greatly exceeded the truth. If they did not, the natives must have been very successful in concealing their treasures from the invaders. Yet much still remained, not only in the great House of the Sun, but in the inferior temples which swarmed in the capital.

Pizarro, on entering Cuzco, had issued an order forbidding any soldier to offer violence to the dwellings of the inhabitants.[38] But the palaces were numerous, and the troops lost no time in plundering them of their contents, as well as in despoiling the religious edifices. The interior decorations supplied them with considerable booty. They stripped off the jewels and rich ornaments that garnished the royal mummies in the temple of Coricancha. Indignant at the concealment of their treasures, they put the inhabitants, in some instances, to the torture, and endeavored to extort from them a confession of their hiding-places.[39] They invaded the repose of the sepulchres, in which the Peruvians often deposited their valuable effects, and compelled the grave to give up its dead. No place was left unexplored by the rapacious Conquerors, and they occasionally stumbled on a mine of wealth that rewarded their labors.

In a cavern near the city they found a number of vases of pure gold, richly embossed with the figures of serpents, locusts, and other animals. Among the spoil were four golden llamas and ten or twelve statues of women, some of gold, others of silver, "which merely to see," says one of the Conquerors, with some *naïveté*, "was truly a great satisfaction." The gold was probably thin, for the figures were all as large as life; and several of them, being reserved for the royal fifth, were not recast, but sent in their original form to Spain.[40] The magazines were stored with curious commodities; richly tinted robes of cotton and feather-work, gold sandals, and slippers of the same material, for the women, and dresses composed entirely of beads of gold.[41] The grain and other articles of food, with which the magazines were filled, were held in contempt by the Con-

---

[38] "Pues mando el marquez dar vn pregon que ningun español fuese á entrar en las casas de los naturales ó tomalles nada." Pedro Pizarro, Descub. y Conq., MS.

[39] Gomara, Hist. de las Ind., cap. 123.

[40] "Et fra l'altre cose singolari, era veder quattro castrati di fin oro molto grandi, et 10 ò 12 statue di dòne, della grandezza delle dòne di quel paese tutte d'oro fino, cosi belle et ben fatte come se fossero viue. . . . . . Queste furono date nel quintc che toccaua a S. M." (Ped. Sancho, Rel., ap. Ramusio, tom. III. fol. 409.) "Muchas estatuas y figuras de oro y plata enteras, hecha la forma toda de una muger, y del tamaño della, muy bien labradas." Relacion del Primer. Descub., MS.

[41] "Avia ansi mismo otras muchas plumas de diferentes colores para este efecto de hacer rropas que vestian los señores y señoras y no otro en los tiempos de sus fiestas; avia tambien mantas hechas de chaquira, de oro, y de plata, que heran vnas quente- citas muy delicadas, que parecia cosa de espanto ver su hechura." Pedro Pizarro, Descub. y Conq., MS.

querors, intent only on gratifying their lust for gold.[42] The time came when the grain would have been of far more value.

Yet the amount of treasure in the capital did not equal the sanguine expectations that had been formed by the Spaniards. But the deficiency was supplied by the plunder which they had collected at various places on their march. In one place, for example, they met with ten planks or bars of solid silver, each piece being twenty feet in length, one foot in breadth, and two or three inches thick. They were intended to decorate the dwelling of an Inca noble.[43]

The whole mass of treasure was brought into a common heap, as in Caxamalca; and after some of the finer specimens had been deducted for the Crown, the remainder was delivered to the Indian goldsmiths to be melted down into ingots of a uniform standard. The division of the spoil was made on the same principle as before. There were four hundred and eighty soldiers, including the garrison of Xauxa, who were each to receive a share, that of the cavalry being double that of the infantry. The amount of booty is stated variously by those present at the division of it. According to some it considerably exceeded the ransom of Atahuallpa. Others state it as less. Pedro Pizarro says that each horseman got six thousand *pesos de oro*, and each one of the infantry half that sum; [44] though the same discrimination was made by Pizarro as before, in respect to the rank of the parties, and their relative services. But Sancho, the royal notary, and secretary of the commander, estimates the whole amount as far less,—not exceeding five hundred and eighty thousand and two hundred *pesos de oro*, and two hundred and fifteen thousand marks of silver.[45] In the absence of the official returns, it is impossible to determine which is correct. But Sancho's narrative is countersigned, it may be remembered, by Pizarro and the royal treasurer Riquelme, and doubtless therefore, shows the actual amount for which the Conquerors accounted to the Crown.

Whichever statement we receive, the sum, combined with that obtained at Caxamalca, might well have satisfied the cravings of the most avaricious. The sudden influx of so much wealth, and that, too, in so transferable a form, among a party of reckless adventurers little accustomed to the possession of money, had its natural effect. It supplied them with the means of gaming, so strong and common a passion with the Spaniards, that it may be considered a national vice. Fortunes were lost and won in a single day, sufficient to render the proprietors independent for life; and many a desperate gamester, by an unlucky throw of the dice or turn of the cards, saw himself stripped in a few hours of the fruits of years of

---

[42] Ondegardo, Rel. Prim., MS.

[43] "Pues andando yo buscando mahiz ó otras cosas para comer, acaso entre en vn buhio donde halle estos tablones de plata que tengo dicho que heran hasta diez y de largo tenian veinte pies y de anchor de vno y de gordor de tres dedos, di noticia dello a! marquez y el y todos los demas que con el estavan entraron á vello." Pedro Pizarro, Descub. y Conq., MS.

[44] Descub. y Conq., MS.

[45] Ped. Sancho, Rel., ap. Ramusio, tom. III. fol. 409.

toil, and obliged to begin over again the business of rapine. Among these, one in the cavalry service is mentioned, named Leguizano, who had received as his share of the booty the image of the Sun, which, raised on a plate of burnished gold, spread over the walls in a recess of the great temple, and which, for some reason or other,—perhaps because of its superior fineness,—was not recast like the other ornaments. This rich prize the spendthrift lost in a single night; whence it came to be a proverb in Spain, *Juega el Sol antes que amanezca*, "Play away the Sun before sunrise." [46]

The effect of such a surfeit of the precious metals was instantly felt on prices. The most ordinary articles were only to be had for exorbitant sums. A quire of paper sold for ten *pesos de oro;* a bottle of wine, for sixty; a sword, for forty or fifty; a cloak, for a hundred,—sometimes more; a pair of shoes cost thirty or forty *pesos de oro*, and a good horse could not be had for less than twenty-five hundred. [47] Some brought a still higher price. Every article rose in value, as gold and silver, the representatives of all, declined. Gold and silver, in short, seemed to be the only things in Cuzco that were not wealth. Yet there were some few wise enough to return contented with their present gains to their native country. Here their riches brought them consideration and competence, and, while they excited the envy of their countrymen, stimulated them to seek their own fortunes in the like path of adventure.

[46] Garcilasso, Com. Real., Parte 1, lib. 3, cap. 20.
[47] Xerez, Conq. del Peru, ap. Barcia, tom. III. p. 233.

CHAPTER IX

New Inca crowned—Municipal Regulations—Terrible March of
Alvarado—Interview with Pizarro—Foundation of Lima—
Hernando Pizarro reaches Spain—Sensation at Court—
Feuds of Almagro and the Pizarros

1534—1535

The first care of the Spanish general, after the division of the booty, was
to place Manco on the throne, and to obtain for him the recognition of
his countrymen. He, accordingly, presented the young prince to them as
their future sovereign, the legitimate son of Huayna Capac, and the true
heir of the Peruvian sceptre. The annunciation was received with enthusiasm by the people, attached to the memory of his illustrious father,
and pleased that they were still to have a monarch rule over them of the
ancient line of Cuzco.

Everything was done to maintain the illusion with the Indian population. The ceremonies of a coronation were studiously observed. The
young prince kept the prescribed fasts and vigils; and on the appointed
day, the nobles and the people, with the whole Spanish soldiery, assembled in the great square of Cuzco to witness the concluding ceremony. Mass was publicly performed by Father Valverde, and the Inca
Manco received the fringed diadem of Peru, not from the hand of the
high-priest of his nation, but from his Conqueror, Pizarro. The Indian
lords then tendered their obeisance in the customary form; after which
the royal notary read aloud the instrument asserting the supremacy of
the Castilian Crown, and requiring the homage of all present to its authority. This address was explained by an interpreter, and the ceremony
of homage was performed by each one of the parties waving the royal
banner of Castile twice or thrice with his hands. Manco then pledged the
Spanish commander in a golden goblet of the sparkling *chicha;* and, the
latter having cordially embraced the new monarch, the trumpets announced the conclusion of the ceremony.[1] But it was not the note of
triumph, but of humiliation; for it proclaimed that the armed foot of the
stranger was in the halls of the Peruvian Incas; that the ceremony of
coronation was a miserable pageant; that their prince himself was but a
puppet in the hands of his Conquerors; and that the glory of the Children of the Sun had departed forever!

[1] Pedro Pizarro, Descub. y Conq., MS.—Ped. Sancho, Rel., ap. Ramusio, tom
III. fol. 407.

Yet the people readily gave in to the illusion, and seemed willing to accept this image of their ancient independence. The accession of the young monarch was greeted by all the usual *fêtes* and rejoicings. The mummies of his royal ancestors, with such ornaments as were still left to them, were paraded in the great square. They were attended each by his own numerous retinue, who performed all the menial offices, as if the object of them were alive and could feel their import. Each ghostly form took its seat at the banquet-table—now, alas! stripped of the magnificent service with which it was wont to blaze at these high festivals—and the guests drank deep to the illustrious dead. Dancing succeeded the carousal, and the festivities, prolonged to a late hour, were continued night after night by the giddy population, as if their conquerors had not been intrenched in the capital! [2]—What a contrast to the Aztecs in the conquest of Mexico!

Pizarro's next concern was to organize a municipal government for Cuzco, like those in the cities of the parent country. Two *alcaldes* were appointed, and eight *regidores*, among which last functionaries were his brothers Gonzalo and Juan. The oaths of office were administered with great solemnity, on the twenty-fourth of March, 1534, in presence both of Spaniards and Peruvians, in the public square; as if the general were willing by this ceremony to intimate to the latter, that, while they retained the semblance of their ancient institutions, the real power was henceforth vested in their conquerors.[3] He invited Spaniards to settle in the place by liberal grants of land and houses, for which means were afforded by the numerous palaces and public buildings of the Incas; and many a cavalier, who had been too poor in his own country to find a place to rest in, now saw himself the proprietor of a spacious mansion that might have entertained the retinue of a prince.[4] From this time, says an old chronicler, Pizarro, who had hitherto been distinguished by his military title of "Captain-General," was addressed by that of "Governor." [5] Both had been bestowed on him by the royal grant.

Nor did the chief neglect the interests of religion. Father Valverde,

---

[2] Pedro Pizarro, Descub. y Conq., MS.

"Luego por la mañana iba al enterramiento donde estaban cada uno por orden embalsamados como es dicho, y asentados en sus sillas, y con mucha veneracion y respeto, todos por orden los sacaban de alli y los trahian á la ciudad, teniendo cada uno su litera, y hombres con su librea, que le trujesen, y ansi desta manera todo el servicio y aderezos como si estubiera vivo." Relacion del Primer. Descub., MS.

[3] Ped. Sancho, Rel., ap. Ramusio, tom. III. fol. 409.—Montesinos, Annales, MS., año 1534.—Actto de la fundacion del Cuzco, MS.

This instrument, which belongs to the collection of Muñoz, records not only the names of the magistrates, but of the *vecinos* who formed the first population of the *Christian* capital.

[4] Actto de la fundacion del Cuzco, MS.—Pedro Pizarro, Descub. y Conq., MS.— Garcilasso, Com. Real., Parte 1, lib. 7, cap. 9, et seq.

When a building was of immense size, as happened with some of the temples and palaces, it was assigned to two or even three of the Conquerors, who each took his share of it. Garcilasso, who describes the city as it was soon after the Conquest, commemorates with sufficient prolixity the names of the cavaliers among whom the buildings were distributed.

[5] Montesinos, Annales, año 1534.

whose nomination as Bishop of Cuzco not long afterwards received the Papal sanction, prepared to enter on the duties of his office. A place was selected for the cathedral of his diocese, facing the *plaza*. A spacious monastery subsequently rose on the ruins of the gorgeous House of the Sun; its walls were constructed of the ancient stones; the altar was raised on the spot where shone the bright image of the Peruvian deity, and the cloisters of the Indian temple were trodden by the friars of St. Dominic.[6] To make the metamorphosis more complete, the House of the Virgins of the Sun was replaced by a Roman Catholic nunnery.[7] Christian churches and monasteries gradually supplanted the ancient edifices, and such of the latter as were suffered to remain, despoiled of their heathen insignia, were placed under the protection of the Cross.

The Fathers of St. Dominic, the Brethren of the Order of Mercy, and other missionaries, now busied themselves in the good work of conversion. We have seen that Pizarro was required by the Crown to bring out a certain number of these holy men in his own vessels; and every succeeding vessel brought an additional reinforcement of ecclesiastics. They were not all like the Bishop of Cuzco, with hearts so seared by fanaticism as to be closed against sympathy with the unfortunate natives.[8] They were, many of them, men of singular humility, who followed in the track of the conqueror to scatter the seeds of spiritual truth, and, with disinterested zeal, devoted themselves to the propagation of the Gospel. Thus did their pious labors prove them the true soldiers of the Cross, and showed that the object so ostentatiously avowed of carrying its banner among the heathen nations was not an empty vaunt.

The effort to Christianize the heathen is an honorable characteristic of the Spanish conquests. The Puritan, with equal religious zeal, did comparatively little for the conversion of the Indian, content, as it would seem, with having secured to himself the inestimable privilege of worshipping God in his own way. Other adventurers who have occupied the New World have often had too little regard for religion themselves, to be very solicitous about spreading it among the savages. But the Spanish missionary, from first to last, has shown a keen interest in the spiritual

[6] Garcilasso, Com. Real., Parte 1, lib. 3, cap. 20; lib. 6, cap. 21.—Naharro, Relacion Sumaria, MS.

[7] Ulloa, Voyage to S. America, book 7, ch. 12.

"The Indian nuns," says the author of the Relacion del Primer. Descub., "lived chastely and in a holy manner."—"Their chastity was all a feint," says Pedro Pizarro, "for they had constant amours with the attendants on the temple." (Descub. y Conq., MS.)—What is truth?—In statements so contradictory, we may accept the most favorable to the Peruvian. The prejudices of the Conquerors certainly did not lie on that side.

[8] Such, however, it is but fair to Valverde to state, is not the language applied to him by the rude soldiers of the Conquest. The municipality of Xauxa, in a communication to the Court, extol the Dominican as an exemplary and learned divine, who had afforded much serviceable consolation to his countrymen. "Es persona de mucho exemplo i Doctrina i con quien todos los Españoles an tenido mucho consuelo." (Carta de la Just. y Reg. de Xauxa, MS.) And yet this is not incompatible with a high degree of insensibility to the natural rights of the natives.

welfare of the natives. Under his auspices, churches on a magnificent scale have been erected, schools for elementary instruction founded, and every rational means taken to spread the knowledge of religious truth, while he has carried his solitary mission into remote and almost inaccessible regions, or gathered his Indian disciples into communities, like the good Las Casas in Cumaná, or the Jesuits in California and Paraguay. At all times, the courageous ecclesiastic has been ready to lift his voice against the cruelty of the conqueror, and the no less wasting cupidity of the colonist; and when his remonstrances, as was too often the case, have proved unavailing, he has still followed to bind up the broken-hearted, to teach the poor Indian resignation under his lot, and light up his dark intellect with the revelation of a holier and happier existence.—In reviewing the blood-stained records of Spanish colonial history, it is but fair, and at the same time cheering, to reflect, that the same nation which sent forth the hard-hearted conqueror from its bosom sent forth the missionary to do the work of beneficence, and spread the light of Christian civilization over the farthest regions of the New World.

While the governor, as we are henceforth to style him, lay at Cuzco, he received repeated accounts of a considerable force in the neighborhood, under the command of Atahuallpa's officer, Quizquiz. He accordingly detached Almagro, with a small body of horse and a large Indian force under the Inca Manco, to disperse the enemy, and, if possible, to capture their leader. Manco was the more ready to take part in the expedition, as the enemy were soldiers of Quito, who, with their commander, bore no good-will to himself.

Almagro, moving with his characteristic rapidity, was not long in coming up with the Indian chieftain. Several sharp encounters followed, as the army of Quito fell back on Xauxa, near which a general engagement decided the fate of the war by the total discomfiture of the natives. Quizquiz fled to the elevated plains of Quito, where he still held out with undaunted spirit against a Spanish force in that quarter, till at length his own soldiers, wearied by these long and ineffectual hostilities, massacred their commander in cold blood.[9] Thus fell the last of the two great officers of Atahuallpa, who, if their nation had been animated by a spirit equal to their own, might long have successfully maintained their soil against the invader.

Some time before this occurrence, the Spanish governor, while in Cuzco, received tidings of an event much more alarming to him than any Indian hostilities. This was the arrival on the coast of a strong Spanish force, under command of Don Pedro de Alvarado, the gallant officer who had served under Cortés with such renown in the war of Mexico. That cavalier, after forming a brilliant alliance in Spain, to which he was entitled by his birth and military rank, had returned to his government of Guatemala, where his avarice had been roused by the magnificent re-

[9] Pedro Pizarro, Descub. y Conq., MS.—Naharro, Relacion Sumaria, MS.—Oviedo, Hist. de las Indias, MS., Parte 3, lib. 8. cap. 20.—Ped. Sancho, Rel., ap Ramusio, tom. III. fol. 408.—Relacion del Primer. Descub., MS.

ports he daily received of Pizarro's conquests. These conquests, he learned, had been confined to Peru; while the northern kingdom of Quito, the ancient residence of Atahuallpa, and, no doubt, the principal depository of his treasures, yet remained untouched. Affecting to consider this country as falling without the governor's jurisdiction, he immediately turned a large fleet, which he had intended for the Spice Islands, in the direction of South America; and in March, 1534, he landed in the bay of Caraques, with five hundred followers, of whom half were mounted, and all admirably provided with arms and ammunition. It was the best equipped and the most formidable array that had yet appeared in the southern seas.[10]

Although manifestly an invasion of the territory conceded to Pizarro by the Crown, the reckless cavalier determined to march at once on Quito. With the assistance of an Indian guide, he proposed to take the direct route across the mountains, a passage of exceeding difficulty, even at the most favorable season.

After crossing the Rio Dable, Alvarado's guide deserted him, so that he was soon entangled in the intricate mazes of the sierra; and, as he rose higher and higher into the regions of winter, he became surrounded with ice and snow, for which his men, taken from the warm countries of Guatemala, were but ill prepared. As the cold grew more intense, many of them were so benumbed, that it was with difficulty they could proceed. The infantry, compelled to make exertions, fared best. Many of the troopers were frozen stiff in their saddles. The Indians, still more sensible to the cold, perished by hundreds. As the Spaniards huddled round their wretched bivouacs, with such scanty fuel as they could glean, and almost without food, they waited in gloomy silence the approach of morning. Yet the morning light, which gleamed coldly on the cheerless waste, brought no joy to them. It only revealed more clearly the extent of their wretchedness. Still struggling on through the winding Puertos Nevados, or Snowy Passes, their track was dismally marked by fragments of dress, broken harness, golden ornaments, and other valuables plundered on their march,—by the dead bodies of men, or by those less fortunate, who were left to die alone in the wilderness. As for the horses, their carcasses were not suffered long to cumber the ground, as they were quickly seized and devoured half raw by the starving soldiers, who, like the famished condors, now hovering in troops above their heads, greedily banqueted on the most offensive offal to satisfy the gnawings of hunger.

Alvarado, anxious to secure the booty which had fallen into his hands at an earlier part of his march, encouraged every man to take what gold he wanted from the common heap, reserving only the royal fifth. But they only answered, with a ghastly smile of derision, "that food was the only gold for them." Yet in this extremity, which might seem to have dissolved the very ties of nature, there are some affecting instances recorded of self-devotion; of comrades who lost their lives in assisting others, and of

[10] The number is variously reported by historians. But from a legal investigation made in Guatemala, it appears that the whole force amounted to 500, of which 230 were cavalry.—Informacion echa en Santiago, Set. 15, 1536, MS.

parents and husbands (for some of the cavaliers were accompanied by their wives) who, instead of seeking their own safety, chose to remain and perish in the snows with the objects of their love.

To add to their distress, the air was filled for several days with thick clouds of earthy particles and cinders, which blinded the men, and made respiration exceedingly difficult.[11] This phenomenon, it seems probable, was caused by an eruption of the distant Cotopaxi, which, about twelve leagues southeast of Quito, rears up its colossal and perfectly symmetrical cone far above the limits of eternal snow,—the most beautiful and the most terrible of the American volcanoes.[12] At the time of Alvarado's expedition, it was in a state of eruption, the earliest instance of the kind on record, though doubtless not the earliest.[13] Since that period, it has been in frequent commotion, sending up its sheets of flame to the height of half a mile, spouting forth cataracts of lava that have overwhelmed towns and villages in their career, and shaking the earth with subterraneous thunders, that, at the distance of more than a hundred leagues, sounded like the reports of artillery![14] Alvarado's followers, unacquainted with the cause of the phenomenon, as they wandered over tracts buried in snow,—the sight of which was strange to them,—in an atmosphere laden with ashes, became bewildered by this confusion of the elements, which Nature seemed to have contrived purposely for their destruction. Some of these men were the soldiers of Cortés, steeled by many a painful march, and many a sharp encounter with the Aztecs. But this war of the elements, they now confessed, was mightier than all.

At length, Alvarado, after sufferings, which even the most hardy, probably, could have endured but a few days longer, emerged from the Snowy Pass, and came on the elevated table-land, which spreads out, at the height of more than nine thousand feet above the ocean, in the neighborhood of Riobamba. But one fourth of his gallant army had been left to feed the condor in the wilderness, besides the greater part, at least two thousand, of his Indian auxiliaries. A great number of his horses, too, had perished; and the men and horses that escaped were all of them more or less injured by the cold and the extremity of suffering.—Such was the terrible passage of the Puertos Nevados, which I have only briefly no-

[11] "It began to rain earthy particles from the heavens," says Oviedo, "that blinded the men and horses, so that the trees and bushes were full of dirt." Hist. de las Indias, MS., Parte 3, lib. 8, cap. 20.

[12] Garcilasso says the shower of ashes came from the "volcano of Quito." (Com. Real., Parte 2, lib. 2, cap. 2.) Cieza de Leon only says from one of the volcanoes in that region. (Cronica, cap. 41.) Neither of them specify the name. Humboldt accepts the common opinion, that Cotopaxi was intended. Researches, I. 123.

[13] A popular tradition among the natives states, that a large fragment of porphyry near the base of the cone was thrown out in an eruption, which occurred at the moment of Atahuallpa's death.—But such tradition will hardly pass for history.

[14] A minute account of this formidable mountain is given by M. de Humboldt, (Researches, I. 118, et seq.,) and more circumstantially by Condamine. (Voyage à l'Equateur, pp. 48-56, 156-160.) The latter philosopher would have attempted to scale the almost perpendicular walls of the volcano, but no one was hardy enough to second him.

ticed as an episode to the Peruvian conquest, but the account of which, in all its details, though it occupied but a few weeks in duration, would give one a better idea of the difficulties encountered by the Spanish cavaliers, than volumes of ordinary narrative.[15]

As Alvarado, after halting some time to restore his exhausted troops, began his march across the broad plateau, he was astonished by seeing the prints of horses' hoofs on the soil. Spaniards, then, had been there before him, and, after all his toil and suffering, others had forestalled him in the enterprise against Quito! It is necessary to say a few words in explanation of this.

When Pizarro quitted Caxamalca, being sensible of the growing importance of San Miguel, the only port of entry then in the country, he despatched a person in whom he had great confidence to take charge of it. This person was Sebastian Benalcazar, a cavalier who afterwards placed his name in the first rank of the South American conquerors, for courage, capacity,—and cruelty. But this cavalier had hardly reached his government, when, like Alvarado, he received such accounts of the riches of Quito, that he determined, with the force at his command, though without orders, to undertake its reduction.

At the head of about a hundred and forty soldiers, horse and foot, and a stout body of Indian auxiliaries, he marched up the broad range of the Andes, to where it spreads out into the table-land of Quito, by a road safer and more expeditious than that taken by Alvarado. On the plains of Riobamba, he encountered the Indian general Ruminavi. Several engagements followed, with doubtful success, when, in the end, science prevailed where courage was well matched, and the victorious Benalcazar planted the standard of Castile on the ancient towers of Atahuallpa. The city, in honor of his general, Francis Pizarro, he named San Francisco del Quito. But great was his mortification on finding that either the stories of its riches had been fabricated, or that these riches were secreted by the natives. The city was all that he gained by his victories,—the shell without the pearl of price which gave it its value. While devouring his chagrin, as he best could, the Spanish captain received tidings of the approach of his superior, Almagro.[16]

No sooner had the news of Alvarado's expedition reached Cuzco, than Almagro left the place with a small force for San Miguel, proposing to

[15] By far the most spirited and thorough record of Alvarado's march is given by Herrera, who has borrowed the pen of Livy describing the Alpine march of Hannibal. (Hist. General, dec. 5, lib. 6, cap. 1, 2, 7, 8, 9.) See also Pedro Pizarro, Descub. y Conq., MS.,—Oviedo, Hist. de las Indias, MS., Parte 3, lib. 8, cap. 20,—and Carta de Pedro de Alvarado al Emperador, San Miguel, 15 de Enero, 1535, MS.

Alvarado, in the letter above cited, which is preserved in the Muñoz collection, explains to the Emperor the grounds of his expedition, with no little effrontery. In this document he touches very briefly on the march, being chiefly occupied by the negotiations with Almagro, and accompanying his remarks with many dark suggestions as to the policy pursued by the Conquerors.

[16] Pedro Pizarro, Descub. y Conq., MS.—Herrera, Hist. General, dec. 5, lib. 4, cap. 11, 18; lib. 6, cap. 5, 6.—Oviedo, Hist. de las Indias, MS., Parte 3, lib. 8, cap. 19.—Carta de Benalcazar, MS.

strengthen himself by a reinforcement from that quarter, and to march at once against the invaders. Greatly was he astonished, on his arrival in that city, to learn the departure of its commander. Doubting the loyalty of his motives, Almagro, with the buoyancy of spirit which belongs to youth, though in truth somewhat enfeebled by the infirmities of age, did not hesitate to follow Benalcazar at once across the mountains.

With his wonted energy, the intrepid veteran, overcoming all the diffi-culties of his march, in a few weeks placed himself and his little company on the lofty plains which spread around the Indian city of Riobamba; though in his progress he had more than one hot encounter with the na-tives, whose courage and perseverance formed a contrast sufficiently striking to the apathy of the Peruvians. But the fire only slumbered in the bosom of the Peruvian. His hour had not yet come.

At Riobamba, Almagro was soon joined by the commander of San Miguel, who disclaimed, perhaps sincerely, any disloyal intent in his un-authorized expedition. Thus reinforced, the Spanish captain coolly await-ed the coming of Alvarado. The forces of the latter, though in a less ser-viceable condition, were much superior in number and appointments to those of his rival. As they confronted each other on the broad plains of Riobamba, it seemed probable that a fierce struggle must immediately follow, and the natives of the country have the satisfaction to see their wrongs avenged by the very hands that inflicted them. But it was Al-magro's policy to avoid such an issue.

Negotiations were set on foot, in which each party stated his claims to the country. Meanwhile Alvarado's men mingled freely with their countrymen in the opposite army, and heard there such magnificent re-ports of the wealth and wonders of Cuzco, that many of them were in-clined to change their present service for that of Pizarro. Their own leader, too, satisfied that Quito held out no recompense worth the sacri-fices he had made, and was like to make, by insisting on his claim, be-came now more sensible of the rashness of a course which must doubtless incur the censure of his sovereign. In this temper, it was not difficult for them to effect an adjustment of difficulties; and it was agreed, as the basis of it, that the governor should pay one hundred thousand *pesos de oro* to Alvarado, in consideration of which the latter was to resign to him his fleet, his forces, and all his stores and munitions. His vessels, great and small, amounted to twelve in number, and the sum he received, though large, did not cover his expenses. This treaty being settled, Al-varado proposed, before leaving the country, to have an interview with Pizarro.[17]

[17] Conq. i Pob. del Piru, MS.—Naharro, Relacion Sumaria, MS.—Pedro Pizarro, Descub. y Conq., MS.—Herrera, Hist. General, dec. 5, lib. 6, cap. 8-10.—Oviedo, Hist. de las Indias, MS., Parte 3, lib. 8, cap. 20.—Carta de Benalcazar, MS.

The amount of the *bonus* paid to Alvarado is stated very differently by writers. But both that cavalier and Almagro, in their letters to the Emperor, which have hitherto been unknown to historians, agree in the sum given in the text. Alvarado complains that he had no choice but to take it, although it was greatly to his own loss, and, by defeating his expedition, as he modestly intimates, to the loss of the

The governor, meanwhile, had quitted the Peruvian capital for the sea-coast, from his desire to repel any invasion that might be attempted in that direction by Alvarado, with whose real movements he was still unacquainted. He left Cuzco in charge of his brother Juan, a cavalier whose manners were such as, he thought, would be likely to gain the good-will of the native population. Pizarro also left ninety of his troops, as the garrison of the capital, and the nucleus of his future colony. Then, taking the Inca Manco with him, he proceeded as far as Xauxa. At this place he was entertained by the Indian prince with the exhibition of a great national hunt,—such as has been already described in these pages,—in which immense numbers of wild animals were slaughtered, and the vicuñas, and other races of Peruvian sheep, which roam over the mountains, driven into inclosures and relieved of their delicate fleeces.[18]

The Spanish governor then proceeded to Pachacamac, where he received the grateful intelligence of the accommodation with Alvarado; and not long afterward he was visited by that cavalier himself, previously to his embarkation.

The meeting was conducted with courtesy and a show, at least, of good-will, on both sides, as there was no longer real cause for jealousy between the parties; and each, as may be imagined, looked on the other with no little interest, as having achieved such distinction in the bold path of adventure. In the comparison, Alvarado had somewhat the advantage; for Pizarro, though of commanding presence, had not the brilliant exterior, the free and joyous manner, which, no less than his fresh complexion and sunny locks, had won for the conqueror of Guatemala, in his campaigns against the Aztecs, the *sobriquet of Tonatiuh*, or "Child of the Sun."

Crown. (Carta de Alvarado al Emperador, MS.)—Almagro, however, states that the sum paid was three times as much as the armament was worth; "a sacrifice," he adds, "which he made to preserve peace, never dear at any price."—Strange sentiment for a Castilian conqueror! Carta de Diego de Almagro al Emperador, MS., Oct. 15, 1534.

[18] Carta de la Just. y Reg. de Xauja, MS.—Relacion del Primer. Descub., MS.—Herrera, Hist. General, dec. 5, lib. 6, cap. 16.—Montesinos, Annales, MS., año 1534.

At this place, the author of the *Relacion del Primer Descubrimiento del Perú*, the MS. so often quoted in these pages, abruptly terminates his labors. He is a writer of sense and observation; and, though he has his share of the national tendency to exaggerate and overcolor, he writes like one who means to be honest, and who has seen what he describes.

At Xauxa, also, the notary Pedro Sancho ends his *Relacion*, which embraces a much shorter period than the preceding narrative, but which is equally authentic. Coming from the secretary of Pizarro, and countersigned by that general himself, this Relation, indeed, may be regarded as of the very highest authority. And yet large deductions must obviously be made for the source whence it springs; for it may be taken as Pizarro's own account of his doings, some of which stood much in need of apology. It must be added, in justice both to the general and to his secretary, that the Relation does not differ substantially from other contemporary accounts, and that the attempt to varnish over the exceptionable passages in the conduct of the Conquerors is not obtrusive.

For the publication of this journal, we are indebted to Ramusio, whose enlightened labors have preserved to us more than one contemporary production of value, though in the form of translation.

Blithe were the revels that now rang through the ancient city of Pachacamac; where, instead of songs, and of the sacrifices so often seen there in honor of the Indian deity, the walls echoed to the noise of tourneys and Moorish tilts of reeds, with which the martial adventurers loved to recall the sports of their native land. When these were concluded, Alvarado reëmbarked for his government of Guatemala, where his restless spirit soon involved him in other enterprises that cut short his adventurous career. His expedition to Peru was eminently characteristic of the man. It was founded in injustice, conducted with rashness, and ended in disaster.[19]

The reduction of Peru might now be considered as, in a manner, accomplished. Some barbarous tribes in the interior, it is true, still held out, and Alonso de Alvarado, a prudent and able officer, was employed to bring them into subjection. Benalcazar was still at Quito, of which he was subsequently appointed governor by the Crown. There he was laying deeper the foundation of the Spanish power, while he advanced the line of conquest still higher towards the north. But Cuzco, the ancient capital of the Indian monarchy, had submitted. The armies of Atahuallpa had been beaten and scattered. The empire of the Incas was dissolved; and the prince who now wore the Peruvian diadem was but the shadow of a king, who held his commission from his conqueror.

The first act of the governor was to determine on the site of the future capital of this vast colonial empire. Cuzco, withdrawn among the mountains, was altogether too far removed from the sea-coast for a commercial people. The little settlement of San Miguel lay too far to the north. It was desirable to select some more central position, which could be easily found in one of the fruitful valleys that bordered the Pacific. Such was that of Pachacamac, which Pizarro now occupied. But, on further examination, he preferred the neighboring valley of Rimac, which lay to the north, and which took its name, signifying in the Quichua tongue "one who speaks," from a celebrated idol, whose shrine was much frequented by the Indians for the oracles it delivered. Through the valley flowed a broad stream, which, like a great artery, was made, as usual by the natives, to supply a thousand finer veins that meandered through the beautiful meadows.

On this river Pizarro fixed the site of his new capital, at somewhat less than two leagues' distance from its mouth, which expanded into a commodious haven for the commerce that the prophetic eye of the founder saw would one day—and no very distant one—float on its waters. The central situation of the spot recommended it as a suitable residence for

[19] Naharro, Relacion Sumaria, MS.—Pedro Pizarro, Descub. y Conq., MS.—Carta de Francisco Pizarro el Señor de Molina, MS.

Alvarado died in 1541, of an injury received from a horse which rolled down on him as he was attempting to scale a precipitous hill in New Galicia. In the same year, by a singular coincidence, perished his beautiful wife, at her own residence in Guatemala, which was overwhelmed by a torrent from the adjacent mountains.

the Peruvian viceroy, whence he might hold easy communication with the different parts of the country, and keep vigilant watch over his Indian vassals. The climate was delightful, and, though only twelve degrees south of the line, was so far tempered by the cool breezes that generally blow from the Pacific, or from the opposite quarter down the frozen sides of the Cordilleras, that the heat was less than in corresponding latitudes on the continent. It never rained on the coast; but this dryness was corrected by a vaporous cloud, which, through the summer months, hung like a curtain over the valley, sheltering it from the rays of a tropical sun, and imperceptibly distilling a refreshing moisture, that clothed the fields in the brightest verdure.

The name bestowed on the infant capital was *Ciudad de los Reyes*, or City of the Kings, in honor of the day, being the sixth of January, 1535, —the festival of Epiphany,—when it was said to have been founded, or more probably when its site was determined, as its actual foundation seems to have been twelve days later.[20] But the Castilian name ceased to be used even within the first generation, and was supplanted by that of Lima, into which the original Indian name of Rimac was corrupted by the Spaniards.[21]

The city was laid out on a very regular plan. The streets were to be much wider than usual in Spanish towns, and perfectly straight, crossing one another at right angles, and so far asunder as to afford ample space for gardens to the dwellings, and for public squares. It was arranged in a triangular form, having the river for its base, the waters of which were to be carried, by means of stone conduits, through all the principal streets, affording facilities for irrigating the grounds around the houses.

No sooner had the governor decided on the site and on the plan of the city, than he commenced operations with his characteristic energy. The Indians were collected from the distance of more than a hundred miles to aid in the work. The Spaniards applied themselves with vigor to the task, under the eye of their chief. The sword was exchanged for the tool of the artisan. The camp was converted into a hive of diligent laborers; and the sounds of war were succeeded by the peaceful hum of a busy population. The *plaza*, which was extensive, was to be surrounded by the cathedral, the palace of the viceroy, that of the municipality, and other public buildings; and their foundations were laid on a scale, and with a solidity, which defied the assaults of time, and, in some instances, even

---

[20] So says Quintana, who follows in this what he pronounces a sure authority, Father Bernabe Cobo, in his book entitled *Fundacion de Lima*. Españoles Celebres, tom. II. p. 250, nota.

[21] The MSS. of the old Conquerors show how, from the very first, the name of Lima superseded the original Indian title. "Y el marquez se passo á Lima y fundo la ciudad de los rreyes que agora es." (Pedro Pizarro, Descub. y Conq., MS.) "Asimismo ordenaron que se pasasen el pueblo que tenian an Xauxa poblado á este Valle de Lima donde agora es esta ciudad de los i aqui se poblo." Conq. i Pob. del Piru, MS.

the more formidable shock of earthquakes, that, at different periods, have laid portions of the fair capital in ruins.[22]

While these events were going on, Almagro, the Marshal, as he is usually termed by chroniclers of the time, had gone to Cuzco, whither he was sent by Pizarro to take command of that capital. He received also instructions to undertake, either by himself or by his captains, the conquest of the countries towards the south, forming part of Chili. Almagro, since his arrival at Caxamalca, had seemed willing to smother his ancient feelings of resentment towards his associate, or, at least, to conceal the expression of them, and had consented to take command under him in obedience to the royal mandate. He had even, in his despatches, the magnanimity to make honorable mention of Pizarro, as one anxious to promote the interests of government. Yet he did not so far trust his companion, as to neglect the precaution of sending a confidential agent to represent his own services, when Hernando Pizarro undertook his mission to the mother-country.

That cavalier, after touching at St. Domingo, had arrived without accident at Seville, in January, 1534. Besides the royal fifth, he took with him gold, to the value of half a million of *pesos*, together with a large quantity of silver, the property of private adventurers, some of whom, satisfied with their gains, had returned to Spain in the same vessel with himself. The custom-house was filled with solid ingots, and with vases of different forms, imitations of animals, flowers, fountains, and other objects, executed with more or less skill, and all of pure gold, to the astonishment of the spectators, who flocked from the neighboring country to gaze on these marvellous productions of Indian art.[23] Most of the manufactured articles were the property of the Crown; and Hernando Pizarro, after a short stay at Seville, selected some of the most gorgeous specimens, and crossed the country to Calatayud, where the emperor was holding the cortes of Aragon.

Hernando was instantly admitted to the royal presence, and obtained a gracious audience. He was more conversant with courts than either of his brothers, and his manners, when in situations that imposed a restraint on the natural arrogance of his temper, were graceful and even attractive. In a respectful tone, he now recited the stirring adventures of his brother and his little troop of followers, the fatigues they had endured, the difficulties they had overcome, their capture of the Peruvian Inca, and his magnificent ransom. He had not to tell of the massacre of the unfortunate prince, for that tragic event, which had occurred since his departure from the country, was still unknown to him. The cavalier expatiated on the productiveness of the soil, and on the civilization of the people, evinced

---

[22] Montesinos, Annales, MS., año 1535.—Conq. i Pob. del Piru, MS.

The remains of Pizarro's palace may still be discerned in the Callejon de Petateros, says Stevenson, who gives the best account of Lima to be found in any modern book of travels which I have consulted. Residence in South America, vol. II. chap. 8.

[23] Herrera, Hist. General, dec. 5, lib. 6, cap. 13.—Lista de todo lo que Hernando Pizarro trajo del Peru, ap. MSS. de Muñoz.

by their proficiency in various mechanic arts; in proof of which he displayed the manufactures of wool and cotton, and the rich ornaments of gold and silver. The monarch's eyes sparkled with delight as he gazed on these last. He was too sagacious not to appreciate the advantages of a conquest which secured to him a country so rich in agricultural resources. But the returns from these must necessarily be gradual and long deferred; and he may be excused for listening with still greater satisfaction to Pizarro's tales of its mineral stores; for his ambitious projects had drained the imperial treasury, and he saw in the golden tide thus unexpectedly poured in upon him the immediate means of replenishing it.

Charles made no difficulty, therefore, in granting the petitions of the fortunate adventurer. All the previous grants to Francis Pizarro and his associates were confirmed in the fullest manner; and the boundaries of the governor's jurisdiction were extended seventy leagues further towards the south. Nor did Almagro's services, this time, go unrequited. He was empowered to discover and occupy the country for the distance of two hundred leagues, beginning at the southern limit of Pizarro's territory.[24] Charles, in proof, still further, of his satisfaction, was graciously pleased to address a letter to the two commanders, in which he complimented them on their prowess, and thanked them for their services. This act of justice to Almagro would have been highly honorable to Hernando Pizarro, considering the unfriendly relations in which they stood to each other, had it not been made necessary by the presence of the marshal's own agents at court, who, as already noticed, stood ready to supply any deficiency in the statements of the emissary.

In this display of the royal bounty, the envoy, as will readily be believed, did not go without his reward. He was lodged as an attendant of the Court; was made a knight of Santiago, the most prized of the chivalric orders in Spain; was empowered to equip an armament, and to take command of it; and the royal officers at Seville were required to aid him in his views and facilitate his embarkation for the Indies.[25]

The arrival of Hernando Pizarro in the country, and the reports spread by him and his followers, created a sensation among the Spaniards such as had not been felt since the first voyage of Columbus. The discovery of the New World had filled the minds of men with indefinite expectations of wealth, of which almost every succeeding expedition had proved the fallacy. The conquest of Mexico, though calling forth general admiration as a brilliant and wonderful exploit, had as yet failed to produce those golden results which had been so fondly anticipated. The splendid promises held out by Francis Pizarro on his recent visit to the country had not revived the confidence of his countrymen, made incredulous by re-

---

[24] The country to be occupied received the name of New Toledo, in the royal grant, as the conquests of Pizarro had been designated by that of New Castile. But the present attempt to change the Indian name was as ineffectual as the former, and the ancient title of Chili still designates that narrow strip of fruitful land between the Andes and the ocean, which stretches to the south of the great continent.

[25] Ibid., loc. cit.

peated disappointment. All that they were assured of was the difficulties of the enterprise; and their distrust of its results was sufficiently shown by the small number of followers, and those only of the most desperate stamp, who were willing to take their chance in the adventure.

But now these promises were realized. It was no longer the golden reports that they were to trust; but the gold itself, which was displayed in such profusion before them. All eyes were now turned towards the West. The broken spendthrift saw in it the quarter where he was to repair his fortunes as speedily as he had ruined them. The merchant, instead of seeking the precious commodities of the East, looked in the opposite direction, and counted on far higher gains, where the most common articles of life commanded so exorbitant prices. The cavalier, eager to win both gold and glory at the point of his lance, thought to find a fair field for his prowess on the mountain plains of the Andes. Ferdinand Pizarro found that his brother had judged rightly in allowing as many of his company as chose to return home, confident that the display of their wealth would draw ten to his banner for every one that quitted it.

In a short time that cavalier saw himself at the head of one of the most numerous and well-appointed armaments, probably, that had left the shores of Spain since the great fleet of Ovando, in the time of Ferdinand and Isabella. It was scarcely more fortunate that this. Hardly had Ferdinand put to sea, when a violent tempest fell on the squadron, and compelled him to return to port and refit. At length he crossed the ocean, and reached the little harbor of Nombre de Dios in safety. But no preparations had been made for his coming, and, as he was detained here some time before he could pass the mountains, his company suffered greatly from scarcity of food. In their extremity, the most unwholesome articles were greedily devoured, and many a cavalier spent his little savings to procure himself a miserable subsistence. Disease, as usual, trod closely in the track of famine, and numbers of the unfortunate adventurers, sinking under the unaccustomed heats of the climate, perished on the very threshold of discovery.

It was the tale often repeated in the history of Spanish enterprise. A few, more lucky than the rest, stumble on some unexpected prize, and hundreds, attracted by their success, press forward in the same path. But the rich spoil which lay on the surface has been already swept away by the first comers, and those who follow are to win their treasure by long-protracted and painful exertion.—Broken in spirit and in fortune, many returned in disgust to their native shores, while others remained where they were, to die in despair. They thought to dig for gold; but they dug only their graves.

Yet it fared not thus with all Pizarro's company. Many of them, crossing the Isthmus with him to Panamá, came in time to Peru, where, in the desperate chances of its revolutionary struggles, some few arrived at posts of profit and distinction. Among those who first reached the Peruvian shore was an emissary sent by Almagro's agents to inform him of the important grant made to him by the Crown. The tidings reached him just as he was making his entry into Cuzco, where he was received with all respect by Juan and Gonzalo Pizarro, who, in obedience to their brother's commands, instantly resigned the government of the capital into the marshal's hands. But Almagro was greatly elated on finding himself now placed by his sovereign in a command that made him independent of the man who had so deeply wronged him; and he intimated that in the exercise of his present authority he acknowledged no superior. In this lordly humor he was confirmed by several of his followers, who insisted that Cuzco fell to the south of the territory ceded to Pizarro, and consequently came within that now granted to the marshal. Among these followers were several of Alvarado's men, who, though of better condition than the soldiers of Pizarro, were under much worse discipline, and had acquired, indeed, a spirit of unbridled license under that unscrupulous chief.[26] They now evinced little concern for the native population of Cuzco; and, not content with the public edifices, seized on the dwellings of individuals, where it suited their conveniences, appropriating their contents without ceremony,—showing as little respect, in short, for person or property, as if the place had been taken by storm.[27]

While these events were passing in the ancient Peruvian capital, the governor was still at Lima, where he was greatly disturbed by the accounts he received of the new honors conferred on his associate. He did not know that his own jurisdiction had been extended seventy leagues further to the south, and he entertained the same suspicion with Almagro, that the capital of the Incas did not rightly come within his present limits. He saw all the mischief likely to result from this opulent city falling into the hands of his rival, who would thus have an almost indefinite means of gratifying his own cupidity, and that of his followers. He felt, that, under the present circumstances, it was not safe to allow Almagro to anticipate the possession of power, to which, as yet, he had no legitimate right; for the despatches containing the warrant for it still remained with Hernando Pizarro, at Panamá, and all that had reached Peru was a copy of a garbled extract.

Without loss of time, therefore, he sent instructions to Cuzco for his

[26] In point of discipline, they presented a remarkable contrast to the Conquerors of Peru, if we may take the word of Pedro Pizarro, who assures us that his comrades would not have plucked so much as an ear of corn without leave from their commander. "Que los que pasamos con el Marquez á la conquista no ovo hombre que osase tomar vna mazorca de mahiz sin licencia." Descub. y Conq., MS.

[27] "Se entraron de paz en la ciudad del Cuzco i los salieron todos los naturales á rescibir i les tomaron la Ciudad con todo quanto habia de dentro llenas las casas de mucha ropa i algunas oro i plata i otras muchas cosas, i las que no estaban bien llenas las enchian de lo que tomaban de las demas casas de la dicha ciudad, sin pensar que en ello hacian ofensa alguna Divina ni humana, i porquesta es una cosa larga i casi incomprehensible, la dexase al juicio de quien mas entiende aunque en el daño rescebido por parte de los naturales cerca deste articulo yo sé harto por mis pecados que no quisiera saber ni haver visto." Conq. i Pob. del Piru, MS.

ʹbrothers to resume the government, while he defended the measure to Almagro on the ground, that, when he should hereafter receive his credentials, it would be unbecoming to be found already in possession of the post. He concluded by urging him to go forward without delay in his expedition to the south.

But neither the marshal nor his friends were pleased with the idea of so soon relinquishing the authority which they now considered as his right. The Pizarros, on the other hand, were pertinacious in reclaiming it. The dispute grew warmer and warmer. Each party had its supporters; the city was split into factions; and the municipality, the soldiers, and even the Indian population, took sides in the struggle for power. Matters were proceeding to extremity, menacing the capital with violence and bloodshed, when Pizarro himself appeared among them.[28]

On receiving tidings of the fatal consequences of his mandates, he had posted in all haste to Cuzco, where he was greeted with undisguised joy by the natives, as well as by the more temperate Spaniards, anxious to avert the impending storm. The governor's first interview was with Almagro, whom he embraced with a seeming cordiality in his manner; and, without any show of resentment, inquired into the cause of the present disturbances. To this the marshal replied, by throwing the blame on Pizarro's brothers; but, although the governor reprimanded them with some asperity for their violence, it was soon evident that his sympathies were on their side, and the dangers of a feud between the two associates seemed greater than ever. Happily, it was postponed by the intervention of some common friends, who showed more discretion than their leaders. With their aid a reconciliation was at length effected, on the grounds substantially of their ancient compact.

It was agreed that their friendship should be maintained inviolate; and, by a stipulation that reflects no great credit on the parties, it was provided that neither should malign nor disparage the other, especially in their despatches to the emperor; and that neither should hold communication with the government without the knowledge of his confederate; lastly, that both the expenditures and the profits of future discovery should be shared equally by the associates. The wrath of Heaven was invoked by the most solemn imprecations on the head of whichever should violate this compact, and the Almighty was implored to visit the offender with loss of property and of life in this world, and with eternal perdition in that to come! [29] The parties further bound themselves to the observance of this contract by a solemn oath taken on the sacrament, as it was held in the hands of Father Bartolomé de Segovia, who con-

---

[28] Pedro Pizarro, Descub. y Conq., MS.—Herrera, Hist. General, dec. 5, lib. 7, cap. 6.—Conq. i Pob. del Piru, MS.

[29] "E suplicamos á su infinita bondad que á qualquier de nos que fuere en contrario de lo asi convenido, con todo rigor de justicia permita la perdicion de su anima, fin y mal acavamiento de su vida, destruicion y perdimientos de su familia, honrras y hacienda." Capitulacion entre Pizarro y Almagro, 12 de Junio, 1535, MS

cluded the ceremony by performing mass. The whole proceeding, and the articles of agreement, were carefully recorded by the notary, in an instrument bearing date June 12, 1535, and attested by a long list of witnesses.[30]

Thus did these two ancient comrades, after trampling on the ties of friendship and honor, hope to knit themselves to each other by the holy bands of religion. That it should have been necessary to resort to so extraordinary a measure might have furnished them with the best proof of its inefficacy.

Not long after this accommodation of their differences, the marshal raised his standard for Chili; and numbers, won by his popular manners, and by his liberal largesses,—liberal to prodigality,—eagerly joined in the enterprise, which they fondly trusted would lead even to greater riches than they had found in Peru. Two Indians, Paullo Topa, a brother of the Inca Manco, and Villac Umu, the high-priest of the nation, were sent in advance, with three Spaniards, to prepare the way for the little army. A detachment of a hundred and fifty men, under an officer named Saavedra, next followed. Almagro remained behind to collect further recruits; but before his levies were completed, he began his march, feeling himself insecure, with his diminished strength, in the neighborhood of Pizarro! [31] The remainder of his forces, when mustered, were to follow him.

Thus relieved of the presence of his rival, the governor returned without further delay to the coast, to resume his labors in the settlement of the country. Besides the principal city of "The Kings," he established others along the Pacific, destined to become hereafter the flourishing marts of commerce. The most important of these, in honor of his birthplace, he named Truxillo, planting it on a site already indicated by Almagro.[32] He made also numerous *repartimientos* both of lands and Indians among his followers, in the usual manner of the Spanish Conquerors; [33]—though here the ignorance of the real resources of the country led to very different results from what he had intended, as the terri-

[30] The original of this remarkable document is preserved in the archives of Simancas.

[31] "El Adelantado Almagro despues que se vido en el Cuzco descarnado de su jente temio al Marquez no le prendiese por las alteraciones pasadas que havia tenido con sus hermanos como ya hemos dicho, i dicen que por ser avisado dello tomó la posta i se fue al pueblo de Paria donde estava su Capitan Saavedra." Conq. i Pob. del Piru, MS.

[32] Carta de F. Pizarro a Molina, MS.

[33] I have before me two copies of grants of *encomiendas* by Pizarro, the one dated at Xauxa, 1534, the other at Cuzco, 1539.—They emphatically enjoin on the colonist the religious instruction of the natives under his care, as well as kind and considerate usage. How ineffectual were the recommendations may be inferred from the lament of the anonymous contemporary often cited, that "from this time forth, the pest of personal servitude was established among the Indians, equally disastrous to body and soul of both the master and the slave." (Conq. i Pob. del Piru, MS.) This honest burst of indignation, not to have been expected in the rude Conqueror, came probably from an ecclesiastic.

tory smallest in extent, not unfrequently, from the hidden treasures in its bosom, turned out greatest in value.[34]

But nothing claimed so much of Pizarro's care as the rising metropolis of Lima; and, so eagerly did he press forward the work, and so well was he seconded by the multitude of laborers at his command, that he had the satisfaction to see his young capital, with its stately edifices and its pomp of gardens, rapidly advancing towards completion. It is pleasing to contemplate the softer features in the character of the rude soldier, as he was thus occupied with healing up the ravages of war, and laying broad the foundations of an empire more civilized than that which he had overthrown. This peaceful occupation formed a contrast to the life of incessant turmoil in which he had been hitherto engaged. It seemed, too, better suited to his own advancing age, which naturally invited to repose. And, if we may trust his chroniclers, there was no part of his career in which he took greater satisfaction. It is certain there is no part which has been viewed with greater satisfaction by posterity; and, amidst the woe and desolation which Pizarro and his followers brought on the devoted land of the Incas, Lima, the beautiful City of the Kings, still survives as the most glorious work of his creation, the fairest gem on the shores of the Pacific.

[34] "El Marques hizo encomiendas en los Españoles, las quales fueron por noticias que ni el sabia lo que dava ni nadie lo que rescebia sino a tiento ya poco mas ó menos y asi muchos que pensaron que se les dava pocos se hallaron con mucho y al contrario." Ondegardo, Rel. Prim., MS.

CHAPTER X

ESCAPE OF THE INCA—RETURN OF HERNANDO PIZARRO—RISING OF TH.
PERUVIANS—SIEGE AND BURNING OF CUZCO—DISTRESSES OF THE
SPANIARDS—STORMING OF THE FORTRESS—PIZARRO'S DISMAY—
THE INCA RAISES THE SIEGE

1535—1536

WHILE the absence of his rival Almagro relieved Pizarro from all immediate disquietude from that quarter, his authority was menaced in another, where he had least expected it. This was from the native population of the country. Hitherto the Peruvians had shown only a tame and
submissive temper, that inspired their conquerors with too much contempt to leave room for apprehension. They had passively acquiesced in
the usurpation of the invaders; had seen one monarch butchered, another
placed on the vacant throne, their temples despoiled of their treasures,
their capital and country appropriated and parcelled out among the Spaniards; but, with the exception of an occasional skirmish in the mountain
passes, not a blow had been struck in defence of their rights. Yet this
was the warlike nation which had spread its conquests over so large a
part of the continent!

In his career, Pizarro, though he scrupled at nothing to effect his object, had not usually countenanced such superfluous acts of cruelty as had
too often stained the arms of his countrymen in other parts of the continent, and which, in the course of a few years, had exterminated nearly
a whole population in Hispaniola. He had struck one astounding blow, by
the seizure of Atahuallpa; and he seemed willing to rely on this to strike
terror into the natives. He even affected some respect for the institutions
of the country, and had replaced the monarch he had murdered by another of the legitimate line. Yet this was but a pretext. The kingdom had
experienced a revolution of the most decisive kind. Its ancient institutions
were subverted. Its heaven-descended aristocracy was levelled almost to
the condition of the peasant. The people became the serfs of the Conquerors. Their dwellings in the capital—at least, after the arrival of Alvarado's officers—were seized and appropriated. The temples were turned into stables; the royal residences into barracks for the troops. The
sanctity of the religious houses was violated. Thousands of matrons and
maidens, who, however erroneous their faith, lived in chaste seclusion in
the conventual establishments, were now turned abroad, and became the

prey of a licentious soldiery.[1] A favorite wife of the young Inca was debauched by the Castilian officers. The Inca, himself treated with contemptuous indifference, found that he was a poor dependant, if not a tool, in the hands of his conquerors.[2]

Yet the Inca Manco was a man of a lofty spirit and a courageous heart; such a one as might have challenged comparison with the bravest of his ancestors in the prouder days of the empire. Stung to the quick by the humiliations to which he was exposed, he repeatedly urged Pizarro to restore him to the real exercise of power, as well as to the show of it. But Pizarro evaded a request so incompatible with his own ambitious schemes, or, indeed, with the policy of Spain, and the young Inca and his nobles were left to brood over their injuries in secret, and await patiently the hour of vengeance.

The dissensions among the Spaniards themselves seemed to afford a favorable opportunity for this. The Peruvian chiefs held many conferences together on the subject, and the high-priest Villac Umu urged the necessity of a rising so soon as Almagro had withdrawn his forces from the city. It would then be comparatively easy, by assaulting the invaders on their several posts, scattered as they were over the country, to overpower them by superior numbers, and shake off their detested yoke before the arrival of fresh reinforcements should rivet it forever on the necks of his countrymen. A plan for a general rising was formed, and it was in conformity to it that the priest was selected by the Inca to bear Almagro company on the march, that he might secure the coöperation of the natives in the country, and then secretly return—as in fact he did—to take a part in the insurrection.

---

[1] So says the author of the *Conquista i Poblacion del Piru*, a contemporary writer, who describes what he saw himself as well as what he gathered from others. Several circumstances, especially the honest indignation he expresses at the excesses of the Conquerors, lead one to suppose he may have been an ecclesiastic, one of the good men who attended the cruel expedition on an errand of love and mercy. It is to be hoped that his credulity leads him to exaggerate the misdeeds of his countrymen.

According to him, there were full six thousand women of rank, living in the convents of Cuzco, served each by fifteen or twenty female attendants, most of whom, that did not perish in the war, suffered a more melancholy fate, as the victims of prostitution.—The passage is so remarkable, and the MS. so rare, that I will cite it in the original.

"De estas señoras del Cuzco es cierto de tener grande sentimiento el que tuviese alguna humanidad en el pecho, que en tiempo de la prosperidad del Cuzco quando los Españoles entraron en el havia grand cantidad de señoras que tenian sus casas i sus asientos mui quietas i sosegadas i vivian mui politicamente i como mui buenas mugeres, cada señora acompañada con quince o veinte mugeres que tenia de servicio en su casa bien traidas i aderezadas, i no salian menos desto i con grand onestidad i gravedad i atavio a su usanza, i es a la cantidad destas señoras principales creo yo que en el . . . . . que avia mas de seis mil sin las de servicio que creo yo que eran mas de veinte mil mugeres sin las de servicio i mamaconas que eran las que andavan como beatas i dende á dos años casi no se allava en el Cuzco i su tierra sino cada qual i qual porque muchas murieron en la guerra que huvo i las otras vinieron las mas á ser malas mugeres. Señor perdone a quien fue la causa desto i aquien no lo remedia pudiendo." Conq. i Pob. del Piru, MS.

[2] Ibid, ubi supra.

To carry their plans into effect, it became necessary that the Inca Manco should leave the city and present himself among his people. He found no difficulty in withdrawing from Cuzco, where his presence was scarcely heeded by the Spaniards, as his nominal power was held in little deference by the haughty and confident Conquerors. But in the capital there was a body of Indian allies more jealous of his movements. These were from the tribe of the Cañares, a warlike race of the north, too recently reduced by the Incas to have much sympathy with them or their institutions. There were about a thousand of this people in the place, and, as they had conceived some suspicion of the Inca's purposes, they kept an eye on his movements, and speedily reported his absence to Juan Pizarro.

That cavalier, at the head of a small body of horse, instantly marched in pursuit of the fugitive, whom he was so fortunate as to discover in a thicket of reeds, in which he sought to conceal himself, at no great distance from the city. Manco was arrested, brought back a prisoner to Cuzco, and placed under a strong guard in the fortress. The conspiracy seemed now at an end; and nothing was left to the unfortunate Peruvians but to bewail their ruined hopes, and to give utterance to their disappointment in doleful ballads, which rehearsed the captivity of their Inca, and the downfall of his royal house.[3]

While these things were in progress, Hernando Pizarro returned to Ciudad de los Reyes, bearing with him the royal commission for the extension of his brother's powers, as well as of those conceded to Almagro. The envoy also brought the royal patent conferring on Francisco Pizarro the title of *marques de los Atavillos,*—a province in Peru. Thus was the fortunate adventurer placed in the ranks of the proud aristocracy of Castile, few of whose members could boast—if they had the courage to boast—their elevation from so humble an origin, as still fewer could justify it by a show of greater services to the Crown.

The new marquess resolved not to forward the commission, at present, to the marshal, whom he designed to engage still deeper in the conquest of Chili, that his attention might be diverted from Cuzco, which, however, his brother assured him, now fell, without doubt, within the newly extended limits of his own territory. To make more sure of this important prize, he despatched Hernando to take the government of the capital into his own hands, as the one of his brothers on whose talents and practical experience he placed greatest reliance.

Hernando, notwithstanding his arrogant bearing towards his countrymen, had ever manifested a more than ordinary sympathy with the Indians. He had been the friend of Atahuallpa; to such a degree, indeed, that it was said, if he had been in the camp at the time, the fate of that unhappy monarch would probably have been averted. He now showed a similar friendly disposition towards his successor, Manco. He caused the

[3] Pedro Pizarro, Descub. y Conq., MS.—Herrera, Hist. General, dec. 5, lib. 8. cap. 1, 2.—Conq. i Pob. del Piru, MS.—Zarate, Conq. dei Peru, lib. 2, cap. 3.

Peruvian prince to be liberated from confinement, and gradually admitted him into some intimacy with himself. The crafty Indian availed himself of his freedom to mature his plans for the rising, but with so much caution, that no suspicion of them crossed the mind of Hernando. Secrecy and silence are characteristic of the American, almost as invariably as the peculiar color of his skin. Manco disclosed to his conqueror the existence of several heaps of treasure, and the places where they had been secreted; and, when he had thus won his confidence, he stimulated his cupidity still further by an account of a statue of pure gold of his father Huayna Capac, which the wily Peruvian requested leave to bring from a secret cave in which it was deposited, among the neighboring Andes. Hernando, blinded by his avarice, consented to the Inca's departure.

He sent with him two Spanish soldiers, less as a guard than to aid him in the object of his expedition. A week elapsed, and yet he did not return, nor were there any tidings to be gathered of him. Hernando now saw his error, especially as his own suspicions were confirmed by the unfavorable reports of his Indian allies. Without further delay, he despatched his brother Juan, at the head of sixty horse, in quest of the Peruvian prince, with orders to bring him back once more a prisoner to his capital.

That cavalier, with his well-armed troops, soon traversed the environs of Cuzco without discovering any vestige of the fugitive. The country was remarkably silent and deserted, until, as he approached the mountain range that hems in the valley of Yucay, about six leagues from the city, he was met by the two Spaniards who had accompanied Manco. They informed Pizarro that it was only at the point of the sword he could recover the Inca, for the country was all in arms, and the Peruvian chief at its head was preparing to march on the capital. Yet he had offered no violence to their persons, but had allowed them to return in safety.

The Spanish captain found this story fully confirmed when he arrived at the river Yucay, on the opposite bank of which were drawn up the Indian battalions to the number of many thousand men, who, with their young monarch at their head, prepared to dispute his passage. It seemed that they could not feel their position sufficiently strong, without placing a river, as usual, between them and their enemy. The Spaniards were not checked by this obstacle. The stream, though deep, was narrow; and plunging in, they swam their horses boldly across, amidst a tempest of stones and arrows that rattled thick as hail on their harness, finding occasionally some crevice or vulnerable point,—although the wounds thus received only goaded them to more desperate efforts. The barbarians fell back as the cavaliers made good their landing; but, without allowing the latter time to form, they returned with a spirit which they had hitherto seldom displayed, and enveloped them on all sides with their greatly superior numbers. The fight now raged fiercely. Many of the Indians were armed with lances headed with copper tempered almost to the hardness of steel, and with huge maces and battle-axes of the same metal. Their defensive armour, also, was in many respects excellent, consisting of stout doublets of quilted cotton, shields covered with skins, and casques richly ornamented with gold and jewels, or sometimes made like those of the Mexicans, in the fantastic shape of the heads of wild animals, garnished with rows of teeth that grinned horribly above the visage of the warrior.[4] The whole army wore an aspect of martial ferocity, under the control of much higher military discipline than the Spaniards had before seen in the country.

The little band of cavaliers, shaken by the fury of the Indian assault, were thrown at first into some disorder, but at length, cheering on one another with the old war-cry of "St. Jago," they formed in solid column, and charged boldly into the thick of the enemy. The latter, incapable of withstanding the shock, gave way, or were trampled down under the feet of the horses, or pierced by the lances of the riders. Yet their flight was conducted with some order; and they turned at intervals, to let off a volley of arrows, or to deal furious blows with their pole-axes and war-clubs. They fought as if conscious that they were under the eye of their Inca.

It was evening before they had entirely quitted the level ground, and withdrawn into the fastnesses of the lofty range of hills which belt round the beautiful valley of Yucay. Juan Pizarro and his little troop encamped on the level at the base of the mountains. He had gained a victory, as usual, over immense odds; but he had never seen a field so well disputed, and his victory had cost him the lives of several men and horses, while many more had been wounded, and were nearly disabled by the fatigues of the day. But he trusted the severe lesson he had inflicted on the enemy, whose slaughter was great, would crush the spirit of resistance. He was deceived.

The following morning, great was his dismay to see the passes of the mountains filled up with dark lines of warriors, stretching as far as the eye could penetrate into the depths of the sierra, while dense masses of the enemy were gathered like thunder-clouds along the slopes and summits, as if ready to pour down in fury on the assailants. The ground, altogether unfavorable to the manœuvres of cavalry, gave every advantage to the Peruvians, who rolled down huge rocks from their elevated position, and sent off incessant showers of missiles on the heads of the Spaniards. Juan Pizarro did not care to entangle himself further in the perilous defile; and, though he repeatedly charged the enemy, and drove them back with considerable loss, the second night found him with men and horses wearied and wounded, and as little advanced in the object of his expedition as on the preceding evening. From this embarrassing position, after a day or two more spent in unprofitable hostilities, he was surprised

---

[4] "Es gente," says Oviedo, "muy belicosa é muy diestra; sus armas son picas, é ondas, porras é Alabardas de Plata é oro é cobre." (Hist. de las Indias, MS., Parte 3, lib. 8, cap. 17.) Xerez has made a good enumeration of the native Peruvian arms. (Conq. del Peru, ap. Barcia, tom. III. p. 200.) Father Velasco has added considerably to this catalogue. According to him they used copper swords, poniards, and other European weapons. (Hist. de Quito, tom. I. pp. 178-180.) He does not insist on their knowledge of fire-arms before the Conquest!

by a summons from his brother to return with all expedition to Cuzco, which was now besieged by the enemy!

Without delay, he began his retreat, recrossed the valley, the recent scene of slaughter, swam the river Yucay, and, by a rapid countermarch, closely followed by the victorious enemy, who celebrated their success with songs or rather yells of triumph, he arrived before nightfall in sight of the capital.

But very different was the sight which there met his eye from what he had beheld on leaving it a few days before. The extensive environs, as far as the eye could reach, were occupied by a mighty host, which an indefinite computation swelled to the number of two hundred thousand warriors.[5] The dusky lines of the Indian battalions stretched out to the very verge of the mountains; while, all around, the eye saw only the crests and waving banners of chieftains, mingled with rich panoplies of feather-work, which reminded some few who had served under Cortés of the military costume of the Aztecs. Above all rose a forest of long lances and battle-axes edged with copper, which, tossed to and fro in wild confusion, glittered in the rays of the setting sun, like light playing on the surface of a dark and troubled ocean. It was the first time that the Spaniards had beheld an Indian army in all its terrors; such an army as the Incas led to battle, when the banner of the Sun was borne triumphant over the land.

Yet the bold hearts of the cavaliers, if for a moment dismayed by the sight, soon gathered courage as they closed up their files, and prepared to open a way for themselves through the beleaguering host. But the enemy seemed to shun the encounter; and, falling back at their approach, left a free entrance into the capital. The Peruvians were, probably, not willing to draw as many victims as they could into the toils, conscious that, the greater the number, the sooner they would become sensible to the approaches of famine.[6]

Hernando Pizarro greeted his brother with no little satisfaction; for he brought an important addition to his force, which now, when all were united, did not exceed two hundred, horse and foot,[7] besides a thousand Indian auxiliaries; an insignificant number, in comparison with the countless multitudes that were swarming at the gates. That night was passed by the Spaniards with feelings of the deepest anxiety, as they looked forward with natural apprehension to the morrow. It was early in February, 1536, when the siege of Cuzco commenced; a siege memorable as calling out the most heroic displays of Indian and European valor.

---

[5] "Pues junta toda la gente quel ynga avia embiado á juntar que á lo que se entendio y los indios dixeron fueron dozientos mil indios de guerra los que vinieron á poner este cerco." Pedro Pizarro, Descub. y Conq., MS.

[6] Pedro Pizarro, Descub. y Conq., MS.—Conq. i Pob. del Piru, MS.—Herrera, Hist. General, dec. 5, lib. 8, cap. 4.—Gomara, Hist. de las Ind., cap. 133.

[7] "Y los pocos Españoles que heramos aun no dozientos todos." Pedro Pizarro, Descub. y Conq., MS.

and bringing the two races in deadlier conflict with each other than had yet occurred in the conquest of Peru.

The numbers of the enemy seemed no less formidable during the night than by the light of day; far and wide their watch-fires were to be seen gleaming over valley and hill-top, as thickly scattered, says an eyewitness, as "the stars of heaven in a cloudless summer night." [8] Before these fires had become pale in the light of the morning, the Spaniards were roused by the hideous clamor of conch, trumpet, and atabal, mingled with the fierce war-cries of the barbarians, as they let off volleys of missiles of every description, most of which fell harmless within the city. But others did more serious execution. These were burning arrows, and red-hot stones wrapped in cotton that had been steeped in some bituminous substance, which, scattered long trains of light through the air, fell on the roofs of the buildings, and speedily set them on fire.[9] These roofs, even of the better sort of edifices, were uniformly of thatch, and were ignited as easily as tinder. In a moment the flames burst forth from the most opposite quarters of the city. They quickly communicated to the wood-work in the interior of the buildings, and broad sheets of flame mingled with smoke rose up towards the heavens, throwing a fearful glare over every object. The rarefied atmosphere heightened the previous impetuosity of the wind, which, fanning the rising flames, they rapidly spread from dwelling to dwelling, till the whole fiery mass, swayed to and fro by the tempest, surged and roared with the fury of a volcano. The heat became intense, and clouds of smoke, gathering like a dark pall over the city, produced a sense of suffocation and almost blindness in those quarters where it was driven by the winds.[10]

The Spaniards were encamped in the great square, partly under awnings, and partly in the hall of the Inca Viracocha, on the ground since covered by the cathedral. Three times in the course of that dreadful day, the roof of the building was on fire; but, although no efforts were made to extinguish it, the flames went out without doing much injury. This miracle was ascribed to the Blessed Virgin, who was distinctly seen by several of the Christian combatants, hovering over the spot on which was to be raised the temple dedicated to her worship.[11]

[8] "Pues de noche heran tantos los fuegos que no parecia sino vn cielo muy sereno lleno de estrellas." Pedro Pizarro, Descub. y Conq., MS.

[9] "Unas piedras rredondas y hechellas en el fuego y hazellas asqua embolvianlas en vnos algodones y poniendolas en hondas las tiravan a las cassas donde no alcan- zavan á poner fuego con las manos, y ansi nos quemavan las cassas sin entendello Otras veces con flechas encendidas tirandolas á las casas que como heran de paja luego se encendian." Ibid., MS.

[10] "I era tanto el humo que casi los oviera de aogar i pasaron grand travajo por esta causa i sino fuera porque de la una parte de la plaza no havia casas i estava desconorado no pudieran escapar porque si por todas partes les diera el humo i el calor siendo tan grande pasaron travajo, pero la divina providencia lo estorvó." Conq. i Pob. del Piru, MS.

[11] The temple was dedicated to Our Blessed Lady of the Assumption. The appari- tion of the Virgin was manifest not only to Christian but to Indian warriors, many

Fortunately, the open space around Hernando's little company sepa-rated them from the immediate scene of conflagration. It afforded a means of preservation similar to that employed by the American hunter, who endeavors to surround himself with a belt of wasted land, when overtaken by a conflagration in the prairies. All day the fire continued to rage, and at night the effect was even more appalling; for by the lurid flames the unfortunate Spaniards could read the consternation depicted in each others' ghastly countenances, while in the suburbs, along the slopes of the surrounding hills, might be seen the throng of besiegers, gazing with fiendish exultation on the work of destruction. High above the town to the north, rose the gray fortress, which now showed ruddy in the glare, looking grimly down on the ruins of the fair city which it was no longer able to protect; and in the distance were to be discerned the shadowy forms of the Andes, soaring up in solitary grandeur into the regions of eternal silence, far beyond the wild tumult that raged so fearfully at their base.

Such was the extent of the city, that it was several days before the fury of the fire was spent. Tower and temple, hut, palace, and hall, went down before it. Fortunately, among the buildings that escaped were the magni-ficent House of the Sun and the neighboring Convent of the Virgins. Their insulated position afforded the means, of which the Indians from motives of piety were willing to avail themselves, for their preservation.[12] Full one half of the capital, so long the chosen seat of Western civiliza-

of whom reported it to Garcilasso de la Vega, in whose hands the marvellous rarely loses any of its gloss. (Com. Real., Parte 2, lib. 2, cap. 25.) It is further attested by Father Acosta, who came into the country forty years after the event. (lib. 7, cap. 27.) Both writers testify to the seasonable aid rendered by St. James, who with his buckler, displaying the device of his Military Order, and armed with his flaming sword, rode his white charger into the thick of the enemy. The patron Saint of Spain might always be relied on when his presence was needed; *dignus vindice nodus*.

[12] Garcilasso, Com. Real., Parte 2, lib. 2, cap. 24.

Father Valverde, Bishop of Cuzco, who took so signal a part in the seizure of Atahuallpa, was absent from the country at this period, but returned the following year. In a letter to the emperor, he contrasts the flourishing condition of the capital when he left it, and that in which he now found it, despoiled, as well as its beautiful suburbs, of its ancient glories. "If I had not known the site of the city," he says, "I should not have recognized it as the same." The passage is too remarkable to be omitted. The original letter exists in the archives of Simancas.—"Certifico á V. M. que si no me acordara del sitio desta Ciudad yo no la conosciera, á lo menos por los edificios y Pueblos della; porque quando el Gobernador D. Franzisco Pizarro entró aqui y entré yo con él estava este valle tan hermoso en edificios y poblazion que en torno tenia que era cosa de admiracion vello, porque aunque la Ciudad en si no ternia mas de 3 o 4000 casas, ternia en torno quasi á vista 19 o 20,000; la fortaleza que estava sobre la Ciudad parescia desde á parte una mui gran fortaleza de las de España: agora la mayor parte de la Ciudad esta toda derivada y quemada; la forta-leza no tiene quasi nada enhiesso; todos los pueblos de alderredor no tienēsino las paredes que por maravilla ai casa cubierta! Las cosa que mas contentamiento me dio en esta Ciudad fue la Iglesia, que para en Indias es harto buena cosa, aunque segun la riqueza a havido en esta tierra pudiera ser mas semejante al Templo de Salomon." Carta del Obispo F. Vicente de Valverde al Emperador, MS., 20 de Marzo, 1539.

tion, the pride of the Incas, and the bright abode of their tutelar deity, was laid in ashes by the hands of his own children. It was some consolation for them to reflect, that it burned over the heads of its conquerors,— their trophy and their tomb!

During the long period of the conflagration, the Spaniards made no attempt to extinguish the flames. Such an attempt would have availed nothing. Yet they did not tamely submit to the assaults of the enemy, and they sallied forth from time to time to repel them. But the fallen timbers and scattered rubbish of the houses presented serious impediments to the movements of horse; and, when these were partially cleared away by the efforts of the infantry and the Indian allies, the Peruvians planted stakes and threw barricades across the path, which proved equally embarrassing.[13] To remove them was a work of time and no little danger, as the pioneers were exposed to the whole brunt of the enemy's archery, and the aim of the Peruvian was sure. When at length the obstacles were cleared away, and a free course was opened to the cavalry, they rushed with irresistible impetuosity on their foes, who, falling back in confusion, were cut to pieces by the riders, or pierced through with their lances. The slaughter on these occasions was great; but the Indians, nothing disheartened, usually returned with renewed courage to the attack, and, while fresh reinforcements met the Spaniards in front, others, lying in ambush among the ruins, threw the troops into disorder by assailing them on the flanks. The Peruvians were expert both with bow and sling; and these encounters, notwithstanding the superiority of their arms, cost the Spaniards more lives than in their crippled condition they could afford to spare,—a loss poorly compensated by that of tenfold the number of the enemy. One weapon, peculiar to South American warfare, was used with some effect by the Peruvians. This was the *lasso*, a long rope with a noose at the end, which they adroitly threw over the rider, or entangled with it the legs of his horse, so as to bring them both to the ground. More than one Spaniard fell into the hands of the enemy by this expedient.[14]

Thus harassed, sleeping on their arms, with their horses picketed by their side, ready for action at any and every hour, the Spaniards had no rest by night or by day. To add to their troubles, the fortress which overlooked the city, and completely commanded the great square in which they were quartered, had been so feebly garrisoned in their false sense of security, that, on the approach of the Peruvians, it had been abandoned without a blow in its defence. It was now occupied by a strong body of the enemy, who, from his elevated position, sent down showers of missiles, from time to time, which added greatly to the annoyance of the be-

[13] Pedro Pizarro, Descub. y Conq., MS.

"Los Indios ganaron el Cuzco casi todo desta manera que enganando la calle hivan haciendo una pared para que los cavallos ni los Españoles no los pudiesen romper." Conq. i Pob. del Piru, MS.

[14] Ibid., MS.—Herrera, Hist. General, dec. 5, lib. 8, cap. 4.

sieged. Bitterly did their captain now repent the improvident security which had led him to neglect a post so important.

Their distresses were still further aggravated by the rumors, which continually reached their ears, of the state of the country. The rising, it was said, was general throughout the land; the Spaniards living on their insulated plantations had all been massacred; Lima and Truxillo and the principal cities were besieged, and must soon fall into the enemy's hands; the Peruvians were in possession of the passes, and all communications were cut off, so that no relief was to be expected from their countrymen on the coast. Such were the dismal stories, (which, however exaggerated, had too much foundation in fact,) that now found their way into the city from the camp of the besiegers. And to give greater credit to the rumors, eight or ten human heads were rolled into the *plaza*, in whose blood-stained visages the Spaniards recognized with horror the lineaments of their companions, who they knew had been dwelling in solitude on their estates! [15]

Overcome by these horrors, many were for abandoning the place at once, as no longer tenable, and for opening a passage for themselves to the coast with their own good swords. There was a daring in the enterprise which had a charm for the adventurous spirit of the Castilian. Better, they said, to perish in a manly struggle for life, than to die thus ignominiously, pent up like foxes in their holes, to be suffocated by the hunter!

But the Pizarros, De Rojas, and some other of the principal cavaliers, refused to acquiesce in a measure which, they said, must cover them with dishonor.[16] Cuzco had been the great prize for which they had contended; it was the ancient seat of empire, and, though now in ashes, would again rise from its ruins as glorious as before. All eyes would be turned on them, as its defenders, and their failure, by giving confidence to the enemy, might decide the fate of their countrymen throughout the land. They were placed in that post as the post of honor, and better would it be to die there than to desert it.

There seemed, indeed, no alternative; for every avenue to escape was cut off by an enemy who had perfect knowledge of the country, and possession of all its passes. But this state of things could not last long. The Indian could not, in the long run, contend with the white man. The spirit of insurrection would die out of itself. Their great army would melt away, unaccustomed as the natives were to the privations incident to a protracted campaign. Reinforcements would be daily coming in from the colonies; and, if the Castilians would be but true to themselves for a season, they would be relieved by their own countrymen, who would never suffer them to die like outcasts among the mountains.

[15] Ibid., ubi supra.—Conq. i Pob. del Piru, MS.

[16] "Pues Hernando Piçarro nunca estuvo en ello y les respondia que todos aviamos de morir y no desamparar el cuzco. Juntavanse á estas consultas Hernando Piçarro y sus hermanos, Graviel de Rojas, Hernan Ponce de Leon, el Thesorero Riquelme." Pedro Pizarro, Descub. y Conq., MS.

The cheering words and courageous bearing of the cavaliers went to the hearts of their followers; for the soul of the Spaniard readily responded to the call of honor, if not of humanity. All now agreed to stand by their leader to the last. But, if they would remain longer in their present position, it was absolutely necessary to dislodge the enemy from the fortress; and, before venturing on this dangerous service, Hernando Pizarro resolved to strike such a blow as should intimidate the besiegers from further attempt to molest his present quarters.

He communicated his plan of attack to his officers; and, forming his little troop into three divisions, he placed them under command of his brother Gonzalo, of Gabriel de Rojas, an officer in whom he reposed great confidence, and Hernan Ponce de Leon. The Indian pioneers were sent forward to clear away the rubbish, and the several divisions moved simultaneously up the principal avenues towards the camp of the besiegers. Such stragglers as they met in their way were easily cut to pieces, and the three bodies, bursting impetuously on the disordered lines of the Peruvians, took them completely by surprise. For some moments there was little resistance, and the slaughter was terrible. But the Indians gradually rallied, and, coming into something like order, returned to the fight with the courage of men who had long been familiar with danger. They fought hand to hand with their copper-headed war-clubs and pole-axes, while a storm of darts, stones, and arrows rained on the well-defended bodies of the Christians.

The barbarians showed more discipline than was to have been expected; for which, it is said, they were indebted to some Spanish prisoners, from several of whom, the Inca, having generously spared their lives, took occasional lessons in the art of war. The Peruvians had, also, learned to manage with some degree of skill the weapons of their conquerors; and they were seen armed with bucklers, helmets, and swords of European workmanship, and even, in a few instances, mounted on the horses which they had taken from the white men.[17] The young Inca, in particular, accoutred in the European fashion, rode a war-horse which he managed with considerable address, and, with a long lance in his hand, led on his followers to the attack.—This readiness to adopt the superior arms and tactics of the Conquerors intimates a higher civilization than that which belonged to the Aztec, who, in his long collision with the Spaniards, was never so far divested of his terrors for the horse as to venture to mount him.

But a few days or weeks of training were not enough to give familiarity with weapons, still less with tactics, so unlike those to which the Peruvians had been hitherto accustomed. The fight, on the present occasion, though hotly contested, was not of long duration. After a gallant struggle, in which the natives threw themselves fearlessly on the horsemen, endeavoring to tear them from their saddles, they were obliged to

[17] Herrera assures us, that the Peruvians even turned the fire-arms of their Conquerors against them, compelling their prisoners to put the muskets in order, and manufacture powder for them. Hist. General, dec. 5, lib. 8, cap. 5, 6.

give way before the repeated shock of their chargers. Many were trampled under foot, others cut down by the Spanish broadswords, while the arquebusiers, supporting the cavalry, kept up a running fire that did terrible execution on the flanks and rear of the fugitives. At length, sated with slaughter, and trusting that the chastisement he had inflicted on the enemy would secure him from further annoyance for the present, the Castilian general drew back his forces to their quarters in the capital.[18]

His next step was the recovery of the citadel. It was an enterprise of danger. The fortress, which overlooked the northern section of the city, stood high on a rocky eminence, so steep as to be inaccessible on this quarter, where it was defended only by a single wall. Towards the open country, it was more easy of approach; but there it was protected by two semicircular walls, each about twelve hundred feet in length, and of great thickness. They were built of massive stones, or rather rocks, put together without cement, so as to form a kind of rustic-work. The level of the ground between these lines of defence was raised up so as to enable the garrison to discharge its arrows at the assailants, while their own persons were protected by the parapet. Within the interior wall was the fortress, consisting of three strong towers, one of great height, which, with a smaller one, was now held by the enemy, under the command of an Inca noble, a warrior of well-tried valor, prepared to defend it to the last extremity.

The perilous enterprise was intrusted by Hernando Pizarro to his brother Juan, a cavalier in whose bosom burned the adventurous spirit of a knight-errant of romance. As the fortress was to be approached through the mountain passes, it became necessary to divert the enemy's attention to another quarter. A little while before sunset Juan Pizarro left the city with a picked corps of horsemen, and took a direction opposite to that of the fortress, that the besieging army might suppose the object was a foraging expedition. But secretly countermarching in the night, he fortunately found the passes unprotected, and arrived before the outer wall of the fortress, without giving the alarm to the garrison.[19]

The entrance was through a narrow opening in the centre of the rampart; but this was now closed up with heavy stones, that seemed to form one solid work with the rest of the masonry. It was an affair of time to dislodge these huge masses, in such a manner as not to rouse the garrison. The Indian nations, who rarely attacked in the night, were not sufficiently acquainted with the art of war even to provide against surprise by posting sentinels. When the task was accomplished, Juan Pizarro and his gallant troop rode through the gateway, and advanced towards the second parapet.

But their movements had not been conducted so secretly as to escape notice, and they now found the interior court swarming with warriors, who, as the Spaniards drew near, let off clouds of missiles that com-

---

[18] Pedro Pizarro, Descub. y Conq., MS.—Conq. i Pob. del Piru, MS.—Herrera, Hist. General, dec. 5, lib. 8, cap. 4, 5.
[19] Conq. i Pob. del Piru, MS.

pelled them to come to a halt. Juan Pizarro, aware that no time was to be lost, ordered one half of his corps to dismount, and, putting himself at their head, prepared to make a breach as before in the fortifications. He had been wounded some days previously in the jaw, so that, finding his helmet caused him pain, he rashly dispensed with it, and trusted for protection to his buckler.[20] Leading on his men, he encouraged them in the work of demolition, in the face of such a storm of stones, javelins, and arrows, as might have made the stoutest heart shrink from encountering it. The good mail of the Spaniards did not always protect them; but others took the place of such as fell, until a breach was made, and the cavalry, pouring in, rode down all who opposed them.

The parapet was now abandoned, and the enemy, hurrying with disorderly flight across the inclosure, took refuge on a kind of platform or terrace, commanded by the principal tower. Here rallying, they shot off fresh volleys of missiles against the Spaniards, while the garrison in the fortress hurled down fragments of rock and timber on their heads. Juan Pizarro, still among the foremost, sprang forward on the terrace, cheering on his men by his voice and example; but at this moment he was struck by a large stone on the head, not then protected by his buckler, and was stretched on the ground. The dauntless chief still continued to animate his followers by his voice, till the terrace was carried, and its miserable defenders were put to the sword. His sufferings were then too much for him, and he was removed to the town below, where, notwithstanding every exertion to save him, he survived the injury but a fortnight, and died in great agony.[21]—To say that he was a Pizarro is enough to attest his claim to valor. But it is his praise, that his valor was tempered by courtesy. His own nature appeared mild by contrast with the haughty temper of his brothers, and his manners made him a favorite of the army. He had served in the conquest of Peru from the first, and no name on the roll of its conquerors is less tarnished by the reproach of cruelty, or stands higher in all the attributes of a true and valiant knight.[22]

Though deeply sensible to his brother's disaster, Hernando Pizarro saw that no time was to be lost in profiting by the advantages already gained. Committing the charge of the town to Gonzalo, he put himself at the head of the assailants, and laid vigorous siege to the fortresses.

---

[20] Pedro Pizarro, Descub. y Conq., MS.

[21] "Y estando batallando con ellos para echallos de alli Joan Piçarro se descuido descubrirse la cabeça con la adarga y con las muchas pedradas que tiravan le acertaron vna en la caveça que le quebraron los cascos y dende á quince dias murio desta herida y ansi herido estuvo forcejando con los yndios y españoles hasta que se gano este terrado y ganado le abaxaron al Cuzco." Pedro Pizarro, Descub. y Conq., MS.

[22] "Hera valiente," says Pedro Pizarro, "y muy animoso, gentil hombre, magnanimo y afable." (Descub. y Conq., MS.) Zarate dismisses him with this brief panegyric:—"Fue gran pèrdida en la Tierra, porque era Juan Piçarro mui valiente, i experimentado en las Guerras de los Indios, i bien quisto, i amado de todos." Conq. del Peru, lib. 3, cap. 3.

One surrendered after a short resistance. The other and more formidable of the two still held out under the brave Inca noble who commanded it. He was a man of an athletic frame, and might be seen striding along the battlements, armed with a Spanish buckler and cuirass, and in his hand wielding a formidable mace, garnished with points or knobs of copper. With this terrible weapon he struck down all who attempted to force a passage into the fortress. Some of his own followers who proposed a surrender he is said to have slain with his own hand. Hernando prepared to carry the place by escalade. Ladders were planted against the walls, but no sooner did a Spaniard gain the topmost round, than he was hurled to the ground by the strong arm of the Indian warrior. His activity was equal to his strength; and he seemed to be at every point the moment that his presence was needed.

The Spanish commander was filled with admiration at this display of valor; for he could admire valor even in an enemy. He gave orders that the chief should not be injured, but be taken alive, if possible.[23] This was not easy. At length, numerous ladders having been planted against the tower, the Spaniards scaled it on several quarters at the same time, and, leaping into the place, overpowered the few combatants who still made a show of resistance. But the Inca chieftain was not to be taken; and, finding further resistance ineffectual, he sprang to the edge of the battlements, and, casting away his war-club, wrapped his mantle around him and threw himself headlong from the summit.[24] He died like an ancient Roman. He had struck his last stroke for the freedom of his country, and he scorned to survive her dishonor.—The Castilian commander left a small force in garrison to secure his conquest, and returned in triumph to his quarters.

Week after week rolled away, and no relief came to the beleaguered Spaniards. They had long since begun to feel the approaches of famine. Fortunately, they were provided with water from the streams which flowed through the city. But, though they had well husbanded their resources, their provisions were exhausted, and they had for some time depended on such scanty supplies of grain as they could gather from the ruined magazines and dwellings, mostly consumed by the fire, or from the produce of some successful foray.[25] This latter resource was attended with no little difficulty; for every expedition led to a fierce encounter with the enemy, which usually cost the lives of several Spaniards, and inflicted a much heavier injury on the Indian allies. Yet it was at least one good result of such loss, that it left fewer to provide for. But the

[23] "Y mando hernando piçarro á los Españoles que subian que no matasen á este yndio sino que se lo tomasen á vida, jurando de no matalle si lo avia bivo." Pedro Pizarro, Descub. y Conq., MS.

[24] "Visto este orejon que se lo avian ganado y le avian ganado y le avian tomado por dos ó tres partes el fuerte, arrojando las armas se tapo la caveça y el rrostro con la manta y se arrojo del cubo abajo mas de cien estados, y ansi se hizo pedazos. Á Hernando Piçarro le peso mucho por no tomalle á vida." Ibid., MS.

[25] Garcilasso, Com. Real., Parte 2, lib. 2, cap. 24.

whole number of the besieged was so small, that any loss greatly increased the difficulties of defence by the remainder.

As months passed away without bringing any tidings of their country-men, their minds were haunted with still gloomier apprehensions as to their fate. They well knew that the governor would make every effort to rescue them from their desperate condition. That he had not succeeded in this made it probable, that his own situation was no better than theirs, or, perhaps, he and his followers had already fallen victims to the fury of the insurgents. It was a dismal thought, that they alone were left in the land, far from all human succour, to perish miserably by the hands of the barbarians among the mountains.

Yet the actual state of things, though gloomy in the extreme, was not quite so desperate as their imaginations had painted it. The insurrection, it is true, had been general throughout the country, at least that portion of it occupied by the Spaniards. It had been so well concerted, that it broke out almost simultaneously, and the Conquerors, who were living in careless security on their estates, had been massacred to the number of several hundreds. An Indian force had sat down before Xauxa, and a considerable army had occupied the valley of Rimac and laid siege to Lima. But the country around that capital was of an open, level character, very favorable to the action of cavalry. Pizarro no sooner saw himself menaced by the hostile array, than he sent such a force against the Peruvians as speedily put them to flight; and, following up his advantage, he inflicted on them such a severe chastisement, that, although they still continued to hover in the distance and cut off his communications with the interior, they did not care to trust themselves on the other side of the Rimac.

The accounts that the Spanish commander now received of the state of the country filled him with the most serious alarm. He was particularly solicitous for the fate of the garrison at Cuzco, and he made repeated efforts to relieve that capital. Four several detachments, amounting to more than four hundred men in all, half of them cavalry, were sent by him at different times, under some of his bravest officers. But none of them reached their place of destination. The wily natives permitted them to march into the interior of the country, until they were fairly entangled in the passes of the Cordilleras. They then enveloped them with greatly superior numbers, and, occupying the heights, showered down their fatal missiles on the heads of the Spaniards, or crushed them under the weight of fragments of rock which they rolled on them from the mountains. In some instances, the whole detachment was cut off to a man. In others, a few stragglers only survived to return and tell the bloody tale to their countrymen at Lima.[26]

[26] Zarate, Conq. del Peru, lib. 4, cap. 5.—Herrera, Hist. General, dec. 5, lib. 8, cap. 5.—Garcilasso, Com. Real., Parte 2, lib. 2, cap. 28.

According to the historians of the Incas, there fell in these expeditions four hun-dred and seventy Spaniards. Cieza de Leon computes the whole number of Chris-tians who perished in the insurrection at seven hundred, many of them, he adds,

Pizarro was now filled with consternation. He had the most dismal forebodings of the fate of the Spaniards dispersed throughout the country, and even doubted the possibility of maintaining his own foothold in it without assistance from abroad. He despatched a vessel to the neighboring colony at Truxillo, urging them to abandon the place, with all their effects, and to repair to him at Lima. The measure was, fortunately, not adopted. Many of his men were for availing themselves of the vessels which rode at anchor in the port to make their escape from the country at once, and take refuge in Panamá. Pizarro would not hearken to so dastardly a counsel, which involved the desertion of the brave men in the interior who still looked to him for protection. He cut off the hopes of these timid spirits by despatching all the vessels then in port on a very different mission. He sent letters by them to the governors of Panamá, Nicaragua, Guatemala, and Mexico, representing the gloomy state of his affairs, and invoking their aid. His epistle to Alvarado, then established at Guatemala, is preserved. He conjures him by every sentiment of honor and patriotism to come to his assistance, and this before it was too late. Without assistance, the Spaniards could no longer maintain their footing in Peru, and that great empire would be lost to the Castilian Crown. He finally engages to share with him such conquests as they may make with their united arms.[27]—Such concessions, to the very man whose absence from the country, but a few months before, Pizarro would have been willing to secure at almost any price, are sufficient evidence of the extremity of his distress. The succours thus earnestly solicited arrived in time, not to quell the Indian insurrection, but to aid him in a struggle quite as formidable with his own countrymen.

It was now August. More than five months had elapsed since the commencement of the siege of Cuzco, yet the Peruvian legions still lay encamped around the city. The siege had been protracted much beyond what was usual in Indian warfare, and showed the resolution of the natives to exterminate the white men. But the Peruvians themselves had for some time been straitened by the want of provisions. It was no easy matter to feed so numerous a host; and the obvious resource of the magazines of grain, so providently prepared by the Incas, did them but little service, since their contents had been most prodigally used, and even dissipated, by the Spaniards, on their first occupation of the country.[28] The season for planting had now arrived, and the Inca well knew, that, if his followers were to neglect it, they would be visited by a scourge even more formidable than their invaders. Disbanding the greater part of his

under circumstances of great cruelty. (Cronica, cap. 82.) The estimate, considering the spread and spirit of the insurrection, does not seem extravagant.

[27] "É crea V. Sᵃ sino somos socorridos se perderá el Cuzco, ques la cosa mas señalada é de mas importancia que se puede descubrir, é luego nos perderémos todos; porque somos pocos é tenemos pocas armas, é los Indios estan atrevidos." Carta de Francisco Pizarro á D. Pedro de Alvarado, desde la Ciudad le los Reyes, 29 de julio 1536, MS.

[28] Ondegardo, Rel. Prim. y Seg., MS

forces, therefore, he ordered them to withdraw to their homes, and, after the labors of the field were over, to return and resume the blockade of the capital. The Inca reserved a considerable force to attend on his own person, with which he retired to Tambo, a strongly fortified place south of the valley of Yucay, the favorite residence of his ancestors. He also posted a large body as a corps of observation in the environs of Cuzco, to watch the movements of the enemy, and to intercept supplies.

The Spaniards beheld with joy the mighty host, which had so long encompassed the city, now melting away. They were not slow in profiting by the circumstance, and Hernando Pizarro took advantage of the temporary absence to send out foraging parties to scour the country, and bring back supplies to his famishing soldiers. In this he was so successful that on one occasion no less than two thousand head of cattle—the Peruvian sheep—were swept away from the Indian plantations and brought safely to Cuzco.[29] This placed the army above all apprehensions on the score of want for the present.

Yet these forays were made at the point of the lance, and many a desperate contest ensued, in which the best blood of the Spanish chivalry was shed. The contests, indeed, were not confined to large bodies of troops, but skirmishes took place between smaller parties, which sometimes took the form of personal combats. Nor were the parties so unequally matched as might have been supposed in these single rencontres; and the Peruvian warrior, with his sling, his bow, and his *lasso*, proved no contemptible antagonist for the mailed horseman, whom he sometimes even ventured to encounter, hand to hand, with his formidable battle-axe. The ground around Cuzco became a battle-field, like the *vega* of Granada, in which Christian and Pagan displayed the characteristics of their peculiar warfare; and many a deed of heroism was performed, which wanted only the song of the minstrel to shed around it a glory like that which rested on the last days of the Moslem of Spain.[30]

But Hernando Pizarro was not content to act wholly on the defensive; and he meditated a bold stroke, by which at once to put an end to the war. This was the capture of the Inca Manco, whom he hoped to surprise in his quarters at Tambo.

For this service he selected about eighty of his best-mounted cavalry, with a small body of foot; and, making a large détour through the less frequented mountain defiles, he arrived before Tambo without alarm to the enemy. He found the place more strongly fortified than he had imagined. The palace, or rather fortress, of the Incas stood on a lofty

---

[29] "Recoximos hasta dos mil cavezas de ganado." Pedro Pizarro, Descub. y Conq., MS.

[30] Pedro Pizarro recounts several of these deeds of arms, in some of which his own prowess is made quite apparent. One piece of cruelty recorded by him is little to the credit of his commander, Hernando Pizarro, who, he says, after a desperate rencontre, caused the right hands of his prisoners to be struck off, and sent them in this mutilated condition back to their countrymen! (Descub. y Conq., MS.) Such atrocities are not often noticed by the chroniclers; and we may hope they were exceptions to the general policy of the Conquerors in this invasion.

eminence, the steep sides of which, on the quarter where the Spaniards approached, were cut into terraces, defended by strong walls of stone and sunburnt brick.[31] The place was impregnable on this side. On the opposite, it looked towards the Yucay, and the ground descended by a gradual declivity towards the plain through which rolled its deep but narrow current.[32] This was the quarter on which to make the assault.

Crossing the stream without much difficulty, the Spanish commander advanced up the smooth *glacis* with as little noise as possible. The morning light had hardly broken on the mountains; and Pizarro, as he drew near the outer defences, which, as in the fortress of Cuzco, consisted of a stone parapet of great strength drawn round the inclosure, moved quickly forward, confident that the garrison were still buried in sleep. But thousands of eyes were upon him; and as the Spaniards came within bowshot, a multitude of dark forms suddenly rose above the rampart, while the Inca, with his lance in hand, was seen on horseback in the inclosure, directing the operations of his troops.[33] At the same moment the air was darkened with innumerable missiles, stones, javelins, and arrows, which fell like a hurricane on the troops, and the mountains rang to the wild war-whoop of the enemy. The Spaniards, taken by surprise, and many of them sorely wounded, were staggered; and, though they quickly rallied, and made two attempts to renew the assault, they were at length obliged to fall back, unable to endure the violence of the storm. To add to their confusion, the lower level in their rear was flooded by the waters, which the natives, by opening the sluices, had diverted from the bed of the river, so that their position was no longer tenable.[34] A council of war was then held, and it was decided to abandon the attack as desperate, and to retreat in as good order as possible.

The day had been consumed in these ineffectual operations; and Hernando, under cover of the friendly darkness, sent forward his infantry and baggage, taking command of the centre himself, and trusting the rear to his brother Gonzalo. The river was happily recrossed without accident, although the enemy, now confident in their strength, rushed out of their defences, and followed up the retreating Spaniards, whom they annoyed with repeated discharges of arrows. More than once they pressed so closely on the fugitives, that Gonzalo and his chivalry were compelled to turn and make one of those desperate charges that effectually punished their audacity, and stayed the tide of pursuit. Yet the victorious foe still

---

[31] "Tambo tan fortalescido que hera cosa de grima, porquel assiento donde Tambo esta es muy fuerte, de andenes muy altos y de muy gran canterias fortalescidos." Pedro Pizarro, Descub. y Conq., MS.

[32] "El rio de yucay ques grande por aquella parte va muy angosto y hondo." Ibid., MS.

[33] "Parecia el Inga à caballo entre su gente, con su lança en la mano." Herrera, Hist. General, dec. 5, lib. 8, cap. 7.

[34] "Pues hechos dos ó tres acometimientos á tomar este pueblo tantas vezes nos hizieron bolver dando de manos. Ansi estuvimos todo este dia hasta puesta de sol; los indios sin entendello nos hechavan el rrio en el llano donde estavamos, y aguardar mas perescieramos aqui todos." Pedro Pizarro, Descub. y Conq., MS.

hung on the rear of the discomfited cavaliers, till they had emerged from the mountain passes, and come within sight of the blackened walls of the capital. It was the last triumph of the Inca.[35]

Among the manuscripts for which I am indebted to the liberality of that illustrious Spanish scholar, the lamented Navarrete, the most remarkable, in connection with this history, is the work of Pedro Pizarro; *Relaciones del Descubrimiento y Conquista de los Reynos del Peru.* But a single copy of this important document appears to have been preserved, the existence of which was but little known till it came into the hands of Señor de Navarrete; though it did not escape the indefatigable researches of Herrera, as is evident from the mention of several incidents, some of them having personal relation to Pedro Pizarro himself, which the historian of the Indies could have derived through no other channel. The manuscript has lately been given to the public as part of the inestimable collection of historical documents now in process of publication at Madrid, under auspices which, we may trust, will insure its success. As the printed work did not reach me till my present labors were far advanced, I have preferred to rely on the manuscrpit copy for the brief remainder of my narrative, as I had been compelled to do for the previous portion of it.

Nothing, that I am aware of, is known respecting the author, but what is to be gleaned from incidental notices of himself in his own history. He was born at Toledo in Estremadura, the fruitful province of adventurers to the New World, whence the family of Francis Pizarro, to which Pedro was allied, also emigrated. When that chief came over to undertake the conquest of Peru, after receiving his commission from the emperor in 1529, Pedro Pizarro, then only fifteen years of age, accompanied him in quality of page. For three years he remained attached to the household of his commander, and afterwards continued to follow his banner as a soldier of fortune. He was present at most of the memorable events of the Conquest, and seems to have possessed in a great degree the confidence of his leader, who employed him on some difficult missions, in which he displayed coolness and gallantry. It is true, we must take the author's own word for all this. But he tells his exploits with an air of honesty, and without any extraordinary effort to set them off in undue relief. He speaks of himself in the third person, and, as his manuscript was not intended solely for posterity, he would hardly have ventured on great misrepresentation, where fraud could so easily have been exposed.

After the Conquest, our author still remained attached to the fortunes of his commander, and stood by him through all the troubles which ensued; and on the assassination of that chief, he withdrew to Arequipa, to enjoy in quiet the *repartimiento* of lands and Indians, which had been bestowed on him as the recompense of his services. He was there on the breaking out of the great rebellion under Gonzalo Pizarro. But he was true to his allegiance, and chose rather, as he tells us, to be false to his name and his lineage than to his loyalty. Gonzalo, in retaliation, seized his estates, and would have proceeded to still further extremities against him, when Pedro Pizarro had fallen into his hands at Lima, but for the interposition of his lieutenant, the famous Francisco de Carbajal, to whom the chronicler had once the good fortune to render an important service. This, Carbajal requited by sparing his life on two occasions,—but on the second coolly remarked, "No man has a right to a brace of lives; and if you fall into my hands a third time, God only can grant you another." Happily, Pizarro did not find occasion to put this menace to the test. After the pacification of the country, he again retired to Arequipa; but, from the querulous tone of his remarks, it would seem he was not fully reinstated in the possessions he had sacrificed by his loyal devotion to government. The last we hear of him is in 1571, the date which he assigns as that of the completion of his history.

Pedro Pizarro's narrative covers the whole ground of the Conquest, from the date of the first expedition that sallied out from Panamá, to the troubles that ensued on the departure of President Gasca. The first part of the work was gathered from the testimony of others, and, of course, cannot claim the distinction of rising to the highest class of evidence. But all that follows the return of Francis Pizarro from Castile, all, in short, which constitutes the conquest of the country, may be said to be reported on his own observation, as an eyewitness and an actor. This gives to his narrative a value to which it could have no pretensions on the score of its literary execution. Pizarro was a soldier, with as little education, probably, as usually falls to those who have been trained from youth in this rough school,—the most unpropitious in the world to both mental and moral progress. He had the good sense, moreover, not to aspire to an excellence which he could not reach. There is no ambition of fine writing in his chronicle; there are none of those affectations of ornament which only make more glaring the beggarly condition of him who assumes them. His object was simply to tell the story of the Conquest, as he had seen it. He was to deal with facts, not with words, which he wisely left to those who came into the field after the laborers had quitted it, to garner up what they could at second hand.

Pizarro's situation may be thought to have necessarily exposed him to party influences, and thus given an undue bias to his narrative. It is not difficult, indeed, to determine under whose banner he had enlisted. He writes like a partisan, and yet like an honest one, who is no further warped from a correct judgment of passing affairs than must necessarily come from preconceived opinions. There is no management to work a conviction in his reader on this side or the other, still less any obvious perversion of fact. He evidently believes what he says, and this is the great point to be desired. We can make allowance for the natural influences of his position. Were he more impartial than this, the critic of the present day, by making allowance for a greater amount of prejudice and partiality, might only be led into error.

Pizarro is not only independent, but occasionally caustic in his condemnation of those under whom he acted. This is particularly the case where their measures bear too unfavorably on his own interests, or those of the army. As to the unfortunate natives, he no more regards their sufferings than the Jews of old did those of the Philistines, whom they considered as delivered up to their swords, and whose lands they regarded as their lawful heritage. There is no mercy shown by the hard Conqueror in his treatment of the infidel.

Pizarro was the representative of the age in which he lived. Yet it is too much to cast such obloquy on the age. He represented more truly the spirit of the fierce warriors who overturned the dynasty of the Incas. He was not merely a crusader, fighting to extend the empire of the Cross over the darkened heathen. Gold was his great object; the estimate by which he judged of the value of the Conquest; the recompense that he asked for a life of toil and danger. It was with these golden visions, far more than with visions of glory, above all, of celestial glory, that the Peruvian adventurer fed his gross and worldly imagination. Pizarro did not rise above his caste. Neither did he rise above it in a mental view, any more than in a moral. His history displays no great penetration, or vigor and comprehension of thought. It is the work of a soldier, telling simply his tale of blood. Its value is, that it is told by him who acted it. And this, to the modern compiler, renders it of higher worth than far abler productions at second hand. It is the rude ore, which, submitted to the regular process of purification and refinement, may receive the current stamp that fits it for general circulation.

Another authority, to whom I have occasionally referred, and whose writings still slumber in manuscript, is the Licentiate Fernando Montesinos. He is, in every respect, the opposite of the military chronicler who has just come under our notice. He flourished about a century after the Conquest. Of course, the value of his writings as an authority for historical facts must depend on his superior opportunities for consulting original documents. For this his advantages were great. He was twice sent in an official capacity to Peru, which required him to visit the different parts of the country. These two missions occupied fifteen years; so that, while his position gave him access to the colonial archives and literary repositories, he was enabled to verify his researches, to some extent, by actual observation of the country.

The result was his two historical works, *Memorias Antiguas Historiales del Peru,* and his *Annales,* sometimes cited in these pages. The former is taken up with the early history of the country,—very early, it must be admitted, since it goes back to the deluge. The first part of this treatise is chiefly occupied with an argument to show the identity of Peru with the golden Ophir of Solomon's time! This hypothesis, by no means original with the author, may give no unfair notion of the character of his mind. In the progress of his work he follows down the line of Inca princes, whose exploits, and names even, by no means coincide with Garcilasso's catalogue; a circumstance, however, far from establishing their inaccuracy. But one will have little doubt of the writer's title to this reproach, that reads the absurd legends told in the grave tone of reliance by Montesinos, who shared largely in the credulity and the love of the marvellous which belong to an earlier and less enlightened age.

These same traits are visible in his Annals, which are devoted exclusively to the Conquest. Here, indeed, the author, after his cloudy flight, has descended on firm ground, where gross violations of truth, or, at least, of probability, are not to be expected. But any one who has occasion to compare his narrative with that of contemporary writers will find frequent cause to distrust it. Yet Montesinos has one merit. In his extensive researches, he became acquainted with original instruments, which he has occasionally transferred to his own pages, and which it would be now difficult to meet elsewhere.

His writings have been commended by some of his learned countrymen, as showing diligent research and information. My own experience would not assign them a high rank as historical vouchers. They seem to me entitled to little praise, either for the accuracy of their statements, or the sagacity of their reflections. The spirit of cold indifference which they manifest to the sufferings of the natives is an odious feature, for which there is less apology in a writer of the seventeenth century than in one of the primitive Conquerors, whose passions had been inflamed by long-protracted hostility. M. Ternaux-Compans has translated the *Memorias Antiguas* with his usual elegance and precision, for his collection of original documents relating to the New World. He speaks in the Preface of doing the same kind office to the *Annales,* at a future time. I am not aware that he has done this; and I cannot but think that the excellent translator may find a better subject for his labors in some of the rich collection of the Muñoz manuscripts in his possession.

BOOK IV

CIVIL WARS OF THE CONQUERORS

CHAPTER I

ALMAGRO'S MARCH TO CHILI—SUFFERING OF THE TROOPS—HE RETURNS
AND SEIZES CUZCO—ACTION OF ABANCAY—GASPAR DE ESPINOSA—
ALMAGRO LEAVES CUZCO—NEGOTIATIONS WITH PIZARRO

1535—1537

WHILE the events recorded in the preceding chapter were passing, the
Marshal Almagro was engaged in his memorable expedition to Chili.
He had set out, as we have seen, with only part of his forces, leaving his
lieutenant to follow him with the remainder. During the first part of the
way, he profited by the great military road of the Incas, which stretched
across the table-land far towards the south. But as he drew near to Chili,
the Spanish commander became entangled in the defiles of the mountains,
where no vestige of a road was to be discerned. Here his progress was impeded by all the obstacles which belong to the wild scenery of the Cordilleras; deep and ragged ravines, round whose sides a slender sheep-path
wound up to a dizzy height over the precipices below; rivers rushing in
fury down the slopes of the mountains, and throwing themselves in stupendous cataracts into the yawning abyss; dark forests of pine that
seemed to have no end, and then again long reaches of desolate table-
land, without so much as a bush or shrub to shelter the shivering traveller from the blast that swept down from the frozen summits of the sierra.
    The cold was so intense, that many lost the nails of their fingers, their
fingers themselves, and sometimes their limbs. Others were blinded by
the dazzling waste of snow, reflecting the rays of a sun made intolerably
brilliant in the thin atmosphere of these elevated regions. Hunger came,
as usual, in the train of woes; for in these dismal solitudes no vegetation
that would suffice for the food of man was visible, and no living thing,
except only the great bird of the Andes, hovering over their heads in expectation of his banquet. This was too frequently afforded by the number
of wretched Indians, who, unable, from the scantiness of their clothing,
to encounter the severity of the climate, perished by the way. Such was
the pressure of hunger, that the miserable survivors fed on the dead

bodies of their countrymen, and the Spaniards forced a similar susten‑
ance from the carcasses of their horses, literally frozen to death in the
mountain passes.[1]—Such were the terrible penalties which Nature im‑
posed on those who rashly intruded on these her solitary and most savage
haunts.

Yet their own sufferings do not seem to have touched the hearts of the
Spaniards with any feeling of compassion for the weaker natives. Their
path was everywhere marked by burnt and desolated hamlets, the inhab‑
itants of which were compelled to do them service as beasts of burden
They were chained together in gangs of ten or twelve, and no infirmity or
feebleness of body excused the unfortunate captive from his full share of
the common toil, till he sometimes dropped dead, in his very chains,
from mere exhaustion! [2] Alvarado's company are accused of having been
more cruel than Pizarro's; and many of Almagro's men, it may be re‑
membered, were recruited from that source. The commander looked with
displeasure, it is said, on these enormities, and did what he could to re‑
press them. Yet he did not set a good example in his own conduct, if it be
true that he caused no less than thirty Indian chiefs to be burnt alive,
for the massacre of three of his followers! [3] The heart sickens at the re‑
cital of such atrocities perpetrated on an unoffending people, or, at least,
guilty of no other crime than that of defending their own soil too well.

There is something in the possession of superior strength most dan‑
gerous, in a moral view, to its possessor. Brought in contact with semi‑
civilized man, the European, with his endowments and effective force so
immeasurably superior, holds him as little higher than the brute, and as
born equally for his service. He feels that he has a natural right, as it
were, to his obedience, and that this obedience is to be measured, not by
the powers of the barbarian, but by the will of his conqueror. Resistance
becomes a crime to be washed out only in the blood of the victim. The
tale of such atrocities is not confined to the Spaniard. Wherever the civil‑

[1] Herrera, Hist. General, dec. 5, lib. 10, cap. 1–3.—Oviedo, Hist. de las Indias,
MS., Parte 3, lib. 9, cap. 4.—Conq. i Pob. del Piru, MS.

[2] Conq. i Pob. del Piru, MS.
The writer must have made one on this expedition, as he speaks from personal
observation. The poor natives had at least one friend in the Christian camp. "I si en
el Real havia algun Español que era buen rancheador i cruel i matava muchos Indios
tenianle por buen hombre i en grand reputacion i el que era inclinado á hacer bien
i a hacer buenos tratamientos a los naturales i los favorecia no era tenido en tan
buena estima, *he apuntado esto que vi con mis ojos i en que por mis pecados anduve*
porque entiendan los que esto leyeren que de la manera que aqui digo i con mayores
crueldades harto se hizo esta jornada i descubrimiento de Chile."

[3] "I para castigarlos por la muerte destos tres Españoles juntolos en un aposento
donde estava aposentado i mandó cavalgar la jente de cavallo i la de apie que
guardasen las puertas i todos estuviesen apercividos i los prendio i en conclusion
hizo quemar mas de 30 señores vivos atados cada uno a su palo." (Conq. i Pob. del
Piru, MS.) Oviedo, who always shows the hard feeling of the colonist, excuses this
on the old plea of necessity,—*fue necesario este castigo*,—and adds, that after this a
Spaniard might send a messenger from one end of the country to the other. with‑
out fear of injury. Hist. de las Indias. MS., Parte 3, lib. 9, cap. 4.

ized man and the savage have come in contact, in the East or in the West, the story has been too often written in blood.

From the wild chaos of mountain scenery the Spaniards emerged on the green vale of Coquimbo, about the thirtieth degree of south latitude. Here they halted to refresh themselves in its abundant plains, after their unexampled sufferings and fatigues. Meanwhile Almagro despatched an officer with a strong party in advance, to ascertain the character of the country towards the south. Not long after, he was cheered by the arrival of the remainder of his forces under his lieutenant Rodrigo de Orgoñez. This was a remarkable person, and intimately connected with the subsequent fortunes of Almagro.

He was a native of Oropesa, had been trained in the Italian wars, and held the rank of ensign in the army of the Constable of Bourbon at the famous sack of Rome. It was a good school in which to learn his iron trade, and to steel the heart against any too ready sensibility to human suffering. Orgoñez was an excellent soldier; true to his commander, prompt, fearless, and unflinching in the execution of his orders. His services attracted the notice of the Crown, and, shortly after this period, he was raised to the rank of Marshal of New Toledo. Yet it may be doubted whether his character did not qualify him for an executive and subordinate station rather than for one of higher responsibility.

Almagro received also the royal warrant, conferring on him his new powers and territorial jurisdiction. The instrument had been detained by the Pizarros to the very last moment. His troops, long since disgusted with their toilsome and unprofitable march, were now clamorous to return. Cuzco, they said, undoubtedly fell within the limits of his government, and it was better to take possession of its comfortable quarters than to wander like outcasts in this dreary wilderness. They reminded their commander that thus only could he provide for the interests of his son Diego. This was an illegitimate son of Almagro, on whom his father doated with extravagant fondness, justified more than usual by the promising character of the youth.

After an absence of about two months, the officer sent on the exploring expedition returned, bringing unpromising accounts of the southern regions of Chili. The only land of promise for the Castilian was one that teemed with gold.[4] He had penetrated to the distance of a hundred leagues, to the limits, probably, of the conquests of the Incas on the river Maule.[5] The Spaniards had fortunately stopped short of the land of Arauco, where the blood of their countrymen was soon after to be poured out like water, and which still maintains a proud independence amidst the general humiliation of the Indian races around it.

---

[4] It is the language of a Spaniard; "i como no le parecio bien la tierra por no ser quajada de oro." Conq. i Pob. del Piru, MS.

[5] According to Oviedo, a hundred and fifty leagues, and very near, as they told him, to the end of the world; *cerca del fin del mundo.* (Hist. de las Indias, MS., Parte 3, lib. 9, cap. 5.) One must not expect to meet with very accurate notions of geography in the rude soldiers of America.

Almagro now yielded, with little reluctance, to the renewed importunities of the soldiers, and turned his face towards the North. It is unnecessary to follow his march in detail. Disheartened by the difficulty of the mountain passage, he took the road along the coast, which led him across the great desert of Atacama. In crossing this dreary waste, which stretches for nearly a hundred leagues to the northern borders of Chili, with hardly a green spot in its expanse to relieve the fainting traveller, Almagro and his men experienced as great sufferings, though not of the same kind, as those which they had encountered in the passes of the Cordilleras. Indeed, the captain would not easily be found at this day, who would venture to lead his army across this dreary region. But the Spaniard of the sixteenth century had a strength of limb and a buoyancy of spirit which raised him to a contempt of obstacles, almost justifying the boast of the historian, that "he contended indifferently, at the same time, with man, with the elements, and with famine!" [6]

After traversing the terrible desert, Almagro reached the ancient town of Arequipa, about sixty leagues from Cuzco. Here he learned with astonishment the insurrection of the Peruvians, and further, that the young Inca Manco still lay with a formidable force at no great distance from the capital. He had once been on friendly terms with the Peruvian prince, and he now resolved, before proceeding farther, to send an embassy to his camp, and arrange an interview with him in the neighborhood of Cuzco.

Almagro's emissaries were well received by the Inca, who alleged his grounds of complaint against the Pizarros, and named the vale of Yucay as the place where he would confer with the marshal. The Spanish commander accordingly resumed his march, and, taking one half of his force, whose whole number fell somewhat short of five hundred men, he repaired in person to the place of rendezvous; while the remainder of his army established their quarters at Urcos, about six leagues from the capital.[7]

The Spaniards in Cuzco, startled by the appearance of this fresh body of troops in their neighborhood, doubted, when they learned the quarter whence they came, whether it betided them good or evil. Hernando Pizarro marched out of the city with a small force, and, drawing near to Urcos, heard with no little uneasiness of Almagro's purpose to insist on his pretensions to Cuzco. Though much inferior in strength to his rival, he determined to resist him.

Meanwhile, the Peruvians, who had witnessed the conference between the soldiers of the opposite camps, suspected some secret understanding between the parties, which would compromise the safety of the Inca. They communicated their distrust to Manco, and the latter, adopting the same sentiments, or perhaps, from the first, meditating a

[6] "Peleando en un tiempo con los Enemigos, con los Elementos, i con la Hambre." Herrera, Hist. General, dec. 5, lib. 10, cap. 2.

[7] Pedro Pizarro, Descub. y Conq., MS.—Conq. i Pob. del Piru, MS.—Oviedo, Hist. de las Indias, MS., Parte 3, lib. 9, cap. 6.

surprise of the Spaniards, suddenly fell upon the latter in the valley of Yucay with a body of fifteen thousand men. But the veterans of Chili were too familiar with Indian tactics to be taken by surprise. And though a sharp engagement ensued, which lasted more than an hour, in which Orgoñez had a horse killed under him, the natives were finally driven back with great slaughter, and the Inca was so far crippled by the blow, that he was not likely for the present to give further molestation.[8]

Almagro, now joining the division left at Urcos, saw no further impediment to his operations on Cuzco. He sent, at once, an embassy to the municipality of the place, requiring the recognition of him as its lawful governor, and presenting at the same time a copy of his credentials from the Crown. But the question of jurisdiction was not one easy to be settled, depending, as it did, on a knowledge of the true parallels of latitude, not very likely to be possessed by the rude followers of Pizarro. The royal grant had placed under his jurisdiction all the country extending two hundred and seventy leagues south of the river at Santiago, situated one degree and twenty minutes north of the equator. Two hundred and seventy leagues on the meridian, by our measurement, would fall more than a degree short of Cuzco, and, indeed, would barely include the city of Lima itself. But the Spanish leagues, of only seventeen and a half to a degree,[9] would remove the southern boundary to nearly half a degree beyond the capital of the Incas, which would thus fall within the jurisdiction of Pizarro.[10] Yet the division-line ran so close to the disputed ground, that the true result might reasonably be doubted, where no careful scientific observations had been made to obtain it; and each party was prompt to assert, as they always are in such cases, that its own claim was clear and unquestionable.[11]

Thus summoned by Almagro, the authorities of Cuzco, unwilling to give umbrage to either of the contending chiefs, decided that they must wait until they could take counsel—which they promised to do at once—with certain pilots better instructed than themselves in the position of the Santiago. Meanwhile, a truce was arranged between the

---

[8] Zarate, Conq. del Peru, lib. 3, cap. 4.—Conq. i Pob. del Piru, MS., Parte 3, lib. 8, cap. 21.

[9] "Contando diez i siete leguas i media por grado." Herrera, Hist. General, dec. 6, lib. 3, cap. 5.

[10] The government had endeavored early to provide against any dispute in regard to the limits of the respective jurisdictions. The language of the original grants gave room to some misunderstanding; and, as early as 1536, Fray Jomás de Berlanga, Bishop of Tierra Firme, had been sent to Lima with full powers to determine the question of boundary, by fixing the latitude of the river of Santiago, and measuring two hundred and seventy leagues south on the meridian. But Pizarro, having engaged Almagro in his Chili expedition, did not care to revive the question, and the Bishop returned, *re infectâ*, to his diocese, with strong feelings of disgust towards the governor. Ibid., dec. 6, lib. 3, cap. 1.

[11] "All say," says Oviedo, in a letter to the emperor, "that Cuzco falls within the territory of Almagro." Oviedo was, probably, the best-informed man in the colonies. Yet this was an error. Carta desde Sto. Domingo, MS., 25 de Oct. 1539.

parties, each solemnly engaging to abstain from hostile measures, and to remain quiet in their present quarters.

The weather now set in cold and rainy. Almagro's soldiers, greatly discontented with their position, flooded as it was by the waters, were quick to discover that Hernando Pizarro was busily employed in strengthening himself in the city, contrary to agreement. They also learned with dismay, that a large body of men, sent by the governor from Lima, under command of Alonso de Alvarado, was on the march to relieve Cuzco. They exclaimed that they were betrayed, and that the truce had been only an artifice to secure their inactivity until the arrival of the expected succours. In this state of excitement, it was not very difficult to persuade their commander—too ready to surrender his own judgment to the rash advisers around him—to violate the treaty, and take possession of the capital.[12]

Under cover of a dark and stormy night (April 8th, 1537), he entered the place without opposition, made himself master of the principal church, established strong parties of cavalry at the head of the great avenues to prevent surprise, and detached Orgoñez with a body of infantry to force the dwelling of Hernando Pizarro. That captain was lodged with his brother Gonzalo in one of the large halls built by the Incas for public diversions, with immense doors of entrance that opened on the *plaza*. It was garrisoned by about twenty soldiers, who, as the gates were burst open, stood stoutly to the defence of their leader. A smart struggle ensued, in which some lives were lost, till at length Orgoñez, provoked by the obstinate resistance, set fire to the combustible roof of the building. It was speedily in flames, and the burning rafters falling on the heads of the inmates, they forced their reluctant leader to an unconditional surrender. Scarcely had the Spaniards left the building, when the whole roof fell in with a tremendous crash.[13]

Almagro was now master of Cuzco. He ordered the Pizarros, with fifteen or twenty of the principal cavaliers, to be secured and placed in confinement. Except so far as required for securing his authority, he does not seem to have been guilty of acts of violence to the inhabitants,[14] and he installed one of Pizarro's most able officers, Gabriel de Rojas, in the government of the city. The municipality, whose eyes were now open to the validity of Almagro's pretensions, made no further scruple to recognize his title to Cuzco.

The marshal's first step was to send a message to Alonso de Alvarado's camp, advising that officer of his occupation of the city, and re-

[12] According to Zarate, Almagro, on entering the capital, found no appearance of the designs imputed to Hernando, and exclaimed that "he had been deceived." (Conq. del Peru, lib. 3, cap. 4.) He was probably easy of faith in the matter.

[13] Carta de Espinall, Tesorero de N. Toledo, 15 de Junio, 1539.—Conq. i Pob. del Piru, MS.—Pedro Pizarro,(Descub. y Conq., MS.—Oviedo, Hist. de las Indias, MS., Parte 3, lib. 8, cap. 21.

[14] So it would appear from the general testimony; yet Pedro Pizarro, one of the opposite faction, and among those imprisoned by Almagro, complains that that thief plundered them of their horses and other property. Descub. y Conq., MS.

quiring his obedience to him as its legitimate master. Alvarado was lying, with a body of five hundred men, horse and foot, at Xauxa, about
thirteen leagues from the capital. He had been detached several months
previously for the relief of Cuzco; but had, most unaccountably, and,
as it proved, most unfortunately for the Peruvian capital, remained at
Xauxa with the alleged motive of protecting that settlement and the
surrounding country against the insurgents.[15] He now showed himself
loyal to his commander; and, when Almagro's ambassadors reached
his camp, he put them in irons, and sent advice of what had been done
to the governor at Lima.

Almagro, offended by the detention of his emissaries, prepared at
once to march against Alonso de Alvarado, and take more effectual
means to bring him to submission. His lieutenant, Orgoñez, strongly
urged him before his departure to strike off the heads of the Pizarros,
alleging, "that, while they lived, his commander's life would never be
safe"; and concluding with the Spanish proverb, "Dead men never
bite." [16] But the marshal, though he detested Hernando in his heart,
shrunk from so violent a measure; and, independently of other considerations, he had still an attachment for his old associate, Francis
Pizarro, and was unwilling to sever the ties between them for ever. Contenting himself, therefore, with placing his prisoners under strong
guard in one of the stone buildings belonging to the House of the Sun,
he put himself at the head of his forces, and left the capital in quest of
Alvarado.

That officer had now taken up a position on the farther side of the
Rio de Abancay, where he lay, with the strength of his little army, in
front of a bridge, by which its rapid waters are traversed, while a strong
detachment occupied a spot commanding a ford lower down the river.
But in this detachment was a cavalier of much consideration in the army,
Pedro de Lerma, who, from some pique against his commander, had entered into treasonable correspondence with the opposite party. By his
advice, Almagro, on reaching the border of the river, established himself against the bridge in face of Alvarado, as if prepared to force a
passage, thus concentrating his adversary's attention on that point.
But, when darkness had set in, he detached a large body under Orgoñez to pass the ford, and operate in concert with Lerma. Orgoñez
executed this commission with his usual promptness. The ford was
crossed, though the current ran so swiftly, that several of his men were
swept away by it, and perished in the waters. Their leader received a
severe wound himself in the mouth, as he was gaining the opposite bank,
but, nothing daunted, he cheered on his men, and fell with fury on the

---

[15] Pizarro's secretary Picado had an *encomienda* in that neighborhood, and Alvarado, who was under personal obligations to him, remained there, it is said, at
his instigation. (Herrera, Hist. General, dec. 5, lib. 8, cap. 7.) Alvarado was a good
officer, and largely trusted, both before and after, by the Pizarros; and we may
presume there was some explanation of his conduct, of which we are not possessed
[16] "El muerto no mordia." Ibid., dec. 6, lib. 2, cap. 8.

enemy. He was speedily joined by Lerma, and such of the soldiers as he had gained over, and, unable to distinguish friend from foe, the enemy's confusion was complete.

Meanwhile, Alvarado, roused by the noise of the attack on this quarter, hastened to the support of his officer, when Almagro, seizing the occasion, pushed across the bridge, dispersed the small body left to defend it, and, falling on Alvarado's rear, that general saw himself hemmed in on all sides. The struggle did not last long; and the unfortunate chief, uncertain on whom he could rely, surrendered with all his force,—those only excepted who had already deserted to the enemy. Such was the battle of Abancay, as it was called, from the river on whose banks it was fought, on the twelfth of July, 1537. Never was a victory more complete, or achieved with less cost of life; and Almagro marched back, with an array of prisoners scarcely inferior to his own army in number, in triumph to Cuzco.[17]

While the events related in the preceding pages were passing, Francisco Pizarro had remained at Lima, anxiously awaiting the arrival of the reinforcements which he had requested, to enable him to march to the relief of the beleaguered capital of the Incas. His appeal had not been unanswered. Among the rest was a corps of two hundred and fifty men, led by the Licentiate Gaspar de Espinosa, one of the three original associates, it may be remembered, who engaged in the conquest of Peru. He had now left his own residence at Panamá, and came in person, for the first time, it would seem, to revive the drooping fortunes of his confederates. Pizarro received also a vessel laden with provisions, military stores, and other necessary supplies, besides a rich wardrobe for himself, from Cortés, the Conqueror of Mexico, who generously stretched forth his hand to aid his kinsman in the hour of need.[18]

With a force amounting to four hundred and fifty men, half of them cavalry, the governor quitted Lima, and began his march on the Inca capital. He had not advanced far, when he received tidings of the return of Almagro, the seizure of Cuzco, and the imprisonment of his brothers; and, before he had time to recover from this astounding intelligence, he learned the total defeat and capture of Alvarado. Filled with consternation at these rapid successes of his rival, he now returned in all haste to Lima, which he put in the best posture of defence, to secure it against the hostile movements, not unlikely, as he thought, to be directed against that capital itself. Meanwhile, far from indulging in impotent sallies of resentment, or in complaints of his ancient comrade, he only lamented that Almagro should have resorted to these violent measures for the settlement of their dispute, and this less—if

[17] Carta de Francisco Pizarro al Obispo de Tierra Firme, MS., 28 de Agosto, 1539. —Pedro Pizarro, Descub. y Conq., MS.—Oviedo, Hist. de las Indias, MS., ubi supra. —Conq. i Pob. del Piru, MS.—Carta de Espinall, MS.

[18] "Fernando Cortès embiò con Rodrigo de Grijalva en vn proprio Navio suio, desde la Nueva España, muchas Armas, Tiros, Jaeces, Adereços, Vestidos de Seda, i vna Ropa de Martas." Gomara, Hist. de las Ind., cap. 136.

we may take his word for it—from personal considerations than from the prejudice it might do to the interests of the Crown.[19]

But, while busily occupied with warlike preparations, he did not omit to try the effect of negotiation. He sent an embassy to Cuzco, consisting of several persons in whose discretion he placed the greatest confidence, with Espinosa at their head, as the party most interested in an amicable arrangement.

The licentiate, on his arrival, did not find Almagro in as favorable a mood for an accommodation as he could have wished. Elated by his recent successes, he now aspired not only to the possession of Cuzco, but of Lima itself, as falling within the limits of his jurisdiction. It was in vain that Espinosa urged the propriety, by every argument which prudence could suggest, of moderating his demands. His claims upon Cuzco, at least, were not to be shaken, and he declared himself ready to peril his life in maintaining them. The licentiate coolly replied by quoting the pithy Castilian proverb, *El vencido vencido, y el vencidor perdido;* "The vanquished vanquished, and the victor undone."

What influence the temperate arguments of the licentiate might eventually have had on the heated imagination of the soldier is doubtful; but unfortunately for the negotiation, it was abruptly terminated by the death of Espinosa himself, which took place most unexpectedly, though, strange to say, in those times, without the imputation of poison.[20] He was a great loss to the parties in the existing fermentation of their minds; for he had the weight of character which belongs to wise and moderate counsels, and a deeper interest than any other man in recommending them.

The name of Espinosa is memorable in history from his early connection with the expedition to Peru, which, but for the seasonable, though secret, application of his funds, could not then have been compassed. He had long been a resident in the Spanish colonies of Tierra Firme and Panamá, where he had served in various capacities, sometimes as a legal functionary presiding in the courts of justice,[21] and not unfrequently as an efficient leader in the early expeditions of conquest and discovery. In these manifold vocations he acquired high reputation for probity, intelligence, and courage, and his death at the present crisis was undoubtedly the most unfortunate event that could befall the country.

All attempt at negotiation was now abandoned; and Almagro announced his purpose to descend to the sea-coast, where he could plant a colony and establish a port for himself. This would secure him the

---

[19] Herrera, Hist. General, dec. 6, lib. 2, cap. 7.

[20] Carta de Pizarro al Obispo de Tierra Firme, MS.—Herrera, Hist. General, dec. 6, lib. 2, cap. 13.—Carta de Espinall, MS.

[21] He incurred some odium as presiding officer in the trial and condemnation of the unfortunate Vasco Nuñez de Balboa. But it must be allowed, that he made great efforts to resist the tyrannical proceedings of Pedrarias, and he earnestly recommended the prisoner to mercy. See Herrera, Hist. General, dec. 2, lib. 2, cap. 21. 22.

means, so essential, of communication with the mother-country, and here he would resume negotiations for the settlement of his dispute with Pizarro. Before quitting Cuzco, he sent Orgoñez with a strong force against the Inca, not caring to leave the capital exposed in his absence to further annoyance from that quarter.

But the Inca, discouraged by his late discomfiture, and unable, perhaps, to rally in sufficient strength for resistance, abandoned his stronghold at Tambo, and retreated across the mountains. He was hotly pursued by Orgoñez over hill and valley, till, deserted by his followers, and with only one of his wives to bear him company, the royal fugitive took shelter in the remote fastnesses of the Andes.[22]

Before leaving the capital, Orgoñez again urged his commander to strike off the heads of the Pizarros, and then march at once upon Lima. By this decisive step he would bring the war to an issue, and for ever secure himself from the insidious machinations of his enemies. But, in the mean time, a new friend had risen up to the captive brothers. This was Diego de Alvarado, brother of that Pedro, who, as mentioned in a preceding chapter, had conducted the unfortunate expedition to Quito. After his brother's departure, Diego had attached himself to the fortunes of Almagro, had accompanied him to Chili, and, as he was a cavalier of birth, and possessed of some truly noble qualities, he had gained deserved ascendency over his commander. Alvarado had frequently visited Hernando Pizarro in his confinement, where, to beguile the tediousness of captivity, he amused himself with gaming,—the passion of the Spaniard. They played deep, and Alvarado lost the enormous sum of eighty thousand gold castellanos. He was prompt in paying the debt, but Hernando Pizarro peremptorily declined to receive the money. By this politic generosity. he secured an important advocate in the council of Almagro. It stood him now in good stead. Alvarado represented to the marshal, that such a measure as that urged by Orgoñez would not only outrage the feelings of his followers, but would ruin his fortunes by the indignation it must excite at court. When Almagro acquiesced in these views, as in truth most grateful to his own nature, Orgoñez, chagrined at his determination, declared that the day would come when he would repent this mistaken lenity. "A Pizarro," he said, "was never known to forget an injury; and that which they had already received from Almagro was too deep for them to forgive." Prophetic words!

On leaving Cuzco, the marshal gave orders that Gonzalo Pizarro and the other prisoners should be detained in strict custody. Hernando he took with him, closely guarded, on his march. Descending rapidly towards the coast, he reached the pleasant vale of Chincha in the latter part of August. Here he occupied himself with laying the foundations of a town bearing his own name, which might serve as a counterpart to the City of the Kings,—thus bidding defiance, as it were, to his rival on his

[22] Pedro Pizarro. Descub. y Conq., MS.—Conq. i Pob. del Piru, MS.

own borders. While occupied in this manner, he received the unwelcome tidings, that Gonzalo Pizarro, Alonso de Alvarado, and the other prisoners, having tampered with their guards, had effected their escape from Cuzco, and he soon after heard of their safe arrival in the camp of Pizarro.

Chafed by this intelligence, the marshal was not soothed by the insinuations of Orgoñez, that it was owing to his ill-advised lenity; that it might have gone hard with Hernando, but that Almagro's attention was diverted by the negotiation which Francisco Pizarro now proposed to resume.

After some correspondence between the parties, it was agreed to submit the arbitration of the dispute to a single individual, Fray Francisco de Bovadilla, a Brother of the Order of Mercy. Though living in Lima, and, as might be supposed, under the influence of Pizarro, he had a reputation for integrity that disposed Almagro to confide the settlement of the question exclusively to him. In this implicit confidence in the friar's impartiality, Orgoñez, of a less sanguine temper than his chief, did not participate.[23]

An interview was arranged between the rival chiefs. It took place at Mala, November 13th, 1537; but very different was the deportment of the two commanders towards each other from that which they had exhibited at their former meetings. Almagro, indeed, doffing his bonnet, advanced in his usual open manner to salute his ancient comrade; but Pizarro, hardly condescending to return the salute, haughtily demanded why the marshal had seized upon his city of Cuzco, and imprisoned his brothers. This led to a recrimination on the part of his associate. The discussion assumed the tone of an angry altercation, till Almagro, taking a hint—or what he conceived to be such—from an attendant, that some treachery was intended, abruptly quitted the apartment, mounted his horse, and galloped back to his quarters at Chincha.[24] The conference closed, as might have been anticipated from the heated temper of their minds when they began it, by widening the breach it was intended to heal. The friar, now left wholly to himself, after some delib-

---

[23] Carta de Gutierrez al Emperador, MS., 10 de Feb. 1539.—Carta de Espinall, MS.—Oviedo, Hist. de las Ind., MS., ubi supra.—Herrera, Hist. General, dec. 6, lib. 2, cap. 8–14.—Pedro Pizarro, Descub. y Conq., MS.—Zarate, Conq. del Peru, lib. 3, cap. 8.—Naharro, Relacion Sumaria, MS.

[24] It was said that Gonzalo Pizarro lay in ambush with a strong force in the neighborhood to intercept the marshal, and that the latter was warned of his danger by an honorable cavalier of the opposite party, who repeated a distich of an old ballad,

"Tiempo es el Caballero
Tiempo es de andar de aqui."

(Herrera, Hist. General, dec. 6, lib. 3, cap. 4.) Pedro Pizarro admits the truth of the design imputed to Gonzalo, which he was prevented from putting into execution by the commands of the governor, who, the chronicler, with edifying simplicity, or assurance, informs us, was a man that scrupulously kept his word. "Porque el marquez don Francisco Piçarro hera hombre que guardava mucho su palabra." Descub. y Conq., MS.

eration, gave his award. He decided that a vessel, with a skilful pilot on board, should be sent to determine the exact latitude of the river of Santiago, the northern boundary of Pizarro's territory, by which all the measurements were to be regulated. In the mean time, Cuzco was to be delivered up by Almagro, and Hernando Pizarro to be set at liberty, on condition of his leaving the country in six weeks for Spain. Both parties were to retire within their undisputed territories, and to abandon all further hostilities.[25]

This award, as may be supposed, highly satisfactory to Pizarro, was received by Almagro's men with indignation and scorn. They had been sold, they cried, by their general, broken, as he was, by age and infirmities. Their enemies were to occupy Cuzco and its pleasant places, while they were to be turned over to the barren wilderness of Charcas. Little did they dream that under this poor exterior were hidden the rich treasures of Potosí. They denounced the umpire as a hireling of the governor, and murmurs were heard among the troops, stimulated by Orgoñez, demanding the head of Hernando. Never was that cavalier in greater danger. But his good genius in the form of Alvarado again interposed to protect him. His life in captivity was a succession of reprieves.[26]

Yet his brother, the governor, was not disposed to abandon him to his fate. On the contrary, he was now prepared to make every concession to secure his freedom. Confessions, that politic chief well knew, cost little to those who are not concerned to abide by them. After some preliminary negotiation, another award, more equitable, or, at all events, more to the satisfaction of the discontented party, was given. The principal articles of it were, that, until the arrival of some definitive instructions on the point from Castile, the city of Cuzco, with its territory, should remain in the hands of Almagro; and that Hernando Pizarro should be set at liberty, on the condition, above stipulated, of leaving the country in six weeks.—When the terms of this agreement were communicated to Orgoñez, that officer intimated his opinion of them, by passing his finger across his throat, and exclaiming, "What has my fidelity to my commander cost me!"[27]

Almagro, in order to do greater honor to his prisoner, visited him in person, and announced to him that he was from that moment free. He expressed a hope, at the same time, that "all past differences would be buried in oblivion, and that henceforth they should live only in the recollection of their ancient friendship." Hernando replied, with apparent cordiality, that "he desired nothing better for himself." He then swore

---

[25] Pedro Pizarro, Descub. y Conq., MS.—Carta de Espinall, MS.

[26] Espinall, Almagro's treasurer, denounces the friar "as proving himself a very devil" by this award. (Carta al Emperador, MS.) And Oviedo, a more dispassionate judge, quotes, without condemning, a cavalier who told the father, that "a sentence so unjust had not been pronounced since the time of Pontius Pilate"! Hist. de las Indias, MS., Parte 3, lib. 8, cap. 21.

[27] "I tomando la barba con la mano izquierda, con la derecha hiço señal de cortarse la cabeça, diciendo: Orgoñez, Orgoñez, por el amistad de Don Diego de Almagro te han de cortar esta." Herrera. Hist. General, dec. 6, lib. 3, cap. 9.

in the most solemn manner, and pledged his knightly honor,—the latter, perhaps, a pledge of quite as much weight in his own mind as the former,—that he would faithfully comply with the terms stipulated in the treaty. He was next conducted by the marshal to his quarters, where he partook of a collation in company with the principal officers; several of whom, together with Diego Almagro, the general's son, afterward escorted the cavalier to his brother's camp, which had been transferred to the neighboring town of Mala. Here the party received a most cordial greeting from the governor, who entertained them with a courtly hospitality, and lavished many attentions, in particular, on the son of his ancient associate. In short, such, on their return, was the account of their reception, that it left no doubt in the mind of Almagro that all was at length amicably settled.[28]—He did not know Pizarro.

[28] Ibid., loc. cit.—Carta de Gutierrez, MS.—Pedro Pizarro, Descub. y Conq., MS. —Zarate, Conq. del Peru, lib. 3, cap. 9.

CHAPTER II

FIRST CIVIL WAR—ALMAGRO RETREATS TO CUZCO—BATTLE OF LAS SAL-
INAS—CRUELTY OF THE CONQUERORS—TRIAL AND EXECUTION OF
ALMAGRO—HIS CHARACTER

1537—1538

SCARCELY had Almagro's officers left the governor's quarters, when the
latter, calling his little army together, briefly recapitulated the many
wrongs which had been done him by his rival, the seizure of his capital,
the imprisonment of his brothers, the assault and defeat of his troops;
and he concluded with the declaration,—heartily echoed back by his
military audience,—that the time had now come for revenge. All the
while that the negotiations were pending, Pizarro had been busily occupied with military preparations. He had mustered a force considerably
larger than that of his rival, drawn from various quarters, but most of
them familiar with service. He now declared, that, as he was too old to
take charge of the campaign himself, he should devolve that duty on
his brothers; and he released Hernando from all his engagements to
Almagro, as a measure justified by necessity. That cavalier, with graceful pertinacity, intimated his design to abide by the pledges he had
given, but, at length, yielded a reluctant assent to the commands of his
brother, as to a measure imperatively demanded by his duty to the
Crown.[1]

The governor's next step was to advise Almagro that the treaty was
at an end. At the same time, he warned him to relinquish his pretensions
to Cuzco, and withdraw into his own territory, or the responsibility of
the consequences would lie on his own head.

Reposing in his false security, Almagro was now fully awakened to
the consciousness of the error he had committed; and the warning voice
of his lieutenant may have risen to his recollection. The first part of
the prediction was fulfilled. And what should prevent the latter from
being so? To add to his distress, he was laboring at this time under a
grievous malady, the result of early excesses, which shattered his constitution, and made him incapable alike of mental and bodily exertion.[2]

---

[1] Herrera, Hist. General, dec. 6, lib. 3, cap. 10.
[2] "Cayó enfermo i estuvo malo a punto de muerte de bubas i dolores." (Carta de
Espinall, MS.) It was a hard penalty, occurring at this crisis, for the sins, perhaps,
of earlier days; but

"The gods are just, and of our pleasant vices
Make instruments to scourge us."

In this forlorn condition, he confided the management of his affairs to Orgoñez, on whose loyalty and courage he knew he might implicitly rely. The first step was to secure the passes of the Guaitara, a chain of hills that hemmed in the valley of Zangalla, where Almagro was at present established. But, by some miscalculation, the passes were not secured in season; and the active enemy, threading the dangerous defiles, effected a passage across the sierra, where a much inferior force to his own might have taken him at advantage. The fortunes of Almagro were on the wane.

His thoughts were now turned towards Cuzco, and he was anxious to get possession of this capital before the arrival of the enemy. Too feeble to sit on horseback, he was obliged to be carried in a litter; and, when he reached the ancient town of Bilcas, not far from Guamanga, his indisposition was so severe that he was compelled to halt and remain there three weeks before resuming his march.

The governor and his brothers, in the mean time, after traversing the pass of Guaitara, descended into the valley of Ica, where Pizarro remained a considerable while, to get his troops into order and complete his preparations for the campaign. Then, taking leave of the army, he returned to Lima, committing the prosecution of the war, as he had before announced, to his younger and more active brothers. Hernando, soon after quitting Ica, kept along the coast as far as Nasca, proposing to penetrate the country by a circuitous route in order to elude the enemy, who might have greatly embarrassed him in some of the passes of the Cordilleras. But unhappily for him, this plan of operations, which would have given him such manifest advantage, was not adopted by Almagro; and his adversary, without any other impediment than that arising from the natural difficulties of the march, arrived, in the latter part of April, 1538, in the neighborhood of Cuzco.

But Almagro was already in possession of that capital, which he had reached ten days before. A council of war was held by him respecting the course to be pursued. Some were for making good the defence of the city. Almagro would have tried what could be done by negotiation. But Orgoñez bluntly replied,—"It is too late; you have liberated Hernando Pizarro, and nothing remains but to fight him." The opinion of Orgoñez finally prevailed, to march out and give the enemy battle on the plains. The marshal, still disabled by illness from taking the command, devolved it on his trusty lieutenant, who, mustering his forces, left the city, and took up a position at Las Salinas, less than a league distant from Cuzco. The place received its name from certain pits or vats in the ground, used for the preparation of salt, that was obtained from a natural spring in the neighborhood. It was an injudicious choice of ground, since its broken character was most unfavorable to the free action of cavalry, in which the strength of Almagro's force consisted. But, although repeatedly urged by the officers to advance into the open country, Orgoñez persisted in his position, as the most favorable for defence, since the front was protected by a marsh, and by a little stream that flowed over the plain. His forces amounted in all to about five hundred, more than half of them horse. His infantry was deficient in firearms, the place of which was supplied by the long pike. He had also six small cannon, or falconets, as they were called, which, with his cavalry, formed into two equal divisions, he disposed on the flanks of his infantry. Thus prepared, he calmly awaited the approach of the enemy.

It was not long before the bright arms and banners of the Spaniards under Hernando Pizarro were seen emerging from the mountain passes. The troops came forward in good order, and like men whose steady step showed that they had been spared in the march, and were now fresh for action. They advanced slowly across the plain, and halted on the opposite border of the little stream which covered the front of Orgoñez. Here Hernando, as the sun had set, took up his quarters for the night, proposing to defer the engagement till daylight.[3]

The rumors of the approaching battle had spread far and wide over the country; and the mountains and rocky heights around were thronged with multitudes of natives, eager to feast their eyes on a spectacle, where, whichever side were victorious, the defeat would fall on their enemies.[4] The Castilian women and children, too, with still deeper anxiety, had thronged out from Cuzco to witness the deadly strife in which brethren and kindred were to contend for mastery.[5] The whole number of the combatants was insignificant; though not as compared with those usually engaged in these American wars. It is not, however, the number of the players, but the magnitude of the stake, that gives importance and interest to the game; and in this bloody game, they were to play for the possession of an empire.

The night passed away in silence, unbroken by the vast assembly which covered the surrounding hill-tops. Nor did the soldiers of the hostile camps, although keeping watch within hearing of one another, and with the same blood flowing in their veins, attempt any communication. So deadly was the hate in their bosoms! [6]

The sun rose bright, as usual in this beautiful climate, on Saturday, the twenty-sixth day of April, 1538.[7] But long before his beams were on the plain, the trumpet of Hernando Pizarro had called his men to arms. His forces amounted in all to about seven hundred. They were drawn

---

[3] Carta de Gutierrez, MS.—Pedro Pizarro, Descub. y Conq., MS.—Herrera, Hist. General, dec. 6, lib. 4, cap. 1–5.—Carta de Espinall, MS.—Zarate, Conq. del Peru, lib. 3, cap. 10, 11.—Garcilasso, Com. Real., Parte 2, lib. 2, cap. 36, 37.

[4] Herrera, Hist. General, dec. 6, lib. 4, cap. 5, 6.

[5] Ibid., ubi supra.

[6] "I fue cosa de notar, que se estuvieron toda la Noche, sin que nadie de la vna i otra parte pensase en mover tratos de Paz: tanta era la ira i aborrecimiento de ambas partes." Ibid., cap. 6.

[7] A church dedicated to Saint Lazarus was afterwards erected on the battle-ground, and the bodies of those slain in the action were interred within its walls. This circumstance leads Garcilasso to suppose that the battle took place on Saturday, the sixth,—the day after the Feast of Saint Lazarus,—and not on the twenty-sixth of April, as commonly reported. Com. Real., Parte 2, lib. 2, cap. 38. See also Montesinos, (Annales, MS., año 1538,)—an indifferent authority for any thing.

from various quarters, the veterans of Pizarro, the followers of Alonso de Alvarado,—many of whom, since their defeat, had found their way back to Lima,—and the late reinforcement from the isles, most of them seasoned by many a toilsome march in the Indian campaigns, and many a hard-fought field. His mounted troops were inferior to those of Almagro; but this was more than compensated by the strength of his infantry, comprehending a well-trained corps of arquebusiers, sent from St. Domingo, whose weapons were of the improved construction recently introduced from Flanders. They were of a large calibre, and threw double-headed shot, consisting of bullets linked together by an iron chain. It was doubtless a clumsy weapon compared with modern firearms, but, in hands accustomed to wield it, proved a destructive instrument.[8]

Hernando Pizarro drew up his men in the same order of battle as that presented by the enemy,—throwing his infantry into the centre, and disposing his horse on the flanks; one corps of which he placed under command of Alonso de Alvarado, and took charge of the other himself. The infantry was headed by his brother Gonzalo, supported by Pedro de Valdivia, the future hero of Arauco, whose disastrous story forms the burden of romance as well as of chronicle.[9]

Mass was said, as if the Spaniards were about to fight what they deemed the good fight of the faith, instead of imbruing their hands in the blood of their countrymen. Hernando Pizarro then made a brief address to his soldiers. He touched on the personal injuries he and his family had received from Almagro; reminded his brother's veterans that Cuzco had been wrested from their possession; called up the glow of shame on the brows of Alvarado's men as he talked of the rout of Abancay, and, pointing out the Inca metropolis that sparkled in the morning sunshine, he told them that there was the prize of the victor. They answered his appeal with acclamations; and the signal being given, Gonzalo Pizarro, heading his battalion of infantry, led it straight across the river. The water was neither broad nor deep, and the soldiers found no difficulty in gaining a landing, as the enemy's horse was prevented by the marshy ground from approaching the borders. But, as they worked their way across the morass, the heavy guns of Orgoñez played with effect on the leading files, and threw them into disorder. Gonzalo and Valdivia threw themselves into the midst of their followers, menacing some, encouraging others, and at length led them gallantly forward to the firm ground. Here the arquebusiers, detaching themselves from the rest of the infantry, gained a small eminence, whence, in their turn, they

[8] Zarate, Conq. del Peru, lib. 3, cap. 8.—Garcilasso, Com. Real., Parte 2, lib. 2, cap. 36.
[9] The Araucana of Ercilla may claim the merit, indeed,—if it be a merit,—of combining both romance and history in one. Surely never did the Muse venture on such a specification of details, not merely poetical, but political, geographical, and statistical, as in this celebrated Castilian epic. It is a military journal done into rhyme

opened a galling fire on Orgoñez, scattering his array of spearmen, and sorely annoying the cavalry on the flanks.

Meanwhile, Hernando, forming his two squadrons of horse into one column, crossed under cover of this well-sustained fire, and, reaching the firm ground, rode at once against the enemy. Orgoñez, whose infantry was already much crippled, advancing his horse, formed the two squadrons into one body, like his antagonist, and spurred at full gallop against the assailants. The shock was terrible; and it was hailed by the swarms of Indian spectators on the surrounding heights with a fiendish yell of triumph, that rose far above the din of battle, till it was lost in distant echoes among the mountains.[10]

The struggle was desperate. For it was not that of the white man against the defenceless Indian, but of Spaniard against Spaniard; both parties cheering on their comrades with their battlecries of *"El Rey y Almagro,"* or *"El Rey y Pizarro,"*—while they fought with a hate, to which national antipathy was as nothing; a hate strong in proportion to the strength of the ties that had been rent asunder.

In this bloody field well did Orgoñez do his duty, fighting like one to whom battle was the natural element. Singling out a cavalier, whom, from the color of the sobre-vest on his armour, he erroneously supposed to be Hernando Pizarro, he charged him in full career, and overthrew him with his lance. Another he ran through in like manner, and a third he struck down with his sword. as he was prematurely shouting "Victory!" But while thus doing the deeds of a paladin of romance, he was hit by a chain-shot from an arquebuse, which, penetrating the bars of his visor, grazed his forehead, and deprived him for a moment of reason. Before he had fully recovered, his horse was killed under him, and though the fallen cavalier succeeded in extricating himself from the stirrups, he was surrounded, and soon overpowered by numbers. Still refusing to deliver up his sword, he asked "if there was no knight to whom he could surrender." One Fuentes, a menial of Pizarro, presenting himself as such, Orgoñez gave his sword into his hands,—and the dastard, drawing his dagger, stabbed his defenceless prisoner to the heart! His head, then struck off, was stuck on a pike, and displayed, a bloody trophy, in the great square of Cuzco, as the head of a traitor.[11] Thus perished as loyal a cavalier, as decided in council, and as bold in action, as ever crossed to the shores of America.

The fight had now lasted more than an hour, and the fortune of the day was turning against the followers of Almagro. Orgoñez being down,

[10] Herrera, Hist. General, dec. 6, lib. 4, cap. 6.—Pedro Pizarro, Descub. y Conq., MS.—Carta de Espinall, MS.—Zarate, Conq. del Peru, lib. 3, cap. 11. Every thing relating to this battle,—the disposition of the forces, the character of the ground, the mode of attack, are told as variously and confusedly, as if it had been a contest between two great armies, instead of a handful of men on either side. It would seem that truth is nowhere so difficult to come at, as on the battle-field.

[11] Pedro Pizarro, Descub. y Conq., MS.—Herrera, Hist. General, ubi supra.— Zarate, Conq. del Peru, ubi supra.

their confusion increased. The infantry, unable to endure the fire of the arquebusiers, scattered and took refuge behind the stone-walls, that here and there straggled across the country. Pedro de Lerma, vainly striving to rally the cavalry, spurred his horse against Hernando Pizarro, with whom he had a personal feud. Pizarro did not shrink from the encounter. The lances of both the knights took effect. That of Hernando penetrated the thigh of his opponent, while Lerma's weapon, glancing by his adversary's saddle-bow, struck him with such force above the groin, that it pierced the joints of his mail, slightly wounding the cavalier, and forcing his horse back on his haunches. But the press of the fight soon parted the combatants, and, in the turmoil that ensued, Lerma was unhorsed, and left on the field covered with wounds.[12]

There was no longer order, and scarcely resistance, among the followers of Almagro. They fled, making the best of their way to Cuzco, and happy was the man who obtained quarter when he asked it. Almagro himself, too feeble to sit so long on his horse, reclined on a litter, and from a neighboring eminence surveyed the battle, watching its fluctuations with all the interest of one who felt that honor, fortune, life itself, hung on the issue. With agony not to be described, he had seen his faithful followers, after their hard struggle, borne down by their opponents, till, convinced that all was lost, he succeeded in mounting a mule, and rode off for a temporary refuge to the fortress of Cuzco. Thither he was speedily followed, taken, and brought in triumph to the capital, where, ill as he was, he was thrown into irons, and confined in the same apartment of the stone building in which he had imprisoned the Pizarros.

The action lasted not quite two hours. The number of killed, variously stated, was probably not less than a hundred and fifty,—one of the combatants calls it two hundred,[13]—a great number, considering the shortness of the time, and the small amount of forces engaged. No account is given of the wounded. Wounds were the portion of the cavalier. Pedro de Lerma is said to have received seventeen, and yet was taken alive from the field! The loss fell chiefly on the followers of Almagro. But the slaughter was not confined to the heat of the action. Such was the deadly animosity of the parties, that several were murdered in cold blood, like

[12] Herrera, Hist. General, ubi supra.—Garcilasso, Com. Real., Parte 2, lib. 2, cap. 36.

Hernando Pizarro wore a surcoat of orange-colored velvet over his armour, according to Garcilasso, and before the battle sent notice of it to Orgoñez, that the latter might distinguish him in the *mêlée*. But a knight in Hernando's suite also wore the same colors, it appears, which led Orgoñez into error.

[13] "Murieron en esta Batalla de las Salinas casi dozientos hombres de vna parte y de otra." (Pedro Pizarro, Descub. y Conq., MS.) Most authorities rate the loss at less. The treasurer Espinall, a partisan of Almagro, says they massacred a hundred and fifty after the fight, in cold blood. "Siguieron el alcance la mas cruelmente que en el mundo se ha visto, porque matavan a los hombres rendidos e desarmados, e por les quitar las armas los mataban si presto no se las quitaban, e trayendo á las ancas de un caballo a un Ruy Diaz viniendo rendido e desarmado le mataron, i desta manera mataron mas de ciento è cinquenta hombres." Carta, MS.

Orgoñez, after they had surrendered. Pedro de Lerma himself, while lying on his sick couch in the quarters of a friend in Cuzco, was visited by a soldier, named Samaniego, whom he had once struck for an act of disobedience. This person entered the solitary chamber of the wounded man took his place by his bed-side, and then, upbraiding him for the insult, told him that he had come to wash it away in his blood! Lerma in vain assured him, that, when restored to health, he would give him the satisfaction he desired. The miscreant, exclaimed "Now is the hour!" plunged his sword into his bosom. He lived several years to vaunt this atrocious exploit, which he proclaimed as a reparation to his honor. It is some satisfaction to know that the insolence of this vaunt cost him his life.[14]—Such anecdotes, revolting as they are, illustrate not merely the spirit of the times, but that peculiarly ferocious spirit which is engendered by civil wars,—the most unforgiving in their character of any, but wars of religion.

In the hurry of the flight of one party, and the pursuit by the other, all pouring towards Cuzco, the field of battle had been deserted. But it soon swarmed with plunderers, as the Indians, descending like vultures from the mountains, took possession of the bloody ground, and, despoiling the dead, even to the minutest article of dress, left their corpses naked on the plain.[15] It has been thought strange that the natives should not have availed themselves of their superior numbers to fall on the victors after they had been exhausted by the battle. But the scattered bodies of the Peruvians were without a leader; they were broken in spirits, moreover, by recent reverses, and the Castilians, although weakened for the moment by the struggle, were in far greater strength in Cuzco than they had ever been before.

Indeed, the number of troops now assembled within its walls, amounting to full thirteen hundred, composed, as they were, of the most discordant materials, gave great uneasiness to Hernando Pizarro. For there were enemies glaring on each other and on him with deadly though smothered rancor, and friends, if not so dangerous, not the less troublesome from their craving and unreasonable demands. He had given the capital up to pillage, and his followers found good booty in the quarters of Almagro's officers. But this did not suffice the more ambitious cavaliers; and they clamorously urged their services, and demanded to be placed in charge of some expedition, nothing doubting that it must prove a golden one. All were in quest of an *El Dorado*. Hernando Pizarro ac-

---

[14] Carta de Espinall, MS.—Garcilasso, Com. Real., Parte 2, lib. 2, cap. 38.

He was hanged for this very crime by the governor of Puerto Viejo, about five years after this time, having outraged the feelings of that officer and the community by the insolent and open manner in which he boasted of his atrocious exploit.

[15] "Los Indios viendo la Batalla fenescida, ellos tambien se dejaron de la suia, iendo los vnos i los otros à desnudar los Españoles muertos, i aun algunos vivos, que por sus heridas no se podian defender, porque com pasò el tropel de la Gente, siguiendo la Victoria, no huvo quien se lo impidiese; de manera que dexaron en cueros à todos los caìdos." Zarate, Conq. del Peru, lib. 3, cap. 11.

quiesced as far as possible in these desires, most willing to relieve himself of such importunate creditors. The expeditions, it is true, usually ended in disaster; but the country was explored by them. It was the lottery of adventure; the prizes were few, but they were splendid; and in the excitement of the game, few Spaniards paused to calculate the chances of success.

Among those who left the capital was Diego, the son of Almagro. Hernando was mindful to send him, with a careful escort, to his brother the governor, desirous to remove him at this crisis from the neighborhood of his father. Meanwhile the marshal himself was pining away in prison under the combined influence of bodily illness and distress of mind. Before the battle of Salinas, it had been told to Hernando Pizarro that Almagro was like to die. "Heaven forbid," he exclaimed, "that this should come to pass before he falls into my hands!"[16] Yet the gods seemed now disposed to grant but half of this pious prayer, since his captive seemed about to escape him just as he had come into his power. To console the unfortunate chief, Hernando paid him a visit in his prison, and cheered him with the assurance that he only waited for the governor's arrival to set him at liberty; adding, "that, if Pizarro did not come soon to the capital, he himself would assume the responsibility of releasing him, and would furnish him with a conveyance to his brother's quarters." At the same time, with considerate attention to his comfort, he inquired of the marshal "what mode of conveyance would be best suited to his state of health." After this he continued to send him delicacies from his own table to revive his faded appetite. Almagro, cheered by these kind attentions, and by the speedy prospect of freedom, gradually mended in health and spirits.[17]

He little dreamed that all this while a process was industriously preparing against him. It had been instituted immediately on his capture, and every one, however humble, who had any cause of complaint against the unfortunate prisoner, was invited to present it. The summons was readily answered; and many an enemy now appeared in the hour of his fallen fortunes, like the base reptiles crawling into light amidst the ruins of some noble edifice; and more than one, who had received benefits from his hands, were willing to court the favor of his enemy by turning on their benefactor. From these loathsome sources a mass of accusations was collected which spread over two thousand folio pages! Yet Almagro was the idol of his soldiers![18]

Having completed the process, (July 8th, 1538,) it was not difficult to obtain a verdict against the prisoner. The principal charges on which

---

[16] "Respondia Hernando Pizarro, que no le haria Dios tan gran mal, que le dexase morir, sin que le huviese á las manos." Herrera, Hist. General, dec. 6, lib. 4, cap. 5.

[17] Ibid., dec. 6, lib. 4, cap. 9.

[18] "De tal manera que los Escrivanos no se davan manos, i iá tenian escritas mas de dos mil hojas." Ibid., dec. 6, lib. 4, cap. 7.

Naharro, Relacion Sumaria, MS.—Conq. i Pob. de Piru, MS.—Carta de Gutierrez, MS.—Pedro Pizarro, Descub. y Conq., MS.—Carta de Espinall, MS.

he was pronounced guilty were those of levying war against the Crown, and thereby occasioning the death of many of his Majesty's subjects; of entering into conspiracy with the Inca; and finally, of dispossessing the royal governor of the city of Cuzco. On these charges he was condemned to suffer death as a traitor, by being publicly beheaded in the great square of the city. Who were the judges, or what was the tribunal that condemned him, we are not informed. Indeed, the whole trial was a mockery; if that can be called a trial, where the accused himself is not even aware of the accusation.

The sentence was communicated by a friar deputed for the purpose to Almagro. The unhappy man, who all the while had been unconsciously slumbering on the brink of a precipice, could not at first comprehend the nature of his situation. Recovering from the first shock, "It was impossible," he said, "that such wrong could be done him,—he would not believe it." He then besought Hernando Pizarro to grant him an interview. That cavalier, not unwilling, it would seem, to witness the agony of his captive, consented; and Almagro was so humbled by his misfortunes, that he condescended to beg for his life with the most piteous supplications. He reminded Hernando of his ancient relations with his brother, and the good offices he had rendered him and his family in the earlier part of their career. He touched on his acknowledged services to his country, and besought his enemy "to spare his gray hairs, and not to deprive him of the short remnant of an existence from which he had now nothing more to fear."—To this the other coldly replied, that "he was surprised to see Almagro demean himself in a manner so unbecoming a brave cavalier; that his fate was no worse than had befallen many a soldier before him; and that, since God had given him the grace to be a Christian, he should employ his remaining moments in making up his account with Heaven!"[19]

But Almagro was not to be silenced. He urged the service he had rendered Hernando himself. "This was a hard requital," he said, "for having spared his life so recently under similar circumstances, and that, too, when he had been urged again and again by those around him to take it away." And he concluded by menacing his enemy with the vengeance of the emperor, who would never suffer this outrage on one who had rendered such signal services to the Crown to go unrequited. It was all in vain; and Hernando abruptly closed the conference by repeating, that "his doom was inevitable, and he must prepare to meet it."[20]

---

[19] "I que pues tuvo tanta gracia de Dios, que le hiço Christiano, ordenase su Alma, i temiese á Dios." Herrera, Hist. General, dec. 6, lib. 5, cap. 1.

[20] Ibid., ubi supra.

The marshal appealed from the sentence of his judges to the Crown, supplicating his conqueror, (says the treasurer Espinall, in his letter to the emperor,) in terms that would have touched the heart of an infidel. "De la qual el dicho Adelantado apelo para ante V. M. i le rogo que por amor de Dios hincado de rodillas le otorgase el apelacion. diciendole que mirase sus canas e vejez e quanto havia servido á V. M i qᵉ el havia sido el primer escalon para que el i sus hermanos subiesen en el estado en que estavan, i diciendole otras muchas palabras de dolor e compasion que despues

Almagro, finding that no impression was to be made on his iron-hearted conqueror, now seriously addressed himself to the settlement of his affairs. By the terms of the royal grant he was empowered to name his successor. He accordingly devolved his office on his son, appointing Diego de Alvarado, on whose integrity he had great reliance, administrator of the province during his minority. All his property and possessions in Peru, of whatever kind, he devised to his master the emperor, assuring him that a large balance was still due to him in his unsettled accounts with Pizarro. By this politic bequest, he hoped to secure the monarch's protection for his son, as well as a strict scrutiny into the affairs of his enemy.

The knowledge of Almagro's sentence produced a deep sensation in the community of Cuzco. All were amazed at the presumption with which one, armed with a little brief authority, ventured to sit in judgment on a person of Almagro's station. There were few who did not call to mind some generous or good-natured act of the unfortunate veteran. Even those who had furnished materials for the accusation, now startled by the tragic result to which it was to lead, were heard to denounce Hernando's conduct as that of a tyrant. Some of the principal cavaliers, and among them Diego de Alvarado, to whose intercession, as we have seen, Hernando Pizarro, when a captive, had owed his own life, waited on that commander, and endeavored to dissuade him from so high-handed and atrocious a proceeding. It was in vain. But it had the effect of changing the mode of execution, which, instead of the public square, was now to take place in prison.[21]

On the day appointed, a strong corps of arquebusiers was drawn up in the *plaza*. The guards were doubled over the houses where dwelt the principal partisans of Almagro. The executioner, attended by a priest, stealthily entered his prison; and the unhappy man, after confessing and receiving the sacrament, submitted without resistance to the *garrote*. Thus obscurely, in the gloomy silence of a dungeon, perished the hero of a hundred battles! His corpse was removed to the great square of the city, where, in obedience to the sentence, the head was severed from the body. A herald proclaimed aloud the nature of the crimes for which he had suffered; and his remains, rolled in their bloody shroud, were borne to the house of his friend Hernan Ponce de Leon, and the next day laid with all due solemnity in the church of Our Lady of Mercy. The

de muerto supe que dixo, que á qualquier hombre, aunque fuera infiel, moviera á piedad." Carta, MS.

[21] Carta de Espinall, MS.—Montesinos, Annales, MS., año 1538.

Bishop Valverde, as he assures the emperor, remonstrated with Francisco Pizarro in Lima, against allowing violence towards the marshal; urging it on him, as an imperative duty, to go himself at once to Cuzco, and set him at liberty. "It was too grave a matter," he rightly added, "to trust to a third party." (Carta al Emperador, MS.) The treasurer Espinall, then in Cuzco, made a similar ineffectual attempt to turn Hernando from his purpose.

Pizarros appeared among the principal mourners. It was remarked, that their brother had paid similar honors to the memory of Atahuallpa.[22]

Almagro, at the time of his death, was probably not far from seventy years of age. But this is somewhat uncertain; for Almagro was a foundling, and his early history is lost in obscurity.[23] He had many excellent qualities by nature; and his defects, which were not few, may reasonably be palliated by the circumstances of his situation. For what extenuation is not authorized by the position of a *foundling*,—without parents, or early friends, or teacher to direct him,—his little bark set adrift on the ocean of life, to take its chance among the rude billows and breakers, without one friendly hand stretched forth to steer or to save it! The name of "foundling" comprehends an apology for much, very much, that is wrong in after life.[24]

He was a man of strong passions, and not too well used to control them.[25] But he was neither vindictive nor habitually cruel. I have mentioned one atrocious outrage which he committed on the natives. But insensibility to the rights of the Indian he shared with many a better-instructed Spaniard. Yet the Indians, after his conviction, bore testimony to his general humanity, by declaring that they had no such friend among the white men.[26] Indeed, far from being vindictive, he was placable and easily yielded to others. The facility with which he yielded, the result of good-natured credulity, made him too often the dupe of the crafty; and it showed, certainly, a want of that self-reliance which belongs to great strength of character. Yet his facility of temper, and the generosity of his nature, made him popular with his followers. No commander was ever more beloved by his soldiers. His generosity was often carried to prodigality. When he entered on the campaign of Chili, he lent a hundred thousand gold ducats to the poorer cavaliers to equip themselves and afterwards gave them up the debt.[27] He was profuse to osten-

[22] Carta de Espinall, MS.—Herrera, Hist. General, loc. cit.—Carta de Valverde al Emperador, MS.—Carta de Gutierrez, MS.—Pedro Pizarro, Descub. y Conq., MS. —Montesinos, Annales, MS., año 1538.
The date of Almagro's execution is not given; a strange omission; but of little moment, as that event must have followed soon on the condemnation.

[23] Ante, p. 836.

[24] Montesinos, for want of a better pedigree, says,—"He was the son of his own great deeds, and such has been the parentage of many a famous hero!" (Annales, MS., año 1538.) It would go hard with a Castilian, if he could not make out something like a genealogy,—however shadowy.

[25] "Hera vn hombre muy profano, de muy mala lengua, que en enojandose tratava muy mal á todos los que con el andavan aunque fuesen cavalleros." (Descub. y Conq., MS.) It is the portrait drawn by an enemy.

[26] "Los Indios lloraban amargamente, diciendo, que de él nunca recibieron mal tratamiento." Herrera, Hist. General, dec. 6, lib. 5, cap. 1.

[27] If we may credit Herrera, he distributed a hundred and eighty loads of silver and twenty of gold among his followers! "Mandò sacar de su Posada mas de ciento i ochenta cargas de Plata i veinte de Oro, i las repartiò." (Dec. 5, lib. 7, cap. 9.) A load was what a man could easily carry. Such a statement taxes our credulity, but

tation. But his extravagance did him no harm among the roving spirits of the camp, with whom prodigality is apt to gain more favor than a strict and well-regulated economy.

He was a good soldier, careful and judicious in his plans, patient and intrepid in their execution. His body was covered with the scars of his battles, till the natural plainness of his person was converted almost into deformity. He must not be judged by his closing campaign, when, depressed by disease, he yielded to the superior genius of his rival; but by his numerous expeditions by land and by water for the conquest of Peru and the remote Chili. Yet it may be doubted whether he possessed those uncommon qualities, either as a warrior or as a man, that, in ordinary circumstances, would have raised him to distinction. He was one of the three, or, to speak more strictly, of the two associates, who had the good fortune and the glory to make one of the most splendid discoveries in the Western World. He shares largely in the credit of this with Pizarro; for, when he did not accompany that leader in his perilous expeditions, he contributed no less to their success by his exertions in the colonies.

Yet his connection with that chief can hardly be considered a fortunate circumstance in his career. A partnership between individuals for discovery and conquest is not likely to be very scrupulously observed, especially by men more accustomed to govern others than to govern themselves. If causes for discord do not arise before, they will be sure to spring up on division of the spoil. But this association was particularly ill-assorted. For the free, sanguine, and confiding temper of Almagro was no match for the cool and crafty policy of Pizarro; and he was invariably circumvented by his companion, whenever their respective interests came in collision.

Still the final ruin of Almagro may be fairly imputed to himself. He made two capital blunders. The first was his appeal to arms by the seizure of Cuzco. The determination of a boundary-line was not to be settled by arms. It was a subject for arbitration; and, if arbitrators could not be trusted, it should have been referred to the decision of the Crown. But, having once appealed to arms, he should not then have resorted to negotiation,—above all, to negotiation with Pizarro. This was his second and greatest error. He had seen enough of Pizarro to know that he was not to be trusted. Almagro did trust him, and he paid for it with his life.

it is difficult to set the proper limits to one's credulity, in what relates to this land of gold.

PIZARRO REVISITS CUZCO—HERNANDO RETURNS TO CASTILE—HIS LONG IMPRISONMENT—COMMISSIONER SENT TO PERU—HOSTILITIES WITH THE INCA—PIZARRO'S ACTIVE ADMINISTRATION—GONZALO PIZARRO

1539—1540

ON the departure of his brother in pursuit of Almagro, the Marquess Francisco Pizarro, as we have seen, returned to Lima. There he anxiously awaited the result of the campaign; and on receiving the welcome tidings of the victory of Las Salinas, he instantly made preparations for his march to Cuzco. At Xauxa, however, he was long detained by the distracted state of the country, and still longer, as it would seem, by a reluctance to enter the Peruvian capital while the trial of Almagro was pending.

He was met at Xauxa by the marshal's son Diego, who had been sent to the coast by Hernando Pizarro. The young man was filled with the most gloomy apprehensions respecting his father's fate, and he besought the governor not to allow his brother to do him any violence. Pizarro, who received Diego with much apparent kindness, bade him take heart, as no harm should come to his father;[1] adding, that he trusted their ancient friendship would soon be renewed. The youth, comforted by these assurances, took his way to Lima, where, by Pizarro's orders, he was received into his house, and treated as a son.

The same assurances respecting the marshal's safety were given by the governor to Bishop Valverde, and some of the principal cavaliers who interested themselves in behalf of the prisoner.[2] Still Pizarro delayed his march to the capital; and when he resumed it, he had advanced no farther than the *Rio de Abancay* when he received tidings of the death of his rival. He appeared greatly shocked by the intelligence, his whole frame was agitated, and he remained for some time with his eyes bent on the ground showing signs of strong emotion.[3]

[1] "I dixo, que no tuviese ninguna pena, porque no consentiria, que su Padre fuese muerto." Herrera, Hist. General, dec. 6, lib. 6, cap. 3.

[2] "Que lo haria asi como lo decia, i que su deseo no era otro, sino ver el Reino en paz; i que en lo que tocaba al Adelantado, perdiese cuidado, que bolveria à tener el antigua amistad con èl." Ibid., dec. 6, lib. 4, cap. 9.

[3] Pedro Pizarro, Descub. y. Conq., MS.

He even shed many tears, *derramó muchas lagrimas,* according to Herrera, who evidently gives him small credit for them. Ibid., dec 6, lib. 6. cap. 7.—Conf. lib. 5, cap. 1.

Such is the account given by his friends. A more probable version of the matter represents him to have been perfectly aware of the state of things at Cuzco. When the trial was concluded, it is said he received a message from Hernando, inquiring what was to be done with the prisoner. He answered in a few words:—"Deal with him so that he shall give us no more trouble."[4] It is also stated that Hernando, afterwards, when laboring under the obloquy caused by Almagro's death, shielded himself under instructions affirmed to have been received from the governor.[5] It is quite certain, that, during his long residence at Xauxa, the latter was in constant communication with Cuzco; and that had he, as Valverde repeatedly urged him,[6] quickened his march to that capital, he might easily have prevented the consummation of the tragedy. As commander-in-chief, Almagro's fate was in his hands; and, whatever his own partisans may affirm of his innocence, the impartial judgment of history must hold him equally accountable with Hernando for the death of his associate.

Neither did his subsequent conduct show any remorse for these proceedings. He entered Cuzco, says one who was present there to witness it, amidst the flourish of clarions and trumpets, at the head of his martial cavalcade, and dressed in the rich suit presented him by Cortés, with the proud bearing and joyous mien of a conqueror.[7] When Diego de Alvarado applied to him for the government of the southern provinces, in the name of the young Almagro, whom his father, as we have seen, had consigned to his protection, Pizarro answered, that "the marshal, by his rebellion, had forfeited all claims to the government." And, when he was still further urged by the cavalier, he bluntly broke off the conversation by declaring that "his own territory covered all on this side of Flanders"![8]—intimating, no doubt, by this magnificent vaunt, that he would endure no rival on this side of the water.

In the same spirit, he had recently sent to supersede Benalcazar, the conqueror of Quito, who, he was informed, aspired to an independent government. Pizarro's emissary had orders to send the offending captain

---

[4] "Respondiò, que hiciese de manera, que el Adelantado no los pusiese en mas alborotos." (Ibid., dec. 6, lib. 6, cap. 7.) "De todo esto," says Espinall, "fue sabidor el dicho Governador Pizarro á lo que mi juicio i el de otros que en ello quisieron mirar alcanzo." Carta de Espinall, MS.

[5] Ibid., dec. 6, lib. 5, cap. 1.
Herrera's testimony is little short of that of a contemporary, since it was derived, he tells us, from the correspondence of the Conquerors, and the accounts given him by their own sons. Lib. 6, cap. 7.

[6] Carta de Valverde al Emperador, MS.

[7] "En este medio tiempo vino á la dicha cibdad del Cuzco el Gobernador D. Franco Pizarro, el qual entro con tronpetas i chirimias vestido con ropa de martas que fue el luto con que entro." Carta de Espinall, MS.

[8] Carta de Espinall, MS.
"Mui asperamente le respondiò el Governador, diciendo, que su Governacion no tenia Termino, i que llegaba hasta Flandes." Herrera, Hist. General, dec. 6, lib. 1, cap. 7.

to Lima; but Benalcazar, after pushing his victorious career far into the
north, had returned to Castile to solicit his guerdon from the emperor.

To the complaints of the injured natives, who invoked his protection,
he showed himself strangely insensible, while the followers of Almagro
he treated with undisguised contempt. The estates of the leaders were
confiscated, and transferred without ceremony to his own partisans.
Hernando had made attempts to conciliate some of the opposite faction
by acts of liberality, but they had refused to accept anything from the
man whose hands were stained with the blood of their commander.[9] The
governor held to them no such encouragement; and many were reduced
to such abject poverty, that, too proud to expose their wretchedness to
the eyes of their conquerors, they withdrew from the city, and sought a
retreat among the neighboring mountains.[10]

For his own brothers he provided by such ample *repartimientos,* as
excited the murmurs of his adherents. He appointed Gonzalo to the command of a strong force destined to act against the natives of Charcas, a
hardy people occupying the territory assigned by the Crown to Almagro.
Gonzalo met with a sturdy resistance, but, after some severe fighting,
succeeded in reducing the province to obedience. He was recompensed,
together with Hernando, who aided him in the conquest, by a large grant
in the neighborhood of Porco, the productive mines of which had been
partially wrought under the Incas. The territory, thus situated, embraced part of those silver hills of Potosí which have since supplied Europe with such stores of the precious metals. Hernando comprehended
the capabilities of the ground, and he began working the mines on a
more extensive scale than that hitherto adopted, though it does not appear that any attempt was then made to penetrate the rich crust of
Potosí.[11] A few years more were to elapse before the Spaniards were to
bring to light the silver quarries that lay hidden in the bosom of its
mountains.[12]

It was now the great business of Hernando to collect a sufficient quantity of treasure to take with him to Castile. Nearly a year had elapsed

[9] "Avia querido hazer amigos de los principales de Chile, y ofrecidoles daria rre-
partimientos y no lo avian aceptado ni querido." Pedro Pizarro, Descub. y Conq.,
MS.

[10] "Viendolas oy en dia, muertos de ambre, fechos pedazos e adeudados, andando
por los montes desesperados por no parecer ante gentes, porque no tienen otra cosa
que se vestir sino ropa de los Indios, ni dineros con que lo comprar." Carta de
Espinall, MS.

[11] "Con la quietud," writes Hernando Pizarro to the emperor, "questa tierra agora
tiene han descubierto i descubren cada dia los vecinos muchas minas ricas de oro
i plata, de que los quintos i rentas reales de V. M. cada dia se le ofrecen i hacer
casa á todo el Mundo." Carta al Emperador, MS., de Puerto Viejo, 6 de Julii, 1539.

[12] Carta de Carbajal al Emperador, MS., del Cuzco, 3 de Nov. 1539.—Pedro Pizarro, Descub. y Conq., MS.—Montesinos, Annales, MS., año 1539.

The story is well known of the manner in which the mines of Potosi were discovered by an Indian, who pulled a bush out of the ground to the fibres of which
a quantity of silver globules was attached. The mine was not registered till 1545.
The account is given by Acosta, lib. 4, cap. 6.

since Almagro's death; and it was full time that he should return and present himself at court, where Diego de Alvarado and other friends of the marshal, who had long since left Peru, were industriously maintaining the claims of the younger Almagro, as well as demanding redress for the wrongs done to his father. But Hernando looked confidently to his gold to dispel the accusations against him.

Before his departure, he counselled his brother to beware of the "men of Chili," as Almagro's followers were called; desperate men, who would stick at nothing, he said, for revenge. He besought the governor not to allow them to consort together in any number within fifty miles of his person; if he did, it would be fatal to him. And he concluded by recommending a strong body-guard; "for I," he added, "shall not be here to watch over you." But the governor laughed at the idle fears, as he termed them, of his brother, bidding the latter take no thought of him, "as every hair in the heads of Almagro's followers was a guaranty for his safety."[13] He did not know the character of his enemies so well as Hernando.

The latter soon after embarked at Lima in the summer of 1539. He did not take the route of Panamá, for he had heard that it was the intention of the authorities there to detain him. He made a circuitous passage, therefore, by way of Mexico, landed in the Bay of Tecoantepec, and was making his way across the narrow strip that divides the great oceans, when he was arrested and taken to the capital. But the Viceroy Mendoza did not consider that he had a right to detain him, and he was suffered to embark at Vera Cruz, and to proceed on his voyage. Still he did not deem it safe to trust himself in Spain without further advices. He accordingly put in at one of the Azores, where he remained until he could communicate with home. He had some powerful friends at court, and by them he was encouraged to present himself before the emperor. He took their advice, and shortly after, reached the Spanish coast in safety.[14]

The Court was at Valladolid; but Hernando, who made his entrance into that city, with great pomp and a display of his Indian riches, met with a reception colder than he had anticipated.[15] For this he was mainly indebted to Diego de Alvarado, who was then residing there, and who, as a cavalier of honorable standing, and of high connections, had considerable influence. He had formerly, as we have seen, by his timely

[13] Herrera, Hist. General, dec. 6, lib. 6, cap. 10.—Zarate, Conq. del Peru, lib. 3, cap. 12.—Gomara, Hist. de las Ind., cap 142.

"No consienta vuestra señoria que se junten diez juntos en cinquenta leguas alrrededor de adonde vuestra señoria estuviere, porque si los dexa juntar le an de matar. Si á Vuestra Señoria matan, yo negociare mal y de vuestra señoria no quedara memoria. Estas palabras dixo Hernando Piçarro altas que todos le oymos. Y abraçando al marquez se partio y se fue." Pedro Pizarro, Descub. y Conq., MS.

[14] Carta de Hernando Pizarro al Emperador, MS.—Herrera, Hist. General, dec. 6 lib. 6, cap 10.—Montesinos, Annales, MS., año 1539.

[15] Gomara, Hist. de las Ind., cap. 143.

interposition, more than once saved the life of Hernando; and he had consented to receive a pecuniary obligation from him to a large amount. But all were now forgotten in the recollection of the wrong done to his commander; and, true to the trust reposed in him by that chief in his dying hour, he had come to Spain to vindicate the claims of the young Almagro.

But although coldly received at first, Hernando's presence, and his own version of the dispute with Almagro, aided by the golden arguments which he dealt with no stinted hand, checked the current of indignation, and the opinion of his judges seemed for a time suspended. Alvarado, a cavalier more accustomed to the prompt and decisive action of a camp than to the tortuous intrigues of a court, chafed at the delay, and challenged Hernando to settle their quarrel by single combat. But his prudent adversary had no desire to leave the issue to such an ordeal; and the affair was speedily terminated by the death of Alvarado himself, which happened five days after the challenge. An event so opportune naturally suggested the suspicion of poison.[16]

But his accusations had not wholly fallen to the ground; and Hernando Pizarro had carried measures with too high a hand, and too grossly outraged public sentiment, to be permitted to escape. He received no formal sentence, but he was imprisoned in the strong fortress of Medina del Campo, where he was allowed to remain for twenty years, when in 1560, after a generation had nearly passed away, and time had, in some measure, thrown its softening veil over the past, he was suffered to regain his liberty.[17] But he came forth an aged man, bent down with infirmities and broken in spirit,—an object of pity, rather than indignation. Rarely has retributive justice been meted out in fuller measure to offenders so high in authority,—most rarely in Castile.[18]

Yet Hernando bore this long imprisonment with an equanimity which, had it been founded on principle, might command our respect. He saw brothers and kindred, all on whom he leaned for support, cut off one after another; his fortune, in part, confiscated, while he was involved in expensive litigation for the remainder;[19] his fame blighted, his career closed in an untimely hour, himself an exile in the heart of his own

[16] "Pero todo lo atajó la repentina muerte de Diego de Alvarado, que sucedió luego en cinco dias, no sin sospecha de veneno." Herrera, Hist. General, dec. 6, lib. 8, cap. 9.

[17] This date is established by Quintana, from a legal process instituted by Hernando's grandson, in vindication of the title of Marquess, in the year 1625.

[18] Naharro, Relacion Sumaria, MS.—Pizarro y Orellana, Varones Ilustres p. 341.— Montesinos, Annales, MS., año 1539.—Gomara, Hist. de las Ind., cap. 142.

[19] Caro de Torres gives a royal *cédula* in reference to the working of the silver mines of Porco, still owned by Hernando Pizarro, in 1555; and another document of nearly the same date, noticing his receipt of ten thousand ducats by the fleet from Peru. (Historia de las Ordenes Militares Madrid, 1629, p. 144.) Hernando's grandson was created by Philip IV. Marquess of the Conquest, *Marques de la Conquista*, with a liberal pension from government. Pizarro y Orellana, Varones Ilustres, p. 342, and Discurso, p. 72.

country;—yet he bore it all with the constancy of a courageous spirit. Though very old when released, he still survived several years, and continued to the extraordinary age of a hundred.[20] He lived long enough to see friends, rivals, and foes all called away to their account before him.

Hernando Pizarro was in many respects a remarkable character. He was the eldest of the brothers, to whom he was related only by the father's side, for he was born in wedlock, of honorable parentage on both sides of his house. In his early years, he received a good education,—good for the time. He was taken by his father, while quite young, to Italy, and there learned the art of war under the Great Captain. Little is known of his history after his return to Spain; but, when his brother had struck out for himself his brilliant career of discovery in Peru, Hernando consented to take part in his adventures.

He was much deferred to by Francisco, not only as his elder brother, but from his superior education and his knowledge of affairs. He was ready in his perceptions, fruitful in resources, and possessed of great vigor in action. Though courageous, he was cautious; and his counsels, when not warped by passion, were wise and wary. But he had other qualities, which more than counterbalanced the good resulting from excellent parts and attainments. His ambition and avarice were insatiable. He was supercilious even to his equals; and he had a vindictive temper, which nothing could appease. Thus, instead of aiding his brother in the Conquest, he was the evil genius that blighted his path. He conceived from the first an unwarrantable contempt for Almagro, whom he regarded as his brother's rival, instead of what he then was, the faithful partner of his fortunes. He treated him with personal indignity, and, by his intrigues at court, had the means of doing him sensible injury. He fell into Almagro's hands, and had nearly paid for these wrongs with his life. This was not to be forgiven by Hernando, and he coolly waited for the hour of revenge. Yet the execution of Almagro was a most impolitic act; for an evil passion can rarely be gratified with impunity. Hernando thought to buy off justice with the gold of Peru. He had studied human nature on its weak and wicked side, and he expected to profit by it. Fortunately, he was deceived. He had, indeed, his revenge; but the hour of his revenge was that of his ruin.

The disorderly state of Peru was such as to demand the immediate interposition of government. In the general license that prevailed there, the rights of the Indian and of the Spaniard were equally trampled under foot. Yet the subject was one of great difficulty; for Pizarro's authority was now firmly established over the country, which itself was too remote from Castile to be readily controlled at home. Pizarro, moreover,

---

[20] *"Multos da, Jupiter, annos"*; the greatest boon, in Pizarro y Orellana's opinion, that Heaven can confer! "Diole Dios, por todo, el premio mayor desta vida, pues fue tan larga, que excedio de cien años." (Varones Ilustres, p. 342.) According to the same somewhat partial authority, Hernando died, as he had lived, in the odor of sanctity! "Viviendo aprender a morir. v saber morir. auando llegò la muerte."

was a man not easy to be approached, confident in his own strength, jealous of interference, and possessed of a fiery temper, which would kindle into a flame at the least distrust of the government. It would not answer to send out a commission to suspend him from the exercise of his authority until his conduct could be investigated, as was done with Cortés, and other great colonial officers, on whose rooted loyalty the Crown could confidently rely. Pizarro's loyalty sat, it was feared, too lightly on him to be a powerful restraint on his movements; and there were not wanting those among his reckless followers, who, in case of extremity, would be prompt to urge him to throw off his allegiance altogether, and set up an independent government for himself.

Some one was to be sent out, therefore, who should possess, in some sort, a controlling, or, at least, concurrent power with the dangerous chief, while ostensibly he should act only in subordination to him. The person selected for this delicate mission, was the Licentiate Vaca de Castro, a member of the Royal Audience of Valladolid. He was a learned judge, a man of integrity and wisdom, and, though not bred to arms, had so much address, and such knowledge of character, as would enable him readily to turn the resources of others to his own account.

His commission was guarded in a way which showed the embarrassment of the government. He was to appear before Pizarro in the capacity of a royal judge; to consult with him on the redress of grievances, especially with reference to the unfortunate natives; to concert measures for the prevention of future evils; and above all, to possess himself faithfully of the condition of the country in all its details, and to transmit intelligence of it to the Court of Castile. But, in case of Pizarro's death, he was to produce his warrant as royal governor, and as such to claim the obedience of the authorities throughout the land.—Events showed the wisdom of providing for this latter contingency.[21]

The licentiate, thus commissioned, quitted his quiet residence at Valledolid, embarked at Seville, in the autumn of 1540, and, after a tedious voyage across the Atlantic, he traversed the Isthmus, and, encountering a succession of tempests on the Pacific, that had nearly sent his frail bark to the bottom, put in with her, a mere wreck, at the northerly port of Buenaventura.[22] The affairs of the country were in a state to require his presence.

The civil war which had lately distracted the land had left it in so unsettled a state, that the agitation continued long after the immediate cause had ceased. This was especially the case among the natives. In the

---

[21] Pedro Pizarro, Descub. y Conq., MS.—Gomara, Hist. de las Ind., cap. 146.—Herrera, Hist. General, dec. 6, lib. 8, cap. 9.—Montesinos, Annales, MS., año 1540.

This latter writer sees nothing short of a "divine mystery" in this forecast of government, so singularly sustained by events. "Prevencion del gran espiritu del Rey, no sin misterio." Ubi supra.

[22] Or, as the port should rather be called, *Mala Ventura*, as Pedro Pizarro punningly remarks. "Tuvo tan mal viaje en la mar que vbo de desembarcar en la Buena Ventura, aunque yo la llamo Mala." Descub. y Conq., MS.

violent transfer of *repartimientos,* the poor Indian hardly knew to whom he was to look as his master. The fierce struggles between the rival chieftains left him equally in doubt whom he was to regard as the rulers of the land. As to the authority of a common sovereign, across the waters, paramount over all, he held that in still greater distrust; for what was the authority which could not command the obedience even of its own vassals?[23] The Inca Manco was not slow in taking advantage of this state of feeling. He left his obscure fastnesses in the depths of the Andes, and established himself with a strong body of followers in the mountain country lying between Cuzco and the coast. From this retreat, he made descents on the neighboring plantations, destroying the houses, sweeping off the cattle, and massacring the people. He fell on travellers, as they were journeying singly or in caravans from the coast, and put them to death—it is told by his enemies—with cruel tortures. Single detachments were sent against him, from time to time, but without effect. Some he eluded, others he defeated; and, on one occasion, cut off a party of thirty troopers, to a man.[24]

At length, Pizarro found it necessary to send a considerable force under his brother Gonzalo against the Inca. The hardy Indian encountered his enemy several times in the rough passes of the Cordilleras. He was usually beaten, and sometimes with heavy loss, which he repaired with astonishing facility; for he always contrived to make his escape, and so true were his followers, that, in defiance of pursuit and ambuscade, he found a safe shelter in the secret haunts of the sierra.

Thus baffled, Pizarro determined to try the effect of pacific overtures. He sent to the Inca, both in his own name, and in that of the Bishop of Cuzco, whom the Peruvian prince held in reverence, to invite him to enter into negotiation.[25] Manco acquiesced, and indicated, as he had formerly done with Almagro, the valley of Yucay, as the scene of it. The governor repaired thither, at the appointed time, well guarded, and, to propitiate the barbarian monarch, sent him a rich present by the hands

---

[23] "Piensan que les mienten los que aca les dizen que ai un gran Señor en Castilla, viendo que aca pelean unos capitanes contra otros; y piensan que no ai otro Rei sino aquel que venze al otro, porque aca entrellos no se acostumbra que un capitan pelee contra otro, estando entrambos debaxo de un Señor." Carta de Valverde al Emperador, MS.

[24] Herrera, Hist. General, dec. 6, lib. 6, cap. 7.—Pedro Pizarro, Descub. y Conq., MS.—Carta de Espinall, MS.—Carta de Valverde al Emperador, MS.

[25] The Inca declined the interview with the bishop, on the ground that he had seen him pay obeisance by taking off his cap to Pizarro. It proved his inferiority to the latter, he said, and that he could never protect him against the governor. The passage in which it is related is curious. "Preguntando a indios del inca que anda alzado que si sabe el inca que yo soi venido á la tierra en nombre de S. M. para defendellos, dixo que mui bien lo sabia; y preguntado que porque no se benia á mi de paz, dixo el indio que dezia el inca que porque yo quando vine hize la mocha al gobernador, que quiere dezir que le quité el Bonete; que no queria venir á mi de paz, que él que no havia de venir de paz sino á uno que viniese de castilla que no hiziese la mocha al gobernador, porque le paresze á él que este lo podrá defender por lo que ha hecho y no otro." Carta de Valverde al Emperador, MS.

of an African slave. The slave was met on the route by a party of the Inca's men, who, whether with or without their master's orders, cruelly murdered him, and bore off the spoil to their quarters. Pizarro resented this outrage by another yet more atrocious.

Among the Indian prisoners was one of the Inca's wives, a young and beautiful woman, to whom he was said to be fondly attached. The governor ordered her to be stripped naked, bound to a tree, and, in presence of the camp, to be scourged with rods, and then shot to death with arrows. The wretched victim bore the execution of the sentence with surprising fortitude. She did not beg for mercy, where none was to be found. Not a complaint, scarcely a groan, escaped her under the infliction of these terrible torments. The iron Conquerors were amazed at this power of endurance in a delicate woman, and they expressed their admiration, while they condemned the cruelty of their commander,—in their hearts.[26] Yet constancy under the most excruciating tortures that human cruelty can inflict is almost the universal characteristic of the American Indian.

Pizarro now prepared, as the most effectual means of checking these disorders among the natives, to establish settlements in the heart of the disaffected country. These settlements, which received the dignified name of cities, might be regarded in the light of military colonies. The houses were usually built of stone, to which were added the various public offices, and sometimes a fortress. A municipal corporation was organized. Settlers were invited by the distribution of large tracts of land in the neighborhood, with a stipulated number of Indian vassals to each. The soldiers then gathered there, sometimes accompanied by their wives and families; for the women of Castile seem to have disdained the impediments of sex, in the ardor of conjugal attachment, or, it may be, of romantic adventure. A populous settlement rapidly grew up in the wilderness, affording protection to the surrounding territory, and furnishing a commercial *dépôt* for the country, and an armed force ready at all times to maintain public order.

Such a settlement was that now made at Guamanga, midway between Cuzco and Lima, which effectually answered its purpose by guarding the communications with the coast.[27] Another town was founded in the min-

---

[26] At least, we may presume they did so, since they openly condemn him in their accounts of the transaction. I quote Pedro Pizarro, not disposed to criticise the conduct of his general too severely. "Se tomo una muger de mango ynga que le queria mucho y se guardo, creyendo que por ella saldria de paz. Esta muger mando matar al marquez despues en Yncay, haziendola varear con varas y flechar con flechas por una burla que mango ynga le hizo que aqui contare, y entiendo yo que por esta crueldad y otra hermana del ynga que mando matar en Lima quando los yndios pusieron cerco sobrella que se llamava Açarpay. me paresce á mi que nuestro señor le castigo en el fin que tuvo." Descub. y Conq., MS.

[27] Cieza de Leon notices the uncommon beauty and solidity of the buildings at Guamanga. "La qual han edificado las mayores y mejores casas que ay en todo el Peru, todas de piedra, ladrillo, y teja, con grandes torres: de manera que no falta aposentos. La plaça esta llena y bien grande." Cronica, cap. 87.

ing district of Charcas, under the appropriate name of the Villa de la Plata, the "City of Silver." And Pizarro, as he journeyed by a circuitous route along the shores of the southern sea towards Lima, planted there the city of Arequipa, since arisen to such commercial celebrity.

Once more in his favorite capital of Lima, the governor found abundant occupation in attending to its municipal concerns, and in providing for the expansive growth of its population. Nor was he unmindful of the other rising settlements on the Pacific. He encouraged commerce with the remoter colonies north of Peru, and took measures for facilitating internal intercourse. He stimulated industry in all its branches, paying great attention to husbandry, and importing seeds of the different European grains, which he had the satisfaction, in a short time, to see thriving luxuriantly in a country where the variety of soil and climate afforded a home for almost every product.[28] Above all, he promoted the working of the mines, which already began to make such returns, that the most common articles of life rose to exorbitant prices, while the precious metals themselves seemed the only things of little value. But they soon changed hands, and found their way to the mother-country, where they rose to their true level as they mingled with the general currency of Europe. The Spaniards found that they had at length reached the land of which they had been so long in search,—the land of gold and silver. Emigrants came in greater numbers to the country, and, spreading over its surface, formed in the increasing population the most effectual barrier against the rightful owners of the soil.[29]

Pizarro, strengthened by the arrival of fresh adventurers, now turned his attention to the remoter quarters of the country. Pedro de Valdivia was sent on his memorable expedition to Chili; and to his own brother Gonzalo the governor assigned the territory of Quito, with instructions to explore the unknown country towards the east, where, as report said, grew the cinnamon. As this chief, who had hitherto acted but a subordinate part in the Conquest, is henceforth to take the most conspicuous, it may be well to give some account of him.

Little is known of his early life, for he sprang from the same obscure origin with Francisco, and seems to have been as little indebted as his elder brother to the fostering care of his parents. He entered early on the career of a soldier; a career to which every man in that iron age, whether cavalier or vagabond, seems, if left to himself, to have most readily inclined. Here he soon distinguished himself by his skill in martial exercises, was an excellent horseman, and, when he came to the New World, was esteemed the best lance in Peru [30]

[28] "I con que ià començaba à haver en aquellas Tierras cosecha de Trigo, Cevada, i otras muchas cosas de Castilla." Herrera, Hist. General, dec. 6, lib. 10, cap. 2.

[29] Carta de Carvajal al Emperador, MS.—Montesinos, Annales, MS., años 1539 et 1541.—Pedro Pizarro, Descub. y Conq., MS.—Herrera, Hist. General, dec. 6, lib. 7, cap. 1.—Cieza de Leon, Cronica, cap. 76 et alibi.

[30] The cavalier Pizarro y Orellana has given biographical notices of each of the brothers. It requires no witchcraft to detect that the blood of the Pizarros flowed in the veins of the writer to his fingers' ends. Yet his facts are less suspicious than his inferences.

In talent and in expansion of views, he was inferior to his brothers. Neither did he discover the same cool and crafty policy; but he was equally courageous, and in the execution of his measures quite as unscrupulous. He had a handsome person, with open, engaging features, a free, soldier-like address, and a confiding temper, which endeared him to his followers. His spirit was high and adventurous, and, what was equally important, he could inspire others with the same spirit, and thus do much to insure the success of his enterprises. He was an excellent captain in *guerilla* warfare, an admirable leader in doubtful and difficult expeditions; but he had not the enlarged capacity for a great military chief, still less for a civil ruler. It was his misfortune to be called to fill both situations.

CHAPTER IV

GONZALO PIZARRO'S EXPEDITION—PASSAGE ACROSS THE MOUNTAINS—
DISCOVERS THE NAPO—INCREDIBLE SUFFERINGS—ORELLANA
SAILS DOWN THE AMAZON—DESPAIR OF THE SPANIARDS—THE
SURVIVORS RETURN TO QUITO

1540—1542

GONZALO PIZARRO received the news of his appointment to the government of Quito with undisguised pleasure; not so much for the possession
that it gave him of this ancient Indian province, as for the field that it
opened for discovery towards the east,—the fabled land of Oriental
spices, which had long captivated the imagination of the Conquerors. He
repaired to his government without delay, and found no difficulty in
awakening a kindred enthusiasm to his own in the bosoms of his followers. In a short time, he mustered three hundred and fifty Spaniards, and
four thousand Indians. One hundred and fifty of his company were
mounted, and all were equipped in the most thorough manner for the
undertaking. He provided, moreover, against famine by a large stock of
provisions, and an immense drove of swine which followed in the rear.[1]

It was the beginning of 1540, when he set out on this celebrated expedition. The first part of the journey was attended with comparatively
little difficulty, while the Spaniards were yet in the land of the Incas;
for the distractions of Peru had not been felt in this distant province,
where the simple people still lived as under the primitive sway of the
Children of the Sun. But the scene changed as they entered the territory
of Quixos, where the character of the inhabitants, as well as of the climate, seemed to be of another description. The country was traversed by
lofty ranges of the Andes, and the adventurers were soon entangled in
their deep and intricate passes. As they rose into the more elevated regions, the icy winds that swept down the sides of the Cordilleras benumbed their limbs, and many of the natives found a wintry grave in
the wilderness. While crossing this formidable barrier, they experienced

---

[1] Herrera, Hist. General, dec. 6, lib. 8, cap. 6, 7.—Garcilasso, Com. Real. Parte
2, lib. 3, cap. 2.—Zarate, Conq. del Peru, lib. 4, cap. 1, 2.—Gomara, Hist. de las
Ind., cap. 143.—Montesinos, Annales, año 1539.

Historians differ as to the number of Gonzalo's forces,—of his men, his horses,
and his hogs. The last, according to Herrera, amounted to no less than 5000; a
goodly supply of bacon for so small a troop, since the Indians, doubtless, lived on
parched corn, *coca*, which usually formed their only support on the longest journeys.

one of those : remendous earthquakes which, in these volcanic regions so often shake the mountains to their base. In one place, the earth was rent asunder by the terrible throes of Nature, while streams of sulphurous vapor issued from the cavity, and a village with some hundreds of houses was precipitated into the frightful abyss![2]

On descending the eastern slopes, the climate changed; and, as they came on the lower level, the fierce cold was succeeded by a suffocating heat, while tempests of thunder and lightning, rushing from out the gorges of the sierra, poured on their heads with scarcely any intermission day or night, as if the offended deities of the place were willing to take vengeance on the invaders of their mountain solitudes. For more than six weeks the deluge continued unabated, and the forlorn wanderers, wet, and weary with incessant toil, were scarcely able to drag their limbs along the soil broken up and saturated with the moisture. After some months of toilsome travel, in which they had to cross many a morass and mountain stream, they at length reached *Canelas,* the Land of Cinnamon.[3] They saw the trees bearing the precious bark, spreading out into broad forests; yet, however valuable an article for commerce it might have proved in accessible situations, in these remote regions it was of little worth to them. But, from the wandering tribes of savages whom they occasionally met in their path, they learned that at ten days' distance was a rich and fruitful land abounding with gold, and inhabited by populous nations. Gonzalo Pizarro had already reached the limits originally proposed for the expedition. But this intelligence renewed his hopes, and he resolved to push the adventure farther. It would have been well for him and his followers, had they been content to return on their footsteps.

Continuing their march, the country now spread out into broad savannas terminated by forests, which, as they drew near, seemed to stretch on every side to the very verge of the horizon. Here they beheld trees of that stupendous growth seen only in the equinoctial regions. Some were so large, that sixteen men could hardly encompass them with extended arms![4] The wood was thickly matted with creepers and par-

[2] Zarate states the number with precision at five hundred houses. "Sobrevino vn tan gran Terremoto, con temblor, i tempestad de Agua, i Relampagos, i Raios, i grandes Truenos, que abriendose la Tierra por muchas partes, se hundieron quinientas Casas." (Conq. del Peru, lib. 4, cap. 2.) There is nothing so satisfactory to the mind of the reader as precise numbers; and nothing so little deserving of his confidence.

[3] *Canela* is the Spanish for cinnamon.

[4] This, allowing six feet for the spread of a man's arms, would be about ninety-six feet in circumference, or thirty-two feet in diameter; larger, probably, than the largest tree known in Europe. Yet it falls short of that famous giant of the forests mentioned by M. de Humboldt as still flourishing in the intendancy of Oaxaca, which, by the exact measurement of a traveller in 1839, was found to be a hundred and twelve feet in circumference at the height of four feet from the ground. This height may correspond with that of the measurement taken by the Spaniards. See a curious and learned article on Forest-trees in No. 124 of the North American Review

asitical vines, which hung in gaudy-colored festoons from tree to tree, clothing them in a drapery beautiful to the eye, but forming an impenetrable network. At every step of their way, they were obliged to hew open a passage with their axes, while their garments, rotting from the effects of the drenching rains to which they had been exposed, caught in every bush and bramble, and hung about them in shreds.[5] Their provisions, spoiled by the weather, had long since failed, and the live stock which they had taken with them had either been consumed or made their escape in the woods and mountain passes. They had set out with nearly a thousand dogs, many of them of the ferocious breed used in hunting down the unfortunate natives. These they now gladly killed, but their miserable carcasses furnished a lean banquet for the famishing travellers; and, when these were gone, they had only such herbs and dangerous roots as they could gather in the forest.[6]

At length the way-worn company came on a broad expanse of water formed by the Napo, one of the great tributaries of the Amazon, and which, though only a third or fourth rate river in America, would pass for one of the first magnitude in the Old World. The sight gladdened their hearts, as, by winding along its banks, they hoped to find a safer and more practicable route. After traversing its borders for a considerable distance, closely beset with thickets which it taxed their strength to the utmost to overcome, Gonzalo and his party came within hearing of a rushing noise that sounded like subterranean thunder. The river, lashed into fury, tumbled along over rapids with frightful velocity, and conducted them to the brink of a magnificent cataract, which, to their wondering fancies, rushed down in one vast volume of foam to the depth

---

[5] The dramatist Molina, in his play of *"Las Amazonas en las Indias,"* has devoted some dozen columns of *redondillas* to an account of the sufferings of his countrymen in the expedition to the Amazon. The poet reckoned confidently on the patience of his audience. The following verses describe the miserable condition to which the Spaniards were reduced by the incessant rains.

> "Sin que el Sol en este tiempo
> Su cara vèr nos permita,
> Ni las nubes taberneras
> Cessen de echamos encima
> Dilubios inagotables,
> *Que hasta el alma nos bautizan.*
> Cayeron los mas enfermos,
> Porque las ropas podridas
> Con el eterno agua và,
> Nos dexò en las carnes vivas."

[6] Capitulacion con Orellana, MS.—Pedro Pizarro, Descub. by Conq., MS.—Gomara, Hist. de las Ind., cap. 143.—Zarate, Conq. del Peru, lib. 4, cap. 2.—Herrera, Hist. General, dec. 6, lib. 8, cap. 6, 7.—Garcilasso, Com. Real., Parte 2, lib. 3, cap. 2.

The last writer obtained his information, as he tells us, from several who were present in the expedition. The reader may be assured that it has lost nothing in coming through his hands.

of twelve hundred feet![7] The appalling sounds which they had heard for the distance of six leagues were rendered yet more oppressive to the spirits by the gloomy stillness of the surrounding forests. The rude warriors were filled with sentiments of awe. Not a bark dimpled the waters. No living thing was to be seen but the wild tenants of the wilderness, the unwieldy boa, and the loathsome alligator basking on the borders of the stream. The trees towering in wide-spread magnificence towards the heavens, the river rolling on in its rocky bed as it had rolled for ages, the solitude and silence of the scene, broken only by the hoarse fall of waters, or the faint rustling of the woods,—all seemed to spread out around them in the same wild and primitive state as when they came from the hands of the Creator.

For some distance above and below the falls, the bed of the river contracted so that its width did not exceed twenty feet. Sorely pressed by hunger, the adventurers determined, at all hazards, to cross to the opposite side, in hopes of finding a country that might afford them sustenance. A frail bridge was constructed by throwing the huge trunks of trees across the chasm, where the cliffs, as if split asunder by some convulsion of nature, descended sheer down a perpendicular depth of several hundred feet. Over this airy causeway the men and horses succeeded in effecting their passage with the loss of a single Spaniard, who, made giddy by heedlessly looking down, lost his footing and fell into the boiling surges below.

Yet they gained little by the exchange. The country wore the same unpromising aspect, and the river-banks were studded with gigantic trees, or fringed with impenetrable thickets. The tribes of Indians, whom they occasionally met in the pathless wilderness, were fierce and unfriendly, and they were engaged in perpetual skirmishes with them. From these they learned that a fruitful country was to be found down the river at the distance of only a few days' journey, and the Spaniards held on their weary way, still hoping and still deceived, as the promised land flitted before them, like the rainbow, receding as they advanced.

At length, spent with toil and suffering, Gonzalo resolved to construct a bark large enough to transport the weaker part of his company and his baggage. The forests furnished him with timber; the shoes of the horses which had died on the road or been slaughtered for food,

---

[7] "Al cabo de este largo camino hallaron que el rio hazia vn salto de una peña de mas de dozientas braças de alto: que hazia tan gran ruydo, que lo oyeron mas de seys leguas antes que llegassen a el." (Garcilasso, Com. Real., Parte 2, lib. 3, cap. 3.) I find nothing to confirm or to confute the account of this stupendous cataract in later travellers, not very numerous in these wild regions. The alleged height of the falls, twice that of the great cataract of the Tequendama in the Bogotá, as measured by Humboldt, usually esteemed the highest in America, is not so great as that of some of the cascades thrown over the precipices in Switzerland. Yet the estimates of the Spaniards, who, in the gloomy state of their feelings, were doubtless keenly alive to impressions of the sublime and the terrible, cannot safely be relied on.

were converted into nails; gum distilled from the trees took the place of pitch; and the tattered garments of the soldiers supplied a substitute for oakum. It was a work of difficulty; but Gonzalo cheered his men in the task, and set an example by taking part in their labors. At the end of two months a brigantine was completed, rudely put together, but strong and of sufficient burden to carry half the company,—the first European vessel that ever floated on these inland waters.

Gonzalo gave the command to Francisco de Orellana, a cavalier from Truxillo, on whose courage and devotion to himself he thought he could rely. The troops now moved forward, still following the descending course of the river, while the brigantine kept alongside; and when a bold promontory or more impracticable country intervened, it furnished timely aid by the transportation of the feebler soldiers. In this way they journeyed, for many a wearisome week, through the dreary wilderness on the borders of the Napo. Every scrap of provisions had been long since consumed. The last of their horses had been devoured. To appease the gnawings of hunger, they were fain to eat the leather of their saddles and belts. The woods supplied them with scanty sustenance, and they greedily fed upon toads, serpents, and such other reptiles as they occasionally found.[8]

They were now told of a rich district, inhabited by a populous nation, where the Napo emptied into a still greater river that flowed towards the east. It was, as usual, at the distance of several days' journey; and Gonzalo Pizarro resolved to halt where he was and send Orellana down in his brigantine to the confluence of the waters to procure a stock of provisions, with which he might return and put them in condition to resume their march. That cavalier, accordingly, taking with him fifty of the adventurers, pushed off into the middle of the river, where the stream ran swiftly, and his bark, taken by the current, shot forward with the speed of an arrow, and was soon out of sight.

Days and weeks passed away, yet the vessel did not return; and no speck was to be seen on the waters, as the Spaniards strained their eyes to the farthest point, where the line of light faded away in the dark shadows of the foliage on the borders. Detachments were sent out, and, though absent several days, came back without intelligence of their comrades. Unable longer to endure this suspense, or, indeed, to maintain themselves in their present quarters, Gonzalo and his famishing followers now determined to proceed towards the junction of the rivers. Two months elapsed before they accomplished this terrible journey,— those of them who did not perish on the way,—although the distance

---

[8] "Yeruas y rayzes, y fruta siluestre, sapos, y culebras, y otras malas sauandijas, si las auia por aquellas montañas que todo les hazia buen estomago a los Españoles; que peor les yua con la falta de cosas tan viles." Garcilasso, Com. Real., Parte 2, lib. 3, cap. 4—Capitulacion con Orellana, MS.—Herrera, Hist. General, dec. 6, lib 3, cap. 7.—Zarate, Conq. del Peru. lib. 4, cap. 3, 4.—Gomara. Hist. de las Ind., cap. 143.

probably did not exceed two hundred leagues; and they at length reached the spot so long desired, where the Napo pours its tide into the Amazon, that mighty stream, which, fed by its thousand tributaries, rolls on towards the ocean, for many hundred miles, through the heart of the great continent,—the most majestic of American rivers.

But the Spaniards gathered no tidings of Orellana, while the country, though more populous than the region they had left, was as little inviting in its aspect, and was tenanted by a race yet more ferocious. They now abandoned the hope of recovering their comrades, who they supposed must have miserably perished by famine or by the hands of the natives. But their doubts were at length dispelled by the appearance of a white man wandering half-naked in the woods, in whose famine-stricken countenance they recognized the features of one of their countrymen. It was Sanchez de Vargas, a cavalier of good descent, and much esteemed in the army. He had a dismal tale to tell.

Orellana, borne swiftly down the current of the Napo, had reached the point of its confluence with the Amazon in less than three days; accomplishing in this brief space of time what had cost Pizarro and his company two months. He had found the country altogether different from what had been represented; and, so far from supplies for his countrymen, he could barely obtain sustenance for himself. Nor was it possible for him to return as he had come, and make head against the current of the river; while the attempt to journey by land was an alternative scarcely less formidable. In this dilemma, an idea flashed across his mind. It was to launch his bark at once on the bosom of the Amazon, and descend its waters to its mouth. He would then visit the rich and populous nations that, as report said, lined its borders, sail out on the great ocean, cross to the neighboring isles, and return to Spain to claim the glory and the guerdon of discovery. The suggestion was eagerly taken up by his reckless companions, welcoming any course that would rescue them from the wretchedness of their present existence, and fired with the prospect of new and stirring adventure,—for the love of adventure was the last feeling to become extinct in the bosom of the Castilian cavalier. They heeded little their unfortunate comrades, whom they were to abandon in the wilderness![9]

This is not the place to record the circumstances of Orellana's extraordinary expedition. He succeeded in his enterprise. But it is marvellous that he should have escaped shipwreck in the perilous and un-

[9] This statement of De Vargas was confirmed by Orellana, as appears from the language of the royal grant made to that cavalier on his return to Castile. The document is preserved entire in the Muñoz collection of MSS.

"Haviendo vos ido con ciertos compañeros un rio abajo á buscar comida, con la corriente fuistes metidos por el dicho rio mas de 200 leguas donde no pudistes dar la buelta é por esta necesidad é por la mucha noticia que tuvistes de la grandeza é riqueza de la tierra, posponiendo vuestro peligro, sin interes ninguno por servir á S. M. os aventurastes á saber lo que havia en aquellas provincias, é ansi descubristes é hallastes grandes poblaciones." Capitulacion con Orellana, MS.

known navigation of that river. Many times his vessel was nearly dashed to pieces on its rocks and in its furious rapids;[10] and he was in still greater peril from the warlike tribes on its borders, who fell on his little troop whenever he attempted to land, and followed in his wake for miles in their canoes. He at length emerged from the great river; and, once upon the sea, Orellana made for the isle of Cubagua; thence passing over to Spain, he repaired to court, and told the circumstances of his voyage,—of the nations of Amazons whom he had found on the banks of the river, the El Dorado which report assured him existed in the neighborhood, and other marvels,—the exaggeration rather than the coinage of a credulous fancy. His audience listened with willing ears to the tales of the traveller; and in an age of wonders, when the mysteries of the East and West were hourly coming to light, they might be excused for not discerning the true line between romance and reality.[11]

He found no difficulty in obtaining a commission to conquer and colonize the realms he had discovered. He soon saw himself at the head of five hundred followers, prepared to share the perils and the profits of his expedition. But neither he, nor his country, was destined to realize these profits. He died on his outward passage, and the lands washed by the Amazon fell within the territories of Portugal. The unfortunate navigator did not even enjoy the undivided honor of giving his name to the waters he had discovered. He enjoyed only the barren glory of the discovery, surely not balanced by the iniquitous circumstances which attended it.[12]

One of Orellana's party maintained a stout opposition to his proceedings, as repugnant both to humanity and honor. This was Sanchez de Vargas; and the cruel commander was revenged on him by abandoning him to his fate in the desolate region where he was now found by his countrymen.[13]

[10] Condamine, who, in 1743, went down the Amazon, has often occasion to notice the perils and perplexities in which he was involved in the navigation of this river, too difficult, as he says, to be undertaken without the guidance of a skilful pilot. See his Relation Abregée d'un Voyage fait dans l'Interieur de l'Amérique Méridionale. (Maestricht, 1778.)

[11] It has not been easy to discern the exact line in later times, with all the lights of modern discovery. Condamine, after a careful investigation, considers that there is good ground for believing in the existence of a community of armed women, once living somewhere in the neighborhood of the Amazon, though they have now disappeared. It would be hard to disprove the fact, but still harder, considering the embarrassments in perpetuating such a community, to believe it. Voyage dans l'Amérique Méridionale, p. 99, et seq.

[12] "His crime is, in some measure, balanced by the glory of having ventured upon a navigation of near two thousand leagues, through unknown nations, in a vessel hastily constructed, with green timber, and by very unskilful hands, without provisions, without a compass, or a pilot." (Robertson, America, (ed. London, 1796,) vol. III. p. 84.) The historian of America does not hold the moral balance with as unerring a hand as usual, in his judgment of Orellana's splendid enterprise. No success, however splendid, in the language of one not too severe a moralist,
"Can blazon evil deeds or consecrate a crime."

[13] An expedition more remarkable than that of Orellana was performed by a

The Spaniards listened with horror to the recital of Vargas, and their blood almost froze in their veins as they saw themselves thus deserted in the heart of this remote wilderness, and deprived of their only means of escape from it. They made an effort to prosecute their journey along the banks, but, after some toilsome days, strength and spirits failed, and they gave up in despair!

Then it was that the qualities of Gonzalo Pizarro, as a fit leader in the hour of despondency and danger, shone out conspicuous. To advance farther was hopeless. To stay where they were, without food or raiment, without defence from the fierce animals of the forest and the fiercer natives, was impossible. One only course remained; it was to return to Quito. But this brought with it the recollection of the past, of sufferings which they could too well estimate,—hardly to be endured even in imagination. They were now at least four hundred leagues from Quito, and more than a year had elapsed since they had set out on their painful pilgrimage. How could they encounter these perils again![14]

Yet there was no alternative. Gonzalo endeavored to reassure his followers by dwelling on the invincible constancy they had hitherto displayed; adjuring them to show themselves still worthy of the name of Castilians. He reminded them of the glory they would for ever acquire by their heroic achievement, when they should reach their own country. He would lead them back, he said, by another route, and it could not be but that they should meet somewhere with those abundant regions of which they had so often heard. It was something, at least, that every step would take them nearer home; and as, at all events, it was clearly the only course now left, they should prepare to meet it like men. The spirit would sustain the body; and difficulties encountered in the right spirit were half vanquished already!

The soldiers listened eagerly to his words of promise and encouragement. The confidence of their leader gave life to the desponding. They felt the force of his reasoning, and, as they lent a willing ear to his as-

delicate female, Madame Godin, who, in 1769, attempted to descend the Amazon in an open boat to its mouth. She was attended by seven persons, two of them her brothers, and two her female domestics. The boat was wrecked, and Madame Godin, narrowly escaping with her life, endeavored with her party to accomplish the remainder of her journey on foot. She saw them perish, one after another, of hunger and disease, till she was left alone in the howling wilderness. Still, like Milton's lady in Comus, she was permitted to come safely out of all these perils, and, after unparalleled sufferings, falling in with some friendly Indians, she was conducted by them to a French settlement. Though a young woman, it will not be surprising that the hardships and terrors she endured turned her hair perfectly white. The details of the extraordinary story are given in a letter to M. de la Condamine by her husband, who tells them in an earnest, unaffected way that engages our confidence. Voyage dans l'Amérique Méridionale, p. 329, et seq.

[14] Garcilasso, Com. Real., Parte 2, lib. 3, cap. 5.—Herrera, Hist. General, dec. 6, lib. 8, cap. 8.—Zarate, Conq. del Peru, lib. 4, cap. 5.—Gomara, Hist. de las Ind., cap. 143.

One must not expect from these wanderers in the wilderness any exact computation of time or distance, destitute, as they were, of the means of making a correct observation of either.

surances, the pride of the old Castilian honor revived in their bosoms, and every one caught somewhat of the generous enthusiasm of their commander. He was, in truth, entitled to their devotion. From the first hour of the expedition, he had freely borne his part in its privations. Far from claiming the advantage of his position, he had taken his lot with the poorest soldier; ministering to the wants of the sick, cheering up the spirits of the desponding, sharing his stinted allowance with his famished followers, bearing his full part in the toil and burden of the march, ever showing himself their faithful comrade, no less than their captain. He found the benefit of this conduct in a trying hour like the present.

I will spare the reader the recapitulation of the sufferings endured by the Spaniards on their retrograde march to Quito. They took a more northerly route than that by which they had approached the Amazon; and, if it was attended with fewer difficulties, they experienced yet greater distresses from their greater inability to overcome them. Their only nourishment was such scanty fare as they could pick up in the forest, or happily meet with in some forsaken Indian settlement, or wring by violence from the natives. Some sickened and sank down by the way, for there was none to help them. Intense misery had made them selfish; and many a poor wretch was abandoned to his fate, to die alone in the wilderness, or, more probably, to be devoured, while living, by the wild animals which roamed over it.

At length, in June, 1542, after somewhat more than a year consumed in their homeward march, the way-worn company came on the elevated plains in the neighborhood of Quito. But how different their aspect from that which they had exhibited on issuing from the gates of the same capital, two years and a half before, with high romantic hope and in all the pride of military array! Their horses gone, their arms broken and rusted, the skins of wild animals instead of clothes hanging loosely about their limbs, their long and matted locks streaming wildly down their shoulders, their faces burned and blackened by the tropical sun, their bodies wasted by famine and sorely disfigured by scars,—it seemed as if the charnel-house had given up its dead, as, with uncertain step, they glided slowly onwards like a troop of dismal spectres! More than half of the four thousand Indians who had accompanied the expedition had perished, and of the Spaniards only eighty, and many of these irretrievably broken in constitution, returned to Quito.[15]

[15] Pedro Pizarro, Descub. y Conq., MS.—Zarate, Conq. del Peru, lib. 4, cap. 5.—Gomara, Hist. de las Ind., cap. 143.—Garcilasso, Com. Real., Parte 2, lib. 3, cap. 15.—Herrera, Hist. General, dec. 7, lib. 3, cap. 14.

The last historian, in dismissing his account of the expedition, passes a panegyric on the courage and constancy of his countrymen, which we must admit to be well deserved.

"Finalemente, Gonçalo Piçarro entró en el Quito, triunfando del valor, i sufrimiento, i de la constancia, recto, é immutable vigor del animo, pues Hombres Humanos no se hallan haver tanto sufrido, ni padecido tantas desventuras." Ibid., ubi supra.

The few Christian inhabitants of the place, with their wives and children, came out to welcome their countrymen. They ministered to them all the relief and refreshment in their power; and, as they listened to the sad recital of their sufferings, they mingled their tears with those of the wanderers. The whole company then entered the capital, where their first act—to their credit be it mentioned—was to go in a body to the church, and offer up thanksgivings to the Almighty for their miraculous preservation through their long and perilous pilgrimage.[16] Such was the end of the expedition to the Amazon; an expedition which, for its dangers and hardships, the length of their duration, and the constancy with which they were endured, stands, perhaps, unmatched in the annals of American discovery.

[16] Zarate, Conq. del Peru, lib. 4, cap. 5.

CHAPTER V

THE ALMAGRO FACTION—THEIR DESPERATE CONDITION—CONSPIRACY
AGAINST FRANCISCO PIZARRO—ASSASSINATION OF PIZARRO—ACTS
OF THE CONSPIRATORS—PIZARRO'S CHARACTER

1541

WHEN Gonzalo Pizarro reached Quito, he received tidings of an event
which showed that his expedition to the Amazon had been even more
fatal to his interests than he had imagined. A revolution had taken place
during his absence, which had changed the whole condition of things in
Peru.

In a preceding chapter we have seen, that, when Hernando Pizarro
returned to Spain, his brother the marquess repaired to Lima, where he
continued to occupy himself with building up his infant capital, and
watching over the general interests of the country. While thus employed,
he gave little heed to a danger that hourly beset his path, and this, too,
in despite of repeated warnings from more circumspect friends.

After the execution of Almagro, his followers, to the number of several hundred, remained scattered through the country; but, however
scattered, still united by a common sentiment of indignation against the
Pizarros, the murderers, as they regarded them, of their leader. The
governor was less the object of these feelings than his brother Hernando, as having been less instrumental in the perpetration of the deed.
Under these circumstances, it was clearly Pizarro's policy to do one of
two things; to treat the opposite faction either as friends, or as open
enemies. He might conciliate the most factious by acts of kindness,
efface the remembrance of past injury, if he could, by present benefits;
in short, prove to them that his quarrel had been with their leader, not
with themselves, and that it was plainly for their interest to come again
under his banner. This would have been the most politic, as well as the
most magnanimous course; and, by augmenting the number of his adherents, would have greatly strengthened his power in the land. But,
unhappily, he had not the magnanimity to pursue it. It was not in the
nature of a Pizarro to forgive an injury, or the man whom he had injured. As he would not, therefore, try to conciliate Almagro's adherents, it was clearly the governor's policy to regard them as enemies,—
not the less so for being in disguise,—and to take such measures as
should disqualify them for doing mischief. He should have followed the

ᴄounsel of his more prudent brother Hernando, and distributed them in different quarters, taking care that no great number should assemble at any one point, or, above all, in the neighborhood of his own residence.

But the governor despised the broken followers of Almagro too heartily to stoop to precautionary measures. He suffered the son of his rival to remain in Lima, where his quarters soon became the resort of the disaffected cavaliers. The young man was well known to most of Almagro's soldiers, having been trained along with them in the camp under his father's eye, and, now that his parent was removed, they naturally transferred their allegiance to the son who survived him.

That the young Almagro, however, might be less able to maintain this retinue of unprofitable followers, he was deprived by Pizarro of a great part of his Indians and lands, while he was excluded from the government of New Toledo, which had been settled on him by his father's testament.[1] Stripped of all means of support, without office or employment of any kind, the men of Chili, for so Almagro's adherents continued to be called, were reduced to the utmost distress. So poor were they, as is the story of the time, that twelve cavaliers, who lodged in the same house, could muster only one cloak among them all; and, with the usual feeling of pride that belongs to the poor *hidalgo*, unwilling to expose their poverty, they wore this cloak by turns, those who had no right to it remaining at home.[2] Whether true or not, the anecdote well illustrates the extremity to which Almagro's faction was reduced. And this distress was rendered yet more galling by the effrontery of their enemies, who, enriched by their forfeitures, displayed before their eyes all the insolent bravery of equipage and apparel that could annoy their feelings.

Men thus goaded by insult and injury were too dangerous to be lightly regarded. But, although Pizarro received various intimations intended to put him on his guard, he gave no heed to them. "Poor devils!" he would exclaim, speaking with contemptuous pity of the men of Chili; "they have had bad luck enough. We will not trouble them further."[3] And so little did he consider them, that he went freely about, as usual, riding without attendants to all parts of the town and to its immediate environs.[4]

News now reached the colony of the appointment of a judge by the Crown to take cognizance of the affairs of Peru. Pizarro, although alarmed by the intelligence, sent orders to have him well entertained on his landing, and suitable accommodations prepared for him on the route. The spirits of Almagro's followers were greatly raised by the tidings. They confidently looked to this high functionary for the redress of their wrongs; and two of their body, clad in suits of mourning, were chosen

---

[1] Carta de Almagro, MS.
[2] Herrera, Hist. General, dec. 6, lib. 8, cap. 0.
[3] Gomara, Hist de las Ind., cap. 144.
[4] Garcilasso, Com. Real., Parte 2, lib. 3, cap. 6.

to go to the north, where the judge was expected to land, and to lay their grievances before him.

But months elapsed, and no tidings came of his arrival, till, at length, a vessel, coming into port, announced that most of the squadron had foundered in the heavy storms on the coast, and that the commissioner had probably perished with them. This was disheartening intelligence to the men of Chili, whose "miseries," to use the words of their young leader, "had become too grievous to be borne."[5] Symptoms of disaffection had already begun openly to manifest themselves. The haughty cavaliers did not always doff their bonnets, on meeting the governor in the street; and on one occasion, three ropes were found suspended from the public gallows, with labels attached to them, bearing the names of Pizarro, Velasquez the judge, and Picado the governor's secretary.[6] This last functionary was peculiarly odious to Almagro and his followers. As his master knew neither how to read nor write, all his communications passed through Picado's hands; and, as the latter was of a hard and arrogant nature, greatly elated by the consequence which his position gave him, he exercised a mischievous influence on the governor's measures. Almagro's poverty-stricken followers were the objects of his open ridicule, and he revenged the insult now offered him by riding before their young leader's residence, displaying a tawdry magnificence in his dress, sparkling with gold and silver, and with the inscription, "For the Men of Chili," set in his bonnet. It was a foolish taunt; but the poor cavaliers who were the object of it, made morbidly sensitive by their sufferings, had not the philosophy to despise it.[7]

At length, disheartened by the long protracted coming of Vaca de Castro, and still more by the recent reports of his loss, Almagro's faction, despairing of redress from a legitimate authority, determined to take it into their own hands. They came to the desperate resolution of assassinating Pizarro. The day named for this was Sunday, the twenty-sixth of June, 1541. The conspirators, eighteen or twenty in number, were to assemble in Almagro's house, which stood in the great square next to the cathedral, and, when the governor was returning from mass, they were to issue forth and fall on him in the street. A white flag, unfurled

[5] "My sufferings," says Almagro, in his letter to the Royal Audience of Panamá, "were enough to unsettle my reason." See his Letter in the original, Appendix, No. 12.

[6] "Hizo Picado el secretario del Marquez mucho daño a muchos, porque el marquez don Francisco Piçarro como no savia ler ni escrivir fiavase del y no hacia mas de lo que el le aconsejava y ansi hizo este mucho mal en estos rreinos, porque el que no andava á su voluntad sirviendole aunque tuviese meritos le destruya y este Picado fue causa de que los de Chile tomasen mas odio al marquez por donde le mataron. Porque queria este que todos lo reverenciasen, y los de chile no hazian caso dél, y por esta causa los perseguia este mucho, y ansi vinieron á hazer lo que hizieron los de Chile." Pedro Pizarro, Descub. y Conq., MS.—Also Zarate, Conq. del Peru, lib. 4, cap. 6.

[7] Pedro Pizarro, Descub. y Conq., MS.—Garcilasso, Com. Real., Parte 2, lib. 3, cap 6.—Herrera, Hist. General, dec. 6, lib. 10, cap. 2.

at the same time from an upper window in the house, was to be the sig‑ nal for the rest of their comrades to move to the support of those im‑ mediately engaged in the execution of the deed.[8]

These arrangements could hardly have been concealed from Almagro, since his own quarters were to be the place of rendezvous. Yet there is no good evidence of his having taken part in the conspiracy.[9] He was, indeed, too young to make it probable that he took a leading part in it. He is represented by contemporary writers to have given promise of many good qualities, though, unhappily, he was not placed in a situa‑ tion favorable for their development. He was the son of an Indian woman of Panamá; but from early years had followed the troubled for‑ tunes of his father, to whom he bore much resemblance in his free and generous nature, as well as in the violence of his passions. His youth and inexperience disqualified him from taking the lead in the perplexing circumstances in which he was placed, and made him little more than a puppet in the hands of others.[10]

The most conspicuous of his advisers was Juan de Herrada, or Rada, as his name is more usually spelt,—a cavalier of respectable family, but who, having early enlisted as a common soldier, had gradually risen to the highest posts in the army by his military talents. At this time he was well advanced in years; but the fires of youth were not quenched in his bosom, and he burned with desire to avenge the wrongs done to his ancient commander. The attachment which he had ever felt for the elder Almagro he seems to have transferred in full measure to his son; and it was apparently with reference to him, even more than to himself, that he devised this audacious plot, and prepared to take the lead in the execution of it.

There was one, however, in the band of conspirators who felt some compunctions of conscience at the part he was acting, and who relieved his bosom by revealing the whole plot to his confessor. The latter lost no time in reporting it to Picado, by whom in turn it was communicated

---

[8] Pedro Pizarro, Descub. y Conq., MS.—Montesinos, Annales, MS., año 1541.— Zarate, Conq. del Peru, lib. 4, cap. 6.

[9] Yet this would seem to be contradicted by Almagro's own letter to the audi‑ ence of Panamá, in which he states, that, galled by intolerable injuries, he and his followers had resolved to take the remedy into their own hands, by entering the governor's house and seizing his person. It is certain, however, that in the full ac‑ counts we have of the affair by writers who had the best means of information, we do not find Almagro's name mentioned as one who took an active part in the tragic drama. His own letter merely expresses that it was his purpose to have taken part in it, with the further declaration, that it was simply to seize, not to slay, Pizarro;—a declaration that no one who reads the history of the transaction will be very ready to credit.

[10] "Mancebo virtuoso, i de grande Animo, i bien enseñado: i especialmente se navia exercitado mucho en cavalgar a Caballo, de ambas sillas, lo qual hacia con mucha gracia, i destreça, i tambien en escrevir, i leer, lo qual hacia mas liberal‑ mente, i mejor de lo que requeria su Profesion. De este tenia cargo, como Aio Juan de Herrada." Zarate, Conq. del Peru, lib. 4, cap. 6.

to Pizarro. But, strange to say, it made little more impression on the governor's mind than the vague warnings he had so frequently received. "It is a device of the priest," said he; "he wants a mitre." [11] Yet he repeated the story to the judge Velasquez, who, instead of ordering the conspirators to be seized, and the proper steps taken for learning the truth of the accusation, seemed to be possessed with the same infatuation as Pizarro; and he bade the governor be under no apprehension, "for no harm should come to him, while the rod of justice," not a metaphorical badge of authority in Castile, "was in his hands." [12] Still, to obviate every possibility of danger, it was deemed prudent for Pizarro to abstain from going to mass on Sunday, and to remain at home on pretence of illness.

On the day appointed, Rada and his companions met in Almagro's house, and waited with anxiety for the hour when the governor should issue from the church. But great was their consternation, when they learned that he was not there, but was detained at home, as currently reported, by illness. Little doubting that their design was discovered, they felt their own ruin to be the inevitable consequence, and that, too, without enjoying the melancholy consolation of having struck the blow for which they had incurred it. Greatly perplexed, some were for disbanding, in the hope that Pizarro might, after all, be ignorant of their design. But most were for carrying it into execution at once, by assaulting him in his own house. The question was summarily decided by one of the party, who felt that in this latter course lay their only chance of safety. Throwing open the doors, he rushed out, calling on his comrades "to follow him, or he would proclaim the purpose for which they had met." There was no longer hesitation, and the cavaliers issued forth, with Rada at their head, shouting, as they went, "Long live the king! Death to the tyrant!" [13]

It was the hour of dinner, which, in this primitive age of the Spanish colonies, was at noon. Yet numbers, roused by the cries of the assailants, came out into the square to inquire the cause. "They are going to kill the marquess," some said very coolly; others replied, "It is Picado." No one stirred in their defence. The power of Pizarro was not seated in the hearts of his people.

As the conspirators traversed the *plaza*, one of the party made a circuit to avoid a little pool of water that lay in their path. "What!"

[11] "Pues un dia antes un sacerdote clerigo llamado Benao fue de noche y avisso a Picado el secreptario y dixole mañana Domingo quando el marquez saliere á misa tienen concertado los de Chile de matar al marquez y á vos y á sus amigos. Esto me a dicho vno en confision para que os venga á avisar. Pues savido esto Picado se fue luego y lo conto al marquez y el le rrespondio. Ese clerigo obispado quiere." Pedro Pizarro, Descub. y Conq., MS.

[12] "El Juan Velazquez le dixo. No tema vuestra señoria que mientras yo tuviere esta vara en la mano nadie se atrevera." Pedro Pizarro, Descub. y Conq., MS.

[13] Herrera, Hist. General, dec. 6, lib. 10, cap. 6.—Pedro Pizarro, Descub. y Conq., MS.—Zarate, Conq. del Peru, lib. 4, cap. 8.—Naharro, Rel. Sumaria, MS.—Carta del Maestro, Martin de Arauco, MS., 15 de Julio, 1541.

exclaimed Rada, "afraid of wetting your feet, when you are to wade up to your knees in blood!" And he ordered the man to give up the enter-prise and go home to his quarters. The anecdote is characteristic.[14]

The governor's palace stood on the opposite side of the square. It was approached by two courtyards. The entrance to the outer one was pro-tected by a massive gate, capable of being made good against a hundred men or more. But it was left open, and the assailants, hurrying through to the inner court, still shouting their fearful battle-cry, were met by two domestics loitering in the yard. One of these they struck down, The other, flying in all haste towards the house, called out, "Help, help! the men of Chili are all coming to murder the marquess!"

Pizarro at this time was at dinner, or, more probably, had just dined. He was surrounded by a party of friends, who had dropped in, it seems, after mass, to inquire after the state of his health, some of whom had remained to partake of his repast. Among these was Don Martinez de Alcantara, Pizarro's half-brother by the mother's side, the judge Velas-quez, the bishop elect of Quito, and several of the principal cavaliers in the place, to the number of fifteen or twenty. Some of them, alarmed by the uproar in the court-yard, left the saloon, and, running down to the first landing on the stairway, inquired into the cause of the disturb-ance. No sooner were they informed of it by the cries of the servant, than they retreated with precipitation into the house; and, as they had no mind to abide the storm unarmed, or at best imperfectly armed, as most of them were, they made their way to a corridor that overlooked the gardens, into which they easily let themselves down without injury. Velas-quez, the judge, the better to have the use of his hands in the descent, held his rod of office in his mouth, thus taking care, says a caustic old chronicler, not to falsify his assurance, that "no harm should come to Pizarro while the rod of justice was in his hands"! [15]

Meanwhile, the marquess, learning the nature of the tumult, called out to Francisco de Chaves, an officer high in his confidence, and who was in the outer apartment opening on the staircase, to secure the door, while he and his brother Alcantara buckled on their armour. Had this order, coolly given, been as coolly obeyed, it would have saved them all, since the entrance could easily have been maintained against a much larger force, till the report of the cavaliers who had fled had brought

---

[14] "Gomez Perez por haver alli agua derramada de una acequia, rodeo algun tanto por no mojarse; reparó en ello Juan de Rada, y entrandose atrevido por el agua le dijo: ¿Bamos á bañarnos en sangre humana, y rehusais mojaros los pies en agua? Ea volveos. hizolo volver y no asistió al hecho." Montesinos, Annales, MS., año 1541.

[15] "En lo qual no paresce haver quebrantado su palabra, porque despues huiendo (como adelante se dirà) a tiempo, que quisieron matar al Marques, se hecho de vna Ventana abajo, à la Huerta, llevando la Vara en la boca." Zarate, Conq. del Peru, lib. 4, cap. 7.

Pedro Pizarro, Descub. y Conq., MS.—Naharro, Relacion Sumaria, MS.—Carta del Maestro, Martin de Arauco, MS.—Carta de Fray Vicente de Valverde a la Audiencia de Panamá, MS., desde Tumbez, 15 Nov. 1541.—Gomara, Hist. de las Ind., cap. 145.

support to Pizarro. But unfortunately, Chaves, disobeying his commander, half opened the door, and attempted to enter into a parley with the conspirators. The latter had now reached the head of the stairs, and cut short the debate by running Chaves through the body, and tumbling his corpse down into the area below. For a moment they were kept at bay by the attendants of the slaughtered cavalier, but these, too, were quickly despatched; and Rada and his companions, entering the apartment, hurried across it, shouting out, "Where is the marquess? Death to the tyrant!"

Martinez de Alcantara, who in the adjoining room was assisting his brother to buckle on his mail, no sooner saw that the entrance to the antechamber had been gained, than he sprang to the doorway of the apartment, and, assisted by two young men, pages of Pizarro, and by one or two cavaliers in attendance, endeavored to resist the approach of the assailants. A desperate struggle now ensued. Blows were given on both sides, some of which proved fatal, and two of the conspirators were slain, while Alcantara and his brave companions were repeatedly wounded.

At length, Pizarro, unable, in the hurry of the moment, to adjust the fastenings of his cuirass, threw it away, and, enveloping one arm in his cloak, with the other seized his sword, and sprang to his brother's assistance. It was too late; for Alcantara was already staggering under the loss of blood, and soon fell to the ground. Pizarro threw himself on his invaders, like a lion roused in his lair, and dealt his blows with as much rapidity and force, as if age had no power to stiffen his limbs. "What ho!" he cried, "traitors! have you come to kill me in my own house?" The conspirators drew back for a moment, as two of their body fell under Pizarro's sword; but they quickly rallied, and, from their superior numbers, fought at great advantage by relieving one another in the assault. Still the passage was narrow, and the struggle lasted for some minutes, till both of Pizarro's pages were stretched by his side, when Rada, impatient of the delay, called out, "Why are we so long about it? Down with the tyrant!" and taking one of his companions, Narvaez, in his arms, he thrust him against the marquess. Pizarro, instantly grappling with his opponent, ran him through with his sword. But at that moment he received a wound in the throat, and reeling, he sank on the floor, while the swords of Rada and several of the conspirators were plunged into his body. "Jesu!" exclaimed the dying man, and, tracing a cross with his finger on the bloody floor, he bent down his head to kiss it, when a stroke, more friendly than the rest, put an end to his existence.[16]

[16] Zarate, Conq. del Peru, lib. 4, cap. 8.—Naharro, Relacion Sumaria, MS.—Pedro Pizarro, Descub. y Conq., MS.—Herrera, Hist. General, dec. 6, lib. 10, cap. 6.—Carta de la Justicia y Regimiento de la Ciudad de los Reyes, MS., 15 de Julio, 1541.—Carta del Maestro, Martin de Arauco, MS.—Carta de Fray Vicente Valverde, desde Tumbez, MS.—Gomara, Hist. de las Ind., ubi supra.—Montesinos, Annales, MS., año 1541.

Pizarro y Orellana seems to have no doubt that his slaughtered kinsman died

The conspirators, having accomplished their bloody deed, rushed into the street, and, brandishing their dripping weapons, shouted out, "The tyrant is dead! The laws are restored! Long live our master the emperor, and his governor, Almagro!" The men of Chili, roused by the cheering cry, now flocked in from every side to join the banner of Rada, who soon found himself at the head of nearly three hundred followers, all armed and prepared to support his authority. A guard was placed over the houses of the principal partisans of the late governor, and their persons were taken into custody. Pizarro's house, and that of his secretary Picado, were delivered up to pillage; and a large booty in gold and silver was found in the former. Picado himself took refuge in the dwelling of Riquelme, the treasurer; but his hiding-place was detected, —betrayed, according to some accounts, by the looks, though not the words, of the treasurer himself,—and he was dragged forth and committed to a secure prison.[17] The whole city was thrown into consternation, as armed bodies hurried to and fro on their several errands, and all who were not in the faction of Almagro trembled lest they should be involved in the proscription of their enemies. So great was the disorder, that the Brothers of Mercy, turning out in a body, paraded the streets in solemn procession, with the host elevated in the air, in hopes by the presence of the sacred symbol to calm the passions of the multitude.

But no other violence was offered by Rada and his followers than to apprehend a few suspected persons, and to seize upon horses and arms wherever they were to be found. The municipality was then summoned to recognize the authority of Almagro; the refractory were ejected without ceremony from their offices, and others of the Chili faction were substituted. The claims of the new aspirant were fully recognized; and young Almagro, parading the streets on horseback, and escorted by a well-armed body of cavaliers, was proclaimed by sound of trumpet governor and captain-general of Peru.

Meanwhile, the mangled bodies of Pizarro and his faithful adherents were left weltering in their blood. Some were for dragging forth the

---

in the odor of sanctity.—"Alli le acabaron los traidores enemigos, dandole cruelis-simas heridas, con que acabó el Julio Cesar Español, estando tan en si que pidi-endo confession con gran acto de contricion, haziendo la señal de la Cruz con su misma sangre, y besandola murió." Varones Ilustres, p. 186.

According to one authority, the mortal blow was given by a soldier named Borregan, who, when Pizarro was down, struck him on the back of the head with a water-jar, which he had snatched from the table. (Herrera, Hist. General, dec. 6, lib. 10, cap 6.) Considering the hurry and confusion of the scene, the different narratives of the catastrophe, though necessarily differing in minute details, have a remarkable agreement with one another.

[17] "No se olvidaron de buscar à Antonio Picado, i iendo en casa del Tesorero Alonso Riquelme, èl mismo iba diciendo: No sè adonde està el Señor Picado, i con los ojos le mostraba, i le hallaron debaxo de la cama." Herrera, Hist. General, dec. 6, lib. 10, cap. 7.

We find Riquelme's name, soon after this, enrolled among the municipality of Lima, showing that he found it convenient to give in his temporary adhesion, at least, to Almagro. Carta de la Justicia y Regimiento de la Ciudad de los Reyes, MS.

governor's corpse to the market-place, and fixing his head upon a gibbet. But Almagro was secretly prevailed on to grant the entreaties of Pizarro's friends, and allow his interment. This was stealthily and hastily performed, in the fear of momentary interruption. A faithful attendant and his wife, with a few black domestics, wrapped the body in a cotton cloth and removed it to the cathedral. A grave was hastily dug in an obscure corner, the services were hurried through, and, in secrecy, and in darkness dispelled only by the feeble glimmering of a few tapers furnished by these humble menials, the remains of Pizarro, rolled in their bloody shroud, were consigned to their kindred dust. Such was the miserable end of the Conqueror of Peru,—of the man who but a few hours before had lorded it over the land with as absolute a sway as was possessed by its hereditary Incas. Cut off in the broad light of day, in the heart of his own capital, in the very midst of those who had been his companions in arms and shared with him his triumphs and his spoils, he perished like a wretched outcast. "There was none, even," in the expressive language of the chronicler, "to say, God forgive him!" [18]

A few years later, when tranquillity was restored to the country, Pizarro's remains were placed in a sumptuous coffin and deposited under a monument in a conspicuous part of the cathedral. And in 1607, when time had thrown its friendly mantle over the past, and the memory of his errors and his crimes was merged in the consideration of the great services he had rendered to the Crown by the extension of her colonial empire, his bones were removed to the new cathedral, and allowed to repose side by side with those of Mendoza, the wise and good viceroy of Peru.[19]

Pizarro was, probably, not far from sixty-five years of age at the time of his death; though this, it must be added, is but loose conjecture, since there exists no authentic record of the date of his birth.[20] He was never married; but by an Indian princess of the Inca blood, daughter of Atahuallpa and granddaughter of the great Huayna Capac, he had two children, a son and a daughter. Both survived him; but the son did not live to manhood. Their mother, after Pizarro's death, wedded a Spanish cavalier, named Ampuero, and removed with him to Spain. Her daughter Francisca accompanied her, and was there subsequently married to her uncle Hernando Pizarro, then a prisoner in the Mota del Medina. Neither the title nor estates of the Marquess Francisco descended to his illegitimate offspring. But in the third generation, in the reign of Philip the Fourth, the title was revived in favor of Don Juan Hernando Pizarro, who, out of gratitude for the services of his ancestor, was created Mar-

---

[18] "Murió pidiendo confesion, i haciendo la Cruz, sin que nadie dijese, Dios te perdone." Gomara, Hist. de las Ind., cap 144.

MS. de Caravantes.—Zarate, Conq. del Peru, lib. 4, cap. 8.—Carta del Maestro, Martin de Arauco, MS.—Carta de Fray Vicente Valverde, desde Tumbez, MS.

[19] "Sus huesos encerrados en una caxa guarnecida de terciopelo morado con nassa manos de oro que yo he visto." MS. de Caravantes.

[20] Ante, Book 2, chap. 2, note 1.

quess of the Conquest, *Marques de la Conquista*, with a liberal pension
from government. His descendants, bearing the same title of nobility,
are still to be found, it is said, at Truxillo, in the ancient province of
Estremadura, the original birthplace of the Pizarros.[21]

Pizarro's person has been already described. He was tall in stature,
well-proportioned, and with a countenance not unpleasing. Bred in
camps, with nothing of the polish of a court, he had a soldier-like bearing, and the air of one accustomed to command. But though not polished, there was no embarrassment or rusticity in his address, which,
where it served his purpose, could be plausible and even insinuating.
The proof of it is the favorable impression made by him, on presenting
himself, after his second expedition—stranger as he was to all its forms
and usages—at the punctilious court of Castile.

Unlike many of his countrymen, he had no passion for ostentatious
dress, which he regarded as an incumbrance. The costume which he
most affected on public occasions was a black cloak, with a white hat,
and shoes of the same color; the last, it is said, being in imitation of the
Great Captain, whose character he had early learned to admire in Italy,
but to which his own, certainly, bore very faint resemblance.[22]

He was temperate in eating, drank sparingly, and usually rose an
hour before dawn. He was punctual in attendance to business, and
shrunk from no toil. He had, indeed, great powers of patient endurance.
Like most of his nation, he was fond of play, and cared little for the
quality of those with whom he played; though, when his antagonist
could not afford to lose, he would allow himself, it is said, to be the loser;
a mode of conferring an obligation much commended by a Castilian
writer, for its delicacy.[23]

Though avaricious, it was in order to spend and not to hoard. His
ample treasures, more ample than those, probably, that ever before fell
to the lot of an adventurer,[24] were mostly dissipated in his enterprises,

[21] MSS. de Caravantes.—Quintana, Españoles Celebres, tom. II., p. 417.

See also the *discurso, Legal y Político*, annexed by Pizarro y Orellana to his bulky
tome, in which that cavalier urges the claims of Pizarro. It is in the nature of a
memorial to Philip IV. in behalf of Pizarro's descendants, in which the writer, after
setting forth the manifold services of the Conqueror, shows how little his posterity
had profited by the magnificent grants conferred on nim by the Crown The argument of the Royal Counsellor was not without its effect.

[22] Gomara, Hist. de las Ind., cap. 144.—Zarate, Conq. del Peru, lib. 4, cap. 9.
The portrait of Pizarro, in the viceregal palace at Lima, represents him in a
citizen's dress, with a sable cloak,—the *capa y espada* of a Spanish gentleman.
Each panel in the spacious *sala de los Vireyes* was reserved for the portrait of a
viceroy. The long file is complete, from Pizarro to Pezuela; and it is a curious fact,
noticed by Stevenson, that the last panel was exactly filled when the reign of the
viceroys was abruptly terminated by the Revolution. (Residence in South America,
vol. I. p. 228.) It is a singular coincidence that the same thing should have oc-
cured at Venice, where, if my memory serves me, the last niche reserved for the
effigies of its doges was just filled, when the ancient aristocracy was overturned.

[23] Garcilasso, Com. Real., Parte 2, lib. 3, cap. 9.

[24] "Halló, i tuvo mas Oro, i Plata, que otro ningun Español de quantos han
pasado á Indias, ni que ninguno de quantos Capitanes han sido por el Mundo."
Gomara, Hist. de las Ind., cap. 144.

his architectural works, and schemes of public improvement, which, in a country where gold and silver might be said to have lost their value from their abundance, absorbed an incredible amount of money. While he regarded the whole country, in a manner, as his own, and distributed it freely among his captains, it is certain that the princely grant of a territory with twenty thousand vassals, made to him by the Crown, was never carried into effect; nor did his heirs ever reap the benefit of it.[25]

To a man possessed of the active energies of Pizarro, sloth was the greatest evil. The excitement of play was in a manner necessary to a spirit accustomed to the habitual stimulants of war and adventure. His uneducated mind had no relish for more refined, intellectual recreation. The deserted foundling had neither been taught to read nor write. This has been disputed by some, but it is attested by unexceptionable authorities.[26] Montesinos says, indeed, that Pizarro, on his first voyage, tried to learn to read; but the impatience of his temper prevented it, and he contented himself with learning to sign his name.[27] But Montesinos was not a contemporary historian. Pedro Pizarro, his companion in arms, expressly tells us he could neither read nor write;[28] and Zarate, another contemporary, well acquainted with the Conquerors, confirms this statement, and adds, that Pizarro could not so much as sign his name.[29] This was done by his secretary—Picado, in his latter years— while the governor merely made the customary *rúbrica* or flourish at the sides of his name. This is the case with the instruments I have examined, in which his signature, written probably by his secretary, or his title of *Marques*, in later life substituted for his name, is garnished with a flourish at the ends, executed in as bungling a manner as if done by the hand of a ploughman. Yet we must not estimate this deficiency as we should in this period of general illumination,—general, at least, in

[25] MS. de Caravantes.—Pizarro y Orellana, Discurso Leg. y Pol., ap. Varones Ilust. Gonzalo Pizarro, when taken prisoner by President Gasca, challenged him to point out any quarter of the country in which the royal grant had been carried into effect by a specific assignment of land to his brother. See Garcilasso, Com. Real., Parte 2, lib. 5, cap. 36.

[26] Even so experienced a person as Muñoz seems to have fallen into this error. On one of Pizarro's letters I find the following copy of an autograph memorandum by this eminent scholar:—*Carta de Francisco Pizarro, su letra i buena letra.*

[27] "En este viage trató Pizarro de aprender á leer; no le dió su viveza lugar á ello; contentose solo con saber firmar, de lo que se veia Almagro, y decia, que firmar sin saber leer era lo mismo que recibir herida, sin poder darla. En adelante firmó siempre Pizarro por si, y por Almagro su Secretario." Montesinos, Annales, MS., año 1525.

[28] "Porque el marquez don Françisco Piçarro como no savia ler ni escrivir." Pedro Pizarro, Descub. y Conq., MS.

[29] "Siendo personas," says the author, speaking both of Pizarro and Almagro, "no solamente, no leidas, pero que de todo punto no sabian leer ni aun firmar, que en ellos fue cosa de gran defecto. . . Fue el Marquès tan confiado de sus Criados, i Amigos, que todos los Despachos, que hacia, asi de Governacion, como de Repartimientos de Indios. libraba haciendo èl dos señales, en medic de las quales Antonio Picado, su Secretario, firmaba el nombre de Francisco Piçarro." Zarate, Conq. del Peru, lib. 4, cap. 9.

our own fortunate country. Reading and writing, so universal now, in the beginning of the sixteenth century might be regarded in the light of accomplishments; and all who have occasion to consult the autograph memorials of that time will find the execution of them, even by persons of the highest rank, too often such as would do little credit to a school-boy of the present day.

Though bold in action and not easily turned from his purpose, Pizarro was slow in arriving at a decision. This gave him an appearance of irresolution foreign to his character.[30] Perhaps the consciousness of this led him to adopt the custom of saying "No," at first, to applicants for favor; and afterwards, at leisure, to revise his judgment, and grant what seemed to him expedient. He took the opposite course from his comrade Almagro, who, it was observed, generally said "Yes," but too often failed to keep his promise. This was characteristic of the careless and easy na-ture of the latter, governed by impulse rather than principle.[31]

It is hardly necessary to speak of the courage of a man pledged to such a career as that of Pizarro. Courage, indeed, was a cheap quality among the Spanish adventurers, for danger was their element. But he pos-sessed something higher than mere animal courage, in that constancy of purpose which was rooted too deeply in his nature to be shaken by the wildest storms of fortune. It was this inflexible constancy which formed the key to his character, and constituted the secret of his success. A re-markable evidence of it was given in his first expedition, among the mangroves and dreary marshes of Choco. He saw his followers pining around him under the blighting malaria, wasting before an invisible enemy, and unable to strike a stroke in their own defence. Yet his spirit did not yield, nor did he falter in his enterprise.

There is something oppressive to the imagination in this war against nature. In the struggle of man against man, the spirits are raised by a contest conducted on equal terms; but in a war with the elements, we feel, that, however bravely we may contend, we can have no power to control. Nor are we cheered on by the prospect of glory in such a con-test; for, in the capricious estimate of human glory, the silent endur-ance of privations, however painful, is little, in comparison with the ostentatious trophies of victory. The laurel of the hero—alas for hu-manity that it should be so!—grows best on the battle-field.

This inflexible spirit of Pizarro was shown still more strongly, when, in the little island of Gallo, he drew the line on the sand, which was to separate him and his handful of followers from their country and from

---

[30] This tardiness of resolve has even led Herrera to doubt his resolution alto-gether; a judgment certainly contradicted by the whole tenor of his history. "Por-que aunque era astuto, i recatado, por la maior parte fue de animo suspenso, i no mui resoluto." Hist. General, dec. 5, lib. 7, cap. 13.

[31] "Tenia por costumbre de quando algo le pedian dezir siempre de no. esto dezia el que hazia por no faltar su palabra, y no obstante que dezia no, correspondia con hazer lo que le pedian no aviendo inconvenimente. . . . Don Diego de Almagro hera á la contra que á todos dezia si, y con pocos lo cumplia." Pedro Pizarro. Descub. y Conq., MS.

civilized man. He trusted that his own constancy would give strength
to the feeble, and rally brave hearts around him for the prosecution of
his enterprise. He looked with confidence to the future, and he did not
miscalculate. This was heroic, and wanted only a nobler motive for its
object to constitute the true moral sublime.

Yet the same feature in his character was displayed in a manner
scarcely less remarkable, when, landing on the coast, and ascertaining
the real strength and civilization of the Incas, he persisted in marching
into the interior at the head of a force of less than two hundred men.
In this he undoubtedly proposed to himself the example of Cortés, so
contagious to the adventurous spirits of that day, and especially to
Pizarro, engaged, as he was, in a similar enterprise. Yet the hazard assumed by Pizarro was far greater than that of the Conqueror of Mexico,
whose force was nearly three times as large, while the terrors of the
Inca name—however justified by the result—were as widely spread as
those of the Aztecs.

It was doubtless in imitation of the same captivating model, that
Pizarro planned the seizure of Atahuallpa. But the situations of the two
Spanish captains were as dissimilar as the manner in which their acts of
violence were conducted. The wanton massacre of the Peruvians resembled that perpetrated by Alvarado in Mexico, and might have been
attended with consequences as disastrous, if the Peruvian character had
been as fierce as that of the Aztecs.[32] But the blow which roused the
latter to madness broke the tamer spirits of the Peruvians. It was a
bold stroke, which left so much to chance, that it scarcely merits the
name of policy.

When Pizarro landed in the country, he found it distracted by a contest for the crown. It would seem to have been for his interest to play
off one party against the other, throwing his own weight into the scale
that suited him. Instead of this, he resorted to an act of audacious violence which crushed them both at a blow. His subsequent career afforded
no scope for the profound policy displayed by Cortés, when he gathered conflicting nations under his banner, and directed them against a
common foe. Still less did he have the opportunity of displaying the
tactics and admirable strategy of his rival. Cortés conducted his military
operations on the scientific principles of a great captain at the head of
a powerful host. Pizarro appears only as an adventurer, a fortunate
knight-errant. By one bold stroke, he broke the spell which had so long
held the land under the dominion of the Incas. The spell was broken,
and the airy fabric of their empire, built on the superstition of ages,
vanished at a touch. This was good fortune, rather than the result of
policy.

Pizarro was eminently perfidious. Yet nothing is more opposed to
sound policy. One act of perfidy fully established becomes the ruin of its
author. The man who relinquishes confidence in his good faith gives up

---

[32] See Conquest of Mexico, Book 4, chap. 8.

the best basis for future operations. Who will knowingly build on a quicksand? By his perfidious treatment of Almagro, Pizarro alienated the minds of the Spaniards. By his perfidious treatment of Atahuallpa, and subsequently of the Inca Manco, he disgusted the Peruvians. The name of Pizarro became a by-word for perfidy. Almagro took his revenge in a civil war; Manco in an insurrection which nearly cost Pizarro his dominion. The civil war terminated in a conspiracy which cost him his life. Such were the fruits of his policy. Pizarro may be regarded as a cunning man; but not, as he has been often eulogized by his countrymen, as a politic one.

When Pizarro obtained possession of Cuzco, he found a country well advanced in the arts of civilization; institutions under which the people lived in tranquillity and personal safety; the mountains and the uplands whitened with flocks; the valleys teeming with the fruits of a scientific husbandry; the granaries and warehouses filled to overflowing; the whole land rejoicing in its abundance; and the character of the nation, softened under the influence of the mildest and most innocent form of superstition, well prepared for the reception of a higher and a Christian civilization. But, far from introducing this, Pizarro delivered up the conquered races to his brutal soldiery; the sacred cloisters were abandoned to their lust; the towns and villages were given up to pillage; the wretched natives were parcelled out like slaves, to toil for their conquerors in the mines; the flocks were scattered, and wantonly destroyed; the granaries were dissipated; the beautiful contrivances for the more perfect culture of the soil were suffered to fall into decay; the paradise was converted into a desert. Instead of profiting by the ancient forms of civilization, Pizarro preferred to efface every vestige of them from the land, and on their ruin to erect the institutions of his own country. Yet these institutions did little for the poor Indian, held in iron bondage. It was little to him that the shores of the Pacific were studded with rising communities and cities, the marts of a flourishing commerce. He had no share in the goodly heritage. He was an alien in the land of his fathers.

The religion of the Peruvian, which directed him to the worship of that glorious luminary which is the best representative of the might and beneficence of the Creator, is perhaps the purest form of superstition that has existed among men. Yet it was much, that, under the new order of things, and through the benevolent zeal of the missionaries, some glimmerings of a nobler faith were permitted to dawn on his darkened soul. Pizarro, himself, cannot be charged with manifesting any overweening solicitude for the propagation of the Faith. He was no bigot, like Cortés. Bigotry is the perversion of the religious principle; but the principle itself was wanting in Pizarro. The conversion of the heathen was a predominant motive with Cortés in his expedition. It was not a vain boast. He would have sacrificed his life for it at any time; and more than once, by his indiscreet zeal, he actually did place his life and the success of his enterprise in jeopardy. It was his great purpose to purify the land from the brutish abominations of the Aztecs, by substituting the religion of Jesus. This gave to his expedition the character of a crusade. It furnished the best apology for the Conquest, and does more than all other considerations towards enlisting our sympathies on the side of the conquerors.

But Pizarro's ruling motives, so far as they can be scanned by human judgment, were avarice and ambition. The good missionaries, indeed, followed in his train to scatter the seeds of spiritual truth, and the Spanish government, as usual, directed its beneficent legislation to the conversion of the natives. But the moving power with Pizarro and his followers was the lust of gold. This was the real stimulus to their toil, the price of perfidy, the true guerdon of their victories. This gave a base and mercenary character to their enterprise; and when we contrast the ferocious cupidity of the conquerors with the mild and inoffensive manners of the conquered, our sympathies, the sympathies even of the Spaniard, are necessarily thrown into the scale of the Indian.[33]

But as no picture is without its lights, we must not, in justice to Pizarro, dwell exclusively on the darker features of his portrait. There was no one of her sons to whom Spain was under larger obligations for extent of empire; for his hand won for her the richest of the Indian jewels that once sparkled in her imperial diadem. When we contemplate the perils he braved, the sufferings he patiently endured, the incredible obstacles he overcame, the magnificent results he effected with his single arm, as it were, unaided by the government,—though neither a good, nor a great man in the highest sense of that term, it is impossible not to regard him as a very extraordinary one.

Nor can we fairly omit to notice, in extenuation of his errors, the circumstances of his early life; for, like Almagro, he was the son of sin and

---

[33] The following vigorous lines of Southey condense, in a small compass, the most remarkable traits of Pizarro. The poet's epitaph may certainly be acquitted of the imputation, generally well deserved, of flattery towards the subject of it.

"FOR A COLUMN AT TRUXILLO.

"Pizarro here was born; a greater name
The list of Glory boasts not. Toil and Pain,
Famine, and hostile Elements, and Hosts
Embattled, failed to check him in his course,
Not to be wearied, not to be deterred,
Not to be overcome. A mighty realm
He overran, and with relentless arm
Slew or enslaved its unoffending sons,
And wealth and power and fame were his rewards
There is another world, beyond the grave,
According to their deeds where men are judged.
O Reader! if thy daily bread be earned
By daily labor,—yea, however low,
However wretched, be thy lot assigned,
Thank thou, with deepest gratitude, the God
Who made thee, that thou art not such as he."

sorrow, early cast upon the world to seek his fortunes as he might. In his young and tender age he was to take the impression of those into whose society he was thrown. And when was it the lot of the needy outcast to fall into that of the wise and the virtuous? His lot was cast among the licentious inmates of a camp, the school of rapine, whose only law was the sword, and who looked on the wretched Indian and his heritage as their rightful spoil.

Who does not shudder at the thought of what his own fate might have been, trained in such a school? The amount of crime does not necessarily show the criminality of the agent. History, indeed, is concerned with the former, that it may be recorded as a warning to mankind; but it is He alone who knoweth the heart, the strength of the temptation, and the means of resisting it, that can determine the measure of the guilt.

CHAPTER VI

MOVEMENTS OF THE CONSPIRATORS—ADVANCE OF VACA DE CASTRO—
PROCEEDINGS OF ALMAGRO—PROGRESS OF THE GOVERNOR—THE
FORCES APPROACH EACH OTHER—BLOODY PLAINS OF CHUPAS—
CONDUCT OF VACA DE CASTRO

1541—1543

THE first step of the conspirators, after securing possession of the capital, was to send to the different cities, proclaiming the revolution which
had taken place, and demanding the recognition of the young Almagro
as governor of Peru. Where the summons was accompanied by a military force, as at Truxillo and Arequipa, it was obeyed without much
cavil. But in other cities a colder assent was given, and in some the
requisition was treated with contempt. In Cuzco, the place of most importance next to Lima, a considerable number of the Almagro faction
secured the ascendency of their party; and such of the magistracy as
resisted were ejected from their offices to make room for others of a
more accommodating temper. But the loyal inhabitants of the city, dissatisfied with this proceeding, privately sent to one of Pizarro's captains, named Alvarez de Holguin, who lay with a considerable force in
the neighborhood; and that officer, entering the place, soon dispos-
sessed the new dignitaries of their honors, and restored the ancient capital to its allegiance.

The conspirators experienced a still more determined opposition
from Alonso de Alvarado, one of the principal captains of Pizarro,—
defeated, as the reader will remember, by the elder Almagro at the
bridge of Abancay,—and now lying in the north with a corps of about
two hundred men, as good troops as any in the land. That officer, on
receiving tidings of his general's assassination, instantly wrote to the
Licentiate Vaca de Castro, advising him of the state of affairs in Peru,
and urging him to quicken his march towards the south.[1]

This functionary had been sent out by the Spanish Crown, as noticed
in a preceding chapter, to coöperate with Pizarro in restoring tranquillity to the country, with authority to assume the government himself, in
case of that commander's death. After a long and tempestuous voyage,
he had landed, in the spring of 1541, at the port of Buena Ventura, and,

[1] Zarate, Conq. del Peru, lib. 4, cap. 13.—Herrera, Hist. General, dec. 6, lib. 10,
cap. 7.—Declaracion de Uscategui, MS.—Carta del Maestro, Martin de Arauco, MS.
—Carta de Fray Vicente Valverde, desde Tumbez, MS.

disgusted with the dangers of the sea, preferred to continue his wearisome journey by land. But so enfeebled was he by the hardships he had undergone, that it was full three months before he reached Popayan, where he received the astounding tidings of the death of Pizarro. This was the contingency which had been provided for, with such judicious forecast, in his instructions. Yet he was sorely perplexed by the difficulties of his situation. He was a stranger in the land, with a very imperfect knowledge of the country, without an armed force to support him, without even the military science which might be supposed necessary to avail himself of it. He knew nothing of the degree of Almagro's influence, or of the extent to which the insurrection had spread,—nothing, in short, of the dispositions of the people among whom he was cast.

In such an emergency, a feebler spirit might have listened to the counsels of those who advised to return to Panamá, and stay there until he had mustered a sufficient force to enable him to take the field against the insurgents with advantage. But the courageous heart of Vaca de Castro shrunk from a step which would proclaim his incompetency to the task assigned him. He had confidence in his own resources, and in the virtue of the commission under which he acted. He relied, too, on the habitual loyalty of the Spaniards; and, after mature deliberation, he determined to go forward, and trust to events for accomplishing the objects of his mission.

He was confirmed in this purpose by the advices he now received from Alvarado; and without longer delay, he continued his march towards Quito. Here he was well received by Gonzalo Pizarro's lieutenant, who had charge of the place during his commander's absence on his expedition to the Amazon. The licentiate was also joined by Benalcazar, the conqueror of Quito, who brought a small reinforcement, and offered personally to assist him in the prosecution of his enterprise. He now displayed the royal commission, empowering him, on Pizarro's death, to assume the government. That contingency had arrived, and Vaca de Castro declared his purpose to exercise the authority conferred on him. At the same time, he sent emissaries to the principal cities, requiring their obedience to him as the lawful representative of the Crown, —taking care to employ discreet persons on the mission, whose character would have weight with the citizens. He then continued his march slowly towards the south.[2]

He was willing by his deliberate movements to give time for his summons to take effect, and for the fermentation caused by the late extraordinary events to subside. He reckoned confidently on the loyalty

[2] Herrera, Hist. General, dec. 6, lib. 10, cap. 4.—Carta de Benalcazar al Emperador, desde Cali, MS., 20 Septiembre, 1542.

Benalcazar urged Vaca de Castro to assume only the title of Judge, and not that of Governor, which would conflict with the pretensions of Almagro to that part of the country known as New Toledo, and bequeathed to him by his father "Porque yo le avisé muchas veces no entrase en la tierra como Governador, sino como Juez de V. M. que venia á desagraviar á los agraviados, porque todos lo rescibirian de buena gana." Ubi supra.

which made the Spaniard unwilling, unless in cases of the last ex=
tremity, to come into collision with the royal authority; and, however
much this popular sentiment might be disturbed by temporary gusts
of passion, he trusted to the habitual current of their feelings for giving
the people a right direction. In this he did not miscalculate; for so deep-
rooted was the principle of loyalty in the ancient Spaniard, that ages
of oppression and misrule could alone have induced him to shake off his
allegiance. Sad it is, but not strange, that the length of time passed under a bad government has not qualified him for devising a good one.

While these events were passing in the north, Almagro's faction at
Lima was daily receiving new accessions of strength. For, in addition
to those who, from the first, had been avowedly of his father's party,
there were many others who, from some cause or other, had conceived
a disgust for Pizarro, and who now willingly enlisted under the banner
of the chief that had overthrown him.

The first step of the young general, or rather of Rada, who directed
his movements, was to secure the necessary supplies for the troops,
most of whom, having long been in indigent circumstances, were wholly
unprepared for service. Funds to a considerable amount were raised, by
seizing on the moneys of the Crown in the hands of the treasurer. Pizarro's secretary, Picado, was also drawn from his prison, and interro-
gated as to the place where his master's treasures were deposited. But,
although put to the torture, he would not—or, as is probable, could not
—give information on the subject; and the conspirators, who had a long
arrear of injuries to settle with him, closed their proceedings by publicly
beheading him in the great square of Lima.[3]

Valverde, Bishop of Cuzco, as he himself assures us, vainly interposed in his behalf. It is singular, that, the last time this fanatical prelate appears on the stage, it should be in the benevolent character of a
supplicant for mercy.[4] Soon afterwards, he was permitted, with the
judge, Velasquez, and some other adherents of Pizarro, to embark from
the port of Lima. We have a letter from him, dated at Tumbez, in November, 1541; almost immediately after which he fell into the hands of
the Indians, and with his companions was massacred at Puná. A violent
death not unfrequently closed the stormy career of the American adventurer. Valverde was a Dominican friar, and, like Father Olmedo in
the suite of Cortés, had been by his commander's side throughout the
whole of his expedition. But he did not always, like the good Olmedo,
use his influence to stay the uplifted hand of the warrior. At least, this

---

[3] Pedro Pizarro, Descub. y Conq., MS.—Carte de Barrio Nuevo, MS.—Carte de
Fray Vicente Valverde, desde Tumbez, MS.

[4] "Siendo informado que andavan ordenando la muerte á Antonio Picado secretario del Marques que tenian preso, fui á Don Diego é á su Capitan General Ioan
de Herrada é á todos sus capitanes, i les puse delante el servicio de Dios i de S. M.
i que bastase en lo fecho por respeto de Dios, humillandome á sus pies porque no
lo matasen: i no bastó que luego dende á pocos dias lo sacaron á la plaza desta
cibdad donde ie cortaron la cabeza." Carte de Fray Vicente de Valverde, desde
Tumbez, MS.

was not the mild aspect in which he presented himself at the terrible massacre of Caxamalca. Yet some contemporary accounts represent him, after he had been installed in his episcopal office, as unwearied in his labors to convert the natives, and to ameliorate their condition; and his own correspondence with the government, after that period, shows great solicitude for these praiseworthy objects. Trained in the severest school of monastic discipline, which too often closes the heart against the common charities of life, he could not, like the benevolent Las Casas, rise so far above its fanatical tenets as to regard the heathen as his brother, while in the state of infidelity; and, in the true spirit of that school, he doubtless conceived that the sanctity of the end justified the means, however revolting in themselves. Yet the same man, who thus freely shed the blood of the poor native to secure the triumph of his faith, would doubtless have as freely poured out his own in its defence. The character was no uncommon one in the sixteenth century.[5]

Almagro's followers, having supplied themselves with funds, made as little scruple to appropriate to their own use such horses and arms, of every description, as they could find in the city. And this they did with the less reluctance, as the inhabitants for the most part testified no good-will to their cause. While thus employed, Almagro received intelligence that Holguin had left Cuzco with a force of near three hundred men, with which he was preparing to effect a junction with Alvarado in the north. It was important to Almagro's success that he should defeat this junction. If to procrastinate was the policy of Vaca de Castro, it was clearly that of Almagro to quicken operations, and to bring matters to as speedy an issue as possible; to march at once against Holguin, whom he might expect easily to overcome with his superior numbers; then to follow up the stroke by the still easier defeat of Alvarado, when the new governor would be, in a manner, at his mercy. It would be easy to beat these several bodies in detail, which, once united, would present formidable odds. Almagro and his party had already arrayed themselves against the government by a proceeding too atrocious, and which struck too directly at the royal authority, for its perpetrators to flatter themselves with the hopes of pardon. Their only chance was boldly to follow up the blow, and, by success, to place themselves in so formidable an attitude as to excite the apprehensions of government. The dread of its too potent vassal might extort terms that would never be conceded to his prayers.

But Almagro and his followers shrunk from this open collision with the Crown. They had taken up rebellion because it lay in their path, not because they had wished it. They had meant only to avenge their per-

---

[5] "Quel Señor obispo Fray Vicente de Balverde como persona que jamas ha tenido fin ni zelo al servicio de Dios ni de S. M. ni menos en la conversion de los naturales en los poner é dotrinar en las cosas de nuestra santa fée catholica, ni menos en entender en la paz é sosiego destos reynos, sino á sus intereses propios dando mal ejemplo á todos." (Carta de Almagro á la Audiencia de Panamá, MS. 8 de Nov. 1541.) The writer, it must be remembered, was his personal enemy.

sonal wrongs on Pizarro, and not to defy the royal authority. When, therefore, some of the more resolute, who followed things fearlessly to their consequences, proposed to march at once against Vaca de Castro, and, by striking at the head, settle the contest by a blow, it was almost universally rejected; and it was not till after long debate that it was finally determined to move against Holguin, and cut off his communication with Alonso de Alvarado.

Scarcely had Almagro commenced his march on Xauxa, where he proposed to give battle to his enemy, than he met with a severe misfortune in the death of Juan de Rada. He was a man somewhat advanced in years; and the late exciting scenes, in which he had taken the principal part, had been too much for a frame greatly shattered by a life of extraordinary hardship. He was thrown into a fever, of which he soon after died. By his death, Almagro sustained an inestimable loss; for, besides his devoted attachment to his young leader, he was, by his large experience, and his cautious though courageous character, better qualified than any other cavalier in the army to conduct him safely through the stormy sea on which he had led him to embark.

Among the cavaliers of highest consideration after Rada's death, the two most aspiring were Christoval de Sotelo, and Garcia de Alvarado; both possessed of considerable military talent, but the latter marked by a bold, presumptuous manner, which might remind one of his illustrious namesake, who achieved much higher renown under the banner of Cortés. Unhappily, a jealousy grew up between these two officers; that jealousy, so common among the Spaniards, that it may seem a national characteristic; an impatience of equality, founded on a false principle of honor, which has ever been the fruitful source of faction among them, whether under a monarchy or a republic.

This was peculiarly unfortunate for Almagro, whose inexperience led him to lean for support on others, and who, in the present distracted state of his council, knew scarcely where to turn for it. In the delay occasioned by these dissensions, his little army did not reach the valley of Xauxa till after the enemy had passed it. Almagro followed close, leaving behind his baggage and artillery that he might move the lighter. But the golden opportunity was lost. The rivers, swollen by autumnal rains, impeded his pursuit; and, though his light troops came up with a few stragglers of the rear-guard, Holguin succeeded in conducting his forces through the dangerous passes of the mountains, and in effecting a junction with Alonso de Alvarado, near the northern seaport of Huaura.

Disappointed in his object, Almagro prepared to march on Cuzco,—the capital, as he regarded it, of his own jurisdiction,—to get possession of that city, and there make preparations to meet his adversary in the field. Sotelo was sent forward with a small corps in advance. He experienced no opposition from the now defenceless citizens; the government of the place was again restored to the hands of the men of Chili, and their young leader soon appeared at the head of his battalions, and established his winter-quarters in the Inca capital.

Here, the jealousy of the rival captains broke out into an open feud. It was ended by the death of Sotelo, treacherously assassinated in his own apartment by Garcia de Alvarado. Almagro, greatly outraged by this atrocity, was the more indignant, as he felt himself too weak to punish the offender. He smothered his resentment for the present, affecting to treat the dangerous officer with more distinguished favor. But Alvarado was not the dupe of this specious behaviour. He felt that he had forfeited the confidence of his commander. In revenge, he laid a plot to betray him; and Almagro, driven to the necessity of self-defence, imitated the example of his officer, by entering his house with a party of armed men, who, laying violent hands on the insurgent, slew him on the spot.[6]

This irregular proceeding was followed by the best consequences. The seditious schemes of Alvarado perished with him. The seeds of insubordination were eradicated, and from that moment Almagro experienced only implicit obedience and the most loyal support from his followers. From that hour, too, his own character seemed to be changed; he relied far less on others than on himself, and developed resources not to have been anticipated in one of his years; for he had hardly reached the age of twenty-two.[7] From this time he displayed an energy and forecast, which proved him, in despite of his youth, not unequal to the trying emergencies of the situation in which it was his unhappy lot to be placed.

He instantly set about providing for the wants of his men, and strained every nerve to get them in good fighting order for the approaching campaign. He replenished his treasury with a large amount of silver which he drew from the mines of La Plata. Saltpetre, obtained in abundance in the neighborhood of Cuzco, furnished the material for gunpowder. He caused cannon, some of large dimensions, to be cast under the superintendence of Pedro de Candia, the Greek, who, it may be remembered, had first come into the country with Pizarro, and who, with a number of his countrymen,—Levantines, as they were called,— was well acquainted with this manufacture. Under their care, fire-arms were made, together with cuirasses and helmets, in which silver was mingled with copper,[8] and of so excellent a quality, that they might vie,

[6] Pedro Pizarro, Descub. y Conq., MS.—Zarate, Conq. del Peru, lib. 4, cap. 10-14.—Gomara, Hist. de las Ind., cap. 147.—Declaracion de Uscategui, MS.—Carta de Barrio Nuevo, MS.—Herrera, Hist. General, dec. 6, lib. 10, cap. 13; dec. 7, lib. 3, cap. 1, 5.

[7] "Hiço mas que su edad requeria, porque seria de edad de veinte i dos años." Zarate, Conq. del Peru, lib. 4, cap. 20.

[8] "Y demas de esto hiço armas para la Gente de su Real, que no las tenia, de pasta de Plata, i Cobre, mezclado, de que salen mui buenos Coseletes: haviendo corregido, demàs de esto, todas las armas de la Tierra; de manera, que el que menos Armas tenia entre su Gente, era Cota, i Coracinas, ò Coselete, i Celadas de la mesma Pasta, que los Indios hacen diestramente, por muestras de las de Milàn." Zarate, Conq. del Peru, lib. 4, cap. 14.

says an old soldier of the time, with those from the workshops of Milan.[5]
Almagro received a seasonable supply, moreover, from a source scarcely
to have been expected. This was from Manco, the wandering Inca, who,
detesting the memory of Pizarro, transferred to the young Almagro
the same friendly feelings which he had formerly borne to his father;
heightened, it may be, by the consideration that Indian blood flowed in
the veins of the young commander. From this quarter Almagro obtained
a liberal supply of swords, spears, shields, and arms and armour of
every description, chiefly taken by the Inca at the memorable seige of
Cuzco. He also received the gratifying assurance, that the latter would
support him with a detachment of native troops when he opened the
campaign.

Before making a final appeal to arms, however, Almagro resolved
to try the effect of negotiation with the new governor. In the spring, or
early in the summer, of 1542, he sent an embassy to the latter, then at
Lima, in which he deprecated the necessity of taking arms against an
officer of the Crown. His only desire, he said, was to vindicate his own
rights; to secure the possession of New Toledo, the province bequeathed
to him by his father, and from which he had been most unjustly excluded by Pizarro. He did not dispute the governor's authority over New
Castile, as the country was designated which had been assigned to the
marquess; and he concluded by proposing that each party should remain within his respective territory until the determination of the Court
of Castile could be made known to them. To this application, couched
in respectful terms, Almagro received no answer.

Frustrated in his hopes of a peaceful accommodation, the young captain now saw that nothing was left but the arbitrament of arms. Assembling his troops, preparatory to his departure from the capital, he
made them a brief address. He protested that the step which he and his
brave companions were about to take was not an act of rebellion against
the Crown. It was forced on them by the conduct of the governor himself. The commission of that officer gave him no authority over the territory of New Toledo, settled on Almagro's father, and by his father
bequeathed to him. If Vaca de Castro, by exceeding the limits of his
authority, drove him to hostilities, the blood spilt in the quarrel would
lie on the head of that commander, not on his. "In the assassination of
Pizarro," he continued, "we took that justice into our own hands which
elsewhere was denied us. It is the same now, in our contest with the royal
governor. We are as true-hearted and loyal subjects of the Crown as he
is." And he concluded by invoking his soldiers to stand by him heart
and hand in the approaching contest, in which they were all equally interested with himself.

The appeal was not made to an insensible audience. There were few
among them who did not feel that their fortunes were indissolubly

---

[5] "Hombres de armas con tan buenas celadas borgoñesas como se hacen en Milan."
Carta de Ventura Beltran al Emperador, MS., desde Vilcas 8 Octubre, 1542.

connected with those of their commander; and while they had little to expect from the austere character of the governor, they were warmly attached to the person of their young chief, who, with all the popular qualities of his father, excited additional sympathy from the circumstances of his age and his forlorn condition. Laying their hands on the cross, placed on an altar raised for the purpose, the officers and soldiers severally swore to brave every peril with Almagro, and remain true to him to the last.

In point of numbers, his forces had not greatly strengthened since his departure from Lima. He mustered but little more than five hundred in all; but among them were his father's veterans, well seasoned by many an Indian campaign. He had about two hundred horse, many of them clad in complete mail, a circumstance not too common in these wars, where a stuffed doublet of cotton was often the only panoply of the warrior. His infantry, formed of pikemen and arquebusiers, was excellently armed. But his strength lay in his heavy ordnance, consisting of sixteen pieces, eight large and eight smaller guns, or falconets, as they were called, forming, says one who saw it, a beautiful park of artillery, that would have made a brave show on the citadel of Burgos.[10] The little army, in short, though not imposing from its numbers, was under as good discipline, and as well appointed, as any that ever fought on the fields of Peru; much better than any which Almagro's own father or Pizarro ever led into the field and won their conquests with. Putting himself at the head of his gallant company, the chieftain sallied forth from the walls of Cuzco about midsummer, in 1542, and directed his march towards the coast in expectation of meeting the enemy.[11]

While the events detailed in the preceding pages were passing, Vaca de Castro, whom we left at Quito in the preceding year, was advancing slowly towards the south. His first act, after leaving that city, showed his resolution to enter into no compromise with the assassins of Pizarro. Benalcazar, the distinguished officer whom I have mentioned as having early given in his adherence to him, had protected one of the principal conspirators, his personal friend, who had come into his power, and had facilitated his escape. The governor, indignant at the proceeding, would listen to no explanation, but ordered the offending officer to return to his own district of Popayan. It was a bold step, in the precarious state of his own fortunes.

As the governor pursued his march, he was well received by the people on the way; and when he entered the cities of San Miguel and of Truxillo, he was welcomed with loyal enthusiasm by the inhabitants, who

---

[10] "El artilleria hera suficiente para hazer bateria en el castillo de Burgos." Dicho del Capitan Francisco de Carvajal sobre la pregunta 38 de la informacion hecha en el Cuzco en 1543, á favor de Vaca de Castro, MS.

[11] Pedro Pizarro, Descub. y Conq., MS.—Declaracion de Uscategui, MS.—Garcilasso, Com. Real., Parte 2, lib. 2, cap. 13.—Carta del Cabildo de Arequipa al Emperador, San Joan de la Frontera, MS., 24 de Sep. 1542.—Herrera, Hist. General, dec. 7, lib. 3, cap. 1, 2.

readily acknowledged his authority, though they showed little alacrity to take their chance with him in the coming struggle.

After lingering a long time in each of these places, he resumed his march and reached the camp of Alonso de Alvarado at Huaura, early in 1542. Holguin had established his quarters at some little distance from his rival; for a jealousy had sprung up, as usual, between these two captains, who both aspired to the supreme command of Captain-General of the army. The office of governor, conferred on Vaca de Castro, might seem to include that of commander-in-chief of the forces. But De Castro was a scholar, bred to the law; and, whatever authority he might arrogate to himself in civil matters, the two captains imagined that the military department he would resign into the hands of others. They little knew the character of the man.

Though possessed of no more military science than belonged to every cavalier in that martial age, the governor knew that to avow his ignorance, and to resign the management of affairs into the hands of others, would greatly impair his authority, if not bring him into contempt with the turbulent spirits among whom he was now thrown. He had both sagacity and spirit, and trusted to be able to supply his own deficiencies by the experience of others. His position placed the services of the ablest men in the country at his disposal, and with the aid of their counsels he felt quite competent to decide on his plan of operations, and to enforce the execution of it. He knew, moreover, that the only way to allay the jealousy of the two parties in the present crisis was to assume himself the office which was the cause of their dissension.

Still he approached his ambitious officers with great caution; and the representations, which he made through some judicious persons who had the most intimate access to them, were so successful, that both were in a short time prevailed on to relinquish their pretensions in his favor. Holguin, the more unreasonable of the two, then waited on him in his rival's quarters, where the governor had the further satisfaction to reconcile him to Alonso de Alvarado. It required some address, as their jealousy of each other had proceeded to such lengths that a challenge had passed between them.

Harmony being thus restored, the licentiate passed over to Holguin's camp, where he was greeted with salvoes of artillery, and loud acclamations of "Viva el Rey" from the loyal soldiery. Ascending a platform covered with velvet, he made an animated harangue to the troops; his commission was read aloud by the secretary; and the little army tendered their obedience to him as the representative of the Crown.

Vaca de Castro's next step was to send off the greater part of his force, in the direction of Xauxa, while, at the head of a small corps, he directed his march towards Lima. Here he was received with lively demonstrations of joy by the citizens, who were generally attached to the cause of Pizarro, the founder and constant patron of their capital. Indeed, the citizens had lost no time after Almagro's departure in expelling his creatures from the municipality, and reasserting their allegiance. With these favorable dispositions towards himself, the governor found no difficulty in obtaining a considerable loan of money from the wealthier inhabitants. But he was less successful, at first, in his application for horses and arms, since the harvest had been too faithfully gleaned, already, by the men of Chili. As, however, he prolonged his stay some time in the capital, he obtained important supplies, before he left it, both of arms and ammunition, while he added to his force by a considerable body of recruits.[12]

As he was thus employed, he received tidings that the enemy had left Cuzco, and was on his march towards the coast. Quitting Los Reyes, therefore, with his trusty followers, Vaca de Castro marched at once to Xauxa, the appointed place of rendezvous. Here he mustered his forces, and found that they amounted to about seven hundred men. The cavalry, in which lay his strength, was superior in numbers to that of his antagonist, but neither so well mounted or armed. It included many cavaliers of birth, and well-tried soldiers, besides a number who, having great interests at stake, as possessed of large estates in the country, had left them at the call of government, to enlist under its banners.[13] His infantry, besides pikes, was indifferently well supplied with firearms; but he had nothing to show in the way of artillery except three or four ill-mounted falconets. Yet, notwithstanding these deficiencies, the royal army, if so insignificant a force can deserve that name, was so far superior in numbers to that of his rival, that the one might be thought, on the whole, to be no unequal match for the other.[14]

The reader, familiar with the large masses employed in European warfare, may smile at the paltry forces of the Spaniards. But in the New World, where a countless host of natives went for little, five hundred well-trained Europeans were regarded as a formidable body. No army, up to the period before us, had ever risen to a thousand. Yet it is not numbers, as I have already been led to remark, that give importance to a conflict; but the consequences that depend on it,—the magnitude of the stake, and the skill and courage of the players. The more limited the means, even, the greater may be the science shown in the use of

[12] Declaracion de Uscategui, MS.—Pedro Pizarro, Descub. y Conq., MS.—Herrera, Hist. General, dec. 7, lib. 1, cap. 1.—Carta de Barrio Nuevo, MS.—Carta de Benalcazar al Emperador, MS.

[13] The Municipality of Arequipa, most of whose members were present in the army, stoutly urge their claims to a compensation for thus promptly leaving their estates, and taking up arms at the call of government. Without such reward, they say, their patriotic example will not often be followed.

[14] Pedro Pizarro, Descub. y Conq., MS.—Zarate, Conq. del Peru, lib. 4, cap. 15.—Carta de Barrio Nuevo, MS.

Carbajal notices the politic manner in which his commander bribed recruits into his service,—paying them with promises and fair words when ready money failed him. "Dando á unos dineros, é á otros armas i caballos, i á otros palabras, i á otros promesas, i á otros graziosas respuestas de lo que con él negoziaban para ten-erlos á todos muy conttentos i presttos en el servicio de S. M. quando fuese menes-tter." Dicho del Capitan Francisco de Carbajal sobre la informacion hecha en el Cuzco en 1543, á favor de Vaca de Castro, MS.

them; until, forgetting the poverty of the materials, we fix our attention on the conduct of the actors, and the greatness of the results.

While at Xauxa, Vaca de Castro received an embassy from Gonzalo Pizarro, returned from his expedition from the "Land of Cinnamon," in which that chief made an offer of his services in the approaching contest. The governor's answer showed that he was not wholly averse to an accommodation with Almagro, provided it could be effected without compromising the royal authority. He was willing, perhaps, to avoid the final trial by battle, when he considered, that, from the equality of the contending forces, the issue must be extremely doubtful. He knew that the presence of Pizarro in the camp, the detested enemy of the Almagrians, would excite distrust in their bosoms that would probably baffle every effort at accommodation. Nor is it likely that the governor cared to have so restless a spirit introduced into his own councils. He accordingly sent to Gonzalo, thanking him for the promptness of his support, but courteously declined it, while he advised him to remain in his province, and repose after the fatigues of his wearisome expedition. At the same time, he assured him that he would not fail to call for his services when occasion required it.—The haughty cavalier was greatly disgusted by the repulse.[15]

The governor now received such an account of Almagro's movements as led him to suppose that he was preparing to occupy Gaumanga, a fortified place of considerable strength, about thirty leagues from Xauxa.[16] Anxious to secure this post, he broke up his encampment, and by forced marches, conducted in so irregular a manner as must have placed him in great danger if his enemy had been near to profit by it, he succeeded in anticipating Almagro, and threw himself into the place while his antagonist was at Bilcas, some ten leagues distant.

At Guamanga, Vaca de Castro received another embassy from Almagro, of similar import with the former. The young chief again deprecated the existence of hostilities between brethren of the same family, and proposed an accommodation of the quarrel on the same basis as before. To these proposals the governor now condescended to reply. It might be thought, from his answer, that he felt some compassion for the youth and inexperience of Almagro, and that he was willing to distinguish between him and the principal conspirators, provided he could detach him from their interests. But it is more probable that he intended only to amuse his enemy by a show of negotiation, while he gained time for tampering with the fidelity of his troops.

He insisted that Almagro should deliver up to him all those immediately implicated in the death of Pizarro, and should then disband his forces. On these conditions the government would pass over his treasonable practices, and he should be reinstated in the royal favor. Together with this mission, Vaca de Castro, it is reported, sent a Spaniard, disguised as an Indian, who was instructed to communicate with certain

[15] Zarate, Conq. del Peru, lib. 4, cap. 15.
[16] Cieza de Leon, Cronica. cap. 85.

officers in Almagro's camp, and prevail on them, if possible, to abandon his cause and return to their allegiance. Unfortunately, the disguise of the emissary was detected. He was seized, put to the torture, and, having confessed the whole of the transaction, was hanged as a spy.

Almagro laid the proceeding before his captains. The terms proffered by the governor were such as no man with a particle of hono.· in his nature could entertain for a moment; and Almagro's indignation, as well as that of his companions, was heightened by the duplicity of their enemy, who could practise such insidious arts, while ostensibly engaged in a fair and open negotiation. Fearful, perhaps, lest the tempting offers of their antagonist might yet prevail over the constancy of some of the weaker spirits among them, they demanded that all negotiation should be broken off, and that they should be led at once against the enemy.[17]

The governor, meanwhile, finding the broken country around Guamanga unfavorable for his cavalry, on which he mainly relied, drew off his forces to the neighboring lowlands, known as the Plains of Chupas. It was the tempestuous season of the year, and for several days the storm raged wildly among the hills, and, sweeping along their sides into the valley, poured down rain, sleet, and snow on the miserable bivouacs of the soldiers, till they were drenched to the skin and nearly stiffened by the cold.[18] At length, on the sixteenth of September, 1542, the scouts brought in tidings that Almagro's troops were advancing, with the intention, apparently, of occupying the highlands around Chupas. The war of the elements had at last subsided, and was succeeded by one of those brilliant days which are found only in the tropics. The royal camp was early in motion, as Vaca de Castro, desirous to secure the heights that commanded the valley, detached a body of arquebusiers on that service, supported by a corps of cavalry, which he soon followed with the rest of the forces. On reaching the eminence, news was brought that the enemy had come to a halt, and established himself in a strong position at less than a league's distance.

It was now late in the afternoon, and the sun was not more than two hours above the horizon. The governor hesitated to begin the action when they must so soon be overtaken by night. But Alonso de Alvarado assured him that "now was the time; for the spirits of his men were hot for fight, and it was better to take the benefit of it than to damp their ardor by delay." The governor acquiesced, exclaiming at the same time, —"O for the might of Joshua, to stay the sun in his course!"[19] He then

[17] Dicho del Capitan Francisco de Carbajal sobre la informacion hecha en el Cuzco en 1543, á favor de Vaca de Castro, MS.—Zarate, Conq. del Peru, lib. 4, cap. 16.—Herrera, Hist. General, dec. 7, lib. 3, cap. 8.—Carta de Ventura Beltran, MS.—Gomara, Hist. de las Ind., cap. 149.

[18] "Tuvieron tan gran tempestad de agua, Truenos, i Nieve, que pensaron perecer; i amaneciendo con dia claro, i sereno." Herrera, Hist. General, dec. 7, lib. 3, cap. 8.

[19] "Yasi Vaca de Castro signió su parescer, temiendo toda via la falta del Dia, i dijo, que quisiera tener el poder de Josue, para deterner el Sol." Zarate, Conq. del Peru, lib. 4, cap. 18.

drew up his little army in order of batle, and made his dispositions for the attack.

In the centre he placed his infantry, consisting of arquebusiers and pikemen, constituting the *battle,* as it was called. On the flanks, he established his cavalry, placing the right wing, together with the royal standard, under charge of Alonso de Alvarado, and the left under Holguin, supported by a gallant body of cavaliers. His artillery, too insignificant to be of much account, was also in the centre. He proposed himself to lead the van, and to break the first lance with the enemy; but from this chivalrous display he was dissuaded by his officers, who reminded him that too much depended on his life to have it thus wantonly exposed. The governor contented himself, therefore, with heading a body of reserve, consisting of forty horse, to act on any quarter as occasion might require. This corps, comprising the flower of his chivalry, was chiefly drawn from Alvarado's troop, greatly to the discontent of that captain. The governor himself rode a coal-black charger, and wore a rich surcoat of brocade over his mail, through which the habit and emblems of the knightly order of St. James, conferred on him just before his departure from Castile, were conspicuous.[20] It was a point of honor with the chivalry of the period to court danger by displaying their rank in the splendor of their military attire and the caparisons of their horses.

Before commencing the assault, Vaca de Castro addressed a few remarks to his soldiers, in order to remove any hesitation that some might yet feel, who recollected the displeasure shown by the emperor to the victors as well as the vanquished after the battle of Salinas. He told them that their enemies were rebels. They were in arms against him, the representative of the Crown, and it was his duty to quell this rebellion and punish the authors of it. He then caused the law to be read aloud, proclaiming the doom of traitors. By this law, Almagro and his followers had forfeited their lives and property, and the governor promised to distribute the latter among such of his men as showed the best claim to it by their conduct in the battle. This last politic promise vanquished the scruples of the most fastidious; and, having completed his dispositions in the most judicious and soldier-like manner, Vaca de Castro gave the order to advance.[21]

[20] "I visto esto por el dicho señor Governador, mandó dar al arma á mui gran priesa, i mando á este testigo que sacase toda la gente al campo, i el se entró en su tienda á se armar, i dende á poco salió della encima de un cavallo morcillo rabicano armado en blanco i con una ropa de brocado encima de las armas con el abito de Santiago en los pechos." Dicho del Capitan Francisco de Carbajal sobre la informacion hecha en el Cuzco en 1543, á favor de Vaca de Castro, MS.

[21] The governor's words, says Carbajal, who witnessed their effect, stirred the heart of the troops, so that they went to the battle as to a ball. "En pocas palabras comprehendió tan grandes cosas que la gente de S. M. Covró tan grande animo con ellas, que tan determinadamente se partieron de alli para ir á los enemigos como si fueron á fiestas donde estuvieran convidados." Dicho del Capitan Francisco de Carbajal, sobre la informacion hecha en el Cuzco en 1543, á favor de Vaca de Castro, MS.

As the forces turned a spur of the hills, which had hitherto screened them from their enemies, they came in sight of the latter, formed along the crest of a gentle eminence, with their snow-white banners, the distinguishing color of the Almagrians, floating above their heads, and their bright arms flinging back the broad rays of the evening sun. Almagro's disposition of his troops was not unlike that of his adversary. In the centre was his excellent artillery, covered by his arquebusiers and spearmen; while his cavalry rode on the flanks. The troops on the left he proposed to lead in person. He had chosen his position with judgment, as the character of the ground gave full play to his guns, which opened an effective fire on the assailants as they drew near. Shaken by the storm of shot, Vaca de Castro saw the difficulty of advancing in open view of the hostile battery. He took the counsel, therefore, of Francisco de Carbajal, who undertook to lead the forces by a circuitous, but safer, route. This is the first occasion on which the name of this veteran appears in these American wars, where it was afterwards to acquire a melancholy notoriety. He had come to the country after the campaigns of forty years in Europe, where he had studied the art of war under the Great Captain, Gonsalvo de Cordova. Though now far advanced in age, he possessed all the courage and indomitable energy of youth, and well exemplified the lessons he had studied under his great commander.

Taking advantage of a winding route that sloped round the declivity of the hills, he conducted the troops in such a manner, that, until they approached quite near the enemy, they were protected by the intervening ground. While thus advancing, they were assailed on the left flank by the Indian battalions under Paullo, the Inca Manco's brother; but a corps of musketeers, directing a scattering fire among them, soon rid the Spaniards of this annoyance. When, at length, the royal troops, rising above the hill, again came into view of Almagro's lines, the artillery opened on them with fatal effect. It was but for a moment, however, as, from some unaccountable cause, the guns were pointed as such an angle, that, although presenting an obvious mark, by far the greater part of the shot passed over their heads. Whether this was the result of treachery, or merely of awkwardness, is uncertain. The artillery was under charge of the engineer, Pedro de Candia. This man, who, it may be remembered, was one of the thirteen that so gallantly stood by Pizarro in the island of Gallo, had fought side by side with his leader through the whole of the Conquest. He had lately, however, conceived some disgust with him, and had taken part with the faction of Almagro. The death of his old commander, he may perhaps have thought, had settled all their differences, and he was now willing to return to his former allegiance. At least, it is said, that, at this very time, he was in correspondence with Vaca de Castro. Almagro himself seems to have had no doubt of his treachery. For, after remonstrating in vain with him on his present conduct, he ran him through the body, and the unfortunate cavalier fell lifeless on the field. Then, throwing himself on one of the guns, Almagro gave it a new direction, and that so successfully, that, when it was discharged, it struck down several of the cavalry.[22]

The firing now took better effect, and by one volley a whole file of the royal infantry was swept off, and though others quickly stepped in to fill up the ranks, the men, impatient of their sufferings, loudly called on the troopers, who had halted for a moment, to quicken their advance.[23] This delay had been caused by Carbajal's desire to bring his own guns to bear on the opposite columns. But the design was quickly abandoned; the clumsy ordnance was left on the field, and orders were given to the cavalry to charge; the trumpets sounded, and, crying their war-cries, the bold cavaliers struck their spurs into their steeds, and rode at full speed against the enemy.

Well had it been for Almagro, if he had remained firm on the post which gave him such advantage. But from a false point of honor, he thought it derogatory to a brave knight passively to await the assault, and, ordering his own men to charge, the hostile squadrons, rapidly advancing against each other, met midway on the plain. The shock was terrible. Horse and rider reeled under the force of it. The spears flew into shivers;[24] and the cavaliers, drawing their swords, or wielding their maces and battle-axes,—though some of the royal troopers were armed only with a common axe,—dealt their blows with all the fury of civil hate. It was a fearful struggle, not merely of man against man, but, to use the words cf an eyewitness, of brother against brother, and friend against friend.[25] No quarter was asked; for the wrench that had been strong enough to tear asunder the dearest ties of kindred left no hold for

---

[22] Pedro Pizarro, Descub. y Conq., MS.—Zarate, Conq. del Peru, lib. 4, cap. 17-19.—Naharro, Relacion Sumaria, MS.—Herrera, Hist. General, dec. 7, lib. 3, cap. 11.—Dicho del Capitan Francisco de Carbajal sobre la informacion hecha en el Cuzco en 1543, á favor de Vaca de Castro, MS.—Carte del Cabildo de Arequipa al Emperador, MS.—Carta de Ventura Beltran, MS.—Declaracion de Uscategui, MS.—Gomara, Hist. de las Ind., cap. 149.

According to Garcilasso, whose guns usually do more execution than those of any other authority, seventeen men were killed by this wonderful shot. See Com, Real., Parte 2, lib. 3, cap. 16.

[23] The officers drove the men, according to Zarate, at the point of their swords, to take the places of their fallen comrades. "Porque vn tiro llevo toda vna hilera, è hiço abrir el Escuadron, i los Capitanes pusieron gran diligencia en hacerlo cerrar, amenaçando de muerte à los Soldados, con las Espadas desenvainadas, i se cerrò." Conq. del Peru, lib. 4, cap. 1.

[24] "Se encontraron de suerte, que casi todas las lanças quebraron, quedando muchos muertos, i caidos de ambas partes." (Ibid., ubi supra.) Zarate writes on this occasion with the spirit and strength of Thucydides. He was not present, but came into the country the following year, when he gleaned the particulars of the battle from the best informed persons there, to whom his position gave him ready access.

[25] It is the language of the Conquerors themselves, who, in their letter to the Emperor, compare the action to the great battle of Ravenna. "Fue tan reñida i porfiada, que despues de la de Rebena, no se ha visto entre tan poca gente mas cruel batalla, donde hermanos á hermanos, ni deudos a deudos, ni amigos á amigos no se davan vida uno á otro." Carta del Cabildo de Arequipa al Emperador, MS.

humanity. The excellent arms of the Almagrians counterbalanced the odds of numbers; but the royal partisans gained some advantage by striking at the horses instead of the mailed bodies of their antagonists.

The infantry, meanwhile, on both sides, kept up a sharp cross-fire from their arquebuses, which did execution on the ranks of the cavaliers, as well as on one another. But Almagro's battery of heavy guns, now well directed, mowed down the advancing columns of foot. The latter, staggering, began to fall back from the terrible fire, when Francisco de Carbajal, throwing himself before them, cried out, "Shame on you, my men! Do you give way now? I am twice as good a mark for the enemy as any of you!" He was a very large man; and, throwing off his steel helmet and cuirass, that he might have no advantage over his followers, he remained lightly attired in his cotton doublet, when, swinging his partisan over his head, he sprang boldly forward through blinding volumes of smoke and a tempest of musket-balls, and, supported by the bravest of his troops, overpowered the gunners, and made himself master of their pieces.

The shades of night had now, for some time been coming thicker and thicker over the field. But still the deadly struggle went on in the darkness, as the red and white badges intimated the respective parties, and their war-cries rose above the din,—"Vaca de Castro y el Rey,"—"Almagro y el Rey,"—while both invoked the aid of their military apostle St. James. Holguin, who commanded the royalists on the left, pierced through by two musket-balls, had been slain early in the action. He had made himself conspicuous by a rich sobre-vest of white velvet over his armour. Still a gallant band of cavaliers maintained the fight so valiantly on that quarter, that the Almagrians found it difficult to keep their ground.[26]

It fared differently on the right, where Alonso de Alvarado commanded. He was there encountered by Almagro in person, who fought worthy of his name. By repeated charges on his opponent, he endeavored to bear down his squadrons, so much worse mounted and worse armed than his own. Alvarado resisted with undiminished courage; but his numbers had been thinned, as we have seen, before the battle, to supply the governor's reserve, and, fairly overpowered by the superior strength of his adversary, who had already won two of the royal banners, he was slowly giving ground. "Take, but kill not!" shouted the generous young chief, who felt himself sure of victory.[27]

But at this crisis, Vaca de Castro, who, with his reserve, had occupied a rising ground that commanded the field of action, was fully aware that the time had now come for him to take part in the struggle. He had long

---

[26] The battle was so equally contested, says Beltran, one of Vaca de Castro's captains, that it was long doubtful on which side victory was to incline. "I la batalla estuvo mui gran rato en peso sin conoscerse vitoria de la una parte á la otra." Carta de Ventura Beltran, MS.

[27] "Gritaba, Victoria; i decia, Prender i no matar." Herrera, Hist. General, dec 7, lib. 3, cap 11.

strained his eyes through the gloom to watch the movements of the combatants, and received constant tidings how the fight was going. He no longer hesitated, but, calling on his men to follow, led off boldly into the thickest of the *mêlée* to the support of his stout-hearted officer. The arrival of a new corps on the field, all fresh for action, gave another turn to the tide.[28] Alvarado's men took heart and rallied. Almagro's, though driven back by the fury of the assault, quickly returned against their assailants. Thirteen of Vaca de Castro's cavaliers fell dead from their saddles. But it was the last effort of the Almagrians. Their strength, though not their spirit, failed them. They gave way in all directions, and, mingling together in the darkness, horse, foot, and artillery, they trampled one another down, as they made the best of their way from the press of their pursuers. Almagro used every effort to stay them. He performed miracles of valor, says one who witnessed them; but he was borne along by the tide, and, though he seemed to court death, by the freedom with which he exposed his person to danger, yet he escaped without a wound.

Others there were of his company, and among them a young cavalier named Gerónimo de Alvarado, who obstinately refused to quit the field; and shouting out,—"We slew Pizarro! we killed the tyrant!" they threw themselves on the lances of their conquerors, preferring death on the battle-field to the ignominious doom of the gibbet.[29]

It was nine o'clock when the battle ceased, though the firing was heard at intervals over the field at a much later hour, as some straggling party of fugitives were overtaken by their pursuers. Yet many succeeded in escaping in the obscurity of night, while some, it is said, contrived to elude pursuit in a more singular way; tearing off the badges from the corpses of their enemies, they assumed them for themselves, and, mingling in the ranks as followers of Vaca de Castro, joined in the pursuit.

That commander, at length, fearing some untoward accident, and that the fugitives, should they rally again under cover of the darkness, might inflict some loss on their pursuers, caused his trumpets to sound, and recalled his scattered forces under their banners. All night they remained under arms on the field, which, so lately the scene of noisy strife, was now hushed in silence, broken only by the groans of the wounded and the dying. The natives, who had hung, during the fight, like a dark cloud, round the skirts of the mountains, contemplating with gloomy satisfaction the destruction of their enemies, now availed themselves of the obscurity to descend, like a pack of famished wolves, upon the plains, where they stripped the bodies of the slain, and even of the liv-

---

[28] The letter of the municipality of Arequipa gives the governor credit for deciding the fate of the day by this movement, and the writers express their "admiration of the gallantry and courage he displayed, so little to have been expected from his age and profession." See the original in *Appendix, No.* 13.

[29] "Se arrojaron en los Enemigos, como desesperados, hiriendo à todas partes, diciendo cada vno por su nombre: Yo soi Fulano, que matè al Marquès; i asi anduvieron hasta. que los hicieron pedaços." Zarate, Conq. del Peru, lib. 4, cap 19.

ing, but disabled wretches, who had in vain dragged themselves into the bushes for concealment. The following morning, Vaca de Castro gave orders that the wounded—those who had not perished in the cold damps of the night—should be committed to the care of the surgeons, while the priests were occupied with administering confession and absolution to the dying. Four large graves or pits were dug, in which the bodies of the slain—the conquerors and the conquered—were heaped indiscriminately together. But the remains of Alvarez de Holguin and several other cavaliers of distinction were transported to Guamanga, where they were buried with the solemnities suited to their rank; and the tattered banners won from their vanquished countrymen waved over their monuments, the melancholy trophies of their victory.

The number of killed is variously reported,—from three hundred to five hundred on both sides.[30] The mortality was greatest among the conquerors, who suffered more from the cannon of the enemy before the action, than the latter suffered in the rout that followed it. The number of wounded was still greater; and full half of the survivors of Almagro's party were made prisoners. Many, indeed, escaped from the field to the neighboring town of Guamanga, where they took refuge in the churches and monasteries. But their asylum was not respected, and they were dragged forth and thrown into prison. Their brave young commander fled with a few followers only to Cuzco, where he was instantly arrested by the magistrates whom he had himself placed over the city.[31]

At Guamanga, Vaca de Castro appointed a commission, with the Licentiate de la Gama at its head, for the trial of the prisoners; and *justice* was not satisfied, till forty had been condemned to death, and thirty others—some of them with the loss of one or more of their members—sent into banishment.[32] Such severe reprisals have been too common with the Spaniards in their civil feuds. Strange that they should so

[30] Zarate estimates the number at three hundred. Uscategui, who belonged to the Almagrian party, and Garcilasso, both rate it as high as five hundred.

[31] The particulars of the action are gathered from Pedro Pizarro, Descub. y Conq., MS.—Carta de Ventura Beltran, MS.—Zarate, Conq. del Peru, lib. 4, cap. 17-20.—Naharro, Relacion Sumaria, MS.—Dicho del Capital Francisco de Carbajal sobre la informacion hecha en el Cuzco en 1543, á favor de Vaca de Castro, MS.—Carta del Cabildo de Arequipa al Emperador, MS.—Carta de Barrio Nuevo, MS.—Gomara, Hist. de las Ind., cap. 149.—Garcilasso, Com. Real., Parte 2; lib. 3, cap. 15-18.—Declaracion de Uscategui, MS.

Many of these authorities were personally present on the field; and it is rare that the details of a battle are drawn from more authentic testimony. The student of history will not be surprised that in these details there should be the greatest discrepancy.

[32] Declaracion de Uscategui, MS.—Carta de Ventura Beltran, MS.—Zarate, Conq. del Peru, lib. 4, cap. 21.

The loyal burghers of Arequipa seem to have been well contented with these executions. "If night had not overtaken us," they say, alluding to the action, in their letter to the emperor, "your Majesty would have had no reason to complain; but what was omitted then is made up now, since the governor goes on quartering every day some one or other of the traitors who escaped from the field." See the original in *Appendix, No.* 13.

blindly plunge into these, with this dreadful doom for the vanquished!

From the scene of this bloody tragedy, the governor proceeded to Cuzco, which he entered at the head of his victorious battalions, with all the pomp and military display of a conqueror. He maintained a corresponding state in his way of living, at the expense of a sneer from some, who sarcastically contrasted this ostentatious profusion with the economical reforms he subsequently introduced into the finances.[33] But Vaca de Castro was sensible of the effect of this outward show on the people generally, and disdained no means of giving authority to his office. His first act was to determine the fate of his prisoner, Almagro. A council of war was held. Some were for sparing the unfortunate chief, in consideration of his youth, and the strong cause of provocation he had received. But the majority were of opinion that such mercy could not be extended to the leader of the rebels, and that his death was indispensable to the permanent tranquillity of the country.

When led to execution in the great square of Cuzco,—the same spot where his father had suffered but a few years before,—Almagro exhibited the most perfect composure, though, as the herald proclaimed aloud the doom of the traitor, he indignantly denied that he was one. He made no appeal for mercy to his judges, but simply requested that his bones might be laid by the side of his father's. He objected to having his eyes bandaged, as was customary on such occasions, and, after confession, he devoutly embraced the cross, and submitted his neck to the stroke of the executioner. His remains, agreeably to his request, were transported to the monastery of La Merced, where they were deposited side by side with those of his unfortunate parent.[34]

There have been few names, indeed, in the page of history, more unfortunate than that of Almagro. Yet the fate of the son excites a deeper sympathy than that of the father; and this, not merely on account of his youth, and the peculiar circumstances of his situation. He possessed many of the good qualities of the elder Almagro, with a frank and manly nature, in which the bearing of the soldier was somewhat softened by the refinement of a better education than is to be found in the license of a camp. His career, though short, gave promise of considerable talent, which required only a fair field for its development. But he was the child of misfortune, and his morning of life was overcast by clouds and tempests. If his character, naturally benignant, sometimes showed the fiery sparkles of the vindictive Indian temper, some apology may be found, not merely in his blood, but in the circumstances of his situation. He was more sinned against than sinning; and, if conspiracy could ever find a justification, it must be in a case like this, where, borne down by injuries heaped on his parent and himself, he could obtain no redress from the only quarter whence he had a right to look for it. With him,

[33] Herrera, Hist. General, dec. 7, lib. 4, cap. 1.

[34] Pedro Pizarro, Descub. y Conq., MS.—Zarate, Conq. del Peru, lib. 4, cap. 21.— Naharro. Relacion Sumaria, MS.—Herrera. Hist. General, dec. 7, lib. 6, cap. 1.

the name of Almagro became extinct, and the faction of Chili, so long the terror of the land, passed away for ever.

While these events were occurring in Cuzco, the governor learned that Gonzalo Pizarro had arrived at Lima, where he showed himself greatly discontented with the state of things in Peru. He loudly complained that the government of the country, after his brother's death, had not been placed in his hands; and, as reported by some, he was now meditating schemes for getting possession of it. Vaca de Castro well knew that there would be no lack of evil counsellors to urge Gonzalo to this desperate step; and, anxious to extinguish the spark of insurrection before it had been fanned by these turbulent spirits into a flame, he detached a strong body to Lima to secure that capital. At the same time he commanded the presence of Gonzalo Pizarro in Cuzco.

That chief did not think it prudent to disregard the summons; and shortly after entered the Inca capital, at the head of a well-armed body of cavaliers. He was at once admitted into the governor's presence, when the latter dismissed his guard, remarking that he had nothing to fear from a brave and loyal knight like Pizarro. He then questioned him as to his late adventures in Canelas, and showed great sympathy for his extraordinary sufferings. He took care not to alarm his jealousy by any allusion to his ambitious schemes, and concluded by recommending him, now that the tranquillity of the country was reëstablished, to retire and seek the repose he so much needed, on his valuable estates at Charcas. Gonzalo Pizarro, finding no ground opened for a quarrel with the cool and politic governor, and probably feeling that he was, at least not now, in sufficient strength to warrant it, thought it prudent to take the advice, and withdrew to La Plata, where he busied himself in working those rich mines of silver that soon put him in condition for more momentous enterprise than any he had yet attempted.[35]

Thus rid of his formidable competitor, Vaca de Castro occupied himself with measures for the settlement of the country. He began with his army, a part of which he had disbanded. But many cavaliers still remained, pressing their demands for a suitable recompense for their services. These they were not disposed to undervalue, and the governor was happy to rid himself of their importunities by employing them on distant expeditions, among which was the exploration of the country watered by the great Rio de la Plata. The boiling spirits of the high-mettled cavaliers, without some such vent, would soon have thrown the whole country again into a state of fermentation.

His next concern was to provide laws for the better government of the colony. He gave especial care to the state of the Indian population; and established schools for teaching them Christianity. By various provisions, he endeavored to secure them from the exactions of their conquerors, and he encouraged the poor natives to transfer their own resi-

[35] Pedro Pizarro, Descub. y Conq., MS.—Herrera, Hist. General, dec. 7, lib. 4. cap. 1: lib. 6, cap. 3.—Zarate, Conq. del Peru, lib. 4, cap. 22.

dence to the communities of the white men. He commanded the caciques
to provide supplies for the *tambos,* or houses for the accommodation
of travellers, which lay in their neighborhood, by which regulation he
took away from the Spaniards a plausible apology for rapine, and
greatly promoted facility of intercourse. He was watchful over the finances, much dilapidated in the late troubles, and in several instances
retrenched what he deemed excessive *repartimientos* among the Conquerors. This last act exposed him to much odium from the objects of it.
But his measures were so just and impartial, that he was supported by
public opinion.[36]

Indeed, Vaca de Castro's conduct, from the hour of his arrival in the
country, had been such as to command respect, and prove him competent to the difficult post for which he had been selected. Without
funds, without troops, he had found the country, on his landing, in a
state of anarchy; yet, by courage and address, he had gradually acquired sufficient strength to quell the insurrection. Though no soldier, he had
shown undaunted spirit and presence of mind in the hour of action, and
made his military preparations with a forecast and discretion that excited the admiration of the most experienced veteran.

If he may be thought to have abused the advantages of victory by
cruelty towards the conquered, it must be allowed that he was not influenced by any motives of a personal nature. He was a lawyer, bred in
high notions of royal prerogative. Rebellion he looked upon as an unpardonable crime; and, if his austere nature was unrelenting in the exaction of justice, he lived in an iron age, when justice was rarely tempered by mercy.

In his subsequent regulations for the settlement of the country, he
showed equal impartiality and wisdom. The colonists were deeply sensible of the benefits of his administration, and afforded the best commentary on his services by petitioning the Court of Castile to continue
him in the government of Peru.[37] Unfortunately, such was not the policy
of the Crown.

---

[36] Ibid., ubi supra.—Herrera, Hist. General, dec. 7, lib. 6, cap. 2.

[37] "I asi lo escrivieron al Rei la Ciudad del Cuzco, la Villa de la Plata, i otras
Comunidades, suplicandole, que los dexase por Governador à Vaca de Castro,
como Persona, que procedia con rectitud, i que ià entendia el Govierno de aquellos
Reinos." Herrera, Ibid., loc. cit.

CHAPTER VII

ABUSES BY THE CONQUERORS—CODE FOR THE COLONIES—GREAT EX-
CITEMENT IN PERU—BLASCO NUÑEZ THE VICEROY—HIS SEVERE
POLICY—OPPOSED BY GONZALO PIZARRO

1543—1544

BEFORE continuing the narrative of events in Peru, we must turn to the
mother-country, where important changes were in progress in respect to
the administration of the colonies.

Since his accession to the Crown, Charles the Fifth had been chiefly
engrossed by the politics of Europe, where a theatre was opened more
stimulating to his ambition than could be found in a struggle with the
barbarian princes of the New World. In this quarter, therefore, an empire
almost unheeded, as it were, had been suffered to grow up, until it had
expanded into dimensions greater than those of his European dominions
and destined soon to become far more opulent. A scheme of government
had, it is true, been devised, and laws enacted from time to time for the
regulation of the colonies. But these laws were often accommodated less
to the interests of the colonies themselves, than to those of the parent
country; and, when contrived in a better spirit, they were but imperfectly executed; for the voice of authority, however loudly proclaimed at
home, too often died away in feeble echoes before it had crossed the
waters.

This state of things, and, indeed, the manner in which the Spanish
territories in the New World had been originally acquired, were most
unfortunate both for the conquered races and their masters. Had the
provinces gained by the Spaniards been the fruit of peaceful acquisition,
—of barter and negotiation,—or had their conquest been achieved under
the immediate direction of government, the interests of the natives
would have been more carefully protected. From the superior civilization
of the Indians in the Spanish American colonies, they still continued
after the Conquest to remain on the ground, and to mingle in the same
communities, with the white men; in this forming an obvious contrast
to the condition of our own aborigines, who, shrinking from the contact
of civilization, have withdrawn, as the latter has advanced, deeper and
deeper into the heart of the wilderness. But the South American Indian
was qualified by his previous institutions for a more refined legislation
than could be adapted to the wild hunters of the forest; and, had the

sovereign been there in person to superintend his conquests, he could never have suffered so large a portion of his vassals to be wantonly sacrificed to the cupidity and cruelty of the handful of adventurers who subdued them.

But, as it was, the affair of reducing the country was committed to the hands of irresponsible individuals, soldiers of fortune, desperate adventurers, who entered on conquest as a game, which they were to play in the most unscrupulous manner, with little care but to win it. Receiving small encouragement from the government, they were indebted to their own valor for success; and the right of conquest, they conceived, extinguished every existing right in the unfortunate natives. The lands, the persons, of the conquered races were parcelled out and appropriated by the victors as the legitimate spoils of victory; and outrages were perpetrated every day, at the contemplation of which humanity shudders.

These outrages, though nowhere perpetrated on so terrific a scale as in the islands, where, in a few years, they had nearly annihilated the native population, were yet of sufficient magnitude in Peru to call down the vengeance of Heaven on the heads of their authors; and the Indian might feel that this vengeance was not long delayed, when he beheld his oppressors, wrangling over their miserable spoil, and turning their swords against each other. Peru, as already mentioned, was subdued by adventurers, for the most part, of a lower and more ferocious stamp than those who followed the banner of Cortés. The character of the followers partook, in some measure, of that of the leaders in their respective enterprises. It was a sad fatality for the Incas; for the reckless soldiers of Pizarro were better suited to contend with the fierce Aztec than with the more refined and effeminate Peruvian. Intoxicated by the unaccustomed possession of power, and without the least notion of the responsibilities which attached to their situation as masters of the land, they too often abandoned themselves to the indulgence of every whim which cruelty or caprice could dictate. Not unfrequently, says an unsuspicious witness, I have seen the Spaniards, long after the Conquest, amuse themselves by hunting down the natives with bloodhounds for mere sport, or in order to train their dogs to the game![1] The most unbounded scope was given to licentiousness. The young maiden was torn without remorse from the arms of her family to gratify the passion of her brutal conqueror.[2] The sacred houses of the Virgins of the Sun were broken open and violated, and the cavalier swelled his harem with a troop of Indian girls making it seem that the Crescent would have been a much more fitting symbol for his banner than the immaculate Cross.[3]

[1] "Españoles hai que crian perros carniceros i los avezan á matar Indios, lo qual procuran á las veces por pasatiempo, i ver si lo hacen bien los perros." Relacion que dió el Provisor Morales sobre las cosas que convenian provarse en el Peru, MS.

[2] "Que los Justicias dan cedulas de Anaconas que por otros terminos los hacen esclavos é vivir contra su voluntad, diciendo: Por la presente damos licencia á vos Fulano, para que os podais servir de tal Indio ó de tal India é lo podais tomar é sacar donde quiera que lo hallaredes." Rel. del Provisor Morales, MS.

[3] "Es general el vicio del amancebamiento con Indias, i algunos tienen cantidad dellas como en serrallo." Ibid., MS.

But the dominant passion of the Spaniard was the lust of gold. For this he shrunk from no toil himself, and was merciless in his exactions of labor from his Indian slave. Unfortunately, Peru abounded in mines which too well repaid this labor; and human life was the item of least account in the estimate of the Conquerors. Under his Incas, the Peruvian was never suffered to be idle; but the task imposed on him was always proportioned to his strength. He had his seasons of rest and refreshment, and was well protected against the inclemency of the weather. Every care was shown for his personal safety. But the Spaniards, while they taxed the strength of the native to the utmost, deprived him of the means of repairing it, when exhausted. They suffered the provident arrangements of the Incas to fall into decay. The granaries were emptied; the flocks were wasted in riotous living. They were slaughtered to gratify a mere epicurean whim, and many a llama was destroyed solely for the sake of the brains,—a dainty morsel, much coveted by the Spaniards.[4] So reckless was the spirit of destruction after the Conquest, says Onde-gardo, the wise governor of Cuzco, that in four years more of these animals perished than in four hundred, in the times of the Incas.[5] The flocks, once so numerous over the broad table-lands, were now thinned to a scanty number, that sought shelter in the fastnesses of the Andes. The poor Indian, without food, without the warm fleece which furnished him a defence against the cold, now wandered half-starved and naked over the plateau. Even those who had aided the Spaniards in the conquest fared no better; and many an Inca noble roamed a mendicant over the lands where he once held rule, and if driven, perchance, by his necessities, to purloin something from the superfluity of his conquerors, he expiated it by a miserable death.[6]

It is true, there were good men, missionaries, faithful to their calling, who wrought hard in the spiritual conversion of the native, and who, touched by his misfortunes, would gladly have interposed their arm to shield him from his oppressors.[7] But too often the ecclesiastic became

---

[4] "Muchos Españoles han muerto i matan increible cantidad de ovejas por comer solo los sesos, hacer pasteles del tuetano i candelas de la grasa. De ai hambre general." Ibid., MS.

[5] "Se puede afirmar que hicieron mas daño los Españoles en solos quatro años que el Inga en quatrocientos." Ondegardo, Rel. Seg., MS.

[6] "Ahora no tienen que comer ni donde sembrar, i asi van á hurtallo como solian, delito por que han aorcado á muchos." Rel. del Provisor Morales, MS.

This, and some of the preceding citations, as the reader will see, have been taken from the MS. of the Bachelor Luis de Morales, who lived eighteen or twenty years in Cuzco; and, in 1541, about the time of Vaca de Castro's coming to Peru, prepared a Memorial for the government, embracing a hundred and nine chapters. It treats of the condition of the country, and the remedies which suggested themselves to the benevolent mind of its author. The emperor's notes on the margin show that it received attention at court. There is no reason, as far as I am aware, to distrust the testimony of the writer, and Muñoz has made some sensible extracts from it for his inestimable collection.

[7] Father Naharro notices twelve missionaries, some of his own order, whose zealous labors and miracles for the conversion of the Indians he deems worthy of comparison with those of the twelve Apostles of Christianity. It is a pity that

infected by the general spirit of licentiousness; and the religious fraternities, who led a life of easy indulgence on the lands cultivated by their
Indian slaves, were apt to think less of the salvation of their souls than
of profiting by the labor of their bodies.[8]

Yet still there were not wanting good and wise men in the colonies,
who, from time to time, raised the voice of remonstrance against these
abuses, and who carried their complaints to the foot of the throne. To
the credit of the government, it must also be confessed, that it was solicitous to obtain such information as it could, both from its own officers,
and from commissioners deputed expressly for the purpose, whose voluminous communications throw a flood of light on the internal condition
of the country, and furnish the best materials for the historian.[9] But it
was found much easier to get this information than to profit by it.

In 1541, Charles the Fifth, who had been much occupied by the affairs of Germany, revisited his ancestral dominions, where his attention
was imperatively called to the state of the colonies. Several memorials in
relation to it were laid before him; but no one pressed the matter so
strongly on the royal conscience as Las Casas, afterwards Bishop of
Chiapa. This good ecclesiastic, whose long life had been devoted to those
benevolent labors which gained him the honorable title of Protector of
the Indians, had just completed his celebrated treatise on the Destruction of the Indies, the most remarkable record, probably, to be found,

history, while it has commemorated the names of so many persecutors of the
poor heathen, should have omitted those of their benefactors.

"Tomó su divina Magestad por instrumento 12 solos religiosos pobres, descalzos
i desconocidos, 5 del orden de la Merced, 4 de Predicadores, i 3 de San Francisco,
obraron lo mismo que los 12 apostolos en la conversion de todo el universo mundo."
Naharro, Relacion Sumaria, MS.

[8] "Todos los conventos de Dominicos i Mercenarios tienen repartimientos. Ninguno dellos ha dotrinado ni convertido un Indio. Procuran sacar dellos quanto
pueden, trabajarles en grangerias; con esto i con otras limosnas enriquecen. Mal
egemplo. Ademas convendrá no pasen frailes sino precediendo diligente examen de
vida i dotrina." (Relacion de las cosas que S. M. deve proveer para los reynos del
Peru, embiada desde los Reyes á la Corte por el Licenciado Martel Santoyo, de
quien va firmáda en principios de 1542, MS.) This statement of the licentiate
shows a different side of the picture from that above quoted from Father Naharro. Yet they are not irreconcilable. Human nature has both its lights and its
shadows.

[9] I have several of these Memorials or *Relaciones*, as they are called, in my
possession, drawn up by residents in answer to queries propounded by government. These queries, while their great object is to ascertain the nature of existing
abuses, and to invite the suggestion of remedies, are often directed to the laws and
usages of the ancient Incas. The responses, therefore, are of great value to the
historical inquirer. The most important of these documents in my possession is that
by Ondegardo, governor of Cuzco, covering near four hundred folio pages, once
forming part of Lord Kingsborough's valuable collection. It is impossible to per-
use these elaborate and conscientious reports without a deep conviction of the
pains taken by the Crown to ascertain the nature of the abuses in the domestic
government of the colonies, and their honest purpose to amend them. Unfortunately, in this laudable purpose they were not often seconded by the colonists
themselves.

of human wickedness, but which, unfortunately, loses much of its effect from the credulity of the writer, and his obvious tendency to exaggerate.

In 1542, Las Casas placed his manuscript in the hands of his royal master. That same year, a council was called at Valladolid, composed chiefly of jurists and theologians, to devise a system of laws for the regulation of the American colonies.

Las Casas appeared before this body, and made an elaborate argument, of which a part only has been given to the public. He there assumes, as a fundamental proposition, that the Indians were by the law of nature free; that, as vassals of the Crown, they had a right to its protection, and should be declared free from that time, without exception and for ever.[10] He sustains this proposition by a great variety of arguments, comprehending the substance of most that has been since urged in the same cause by the friends of humanity. He touches on the ground of expediency, showing, that, without the interference of government, the Indian race must be gradually exterminated by the systematic oppression of the Spaniards. In conclusion, he maintains, that, if the Indians, as it was pretended, would not labor unless compelled, the white man would still find it for his interest to cultivate the soil; and that if he should not be able to do so, that circumstance would give him no right over the Indian, since *God does not allow evil that good may come of it*.[11]—This lofty morality, it will be remembered, was from the lips of a Dominican, in the sixteenth century, one of the order that founded the Inquisition, and in the very country where the fiery tribunal was then in most active operation![12]

The arguments of Las Casas encountered all the opposition naturally to be expected from indifference, selfishness, and bigotry. They were also resisted by some persons of just and benevolent views in his audience, who, while they admitted the general correctness of his reasoning, and felt deep sympathy for the wrongs of the natives, yet doubted whether

[10] The perpetual emancipation of the Indians is urged in the most emphatic manner by another bishop, also a Dominican, but bearing certainly very little resemblance to Las Casas. Fray Valverde makes this one of the prominent topics in a communication, already cited, to the government, the general scope of which must be admitted to do more credit to his humanity than some of the passages recorded of him in history.—"A V. M. representarán alla los conquistadores muchos servicios, dandalos por causa para que los dexen servir de los indios como de esclavos: V. M. se los tiene mui bien pagados en los provechos que han avido desta tierra, y no los ha de pagar con hazer á sus vasallos esclavos." Carta de Valverde al Emperador, MS.

[11] "La loi de Dieu défend de faire le mal pour qu'il en résulte du bien." Œuvres de Las Casas, évêque de Chiapa, trad. par Llorente, (Paris, 1822,) tom. I, p. 251.

[12] It is a curious coincidence, that this argument of Las Casas should have been first published—in a translated form, indeed—by a secretary of the Inquisition, Llorente. The original still remains in MS. It is singular that these volumes, containing the views of this great philanthropist on topics of such interest to humanity, should not have been more freely consulted, or at least cited, by those who have since trod in his footsteps. They are an arsenal from which many a serviceable weapon for the good cause might be borrowed.

his scheme of reform was not fraught with greater evils than those it was intended to correct. For Las Casas was the uncompromising friend of freedom. He intrenched himself strongly on the ground of natural right; and, like some of the reformers of our own day, disdained to calculate the consequences of carrying out the principle to its full and unqualified extent. His earnest eloquence, instinct with the generous love of humanity, and fortified by a host of facts, which it was not easy to assail, prevailed over his auditors. The result of their deliberations was a code of ordinances, which, however, far from being limited to the wants of the natives, had particular reference to the European population, and the distractions of the country. It was of general application to all the American colonies. It will be necessary here only to point out some of the provisions having immediate reference to Peru.

The Indians were declared true and loyal vassals of the Crown, and their freedom as such was fully recognized. Yet, to maintain inviolate the guaranty of the government to the Conquerors, it was decided, that those lawfully possessed of slaves might retain them; but, at the death of the present proprietors, they were to revert to the Crown.

It was provided, however, that slaves, in any event, should be forfeited by all those who had shown themselves unworthy to hold them by neglect or ill-usage; by all public functionaries, or such as had held offices under the government; by ecclesiastics and religious corporations; and lastly,—a sweeping clause,—by all who had taken a criminal part in the feuds of Almagro and Pizarro.

It was further ordered, that the Indians should be moderately taxed; that they should not be compelled to labor where they did not choose, and that where, from particular circumstances, this was made necessary, they should receive a fair compensation. It was also decreed, that, as the *repartimientos* of land were often excessive, they should in such cases be reduced; and that, where proprietors had been guilty of a notorious abuse of their slaves, their estates should be forfeited altogether.

As Peru had always shown a spirit of insubordination, which required a more vigorous interposition of authority than was necessary in the other colonies, it was resolved to send a viceroy to that country, who should display a state, and be armed with powers, that might make him a more fitting representative of the sovereign. He was to be accompanied by a Royal Audience, consisting of four judges, with extensive powers of jurisdiction, both criminal and civil, who, besides a court of justice, should constitute a sort of council to advise with and aid the viceroy. The Audience of Panamá was to be dissolved, and the new tribunal, with the vice-king's court, was to be established at Los Reyes, or Lima, as it now began to be called,—henceforth the metropolis of the Spanish empire on the Pacific.[13]

___

[13] The provisions of this celebrated code are to be found, with more or less— generally less—accuracy, in the various contemporary writers. Herrera gives them *in extenso*. Hist. General, dec. 7, lib. 6, cap. 5.

Such were some of the principal features of this remarkable code, which, touching on the most delicate relations of society, broke up the very foundations of property, and, by a stroke of the pen, as it were, converted a nation of slaves into freemen. It would have required, we may suppose, but little forecast to divine, that in the remote regions of America, and especially in Peru, where the colonists had been hitherto accustomed to unbounded license, a reform, so salutary in essential points, could be enforced thus summarily only at the price of a revolution.—Yet the ordinances received the sanction of the emperor that same year, and in November, 1543, were published at Madrid.[14]

No sooner was their import known than it was conveyed by numerous letters to the colonists, from their friends in Spain. The tidings flew like wildfire over the land, from Mexico to Chili. Men were astounded at the prospect of the ruin that awaited them. In Peru, particularly, there was scarcely one that could hope to escape the operation of the law. Few there were who had not taken part, at some time or other, in the civil feuds of Almagro and Pizarro; and still fewer of those that remained that would not be entangled in some one or other of the insidious clauses that seemed spread out, like a web, to ensnare them.

The whole country was thrown into commotion. Men assembled tumultuously in the squares and public places, and, as the regulations were made known they were received with universal groans and hisses. "Is this the fruit," they cried, "of all our toil? Is it for this that we have poured out our blood like water? Now that we are broken down by hardships and sufferings, to be left at the end of our campaigns as poor as at the beginning! Is this the way government rewards our services in winning for it an empire? The government has done little to aid us in making the conquest, and for what we have we may thank our own good swords; and with these same swords," they continued, warming into menace, "we know how to defend it." Then, stripping up his sleeve, the war-worn veteran bared his arm, or, exposing his naked bosom, pointed to his scars, as the best title to his estates.[15]

The governor, Vaca de Castro, watched the storm thus gathering from all quarters, with the deepest concern. He was himself in the very heart

[14] Las Casas pressed the matter home on the royal conscience, by representing that the Papal See conceded the right of conquest to the Spanish sovereigns on the exclusive condition of converting the heathen, and that the Almighty would hold him accountable for the execution of this trust. Œuvres de Las Casas, ubi supra.

[15] Carta de Gonzalo Pizarro a Pedro de Valdivia, MS., desde Los Reyes, 31 de Oct., 1538.—Zarate, Conq. del Peru, lib. 5, cap. 1.—Herrera, Hist. General, dec. 7, lib. 6, cap. 10, 11.

Benalcazar, in a letter to Charles the Fifth, indulges in a strain of invective against the ordinances, which, by stripping the planters of their Indian slaves, must inevitably reduce the country to beggary. Benalcazar was a conqueror, and one of the most respectable of his caste. His argument is a good specimen of the reasoning of his party on this subject, and presents a decided counterblast to that of Las Casas. Carta de Benalcazar al Emperador, MS., desde Cali, 20 de Diciembre, 1544.

of disaffection; for Cuzco, tenanted by a mixed and lawless population, was so far removed into the depths of the mountains, that it had much less intercourse with the parent country, and was consequently much less under her influence, than the great towns on the coast. The people now invoked the governor to protect them against the tyranny of the Court; but he endeavored to calm the agitation by representing, that by these violent measures they would only defeat their own object. He counselled them to name deputies to lay their petition before the Crown, stating the impracticability of the present scheme of reform, and praying for the repeal of it; and he conjured them to wait patiently for the arrival of the viceroy, who might be prevailed on to suspend the ordinances till further advices could be received from Castile.

But it was not easy to still the tempest; and the people now eagerly looked for some one whose interests and sympathies might lie with theirs, and whose position in the community might afford them protection. The person to whom they naturally turned in this crisis was Gonzalo Pizarro, the last in the land of that family who had led the armies of the Conquest,—a cavalier whose gallantry and popular manners had made him always a favorite with the people. He was now beset with applications to interpose in their behalf with the government, and shield them from the oppressive ordinances.

But Gonzalo Pizarro was at Charcas, busily occupied in exploring the rich veins of Potosí, whose silver fountains, just brought into light, were soon to pour such streams of wealth over Europe. Though gratified with this appeal to his protection, the cautious cavalier was more intent on providing for the means of enterprise than on plunging prematurely into it; and, while he secretly encouraged the malecontents, he did not commit himself by taking part in any revolutionary movement. At the same period, he received letters from Vaca de Castro,—whose vigilant eye watched all the aspects of the time,—cautioning Gonzalo and his friends not to be seduced, by any wild schemes of reform, from their allegiance. And, to check still further these disorderly movements, he ordered his alcaldes to arrest every man guilty of seditious language, and bring him at once to punishment. By this firm yet temperate conduct the minds of the populace were overawed, and there was a temporary lull in the troubled waters, while all looked anxiously for the coming of the viceroy.[16]

The person selected for this critical post was a knight of Avila, named Blasco Nuñez Vela. He was a cavalier of ancient family, handsome in person, though now somewhat advanced in years, and reputed brave and devout. He had filled some offices of responsibility to the satisfaction of Charles the Fifth, by whom he was now appointed to this post in Peru. The selection did no credit to the monarch's discernment.

---

[16] Ibid., ubi supra.—Zarate, Conq. del Peru, ubi supra.—Pedro Pizarro, Descub y Conq., MS.—Carta de Gonzalo Pizarro a Valdivia. MS.—Montesinos, Annales MS., año 1543

It n.ay seem strange that this important place should not have been bestowed on Vaca de Castro, already on the spot, and who had shown himself so well qualified to fill it. But ever since that officer's mission to Peru, there had been a series of assassinations, insurrections, and civil wars, that menaced the wretched colony with ruin; and, though his wise administration had now brought things into order, the communication with the Indies was so tardy, that the results of his policy were not yet fully disclosed. As it was designed, moreover, to make important innova-tions in the government, it was thought better to send some one who would have no personal prejudices to encounter, from the part he had already taken, and who, coming directly from the Court, and clothed with extraordinary powers, might present himself with greater authority than could one who had become familiar to the people in an inferior capacity. The monarch, however, wrote a letter with his own hand to Vaca de Castro, in which he thanked that officer for his past services, and directed him, after aiding the new viceroy with the fruits of his large experience, to return to Castile, and take his seat in the Royal Council. Letters of a similar complimentary kind were sent to the loyal colonists who had stood by the governor in the late troubles of the country. Freighted with these testimonials, and with the ill-starred ordinances, Blasco Nuñez embarked at San Lucar, on the 3d of November, 1543. He was attended by the four judges of the Audience, and by a numerous retinue, that he might appear in the state befitting his distinguished rank.[17]

About the middle of the following January, 1544, the viceroy, after a favorable passage, landed at Nombre de Dios. He found there a vessel laden with silver from the Peruvian mines, ready to sail for Spain. His first act was to lay an embargo on it for the government, as containing the proceeds of slave labor. After this extraordinary measure, taken in opposition to the advice of the Audience, he crossed the Isthmus to Panamá. Here he gave sure token of his future policy, by causing more than three hundred Indians, who had been brought by their owners from Peru, to be liberated and sent back to their own country. This high-handed measure created the greatest sensation in the city, and was strongly resisted by the judges of the Audience. They besought him not to begin thus precipitately to execute his commission, but to wait till his arrival in the colony, when he should have taken time to acquaint him-self somewhat with the country, and with the temper of the people. But Blasco Nuñez coldly replied, that "he had come, not to tamper with the laws, nor to discuss their merits, but to execute them,—and execute them he would, to the letter, whatever might be the consequence."[18] This

[17] Carta de Gonzalo Pizarro a Valdivia, MS.—Herrera, Hist. General, dec. 7, lib. 6, cap. 9.—Fernandez, Hist. del Peru, Parte 1, lib. 1, cap. 6.--Zarate, MS.

[18] "Estas y otras cosas le dixo el Licenciado Çarate: que no fueron al gusto del Virey: antes se enojò mucho por ello, y respondio con alguna aspereza: jurando. que auia de executar las ordenanças como en ellas se contenia: sin esperar para ello terminos algunos, ni dilaciones." Fernandez, Hist. del Peru, Parte 1, lib. 1, cap. 6.

answer, and the peremptory tone in which it was delivered, promptly ad-
journed the debate; for the judges saw that debate was useless with one
who seemed to consider all remonstrance as an attempt to turn him from
his duty, and whose ideas of duty precluded all discretionary exercise of
authority, even where the public good demanded it.

Leaving the Audience, as one of its body was ill, at Panamá, the viceroy proceeded on his way, and, coasting down the shores of the Pacific,
on the fourth of March he disembarked at Tumbez. He was well received
by the loyal inhabitants; his authority was publicly proclaimed, and the
people were overawed by the display of a magnificence and state such
as had not till then been seen in Peru. He took an early occasion to intimate his future line of policy by liberating a number of Indian slaves
on the application of their caciques. He then proceeded by land towards
the south, and showed his determination to conform in his own person
to the strict letter of the ordinances, by causing his baggage to be carried
by mules, where it was practicable; and where absolutely necessary to
make use of Indians, he paid them fairly for their services.[19]

The whole country was thrown into consternation by reports of the
proceedings of the viceroy, and of his conversations, most unguarded,
which were eagerly circulated, and, no doubt, often exaggerated. Meetings were again called in the cities. Discussions were held on the expediency of resisting his further progress, and a deputation of citizens
from Cuzco, who were then in Lima, strongly urged the people to close
the gates of that capital against him. But Vaca de Castro had also left
Cuzco for the latter city, on the earliest intimation of the viceroy's approach, and, with some difficulty, he prevailed on the inhabitants not to
swerve from their loyalty, but to receive their new ruler with suitable
honors, and trust to his calmer judgment for postponing the execution
of the law till the case could be laid before the throne.

But the great body of the Spaniards, after what they had heard, had
slender confidence in the relief to be obtained from this quarter. They
now turned with more eagerness than ever towards Gonzalo Pizarro; and
letters and addresses poured in upon him from all parts of the country,
inviting him to take on himself the office of their protector. These applications found a more favorable response than on the former occasion.

There were, indeed, many motives at work to call Gonzalo into action.
It was to his family, mainly, that Spain was indebted for this extension
of her colonial empire; and he had felt deeply aggrieved that the government of the colony should be trusted to other hands than his. He had felt
this on the arrival of Vaca de Castro, and much more so when the appointment of a viceroy proved it to be the settled policy of the Crown to
exclude his family from the management of affairs. His brother Hernando still languished in prison, and he himself was now to be sacrificed
as the principal victim of the fatal ordinances. For who had taken so

[19] Zarate, Conq. del Peru, lib. 5, cap. 2.—Fernandez, Hist. del Peru, ubi supra.
--Carta de Gonzalo Pizarro a Valdivia, MS.—Montesinos, Annales, MS., año 1544

prominent a part in the civil war with the elder Almagro? And the vice-roy was currently reported—it may have been scandal—to have inti-mated that Pizarro would be dealt with accordingly.[20] Yet there was no one in the country who had so great a stake, who had so much to lose by the revolution. Abandoned thus by the government, he conceived that it was now time to take care of himself.

Assembling together some eighteen or twenty cavaliers in whom he most trusted, and taking a large amount of silver, drawn from the mines, he accepted the invitation to repair to Cuzco. As he approached this capital, he was met by a numerous body of the citizens, who came out to welcome him, making the air ring with their shouts, as they saluted him with the title of Procurator-General of Peru. The title was speedily con-firmed by the municipality of the city, who invited him to head a depu-tation to Lima, in order to state their grievances to the viceroy, and solicit the present suspension of the ordinances.

But the spark of ambition was kindled in the bosom of Pizarro. He felt strong in the affections of the people; and, from the more elevated position in which he now stood, his desires took a loftier and more un-bounded range. Yet, if he harbored a criminal ambition in his breast, he skilfully veiled it from others—perhaps from himself. The only ob-ject he professed to have in view was the good of the people;[21] a sus-picious phrase, usually meaning the good of the individual. He now de-manded permission to raise and organize an armed force, with the fur-ther title of Captain-General. His views were entirely pacific; but it was not safe, unless strongly protected, to urge them on a person of the viceroy's impatient and arbitrary temper. It was further contended by Pizarro's friends, that such a force was demanded, to rid the country of their old enemy, the Inca Manco, who hovered in the neighboring mountains with a body of warriors, ready, at the first opportunity, to descend on the Spaniards. The municipality of Cuzco hesitated, as well it might, to confer powers so far beyond its legitimate authority. But Pizarro avowed his purpose, in case of refusal, to decline the office of Procurator; and the efforts of his partisans, backed by those of the people, at length silenced the scruples of the magistrates, who bestowed on the ambitious chief the military command to which he aspired. Pi-zarro accepted it with the modest assurance, that he did so "purely from

[20] "It was not fair," the viceroy said, "that the country should remain longer in the hands of muleteers and swineherds, (alluding to the origin of the Pizarros,) and he would take measures to restore it to the Crown."

"Que asi me la havia de cortar á mi i á todos los que havian seido notablemente, como el decia, culpados en la batalla de las Salinas i en las diferencias de Almagro, i que una tierra como esta no era justo que estuviese en poder de gente tan vaxa que llamava el á los desta tierro porqueros i arrieros, sino que estuviese toda en la Corona real." Carta de Gonzalo Pizarro a Valdivia, MS.

[21] "Diciendo que no queria nada para si, sino para el beneficio universal, i que por todos havia de poner todas sus fuerças." Herrera, Hist. General, dec. 7. lib. 7 cap. 20.

regard to the interests of the king, of the Indies, and, above all, of Peru!" [22]

[22] "Acepté lo por ver que en ello hacia servicio á Dios i á S. M. i gran bien á esta tier: : i generalmente á todas las Indias." Carta de Gonzalo Pizarro a Valdivia, MS.

Herrera, Hist. General, dec. 7, lib. 7, cap. 19, 20.—Zarate, Conq. del Peru, lib. 5, cap. 4, 8.—Fernandez, Hist. del Peru, Parte 1, lib. 1, cap. 8.—Carta de Gonzalo Pizarro a Valdivia, MS.—Montesinos, Annales, MS., año 1544.

CHAPTER VIII

THE VICEROY ARRIVES AT LIMA—GONZALO PIZARRO MARCHES FROM CUZCO—DEATH OF THE INCA MANCO—RASH CONDUCT OF THE VICEROY—SEIZED AND DEPOSED BY THE AUDIENCE—GONZALO PROCLAIMED GOVERNOR OF PERU

1544

WHILE the events recorded in the preceding pages were in progress, Blasco Nuñez had been journeying towards Lima. But the alienation which his conduct had already caused in the minds of the colonists was shown in the cold reception which he occasionally experienced on the route, and in the scanty accommodations provided for him and his retinue. In one place where he took up his quarters, he found an ominous inscription over the door:—"He that takes my property must expect to pay for it with his life."[1] Neither daunted, nor diverted from his purpose, the inflexible viceroy held on his way towards the capital, where the inhabitants, preceded by Vaca de Castro and the municipal authorities, came out to receive him. He entered in great state, under a canopy of crimson cloth, embroidered with the arms of Spain, and supported by stout poles or staves of solid silver, which were borne by the members of the municipality. A cavalier, holding a mace, the emblem of authority, rode before him; and after the oaths of office were administered in the council-chamber, the procession moved towards the cathedral, where Te Deum was sung, and Blasco Nuñez was installed in his new dignity of viceroy of Peru.[2]

[1] "A quien me viniere à quitar mi hacienda, quitarle he la vida." Herrera, Hist. General, dec. 7, lib. 7, cap. 18.

[2] "Entró en la cibdad de Lima á 17 de Mayo de 1544: saliole á recibir todo el pueblo á pie y á caballo dos tiros de ballesta del pueblo, y á la entrada de la cibdad estaba un arco triunfal de verde con las Armas de España, y las de la misma cibdad; estaban le esperando el Regimiento y Justicia, y oficiales del Rey con ropas largas, hasta en pies de carmesi, y un palio del mesmo carmesi aforrado en lo mesmo, con ocho baras guarnecidas de plata y tomaronle debajo todos á pie, cada Regidor y justicia con una bara del palio, y el Virrey en su caballo con las mazas delante tomaronle juramento en un libro misal, y juró de las guardar y cumplir todas sus libertades y provisiones de S. M.; y luego fueron desta manera hasta la iglesia, salieron los clerigos con la cruz á la puerta y le metieron dentro cantando Te deum laudamus, y despues que obo dicho su oracion, fué con el cabildo y toda la ciudad á su palacio donde fué recebido y hizo un parlamento breve en que contentó á toda la gente." Relacion de los sucesos del Peru desde que entró el virrey Blasco Nuñez acaecidos en mar y tierra, MS.

His first act was to proclaim his determination in respect to the ordinances. He had no warrant to suspend their execution. He should fulfil his commission; but he offered to join the colonists in a memorial to the emperor, soliciting the repeal of a code which he now believed would be for the interests neither of the country nor of the Crown.[3] With this avowed view of the subject, it may seem strange that Blasco Nuñez should not have taken the responsibility of suspending the law until his sovereign could be assured of the inevitable consequences of enforcing it. The pacha of a Turkish despot, who had allowed himself this latitude for the interests of his master, might, indeed, have reckoned on the bowstring. But the example of Mendoza, the prudent viceroy of Mexico, who adopted this course in a similar crisis, and precisely at the same period, showed its propriety under existing circumstances. The ordinances were suspended by him till the Crown could be warned of the consequences of enforcing them,—and Mexico was saved from revolution.[4] But Blasco Nuñez had not the wisdom of Mendoza.

The public apprehension was now far from being allayed. Secret cabals were formed in Lima, and communications held with the different towns. No distrust, however, was raised in the breast of the viceroy, and, when informed of the preparations of Gonzalo Pizarro, he took no other step than to send a message to his camp, announcing the extraordinary powers with which he was himself invested, and requiring that chief to disband his forces. He seemed to think that a mere word from him would be sufficient to dissipate rebellion. But it required more than a breath to scatter the iron soldiery of Peru.

Gonzalo Pizarro, meanwhile, was busily occupied in mustering his army. His first step was to order from Guamanga sixteen pieces of artillery, sent there by Vaca de Castro, who, in the present state of excitement, was unwilling to trust the volatile people of Cuzco with these implements of destruction. Gonzalo, who had no scruples as to Indian labor, appropriated six thousand of the natives to the service of transporting this train of ordnance across the mountains.[5]

By his exertions and those of his friends, the active chief soon mustered a force of nearly four hundred men, which, if not very imposing in the outset, he conceived would be swelled, in his descent to the coast, by tributary levies from the towns and villages on the way. All his own funds were expended in equipping his men and providing for the march; and, to supply deficiencies, he made no scruple—since, to use his words, it was for the public interest—to appropriate the moneys in the royal treasury. With this seasonable aid, his troops, well mounted and thoroughly equipped, were put in excellent fighting order; and, after making them a brief harangue, in which he was careful to insist on the pacific character of his enterprise, somewhat at variance with its military

---

[3] "Porque llanamente el confesaba, que asi para su Magestad, como para aquellos Reinos, eran perjudiciales." Zarate, Conq. del Peru, lib. ᴄ cap. 5.

[4] Fernandez, Hist. del Peru, Parte 1, lib. 1, cap ⁻ ᴄ.

[5] Zarate, Conq. del Peru, lib. 5, cap. 8.

preparations, Gonzalo Pizarro sallied forth from the gates of the capital.

Before leaving it, he received an important accession of strength in the person of Francisco de Carbajal, the veteran who performed so conspicuous a part in the battle of Chupas. He was at Charcas when the news of the ordinances reached Peru; and he instantly resolved to quit the country and return to Spain, convinced that the New World would be no longer the land for him,—no longer the golden Indies. Turning his effects into money, he prepared to embark them on board the first ship that offered. But no opportunity occurred, and he could have little expectation now of escaping the vigilant eye of the viceroy. Yet, though solicited by Pizarro to take command under him in the present expedition, the veteran declined, saying, he was eighty years old, and had no wish but to return home, and spend his few remaining days in quiet.[6] Well had it been for him, had he persisted in his refusal. But he yielded to the importunities of his friend; and the short space that yet remained to him of life proved long enough to brand his memory with perpetual infamy.

Soon after quitting Cuzco, Pizarro learned the death of the Inca Manco. He was massacred by a party of Spaniards, of the faction of Almagro, who, on the defeat of their young leader, had taken refuge in the Indian camp. They, in turn, were all slain by the Peruvians. It is impossible to determine on whom the blame of the quarrel should rest, since no one present at the time has recorded it.[7]

The death of Manco Inca, as he was commonly called, is an event not to be silently passed over in Peruvian history; for he was the last of his race that may be said to have been animated by the heroic spirit of the ancient Incas. Though placed on the throne by Pizarro, far from remaining a mere puppet in his hands, Manco soon showed that his lot was not to be cast with that of his conquerors. With the ancient institutions of his country lying a wreck around him, he yet struggled bravely, like Guatemozin, the last of the Aztecs, to uphold her tottering fortunes, or to bury his oppressors under her ruins. By the assault on his own capital of Cuzco, in which so large a portion of it was demolished, he gave a check to the arms of Pizarro, and, for a season, the fate of the Conquerors trembled in the balance. Though foiled, in the end, by the superior science of his adversary, the young barbarian still showed the same unconquerable spirit as before. He withdrew into the fastnesses of his native mountains, whence sallying forth as occasion offered, he fell on the caravan of the traveller, or on some scattered party of the military; and, in the event of a civil war, was sure to throw his own weight into the weaker scale, thus prolonging the contest of his enemies, and feeding his revenge by the sight of their calamities. Moving lightly from spot to spot, he eluded pursuit amidst the wilds of the Cordilleras; and, hovering in the neighborhood of the towns, or lying in ambush on the

[6] Herrera, Hist. General, dec. 7, lib. 7, cap. 22.
[7] Pedro Pizarro, Descub. y Conq., MS.—Garcilasso, Com. Real., Parte 2, lib. 4, cap. 7.

great thoroughfares of the country, the Inca Manco made his name a terror to the Spaniards. Often did they hold out to him terms of accommodation; and every succeeding ruler, down to Blasco Nuñez, bore instructions from the Crown to employ every art to conciliate the formidable warrior. But Manco did not trust the promises of the white man; and he chose rather to maintain his savage independence in the mountains, with the few brave spirits around him, than to live a slave in the land which had once owned the sway of his ancestors.

The death of the Inca removed one of the great pretexts for Gonzalo Pizarro's military preparations; but it had little influence on him, as may be readily imagined. He was much more sensible to the desertion of some of his followers, which took place early on the march. Several of the cavaliers of Cuzco, startled by his unceremonious appropriation of the public moneys, and by the belligerent aspect of affairs, now for the first time seemed to realize that they were in the path of rebellion. A number of these, including some principal men of the city, secretly withdrew from the army, and, hastening to Lima, offered their services to the viceroy. The troops were disheartened by this desertion, and even Pizarro for a moment faltered in his purpose, and thought of retiring with some fifty followers to Charcas, and there making his composition with government. But a little reflection, aided by the remonstrances of the courageous Carbajal, who never turned his back on an enterprise which he had once assumed, convinced him that he had gone too far to recede,—that his only safety was to advance.

He was reassured by more decided manifestations, which he soon after received, of the public opinion. An officer named Puelles, who commanded at Guanuco, joined him, with a body of horse with which he had been intrusted by the viceroy. This defection was followed by that of others, and Gonzalo, as he descended the sides of the table-land, found his numbers gradually swelled to nearly double the amount with which he had left the Indian capital.

As he traversed with a freer step the bloody field of Chupas, Carbajal pointed out the various localities of the battle-ground, and Pizarro might have found food for anxious reflection, as he meditated on the fortunes of a rebel. At Guamanga he was received with open arms by the inhabitants, many of whom eagerly enlisted under his banner; for they trembled for their property, as they heard from all quarters of the inflexible temper of the viceroy.[8]

That functionary began now to be convinced that he was in a critical position. Before Puelles's treachery, above noticed, had been consummated, the viceroy had received some vague intimation of his purpose. Though scarcely crediting it, he detached one of his company, named Diaz, with a force to intercept him. But, although that cavalier undertook the mission with alacrity, he was soon after prevailed on to follow the ex-

[8] Fernandez, Hist. del Peru, Parte 1, lib. 1, cap. 14, 16.—Zarate, Conq. del Peru, lib. 5, cap. 9, 10.—Herrera, Hist. General, dec. 7, lib. 8, cap. 5-9.—Carta de Gonzalo Pizarro a Valdivia, MS.—Relacion de los Sucesos del Peru, MS.

ample of his comrade, and, with the greater part of the men under his command, went over to the enemy. In the civil feuds of this unhappy land, parties changed sides so lightly, that treachery to a commander had almost ceased to be a stain on the honor of a cavalier. Yet all, on whichever side they cast their fortunes, loudly proclaimed their loyalty to the Crown.

Thus betrayed by his own men, by those apparently most devoted to his service, Blasco Nuñez became suspicious of every one around him. Unfortunately, his suspicions fell on some who were most deserving of his confidence. Among these was his predecessor, Vaca de Castro. That officer had conducted himself, in the delicate situation in which he had been placed, with his usual discretion, and with perfect integrity and honor. He had frankly communicated with the viceroy, and well had it been for Blasco Nuñez, if he had known how to profit by it. But he was too much puffed up by the arrogance of office, and by the conceit of his own superior wisdom, to defer much to the counsels of his experienced predecessor. The latter was now suspected by the viceroy of maintaining a secret correspondence with his enemies at Cuzco,—a suspicion which seems to have had no better foundation than the personal friendship which Vaca de Castro was known to entertain for these individuals. But, with Blasco Nuñez, to suspect was to be convinced; and he ordered De Castro to be placed under arrest, and confined on board of a vessel lying in the harbor. This high-handed measure was followed by the arrest and imprisonment of several other cavaliers, probably on grounds equally frivolous.[9]

He now turned his attention towards the enemy. Notwithstanding his former failure, he still did not altogether despair of effecting something by negotiation, and he sent another embassy, having the bishop of Lima at its head, to Gonzalo Pizarro's camp, with promises of a general amnesty, and some proposals of a more tempting character to the commander. But this step, while it proclaimed his own weakness, had no better success than the preceding.[10]

The viceroy now vigorously prepared for war. His first care was to put the capital in a posture of defence, by strengthening its fortifications, and throwing barricades across the streets. He ordered a general enrolment of the citizens, and called in levies from the neighboring towns,— a call not very promptly answered. A squadron of eight or ten vessels was got ready in the port to act in concert with the land forces. The bells were taken from the churches, and used in the manufacture of muskets;[11] and funds were procured from the fifths which had accumulated

[9] Zarate, Conq. del Peru, lib. 5, cap. 3.—Pedro Pizarro, Descub. y Conq., MS.— Fernandez, Hist. del Peru, Parte 1, lib. 1, cap. 10.

[10] Loaysa, the bishop, was robbed of his despatches, and not even allowed to enter the camp, lest his presence should shake the constancy of the soldiers. (See Relacion de los Sucesos del Peru, MS.) The account occupies more space than it deserves in most of the authorities.

[11] "Hiço hacer gran Copia de Arcabuces, asi de Hierro, como de Fundicion, de ciertas Campanas de la Iglesia Maior, que para ello quitó." Zarate, Conq. del Peru, lib. 5, cap. 6

in the royal treasury. The most extravagant bounty was offered to the soldiers, and prices were paid for mules and horses, which showed that gold, or rather silver, was the commodity of least value in Peru.[12] By these efforts, the active commander soon assembled a force considerably larger than that of his adversary. But how could he confide in it?

While these preparations were going forward, the judges of the Audience arrived at Lima. They had shown, throughout their progress, no great respect either for the ordinances, or the will of the viceroy; for they had taxed the poor natives as freely and unscrupulously as any of the Conquerors. We have seen the entire want of cordiality subsisting between them and their principal in Panamá. It became more apparent, on their landing at Lima. They disapproved of his proceedings in every particular; of his refusal to suspend the ordinances,—although, in fact, he had found no opportunity, of late, to enforce them; of his preparations for defence, declaring that he ought rather trust to the effect of negotiation; and, finally, of his imprisonment of so many loyal cavaliers, which they pronounced an arbitrary act, altogether beyond the bounds of his authority; and they did not scruple to visit the prison in person, and discharge the captives from their confinement.[13]

This bold proceeding, while it conciliated the good-will of the people, severed, at once, all relations with the viceroy. There was in the Audience a lawyer, named Cepeda, a cunning, ambitious man, with considerable knowledge in the way of his profession, and with still greater talent for intrigue. He did not disdain the low arts of a demagogue to gain the favor of the populace, and trusted to find his own account in fomenting a misunderstanding with Blasco Nuñez. The latter, it must be confessed, did all in his power to aid his counsellor in this laudable design.

A certain cavalier in the place, named Suarez de Carbajal, who had long held an office under government, fell under the viceroy's displeasure, on suspicion of conniving at the secession of some of his kinsmen, who had lately taken part with the malecontents. The viceroy summoned Carbajal to attend him at his palace, late at night; and when conducted to his presence, he bluntly charged him with treason. The latter stoutly denied the accusation, in tones as haughty as those of his accuser. The altercation grew warm, until, in the heat of passion, Blasco Nuñez struck him with his poniard. In an instant, the attendants, taking this as a signal, plunged their swords into the body of the unfortunate man, who fell lifeless on the floor.[14]

---

[12] Blasco Nuñez paid, according to Zarate, who had the means of knowing, twelve thousand ducats for thirty-five mules.—"El Visorrei les mandó comprar, de la Hacienda Real, treinta i cinco Machos, en que hiciesen la Jornada, que costaron mas de doce mil ducados." (Zarate, Conq. del Peru, lib. 5, cap. 10.) The South-American of our day might well be surprised at such prices for animals since so abundant in his country.

[13] Fernandez, Hist. del Peru, Parte 1, lib. 1, cap. 10.—Herrera, Hist. General, dec. 7, lib. 8, cap. 2, 10.—Carta de Gonzalo Pizarro a Valdivia, MS.

[14] "He struck him in the bosom with his dagger, as some say, but the viceroy denies it."—So says Zarate, in the *printed* copy of his history. (Lib. 5, cap. 11.) In

Greatly alarmed for the consequences of his rash act,—for Carbajal was much beloved in Lima,—Blasco Nuñez ordered the corpse of the murdered man to be removed by a private stairway from the house, and carried to the cathedral, where, rolled in his bloody cloak, it was laid in a grave hastily dug to receive it. So tragic a proceeding, known to so many witnesses, could not long be kept secret. Vague rumors of the fact explained the mysterious disappearance of Carbajal. The grave was opened, and the mangled remains of the slaughtered cavalier established the guilt of the viceroy.[15]

From this hour Blasco Nuñez was held in universal abhorrence; and his crime, in this instance, assumed the deeper dye of ingratitude, since the deceased was known to have had the greatest influence in reconciling the citizens early to his government. No one knew where the blow would fall next, or how soon he might himself become the victim of the ungovernable passions of the viceroy. In this state of things, some looked to the Audience, and yet more to Gonzalo Pizarro, to protect them.

That chief was slowly advancing towards Lima, from which, indeed, he was removed but a few days' march. Greatly perplexed, Blasco Nuñez now felt the loneliness of his condition. Standing aloof, as it were, from his own followers, thwarted by the Audience, betrayed by his soldiers, he might well feel the consequences of his misconduct. Yet there seemed no other course for him, but either to march out and meet the enemy, or to remain in Lima and defend it. He had placed the town in a posture of defence, which argued this last to have been his original purpose. But he felt he could no longer rely on his troops, and he decided on a third course, most unexpected.

This was to abandon the capital, and withdraw to Truxillo, about eighty leagues distant. The women would embark on board the squadron, and, with the effects of the citizens, be transported by water. The troops, with the rest of the inhabitants, would march by land, laying waste the country as they proceeded. Gonzalo Pizarro, when he arrived at Lima, would find it without supplies for his army, and, thus straitened he would not care to take a long march across a desert in search of his enemy.[16]

What the viceroy proposed to effect by this movement is not clear, unless it were to gain time; and yet the more time he had gained, thus

---

the original manuscript of this work, still extant at Simancas, he states the fact without any qualification at all. "Luego el dicho Virrei echó mano á una daga, i arremetió con él, i le dió una puñalada, i á grandes voces mandó que le matasen." (Zarate, MS.) This was doubtless his honest conviction, when on the spot soon after the event occurred. The politic historian thought it prudent to qualify his remark before publication.—"They say," says another contemporary, familiar with these events and friendly to the viceroy, "that he gave him several wounds with his dagger." And he makes no attempt to refute the charge. (Relacion de los Sucesos del Peru, MS.) Indeed, this version of the story seems to have been generally received at the time by those who had the best means of knowing the truth.

[15] Zarate, Conq. del Peru, ubi supra.

[16] Ibid., lib. 5, cap. 12.—Fernandez, Parte 1, lib. 1, cap. 18.

far, the worse it had proved for him. But he was destined to encounter a decided opposition from the judges. They contended that he had no warrant for such an act, and that the Audience could not lawfully hold its sessions out of the capital. Blasco Nuñez persisted in his determination, menacing that body with force, if necessary. The judges appealed to the citizens to support them in resisting such an arbitrary measure. They mustered a force for their own protection, and that same day passed a decree that the viceroy should be arrested.

Late at night, Blasco Nuñez was informed of the hostile preparations of the judges. He instantly summoned his followers, to the number of more than two hundred, put on his armour, and prepared to march out at the head of his troops against the Audience. This was the true course; for in a crisis like that in which he was placed, requiring promptness and decision, the presence of the leader is essential to insure success. But, unluckily, he yielded to the remonstrances of his brother and other friends, who dissuaded him from rashly exposing his life in such a venture.

What Blasco Nuñez neglected to do was done by the judges. They sallied forth at the head of their followers, whose number, though small at first, they felt confident would be swelled by volunteers as they advanced. Rushing forward, they cried out,—"Liberty! Liberty! Long live the king and the Audience!" It was early dawn, and the inhabitants, startled from their slumbers, ran to the windows and balconies, and, learning the object of the movement, some snatched up their arms and joined in it, while the women, waving their scarfs and kerchiefs, cheered on the assault.

When the mob arrived before the viceroy's palace, they halted for a moment, uncertain what to do. Orders were given to fire on them from the windows, and a volley passed over their heads. No one was injured; and the greater part of the viceroy's men, with most of the officers,— including some of those who had been so anxious for his personal safety, —now openly joined the populace. The palace was then entered, and abandoned to pillage. Blasco Nuñez, deserted by all but a few faithful adherents, made no resistance. He surrendered to the assailants, was led before the judges, and by them was placed in strict confinement. The citizens, delighted with the result, provided a collation for the soldiers; and the affair ended without the loss of a single life. Never was there so bloodless a revolution.[17]

The first business of the judges was to dispose of the prisoner. He was sent, under a strong guard, to a neighboring island, till some measures could be taken respecting him. He was declared to be deposed from his

---

[17] Relacion de los Sucesos del Peru, MS.—Relacion Anonima, MS.—Pedro Pizarro, Descub. y Conq., MS.—Fernandez, Hist. del Peru, Parte 1, lib. 1, cap. 19.— Zarate, Conq. del Peru, lib. 5, cap. 11.—Carta de Gonzalo Pizarro a Valdivia, MS.

Gonzalo Pizarro devoutly draws a conclusion from this, that the revolution was clearly brought about by the hand of God for the good of the land. "En hizóse sin que muriese un hombre, ni fuese herido, como obra que Dios la guiava para el bien besta tierra." Carta, MS., ubi supra.

office; a provisional government was established, consisting of their own body, with Cepeda at its head, as president; and its first act was to pronounce the detested ordinances suspended, till instructions could be received from Court. It was also decided to send Blasco Nuñez back to Spain with one of their own body, who should explain to the emperor the nature of the late disturbances, and vindicate the measures of the Audience. This was soon put in execution. The Licentiate Alvarez was the person selected to bear the viceroy company; and the unfortunate commander, after passing several days on the desolate island, with scarcely any food, and exposed to all the inclemencies of the weather, took his departure for Panamá.[18]

A more formidable adversary yet remained in Gonzalo Pizarro, who had now advanced to Xauxa, about ninety miles from Lima. Here he halted, while numbers of the citizens prepared to join his banner, choosing rather to take service under him than to remain under the self-constituted authority of the Audience. The judges, meanwhile, who had tasted the sweets of office too short a time to be content to resign them, after considerable delay, sent an embassy to the Procurator. They announced to him the revolution that had taken place, and the suspension of the ordinances. The great object of his mission had been thus accomplished; and, as a new government was now organized, they called on him to show his obedience to it, by disbanding his forces, and withdrawing to the unmolested enjoyment of his estates. It was a bold demand,—though couched in the most courteous and complimentary phrase,—to make of one in Pizarro's position. It was attempting to scare away the eagle just ready to stoop on his prey. If the chief had faltered, however, he would have been reassured by his lion-hearted lieutenant. "Never show faint heart," exclaimed the latter, "when you are so near the goal. Success has followed every step of your path. You have now only to stretch forth your hand, and seize the government. Every thing else will follow."—The envoy who brought the message from the judges was sent back with the answer, that "the people had called Gonzalo Pizarro to the government of the country, and, if the Audience did not at once invest him with it, the city should be delivered up to pillage." [19]

The bewildered magistrates were thrown into dismay by this decisive answer. Yet loth to resign, they took counsel in their perplexity of Vaca de Castro, still detained on board of one of the vessels. But that commander had received too little favor at the hands of his successors to

---

[18] Carta de Gonzalo Pizarro a Valdivia, MS.—Relacion de los Sucesos del Peru, MS.

The story of the seizure of the viceroy is well told by the writer of the last MS., who seems here, at least, not unduly biased in favor of Blasco Nuñez, though a partisan.

[19] Zarate, Conq. del Peru, lib. 5, cap. 13.

It required some courage to carry the message of the Audience to Gonzalo and his desperate followers. The historian Zarate, the royal comptroller, was the envoy; not much, as it appears, to his own satisfaction. He escaped, however, unharmed, and has made a full report of the affair in his chronicle.

think it necessary to peril his life on their account by thwarting the plans of Pizarro. He maintained a discreet silence, therefore, and left the matter to the wisdom of the Audience.

Meanwhile, Carbajal was sent into the city to quicken their deliberations. He came at night, attended only by a small party of soldiers, intimating his contempt of the power of the judges. His first act was to seize a number of cavaliers, whom he dragged from their beds, and placed under arrest. They were men of Cuzco, the same already noticed as having left Pizarro's ranks soon after his departure from that capital. While the Audience still hesitated as to the course they should pursue, Carbajal caused three of his prisoners, persons of consideration and property, to be placed on the backs of mules, and escorted out of town to the suburbs, where, with brief space allowed for confession, he hung them all on the branches of a tree. He superintended the execution himself, and tauntingly complimented one of his victims, by telling him, that, "in consideration of his higher rank, he should have the privilege of selecting the bough on which to be hanged!"[20] The ferocious officer would have proceeded still further in his executions, it is said, had it not been for orders received from his leader. But enough was done to quicken the perceptions of the Audience as to their course, for they felt their own lives suspended by a thread in such unscrupulous hands. Without further delay, therefore, they sent to invite Gonzalo Pizarro to enter the city, declaring that the security of the country and the general good required the government to be placed in his hands.[21]

That chief had now advanced within half a league of the capital, which soon after, on the twenty-eighth of October, 1544, he entered in battle-array. His whole force was little short of twelve hundred Spaniards, besides several thousand Indians, who dragged his heavy guns in the advance.[22] Then came the files of spearmen and arquebusiers, making a formidable corps of infantry for a colonial army; and lastly, the cavalry, at the head of which rode Pizarro himself, on a powerful

---

[20] "Le queria dar su muerte con una preëminencia señalada, que escogiese en qual de las Ramas de aquel Arbol queria que le colgasen." Zarate, Conq. del Peru, lib. 5, cap. 13.—See also Relacion Anonima, MS.—Fernandez, Parte 1, lib. 1, cap. 25.

[21] According to Gonzalo Pizarro, the Audience gave this invitation in obedience to the demands of the representatives of the cities.—"Y á esta sazon llegué yo á Lima, i todos los procuradores de las cibdades destos reynos suplicaron al Audiencia me hiciesen Governador para resistir los robos é fuerzas que Blasco Nuñez andava faciendo, i para tener la tierra en justicia hasta que S. M. proveyese lo que mas á su real servicio convenia. Los Oydores visto que asi convenia al servicio de Dios i al de S. M. i al bien destos reynos," &c. (Carta de Gonzalo Pizarro a Valdivia, MS.) But Gonzalo's account of himself must be received with more than the usual grain of allowance. His letter, which is addressed to Valdivia, the celebrated conqueror of Chili, contains a full account of the rise and progress of his rebellion. It is the best vindication, therefore, to be found of himself, and, as a counterpoise to the narratives of his enemies, is of inestimable value to the historian.

[22] He employed twelve thousand Indians on this service, says the writer of the Relacion Anónima, MS. But this author, although living in the colonies at the time, talks too much at random to gain our implicit confidence.

charger, gaily caparisoned. The rider was in complete mail, over which floated a richly embroidered surcoat, and his head was protected by a crimson cap, highly ornamented,—his showy livery setting off his handsome, soldierlike person to advantage.[23] Before him was borne the royal standard of Castile; for every one, royalist or rebel, was careful to fight under that sign. This emblem of loyalty was supported on the right by a banner, emblazoned with the arms of Cuzco, and by another on the left, displaying the armorial bearings granted by the Crown to the Pizarros. As the martial pageant swept through the streets of Lima, the air was rent with acclamations from the populace, and from the spectators in the ablconies. The cannon sounded at intervals, and the bells of the city—those that the viceroy had spared——rang out a joyous peal, as if in honor of a victory!

The oaths of office were duly administered by the judges of the Royal Audience, and Gonzalo Pizarro was proclaimed Governor and Captain-General of Peru, till his Majesty's pleasure could be known in respect to the government. The new ruler then took up his quarters in the palace of his brother,—where the stains of that brother's blood were not yet effaced. *Fêtes*, bull-fights, and tournaments graced the ceremony of inauguration, and were prolonged for several days, while the giddy populace of the capital abandoned themselves to jubilee, as if a new and more auspicious order of things had commenced for Peru! [24]

---

[23] "Y el armado y con una capa de grana cubierta con muchas guarniciones de oro é con sayo de brocado sobre las armas." Relacion de los Sucesos del Peru, MS.—Also Zarate, Conq. del Peru, lib. 5, cap. 13.

[24] For the preceding pages relating to Gonzalo Pizarro, see Relacion Anonima, MS.—Fernandez, Hist. del Peru, Parte 1, lib. 1, cap. 25.—Pedro Pizarro, Descub. y Conq., MS.—Carta de Gonzalo Pizarro a Valdivia, MS.—Zarate, loc. cit.—Herrera. Hist. General, dec. 7, lib. 8, cap. 16–19.—Relacion de los Sucesos del Peru, MS.—Montesinos, Annales, MS., año 1544.

CHAPTER IX

MEASURES OF GONZALO PIZARRO—ESCAPE OF VACA DE CASTRO—RE-APPEARANCE OF THE VICEROY—HIS DISASTROUS RETREAT—DEFEAT AND DEATH OF THE VICEROY—GONZALO PIZARRO LORD OF PERU

1544—1546

THE first act of Gonzalo Pizarro was to cause those persons to be apprehended who had taken the most active part against him in the late troubles. Several he condemned to death; but afterwards commuted the sentence, and contented himself with driving them into banishment and confiscating their estates.[1] His next concern was to establish his authority on a firm basis. He filled the municipal government of Lima with his own partisans. He sent his lieutenants to take charge of the principal cities. He caused galleys to be built at Arequipa to secure the command of the seas; and brought his forces into the best possible condition, to prepare for future emergencies.

The Royal Audience existed only in name; for its powers were speedily absorbed by the new ruler, who desired to place the government on the same footing as under the marquess, his brother. Indeed, the Audience necessarily fell to pieces, from the position of its several members. Alvarez had been sent with the viceroy to Castile. Cepeda, the most aspiring of the court, now that he had failed in his own schemes of ambition, was content to become a tool in the hands of the military chief who had displaced him. Zarate, a third judge, who had, from the first, protested against the violent measures of his colleagues, was confined to his house by a mortal illness;[2] and Tepeda, the remaining magistrate, Gonzalo now proposed to send back to Castile with such an account of the late transactions as should vindicate his own conduct in the eyes of the emperor. This step was opposed by Carbajal, who bluntly told his commander that "he had gone too far to expect favor from the Crown; and

---

[1] Pedro Pizarro, Descub. y Conq., MS.

The honest soldier, who tells us this, was more true to his king than to his kindred. At last, he did not attach himself to Gonzalo's party, and was among those who barely escaped hanging on this occasion. He seems to have had little respect for his namesake.

[2] Zarate, the judge, must not be confounded with Zarate, the historian, who went out to Peru with the Court of Audience, as *contador real*, royal comptroller,—having before filled the office of secretary of the royal council in Spain.

that he had better rely for his vindication on his pikes and muskets!"[3]

But the ship which was to transport Tepeda was found to have suddenly disappeared from the port. It was the same in which Vaca de Castro was confined; and that officer, not caring to trust to the forbearance of one whose advances, on a former occasion, he had so unceremoniously repulsed, and convinced, moreover, that his own presence could profit nothing in a land where he held no legitimate authority, had prevailed on the captain to sail with him to Panamá. He then crossed the Isthmus, and embarked for Spain. The rumors of his coming had already preceded him, and charges were not wanting against him from some of those whom he had offended by his administration. He was accused of having carried measures with a high hand, regardless of the rights, both of the colonist and of the native; and, above all, of having embezzled the public moneys, and of returning with his coffers richly freighted to Castile. This last was an unpardonable crime.

No sooner had the governor set foot in his own country than he was arrested, and hurried to the fortress of Arevalo; and, though he was afterwards removed to better quarters, where he was treated with the indulgence due to his rank, he was still kept a prisoner of state for twelve years, when the tardy tribunals of Castile pronounced a judgment in his favor. He was acquitted of every charge that had been brought against him, and, so far from peculation, was proved to have returned home no richer than he went. He was released from confinement, reinstated in his honors and dignities, took his seat anew in the royal council, and Vaca de Castro enjoyed, during the remainder of his days, the consideration to which he was entitled by his deserts.[4] The best eulogium on the wisdom of his administration was afforded by the troubles brought on the colonies by that of his successor. The nation became gradually sensible of the value of his services; though the manner in which they were requited by the government must be allowed to form a cold commentary on the gratitude of princes.

Gonzalo Pizarro was doomed to experience a still greater disappointment than that caused by the escape of Vaca de Castro, in the return of Blasco Nuñez. The vessel which bore him from the country had hardly left the shore, when Alvarez, the judge, whether from remorse at the part which he had taken, or apprehensive of the consequences of carrying back the viceroy to Spain, presented himself before that dignitary, and announced that he was no longer a prisoner. At the same time he excused himself for the part he had taken, by his desire to save the life of Blasco Nuñez, and extricate him from his perilous situation. He now placed the vessel at his disposal, and assured him it should take him wherever he chose.

[3] Gomara, Hist. de las Ind., cap. 172.—Garcilasso, Com. Real., Parte 2, lib. 4, cap. 21.

[4] Zarate, Conq. del Peru, lib. 5, cap. 15.—Relacion Anonima, MS.—Relacion de los Sucesos del Peru, MS.—Montesinos, Annales, MS., año 1545.—Fernandez, Hist. del Peru, Parte 1, lib. 1, cap. 28.

The viceroy, whatever faith he may have placed in the judge's explanation, eagerly availed himself of his offer. His proud spirit revolted at the idea of returning home in disgrace, foiled, as he had been, in every object of his mission. He determined to try his fortune again in the land, and his only doubt was, on what point to attempt to rally his partisans around him. At Panamá he might remain in safety, while he invoked assistance from Nicaragua, and other colonies at the north. But this would be to abandon his government at once; and such a confession of weakness would have a bad effect on his followers in Peru. He determined, therefore, to direct his steps towards Quito, which, while it was within his jurisdiction, was still removed far enough from the theatre of the late troubles to give him time to rally, and make head against his enemies.

In pursuance of this purpose, the viceroy and his suite disembarked at Tumbez, about the middle of October, 1544. On landing, he issued a manifesto setting forth the violent proceedings of Gonzalo Pizarro and his followers, whom he denounced as traitors to their prince, and he called on all true subjects in the colony to support him in maintaining the royal authority. The call was not unheeded; and volunteers came in, though tardily, from San Miguel, Puerto Viejo, and other places on the coast, cheering the heart of the viceroy with the conviction that the sentiment of loyalty was not yet extinct in the bosoms of the Spaniards.

But, while thus occupied, he received tidings of the arrival of one of Pizarro's captains on the coast, with a force superior to his own. Their number was exaggerated; but Blasco Nuñez, without waiting to ascertain the truth, abandoned his position at Tumbez, and, with as much expedition as he could make across a wild and mountainous country half-buried in snow, he marched to Quito. But this capital, situated at the northern extremity of his province, was not a favorable point for the rendezvous of his followers; and, after prolonging his stay till he had received assurance from Benalcazar, the loyal commander at Popayan, that he would support him with all his strength in the coming conflict, he made a rapid countermarch to the coast, and took up his position at the town of San Miguel. This was a spot well suited to his purposes, as lying on the great high road along the shores of the Pacific, besides being the chief mart for commercial intercourse with Panamá and the north.

Here the viceroy erected his standard, and in a few weeks found himself at the head of a force amounting to nearly five hundred in all, horse and foot, ill provided with arms and ammunition, but apparently zealous in the cause. Finding himself in sufficient strength to commence active operations, he now sallied forth against several of Pizarro's captains in the neighborhood, over whom he obtained some decided advantages, which renewed his confidence, and flattered him with the hopes of reëstablishing his ascendency in the country.[5]

[5] Carta de Gonzalo Pizarro a Valdivia, MS.—Zarate, Conq. del Peru, lib. 5, cap. 14, 15.—Herrera, Hist. General, dec. 7, lib. 8, cap. 19, 20.—Relacion Anonima, MS

During this time, Gonzalo Pizarro was not idle. He had watched with anxiety the viceroy's movements; and was now convinced that it was time to act, and that, if he would not be unseated himself, he must dislodge his formidable rival. He accordingly placed a strong garrison under a faithful officer in Lima, and, after sending forward a force of some six hundred men by land to Truxillo, he embarked for the same port himself, on the 4th of March, 1545, the very day on which the viceroy had marched from Quito.

At Truxillo, Pizarro put himself at the head of his little army, and moved without loss of time against San Miguel. His rival, eager to bring their quarrel to an issue, would fain have marched out to give him battle; but his soldiers, mostly young and inexperienced levies, hastily brought together, were intimidated by the name of Pizarro. They loudly insisted on being led into the upper country, where they would be reinforced by Benalcazar; and their unfortunate commander, like the rider of some unmanageable steed, to whose humors he is obliged to submit, was hurried away in a direction contrary to his wishes. It was the fate of Blasco Nuñez to have his purposes baffled alike by his friends and his enemies.

On arriving before San Miguel, Gonzalo Pizarro found, to his great mortification, that his antagonist had left it. Without entering the town, he quickened his pace, and, after traversing a valley of some extent, reached the skirts of a mountain chain, into which Blasco Nuñez had entered but a few hours before. It was late in the evening; but Pizarro, knowing the importance of despatch, sent forward Carbajal with a party of light troops to overtake the fugitives. That captain succeeded in coming up with their lonely bivouac among the mountains at midnight, when the weary troops were buried in slumber. Startled from their repose by the blast of the trumpet, which, strange to say, their enemy had incautiously sounded,[6] the viceroy and his men sprang to their feet, mounted their horses, grasped their arquebuses, and poured such a volley into the ranks of their assailants, that Carbajal, disconcerted by his reception, found it prudent, with his inferior force, to retreat. The viceroy followed, till, fearing an ambuscade in the darkness of the night, he withdrew, and allowed his adversary to rejoin the main body of the army under Pizarro.

This conduct of Carbajal, by which he allowed the game to slip

—Fernandez, Hist. del Peru, Parte 1, lib. 1, cap. 23.—Relacion de los Sucesos deⁱ Peru, MS.

The author of the document last cited notices the strong feeling for the Crown existing in several of the cities; and mentions also the rumor of a meditated assault on Cuzco by the Indians.—The writer belonged to the discomfited party of Blasco Nuñez; and the facility with which exiles credit reports in their own favor is proverbial.

[6] "Mas Francisco Caruajal q̄ los yua siguiendo, llegó quatro horas de la noche á dōde estauan: y con vna Trompeta que lleuaua les tocó arma: y sentido por el Virey se leuantó luego el primero." Fernandez, Hist. del Peru, Parte 1, lib. 1, cap. 40.

through his hands, from mere carelessness, is inexplicable. It forms a singular exception to the habitual caution and vigilance displayed in his military career. Had it been the act of any other captain, it would have cost him his head. But Pizarro, although greatly incensed, set too high a value on the services and well-tried attachment of his lieutenant, to quarrel with him. Still it was considered of the last importance to overtake the enemy, before he had advanced much farther to the north, where the difficulties of the ground would greatly embarrass the pursuit. Carbajal, anxious to retrieve his error, was accordingly again placed at the head of a corps of light troops, with instructions to harass the enemy's march, cut off his stores, and keep him in check, if possible, till the arrival of Pizarro.[7]

But the viceroy had profited by the recent delay to gain considerably on his pursuers. His road led across the valley of Caxas, a broad, uncultivated district, affording little sustenance for man or beast. Day after day, his troops held on their march through this dreary region, intersected with *barrancas* and rocky ravines that added incredibly to their toil. Their principal food was the parched corn, which usually formed the nourishment of the travelling Indians, though held of much less account by the Spaniards; and this meagre fare was reinforced by such herbs as they found on the way-side, which, for want of better utensils, the soldiers were fain to boil in their helmets.[8] Carbajal, meanwhile, pressed on them so close, that their baggage, ammunition, and sometimes their mules, fell into his hands. The indefatigable warrior was always on their track, by day and by night, allowing them scarcely any repose. They spread no tent, and lay down in their arms, with their steeds standing saddled beside them; and hardly had the weary soldier closed his eyes, when he was startled by the cry that the enemy was upon him.[9]

At length, the harassed followers of Blasco Nuñez reached the *depoblado*, or desert of Paltos, which stretches towards the north for many a dreary league. The ground, intersected by numerous streams, has the character of a great quagmire, and men and horses floundered about in the stagnant waters, or with difficulty worked their way over the marsh, or opened a passage through the tangled underwood that shot up in rank luxuriance from the surface. The wayworn horses, without food, except such as they could pick up in the wilderness, were often spent with travel, and, becoming unserviceable, were left to die on the road, with

---

[7] Ibid., ubi supra.—Herrera, Hist. General, dec. 7, lib. 9, cap. 22.—Garcilasso, Com. Real., lib. 4, cap. 26.

[8] "Caminando, pues, comiendo algunas Jervas, que cocian en las Celadas, quando paraban à dar aliento a los Caballos." Herrera, Hist. General, dec. 7, lib. 9, cap. 24.

[9] "I sin que en todo el camino los vnos, ni los otros, quitasen las Sillas à los Caballos, aunque en este caso estaba mas alerta la Gente del Visorei, porque si algun pequeño rato de la Noche reposaban, era vestidos, i teniendo siempre los Caballos del Cabestro, sin esperar à poner Toldos, ni à adereçar las otras formas, que se suelen tener para atar los Caballos de Noche." Zarate, Conq. del Peru, lib. 5, cap. 29.

their hamstrings cut, that they might be of no use to the enemy; though more frequently they were despatched to afford a miserable banquet to their masters.[10] Many of the men now fainted by the way from mere exhaustion, or loitered in the woods, unable to keep up with the march. And woe to the straggler who fell into the hands of Carbajal, at least if he had once belonged to the party of Pizarro. The mere suspicion of treason sealed his doom with the unrelenting soldier.[11]

The sufferings of Pizarro and his troop were scarcely less than those of the viceroy; though they were somewhat mitigated by the natives of the country, who, with ready instinct, discerned which party was the strongest, and, of course, the most to be feared. But, with every alleviation, the chieftain's sufferings were terrible. It was repeating the dismal scenes of the expedition to the Amazon. The soldiers of the Conquest must be admitted to have purchased their triumphs dearly.

Yet the viceroy had one source of disquietude, greater, perhaps, than any arising from physical suffering. This was the distrust of his own followers. There were several of the principal cavaliers in his suite whom he suspected of being in correspondence with the enemy, and even of designing to betray him into their hands. He was so well convinced of this, that he caused two of these officers to be put to death on the march; and their dead bodies, as they lay by the roadside, meeting the eye of the soldier, told him that there were others to be feared in these frightful solitudes besides the enemy in his rear.[12]

Another cavalier, who held the chief command under the viceroy, was executed, after a more formal investigation of his case, at the first place where the army halted. At this distance of time, it is impossible to determine how far the suspicions of Blasco Nuñez were founded on truth. The judgments of contemporaries are at variance.[13] In times of political ferment, the opinion of the writer is generally determined by the complexion of his party. To judge from the character of Blasco Nuñez, jealous and irritable, we might suppose him to have acted without sufficient cause. But this consideration is counterbalanced by that

[10] "I en cansandose el Caballo, le desjarretaba, i le dexaba, porque sus contrarios no se aprovechasen de èl." Ibid., loc. cit.

[11] "Had it not been for Gonzalo Pizarro's interference," says Fernandez, "many more would have been hung up by his lieutenant, who *pleasantly* quoted the old Spanish proverb,—'The fewer of our enemies the better.'" *De los enemigos, los menos.* Hist. del Peru, Parte 1, lib. 1, cap. 40.

[12] "Los afligidos Soldados, que por el cansancio de los Caballos iban à pie con terrible angustia, por la persecucion de los Enemigos, que iban cerca, i por la fatiga de la hambre, quando vieron los Cuerpos de los dos Capitanes muertos en aquel camino quedaron atonitos." Herrera, Hist. General, dec. 7, lib. 9, cap. 25.

[13] Fernandez, who held a loyal pen, and one sufficiently friendly to the viceroy, after stating that the officers, whom the latter put to death, had served him to that time with their lives and fortunes, dismisses the affair with the temperate reflection, that men formed different judgments on it. "Sobre estas muertes uuo en el Perù varios y contrarios juyzios y opiniones, de culpa y de su descargo." (Hist. del Peru, Parte 1, lib. 1, cap. 41.) Gomara says, more unequivocally, "All condemned it." (Hist. de las Ind., cap. 167.) The weight of opinion seems to have been against the viceroy.

of the facility with which his followers swerved from their allegiance to their commander, who seems to have had so light a hold on their affections, that they were shaken off by the least reverse of fortune. Whether his suspicions were well or ill founded, the effect was the same on the mind of the viceroy. With an enemy in his rear whom he dared not fight, and followers whom he dared not trust, the cup of his calamities was nearly full.

At length, he issued forth on firm ground, and, passing through Tomebamba, Blasco Nuñez reëntered his northern capital of Quito. But his reception was not so cordial as that which he had before experienced. He now came as a fugitive, with a formidable enemy in pursuit; and he was soon made to feel that the surest way to receive support is not to need it.

Shaking from his feet the dust of the disloyal city, whose superstitious people were alive to many an omen that boded his approaching ruin,[14] the unfortunate commander held on his way towards Pastos, in the jurisdiction of Benalcazar. Pizarro and his forces entered Quito not long after, disappointed, that, with all his diligence, the enemy still eluded his pursuit. He halted only to breathe his men, and, declaring that "he would follow up the viceroy to the North Sea but he would overtake him," [15] he resumed his march. At Pastos, he nearly accomplished his object. His advance-guard came up with Blasco Nuñez as the latter was halting on the opposite bank of a rivulet. Pizarro's men, fainting from toil and heat, staggered feebly to the water-side, to slake their burning thirst, and it would have been easy for the viceroy's troops, refreshed by repose, and superior in number to their foes, to have routed them. But Blasco Nuñez could not bring his soldiers to the charge. They had fled so long before their enemy, that the mere sight of him filled their hearts with panic, and they would have no more thought of turning against him than the hare would turn against the hound that pursues her. Their safety, they felt, was to fly, not to fight, and they profited by the exhaustion of their pursuers only to quicken their retreat.

Gonzalo Pizarro continued the chase some leagues beyond Pastos; when, finding himself carried farther than he desired into the territories of Benalcazar, and not caring to encounter this formidable captain at disadvantage, he came to a halt, and, notwithstanding his magnificent vaunt about the North Sea, ordered a retreat, and made a rapid countermarch on Quito. Here he found occupation in repairing the wasted spirits of his troops, and in strengthening himself with fresh reinforcements, which much increased his numbers; though these were again diminished by a body that he detached under Carbajal to suppress an

---

[14] Some of these omens recorded by the historian—as the howling of dogs—were certainly no miracles. "En esta lamentable, i angustiosa partida, muchos afirmaron, haver visto por el Aire muchos Cometas, i que quadrillas de Perros andaban por las Calles, dando grandes i temerosos ahullidos, i los Hombres andaban asombrados, i fuera de si." Herrera, Hist. General, dec. 7, lib. 10, cap. 4.

[15] Ibid., ubi supra.

insurrection, which he now learned had broken out in the south. It was headed by Diego Centeno, one of his own officers, whom he had established in La Plata, the inhabitants of which place had joined in the revolt and raised the standard for the Crown. With the rest of his forces, Pizarro resolved to remain at Quito, waiting the hour when the viceroy would reënter his dominions; as the tiger crouches by some spring in the wilderness, patiently waiting the return of his victims.

Meanwhile Blasco Nuñez had pushed forward his retreat to Popayan, the capital of Benalcazar's province. Here he was kindly received by the people; and his soldiers, reduced by desertion and disease to one fifth of their original number, rested from the unparalleled fatigues of a march which had continued for more than two hundred leagues.[16] It was not long before he was joined by Cabrera, Benalcazar's lieutenant, with a stout reinforcement, and, soon after, by that chieftain himself. His whole force now amounted to near four hundred men, most of them in good condition, and well trained in the school of American warfare. His own men were sorely deficient both in arms and ammunition; and he set about repairing the want by building furnaces for manufacturing arquebuses and pikes.[17]—One familiar with the history of these times is surprised to see the readiness with which the Spanish adventurers turned their hands to various trades and handicrafts usually requiring a long apprenticeship. They displayed the dexterity so necessary to settlers in a new country, where every man must become in some degree his own artisan. But this state of things, however favorable to the ingenuity of the artist, is not very propitious to the advancement of the art; and there can be little doubt that the weapons thus made by the soldiers of Blasco Nuñez were of the most rude and imperfect construction.

As week after week rolled away, Gonzalo Pizarro, though fortified with the patience of a Spanish soldier, felt uneasy at the protracted stay of Blasco Nuñez in the north, and he resorted to stratagem to decoy him from his retreat. He marched out of Quito with the greater part of his forces, pretending that he was going to support his lieutenant in the south, while he left a garrison in the city under the command of Puelles, the same officer who had formerly deserted from the viceroy. These tidings he took care should be conveyed to the enemy's camp. The artifice succeeded as he wished. Blasco Nuñez and his followers, confident in their superiority over Puelles, did not hesitate for a moment to profit by

[16] This retreat of Blasco Nuñez may undoubtedly compare, if not in duration, at least in sharpness of suffering, with any expedition in the New World,—save, indeed, that of Gonzalo Pizarro himself to the Amazon. The particulars of it may be found, with more or less amplification, in Zarate, Conq. del Peru, lib. 5, cap. 19, 29.—Carta de Gonzalo Pizarro a Valdivia, MS.—Herrera, Hist. General, dec. 7, lib. 9, cap. 20-26.—Fernandez, Hist. del Peru, Parte 1, lib. 1, cap. 49, et seq.—Relacion de los Sucesos del Peru, MS.—Relacion Anonima, MS.—Montesinos, Annales, MS., año 1545.

[17] "Proveió, que se tragese alli todo el hierro que se pudo haver en la Provincia. i buscó Maestros, i hiço adereçar Fraguas, i en breve tiempo se forjaron en ellas docientos Arcabuces. con todos sus aparejos." Zarate, Conq. del Peru, lib. 5, cap 34

the supposed absence of Pizarro. Abandoning Popayan, the viceroy, early in January, 1546, moved by rapid marches towards the south. But before he reached the place of his destination, he became appraised of the snare into which he had been drawn. He communicated the fact to his officers; but he had already suffered so much from suspense, that his only desire now was, to bring his quarrel with Pizarro to the final arbitrament of arms.

That chief, meanwhile, had been well informed, through his spies, of the viceroy's movements. On learning the departure of the latter from Popayan, he had reëntered Quito, joined his forces with those of Puelles, and, issuing from the capital, had taken up a strong position about three leagues to the north, on a high ground that commanded a stream, across which the enemy must pass. It was not long before the latter came in sight, and Blasco Nuñez, as night began to fall, established himself on the opposite bank of the rivulet. It was so near to the enemy's quarters, that the voices of the sentinels could be distinctly heard in the opposite camps, and they did not fail to salute one another with the epithet of "traitors." In these civil wars, as we have seen, each party claimed for itself the exclusive merit of loyalty.[18]

But Benalcazar soon saw that Pizarro's position was too strong to be assailed with any chance of success. He proposed, therefore, to the viceroy, to draw off his forces secretly in the night; and, making a détour round the hills, to fall on the enemy's rear, where he would be least prepared to receive them. The counsel was approved; and, no sooner were the two hosts shrouded from each other's eyes by the darkness, than, leaving his camp-fires burning to deceive the enemy, Blasco Nuñez broke up his quarters, and began his circuitous march in the direction of Quito. But either he had been misinformed, or his guides misled him; for the roads proved so impracticable, that he was compelled to make a circuit of such extent, that dawn broke before he drew near the point of attack. Finding that he must now abandon the advantage of a surprise, he pressed forward to Quito, where he arrived with men and horses sorely fatigued by a night-march of eight leagues, from a point which, by the direct route, would not have exceeded three. It was a fatal error on the eve of an engagement.[19]

[18] "Que se llegaron à hablar los Corredores de ambas partes, llamandose Traidores los vnos à los otros, fundando, que cada vno sustentaba la voz del Rei, i asi estuvieron toda aquella noche aguardando." Ibid., ubi supra.

[19] For the preceding pages, see Zarate, Conq. del Peru, lib. 5, cap. 34, 35.—Gomara, Hist. de las Ind., cap. 167.—Carta de Gonzalo Pizarro a Valdivia, MS.—Montesinos, Annales, MS., año 1546.—Fernandez, Hist. del Peru, Parte 1, lib. 1, cap. 50-52.

Herrera, in his account of these transactions, has fallen into a strange confusion of dates, fixing the time of the viceroy's entry into Quito on the 10th of January, and that of his battle with Pizarro nine days later. (Hist. General, dec. 8, lib. 1, cap. 1.) This last event, which, by the testimony of Fernandez, was on the eighteenth of the month, was, by the agreement of such contemporary authorities as I have consulted,—as stated in the text,—on the evening of the same day in which the viceroy entered Quito. Herrera, though his work is arranged on the chrono-

He found the capital nearly deserted by the men. They had all joined the standard of Pizarro; for they had now caught the general spirit of disaffection, and looked upon that chief as their protector from the oppressive ordinances. Pizarro was the representative of the people. Greatly moved at this desertion, the unhappy viceroy, lifting his hands to heaven, exclaimed, —"Is it thus, Lord, that you abandonest thy servants?" The women and children came out, and in vain offered him food, of which he stood obviously in need, asking him, at the same time, "Why he had come there to die?" His followers, with more indifference than their commander, entered the houses of the inhabitants, and unceremoniously appropriated whatever they could find to appease the cravings of appetite.

Benalcazar, who saw the temerity of giving battle, in their present condition, recommended the viceroy to try the effect of negotiation, and offered himself to go to the enemy's camp, and arrange, if possible, terms of accommodation with Pizarro. But Blasco Nuñez, if he desponded for a moment, had now recovered his wonted constancy, and he proudly replied,—"There is no faith to be kept with traitors. We have come to fight, not to parley; and we must do our duty like good and loyal cavaliers. I will do mine," he continued, "and be assured I will be the first man to break a lance with the enemy." [20]

He then called his troops together, and addressed to them a few words preparatory to marching. "You are all brave men," he said, "and loyal to your sovereign. For my own part, I hold life as little in comparison with my duty to my prince. Yet let us not distrust our success; the Spaniard, in a good cause, has often overcome greater odds than these. And we are fighting for the right; it is the cause of God.—the cause of God," [21] he concluded, and the soldiers, kindled by his generous ardor, answered him with huzzas that went to the heart of the unfortunate commander, little accustomed of late to this display of enthusiasm.

It was the eighteenth of January, 1546, when Blasco Nuñez marched out at the head of his array, from the ancient city of Quito. He had proceeded but a mile,[22] when he came in view of the enemy, formed along the crest of some high lands, which, by a gentle swell, rose gradually from the plains of Añaquito. Gonzalo Pizarro, greatly chagrined on ascertaining the departure of the viceroy, early in the morning, had broken up his camp, and directed his march on the capital, fully resolved that his enemy should not escape him.

The viceroy's troops, now coming to a halt, were formed in order of

logical system of annals, is by no means immaculate as to his dates. Quintana has exposed several glaring anachronisms of the historian in the earlier period of the Peruvian conquest. See his Españoles Celebres, tom. II, Appendix, *No. 7.*

[20] "Yo os prometo, que la primera láça que se rompa en los enemigos, sea la mia (y assi lo cumplio)." Fernandez, Hist. del Peru, Parte 1, lib. 1, cap. 53.

[21] "Que de Dios es la causa, de Dios es la causa, de Dios es la causa." Zarate, Conq. del Peru, lib. 5, cap. 35.

[22] "Un quarto de legua de la ciudad." Carta de Gonzalo Pizzaro a Valdivia, MS.

battle. A small body of arquebusiers was stationed in the advance to begin the fight. The remainder of that corps was distributed among the spearmen, who occupied the centre, protected on the flanks by the horse drawn up in two nearly equal squadrons. The cavalry amounted to about one hundred and forty, being little inferior to that on the other side, though the whole number of the viceroy's forces, being less than four hundred, did not much exceed the half of his rival's. On the right, and in front of the royal banner, Blasco Nuñez, supported by thirteen chosen cavaliers, took his station, prepared to head the attack.

Pizarro had formed his troops in a corresponding manner with that of his adversary. They mustered about seven hundred in all, well appointed, in good condition, and officered by the best knights in Peru.[23] As, notwithstanding his superiority of numbers, Pizarro, did not seem inclined to abandon his advantageous position, Blasco Nuñez gave orders to advance. The action commenced with the arquebusiers, and in a few moments the dense clouds of smoke, rolling over the field, obscured every object; for it was late in the day when the action began, and the light was rapidly fading.

The infantry, now leveling their pikes, advanced under cover of the smoke, and were soon hotly engaged with the opposite files of spearmen. Then came the charge of the cavalry, which—notwithstanding they were thrown into some disorder by the fire of Pizaro's arquebusiers, far superior in number to their own—was conducted with such spirit that the enemy's horse were compelled to reel and fall back before it. But it was only to recoil with greater violence, as, like an overwhelming wave, Pizarro's troopers rushed on their foes, driving them along the slope, and bearing down man and horse in indiscriminate ruin. Yet these, in turn, at length rallied, cheered on by the cries and desperate efforts of their officers. The lances were shivered, and they fought hand to hand with swords and battle-axes mingled together in wild confusion. But the struggle was of no long duration; for, though the numbers were nearly equal, the viceroy's cavalry, jaded by the severe march of the previous night,[24] were no match for their antagonists. The ground was strewn with the wreck of their bodies; and horses and riders, the dead and the dying, lay heaped on one another. Cabrera, the brave lieutenant of Benalcazar, was slain, and that commander was thrown under his horse's feet, covered with wounds, and left for dead on the field. Alvarez, the judge, was mortally wounded. Both he and his colleague Cepeda were in the action, though ranged on opposite sides, fighting as if they had been bred to arms, not to the peaceful profession of the law.

[23] The amount of the numbers on both sides is variously given, as usual, making however, more than the usual difference in the relative proportions, since the sum total is so small. I have conformed to the statements of the best-instructed writers. Pizzaro estimates his adversary's force at four hundred and fifty men, and his own at only six hundred; an estimate, it may be remarked, that does not make that given in the text any less credible.

[24] Zarate, Conq. del Peru, lib. 5, cap. 35.

Yet Blasco Nuñez and his companions maintained a brave struggle on the right of the field. The viceroy had kept his word by being the first to break his lance against the enemy, and by a well-directed blow had borne a cavalier, named Alonso de Montalvo, clean out of his saddle. But he was at length overwhelmed by numbers, and, as his companions, one after another, fell by his side, he was left nearly unprotected. He was already wounded, when a blow on the head from the battle-axe of a soldier struck him from his horse, and he fell stunned on the ground. Had his person been known, he might have been taken alive, but he wore a sobre-vest of Indian cotton over his armour, which concealed the military order of St. James, and the other badges of his rank.[25]

His person, however, was soon recognized by one of Pizarro's followers, who, not improbably, had once followed the viceroy's banner. The soldier immediately pointed him out to the Licentiate Carbajal. This person was the brother of the cavalier whom, as the reader may remember, Blasco Nuñez had so rashly put to death in his palace at Lima. The licentiate had afterwards taken service under Pizarro, and, with several of his kindred, was pledged to take vengeance on the viceroy. Instantly riding up, he taunted the fallen commander with the murder of his brother, and was in the act of dismounting to despatch him with his own hand, when Puelles remonstrating on this, as an act of degradation, commanded one of his attendants, a black slave, to cut off the viceroy's head. This the fellow executed with a single stroke of his sabre, while the wretched man, perhaps then dying of his wounds, uttered no word, but with eyes imploringly turned up towards heaven, received the fatal blow.[26] The head was then borne aloft on a pike, and some were brutal enough to pluck out the grey hairs from the beard and set them in their caps, as grisly trophies of their victory.[27] The fate of the day was now decided. Yet still the infantry made a brave stand, keeping Pizarro's horse at bay with their bristling array of pikes. But

[25] He wore this dress, says Garcilasso de la Vega, that he might fare no better than a common soldier, but take his chance with the rest. (Com. Real., Parte 2, lib. 4, cap. 34.) Pizarro gives him credit for no such magnanimous intent. According to him, the viceroy assumed this disguise, that, his rank being unknown, he might have the better chance for escape.—It must be confessed that this is the general motive for a disguise. "I Blasco Nuñez puso mucha diligencia por poder huirse si pudiera, porque venia vestido con una camiseta de Yndios por no ser conocido, i no quiso Dios porque pagase quantos males por su causa se havian hecho." Carta de Gonzalo Pizarro a Valdivia, MS.

[26] Fernandez, Hist. del Peru, Parte 1, lib. 1, cap. 54.—Zarate, Conq. del Peru, lib. 5, cap. 35.

"Mandò à un Negro que traìa, que le cortase la Cabeça, i en todo esto no se conoció flaqueça en el Visorrei, ni hablò palabra, ni hiço mas movimiento, que alçar los ojos al Cielo, dando muestras de mucha Christiandad, i constancia." Herrera, Hist. General, dec. 8, lib. 1, cap. 3.

[27] "Aviendo algunos capitanes y personas arrancado y pelado algunas de sus blancas y leales baruas, para traer por empresa, y Juã de la Torre las traxo despues publicamente en la gorra por la ciudad de los Reyes." Fernandez, Hist. del Peru, Parte 1, lib. 1, cap. 54.

their numbers were thinned by the arquebusiers; and, thrown into **dis**order, they could no longer resist the onset of the horse, who broke into their column, and soon scattered and drove them off the ground. The pursuit was neither long nor bloody; for darkness came on, and Pizarro bade his trumpets sound, to call his men together under their banners.

Though the action lasted but a short time, nearly one third of the viceroy's troops had perished. The loss of their opponents was inconsiderable.[28] Several of the vanquished cavaliers took refuge in the churches of Quito. But they were dragged from the sanctuary, and some —probably those who had once espoused the cause of Pizarro—were led to execution, and others banished to Chili. The greater part were pardoned by the conqueror. Benalcazar, who recovered from his wounds, was permitted to return to his government, on condition of no more bearing arms against Pizarro. His troops were invited to take service under the banner of the victor, who, however, never treated them with the confidence shown to his ancient partisans. He was greatly displeased at the indignities offered to the viceroy; whose mangled remains he caused to be buried with the honors due to his rank in the cathedral of Quito. Gonzalo Pizarro, attired in black, walked as chief mourner in the procession.—It was usual with the Pizarros, as we have seen, to pay these obituary honors to their victims.[29]

Such was the sad end of Blasco Nuñez Vela, first viceroy of Peru. It was less than two years since he had set foot in the country, a period of unmitigated disaster and disgrace. His misfortunes may be imputed partly to circumstances, and partly to his own character. The minister of an odious and oppressive law, he was intrusted with no discretionary power in the execution of it.[30] Yet every man may, to a certain extent, claim the right to such a power; since, to execute a commission, which

---

[28] The estimates of killed and wounded in this action are as discordant as usual. Some carry the viceroy's loss to two hundred, while Gonzalo Pizarro rates his own at only seven killed and but a few wounded. But how rarely is it that a faithful bulletin is issued by the parties engaged in the action!

[29] For the accounts of the battle of Añaquito, rather summarily despatched by most writers, see Carta de Gonzalo Pizarro a Valdivia, MS.—Gomara, Hist. de las Ind., cap. 170.—Herrera, Hist. General, dec. 8, lib. 1, cap. 1-3.—Pedro Pizarro, Descub. y Conq., MS.—Zarate, Conq. del Peru, lib. 5, cap. 35.—Montesinos, Annales, MS., año 1546.—Garcilasso, Com. Real., Parte 2, lib. 4, cap. 33-35.—Fernandez, Hist. del Peru, Parte 1, lib. 1, cap. 53, 54.

Gonzalo Pizarro seems to regard the battle as a sort of judicial trial by combat, in which Heaven, by the result, plainly indicated the right. His remarks are edifying. "Por donde parecerá claramente que Nuestro Señor fuè servido este se viniese á meter en las manos para quitarnos de tantos cuidados, i que pagase quantos males havia fecho en la tierra, la qual quedó tan asosegada i tan en paz i servicio de S. M. como lo estuvo en tiempo del Marques mi hermano." Carta de Gonzalo Pizarro a Valdivia, MS.

[30] Garcilasso's reflections on this point are commendably tolerant. "Assi acabò este buen cauallero, por querer porfiar tanto en la execucion de lo que ni a su Rey ni a aquel Reyno conuenia: donde se causaron tantas muertes y daños de Españoles, y de Yndios: aunque no tuuo tanta culpa como se le atribuye, porque lleuó preciso mandato de lo que hizó." Com. Real., Parte 2. lib. 4, cap. 34.

circumstances show must certainly defeat the object for which it was designed, would be absurd. But it requires sagacity to determine the existence of such a contingency, and moral courage to assume the responsibility of acting on it. Such a crisis is the severest test of character. To dare to disobey from a paramount sense of duty is a paradox that a little soul can hardly comprehend. Unfortunately, Blasco Nuñez was a pedantic martinet, a man of narrow views, who could not feel himself authorized under any circumstances to swerve from the letter of the law. Puffed up by his brief authority, moreover, he considered opposition to the ordinances as treason to himself; and thus, identifying himself with his commission, he was prompted by personal feelings, quite as much as by those of a public and patriotic nature.

Neither was the viceroy's character of a kind that tended to mitigate the odium of his measures, and reconcile the people to their execution. It afforded a strong contrast to that of his rival, Pizarro, whose frank, chivalrous bearing, and generous confidence in his followers, made him universally popular, blinding their judgments, and giving to the worse the semblance of the better cause. Blasco Nuñez, on the contrary, irritable and suspicious, placed himself in a false position with all whom he approached; for a suspicious temper creates an atmosphere of distrust around it that kills every kindly affection. His first step was to alienate the members of the Audience who were sent to act in concert with him. But this was their fault as well as his, since they were as much too lax, as he was too severe, in the interpretation of the law.[31] He next alienated and outraged the people whom he was appointed to govern. And, lastly, he disgusted his own friends, and too often turned them into enemies; so that, in his final struggle for power and for existence, he was obliged to rely on the arm of the stranger. Yet in the catalogue of his qualities we must not pass in silence over his virtues. There are two to the credit of which he is undeniably entitled,—a loyalty, which shone the brighter amidst the general defection around him, and a constancy under misfortune, which might challenge the respect even of his enemies. But with the most liberal allowance for his merits, it can scarcely be doubted that a person more incompetent to the task assigned him could not have been found in Castile.[32]

[31] Blasco Nuñez characterized the four judges of the Audience in a manner more concise than complimentary,—a boy, a madman, a booby, and a dunce! "Decia muchas vecces Blasco Nuñez, que le havian dado el Emperador, i su Consejo de Indias vn Moço, un Loco, un Necio, vn Tonto por Oidores, que asi lo havian hecho como ellos eran. Moço era Cepeda, i llamaba Loco a Juan Alvarez, i Necio à Tejada, que no sabia Latin." Gomara, Hist. de las Ind., cap. 171.
[32] The account of Blasco Nuñez Vela rests chiefly on the authority of loyal writers, some of whom wrote after their return to Castile. They would, therefore, more naturally lean to the side of the true representative of the Crown, than to that of the rebel. Indeed, the only voice raised decidedly in favor of Pizarro is his own,— a very suspicious authority. Yet, with all the *prestiges* in his favor, the administration of Blasco Nuñez, from universal testimony, was a total failure. And there is little to interest us in the story of the man, except his unparalleled misfortunes and the firmness with which he bore them.

The victory of Añaquito was received with general joy in the neighboring capital; all the cities of Peru looked on it as sealing the downfall of the detested ordinances, and the name of Gonzalo Pizarro was sounded from one end of the country to the other as that of its deliverer. That chief continued to prolong his stay in Quito during the wet season, dividing his time between the licentious pleasures of the reckless adventurer and the cares of business that now pressed on him as ruler of the state. His administration was stained with fewer acts of violence than might have been expected from the circumstances of his situation. So long as Carbajal, the counsellor in whom he unfortunately placed greatest reliance, was absent, Gonzalo sanctioned no execution, it was observed, but according to the forms of law.[33] He rewarded his followers by new grants of land, and detached several on expeditions, to no greater distance, however, than would leave it in his power readily to recall them. He made various provisions for the welfare of the natives, and some, in particular, for instructing them in the Christian faith. He paid attention to the faithful collection of the royal dues, urging on the colonists that they should deport themselves so as to conciliate the goodwill of the Crown, and induce a revocation of the ordinances. His administration, in short, was so conducted, that even the austere Gasca, his successor, allowed "it was a good government,—for a tyrant." [34]

At length, in July, 1546, the new governor bade adieu to Quito, and, leaving there a sufficient garrison under his officer Puelles, began his journey to the south. It was a triumphal progress, and everywhere he was received on the road with enthusiasm by the people. At Truxillo, the citizens came out in a body to welcome him, and the clergy chanted anthems in his honor, extolling him as the "victorious prince," and imploring the Almighty "to lengthen his days, and give him honor."[35] At Lima, it was proposed to clear away some of the buildings, and open a new street for his entrance, which might ever after bear the name of the victor. But the politic chieftain declined this flattering tribute, and modestly preferred to enter the city by the usual way. A procession was formed of the citizens, the soldiers, and the clergy, and Pizarro made his entry into the capital with two of his principal captains on foot, holding the reins of his charger, while the archbishop of Lima, and the bishops of Cuzco, Quito, and Bogotá, the last of whom had lately come to the city to be consecrated, rode by his side. The streets were strewn with boughs, the walls of the houses hung with showy tapestries, and

---

[33] "Nunca Piçarro, en ausencia de Francisco de Carvajal, su Maestre de Campo, matò, ni consintió matar Español, sin que todos, los mas de su Consejo, lo aprobasen: i entonces con Proceso en forma de Derecho, i confesados primero." Gomara, Hist. de las Ind., cap. 172.

[34] Ibid., ubi supra.—Fernandez gives a less favorable picture of Gonzalo's administration. (Hist. del Peru, Parte 1, lib. 1, cap. 54; lib. 2, cap. 13.) Fernandez wrote at the instance of the Court; Gomara, though present at court, wrote to please himself. The praise of Gomara is less suspicious than the censure of Fernandez.

[35] "Victorioso Principe, hagate Dios dichoso, i bienaventurado, èl te mantenga, i te conserve." Herrera, Hist. General, dec. 8. lib. 2, cap. 9.

triumphal arches were thrown over the way in honor of the victor. Every balcony, veranda, and house-top was crowded with spectators, who sent up huzzas, loud and long, saluting the victorious soldier with the titles of "Liberator, and Protector of the people." The bells rang out their joyous peal, as on his former entrance into the capital; and amidst strains of enlivening music, and the blithe sounds of jubilee, Gonzalo held on his way to the palace of his brother. Peru was once more placed under the dynasty of the Pizarros.[36]

Deputies came from different parts of the country, tending the congratulations of their respective cities; and every one eagerly urged his own claims to consideration for the services he had rendered in the revolution. Pizarro, at the same time, received the welcome intelligence of the success of his arms in the south. Diego Centeno, as before stated, had there raised the standard of rebellion, or rather, of loyalty to his sovereign. He had made himself master of La Plata, and the spirit of insurrection had spread over the broad province of Charcas. Carbajal, who had been sent against him from Quito, after repairing to Lima, had passed at once to Cuzco, and there, strengthening his forces, had descended by rapid marches on the refractory district. Centeno did not trust himself in the field against this formidable champion. He retreated with his troops into the fastnesses of the sierra. Carbajal pursued, following on his track with the pertinacity of à bloodhound; over mountain and moor, through forests and dangerous ravines, allowing him no respite, by day or by night. Eating, drinking, sleeping in his saddle, the veteran, eighty years of age, saw his own followers tire one after another, while he urged on the chase, like the wild huntsman of Bürger, as if endowed with an unearthly frame, incapable of fatigue! During this terrible pursuit, which continued for more than two hundred leagues over a savage country, Centeno found himself abandoned by most of his followers. Such of them as fell into Carbajal's hands were sent to speedy execution; for that inexorable chief had no mercy on those who had been false to their party.[37] At length, Centeno, with a handful of men, arrived on the borders of the Pacific, and there, separating from one another, they provided, each in the best way he could, for their own safety. Their leader found an asylum in a cave in the mountains, where he was secretly fed by an Indian curaca, till the time again for him to unfurl the standard of revolt.[38]

---

[36] For an account of this pageant, see Pedro Pizarro, Descub. y Conq., MS.— Herrera, Hist. General, dec. 8, lib. 2, cap. 9.—Zarate, Conq. del Peru, lib. 6, cap. 5. —Carta de Gonzalo Pizarro a Valdivia, MS.

[37] *Poblando los arboles con sus cuerpos*, "peopling the trees with their bodies," says Fernandez, strongly; alluding to the manner in which the ferocious officer hung up his captives on the branches.

[38] For the expedition of Carbajal, see Herrera, Hist. General, dec. 8, lib. 1, cap. 9, et seq.—Zarate, Conq. del Peru, lib. 6, cap. 1.—Garcilasso, Com. Real., Parte 2, lib. 4, cap. 28, 29, 36, 39.—Fernandez, Hist. del Peru, Parte 1, lib. 2, cap. 1, et seq.—Carta de Gonzalo Pizarro a Valdivia, MS.

It is impossible to give, in a page or two, any adequate idea of the hairbreadth

Carbajal, after some further decisive movements, which fully established the ascendency of Pizarro over the south, returned in triumph to La Plata. There he occupied himself with working the silver mines of Potosí, in which a vein, recently opened, promised to make richer returns than any yet discovered in Mexico or Peru;[39] and he was soon enabled to send large remittances to Lima, deducting no stinted commission for himself,—for the cupidity of the lieutenant was equal to his cruelty.

Gonzalo Pizarro was now undisputed master of Peru. From Quito to the northern confines of Chili, the whole country acknowledged his authority. His fleet rode triumphant on the Pacific, and gave him the command of every city and hamlet on its borders. His admiral, Hinojosa, a discreet and gallant officer, had secured him Panamá, and, marching across the Isthmus, had since obtained for him the possession of Nombre de Dios,—the principal key of communication with Europe. His forces were on an excellent footing, including the flower of the warriors who had fought under his brother, and who now eagerly rallied under the name of Pizarro; while the tide of wealth that flowed in from the mines of Potosí supplied him with the resources of an European monarch.

The new governor now began to assume a state correspondent with his full-blown fortunes. He was attended by a body-guard of eighty soldiers. He dined always in public, and usually with not less than a hundred guests at table. He even affected, it was said, the most decided etiquette of royalty, giving his hand to be kissed, and allowing no one, of whatever rank, to be seated in his presence.[40] But this is denied by others. It would not be strange that a vain man like Pizarro, with a superficial, undisciplined mind, when he saw himself thus raised from an humble condition to the highest post in the land, should be somewhat intoxicated by the possession of power, and treat with superciliousness those whom he had once approached with deference. But one who had often seen him in his prosperity assures us, that it was not so, and that the governor continued to show the same frank and soldierlike bearing as before his elevation, mingling on familiar terms with his comrades,

---

escapes and perilous risks of Carbajal, not only from the enemy, but from his own men, whose strength he overtasked in the chase. They rival those of the renowned Scanderbeg, or our own Kentucky hero, Colonel Boone. They were, indeed, far more wonderful than theirs, since the Spanish captain had reached an age when the failing energies usually crave repose. But the veteran's body seems to have been as insensible as his soul.

[39] The vein now discovered at Potosí was so rich, that the other mines were comparatively deserted in order to work this. (Zarate, Conq. del Peru, lib. 6, cap. 4.) The effect of the sudden influx of wealth was such, according to Garcilasso, that in ten years from this period an iron horseshoe, in that quarter, came to be worth nearly its weight in silver. Com. Real., Parte 1, lib. 8, cap. 24.

[40] "Traia Guarda de ochenta Alabarderos, i otros muchos de Caballo, que le acompañaban, i ià en su presencia ninguno se sentaba. i à mui pocos quitaba la Gorra." Zarate, Conq. del Peru, lib. 6, cap. 5.

and displaying the same qualities which had hitherto endeared him to the people.[41]

However this may be, it is certain there were not wainting those who urged him to throw off his allegiance to the Crown, and set up an independent government for himself. Among these was his lieutenant, Carbajal, whose daring spirit never shrunk from following things to their consequences. He plainly counselled Pizarro to renounce his allegiance at once. "In fact, you have already done so," he said. "You have been in arms against a viceroy, have driven him from the country, beaten and slain him in battle. What favor, or even mercy, can you expect from the Crown? You have gone too far either to halt, or to recede. You must go boldly on, proclaim yourself king; the troops, the people, will support you." And he concluded, it is said, by advising him to marry the Coya, the female representative of the Incas, that the two races might henceforth repose in quiet under a common sceptre! [42]

The advice of the bold counsellor was, perhaps, the most politic that could have been given to Pizarro under existing circumstances. For he was like one who had heedlessly climbed far up a dizzy precipice,—too far to descend safely, while he had no sure hold where he was. His only chance was to climb still higher, till he had gained the summit. But Gonzalo Pizarro shrunk from the attitude, in which this placed him, of avowed rebellion. Notwithstanding the criminal course into which he had been, of late, seduced, the sentiment of loyalty was too deeply implanted in his bosom to be wholly eradicated. Though in arms against the measures and ministers of his sovereign, he was not prepared to raise the sword against the sovereign himself. He, doubtless, had conflicting emotion in his bosom; like Macbeth, and many a less noble nature,

> "Would not play false,
> And yet would wrongly win."

[41] Garcilasso, Com. Real., Parte 2, lib. 4, cap. 42.

Garcilasso had opportunities of personal acquaintance with Gonzalo's manner of living; for, when a boy, he was sometimes admitted, as he tells us, to a place at his table. This courtesy, so rare from the Conquerors to any of the Indian race, was not lost on the historian of the Incas, who has depicted Gonzalo Pizarro in more favorable colors than most of his own countrymen.

[42] Ibid., Parte 2, lib. 4, cap. 40.—Gomara, Hist. de las Ind., cap. 172.—Fernandez, Hist. del Peru, Parte 1, lib. 2, cap. 13.

The poet Molina has worked up this scene between Carbajal and his commander with good effect, in his *Amazonas en las Indias*, where he uses something of a poet's license in the homage he pays to the modest merits of Gonzalo. Julius Cæsar himself was not more magnanimous.

> "Sepa mi Rey, sepa España,
> Que muero por no ofenderla,
> Tan facil de conservarla,
> Que pierdo por no agraviarla,
> Quanto infame en poseerla,
> Una Corona ofrecida."

And however grateful to his vanity might be the picture of the air-drawn sceptre thus painted to his imagination, he had not the audacity—we may, perhaps, say, the criminal ambition—to attempt to grasp it.

Even at this very moment, when urged to this desperate extremity, he was preparing a mission to Spain, in order to vindicate the course he had taken, and to solicit an amnesty for the past, with a full confirmation of his authority, as successor to his brother in the government of Peru.— Pizarro did not read the future with the calm, prophetic eye of Carbajal.

Among the biographical notices of the writers on Spanish colonial affairs, the name of Herrera, who has done more for this vast subject than any other author, should certainly not be omitted. His account of Peru takes its proper place in his great work, the *Historia General de las Indias,* according to the chronological plan on which that history is arranged. But as it suggests reflections not different in character from those suggested by other portions of the work, I shall take the liberty to refer the reader to the Postscript to Book Third of the *Conquest of Mexico,* for a full account of these volumes and their learned author.

Another chronicler, to whom I have been frequently indebted in the progress of the narrative, is Francisco Lopez de Gomara. The reader will also find a notice of this author in the *Conquest of Mexico,* Book 5, Postscript. But as the remarks on his writings are there confined to his *Crónica de Nueva España,* it may be well to add here some reflections on his greater work, *Historia de las Indias,* in which the Peruvian story bears a conspicuous part.

The "History of the Indies" is intended to give a brief view of the whole range of Spanish conquest in the islands and on the American continent, as far as had been achieved by the middle of the sixteenth century. For this account, Gomara, though it does not appear that he ever visited the New World, was in a situation that opened to him the best means of information. He was well acquainted with the principal men of the time, and gathered the details of their history from their own lips; while, from his residence at court, he was in possession of the state of opinion there, and of the impression made by passing events on those most competent to judge of them. He was thus enabled to introduce into his work many interesting particulars, not to be found in other records of the period. His range of inquiry extended beyond the mere doings of the Conquerors, and led him to a survey of the general resources of the countries he describes, and especially of their physical aspect and productions. The conduct of his work, no less than its diction, shows the cultivated scholar, practised in the art of composition. Instead of the *naïveté,* engaging, but childlike, of the old military chroniclers, Gomara handles his various topics with the shrewd and piquant criticism of a man of the world; while his descriptions are managed with a comprehensive brevity that forms the opposite to the long-winded and rambling paragraphs of the monkish annalist. These literary merits, combined with the knowledge of the writer's opportunities for information, secured his productions from the oblivion which too often awaits the unpublished manuscript; and he had the satisfaction to see them pass into more than one edition in his own day. Yet they do not bear the highest stamp of authenticity. The author too readily admits accounts into his pages which are not supported by contemporary testimony. This he does, not from credulity, for his mind rather leans in an opposite direction, but from a want, apparently, of the true spirit of historic conscientiousness. The imputation of carelessness in his statements—to use a temperate phrase—was brought against Gomara in his own day; and Garcilasso tells us, that, when called to account by some of the Peruvian cavaliers for misstatements which bore hard on themselves, the historian made but an awkward explanation. This is a great blemish on his productions, and renders them of far less value to the modern compiler, who seeks for the well of truth undefiled, than many an humbler but less unscrupulous chronicle.

There is still another authority used in this work, Gonzalo Fernandez de Oviedo, of whom I have given an account elsewhere; and the reader curious in the matter will permit me to refer him for a critical notice of his life and writings to the *Conquest of Mexico*, Book 4, Postscript.—His account of Peru is incorporated into his great work, *Natural é General Historia de las Indias, MS.*, where it forms the forty-sixth and forty-seventh books. It extends from Pizarro's landing at Tumbez to Almagro's return from Chili, and thus covers the entire portion of what may be called the conquest of the country. The style of its execution, corresponding with that of the residue of the work to which it belongs, affords no ground for criticism different from that already passed on the general character of Oviedo's writings.

This eminent person was at once a scholar and a man of the world. Living much at court, and familiar with persons of the highest distinction in Castile, he yet passed much of his time in the colonies, and thus added the fruits of personal experience to what he had gained from the reports of others. His curiosity was indefatigable, extending to every department of natural science, as well as to the civil and personal history of the colonists. He was, at once, their Pliny and their Tacitus. His works abound in portraitures of character, sketched with freedom and animation. His reflections are piquant, and often rise to a philosophic tone, which discards the usual trammels of the age; and the progress of the story is varied by a multiplicity of personal anecdotes, that give a rapid insight into the characters of the parties.

With his eminent qualifications, and with a social position that commanded respect, it is strange that so much of his writings—the whole of his great *Historia de las Indias,* and his curious *Quincuagenas*—should be so long suffered to remain in manuscript. This is partly chargeable to the caprice of fortune; for the History was more than once on the eve of publication, and is even now understood to be prepared for the press. Yet it has serious defects, which may have contributed to keep it in its present form. In its desultory and episodical style of composition, it resembles rather notes for a great history, than history itself. It may be regarded in the light of commentaries, or as illustrations of the times. In that view his pages are of high worth, and have been frequently resorted to by writers who have not too scrupulously appropriated the statements of the old chronicler, with slight acknowledgments to their author.

It is a pity that Oviedo should have shown more solicitude to tell what was new, than to ascertain how much of it was strictly true. Among his merits will scarcely be found that of historical accuracy. And yet we may find an apology for this, to some extent, in the fact, that his writings, as already intimated, are not so much in the nature of finished compositions, as of loose memoranda, where everything, rumor as well as fact,—even the most contradictory rumors,—are all set down at random, forming a miscellaneous heap of materials, of which the discreet historian may avail himself to rear a symmetrical fabric on foundations of greater strength and solidity.

Another author worthy of particular note is Pedro Cieza de Leon. His *Crónica del Peru* should more properly be styled an Itinerary, or rather Geography, of Peru. It gives a minute topographical view of the country at the time of the Conquest; of its provinces and towns, both Indian and Spanish; its flourishing sea-coast; its forests, valleys, and interminable ranges of mountains in the interior; with many interesting particulars of the existing population,—their dress, manners, architectural remains, and public works, while, scattered here and there, may be found notices of their early history and social polity. It is, in short, a lively picture of the country in its physical and moral relations, as it met the eye at the time of the Conquest, and in that transition period when it was first subjected to European influences. The conception of a work, at so early a period, on this philosophical plan, reminding us of that of Malte-Brun in our own time,—*parva componere magnis,*—was, of itself, indicative of great comprehensiveness of mind in its author. It was a task of no little difficulty, where there was yet no pathway opened by the labors of the antiquarian; no hints from the sketch-book of the traveller, or the measurements of the scientific explorer. Yet the distances from place to place are all carefully jotted down by the industrious compiler, and the bearings of the different places and their peculiar features are exhibited with sufficient precision, considering the nature of the obstacles he had to encounter. The literary execution of the work, moreover, is highly respectable, sometimes even rich and picturesque; and the author describes the grand and beautiful scenery of the Cordilleras with a sensibility to its charms, not often found in the tasteless topographer, still less ofter in the rude Conqueror.

Cieza de Leon came to the New World, as he informs us, at the early age of thirteen. But it is not till Gasca's time that we find his name enrolled among the actors in the busy scenes of civil strife, when he accompanied the president in his campaign against Gonzalo Pizarro. His Chronicle, or, at least, the notes for it, was compiled in such leisure as he could snatch from his more stirring avocations; and after ten years from the time he undertook it, the First Part—all we have—was completed in 1550, when the author had reached only the age of thirty-two. It appeared at Seville in 1553, and the following year at Antwerp; while an Italian translation, printed at Rome, in 1555, attested the rapid celebrity of the work. The edition of Antwerp—the one used by me in this compilation—is in the duodecimo form, exceedingly well printed, and garnished with wood-cuts, in which Satan,— for the author had a full measure of the ancient credulity,—with his usual bugbear accompaniments frequently appears in bodily presence. In the Preface, Cieza announces his purpose to continue the work in three other parts, illustrating respectively the ancient history of the country under the Incas, its conquest by the Spaniards, and the civil wars which ensued. He even gives, with curious minuteness, the contents of the several books of the projected history. But the First Part, as already noticed, was alone completed; and the author, having returned to Spain, died there in 1560, at the premature age of forty-two, without having covered any portion of the magnificent ground-plan which he had thus confidently laid out. The deficiency is much to be regretted, considering the talent of the writer, and his opportunities for personal observation. But he has done enough to render us grateful for his labors. By the vivid delineation of scenes and scenery, as they were presented fresh to his own eyes, he has furnished us with a background to the historic picture,—the landscape, as it were, in which the personages of the time might be more fitly portrayed. It would have been impossible to exhibit the ancient topography of the land so faithfully at a subsequent period, when old things had passed away, and the Conqueror, breaking down the landmarks of ancient civilization, had effaced many of the features even of the physical aspect of the country, as it existed under the elaborate culture of the Incas.

BOOK V

SETTLEMENT OF THE COUNTRY

CHAPTER I

GREAT SENSATION IN SPAIN—PEDRO DE LA GASCA—HIS EARLY LIFE—
HIS MISSION TO PERU—HIS POLITIC CONDUCT—HIS OFFERS TO
PIZARRO—GAINS THE FLEET

1545—1547

WHILE the important revolution detailed in the preceding pages was
going forward in Peru, rumors of it, from time to time, found their way
to the mother-country; but the distance was so great, and opportunities
for communication so rare, that the tidings were usually very long behind the occurrence of the events to which they related. The government
heard with dismay of the troubles caused by the ordinances and the
intemperate conduct of the viceroy; and it was not long before it
learned that this functionary was deposed and driven from his capital,
while the whole country, under Gonzalo Pizarro, was arrayed in arms
against him. All classes were filled with consternation at this alarming
intelligence; and many that had before approved the ordinances now
loudly condemned the ministers, who, without considering the inflammable temper of the people, had thus rashly fired a train which menaced
a general explosion throughout the colonies.[1] No such rebellion, within
the memory of man, had occurred in the Spanish empire. It was compared with the famous war of the *comunidades*, in the beginning of
Charles the Fifth's reign. But the Peruvian insurrection seemed the more
formidable of the two. The troubles of Castile, being under the eye of
the Court, might be the more easily managed; while it was difficult to
make the same power felt on the remote shores of the Indies. Lying
along the distant Pacific, the principle of attraction which held Peru to
the parent country was so feeble, that this colony might, at any time,
with a less impulse than that now given to it, fly from its political orbit.

[1] "Que aquello era contra una cédula que tenian del Emperador que les daba el
repartimiento de los indios de su vida, y del hijo mayor, y no teniendo hijos á
sus mugeres, con mandarles espresamente que se casasen como lo habian ya hecho
los mas de ellos; y que tambien era contra otra cédula real que ninguno podia ser
despojado de sus indios sin ser primero oido á justicia y condenado." Historia de
Don Pedro Gasca, Obispo de Siguenza, MS.

It seemed as if the fairest of its jewels was about to fall from the imperial diadem!

Such was the state of things in the summer of 1545, when Charles the Fifth was absent in Germany, occupied with the religious troubles of the empire. The government was in the hands of his son, who, under the name of Philip the Second, was soon to sway the sceptre over the largest portion of his father's dominions, and who was then holding his court at Valladolid. He called together a council of prelates, jurists, and military men of greatest experience, to deliberate on the measures to be pursued for restoring order in the colonies. All agreed in regarding Pizarro's movement in the light of an audacious rebellion; and there were few, at first, who were not willing to employ the whole strength of government to vindicate the honor of the Crown,—to quell the insurrection, and bring the authors of it to punishment.[2]

But, however desirable this might appear, a very little reflection showed that it was not easy to be done, if, indeed, it were practicable. The great distance of Peru required troops to be transported not merely across the ocean, but over the broad extent of the great continent. And how was this to be effected, when the principal posts, the keys of communication with the country, were in the hands of the rebels, while their fleet rode in the Pacific, the mistress of its waters, cutting off all approach to the coast? Even if a Spanish force could be landed in Peru, what chance would it have, unaccustomed, as it would be, to the country and the climate, of coping with the veterans of Pizarro, trained to war in the Indies and warmly attached to the person of their commander? The new levies thus sent out might become themselves infected with the spirit of insurrection, and cast off their own allegiance.[3]

Nothing remained, therefore, but to try conciliatory measures. The government, however mortifying to its pride, must retrace its steps. A free grace must be extended to those who submitted, and such persuasive arguments should be used, and such politic concessions made, as would convince the refractory colonists that it was their interest, as well as their duty, to return to their allegiance.

But to approach the people in their present state of excitement, and to make those concessions without too far compromising the dignity and permanent authority of the Crown, was a delicate matter, for the success of which they must rely wholly on the character of the agent. After much deliberation, a competent person, as it was thought, was found in an ecclesiastic, by the name of Pedro de la Gasca,—a name which,

---

[2] MS. de Caravantes.—Hist. de Don Pedro Gasca, MS.
One of this council was the great Duke of Alva, of such gloomy celebrity afterwards in the Netherlands. We may well believe his voice was for coercion.

[3] "Ventilose la forma del remedio de tan grave caso en que huvo dos opiniones; la una de imbiar un gran soldado con fuerza de gente á la demostracion de este castigo; la otra que se llevase el negocio por prudentes y suaves medios, por la imposibilidad y falto de dinero para llevar gente, cavallos, armas, municiones y vastimentos, y para sustentarlos en tierra firme y pasarlos al Pirú." MS. de Caravantes

brighter by contrast with the gloomy times in which it first appeared, still shines with undiminished splendor after the lapse of ages.

Pedro de la Gasca was born, probably, towards the close of the fifteenth century, in a small village in Castile named Barco de Avila. He came, both by father and mother's side, from an ancient and noble lineage; ancient indeed, if, as his biographers contend, he derived his descent from Casca, one of the conspirators against Julius Cæsar![4] Having the misfortune to lose his father early in life, he was placed by his uncle in the famous seminary of Alcalá de Henares, founded by the great Ximénes. Here he made rapid proficiency in liberal studies, especially in those connected with his profession, and at length received the degree of Master of Theology.

The young man, however, discovered other talents than those demanded by his sacred calling. The war of the *comunidades* was then raging in the country; and the authorities of his college showed a disposition to take the popular side. But Gasca, putting himself at the head of an armed force, seized one of the gates of the city, and, with assistance from the royal troops, secured the place to the interests of the Crown. This early display of loyalty was probably not lost on his vigilant sovereign.[5]

From Alcalá, Gasca was afterwards removed to Salamanca; where he distinguished himself by his skill in scholastic disputation, and obtained the highest academic honors in that ancient university, the fruitful nursery of scholarship and genius. He was subsequently intrusted with the management of some important affairs of an ecclesiastical nature, and made a member of the Council of the Inquisition.

In this latter capacity he was sent to Valencia, about 1540, to examine into certain alleged cases of heresy in that quarter of the country. These were involved in great obscurity; and, although Gasca had the assistance of several eminent jurists in the investigation, it occupied him nearly two years. In the conduct of this difficult matter, he showed so much penetration, and such perfect impartiality, that he was appointed by the Cortes of Valencia to the office of *visitador* of that kingdom; a highly responsible post, requiring great discretion in the person who filled it, since it was his province to inspect the condition of the courts of justice

---

[4] "Pasando á España vinieron á tierra de Avila y quedó del nombre dellos el lugar y familia de Gasca; mudandose por la afinidad de la pronunciacion, que hay entre las dos letras consonantes *c. y. g.* el nombre de Casca en Gasca." Hist. de Don Pedro Gasca, MS.

Similarity of name is a peg quite strong enough to hang a pedigree upon in Castile.

[5] This account of the early history of Gasca I have derived chiefly from a manuscript biographical notice written in 1465, during the prelate's life. The name of the author, who speaks apparently from personal knowledge, is not given; but it seems to be the work of a scholar, and is written with a certain pretension to elegance. The original MS. forms part of the valuable collection of Don Pascual de Gayangos of Madrid. It is of much value for the light it throws on the early career of Gasca, which has been passed over in profound silence by Castilian historians. It is to be regretted that the author did not continue his labors beyond the period when the subject of them received his appointment to the Peruvian mission.

and of finance, throughout the land, with authority to reform abuses
It was proof of extraordinary consideration, that it should have been
bestowed on Gasca; since it was a departure from the established usage
—and that in a nation most wedded to usage—to confer the office on
any but a subject of the Aragonese crown.[6]

Gasca executed the task assigned to him with independence and abil·
ity. While he was thus occupied, the people of Valencia were thrown into
consternation by a meditated invasion of the French and the Turks,
who, under the redoubtable Barbarossa, menaced the coast and the
neighboring Balearic isles. Fears were generally entertained of a rising
of the Morisco population; and the Spanish officers who had command
in that quarter, being left without the protection of a navy, despaired
of making head against the enemy. In this season of general panic,
Gasca alone appeared calm and self-possessed. He remonstrated with
the Spanish commanders on their unsoldierlike despondency; encouraged them to confide in the loyalty of the Moriscos; and advised the immediate erection of fortifications along the shores for their protection.
He was, in consequence, named one of a commission to superintend
these works, and to raise levies for defending the sea-coast; and so faithfully was the task performed, that Barbarossa, after some ineffectual
attempts to make good his landing, was baffled at all points, and compelled to abandon the enterprise as hopeless. The chief credit of this
resistance must be assigned to Gasca, who superintended the construction of the defences, and who was enabled to contribute a large part of
the requisite funds by the economical reforms he had introduced into
the administration of Valencia.[7]

It was at this time, the latter part of the year 1545, that the council
of Philip selected Gasca as the person most competent to undertake the
perilous mission to Peru.[8] His character, indeed, seemed especially suited to it. His loyalty had been shown through his whole life. With great
suavity of manners he combined the most intrepid resolution. Though
his demeanor was humble, as beseemed his calling, it was far from abject; for he was sustained by a conscious rectitude of purpose, that impressed respect on all with whom he had intercourse. He was acute in

---

[6] "Era tanta la opinion que en Valencia tenian de la integridad y prudencia de
Gasca, que en las Cortes de Monzon los Estados de aquel Reyno le pidieron por
Visitador contra la costumbre y fuero de aquel Reyno, que no puede serlo sino
fuere natural de la Corona de Araugon, y consintiendo que aquel fuero se derogase
el Emperador lo concedió á instancia y peticion dellos." Hist. de Don Pedro Gasca,
MS.

[7] "Que parece cierto," says his enthusiastic biographer, "que por disposicion Divina vino á hallarse Gasca entónces en la Ciudad de Valencia, para remedio de
aquel Reyno y Islas de Mallorca y Menorca é Iviza, segun la órden, prevencion y
diligencia que en la defensa contra las armadas del Turco y Francia tuvo, y las
provisiones que para ello hizo." Hist. de Don Pedro Gasca, MS.

[8] "Finding a lion would not answer, they sent a lamb," says Gomara;—"Finalmente, quiso embiar una Oveja, pues un Leon no aprovecho; y asi escogió al Licenciado Pedro Gasca." Hist. de las Ind., cap. 174.

his perceptions, had a shrewd knowledge of character, and, though bred to the cloister, possessed an acquaintance with affairs, and even with military science, such as was to have been expected only from one reared in courts and camps.

Without hesitation, therefore, the council unanimously recommended him to the emperor, and requested his approbation of their proceedings. Charles had not been an inattentive observer of Gasca's course. His attention had been particularly called to the able manner in which he had conducted the judicial process against the heretics of Valencia.[9] The monarch saw, at once, that he was the man for the present emergency; and he immediately wrote to him, with his own hand, expressing his entire satisfaction at the appointment, and intimating his purpose to testify his sense of his worth by preferring him to one of the principal sees then vacant.

Gasca accepted the important mission now tendered to him without hesitation; and, repairing to Madrid, received the instructions of the government as to the course to be pursued. They were expressed in the most benign and conciliatory tone, perfectly in accordance with the suggestions of his own benevolent temper.[10] But, while he commended the tone of the instructions, he considered the powers with which he was to be intrusted as wholly incompetent to their object. They were conceived in the jealous spirit with which the Spanish government usually limited the authority of its great colonial officers, whose distance from home gave peculiar cause for distrust. On every strange and unexpected emergency, Gasca saw that he should be obliged to send back for instructions. This must cause delay, where promptitude was essential to success. The Court, moreover, as he represented to the council, was, from its remoteness from the scene of action, utterly incompetent to pronounce as to the expediency of the measures to be pursued. Some one should be sent out in whom the king could implicitly confide, and who should be invested with powers competent to every emergency; powers not merely to decide on what was best, but to carry that decision into execution; and he boldly demanded that he should go not only as the representative of the sovereign, but clothed with all the authority of the sovereign himself. Less than this would defeat the very object for which he was to be sent. "For myself," he concluded, "I ask neither salary nor compensation of any kind. I covet no display of state or military array. With

---

[9] Gasca made what the author calls *una breve y copyosa relacion* of the proceedings to the emperor in Valencia; and the monarch was so intent on the inquiry, that he devoted the whole afternoon to it, notwithstanding his son Philip was waiting for him to attend a *fiesta!* irrefragable proof, as the writer conceives, of his zeal for the faith.—"Queriendo entender muy de raizo todo lo que pasaba, como Principe tan zeloso que era de las cosas de la religion." Hist. de Don Pedro Gasca, MS.

[10] These instructions, the patriarchal tone of which is highly creditable to the government, are given *in extenso* in the MS. of Caravantes, and in no other work which I have consulted.

my stole and breviary I trust to do the work that is committed to me.¹¹ Infirm as I am in body, the repose of my own home would have been more grateful to me than this dangerous mission; but I will not shrink from it at the bidding of my sovereign, and if, as is very probable, I may not be permitted again to see my native land, I shall, at least, be cheered by the consciousness of having done my best to serve its interests." ¹²

The members of the council, while they listened with admiration to the disinterested avowal of Gasca, were astounded by the boldness of his demands. Not that they distrusted the purity of his motives, for these were above suspicion. But the powers for which he stipulated were so far beyond those hitherto delegated to a colonial viceroy, that they felt they had no warrant to grant them. They even shrank from soliciting them from the emperor, and required that Gasca himself should address the monarch, and state precisely the grounds on which demands so extraordinary were founded.

Gasca readily adopted the suggestion, and wrote in the most full and explicit manner to his sovereign, who had then transferred his residence to Flanders. But Charles was not so tenacious, or, at least, so jealous, of authority, as his ministers. He had been too long in possession of it to feel that jealousy; and, indeed, many years were not to elapse, before, oppressed by its weight, he was to resign it altogether into the hands of his son. His sagacious mind, moreover, readily comprehended the difficulties of Gasca's position. He felt that the present extraordinary crisis was to be met only by extraordinary measures. He assented to the force of his vassal's arguments, and, on the sixteenth of February, 1546, wrote him another letter expressive of his approbation, and intimated his willingness to grant him powers as absolute as those he had requested.

Gasca was to be styled President of the Royal Audience. But, under this simple title, he was placed at the head of every department in the colony, civil, military, and judicial. He was empowered to make new *repartimientos*, and to confirm those already made. He might declare war, levy troops, appoint to all offices, or remove from them, at pleasure. He might exercise the royal prerogative of pardoning offences, and was especially authorized to grant an amnesty to all, without exception, implicated in the present rebellion. He was, moreover, to proclaim at once the revocation of the odious ordinances. These two last provisions might be said to form the basis of all his operations.

Since ecclesiastics were not to be reached by the secular arm, and yet were often found fomenting troubles in the colonies, Gasca was permitted to banish from Peru such as he thought fit. He might even send

---

¹¹ "De suerte que juzgassen que la mas fuerça que lleuaua, era su abito de clerigo y breuiario." Fernandez, Hist. del Peru, Parte 1, lib. 2, cap. 16.

¹² MS. de Caravantes.—Hist. de Don Pedro Gasca, MS.—Fernandez, Hist. del Peru, Parte 1, lib. 2, cap. 16, 17.

Though not for himself, Gasca did solicit one favor of the emperor,—the appointment of his brother, an eminent jurist, to a vacant place on the bench of one of the Castilian tribunals.

home the viceroy, if the good of the country required it. Agreeably to his own suggestion, he was to receive no specified stipend; but he had unlimited orders on the treasuries both of Panamá and Peru. He was furnished with letters from the emperor to the principal authorities, not only in Peru, but in Mexico and the neighboring colonies, requiring their countenance and support; and, lastly, blank letters, bearing the royal signature, were delivered to him, which he was to fill up at his pleasure.[13]

While the grant of such unbounded powers excited the warmest sentiments of gratitude in Gasca towards the sovereign who could repose in him so much confidence, it seems—which is more extraordinary—not to have raised corresponding feelings of envy in the courtiers. They knew well that it was not for himself that the good ecclesiastic had solicited them. On the contrary, some of the council were desirous that he should be preferred to the bishopric, as already promised him, before his departure; conceiving that he would thus go with greater authority than as an humble ecclesiastic, and fearing, moreover, that Gasca himself, were it omitted, might feel some natural disappointment. But the president hastened to remove these impressions. "The honor would avail me little," he said, "where I am going; and it would be manifestly wrong to appoint me to an office in the Church, while I remain at such a distance that I cannot discharge the duties of it. The consciousness of my insufficiency," he continued, "should I never return, would lie heavy on my soul in my last moments."[14] The politic reluctance to accept the mitre has passed into a proverb. But there was no affectation here; and Gasca's friends, yielding to his arguments, forbore to urge the matter further.

The new president now went forward with his preparation. They were few and simple; for he was to be accompanied by a slender train of followers, among whom the most conspicuous was Alonso de Alvarado, the gallant officer who, as the reader may remember, long commanded under Francisco Pizarro. He had resided of late years at court; and now at Gasca's request accompanied him to Peru, where his presence might facilitate negotiations with the insurgents, while his military experience would prove no less valuable in case of an appeal to arms.[15] Some delay necessarily occurred in getting ready his little squadron, and it was not till the 26th of May, 1546, that the president and his suite embarked at San Lucar for the New World.

After a prosperous voyage, and not a long one for that day, he landed, about the middle of July, at the port of Santa Martha. Here he received

---

[13] Zarate, Conq. del Peru, lib. 6, cap. 6.—Herrera, Hist. General, dec. 8, lib. 1, cap. 6.—MS. de Caravantes.—Fernandez, Hist. del Peru, Parte 1, lib. 2, cap. 17, 18 —Gomara, Hist. de las Ind., cap. 174.—Hist. de Don Pedro Gasca, MS.

[14] "Especialmente, si alla muriesse ó le matassen: que entōces de nada le podria ser buena, sino para partir desta vida, con mas congoxa y pena de la poca cuenta que daua de la prouision que auia aceptado." Fernandez, Hist. de Peru, Parte 1, lib. 2, cap. 18.

[15] From this cavalier descended the noble house of the counts of Villamor in Spain. MS. de Caravantes.

the astounding intelligence of the battle of Añaquito, of the defeat and death of the viceroy, and of the manner in which Gonzalo Pizarro had since established his absolute rule over the land. Although these events had occurred several months before Gasca's departure from Spain, yet, so imperfect was the intercourse, no tidings of them had then reached that country.

They now filled the president with great anxiety; as he reflected that the insurgents, after so atrocious an act as the slaughter of the viceroy, might well despair of grace, and become reckless of consequences. He was careful, therefore, to have it understood, that the date of his commission was subsequent to that of the fatal battle, and that it authorized an entire amnesty of all offences hitherto committed against the government.[16]

Yet, in some points of view, the death of Blasco Nuñez might be regarded as an auspicious circumstance for the settlement of the country. Had he lived till Gasca's arrival, the latter would have been greatly embarrassed by the necessity of acting in concert with a person so generally detested in the colony, or by the unwelcome alternative of sending him back to Castile. The insurgents, moreover, would, in all probability, be now more amenable to reason, since all personal animosity might naturally be buried in the grave of their enemy.

The president was much embarrassed by deciding in what quarter he should attempt to enter Peru. Every port was in the hands of Pizarro, and was placed under the care of his officers, with strict charge to intercept any communications from Spain, and to detain such persons as bore a commission from that country until his pleasure could be known respecting them. Gasca, at length, decided on crossing over to Nombre de Dios, then held with a strong force by Hernan Mexia, an officer to whose charge Gonzalo had committed this strong gate to his dominions, as to a person on whose attachment to his cause he could confidently rely.

Had Gasca appeared off this place in a menacing attitude, with a military array, or, indeed, with any display of official pomp that might have awakened distrust in the commander, he would doubtless have found it no easy matter to effect a landing. But Mexia saw nothing to apprehend in the approach of a poor ecclesiastic, without an armed force, with hardly even a retinue to support him, coming solely, as it seemed, on an errand of mercy. No sooner, therefore, was he acquainted with the character of the envoy, and his mission, than he prepared to receive him with the honors due to his rank, and marched out at the head of his soldiers, together with a considerable body of ecclesiastics resident in the place. There was nothing in the person of Gasca, still less in his humble clerical attire and modest retinue, to impress the vulgar spectator with feelings of awe or reverence. Indeed, the poverty-stricken aspect, as it seemed, of himself and his followers, so different from the usual state affected by the Indian viceroys, excited some merriment

[16] Fernandez, Hist. del Peru, Parte 1, lib. 2, cap. 21.

among the rude soldiery, who did not scruple to break their coarse jests on his appearance, in hearing of the president himself.[17] "If this is the sort of governor his Majesty sends over to us," they exclaimed, "Pizarro need not trouble his head much about it."

Yet the president, far from being ruffled by this ribaldry, or from showing resentment to its authors, submitted to it with the utmost humility, and only seemed the more grateful to his own brethren, who, by their respectful demeanor, appeared anxious to do him honor.

But, however plain and unpretending the manners of Gasca, Mexia, on his first interview with him soon discovered that he had no common man to deal with. The president, after briefly explaining the nature of his commission, told him that he had come as a messenger of peace; and that it was on peaceful measures he relied for his success. He then stated the general scope of his commission, his authority to grant a free pardon to all, without exception, who at once submitted to government, and, finally, his purpose to proclaim the revocation of the ordinances. The objects of the revolution were thus attained. To contend longer would be manifest rebellion, and that without a motive; and he urged the commander by every principle of loyalty and patriotism to support him in settling the distractions of the country, and bringing it back to its allegiance.

The candid and conciliatory language of the president, so different from the arrogance of Blasco Nuñez, and the austere demeanor of Vaca de Castro, made a sensible impression on Mexia. He admitted the force of Gasca's reasoning, and flattered himself that Gonzalo Pizarro would not be insensible to it. Though attached to the fortunes of that leader, he was loyal in heart, and, like most of the party, had been led by accident, rather than by design, into rebellion; and now that so good an opportunity occurred to do it with safety, he was not unwilling to retrace his steps, and secure the royal favor by thus early returning to his allegiance. This he signified to the president, assuring him of his hearty coöperation in the good work of reform.[18]

This was an important step for Gasca. It was yet more important for him to secure the obedience of Hinojosa, the governor of Panamá, in the harbor of which city lay Pizarro's navy, consisting of two-and-twenty vessels. But it was not easy to approach this officer. He was a person of much higher character than was usually found among the reckless adventurers in the New World. He was attached to the interests of Pizarro, and the latter had requited him by placing him in command of his armada and of Panamá, the key to his territories on the Pacific.

The president first sent Mexia and Alonso de Alvarado to prepare the

---

[17] "Especialmente muchos de los soldados, que estauan desacatados, y decian palabras feas, y desuergōçadas. A lo qual el Presidente (viendo que era necessario) hazia las orejas sordas." Ibid., Parte 1, lib. 2, cap. 23.

[18] Ibid., ubi supra.—Carta de Gonzalo Pizarro a Valdivia, MS.—Montesinos, Annales, MS. año 1546.—Zarate, Conq. del Peru. lib. 6, cap. 6.—Herrera, Hist. General, dec. 8, lib. 2, cap. 5.

way for his own coming, by advising Hinojosa of the purport of his mission. He soon after followed, and was received by that commander with every show of outward respect. But while the latter listened with deference to the representations of Gasca, they failed to work the change in him which they had wrought in Mexia; and he concluded by asking the president to show him his powers, and by inquiring whether they gave him authority to confirm Pizarro in his present post, to which he was entitled no less by his own services than by the general voice of the people.

This was an embarrassing question. Such a concession would have been altogether too humiliating to the Crown; but to have openly avowed this at the present juncture to so stanch an adherent of Pizarro might have precluded all further negotiation. The president evaded the question, therefore, by simply stating, that the time had not yet come for him to produce his powers, but that Hinojosa might be assured they were such as to secure an ample recompense to every loyal servant of his country.[19]

Hinojosa was not satisfied; and he immediately wrote to Pizarro, acquainting him with Gasca's arrival and with the object of his mission, at the same time plainly intimating his own conviction that the president had no authority to confirm him in the government. But before the departure of the ship, Gasca secured the services of a Dominican friar, who had taken his passage on board for one of the towns on the coast. This man he intrusted with manifestoes, setting forth the purport of his visit, and proclaiming the abolition of the ordinances, with a free pardon to all who returned to their obedience. He wrote, also, to the prelates and to the corporations of the different cities. The former he requested to coöperate with him in introducing a spirit of loyalty and subordination among the people, while he intimated to the towns his purpose to confer with them hereafter, in order to devise some effectual measures for the welfare of the country. These papers the Dominican engaged to distribute, himself, among the principal cities of the colony; and he faithfully kept his word, though, as it proved, at no little hazard of his life. The seeds thus scattered might many of them fall on barren ground. But the greater part, the president trusted, would take root in the hearts of the people; and he patiently waited for the harvest.

Meanwhile, though he failed to remove the scruples of Hinojosa, the courteous manners of Gasca, and his mild, persuasive discourse, had a visible effect on other individuals with whom he had daily intercourse. Several of these, and among them some of the principal cavaliers in Panamá, as well as in the squadron, expressed their willingness to join the royal cause, and aid the president in maintaining it. Gasca profited by their assistance to open a communication with the authorities of Guatemala and Mexico, whom he advised of his mission, while he ad-

[19] Fernandez, Hist. del Peru, Parte 1, lib 2, cap. 25.—Zarate, Conq. del Peru, lib. 6, cap. 7.—MS. de Caravantes.

monished them to allow no intercourse to be carried on with the insurgents on the coast of Peru. He, at length, also prevailed on the governor of Panamá to furnish him with the means of entering into communication with Conzalo Pizarro himself; and a ship was despatched to Lima, bearing a letter from Charles the Fifth, addressed to that chief, with an epistle also from Gasca.

The emperor's communication was couched in the most condescending and even conciliatory terms. Far from taxing Gonzalo with rebellion, his royal master affected to regard his conduct as in a manner imposed on him by circumstances, especially by the obduracy of the viceroy Nuñez in denying the colonists the inalienable right of petition. He gave no intimation of an intent to confirm Pizarro in the government, or, indeed, to remove him from it; but simply referred him to Gasca as one who would acquaint him with the royal pleasure, and with whom he was to coöperate in restoring tranquillity to the country.

Gasca's own letter was pitched on the same politic key. He remarked, however, that the exigencies which had hitherto determined Gonzalo's line of conduct existed no longer. All that had been asked was conceded. There was nothing now to contend for; and it only remained for Pizarro and his followers to show their loyalty and the sincerity of their principles by obedience to the Crown. Hitherto, the president said, Pizarro had been in arms against the viceroy; and the people had supported him as against a common enemy. If he prolonged the contest, that enemy must be his sovereign. In such a struggle, the people would be sure to desert him; and Gasca conjured him, by his honor as a cavalier, and his duty as a loyal vassal, to respect the royal authority, and not rashly provoke a contest which must prove to the world that his conduct hitherto had been dictated less by patriotic motives than by selfish ambition.

This letter, which was conveyed in language the most courteous and complimentary to the subject of it, was of great length. It was accompanied by another much more concise, to Cepeda, the intriguing lawyer, who, as Gasca knew, had the greatest influence over Pizarro, in the absence of Carbajal, then employed in reaping the silver harvest from the newly discovered mines of Potosí.[20] In this epistle, Gasca affected to defer to the cunning politician as a member of the Royal Audience, and he conferred with him on the best manner of supplying a vacancy in that body. These several despatches were committed to a cavalier, named Paniagua, a faithful adherent of the president, and one of those who had accompanied him from Castile. To this same emissary he also gave manifestos and letters, like those intrusted to the Dominican, with orders secretly to distribute them in Lima, before he quitted that capital.[21]

---

[20] "El Licenciado Cepeda que tengo yo agora por teniente, de quien yo hago mucho caso i le quiero mucho." Carta de Gonzalo Pizarro a Valdivia, MS.

[21] The letters noticed in the text may be found in Zarate, Conq. del Peru, lib. 6, cap. 7, and Fernandez, Hist. del Peru, Parte 1, lib. 2, cap. 29, 30. The president's letter covers several pages. Much of it is taken up with historic precedents and

Weeks and months rolled away, while the president still remained at Panamá, where, indeed, as his communications were jealously cut off with Peru, he might be said to be detained as a sort of prisoner of state. Meanwhile, both he and Hinojosa were looking with anxiety for the arrival of some messenger from Pizarro, who should indicate the manner in which the president's mission was to be received by that chief. The governor of Panamá was not blind to the perilous position in which he was himself placed, nor to the madness of provoking a contest with the Court of Castile. But he had a reluctance—not too often shared by the cavaliers of Peru—to abandon the fortunes of the commander who had reposed in him so great confidence. Yet he trusted that this commander would embrace the opportunity now offered, of placing himself and the country in a state of permanent security.

Several of the cavaliers who had given in their adhesion to Gasca, displeased by this obstinacy, as they termed it, of Hinojosa, proposed to seize his person and then get possession of the armada. But the president at once rejected this offer. His mission, he said, was one of peace, and he would not stain it at the outset by an act of violence. He even respected the scruples of Hinojosa; and a cavalier of so honorable a nature, he conceived, if once he could be gained by fair means, would be much more likely to be true to his interests, than if overcome either by force or fraud. Gasca thought he might safely abide his time. There was policy, as well as honesty, in this; indeed, they always go together.

Meantime, persons were occasionally arriving from Lima and the neighboring places, who gave accounts of Pizarro, varying according to the character and situation of the parties. Some represented him as winning all hearts by his open temper and the politic profusion with which, though covetous of wealth, he distributed *repartimientos* and favors among his followers. Others spoke of him as carrying matters with a high hand, while the greatest timidity and distrust prevailed among the citizens of Lima. All agreed that his power rested on too secure a basis to be shaken; and that, if the president should go to Lima, he must either consent to become Pizarro's instrument and confirm him in the government, or forfeit his own life.[22]

It was undoubtedly true, that Gonzalo, while he gave attention, as his friends say, to the public business, found time for free indulgence in those pleasures which wait on the soldier of fortune in his hour of triumph. He was the object of flattery and homage; courted even by those who hated him. For such as did not love the successful chieftain had good cause to fear him; and his exploits were commemorated in

illustrations, to show the folly, as well as wickedness, of a collision with the imperial authority. The benignant tone of this homily may be inferred from its concluding sentence; "Nuestro señor por su infinita bõdad alumbre a vuestra merced, y a todos los demas para que acierten a hazer en este negocio lo que cõuiene a sus almas, honras, vidas y haziendas: y guarde en su sancto servicio la Illustre persona de vuestra merced."

[22] Fernandez, Hist. del Peru, Parte 1, lib. 2, cap. 27.—Herrera, Hist. General, dec. 8, lib. 2, cap. 7.—MS. de Caravantes.

romances or ballads, as rivalling—it was not far from truth—those of the most doughty paladins of chivalry.[23]

Amidst this burst of adulation, the cup of joy commended to Pizarro's lips had one drop of bitterness in it that gave its flavor to all the rest; for, notwithstanding his show of confidence, he looked with unceasing anxiety to the arrival of tidings that might assure him in what light his conduct was regarded by the government at home. This was proved by his jealous precautions to guard the approaches to the coast, and to detain the persons of the royal emissaries. He learned, therefore, with no little uneasiness, from Hinojosa, the landing of President Gasca, and the purport of his mission. But his discontent was mitigated, when he understood that the new envoy had come without military array, without any of the ostentatious trappings of office to impose on the minds of the vulgar, but alone, as it were, in the plain garb of an humble missionary.[24] Pizarro could not discern, that under this modest exterior lay a moral power, stronger than his own steel-clad battalions, which, operating silently on public opinion,—the more sure than it was silent,—was even now undermining his strength, like a subterraneous channel eating away the foundations of some stately edifice, that stands secure in its pride of place!

But, although Gonzalo Pizarro could not foresee this result, he saw enough to satisfy him that it would be safest to exclude the president from Peru. The tidings of his arrival, moreover, quickened his former purpose of sending an embassy to Spain to vindicate his late proceedings, and request the royal confirmation of his authority. The person placed at the head of this mission was Lorenzo de Aldana, a cavalier of discretion as well as courage, and high in the confidence of Pizarro, as one of his most devoted partisans. He had occupied some important posts under that chief, one secret of whose successes was the sagacity he showed in the selection of his agents.

Besides Aldana and one or two cavaliers, the bishop of Lima was joined in the commission, as likely, from his position, to have a favorable influence on Gonzalo's fortunes at court. Together with the despatches for the government, the envoys were intrusted with a letter to Gasca from the inhabitants of Lima; in which, after civilly congratulating the president on his arrival, they announce their regret that he had come too late. The troubles of the country were now settled by the overthrow of the viceroy, and the nation was reposing in quiet under the

---

[23] "Y con esto, estaua siempre en fiestas y recozijo, holgandose mucho que le diessen musicas, cantando romances, y coplas, de todo lo que auia hecho: encaresciendo sus hazañas, y victorias. En lo qual mucho se deleytaua como hombre de gruesso entēdimiento." Fernandez, Hist del Peru, Parte 1, lib. 2, cap. 32.

[24] Gonzalo, in his letter to Valdivia, speaks of Gasca as a clergyman of a godly reputation, who, without recompense, in the true spirit of a missionary, had come over to settle the affairs of the country. "Dicen ques mui buen christiano i hombre de buena vida i clerigo, i dicen que viene a estas partes con buena intencion i no quiso salario ninguno del Rey sino venir para poner paz en estos reynos con sus cristiandades." Carta de Gonzalo Pizarro a Valdivia, MS.

rule of Pizarro. An embassy, they stated, was on its way to Castile, *not to solicit pardon,* for they had committed no crime,[25] but to petition the emperor to confirm their leader in the government, as the man in Peru best entitled to it by his virtues.[26] They expressed the conviction that Gasca's presence would only serve to renew the distractions of the country, and they darkly intimated that his attempt to land would probably cost him his life.—The language of this singular document was more respectful than might be inferred from its import. It was dated the 14th of October, 1546, and was subscribed by seventy of the principal cavaliers in the city. It was not improbably dictated by Cepeda, whose hand is visible in most of the intrigues of Pizarro's little court. It is also said, —the authority is somewhat questionable,—that Aldana received instructions from Gonzalo secretly to offer a bribe of fifty thousand *pesos de oro* to the president, to prevail on him to return to Castile; and in case of his refusal, some darker and more effectual way was to be devised to rid the country of his presence.[27]

Aldana, fortified with his despatches, sped swiftly on his voyage to Panamá. Through him the governor learned the actual state of feeling in the councils of Pizarro; and he listened with regret to the envoy's conviction, that no terms would be admitted by that chief or his companions, that did not confirm him in the possession of Peru.[28]

Aldana was soon admitted to an audience by the president. It was attended with very different results from what had followed from the conferences with Hinojosa; for Pizarro's envoy was not armed by nature with that stubborn panoply which had hitherto made the other proof against all argument. He now learned with surprise the nature of Gasca's

[25] "Porque perdō ninguno de nosotros le pide, porque no entendemos que emos errado, sino seruido à su Magestad: conseruādo nuestro derecho; que por sus leyes Reales à sus vasallos es permitido." Fernandez, Hist. del Peru, Parte 1, lib. 2, cap. 33.

[26] "Porque el por sus virtudes es muy amado de todos: y tenido por padre del Perú." Ibid., ubi supra.

[27] Ibid., loc. cit.—Herrera, Hist. General, dec. 8, lib. 2, cap. 10.—Zarate, Conq. del Peru, lib. 6, cap. 8.—Gomara, Hist. de las Ind., cap. 177.—Montesinos, Annales, MS., año 1546.

Pizarro, in his letter to Valdivia, notices this remonstrance to Gasca, who, with all his *reputation as a saint, was as deep as any man in Spain,* and had now come to send him home, as a reward, no doubt, of his faithful services. "But I and the rest of the cavaliers," he concludes, "have warned him not to set foot here." "Y agora que yo tenia puesta esta tierra en sosiego embiava su parte al de la Gasca, que aunque arriba digo que dicen ques un santo, es un hombre mas mañoso que havia en toda España é mas sabio; é asi venia por presidente é Governador, é todo quanto el quiera; é para poderme embiar á mi á España, i á cabo de dos años que andavamos fuera de nuestras casas queria el Rey darme este pago, mas yo con todos los cavalleros deste Reyno le embiavamos á decir que se vaya, sino que harémos con él como con Blasco Nuñez." Carta de Gonzalo Pizarro a Valdivia, MS.

[28] With Aldana's mission to Castile Gonzalo Pizarro closes the important letter, so often cited in these pages, and which may be supposed to furnish the best arguments for his own conduct. It is a curious fact, that Valdivia, the conqueror of Chili, to whom the epistle is addressed, soon after this openly espoused the cause of Gasca, and his troops formed part of the forces who contended with Pizarro, not long afterwards, at Huarina. Such was the friend on whom Gonzalo relied!

powers, and the extent of the royal concessions to the insurgents. He had embarked with Gonzalo Pizarro on a desperate venture, and he found that it had proved successful. The colony had nothing more, in reason, to demand; and, though devoted in heart to his leader, he did not feel bound by any principle of honor to take part with him, solely to gratify his ambition, in a wild contest with the Crown that must end in inevitable ruin. He consequently abandoned his mission to Castile, probably never very palatable to him, and announced his purpose to accept the pardon proffered by government, and support the president in settling the affairs of Peru. He subsequently wrote, it should be added, to his former commander in Lima, stating the course he had taken, and earnestly recommending the latter to follow his example.

The influence of this precedent in so important a person as Aldana, aided, doubtless, by the conviction that no change was now to be expected in Pizarro, while delay would be fatal to himself, at length prevailed over Hinojosa's scruples, and he intimated to Gasca his willingness to place the fleet under his command. The act was performed with great pomp and ceremony. Some of Pizarro's stanchest partisans were previously removed from the vessels; and on the nineteenth of November, 1546, Hinojosa and his captains resigned their commissions into the hands of the president. They next took the oaths of allegiance to Castile; a free pardon for all past offences was proclaimed by the herald from a scaffold erected in the great square of the city; and the president, greeting them as true and loyal vassals of the Crown, restored their several commissions to the cavaliers. The royal standard of Spain was then unfurled on board the squadron, and proclaimed that this stronghold of Pizarro's power had passed away from him for ever.[29]

The return of their commissions to the insurgent captains was a politic act in Gasca. It secured the services of the ablest officers in the country, and turned against Pizarro the very arm on which he had most leaned for support. Thus was this great step achieved, without force or fraud, by Gasca's patience and judicious forecast. He was content to bide his time; and he now might rely with well-grounded confidence on the ultimate success of his mission.

[29] Pedro Pizarro, Descub. y Conq., MS.—Zarate, Conq. del Peru, lib. 6, cap. 9.—Fernandez, Hist. del Peru, Parte 1, lib. 2, cap. 38, 42.—Gomara, Hist. de las Indias, cap. 178.—MS. de Caravantes.

Garcilasso de la Vega,—whose partiality for Gonzalo Pizarro forms a wholesome counterpoise to the unfavorable views taken of his conduct by most other writers, —in his notice of this transaction, seems disposed to allow little credit to that loyalty which is shown by the sacrifice of a benefactor. Com. Real., Parte 2, lib. 5, cap. 4.

CHAPTER II

GASCA ASSEMBLES HIS FORCES—DEFECTION OF PIZARRO'S FOLLOWERS
—HE MUSTERS HIS LEVIES—AGITATION IN LIMA—HE ABANDONS
THE CITY—GASCA SAILS FROM PANAMA—BLOODY BATTLE OF
HUARINA

1547

No sooner was Gasca placed in possession of Panamá and the fleet, than he entered on a more decisive course of policy than he had been hitherto allowed to pursue. He raised levies of men, and drew together supplies from all quarters. He took care to discharge the arrears already due to the soldiers, and promised liberal pay for the future; for, though mindful that his personal charges should cost little to the Crown, he did not stint his expenditure when the public good required it. As the funds in the treasury were exhausted, he obtained loans on the credit of the government from the wealthy citizens of Panamá, who, relying on his good faith, readily made the necessary advances. He next sent letters to the authorities of Guatemala and Mexico, requiring their assistance in carrying on hostilities, if necessary, against the insurgents; and he despatched a summons, in like manner, to Benalcazar, in the provinces north of Peru, to meet him, on his landing in that country, with his whole available force.

The greatest enthusiasm was shown by the people of Panamá in getting the little navy in order for his intended voyage; and prelates and commanders did not disdain to prove their loyalty by taking part in the good work, along with the soldiers and sailors.[1] Before his own departure, however, Gasca proposed to send a small squadron of four ships under Aldana, to cruise off the port of Lima, with instructions to give protection to those well affected to the royal cause, and receive them, if need be, on board his vessels. He was also intrusted with authenticated copies of the president's commission, to be delivered to Gonzalo Pizarro, that the chief might feel, there was yet time to return before the gates of mercy were closed against him.[2]

[1] "Y ponia sus fuerças con tanta llaneza y obediencia, que los Obispos y clerigos y los capitanes y mas principales personas eran los que primero echauan mano, y tirauan de las gumenas y cables de los nauios, para los sacar à la costa." Fernandez, Hist. del Peru, Parte 1, lib. 2, cap. 70.

[2] Ibid., ubi supra.—Montesinos, Annales, MS., año 1546.—Gomara, Hist. de las Ind., cap. 178.—Zarate, Conq. del Peru, lib. 6, cap. 9.—Herrera, Hist. General, dec. 9, lib. 3, cap. 3.

While these events were going on, Gasca's proclamations and letters were doing their work in Peru. It required but little sagacity to perceive that the nation at large, secured in the protection of person and property, had nothing to gain by revolution. Interest and duty, fortunately, now lay on the same side; and the ancient sentiment of loyalty, smothered for a time, but not extinguished, revived in the breasts of the people. Still this was not manifested, at once, by any overt act; for, under a strong military rule, men dared hardly think for themselves, much less communicate their thoughts to one another. But changes of public opinion, like changes in the atmosphere that come on slowly and imperceptibly, make themselves more and more widely felt, till, by a sort of silent sympathy, they spread to the remotest corners of the land. Some intimations of such a change of sentiment at length found their way to Lima, although all accounts of the president's mission had been jealously excluded from that capital. Gonzalo Pizarro himself became sensible of these symptoms of disaffection, though almost too faint and feeble, as yet, for the most experienced eye to descry in them the coming tempest.

Several of the president's proclamations had been forwarded to Gonzalo by his faithful partisans; and Carbajal, who had been summoned from Potosí, declared they were "more to be dreaded than the lances of Castile." [3] Yet Pizarro did not, for a moment, lose his confidence in his own strength; and with a navy like that now in Panamá at his command, he felt he might bid defiance to any enemy on his coasts. He had implicit confidence in the fidelity of Hinojosa.

It was at this period that Paniagua arrived off the port with Gasca's despatches to Pizarro, consisting of the emperor's letter and his own. They were instantly submitted by that chieftain to his trusty counsellors, Carbajal and Cepeda, and their opinions asked as to the course to be pursued. It was the crisis of Pizarro's fate.

Carbajal, whose sagacious eye fully comprehended the position in which they stood, was in favor of accepting the royal grace on the terms proposed; and he intimated his sense of their importance by declaring, that "he would pave the way for the bearer of them into the capital with ingots of gold and silver." [4] Cepeda was of a different way of thinking. He was a judge of the Royal Audience; and had been sent to Peru as the immediate counsellor of Blasco Nuñez. But he had turned against the viceroy, had encountered him in battle, and his garments might be said to be yet wet with his blood! What grace was there, then, for him? Whatever respect might be shown to the letter of the royal provisions, in point of fact, he must ever live under the Castilian rule a ruined man. He accordingly, strongly urged the rejection of Gasca's offers. "They will cost you your government," he said to Pizarro; "the smooth-tongued priest is not so simple a person as you take him to be. He is deep

[3] "Que eran mas de temer aquellas cartas que a las lāças del Rey de Castilla." Fernandez, Hist. del Peru, Parte I, lib. 2, cap. 45.

[4] "Y le enladrillen los caminos por do viniere con barras de plata, y tejos de Oro." Garcilasso, Com. Real., Parte 2, lib. 5, cap. 5.

and politic.[5] He knows well what promises to make; and, once master of the country, he will know, too, how to keep them."

Carbajal was not shaken by the arguments or the sneers of his companions; and as the discussion waxed warm, Cepeda taxed his opponent with giving counsel suggested by fears for his own safety,—a foolish taunt, sufficiently disproved by the whole life of the doughty old warrior. Carbajal did not insist further on his own veiws, however, as he found them unwelcome to Pizarro, and contented himself with coolly remarking, that "he had, indeed, no relish for rebellion; but he had as long a neck for a halter, he believed, as any of his companions; and as he could hardly expect to live much longer, at any rate, it was, after all, of little moment to him." [6]

Pizarro, spurred on by a fiery ambition that overleaped every obstacle,[7] did not condescend to count the desperate chances of a contest with the Crown. He threw his own weight into the scale with Cepeda. The offer of grace was rejected; and he thus cast away the last tie which held him to his country, and, by the act, proclaimed himself a rebel.[8]

It was not long after the departure of Paniagua, that Pizarro received tidings of the defection of Aldana and Hinojosa, and of the surrender of the fleet, on which he had expended an immense sum, as the chief bulwark of his power. This unwelcome intelligence was followed by accounts of the further defection of some of the principal towns in the north, and of the assassination of Puelles, the faithful lieutenant to whom he had confided the government of Quito. It was not very long, also, before he found his authority assailed in the opposite quarter at Cuzco; for Centeno, the loyal chieftain who, as the reader may remember, had been driven by Carbajal to take refuge in a cave near Arequipa, had issued from his concealment after remaining there a year, and, on learning the arrival of Gasca, had again raised the royal standard. Then collecting a small body of followers, and falling on Cuzco by night, he made himself master of that capital, defeated the garrison who held it, and secured it for the Crown. Marching soon after into the province of

[5] "Que no lo embiauan por hombre sencillo y llano, sino de grandes cautelas, astucias, falsedades y engaños." Ibid., loc. cit.

[6] Por lo demas, quãdo acaezca otra cosa, ya yo he viuido muchos años, y tengo tan buẽ palmo de pescueço para la soga, como cada uno de vuesas mercedes." Ibid., loc. cit.

[7] "Loca y luciferina soberuia," as Fernandez characterizes the aspiring temper of Gonzalo. Hist. del Peru, Parte 1, lib. 2, cap. 15.

[8] MS. de Caravantes.

According to Garçilasso, Paniagua was furnished with secret instructions by the president, empowering him, in case he judged it necessary to the preservation of the royal authority, to confirm Pizarro in the government, "it being little matter if the Devil ruled there, provided the country remained to the Crown!" The fact was so reported by Paniagua, who continued in Peru after these events. (Com. Real., Parte 2, lib. 5, cap. 5.) This is possible. But it is more probable that a credulous gossip, like Garcilasso, should be in error, than that Charles the Fifth should have been prepared to make such an acknowledgment of his imbecility, or that the man selected for Gasca's confidence should have so indiscreetly betrayed his trust.

Charcas, the bold chief allied himself with the officer who commanded for Pizarro in La Plata; and their combined forces, to the number of a thousand, took up a position on the borders of Lake Titicaca, where the two cavaliers coolly waited an opportunity to take the field against their ancient commander.

Gonzalo Pizarro, touched to the heart by the desertion of those in whom he most confided, was stunned by the dismal tidings of his losses coming so thick upon him. Yet he did not waste his time in idle crimination or complaint; but immediately set about making preparations to meet the storm with all his characteristic energy. He wrote, at once, to such of his captains as he believed still faithful, commanding them to be ready with their troops to march to his assistance at the shortest notice. He reminded them of their obligations to him, and that their interests were identical with his own. The president's commission, he added, had been made out before the news had reached Spain of the battle of Añaquito, and could never cover a pardon to those concerned in the death of the viceroy.[9]

Pizarro was equally active in enforcing his levies in the capital, and in putting them in the best fighting order. He soon saw himself at the head of a thousand men, beautifully equipped, and complete in all their appointments; "as gallant an array," says an old writer, "though so small in number, as ever trod the plains of Italy,"—displaying in the excellence of their arms, their gorgeous uniforms, and the caparisons of their horses, a magnificence that could be furnished only by the silver of Peru.[10] Each company was provided with a new stand of colors, emblazoned with its peculiar device. Some bore the initials and arms of Pizarro, and one or two of these were audaciously surmounted by a crown, as if to intimate the rank to which their commander might aspire.[11]

Among the leaders most conspicuous on this occasion was Cepeda, "who," in the words of a writer of his time, "had exchanged the robe of the licentiate for the plumed casque and mailed harness of the war-

---

[9] Pedro Pizarro, Descub. y Conq., MS.—Zarate, Conq. del Peru, lib. 6, cap. 11, 13.—Fernandez, Hist. del Peru, Parte 1, lib. 2, cap. 45, 59.—Montesinos, Annales, MS., año 1547.

[10] "Mil Hombres tan bien armados i adereçados, como se han visto en Italia, en la maior prosperidad, porque ninguno havia, demas de las Armas, que no llevase Calças, i Jubon de Seda, i muchos de Tela de Oro, i de Brocado, i otros bordados, i recamados de Oro, i Plata, con mucha Chaperia de Oro por los Sombreros, i especialmente por Frascos, i Caxas de Arcubuces." Zarate, Conq. del Peru, lib. 6, cap. 11.

[11] Ibid., ubi supra.

Some writers even assert that Pizarro was preparing for his coronation at this time, and that he had actually despatched his summons to the different towns to send their deputies to assist at it. "Queria apresurar su coronacion, y para ello despachó cartas á todas las ciudades del Perú." (Montesinos, Annales, MS., año 1547.) But it is hardly probable he could have placed so blind a confidence in the colonists at this crisis, as to have meditated so rash a step. The loyal Castilian historians are not slow to receive reports to the discredit of the *rebel*.

rior." [12] But the cavalier to whom Pizarro confided the chief care of organizing his battalions was the veteran Carbajal, who had studied the art of war under the best captains of Europe, and whose life of adventure had been a practical commentary on their early lessons. It was on his arm that Gonzalo most leaned in the hour of danger; and well had it been for him, if he had profited by his counsels at an earlier period.

It gives one some idea of the luxurious accommodations of Pizarro's forces, that he endeavored to provide each of his musketeers with a horse. The expenses incurred by him were enormous. The immediate cost of his preparations, we are told, was not less than half a million of *pesos de oro;* and his pay to the cavaliers, and, indeed, to the common soldiers, in his little army, was on an extravagant scale, nowhere to be met with but on the silver soil of Peru.[13]

When his own funds were exhausted, he supplied the deficiency by fines imposed on the rich citizens of Lima as the price of exemption from service, by forced loans, and various other schemes of military exaction.[14] From this time, it is said, the chieftain's temper underwent a visible change.[15] He became more violent in his passions, more impatient of control, and indulged more freely in acts of cruelty and license. The desperate cause in which he was involved made him reckless of consequences. Though naturally frank and confiding, the frequent defection of his followers filled him with suspicion. He knew not in whom to confide. Every one who showed himself indifferent to his cause, or was suspected of being so, was dealt with as an open enemy. The greatest distrust prevailed in Lima. No man dared confide in his neighbor. Some concealed their effects; others contrived to elude the vigilance of the sentinels, and hid themselves in the neighboring woods and mountains.[16] No one was allowed to enter or leave the city without a license. All commerce, all intercourse, with other places was cut off. It was long since the fifth belonging to the Crown had been remitted to Castile; as Pizarro had appropriated them for his own use. He now took possession of the mints, broke up the royal stamps, and issued a debased coin, emblazoned with his own cipher.[17] It was the most decisive act of sovereignty.

[12] "El qual en este tiempo, oluidado de lo que conuenia a sus letras, y profession, y officio de Oydor; salio en calças jubon, y cuera, de muchos recamados: y gorra con plumas." Fernandez, Hist. del Peru, Parte 1, lib. 2, cap. 62.

[13] Ibid., ubi supra.—Zarate, Conq. del Peru, lib. 6, cap. 11.—Herrera, Hist. General, dec. 8, lib. 3, cap. 5.—Montesinos, Annales, año 1547.

[14] Fernandez, Parte 1, lib. 2, cap. 62.—Montesinos, Annales, MS., año 1547.

[15] Gomara, Hist. de las Ind., cap. 172.

[16] "Andaba la Gente tan asombrada con el temor de la muerte, que no se podian entender, ni tenian animo para huir, i algunos, que hallaron mejor aparejo, se escondieron por los Cañaverales, i Cuevas, enterrando sus Haciendas." Zarate, Conq. del Peru, lib. 6, cap. 15.

[17] Rel. Anonima, MS.—Montesinos, Annales, MS., año 1547. "Assi mismo echó Gõzalo Piçarro a toda la plata que gastaua y destribuya su marca, que era una G. rebuelta en una P. y pregonò que so pena de muerte, todos recibiessen por plata fina

At this gloomy period, the lawyer Cepeda contrived a solemn farce, the intent of which was to give a sort of legal sanction to the rebel cause in the eyes of the populace. He caused a process to be prepared against Gasca, Hinojosa, and Aldana, in which they were accused of treason against the existing government of Peru, were convicted, and condemned to death. This instrument he submitted to a number of jurists in the capital, requiring their signatures. But they had no mind thus inevitably to implicate themselves, by affixing their names to such a paper; and they evaded it by representing, that it would only serve to cut off all chance, should any of the accused be so disposed, of their again embracing the cause they had deserted. Cepeda was the only man who signed the document. Carbajal treated the whole thing with ridicule. "What is the object of your process?" said he to Cepeda. "Its object," replied the latter, "is to prevent delay, that, if taken at any time, the guilty party may be at once led to execution." "I cry you mercy," retorted Carbajal; "I thought there must be some virtue in the instrument, that would have killed them outright. Let but one of these same traitors fall into my hands, and I will march him off to execution, without waiting for the sentence of a court, I promise you!" [18]

While this paper war was going on, news was brought that Aldana's squadron was off the port of Callao. That commander had sailed from Panamá, the middle of February, 1547. On his passage down the coast he had landed at Truxillo, where the citizens welcomed him with enthusiasm, and eagerly proclaimed their submission to the royal authority. He received, at the same time, messages from several of Pizarro's officers in the interior, intimating their return to their duty, and their readiness to support the president. Aldana named Caxamalca as a place of rendezvous, where they should concentrate their forces, and wait the landing of Gasca. He then continued his voyage towards Lima.

No sooner was Pizarro informed of his approach, than, fearful lest it might have a disastrous effect in seducing his followers from their fidelity, he marched them about a league out of the city, and there encamped. He was two leagues from the coast, and he posted a guard on the shore to intercept all communication with the vessels. Before leaving the capital, Cepeda resorted to an expedient for securing the inhabitants more firmly, as he conceived, in Pizarro's interests. He caused the citizens to be assembled, and made them a studied harangue, in which he expatiated on the services of their governor, and the security which the

la que tuuiesse aquella marca: sin ensayo, ni otra diligencia alguna. Y desta suerte hizo passar mucha plata de ley baja por fina." Fernandez, Hist. del Peru, Parte 1, lib. 2, cap. 62.

[18] "Riose mucho entonces Caruajal y dixo que segũ auia hecho la instancia, que auia entendido, que la justicia como rayo, auia de yr luego a justiciarlos. Y dezia que si el los tuuiesse presos, no se le daria vn clauo por su sentẽcia, ni firmas." (Ibid., Parte 1, lib. 2, cap. 55.) Among the jurists in Lima who thus independently resisted Cepeda's requisition to sign the paper was the Licentiate Polo Ondegardo, a man of much discretion, and one of the best authorities for the ancient institutions of the Incas.

country had enjoyed under his rule. He then told them that every man
was at liberty to choose for himself; to remain under the protection of
their present ruler, or, if they preferred, to transfer their allegiance to
his enemy. He invited them to speak their minds, but required every
one who would still continue under Pizarro to take an oath of fidelity to
his cause, with the assurance, that, if any should be so false hereafter as
to violate this pledge, he should pay for it with his life.[19] There was no
one found bold enough—with his head thus in the lion's mouth—to
swerve from his obedience to Pizarro; and every man took the oath prescribed, which was administered in the most solemn and imposing form
by the licentiate. Carbajal, as usual, made a jest of the whole proceeding. "How long," he asked his companion, "do you think these same
oaths will stand? The first wind that blows off the coast after we are
gone will scatter them in air!" His prediction was soon verified.

Meantime, Aldana anchored off the port, where there was no vessel of
the insurgents to molest him. By Cepeda's advice, some four or five had
been burnt a short time before, during the absence of Carbajal, in order
to cut off all means by which the inhabitants could leave the place. This
was deeply deplored by the veteran soldier on his return. "It was
destroying," he said, "the guardian angels of Lima." [20] And certainly,
under such a commander, they might now have stood Pizarro in good
stead; but his star was on the wane.

The first act of Aldana was to cause the copy of Gasca's powers, with
which he had been intrusted, to be conveyed to his ancient commander,
by whom it was indignantly torn in pieces. Aldana next contrived, by
means of his agents, to circulate among the citizens, and even the soldiers of the camp, the president's manifestoes. They were not long in
producing their effect. Few had been at all aware of the real purport of
Gasca's mission, of the extent of his powers, or of the generous terms offered by government. They shrunk from the desperate course into which
they had been thus unwarily seduced, and they sought only in what way
they could, with least danger, extricate themselves from their present
position, and return to their allegiance. Some escaped by night from the
camp, eluded the vigilance of the sentinels, and effected their retreat on
board the vessels. Some were taken, and found no quarter at the hands
of Carbajal and his merciless ministers. But, where the spirit of disaffection was abroad, means of escape were not wanting.

As the fugitives were cut off from Lima and the neighboring coast,
they secreted themselves in the forests and mountains, and watched
their opportunity for making their way to Truxilla and other ports at a
distance; and so contagious was the example, that it not unfrequently

[19] Pedro Pizarro, Descub. y Conq., MS.—Fernandez, Hist. del Peru, Parte 1, lib.
2, cap. 61.—Montesinos, Annales, MS., año 1547.—Zarate, Conq. del Peru, lib. 6,
cap. 11, 14.

[20] "Entre otras cosas dixo a Gonçalo Piçarro vuesa Señoria mandò quemar cinco
angeles que tenia en su puerto para guarda y defensa de la costa del Peru." Garcilasso, Parte 2 lib. 5, cap. 6.

happened that the very soldiers sent in pursuit of the deserters joined with them. Among those that fled was the Licentiate Carbajal, who must not be confounded with his military namesake. He was the same cavalier whose brother had been put to death in Lima by Blasco Nuñez, and who revenged himself, as we have seen, by imbruing his own hands in the blood of the viceroy. That a person thus implicated should trust to the royal pardon showed that no one need despair of it; and the example proved most disastrous to Pizarro.[21]

Carbajal, who made a jest of every thing, even of the misfortunes which pinched him the sharpest, when told of the desertion of his comrades, amused himself by humming the words of a popular ditty:—

> "The wind blows the hairs off my head, mother;
> Two at a time, it blows them away!"[22]

But the defection of his followers made a deeper impression on Pizarro, and he was sorely distressed as he beheld the gallant array, to which he had so confidently looked for gaining his battles, thus melting away like a morning mist. Bewildered by the treachery of those in whom he had most trusted, he knew not where to turn, nor what course to take. It was evident that he must leave his present dangerous quarters without loss of time. But whither should he direct his steps? In the north, the great towns had abandoned his cause, and the president was already marching against him; while Centeno held the passes of the south, with a force double his own. In this emergency, he at length resolved to occupy Arequipa, a seaport still true to him, where he might remain till he had decided on some future course of operations.

After a painful but rapid march, Gonzalo arrived at this place, where he was speedily joined by a reinforcement that he had detached for the recovery of Cuzco. But so frequent had been the desertions from both companies,—though in Pizarro's corps these had greatly lessened since the departure from the neighborhood of Lima,—that his whole number did not exceed five hundred men, less than half of the force which he had so recently mustered in the capital. To such humble circumstances was the man now reduced, who had so lately lorded it over the land with unlimited sway! Still the chief did not despond. He had gathered new spirit from the excitement of his march and his distance from Lima; and he seemed to recover his former confidence, as he exclaimed,—"It is misfortune that teaches us who are our friends. If but ten only remain true to me, fear not but I will again be master of Peru!"[28]

[21] Pedro Pizarro, Descub. y Conq., MS.—Gomara, Hist. de las Ind., cap. 180.— Fernandez, Hist. del Peru, Parte 1, lib. 2, cap. 63, 65.—Zarate, Conq. del Peru, lib. 6, cap. 15, 16.

> "Estos mis Cabellicos, Madre,
> Dos a dos me los lleva el Aire."

Gomara, Hist. de las Ind., cap. 180.

[28] "Aunque siempre dijo: que con diez Amigos que le quedasen, havia de conservarse, i conquistar de nuevo el Perù: tanta era su saña, ò su sobervia." Ibid., loc. cit.

No sooner had the rebel forces withdrawn from the neighborhood of Lima, than the inhabitants of that city, little troubled, as Carbajal had predicted, by their compulsory oaths of allegiance to Pizarro, threw open their gates to Aldana, who took possession of this important place in the name of the president. That commander, meanwhile, had sailed with his whole fleet from Panamá, on the tenth of April, 1547. The first part of his voyage was prosperous; but he was soon perplexed by contrary currents, and the weather became rough and tempestuous. The violence of the storm continuing day after day, the sea was lashed into fury, and the fleet was tossed about on the billows, which ran mountain high, as if emulating the wild character of the region they bounded. The rain descended in torrents, and the lightning was so incessant, that the vessels, to quote the lively language of the chronicler, "seemed to be driving through seas of flame!" [24] The hearts of the stoutest mariners were filled with dismay. They considered it hopeless to struggle against the elements, and they loudly demanded to return to the continent, and postpone the voyage till a more favorable season of the year.

But the president saw in this the ruin of his cause, as well as of the loyal vassals who had engaged, on his landing, to support it. "I am willing to die," he said, "but not to return"; and, regardless of the remonstrances of his more timid followers, he insisted on carrying as much sail as the ships could possibly bear, at every interval of the storm. [25] Meanwhile, to divert the minds of the seamen from their present danger, Gasca amused them by explaining some of the strange phenomena exhibited by the ocean in the tempest, which had filled their superstitious minds with mysterious dread. [26]

Signals had been given for the ships to make the best of their way, each for itself, to the island of Gorgona. Here they arrived, one after another, with but a single exception, though all more or less shattered by the weather. The president waited only for the fury of the elements to spend itself, when he again embarked, and, on smoother waters, crossed over to Manta. From this place he soon after continued his voyage to Tumbez, and landed at that port on the thirteenth of June. He was everywhere received with enthusiasm, and all seemed anxious to efface the remembrance of the past by professions of future fidelity to the

[24] "Y los truenos y relápagos eran tantos y tales; que siempre parecia que estauan en llamas, y que sobre ellos venian Rayos (que en todas aquellas partes caen muchos)." (Fernandez, Hist. del Peru, Parte 1, lib. 2, cap. 71.) The vivid coloring of the old chronicler shows that he had himself been familiar with these tropical tempests on the Pacific.

[25] "Y con lo poco que en aquella sazon, el Presidente estimaua la vida si no auia de hazer la jornada: y el gran desseo que tenia de hazerla se puso cōtra ellos diziendo, que qual quiera que le tocasse en abaxar vela, le costaria la vida." Fernandez, Parte 1, lib. 2, cap. 71.

[26] The phosphoric lights, sometimes seen in a storm at sea, were observed to hover round the masts and rigging of the president's vessel; and he amused the seamen, according to Fernandez, by explaining the phenomenon, and telling the fables to which they had given rise in ancient mythology.—This little anecdote affords a key to Gasca's popularity with even the humblest classes.

Crown. Gasca received, also, numerous letters of congratulation from cavaliers in the interior, most of whom had formerly taken service under Pizarro. He made courteous acknowledgments for their offers of assistance, and commanded them to repair to Caxamalca, the general place of rendezvous.

To this same spot he sent Hinojosa, so soon as that officer had disembarked with the land forces from the fleet, ordering him to take command of the levies assembled there, and then join him at Xauxa. Here he determined to establish his headquarters. It lay in a rich and abundant territory, and by its central position afforded a point for acting with greatest advantage against the enemy.

He then moved forward, at the head of a small detachment of cavalry, along the level road on the coast towards Truxillo. After halting for a short time in that loyal city, he traversed the mountain range on the southeast, and soon entered the fruitful valley of Xauxa. There he was presently joined by reinforcements from the north, as well as from the principal places on the coast; and, not long after his arrival, received a message from Centeno, informing him that he held the passes by which Gonzalo Pizarro was preparing to make his escape from the country, and that the insurgent chief must soon fall into his hands.

The royal camp was greatly elated by these tidings. The war, then, was at length terminated, and that without the president having been called upon so much as to lift his sword against a Spaniard. Several of his counsellors now advised him to disband the greater part of his forces, as burdensome and no longer necessary. But the president was too wise to weaken his strength before he had secured the victory. He consented, however, to countermand the requisition for levies from Mexico and the adjoining colonies, as now feeling sufficiently strong in the general loyalty of the country. But, concentrating his forces at Xauxa, he established his quarters in that town, as he had first intended, resolved to await there tidings of the operations in the south. The result was different from what he had expected.[27]

Pizarro, meanwhile, whom we left at Arequipa, had decided, after much deliberation, to evacuate Peru, and pass into Chili. In this territory, beyond the president's jurisdiction, he might find a safe retreat. The fickle people, he thought, would soon weary of their new ruler; and he would then rally in sufficient strength to resume active operations for the recovery of his domain. Such were the calculations of the rebel chieftain. But how was he to effect his object, while the passes among the mountains, where his route lay, were held by Centeno with a force more

[27] For the preceding pages, see Pedro Pizarro, Descub. y Conq., MS.—Zarate, Conq. del Peru, lib. 7, cap. 1.—Herrera, Hist. General, dec. 8, lib. 3, cap. 14, et seq. —Fernandez, Hist. del Peru, Parte 1, lib. 2, cap. 71-77.—MS. de Caravantes.

This last writer, who held an important post in the department of colonial finance, had opportunities of information which have enabled him to furnish several particulars not to be met with elsewhere, respecting the principal actors in these turbulent times. His work, still in manuscript, which formerly existed in the archives of the University of Salamanca, has been transferred to the King's library at Madrid

than double his own? He resolved to try negotiation; for that captain had once served under him, and had, indeed, been most active in persuading Pizarro to take on himself the office of procurator. Advancing, accordingly, in the direction of Lake Titicaca, in the neighborhood of which Centeno had pitched his camp, Gonzalo despatched an emissary to his quarters to open a negotiation. He called to his adversary's recollection the friendly relations that had once subsisted between them; and reminded him of one occasion in particular, in which he had spared his life, when convicted of a conspiracy against himself. He harbored no sentiments of unkindness, he said, for Centeno's recent conduct, and had not now come to seek a quarrel with him. His purpose was to abandon Peru; and the only favor he had to request of his former associate was to leave him a free passage across the mountains.

To this communication Centeno made answer in terms as courtly as those of Pizarro himself, that he was not unmindful of their ancient friendship. He was now ready to serve his former commander in any way not inconsistent with honor, or obedience to his sovereign. But he was there in arms for the royal cause, and he could not swerve from his duty. If Pizarro would but rely on his faith and surrender himself up, he pledged his knightly word to use all his interest with the government, to secure as favorable terms for him and his followers as had been granted to the rest of their countrymen.—Gonzalo listened to the smooth promises of his ancient comrade with bitter scorn depicted in his countenance, and, snatching the letter from his secretary, cast it away from him with indignation. There was nothing left but an appeal to arms.[28]

He at once broke up his encampment, and directed his march on the borders of Lake Titicaca, near which lay his rival. He resorted, however, to stratagem, that he might still, if possible, avoid an encounter. He sent forward his scouts in a different direction from that which he intended to take, and then quickened his march on Huarina. This was a small town situated on the southeastern extremity of Lake Titicaca, the shores of which, the seat of the primitive civilization of the Incas, were soon to resound with the murderous strife of their more civilized conquerors!

But Pizarro's movements had been secretly communicated to Centeno, and that commander, accordingly, changing his ground, took up a position not far from Huarina, on the same day on which Gonzalo reached this place. The videttes of the two camps came in sight of each other that evening, and the rival forces, lying on their arms, prepared for action on the following morning.

It was the twenty-sixth of October, 1547, when the two commanders, having formed their troops in order of battle, advanced to the encounter on the plains of Huarina. The ground, defended on one side by a bold spur of the Andes, and not far removed on the other from the waters of Titicaca, was an open and level plain, well suited to military manœuvres. It seemed as if prepared by Nature as the lists for an encounter.

[28] Pedro Pizarro, Descub. y Conq., MS.—Garcilasso, Com. Real., Parte 2, lib. 5, cap. 16.—Zarate, Conq. del Peru, lib. 7

Centeno's army amounted to about a thousand men. His cavalry consisted of near two hundred and fifty, well equipped and mounted. Among them were several gentlemen of family, some of whom had once followed the banners of Pizarro; the whole forming an efficient corps, in which rode some of the best lances of Peru. His arquebusiers were less numerous, not exceeding a hundred and fifty, indifferently provided with ammunition. The remainder, and much the larger part of Centeno's army, consisted of spearmen, irregular levies hastily drawn together, and possessed of little discipline.[29]

This corps of infantry formed the centre of his line, flanked by the arquebusiers in two nearly equal divisions, while his cavalry were also disposed in two bodies on the right and left wings. Unfortunately, Centeno had been for the past week ill of a pleurisy,—so ill, indeed, that on the preceding day he had been bled several times. He was now too feeble to keep his saddle, but was carried in a litter, and when he had seen his men formed in order, he withdrew to a distance from the field, unable to take part in the action. But Solano, the militant bishop of Cuzco, who, with several of his followers, took part in the engagement,—a circumstance, indeed, of no strange occurrence,—rode along the ranks with the crucifix in his hand, bestowing his benediction on the soldiers, and exhorting each man to do his duty.

Pizarro's forces were less than half of his rival's, not amounting to more than four hundred and eighty men. The horse did not muster above eighty-five in all, and he posted them in a single body on the right of his battalion. The strength of his army lay in his arquebusiers, about three hundred and fifty in number. It was an admirable corps, commanded by Carbajal, by whom it had been carefully drilled. Considering the excellence of its arms, and its thorough discipline, this little body of infantry might be considered as the flower of the Peruvian soldiery, and on it Pizarro mainly relied for the success of the day.[30] The remainder of his force, consisting of pikemen, not formidable for their numbers, though, like the rest of the infantry, under excellent discipline, he distributed on the left of his musketeers, so as to repel the enemy's horse.

Pizarro himself had charge of the cavalry, taking his place, as usual, in the foremost rank. He was superbly accoutred. Over his shining mail he wore a sobre-vest of slashed velvet of a rich crimson color; and he rode a high-mettled charger, whose gaudy caparisons, with the showy livery of his rider, made the fearless commander the most conspicuous object in the field.

His lieutenant, Carbajal, was equipped in a very different style. He wore armor of proof of the most homely appearance, but strong and

---

[29] In the estimate of Centeno's forces,—which ranges, in the different accounts, from seven hundred to twelve hundred,—I have taken the intermediate number of a thousand adopted by Zarate, as, on the whole, more probable than either extreme.

[30] *Flor de la milicia del Peru,* says Garcilasso de la Vega, who compares Carbajal to an expert chess-player, disposing his pieces in such a manner as must infallibly secure him the victory. Com. Real., Parte 2, lib. 5, cap. 18.

serviceable; and his steel bonnet, with its closely barred visor of the same material, protected his head from more than one desperate blow on that day. Over his arms he wore a surcoat of a greenish color, and he rode an active, strong-boned jennet, which, though capable of enduring fatigue, possessed neither grace nor beauty. It would not have been easy to distinguish the veteran from the most ordinary cavalier.

The two hosts arrived within six hundred paces of each other, when they both halted. Carbajal preferred to receive the attack of the enemy, rather than advance further; for the ground he now occupied afforded a free range for his musketry, unobstructed by the trees or bushes that were sprinkled over some other parts of the field. There was a singular motive, in addition, for retaining his present position. The soldiers were encumbered, some with two, some with three, arquebuses each, being the arms left by those who, from time to time, had deserted the camp. This uncommon supply of muskets, however serious an impediment on a march, might afford great advantage to troops waiting an assault; since, from the imperfect knowledge as well as construction of fire-arms at that day, much time was wasted in loading them.[31]

Preferring, therefore, that the enemy should begin the attack, Carbajal came to a halt, while the opposite squadron, after a short respite, continued their advance a hundred paces farther. Seeing that they then remained immovable. Carbajal detached a small party of skirmishers to the front, in order to provoke them; but it was soon encountered by a similar party of the enemy, and some shots were exchanged, though with little damage to either side. Finding this manœuvre fail, the veteran ordered his men to advance a few paces, still hoping to provoke his antagonist to the charge. This succeeded. "We lose honor," exclaimed Centeno's soldiers; who, with a bastard sort of chivalry, belonging to undisciplined troops, felt it a disgrace to await an assault. In vain their officers called out to them to remain at their post. Their commander was absent, and they were urged on by the cries of a frantic friar, named Damingo Ruiz, who, believing the Philistines were delivered into their hands, called out,—"Now is the time! Onward, onward, fall on the enemy!" [32] There needed nothing further, and the men rushed forward in tumultuous haste, the pikemen carrying their levelled weapons so heedlessly as to interfere with one another, and in some instances to wound their comrades. The musketeers, at the same time, kept up a disorderly fire as they advanced, which, from their rapid motion and the distance, did no execution.

Carbajal was well pleased to see his enemies thus wasting their am-

---

[31] Garcilasso, Com. Real., ubi supra.

The historian's father—of the same name with himself—was one of the few noble cavaliers who remained faithful to Gonzalo Pizarro, in the wane of his fortunes. He was present at the battle of Huarina; and the particulars which he gave his son enabled the latter to supply many deficiencies in the reports of historians.

[32] "A las manos, á las manos· á ellos, á ellos." Fernandez Hist. del Perú. Parte 1, lib. 2, cap. 75

munition. Though he allowed a few muskets to be discharged, in order to stimulate his opponents the more, he commanded the great body of his infantry to reserve their fire till every shot could take effect. As he knew the tendency of marksmen to shoot above the mark, he directed his men to aim at the girdle, or even a little below it; adding, that a shot that fell short might still do damage, while one that passed a hair's breadth above the head was wasted.[33]

The veteran's company stood calm and unmoved, as Centeno's rapidly advanced; but when the latter had arrived within a hundred paces of their antagonists, Carbajal gave the word to fire. An instantaneous volley ran along the line, and a tempest of balls was poured into the ranks of the assailants, with such unerring aim, that more than a hundred fell dead on the field, while a still greater number were wounded. Before they could recover from their disorder, Carbajal's men, snatching up their remaining pieces, discharged them with the like dreadful effect in, to the thick of the enemy. The confusion of the latter was now complete. Unable to sustain the incessant shower of balls which fell on them from the scattering fire kept up by the arquebusiers, they were seized with a panic, and fled, scarcely making a show of further fight, from the field.

But very different was the fortune of the day in the cavalry combat. Gonzalo Pizarro had drawn up his troop somewhat in the rear of Carbajal's right, in order to give the latter a freer range for the play of his musketry. When the enemy's horse on the left galloped briskly against him, Pizarro, still favoring Carbajal,—whose fire, moreover, inflicted some loss on the assailants,—advanced but a few rods to receive the charge. Centeno's squadron, accordingly, came thundering on in full career, and, notwithstanding the mischief sustained from their enemy's musketry, fell with such fury on their adversaries as to overturn them, man and horse, in the dust; "riding over their prostrate bodies," says the historian, "as if they had been a flock of sheep!" [34] The latter, with great difficulty recovering from the first shock, attempted to rally and sustain the fight on more equal terms.

Yet the chief could not regain the ground he had lost. His men were driven back at all points. Many were slain, many more wounded, on both sides, and the ground was covered with the dead bodies of men and horses. But the loss fell much the most heavily on Pizarro's troop; and the greater part of those who escaped with life were obliged to surrender as prisoners. Cepeda, who fought with the fury of despair, received a severe cut from a sabre across the face, which disabled him and forced him to yield.[35] Pizarro, after seeing his best and bravest fall

---

[33] Garcilasso, Com. Real., ubi supra.

[34] "Los de Diego Centeno, como yuan con la pujança de vna carrera larga, lleuaron a los de Gonçalo Piçarro de encuentro, y los tropellaron como si fueran ouejas, y cayeron cauallos y caualleros." Ibid., Parte 2, lib. 5, cap. 19.

[35] Cepeda's wound laid open his nose, leaving so hideous a scar that he was obliged afterwards to cover it with a patch. as Garcilasso tells us, who frequently saw him in Cuzco.

around him, was set upon by three or four cavaliers at once. Disentangling himself from the *mêlée*, he put spurs to his horse, and the noble animal, bleeding from a severe wound across the back, outstripped all his pursuers except one, who stayed him by seizing the bridle. It would have gone hard with Gonzalo, but, grasping a light battle-axe, which hung by his side, he dealt such a blow on the head of his enemy's horse that he plunged violently, and compelled his rider to release his hold. A number of arquebusiers, in the mean time, seeing Pizarro's distress, sprang forward to his rescue, slew two of his assailants who had now come up with him, and forced the others to fly in their turn.[36]

The rout of the cavalry was complete; and Pizarro considered the day as lost, as he heard the enemy's trumpet sending forth the note of victory. But the sounds had scarcely died away, when they were taken up by the opposite side. Centeno's infantry had been discomfited, as we have seen, and driven off the ground. But his cavalry on the right had charged Carbajal's left, consisting of spearmen mingled with arquebusiers. The horse rode straight against this formidable phalanx. But they were unable to break through the dense array of pikes, held by the steady hands of troops who stood firm and fearless on their post; while, at the same time, the assailants were greatly annoyed by the galling fire of the arquebusiers in the rear of the spearmen. Finding it impracticable to make a breach, the horsemen rode round the flanks in much disorder, and finally joined themselves with the victorious squadron of Centeno's cavalry in the rear. Both parties now attempted another charge on Carbajal's battalion. But his men facing about with the promptness and discipline of well-trained soldiers, the rear was converted into the front. The same forest of spears was presented to the attack; while an incessant discharge of balls punished the audacity of the cavaliers, who, broken and completely dispirited by their ineffectual attempt, at length imitated the example of the panic-struck foot, and abandoned the field.

Pizarro and a few of his comrades still fit for action followed up the pursuit for a short distance only, as, indeed, they were in no condition themselves, nor sufficiently strong in numbers, long to continue it. The victory was complete, and the insurgent chief took possession of the deserted tents of the enemy, where an immense booty was obtained in silver;[37] and where he also found the tables spread for the refreshment

[36] According to most authorities, Pizarro's horse was not only wounded but slain in the fight, and the loss was supplied by his friend Garcilasso de la Vega, who mounted him on his own. This timely aid to the rebel did no service to the generous cavalier in after times, but was urged against him by his enemies as a crime. The fact is stoutly denied by his son, the historian, who seems anxious to relieve his father from this honorable imputation, which threw a cloud over both their fortunes. Ibid., Parte 2, lib. 5, cap. 23.

[37] The booty amounted to no less than one million four hundred thousand *pesos*, according to Fernandez. "El saco que vuo fue grande: que se dixo ser de mas de vn millon y quatrociẽtos mil pesos." (Hist. del Peru, Parte 1, lib. 2, cap. 79.) The amount is, doubtless, grossly exaggerated. But we get to be so familiar with the golden wonders of Peru, that, like the reader of the "Arabian Nights," we become of too easy faith to resort to the vulgar standard of probability.

of Centeno's soldiers after their return from the field. So confident were they of success! The repast now served the necessities of their conquerors. Such is the fortune of war! It was, indeed, a most decisive action; and Gonzalo Pizarro, as he rode over the field strewed with the corpses of his enemies, was observed several times to cross himself and exclaim,—"Jesu! what a victory!"

No less than three hundred and fifty of Centeno's followers were killed, and the number of wounded was even greater. More than a hundred of these are computed to have perished from exposure during the following night; for, although the climate in this elevated region is temperate, yet the night winds blowing over the mountains are sharp and piercing, and many a wounded wretch, who might have been restored by careful treatment, was chilled by the damps, and found a stiffened corpse at sunrise. The victory was not purchased without a heavy loss on the part of the conquerors, a hundred or more of whom were left on the field. Their bodies lay thick on that part of the ground occupied by Pizarro's cavalry, where the fight raged hottest. In this narrow space were found, also, the bodies of more than a hundred horses, the greater part of which, as well as those of their riders, usually slain with them, belonged to the victorious army. It was the most fatal battle that had yet been fought on the blood-stained soil of Peru.[38]

The glory of the day—the melancholy glory—must be referred almost wholly to Carbajal and his valiant squadron. The judicious arrangements of the old warrior, with the thorough discipline and unflinching courage of his followers, retrieved the fortunes of the fight, when it was nearly lost by the cavalry, and secured the victory.

Carbajal, proof against all fatigue, followed up the pursuit with those of his men that were in condition to join him. Such of the unhappy fugitives as fell into his hands—most of whom had been traitors to the cause of Pizarro—were sent to instant execution. The laurels he had won in the field against brave men in arms, like himself, were tarnished by cruelty towards his defenceless captives. Their commander, Centeno, more fortunate, made his escape. Finding the battle lost, he quitted his litter, threw himself upon his horse, and, notwithstanding his illness, urged on by the dreadful doom that awaited him, if taken, he succeeded in making his way into the neighboring sierra. Here he vanished from his pursuers, and, like a wounded stag, with the chase close upon his track, he still contrived to elude it, by plunging into the depths of the

---

[38] "La mas sangrienta batalla que vuo en el Perù." Ibid., loc. cit.

In the accounts of this battle there are discrepancies, as usual, which the historian must reconcile as he can. But on the whole, there is a general conformity in the outline and in the prominent points. All concur in representing it as the bloodiest fight that had yet occurred between the Spaniards in Peru, and all assign to Carbajal the credit of the victory.—For authorities, besides Garcilasso and Fernandez, repeatedly quoted, see Pedro Pizarro, Descub. y Conq., MS. (He was present in the action.)—Zarate, Conq. del Peru, lib. 7, cap. 3.—Herrera, Hist. General, dec. 8, lib. 4, cap. 2.—Gomara, Hist. de las Indias. cap. 181.—Montesinos, Annales, MS., año 1547.

forests, till, by a circuitous route, he miraculously succeeded in effecting his escape to Lima. The bishop of Cuzco, who went off in a different direction, was no less fortunate. Happy for him that he did not fall into the hands of the ruthless Carbajal, who, as the bishop had once been a partisan of Pizarro, would, to judge from the little respect he usually showed those of his cloth, have felt as little compunction in sentencing him to the gibbet as if he had been the meanest of the common file.[39]

On the day following the action, Gonzalo Pizarro caused the bodies of the soldiers, still lying side by side on the field where they had been so lately engaged together in mortal strife, to be deposited in a common sepulchre. Those of higher rank—for distinctions of rank were not to be forgotten in the grave—were removed to the church of the village of Huarina, which gave its name to the battle. There they were interred with all fitting solemnity. But in later times they were transported to the cathedral church of La Paz, "The City of Peace," and laid under a mausoleum erected by general subscription in that quarter. For few there were who had not to mourn the loss of some friend or relative on that fatal day.

The victor now profited by his success to send detachments to Arequipa, La Plata, and other cities in that part of the country, to raise funds and reinforcements for the war. His own losses were more than compensated by the number of the vanquished party who were content to take service under his banner. Mustering his forces, he directed his march to Cuzco, which capital, though occasionally seduced into a display of loyalty to the Crown, had early manifested an attachment to his cause.

Here the inhabitants were prepared to receive him in triumph, under arches thrown across the streets, with bands of music, and minstrelsy commemorating his successes. But Pizarro, with more discretion, declined the honors of an ovation while the country remained in the hands of his enemies. Sending forward the main body of his troops, he followed on foot, attended by a slender retinue of friends and citizens, and proceeded at once to the cathedral, where thanksgivings were offered up, and *Te Deum* was chanted in honor of his victory. He then withdrew to his residence, announcing his purpose to establish his quarters, for the present, in the venerable capital of the Incas.[40]

All thoughts of a retreat into Chili were abandoned; for his recent success had kindled new hopes in his bosom, and revived his ancient confidence. He trusted that it would have a similar effect on the vacillat-

[39] Pedro Pizarro, Descub. y Conq., MS.—Fernandez, Hist. del Peru, ubi supra.—Zarate, lib. 7, cap. 3.—Garcilasso, Com. Real., Parte 2, lib. 5, cap. 21, 22.
[40] Ibid., Parte 2, lib. 5, cap. 27.—Pedro Pizarro, Descub. y Conq., MS.—Zarate, Conq. del Peru, lib. 7, cap. 3.
Garcilasso de la Vega, who was a boy at the time, witnessed Pizarro's entry into Cuzco. He writes therefore, from memory; though after an interval of many years. In consequence of his father's rank, he had easy access to the palace of Pizarro; and this portion of his narrative may claim the consideration due not merely to a contemporary, but to an eyewitness.

ing temper of those whose fidelity had been shaken by fears for their own safety, and their distrust of his ability to cope with the president. They would now see that his star was still in the ascendant. Without further apprehensions for the event, he resolved to remain in Cuzco, and there quietly await the hour when a last appeal to arms should decide which of the two was to remain master of Peru.

CHAPTER III

DISMAY IN GASCA'S CAMP—HIS WINTER QUARTERS—RESUMES HIS
MARCH—CROSSES THE APURIMAC—PIZARRO'S CONDUCT IN CUZCO
HE ENCAMPS NEAR THE CITY—ROUT OF XAQUIXAGUANA

1547—1548

WHILE the events recorded in the preceding chapter were passing, President Gasca had remained at Xauxa, awaiting further tidings from Centeno, little doubting that they would inform him of the total discomfiture of the rebels. Great was his dismay, therefore, on learning the issue of the fatal conflict in Haurina,—that the royalists had been scattered far and wide before the sword of Pizarro, while their commander had vanished like an apparition,[1] leaving the greatest uncertainty as to his fate.

The intelligence spread general consternation among the soldiers, proportioned to their former confidence; and they felt it was almost hopeless to contend with a man who seemed protected by a charm that made him invincible against the greatest odds. The president, however sore his disappointment, was careful to conceal it, while he endeavored to restore the spirits of his followers. "They had been too sanguine," he said, "and it was in this way that Heaven rebuked their persumption. Yet it was but in the usual course of events that Providence, when it designed to humble the guilty, should allow him to reach as high an elevation as possible, that his fall might be the greater!"

But while Gasca thus strove to reassure the superstitious and the timid, he bent his mind, with his usual energy, to repair the injury which the cause had sustained by the defeat at Huarina. He sent a detachment under Alvarado to Lima, to collect such of the royalists as had fled thither from the field of battle, and to dismantle the ships of their cannon, and bring them to the camp. Another body was sent to Guamanga, about sixty leagues from Cuzco, for the similar purpose of protecting the fugitives, and also of preventing the Indian caciques from forwarding supplies to the insurgent army in Cuzco. As his own forces now amounted to considerably more than any his opponent could bring against him,

---

[1] "Y salio a la Ciudad de los Reyes, sin que Carbajal, ni alguno de los suyos supiesse por donde fue, sino que parecio encantamiento." Garcilasso, Com. Real., Parte 2, lib. 5, cap. 22.

Gasca determined to break up his camp without further delay, and march on the Inca capital.[2]

Quitting Xauxa, December 29, 1547, he passed through Guamanga, and after a severe march, rendered particularly fatiguing by the inclement state of the weather and the badness of the roads, he entered the province of Andaguaylas. It was a fair and fruitful country, and since the road beyond would take him into the depths of a gloomy sierra, scarcely passable in the winter snows, Gasca resolved to remain in his present quarters until the severity of the season was mitigated. As many of the troops had already contracted diseases from exposure to the incessant rains, he established a camp hospital; and the good president personally visited the quarters of the sick, ministering to their wants, and winning their hearts by his sympathy.[3]

Meanwhile, the royal camp was strengthened by the continual arrival of reinforcements; for notwithstanding the shock that was caused throughout the country by the first tidings of Pizarro's victory, a little reflection convinced the people that the right was the strongest, and must eventually prevail. There came, also, with these levies, several of the most distinguished captains in the country. Centeno, burning to retrieve his late disgrace, after recovering from his illness, joined the camp with his followers from Lima. Benalcazar, the conqueror of Quito, who, as the reader will remember, had shared in the defeat of Blasco Nuñez in the north, came with another detachment; and was soon after followed by Valdivia, the famous conqueror of Chili, who, having returned to Peru to gather recruits for his expedition, had learned the state of the country, and had thrown himself, without hesitation, into the same scale with the president, though it brought him into collision with his old friend and comrade, Gonzalo Pizarro. The arrival of this last ally was greeted with general rejoicing by the camp; for Valdivia, schooled in the Italian wars, was esteemed the most accomplished soldier in Peru; and Gasca complimented him by declaring "he would rather see him than a reinforcement of eight hundred men!"[4]

Besides these warlike auxiliaries, the president was attended by a train of ecclesiastics and civilians, such as was rarely found in the martial fields of Peru. Among them were the bishops of Quito, Cuzco,

---

[2] Gasca, according to Ondegardo, supported his army, during his stay at Xauxa, from the Peruvian granaries in the valley, as he found a quantity of maize still remaining in them sufficient for several years' consumption. It is passing strange that these depositaries should have been so long respected by the hungry Conquerors.— "Cuando el Señor Presidente Gasca passó con la gente de castigo de Gonzalo Pizarro por el Valle de Jauja, estuvo alli siete semanas á lo que me acuerdo, se hallaron en deposito maiz de cuatro y de tres y de dos años mas de 15,000 hanegas junto al camino, é alli comió la gente." Ondegardo, Rel. Seg., MS.

[3] Zarate, Conq. del Peru, lib. 7, cap. 4.—Fernandez, Hist. del Peru, Parte 1, lib 2, cap. 82–85.—Pedro Pizarro, Descub. y Conq., MS.—Cieza de Leon, cap. 90.

[4] At least, so says Valdivia in his letter to the emperor. "I dixo publico que estimara mas mi persona que á los mejores ochocientos hombres de guerra que le pudieran venir aquella hora." Carta de Valdivia, MS.

and Lima, the four judges of the new Audience, and a considerable number of churchmen and monkish missionaries.[5] However little they might
serve to strengthen his arm in battle, their presence gave authority and
something of a sacred character to the cause, which had their effect on
the minds of the soldiers.

The wintry season now began to give way before the mild influence
of spring, which makes itself early felt in these tropical, but from their
elevation temperate, regions; and Gasca, after nearly three months'
detention in Andaguaylas, mustered his levies for the final march upon
Cuzco.[6] Their whole number fell little short of two thousand,—the
largest European force yet assembled in Peru. Nearly half were provided with fire-arms; and infantry were more available than horse in
the mountain countries which they were to traverse. But his cavalry was
also numerous, and he carried with him a train of eleven heavy guns.
The equipment and discipline of the troops were good; they were well
provided with ammunition and military stores; and were led by officers
whose names were associated with the most memorable achievements
in the New World. All who had any real interest in the weal of the country were to be found, in short, under the president's banner, making a
striking contrast to the wild and reckless adventurers who now swelled
the ranks of Pizarro.

Gasca, who did not affect a greater knowledge of military affairs than
he really possessed, had given the charge of his forces to Hinojosa,
naming the Marshal Alvarado as second in command. Valdivia, who
came after these dispositions had been made, accepted a colonel's commission, with the understanding that he was to be consulted and employed in all matters of moment.[7]—Having completed his arrangements,
the president broke up his camp in March, 1548, and moved upon
Cuzco.

The first obstacle of his progress was the river Abancay, the bridge
over which had been broken down by the enemy. But as there was no
force to annoy them on the opposite bank, the army was not long in
preparing a new bridge, and throwing it across the stream, which in this
place had nothing formidable in its character. The road now struck into

---

[5] Zarate, MS.

[6] Cieza de Leon, Cronica, cap. 90.
The old chronicler, or rather geographer, Cieza de Leon, was present in the campaign, he tells us; so that his testimony, always good, becomes for the remaining
events of more than usual value.

[7] Valdivia, indeed, claims to have had the whole command intrusted to him by
Gasca. "Luego me dio el autoridad toda que traia de parte de V. M. para en los casos
tocantes à la guerra, i me encargó todo el exercito, i le puso baxo de mi mano
rogando i pidiendo por merced de su parte á todos aquellos caballeros capitanes e
gente de guerra, i de la de V. M. mandandoles me obedesciesen en todo lo que les
mandase acerca de la guerra, i cumpliesen mis mandamientos como los suyos."
(Carta de Valdivia, MS.) But other authorities state it, with more probability, as
given in the text. Valdivia, it must be confessed, loses nothing from modesty. The
whole of his letter to the emperor is written in a strain of self-glorification, rarely
matched even by a Castilian hidalgo.

the heart of a mountain region, where woods, precipices, and ravines were mingled together in a sort of chaotic confusion, with here and there a green and sheltered valley, glittering like an island of verdure amidst the wild breakers of a troubled ocean! The bold peaks of the Andes, rising far above the clouds, were enveloped in snow, which, descending far down their sides, gave a piercing coldness to the winds that swept over their surface, until men and horses were benumbed and stiffened under their influence. The roads, in these regions, were in some places so narrow and broken, as to be nearly impracticable for cavalry. The cavaliers were compelled to dismount; and the president, with the rest, performed the journey on foot, so hazardous, that, even in later times, it has been no uncommon thing for the sure-footed mule to be precipitated, with its cargo of silver, thousands of feet down the sheer sides of a precipice.[8]

By these impediments of the ground, the march was so retarded, that the troops seldom accomplished more than two leagues a day.[9] Fortunately, the distance was not great; and the president looked with more apprehension to the passage of the Apurimac, which he was now approaching. This river, one of the most formidable tributaries of the Amazon, rolls its broad waters through the gorges of the Cordilleras, that rise up like an immense rampart of rock on either side, presenting a natural barrier which it would be easy for an enemy to make good against a force much superior to his own. The bridges over this river, as Gasca learned before his departure from Andaguaylas, had been all destroyed by Pizarro. The president, accordingly, had sent to explore the banks of the stream, and determine the most eligible spot for reëstablishing communications with the opposite side.

The place selected was near the Indian village of Cotapampa, about nine leagues from Cuzco; for the river, though rapid and turbulent from being compressed within more narrow limits, was here less than two hundred paces in width; a distance, however, not inconsiderable. Directions had been given to collect materials in large quantities in the neighborhood of this spot as soon as possible; and at the same time, in order to perplex the enemy and compel him to divide his forces, should he be disposed to resist, materials in smaller quantities were assembled on three other points of the river. The officer stationed in the neighborhood of Cotapampa was instructed not to begin to lay the bridge, till the arrival of a sufficient force should accelerate the work, and insure its success.

The structure in question, it should be remembered, was one of those suspension bridges formerly employed by the Incas, and still used in crossing the deep and turbulent rivers of South America. They are made of osier withes, twisted into enormous cables, which, when stretched across the water, are attached to heavy blocks of masonry, or, where it will serve, to the natural rock. Planks are laid transversely across these

[8] Cieza de Leon, Cronica, cap. 91.
[9] MS. de Caravantes.

cables, and a passage is thus secured, which, notwithstanding the light and fragile appearance of the bridge, as it swings at an elevation sometimes of several hundred feet above the abyss, affords a tolerably safe means of conveyance for men, and even for such heavy burdens as artillery.[10]

Notwithstanding the peremptory commands of Gasca, the officer intrusted with collecting the materials for the bridge was so anxious to have the honor of completing the work himself, that he commenced it at once. The president, greatly displeased at learning this, quickened his march, in order to cover the work with his whole force. But, while toiling through the mountain labyrinth, tidings were brought him that a party of the enemy had demolished the small portion of the bridge already made, by cutting the cables on the opposite bank. Valdivia, accordingly, hastened forward at the head of two hundred arquebusiers, while the main body of the army followed with as much speed as practicable.

That officer, on reaching the spot, found that the interruption had been caused by a small party of Pizarro's followers, not exceeding twenty in number, assisted by a stronger body of Indians. He at once caused *balsas*, broad and clumsy barks, or rather rafts, of the country, to be provided, and by this means passed his men over, without opposition, to the other side of the river. The enemy, disconcerted by the arrival of such a force, retreated and made the best of their way to report the affair to their commander at Cuzco. Meanwhile, Valdivia, who saw the importance of every moment in the present crisis, pushed forward the work with the greatest vigor. Through all that night his weary troops continued the labor, which was already well advanced, when the president and his battalions, emerging from the passes of the Cordilleras, presented themselves at sunrise on the opposite bank.

Little time was given for repose, as all felt assured that the success of their enterprise hung on the short respite now given them by the improvident enemy. The president, with his principal officers, took part in the labor with the common soldiers;[11] and before ten o'clock in the evening, Gasca had the satisfaction to see the bridge so well secured, that the leading files of the army, unencumbered by their baggage, might venture to cross it. A short time sufficed to place several hundred men on the other bank. But here a new difficulty, not less formidable than that of the river, presented itself to the troops. The ground rose up with an abrupt, almost precipitous, swell from the river-side, till, in the

---

[10] Fernandez, Hist. del Peru, Parte 1, lib. 2, cap. 86, 87.—Zarate, Conq. del Peru, lib. 7, cap. 5.—Pedro Pizarro, Descub. y Conq., MS.—MS. de Caravantes.—Carta de Valdivia, MS.—Relacion del Lic. Gasca, MS.

[11] "La gente que estaua, de la vna parte y de la otra, todos tirauan y trabajauan al poner, y apretar de las Criznejas: sin que el Presidente ni Obispos, ni otra persona quisiesse tener preuilegio para dexar de trabajar." Fernandez, Hist del Peru, Parte 1, lib. 2, cap. 87

highest peaks, it reached an elevation of several thousand feet. This steep ascent, though not to its full height, indeed, was now to be surmounted. The difficulties of the ground, broken up into fearful chasms and water-courses, and tangled with thickets, were greatly increased by the darkness of the night; and the soldiers, as they toiled slowly upward, were filled with apprehension, akin to fear, from the uncertainty whether each successive step might not bring them into an ambuscade, for which the ground was so favorable. More than once, the Spaniards were thrown into a panic by false reports that the enemy were upon them. But Hinojosa and Valdivia were at hand to rally their men, and cheer them on, until, at length, before dawn broke, the bold cavaliers and their followers placed themselves on the highest point traversed by the road, where they waited the arrival of the president. This was not long delayed; and in the course of the following morning, the royalists were already in sufficient strength to bid defiance to their enemy.

The passage of the river had been effected with less loss than might have been expected, considering the darkness of the night, and the numbers that crowded over the aërial causeway. Some few, indeed, fell into the water, and were drowned; and more than sixty horses, in the attempt to swim them across the river, were hurried down the current, and dashed against the rocks below.[12] It still required time to bring up the heavy train of ordnance and the military wagons; and the president encamped on the strong ground which he now occupied, to await their arrival, and to breathe his troops after their extraordinary efforts. In these quarters we must leave him, to acquaint the reader with the state of things in the insurgent army, and with the cause of its strange remissness in guarding the passes of the Apurimac.[13]

From the time of Pizarro's occupation of Cuzco, he had lived in careless luxury in the midst of his followers, like a soldier of fortune in the hour of prosperity; enjoying the present, with as little concern for the future as if the crown of Peru were already fixed irrevocably upon his head. It was otherwise with Carbajal. He looked on the victory at Huarina as the commencement, not the close, of the struggle for empire; and he was indefatigable in placing his troops in the best condition for maintaining their present advantage. At the first streak of dawn, the veteran might be seen mounted on his mule, with the garb and air of a common soldier, riding about in the different quarters of the capital, sometimes superintending the manufacture of arms, or providing mili-

---

[12] "Aquel dia pasaron mas de quatrocientos Hombres, llevando los Caballos à nado, encima de ellos atadas sus armas, i arcabuces, caso que se perdieron mas de sesenta Caballos, que con la corriente grande se desataron, i luego daban en vnas peñas, donde se hacian pedaços, sin darles lugar el impetu del rio, à que pudiesen nadar." Zarate, Conq. del Peru, lib. 7, cap. 5.—Gomara, Hist. de las Indias, cap. 184.

[13] Ibid., ubi supra.—Fernandez, Hist. del Peru, Parte 1, lib. 2, cap. 87.—Zarate, Conq. del Peru, lib. 7, cap. 5.—Pedro Pizarro, Descub. y Conq., MS.—MS. de Caravantes.—Carta de Valdivia, MS.—Cieza de Leon, Cronica, cap. 91.—Relacion del Lic. Gasca, MS.

tary stores, and sometimes drilling his men, for he was most careful always to maintain the strictest discipline.[14] His restless spirit seemed to find no pleasure but in incessant action; living, as he had always done, in the turmoil of military adventure, he had no relish for any thing unconnected with war, and in the city saw only the materials for a well-organized camp.

With these feelings, he was much dissatisfied at the course taken by his younger leader, who now professed his intention to abide where he was, and, when the enemy advanced, to give him battle. Carbajal advised a very different policy. He had not that full confidence, it would seem, in the loyalty of Pizarro's partisans, at least, not of those who had once followed the banner of Centeno. These men, some three hundred in number, had been in a manner compelled to take service under Pizarro. They showed no heartiness in the cause, and the veteran strongly urged his commander to disband them at once; since it was far better to go to battle with a few faithful followers than with a host of the false and faint-hearted.

But Carbajal thought, also, that his leader was not sufficiently strong in numbers to encounter his opponent, supported as he was by the best captains of Peru. He advised, accordingly, that he should abandon Cuzco, carrying off all the treasure, provisions, and stores of every kind from the city, which might, in any way, serve the necessities of the royalists. The latter, on their arrival, disappointed by the poverty of a place where they had expected to find so much booty, would become disgusted with the service. Pizarro, meanwhile, might take refuge with his men in the neighboring fastnesses, where, familiar with the ground, it would be easy to elude the enemy; and if the latter persevered in the pursuit, with numbers diminished by desertion, it would not be difficult in the mountain passes to find an opportunity for assailing him at advantage.—Such was the wary counsel of the old warrior. But it was not to the taste of his fiery commander, who preferred to risk the chances of a battle, rather than turn his back on a foe.

Neither did Pizarro show more favor to a proposition, said to have been made by the Licentiate Cepeda,—that he should avail himself of his late success to enter into negotiations with Gasca. Such advice, from the man who had so recently resisted all overtures of the president, could only have proceeded from a conviction, that the late victory placed Pizarro on a vantage-ground for demanding terms far better than would have been before conceded to him. It may be that subsequent experience had also led him to distrust the fidelity of Gonzalo's followers, or, possibly, the capacity of their chief to conduct them through the present crisis. Whatever may have been the motives of the slippery

[14] "Andaua siempre en vna mula crescida de color entre pardo y bermejo, yo no le vi en otra caualgadura en todo el tiempo que estuuo en el Cozco antes de la Batalla de Sacsahuana. Era tan contino y diligēte en solicitar lo que a su exercito conuenia, que a todas horas del dia y de la noche le topauan sus soldados haziendo su oficio, y los agenos." Garcilasso, Com. Real., Parte I, lib. 5, cap. 27.

counsellor, Pizarro gave little heed to the suggestion, and even showed some resentment, as the matter was pressed on him. In every contest, with Indian or European, whatever had been the odds, he had come off victorious. He was not now for the first time to despond; and he resolved to remain in Cuzco, and hazard all on the chances of a battle. There was something in the hazard itself captivating to his bold and chivalrous temper. In this, too, he was confirmed by some of the cava· liers who had followed him through all his fortunes; reckless young adventurers, who, like himself, would rather risk all on a single throw of the dice, than adopt the cautious, and, as it seemed to them, timid, policy of graver counsellors. It was by such advisers, then, that Pizarro's future course was to be shaped.[16]

Such was the state of affairs in Cuzco, when Pizarro's soldiers returned with the tidings, that a detachment of the enemy had crossed the Apurimac, and were busy in reëstablishing the bridge. Carbajal saw at once the absolute necessity of maintaining this pass. "It is my affair," he said; "I claim to be employed on this service. Give me but a hundred picked men, and I will engage to defend the pass against an army, and bring back the *chaplain*—the name by which the president was known in the rebel camp—a prisoner to Cuzco." [16] "I cannot spare you, father," said Gonzalo, addressing him by this affectionate epithet, which he usually applied to his aged follower,[17] "I cannot spare you so far from my own person"; and he gave the commission to Juan de Acosta, a young cavalier warmly attached to his commander, and who had given undoubted evidence of his valor on more than one occasion, but who, as the event proved, was signally deficient in the qualities de· manded for so critical an undertaking as the present. Acosta, accord· ingly, was placed at the head of two hundred mounted musketeers, and, after much wholesome counsel from Carbajal, set out on his expedition.

But he soon forgot the veteran's advice, and moved at so dull a pace over the difficult roads, that, although the distance was not more than nine leagues, he found, on his arrival, the bridge completed, and so large a body of the enemy already crossed, that he was in no strength to attack them. Acosta did, indeed, meditate an ambuscade by night; but the design was betrayed by a deserter, and he contented himself with retreating to a safe distance, and sending for a further reinforcement from Cuzco. Three hundred men were promptly detached to his support; but when they arrived, the enemy was already planted in full force on the crest of the eminence. The golden opportunity was irrecoverably

[15] Garcilasso, Com. Real., Parte 2, lib. 5, cap. 27.—Gomara, Hist. de las Indias, cap. 182.—Fernandez, Hist. del Peru, Parte 1, lib. 2, cap. 88.

"Finalmente, Gonçalo Pizarro dixo que queria prouar su ventura: pues siempre auia sido vencedor, y jamas vencido." Ibid., ubi supra.

[16] "Paresceme vuestra Señoria se vaya á la vuelta del Collao y me deje cien hom· bres, los que yo escojiere, que yo me iré á vista deste capellan, que ansi llamaba él al presidente." Pedro Pizarro, Descub. y Conq., MS.

[17] Garcilasso, Com. Real., Parte 2, lib. 5, cap. 31.

lost; and the disconsolate cavalier rode back in all haste to report the failure of his enterprise to his commander in Cuzco.[18]

The only question now to be decided was as to the spot where Gonzalo Pizarro should give battle to his enemies. He determined at once to abandon the capital, and wait for his opponents in the neighboring valley of Xaquixaguana. It was about five leagues distant, and the reader may remember it as the place where Francis Pizarro burned the Peruvian general Challcuchima, on his first occupation of Cuzco. The valley, fenced round by the lofty rampart of the Andes, was, for the most part, green and luxuriant, affording many picturesque points of view; and, from the genial temperature of the climate, had been a favorite summer residence of the Indian nobles, many of whose pleasure-houses still dotted the sides of the mountains. A river, or rather stream, of no great volume, flowed through one end of this inclosure, and the neighboring soil was so wet and miry as to have the character of a morass.

Here the rebel commander arrived, after a tedious march over roads not easily traversed by his train of heavy wagons and artillery. His forces amounted in all to about nine hundred men, with some half-dozen pieces of ordnance. It was a well-appointed body, and under excellent discipline, for it had been schooled by the strictest martinet in the Peruvian service. But it was the misfortune of Pizarro that his army was composed, in part, at least, of men on whose attachment to his cause he could not confidently rely. This was a deficiency which no courage nor skill in the leader could supply.

On entering the valley, Pizarro selected the eastern quarter of it, towards Cuzco, as the most favorable spot for his encampment. It was crossed by the stream above mentioned, and he stationed his army in such a manner, that, while one extremity of the camp rested on a natural barrier formed by the mountain cliffs that here rose up almost perpendicularly, the other was protected by the river. While it was scarcely possible, therefore, to assail his flanks, the approaches in front were so extremely narrowed by these obstacles, that it would not be easy to overpower him by numbers in that direction. In the rear, his communications remained open with Cuzco, furnishing a ready means for obtaining sup-

[18] Pedro Pizarro, Descub. y Conq., MS.—Fernandez, Hist. del Peru, Parte 1, lib. 2, cap. 88.—Zarate, Conq. del Peru, lib. 7, cap. 5.—Carta de Valdivia, MS.

Valdivia's letter to the emperor, dated at Concepcion, was written about two years after the events above recorded. It is chiefly taken up with his Chilian conquests, to which his campaign under Gasca, on his visit to Peru, forms a kind of brilliant episode. This letter, the original of which is preserved in Simancas, covers about seventy folio pages in the copy belonging to me. It is one of that class of historical documents, consisting of the despatches and correspondence of the colonial governors, which from the minuteness of the details and the means of information possessed by the writers, are of the highest worth. The despatches addressed to the Court, particularly, may compare with the celebrated *Relazioni* made by the Venetian ambassadors to their republic, and now happily in the course of publication, at Florence, under the editorial auspices of the learned Albèri.

plies. Having secured this strong position, he resolved patiently to wait the assault of the enemy.[19]

Meanwhile, the royal army had been toiling up the steep sides of the Cordilleras, until, at the close of the third day, the president had the satisfaction to find himself surrounded by his whole force, with their guns and military stores. Having now sufficiently refreshed his men, he resumed his march, and all went forward with the buoyant confidence of bringing their quarrel with the *tyrant*, as Pizarro was called, to a speedy issue.

Their advance was slow, as in the previous part of the march, for the ground was equally embarrassing. It was not long, however, before the president learned that his antagonist had pitched his camp in the neighboring valley of Xaquixaguana. Soon afterward, two friars, sent by Gonzalo himself, appeared in the army, for the ostensible purpose of demanding a sight of the powers with which Gasca was intrusted. But as their conduct gave reason to suspect they were spies, the president caused the holy men to be seized, and refused to allowed them to return to Pizarro. By an emissary of his own, whom he despatched to the rebel chief, he renewed the assurance of pardon already given him, in case he would lay down his arms and submit. Such an act of generosity, at this late hour, must be allowed to be highly creditable to Gasca, believing, as he probably did, that the game was in his own hands.—It is a pity that the anecdote does not rest on the best authority.[20]

After a march of a couple of days, the advanced guard of the royalists came suddenly on the outposts of the insurgents, from whom they had been concealed by a thick mist, and a slight skirmish took place between them. At length, on the morning of the eighth of April, the royal army, turning the crest of the lofty range that belts round the lovely valley of Xaquixaguana, beheld far below on the opposite side the glittering lines of the enemy, with their white pavilions, looking like clusters of wild fowl nestling among the cliffs of the mountains. And still further off might be descried a host of Indian warriors, showing gaudily in their variegated costumes; for the natives, in this part of the country, with little perception of their true interests, manifested great zeal in the cause of Pizarro.

Quickening their step, the royal army now hastily descended the steep sides of the sierra; and notwithstanding every effort of their officers, they moved in so little order, each man picking his way as he

[19] Carta de Valdivia, MS.—Garcilasso, Com. Real., Parte 2, lib. 5, cap. 33, 34.—Pedro Pizarro, Descub. y Conq., MS.—Gomara, Hist. de las Indias, cap. 185.—Fernandez, Hist. del Peru, Parte 1, lib. 2, cap. 88.

[20] The fact is not mentioned by any of the parties present at these transactions. It is to be found, with some little discrepancy of circumstances, in Gomara (Hist. de las Indias,, cap. 185) and Zarate (Conq. del Peru, lib. 7, cap. 6); and their positive testimony may be thought by most readers to outweigh the negative afforded by the silence of other contemporaries.

could, that the straggling column presented many a vulnerable point to the enemy; and the descent would not have been accomplished without considerable loss, had Pizarro's cannon been planted on any of the favorable positions which the ground afforded. But that commander, far from attempting to check the president's approach, remained doggedly in the strong position he had occupied, with the full confidence that his adversaries would not hesitate to assail it, strong as it was, in the same manner as they had done at Huarina.[21]

Yet he did not omit to detach a corps of arquebusiers to secure a neighboring eminence or spur of the Cordilleras, which in the hands of the enemy might cause some annoyance to his own camp, while it commanded still more effectually the ground soon to be occupied by the assailants. But his manœuvre was noticed by Hinojosa; and he defeated it by sending a stronger detachment of the royal musketeers, who repulsed the rebels, and, after a short skirmish, got possession of the heights. Gasca's general profited by this success to plant a small battery of cannon on the eminence, from which, although the distance was too great for him to do much execution, he threw some shot into the hostile camp. One ball, indeed, struck down two men, one of them Pizarro's page, killing a horse, at the same time, which he held by the bridle; and the chief instantly ordered the tents to be struck, considering that they afforded too obvious a mark for the artillery.[22]

Meanwhile, the president's forces had descended into the valley, and as they came on the plain were formed into line by their officers. The ground occupied by the army was somewhat lower than that of their enemy, whose shot, as discharged, from time to time, from his batteries, passed over their heads. Information was now brought by a deserter, one of Centeno's old followers, that Pizarro was getting ready for a night attack. The president, in consequence, commanded his whole force to be drawn up in battle array, prepared, at any instant, to repulse the assault. But if such were meditated by the insurgent chief, he abandoned it,—and, as it is said, from a distrust of the fidelity of some of the troops, who, under cover of the darkness, he feared, would go over to the opposite side. If this be true, he must have felt the full force of Carbajal's admonition, when too late to profit by it. The unfortunate commander was in the situation of some bold, high-mettled cavalier, rushing to battle on a war-horse whose tottering joints threaten to give way

---

[21] "Salió á Xaquixaguana con toda su gente y allí nos aguardó en un llano junto á un cerro alto por donde bajábamos; y cierto nuestro Señor le cegó el entendimiento, porque si nos aguardaran al pie de la bajada, hicieran mucho daño á nosotros. Retiráronse á un llano junto á una ciénaga, creyendo que nuestro campo allí les acometiera y con la ventaja que nos tenian del puesto nos vencieran." Pedro Pizarro, Descub. y Conq., MS.—Carta de Valdivia, MS.—Relacion del Lic. Gasca, MS.

[22] "Porq̃. muchas pelotas dieron en medio de la gente, y una dellas matò jũto á Gonçalo Pizarro vn criado suyo que se estaua armando: y matò otro hombre y vn cauallo: que puso grande alteracion en el campo, y abatieron todas las tiẽdas y toldos." Fernandez, Hist. del Peru, Parte 1, lib. 2, cap. 89.—Carta de Valdivia, MS.—Relacion del Lic. Gasca, MS.

under him at every step, and leave his rider to the mercy of his enemies!

The president's troops stood to their arms the greater part of the night, although the air from the mountains was so keen, that it was with difficulty they could hold their lances in their hands.[23] But before the rising sun had kindled into a glow the highest peaks of the sierra, both camps were in motion, and busily engaged in preparations for the combat. The royal army was formed into two battalions of infantry, one to attack the enemy in front, and the other, if possible, to operate on his flank. These battalions were protected by squadrons of horse on the wings and in the rear, while reserves both of horse and arquebusiers were stationed to act as occasion might require. The dispositions were made in so masterly a manner, as to draw forth a hearty eulogium from old Carbajal, who exclaimed, "Surely the Devil or Valdivia must be among them!" an undeniable compliment to the latter, since the speaker was ignorant of that commander's presence in the camp.[24]

Gasca, leaving the conduct of the battle to his officers, withdrew to the rear with his train of clergy and licentiates, the last of whom did not share in the ambition of their rebel brother, Cepeda, to break a lance in the field.

Gonzalo Pizarro formed his squadron in the same manner as he had done on the plains of Huarina; except that the increased number of his horse now enabled him to cover both flanks of his infantry. It was still on his fire-arms, however, that he chiefly relied. As the ranks were formed, he rode among them, encouraging his men to do their duty like brave cavaliers, and true soldiers of the Conquest. Pizarro was superbly armed, as usual, and wore a complete suit of mail, of the finest manufacture, which, as well as his helmet, was richly inlaid with gold.[25] He rode a chestnut horse of great strength and spirit, and as he galloped along the line, brandishing his lance, and displaying his easy horsemanship, he might be thought to form no bad personification of the Genius of Chivalry. To complete his dispositions, he ordered Cepeda to lead up the infantry; for the licentiate seems to have had a larger share in the conduct of his affairs of late, or at least in the present military arrangements, than Carbajal. The latter, indeed, whether from disgust at the course taken by his leader, or from a distrust, which, it is said, he did

[23] "I asi estuvo el Campo toda la Noche en Arma, desarmadas las Tiendas, padesciendo mui gran frio que no podian tener las Lanças en las manos." Zarate, Conq. del Peru, lib. 7, cap. 6.

[24] "Y assi Quando vio Francisco de Caruajal el campo Real; pareciendole que los esquadrones venian bie ordenados dixo, Valdiuia està en la tierra, y rige el campo, ò el diablo." Fernandez, Hist. del Peru, Parte 1, lib. 2, cap. 89.—Relacion del Lic. Gasca, MS.—Carta de Valdivia, MS.—Gomara, Hist. de las Indias, cap. 185.— Zarate, Conq. del Peru, lib. 7, cap. 6.—Garcilasso, Com. Real., Parte 2, lib. 5, cap. 34.—Pedro Pizarro, Descub. y Conq., MS.

[25] "Iba mui galàn, i gentil hombre sobre vn poderoso caballo castaño, armado de Cota, i Coracinas ricas, con vna sobre ropa de Raso bien golpeada, i vn Capacete de Oro en la cabeca, con su barbote de lo mismo." Gomara, Hist. de las Indias, cap. 185.

not affect to conceal, of the success of the present operations, disclaimed all responsibility for them, and chose to serve rather as a private cavalier than as a commander.[26] Yet Cepeda, as the event showed, was no less shrewd in detecting the coming ruin.

When he had received his orders from Pizarro, he rode forward as if to select the ground for his troops to occupy; and in doing so disappeared for a few moments behind a projecting cliff. He soon reappeared, however, and was seen galloping at full speed across the plain. His men looked with astonishment, yet not distrusting his motives, till, as he continued his course direct towards the enemy's lines, his treachery became apparent. Several pushed forward to overtake him, and among them a cavalier, better mounted than Cepeda. The latter rode a horse of no great strength or speed, quite unfit for this critical manœuvre of his master. The animal, was, moreover, encumbered by the weight of the caparisons with which his ambitious rider had loaded him, so that, on reaching a piece of miry ground that lay between the armies, his pace was greatly retarded.[27] Cepeda's pursuers rapidly gained on him, and the cavalier above noticed came, at length, so near as to throw a lance at the fugitive, which, wounding him in the thigh, pierced his horse's flank, and they both came headlong to the ground. It would have fared ill with the licentiate, in this emergency, but fortunately a small party of troopers on the other side, who had watched the chase, now galloped briskly forward to the rescue, and, beating off his pursuers, they recovered Cepeda from the mire, and bore him to the president's quarters.

He was received by Gasca with the greatest satisfaction,—so great, that, according to one chronicler, he did not disdain to show it by saluting the licentiate on the cheek.[28] The anecdote is scarcely reconcilable with the characters and relations of the parties, or with the president's subsequent conduct. Gasca, however, recognized the full value of his prize, and the effect which his desertion at such a time must have on the spirits of the rebels. Cepeda's movement, so unexpected by his own party, was the result of previous deliberation, as he had secretly given assurance, it is said, to the prior of Arequipa, then in the royal camp, that, if Gonzalo Pizarro could not be induced to accept the pardon offered him, he would renounce his cause.[29] The time selected by the crafty counsellor for doing so was that most fatal to the interests of his commander.

[26] "Porque el Maesse de campo Francisco de Caruajal, como hombre desdeñado de que Gonçalo Piçarro no huuiesse querido seguir su parecer y consejo (dandose ya por vencido), no quiso hazer oficio de Maesse de campo, como solia, y assi fue a ponerse en el esquadron con su compañia, como vno de los capitanes de ynfanteria." Garcilasso, Com. Real., Parte 2, lib. 5, cap. 35.

[27] Ibid., ubi supra.

[28] "Gasca abraçò, i besò en el carrillo à Cepeda, aunque lo llevaba encenagado, teniendo por vencido à Piçarro, con su falta." Gomara, Hist. de las Indias, cap. 185.

[29] "Ça, segun pareciò, Cepeda le huvo avisado con Fr. Antonio de Castro, Prior de Santo Domingo en Arequipa; que si Piçarro no quisiesse concierto ninguno, èl se pasaria al servicio del Emperador i. tiempo que le deshiciese." Ibid., ubi supra.

The example of Cepeda was contagious. Garcilasso de la Vega, father of the historian, a cavalier of old family, and probably of higher consideration than any other in Pizarro's party, put spurs to his horse, at the same time with the licentiate, and rode over to the enemy. Ten or a dozen of the arquebusiers followed in the same direction, and succeeded in placing themselves under the protection of the advanced guard of the royalists.

Pizarro stood aghast at this desertion, in so critical a juncture, of those in whom he had most trusted. He was, for a moment, bewildered. The very ground on which he stood seemed to be crumbling beneath him. With this state of feeling among his soldiers, he saw that every minute of delay was fatal. He dared not wait for the assault, as he had intended, in his strong position, but instantly gave the word to advance. Gasca's general, Hinojosa, seeing the enemy in motion, gave similar orders to his own troops. Instantly the skirmishers and arquebusiers on the flanks moved rapidly forward, the artillery prepared to open their fire, and "the whole army," says the president in his own account of the affair, "advanced with steady step and perfect determination." [30]

But before a shot was fired, a column of arquebusiers, composed chiefly of Centeno's followers, abandoned their post, and marched directly over to the enemy. A squadron of horse, sent in pursuit of them, followed their example. The president instantly commanded his men to halt, unwilling to spill blood unnecessarily, as the rebel host was like to fall to pieces of itself.

Pizarro's faithful adherents were seized with a panic, as they saw themselves and their leader thus betrayed into the enemy's hands. Further resistance was useless. Some threw down their arms and fled in the direction of Cuzco. Others sought to escape to the mountains; and some crossed to the opposite side, and surrendered themselves prisoners, hoping it was not too late to profit by the promises of grace. The Indian allies, on seeing the Spaniards falter, had been the first to go off the ground.[31]

Pizarro, amidst the general wreck, found himself left with only a few cavaliers who disdained to fly. Stunned by the unexpected reverse of fortune, the unhappy chief could hardly comprehend his situation. "What remains for us?" said he to Acosta, one of those who still adhered to him. "Fall on the enemy, since nothing else is left," answered the

[30] "Visto por Gonzalo Pizarro i Caravajal su Maestre de Campo que se les iva gente procuraron de caminar en su orden hacia el campo de S. M. i que viendo esto los lados i sobre salientes del exercito real se empezaron á llegar á ellos i á disparar en ellos i que lo mesmo hizo la artilleria, i todo el campo con paso bien concertado i entera determinacion se llegó á ellos." Relacion del Lic. Gasca, MS.

[31] "Los Indios que tenian los enemigos que diz que eran mucha cantidad huyeron mui á furia." (Relacion del Lic. Gasca, MS.) For the particulars of the battle, more or less minute, see Carta de Valdivia, MS.—Garcilasso, Com. Real., Parte 2, lib. 5, cap. 35.—Pedro Pizarro, Descub. y Conq., MS.—Gomara, Hist. de las Indias, cap. 185.—Fernandez, Hist. del Peru, Parte 1, lib. 2, cap. 90.—Zarate, Conq. del Peru, lib. 7, cap. 7 —Herrera, Hist. General, dec. 8, lib. 4, cap. 16.

ñon-hearted soldier, "and die like Romans!" "Better to die like Christians," replied his commander; and, slowly turning his horse, he rode
off in the direction of the royal army.[32]

He had not proceeded far, when he was met by an officer, to whom,
after ascertaining his name and rank, Pizarro delivered up his sword,
and yielded himself prisoner. The officer, overjoyed at his prize, conducted him, at once, to the president's quarters. Gasca was on horseback,
surrounded by his captains, some of whom, when they recognized the
person of the captive, had the grace to withdraw, that they might not
witness his humiliation.[33] Even the best of them, with a sense of right
on their side, may have felt some touch of compunction at the thought
that their desertion had brought their benefactor to this condition.

Pizarro kept his seat in his saddle, but, as he approached, made a respectful obeisance to the president, which the latter acknowledged by a
cold salute. Then, addressing his prisoner in a tone of severity, Gasca
abruptly inquired,—"Why he had thrown the country into such confusion;—raising the banner of revolt; killing the viceroy; usurping the
government; and obstinately refusing the offers of grace that had been
repeatedly made him?"

Gonzalo attempted to justify himself by referring the fate of the
viceroy to his misconduct, and his own usurpation, as it was styled, to
the free election of the people, as well as that of the Royal Audience.
"It was my family," he said, "who conquered the country; and, as their
representative here, I felt I had a right to the government." To this
Gasca replied, in a still severer tone, "Your brother did, indeed, conquer the land; and for this the emperor was pleased to raise both him
and you from the dust. He lived and died a true and loyal subject; and
it only makes your ingratitude to your sovereign the more heinous."
Then, seeing his prisoner about to reply, the president cut short the conference, ordering him into close confinement. He was committed to the
charge of Centeno, who had sought the office, not from any unworthy
desire to gratify his revenge,—for he seems to have had a generous
nature,—but for the honorable purpose of ministering to the comfort of
the captive. Though held in strict custody by this officer, therefore,
Pizarro was treated with the deference due to his rank, and allowed
every indulgence by his keeper, except his freedom.[34]

In this general wreck of their fortunes, Francisco de Carbajal fared
no better than his chief. As he saw the soldiers deserting their posts and

---

[32] "Gonçalo Piçarro boluiendo el rostro, a Juan de Acosta, que estaua cerca del,
le dixo, que haremos hermano Juan? Acosta presumiendo mas de valiente que de
discreto respondiò, Señor arremetamos, y muramos como los antiguos Romanos.
Gonçalo Piçarro dixo mejor es morir como Cristianos." Garcilasso, Com. Real.,
Parte 2, lib. 5, cap. 36.—Zarate, Conq. del Peru, lib. 7, cap. 7.

[33] Garcilasso, Com. Real., ubi supra.

[34] Fernandez, Hist. del Peru, Parte 1, lib. 2, cap. 90.

Historians, of course, report the dialogue between Gasca and his prisoner with
some variety. See Gomara, Hist. de las Indias, cap. 185.—Garcilasso, Com. Real.,
Parte 2, lib. 5, cap. 36.—Relacion del Lic. Gasca, MS.

going over to the enemy, one after another, he coolly hummed the words of his favorite old ballad,—

"The wind blows the hairs off my head, mother!"

But when he found the field nearly empty, and his stout-hearted followers vanished like a wreath of smoke, he felt it was time to provide for his own safety. He knew there could be no favor for him; and, putting spurs to his horse, he betook himself to flight with all the speed he could make. He crossed the stream that flowed, as already mentioned, by the camp, but, in scaling the opposite bank, which was steep and stony, his horse, somewhat old, and oppressed by the weight of his rider, who was large and corpulent, lost his footing and fell with him into the water. Before he could extricate himself, Carbajal was seized by some of his own followers, who hoped, by such a prize, to make their peace with the victor, and hurried off towards the president's quarters.

The convoy was soon swelled by a number of the common file from the royal army, some of whom had long arrears to settle with the prisoner; and, not content with heaping reproaches and imprecations on his head, they now threatened to proceed to acts of personal violence, which Carbajal, far from deprecating, seemed rather to court, as the speediest way of ridding himself of life.[35] When he approached the president's quarters, Centeno, who was near, rebuked the disorderly rabble, and compelled them to give way. Carbajal, on seeing this, with a respectful air demanded to whom he was indebted for this courteous protection. To which his ancient comrade replied, "Do you not know me?— Diego Centeno!" "I crave your pardon," said the veteran, sarcastically alluding to his long flight in the Charcas, and his recent defeat at Huarina; "it is so long since I have seen any thing but your back, that I had forgotten your face!" [36]

Among the president's suite was the martial bishop of Cuzco, who, it will be remembered, had shared with Centeno in the disgrace of his defeat. His brother had been taken by Carbajal, in his flight from the field, and instantly hung up by that fierce chief, who, as we have had more than one occasion to see, was no respecter of persons. The bishop now reproached him with his brother's murder, and, incensed by his cool replies, was ungenerous enough to strike the prisoner on the face. Carbajal made no attempt at resistance. Nor would he return a word to

---

[35] "Luego llevaron antel dicho Licenciado Caravajal Maestre de campo del dicho Pizarro i tan cercado de gentes que del havian sido ofendidas que le querian matar, el qual diz que mostrava que olgara que le matáran alli." Relacion del Lic. Gasca, MS.

[36] "Diego Centeno reprehendia mucho à los que le offendian. Por lo qual Caruajal le mirò, y le dixo, Señor quien es vuestra merced que tanta merced me haze? à lo qual Centeno respondio, Que no conoce vuestra merced a Diego Centeno? Dixo entonces Caruajal, Por Dios señor que como siempre vi à vuestra merced de espaldas, que agora teniendo le de cara, no le conocia." Fernandez, Hist. del Peru, Parte 1, lib. 2, cap. 90.

the queries put to him by Gasca; but, looking haughtily round on the circle, maintained a contemptuous silence. The president, seeing that nothing further was to be gained from his captive, ordered him, together with Acosta, and the other cavaliers who had surrendered, into strict custody, until their fate should be decided.[37]

Gasca's next concern was to send an officer to Cuzco, to restrain his partisans from committing excesses in consequence of the late victory,— if victory that could be called, where not a blow had been struck. Every thing belonging to the vanquished, their tents, arms, ammunition, and military stores, became the property of the victors. Their camp was well victualled, furnishing a seasonable supply to the royalists, who had nearly expended their own stock of provisions. There was, moreover, considerable booty in the way of plate and money; for Pizarro's men, as was not uncommon in those turbulent times, went, many of them, to the war with the whole of their worldly wealth, not knowing of any safe place in which to bestow it. An anecdote is told of one of Gasca's soldiers, who, seeing a mule running over the field, with a large pack on his back, seized the animal, and mounted him, having first thrown away the burden, supposing it to contain armour, or something of little worth. Another soldier, more shrewd, picked up the parcel, as his share of the spoil, and found it contained several thousand gold ducats! It was the fortune of war.[38]

Thus terminated the battle, or rather rout, of Xaquixaguana. The number of killed and wounded—for some few perished in the pursuit— was not great; according to most accounts, not exceeding fifteen killed on the rebel side, and one only on that of the royalists! and that one, by the carelessness of a comrade.[39] Never was there a cheaper victory; so bloodless a termination of a fierce and bloody rebellion! It was gained not so much by the strength of the victors as by the weakness of the

[37] Ibid., ubi supra.

It is but fair to state that Garcilasso, who was personally acquainted with the bishop of Cuzco, doubts the fact of the indecorous conduct imputed to him by Fernandez, as inconsistent with the prelate's character. Com. Real., Parte 2, lib. 5, cap. 39.

[38] Zarate, Conq. del Peru, lib. 7, cap. 8.

[39] "Temióse que en esta batalla muriria mucha gente de ambas partes por haver en ellas mill i quatrocientos arcabuceros i seiscientos de caballo i mucho numero de piqueros i diez i ocho piezas de artilleria, pero plugo á Dios que solo murió un hombre del campo de S. M. i quince de los contrarios como está dicho." Relacion del Lic. Gasca, MS.

The MS. above referred to is supposed by Muños to have been written by Gasca, or rather dictated by him to his secretary. The original is preserved at Simancas, without date, and in the character of the sixteenth century. It is principally taken up with the battle, and the events immediately connected with it; and although very brief, every sentence is of value as coming from so high a source. Alcedo, in his *Biblioteca Americana, MS.*, gives the title of a work from Gasca's pen, which would seem to be an account of his own administration, *Historia del Peru, y de su Pacificacion*, 1576, fol.—I have never met with the work, or with any other allusion to it.

vanquished. They fell to pieces of their own accord, because they had no sure ground to stand on. The arm, not nerved by the sense of right, became powerless in the hour of battle. It was better that they should thus be overcome by moral force than by a brutal appeal to arms. Such a victory was more in harmony with the beneficent character of the conqueror and of his cause. It was the triumph of order; the best homage to law and justice.

CHAPTER IV

EXECUTION OF CARBAJAL—GONZALO PIZARRO BEHEADED—SPOILS OF
VICTORY—WISE REFORMS BY GASCA—HE RETURNS TO SPAIN—
HIS DEATH AND CHARACTER

1548—1550

IT was now necessary to decide on the fate of the prisoners; and Alonso
de Alvarado, with the Licentiate Cianca, one of the new Royal Audience, was instructed to prepare the process. It did not require a long
time. The guilt of the prisoners was too manifest, taken, as they had
been, with arms in their hands. They were all sentenced to be executed,
and their estates were confiscated to the use of the Crown. Gonzalo
Pizarro was to be beheaded, and Carbajal to be drawn and quartered.
No mercy was shown to him who had shown none to others. There was
some talk of deferring the execution till the arrival of the troops in
Cuzco; but the fear of disturbances from those friendly to Pizarro determined the president to carry the sentence into effect the following
day, on the field of battle.[1]

When his doom was communicated to Carbajal, he heard it with his
usual indifference. "They can but kill me," he said, as if he had already
settled the matter in his own mind.[2] During the day, many came to see
him in his confinement; some to upbraid him with his cruelties; but
most, from curiosity to see the fierce warrior who had made his name
so terrible through the land. He showed no unwillingness to talk with
them, though it was in those sallies of caustic humor in which he usually indulged at the expense of his hearer. Among these visitors was a
cavalier of no note, whose life, it appears, Carbajal had formerly spared,
when in his power. This person expressed to the prisoner his strong desire to serve him; and as he reiterated his professions, Carbajal cut
them short by exclaiming,—"And what service can you do me? Can you
set me free? If you cannot do that, you can do nothing. If I spared your
life, as you say, it was probably because I did not think it worth while
to take it."

Some piously disposed persons urged him to see a priest, if it were
only to unburden his conscience before leaving the world. "But of

---

[1] The sentence passed upon Pizarro is given at length in the *manuscript* copy of
Zarate's History, to which I have had occasion more than once to refer. The historian omitted it in his printed work.
[2] "Basta matar." Fernandez, Hist. del Peru, Parte 1, lib. 2, cap. 91.

what use would that be?" asked Carbajal. "I have nothing that lies
heavy on my conscience, unless it be, indeed, the debt of half a real to a
shopkeeper in Seville, which I forgot to pay before leaving the country!" [3]

He was carried to execution on a hurdle, or rather in a basket, drawn
by two mules. His arms were pinioned, and, as they forced his bulky
body into this miserable conveyance, he exclaimed,—"Cradles for infants, and a cradle for the old man too, it seems!" [4] Notwithstanding
the disinclination he had manifested to a confessor, he was attended by
several ecclesiastics on his way to the gallows; and one of them repeatedly urged him to give some token of penitence at this solemn hour,
if it were only by repeating the *Pater Noster* and *Ave Maria*. Carbajal,
to rid himself of the ghostly father's importunity, replied by coolly repeating the words, "*Pater Noster*," "*Ave Maria*"! He then remained
obstinately silent. He died, as he had lived, with a jest, or rather a scoff,
upon his lips. [5]

Francisco de Carbajal was one of the most extraordinary characters
of these dark and turbulent times; the more extraordinary from his
great age; for, at the period of his death, he was in his eighty-fourth
year;—an age when the bodily powers, and, fortunately, the passions,
are usually blunted; when, in the witty words of the French moralist,
"We flatter ourselves we are leaving our vices, whereas it is our vices
that are leaving us." [6] But the fires of youth glowed fierce and unquenchable in the bosom of Carbajal.

The date of his birth carries us back towards the middle of the fifteenth century, before the times of Ferdinand and Isabella. He was of
obscure parentage, and born, as it is said, at Arevalo. For forty years he
served in the Italian wars, under the most illustrious captains of the day,
Gonsalvo de Córdova, Navarro, and the Colonnas. He was an ensign at
the battle of Ravenna; witnessed the capture of Francis the First at
Pavia; and followed the banner of the ill-starred Bourbon at the sack
of Rome. He got no gold for his share of the booty, on this occasion, but
simply the papers of a notary's office, which, Carbajal shrewdly thought,
would be worth gold to him. And so it proved; for the notary was fain
to redeem them at a price which enabled the adventurer to cross the
seas to Mexico, and seek his fortune in the New World. On the insurrection of the Peruvians, he was sent to the support of Francis Pizarro,

[3] "En esso no tengo que confessar: porque juro à tal, que no tengo otro cargo, si
no medio real que deuo en Seuilla à vna bodegonera de la puerta del Arenal, del
tiempo que passè a Indias." Ibid., ubi supra.

[4] "Niño en cuna, y viejo en cuna." Ibid., loc. cit.

[5] "Murió como gentil, porque dicen, que yo no le quise ver, que ansí le dí la
palabra de no velle; mas á la postrer vez que me habló llevandole á matar le decia
el sacerdote que con él iba, que se encomendase á Dios y dijese el Pater Noster y el
Ave María, y dicen que dijo Pater Noster, Ave María, y que no dijo otra palabra."
Pedro Pizarro, Descub. y Conq., MS.

[6] I quote from memory, but believe the reflection may be found in that admirable digest of worldly wisdom, The Characters of La Bruyère.

and was rewarded by that chief with a grant of land in Cuzco. Here he remained for several years, busily employed in increasing his substance; for the love of lucre was a ruling passion in his bosom. On the arrival of Vaca de Castro, we find him doing good service under the royal banner; and at the breaking out of the great rebellion under Gonzalo Pizarro, he converted his property into gold, and prepared to return to Castile. He seemed to have a presentiment that to remain where he was would be fatal. But, although he made every effort to leave Peru, he was unsuccessful, for the viceroy had laid an embargo on the shipping.[7] He remained in the country, therefore, and took service, as we have seen, though reluctantly, under Pizarro. It was his destiny.

The tumultuous life on which he now entered roused all the slumbering passions of his soul, which lay there, perhaps unconsciously to himself; cruelty, avarice, revenge. He found ample exercise for them in the war with his countrymen; for civil war is proverbially the most sanguinary and ferocious of all. The atrocities recorded of Carbajal, in his new career, and the number of his victims, are scarcely credible. For the honor of humanity, we may trust the accounts are greatly exaggerated; but that he should have given rise to them at all is sufficient to consign his name to infamy.[8]

He even took a diabolical pleasure, it is said, in amusing himself with the sufferings of his victims, and in the hour of execution would give utterance to frightful jests, that made them taste more keenly the bitterness of death! He had a sportive vein, if such it could be called, which he freely indulged on every occasion. Many of his sallies were preserved by the soldiery; but they are, for the most part, of a coarse, repulsive character, flowing from a mind familiar with the weak and wicked side of humanity, and distrusting every other. He had his jest for every thing,—for the misfortunes of others, and for his own. He looked on life as a farce,—though he too often made it a tragedy.

Carbajal must be allowed one virtue; that of fidelity to his party. This made him less tolerant to perfidy in others. He was never known to show mercy to a renegade. This undeviating fidelity, though to a bad cause, may challenge something like a feeling of respect, where fidelity was so rare.[9]

---

[7] Pedro Pizarro bears testimony to Carbajal's endeavors to leave the country, in which he was aided, though ineffectually, by the chronicler, who was, at that time, in the most friendly relations with him. Civil war parted these ancient comrades; but Carbajal did not forget his obligations to Pedro Pizarro, which he afterwards repaid by exempting him on two different occasions from the general doom of the prisoners who fell into his hands.

[8] Out of three hundred and forty executions, according to Fernandez, three hundred were by Carbajal. (Hist. del Peru, Parte 1, lib. 2, cap. 91.) Zarate swells the number of these executions to five hundred. (Conq. del Peru, lib. 7, cap. 1.) The discrepancy shows how little we can confide in the accuracy of such estimates.

[9] Fidelity, indeed, is but one of many virtues claimed for Carbajal by Garcilasso, who considers most of the tales of cruelty and avarice circulated of the veteran, as well as the hardened levity imputed to him in his latter moments, as inventions of his enemies. The Inca chronicler was a boy when Gonzalo and his chivalry oc-

As a military man, Carbajal takes a high rank among the soldiers of the New World. He was strict, even severe, in enforcing discipline, so that he was little loved by his followers. Whether he had the genius for military combinations requisite for conducting war on an extended scale may be doubted; but in the shifts and turns of guerilla warfare he was unrivalled. Prompt, active, and persevering, he was insensible to danger or fatigue, and, after days spent in the saddle, seemed to attach little value to the luxury of a bed.[10]

He knew familiarly every mountain pass, and, such were the sagacity and the resources displayed in his roving expeditions, that he was vulgarly believed to be attended by a *familiar*.[11] With a character so extraordinary, with powers prolonged so far beyond the usual term of humanity, and passions so fierce in one tottering on the verge of the grave, it was not surprising that many fabulous stories should be eagerly circulated respecting him, and that Carbajal should be clothed with mysterious terrors as a sort of supernatural being,—the demon of the Andes!

Very different were the circumstances attending the closing scene of Gonzalo Pizarro. At his request, no one had been allowed to visit him in his confinement. He was heard pacing his tent during the greater part of the day, and when night came, having ascertained from Centeno that his execution was to take place on the following noon, he laid himself down to rest. He did not sleep long, however, but soon rose, and continued to traverse his apartment, as if buried in meditation, till dawn. He then sent for a confessor, and remained with him till after the hour of noon, taking little or no refreshment. The officers of justice became impatient; but their eagerness was sternly rebuked by the soldiery, many of whom, having served under Gonzalo's banner, were touched with pity for his misfortunes.

When the chieftain came forth to execution, he showed in his dress the same love of magnificence and display as in happier days. Over his doublet he wore a superb cloak of yellow velvet, stiff with gold embroidery, while his head was protected by a cap of the same materials, richly decorated, in like manner, with ornaments of gold.[12] In this gaudy attire

cupied Cuzco; and the kind treatment he experienced from them, owing, doubtless, to his father's position in the rebel army, he has well repaid by depicting their portraits in the favorable colors in which they appeared to his young imagination. But the garrulous old man has recorded several individual instances of atrocity in the career of Carbajal, which form but an indifferent commentary on the correctness of his general assertions in respect to his character.

[10] "Fue maior sufridor de trabajos, que requeria su edad, porque à maravilla se quitaba las Armas de Dia, ni de Noche, i quando era necesario, tampoco se acostaba, ni dormia mas de quanto recostado en vna Silla, se le cansaba la mano en que arrimaba la Cabeça." Zarate, Conq. del Peru, lib. 5, cap. 14.

[11] Pedro Pizarro, who seems to have entertained feelings not unfriendly to Carbajal, thus sums up his character in a few words. "Era mui lenguaz: hablaba muy discretamente y á gusto de los que le oian: era hombre sagaz, cruel, bien entendido en la guerra. . . . . . Este Carbajal era tan sabio que decian tenia familiar." Descub. y Conq., MS.

[12] "Al tiempo que lo mataron, diò al Verdugo toda la Ropa, que traìa que era

he mounted his mule, and the sentence was so far relaxed that his arms were suffered to remain unshackled. He was escorted by a goodly number of priests and friars, who held up the crucifix before his eyes, while he carried in his own hand an image of the Virgin. She had ever been the peculiar object of Pizarro's devotion; so much so, that those who knew him best in the hour of his prosperity were careful, when they had a petition, to prefer it in the name of the blessed Mary.

Pizarro's lips were frequently pressed to the emblem of his divinity, while his eyes were bent on the crucifix in apparent devotion, heedless of the objects around him. On reaching the scaffold, he ascended it with a firm step, and asked leave to address a few words to the soldiery gathered round it. "There are many among you," said he, "who have grown rich on my brother's bounty, and my own. Yet, of all my riches, nothing remains to me but the garments I have on; and even these are not mine, but the property of the executioner. I am without means, therefore, to purchase a mass for the welfare of my soul; and I implore you, by the remembrance of past benefits, to extend this charity to me when I am gone, that it may be well with you in the hour of death." A profound silence reigned throughout the martial multitude, broken only by sighs and groans, as they listened to Pizarro's request; and it was faithfully responded to, since, after his death, masses were said in many of the towns for the welfare of the departed chieftain.

Then, kneeling down before a crucifix placed on a table, Pizarro remained for some minutes absorbed in prayer; after which, addressing the soldier who was to act as the minister of justice, he calmly bade him "do his duty with a steady hand." He refused to have his eyes bandaged, and, bending forward his neck, submitted it to the sword of the executioner, who struck off the head with a single blow, so true that the body remained for some moments in the same erect posture as in life.[13] The head was taken to Lima, where it was set in a cage or frame, and then fixed on a gibbet by the side of Carbajal's. On it was placed a label, bearing,—"This is the head of the traitor Gonzalo Pizarro, who rebelled in Peru against his sovereign, and battled in the cause of tyranny and treason against the royal standard in the valley of Xaquixaguana."[14] His large estates, including the rich mines in Potosí, were confiscated; his mansion in Lima was razed to the ground, the place strewed with

mui rica, i de mucho valor, porque tenia vna Ropa de Armas de Terciopelo amarillo, casi toda cubierta de Chaperia de Oro, i vn Chapeo de la misma forma." Zarate, Conq. del Peru, lib. 7, cap. 8.

[13] "The executioner," says Garcilasso, with a simile more expressive than elegant, "did his work as cleanly as if he had been slicing off a head of lettuce!" "De vn reues le cortò la cabeça con tanta facilidad, como si fuera vna hoja de lechuga, y se quedò con ella en la mano, y tardò el cuerpo algun espacio en caer en el suelo." Garcilasso, Com. Real., Parte 2, lib. 5, cap. 43.

[14] "Esta es la cabeza del traidor de Gonzalo Pizarro que se hizo justicia del en el valle de Aquixaguana, donde dió batalla campal contra el estandarte real queriendo defender su traicion e tirania: ninguno sea osado de la quitar de aqui so pena de muerte natural." Zarate, MS.

salt, and a stone pillar set up, with an inscription interdicting any one from building on a spot which had been profaned by the residence of a traitor.

Gonzalo's remains were not exposed to the indignities inflicted on Carbajal's, whose quarters were hung in chains on the four great roads leading to Cuzco. Centeno saved Pizarro's body from being stripped, by redeeming his costly raiment from the executioner, and in this sumptuous shroud it was laid in the chapel of the convent of Our Lady of Mercy in Cuzco. It was the same spot where, side by side, lay the bloody remains of the Almagros, father and son, who in like manner had perished by the hand of justice, and were indebted to private charity for their burial. All these were now consigned "to the same grave," says the historian, with some bitterness, "as if Peru could not afford land enough for a burial-place to its conquerors." [15]

Gonzalo Pizarro had reached only his forty-second year at the time of his death,—being just half the space allotted to his follower Carbajal. He was the youngest of the remarkable family to whom Spain was indebted for the acquisition of Peru. He came over to the country with his brother Francisco, on the return of the latter from his visit to Castile. Gonzalo was present in all the remarkable passages of the Conquest. He witnessed the seizure of Atahuallpa, took an active part in suppressing the insurrection of the Incas, and especially in the reduction of Charcas. He afterwards led the disastrous expedition to the Amazon; and, finally, headed the memorable rebellion which ended so fatally to himself. There are but few men whose lives abound in such wild and romantic adventure, and, for the most part, crowned with success. The space which he occupies in the page of history is altogether disproportioned to his talents. It may be in some measure ascribed to fortune, but still more to those showy qualities which form a sort of substitute for mental talent, and which secured his popularity with the vulgar.

He had a brilliant exterior; excelled in all martial exercises; rode well, fenced well, managed his lance to perfection, was a first-rate marksman with the arquebuse, and added the accomplishment of being an excellent draughtsman. He was bold and chivalrous, even to temerity; courted adventure, and was always in the front of danger. He was a knight-errant, in short, in the most extravagant sense of the term, and, "mounted on his favorite charger," says one who had often seen him, "made no more account of a squadron of Indians than of a swarm of flies." [16]

---

[15] "Y las sepolturas vna sola auiendo de ser tres: que aun la tierra parece que les faltò para auer los de cubrir." Garcilasso, Com. Real., Parte 2, lib. 5, cap. 43.

For the tragic particulars of the preceding pages, see Ibid., cap. 39-43.—Relacion del Lic. Gasca, MS.—Carta de Valdivia, MS.—MS. de Caravantes.—Pedro Pizarro, Descub. y Conq., MS.—Gomara, Hist. de las Indias, cap. 186.—Fernandez, Hist. del Peru, Parte 1, lib. 2, cap. 91.—Zarate, Conq. del Peru, lib. 7, cap. 8.—Herrera, Hist. General, dec. 8, lib. 4, cap. 16.

[16] "Quando Gonçalo Pizarro, que aya gloria, se veya en su zaynillo, no hazia mas

While thus, by his brilliant exploits and showy manners, he captivated the imaginations of his countrymen, he won their hearts no less by his soldier-like frankness, his trust in their fidelity,—too often abused,— and his liberal largesses; for Pizarro, though avaricious of the property of others, was, like the Roman conspirator, prodigal of his own. This was his portrait in happier days, when his heart had not been corrupted by success; for that some change was wrought on him by his prosperity is well attested. His head was made giddy by his elevation; and it is proof of a want of talent equal to his success, that he knew not how to profit by it. Obeying the dictates of his own rash judgment, he rejected the warnings of his wisest counsellors, and relied with blind confidence on his destiny. Garcilasso imputes this to the malignant influence of the stars.[17] But the superstitious chronicler might have better explained it by a common principle of human nature; by the presumption nourished by success; the insanity, as the Roman, or rather Grecian, proverb calls it, with which the gods afflict men when they design to ruin them.[18]

Gonzalo was without education, except such as he had picked up in the rough school of war. He had little even of that wisdom which springs from natural shrewdness and insight into character. In all this he was inferior to his elder brothers, although he fully equalled them in ambition. Had he possessed a tithe of their sagacity, he would not have madly persisted in rebellion, after the coming of the president. Before this period, he represented the people. Their interests and his were united. He had their support, for he was contending for the redress of their wrongs. When these were redressed by the government, there was nothing to contend for. From that time, he was battling only for himself. The people had no part nor interest in the contest. Without a common sympathy to bind them together, was it strange that they should fall off from him, like leaves in winter, and leave him exposed, a bare and sapless trunk, to the fury of the tempest?

Cepeda, more criminal than Pizarro, since he had both superior education and intelligence, which he employed only to mislead his commander, did not long survive him. He had come to the country in an office of high responsibility. His first step was to betray the viceroy whom he was sent to support; his next was to betray the Audience with whom he should have acted; and lastly, he betrayed the leader whom he most affected to serve. His whole career was treachery to his own government. His life was one long perfidy.

---

caso de esquadrones de Yndios, que si fueran de moscas." Garcilasso, Parte 2, lib. 5, cap. 43.

[17] "Dezian que no era falta de entendimiento, pues lo tenia bastante, sino que deuia de ser sobra de influencia de signos y planetas, que le cegauan y forcauan a que pusiesse la garganta al cuchillo." Garcilasso, Com. Real., Parte 2, lib. 5, cap. 33.

[18] " Ὅταν δὲ Δαίμων ἀνδρὶ πορσύνῃ κακὰ,
Τὸν νοῦν ἔβλαψε πρῶτον."
Eurip. Fragmenta.

After his surrender, several of the cavaliers, disgusted at his cold-blooded apostasy, would have persuaded Gasca to send him to execution along with his commander; but the president refused, in consideration of the signal service he had rendered the Crown by his defection. He was put under arrest, however, and sent to Castile. There he was arraigned for high-treason. He made a plausible defence, and as he had friends at court, it is not improbable he would have been acquitted; but, before the trial was terminated, he died in prison. It was the retributive justice not always to be found in the affairs of this world.[19]

Indeed, it so happened, that several of those who had been most forward to abandon the cause of Pizarro survived their commander but a short time. The gallant Centeno, and the Licentiate Carbajal, who deserted him near Lima, and bore the royal standard on the field of Xaquixaguana, both died within a year after Pizarro. Hinojosa was assassinated but two years later in La Plata; and his old comrade Valdivia, after a series of brilliant exploits in Chili, which furnished her most glorious theme to the epic Muse of Castile, was cut off by the invincible warriors of Arauco. The Manes of Pizarro were amply avenged.

Acosta, and three or four other cavaliers who surrendered with Gonzalo, were sent to execution on the same day with their chief; and Gasca, on the morning following the dismal tragedy, broke up his quarters and marched with his whole army to Cuzco, where he was received by the politic people with the same enthusiasm which they had so recently shown to his rival. He found there a number of the rebel army who had taken refuge in the city after their late defeat, where they were immediately placed under arrest. Proceedings, by Gasca's command, were instituted against them. The principal cavaliers, to the number of ten or twelve, were executed; others were banished or sent to the galleys. The same rigorous decrees were passed against such as had fled and were not yet taken; and the estates of all were confiscated. The estates of the rebels supplied a fund for the recompense of the loyal.[20] The execution of justice may seem to have been severe; but Gasca was willing that the rod should fall heavily on those who had so often rejected his proffers of grace. Lenity was wasted on a rude, licentious soldiery, who hardly recognized the existence of government, unless they felt its rigor.

A new duty now devolved on the president,—that of rewarding his faithful followers,—not less difficult, as it proved, than that of punishing the guilty. The applicants were numerous; since every one who had raised a finger in behalf of the government claimed his reward. They

---

[19] The cunning lawyer prepared so plausible an argument in his own justification, that Yllescas, the celebrated historian of the Popes, declares that no one who read the paper attentively, but must rise from the perusal of it with an entire conviction of the writer's innocence, and of his unshaken loyalty to the Crown. See the passage quoted by Garcilasso, Com. Real., Parte 2, lib. 6, cap. 10.

[20] Pedro Pizarro, Descub. y Conq., MS.—Fernandez, Hist. del Peru, Parte 1, lib 2, cap. 91.—Carta de Valdivia, MS.—Zarate, Conq. del Peru, lib. 7, cap. 8.—Relacion del Lic. Gasca, MS.

urged their demands with a clamorous importunity which perplexed the good president, and consumed every moment of his time.

Disgusted with this unprofitable state of things, Gasca resolved to rid himself of the annoyance at once, by retiring to the valley of Guaynarima, about twelve leagues distant from the city, and there digesting, in quiet, a scheme of compensation, adjusted to the merits of the parties. He was accompanied only by his secretary, and by Loaysa, now archbishop of Lima, a man of sense, and well acquainted with the affairs of the country. In this seclusion the president remained three months, making a careful examination into the conflicting claims, and apportioning the forfeitures among the parties according to their respective services. The *repartimientos*, it should be remarked, were usually granted only for life, and, on the death of the incumbent, reverted to the Crown, to be reassigned or retained at its pleasure.

When his arduous task was completed, Gasca determined to withdraw to Lima, leaving the instrument of partition with the archbishop, to be communicated to the army. Notwithstanding all the care that had been taken for an equitable adjustment, Gasca was aware that it was impossible to satisfy the demands of a jealous and irritable soldiery, where each man would be likely to exaggerate his own deserts, while he underrated those of his comrades; and he did not care to expose himself to importunities and complaints that could serve no other purpose than to annoy him.

On his departure, the troops were called together by the archbishop in the cathedral, to learn the contents of the schedule intrusted to him. A discourse was first preached by a worthy Dominican, the prior of Arequipa, in which the reverend father expatiated on the virtue of contentment, the duty of obedience, and the folly, as well as wickedness, of an attempt to resist the constituted authorities,—topics, in short, which he conceived might best conciliate the good-will and conformity of his audience.

A letter from the president was then read from the pulpit. It was addressed to the officers and soldiers of the army. The writer began with briefly exposing the difficulties of his task, owing to the limited amount of the gratuities, and the great number and services of the claimants. He had given the matter the most careful consideration, he said, and endeavored to assign to each his share, according to his deserts, without prejudice or partiality. He had, no doubt, fallen into errors, but he trusted his followers would excuse them, when they reflected that he had done according to the best of his poor abilities; and all, he believed, would do him the justice to acknowledge he had not been influenced by motives of personal interest. He bore emphatic testimony to the services they had rendered to the good cause, and concluded with the most affectionate wishes for their future prosperity and happiness. The letter was dated at Guaynarima, August 17, 1548, and bore the simple signature of the Licentiate Gasca.[21]

---

[21] MS. de Caravantes.—Pedro Pizarro, Descub. y Conq., MS.—Zarate, Conq. del Peru, lib. 7, cap. 9.—Fernandez, Hist. del Peru, Parte 1, lib. 2, cap. 92.

The archbishop next read the paper containing the president's award. The annual rent of the estates to be distributed amounted to a hundred and thirty thousand *pesos ensayados;*[22] a large amount, considering the worth of money in that day,—in any other country than Peru, where money was a drug.[23]

The *repartimientos* thus distributed varied in value from one hundred to thirty-five hundred *pesos* of yearly rent; all, apparently, graduated with the nicest precision to the merits of the parties. The number of pensioners was about two hundred and fifty; for the fund would not have sufficed for general distribution, nor were the services of the greater part deemed worthy of such a mark of consideration.[24]

The effect produced by the document, on men whose minds were filled with the most indefinite expectations, was just such as had been anticipated by the president. It was received with a general murmur of disapprobation. Even those who had got more than they expected were discontented, on comparing their condition with that of their comrades, whom they thought still better remunerated in proportion to their deserts. They especially inveighed against the preference shown to the old partisans of Gonzalo Pizarro—as Hinojosa, Centeno, and Aldana—over those who had always remained loyal to the Crown. There was some ground for such a preference; for none had rendered so essential services in crushing the rebellion; and it was these services that Gasca proposed to recompense. To reward every man who had proved himself

[22] The *peso ensayado,* according to Garcilasso, was one fifth more in value than the Castilian ducat. Com. Real., Parte 2, lib. 6, cap. 3.

[23] "Entre los cavalleros capitanes y soldados que le ayudaron en esta ocasion repartió el Presidente Pedro de la Gasca 135,000 pesos ensayados de renta que estaban vacos, y no un millon y tantos mil pesos, como dize Diego Fernandez, que escrivió en Palencia estas alteraciones, y de quien lo tomó Antonio de Herrera: y porque esta ocasion fué la segunda en que los benemeritos del Pirú fundan con razon los servicios de sus pasados, porque mediante esta batalla aseguro la corona de Castilla las provincias mas ricas que tiene en America, pondré sus nombres para que se conserbe con certeza su memoria como pareze en el auto original que proveyó en el asiento de Guainarima cerca de la ciudad del Cuzco en diez y siete de Agosto de 1548, que está en los archivos del govierno." MS. de Caravantes.

The sum mentioned in the text, as thus divided among the army, falls very far short of the amount stated by Garcilasso, Fernandez, Zarate, and, indeed, every other writer on the subject, none of whom estimate it at less than a million of *pesos.* But Caravantes, from whom I have taken it, copies the original act of partition preserved in the royal archives. Yet Garcilasso de la Vega ought to have been well informed of the value of these estates, which, according to him, far exceeded the estimate given in the schedule. Thus, for instance, Hinojosa, he says, obtained from the share of lands and rich mines assigned to him from the property of Gonzalo Pizarro no less than 200,000 *pesos* annually, while Aldana, the Licentiate Carbajal, and others, had estates which yielded them from 10,000 to 50,000 *pesos.* (Ibid., ubi supra.) It is impossible to reconcile these monstrous discrepancies. No sum seems to have been too large for the credulity of the ancient chronicler; and the imagination of the reader is so completely bewildered by the actual riches of this El Dorado, that it is difficult to adjust his faith by any standard of probability.

[24] Caravantes has transcribed from the original act a full catalogue of the pensioners, with the amount of the sums set against each of their names.

loyal, simply for his loyalty, would have frittered away the donative into fractions that would be of little value to any.[25]

It was in vain, however, that the archbishop, seconded by some of the principal cavaliers, endeavored to infuse a more contented spirit into the multitude. They insisted that the award should be rescinded, and a new one made on more equitable principles; threatening, moreover, that, if this were not done by the president, they would take the redress of the matter into their own hands. Their discontent, fomented by some mischievous persons who thought to find their account in it, at length proceeded so far as to menace a mutiny; and it was not suppressed till the commander of Cuzco sentenced one of the ringleaders to death, and several others to banishment. The iron soldiery of the Conquest required an iron hand to rule them.

Meanwhile, the president had continued his journey towards Lima; and on the way was everywhere received by the people with an enthusiasm, the more grateful to his heart that he felt he had deserved it. As he drew near the capital, the loyal inhabitants prepared to give him a magnificent reception. The whole population came forth from the gates, led by the authorities of the city, with Aldana as corregidor at their head. Gasca rode on a mule, dressed in his ecclesiastical robes. On his right, borne on a horse richly caparisoned, was the royal seal, in a box curiously chased and ornamented. A gorgeous canopy of brocade was supported above his head by the officers of the municipality, who, in their robes of crimson velvet, walked bareheaded by his side. Gay troops of dancers, clothed in fantastic dresses of gaudy-colored silk, followed the procession, strewing flowers and chanting verses as they went, in honor of the president. They were designed as emblematical of the different cities of the colony; and they bore legends or mottoes in rhyme on their caps, intimating their loyal devotion to the Crown, and evincing much more loyalty in their composition, it may be added, than poetical merit.[26] In this way, without beat of drum, or noise of artillery, or any of the rude accompaniments of war, the good president made his peaceful entry into the City of the Kings, while the air was rent with the acclamations of the people, who hailed him as their "Father and Deliverer, the Saviour of their country!" [27]

But, however grateful was this homage to Gasca's heart, he was not a

---

[25] The president found an ingenious way of remunerating several of his followers, by bestowing on them the hands of the rich widows of the cavaliers who had perished in the war. The inclinations of the ladies do not seem to have been always consulted in this politic arrangement. See Garcilasso, Com. Real., Parte 2, lib. 6, cap. 3.

[26] Fernandez has collected these flowers of colonial poesy, which prove that the old Conquerors were much more expert with the sword than with the pen. Hist. del Peru, Parte 1, lib. 2, cap. 93.

[27] "Fue recibimiento mui solemne, con universal alegria del Pueblo, por verse libre de Tiranos; i toda la Gente, à voces, bendecia al Presidente, i le llamaban: Padre, Restaurador, i Pacificador, dando gracias à Dios, por haver vengado las injurias hechas à su Divina Magestad." Herrera, Hist. General, dec. 8, lib. 4, cap. 17.

man to waste his time in idle vanities. He now thought only by what means he could eradicate the seeds of disorder which shot up so readily in this fruitful soil, and how he could place the authority of the government on a permanent basis. By virtue of his office, he presided over the Royal Audience, the great judicial, and, indeed, executive tribunal of the colony; and he gave great despatch to the business, which had much accumulated during the late disturbances. In the unsettled state of property, there was abundant subject for litigation; but, fortunately, the new Audience was composed of able, upright judges, who labored diligently with their chief to correct the mischief caused by the misrule of their predecessors.

Neither was Gasca unmindful of the unfortunate natives; and he occupied himself earnestly with that difficult problem,—the best means practicable of ameliorating their condition. He sent a number of commissioners, as visitors, into different parts of the country, whose business it was to inspect the *encomiendas*, and ascertain the manner in which the Indians were treated, by conversing not only with the proprietors, but with the natives themselves. They were also to learn the nature and extent of the tributes paid in former times by the vassals of the Incas.[28]

In this way, a large amount of valuable information was obtained, which enabled Gasca, with the aid of a council of ecclesiastics and jurists, to digest a uniform system of taxation for the natives, lighter even than that imposed on them by the Peruvian princes. The president would gladly have relieved the conquered races from the obligations of personal service; but, on mature consideration, this was judged impracticable in the present state of the country, since the colonists, more especially in the tropical regions, looked to the natives for the performance of labor, and the latter, it was found from experience, would not work at all, unless compelled to do so. The president, however, limited the amount of service to be exacted with great precision, so that it was in the nature of a moderate personal tax. No Peruvian was to be required to change his place of residence, from the climate to which he had been accustomed, to another; a fruitful source of discomfort, as well as of disease, in past times. By these various regulations, the condition of the natives, though not such as had been contemplated by the sanguine philanthropy of Las Casas, was improved far more than was compatible with the craving demands of the colonists; and all the firmness of the Audience was required to enforce provisions so unpalatable to the latter. Still they were enforced. Slavery, in its most odious sense, was no longer tolerated in Peru. The term "slave" was not recognized as having rela-

---

[28] "El Presidente Gasca mando visitar todas las provincias y repartimientos deste reyno, nombrando para ello personas de autoridad y de quien se tenia entendido que tenian conoscimiento de la tierra que se les encargavan, que ha de ser la principal calidad, que se ha buscar en la persona, a quien se comete semejante negocio despues que sea Cristiana: lo segundo se les dio instruccion de lo que hauian de averiguar, que fueron muchas cosas: el numero, las haciendas, los tratos y grangerias, la calidad de la gente y de sus tierras y comarca, y lo que davan de tributo." Ondegardo, Rel. Prim., MS.

tion to her institutions; and the historian of the Indies makes the proud boast,—it should have been qualified by the limitations I have noticed, —that every Indian vassal might aspire to the rank of a freeman.[29]

Besides these reforms, Gasca introduced several in the municipal government of the cities, and others yet more important in the management of the finances, and in the mode of keeping the accounts. By these and other changes in the internal economy of the colony, he placed the administration on a new basis, and greatly facilitated the way for a more sure and orderly government by his successors. As a final step, to secure the repose of the country after he was gone, he detached some of the more aspiring cavaliers on distant expeditions, trusting that they would draw off the light and restless spirits, who might otherwise gather together and disturb the public tranquillity; as we sometimes see the mists which have been scattered by the genial influence of the sun become condensed, and settle into a storm, on his departure.[30]

Gasca had been now more than fifteen months in Lima, and nearly three years had elapsed since his first entrance into Peru. In that time, he had accomplished the great objects of his mission. When he landed, he found the colony in a state of anarchy, or rather organized rebellion under a powerful and popular chief. He came without funds or forces to support him. The former he procured through the credit which he established in his good faith; the latter he won over by argument and persuasion from the very persons to whom they had been confided by his rival. Thus he turned the arms of that rival against himself. By a calm appeal to reason he wrought a change in the hearts of the people; and, without costing a drop of blood to a single loyal subject, he suppressed a rebellion which had menaced Spain with the loss of the wealthiest of her provinces. He had punished the guilty, and in their spoils found the means to recompense the faithful. He had, moreover, so well husbanded the resources of the country, that he was enabled to pay off the large loan he had negotiated with the merchants of the colony, for the expenses of the war, exceeding nine hundred thousand *pesos de oro*.[31] Nay, more, by his economy he had saved a million and a half of ducats for the government, which for some years had received nothing from Peru; and he now proposed to carry back this acceptable treasure to swell the royal coffers.[32] All this had been accomplished without the cost of out-

[29] "El Presidente, i el Audiencia dieron tales ordenes, que este negocio se asentò, de manera, que para adelante no se platicò mas este nombre de Esclavos, sino que la libertad fue general por todo el Reino." Herrera, Hist. Gen., dec. 8, lib. 5, cap. 7

[30] MS. de Caravantes.—Gomara, Hist. de las Indias, cap. 187.—Fernandez, Hist. del Peru, Parte 1, lib. 2, cap. 93-95.—Zarate, Conq. del Peru, lib. 7, cap. 10.

[31] "Recogiò tanta suma de dinero, que pagò novecientos mil pesos de Oro, que se hallò haver gastado, desde el Dia que entrò en Panamá, hasta que se acabò la Guerra, los quales tomò prestados." Herrera, Hist. General, dec. 8, lib. 5, cap. 7.—Zarate, Conq. del Peru, lib. 7, cap. 10.

[32] "Aviendo pagado el Presidente las costas de la guerra que fueron muchas, remitió á S. M. y lo llevó consigo 264,422 marcos de plata, que á seis ducados valieron 1 million 588,332 ducados." MS., de Caravantes.

fit or salary, or any charge to the Crown except that of his own frugal expenditure.[33] The country was now in a state of tranquillity. Gasca felt that his work was done; and that he was free to gratify his natural long-ing to return to his native land.

Before his departure, he arranged a distribution of those *repartimien-tos* which had lapsed to the Crown during the past year by the death of the incumbents. Life was short in Peru; since those who lived by the sword, if they did not die by the sword, too often fell early victims to the hardships incident to their adventurous career. Many were the ap-plicants for the new bounty of government; and, as among them were some of those who had been discontented with the former partition, Gasca was assailed by remonstrances, and sometimes by reproaches couched in no very decorous or respectful language. But they had no power to disturb his equanimity; he patiently listened, and replied to all in the mild tone of expostulation best calculated to turn away wrath; "by this victory over himself," says an old writer, "acquiring more real glory, than by all his victories over his enemies." [34]

An incident occurred on the eve of his departure, touching in itself, and honorable to the parties concerned. The Indian caciques of the neighboring country, mindful of the great benefits he had rendered their people, presented him with a considerable quantity of plate in token of their gratitude. But Gasca refused to receive it, though in doing so he gave much concern to the Peruvians, who feared they had un-wittingly fallen under his displeasure.

Many of the principal colonists, also, from the same wish to show their sense of his important services, sent to him, after he had em-barked, a magnificent donative of fifty thousand gold *castellanos*. "As he had taken leave of Peru," they said, "there could be no longer any ground for declining it." But Gasca was as decided in his rejection of this present, as he had been of the other. "He had come to the country," he remarked, "to serve the king, and to secure the blessings of peace to the inhabitants; and now that, by the favor of Heaven, he had been permitted to accomplish this, he would not dishonor the cause by any act that might throw suspicion on the purity of his motives." Notwith-standing his refusal, the colonists contrived to secrete the sum of twenty thousand *castellanos* on board his vessel, with the idea, that, once in his own country, with his mission concluded, the president's scruples would be removed. Gasca did, indeed, accept the donative; for he felt that it would be ungracious to send it back; but it was only till he could ascer-

---

[33] "No tubo ni quiso salario el Presidente Gasca sino cedula para que á un mayor-domo suyo diosen los Oficiales reales lo necesario de la real Hacienda, que como pareze de los quadernos de su gasto fué muy moderado." (MS. de Caravantes.) Gasca, it appears, was most exact in keeping the accounts of his disbursements for the expenses of himself and household, from the time he embarked for the colonies.

[34] "En lo qual hizo mas que en vencer y ganar todo aquel Ymperio: porque fue vencerse assi proprio." Garcilasso, Com. Real., Parte 2, lib. 6, cap. 7.

tain the relatives of the donors, when he distributed it among the most needy.[35]

Having now settled all his affairs, the president committed the government, until the arrival of a viceroy, to his faithful partners of the Royal Audience; and in January, 1550, he embarked with the royal treasure on board of a squadron for Panamá. He was accompanied to the shore by a numerous crowd of the inhabitants, cavaliers and common people, persons of all ages and conditions, who followed to take their last look of their benefactor, and watch with straining eyes the vessel that bore him away from their land.

His voyage was prosperous, and early in March the president reached his destined port. He stayed there only till he could muster horses and mules sufficient to carry the treasure across the mountains; for he knew that this part of the country abounded in wild, predatory spirits, who would be sorely tempted to some act of violence by a knowledge of the wealth which he had with him. Pushing forward, therefore, he crossed the rugged Isthmus, and, after a painful march, arrived in safety at Nombre de Dios.

The event justified his apprehensions. He had been gone but three days, when a ruffian horde, after murdering the bishop of Guatemala, broke into Panamá with the design of inflicting the same fate on the president, and of seizing the booty. No sooner were the tidings communicated to Gasca, than, with his usual energy, he levied a force and prepared to march to the relief of the invaded capital. But Fortune—or, to speak more correctly, Providence—favored him here, as usual; and, on the eve of his departure, he learned that the marauders had been met by the citizens, and discomfited with great slaughter. Disbanding his forces, therefore, he equipped a fleet of nineteen vessels to transport himself and the royal treasure to Spain, where he arrived in safety, entering the harbor of Seville after a little more than four years from the period when he had sailed from the same port.[36]

Great was the sensation throughout the country caused by his arrival. Men could hardly believe that results so momentous had been accomplished in so short a time by a single individual,—a poor ecclesiastic, who, unaided by government, had, by his own strength, as it were, put down a rebellion which had so long set the arms of Spain at defiance!

The emperor was absent in Flanders. He was overjoyed on learning the complete success of Gasca's mission; and not less satisfied with the tidings of the treasure he had brought with him; for the exchequer, rarely filled to overflowing, had been exhausted by the recent troubles in Germany. Charles instantly wrote to the president, requiring his presence at court, that he might learn from his own lips the particulars of his expedition. Gasca, accordingly, attended by a numerous retinue

[35] Fernandez, Hist. del Peru, Parte 1, lib. 2, cap. 95.
[36] MS. de Caravantes.—Gomara, Hist. de las Indias, cap. 183.—Fernandez, Hist. del Peru, Parte 2, lib. 1, cap. 10.—Zarate, Conq. del Peru, lib. 7, cap. 13.—Herrera, Hist. General, dec. 8, lib. 6, cap. 17.

of nobles and cavaliers,—for who does not pay homage to him whom the king delighteth to honor?—embarked at Barcelona, and, after a favorable voyage, joined the Court in Flanders.

He was received by his royal master, who fully appreciated his services, in a manner most grateful to his feelings; and not long afterward he was raised to the bishopric of Palencia,—a mode of acknowledgment best suited to his character and deserts. Here he remained till 1561, when he was promoted to the vacant see of Siguenza. The rest of his days he passed peacefully in the discharge of his episcopal functions; honored by his sovereign, and enjoying the admiration and respect of his countrymen.[37]

In his retirement, he was still consulted by the government in matters of importance relating to the Indies. The disturbances of that unhappy land were renewed, though on a much smaller scale than before, soon after the president's departure. They were chiefly caused by discontent with the *repartimientos*, and with the constancy of the Audience in enforcing the benevolent restrictions as to the personal services of the natives. But these troubles subsided, after a very few years, under the wise rule of the Mendozas,—two successive viceroys of that illustrious house which has given so many of its sons to the service of Spain. Under their rule, the mild yet determined policy was pursued, of which Gasca had set the example. The ancient distractions of the country were permanently healed. With peace, prosperity returned within the borders of Peru; and the consciousness of the beneficent results of his labors may have shed a ray of satisfaction, as it did of glory, over the evening of the president's life.

That life was brought to a close in November, 1567, at an age, probably not far from the one fixed by the sacred writer as the term of human existence.[38] He died at Valladolid, and was buried in the church of Santa Maria Magdalena, in that city, which he had built and liberally endowed. His monument, surmounted by the sculptured effigy of a priest in his sacerdotal robes, is still to be seen there, attracting the admiration of the traveller by the beauty of its execution. The banners taken from Gonzalo Pizarro on the field of Xaquixaguana were suspended over his tomb, as the trophies of his memorable mission to Peru.[39] The banners have long since mouldered into dust, with the remains of him who slept

---

[37] Ibid., ubi supra.—MS. de Caravantes.—Gomara, Hist. de las Indias, cap. 182.—Fernandez, Hist. del Peru, Parte 2, lib. 1, cap. 10.—Zarate, Conq. del Peru, lib. 7, cap. 13.

[38] I have met with no account of the year in which Gasca was born; but an inscription on his portrait in the sacristy of St. Mary Magdalene at Valladolid, from which the engraving prefixed to this volume is taken, states that he died in 1567, at the age of seventy-one. This is perfectly consistent with the time of life at which he had probably arrived when we find him a collegiate at Salamanca, in the year 1522.

[39] "Murió en Valladolid, donde mandó enterrar su cuerpo en la Iglesia de la advocacion de la Magdalena, que hizo edificar en equalla ciudad, donde se pusieron las vanderas que ganó á Gonzalo Pizarro." MS de Caravantes.

beneath them; but the memory of his good deeds will endure for ever.[4]

Gasca was plain in person, and his countenance was far from comely. He was awkward and ill-proportioned; for his limbs were too long for his body,—so that when he rode, he appeared to be much shorter than he really was.[41] His dress was humble, his manners simple, and there was nothing imposing in his presence. But, on a nearer intercourse, there was a charm in his discourse that effaced every unfavorable impression produced by his exterior, and won the hearts of his hearers.

The president's character may be thought to have been sufficiently portrayed in the history already given of his life. It presented a combination of qualities which generally serve to neutralize each other, but which were mixed in such proportions in him as to give it additional strength. He was gentle, yet resolute; by nature intrepid, yet preferring to rely on the softer arts of policy. He was frugal in his personal expenditure, and economical in the public; yet caring nothing for riches on his own account, and never stinting his bounty when the public good required it. He was benevolent and placable, yet could deal sternly with the impenitent offender; lowly in his deportment, yet with a full measure of that self-respect which springs from conscious rectitude of purpose; modest and unpretending, yet not shrinking from the most difficult enterprises; deferring greatly to others, yet, in the last resort, relying mainly on himself; moving with deliberation,—patiently waiting his time; but, when that came, bold, prompt, and decisive.

Gasca, was not a man of genius, in the vulgar sense of that term. At least, no one of his intellectual powers seems to have received an extraordinary development, beyond what is found in others. He was not a great writer, nor a great orator, nor a great general. He did not affect to be either. He committed the care of his military matters to military men; of ecclesiastical to the clergy; and his civil and judicial concerns he reposed on the members of the Audience. He was not one of those little great men who aspire to do every thing themselves, under the conviction that nothing can be done so well by others. But the president was a keen judge of character. Whatever might be the office, he selected the best man for it. He did more. He assured himself of the fidelity of his

---

[40] The memory of his achievements has not been left entirely to the care of the historian. It is but a few years since the character and administration of Gasca formed the subject of an elaborate panegyric from one of the most distinguished statesmen in the British parliament. (See Lord Brougham's speech on the maltreatment of the North American colonies, February, 1838.) The enlightened Spaniard of our day, who contemplates with sorrow the excesses committed by his countrymen of the sixteenth century in the New World, may feel an honest pride, that in this company of dark spirits should be found one to whom the present generation may turn as to the brightest model of integrity and wisdom.

[41] "Era muy pequeño de cuerpo con estraña hechura, que de la cintura abaxo tenia tanto cuerpo, como qualquiera hombre alto, y de la cintura al hombro no tenia vna tercia. Andando a cauallo parescia a vn mas pequeño de lo que era, porque todo era piernas: de rostro era muy feo: pero lo que la naturaleza le nego de las dotes del cuerpo, se los dobló en los del animo." Garcilasso, Com. Real., Parte 2, lib. 5 cap. 2.

agents, presided at their deliberations; dictated a general line of policy, and thus infused a spirit of unity into their plans, which made all move in concert to the accomplishment of one grand result.

A distinguishing feature of his mind was his common sense,—the best substitute for genius in a ruler who has the destinies of his fellow-men at his disposal, and more indispensable than genius itself. In Gasca, the different qualities were blended in such harmony, that there was no room for excess. They seemed to regulate each other. While his sympathy with mankind taught him the nature of their wants, his reason suggested to what extent these were capable of relief, as well as the best mode of effecting it. He did not waste his strength on illusory schemes of benevolence, like Las Casas, on the one hand; nor did he countenance the selfish policy of the colonists, on the other. He aimed at the practicable,—the greatest good praticable.

In accomplishing his objects, he disclaimed force equally with fraud. He trusted for success to his power over the convictions of his hearers; and the source of this power was the confidence he inspired in his own integrity. Amidst all the calumnies of faction, no imputation was ever cast on the integrity of Gasca.[42] No wonder that a virtue so rare should be of high price in Peru.

There are some men whose characters have been so wonderfully adapted to the peculiar crisis in which they appeared, that they seem to have been specially designed for it by Providence. Such was Washington, in our own country, and Gasca in Peru. We can conceive of individuals with higher qualities, at least with higher intellectual qualities, than belonged to either of these great men. But it was the wonderful conformity of their characters to the exigencies of their situation, the perfect adaptation of the means to the end, that constituted the secret of their success; that enabled Gasca so gloriously to crush revolution, and Washington still more gloriously to achieve it.

Gasca's conduct on his first coming to the colonies affords the best illustration of his character. Had he come backed by a military array, or even clothed in the paraphernalia of authority, every heart and hand would have been closed against him. But the humble ecclesiastic excited no apprehension; and his enemies were already disarmed, before he had begun his approaches. Had Gasca, impatient of Hinojosa's tardiness, listened to the suggestions of those who advised his seizure, he would have brought his cause into jeopardy by this early display of violence. But he wisely chose to win over his enemy by operating on his conviction.

In like manner, he waited his time for making his entry into Peru. He suffered his communications to do their work in the minds of the people, and was careful not to thrust in the sickle before the harvest was ripe.

---

[42] "Fue tan recatado y estremado en esta virtud, que puesto que de muchos quedò mal quisto, quando del Perù se partio para España, por el repartimiento que hizo: con todo esso, jamas nadie dixo del, ni sospechò; que en esto, ni otra cosa, se vuiesse mouido por codicia." Fernandez, Hist. del Peru, Parte 1, lib. 2, cap. 95.

In this way, wherever he went, every thing was prepared for his coming; and when he set foot in Peru, the country was already his own.

After the dark and turbulent spirits with which we have been hitherto occupied, it is refreshing to dwell on a character like that of Gasca. In the long procession which has passed in review before us, we have seen only the mail-clad cavalier, brandishing his bloody lance, and mounted on his war-horse, riding over the helpless natives, or battling with his own friends and brothers; fierce, arrogant, and cruel, urged on by the lust of gold, or the scarce more honorable love of a bastard glory. Mingled with these qualities, indeed, we have seen sparkles of the chivalrous and romantic temper which belongs to the heroic age of Spain. But, with some honorable exceptions, it was the scum of her chivalry that resorted to Peru, and took service under the banner of the Pizarros. At the close of this long array of iron warriors, we behold the poor and humble missionary coming into the land on an errand of mercy, and everywhere proclaiming the glad tidings of peace. No warlike trumpet heralds his approach, nor is his course to be tracked by the groans of the wounded and the dying. The means he employs are in perfect harmony with his end. His weapons are argument and mild persuasion. It is the reason he would conquer, not the body. He wins his way by conviction, not by violence. It is a moral victory to which he aspires, more potent, and happily more permanent, than that of the blood-stained conqueror. As he thus calmly, and imperceptibly, as it were, comes to his great results, he may remind us of the slow, insensible manner in which Nature works out her great changes in the material world, that are to endure when the ravages of the hurricane are passed away and forgotten.

With the mission of Gasca terminates the history of the Conquest of Peru. The Conquest, indeed, strictly terminates with the suppression of the Peruvian revolt, when the strength, if not the spirit, of the Inca race was crushed for ever. The reader, however, might feel a natural curiosity to follow to its close the fate of the remarkable family who achieved the Conquest. Nor would the story of the invasion itself be complete without some account of the civil wars which grew out of it; which serve, moreover, as a moral commentary on preceding events, by showing that the indulgence of fierce, unbridled passions is sure to recoil, sooner or later, even in this life, on the heads of the guilty.

It is true, indeed, that the troubles of the country were renewed on the departure of Gasca. The waters had been too fearfully agitated to be stilled, at once, into a calm; but they gradually subsided, under the temperate rule of his successors, who wisely profited by his policy and example. Thus the influence of the good president remained after he was withdrawn from the scene of his labors; and Peru, hitherto so distracted, continued to enjoy as large a share of repose as any portion of the colonial empire of Spain. With the benevolent mission of Gasca, then, the historian of the Conquest may be permitted to terminate his labors, —with feelings not unlike those of the traveller who, having long

journeyed among the dreary forests and dangerous defiles of the mountains, at length emerges on some pleasant landscape smiling in tranquillity and peace.

Augustin de Zarate—a highly respectable authority, frequently cited in the later
portion of this work—was *Contador de Mercedes,* Comptroller of Accounts, for
Castile. This office he filled for fifteen years; after which he was sent by the government to Peru to examine into the state of the colonial finances, which had been
greatly deranged by the recent troubles, and to bring them, if possible, into order.

Zarate went out accordingly in the train of the viceroy Blasco Nuñez, and found
himself, through the passions of his imprudent leader, entangled, soon after his arrival, in the inextricable meshes of civil discord. In the struggle which ensued, he
remained with the Royal Audience; and we find him in Lima, on the approach
of Gonzalo Pizarro to that capital, when Zarate was deputed by the judges to wait
on the insurgent chief, and require him to disband his troops and withdraw to his
own estates. The historian executed the mission, for which he seems to have had
little relish, and which certainly was not without danger. From this period, we rarely
hear of him in the troubled scenes that ensued. He probably took no further part in
affairs than was absolutely forced on him by circumstances; but the unfavorable
bearing of his remarks on Gonzalo Pizarro intimates, that, however he may have
been discontented with the conduct of the viceroy, he did not countenance, for a
moment, the criminal ambition of his rival. The times were certainly unpropitious
to the execution of the financial reforms for which Zarate had come to Peru. But he
showed so much real devotion to the interests of the Crown, that the emperor, on
his return, signified his satisfaction by making him Superintendent of the Finances
in Flanders.

Soon after his arrival in Peru, he seems to have conceived the idea of making his
countrymen at home acquainted with the stirring events passing in the colony,
which, moreover, afforded some striking passages for the study of the historian.
Although he collected notes and diaries, as he tells us, for this purpose, he did not
dare to avail himself of them till his return to Castile. "For to have begun the history in Peru," he says, "would have alone been enough to put my life in jeopardy;
since a certain commander, named Francisco de Carbajal, threatened to take vengeance on any one who should be so rash as to attempt the relation of his exploits,
—far less deserving, as they were, to be placed on record, than to be consigned to
eternal oblivion." In this same commander, the reader will readily recognize the
veteran lieutenant of Gonzalo Pizarro.

On his return home, Zarate set about the compilation of his work. His first purpose was to confine it to the events that followed the arrival of Blasco Nuñez; but
he soon found, that, to make these intelligible, he must trace the stream of history
higher up towards its sources. He accordingly enlarged his plan, and, beginning
with the dscovery of Peru, gave an entire view of the conquest and subsequent occupation of the country, bringing the narrative down to the close of Gasca's mission. For the earlier portion of the story, he relied on the accounts of persons who
took a leading part in the events. He disposes more summarily of this portion than
of that in which he himself was both a spectator and an actor; where his testimony, considering the advantages his position gave him for information, is of the
highest value.

Alcedo in his *Biblioteca Americana, MS.,* speaks of Zarate's work as "containing
much that is good, but as not entitled to the praise of exactness." He wrote under
the influence of party heat, which necessarily operates to warp the fairest mind
somewhat from its natural bent. For this we must make allowance, in perusing accounts of conflicting parties. But there is no intention, apparently, to turn the truth
aside in support of his own cause; and his access to the best sources of knowledge
often supplies us with particulars not within the reach of other chroniclers. His narrative is seasoned, moreover, with sensible reflections and passing comments, that
open gleams of light into the dark passages of that eventful period. Yet the style

of the author can make but moderate pretensions to the praise of elegance or exact. ness; while the sentences run into that tedious, interminable. length which belongs to the garrulous compositions of the regular thoroughbred chronicler of the olden time.

The personalities, necessarily incident, more or less, to such a work, led its author to shrink from publication, at least during his life. By the jealous spirit of the Castilian cavalier, "censure," he says, "however light, is regarded with indignation, and even praise is rarely dealt out in a measure satisfactory to the subject of it." And he expresses his conviction that those do wisely, who allow their accounts of their own times to repose in the quiet security of manuscript, till the generation that is to be affected by them has passed away. His own manuscript, however, was submitted to the emperor; and it received such commendation from this royal authority, that Zarate, plucking up a more courageous spirit, consented to give it to the press. It accordingly appeared at Antwerp, in 1555, in octavo; and a second edition was printed, in folio, at Seville, in 1577. It has since been incorporated in Barcia's valuable collection; and, whatever indignation or displeasure it may have excited among contemporaries, who smarted under the author's censure, or felt themselves defrauded of their legitimate guerdon, Zarate's work has taken a permanent rank among the most respectable authorities for a history of the time.

The name of Zarate naturally suggests that of Fernandez, for both were laborers in the same field of history. Diego Fernandez de Palencia, or *Palentino*, as he is usually called, from the place of his birth, came over to Peru, and served as a private in the royal army raised to quell the insurrections that broke out after Gasca's return to Castile. Amidst his military occupations, he found leisure to collect materials for a history of the period, to which he was further urged by the viceroy, Mendoza, Marques de Cañete, who bestowed on him, as he tells us, the post of Chronicler of Peru. This mark of confidence in his literary capacity intimates higher attainments in Fernandez than might be inferred from the humble station that he occupied. With the fruits of his researches the soldier-chronicler returned to Spain, and, after a time, completed his narrative of the insurrection of Giron.

The manuscript was seen by the President of the Council of the Indies, and he was so much pleased with its execution, that he urged the author to write the account, in like manner, of Gonzalo Pizarro's rebellion, and of the administration of Gasca. The historian was further stimulated, as he mentions in his dedication to Philip the Second, by the promise of a guerdon from that monarch, on the completion of his labors; a very proper, as well as politic, promise, but which inevitably suggests the idea of an influence not altogether favorable to severe historic impartiality. Nor will such an inference be found altogether at variance with truth; for while the narrative of Fernandez studiously exhibits the royal cause in the most favorable aspect to the reader, it does scanty justice to the claims of the opposite party. It would not be meet, indeed, that an apology for rebellion should be found in the pages of a royal pensioner; but there are always mitigating circumstances, which, however we may condemn the guilt, may serve to lessen our indignation towards the guilty. These circumstances are not to be found in the pages of Fernandez. It is unfortunate for the historian of such events, that it is so difficult to find one disposed to do even justice to the claims of the unsuccessful rebel. Yet the Inca Garcilasso has not shrunk from this, in the case of Gonzalo Pizarro; and even Gomara, though living under the shadow, or rather in the sunshine, of the Court, has occasionally ventured a generous protest in his behalf.

The countenance thus afforded to Fernandez from the highest quarter opened to him the best fountains of intelligence,—at least, on the government side of the quarrel. Besides personal communication with the royalist leaders, he had access to their correspondence, diaries, and official documents. He industriously profited by his opportunities; and his narrative, taking up the story of the rebellion from its birth, continues it to its final extinction, and the end of Gasca's administration. Thus the First Part of his work, as it was now called, was brought down to the commencement of the Second, and the whole presented a complete picture of the distractions of the nation, till a new order of things was introduced, and tranquillity was permanently established throughout the country.

The diction is sufficiently plain, not aspiring to rhetorical beauties beyond the reach of its author, and out of keeping with the simple character of a chronicle. The sentences are arranged with more art than in most of the unwieldy compositions of the time; and, while there is no attempt at erudition or philosophic speculation, the current of events flows on in an orderly manner, tolerably prolix, it is true, but leaving a clear and intelligible impression on the mind of the reader. No history of that period compares with it in the copiousness of its details; and it has accordingly been resorted to by later compilers, as an inexhaustible reservoir for the supply of their own pages; a circumstance that may be thought of itself to bear no slight testimony to the general fidelity, as well as fulness, of the narrative.—The Chronicle of Fernandez, thus arranged in two parts, under the general title of *Historia del Peru*, was given to the world in the author's lifetime, at Seville, in 1571, in one volume, folio, being the edition used in the preparation of this work.

INDEX
THE CONQUEST OF MEXICO

A.

ABDERAHMAN, on the palm-tree, 99, *note.*
Ablutions at table, 88, 323.
Aborigines of America, origin of the, 689, 690, 703; of their civilization, 691. Peculiarities in their organization, 704. See *Indians* and *Mankind.*
Absolution, Aztec rite of, 43.
Achilles, shade of, cited, 40, *note.*
Acolhuans. See *Tezcucans.*
Acolman, 543. Dispute there, 553.
Aculan, Spaniards at the capital of, 650.
Adelantado, 138, *note*, 374.
Adrian of Utrecht, regent of Spain, 544, 625. Warrant by, 626. Pope, 628.
Adultery, charge respecting, 716.
Agave Americana, or aloe, or maguey, 11. Paper from the, 59, 80. Various uses made of the, 59, *note*, 79, 90. Dresden Codex made of the, 61, *note.* Account of it, 80. Nezahualcoyotl concealed under fibres of, 95.
Agriculture, tax on, among the Aztecs, 28, 78. Remarks on, 77. Of North American Indians, 78. Among the Mexicans, 78. Articles of Aztec, 79. Encouraged by Nezahualcoyotl, 100. Tlascalan, 222. Cholulan, 265. Near the lake of Chalco, 291. Attention to, after the Conquest, 639, 671.
Aguilar, Jerónimo de, a Christian captive, account of, 150. Cortés' reception of, 151. An interpreter, 151. In the retreat from Mexico, 449. At Chalco, 529.
Ahualco, crossed by Spaniards, 286.
Ahuitzotl, 18, 49, *note.*
Ajotzinco, city of, 290.
Alaminos, Antonio de, chief pilot of the armada, 144, 177. Despatched to Spain, 199. Anchors at Cuba, 199.
Alderete, Julian de, royal treasurer, 528. At Tacuba, 541. Advice of, as to attack, 572. His division for assaulting Mexico, 573, *note.* Too eager and in peril, 574, 575. Urges the torture of Guatemozin, 621, 629.
Alexander the Great, 470, *note.*
Alexander VI., Pope, bull of partition by, 276, *note.* Enjoins conversion of the heathen, 276, *note.*

Algiers, expedition against, 675.
Alms-giving, Aztec, 44.
Aloe. See *Agave Americana.*
Alphabet, Egyptian, 55, *note.* Nearest approach to, 55. European, introduced into Mexico, 57.
Alvarado, Jorge de, 573.
Alvarado, Pedro de, enters the river Alvarado, 125, 161. His return to Cuba with treasures, 126, 134. Joins Cortés, 141. Marches across Cuba, 142. Reprimanded, 147. In the battles near the Tabasco, 154, 155. On a foraging party, 183. Cuts down the body of Morla, 193. Despatched to Cempoalla, 201. Troops put under, 210. At Tlascala, 256. Doña Luisa given to, 258. Visits Montezuma with Cortés, 303. Aids in seizing Montezuma, 343. Montezuma pleased with, 354. Takes command at Mexico, 382. Instructions to, 382. Forces under, 383, 408, *note.* Assault on, 400, 404, 405. Blockaded, 402, 407. Joined by Cortés, 403. Aztecs massacred by, 404, 589. Character of, 407. Cortés' dissatisfaction with, 407. Chivalrous, 419. Storms the great temple, 425. Overpowered at the Mexican bridges, 432. Acts at the evacuation of Mexico, 443, 449. Unhorsed, 447, 448. At the battle of Otumba, 463. Accompanies Duero and Bermudez to Vera Cruz, 483. Sandoval and, 514. Reconnoitres Mexico, 518. Conspiracy against, 545. To command the point Tacuba, 550. Demolishes the aqueduct, 553, 554. Enmity of Olid and, 554. Operations of, 563. Protects breaches, 567. Sandoval to join, 572. His neglect to secure a retreat, 573. Rebuked, 573. His fortune at the assault, 578. Cortés' opinion of, 580. Temple burnt by, 593. Meeting of Cortés and, 595. In the murderous assault, 600, 602. To occupy the market-place, 603. Detached to Oaxaca, 623. Conquers Guatemala, 641.
Alvarado's Leap, 448.
Amadis de Gaula, 292, *note.*
Amaquemecan, Spaniards at, 289.
Ambassadors, persons of, held sacred, 30.
Ammunition, 586. See *Gunpowder.*

of future life, 40. Their claims to civilization, 50, 612. Compared with Europeans of the sixteenth century, 50. Their law of honor, 51, *note*. Their manuscripts, 59. The Teoamoxtli, or divine book of the, 63, *note*. Their literary culture, 63. Measurement of time, 64. Their cycle called "an old age," 66, *note*. Astrology, 70. Astronomy, 71. Their festival at the termination of the great cycle, 73. Their agriculture, 78. Acquaintance of, with plants, 80; with minerals, 81; with the mechanical arts, 81, 83. Their domestic manners, 87. Differ from North American Indians, 91, 704, *note*. Character of the, original and unique, 91. Nezahualcoyotl unites his forces with the, 96. Beat and sacrifice Maxtla, 96. Transfer of power to, from the Tezcucans, 114. The first communication with them, 125, 126. Orders to Cortés respecting the treatment of them, 137. Their condition, and disgust with Montezuma, at the time of Cortés' arrival, 170. Defeated by Tlascalans, 224. Aid in a Cholulan conspiracy, 267, 269. Number of, in the Mexican market, 330. Enraged at the profanation of their temples, 369. Aid in burning vessels at Vera Cruz, 370, 379. Insurrection by the, 406. Their assaults on the Spanish quarters, 413, 420. Sally against them, 416. Addressed by Montezuma, 421. Insult Montezuma, 422. Their spirit at the storming of the great temple, 425. Cortés' address to, 428. Their reply, 428. Their combatant spirit, 431, 432. Assault the retreating Spaniards, 445. Measures for rallying, 473. Tlascalan alliance with, rejected, 474. Guatemozin emperor of the, 489. Proceeded against as rebels, 491. Want of cohesion among them, 513. Deride Cortés, 522. Fights with, on the Sierra, 530. At Xochimilco, 538. Defend the aqueduct of Chapoltepec, 554. At Iztapalapan, 556. Defeat of their flotilla, 557. Fight on the causeways, 559. Their exasperation, 566. Their hatred of white men, 571, 592. Their bravery at the general assault, 575. Attack Alvarado and Sandoval, 578. Their spirit and sufferings, 587, 590, 592, 598, 603. Sortie of, 589. Do not bury their dead, 592, 599. Assault on, at the marketplace, 601. Effect of Guatemozin's capture on, 606. Evacuate the city, 609. Remarks on the fall of their empire,

612. Essay on the origin of the civilization of the, 689. Traditions respecting their origin, 702. See *Guatemozin* and *Montezuma*.

B.

Babel, coincidences of the tower of, and the temple of Cholula, 694.
Bachelors subject to penalties, 635.
Badajoz, British atrocities at, 277.
Badajoz, Gutierre de, storms the great *teocalli*, 593.
Bahama Islands, 121. Expedition to, for slaves, 123.
Balboa, Nuñez de, 121, 132. Transports brigantines, 517, *note*.
Banana, 79. The forbidden fruit, 79, *note*.
Banner of Cortés, 142, 244, *note*. Lost and recovered, 577. See *Standard*.
Banners, River of, 125, 161.
Baptism, Aztec and Pagan, 41, 696, 697.
Barante, on a disclosure in the reign of Louis the Eleventh, 547.
Barba, Don Pedro, governor of Havana, ordered to seize Cortés, 143.
Barba, Pedro, killed, 569.
Barbers, Aztec, 254, 329.
Barca, Madame Calderon de la, on Mexican love of flowers, 186, *note*. On Tacuba, 554, *note*. On Cuernavaca, 671, *note*.
Barks at Ajotzinco, 290. See *Canoes*.
Barracks built at Mexico, 570.
Barrio de San Jago, 596.
Barter, Grijalva's, at the River of Banners, 125, 161. Object of Cortés' expedition, 137. At Cozumel, 147. With the Tabascans, 158. See *Traffic*.
Basque language, 702, *note*.
Bas-reliefs destroyed, 82, 321.
Baths of Montezuma, 104, 322.
Battles, Aztecs avoided slaying their enemies in, 50. Of Tabasco, 153, 154. Of Ceutla, 156. Between Aztecs and Tlascalans, 224, 225; Spaniards and Tlascalans, 227, 228, 230, 235, 237, 241; Escalante and Quauhpopoca, 342; Cortés and Narvaez, 392. At the Aztec insurrection, 414, 417. At the great temple, 425. On leaving Mexico, 431, 432. Of the Melancholy Night, 445. Of Otumba, 460. Of Quauhquechollan, 478. Of Iztapalapan, 508, 509, 556. Near Chalco, 510. At Xaltocan, 518. At Tlacopan, 520. Of Jacapichtla, 525. On the rocks of the Sierra, 530. At Cuernavaca, 534. At Xochimilco, 535, 538. At the aqueduct of Chapoltepec,

William H. Prescott was born in 1796 in Salem, Massachusetts, the grandson of an eminent Revolutionary War hero. He was educated at Harvard College, where he suffered an injury that destroyed the sight of his left eye and subsequently weakened his right eye, leaving him almost totally blind. After graduation, and as increasing blindness plagued him, he abandoned the practice of law and turned his attention to research in Spanish history and to writing. His first published work was the *History of the Reign of Ferdinand and Isabella the Catholic* (1838). His monumental *History of the Conquest of Mexico* (1843) and *History of the Conquest of Peru* (1847) have become classics. Three volumes of the unfinished *History of the Reign of Philip II* were published before his death in 1859.